KU-659-554

CHAMBERS
ANAGRAMS

CHAMBERS ANAGRAMS

for crosswords, Scrabble®
and all wordgames

New edition

Compiled by
Chaz R Pewters, Zac Wherpster
and Esther C Zwarp

Chambers

CHAMBERS
An imprint of Larousse plc
43–45 Annandale Street
Edinburgh, EH7 4AZ

This edition first published by Chambers 1994
Earlier edition by W & R Chambers Ltd 1985

10 9 8 7 6 5 4 3 2

We have made every effort to mark as such all words which we believe to be trademarks. We should also like to make it clear that the presence of a word in the book, whether marked or unmarked, in no way affects its legal status as a trademark.

A CIP catalogue record for this book is available from the British Library

ISBN 0-550-19048-1

Typeset by In Production Ltd, Edinburgh
Printed in England by Clays Ltd, St Ives plc

Introduction

This newly compiled edition of *Chambers Anagrams,* listing 140 000 solutions to anagrams, is based on the latest (1993) edition of *The Chambers Dictionary.* Like its companion volume, *Chambers Words,* it reflects the huge vocabulary coverage of its parent, and is an essential addition to the library of every word-puzzler.

The letter groupings are listed according to length (of from 3 to 15 letters), and then alphabetically within each length, all possible anagram solutions being clearly presented beside them. This means that all the 6-letter groupings, for example, are listed together, with their solutions. For quick reference, each page of *Anagrams* is clearly marked with the letter lengths and a guide to the letter combinations.

All you have to do to find an anagram solution is to decide which letters make up the anagram, put these letters in alphabetical order — hyphens, accents, capital letters, etc should be ignored — and look up this combination of letters in the book.

For example, if the anagram you wish to solve is OPEN A RIOT (9 letters), arrange these letters into alphabetical order to give AEINOOPRT, then look for this combination in the 9-letter section where you will find the answer: OPERATION. Sometimes more than one solution is given under a letter combination, for example ACCEEIRTV = CREATIVE or REACTIVE, but in these cases the correct answer should be obvious from the wording of the clue and the letters already on the crossword grid.

A fixed-space font has been used, which is particularly important in the solutions. This means that the fourth letter (say) always appears in the same position (except when there are hyphens or apostrophes, which are of course retained in the solutions).

To retain information which may help with crossword clues, the solution words are listed as they appear in the dictionary (not in capitals, as in some word-books); words genuinely beginning with a capital can therefore be recognized. Where *The Chambers Dictionary* indicates that a word can be spelled with or without an initial capital letter, often with different meanings, this is shown by the symbol △ (eg 'Moor' and 'moor', and 'Cabinet' and 'cabinet') even when, as in the latter case, the capitalized form is not shown in bold in the dictionary but is only indicated in the definition. Accents have been retained since they often point to separate meanings (eg 'pate' and 'pâté') or to the foreign origin of a word.

Although phrases are not included as solutions, some words listed in the dictionary only as parts of phrases are included if they are considered as meaningful in their own right, eg 'Alzheimer's' and 'Dresden'. Abbreviations are included if they are commonly used instead of the full form, eg 'viz' and 'rehab'.

Irregular plurals, and irregular verb and adjectival forms, are listed as solutions. Plurals, even when regular, are listed if they are mentioned in definitions in the dictionary, often as having separate meanings, eg 'briefs' or 'kangaroos' (the latter in the sense of Australian mining shares).

The already wide scope of this book may be extended by taking into account the possibility of adding 's', 'es', 'ing', 'd', 'ed', 'er', 'est' or 'ly'. Such possibilities are usually implied by the crossword clue, which may suggest a plural, a past tense, a comparative or superlative, or an adverb. In these cases, you should remove the expected 'ending' letter or letters from the letter combination and look up the 'basic' word in *Anagrams*. Once you have found the required basic word, the 'ending' letter or letters should be replaced. For example, in the clue

Obtained pure cord strangely (8)

'strangely' suggests an anagram of 'pure cord', with 'obtained' hinting at a solution in the past tense. This suggests removing 'D', leaving the letter combination CEOPRRU = PROCURE. Replacing 'D' gives the solution, PROCURED.

Scrabble® players will find *Anagrams* particularly helpful in checking what combinations of letters form useful words, although *Official Scrabble® Words* is of course the final authority.

A

AAB	aba
	baa
AAC	caa'
AAD	Ada
AAG	aga
AAH	aha
AAI	aia
AAK	aka
AAL	ala
AAM	maa
AAN	ana
AAV	ava
	ava'
AAW	awa
	awa'
ABB	abb
ABC	ABC
	cab
ABD	bad
	dab
ABF	fab
ABG	bag
	gab
ABH	bah
ABJ	jab
ABL	alb
	lab
ABM	bam
	Mab
ABN	△ban
	nab
ABO	Abo
	AOB
	△boa
	oba
ABP	bap
ABR	arb
	△bar
	bra
ABS	sab
ABT	bat
	tab
ABY	aby
	bay
ACD	cad
ACE	ace
ACH	ach
	cha
ACI	CIA
ACL	lac
ACM	cam
	△mac
ACN	can
ACO	oca
ACP	cap
ACR	arc
	car
ACS	sac
ACT	act
	cat
ACV	vac
ACW	caw
ACY	cay
ADD	add
	dad
ADE	dae
ADF	fad
ADG	dag
	gad
ADH	dah
	had
ADI	aid
ADK	dak
ADL	dal
	lad
ADM	dam
	mad
ADN	AND
	and
	△dan
	DNA
ADO	ado
	oda
ADP	dap
	pad
ADR	ard
	△rad
ADS	sad
ADT	tad
ADW	daw
	wad
ADY	day
ADZ	adz
AEG	age
	gae
AEH	hae
AEK	ake
	kae
	kea
AEL	ale
	e-la
	lea
AEM	mae
AEN	ane
	ean
	nae
AEP	ape
	pea
AER	are
	ear
	era
AES	sae
	sea
AET	△ate
	eat
	△eta
	tae
	tea
AEU	eau
AEV	ave
	vae
AEW	awe
	wae
AEX	axe
AEY	aye
	yea
AEZ	△zea
AFG	fag
AFH	fah
AFL	Alf
AFN	fan
AFO	oaf
AFP	fap
AFR	far
	fra
AFT	aft
	fat
AFU	auf
AFW	faw
AFX	fax
AFY	fay
AGG	gag
AGH	hag
AGJ	△jag
AGL	gal
	lag
AGM	AGM
	gam
	mag
AGN	gan
	nag
AGO	ago
	△goa
AGP	gap
AGR	gar
	rag
AGS	gas
	sag
AGT	gat
	tag
AGU	gau
AGW	wag
AGY	gay
AGZ	zag
AHH	hah
AHJ	haj
	Jah
AHL	lah
AHM	ham
AHN	△han
AHO	hoa
AHP	hap
	pah
AHR	rah
	'rah
AHS	ash
	has
AHT	hat
AHW	haw
	wha
AHY	hay
	yah
AIK	kai
AIL	ail
AIM	aim
	ami
AIN	ain
	ani
AIP	IPA
	pia
AIR	air
	△rai
	ria
AIS	sai
AIT	ait
	ita
	△tai
	△t'ai
AIV	△via
	viâ
AJK	jak
AJM	jam
AJP	△jap
AJR	jar
	△raj
AJT	Jat
	taj
AJW	jaw
AJY	jay
AKM	kam
	mak
AKO	koa
	oak
AKR	△ark
AKS	ask
	ska
AKT	kat
	tak
AKU	auk
AKW	kaw
AKY	kay
	yak
ALL	all
ALM	lam
	mal
ALO	Lao
ALP	alp
	lap
	pal
ALR	lar
ALS	als
	sal
ALT	alt
	lat
ALV	lav
ALW	awl
	△law
ALX	lax
ALY	lay
AMM	△mam
AMN	△man
	mna
	nam
AMO	moa
AMP	amp
	map
	pam
AMR	arm
	mar
	RAM
	ram
AMS	△mas
	sam
	sma
AMT	mat
	tam
AMW	maw
AMX	max
AMY	△may
	Mya
	yam
ANN	ann
	nan
ANP	nap
	△pan
ANR	ran
	RNA
ANS	nas
	san
ANT	ant
	an't
	△nat
	tan
ANV	van
ANW	awn
	wan
ANY	any
	nay
AOP	OAP
	poa
AOR	oar
AOT	oat
	Tao
AOV	ova
AOZ	zoa
APP	pap
APR	par
	rap
APS	asp
	pas
	sap
	spa
APT	apt
	△pat
	tap
APW	paw
	wap
APX	pax
APY	pay
	yap
APZ	zap
AQT	qat
AQU	qua
ARS	ras
	sar
	sa'r
ART	art
	rat
	tar
ARW	raw
	war
ARX	rax
ARY	ary
	ray
	rya
ASS	ass
AST	Ats
	sat
ASV	vas
ASW	saw
	was
ASX	sax
ASY	say
ASZ	saz
ATT	tat
ATU	tau
ATV	△vat
ATW	taw
	twa
	wat
ATX	tax
ATY	tay
AUV	uva
	vau
AUY	ayu
AWW	waw
AWX	wax
AWY	△way
	'way
	yaw
AXZ	zax

B

BBE	ebb
BBI	bib
BBO	bob
BBU	bub
BCJ	JCB
BCO	cob
BCU	△cub
BDE	bed
	deb
BDI	bid
	dib
BDO	bod
	dob
BDU	bud
	dub
BEE	bee
BEG	beg
BEK	keb
BEL	bel
BEN	ben
	neb
BES	BSE
BET	bet
BEW	web

BEY	bey
	bye
BEZ	bez
BFI	FBI
	fib
BFO	fob
BFU	fub
BGH	GBH
BGI	△big
	△gib
BGO	bog
	gob
BGU	bug
	gub
BHO	boh
	hob
BHU	hub
BIJ	jib
BIL	△lib
BIM	Bim
BIN	bin
	nib
BIO	bio
	Ibo
	obi
BIR	rib
BIS	bis
	bi's
	sib
BIT	bit
	Tib
BIZ	biz
BJO	△job
BKO	△bok
	kob
BLO	lob
BMO	△mob
BMU	bum
BNO	bon
	nob
BNU	bun
	nub
BOO	boo
	obo
BOP	bop
BOR	bor
	bro
	orb
	rob
BOS	bos
	sob
BOT	bot
BOW	bow
BOX	box
BOY	boy
	yob
BPU	pub
BRU	bur
	rub
BSU	bus
	'bus
	sub
BSY	bys
BTU	but
	tub
BUY	buy

C

CDI	CID
	△cid
CDO	cod
	doc
CDU	cud
CEE	cee
CEG	ECG
	GCE
CEH	che
	ech
CEI	ice
CEL	cel
CEO	eco
CEP	cep
	pec
CER	rec
CES	sec
CET	'tec
CEU	cue
	△ecu
	écu
CGI	cig
CGO	cog
CHI	chi
	ch'i
	hic
	ich
CHO	hoc
	och
CIP	pic
CIS	sic
CIT	cit
	tic
CIY	icy
CLO	col
CLY	cly
CMU	cum
CMW	cwm
CNO	con
COO	coo
COP	cop
COR	cor
	orc
	roc
COS	cos
	'cos
	soc
COT	cot
	toc
COW	cow
COX	cox
COY	coy
COZ	coz
CPU	cup
CRU	cru
	cur
	ruc
CRY	cry
CTU	cut
CUZ	cuz

D

DDI	did
DDO	dod
	odd
	OD'd
DDU	dud
DEE	dee
DEF	def
	△fed
DEG	ged
DEH	edh
	he'd
DEI	dei
	die
	ide
DEK	ked
DEL	del
	eld
	LED
	led
DEM	Med
DEN	den
	end
	ned
DEO	Deo
	doe
	ode
DEP	ped
DER	red
DES	sed
	se'd
DET	△ted
DEU	due
DEW	dew
	wed
	we'd
DEY	dey
	dye
DEZ	zed
DFI	fid
DFU	fud
DGI	dig
	gid
DGO	dog
	△god
DGU	dug
DHI	hid
DHO	doh
	hod
DIK	kid
DIL	lid
DIM	dim
	mid
	'mid
DIN	DIN
	din
	Ind
	nid
DIO	Ido
DIP	dip
DIR	rid
DIS	Dis
DIT	dit
	tid
DIV	div
	vid
DIY	Yid
DJU	jud
DKO	KO'd
	OK'd
DLO	old
DLS	LSD
DLU	lud
DMO	Dom
	△mod
DMU	mud
DNO	△don
	△nod
DNU	dun
DNY	Ynd
DOO	doo
DOP	dop
	pod
DOR	dor
	ord
	rod
DOS	dos
	do's
	dso
	sod
DOT	dot
	tod
DOU	duo
	udo
DOW	dow
DOY	yod
DOZ	dzo
DPU	dup
	pud
DRU	rud
	urd
DRY	△dry
DST	'dst
	DTs
	dt's
DSU	sud
	uds
DUW	wud
DUX	dux

E

EEF	fee
	fée
EEG	gee
EEJ	jee
EEK	eek
	eke
EEL	eel
	lee
EEM	eme
EEN	een
	e'en
	ene
	née
EEP	pee
EER	e'er
	ere
	ree
EES	see
EET	tee
EEV	△eve
	vee
EEW	ewe
	wee
EEY	eye
EEZ	zee
EFF	eff
EFI	fie
EFK	kef
EFL	elf
EFN	fen
	nef
EFO	foe
EFR	erf
	ref
EFT	eft
	fet
	tef
EFU	feu
EFW	few
EFY	fey
EFZ	fez
EGG	egg
EGI	gie
EGK	keg
EGL	gel
	leg
EGM	gem
	meg
EGN	eng
	gen
EGO	ego
	geo
	goe
EGP	peg
EGR	erg
EGS	seg
EGT	get
	teg
EGU	gue
EGV	veg
EGY	gey
EHI	hie
EHL	Hel
EHM	hem
EHN	hen
EHO	hoe
EHP	hep
EHR	her
	reh
EHS	hes
	he's
	she
EHT	eth
	het
	the
EHU	hue
EHW	hew
EHX	hex
EHY	hey
	hye
EIK	eik
EIL	lei
	lie
EIN	nie
EIP	pie
EIR	ire
EIS	sei
EIT	tie
EIV	I've
	vie
EJO	△joe
EJT	jet
EJU	jeu
EJW	△jew
EKL	elk
	lek
EKN	ken
	nek
EKO	oke
EKP	kep
EKR	erk
EKT	ket
EKU	euk
	uke
EKW	ewk
EKX	kex
EKY	key
	kye
EKZ	zek
ELL	ell
ELM	elm
	mel
ELN	len'
ELO	Elo
	Leo
	lo'e
	olé
ELP	lep
ELS	les
	sel
ELT	elt
	let
	tel
ELU	leu
	ule
ELV	lev
ELW	lew
ELX	lex

Words marked △ may be spelled also with a capital letter

ELY ley
lye
ELZ lez
zel
EMN △men
EMO moe
EMR rem
EMS △mes
EMT △met
EMU emu
meu
EMW mew
wem
ENO eon
Neo
one
ENP nep
pen
ENR ern
ren
ENS ens
sen
ENT net
ten
ENW new
wen
ENY nye
yen
ENZ Zen
EOP ope
EOR o'er
ore
öre
øre
o're
roe
EOS △oes
EOT toe
EOV voe
EOW owe
woe
EOY oye
EPP pep
EPR per
pre
rep
EPT pet
EPW pew
EPY pye
yep
ERR err
ERS ers
res
ERT ret
ERU rue
ure
ERV △rev
ERW rew
ERX △rex
ERY rye
ERZ rez
ESS ess
EST est
set
ESU sue
use
ESW sew
ESX ex's
sex
ESY sey
sye
yes
ESZ sez
ETT Tet
ETU △ute
ETV vet
ETW ewt
tew
wet
ETY tye
yet
EUY uey
EVX vex
EWX wex
EWY wey
wye
yew
EXY yex
EXZ zex

F

FFI iff
FFO off
FGI fig
gif
FGO fog
FGU fug
FHO foh
Hof
FIK kif
FIL fil
FIN fin
FIR fir
FIS ifs
FIT fit
FIX fix
FIZ fiz
FLU flu
FLY fly
FMU fum
FNO fon
FNU fun
FOO oof
FOP fop
FOR for
fro
orf
FOT oft
FOU fou
ufo
FOX fox
FOY foy
FRU fur
FRY fry

G

GGI gig
GGO Gog
GHI ghi
GHO hog
GHU hug
ugh
GHV HGV
GIJ jig
GIL lig
GIM MiG
GIN gin
GIO gio
GIP gip
pig
GIR rig
GIT git
tig
GIW wig
GIZ Giz
zig
GJO jog
GJU gju
jug
GLO log
GLU lug
GMO mog
GMU gum
mug
GMY gym
GNO gon
nog
GNU gnu
gun
GOO goo
GOS sog
GOT got
tog
GOV gov
GOW wog
GOY goy
ygo
GPU gup
△pug
GPY gyp
GRU gur
rug
GTU gut
tug
GTY tyg
GUV guv
vug
GUY guy
yug

H

HHO hoh
HHU huh
HIM him
HIN hin
HIO hoi
HIP hip
phi
HIS his
ish
HIT hit
HIU hui
HIV HIV
HMO mho
ohm
HMU hum
HNO △hon
△noh
HNT nth
HNU Hun
HOO hoo
oho
ooh
HOP hop
pho
poh
HOR rho
HOS hos
soh
HOT hot
tho
tho'
HOW how
who
HOX hox
HOY hoy
HOZ zho
HPU hup
puh
HPY hyp
HRY rhy
HSS sh's
HSY shy
HTU hut
HTY thy
HWY why

I

IJZ jiz
IKL ilk
IKN ink
kin
IKO oik
IKP kip
IKR irk
kir
k'ri
IKS ski
IKT kit
ILL ill
I'll
ILM mil
ILN lin
nil
ILO oil
ILP lip
ILS lis
ILT lit
til
ILV vil
IMM mim
IMN nim
IMO moi
IMP imp
IMR △mir
rim
IMS ism
mis
sim
IMV vim
IMX mix
IMZ miz
INN inn
INO ion
INP △nip
pin
INR rin
INS ins
nis
n'is
sin
sin'
INT nit
tin
INU uni
INV vin
INW win
INX nix
INY △yin
IOP poi
IOS ios
iso
IOU IOU
IPP pip
IPR △pir
rip
IPS psi
sip
IPT pit
tip
IPU più
IPX pix
IPY yip
IPZ zip
IRS △sir
Sri
IRT rit
IRZ riz
ISS sis
IST its
it's
sit
'tis
ISU sui
ISV vis
ISW wis
ISX six
ITT tit
ITU Tiu
tui
ITW Tiw
Twi
wit
ITZ zit
IUZ Uzi
IVY ivy
IVZ viz
IZZ ziz

J

JOR jor
JOT jot
JOW jow
JOY joy
JSU jus
JTU jut

K

KNO kon
KOP △kop
KOR rok
KOS kos
KO's
OKs
OK's
KOU ouk
KOW kow
wok
KOY yok
KRU Kru
KSU suk
KSY sky
KUY kyu
yuk

L

LMO olm
LMU lum
LMY lym
LOO loo
LOP lop
LOR lor
lor'
LOS los
△sol
LOT lot
LOV vol
LOW low
owl
LOX lox
LOY loy
LPY ply
LRU lur
LSY sly
LUV luv
LUX lux
LUZ luz
LVY vly

M

MMO mom
MMU mum
MNO mon
nom
MNU mun
MOO moo
oom
MOP mop
△pom
MOR mor
ROM
rom
MOT MOT
mot
△tom
MOU mou
mou'
MOW mow
MOY moy
MOZ moz
MPT PMT
MRS Mrs
MRU rum
MSU sum
MTU tum
MUV vum
MUX mux

N

NNO non
NNU nun
NOO oon
NOP 'pon
NOR NOR
nor
nor'
NOS nos
△son
NOT NOT
not
ton
NOW now
own
won
NOX △nox
NOY noy
yon
NPU pun
NRU nur
run
urn
NSU △sun
NSY nys
sny
NTU nut
tun
NWY wyn

O

OOP oop
poo
OOR oor
roo
OOT too
OOW woo
OOZ △zoo
OPP pop
OPR pro
OPS pos
sop
OPT opt
pot
top
OPU oup
upo'
OPW pow
wop
OPX pox
OPZ poz
OQU quo'
ORT ort
rot
tor
ORU our
ORV △vor
ORW row
ORY Roy
OSS SOS
OST sot
OSU sou
OSV sov
OSW sow
wos
OSX sox
OSY soy
yos
OTT tot
OTU out
OTW owt
tow
two
wot
OTY toy
OUY you
OVW vow
OVX vox
OWW wow
OWX wox
OWY yow

P

PPU pup
PRU pur
PRY pry
PST pst
PSU pus
sup
PSY spy
PTU put
tup
PTW twp
PUY puy
yup
PXY pyx

Q

QSU suq

R

RSU sur
RTU rut
RTY try
Tyr
RWY wry

S

SST st's
SSU sus
STY sty
SUW wus
SWY swy

T

TTU tut
TUU utu
TUX tux

U

UZZ zuz

4 AAB

A

AABB abba
baba
AABC abac
caba
AABL Baal
AABR Arab
arba
AABS baas
Saba
AACM Cama
AACP capa
paca
AACR raca
AACS casa
AACT acta
AACW Waac
AADD Dada
AADM Adam
AADN nada
AADR Adar
AADT data
AADW adaw
AAEG Gaea
AAEL alae
AAER area
AAFH haaf
AAFL alfa
fa-la
AAFR afar
AAFW Waaf
AAGG gaga
AAGH agha
AAGI Gaia
AAGL alga
gala
AAGM agma
AAGN naga
AAGR agar
raga
AAGS saga
AAHH ha-ha
AAHK haka
AAHM amah
AAHR haar
AAHT taha
AAHY ayah
AAIN Naia
AAIR aria
AAJN Naja
AAJR ajar
raja
AAJV Java
AAJX Ajax
AAKK kaka
AAKM △kama
AAKN kana
AAKR arak
kara
AAKT kata
taka
AAKV kava
AAKW waka
AALL la-la
AALM alma
amla
△lama
AALN anal
lana
nala
AALP alap
AALR △alar
AALS alas
AALT Taal
tala
AALU aula
AALV aval
lava
AALY alay
AAMM ma'am
mama
AAMN mana
naam
AAMR maar
mara
Rama
AAMS masa
Saam
sama
AAMY △maya
Yama
AANN anan
anna
naan
nana
AANO anoa
AANP napa
AANR Aran
arna
△rana
AANS anas
ana's
AANT anta
tana
AANZ azan
AAPP papa
AAPR Pará
para
AAPT atap
tapa
AAPU paua
AAPW pawa
AAPY apay
AAQU aqua
AARR arar
ra-ra
AARS åsar
AART rata
tara
AARU aura
AARV vara
AASV vasa
AATT ta-ta
AATV tava
AATW tawa
AATX taxa
AAWY away
ABBE abbé
babe
ABBI Abib
Babi
ABBL blab
ABBO boba
ABBR barb
ABBU babu
buba
ABBY baby
ABCH △bach
ABCK back

ABCN	banc
ABCR	carb
	△crab
ABCS	scab
ABDE	abed
	bade
	bead
ABDI	abid
ABDL	bald
	blad
ABDN	△band
ABDO	doab
ABDR	△bard
	brad
	drab
ABDS	Dabs
ABDU	baud
	daub
ABDW	bawd
ABEK	bake
	beak
ABEL	able
	albe
	bael
	bale
	blae
ABEM	beam
	bema
ABEN	bane
	bean
ABEP	peba
ABER	bare
	bear
	brae
ABES	base
ABET	abet
	bate
	beat
	△beta
ABEU	beau
ABEY	abye
	baye
ABFF	baff
ABFL	flab
ABFR	barf
	frab
ABFT	baft
ABGI	biga
ABGL	blag
ABGM	gamb
ABGN	bang
ABGR	brag
	garb
	grab
ABGS	bags
ABGY	gaby
ABHL	blah
ABHS	bash
ABHT	baht
	△bath
ABIL	bail
ABIM	iamb
ABIN	bani
ABIO	obia
ABIR	rabi
ABIS	bias
ABIT	bait
	tabi
ABIX	Bixa
ABJM	jamb
ABJU	baju
	juba
ABKL	balk
ABKN	bank
	nabk
ABKO	boak
ABKR	bark
	krab
ABKS	bask
ABKU	bauk
ABLL	ball
ABLM	balm
	△lamb
ABLS	slab
ABLT	Balt
	blat
ABLU	balu
ABLW	bawl
ABLY	ably
	blay
ABMO	ambo
	boma
ABMR	barm
ABNO	bona
ABNR	barn
	bran
ABNS	nabs
	snab
ABNT	bant
ABNU	buna
ABNW	bawn
ABOR	boar
	bora
ABOS	Abos
ABOT	boat
ABPR	barp
ABPU	bapu
ABRS	bars
	bras
ABRT	brat
	T-bar
ABRU	baur
ABRW	bawr
	braw
ABRY	△bray
ABSS	bass
ABST	bast
	bats
	stab
	tabs
ABSW	swab
ABSY	bays
ABTT	batt
ABTU	abut
	buat
	tabu
	tuba
ABTY	bayt
ACCD	AC/DC
ACCE	ceca
ACCO	coca
ACDE	cade
	dace
	ecad
ACDH	△chad
ACDI	acid
	cadi
ACDL	clad
ACDO	coda
ACDR	card
ACDS	scad
ACEF	cafe
	café
	face
ACEG	cage
ACEH	ache
	each
ACEK	cake
ACEL	lace
ACEM	acme
	came
	Mace®
	mace
ACEN	acne
	ance
	cane
ACEP	△cape
	△pace
ACER	acer
	acre
	care
	race
ACES	aesc
	case
	ceas
ACET	cate
	tace
ACEV	cave
ACFF	caff
ACFL	calf
ACFT	fact
ACFU	cauf
ACGL	clag
ACGN	cang
ACGR	crag
ACGS	scag
ACGY	cagy
ACHI	chai
ACHK	hack
ACHL	chal
ACHM	cham
	Mach
ACHN	nach
ACHP	chap
ACHR	arch
	char
	rach
ACHS	cash
ACHT	chat
	tach
ACHW	chaw
ACHY	achy
	chay
ACIL	laic
ACIM	mica
ACIN	△cain
	Inca
ACIO	ciao
ACIP	capi
	△pica
ACIS	asci
	saic
ACJK	△jack
ACKL	calk
	lack
ACKM	mack
ACKP	pack
ACKR	cark
	rack
ACKS	cask
	sack
ACKT	tack
ACKU	cauk
ACKW	cawk
	wack
ACKY	caky
	yack
ACKZ	zack
ACLL	call
ACLM	calm
	clam
ACLN	clan
ACLO	coal
	△cola
ACLP	calp
	clap
ACLR	carl
ACLT	clat
	talc
ACLU	caul
ACLW	claw
ACLX	calx
ACLY	acyl
	clay
	lacy
ACMO	coma
ACMP	camp
ACMR	cram
	marc
ACMS	scam
ACMU	caum
ACMY	cyma
ACNN	cann
ACNR	cran
	narc
ACNS	cans
	scan
ACNT	cant
	can't
ACNY	cany
	cyan
ACOP	capo
	paco
ACOR	arco
	orca
ACOS	soca
ACOT	atoc
	coat
	octa
	taco
ACOX	coax
	co-ax
	coxa
ACPR	carp
	crap
ACPS	caps
ACPT	pact
ACPU	caup
ACPY	pacy
ACRR	carr
ACRS	scar
ACRT	cart
ACRW	craw
ACRY	racy
ACRZ	czar
ACST	cast
	cats
	scat
ACSW	scaw
ACTT	tact
ACUY	yuca
ACVY	cavy
ADDE	dead
	Edda
ADDO	dado
ADDR	Dard
	drad
ADDU	daud
	duad
ADDW	dawd
	wadd
ADDY	D-day
	dyad
ADEF	deaf
	fade
ADEG	aged
	egad
	gade
	gaed
ADEH	hade
	head
ADEI	aide
	idea
ADEJ	jade
ADEK	kade

ADEL dale deal lade lead
ADEM dame Edam made mead
ADEN Dane △dean
ADEO odea
ADER ared dare dear eard rade read
ADES Ades sade
ADET date tea'd
ADEV deva vade Veda
ADEW awed deaw wade
ADEY yead
ADEZ adze daze
ADFF daff
ADFN fand
ADFO fado
ADFR fard
ADFT daft
ADFW Wafd
ADFY fady
ADGI gadi gaid igad
ADGL glad
ADGN dang
ADGO dago goad
ADGR darg drag grad rag'd
ADGU gaud
ADGW gawd
ADHJ hadj
ADHK dhak
ADHL dahl dhal
ADHN hand
ADHR hard
ADHS dash shad
ADHU haud
ADIK dika kadi kaid
ADIL Dáil dali dial laid
ADIM amid maid
ADIN Dian
ADIP paid
ADIQ qadi
ADIR arid dari raid
ADIS AIDS dais disa said sida
ADIT adit dita
ADIV avid diva
ADIW wadi waid
ADKN dank
ADKR dark
ADKW dawk
ADKY Dyak
ADLN △land
ADLO alod load odal
ADLR lard
ADLT dalt
ADLU auld dual laud udal
ADLW awdl wald
ADLY △lady yald
ADMN damn mand
ADMP damp
ADMR DRAM dram mard
ADMS dams
ADMU duma maud
ADMW dwam
ADNN NAND
ADNO Doña dona
ADNP pand
ADNR darn nard △rand
ADNS sand
ADNT dant
ADNU duan
ADNW dawn wand wan'd
ADOP apod dopa
ADOR Dora road
ADOS ados soda
ADOT doat toad
ADOW woad
ADPR drap pard prad
ADPS pads
ADQU △quad
ADRS △sard
ADRT dart drat trad
ADRU daur duar dura
ADRW draw ward
ADRY adry dray △yard
ADSW swad
ADSY days
ADTU daut
ADTW dawt wadt
ADUY yaud
ADVY Davy V-day
ADWY wady
AEEG agee
AEEJ ajee
AEEK akee
AEEL alee eale
AEES ease
AEFK fake
AEFL feal flea leaf
AEFM fame
AEFN fane
AEFR fare fear frae
AEFS safe
AEFT fate feat feta
AEFV fave
AEFZ faze
AEGG gage
AEGL egal Gael gale geal
AEGM egma game mage mega
AEGN agen gane gean gena
AEGP gape page peag
AEGR areg gare gear rage
AEGS ages sage
AEGT gate geat geta
AEGU ague
AEGV gave △vega
AEGW wage
AEGZ gaze
AEHK hake
AEHL hale heal
AEHM ahem haem hame
AEHP epha heap
AEHR hare hear △rhea
AEHS shea
AEHT eath haet hate heat thae Thea
AEHV have
AEHY yeah
AEHZ haze
AEIK kaie
AEIL ilea
AEIM amie
AEIN aîné
AEJK jake
AEJN △jane jean Jena
AEJP jape
AEJT jeat
AEKK ekka
AEKL kale lake leak
AEKM kame make
AEKP peak
AEKR rake reak
AEKS sake saké
AEKT keta take teak
AEKW wake weak weka
AELL △leal
AELM alme lame lamé leam male meal mela
AELN élan △lane lean neal
AELO △aloe Olea
AELP leap △pale peal pela plea
AELR arle △earl laer lare lear rale râle real
AELS lase sale seal slae
AELT late leat tael tale teal tela
AELV lave leva vale veal △vela
AELW alew wale weal

Words marked △ may be spelled also with a capital letter

AELX	axel
	axle
AELY	Yale®
	yale
AELZ	laze
	zeal
AEMM	emma
AEMN	△amen
	mane
	mean
	△name
AEMR	mare
	ream
AEMS	mase
	mesa
	same
	seam
AEMT	mate
	maté
	meat
	tame
	team
AEMW	wame
AEMX	Amex
	exam
	Xema
AEMZ	maze
AENO	aeon
	eoan
AENP	nape
	neap
	pane
	pean
AENR	earn
	nare
	near
	rean
AENS	sane
	sean
	sena
AENT	ante
	etna
	neat
	ta'en
	tane
	ta'ne
	Tean
AENU	aune
AENV	nave
	vane
	vena
AENW	anew
	wane
	wean
AENY	yean
AENZ	naze
AEOR	aero
AEOT	toea
AEOZ	zoea
AEPP	pape
AEPR	pare
	pear
	rape
	reap
AEPS	apes
	apse
	peas
	spae
AEPT	pate
	pâté
	peat
	tape
AEPV	pave
	pavé
AEPX	△apex
AEPY	PAYE
AERR	rare
	rear
AERS	Ares
	arse
	ears
	rase
	sear
	sera
AERT	aret
	rate
	tare
	tear
AERU	urea
AERV	aver
	rave
	vare
	Vera
AERW	arew
	ware
	wear
AERY	aery
	ayre
	eyra
	yare
	year
AERZ	raze
AESS	seas
AEST	△east
	eats
	sate
	seat
	seta
AESV	Aves
	save
	vase
AESW	wase
AESX	axes
	Saxe
AESY	ayes
	easy
	eyas
AETT	état
	tate
	teat
AETW	twae
	wate
	weta
AETY	yate
AETZ	zeta
AEUV	uvea
AEVW	wave
AEWW	wawe
AFFF	faff
AFFG	gaff
AFFH	haff
AFFN	naff
AFFR	raff
AFFW	waff
AFFY	affy
	yaff
AFGL	flag
AFGN	fang
AFGO	goaf
AFGR	frag
	Graf
AFHL	half
AFHS	fash
AFHT	haft
AFIK	faik
	kaif
AFIL	fail
AFIN	fain
	naif
	naïf
AFIR	fair
	fiar
AFIT	fiat
AFIW	waif
AFIX	faix
AFKL	flak
AFKN	fank
AFKW	△wakf
AFLL	fall
AFLM	flam
AFLN	flan
AFLO	foal
	loaf
AFLP	flap
AFLR	farl
AFLT	flat
AFLU	lauf
AFLW	flaw
AFLX	falx
	flax
AFLY	flay
AFMO	foam
AFMR	farm
AFNO	anfo
AFNU	faun
AFNW	fawn
AFOR	△afro
	faro
	fora
AFOS	oafs
	sofa
AFOY	ofay
AFPR	frap
AFQW	△waqf
AFRT	fart
	raft
AFRU	△frau
AFRY	fray
AFRZ	zarf
AFST	fast
AFTU	tufa
AFTW	waft
AFUX	faux
AGGH	hagg
AGGI	giga
AGGM	magg
AGGN	gang
AGGO	agog
AGGR	ragg
AGGU	guga
AGHN	hang
AGHS	gash
	shag
AGHT	gath
	ghat
AGIL	gila
	glia
AGIM	magi
AGIN	agin
	gain
AGIO	agio
AGIR	gair
	ragi
AGIT	gait
	Taig
AGIV	vagi
AGIY	△yagi
AGJO	gajo
AGJU	juga
AGKN	kang
	knag
AGKO	kago
AGKS	skag
AGKW	gawk
AGLL	gall
AGLM	glam
AGLN	lang
AGLO	gaol
	goal
AGLS	lags
	slag
AGLU	Gaul
	gula
AGLY	gyal
AGMN	G-man
	mang
AGMO	ogam
AGMP	gamp
AGMR	gram
	marg
AGMS	mags
AGMU	gaum
AGMY	gamy
AGNO	agon
	Goan
AGNP	pang
AGNR	gnar
	gran
	rang
AGNS	sang
	snag
AGNT	gant
	gnat
	△tang
	T'ang
AGNU	gaun
	guan
AGNV	vang
AGNW	gnaw
	wang
AGNY	△yang
AGOP	gapó
AGOR	Argo
AGOS	sago
AGOT	△goat
	toga
AGOY	yoga
AGPS	gasp
	spag
AGPU	gaup
AGPW	gawp
AGQU	quag
AGRS	rags
AGRT	gart
	grat
AGRU	gaur
	guar
AGRY	gray
AGST	gast
	stag
	tags
AGSW	swag
AGSY	sagy
AGUY	yuga
AGYZ	gazy
AHHS	hash
	shah
AHHT	hath
AHIJ	haji
AHIK	haik
AHIL	hail
	hila
AHIN	hain
AHIR	hair
AHIS	Shia
AHIT	ha'it
	Thai
AHIU	huia
AHIY	hiya
AHJJ	hajj
AHKL	lakh
AHKN	ankh
	hank
	△khan
AHKR	hark

AHKS	hask
AHKT	khat
AHKW	hawk
AHLL	hall
AHLM	halm
AHLO	halo
AHLR	harl
AHLS	lash
AHLT	halt
	lath
AHLU	haul
	hula
AHMR	harm
AHMS	mash
	sham
AHMT	math
AHMU	huma
AHMW	hawm
	wham
AHNR	harn
AHNS	△shan
AHNT	ha'n't
	tanh
	than
AHOP	opah
AHOR	haro
	hoar
AHOS	hoas
AHOT	oath
AHOV	Hova
AHOW	whoa
AHOX	hoax
AHOY	ahoy
	hoya
AHPR	harp
AHPS	hasp
	pash
AHPT	path
AHPW	whap
AHRS	rash
AHRT	hart
	rath
	tahr
	thar
AHRU	Rahu
AHSS	hass
	sash
AHST	hast
	shat
	tash
AHSW	shaw
	shwa
	wash
AHSY	ashy
	shay
AHTT	tath
	that
AHTU	haut
AHTW	thaw
	what
AHYZ	hazy
AIIL	ilia
AIIN	inia
AIIX	ixia
AIJL	jail
AIJN	Jain
AIJO	jiao
AIJW	Jawi
AIKK	kaki
AIKL	ilka
	kail
	△kali
	laik
AIKM	kaim
	kami
	maik
AIKN	akin
	kain
	kina
	naik
AIKP	paik
	Paki
	pika
AIKR	raik
	raki
AIKS	saki
	sika
AIKT	ikat
	kati
	taki
	tika
AIKV	kiva
AIKZ	kazi
AILM	lima
	mail
	mali
AILN	anil
	lain
	nail
AILP	pail
	Pali
	pila
AILR	aril
	lair
	liar
	lira
	rail
	rial
AILS	Lias
	sail
	sial
AILT	alit
	tail
	tali
AILV	vail
	vali
	vial
AILW	wail
	wali
AILX	axil
AILZ	zila
AIMM	△imam
	maim
AIMN	△main
	mani
	mina
AIMR	amir
	mair
	Mira
	rami
	rima
AIMS	amis
	saim
	Sami
	sima
AIMX	maxi
AINN	nain
AINP	△nipa
	△pain
	piña
AINR	airn
	Nair
	rain
	rani
AINS	anis
	sain
AINT	ain't
	anti
AINU	Ainu
AINV	vain
	vina
AINW	△wain
AINX	Xian
AINZ	Nazi
AIOT	iota
AIPP	pipa
AIPR	pair
AIPS	pais
AIPT	pita
AIRS	airs
	aris
	sair
	sari
AIRT	airt
	rait
	tiar
AIRV	riva
	vair
AIRY	airy
AIRZ	riza
AIST	Asti
	sati
AISV	Siva
	visa
AISX	axis
AITT	tait
AITU	aitu
AITV	Vita®
	vita
AITW	wait
AITX	taxi
AITZ	zati
AIVV	viva
AJKR	jark
AJLR	jarl
AJNN	jann
AJNO	Joan
AJOS	soja
AJOT	jato
	jota
AJPS	jasp
AJPU	jaup
	puja
AJRU	△jura
AJSS	jass
AJSW	jaws
AJSY	jasy
AJYZ	jazy
AJZZ	jazz
AKLN	lank
AKLO	kola
AKLR	lark
AKLS	Salk
AKLT	talk
AKLW	lawk
	walk
AKLY	alky
	laky
AKMO	amok
	mako
AKMR	mark
AKMS	mask
AKMW	mawk
AKNO	kaon
	koan
AKNP	knap
AKNR	knar
	nark
	rank
AKNS	kans
	sank
AKNT	kant
	tank
AKNW	wank
AKNY	△yank
AKOR	kora
	okra
AKOS	Oaks
	soak
AKOT	atok
	okta
AKOY	kayo
	oaky
	okay
AKPR	△park
AKPW	pawk
AKRS	ksar
	sark
AKRT	kart
AKRU	raku
AKRW	wark
AKST	skat
	task
AKSU	skua
AKSW	skaw
AKTY	kyat
	taky
AKUW	wauk
ALLM	mall
ALLO	olla
ALLP	pall
ALLS	alls
ALLT	tall
ALLW	△wall
ALLY	ally
	y'all
ALMM	malm
ALMO	loam
	loma
	mola
ALMP	lamp
	palm
ALMR	marl
ALMS	alms
	slam
ALMT	malt
ALMU	alum
	maul
ALMY	amyl
	lyam
	myal
ALNO	loan
ALNP	plan
ALNR	larn
ALNT	lant
ALNU	luna
	ulna
ALNW	lawn
ALNX	lanx
ALOP	opal
ALOR	oral
ALOS	also
	sola
ALOT	alto
	lota
	tola
ALOV	oval
	vola
ALOW	alow
	AWOL
ALOZ	lazo
ALPP	Lapp
	palp
	plap
ALPS	Alps
	salp
	slap
ALPT	plat
ALPU	paul
	pula
ALPW	pawl
ALPY	paly
	play
ALRU	Ural
ALRY	aryl
	Lyra
	ryal
ALSS	lass

ALST last
salt
slat
ALSU saul
ALSV Slav
ALSW slaw
ALSY slay
ALTW twal
ALUU luau
ALUV ulva
ALUW waul
ALWW wawl
ALWY waly
yawl
ALYZ lazy
AMMO ammo
AMMR marm
AMNO mano
moan
mona
noma
AMNU maun
AMNX Manx
AMNY many
myna
AMOR mora
roam
roma
AMOS △soma
AMOT atom
moat
AMOW mowa
AMOX moxa
AMOY moya
AMPR pram
ramp
AMPS samp
Spam®
AMPT tamp
AMPU puma
AMPV vamp
AMRS arms
Mars
rams
AMRT mart
tram
AMRU arum
AMRW mawr
warm
AMRY △army
△mary
AMSS △mass
AMST mast
AMSU masu
Musa
AMSW swam
wasm
AMSX Xmas
AMTT matt
AMTY maty
AMWY M-way

AMYZ azym
mazy
ANNO anno
anon
ANOR roan
ANOS naos
ANOT Nato
ANOV nova
ANOW anow
ANOX axon
ANOZ zona
ANPS snap
span
ANPT pant
ANPU puna
ANPW pawn
ANRS snar
ANRT rant
tarn
ANRU raun
ANRW rawn
warn
ANRY nary
yarn
ANSS sans
ANST ants
△sant
ANSU anus
ANSW sawn
swan
ANSY nyas
ANTU △aunt
tuan
tuna
ANTV vant
ANTW want
ANUU unau
ANUY yuan
ANVY △navy
ANWY awny
wany
yawn
ANYZ zany
AOPR proa
AOPS soap
AOPT atop
AOPV Pavo
AORR orra
roar
AORS Rosa
soar
sora
AORT △rota
taro
AORU urao
AORV arvo
voar
AORW arow
a-row
AORY oary
AOSS ossa

AOST oast
oats
stoa
tosa
AOSX Xosa
AOSY Soay
soya
AOTU auto
AOVW avow
APPR parp
APPU pupa
APPY yapp
APRR parr
APRS rasp
spar
APRT part
prat
rapt
tarp
trap
APRU prau
APRW warp
wrap
APRY pray
APSS pass
APST past
spat
stap
taps
APSU upas
APSW spaw
swap
wasp
APSY pays
spay
APTU tapu
APTY pyat
APUY yaup
APUZ zupa
APWY yawp
AQTU quat
AQUY quay
ARRY 'Arry
yarr
ARST △arts
rast
rats
star
tsar
ARSU rusa
sura
Ursa
ARTT tart
trat
ARTU ratu
Ruta
ARTW wart
ARTY arty
tray
ARTZ tzar
ARUV urva
ARUW waur

ARVY vary
ARWY awry
wary
ARXY X-ray
ARZZ razz
ASSS sass
ASST tass
ASSY says
ASTU saut
utas
ASTV vast
ASTW staw
swat
taws
'twas
wast
wats
ASTY stay
ASWY sway
ways
yaws
ATTT tatt
ATTU tatu
taut
ATTW tawt
twat
watt
ATUV vatu
vaut
ATWY tway
AVWY wavy
AWXY waxy
AWYY yawy

B

BBCO cobb
BBEE Beeb
BBEL bleb
BBIS sibb
BBLO blob
BBLU blub
bulb
BBMO bomb
BBOO boob
BBOS bobs
BBOU △bubo
BCEI bice
BCEK beck
BCEU cube
BCHU chub
BCIR crib
BCKO bock
BCKU buck
BCLO bloc
BCLU club
BCMO comb
BCRU curb
BDEE bede
BDEI bide
dieb
BDEL bled
BDEN bend

BDEO bode
BDER bred
BDET debt
BDEU Bedu
BDIN bind
BDIR bird
drib
BDIS dibs
BDLO bold
BDMU dumb
BDNO bond
BDNU △bund
BDOO doob
BDOR bord
brod
BDOU budo
BDOY body
BDRU burd
drub
BDSU dubs
BDUZ 'zbud
BEEF beef
BEEH △hebe
BEEL blee
BEEN been
bene
BEEP beep
BEER beer
bere
bree
BEES bees
BEET beet
bete
bête
BEGI gibe
BEGO bego
BEGR berg
BEGY gybe
BEHL bhel
BEHR herb
BEHT beth
BEIJ jibe
BEIK bike
kibe
BEIL bile
BEIN bein
beni
bien
bine
BEIR bier
Brie
BEIS bise
BEIT bite
BEIX ibex
BEJN benj
BEJO jobe
BEJU jube
BEKM kemb
BEKO boke
BEKR berk
kerb
BEKU buke

BEKY byke
BELL bell
BELO bole
lobe
BELP pleb
BELT belt
blet
BELU blue
BELW blew
BELY bley
BEMR berm
BEMW wemb
BENO bone
ebon
BENR △bren
BENS sneb
BENT bent
BENU unbe
BEOO oboe
BEOR Boer
bore
robe
'robe
BEOT to-be
BEOY obey
BERR brer
BERS Serb
BERU rube
BERV verb
BERW brew
BERY byre
BEST best
BESY byes
BETU △bute
△tube
BETY byte
ybet
BEUZ zebu
BEVY bevy
BFFI biff
BFFO boff
BFFU buff
BFLU flub
BFMU bumf
BFOR forb
BFOU bufo
BGGI bigg
BGIL glib
BGIN bing
BGIO biog
Igbo
BGIR brig
BGLO glob
BGNO bong
BGNU bung
BGOO gobo
BGOR brog
BGOY bogy
boyg
goby
go-by
BGRU burg
△grub
BHIS bish
BHLU buhl
BHOO booh
hobo
BHOS bosh
BHOT both
BHSU bush
BIIS ibis
BIKL bilk
BIKN bink
BIKR birk
BIKS bisk
BIKU buik
BILL △bill
BILM limb
BILN blin
BILO boil
lobi
BILP blip
BILR birl
BIMN nimb
BIMR brim
BIMZ zimb
BINS nibs
snib
BINT bint
BINY inby
BIOR Biro®
brio
BIOS bios
Ibos
BIOT bito
obit
BIRR birr
BIRT △brit
BIRX Brix
BIST bits
BISV vibs
BITT bitt
BJOS jobs
BKLU bulk
BKNO bonk
knob
BKNU bunk
knub
BKOO boko
△book
BKOS bosk
BKOU bouk
BKRU burk
BKSU busk
BLLO boll
BLLU △bull
BLOO bolo
bool
lobo
obol
BLOS slob
BLOT blot
bolt
BLOW blow
bowl
BLRU blur
burl
BLSU slub
BLTU Blut
BMNU numb
BMOO boom
BMOT tomb
BMOU ombu
ombú
umbo
BMOW womb
BMPU bump
BMRU Brum
BNOO boon
BNOR born
BNOS bo's'n
bos'n
snob
BNOU boun
BNOY bony
BNRU burn
BNSU snub
BNTU bunt
BOOR boor
broo
BOOS obos
BOOT boot
BOOY boyo
BOOZ bozo
zobo
BOPR prob
BORS △sorb
BORT bort
BORW bowr
brow
BORY orby
BOSS boss
BOST bots
stob
BOSW bows
swob
BOSY boys
sybo
BOTT bott
BOTU bout
BOTY △toby
BOUY buoy
BOUZ zobu
BOXY boxy
BPRU burp
BPUY upby
BRRR brrr
BRRU burr
BRTU brut
BRUY bury
ruby
BSSU buss
BSTU bust
buts
stub
BSUY busy
BTTU butt
BUZZ buzz

C

CCEE ecce
CCEO ecco
CCHI chic
CCHO choc
CCKO cock
CCOO coco
CCOR croc
CDEE cede
CDEI cedi
dice
iced
CDEK deck
CDEO code
coed
△deco
ecod
CDER cred
CDEU cued
duce
CDHI chid
dich
CDIK △dick
CDIO odic
CDIS disc
CDIT dict
CDKO dock
CDKU duck
CDLO clod
cold
CDNO cond
CDOR cord
CDOU douc
CDRU crud
curd
CDSU △scud
CDTU duct
CEEH eche
eech
CEER cere
△cree
CEET cete
CEFH chef
CEFK feck
CEFL clef
CEGK geck
CEGL cleg
CEHH hech
CEHK heck
CEHL lech
CEHO echo
oche
CEHP pech
CEHR cher
CEHS sech
CEHT echt
etch
tech
CEHW chew
CEHY yech
CEHZ chez
CEIL ceil
ciel
lice
CEIM mice
CEIN cine
ciné
nice
CEIP epic
pice
CEIR ciré
eric
icer
rice
CEIS sice
CEIT cite
tice
CEIV cive
△vice
CEIW wice
CEKK keck
CEKN neck
CEKO △coke
CEKP peck
CEKR reck
CELL cell
CELM clem
CELO ceòl
cole
CELT △celt
CELU clue
luce
CELW clew
CEMO come
CEMR merc
CEMY cyme
CENO cone
once
CENS cens
CENT cent
CENU unce
CEOP cope
CEOR core
CEOS cose
seco
CEOT cote
CEOV cove
CEOZ coze
CEPS pecs
spec
CEPU puce
CERT cert
CERU cure
curé
ecru
CERW crew
CESS cess
CEST sect
CESY scye
syce

CETU	cute
CFFO	coff
CFFU	cuff
CFIL	flic
CFIO	coif
	fico
	foci
CFIS	fisc
CFIU	cuif
	fuci
CFKU	fuck
CFOO	coof
CFOR	corf
CFOT	coft
CFSU	fusc
CGHU	chug
CGKU	guck
CGLO	clog
CGOS	scog
CGSU	scug
CHIK	chik
	hick
CHIL	lich
CHIN	chin
	inch
CHIP	chip
CHIR	rich
CHIS	sich
CHIT	chit
	itch
	△tich
CHIV	chiv
CHIW	wich
CHIZ	chiz
CHKO	△hock
CHKU	huck
CHLO	loch
CHMO	moch
CHMU	chum
	much
CHNO	chon
CHOO	coho
CHOP	chop
CHOR	roch
CHOS	cosh
CHOT	coth
CHOU	chou
	ouch
CHOW	△chow
CHSU	cush
	such
CHTU	chut
CHWY	wych
CIKK	kick
CIKL	lick
CIKM	mick
CIKN	△nick
CIKP	pick
CIKR	rick
CIKS	sick
CIKT	tick
CIKW	wick
CIKY	icky
CILL	cill
CILO	Clio
	coil
	loci
CILP	clip
CILR	cirl
CIMO	mico
CIMR	crim
CINO	cion
	coin
	icon
CINU	unci
CINZ	zinc
CIOR	coir
CIOT	cito
	coit
	otic
	Tico
CIOZ	zoic
CIPS	pics
	spic
CIPT	Pict
CIRT	crit
CIRU	uric
CIRY	ricy
CIST	cist
	cits
CITU	cuit
CITY	△city
CJKO	△jock
CJOO	joco
CKLO	lock
CKLU	luck
CKMO	mock
CKMU	△muck
CKNO	conk
	nock
CKOO	cook
CKOP	pock
CKOR	cork
	△rock
CKOS	sock
CKOT	tock
CKOW	wock
CKOY	coky
	yock
CKPU	△puck
CKRU	ruck
CKSU	cusk
	suck
CKTU	tuck
CKUY	yuck
CLLO	coll
CLLU	cull
CLMU	△culm
CLOO	cool
	loco
CLOP	clop
CLOT	clot
	Colt®
	colt
CLOU	clou
CLOW	clow
	cowl
CLOY	cloy
CLRU	curl
CLSU	scul
CLTU	cult
CMOO	coom
CMOP	comp
CMOR	corm
CMOS	coms
CMSU	scum
CNNO	conn
CNOO	coon
CNOR	corn
CNOS	cons
CNOU	unco
CNOY	cony
CNRU	curn
CNSY	sync
CNTU	cunt
COOP	coop
	co-op
	poco
COOT	coot
	toco
COPR	crop
COPS	scop
COPT	Copt
COPU	coup
COPW	cowp
COPY	copy
CORT	torc
CORU	cour
CORW	crow
CORY	cory
COSS	coss
COST	△cost
	scot
COSW	cows
	scow
COSX	Cox's
COSY	cosy
COTT	cott
COXY	coxy
COYZ	cozy
CPSU	cups
	cusp
	scup
CRRU	curr
CRSU	scur
CRSY	scry
CRTU	curt
CRUX	crux
CSSU	cuss
CSTU	scut
CSTY	cyst

D

DDEE	deed
DDEI	deid
	died
DDEO	eddo
DDER	redd
DDEU	dude
DDEY	dyed
	eddy
DDIO	dido
DDOO	dodo
DDOS	dods
	odds
DDOW	dowd
DDRU	rudd
DDSU	duds
	sudd
DEEF	feed
	fee'd
DEEG	edge
DEEH	heed
DEEI	idée
DEEK	deek
DEEL	dele
DEEM	deem
	deme
	Mede
	meed
DEEN	deen
	dene
	Eden
	need
DEEP	△deep
DEER	deer
	dere
	dree
	rede
	reed
DEES	seed
DEET	teed
	tee'd
DEEV	deev
DEEW	weed
DEEY	eyed
	yede
	yeed
DEFL	delf
	fled
DEFN	fend
DEFO	feod
DEFT	deft
DEFU	feud
DEFY	defy
DEGI	gied
DEGL	geld
	gled
DEGO	doge
DEGR	dreg
DEGU	gude
DEGY	edgy
DEHI	heid
	hide
	hied
DEHL	held
DEHN	hend
DEHO	hoed
DEHR	herd
DEHS	shed
	she'd
DEHU	hued
DEIK	dike
DEIL	deil
	deli
	eild
	idle
	Lide
	lied
DEIM	dime
	idem
DEIN	dine
	nide
DEIP	pied
DEIR	dire
	ride
DEIS	dies
	△ides
	side
DEIT	△diet
	dite
	edit
	tide
	tied
DEIU	Dieu
DEIV	Devi
	dive
	vide
	vied
DEIW	weid
	wide
DEKO	doek
	OKed
DEKR	drek
DEKS	desk
DEKU	△duke
DEKY	dyke
DELL	dell
DELM	meld
DELN	lend
DELO	dole
	lode
DELP	pled
DELS	seld
	sled
DELT	delt
	teld
DELU	duel
	dule
DELV	veld
DELW	lewd
	weld
DELY	yeld
DEMN	mend
DEMO	demo
	dome
	mode
DEMR	derm
DEMY	demy

DENO doen
done
node
DENP pend
DENR dern
nerd
rend
DENS ends
send
sned
DENT dent
tend
DENU dune
nude
unde
undé
DENV vend
DENW △wend
DENY deny
dyne
DENZ Zend
DEOP dope
DEOR doer
redo
rode
roed
DEOS does
dose
DEOT dote
toed
DEOV dove
DEOW owed
DEOY yode
DEOZ doze
DEPS sped
DEPU dupe
DERS reds
DERU dure
rude
rued
urdé
DERV derv
DERW drew
DERY drey
dyer
yerd
DEST sted
DESU deus
dues
sued
used
DETU duet
DETY tedy
tyde
DEWY dewy
DFFO doff
DFFU duff
DFIN find
DFIO Fido
foid
DFLO fold
DFNO fond
DFNU fund
DFOO food
DFOR ford
DFOU foud
DFOW dowf
DFRY fyrd
DGIL gild
glid
DGIN ding
DGIR gird
grid
DGIS digs
DGIU guid
DGLO gold
DGNO dong
DGNU dung
DGOO △good
DGOS dogs
gods
DGOW gowd
DGOY dogy
DGRU drug
DHIL hild
DHIN hind
DHIS dish
DHIW whid
DHKU khud
DHLO hold
DHNO hond
DHOO hood
DHOS dohs
dosh
shod
DHOT doth
DHOW dhow
who'd
DHOZ dzho
DHSU dush
DHTU thud
DIIM △midi
DIIN nidi
DIIR irid
DIIV divi
DIIX dixi
DIJR jird
DIKL kild
DIKN dink
kind
DIKR dirk
DIKS disk
skid
ski'd
DILL dill
DILM mild
DILN lind
DILO idol
lido
loid
olid
DILR dirl
DILS sild
slid
'slid
DILV vild
DILW △wild
DILY idly
idyl
DIMN mind
DIMO modi
DIMU muid
DINO nodi
Odin
DINR rind
DINS sind
DINT dint
tind
DINW wind
DIOT doit
DIOV void
DIPR drip
DIQU quid
DIRT dirt
DIRY yird
DISS diss
DISU suid
DITT ditt
DITY tidy
DIVY ivy'd
DIXY dixy
DJOO dojo
DJOU judo
DJUY △judy
DKNO kond
DKNU dunk
DKNY kynd
DKOO dook
DKOR dork
DKRU Kurd
DKSU dusk
DKUU kudu
DLLO doll
DLLU dull
DLMO mold
DLOO dool
DLOP plod
DLOR △lord
DLOS olds
sold
DLOT dolt
told
DLOU loud
ludo
ould
DLOW dowl
wold
DLOY odyl
oldy
yold
DLUY duly
DMOO doom
mood
DMOR dorm
DMOS △mods
DMOT MOT'd
DMOY domy
DMPU dump
DMRU drum
DNOP △pond
DNOS snod
DNOT don't
DNOU undo
DNOW down
DNOY yond
DNRU durn
nurd
rund
DNRY rynd
DNSY synd
DNTU dunt
tund
DNTY tynd
tyn'd
DNWY wynd
DOOP pood
DOOR door
odor
△rood
DOOS odso
DOOT to-do
DOOW wood
DOPR dorp
drop
△prod
DOPU doup
DOPW dowp
DOPY dopy
DOQU quod
DORR dorr
DORS sord
DORT dort
trod
DORU dour
duro
DORW drow
△word
DORY dory
DOSS doss
sods
DOST dost
DOSU duos
udos
DOSW dows
DOTU dout
DOTW dowt
DOTY doty
tody
DOUY you'd
DOXY doxy
DOYZ dozy
DPSU spud
DPUU pudu
DRSU surd
DRTU turd
DRUU Urdu
DRUY urdy
DRUZ Druz
DSSU suds
DSTU dust
stud
DTUY duty

E

EEEP épée
EEFL feel
flee
EEFM feme
EEFR feer
fere
free
reef
EEFT feet
fête
EEGH ghee
EEGK geek
EEGL glee
EEGN gene
gêne
EEGO ogee
EEGP geep
EEGR eger
gere
gree
EEGU euge
EEGZ Geëz
EEHH he-he
EEHL heel
hele
EEHM heme
EEHR here
EEHT ethe
hete
thee
EEHW whee
EEIN eine
EEJL jeel
EEJP Jeep
EEJR jeer
EEJT jeté
EEJZ Jeez
EEKK keek
EEKL keel
leek
leke
EEKM meek
EEKN keen
knee
EEKP keep
peek
peke
EEKR reek
reke
EEKS seek
EEKW week
EELM leme

EELP	leep
	peel
	△pele
EELR	leer
	lere
	reel
EELS	else
	lees
	lese
	seel
	sele
	slee
EELT	leet
	teel
EELV	leve
	vele
EELW	weel
EELY	eely
EELZ	leze
EEMN	mene
	neem
EEMR	meer
	mere
EEMS	mese
	seem
	semé
	smee
EEMT	meet
	mete
	teem
	teme
EEMU	emeu
EEMV	meve
EEMW	weem
EEMZ	meze
	mézé
	mzee
EENN	nene
EENP	neep
	peen
	pene
EENR	erne
	ne'er
	reen
EENS	esne
	seen
	snee
EENT	eten
	nete
	teen
	tene
EENV	eevn
	eev'n
	even
	névé
EENW	enew
	ween
EENY	eyne
EEOV	evoe
EEPP	peep

EEPR	peer
	père
	pree
EEPS	seep
EEPV	veep
EEPW	weep
EERS	Erse
	seer
	sere
EERT	rete
	teer
	tree
EERV	ever
	veer
EERW	ewer
	were
	we're
EERY	eery
	eyre
EESS	esse
	sese
EESW	swee
EESX	exes
EESY	eyes
EETT	tête
EETV	evet
EETW	twee
	weet
EEVW	we've
EEVY	yeve
EEWX	wexe
EEZZ	zeze
EFFI	fief
	fife
EFFJ	jeff
EFFT	teff
EFGL	fleg
EFGS	fegs
EFHM	△fehm
EFHT	heft
EFIK	Efik
	fike
EFIL	file
	lief
	life
EFIN	feni
	fine
	neif
	nief
	nife
EFIR	fire
	reif
	rife
EFIS	feis
	seif
EFIT	E-fit®
EFIV	five
EFIW	wife
EFKR	kerf
EFKY	fyke
EFLL	fell
EFLO	floe

EFLP	pelf
EFLS	self
EFLT	felt
	△left
EFLU	flue
	fuel
EFLW	flew
EFLX	flex
EFLY	fley
	fyle
EFMR	ferm
EFMU	fume
EFNO	foen
	fone
EFNR	fern
EFNT	fent
EFOR	fore
	orfe
EFOS	foes
EFRS	serf
EFRT	fret
	reft
	terf
	tref
EFRY	ryfe
EFSS	fess
EFST	fest
EFSU	fuse
EFTT	fett
EFTW	weft
EFUZ	fuze
EGGL	gleg
EGGS	eggs
EGGT	tegg
EGGY	eggy
	yegg
EGHP	pegh
EGHU	eugh
	huge
EGIL	glei
EGIN	gien
EGIS	egis
EGIT	geit
	gite
	gîte
	tige
EGIV	give
EGKS	skeg
EGLN	glen
	leng
EGLO	goel
	gole
	Lego®
	loge
	ogle
EGLT	gelt
EGLU	glue
	gule
	luge
EGLY	gley
EGMN	meng
EGMR	germ

EGMU	△geum
EGNO	gone
	Ogen
EGNR	gren
EGNS	gens
EGNT	gent
EGNU	genu
EGOR	ergo
	goer
	gore
	ogre
	rego
EGOS	geos
	goes
	sego
EGOT	toge
EGOY	goey
	ygoe
EGRS	ergs
EGRU	grue
	urge
EGRW	grew
EGRY	grey
	gyre
EGST	gest
EGTU	tegu
EGTY	gyte
EGVY	gyve
EHIK	hike
EHIL	heil
EHIR	heir
	hire
EHIV	hive
EHJU	Jehu
EHKO	hoke
EHKS	kesh
EHKY	hyke
EHLL	△hell
	he'll
EHLM	helm
EHLO	hole
EHLP	help
EHLR	herl
	lehr
EHLU	hule
EHLY	hyle
EHMO	home
EHMP	hemp
EHMR	herm
EHMS	mesh
EHMT	them
EHMV	△vehm
EHNO	hone
EHNR	hern
EHNS	nesh
EHNT	hent
	then
EHNW	hewn
	when
EHNY	hyen
EHOP	hope

EHOR	△hero
	hoer
	hore
EHOS	hose
	shoe
EHOT	hote
EHOV	hove
EHOW	howe
EHPS	hesp
EHPT	hept
EHPW	phew
EHPY	hype
EHRR	Herr
EHRS	hers
EHRT	tehr
EHRU	huer
EHRW	whe'r
EHRY	hery
EHSS	shes
	she's
EHST	Esth
	hest
	shet
EHSW	shew
EHTW	thew
	whet
EHTY	they
EHWW	whew
EHWY	whey
EIJV	jive
EIKK	kike
EIKL	like
EIKM	mike
EIKN	kine
	Nike
EIKP	kepi
	kipe
	pike
EIKR	keir
	kier
	reik
EIKS	seik
	sike
EIKT	kite
	tike
EIKY	yike
EILM	lime
	mile
EILN	lien
	△line
EILP	pile
	plié
EILR	leir
	lier
	lire
	riel
	rile
EILS	isle
	seil
	sile

Words marked △ may be spelled also with a capital letter

EILT	lite
	teil
	tile
EILU	lieu
EILV	evil
	live
	veil
	vile
	vlei
EILW	weil
	wiel
	wile
EILX	ilex
EIMM	mime
EIMN	mein
	mien
	mine
EIMR	emir
	meri
	mire
	riem
	rime
EIMS	mise
	semi
EIMT	emit
	item
	mite
	△time
EINN	△nine
EINP	pein
	peni
	pine
EINR	rein
	rine
EINS	sien
	sine
EINT	nite
	tine
EINV	nevi
	vein
	vine
EINW	wine
EINZ	zein
EIOU	euoi
EIPP	pipe
EIPR	peri
	pier
	ripe
EIPS	pisé
	sipe
	spie
EIPT	piet
EIPW	wipe
EIPZ	pize
EIRS	reis
	rise
	seir
	sire
EIRT	rite
	tier
	tire
	trie
EIRU	iure
EIRV	rive
	vier
	vire
EIRW	weir
	wire
EIST	site
	stie
EISV	vise
	visé
EISW	wise
EISZ	size
EITT	tite
EITU	étui
EITV	vite
EITW	wite
EITX	△exit
EITY	yeti
	yite
EITZ	zite
EIVV	vive
EIVW	△view
	wive
EJKO	joke
EJKR	jerk
EJKU	juke
EJLL	jell
EJLO	jole
EJMS	Sejm
EJNP	J-pen
EJNU	June
EJOS	joes
EJOV	Jove
EJOY	△joey
EJRU	jure
EJSS	jess
EJST	jest
EJSU	Jesu
EJTU	△jute
EJUV	juve
EJUX	jeux
EKLL	kell
EKLO	loke
EKLP	kelp
EKLT	△kelt
EKLU	luke
EKLW	welk
EKLY	kyle
	yelk
	ylke
EKMO	moke
EKMP	kemp
EKMR	merk
EKNO	keno
EKNP	penk
EKNR	kern
	nerk
EKNT	kent
EKNU	neuk
	nuke
EKNW	knew
EKNY	kyne
EKOP	poke
EKOR	kore
	roke
EKOS	skeo
	soke
EKOT	toke
EKOW	woke
EKOY	yoke
EKPR	perk
EKPS	skep
	spek
EKPT	kept
EKPU	puke
EKRS	serk
	sker
EKRT	trek
EKRY	ryke
	yerk
EKST	kest
	△sekt
EKSW	skew
EKSY	Esky®
	esky
	△keys
	Skye
	syke
	yesk
EKTY	kyte
	tyke
EKUY	yeuk
	yuke
ELLM	mell
ELLP	pell
ELLS	sell
ELLT	tell
ELLU	Elul
ELLV	vell
ELLW	well
	we'll
ELLY	yell
ELMO	lome
	mole
ELMR	merl
ELMT	melt
ELMU	mule
ELMW	mewl
ELMY	elmy
	lyme
	yelm
	ylem
ELNO	leno
	lone
	Noel
	Noël
	nole
ELNS	△lens
ELNT	△lent
ELNU	lune
ELNY	lyne
ELOO	oleo
ELOP	lope
	olpe
	△pole
ELOR	eorl
	lore
	orle
	role
	rôle
ELOS	lose
	sloe
	sole
ELOT	lote
	tole
ELOV	love
	vole
ELOW	lowe
ELPR	lerp
ELPT	pelt
ELPU	pule
ELPY	yelp
ELRU	lure
	rule
ELRY	lyre
	rely
ELSS	less
	'less
ELST	lest
ELSU	lues
	slue
ELSW	slew
ELSY	lyse
	sley
ELTT	Lett
	telt
ELTU	lute
	tule
ELTW	△welt
ELTY	lyte
	yelt
ELUX	exul
	luxe
	ulex
ELUY	△yule
ELVY	levy
ELZZ	lezz
EMMO	memo
	mome
EMMY	Emmy
EMNN	nemn
EMNO	nome
	omen
EMNT	ment
EMNU	menu
	neum
EMOP	mope
	poem
	pome
EMOR	more
	omer
	Rome
EMOS	mose
	some
EMOT	mote
	tome
EMOU	moue
EMOV	move
EMOW	meow
EMOZ	moze
EMPR	perm
EMPT	temp
EMPY	ympe
EMRT	term
EMRU	mure
	rume
EMSS	△mess
EMST	stem
	tems
EMSU	△muse
EMSW	mews
	smew
EMSY	emys
EMTU	mute
EMYZ	zyme
ENNO	neon
	none
ENNV	Venn
ENOP	nope
	△open
	peon
	pone
ENOR	oner
	rone
ENOS	noes
	nose
	sone
ENOT	Eton
	note
	n'ote
	no'te
	tone
ENOV	oven
ENOW	enow
ENOX	exon
	oxen
ENOZ	zone
ENPR	pern
ENPS	EPNS
ENPT	pent
ENPU	Nupe
ENPY	pyne
ENRT	rent
	tern
ENRU	rune
ENRW	△wren
ENRY	reny
ENSS	ness
	sens
ENST	nest
	nets
	sent
	△sten
ENSW	news
	sewn

ENSY snye
syen
syne
ENTT nett
tent
ENTU tune
ENTV vent
ENTW newt
went
ENTX next
ENTY tyne
ENVY envy
EOOS oose
EOOZ ooze
EOPP pepo
△pope
EOPR pore
repo
rope
EOPS EPOS
epos
peso
pose
posé
EOPT poet
pote
tope
EOPX expo
EORR rore
EORS Eros
rose
rosé
sore
EORT rote
tore
EORU euro
roué
EORV over
rove
EORW ower
owre
wore
EORX oxer
EORY oyer
yore
EORZ zero
EOST toes
tose
EOSW woes
EOSY oyes
EOTT tote
EOTV veto
vote
EOTY eyot
toey
EOTZ toze
EOVW wove
EOWY yowe
EOYZ oyez
EPPR prep
repp
EPQU quep
EPRS reps
EPRT pert
EPRU Peru
puer
pure
EPRV perv
EPRX prex
EPRY prey
pyre
rype
EPSS seps
EPST pest
sept
△spet
step
EPSU spue
supe
EPSW spew
EPSY espy
sype
EPTW wept
EPTY pyet
type
EQUY quey
ERRS serr
ERST erst
rest
très
ERSU ruse
rusé
suer
sure
user
ERSV vers
ERTT tret
ERTU true
ERTV vert
ERTW trew
wert
ERTY trey
trye
tyre
ERTZ trez
ERVY △very
ERYY eyry
ESSS sess
ESSU uses
ESSY yes's
ESTT sett
stet
test
ESTU suet
Utes
ESTV vest
ESTW stew
△west
ESTX sext
ESTY stey
stye
yest
ESTZ zest
ESUZ Zeus
ESWY swey
ESXY sexy
ETTX text
ETTY tyte
yett
ETVX vext
ETWY wyte

F

FFFU fuff
FFGO goff
FFGU guff
FFHU huff
FFIJ jiff
FFIM miff
FFIN niff
FFIR riff
FFIT tiff
FFIY iffy
FFIZ ziff
FFKO koff
FFLU luff
FFMU muff
FFNU nuff
FFOT toff
FFPU puff
FFRU ruff
FFTU tuff
FGIO figo
FGIR frig
FGIT gift
FGLO flog
golf
FGLU △gulf
FGNU fung
FGOO goof
FGOR △frog
FGOW gowf
FGOY fogy
FHII hi-fi
FHIS fish
FHMU humf
FHNO föhn
FHOO hoof
FHOU houf
FHOW howf
FIIN fini
FIKN fink
FIKR firk
FIKS fisk
FIKY fiky
FILL fill
FILM film
FILO filo
foil
lo-fi
FILP flip
FILS fils
FILT flit
lift
FILX flix
FIMR firm
FINN Finn
FINO fino
foin
info
FINR firn
FIOS Sofi
FIRS fris
FIRT frit
rift
FIRZ friz
FIST fist
fits
sift
FISU Sufi
FITT fitt
tift
FIZZ fizz
FKLO folk
FKNU funk
FKOR fork
FLLU full
FLOO fool
loof
FLOP flop
FLOR flor
FLOT loft
FLOU foul
FLOW flow
fowl
wolf
FLOX flox
FLRU furl
FLUX flux
FMOR form
from
FMUY fumy
FNOT font
FOOP poof
FOOR roof
FOOT foot
FOOW woof
FOOY yoof
FOPR △prof
FOPU pouf
FORT fort
FORU four
FORW frow
FOSS foss
FOST soft
FOSU ufos
FOSW sowf
FOTT toft
FOTU tofu
FOWW wowf
FOXY foxy
FOYZ fozy
FRRU furr
FRSU surf
FRTU turf
FRUY △fury
FRUZ zurf
FSSU fuss
FSTU fust
FTTU tuft
FTUY yuft
FUZZ fuzz

G

GGHO hogg
GGIN ging
GGIR grig
rigg
GGLU glug
GGNO gong
nogg
GGOO gogo
go-go
GGOR grog
GHHI high
GHHO hogh
GHIN hing
nigh
GHIS sigh
GHIT thig
GHIW △whig
GHNO hong
GHNU hung
GHOS gosh
shog
GHOT Goth
GHOY yogh
GHPU pugh
GHSU gush
GHTU thug
GHUY hugy
GIKN gink
△king
GILL gill
GILM glim
GILN ling
GILR girl
GILS Glis
GILT gilt
glit
GILU ugli®
GIMN △ming
GIMP gimp
GIMR grim
GIMS gism
GINN ginn
GINO ingo
GINP ping
GINR girn
grin
ring
GINS sign
sing
snig
GINT ting
GINW wing
GINZ zing
GIOR △giro
GIOS gios
GIOY yogi

GIPR	grip
	prig
GIRR	girr
GIRS	gris
GIRT	girt
	grit
	trig
GIST	gist
GISW	swig
GITW	twig
GIZZ	gizz
GKNO	Gonk®
	gonk
GKNU	gunk
GKOO	gook
GKOU	gouk
GKOW	gowk
GKSU	skug
GLLU	gull
GLMO	glom
GLMU	glum
GLNO	long
GLNU	lung
GLOO	gool
	logo
GLOP	glop
	golp
GLOS	slog
GLOW	glow
	gowl
GLOY	logy
GLPU	gulp
	plug
GLRU	gurl
GLSU	slug
GLTU	glut
GLUY	guly
	ugly
GMNO	mong
	'mong
GMNU	mung
GMOO	Moog®
GMOR	gorm
GMOS	smog
GMPU	gump
GMPY	gymp
GMRU	grum
GMSU	smug
GNNO	nong
GNOO	goon
	no-go
GNOP	pong
GNOR	rong
GNOS	snog
	song
GNOT	tong
GNOW	gown
GNRU	gurn
	rung
GNSU	gnus
	guns
	snug
	△sung
GNUZ	Günz
GNYY	gyny
GOOP	goop
	pogo
GOOR	goor
GOPR	gorp
	prog
GOPU	Ogpu
	upgo
GORT	grot
	trog
GORW	grow
GORY	gory
	gyro
	orgy
GOSS	Goss
GOST	togs
GOSY	goys
GOTU	gout
	goût
GRTU	trug
GRUU	guru
GSTU	gust
	guts
GSUY	guys

H

HHIS	hish
HHOP	phoh
HHOS	hohs
HHSU	hush
HIIL	hili
HIKO	hoik
	hoki
HIKS	kish
	Sikh
HIKT	kith
HILL	hill
HILO	Holi
HILT	hilt
	lith
HIMS	shim
HIMW	whim
HINS	hisn
	his'n
	shin
	sinh
HINT	hint
	thin
HINW	whin
HIPS	pish
	ship
HIPT	hipt
	pith
HIPW	whip
HIPZ	phiz
HIRS	shir
	Shri
HIRT	thir
HIRW	whir
HISS	hiss
HIST	hist
	shit
	sith
	this
	Tshi
HISU	huis
HISV	shiv
HISW	wish
HITW	△whit
	with
HIWZ	whiz
HIZZ	hizz
HJNO	△john
HJOS	josh
HKLO	kohl
HKLU	hulk
HKNO	honk
HKNU	hunk
HKOO	hook
HKOP	koph
HKOR	khor
HKOW	howk
HKRU	rukh
HKSU	husk
	sukh
HLLU	hull
HLMO	holm
HLOP	holp
HLOS	hols
	losh
HLOT	holt
	loth
HLOW	howl
HLOY	holy
HLRU	hurl
HLSU	lush
	shul
HLWY	hwyl
HMNY	hymn
HMOO	△homo
	Moho
HMOR	mohr
HMOS	mhos
	Mohs
	shmo
HMOT	moth
HMOW	whom
HMOY	homy
HMPU	hump
	umph
HMSU	mush
HMTY	myth
HNOO	hoon
HNOP	phon
HNOR	horn
HNOS	nosh
HNOT	thon
HNOU	Huon
HNSU	shun
	'shun
HNTU	hunt
HOOP	hoop
	pooh
HOOS	ohos
	shoo
	soho
	so-ho
HOOT	hoot
	toho
HOOY	yo-ho
HOPQ	qoph
HOPS	hops
	phos
	posh
	△shop
	soph
HOPT	phot
HOPU	ouph
HOPW	whop
HOPY	hypo
HORS	hors
	rhos
HORT	Thor
	thro
	thro'
HORU	hour
HOSS	hoss
HOST	△host
	hots
	shot
	tosh
HOSU	huso
HOSW	show
	who's
HOTU	hout
	thou
HOTW	whot
HOWW	whow
HPRU	pruh
HPSU	push
HPTU	phut
HRSU	rhus
	rush
HRTU	hurt
	ruth
	thru
HSSU	huss
HSTU	shut
	thus
	tush

I

IIKT	tiki
IIKW	kiwi
IILP	pili
IILW	wili
IIMN	mini
IIMP	impi
IIMR	miri
IIMS	simi
IINS	nisi
IINT	inti
IIPP	pipi
IIPT	tipi
IIRS	iris
	siri
IISW	iwis
IITT	titi
IITZ	ziti
IJKN	jink
IJLL	jill
IJLT	jilt
IJMP	jimp
IJMS	jism
IJNN	jinn
IJNO	join
IJNX	jinx
IJOR	roji
IJOS	sijo
IJZZ	jizz
IKKN	kink
IKKR	△kirk
IKLL	kill
IKLM	milk
IKLN	kiln
	link
IKLO	kilo
	Loki
IKLP	kilp
IKLR	lirk
IKLS	lisk
	silk
IKLT	kilt
IKMN	mink
IKMO	moki
IKMR	mirk
IKMS	skim
IKNO	ikon
	kino
	oink
IKNP	pink
IKNR	kirn
	rink
IKNS	sink
	skin
IKNT	knit
	tink
IKNW	wink
IKNY	inky
IKOS	skio
IKPP	△kipp
IKPS	skip
	spik
IKRS	kris
	risk
IKRU	kuri
IKRY	yirk
IKSS	kiss
	skis
IKST	kist
	skit
ILLL	lill

ILLM	mill
ILLN	nill
	n'ill
ILLO	Lilo®
	lilo
ILLP	pill
ILLR	rill
ILLS	sill
ILLT	it'll
	lilt
	till
ILLV	vill
ILLW	will
ILLY	illy
	lily
	yill
ILMN	limn
ILMO	limo
	milo
	moil
ILMP	limp
	plim
ILMS	△slim
ILMT	milt
ILMU	muil
ILMY	limy
ILNN	linn
ILNO	lino
	△lion
	loin
	noil
ILNR	nirl
ILNT	lint
ILNY	inly
	liny
ILOO	olio
ILOR	loir
	roil
ILOS	oils
	silo
	soil
	soli
ILOT	toil
ILOV	viol
ILOY	oily
ILPR	pirl
ILPS	lips
	△lisp
	Pils
	slip
ILRT	tirl
ILRV	virl
	vril
ILST	list
	'list
	silt
	slit
ILTT	tilt
ILTU	luit
ILTW	wilt
ILWY	wily
IMNO	mino
IMNT	mint
IMNX	minx
IMNY	miny
IMOO	mooi
IMOS	miso
IMOT	moit
	omit
IMPP	pimp
IMPR	prim
IMPS	simp
IMPU	pium
IMPW	wimp
IMQU	quim
IMRS	mirs
	smir
IMRT	trim
IMRU	muir
	rimu
	Urim
IMRV	MIRV
	mirv
IMRY	miry
	rimy
IMSS	△miss
IMST	mist
	smit
IMSU	Sium
IMSW	swim
IMTT	mitt
IMTU	muti
IMTX	mixt
IMTY	mity
IMXY	mixy
IMZZ	mizz
INNW	winn
INOP	pion
INOR	inro
	△iron
	nori
	roin
INOT	into
	not-I
	oint
INOU	Unio
INOV	vino
INOW	wino
INOY	yoni
INOZ	Zion
INPR	pirn
INPS	pins
	snip
	spin
INPT	pint
INPY	piny
INQU	quin
INRT	trin
INRU	ruin
INST	inst
	isn't
INTT	tint
INTU	unit
INTV	vint
INTW	twin
	win't
INTY	tiny
INUZ	Zuni
	Zuñi
INVY	viny
INWY	winy
INXY	Iynx
	nixy
IOPT	topi
IOPY	pioy
IORS	sori
IORT	riot
	roti
	tiro
	tori
	trio
IORV	rivo
IOVV	vivo
IPPR	ripp
IPPS	pips
IPPY	pipy
IPQU	quip
IPRS	risp
IPRT	ript
	trip
IPRU	puir
	puri
IPRX	Prix
IPSS	piss
IPST	pits
	spit
IPSV	spiv
IPSW	wisp
IPSY	I-spy
	yips
IPTT	tipt
IPTU	Tupi
	Tupí
IPTY	pity
IPXY	pixy
IQTU	quit
IQUZ	quiz
IRRT	tirr
IRSS	Riss
IRST	stir
IRTT	ritt
IRTW	writ
IRTZ	△ritz
IRWY	wiry
ISSS	siss
ISST	sist
ISTT	tits
ISTU	suit
	utis
ISTW	wist
	wits
ISUZ	Uzis
ISWY	ywis
ISWZ	swiz
ISYZ	sizy
ITTW	twit
ITZZ	tizz
IVYZ	vizy
IZZZ	zizz

J

JJUU	juju
	ju-ju
JKNU	junk
JKOO	jook
JKOU	jouk
JKOY	joky
JLLO	joll
JLOT	jolt
JLOW	jowl
JLUY	July
JMOO	jomo
	mojo
JMPU	jump
JNOU	Juno
JNXY	△jynx
JORU	jour
JOSS	joss
JRUY	jury
JSTU	just

K

KKNO	konk
KKOO	kook
KKUU	kuku
KLOO	kolo
	look
KLOP	polk
KLOS	skol
KLOU	oulk
KLOV	volk
KLOY	yolk
KLPU	pulk
KLRU	lurk
KLSU	lusk
	sulk
KMNO	monk
KMOO	moko
	mook
KMRU	murk
KMSU	musk
KNOO	nook
KNOP	knop
	ponk
KNOR	nork
KNOT	knot
	tonk
KNOW	know
KNOZ	zonk
KNPU	punk
KNRU	knur
KNSU	sunk
KNTU	knut
KOOP	pook
KOOR	Kroo
	rook
KOOS	sook
KOOT	koto
	toko
	took
KOPR	pork
KOPU	pouk
KOPY	poky
KORW	work
KORY	roky
	york
KOSS	koss
KOSU	souk
KOTU	touk
KOUY	youk
	yuko
KOUZ	zouk
KPUU	puku
KRSU	rusk
KRSY	skry
	skyr
KRTU	△turk
KRUU	kuru
KSTU	tusk
KUYY	yuky

L

LLLO	loll
LLLU	lull
LLMO	moll
LLMU	mull
LLNO	noll
LLNU	null
LLOP	△poll
LLOR	roll
LLOT	toll
LLPU	pull
LLUU	lulu
LLUW	wull
LMOO	loom
	mool
LMOT	molt
LMOY	moly
	moyl
LMPU	lump
	plum
LMRU	murl
LMSU	slum
LNOO	loon
LNOR	lorn
LNOU	loun
	noul
LNOW	lown
	nowl
LNOY	Lyon
	only
LNRU	nurl
LNTU	lunt
LNUV	vuln
LNXY	lynx
LOOP	loop
	polo
	pool
LOOR	loor

LOOS	loos
	solo
LOOT	loot
	loto
	tool
LOOW	wool
LOPP	plop
LOPS	slop
LOPT	plot
	polt
LOPU	loup
LOPW	△plow
LOPY	ploy
	poly
LORT	rotl
LORU	lour
	roul
LORY	lory
LOSS	loss
	löss
	sols
LOST	lost
	lots
	slot
	STOL
LOSU	soul
LOSW	slow
	sowl
LOTT	tolt
LOTU	lout
	△tolu
LOTV	volt
	VTOL
LOTW	lowt
LOWY	owly
	yowl
LPPU	pulp
LPRU	purl
LPSU	plus
LPUU	pulu
LPUY	puly
LRSU	slur
LRUY	ruly
LSTU	lust
	slut
LSUU	△sulu
LTUZ	lutz
LUUZ	△zulu

M

MMMU	mumm
MMPU	mump
MNOO	mono
	△moon
MNOR	morn
	norm
MNOU	muon
MNOW	mown
MNOY	mony
MNTU	munt
MOOP	moop
MOOR	△moor
	Moro
	room
MOOS	soom
MOOT	moot
	toom
MOOZ	zoom
MOPP	Mopp
	pomp
MOPR	PROM
	prom
	romp
MOPU	moup
MOPY	mopy
	yomp
MORT	mort
MORU	roum
MORW	worm
MOSS	moss
MOST	most
MOSU	muso
	soum
	sumo
MOSW	sowm
MOTT	mott
MOTU	△motu
MOUV	ovum
MOZZ	mozz
MPPU	pump
MPRU	△rump
MPSU	sump
MPTU	tump
MPTY	tymp
	ympt
MPUY	pumy
	yump
MRSU	smur
MRTU	turm
MRUW	Würm
MSSU	muss
MSTU	must
	smut
	stum
MSUW	swum
MTTU	mutt

N

NNOO	no-no
	noon
NNOR	Norn
NNOU	non-U
	noun
NNOW	nown
NNSU	sunn
NNWY	wynn
NOOP	noop
	poon
NOOR	roon
NOOS	oons
	soon
NOOT	onto
	oont
	toon
NOOW	woon
NOOZ	zoon
NOPR	porn
NOPS	pons
NOPT	pont
NOPU	noup
	upon
NOPW	pown
NOPY	pony
NORS	sorn
NORT	ront
	torn
	tron
NORU	ourn
NORW	worn
NOST	onst
	snot
	tons
NOSU	nous
	onus
NOSW	snow
	sown
NOSY	nosy
NOTT	nott
NOTU	nout
	toun
	unto
NOTW	nowt
	town
	wont
	won't
NOTY	△tony
	yont
NOWY	nowy
NOXY	onyx
NPSU	spun
NPTU	punt
NPUY	puny
NPXY	Pnyx
NRRU	nurr
NRSU	runs
NRTU	runt
	turn
NSTU	nuts
	stun
NTUY	tuny
NUXY	yunx

O

OOPP	oppo
	poop
OOPR	poor
	proo
	roop
OOPS	oops
	soop
OOPT	poot
OOPY	yoop
OORR	ro-ro
OORT	root
OOSS	so-so
OOST	soot
OOSY	oosy
OOTT	otto
	toot
OOTW	woot
	woo't
OOUZ	ouzo
OOYY	yo-yo
OOYZ	oozy
OPPR	prop
OPPS	pops
OPPZ	zopp
OPQU	quop
OPRS	pros
OPRT	port
OPRU	pour
	roup
OPRW	prow
OPRY	pory
	pyro
	ropy
OPSS	poss
OPST	post
	pots
	spot
	stop
	tops
OPSU	opus
	soup
OPSW	sowp
	swop
OPSY	posy
OPTT	pott
OPTU	pout
OPTY	pyot
	typo
OPXY	poxy
OPZZ	pozz
ORRT	rort
	torr
ORRY	rory
ORST	orts
	rost
	sort
ORSU	ours
	sour
ORSY	rosy
ORTT	tort
	△trot
ORTU	rout
	tour
ORTW	rowt
	trow
	wort
ORTY	ryot
	Tory
	troy
	tyro
ORUX	roux
ORUY	your
ORVW	vrow
ORXY	oryx
OSSS	soss
OSST	toss
OSSU	sous
OSTT	stot
	tost
OSTU	oust
	outs
	sout
OSTW	stow
	swot
	wost
	wots
OTTU	tout
OTTW	towt
OTWY	towy

P

PRRU	purr
	rurp
PRSU	spur
PRSY	prys
	spry
PRTY	tryp
PSST	psst
PSSU	puss
PSUY	upsy
PTTU	putt
PTUZ	putz

R

RRUU	ruru
RSSU	Russ
RSTU	rust
RSUU	urus
RTUY	yurt

S

SSSU	suss
SSUU	Susu
SSUW	wuss
STTU	tuts
STXY	xyst

T

TTUU	tutu
TUZZ	tuzz

A

AAABC	abaca
	Caaba
AAABK	Kaaba
AAABR	araba
AAABY	abaya
AAAFR	afara
AAAGM	Agama
AAAKM	kaama
AAALP	alaap
	alapa
AAANN	anana
AAANS	asana
AABBK	kabab
AABCC	bacca
AABCI	abaci
AABCK	aback
AABCL	cabal
AABCR	barca
AABCS	cabas
AABDL	labda
AABDN	aband
	banda
AABEM	abeam
	ameba
AABER	abear
AABES	abase
AABET	abate
AABFT	abaft
AABGM	gamba
AABHI	Bahai
	Baha'i
AABHS	abash
AABIL	labia
AABIN	△bania
AABJN	△bajan
AABJR	bajra
AABJU	Bajau
AABKS	abask
AABLN	Alban
	banal
	nabla
AABLR	labra
AABLS	balas
	balsa
	basal
	Sabal
AABLT	tabla
AABMM	mamba
AABMN	amban
AABMR	abram
AABMS	samba
AABNS	basan
AABNT	Banat
AABNU	abuna
AABNW	bwana
	nawab
AABOR	aroba
AABRS	sabra
AABRT	rabat
AABRV	brava
AABRY	abray
	Araby
AABRZ	bazar
	zabra
AABST	basta
AABSU	sauba
AABTT	batta
AACCE	caeca
AACCO	cacao
AACCY	yacca
AACDH	dacha
AACEI	aecia
AACEP	apace
AACER	areca
AACFI	facia
AACHK	kacha
AACHP	△pacha
AACHR	chara
AACHY	chaya
AACIR	acari
AACKL	alack
AACLL	calla
AACLN	canal
AACLP	calpa
AACLS	scala
AACMN	caman
AACMS	camas
AACMW	macaw
AACNN	canna
AACNT	△tacan
AACNZ	Anzac
AACPR	carap
	Parca
AACPS	scapa
AACRS	sacra
AACRT	carat
	carta
AACSU	causa
AACSW	AWACS
AACUV	vacua
AADDR	adrad
AADDX	addax
AADEG	adage
AADEH	ahead
AADEL	aldea
AADER	Ardea
	aread
AADFL	afald
AADFR	daraf
	fa'ard
	farad
AADGG	dagga
AADGR	darga
	garda
AADHL	hadal
AADIN	Diana
	naiad
AADIP	apaid
AADKY	Dayak
AADLN	aland
AADLS	salad
AADLT	datal
AADMM	△madam
AADMN	adman
	ad-man
	daman
AADMP	padma
AADMR	damar
	drama
AADMS	Adam's
AADNP	panda
AADOR	A-road
AADPT	adapt
AADPY	apayd
AADRR	radar
AADRS	Ardas
AADRW	award
AADSY	adays
AADSZ	sadza
AADTY	adyta
AAEFR	afear
AAEGL	△algae
	galea
AAEGP	agape
	apage
AAEGT	agate
	a'gate
AAEGV	agave
AAEGZ	agaze
AAEHP	aheap
AAEKL	Akela
AAEKP	apeak
AAEKW	awake
AAELP	palea
AAELR	areal
AAELT	alate
	talea
AAELV	avale
AAEMR	arame
	marae
AAEMS	Saame
AAEMT	amate
AAEMZ	amaze
AAENP	apnea
	△paean
AAENR	anear
	arena
AAENT	antae
AAENV	Avena
AAERR	arear
AAERS	rasae
AAERT	reata
AAERU	aurae
AAERW	aware
AAEVW	awave
AAFFJ	Jaffa
AAFHL	halfa
AAFIM	△mafia
AAFIN	Naafi
AAFIT	tafia
AAFJL	aflaj
	falaj
AAFLN	fanal
AAFLT	fatal
AAFNU	fauna
AAFRY	yarfa
AAFTW	fatwa
AAGHL	galah
AAGIL	agila
AAGIM	agami
AAGIN	again
AAGIS	saiga
AAGIT	taiga
AAGJN	ganja
AAGKN	kanga
AAGLL	algal
AAGLM	Galam
AAGLN	alang
	lagan
AAGLR	argal
	graal
AAGLV	vagal
AAGLY	gayal
AAGLZ	gazal
AAGMM	gamma
	magma
AAGMN	manga
AAGMR	grama
AAGMT	tagma
AAGMY	gamay
AAGNN	ngana
AAGNP	pagan
	panga
AAGNR	argan
AAGNT	tanga
AAGNU	guana
AAGOR	agora
AAGPR	Apgar
AAGRT	targa
AAGST	agast
AAGSV	avgas
AAGUV	guava
AAHHT	hatha
AAHJL	jhala
AAHJR	rajah
AAHKL	kahal
AAHKM	hakam
AAHKS	kasha
AAHKY	khaya
AAHLL	Allah
	halal
AAHLM	almah
	halma
	hamal
AAHLN	△nahal
AAHLO	aloha
AAHLP	alpha
AAHLR	lahar
AAHLV	halva
AAHMO	△haoma
AAHMR	haram
	marah
AAHMS	shama
AAHMU	mahua
AAHMW	mahwa
AAHMZ	hamza

Words marked △ may be spelled also with a capital letter

AAHNP hanap
AAHNS Hansa
AAHNT thana
AAHPS △pasha
AAHRR arrah
AAHRY rayah
AAHST hasta
AAHSU Hausa
AAHSW awash
sawah
AAHSY shaya
AAHTV tavah
AAIJN Jaina
AAIKK kaiak
AAIKL laika
AAIKS Sakai
sakia
AAILM lamia
AAILN liana
AAILS alias
AAILT Itala
AAILV avail
AAILX axial
AAILY aliya
AAIMN amain
amnia
anima
mania
AAIMR maria
AAIMS Masai
AAIMT Amati
AAIMZ zamia
AAINP apian
AAINR Arian
naira
AAINS Asian
Naias
AAINV avian
AAIPS paisa
AAIRT Arita
atria
raita
riata
taira
tiara
AAISS assai
AAISV Saiva
AAITW await
AAJLP jalap
AAJNN jnana
AAJNP japan
AAJNV Javan
AAJNW ajwan
jawan
AAJNZ zanja
AAJQR Qajar
AAJRT jarta
AAKKN Kanak
AAKKP pakka
AAKKS akkas
AAKKY kayak
yakka

AAKKZ Kazak
AAKLO koala
AAKLP kalpa
AAKLR kraal
AAKLT talak
AAKMR karma
makar
AAKNT △tanka
AAKOP poaka
AAKPP kappa
AAKPR parka
AAKRT karat
AAKST Sakta
AAKTZ zakat
AALLM llama
AALLN nalla
AALLP palla
AALLS salal
AALLU alula
AALLW walla
AALLY allay
AALMR alarm
malar
ramal
AALMT Malta
talma
tamal
AALMV malva
AALMX malax
AALMY Malay
AALNN annal
AALNS nasal
AALNT natal
AALNV naval
AALNY nyala
AALPP appal
△papal
AALPS palas
salpa
AALPT △talpa
AALPY palay
playa
AALPZ plaza
AALQT talaq
AALRT altar
artal
talar
tra-la
AALRU aural
laura
AALRV △arval
larva
lavra
AALRY alary
AALRZ lazar
AALSS Lassa
salsa
AALST △atlas
AALSV lavas
vasal
AALWY alway
AAMMM mamma

AAMMN amman
AAMNN manna
AAMNS saman
AAMNT atman
△manta
AAMNX axman
AAMNY Mayan
AAMNZ zaman
AAMOR aroma
AAMOS omasa
AAMPP pampa
AAMPR Parma
praam
AAMSS amass
massa
AAMTZ matza
AANNN nanna
AANNO Anona
AANNT annat
tanna
AANNW wanna
AANOX xoana
AANPP nappa
AANPR prana
AANPS sapan
AANPT Patna
AANPV pavan
AANPX panax
AANQT qanat
AANRS naras
Saran®
AANRT antar
antra
ratan
AANRU Anura
ruana
AANRV varan
varna
AANRW awarn
AANRY Aryan
Nayar
AANSS sansa
AANST Santa
Satan
AANSU sauna
AANTV avant
AAORT aorta
AAPPT tappa
AAPPW papaw
AAPPY appay
AAPRT apart
AAPST pasta
tapas
AAPTT attap
AAPTW watap
AAPWW pawaw
AARRS arras
AARRY array
AARST △rasta
tasar
AARSU auras

AARTT attar
Tatar
AARTY tayra
yarta
AASSY assay
AASTV avast
AASTY satay
AASWY asway
aways
AATXY ataxy
AATZZ tazza
ABBCO bobac
cabob
ABBCY cabby
ABBEE Babee
ABBEK kebab
ABBEL △babel
ABBER barbe
ABBEY abbey
ABBGY gabby
ABBIR △rabbi
ABBKO bobak
kabob
ABBLU babul
bubal
ABBMO A-bomb
ABBNO nabob
ABBOO baboo
ABBOT abbot
ABBQR bar-b-q
ABBRS barbs
ABBTY tabby
ABBYY yabby
ABCCO bacco
bocca
caboc
ABCCY baccy
ABCEE abcee
ABCEH beach
ABCEL cable
ABCER acerb
brace
caber
cabré
ABCHO cohab
ABCHR brach
ABCHT batch
ABCIN Binca®
cabin
ABCIO cobia
ABCIR baric
Carib
rabic
ABCIS △basic
ABCJO Jacob
ABCKL △black
ABCKR brack
ABCKS Backs
ABCNO bacon
banco
ABCNU Cuban

ABCOR	carob
	coarb
	cobra
ABCOV	vocab
ABCOZ	cobza
ABCRS	scrab
ABCRT	bract
ABCRY	carby
ABCSU	scuba
ABDDE	bedad
ABDDY	baddy
ABDEG	badge
	begad
	debag
ABDEI	abide
ABDEK	baked
ABDEL	abled
	blade
ABDEM	bemad
ABDEN	Bände
ABDEO	abode
	adobe
ABDER	ardeb
	beard
	bread
	debar
ABDES	based
	beads
ABDET	bated
ABDEU	daube
ABDEY	beady
ABDIL	ad-lib
ABDIR	braid
	rabid
ABDIT	tabid
ABDKL	balk'd
ABDLN	bland
ABDLU	blaud
ABDLY	badly
	baldy
ABDNR	brand
ABDNS	bands
ABDNY	bandy
ABDOR	abord
	bardo
	board
	broad
ABDOY	a'body
ABDRS	bards
	drabs
ABDRY	bardy
	Darby
ABDUY	dauby
ABDWY	bawdy
ABEEL	abele
	albee
ABEER	beare
ABEFL	fable
ABEGI	bigae
ABEGL	bagel
	belga
	gable
ABEGN	began
ABEGR	barge
	begar
	garbe
ABEGT	begat
ABEHJ	hejab
ABEHK	bekah
ABEHL	belah
	hable
ABEHM	H-beam
ABEHO	bohea
	obeah
ABEHR	rehab
ABEHS	Sheba
ABEHT	bathe
	beath
ABEIM	I-beam
ABEIR	erbia
ABEIS	abies
ABEIZ	baize
ABEJL	jelab
ABEJM	jambe
ABEKL	bleak
ABEKN	baken
ABEKR	△baker
	brake
	break
ABEKY	beaky
ABELL	all-be
	be-all
	label
ABELM	amble
	blame
	△melba
ABELR	abler
	baler
	blare
	blear
ABELS	blaes
	blasé
	sable
ABELT	ablet
	blate
	bleat
	table
ABELY	bayle
	belay
ABELZ	blaze
ABEMR	amber
	brame
	bream
	embar
ABEMS	Sabme
ABEMW	weamb
ABEMY	beamy
	embay
	maybe
ABENO	beano
ABENU	abune
ABEOR	abore
ABEOT	E-boat
ABEOV	above
ABEPT	bepat
ABERR	barre
	barré
	re-bar
ABERS	saber
	sabre
ABERV	brave
ABERY	barye
	beray
	yerba
ABERZ	braze
	zebra
ABESS	bases
	basse
ABEST	baste
	△beast
	Sebat
	tabes
ABESU	abuse
ABESY	absey
ABETU	beaut
	Butea
	taube
	tubae
ABEUX	beaux
ABEUZ	buaze
ABFFU	buffa
ABFFY	baffy
ABGGY	baggy
ABGHI	bigha
ABGHN	bhang
ABGIN	ba'ing
ABGMO	gambo
ABGNO	bogan
	obang
ABGNS	bangs
ABGNU	unbag
ABGOR	garbo
	gobar
ABGRS	grabs
ABHIJ	hijab
ABHIS	△sahib
ABHIT	habit
ABHLS	blash
ABHOR	abhor
ABHOS	basho
ABHRS	brash
ABHST	baths
ABHSU	subah
ABHTU	bahut
ABIIL	alibi
ABIIM	iambi
ABIIT	tibia
ABIJR	bajri
ABIKT	batik
ABILN	blain
ABILO	aboil
ABILQ	qibla
ABILR	brail
	△libra
ABILS	basil
	labis
ABIMR	abrim
	imbar
	mbira
ABIMS	Sabmi
ABIMT	ambit
ABINR	abrin
	bairn
	brain
ABINS	basin
	sabin
ABINU	bunia
	nubia
ABINV	bavin
ABIOT	biota
ABIRR	briar
ABIRU	△rubai
	Rubia
ABIRV	bravi
ABISS	basis
	bassi
ABIST	absit
ABIWZ	bwazi
ABJMO	jambo
ABJMU	jambu
ABJNO	banjo
ABJOT	jabot
ABKLN	blank
ABKLS	balks
ABKLU	baulk
ABKLY	balky
ABKNO	koban
ABKNR	brank
ABKOR	borak
ABKRU	burka
ABKRY	barky
	braky
ABLLS	balls
ABLLU	△bulla
ABLLY	bally
ABLMU	album
ABLMY	balmy
ABLOO	baloo
ABLOR	labor
	lobar
ABLOS	bolas
ABLOT	bloat
ABLOW	ablow
ABLRU	lubra
ABLRW	brawl
ABLST	blast
ABLTT	blatt
ABLTU	tubal
ABLWY	bylaw
ABLYY	lay-by
ABMMO	mambo
ABMOS	ambos
	sambo
ABMOZ	zambo
ABMRU	rumba
	umbra
ABMRY	ambry
	barmy

ABMSY abysm
ABNNS banns
ABNOR baron
ABNOS bason
ABNOT baton
ABNOZ bonza
ABNRU buran
unbar
urban
ABNRW brawn
ABNTU △bantu
△tabun
ABNUY bunya
ABOOT taboo
ABOOY ya-boo
ABOQT Q-boat
ABORR △arbor
ABORT abort
boart
tabor
ABORV bravo
ABORX borax
ABORY boyar
ABOSS basso
ABOST basto
boast
sabot
ABOTU about
U-boat
ABOTW bowat
ABOUY bayou
boyau
ABQRU burqa
ABQSU squab
ABRSS brass
ABRST Bart's
brast
ABRSU Abrus
bursa
ABRSW braws
ABRTU tubar
ABRTY rybat
ABRWY warby
ABRXY braxy
ABSSY abyss
bassy
ABSTT batts
ABSTU tabus
tsuba
tubas
ABTTY batty
ABUZZ abuzz
ABWYY byway
ACCDE Decca®
ACCDY cycad
ACCEH cache
chace
ACCEL cecal
ACCEM Mecca
ACCHI chica
ACCHK chack
ACCHO chaco
coach
ACCHT catch
ACCIR circa
ACCIT cacti
ticca
ACCIW △wicca
ACCKL clack
ACCKO acock
ACCKR crack
ACCMO occam
ACCOO cocoa
ACCOS casco
ACCOT coact
ACCOY accoy
ACCUY yucca
ACDDE decad
ACDDY caddy
ACDEE cadee
ACDEF faced
ACDEG cadge
caged
ACDEI cadie
ACDEL clade
decal
laced
ACDEN dance
ACDEP paced
ACDER acred
arced
cadre
cedar
ACDET cadet
ACDEY decay
ACDGY cadgy
ACDHR chard
ACDIL calid
ACDIN canid
cnida
nicad
ACDIR acrid
caird
cardi
daric
ACDIS Asdic
ACDIT diact
dicta
ACDLO acold
ACDLS scald
ACDLU cauld
ducal
ACDLY yclad
ACDNS scand
ACDNU adunc
Candu
ACDNY candy
ACDOR Draco
ACDOT octad
ACDRS cards
ACDRY cardy
darcy
ACDSS scads
ACDSU scaud
ACDTU ducat
ACEEK ackee
ACEEP peace
ACEES caese
cease
ACEEZ ceaze
ACEFH chafe
ACEFL fecal
ACEFR facer
farce
ACEFT facet
ACEGL glacé
ACEGR △grace
ACEGY cagey
ACEHK △cheka
haček
ACEHL chela
leach
ACEHN caneh
hance
nache
ACEHP chape
cheap
peach
ACEHR chare
rache
reach
ACEHS chase
ACEHT cheat
Hecat
tache
teach
theca
ACEHV chave
ACEIL Alice
ileac
ACEIM amice
ACEIN eniac
ACEIP Picea
ACEIR ceria
erica
ACEIS saice
ACEIV cavie
ACEKR crake
creak
ACEKS cakes
ACEKW wacke
ACEKY cakey
ACELL cella
ACELM camel
clame
macle
ACELN ancle
clean
lance
ACELP caple
△place
ACELR Clare
clear
recal
ACELS claes
△scale
ACELT cleat
éclat
lacet
ACELV calve
cavel
clave
ACELY lacey
ACEMO cameo
comae
ACEMR crame
cream
macer
ACENN △nance
ACENO canoe
ocean
ACENP pance
pecan
ACENR crane
crena
nacre
rance
ACENS scena
ACENT enact
ACEOR ocrea
ACEOT coate
ACEOX coxae
ACEPR caper
crape
pacer
Perca
recap
ACEPS paces
scape
'scape
space
ACEPT epact
ACEPY pacey
ACERR carer
crare
racer
ACERS acres
carse
races
scare
scrae
serac
sérac
ACERT caret
carte
cater
crate
react
recta
trace
ACERU Eruca
ACERV carve
caver
crave
varec
ACERX carex

ACERY	Carey
ACERZ	craze
ACEST	caste
	cates
	sceat
ACESU	cause
	'cause
	sauce
ACETT	tacet
ACETU	acute
ACETX	exact
ACETZ	Aztec
ACFFH	chaff
ACFFS	scaff
ACFHT	chaft
ACFHU	chufa
ACFIL	calif
ACFIM	mafic
ACFIR	Afric
	farci
ACFIS	fasci
ACFKL	flack
ACFKR	frack
ACFLO	focal
ACFLS	calfs
ACFNR	franc
ACFNY	fancy
ACFRS	scarf
ACFRT	craft
	fract
ACFRY	farcy
ACGHN	ganch
ACGIM	gamic
	magic
ACGIR	cigar
	craig
ACGLN	clang
ACGNO	conga
ACGOR	cargo
ACGOT	cagot
ACGOU	guaco
ACGRS	scrag
ACGUY	gaucy
ACGWY	gawcy
ACHHN	hanch
ACHHT	hatch
ACHIK	haick
ACHIN	chain
	Chian
	△china
ACHIO	chiao
ACHIR	chair
ACHIT	aitch
ACHKL	△chalk
ACHKN	chank
ACHKR	chark
ACHKS	shack
ACHKT	thack
ACHKW	whack
ACHLN	lanch
ACHLO	loach
ACHLR	larch
ACHLS	clash
ACHLT	latch
ACHLU	lauch
ACHLV	Vlach
ACHMO	macho
	△mocha
ACHMP	champ
ACHMR	charm
	△march
ACHMS	chasm
ACHMT	match
ACHNO	nacho
ACHNR	ranch
ACHNT	chant
	natch
ACHNU	nucha
ACHOP	△phoca
	poach
ACHOR	orach
	roach
ACHOS	chaos
	oshac
ACHOT	chota
	tacho
ACHOV	havoc
ACHPR	parch
ACHPS	chaps
	Pasch
ACHPT	patch
ACHRR	charr
ACHRS	chars
	crash
ACHRT	chart
	ratch
ACHRY	chary
ACHST	scath
ACHSU	sauch
ACHSW	schwa
ACHTW	watch
ACHTY	yacht
ACIIL	cilia
	△iliac
ACIIM	amici
ACIIN	acini
ACIIS	ASCII
ACIKS	saick
ACILL	lilac
ACILM	claim
	malic
ACILN	linac
ACILP	plica
ACILS	△salic
	scail
ACILT	cital
	ictal
	tical
ACILU	△aulic
ACILV	cavil
ACILX	calix
ACIMN	manic
	Nicam
ACIMR	cimar
	micra
ACIMS	camis
	micas
	misca'
ACINN	Incan
ACINO	conia
ACINP	panic
ACINR	cairn
	in-car
ACINS	Canis
	Sican
ACINT	actin
	antic
ACINV	vinca
ACIOS	ciaos
ACIOT	coati
ACIOZ	azoic
ACIPR	Capri
	carpi
	picra
ACIPS	aspic
	scapi
	spica
ACIPZ	capiz
ACIRT	artic
ACIRU	auric
	curia
ACIRV	△vicar
	vraic
ACITT	△attic
	tacit
ACITV	vatic
ACJKS	jacks
ACJKY	Jacky
ACJNU	△cajun
ACKKN	knack
ACKLN	clank
ACKLO	cloak
ACKLP	plack
ACKLS	slack
ACKLU	caulk
ACKMS	smack
ACKMU	amuck
ACKNR	crank
ACKNS	snack
ACKOR	croak
ACKOW	wacko
ACKPU	pucka
ACKQU	quack
ACKRT	track
ACKRW	wrack
ACKST	stack
ACKSW	swack
ACKTY	tacky
ACKWY	wacky
ACLLO	local
ACLLS	scall
ACLMO	cloam
	comal
ACLMP	clamp
ACLMS	calms
ACLMY	calmy
ACLNU	Lucan
ACLOP	copal
ACLOR	△calor
	carol
	claro
	△coral
ACLOS	coals
ACLOT	octal
ACLOV	vocal
ACLOW	cowal
ACLOX	coxal
ACLOY	coaly
ACLOZ	colza
ACLPS	clasp
	scalp
ACLPU	capul
ACLRT	clart
ACLRW	crawl
ACLRY	clary
	Lycra®
ACLSS	class
ACLSV	Sclav
ACLSY	scaly
ACLTU	claut
ACLTY	talcy
ACLXY	calyx
ACMMO	comma
ACMNO	Mâcon
	macon
ACMOP	campo
ACMOR	carom
	coram
	macro
ACMPR	cramp
ACMPS	scamp
ACMPY	campy
ACMRS	scram
ACMRY	cymar
ACMSU	camus
	Musca
	sumac
ACNNO	ancon
	canon
	cañon
ACNNY	canny
	△nancy
ACNOP	capon
ACNOR	acorn
	narco
	racon
ACNOS	Oscan
ACNOT	acton
	canto
ACNOW	cowan
ACNOX	caxon
ACNPU	uncap
ACNRS	narcs
	scran
ACNRY	carny
ACNST	canst
	scant

ACNTY	canty
ACOPR	copra
ACOPS	capos
	pacos
	scopa
ACOPT	capot
	coapt
ACORS	Oscar
ACORT	actor
	Croat
	taroc
ACORY	oracy
ACOST	ascot
	△coast
	costa
	tacos
ACOTT	cotta
ACPPU	cuppa
ACPRS	craps
	scarp
	scrap
ACPRY	crapy
ACPSU	scaup
ACPSY	spacy
ACPTU	caput
ACRRY	carry
ACRSS	crass
ACRST	scart
	scrat
ACRSU	arcus
	scaur
ACRSW	scraw
ACRSY	scary
	scray
ACRTT	T-cart
	tract
ACRTU	curat
ACRVY	carvy
ACRYZ	crazy
ACSSU	ascus
ACSTT	scatt
ACSTU	scuta
ACSUY	saucy
ACTTY	catty
ADDDY	daddy
ADDEI	aided
ADDEJ	jaded
ADDEL	addle
	dedal
	laded
ADDER	adder
	adred
	aredd
	dared
	dread
ADDET	dated
ADDEV	Vedda
ADDEZ	dazed
ADDFY	faddy
ADDIM	madid
ADDIO	addio
ADDIV	David
ADDNO	add-on
ADDNY	dandy
ADDOR	dorad
ADDOS	dados
ADDOT	add-to
ADDPY	△paddy
ADDRY	dryad
	ydrad
ADDWY	waddy
ADEEM	adeem
	edema
ADEER	arede
	deare
	eared
ADEES	aedes
ADEET	teade
	teaed
ADEEV	deave
	evade
ADEFG	fadge
ADEFM	famed
ADEFR	fader
ADEFT	defat
	fated
ADEFZ	fazed
ADEGG	gadge
ADEGJ	gadje
ADEGL	glade
ADEGM	madge
ADEGR	grade
	radge
	ragde
	raged
ADEGS	degas
ADEGT	gated
ADEGU	agued
ADEHJ	jehad
ADEHK	kheda
ADEHL	heald
ADEHR	heard
ADEHS	Hades
	heads
	sadhe
	shade
ADEHT	death
ADEHX	hexad
ADEHY	heady
ADEIL	eliad
	ideal
ADEIM	amide
	media
ADEIN	Adeni
	daine
ADEIR	aider
	irade
	redia
ADEIS	aside
	A-side
ADEIU	adieu
ADEIW	waide
ADEIZ	azide
ADEJW	jawed
ADEKL	Dalek
ADEKN	knead
	naked
ADEKR	daker
	drake
ADEKW	waked
ADELL	dalle
	ladle
ADELM	meal'd
	medal
ADELN	eland
	laden
	lande
ADELO	aloed
ADELP	padle
	pedal
	plead
ADELR	alder
ADELS	leads
	slade
ADELT	Datel®
	dealt
	delta
	lated
ADELW	dwale
	△weald
ADELY	delay
	leady
ADEMM	damme
ADEMN	amend
	deman
	maned
	named
ADEMR	armed
	derma
	dream
	mear'd
ADEMU	Medau
ADEMW	wamed
ADENN	an-end
ADENO	anode
ADENP	paned
ADENR	dearn
	redan
ADENS	sedan
	snead
ADENV	daven
	vaned
ADENW	awned
	dewan
	waned
ADENY	denay
ADEOP	apode
ADEOR	adore
	oared
	oread
ADEPR	drape
	padre
ADEPS	sepad
	spade
ADEPT	adept
	pated
ADEPU	eupad
ADEPV	paved
ADEPY	payed
ADERR	darre
	drear
ADERS	dares
	rased
	sared
ADERT	dater
	rated
	trade
	tread
ADERV	drave
ADERW	dewar
	wader
ADERY	deary
	deray
	rayed
	ready
	yeard
ADERZ	dazer
	razed
	zerda
ADEST	sated
	stade
	stead
ADESV	saved
	Vedas
ADESW	sawed
ADETX	taxed
ADEVW	advew
	waved
ADEWX	waxed
ADEWY	deawy
ADFFR	draff
ADFFY	daffy
ADFIV	vifda
ADFNO	fonda
ADFOS	fados
ADFRT	draft
ADFRU	faurd
	fraud
ADFRW	dwarf
ADGGY	daggy
ADGIL	algid
ADGLN	gland
ADGLY	glady
ADGMO	dogma
ADGNO	Dagon
	donga
	gonad
ADGNR	grand
ADGNW	dwang
ADGNY	gandy
ADGOO	agood
ADGOP	pagod
ADGOS	dagos
	gadso
ADGOT	toga'd
ADGOU	Gouda
ADGRU	guard
ADGSU	Gadus

ADGUY	gaudy
ADHIJ	hadji
	jihad
ADHIK	khadi
ADHIM	Mahdi
ADHIN	ahind
ADHIP	aphid
ADHIS	Hasid
	sidha
ADHJO	hodja
ADHLO	ahold
	halo'd
ADHLU	hauld
ADHNO	donah
ADHNS	hands
	shand
ADHNT	hadn't
ADHNY	handy
ADHOR	hoard
ADHRS	hards
	shard
	shar'd
ADHRY	hardy
	△hydra
ADHST	hadst
ADHSU	sadhu
ADHSY	Hyads
	shady
ADIIL	Iliad
ADIIN	I-and-I
ADIIO	Iai-do
	oidia
ADIIR	radii
ADIKN	kinda
ADIKU	aduki
ADILN	Ladin
	nidal
ADILO	dolia
ADILP	plaid
ADILR	drail
	laird
	liard
ADILS	slaid
ADILT	dital
	tidal
ADILU	dulia
ADILV	valid
ADILY	daily
ADIMN	admin
ADIMR	marid
ADIMS	Midas
ADIMT	admit
ADIMX	admix
ADINN	Nandi
ADINO	danio
ADINR	dinar
	drain
	Indra
	nadir
ADINT	daint
	Datin
ADINV	divan
	viand
ADINW	diwan
ADIOP	podia
ADIOR	aroid
	radio
ADIOS	adiós
	aidos
ADIOT	diota
ADIOU	audio
ADIOV	avoid
ADIOX	axoid
ADIOZ	diazo
ADIPR	pardi
	rapid
ADIPS	sapid
ADIPV	pavid
	vapid
ADIRR	ardri
	ard-ri
	raird
ADIRT	△triad
ADIRX	radix
ADIRY	dairy
	diary
ADIRZ	darzi
	izard
ADIST	staid
ADISY	daisy
	sayid
ADITU	audit
ADITV	davit
ADIVV	vivda
ADJSU	△judas
ADKKO	Kodak®
ADKLS	skald
ADKLY	alkyd
ADKMR	D-mark
ADKMU	dumka
ADKNR	drank
ADKNY	kandy
ADKOV	vodka
ADKRY	darky
ADKTU	Datuk
ADLLO	allod
	do-all
ADLLY	dally
	laldy
ADLMO	dolma
	domal
	modal
ADLMW	dwalm
ADLMY	madly
ADLNO	nodal
ADLNU	laund
ADLOP	L-dopa
	podal
ADLOS	loads
ADLOT	dotal
ADLOU	aloud
ADLPS	spald
ADLRU	dural
ADLRW	drawl
ADLRY	lardy
ADLST	stal'd
ADLSU	lauds
ADLSY	sadly
ADLTU	adult
	dault
	tauld
ADLUY	yauld
ADMNO	monad
	nomad
ADMNU	maund
	Munda
	undam
ADMOU	douma
ADMPY	dampy
ADMRU	mudra
ADMRY	mardy
ADMSU	adsum
ADMTU	datum
ADMUW	dwaum
ADNNO	Donna
ADNNU	nandu
ADNOO	doona
ADNOR	adorn
	radon
ADNOT	Donat
ADNOW	adown
	downa
	Wodan
ADNOZ	zonda
ADNPY	pandy
ADNRS	rands
ADNRT	drant
ADNRW	drawn
ADNRY	randy
ADNSS	sands
ADNST	stand
ADNSY	△sandy
	sdayn
ADNTU	daunt
ADNTY	daynt
ADOPS	spado
ADOPT	adopt
ADOQU	quoad
ADORR	ardor
ADORS	Doras
	dorsa
	roads
	sarod
	sorda
ADORT	troad
ADORU	douar
	doura
ADORW	dowar
ADOTY	toady
	today
ADOUY	Douay
ADPRS	spard
	sprad
ADPRY	pardy
ADPSY	paysd
	spayd
ADQSU	squad
ADQUY	quayd
ADRRU	durra
ADRST	darts
	strad
ADRSU	rudas
	Sudra
ADRSW	sward
ADRTY	tardy
ADRVY	vardy
ADSTU	adust
AEEFN	neafe
AEEFR	feare
AEEGL	aglee
	eagle
AEEGN	agene
AEEGR	agree
	eager
	eagre
	geare
	ragee
AEEGT	étage
AEEHM	heame
AEEHR	heare
AEEHT	eathe
AEEHV	heave
	△hevea
AEEIN	aînée
AEEIR	aerie
AEEKN	akene
AEEKP	apeek
AEEKR	rakee
AEEKW	a-week
AEELL	allée
AEELN	anele
AEELR	leare
	leear
AEELS	easel
	easle
	lease
AEELT	elate
	telae
AEELV	leave
	veale
AEELW	aweel
AEELY	aleye
AEELZ	leaze
AEEMM	mamee
AEEMN	amene
	enema
	meane
AEEMR	ameer
	meare
	ramee
	reame
AEEMS	mease
	seame
AEENR	ranee
AEENT	eaten
	enate

AEENV	naeve
	veena
	venae
AEEOZ	zoeae
AEEPR	peare
AEEPS	pease
AEEPT	étape
AEEPY	payee
AEEPZ	peaze
AEERR	arere
AEERS	erase
	saree
	seare
AEERT	arête
	eater
	reate
AEERV	reave
AEERZ	razee
AEESS	sease
AEEST	setae
	tease
AEESV	eaves
AEESZ	seaze
AEETX	exeat
AEETZ	teaze
AEEVW	weave
AEFFG	gaffe
AEFHS	sheaf
AEFIN	faine
AEFIR	afire
AEFKL	flake
AEFKN	kenaf
AEFKR	faker
	freak
AEFKS	fakes
AEFLL	fella
AEFLM	femal
	flame
	fleam
AEFLR	farle
	feral
	flare
AEFLS	false
AEFLT	aleft
	fetal
AEFLV	favel
AEFLY	leafy
AEFMR	frame
AEFNR	frena
AEFNY	fayne
AEFOR	afore
AEFOV	fovea
AEFRS	farse
AEFRT	after
	frate
	trefa
AEFRU	feuar
AEFRW	wafer
AEFRY	arefy
	faery
	fayre
AEFST	Fates
	feast
	festa
AEFTT	fetta
AEFTW	fetwa
AEFUV	Fauve
AEFUW	waefu'
AEGGO	agoge
AEGGR	agger
	eggar
AEGGU	gauge
AEGHP	phage
AEGHR	gerah
AEGIL	agile
AEGIM	image
AEGIR	Argie
AEGIS	aegis
AEGJR	jäger
AEGJU	gauje
AEGLL	legal
AEGLM	gleam
AEGLN	angel
	△angle
	genal
	glean
AEGLP	pagle
	plage
AEGLR	glare
	lager
	large
	regal
AEGLT	aglet
AEGLV	gavel
AEGLY	agley
AEGLZ	glaze
AEGMM	gamme
	gemma
AEGMN	mange
AEGMO	omega
AEGMR	grame
	marge
	regma
AEGMS	△games
AEGMY	gamey
AEGNO	agone
	△genoa
AEGNR	anger
	range
	renga
AEGNT	agent
AEGNU	nugae
AEGNV	△vegan
AEGNY	geyan
	gynae
AEGOS	Osage
AEGPR	gaper
	grape
	pager
	parge
AEGPS	gapes
	pages
AEGRR	garre
	rager
	regar
AEGRS	sarge
	segar
AEGRT	grate
	great
	targe
	terga
AEGRU	argue
	auger
AEGRV	grave
AEGRW	wager
AEGRY	aygre
	gayer
	yager
AEGRZ	gazer
	graze
AEGSS	gases
AEGST	getas
	stage
AEGSU	usage
AEGSW	swage
	wages
AEGUV	vague
AEGUZ	gauze
AEHHP	ephah
AEHHT	heath
AEHJR	hejra
AEHKN	kaneh
AEHKS	shake
AEHLM	almeh
	hemal
AEHLP	aleph
AEHLR	haler
AEHLS	halse
	leash
	selah
	shale
	sheal
AEHLT	ethal
	lathe
AEHLV	halve
AEHLW	△whale
	wheal
AEHLY	hayle
AEHLZ	hazel
AEHMN	he-man
	maneh
AEHMO	mahoe
AEHMR	harem
	herma
AEHMS	shame
	Shema
AEHMT	meath
	thema
AEHNN	henna
AEHNS	ashen
	Hanse
AEHNT	ahent
	neath
	'neath
	thane
AEHNV	haven
AEHNY	hyena
AEHPR	hepar
	phare
	raphe
	raphé
AEHPS	heaps
	Pesah
	phase
	shape
AEHPY	heapy
AEHRS	share
	shear
AEHRT	△earth
	hater
	heart
	rathe
	thrae
AEHRV	haver
AEHRW	whare
	whear
AEHRZ	hazer
AEHSS	△ashes
AEHST	ashet
	haste
	heast
AEHSU	hause
AEHSV	haves
	shave
	sheva
AEHSW	hawse
AEHTT	theta
AEHTU	haute
AEHTW	wheat
AEHVY	heavy
	Yahve
AEHWY	Yahwe
AEIKL	alike
	alkie
AEILM	e-la-mi
	△e-mail
	maile
	Melia
AEILN	alien
	aline
	A-line
	anile
	Elian
	liane
AEILP	pilea
AEILR	△ariel
	raile
AEILS	aisle
AEILT	telia
AEILV	alive
AEILX	axile
AEILZ	aizle

AEIMN	amine
	anime
	animé
	minae
AEIMR	maire
	ramie
	rimae
AEIMS	maise
AEIMZ	maize
AEINN	inane
AEINR	raine
AEINS	anise
	saine
AEINT	entia
	Teian
	tenia
	△tinea
AEINV	avine
	naevi
	naive
	naïve
AEINX	xenia
AEINZ	azine
AEIPR	paire
	perai
AEIPS	paise
	sepia
AEIPT	pietà
AEIRR	airer
AEIRS	aesir
	Aries
	arise
	raise
	serai
AEIRT	irate
	terai
AEIRU	aurei
AEIRV	vairé
AEIRY	aiery
	ayrie
AEIRZ	Azeri
	zaire
AEISV	avise
AEITT	tatie
AEITW	tawie
	waite
AEIVW	waive
AEIVZ	avize
AEJKS	jakes
AEJLP	lapje
AEJLV	△javel
AEJMS	james
AEJNS	jeans
AEJPR	japer
AEJPS	jaspe
	jaspé
AEJSY	jasey
AEKLN	ankle
AEKLR	laker
AEKLS	slake
AEKLT	latke
AEKLW	kwela
AEKLY	kayle
	leaky
AEKMM	kamme
AEKMR	△maker
AEKNO	oaken
AEKNP	pekan
AEKNR	anker
	Karen
	naker
	nerka
	ranke
AEKNS	skean
	snake
	sneak
AEKNT	taken
AEKNV	knave
AEKNW	waken
AEKOP	poake
AEKOR	oaker
AEKOT	atoke
AEKOW	awoke
AEKPS	spake
	speak
AEKPY	peaky
AEKQU	quake
AEKRR	raker
AEKRS	asker
	eskar
	kesar
	reaks
	saker
	skear
AEKRT	taker
AEKRW	waker
	wreak
AEKST	skate
	stake
	steak
AEKSU	ukase
AEKSW	askew
	wakes
AEKTW	tweak
AELLL	allel
AELLN	Allen
AELLP	lapel
AELLS	salle
	sella
AELLY	alley
AELMM	lemma
AELMN	leman
	Lemna
AELMP	ample
	△maple
	pelma
AELMR	marle
	realm
AELMS	mesal
	samel
AELMT	metal
AELMU	ulema
AELMY	mealy
	yealm
AELNO	alone
AELNP	panel
	penal
	plane
	'plane
AELNR	learn
	Lerna
	renal
AELNS	Elsan®
	slane
AELNT	laten
	leant
AELNU	ulnae
AELNV	elvan
	navel
	venal
AELNW	wanle
AELNY	leany
AELOR	realo
AELOS	aloes
AELOV	loave
	volae
AELOW	alowe
AELOZ	zoeal
AELPP	appel
	apple
AELPR	lepra
	parle
	pearl
	repla
AELPS	Elaps
	lapse
	leaps
	salep
	sepal
	spale
	speal
AELPT	leapt
	lepta
	palet
	pelta
	petal
	plate
	pleat
	tepal
AELPY	ayelp
AELQU	equal
	quale
AELRS	arles
	lares
	laser
	seral
AELRT	alert
	alter
	artel
	later
	ratel
	taler
AELRU	alure
	ureal
AELRV	laver
	ravel
	velar
AELRW	waler
AELRX	relax
AELRY	early
	layer
	leary
	rayle
	relay
AELSS	sales
	salse
AELST	least
	salet
	slate
	stale
	steal
	stela
	tales
	teals
	tesla
AELSU	salue
AELSV	salve
	selva
	slave
	vales
	valse
AELSW	swale
	sweal
	wales
AELTV	valet
AELTX	exalt
	latex
AELUV	uveal
	value
AELVV	valve
AELVY	leavy
	vealy
AEMNR	enarm
	namer
	ramen
	reman
AEMNS	manes
	manse
	means
	Mensa
	names
	samen
AEMNT	ament
	manet
	meant
AEMNV	maven
AEMNY	meany
	yamen
AEMOR	Moera
AEMOV	amove
AEMPX	Ampex®
AEMRR	rearm
AEMRS	maser
	reams
	smear

AEMRT	armet
	mater
	tamer
	trema
AEMRY	reamy
AEMRZ	mazer
AEMSS	massé
AEMST	steam
AEMSU	amuse
AEMSY	samey
	seamy
	ysame
AEMTT	matte
AEMTY	etyma
	matey
	meaty
AEMUV	mauve
AEMYZ	△azyme
AENNP	panne
	penna
AENNS	senna
AENNT	anent
AENNX	annex
AENOP	paeon
AENOT	atone
	oaten
AENOV	novae
AENOZ	zonae
AENPP	nappe
AENPS	aspen
	sneap
	spane
	spean
AENPT	paten
	tapen
AENPV	paven
AENQU	quean
	quena
AENRR	narre
AENRS	nares
	snare
AENRT	antre
	aren't
AENRU	urena
AENRV	raven
AENRW	awner
AENRY	rayne
	renay
	yearn
AENSS	sensa
AENST	nates
	stane
	stean
AENSU	usnea
AENSV	avens
AENSY	sayne
AENSZ	senza
AENTX	Texan
AENTY	yenta
AENTZ	△zante
AENVW	navew
AENWX	waxen
AENWY	waney
AENWZ	wanze
AENZZ	zanze
AEOOZ	zooea
AEOPR	opera
	opéra
	pareo
AEOPS	paseo
AEORS	arose
	soare
AEORT	Erato
	oater
	orate
	roate
AEOSS	oases
AEOST	stoae
AEOSV	oaves
	Soave
AEOSZ	zoeas
AEOTV	ovate
AEOTW	aweto
AEOTZ	azote
	toaze
AEPPR	paper
AEPPU	pupae
AEPRR	parer
	raper
AEPRS	après
	asper
	parse
	prase
	presa
	spaer
	spare
	spear
AEPRT	apert
	pater
	peart
	petar
	prate
	taper
	trape
AEPRU	pareu
AEPRV	paver
AEPRY	apery
	payer
	repay
AEPSS	passé
AEPST	paste
	septa
	spate
	speat
AEPSU	pause
AEPSV	vespa
AEPTT	patte
	patté
	tapet
AEPTU	taupe
AEPTX	expat
AEPTY	peaty
AEPVY	peavy
AEQRU	quare
AERRS	rears
	serra
AERRT	arrêt
	rater
	tarre
	terra
AERRV	raver
AERRW	warre
AERSS	arses
	rasse
AERST	aster
	earst
	rates
	reast
	resat
	stare
	stear
	strae
	Taser®
	taser
	tears
	teras
AERSV	saver
AERSW	sawer
	sware
	swear
	wares
AERSY	resay
	sayer
	years
AERTT	arett
	tater
	tetra
	treat
AERTU	urate
AERTV	avert
	taver
	trave
AERTW	tawer
	water
	wrate
AERTX	extra
	taxer
AERTY	teary
AERUZ	azure
AERVV	varve
AERVW	waver
AERWX	waxer
AERWY	weary
AESSS	asses
	sasse
	sessa
AESST	asset
	tasse
AESSY	essay
AESTT	state
	taste
	testa
AESTU	sauté
AESTV	stave
	vesta
AESTW	sweat
	tawse
	waste
AESTX	taxes
	△texas
AESTY	as-yet
	yeast
AESUV	suave
AESVW	waves
AESVY	savey
AETUV	vaute
AETVW	vawte
AETZZ	tazze
AEVWY	wavey
AEVYZ	avyze
AEWYY	yawey
AFFFL	flaff
AFFGR	graff
AFFIX	affix
AFFLO	offal
AFFLU	luffa
AFFNY	nyaff
AFFQU	quaff
AFFST	staff
AFFTY	△taffy
AFFUW	wauff
AFGHU	faugh
AFGIN	Fagin
AFGLO	oflag
AFGLU	fugal
AFGNO	fango
AFGOT	fagot
AFGRT	graft
AFGSU	Fagus
AFHIT	faith
AFHLS	flash
	halfs
AFHRW	wharf
AFHST	shaft
AFIKL	kalif
AFIKR	fakir
	Kafir
AFILL	flail
AFILN	final
AFILO	folia
AFILR	filar
	flair
	frail
AFIMR	fraim
AFINR	infra
AFINS	fains
AFINT	faint
	Fanti
AFIRR	friar
AFIRS	Farsi
	fiars
AFIRT	afrit
	frati
AFIRY	fairy
AFIST	fasti
AFISW	waifs
AFITW	waift

AFKLN	flank
AFKLS	flask
AFKLY	flaky
AFKNR	△frank
AFKOT	kofta
AFKRT	kraft
AFLMM	flamm
AFLMY	flamy
AFLNW	flawn
AFLOO	aloof
	loofa
AFLOR	flora
AFLOS	sol-fa
AFLOT	aloft
	float
	flota
AFLOU	afoul
AFLRU	fural
AFLRY	flary
AFLST	flats
AFLSU	sulfa
AFLTU	fault
AFLTY	fatly
AFLUW	awful
AFLWY	flawy
AFLXY	flaxy
AFMOX	Oxfam
AFMOY	foamy
AFMSU	samfu
AFNNO	fanon
AFNNY	fanny
AFNRU	furan
AFNSU	snafu
AFOOT	afoot
AFORS	sofar
AFORV	favor
AFORY	foray
AFOSS	△fossa
AFOST	fatso
	softa
AFOTU	fouat
AFRSS	frass
AFRSW	swarf
AFSUV	favus
AFTTY	fatty
AGGIN	aging
AGGIR	aggri
AGGJY	jaggy
AGGLU	gulag
AGGMO	Magog
AGGMS	maggs
AGGNU	ungag
AGGNY	naggy
AGGOR	aggro
AGGRY	aggry
	raggy
AGGSY	saggy
AGGTY	taggy
AGHHI	ahigh
AGHHU	haugh
AGHIL	laigh
AGHIN	anigh
AGHIT	thagi
AGHIZ	ghazi
AGHKU	kaugh
AGHLU	laugh
AGHMO	ogham
AGHNO	hogan
AGHNP	phang
AGHNS	gnash
	Shang
AGHNW	whang
AGHPR	graph
AGHRT	garth
AGHST	ghast
AGHSU	saugh
AGHTU	aught
	ghaut
AGHUW	waugh
AGIIV	vigia
AGIJR	jagir
	jirga
AGIKL	glaik
AGIKN	kiang
AGILL	glial
AGILN	algin
	align
	liang
	ligan
	linga
AGILO	logia
AGILR	argil
	glair
	△grail
AGILS	sigla
AGILW	wilga
AGILY	gaily
AGIMN	gamin
AGIMO	amigo
	imago
AGIMS	sigma
AGINN	ingan
AGINO	gonia
	ngaio
AGINR	agrin
	garni
	grain
AGINS	gains
AGINT	giant
	tangi
AGINW	a-wing
	wigan
AGINZ	zigan
AGIOP	igapó
AGIOR	orgia
AGIOS	agios
AGIPR	graip
	pagri
AGIRT	tragi
AGIRV	virga
AGIST	agist
	staig
AGITT	gaitt
AGITU	aguti
AGJLU	jugal
AGJOS	gajos
AGKLN	klang
AGKNR	krang
AGKNY	kyang
AGKOP	gopak
AGKOS	kagos
AGKWY	gawky
AGLLO	Algol
AGLLY	gally
AGLMU	algum
	almug
	glaum
	mulga
AGLNO	along
	Anglo
	logan
	longa
AGLNR	gnarl
AGLNS	glans
	slang
AGLOP	galop
AGLOR	argol
	goral
	largo
	rolag
AGLOS	goals
	Lagos
AGLOT	gloat
AGLOW	aglow
AGLPY	pygal
AGLRU	glaur
	gular
AGLRY	glary
	gyral
AGLSS	glass
AGLSU	gusla
AGLTU	△galut
	△gault
AGLUX	Glaux
AGLYZ	glazy
	zygal
AGMMU	gumma
AGMMY	gammy
AGMNO	among
	mango
AGMNY	mangy
AGMOP	gompa
AGMOR	groma
AGMOT	magot
AGMRU	garum
AGMSU	△magus
	sagum
AGMTU	gamut
AGMUY	gaumy
AGNNO	gonna
AGNNW	gnawn
AGNOP	ponga
AGNOR	argon
	groan
	nagor
	orang
	organ
AGNOT	tango
	tonga
AGNOU	guano
AGNOW	gowan
	△wagon
	wonga
AGNOY	agony
AGNOZ	gazon
AGNPR	prang
AGNPS	spang
AGNPU	punga
AGNRR	gnarr
AGNRT	grant
AGNRY	angry
	rangy
AGNST	△angst
	stang
AGNSW	swang
AGNTT	Gantt
AGNTU	gaunt
AGNTW	twang
AGNTY	tangy
AGOOZ	gazoo
AGOPS	gapós
AGORS	sargo
AGORT	argot
	groat
AGORU	△goura
AGORY	goary
AGOST	goats
AGOTT	gotta
AGOTY	goaty
AGPPY	gappy
AGPRS	grasp
	sprag
AGPRY	grapy
AGPSY	gaspy
AGRSS	grass
AGRSU	△argus
	sugar
AGRTU	tugra
AGRUU	augur
AGRVY	gravy
AGSSU	gauss
AGSSY	gassy
AGSTU	Tsuga
AGSTY	stagy
AGSUV	vagus
AGSWY	gawsy
AGTTU	gutta
AGUYZ	gauzy
AGYYZ	azygy
AHHIK	Haikh
AHHIS	Shiah
AHHIT	haith
	hi-hat
AHHOO	hoo-ha

Words marked △ may be spelled also with a capital letter

AHHPY	hypha
AHHRS	harsh
AHHSS	shash
AHHSY	hashy
AHIJJ	hajji
AHIJR	hijra
AHIKK	khaki
AHIKM	hakim
AHIKT	takhi
AHIKU	haiku
AHILP	phial
AHILR	hilar
AHILT	laith
	lathi
AHILY	haily
AHIMR	harim
	ihram
AHIMS	Amish
AHIMT	thaim
AHINT	ahint
	hiant
AHIPS	aphis
	apish
	spahi
AHIRS	arish
AHIRY	hairy
AHIST	saith
	taish
AHISV	Shiva
AHITU	hutia
AHJKO	khoja
AHJNO	Jonah
AHJTU	thuja
AHKNS	shank
AHKNT	thank
AHKNY	hanky
AHKOO	hooka
AHKOS	shako
	sokah
AHKRS	shark
AHKST	shakt
AHKSW	hawks
AHKSY	shaky
AHLLO	hallo
	holla
AHLLS	halls
	shall
AHLLU	ahull
AHLMO	omlah
AHLMS	shalm
AHLMU	haulm
AHLNO	halon
AHLNU	uhlan
AHLOR	horal
AHLOS	halos
	shoal
	shola
	solah
AHLOT	loath
	lotah
AHLPR	Ralph
AHLPS	plash
AHLPY	haply
	phyla
AHLSS	slash
AHLST	laths
	shalt
AHLSW	shawl
AHLSY	shaly
AHLTU	hault
AHLTY	lathy
AHMMY	hammy
AHMNU	human
AHMNY	mynah
AHMOR	omrah
AHMPS	pashm
AHMRS	marsh
AHMSS	smash
AHMST	maths
AHMSU	musha
AHMSW	shawm
AHMSY	mashy
AHNOS	Shona
AHNRS	harns
	sharn
AHNSS	snash
AHNST	hasn't
	sha'n't
	shan't
	snath
AHNTU	haunt
	unhat
AHOOW	wahoo
AHOOY	△yahoo
AHORS	haros
AHORT	Torah
AHORY	hoary
AHORZ	Zohar
AHOST	hoast
	hosta
	oaths
	shoat
AHOSV	Hovas
AHOSX	Xhosa
AHOTZ	azoth
AHPPY	happy
AHPRS	sharp
AHPRU	prahu
AHPRY	harpy
AHPSS	shaps
AHPST	paths
	staph
AHPSW	pshaw
AHPTY	Typha
AHPUW	whaup
AHQSU	quash
AHRRU	hurra
AHRRY	harry
AHRST	trash
AHRSU	shura
	surah
AHRSY	△syrah
AHRTW	thraw
	wrath
AHRTY	rhyta
AHRUW	whaur
AHRXY	△hyrax
AHSST	stash
AHSSW	swash
AHSTW	swath
AHSTY	hasty
AHSWY	washy
AHTTU	tuath
AHTUY	thuya
AHTWY	thawy
AHUZZ	huzza
AIILN	Ilian
AIILO	aioli
	aïoli
AIILT	Tilia
AIIMR	△imari
AIIPR	pirai
AIIQR	Iraqi
AIJKN	kanji
AIJKT	Tajik
AIJLW	wilja
AIJNN	△ninja
AIJOR	Rioja
AIJOU	Ouija®
	ouija
AIJPW	pi-jaw
AIKKM	kamik
AIKKT	tikka
AIKLM	malik
AIKLN	lakin
AIKLP	palki
AIKLS	kails
	skail
AIKLV	vakil
AIKMO	maiko
AIKMR	mikra
AIKMS	kamis
	smaik
AIKMU	umiak
AIKNS	kisan
	Nasik
AIKNT	takin
AIKNU	nikau
AIKOP	okapi
AIKPP	kippa
AIKPR	parki
AIKPS	paiks
AIKRR	karri
AIKRT	krait
	traik
AIKRU	kauri
AIKST	Sakti
	Sitka
AIKTT	katti
AILLN	all-in
AILLS	allis
AILLV	villa
AILMM	limma
AILMR	armil
AILMS	Islam
	salmi
AILMT	Tamil
AILMU	aumil
	miaul
AILMX	limax
AILNP	plain
AILNS	slain
	snail
AILNT	Intal®
	Latin
AILNU	inula
AILNV	anvil
	nival
	vinal
AILNW	in-law
	lawin
AILNY	inlay
AILOP	apiol
	paoli
AILOU	auloi
AILOV	Oliva
	viola
	voilà
AILPP	palpi
	pipal
AILPR	April
	prial
AILPS	lapis
	spial
AILPT	plait
AILPU	pilau
AILPW	pilaw
AILQU	quail
AILRS	liras
	rails
AILRT	liart
	trail
	T-rail
	△trial
AILRU	urali
	urial
AILRV	rival
	viral
AILRY	lairy
	riyal
AILSS	lassi
	sisal
AILST	tails
AILSV	silva
	vails
AILSX	salix
AILTT	atilt
AILTV	vital
AILTY	△laity
AILZZ	lazzi
AIMMS	miasm
AIMMU	imaum
AIMMX	△maxim
AIMNO	amino
AIMNP	panim
AIMNR	inarm
	minar
	ramin

AIMNS	mains
	Manis
	minas
AIMNT	matin
	tamin
AIMNV	mavin
AIMNZ	△nizam
AIMOR	Maori
	Moira
	moria
AIMOW	miaow
AIMOX	axiom
AIMPR	prima
AIMPS	apism
	sampi
AIMQU	maqui
AIMRS	simar
AIMRT	amrit
AIMRZ	Mirza
AIMSS	amiss
	△missa
AIMST	Samit
	tamis
AIMSV	mavis
AIMSW	aswim
	△swami
AIMTY	amity
	atimy
AINNO	anion
AINNP	△pinna
AINNS	Nisan
AINNW	winna
AINOP	piano
AINOR	noria
AINOT	Taino
AINOV	avion
AINPS	pains
	spain
	spina
AINPT	inapt
	paint
	patin
	pinta
	tap-in
AINPV	pavin
AINQU	quina
AINRS	rains
	sarin
AINRT	intra
	riant
	train
AINRV	Invar®
	ravin
AINRY	rainy
AINRZ	nazir
AINSS	sasin
AINST	△saint
	satin
	stain
AINSV	savin
	Sivan
AINSW	swain
AINTT	taint
	'taint
	tanti
	△tatin
	△titan
AINTU	Uniat
AINTW	twain
	witan
AINUX	auxin
AIOPT	patio
AIORT	ariot
	ratio
AIORY	Oriya
AIOSS	△oasis
	ossia
AIOST	ostia
	stoai
AIOSV	aviso
AIPPU	appui
AIPRS	pairs
	Paris
	Parsi
AIPRT	atrip
	parti
	tapir
AIPRU	rupia
AIPSS	apsis
AIPST	stipa
	tapis
AIPSV	pavis
AIPTT	△pitta
AIPZZ	pizza
AIQRU	quair
AIQSU	quasi
AIRRS	arris
AIRRU	urari
AIRSS	arsis
AIRST	astir
	sitar
	stair
	stria
	tarsi
	Trias
AIRSZ	sizar
AIRTT	trait
AIRVX	varix
AIRVY	vairy
AIRWZ	wazir
AIRYY	Iyyar
AISST	saist
AISTT	Sitta
AISTV	vista
	vitas
AISTW	waist
	waits
AISTX	taxis
AISWZ	Swazi
AITTV	vitta
AITVV	vivat
AITZZ	izzat
AJKOT	Tokaj
AJLOU	joual
AJLRU	jarul
	jural
AJMMY	jammy
AJMOR	joram
	△major
AJMRU	jumar
AJNOY	yojan
AJNSU	Janus
AJNTU	jaunt
	junta
AJNTY	janty
AJOOP	pooja
AJORW	jowar
AJOST	jatos
AJOSU	sajou
AJRTU	jurat
AJYZZ	jazzy
AKKLU	kulak
AKKNS	skank
AKKOP	kapok
AKKOR	kokra
AKKPU	pukka
AKLLY	alkyl
AKLNP	plank
AKLNR	knarl
AKLNU	kulan
AKLNY	lanky
AKLOP	pokal
	polka
AKLOS	skoal
AKLPU	pulka
AKLRY	larky
AKLST	stalk
	talks
AKLSW	lawks
	walks
AKLTU	taluk
AKLTY	talky
AKLUW	waulk
AKMNY	manky
AKMOP	Pomak
AKMOR	korma
AKMOS	makos
AKMOU	oakum
AKMRS	marks
AKMSU	Musak
AKMUZ	Muzak®
AKMWY	mawky
AKNOR	Koran
	krona
	króna
AKNOS	kaons
	sanko
AKNPR	prank
AKNPS	spank
AKNPU	punka
AKNRS	krans
	ranks
	skran
	snark
AKNRY	narky
AKNRZ	kranz
AKNST	stank
AKNSU	ankus
AKNSW	swank
AKNSY	snaky
AKNTW	twank
AKNTY	tanky
AKNUZ	kanzu
AKNWY	wanky
AKOOP	pooka
AKOOR	Karoo
AKOOZ	kazoo
AKOPP	koppa
AKOPY	yapok
AKORT	tarok
AKORW	awork
AKOSY	kayos
	okays
AKOTY	△tokay
AKOWY	yakow
AKPRS	spark
AKPRY	parky
AKPTU	kaput
	uptak
AKPWY	pawky
AKQRU	quark
AKQUY	quaky
AKRST	karst
	skart
	stark
AKRSY	karsy
	sarky
AKRTU	△kraut
	kurta
AKRYZ	karzy
AKSSV	kvass
AKSTT	skatt
AKTUY	Yakut
ALLLY	allyl
ALLMO	molal
	molla
ALLMS	small
ALLMY	myall
ALLNO	llano
ALLNU	nulla
ALLOR	loral
ALLOT	allot
	all-to
	atoll
ALLOV	ollav
ALLOW	allow
ALLOY	alloy
	loyal
ALLPS	spall
ALLPU	all-up
ALLPY	pally
ALLRY	rally
ALLST	stall
ALLSW	walls
ALLSY	sally
ALLTY	tally
ALLWY	△wally
ALLXY	laxly

ALMMS	smalm
ALMMY	lammy
ALMNO	monal
ALMNU	manul
ALMNY	manly
ALMOO	moola
ALMOR	molar
	moral
	romal
ALMOS	molas
	Salmo
ALMOT	matlo
ALMOY	loamy
ALMPS	plasm
	psalm
ALMPU	ampul
ALMPY	amply
	palmy
ALMQU	qualm
ALMRS	marls
ALMRU	larum
	mural
	rumal
ALMRY	marly
ALMST	smalt
ALMTY	malty
ALNNU	annul
ALNOP	nopal
ALNOR	loran
ALNOS	△salon
	sloan
	solan
ALNOT	notal
	talon
	tonal
ALNOW	lowan
ALNOX	noxal
ALNOZ	zonal
ALNPT	plant
ALNRS	snarl
ALNRU	lunar
	ulnar
	urnal
ALNST	slant
ALNSU	Alnus
ALNUW	unlaw
ALNUY	unlay
	yulan
ALNWY	lawny
	wanly
ALOOP	paolo
ALOPR	parol
	polar
	poral
ALOPS	salop
ALOPT	ploat
ALORR	roral
ALORS	solar
	soral
ALORT	rotal

ALORV	orval
	valor
	volar
ALORY	royal
ALOSS	lasso
ALOST	altos
	loast
	salto
ALOSU	aulos
ALOSV	salvo
ALOTT	total
ALOTV	lovat
	volta
ALOTX	△taxol
ALOVV	volva
ALOZZ	lazzo
ALPPU	pupal
ALPPY	apply
ALPRY	parly
	pyral
ALPST	plast
	spalt
	splat
ALPSU	spaul
ALPSW	spawl
ALPSY	palsy
	splay
	spyal
ALPTY	aptly
	patly
	platy
	typal
ALPUY	lay-up
	uplay
ALRRU	rural
ALRSU	Larus
	sural
	Urals
ALRTU	ultra
ALRTW	trawl
ALRTY	lyart
ALRWW	wrawl
ALRWY	rawly
ALSST	salts
ALSSU	lassu
ALSSY	lyssa
ALSTU	sault
	talus
ALSTY	salty
	slaty
ALSUU	usual
ALSVY	sylva
ALSWY	swaly
	swayl
ALTTY	lytta
ALTUV	vault
ALTWY	walty
ALTWZ	waltz
ALUUV	uvula
ALUVV	vulva
AMMMO	momma
AMMMY	mammy

AMMNO	△ammon
AMMOY	myoma
AMMRS	smarm
AMMRY	rammy
AMMSU	summa
AMMSY	Sammy
AMMTY	tammy
AMNNO	no-man
AMNNU	unman
AMNOR	manor
	maron
	△norma
	△roman
AMNOS	manos
	mason
	△monas
	soman
AMNOT	manto
	toman
AMNOW	△woman
AMNOY	anomy
AMNRU	Ruman
	unarm
	urman
AMNSU	manus
AMNTY	manty
AMOPR	pro-am
AMORR	armor
	maror
	morra
AMORS	romas
AMORT	amort
	morat
AMORU	amour
AMORW	mowra
AMORY	△mayor
	moray
AMOSS	somas
AMOST	stoma
AMOTY	atomy
AMOTZ	matzo
	motza
AMPRT	tramp
AMPSS	spasm
AMPST	stamp
AMPSU	pumas
AMPSW	swamp
AMRRU	murra
AMRRY	marry
AMRST	smart
AMRSU	ramus
	rusma
	Sarum
AMRSW	swarm
AMRSY	symar
AMRUV	murva
AMRWY	awmry
AMSSY	massy
AMSTY	masty
	mayst
AMSUW	wamus
AMTUZ	mazut

ANNNY	nanny
ANNOR	Norna
ANNOY	annoy
ANNSU	Sunna
ANNTU	naunt
ANNTZ	Nantz
ANOOP	napoo
ANOPR	apron
ANOPT	panto
ANOPW	powan
ANOPY	yapon
ANOQR	Qoran
ANORS	arson
	△sonar
ANORT	orant
	toran
	trona
ANORW	rowan
ANORY	rayon
ANOSV	novas
ANOSX	Saxon
ANOSY	sayon
ANOTT	tanto
ANOTW	Wotan
ANOTX	taxon
ANOTY	atony
	ayont
ANOUY	noyau
ANOWY	noway
ANPPY	nappy
ANPRW	prawn
ANPSS	snaps
ANPST	pants
ANPSW	spawn
ANPSY	pansy
ANPTU	unapt
ANPTY	panty
ANPUY	unpay
ANPUZ	zupan
ANQRU	Quran
	Qur'an
ANQTU	quant
ANRST	starn
ANRSY	snary
ANRTT	trant
ANRTU	arnut
ANRTY	tyran
ANRUZ	azurn
ANSSY	nyssa
ANSTU	astun
	saunt
	tunas
ANSTW	wants
ANSTY	nasty
	tansy
ANSUY	unsay
ANSWY	Sawny
ANTTU	taunt
ANTTY	natty
ANTUV	vaunt
ANTUX	untax
ANTUY	aunty

Words marked △ may be spelled also with a capital letter

ANTWY	tawny
	wanty
ANVVY	navvy
ANWYY	yawny
AOOPP	apoop
AOORS	roosa
AOORT	ratoo
AOORZ	razoo
AOPPP	poppa
AOPPR	appro
AOPRS	psora
	sapor
	sopra
AOPRT	aport
	porta
AOPRV	Parvo
	vapor
AOPSS	psoas
AOPSY	soapy
AOPTY	atopy
AOPTZ	topaz
AOQTU	quota
AORRS	sorra
AORRW	arrow
AORRY	roary
AORRZ	razor
AORSS	saros
AORST	roast
	taros
AORSV	arvos
	savor
AORSW	sowar
AORTT	ottar
	tarot
	troat
AORTX	taxor
AORTY	otary
	yarto
AORVY	ovary
AORYZ	Oryza
AOSST	assot
	stoas
AOSSY	say-so
AOSTT	stoat
	toast
AOSTU	autos
AOSVY	△savoy
AOTTU	tatou
APPPY	pappy
APPSU	pupas
APPSY	paspy
	sappy
APPUY	appuy
APPYY	yappy
APPYZ	zappy
APRRY	parry
APRST	parts
	spart
	sprat
	strap
	traps
APRSW	wraps
APRSY	raspy
	spray
APRTT	pratt
APRTU	U-trap
APRTW	wrapt
APRTY	party
	praty
	yrapt
APSTU	sputa
	stupa
APSTW	swapt
APSTY	pasty
	patsy
APSWY	waspy
APTTY	patty
APZZZ	pzazz
AQRTU	quart
AQSTU	squat
AQSUW	squaw
ARRST	starr
ARRSU	surra
ARRTY	tarry
ARSST	stars
	trass
ARSSU	sarus
ARSTT	start
ARSTU	surat
	sutra
ARSTW	straw
	swart
	warst
	wrast
ARSTY	artsy
	satyr
	stray
ARSUV	varus
ARSUY	saury
	Surya
ARSXY	X-rays
ARTTT	tratt
ARTTU	tuart
ARTTY	ratty
	tarty
ARTWY	warty
ARUYZ	azury
ASSSY	sassy
ASSTW	swats
ASSTY	sayst
	stays
ASTTT	Tatts
ASTTY	tasty
ASTUX	Taxus
ASTVY	vasty
ASVVY	savvy
ATTTY	tatty

B

BBBIY	Bibby
BBBOY	bobby
BBBUY	bubby
BBCEU	cubeb
BBCHU	Chubb®
BBCOY	cobby
BBCUY	cubby
BBDEY	debby
BBDIS	dibbs
BBDOY	dobby
BBEER	△rebbe
BBEIL	△bible
BBEIR	bribe
BBEKO	kebob
BBEMO	bombe
	bombé
BBEOP	bebop
BBEOR	berob
BBESY	sybbe
BBEUZ	zebub
BBEWY	webby
BBFUY	fubby
BBGIO	gobbi
BBGOO	gobbo
BBHMO	H-bomb
BBHOY	hobby
BBHUY	hubby
BBILO	bilbo
BBIMO	bimbo
BBIRY	ribby
BBLOY	lobby
BBLRU	blurb
BBLSU	slubb
BBMOO	bombo
BBMOU	bumbo
BBMOY	mobby
BBNOY	nobby
BBNUY	nubby
BBOOS	boobs
BBOOY	booby
	yobbo
BBSUY	busby
	subby
BBTUY	tubby
BCCIU	cubic
BCCIY	biccy
BCEEH	beech
BCEEK	becke
BCEEL	celeb
BCEER	rebec
BCEEX	xebec
BCEEZ	zebec
BCEHL	belch
BCEHN	bench
BCEHO	boche
BCELO	coble
BCEMO	combe
BCENO	bonce
BCENU	bunce
BCEOR	corbe
BCESU	Cebus
BCHIM	chimb
BCHIR	birch
BCHIT	bitch
BCHNU	bunch
BCHOR	broch
BCHOT	botch
BCHTU	butch
BCHUU	buchu
BCIKR	brick
BCILM	climb
BCILO	cibol
BCIOR	boric
BCIPU	pubic
BCITU	cubit
BCKLO	block
BCKOR	brock
BCKOU	bucko
BCKUU	bucku
BCLMO	clomb
BCLOO	Cobol
BCLSU	clubs
BCMOO	combo
	coomb
BCMOR	cromb
BCMOS	combs
BCMOY	comby
BCMRU	crumb
BCNOU	bunco
BCORU	courb
BCRSU	scrub
BDDEI	bided
BDDIY	biddy
BDDUY	buddy
BDEEL	bedel
	bleed
	debel
BDEEM	embed
BDEEN	Deneb
BDEER	brede
	breed
BDEEW	bedew
	dweeb
BDEEY	bedye
	Debye
BDEGO	bodge
BDEGU	budge
	debug
BDEIL	bield
BDEIM	bedim
	imbed
BDEIP	biped
BDEIR	bride
	rebid
BDEIS	B-side
BDEIT	betid
	bidet
	debit
BDELN	blend
BDELO	bodle
	lobed
BDELU	blude
BDEMO	demob
BDEMU	bemud
BDENO	boned
BDENS	bends
BDENU	U-bend
	unbed

Words marked △ may be spelled also with a capital letter

BDENY	bendy
	by-end
BDENZ	Z-bend
BDEOR	borde
	orbed
BDEOW	bowed
BDERY	△derby
BDESU	debus
BDETU	debut
	début
	tubed
BDFII	bifid
BDHIO	bodhi
	dhobi
BDILN	blind
BDILU	bluid
	build
BDINO	bidon
BDINU	unbid
BDIOP	bipod
BDIOV	bovid
BDIRS	birds
	dribs
BDLNO	blond
BDLOO	blood
BDLOY	Dolby®
BDLUY	bludy
BDMOU	dumbo
BDNOR	brond
BDNOS	bonds
BDNOU	bound
BDNUU	bundu
BDNUY	Bundy®
BDOOR	boord
	brood
	Dobro®
BDOOS	dsobo
BDOOY	boody
BDORU	bourd
BDOSU	budos
BDOTU	doubt
BDOXY	X-body
BEEEL	belee
BEEES	besee
BEEFS	beefs
BEEFY	beefy
BEEGI	beige
BEEGL	glebe
BEEGM	begem
BEEGR	gerbe
	grebe
BEEGT	beget
BEEHN	heben
BEEIL	belie
BEEJL	jebel
BEEKN	nebek
BEELL	belle
BEELN	nebel
BEELP	bleep
BEELR	rebel
BEELT	betel
BEELV	bevel
BEELZ	bezel
BEEMN	neemb
BEEMR	breem
	breme
	ember
BEENN	benne
BEENT	benet
BEEOR	boree
BEEOS	obese
BEERR	breer
	brere
BEERT	beret
BEERV	bever
	breve
BEERW	weber
BEERY	beery
BEEST	beset
BEETT	Tebet
BEETW	bewet
BEEUV	bevue
BEFFU	buffe
BEFGO	befog
BEFIR	brief
	fiber
	fibre
BEFIT	befit
BEGIL	bilge
	gibel
BEGIN	begin
	△being
	binge
BEGIO	bogie
BEGIR	giber
BEGIW	bewig
BEGLO	bogle
	globe
BEGLU	bugle
	bulge
BEGLY	gleby
BEGMO	embog
BEGMU	begum
BEGNU	begun
BEGOT	begot
BEGOU	bouge
BEGOY	bogey
BEGRU	gebur
BEGUZ	Uzbeg
BEHOW	howbe
BEHRT	berth
BEHRY	herby
BEIIK	bikie
BEIJR	jiber
BEIKR	biker
BEILL	libel
BEILO	obeli
BEILR	birle
	liber
BEILS	Eblis
BEILT	blite
BEILV	blive
BEIMO	biome
BEIMU	imbue
BEINN	benni
BEINO	bonie
	Niobe
BEINR	brine
BEINV	Bevin
BEINY	inbye
BEINZ	zineb
BEIOW	bowie
BEIRR	brier
BEIRS	birse
	brisé
	Ribes
BEIRT	biter
	tribe
BEIRZ	brize
BEIST	besit
BEISV	vibes
BEITT	bitte
	Tibet
BEITZ	zibet
BEIVX	vibex
BEJNU	bunje
BEJOT	objet
BEKLO	bloke
BEKMO	kembo
BEKOR	broke
BEKRU	burke
BEKUZ	Uzbek
BELLS	bells
BELLY	belly
BELMO	moble
BELMU	umbel
BELNO	Nobel
	noble
BELNT	blent
BELOR	blore
	borel
	roble
BELOS	lesbo
BELOT	botel
BELOU	boule
BELOW	below
	bowel
	elbow
BELPS	plebs
BELRU	brûlé
	ruble
BELRY	beryl
BELSS	bless
BELST	blest
BELSU	△blues
	bulse
BELUY	bluey
BEMOP	pombe
BEMOR	ombre
	ombré
BEMOS	besom
	mebos
BEMOW	embow
BEMOX	embox
BEMRU	brume
	umber
	umbre
BEMSU	embus
	sebum
BENNO	bonne
BENNY	benny
BENOR	boner
	borne
	borné
BENOS	bones
BENOT	béton
	T-bone
BENOW	bowne
BENOX	boxen
BENOY	ebony
BENOZ	bonze
BENRT	brent
BENTY	benty
BEOOS	boose
BEOOZ	booze
BEOPR	probe
BEORR	borer
BEORS	brose
	robes
	sober
BEORW	bower
BEORX	△boxer
BEORY	o'erby
	ybore
BEOST	besot
BEOSU	bouse
BEOSW	bowes
	bowse
BEOSY	syboe
BEOTT	botte
BEOTW	bowet
BEPSU	pubes
BEPUY	upbye
BERRY	berry
BERSU	burse
	rebus
	suber
BERTU	brute
	buret
	rebut
	△tuber
BERUX	exurb
BERUY	buyer
BESSU	buses
BESTU	tubes
BETTU	butte
BETTY	betty
BETUU	U-tube
BEVVY	bevvy
BFFIU	buffi
BFFLU	bluff
BFFOU	buffo
BFFSU	buffs
BFIOR	fibro
BFLYY	fly-by
BFORY	forby

BFSUY	fubsy
BGGIY	biggy
BGGOY	boggy
BGGUY	buggy
BGHIT	bight
BGHOR	brogh
BGHOU	bough
BGHRU	burgh
BGILY	bilgy
BGINO	bingo
	boing
BGINR	bring
BGINY	bingy
BGIOT	bigot
BGISU	gibus
BGLOY	globy
BGLUY	bulgy
BGMOO	gombo
BGMOU	△gumbo
BGNOO	bongo
	boong
BGNUY	bungy
BGOOR	borgo
BGOOS	gobos
BGORU	bourg
BGOSU	bogus
BGRUY	△rugby
BHIRT	birth
BHLSU	blush
BHMOR	rhomb
BHMPU	bumph
BHMRU	rhumb
BHMTU	thumb
BHOOS	hobos
BHOOT	booth
BHORT	broth
	throb
BHOTY	bothy
BHRSU	brush
	shrub
BHSUY	bushy
BIILM	Limbi
BIILN	blini
BIILS	Iblis
BIIMN	nimbi
BIIMZ	zimbi
BIIOR	oribi
BIIOT	obiit
BIJOU	bijou
BIKLN	blink
BIKMO	kimbo
BIKNO	boink
BIKNR	brink
BIKRS	brisk
BILLR	brill
BILLY	billy
BILMO	△limbo
BILMP	△blimp
BILMY	blimy
BILOO	oboli
BILOR	broil
	Libor

BILOX	bolix
BILSS	bliss
BILST	blist
	stilb
BILSY	△sibyl
	△sybil
BILTU	built
BILTZ	blitz
BIMNY	Nimby
BIMOT	timbó
BIMOZ	△zombi
BINOR	inorb
	robin
BINOS	bison
BINOT	biont
BINRU	Bruin
	burin
	rubin
BINRY	briny
BINUY	buy-in
BIOOT	oobit
BIORS	Biros
BIORT	orbit
BIOST	bitos
BIOTT	Tobit
BIOTU	oubit
BIPSU	pubis
BIQSU	squib
BIRSY	birsy
BIRTU	bruit
BISTT	bitts
BISTU	buist
BISTY	bitsy
BITTY	bitty
BIVVY	bivvy
BJMOU	jumbo
BJMUY	jumby
BJNOO	on-job
BJNUY	bunjy
BKLNU	blunk
BKLUY	bulky
BKMOU	kombu
BKNOU	bunko
BKOOR	brook
BKOOS	bokos
	books
BKOOY	booky
BKOSY	bosky
BKSUY	busky
BLLUY	bully
BLMOO	bloom
BLMPU	plumb
BLNOW	blown
BLNOY	nobly
BLNTU	blunt
BLOOP	bloop
BLOOR	brool
BLOOS	bolos
BLOOY	looby
BLOST	bolts
BLOSU	bolus
	lobus

BLOSW	blows
	bowls
BLOTU	boult
	U-bolt
BLOWY	blowy
BLRSU	slurb
BLRTU	blurt
BLRUY	burly
BLTUY	butyl
BMOOR	broom
BMOOS	bosom
BMORU	rumbo
BMOSU	ombus
	ombús
	umbos
BMOUX	buxom
BMOWY	womby
BMPSU	bumps
BMPUY	bumpy
BNNOY	bonny
BNNUY	bunny
BNOOR	boron
BNOOS	boson
BNORU	bourn
BNORW	brown
BNORX	Bronx
BNOSU	bonus
	bosun
	bo'sun
BNOUX	unbox
BNRTU	brunt
	burnt
BNTUY	bunty
BOORS	sorbo
BOORT	robot
BOORU	buroo
BOOST	boost
	boots
BOOTX	ox-bot
BOOTY	booty
BOOWX	ox-bow
BOOYZ	boozy
BOPUW	up-bow
BORRU	burro
BORTU	turbo
BOSSY	bossy
BOSTT	botts
BOSUY	bousy
BOSWY	sybow
BOTTY	botty
BOTUY	outby
BPPUY	buppy
BRRUY	burry
BRSTU	brust
	burst
BRSUU	Rubus
BRUUU	urubu
BSSTU	stubs
BSSUU	bussu
BSTUY	busty
BTTUY	butty
BUYZZ	buzzy

C

CCCIO	cocci
CCCOO	cocco
CCEER	recce
CCEHK	check
CCEHZ	Czech
CCEIR	cerci
	ceric
CCEKL	cleck
CCELY	cycle
CCEMU	cecum
	cumec
CCEOR	recco
CCEOS	cosec
	secco
CCERY	reccy
CCESU	cusec
CCFIU	Cufic
CCHHI	chich
CCHIK	chick
CCHIN	cinch
CCHIO	chico
CCHKO	chock
CCHKU	chuck
CCHLU	culch
CCHNO	conch
CCHOO	choco
CCHOU	couch
CCHRU	curch
CCHTU	cutch
CCIIT	ictic
CCIIV	civic
CCIKL	click
CCIKR	crick
CCILO	colic
CCIMO	comic
CCIMU	mucic
CCINO	conic
CCINT	cinct
CCINY	△cynic
CCIOS	cisco
CCIPY	piccy
CCIRS	circs
CCISU	succi
CCKLO	clock
CCKLU	cluck
CCKOR	crock
CCKOY	cocky
CCKRU	cruck
CCLOY	cyclo
CCMOY	McCoy
CCOOS	cocos
CCOOZ	zocco
CCORU	occur
CDDEI	diced
	Eddic
CDDUY	cuddy
CDEEI	de-ice
CDEER	△creed
CDEEU	deuce
	educe

Words marked △ may be spelled also with a capital letter

CDEHI	chide
CDEHO	chode
CDEIM	demic
	△medic
CDEIR	cider
	cried
	dicer
CDEIS	cedis
CDEIT	edict
CDEIV	Vedic
CDEIY	dicey
CDEKO	decko
CDEKR	dreck
CDEKS	decks
CDELO	dolce
CDELY	ycled
CDEMO	Médoc
CDENS	scend
	'scend
CDENU	dunce
CDEOO	cooed
CDEOR	cored
	△credo
	decor
	décor
CDEOU	coudé
	douce
CDEOV	coved
CDEOW	cowed
CDEOX	codex
	coxed
CDEOY	decoy
CDERU	crude
CDERY	cyder
	decry
CDETU	educt
CDHIL	child
CDHIT	dicht
	ditch
CDHNU	dunch
CDHNY	chynd
CDHOR	chord
CDHOT	docht
CDHTU	△dutch
CDHUY	duchy
CDIIN	dinic
	Indic
CDIIO	iodic
CDIKY	dicky
CDILU	lucid
	ludic
CDIMU	mucid
CDIOR	Doric
CDIOS	disco
	sodic
CDIOT	dicot
CDIPU	△cupid
	pudic
CDISU	scudi
CDITY	dicty
CDKOS	docks
CDKSU	ducks
CDKUY	ducky
CDLOS	scold
CDLOU	cloud
	could
CDMOR	CD-ROM
CDNOO	codon
	condo
CDNOT	contd
CDNOY	ycond
CDNUY	cundy
CDORS	cords
	scrod
CDORU	courd
CDORW	crowd
CDOSU	scudo
CDRUY	curdy
CDSSU	scuds
CEEEM	emcee
CEEEP	peece
CEEFN	fence
CEEFS	feces
CEEGR	cerge
	grece
CEEHK	cheek
	keech
CEEHL	leech
CEEHN	hence
CEEHP	cheep
CEEHR	cheer
	chère
	reech
CEEIN	niece
CEEIP	piece
	pièce
CEEJT	eject
CEEKL	cleek
CEEKP	pecke
CEEKR	△creek
CEELP	cleep
	clepe
CEELR	creel
CEELT	elect
CEELV	cleve
CEELX	excel
CEELY	lycée
CEEMR	creme
	crème
	crême
CEENP	pence
CEENR	cerne
CEENS	cense
	scene
CEENT	ctene
CEEOO	cooee
CEEPR	creep
	crepe
	crêpe
	perce
CEERS	Ceres
	scree
CEERT	erect
	terce
CEERW	crewe
CEESS	cesse
CEESY	sycee
CEEUV	cuvée
CEFFL	F-clef
CEFGL	G-clef
CEFHI	chief
	fiche
CEFHT	fecht
	fetch
CEFIT	fecit
CEFKL	fleck
CEFLT	cleft
CEFOR	△force
CEGIN	genic
CEGIO	cogie
CEGIR	grice
CEGKO	△gecko
CEGNO	congé
CEGOU	cogue
CEGRY	gryce
CEHHT	hecht
CEHHU	heuch
CEHIL	chiel
	△chile
	elchi
CEHIM	chime
	hemic
	miche
CEHIN	chine
	chiné
	niche
CEHIR	Reich
CEHIT	ethic
	hi-tec
	theic
CEHIV	chive
CEHKO	choke
CEHKT	ketch
CEHLT	letch
CEHLU	leuch
CEHLW	△welch
CEHLY	chyle
CEHMY	chyme
CEHNT	tench
CEHNW	wench
CEHOO	cohoe
CEHOP	epoch
CEHOR	chore
	ocher
	ochre
CEHOS	chose
CEHOW	owche
CEHPR	perch
CEHPT	Pecht
CEHRT	chert
	retch
CEHRU	ruche
CEHSS	chess
CEHST	chest
CEHSU	chuse
CEHTU	chute
	teuch
CEHTV	vetch
CEHTW	wecht
CEHTY	techy
	Tyche
CEHVY	chevy
CEHWY	chewy
CEIIL	ceili
CEIIN	Iceni
CEIJU	juice
CEIKR	erick
	icker
CEILM	clime
	melic
CEILN	cline
	incle
CEILO	Eolic
	oleic
CEILP	clipe
CEILR	relic
CEILS	Sicel
	slice
CEILT	telic
CEIMN	mince
CEIMR	crime
CEIMS	mesic
CEIMT	metic
CEIMX	cimex
CEINR	crine
CEINS	since
CEINW	wince
CEINY	yince
CEINZ	Zenic
CEIOV	voice
CEIPR	price
CEIPS	spice
CEIRR	crier
	ricer
CEIRS	cries
	crise
	△seric
CEIRT	citer
	récit
	recti
	trice
CEIRU	curie
	ureic
CEIRX	xeric
CEIRY	ricey
CEITU	cutie
CEITV	civet
	evict
CEITW	twice
CEKKS	kecks
CEKLO	cloke
CEKLR	clerk
CEKNS	sneck
CEKNV	V-neck
CEKOR	△ocker
CEKOS	cokes
CEKPS	speck

CEKRT	treck
CEKRW	wreck
CELLO	cello
	'cello
CELLT	T-cell
CELMO	celom
CELNO	clone
CELNU	△uncle
CELOR	ceorl
CELOS	△close
	socle
CELOT	clote
CELOV	clove
CELOY	coley
CELOZ	cloze
CELPT	P-Celt
CELPU	cupel
CELPY	clype
CELQT	Q-Celt
CELRU	cruel
	lucre
	ulcer
CELSU	luces
CELTU	culet
CELTY	cetyl
CELUX	culex
CEMOR	△comer
	crome
CEMOT	comet
CEMRY	mercy
CENNO	conne
	nonce
CENOP	ponce
CENOR	crone
	oncer
CENOS	scone
	sonce
CENOT	cento
	Conté
	conte
	conté
CENOU	ounce
CENOV	coven
CENOY	coney
CENOZ	cozen
CENPU	punce
CENST	scent
CEOOY	cooey
CEOPR	coper
CEOPS	copse
	scope
CEOPU	coupe
	coupé
CEORR	corer
	crore
CEORS	corse
	score
CEORT	recto
CEORU	coure
CEORV	cover
CEORW	cower
CEORY	corey
CEORZ	croze
CEOST	coset
	coste
	escot
	estoc
CEOSU	souce
CEOSV	voces
CEOSW	sowce
CEOSX	Coxes
CEOTT	octet
CEOTV	covet
CEOVY	covey
CEPRT	crept
CEPRU	Pruce
CEPRY	crepy
	crêpy
CEPSS	specs
CERRU	curer
	recur
CERSS	cress
CERST	crest
CERSU	cruse
	curse
	sucre
CERSW	screw
CERTU	cruet
	eruct
	truce
CERTY	certy
CERUV	cruve
	curve
CESSU	scuse
	'scuse
CESTU	scute
CETUY	cutey
CFFHU	chuff
CFFIL	cliff
CFFLO	cloff
CFFOS	scoff
CFFOU	cuffo
CFFSU	scuff
CFHIL	filch
CFHIN	finch
CFHIT	fitch
CFHIU	fichu
CFHOO	choof
CFIIS	sci-fi
CFIKL	flick
CFIKU	Kufic
CFILO	folic
CFILT	clift
CFIOS	ficos
CFISU	ficus
	Sufic
CFKLO	flock
CFKOR	frock
CFMOY	comfy
CFORT	croft
CFOSU	focus
CFRSU	scurf
CFSTU	scuft
CFSUU	fucus
CGGIY	ciggy
CGHLU	gulch
CGHOO	cohog
CGHOU	cough
CGIIN	icing
CGIIT	ci-gît
CGILN	cling
CGILO	logic
CGIMO	ogmic
CGINO	coign
CGINU	cuing
CGIOR	corgi
	orgic
CGIOY	yogic
CGIRU	Ugric
CGKUY	gucky
CGLNU	clung
CGNOO	congo
CGOOS	scoog
CGORS	scrog
CGOSU	scoug
CHHIL	hilch
CHHIS	shchi
CHHIT	hitch
CHHIW	which
CHHNU	hunch
CHHOO	hooch
CHHOT	hotch
CHHTU	hutch
CHIIL	chili
	lichi
CHIKN	△chink
CHIKO	hoick
CHIKR	chirk
CHIKT	thick
CHILL	chill
CHILM	milch
CHILN	linch
CHILO	choli
CHILP	pilch
CHILR	chirl
CHILT	licht
CHILY	hylic
CHILZ	zilch
CHIMO	chimo
	ohmic
CHIMP	chimp
CHIMR	chirm
CHIMT	mitch
CHIMU	humic
CHINO	chino
CHINP	pinch
CHINW	winch
CHIOR	choir
	ichor
CHIPR	chirp
CHIPS	chips
CHIPT	pitch
CHIQU	quich
CHIRR	chirr
CHIRT	chirt
	crith
	richt
CHIST	stich
CHISU	cuish
CHITT	△titch
CHITW	witch
CHITY	itchy
	tichy
CHIVY	chivy
	△vichy
CHIZZ	chizz
CHKNU	chunk
CHKOO	choko
	chook
CHKOS	shock
CHKOY	choky
CHKSU	shuck
CHKTU	kutch
CHLMU	mulch
CHLNU	lunch
CHLNY	lynch
CHLOT	cloth
CHLRU	churl
	lurch
CHMNU	munch
CHMOO	△choom
	mooch
CHMOP	chomp
CHMOS	schmo
CHMOU	mouch
CHMOY	mochy
CHMPU	chump
CHMTU	mutch
CHNOT	notch
CHNPU	△punch
CHNRU	churn
	runch
CHNSY	synch
CHOOP	pooch
CHOOS	cohos
CHOPR	porch
CHOPS	chops
CHOPT	potch
CHOPU	pouch
CHORT	rotch
	torch
CHORY	ochry
CHOSU	hocus
CHOTT	chott
CHOTU	chout
	couth
	oucht
	touch
CHOUV	vouch
CHOUX	choux
CHPSY	psych
CHRRU	churr
CHRSU	crush
CHRTW	crwth
CHSUY	cushy
CIILT	licit

Words marked △ may be spelled also with a capital letter

CIILV	civil
CIILY	icily
CIIMM	mimic
CIINO	△ionic
CIINR	ricin
CIINS	Sinic
CIIPP	cippi
CIIRR	cirri
CIJUY	juicy
CIKKS	kicks
CIKLN	clink
CIKLS	licks
	slick
CIKMY	micky
CIKNS	snick
CIKOS	sicko
CIKOY	yoick
CIKPR	prick
CIKPS	spick
CIKPY	picky
CIKQU	quick
CIKRT	trick
CIKRW	wrick
CIKST	stick
	ticks
CIKTY	ticky
CIKWY	wicky
CILMS	sclim
CILNO	colin
	△nicol
CILNT	clint
CILOR	loric
CILOT	lotic
CILOU	oculi
CILOW	wilco
CILPT	clipt
CILPU	picul
CILRY	lyric
CILSU	sulci
CILXY	cylix
	xylic
CIMNO	nomic
CIMNU	cumin
	mucin
CIMOR	micro
	Romic
CIMOS	micos
	osmic
CIMPR	crimp
CIMRS	scrim
CIMSU	Musci
	music
CIMYZ	zymic
CINNO	conin
CINOR	corni
	orcin
CINOS	scion
	sonic
CINOT	tonic
CINOV	covin
CINOZ	zinco
CINPU	Punic
CINRU	incur
	runic
CINSU	incus
CINTT	tinct
CINTU	cutin
	cut-in
	incut
	tunic
CINYZ	zincy
CIOPT	Optic®
	optic
	picot
	topic
CIORR	roric
CIORS	siroc
CIORT	toric
	Troic
CIORU	curio
CIOST	△stoic
	Ticos
CIOTX	toxic
CIPRS	crisp
	scrip
CIPRY	pricy
CIPSU	Picus
CIPSY	spicy
CIPTY	typic
CIRSU	cursi
CISSY	cissy
CISTU	cutis
	ictus
CIVVY	civvy
CJKOO	jocko
CJNOU	junco
CKKNO	knock
CKLNO	clonk
CKLNU	clunk
CKLOS	locks
CKLPU	pluck
CKLSU	sculk
CKLUY	△lucky
CKMOS	mocks
	smock
CKMUY	mucky
CKNOR	cronk
CKNOY	conky
CKNSU	snuck
CKOOR	crook
CKOOS	socko
CKOOY	cooky
CKOPY	pocky
CKORS	rocks
CKORT	trock
CKORY	corky
	rocky
CKOSS	socks
CKOST	stock
CKRTU	truck
CKSSU	sucks
CKSTU	stuck
CKUYY	yucky
CLLOY	colly
CLLSU	scull
CLLUY	cully
CLMOP	clomp
CLMOU	locum
CLMPU	clump
CLMTU	mulct
CLNOO	colon
CLNOW	clown
CLOOP	cloop
CLOOR	color
CLOOS	locos
CLOOT	cloot
CLOOY	cooly
CLORU	clour
CLOSU	locus
CLOSW	scowl
CLOTU	clout
CLOYY	coyly
CLPSU	sculp
CLRUY	curly
CMMOO	commo
CMMOS	comms
CMMOY	commy
CMOOP	compo
CMOOY	coomy
CMOPT	compt
CMORU	mucor
	mucro
CMOSU	△comus
CMPRU	crump
CMRSU	scrum
CMRYY	Cymry
CMSUU	mucus
CNOOR	corno
	croon
CNOOT	conto
CNOOV	convo
CNOPY	poncy
CNORS	scorn
CNORT	tronc
CNORU	cornu
CNORW	△crown
CNORY	corny
	crony
CNOSU	oncus
	uncos
CNOTU	count
CNOTY	cyton
CNRUY	curny
CNSUU	uncus
CNTUU	uncut
COOPS	scoop
COOPT	coopt
	co-opt
COORS	corso
COOST	coost
	scoot
	tocos
COPPY	coppy
COPRS	corps
COPRU	croup
COPSS	Scops
COPSU	scoup
COPSW	scowp
COPSY	copsy
COPUY	coypu
CORRU	cruor
CORSS	△cross
CORSU	scour
CORSW	scrow
CORTU	court
	crout
	Turco
CORWY	cowry
COSST	costs
	Scots
COSTU	△scout
	souct
COTTU	cutto
CPRTY	crypt
CPTUU	cut-up
CRRUY	curry
CRSTU	crust
	curst
CRSUY	crusy
CRUVY	curvy
CSUZZ	scuzz
CTTUY	cutty

D

DDDIY	diddy
DDDOY	doddy
DDDUY	duddy
DDEEG	edged
DDEEN	ended
DDEEY	deedy
DDEGO	dodge
DDEIO	diode
DDEIR	dried
	redid
DDEIS	sided
DDEIV	dived
DDEMO	domed
DDENY	△neddy
DDEOT	doted
	todde
DDEOW	dowed
DDEOZ	dozed
DDERU	udder
DDERY	reddy
	ydred
DDEST	stedd
DDETY	△teddy
DDGIY	giddy
DDGOY	dodgy
DDIKO	kiddo
DDIKY	kiddy
DDILO	dildo
DDIMY	middy
DDINU	undid
DDIOS	didos
DDIRU	△druid
DDIST	didst
DDITY	tiddy

DIWY	widdy
DLOY	oddly
DMUY	muddy
DNOY	noddy
DOOS	dodos
DOPY	poddy
DOSY	soddy
DOTY	toddy
DOWY	dowdy
DPUY	puddy
DRUY	ruddy
EEER	deere
	reede
EEEV	deeve
EEFR	defer
	freed
EEGH	hedge
EEGK	kedge
EEGL	glede
	gleed
	ledge
EEGO	geode
	ogee'd
EEGR	edger
	greed
EEGS	sedge
EEGW	wedge
EEHW	hewed
EEHY	heedy
EEIL	edile
	elide
EEIN	diene
EEIR	eider
EEKN	kneed
	knee'd
EEKY	keyed
EELM	medle
EELN	neeld
EELR	elder
EELS	seeld
EELU	elude
EELV	delve
	devel
EEMN	emend
EEMR	mered
EEMT	meted
	temed
EENO	donee
EENS	dense
	needs
EENT	teend
EENU	endue
	undee
	undée
EENW	endew
EENY	needy
EENZ	Enzed
EEOP	epode
EEOR	doree
	erode
EEOX	exode
EEPS	speed
DEERR	drere
	erred
DEERS	Seder
DEERT	deter
DEERU	urdee
	urdée
DEERY	reedy
DEESS	desse
	sedes
DEEST	stede
	steed
DEESU	suede
	suède
DEESW	sewed
	△swede
	weeds
DEESX	desex
	sexed
DEESY	seedy
DEETU	étude
DEETW	tweed
DEEUX	exude
DEEVX	vexed
DEEWY	Dewey
	weedy
DEFGI	fidge
DEFGU	fudge
DEFIL	felid
	field
	filed
DEFIN	fiend
DEFIR	fired
	fried
DEFIT	fetid
DEFIX	fixed
DEFIY	deify
	edify
DEFLS	delfs
DEFLT	delft
DEFMR	fremd
DEFNU	unfed
DEFNY	fendy
DEFOX	foxed
DEGGU	ugged
DEGHO	Hodge
DEGHY	hedgy
DEGIK	kidge
DEGIL	gelid
	glide
DEGIM	midge
DEGIN	deign
	dinge
DEGIO	dogie
	geoid
DEGIR	derig
	dirge
	gride
	ridge
DEGIU	△guide
DEGJU	judge
DEGKY	kedgy
DEGLO	glode
	lodge
DEGLU	glued
DEGLY	gyeld
	ledgy
DEGMU	degum
	mudge
DEGNU	nudge
DEGOP	podge
DEGOT	godet
	toged
DEGOW	wodge
DEGPU	pudge
DEGRS	dregs
DEGRY	gryde
DEGSY	sedgy
DEGWY	wedgy
DEHIM	Mehdi
DEHIR	hider
	hired
DEHIS	shied
DEHLO	dhole
DEHLP	delph
DEHNS	shend
DEHNY	hynde
DEHOP	ephod
DEHOR	horde
DEHOS	doseh
	hosed
	shoed
DEHOT	doeth
DEHPT	depth
DEHRS	sherd
	shred
DEHRT	derth
DEHTY	they'd
DEIIM	imide
DEIIN	indie
DEIIV	ivied
DEIIX	dixie
DEIJR	jerid
DEIKL	kidel
DEIKP	piked
DEIKR	diker
	dirke
DEIKS	skied
DEIKY	dikey
DEILN	eldin
	lined
DEILO	oiled
	oldie
DEILP	lepid
	piel'd
	plied
DEILR	idler
DEILS	sidle
	sield
	slide
DEILT	tilde
	tiled
DEILV	△devil
	lived
	vilde
DEILW	dwile
	wield
DEILY	yield
DEIMN	denim
DEIMR	dimer
	rimed
DEIMS	deism
	disme
DEIMT	demit
	timed
DEIMX	mixed
DEINP	piend
DEINR	diner
DEINS	sdein
	snide
DEINT	teind
	tined
DEINU	indue
	nudie
DEINW	dwine
	indew
	widen
DEINX	index
DEINZ	dizen
DEIOV	dovie
	video
DEIOW	dowie
DEIOX	oxide
DEIPP	piped
DEIPR	pride
	pried
	redip
DEIPS	spide
	spied
DEIPT	tepid
DEIQU	equid
DEIRR	drier
	reird
	rider
DEIRS	dries
	sider
DEIRT	tired
	tride
	tried
DEIRU	rudie
DEIRV	diver
	drive
	rived
DEIRW	weird
	wired
DEISS	sides
DEIST	deist
	stied
DEISV	Dives
DEISZ	sized
DEITY	△deity
DEIVX	ex-div
DEIYZ	Yezdi
DEJLO	jodel

DEJOY	joyed
DEKKO	dekko
DEKNO	kendo
DEKNU	unked
DEKNY	kynde
DEKOP	poked
DEKYY	dykey
DELLT	tell'd
DELLW	dwell
DELMO	model
DELMU	ledum
DELNO	loden
	olden
DELNU	unled
DELOO	doole
DELOR	drôle
	older
DELOS	solde
DELOW	dowel
	dowle
DELOY	odyle
	yodel
	yodle
DELPS	speld
DELPU	duple
	upled
DELRY	redly
DELSU	dulse
	slued
DELTV	veldt
DELTW	dwelt
DEMMO	modem
DEMNO	demon
DEMNS	mends
DEMOP	moped
DEMOR	drome
	moder
DEMOS	demos
DEMOT	moted
DEMOU	odeum
DEMOV	moved
DEMOW	mowed
DEMPT	dempt
DEMRU	demur
DEMSU	mused
	sedum
DEMTU	muted
DENNO	donne
	donné
	end-on
DENOO	odeon
DENOR	drone
	ronde
DENOS	nosed
	sonde
DENOT	Donet
	noted
	toned
DENOV	Devon
DENOW	endow
	nowed
	Woden
DENOY	doyen
DENOZ	dozen
	zoned
DENPS	spend
DENPU	upend
	up-end
DENRT	drent
	trend
DENRU	runed
	under
	unred
	urned
DENRY	nerdy
DENST	stend
DENTU	tuned
DENTY	tynde
	tyned
DENUU	undue
DENUW	unwed
DEOOR	rodeo
DEOOW	wooed
DEOPR	doper
	pedro
	roped
DEOPS	△spode
DEOPT	depot
DEOPX	podex
DEOPY	dopey
DEORR	order
DEORS	dorse
	rosed
DEORT	doter
	trode
DEORU	uredo
DEORV	dover
	drove
DEORW	dower
DEORX	redox
DEORZ	dozer
DEOST	doest
DEOSU	douse
DEOSW	dowse
	sowed
DEOTU	outed
DEOTV	dévot
DEOTX	detox
DEOVW	vowed
DEPPU	upped
DEPRS	spred
DEPRU	drupe
	duper
	perdu
	prude
DEPRY	perdy
	predy
DEPSU	pseud
DERRY	derry
	dryer
DERSS	dress
DERST	drest
DERSU	△druse
DERTY	tyred
DERUZ	Druze
DESTU	duets
DESTY	styed
DETTU	duett
DETUV	duvet
DFILU	fluid
DFINU	fundi
DFIOR	fiord
DFIRT	drift
DFJOR	fjord
DFLOO	△flood
DFNOR	frond
DFNOS	fonds
DFNOU	found
DFNSU	funds
DFNUY	fundy
DFOOR	fordo
DFOOY	foody
DFORW	F-word
DGGOO	doggo
DGGOY	doggy
DGHIT	dight
DGHOU	dough
DGIIR	rigid
DGIIT	digit
DGILU	guild
DGINO	dingo
	doing
	OD'ing
DGINR	D-ring
	grind
DGINY	dingy
	dying
DGIOP	pi-dog
DGIRY	ridgy
DGLOO	goold
DGLOY	godly
	goldy
DGNOU	ungod
DGNUU	undug
DGNUY	dungy
	gundy
DGOOO	good-o
DGOOR	droog
DGOOS	godso
	goods
DGOOY	goody
DGOPY	podgy
DGORU	gourd
DGORY	grody
DGPUY	pudgy
DGRSU	drugs
DGRUY	durgy
DHIIN	Hindi
DHIMU	humid
DHINU	Hindu
DHIOT	dhoti
DHIOY	hyoid
DHIRT	third
	thrid
DHISY	dishy
DHITW	width
DHLLO	dholl
DHNOU	hound
DHNSU	dunsh
DHOOR	hoord
DHOOY	dohyo
DHORY	hydro
	rhody
DHOTU	thou'd
DHOVZ	vozhd
DHOWY	howdy
DHRSU	hurds
DIILL	dilli
DIILP	lipid
DIILV	livid
DIIMO	idiom
	modii
DIIMT	timid
DIINR	indri
DIINS	Sindi
DIINT	nitid
DIIOT	idiot
DIIRV	virid
DIIST	Idist
DIIVV	vivid
DIJNN	djinn
DIKNO	kid-on
DIKNR	drink
DIKNU	unkid
DIKNY	dinky
	kindy
DIKSS	skids
DILLR	drill
DILLY	dilly
	idyll
DILMY	dimly
DILNO	indol
DILNU	unlid
DILOR	droil
DILOS	lidos
	silo'd
	sloid
	soldi
	solid
DILOT	doilt
DILOV	viold
DILOY	doily
DILRT	trild
DILRU	lurid
DILRY	drily
DILSW	wilds
DIMNO	mid-on
DIMNS	minds
DIMOS	misdo
	odism
DIMOU	duomi
	odium
DIMOY	myoid
DIMRU	mudir
DIMST	midst
	'midst
DIMTU	tumid
DINOP	poind

Words marked △ may be spelled also with a capital letter

DINOR nidor
DINOT on-dit
tondi
DINRU unrid
DINRY rindy
DINSU nidus
DINSW winds
DINWY windy
DIOOV ovoid
DIOOZ zooid
DIOPS dipso
DIOPY pyoid
DIORR rorid
DIORS Doris
DIORT droit
DIOST odist
DIOTT ditto
DIOTV divot
DIOWW △widow
DIPPY dippy
DIPTU putid
DIQSU quids
squid
DIRTY dirty
DIRVY yrivd
DISTY ditsy
DITTY ditty
DITYZ ditzy
DIVVY divvy
DIYZZ dizzy
DJOOS dojos
DKMUY dumky
DKNRU drunk
DKOOR drook
DKORU drouk
DKORY dorky
DKOSU kudos
DKSTY kydst
DKSUY dusky
DKUUZ kudzu
DLLOR droll
DLLOY dolly
DLLUY dully
DLMOU mould
DLNOU lound
nould
n'ould
DLNOW lownd
DLOOR dolor
drool
loord
DLOOS soldo
DLOOW woold
DLORS Lords
DLORW △world
DLORY lordy
DLOSU ludos
DLOSY sloyd
DLOUW would
DLOYY doyly
DLPUY duply
DLRYY dryly

DMMUY dummy
DMNOO mondo
DMNOU mound
DMOOS dooms
dsomo
Sodom
DMOOU duomo
DMOOY doomy
moody
DMORY dormy
DMOSU modus
DMPSU dumps
DMPUY dumpy
DMRUU durum
DNNOU dunno
DNNUY dunny
DNOOR donor
doorn
rondo
DNOOS snood
DNOOT tondo
DNOPU pound
DNOPW pownd
DNORU round
DNORW drown
rownd
DNORY drony
DNOST don'ts
stond
DNOSU nodus
sound
unsod
DNOSW △downs
sownd
DNOSY △synod
DNOTU donut
DNOUW wound
DNOUY oundy
DNOWY downy
DOOPR droop
DOORS sordo
DOORU odour
DOOSS odsos
DOOST stood
to-dos
DOOSW woods
DOOTU outdo
DOOWY woody
DOPRS drops
sprod
DOPRU proud
pudor
DORSS dross
DORST dorts
DORSU duros
sudor
DORSW sword
words
DORTU Tudor
DORTY dorty
DORUY duroy

DORWY dowry
rowdy
wordy
DOTTY dotty
DPPUY duppy
DPSUY pudsy
DRSTU durst
DRSUY drusy
DRUXY druxy
DSSUY sudsy
DSTUY dusty
study

E

EEEFS feese
EEEFZ feeze
EEEGS geese
EEEHT te-hee
EEEHZ heeze
EEEIR eerie
EEEJZ Jeeze
EEEKV keeve
EEEKW weeke
EEELM mêlée
EEELN neele
EEELP elpee
EEELS leese
EEELV levee
EEELZ leeze
EEEMR emeer
EEEMS semée
EEEMX exeem
exeme
EEENS neese
EEENT teene
EEENV eeven
EEENZ neeze
EEEPP peepe
EEEPT tepee
EEEPV peeve
EEERV reeve
EEETW etwee
weete
EEFHM △fehme
EEFHT hefte
EEFIR fiere
EEFLM fleme
EEFLR fleer
refel
EEFLT △fleet
lefte
EEFMM femme
EEFRR freer
frère
refer
EEFRT freet
terfe
EEFRV fever
EEFRY yfere
EEFSS fesse
EEFSU fusee
EEFSZ fezes

EEFTW wefte
EEFUZ fuzee
EEGGL legge
EEGGR egger
grège
EEGHN henge
EEGIL liege
EEGIN eigne
genie
EEGIR régie
EEGIS siege
EEGIV vegie
EEGKL gleek
EEGKR Greek
EEGKY geeky
EEGLM gemel
EEGLO éloge
EEGLR gerle
leger
EEGLT gleet
EEGLY elegy
EEGMN menge
EEGMR merge
EEGNR genre
gerne
△green
EEGNT genet
EEGNV venge
EEGNW ngwee
EEGRS grees
grese
Seger
serge
EEGRT egret
greet
EEGRV greve
verge
EEGSS gesse
EEGST egest
geste
EEGSU segue
EEHKT theek
EEHLS sheel
EEHLT Lethe
EEHLV helve
EEHLW wheel
EEHMT theme
EEHMV △vehme
EEHNP phene
EEHNS sheen
EEHNW wheen
EEHOR heroe
EEHOV evhoe
evohe
EEHPR pheer
EEHPS phese
sheep
EEHRS herse
sheer
shere

EEHRT	ether
	there
	three
EEHRW	hewer
	where
EEHRY	herye
EEHST	sheet
	these
EEHTT	teeth
	thete
EEIKV	kieve
EEILM	elemi
EEILR	relie
EEILS	eisel
	esile
EEILT	elite
	élite
EEILV	lieve
EEILX	△exile
EEIMS	semie
EEIMV	mieve
EEINP	penie
EEINR	Ernie
EEINS	seine
EEINV	neive
	nieve
EEINX	exine
EEIPS	peise
EEIPZ	peize
EEIRT	retie
EEIRV	reive
	revie
	rieve
EEIRY	eyrie
EEISS	seise
EEISV	sieve
EEISW	weise
EEISX	exies
EEISZ	seize
EEITV	evite
EEITY	Eyeti
	Eytie
EEIWZ	weize
EEJLW	jewel
EEJLY	jeely
EEJNU	jeune
EEJSS	Jesse
EEJSU	sujee
EEKLN	kneel
EEKLS	sleek
EEKLV	kevel
EEKLW	welke
EEKMS	smeek
EEKNR	kerne
EEKNS	skene
EEKNT	kente
EEKOP	pekoe
EEKOV	evoke
EEKPS	keeps
EEKRS	esker
	skeer
EEKRT	△terek
EEKRV	kerve
EEKRY	reeky
EEKST	skeet
	steek
EEKSW	weeks
EELLM	lemel
EELLS	selle
EELLV	level
EELMN	elmen
EELMR	merel
	merle
EELMS	mesel
EELMU	emule
EELNO	leone
EELNR	Lerne
EELNS	lenes
EELNV	nevel
EELNW	newel
EELOP	elope
EELPR	leper
	repel
EELPS	sleep
	speel
EELPX	expel
EELRS	reels
EELRT	relet
EELRV	elver
	lever
	revel
EELRY	leery
EELST	sleet
	steel
	stele
EELSV	elves
EELSW	sewel
	sweel
EELSY	seely
EELTT	ettle
EELTU	elute
EELTW	tewel
	tweel
EELTX	telex
	Texel
EEMMN	mneme
EEMMR	emmer
EEMMT	emmet
EEMMW	emmew
EEMNR	remen
EEMNS	mense
	mesne
	semen
EEMNU	neume
EEMNW	enmew
EEMNY	enemy
EEMOT	emote
EEMOV	emove
EEMPT	Tempe
EEMQU	queme
EEMRS	merse
EEMRT	meter
	metre
EEMRU	emure
EEMRX	remex
EEMRY	emery
EEMST	steem
	steme
	temse
EEMSU	meuse
EEMZZ	mezze
EENNP	penne
EENNR	renne
EENNT	tenné
EENOR	one-er
EENPR	neper
	preen
EENPS	penes
EENQU	△queen
EENRS	sneer
EENRT	enter
	rente
	terne
	treen
EENRU	enure
EENRV	erven
	nerve
	never
EENRW	renew
EENRY	reney
EENRZ	Zener
EENSS	sense
EENST	steen
	teens
	tense
EENSU	ensue
EENSV	evens
	seven
EENSW	ensew
	sewen
EENSY	seyen
EENTT	tenet
EENTU	tenue
EENTV	event
EENTW	'tween
EENTY	teeny
EENUV	venue
EENVY	veney
	yeven
EENWY	weeny
	yewen
EEOPP	opepe
EEOPT	topee
EEOPY	peeoy
EEORS	erose
	soree
EEOWW	wowee
EEOXY	ox-eye
EEPRS	perse
	prese
	speer
	spree
EEPRT	peter
	petre
EEPRU	puree
	purée
	rupee
EEPRV	perve
	preve
EEPRY	peery
EEPST	steep
EEPSU	upsee
EEPSW	sweep
EEPSY	peyse
	seepy
EEPWY	weepy
EEQRU	queer
EEQUU	queue
EERRS	serre
EERST	ester
	reest
	reset
	steer
	stere
	teres
	terse
EERSU	reuse
EERSV	serve
	sever
	verse
EERSW	sewer
	sweer
EERSX	sexer
	Xeres
EERTV	evert
	revet
EERTW	tweer
	'twere
EERTX	exert
EERUV	revue
EERVV	verve
EERVX	vexer
EERVY	every
	veery
EESSS	esses
EESSX	Essex
EESSY	sesey
	yeses
EESTT	teste
EESTW	ewest
	sweet
EETTU	tutee
EETTV	Tevet
EETTW	tweet
EFFFO	feoff
EFFIR	fifer
EFFOR	offer
	reffo
EFFRU	ruffe
EFFTU	tuffe
EFGIN	feign
EFGIR	grief
EFGIU	fugie
EFGLO	fogle
EFGLU	fugle
	Guelf

EFGOR	forge
	gofer
EFGOY	fogey
EFGRU	grufe
EFGUU	fugue
EFHIT	thief
EFHLO	f-hole
EFHLS	flesh
	shelf
EFHLT	thelf
EFHNO	foehn
EFHRS	fresh
EFHTT	theft
EFHTW	wheft
EFHTY	hefty
EFIIW	wifie
EFIKN	knife
EFIKR	kefir
EFILL	fille
EFILN	elfin
EFILO	folie
EFILR	filer
	flier
	lifer
	rifle
EFILS	Felis
	flies
	'slife
EFILT	filet
	flite
EFIMR	fermi
EFIMT	△metif
EFINR	finer
	infer
EFINS	fines
EFINT	feint
	fient
EFINX	enfix
EFIPR	preif
	prief
EFIRR	firer
	frier
EFIRS	fries
	serif
EFIRT	freit
	refit
	rifte
	treif
EFIRV	fiver
EFIRX	fixer
EFIRY	fiery
	reify
EFIRZ	frize
EFISV	fives
EFITT	fitte
EFKLS	skelf
EFKLU	fluke
EFKNS	fenks
EFLLY	felly
EFLMU	flume
EFLNO	felon
EFLOR	forel
EFLOT	flote
EFLOU	foulé
EFLOY	foyle
EFLPY	flype
EFLRY	ferly
	flyer
EFLSS	selfs
EFLSW	flews
EFLTU	flute
EFLTY	felty
	flyte
	lefty
EFLUY	fluey
EFMOR	forme
EFMOS	fomes
EFMRU	femur
EFMSU	fumes
EFMTU	fumet
EFNNY	fenny
EFNOR	Freon®
	freon
EFNOT	often
EFNOY	foyne
EFNRY	ferny
EFORR	frore
EFORT	fetor
	forte
EFORU	fuero
EFORX	forex
EFORY	foyer
EFORZ	froze
EFOSS	fosse
EFOTU	fouet
EFRRY	ferry
	fryer
EFRSS	serfs
EFRSW	swerf
EFRUZ	furze
EFSTU	fetus
EFTTY	fytte
EGGIL	ligge
EGGIU	gigue
EGGKS	skegg
EGGLY	leggy
EGGNU	gunge
EGGOP	pogge
EGGOR	gorge
	grego
	reggo
EGGOU	gouge
EGGPY	peggy
EGGRU	gurge
EGHHI	heigh
EGHHU	heugh
EGHHW	hewgh
EGHIN	hinge
	neigh
EGHIT	eight
EGHIW	weigh
EGHLU	leugh
EGHLY	hyleg
EGHNO	hogen
EGHNT	thegn
EGHPT	Peght
EGHST	ghest
EGHTU	teugh
EGIIN	genii
EGIJR	rejig
	re-jig
EGIKL	glike
EGIKR	grike
EGILN	Elgin
	ingle
	ligne
EGILO	logie
EGILR	liger
	Rigel
EGILT	gilet
	legit
EGILU	guile
EGIMM	gimme
EGIMN	minge
EGIMR	grime
EGINP	genip
EGINR	grein
	niger
	reign
	renig
EGINS	singe
EGINT	tinge
EGINV	given
EGINW	winge
EGINY	eying
	gynie
EGIOV	ogive
	vogie
EGIPR	gripe
EGIRS	grise
EGIRT	tiger
EGIRV	giver
	virge
EGIRZ	grize
EGIST	geist
EGISU	guise
EGKNR	kreng
EGKRY	gryke
EGLLY	gelly
EGLMO	golem
EGLMU	glume
EGLNO	longe
EGLNT	glent
EGLNU	lunge
EGLOP	golpe
EGLOR	ogler
EGLOS	segol
EGLOV	glove
EGLOY	elogy
EGLOZ	gloze
EGLRU	gluer
	gruel
	Luger®
	luger
EGLSU	gules
	gusle
EGLUY	gluey
	guyle
EGMMY	gemmy
EGMNO	emong
	genom
	gnome
EGMOT	gemot
EGMRU	grume
EGNOR	ergon
	Genro
	goner
	grone
	△negro
EGNOS	segno
EGNPU	unpeg
EGNST	gents
	gents'
EGNSU	genus
	△negus
EGNTU	unget
EGNTY	genty
EGOOS	goose
EGOOY	gooey
EGOPR	grope
	porge
EGORR	△roger
EGORS	gorse
	soger
EGORT	ergot
EGORU	orgue
	rogue
	rouge
EGORV	△grove
EGOSS	gesso
	gosse
	segos
EGOTU	togue
EGOTY	goety
EGOUV	vogue
	vouge
EGPRU	purge
EGPRY	grype
EGPTU	get-up
EGPTY	Egypt
EGQSU	squeg
EGRRU	regur
	urger
EGRRY	Gerry
EGRSU	surge
EGRSY	Greys
EGSSU	guess
EGSTU	guest
EGSUY	guyse
EGUUX	Gueux
EHHIT	hithe
EHHTY	hythe
EHIKR	hiker
EHIKS	sheik
EHIKT	kithe
EHILS	leish
	shiel
EHILT	lithe

EHILW	while
EHILX	△helix
EHIMN	hemin
EHIMR	rhime
EHIMS	hiems
EHIMT	meith
EHINR	△rhine
EHINS	shine
EHINT	thine
EHINW	whine
EHINZ	△hizen
EHIOS	hoise
EHIRR	hirer
EHIRS	shier
	shire
EHIRT	their
EHIRV	hiver
EHISS	shies
EHIST	heist
	shite
	sieth
	sithe
EHISV	hives
	shive
EHITT	tithe
EHITW	△white
	withe
EHKLW	whelk
EHKMR	Khmer
EHKMS	shmek
EHKOY	hokey
EHKTY	kythe
EHLLO	hello
EHLLS	shell
	she'll
EHLMO	mohel
EHLMW	whelm
EHLOS	△sheol
	△she'ol
EHLOT	helot
	hotel
	thole
EHLOV	hovel
EHLOW	whole
EHLOY	holey
EHLPS	plesh
	shlep
EHLPW	whelp
EHLPY	phyle
EHLSU	shule
EHLSW	△welsh
EHLTU	Thule
EHLTY	△ethyl
	lythe
EHMMO	homme
EHMNS	mensh
EHMNY	△hymen
EHMOR	homer
	horme
EHMOS	shmoe
EHMOY	homey
EHMPY	hempy

EHMRS	herms
EHMRT	therm
EHMRU	△rheum
EHMRY	rhyme
EHMST	meths
EHMSY	meshy
EHMTY	thyme
EHNNY	henny
EHNOO	ohone
EHNOP	pheon
	phone
	'phone
EHNOR	heron
	honer
	rhone
EHNOS	hosen
	shone
EHNOT	hoten
EHNOV	hoven
EHNOY	honey
EHNRY	△henry
	rhyne
	yrneh
EHNST	shent
EHNSW	shewn
EHNTT	tenth
EHNTU	uneth
EHOOV	hoove
EHOOY	hooey
EHOPR	ephor
	hoper
EHOPS	shope
EHOPU	ouphe
EHORS	horse
	shoer
	shore
EHORT	other
	throe
EHORV	hover
EHORW	howre
	whore
EHOSS	hoses
	shoes
EHOST	ethos
	shote
	those
EHOSU	△house
EHOSV	shove
EHOSW	whose
EHOTW	theow
EHOVW	who've
EHOWW	ewhow
EHPRY	hyper
EHRRY	herry
EHRSU	usher
EHRSW	shrew
	wersh
EHRSY	shyer
EHRTW	rewth
	threw
EHRTZ	hertz
EHSTU	shute

EHSTW	thews
EHSTY	sythe
EHTTY	tythe
EHTWY	thewy
EIIJM	Meiji
EIILN	lie-in
EIILP	pilei
EIIMN	imine
	Minié
EIINS	nisei
EIINT	tie-in
EIINX	nixie
EIIPX	pixie
EIISS	issei
EIISV	visie
EIJMO	ojime
EIJRV	jiver
EIKLM	kelim
	melik
EIKLN	inkle
	liken
EIKLR	liker
EIKLS	Sikel
EIKLY	kiley
	kylie
	ylike
EIKMN	minke
EIKNO	eikon
	enoki
	△koine
EIKNP	Pekin
EIKNR	inker
EIKNS	Neski
	skein
EIKNV	knive
EIKNZ	zinke
EIKOZ	ozeki
EIKPR	piker
EIKPS	spike
EIKRS	skier
EIKRT	trike
EIKRY	Kyrie
EIKSS	skies
EIKST	skite
EIKSV	skive
EIKSY	skiey
	yikes
EILLM	mille
EILLR	rille
EILLS	lisle
EILMN	limen
EILMP	impel
EILMR	meril
	miler
EILMS	limes
	slime
	smile
EILMU	ileum
EILMY	limey
EILNN	linen
EILNO	eloin
	olein

EILNR	liner
EILNS	elsin
	lenis
	lines
	nelis
	silen
EILNT	inlet
	lenti
EILNV	levin
	liven
EILNY	liney
EILOP	loipe
EILOR	oiler
	oriel
EILOT	toile
EILOV	olive
	voile
EILPR	peril
	piler
	plier
EILPS	piles
	plies
	slipe
	spiel
	spile
EILPX	pixel
EILRS	siler
	slier
EILRT	liter
	litre
	tiler
EILRV	liver
	livre
	rivel
EILRY	△riley
EILST	islet
	istle
	steil
	stile
	tiles
EILSU	ileus
EILSV	Levis®
	levis
	lives
	slive
EILSW	△lewis
	wiles
EILSX	lexis
	silex
EILSZ	sizel
EILTT	title
EILTU	utile
EILTX	ixtle
EILUY	ulyie
EILUZ	ulzie
EILVY	veily
EILZZ	zizel
EIMMR	mimer
EIMMW	immew
EIMNR	inerm
	miner
EIMNT	meint

EIMNX	mixen
EIMNY	meiny
EIMNZ	mizen
EIMOR	moire
	moiré
EIMOV	movie
EIMOX	moxie
	oxime
EIMPR	prime
EIMPT	tempi
EIMPU	pumie
EIMRR	rimer
EIMRS	miser
EIMRT	merit
	miter
	mitre
	remit
	timer
EIMRX	mixer
	remix
EIMSS	seism
	semis
EIMST	Metis
	△métis
	smite
	stime
	△times
EINNR	inner
	renin
EINNU	ennui
EINNV	venin
EINOP	opine
EINOS	eosin
	noise
EINOT	toe-in
EINOV	envoi
	ovine
EINPR	ripen
EINPS	penis
	snipe
	spine
EINPT	inept
	nepit
EINPY	piney
EINQU	quine
EINRS	reins
	resin
	rinse
	risen
	serin
	△siren
EINRT	inert
	inter
	niter
	nitre
	trine
EINRU	inure
	urine
EINRV	riven
	viner
EINSS	nisse
EINST	inset
	neist
	sient
	stein
EINSV	visne
EINSW	sewin
	sinew
	swine
EINSX	nixes
EINTT	ettin
EINTU	unite
	untie
EINTW	twine
EINVW	vinew
EINVX	vixen
EINVY	veiny
EINWY	winey
EINWZ	winze
	wizen
EIOOR	oorie
EIOPS	poise
EIOPY	pioye
EIOPZ	piezo
EIORR	rorie
EIORS	osier
EIORU	ourie
EIORV	vireo
EIORW	owrie
EIOSS	Ossie
EIOST	toise
EIOTZ	tozie
EIOWY	yowie
EIOWZ	△zowie
EIPPR	△piper
EIPPS	pipes
EIPQU	equip
	pique
	piqué
EIPRR	prier
	riper
EIPRS	épris
	pries
	prise
	speir
	spire
EIPRT	△petri
	piert
	tripe
EIPRV	viper
EIPRW	wiper
EIPRZ	prize
EIPSS	spies
EIPST	piste
	spite
	stipe
EIPSW	swipe
EIPTT	petit
EIPTU	tie-up
	uptie
EIPTW	pewit
EIPTY	piety
EIQRU	quire
EIQTU	quiet
	quite
EIRRS	riser
EIRRT	trier
EIRRV	river
EIRRW	wirer
	wrier
EIRST	reist
	resit
	rites
	stire
	tries
EIRSV	siver
	vires
EIRSW	sweir
	swire
	wires
EIRSX	sixer
EIRSZ	sizer
EIRTT	titer
	titre
	trite
EIRTU	urite
	uteri
EIRTV	rivet
EIRTW	twier
	twire
	write
EIRVV	viver
EIRVZ	vezir
EISST	sties
EISSU	issue
EISSX	sixes
EISTU	suite
EISTV	stive
EISTX	exist
	exits
	sixte
EISTY	seity
EISVV	vives
EISVW	swive
	wives
EITTW	tewit
	twite
EITVX	vitex
EIVWY	viewy
EJKOP	kopje
EJKOR	joker
EJKOY	jokey
EJKRS	jerks
EJKRY	jerky
EJLLO	jello
EJLLY	jelly
EJLOU	joule
EJLPU	julep
EJMMY	jemmy
EJNNY	△jenny
EJNOR	rejón
EJNOT	jeton
EJNOY	enjoy
EJPTU	upjet
EJRRY	△jerry
EJRWY	Jewry
EJSSU	Jesus
	jésus
EJTTY	jetty
EKKOR	koker
EKLLN	knell
EKLLS	skell
EKLLY	kelly
EKLMS	skelm
EKLNT	knelt
EKLOY	kyloe
	yokel
EKLPS	skelp
	spelk
EKLPT	P-Kelt
EKLPY	kelpy
EKLQT	Q-Kelt
EKLTW	welkt
EKLTY	kelty
EKMOS	△smoke
EKMPS	kemps
EKMPT	kempt
EKNNO	ken-no
EKNOR	krone
EKNOS	snoek
	snoke
	soken
EKNOT	token
EKNOW	knowe
	woken
EKNSY	ensky
EKNTU	unket
EKOPR	poker
	proke
EKOPS	pokes
	spoke
EKOPT	topek
EKOPU	pouke
EKOPY	pokey
EKORR	roker
EKORT	troke
EKORW	wroke
EKOSS	sekos
	skeos
EKOST	stoke
EKPRU	puker
EKPRY	perky
EKPSY	pesky
EKPTU	tupek
EKRRU	kurre
EKRSY	skyer
	skyre
	syker
EKSTY	skyte
EKSYY	skyey
ELLMS	smell
ELLNS	snell
ELLNY	nelly
ELLOR	lorel
ELLOS	losel
ELLPS	spell
ELLQU	quell

Words marked △ may be spelled also with a capital letter

ELLSS sells
ELLST stell
ELLSW swell
ELLTU tulle
ELLTY telly
ELLWY welly
ELMMU lumme
ELMNO lemon
melon
Monel®
ELMNU lumen
ELMOR morel
ELMOS Mosel
ELMOT metol
motel
ELMOU oleum
ELMOY moyle
ELMPU plume
ELMRU lemur
ELMST smelt
ELMSU mulse
ELMUV mvule
velum
ELMUY muley
ELMXY xylem
ELNOP pleon
ELNOR enrol
loner
ELNOS lenos
losen
ELNOT lento
olent
ELNOU noule
ELNOV novel
ELNOW lowne
△nowel
ELNOY onely
ELNOZ lozen
ELNTU unlet
ELNWY newly
ELOOS loose
oleos
soole
ELOPR loper
poler
prole
ELOPS △elops
poles
slope
ELOPU loupe
poule
ELOPY poley
ELORS loser
soler
sorel
ELORU loure
roule
ELORV lover
ELORW △lower
owler
rowel

ELOSS loess
soles
ELOST los'te
stole
telos
ELOSU eusol
louse
ousel
ELOSV slove
solve
ELOSW lowse
sowle
ELOSY soyle
ELOTV volet
volte
ELOTW owlet
towel
ELOTX extol
ELOUV ovule
ELOUZ ouzel
ELOVV volve
ELOVW vowel
wolve
ELOVY lovey
ELPRU puler
ELPRY reply
ELPST slept
spelt
ELPSU pulse
pusle
spule
ELPSY slype
ELPTU let-up
ELPUX Pulex
ELPUZ puzel
ELRRU ruler
ELRSU △rules
ELRSY slyer
ELRTU luter
ELRTY tyler
ELRUX Lurex®
ELSSU sluse
ELSTW swelt
ELSTY style
ELSUX luxes
ELTUX exult
ELTWY wetly
ELYZZ lezzy
EMMOS memos
EMMRY rymme
EMMSY Emmys
EMNNO nomen
EMNNU numen
EMNOR enorm
moner
morne
morné
EMNOS meson
EMNOT mento
monte
moten
EMNOV venom

EMNOW women
EMNOY money
EMNPT nempt
EMNRU rumen
EMNTU unmet
EMNTY meynt
EMNUW unmew
EMOOR Romeo
EMOOS moose
EMOOT me-too
EMOOV moove
EMOPR EPROM
eprom
moper
proem
EMOPS Epsom
mopes
EMOPT tempo
EMOPY mopey
myope
EMORR ormer
EMORS mores
△morse
smore
EMORT △metro
△métro
EMORV mover
vomer
EMORW mower
rowme
EMOSS Moses
EMOST mesto
smote
EMOSU mouse
EMOSY mosey
EMOTT motet
motte
totem
EMOTY motey
EMOZZ mezzo
EMPRS sperm
EMPRT mpret
EMPRY premy
EMPSU spume
EMPTT tempt
'tempt
EMPTY empty
EMRRU murre
EMRRY merry
EMRST terms
EMRSU muser
serum
EMRTU turme
EMRUX murex
Rumex
EMSSU musse
EMSSY messy
EMSTU muset
EMSTY styme
ENNOO no-one
ENNOR ronne

ENNOS △nones
sonne
ENNOT nonet
tenno
tenon
tonne
ENNOX xenon
ENNPU unpen
ENNPY penny
ENNTY tenny
ENNWY wenny
ENOOR Roneo®
roneo
ENOOS noose
ENOOZ ozone
ENOPR prone
ENOPY peony
poney
ENORS Norse
noser
Señor
seron
snore
ENORT noter
ronte
tenor
toner
trone
ENORW owner
rowen
ENORY royne
ENOSS sonse
ENOST Etons
onset
seton
stone
ENOSW owsen
sowne
swone
ENOSY nosey
noyes
ENOSZ Zeno's
ENOTY toney
ENOVW woven
ENOVY envoy
ENOWX woxen
ENPRT prent
ENPRU prune
ENPST spent
ENPSU Nupes
ENPTY n-type
ENQRU quern
ENQUY queyn
ENRRU rerun
ENRST stern
ENRSU nurse
ENRSY syren
ENRTU tuner
urent
ENRTY entry
yrent
ENRVY nervy

ENSTT	stent
ENSTU	unset
	usen't
ENSUV	nevus
	△venus
ENSUW	unsew
ENSUX	nexus
	unsex
ENSVY	senvy
ENSWY	newsy
ENTTY	netty
	tenty
ENTUW	unwet
EOOPV	poove
EOORS	roose
EOORW	wooer
EOOST	soote
EOPPS	pepos
EOPPT	epopt
EOPPU	poupe
EOPRR	porer
	prore
	repro
	roper
EOPRS	poser
	prose
	repos
	ropes
	spore
EOPRT	opter
	Porte
	repot
	toper
	trope
EOPRV	prove
EOPRW	power
	powre
EOPRY	ropey
EOPSS	pesos
	posse
	speos
EOPST	estop
	pesto
	stoep
	stope
EOPSX	expos
EOPSY	poesy
	posey
	poyse
	sepoy
EOPXY	epoxy
EOQRU	roque
EOQTU	quote
	toque
EORRR	error
EORRT	△retro
EORRV	rover
EORRW	rower
EORSS	△roses
EORST	estro
	roset
	store
	torse
EORSU	euros
	rouse
EORSV	servo
	verso
EORSW	serow
	sower
	swore
	worse
EORSX	sorex
EORSZ	zeros
EORTT	otter
	torte
EORTU	outer
	outré
	route
EORTV	overt
	voter
EORTW	tower
	twoer
	wrote
EORTX	oxter
EORTY	toyer
EORTZ	rozet
EORUY	you're
EORVW	vower
EORXX	Xerox®
EOSSU	souse
EOSSW	sowse
EOSTT	set-to
EOSTU	touse
EOSTV	stove
EOSTW	towse
EOTUZ	touze
EOTWZ	towze
EOUVY	you've
EPPPY	peppy
EPPRU	upper
EPPTY	p-type
EPRRY	perry
	pryer
	ryper
EPRSS	△press
	Serps
EPRST	perst
	prest
	strep
EPRSU	△purse
	sprue
	super
EPRSW	sprew
EPRSY	pryse
	spyre
EPRTU	erupt
EPRTW	twerp
EPRUX	Purex
EPRXY	prexy
	Pyrex®
EPSST	steps
EPSTT	stept
EPSTU	set-up
	stupe
	upset
EPSTW	swept
EPSUY	upsey
EPSWY	spewy
EPTTY	△petty
EQRUY	query
EQSTU	quest
EQSUU	Equus
EQTUU	tuque
EQTUY	quyte
ERRSY	serry
ERRTY	retry
	terry
	tryer
ERRVY	verry
ERRWY	wryer
ERSST	tress
ERSTT	terts
	trest
ERSTU	sture
ERSTV	verst
ERSTW	strew
	trews
	wrest
ERSTY	resty
	styre
ERSUU	Eurus
	usure
ERSVY	syver
ERTTU	utter
ERTUV	vertu
ERTWY	twyer
ESSTW	stews
ESSTY	styes
ESTTX	texts
ESTTY	styte
	testy
ESTUY	suety
ESTWY	stewy
ESTYY	yesty
ESTYZ	zesty

F

FFFLU	fluff
FFFUY	fuffy
FFGIL	gliff
FFGIR	griff
FFGOO	go-off
FFGRU	gruff
FFHIT	△fifth
FFHIW	whiff
FFHOU	houff
FFHOW	howff
FFHUY	huffy
FFIJY	jiffy
FFIKS	skiff
FFIMY	miffy
FFINO	in-off
FFINS	sniff
FFINY	niffy
FFIPS	spiff
FFIQU	quiff
FFIRT	triff
FFIST	stiff
FFITY	fifty
FFKOS	skoff
FFLPU	pluff
FFNOO	on-off
FFNSU	snuff
FFOSW	sowff
FFOTY	toffy
FFPUY	puffy
FFSTU	stuff
FGGOY	foggy
FGGUY	fuggy
FGHIT	fight
FGILN	fling
FGILT	glift
FGINU	fungi
FGIOS	figos
FGIRT	grift
FGLNO	flong
FGLNU	flung
FGLUY	gulfy
FGOOR	forgo
	groof
FGOOY	goofy
FGORU	grouf
FHILT	filth
FHIRT	firth
	frith
FHIST	shift
FHISY	fishy
FHITW	whift
FHLOS	flosh
FHLSU	flush
FHOOS	hoofs
FHORT	forth
	froth
FHOTT	thoft
FHOTU	fouth
FHOTW	fowth
FHRSU	frush
FHRTU	furth
FIINS	finis
FIINX	infix
FIKLS	flisk
FIKNS	finks
FIKRS	frisk
FILLR	frill
FILLY	filly
FILMP	flimp
FILMS	films
FILMY	filmy
FILNT	flint
FILOO	folio
FILRT	flirt
FILSU	fusil
FILTT	flitt
FILTY	fitly
FIMOT	motif

FIMTU	△mufti
FIMTY	mifty
FINNY	finny
FINOS	finos
FINST	snift
FINTU	unfit
FINTY	nifty
FINUX	unfix
FINUY	unify
FIOQU	quoif
FIOST	foist
FIPTU	fit-up
FIRRY	firry
FIRST	first
	frist
FIRTU	fruit
FIRTY	rifty
FIRTZ	fritz
FIRZZ	frizz
FISSU	Sufis
FISTW	swift
FISTY	fisty
FIYZZ	fizzy
FKLNU	flunk
FKLOO	kloof
FKLOS	folks
FKLUY	fluky
FKNUY	funky
FKORY	forky
FLLOY	folly
FLLUY	fully
FLMOY	Flymo®
FLMPU	flump
FLNOU	Fluon®
FLNOW	flown
FLNOY	fonly
FLOOR	floor
FLOOS	loofs
FLOOW	Wolof
FLORU	flour
	fluor
	furol
FLORY	flory
FLOSS	floss
FLOSW	fowls
FLOTU	flout
FLOTY	lofty
FLOUW	woful
FLRRU	flurr
FLTUY	fluty
FMOOR	M-roof
FMORU	forum
FMPRU	frump
FNNUY	funny
FNORR	frorn
FNORT	front
FNORW	frown
FNOTU	fount
	futon
FOOPR	proof
FOOPS	spoof
FOOPY	poofy
FOORS	roofs
FOORY	roofy
FOOST	foots
	'sfoot
FOOTY	footy
FOOWY	woofy
FOPST	f-stop
FORRU	furor
FORRY	frory
FORST	frost
FORSU	fours
FORTY	△forty
FORWY	frowy
FOSST	softs
FOSTY	softy
FPRUY	fry-up
FRRUY	furry
FRSTU	frust
	turfs
FRSUY	surfy
FRTUY	turfy
FRUYZ	furzy
FSSUU	Fusus
FSSUY	fussy
FSTUY	fusty
FTTUY	tufty
FUYZZ	fuzzy

G

GGGLO	glogg
GGINO	going
	oggin
GGIOT	gigot
GGIPY	piggy
GGMOY	moggy
GGMUY	muggy
GGNUY	gungy
GGOSY	soggy
GGPUY	puggy
GGRUY	ruggy
GGUVY	vuggy
GHHIT	hight
	thigh
GHHOU	hough
GHIKT	kight
GHILT	light
GHIMT	might
GHINO	hongi
GHINT	night
	thing
GHINY	hying
GHIOS	shogi
GHIPT	pight
GHIRT	girth
	grith
	△right
GHIST	sight
GHITT	tight
GHITW	wight
GHLLY	ghyll
GHLOU	ghoul
	lough
GHLPU	gulph
GHLPY	glyph
GHNOT	thong
GHORU	rough
GHOST	ghost
	gosht
GHOSU	sough
GHOTU	ought
	tough
GHRSU	shrug
GHSUY	gushy
GIILR	Rigil
GIILS	sigil
GIILV	vigil
GIJNO	△jingo
GIJOT	jigot
GIKLS	glisk
GIKNO	KOing
GIKNS	Kings
GILLR	grill
GILLY	gilly
GILNO	lingo
GILNP	pling
GILNS	sling
GILNT	glint
GILNU	Luing
	lungi
GILNY	lingy
	lying
GILOO	igloo
GILOR	rigol
GILPU	pugil
GILPY	gilpy
GILRU	△lurgi
GILRY	girly
GILST	gilts
GILSU	gusli
GILTU	guilt
GILTZ	glitz
GIMNY	mingy
GIMOS	gismo
	misgo
GIMOY	goyim
GIMOZ	gizmo
GIMPU	guimp
GIMPY	gimpy
	pigmy
GIMRY	grimy
GINNO	Ngoni
GINNU	Nguni
GINNY	ginny
	nying
GINOP	pingo
GINOR	giron
	groin
	O-ring
GINOT	ingot
	tigon
	toing
GINOW	owing
	wongi
GINOY	yogin
GINRU	ruing
	unrig
GINRW	wring
GINSS	signs
GINST	sting
GINSU	suing
GINSV	V-sign
GINSW	△swing
	wings
GINTY	tying
GINVY	vying
GINWY	wingy
GINYZ	zingy
GIOPP	gippo
GIORR	rigor
GIORS	giros
GIORT	griot
GIORU	guiro
GIORV	vigor
	Virgo
GIPPY	gippy
GIPRS	grips
	sprig
GIPSY	gipsy
GIRST	grist
	grits
	strig
GIRSY	grisy
GISTU	giust
	g-suit
GJMUU	jugum
GJOSU	jougs
GLLOO	lolog
GLLOY	golly
GLLUY	gully
GLMOO	gloom
GLMOU	△mogul
GLNOP	plong
GLNOS	longs
GLNOU	gluon
GLNSU	slung
GLOOP	gloop
GLOOS	△logos
GLOOY	gooly
	ology
GLORW	growl
GLORY	glory
GLOSS	gloss
GLOTU	glout
GLOUV	vulgo
GLRUY	gurly
	lurgy
GMMUY	gummy
GMNOO	moong
GMNOU	mungo
GMNUU	ungum
GMOOR	groom
GMORY	gormy
GMPRU	grump
GMPYY	pygmy
GNNUY	gunny
GNNYY	gynny

GNOOP	pongo
GNOOZ	gonzo
GNOPR	prong
GNOPY	pongy
GNORW	grown
	wrong
GNORY	gyron
GNOST	stong
	tongs
GNOSY	gonys
GNOTU	ungot
GNOUY	young
GNOYZ	zygon
GNRTU	grunt
GNRUW	wrung
GNSTU	stung
GNSUW	swung
GOOPY	goopy
GOORS	sorgo
GOOSY	goosy
GOOTU	outgo
GOPPY	gyppo
GOPRS	sprog
GOPRU	group
GOPRY	porgy
GORSS	gross
GORSY	gorsy
GORTU	grout
GORUY	roguy
GOSTU	gusto
GOSTY	stogy
GOTUY	gouty
	guyot
GPPUY	guppy
GPPYY	gyppy
GPRSU	sprug
GPRTY	grypt
GPSYY	gypsy
GRRUY	gurry
GRSUY	gyrus
	surgy
GSSUY	gussy
GSTUY	gusty
	gutsy
GTTUY	gutty

H

HHHUU	uh-huh
HHISW	whish
HHMOU	ho-hum
HHMPU	humph
HHOOS	hoosh
HHOTT	Thoth
HHSSU	shush
HHSUY	hushy
HIILN	nihil
HIIMS	imshi
HIIQU	qui-hi
HIIRS	Irish
	rishi
	sirih
HIJOS	shoji
HIKLT	thilk
HIKLW	whilk
HIKNS	knish
HIKNT	think
HIKRS	shirk
HIKSW	whisk
HILLO	hillo
HILLS	shill
HILLT	illth
	thill
HILLY	hilly
HILMU	hilum
HILOT	litho
	thiol
	tholi
HILRT	thirl
HILRW	whirl
HILSS	slish
HILST	hilts
HILSU	hilus
HILSY	shily
HILTT	tilth
HIMRT	mirth
HIMST	smith
HIMSY	imshy
HIMTY	thymi
HINNT	ninth
HINNY	hinny
HINOR	rhino
HINPU	unhip
HINSY	shiny
HINWY	whiny
HIOPP	hippo
HIOPS	Sophi
HIOPT	tophi
HIORU	houri
HIOST	hoist
HIPPY	hippy
HIPQS	Q-ship
HIPTW	whipt
HIPTY	pithy
HIRRS	shirr
HIRRW	whirr
HIRST	shirt
HISST	shits
HISSU	sushi
HISSW	swish
	whiss
HISTW	swith
	whist
HISTX	sixth
HITWY	△whity
	withy
HIWZZ	whizz
HKKOU	hokku
HKLSU	hulks
HKLUY	hulky
HKMOU	hokum
HKNOY	honky
HKNSU	hunks
HKNUY	hunky
HKOOS	shook
HKOOY	hooky
HKSSU	husks
HKSUY	husky
HLLOO	hollo
HLLOU	hullo
HLLOW	who'll
HLLOY	holly
HLLUY	hully
HLMPY	lymph
HLMSU	mulsh
HLNSU	shuln
HLOOS	shool
HLOOY	hooly
HLOPX	△phlox
HLORW	whorl
HLOSS	slosh
HLOST	sloth
HLOTW	thowl
HLOTY	hotly
HLPSU	plush
HLPSY	sylph
HLRUY	hurly
HLSSU	shuls
	slush
HLSUY	lushy
HLSYY	shyly
HMNOT	month
HMNPY	nymph
HMOOP	oomph
HMOOS	homos
HMOOZ	zhomo
HMOPR	morph
HMORR	mhorr
HMORU	humor
	mohur
HMOST	moths
HMOTU	mouth
HMOTY	mothy
	Y-moth
HMPSU	sumph
HMPTU	thump
HMPUY	humpy
HMRRY	myrrh
HMRTU	thrum
HMSTU	musth
	shtum
HMSUU	humus
HMSUY	mushy
HMTYY	thymy
HNOOR	honor
HNOOS	shoon
HNOOW	nohow
HNOPY	phony
HNORS	horns
	shorn
HNORT	△north
	thorn
HNORY	horny
HNOSW	shown
HNOSY	hyson
HNSSU	snush
HNSTU	shunt
HNSTY	synth
HOOOO	hoo-oo
HOOPT	photo
HOOPW	whoop
HOORT	ortho
HOOST	shoot
	sooth
	Sotho
	tohos
HOOSW	howso
	whoso
	woosh
HOOTT	tooth
HOOTW	how-to
	whoot
HOPPY	hoppy
HOPRT	thorp
HOPSS	sposh
HOPSY	hypos
	Sophy
HOQTU	quoth
HORST	horst
	short
HORSU	Horus
	hours
HORSW	shrow
HORSY	horsy
HORTT	troth
HORTU	routh
HORTW	rowth
	throw
	whort
	worth
	wroth
HOSSU	husos
HOSTT	shott
HOSTU	shout
	△south
	thous
HOSTW	sowth
HOSTY	toshy
HOSUY	shoyu
HOSWY	showy
HOTUY	youth
HPSTU	shtup
HPSUY	pushy
HRRUY	hurry
HRSTU	hurst
HRSUY	rushy
HRTTU	truth
HRUUU	uhuru
HSSUY	hussy
HSTUY	tushy
HSUUW	△wushu
HUYZZ	huzzy

I

IIJNN	jinni
IIKKO	kikoi
IIKLM	kilim
IIKLN	likin
IIKNN	kinin

IIKRR	kirri
IILLV	villi
IILMT	limit
IILMU	△ilium
IILNN	linin
IILNT	intil
IIMMN	minim
IIMMT	immit
IIMMX	immix
IIMNR	mirin
IIMNX	mix-in
IIMPS	impis
IINNO	inion
IINPZ	zip-in
IINST	sit-in
IINTU	Inuit
IINTW	inwit
IIORT	torii
IIPPT	pipit
IIRST	Tisri
IIRVZ	vizir
IISTV	visit
	Vitis
IJKMU	mujik
IJKNS	jinks
IJMMY	△jimmy
IJMPY	jimpy
IJNNS	jinns
IJNNU	Injun
IJNOT	joint
IJOST	joist
IKKNS	skink
IKKNY	kinky
IKKOS	kiosk
IKKRS	skrik
IKKRU	kukri
IKLLR	krill
IKLLS	skill
IKLMO	milko
IKLMS	sklim
IKLMY	milky
IKLNP	plink
IKLNS	links
	slink
IKLNY	kylin
IKLOS	kilos
IKLPU	pikul
IKLRS	skirl
IKLSY	silky
IKLTY	kilty
IKLXY	kylix
IKMPS	skimp
IKMRS	smirk
IKMRY	mirky
IKNOP	pinko
IKNOS	kinos
IKNPR	prink
IKNPS	spink
IKNPY	pinky
IKNST	skint
	stink
IKNSW	swink
	winks
IKNSY	sinky
IKNTW	twink
IKNYZ	zinky
IKOOR	iroko
	koori
IKOSS	skios
IKPSY	pisky
	spiky
IKPTU	tupik
IKPUY	Yupik
IKQRU	quirk
IKRRS	skirr
IKRST	skirt
	stirk
IKRSY	risky
IKRTU	Turki
IKSVY	skivy
IKTTY	kitty
ILLPR	prill
ILLPS	pills
	spill
ILLQU	quill
ILLRT	trill
ILLST	still
ILLSW	swill
	wills
ILLSY	silly
	slily
ILLTW	twill
	'twill
ILLTY	tilly
ILLWY	willy
ILMNU	ulmin
ILMOO	mooli
ILMOR	milor
ILMOS	limos
	milos
ILMOU	Mouli®
ILMPU	pilum
ILMPY	imply
ILMRY	mirly
ILMSU	simul
ILMSY	slimy
ILMTZ	miltz
ILNNY	linny
ILNOS	linos
	Lions
	loins
	noils
ILNOT	Nilot
ILNPU	lupin
ILNRY	nirly
ILNSY	lysin
ILNTU	unlit
	until
ILNTY	linty
ILNVY	vinyl
ILOOP	polio
ILOOS	olios
ILOOV	ovoli
ILOPS	spoil
ILOPT	pilot
ILOPU	poilu
ILOPW	pilow
ILOPX	oxlip
ILORS	loris
ILORV	livor
ILORY	roily
ILORZ	zoril
ILOSS	silos
ILOST	toils
ILOSU	louis
ILOSY	soily
ILPPU	pipul
	pupil
ILPPY	lippy
ILPSS	slips
ILPST	slipt
	spilt
	split
ILPSU	pilus
ILPTU	tulip
ILQTU	quilt
ILRSW	swirl
ILRTW	twirl
ILSST	lists
ILSSY	lysis
ILSTT	stilt
ILSTU	sluit
ILSTY	silty
	styli
ILTTW	twilt
IMMSU	Mimus
IMMSY	mimsy
IMNOO	nomoi
IMNOR	△minor
IMNOS	minos
IMNOT	△timon
IMNSU	minus
IMNTY	minty
IMOPR	primo
IMOPT	impot
IMOPU	opium
IMOSS	misos
IMOST	moist
IMOSU	Suomi
IMOSZ	zoism
IMOTV	vomit
IMPPR	primp
IMPRS	prism
IMPRU	purim
IMPRY	primy
IMPST	timps
IMPUX	mix-up
IMPWY	Wimpy®
	wimpy
IMRRS	smirr
IMSSY	missy
IMSTU	muist
	musit
	tuism
IMSTY	misty
	stimy
IMTTY	Mitty
INNNO	ninon
INNNY	ninny
INNOO	onion
INNOP	piñon
INNOT	niton
	noint
	'noint
INNOU	△union
INNOW	no-win
INNPU	unpin
INNPY	pinny
INNRU	inurn
	run-in
INNSU	Sunni
INNTU	untin
INNTY	tinny
INOOR	Orion
INOPP	ippon
INOPR	orpin
	prion
	proin
INOPS	pions
	psion
INOPT	△pinot
	pinto
	piton
	point
	potin
INOPW	powin
INOPY	piony
INOPZ	zip-on
INOQU	quoin
INORS	irons
	ornis
	rosin
INORT	intro
INORY	irony
INOSV	vinos
	vison
INOSW	winos
INOSY	noisy
INOTX	toxin
INPPU	pin-up
INPPY	△nippy
INPRT	print
INPRU	purin
	unrip
INPSS	snips
INPSY	snipy
	spiny
INPTU	input
	put-in
INPUZ	unzip
INQTU	quint
INRST	snirt
INRSU	ruins
INRTU	rutin
INRTY	nitry

Words marked △ may be spelled also with a capital letter

INSSU	nisus
	sinus
INSTT	stint
	'tisn't
INSTU	inust
	suint
INSTW	Twins
INTTY	nitty
	tinty
INTUW	unwit
INTUY	unity
INTWY	twiny
IOOPR	poori
IOOPT	topoi
IOPPZ	zippo
IOPQU	quipo
IOPRR	prior
IOPST	posit
IOPSU	pious
IOPTV	pivot
IOQTU	quoit
IORRS	orris
IORRT	trior
IORST	roist
	rosit
	rotis
	△tiros
	torsi
	trios
IORSV	rivos
	visor
IORTZ	rozit
IORVY	ivory
IORVZ	vizor
IOSTT	stoit
IOSTV	ovist
	visto
IOSTZ	zoist
IOSUX	Sioux
IPPPY	pippy
IPPTU	tip-up
IPPTY	tippy
IPPYY	yippy
IPPYZ	zippy
IPQUU	quipu
IPRST	spirt
	sprit
	stirp
	strip
IPRSU	sirup
IPRSY	spiry
IPRTW	twirp
IPRTY	tripy
IPRVY	△privy
IPSTY	tipsy
IPSTZ	spitz
IPSWY	wispy
IPSXY	pyxis
IPTTU	putti
	titup
IQRTU	quirt
IQSTU	quist
	quits
	squit
IQSUZ	squiz
IRSSU	risus
IRSTT	trist
IRSTW	wrist
IRSUV	virus
IRSXY	Xyris
IRTUV	virtu
IRTYZ	ritzy
ISSSW	Swiss
ISSSY	sissy
ISSTU	situs
	suits
ISSTW	swits
ISTTU	Tutsi
ISTTW	twist
ISTVY	stivy
ISTXY	sixty
	xysti
ITTTU	tutti
ITTTY	titty
ITTWX	'twixt
ITTWY	witty
ITYZZ	tizzy

J

JKLOO	jokol
JKNUY	junky
JLLOY	jolly
JLOTY	jolty
JLOWY	jowly
JMOOS	mojos
JMORU	jorum
JMPSU	jumps
JMPUY	jumpy
JNOPU	jupon
JNOTU	jotun
	junto
JNOTY	jonty
JORRU	juror
JOSTU	joust
JTTUY	jutty

K

KKLSU	skulk
KKMOU	kokum
KKNSU	skunk
KKOOY	kooky
KKUYY	yukky
KLLNO	knoll
KLLSU	skull
KLNOP	plonk
KLNPU	plunk
KLNRU	knurl
KLNSU	slunk
KLOOP	plook
KLOOS	kolos
	looks
KLOPU	plouk
KLOUY	yokul
KLOYY	yolky
KLSSU	sulks
KLSUY	sulky
KLTUZ	klutz
KMOOS	mokos
	smoko
KMOSY	smoky
KMRUY	murky
KMSUY	musky
KNNOW	known
KNOOS	snook
KNOOY	nooky
KNOPR	pronk
KNOPS	knosp
KNOQU	quonk
KNOST	stonk
KNOSU	onkus
KNOSW	snowk
KNOSY	yonks
KNOTU	knout
KNOWY	wonky
KNPSU	spunk
KNRRU	knurr
KNRTU	trunk
KNSTU	stunk
KNTUU	Tunku
KOOPS	spook
KOORY	rooky
KOOST	kotos
	stook
	tokos
KOOSZ	zooks
KOOTW	kotow
KOPRY	porky
KORST	stork
	torsk
KORSW	works
KORSY	Yorks
KOSTY	Kotys
KOUUY	Kuo-yü
KSTUY	tusky

L

LLLOY	lolly
LLMOY	molly
LLOPR	proll
LLOPS	polls
LLOPY	△polly
LLOQU	quoll
LLORS	Rolls
LLORT	troll
LLOSY	lysol
LLOUY	you'll
LLOWY	lowly
	wolly
LLOXY	xylol
LLRTU	trull
LLSTU	stull
LLSUY	sully
LLSYY	slyly
LLXYY	xylyl
LMMUY	lummy
LMOOS	mools
	slo-mo
	sloom
LMOOT	molto
LMOOY	mooly
LMOPU	pulmo
LMOST	smolt
LMOSU	mouls
	solum
LMOTU	moult
LMOTY	ymolt
LMPPU	plump
LMPSU	slump
LMPUY	lumpy
	plumy
LMRUY	murly
	rumly
LMSTU	stulm
LMSUU	Ulmus
LNNOY	nylon
LNOOR	Orlon®
LNOOS	loons
	snool
	Solon
LNOOY	loony
LNOPY	pylon
LNOST	stoln
LNOSW	swoln
LOOOV	ovolo
LOOPR	orlop
LOOPS	polos
	pools
	sloop
	spool
LOOPY	loopy
LOOSS	solos
LOOST	lotos
	sloot
	stool
	tools
LOOTT	lotto
LOPPU	poulp
LOPPY	polyp
LOPRU	proul
LOPRW	prowl
LOPSS	slops
LOPSY	polys
	slopy
LOPTU	Pluto
	poult
LORRY	lorry
LORST	rotls
LORUY	loury
LOSSU	solus
LOSSY	lossy
LOSTU	△lotus
LOSTY	stylo
LOSUY	lousy
LOTYZ	zloty
LOUUV	voulu
LPPUY	pulpy
LPRSU	slurp

LPSUU	△lupus
LRRUY	lurry
LRSUY	surly
LRTUY	truly
LRWYY	wryly
LSTUY	lusty

M

MMMOY	mommy
MMMUY	mummy
MMOPY	pommy
MMOSU	Momus
MMOTY	△tommy
MMPSU	mumps
MMRUY	rummy
MMSTU	stumm
MMSUY	mumsy
MMTUY	tummy
MMUYY	yummy
MNOOR	moron
MNOOS	monos
	nomos
MNOOY	moony
MNORU	mourn
	Munro
MNOTU	△mount
	muton
	notum
MNOUV	novum
MNTUU	muntu
MNTUZ	Muntz
MOOPR	promo
MOOPS	spoom
MOORR	morro
MOORS	Moros
	rooms
	smoor
MOORT	motor
MOORV	vroom
MOORY	moory
	roomy
MOOST	smoot
MOOTT	motto
MOPPU	mop-up
MOPPY	moppy
MOPRS	Proms
MOPRT	tromp
MOPST	stomp
MOPSU	mopus
MOPSY	mopsy
	myops
MORRU	rumor
MORST	storm
MORSU	Morus
MORSW	worms
MORTU	tumor
MORWY	wormy
MOSSU	musos
	sumos
MOSSY	mossy
MOSTU	△motus
	moust
	smout
MOSTW	smowt
MOSUY	mousy
MOTTY	motty
MPRTU	trump
MPRUY	rumpy
MPSTU	stump
MPSUY	spumy
MPTUY	tumpy
	umpty
MRRUY	murry
MRSTU	strum
MSSUY	mussy
MSTUY	musty
MUYZZ	muzzy

N

NNNOY	nonny
NNOOS	no-nos
	no-no's
NNORU	run-on
NNOST	stonn
NNOSU	nouns
NNOSY	sonny
NNOUW	unwon
NNOUY	nouny
NNRUY	runny
NNSUY	sunny
NNTUY	tunny
NOOPR	porno
NOOPS	snoop
	spoon
NOOST	snoot
NOOSW	swoon
NOOSZ	zoons
NOPRY	proyn
NOPTU	punto
	put-on
	ton-up
NOPTY	ponty
	poynt
NOPUY	yupon
NOPWY	powny
NOQRU	Quorn®
NORST	snort
NORSU	urson
NORSW	sworn
NORTY	try-on
NORUY	yourn
NOSSY	sonsy
NOSTU	Notus
	snout
	stoun
	tonus
NOSTW	stown
NOSTY	stony
	Tonys
NOSUW	swoun
NOSWY	snowy
NOTWY	towny
NPRSU	spurn
NPRTU	prunt
NPRUU	run-up
	uprun
NPSUU	sunup
NPTUY	punty
NRTUU	U-turn
NRTUY	runty
NSTTU	stunt
NTTUY	nutty

O

OOOPT	potoo
OOPPS	oppos
OOPPZ	zoppo
OOPRS	proso
	sopor
	spoor
OOPRT	poort
	Proto®
	△proto
	troop
OOPRV	Provo
OOPRY	roopy
OOPST	spoot
	stoop
	topos
OOPSW	swoop
OOPTT	potto
OOPVY	poovy
OORRS	ro-ros
OORRT	rotor
OORRZ	zorro
OORST	roost
	roots
	stoor
	torso
OORTW	wroot
OORTY	rooty
OOSTT	toots
OOSTY	sooty
OOSUZ	ouzos
OOTWZ	wootz
OOWYZ	woozy
OPPPU	pop-up
OPPPY	poppy
OPPRS	props
OPPSY	popsy
	psyop
	soppy
OPPTU	poupt
	top-up
OPRST	sport
	strop
OPRSY	prosy
OPRTY	porty
OPRUY	roupy
OPRXY	proxy
OPSST	spots
OPSSY	sysop
OPSTU	spout
	stoup
OPSTW	swopt
OPSTY	Topsy
	typos
OPSUY	soupy
OPTTU	putto
OPTTY	potty
	typto
OPTUW	two-up
OPTUY	pouty
OPYZZ	pozzy
OQRST	Q-sort
ORRSY	sorry
ORRTY	rorty
ORRWY	worry
ORSST	sorts
ORSSU	sorus
ORSTT	trots
ORSTU	roust
	stour
	sutor
	torus
ORSTW	strow
	worst
ORSTY	royst
	story
	stroy
	tyros
ORSUY	yours
ORTTU	trout
	tutor
ORTUY	yourt
ORUVW	vrouw
OSSST	stoss
OSSTY	tossy
OSTTU	stout
OSTTY	ytost
OSTUY	tousy
OSTWY	towsy
OSUYZ	Soyuz
OTTTY	totty
OTUYZ	touzy
OTWYZ	towzy

P

PPPUY	puppy
PPRUY	purpy
PPTUU	put-up
PPUYY	yuppy
PRSSU	spurs
PRSTU	spurt
	turps
PRSUU	usurp
PRSUY	pursy
	Pyrus
	syrup
PRTUY	purty
PSSUY	pussy
PSUWY	swy-up
PTTUY	putty

R

RSSTU	truss

RSSUU	Ursus
RSTTU	strut
	sturt
	trust
RSTTY	tryst
RSTUW	wurst
RSTUY	rusty
RSUUY	usury
RTTUY	rutty

T

TTTUY	tutty

A

AAABCL	cabala
AAABCN	cabana
AAABDG	dagaba
AAABDH	bahada
AAABDJ	bajada
AAABKL	kabala
AAABKY	kabaya
AAABLM	Balaam
AAABLT	albata
	atabal
	balata
AAABNN	banana
AAABNS	anabas
AAABRZ	baraza
	bazaar
AAABTT	batata
AAACCI	acacia
AAACDN	cañada
AAACJN	jacana
	jaçana
AAACLP	alpaca
AAACMR	maraca
AAACNR	arcana
AAACPR	Carapa
AAACPT	pataca
AAADGH	Agadah
AAADMR	armada
AAADNP	panada
AAAEGP	agapae
AAAELZ	azalea
AAAENR	Aranea
AAAGIL	Aglaia
AAAGLM	Malaga
AAAGLR	argala
AAAGNN	nagana
AAAGNP	pa'anga
AAAHIT	taiaha
AAAHNV	Havana
AAAILL	alalia
AAAILR	aralia
AAAINZ	Azania
AAAITX	ataxia
AAAJKT	jataka
AAAJMU	ujamaa
AAAKKN	△kanaka
AAAKKR	karaka
AAAKLM	kamala
AAAKNT	katana
AAALMP	palama
AAALMS	salaam
AAAMNN	mañana
AAAMNP	△panama
AAAMNS	samaan
AAAMNT	ataman
AAAMRS	samara
AAAMRT	tamara
AAAMRY	Aymara
AAANNS	ananas
AAANPR	Paraná
AAANRT	antara
AAANTT	anatta
AAAPPY	papaya
AAAPTZ	zapata
AAARST	satara
AAARTV	avatar
AABBBO	baobab
AABBCO	babaco
AABBCY	abbacy
AABBDS	abdabs
AABBHL	bablah
AABBKS	kababs
AABBLL	lablab
AABBLO	balboa
AABBST	sabbat
AABCHS	casbah
AABCIM	cambia
AABCIR	△arabic
AABCKR	backra
AABCMN	cabman
AABCMT	tambac
AABCRS	scarab
AABCSU	abacus
AABCUU	aucuba
AABDER	abrade
AABDES	abased
AABDET	abated
AABDEU	aubade
AABDGO	dagoba
AABDIN	indaba
AABDIR	abraid
AABDLL	ballad
AABDLM	lambda
AABDMN	badman
AABDNR	bandar
AABDOR	aboard
	abroad
AABDRT	tabard
AABDRY	△bayard
AABDSS	badass
AABEFN	befana
AABEGM	ambage
AABEGT	atabeg
AABEIL	abelia
AABEKT	atabek
AABELR	arable
AABELT	ablate
AABELZ	ablaze
AABEMO	amoeba
AABENS	Sabean
AABENT	Banate
AABERU	bauera
AABERZ	zareba
AABETU	bateau
AABETZ	zabeta
AABFIN	Fabian
AABGGR	ragbag
AABGGS	gasbag
AABGIN	baaing
AABGMN	bagman
AABGRT	ratbag
AABHIS	sahiba
AABHIW	Wahabi
AABHJN	bhajan
AABHKS	kasbah
	sabkha
AABHLR	bharal
AABHMR	Brahma
AABHMS	shamba
AABHRT	Bharat
AABHSW	bashaw
AABILL	labial
AABILM	Baalim
AABILU	abulia
AABILX	biaxal
AABIMN	Bimana
AABIMR	Bairam
AABINN	banian
AABINR	arabin
AABINS	Sabian
AABINW	wabain
AABINZ	banzai
	Zabian
AABIRS	arabis
AABIRZ	zariba
AABIST	abatis
AABJNX	banjax
AABKNR	barkan
AABLLN	ballan
AABLLO	abolla
AABLLT	ballat
AABLMS	balsam
	sambal
AABLNY	Albany
AABLOR	aboral
AABLOV	lavabo
AABLST	basalt
AABLTU	ablaut
	tabula
AABMNR	barman
AABMNT	bantam
	batman
AABMOR	Abroma
AABMRS	sambar
AABMST	tsamba
AABNNT	Bannat
AABNNY	banyan
AABORR	arroba
AABORT	abator
	rabato
AABORZ	abrazo
AABRRT	barrat
AABRTY	baryta
AABTTU	abattu
AABZZZ	bazazz
AACCDI	cicada
AACCDU	caduac
AACCEL	caecal
AACCHH	cha-cha
AACCHK	kaccha
AACCHM	chacma
AACCIL	Alcaic
	cicala
AACCIM	caimac
AACCIR	Carica
AACCKK	ack-ack
AACCKR	carack
AACCLO	cloaca
AACCLP	calpac
AACCLR	calcar
AACCMO	macaco
AACCNN	cancan
AACCRT	caract
AACDDU	caudad
AACDEF	facade
	façade
AACDEI	acedia
AACDER	arcade
AACDEU	cadeau

AACDFR	cafard
AACDGI	Agadic
AACDHR	chadar
AACDIM	Adamic
AACDIR	acarid
AACDLU	caudal
AACDMP	madcap
AACDNR	canard
AACDRY	Arcady
AACEFL	faecal
AACEFR	carafe
AACEGH	achage
AACEHP	△apache
AACEHR	areach
AACEHT	chaeta
AACELN	anlace
AACELP	palace
AACELS	scalae
AACELT	acetal
AACEMR	camera
AACENN	cannae
AACENP	canapé
AACENR	arcane
AACENT	catena
AACEPR	ear-cap
	Parcae
AACERS	△caesar
AACERT	acater
AACEST	acates
AACETV	caveat
	vacate
AACFIL	cafila
	facial
AACFIS	fascia
AACFLU	facula
	faucal
AACFNT	caftan
AACFRS	fracas
AACFRX	carfax
AACFTT	fat-cat
AACGHN	chagan
AACGIM	agamic
AACGIR	agaric
AACHKN	achkan
AACHKP	chapka
	pachak
AACHKR	chakra
	charka
AACHKW	kwacha
AACHLN	chalan
AACHLS	calash
AACHLT	caltha
AACHMN	machan
AACHMS	camash
AACHNO	choana
AACHNR	anarch
AACHNS	ash-can
AACHNT	acanth
	Tanach
AACHRS	charas
AACHRT	Cathar
	charta
AACHSW	cashaw
AACHTT	attach
	chatta
AACHTW	awatch
AACILL	laical
AACILM	calami
	calima
AACILP	apical
AACILR	racial
AACILT	Altaic
AACIMN	caiman
	maniac
AACINR	arnica
	△carina
	crania
AACINS	ascian
	sancai
AACIOT	atocia
	coaita
AACIPS	capias
AACIPT	capita
AACIRR	air-car
AACIRS	air-sac
AACIRV	caviar
AACISS	△cassia
AACITX	ataxic
AACJKL	jackal
AACJOU	acajou
AACKPZ	czapka
AACKRR	arrack
AACKRW	awrack
AACKTT	attack
AACLLN	callan
AACLMU	macula
AACLNR	carnal
AACLNT	Cantal
AACLNU	canula
	lacuna
AACLOT	catalo
AACLPR	carpal
AACLPS	pascal
AACLPT	cat-lap
AACLRS	lascar
	rascal
	sacral
	scalar
AACLRW	acrawl
AACLSU	△casual
	causal
AACLTU	actual
AACMNR	carman
	Marcan
AACMNY	cayman
AACMOY	macoya
AACMRT	ramcat
	Tarmac®
	tarmac
AACMSS	camass
AACNNO	Ancona
AACNOR	ancora
AACNPT	captan
	catnap
AACNRT	arctan
	cantar
AACNRX	Caranx
AACNRY	canary
AACNSV	canvas
AACNTV	vacant
AACPPY	papacy
AACPRS	scarpa
AACRRT	carrat
AACRRU	curara
AACRSU	acarus
AACRTV	cravat
AACSSV	cavass
AADDEL	daedal
AADDER	adread
AADDIL	alidad
	la-di-da
AADDLN	adland
AADDNR	Dardan
AADDOU	aoudad
AADDRW	adward
AADDST	stadda
AADEFL	aefald
AADEFR	afeard
AADEGL	gelada
AADEGM	damage
AADEGN	agenda
AADEGZ	agazed
AADEHK	akedah
AADEKM	medaka
AADEKW	awaked
AADELS	salade
AADELT	alated
AADEMM	△madame
AADEMN	anadem
	maenad
AADENN	Andean
AADENS	Seanad
AADENT	adnate
AADEPR	parade
AADEPS	espada
AADERV	Veadar
AADFIR	afraid
AADFLW	afawld
AADFNR	farand
AADFNT	fantad
AADFRT	daftar
AADFTW	fatwa'd
AADGIM	agamid
AADGIO	adagio
AADGIR	gardai
AADGNP	padang
	pad-nag
AADGNR	argand
AADGOP	pagoda
AADGRS	Asgard
AADGRU	△garuda
AADHIL	dahlia
AADHMR	dharma
AADHNR	dharna
AADHRZ	hazard
AADILL	Dalila
AADILR	radial
AADIMN	maidan
AADINO	Adonai
	Adonia
AADINR	radian
AADINS	naiads
AADINT	aidant
AADINV	navaid
AADIPP	appaid
AADIQS	qasida
AADIRT	tiara'd
AADIST	stadia
AADJLN	jandal®
AADKMS	damask
AADKPU	padauk
AADLLS	sallad
AADLLY	all-day
AADLMP	lampad
AADLMW	wadmal
AADLMY	malady
AADLNO	anodal
AADLNS	sandal
AADLNU	landau
AADLNV	△vandal
AADLOP	apodal
AADLPR	pardal
AADLRU	radula
AADLWY	law-day
AADLYY	lay-day
AADMMN	madman
AADMMR	am-dram
	dammar
AADMMS	madams
AADMNY	man-day
AADMOU	amadou
AADMRS	madras
AADMRU	maraud
AADMRZ	mazard
AADMSS	admass
	ad-mass
AADMYY	mayday
AADNNR	randan
AADNPR	pandar
AADNPU	Paduan
AADNRS	nasard
AADNRT	tarand
AADOPS	posada
AADPPY	appayd
AADPSW	padsaw
AADPSY	spayad
AADPYY	pay-day
AADRTU	datura
AADRTY	datary
AADRVW	vaward
AAEEGR	Graeae
AAEEGT	eatage
AAEELP	paleae
AAEELT	taleae
AAEERT	aerate
AAEEYY	aye-aye
AAEFFR	affear
AAEFLM	aflame

AAEFLR rafale
AAEFLV favela
AAEFNR fraena
AAEFNU faunae
AAEGGL galage
AAEGGR garage
AAEGGV gavage
AAEGIR Graiae
AAEGLM agleam
AAEGLN alnage
anlage
galena
lagena
AAEGLR alegar
laager
AAEGLT algate
AAEGLV lavage
AAEGMN agname
manage
AAEGMR Gemara
AAEGNP Pangea
AAEGNS Ganesa
AAEGNT agnate
AAEGNU Augean
AAEGOR oarage
AAEGPR parage
AAEGPV pavage
AAEGRV ravage
AAEGSV savage
AAEGTU gateau
gâteau
AAEHKP pakeha
AAEHKS ashake
AAEHKT takahe
AAEHLM haemal
AAEHLT althea
AAEHMS ashame
AAEHMT hamate
AAEHNT aneath
Athena
AAEHNY hyaena
AAEHPW awhape
AAEILM amelia
AAEILR aerial
realia
AAEILV availe
AAEILX alexia
AAEIMN anemia
AAEINT taenia
AAEIRS air-sea
araise
AAEIRT Raetia
AAEITV aviate
AAEKLM kamela
AAEKLN alkane
AAEKLS aslake
AAEKNN ananke
AAEKNW awaken
wakane
AAEKRS keasar
AAEKRT karate

AAELLP paella
pallae
AAELMP Palmae
AAELMR rameal
AAELMT malate
meatal
tamale
AAELNN anneal
AAELNT lanate
AAELOR areola
AAELPP appeal
AAELPR earlap
AAELPS salpae
AAELPT palate
AAELRV larvae
AAELRZ Azrael
AAELTV valeta
AAELTZ alteza
AAEMMM mammae
AAEMNP apeman
AAEMNR Ramean
AAEMNS seaman
AAEMNT amenta
AAEMNX axeman
AAEMRS asmear
AAEMRT ramate
retama
AAEMTX meat-ax
AAENNS Saanen
AAENNZ zenana
AAENOP apnoea
AAENOZ ozaena
AAENPV pavane
AAENST ansate
AAENSU nausea
AAEPPR appear
AAEPRS pasear
sarape
AAEPRT patera
petara
AAEPRZ zarape
AAEPTT tapeta
AAERRR arrear
AAERRT errata
AAERST astare
searat
AAERSY arayse
AAERTT terata
AAERTU aurate
AAERWX earwax
AAERWY aweary
AAESTV Avesta
savate
AAESWY awayes
seaway
AAFFIM △maffia
AAFFIR affair
raffia
AAFFIT taffia
AAFFPR affrap
AAFFRY affray

AAFGHN △afghan
AAFHTW fatwah
AAFIKL kafila
AAFIKS sifaka
AAFINR farina
AAFIRS safari
AAFIST fatsia
AAFKNT kaftan
AAFLLL fallal
AAFLNU faunal
AAFLOT afloat
AAFNNT fan-tan
AAFNSU faunas
AAGGKU gagaku
AAGGLO galago
AAGGMN gagman
mganga
AAGGQU quagga
AAGGRS saggar
AAGGRT ragtag
tagrag
AAGHIL Alhagi
AAGHKN kangha
khanga
AAGHLZ ghazal
AAGHMR graham
AAGHMS gamash
AAGHNR arghan
hangar
AAGHST aghast
AAGILN agnail
AAGILO alogia
AAGILP palagi
AAGILR argali
garial
AAGILV gavial
AAGIMN magian
AAGINN angina
AAGINR nagari
AAGINT gitana
AAGINU iguana
AAGINV vagina
AAGIPR airgap
AAGIRS air-gas
AAGIRU Auriga
AAGJNR garjan
AAGJRU jaguar
AAGLLN lalang
AAGLLP plagal
AAGLMM malmag
AAGLMN mangal
AAGLNO analog
△angola
AAGLNR raglan
AAGLNT galant
AAGLST stalag
AAGLXY △galaxy
AAGMMN gnamma
AAGMMR gramma
AAGMMS magmas
AAGMNR ragman
AAGMNS gasman

AAGMNZ zamang
AAGMRY △magyar
margay
AAGNNO goanna
AAGNNW wangan
AAGNOR △angora
Onagra
organa
AAGNPR parang
AAGNRR garran
AAGNRS sangar
AAGNRY angary
AAGNST satang
AAGNTU taguan
AAGOTU agouta
AAGPPR grappa
AAGRRY garrya
AAGRST gas-tar
AAGRSV Svarga
AAGRSW Swarga
AAGRVY vagary
AAHHLV halvah
AAHHMZ hamzah
AAHHNT thanah
AAHHPT aphtha
AAHHWW haw-haw
wah-wah
AAHIIK haikai
AAHILT Thalia
AAHILY aliyah
AAHIMS ahimsa
AAHINT tahina
AAHIPR Pahari
pariah
△raphia
AAHIRS △sharia
AAHIRV vihara
AAHISV Shaiva
AAHJNR hanjar
AAHJRR jarrah
AAHJRS Jashar
AAHKKL Khalka
AAHKKT kathak
AAHKKZ Kazakh
AAHKLS Khalsa
AAHKLT khalat
AAHKNT kantha
AAHKST Shakta
AAHLLL hallal
AAHLLN hallan
nallah
AAHLLO halloa
AAHLLP pallah
AAHLLW wallah
AAHLMM hammal
mahmal
AAHLMT maltha
AAHLRS ashlar
AAHLRT hartal
AAHMMM hammam
AAHMNR harman
AAHMNS shaman

AAHMPS	Phasma
AAHMPY	mayhap
AAHMRS	ashram
AAHMST	asthma
AAHMSU	mashua
AAHMTZ	matzah
AAHNNT	tannah
	thanna
AAHNOV	Navaho
AAHNPS	ash-pan
AAHNPT	Pathan
AAHNST	Sathan
AAHNTW	whatna
AAHPPR	paraph
AAHPRY	yarpha
AAHPTY	apathy
AAHRSS	harass
	hassar
AAHRSU	Ashura
AAHSSY	sashay
AAIIKK	kaikai
AAIIMM	mia-mia
AAIJNT	tinaja
AAIJRW	jawari
AAIKLL	alkali
AAIKLM	kalmia
	kamila
AAIKLN	kalian
AAIKNO	aikona
AAIKNT	tankia
AAIKOR	kia-ora
AAIKPT	Pitaka
AAIKRS	askari
AAIKRT	karait
AAIKRU	uakari
AAILLP	pallia
AAILLX	axilla
AAILMN	△almain
	animal
	lamina
	Malian
	△manila
AAILMP	impala
AAILMS	alisma
	salami
AAILMU	aumail
AAILNR	narial
AAILNS	Salian
	salina
AAILNT	△antlia
	Latian
	Latina
AAILNW	Walian
AAILNY	inyala
AAILPR	parial
AAILQU	Aquila
	qualia
AAILRT	Altair
	atrial
	lariat
	latria
AAILSS	assail
AAILSV	avails
	saliva
	salvia
AAILTV	avital
AAIMMS	miasma
AAIMMX	maxima
AAIMNR	airman
	Marian
	marina
AAIMNS	Samian
AAIMNT	manati
AAIMNV	vimana
AAIMRR	air-arm
	ram-air
AAIMRT	amrita
	tamari
AAIMTT	tatami
AAINNO	Aonian
AAINNT	naiant
AAINOX	anoxia
AAINPP	papain
AAINPR	Parian
	piraña
AAINPT	patina
	piñata
	taipan
AAINRT	antiar
AAINRU	anuria
	Urania
AAINTT	attain
AAINTV	Ativan®
	avanti
AAINTW	atwain
AAIOPR	aporia
AAIPPR	appair
AAIPRT	pitara
AAIPRY	apiary
	piraya
AAIPTU	Tupaia
AAIPZZ	piazza
AAIRST	arista
	tarsia
AAIRTY	raiyat
AAIRVY	aviary
AAIRWY	airway
AAIRZZ	razzia
AAISVY	Vaisya
AAJJMR	jamjar
AAJKNS	sanjak
AAJMNP	jampan
AAJMPY	pyjama
AAJNNO	joanna
AAJNNY	Nyanja
AAJNOV	Navajo
AAJNOW	ajowan
AAJNOY	yojana
AAJRSW	swaraj
AAKKLP	kalpak
AAKKMR	markka
AAKKOP	kakapo
AAKLOT	atokal
	Lakota
AAKLTU	taluka
AAKMNU	manuka
AAKMRT	Amtrak
AAKMRU	kumara
AAKNOR	anorak
AAKNRT	kantar
AAKNST	askant
	tankas
AAKNWZ	kwanza
AAKOPR	pakora
AAKSSV	kavass
	vakass
AAKSTT	attask
AAKTUY	yukata
AAKUYZ	yakuza
AALLLN	lallan
AALLLS	sallal
AALLMM	mallam
AALLNY	anally
AALLOR	arolla
AALLOZ	azolla
AALLPP	palpal
AALLPS	Pallas
AALLRV	larval
	vallar
AALLTT	atlatl
	tallat
AALLVV	valval
AALMMM	mammal
AALMMS	Lammas
AALMNP	napalm
AALMNU	alumna
	manual
AALMNW	lawman
	law-man
AALMNY	Almany
	layman
AALMOR	amoral
AALMOS	omasal
AALMOT	amatol
AALMPR	palmar
AALMPS	lampas
	plasma
AALMRS	alarms
AALMRU	alarum
AALMSU	masula
AALMTY	Amytal®
	amytal
AALNNS	annals
AALNNU	annual
AALNOT	atonal
AALNOZ	azonal
AALNPR	planar
AALNPT	planta
	platan
AALNRT	tarnal
AALNRU	ranula
AALNRX	larnax
AALNST	aslant
	santal
AALNSY	nyalas
AALNTT	talant
AALOPR	oar-lap
AALOPY	payola
AALORT	aortal
AALOVW	avowal
AALPPU	papula
AALPRR	parral
AALPRY	parlay
AALPSS	salpas
AALPSU	pausal
AALPTU	Laputa
AALRST	astral
	tarsal
AALRSV	varsal
AALRSY	salary
AALRVV	valvar
AALSSV	vassal
AALSTT	statal
AALSUX	saxaul
AALSWY	always
AALTUV	valuta
AALWYY	waylay
AAMMNT	amtman
AAMMRR	marram
AAMMRT	tammar
AAMMTT	tam-tam
AAMMUZ	mazuma
AAMNNU	maunna
AAMNOO	manoao
AAMNOZ	△amazon
AAMNPS	sampan
AAMNRT	mantra
AAMNRW	warman
AAMNTU	mantua
	tamanu
AAMNTV	△vatman
AAMNTX	taxman
AAMOPR	paramo
AAMORS	Masora
AAMOSS	samosa
AAMOST	somata
AAMPPS	pampas
AAMPTY	Pamyat
AAMQSU	squama
AAMRSU	asarum
AAMRSW	aswarm
AAMRTU	trauma
AAMSTZ	matzas
AANNNO	Annona
AANNPS	sanpan
AANNTT	natant
AANNYZ	nyanza
AANOQY	yaqona
AANORT	torana
AANORU	Anoura
AANOST	sonata
AANOTT	anatto
AANPPS	sappan
AANPPU	Papuan
AANPRT	partan
	tarpan
	trapan
AANPRU	Purana

AANPRY	panary
AANQTU	quanta
AANRRS	narras
AANRRT	arrant
AANRRW	warran
AANRTT	rattan
	△tantra
	Tartan®
	tartan
AANRTU	Arnaut
	natura
AANRTZ	Tarzan
AANRUV	Varuna
AANSTV	satnav
	savant
AANSTW	Tswana
AANSTZ	stanza
AANSYY	nay-say
AANTTV	tan-vat
AANTUV	avaunt
AANWYY	anyway
AAOPRT	Atropa
AAOPST	sapota
AAORRU	△aurora
AAORRV	△varroa
AAORTT	totara
AAOTTV	ottava
AAPPWW	pawpaw
AAPQUW	Quapaw
AAPRST	satrap
	Sparta
AAPRTT	attrap
AAPWXX	paxwax
AAPZZZ	pazazz
AAQRSU	quasar
AAQSTU	asquat
AARRST	tarras
AARRTT	△tartar
AARRWY	warray
AARSST	assart
AARSTT	astart
	strata
AARSTY	astray
	satyra
AARTTT	rat-tat
AARTTY	Tatary
AASTTU	statua
AASTZZ	tazzas
ABBBEL	babble
ABBBLY	babbly
ABBCEI	cabbie
ABBCIR	bicarb
ABBCOS	cabobs
ABBCOT	bobcat
ABBCRY	crabby
ABBCSY	scabby
ABBDDE	dabbed
ABBDEG	gabbed
ABBDEL	dabble
ABBDEN	nabbed
ABBDER	barbed
	dabber
ABBDET	tabbed
	tebbad
ABBDEU	bedaub
ABBDRY	drabby
ABBEEW	bawbee
ABBEGL	gabble
ABBEGR	gabber
ABBEIR	△barbie
ABBEIY	yabbie
ABBEJL	jabble
ABBEJR	jabber
ABBEKS	kebabs
ABBELR	barbel
	rabble
ABBELU	bauble
ABBELW	bawble
	wabble
ABBENR	nabber
ABBEOR	earbob
ABBERR	barber
ABBERT	barbet
	rabbet
ABBERY	yabber
ABBESS	abbess
ABBESY	abbeys
ABBFLY	flabby
ABBGHU	gubbah
ABBGIN	bin-bag
ABBGMU	bumbag
ABBGOR	gabbro
ABBHIJ	jibbah
ABBHJU	jubbah
ABBHOO	haboob
ABBHSY	shabby
ABBILL	Lib-Lab
ABBIMS	Babism
ABBINR	rabbin
ABBIRS	rabbis
ABBIRT	rabbit
ABBIST	Babist
ABBITW	wabbit
ABBKOS	kabobs
ABBLRU	bulbar
ABBLSY	slabby
ABBMOO	bamboo
ABBMOX	bombax
ABBNOO	baboon
ABBORS	absorb
ABBRSU	bus-bar
ABBSWY	swabby
ABCCIU	cubica
ABCCLU	buccal
ABCDEK	backed
ABCDER	decarb
ABCDEU	abduce
ABCDHO	bodach
ABCDIR	bardic
ABCDTU	abduct
ABCEEL	belace
ABCEEM	became
	embace
ABCEGO	bocage
ABCEGU	cubage
ABCEHL	bleach
ABCEHR	breach
ABCEHY	beachy
ABCEIM	amebic
ABCEIR	cabrie
	caribe
ABCEJT	abject
ABCEKR	backer
	reback
ABCEKT	backet
ABCELL	becall
ABCELM	becalm
ABCELT	cablet
ABCEMR	camber
	cembra
ABCEMX	excamb
ABCENO	beacon
ABCERR	bracer
ABCERS	braces
ABCFIR	fabric
ABCFNO	confab
ABCGIT	gib-cat
ABCHLN	blanch
ABCHLU	Baluch
ABCHNR	branch
ABCHOR	broach
ABCHPU	hub-cap
ABCIIM	iambic
ABCIIR	Cabiri
ABCILT	Baltic
ABCIRT	cabrit
ABCISS	basics
ABCITT	Tib-cat
ABCKLS	blacks
ABCKOR	barock
ABCKPU	back-up
ABCKRU	buckra
ABCLMY	cymbal
ABCLNO	blanco
ABCLOT	cobalt
ABCMOP	mob-cap
ABCMOR	comarb
	crambo
ABCMOT	combat
	tombac
ABCMRS	scramb
ABCNOR	carbon
	corban
ABCORX	boxcar
ABCORY	carboy
ABCSTU	subact
ABDDEE	beaded
ABDDEI	abided
	baddie
ABDDEL	bladed
ABDDEN	banded
ABDDER	barded
ABDDEY	day-bed
ABDDHU	△buddha
ABDEEH	behead
ABDEEJ	bejade
ABDEEK	beaked
ABDEEL	beadle
ABDEES	debase
	seabed
ABDEET	debate
ABDEEZ	bedaze
ABDEFL	fabled
ABDEGG	bagged
ABDEGL	gabled
ABDEGN	banged
ABDEGO	bodega
ABDEGR	△badger
ABDEHS	bedash
ABDEIL	diable
ABDEIR	air-bed
	braide
ABDEIS	biased
ABDEKR	debark
ABDELL	balled
ABDELM	△bedlam
	beldam
	blamed
ABDELO	albedo
	doable
ABDELR	bedral
ABDELS	blades
ABDELT	tabled
ABDELU	belaud
ABDELY	dyable
ABDELZ	blazed
ABDENP	bedpan
ABDENT	tan-bed
ABDERR	barred
ABDERS	serdab
ABDERT	taberd
ABDERU	dauber
ABDERV	adverb
ABDEST	bestad
ABDETT	batted
ABDETU	tabued
ABDFOR	forbad
ABDGNO	bandog
ABDGOR	bodrag
ABDHOY	hobday
ABDILR	bridal
	labrid
	ribald
ABDINR	riband
ABDINT	bandit
ABDIRR	braird
	Briard
ABDIRS	disbar
ABDIRU	ribaud
ABDLLY	baldly
ABDLRY	drably
ABDNOU	abound
ABDNRY	brandy
ABDORR	bordar
ABDORS	adsorb
	boards
ABDORY	byroad
ABDOXY	box-day

ABDOYY	day-boy
ABDRRU	durbar
ABDRSU	absurd
ABDRWY	bawdry
	dawbry
ABEEES	Seabee
ABEEGH	beegah
	bhagee
ABEEGL	beagle
ABEEGR	abrégé
	barege
	barège
	bargee
ABEEHJ	bhajee
ABEEHN	beenah
ABEEHV	behave
ABEEIL	bailee
ABEEIN	beanie
ABEEJM	jambee
ABEEJR	bajree
ABEEKL	kabele
ABEEKR	beaker
ABEEKT	betake
ABEELM	embale
ABEELN	baleen
	enable
ABEELT	belate
	let-a-be
ABEEMN	bemean
	bename
ABEEMR	beamer
ABEEMS	embase
ABEENR	Berean
ABEENT	beaten
ABEENU	Beaune
ABEEOR	aerobe
ABEERR	bearer
	breare
ABEERT	beater
	berate
	rebate
ABEERV	beaver
ABEERW	beware
ABEERZ	zereba
ABEEST	sebate
ABEFFL	baffle
ABEFHL	behalf
ABEFIL	faible
ABEFLL	befall
ABEFLM	flambé
ABEFLR	fabler
ABEFMO	befoam
ABEFPR	prefab
ABEFTY	tabefy
ABEGGR	beggar
ABEGHI	abeigh
ABEGLM	gamble
	△lambeg
ABEGLN	bangle
	Bengal
ABEGLR	garble
ABEGLT	gablet
ABEGLU	beluga
	blague
ABEGMR	bregma
ABEGMT	gambet
ABEGNR	banger
	graben
ABEGNT	bag-net
ABEGNW	begnaw
ABEGOR	borage
ABEGOZ	gazebo
ABEGTU	tubage
ABEHIL	habile
ABEHKL	keblah
ABEHLM	hamble
ABEHLR	herbal
ABEHLU	Beulah
ABEHNO	hebona
ABEHNT	Theban
ABEHRR	herbar
ABEHRS	basher
ABEHRT	bather
	△bertha
	breath
ABEHST	Shebat
ABEIIL	bailie
ABEIIT	tibiae
ABEILL	Belial
	labile
	liable
ABEILM	embail
	lambie
ABEILR	bailer
ABEILS	abseil
	blaise
	isabel
ABEILT	albeit
	albite
	libate
ABEILV	viable
ABEILW	bewail
ABEILY	△bailey
ABEILZ	blaize
ABEIMS	imbase
ABEINS	Sabine
ABEINT	binate
ABEIOT	boatie
ABEIRS	braise
	rabies
ABEIRT	baiter
	barite
ABEIRZ	braize
	zeriba
ABEJMN	enjamb
ABEJMR	jamber
ABEJNT	bejant
ABEJOR	jerboa
ABEJRS	jabers
ABEJRU	abjure
ABEJTU	jubate
ABEKLR	balker
ABEKLY	bleaky
	Kabyle
ABEKMN	embank
ABEKMR	embark
ABEKNR	banker
	barken
ABEKNT	banket
ABEKRR	barker
ABEKRY	bakery
ABEKST	basket
ABELLM	emball
ABELLT	ballet
ABELLU	bullae
ABELMM	embalm
ABELMR	ambler
	lamber
	marble
	ramble
ABELMU	bemaul
ABELMW	wamble
ABELMY	belamy
ABELNR	branle
ABELNU	nebula
	unable
ABELNY	by-lane
ABELNZ	benzal
ABELOR	△boreal
ABELOT	boatel
	lobate
	oblate
ABELRR	barrel
ABELRT	albert
	batler
	labret
ABELRV	verbal
ABELRW	bawler
	warble
ABELRY	barely
	barley
	bleary
ABELRZ	blazer
ABELSS	sables
ABELST	ablest
	bastle
	stable
	tables
ABELSU	suable
	usable
ABELSY	basely
ABELSZ	blazes
ABELTT	batlet
	battel
	battle
	tablet
ABELTU	Betula
ABELTY	baetyl
ABELWY	bawley
	bye-law
ABELYY	lay-bye
ABEMMR	bammer
ABEMNO	bemoan
ABEMNY	byname
	by-name
ABEMRT	tamber
ABEMRU	umbrae
ABEMRY	ambery
ABENNR	banner
ABENOR	aborne
	borane
ABENOS	beanos
ABENRR	barren
ABENRT	banter
ABENRU	unbare
	unbear
	urbane
ABENRY	barney
	near-by
ABENRZ	brazen
ABENST	absent
	basnet
ABENTT	batten
ABENTU	butane
ABENTZ	bezant
ABEORS	Boreas
ABEORT	boater
	borate
	rebato
ABEORZ	bezoar
ABEOTV	bovate
ABEPRU	upbear
ABEPST	bespat
ABEPTU	beat-up
	upbeat
	up-beat
ABEQRU	barque
ABEQSU	△basque
ABERRT	barret
	barter
ABERRY	brayer
ABERST	baster
	bestar
	breast
ABERSU	abuser
	bursae
ABERTT	batter
	tabret
ABERTU	arbute
ABERTX	baxter
ABERTY	betray
ABERUU	bureau
ABERWY	bewray
ABESST	basset
ABESSU	subsea
ABETTU	battue
	tubate
ABETUY	beauty
ABEZZZ	bezazz
ABFGLU	bagful
ABFGOW	gowf-ba'
ABFILU	fibula
ABFLRU	barful
ABFLRY	barfly
ABFOTX	fox-bat
ABGGIT	baggit
	gag-bit
ABGGIW	bagwig

Words marked △ may be spelled also with a capital letter

ABGGNO	gobang
ABGGNU	buggan
ABGHRU	ghubar
ABGHTU	hagbut
ABGIKN	baking
	ink-bag
ABGIKT	kit-bag
ABGILM	gimbal
ABGIMR	gambir
ABGIMT	gambit
ABGIMY	bigamy
ABGINO	bagnio
	gabion
ABGINS	basing
ABGINT	bating
ABGIOS	biogas
ABGIOU	baguio
ABGKNO	kobang
ABGKOO	bogoak
ABGLLO	global
ABGLMO	gambol
ABGLMY	gymbal
ABGLOR	brolga
ABGLOU	albugo
ABGLRU	Bulgar
ABGLRY	bragly
ABGNOR	barong
	brogan
ABGNPU	bang-up
ABGORS	garbos
ABHHIS	shibah
ABHIIR	Bihari
ABHIKL	kiblah
ABHIKT	bhakti
ABHIMR	Brahmi
	mihrab
ABHIMZ	mazhbi
ABHINS	ash-bin
	banish
ABHIOP	phobia
ABHIRS	barish
ABHLSU	ablush
ABHLSY	blashy
ABHMRU	rhumba
ABHMSU	ambush
ABHNOT	bothan
ABHOOY	yah-boo
ABHORR	harbor
ABHORT	athrob
ABHOST	bathos
	boshta
ABHOTX	hatbox
ABHOXY	haybox
ABHPTY	bypath
ABHRSY	brashy
ABIILL	bailli
ABIILN	bilian
ABIILT	tibial
ABIINN	bainin
ABIIST	tibias
ABIJOW	Ojibwa
ABIJRU	jabiru
ABIKKU	kabuki
ABIKMO	akimbo
ABIKMR	imbark
ABILMT	timbal
ABILMU	labium
	Malibu
ABILNO	albino
	Albion
ABILNS	ablins
ABILNT	libant
ABILNY	Libyan
ABILOR	bailor
ABILOT	obital
ABILRS	brails
ABILRT	tribal
ABILRU	burial
ABILRZ	△brazil
ABIMMR	mimbar
ABIMNN	binman
ABIMNO	obi-man
ABIMNR	minbar
ABIMPT	bitmap
ABIMRS	bismar
ABIMRU	barium
ABIMRV	Vibram®
ABIMSU	iambus
ABINNU	bunnia
ABINOS	bonsai
ABINOT	obtain
ABINRS	brains
ABINRY	binary
	brainy
ABINSU	Anubis
	unbias
ABIORR	barrio
ABIORS	isobar
ABIORT	orbita
ABIRSU	Air-bus®
	air-bus
ABIRTU	rubati
ABIZZZ	bizazz
ABJJOO	jojoba
ABJKMO	jambok
ABJLMU	jambul
	jumbal
ABJMOS	jambos
ABJNOS	banjos
ABJOWX	jawbox
ABKLMO	Bokmål
ABKLNY	blanky
ABKLSY	△skylab
ABKMOT	tombak
ABKMUZ	△zambuk
ABKNRS	branks
ABKNRU	unbark
ABKNRY	branky
ABKOOR	boorka
ABLLNO	ballon
	no-ball
ABLLOT	ballot
ABLLOW	ballow
ABLLPU	ballup
ABLLSY	ballsy
ABLMOO	abloom
ABLMOP	aplomb
ABLMOU	bumalo
ABLMOW	mob-law
ABLMRU	brumal
	labrum
	lumbar
	umbral
ABLMRY	marbly
ABLMSU	albums
ABLMTY	tymbal
ABLMWY	wambly
ABLNOZ	blazon
ABLNTU	buntal
	tulban
ABLOOR	robalo
ABLORU	△labour
ABLOST	oblast
ABLOTT	talbot
ABLOTV	abvolt
ABLPRU	burlap
ABLPYY	by-play
ABLRSU	bursal
	Labrus
ABLRSY	labrys
ABLRTU	brutal
ABLRWY	brawly
	byrlaw
ABLSSY	byssal
ABLSTY	stably
ABLSUY	suably
	usably
ABLSYY	lay-bys
ABMMOS	mambos
ABMNOW	bowman
ABMNRU	Burman
ABMNSU	busman
	subman
ABMNTU	numbat
ABMNUY	ynambu
ABMOOW	waboom
ABMOPT	bampot
ABMOSS	sambos
ABMOSZ	zambos
ABMOTW	wombat
ABMRSU	sambur
	umbras
ABMRUY	aumbry
ABNNRY	branny
ABNOOT	batoon
ABNORT	barton
ABNORY	barony
	baryon
ABNOTY	△botany
ABNRTU	turban
ABNRUU	auburn
ABNRUY	anbury
ABNRWY	brawny
ABNTYZ	byzant
ABOORW	bow-oar
ABOOST	taboos
ABOPXY	pay-box
ABORRU	arbour
ABORRW	barrow
ABORSV	bravos
ABORTU	outbar
	rubato
	tabour
ABORTW	towbar
ABORTX	tar-box
ABORTY	tarboy
ABORUY	Yoruba
ABOSSS	bassos
ABOSST	bastos
ABOSTU	abouts
	Basuto
ABOSWW	bow-saw
ABOUXY	boyaux
ABPRTU	abrupt
ABPRUY	upbray
ABPSSY	bypass
ABPSTY	by-past
ABRRSU	bursar
ABRSSY	brassy
ABRSTU	aburst
ABRTTY	bratty
ABSTUU	Basutu
ABSUWY	subway
ACCCIL	calcic
ACCCLO	coccal
ACCDEE	accede
ACCDEL	calced
ACCDEN	accend
ACCDHI	Chadic
ACCDII	acidic
ACCDOR	accord
ACCEHN	chance
ACCEHR	creach
ACCEHT	cachet
ACCEIL	celiac
ACCEIP	icecap
	ipecac
ACCEIT	accite
	acetic
ACCEKL	cackle
ACCELN	cancel
ACCELR	cercal
ACCELS	calces
ACCEMU	caecum
ACCENR	△cancer
ACCENT	accent
ACCEPT	accept
ACCERS	scarce
ACCERU	accrue
ACCERW	accrew
ACCESS	Access®
	access
ACCESU	accuse
ACCGNO	Cognac
ACCHHI	chicha
ACCHIK	chiack
ACCHKY	chyack
ACCHLT	clatch

ACCHNO	concha
ACCHNR	cranch
ACCHNY	chancy
ACCHOU	cachou
ACCHOY	coachy
ACCHRT	cratch
ACCHST	scatch
ACCHSU	succah
ACCHTT	catcht
ACCHTU	cutcha
ACCHTY	catchy
ACCIIR	Riccia
ACCILO	accoil
	calico
ACCILT	lactic
ACCIMM	Micmac
ACCINS	siccan
ACCINW	wiccan
ACCINY	cyanic
ACCIPR	capric
ACCIRR	circar
	ric-rac
ACCIRS	siccar
ACCIRT	△arctic
ACCITT	tactic
	tic-tac
ACCITU	cicuta
ACCKNU	Canuck
ACCLOU	coucal
ACCLOY	accloy
ACCMOY	occamy
ACCNOO	cacoon
ACCORS	arccos
	corsac
ACCOSS	cascos
	saccos
ACCOST	accost
ACCRUY	curacy
ACCSTU	cactus
ACCSUU	caucus
ACDDEE	decade
ACDDEI	caddie
	Eddaic
ACDDEU	adduce
ACDDII	diacid
ACDDIN	candid
ACDDIR	Dardic
ACDDIS	caddis
ACDDIT	addict
ACDDIY	dyadic
ACDDTU	adduct
ACDEEF	deface
ACDEEN	decane
ACDEER	decare
ACDEFF	decaff
ACDEGR	cadger
	graced
ACDEHR	arched
	chared
ACDEHT	detach
ACDEIN	candie
	cnidae
	decani
ACDEIT	dacite
ACDEIV	advice
ACDEKR	arcked
	dacker
	racked
ACDEKT	tacked
ACDEKV	vacked
ACDELM	calmed
	macled
ACDELN	candle
ACDELP	placed
ACDELR	cradle
	credal
ACDELS	scaled
ACDELT	talced
ACDELU	caudle
	cedula
ACDELW	clawed
ACDELY	clayed
	lac-dye
ACDEMP	decamp
ACDENN	canned
ACDENO	deacon
ACDENR	cedarn
	dancer
	nacred
ACDENS	ascend
ACDENT	cadent
	canted
	decant
ACDEOP	peacod
ACDEPP	capped
ACDEPR	redcap
ACDEPS	spaced
ACDERR	carder
ACDERS	sacred
	scared
ACDERT	Dectra®
	redact
ACDERV	carved
ACDERZ	crazed
ACDEST	casted
ACDEUX	caudex
ACDHIR	diarch
ACDHIS	Chasid
ACDHMR	drachm
ACDHOR	chador
	chorda
ACDIIP	adipic
ACDIJU	Judaic
	Judica
ACDILL	callid
ACDILP	placid
ACDILS	discal
ACDILY	acidly
ACDINO	Adonic
	anodic
ACDINR	rancid
ACDINW	windac
ACDIOS	sodaic
ACDIOT	dacoit
ACDIOZ	zodiac
ACDIPR	caprid
ACDIPS	capsid
ACDIRU	raucid
ACDIST	dicast
ACDLNU	unclad
ACDLTY	dactyl
ACDMTU	mudcat
ACDNOR	candor
	Dacron®
ACDORS	Dorcas
ACDORW	coward
ACDRRS	scarr'd
ACDRSY	darcys
ACEEFF	efface
ACEEFN	enface
ACEEFR	reface
ACEEFS	faeces
ACEEFT	facete
ACEEFX	Ceefax®
ACEEGN	encage
ACEEHK	hackee
ACEEHL	chelae
ACEEHN	achene
ACEEHT	eatche
	Hecate
	thecae
ACEEIP	apiece
ACEEJT	ejecta
ACEELL	cellae
ACEELN	elance
	enlace
ACEELR	alerce
	cereal
ACEELV	cleave
ACEEMN	menace
ACEEMR	amerce
	△carême
	raceme
ACEEMS	camese
ACEEMZ	eczema
ACEENR	careen
	enrace
ACEENS	encase
	séance
	Seneca
ACEENT	cetane
	tenace
ACEENV	encave
ACEEOR	ocreae
ACEEOT	coatee
ACEEPR	pearce
	preace
ACEEPS	escape
ACEERR	career
ACEERS	crease
	searce
ACEERT	cerate
	create
	écarté
ACEFFR	Caffre
ACEFFT	affect
ACEFHR	chafer
ACEFHU	chaufe
ACEFIL	facile
	fecial
ACEFIN	fiancé
ACEFIR	fiacre
ACEFIS	facies
ACEFLS	falces
ACEFLU	fecula
ACEFLY	calefy
ACEFSS	fasces
ACEFSU	fauces
ACEFTU	faucet
ACEGHN	change
	'change
ACEGHR	charge
	chargé
	creagh
ACEGHU	gauche
ACEGIL	Gaelic
ACEGIN	incage
ACEGIU	gaucie
ACEGLN	cangle
	glance
ACEGLY	legacy
ACEGNU	cangue
	uncage
ACEGNY	agency
ACEGOS	socage
ACEGOW	cowage
ACEGRS	△graces
ACEHHT	chetah
ACEHIL	heliac
ACEHIM	haemic
ACEHIN	chaîné
ACEHIP	phaeic
ACEHIR	Archie
	cahier
	eriach
ACEHIS	chaise
ACEHKL	hackle
ACEHKR	hacker
ACEHLP	chapel
	pleach
ACEHLS	laches
	sealch
ACEHLT	chalet
	thecal
	Thecla
ACEHLY	leachy
ACEHMN	manche
ACEHMS	sachem
	schema
ACEHNR	chenar
	enarch
ACEHNS	encash
ACEHNU	nuchae
ACEHOP	cheapo
	epocha
	phocae

ACEHOR	chorea
	ochrea
	orache
ACEHPR	eparch
	preach
ACEHPS	Pesach
ACEHPT	hep-cat
ACEHPY	cheapy
	peachy
ACEHQU	queach
ACEHRR	archer
ACEHRS	△arches
	chaser
	eschar
	search
ACEHRT	charet
ACEHRV	varech
ACEHRX	exarch
ACEHSS	chasse
	chassé
ACEHST	chaste
	sachet
	scathe
ACEHSW	cashew
ACEHTX	hexact
ACEIKR	eirack
ACEILL	allice
	caille
ACEILM	maleic
	malice
ACEILN	ancile
	inlace
ACEILO	Aeolic
ACEILP	epical
	plaice
	plicae
ACEILR	éclair
ACEILV	clavie
ACEILX	alexic
ACEIMN	anemic
	cinema
ACEIMS	camise
ACEIMT	acmite
	micate
ACEIMU	aecium
ACEINN	canine
	neanic
ACEINS	casein
	incase
ACEINT	anetic
ACEINU	eucain
ACEINV	cave-in
	incave
ACEIPS	apices
	spicae
ACEIQU	caique
	caïque
ACEIRS	caries
ACEISV	vesica
ACEITT	tietac
ACEITV	active
ACEIVV	vivace
ACEJKT	jacket
ACEJLO	cajole
ACEJNT	jacent
ACEJNU	jaunce
ACEJQU	Jacque
ACEKLM	mackle
ACEKLR	calker
	lacker
ACEKLT	tackle
ACEKLY	lackey
ACEKNO	nocake
ACEKNR	canker
	reckan
ACEKNT	nacket
ACEKNW	acknew
ACEKPR	packer
	repack
ACEKPT	packet
ACEKRR	racker
ACEKRS	ackers
	sacker
	screak
ACEKRT	racket
	tacker
ACEKRU	cauker
ACEKRW	cawker
	wacker
ACEKRY	creaky
	yacker
ACEKST	casket
ACEKTT	tacket
ACELLO	locale
ACELLR	caller
	cellar
	recall
ACELLT	callet
ACELMN	encalm
ACELMP	cample
ACELMR	△marcel
ACELMS	mascle
	mescal
	scamel
ACELMT	camlet
ACELMU	almuce
	macule
ACELNN	cannel
ACELNR	lancer
	rancel
ACELNS	lances
ACELNT	cantle
	cental
	lancet
ACELNU	cuneal
	launce
	unlace
ACELOR	coaler
	△oracle
ACELOS	solace
ACELOT	Alecto
	locate
ACELOV	alcove
	coeval
ACELPR	carpel
	craple
	parcel
	placer
ACELPT	caplet
	placet
ACELPU	Clupea
ACELQU	calque
	claque
ACELRR	carrel
ACELRS	scaler
	sclera
ACELRT	cartel
	claret
	rectal
	tarcel
ACELRU	raucle
ACELRV	calver
	carvel
	claver
ACELSS	△scales
ACELST	castle
	sclate
ACELSU	caules
	clause
ACELSV	calves
	claves
	sclave
ACELSX	calxes
ACELTT	cattle
ACELTU	cautel
ACELTY	acetyl
ACELYY	clayey
ACEMNO	ancome
ACEMNP	encamp
ACEMNU	acumen
ACEMOP	pomace
ACEMOR	amorce
ACEMOS	cameos
	cosmea
ACEMOT	camote
	comate
ACEMPR	camper
ACEMRS	scream
ACEMRT	mercat
ACEMRY	creamy
ACEMSU	muscae
ACEMTU	mucate
ACENNR	canner
ACENNU	nuance
ACENOR	cornea
	earcon
ACENOT	octane
ACENPR	prance
ACENPT	catnep
ACENPU	paunce
	uncape
ACENPW	pawnce
ACENRS	casern
ACENRT	canter
	carnet
	centra
	creant
	Cretan
	nectar
	recant
	tanrec
	trance
ACENRV	carven
	cavern
	craven
ACENRY	carney
ACENRZ	zarnec
ACENST	ascent
	secant
	stance
ACENSU	causen
	uncase
	usance
ACENTU	uncate
ACENUV	vaunce
ACEOPR	Pecora
ACEOPS	scopae
ACEOPT	capote
	toecap
ACEOPW	cowpea
ACEORS	coarse
	rosace
ACEORT	coater
ACEORX	coaxer
ACEOST	costae
ACEOTU	coteau
ACEOTV	avocet
	octave
ACEPPR	capper
ACEPRR	carper
ACEPRS	capers
	escarp
	parsec
	scrape
	spacer
ACEPRT	carpet
ACEPRU	aperçu
ACEPST	aspect
ACEPSU	auceps
ACEPSY	spacey
ACEPTU	teacup
ACEQSU	casque
	sacque
ACERRS	scarer
	scarre
ACERRT	arrect
	carter
	crater
	tracer
ACERRU	curare
ACERRV	carver
	craver
ACERRY	crayer
ACERSS	caress
	crases

ACERST	caster
	recast
	traces
ACERSU	causer
	cesura
	saucer
ACERSY	carsey
	creasy
	scarey
	scraye
ACERTU	acture
	cauter
	curate
ACESTT	sceatt
	stacte
ACESTU	cuesta
ACESTY	cytase
ACESUV	cauves
ACESUY	causey
	cayuse
ACFFHU	chauff
ACFFLS	sclaff
ACFGIN	facing
ACFHLN	flanch
ACFHRT	fratch
ACFHST	chafts
ACFILN	in-calf
ACFILS	fiscal
ACFINN	finnac
ACFINR	farcin
ACFIOS	fascio
	fiasco
ACFIPY	pacify
ACFIST	factis
ACFLNO	falcon
	flacon
ACFLNU	canful
ACFLOT	olfact
ACFLPU	capful
ACFLRU	fulcra
	furcal
ACFMOR	Corfam®
ACFMTU	factum
ACFNOR	franco
ACFNTU	unfact
ACFORT	factor
	forçat
ACFORX	carfox
ACFRSS	scarfs
ACFRTX	X-craft
ACFRTY	crafty
ACGGIN	caging
ACGGIO	agogic
ACGGLY	claggy
ACGGRY	craggy
ACGHIN	aching
ACGHNU	gaunch
ACGHOU	gaucho
ACGHTU	caught
ACGIKN	caking
ACGILL	△gallic
ACGILN	lacing
ACGILO	caligo
ACGILR	garlic
ACGILS	glacis
ACGILY	cagily
ACGIMO	ogamic
ACGINN	caning
ACGINO	agonic
	angico
ACGINR	arcing
	caring
	racing
ACGINS	casing
ACGINT	acting
ACGINV	caving
ACGINW	cawing
ACGIRT	tragic
ACGLOU	cagoul
ACGNOR	garçon
ACGNOS	△gascon
	Scogan
ACGORT	go-cart
ACGORU	cougar
ACGOSU	guacos
ACGTTU	catgut
ACHHIN	hainch
ACHHIS	hachis
ACHHNU	haunch
ACHHTT	thatch
ACHIIS	ischia
ACHIJK	hijack
ACHILO	lochia
ACHILP	caliph
ACHILR	archil
	chiral
ACHILT	chital
ACHIMS	chiasm
ACHINR	chinar
	inarch
ACHINS	chains
ACHINT	canthi
ACHIOR	choria
ACHIPS	phasic
ACHIPT	haptic
	pathic
	phatic
ACHIQU	quaich
ACHIRS	Charis
	rachis
ACHIST	scaith
	taisch
ACHISU	chiaus
ACHITT	chatti
ACHKKU	chukka
ACHKLY	chalky
	hackly
ACHKOR	chokra
ACHKOS	shacko
ACHKOW	whacko
ACHKRU	chukar
ACHKTU	kutcha
ACHKTW	thwack
ACHKWY	whacky
ACHLNO	lochan
ACHLNP	planch
ACHLNU	launch
	nuchal
ACHLOR	choral
	lorcha
ACHLRY	archly
ACHLST	slatch
ACHMMY	chammy
ACHMNU	Manchu
ACHMOR	chroma
ACHMOS	camsho
	machos
ACHMRS	charms
ACHMST	smatch
ACHMSU	sumach
ACHMSY	chasmy
ACHNOR	anchor
	archon
	Charon
	rancho
ACHNOS	nachos
	sancho
ACHNOT	chaton
ACHNOY	onycha
ACHNPU	paunch
ACHNRU	raunch
ACHNST	snatch
	stanch
ACHNTU	chaunt
	nautch
ACHNTY	chanty
ACHOPS	phocas
ACHOPY	poachy
	pochay
	po'chay
ACHORT	orchat
ACHOST	tachos
ACHOUV	avouch
ACHPPY	chappy
ACHPRS	scarph
ACHPTY	patchy
ACHQTU	quatch
ACHRRY	charry
ACHRST	charts
	scarth
	starch
ACHSTU	cushat
ACHSTW	swatch
ACHSUW	cushaw
ACHTTY	chatty
ACHTUW	waucht
ACIILS	sialic
	silica
ACIILT	△italic
ACIILV	clivia
ACIINN	niacin
ACIINV	incavi
ACIIST	Iastic
ACIKLN	calkin
ACIKMR	karmic
ACIKNP	ink-cap
	panick
ACIKNR	nickar
ACIKNS	ink-sac
ACIKNT	antick
	catkin
ACIKOP	paiock
ACIKPS	aspick
ACIKRT	kit-car
ACIKTT	Kit-Cat
	kit-cat
ACILLP	plical
ACILLS	scilla
ACILMX	climax
ACILNO	oilcan
ACILNP	caplin
ACILNR	crinal
ACILNT	tincal
ACILNU	Lucina
	uncial
ACILOR	caroli
	lorica
ACILOS	scolia
	social
ACILOT	coital
ACILOX	oxalic
ACILPT	placit
ACILRT	rictal
ACILRU	lauric
	uracil
	Uralic
ACILRY	racily
ACILSU	caulis
	clusia
ACILSV	clavis
	Slavic
ACIMNO	anomic
	camion
	conima
	manioc
ACIMNT	mantic
ACIMOO	oomiac
ACIMOR	Romaic
ACIMOS	△mosaic
ACIMOT	atomic
	matico
ACIMOV	vomica
ACIMPS	scampi
ACIMPT	impact
ACIMRS	racism
ACIMRT	matric
ACIMRY	Myrica
ACIMST	mastic
ACINNT	tannic
ACINNY	cyanin
ACINOS	casino
ACINOT	action
	atonic
	cation
ACINOV	incavo
ACINOX	anoxic
ACINOZ	azonic

ACINPS	panisc
ACINPT	catnip
ACINPU	Punica
ACINPY	Naypic
ACINRS	arcsin
ACINRT	criant
ACINRU	uranic
ACINRY	riancy
ACINST	antics
	nastic
ACINSU	acinus
ACINTT	intact
ACINTU	anicut
	nautic
ACINUV	vicuña
ACIOPT	atopic
	copita
ACIORS	scoria
ACIORT	aortic
ACIOST	△scotia
ACIOSV	ovisac
ACIOTZ	azotic
ACIPRS	Capris
ACIPRY	piracy
ACIPSS	spicas
ACIPTT	tipcat
ACIQTU	acquit
ACIRRS	sircar
ACIRRT	tricar
ACIRRU	curari
ACIRSS	crasis
	crissa
ACIRST	crista
	racist
ACIRSY	Syriac
ACIRTT	triact
ACIRTU	tauric
	urtica
ACIRVY	vicary
ACISSS	cassis
ACISTT	static
ACITUY	acuity
ACITVY	cavity
ACJKOP	pajock
ACJKPU	jack-up
ACJKSY	jacksy
ACKKNU	Kanuck
ACKKNY	knacky
ACKLOP	Polack
ACKLSS	slacks
ACKLTY	talcky
ACKNOW	acknow
ACKNPR	pranck
ACKNPU	unpack
ACKNRY	cranky
ACKNST	stanck
ACKNTU	untack
ACKOPY	yapock
ACKORY	croaky
ACKPRS	sprack
ACKRST	tracks
ACKRTY	Y-track
ACLLMY	calmly
ACLLNO	clonal
ACLLOR	collar
ACLLOW	callow
	low-cal
ACLLPU	call-up
ACLLSU	callus
	sulcal
ACLLSY	Scylla
ACLMMY	clammy
ACLMOR	clamor
	Colmar
ACLMPY	camply
ACLMSU	lacmus
ACLMTU	talcum
ACLMUU	lucuma
ACLNOS	Caslon
ACLNUV	△vulcan
ACLNUY	lunacy
ACLOPU	copula
	cupola
ACLORR	corral
ACLORS	claros
	corals
ACLORT	carlot
	crotal
ACLORU	ocular
	rucola
ACLORW	owl-car
ACLORY	△calory
ACLOST	costal
ACLOSU	oscula
ACLOSV	vocals
ACLOSY	Lycosa
ACLOTW	cotwal
ACLRRU	crural
ACLRST	clarts
ACLRSU	cursal
ACLRSW	scrawl
ACLRTU	curtal
ACLRTY	clarty
ACLRWY	crawly
ACLSST	clasts
ACLSSY	classy
ACLSTU	scutal
ACMNOR	macron
ACMNOS	mascon
	socman
ACMNOT	monact
ACMNOW	cowman
ACMNPU	cupman
ACMNSU	mancus
ACMOPS	campos
ACMORS	macros
ACMORT	comart
ACMOST	comsat
	mascot
ACMOSU	mucosa
ACMOTT	tomcat
ACMOTU	motuca
ACMPRS	cramps
ACMPRY	crampy
ACMPSU	campus
ACMPTU	pactum
ACMRSU	sacrum
ACMRSW	scrawm
ACMSTU	muscat
ACMTUU	mutuca
ACMUUV	vacuum
ACNNNO	cannon
ACNNOT	cannot
	canton
ACNNOY	canyon
ACNNRY	cranny
ACNOOP	poonac
ACNOOR	corona
	racoon
ACNOPY	canopy
ACNORR	carron
	rancor
ACNORS	narcos
ACNORT	cantor
	carton
	contra
	craton
ACNORU	cornua
ACNORY	crayon
ACNOST	cantos
	Octans
	Sno-cat®
ACNOSZ	scazon
ACNOTT	octant
ACNOTU	△noctua
	toucan
ACNOTX	Caxton
ACNPTU	puncta
ACNRST	crants
ACNRTU	uncart
ACNSTU	cantus
	Tuscan
ACNSTY	scanty
ACOOTV	octavo
ACOPRT	captor
ACOPSS	scopas
ACOPTW	cowpat
ACORRT	carrot
	trocar
ACORSS	across
ACORST	△castor
	co-star
ACORSU	Acorus
ACORTT	cottar
ACORTU	turaco
ACORTV	cavort
ACORVY	covary
ACORYZ	coryza
ACPPRY	crappy
ACPRSU	carpus
ACPSSU	scapus
ACPSTU	catsup
	upcast
ACRRSY	scarry
ACRRTU	cratur
ACRSSU	Scarus
ACRSTU	crusta
ACRSUY	scaury
ACSTTY	scatty
ADDDEG	gadded
ADDDEL	addled
	daddle
ADDDEN	addend
ADDDEP	padded
ADDDEW	wadded
ADDDOO	doodad
ADDEEH	headed
ADDEEL	leaded
ADDEEM	addeem
ADDEEN	deaden
ADDEER	deader
ADDEFL	faddle
ADDEFN	fanded
ADDEGR	gadder
ADDEHI	haddie
ADDEHK	keddah
ADDEHN	hadden
	handed
ADDEHS	shaded
ADDEIL	daidle
	dialed
	laddie
ADDEIM	diadem
ADDEIN	Dandie
ADDEIT	taddie
ADDEIW	waddie
ADDELN	dandle
	landed
ADDELO	loaded
ADDELP	paddle
ADDELR	ladder
	raddle
ADDELS	saddle
ADDELW	dawdle
	waddle
ADDELY	deadly
ADDEMM	dammed
ADDEMN	damned
	demand
	madden
ADDEMR	madder
	red-mad
ADDENO	dead-on
ADDENR	dander
	darned
ADDENS	dedans
	sadden
	sanded
ADDENU	undead
ADDEOR	deodar
ADDEOS	dadoes
ADDEOW	woaded
ADDEPR	draped
	padder
	parded
ADDERR	darred
ADDERS	sadder
ADDERT	traded

ADDERW	warded
ADDGIO	gadoid
ADDGIP	giddap
ADDGMO	goddam
ADDGOO	ogdoad
ADDHIS	siddha
ADDHOO	doodah
ADDHSU	saddhu
ADDIKZ	zaddik
ADDIMR	dirdam
ADDIMY	midday
ADDIOS	addios
ADDLOY	day-old
ADDMNO	dodman
	odd-man
ADDMOO	addoom
ADDNOS	add-ons
ADDOOR	△dorado
ADDORT	dotard
ADDRSY	dryads
ADDSWY	swaddy
ADEEFL	leafed
ADEEFM	defame
ADEEFN	deafen
ADEEFR	feared
ADEEFT	defeat
ADEEGG	dégagé
ADEEGR	agreed
	dragée
	geared
ADEEHR	adhere
	header
	Hedera
ADEEHT	heated
ADEEHV	heaved
ADEEIL	aedile
ADEEIM	mediae
ADEEIN	Aeneid
ADEEIR	dearie
	rediae
ADEEIT	ideate
ADEEIW	deawie
ADEEJY	deejay
	dee-jay
ADEEKP	peaked
ADEELN	leaden
	leaned
ADEELO	Elodea
ADEELP	leaped
ADEELR	dealer
	leader
	redeal
ADEELS	sealed
ADEELT	delate
	tele-ad
ADEELV	leaved
ADEEMN	amende
	demean
ADEEMO	oedema
ADEEMR	remade
	remead
ADEEMT	teamed
ADEENN	ennead
	Na-Dene
ADEENP	neaped
ADEENR	deaner
	endear
ADEENV	advene
ADEEPS	pesade
ADEEPT	pedate
ADEERR	dreare
	reader
	reread
ADEERS	erased
	Reseda
	réséda
	seared
ADEERT	derate
	redate
ADEERV	evader
ADEERW	drawee
ADEERX	exedra
ADEEST	seated
	sedate
ADEETT	teated
ADEEVW	weaved
ADEFFI	affied
ADEFFY	affyde
ADEFGG	fagged
ADEFGN	fag-end
	fanged
ADEFIL	afield
	failed
ADEFIN	fade-in
ADEFIT	daftie
ADEFLM	flamed
ADEFLO	feodal
ADEFLR	fardel
ADEFLU	feudal
ADEFLW	flawed
ADEFLY	deafly
	flayed
ADEFMY	madefy
ADEFNN	fanned
ADEFNR	farden
ADEFNU	undeaf
ADEFOR	fedora
ADEFPU	fade-up
ADEFRU	fadeur
ADEFRY	defray
ADEFST	defast
ADEFTT	fatted
ADEFTW	wafted
ADEGGG	gagged
ADEGGH	hagged
ADEGGI	gadgie
ADEGGJ	jagged
ADEGGL	daggle
	lagged
ADEGGN	nagged
ADEGGR	dagger
	ragged
ADEGGS	sagged
ADEGGT	gadget
	tagged
ADEGGW	wagged
ADEGGZ	zagged
ADEGHI	hidage
ADEGHL	Gadhel
ADEGHN	hagden
	hanged
ADEGIM	mid-age
ADEGLN	angled
	dangle
	lag-end
ADEGLO	age-old
	old-age
ADEGLR	dargle
ADEGLZ	glazed
ADEGNR	danger
	gander
	garden
	grande
ADEGNT	tag-end
	tanged
ADEGNW	gnawed
ADEGOP	dog-ape
ADEGOR	dog-ear
	O-grade
ADEGOS	dagoes
	dosage
ADEGOT	dogate
	dotage
	togaed
ADEGRR	garred
	grader
	regard
ADEGRS	degras
	grades
ADEGRT	grated
ADEGRV	graved
ADEGSS	gassed
ADEGST	staged
ADEHIL	halide
ADEHIN	hained
ADEHIR	haired
ADEHIS	eadish
ADEHKS	shaked
ADEHKW	hawked
ADEHLN	handle
ADEHLO	haloed
ADEHLR	hareld
	herald
ADEHLS	halsed
ADEHMR	derham
ADEHMS	shamed
ADEHNO	head-on
ADEHNP	daphne
ADEHNR	hander
	harden
ADEHNU	unhead
ADEHOX	oxhead
ADEHPP	happed
ADEHPS	phased
	shaped
ADEHPT	heptad
ADEHPU	head-up
ADEHRS	dasher
	shared
ADEHRT	dearth
	hatred
	red-hat
	thread
ADEHSS	shades
ADEHST	'sdeath
ADEHSV	shaved
ADEHSW	washed
ADEHSY	Hyades
ADEHTT	hatted
ADEHTY	deathy
ADEHYY	heyday
ADEIKR	daiker
	darkie
ADEILL	allied
	laldie
ADEILM	maelid
	mailed
	medial
ADEILN	Aldine
	Daniel
	Delian
	denial
	lead-in
	nailed
ADEILO	eidola
ADEILP	aliped
	paidle
	Pleiad
ADEILR	derail
	redial
	relaid
ADEILS	aisled
	deasil
	ladies
	ladies'
	sailed
ADEILT	detail
	dilate
	tailed
ADEILU	audile
ADEILW	Dewali
ADEILY	eyliad
ADEIMM	maimed
ADEIMN	daimen
	demain
	△maiden
	△median
	medina
ADEIMR	admire
ADEIMS	mid-sea
ADEIMV	vidame
ADEINN	Andine
ADEINP	pained
ADEINR	randie
	read-in
ADEINS	sdaine

ADEINT	Danite
	detain
ADEINV	invade
ADEINW	dewani
ADEIOR	roadie
ADEIOT	iodate
ADEIPR	diaper
	paired
	pardie
	repaid
ADEIRR	arride
	raider
ADEIRS	resaid
ADEIRT	raited
	tirade
ADEIRU	uredia
ADEIRV	varied
ADEIRY	Yardie
ADEISS	dassie
ADEISU	adieus
	Suidae
ADEISV	advise
	visaed
ADEITU	dautie
ADEITV	dative
ADEITW	dawtie
ADEITX	taxied
ADEIUX	adieux
ADEJMM	jammed
ADEJNU	Judean
ADEJRR	jarred
ADEJRU	adjure
ADEJRY	jadery
ADEKLN	ankled
ADEKLR	darkle
ADEKLW	wealk'd
ADEKMO	make-do
ADEKMR	demark
	marked
ADEKMS	masked
ADEKNR	darken
	narked
	ranked
ADEKNT	tanked
ADEKOS	soaked
ADEKOY	kayoed
	okayed
ADEKPY	keypad
ADEKRS	drakes
ADEKRY	darkey
ADELLN	end-all
ADELLP	palled
ADELLR	all-red
ADELLS	dalles
ADELLU	allude
	aludel
ADELLV	devall
ADELLW	walled
ADELMP	palmed
ADELMR	dermal
	marled
	medlar
ADELMS	damsel
ADELMT	malted
ADELNO	enodal
	loaden
ADELNR	aldern
	darnel
	enlard
	Länder
	lander
ADELNS	sendal
ADELNT	dental
ADELNU	unlade
	unlead
ADELNW	wandle
ADELOP	opaled
	pedalo
ADELOR	loader
	ordeal
	reload
ADELOS	aldose
ADELPP	dapple
	lapped
ADELPR	pedlar
ADELPS	lapsed
ADELPT	plated
ADELPU	uplead
ADELPW	dewlap
ADELPY	played
ADELRR	larder
ADELRS	sardel
ADELRT	dartle
ADELRU	lauder
ADELRY	dearly
ADELRZ	drazel
ADELST	desalt
	salted
	slated
ADELSU	salue'd
ADELSV	salve'd
ADELSW	salewd
ADELSY	slayed
ADELUV	valued
ADELVV	valved
ADELZZ	dazzle
ADEMMR	dammer
	rammed
ADEMNN	manned
ADEMNO	daemon
	modena
	nomade
ADEMNP	dampen
ADEMNR	manred
	randem
	red-man
	remand
ADEMNS	amends
	desman
ADEMNT	tandem
ADEMNU	unmade
ADEMOP	apedom
	pomade
ADEMOR	radome
ADEMOS	Samoed
ADEMOT	moated
ADEMOW	meadow
ADEMPP	mapped
ADEMPR	damper
ADEMRR	marred
ADEMRT	dreamt
ADEMRU	remuda
ADEMRW	warmed
ADEMRY	dreamy
ADEMST	masted
ADEMSU	amused
	△medusa
ADEMTT	matted
ADEMWY	May-dew
ADENNP	panned
ADENNT	tanned
ADENNU	duenna
ADENNV	vanned
ADENNW	wanned
ADENOT	donate
ADENOU	douane
ADENOY	noyade
	one-day
ADENPP	append
	napped
ADENPR	pander
	repand
ADENPT	pedant
	pentad
ADENPX	expand
ADENRR	darner
	errand
ADENRS	sander
ADENRT	ardent
	endart
ADENRU	dauner
	undear
	unread
ADENRW	Andrew
	dawner
	wander
	warden
ADENRY	denary
ADENRZ	zander
ADENSU	sundae
ADENSW	new-sad
	wesand
ADENTT	attend
ADENTU	undate
ADENTV	△advent
ADENTW	wanted
ADENUW	unawed
ADENWZ	wezand
ADEOPP	peapod
ADEORR	adorer
ADEORS	oreads
ADEORT	doater
	troade
ADEORW	redowa
ADEOSV	vadose
ADEOVW	avowed
ADEPPR	dapper
	rapped
ADEPPS	sapped
ADEPPT	tapped
ADEPPW	wapped
ADEPRR	draper
ADEPRS	drapes
	spader
	spread
ADEPRT	depart
	drapet
	parted
	petard
ADEPRW	warped
ADEPRY	prayed
ADEPSS	passed
	spades
ADEPTT	patted
ADEPTU	update
ADEPTY	pet-day
ADERRT	darter
	dartre
	retard
	tarred
	trader
ADERRW	drawer
	redraw
	reward
	warder
	warred
ADERRY	dreary
ADERST	steard
	trades
ADERSW	sawder
	sweard
	waders
ADERTT	ratted
	tetrad
ADERTV	advert
ADERTW	warted
ADERTX	X-rated
ADERUW	waured
ADERVV	varved
ADERWX	wax-red
ADERWY	weyard
ADESTT	stated
	tasted
ADESTU	sudate
ADESTV	staved
ADESTW	stawed
	wadset
	wasted
ADESTY	stayed
	steady
ADESWY	swayed
ADETTV	vatted
ADETUV	veduta
ADFFOR	afford
ADFFOY	off-day
ADFFRY	draffy
ADFGIN	fading
ADFGLY	gadfly

ADFHSU	shaduf
ADFILU	aidful
ADFILY	ladify
ADFINR	friand
ADFIRT	adrift
ADFIRY	Friday
ADFLOS	sol-fa'd
ADFLTY	daftly
ADFLYY	day-fly
	ladyfy
ADFMNO	fandom
ADFMOU	fumado
ADFNOT	fantod
ADFORR	forrad
ADFRST	drafts
ADFRSW	dwarfs
ADFRTY	drafty
ADGGRY	draggy
ADGHNO	hagdon
ADGIIN	aiding
ADGILN	lading
	ligand
ADGILO	algoid
	dialog
ADGIMY	digamy
ADGINO	ganoid
ADGINR	daring
	gradin
ADGINT	dating
ADGINW	wading
ADGIRV	gravid
ADGLLY	gladly
ADGLNS	glands
ADGLNU	unglad
ADGLNY	dangly
ADGLOP	lapdog
ADGLOY	dayglo
	Day-Glo
ADGNOO	goonda
ADGNOR	△dragon
ADGNRU	durgan
ADGORW	wardog
ADGOSS	gadsos
ADGPRU	updrag
ADGRSU	gradus
	△guards
ADGRTU	Utgard
ADHHIT	Hadith
ADHHIW	whidah
ADHHOU	houdah
ADHHOW	howdah
ADHHWY	whydah
ADHIJS	jadish
ADHIKU	haiduk
ADHILL	all-hid
ADHILO	haloid
ADHIMR	dirham
ADHINN	hand-in
ADHINS	Danish
	sandhi
ADHIOR	hairdo
ADHIPS	aphids
ADHIRS	radish
ADHIRY	hydria
ADHISS	Hassid
ADHISW	dawish
ADHJKO	khodja
ADHLOT	old-hat
ADHLRY	hardly
ADHMNO	hodman
ADHMNU	numdah
ADHMRU	Durham
ADHNNU	nhandu
	unhand
ADHNOR	hadron
	hard-on
ADHNOU	houdan
ADHNPU	uphand
ADHNSY	shandy
ADHOSW	shadow
ADHPRU	hard-up
	purdah
ADHPUU	uphaud
ADHRRU	dhurra
ADHUZZ	huzza'd
ADIIKO	aikido
ADIILL	illiad
ADIILM	miladi
ADIILN	inlaid
ADIILR	iridal
ADIILV	Divali
ADIILW	Diwali
ADIIMO	daimio
ADIIMR	midair
ADIINN	Indian
ADIINV	avidin
ADIINZ	dizain
ADIIPR	diapir
ADIJKT	Tadjik
ADIJMS	masjid
ADIJNO	adjoin
ADIKKO	Kodiak
ADIKMO	mikado
ADIKNO	daikon
ADIKNP	kidnap
ADIKNS	Danisk
ADIKOT	dakoit
ADIKST	dikast
ADIKSU	adsuki
ADIKTT	diktat
ADIKUZ	adzuki
ADILLP	pallid
ADILLY	laidly
ADILMO	Amidol®
ADILMS	△dismal
ADILMY	diamyl
	milady
ADILNN	inland
ADILNO	dolina
	Ladino
ADILNR	aldrin
ADILNS	island
ADILNT	tindal
ADILNU	dualin
	unlaid
ADILNY	Lydian
ADILOO	ooidal
ADILOP	podial
ADILOR	laroid
ADILOZ	Ozalid®
ADILPT	pat-lid
ADILRY	aridly
ADILRZ	△lizard
ADILST	distal
ADILSU	Lusiad
ADILUV	vidual
ADILVY	avidly
ADIMMT	dammit
ADIMNO	daimon
	domain
ADIMNR	mandir
ADIMNS	disman
ADIMNT	mantid
ADIMOT	diatom
ADIMQU	quidam
ADIMRS	disarm
ADIMRU	radium
ADIMRY	myriad
ADIMSS	sadism
ADIMST	amidst
ADIMSY	dismay
ADIMWY	midway
ADINNU	induna
ADINOR	Dorian
	inroad
	ordain
ADINOS	Adonis
	danios
	sodain
ADINOX	diaxon
	dioxan
ADINPT	pandit
ADINPU	unpaid
ADINRT	indart
ADINRU	durian
ADINRV	ravin'd
ADINRW	inward
ADINSU	unsaid
ADINSV	viands
ADINSW	windas
ADINTY	dainty
ADIORS	radios
ADIORT	adroit
ADIOSU	audios
ADIOSZ	diazos
ADIPPU	paid-up
ADIPRS	rapids
	sparid
	spraid
ADIPSS	dipsas
ADIPSX	spadix
ADIRRS	sirdar
ADIRRY	air-dry
ADIRRZ	rizard
ADIRSU	radius
ADIRSW	wisard
ADIRVZ	vizard
ADIRWZ	wizard
ADIRZZ	izzard
ADISST	sadist
	saidst
ADISTV	vista'd
ADISXY	six-day
ADISYY	sayyid
ADITTY	dittay
ADJKOU	judoka
ADJNOR	△jordan
ADJSTU	adjust
ADKLRY	darkly
ADKOPU	padouk
ADLLOP	dallop
ADLLOR	dollar
ADLLUY	dually
ADLMNO	almond
	dolman
	old-man
ADLMOS	dolmas
ADLMOW	wadmol
ADLMPY	damply
ADLMTU	△talmud
ADLNOP	Poland
ADLNOR	Dralon®
	lardon
	Roland
ADLNOS	soldan
ADLNOT	dalton
ADLNOU	unload
ADLNOX	oxland
ADLNPU	upland
ADLNRU	lurdan
ADLORS	dorsal
ADLOSS	dossal
ADLOSW	dowlas
ADLPSU	spauld
ADMMNO	mandom
ADMNOR	random
	rodman
ADMNOS	damson
ADMNOW	woman'd
ADMNOY	dynamo
	Monday
	nomady
ADMNRU	unmard
ADMNUY	△maundy
ADMORR	ramrod
ADMORZ	Ormazd
ADMOSS	Mossad
ADMTUY	adytum
ADNNOO	nandoo
ADNNOR	randon
ADNNOT	danton
	donnat
ADNNOU	adnoun
ADNOOR	nardoo
ADNOOW	wandoo
ADNOPR	pardon
ADNOPT	dopant

ADNORU	around
ADNORW	onward
ADNORY	donary
ADNOTT	dotant
ADNRST	strand
ADNRSU	sundra
ADNRTU	draunt
	durant
	tundra
ADNRUW	undraw
ADNSTY	dynast
ADNSUY	Sunday
ADOORS	adoors
ADOOUV	vaudoo
ADOPRU	Podura
ADOPRY	parody
ADOPSS	spados
ADORRU	ardour
ADORTW	toward
ADORWY	ayword
ADPPRY	drappy
ADPRUW	updraw
	upward
ADRSUW	usward
ADRSUY	sudary
ADRSWY	swardy
ADRTWY	tawdry
AEEFFN	neaffe
AEEFFR	affeer
AEEFGU	feague
AEEFIR	faerie
AEEFLM	female
AEEFNT	Fantee
AEEFOV	foveae
AEEFRT	afreet
	terefa
AEEGGL	alegge
AEEGGM	Gamgee®
	gamgee
AEEGGN	engage
	engagé
AEEGGR	agrégé
	raggee
	reggae
AEEGGT	taggee
AEEGGW	geegaw
AEEGIR	Egeria
AEEGJR	Jaeger®
	jaeger
AEEGLL	allege
AEEGLP	pelage
AEEGLR	galère
	regale
AEEGLT	eaglet
	legate
	teagle
	telega
AEEGLU	league
AEEGLV	gleave
AEEGMM	gemmae
AEEGMN	manège
	menage
	ménage
AEEGMR	meagre
AEEGMT	gamete
	metage
AEEGNN	ennage
AEEGNR	enrage
	enragé
	genera
AEEGNS	sagene
	senega
AEEGNT	negate
AEEGNV	avenge
	geneva
AEEGNW	New-Age
	new-age
AEEGOP	apogee
AEEGOT	goatee
AEEGRS	grease
AEEGRT	ergate
AEEGRV	greave
AEEGST	egesta
AEEGSW	sewage
AEEGTU	Teague
AEEHHW	heehaw
AEEHIR	hearie
AEEHLR	healer
AEEHLT	lathee
AEEHLW	awheel
AEEHLX	exhale
AEEHMR	hareem
	hermae
AEEHMT	meathe
AEEHMU	heaume
AEEHNP	pea-hen
AEEHNT	Athene
	ethane
AEEHNV	△heaven
AEEHNX	hexane
AEEHPS	spahee
AEEHRR	hearer
	rehear
AEEHRS	hearse
AEEHRT	aether
	heater
	hereat
	reheat
AEEHRV	heaver
AEEHRW	a'where
	wheare
AEEHST	heaste
AEEHSV	heaves
	sheave
AEEHTV	theave
AEEIKV	keavie
AEEILM	mealie
AEEILS	Elaeis
	laesie
AEEIMN	meanie
AEEIMS	semeia
AEEINT	teniae
AEEIPR	epeira
	pereia
AEEJMS	Jeames
AEEJNT	jantee
AEEJRV	evejar
AEEKLN	alkene
AEEKLP	palkee
AEEKLR	leaker
AEEKLV	vakeel
AEEKMR	remake
AEEKMS	kamees
AEEKMZ	kameez
AEEKNW	weaken
AEEKNY	Yankee
AEEKPR	parkee
AEEKRT	retake
AEEKRU	eureka
AEELLL	allele
AEELLM	mallee
AEELLS	sallee
AEELMN	enamel
AEELMP	empale
AEELMR	mealer
AEELMS	measle
AEELMU	aemule
AEELMZ	meazel
AEELNP	alpeen
AEELNS	enseal
AEELNT	elanet
	lateen
AEELNV	leaven
AEELNW	weanel
AEELOR	areole
AEELOT	oleate
AEELPR	leaper
	△repeal
AEELPS	asleep
	elapse
	please
	sapele
AEELPU	epaule
AEELQU	quelea
AEELRS	leaser
	resale
	reseal
	sealer
AEELRT	elater
	relate
AEELRV	laveer
	leaver
	reveal
	vealer
AEELRY	E-layer
AEELSS	eassel
AEELST	steale
	stelae
	teasel
AEELSV	leaves
	sleave
AEELSW	weasel
AEELSZ	sleaze
AEELTU	eluate
AEELTV	valete
	velate
	veleta
AEELTW	atweel
AEELTY	eyalet
AEELTZ	teazel
	teazle
AEELWY	leeway
AEEMMM	mammee
AEEMNN	Nemean
AEEMNR	rename
AEEMNS	enemas
	enseam
AEEMNT	entame
AEEMNX	examen
AEEMOR	Moerae
AEEMPR	ampere
	ampère
	empare
AEEMPW	wampee
AEEMRR	reamer
AEEMRS	seamer
AEEMRT	teamer
AEEMSS	sesame
AEEMST	meseta
AEEMSW	meawes
AEEMTT	metate
AEENNP	pennae
AEENNT	Etnean
	neaten
AEENNX	annexe
AEENPT	nepeta
AEENPW	△pawnee
AEENRR	earner
	nearer
AEENRS	ensear
AEENRT	entera
AEENRW	weaner
AEENSS	aneses
AEENST	ensate
	sateen
	senate
	steane
AEENSU	unease
AEENSV	naeves
AEENTW	atween
AEENUV	△avenue
AEENWZ	weazen
AEEOUU	euouae
AEEOVV	evovae
AEEPPR	rappee
AEEPRR	reaper
AEEPRS	a-per-se
	Parsee
	prease
	serape
AEEPRT	repeat
AEEPSS	passée
AEEPST	peseta
AEEPSW	pesewa
AEEPSX	apexes
AEEPTT	pattée

AEEPVY	peavey
AEEQRU	quaere
AEEQTU	equate
AEERRR	rearer
AEERRS	eraser
	serrae
AEERRT	tearer
	terrae
AEERRV	reaver
AEERRW	wearer
AEERST	△easter
	reseat
	saeter
	seater
	steare
	teaser
AEERSU	réseau
AEERSV	averse
AEERTY	eatery
AEERVW	weaver
AEESSW	seesaw
AEESTT	estate
AEFFGR	gaffer
AEFFHT	haffet
AEFFIN	affine
AEFFIP	piaffe
AEFFKR	△kaffer
AEFFLR	raffle
AEFFLW	waffle
AEFFLY	yaffle
AEFFRT	affret
	farfet
AEFFRY	effray
AEFFRZ	zaffer
	zaffre
AEFGLN	fangle
	flange
AEFGLR	reflag
AEFGMU	fumage
AEFGOR	forage
AEFGRU	gaufer
	gaufre
AEFGRY	fegary
AEFHLL	fellah
AEFHLN	halfen
AEFHNT	fat-hen
AEFHRS	afresh
AEFHRT	△father
AEFHSY	sheafy
AEFIJO	feijoa
AEFIKS	faikes
AEFILL	faille
AEFILN	finale
AEFILR	ferial
AEFILS	falsie
AEFILT	fetial
AEFIMN	famine
	infame
AEFINN	Fenian
AEFINR	infare
AEFIRS	fraise
AEFIST	fiesta
AEFITX	fixate
AEFJNT	fan-jet
AEFKLN	fankle
AEFKLS	flakes
AEFKRY	fakery
	freaky
AEFLLN	fallen
AEFLLR	faller
AEFLLV	△favell
AEFLMN	flamen
AEFLNN	fannel
AEFLNU	flaune
AEFLNX	flaxen
AEFLOR	florae
	loafer
AEFLOT	foetal
	folate
AEFLOV	foveal
AEFLRS	falser
	flares
	flaser
AEFLRT	falter
AEFLRU	earful
	△ferula
AEFLRY	flayer
AEFLST	festal
AEFLSY	safely
AEFLTU	fluate
AEFLTY	fealty
	featly
AEFLUW	waeful
AEFMNN	fenman
AEFMNO	foeman
AEFMOR	femora
AEFMRR	farmer
	framer
AEFNNR	fanner
AEFNNT	enfant
AEFNOR	forane
AEFNRR	farren
AEFNRU	furane
AEFNRW	fawner
AEFNST	fasten
	nefast
AEFNSU	unsafe
AEFNTT	fatten
AEFOSS	fossae
AEFOSV	favose
AEFPPR	frappé
AEFPRY	perfay
AEFRRT	frater
	rafter
AEFRRY	rarefy
AEFRST	afters
	faster
	strafe
AEFRTT	fatter
AEFRTW	wafter
AEFRWY	wafery
AEFSTY	safety
AEGGGL	gaggle
AEGGGR	gagger
AEGGHL	haggle
AEGGIN	ageing
AEGGJR	jagger
AEGGLN	laggen
AEGGLR	gargle
	lagger
	raggle
AEGGLW	waggle
AEGGNR	ganger
	grange
	nagger
AEGGNU	gangue
AEGGRS	sagger
	seggar
AEGGRT	garget
	tagger
AEGGRU	gauger
AEGGRY	yagger
AEGGWW	gewgaw
AEGHIR	hegira
	hirage
AEGHIS	geisha
AEGHIW	aweigh
AEGHLS	sealgh
AEGHLT	haglet
AEGHLZ	ghazel
AEGHMO	homage
	ohmage
AEGHNR	hanger
	rehang
AEGHOR	gherao
AEGHOS	seahog
AEGHPT	hatpeg
AEGHRT	gather
AEGILM	milage
AEGILN	genial
	linage
AEGILO	goalie
AEGILP	paigle
AEGILR	graile
	lea-rig
AEGILS	ligase
	silage
AEGILT	aiglet
	gelati
	ligate
	taigle
AEGILV	glaive
	vagile
AEGIMN	△enigma
	gamine
AEGIMP	magpie
AEGIMR	maigre
	mirage
AEGIMS	ageism
AEGINR	earing
	gainer
	graine
	regain
	△regina
AEGINS	agnise
AEGINT	eating
	ingate
	tangie
	teaing
AEGINU	guinea
AEGINZ	agnize
AEGIPP	pipage
AEGIPS	sea-pig
AEGIRS	agrise
AEGIRT	gaiter
	triage
AEGIRV	Argive
	garvie
	rivage
AEGIRW	earwig
AEGIRZ	agrize
AEGIST	ageist
AEGISU	aguise
AEGISV	visage
AEGITU	augite
AEGITY	gaiety
AEGIUZ	aguize
AEGJLN	jangle
AEGJLT	jet-lag
AEGJTU	jugate
AEGKLR	grakle
AEGKRW	gawker
AEGKST	gasket
AEGLLN	leglan
AEGLLT	gallet
AEGLLU	ullage
AEGLLY	egally
	galley
AEGLMN	leg-man
	mangel
	mangle
AEGLMR	malgre
	malgré
AEGLMV	maglev
AEGLMY	gamely
	gleamy
	mygale
AEGLNO	engaol
AEGLNR	angler
	largen
	regnal
AEGLNT	tangle
AEGLNU	lagune
	langue
AEGLNW	wangle
AEGLNY	lynage
AEGLNZ	glazen
AEGLOR	galore
	gaoler
AEGLOT	gelato
	legato
AEGLOV	lovage
	volage
AEGLPR	graple
AEGLPU	plague
AEGLRT	tergal
AEGLRU	regula

Words marked △ may be spelled also with a capital letter

AEGLRV	gravel
AEGLRY	argyle
	grayle
AEGLRZ	glazer
AEGLSU	saulge
AEGLSY	sagely
AEGLTU	tegula
AEGLTW	talweg
AEGMMN	gemman
AEGMMR	gammer
	gramme
AEGMMS	smegma
AEGMNO	gnomae
AEGMNR	engram
	△german
	manger
AEGMNS	magnes
AEGMNT	magnet
AEGMNY	mangey
AEGMOR	romage
AEGMPS	sepmag
AEGMRU	maugre
	murage
AEGMSS	megass
AEGMSY	gamesy
AEGMUY	maguey
AEGMUZ	zeugma
AEGNNO	nonage
AEGNNP	pangen
AEGNNT	gannet
AEGNOR	onager
	△orange
AEGNOS	geason
AEGNRR	garner
	△ranger
AEGNRS	serang
AEGNRT	argent
	garnet
AEGNRU	raunge
	ungear
AEGNRV	graven
AEGNRW	gnawer
AEGNSY	gansey
AEGOPS	sapego
AEGOPT	potage
AEGORS	sorage
AEGORT	orgeat
	toerag
AEGOTT	togate
AEGOTU	outage
AEGOTW	towage
AEGOTX	oxgate
AEGOVY	voyage
AEGPRS	gasper
	grapes
	sparge
AEGPRT	parget
AEGPRU	gauper
AEGPRW	gawper
AEGPRY	grapey
AEGPTY	Aegypt
AEGPUZ	upgaze
AEGRRT	garret
	△garter
	grater
AEGRRU	arguer
AEGRRV	graver
AEGRRZ	grazer
AEGRSS	gasser
AEGRST	gaster
	graste
	Greats
	stager
	Strega®
AEGRSU	sauger
	usager
AEGRSV	△graves
AEGRSW	Swerga
AEGRSY	greasy
AEGRTT	target
AEGRTU	argute
	rugate
	Tuareg
AEGRTY	gyrate
AEGRYZ	agryze
AEGSSU	usages
AEGSTY	gayest
	stagey
AEGTTU	guttae
AEHHJV	Jahveh
AEHHLT	health
AEHHPR	rhaphe
AEHHPY	hyphae
AEHHRS	rehash
AEHHRT	hearth
AEHHST	sheath
AEHHTY	heathy
AEHHVY	Yahveh
AEHHWY	Yahweh
AEHIJR	hejira
AEHIKN	hankie
AEHIKS	sakieh
AEHIKW	hawkie
AEHILM	hiemal
AEHILN	Hielan'
	inhale
AEHILR	hailer
AEHILS	sheila
AEHILT	halite
AEHILW	awhile
AEHIMN	haemin
	hemina
AEHIMS	mashie
AEHIMT	Hamite
AEHINR	hernia
AEHINS	ashine
AEHINV	vahine
AEHINW	wahine
AEHIQU	haique
AEHIRS	△sheria
AEHIRT	Theria
AEHIST	saithe
AEHISV	shavie
AEHJRS	Jasher
AEHKMS	samekh
AEHKNR	hanker
	harken
AEHKNS	shaken
AEHKOS	she-oak
AEHKPR	phreak
AEHKRS	shaker
AEHKRW	hawker
AEHKSY	ash-key
AEHKWY	hawkey
AEHLLT	lethal
AEHLMP	△pelham
AEHLMT	hamlet
AEHLNO	enhalo
AEHLNS	hansel
AEHLNT	hantle
	lathen
AEHLNU	unheal
AEHLOS	haloes
AEHLOT	loathe
AEHLRS	ashler
	halser
	lasher
AEHLRT	halter
	lather
	thaler
AEHLRU	hauler
AEHLRV	halver
AEHLRW	whaler
AEHLSS	hassle
AEHLST	haslet
	Shelta
AEHLSV	halves
AEHLSY	haysel
AEHLTW	wealth
AEHLTY	eathly
	hyetal
AEHMMR	hammer
AEHMMY	mayhem
AEHMNT	anthem
	hetman
AEHMNU	humane
	Humean
AEHMOS	hamose
AEHMOT	at-home
AEHMPR	hamper
AEHMRS	masher
	shamer
AEHMST	smeath
AEHNOV	have-on
AEHNPP	happen
AEHNPS	shapen
AEHNPT	hapten
AEHNRT	anther
	harten
	thenar
AEHNST	hasten
	snathe
	sneath
AEHNSV	Hesvan
	shaven
AEHNSW	washen
	whenas
AEHNSZ	sazhen
AEHNTU	uneath
AEHNTV	haven't
AEHNTW	whaten
AEHNUY	haüyne
AEHORS	ahorse
	ashore
	hoarse
AEHORX	hoaxer
AEHPPU	upheap
AEHPRR	harper
AEHPRS	phrase
	seraph
	shaper
	△sherpa
	sphaer
	sphear
AEHPRT	tephra
	teraph
	threap
AEHPSS	phases
AEHPST	spathe
AEHPSV	V-shape
AEHPSW	peshwa
AEHPTY	hypate
AEHRRS	rasher
	sharer
AEHRRT	rather
AEHRSS	shares
	shears
AEHRST	hearts
	'sheart
AEHRSV	havers
	shaver
AEHRSW	hawser
	washer
AEHRSY	ashery
	hearsy
AEHRTT	hatter
	threat
AEHRTV	thrave
AEHRTW	thawer
	wreath
AEHRTY	earthy
	hearty
AEHRVW	wharve
AEHSSS	she-ass
AEHSTW	swathe
AEIIKS	saikei
AEIILS	liaise
AEIJLR	jailer
AEIJLZ	jezail
AEIJMM	jemima
AEIJNR	injera
AEIJNT	tajine
AEIJRV	jarvie
AEIKLR	laiker
AEIKLS	alsike
AEIKLT	talkie
AEIKMN	kinema

AEIKNS	kinase
AEIKNT	intake
	△kentia
	take-in
AEIKNY	yankie
AEIKPR	parkie
AEIKRR	△kerria
AEIKRS	kaiser
AEIKRT	arkite
	karite
AEILLN	lienal
	lineal
AEILLS	allies
AEILLT	taille
	telial
AEILLW	wallie
AEILMM	lammie
AEILMN	menial
AEILMP	impale
	palmie
AEILMR	mailer
AEILMS	mesail
	mesial
	samiel
AEILMZ	mezail
AEILNO	Eolian
AEILNP	△alpine
	Nepali
	penial
	pineal
AEILNR	larine
	linear
	nailer
AEILNS	saline
	silane
AEILNT	entail
	tenail
	tineal
AEILNV	alevin
	alvine
	valine
	venial
AEILNX	alexin
	xenial
AEILOP	leipoa
AEILPP	lappie
AEILPS	espial
	lipase
AEILPT	aplite
AEILRR	railer
	rerail
AEILRS	sailer
	serail
	serial
AEILRT	retail
	retial
AEILRW	wailer
AEILSS	eassil
	laisse
	lassie
AEILSU	saulie
AEILSV	silvae
	valise
AEILSW	walise
AEILSY	easily
AEILTY	tailye
AEIMMN	immane
AEIMNO	anomie
AEIMNP	pieman
AEIMNR	marine
	remain
AEIMNS	inseam
	mesian
AEIMNT	inmate
	tamine
AEIMPR	premia
AEIMPV	impave
AEIMPY	pyemia
AEIMRT	imaret
AEIMRU	uremia
AEIMRW	awmrie
AEIMST	samite
	tamise
AEIMTT	mattie
AEIMXX	maxixe
AEINNP	pinnae
AEINNR	narine
	ranine
AEINNS	insane
	sannie
	sienna
AEINNT	innate
AEINNZ	enzian
AEINOZ	azione
AEINPR	rapine
AEINPS	aspine
AEINPT	patine
	pineta
AEINPV	Evipan®
AEINRS	arisen
	arsine
	sarnie
AEINRT	Nerita
	ratine
	ratiné
	retain
	retina
AEINRV	avenir
	ravine
AEINSS	anesis
	sanies
	sansei
	sasine
AEINST	tisane
AEINSV	savine
AEINTU	△auntie
	Uniate
AEINTV	native
AEIOPS	soapie
AEIOPT	opiate
AEIOPZ	epizoa
AEIORR	roarie
AEIPPY	yappie
AEIPRR	rapier
	repair
AEIPRS	aspire
	praise
	spirea
AEIPRT	pirate
	pratie
	pteria
AEIPST	pe-tsai
AEIPSV	pavise
	spavie
AEIPSW	waspie
AEIPTT	tapeti
AEIPTU	taupie
AEIPTW	tawpie
AEIPZZ	Peziza
AEIQSU	saique
AEIRRS	raiser
	sierra
AEIRRT	'Arriet
AEIRRV	arrive
	varier
AEIRST	satire
	striae
AEIRTT	attire
	ratite
	tertia
AEIRTV	taiver
AEIRTW	waiter
AEIRVW	waiver
AEISST	siesta
	tassie
AEISSU	Aussie
AEISSX	axises
AEISSZ	assize
AEISTV	sative
AEISTX	taxies
AEISTY	aseity
AEITTT	tattie
AEITTV	vittae
AEITTW	tawtie
	twaite
AEJKNR	janker
AEJMMR	jammer
AEJMRT	ramjet
AEJMST	jetsam
	matjes
AEJNST	sejant
AEJNSU	jaunse
AEJPRS	jasper
AEJRVY	jarvey
AEJRZZ	jazzer
AEKKNR	kraken
AEKKRY	yakker
AEKLNO	Ankole
AEKLNR	rankle
AEKLNT	anklet
AEKLNW	knawel
	wankle
AEKLNY	alkyne
AEKLRR	larker
AEKLRT	talker
AEKLRV	Kevlar®
AEKLRW	△walker
AEKLST	lasket
	sklate
AEKLTU	auklet
AEKLWY	weakly
AEKMNU	unmake
AEKMOT	matoke
AEKMPU	make-up
	upmake
AEKMRR	marker
	remark
	re-mark
AEKMRS	masker
AEKMRT	market
AEKNNR	enrank
AEKNNT	kanten
AEKNOR	Korean
AEKNOS	soaken
AEKNOW	awoken
AEKNRR	ranker
AEKNRT	tanker
AEKNRU	unrake
AEKNRW	wanker
AEKNRY	yanker
AEKNSY	sneaky
AEKORS	arkose
	soaker
AEKOSY	kayoes
AEKPRR	parker
AEKPRS	sparke
AEKPTU	take-up
	uptake
AEKPUW	wake-up
AEKQRU	△quaker
AEKQSU	squeak
AEKRRT	karter
	krater
AEKRRY	rakery
AEKRST	skater
	strake
	streak
	tasker
AEKRSY	karsey
	skeary
AEKRUW	wauker
AEKSST	skates
	stakes
AEKWYY	key-way
AELLLY	leally
AELLMT	mallet
AELLMY	lamely
	mellay
AELLNU	unleal
AELLNW	enwall
AELLNY	leanly
AELLPP	lappel
AELLPS	spalle
AELLPT	L-plate
	pallet
AELLPY	palely
AELLRT	tellar

Words marked △ may be spelled also with a capital letter

AELLRU allure
laurel
AELLRW waller
AELLRY rallye
really
re-ally
AELLST sallet
AELLSY alleys
AELLTT tallet
AELLTU luteal
AELLTW wallet
AELLTY lately
lealty
AELLVY valley
AELMMR lammer
AELMMS lemmas
AELMNO melano
AELMNS lemans
mensal
AELMNT lament
mantel
mantle
mental
AELMNY meanly
namely
AELMOR morale
AELMPR emparl
palmer
AELMPS sample
AELMPU ampule
AELMRT armlet
martel
AELMRV marvel
vermal
AELMRY almery
AELMST metals
samlet
AELMSY measly
samely
AELMTU amulet
AELMTY tamely
AELNNP pennal
AELNNR lanner
AELNNW wannel
AELNOS lanose
Sloane
AELNOT etalon
lean-to
AELNPP pen-pal
AELNPR planer
replan
AELNPT planet
platen
AELNPU uplean
AELNRS ransel
AELNRT altern
antler
learnt
rental
ternal
AELNRU neural
ulnare
unreal
AELNRV nerval
vernal
AELNRY anerly
nearly
AELNRZ ranzel
AELNSU Elanus
unseal
AELNSY sanely
AELNTT latent
latten
talent
AELNTU eluant
lunate
AELNTV △levant
AELNTY neatly
AELNTZ zelant
AELNUW unweal
AELOOZ zooeal
AELOPR parole
AELOPS aslope
AELOPT pelota
AELOPX pole-ax
AELORS realos
roseal
solera
AELORT lorate
AELORY o'erlay
AELOST osteal
AELOSV loaves
AELOSW leasow
AELOTZ △zealot
AELPPR lapper
rappel
AELPPS apples
sapple
AELPPT lappet
AELPPU papule
upleap
AELPQU plaque
AELPRR parrel
AELPRT palter
plater
AELPRU pleura
AELPRW prawle
AELPRY parley
pearly
player
replay
AELPST pastel
plaste
plates
septal
staple
AELPTT pattle
T-plate
AELPTU puteal
AELQRU quar'le
AELQSU lasque
squeal
AELRRT retral
AELRRY rarely
rearly
AELRST estral
laster
salter
slater
stelar
tarsel
AELRSU saurel
AELRSV salver
serval
slaver
versal
AELRSW warsle
AELRSY slayer
AELRTT latter
rattle
tatler
AELRTV travel
varlet
AELRTY elytra
lyrate
raylet
realty
telary
AELRUV valuer
AELRVV varvel
AELRWX wraxle
AELRWY lawyer
AELRYY yarely
yearly
AELRZZ razzle
AELSST tassel
AELSSV selvas
AELSTT latest
stealt
taslet
AELSTU salute
AELSTV △vestal
AELSTW wastel
AELSTY astely
AELSUV avulse
values
AELSUX sexual
AELSVY slavey
sylvae
AELSYZ sleazy
AELTTT tattle
AELTTW wattle
AELTUX luxate
AELUUV uvulae
AEMMMR mammer
marmem
AEMMMT mammet
AEMMNR merman
AEMMRR rammer
AEMMRY yammer
AEMMRZ mamzer
AEMMST stemma
AEMMSU summae
AEMMTU maumet
AEMMTW mawmet
AEMNNO one-man
AEMNNP penman
AEMNNR manner
AEMNNT manent
AEMNOP mopane
AEMNOR enamor
moaner
monera
AEMNOT omenta
to-name
AEMNOY yeoman
AEMNPU pneuma
AEMNQU manqué
AEMNRT marten
AEMNRU manure
murena
AEMNSS messan
AEMNST stamen
AEMNSU unseam
AEMNSY yes-man
AEMNTU untame
unteam
AEMOOV amoove
AEMOPZ apozem
AEMORR remora
roamer
AEMORS ramose
AEMORT amoret
omerta
omertà
AEMORW womera
AEMORX xeroma
AEMOST osmate
AEMOSV vamose
AEMOSW awsome
AEMPPR mapper
pamper
preamp
AEMPRR ramper
AEMPRT empart
tamper
AEMPRV revamp
vamper
AEMPSU △empusa
AEMQRU marque
AEMQSU masque
squame
AEMRRU armure
AEMRRV marver
AEMRRW warmer
AEMRST △master
stream
AEMRSU amuser
Mauser
AEMRSY smeary
AEMRTT matter
AEMRTU mature
AEMSSS masses
AEMSSU assume
AEMSTU meatus

AEMSTY	mayest
	steamy
AEMSYZ	zymase
AEMTTU	mutate
AEMUZZ	mezuza
AENNNO	nonane
AENNOS	nosean
AENNOV	novena
AENNOY	anyone
AENNRT	tanner
AENNRV	vanner
AENNTT	tenant
AENOPS	peason
AENOPV	pavone
AENOPW	weapon
AENOPY	paeony
AENORS	reason
	Señora
AENORT	atoner
	ornate
AENOSS	season
AENOST	astone
AENOTT	attone
	notate
AENOTZ	zonate
AENOWY	one-way
AENPPR	napper
	parpen
AENPRT	arpent
	enrapt
	entrap
	panter
	parent
	trepan
AENPRW	enwrap
	pawner
AENPRY	napery
AENPRZ	panzer
AENPST	pesant
AENPTT	patent
	patten
AENPTU	peanut
AENPTZ	pezant
AENQTU	equant
AENRRS	serran
	snarer
AENRRT	errant
	ranter
	Terran
AENRRW	warner
	warren
AENRSS	sarsen
AENRST	astern
	transe
AENRSW	answer
AENRSY	sarney
	senary
AENRTT	natter
	ratten
AENRTU	aunter
	△nature
AENRTV	tavern
AENRTW	wanter
AENRTY	trayne
AENRUW	unware
AENSST	assent
	snaste
AENSTU	nasute
	unseat
AENSTX	sextan
AENSTY	stayne
AENSTZ	stanze
AENSUV	naevus
AENSUY	uneasy
AENSWY	△sawney
AENTTT	attent
AENTTU	attune
	nutate
	tauten
AENTTX	extant
AENTTY	tetany
AENTWY	tawney
AEOPPS	appose
AEOPQU	opaque
AEOPRS	soaper
AEOPRT	protea
AEOPTT	aptote
	teapot
AEOPTY	teapoy
AEORRR	roarer
AEORRS	soarer
AEORSS	serosa
AEORST	Ostrea
AEORSU	arouse
AEORTT	rotate
	to-tear
AEORUV	avoure
AEORVW	avower
AEORVY	avoyer
AEOSTV	avoset
AEOSTW	awetos
AEOTTU	outeat
AEOUVZ	Zouave
AEPPRR	rapper
AEPPRS	papers
	sapper
AEPPRT	tapper
AEPPRU	pauper
AEPPRW	wapper
AEPPRY	papery
	prepay
	yapper
AEPPRZ	zapper
AEPPSY	apepsy
AEPPTT	tappet
AEPPTU	pupate
AEPRRS	parser
	rasper
	sparer
	sparre
AEPRRT	parter
	prater
AEPRRU	parure
	uprear
AEPRRW	pre-war
	rewrap
	warper
AEPRRY	prayer
AEPRSS	passer
	repass
	sparse
AEPRST	paster
	pearst
	repast
	trapes
AEPRSU	pauser
AEPRSY	speary
AEPRTT	patter
AEPRTU	uprate
	uptear
AEPRTX	pre-tax
AEPRTY	petary
AEPRTZ	patzer
AEPRUV	rave-up
AEPRWY	yawper
AEPSST	stapes
AEQRSU	△square
AEQRTU	quarte
AEQRUV	quaver
AEQSUY	queasy
AEQUYZ	queazy
AERRSS	serras
AERRST	arrest
	raster
	starer
	terras
AERRSU	rasure
AERRTT	ratter
AERRTY	artery
AERRUZ	razure
AERRWY	warrey
AERSST	assert
AERSSU	assure
AERSSW	wrasse
AERSTT	astert
	stater
	taster
AERSTU	Auster
AERSTV	starve
	tavers
AERSTW	waster
	waters
AERSTX	Astrex
AERSTY	estray
	reasty
	stayer
	stayre
AERSTZ	ersatz
AERSUU	aureus
	uraeus
AERSVW	swarve
AERSWY	sawyer
	swayer
AERTTT	tatter
AERTTV	tavert
	vatter
AERTTW	tewart
AERTTY	treaty
	yatter
AERTUU	auteur
AERTWY	tawery
	watery
AERVWY	wavery
AESSSS	assess
AESSST	assets
AESSTT	△states
	tasset
AESSTU	sautés
AESSTV	staves
	vestas
AESSTW	wastes
AESSTY	sayest
AESTTT	attest
AESTTU	astute
	statue
AESTWY	sweaty
AESTXY	extasy
AESTYY	yeasty
AESVVY	savvey
AETUXY	eutaxy
AFFFOR	far-off
AFFGUW	guffaw
AFFHIT	haffit
AFFIKR	△kaffir
AFFILP	pilaff
AFFIMR	affirm
AFFIOR	off-air
AFFIRT	tariff
AFFLNY	naffly
AFFLOY	lay-off
AFFLUX	afflux
AFFLWY	waffly
AFFOPY	pay-off
AFFRST	straff
AFFSST	staffs
AFGGLY	flaggy
AFGGOT	faggot
AFGHOS	fogash
AFGINN	fingan
AFGINR	Gräfin
AFGISY	gasify
AFGLNO	flagon
AFGLNU	fungal
AFGLRU	frugal
AFGMNO	fogman
AFGMOR	fogram
AFGNOS	fangos
AFGNPU	pang-fu'
AFGORR	fragor
AFGORT	forgat
AFGOTU	fugato
AFGRUY	argufy
AFHIKL	khalif
AFHIKR	kharif
AFHIMS	famish
AFHIOS	oafish
AFHIRS	sharif
AFHLMU	fulham

AFHLOO	loofah
AFHLSY	flashy
AFHLTU	hatful
AFHMOT	fathom
AFHORS	shofar
AFHRSW	wharfs
AFIILL	filial
AFIILN	finial
AFIJNN	finjan
AFIKNU	funkia
AFIKRS	friska
AFILLN	fall-in
	infall
AFILMY	family
AFILNO	in-foal
AFILNS	finals
AFILNU	infula
AFILNV	flavin
AFILNY	fainly
AFILOR	foliar
AFILRY	fairly
AFILRZ	frazil
AFILSY	salify
AFIMNR	farm-in
	firman
AFIMNY	infamy
AFIMRY	ramify
AFIMSS	massif
AFIMSV	favism
AFINNN	finnan
AFINNO	fanion
AFINNT	infant
AFINRU	unfair
AFINRY	fin-ray
AFINST	faints
AFINSU	fusain
AFINSY	sanify
AFINTU	fiaunt
AFINTY	fainty
AFINYZ	Nazify
AFIORT	faitor
AFIQRU	faquir
AFIRRY	friary
AFIRTY	ratify
AFIRUY	aurify
AFJLRU	jarful
AFLLMU	fullam
AFLLNO	onfall
AFLLNU	fullan
AFLLOR	floral
AFLLOT	to-fall
AFLLOW	fallow
AFLLPU	lapful
AFLLTY	flatly
AFLLUW	lawful
AFLMNU	manful
AFLMNY	fly-man
AFLMOR	formal
AFLMRU	armful
	fulmar
AFLMYY	mayfly
AFLNOT	fontal
AFLNPU	panful
AFLNTU	flaunt
AFLORS	floras
AFLORV	flavor
AFLOTW	low-fat
AFLOTY	floaty
AFLPPY	flappy
AFLPSU	sapful
AFLRTU	artful
AFLSTU	flatus
AFLSTY	fastly
AFLSWY	saw-fly
AFLTUV	vatful
AFLTUY	faulty
AFLWYY	flyway
AFMNOT	fantom
AFMOOS	samfoo
AFMORT	format
AFMOSU	famous
AFMTTU	Muftat
AFNNOT	non-fat
AFNORT	afront
AFNRYZ	franzy
AFOORT	footra
AFORRW	farrow
AFORRY	forray
AFORSY	forsay
AFORTU	far-out
	fautor
	foutra
AFORUV	favour
AFOSST	fatsos
AFOSSU	foussa
AFOSUV	favous
AFPTUW	upwaft
AFRRTY	fratry
AFRSTU	frusta
AGGHIS	haggis
AGGHSY	shaggy
AGGIIL	gilgai
AGGILN	gingal
	laggin
AGGILO	loggia
AGGIMN	gaming
	gigman
AGGINO	agoing
	a-going
AGGINP	gaping
	paging
AGGINR	raging
AGGINT	gating
AGGIOR	gorgia
AGGIWW	wigwag
AGGIZZ	zigzag
AGGKNY	knaggy
AGGLNY	gangly
AGGLOT	loggat
AGGLSY	slaggy
AGGLWY	waggly
AGGMNO	moggan
AGGMOT	maggot
AGGNOU	guango
AGGNOW	waggon
AGGNOX	oxgang
AGGNPU	upgang
AGGNRU	nuggar
AGGNSY	snaggy
AGGPRY	pygarg
AGGQUY	quaggy
AGHHTU	haught
AGHIJR	jaghir
AGHIKU	kiaugh
AGHILT	alight
AGHINT	anight
	a'thing
AGHINV	having
AGHINY	haying
AGHINZ	hazing
AGHIQU	quaigh
AGHIRR	gharri
AGHIRS	garish
AGHIRT	aright
	graith
AGHISU	aguish
AGHKRU	Gurkha
AGHLLU	Gullah
AGHLMU	Mughal
AGHLOS	galosh
AGHLSY	gashly
AGHLTU	galuth
AGHLUY	laughy
AGHNNU	unhang
AGHNOU	anough
AGHNPU	hang-up
	uphang
AGHNRT	Granth
	thrang
AGHNRU	nurhag
AGHNTU	naught
AGHNUY	gunyah
AGHOQU	quahog
AGHORT	hog-rat
AGHRRU	gurrah
AGHRRY	gharry
AGHRTU	raught
	tughra
AGHTTU	taught
AGHTUW	waught
AGIIJN	gaijin
AGIILN	ailing
	nilgai
AGIINR	airing
	ragini
AGIJLN	jingal
AGIJNP	japing
AGIJNW	jawing
AGIJSW	jigsaw
AGIKLS	glaiks
AGIKMN	making
AGIKNR	raking
AGIKNS	gaskin
AGIKNT	taking
AGIKNW	waking
AGILLO	Gallio
AGILLU	ligula
AGILMM	gimmal
AGILMN	lingam
	malign
AGILMO	glioma
AGILMP	magilp
AGILNP	paling
AGILNS	lasing
	signal
AGILNU	lingua
	nilgau
AGILNW	lawing
AGILNY	gainly
	laying
AGILOR	gloria
AGILOS	golias
	oil-gas
AGILOT	galiot
AGILOV	ogival
AGILRS	slairg
AGILRU	arguli
AGILRY	glairy
AGILST	gaslit
AGIMMS	magism
AGIMNN	naming
AGIMNP	pig-man
AGIMNR	ingram
	margin
AGIMNT	taming
AGIMNY	maying
AGIMOS	amigos
	imagos
AGIMRU	gurami
AGIMST	stigma
AGIMWW	wigwam
AGINNO	ganoin
AGINNT	anting
AGINNU	ungain
AGINNW	awning
	waning
AGINOR	ignaro
	origan
AGINOS	ngaios
	sagoin
AGINOT	gitano
AGINPR	paring
	raping
AGINPS	spaing
AGINPV	paving
AGINPY	paying
AGINRR	raring
AGINRS	grains
	saring
AGINRT	gratin
	rating
	taring
AGINRU	air-gun
	Ugrian
AGINRV	raving
AGINRW	rawing
AGINRY	grainy
AGINSS	assign

AGINST	'gainst
AGINSU	Anguis
	saguin
AGINSV	saving
AGINSW	aswing
	sawing
AGINSY	saying
AGINTW	tawing
AGINTX	taxing
AGINVW	waving
AGINWX	waxing
AGIORU	giaour
AGIORV	virago
AGIOTU	agouti
AGIPRT	pig-rat
AGIQRU	Griqua
AGIRST	gratis
	striga
AGIRTU	guitar
AGITTW	witgat
AGJLMO	log-jam
AGJLNY	jangly
AGJNOR	jargon
AGKLNO	kalong
AGKLOT	kgotla
AGKNOU	nogaku
AGKNRU	kurgan
AGKORT	go-kart
AGLLNO	gallon
	gollan
AGLLOP	gallop
AGLLOR	gollar
AGLLOW	gallow
AGLLRY	Argyll
AGLLSU	gallus
AGLMMY	gymmal
AGLMNO	log-man
AGLMOR	glamor
AGLNNO	longan
AGLNOO	lagoon
AGLNOS	Anglos
	slogan
AGLNOU	lanugo
AGLNOW	gowlan
AGLNRU	langur
AGLNRY	gnarly
AGLNSS	slangs
AGLNSY	slangy
AGLNTY	tangly
AGLNUU	ungual
	ungula
AGLOOT	galoot
AGLORS	largos
AGLOSS	glossa
AGLOSW	log-saw
AGLOTY	otalgy
AGLPUY	plaguy
AGLRSU	guslar
AGLRUV	vulgar
AGLRUY	glaury
	raguly
AGLSSY	glassy
AGLSUV	valgus
AGMMNO	gammon
AGMMNU	magnum
AGMMRY	Grammy
AGMNNO	magnon
AGMNNU	gunman
AGMNOR	Morgan
AGMNOX	Magnox®
	magnox
AGMNSU	musang
AGMNUY	maungy
AGMOOY	oogamy
AGMORS	orgasm
AGMORV	vagrom
AGMORY	goramy
	morgay
AGMOYZ	zygoma
AGMPUZ	gazump
AGMRTU	Targum
AGNNOT	tonnag
AGNNRY	granny
AGNNTU	tangun
AGNNUW	wangun
AGNOOZ	gazoon
AGNOQU	quango
AGNORR	garron
AGNORS	sarong
AGNORW	awrong
AGNOSS	gossan
AGNOST	sontag
	tangos
AGNOSU	guanos
AGNOTU	nougat
AGNOWY	gowany
AGNOZZ	gozzan
AGNPRS	sprang
AGNRSU	sungar
AGNRTY	gantry
	gyrant
AGNSSY	syngas
AGNTWY	twangy
AGOORT	agorot
AGOORV	vorago
AGOPRT	ragtop
AGOPRU	gopura
AGORRT	garrot
AGORSS	sargos
AGORST	groats
AGORSY	argosy
AGORTU	ragout
	rag-out
AGORTW	tow-rag
AGOSTU	outgas
AGOSYZ	azygos
AGOTTU	tautog
AGOTUY	agouty
AGOUYY	gay-you
AGPSUU	gaupus
AGPSUW	gawpus
AGRSSU	sargus
AGRSSY	grassy
AGRSTU	tragus
AGRSUY	sugary
AGRUUY	augury
AGSTUU	△august
AHHHOO	hoo-hah
AHHIJR	hijrah
AHHIKS	shaikh
AHHIRS	harish
AHHISV	shivah
AHHKOO	hookah
AHHLPY	hyphal
AHHOOR	hoorah
AHHORT	Thorah
AHHPPU	huppah
AHHRRU	hurrah
AHHRST	thrash
AHIILT	lithia
AHIINT	tahini
AHIKLS	lakish
AHIKLT	khilat
AHIKNS	Naskhi
AHIKOW	kowhai
AHIKRS	rakish
	shikar
AHIKSS	shiksa
AHIKST	Shakti
	skaith
AHIKTW	hawkit
AHILLP	phalli
AHILLS	shalli
AHILLT	thalli
AHILLZ	zillah
AHILMO	holmia
AHILMS	lamish
AHILMU	hamuli
AHILNR	rhinal
AHILNU	inhaul
AHILNY	linhay
AHILPS	palish
AHILPT	Lapith
AHILRY	Hilary
AHILSS	Salish
AHILST	latish
	tahsil
AHILSV	lavish
AHILTU	thulia
AHILTW	withal
AHILYZ	hazily
AHIMNR	harmin
AHIMNS	Mishna
AHIMNT	hit-man
AHIMNU	Humian
AHIMOR	mohair
AHIMPS	mishap
	pashim
AHIMRS	mahsir
	marish
AHIMRT	Mithra
	thairm
	thiram
AHIMVZ	mizvah
AHINPT	hatpin
AHINRS	arshin
	shairn
AHINRU	unhair
AHINSV	vanish
AHINSW	wash-in
AHIORT	hot-air
	thoria
AHIPPS	papish
AHIPRS	parish
	raphis
AHIPRU	rupiah
AHIPSS	phasis
AHIPST	ash-pit
AHIPTY	Pythia
AHIRRS	arrish
	shirra
	sirrah
AHIRST	hairst
	Ishtar
AHIRSV	ravish
AHIRSW	rawish
AHIRSZ	Shiraz
AHIRTW	wraith
AHISSW	△siwash
AHISTT	staith
AHISTU	hiatus
AHJOOP	poojah
AHKKSU	sukkah
AHKLOO	koolah
AHKLPU	pulkha
AHKMNU	khanum
AHKMOW	△mohawk
AHKNPU	punkah
AHKNRS	shrank
AHKNST	thanks
AHKOPT	Pakhto
AHKOSS	shakos
AHKPTU	Pakhtu
AHKRST	skarth
AHKRTU	khurta
AHLLMO	mollah
	ollamh
AHLLMU	mullah
AHLLNU	nullah
AHLLOO	halloo
	holloa
AHLLOS	hallos
AHLLOW	hallow
AHLLRT	thrall
AHLLUX	hallux
AHLLWY	whally
AHLMNY	hymnal
AHLMOO	moolah
AHLMOS	shalom
AHLMTU	lum-hat
AHLNOP	phonal
AHLNSU	unlash
AHLOOP	hoop-la
AHLOPS	△pholas
AHLORT	harlot
AHLOST	shalot
AHLOSY	shoaly

Words marked △ may be spelled also with a capital letter

AHLOTY	loathy
AHLPSS	splash
AHLPSU	lash-up
	sulpha
AHLPSY	plashy
AHLRSY	rashly
AHLSTU	haulst
AHMMOW	whammo
AHMMSY	shammy
AHMMWY	whammy
AHMNNU	numnah
AHMNOS	hansom
AHMNOU	Mahoun
AHMOOP	oompah
AHMORZ	mahzor
AHMOSU	hamous
AHMOSV	moshav
AHMOSY	shamoy
AHMOTU	mahout
AHMOTZ	matzoh
AHMOWY	haymow
AHMRRU	murrha
AHMRSY	marshy
AHMRTW	warmth
AHMSSU	samshu
	shamus
AHNNSU	Sunnah
AHNNSY	shanny
AHNOPR	orphan
AHNOPY	aphony
AHNORS	△sharon
	shoran
AHNOSX	Xhosan
AHNOWY	anyhow
AHNPRU	Nuphar
AHNPSU	unhasp
AHNRSY	sharny
AHNRTW	thrawn
AHNSTU	sunhat
AHNSTY	shanty
AHNTUW	unthaw
AHOORY	hooray
AHOPPS	Sappho
AHOPRS	pharos
AHOPST	Pashto
	pathos
	potash
	pot-ash
AHOPTT	top-hat
AHOQTU	quotha
AHORRW	harrow
AHORRY	horary
AHORTT	throat
AHORTU	author
AHORTW	wroath
AHORTX	thorax
AHOSTW	whatso
AHOTWZ	howzat
AHPRSS	sharps
AHPRST	sparth
AHPRSY	phrasy
AHPSTU	Pashtu
AHPSUW	wash-up
AHQSSU	squash
AHRRUY	hurray
AHRSSU	hussar
AHRSTT	strath
AHRSTW	swarth
	thraws
AHRSTY	trashy
AHRTTW	thwart
AHRTWY	wrathy
AHSSTU	tussah
AHSSWY	swashy
AHSTWY	swathy
AIIKKW	wakiki
AIILLM	limail
AIILLR	arilli
AIILMS	simial
AIILNP	Alpini
AIILRY	airily
AIIMMN	minima
AIIMMS	misaim
AIIMNP	painim
AIIMNS	simian
AIIMNT	intima
AIIMOR	Moirai
AIIMPR	impair
AIIMPS	simpai
AIIMST	samiti
AIINNO	Ionian
AIINNZ	zinnia
AIINRS	raisin
	Sirian
AIINST	isatin
AIINSX	sixain
AIINTT	△titian
AIIORS	ariosi
AIIPTW	wapiti
AIIRTV	trivia
AIISST	Isatis
AIJJMM	jimjam
AIJKNS	kanjis
AIJLMS	△majlis
AIJLNU	Julian
AIJLOR	jailor
AIJLOV	△jovial
AIJLTW	wiltja
AIJNNS	ninjas
AIJNOV	Jovian
AIJORW	jowari
AIJPSS	jaspis
AIJPTU	jupati
AIKLLS	killas
AIKLMN	malkin
AIKLMU	kalium
AIKLNO	kaolin
AIKLNT	talk-in
AIKLNW	walk-in
AIKLOS	skolia
AIKLPS	kalpis
AIKLSU	saluki
AIKMMS	immask
AIKMNR	Kirman
AIKMNS	kamsin
AIKMNW	mawkin
AIKMOO	oomiak
AIKMOS	maikos
AIKMPR	impark
AIKMRU	kumari
AIKNNN	nankin
AIKNNP	napkin
AIKNOT	kation
AIKNPR	kirpan
	parkin
AIKNPS	panisk
AIKOPS	okapis
AIKOPT	katipo
AIKORT	troika
AIKOST	Ostiak
AIKRRS	sirkar
AIKRST	at-risk
	straik
AILLMU	allium
AILLNV	villan
AILLNW	inwall
AILLPR	pillar
AILLPU	pillau
	pilula
AILLRV	villar
AILLRY	railly
AILLYZ	lazily
AILMMS	malism
AILMNO	monial
	oilman
AILMNR	marlin
AILMNS	maslin
AILMNU	alumni
	lumina
AILMNY	mainly
AILMOP	lipoma
AILMOT	tomial
AILMPR	imparl
	primal
AILMRT	mitral
AILMRU	ramuli
AILMSS	missal
	salmis
AILMST	malist
	smalti
AILMSX	laxism
	smilax
AILMSY	mislay
AILMTU	ultima
AILMTY	matily
AILMUV	maulvi
	Valium®
AILMYZ	mazily
AILNNU	annuli
	unnail
AILNOP	Alpino
	oil-pan
AILNOS	sialon
AILNOT	Latino
	talion
AILNOV	Novial
AILNPS	△plains
	spinal
AILNPT	plaint
	pliant
AILNRT	ratlin
	trinal
AILNRU	urinal
AILNSS	'snails
AILNST	instal
AILNSU	insula
AILNSV	silvan
AILNSW	in-laws
AILNSY	snaily
AILNTU	unital
AILNTY	litany
AILNUV	unvail
AILNVY	vainly
AILOOR	oorial
AILORS	sailor
AILORT	Rialto
	tailor
AILORU	ourali
AILOSS	assoil
AILOST	ostial
AILOSX	oxalis
AILOTX	oxtail
AILPRS	spiral
AILPST	pastil
	spital
AILPTU	tipula
	Tulipa
AILQSU	squail
AILRST	trials
AILRSW	aswirl
AILRTU	ritual
AILRWY	warily
AILSSV	silvas
AILSTU	situla
AILSTV	vistal
	vitals
AILSTX	laxist
AILSUV	visual
AILSVY	sylvia
AILSVZ	vizsla
AILTXY	laxity
AILVWY	wavily
AILWXY	waxily
AIMMMU	mummia
AIMMOS	Maoism
	mimosa
AIMMRS	Ramism
AIMMSS	miasms
AIMNNO	amnion
	Minoan
	nomina
AIMNNP	pin-man
AIMNNS	nanism
AIMNNT	tinman
AIMNNU	numina
AIMNNY	minyan
AIMNOP	mopani

Words marked △ may be spelled also with a capital letter

AIMNOR	mainor
	Romani
AIMNOT	manito
AIMNPP	map-pin
AIMNPT	pitman
AIMNPW	impawn
AIMNPY	paynim
AIMNRT	martin
AIMNRU	rumina
AIMNST	mantis
	△matins
AIMNSU	animus
AIMNSZ	Nazism
AIMNUV	mauvin
AIMOPT	optima
AIMOPY	myopia
AIMORS	Maoris
AIMOST	Maoist
	Samiot
	Taoism
AIMPPS	papism
AIMPRT	armpit
	impart
	partim
AIMPSS	passim
AIMPSU	Sapium
AIMQSU	△maquis
AIMRST	Marist
	Ramist
AIMRTU	atrium
AIMRTX	matrix
AIMSSY	missay
AIMSTT	statim
AIMSTU	autism
AINNNT	tannin
AINNOS	nasion
AINNOT	anoint
	nation
AINNOW	wanion
AINNPS	inspan
AINNRU	uranin
AINNUZ	Zunian
	Zuñian
AINOOZ	Aizoon
AINOPP	Popian
AINOPS	pianos
AINOQU	quinoa
AINORT	aroint
	ration
AINOSS	Ossian
AINOST	Tainos
AINOSU	Siouan
AINOTW	wait-on
AINPRS	spinar
	sprain
AINPRU	pruina
AINPRW	inwrap
AINPST	ptisan
AINPSV	spavin
AINPTT	tan-pit
AINPTU	Tupian
AINPTY	painty
AINQRT	qintar
	Q-train
AINQTU	quaint
	quinta
AINQUY	yanqui
AINRST	instar
	santir
	strain
AINRSY	Syrian
AINRTU	nutria
AINRTY	in-tray
	Tyrian
AINRYZ	Zyrian
AINSTT	tanist
AINSTY	sanity
	satiny
AINTVY	vanity
AIOORS	arioso
AIOPRV	pavior
AIOPST	patios
	patois
AIOPTU	△utopia
AIORRU	ourari
AIORST	aorist
	aristo
	ratios
	satori
AIORSU	souari
AIORTV	viator
AIOSSV	avisos
AIOSTT	Taoist
AIPPRR	riprap
	rip-rap
AIPPRY	papyri
AIPPST	papist
AIPPTT	pit-pat
	tappit
AIPRST	rapist
AIPRSV	parvis
AIPRSW	rip-saw
AIPRSX	praxis
AIPRTT	rat-pit
AIPRTY	parity
AIPRUY	pyuria
AIPSST	pastis
AIPSTT	tapist
AIPSTW	pit-saw
	sawpit
AIPZZZ	pizazz
AIRRST	stirra
AIRRTY	rarity
AIRRZZ	rizzar
AIRSST	sistra
	stairs
AIRSSU	△russia
AIRSTT	artist
	sittar
	strait
AIRSTU	aurist
AIRSTV	travis
AIRTTT	attrit
AIRTTY	yttria
AIRVVY	vivary
AISSST	assist
	stasis
AISSTW	tiswas
AISTWZ	tizwas
AITTTU	tautit
AITTWX	atwixt
AJKNSY	jansky
AJLOOR	jarool
AJLOPY	jalopy
AJMOPT	jampot
AJMORS	majors
AJMRTU	jumart
AJNORT	Trojan
AJNRTU	jurant
AJNTUY	jaunty
AJPRTU	Rajput
AKKNRU	kunkar
AKKOQU	quokka
AKKOSS	sakkos
AKLLNY	lankly
AKLNOU	koulan
AKLNOW	walk-on
AKLNOX	△klaxon
AKLNRY	rankly
AKLOST	stalko
AKLOSV	Slovak
AKLOTW	kotwal
AKLPRY	parkly
AKLPUW	walk-up
AKLSTY	stalky
AKMNSU	unmask
AKMNSY	skyman
AKMPRU	mark-up
AKMUYZ	muzaky
AKNORU	koruna
AKNORY	karyon
	ryokan
AKNOSS	sankos
AKNOTU	oak-nut
AKNPRY	pranky
AKNRTZ	krantz
AKNSWY	swanky
AKNTUU	Tuanku
AKOORR	Karroo
	korora
AKORSS	kaross
AKOSTU	out-ask
AKOSTY	Ostyak
AKPRSS	sparks
AKPRSY	sparky
AKPTTU	kaputt
AKQSUW	squawk
AKRSTU	tuskar
AKSWYY	skyway
ALLMOR	morall
ALLMOS	slalom
ALLMOW	mallow
ALLMSS	smalls
ALLMUV	vallum
ALLNOP	pollan
ALLNOS	allons
	llanos
ALLNUU	lunula
ALLOOP	△apollo
	palolo
ALLOPR	pallor
ALLOPW	wallop
ALLORS	sollar
ALLORY	orally
ALLOSW	sallow
ALLOTT	tallot
ALLOTU	all-out
ALLOTV	lavolt
ALLOTW	tallow
ALLOUY	you-all
ALLOVY	ovally
ALLOWW	wallow
ALLOYY	Y-alloy
ALLPRU	plural
ALLPSY	psylla
ALLQSU	squall
ALLRSU	Rallus
ALLRUY	lauryl
ALLSST	stalls
ALLSTY	lastly
	saltly
ALLUUZ	Luzula
ALLUVV	vulval
ALMMSY	smalmy
ALMMUY	amylum
ALMNOR	normal
ALMNOS	salmon
ALMNOU	monaul
ALMNRU	murlan
ALMORS	morals
	morsal
	samlor
ALMORT	mortal
ALMORU	morula
ALMOST	almost
	matlos
	smalto
	stomal
ALMOSU	almous
ALMOTW	matlow
ALMOXY	xyloma
ALMPSS	Psalms
ALMQUY	qualmy
ALMRWY	warmly
ALMSUY	asylum
ALMTUU	mutual
	umlaut
ALNNOR	norlan'
ALNNOU	nounal
ALNOOS	alsoon
	saloon
	solano
ALNOOZ	zoonal
ALNOPT	pontal
ALNORT	latron
ALNOSV	Volans
ALNOSY	Syalon®

ALNOTV	volant
ALNOUZ	zonula
ALNPTU	pultan
ALNRSY	snarly
ALNRUY	lunary
	uranyl
ALNRXY	larynx
ALNSTU	sultan
	unlast
ALNSVY	sylvan
ALNTUW	walnut
ALNTUY	auntly
ALOOPS	saloop
ALOPPR	poplar
ALOPPT	laptop
ALOPRR	parlor
ALOPRT	patrol
	portal
ALOPRV	vorpal
ALOPRY	Pyrola
ALOPST	postal
ALOQTU	loquat
ALORRW	worral
ALORSU	rosula
ALORSV	salvor
ALORSY	△royals
ALORTU	rotula
	torula
ALORTW	low-tar
ALORUV	ovular
	valour
ALORVY	volary
ALOSSS	lassos
ALOSST	saltos
ALOSSV	salvos
ALOTUW	outlaw
ALOTUY	layout
	outlay
ALPPSU	palpus
	slap-up
ALPRRU	larrup
ALPRSU	pulsar
ALPRSW	sprawl
ALPRTY	paltry
	partly
	raptly
ALPRUW	pulwar
ALPSSU	lapsus
ALPSTY	yplast
ALRSTU	lustra
ALRSTY	stylar
ALRSUU	Laurus
ALRSUW	walrus
ALRTTY	rattly
	tartly
ALRTUW	tulwar
ALRUUV	uvular
ALRUVV	vulvar
ALSSTU	saltus
	tussal
ALSSVY	sylvas
ALSTVY	vastly
ALSUUV	uvulas
ALTTUY	tautly
ALTUVY	vaulty
AMMMNO	△mammon
AMMMOU	amomum
AMMORT	marmot
AMMOSU	omasum
AMMOXY	myxoma
AMMPSY	spammy
AMMPUW	wampum
AMMRRU	marrum
	murram
AMMRSU	summar
AMMRSY	smarmy
AMMSTU	summat
AMMSUW	wammus
AMMTUZ	Tammuz
AMNNOR	△norman
AMNNOY	anonym
AMNOOP	Pomona
AMNOOR	maroon
AMNOPT	potman
	tampon
	topman
AMNORS	ramson
	ransom
AMNORT	matron
AMNORU	Rouman
AMNORY	mornay
	Romany
AMNOSS	Samson
AMNOST	mantos
AMNOTU	amount
	moutan
	outman
AMNOTY	toyman
AMNPTY	tympan
AMNRTU	antrum
AMNTTU	mutant
	tutman
AMNTUU	autumn
AMOOPT	pomato
AMOORV	moorva
AMOOTT	tomato
AMORRT	mortar
AMORRU	armour
AMORRW	marrow
AMORRY	armory
AMORSS	morass
AMORST	stroam
	stroma
AMORSU	amours
	ramous
AMOSTZ	matzos
AMOSUW	awmous
AMOTTZ	matzot
AMOTUZ	mazout
AMPRST	stramp
AMPRUW	warm-up
AMPSUW	mawpus
	wampus
AMPSWY	swampy
AMRRTY	martyr
AMRRUY	murray
AMRSTU	struma
AMRSTY	smarty
ANNOOX	xoanon
ANNOPR	napron
ANNOPT	panton
ANNORT	natron
ANNORY	nonary
ANNOST	santon
	sonant
ANNOTT	tonant
ANNOTW	wanton
ANNOTY	Tannoy®
	tannoy
ANNPSU	pannus
	sannup
	unsnap
ANNPTU	pantun
ANNRTY	tranny
ANNSTU	suntan
ANNSTY	syntan
ANNSWY	swanny
ANNTTU	nutant
ANOORT	ratoon
ANOOSW	aswoon
ANOPRS	parson
ANOPRT	parton
	patron
	tarpon
ANOPST	pantos
ANOPTT	optant
ANOPUY	yaupon
ANORRW	narrow
ANORSV	sovran
ANORTT	attorn
	ratton
	rottan
ANORTV	vorant
ANORTY	aroynt
	notary
	Troyan
ANORWY	Norway
ANORYZ	zonary
ANOSSW	sowans
ANOSTY	astony
	stay-on
ANOSTZ	stanzo
ANOSWY	noways
ANOSXY	△saxony
ANPPSY	snappy
ANPRSU	unspar
ANPRTY	pantry
ANPRUW	unwrap
ANPRUY	unpray
ANPSUW	supawn
ANPSWY	spawny
ANRRTU	rat-run
ANRSTU	santur
	Saturn
ANRSTW	strawn
ANRSUU	Uranus
ANRSUY	sunray
ANRTTU	truant
ANRTTY	tyrant
ANRUWY	runway
	unwary
ANSTTU	tutsan
ANSTXY	syntax
ANSYZZ	snazzy
ANTUVY	vaunty
AOOPST	astoop
AOOPTT	potato
AOORRT	orator
AOORRY	arroyo
AOORTT	tooart
AOORTV	ovator
AOOTTT	tattoo
AOPPRT	apport
AOPRRT	parrot
	raptor
AOPRRU	uproar
AOPRST	asport
	pastor
	portas
AOPRUV	vapour
AOPSST	potass
AOPSTU	aspout
AOPTUY	pay-out
AOPWWW	powwaw
AOQRTU	quarto
AOQSTU	quotas
AORRST	rostra
	sartor
AORRSW	arrows
AORRSY	rosary
AORRTW	tarrow
AORRTY	△rotary
AORRWY	arrowy
	yarrow
AORSST	assort
AORSTT	stator
	tarots
AORSTU	soutar
AORSTX	storax
AORSUU	aurous
AORSUV	savour
AORSVY	savory
AORTUY	yaourt
AORTVY	votary
AORVWY	avowry
AOSSTT	assott
AOSTTY	toasty
AOTTTW	tattow
AOTUWY	way-out
AOTWWY	two-way
APPPSU	pappus
APPRTY	trappy
APPRUW	upwrap
APRRSY	sparry
APRSTT	T-strap
APRSTY	pastry
APRSWY	psywar
APSSSU	passus

Words marked △ may be spelled also with a capital letter

APSTUY	upstay
APSUWY	upsway
AQRRUY	quarry
AQRTUZ	quartz
ARRSTY	starry
ARSSST	strass
ARSSTT	starts
ARSSTU	tarsus
ARSSTY	strays
ARSTTU	astrut
ARSTUU	Taurus
ARSTUW	waurst
ARSTUX	surtax
ARSTWY	strawy
	swarty
	wastry
ARSTXY	styrax
ASSTTU	status

B

BBBDEO	bobbed
BBBEIR	bibber
BBBELO	bobble
BBBELU	bubble
BBBHUU	hubbub
BBBINO	bobbin
BBBLOY	bobbly
BBBLUY	bubbly
BBCDEU	cubbed
BBCELO	cobble
BBCEOR	cobber
BBCEOW	cobweb
BBCHUY	chubby
BBCLUY	clubby
BBDDEI	dibbed
BBDDEO	dobbed
BBDDEU	dubbed
BBDEEN	nebbed
BBDEEW	webbed
BBDEFI	fibbed
BBDEGI	gibbed
BBDEGU	bedbug
BBDEIJ	jibbed
BBDEIL	dibble
BBDEIN	nibbed
BBDEIO	dobbie
BBDEIR	dibber
	ribbed
BBDEJO	jobbed
BBDELO	lobbed
BBDELU	bulbed
BBDEMO	mobbed
BBDEOR	dobber
	robbed
BBDEOS	sobbed
BBDEOX	box-bed
BBDERU	rubbed
BBDESU	subbed
BBDGIU	big-bud
BBDINO	dobbin
BBDINU	dubbin
BBDKUY	dybbuk
BBEEIK	kebbie
BBEEKL	lebbek
BBEELP	pebble
BBEEMU	bum-bee
BBEEMX	△bembex
BBEENN	neb-neb
BBEENS	snebbe
BBEERR	Berber
BBEEYY	bye-bye
BBEFIR	fibber
BBEGIR	gibber
BBEGIT	gibbet
BBEGLO	gobble
BBEGNU	bebung
BBEGOT	gobbet
BBEHLO	hobble
BBEIIM	imbibe
BBEIIR	ribibe
BBEIJO	jobbie
BBEIJR	jibber
BBEIKL	kibble
BBEILN	nibble
BBEILR	libber
BBEIMO	mobbie
BBEIMX	△bembix
BBEIRR	briber
BBEISU	subbie
BBEJOR	jobber
BBEKNU	nebbuk
BBEKOS	kebobs
BBELLU	bulbel
BBELMO	mobble
BBELMU	△bumble
BBELNO	nobble
BBELNU	nubble
BBELNY	nybble
BBELOW	wobble
BBELPY	pebbly
	plebby
BBELRU	burble
	lubber
	rubble
BBEMNU	benumb
BBEMOR	bomber
BBENSU	snubbe
BBEORR	robber
BBEOSU	buboes
BBERRU	rubber
BBERTU	rubbet
	tubber
BBFILU	bibful
BBFLOY	bob-fly
BBGINO	gibbon
BBGIOW	bobwig
BBGLOY	globby
BBGRUY	grubby
BBHIOT	hobbit
BBHJOO	hobjob
BBHNOO	hobnob
BBIKOS	skibob
BBILLU	bulbil
BBILOS	bilbos
BBIMOS	bimbos
BBINNU	nubbin
BBINOR	ribbon
BBIRTU	rubbit
BBKNOY	knobby
BBKNUY	knubby
BBKOOS	bosbok
BBLLUU	bulbul
BBLNUY	nubbly
BBLOSY	slobby
BBLOWY	by-blow
	wobbly
BBLRUY	rubbly
BBLSUY	slubby
BBMOOS	bombos
BBMOSU	bumbos
BBMOXY	Bombyx
BBMRUY	brumby
BBNNOO	bonbon
BBNOSY	snobby
BBNOTU	nobbut
BBNSUY	snubby
BBOOOO	booboo
BBOOSY	yobbos
BBOOWY	bow-boy
BBORTU	burbot
BBOSUY	busboy
BBRSUU	suburb
BBSTUY	stubby
BCCDEU	C-cubed
BCCIOR	cobric
BCDEEK	bedeck
BCDEIO	bodice
BCDEKU	beduck
BCDEMO	combed
BCDIOU	cuboid
BCDIRY	cybrid
BCDNOU	bonduc
BCEEHO	obeche
BCEEHR	breech
BCEEKN	nebeck
BCEEKR	rebeck
BCEEKT	becket
BCEEKZ	zebeck
BCEELO	ecbole
BCEELY	Cybele
BCEEMO	become
BCEGIL	Belgic
BCEHLN	blench
BCEHOR	broché
BCEHOS	△bosche
BCEHOU	bouche
	bouché
BCEHRU	cherub
BCEIIS	ibices
BCEIKR	bicker
BCEIKU	buckie
BCEILM	emblic
	limbec
BCEILR	criblé
BCEILS	lesbic
BCEIOR	corbie
BCEIOX	icebox
BCEIPS	biceps
BCEIRS	scribe
BCEIRT	terbic
BCEIST	bisect
BCEJOT	object
BCEKLU	buckle
BCEKMO	bemock
BCEKNO	beckon
BCEKRU	Brücke
	bucker
BCEKTU	bucket
BCELMO	comble
BCELOR	corbel
BCELOU	bouclé
BCELRU	becurl
BCEMOO	coombe
BCEMOR	comber
BCEMRU	cumber
BCENOU	bounce
BCEORS	scrobe
BCEOTT	obtect
BCGORU	çoburg
BCGORY	cyborg
BCHILO	chibol
BCHIOP	phobic
BCHITY	bitchy
BCHLOT	blotch
BCHNRU	brunch
BCHNUY	bunchy
BCHOOR	brooch
BCHORS	borsch
BCHOTY	botchy
BCHRSU	Bursch
BCIILM	limbic
BCIINO	bionic
	niobic
BCIINU	incubi
BCIIOP	biopic
BCIIOT	biotic
BCIKNO	kincob
BCIKRY	bricky
BCILOO	colobi
BCILPU	public
BCILRU	lubric
BCIMOR	bromic
BCIMOT	tombic
BCIMSU	cubism
BCINOR	bicorn
BCIRRU	rubric
BCISTU	cubist
BCKLOS	blocks
BCKLOY	blocky
BCMOOS	combos
BCMOOT	tomboc
BCMORY	corymb
BCMRSU	crumbs
BCMRUY	crumby
BCNOOR	bronco
BCNOSU	buncos
BCNOTU	cobnut
BCNOUY	bouncy

BCOOWY	cowboy
BCRSSU	Scrubs
BDDDEE	bedded
BDDDEU	budded
BDDEEI	bedide
BDDEEN	bended
BDDEER	bedder
BDDEET	debted
BDDEEY	bedyde
	bedyed
BDDEIN	bidden
BDDEIO	bodied
BDDEIR	bedrid
	bidder
BDDELO	boddle
BDDELU	buddle
BDDENO	bonded
BDDERU	redbud
BDDISU	disbud
BDDJOO	odd-job
BDEEEN	bendee
	need-be
BDEEET	debtee
BDEEFL	befeld
BDEEGG	begged
BDEEGO	dog-bee
BDEEHL	beheld
BDEEIL	belied
	debile
	edible
BDEEIS	beside
BDEEIT	betide
BDEEJL	djebel
BDEEKY	bed-key
BDEELL	bedell
	belled
BDEELN	blende
BDEELT	belted
BDEENR	bender
BDEEPS	besped
BDEEST	bested
BDEETT	betted
BDEFIR	fibred
BDEGGU	bugged
BDEGIL	begild
BDEGIO	bodgie
BDEGIP	pig-bed
BDEGIR	begird
	bridge
BDEGIU	budgie
BDEGLO	globed
BDEGLU	bludge
BDEGNU	bedung
BDEGOR	bodger
BDEGRU	budger
BDEGTU	△budget
BDEHIN	behind
BDEHIR	Hebrid
BDEHLO	behold
BDEHOS	debosh
BDEHOT	hotbed
BDEHSU	bushed
BDEIIM	ibidem
BDEIIR	birdie
	bridie
BDEILL	billed
BDEILM	dimble
	limbed
BDEILO	boiled
	bolide
BDEILR	bridle
BDEILU	bludie
BDEILY	bieldy
BDEIMN	nimbed
BDEINN	binned
BDEINR	binder
	inbred
	rebind
BDEINT	bident
BDEINU	△beduin
BDEIOO	boodie
BDEIOR	boride
BDEIOS	bodies
BDEIRR	birder
BDEIRS	debris
	débris
BDEIRU	burdie
	buried
	rubied
BDEIRV	verbid
BDEIST	bed-sit
BDEISU	busied
BDEITT	bitted
BDEKNU	debunk
BDEKSU	busked
BDELLO	bolled
BDELMO	mobled
BDELNO	blonde
	blonde®
	bolden
BDELNU	bundle
BDELOO	boodle
BDELOR	bordel
BDELOU	double
BDELOW	blowed
	bowled
BDELRU	de-blur
BDEMMU	bummed
BDEMNU	numbed
BDEMOW	wombed
BDEMOY	embody
BDENNU	unbend
BDENOR	bonder
BDENOT	obtend
BDENOY	△beyond
BDENRU	burden
	burned
	unbred
BDENSU	sunbed
BDENTU	bunted
	but-end
BDEOOR	boorde
BDEOOT	booted
BDEOOZ	boozed
BDEOPR	bedrop
BDEORR	△border
BDEORS	desorb
BDEORT	betrod
	debtor
BDEORU	obdure
BDEORX	red-box
BDEOSS	bossed
	deboss
BDEOWW	dew-bow
BDERSU	surbed
BDESTU	bedust
	bestud
	busted
BDESUU	subdue
BDESUW	subdew
BDFILO	bifold
BDFIOR	forbid
BDGIIN	biding
BDGIIO	gobiid
BDGINO	boding
BDGORU	dor-bug
BDHIIN	bhindi
BDHIRY	hybrid
BDIILO	libido
BDIIMR	midrib
BDIITT	tidbit
BDIKNO	bodkin
BDILOY	bodily
BDILUY	bluidy
BDIMOR	morbid
BDIMOY	imbody
BDINNO	in-bond
BDINNU	unbind
BDINPU	upbind
BDIORX	ox-bird
BDIOTU	outbid
BDIRTU	turbid
BDKLOO	kobold
BDLLOY	boldly
BDLMUY	dumbly
BDLOOS	'sblood
BDLOOY	bloody
	Old-Boy
	old-boy
BDLOUY	doubly
BDMRUU	rum-bud
BDNOOY	nobody
BDNOSU	bounds
BDNOTU	obtund
BDNOUY	ybound
BDOORY	broody
BDORWY	byword
BEEEFL	feeble
BEEEHP	ephebe
BEEEKL	kebele
BEEELT	△beetle
BEEEMS	beseem
BEEEMT	bemete
	beteem
BEEENS	beseen
BEEEPR	beeper
BEEEPW	beweep
BEEERS	breese
BEEERZ	breeze
BEEESV	beeves
BEEFIL	belief
BEEFLL	befell
BEEFLY	bee-fly
	feebly
BEEFOR	before
BEEFRT	bereft
BEEGHR	Gheber
	Ghebre
BEEGIL	beigel
BEEGNO	begone
	engobe
BEEGNU	bungee
BEEGRU	burgee
	Gueber
	Guebre
BEEHIP	ephebi
BEEHLT	bethel
BEEHNS	Benesh
BEEHOP	△phoebe
BEEHOT	behote
BEEHOV	behove
BEEHRT	berthe
BEEHRW	Hebrew
BEEHRY	hereby
BEEHST	behest
	Thebes
BEEHTT	Tebeth
BEEIKL	belike
BEEILR	belier
BEEILV	belive
BEEIMR	bemire
	bireme
BEEIMT	betime
BEEIRT	rebite
BEEIST	bêtise
BEEISX	ibexes
BEEJNU	bunjee
BEEKOR	reebok
BEEKRS	breeks
BEEKRU	rebuke
BEELMM	emblem
BEELMR	remble
BEELMS	semble
BEELNO	Belone
BEELNU	nebule
	nebulé
BEELOV	belove
BEELPT	bepelt
BEELRT	belter
	treble
BEELRY	berley
BEELZZ	bezzle
BEEMMR	member
BEEMRS	embers
BEEMRU	embrue
BEEMSU	bemuse
BEENNR	brenne
BEENNT	bennet

BEENOR	boreen
	enrobe
BEENTU	butene
BEEOOT	bootee
BEEOPP	bo-peep
BEEORR	rebore
BEEORY	obeyer
BEEPRU	beer-up
BEEPTW	bewept
BEERRT	berret
BEERRU	beurre
	beurré
BEERRV	reverb
BEERRW	brewer
BEERSU	Erebus
BEERTT	better
BEERTV	brevet
BEERYZ	breezy
BEESTU	bustee
BEFFOU	bouffe
BEFFPU	bepuff
BEFFRU	buffer
	rebuff
BEFFTU	buffet
BEFGIT	begift
BEFHOO	behoof
BEFILM	fimble
BEFILO	foible
BEFIRS	briefs
BEFLMU	beflum
	fumble
BEFLOO	befool
BEFLOU	befoul
BEFLRY	belfry
BEFORY	forbye
	foreby
BEFRUY	rubefy
BEFSUU	subfeu
BEGGII	biggie
BEGGIR	bigger
BEGGLO	boggle
BEGGOX	egg-box
BEGGRU	△bugger
BEGHIS	besigh
BEGIIL	Liebig
BEGILN	bingle
BEGILO	oblige
BEGILR	gerbil
BEGILS	bilges
BEGILT	giblet
BEGINN	benign
BEGINO	biogen
BEGINR	binger
BEGINS	besing
BEGINU	beguin
	béguin
	bungie
BEGIOO	boogie
BEGIOS	bogies
BEGIOU	bougie
BEGIRT	begirt
BEGIRU	brigue
BEGKNU	begunk
BEGLNO	belong
BEGLNU	blunge
	bungle
BEGLOT	goblet
BEGLOW	bow-leg
BEGLRU	bugler
	bulger
	burgle
BEGLTU	buglet
BEGNOY	bygone
BEGNSU	besung
BEGNUY	bungey
BEGOOR	bog-ore
	goober
BEGOOS	goboes
BEGOPX	peg-box
BEGORU	brogue
BEGOSY	bogeys
BEGOTU	bouget
BEGOTW	bowget
BEGRRU	burger
BEHIKR	kirbeh
BEHILT	blithe
	thible
BEHINS	nebish
BEHINT	hen-bit
BEHIOT	bothie
BEHITT	△thibet
BEHLMU	humble
BEHLOW	behowl
BEHLRU	burhel
BEHLSU	bushel
BEHMOR	hombre
BEHNOR	△brehon
BEHOOS	hoboes
BEHORT	bother
BEIIKR	birkie
BEIILL	billie
BEIIRS	iberis
BEIITT	bittie
BEIJLR	jerbil
	jirble
BEIJMU	jumbie
BEIJNU	bunjie
BEIKLN	libken
BEIKLR	bilker
BEIKNR	birken
BEIKOO	bookie
BEIKSS	bekiss
BEILLT	billet
BEILMN	nimble
BEILMO	bemoil
	emboil
	mobile
BEILMR	limber
BEILMW	wimble
BEILMY	blimey
BEILNO	ben-oil
BEILNR	berlin
BEILNU	nubile
BEILNY	byline
BEILNZ	benzil
BEILOR	boiler
	libero
	reboil
BEILOT	betoil
	boleti
BEILOW	blowie
BEILRR	birler
BEILRS	birsle
BEILRT	riblet
BEILVY	bylive
BEIMOS	obeism
BEIMOV	B-movie
BEIMOZ	zombie
BEIMRT	betrim
	timber
	timbre
BEIMRU	erbium
	imbrue
BEIMRX	imbrex
BEIMTY	by-time
BEINNO	bonnie
BEINNP	pen-nib
BEINNT	inbent
BEINOS	besoin
BEINOV	bovine
BEINOX	bonxie
BEINOZ	bizone
BEINRS	nebris
BEINRU	rubine
BEINRY	byrnie
BEINTT	bitten
BEIORS	ribose
BEIORT	obiter
BEIORU	ourebi
BEIOST	sobeit
	stobie
BEIPST	bespit
BEIPTY	bepity
BEIQSU	bisque
BEIQUU	ubique
BEIRRY	briery
BEIRST	bestir
	bister
	bistre
BEIRSU	bruise
	rubies
BEIRSW	brewis
BEIRTT	bitter
	Tibert
BEITUY	ubiety
BEJJUU	jujube
BEJLMU	jumble
BEJORU	objure
BEKLRU	bulker
BEKNOR	broken
BEKNRU	bunker
BEKOOT	betook
BEKORR	broker
BEKORS	bosker
BEKOST	bosket
BEKRSU	busker
BEKSTU	busket
BELLNO	bollen
BELLOU	boulle
	lobule
BELLOW	bellow
BELLRU	buller
BELLSY	sell-by
BELLTU	bullet
BELLUY	bluely
BELMMU	bummel
	bummle
	mumble
BELMOY	emboly
BELMRU	lumber
	rumble
	umbrel
BELMSU	umbles
BELMTU	tumble
BELNNY	blenny
BELNOZ	benzol
BELNTU	unbelt
BELNTY	yblent
BELNUY	nebuly
BELNYZ	benzyl
BELOOR	bolero
BELOOS	lobose
	sobole
BELOPU	△pueblo
BELORR	borrel
BELORT	bolter
BELORU	rouble
BELORW	blower
	bowler
BELOSS	lesbos
BELOSU	blouse
	boules
	obelus
BELOSW	blowse
	bowels
BELOTT	bottle
BELOWZ	blowze
BELRRU	burler
	burrel
BELRTU	butler
BELRTY	trebly
BELRUY	burley
BELSTU	bustle
	sublet
	subtle
BELSUY	bluesy
BELTTU	buttle
BELTUU	tubule
BEMMRU	bummer
BEMNOT	entomb
BEMNOW	enwomb
BEMNRU	number
BEMOOR	boomer
BEMORS	somber
	sombre
BEMORY	embryo
BEMOSS	emboss
BEMOST	embost

BEMPRU	bumper
BEMRUY	umbery
BEMSTU	besmut
BEMSUY	embusy
BENNOT	bonnet
BENNOU	unbone
BENNSU	△bunsen
BENNTU	ben-nut
	unbent
BENOOR	Oberon
BENOOT	botoné
BENORR	reborn
BENORT	△breton
BENORU	bourne
	unrobe
BENORZ	bonzer
	bronze
BENOTY	betony
BENRRU	burner
BENRTU	brunet
	△bunter
	burnet
BENRTY	ybrent
BEOORS	broose
BEOORZ	boozer
BEOOST	Boötes
BEOOYZ	boozey
BEOPPR	bopper
BEOPRR	prober
BEOPST	bespot
BEORRS	resorb
BEORST	besort
	sorbet
	strobe
BEORSU	△bourse
BEORSW	△bowser
	browse
BEORTT	bettor
BEORTV	obvert
BEORUZ	brouze
BEORVV	bovver
BEORVY	overby
BEORWY	△bowery
	bowyer
	owerby
BEOSSS	obsess
BEOSST	betoss
BEOSSY	syboes
BEOSTT	obtest
BEOSTU	obtuse
BEOSTW	bestow
BEOTUY	outbye
BEPRSU	superb
BEPRUW	brew-up
BEPRUY	pre-buy
BERRTU	bruter
BERRUY	rebury
BERSTU	buster
	surbet
BERTTU	butter
BERTUY	uberty
BERUZZ	buzzer
BESSSU	busses
BESSTU	subset
BESTUY	yes-but
BFFIIN	biffin
BFFINO	boffin
BFFJOO	off-job
BFGOOW	fog-bow
BFIILR	fibril
BFIINR	fibrin
BFIMOR	biform
BFINOW	bowfin
BFIORS	fibros
BFIRUY	rubify
BFLOTY	botfly
BFLOUX	boxful
BFLTUU	tubful
BFMORY	by-form
BFNOSY	fynbos
BFOORS	Bofors
BGGIIN	biggin
BGGIIW	bigwig
BGGINU	buggin
BGGLUY	bluggy
BGGNOO	bogong
BGGNOU	bugong
BGHIIN	△binghi
BGHILT	blight
BGHIRT	bright
BGHMUU	humbug
BGHORU	brough
BGHOTU	bought
BGIIKN	biking
BGIINT	biting
BGILLY	glibly
BGILNO	globin
	goblin
	lobing
BGILNU	bluing
BGINNO	boning
BGINOR	boring
	robing
BGINOS	bingos
	obsign
BGINOW	bowing
BGINOX	boxing
BGINSU	busing
BGINTU	tubing
BGINUY	buying
BGIOSS	gossib
BGLNOO	oblong
BGLRUU	bulgur
BGMOSU	gumbos
BGMSUU	subgum
BGNOOS	bongos
BGNOOY	gobony
BGOORS	borgos
BGOORU	burgoo
BGOTUU	bug-out
BHHIKT	k'thibh
BHIIST	bhisti
BHIKOS	kibosh
BHIKSU	bukshi
BHILSU	bluish
BHIMOR	rhombi
BHIOPS	bishop
BHIOSY	boyish
BHIRSU	hubris
BHIRSY	hybris
BHKNOU	bohunk
BHKOSY	kybosh
BHLMUY	humbly
BHLOSY	bolshy
BHMTUY	thumby
BHOOOO	boo-hoo
BHRSUY	brushy
BIIIKN	bikini
BIIKTZ	kibitz
BIILNS	blinis
BIIMOS	obiism
BIIMUV	bivium
BIINOT	biotin
BIIORV	vibrio
BIIRRS	sbirri
BIIRTU	buriti
BIISTV	vibist
BIITTT	titbit
BIJOUX	bijoux
BIKLNS	blinks
BIKMNU	bumkin
BIKMOS	imbosk
BIKNSU	buskin
BIKRSY	brisky
BILLNO	billon
BILLOU	lobuli
BILLOW	billow
BILLOX	bollix
BILLOY	billy-o
BILMNY	nimbly
BILMOS	△limbos
BILMRU	umbril
BILMSU	Limbus
BILMUY	bulimy
BILNOS	Lisbon
BILNTZ	blintz
BILOPU	upboil
BILORV	Bovril®
BILRTY	trilby
BILSTU	subtil
BILSUY	busily
BIMMOO	miombo
BIMNOS	bonism
BIMNOT	intomb
BIMNSU	nimbus
BIMOSS	imboss
BIMOST	timbós
BIMSTU	submit
BINNOR	inborn
BINNOU	bunion
BINOOT	bonito
BINORT	Briton
BINORY	briony
BINOSS	bisson
BINOST	bonist
BINPUY	bunyip
BINTTU	unbitt
BIOORZ	borzoi
BIOOST	oboist
BIOOSV	ovibos
BIOPRT	probit
BIOPSY	biopsy
BIORRS	sbirro
BIORST	bistro
BIORTT	bittor
BIORTY	orbity
BIOSTU	subito
BIOTTW	two-bit
BIOTUW	woubit
BIRTTU	bittur
	turbit
BJLMUY	jumbly
BJLOOT	job-lot
BJMOSU	jumbos
BKMNUU	bunkum
BKNOSU	bunkos
BKOOSY	booksy
BKORWY	by-work
BLLORY	brolly
BLMNUY	numbly
BLMOOY	bloomy
BLMOSY	symbol
BLMRUY	rumbly
BLNOOT	bolt-on
BLNOTU	unbolt
BLOOSU	obolus
BLOOTT	blotto
BLOOWY	lowboy
BLOPTY	by-plot
BLOPUW	blow-up
	upblow
BLOSWY	blowsy
BLOTTY	blotty
BLOWYZ	blowzy
BLSTUY	subtly
BMNOTU	untomb
BMOORY	broomy
	byroom
BMOOSS	bosoms
BMOOSY	bosomy
BMOOTT	bottom
BMOOTY	tomboy
BMORST	stromb
BMORSU	morbus
	rumbos
BNNORU	unborn
BNOOST	boston
BNOOTU	bouton
	unboot
BNORSU	suborn
BNORTU	△burton
BNORWY	browny
BNORYY	bryony
BNORYZ	bronzy
BNOSUW	sunbow
BNOTTU	button
BNOTUY	bounty
BNPRUU	burn-up

BNRTUY Tyburn
BNRUUY unbury
BNSUUY unbusy
BOOPTW bowpot
BOOPTY potboy
BOORRW borrow
BOOTUW woobut
BOOTUX outbox
BOOWWW bowwow
BORRSU burros
BORRUW burrow
BORSSU sorbus
BORSTU robust
turbos
BORSTW browst
BORSWY browsy
BORTTU turbot
BORTUU rubout
BOSSWY sybows
BOTUUY buy-out
BPSTUU bust-up
BRSTUU Brutus
BSSSUY byssus

C

CCCDIO coccid
CCCHOY choccy
CCCILY cyclic
CCCOOS coccos
CCCOSU coccus
CCCOXY coccyx
CCDEEI △deccie
CCDEER recced
CCDEKO cocked
CCDEOT decoct
CCEEHL cleché
CCEEHR △crèche
CCEELS Eccles
CCEEOR coerce
CCEERS recces
CCEHIL chicle
cliché
CCEHIM chemic
CCEHIO choice
echoic
CCEHIT hectic
CCEHKY checky
CCEHLN clench
CCEHLO cloche
CCEHLU cleuch
CCEHNO conche
CCEHOR croche
CCEHOS cosech
CCEHOU couché
CCEIIL cilice
icicle
CCEILR circle
cleric
CCEILS cecils
CCEILT Celtic
CCEILY cicely
CCEIMO comice
CCEINS scenic
CCEIOR △cicero
CCEIPT pectic
CCEIRT △cretic
CCEIRU erucic
CCEITY cecity
CCEKLO cockle
CCEKOP copeck
CCEKOR △cocker
CCEKOT cocket
CCELRY cycler
CCENOS sconce
CCEORS escroc
reccos
soccer
CCEOSS seccos
CCEPSY speccy
CCERSU cercus
cruces
CCESSU succès
CCFILO flocci
CCHHII chichi
chi-chi
CCHHIN chinch
CCHHOO chocho
CCHHRU △church
CCHIKT tchick
CCHILN clinch
CCHILO cholic
CCHILY chicly
CCHINO chicon
Cochin
CCHIOR choric
CCHIPU hiccup
CCHKOO chocko
CCHKSU chucks
CCHLNU clunch
CCHLTU clutch
cultch
CCHNOS conchs
CCHNOY conchy
CCHNRU crunch
CCHORS scorch
CCHORT crotch
CCHORU crouch
CCHOST △scotch
CCHRTU crutch
CCHSTU scutch
CCIILN clinic
CCIILT clitic
CCIINO iconic
CCIINP picnic
CCIIPR picric
CCIIRT citric
critic
CCIIST cistic
CCIISV civics
CCIKRY cricky
CCILNO clonic
CCILTU cultic
CCIMOS cosmic
CCIMRY Cymric
CCINOS conics
CCINPY pycnic
CCIOPT Coptic
CCIORS sciroc
CCIOSS ciscos
CCIOST Scotic
CCIPRU cupric
CCIRSU circus
CCISTY cystic
CCKLOO o'clock
CCKLUY clucky
CCKMOO mocock
CCKMOU mocuck
CCKNOU uncock
CCKOOU cuckoo
CCKOPU cock-up
CCKOSY cocksy
CCLMUU mucluc
CCLOSY cyclos
CCLOTU occult
CCLSUY cyclus
CCNOOO cocoon
CCNORU concur
CCOOOR rococo
CCOOSZ zoccos
CCOOUU cou-cou
CCOPUY occupy
CCORSU crocus
succor
CCOSTU stucco
CCSSUU cuscus
succus
CDDDEO codded
CDDEEI decide
CDDEEK decked
CDDEEO decode
CDDEEU deduce
deuced
CDDEHI chided
CDDEIU cuddie
CDDELO coddle
CDDELU cuddle
CDDENU cudden
CDDEOR codder
corded
CDDETU deduct
CDDHUY chuddy
CDDINU cuddin
CDDLOY cloddy
CDDLUY cuddly
CDDRUY cruddy
CDEEER decree
recede
re-cede
CDEEES secede
CDEEEX exceed
CDEEFN fenced
CDEEFT defect
CDEEHO echoed
CDEEIL ceiled
delice
CDEEIM décime
CDEEIN Edenic
incede
CDEEIR de-icer
CDEEIT deceit
CDEEIV device
CDEEIX excide
CDEEJT deject
CDEEKL deckle
CDEEKN necked
CDEEKO decoke
CDEEKR decker
recked
CDEELL celled
CDEELU Culdee
CDEENO encode
CDEENR cendré
decern
CDEENT decent
CDEEOR recode
CDEEOT Docete
CDEERS screed
CDEERU reduce
CDEERW decrew
CDEESU seduce
CDEETT dectet
detect
CDEFFO coffed
CDEFII deific
CDEFKU fucked
CDEFNU fecund
CDEFOR forced
CDEGGO cogged
CDEGIO geodic
CDEGLU cudgel
CDEGOR codger
CDEHIL chield
childe
CDEHIN inched
niched
CDEHIR chider
dreich
herdic
CDEHKO choked
CDEHLY chylde
CDEHNR drench
CDEHOU douche
CDEIIK dickie
CDEIJU juiced
CDEIKM medick
CDEIKP picked
CDEIKR dicker
ricked
CDEIKT ticked
CDEIKW wicked
CDEIKY dickey
CDEILO docile
CDEILT delict
CDEIMN minced
CDEIMO medico
CDEIMR dermic
CDEINO condie
CDEINR cinder

CDEINU	induce
CDEINW	Wendic
CDEINZ	zinced
CDEIOP	copied
	epodic
CDEIOV	voiced
CDEIOX	exodic
CDEIPR	priced
CDEIPS	spiced
CDEIPT	depict
CDEIRS	scried
CDEIRT	credit
	direct
CDEIRV	cervid
CDEIRY	cidery
CDEIST	cisted
CDEKNO	docken
CDEKNU	undeck
CDEKOP	pocked
CDEKOR	corked
	docker
CDEKOS	deckos
CDEKOT	docket
CDEKRU	ducker
CDEKRY	drecky
CDEKSU	sucked
CDELOO	locoed
CDELOS	closed
CDELOW	cowled
CDELOY	cloyed
CDELRU	curdle
	curled
CDELTU	dulcet
CDEMOO	comedo
CDEMOY	comedy
CDENNO	conned
CDENOR	conder
	corned
CDENOS	second
CDENOT	docent
CDENSU	secund
CDEOOP	opcode
CDEOPP	copped
CDEOPU	couped
CDEORR	record
CDEORS	credos
CDEORW	crowed
CDEOST	costed
CDEOSU	escudo
CDEOTT	cotted
CDEOTU	doucet
CDEOTY	cytode
CDEPPU	cupped
CDEPSU	cusped
CDERSU	cursed
CDERSY	descry
	scryde
CDERUV	curved
CDERUY	decury
CDESSU	cussed
CDFIOU	fucoid
CDFIOY	codify
CDGIIN	dicing
CDGINO	coding
CDHIOR	droich
	orchid
	rhodic
CDHIRY	hydric
CDIIIM	imidic
CDIIIR	iridic
CDIINT	indict
CDIIOY	idiocy
CDIISV	viscid
CDIKTY	dickty
CDILNO	codlin
CDIMNU	mundic
CDIMOR	dromic
CDIMOU	mucoid
CDIMOY	cymoid
CDIMSU	muscid
CDIMTU	dictum
CDINOO	conoid
CDINOR	Nordic
CDINSY	syndic
CDINTU	induct
CDIOPS	psocid
CDIORS	roscid
CDIORV	corvid
CDIOSS	discos
CDIOST	codist
CDIOTT	cottid
CDIOTY	cytoid
CDIPRY	cyprid
CDIPSU	cuspid
CDISSU	△discus
CDISTY	cystid
CDJNOU	jocund
CDKNOU	undock
CDLLOY	clodly
	coldly
CDLOUY	cloudy
CDMNOO	condom
CDMOOO	comodo
CDNOOR	condor
	con-rod
	cordon
CDNORU	uncord
CDNOUW	dun-cow
CDOOOT	doocot
CDOORT	doctor
CDOORY	corody
CEEEFL	fleece
CEEEGN	egence
CEEEGR	greece
CEEEHL	elchee
CEEEHS	cheese
CEEELV	cleeve
CEEENO	Eocene
CEEERS	creese
CEEFFO	coffee
CEEFFT	effect
CEEFHL	flèche
	fleech
CEEFIR	fierce
CEEFLY	fleecy
CEEFNN	fennec
CEEFNR	fencer
CEEFNS	fences
CEEFRT	refect
CEEFSU	fescue
CEEGIR	cierge
	griece
CEEGNO	congee
CEEGNY	egency
CEEHHW	wheech
CEEHIL	lichee
CEEHIN	△chinee
CEEHIR	rechie
CEEHIS	seiche
CEEHIW	chewie
CEEHKL	heckle
CEEHKY	cheeky
CEEHLN	elench
CEEHLR	lecher
CEEHLS	sleech
CEEHLW	lechwe
CEEHLY	lychee
CEEHMS	scheme
	smeech
CEEHNT	chenet
	thence
CEEHNV	cheven
CEEHNW	whence
CEEHOR	choree
	cohere
	echoer
	re-echo
CEEHOS	echoes
CEEHPS	speech
CEEHQU	cheque
CEEHRS	cheers
	creesh
CEEHRT	etcher
CEEHRU	euchre
CEEHRV	chèvre
CEEHRW	chewer
CEEHRY	cheery
	reechy
CEEHSS	secesh
CEEHSW	eschew
CEEHSY	cheesy
CEEHTV	chevet
CEEHTW	chewet
CEEIMR	eremic
CEEIMT	emetic
CEEINN	Nicene
CEEINP	picene
	piecen
CEEINT	entice
CEEINV	evince
	Venice
CEEIPR	piecer
	pierce
	recipe
CEEIPS	pieces
	specie
CEEIRS	cerise
CEEIRT	cerite
	certie
	recite
	tierce
	tiercé
CEEIRU	écurie
CEEISX	excise
CEEITX	excite
CEEJNO	conjee
CEEJRT	reject
CEEKKL	keckle
CEEKLS	seckel
	seckle
CEEKLT	teckel
CEEKPR	pecker
CEEKRY	creeky
CEELNP	pencel
CEELNR	crenel
CEELOR	△creole
CEELOS	eclose
CEELOU	coulée
CEELOV	veloce
CEELRS	sclere
CEELRT	tercel
CEELRU	cerule
	recule
CEELRV	clever
CEELRW	crewel
CEELRY	celery
CEELST	select
CEEMNT	cement
CEEMRR	mercer
CEEMRT	cermet
CEENOR	encore
CEENOT	cenote
CEENPR	percen
CEENPS	spence
CEENPT	pecten
CEENRS	censer
	scerne
	screen
	secern
CEENRT	center
	centre
	△recent
	tenrec
CEENSY	esnecy
CEEOPU	coupee
CEEORV	corvée
CEEOTX	Exocet®
CEEPRT	recept
CEEPRY	creepy
	crepey
CEEPTX	except
	expect
CEEPTY	ectype
CEEPUY	eye-cup
CEERRU	recure
CEERSS	cesser
	recess

CEERST	certes
	resect
	secret
CEERSU	cereus
	ceruse
	cesure
	recuse
	rescue
	secure
CEERTT	tercet
CEESSX	excess
CEESSY	cyeses
CEESTX	exsect
CEESUX	excuse
CEFFIO	office
CEFFLO	coffle
CEFFLU	cuffle
CEFFOR	coffer
CEFHIM	△fehmic
CEFHIT	fetich
	fitché
CEFHLN	flench
CEFHLT	fletch
CEFHNR	△french
CEFIKL	fickle
CEFILS	felsic
CEFINT	infect
CEFIRR	ferric
CEFKLY	feckly
CEFKRU	fucker
CEFLOS	fo'c'sle
CEFNOR	confer
CEFORR	forcer
CEFORS	△forces
	fresco
CEFRUW	curfew
CEGGII	ciggie
CEGGIO	coggie
CEGGLO	coggle
CEGGOR	cogger
CEGGPU	eggcup
CEGHIO	chigoe
CEGHIR	chigre
CEGHLU	cleugh
CEGINO	coigne
CEGINR	cringe
CEGINU	cueing
CEGIOT	goetic
CEGIRR	gricer
CEGIRS	grices
CEGIST	gestic
CEGKOS	geckos
CEGLRY	clergy
CEGNOR	conger
CEGNOT	cogent
CEGNSU	scunge
CEGNTY	cygnet
CEGORR	grocer
CEHHSU	sheuch
CEHHTT	thetch
CEHIKY	hickey
CEHILN	lichen
CEHILS	chesil
	chisel
CEHILT	eltchi
CEHIMO	mochie
CEHIMR	chimer
	micher
CEHIMS	chimes
CEHIMV	△vehmic
CEHINP	phenic
CEHINR	enrich
	nicher
	richen
CEHINS	inches
CEHINT	ethnic
CEHINV	chevin
CEHINX	chenix
CEHIOR	coheir
	heroic
CEHIPR	ceriph
	cipher
CEHIQU	quiche
CEHIRR	chirre
CEHIRS	riches
CEHIRT	cither
	thrice
CEHIST	ethics
CEHITT	thetic
CEHKLU	huckle
CEHKNU	Kuchen
CEHKOR	choker
	hocker
CEHKOY	chokey
	hockey
CEHKST	sketch
CEHKTV	kvetch
CEHLMO	Molech
CEHLMS	schelm
CEHLMU	muchel
CEHLNO	nochel
CEHLOR	choler
	orchel
CEHLOT	clothe
CEHLOU	louche
CEHLPS	schlep
CEHLPU	pleuch
CEHLQU	quelch
CEHMMY	chemmy
CEHMNS	mensch
CEHMOR	chrome
CEHMTU	humect
CEHNOO	ochone
CEHNOS	chosen
CEHNOT	no-tech
	techno
CEHNOU	cohune
CEHNQU	quench
CEHNRT	trench
CEHNRW	wrench
CEHNST	stench
CEHNUU	eunuch
CEHOOS	choose
	cohoes
CEHOPT	potche
CEHORS	cosher
CEHORT	hector
	rochet
	rotche
	tocher
	troche
CEHORY	ochery
	ochrey
CEHOSU	chouse
CEHOTU	touché
CEHPRU	cherup
CEHPRY	chypre
	cypher
CEHPST	spetch
CEHPSY	△psyche
CEHQTU	quetch
CEHQUY	chequy
CEHRRY	cherry
CEHRTW	wretch
CEHRTY	cherty
CEHSTU	tusche
CEHSTY	chesty
	scythe
CEHTTY	tetchy
CEHTVY	vetchy
CEIIKS	sickie
CEIILM	Milice
CEIILS	ilices
CEIILT	elicit
CEIILX	exilic
CEIIMR	cimier
CEIINP	picine
CEIINR	irenic
CEIINS	incise
CEIINT	incite
CEIJNT	inject
CEIJRU	juicer
CEIKKR	kicker
CEIKLM	mickle
CEIKLN	nickel
CEIKLP	pickle
CEIKLR	licker
	rickle
CEIKLS	sickle
CEIKLT	Keltic
	tickle
CEIKLU	luckie
CEIKMY	△mickey
CEIKNR	nicker
CEIKNS	sicken
CEIKNT	ticken
CEIKNW	wicken
CEIKOO	cookie
CEIKPR	picker
	ripeck
CEIKPT	picket
CEIKRR	ricker
CEIKRS	scrike
	sicker
CEIKRT	ticker
CEIKRW	wicker
CEIKRY	crikey
	yicker
CEIKTT	ticket
CEIKTW	wicket
CEIKTY	tickey
CEILLO	collie
	ocelli
CEILNO	cineol
CEILNP	pencil
CEILNT	client
	lectin
	lentic
CEILNU	leucin
	nuclei
CEILNY	nicely
CEILOO	coolie
CEILOP	police
CEILOR	recoil
CEILOT	citole
CEILPS	splice
CEILPV	pelvic
CEILQU	clique
CEILRS	relics
	slicer
CEILRT	relict
CEILSU	sluice
CEILSV	clevis
CEILTT	Lettic
CEILTU	Lucite®
	luetic
CEIMMN	mnemic
CEIMMO	commie
CEIMNO	income
CEIMNR	crimen
	mincer
CEIMPU	pumice
CEIMPY	pyemic
CEIMRT	metric
CEIMRU	cerium
	uremic
CEIMSU	cesium
	miscue
CEIMTY	etymic
CEINNO	conine
CEINOR	coiner
	orcein
	orcine
	recoin
CEINOS	cosine
	oscine
CEINOT	noetic
	notice
CEINOV	novice
CEINOX	exonic
CEINPR	pincer
	prince
CEINPT	incept
	pectin
	peinct
CEINQU	cinque
	quince
CEINRS	scrine

Words marked △ may be spelled also with a capital letter

CEINRT	cretin
CEINRW	wincer
CEINST	incest
	insect
	scient
CEINSU	incuse
CEINTY	nicety
CEINWY	wincey
CEIOOT	cootie
CEIOOZ	Eozoic
CEIOPR	copier
CEIOPT	picoté
	poetic
CEIORR	corrie
CEIORS	cosier
CEIORT	erotic
	tercio
CEIORV	voicer
CEIORW	cowrie
CEIORZ	cozier
CEIOSS	cessio
	cossie
CEIOST	cotise
	oecist
CEIOTX	exotic
CEIOTZ	zoetic
CEIPPT	peptic
CEIPRR	pricer
CEIPRS	cripes
	Persic
	précis
	spicer
CEIPRY	pricey
CEIPSS	Pisces
CEIPST	septic
CEIPTU	cup-tie
CEIPTY	etypic
CEIQRU	cirque
CEIRRS	cerris
CEIRRU	currie
CEIRSS	crises
CEIRST	steric
CEIRSU	cruise
	crusie
CEIRSV	scrive
CEIRTU	cuiter
	curiet
	uretic
CEIRTW	twicer
CEIRUV	cruive
CEIRVX	cervix
CEISST	citess
CEISSU	cuisse
CEISSY	cyesis
CEISTU	cestui
	cueist
CEJKOY	jockey
CEJNOU	jounce
CEJOOS	jocose
CEJRUV	J-curve
CEKKOP	kopeck
CEKKSY	kecksy
CEKLMU	muckle
CEKLNO	enlock
CEKLNU	lucken
CEKLOR	locker
CEKLOT	locket
CEKLPU	puckle
CEKLRU	ruckle
CEKLSU	suckle
CEKMOR	mocker
CEKMRU	△mucker
CEKNOR	conker
	reckon
CEKNOT	nocket
CEKNSU	sucken
CEKOOR	cooker
CEKOPT	pocket
CEKORR	corker
	△rocker
CEKORT	rocket
CEKOST	socket
CEKPRU	pucker
CEKPRY	rypeck
CEKPSS	specks
CEKPSY	specky
CEKRSU	sucker
	uckers
CEKRTU	tucker
CEKRUY	yucker
CEKSTU	sucket
CEKTTU	tucket
CELLOS	cellos
CELLOT	collet
CELLOU	locule
CELLRU	culler
CELLSU	sculle
CELLTU	cullet
CELMNU	culmen
CELMOO	coelom
CELMOP	compel
CELMOR	cormel
CELMOY	comely
CELMSU	muscle
CELMUY	△lyceum
CELNNU	nuncle
CELNOR	cornel
CELNOV	cloven
CELNOY	Ceylon
CELNRU	lucern
CELNTU	lucent
CELNUU	nucule
CELNUW	unclew
CELOOR	cooler
CELOOS	locoes
CELOOT	ocelot
CELOPP	copple
CELOPU	couple
CELOQU	cloqué
CELORS	closer
	cresol
	escrol
CELORT	colter
	lector
CELORU	colure
CELORV	clover
	Velcro®
CELOST	closet
CELOSU	coleus
	oscule
CELOSV	cloves
CELOSX	scolex
CELOTT	Toltec
CELOTY	cotyle
CELOUV	vocule
CELPRU	curpel
CELPTY	yclept
CELPUU	cupule
CELRRU	curler
CELRSU	cruels
CELRTU	culter
	cutler
	reluct
CELRUU	curule
CELRUV	culver
CELRUW	curlew
CELTTU	cutlet
	cuttle
CELTUY	cutely
CEMMOR	commer
CEMMRU	cummer
CEMNOO	come-on
	oncome
CEMNRU	crumen
CEMNTU	centum
CEMOOS	comose
CEMOPR	comper
CEMOPU	upcome
CEMORR	cremor
CEMOSY	cymose
CEMRTU	rectum
CEMTTU	tectum
CENNOR	conner
CENNOT	nocent
CENNRU	cunner
CENOOP	poonce
CENOOR	ceroon
CENOPR	crepon
CENOPU	pounce
	uncope
CENOPY	poncey
CENORR	corner
CENORS	censor
CENORT	cornet
	cronet
CENORU	conure
	rounce
CENOST	centos
CENOTU	econut
CENOTV	covent
CENOVX	convex
CENOVY	convey
	covyne
CENRSY	scryne
CENRTY	centry
CENRUY	curney
CENSSU	census
CENSTY	encyst
CEOOPR	cooper
CEOORS	cooser
CEOORV	croove
CEOOTY	coyote
	oocyte
CEOPPR	copper
CEOPRS	corpse
CEOPRT	copter
CEOPRU	couper
	croupe
	recoup
CEOPTY	ectopy
CEOQTU	coquet
CEORRS	scorer
CEORRT	rector
CEORSS	crosse
	scorse
CEORST	corset
	Cortes
	coster
	escort
	rectos
	scoter
	sector
CEORSU	cerous
	course
	crouse
	source
CEORSV	corves
	covers
CEORSW	escrow
CEORTT	cotter
CEORTU	couter
	croûte
CEORTV	corvet
	covert
	vector
CEORTX	cortex
CEOSST	cestos
	cosset
CEOSSU	△scouse
CEOTTT	octett
CEOTTU	cuttoe
CEPPRU	cupper
CEPRSU	spruce
CEPRTU	precut
CERRSU	curser
CERRSY	scryer
CERSSU	cusser
CERSTU	cruset
	rectus
CERSUV	curves
CERSUX	cruxes
CERSUZ	scruze
CERSWY	screwy
CERTTU	cutter
CERTUV	curvet
CESSTU	cestus
CESTUY	cutesy
CFFHUY	chuffy

CFFILS	scliff
CFFILY	cliffy
CFFINO	coffin
CFFINU	cuffin
CFFOTU	cut-off
	offcut
CFFRSU	scruff
CFHILN	flinch
CFHILT	flitch
CFHIRT	fricht
CFHITY	fitchy
CFHLSY	△flysch
CFIILM	filmic
CFIINN	Finnic
CFIINU	unific
CFIIST	fistic
CFIITY	citify
CFIKLS	flicks
CFILOR	frolic
CFILTY	clifty
CFIMOR	formic
CFIMOT	comfit
CFINOT	confit
CFINOX	confix
CFIORT	fictor
CFIRTU	fruict
CFISTU	fustic
CFITYY	cityfy
CFKLOS	flocks
CFKPUU	fuck-up
CFLPUU	cupful
CFOSTU	fustoc
CFRSUY	scurfy
CGGLOY	cloggy
	coggly
CGHHOU	chough
CGHILT	glitch
CGHIOT	△gothic
CGHLOU	clough
CGHORU	grouch
CGHRTU	grutch
CGILNY	clingy
	glycin
CGILPU	gilcup
CGIMNO	coming
	gnomic
CGIMNY	gymnic
CGINOO	cooing
CGINOP	coping
CGINOV	coving
CGINRY	crying
CGLLOY	glycol
CGLNOU	unclog
CGLOOU	colugo
CGNOOU	congou
CGNSUY	scungy
CHHIOR	△chi-rho
CHHIST	shtchi
CHHITY	hitchy
CHHNOO	honcho
CHHOOT	hootch
CHIIKM	kimchi
CHIILL	chilli
CHIILT	litchi
	lithic
CHIINS	nicish
CHIINT	chitin
CHIIPP	hippic
CHIIRZ	rhizic
CHIKNS	chinks
CHIKNT	knitch
CHIKNY	△chinky
CHIKOR	chikor
	chokri
CHIKOS	hoicks
CHIKOT	thicko
CHIKRS	kirsch
CHIKST	kitsch
	schtik
	shtick
CHIKTY	thicky
CHILLY	chilly
CHILMO	holmic
CHILNU	unlich
CHILOR	orchil
CHILRY	richly
CHIMNU	Munich
CHIMNY	hymnic
CHIMOR	hormic
CHIMRS	chrism
	smirch
CHIMSS	schism
CHIMTY	mythic
	thymic
CHINNU	Hunnic
CHINOP	chopin
	phonic
CHINOR	Chiron
CHINOS	chinos
CHINOT	chiton
CHINPY	hypnic
CHINRU	urchin
CHINST	snitch
CHINTZ	chintz
CHIOPR	Orphic
CHIOPT	photic
CHIORS	△orchis
CHIORT	rhotic
CHIORW	chowri
CHIOST	Sothic
CHIOSW	cowish
CHIOSZ	schizo
CHIPPY	chippy
CHIPRY	chirpy
CHIPSY	physic
	scyphi
CHIPTY	pitchy
	Pythic
CHIQTU	quitch
CHIRST	Christ
	strich
CHISST	schist
CHISTT	stitch
CHISTU	schuit
CHISTW	switch
CHITTW	twitch
CHITTY	chitty
	titchy
CHITWY	witchy
CHIVVY	chivvy
CHKLOO	klooch
CHKLOS	shlock
CHKMOO	Mohock
CHKMOS	shmock
CHKMSU	shmuck
CHKNUY	chunky
CHKORU	chukor
CHKSSU	shucks
CHKSTU	shtuck
CHLMOO	△moloch
CHLMUY	muchly
CHLOOS	school
CHLOOT	Clotho
	coolth
CHLORS	schorl
CHLOST	cloths
CHLOSU	slouch
CHLOTT	T-cloth
CHMMUY	chummy
CHMOOR	chromo
CHMOOS	smooch
CHMOSU	smouch
CHMSTU	smutch
CHNOOP	poncho
CHNOOR	cohorn
CHNOTY	notchy
CHNPUY	punchy
CHNTUU	tuchun
CHOORT	cohort
CHOOST	co-host
CHOOSY	choosy
CHOPPY	choppy
CHOPSY	psycho
CHOPUY	pouchy
CHORSU	chorus
CHORWY	chowry
CHOSTU	schout
	scouth
CHOSTW	scowth
CHOTUY	couthy
	touchy
CHPSTU	putsch
CHSSSU	schuss
CHSTUY	schuyt
CIIIRT	iritic
CIIKNW	inwick
CIIKST	tisick
CIILMU	cilium
CIILNP	inclip
CIIMOT	miotic
CIIMSV	civism
CIIMTV	victim
CIINNU	uncini
CIINOP	pionic
CIINOR	ironic
	oniric
CIINQU	quinic
CIINRT	citrin
	nitric
CIINSV	viscin
CIIPRS	spiric
CIIRSS	crisis
CIIRTV	vitric
CIISTY	cytisi
CIJNOO	cojoin
CIKKNS	knicks
CIKKPU	kick-up
CIKLNO	inlock
CIKLRY	rickly
CIKLSY	sickly
CIKLTY	tickly
CIKMNU	nickum
CIKNPU	unpick
CIKNPY	pyknic
CIKNSU	suck-in
CIKNTU	tuck-in
CIKNYZ	zincky
CIKORR	corkir
CIKOSY	yoicks
CIKPPU	pick-up
CIKRST	tricks
CIKRTU	Turkic
CIKRTY	tricky
CIKSST	sticks
CIKSTY	sticky
CILLOU	loculi
CILLSU	cullis
CILMUU	cumuli
CILNOP	clip-on
CILNOU	ulicon
	uncoil
CILNST	clints
CILNTU	incult
CILOPU	oil-cup
	upcoil
CILOPY	policy
CILORT	lictor
CILOSU	coulis
CILOSY	cosily
CILOTU	coutil
	toluic
CILQUY	cliquy
CILRSY	lyrics
CILSUY	sluicy
CIMMNU	cummin
CIMMOS	commis
CIMMOT	commit
CIMMOX	commix
CIMNNO	nincom
CIMNNU	nincum
CIMNOR	micron
CIMNOU	muonic
CIMNRU	crinum
CIMOPY	myopic
CIMORS	micros
CIMORU	corium
CIMOST	sitcom
CIMOSU	Suomic

Words marked △ may be spelled also with a capital letter

CIMOTY	comity
	myotic
CIMPRS	scrimp
CIMPRY	crimpy
CIMRUU	curium
CIMSTY	mystic
CIMSUV	△viscum
CINNOU	nuncio
CINNOY	incony
CINOOZ	zoonic
CINOPP	coppin
CINOPT	△pontic
CINORT	citron
CINORZ	zircon
CINOSS	sonics
CINOST	tocsin
CINOSU	cousin
CINOSZ	zincos
CIOORT	octroi
CIOPRS	psoric
CIOPRT	tropic
CIOPST	optics
CIORSU	curios
CIORTT	tricot
CIORTV	victor
CIOSTU	coitus
CIPPSU	cippus
CIPRSS	crisps
CIPRST	script
CIPRSY	crispy
	cypris
CIRRSU	cirrus
CIRSTT	strict
CIRSTU	△citrus
	rictus
	rustic
CIRTTY	yttric
CISSSU	cissus
CISSTU	cistus
CISSUV	viscus
CJKOOS	jockos
CJNOSU	juncos
CJNSUU	juncus
CKLNOU	unlock
CKLOPU	lock-up
	uplock
CKLPUY	plucky
CKMOPU	mock-up
CKMPUU	muck-up
CKNORU	uncork
CKNTUU	untuck
CKOSST	stocks
CKOSTY	stocky
CKRSTU	struck
CKRSUU	ruckus
CLLOOP	collop
CLLOOY	coolly
CLLORS	scroll
CLLSSU	sculls
CLMNOU	column
CLMOPY	comply
CLMOSU	locums
CLMOUU	lucumo
CLMPSU	clumps
CLMPUY	clumpy
CLMSUY	clumsy
	muscly
CLNOOS	colons
CLNOOU	uncool
CLNOOY	colony
CLNOSU	clonus
	consul
CLNOTU	uncolt
CLNOUW	uncowl
CLNRUU	uncurl
CLOORS	colors
CLOORU	colour
CLOOST	Cloots
CLORSW	scrowl
CLOSTU	locust
CLOSTY	costly
CLOSUU	oculus
CLOTTY	clotty
CLOTUW	low-cut
CLPRUU	upcurl
CLPSTU	sculpt
CLRTUY	curtly
CLSSUU	sulcus
CLSTUU	cultus
CMMNOO	common
CMMOOS	commos
CMMOOT	commot
CMMRUY	crummy
CMMSUY	scummy
CMNNOO	non-com
CMNOSY	Syncom
CMOOOW	moo-cow
CMOOPS	compos
CMOOPT	compot
CMOOSS	cosmos
CMOOSU	comous
CMORSU	cormus
	mucros
CMOSTU	custom
CMOSUU	mucous
CMOSUY	cymous
CMPRSU	scrump
CMPRUY	crumpy
CMSTUU	scutum
CNNNOO	non-con
CNNOPY	pycnon
CNOOPU	coupon
CNOORT	croton
CNOOST	contos
	nostoc
	oncost
CNOOTT	cotton
CNOOTY	coonty
	tycoon
CNOOVY	convoy
CNOPTU	puncto
CNORSY	synroc
CNORUY	rouncy
CNOTUY	county
CNRSTU	scrunt
COOORZ	corozo
COOPRS	scroop
COOPTU	cop-out
COOPWX	cowpox
COORSS	corsos
COORTU	octuor
COORUU	roucou
COPPRY	croppy
COPRSU	corpus
COPRTY	crypto
COPRUY	croupy
CORRSU	cursor
CORSST	T-cross
CORSSW	scrows
CORSTU	scruto
	Turcos
CORSUV	△corvus
CORTUY	outcry
COSSTU	costus
	custos
COSTTU	cottus
COSTTY	Scotty
COTTUU	cut-out
CPRSUY	cyprus
CRRSUY	scurry
CRSSUU	cursus
	ruscus
CRSTUY	crusty
	curtsy
CRSUVY	scurvy
CSUYZZ	scuzzy

D

DDDDEO	dodded
DDDEEI	eddied
DDDEET	tedded
DDDEEW	wedded
DDDEGO	godded
DDDEIK	kidded
DDDEIL	diddle
	lidded
DDDEIR	didder
	ridded
DDDEIU	duddie
DDDELO	doddle
DDDENO	nodded
DDDEOP	podded
DDDEOR	dodder
	rodded
DDDERU	dudder
	rudded
DDEEEM	deemed
DDEEER	reeded
DDEEES	seeded
DDEEEW	weeded
DDEEFI	defied
DDEEFN	defend
DDEEGL	gelded
DDEEGR	dredge
DDEEGS	sedged
DDEEGW	wedged
DDEEHL	heddle
DDEEIN	denied
	indeed
DDEEIR	deride
	dièdre
DDEEIT	teddie
DDEELM	meddle
DDEELN	ledden
DDEELP	peddle
DDEELR	reddle
DDEELS	sleded
DDEELU	delude
DDEEMO	démodé
DDEENP	depend
DDEENR	redden
DDEENS	sended
DDEENT	tended
DDEENU	denude
	dudeen
	duende
DDEENW	wended
DDEEOR	eroded
DDEEOS	eddoes
DDEEPR	pedder
DDEERR	redder
DDEERT	tedder
DDEERW	wedder
DDEEST	stedde
DDEFIL	fiddle
DDEFLU	fuddle
DDEFNO	fonded
DDEFNU	funded
DDEFOR	fodder
DDEFSU	defus'd
DDEGGI	digged
DDEGGO	dogged
DDEGIL	gilded
DDEGIN	dinged
DDEGIR	girded
	ridged
DDEGIT	geddit
DDEGLU	guddle
DDEGMO	Dodgem®
DDEGNO	dog-end
	godden
	god-den
DDEGOR	dodger
	red-dog
DDEGRU	drudge
DDEHIN	hidden
DDEHIR	hidder
DDEHIS	dished
	eddish
DDEHLO	hoddle
DDEHLU	huddle
DDEHNO	hodden
DDEHNU	hudden
DDEHOO	hooded
DDEIIO	iodide
DDEIIT	tidied
DDEIIV	divide
DDEIKL	kiddle

DDEIKR	kidder
DDEILM	△middle
DDEILN	dindle
DDEILO	dildoe
	doiled
DDEILP	piddle
DDEILR	riddle
DDEILS	slided
DDEILT	tiddle
DDEILW	widdle
DDEIMM	dimmed
DDEIMN	midden
	minded
DDEIMS	desmid
DDEINN	dinned
DDEINR	ridden
	rinded
DDEINT	tinded
DDEINW	winded
DDEIOS	didoes
DDEIOT	doited
DDEIOV	devoid
	voided
DDEIPP	dipped
DDEIRR	ridder
DDEITT	ditted
DDEITU	dutied
DDEJRU	judder
DDEKNY	kynded
DDELMU	muddle
DDELNO	noddle
DDELOO	doodle
DDELOT	toddle
DDELPU	puddle
DDELRU	ruddle
DDEMOO	doomed
DDEMRU	mudder
DDENNO	donned
DDENNU	dunned
DDENOR	donder
	nodder
DDENOS	sodden
DDENOW	downed
DDENOY	dynode
DDENPU	pudden
DDENRU	dunder
DDENSU	sudden
DDENUY	undyed
DDEOOS	dodoes
DDEOOW	wooded
DDEORW	worded
DDEOTT	dotted
DDEPRS	spredd
DDEPRU	pudder
DDERRU	rudder
DDERSU	sudder
DDERUW	red-wud
DDESTY	steddy
DDFILY	fiddly
DDFIOR	fordid
DDGIPU	giddup
DDHIIS	siddhi
DDHIOS	oddish
DDHISU	dudish
DDHOSY	shoddy
DDHPUU	huddup
DDIIKK	dik-dik
DDIIMS	misdid
DDIKNO	dodkin
DDILNR	dirndl
DDILOS	dildos
DDILTY	tiddly
DDIMRU	dirdum
DDIMSU	dudism
DDIMSY	smiddy
DDINNO	nid-nod
DDINOO	Diodon
DDIOOS	dosi-do
DDIOPY	dipody
DDIORS	sordid
DDIOTY	oddity
DDIRSU	siddur
DDLPUY	puddly
DDMMUU	dumdum
DDMRUU	durdum
DDNOOS	odds-on
DDPSUY	spuddy
DEEEFR	feeder
DEEEGR	degree
DEEEHL	heeled
DEEEIP	deepie
DEEEJR	jereed
DEEEKL	keeled
DEEELN	needle
DEEELP	peeled
DEEELT	delete
DEEEMR	meered
	redeem
	remede
DEEEMS	seméed
DEEEMT	teemed
DEEENP	deepen
DEEENR	needer
	reeden
DEEENV	vendee
DEEEPV	peeved
DEEERR	reeder
DEEERS	seeder
DEEERV	reeved
DEEERW	weeder
DEEERY	red-eye
DEEFFR	reffed
DEEFGL	fledge
DEEFIL	defile
DEEFIN	define
DEEFIR	defier
DEEFIS	defies
DEEFLW	flewed
DEEFLX	deflex
DEEFNR	fender
DEEFNU	unfeed
DEEFRZ	freez'd
DEEFSU	defuse
DEEFUZ	defuze
DEEFZZ	fezzed
DEEGGI	gidgee
DEEGGL	gledge
	legged
DEEGGP	pegged
DEEGHR	hedger
DEEGIJ	gidjee
DEEGIW	wedgie
DEEGKR	kedger
DEEGLL	gelled
DEEGLN	legend
DEEGLP	pledge
DEEGLR	gelder
	ledger
	redleg
DEEGLS	sledge
DEEGLU	deluge
DEEGLY	gleyed
DEEGMM	gemmed
DEEGMN	menged
DEEGNR	gender
DEEGNU	dengue
	unedge
DEEGRY	greedy
DEEGSU	segued
DEEHLM	helmed
DEEHLP	helped
DEEHMM	hemmed
DEEHMT	themed
DEEHNR	herden
DEEHRS	hersed
DEEHRT	three-D
DEEHSW	shewed
DEEHTW	thewed
DEEILR	lieder
	relide
	relied
DEEILS	diesel
	sedile
DEEILV	levied
	veiled
DEEILY	eyelid
DEEIMP	impede
DEEIMR	remeid
DEEIMS	demies
	demise
	Medise
DEEIMZ	Medize
DEEINN	indene
DEEINR	denier
	△nereid
	renied
DEEINS	desine
DEEINT	eident
	endite
DEEINV	endive
	envied
	veined
DEEIOR	oreide
DEEIOV	voidee
DEEIPR	perdie
DEEIPS	espied
DEEIRS	desire
	reside
DEEIRT	dieter
	re-edit
	tiered
DEEIRU	ureide
DEEIRV	derive
	revied
DEEISS	dieses
	seised
DEEISV	devise
	viséed
DEEITX	exited
DEEJSS	jessed
DEEJTT	jetted
DEEKNN	kenned
DEEKSW	skewed
DEELMR	melder
DEELMT	melted
DEELMY	medley
DEELNR	lender
DEELNT	dentel
DEELNW	△wedeln
DEELNY	needly
DEELOP	delope
DEELPP	lepped
DEELPY	deeply
DEELRU	eluder
DEELRV	delver
DEELRW	welder
DEELST	eldest
	steeld
DEELSV	delves
DEELSW	slewed
DEELTT	letted
DEELTU	teledu
DEELVV	devvel
DEEMNO	omened
DEEMNR	mender
DEEMNT	dement
DEEMOT	demote
DEEMPR	premed
DEEMRT	metred
DEEMRU	demure
DEEMRY	remedy
DEEMSY	emydes
DEENNO	donnée
DEENNP	penned
DEENNT	dennet
DEENOP	depone
DEENOR	redone
DEENOT	denote
DEENPX	expend
DEENRR	render
DEENRS	sender
DEENRT	tender
	tendre
DEENRU	endure
DEENRV	nerved
	vender
DEENRZ	dzeren
DEENSS	sensed

Words marked △ may be spelled also with a capital letter

DEENST	sedent
DEENSU	ensued
DEENSY	desyne
DEENTT	detent
	netted
	tented
DEENTU	détenu
	detune
DEENTV	vented
DEENTX	dentex
	extend
DEENUV	vendue
DEENUY	uneyed
DEEOPS	depose
	speedo
DEEORT	teredo
DEEORZ	zeroed
DEEOTV	devote
	dévote
DEEOXY	ox-eyed
DEEPPR	repped
DEEPRU	éperdu
	perdue
DEEPSY	speedy
DEEPTT	petted
DEEPTU	depute
DEEQUU	queued
DEERST	desert
DEERSV	versed
DEERTT	retted
DEERTV	verdet
DEERTX	dexter
DEERVV	revved
DEESTT	detest
DEESTV	devest
	vested
DEESTW	stewed
	tweeds
DEESTY	steedy
DEETTV	vetted
DEETTW	wetted
DEETUV	vedute
DEETWY	tweedy
DEFFIM	miffed
DEFFIR	differ
DEFFLU	duffel
	duffle
DEFFLY	deffly
DEFFNO	offend
DEFFOR	doffer
DEFFPU	puffed
DEFFRU	duffer
	ruffed
DEFGGI	figged
DEFGGO	fogged
DEFGIR	fridge
DEFGIT	fidget
	gifted
DEFGLY	fledgy
DEFHOO	hoofed
DEFILO	foiled
DEFIMS	misfed
DEFINN	finned
DEFINR	finder
	friend
DEFINU	fundie
DEFIOO	foodie
DEFIOT	foetid
DEFIRV	fervid
DEFISX	sexfid
DEFITT	fitted
DEFIZZ	fizzed
DEFKOR	forked
DEFLMY	medfly
DEFLNO	enfold
	fondle
DEFLOR	folder
DEFLOT	lofted
DEFLOU	defoul
DEFLOW	flowed
DEFLTU	fluted
DEFLTY	deftly
DEFLUU	dueful
DEFMOR	deform
	formed
DEFNOR	Fronde
DEFNOU	fondue
DEFNRU	funder
	refund
	re-fund
DEFOOR	roofed
DEFOOT	footed
DEFOOW	woofed
DEFOPU	poufed
DEFOSS	fossed
DEFRRU	furder
	furred
DEFRTU	turfed
DEFTTU	tufted
DEGGGI	gigged
DEGGHO	hogged
DEGGHU	hugged
DEGGIJ	jigged
DEGGIN	edging
DEGGIO	doggie
DEGGIP	pigged
DEGGIR	digger
	rigged
DEGGIT	tigged
DEGGIW	wigged
DEGGIZ	zigged
DEGGJO	jogged
DEGGJU	jugged
DEGGLO	dog-leg
	logged
DEGGLU	lugged
DEGGNO	nogged
DEGGOR	△dogger
	gorged
DEGGOS	sogged
DEGGOT	togged
DEGGRU	grudge
	rugged
DEGGRY	dreggy
DEGGTU	tugged
DEGHIN	hinged
DEGHOP	dog-hep
DEGIIK	kidgie
DEGIIR	dirige
DEGIIW	widgie
DEGILM	mid-leg
DEGILN	dingle
	elding
	engild
	gilden
DEGILO	Goidel
DEGILR	gilder
	girdle
	glider
	lidger
	ridgel
DEGILU	guiled
DEGIMN	minged
DEGIMT	midget
DEGINN	ending
	ginned
DEGINO	Gideon
DEGINR	dinger
	engird
	ringed
DEGINS	design
	dinges
	sdeign
	singed
DEGINT	nidget
DEGINW	winged
DEGINY	dingey
	dyeing
DEGIOP	pie-dog
DEGIRR	girder
	ridger
DEGIRU	△guider
DEGIST	digest
DEGITW	widget
DEGJSU	Judges
DEGKLU	kludge
DEGLNO	dongle
	golden
DEGLNU	gulden
	lunged
DEGLNY	gylden
DEGLOR	lodger
DEGLOV	gloved
DEGLSU	sludge
DEGMMU	gummed
DEGMRU	mudger
	red-gum
DEGMSU	smudge
DEGNOW	gowned
DEGNRU	gerund
	nudger
DEGNSU	snudge
DEGOPY	pye-dog
DEGORR	droger
DEGORS	sodger
DEGORU	drogue
	gourde
DEGOST	stodge
DEGOTU	dégoût
DEGPPY	gypped
DEGRTU	trudge
DEGSTU	degust
	gutsed
DEGTTU	gutted
DEHHSU	hushed
DEHILL	hilled
DEHILS	shield
DEHIMR	dirhem
DEHINO	hoiden
	honied
DEHINR	hinder
DEHINS	shined
DEHIOO	hoodie
DEHIOR	rhodie
DEHIOS	hoised
DEHIOW	howdie
DEHIPP	hipped
DEHIRT	dither
DEHIST	shited
DEHITT	tithed
DEHITW	whited
DEHKLW	whelk'd
DEHKOO	hooked
DEHKSU	husked
DEHLNO	holden
DEHLOR	holder
DEHLOW	howled
DEHLPS	delphs
DEHLPU	upheld
DEHLRU	hurdle
DEHMMU	hummed
DEHMNY	hymned
DEHMOT	method
	mothed
DEHMPU	humped
DEHMRY	rhymed
DEHNOR	dehorn
	horned
DEHNOY	hoyden
DEHNRU	hurden
DEHNSU	unshed
DEHNSY	yshend
DEHNYY	hydyne
DEHOPP	hopped
DEHORS	Rhodes
	shoder
DEHORT	dehort
	red-hot
DEHOSW	showed
DEHOTT	hotted
DEHPST	depths
DEHPSU	pushed
DEHRSW	shrewd
DEHTTU	hutted
DEIILL	lilied
DEIILP	lipide
DEIINO	iodine

DEIINS	Indies
	inside
DEIINT	indite
	tineid
DEIINV	divine
DEIIOS	iodise
DEIIOZ	iodize
DEIIPR	pierid
DEIIPT	pitied
DEIIRS	irides
	irised
DEIISS	diesis
DEIISX	deixis
DEIIYZ	Yezidi
DEIJNX	jinxed
DEIKLN	kindle
DEIKLO	keloid
DEIKLT	kidlet
	kilted
DEIKNP	pinked
DEIKNR	kinder
	kinred
DEIKNY	kidney
DEIKNZ	zendik
	zinked
DEIKPS	spiked
DEIKPU	duikep
DEIKRU	duiker
DEILLM	milled
DEILLN	nilled
DEILLU	illude
DEILLW	willed
DEILMN	milden
	Mindel
DEILMP	dimple
DEILMS	misled
DEILMW	mildew
DEILNN	dinnle
	linden
DEILNO	doline
	indole
	Leonid
DEILNR	nirled
DEILNT	dentil
DEILNW	windle
DEILOO	doolie
DEILOP	diploe
	dipole
	peloid
DEILOS	siloed
	soiled
DEILOT	toiled
DEILPP	lipped
DEILPS	dispel
	disple
DEILPX	diplex
DEILRS	slider
DEILRV	drivel
DEILRW	wilder
DEILST	listed
DEILSV	slived
DEILTT	tilted
	titled
DEILTU	dilute
DEILWY	dewily
	widely
	wieldy
DEIMMN	nimmed
DEIMMR	dimmer
	rimmed
DEIMMS	Medism
DEIMMU	medium
DEIMNO	monied
DEIMNP	impend
DEIMNR	minder
	remind
DEIMNS	denims
DEIMOR	dormie
	moider
DEIMRS	dermis
DEIMSS	demiss
DEIMST	demist
DEIMSU	medius
DEIMSV	Vedism
DEIMTU	tedium
DEINNO	ondine
DEINNP	pinned
DEINNR	dinner
DEINNS	sinned
DEINNT	dentin
	indent
	intend
	tinned
DEINNU	undine
DEINNW	enwind
DEINOP	pioned
DEINOS	donsie
	no-side
	onside
	side-on
DEINOT	ditone
	intoed
	in-toed
DEINOW	Downie®
DEINPP	nipped
DEINPR	pinder
DEINPS	spined
DEINPT	dip-net
DEINPU	uniped
DEINRT	rident
	tinder
DEINRU	ruined
DEINRV	driven
	verdin
DEINRW	rewind
	winder
DEINSU	undies
DEINSV	vendis
DEINTT	tinted
DEINTU	dunite
	united
	untied
DEINTW	twined
DEIOOR	oroide
DEIOOW	woodie
DEIOPP	doppie
DEIOPR	period
DEIOPS	poised
DEIOPT	pioted
	podite
DEIORS	dorise
DEIORT	editor
	tierod
	triode
DEIORV	devoir
	voider
DEIORW	weirdo
DEIORZ	dorize
DEIOSV	videos
DEIPPP	pipped
DEIPPR	△dipper
	ripped
DEIPPS	sipped
DEIPPT	tipped
DEIPPZ	zipped
DEIPRS	spider
	spired
DEIPRT	trepid
DEIPRZ	prized
DEIPSS	pissed
DEIPSU	upside
DEIPTT	pitted
DEIQTU	quited
DEIRRS	derris
	sirred
DEIRRU	durrie
DEIRRV	driver
DEIRST	driest
	stride
DEIRSU	diseur
DEIRSV	divers
DEIRSW	Weirds
DEIRTU	reduit
DEIRTV	divert
	verdit
DEISST	desist
DEISSU	disuse
DEISTU	suited
DEISTV	divest
	stived
	Vedist
DEITTU	duetti
DEITTW	dewitt
	witted
DEJLOW	jowled
DEJOTT	jotted
DEJTTU	jutted
DEKKOS	dekkos
DEKLOY	yolked
DEKMOS	smoked
DEKMSU	musked
DEKNOT	token'd
DEKNOY	donkey
DEKNOZ	zonked
DEKNRU	△dunker
DEKNSU	dusken
DEKOOT	dooket
DEKORW	worked
DEKRUY	dukery
	duyker
DEKSTU	tusked
DELLMU	mulled
DELLOP	polled
DELLOR	rolled
DELLOU	duello
DELLWY	lewdly
DELMNO	dolmen
DELMOS	seldom
DELMOU	module
DELMOY	melody
DELMPU	dumple
	plumed
DELNNO	on-lend
DELNOO	noodle
DELNOR	rondel
DELNOT	dolent
DELNOU	louden
	nodule
	noulde
DELNOW	dowlne
	new-old
DELNOZ	donzel
DELNRU	lurden
	nurdle
	rundle
DELNRY	dernly
DELNUV	vulned
DELNUY	nudely
DELOOP	looped
	poodle
DELOOS	oodles
DELOOT	Toledo
DELOPP	lopped
DELOPR	polder
DELOPY	deploy
	podley
DELORS	dorsel
	resold
	solder
DELORT	retold
DELORW	weldor
DELORY	yodler
DELOSS	dossel
DELOST	oldest
	stoled
DELOSU	souled
DELOTT	dottle
	lotted
DELOTX	extold
DELOYY	doyley
DELPRU	drupel
DELPSU	plused
	pulsed
DELPTU	duplet
DELPUX	duplex
DELRUY	rudely
DEMMMU	mummed

Words marked △ may be spelled also with a capital letter

DEMMSU	summed
DEMNOO	mooned
DEMNOR	△modern
	morned
DEMNOS	demons
DEMOOR	droome
	roomed
DEMOPP	mopped
DEMORR	dormer
DEMORU	remoud
DEMORW	wormed
DEMOST	modest
DEMOSU	dumose
	odeums
DEMOTT	domett
DEMPPU	pumped
DEMPRU	dumper
DEMRRU	murder
DENNOS	donnés
DENNOT	tendon
DENNOU	undone
DENNOW	wonned
DENNPU	punned
DENNRU	undern
DENNSU	sunned
DENOOS	nodose
DENOOW	wooden
DENOPR	Pernod®
	ponder
DENORT	rodent
	to-rend
DENORU	undoer
DENORV	vendor
DENORW	downer
	wonder
DENORY	yonder
DENOSS	endoss
DENOST	stoned
DENOSZ	dozens
DENOTU	deuton
DENOTW	wonted
DENOUW	unowed
DENPSU	send-up
	unsped
	upsend
DENPTU	pudent
DENRSU	sunder
DENRTU	retund
	runted
	turned
DENRTY	trendy
DENRUU	unrude
DENRUY	unredy
DENSTU	usedn't
DENSTY	syndet
DENSUU	unused
DENSUW	sundew
DENTTU	nutted
DEOOPP	pooped
DEOOPX	exopod
DEOORS	rodeos
DEOORT	rooted
DEOORV	overdo
DEOPPR	△dopper
DEOPPS	sopped
DEOPPT	topped
DEOPPW	wopped
DEOPRT	deport
	redtop
DEOPRU	pouder
	poudre
DEOPRV	proved
DEOPRW	powder
DEOPST	despot
DEOPSU	pseudo
DEOPTT	potted
DEORRS	dorser
	orders
DEORRT	dorter
	retrod
DEORRU	ordure
DEORRV	drover
DEORRW	reword
DEORSS	dosser
DEORST	strode
DEORSU	douser
DEORSW	dowser
	drowse
	sowder
DEORTT	detort
	rotted
DEORTU	detour
	douter
	outred
	routed
DEORUV	devour
DEORVY	verdoy
DEOSST	tossed
DEOSSU	soused
DEOSTT	sotted
DEOSTW	dowset
DEOSUX	△exodus
DEOTTT	totted
DEOTTU	duetto
DEOTTW	wotted
DEOTUV	devout
DEOTUX	tuxedo
DEPPPU	pupped
DEPPSU	supped
DEPPTU	tupped
DEPRUY	dupery
	Purdey®
DEPSUU	used-up
DEPSUY	pudsey
DEPTTU	putted
DEPTUY	deputy
DERRUY	rudery
DERSSU	duress
	sudser
DERSSY	dressy
DERSTU	duster
	rusted
DERTTU	rutted
DESSSU	sussed
DESTTU	duetts
DESTUV	duvets
DETTTU	tutted
DFFIMO	mid-off
DFGGOO	fog-dog
DFGIIR	frigid
DFGILU	fulgid
DFGOOX	dogfox
DFIINY	nidify
DFIIRT	trifid
DFIKOX	kid-fox
DFILNO	infold
DFILNU	dinful
DFILOR	florid
DFILUV	fulvid
DFIMOY	modify
DFIRTY	drifty
DFLNOU	unfold
DFLNOY	fondly
DFLORY	dor-fly
DFLRYY	dry-fly
DFNSUU	fundus
DFOORX	△oxford
DGGNOU	dugong
DGGOPU	pug-dog
DGGRUY	druggy
DGHIIN	hiding
DGHINY	dinghy
DGHIOP	dog-hip
DGHOOO	good-oh
DGHOOP	hopdog
DGHOOT	hot-dog
DGHOTU	dought
DGHOUY	doughy
DGIILR	ridgil
DGIINN	indign
	niding
DGIINO	indigo
DGIINP	pidgin
DGIINR	△riding
DGIINS	siding
DGIINV	diving
DGIJOU	judogi
DGILNU	ungild
DGILOT	diglot
DGIMTU	mid-gut
DGINNO	doning
	onding
DGINOP	doping
	pongid
DGINOR	roding
DGINOS	doings
DGINOT	doting
DGINOU	guidon
DGINOZ	dozing
DGINRU	during
	ungird
DGINRY	drying
DGINSU	dingus
DGIOTW	godwit
DGIRTU	turgid
DGLNOP	plongd
DGLOOY	goodly
DGLSUY	sludgy
DGMSUY	smudgy
DGNOOO	no-good
DGNOOR	drongo
DGNOOS	godson
DGNOOW	godown
	go-down
DGNORU	ground
	ungord
DGNOSU	sundog
	sun-god
DGORSU	gourds
DGORUY	gourdy
DGOSTY	stodgy
DGOTUU	dugout
DHIINS	Sindhi
DHIIPS	hispid
DHIISW	widish
DHILOS	oldish
DHILPU	uphild
DHIMOS	modish
DHINOO	Hindoo
DHINSY	shindy
DHIOOT	dhooti
DHIOPY	hypoid
DHIORR	horrid
DHIOST	dotish
DHIOSV	dovish
DHIRSU	rudish
DHIRSY	dryish
DHLOOY	dhooly
DHLOPU	hold-up
	uphold
DHLOSU	should
DHNOOU	unhood
DHNOSU	hounds
	unshod
DHOOOO	hoodoo
DHORSU	△shroud
DHORSW	shrowd
DHORSY	hydros
DHORTU	drouth
DIIJNN	djinni
DIILMP	limpid
DIILOP	lipoid
DIILOS	solidi
DIILQU	liquid
DIILST	distil
DIILTY	tidily
DIIMNU	indium
DIIMOS	iodism
DIIMOU	oidium
DIIMTW	dimwit
DIIMTY	dimity
DIINNW	inwind
DIINOP	Dipnoi
DIINOX	dioxin
DIINRS	indris
DIINSV	invis'd
DIIOOP	opioid
DIIORV	viroid

Words marked △ may be spelled also with a capital letter

DIIOST	Idoist
DIIOTT	doitit
DIITTT	dittit
DIKKOP	dikkop
DIKLNY	kindly
DIKMNU	dinkum
DIKMSY	mid-sky
DIKNNU	nudnik
	unkind
DIKOOS	skidoo
	Ski-doo®
DILLMY	mildly
DILLVY	vildly
DILLWY	wildly
DILMOR	milord
DILMOU	dolium
	idolum
	moduli
DILMPY	dimply
DILNNU	dunlin
DILNOP	diplon
DILNTU	indult
DILOPT	pot-lid
DILOPY	ploidy
DILOSS	dossil
DILOST	stolid
DILOXY	xyloid
DIMNOO	domino
DIMNOR	Nimrod
DIMNSU	nudism
DIMOOR	dromoi
DIMOPU	podium
DIMORS	Dorism
DIMOST	modist
DIMOSU	modius
	sodium
DIMOSW	△wisdom
DIMOTU	dim-out
DIMOYZ	zymoid
DINNOS	sindon
DINNUW	unwind
DINOOR	indoor
DINOOZ	zonoid
DINOPR	drop-in
DINOPU	dupion
	unipod
DINORU	durion
DINORW	in-word
DINOST	on-dits
DINOSW	disown
DINOWW	△window
DINPSU	unspi'd
DINPTU	pundit
DINPUW	upwind
	up-wind
	wind-up
DINRSU	sundri
DINSTU	nudist
DINTUY	nudity
	untidy
DIOOPS	isopod
DIOORT	toroid
DIOOSU	iodous
	odious
DIOOTX	toxoid
DIOPRT	torpid
	tripod
DIOPSS	dipsos
DIORRT	torrid
DIOSTT	dittos
DIOSTU	studio
DIPPRY	drippy
DIPRTU	putrid
DIPSTU	stupid
DIQSSU	squids
DJLMOY	jymold
DJNNOO	donjon
DKLSUY	duskly
DKNOOP	pondok
DKNOPU	Podunk
DKOOOO	koodoo
DKORSY	drosky
DLLOOP	dollop
DLLORY	drolly
	lordly
DLLOUY	loudly
DLMOOU	modulo
DLMOSU	moulds
DLMOUY	mouldy
DLMRUY	drumly
DLNOPU	Dunlop
DLNORU	unlord
DLNOSU	unsold
DLNOTU	untold
DLNUUY	unduly
DLOOPS	podsol
DLOOPZ	podzol
DLOORU	dolour
DLOTUW	'twould
DMNOOR	dromon
DMNOOY	monody
DMNOSU	osmund
DMOORS	dromos
DMOOSU	duomos
DMOOSY	sodomy
DMOOTT	motto'd
DMORSU	dorsum
DMORUZ	Ormuzd
DMOSUU	dumous
DNNOOT	donnot
DNNTUU	tundun
DNOORS	rondos
DNOOST	tondos
DNOOSU	nodous
DNOPSU	pounds
DNORST	strond
DNORSU	rounds
DNORTU	rotund
	untrod
DNOSSU	sounds
DNOSTU	stound
DNOSTW	stownd
DNOSUW	swound
DNOSUZ	zounds
DNOSWW	swownd
DNOUWY	woundy
DNRSUY	sundry
DOOOOV	voodoo
DOOOPW	doo-wop
DOOPRU	uropod
DOOPRY	droopy
DOORWW	row-dow
DOOSWY	woodsy
DOOUUV	voudou
DOPRSY	dropsy
DORRTY	dry-rot
DORSSW	swords
DORSSY	drossy
DORSTU	stroud
DORSWY	drowsy
DORUVY	dyvour
DPSTUU	dust-up
DRSTUU	Turdus
DRSTUY	sturdy
DRSUYY	dysury

E

EEEEGG	gee-gee
EEEEHT	tee-hee
EEEEPT	teepee
EEEEPW	peewee
EEEETT	tee-tee
EEEEWW	wee-wee
EEEFFR	effere
EEEFFT	effete
EEEFIR	féerie
EEEFLR	feeler
EEEFNR	enfree
EEEFRR	reefer
EEEFRZ	freeze
EEEGMR	emerge
EEEGNP	peenge
EEEGNR	renege
EEEGRS	greese
EEEGRT	greete
EEEGRZ	geezer
EEEGTV	vegete
EEEHIZ	heezie
EEEHLR	heeler
	reheel
EEEHLT	lethee
EEEHNT	ethene
EEEHNX	hexene
EEEHPR	pheere
EEEHPS	pheese
EEEHPZ	pheeze
EEEHST	seethe
EEEHTT	teethe
EEEHWZ	wheeze
EEEIJL	jeelie
EEEIKL	keelie
EEEIKR	reekie
EEEILR	Leerie
EEEIMM	meemie
EEEIPR	peerie
EEEIPW	weepie
EEEITY	Eyetie
EEEJRR	jeerer
EEEJST	jestee
EEEKKR	keeker
EEEKLR	keeler
EEEKLU	ekuele
EEEKMN	meeken
EEEKNR	keener
EEEKPR	keeper
EEEKRS	kreese
	△seeker
EEELLT	leetle
EEELMX	lexeme
EEELNV	eleven
	enlevé
EEELPR	peeler
EEELRR	reeler
EEELSS	lessee
EEELST	eel-set
EEELSV	sleeve
EEELTY	eyelet
EEEMMS	sememe
EEEMNR	meneer
EEEMNT	mentee
EEEMRS	seemer
EEEMRT	teemer
EEEMST	esteem
	mestee
EEEMTU	émeute
EEENPS	pensée
EEENRS	△serene
EEENRT	entrée
	eterne
	retene
EEENRV	enerve
	evener
	veneer
EEENSS	Essene
EEENSZ	sneeze
EEENTT	entêté
EEENTW	weeten
EEENVW	venewe
EEEOPP	epopee
EEEPPR	peeper
EEEPRV	peever
	preeve
EEEPRW	weeper
EEERRT	retree
EEERRV	revere
EEERSV	severe
EEERTT	teeter
	terete
EEERVW	weever
EEESTT	settee
	testee
EEESTV	steeve
EEETWZ	tweeze
EEFFIR	effeir
EEFFKL	keffel
EEFFOT	tee-off
	toffee
EEFFSU	effuse

EEFGIN	feeing
EEFGRU	refuge
EEFHIR	heifer
EEFHOR	hereof
EEFILN	feline
EEFILR	liefer
	relief
EEFILT	leftie
EEFINR	enfire
	feerin
	ferine
	fineer
	infere
	refine
EEFINW	Newfie
EEFIPR	preife
	priefe
EEFIRS	frisée
EEFIRZ	frieze
EEFLLO	felloe
EEFLLR	feller
EEFLNN	fennel
EEFLNS	flense
EEFLRR	ferrel
EEFLRT	felter
	reflet
	telfer
EEFLRU	ferule
	refuel
EEFLRX	reflex
EEFLRY	freely
EEFLTT	fettle
EEFLUY	eyeful
EEFMNO	foemen
EEFMTW	fewmet
EEFNNR	frenne
EEFNRU	unfree
EEFPRR	prefer
EEFPRT	perfet
EEFPTY	tepefy
EEFQRV	Q-fever
EEFRRT	ferret
EEFRST	fester
	freest
EEFRSU	refuse
EEFRTT	fetter
EEFRTU	feutre
	refute
EEFRTW	fewter
EEFRTY	freety
EEFSTT	eftest
EEFSTW	ewftes
EEFSZZ	fezzes
EEGGIR	greige
EEGGIV	veggie
EEGGLP	peg-leg
EEGGLR	eggler
	legger
EEGGMU	muggee
EEGGOR	George
EEGGRY	eggery
EEGHNU	eughen
EEGHNW	ewghen
EEGHSS	ghesse
EEGILR	leiger
	lieger
EEGILT	elegit
EEGIMR	émigré
	regime
	régime
EEGINN	engine
EEGINS	seeing
EEGINT	teeing
EEGINY	eyeing
EEGIRS	sieger
EEGIRV	grieve
	regive
EEGISV	vegies
EEGLLN	leglen
EEGLLT	leglet
EEGLMU	emulge
	legume
EEGLNN	gennel
EEGLNR	lenger
EEGLNT	gentle
EEGLRT	reglet
EEGLTU	Telegu
EEGLTY	gleety
EEGMMN	gemmen
EEGMNO	genome
EEGMNR	germen
EEGMNT	tegmen
EEGMNU	emunge
EEGMRR	merger
EEGMUW	mug-ewe
EEGNNT	gennet
EEGNOP	pongee
EEGNOR	engore
EEGNOX	exogen
EEGNRS	greens
EEGNRT	erg-ten
	gerent
	regent
EEGNRV	venger
EEGNRY	energy
	greeny
EEGNST	gentes
EEGOOS	soogee
EEGRRT	regret
EEGRRU	reurge
EEGRRV	verger
EEGRSS	egress
EEGRST	regest
EEGRSY	geyser
EEGRTT	getter
EEHHRT	hether
EEHHSW	wheesh
EEHINR	herein
	inhere
EEHINT	theine
EEHIRT	either
EEHITV	thieve
EEHKLS	shekel
EEHKRS	shreek
EEHLLR	heller
EEHLMT	helmet
EEHLNU	unhele
EEHLPR	helper
EEHLSV	shelve
EEHLSW	shewel
	wheels
EEHLWY	wheely
EEHMMS	emmesh
EEHMNP	hempen
EEHMNS	enmesh
EEHMPT	tempeh
EEHMRS	Hermes
EEHMST	smeeth
EEHMUX	exhume
EEHNNP	hen-pen
EEHNNR	henner
EEHNOR	hereon
EEHNOT	eothen
EEHNPS	sephen
	sphene
EEHNPW	nephew
EEHNRR	Herren
EEHNRT	nether
	threne
EEHNSS	sneesh
EEHNSY	△sheeny
EEHNTY	ethyne
EEHOPS	sheepo
EEHORR	Herero
EEHORS	heroes
EEHORT	hereto
	hetero
EEHORW	howe'er
EEHOSX	hexose
EEHOTW	towhee
EEHPRS	herpes
	Hesper
	sphere
EEHPRT	pether
	threep
EEHPSY	sheepy
EEHQTU	quethe
EEHRSS	sheers
EEHRSU	rushee
EEHRSY	heresy
EEHRTT	tether
EEHRTW	wether
	wrethe
EEHRTY	they're
EEHSST	sheets
	theses
EEHSTW	thewes
EEHSTY	sheety
EEHTVY	they've
EEHWYY	wheyey
EEHWYZ	wheezy
EEIIKK	kie-kie
EEIIKR	kierie
EEIIMN	meinie
EEIINW	wienie
EEIJNN	jinnee
EEIJSS	△jessie
EEIKLP	kelpie
EEIKLS	selkie
EEIKLT	keltie
EEIKNP	Kneipe
EEIKPW	kewpie
EEILLN	nellie
EEILLS	eisell
EEILLV	vielle
EEILLW	wellie
EEILNP	penile
EEILNR	lierne
	reline
EEILNS	enisle
	ensile
	nelies
	senile
	silene
EEILOT	étoile
EEILPT	pelite
EEILRR	relier
EEILRS	resile
EEILRT	retile
EEILRV	liever
	relive
	revile
EEILRY	eerily
EEILSS	seseli
EEILSX	ilexes
EEILTV	△levite
EEILVW	weevil
EEIMMS	Emmies
EEIMNR	ermine
EEIMNS	inseem
EEIMNT	emetin
EEIMNY	meiney
	menyie
	Yemeni
EEIMPR	△empire
	epimer
	premie
EEIMRS	misère
	remise
EEIMRT	métier
	retime
	tremie
	trémie
EEIMSS	emesis
	missee
EEIMST	Semite
EEINNR	nerine
EEINPR	repine
EEINQU	equine
EEINRS	seiner
	serein
	serine
EEINRT	entire
	nerite
EEINRV	envier
	venire
	Verein
EEINRW	Wiener

Words marked △ may be spelled also with a capital letter

EEINST	seiten
EEINTT	tentie
EEINTV	venite
EEINTX	extine
EEIORS	soirée
EEIPPY	yippee
EEIPQU	équipe
EEIPRS	éprise
EEIPRV	prieve
EEIPRX	expire
EEIPSS	espies
EEIPSU	épuisé
EEIPTT	petite
EEIPTW	peewit
EEIPTY	eye-pit
EEIRRS	sirree
EEIRRT	étrier
	reiter
	retire
EEIRRV	reiver
	riever
	verier
EEIRRW	rewire
EEIRSS	series
EEIRST	re-site
EEIRSV	revise
EEIRSZ	seizer
EEIRTT	ti-tree
EEIRVV	revive
EEIRVW	review
	re-view
	viewer
EEISSV	essive
EEISTV	stieve
EEISTW	Westie
EEJJNU	jejune
EEJKRR	jerker
EEJNNT	jennet
EEJQRU	jerque
EEJRST	jester
EEJRSY	△jersey
EEJSSW	△jewess
EEKKSY	keksye
EEKLMP	kemple
EEKLMY	meekly
EEKLNN	kennel
EEKLNR	kernel
EEKLNY	keenly
EEKLPR	△kelper
EEKLRT	kelter
EEKLSY	skeely
	sleeky
EEKLSZ	Szekel
EEKLTT	kettle
EEKLWY	weekly
EEKMNU	unmeek
EEKMPR	kemper
EEKMRS	kermes
EEKNNR	kenner
EEKNNT	kennet
EEKNOT	ketone
EEKNRS	skreen
EEKORV	evoker
	revoke
EEKOST	ketose
EEKPPU	upkeep
EEKPRU	Keuper
	peruke
EEKRST	streek
EEKRSU	reskue
EEKRSW	reskew
	skewer
EEKRSY	kersey
	skeery
EELLMR	merell
EELLNT	tellen
EELLNW	newell
EELLOV	O-level
EELLPT	pellet
EELLRS	resell
	seller
EELLRT	retell
	teller
EELLRU	ruelle
EELLTV	vellet
EELLVY	Y-level
EELMOT	omelet
EELMPS	semple
EELMPT	pelmet
	△temple
EELMRS	merels
EELMRU	relume
EELMRY	merely
EELMST	telesm
EELMSY	seemly
EELMTT	mettle
EELMTY	meetly
EELNNT	△lenten
EELNNV	vennel
EELNOV	elevon
EELNPS	pensel
	spleen
EELNPT	Pentel®
	pentel
EELNRT	relent
EELNRU	unreel
EELNSS	lenses
	lessen
EELNST	nestle
EELNSU	unseel
EELNTT	nettle
EELNTU	eluent
EELNUV	venule
EELNVY	evenly
EELNXY	xylene
EELOPP	people
EELOPR	eloper
EELORS	resole
EELOUV	évolué
EELOVV	evolve
EELPPU	peepul
EELPRT	pelter
	petrel
	pre-let
EELPRY	yelper
EELPST	pestle
EELPSV	pelves
EELPSY	sleepy
EELPTT	pettle
EELQSU	sequel
EELRRV	verrel
EELRSS	lesser
EELRST	streel
EELRSV	revels
EELRTT	letter
	lettre
EELRTW	welter
EELRUV	velure
EELRVV	vervel
EELSST	steels
EELSSV	selves
	vessel
EELSTT	settle
EELSTU	setule
EELSTV	svelte
EELSTY	sleety
	steely
EELSUV	evulse
EELSYZ	sleezy
EELTVV	velvet
EELTVW	△twelve
EELTWY	tweely
EEMMOR	merome
EEMMOV	emmove
EEMMSS	semsem
EEMMST	stemme
EEMNOR	moreen
EEMNOT	toneme
EEMNOV	enmove
EEMNOY	yeomen
EEMNSS	menses
EEMNTU	unmeet
EEMNYZ	enzyme
EEMOPT	metope
EEMORR	roemer
EEMORT	meteor
	remote
EEMORV	remove
EEMPRS	semper
	sempre
EEMPRT	temper
EEMPRY	empery
EEMPSU	empuse
EEMPTX	exempt
EEMRRT	termer
EEMRST	restem
	Termes
EEMRSU	resume
	résumé
EEMRSV	△vermes
EEMRSY	Mersey
EEMSST	tmeses
EEMSSU	smeuse
EEMSSW	mewses
EEMSTU	mustee
EEMSTX	Semtex®
EEMTXX	Tex-Mex
EENNOO	one-one
EENNOZ	enzone
EENNPR	penner
EENNRT	rennet
	tenner
EENNST	sennet
EENNSU	unseen
EENNUV	uneven
EENNUY	ennuyé
EENOPR	opener
	perone
	reopen
	repone
EENOPT	poteen
EENORW	erenow
EENORY	oneyer
	oneyre
EENORZ	rezone
EENOSS	enoses
EENOSV	venose
EENOTV	voteen
EENOTW	townee
EENOVZ	evzone
EENPRT	repent
EENPRY	pyrene
EENPTU	puntee
EENQUY	queeny
EENRRT	renter
EENRRV	nerver
EENRST	nester
	rentes
	resent
	strene
EENRSU	ensure
EENRSV	nerves
EENRSY	sneery
EENRTT	tenter
EENRTU	neuter
	retune
	tenure
	tureen
EENRTV	venter
	ventre
EENRTX	extern
EENRTZ	entrez
EENRVV	verven
EENRVY	venery
EENSSS	senses
EENSSV	sevens
EENSTU	tenues
EENSTV	steven
EENSTY	teensy
EENSVW	sweven
EENSWY	sweeny
EENSYZ	sneezy
EENTTX	extent
EENTTY	teenty
EENTUX	exeunt
EENTWY	tweeny
EEOOTT	toetoe
EEOPPY	pop-eye

Words marked △ may be spelled also with a capital letter

EEOPRS	repose
EEOPSS	eposes
EEOPSX	expose
	exposé
EEOPTU	toupee
EEOPTY	peyote
EEORST	stereo
EEORSV	soever
EEORUV	oeuvre
EEOSST	setose
EEOSTV	vetoes
EEPPPR	pepper
EEPPST	steppe
EEPRRS	sperre
EEPRRU	repure
EEPRSS	preses
	sperse
EEPRST	pester
	preset
EEPRSU	persue
	peruse
EEPRSV	△vesper
EEPRSW	spewer
EEPRTT	petter
EEPRTU	repute
EEPRTW	pewter
EEPRTX	expert
EEPRTY	re-type
EEPRUV	prevue
EEPSSS	sepses
EEPSTT	septet
EEPSTY	steepy
EEPSWY	sweepy
EEPTTU	puttee
EEQSTU	queest
EEQUXY	exequy
EERRST	rester
EERRSV	revers
	server
	verser
EERRTT	terret
EERRTU	ureter
EERRTV	revert
EERRUV	rêveur
EERRVY	revery
	verrey
EERSSV	Sèvres
EERSTT	setter
	△street
	tester
EERSTU	retuse
	Sûreté
EERSTV	revest
	sterve
	verset
EERSTW	stewer
	sweert
	wester
EERSTX	exsert
EERSTY	reesty
	steery
	yester
EERSTZ	zester
EERSVW	swerve
EERSVY	severy
EERTTT	tetter
EERTUV	vertue
EERTUY	tuyère
EERTVV	vervet
EERTVX	vertex
EERTWY	twyere
EESSSY	yesses
EESSTT	sestet
	testes
	tsetse
EESSTW	sweets
EESTTU	suttee
EESTTX	sextet
EESTTZ	tzetse
EESTWY	sweety
EFFGIN	effing
EFFGIR	griffe
EFFGIU	guffie
EFFGIY	effigy
EFFGOR	goffer
EFFILP	piffle
EFFILR	riffle
EFFILS	siffle
EFFINR	niffer
EFFINT	infeft
EFFIRS	Fifers
EFFKOY	off-key
EFFLMU	muffle
EFFLOP	poffle
EFFLOT	let-off
EFFLRU	ruffle
EFFLUX	efflux
EFFNOO	one-off
EFFOPU	pouffe
EFFORS	reffos
EFFORT	effort
EFFORX	forfex
EFFOST	offset
	set-off
EFFPRU	puffer
EFFRSU	suffer
EFFTTU	tuffet
EFGGOR	fogger
EFGINR	finger
	fringe
EFGIOS	fogies
EFGIRU	figure
EFGLLU	flugel
	flügel
EFGLNU	engulf
EFGLOR	golfer
EFGOOR	forego
EFGORR	forger
EFGORT	forget
EFGORW	gowfer
EFGOSY	fogeys
EFHILS	elfish
EFHIRS	fisher
	sherif
EFHISS	fishes
EFHIST	fetish
EFHLSY	fleshy
	shelfy
EFHMUY	humefy
EFHOOR	hoofer
EFHORT	fother
EFHRRU	Führer
EFIINT	finite
EFIIVX	fixive
EFIKLO	folkie
EFIKRY	fikery
EFILLR	filler
	refill
EFILLT	fillet
EFILMT	flemit
EFILNO	olefin
EFILNT	infelt
EFILNY	finely
	lenify
EFILOS	filose
EFILPP	fipple
EFILPR	pilfer
EFILRR	rifler
EFILRT	filter
	filtre
	lifter
	trifle
EFILRU	ireful
EFILRY	rifely
EFILSS	fissle
EFILST	itself
	stifle
EFILSU	fusile
EFILTU	futile
EFILWY	wifely
EFILZZ	fizzle
EFIMRR	firmer
EFIMRT	fremit
EFINNR	finner
EFINNU	unfine
EFINRY	finery
EFINST	feints
	infest
EFINSU	infuse
EFINZZ	fizzen
EFIOOT	footie
EFIORS	froise
EFIORW	frowie
EFIORX	orifex
EFIOST	softie
EFIPRX	prefix
EFIRST	sifter
	strife
EFIRSU	surfie
EFIRTT	fitter
	titfer
EFIRTY	ferity
	freity
EFIRUX	fixure
EFIRVY	verify
EFIRZZ	fizzer
EFISTY	feisty
EFKLUY	flukey
EFKORR	forker
EFLLOT	flotel
EFLLOW	△fellow
EFLLRU	fuller
EFLMSY	myself
EFLNNU	funnel
EFLNOT	Teflon®
EFLNOY	felony
EFLNPU	penful
EFLNSU	unself
EFLNTU	fluent
	netful
	unfelt
EFLOOT	footle
EFLOOZ	foozle
EFLORR	△rolfer
EFLORT	floret
	lofter
EFLORU	furole
EFLORW	flower
	fowler
	reflow
	wolfer
EFLORX	flexor
EFLOSU	flouse
EFLOUW	woeful
EFLPPU	pepful
EFLPRU	purfle
EFLRTU	fluter
EFLRUU	rueful
EFLRUX	reflux
EFLRUY	fleury
EFLSUU	useful
EFLTWY	wet-fly
EFLUZZ	fuzzle
EFMNOR	enform
EFMNOT	foment
EFMNRU	frenum
EFMORR	former
	reform
	re-form
EFMRSU	femurs
EFMSTU	fumets
EFMTUY	tumefy
EFNORR	forren
	froren
	frorne
EFNORZ	frozen
EFNOST	soften
EFNRTU	turfen
EFNRYZ	frenzy
EFNSTU	funest
EFOORR	re-roof
	roofer
EFOORT	foetor
	footer
	refoot
	tofore
EFOORW	woofer
EFOPRT	forpet

EFOPST	Eftpos
EFORRU	furore
EFORST	forest
	fortes
	foster
EFORSU	fueros
EFORTU	fouter
	foutre
EFOSTU	foetus
EFRRSU	surfer
EFRRTU	returf
EFRRUU	fureur
EFRSSU	fusser
EFRTTU	tufter
EFRTTY	fretty
EFRTUU	future
EFRTUX	frutex
EFSTTU	fustet
EGGGIL	giggle
EGGGLO	goggle
EGGGLU	guggle
EGGGNO	eggnog
EGGHIL	higgle
EGGHOR	hogger
EGGHOT	hogget
EGGIIL	gilgie
EGGIIP	piggie
EGGIJL	jiggle
EGGIJR	jigger
EGGILN	gingle
	liggen
	niggle
EGGILO	loggie
EGGILR	ligger
EGGILT	giglet
EGGILU	luggie
EGGILW	wiggle
EGGIMO	moggie
EGGINR	ginger
	nigger
EGGIPU	puggie
EGGIRR	rigger
EGGJLO	joggle
EGGJLU	juggle
EGGJOR	jogger
EGGLOO	google
EGGLOR	logger
EGGLOT	goglet
	toggle
EGGLOW	woggle
EGGLPU	puggle
EGGLRU	gurgle
	lugger
EGGMRU	mugger
EGGNRU	grunge
EGGNTU	nugget
EGGORS	gregos
EGGORT	gorget
EGGRRU	rugger
EGGRTU	tugger
EGHHIR	△higher
EGHHIT	eighth
	height
EGHHSU	sheugh
EGHHUW	wheugh
EGHIIN	hieing
EGHIKS	skeigh
EGHIKT	keight
EGHILS	sleigh
EGHINO	hoeing
EGHINW	hewing
	whinge
EGHINX	hexing
EGHIOT	hogtie
EGHIRS	sigher
EGHIST	eights
EGHITW	weight
EGHITY	eighty
EGHLMP	phlegm
EGHLNT	length
EGHLOS	seghol
EGHLPU	Guelph
	pleugh
EGHLUY	hugely
EGHMMO	megohm
EGHNOP	hog-pen
EGHNOS	Goshen
EGHNOU	enough
EGHNRU	hunger
	rehung
EGHOPR	gopher
EGHOTT	ghetto
EGHRSU	gusher
EGIIJL	jilgie
EGIILL	gillie
EGIILR	girlie
EGIIMN	△gemini
EGIINN	ingine
EGIINP	pieing
EGIINR	girnie
EGIINT	ignite
EGIITW	tie-wig
EGIJLN	jingle
EGIKLN	kingle
EGIKLR	kilerg
EGILLN	leglin
	lingel
	lingle
EGILLR	grille
EGILLT	gillet
EGILLU	ligule
EGILMN	mingle
EGILMP	megilp
EGILMT	gimlet
EGILNN	ginnel
EGILNO	eloign
	△legion
EGILNP	pingle
	pin-leg
EGILNR	girnel
	linger
EGILNS	single
EGILNT	tingle
EGILNU	lungie
EGILNZ	zingel
EGILOO	goolie
EGILOP	epilog
EGILOR	gloire
EGILOU	ouglie
EGILPR	griple
EGILPT	piglet
EGILPY	gilpey
EGILRS	Glires
	grilse
EGILRU	guiler
	ligure
EGILRV	verlig
EGILST	legist
EGILTU	glutei
EGIMMR	gimmer
	megrim
EGIMMS	gimmes
EGIMNR	germin
EGIMNY	geminy
EGIMOS	egoism
EGIMST	stigme
EGINNR	enring
	ginner
EGINNS	ensign
EGINNU	ingénu
EGINOP	epigon
	pigeon
EGINOR	eringo
	ignore
	region
EGINOS	ingoes
	soigné
EGINOT	toeing
EGINOW	wigeon
EGINPP	pigpen
EGINPR	Pinger®
	pinger
EGINPS	gipsen
EGINPY	pyeing
EGINRR	erring
	girner
	ringer
EGINRS	resign
	re-sign
	signer
	singer
EGINRT	engirt
EGINRU	rueing
EGINRW	winger
EGINRZ	zinger
EGINSS	gneiss
EGINST	ingest
	signet
EGINSU	genius
EGINSW	sewing
	swinge
EGINTU	gunite
EGINTW	twinge
EGINVX	vexing
EGINZZ	gizzen
EGIOOS	soogie
EGIOPR	porgie
EGIORS	orgies
EGIORT	goiter
	goitre
EGIOST	egoist
	stogie
EGIOTY	egoity
EGIPPR	grippe
EGIPPY	gyppie
EGIPRR	griper
EGIPRS	gripes
EGIRRV	virger
EGIRSU	guiser
	regius
EGIRSY	griesy
	grysie
EGIRTV	grivet
EGIRTY	tigery
EGIRUZ	guizer
EGISSU	gussie
EGISTU	gustie
EGJLNU	jungle
EGJLTU	juglet
EGKMSU	muskeg
EGKNOY	kyogen
EGKNTU	Tengku
EGLLOR	goller
EGLLOS	solgel
	sol-gel
EGLLRU	guller
EGLLTU	gullet
EGLLUY	gulley
EGLNNU	gunnel
EGLNOP	plonge
EGLNOR	longer
EGLNOU	lounge
EGLNPU	plunge
EGLNSU	gunsel
EGLNTU	englut
	gluten
EGLNTY	gently
EGLNUU	unglue
EGLOOY	gooley
EGLOPR	proleg
EGLOPS	gospel
EGLORU	Regulo®
	regulo
EGLORV	glover
	grovel
EGLORW	glower
EGLOST	goslet
EGLOSV	gloves
EGLOSY	gelosy
EGLOUV	voulge
EGLOUY	eulogy
EGLPRU	gulper
EGLRTU	gurlet
EGLRUY	guyler
EGLRYY	greyly
EGLTTU	guttle
EGLTUU	Telugu

Words marked △ may be spelled also with a capital letter

EGLUZZ	guzzle
EGMNOR	monger
	morgen
EGMNOS	gnomes
EGMNOY	gemony
	myogen
EGMNTU	Gnetum
	nutmeg
EGMORT	gromet
EGMORU	morgue
EGMOSU	ugsome
EGMOSY	Geomys
EGMRTU	tergum
EGNNOO	non-ego
EGNNOU	guenon
EGNNPU	pen-gun
EGNNRU	gunner
EGNNYY	gynney
EGNOOR	orgone
	orogen
EGNOOT	△gentoo
EGNOOY	gooney
	oogeny
EGNOPR	Progne
EGNOPS	sponge
EGNOPW	gowpen
EGNORV	govern
EGNORY	eryngo
	groyne
EGNOSS	gnoses
	segnos
EGNOTT	gotten
EGNOTU	tongue
EGNOXY	oxygen
EGNPRU	repugn
EGNPSU	spunge
EGNPUX	expugn
EGNRTU	gunter
	gurnet
	urgent
EGNRTY	gentry
EGNRUY	gurney
EGNSUU	ungues
EGNUVY	ungyve
EGOOPY	poogye
EGOORV	groove
	overgo
EGOOSS	gooses
EGOOST	stooge
EGOOSY	goosey
EGOPPT	peg-top
EGOPRR	groper
EGORRS	groser
EGORRW	grower
EGORSS	ogress
EGORST	groset
	storge
EGORSU	grouse
	rugose
EGORSY	gyrose
EGORTV	grovet
EGORUV	voguer
EGOSTY	stogey
EGOSYZ	zygose
EGOTTU	get-out
	goutte
EGOTYZ	zygote
EGOUVY	voguey
EGPRRU	purger
EGPRSU	spurge
EGPRUW	upgrew
EGRSTU	gutser
EGRSYY	gryesy
EGRTTU	gutter
EGRTUZ	gutzer
EGSSTU	gusset
EHHIKS	sheikh
EHHIRT	hither
EHHNPY	hyphen
EHHRST	thresh
EHHRSU	husher
EHIIMS	meishi
EHIIPP	hippie
EHIIST	histie
	Shiite
EHIJSW	Jewish
EHIKKS	kishke
EHIKNO	honkie
EHIKNS	Neskhi
EHIKPR	kephir
EHIKRS	shreik
	shriek
	shrike
EHIKSS	shikse
EHILMO	Elohim
EHILMP	Philem
EHILMU	helium
	humlie
EHILNS	elshin
EHILOS	holies
	isohel
EHILOT	eolith
EHILPR	hirple
EHILRS	hirsel
	hirsle
	relish
EHILRT	Hitler
	lither
EHILSV	elvish
EHILSW	whiles
EHILTV	thivel
EHIMMS	immesh
EHIMNR	menhir
EHIMNS	inmesh
EHIMNU	inhume
EHIMRT	hermit
	mither
EHIMRU	humeri
EHIMST	theism
	Themis
EHIMTU	humite
EHINNN	hennin
EHINNS	shinne
EHINOR	heroin
	Hornie
EHINRS	shiner
	shrine
EHINRW	whiner
EHINST	sithen
EHINSW	newish
EHINTW	whiten
EHINTY	thyine
EHINTZ	zenith
EHINUV	unhive
EHIOPT	Ethiop
	△ophite
EHIORS	hosier
EHIORT	heriot
EHIOTT	hottie
EHIPRS	perish
	reship
	seriph
EHIQUY	qui-hye
EHIRSS	Shires
EHIRST	theirs
EHIRSV	shiver
	shrive
EHIRSW	wisher
EHIRSX	rhexis
EHIRTT	hitter
	tither
EHIRTV	thrive
EHIRTW	wither
	writhe
EHIRTZ	zither
EHISST	shiest
	sithes
	thesis
EHISSV	shives
EHISSW	wishes
EHISTT	theist
EHISTU	tushie
EHISTW	whites
EHITTW	tewhit
EHITWY	△whitey
EHJOPS	△joseph
EHJORS	josher
EHKLPT	klepht
EHKLWY	whelky
EHKNOR	honker
EHKNRU	hunker
EHKOOR	hooker
EHKOOY	hookey
EHKORS	kosher
EHKORW	howker
EHKORY	horkey
EHKRSU	husker
EHLLOR	holler
EHLLOS	hellos
EHLLSY	shelly
EHLLTY	they'll
EHLMMU	hummel
	hummle
EHLMNU	unhelm
EHLMOP	phloem
EHLMOY	homely
EHLMPU	Phleum
EHLMTY	methyl
EHLNOP	holpen
	phenol
EHLNPY	phenyl
EHLOOS	shoole
EHLOOY	hooley
EHLOPP	hopple
EHLORW	howler
EHLOST	hostel
EHLOSU	housel
EHLOSV	shovel
EHLOTW	howlet
	thowel
EHLRRU	hurler
EHLRSU	lusher
EHLRTU	hurtle
EHLRUY	hurley
EHLSTT	shtetl
EHLSTU	hustle
	sleuth
EHLSTY	shelty
EHLSVY	shelvy
EHMMRU	hummer
EHMNOP	phenom
EHMNOT	moneth
EHMNPU	△humpen
EHMORT	mother
EHMOSS	shmoes
EHMPRU	humper
EHMRRY	rhymer
EHMRST	therms
EHMRSU	musher
	rheums
EHMRUY	rheumy
EHNNRU	hen-run
EHNNUW	unhewn
EHNOOP	no-hope
EHNOOR	heroon
EHNOOV	hooven
EHNOPR	phoner
EHNOPU	euphon
EHNOPY	phoney
EHNORR	horner
EHNORS	nosher
	Senhor
EHNORT	hornet
	throne
EHNOST	honest
EHNOSU	unshoe
EHNRSU	rushen
EHNRSY	henrys
EHNRTU	hunter
EHOOOP	hoopoe
EHOOPR	hooper
EHOOPY	phooey
EHOORT	hooter
EHOORV	Hoover®
	hoover
EHOOST	soothe
EHOOSV	hooves

Words marked △ may be spelled also with a capital letter

EHOPPR	hopper
EHOPRT	pother
	thorpe
EHOPRU	uphroe
EHOPTT	Tophet
EHORRS	shorer
EHORRT	rhetor
	rother
EHORSS	horses
EHORST	others
	throes
	tosher
EHORSV	shover
	△shrove
EHORSW	shower
EHORSY	horsey
EHORTT	hotter
	tother
	t'other
EHORTU	outher
EHORTV	throve
EHORTW	throwe
EHORTX	exhort
EHORTY	theory
EHORTZ	zeroth
EHOSSU	houses
EHOSTT	shotte
EHPRSU	pusher
EHPRSY	sphery
	sypher
EHPRYZ	△zephyr
EHRRSU	rusher
EHRRSY	sherry
EHRRTU	hurter
EHRRWY	wherry
EHRSSU	△rhesus
	rushes
EHRSTY	thyrse
EHRTUW	wuther
EHSSTU	tusseh
EHSSTY	shyest
	sythes
EHSTTY	Tethys
EIIKKN	Nikkei
EIIKLS	silkie
EIIKLT	kiltie
EIIKNP	pinkie
EIIKSV	skivie
EIILLN	nielli
EIILLP	illipe
EIILLT	illite
EIILLW	willie
EIILMS	simile
EIILMU	milieu
EIILNN	in-line
EIILNR	inlier
	nirlie
EIILNS	inisle
	△sileni
EIILNT	lintie
EIILNV	live-in
EIILOT	iolite
EIILPP	lippie
EIILRV	virile
EIILRX	elixir
EIILSV	visile
EIIMNN	minnie
EIIMNT	intime
EIIMPS	impies
EIIMST	stimie
EIINNP	pinnie
EIINNT	intine
	tinnie
EIINNX	nix-nie
EIINOS	△ionise
EIINOZ	△ionize
EIINPP	Nippie
EIINPR	pirnie
EIINPT	pinite
	tiepin
EIINQU	quinie
EIINRT	intire
	tinier
EIINSS	seisin
EIINST	tinies
EIINSZ	seizin
EIINTV	invite
EIIPRS	Pieris
EIIPRT	periti
	pitier
EIIRSS	irises
EIIRSV	visier
EIIRVZ	vizier
EIIRWZ	wizier
EIISTV	visite
EIISVV	visive
EIIVZZ	vizzie
EIJKNO	in-joke
EIJKNR	jerkin
	jinker
EIJKNU	junkie
EIJKST	jet-ski
EIJLLT	jillet
EIJLMS	Mejlis
EIJLTU	juliet
EIJNNO	enjoin
EIJNOR	joiner
	rejoin
EIJNRU	injure
EIJNTY	jitney
EIJRTT	jitter
	tri-jet
EIJSTU	Jesuit
EIKKLN	kinkle
EIKKOO	kookie
EIKKRY	yikker
EIKLLR	killer
EIKLLY	likely
EIKLMN	milken
EIKLMR	milker
EIKLNN	enlink
EIKLNR	linker
EIKLNS	silken
EIKLNT	tinkle
EIKLNU	unlike
EIKLNV	△kelvin
EIKLNW	welkin
	winkle
EIKLRT	kilter
	kirtle
EIKLSS	kissel
EIKLSU	Kisleu
EIKLSV	Kislev
EIKLTT	kittle
EIKMMR	kimmer
EIKMNR	merkin
EIKMNS	misken
EIKMOS	Eskimo
EIKMRS	kermis
EIKMSS	kiss-me
EIKMST	kismet
EIKMSY	miskey
EIKNNO	kinone
EIKNOO	nookie
EIKNOV	invoke
EIKNPR	perkin
EIKNRS	sinker
EIKNRT	tinker
EIKNRW	winker
EIKNSU	sunkie
EIKNSV	knives
EIKNTT	kitten
EIKOOR	rookie
EIKOPP	koppie
EIKOPS	pokies
EIKORY	△yorkie
EIKOUY	ukiyo-e
EIKPPR	kipper
EIKPPT	keppit
EIKPSS	spikes
EIKRRS	risker
EIKRSS	kisser
	krises
EIKRST	strike
EIKRSV	skiver
EIKSTW	wisket
EILLMO	mollie
EILLMR	miller
EILLMT	millet
EILLMU	illume
EILLNO	lionel
	niello
EILLNT	lentil
	lintel
	tellin
EILLOT	oillet
EILLPU	pilule
EILLRS	siller
EILLRT	rillet
	tiller
EILLRW	willer
EILLST	listel
EILLSU	ill-use
EILLTT	little
EILLTU	tuille
EILLTW	willet
EILLVY	evilly
	lively
	vilely
EILLWY	willey
EILMMR	limmer
EILMNO	moline
EILMNR	limner
	merlin
EILMNS	simnel
EILMNU	lumine
	unlime
EILMNY	myelin
EILMOR	moiler
EILMOS	smoile
EILMOT	motile
EILMPP	pimple
EILMPR	prelim
EILMPS	simple
EILMPT	limpet
EILMPU	pileum
EILMPW	wimple
EILMPX	implex
EILMRS	merils
	smiler
EILMRT	milter
EILMRV	vermil
EILMSS	missel
	slimes
EILMST	mistle
	smilet
EILMSU	muesli
EILMSY	milsey
EILMTU	telium
EILMTY	timely
EILMUV	Vimule®
EILMZZ	mizzle
EILNNO	on-line
EILNNT	linnet
EILNNU	unline
EILNNW	winnle
EILNNY	linney
EILNOO	loonie
EILNOP	loipen
	pinole
EILNOR	neroli
EILNOS	esloin
	insole
	lesion
	solein
EILNOT	entoil
	lionet
	Nilote
EILNOV	love-in
EILNPP	lippen
	nipple
EILNPS	pensil
	spinel
	spline
EILNPT	pintle
EILNPU	line-up
	lupine
	up-line

EILNRT	linter
EILNST	enlist
	listen
	silent
	tinsel
EILNSV	sliven
	snivel
EILNSY	linsey
	lysine
EILNTT	litten
EILNTU	luiten
	lutein
	untile
EILNTV	ventil
EILNTW	wintle
EILNTY	lenity
EILNUV	unlive
	unveil
EILNUY	lunyie
EILOOR	oriole
EILOOT	△oolite
EILOPS	pilose
EILOPT	piolet
	polite
EILORS	oilers
EILORT	loiter
	toiler
EILORV	△oliver
	violer
EILORW	Lowrie
EILORY	oilery
EILOSV	solive
EILOTT	toilet
EILOTU	outlie
EILOTV	olivet
	violet
EILPPR	ripple
EILPPS	sipple
EILPPT	tipple
EILPPU	pile-up
EILPRS	lisper
	pliers
EILPRT	triple
EILPRY	ripely
EILPSS	plissé
EILPST	stipel
EILPSU	epulis
	pileus
EILPSV	pelvis
EILPTU	puteli
EILPZZ	pizzle
EILRST	lister
EILRSV	silver
	sliver
EILRTT	litter
	tilter
	titler
EILRTU	rutile
EILRTY	tilery
EILRVY	livery
	verily
EILSSS	lisses
EILSST	sliest
EILSTT	stilet
	titles
EILSTU	sutile
EILSVW	swivel
EILSWY	wisely
EILSZZ	sizzle
EILTTT	tittle
EILTTU	titule
EILTTV	vittle
EILTTY	titely
EILTVY	levity
EILVVY	vively
EILVWY	viewly
EIMMNR	nimmer
EIMMNU	immune
EIMMOR	memoir
EIMMRS	merism
	simmer
EIMMRU	immure
EIMMRZ	Zimmer®
	zimmer
EIMMST	semmit
EIMMSY	mimsey
EIMNNX	meninx
EIMNOO	Moonie
EIMNOP	impone
EIMNOR	merino
EIMNOS	eonism
	monies
EIMNPT	piment
EIMNRT	minter
	remint
EIMNRU	murine
	Nerium
EIMNRV	vermin
EIMNTT	mitten
EIMNTU	minuet
	minute
	munite
	mutine
EIMNTY	enmity
EIMNUX	xenium
EIMNZZ	mizzen
EIMOOR	roomie
EIMOPS	impose
EIMOPT	optime
EIMORS	isomer
	moiser
	rimose
EIMOSS	mossie
EIMOST	somite
EIMOSU	mousie
EIMOSV	movies
EIMOSX	exomis
EIMOTV	motive
EIMOTY	moiety
EIMOZZ	mozzie
EIMPRR	primer
EIMPRS	simper
EIMPRT	permit
EIMPRU	impure
	umpire
EIMPRX	premix
EIMPSU	sepium
EIMPTU	impute
EIMPUY	△yumpie
EIMRRT	retrim
	trimer
EIMRSS	remiss
EIMRST	merits
	△mister
	smiter
EIMRSV	verism
	vermis
EIMRSY	misery
EIMRTU	iterum
EIMSSS	misses
EIMSST	misset
	tmesis
EIMSSU	misuse
EIMSSX	sexism
EIMSTY	stymie
EIMSUV	musive
EIMTYZ	zymite
EINNNR	rennin
EINNOO	ionone
EINNOT	intone
EINNPR	pinner
EINNPT	pinnet
	tenpin
EINNRS	sinner
EINNRT	intern
	tinner
EINNRU	unrein
EINNRW	winner
EINNSS	Nissen
EINNST	sennit
	sinnet
	tennis
EINNTT	intent
EINNTV	invent
EINNTY	ninety
EINOPP	pepino
EINOPR	orpine
	pioner
	proine
EINOPT	pointe
	pontie
EINOPW	pownie
EINOPY	pioney
EINORR	ironer
EINORS	senior
	soneri
EINORT	norite
	△orient
EINORV	renvoi
EINOSS	enosis
	essoin
	noesis
	noises
	ossein
	sonsie
EINOST	Nesiot
	on-site
	Tonies
EINOSV	Nivôse
EINOSW	nowise
EINOTT	tonite
EINOTW	townie
EINOVW	inwove
EINPPR	nipper
EINPPS	pepsin
EINPPW	wippen
EINPRS	sniper
EINPRT	nipter
	pterin
EINPRU	pruine
	punier
	purine
	unripe
EINPRY	pinery
EINPST	instep
	spinet
	step-in
EINPSU	puisne
	supine
EINPTT	pitten
EINQSU	sequin
EINQTU	queint
	quinte
EINQUU	unique
EINQUZ	quinze
EINRRS	rinser
EINRRU	ruiner
EINRST	insert
	sinter
	Strine
EINRSU	insure
	rusine
	ursine
EINRSV	versin
EINRSY	Erinys
EINRTT	tinter
EINRTU	triune
	uniter
EINRTV	invert
	virent
EINRTW	twiner
	winter
EINRTY	nitery
EINRUW	unwire
EINRVW	wivern
EINRVY	vinery
EINRWY	winery
EINSSS	nisses
EINSSU	Senusi
EINSTU	intuse
	tenuis
EINSTV	invest
EINSTW	wisent
EINSTY	tinsey
EINSTZ	Zenist
EINSUW	unwise
EINSUX	unisex

EINSWY	sinewy
	winsey
EINTTY	entity
EINUVW	unwive
EIOORT	toorie
EIOOST	otiose
EIOPRS	poiser
EIOPRU	pourie
EIOPSS	possie
EIOPST	postie
	sopite
EIOPTT	tiptoe
EIORRS	rosier
EIORRT	rioter
EIORST	sortie
	tiroes
EIORSV	vireos
	virose
EIORSX	orexis
EIORSY	osiery
EIORTU	tourie
EIOSTV	△soviet
EIOTTT	tottie
EIOTTU	toutie
EIOTUV	outvie
EIOTVV	votive
EIPPRR	ripper
EIPPRS	sipper
EIPPRT	tipper
EIPPRU	purpie
EIPPRY	yipper
EIPPRZ	zipper
EIPPST	sippet
EIPPTT	tippet
EIPPTX	Tippex
	Tipp-Ex®
EIPPUY	△yuppie
EIPQTU	piquet
EIPRRS	priser
EIPRRZ	prizer
EIPRST	esprit
	pierst
	priest
	Pteris
	sitrep
	sprite
	stripe
EIPRSU	uprise
EIPRSW	swiper
EIPRTT	pitter
EIPRTV	privet
EIPRTX	extirp
EIPRTY	pyrite
	tripey
EIPRXY	expiry
EIPSSS	sepsis
	speiss
EIPSST	stipes
EIPSSW	swipes
EIPSTT	pet-sit
EIPSWY	swipey
EIPTTU	puttie
EIQRSU	risque
	risqué
	squier
	squire
EIQRTU	requit
EIQRUV	quiver
EIQTUY	equity
EIRRST	stirre
EIRRTT	ritter
	territ
EIRRTW	writer
EIRRVY	rivery
EIRRZZ	rizzer
EIRSST	resist
	sister
EIRSSU	issuer
	uresis
EIRSTT	sitter
	triste
EIRSTV	stiver
	strive
	trevis
	verist
EIRSTW	sweirt
	wriest
EIRSVV	vivers
	vivres
EIRTTT	titter
EIRTTV	trivet
EIRTTW	witter
EIRTUV	virtue
EIRTVY	verity
EISSTT	testis
EISSTU	tissue
EISSTX	sexist
EISTTY	tystie
EISTVW	swivet
EISUVZ	suivez
EITTTX	tettix
EJKLSU	Seljuk
EJKNRU	△junker
EJKNTU	junket
EJLLOS	jellos
EJLLOY	jolley
EJLORT	jolter
EJLORW	jowler
EJLOST	jostle
EJLSTU	justle
EJMOOS	mojoes
EJMOST	jetsom
EJMPRU	jumper
EJNOST	jetson
EJNOTT	jetton
EJOOSY	soojey
EJORSS	josser
EJORTT	jotter
EJOTTU	outjet
EKKOPU	pukeko
EKLLSY	skelly
EKLMMU	kümmel
EKLMSU	muskle
	skelum
EKLNOS	kelson
	sloken
EKLNRU	lunker
	runkle
EKLNST	sklent
EKLOOR	looker
EKLOWY	low-key
EKLRRU	lurker
EKMNOY	monkey
EKMOOP	mopoke
EKMORS	smoker
EKMSTU	musket
EKNNOR	kronen
EKNNOT	nekton
EKNNSU	sunken
EKNNTU	unkent
EKNOPS	spoken
EKNORR	kroner
EKNORT	tonker
EKNORW	knower
	wroken
EKNORY	yonker
EKNOUY	unyoke
EKNPTU	unkept
EKNRTU	Tunker
EKNSTU	sunket
EKOOQU	quooke
EKOORR	korero
EKOORT	retook
EKOPRR	porker
	proker
EKOPSY	pokeys
EKORRW	rework
	worker
EKORRY	yorker
EKORST	stoker
	stroke
EKORTX	trek-ox
EKORWY	ywroke
EKOSST	stokes
EKRRSY	skerry
	skryer
EKRSTU	tusker
EKRTUY	turkey
EKRUVY	kurvey
ELLLOR	loller
ELLLOZ	lozell
ELLMOW	mellow
ELLMRU	muller
ELLMSY	smelly
ELLMTU	mullet
ELLMUV	vellum
ELLMUY	mulley
ELLNOP	pollen
ELLNOR	enroll
ELLNOV	vellon
ELLNOW	Nowell
ELLNOY	lonely
ELLNSU	sullen
ELLNSY	snelly
ELLNUU	lunule
ELLNUW	unwell
ELLOPR	poller
ELLOPS	ellops
ELLOPX	pollex
ELLORR	△roller
ELLORS	soller
	sorell
ELLORT	toller
ELLOST	tolsel
ELLOSY	solely
ELLOVY	lovely
	volley
ELLOWY	yellow
ELLPRU	puller
ELLPTU	pullet
ELLPUW	upwell
ELLPUY	pulley
ELLSTU	△tellus
ELMMOP	pommel
ELMMOS	Moslem
ELMMPU	pummel
ELMNOR	merlon
ELMNOS	solemn
ELMNOT	loment
	melton
	molten
ELMNOY	lemony
	myelon
ELMNPU	lumpen
	plenum
ELMNSU	lumens
ELMOOP	pomelo
ELMOPU	pumelo
ELMOPY	employ
ELMORS	morsel
ELMORT	Merlot
ELMOST	molest
ELMOSU	mousle
ELMOSY	smoyle
ELMOTT	mottle
ELMOTY	motley
ELMOUV	volume
ELMOXY	oxymel
ELMOZZ	mozzle
ELMPPU	peplum
ELMPRU	lumper
	replum
	rumple
ELMRSU	lemurs
ELMRTY	myrtle
	termly
ELMSSU	mussel
ELMTUU	mutule
ELMTUY	mutely
ELMUZZ	muzzle
ELNNOS	nelson
ELNNRU	runnel
ELNNTU	△tunnel
ELNOOS	loosen
ELNOOT	looten
ELNOOW	woolen
ELNOPT	lepton
ELNOPU	loupen

ELNOPY	openly
	poleyn
ELNORS	norsel
ELNORT	lentor
ELNOSS	lesson
ELNOST	lentos
	stolen
	telson
ELNOSU	ensoul
	nousle
	Olenus
ELNOSV	novels
	sloven
	volens
ELNOTT	tonlet
ELNOUV	unlove
ELNOUZ	zonule
ELNOVY	lenvoy
ELNOZZ	nozzle
ELNPPU	luppen
ELNPTU	penult
ELNPTY	plenty
ELNRSU	nursle
ELNRTU	runlet
ELNRUU	unrule
ELNRUZ	luzern
ELNSSU	unless
ELNSXY	lynxes
ELNTTU	lutten
	nutlet
ELNTTY	nettly
ELNTXY	nextly
ELNUZZ	nuzzle
ELOOPR	looper
ELOORT	looter
	retool
	rootle
	tooler
ELOOSV	looves
ELOOSW	woosel
ELOOSZ	zeloso
ELOOTT	tootle
ELOPPP	popple
ELOPPR	lopper
	propel
ELOPPS	peplos
ELOPPT	topple
ELOPPU	poulpe
ELOPPY	polype
ELOPRR	proler
ELOPRS	splore
ELOPRT	petrol
ELOPRV	plover
ELOPRX	plexor
ELOPRY	pelory
ELOPSU	souple
ELOPTT	pottle
ELOPTU	tupelo
ELORRS	sorrel
ELORRW	worrel
ELORSS	lessor

ELORST	ostler
	sterol
	torsel
ELORSV	solver
ELORSY	sorely
ELORTT	tolter
ELORTU	elutor
	outler
	troule
ELORTV	revolt
ELORTW	trowel
	wortle
ELORTY	troely
ELORUV	louver
	louvre
	velour
ELORVW	wolver
ELORVY	overly
	volery
ELORWY	lowery
	owlery
ELOSSU	louses
	soleus
ELOSTU	solute
	tousle
ELOSTW	lowest
ELOSTY	tolsey
ELOSVW	vowels
	wolves
ELOSXY	xylose
ELOSZZ	sozzle
ELOTTU	let-out
	outlet
ELOTTY	tylote
ELOTUV	volute
ELOTUZ	touzle
ELOTWY	owelty
ELOTYZ	tolzey
ELOWYY	yowley
ELPPRU	pulper
	purple
	repulp
ELPPSU	peplus
	supple
ELPQUU	pulque
ELPRRU	purler
ELPRTY	peltry
	pertly
ELPRUV	pulver
ELPRUY	purely
ELPSSU	pluses
	pussel
ELPSUV	Vulpes
ELPSUX	plexus
ELPSUY	spulye
ELPUZZ	puzzel
	puzzle
ELRSSU	russel

ELRSTU	luster
	lustre
	result
	rustle
	sutler
	ulster
ELRSUY	surely
ELRSYY	syrlye
ELRTTU	turtle
ELRTTY	tetryl
ELRUWY	wurley
ELSSTU	tussle
ELSSTY	slyest
ELSTTU	suttle
ELSTTY	stylet
ELUWZZ	wuzzle
EMMMOT	mommet
EMMMRU	mummer
EMMNNO	Memnon
	mnemon
EMMNOT	moment
	montem
EMMNTU	mentum
EMMORY	memory
EMMORZ	momzer
EMMOSU	mousmé
EMMOYZ	zymome
EMMPRU	mumper
EMMRRU	rummer
EMMRSU	summer
EMMSUU	museum
EMNOOR	mooner
EMNOPY	eponym
EMNORS	sermon
EMNORT	mentor
	montre
EMNOST	mentos
	Ostmen
EMNOSY	moneys
EMNOTY	etymon
EMNOXY	exonym
EMNPSU	pensum
EMNRRU	murren
EMNRSU	Mensur
EMNSSU	sensum
EMOORR	roomer
EMOORS	morose
	Romeos
EMOORT	mooter
EMOOSS	osmose
EMOPPR	mopper
EMOPPT	moppet
EMOPPY	△pompey
EMOPRR	romper
EMOPRS	Merops
EMOPRT	trompe
EMOPRU	Euro-MP
EMOPST	tempos
EMOQSU	mosque
EMORRT	termor
	tremor
EMORRW	wormer

EMORST	métros
	motser
EMORSU	mouser
EMORSV	movers
EMORTU	mouter
EMOSSU	mousse
	smouse
EMOSUY	mousey
EMOSZZ	mezzos
EMOTTT	motett
EMPPRU	pumper
EMPRRU	Rumper
EMPSSU	mess-up
EMPSTU	septum
EMRRUY	murrey
EMRSSU	serums
EMRSTU	estrum
	muster
	stumer
EMRTTU	mutter
EMSSTY	△system
EMSSWY	Wemyss
ENNNOP	pennon
ENNNOT	non-net
ENNOOR	nooner
ENNOOS	no-noes
ENNOPT	ponent
ENNORU	neuron
ENNORW	renown
ENNOST	sonnet
	stonen
	stonne
	tenson
ENNOSV	ven'son
ENNOTW	newton
ENNOTZ	tenzon
ENNPRU	punner
ENNPTU	punnet
	unpent
ENNRRU	runner
ENNRST	Nernst
ENNRTU	runnet
	unrent
ENNRUW	wunner
ENNSTU	unnest
	unsent
ENNSUW	unsewn
ENNTTU	untent
ENNTUU	untune
ENOOOZ	Eozoon
ENOOPR	operon
ENOORS	Roneos
	seroon
	sooner
ENOORT	enroot
ENOOSZ	snooze
ENOOTW	one-two
ENOPPU	unpope
ENOPRR	perron
ENOPRS	person
ENOPRU	unrope
ENOPRV	proven

ENOPRY proyne
pyoner
ENOPST pontes
posnet
ENOPTT potent
ENOPWY powney
ENORRS snorer
sorner
ENORRY ornery
ENORSS sensor
ENORST Nestor
stoner
tensor
ENORSW worsen
ENORTT rotten
to-rent
torten
ENORTU tenour
ENORUZ zonure
ENORVY renvoy
ENORZZ nozzer
ENOSST seston
tossen
ENOSSW sowens
ENOSTT ostent
teston
ENOSTX sexton
ENOSUV venous
ENOSUW swoune
ENOSWW swowne
ENOTTU tenuto
Teuton
ENOTTW tow-net
ENPPTU pent-up
ENPRRU pruner
ENPRST sprent
ENPRSU prunes
spurne
ENPRTU punter
ENPRUY penury
ENPRWY prewyn
ENPSTU unstep
ENPTTU putten
ENPTUW unwept
ENRRSU nurser
ENRRTU return
re-turn
turner
ENRSTU unrest
ENRSTW strewn
ENRSTY sentry
ENRSUU unsure
ENRTTU nutter
ENRTUU untrue
ENRUZZ nuzzer
ENRVWY wyvern
ENSSTU sunset
ENTTWY twenty
EOOPPS oppose
EOOPRS porose
EOOPRT △pooter
EOOPST stoope
EOORRT rooter
torero
EOORST torose
EOORTT tooter
EOPPPR popper
EOPPPT poppet
EOPPRR proper
EOPPRT topper
EOPPRY popery
pyrope
yopper
EOPRRS proser
repros
EOPRRT porter
pretor
report
EOPRRU pourer
EOPRRV prover
EOPRRY ropery
EOPRSS posser
EOPRST poster
presto
repost
EOPRSU poseur
souper
uprose
EOPRSW powers
EOPRSY osprey
EOPRTT potter
EOPRTU pouter
troupe
EOPRTW powter
EOPRTX export
EOPRTY poetry
EOPRUV up-over
EOPSST posset
ptoses
EOPSSU opuses
pousse
spouse
EOPSTX sexpot
EOPTTU toupet
EOQRTU quoter
roquet
torque
EOQSTU quotes
EORRRT rorter
△terror
EORRRY orrery
EORRSS rosser
EORRST resort
retros
roster
sorter
storer
EORRSU rouser
EORRSW worser
EORRSY rosery
EORRTT retort
rotter
torret
EORRTU retour
router
tourer
EORRTV trover
EORRZZ rozzer
EORSST sortes
stores
tosser
EORSSU serous
sourse
EORSSV versos
EORSTT tortes
EORSTU ouster
souter
touser
trouse
EORSTV stover
strove
EORSTW sowter
stower
stowre
△towser
EORSTY oyster
rosety
storey
tyroes
EORSTZ zoster
EORSWW wowser
EORTTT totter
EORTTU touter
EORTTX extort
EORTUV ouvert
EORTVX vortex
EORTWY towery
EORUVY voyeur
EOSSSU souses
EOSSSW sowsse
EOSSTT set-tos
set-to's
EOSSVW vowess
EOSTTU outset
set-out
EOSUUV uveous
EPPPRY preppy
EPPPTU puppet
EPPRSU supper
uppers
EPPSTU step-up
EPRRSU purser
EPRRSY spryer
EPRSST sperst
EPRSSU pusser
EPRSTU uprest
EPRSUU pursue
EPRSUW pursew
EPRTTU putter
EPRTTY pretty
EPRTUU puture
EPRUVY purvey
EPSTUZ putzes
EQRTWY qwerty
ERRSTU rustre
ERRSUU usurer
ERRSUY surrey
ERRTTU rutter
turret
ERSSST stress
ERSSTU estrus
russet
tusser
ERSSTY syrtes
tressy
ERSSUU uruses
ERSSUV versus
ERSTUU suture
uterus
ERSTUV turves
ERSTUY surety
ERSTVY vestry
ERSTWY wryest
ERSTXY xyster
ERSUVW survew
ERSUVY survey
ERTTUX urtext

F

FFFLUY fluffy
FFGINO offing
FFHIIS Fifish
FFHIOS offish
FFHIWY whiffy
FFHOOP hop-off
FFHORS shroff
FFIINT tiffin
FFIKLS skliff
FFILLO ill-off
FFILLU fulfil
FFILOT filfot
FFILPS spliff
FFILTU fitful
FFIMNU muffin
FFINNU nuffin
FFINPU puffin
FFINRU ruffin
FFINSY sniffy
FFIOPR rip-off
FFIOPT tip-off
FFIOPZ zip-off
FFIOST soffit
FFIPSY spiffy
FFIQSU squiff
FFISUX suffix
FFLOTY fylfot
FFLPUY pluffy
FFNORU run-off
FFNSUY snuffy
FFOPSY spoffy
FFOPTU offput
put-off
FFRRUU furfur
FFSTUY stuffy
FGGIIS fisgig
FGGIIZ fizgig
FGGORY △froggy

FGHILT	flight
FGHIRT	fright
FGHOTU	fought
FGIILN	filing
FGIINN	fining
FGIINR	firing
FGIINX	fixing
FGILNU	ingulf
FGILNY	flying
FGILUY	uglify
FGINOR	froing
FGINOX	foxing
FGINRY	fringy
	frying
FGIORT	frigot
FGJLUU	jugful
FGLMUU	mugful
FGLORU	fulgor
FGLTUU	gutful
FGNORY	gryfon
FGNSUU	fungus
FGOORT	forgot
FHIIKS	fikish
FHIINS	finish
FHILTY	filthy
FHIMUY	humify
FHIRST	shrift
FHIRTT	thrift
FHISSU	hussif
FHISTU	shufti
FHISTY	shifty
FHLOPY	hop-fly
FHLOSU	floush
FHLSUY	flushy
FHOOOR	forhoo
FHOORW	forhow
FHORTU	fourth
FHORTY	forthy
	frothy
FHORWY	forwhy
FHPRUY	furphy
FHSTUY	shufty
FIIKNR	firkin
FIILLN	fill-in
	infill
FIILLP	fillip
FIILVY	vilify
FIIMNR	infirm
FIIMNY	minify
FIIMST	misfit
FIINOR	fiorin
FIIOST	tifosi
FIITXY	fixity
FIIVVY	vivify
FIJLOR	frijol
FIKLSY	flisky
FIKNOS	finsko
FIKRSY	frisky
FILLLU	lifull
FILLPU	upfill
FILLRS	frills
FILLRY	frilly
FILLUW	wilful
FILMOU	folium
FILMRY	firmly
FILMSY	flimsy
FILNOR	florin
FILNOW	inflow
FILNSU	sinful
FILNTU	tinful
FILNTY	flinty
FILNUX	influx
FILOOS	folios
FILORT	firlot
FILORV	frivol
FILOSS	fossil
FILOUZ	zufoli
FILPTU	uplift
FILRTY	flirty
FIMNOR	inform
FIMNOY	omnify
FIMNRU	unfirm
FIMNUY	munify
FIMOSS	Sofism
FIMSSU	Sufism
FIMSTU	Muftis
FINOOS	foison
FINOPR	fripon
FINORT	forint
FINORX	fornix
FINOSU	fusion
FINOTY	notify
FINSTY	snifty
FIOOST	tifoso
FIOPRT	forpit
	profit
FIORRT	forrit
FIORST	fortis
FIORTY	Torify
FIOSSY	ossify
FIOTTU	fit-out
	outfit
FIPRUY	purify
FIPTYY	typify
FIRSTT	strift
FIRSTU	fruits
FIRTUY	fruity
FIRYZZ	frizzy
FJLOUY	joyful
FKLNUY	flunky
FKLOSY	folksy
FKNOTY	konfyt
FLLLUY	lyfull
FLLOOW	follow
FLLOUY	foully
FLMNOU	muflon
FLMOOR	formol
FLNOOU	unfool
FLNOOW	flow-on
	onflow
FLNRUU	unfurl
	urnful
FLOOSY	floosy
FLOOUZ	zufolo
FLOOYZ	floozy
FLOPPY	floppy
FLOPTU	potful
FLOPUU	foul-up
FLOPUW	upflow
FLORUY	floury
FLOSSY	flossy
FLOSTY	softly
FLOTUY	outfly
FLPRUU	upfurl
FLPRUY	purfly
FLRRUY	flurry
FLRSUU	sulfur
FMNORU	unform
FMORSU	forums
FMOSUU	fumous
FMPRUY	frumpy
FNOORU	unroof
FNOSTU	unsoft
FNRTUU	unturf
FOOPRS	proofs
FOORSS	fossor
FOOTUX	outfox
FORRUW	furrow
FORSTW	frowst
FORSTY	frosty
FORSUU	rufous
FORSWY	frowsy
FORTYY	Toryfy
FORWYZ	frowzy
FOSTUY	fousty
G	
GGGIIT	giggit
GGGILY	giggly
GGGLOY	goggly
GGGORY	groggy
GGHINO	hoggin
GGHNOU	gung-ho
GGHORU	grough
GGHOTU	thuggo
GGIIJJ	jigjig
	jig-jig
GGIINP	piggin
GGIINV	giving
GGIIRR	grigri
GGIJJO	jig-jog
GGIJLY	jiggly
GGIKNO	gingko
	ginkgo
GGILNO	ogling
GGILNU	gluing
	luging
GGILNY	niggly
GGILOO	gigolo
GGILOT	giglot
GGILWY	wiggly
GGINNO	nig-nog
	noggin
GGINOQ	qigong
GGINOR	goring
	gringo
GGINRU	urging
GGIOOR	gorgio
GGITWY	twiggy
GGJJUU	jug-jug
GGLLOO	loglog
GGLOOO	googol
GGLOOY	googly
GGMOSY	smoggy
GGNOOR	△gorgon
	grog-on
GGNRUY	grungy
GGOPRU	grog-up
GGORST	troggs
GGRRUU	gru-gru
GGSTUY	stuggy
GHHHIT	highth
GHHILY	highly
GHHIPU	high-up
GHHOSU	shough
GHHOTU	though
GHIINR	hiring
GHIKNT	knight
GHILNO	holing
GHILNY	nighly
GHILPT	plight
GHILST	lights
	slight
	'slight
GHILSU	gluish
GHIMNO	homing
GHIMST	smight
GHIMTY	mighty
GHINNO	nigh-on
GHINST	nights
	things
GHINSY	shying
GHINTY	nighty
	thingy
GHIOPZ	phizog
GHIORS	ogrish
GHIORT	righto
GHIOSY	goyish
GHIPST	spight
GHIPTY	ypight
GHIQTU	quight
GHIRST	rights
GHIRTW	wright
GHISTT	tights
GHITTW	twight
GHLOOS	golosh
GHLOPU	△plough
GHLOSU	slough
GHLOTU	log-hut
GHLOUY	oughly
GHMOTU	mought
GHMPRU	grumph
GHNNUU	unhung
GHNORT	throng
GHNOSU	shogun
GHNOTU	nought
GHNRUY	hungry
GHNSUY	gun-shy

Words marked △ may be spelled also with a capital letter

GHOORS	sorgho
GHORTU	rought
	trough
GHORTW	growth
GHORUY	roughy
GHOSTU	sought
GHOSTY	ghosty
GHPSUU	upgush
GIIKLN	liking
GIIKNR	girkin
GIIKNS	skiing
GIIKNT	kiting
GIIKNV	△viking
GIILMN	liming
GIILNN	lignin
	lining
GIILNP	piling
GIILNR	riglin
GIILNT	tiling
GIILNV	living
GIIMNN	mingin
	mining
GIIMNT	timing
GIINNN	inning
GIINOR	origin
GIINOY	yogini
GIINPP	piping
GIINPW	wiping
GIINRS	rising
GIINRT	tiring
GIINRV	△virgin
GIINRW	wiring
GIINSZ	sizing
GIJLNU	jungli
GIJLNY	jingly
GIJNOY	joying
GIKLNY	kingly
GIKNNU	unking
GIKNOP	poking
GIKNOY	yoking
GIKNSY	skying
GIKRTU	tugrik
GILLNU	ulling
GILLOO	loligo
GILLOR	rigoll
GILLOT	ill-got
GILLUY	uglily
GILMNU	lignum
GILMRY	grimly
GILNOO	logion
GILNOP	loping
	poling
GILNOR	loring
GILNOS	losing
GILNOT	lingot
	tiglon
	toling
GILNOV	loving
GILNOW	lowing
GILNPU	plug-in
	puling
GILNPY	plying
GILNRU	ruling
GILNSY	singly
GILNTU	luting
	ungilt
GILNTY	tingly
GILORY	gorily
GILRSY	grisly
GILRTY	trigly
GILTUY	guilty
GILTYZ	glitzy
GIMMOR	gimmor
GIMNNO	mignon
GIMNOV	moving
GIMNOW	mowing
GIMNOY	ignomy
GIMNPU	impugn
GIMNRU	ingrum
GIMNSU	musing
GIMORS	simorg
GIMOSS	gismos
GIMOSY	yogism
GIMOSZ	gizmos
GIMOTU	gomuti
GIMRSU	simurg
GINNOO	gonion
GINNOS	nosing
GINNOT	toning
GINNOW	woning
GINNOZ	zoning
GINNRU	urning
GINNSU	Ngunis
GINNTU	tuning
GINOOS	isogon
GINOOW	wooing
GINOPR	proign
	proing
	roping
GINOPS	pingos
	posing
GINORS	grison
	△signor
GINORT	trigon
GINORV	roving
GINORW	rowing
GINOSS	gnosis
GINOST	stingo
GINOSW	sowing
GINOTU	outing
GINOTW	towing
GINOTY	toying
GINPPU	upping
GINPRS	△spring
GINPRY	prying
GINPSY	pigsny
	spying
GINPTU	pignut
GINPTY	typing
GINRRU	runrig
GINRST	string
GINRTU	ungirt
GINRTY	trying
GINSTY	stingy
	stying
GINSUU	unguis
GINSUX	six-gun
GINSWY	swingy
GIOORV	vigoro
GIOPPS	gippos
GIOPSS	gossip
GIOPST	spigot
GIORRU	rigour
GIORSU	guiros
GIORTU	rig-out
GIORUV	vigour
GIOSTU	giusto
GIPPRY	grippy
GIPSTY	pigsty
GIRTTY	gritty
GJLNUY	jungly
GJNRUU	gurjun
GKMOOU	gomoku
GLLMUY	glumly
GLLNOY	longly
GLLOOP	gollop
GLMNOO	△mongol
GLMOOY	gloomy
GLMOSU	moguls
GLMPSU	glumps
GLMPUY	glumpy
GLMRUY	grumly
GLMSUY	smugly
GLNOOO	oolong
GLNOOS	so-long
GLNOOU	oulong
GLNPUU	unplug
GLNSUY	snugly
GLOOOY	oology
GLOOPY	gloopy
GLOORY	grooly
GLOOSW	go-slow
GLOPTU	putlog
GLORWY	growly
GLOSSY	glossy
GLSUUV	vulgus
GMNNOO	gnomon
GMNOST	'mongst
GMNOSU	mungos
GMNTUU	gumnut
GMNUUZ	mzungu
GMOOPR	pogrom
GMOOTU	gomuto
GMPRSU	grumps
GMPRUY	grumpy
GMPSUY	gypsum
GNNOUW	ungown
GNNSUU	unsung
GNOOPS	pongos
GNOORT	trogon
GNOPPU	oppugn
	pop-gun
GNOPRS	sprong
GNOPSY	spongy
GNOPTU	potgun
GNORST	strong
GNORTY	Trygon
GNOTUU	outgun
GNPRSU	sprung
GNRSTU	strung
GNSTUU	Tungus
GOOOOR	gooroo
GOOPST	stop-go
GOORSS	sorgos
GOORTT	grotto
GOORVY	groovy
GOPPSY	gyppos
GOPRTU	T-group
GOPRUW	upgrow
GOPRUY	groupy
GORRTU	turgor
GORSUU	rugous
GORSUY	gyrous
GORTTU	gutrot
	rotgut
GORTTY	grotty
GORTUY	grouty
	yogurt
GOSTUY	gousty
GSYYYZ	syzygy

H

HHIOPP	hip-hop
HHISSY	shyish
HHISTW	whisht
HHMMUU	humhum
HHMRTY	rhythm
HHOOOY	yo-ho-ho
HHOOSW	whoosh
HHRSTU	thrush
HIIKLM	khilim
HIIMMS	mishmi
HIIMNS	minish
HIIMPS	impish
HIIMSS	Shiism
HIIMST	mishit
HIINPS	inship
HIINTW	inwith
	within
HIIRST	Tishri
HIITTW	with-it
HIJOSS	shojis
HIKMUZ	muzhik
HIKNRS	shrink
HIKSSY	skyish
HIKSTY	tykish
HIKSWY	whisky
HILLOY	holily
HILLPU	uphill
HILLRS	shrill
HILLRT	thrill
HILLWY	whilly
HILMOS	holism
HILMOW	whilom
HILMOY	homily
HILMSU	mulish
HILMSY	hylism

HILNPT plinth
HILNTY thinly
HILOOT tholoi
HILOPS △polish
HILOST holist
lithos
HILOSW owlish
HILPST spilth
HILRWY whirly
HILSSY slyish
HILSTW whilst
HILSTY hylist
HIMMSU Humism
HIMMSY shimmy
HIMMWY whimmy
HIMNOY hominy
HIMNSU munshi
HIMOPS mopish
Ophism
HIMORS morish
Romish
HIMPRS shrimp
HIMSTU Humist
HIMSTY smithy
HIMSWY whimsy
HINNSY shinny
HINNTU thin'un
HINNWY whinny
HINOOP inhoop
HINOOS shoo-in
HINOPS siphon
HINORS rhinos
HINOST Shinto
tonish
HINPSU punish
unship
HINPSX △sphinx
HINRSU inrush
HINSTU shut-in
HINSTY shinty
HINSUV Vishnu
HINSUW unwish
HIOOSV shivoo
HIOPPS hippos
popish
shippo
HIOPRT trophi
HIOPST pithos
HIOPSY physio
HIOSTY toyish
HIOTTU outhit
HIPPSU hippus
uppish
HIPPWY whippy
HIPRST thrips
HIQSSU squish
HIRRWY whirry
HIRSTT thirst
thrist
T-shirt
HIRSTY shirty
thyrsi

HIRTTY thirty
HISSWY swishy
HISTTY shitty
stithy
HJNNOY △johnny
HKNOOU unhook
HKNOSY shonky
HKNRSU shrunk
HKNSUU unhusk
HKOOPU hook-up
HKOOSS skoosh
HKOOST shtook
HKOSSY Hyksos
HLLOOS hollos
HLLOOW hollow
HLLOPY phyllo
HLLOSU hullos
HLLOWY wholly
HLLSUY lushly
HLMOOS sholom
HLMOTY thymol
HLMPUY phylum
HLNOUY unholy
HLOOSS sloosh
HLOOST tholos
HLOPSS splosh
HLOPSY poshly
HLORUY hourly
HLOSSY sloshy
HLOSTU tholus
HLPRUU uphurl
HLPSUY plushy
HLPSYY sylphy
HLSSUY slushy
HMMMUU hummum
HMMSTU shtumm
HMMSUU hummus
HMNOPY nympho
HMNOST months
HMNPUY hypnum
HMOOPR morpho
HMOOST shtoom
smooth
HMORUU humour
HMOSTU mouths
HMOSTY mythos
HMOSUU houmus
humous
HMOTUY mouthy
HMPRUY murphy
HMPTUY humpty
tumphy
HMSTUY mythus
thymus
HMSUUY humusy
HMTUYZ zythum
HNNOOP phonon
HNOOPT photon
HNOOPU unhoop
HNOORS horson
HNOORT thoron
HNOORU honour

HNOOSW no-show
HNOPSU nosh-up
HNOPSY Hypnos
syphon
HNOPTY phyton
△python
△typhon
HNORSU onrush
HNORTW thrown
HNORTY rhyton
thorny
HNOSTU unshot
HNOTWY why-not
HNRTUU unhurt
HNSTUU unshut
HOOOOR hooroo
HOOOOY yoo-hoo
HOOPST photos
HOOPSW whoops
HOOPTT hotpot
HOORRR horror
HOORST orthos
HOORUZ huzoor
HOOSSW swoosh
HOOTTY toothy
HOOTUW tu-whoo
HOPPSY shoppy
HOPRTY trophy
HOPSSY hyssop
phossy
sposhy
HOPSTU Pushto
tophus
upshot
HORSST shorts
HORSTY hostry
shorty
HORTWY worthy
HOSSTU stoush
HOSTTU stouth
HOSTUY youths
HOTUYY youthy
HPPSUU push-up
HPRSSU sprush
HPRSUU uprush
HPSTUU Pushtu
HPSTUY typhus
HRSTTU thrust
HRTTUY truthy

I

IIIMRT miriti
IIIRST iritis
IIJMNY jiminy
IIKKNR kirkin'
IIKMNS simkin
IIKNPP pipkin
IIKNSS siskin
IIKOST oikist
IIKOTT titoki
IILLMU Lilium
IILLOT til-oil

IILLOY oilily
IILLPU illupi
IILLWY wilily
IILMNO nim-oil
IILMST limits
IILNNU inulin
IILNOV violin
IILNRT nirlit
IILNRV rivlin
IILNST instil
IILNTY tinily
IILPST pistil
IILRWY wirily
IILSTU ulitis
IILTTW twilit
IIMMNU minium
IIMNNO minion
IIMNOS Ionism
IIMNOU ionium
IIMOSS miosis
IIMSSS missis
IIMSSZ sizism
IIMSTT timist
IINNOP pinion
IINNPY Pinyin
IINNTU Innuit
IINORV virino
virion
IINOST Ionist
IINOSV vision
IINPPP pippin
IINPRT pirnit
IINPTX pinxit
IINSST insist
IINSTU in-situ
IINTTU intuit
IINTTW nitwit
IIOOTT toitoi
IIORSS Osiris
IIOSTT otitis
IIPPUU piupiu
IIPRST △spirit
IIPRTU pituri
IIQTUV qiviut
IIRRTT tirrit
IIRSSU Sirius
IISSTZ sizist
IJKMOU moujik
IJKNOS joskin
IJLMPY jimply
IJMOSS jissom
IJNORU △junior
IJNRUY injury
IJRSTU jurist
IKKORR korkir
IKKUUY △kikuyu
IKLLSS skills
IKLLSY skilly
IKLLTU killut
IKLNNU unlink
IKLNOO look-in
IKLNOU ulikon

IKLNPU	link-up
	uplink
IKLNSY	slinky
IKLNTY	tinkly
IKLSSU	suslik
IKLTTU	kittul
IKLTTY	kittly
IKMNOO	kimono
IKMNOR	mikron
	morkin
IKMNRU	rumkin
IKMORS	Morisk
IKMPRS	skrimp
IKMPSY	skimpy
IKMRSY	smirky
IKMSSU	kumiss
IKNNSY	skinny
IKNNTU	unknit
IKNOPS	pinkos
IKNOPT	inkpot
IKNORW	inwork
	work-in
IKNOST	stinko
IKNPTU	upknit
IKNSST	stinks
IKNSSU	unkiss
IKNSTW	swink't
IKOOPT	pookit
IKOORS	irokos
IKOPTU	poukit
IKPPSY	skippy
IKPRSU	△prusik
	spruik
IKQRUY	quirky
IKRSSU	Russki
IKRSTU	turkis
IKSVVY	skivvy
ILLMOU	lolium
ILLMPY	limply
ILLMSY	slimly
ILLNOY	lionly
ILLNPU	pull-in
ILLNUW	unwill
ILLOPW	pillow
ILLORT	trillo
ILLOWW	willow
ILLPTU	up-till
ILLPUV	pulvil
ILLQSU	squill
ILLSTY	stilly
ILLSUV	villus
ILLTWY	twilly
ILMMSU	Muslim
ILMNOU	moulin
ILMNRU	murlin
ILMNSU	muslin
ILMOSS	lissom
ILMOSU	limous
ILMOTU	ultimo
ILMPPY	pimply
ILMPRY	primly
ILMPSY	simply
ILMRSY	lyrism
ILMRTY	trimly
ILMSSY	slimsy
ILMSTU	litmus
ILMSUV	Milvus
ILMTUU	tumuli
ILMYZZ	mizzly
ILNOOS	solion
ILNOOT	lotion
ILNOPP	poplin
ILNOPS	slip-on
ILNOPT	pontil
ILNOQU	quinol
ILNOST	Nilots
	tonsil
ILNOSU	insoul
ILNOSY	nosily
ILNOTU	oilnut
	ultion
ILNOTW	Wilton
ILNPRU	purlin
ILNPST	splint
ILNPUY	punily
ILNRTY	nitryl
ILNSTU	insult
	sunlit
ILOOPS	polios
ILOORT	loriot
ILOOST	solito
ILOOYZ	oozily
ILOPPY	polypi
ILOPRX	prolix
ILOPRY	ropily
ILOPSS	spoils
ILOPST	pistol
	postil
	spoilt
ILOPSU	pilous
ILOPSX	oxslip
ILOPTU	loupit
ILOPTY	polity
ILOQRU	liquor
ILORSY	rosily
ILORTU	toruli
ILOSSU	ulosis
ILOSTW	lowsit
ILOTTW	wittol
ILPPRY	ripply
ILPPSU	slip-up
ILPPSY	slippy
ILPPTU	pulpit
ILPRTY	triply
ILPSST	splits
ILPTTU	uptilt
ILRSTU	trisul
ILRSTY	lyrist
ILRSWY	swirly
ILRTWY	twirly
ILSTTU	lutist
ILSTTY	stilty
ILSTUU	lituus
ILSTWY	wistly
IMMNOS	monism
	nomism
	'simmon
IMMNOU	omnium
IMMOOS	simoom
IMMOSU	osmium
IMMOTU	tomium
IMMSTU	mutism
	summit
IMMSWY	swimmy
IMNNOW	minnow
IMNNTU	muntin
IMNOOR	morion
IMNOOS	simoon
IMNOOT	motion
IMNORS	minors
IMNOST	inmost
	monist
IMNOSY	myosin
	simony
IMNRRU	murrin
IMNRTU	untrim
IMNRUY	unmiry
IMNTUY	mutiny
IMOOTV	vomito
IMOPRS	porism
	primos
IMOPRT	import
IMOPRV	improv
IMOPST	impost
IMORRR	mirror
IMORRS	morris
IMORSU	rimous
IMOSSY	myosis
IMOSTU	ostium
	timous
IMOTTT	tomtit
IMOTYY	moyity
IMPRSS	prisms
IMPRSU	Primus®
	primus
	purism
IMPRSY	prismy
IMPSTU	sumpit
IMQRSU	squirm
IMRRSY	smirry
IMRSSY	Syrism
IMRSTU	truism
IMRSUU	miurus
IMSSSU	missus
IMSSTU	misust
INNOOT	notion
INNOOY	oniony
INNOPP	Nippon
INNORT	intron
INNORW	inworn
INNOSU	unison
INNOTW	intown
INNOWW	winnow
INNPSY	spinny
INNRTU	turn-in
INOOPS	poison
INOOPT	option
	potion
INOORS	orison
INOORZ	zorino
INOOST	toison
INOPPR	poprin
	Rippon
INOPRS	prison
INOPST	pintos
	piston
	points
INOPTT	tinpot
INOPTY	pointy
INORST	intros
INORSY	rosiny
INORTT	△triton
INORTU	turion
INOSTU	ustion
INOSUV	vinous
INOTUW	outwin
INOTVY	novity
INPPSY	snippy
INPRST	sprint
INPRTU	turnip
INPSUY	puisny
INQSTU	squint
INQSUY	quinsy
	squiny
INRSXY	syrinx
INRTVY	vintry
INRTWY	wintry
INSTTY	stinty
INSTUU	unsuit
INSTUW	unwist
IOOPRT	roopit
IOOSSS	sissoo
IOPPPT	poppit
IOPPTT	tiptop
IOPPTZ	ziptop
IOPQSU	quipos
IOPRRY	priory
IOPRST	prosit
	tripos
IOPRTU	roupit
IOPSST	ptosis
IOPSTU	putois
IOQSTU	quoist
	quoits
IORRTW	worrit
IORRTY	riotry
IORRZZ	rizzor
IORSSU	urosis
IORSTU	suitor
IORSUV	virous
IOSSTT	tsotsi
IOSSTV	vistos
IOSTTU	outsit
IOSTXY	xystoi
IOTTUW	outwit
IPPSSU	piss-up
IPPTUY	uppity
IPRRTU	irrupt

IPRSST stirps
IPRSSY prissy
IPRSTU purist
spruit
uprist
IPRSTY stripy
IPRTUY purity
IPSTTY typist
IPSTXY ptyxis
IPSVVY spivvy
IPTTTU tittup
IPTTUY titupy
IQRRSU squirr
IQRSTU squirt
IRSSTU tsuris
IRSSTY syrtis
IRSTWY wristy
IRTTUX tutrix
ISSSTU tussis
ISTTWY twisty

J

JLSTUY justly
JMPPUU jump-up
JNNOTU jötunn
JNOORU journo
JNOSTU juntos
JNSTUU unjust
JOOPPY joy-pop
popjoy
JOOSUY joyous
JOTTUU outjut

K

KKLMUU mukluk
KKLUUX Ku-Klux
KKNRUU kunkur
KKOSTU Sukkot
KLLOSY skolly
KLNOPY plonky
KLNRUY knurly
KLOOPU uplook
KLRTUU Kultur
KMOOSS kosmos
smokos
KMPRSU skrump
KNNOTU unknot
KNOORR kronor
KNOORS Kronos
KNOOSS snooks
KNORRU krónur
KNORUW unwork
KNOTTY knotty
KNPSUY spunky
KNRSTU trunks
KOOPSY spooky
KOORST strook
KOORSU kouros
KOOTWW kowtow
KRRSUY skurry
KRSSUY Russky

L

LLLOOP lollop
LLLOOT tol-lol
LLMMUU mulmul
LLNOOR roll-on
LLNOPU pull-on
LLNORU unroll
LLOOTU toluol
LLOOWY woolly
LLOPRU roll-up
uproll
LLOPUX Pollux
LLORST stroll
LLORTY trolly
LLOSWY slowly
LLPPUU pull-up
LMMOUX lummox
LMMPUY plummy
LMMSUY slummy
LMMTUU multum
LMOORU ormolu
LMOOSY sloomy
LMORSU musrol
LMOSTY mostly
LMPPUY plumpy
LMPSUY slumpy
LMTTUU tumult
LNOOPY polony
LNOOST stolon
LNOPSY pylons
LNOPTU pluton
pulton
LNOSTU unlost
LNOSUU unsoul
LNOTWY townly
LNPTUU pultun
LNRUUY unruly
LNSSTU stuns'l
LOOORT rotolo
LOOPRY poorly
LOOSST stools
LOOSTT lottos
LOOSTV volost
LOOVVX volvox
LOPPPY popply
LOPPRY propyl
LOPPSY polyps
sloppy
LOPRTY portly
protyl
LOPSUU opulus
LOPSUW slow-up
LOPTTY plotty
LOPTWY two-ply
LORSUY sourly
LORTTY trotyl
LOSSTY stylos
LOSTYZ zlotys
LOSYZZ sozzly
LPPRUY purply
LPPSUY supply
LPRSYY spryly
LRRSUY slurry
LRSTUY sultry
LRUUXY luxury
LSSTUY stylus
LSTTUY suttly

M

MMNOOR Mormon
MMNOSU musmon
summon
MMOOPP pompom
MMOOTT motmot
tom-tom
MMRRUU murmur
MMTTUU tum-tum
MMTUUU mutuum
MMUUUU muu-muu
MMUUYY yum-yum
MNNOUW unmown
MNOOPP pompon
MNOOPT tompon
MNOORU unmoor
MNOOSY monosy
MNOOTU mouton
MNOOTW Motown®
towmon
MNORSU Munros
MNOTTU mutton
MNOTUY Mounty
MNPTUY numpty
MOOPRS promos
MOOPRY pomroy
MOORRS morros
MOORRW morrow
MOORTY motory
MOOSSU osmous
MOPPRT prompt
MOPSSU Possum®
possum
'possum
MOPSTU upmost
MOQRUU quorum
MOQTUU quotum
MORRUU rumour
MORSTY stormy
MORTUU tumour
MOSTTU utmost
MOSTUU outsum
MPRSTU trumps
MPRSUU rumpus
MPSSTU stumps
MPSTUU sputum
MPSTUY stumpy
MRRSUY smurry
MRSTUY Myrtus
MSTTUY smutty

N

NNOOPT ponton
NNOORY ronyon
NNORTU turn-on
untorn
NNORUW unworn
NNOSUW unsown
NNOTUW unwont
NNPSUU unspun
NNRTUU unturn
NOOPRT pronto
proton
NOOPST spot-on
NOOPSY poyson
snoopy
spoony
NOORRY Norroy
NOORST tonsor
NOORTU notour
unroot
NOOSST nostos
NOOSTY snooty
NOOSUY noyous
NOOSYZ snoozy
NOOTTU not-out
NOPPRU unprop
NOPRTU uptorn
NOPSTU puntos
unstop
NOPTUW uptown
NORSTW strown
NORSTY snorty
NORTUU outrun
NOSTTY snotty
NOSTUW unstow
NOSTUY snouty
NPRSUU prunus
NPRTUU turn-up
upturn
NRSTTU strunt

O

OOOOPP poo-poo
OOOOTT too-too
OOOOZZ zoozoo
OOPPRT troppo
OOPRRT torpor
OOPRST troops
OOPRSU porous
OOPRSV Provos
OOPRTU uproot
OOPSTT pottos
OOPTTU opt-out
outtop
OOPWWW powwow
OORRSW sorrow
OORRSZ zorros
OORSST torsos
OORSTU torous
OORSTY rootsy
OOSTTY tootsy
OOUUWW wou-wou
OOWWWW wow-wow
OPRSST sports

OPRSTU	sprout
	stroup
	stupor
OPRSTY	sporty
OPSSTU	toss-up
OPSTTY	spotty
OPSTUY	spouty
OPTTUU	output
ORSTTU	strout
	trouts
ORSTUY	stoury
ORTTUY	trouty
	try-out
OSSTXY	xystos

P

PPTTUU	put-put
PRRSUY	spurry
PRSTUY	upryst
PRSUYY	syrupy

R

RSTTUY	trusty

S

SSTUXY	xystus

T

TTTTUU	tut-tut

7AAA

A

AAAADNP	apadana
AAAALTY	atalaya
AAABBCL	cabbala
AAABBKL	kabbala
AAABCCR	baccara
AAABCIR	arabica
AAABCLV	baclava
AAABCMR	caramba
AAABCNR	baracan
AAABCOR	carabao
AAABCTW	catawba
AAABDLM	lambada
AAABDNN	bandana
AAABEGL	galabea
AAABENS	Sabaean
AAABFLL	falbala
AAABGIL	galabia
AAABHLQ	qabalah
AAABHNS	Sabahan
AAABILX	abaxial
AAABINR	Arabian
AAABKLV	baklava
AAABLLW	wallaba
AAABLPR	palabra
AAABMOS	abomasa
AAABMST	mastaba
AAABNNR	rabanna
AAABNNS	bananas
AAABNPR	Pan-Arab
AAABORR	araroba
AAABRSX	△abraxas
AAACCIS	acacias
AAACCLR	caracal
AAACCRS	cascara
AAACDIN	Acadian
AAACDIR	Acarida
AAACDLU	acaudal
AAACDMM	macadam
AAACEER	Araceae
AAACEHN	Achaean
AAACENP	panacea
AAACGNT	agaçant
AAACHHL	Halacha
AAACHIN	Achaian
AAACHLZ	chalaza
AAACHNT	acantha
AAACHRY	acharya
AAACIJM	Jamaica
AAACILM	malacia
AAACIMR	Aramaic
	cariama
AAACINP	acapnia
AAACINR	acarian
	Acarina
AAACINT	Cataian
AAACJMR	jacamar
AAACJNN	Canajan
AAACLLV	cavalla
AAACLMN	almanac
	mancala
AAACLNT	cantala
	Catalan
AAACLPT	catalpa
AAACLRZ	alcázar
AAACMNP	campana
AAACMRS	maracas
	mascara
AAACNNR	caranna
AAACNPT	catapan
AAACNRT	nacarat
AAACNRU	carauna
AAACNRV	caravan
AAACNST	canasta
AAACNTT	cantata
AAACNTY	Catayan
AAACRWY	caraway
AAACSST	cassata
AAACSSV	cassava
AAACSTT	catasta
AAADELM	alameda
AAADFRY	faraday
AAADGGH	Haggada
AAADGHL	Galahad
AAADHMR	adharma
AAADILX	adaxial
AAADIRT	dataria
	△radiata
AAADJMR	jamadar
AAADKNN	Kannada
AAADLMN	mandala
AAADLMW	wadmaal
AAADMNR	Ramadan
AAADMNT	adamant
AAADMRS	madrasa
AAADNRS	sardana
AAADNRT	tanadar
AAAEENR	Araneae
AAAEGLT	galatea
AAAEGNP	apanage
	Pangaea
AAAEHLT	althaea
AAAEIMN	anaemia
AAAELMP	palamae
AAAENST	anatase
AAAERWY	areaway
AAAFFLL	alfalfa
AAAFHLS	Falasha
AAAFIRT	ratafia
AAAFNRS	sarafan
AAAFRWY	faraway
AAAGGLN	galanga
AAAGHIP	aphagia
AAAGHLN	langaha
AAAGHNT	ataghan
AAAGHPR	agrapha
AAAGINP	Panagia
AAAGINZ	gazania
AAAGIPT	patagia
AAAGISS	assagai
AAAGLMM	amalgam
AAAGLMN	nagmaal
AAAGLNS	lasagna
AAAGMMT	magmata
AAAGMNR	anagram
AAAGMNS	sagaman
AAAGMTT	tagmata
AAAGNPR	pargana
AAAGNRT	△tanagra
AAAGNRU	guaraná
AAAGNTY	yatagan
AAAHHKL	Halakah
AAAHHLV	halavah
AAAHIKW	kahawai

AAAHIPS	aphasia
AAAHJKW	kajawah
AAAHLMR	harmala
AAAHLNN	alannah
AAAHMMT	mahatma
AAAHMRS	ashrama
AAAHMRT	Maratha
AAAHMST	tamasha
AAAHNRS	Saharan
AAAHPRT	paratha
AAAHRTW	waratah
AAAIKLT	Latakia
AAAILMR	malaria
AAAILNX	anaxial
AAAILPS	aplasia
AAAILRT	talaria
AAAILST	Alsatia
AAAIMNT	amanita
AAAINNS	Ananias
AAAINNZ	Azanian
AAAIPRX	apraxia
AAAIPSS	Aspasia
AAAIQRU	aquaria
AAAIRWZ	waza-ari
AAAJMPS	pajamas
AAAKKMR	markkaa
AAALLPT	palatal
AAALMMY	Malayam
AAALMNY	Malayan
AAALMRS	Marsala
AAALMSS	salaams
AAALNNT	lantana
AAALNPT	aplanat
AAALRRY	arrayal
AAALWYY	layaway
AAAMNRT	amarant
	Maranta
AAAMNRY	Aymaran
AAAMNST	atamans
AAAMNTY	manyata
AAAMORT	tamarao
AAAMPRT	patamar
AAAMRRZ	zamarra
AAAMRSS	samsara
AAAMRSY	Aymaras
AAAMRTU	tamarau
AAANNSV	savanna
AAANNTT	annatta
AAANRTT	tantara
	tartana
AAANSST	Satanas
AAAOPRZ	△parazoa
AAAPPRT	apparat
AAAPRSS	apsaras
AAARTTT	rat-a-tat
AAARTTU	tuatara
AAARTXY	ataraxy
AABBCEG	cabbage
AABBCGY	cabbagy
AABBDGR	gabbard
AABBDHS	habdabs
AABBDIS	Abbasid
AABBEGN	beanbag
AABBEIS	Babesia
AABBELT	batable
AABBERT	barbate
AABBGGR	grab-bag
AABBGRT	gabbart
AABBGRY	rag-baby
AABBHST	Sabbath
AABBLOR	barbola
AABBNRY	Barnaby
AABBRRY	Barbary
AABBRSS	bass-bar
AABBSSU	babassu
AABCCEH	Bacchae
AABCCEL	accablé
AABCCER	baccare
AABCCET	baccate
AABCCIR	braccia
AABCDIR	carabid
AABCEKR	backare
AABCELN	△balance
	balancé
AABCELP	capable
	pacable
AABCELT	actable
AABCEMR	macabre
AABCEMS	ambs-ace
AABCEPR	pea-crab
AABCERR	barrace
AABCERT	abreact
	bear-cat
	cabaret
AABCHMT	ambatch
AABCHNR	barchan
AABCHOR	abroach
AABCILM	cambial
AABCILN	Caliban
AABCINR	carabin
	Cariban
AABCIOP	copaiba
AABCITX	taxicab
AABCKLY	layback
AABCKNN	canbank
AABCKNR	cab-rank
AABCKPY	backpay
	payback
AABCKRR	barrack
AABCKSW	backsaw
AABCLMU	calumba
AABCLSY	scybala
AABCMSU	sambuca
AABCORT	abactor
	acrobat
AABCOST	Tabasco®
AABCOTT	catboat
AABCRSU	Carabus
AABCTTU	cattabu
AABDDIK	kabaddi
AABDDIN	Band-aid®
	band-aid
AABDDNO	Abaddon
AABDEFL	fadable
AABDEGN	bandage
AABDEHS	abashed
AABDEIS	diabase
AABDELL	ballade
AABDELT	datable
AABDEMN	beadman
AABDENU	bandeau
AABDGHN	handbag
AABDGMO	gambado
AABDGNS	sandbag
AABDGRR	drag-bar
AABDHMS	badmash
AABDHNT	hatband
AABDHNY	hayband
AABDHRS	bardash
AABDHRU	Bahadur
AABDIIS	basidia
AABDIKR	bidarka
AABDILN	baladin
AABDIMR	barmaid
AABDINT	tabanid
AABDIOT	biodata
AABDLNS	salband
AABDLRW	bradawl
AABDMNR	armband
AABDNNO	abandon
AABDNOR	bandora
AABDNRU	bandura
AABDNSW	band-saw
AABDORV	bravado
AABDOTY	day-boat
AABDRRW	drawbar
AABDRST	bastard
AABDRSU	subadar
AABDSTU	databus
AABEEHW	Wahabee
AABEELT	eatable
AABEEMO	amoebae
AABEERZ	zareeba
AABEEST	sea-beat
AABEFFL	affable
AABEFFN	beffana
AABEFGL	flea-bag
AABEFGU	aufgabe
AABEGGG	baggage
AABEGGR	garbage
AABEGLR	algebra
AABEGMR	bergama
	megabar
AABEGMS	ambages
AABEGRR	bagarre
	barrage
AABEGSS	bagasse
AABEGSU	abusage
AABEHIT	Bahaite
AABEHLT	hatable
AABEHNT	abthane
AABEHRS	earbash
AABEIKN	ikebana
AABEILM	amabile
	amiable

Words marked △ may be spelled also with a capital letter

AABEILT	Baalite
	labiate
AABEIRS	airbase
	arabise
AABEIRZ	arabize
AABEJLL	jellaba
AABEJMU	jambeau
AABEKLM	makable
AABEKLT	takable
AABEKNS	seabank
AABELLL	labella
AABELLM	lamb-ale
AABELLN	balneal
AABELLS	sabella
	salable
AABELMN	namable
AABELMT	tamable
AABELNO	abalone
AABELPP	papable
AABELPR	parable
AABELPY	payable
AABELRT	ratable
AABELST	astable
AABELSV	savable
AABELSY	sayable
AABELTT	abettal
AABELTU	tableau
	tabulae
AABELTV	vatable
AABELTX	taxable
AABEMNS	baseman
AABEMOS	amoebas
AABENNW	wannabe
AABENRT	antbear
AABENTY	abeyant
AABERST	abreast
AABERSU	subarea
AABERTT	rabatte
	tabaret
AABERTU	abature
AABETUX	bateaux
AABFFLY	affably
AABFILU	fabliau
AABFLRU	fabular
AABGHNR	bhangra
AABGHNS	gabnash
	nashgab
AABGHPU	Buphaga
AABGHSW	bagwash
AABGIIL	abigail
AABGILM	mailbag
AABGINR	bargain
AABHHIS	sahibah
AABHHKS	sabkhah
AABHHRU	bruhaha
AABHIMS	Bahaism
AABHIRT	air-bath
	Bharati
AABHIST	Bahaist
AABHITT	habitat
AABHKNR	barkhan
AABHKST	sabkhat
AABHLTY	bathyal
AABHMNR	Brahman
AABHOST	Sabaoth
AABHSUU	Bauhaus
AABIIKS	Baisaki
AABIILX	biaxial
AABIJMY	jambiya
AABIJNP	Panjabi
AABIKNS	banksia
AABILLR	barilla
AABILMN	bimanal
AABILMS	Baalism
AABILMY	amiably
AABILOU	aboulia
AABILRS	basilar
AABILST	balista
AABIMMR	marimba
AABIMNO	bonamia
AABIMNZ	Zambian
AABIMRS	Arabism
AABIMSS	Sabaism
AABIMST	basmati
AABINOU	ouabain
AABINRT	atabrin
AABINST	abstain
	Tsabian
AABIPUX	paxiuba
AABIRST	Arabist
AABIRSV	Bravais
AABISTT	abattis
AABKNRT	tanbark
AABKOOZ	bazooka
AABLLNT	ballant
AABLLNY	banally
AABLLPT	patball
AABLLST	ballast
AABLLSY	salably
AABLLWY	wallaby
AABLMRU	labarum
AABLMST	lambast
AABLMSY	abysmal
	balsamy
AABLNSU	Balanus
AABLNTT	blatant
AABLORT	ablator
AABLOSV	lavabos
AABLPRU	pabular
AABLRST	arblast
AABLRTU	tabular
AABLRTY	ratably
AABLSSY	abyssal
AABLTTU	abuttal
AABLTXY	taxably
AABMNOT	boatman
AABMNST	batsman
AABMORU	marabou
AABMORZ	Mozarab
AABMRTU	tambura
AABMSSY	ambassy
AABNNOZ	bonanza
AABNOST	sabaton
AABNRSY	Ray-Bans®
AABNSTU	Tabanus
AABOPPT	pap-boat
AABORSZ	abrazos
AABOTTY	attaboy
AABQSUU	subaqua
	sub-aqua
AABRRSU	saburra
AABRRUV	bravura
AABSSSY	sassaby
AABTTTU	battuta
AABZZZZ	bazzazz
AACCDEM	medacca
AACCDES	cascade
	saccade
AACCDIR	cardiac
AACCEET	Cetacea
AACCEIR	Circaea
AACCEKR	carcake
AACCELO	cloacae
AACCENV	vacance
AACCEPS	cap-case
AACCERS	carcase
AACCEST	saccate
AACCHHK	kachcha
AACCHIN	chicana
AACCHIR	archaic
AACCHLN	clachan
AACCHMP	champac
AACCHNN	cannach
AACCILM	acclaim
AACCILS	Alcaics
AACCIOR	△carioca
AACCITT	atactic
AACCKLP	calpack
AACCKRR	carrack
AACCLLO	cloacal
AACCLLT	catcall
AACCLOP	polacca
AACCLOR	caracol
AACCLPT	placcat
AACCLRU	accrual
	caracul
AACCLSU	accusal
AACCLTU	Lactuca
AACCMOS	macacos
AACCNVY	vacancy
AACCORT	car-coat
AACCORU	curaçao
	curaçoa
AACCOST	accoast
AACCOTT	toccata
AACCRRT	carract
AACCRSS	carcass
AACDDEL	decadal
AACDDER	arcaded
AACDDET	dead-cat
AACDDHR	chaddar
AACDDIN	candida
AACDEEM	academe
AACDEFL	falcade
AACDEHM	chamade
AACDEHR	charade

AACDEHT	cathead
AACDEII	aecidia
AACDEIL	alcaide
AACDEIN	aidance
	Canidae
AACDELL	alcalde
AACDELN	candela
	decanal
AACDELR	caldera
AACDELS	scalade
AACDELY	alcayde
AACDEMN	Cadmean
AACDEMY	academy
AACDENV	advance
AACDENZ	cadenza
AACDERV	cadaver
AACDETU	caudate
AACDEUX	cadeaux
AACDFIR	faradic
AACDHMR	drachma
AACDHNR	handcar
AACDIIS	ascidia
AACDIJU	Judaica
AACDILR	△radical
AACDINT	antacid
AACDINV	vanadic
AACDIOR	acaroid
AACDIRS	ascarid
AACDJKW	jackdaw
AACDLNO	calando
AACDLNS	scandal
AACDLOR	carload
AACDLOS	scalado
AACDLOY	day-coal
AACDLPR	placard
AACDNRS	cadrans
AACDOOV	avocado
AACDRSS	csárdás
AACDRST	dart-sac
AACDRSZ	czardas
AACEEGR	acreage
AACEEHR	earache
AACEEHT	chaetae
AACEELM	mace-ale
AACEELN	anelace
AACEEMR	camerae
AACEEMS	ames-ace
AACEENT	catenae
AACEERT	acerate
AACEETT	acetate
AACEFFT	fat-face
AACEFLT	falcate
AACEFLU	faculae
AACEFMN	faceman
AACEFRR	carfare
AACEGGR	aggrace
AACEGKP	package
AACEGKS	sackage
AACEGNR	carnage
	cranage
AACEGRT	cartage
AACEGSV	scavage
AACEHLP	acaleph
AACEHLR	alchera
AACEHNO	choanae
AACEHNP	panache
AACEHNR	acharné
AACEHNS	Aeschna
AACEHPP	appeach
AACEHPU	chapeau
AACEHRT	trachea
AACEHST	△achates
AACEHTT	attaché
AACEHTU	château
AACEHWY	each-way
AACEIMN	anaemic
AACEIMU	camaïeu
AACEINN	Nicaean
AACEINR	acarine
AACEIPP	cap-a-pie
	cap-à-pie
AACEIRV	avarice
	caviare
AACEKLL	lac-lake
AACEKMM	ack-emma
AACEKNP	pancake
AACEKNS	askance
AACEKOT	oatcake
AACELLN	canella
AACELLP	Capella
AACELLS	sacella
AACELLT	lacteal
AACELMN	lace-man
	manacle
AACELMR	cameral
	caramel
	ceramal
AACELMU	maculae
AACELNU	canulae
	lacunae
AACELNV	valance
AACELNY	Lycaena
AACELPT	placate
AACELRT	Lacerta
AACELRV	caravel
AACELST	lactase
AACELSW	case-law
AACELTT	lactate
AACELTV	clavate
AACEMMR	macramé
AACEMNS	caseman
AACEMNV	caveman
AACEMPR	paracme
AACEMQU	macaque
AACEMRS	cameras
AACENOT	Actaeon
AACENRS	Saracen
AACENRT	cateran
AACENST	catenas
AACENTT	cantate
AACENTY	cyanate
AACEOPT	pea-coat
AACEORS	rosacea
AACEPRT	caprate
	rate-cap
AACEPRU	capuera
AACEPRV	precava
AACERST	cat's-ear
AACERSU	caesura
AACERSZ	sazerac®
AACERTU	arcuate
AACERWY	raceway
AACETTU	actuate
AACETUV	vacuate
AACFFIL	caffila
AACFHLP	half-cap
AACFILS	fascial
AACFILU	faucial
AACFINR	African
AACFINT	fanatic
AACFLLU	falcula
AACFLLW	law-calf
AACFLLY	fallacy
AACFLPT	cat-flap
	flat-cap
AACFLRT	fractal
AACFLRU	facular
AACFLTU	factual
AACFRRU	farruca
AACGILL	glacial
AACGILM	magical
AACGILS	scaglia
AACGINT	agnatic
AACGIRV	agravic
AACGLOS	gas-coal
AACGLOT	catalog
AACGNOU	guanaco
AACHHKR	charkha
AACHHLL	challah
AACHIKN	kachina
AACHIKR	chikara
AACHILR	rachial
AACHILT	calathi
AACHIMN	Mahican
AACHIMR	Amharic
	machair
AACHIMS	chiasma
AACHIPS	aphasic
AACHIPT	chapati
AACHIRS	arachis
AACHIRT	Cathari
	cithara
AACHKMP	champak
AACHKRT	hatrack
AACHKSW	hack-saw
AACHLLN	challan
AACHLMS	chasmal
AACHLPP	chappal
AACHLPS	paschal
AACHLSU	acushla
AACHMNP	chapman
AACHNOP	panocha
AACHNOS	choanas
AACHNOU	huanaco
AACHNPX	panchax

AACHNRV	navarch
AACHNRY	anarchy
AACHRRT	catarrh
AACHRST	Cathars
AACHRSW	car-wash
AACHRWY	archway
AACIILN	lacinia
AACIILT	Ciliata
AACIINP	△apician
AACIINS	Asianic
AACIINT	actinia
AACIIST	Asiatic
AACIITV	viatica
AACIJLP	jalapic
AACIKLR	clarkia
AACIKNN	canakin
AACILMR	mail-car
AACILNR	Acrilan®
	clarain
	cranial
AACILNT	actinal
	alicant
AACILNZ	Zincala
AACILOS	asocial
AACILOX	coaxial
AACILPS	spacial
AACILPT	capital
	placita
AACILRR	rail-car
AACILUV	Avicula
AACIMMR	macrami
AACIMOR	acromia
AACIMPR	Campari
	picamar
AACINNT	cantina
AACINOR	Aaronic
	conaria
	ocarina
AACINPS	Capsian
AACINPT	capitan
	△captain
AACINRZ	czarina
AACINST	△satanic
AACINTV	Vatican
AACIOPT	tapioca
AACIOPV	copaiva
AACIPRS	Sarapic
AACIQTU	aquatic
AACIRSS	ascaris
AACIRST	caritas
AACIRTT	Tataric
AACISTT	astatic
AACJKMN	jackman
	manjack
	man-jack
AACJKSS	jackass
AACKLLL	lack-all
AACKLTW	cat-walk
AACKMNP	manpack
	packman
AACKMRT	amtrack
AACKNRS	ransack
AACKNRT	tank-car
AACKPRR	carpark
AACKPRT	pack-rat
	ratpack
AACKPWY	packway
AACLLNT	callant
AACLLNU	calluna
	lacunal
AACLLOR	coralla
AACLLSU	clausal
AACLLVY	cavally
AACLMNO	coalman
AACLMNT	calmant
	clamant
AACLMPR	arc-lamp
AACLMPT	palm-cat
AACLMRU	macular
AACLMSU	△calamus
AACLNNU	cannula
AACLNOR	Alcoran
AACLNPY	claypan
AACLNRU	lacunar
AACLNSU	Calanus
	canulas
AACLOPR	caporal
AACLOPT	octapla
AACLORT	coaltar
	coal-tar
	crotala
AACLORZ	alcorza
AACLOST	catalos
	coastal
AACLOTT	cattalo
AACLOTV	octaval
AACLPRT	caltrap
AACLPSU	pascual
	scapula
AACLPTY	play-act
AACLRST	castral
AACLRVY	△calvary
	cavalry
AACLSSU	casuals
AACLSTT	saltcat
AACLSUV	vascula
AACLTTU	tactual
AACMNOR	camaron
AACMNRU	arcanum
AACMNSY	caymans
AACMORR	△camorra
AACMORS	sarcoma
AACMORT	marcato
AACMRRT	tramcar
AACMRRU	Macrura
AACMRSS	sarcasm
AACNNOZ	canzona
AACNOST	sacaton
AACNPST	capstan
AACNRTU	curtana
AACNSSV	canvass
AACNSTU	ascaunt
AACORST	ostraca
AACORTU	acatour
	autocar
AACOTUV	autovac
AACPSTW	cat's-paw
AACRTTT	attract
AACRTUV	vacatur
AACRTUY	actuary
AACRTWY	cartway
AACTUWY	cutaway
AADDDEN	addenda
AADDEFI	deaf-aid
AADDEGI	Gadidae
AADDEIL	alidade
AADDENP	deadpan
AADDEPT	adapted
AADDEPY	dead-pay
AADDGNR	graddan
	grandad
AADDHKR	khaddar
AADDHRS	sraddha
AADDIIK	didakai
AADDIIV	davidia
AADDIMS	Dadaism
AADDIST	Dadaist
AADDNVV	dvandva
AADDRST	dastard
AADEEGH	headage
AADEEHX	axe-head
AADEFFR	affeard
	affear'd
AADEFGL	faldage
AADEFGR	fardage
AADEFHT	fat-head
AADEFIS	fadaise
AADEFLU	aefauld
AADEFNZ	fazenda
AADEGGR	aggrade
AADEGHO	go-ahead
AADEGHR	raghead
AADEGMN	agnamed
AADEGMR	megarad
AADEGMS	damages
AADEGRT	gradate
AADEGRY	drayage
	yardage
AADEHIR	airhead
AADEHMN	headman
AADEHMS	ashamed
AADEHPS	saphead
AADEHRW	rawhead
	warhead
AADEHWY	headway
AADEILR	Laridae
	radiale
AADEILV	vedalia
AADEIMR	Madeira
AADEIMS	seamaid
AADEIMT	Adamite
AADEINO	Dionaea
AADEINR	araneid
	Ranidae
AADEINS	naiades

AADEIPS	diapase
AADEIRT	radiate
	tiaraed
AADEIWY	die-away
AADEJMR	jemadar
AADEJNU	Judaean
AADEKMR	kamerad
AADELLP	padella
AADELMO	alamode
AADELMR	alarmed
AADELNR	adrenal
AADELNW	△danelaw
AADELPR	pardale
AADELRU	radulae
AADELRY	already
AADELTU	adulate
AADELTY	daytale
AADEMMN	man-made
AADEMNO	adenoma
AADEMNT	△mandate
AADEMNY	name-day
AADEMNZ	Mazdean
AADENNP	Pandean
AADENNT	andante
	Dantean
AADENRV	veranda
AADENST	ansated
AADENSW	weasand
AADENTV	Vedanta
AADENWZ	weazand
AADEPRR	para-red
AADEPRS	aspread
AADEPRT	adapter
	readapt
AADEPSS	passade
AADERRS	arrased
AADERSW	seaward
AADERSY	daresay
AADERTU	aurated
AADFGLY	flag-day
AADFHLY	half-day
AADFIRY	fair-day
AADFLTW	twafald
AADFNRR	farrand
AADFNST	fantads
AADFSTY	fast-day
AADGGHR	haggard
AADGGLR	laggard
AADGGRS	saggard
AADGHIL	hidalga
AADGIIR	Giardia
AADGIMM	digamma
AADGIMO	agamoid
AADGIMR	diagram
AADGIOS	adagios
AADGLLW	gadwall
AADGLMY	amygdal
AADGLNO	gonadal
AADGLNR	garland
AADGLNS	sladang
AADGLNT	Landtag
AADGLRU	gradual
AADGMNR	drag-man
	grandam
	grandma
AADGMNS	gadsman
AADGMRS	smaragd
AADGNPR	grandpa
AADGNRT	gardant
AADGNRY	yardang
AADGOPR	podagra
AADHILL	Dalilah
AADHIMS	samadhi
AADHINP	Daphnia
AADHJNR	handjar
AADHKNY	yakhdan
AADHLRY	halyard
AADHNPR	hard-pan
AADHNRS	darshan
	Hansard
AADHNSW	handsaw
AADHRWY	hayward
AADHSWY	washday
AADIILR	diarial
AADIINR	diarian
AADIIPS	aspidia
AADIIRR	air-raid
AADIJMN	jamdani
AADIKLY	ilkaday
AADILLO	alodial
AADILMR	admiral
	amildar
AADILMT	Matilda
AADILNP	paladin
AADILNR	laniard
AADILPS	apsidal
AADILRT	tailard
AADILST	stadial
AADILTV	datival
AADILWY	waylaid
AADIMNR	mandira
AADIMOR	diorama
AADIMOT	domatia
AADIMRR	ram-raid
AADINRR	darrain
AADINRT	intrada
	radiant
AADINRV	viranda
AADINRW	Wardian
AADIRRW	airward
AADJMPY	pyjama'd
AADKMRY	daymark
AADKNRT	tankard
AADKRWW	awkward
AADLLMR	mallard
AADLLNW	land-law
	lawland
AADLLPU	paludal
AADLMNN	landman
AADLMNO	mandola
AADLMNU	ladanum
AADLMYY	May-lady
AADLNOP	Panadol®
AADLNRT	land-rat
AADLNRY	lanyard
AADLNTX	land-tax
AADLOPY	pay-load
AADLPPU	applaud
AADLPYY	play-day
AADLRRU	radular
AADMNNO	Madonna
AADMNNS	sandman
AADMNNW	dawn-man
AADMNOR	madroña
	mandora
	monarda
	roadman
AADMNRS	mansard
AADMNRY	drayman
	yardman
AADMNSY	daysman
	man-days
AADMNTU	mutanda
	tamandu
AADMOPR	road-map
AADMOQU	madoqua
AADMORT	matador
AADMOSY	Asmoday
AADMRRY	yard-arm
AADMRZZ	mazzard
AADNNOT	notanda
AADNOOT	Odonata
AADNOPR	△pandora
AADNORT	ondatra
AADNORY	anyroad
AADNPRU	pandura
AADNRRW	warrand
AADNRRY	darrayn
AADNRST	astrand
	tar-sand
AADNRTY	tanyard
AADNRVW	vanward
AADNRWY	nayward
AADOPRR	parador
AADOPRS	parados
AADOPRT	adaptor
AADOPRX	paradox
AADOPSS	passado
AADOPTT	dopatta
AADORWY	roadway
AADOSTT	tostada
AADPTTU	dupatta
AADQRTU	quadrat
AADRSTY	daystar
AADRWWY	wayward
AAEEFFR	affeare
AAEEFGL	leafage
AAEEGKL	leakage
AAEEGLT	étalage
	galeate
AAEEGMN	amenage
AAEEGMR	Megaera
AAEEGNO	Neogaea
AAEEGRV	average
AAEEHRT	hetaera
AAEEINT	taeniae

AAEEKLS	seakale
AAEEKRW	reawake
AAEELMT	maleate
AAEELOR	areolae
AAEELRT	laetare
AAEEMNT	emanate
	enemata
	manatee
AAEEMTT	meat-tea
AAEEMTX	meat-axe
AAEENNT	Aetnean
AAEEPPS	appease
AAEEPRT	paterae
AAEERSW	seaware
AAEERTU	aureate
AAEERTX	exarate
AAEFFGR	agraffe
AAEFFIR	affaire
AAEFFLL	falafel
AAEFFNR	fanfare
AAEFFTT	taffeta
AAEFGLN	Falange
AAEFGTW	waftage
AAEFHLP	half-ape
AAEFHNT	haaf-net
AAEFKLO	oakleaf
AAEFLPR	earflap
	parafle
AAEFLRT	rat-flea
AAEFMRT	fermata
AAEFQRU	aquafer
AAEFRRR	Ferrara
AAEFRRW	warfare
AAEFRWY	wayfare
AAEGGNO	anagoge
AAEGGOP	apagoge
AAEGGRT	aggrate
AAEGHLU	haulage
AAEGHNS	Ganesha
AAEGHNT	thanage
AAEGHOV	have-a-go
AAEGHPT	peat-hag
AAEGILR	lairage
	regalia
AAEGILS	algesia
AAEGINP	nagapie
AAEGINV	vaginae
AAEGINW	wainage
AAEGIPR	igarapé
AAEGIRR	arriage
AAEGISS	assegai
AAEGITT	agitate
AAEGJTU	ajutage
AAEGKNT	tankage
AAEGKOS	soakage
AAEGKRW	Gaekwar
AAEGLLR	glareal
	Grallae
AAEGLLT	gallate
	tallage
AAEGLMN	gamelan
AAEGLMT	gametal
AAEGLNR	alnager
AAEGLNS	lasagne
AAEGLNU	aulnage
AAEGLOP	apogeal
AAEGLRR	realgar
AAEGLST	agelast
	algates
	lastage
AAEGLSV	salvage
AAEGMMY	May-game
AAEGMNR	manager
AAEGMNT	gateman
	magenta
	magnate
AAEGMPR	rampage
AAEGMRT	regmata
AAEGMSS	massage
AAEGNNP	pannage
AAEGNNT	tannage
AAEGNOP	apogean
AAEGNPT	pageant
AAEGNRR	arrange
AAEGNRT	tanager
AAEGNTV	vantage
AAEGNTW	wantage
AAEGNYZ	Zygaena
AAEGPRR	parerga
AAEGPSS	passage
AAEGPSY	paysage
AAEGQUY	quayage
AAEGRRV	ravager
AAEGRST	agraste
	tear-gas
AAEGRTT	regatta
AAEGSSU	assuage
	sausage
AAEGSSW	asswage
AAEGSTU	gateaus
AAEGSTW	wastage
AAEGTTW	wattage
AAEGTUX	gâteaux
AAEGTWY	gateway
	getaway
AAEHHPS	ash-heap
AAEHHPT	aphthae
AAEHILP	aphelia
AAEHIRT	hetaira
	Rhaetia
AAEHKNT	khanate
AAEHKSW	seahawk
AAEHLLL	allheal
	heal-all
AAEHLPX	hexapla
AAEHLRT	trehala
AAEHLTT	athleta
AAEHMTT	themata
AAEHNPR	hanaper
AAEHNPS	saphena
AAEHPRZ	pheazar
AAEHRSY	hearsay
AAEHSTT	hastate
AAEIKRT	Karaite
AAEILLX	axillae
AAEILMN	Almaine
	laminae
	Limnaea
AAEILMS	malaise
AAEILNN	alanine
AAEILNO	△aeolian
AAEILNR	air-lane
AAEILNT	antliae
AAEILOR	olearia
AAEILPX	epaxial
AAEILRU	aurelia
AAEILRV	velaria
AAEILSS	aliases
AAEIMMT	imamate
AAEIMNS	amnesia
AAEIMNT	amentia
	animate
AAEIMPY	pyaemia
AAEIMRU	uraemia
AAEIMTV	amative
AAEINNO	aeonian
AAEINNS	Sinaean
AAEINRT	Raetian
AAEINRZ	Zairean
AAEINST	taenias
AAEIPPS	apepsia
AAEIPRR	pareira
AAEIPRS	spiraea
AAEIPRT	apteria
AAEIPTT	apatite
AAEIRST	asteria
	atresia
AAEIRSX	xerasia
AAEIRTT	arietta
	Ratitae
AAEIRTV	variate
AAEIRVW	airwave
AAEISTT	satiate
AAEJMST	maatjes
AAEJNRT	naartje
AAEKKOR	karaoke
AAEKLMR	meal-ark
AAEKLNT	alkanet
	kantela
AAEKMNW	wakeman
AAEKMRR	earmark
AAEKMRS	seamark
AAEKPRT	partake
AAELLLM	lamella
AAELLNZ	zanella
AAELLPR	parella
AAELLPT	△patella
AAELLRT	lateral
AAELLRY	allayer
AAELLSV	save-all
AAELMMN	meal-man
AAELMMT	lemmata
AAELMNS	Ameslan
AAELMNT	amental
AAELMNU	alumnae
AAELMNY	Lymnaea

Words marked △ may be spelled also with a capital letter

AAELMOT	oatmeal
AAELMPT	palmate
AAELMST	maltase
AAELMSY	amylase
AAELNOV	valonea
AAELNPT	platane
AAELNPU	paenula
AAELNRS	arsenal
AAELNRT	Lateran
AAELNST	sealant
AAELNSY	analyse
AAELNTT	tetanal
AAELNTZ	zealant
AAELNWY	laneway
AAELNYZ	analyze
AAELORR	areolar
AAELORU	aureola
AAELOTX	oxalate
AAELPPR	apparel
AAELPPT	palpate
AAELPPU	papulae
AAELPRT	apteral
AAELPRV	palaver
AAELPTT	tapetal
AAELPTU	plateau
AAELPTY	apetaly
AAELRST	tar-seal
AAELRTV	larvate
AAELRTZ	lazaret
AAELRVY	alveary
AAELSST	atlases
AAELSTT	saltate
AAELSUX	asexual
AAELSWX	sealwax
AAELTUV	valuate
AAELTVV	valvate
AAELTZZ	altezza
AAELWWY	welaway
AAEMMMR	maremma
AAEMMMT	mammate
AAEMMNT	meat-man
AAEMMNU	manumea
AAEMMOT	ommatea
AAEMNNT	emanant
AAEMNPP	pampean
AAEMNPS	spaeman
AAEMNPT	peatman
AAEMNRT	ramenta
AAEMNRU	△muraena
AAEMNRY	man-year
AAEMNST	namaste
AAEMNTU	manteau
AAEMOTZ	△metazoa
AAEMPPT	pap-meat
AAEMQSU	squamae
AAEMRST	amearst
AAEMRTU	amateur
AAENNNT	antenna
AAENNST	annates
AAENNTT	tannate
AAENNTV	ventana
AAENPPR	parpane
AAENPST	anapest
	peasant
AAENPTT	épatant
AAENRRT	narrate
AAENRST	Antares
AAENRTT	tartane
AAENRTU	△taurean
AAENRTV	taverna
AAENRUW	unaware
AAENRUZ	azurean
AAENSSV	vanessa
AAENSTV	Avestan
AAEORRT	aerator
AAEORRU	aurorae
AAEPPRT	parapet
AAEPPRV	Papaver
AAEPRTY	peatary
AAERRRS	arrears
AAERRRY	arrayer
AAERRTT	△tartare
AAERSSY	assayer
AAERSTT	Astarte
AAETTUW	Watteau
AAFFINS	saffian
AAFFIRS	affairs
AAFGIRR	rag-fair
AAFGORR	farrago
AAFHIKL	khalifa
AAFHLPY	half-pay
AAFHLWY	halfway
AAFIILR	△filaria
AAFIJST	fajitas
AAFILNT	fantail
AAFILNV	Flavian
AAFILQU	alfaquí
AAFIMRU	Fumaria
AAFIMRY	Mayfair
AAFINNT	infanta
AAFIPRT	parfait
AAFIRUY	rufiyaa
AAFIRWY	fairway
AAFJLLW	jawfall
AAFJLOR	alforja
AAFLLTY	fatally
AAFLMPR	frampal
AAFLNOR	forlana
AAFLNRU	furlana
AAFLSTT	salt-fat
AAFLWYY	flyaway
AAFMNRT	raftman
AAFMNST	fantasm
AAFNRRT	farrant
AAFNSTT	fantast
AAFNSTY	fantasy
AAGGILN	ganglia
AAGGLMO	magalog
AAGGLOS	galagos
AAGGLOT	Tagalog
	Tagálog
AAGGNOY	anagogy
AAGGNWY	gangway
AAGHILR	gharial
AAGHLNT	gnathal
AAGHLOS	gasahol
AAGHMNN	hangman
AAGHMNW	whangam
AAGHMRS	gramash
AAGHQUU	quahaug
AAGHRSW	washrag
AAGHSTY	sagathy
AAGIKNW	awaking
AAGIKNZ	ziganka
AAGIKRW	Gaikwar
AAGILMY	myalgia
AAGILNN	anginal
	Anglian
AAGILNO	logania
AAGILNP	paginal
AAGILNV	vaginal
AAGILOT	otalgia
AAGILTT	tag-tail
AAGILTW	wagtail
AAGIMNO	angioma
AAGIMNS	siamang
AAGIMNZ	amazing
AAGINNW	wanigan
AAGINNZ	Zingana
AAGINOS	agnosia
AAGINRR	arraign
AAGINRS	sangria
	sarangi
AAGINRT	granita
AAGINRU	Guaraní
	guarani
AAGINRZ	Zingara
AAGINST	against
AAGINSV	vaginas
AAGINSY	gainsay
AAGINTY	antigay
AAGIOTT	agitato
AAGIPRU	piragua
AAGIRRY	argyria
AAGISTT	△sagitta
AAGKLLO	oak-gall
AAGKOOZ	gazooka
AAGKORT	katorga
AAGLLNT	gallant
AAGLNNO	Angolan
AAGLNOR	granola
AAGLNOY	analogy
AAGLNPS	lapsang
AAGLNRU	angular
AAGLRUU	arugula
	augural
AAGLRVX	gravlax
AAGMMNS	magsman
AAGMMRR	grammar
AAGMMTU	gummata
AAGMNNR	grannam
AAGMNOS	sangoma
AAGMNPR	pangram
AAGMNPY	pangamy
AAGMNRT	tangram
	trangam

AAGMNSW	swagman
AAGMOPY	apogamy
AAGMORS	margosa
AAGMOSU	agamous
AAGMRRY	gramary
AAGNOPR	paragon
AAGNORZ	organza
AAGNRRY	Granary®
	granary
AAGNRTV	vagrant
AAGOPSS	sapsago
AAGORSU	saguaro
AAHHNNT	thannah
AAHHNPT	naphtha
AAHHOPR	Pharaoh
AAHIINT	Haitian
AAHIJNR	Harijan
AAHIKNT	Inkatha
AAHIKRT	kithara
AAHILLL	all-hail
	hallali
AAHILLN	hallian
AAHILMR	almirah
AAHILMS	shimaal
AAHILMT	thalami
AAHILNS	Sinhala
AAHILNT	thalian
AAHILPV	Pahlavi
AAHIMNO	mahonia
AAHIMNR	Ahriman
AAHIMRT	Marathi
AAHINOP	aphonia
AAHINPP	Paphian
AAHINPR	piranha
AAHINST	△shaitan
AAHINSV	Shavian
AAHINTW	taniwha
AAHIPRT	pitarah
AAHIPTZ	zaptiah
AAHIRST	△shariat
AAHISVY	Vaishya
AAHJKNR	khanjar
AAHKLRS	lashkar
AAHKMSY	yashmak
AAHKNSY	Sankhya
AAHKRSS	rakshas
AAHLLWY	hallway
AAHLMMS	mashlam
AAHLMRS	marshal
AAHLMRU	hamular
AAHLNPX	phalanx
AAHLNRW	narwhal
AAHLNTU	Nahuatl
AAHLPRS	phrasal
AAHLPST	asphalt
	taplash
AAHLRSW	shalwar
AAHMMNS	mashman
AAHMNNU	hanuman
AAHMNRS	harmans
AAHMNSS	shamans
AAHMNTX	xantham
AAHMOPR	amphora
AAHMORS	Masorah
AAHMQSU	quamash
AAHMSTV	mash-vat
AAHMSTZ	matzahs
AAHNNOS	hosanna
AAHNNPR	harn-pan
AAHNNTX	xanthan
AAHNORT	athanor
AAHNORV	navarho
AAHNOSV	Navahos
AAHNRTX	anthrax
AAHNRTY	rhatany
AAHPRTW	warpath
AAHPTWY	pathway
AAHRSST	shastra
AAHRSTY	ash-tray
AAHRTTW	athwart
AAIILLP	Palilia
AAIILMR	airmail
AAIILNT	Italian
AAIILNV	Vinalia
AAIILNZ	Azilian
AAIILPR	pairial
AAIILPT	tilapia
AAIILRR	air-rail
AAIILRZ	alizari
AAIINNR	Iranian
AAIINNZ	anziani
AAIINTT	Titania
AAIINZZ	zizania
AAIIRVV	vivaria
AAIJLNP	jalapin
AAIJMNP	jampani
AAIJNRZ	janizar
AAIJPPY	jipyapa
AAIKLLM	Kallima
AAIKLLS	alkalis
AAIKLPT	kail-pat
AAIKMNN	manakin
AAIKMNR	ramakin
AAIKMOR	romaika
AAIKMRS	karaism
AAIKNNT	Kantian
AAIKORU	ouakari
AAIKPPR	paprika
AAIKRSS	askaris
AAIKSTT	astatki
AAIKTVV	akvavit
AAILLLP	pallial
AAILLMM	mamilla
AAILLMN	△manilla
AAILLMR	armilla
AAILLMX	maxilla
AAILLNV	vanilla
AAILLPP	papilla
AAILLRX	axillar
AAILLSV	salival
AAILLUV	alluvia
AAILLXY	axially
AAILMMN	mailman
AAILMMR	ammiral
AAILMMS	Lamaism
	miasmal
AAILMMX	maximal
AAILMNR	laminar
	railman
AAILMNT	matinal
AAILMNU	alumina
AAILMNV	mailvan
AAILMPS	impalas
AAILMRT	marital
	martial
AAILMSS	salamis
AAILMST	Lamaist
AAILMWW	Mawlawi
AAILNOP	Pianola®
AAILNOT	ailanto
	Laotian
AAILNOV	novalia
	△valonia
AAILNPS	salpian
AAILNPT	platina
AAILNPU	Paulian
AAILNRU	ulnaria
	Uralian
AAILNRY	laniary
AAILNSS	Nasalis
AAILNTV	Latvian
	valiant
AAILORS	rosalia
AAILORU	raoulia
AAILORV	variola
AAILOST	solatia
AAILPPT	appalti
AAILPRT	partial
	patrial
AAILPST	spatial
AAILPTT	talipat
AAILPZZ	palazzi
AAILRRV	arrival
AAILRTT	rat-tail
AAILRTV	travail
AAILRWY	railway
AAILSSV	vassail
AAILSSW	wassail
AAILTTT	latitat
AAIMMNO	ammonia
AAIMMSS	miasmas
AAIMNNO	omniana
AAIMNOS	anosmia
AAIMNOT	amation
AAIMNRT	Martian
	tamarin
AAIMNRX	Marxian
AAIMNRZ	Mazarin
AAIMNST	stamina
AAIMNTX	taximan
AAIMPRS	Arimasp
AAIMRSU	samurai
AAIMRTU	timarau
AAIMRTX	Tamarix
AAIMSST	stasima
AAIMSTV	atavism

AAIMSUV	mauvais
AAINNRU	△uranian
AAINNRV	navarin
	△nirvana
AAINOPS	paisano
AAINORR	orarian
AAINORV	ovarian
AAINPRT	Patarin
AAINRST	artisan
	tsarina
AAINRSU	saurian
AAINRSV	savarin
AAINRTV	variant
AAINRTW	antiwar
AAINSTV	vanitas
AAINTTT	attaint
AAINTTU	tutania
AAIOPRR	pair-oar
AAIOPRT	atropia
AAIORSU	saouari
AAIORTV	aviator
AAIPPRU	puparia
AAIPPTT	pitapat
AAIPRRT	air-trap
AAIPRSS	Sarapis
AAIPRTT	partita
AAIQSSU	quassia
AAIQTUV	aquavit
AAITWXY	taxiway
AAJKLWY	jaywalk
AAJKMNR	jarkman
AAJMNZZ	jazzman
AAJMORT	majorat
AAJMPSY	pyjamas
AAJNNSY	Nyanjas
AAJNOSV	Navajos
AAJNRUY	January
AAJOPSU	sapajou
AAKKLRU	△karakul
AAKKMOT	tokamak
AAKKMRS	markkas
AAKKOPS	kakapos
AAKKSUZ	zakuska
AAKLMNW	Walkman®
AAKLMPU	lampuka
AAKLMRY	malarky
AAKLMUY	yamulka
AAKLNOO	oolakan
AAKLNOR	Alkoran
AAKLNOU	oulakan
AAKLOOP	palooka
AAKLOOT	talooka
AAKLRSU	kursaal
	rusalka
AAKLSSU	saksaul
AAKLWWY	walkway
AAKMMNR	markman
AAKMOST	oak-mast
AAKMOSU	mousaka
AAKMRUZ	mazurka
AAKMRWY	waymark
AAKNNTU	nunatak
AAKNTWY	twankay
AAKOOPP	pakapoo
AAKORST	ostraka
AAKPRWY	parkway
AAKRTUY	autarky
AAKSTTT	attaskt
AALLLNS	Lallans
AALLMPU	ampulla
AALLNPU	planula
AALLNSY	nasally
AALLOSS	Salsola
AALLOTV	lavolta
AALLPPY	papally
AALLRST	all-star
AALLRUY	aurally
AALLRVY	vallary
AALLTWY	ally-taw
AALLUVV	valvula
AALMMNO	ammonal
AALMMNS	alms-man
AALMMNT	maltman
AALMNOS	salamon
AALMNOY	anomaly
AALMORT	alamort
AALMORY	mayoral
AALMPRY	palmary
	palmyra
AALMRRU	ramular
AALMRSU	alarums
AALMTTU	mulatta
AALNNRU	annular
AALNORS	also-ran
AALNPRT	plantar
AALNPSV	Pan-Slav
AALNPTU	Laputan
AALNPUU	punalua
AALNQTU	quantal
AALNRTT	latrant
AALNRTU	natural
AALNSTT	saltant
AALNSTU	sultana
AALNSTY	analyst
AALNTTU	talaunt
AALOPPT	appalto
AALOPRS	parasol
AALOPVV	△pavlova
AALOPZZ	palazzo
AALORRU	auroral
AALORSU	arousal
AALORTX	laxator
AALOSTT	saltato
AALOTTY	talayot
AALPPRU	papular
AALPRSW	asprawl
AALPSTU	spatula
AALPWYY	play-way
AALRSTU	△austral
AALRSTY	astylar
	satyral
AALRWYY	lyra-way
AALSSTU	assault
AAMMMRY	mammary
AAMMNNX	Manxman
AAMMNRT	mantram
AAMMNTY	Tammany
AAMMRST	ramstam
AAMNNOY	anonyma
AAMNNTU	Mantuan
AAMNOOS	manoaos
AAMNORR	Marrano
AAMNORS	oarsman
AAMNORT	amorant
AAMNORW	man-o'-war
AAMNOTY	anatomy
AAMNPRT	mantrap
	rampant
AAMNPRY	paranym
AAMNPSS	passman
AAMNPST	tapsman
AAMNPTY	tympana
AAMNRST	artsman
AAMOORS	amorosa
AAMOPRS	paramos
AAMORRZ	zamarro
AAMORSS	Massora
AAMORSV	samovar
AAMORTY	amatory
AAMOSSS	samosas
AAMOSTT	stomata
AAMOTTU	automat
AAMPRRT	rampart
AAMPSSY	ampassy
AAMRSST	matrass
AAMRSTU	sumatra
	traumas
AAMRTWY	tramway
AAMSSTU	△satsuma
AANNOTT	annatto
AANORTU	Arnaout
AANOSTT	anattos
AANPRST	△spartan
AANPSST	passant
AANQRTU	quartan
AANRRTW	warrant
AANRSUV	Varanus
AANRUWY	runaway
AANSSTW	Tswanas
AANSTTT	statant
AANSWYY	anyways
AAOORRW	woorara
AAOPSST	potassa
AAORRSU	auroras
AAOTTUY	tatouay
AAPQSUW	Quapaws
AAPRRTT	rat-trap
AAPRSTY	satrapy
AAPZZZZ	pazzazz
AARRTTY	Tartary
ABBBDEL	blabbed
ABBBELR	babbler
	blabber
	brabble
ABBBITT	△babbitt
ABBCDER	crabbed

ABBCDES scabbed
ABBCEHI babiche
ABBCEHU babuche
ABBCELR clabber
ABBCELS scabble
ABBCERR crabber
ABBCKUY buy-back
ABBCRYY crybaby
ABBDEGR grabbed
ABBDEHT bed-bath
ABBDEIT tabbied
ABBDEKR bark-bed
ABBDELR dabbler
drabble
ABBDELS slabbed
ABBDERR drabber
ABBDERT drabbet
ABBDEST stabbed
ABBDESW swabbed
ABBDGIN big-band
dabbing
ABBDGOY body-bag
ABBDHIJ djibbah
ABBDILO Bobadil
ABBDILR libbard
ABBDINR ribband
ABBDITY dabbity
ABBDLRU lubbard
ABBDMOR bombard
ABBDMOU babudom
ABBDNOX band-box
ABBDNYY by-and-by
ABBEESW bawbees
ABBEGLR gabbler
grabble
ABBEGNO bogbean
ABBEGNU bugbane
ABBEGRR grabber
ABBEGRU bugbear
ABBEHLS shabble
ABBELLR bar-bell
ABBELMR bramble
ABBELNS snabble
ABBELOR belabor
ABBELPR prabble
ABBELRR rabbler
ABBELRS slabber
ABBELRU barbule
ABBELRW wabbler
ABBELSU bas-bleu
ABBELUY buyable
ABBEMUZ bumbaze
ABBERST stabber
ABBERSW swabber
ABBESSU subbase
ABBFIRT frabbit
ABBGGIN gabbing
ABBGINN nabbing
ABBGINT tabbing
ABBGINU bubinga
ABBGOOU bugaboo
ABBGORS gabbros
ABBGORY Babygro®
ABBHINO Hobbian
ABBHISY babyish
ABBHNOO hob-a-nob
ABBHOOS baboosh
ABBHRRU rhubarb
ABBHTTU bathtub
ABBIIMN bambini
ABBIIMS Babiism
ABBILOR bilobar
ABBILOT bobtail
ABBILSU bubalis
ABBIMNO bambino
ABBIMSU babuism
ABBINOR rabboni
ABBINRS rabbins
ABBIRST rabbits
ABBIRTY rabbity
ABBISTY baby-sit
ABBKLOU blaubok
ABBLLOY ball-boy
ABBLLRU bullbar
ABBLLTU bullbat
ABBLMRY brambly
ABBLNOY Babylon
ABBLSUU Bubalus
ABBMOOR bombora
ABBMOST bombast
ABBMOTU bum-boat
ABBNRTU bran-tub
ABBNRUY Banbury
ABBORRU Barbour®
ABBQSUY squabby
ABCCCHI △bacchic
ABCCEER Rebecca
ABCCEIR acerbic
breccia
ABCCEIS sebacic
ABCCHII bacchii
ABCCHOR choc-bar
ABCCHSU Bacchus
ABCCHTY bycatch
ABCCIIR Cabiric
ABCCILU cubical
ABCCIMR cambric
ABCCINU buccina
ABCCIOR boracic
braccio
ABCCKOW bawcock
ABCCKTU cutback
ABCCOOR barocco
ABCCOOT tobacco
ABCCSUU succuba
ABCDEEH beached
ABCDEEI Cebidae
ABCDEEL debacle
débâcle
ABCDEHU debauch
ABCDEIK dieback
ABCDEIP pedicab
ABCDEIR carbide
ABCDEKN back-end
ABCDEKR redback
ABCDELO coal-bed
ABCDEMP camp-bed
ABCDEOR brocade
ABCDERU cudbear
ABCDGOR dog-crab
ABCDHIO ichabod
ABCDHOR chobdar
ABCDIIS dibasic
ABCDILR baldric
ABCDINS abscind
ABCDIRS scabrid
ABCDIRT catbird
ABCDIRU baudric
ABCDISU subacid
ABCDNOS abscond
ABCDOOR córdoba
ABCDORR brocard
ABCEEHU ébauche
ABCEEMR embrace
ABCEENS absence
ABCEERR cerebra
rebrace
ABCEERU berceau
ABCEESS bécasse
ABCEESU because
ABCEGIR ribcage
ABCEGMO camboge
ABCEGOR brocage
ABCEGOS boscage
ABCEHIR Hebraic
ABCEHIT Thebaic
ABCEHKO backhoe
ABCEHLU bauchle
ABCEHMR becharm
brecham
chamber
chambré
ABCEHOS basoche
ABCEHRT brachet
ABCEIIR Cabeiri
ABCEIKT tieback
ABCEILL iceball
ABCEILM alembic
cembali
ABCEILR caliber
calibre
ABCEILT citable
ABCEIMO amoebic
ABCEINO cenobia
ABCEINR carbine
ABCEINT △cabinet
ABCEIOR aerobic
ABCEIOT iceboat
ABCEIRS ascribe
ABCEISS abscise
scabies
ABCEITT tabetic
ABCEKLN blacken
ABCEKNR bracken
ABCEKRT bracket

ABCEKST	backset
	setback
ABCEKSY	backsey
ABCEKTW	wetback
ABCELLU	bullace
ABCELMO	cembalo
ABCELMR	cambrel
	clamber
ABCELMS	scamble
ABCELOP	placebo
ABCELOV	vocable
ABCELPU	bluecap
ABCELPY	byplace
ABCELRU	curable
ABCELSU	bascule
ABCENOR	baconer
ABCENOW	cowbane
ABCENRU	unbrace
ABCEOOS	caboose
ABCEORU	corbeau
ABCESSS	abscess
ABCFIKN	finback
ABCFILO	bifocal
ABCFLOO	cobloaf
ABCFLOX	box-calf
ABCGHKO	hogback
ABCGIKN	backing
ABCGILN	cabling
ABCGINR	bracing
ABCGKLO	backlog
ABCGMSU	scumbag
ABCHHII	hibachi
ABCHILS	Chablis
ABCHILU	Baluchi
ABCHIMT	bathmic
ABCHIOT	cohabit
ABCHKOU	chabouk
ABCHKTU	hackbut
ABCHKUW	hawbuck
ABCHNOR	brochan
ABCHNRU	braunch
ABCHNRY	branchy
ABCHOSX	cash-box
ABCHSTU	bush-cat
ABCIILL	bacilli
ABCIILN	albinic
ABCIILT	albitic
ABCIIMN	minicab
ABCIIMS	iambics
ABCIIOR	ciboria
ABCIIOT	abiotic
ABCIJNO	△jacobin
ABCILOR	crab-oil
ABCILRS	scribal
ABCILTU	cubital
ABCIMMS	cambism
ABCIMMU	cambium
ABCIMST	cambist
ABCINOT	botanic
ABCIORR	barrico
ABCIORU	caribou
ABCIOUV	bivouac
ABCIRTY	barytic
ABCISSS	absciss
ABCJOSU	jacobus
ABCKLLY	blackly
ABCKLOT	backlot
ABCKMRU	buckram
ABCKMUZ	zambuck
ABCKNNO	bannock
ABCKNRU	runback
ABCKORW	back-row
ABCKOSW	sowback
ABCKOTU	outback
ABCKSTU	sackbut
	subtack
ABCKSUW	bucksaw
	sawbuck
ABCLLOX	call-box
ABCLLOY	call-boy
ABCLLUW	club-law
ABCLMNU	clubman
ABCLMOU	Columba
ABCLMOY	cymbalo
ABCLMUU	baculum
ABCLNOY	balcony
ABCLOOX	coal-box
ABCNOSW	cob-swan
ABCOOTX	box-coat
ABCORRW	crowbar
ABCOTTU	cab-tout
ABDDEER	bearded
	breaded
ABDDEES	debased
ABDDEEZ	bedazed
ABDDEIN	abidden
	bandied
ABDDEIR	braided
ABDDEIS	baddies
ABDDELR	bladder
ABDDEMR	mad-bred
ABDDENR	branded
ABDDEOR	road-bed
ABDDERW	bedward
ABDDHIS	baddish
ABDDINS	disband
ABDDLLO	oddball
ABDDMOR	dambrod
ABDEEHV	behaved
ABDEEIL	lie-abed
ABDEEIR	beardie
ABDEELM	beldame
	bemedal
ABDEELR	bederal
	bleared
ABDEELT	belated
ABDEELY	belayed
	dyeable
ABDEEMN	bedeman
	benamed
ABDEEMR	ambered
	embread
ABDEEMS	embased
ABDEEMZ	bemazed
ABDEEPT	peat-bed
ABDEERS	debaser
ABDEERT	betread
	debater
ABDEEST	bestead
ABDEETT	abetted
ABDEFLT	flatbed
ABDEFLU	leafbud
ABDEFOR	forbade
ABDEFRW	bedwarf
ABDEFST	bedfast
ABDEGGR	bragged
ABDEGHI	big-head
ABDEGHR	beghard
ABDEGIN	beading
ABDEGIR	abridge
	brigade
ABDEGIW	wide-gab
ABDEGLN	bangled
ABDEGLR	belgard
	garbled
ABDEGNO	bondage
	dogbane
ABDEHIT	habited
	Thebaid
ABDEHLR	halberd
ABDEHOW	bowhead
ABDEHRS	berdash
ABDEHRT	breadth
ABDEHSU	subhead
ABDEILN	nail-bed
ABDEILP	bipedal
	piebald
ABDEILR	railbed
	ridable
ABDEILS	disable
ABDEILU	audible
ABDEIMR	embraid
ABDEINR	brained
ABDEINW	Bedawin
ABDEIOV	Bovidae
ABDEIRR	briared
ABDEIRS	darbies
	seabird
	sidebar
	side-bar
ABDEIRT	tribade
ABDEISS	biassed
ABDEIST	bastide
ABDEJOU	j'adoube
ABDEKNU	unbaked
ABDELMR	marbled
ABDELMY	embayld
ABDELOS	albedos
ABDELOT	bloated
ABDELOW	dowable
ABDELPU	dupable
ABDELPY	pyebald
ABDELRR	drabler
ABDELRU	durable
ABDELST	blasted
ABDELTT	blatted

ABDELYZ	lazy-bed
ABDEMNO	abdomen
ABDEMRU	Bermuda
ABDENOR	bandore
	broaden
ABDENOY	naebody
ABDENRR	brander
ABDENRW	brawned
ABDENSS	badness
ABDENSU	subdean
ABDENTU	unbated
ABDEOOT	tabooed
ABDEORR	boarder
ABDEOST	boasted
ABDEOTU	boutade
ABDEQSU	basqued
ABDERST	dabster
ABDERSU	subedar
ABDERTY	drybeat
ABDERUY	daubery
ABDETTU	abutted
ABDGGOR	boggard
ABDGIIN	abiding
ABDGILN	balding
ABDGINN	banding
ABDGINR	brigand
ABDGINT	dingbat
ABDGINU	daubing
ABDGINW	windbag
ABDGLNO	bogland
ABDGLUY	ladybug
ABDHHOS	dobhash
ABDHIIT	adhibit
ABDHILS	baldish
ABDHMOR	rhabdom
ABDHMSU	budmash
ABDHMTU	mudbath
ABDHNOR	bodhrán
ABDHNOW	bow-hand
ABDHNSU	husband
ABDHRSU	burdash
	rhabdus
ABDIKNW	bawdkin
ABDIKRS	disbark
ABDILMO	bimodal
ABDILNW	Baldwin
ABDILOO	diabolo
ABDILOR	labroid
ABDILOT	tabloid
ABDILRW	awlbird
ABDILRY	rabidly
ABDILUY	audibly
ABDILWY	bawdily
ABDIMNR	birdman
ABDIMOR	ambroid
ABDIMRY	may-bird
ABDINOR	inboard
ABDINRT	antbird
ABDINST	bandits
ABDIOSU	badious
ABDIPRU	upbraid
ABDIRSU	subarid
ABDIRTY	tribady
ABDKNOO	bandook
ABDKOOY	day-book
ABDLLNY	blandly
ABDLLOR	bollard
ABDLMOR	Lombard
ABDLNOR	bandrol
ABDLORY	broadly
ABDLRUY	durably
	rybauld
ABDLRYY	byrlady
ABDLSUU	subdual
ABDMNNO	bondman
ABDMNOY	man-body
ABDMOTU	mud-boat
ABDMRUY	marybud
ABDNOOR	onboard
	on-board
ABDNOPR	proband
ABDNOSU	bausond
ABDNOSX	sandbox
ABDNOSY	sandboy
ABDNOYY	anybody
ABDNRTU	turband
ABDNSTY	stand-by
ABDOORW	barwood
ABDORWY	draw-boy
ABDRSTU	bustard
ABDRUZZ	buzzard
ABEEEFT	beef-tea
ABEEEGR	beerage
ABEEELS	seeable
ABEEEMY	eye-beam
ABEEERV	bereave
ABEEFFL	effable
ABEEFGR	Fabergé
ABEEFHM	beef-ham
ABEEFLO	beefalo
ABEEFTU	beaufet
ABEEGHR	herbage
ABEEGLL	gabelle
ABEEGLR	beagler
ABEEGRR	△gerbera
ABEEGRU	auberge
ABEEGRW	brewage
ABEEHMS	beshame
ABEEHMT	embathe
ABEEHNN	henbane
ABEEHNS	banshee
	has-been
ABEEHNT	beneath
ABEEHRS	she-bear
ABEEHRT	breathe
ABEEHTY	eye-bath
ABEEINT	betaine
ABEEIRT	ebriate
ABEEIST	beastie
ABEEKNT	betaken
ABEEKNV	beknave
ABEEKOP	peekabo
ABEEKPS	bespake
	bespeak
ABEEKRR	breaker
ABEELLY	eyeball
ABEELMM	emblema
ABEELMT	beamlet
ABEELMW	ewe-lamb
ABEELMZ	emblaze
ABEELNP	plebean
ABEELNR	enabler
ABEELNT	Beltane
	tenable
ABEELNU	nebulae
ABEELOR	earlobe
ABEELPR	bepearl
ABEELQU	equable
ABEELRR	errable
ABEELRT	bleater
	retable
ABEELSU	sea-blue
	sueable
ABEELSV	beslave
ABEEMRS	besmear
ABEEMRT	beer-mat
ABEEMRV	embrave
ABEEMST	embaste
ABEENOR	ear-bone
ABEENRV	verbena
ABEENRY	beanery
ABEEPST	bespate
ABEERRT	rebater
	tabrere
	△terebra
ABEERTT	abetter
ABEERVY	beavery
ABEESWX	beeswax
ABEFFLR	baffler
ABEFFMO	off-beam
ABEFFOT	offbeat
ABEFGIL	filabeg
ABEFGST	gabfest
ABEFILN	finable
ABEFILR	friable
ABEFILX	fixable
ABEFINU	beaufin
ABEFIRR	fire-bar
ABEFIRV	five-bar
ABEFITY	beatify
ABEFLLU	baleful
ABEFLLY	flyable
ABEFLNU	baneful
ABEFLNY	flybane
ABEFORR	forbear
ABEFRSU	bus-fare
ABEGGIS	baggies
ABEGGLR	blagger
ABEGGMO	gamboge
ABEGGNU	buggane
ABEGGNY	gang-bye
ABEGGRU	burgage
ABEGGRY	beggary
ABEGHMR	Maghreb
ABEGHNS	shebang

ABEGILN	Belgian
	Bengali
ABEGIMN	beaming
ABEGIMR	gambier
ABEGIMT	megabit
ABEGINO	begonia
ABEGINR	bearing
ABEGINT	beating
ABEGIPP	bagpipe
ABEGKOR	brokage
ABEGKOS	boskage
ABEGLMR	gambler
	gambrel
ABEGLNR	brangle
ABEGLOR	albergo
ABEGLOT	globate
ABEGLRR	garbler
ABEGMOR	embargo
ABEGMRU	umbrage
ABEGNNT	banteng
ABEGNOS	nosebag
ABEGOPT	peat-bog
ABEGOPY	page-boy
ABEGORR	begorra
ABEGORX	gearbox
ABEGOSZ	gazebos
ABEGOTT	bottega
ABEGOUY	buoyage
ABEGRRU	garbure
ABEGRST	bargest
ABEHILR	hirable
ABEHILS	Belisha
ABEHIMS	beamish
ABEHIMT	imbathe
ABEHIRS	bearish
ABEHISU	beauish
ABEHITU	habitué
ABEHITZ	zabtieh
ABEHKRU	hauberk
ABEHKTU	Ketubah
ABEHLMS	shamble
ABEHLNU	unhable
ABEHLRT	blather
	halbert
ABEHLSU	ale-bush
ABEHNOS	bone-ash
ABEHOTY	hay-bote
ABEHRRY	herbary
ABEHRST	bathers
ABEHRTY	breathy
ABEIILL	baillie
ABEIINR	Iberian
ABEIINT	bainite
ABEIJMR	jambier
ABEIJNS	basenji
ABEIKLL	likable
ABEIKLS	skiable
ABEIKNR	break-in
	inbreak
ABEIKNT	beatnik
ABEIKWY	bikeway
ABEILLO	lobelia
ABEILLP	pliable
ABEILLR	air-bell
	Braille
	△liberal
ABEILLV	livable
ABEILMR	mirable
	remblai
ABEILMT	limbate
	timbale
ABEILMX	mixable
ABEILMY	beamily
ABEILNP	biplane
ABEILNS	△lesbian
ABEILNY	bay-line
ABEILPS	ba'spiel
ABEILPT	patible
ABEILRT	Alberti
	librate
	tablier
	triable
ABEILST	astilbe
	bestial
	stabile
ABEILSZ	sizable
ABEILVV	bivalve
ABEIMNR	mirbane
ABEIMNT	ambient
ABEIMOT	Moabite
ABEINNO	Niobean
ABEINOT	niobate
ABEINPR	bran-pie
ABEINPT	bepaint
ABEINRS	Serbian
ABEINRT	atebrin
ABEINRZ	zebrina
ABEINST	basinet
	besaint
	bestain
ABEINTT	tabinet
	Tibetan
ABEINTY	bay-tine
ABEIORS	isobare
ABEIOSS	isobase
ABEIOTV	obviate
ABEIPST	baptise
ABEIPTZ	baptize
ABEIRRR	barrier
ABEIRRS	brasier
ABEIRRT	arbiter
	rarebit
ABEIRRZ	bizarre
	brazier
ABEIRSS	brassie
ABEIRTT	biretta
	bit-rate
ABEIRTV	vibrate
ABEIRUX	exurbia
ABEISTT	batiste
ABEISUV	abusive
ABEITUX	bauxite
ABEJLLR	bell-jar
ABEJMNO	jambone
ABEJMUX	jambeux
ABEJNOS	banjoes
ABEJNOW	jawbone
ABEJRRU	abjurer
ABEKLLY	bleakly
ABEKLNT	blanket
ABEKNSU	sunbake
ABEKOOR	abrooke
ABEKORT	to-brake
	to-break
ABEKPRU	break-up
	upbreak
ABELLMN	bellman
ABELLNO	Bellona
ABELLNT	netball
ABELLOS	losable
ABELLOV	lovable
	volable
ABELLRU	rubella
	rulable
ABELLTU	bullate
ABELMMR	membral
ABELMNT	beltman
	lambent
ABELMNU	albumen
ABELMOV	movable
ABELMRR	marbler
	rambler
ABELMRS	marbles
ABELMRT	lambert
ABELMTU	mutable
ABELNOO	Boolean
ABELNOT	notable
ABELNOY	baloney
ABELNRS	bransle
ABELNRT	brantle
ABELNRU	nebular
ABELNRY	blarney
ABELNSU	nebulas
ABELNTU	tunable
ABELOPR	ropable
ABELOPT	potable
ABELORS	labrose
ABELORT	bloater
ABELORU	rubeola
ABELORW	rowable
ABELOSV	absolve
ABELOTW	towable
ABELOXX	axle-box
ABELPRU	puberal
ABELQUY	equably
ABELRRW	brawler
	warbler
ABELRSS	braless
ABELRST	blaster
	stabler
ABELRSV	verbals
ABELRTT	battler
	blatter
	brattle
ABELRTW	blewart
ABELRUZ	zebrula

Words marked △ may be spelled also with a capital letter

ABELRVY bravely
ABELSST stables
ABELSTT battels
ABELSTU sublate
ABELSTY beastly
ABELTWY beltway
ABEMNOS ambones
ABEMNRY byreman
myrbane
ABEMNSU sunbeam
ABEMORT bromate
ABEMSSY embassy
ABEMTTU meat-tub
ABENNOR baronne
ABENNRW bran-new
ABENORS sea-born
ABENORT baronet
reboant
ABENORW rawbone
ABENOTY bayonet
ABENQTU banquet
ABENRRS Barrens
ABENRUX exurban
ABENSTT test-ban
ABENSTU sunbeat
ABEOOTV obovate
ABEOPRS saprobe
ABEOPRT probate
ABEOQRU baroque
ABEORRS brasero
ABEORRT arboret
taborer
ABEORST Barotse
boaster
sorbate
ABEORSU aerobus
ABEORSV bravoes
ABEORSY rosebay
ABEORTT abettor
battero
taboret
ABEOSTX box-seat
ABEOVWW bow-wave
ABEPRTY type-bar
ABERRSU Bursera
sabreur
ABERRVY bravery
ABERSST brasset
ABERSSU surbase
ABERSSZ zebrass
ABERSTU surbate
ABERSTW wabster
ABERSTY barytes
ABERSUU bureaus
ABERTTU abutter
ABERTTY battery
ABERUUX bureaux
ABEZZZZ bezzazz
ABFFIIL bailiff
ABFFLOU buffalo
ABFGILN fabling
ABFGKNO fog-bank

ABFGLSU bagfuls
ABFHIST batfish
ABFHLSU bashful
ABFIILR bifilar
ABFIIMR fimbria
ABFILRU fibular
ABFIMOR fibroma
ABFLOTY boat-fly
flyboat
ABFOORT footbar
ABFSTTU tubfast
ABGGGIN bagging
ABGGILY baggily
ABGGINN banging
ABGGORT boggart
ABGGORW grow-bag
ABGHIMR Maghrib
ABGHINS bashing
ABGHLOT hagbolt
ABGHLRU burghal
ABGHMRU Hamburg
ABGHOTU abought
ABGHRSU rag-bush
ABGIINS biasing
ABGIINT baiting
ABGIKLN balking
ABGIKNN banking
ABGIKNR barking
ABGILLN balling
ABGILMN ambling
ABGILMS gimbals
ABGILNT tabling
ABGILNW bawling
ABGILOR garboil
ABGIMST gambist
ABGINNT banting
ABGINOR Grobian
ABGINOS bagnios
ABGINOT boating
ABGINRR barring
ABGINST basting
ABGINTT batting
ABGINTU tabuing
ABGINTW batwing
ABGIOPT pigboat
ABGIOSU baguios
ABGKMSU musk-bag
ABGKOOR rag-book
ABGKORW workbag
ABGLMMU mug-lamb
ABGLMNU lumbang
ABGLMOU lumbago
ABGLNOO Bologna
ABGLOOT toolbag
ABGLORT ragbolt
ABGLOSU albugos
subgoal
ABGLRRU burglar
ABGMNOY bogy-man
ABGNOPR probang
ABGNOTU gunboat
ABGNOWY bowyang

ABGOORT botargo
ABGOPST postbag
ABGORRU goburra
ABGORTU outbrag
ABGOSUY gas-buoy
ABGOTTU tugboat
ABHHIPT hip-bath
ABHHKOT khotbah
ABHHKTU khutbah
ABHHOOP Pooh-Bah
ABHHSUY hushaby
ABHIINT inhabit
ABHIKLS bashlik
ABHIKTW hawkbit
ABHILNO hobnail
ABHILOS abolish
ABHILOT oil-bath
ABHILTU halibut
ABHIMNR △brahmin
ABHINST absinth
ABHIORS boarish
ABHIOST isobath
ABHISTU habitus
ABHKORU bourkha
ABHKRSU kurbash
ABHLMSY shambly
ABHLOUX box-haul
ABHLRTU hurlbat
ABHMNSU △bushman
ABHMSTU mash-tub
ABHNSTU sunbath
ABHORRU harbour
ABHOTUY hautboy
ABHRSTU tarbush
ABHSTUW washtub
ABIIJLS jib-sail
ABIIKKT kibitka
ABIILMU bulimia
ABIILNQ inqilab
ABIILNS aiblins
ABIILRY biliary
ABIILST stibial
ABIILTY ability
ABIIMST iambist
ABIINOR △robinia
ABIINRY biryani
ABIIOSS abiosis
ABIJLNR brinjal
ABIJNOT abjoint
ABIJNPU Punjabi
ABIJOSW Ojibwas
ABIKLMN lambkin
ABIKLMR milk-bar
ABIKLOR kilobar
ABIKMNR barmkin
ABIKOTT kit-boat
ABIKOUZ bazouki
ABIKRST britska
ABIKRTZ britzka
ABILLMN billman
ABILLMU ballium
ABILLMY balmily

ABILLNP	pinball
ABILLPY	pay-bill
	pliably
ABILLSW	sawbill
ABILLSY	syllabi
ABILLTT	battill
ABILLWX	waxbill
ABILLWY	waybill
ABILMNU	albumin
ABILMOX	mailbox
ABILNOS	albinos
ABILNOT	bitonal
ABILNOZ	bizonal
ABILNRY	bairnly
ABILOPR	bipolar
	parboil
ABILORT	orbital
ABILORV	bolivar
ABILOTU	bail-out
	obitual
ABILRRY	library
ABILRSU	railbus
ABIMNOU	Anobium
ABIMNRU	Umbrian
ABIMOSS	biomass
ABIMPST	baptism
ABIMRST	imbrast
ABIMRTT	trimtab
ABIMTTY	ambitty
ABINOOR	boronia
ABINORR	bar-iron
ABINORS	Sorbian
ABINORT	taborin
ABINORW	rainbow
ABINOST	bastion
ABINOSU	abusion
ABINRTV	vibrant
ABIORRS	barrios
ABIORTV	vibrato
ABIPRTT	bit-part
ABIPSTT	△baptist
ABIRTTY	traybit
ABISSST	bassist
ABIZZZZ	bizzazz
ABJKMOS	sjambok
ABJLMOO	jambool
ABKLLNY	blankly
ABKLOOW	law-book
ABKLRUW	bulwark
ABKMNOO	bookman
ABKNRUU	bunraku
ABLLLUY	lullaby
ABLLNOO	balloon
ABLLOPR	proball
ABLLORR	roll-bar
ABLLORU	lobular
ABLLOTY	tallboy
ABLLPSU	balls-up
ABLLPTU	pull-tab
ABLLRUY	bullary
ABLMMOU	bummalo
ABLMNOU	umbonal
ABLMOOT	tombola
ABLMOSY	lamboys
ABLMOVY	movably
ABLMPUU	pabulum
ABLMTUY	mutably
ABLNOTU	butanol
ABLNOTY	notably
ABLNTUY	tunably
ABLOORS	robalos
ABLOORT	toolbar
ABLOORY	obolary
ABLOPTT	tap-bolt
ABLOPXY	play-box
ABLOPYY	playboy
ABLORST	borstal
ABLORTW	blawort
ABLORUW	bourlaw
ABLOSTX	saltbox
ABLPRSU	burlaps
ABLPSUY	playbus®
ABLRTUU	tubular
ABMMNOS	mobsman
ABMOORR	bar-room
ABMORTU	tambour
ABMOSTU	subatom
ABNOORS	soroban
ABNOORZ	borazon
ABNOOSS	bassoon
ABNORTY	baryton
ABNORUY	Yoruban
ABNOSSU	bonasus
ABNOTUY	buoyant
ABNRTTU	turbant
ABOOPSX	soapbox
ABOORTW	rowboat
ABOORYZ	Bryozoa
ABOOTTW	towboat
ABORSTU	robusta
	rubatos
ABOSSTU	Basutos
ABOSTUU	autobus
ABPRSTU	upbrast
ABRRSUY	bursary
ABRRTUY	turbary
ABRSTUU	arbutus
ABSUWZZ	buzz-saw
ACCCILY	acyclic
ACCDDEI	caddice
ACCDDOR	d'accord
ACCDEEN	cadence
ACCDEER	acceder
ACCDEHT	catched
ACCDEII	accidie
ACCDEIO	accoied
ACCDEIU	caducei
ACCDEKO	cockade
ACCDEKR	cracked
ACCDENY	cadency
ACCDEOY	accoyed
ACCDERU	cardecu
ACCDESU	accused
	succade
ACCDFIL	flaccid
ACCDHIL	chalcid
ACCDILS	scaldic
ACCDINS	Scandic
ACCDIOT	octadic
ACCDKNO	candock
ACCDKOW	dawcock
ACCDLOY	accoyld
	cacodyl
ACCEEHO	coachee
ACCEELN	cenacle
ACCEENR	creance
ACCEERT	accrete
ACCEFIT	factice
ACCEFLU	felucca
ACCEGIN	accinge
ACCEGNO	Cocagne
ACCEGOS	soccage
ACCEGPU	cage-cup
ACCEHHI	chéchia
ACCEHIL	caliche
	chalice
ACCEHIM	macchie
ACCEHIN	chicane
ACCEHLN	chancel
ACCEHLO	cochlea
ACCEHLT	Caltech
ACCEHNO	conchae
ACCEHNR	chancer
	chancre
ACCEHNS	chances
ACCEHNT	catchen
ACCEHNU	chaunce
ACCEHNY	chancey
ACCEHOR	caroche
	coacher
ACCEHPU	capuche
ACCEHRT	catcher
	recatch
ACCEHTU	catechu
ACCEHXY	cachexy
ACCEIKP	icepack
ACCEILL	calicle
ACCEILN	calcine
ACCEILO	coeliac
ACCEILS	calices
ACCEILT	calcite
ACCEIMR	ceramic
	racemic
ACCEINO	cocaine
	oceanic
ACCEINR	Circean
ACCEINV	vaccine
ACCEIPR	caprice
ACCEIPV	peccavi
ACCEIQU	cacique
ACCEIRS	carices
ACCEIRT	creatic
ACCEIST	ascetic
ACCEKLR	cackler
	clacker
	crackle

ACCEKMO meacock
ACCEKOP peacock
ACCEKOS seacock
ACCEKPU cupcake
ACCEKRR cracker
ACCELLY calycle
ACCELNO conceal
ACCELOR coracle
ACCELOT cacolet
ACCELSU saccule
ACCELSY calyces
ACCEMNO Meccano®
ACCENOR conacre
ACCENOS asconce
ACCENOV concave
ACCENPT peccant
ACCENST accents
ACCEOPY cacoepy
ACCEPRU race-cup
ACCEPRY peccary
ACCERRT carrect
ACCERSU accurse
accuser
ACCFIIP △pacific
ACCFILY calcify
ACCFLOW cow-calf
ACCGHIO Chicago
ACCHHKU kuchcha
ACCHIMS chasmic
ACCHINO △chicano
Noachic
ACCHIOR co-chair
ACCHIOT chaotic
ACCHIOU acouchi
ACCHIRS scraich
ACCHJSU jacchus
ACCHKOY haycock
ACCHLNO conchal
ACCHLTU claucht
ACCHNRS scranch
ACCHNRU craunch
ACCHOPU capouch
ACCHOTW △choctaw
ACCHOUY acouchy
ACCHPTU catchup
upcatch
ACCHRRU currach
ACCHRST △scratch
ACCHRSU scrauch
ACCIILN aclinic
ACCIINT actinic
ACCIIST ascitic
sciatic
ACCIKRR carrick
ACCIKRS car-sick
ACCILLU calculi
ACCILMO comical
ACCILMU calcium
ACCILNO conical
△laconic
ACCILNU Cluniac
ACCILNY cynical
ACCILOR caloric
ACCILOS calicos
ACCILOV vocalic
ACCILRU crucial
ACCILRY acrylic
ACCILSS classic
ACCILST clastic
ACCILSU sacculi
ACCIMOZ zimocca
ACCINNO canonic
ACCINOP Canopic
ACCINOT cantico
ACCINRU crucian
ACCIOPR caproic
ACCIORS scoriac
ACCIPRT practic
ACCISTT tactics
ACCISTU caustic
ACCKLMU Calmuck
ACCKLOR carlock
ACCKLRY crackly
ACCKMOR cromack
ACCKOSS cassock
Cossack
ACCKOST castock
ACCMOPT accompt
compact
ACCMRUU curcuma
ACCNNOO cooncan
ACCNOOP cocopan
ACCNOOR raccoon
ACCNOTT contact
ACCNOTU account
ACCOPTY copycat
ACCOQSU squacco
ACCORSS corcass
ACCORTU accourt
ACCRSTU accurst
ACDDDKO daddock
ACDDEER cedared
ACDDEEY decayed
ACDDEHR Cheddar
ACDDEIL dedalic
ACDDEIN candied
ACDDEIU decidua
ACDDELO cladode
ACDDELR cladder
ACDDEMU ducdame
ACDDEOP decapod
ACDDERU adducer
ACDDHHU chuddah
ACDDHIS caddish
ACDDHKO haddock
ACDDHOR chaddor
ACDDHRU chuddar
ACDDINU Dunciad
ACDDIRS discard
ACDDKMO Maddock
ACDDKOP paddock
ACDDSSY caddyss
ACDEEES decease
ACDEEFR defacer
ACDEEFT faceted
ACDEEGL glacéed
ACDEEHL Chaldee
ACDEEHR reached
ACDEEIR deciare
ACDEEJT dejecta
ACDEELL cadelle
ACDEELR Cedrela
creedal
declare
ACDEELS descale
seed-lac
ACDEELV cleaved
ACDEEMR racemed
ACDEENV vendace
ACDEEOT Docetae
ACDEERT cedrate
cerated
ACDEEST tedesca
ACDEETU educate
ACDEETY cat-eyed
ACDEFIN fancied
ACDEFIR farcied
ACDEFOP po-faced
ACDEFRS scarfed
ACDEFRT fracted
ACDEGGL clagged
ACDEGGR cragged
ACDEGHR charged
ACDEGIS discage
ACDEGKO dockage
ACDEGNO decagon
ACDEGOR cordage
ACDEHIN chained
echidna
ACDEHIP edaphic
ACDEHIX hexadic
ACDEHKW whacked
ACDEHLR chalder
ACDEHMR charmed
ACDEHMS chasmed
ACDEHMT matched
ACDEHNR endarch
ranched
ACDEHOR chordae
ACDEHOT cathode
ACDEHPP chapped
ACDEHPR parched
ACDEHPT patched
ACDEHPU cuphead
ACDEHRR charred
ACDEHTT chatted
ACDEIIO Dioecia
ACDEILL cedilla
ACDEILM camelid
decimal
declaim
medical
ACDEILN Iceland
ACDEILR decrial
radicel
radicle

ACDEILS	Alcides
ACDEILT	citadel
	deltaic
	dialect
	edictal
ACDEIMY	mediacy
ACDEINO	△oceanid
ACDEINR	cairned
ACDEINS	candies
ACDEINY	cyanide
ACDEIPR	epacrid
ACDEIPS	dispace
ACDEIRR	carried
ACDEIRS	darcies
	radices
	sidecar
ACDEIRU	decuria
ACDEISS	discase
ACDEIST	die-cast
ACDEISV	advices
ACDEITT	dictate
ACDEITY	edacity
ACDEKLT	tackled
	talcked
ACDEKRT	tracked
ACDEKRW	wracked
ACDEKST	stacked
ACDELLS	scalled
ACDELMM	clammed
ACDELMS	mascled
ACDELNO	celadon
ACDELNS	calends
ACDELPP	clapped
ACDELPY	ycleap'd
ACDELRS	scalder
ACDELSS	classed
	declass
ACDELST	castled
ACDELWW	dew-claw
ACDEMMR	crammed
ACDEMNU	decuman
ACDEMOR	comrade
ACDEMPR	cramped
ACDENNS	scanned
ACDENNT	candent
ACDENNU	nuanced
ACDENOR	acorned
	Dracone®
	dracone
ACDENPT	pandect
ACDENPU	unpaced
ACDENRT	cantred
	tranced
ACDENRU	durance
	unraced
ACDENRY	ardency
ACDENST	descant
ACDENTU	unacted
ACDEOPS	peascod
ACDEORR	corrade
ACDEORS	sarcode
ACDEORT	cordate
	redcoat
ACDEOTT	codetta
ACDEOUV	couvade
ACDEPRS	scarped
ACDERRS	scarred
ACDERSU	crusade
ACDERTT	detract
ACDERTU	traduce
ACDESTT	scatted
ACDFIIY	acidify
ACDFIOT	factoid
ACDGINN	dancing
ACDGINO	gonadic
ACDGKLO	daglock
ACDGNOT	cantdog
ACDGORT	dogcart
ACDHIIL	chiliad
ACDHIIS	Hasidic
ACDHIOP	phacoid
ACDHIRY	diarchy
ACDHISS	Chassid
ACDHKOY	Hock-day
ACDHLOR	chordal
	dorlach
ACDHNOW	cowhand
ACDHOOT	cathood
ACDHOPR	pochard
ACDHORR	orchard
ACDHRUY	duarchy
ACDHRYY	dyarchy
ACDIIIN	indicia
ACDIINN	indican
ACDIINO	conidia
ACDIINR	acridin
ACDIIRS	△cidaris
	sciarid
ACDIIRT	arctiid
	triacid
	triadic
ACDIITY	acidity
ACDIKLS	skaldic
ACDILLO	codilla
ACDILMO	domical
ACDILMS	cladism
ACDILNO	nodical
ACDILNU	dulcian
ACDILOP	placoid
	podalic
ACDILOR	cordial
ACDILOT	cotidal
ACDILPU	paludic
ACDILST	cladist
ACDILTW	wildcat
ACDIMMU	cadmium
ACDIMNO	mandioc
	monacid
	monadic
	nomadic
ACDIMNY	dynamic
ACDINRU	iracund
ACDINST	discant
ACDINSU	Sudanic
ACDIOPR	parodic
	picador
ACDIORR	corrida
ACDIORS	sarcoid
ACDIORT	arctoid
	carotid
ACDIOST	Sotadic
ACDIOTY	dacoity
ACDIOXY	oxy-acid
ACDIQRU	quadric
ACDIRST	drastic
ACDITUV	viaduct
ACDJNTU	adjunct
ACDKLOP	padlock
ACDKLSY	skyclad
ACDKMOO	mockado
ACDKMPU	mudpack
ACDKNTU	duck-ant
ACDKOPR	pockard
ACDLLOR	collard
ACDLLUY	ducally
ACDLNOR	caldron
ACDLNOT	cotland
ACDLNSU	sun-clad
ACDLOPU	cupola'd
ACDLOWY	ladycow
ACDMMNO	command
ACDMOOW	camwood
ACDMORZ	czardom
ACDNOOR	cardoon
ACDNORU	candour
	caudron
ACDORST	costard
ACDORSU	crusado
ACDORUZ	cruzado
ACDRSTU	custard
ACDRSUU	carduus
ACEEEPS	escapee
ACEEEUV	evacuee
ACEEFFT	A-effect
ACEEFHN	enchafe
ACEEFIN	faience
	faïence
	fiancée
ACEEFNY	fayence
ACEEFPR	preface
ACEEGGP	pace-egg
ACEEGGS	egg-case
ACEEGIL	elegiac
ACEEGNR	engrace
ACEEGNT	centage
ACEEGSU	escuage
ACEEHHT	cheetah
ACEEHIP	cheapie
ACEEHIT	hicatee
	teachie
ACEEHIV	achieve
ACEEHKO	hoe-cake
ACEEHLR	relâche
ACEEHLS	Chelsea
ACEEHLT	chelate

ACEEHMP	empeach
ACEEHMR	machree
ACEEHMT	machete
ACEEHNN	enhance
ACEEHNP	cheapen
	ha'pence
ACEEHNS	enchase
ACEEHOR	ochreae
ACEEHPP	échappé
ACEEHPR	peacher
ACEEHRR	reacher
ACEEHRT	cheater
	hectare
	rechate
	recheat
	teacher
ACEEHST	escheat
ACEEHTT	thecate
ACEEHTX	excheat
ACEEILP	calipee
ACEEILT	Eleatic
ACEEIMT	emicate
ACEEINR	Cairene
	cinerea
ACEEINU	eucaine
ACEEIRR	cariere
ACEEISV	vesicae
ACEEJKN	△jackeen
ACEEKNP	kneecap
	knee-cap
ACEELLN	nacelle
ACEELMP	emplace
ACEELMR	réclame
ACEELNR	cleaner
ACEELNS	cleanse
	scalene
ACEELNT	latence
ACEELNV	enclave
	valence
ACEELPR	percale
	replace
ACEELPT	capelet
ACEELRR	clearer
ACEELRS	rescale
	re-scale
ACEELRT	treacle
ACEELRU	caerule
ACEELRV	cleaver
ACEELST	celesta
ACEELSU	euclase
ACEELVX	exclave
ACEEMNR	menacer
ACEEMRR	creamer
ACEEMRT	cremate
	meercat
ACEENNP	penance
ACEENNR	narceen
ACEENNS	Senecan
ACEENNT	canteen
ACEENNY	cayenne
ACEENOT	acetone
ACEENPS	pen-case
ACEENRS	caserne
ACEENRT	centare
	crenate
	re-enact
ACEENTU	cuneate
ACEEORS	acerose
ACEEORT	ocreate
ACEEOST	acetose
ACEEOTV	evocate
ACEEPRR	caperer
ACEEPRS	escaper
	percase
ACEERRS	creaser
ACEERRT	caterer
	retrace
	terrace
ACEERST	secreta
ACEERTX	exacter
	excreta
ACEESST	ectases
ACEESTY	cat's-eye
ACEFFFO	face-off
ACEFFHI	affiche
ACEFFHR	chaffer
ACEFFIN	caffein
ACEFFIS	scaffie
ACEFFOR	afforce
ACEFGOT	geofact
ACEFHMR	chamfer
ACEFHOR	arch-foe
ACEFHRU	chaufer
ACEFIIL	felicia
ACEFILM	malefic
ACEFILR	filacer
ACEFINN	finance
ACEFINR	fancier
ACEFINS	fascine
ACEFITV	factive
ACEFITY	acetify
ACEFKLR	flacker
ACEFKLT	flacket
ACEFLRU	careful
ACEFNNO	façonné
ACEFNRT	cantref
ACEFNRU	furnace
ACEFOPR	proface
ACEFORR	forecar
ACEFOTU	outface
ACEFRRT	refract
ACEFRRU	farceur
ACEFRSU	surface
ACEFRTU	facture
	furcate
ACEGHLO	galoche
ACEGHNR	changer
ACEGHNS	changes
ACEGHNU	chaunge
ACEGHOU	gouache
ACEGHOW	cowhage
ACEGHRR	charger
ACEGHRS	charges
ACEGHRT	gertcha
ACEGILL	ellagic
	△gallice
ACEGILN	angelic
	△anglice
	Galenic
ACEGILP	pelagic
ACEGILR	glacier
	gracile
ACEGIMO	camogie
ACEGIMR	grimace
ACEGIMT	gametic
ACEGINO	coinage
ACEGINR	△grecian
ACEGINS	ceasing
ACEGINV	veganic
ACEGKLO	lockage
ACEGKLR	grackle
ACEGKMO	mockage
ACEGKOR	corkage
ACEGKOS	gas-coke
ACEGLLO	collage
ACEGLNO	congeal
ACEGLNR	clanger
ACEGLOT	catelog
ACEGLOU	cagoule
ACEGMOP	compage
ACEGNOR	acrogen
	cornage
ACEGNOT	co-agent
	cognate
ACEGORS	cargoes
	corsage
	socager
ACEGORU	courage
ACEGOTT	cottage
ACEGRTU	trucage
ACEGSTU	scutage
ACEHHLT	hatchel
ACEHHRT	hatcher
ACEHHRU	hachure
ACEHHRX	hexarch
ACEHHST	hatches
ACEHHTT	hatchet
ACEHIKR	kacheri
ACEHILL	challie
	helical
ACEHILN	Chilean
ACEHILR	△charlie
ACEHILT	ethical
ACEHIMN	machine
ACEHIMP	impeach
ACEHIMR	chimera
ACEHIMS	chamise
ACEHIMT	hematic
ACEHINN	enchain
ACEHINS	inchase
ACEHINT	chantie
	teach-in
ACEHINY	hyacine
ACEHIPP	chappie
ACEHIPR	charpie

Words marked △ may be spelled also with a capital letter

ACEHIPT	aphetic
	hepatic
ACEHIRS	cashier
ACEHIRT	Rhaetic
	theriac
ACEHIRV	archive
ACEHIST	aitches
ACEHITY	yachtie
ACEHKLR	hackler
ACEHKLS	hackles
	shackle
ACEHKLT	hacklet
ACEHKNY	hackney
ACEHKRW	whacker
ACEHKRY	hackery
ACEHLLP	pellach
ACEHLLS	shellac
ACEHLLT	hell-cat
ACEHLMT	chamlet
ACEHLMY	alchemy
ACEHLNN	△channel
ACEHLNO	chalone
ACEHLNR	charnel
	larchen
ACEHLOP	epochal
ACEHLOR	cholera
	chorale
ACEHLOS	oscheal
ACEHLOT	cathole
ACEHLPT	chaplet
ACEHLPY	cheaply
ACEHLRS	clasher
	raschel
ACEHLRT	archlet
ACEHLRY	△charley
ACEHLST	satchel
ACEHLTT	chattel
	latchet
ACEHMNR	encharm
	Märchen
ACEHMNT	manchet
ACEHMRR	charmer
	marcher
ACEHMRS	marches
	mesarch
ACEHMRT	matcher
	rematch
ACEHMRU	chaumer
ACEHMTY	ecthyma
ACEHNNR	channer
ACEHNNT	enchant
ACEHNOR	Acheron
ACEHNRR	rancher
ACEHNRT	chanter
	tranche
ACEHNSS	schanse
ACEHNST	chasten
ACEHNSV	Chesvan
ACEHNSZ	schanze
ACEHNTT	etchant
ACEHNTU	unteach
ACEHNTY	chantey
ACEHOPR	poacher
ACEHOTY	chayote
ACEHPPS	schappe
ACEHPRT	chapter
	patcher
ACEHPRY	eparchy
	preachy
ACEHPSS	chapess
ACEHQUU	Quechua
ACEHQUY	queachy
ACEHRRT	charter
	rechart
ACEHRRX	xerarch
ACEHRRY	archery
ACEHRSU	△archeus
ACEHRSY	hyraces
ACEHRTT	chatter
	ratchet
ACEHRTW	watcher
ACEHRTY	yachter
ACEHRXY	exarchy
ACEHSTW	watches
ACEHTTU	teuchat
ACEHTTW	watchet
ACEIILM	cimelia
ACEIILS	laicise
ACEIILT	ciliate
ACEIILZ	laicize
ACEIINT	Cainite
ACEIITV	caitive
	viciate
ACEIJKS	jacksie
ACEIKLO	oil-cake
ACEIKLS	saclike
ACEIKLT	catlike
ACEIKMR	keramic
ACEIKNT	anticke
ACEIKOP	paiocke
ACEIKPR	earpick
ACEIKPX	pickaxe
ACEIKSS	seasick
ACEIKTT	tietack
ACEILLM	limacel
	micella
ACEILLR	air-cell
ACEILLX	lexical
ACEILMN	cnemial
	melanic
ACEILMR	claimer
	miracle
	reclaim
ACEILMS	limaces
ACEILMT	climate
	metical
ACEILMX	exclaim
ACEILMY	mycelia
ACEILNP	capelin
	panicle
	pelican
ACEILNR	carline
ACEILNS	sanicle
	scaleni
ACEILNU	cauline
ACEILOR	△calorie
	cariole
	loricae
ACEILOS	coalise
ACEILOT	aloetic
	Coalite®
ACEILOZ	coalize
ACEILPP	pile-cap
ACEILPR	caliper
	replica
ACEILPS	special
ACEILPT	plicate
ACEILRR	cerrial
ACEILRS	Sercial
ACEILRT	article
	recital
ACEILRU	auricle
ACEILRV	caliver
	clavier
	valeric
	velaric
ACEILSS	salices
ACEILST	astelic
	Castile
	elastic
	latices
	salicet
ACEILSV	vesical
ACEILTT	lattice
	tactile
ACEIMMS	Acmeism
ACEIMNO	encomia
ACEIMNP	pemican
ACEIMNR	carmine
ACEIMNS	amnesic
ACEIMNT	emicant
	nematic
ACEIMNX	Mexican
ACEIMPY	pyaemic
ACEIMRT	matrice
ACEIMRU	uraemic
ACEIMST	Acmeist
	etacism
	sematic
ACEIMSU	caesium
ACEINNP	pinnace
ACEINNS	Nancies
ACEINNT	ancient
ACEINNY	cyanine
ACEINOP	paeonic
ACEINOS	acinose
ACEINOT	aconite
	anoetic
ACEINPR	caprine
ACEINPS	inscape
	pincase
ACEINRS	arsenic
	cerasin

ACEINRT	certain
	creatin
	crinate
	nacrite
ACEINST	cineast
	Insecta
ACEINSY	cyanise
ACEINTT	nictate
	tetanic
ACEINTV	Vectian
	venatic
ACEINTX	inexact
ACEINTY	cyanite
ACEINYZ	cyanize
ACEIOOZ	zooecia
ACEIOPT	ectopia
ACEIORS	scoriae
ACEIORT	erotica
ACEIOST	sociate
ACEIOTX	exotica
ACEIPPR	epicarp
ACEIPPT	tappice
ACEIPRS	epacris
	scrapie
	Serapic
ACEIPRT	paretic
	picrate
ACEIPST	aseptic
	spicate
ACEIPSU	auspice
ACEIPSZ	capsize
ACEIPTV	captive
ACEIQRU	acquire
ACEIQTU	acquite
ACEIQUZ	cazique
ACEIRRR	carrier
ACEIRRT	cirrate
	erratic
ACEIRRW	air-crew
ACEIRST	cristae
	stearic
ACEIRSU	saucier
	uricase
ACEIRSV	varices
	viscera
ACEIRSZ	crazies
ACEIRTT	citrate
ACEISSS	ascesis
ACEISST	ascites
	ectasis
ACEISTT	statice
ACEISTV	Avestic
ACEITTV	cavetti
ACEITTX	extatic
ACEITUX	auxetic
ACEJKOP	pajocke
ACEJLOR	cajoler
ACEJNOT	jaconet
ACEJNOY	joyance
	Joycean
ACEJNTU	juncate
ACEJPTU	cajeput
ACEJRTT	traject
ACEKKNR	knacker
ACEKLLP	pellack
ACEKLNR	crankle
ACEKLNS	slacken
ACEKLOR	earlock
ACEKLPT	placket
ACEKLQU	quackle
ACEKLRS	slacker
ACEKLRT	tackler
ACEKLRU	caulker
ACEKLSY	lackeys
ACEKMRS	smacker
ACEKNPR	prancke
ACEKNRY	cankery
ACEKORR	croaker
ACEKPPR	prepack
ACEKQRU	quacker
ACEKRRT	tracker
ACEKRST	rackets
	stacker
ACEKRSY	screaky
ACEKRTT	rackett
ACEKRTY	rackety
ACEKSTT	stacket
ACEKTTY	tackety
ACELLMO	calomel
ACELLNU	nucleal
ACELLNY	cleanly
ACELLOR	corella
	ocellar
ACELLOT	collate
ACELLPS	scalpel
ACELLPY	clypeal
ACELLRR	carrell
ACELLRS	scleral
ACELLRU	cure-all
ACELLRY	clearly
ACELMOR	caromel
ACELMOT	camelot
ACELMOU	caulome
	leucoma
ACELMPR	clamper
ACELMRY	camelry
ACELMTU	calumet
ACELNNU	unclean
ACELNNY	lyncean
ACELNOR	corneal
ACELNOS	Seconal®
ACELNOT	lactone
ACELNOZ	calzone
ACELNPS	enclasp
	spancel
ACELNPT	clapnet
ACELNPU	clean-up
	unplace
ACELNRS	lancers
ACELNRT	central
ACELNRU	lucarne
	nuclear
	unclear
ACELNRY	larceny
ACELNST	scantle
ACELNSU	censual
	unscale
ACELNTT	cantlet
ACELNTY	latency
ACELNVY	valency
ACELOPR	polacre
ACELOPS	escalop
ACELOPT	polecat
ACELOQU	coequal
ACELORS	claroes
	escolar
ACELORY	caloyer
ACELOST	alecost
	lactose
	scatole
	talcose
ACELOTT	calotte
ACELOTU	oculate
ACELOTY	acolyte
	cotylae
ACELOUV	vacuole
ACELPPR	clapper
ACELPPS	scapple
ACELPRS	clasper
	scalper
ACELPRT	plectra
ACELPRY	prelacy
ACELPSU	capsule
	lace-ups
	specula
	upscale
ACELPSY	cypsela
ACELPTY	ectypal
ACELQRU	lacquer
ACELQUY	lacquey
ACELRRW	crawler
ACELRST	scarlet
ACELRSU	cesural
	secular
ACELRTT	clatter
ACELRTY	treacly
ACELSSS	sacless
ACELSTU	sulcate
ACELSTY	scytale
ACELSUU	aculeus
ACELSUX	excusal
ACELSXY	calyxes
ACELTUY	acutely
ACELTXY	exactly
ACEMMRR	crammer
ACEMNOR	△cremona
	△romance
ACEMOPR	compare
	compear
ACEMORU	morceau
ACEMOSU	mucosae
ACEMPRS	scamper
ACEMPRT	crampet
ACEMRSY	cramesy
ACEMSTT	metcast

ACENNOS	ancones
	sonance
ACENNOT	connate
ACENNOY	noyance
ACENNOZ	canzone
ACENNRS	scanner
ACENNRY	cannery
ACENNST	nascent
ACENNTY	tenancy
ACENOOR	coronae
ACENOPT	patonce
ACENOPU	ponceau
ACENORS	carnose
	coarsen
ACENORT	enactor
ACENOSS	cassone
ACENOST	costean
ACENOTT	attonce
ACENOTV	centavo
ACENPRR	prancer
ACENPRU	praunce
ACENPTT	pentact
ACENPTY	patency
ACENRSS	ancress
ACENRSU	surance
ACENRSY	carneys
	scenary
ACENRTT	tranect
ACENRTU	centaur
	uncrate
	untrace
ACENRTY	encraty
	nectary
ACENSTU	nutcase
ACENSTW	stew-can
ACEOOPP	apocope
ACEOOTZ	ectozoa
ACEOPRR	crop-ear
ACEOPRX	exocarp
ACEOPST	scopate
ACEOPTU	outpace
ACEORRT	acroter
	△creator
	reactor
ACEORST	△coaster
ACEORSU	acerous
	carouse
ACEORTU	outrace
ACEORTV	overact
ACEORTX	exactor
ACEOSSU	caseous
ACEOSTT	costate
ACEOSTU	acetous
ACEOTTV	cavetto
ACEOTUU	autocue
ACEOTUX	coteaux
ACEPRRS	scarper
	scraper
ACEPRST	precast
	spectra
ACEPRSU	scauper
ACEPRTU	capture
ACEPRUV	carve-up
ACEPSTU	cuspate
ACEQRTU	racquet
ACEQSTU	acquest
ACERRTT	retract
ACERRTY	tracery
ACERRUV	verruca
ACERRVY	carvery
ACERSST	actress
ACERSSU	cesuras
	sucrase
ACERSSV	scarves
ACERSTT	scatter
ACERSTU	crustae
ACERSTY	sectary
ACERTTT	tetract
ACERTTU	curtate
	cut-rate
ACERTTX	extract
ACERTTY	cattery
ACERTUV	curvate
ACERTUY	cautery
ACESSTU	caestus
ACESSTY	△ecstasy
ACESTTU	scutate
ACESTTY	testacy
ACESTUY	eustacy
ACFFHPU	huff-cap
ACFFIIT	caitiff
ACFFIKM	maffick
ACFFILT	afflict
ACFFIRT	traffic
ACFFIRY	farcify
ACFFOST	cast-off
ACFGINR	farcing
ACFHIST	catfish
ACFHISU	fuchsia
ACFHLNU	flaunch
ACFHLTU	half-cut
ACFHNOU	fauchon
ACFHRTY	fratchy
ACFIILN	finical
ACFIKNN	finnack
ACFILNO	folacin
ACFILRY	clarify
ACFIMOR	aciform
	Formica®
ACFIMRU	fumaric
ACFIMSS	△fascism
ACFINNY	infancy
ACFINOT	faction
ACFINRT	frantic
	infarct
	infract
ACFINRY	carnify
ACFIOSS	fiascos
ACFIPRY	caprify
ACFIRSY	sacrify
	scarify
ACFISST	△fascist
ACFKLSU	sackful
ACFLLOY	focally
ACFLNSU	canfuls
ACFLRUU	furcula
ACFLTTU	tactful
ACFLTUY	faculty
ACFORTX	X-factor
ACFORTY	factory
ACGGIOS	agogics
ACGGRSY	scraggy
ACGHIKN	hacking
ACGHIMO	oghamic
ACGHINR	chagrin
	charing
ACGHINS	chasing
ACGHINT	gnathic
ACGHINW	chinwag
ACGHIPR	graphic
ACGHIRS	scraigh
ACGHKLO	hack-log
ACGHLOY	Chogyal
ACGHLTU	claught
ACGHNRU	graunch
ACGHOSU	gauchos
ACGHRRU	curragh
ACGHRSU	scraugh
ACGIILN	alginic
ACGIITU	augitic
ACGIKLN	lacking
ACGIKNP	packing
ACGIKNR	arcking
	carking
	racking
ACGIKNS	sacking
ACGIKNT	tacking
ACGIKNV	vacking
ACGILLN	calling
ACGILLO	logical
ACGILMY	myalgic
ACGILNP	placing
ACGILNR	carling
ACGILNS	scaling
ACGILNT	catling
	talcing
ACGILNU	glucina
ACGIMNO	coaming
ACGINNN	canning
ACGINNT	canting
ACGINOR	organic
ACGINOS	angicos
ACGINOT	coating
	cotinga
ACGINPP	capping
ACGINPR	carping
ACGINPS	spacing
ACGINRS	sacring
ACGINRT	tracing
ACGINRV	carving
	craving
ACGINST	casting
ACGIRST	gastric
ACGKMMO	gammock
ACGKORV	garvock
ACGLLPU	cupgall

ACGLNOR clangor
ACGLSUU Glaucus
ACGNNOR crannog
ACGNOOT octagon
ACGORRY gyrocar
ACGORUU couguar
ACHHIRS rhachis
ACHHOST toshach
ACHHPPU chuppah
ACHHTTT thatcht
ACHIIKM kamichi
ACHIILN Chilian
ACHIILS ischial
ACHIIMS chiasmi
ACHIIMT Hamitic
ACHIINT Chianti
ACHIIPS pachisi
ACHIJNT jacinth
ACHIKOP pak-choi
ACHIKRS ricksha
ACHIKRY hayrick
ACHIKSS shicksa
ACHILLO lochial
ACHILLP phallic
ACHILLS challis
ACHILLT thallic
ACHILMO malicho
ACHILOR chorial
ACHILOS scholia
ACHILRS carlish
ACHILRY charily
ACHILSY clayish
ACHILWY lichway
ACHIMNO manihoc
Mohican
ACHIMOS chamiso
chamois
ACHIMRS charism
ACHIMSS chiasms
schisma
ACHIMST mastich
tachism
ACHINNU unchain
ACHINOP aphonic
ACHINOY onychia
ACHINPS spinach
ACHINRZ zarnich
ACHINTX xanthic
ACHINUV chauvin
ACHIOPT aphotic
ACHIORT chariot
haricot
ACHIPPS △sapphic
ACHIPST haptics
spathic
ACHIPTU chupati
ACHIPTW whipcat
ACHIQRU charqui
ACHIQUU Quichua
ACHIRRT triarch
ACHIRTU haircut
ACHIRTY charity

ACHISSS chassis
ACHISTT cattish
tachist
ACHKMMO hammock
ACHKOPS hopsack
hop-sack
ACHKOSS hassock
ACHKOSW whackos
ACHKOTT hattock
ACHLLOO alcohol
ACHLLOR chloral
ACHLMSY chlamys
ACHLMYY alchymy
ACHLNOY halcyon
ACHLNTU tulchan
unlatch
ACHLOPR raploch
ACHLOPT potlach
ACHLORS scholar
ACHLORT trochal
ACHLOSW salchow
ACHLOTY acolyth
ACHLPST splatch
ACHLTUZ chalutz
ACHMNOO Manchoo
ACHMNOR monarch
nomarch
ACHMNRU uncharm
ACHMOPR camphor
ACHMORZ machzor
ACHMOST stomach
ACHMSUW cumshaw
ACHNNOS chanson
ACHNORS ranchos
ACHNORT chantor
ACHNOSS sanchos
ACHNOTY tachyon
ACHNOUY chanoyu
ACHNOVY anchovy
ACHNPSS schnaps
ACHNPUY paunchy
ACHNRTY chantry
ACHNRUY raunchy
unchary
ACHNSTU canthus
staunch
ACHNSTY snatchy
ACHOOST cahoots
ACHOPRT toparch
ACHOPRY charpoy
Corypha
ACHORSU aurochs
ACHPPTU patch-up
ACHRSTY starchy
ACHRSUU urachus
ACHSSTY stachys
ACHSTUY cyathus
ACIIKNN canikin
ACIIKRS airsick
ACIILMM mimical
ACIILMS Islamic
ACIILMT Tamilic

ACIILNR clarini
ACIILNS salicin
sinical
ACIILNV vicinal
ACIILNZ Zincali
ACIILOV viliaco
ACIILRY ciliary
ACIILSS Liassic
ACIILST italics
ACIILSU iliacus
ACIILTY laicity
ACIIMMN minicam
ACIIMMS miasmic
ACIIMNR crimina
mini-car
ACIIMOT comitia
ACIIMST ismatic
itacism
ACIINNO anionic
ACIINOS asinico
ACIINOV avionic
ACIINPS piscina
ACIINTT △titanic
ACIIPPR △priapic
ACIIPRT piratic
ACIIRST satiric
ACIIRTT triatic
ACIJNOP Japonic
ACIJUZZ Jacuzzi®
jacuzzi
ACIKKPT tap-kick
ACIKLNO Lockian
ACIKLOR airlock
air-lock
ACIKLTY tackily
ACIKMOO oomiack
ACIKMPR rampick
ACIKMPW pickmaw
ACIKNNP pannick
ACIKNOR Koranic
ACIKNPY panicky
ACIKNST catskin
ACIKNTT tintack
ACIKPRT patrick
ACIKPSX six-pack
ACIKRST karstic
ACILLMS miscall
ACILLRY lyrical
ACILMNO limaçon
malonic
ACILMOT comital
ACILMPS plasmic
ACILMRS Carlism
ACILMSU musical
ACILMTU Tamulic
ACILNNY cannily
ACILNOR clarino
clarion
Locrian
ACILNOZ calzoni
Zincalo
ACILNPS inclasp

ACILNPY	pliancy
ACILNTU	lunatic
ACILNUV	vincula
ACILOOR	air-cool
ACILOPT	Capitol
	optical
	pit-coal
	topical
ACILORR	racloir
ACILORV	corival
ACILOST	△stoical
ACILOTV	volatic
	voltaic
ACILOTX	toxical
ACILPST	plastic
ACILPSU	spicula
ACILPTY	clay-pit
	typical
ACILRST	Carlist
ACILRTU	curtail
	trucial
ACILRTY	clarity
ACILRYZ	crazily
ACILSSS	classis
ACILSUY	saucily
ACILTTY	cattily
	tacitly
ACILTUV	victual
ACIMNOP	campion
ACIMNOR	Marconi®
	marconi
	Minorca
	Romanic
ACIMNOS	masonic
ACIMNOT	Comtian
ACIMNPU	Panicum
ACIMNRU	cranium
	cumarin
ACIMNTT	catmint
ACIMOPT	cami-top
	potamic
	Tampico
ACIMORR	Armoric
ACIMOST	maticos
	somatic
ACIMPRT	crampit
	ptarmic
ACIMPRY	primacy
ACIMPSS	spasmic
ACIMRSZ	czarism
ACIMSST	miscast
ACIMSTT	tactism
ACINNOT	actinon
	cantion
	contain
ACINNOZ	canzoni
	Cinzano®
ACINNST	stannic
ACINNTU	annicut
ACINOPT	caption
	paction
ACINOQU	coquina
ACINORR	carrion
ACINORS	Roscian
	saronic
ACINORT	carotin
ACINOSS	caisson
	casinos
	cassino
ACINOST	Scotian
ACINOSU	acinous
ACINOSX	Saxonic
ACINOTT	taction
ACINOTU	auction
	caution
ACINPRT	cantrip
ACINPRU	Puranic
ACINPRY	△cyprian
ACINQTU	quantic
ACINRSU	crusian
ACINRTT	△tantric
ACINRTU	curtain
	turacin
ACINSTU	nautics
ACIOPRS	prosaic
ACIOPRT	apricot
	parotic
	patrico
ACIOPTT	aptotic
ACIOPTY	opacity
ACIORRS	corsair
ACIORSU	carious
	curiosa
ACIORTT	ricotta
ACIPRSY	piscary
ACIPRTT	tip-cart
ACIPRVY	privacy
ACIPSST	spastic
ACIPTUY	paucity
ACIQRTU	quartic
ACIQSTU	acquist
ACIRSST	sacrist
ACIRSSU	cuirass
ACIRSTT	astrict
ACIRSTU	Austric
ACIRSTW	twiscar
ACIRSTY	satyric
ACIRSTZ	czarist
ACISSTT	statics
ACISSTU	casuist
ACISTTU	catsuit
ACISTUV	vacuist
ACITUVY	vacuity
ACJKKSY	skyjack
ACJKLOW	lockjaw
ACJKNNO	jannock
ACJKOPT	jackpot
ACJLORU	jocular
ACJMNTU	muntjac
ACJPTUU	cajuput
ACKKLMU	Kalmuck
ACKLLOP	pollack
ACKLLOY	laylock
ACKLLSY	slackly
ACKLMNO	lockman
ACKLMOR	armlock
	lockram
ACKLNOU	uncloak
ACKLOOR	oar-lock
ACKLORW	warlock
ACKLORY	rocklay
ACKLOSS	lassock
ACKLOSY	yolk-sac
ACKMMMO	mammock
ACKMOTT	mattock
ACKMSSU	musk-sac
ACKMSTU	musk-cat
ACKNNOW	acknown
ACKNSTU	unstack
ACKOPRR	parrock
ACKORRT	rock-tar
	tarrock
ACLLLOY	locally
ACLLOOR	corolla
ACLLOPS	scallop
ACLLORU	locular
ACLLOSU	callous
ACLLOTU	call-out
ACLLOVY	vocally
ACLMNOO	locoman
ACLMNUY	calumny
ACLMORU	clamour
ACLMSUY	masculy
ACLNOOR	coronal
ACLNOOT	coolant
ACLNOOV	volcano
ACLNORU	cornual
	courlan
ACLNOUV	unvocal
ACLNPSU	unclasp
ACLNRTU	truncal
ACLNSTY	scantly
ACLOPRT	caltrop
	proctal
ACLOPRU	copular
	cupolar
ACLOPSU	scopula
ACLOPSY	calypso
ACLOPTY	polyact
ACLORST	scrotal
	slot-car
ACLORSU	carolus
	oscular
ACLORUV	vocular
ACLOSTU	△locusta
	talcous
ACLPRTY	cryptal
ACLPRUU	cupular
ACLRSSY	crassly
ACLRSTU	crustal
ACLRSTY	crystal
ACLRSWY	scrawly
ACLSSTU	cutlass
ACMNOPR	crampon
ACMNOPY	company
ACMNORY	acronym

ACMNSTU	sanctum
ACMOOST	scotoma
ACMOPRT	compart
ACMOPSS	compass
ACMOPST	compast
ACMORTW	catworm
ACMQTUU	cumquat
ACMSUUV	vacuums
ACNNNOS	cannons
ACNNNUY	uncanny
ACNNORY	△canonry
ACNNOSY	sonancy
ACNNRSY	scranny
ACNOORS	coronas
ACNOORT	cartoon
	coranto
ACNOPSU	Canopus
ACNOPSW	snowcap
ACNORRU	rancour
ACNORRY	carry-on
ACNORSU	nacrous
ACNORTT	contrat
ACNORTU	courant
ACNOSSZ	scazons
ACNOSTU	conatus
ACNPRSY	syncarp
ACNRRTU	currant
ACNRSUY	unscary
ACNRSWY	scrawny
ACNRTUY	truancy
ACNSSTU	Sanctus
ACOOPRR	corpora
ACOOPRT	root-cap
ACOOPSU	opacous
ACOOPTT	topcoat
ACOORTU	touraco
ACOOSTV	octavos
ACOPRRT	carport
ACOPSTU	upcoast
ACORRTT	tractor
ACORRTU	curator
ACORRTY	carroty
ACORSSU	sarcous
ACORSTU	surcoat
	turacos
ACORSTY	castory
ACORSUU	raucous
ACOSTTU	outcast
ACOSUUV	vacuous
ACPPRSY	scrappy
ACPRTTU	trap-cut
ACPSTUU	usucapt
ACRSTTU	tractus
ADDDDOR	doddard
ADDDEEN	dead-end
ADDDEER	dreaded
ADDDEGL	gladded
ADDDELR	raddled
ADDDENO	deodand
ADDEEEY	dead-eye
ADDEEGR	degrade
ADDEEHR	redhead
ADDEELM	medaled
ADDEELN	delenda
ADDEELP	pedaled
	pleaded
ADDEELY	delayed
ADDEEMN	dead-men
ADDEEMR	dreamed
ADDEEOT	deodate
ADDEERR	dreader
ADDEEST	dead-set
	steaded
ADDEESY	sad-eyed
ADDEFLY	fadedly
ADDEFNU	unfaded
ADDEFRU	defraud
ADDEFRW	dwarfed
ADDEGGR	dragged
ADDEGHO	dog-head
	△godhead
ADDEGIL	gladdie
ADDEGJU	adjudge
ADDEGLN	gladden
ADDEGRU	guarded
ADDEHIR	die-hard
ADDEHLN	handled
ADDEHRS	sharded
ADDEIIK	didakei
ADDEIIS	daisied
ADDEILL	dialled
ADDEILP	plaided
ADDEILR	diedral
ADDEILT	dilated
ADDEINO	adenoid
ADDEINU	unaided
	unidea'd
ADDEINV	videnda
ADDEIOT	toadied
ADDEISV	advised
ADDEJLY	jadedly
ADDEJNU	unjaded
ADDEJRT	Jeddart
ADDELNR	dandler
ADDELPP	dappled
ADDELPR	paddler
ADDELRS	saddler
ADDELRW	dawdler
	waddler
ADDELRY	dreadly
	laddery
ADDELST	staddle
ADDELSW	swaddle
ADDELTW	twaddle
ADDELYZ	dazedly
ADDEMST	maddest
ADDENOR	road-end
ADDENOT	nodated
ADDENOU	duodena
ADDENPU	pudenda
ADDENRU	daunder
ADDENSU	asudden
ADDENTU	undated
ADDEOPT	adopted
ADDERSS	address
ADDERST	addrest
ADDERSW	swarded
ADDERSY	dryades
ADDERTT	dratted
ADDESST	saddest
ADDFHIS	faddish
ADDFIMS	faddism
ADDFINY	dandify
ADDFIST	faddist
ADDGGIN	gadding
ADDGIIR	diagrid
ADDGIMN	madding
ADDGIMR	Midgard
ADDGINP	padding
ADDGINW	wadding
ADDGLNO	gladdon
ADDGMNO	goddamn
ADDGOOW	dagwood
ADDGOOY	good-day
ADDGORW	godward
ADDGOSY	dogdays
ADDHIKS	Kaddish
ADDHINP	daphnid
ADDHIQS	Qaddish
ADDHISS	saddish
ADDHITY	hydatid
ADDIINS	disdain
ADDIKST	tsaddik
ADDIKSZ	zaddiks
ADDIKTY	katydid
ADDIKTZ	tzaddik
ADDILMN	△midland
ADDILNY	dandily
ADDILOS	disload
ADDIMNO	diamond
ADDIMOR	diadrom
ADDIMSY	dismayd
ADDINOR	android
ADDINRY	diandry
ADDIPRS	disprad
ADDIQST	tsaddiq
ADDIQTZ	tzaddiq
ADDIRZZ	dizzard
ADDLLRU	dullard
ADDLOOS	soldado
ADDLTWY	twaddly
ADDMNOS	oddsman
ADDNNOR	donnard
ADDNOOW	downa-do
ADDOORS	dorados
ADDOOSS	dos-à-dos
ADDOPSY	dasypod
ADDQSUY	squaddy
ADEEEFY	fedayee
ADEEEMN	demeane
ADEEEPS	deep-sea
ADEEERR	arreede
ADEEERX	exedrae
ADEEESW	seaweed
ADEEFIL	Felidae
ADEEFIR	fedarie

ADEEFLR	federal
ADEEFLT	deflate
ADEEFPR	prefade
ADEEFRT	draftee
ADEEFST	defaste
ADEEGGH	egghead
ADEEGGN	engaged
ADEEGHS	hag-seed
ADEEGHW	hag-weed
ADEEGLL	alledge
	alleged
ADEEGMN	endgame
ADEEGNR	derange
	enraged
	grandee
	grenade
ADEEGNV	vendage
ADEEGOT	dogeate
	goateed
ADEEGRR	regrade
ADEEGRU	guardee
ADEEGRW	ragweed
ADEEGSW	saw-edge
ADEEHLO	Helodea
ADEEHLR	hederal
ADEEHNN	hennaed
ADEEHNS	dasheen
ADEEHNV	havened
ADEEHPR	ephedra
ADEEHRR	adherer
ADEEHRS	sheared
ADEEHRT	hearted
ADEEHRX	exhedra
ADEEHST	headset
ADEEHSV	sheaved
ADEEHSY	hayseed
ADEEIIR	Irideae
ADEEIJT	jadeite
ADEEILM	limeade
ADEEILN	aliened
	delaine
ADEEILP	Pléiade
ADEEILS	deiseal
ADEEILY	eyeliad
ADEEIMN	demaine
ADEEIMT	mediate
ADEEINN	adenine
ADEEINS	aniseed
ADEEIQU	Equidae
ADEEIRR	readier
ADEEIRS	readies
ADEEIRW	wearied
ADEEISS	disease
	seaside
ADEEITV	deviate
ADEEKNP	knee-pad
ADEEKNR	kneader
ADEEKNS	sneaked
ADEEKNW	wakened
ADEEKRW	wreaked
ADEEKWY	weekday
ADEELLS	allseed
ADEELLY	alleyed
ADEELMR	emerald
ADEELMS	measled
ADEELMT	medalet
	metaled
ADEELNP	deplane
ADEELNR	Laender
	learned
ADEELNT	edental
ADEELNW	Wealden
ADEELPR	pearled
	pleader
ADEELPS	delapse
	pleased
ADEELPT	pleated
ADEELRT	altered
	related
	treadle
ADEELRW	leeward
ADEELRY	delayer
	layered
	relayed
ADEELST	stealed
ADEELSV	sleaved
ADEELTV	velated
ADEELTX	exalted
ADEELUV	devalue
ADEEMNR	amender
	enarmed
	meander
	reamend
ADEEMNW	new-made
ADEEMNY	demayne
ADEEMRR	dreamer
ADEEMST	steamed
ADEEMSU	medusae
ADEEMSW	mawseed
ADEEMTW	matweed
ADEEMWY	mayweed
ADEENNV	Vendean
ADEENRU	uneared
ADEENRY	deanery
	△ne'erday
	renayed
	year-end
ADEENST	standee
ADEENTT	dentate
ADEEORS	oreades
ADEEORW	oarweed
ADEEPPY	day-peep
ADEEPRS	speared
ADEEPRT	pad-tree
	predate
	red-tape
	tapered
ADEEPRV	deprave
	pervade
ADEERRS	redsear
ADEERRT	retread
	treader
ADEERRV	averred
ADEERST	estrade
	Tasered
ADEERSV	adverse
ADEERTV	averted
ADEERTW	dewater
	tarweed
	watered
ADEESSY	essayed
ADEESTU	sautéed
ADEESTW	sweated
ADEETUX	exudate
ADEFFIN	affined
ADEFFLM	maffled
ADEFGGL	flagged
ADEFGGR	fragged
ADEFGLN	fangled
	flanged
ADEFGOU	fougade
ADEFHST	shafted
ADEFILS	disleaf
ADEFIMS	disfame
ADEFINR	friande
ADEFINT	defiant
	fainted
ADEFIVY	five-day
ADEFLLN	elfland
ADEFLLW	dew-fall
ADEFLNN	fenland
ADEFLOS	sol-faed
ADEFLPP	flapped
ADEFLRU	dareful
ADEFLTT	flatted
ADEFLTU	default
ADEFMNU	unfamed
ADEFMST	mast-fed
ADEFNUZ	unfazed
ADEFOOS	seafood
ADEFORV	favored
ADEFORY	feodary
	fore-day
ADEFOTU	fade-out
ADEFPPR	frapped
ADEFPRR	prefard
ADEFRRT	drafter
	redraft
ADEFRUY	feudary
ADEGGHS	shagged
ADEGGIU	gaudgie
	guidage
ADEGGLR	draggle
ADEGGLS	slagged
ADEGGNS	snagged
ADEGGRS	daggers
ADEGGRY	raggedy
ADEGGSW	swagged
ADEGHIN	heading
ADEGHIR	hag-ride
	headrig
ADEGHJU	jughead
ADEGHLO	log-head
ADEGILN	dealing
	leading

ADEGILO	geoidal
ADEGILP	pig-lead
ADEGILV	glaived
ADEGINR	deraign
	gradine
	grained
	reading
ADEGINW	windage
ADEGIOT	△godetia
ADEGIRS	agrised
ADEGIRV	Rigveda
ADEGISV	visaged
ADEGIUV	viduage
ADEGLMO	Gaeldom
ADEGLNN	endlang
ADEGLNR	dangler
	gnarled
ADEGLNS	glandes
ADEGLNT	tangled
ADEGLNU	langued
ADEGLRU	raguled
ADEGLRY	gradely
ADEGMNU	gudeman
ADEGNNO	nonaged
ADEGNNU	dunnage
ADEGNOP	pondage
ADEGNOS	sondage
ADEGNOT	tangoed
ADEGNOV	dogvane
ADEGNOW	gowaned
ADEGNPU	unpaged
ADEGNRR	gnarred
ADEGNRS	△gardens
ADEGNRT	dragnet
	granted
ADEGNRU	enguard
ADEGNUW	unwaged
ADEGNUZ	ungazed
ADEGORS	dog's-ear
ADEGORW	dowager
	wordage
ADEGOTT	togated
ADEGPRS	spadger
ADEGPRU	upgrade
ADEGRRS	regards
ADEGRSU	sugared
ADEGRTY	tragedy
ADEGRUY	gaudery
ADEGSSU	degauss
ADEHHOP	hop-head
ADEHHOT	hothead
ADEHIKS	dasheki
ADEHIKV	khediva
ADEHILL	Delilah
ADEHILN	Hieland
ADEHILP	helipad
ADEHILY	headily
ADEHINP	pinhead
ADEHINR	handier
ADEHIPR	raphide
ADEHIPS	aphides
ADEHIPT	pithead
ADEHIRR	harried
ADEHIRW	rawhide
ADEHIRY	hayride
ADEHKNS	shanked
ADEHKOR	hardoke
ADEHKOT	kathode
ADEHLLP	lapheld
ADEHLMU	lum-head
ADEHLNR	handler
ADEHLNS	handsel
ADEHLOT	loathed
ADEHLSS	slashed
ADEHLTY	deathly
ADEHMMS	shammed
ADEHMMW	whammed
ADEHMNR	herdman
ADEHMOP	mophead
ADEHMOR	hadrome
ADEHMSS	smashed
ADEHNRU	unheard
ADEHNST	handset
ADEHNTU	haunted
ADEHOOP	apehood
ADEHOPT	pot-head
ADEHOPX	hexapod
ADEHORR	hoarder
ADEHOTW	tow-head
ADEHPPW	whapped
ADEHPST	spathed
	T-shaped
ADEHPSU	U-shaped
ADEHPSV	V-shaped
ADEHRST	hard-set
	threads
ADEHRTY	hydrate
	thready
ADEHUZZ	huzzaed
ADEIILR	deliria
	irideal
ADEIILS	dailies
	sedilia
ADEIINR	denarii
ADEIIRS	airside
	diarise
ADEIIRZ	diarize
ADEIJMR	jemidar
ADEIJSU	Judaise
ADEIJUZ	Judaize
ADEIKLN	knaidel
ADEIKLZ	Zadkiel
ADEILLN	Daniell
ADEILLR	dallier
	dialler
	rallied
ADEILLS	disleal
	sallied
ADEILLT	tallied
ADEILLV	vialled
ADEILLY	ideally
ADEILMM	dilemma
ADEILMP	implead
ADEILMS	misdeal
	mislead
ADEILNN	annelid
	lindane
ADEILNT	tail-end
ADEILNU	aliunde
	unideal
ADEILNV	andvile
ADEILNW	new-laid
ADEILNX	indexal
ADEILOP	Oedipal
ADEILOR	dariole
ADEILOS	deasoil
ADEILOU	douleia
ADEILPP	applied
ADEILPR	lip-read
	pedrail
	predial
ADEILPS	palsied
	Pleiads
ADEILPT	plaited
	taliped
ADEILRS	sideral
ADEILRT	dilater
ADEILRY	readily
ADEILSS	aidless
ADEILSU	deasiul
ADEILSV	devisal
ADEILSY	dialyse
ADEILYZ	dialyze
ADEIMMR	mermaid
ADEIMMS	mismade
ADEIMNR	adermin
	Amerind
ADEIMNS	sideman
ADEIMNT	mediant
ADEIMNU	unaimed
ADEIMRR	admirer
	married
ADEIMRS	misread
	sidearm
ADEIMRT	readmit
ADEIMRU	Muridae
ADEIMRY	mid-year
ADEIMST	misdate
ADEIMTU	taedium
ADEIMTY	daytime
ADEINNN	nandine
	nannied
ADEINOR	aneroid
ADEINOS	adonise
	anodise
	Diasone®
	sodaine
ADEINOV	naevoid
ADEINOX	dioxane
ADEINOZ	adonize
	anodize
ADEINPR	pardine
ADEINPS	pansied

ADEINPT	depaint
	painted
	patined
ADEINRR	drainer
ADEINRS	sardine
ADEINRT	detrain
	tan-ride
	trade-in
	trained
ADEINRU	unaired
	uranide
ADEINRV	invader
	ravined
ADEINST	instead
	sainted
	stained
ADEINTT	tainted
ADEINTU	audient
ADEINTV	deviant
ADEINVV	navvied
ADEIOPS	adipose
ADEIOPT	opiated
ADEIORS	soredia
ADEIORX	exordia
ADEIOSX	oxidase
ADEIOSZ	diazoes
ADEIOTX	oxidate
ADEIOVV	vaivode
ADEIOVW	waivode
ADEIOWW	waiwode
ADEIPPR	drappie
	prepaid
ADEIPPU	appuied
ADEIPRR	drapier
	parried
ADEIPRS	despair
	prisade
ADEIPRT	△diptera
ADEIPSS	apsides
ADEIRRT	tarried
ADEIRST	asterid
	astride
	diaster
	disrate
	staired
ADEIRSU	residua
ADEIRSV	adviser
ADEIRTV	tardive
ADEIRTY	dietary
ADEISST	disseat
	saidest
ADEISTV	vistaed
ADEISTW	waisted
ADEISWY	wayside
ADEITUZ	Deutzia
ADEITWY	tideway
ADEJMRU	mudéjar
ADEJOPR	jeopard
ADEKLNS	kalends
ADEKLNY	nakedly
ADEKLST	stalked
ADEKLSY	yslaked
ADEKMUY	may-duke
ADEKNPP	knapped
ADEKNRR	knarred
ADEKNRS	Dansker
ADEKNRU	unraked
ADEKNSU	unasked
ADEKNUW	unwaked
ADEKNVY	△vandyke
ADEKPSY	pay-desk
ADELLMU	medulla
ADELLNR	ländler
ADELLNW	ellwand
ADELLOR	odaller
ADELLOW	allowed
ADELLRU	udaller
ADELLST	stalled
ADELMMS	slammed
ADELMNR	mandrel
ADELMOR	earldom
ADELMOS	damosel
ADELMOZ	damozel
ADELNNP	planned
ADELNNU	unladen
ADELNOR	ladrone
ADELNOT	taloned
ADELNOY	yealdon
ADELNRS	slander
	snarled
ADELNRU	launder
	lurdane
	rundale
ADELNRY	dearnly
ADELNST	slanted
ADELNTU	lunated
	undealt
ADELNTW	wetland
ADELOPR	leopard
ADELOPS	deposal
	pedalos
ADELOPT	tadpole
ADELORT	delator
	leotard
ADELORU	roulade
	Urodela
ADELOSS	lassoed
ADELOST	saltoed
ADELOTU	lead-out
ADELOVY	love-day
ADELPPS	slapped
ADELPRY	pedlary
ADELPST	spalted
ADELPTT	platted
ADELPTW	dewlapt
ADELPTY	adeptly
ADELRRU	ruderal
ADELRRW	drawler
ADELRST	star-led
ADELRTX	dextral
ADELRTY	lyrated
ADELRZZ	dazzler
ADELSTT	slatted
ADELTTW	wattled
ADELTUV	vaulted
ADEMMRT	trammed
ADEMNNU	mundane
	unnamed
ADEMNOR	madrone
ADEMNRU	duramen
	maunder
	unarmed
ADEMNSS	madness
ADEMNSU	medusan
	sudamen
ADEMNTU	unmated
	untamed
ADEMOSY	Samoyed
	someday
ADEMOWY	meadowy
ADEMRRU	eardrum
ADEMSSU	assumed
	medusas
ADENNOY	annoyed
	anodyne
ADENNPS	spanned
ADENNPT	pendant
ADENNST	standen
ADENNWY	dewanny
ADENOOZ	endozoa
ADENOPR	operand
	padrone
	pandore
ADENOPS	dapsone
ADENOPT	note-pad
	tonepad
ADENORT	tornade
ADENORU	rondeau
ADENOST	onstead
ADENOTZ	zonated
ADENPPR	parpend
ADENPPS	snapped
ADENPPW	wappend
ADENPRR	pardner
ADENPRU	unpared
ADENPRW	predawn
ADENPSX	△spandex
ADENPSY	dyspnea
ADENPUV	unpaved
ADENRRS	errands
ADENRRY	△reynard
ADENRSS	sanders
	sarsden
ADENRST	stander
ADENRSU	asunder
	danseur
ADENRTU	daunter
	natured
	unrated
	untread
ADENRTV	verdant
ADENRTW	draw-net
ADENRTX	dextran
ADENRTY	dentary
	rent-day
ADENRUY	unready

Words marked △ may be spelled also with a capital letter

ADENSSS	sadness
ADENSTU	unsated
ADENSUV	unsaved
ADENSWY	endways
ADENTUV	vaunted
ADENTUX	untaxed
ADENUWY	unwayed
ADEOORT	odorate
ADEOPRR	eardrop
	padrero
ADEOPRT	adopter
	readopt
ADEOPSS	spadoes
ADEOPST	podestà
ADEORRS	drosera
	rear-dos
ADEORST	torsade
ADEORTU	outdare
	read-out
ADEORWY	rodeway
ADEORYZ	zedoary
ADEOSTT	toasted
ADEOTTU	outdate
ADEOWWY	waywode
ADEPPRT	trapped
ADEPPRW	wrapped
ADEPPSW	swapped
ADEPPUY	appuyed
ADEPRRS	sparred
ADEPRRY	drapery
ADEPRSS	adpress
ADEPRSY	sprayed
ADEQRSU	squared
ADERRST	starred
ADERRSW	drawers
ADERSSU	assured
ADERSTV	starved
ADERSTW	steward
	strawed
ADERSTY	rest-day
	strayed
ADERSUY	dasyure
ADERSVW	dwarves
ADERWWY	weyward
ADESTTU	statued
ADESTTW	swatted
	wadsett
ADESTUY	Tuesday
ADFFGIN	daffing
ADFFHNO	hand-off
	offhand
ADFFIST	distaff
ADFFLNO	fanfold
ADFFLOO	offload
ADFFOOR	affoord
	off-road
ADFFORW	off-ward
ADFGINR	farding
ADFGLLU	gladful
ADFHISY	fish-day
ADFHLNU	handful
ADFHOOS	shadoof
ADFIIMT	Fatimid
ADFILLU	fluidal
ADFIMNR	findram
ADFIMNY	damnify
ADFINRT	indraft
ADFLLYY	ladyfly
ADFLMOO	damfool
ADFLMPU	mudflap
ADFLMTU	mudflat
ADFLNOP	plafond
ADFLNSY	sandfly
ADFLORU	foulard
ADFMOSU	fumados
ADFNNOT	fondant
ADFNOST	fantods
ADFOOPT	footpad
ADFORRW	forward
	froward
ADFORTX	draft-ox
ADGGHNO	hangdog
ADGGILN	gadling
ADGGILR	riggald
ADGGINR	niggard
ADGGIRS	Rigsdag
ADGGOOT	goat-god
ADGHILO	hidalgo
ADGHINS	dashing
	shading
ADGHIPR	digraph
ADGHIRR	ardrigh
	ard-righ
ADGHIRS	dish-rag
ADGHNNU	handgun
ADGHNOS	sand-hog
ADGHNOW	hagdown
ADGHOOR	road-hog
ADGHORT	hard-got
ADGHORW	hogward
ADGHRTU	draught
ADGIILN	dialing
	gliadin
ADGIILT	digital
ADGIINO	gonidia
ADGIINR	gradini
ADGIINU	iguanid
ADGIINW	gwiniad
ADGIINY	Digynia
ADGIKRS	Riksdag
ADGILMN	madling
ADGILNN	landing
ADGILNO	digonal
	loading
ADGILNR	darling
ADGILNU	languid
ADGILOR	goliard
ADGILRY	day-girl
ADGILSU	gladius
ADGILUY	gaudily
ADGIMMN	damming
ADGIMNN	damning
ADGIMNP	damping
ADGIMNR	mridang
ADGINNR	darning
ADGINNS	sanding
ADGINNW	dawning
ADGINOR	Gordian
	gradino
	roading
ADGINOT	doating
ADGINRT	darting
	trading
ADGINRW	drawing
	warding
ADGINWY	gwyniad
ADGIPRU	pagurid
ADGIRSU	guisard
ADGIRZZ	gizzard
ADGLLNO	golland
ADGLLOO	all-good
ADGLLOR	rag-doll
ADGLMNO	mangold
ADGLNOO	gondola
ADGLNOR	goldarn
ADGLNOW	gowland
ADGLNOY	daylong
	long-day
ADGLNRY	grandly
ADGMNOO	△goodman
	Mogadon®
ADGMNOR	gormand
ADGNOOR	dragoon
	gadroon
ADGNORU	aground
ADGNRRU	gurnard
ADGNRUU	unguard
ADGORST	Dogstar
ADGRSTU	rag-dust
ADHHIRS	hardish
ADHHIRT	hard-hit
ADHIIJT	ijtihad
ADHIIKS	dashiki
ADHIIMS	Hasidim
	maidish
ADHIIOP	Ophidia
ADHIKNS	dankish
ADHIKRS	darkish
ADHIKTZ	Tadzhik
ADHILMO	halidom
ADHILNY	handily
ADHILOP	haploid
ADHILOY	holiday
	hyaloid
ADHILRY	hardily
ADHILSY	ladyish
	shadily
ADHIMMS	Mahdism
ADHIMPS	dampish
	phasmid
ADHIMRS	Midrash
ADHIMST	Mahdist
ADHINOR	Rhodian
ADHINOT	anthoid
ADHINPU	dauphin
ADHIORS	hairdos

ADHKORW	dorhawk	ADIKMOS	mikados	ADINOPP	oppidan
ADHKOSU	shakudo	ADIKMSS	dismask	ADINOPR	padroni
ADHLLLO	hold-all	ADIKNPS	skidpan		poniard
ADHLLNO	holland	ADIKNRS	disrank	ADINOPT	pintado
ADHLMOY	holydam	ADIKPRS	dispark	ADINORR	ordinar
ADHLMPY	lymphad	ADILLMM	milldam	ADINORS	inroads
ADHMNOO	hoodman	ADILLSY	disally		sadiron
	manhood	ADILLVY	validly	ADINORV	virando
ADHMNOR	horn-mad	ADILLYY	day-lily	ADINOTX	oxidant
ADHMNOU	Mahound	ADILMNO	mondial	ADINPST	sandpit
ADHNNOS	hands-on	ADILMNR	mandril	ADINRRT	tridarn
ADHNNUY	unhandy	ADILMNU	maudlin	ADINRSU	Drusian
ADHNORU	unhoard	ADILMOO	Modiola		sundari
ADHNORW	hard-won	ADILMOP	diploma	ADINRSW	inwards
ADHNOTU	handout	ADILMOU	alodium	ADINRTU	triduan
	hand-out	ADILMOY	amyloid		unitard
ADHNOTW	two-hand	ADILMPS	plasmid	ADINSTT	Dantist
ADHNRRU	hard-run	ADILMSS	△dismals		distant
ADHNRSY	shandry	ADILMSU	dualism	ADINSTU	unstaid
ADHNRTY	hydrant	ADILMSY	dismayl	ADINSUW	unswai'd
ADHNRUY	unhardy		ladyism	ADINTTY	dittany
ADHOORR	rhodora	ADILNOR	nail-rod	ADIOOPS	Isopoda
ADHOPRT	hardtop		ordinal	ADIOOSW	woodsia
ADHOPRU	uphoard	ADILNOS	Ladinos	ADIOPRR	air-drop
ADHOPRY	hop-yard	ADILNRU	diurnal	ADIOPRS	prisado
ADHOPST	dash-pot	ADILNSU	sundial		sparoid
ADHOSWY	shadowy	ADILOOV	ovoidal	ADIOPRT	parotid
ADHRSWY	dry-wash	ADILOOZ	zooidal	ADIOPRV	privado
ADIIILR	iridial	ADILOPR	dipolar	ADIORST	astroid
ADIIINR	iridian	ADILOPW	low-paid	ADIORSU	sauroid
ADIIKLO	dika-oil	ADILORT	dilator	ADIORSV	advisor
ADIIKOT	dakoiti	ADILPRY	pyralid	ADIORTU	auditor
ADIILMS	misdial		rapidly	ADIOSUV	Vaudois
	mislaid	ADILPST	plastid	ADIOSVW	disavow
ADIILNO	lianoid	ADILPSY	display	ADIPPRT	dip-trap
ADIILNV	invalid	ADILPTU	plaudit	ADIPRST	dispart
ADIILOS	sialoid	ADILPVY	vapidly	ADIPRTY	pay-dirt
ADIILST	dialist	ADILQSU	squalid	ADIRSSU	sardius
ADIIMMS	maidism	ADILRTY	tardily	ADIRSTY	satyrid
ADIIMOS	daimios	ADILSSU	Lusiads	ADIRSUY	dysuria
ADIIMPV	impavid	ADILSTU	dualist	ADJNORU	adjourn
ADIIMRU	mudiria	ADILSTY	staidly	ADKKLOY	kakodyl
ADIIMSS	missaid	ADILTUY	duality	ADKLMRU	mudlark
ADIINNN	in-and-in	ADIMNNO	mondain	ADKNNSU	unskan'd
ADIINOV	Ovidian	ADIMOOS	isodoma	ADKOOOW	oak-wood
ADIINPR	pindari	ADIMORR	mirador	ADKORWY	day-work
	pridian	ADIMOST	mastoid		workday
ADIINST	distain	ADIMOTT	mattoid	ADKRSWY	skyward
ADIINSU	indusia	ADIMPRY	pyramid	ADLLLOR	Lollard
	suidian	ADIMQSU	quidams	ADLLMOW	wadmoll
ADIIPXY	pyxidia	ADIMRSW	misdraw	ADLLMOY	modally
ADIIQRU	daquiri	ADIMSST	dismast	ADLLNOW	lowland
ADIIRST	diarist	ADIMSTU	dumaist	ADLLNOY	nodally
ADIIRTY	aridity		stadium	ADLLOPR	pollard
ADIITVY	avidity	ADINNOP	dipnoan	ADLMMPU	dum-palm
ADIJMSU	Judaism		Pandion	ADLMORU	modular
ADIJNOT	adjoint	ADINNOR	andiron	ADLMORY	May-lord
ADIJSTU	Judaist	ADINNRS	innards	ADLMOSV	Slavdom
ADIKLNY	ladykin	ADINNRW	indrawn	ADLNNOR	norland
ADIKLOS	odalisk	ADINNRY	innyard	ADLNOOR	lardoon
ADIKLPS	klipdas	ADINNST	stand-in	ADLNOPU	poundal
ADIKMNN	mankind	ADINOOP	poinado	ADLNORU	nodular

ADLNOSU	souldan
ADLNOSY	synodal
ADLNOTU	outland
ADLNOWY	lay-down
ADLNRUY	laundry
ADLNTWY	Tynwald
ADLOPRU	poulard
ADLORRW	warlord
ADLORSU	sudoral
ADLRSTY	dry-salt
ADMMNSU	summand
ADMNOOR	madroño
ADMNOOW	woodman
ADMNOOZ	madzoon
ADMNOQU	quondam
ADMNORS	rodsman
ADMNORT	dormant
	mordant
ADMNOSU	osmunda
ADMNOSY	dynamos
ADMNSTU	dustman
ADMOORT	doormat
ADMOPPU	popadum
ADMORST	stardom
	tsardom
ADMORTW	madwort
ADMRSTU	durmast
	mustard
ADNNOOY	noonday
ADNNORT	donnart
ADNNOTU	daunton
ADNNRTU	dunnart
ADNOOPR	pandoor
ADNOORT	donator
	odorant
	tandoor
	tornado
ADNOOSS	so-and-so
ADNOPRU	pandour
ADNOPRV	provand
ADNORRW	norward
	nor'ward
ADNORSW	onwards
ADNORTU	rotunda
ADNORWY	nayword
ADNOSTT	stand-to
ADNOSTU	astound
ADNPRUW	updrawn
ADNPSTU	dust-pan
	stand-up
	upstand
ADNRSUW	sunward
ADNSTYY	dynasty
ADOOPSU	apodous
ADOOPSW	sapwood
ADOORWY	doorway
ADOOWWX	woodwax
ADOPRRW	wardrop
ADOPRTW	draw-top
ADORSTW	towards
ADORSUU	arduous
ADORTUW	outward
ADOUUVX	vaudoux
ADPRSUW	upwards
ADPSSUY	Dasypus
ADSSTUW	sawdust
AEEEFLR	eelfare
AEEEGGL	lee-gage
AEEEGKL	keelage
AEEEGLT	legatee
AEEEGNT	teenage
AEEEGPR	peerage
AEEEGPS	seepage
AEEEGRT	étagère
AEEEILN	alienee
AEEELLN	lee-lane
AEEELRS	release
AEEELTV	elevate
AEEFFLL	felafel
AEEFFMR	fee-farm
AEEFGNT	fanteeg
AEEFGRS	serfage
AEEFGTW	weftage
AEEFHRT	feather
	terefah
AEEFILN	Felinae
AEEFILW	alewife
AEEFIRS	freesia
	sea-fire
AEEFISW	seawife
AEEFLLT	fellate
	leaflet
AEEFLMN	enflame
AEEFLMS	alms-fee
AEEFLPY	eye-flap
AEEFLRT	reflate
AEEFLRW	welfare
AEEFLRY	leafery
AEEFLRZ	alférez
AEEFLSU	easeful
AEEFLTX	telefax
AEEFMNR	enframe
	freeman
AEEFMRR	free-arm
	reframe
AEEFMRT	fermate
AEEFOTV	foveate
AEEFPPR	frappée
AEEFRRT	ferrate
AEEFRST	feaster
AEEFRTU	feature
AEEFRTX	tax-free
AEEFRWY	freeway
AEEGGLL	allegge
AEEGGLR	gregale
AEEGGLT	gateleg
AEEGGNR	△engager
AEEGGOP	epagoge
AEEGHIR	hireage
AEEGHNN	Gehenna
AEEGHNW	whangee
AEEGILL	galilee
AEEGILM	mileage
AEEGILN	lineage
AEEGILP	epigeal
AEEGILW	weigela
AEEGINP	epigean
AEEGINU	eugenia
AEEGIPR	pierage
AEEGISS	assiege
AEEGLLR	alleger
AEEGLLZ	gazelle
AEEGLMN	gleeman
	melange
	mélange
AEEGLNR	enlarge
	△general
	gleaner
AEEGLNT	elegant
AEEGLNU	Euglena
AEEGLNV	evangel
AEEGLPR	peregal
AEEGLRU	△leaguer
	regulae
AEEGLRW	legwear
AEEGLRY	eagerly
AEEGLSS	ageless
AEEGLSV	selvage
AEEGLTT	galette
AEEGLTU	tegulae
AEEGLTV	vegetal
AEEGMMT	gemmate
	tagmeme
AEEGMNR	germane
AEEGMRU	remuage
AEEGMSS	megasse
	message
AEEGNNP	pangene
AEEGNNR	enrange
AEEGNNV	Genevan
AEEGNOP	peonage
AEEGNOS	Goanese
AEEGNPP	genappe
AEEGNRT	grantee
	greaten
	reagent
AEEGNRU	renague
AEEGNRV	avenger
	engrave
AEEGNTT	tentage
AEEGNTV	ventage
AEEGNTW	Newgate
AEEGORV	overage
	over-age
AEEGPRS	asperge
	presage
AEEGRRS	greaser
AEEGRRT	greater
	regrate
AEEGRRW	wagerer
AEEGRST	ergates
	restage
AEEGRSV	greaves
AEEGRTU	treague
AEEGRUZ	guereza

AEEGSTT	gestate
	tagetes
AEEGTTZ	△gazette
AEEHHNT	heathen
AEEHHOV	heave-ho
AEEHHRT	heather
AEEHHST	sheathe
AEEHILR	hair-eel
AEEHIRV	heavier
AEEHIST	atheise
AEEHISV	heavies
AEEHITZ	atheize
AEEHKNR	hearken
AEEHKNT	thankee
AEEHKRU	heureka
AEEHLNT	lethean
AEEHLOR	ear-hole
AEEHLPT	heel-tap
AEEHLRT	leather
	tar-heel
AEEHLRV	haverel
AEEHLSW	awheels
AEEHLSY	eyelash
AEEHLTT	athlete
AEEHMNT	methane
AEEHMRS	mahseer
AEEHMRT	erathem
	thermae
AEEHNPT	heptane
	phenate
AEEHNRS	arsheen
AEEHNRT	earthen
	hearten
AEEHNSV	heavens
AEEHNSW	Shawnee
AEEHNTW	wheaten
AEEHPRS	reshape
	sphaere
	spheare
AEEHPRT	preheat
AEEHPUV	upheave
AEEHQSU	△quashee
AEEHRRS	shearer
AEEHRSW	whereas
AEEHRTT	theater
	theatre
	thereat
AEEHRTV	threave
AEEHRTW	weather
	whate'er
	whereat
	wreathe
AEEHSSV	sheaves
AEEHSWY	eye-wash
AEEIJNT	Janeite
AEEIKLS	sea-like
AEEILLR	reallie
AEEILMS	mealies
AEEILNP	alepine
AEEILNS	sealine
AEEILNT	lineate

AEEILPT	epilate
	pileate
AEEILRR	earlier
AEEILRS	earlies
	realise
AEEILRT	atelier
	realtie
AEEILRZ	realize
AEEILTT	ailette
AEEILTV	elative
AEEIMNR	remanié
AEEIMNS	nemesia
AEEIMNT	matinee
	matinée
AEEIMNX	examine
AEEIMPR	empaire
AEEIMRS	seriema
AEEIMRT	emirate
AEEIMSS	misease
	△siamese
AEEIMST	steamie
AEEIMSZ	siameze
AEEIMTT	teatime
AEEINNP	Peneian
AEEINRT	retinae
	trainee
AEEINST	etesian
AEEINTT	teniate
AEEINTV	naïveté
	naiveté
AEEINVW	inweave
AEEIORT	etaerio
AEEIPRR	pereira
AEEIPTX	expiate
AEEIRRR	arriéré
AEEIRRS	rearise
AEEIRST	seriate
AEEIRTT	ariette
	iterate
AEEIRTV	evirate
AEEISVV	evasive
AEEITTV	aviette
	evitate
AEEITUX	eutexia
AEEIUVX	exuviae
AEEJLLV	Javelle
AEEJNST	sejeant
AEEJNTU	jauntee
AEEJRSW	Jew's-ear
AEEKKNO	kokanee
AEEKLLT	lakelet
AEEKLMN	keelman
AEEKLNT	kantele
AEEKMNS	kamseen
AEEKMNW	man-week
AEEKMRT	meerkat
AEEKNNN	nankeen
AEEKNNP	knee-pan
AEEKNRS	sneaker
AEEKNRT	retaken
AEEKNRW	wakener
AEEKORT	oak-tree

AEEKPRS	respeak
	speaker
AEEKPRT	pertake
AEEKRRT	retaker
AEEKRRW	wreaker
AEEKRST	sakeret
AEEKSTY	key-seat
AEELLOP	ale-pole
AEELLOV	alveole
AEELLPR	parelle
AEELLRS	all-seer
AEELLWY	wall-eye
AEELMNP	empanel
	emplane
AEELMNR	reelman
AEELMNT	manteel
AEELMNV	velamen
AEELMNY	amylene
AEELMPX	example
	exempla
AEELMRT	lameter
AEELMSS	measles
AEELMST	△maltese
AEELMTU	emulate
AEELNNP	enplane
AEELNNR	lernean
AEELNPS	spelean
AEELNRR	learner
AEELNRT	alterne
	enteral
	△eternal
AEELNRW	renewal
AEELNSV	enslave
AEELNTY	entayle
AEELOPR	parolee
AEELOPX	pole-axe
AEELORU	aureole
AEELOSW	leasowe
AEELPRR	pearler
AEELPRS	pleaser
	relapse
AEELPRT	pleater
	prelate
AEELPRU	pleurae
AEELPTT	palette
	peltate
AEELPTU	epaulet
AEELQSU	sequela
AEELRRT	re-alter
	relater
AEELRSS	earless
AEELRST	stealer
AEELRSU	leasure
AEELRSV	several
AEELRSY	sealery
AEELRUV	revalue
AEELSST	altesse
AEELSSU	Auslese
AEELSSW	aweless
AEELSTU	setuale
AEELSTV	salvete
AEELSTX	latexes

AEELTTY	layette
AEELTVW	wavelet
AEEMMPY	empyema
AEEMMRT	ammeter
	metamer
AEEMNNO	anemone
AEEMNPT	Tempean
AEEMNRT	remanet
AEEMORT	erotema
AEEMOSW	awesome
	waesome
AEEMPRT	tempera
AEEMPRY	empayre
AEEMPTU	amputee
AEEMQRU	marquee
AEEMRST	steamer
AEEMRSU	measure
AEEMRTY	métayer
AEEMSST	seamset
AEENNOT	neonate
AEENNPT	pennate
	pentane
AEENNRS	ensnare
AEENNRX	reannex
AEENNTU	uneaten
AEENOPR	peraeon
AEENOSS	anoeses
AEENOSU	aeneous
AEENPST	penates
	pesante
AEENPSX	expanse
AEENRRT	terrane
AEENRRV	ravener
AEENRRY	yearner
AEENRST	earnest
	eastern
	nearest
AEENRTT	entreat
	ratteen
	ternate
AEENRTV	aventre
	nervate
	veteran
AEENRUV	unreave
AEENSST	sensate
AEENSSW	waeness
AEENTTV	navette
AEENUVW	unweave
AEENVWW	New-Wave
	new-wave
AEEOPRT	operate
AEEORSS	serosae
AEEORST	roseate
AEEORSV	oversea
AEEORTV	overeat
AEEORVW	overawe
AEEPPRR	paperer
	prepare
	repaper
AEEPRRT	taperer
AEEPRSS	asperse
	praeses
	preasse
AEEPRSZ	spreaze
AEEPRTU	epurate
AEEPRTY	peatery
AEEPRTZ	trapeze
AEEPSSS	asepses
AEEPSSW	pesewas
AEEPSTT	septate
	spattee
AEERRST	serrate
AEERRSU	erasure
AEERRSW	swearer
AEERRTT	retrate
	retreat
	re-treat
	treater
AEERRTW	waterer
AEERRVW	waverer
AEERSST	tessera
AEERSSU	réseaus
	seasure
AEERSSV	assever
AEERSSY	essayer
AEERSTT	estreat
	restate
AEERSTU	austere
AEERSTW	sweater
AEERSUV	vareuse
AEERSUX	réseaux
AEERTTX	extreat
AEERTWW	wetware
AEESTTT	testate
AEFFFLR	flaffer
AEFFGIL	fig-leaf
AEFFGIR	giraffe
AEFFGNR	engraff
AEFFGRU	gauffer
AEFFIPR	piaffer
AEFFKOP	offpeak
	off-peak
AEFFKOR	rake-off
AEFFKOT	offtake
	take-off
AEFFKRS	Kaffers
AEFFLLY	flyleaf
AEFFLMW	flamfew
AEFFLNS	snaffle
AEFFLRR	raffler
AEFFLRU	fearful
AEFFLRW	waffler
AEFFLTU	fateful
AEFFQRU	quaffer
AEFFRST	restaff
	staffer
AEFFTTY	taffety
AEFGGGO	foggage
AEFGGMO	megafog
AEFGGRY	faggery
AEFGILN	finagle
	leafing
AEFGILO	foliage
AEFGILR	fragile
AEFGIRT	frigate
AEFGIRU	refugia
AEFGITU	ague-fit
	fatigue
AEFGLLU	fullage
AEFGLOT	flotage
AEFGLOW	flowage
AEFGLRU	rageful
AEFGLUZ	gazeful
AEFGNRR	granfer
AEFGNRT	engraft
AEFGOOT	footage
AEFGORR	forager
AEFGORV	forgave
AEFGRRT	grafter
AEFHLLS	fellahs
AEFHLNO	half-one
AEFHLOO	ale-hoof
AEFHLOP	hop-flea
AEFHLOR	fahlore
AEFHLRS	flasher
AEFHLRT	farthel
AEFHLRZ	fahlerz
AEFHLTU	hateful
AEFHRRT	farther
AEFHRST	fathers
	shafter
AEFHRSY	fashery
AEFIILT	filiate
AEFIIMN	infimae
AEFIJLO	jeofail
AEFILMN	feminal
	inflame
AEFILNT	inflate
AEFILNU	infulae
AEFILNV	flavine
AEFILOT	foliate
AEFILPT	fleapit
AEFILRU	failure
AEFILRV	favrile
AEFILRZ	filazer
AEFILSS	falsies
	filasse
AEFIMNR	fireman
AEFIMRR	firearm
AEFIMRS	misfare
AEFINNT	infante
AEFINNZ	fanzine
AEFINPR	firepan
AEFINRR	refrain
AEFINRS	serafin
AEFINRT	fenitar
AEFINRX	xerafin
AEFINSW	fan-wise
AEFINTX	antefix
AEFIQRU	aquifer
AEFIRRR	farrier
AEFKLNR	flanker
AEFKLOS	seafolk
AEFKLRT	fartlek

AEFKLST	flasket
AEFKLUW	wakeful
AEFKNOR	oak-fern
AEFKORS	forsake
AEFLLNN	fannell
	flannel
AEFLLOR	Floréal
AEFLLOT	floatel
AEFLLSY	falsely
AEFLLTT	flatlet
AEFLLTU	taleful
AEFLLUZ	zealful
AEFLMOR	femoral
AEFLMTY	meat-fly
AEFLMUW	wameful
AEFLMUZ	mazeful
AEFLNNN	flannen
AEFLNOV	flavone
AEFLNRS	salfern
AEFLNRU	flâneur
	frenula
	funeral
AEFLNTT	flatten
AEFLOOV	foveola
AEFLOPW	peafowl
AEFLORS	safrole
AEFLORT	floater
	floreat
	refloat
AEFLORU	four-ale
AEFLORY	forelay
AEFLOSW	seafowl
	sea-wolf
AEFLPPR	flapper
AEFLPRS	felspar
AEFLPRU	flare-up
AEFLPRY	palfrey
AEFLRSU	fur-seal
	refusal
AEFLRTT	flatter
AEFLRTU	refutal
	tearful
AEFLRZZ	frazzle
AEFLSTU	sulfate
AEFLTTU	fat-lute
AEFMNOR	foramen
	foreman
AEFMNRU	fraenum
AEFMORR	forearm
AEFMORT	formate
AEFMPRU	frame-up
AEFMRRY	farmery
AEFNOPR	profane
AEFNOPY	payfone
AEFNORR	foreran
AEFNRSS	farness
AEFNSST	Fastens
	fatness
AEFOPRW	forepaw
AEFORRV	favorer
	overfar
AEFORRY	forayer
AEFORSW	foresaw
AEFORSY	foresay
AEFOSST	fatsoes
AEFOSTU	featous
AEFRRTY	fratery
AEFRSTW	fretsaw
AEFRTTU	Tartufe
AEFRTUW	wafture
AEFSTTT	fattest
AEFSTTX	Fastext
AEGGGLU	luggage
AEGGHLR	haggler
AEGGHSW	eggwash
AEGGILN	lignage
AEGGINR	gag-rein
	gearing
AEGGINS	signage
AEGGIOS	isagoge
AEGGIRU	garigue
AEGGISW	swaggie
AEGGJRY	jaggery
AEGGLNO	agelong
AEGGLNR	gangrel
AEGGLRY	grey-lag
AEGGMNY	yeggman
AEGGMSS	eggmass
AEGGNNU	gunnage
AEGGNOR	o'ergang
AEGGNRR	granger
AEGGNST	ant-eggs
	G-agents
AEGGRRY	raggery
AEGGRSS	aggress
AEGGRST	gagster
	stagger
	taggers
AEGGRSW	swagger
AEGGRTY	gargety
AEGGRWY	waggery
AEGHHIT	aheight
AEGHIJR	jaghire
AEGHILN	healing
AEGHINP	heaping
AEGHINR	hearing
AEGHINT	gahnite
	heating
AEGHINV	heaving
AEGHINY	Hygeian
AEGHINZ	genizah
AEGHISS	geishas
AEGHLNO	halogen
AEGHLNT	alength
AEGHLRU	laugher
AEGHLTW	thalweg
AEGHMNO	hog-mane
	Mohegan
AEGHMOR	homager
AEGHMSU	meshuga
AEGHNOX	hexagon
AEGHNRS	gnasher
AEGHNRU	nuraghe
AEGHNST	stengah
AEGHOPY	hypogea
AEGHORS	gheraos
AEGHOST	hostage
AEGHPRS	spreagh
AEGHRST	gathers
AEGIIMN	imagine
AEGIKLN	linkage
AEGIKLT	glaiket
AEGIKNP	peaking
AEGIKNS	sinkage
AEGIKPP	kippage
AEGIKPR	garpike
AEGILLL	illegal
AEGILLN	nigella
AEGILLP	pillage
AEGILLS	gallise
AEGILLT	tillage
AEGILLV	village
AEGILLY	agilely
AEGILLZ	gallize
AEGILMR	gremial
	lamiger
AEGILMS	gas-lime
AEGILNN	eanling
	leaning
AEGILNP	leaping
AEGILNR	engrail
	nargile
	realign
	reginal
AEGILNS	leasing
	sealing
AEGILNT	atingle
	gelatin
	genital
AEGILNV	leaving
AEGILOS	soilage
AEGILOU	eulogia
AEGILRZ	glazier
AEGILSS	algesis
AEGILTU	glutaei
AEGILTY	egality
AEGIMNN	meaning
AEGIMNP	pigmean
AEGIMNR	germain
	reaming
AEGIMNT	mintage
	teaming
	tegmina
AEGIMOS	imagoes
AEGIMPR	epigram
	primage
AEGIMPT	pigmeat
AEGIMRR	armiger
AEGIMRS	gisarme
AEGIMRT	migrate
	ragtime
AEGIMRY	imagery
AEGIMST	sigmate
AEGIMSV	misgave
AEGINNO	ganoine

AEGINNR	aginner
	earning
	engrain
	grannie
AEGINNT	antigen
	gentian
AEGINNU	anguine
	guanine
AEGINNV	Angevin
AEGINNZ	Zingane
AEGINOR	origane
AEGINOS	agonise
AEGINOZ	agonize
AEGINPP	genipap
AEGINRR	earring
	grainer
AEGINRS	searing
	seringa
AEGINRT	granite
	gratiné
	ingrate
	tearing
AEGINRV	vinegar
AEGINRW	wearing
AEGINRZ	Zingare
AEGINST	easting
	genista
	ingesta
	seating
	teasing
	tsigane
AEGINTV	vintage
AEGINVW	weaving
AEGIPRS	prisage
	spairge
AEGIRRZ	grazier
AEGIRST	agister
	gaiters
	sea-girt
	strigae
AEGIRTV	virgate
	vitrage
AEGISTY	gaseity
AEGJLNR	jangler
AEGJRSU	jug-ears
AEGKKNO	angekok
AEGKLOU	kagoule
AEGKMRY	kerygma
AEGLLLY	legally
AEGLLNO	allonge
	galleon
AEGLLNR	langrel
AEGLLOR	allegro
AEGLLOT	tollage
AEGLLRY	allergy
	gallery
	largely
	regally
AEGLLSU	seagull
	sullage
AEGLLTU	gluteal
AEGLMNR	mangler
AEGLMOR	gomeral
AEGLMOU	moulage
AEGLMPU	plumage
AEGLMRU	maulgre
AEGLNOT	tangelo
AEGLNPR	grapnel
AEGLNPS	spangle
AEGLNRS	slanger
AEGLNRT	tangler
	trangle
AEGLNRU	granule
AEGLNRW	wangler
	wrangle
AEGLNRY	angerly
AEGLNSS	glassen
AEGLNSU	angelus
AEGLNTT	gantlet
AEGLNTU	languet
AEGLNTW	twangle
AEGLNUU	ungulae
AEGLNUW	gunwale
AEGLOPR	pergola
AEGLORT	gloater
	legator
AEGLORW	low-gear
AEGLOST	legatos
AEGLOSU	gealous
AEGLOTV	voltage
AEGLPPR	grapple
AEGLPRU	earplug
	graupel
AEGLPSU	plusage
AEGLPUY	plaguey
AEGLRRU	regular
AEGLRSS	largess
AEGLRSV	verglas
AEGLRTU	gaulter
	tegular
	tragule
AEGLRTY	greatly
AEGLRVY	gravely
AEGLSSS	glasses
AEGLSTT	△gestalt
AEGLTUV	△vulgate
AEGLUUY	guayule
AEGLUVY	vaguely
AEGMMRU	rummage
AEGMNNO	agnomen
AEGMNOR	megaron
AEGMNOS	mangoes
AEGMNOT	geomant
	magneto
	megaton
	montage
AEGMNPY	pygmean
AEGMNRS	Germans
AEGMNRT	garment
	margent
	ragment
AEGMNTU	augment
	mutagen
AEGMOOR	moorage
AEGMOSY	gaysome
AEGMOXY	exogamy
AEGNNOT	tonnage
AEGNNRT	regnant
AEGNNRU	gunnera
AEGNNTT	tangent
AEGNNTU	tunnage
AEGNOOR	oregano
AEGNOPT	pontage
AEGNORR	groaner
AEGNORS	nose-rag
AEGNORW	wagoner
AEGNORY	orangey
AEGNOST	on-stage
AEGNOSV	Vosgean
AEGNOSY	nosegay
AEGNOWY	waygone
AEGNPRS	engrasp
AEGNPRT	trepang
AEGNRRS	garners
	Rangers
AEGNRRT	granter
	regrant
AEGNRST	strange
AEGNSSY	gayness
AEGNSTT	gestant
AEGNSTV	V-agents
AEGNTTU	tutenag
AEGOORT	rootage
AEGOPPR	propage
AEGOPRT	portage
	potager
AEGOPST	△gestapo
	postage
AEGOPTT	pottage
AEGORRT	garrote
AEGORST	storage
AEGORTT	garotte
AEGORTU	outrage
AEGORUV	ouvrage
AEGORVY	voyager
AEGOSSU	gaseous
AEGOSTW	stowage
AEGOTTU	outgate
AEGOTTV	gavotte
AEGPRRS	grasper
	sparger
AEGPRRY	grapery
AEGPSSU	△pegasus
AEGPSTU	upstage
AEGRRSS	grasser
AEGRRST	garters
AEGRRUU	augurer
AEGRRUV	gravure
	verruga
AEGRSSU	arguses
AEGRSTY	stagery
AEGRSUV	sevruga
AEGSTUU	auguste
AEGTTTU	guttate
AEHHIKS	sheikha
AEHHIST	shehita

AEHHJOV	Jehovah	AEHKOSS	shakoes	AEHNOPW	wanhope
AEHHLOS	ash-hole	AEHKPSU	shake-up	AEHNORS	hoarsen
AEHHLTY	healthy	AEHKRRS	sharker		Senhora
AEHHNRS	harshen	AEHKRSS	△shakers	AEHNORT	another
AEHHNSV	Heshvan	AEHLLOV	hellova	AEHNOTV	have-not
AEHHSST	sheaths	AEHLLOY	holy-ale	AEHNPRS	sharpen
AEHHSTY	sheathy	AEHLLRS	hersall	AEHNPRT	panther
AEHIKSY	sakiyeh	AEHLLUV	helluva	AEHNPSU	unshape
AEHILMN	heliman	AEHLLYZ	hazelly	AEHNRSS	harness
AEHILMO	hemiola	AEHLMNO	manhole	AEHNRTU	haunter
AEHILMS	Ishmael	AEHLMNY	hymenal		unearth
AEHILNR	hernial	AEHLMOR	armhole		unheart
	inhaler	AEHLMPW	whample		urethan
AEHILNT	Hielant	AEHLMRT	thermal	AEHNRTX	△narthex
AEHILNY	hyaline	AEHLMRU	humeral	AEHNSTY	shantey
AEHILOR	airhole	AEHLNOT	ethanol	AEHNTTW	whatten
AEHILPR	hare-lip	AEHLNRT	enthral	AEHOORT	toheroa
AEHILRU	haulier	AEHLNSU	Hulsean	AEHOPST	tap-shoe
AEHILSW	shawlie		unleash	AEHORST	asthore
	whaisle		unshale		earshot
AEHILTT	lithate	AEHLORT	loather		haroset
	tile-hat		rat-hole	AEHORUV	haveour
AEHILTY	hyalite	AEHLOSS	asshole	AEHOSTU	atheous
AEHILUV	vihuela	AEHLPRS	spheral	AEHPPRS	perhaps
AEHILVY	heavily	AEHLPSS	hapless	AEHPPSU	shape-up
AEHILWZ	whaizle	AEHLPST	plashet	AEHPRRS	phraser
AEHIMNR	harmine	AEHLPSY	shapely		sharper
AEHIMNT	hematin	AEHLRSS	slasher	AEHPRSS	seraphs
AEHIMPS	phaeism	AEHLRST	harslet		Sherpas
AEHIMRS	mishear		slather	AEHPRST	sparthe
AEHIMSS	△messiah	AEHLRSV	halvers	AEHPRSW	pre-wash
AEHIMST	atheism	AEHLRTY	earthly	AEHPRTY	therapy
AEHINPR	heparin		hartely	AEHPSSY	hey-pass
AEHINPS	inphase		heartly	AEHRRTU	urethra
AEHINPT	penthia		lathery	AEHRSST	shaster
AEHINRS	arshine	AEHLRWY	whalery	AEHRSSW	swasher
AEHINRT	hairnet	AEHLSST	hatless		washers
	inearth	AEHLSTT	stealth	AEHRSTT	rathest
	therian	AEHLSWY	shawley		shatter
AEHINSS	△hessian	AEHLTWY	wealthy	AEHRSTV	harvest
AEHINSV	evanish	AEHMMRS	shammer	AEHRSTW	wreaths
AEHIPPT	epitaph	AEHMMSS	shammes	AEHRSVW	wharves
AEHIPRS	Shar-Pei	AEHMNOR	△menorah	AEHRSWY	washery
	sharpie	AEHMNOS	hoseman	AEHRSXY	hyraxes
AEHIPSS	aphesis	AEHMNOT	nathemo	AEHRTUU	hauteur
AEHIPST	ape-shit	AEHMNOY	haemony	AEHRTWY	wreathy
AEHIPSW	peishwa	AEHMNPY	nymphae	AEHSTUX	exhaust
AEHIPTZ	zaptieh	AEHMNST	hetmans	AEIIKNT	kainite
AEHIQSU	△quashie	AEHMOPT	apothem	AEIILLT	taillie
AEHIRRR	harrier	AEHMOTT	moth-eat	AEIILMR	Ramilie
AEHIRST	△sheriat	AEHMPTY	empathy	AEIILNN	aniline
AEHIRSV	ashiver	AEHMRSS	smasher	AEIILNR	airline
AEHIRSW	wearish	AEHMRST	hamster	AEIILNX	exilian
AEHIRWY	haywire	AEHMRTU	mauther	AEIILRS	Israeli
AEHISST	stashie	AEHMRTW	mawther		lairise
AEHISTT	atheist	AEHMUZZ	mezuzah	AEIILRZ	lairize
	staithe	AEHNNPY	ha'penny	AEIILSS	silesia
AEHISVY	yeshiva	AEHNNTU	unneath	AEIILSW	lewisia
AEHITTW	thwaite	AEHNNWY	anywhen	AEIILTZ	tailzie
AEHJLOW	jawhole	AEHNOPR	Orphean	AEIIMNT	intimae
AEHJRTT	Jethart	AEHNOPT	phaeton		miniate
AEHKNRT	thanker		phonate	AEIIMPR	imperia

AEIIMRT	airtime
AEIIMRV	viremia
AEIIMTT	imitate
AEIINNS	asinine
	insanie
AEIINPR	Pierian
AEIINQU	equinia
AEIINRS	senarii
	Sirenia
AEIINRT	inertia
AEIINST	isatine
AEIINSX	sixaine
AEIINTX	axinite
AEIIPRR	prairie
AEIIRRV	riviera
AEIIRST	irisate
AEIISTV	Saivite
	Sivaite
AEIITTV	vitiate
AEIJLNV	javelin
AEIJMNS	jasmine
AEIJNRS	Jersian
AEIJNRT	nartjie
AEIJNTU	jauntie
AEIJSSV	jive-ass
AEIKLMN	man-like
AEIKLNO	kaoline
AEIKLNU	unalike
AEIKLOT	keitloa
AEIKLOV	live-oak
AEIKLRS	serkali
AEIKLRV	klavier
AEIKLRW	warlike
AEIKLST	talkies
AEIKMMS	mismake
AEIKMNP	pikeman
AEIKMNR	ramekin
AEIKMPR	rampike
AEIKMST	mistake
AEIKNNR	Karenni
	Rankine
AEIKNRT	keratin
AEIKNSW	swankie
AEIKNSY	kyanise
AEIKNTY	kyanite
AEIKNYZ	kyanize
AEIKPRS	sparkie
AEIKSSS	askesis
AEILLMN	manille
AEILLMT	all-time
	Tellima
AEILLNR	ralline
AEILLNU	uillean
AEILLOV	alveoli
AEILLPS	illapse
AEILLQU	Lalique
AEILLRR	rallier
AEILLRT	literal
	tallier
AEILLRU	ruellia
AEILLST	tailles
	tallies
AEILLSW	wallies
AEILLUV	eluvial
AEILLVX	vexilla
AEILLVY	Viyella®
AEILMMS	melisma
AEILMNN	Lemnian
	lineman
	melanin
AEILMNO	mineola
AEILMNP	impanel
	maniple
AEILMNR	marline
	mineral
AEILMNS	isleman
	Malines
	seminal
AEILMNT	ailment
	aliment
AEILMPR	impearl
	lempira
AEILMPT	implate
	palmiet
AEILMRR	larmier
AEILMRS	△realism
AEILMRT	lamiter
AEILMRU	Lemuria
AEILMSS	aimless
	seismal
AEILMTY	laytime
	meatily
AEILNNN	Linnean
AEILNNS	nainsel'
AEILNNY	inanely
AEILNOP	opaline
AEILNOR	aileron
	alerion
	alienor
AEILNOT	elation
	toenail
AEILNOZ	Zoilean
AEILNPR	pearlin
	praline
AEILNPS	Nepalis
	spaniel
AEILNPT	pantile
AEILNPU	Pauline
AEILNPX	explain
AEILNQU	equinal
AEILNRT	entrail
	Latiner
	latrine
	ratline
	reliant
	retinal
	trenail
AEILNRV	ravelin
AEILNRX	relaxin
AEILNRY	inlayer
	nailery
AEILNST	eastlin
	elastin
	salient
	slàinte
	staniel
AEILNSU	inulase
AEILNSY	Elysian
AEILNTU	alunite
AEILNTV	ventail
AEILNUV	unalive
	unvaile
AEILNUW	lauwine
AEILNVY	naively
	naïvely
AEILOPR	peloria
AEILORV	variole
AEILOST	isolate
AEILOTV	violate
AEILPPR	apperil
	applier
	aripple
AEILPRT	plaiter
AEILPRV	prevail
AEILPST	talipes
AEILPSY	paisley
AEILQSU	Salique
AEILQTU	liquate
	tequila
AEILRRT	retiral
	retrial
	trailer
AEILRSS	airless
AEILRST	realist
	saltier
	saltire
AEILRSV	revisal
AEILRTT	tertial
AEILRTU	uralite
AEILRTY	irately
	reality
AEILRVV	revival
AEILRVY	virelay
AEILRWY	wearily
AEILSSV	vessail
AEILSTU	situlae
AEILSTV	estival
AEILTVY	vilayet
AEILUVX	exuvial
AEIMMNS	misname
AEIMMRT	Marmite®
	marmite
AEIMMST	mismate
AEIMMTY	Maytime
AEIMMZZ	mizmaze
AEIMNNT	mannite
AEIMNOR	moraine
AEIMNOU	moineau
AEIMNPR	Permian
AEIMNRR	mariner
	rein-arm

AEIMNRS	marines
	remains
	seminar
	sirname
AEIMNRT	minaret
	raiment
AEIMNRV	Minerva
	vermian
AEIMNRW	wireman
AEIMNSS	samisen
AEIMNST	mista'en
	Samnite
AEIMNSZ	man-size
AEIMNTV	Vietnam
AEIMNTY	amenity
	anytime
AEIMNUV	mauvein
	mauvine
AEIMOOP	ipomoea
AEIMOPR	emporia
AEIMORR	armoire
AEIMOST	amosite
	atomise
	osmiate
	Samiote
AEIMOTX	toxemia
AEIMOTZ	atomize
AEIMPRR	rampire
AEIMPRS	impresa
	sampire
AEIMPRT	primate
AEIMPRV	vampire
AEIMPSS	impasse
	pessima
AEIMPST	impaste
	pastime
AEIMPSW	mapwise
AEIMRRR	marrier
AEIMRRS	simarre
AEIMRST	maestri
	maister
	misrate
	semitar
	smartie
AEIMRTU	muriate
AEIMRTW	wartime
AEIMSSS	△messias
AEIMSST	asteism
AEIMSSV	massive
AEIMSTZ	mestiza
AEIMSUV	amusive
AEIMTYZ	azymite
AEINNNS	nannies
AEINNOT	enation
	Etonian
	Noetian
AEINNOW	Owenian
AEINNOZ	neo-Nazi
AEINNPR	pannier
AEINNPT	pantine
	pinnate
AEINNRS	insnare
AEINNRT	entrain
	trannie
AEINNRU	aneurin
AEINNTT	antient
AEINOPR	open-air
	pea-iron
AEINOPZ	apiezon
	epizoan
AEINORS	erasion
AEINORT	otarine
AEINOSS	anoesis
AEINOSV	evasion
AEINOXZ	oxazine
AEINPPS	nappies
AEINPRS	Persian
AEINPRT	painter
	pertain
	repaint
AEINPST	panties
	sapient
	spinate
AEINPSW	wine-sap
AEINPTT	patient
AEINPTU	△petunia
AEINPTY	paneity
AEINQTU	antique
	quinate
AEINRRS	sierran
AEINRRT	retrain
	terrain
	trainer
AEINRST	resiant
	retinas
	retsina
	stainer
	starnie
	stearin
AEINRSV	Servian
AEINRTT	intreat
	iterant
	nitrate
	tartine
	tertian
AEINRTU	ruinate
	taurine
	uranite
	urinate
AEINRTV	Avertin®
AEINRTW	tinware
AEINRUV	vaurien
AEINRUW	unwarie
AEINRUZ	azurine
AEINRVV	vervain
AEINSST	entasis
	sestina
AEINSSV	vinasse
AEINSTT	instate
	satinet
AEINSTU	sinuate
AEINSWY	anywise
AEINTVY	naivety
	naïvety
AEINTXY	anxiety
AEINUXZ	Zeuxian
AEIOQSU	sequoia
AEIORRR	arriero
AEIORST	otaries
AEIOSTT	ostiate
	toastie
AEIOSTZ	azotise
AEIOTZZ	azotize
AEIPPRS	apprise
AEIPPRT	periapt
	Rappite
AEIPPRZ	apprize
AEIPRRS	praiser
AEIPRSS	paresis
	praises
	Serapis
AEIPRST	piastre
	traipse
AEIPRSU	spuriae
	upraise
AEIPRSV	parvise
AEIPRTT	partite
AEIPRTV	private
AEIPRTW	wiretap
AEIPRXY	pyrexia
AEIPSSS	asepsis
AEIPSST	pasties
AEIPSSV	passive
AEIPTXY	epitaxy
AEIQRUV	aquiver
AEIRRRT	tarrier
AEIRRST	tarsier
AEIRRTT	retrait
AEIRRTU	Etruria
AEIRRTY	retiary
AEIRRVV	△viverra
AEIRSST	tirasse
AEIRSSZ	assizer
AEIRSTT	artiste
	striate
AEIRSTV	taivers
AEIRSTW	waister
AEIRTTT	attrite
	titrate
AEIRTTV	taivert
AEIRTTX	extrait
AEIRTUY	aureity
AEIRTUZ	azurite
AEIRTVY	variety
AEIRWWY	wireway
AEISSSZ	assizes
AEISSUV	suasive
AEISSUX	auxesis
AEISTTU	situate
AEISTTV	stative
AEISTTY	satiety
AEITTTU	attuite
AEITTTV	vittate
AEJKNRS	jankers
AEJLNUV	juvenal

Words marked △ may be spelled also with a capital letter

AEJLOSU	jalouse
	jealous
AEJLOUZ	azulejo
AEJMSSY	jessamy
AEJMSTY	majesty
AEJNNOS	joannes
AEJNORZ	zanjero
AEJNSST	jessant
AEJPRSY	jaspery
AEKLLRT	Kartell
AEKLLTU	kellaut
AEKLMOU	leukoma
AEKLNPP	knapple
AEKLNPR	prankle
AEKLNST	asklent
AEKLORY	rokelay
AEKLOST	skatole
AEKLPRS	sparkle
AEKLRST	stalker
AEKLRUW	waulker
AEKMNOS	sokeman
AEKMOOT	matooke
AEKMPRU	upmaker
AEKNNTU	untaken
AEKNPPR	knapper
AEKNPRS	spanker
AEKNPSU	sneak-up
	unspeak
AEKNRST	starken
AEKNRSW	swanker
AEKNRVY	knavery
AEKNSWY	swankey
AEKORRS	rosaker
AEKOTTU	outtake
	out-take
	takeout
AEKPPSU	upspake
	upspeak
AEKPSSY	passkey
AEKQSUY	squeaky
AEKRSTY	streaky
AELLMNU	lumenal
AELLMSU	malleus
AELLMSY	mesally
AELLMTY	metally
AELLMWX	maxwell
AELLNOP	pallone
AELLNOR	llanero
AELLNOV	novella
AELLNOY	alonely
AELLNPY	penally
AELLNRT	entrall
AELLNSS	allness
AELLNTT	tallent
AELLNVY	venally
AELLOPX	poll-axe
AELLORS	rosella
AELLORT	reallot
AELLORV	all-over
	overall
	over-all
AELLPRU	pleural
AELLPTU	pluteal
AELLPTY	playlet
AELLQUY	equally
AELLRRU	allurer
AELLRST	stellar
AELLRSU	laurels
AELLRTY	alertly
	elytral
AELLSST	tassell
AELLSSW	lawless
AELLSTW	setwall
	swallet
AELLSTY	stalely
AELLSVY	valleys
AELLTUU	ululate
AELLUVV	valvule
AELMMNO	mamelon
AELMMOY	myeloma
AELMMRS	slammer
AELMMRT	trammel
AELMMST	stammel
AELMMSY	malmsey
AELMNNS	lensman
AELMNOR	almoner
	nemoral
AELMNOS	melanos
AELMNOT	lomenta
	omental
	telamon
AELMNPR	lampern
AELMNRU	numeral
AELMNSU	mensual
AELMNTT	mantlet
AELMNTU	nutmeal
AELMOPR	pleroma
AELMOPU	ampoule
AELMOPY	maypole
AELMORT	molerat
AELMORV	removal
AELMOSS	Molasse
AELMOST	maltose
AELMOTT	matelot
AELMPRS	lampers
	sampler
AELMPRT	△templar
	trample
AELMPRY	lamprey
AELMPTU	plumate
AELMRRS	marrels
AELMRSS	armless
AELMRSU	maulers
AELMRTT	martlet
AELMSSU	Musales
AELMSTU	Mustela
AELNNPR	planner
AELNNPU	unpanel
AELNNRS	ensnarl
AELNNRT	lantern
AELNNRU	unlearn
AELNNST	stannel
AELNNTU	annulet
AELNOOS	alsoone
AELNOPT	polenta
AELNORS	orleans
AELNORU	aleuron
AELNORV	Veronal®
	veronal
AELNOST	lean-tos
AELNOTV	volante
AELNPPY	playpen
AELNPRT	pantler
	planter
	replant
AELNPRY	plenary
AELNPSS	napless
AELNPTX	explant
AELNPTY	aplenty
	net-play
	penalty
AELNQUU	unequal
AELNRRS	snarler
AELNRST	saltern
	sternal
AELNRTT	trental
AELNRTU	neutral
AELNRTV	ventral
AELNRUV	unravel
AELNSSU	sensual
AELNSSW	awnless
AELNSSX	laxness
AELNSTU	unlaste
AELNSTY	stanyel
AELNTUV	envault
AELOORS	aerosol
	roseola
AELOPPR	propale
AELOPPX	apoplex
AELOPRR	preoral
AELOPRS	reposal
AELOPRT	prolate
AELOPRV	overlap
AELOPST	△apostle
AELOPSX	exposal
AELOPTT	paletot
AELOPTU	outleap
AELORRT	Realtor®
	realtor
	relator
AELORSS	oarless
AELORST	oestral
AELORTU	torulae
AELORTV	levator
AELORTY	royalet
AELORTZ	zelator
AELORUU	rouleau
AELORVY	overlay
AELORWY	owre'lay
AELOSSS	lassoes
AELOSSV	salvoes
AELOSTV	solvate
AELOSUZ	zealous
AELOSVY	saveloy
AELOTTU	toluate
AELOTUV	ovulate

Words marked △ may be spelled also with a capital letter

AELOTVV	volvate
AELPPRS	slapper
AELPPRY	reapply
AELPPSS	sapples
AELPPST	stapple
AELPPSU	appulse
	papules
AELPRST	plaster
	△psalter
	stapler
AELPRSU	perusal
	serpula
AELPRSY	parsley
	sparely
AELPRTT	△partlet
	platter
	prattle
AELPRTY	peartly
	prelaty
	pteryla
AELPRUY	epulary
AELPSSS	sapless
AELPSTT	peltast
AELPSTU	pulsate
	spatule
AELPUUV	upvalue
AELQRRU	quarrel
AELQTUZ	quetzal
AELRRSU	surreal
AELRRTT	rattler
AELRRTW	trawler
AELRSST	artless
AELRSSY	rayless
AELRSTT	slatter
	starlet
	startle
	Telstar
AELRSTU	saluter
AELRSTV	travels
	vestral
AELRSTW	wastrel
AELRSVY	slavery
AELRTTT	tartlet
	tattler
AELRTTU	tutelar
AELRTUV	vaulter
AELRTWZ	waltzer
AELSSTX	taxless
AELSSWY	wayless
AELSTTW	wattles
AELSTTY	stately
	stylate
AELSUVY	suavely
AELSWZZ	swazzle
AELTTTW	twattle
AELTTUX	textual
AELTUVV	vulvate
AEMMNOT	momenta
AEMMNTU	amentum
AEMMORS	marmose
AEMMRST	stammer
AEMMRSZ	mamzers
AEMMSTU	summate
AEMNNOS	mannose
	name-son
AEMNNOT	montane
AEMNNOU	noumena
AEMNNRS	manners
AEMNNRT	manrent
	remnant
AEMNNSW	newsman
AEMNNTU	unmeant
AEMNOPR	repoman
AEMNOPZ	zampone
AEMNORS	Romanes
AEMNORT	tone-arm
AEMNORU	enamour
	neuroma
AEMNORV	overman
AEMNORW	men-o'-war
AEMNORY	romneya
AEMNOST	mantoes
AEMNOTU	notaeum
	outname
AEMNPST	enstamp
AEMNPTU	putamen
AEMNPTY	payment
AEMNRRU	manurer
AEMNRST	sarment
	smarten
AEMNRSU	surname
AEMNRTU	trueman
AEMNRTV	varment
AEMNSST	stamens
AEMNSTY	amnesty
AEMNTTX	text-man
AEMNTWY	wayment
AEMOORW	woomera
AEMOOST	osteoma
AEMOOSV	vamoose
AEMOOSZ	Mesozoa
AEMOPPR	pampero
AEMORRV	overarm
AEMORST	maestro
AEMORSU	rameous
AEMORSW	seaworm
AEMORSX	xeromas
AEMORTU	Euratom
AEMOSTW	twasome
AEMOSUZ	zamouse
AEMOSWY	someway
AEMOTTZ	mozetta
AEMPPRY	mappery
AEMPRRT	tramper
AEMPRRW	prewarm
AEMPRST	stamper
AEMPRSW	swamper
AEMPRTT	trampet
AEMPRTU	tempura
AEMPTTT	attempt
AEMPTTU	tapetum
AEMQRSU	masquer
AEMRRRY	remarry
AEMRRST	arm-rest
AEMRRSW	swarmer
AEMRRTU	erratum
AEMRRUU	Réaumur
AEMRSSU	masseur
AEMRSTT	smatter
AEMRSTU	strumae
AEMRSTY	mastery
	mayster
	streamy
AEMRTTX	martext
AEMRTTY	mattery
AEMRTUU	trumeau
AEMSTVZ	zemstva
AENNNPT	pennant
AENNOPS	pannose
AENNORT	norteña
AENNORY	annoyer
AENNOTU	tonneau
AENNPRS	spanner
AENNQTU	quannet
AENNRTT	entrant
AENNRTV	vernant
AENNRTY	tannery
	tyranne
AENNSSW	wanness
AENOOTZ	entozoa
	tan-ooze
AENOPPR	propane
AENOPRS	persona
AENOPRT	operant
	pronate
	△protean
AENOPSU	posaune
AENORRV	overran
AENORST	nor'-east
	senator
	treason
AENORSW	sea-worn
AENORTV	venator
AENORXY	anorexy
AENOSTT	attones
AENOSTU	soutane
AENOSVW	waveson
AENOUUV	nouveau
AENPPRS	parsnep
	snapper
AENPPRT	parpent
AENPPRU	unpaper
AENPRRT	partner
AENPRRW	prewarn
AENPRST	pastern
	persant
AENPRSW	spawner
AENPRTT	pattern
	reptant
AENPRUV	parvenu
AENPSST	aptness
	patness
AENPSSY	synapse
AENPSTU	peanuts
	pesaunt
AENPSTW	stewpan

AENPSTY	synapte
AENRRTT	tranter
AENRRTY	ternary
AENRSST	sarsnet
AENRSSW	rawness
AENRSTU	saunter
AENRSTV	servant
	versant
AENRSTW	strawen
AENRSUV	Avernus
AENRSUW	unswear
	unwares
AENRTTU	taunter
AENRTTY	nattery
AENRTUV	vaunter
AENRTUW	unwater
AENRUWY	unweary
AENSSTU	△senatus
AENSSTX	△sextans
AENSTTU	tetanus
	unstate
AENSTTX	△sextant
AENTTTU	attuent
AEOOPPS	papoose
AEOOPRS	oropesa
AEOPPPS	pappose
AEOPPRS	apposer
AEOPPRV	approve
AEOPPSU	pea-soup
AEOPRRT	patrero
	praetor
	prorate
AEOPRST	esparto
	seaport
AEOPRTT	portate
AEOPRVY	overpay
AEOPRWY	ropeway
AEOQRTU	equator
	quorate
AEOQRUV	vaquero
AEOQSUU	aqueous
AEORRSS	Rasores
AEORRST	roaster
AEORRSU	arouser
AEORSSS	serosas
AEORSTT	Rosetta
	toaster
AEORSTZ	Zostera
AEORTTU	outrate
AEORTUW	outwear
AEORTVX	overtax
AEOSSYY	easy-osy
AEPPRRT	trapper
AEPPRRW	wrapper
AEPPRSS	appress
AEPPRSU	upspear
AEPPRSW	swapper
AEPPSTU	paste-up
AEPQRTU	parquet
AEPRRRS	sparrer
AEPRRSY	prayers
	respray
	sprayer
AEPRRTU	parture
	rapture
AEPRRTY	petrary
AEPRSSY	pessary
AEPRSTT	spatter
	tapster
AEPRSTU	pasture
	upstare
AEPRSTY	yapster
AEPRSYY	sprayey
AEPRTXY	apteryx
AEPSSTU	petasus
AEPSTTU	upstate
AEQRRSU	squarer
AEQRRTU	quarter
AEQRSTU	T-square
AEQRTTU	quartet
AEQRUVY	quavery
AERRSST	starers
AERRSSU	assurer
AERRSTT	△restart
	starter
AERRSTY	strayer
AERRTTY	rattery
AERSSTT	starets
AERSTTT	stretta
	tatters
AERSTTU	stature
AERSTTW	swatter
AERSTTZ	staretz
AERSTUY	estuary
AERSTWY	wastery
AERTTTY	tattery
AERTTUV	vettura
AESSTUY	eustasy
AESTTTU	statute
AFFGGIN	gaffing
AFFGHIS	fish-fag
AFFGINN	naffing
AFFGINY	affying
AFFHILN	hafflin
AFFHIRS	raffish
AFFHLLY	fly-half
AFFIKRS	Kaffirs
AFFILMN	mafflin
AFFILOX	Filofax®
AFFILSY	falsify
AFFIMST	mastiff
AFFINRU	funfair
	ruffian
AFFINTY	△tiffany
AFFIORR	forfair
AFFIRRU	furfair
AFFLLPY	fly-flap
AFFLNOP	off-plan
AFFLOPY	play-off
AFFNORS	saffron
AFFNORT	affront
AFFNOSW	sawn-off
AFFOPRT	part-off
AFGGGIN	fagging
AFGGIOT	goat-fig
AFGHHIS	hagfish
AFGHIRS	garfish
AFGHLSU	gashful
AFGHLTU	flaught
AFGHOST	Gasthof
AFGHRTU	fraught
AFGIILN	failing
AFGIINR	fairing
AFGILLN	falling
AFGILMN	flaming
AFGILNO	loafing
AFGILNR	flaring
AFGILNT	fatling
AFGILNU	gainful
AFGILNY	anglify
	flaying
AFGILRU	figural
AFGIMNO	foaming
AFGIMNR	farming
	framing
AFGIMNY	magnify
AFGINNN	fanning
AFGINNW	fawning
AFGINRT	ingraft
AFGINRY	fraying
AFGINST	fasting
AFGINTT	fatting
AFGINTW	wafting
AFGIOTT	fagotti
AFGIRTY	gratify
AFGKNOP	pakfong
AFGKORT	koftgar
AFGLLLY	gallfly
AFGLLUY	fall-guy
	fugally
AFGLMOP	fog-lamp
AFGLRYY	grayfly
AFGMNOR	frogman
AFGOOTT	fagotto
AFGOSTU	fugatos
AFHIIRS	fairish
AFHIKUY	kufiyah
AFHILLN	halflin
AFHILSS	falsish
AFHILTU	laithfu'
AFHILTW	halfwit
AFHIMNU	hafnium
AFHINOS	fashion
AFHINTU	unfaith
AFHISST	fastish
AFHISSW	sawfish
AFHISTT	fattish
AFHISWY	fish-way
AFHKORY	hayfork
AFHKRTU	futhark
AFHLMRU	harmful
AFHLOTU	out-half
AFHLOTY	hayloft
AFHLSTU	hatfuls

AFHMOST	fathoms
AFHOOPT	pooftah
AFHOPTU	pouftah
AFHORSS	shofars
AFIILOR	airfoil
AFIILRT	airlift
AFIILRY	fairily
AFIIMOS	△mafiosi
AFIINRS	Frisian
AFIKLOT	flokati
AFIKNRT	ratfink
AFILLMS	misfall
AFILLNY	finally
AFILLPT	pitfall
AFILLPU	pailful
AFILLRY	frailly
AFILLTY	tail-fly
AFILLUV	fluvial
	vialful
AFILLUW	wailful
AFILMNT	lift-man
AFILMOR	aliform
AFILMOY	foamily
AFILMPY	amplify
AFILMSS	falsism
AFILNOW	Wolfian
AFILNPU	painful
AFILNTU	flutina
AFILNTY	faintly
AFILORW	airflow
AFILOTX	fox-tail
AFILQUY	qualify
AFILRRY	friarly
AFILRTY	frailty
AFILSSY	salsify
AFILSTU	fistula
AFILSTW	fist-law
AFILSTY	falsity
AFILSVY	Slavify
AFIMOOS	△mafioso
AFIMORV	aviform
AFIMSUV	Fauvism
AFIMTTU	Muftiat
AFINNOR	franion
AFINORS	insofar
AFINSTU	faunist
	fustian
	infaust
AFIORTU	faitour
AFIORTZ	forzati
AFISSTT	sitfast
AFISSTY	satisfy
AFISTUV	Fauvist
AFITTUY	fatuity
AFJLRSU	jarfuls
AFJOOTW	foot-jaw
	jaw-foot
AFKLNRY	frankly
AFKLNTU	tankful
AFKLOWY	folkway
AFKMORX	fox-mark
AFKRRTU	Fraktur
AFLLMPU	palmful
AFLLMPY	lamp-fly
AFLLOOY	aloofly
AFLLOTU	fallout
	fall-out
	outfall
AFLLPUY	playful
AFLLUWY	awfully
AFLMNNO	non-flam
AFLMNOU	moanful
AFLMORU	formula
AFLMORW	wolfram
AFLMOST	flotsam
AFLMRSU	armfuls
AFLMSTU	mastful
AFLMSUU	famulus
AFLNORT	frontal
AFLNOTT	flotant
AFLNOTU	no-fault
AFLNPSU	panfuls
AFLNRTU	runflat
AFLNTUY	flaunty
AFLOOTW	woolfat
AFLORSU	fusarol
AFLORUV	flavour
AFLORWW	warwolf
AFLOSSU	fossula
AFLPRTY	flytrap
AFLPSTY	fly-past
AFLRSTU	Flustra
AFLRTUY	trayful
AFLSTUV	vatfuls
AFMNOOT	footman
AFMNORT	formant
AFMNRSU	surfman
AFMNRTU	turfman
AFMORST	farmost
AFMORTU	foumart
AFMOSTT	aftmost
AFMOSTU	sfumato
AFNORRT	Fortran
AFNORRW	forwarn
AFNSSTU	sunfast
AFOOPPR	approof
AFOORRU	four-oar
AFOORTZ	forzato
AFOOTWY	footway
AFOPRTX	fox-trap
AFORSUV	favours
AFOSTUU	fatuous
AGGGGIN	gagging
AGGGIJN	jagging
AGGGILN	lagging
AGGGINN	ganging
	nagging
AGGGINR	ragging
AGGGINS	sagging
AGGGINT	tagging
AGGGINU	gauging
AGGGINW	wagging
AGGGINZ	zagging
AGGHHIS	haggish
AGGHIIL	ghilgai
AGGHIMN	gingham
AGGHINN	hanging
AGGHISW	waggish
AGGIIJJ	jigajig
	jig-a-jig
AGGIILM	mail-gig
AGGIIMN	imaging
AGGIJJO	jigajog
AGGILLN	galling
	gingall
AGGILNN	angling
AGGILNR	glaring
AGGILNT	gatling
	Lagting
AGGILNZ	glazing
AGGILOS	loggias
AGGINNP	panging
AGGINOY	Ogygian
AGGINPS	gasping
AGGINRS	sirgang
AGGINRT	grating
AGGINRV	graving
AGGINRZ	grazing
AGGINSS	gassing
AGGINST	staging
AGGLNOO	long-ago
AGGLOST	loggats
AGGMORR	grogram
AGGMOTY	maggoty
AGGNOSU	guangos
AGHHHIT	high-hat
AGHHIMN	highman
AGHHIWY	highway
AGHHOSW	hogwash
AGHHTUY	haughty
AGHIINN	haining
AGHIKNS	shaking
AGHIKNW	hawking
AGHILLN	halling
AGHILNR	harling
AGHILNS	lashing
AGHILNT	Althing
	halting
	lathing
AGHILNW	whaling
AGHILOT	△goliath
AGHILRS	largish
AGHILRT	alright
AGHILSU	Gaulish
AGHIMNS	mashing
AGHIMPS	gampish
AGHINNO	nihonga
AGHINNT	tanghin
AGHINPP	happing
AGHINPS	shaping
AGHINRS	garnish
	sharing
AGHINRT	Granthi
AGHINRU	nuraghi
AGHINSU	anguish

AGHINSV	havings
	shaving
AGHINSW	washing
AGHINTT	hatting
AGHINTW	thawing
AGHIOST	goatish
AGHIPRS	Graphis
AGHIPSW	pigwash
AGHIRST	a-rights
AGHIRSU	guarish
AGHJMNO	mah-jong
AGHKOOR	Goorkha
AGHKOSW	goshawk
AGHLMPU	galumph
AGHLNOT	Loghtan
AGHLNUY	nylghau
AGHLOOS	gasohol
AGHLOSU	goulash
AGHLPTU	plug-hat
AGHLSTY	ghastly
AGHMOSS	moss-hag
AGHNOTU	hangout
	tohunga
AGHNRSU	nurhags
AGHNRUY	ahungry
	Hungary
AGHNTUY	naughty
AGHORTW	warthog
AGHPSUW	Pugwash
AGHPTUY	paughty
AGHRSTY	gytrash
AGIIKLT	glaikit
AGIILMN	mailing
AGIILNN	nailing
AGIILNR	glairin
	railing
AGIILNS	aisling
	nilgais
	sailing
AGIILNT	tailing
AGIILNW	wailing
AGIILOV	viliago
AGIILPT	pigtail
AGIILTY	agility
AGIIMMN	maiming
AGIIMMS	△imagism
AGIIMOR	origami
AGIIMST	imagist
AGIINNR	ingrain
AGIINNZ	Zingani
AGIINPR	pairing
AGIINPT	T'ai-p'ing
AGIINRS	raising
AGIINRT	raiting
AGIINRZ	Zingari
AGIINTW	waiting
AGIINTX	taxiing
AGIJMMN	jamming
AGIJNNU	Jungian
AGIJNRR	jarring
AGIKLNO	oakling
AGIKLNR	Karling
AGIKLNT	talking
AGIKLNW	walking
AGIKMNR	marking
AGIKMNS	makings
AGIKNNR	ranking
AGIKNNT	tanking
AGIKNNU	unaking
AGIKNNY	yanking
AGIKNOS	soaking
AGIKNOY	kayoing
	okaying
AGIKNPR	parking
AGIKNQU	quaking
AGIKNRS	sarking
AGIKNRT	karting
AGIKNSS	gaskins
AGIKNST	skating
	takings
	tasking
AGILLLN	lalling
AGILLMN	malling
AGILLMU	gallium
AGILLNP	palling
AGILLNU	lingual
	△lingula
AGILLNW	all-wing
	walling
AGILLNY	allying
AGILLOR	gorilla
AGILLOS	Gallios
AGILLOT	galliot
AGILLRU	ligular
AGILLSU	lugsail
AGILMMN	lamming
AGILMNP	lamping
AGILMNR	marling
AGILMNT	malting
AGILMOS	gliomas
AGILMPU	plagium
AGILNNO	loaning
AGILNNS	linsang
AGILNNT	tanling
AGILNOP	galopin
AGILNOR	rangoli
AGILNOT	antilog
AGILNPP	lapping
AGILNPS	sapling
AGILNPT	plating
AGILNPW	lapwing
AGILNPY	playing
AGILNRT	ratling
AGILNRW	warling
AGILNRY	angrily
	nargily
AGILNST	anglist
	lasting
	salting
	slating
AGILNSU	nilgaus
AGILNSV	salving
AGILNSW	swaling
AGILNTY	giantly
AGILNUW	wauling
AGILNWW	wawling
AGILOPT	galipot
AGILORS	girasol
AGILOST	saligot
AGILSTY	stagily
AGIMMNR	ramming
AGIMNNN	manning
AGIMNNR	ringman
AGIMNOR	Moringa
	roaming
AGIMNPP	mapping
AGIMNPR	ramping
AGIMNPT	tamping
AGIMNPV	vamping
AGIMNRR	marring
AGIMNRT	migrant
AGIMNRW	warming
AGIMNRY	myringa
AGIMNSU	amusing
AGIMNTT	matting
AGIMORS	isogram
AGIMORU	gourami
AGIMOSY	isogamy
AGIMRRT	trigram
AGIMRTY	trigamy
AGIMSST	stigmas
AGINNNP	panning
AGINNNT	tanning
AGINNNV	vanning
AGINNOZ	Zingano
AGINNPP	napping
AGINNPT	panting
AGINNRS	snaring
AGINNRT	ranting
AGINNRW	warning
AGINNTW	wanting
AGINNUZ	Günzian
AGINNWY	yawning
AGINOOO	oogonia
AGINORR	roaring
AGINORS	ignaros
	△signora
	soaring
AGINORT	Grotian
AGINORV	Virgoan
AGINORZ	Zingaro
AGINOST	agonist
	gitanos
AGINOSU	sagouin
AGINOSV	Vosgian
AGINPPR	rapping
AGINPPS	sapping
AGINPPT	tapping
AGINPPW	wapping
AGINPRS	parsing
	rasping
	sparing
AGINPRT	parting
	prating
AGINPRW	warping
AGINPRY	praying

AGINPSS	passing
AGINPST	pasting
AGINPSU	pausing
AGINPTT	patting
AGINRRT	tarring
AGINRRW	warring
AGINRST	gastrin
	ratings
	staring
AGINRSY	signary
	△syringa
AGINRTT	ratting
AGINRTW	ring-taw
AGINRTY	giantry
AGINRUW	wauring
AGINRVY	varying
AGINRWY	ringway
AGINSSS	assigns
AGINSSV	savings
AGINSTT	tasting
AGINSTW	wasting
AGINSTY	staying
	Stygian
AGINSWY	swaying
AGINTTT	tatting
AGINTTV	vatting
AGINTXY	taxying
AGINTYZ	tzigany
AGINWWX	waxwing
AGIORST	agistor
	orgiast
AGIORSV	viragos
AGIRTVY	gravity
AGISTUV	vagitus
AGJLNSU	Juglans
AGJLRUU	jugular
AGJNOOR	jargoon
AGKLNNO	anklong
AGKLNNU	anklung
AGKMNOP	kampong
AGKNOPT	paktong
AGKORRW	ragwork
AGLLNOO	galloon
AGLLNTU	gallnut
	nutgall
AGLLOSS	glossal
AGLLOSW	gallows
AGLLOTT	glottal
AGLLPTY	glyptal
AGLLRYY	gyrally
AGLMOPY	polygam
AGLMORU	glamour
AGLMORY	Morglay
AGLNOPS	Gosplan
AGLNOPU	up-along
AGLNORU	languor
AGLNOST	alongst
AGLNOSU	lanugos
AGLNPSY	spangly
AGLNPUY	gunplay
AGLNTUY	gauntly
AGLOOPY	apology
AGLOORW	rag-wool
AGLOPSU	Solpuga
AGLOSUV	valgous
AGLRSUU	argulus
AGMMNSU	magnums
AGMMORY	myogram
AGMNNOS	songman
AGMNNOW	gownman
AGMNORU	organum
AGMNOST	amongst
AGMNSTU	mustang
AGMNSTY	gymnast
	syntagm
AGMNSYY	syngamy
AGMOOYZ	zoogamy
AGMOPRR	program
AGMOPRU	gopuram
AGMORRW	ragworm
AGMOSYZ	zygomas
AGMPRSU	grampus
AGMRSSU	grassum
AGMRSTU	Targums
AGNNNOO	nonagon
AGNNOOR	organon
AGNOQSU	quangos
AGNORRT	grantor
AGNORST	art-song
AGNRTUY	gauntry
AGOPPST	stopgap
AGORRTW	ragwort
AGOSUYZ	azygous
AHHHISS	hashish
AHHIKSW	hawkish
AHHIMNS	Mishnah
AHHIMNU	hahnium
AHHIPRS	rhaphis
AHHISTT	shittah
AHHLLOO	holla-ho
AHHLRSY	harshly
AHHOOPS	hoop-ash
AHHOPRS	shophar
AHHOPRT	hap'orth
AHHPTUZ	hutzpah
AHIIKRS	shikari
AHIILPS	silphia
AHIILSW	Swahili
AHIIMNT	thiamin
AHIIMSS	sashimi
AHIINPR	hairpin
AHIINTU	huitain
AHIIPRS	airship
AHIIPSX	Xiphias
AHIJMSV	Jahvism
AHIJNNO	Johnian
AHIJSTV	Jahvist
AHIKLMS	Lakshmi
AHIKLRS	larkish
AHIKLSY	shakily
AHIKMNS	khamsin
AHIKMRS	△kashmir
AHIKMSW	mawkish
AHIKNRS	Krishna
AHIKNSS	snakish
AHIKNSV	knavish
AHIKPRS	parkish
AHILLNO	hallion
AHILLNP	phallin
AHILLNT	ant-hill
AHILLRT	athrill
AHILLST	tallish
AHILLTT	tallith
AHILMMS	mashlim
AHILMMY	hammily
AHILMNS	mashlin
AHILMOT	halimot
AHILMSU	alumish
AHILNPS	planish
AHILNRS	shrinal
AHILNRT	inthral
AHILORY	hoarily
AHILPPS	Lappish
	shiplap
AHILPPY	happily
AHILPST	Lapiths
AHILPSY	apishly
AHILSST	saltish
AHILSSV	slavish
AHILSTU	halitus
AHILSTY	hastily
AHIMMRS	rammish
AHIMNNS	mannish
AHIMNNU	inhuman
AHIMNOT	Manihot
AHIMNPS	shipman
AHIMOPR	morphia
AHIMPST	mishapt
AHIMPSV	vampish
AHIMPSW	wampish
AHIMRST	Mithras
	thrimsa
AHIMRSW	warmish
AHIMSTV	mitsvah
AHIMTUZ	azimuth
AHIMTVZ	mitzvah
AHINNSW	wannish
AHINNTX	xanthin
AHINORT	orthian
AHINOTZ	hoatzin
AHINPSS	Spanish
AHINPTY	Pythian
AHINRST	tarnish
AHINRSV	varnish
AHINRTY	rhytina
AHINSTU	inhaust
AHIOOST	atishoo
	a-tishoo
AHIOPRU	ophiura
AHIOPXY	hypoxia
AHIORUV	haviour
AHIPRST	harpist
AHIPRSU	rupiahs
AHIPRSW	warship
AHIPSSW	waspish
AHIPSWW	whipsaw

AHIPSWY	shipway
AHIRRST	stirrah
AHIRRSY	'Arryish
AHIRSTT	athirst
	rattish
	tartish
AHIRSTW	trishaw
AHISSTU	shiatsu
	thiasus
AHISSTW	whatsis
AHISTTW	whatsit
AHISTUZ	shiatzu
AHISTVY	Yahvist
AHISTWY	Yahwist
AHITTWW	whittaw
AHJMNOS	Mas-John
AHKLMOO	holm-oak
AHKMORR	markhor
AHKMRTU	mukhtar
AHKNPTU	Pakhtun
AHKRSSU	△kashrus
AHKRSTU	△kashrut
	tushkar
AHKRSUU	Kurhaus
AHLLNOS	shallon
AHLLNOY	hallyon
AHLLOPS	shallop
AHLLOST	shallot
AHLLOSW	shallow
AHLLOTY	loathly
	tally-ho
AHLLPSU	△phallus
AHLLPYY	aphylly
AHLLSTU	thallus
AHLMMSU	mashlum
AHLMNPY	nymphal
AHLMNUY	humanly
AHLMORU	humoral
AHLMSTZ	shmaltz
AHLMSUU	hamulus
AHLNOPR	alphorn
AHLNORT	althorn
AHLOSTU	outlash
AHLOTUU	outhaul
AHLPRSY	sharply
AHLPRUY	hypural
AHLPSSY	splashy
AHMMMOT	mammoth
AHMMMUU	hummaum
AHMMTUZ	Thammuz
AHMNNTU	manhunt
AHMNNUU	unhuman
AHMNOPS	shopman
AHMNOPT	phantom
AHMNORS	Romansh
AHMNORU	man-hour
AHMNORY	harmony
AHMNOSW	showman
AHMNRSU	Rhamnus
AHMNRYY	hymnary
AHMNSTU	mash-tun
AHMOOPS	shampoo

AHMOOSS	samshoo
AHMORRU	morrhua
AHMORST	harmost
AHMOTTZ	matzoth
AHMPSSU	smash-up
AHMRSTY	thrymsa
AHNNOTY	Anthony
AHNOOPR	harpoon
AHNORSX	saxhorn
AHNOTTW	whatnot
AHNPPUU	pupunha
AHNPPUY	unhappy
AHNPRXY	pharynx
AHNPSTU	Pashtun
AHNSTUY	unhasty
AHOOPST	hop-oast
AHOPRTY	atrophy
AHOPSTW	washpot
AHOPTTW	towpath
AHORTTY	throaty
AHOSTUV	Shavuot
AHOSTUW	outwash
	washout
	wash-out
AHPRRTY	phratry
AHPSXYY	asphyxy
AHQSSUY	squashy
AHRSTWY	swarthy
AHRTUWY	thruway
AIIILMS	Ismaili
AIIILMT	militia
AIIILNT	initial
AIIIMRS	saimiri
AIIJMNS	Jainism
AIIJNST	Jainist
AIIKMMS	skimmia
AIIKMNN	manikin
AIIKRTT	traikit
AIILLLP	lapilli
AIILLMN	liminal
	Millian
AIILLNV	villain
AIILLQU	quillai
AIILMMN	minimal
AIILMNO	monilia
AIILMRS	similar
AIILMRT	militar
AIILMRY	miliary
AIILNOS	liaison
AIILNPT	pintail
AIILNPU	nauplii
AIILNTU	nautili
AIILNTY	anility
AIILOPP	△papilio
AIILORV	ravioli
AIILOTT	Italiot
AIILQSU	siliqua
AIILRTV	trivial
	vitrail
AIIMMNS	animism
AIIMMNX	maximin
	minimax

AIIMNOR	amorini
AIIMNPS	pianism
AIIMNPT	impaint
	timpani
AIIMNRT	Martini
	Martini®
	martini
AIIMNST	animist
AIIMNSZ	Naziism
AIIMNTT	imitant
AIIMNTU	minutia
AIIMNTV	vitamin
AIIMRSS	air-miss
AIIMRST	simitar
AIIMSSV	Saivism
	Sivaism
AIIMSSY	myiasis
AIINNOP	pianino
AIINNRT	Nitrian
AIINNTY	inanity
AIINOPS	sinopia
AIINORS	Osirian
AIINORV	Ivorian
AIINOTT	notitia
AIINPRS	aspirin
AIINPST	pianist
AIINRSS	Rissian
AIINRTV	vitrain
	Vitrina
AIINSTT	△titanis
AIINSTV	naivist
AIIPRST	piarist
AIIPTTU	pituita
AIISSVV	vis-à-vis
AIJJMMS	jimjams
AIJKLPS	Jap-silk
AIJLYZZ	jazzily
AIJNORT	janitor
AIKKMOT	komatik
AIKKSUZ	zakuski
AIKLLNY	lankily
AIKLMMN	milkman
AIKLMNN	linkman
AIKLMNP	milk-pan
AIKLMNS	silk-man
AIKLMPU	lampuki
AIKLNSY	snakily
AIKLOPT	kail-pot
AIKLPWY	pawkily
AIKLRTT	titlark
AIKLSSY	skysail
AIKMNNS	kinsman
AIKMNST	Kantism
AIKMSST	Saktism
AIKNSTT	Kantist
AIKPRRT	Prakrit
AILLLOT	tall-oil
AILLMNU	luminal
AILLMOP	oil-palm
	palm-oil
AILLMOT	maillot
AILLMPU	pallium

AILLMSW sawmill
AILLMSY misally
AILLMYY may-lily
AILLNNO lanolin
AILLNOP paillon
AILLNPY plainly
AILLNST install
AILLNTU Tullian
AILLNVY villany
AILLPRU pilular
AILLPUV pluvial
AILLQSU squilla
AILLRSU arillus
AILLSTW law-list
AILLSTY saltily
AILLTVY vitally
AILLTWW witwall
AILMMOR immoral
AILMMSY myalism
AILMMUU alumium
AILMNNO nominal
AILMNOP lampion
AILMNOS malison
Osmanli
somnial
AILMNOY alimony
AILMNPS plasmin
AILMNPT implant
AILMNRU murlain
AILMOOV Moviola®
AILMOPT optimal
AILMOPY Olympia
AILMORS oralism
AILMOST somital
AILMOSZ Zolaism
AILMPRT marl-pit
AILMPRU primula
AILMPST palmist
AILMPSY misplay
AILMRST mistral
AILMRSU simular
AILMSSV Slavism
AILNNOT antlion
AILNNPT Plantin
AILNNPU pinnula
AILNNSU unslain
AILNOOP Polonia
AILNOPY polynia
AILNOQU △aquilon
AILNPRW prawlin
AILNPSX salpinx
AILNPTU nuptial
patulin
unplait
AILNPTY inaptly
ptyalin
AILNQTU quintal
AILNRSU insular
AILNRTT rattlin
AILNSTU unalist
AILNSTY nastily
saintly

AILNSVY Sylvian
AILNTTY nattily
AILNTUV unvital
AILOORW woorali
AILOPRS Polaris
AILOPST apostil
topsail
AILOPSY soapily
AILOPTT talipot
AILOPTV pivotal
AILOPXY Xylopia
AILOQTU aliquot
AILORTY orality
AILORUW wourali
AILORUX uxorial
AILORVY olivary
AILOSTU outsail
AILPPRU pupilar
AILPPSY payslip
AILPQSU Pasquil
AILPRSU parulis
uprisal
AILPRSY △pyralis
AILPSTY pay-list
AILPSWY slipway
AILQSSU squails
AILQTTU quittal
AILQTUY quality
AILRRVY rivalry
AILRSTT starlit
AILRSTU trisula
AILRSTY trysail
AILRTTU titular
AILRTUV virtual
vitular
AILSSUV visuals
AILSTTY tastily
AILSTUW lawsuit
AILTTTY tattily
AIMMMUX maximum
AIMMNNT mint-man
AIMMNTU manumit
AIMMORS amorism
AIMMOSS Mosaism
AIMMOST atomism
AIMMRSX Marxism
AIMNNOS mansion
onanism
AIMNNSY minyans
AIMNOOR amorino
AIMNOPR rampion
AIMNOPT maintop
tampion
timpano
AIMNOPZ zamponi
AIMNORT tormina
AIMNORU mainour
AIMNORW Wormian
AIMNOST stamnoi
AIMNOTU manitou
tinamou
AIMNPTY tympani

AIMNRRU murrain
AIMNRSU suramin
Surinam
uranism
AIMNRTU natrium
AIMNRTV varmint
AIMNRUU uranium
AIMNRUW Würmian
AIMNSTT mattins
AIMNSTU tsunami
AIMNSYZ zanyism
AIMOPST impasto
AIMORRU orarium
AIMORST amorist
AIMORTT Tritoma
AIMORUZ zoarium
AIMOSTT atomist
AIMOSTU Mao-suit
AIMPPRU air-pump
AIMPPST mappist
AIMPRRY △primary
AIMPRSS Parsism
AIMPRSY pyramis
AIMQRSU marquis
AIMRSST tsarism
AIMRSSY Syriasm
AIMRSTU atriums
matsuri
Maurist
AIMRSTX Marxist
S-matrix
AIMRSTY maistry
symitar
AIMSSTT statism
AINNNOW wannion
AINNOOX Oxonian
AINNOPR iron-pan
AINNOPS saponin
AINNOST nations
onanist
AINNPTU unpaint
AINNQTU quinnat
quintan
AINNRTT intrant
AINNRTU urinant
AINNSTT instant
AINNSTU unsaint
AINNTUY annuity
AINOOPR pronaoi
AINOORR orarion
AINOORT oration
AINOOTV ovation
AINOPPT appoint
AINOPRS parison
soprani
AINOPRT atropin
AINOPSS △passion
AINOPTU opuntia
△utopian
AINORST rations
AINORSW warison
AINORTX triaxon

AINOSSU	sanious
	suasion
AINOSTT	station
AINOSUX	anxious
AINOSVY	synovia
AINOTTZ	Zantiot
AINPPRS	parsnip
AINPQSU	Pasquin
AINPQTU	piquant
AINPRST	spirant
	spraint
AINPRTU	△puritan
	uptrain
	up-train
AINQRUY	quinary
AINQSTU	asquint
AINRRTY	trinary
AINRRUY	urinary
AINRSSU	Russian
AINRSTT	straint
	transit
AINRTUY	unitary
AINSSTU	issuant
	sustain
AINSSXY	synaxis
AINTTVY	tantivy
AINTTWW	want-wit
AIOORSS	ariosos
AIOPRRT	airport
	paritor
AIOPRST	airstop
	parotis
AIOPRTT	patriot
AIOPRTW	two-pair
AIOPRTY	topiary
AIOPRUV	paviour
AIORRRW	warrior
AIORRTT	traitor
AIORRTX	oratrix
AIORSST	aristos
AIORSTU	sautoir
AIORSTV	travois
AIORSTY	ostiary
AIORSUV	△saviour
	various
AIPPRST	Rappist
AIPPRSU	Priapus
AIPRSTU	upstair
AIPRTVY	pravity
AIPZZZZ	pizzazz
AIRRTZZ	rizzart
AIRSSTT	straits
	tsarist
AIRSSTU	Tarsius
AIRSTTT	attrist
AIRSTVY	varsity
AIRSUUV	uva-ursi
AIRTUVX	vitraux
AISSTTT	statist
AISTTVY	vastity
AISTUVY	suavity
AJKMNNU	junkman

AJKMNTU	muntjak
AJKNSSY	janskys
AJLLRUY	jurally
AJLNORU	journal
AJLOPPY	jaloppy
AJMNRUY	juryman
AJOOPRT	Rajpoot
AJOPPZZ	jazz-pop
AKKKORU	rokkaku
AKKLRSY	skylark
AKLLNOW	know-all
AKLLORW	all-work
AKLMOPU	oak-lump
AKLOPRW	lapwork
AKLOPUV	Volapük
AKLOTTU	outtalk
AKLOTUW	outwalk
	walk-out
AKLPRSY	sparkly
AKLRSTY	starkly
AKMNOOR	Kroo-man
AKMNORW	workman
AKMNRTU	trankum
	Turkman
AKMOORT	mooktar
AKMORST	Ostmark
AKMQTUU	kumquat
AKMRSTU	muskrat
AKNORTU	outrank
AKOOPRT	partook
AKOOSTU	atokous
AKORRTW	artwork
AKORWWX	waxwork
AKQSUWY	squawky
ALLLOYY	loyally
ALLMNOP	pollman
ALLMNOT	tollman
ALLMNOY	allonym
ALLMNPU	Pullman
ALLMORY	morally
ALLMPUU	plumula
ALLNOOW	Walloon
ALLNOTY	tonally
ALLNRTU	Trullan
ALLNRUU	lunular
ALLNSTY	slantly
ALLNTUU	ululant
ALLOOPS	apollos
	palolos
ALLOOTX	axolotl
ALLOPRY	payroll
	pay-roll
ALLOPTX	poll-tax
ALLORTY	ally-tor
ALLORYY	royally
ALLOSWW	swallow
ALLOSWY	sallowy
ALLOTTY	totally
ALLOTUW	out-wall
ALLOTWY	tallowy
ALLOTYY	loyalty
ALLQSUY	squally

ALLRRUY	rurally
ALLRSTU	lustral
ALLSUUY	usually
ALMNNUY	unmanly
ALMNOOP	lampoon
ALMNOOT	toolman
ALMNOOW	woolman
ALMNORU	unmoral
ALMNORY	almonry
ALMNOSS	salmons
ALMNOSU	solanum
ALMNOWY	womanly
ALMNPSU	sunlamp
ALMNSUU	alumnus
ALMOOPY	polyoma
ALMOPPT	palmtop
ALMOPRT	marplot
ALMORRU	morular
ALMOSST	smaltos
ALMOSTW	matlows
ALMOSXY	xylomas
ALMOTTU	mulatto
ALMRSTY	smartly
ALMRSUU	ramulus
ALMRTUU	tumular
ALMSSUY	alyssum
	asylums
ALNNRSU	unsnarl
ALNNSUU	annulus
ALNOOPR	polaron
ALNOOPT	platoon
ALNOORT	ortolan
ALNOOSS	solanos
ALNOPPY	panoply
ALNOPSS	sponsal
ALNOPYY	polynya
ALNORUY	unroyal
ALNORUZ	zonular
ALNPRSU	snarl-up
ALNPRUY	planury
ALNPTUY	unaptly
ALNPTXY	planxty
ALNSUUU	unusual
ALOOPRW	poor-law
ALOOPYZ	Polyzoa
ALOORRS	sororal
ALOPPRU	popular
ALOPPRY	propyla
ALOPRRU	parlour
ALOPRSU	parlous
ALOPSSU	spousal
ALOPSUV	△völuspa
ALOPTUY	outplay
ALOQRRU	rorqual
ALOQRSU	squalor
ALORRST	rostral
ALORTYY	royalty
ALOSTTU	outlast
ALOSTXY	oxy-salt
ALPRSUU	pursual
ALPRSWY	sprawly
ALRSTTY	startly

ALRSTUU	sutural
AMMNOOR	moorman
AMMNOOT	mootman
AMMNORY	May-morn
	Rommany
AMMNRUY	nummary
AMMOORR	maormor
	mormaor
AMMOPTU	pomatum
AMMORWW	maw-worm
AMMRSUY	summary
AMNNOOX	monaxon
AMNNORS	Normans
AMNNOSW	snowman
AMNNOTT	montant
AMNNOTY	antonym
AMNNOUW	unwoman
AMNOOPP	pompano
AMNOOPR	moor-pan
AMNOOTT	△ottoman
AMNOOTZ	matzoon
AMNOPRT	portman
AMNOPRY	paronym
AMNOPST	postman
	topsman
AMNOPTU	pantoum
AMNOPTY	tympano
AMNORSS	ramsons
AMNORST	transom
AMNORSY	masonry
AMNORTU	romaunt
AMNOSST	stamnos
AMNOTUX	Mantoux
AMNOTUY	autonym
AMNPTYY	tympany
AMNQTUU	quantum
AMNRRUY	unmarry
AMNRSTU	unsmart
AMNRTTU	tantrum
AMNTUUY	autumny
AMOOORS	amoroso
AMOOPRT	taproom
AMOORSU	amorous
AMOPSTT	topmast
AMORRUY	armoury
AMORRWY	marrowy
AMORSST	matross
AMORSSY	morassy
AMOSUYZ	azymous
AMPRSUW	upswarm
AMRRSTU	rastrum
AMRRTYY	martyry
AMRSTTU	stratum
ANNOPTY	poynant
ANNOTTY	tantony
ANNRTYY	tyranny
ANNSSTU	suntans
ANOOPRS	pronaos
	soprano
ANOOPRT	patroon
	pronota
ANOORTT	arnotto
ANOPRRS	sporran
ANOPRSY	spray-on
ANOPRTV	provant
ANOPSTU	outspan
ANORRSW	narrows
ANORRWW	war-worn
ANORSTU	rousant
	santour
ANORSUU	anurous
	uranous
ANORWWY	wayworn
ANOSSTZ	stanzos
ANOSTTU	totanus
ANPPSUW	suppawn
ANPRSTU	suntrap
	unstrap
AOOPPRS	apropos
AOOPRST	Atropos
AOOPRTT	taproot
AOORRSY	arroyos
AOORRTT	rotator
AOORRTU	outroar
AOORRTY	△oratory
AOORSTU	outsoar
AOOSTUZ	azotous
AOOTXYZ	zootaxy
AOPPPSU	pappous
AOPPRRT	rapport
AOPPRST	apports
AOPRRSW	sparrow
AOPRRTY	parroty
	portray
AOPRSTT	tar-spot
AOPRSTU	asprout
AOPRSTW	postwar
AOPRSUV	vapours
AOPRTTU	outpart
AOPRTTW	two-part
AOPRTUY	outpray
AOPRUVY	vapoury
AOPSSTU	passout
AOPSTUY	autopsy
AOPSTWY	waypost
AOQRSTU	quartos
AORRSWY	sowarry
AORSSUY	ossuary
	suasory
AORSTWW	saw-wort
AORSUVY	savoury
AORTTUY	out-tray
AORTUVY	avoutry
AOSTTUY	outstay
APPRRUU	△purpura
APPRSTY	strappy
APPRSUY	papyrus
APRSSSU	surpass
APRSTTU	start-up
	upstart
APRSTTY	tapstry
APRSUWY	spurway
AQRTUYZ	quartzy
AQSTTUY	squatty
ARSSTTU	stratus

B

BBBDELU	blubbed
BBBELOS	bobbles
BBBELRU	blubber
BBBEORY	bobbery
BBBGINO	bobbing
BBBHIOS	bobbish
BBCCIKO	bibcock
BBCDEIR	cribbed
BBCDELU	clubbed
BBCEEIR	Berbice
BBCEHIN	nebbich
BBCEILR	cribble
BBCEKKO	kebbock
BBCEKKU	kebbuck
BBCELOR	clobber
	cobbler
BBCELRU	clubber
BBCGINU	cubbing
BBCHISU	cubbish
BBCINOU	bubonic
BBCJLOU	Jobclub
BBCRSUY	scrubby
BBDDERU	drubbed
BBDEEIT	ebbtide
BBDEELP	pebbled
BBDEENO	bone-bed
BBDEFLU	flubbed
BBDEGRU	grubbed
BBDEILO	bilobed
BBDEILR	dibbler
	dribble
BBDEIRR	dribber
BBDEKNO	knobbed
BBDELOS	bobsled
BBDELSU	slubbed
BBDENSU	snubbed
BBDESTU	stubbed
BBDGIIN	dibbing
BBDGINO	dobbing
BBDGINU	dubbing
BBDILRY	dribbly
BBDOOSS	od's-bobs
BBEEERU	bebeeru
BBEELSS	ebbless
BBEESYY	bye-byes
BBEFILR	fribble
BBEFIRY	fibbery
BBEFRUY	fubbery
BBEGILR	gribble
BBEGINW	webbing
BBEGIOS	gibbose
BBEGLOR	gobbler
BBEGLRU	grubble
BBEGRRU	grubber
BBEHINS	nebbish
BBEHLOR	hobbler
BBEHMTU	bethumb
BBEIILR	ribible
BBEIIMR	imbiber

BBEILNR nibbler
BBEILOS bilboes
BBEILOT bibelot
BBEILPR pribble
BBEILQU quibble
BBEILRT tribble
BBEILST stibble
BBEILSY yibbles
BBEINOR rib-bone
BBEIRRY bribery
BBEJORY jobbery
BBEKLNO knobble
BBEKLNU knubble
BBEKLOS blesbok
BBEKLUU bubukle
BBEKNOR knobber
BBELLOY bell-boy
BBELMOT bomblet
BBELMRU bumbler
BBELNOR nobbler
BBELORS slobber
BBELORW wobbler
BBELORY lobbyer
BBELRRU burbler
BBELRSU slubber
BBELSTU stubble
BBENOTW bowbent
BBENRSU snubber
BBEOOSY yobboes
BBEORRY robbery
BBEORSW swobber
BBEORYY yobbery
BBEPRUW brewpub
BBERRSU rubbers
BBERRUY rubbery
BBFGIIN fibbing
BBGGIIN gibbing
BBGIIJN jibbing
BBGIINN nibbing
BBGIINR ribbing
BBGIJNO jobbing
BBGIMNO mobbing
BBGINOR robbing
BBGINOS sobbing
BBGINRU rubbing
BBGINSU gubbins
subbing
BBGINTU tubbing
BBGIOSU gibbous
BBHHIOS hobbish
BBHIMOS Hobbism
mobbish
BBHIOST Hobbist
BBHIOSY yobbish
BBHIRSU rubbish
BBHISTU tubbish
BBHOOUW whoobub
BBHRSUY shrubby
BBIIILM bilimbi
BBIILST biblist
BBIJMOO jib-boom
BBIKTUZ kibbutz
BBILLUU lulibub
BBILNOY nobbily
BBIMOSY yobbism
BBINORS ribbons
BBINORY ribbony
BBJLOOW blowjob
BBKLNOY knobbly
BBKLNUY knubbly
BBKLOOU bloubok
BBKOOOO boobook
BBLOSUU bulbous
BBLSTUY stubbly
BBMOOOX boom-box
BBNOORU △bourbon
BBNRUUY Bunbury
BBRSSUU suburbs
BCCEIIS biccies
BCCEILO ecbolic
BCCEILU cubicle
BCCEILY bicycle
BCCILOU bucolic
BCCINOO obconic
BCCISUU succubi
BCCMOOX coxcomb
BCCMSUU succumb
BCDEEIL decibel
BCDEHNU bunched
BCDEHOU debouch
BCDEIIO biocide
BCDEIKS sickbed
BCDEIKT bedtick
BCDEILM climbed
BCDEILO docible
BCDEIOX dice-box
BCDEKLO blocked
BCDEKOR bedrock
brocked
BCDELOU becloud
BCDESUU subduce
BCDHIOR bichord
BCDHIRU bruchid
BCDHOOU cubhood
BCDILOO colobid
BCDIORW cowbird
BCDKORU burdock
BCDSTUU subduct
BCEEEHN beechen
BCEEEHS beseech
BCEEFIN benefic
BCEEGIR iceberg
BCEEHIP ephebic
BCEEHLR belcher
BCEEHNR bencher
BCEEHOU bouchée
BCEEHRS Becher's
BCEEILT ice-belt
BCEEILU ice-blue
BCEEIPS bespice
BCEEIRS escribe
BCEEKNU buckeen
BCEEKUY buck-eye
BCEENOS obscene
BCEENRU crubeen
BCEFIIS sebific
BCEHINR birchen
BCEHINT benthic
BCEHIOR brioche
BCEHITW bewitch
BCEHLRU blucher
BCEHNSU bunches
BCEHORT botcher
BCEHORW cowherb
BCEHRSU cherubs
BCEHRTU butcher
BCEIIKR brickie
BCEIISV vibices
BCEIKLM limbeck
BCEIKLR brickle
BCEIKNR bricken
BCEIKST bestick
BCEILMO embolic
BCEILMR climber
reclimb
BCEILNO binocle
BCEILOR bricole
corbeil
BCEIMNO combine
BCEIMOR crombie
microbe
BCEINOR bicorne
BCEINOZ benzoic
BCEINRU brucine
BCEIOPP cob-pipe
BCEIRRS scriber
BCEIRSU suberic
BCEIRTU brucite
BCEJSTU subject
BCEKLOR blocker
BCEKLRU bruckle
buckler
BCEKNOR Brocken
BCEKORT brocket
BCEKORU roebuck
BCEKOSU buckoes
BCEKOTY bycoket
BCEKPRU Purbeck
BCEKSTU bestuck
BCELLOW cowbell
BCELMRU clumber
crumble
BCELMSU scumble
BCELSSU cubless
BCEMNTU cumbent
BCEMORS Scomber
BCEMRSU scumber
BCENORU bouncer
BCEOORT October
BCEORSU obscure
BCEORTT Corbett
BCFSSUU subfusc
BCGIKNU bucking
BCHIIOT cohibit
BCHIKOU chibouk
BCHIKSU buckish

BCHIMOR	rhombic
BCHINOR	bronchi
BCHIOPR	pibroch
BCHLOTY	blotchy
BCHNOOR	broncho
BCHORST	borscht
	bortsch
BCIIKLN	niblick
BCIILMU	bulimic
BCIILOR	colibri
BCIILSY	sibylic
BCIINOS	bionics
BCIINOT	biontic
BCIISTU	biscuit
BCIKORT	brockit
BCIKOTT	bittock
BCILMPU	plumbic
	upclimb
BCILNOU	lion-cub
BCINORU	△rubicon
BCINORY	Byronic
BCINSUU	incubus
BCIOORT	robotic
BCIORST	strobic
BCIOSTY	sybotic
BCIRTUY	butyric
BCISTUU	cubitus
BCJKMUU	jumbuck
BCKLLOO	bollock
BCKLLOU	bullock
BCKLNOU	unblock
BCKMMOU	bummock
BCKMOSU	bucksom
BGKOTTU	buttock
BCLMOOU	coulomb
BCLMRUY	crumbly
BCLOOSU	colobus
	subcool
BCLORTU	clotbur
BCMOOTU	comb-out
BCMOSTU	combust
BCNOORS	broncos
BCOOTTY	boycott
BDDDEOR	brodded
BDDEEER	reedbed
BDDEEES	seedbed
BDDEEIR	débride
BDDEEIS	bedside
BDDEEIT	betided
BDDEELN	blended
BDDEGIN	bedding
BDDEILN	blinded
BDDEILR	bridled
BDDEILU	builded
BDDEINR	brinded
BDDEIOO	boodied
BDDEIRR	redbird
BDDEIRT	dirt-bed
BDDELOO	blooded
BDDENOU	bounded
BDDENOW	down-bed
BDDEOTU	doubted
BDDESUU	subdued
BDDGIIN	bidding
BDDGINU	budding
BDDGIOR	bird-dog
BDDINRU	dun-bird
BDEEELL	deleble
BDEEELR	bleeder
BDEEEPS	bespeed
BDEEERR	breeder
BDEEFIR	debrief
	fibered
BDEEGOR	begored
BDEEGUY	bug-eyed
BDEEIKN	beinked
BDEEILL	bellied
	delible
BDEEILV	bedevil
BDEEIMR	bemired
BDEEIMT	bedtime
BDEEINR	inbreed
BDEEINZ	bedizen
BDEEIRR	berried
	briered
BDEEIRT	bed-rite
BDEEISS	besides
BDEEIVV	bevvied
BDEELNR	blender
BDEELNT	bendlet
BDEELOV	beloved
BDEELSS	△blessed
BDEELTT	bletted
BDEEMOS	besomed
BDEEMOW	embowed
BDEEMRU	umbered
BDEEMSU	bemused
BDEENPR	prebend
BDEENTT	tent-bed
BDEEORS	bedsore
BDEEOSX	seedbox
BDEEOTW	web-toed
BDEERRU	bur-reed
BDEERST	bed-rest
BDEERTT	Debrett
BDEERUW	burweed
BDEESTT	test-bed
BDEFILR	filberd
BDEFLOU	bodeful
BDEFOOR	forbode
BDEGGIR	egg-bird
BDEGGOR	brogged
BDEGHIT	bedight
BDEGINN	bending
BDEGIOO	boogied
BDEGIOT	bigoted
BDEGLOT	dog-belt
BDEGLRU	bludger
BDEGOOY	good-bye
BDEGORU	budgero
BDEHMTU	thumbed
BDEHORY	herdboy
BDEHRSU	brushed
BDEIIIN	bidie-in
BDEIKLN	blinked
BDEIKMO	kimboed
BDEILLR	ill-bred
BDEILLU	bullied
BDEILNR	blinder
	brindle
BDEILOP	lobiped
BDEILRR	bridler
BDEILRT	driblet
BDEILRU	builder
	rebuild
BDEIMMR	brimmed
BDEIMOR	bromide
BDEIMTU	bitumed
BDEINOU	△bedouin
BDEINRY	bindery
BDEIOPR	poe-bird
BDEIORR	broider
BDEIORS	disrobe
BDEIORT	debitor
BDEIORV	overbid
BDEIORZ	zebroid
BDEIOSW	bow-side
BDEIOSY	disobey
BDEIOTW	bow-tied
BDEIRST	bestrid
	bistred
BDEISSU	subside
BDEISTU	subedit
BDEITUY	dubiety
BDEKNOO	book-end
BDEKOOR	red-book
BDEKORW	bed-work
BDEKRSY	sky-bred
BDELLOR	bed-roll
BDELMRU	drumble
BDELNRU	blunder
BDELORU	boulder
	doubler
BDELORW	bowlder
	low-bred
BDELOSU	doubles
BDELOSW	blowsed
BDELOTT	blotted
	bottled
BDELOTU	doublet
BDELOUU	double-u
BDELOUW	would-be
BDELOWZ	blowzed
BDELRRU	blurred
BDELSSU	budless
BDELSWY	lewdsby
BDEMNOU	embound
BDEMOOR	bedroom
	boredom
BDEMOOS	bosomed
BDENNOU	bounden
BDENORU	bounder
	rebound
BDENORY	bone-dry
BDENORZ	bronzed
BDENOUW	unbowed

BDENRSU	burdens
BDENSTU	subtend
BDENSUY	sebundy
BDENTTU	butt-end
BDEOORR	brooder
BDEOPRT	bedropt
BDEOPST	bedpost
BDEORRS	Borders
BDEORRU	bordure
	bourder
BDEORSU	rosebud
BDEORTU	doubter
	obtrude
	outbred
	redoubt
BDERRUY	ruby-red
BDERSTU	bursted
BDERSUU	subduer
BDERSUY	rudesby
BDFGIIR	fig-bird
BDFIIOR	fibroid
BDFIISU	fidibus
BDGGLOU	gold-bug
BDGIINN	binding
BDGIINR	birding
BDGIIOO	gobioid
BDGILOO	globoid
BDGINNO	bonding
BDGINOY	bodying
BDGLLOU	△bulldog
BDGLOOT	dogbolt
BDGORUW	bug-word
BDHINOP	hopbind
BDHIOSU	bushido
BDHMOOO	hobodom
BDHOOOY	boyhood
BDIIKNO	bodikin
BDIILMS	dislimb
BDIILOR	oil-bird
BDIILOS	libidos
BDIJOOR	jib-door
BDIKNOR	brodkin
BDILLNY	blindly
BDILNNU	unblind
BDILNUU	unbuild
BDILPUU	build-up
	upbuild
BDILRUY	buirdly
BDILTUY	dibutyl
BDIMNPU	dumpbin
BDINNOU	inbound
BDINOOR	bridoon
BDINRSU	sunbird
BDINSTU	dustbin
BDIOOOV	obovoid
BDIOORU	boudoir
BDIOPRY	poy-bird
BDIORSW	wosbird
BDIOSSY	byssoid
BDIOSUU	dubious
BDIRSTU	disturb
BDISSUY	subsidy
BDKNOOU	bundook
BDLOOOX	oxblood
BDLORWY	blow-dry
BDMORUW	budworm
BDNNOUU	unbound
BDNOORU	△bourdon
BDNOOWW	downbow
BDNOPUU	upbound
BDNORTU	turbond
BDNORUW	rubdown
BDOOORW	boo-word
BDOOOWX	boxwood
BDORSTU	to-brusd
BEEEEFR	freebee
BEEEEKS	beseeke
BEEEEMT	beteeme
BEEEFIR	freebie
BEEEGIS	besiege
BEEEGLU	bee-glue
BEEEGRR	bergère
BEEEHIV	beehive
	hive-bee
BEEEHNS	shebeen
BEEEHPS	ephebes
BEEEIKT	bee-kite
BEEEILL	libelee
BEEEILN	beeline
BEEEILV	believe
BEEEJLW	bejewel
BEEEJLZ	Jezebel
BEEEKPS	bee-skep
BEEELPR	bleeper
BEEELUY	blue-eye
BEEEMOS	beesome
BEEEMRW	embrewe
BEEENNZ	benzene
BEEENTW	between
BEEERTV	breveté
BEEFILR	febrile
	Félibre
BEEFINT	benefit
BEEFIRS	Frisbee®
BEEFLOR	Froebel
BEEFLTY	beet-fly
BEEFNRU	funèbre
BEEGGNU	geebung
BEEGILL	legible
BEEGILO	obligee
BEEGILU	beguile
BEEGIMR	begrime
BEEGINN	beginne
BEEGINR	bigener
BEEGINT	beignet
BEEGINU	beguine
	béguine
BEEGLNO	englobe
BEEGMNO	gombeen
BEEGMOU	embogue
BEEGNTU	unbeget
BEEHINS	beshine
BEEHIST	bhistee
BEEHKSU	bukshee
BEEHLRT	blether
	herblet
BEEHMOT	bee-moth
BEEHNNO	hebenon
BEEHNOS	beshone
BEEHOOV	behoove
BEEHOPS	ephebos
BEEHORS	herbose
BEEHORW	bewhore
BEEHPSU	ephebus
BEEHRST	sherbet
BEEHRSW	beshrew
BEEHRTY	thereby
BEEHRWY	whereby
BEEHSTY	bheesty
BEEIJLU	jubilee
BEEILLR	libeler
BEEILNR	berline
BEEILOS	obelise
BEEILOZ	obelize
BEEILTT	betitle
BEEIMST	betimes
BEEINNZ	benzine
BEEINOS	ebonise
BEEINOT	ebonite
BEEINOZ	ebonize
BEEINPR	pébrine
BEEINRZ	zebrine
BEEINTZ	bez-tine
BEEIORS	ebriose
BEEIQUZ	bezique
BEEIRRV	brevier
BEEIRTY	ebriety
BEEKNOT	betoken
BEEKOPS	bespoke
BEEKRRS	berserk
BEEKRRU	rebuker
BEELLOT	lobelet
BEELMOW	embowel
BEELMRT	tremble
BEELNNO	ennoble
BEELNOZ	benzole
BEELNUX	Benelux
BEELOTY	eyebolt
BEELRUZ	zebrule
BEELTTU	bluette
BEEMNPT	benempt
BEEMORW	embower
BEEMRRU	umbrere
BEEMRSU	Burmese
BEEMRTU	embrute
BEENOST	boneset
BEENSTU	subteen
BEEOPRS	beprose
BEEORRU	bourrée
BEEORSV	observe
	obverse
	verbose
BEEORTX	box-tree
BEEORWY	eyebrow
BEEPRRV	preverb
BEEQSTU	bequest

Words marked △ may be spelled also with a capital letter

BEERRSW	brewers'
BEERRWY	brewery
BEERSSU	rebuses
	subsere
BEERSTT	betters
BEERSTW	bestrew
	webster
BEERTTU	burette
BEETTUV	buvette
BEFFLRU	bluffer
BEFGIIL	filibeg
BEFGIRU	firebug
BEFGLLO	fog-bell
BEFILPY	plebify
BEFILRT	filbert
BEFILRY	briefly
BEFILSU	fusible
BEFINOR	bonfire
BEFIORS	fibrose
BEFIORX	firebox
BEFIRST	fibster
BEFIRVY	verbify
BEFITUX	tubifex
BEFLLOT	elf-bolt
BEFLLTY	flybelt
BEFLMRU	fumbler
BEFLTUU	tubeful
BEFMNRU	f-number
BEFOORR	forbore
BEFOOTW	webfoot
BEGGGIN	begging
BEGGIST	biggest
BEGGLOR	boggler
BEGGRUY	buggery
BEGHHIT	behight
BEGHINT	benight
BEGHITT	betight
BEGHRRU	△burgher
BEGIIMT	big-time
BEGIINN	inbeing
BEGILLY	legibly
BEGILNO	Gobelin
	ignoble
	inglobe
BEGILNT	belting
BEGILNU	blueing
	bulgine
BEGILNY	belying
BEGILRT	gilbert
BEGILST	giblets
BEGINNU	unbeing
BEGINOT	big-note
BEGINOY	biogeny
BEGINRR	bringer
BEGINRW	brewing
BEGINSS	bigness
BEGINTT	betting
BEGKMOS	gemsbok
BEGLLOU	globule
BEGLMOO	begloom
BEGLMRU	grumble
BEGLNRU	blunger
	bungler
BEGLOOS	globose
BEGLOOT	bootleg
BEGLOSU	glebous
BEGLRTY	bergylt
BEGNNUU	unbegun
BEGNORU	burgeon
BEGNOSY	bygones
BEGNOTU	unbegot
BEGORSU	rose-bug
BEGRSSU	burgess
BEHHKOT	khotbeh
BEHIITX	exhibit
BEHIKNT	bethink
BEHILMS	blemish
BEHILMT	thimble
BEHILOS	bolshie
BEHILPT	hip-belt
BEHILRT	blither
BEHILSU	helibus
BEHINOP	hip-bone
	hopbine
BEHIOTW	howbeit
BEHIRRT	rebirth
BEHIRST	herbist
BEHLLOP	bellhop
BEHLLOX	hell-box
BEHLMOW	whomble
BEHLMSU	humbles
BEHLOOT	bothole
BEHLORT	brothel
BEHLRRU	burrhel
BEHLRSU	blusher
BEHLSTU	blushet
BEHMOTU	bemouth
BEHMPTU	bethump
BEHNOST	benthos
BEHNRTU	burthen
BEHOORT	theorbo
BEHOPSU	Phoebus
BEHORRT	brother
BEHORST	boshter
BEHORSU	herbous
BEHORTT	betroth
BEHRRSU	brusher
BEIIKLR	riblike
BEIILLS	billies
BEIILRS	risible
BEIILSV	visible
BEIINOT	niobite
BEIINST	stibine
BEIIOTT	biotite
BEIKLNR	blinker
BEIKLOS	obelisk
BEIKNRS	brisken
BEIKOOS	booksie
BEIKOTX	box-kite
BEIKRST	brisket
BEILLNR	Brinell
BEILLOT	oil-belt
BEILLST	bestill
BEILMOR	embroil
BEILMRS	limbers
BEILMRT	timbrel
BEILMRW	wimbrel
BEILMSU	sublime
BEILNOO	bone-oil
	obelion
BEILNOW	bowline
BEILNTZ	blintze
BEILOQU	oblique
BEILORR	broiler
BEILORS	liberos
BEILORT	trilobe
BEILORY	boilery
BEILOVX	live-box
BEILRSS	ribless
BEILRST	blister
	bristle
BEILRTT	brittle
	triblet
BEILRTY	liberty
BEILRUY	brulyie
BEILRUZ	brulzie
BEILSST	bitless
BEILSTU	subtile
BEILSTW	blewits
BEIMMRR	brimmer
BEIMMRU	Brummie
BEIMNOR	bromine
BEIMNTU	bitumen
BEIMORW	imbower
BEIMRST	timbers
BEIMRSU	imburse
BEIMRTU	imbrute
	terbium
BEINNOS	benison
BEINNOZ	benzoin
BEINOOS	boonies
BEINORT	bornite
BEINORW	△brownie
	Brownie®
BEINOST	ebonist
BEINOTT	bottine
BEINRSU	suberin
BEINRTT	bittern
BEINRTU	tribune
	turbine
BEINSSY	byssine
BEIOPTY	biotype
BEIORRT	orbiter
BEIORST	sorbite
BEIOSSU	soubise
BEIOSTY	obesity
BEIPSSU	pubises
BEIQRTU	briquet
BEIRRSU	brisure
	bruiser
BEIRSTT	bitters
BEIRSTU	bustier
BEIRTTU	tribute
BEIRTTY	treybit
BEIRTVY	brevity

BEITTWX	betwixt
BEJKOUX	juke-box
BEJLMRU	jumbler
BEJLOSS	jobless
BEKLNRU	blunker
BEKLOOT	booklet
BEKLSUY	blue-sky
	sky-blue
BEKMOST	stembok
BEKNNOW	beknown
BEKNORS	bonkers
BEKNORU	unbroke
BEKORRY	brokery
BELLLOW	low-bell
BELLNPU	bull-pen
BELLORR	borrell
BELLOSU	soluble
BELLOSW	bellows
BELLOUV	voluble
BELLRRU	burrell
BELMMOO	embloom
BELMMRU	mumbler
BELMNOS	nombles
BELMNOU	nelumbo
BELMNSU	numbles
BELMOOR	bloomer
	rebloom
BELMOOS	bloosme
BELMOOT	boomlet
BELMOPR	problem
BELMORT	temblor
BELMOSU	embolus
BELMOSY	symbole
BELMPRU	plumber
BELMRRU	rumbler
BELMRSU	slumber
BELMRTU	tumbler
	tumbrel
BELMRTY	trembly
BELMSTU	stumble
BELNNOU	unnoble
BELNNTU	unblent
BELNOOY	boloney
BELNOYZ	benzoyl
BELNSSU	unbless
BELNSTU	△sunbelt
	unblest
BELOOPR	blooper
BELOORS	boleros
BELOOSS	soboles
BELOOTT	bottle-o
BELOPSU	pueblos
BELORST	bolster
	lobster
BELORSY	soberly
BELORTT	blotter
	bottler
BELORTU	blue-rot
	boulter
	trouble
BELOSSU	boluses
BELOSTU	△boletus
BELRSTU	bluster
	bustler
BELRTUY	butlery
BEMMOOS	embosom
BEMMORR	brommer
BEMMRRU	brummer
BEMNORW	embrown
BEMNORY	embryon
BEMNOSU	umbones
BEMNPTY	bynempt
BEMNRSU	△numbers
BEMNTTU	butment
BEMORST	bestorm
	mobster
BEMORSU	umbrose
BEMORSY	embryos
BEMORWW	webworm
BEMOTUY	myotube
BEMSSUU	subsume
BENNORW	newborn
BENNORZ	bronzen
BENOPRR	preborn
BENORRZ	bronzer
BENORST	sorbent
BENORWY	bywoner
BENOSUZ	subzone
BENOSWY	newsboy
BENRSTU	bursten
BEOOPUZ	booze-up
BEOORST	booster
BEOPRRV	proverb
BEOPRST	besport
BEOPSTU	bespout
BEOQSTU	bosquet
BEOQSUY	obsequy
BEOQTUU	bouquet
BEORRSW	browser
BEORSUU	uberous
BEORSUZ	subzero
BEORUVY	overbuy
BEPRRTU	perturb
BEPRTUY	puberty
BEPSTUY	subtype
BEQRSUU	brusque
BERRSTU	burster
BERSTUV	subvert
BERTTUY	buttery
BESTTUX	subtext
BFFGINU	buffing
BFFLLUY	bluffly
BFFLOOW	blow-off
BFFNOOU	buffoon
BFFOPUX	puff-box
BFGIOOT	bigfoot
BFGIORT	frogbit
BFHILSU	lubfish
BFHIRSU	furbish
BFHISTU	tubfish
BFHLSUY	bush-fly
BFIINOR	fibroin
BFILMRU	brimful
BFILOTY	lift-boy
BFIMOYZ	zombify
BFIORSU	fibrous
BFIRTUY	brutify
BFKLOOU	bookful
BFKLOOY	flybook
BFKSSUU	subfusk
BFLLOUW	bowlful
BFLLOWY	blowfly
	flyblow
BFLOSUX	boxfuls
BFLSTUU	tubfuls
BFOOOTY	footboy
BGGGINU	bugging
BGGHIIS	biggish
BGGILNU	bulging
BGGINOY	by-going
BGHHIOY	highboy
BGHILTY	blighty
BGHINOR	bighorn
BGHINSU	bushing
BGHINTY	by-thing
BGHLRUU	bulghur
	burghul
BGHMORU	Homburg
BGHNORU	hornbug
BGHOORU	borough
BGHORTU	brought
BGIILLN	billing
BGIILNO	boiling
BGIILNR	birling
BGIILNS	sibling
BGIIMNR	briming
BGIINNN	binning
BGIINNR	inbring
BGIINRT	ringbit
BGIINTT	bitting
BGIKNOO	booking
BGIKNOR	broking
BGIKNSU	busking
BGILLNU	bulling
BGILLPU	pill-bug
BGILMOU	gumboil
BGILNOT	biltong
	bolting
BGILNOW	blowing
	bowling
BGILNOY	ignobly
BGILOOR	obligor
BGILOOY	biology
BGILORY	boy-girl
BGILRSU	busgirl
BGIMMNU	bumming
BGIMNNU	numbing
BGIMNOO	booming
BGIMNPU	bumping
BGIMOSY	bogyism
BGINNRU	burning
BGINNTU	bunting
BGINOOR	bog-iron
BGINOOZ	boozing
BGINORS	borings

BGINOSU bousing
BGINPRU upbring
BGINRSU subring
BGINRTU bruting
BGINRUY burying
rubying
BGINSSU bussing
BGINSTU busting
BGINSUY busying
BGINSWY swing-by
BGINUZZ buzzing
BGIORTY bigotry
BGIUWZZ buzz-wig
BGJOTUY △toby-jug
BGKLOOO logbook
BGKORSY grysbok
BGLMRUY grumbly
BGLNOOW longbow
BGLNOUW blowgun
BGLOOSU globous
BGLOSSU bugloss
BGMOOSS bog-moss
BGMOOTU gumboot
BGNOOWY gownboy
BGNOSSU subsong
BGORTUW bugwort
BHIIINT inhibit
BHIINRS brinish
BHIIPSS sibship
BHIIRST British
BHIKNOP hip-knob
BHIKOOS bookish
BHILLOY billy-oh
BHILLSU bullish
BHILOTU holibut
BHILPSU publish
BHIMOOR rhomboi
BHIMOOS hoboism
BHIMOPS phobism
BHIMORT thrombi
BHIMSTU bismuth
BHINRSU burnish
BHIOOPR biophor
BHIOORS boorish
BHIOPST phobist
BHIORSS Sorbish
BHIOSWZ showbiz
BHIRSTU brutish
BHIRTTU turbith
BHISTTU bush-tit
BHISUVY ivy-bush
BHLRSUU bulrush
BHMOORS rhombos
BHMORSU rhombus
BHMUUZZ humbuzz
BHNOOSS Hobson's
BHNORTY Brython
BHOOPSY shop-boy
BHOOSTW bowshot
BHOOSWX showbox
BHPRSUU brush-up
BIIKLOT kilobit

BIILLNO billion
BIILLOU bouilli
BIILLTW twibill
BIILMRU Librium®
BIILNNR birlinn
BIILNQU quiblin
BIILNTU built-in
in-built
BIILOSU bilious
BIILSVY visibly
BIIMNOU niobium
BIIMNSU minibus
mini-sub
BIIMSTU stibium
BIIORSV vibrios
BIIOSUV bivious
BIJNOSU subjoin
BIKLLUY bulkily
BIKLNOT ink-blot
BIKLNOY linkboy
BIKLRSY briskly
BIKMNPU bumpkin
BIKORRW ribwork
BILLNOU bullion
BILLOOY loobily
BILLOPX pill-box
BILLOUV volubil
BILLOWY billowy
BILLRWY wrybill
BILMNOR nombril
BILMOSU limbous
BILMPUY bumpily
BILMRTU tumbril
BILMSUU bulimus
BILNNOY bonnily
BILNTUU tubulin
unbuilt
BILOOYZ boozily
BILORST Bristol
BILOSSU subsoil
BILOSSY bossily
BILPTUU built-up
BILRSTY bristly
trilbys
BILRTTY brittly
BILRTUY tilbury
BIMMOOS imbosom
miombos
BIMMORS bromism
BIMNORS misborn
BIMNORW imbrown
BIMNOSU omnibus
BIMRSUX bruxism
BIMSSSU submiss
BINOORS bonsoir
BINOORX box-iron
BINOOST bonitos
BINOOSU niobous
BINORST ribston
BINRSTU inburst
BINSTUU subunit
BINTTUW twin-tub

BIOOSUV obvious
BIOPRTY probity
BIORRTU burrito
BIORRTW ribwort
BIORSST bistros
BIORSTT bistort
BIORSUU rubious
BIORTTU bittour
BISSSTU subsist
BJNOORU bonjour
BJORUXY jury-box
BKNOOTW bowknot
BKNORSY skyborn
BKOOORY Kroo-boy
BKOORWX workbox
BLLNTUY bluntly
BLLOSUU lobulus
BLLOUVY volubly
BLLPPUU bull-pup
BLMMPUU plumbum
BLMNPUU unplumb
BLMOOOT tombolo
BLMOORW lobworm
BLMOOSS blossom
BLMRSUY slumbry
BLMSTUY stumbly
BLNNOUW unblown
BLNOORW low-born
BLNOOSU blouson
BLNOPUW upblown
BLOOOTX toolbox
BLOOQUY obloquy
BLOORWW low-brow
BLOOTUW blow-out
BLOPSTU subplot
BMNOOOW moon-bow
BMNOOSU unbosom
BMNORUW mowburn
BMOOORX boxroom
BMOOSTT bottoms
BMORSUU brumous
umbrous
BNNOUUY nun-buoy
BNNRSUU sunburn
BNNRTUU unburnt
BNOOTTY bottony
BNORSUU burnous
BNORTUU burn-out
outburn
BNOSTTU buttons
BNOTTUY buttony
BOOOPRX poor-box
BOOOPTT top-boot
BOOPSTX postbox
BOPSSTU postbus
BORSTXY bostryx
BPRSTUU burst-up
upburst

C

CCCDIOO coccoid
CCCEHIO choc-ice

CCCEHIZ Czechic
CCCNOOT concoct
CCDEEER recceed
CCDEEIO ecocide
CCDEEIR reccied
CCDEENO concede
CCDEENY decency
CCDEESU succeed
CCDEHIL cliché'd
CCDEIIT deictic
CCDEILO ice-cold
CCDEILR circled
CCDEIMO comedic
CCDEIOS codices
CCDEIOT Docetic
CCDEKLO clocked
cockled
CCDEKOR crocked
CCDELOU occlude
CCDENOO concedo
CCDENOU conduce
CCDHIIL cichlid
CCDIILO codicil
CCDIILU culicid
CCDIIOR cricoid
CCDILOY cycloid
CCDKLOU cuckold
CCDKOOR rock-cod
CCDKOUY duck-coy
CCDNOOR concord
CCDNOTU conduct
CCDOSTU stucco'd
CCEEGNO cogence
CCEEHHN Chechen
CCEEHIV ceviche
CCEEHKR checker
recheck
CCEEHOR écorché
CCEEHOU couchee
couchée
CCEEHRS screech
CCEEILN licence
CCEEINR eccrine
CCEEINS △science
CCEEIRV crevice
CCEEKOY cockeye
CCEELRY recycle
CCEENRY recency
CCEERSY secrecy
CCEFNOT confect
CCEGNOY cogency
CCEHIKN check-in
chicken
CCEHIKU chuckie
CCEHILU culchie
CCEHINO conchie
CCEHINT technic
CCEHIOR choreic
CCEHIRS screich
scriech
CCEHKLU chuckle
CCEHKMS schmeck
CCEHKNU uncheck
CCEHKOR chocker
CCEHKPU check-up
CCEHLRU cleruch
CCEHNOS conches
CCEHORT crochet
CCEIIMS cimices
CCEIIPS piccies
CCEIIRT icteric
CCEIIST cecitis
CCEIKLR clicker
CCEIKLT clicket
CCEIKRT cricket
CCEIKRY crickey
CCEILMO celomic
CCEILNU nucleic
CCEILOT coctile
CCEILPT P-Celtic
CCEILQT Q-Celtic
CCEILRR circler
CCEILRS circles
CCEILRT circlet
CCEILSU culices
CCEILSY cylices
CCEILTU cuticle
CCEIMNO meconic
CCEIMOT cometic
CCEIMST smectic
CCEINOR cornice
crocein
CCEINOS concise
CCEINOT conceit
CCEINRT centric
CCEIOPP coppice
CCEIOPT ectopic
CCEIORT cerotic
orectic
CCEIOSS ciscoes
CCEIOST Scotice
CCEIPST △sceptic
CCEISSU succise
CCEJNOT conject
CCEKLOR clocker
CCEKLOS cockles
CCEKNOT conteck
CCEKNOY △cockney
CCEKOPT petcock
CCEKORT crocket
CCELLOT collect
CCELNOY cyclone
CCELNUY lucency
CCEMNOO Comecon
CCENNOR concern
CCENNOT concent
connect
CCENOPT concept
CCENORT concert
CCENORW concrew
CCEOOTT cocotte
CCEOPRT percoct
CCEORRT correct
CCEORTW twoccer
CCEOSSU succose
CCESSSU success
CCFIRUY crucify
CCFLOSU floccus
CCGHINO gnocchi
CCGIKNU cucking
CCGILNY cycling
CCGKOOR gorcock
CCHHIIT ichthic
CCHHILS schlich
CCHHRUY churchy
CCHIIST stichic
CCHIKST schtick
CCHILNY Lychnic
CCHILOR chloric
CCHIMOR chromic
CCHINOR chronic
CCHINSU scuchin
CCHIORY chicory
CCHIOTW cowitch
CCHIPSY psychic
CCHIPUY hiccupy
CCHIRST scritch
CCHKLOS schlock
CCHKMOS schmock
CCHKMSU schmuck
CCHKOSY cockshy
shy-cock
CCHKPUU upchuck
CCHKSTU schtuck
CCHNRSU scrunch
CCHNRUY crunchy
CCHOSTU Succoth
CCHOSTY Scotchy
CCIIILS silicic
CCIILPR circlip
CCIIRTU circuit
CCIISTY siccity
CCIKLOW cowlick
CCIKLOY cockily
colicky
CCIKOPT cockpit
CCILNOO colonic
CCILNOU council
CCILOOP piccolo
CCILSTY cyclist
CCIMOTY mycotic
CCINOOT coction
CCINORY cryonic
CCINOTV convict
CCIOORS sirocco
CCIOPTU occiput
CCIPRTY cryptic
CCIRSUY circusy
CCKOSTU custock
CCLOOOZ zoccolo
CCLOPSY △cyclops
CCMOOOR morocco
CCNOOPU puccoon
CCNOOTU coconut
CCNOPUY concupy
CCNOSSU concuss

CCOOORS	rococos
CCORSUU	succour
CCORSUY	succory
CCOSSTU	stuccos
CCOSSUU	succous
CCSSSUU	succuss
CDDDEEI	decided
CDDDELO	clodded
CDDDESU	scudded
CDDEEER	decreed
CDDEEII	deicide
CDDEEIR	decider
	decried
CDDEEKL	deckled
CDDEENS	descend
CDDEEOR	decoder
CDDEERU	reduced
CDDEEUW	cudweed
CDDEHIL	childed
CDDEHIN	chidden
CDDEIIS	discide
CDDEIOS	discoed
CDDEIRY	dry-iced
CDDELOU	clouded
CDDELRU	cruddle
CDDELSU	scuddle
CDDEORW	crowded
CDDERSU	scudder
CDDGINO	codding
CDDHIOR	dichord
CDDIIIO	didicoi
CDDIINO	Indocid®
CDDIIOS	discoid
CDDIIOY	didicoy
CDDIIRU	druidic
CDDIKOP	piddock
CDDIORS	discord
CDDKOPU	puddock
CDDKORU	ruddock
CDDKORY	dry-dock
CDEEEFL	fleeced
CDEEEFN	defence
CDEEEHP	dépêche
CDEEEHS	cheesed
CDEEEIP	epicede
CDEEEIV	deceive
CDEEEKL	cleeked
CDEEEPR	precede
CDEEERS	seceder
CDEEERT	decreet
	erected
CDEEFII	edifice
CDEEFKL	flecked
CDEEFLT	deflect
CDEEFOR	deforce
CDEEGIR	grieced
CDEEHIP	Cepheid
CDEEHIS	dehisce
CDEEHOR	chordee
CDEEHPR	perched
CDEEHRU	euchred
CDEEHST	chested
CDEEIIT	eidetic
CDEEILN	decline
CDEEILP	pedicel
	pedicle
CDEEIMN	endemic
CDEEINO	codeine
CDEEINR	cedrine
CDEEIOS	diocese
CDEEIOV	devoice
CDEEIPR	pierced
CDEEIPT	pedetic
CDEEIRR	decrier
CDEEIRT	tierced
CDEEITX	excited
CDEEKNR	redneck
CDEEKNV	V-necked
CDEELPU	cupeled
	decuple
CDEELPY	ycleped
CDEELRU	ulcered
CDEELSU	scedule
	seclude
CDEELUX	exclude
CDEENOS	seconde
CDEENRT	centred
	credent
CDEENST	descent
	scented
CDEEOPR	proceed
CDEEORV	covered
CDEEOST	cestode
	tedesco
CDEEOTV	coveted
CDEEOWW	cow-weed
CDEERRU	reducer
CDEERST	crested
CDEERSU	rescued
	seducer
CDEERSW	screwed
CDEERUV	decurve
CDEFFHU	chuffed
CDEFFIL	cliffed
CDEFHIN	finched
CDEFIIT	deficit
CDEFILP	clip-fed
CDEFILT	clifted
CDEFINO	confide
CDEFKOR	defrock
	frocked
CDEFNOR	corn-fed
CDEFNTU	defunct
CDEFOOR	od-force
CDEFOSU	focused
CDEFRTU	fructed
CDEFSUU	fucused
CDEGGLO	clogged
CDEGIKN	decking
CDEGILU	cludgie
CDEGIOR	ergodic
CDEGLSU	cudgels
CDEHIIL	ceilidh
CDEHILL	chilled
CDEHILO	cheloid
	helcoid
CDEHILP	△delphic
CDEHILR	childer
CDEHINO	hedonic
CDEHINP	pinched
CDEHIOW	cowhide
CDEHIPP	chipped
CDEHIPT	pitched
CDEHIRT	ditcher
CDEHKOS	shocked
CDEHKUY	heyduck
CDEHLOT	clothed
CDEHNOR	chondre
CDEHNOT	notched
CDEHNRU	chunder
CDEHOPP	chopped
CDEHOPU	pouched
CDEHORW	chowder
	cowherd
CDEHOSU	hocused
CDEHOSW	cowshed
CDEHOTU	touched
CDEHRSU	crushed
CDEHSSU	duchess
CDEHSTY	scythed
CDEIIMR	dimeric
CDEIINS	incised
	indices
CDEIINT	identic
CDEIIOR	ericoid
CDEIIOV	ovicide
CDEIIRT	icterid
CDEIIST	deistic
CDEIISU	suicide
CDEIJST	disject
CDEIKLP	pickled
CDEIKLS	sickled
CDEIKNS	dickens
CDEIKNZ	zincked
CDEIKOS	dockise
CDEIKOZ	dockize
CDEIKRR	derrick
CDEIKST	sticked
CDEILLO	codille
	collide
CDEILLU	cullied
CDEILMO	melodic
CDEILNU	include
	nuclide
CDEILOO	oceloid
CDEILPP	clipped
CDEILPU	clupeid
CDEILTU	ductile
	dulcite
CDEIMNO	demonic
CDEIMOR	dormice
CDEIMOS	medicos
CDEIMOT	demotic
CDEINOS	secondi

CDEINOT	ctenoid
	deontic
	D-notice
CDEINOU	doucine
CDEINOZ	zincode
CDEINRS	discern
	rescind
CDEINRU	inducer
CDEINRY	cindery
CDEINSU	incudes
CDEINSX	exscind
CDEINTU	uncited
CDEIOPR	percoid
CDEIORS	discoer
CDEIORT	cordite
CDEIORV	divorce
	divorcé
CDEIORW	crowdie
CDEIOST	cestoid
CDEIPRS	discerp
CDEIPRT	predict
CDEIPST	discept
CDEIPTU	cup-tied
CDEIRRU	curried
CDEIRST	credits
CDEIRSU	discure
CDEIRTV	verdict
CDEISST	dissect
CDEISSY	ecdysis
CDEITUX	excudit
CDEKLOW	wedlock
CDEKLOY	key-cold
CDEKLPU	plucked
CDEKNRU	drucken
CDEKNSU	sundeck
CDEKOOR	crooked
CDELLOU	collude
CDELLRY	dry-cell
CDELMSU	muscled
CDELMTU	mulcted
CDELNOO	condole
CDELNOU	encloud
CDELNOY	condyle
CDELOOR	croodle
	decolor
CDELORS	scolder
CDELORW	clowder
	red-cowl
CDELOSU	dulcose
CDELOTT	clotted
CDELOTU	clouted
CDELOUY	doucely
CDELPUU	clued-up
CDELRSU	scudler
CDELRUY	crudely
CDEMMNO	commend
CDEMMOO	commode
CDEMMSU	scummed
CDEMNNO	condemn
CDEMNOU	mud-cone
CDEMOOS	comedos
CDEMORU	decorum
CDENNOO	condone
CDENNOT	contend
CDENOOS	secondo
CDENOPU	pounced
CDENORS	corsned
CDENORW	crowned
	decrown
CDENOSS	seconds
CDENOTU	counted
CDENPUY	pudency
CDENRUU	uncured
CDENRUY	duncery
CDEOOPP	copepod
CDEOOPS	scooped
CDEOORR	corrode
CDEOORV	vocoder
CDEOOTV	dovecot
CDEOPPR	cropped
CDEOPRU	produce
CDEOQTU	docquet
CDEORRW	crowder
CDEORSS	crossed
CDEORSW	scowder
CDEORTU	eductor
CDEORUU	douceur
CDEOSSU	escudos
CDEOSTU	doucets
CDEOSTW	dowcets
CDEPRTY	decrypt
CDERRUY	dry-cure
CDFHIOS	codfish
CDFIILU	fluidic
CDFIISU	fusidic
CDFILUY	dulcify
CDFIOOT	octofid
CDGHIIN	chiding
CDGIINO	gonidic
CDGIKNO	docking
CDGIKNU	ducking
CDGIKOS	dog-sick
CDGIKOT	dog-tick
CDGILNO	codling
CDGINNO	condign
CDGINOR	cording
CDGNOOO	coondog
CDGNOUW	cow-dung
CDHIINT	△chindit
CDHIIST	distich
CDHILLY	childly
CDHILNU	unchild
CDHILOS	coldish
CDHINOR	chondri
CDHIOOR	choroid
	ochroid
CDHIORY	droichy
CDHIPTY	diptych
CDHKOOR	hordock
CDIIIOT	idiotic
CDIIJRU	juridic
CDIILLY	idyllic
CDIILMO	domicil
CDIINOR	crinoid
CDIINOT	diction
CDIINOV	Vidicon®
CDIINOZ	zincoid
CDIIORS	cirsoid
CDIIOSS	cissoid
CDIIOTY	idiotcy
CDIKLOP	Diplock
CDIKNOR	dornick
CDIKNOW	windock
CDILLOO	colloid
CDILLUY	lucidly
CDILOTU	dulotic
CDIMMOU	modicum
CDIMNOO	monodic
CDIMOSU	muscoid
CDINOOT	odontic
CDINOSY	synodic
CDINOTU	conduit
	noctuid
CDIOOTT	cottoid
CDIOPRR	rip-cord
CDIOSTY	cystoid
CDIOTUV	oviduct
CDIRSUY	dysuric
CDIRTUY	crudity
CDISSSU	discuss
CDISTUY	Dyticus
CDKMOSU	musk-cod
CDKNNOU	dunnock
CDLNOUU	uncloud
CDLOOPY	lycopod
CDMMOOO	commodo
CDMOSUW	mudscow
CDNNOTU	contund
CDNOORY	Corydon
CDOOOPT	octopod
CDOOPST	post-doc
CDOORRY	corrody
CDOORST	doctors
CDOOTUW	woodcut
CDOPRTU	product
CDOSTUY	custody
CEEEEGH	geechee
CEEEEHL	leechee
CEEEFIR	ice-free
CEEEFLR	fleecer
CEEEGNR	regence
CEEEHIR	reechie
CEEEHNR	encheer
CEEEHPR	cheeper
CEEEHRR	cheerer
CEEEINP	epicene
CEEEIPR	creepie
CEEEIRV	receive
CEEEKNW	ewe-neck
CEEELLU	écuelle
CEEELPY	ycleepe
CEEELRT	re-elect
CEEELST	celeste
CEEEMPR	emperce
CEEENRS	recense
CEEENSS	essence

CEEEPRR	creeper
CEEERRT	erecter
	re-erect
CEEERST	secrete
CEEERSV	screeve
CEEERTX	excrete
CEEETUX	execute
CEEFFNO	offence
CEEFFOR	efforce
CEEFFST	effects
CEEFHIR	chiefer
CEEFHIT	fetiche
	fitchée
CEEFHRT	fechter
CEEFINV	venefic
CEEFKLR	flecker
	freckle
CEEFLNU	fluence
CEEFLRT	reflect
CEEFNOR	enforce
CEEFNOX	ox-fence
CEEFPRT	perfect
	prefect
CEEGGLL	egg-cell
CEEGINR	energic
	generic
CEEGINT	genetic
CEEGINU	eugenic
CEEGIRS	△grecise
CEEGIRZ	△grecize
CEEGKOS	geckoes
CEEGLLO	college
CEEGLNT	neglect
CEEGLOU	eclogue
CEEGNOR	cogener
	congree
CEEGNRU	urgence
CEEGNRY	regency
CEEGORT	cortège
CEEGQRU	grecque
CEEHILN	elenchi
CEEHILS	helices
CEEHILV	vehicle
CEEHIMR	chimere
CEEHIMS	chemise
CEEHINR	inherce
CEEHINS	△chinese
CEEHIOR	cheerio
CEEHIOS	echoise
CEEHIOZ	echoize
CEEHIRT	etheric
	heretic
CEEHKLR	heckler
CEEHKNP	henpeck
CEEHLNO	chelone
	echelon
CEEHLNU	leuchen
CEEHLOW	cowheel
CEEHLRW	welcher
CEEHLRY	cheerly
	lechery
CEEHLSS	chessel
CEEHLSY	sleechy
CEEHMRS	schemer
CEEHMRT	merchet
CEEHNPU	penuche
CEEHNRW	wencher
CEEHOPR	pre-echo
CEEHORR	coherer
CEEHORT	trochee
CEEHOUV	vouchee
CEEHPRR	percher
CEEHPRU	upcheer
CEEHPSU	Cepheus
CEEHQRU	chequer
CEEHQUY	queechy
CEEHRSY	creeshy
CEEHSSS	chesses
CEEIINR	eirenic
CEEIIPR	épicier
CEEIJOR	rejoice
CEEIKLT	cleekit
CEEIKNT	necktie
	tie-neck
CEEIKPR	pickeer
CEEILLM	micelle
CEEILNO	cineole
CEEILNR	recline
CEEILNS	license
	selenic
	silence
CEEILNU	leucine
CEEILPS	eclipse
CEEILRT	reticle
	tiercel
CEEILRU	recuile
CEEILST	sectile
CEEILSV	vesicle
CEEILTU	leucite
CEEIMNO	Miocene
CEEIMNT	centime
CEEINNS	incense
CEEINOS	senecio
CEEINPR	percine
CEEINPT	pentice
CEEINRS	ceresin
	scriene
	sincere
CEEINRT	enteric
	enticer
CEEINRV	cervine
CEEIOPT	picotee
CEEIORT	coterie
CEEIPRR	piercer
CEEIPRS	precise
	recipes
CEEIPRT	receipt
CEEIPRU	epicure
CEEIPSS	species
CEEIPST	pectise
CEEIPTZ	pectize
CEEIQSU	quiesce
CEEIRRT	reciter
CEEIRSV	scrieve
	service
CEEIRTT	tiercet
CEEIRTU	eucrite
CEEIRTX	exciter
CEEITTZ	zetetic
CEEJORT	ejector
CEEKLNT	necklet
CEEKLPS	speckle
CEEKOSY	sockeye
CEEKPRY	ryepeck
CEEKRRW	wrecker
CEELLLU	cellule
CEELLNO	colleen
CEELLNT	Cellnet®
CEELLOS	cellose
CEELLPU	△pucelle
CEELMNT	clement
CEELMOT	telecom
CEELMOW	welcome
CEELNOS	enclose
CEELNRT	lectern
CEELNRU	lucerne
CEELORS	reclose
CEELORT	△elector
	electro
CEELORY	recoyle
CEELOTU	elocute
CEELOTV	covelet
CEELPRT	plectre
	prelect
CEELRSU	recluse
CEELRSW	crewels
CEELRTU	lecture
CEELRTY	erectly
CEELTTU	lettuce
CEEMMOR	commère
CEEMNOW	newcome
CEEMNRU	cerumen
CEEMOOR	o'ercome
CEEMOPR	compeer
	compère
CEEMOPT	compete
CEEMRRY	mercery
	remercy
CEEMSTU	tumesce
CEEMSTY	△mycetes
CEENNOU	enounce
CEENNOV	convene
CEENNRT	centner
CEENOPT	potence
	potencé
CEENORS	necrose
CEENORZ	cozener
CEENPRS	spencer
CEENRSU	censure
CEENRSY	scenery
CEENTTU	cunette
CEEOPST	pectose
CEEOPTY	ecotype
CEEORRS	rescore
CEEORRT	erector

CEEORRU	recoure
CEEORRV	recover
	re-cover
CEEORRW	recower
CEEORSU	cereous
CEEORTW	cowtree
CEEOTTT	octette
CEEPPRT	percept
	precept
CEEPPRU	prepuce
CEEPRSS	precess
CEEPRST	respect
	scepter
	sceptre
	specter
	spectre
CEEPRTX	excerpt
CEERRSU	rescuer
	securer
CEERRSW	screwer
CEERRUV	recurve
CEERSST	cresset
	secrets
CEERSSU	cesures
CEERSUX	excurse
	excuser
CEERTTU	curette
CEETTUV	cuvette
CEFFIOR	officer
CEFFIOS	offices
CEFFISU	suffice
CEFFLSU	scuffle
CEFFMOO	come-off
	off-come
CEFFORS	scoffer
CEFFORT	coffret
CEFFSTU	suffect
CEFGILU	Guelfic
CEFGINN	fencing
CEFHILR	filcher
CEFHILY	chiefly
CEFHIRY	chiefry
CEFHITT	fitchet
CEFHITW	fitchew
CEFHLTU	futchel
CEFHNRY	Frenchy
CEFIILS	Filices
CEFIILT	fictile
CEFIIOR	orifice
CEFIIRS	Friesic
CEFIITV	fictive
CEFIKLR	flicker
CEFILNT	inflect
CEFILNU	funicle
CEFILRU	△lucifer
CEFIMRY	mercify
CEFINNO	confine
CEFINOR	conifer
	fir-cone
	inforce
CEFIOOT	ice-foot
CEFIPSY	specify
CEFIRSS	sferics
CEFIRTY	certify
	rectify
CEFKLOT	fetlock
CEFKLRY	freckly
CEFLNOU	flounce
CEFLNUY	fluency
CEFMORY	comfrey
CEFNORU	frounce
CEFNOSS	confess
CEFNOST	confest
CEFNOSU	confuse
CEFNOTU	confute
CEFOPRS	forceps
CEFORRT	crofter
CEFORSS	frescos
CEFORSU	refocus
CEFOSSU	focuses
CEFSSUU	fucuses
CEGGHIR	chigger
CEGGIOR	georgic
CEGGLOR	clogger
CEGGOSY	egg-cosy
CEGHINO	echoing
CEGHINT	etching
CEGHIRS	screigh
CEGHITU	guichet
CEGHORU	cougher
CEGHRTU	gutcher
CEGIILN	ceiling
	cieling
CEGIKNN	necking
CEGIKNP	pecking
CEGILNR	clinger
	cringle
CEGILNU	lucigen
CEGILNY	glycine
CEGIMNO	genomic
CEGIMNU	mucigen
CEGIMRS	Grecism
CEGINOS	cognise
CEGINOZ	cognize
CEGINRR	cringer
CEGKLNO	genlock
CEGKLOR	grockle
CEGLNOO	cologne
CEGLOOY	ecology
CEGLOSU	glucose
CEGLOSY	glycose
CEGNNOO	oncogen
CEGNORU	congrue
CEGNORY	cryogen
CEGNOST	congest
CEGNRUY	urgency
CEGOORS	△scrooge
CEGORRY	grocery
CEGORSU	scourge
	scrouge
CEHHIRS	cherish
	shriech
CEHHIRT	hitcher
CEHHOST	shochet
CEHIIKN	△chinkie
CEHIINR	hircine
CEHIINS	niceish
CEHIINT	ichnite
CEHIIPP	chippie
CEHIJOR	Jericho
CEHIKNT	chetnik
	kitchen
	thicken
CEHIKNW	chewink
CEHIKOO	chookie
CEHIKPS	peckish
CEHIKRS	shicker
	skriech
CEHIKRW	whicker
CEHIKST	chekist
CEHIKTT	thicket
CEHILLR	chiller
CEHILMN	Mechlin
CEHILMY	chimley
CEHILNO	choline
	helicon
CEHILNT	linchet
	tinchel
CEHILPR	pilcher
CEHILRV	chervil
CEHILSV	Chislev
CEHILTY	techily
CEHIMMS	chemism
CEHIMNY	chimney
CEHIMOR	Homeric
	moriche
CEHIMOS	echoism
CEHIMRT	thermic
CEHIMST	chemist
CEHINOP	chopine
	phocine
CEHINOR	chorine
CEHINOT	henotic
CEHINOX	choenix
CEHINPR	nephric
	phrenic
	pincher
CEHINPS	sphenic
CEHINPU	penuchi
CEHINQU	quinche
CEHINRT	cithern
CEHINST	sthenic
CEHINSU	echinus
CEHINTW	witchen
CEHIOPS	hospice
CEHIOPT	potiche
CEHIORS	heroics
CEHIORT	rotchie
	theoric
CEHIOST	echoist
	toisech
CEHIOTU	couthie
CEHIOTV	Cheviot
CEHIPPR	chipper
CEHIPRR	chirper
CEHIPRS	spheric

Words marked △ may be spelled also with a capital letter

CEHIPRT	pitcher
CEHIRRT	Richter
CEHIRST	estrich
CEHIRSZ	scherzi
CEHIRTT	chitter
CEHISTU	Cushite
CEHKKRU	chukker
CEHKLMO	hemlock
CEHKORS	shocker
CEHKPTU	ketchup
CEHKRSU	shucker
CEHKSTY	sketchy
CEHLLMO	mochell
CEHLLMU	muchell
CEHLLNS	schnell
CEHLLOY	yelloch
CEHLMOR	chromel
CEHLMSZ	schmelz
CEHLMUY	chumley
CEHLMWY	wych-elm
CEHLNNU	△chunnel
CEHLNOT	cholent
	notchel
CEHLNRU	luncher
CEHLNTY	lynchet
CEHLOOS	schoole
CEHLORT	chortle
CEHLOST	clothes
CEHLOTW	low-tech
CEHLPPS	schlepp
CEHLQSU	squelch
CEHLRRU	lurcher
CEHMNRU	muncher
CEHMOOR	moocher
CEHMORU	moucher
CEHMOSS	schmoes
CEHNNRU	chunner
CEHNOOP	hen-coop
CEHNOOR	coehorn
CEHNORT	notcher
CEHNORV	chevron
CEHNPRU	puncher
	unperch
CEHNPST	pschent
CEHNRTU	chunter
CEHNSTU	chesnut
CEHNSTY	stenchy
CEHNTUY	chutney
CEHOORS	chooser
	soroche
CEHOORT	cheroot
CEHOOSY	choosey
CEHOPPR	chopper
CEHOPRT	potcher
CEHOPRY	coryphe
CEHORRT	torcher
CEHORSU	choreus
CEHORSY	coshery
CEHORSZ	scherzo
CEHORTU	retouch
	toucher
CEHORTW	wotcher
CEHORUV	voucher
CEHPRTU	putcher
CEHQSTU	quetsch
CEHRRSU	crusher
CEHRSTT	stretch
CEHRSTY	scyther
CEIIKLS	siclike
CEIIKNT	kinetic
CEIIKQU	quickie
CEIIKST	ekistic
CEIILLS	silicle
CEIILNN	incline
CEIILPP	clippie
CEIILPT	pelitic
CEIILTV	levitic
CEIIMMT	mimetic
CEIIMNR	crimine
CEIIMNS	menisci
CEIIMOT	meiotic
CEIIMPR	empiric
CEIIMPS	epicism
CEIIMRV	viremic
CEIIMSS	seismic
CEIIMST	Semitic
CEIIMTT	titmice
CEIINNO	coniine
	inconie
CEIINNR	cinerin
CEIINOR	oneiric
CEIINOS	iconise
CEIINOV	invoice
CEIINOZ	iconize
CEIINPS	piscine
CEIINRS	irenics
	sericin
	sirenic
CEIINRT	citrine
	crinite
	inciter
	neritic
CEIINSS	iciness
CEIINSU	cuisine
CEIINTZ	citizen
	zincite
CEIIOPZ	epizoic
CEIIPPR	piperic
CEIIPRR	pricier
CEIIPRT	picrite
CEIIPST	epicist
CEIIRST	eristic
CEIIRSU	cruisie
CEIISVV	civvies
CEIITUV	uveitic
CEIJSTU	justice
CEIKKNN	Kennick
CEIKKNR	knicker
CEIKLNR	clinker
	crinkle
CEIKLNS	slicken
CEIKLPR	pickler
	prickle
CEIKLPS	pickles
CEIKLPT	P-Keltic
CEIKLQT	Q-Keltic
CEIKLRS	slicker
CEIKLRT	tickler
	trickle
CEIKLST	stickle
CEIKLSY	kylices
CEIKMRS	smicker
CEIKMST	smicket
CEIKNOT	kenotic
CEIKNPZ	zip-neck
CEIKNQU	quicken
CEIKNRS	snicker
CEIKNST	snicket
CEIKORR	rockier
CEIKORS	Rockies
CEIKPRR	pricker
CEIKPRT	pricket
CEIKPRY	pickery
CEIKPST	skeptic
CEIKRRT	tricker
CEIKRST	rickets
	sticker
CEIKRTU	truckie
CEIKRTY	rickety
CEILLNO	lioncel
CEILLNU	nucelli
CEILLOR	collier
CEILLST	cellist
	'cellist
CEILMOP	compile
	polemic
CEILMPR	crimple
CEILNNU	nuclein
CEILNOP	pinocle
CEILNOS	close-in
	conseil
	inclose
CEILNOT	lection
CEILNOX	lexicon
CEILNPS	splenic
CEILNST	stencil
CEILNTU	cutline
	tunicle
CEILOOT	△clootie
CEILOPR	peloric
CEILOPT	toeclip
CEILORT	cortile
CEILOSS	ossicle
CEILOTT	coletit
CEILPPR	clipper
	cripple
CEILPRS	splicer
CEILPSU	spicule
CEILQUY	cliquey
CEILRSU	curlies
CEILRSV	clivers
CEILRSY	clerisy
CEILRTT	clitter
CEILRTU	utricle
CEILSSS	scissel
CEILSSU	Celsius

CEILTTU	cuittle
CEIMMRR	crimmer
CEIMNNO	meconin
CEIMNOR	incomer
CEIMNOS	mesonic
CEIMNOT	centimo
	entomic
	Metonic
	tonemic
CEIMNRS	cremsin
CEIMNRU	minceur
	numeric
CEIMNYZ	enzymic
CEIMOPT	metopic
CEIMOQU	comique
CEIMORR	morrice
CEIMORT	mortice
CEIMOSU	Couéism
CEIMOTT	totemic
CEIMOTV	vicomte
CEIMOTX	toxemic
CEIMPRR	crimper
CEIMPRS	spermic
CEIMRST	cretism
	metrics
CEIMRSU	murices
CEINNOR	Neronic
CEINNOV	connive
CEINOOT	coontie
CEINOOZ	Neozoic
CEINOPR	pericon
	porcine
CEINOPT	entopic
	nepotic
CEINORS	crinose
	sericon
CEINORT	rection
CEINORU	nourice
CEINORV	corvine
CEINORY	oriency
CEINOSS	cession
	Oscines
CEINOST	section
CEINOSW	snow-ice
CEINOTT	entotic
	tonetic
CEINOTX	exciton
CEINOUV	unvoice
CEINOVV	convive
CEINPRS	pincers
CEINPRY	cyprine
CEINPST	inspect
CEINPTY	pycnite
CEINRST	cistern
CEINRSV	crivens
CEINRTT	cittern
CEINRUV	incurve
CEINSTY	cystine
CEINTTX	extinct
CEINVVY	vivency
CEIOOPR	oporice
CEIOPRS	persico
CEIOPRT	pteroic
CEIOPST	poetics
CEIOPSU	piceous
CEIORRS	cirrose
	crosier
CEIORRU	courier
CEIORRZ	crozier
CEIORST	tercios
CEIORSU	scourie
CEIORSV	corsive
CEIORSW	scowrie
CEIORTT	cottier
CEIORTV	evictor
CEIORTW	co-write
CEIORTX	excitor
	xerotic
CEIORVY	viceroy
CEIOSSV	viscose
CEIOSTT	cottise
	Scottie
CEIOSTU	Couéist
CEIOSTV	costive
CEIOSTX	coexist
CEIOSTY	society
CEIPPST	peptics
CEIPQTU	picquet
CEIPRRS	crisper
CEIPRST	triceps
CEIPRSY	spicery
CEIPRTU	cuprite
	picture
CEIPRTY	pyretic
CEIPRXY	pyrexic
CEIPSSS	scepsis
CEIPSST	cesspit
CEIRRRU	currier
CEIRRSU	cruiser
	sucrier
CEIRRTT	critter
CEIRRTU	recruit
CEIRRTX	rectrix
CEIRSSU	cuisser
CEIRSTT	trisect
CEIRSTU	icterus
CEIRSUV	cursive
CEIRTTX	tectrix
CEISSTU	ictuses
CEJNOOS	cojones
CEJNORU	conjure
CEJNOSU	juncoes
CEJOPRT	project
CEKKLNU	knuckle
CEKKNOR	knocker
CEKLLOP	pellock
CEKLLRY	clerkly
CEKLMOR	rock-elm
CEKLNOS	slocken
CEKLNOW	Wenlock
CEKLNRU	crunkle
CEKLOSU	suck'ole
CEKLPRU	plucker
CEKLRSU	suckler
CEKLRTU	truckle
CEKMORS	mockers
CEKMORY	mockery
CEKNNSU	unsneck
CEKNOOV	convoke
CEKNORS	conkers
CEKNORT	trocken
CEKNRWY	wryneck
CEKOOPR	precook
CEKOOPW	cowpoke
CEKOORY	cookery
CEKORRY	rockery
CEKORST	restock
	stocker
CEKPRUY	puckery
CEKRRTU	trucker
CELLMOU	columel
CELLNOO	△colonel
CELLORS	escroll
CELLOSU	locules
	ocellus
CELLOSY	closely
CELLRRU	cruller
CELLRSU	cruells
	sculler
CELLRUY	cruelly
CELMMSU	mesclum
CELMNOO	monocle
CELMNSU	mesclun
CELMOPX	complex
CELMPRU	clumper
	crumple
CELMSUU	seculum
CELMSUY	lyceums
CELNNOU	nucleon
CELNOOS	colones
	console
CELNOSU	counsel
	unclose
CELNOTU	noctule
CELNRTU	lecturn
CELNSUU	nucleus
CELOOPR	precool
CELOORS	creosol
CELOPRU	coupler
CELOPSU	close-up
	opuscle
	upclose
CELOPTU	couplet
	octuple
CELORST	corslet
	costrel
CELORSU	closure
CELORSW	scrowle
CELORSY	scroyle
CELORTT	clotter
	crottle
CELORTU	cloture
	clouter
	coulter
CELORVY	clovery
CELOSTY	cotyles

CELPRSU	scruple
CELPSUY	clypeus
CELRSTU	cluster
	custrel
CELRSTY	clyster
CELRTTU	clutter
CELRTUU	culture
CELRTUV	culvert
CELRTUY	cruelty
	cutlery
CELSTTU	scuttle
CEMMNOT	comment
CEMMNOU	commune
CEMMOOT	commote
CEMMOOV	commove
CEMMOTU	commute
CEMMRSU	scummer
CEMNNOO	non-come
CEMNNOT	contemn
CEMNOOP	componé
CEMNOOY	economy
CEMNOSU	consume
	muscone
CEMNRTU	centrum
CEMOOPS	compose
CEMOOPT	compote
CEMOORS	Moresco
CEMOOTU	outcome
CEMOPRT	compter
CEMOPTU	compute
CEMOSSU	muscose
CEMOSTU	costume
CEMPRTU	crumpet
CEMRRUY	△mercury
CEMRSTU	rectums
CENNOOT	connote
CENNOST	consent
CENNOTT	content
CENNOTV	convent
CENNRSU	scunner
CENOORR	coroner
	crooner
CENOORS	no-score
CENOORT	coronet
CENOPSY	syncope
CENOPTU	pouncet
CENOPTY	potency
CENOQRU	conquer
CENORRS	scorner
CENORRW	crowner
CENORST	conster
	creston
CENORTT	cornett
CENORTU	cornute
	counter
	recount
	re-count
	trounce
CENORTV	convert
CENORTW	crownet
CENORUV	uncover
CENOSSY	coyness
CENOSTT	contest
CENOSTU	contuse
CENOTTX	context
CENPRTY	encrypt
CENPTUX	expunct
CENRRTU	current
CENRSTU	encrust
CENRSUU	uncurse
CENRSUW	unscrew
CENRTUY	century
CEOOPRS	scooper
CEOOPRY	coopery
CEOORST	scooter
CEOORTW	crow-toe
CEOOSTY	coyotes
CEOPPRR	cropper
CEOPPRY	coppery
CEOPRRS	scorper
CEOPRRT	porrect
CEOPRRU	crouper
	procure
CEOPRSS	process
CEOPRTT	protect
CEOPRUU	coupure
CEOPRUV	cover-up
CEOQRTU	croquet
	rocquet
CEORRSS	recross
	scorser
CEORRSU	courser
	cruores
	scourer
CEORRSW	scowrer
CEORRSY	sorcery
CEORRTY	rectory
CEORSSS	crosses
CEORSSU	courses
	Croesus
	scourse
	scouser
	sucrose
CEORSTU	rose-cut
	scouter
CEORTUU	couture
CEORTUV	couvert
	cut-over
CEOSTTU	cuttoes
CEPPRRU	crupper
CEPPRSU	scupper
CEPRSSU	percuss
CEPRSSY	cypress
CEPRSTY	sceptry
CEPRSUW	screw-up
CEPSSTU	suspect
CEPSTTU	step-cut
CEQRSUU	Quercus
CERSTTU	scutter
CERSTUY	curtesy
	curtsey
CFFHINO	chiffon
CFFIIRT	triffic
CFFIKKO	kick-off
CFFMOSU	offscum
CFFRSUY	scruffy
CFGIKNU	fucking
CFHILYY	chylify
CFHIMYY	chymify
CFHIOSW	cowfish
CFHORTU	futhorc
CFIIIMR	mirific
CFIIIVV	vivific
CFIIKNY	finicky
CFIILNT	inflict
CFIIMNO	omnific
CFIINOT	fiction
CFIINOY	iconify
CFIINYZ	zincify
CFIIOSS	ossific
CFIKKLY	fly-kick
CFIKNNO	finnock
CFIKOSS	fossick
CFILORU	fluoric
CFIMNOR	confirm
CFIOORT	Corfiot
CFIORSY	scorify
CFIOSTY	Scotify
CFKLLOU	lockful
CFKLOOT	cot-folk
CFKNORU	unfrock
CFKOTTU	futtock
CFLMRUU	fulcrum
CFLNORY	cornfly
CFLNOUX	conflux
CFLNOUY	flouncy
CFLOPRU	cropful
CFLPSUU	cupfuls
CFMNOOR	conform
CFMOORT	comfort
CFOSSUU	fuscous
CGGGINO	cogging
CGGIINR	gricing
CGGINOS	Scoggin
CGGORSY	scroggy
CGHIIMN	miching
CGHIKOT	Gothick
CGHILOP	log-chip
CGHILPY	glyphic
CGHINNO	chignon
CGHINRU	ruching
CGHIOSY	goyisch
CGHOORT	torgoch
CGHORUY	grouchy
CGIIKLN	licking
CGIIKMM	gimmick
CGIIKNP	picking
CGIIKNT	ticking
CGIILLO	illogic
CGIILNS	slicing
CGIIMNN	mincing
CGIINNO	coining
CGIINNW	wincing
CGIINNZ	zincing
CGIINOR	gironic
CGIINOV	voicing

Words marked △ may be spelled also with a capital letter

CGIKMNO mocking
CGIKNOR corking
rocking
CGIKNOS socking
CGIKNPU kingcup
CGIKNSU sucking
CGILLNO colling
CGILLNU culling
CGILNOS closing
CGILNOW cowling
CGILNOY cloying
CGILNRU curling
CGILORW cowgirl
CGILOSS Glossic
CGILOTT glottic
CGILPTU giltcup
CGILPTY glyptic
CGIMNOP comping
CGINNNO conning
CGINNNU cunning
CGINNOS consign
CGINOPY copying
CGINORS scoring
CGINORY gyronic
CGINOST △gnostic
CGINOSU congius
CGINPPU cupping
CGINPRS c-spring
CGINRSU cursing
CGINRSY scrying
CGINRUV curving
CGINTTU cutting
CGIOOOS giocoso
CGIOTYZ zygotic
CGKLNOU gunlock
CGLOOSU colugos
CGOORRW gorcrow
CHHIKOR chikhor
CHHINOR rhonchi
CHHINTU unhitch
CHHIRST shritch
CHHISTY ichthys
CHHRTTU thrutch
CHIIIST Shiitic
CHIIKNN kinchin
CHIIKSS sickish
CHIILLS chillis
CHIILOR oil-rich
CHIIMNS Mishnic
CHIIMSU ischium
CHIINNP inchpin
CHIIOPT △ophitic
CHIIOST stichoi
CHIIPST Pictish
CHIKLLO hillock
CHIKLOP hip-lock
CHIKLTY thickly
CHIKNOO △chinook
CHIKNTU thick'un
CHIKORY hickory
CHIKOST thickos
CHIKPSU puckish
CHIKSTY kitschy
CHILLMU chillum
CHILLOW lich-owl
CHILLTY lichtly
CHILNOR chlorin
CHILNOU ulichon
CHILNSY lychnis
CHILOOS coolish
CHILOST coltish
CHILSTU cultish
CHIMNPY nymphic
CHIMOPR morphic
CHIMORS chorism
chrisom
CHIMRRY myrrhic
CHIMSTY tychism
CHINOOR chorion
CHINOPS phonics
CHINOPT to-pinch
CHINORS Cornish
CHINORT Corinth
CHINOSU cushion
CHINOTW two-inch
CHINQSU squinch
CHINTUW unwitch
CHINTYZ chintzy
CHIOOPR pochoir
CHIOORS isochor
CHIOORZ chorizo
CHIOPRT trophic
CHIOPST photics
CHIOPXY hypoxic
CHIORST chorist
ostrich
CHIOSST stichos
CHIOSSZ schizos
CHIPRRU chirrup
CHIPRRY △pyrrhic
CHIPSSY physics
CHIQSTU squitch
CHIRRSU currish
CHIRSTY △christy
CHISTTU chutist
CHISTWY switchy
CHITTWY twitchy
CHKLOOO hoolock
CHKLOOT klootch
CHKLOSY Shylock
CHKMMOO hommock
CHKMMOU hummock
CHKNOOS schnook
CHKOOST schtook
CHKPTUU putchuk
CHLOOSS schools
CHLOPST splotch
CHLORTY choltry
CHLOSSS schloss
CHLOSUY slouchy
CHMOORS chromos
CHMOOST schtoom
CHMOOSZ schmooz
CHMOSUY chymous
CHNNOOR chronon
CHNNOSU nonsuch
CHNOOPS ponchos
CHNOORT torchon
CHNORRS schnorr
CHNORSY synchro
CHNORTU cothurn
CHNOTUU uncouth
CHNPPUU punch-up
CHOOPPS copshop
CHOORSU ochrous
CHOPSSY psychos
CHORSTU △trochus
CHPPSUY psych-up
CHPSSUY scyphus
CHRRSUU churrus
CIIILLT illicit
CIIILNV incivil
CIIIMNR crimini
CIIINPT incipit
CIIKKLL killick
CIIKMMM mimmick
CIIKMNN minnick
CIIKNPT nit-pick
CIIKNTU cutikin
CIIKPUW wickiup
CIIKSTT stickit
CIILLTY licitly
CIILLVY civilly
CIILNOP cipolin
CIILNOS silicon
CIILNOT Nilotic
CIILNUV uncivil
CIILOOT oolitic
CIILOPT politic
CIILORT cortili
CIILOST colitis
solicit
CIILPSY spicily
CIILSSS scissil
CIIMMRY mimicry
CIIMNNO nimonic
CIIMNOT miction
CIIMOST mistico
somitic
CIIMOTT mitotic
CIIMOTV motivic
CIINNTU tunicin
CIINOOT coition
CIINOPS psionic
CIINORS incisor
CIINPRS crispin
CIINQTU quintic
CIINRSU Ricinus
CIINTUY unicity
CIIORST soritic
CIIOSUV vicious
CIIPRTY pyritic
CIIRSTV vitrics
CIIRTVX victrix
CIJMORW jim-crow
CIJNNOO conjoin

CIJNNTU	injunct
CIKKLLO	killock
CIKLLOP	pillock
CIKLLOR	rollick
CIKLLOS	sillock
CIKLLOW	killcow
CIKLLSY	slickly
CIKLLUY	luckily
CIKLMOR	rim-lock
CIKLMOW	milk-cow
CIKLMSU	misluck
CIKLMSY	smickly
CIKLNRY	crinkly
CIKLOOR	rock-oil
CIKLOPZ	ziplock
CIKLORY	rockily
CIKLOST	Lockist
CIKLPRY	prickly
CIKLQUY	quickly
CIKLRTY	trickly
CIKLSTU	lustick
CIKMNNO	minnock
CIKNNOP	pinnock
CIKNNOW	winnock
CIKNSTU	unstick
CIKOPPT	pockpit
CIKOPST	pot-sick
CIKOSTU	sick-out
CIKOTUW	outwick
CIKPSTU	stick-up
CIKRSTY	tricksy
CILLNOS	Collins
CILLNOU	cullion
CILLOOR	criollo
CILLOPY	pollicy
CILMNOP	△complin
CILMOPY	Olympic
CILMSTU	cultism
CILNOOR	orcinol
CILNOOS	cloison
	scolion
CILNOPR	pilcorn
CILNOPS	clip-ons
CILNORY	lyricon
CILNOTU	linocut
CILNOXY	xylonic
CILNPSU	insculp
	sculpin
CILNPSY	lip-sync
CILNPTU	unclipt
CILNSTU	linctus
CILOOPT	copilot
	co-pilot
CILOORU	couloir
CILOOSS	colossi
CILOOST	sciolto
CILOPRW	pilcrow
CILOPRY	pyloric
CILOPSW	cowslip
CILOSTU	oculist
CILPRSY	crisply
CILPRTU	culprit
CILRRSU	scurril
CILSTTU	cultist
CIMMOSS	cosmism
CIMMOST	Comtism
CIMNOOR	moronic
	omicron
CIMNORS	crimson
	microns
CIMOORS	△morisco
CIMOOST	osmotic
CIMOPSY	copyism
	miscopy
CIMOSST	cosmist
	Scotism
CIMOSSY	mycosis
CIMOSTT	Comtist
CIMOTYZ	zymotic
CIMPRSY	scrimpy
CIMRSSU	crissum
CINNNOU	inconnu
CINNORU	△unicorn
CINNOSU	nuncios
CINNOTU	unction
CINNSUU	uncinus
CINOOPS	opsonic
CINOORS	coronis
CINOPRX	princox
CINORRT	tricorn
CINORSS	incross
CINORST	cistron
	cornist
CINORTU	ruction
CINOSST	consist
CINOSSU	Oniscus
CINOSTU	suction
CINOSUZ	zincous
CINRSTU	incrust
	scrutin
CIOOPRS	Scorpio
CIOOPRT	portico
	prootic
CIOOPSU	copious
CIOOQTU	coquito
CIOORSU	corious
CIOPRST	tropics
CIOPRTY	Cypriot
CIOPSTY	copyist
CIOQRSU	croquis
CIORRSU	cirrous
CIORSSS	scissor
CIORSSU	Roscius
CIORSTU	citrous
CIORSUU	curious
CIORTVY	△victory
CIOSSSY	sycosis
CIOSSTT	Scotist
CIOSSUV	viscous
CIPRSSU	prussic
	Scirpus
CIPRTTY	tryptic
CIPRUVY	pyruvic
CIPSTTY	styptic
CIRRTTU	crittur
CIRSSUU	Sciurus
CIRTUVY	curvity
CISSTUY	cytisus
CJMPTUU	jump-cut
CJNORUY	conjury
CKKLNUY	knuckly
CKKNNOO	knock-on
CKKNOPU	knock-up
CKLLMOU	mullock
CKLLOOP	pollock
CKLLOOR	rollock
CKLLORU	rullock
CKLNOTU	lock-nut
CKLNUUY	unlucky
CKLOOOY	olycook
CKLOOPR	Porlock
CKLOORW	rowlock
CKLOOTU	lockout
CKLOPTU	putlock
CKMMMOU	mummock
CKNOSTU	unstock
CKNSTUU	unstuck
CKOOOTU	cookout
CKOORSU	sourock
CKOPTTU	puttock
CKORTUW	cutwork
CKOSSTU	tussock
CKOTTUU	tuck-out
CKPSTUU	stuck-up
CLLMOSU	mollusc
CLLOOPS	collops
	scollop
CLLOSUU	loculus
CLMOOPT	complot
CLMOPTU	plumcot
CLMOSUU	lucumos
	osculum
CLMSUUU	cumulus
CLNOORT	control
CLNOOSS	consols
CLNOSTU	consult
CLOORSU	colours
CLOORUY	coloury
CLOOSTW	low-cost
CLORSSY	crossly
CLORSUY	corylus
CLORTUY	courtly
CMMNOOS	△commons
CMMRSUY	scrummy
CMNOOOT	monocot
CMNOOPY	compony
CMNPTUU	punctum
CMOOPRT	comport
CMOOPST	compost
CMOORSU	cormous
CMOOSTY	scotomy
CMORSTU	scrotum
CMORTUW	cutworm
CMOSSTU	customs
CMOSUVY	△muscovy
CMPRSUY	scrumpy

CNNORTU nocturn
CNNORUW uncrown
CNOOPPR popcorn
CNOOPRU croupon
CNOOPRY Procyon
CNOOPSU soupçon
CNOORRW cornrow
CNOORST consort
CNOORTT contort
CNOORTU contour
cornuto
croûton
CNOOSST oncosts
CNOOSUU nocuous
CNOOTTW cottown
CNOOTTY cottony
CNOPRTY crypton
CNOPSTU punctos
CNORSSU uncross
CNORTUY country
CNRSTUY scrunty
COOORSZ corozos
COOPRRT proctor
COOPRTU outcrop
COOPSTU octopus
COOSTTY otocyst
COPRRTU corrupt
COPRSUU cuprous
CORRSUY cursory
CORSSTU scrutos

D

DDDEELS sledded
DDDEELU deluded
DDDEEMO demoded
DDDEERU uddered
DDDEFLU fuddled
DDDEHIW whidded
DDDEHLU huddled
DDDEHTU thudded
DDDEIKS skidded
DDDEILR diddler
DDDEILT tiddled
DDDEIMU muddied
DDDEIOV Veddoid
DDDEIRU ruddied
DDDELOP plodded
DDDENOS snodded
DDDEOPR prodded
DDDEORY doddery
DDDERUY duddery
DDDESTU studded
DDEEEOY doe-eyed
DDEEEPS speeded
DDEEFGL fledged
DDEEFII deified
edified
DDEEFIL fielded
DDEEFLU deedful
DDEEGIS disedge
DDEEGRR dredger
DDEEHNU dudheen
DDEEHRS shedder
DDEEILS sleided
DDEEILV deviled
DDEEILY deedily
DDEEIMS misdeed
DDEEIOV videoed
DDEEIPS depside
DDEEIRR derider
ridered
DDEELLU duelled
DDEELLW dwelled
DDEELMO modeled
DDEELMR meddler
DDEELPR peddler
DDEELRT treddle
DDEELRU deluder
DDEENOV even-odd
odd-even
DDEENOW endowed
DDEENRS Dresden
DDEENSU duendes
DDEEOTV devoted
DDEEPRS spredde
DDEERSS dressed
DDEERST reddest
DDEERTU detrude
DDEERYY dry-eyed
DDEETTU duetted
DDEFILR fiddler
DDEFILY fiddley
DDEFLOO flooded
DDEFLRU fuddler
DDEFNOR fronded
DDEGGRU drugged
DDEGILR girdled
glidder
griddle
DDEGIMO demigod
DDEGINR grinded
redding
DDEGINT tedding
DDEGINW wedding
DDEGINY eddying
DDEGIRR gridder
DDEGLOS dogsled
DDEGMOS Dodgems®
dodgems
DDEGNOO good-den
DDEGNOS godsend
DDEGNOU dudgeon
DDEGORS △gorsedd
DDEGORY dodgery
DDEGOSS △goddess
DDEGRRU drudger
DDEHIRS reddish
shidder
DDEHIRW whidder
DDEHIRY hydride
DDEHNRU hundred
DDEHRSU shudder
DDEHRSY shreddy
DDEIIKR kiddier
DDEIIKS kiddies
DDEIIOX dioxide
DDEIIRT dirtied
DDEIIRV divider
DDEIIST stiddie
DDEIIVV divvied
DDEIIZZ dizzied
DDEIKLO odd-like
DDEIKNR kindred
DDEIKRS skidder
DDEILLO dollied
DDEILMP dimpled
DDEILNS slidden
DDEILNW dwindle
DDEILOS dildoes
DDEILOT deltoid
DDEILPR piddler
DDEILQU quiddle
DDEILRR riddler
DDEILRS slidder
DDEILRT tiddler
DDEILTU Luddite
DDEILTW twiddle
DDEILTY lyddite
tiddley
DDEIMNU mueddin
DDEIMOR dermoid
DDEIMOS desmoid
DDEIMST middest
DDEIMSU dedimus
DDEINOT dentoid
DDEINPS dispend
DDEINRU undried
DDEINST distend
DDEINSW swidden
DDEIOOR do-or-die
DDEIOTT dittoed
DDEIPPR dripped
DDEIPRS dispred
DDEIRRU ruddier
DDEISSU disused
DDEISTU studied
DDEKMOU dukedom
DDELMRU muddler
DDELNOU noduled
DDELNRU rundled
DDELOOR doodler
DDELOOW woolded
DDELOPR plodder
DDELORT toddler
DDELORW worlded
DDELOTT dottled
DDELPRU puddler
DDELSTU studdle
DDEMMRU drummed
DDEMMSU smeddum
DDEMNOT oddment
DDENNOR dendron
donnerd
DDENOOS snooded
DDENOPS despond
DDENOPW dew-pond

DDENORT	trodden
DDENORU	redound
	rounded
	underdo
DDENORW	wondred
DDENOSS	oddness
DDENSTU	studden
DDEOORU	odoured
DDEOORW	redwood
	red-wood
DDEOOWY	dye-wood
DDEOPPR	dropped
DDEOPRW	dew-drop
DDGGINO	dodging
DDGHOOO	godhood
DDGIIKN	kidding
DDGIILY	giddily
DDGIINR	ridding
DDGINNO	nodding
DDGINOP	podding
DDGINOR	rodding
DDGINOS	sodding
DDGINPU	pudding
DDGIPUY	giddy-up
DDGOOOW	dogwood
DDHIISS	Siddhis
DDHIISY	Yiddish
DDHIKSU	kiddush
DDHIORY	hydroid
DDHOOWY	howdy-do
DDHORSY	dry-shod
DDIIKNY	dinky-di
DDIILOP	diploid
DDIIQTU	quiddit
DDILMSU	Luddism
DDILMUY	muddily
DDILOSY	dysodil
DDILOWY	dowdily
DDILRUY	ruddily
DDILTWY	twiddly
DDINOST	snoddit
DDIOOSS	dosi-dos
DDIORTU	turdoid
DDIPRRY	drip-dry
DDLLMOO	dolldom
DDMNOOR	dromond
DDORSTY	drostdy
DEEEEHT	tee-heed
DEEEEWW	wee-weed
DEEEFNS	defense
DEEEFPT	deep-fet
DEEEFRV	fevered
DEEEGLP	pledgee
DEEEGMR	demerge
DEEEGRR	regrede
DEEEGRT	deterge
	greeted
DEEEHLW	wheedle
	wheeled
DEEEHST	seethed
	sheeted
DEEEIPY	pie-eyed
DEEEISV	devisee
DEEEIYZ	Yezidee
DEEEIZZ	Zezidee
DEEEJNU	dejeune
DEEEKLN	kneeled
DEEEKNW	weekend
DEEELMS	meseled
DEEELNR	needler
DEEELNS	needles
DEEELPT	deplete
DEEELRT	deerlet
DEEELST	steeled
DEEELSV	sleeved
DEEELTW	tweedle
DEEEMNS	demesne
DEEEMRS	demerse
	emersed
DEEENOY	one-eyed
DEEENTT	détente
DEEENTU	détenue
DEEEORR	roe-deer
DEEEORW	oreweed
DEEEOTV	devotee
DEEEPRS	speeder
DEEEPRU	éperdue
DEEEPST	deep-set
DEEERSV	deserve
DEEERSW	sweered
DEEERWY	weedery
DEEETTV	vedette
DEEFFIN	effendi
DEEFFLS	self-fed
DEEFFOR	offered
DEEFGIN	feeding
	feigned
DEEFGIP	pigfeed
DEEFHLS	fleshed
DEEFHLU	heedful
DEEFIIR	deifier
	edifier
DEEFIKN	ink-feed
DEEFILN	Enfield
	enfiled
DEEFILR	defiler
	fielder
DEEFIMS	misfeed
DEEFINR	definer
	refined
DEEFIRR	ferried
DEEFIRY	re-edify
DEEFIRZ	friezed
DEEFLLU	fuelled
DEEFLLW	well-fed
DEEFLNS	self-end
DEEFLNU	needful
DEEFLOT	feedlot
DEEFMOR	freedom
DEEFNOR	fore-end
DEEFNRU	unfreed
DEEFNUU	unfeued
DEEFORV	overfed
DEEFPRY	deep-fry
DEEFRTT	fretted
DEEGHIW	weighed
DEEGHOR	hog-deer
DEEGHOW	hogweed
DEEGHSS	ghessed
DEEGILR	leidger
DEEGILS	leg-side
DEEGINR	energid
	reeding
DEEGINS	sdeigne
	seeding
DEEGINW	weeding
DEEGIOR	Geordie
DEEGIPR	pig-deer
DEEGIPW	pigweed
DEEGIPY	pig-eyed
DEEGIRV	diverge
DEEGJRU	rejudge
DEEGLOY	goldeye
DEEGLPR	pledger
DEEGLPT	pledget
DEEGLRS	sledger
DEEGLRU	guelder
DEEGNNO	endogen
DEEGNOO	good-e'en
DEEGOSY	geodesy
DEEGOTU	outedge
DEEHIKV	khedive
DEEHILT	lethied
DEEHKLW	whelked
DEEHLLS	shelled
DEEHLOV	hoveled
DEEHMRU	rheumed
DEEHNOT	hen-toed
DEEHNOY	honeyed
DEEHNPR	prehend
DEEHNUY	unheedy
DEEHPRS	sphered
DEEHRSS	herdess
DEEHTTW	whetted
DEEIINT	dietine
DEEIIPR	epeirid
DEEIIRW	weirdie
DEEIJLL	jellied
DEEIJMM	jemmied
DEEIJTT	jettied
DEEIKLL	killdee
DEEIKMW	△mid-week
DEEIKNN	in-kneed
DEEIKOV	dovekie
DEEILNR	red-line
DEEILNS	linseed
DEEILNY	dyeline
	needily
DEEILOS	oil-seed
	seed-oil
DEEILPP	lip-deep
DEEILPR	replied
DEEILPS	seedlip
DEEILRT	tile-red
DEEILRV	deliver
DEEILRW	wielder

Words marked △ may be spelled also with a capital letter

DEEILRY yielder
DEEILSS idlesse
DEEILST til-seed
DEEILSY seedily
DEEILTU dilutee
DEEILTV devilet
DEEIMMS misdeem
DEEIMNO dominee
DEEIMNR ermined
DEEIMNS desmine
sidemen
DEEIMNT démenti
DEEIMPR demirep
DEEIMPS semiped
DEEIMPT emptied
DEEIMRT demerit
dimeter
DEEIMTT emitted
DEEINNP pennied
DEEINNT dentine
DEEINNU ennuied
DEEINNZ denizen
DEEINOR ordinee
DEEINPY pin-eyed
DEEINRR dernier
DEEINRS nereids
DEEINRU uredine
DEEINRW widener
DEEINRX indexer
DEEINST destine
DEEINSW endwise
sinewed
DEEINSX indexes
DEEINTT dinette
DEEINTU detinue
DEEINTV evident
DEEINVW vinewed
DEEINVX invexed
DEEINWZ wizened
DEEIOPS episode
DEEIOPT epidote
DEEIOPX epoxide
DEEIORS osiered
DEEIPPT peptide
DEEIPRS Perseid
preside
DEEIPRV deprive
DEEIPRX expired
DEEIPSS despise
pedesis
DEEIPST despite
DEEIQRU queried
DEEIRRS desirer
resider
serried
DEEIRRT retired
retried
DEEIRRV redrive
rivered
DEEIRSU residue
DEEIRSV deviser
diverse
DEEIRTU erudite
DEEIRTV riveted
verdite
DEEISSU diseuse
DEEITTV vidette
DEEKKRT trekked
DEEKKSY key-desk
DEEKLRS skelder
DEEKPPS skepped
DEEKPRU peruked
DEELLMS smelled
DEELLPS spelled
DEELLRU dueller
DEELLRW dweller
DEELLRY elderly
DEELLST stelled
DEELLSW swelled
DEELMOR modeler
remodel
DEELMPT templed
DEELMPU deplume
DEELMTT mettled
DEELNOS nose-led
DEELNRS slender
DEELNSS endless
DEELNSY densely
DEELOPR deplore
DEELOPV develop
DEELOPX explode
DEELORU urodele
DEELORV lovered
DEELOSU delouse
DEELOTV dovelet
DEELOTW toweled
DEELOVV devolve
DEELOWY owl-eyed
DEELPRS spelder
DEELPRU prelude
DEELSTT settled
DEELSTW swelted
DEELVXY vexedly
DEEMMST stemmed
DEEMNOV venomed
DEEMNOY moneyed
DEEMNTU unmeted
DEEMORS emerods
DEEMORV removed
DEEMORX exoderm
DEENNOP open-end
DEENNOR enderon
DEENNOS données
DEENNOY doyenne
DEENNPT pendent
DEENNTZ tendenz
DEENNUY ennuyed
DEENOPS spondee
DEENOPT pentode
DEENORS endorse
DEENORT erodent
DEENORW endower
re-endow
DEENPPR perpend
DEENPRS spender
DEENPRT pretend
DEENRRU endurer
DEENRSS redness
DEENRSU end-user
DEENRTU denture
tenured
DEENSUW unsewed
DEENSUX unsexed
DEENUVX unvexed
DEEOPPW pop-weed
DEEOPPY pop-eyed
DEEOPRR pedrero
DEEOPRS deposer
reposed
DEEOPRW powered
DEEOPRY eye-drop
DEEOPSS speedos
DEEOPSX exposed
DEEORRR orderer
reorder
DEEORRS reredos
rose-red
DEEORRV overred
DEEORST oersted
teredos
DEEORTT tetrode
DEEORTW towered
DEEORUV overdue
DEEORVY overdye
DEEOTUW outweed
DEEOTWY two-eyed
DEEPPPR prepped
DEEPPST stepped
DEEPPSU speed-up
DEEPRRU perdure
DEEPRSS depress
pressed
spersed
DEEPRTU reputed
DEEPSUX sexed-up
DEERRSS dresser
redress
re-dress
DEERRUV verdure
DEERSST dessert
tressed
DEERSSU duresse
DEERSTW strewed
DEERSTY dyester
DEERTUX extrude
DEESTTT stetted
DEFFIMO fiefdom
DEFFIOS offside
DEFFISU diffuse
DEFFLLU full-fed
DEFFLMU muffled
DEFFLRU ruffled
DEFFNOR forfend
DEFFNOS send-off
DEFFOPU pouffed
DEFFSTU stuffed

DEFGGIR	frigged
DEFGGLO	flogged
DEFGGOR	frogged
DEFGHHI	high-fed
DEFGINR	fringed
DEFGINU	feuding
DEFGINY	defying
DEFGIOR	firedog
DEFGIRU	figured
DEFGIST	fidgets
DEFGITY	fidgety
DEFGRTU	grufted
DEFHIRS	redfish
DEFHIST	shifted
DEFHLOO	elfhood
DEFHLSU	flushed
DEFIILM	mid-life
DEFIILN	infidel
	infield
DEFIIMS	fideism
DEFIIMW	midwife
DEFIINU	unified
DEFIIST	fideist
DEFILNR	flinder
DEFILNU	unfilde
	unfiled
DEFILOO	folioed
DEFILOS	od's-life
DEFILRU	direful
DEFILST	stifled
DEFILSU	sulfide
DEFILTT	flitted
DEFILXY	fixedly
DEFIMOR	deiform
DEFINOT	fin-toed
DEFINRS	finders
	Friends
DEFINRU	unfired
DEFINSY	densify
DEFINUX	unfixed
DEFINUY	undeify
DEFIORU	foudrie
DEFIPRY	perfidy
DEFIRRT	drifter
DEFIRTT	fritted
DEFIRTU	fruited
DEFIRZZ	frizzed
DEFISTU	feudist
DEFLLOU	doleful
DEFLLUW	dewfull
DEFLNOO	onefold
DEFLNOP	penfold
DEFLNOR	fondler
	forlend
DEFLNOT	tenfold
DEFLNRU	dernful
DEFLOOR	floored
DEFLORU	foulder
DEFLPRU	purfled
DEFLRUU	dureful
DEFMNUU	unfumed
DEFMORS	serfdom
DEFMPRU	rump-fed
DEFNOOR	fordone
DEFNORT	fronted
DEFNORU	founder
	refound
DEFNOSW	snow-fed
DEFORST	defrost
	frosted
DEGGGLO	goggled
DEGGGLU	glugged
DEGGHIN	hedging
DEGGHIW	whigged
DEGGHOS	shogged
DEGGILN	gelding
DEGGINW	wedging
DEGGIPR	prigged
DEGGIRU	druggie
DEGGISW	swigged
DEGGJLO	joggled
DEGGLOR	doggrel
DEGGLOS	slogged
DEGGLPU	plugged
	puggled
DEGGNOO	doggone
DEGGNOU	gudgeon
DEGGNSU	snugged
DEGGORT	trogged
DEGGORY	doggery
DEGGOSS	doggess
DEGGRRU	drugger
DEGGRTU	drugget
DEGHILN	hindleg
DEGHILT	delight
	lighted
DEGHINT	nighted
DEGHIPR	pig-herd
DEGHIST	sighted
DEGHLOO	doghole
DEGHNOT	thonged
DEGHORR	drogher
DEGIILN	eilding
DEGIIMN	Geminid
DEGIKLO	godlike
DEGILLR	grilled
DEGILLU	gullied
DEGILLY	gelidly
DEGILNN	lending
DEGILNO	glenoid
DEGILNU	indulge
DEGILNV	devling
DEGILNW	welding
	wing-led
DEGILOR	gloried
DEGILOV	go-devil
DEGILRR	girdler
DEGILRS	grisled
DEGILRU	guilder
DEGILRW	wergild
DEGILUV	divulge
DEGIMNN	mending
DEGIMNS	smidgen
DEGINNP	pending
DEGINNR	grinned
DEGINNS	sending
DEGINNY	denying
DEGINOP	pidgeon
DEGINOR	groined
	△negroid
DEGINOS	dingoes
DEGINOW	wendigo
	widgeon
	wongied
DEGINRR	grinder
	regrind
DEGINRW	redwing
	wringed
DEGINST	stinged
DEGINSW	swindge
DEGIOOS	goodies
DEGIORR	grodier
DEGIORT	goitred
DEGIPPR	gripped
DEGIQSU	squidge
DEGIRSS	digress
DEGISST	disgest
DEGLMMO	glommed
DEGLMOU	moguled
DEGLNNO	endlong
DEGLNUU	unglued
	unguled
DEGLOPR	pledgor
DEGLOPS	splodge
DEGLOSS	godless
DEGLTTU	glutted
DEGMRSU	smudger
DEGNNOU	dungeon
DEGNOPR	pronged
DEGNORU	guerdon
	undergo
	ungored
DEGNOTU	tongued
DEGNRTU	trudgen
DEGNRUU	unurged
DEGNUVY	ungyved
DEGORST	stodger
DEGORTU	droguet
DEGRRTU	trudger
DEHIIPS	piedish
DEHILMS	dishelm
DEHILNP	delphin
DEHILTY	diethyl
DEHIMMW	whimmed
DEHIMOR	heirdom
	Homerid
DEHIMOS	dishome
DEHIMOT	ethmoid
DEHINNT	thinned
DEHINOP	diphone
DEHINOR	hordein
DEHINPS	endship
DEHINPT	in-depth
DEHINRU	unhired
DEHINSW	Wendish
DEHIORT	theroid

Words marked △ may be spelled also with a capital letter

DEHIOSU	hideous
DEHIOSV	doveish
DEHIOTU	hideout
DEHIPPS	shipped
DEHIPPW	whipped
DEHIRRS	shirred
DEHIRRU	dhurrie
	hurried
DEHIRRW	whirred
DEHIRSU	hurdies
DEHIRSV	△dervish
	shrived
DEHIRTV	thrived
DEHIRTY	dithery
DEHISSW	Swedish
DEHISTT	shitted
DEHIWZZ	whizzed
DEHLMOU	mudhole
DEHLOOT	toehold
DEHLORW	whorled
DEHLOSS	sloshed
DEHLRRU	hurdler
DEHLRSU	hurdles
DEHMORU	Hordeum
DEHMOTY	Methody
DEHNNSU	shunned
DEHNOOW	hoedown
DEHNOPU	unhoped
DEHNORT	thonder
	thorned
	throned
DEHNOTZ	dozenth
DEHNRTU	thunder
DEHOOTT	toothed
DEHOPPS	shopped
DEHOPPW	whopped
DEHOSTT	shotted
DEHOSTW	wet-shod
DEHPPUY	hyped-up
DEIIIRS	iridise
DEIIIRZ	iridize
DEIIKLS	dislike
DEIIKNS	dinkies
DEIILMP	implied
DEIILMT	delimit
	limited
DEIILNV	lived-in
DEIILOS	idolise
DEIILOZ	idolize
DEIIMNO	dominie
DEIIMST	misdiet
DEIIMSZ	midsize
DEIIMVW	midwive
DEIINOT	edition
	tenioid
DEIINRS	insider
DEIINRT	inditer
	nitride
DEIINRU	uridine
DEIINRV	diviner
	drive-in
DEIINSS	insides
DEIINSW	Windies
DEIIORT	diorite
DEIIORV	ivoried
DEIIOSX	oxidise
DEIIOXZ	oxidize
DEIIPPP	dip-pipe
DEIIPRT	dirt-pie
	riptide
	tide-rip
DEIIRTT	tritide
DEIISTT	dietist
DEIJNOR	joinder
DEIJNOT	jointed
DEIJNSU	disjune
DEIJORY	joy-ride
DEIKLLS	deskill
	skilled
DEIKLNR	kindler
DEIKLOR	rodlike
DEIKLRT	kirtled
DEIKMMS	skimmed
DEIKNNS	skinned
DEIKNOS	doe-skin
DEIKNRR	drinker
DEIKNRS	redskin
DEIKNSW	swinked
DEIKNTT	knitted
DEIKORW	die-work
DEIKOSY	disyoke
DEIKPPS	skipped
DEIKRST	skirted
DEILLMO	modelli
DEILLNW	indwell
DEILLOR	dollier
DEILLOV	livelod
DEILLPS	spilled
DEILLQU	quilled
DEILLRR	driller
DEILLRT	trilled
DEILLRV	drevill
DEILLSS	lidless
DEILLSU	ill-used
	sullied
DEILLTW	twilled
DEILMMS	slimmed
DEILMNT	mid-Lent
DEILMNU	unlimed
DEILMOP	implode
DEILMOT	old-time
DEILMOY	myeloid
DEILMPP	pimpled
DEILMWY	mildewy
DEILMXY	mixedly
DEILNNU	unlined
DEILNOO	eidolon
DEILNOS	sondeli
DEILNOT	lentoid
DEILNOU	unoiled
DEILNOW	lie-down
DEILNPS	speldin
	spindle
DEILNRT	tendril
	trindle
DEILNSW	swindle
DEILNSY	snidely
DEILNTU	diluent
	untiled
DEILNTW	indwelt
DEILOPP	Pelopid
DEILOPS	despoil
	soliped
	spoiled
DEILORS	soldier
DEILPPS	slipped
DEILPPU	uppiled
DEILPRU	preludi
DEILPTY	tepidly
DEILPXY	pixy-led
DEILQTU	quilted
DEILRTU	diluter
DEILRTY	tiredly
DEILRVY	devilry
DEILRWY	weirdly
DEILRWZ	wrizled
DEILRZZ	drizzle
DEILSTT	stilted
DEILSTY	distyle
DEIMMMU	mummied
DEIMMPR	primmed
DEIMMRT	midterm
	trimmed
DEIMMSU	mediums
DEIMNNU	minuend
DEIMNOS	misdone
DEIMNRU	unrimed
DEIMNSS	dimness
	missend
DEIMNST	mindset
DEIMNSW	miswend
DEIMNUX	unmixed
DEIMOOR	moidore
DEIMORS	misdoer
DEIMORU	erodium
DEIMOST	modiste
DEIMOTT	omitted
DEIMOTV	vomited
DEIMPRT	dirempt
DEIMPUX	mixed-up
DEIMRUU	uredium
DEIMSTW	Midwest
DEIMSTY	stymied
DEINNNU	nundine
DEINNOP	pinnoed
DEINNOR	endiron
DEINNTU	dunnite
DEINNTW	twinned
DEINOPR	poinder
DEINOPS	dispone
	spinode
DEINOPT	pointed
DEINORS	indorse
	rosined
DEINORU	dourine

DEINORV on-drive
vine-rod
DEINORW windore
DEINOST stonied
DEINPPS snipped
DEINPST stipend
DEINPSU unspide
unspied
DEINPSV pensiv'd
DEINPUW unwiped
DEINRSU insured
DEINRTT trident
DEINRTU intrude
turdine
untired
untride
untried
DEINRTX dextrin
DEINRTY tindery
DEINSST disnest
dissent
DEINSSV vendiss
DEINSTT dentist
distent
stinted
DEINSTU distune
DEINSTY density
destiny
DEINSUZ unsized
DEINUVW unwived
DEIOOST osteoid
DEIOOVV voivode
DEIOOWW woiwode
DEIOPPP poppied
DEIOPRS periods
DEIOPRT diopter
dioptre
peridot
proteid
DEIOPRV provide
DEIOPSS dispose
DEIOPST deposit
posited
topside
DEIOPSU Oedipus
DEIOPSV vespoid
DEIOPTT tiptoed
DEIOPTV pivoted
DEIORRW worried
DEIORSS dossier
DEIORST steroid
storied
DEIORSV devisor
devoirs
visored
DEIORSW weirdos
DEIORTU étourdi
ioduret
outride
DEIORVZ vizored
DEIORWW widower

DEIOSTU outside
tedious
DEIOSTX exodist
DEIOSUV devious
DEIPPRT tripped
DEIPRST striped
DEIPRSY spidery
DEIPSSU upsides
DEIPSTT spitted
DEIPSTU dispute
DEIPSXY pyxides
DEIPTTU puttied
tituped
DEIQTTU quitted
DEIQUZZ quizzed
DEIRRST stirred
DEIRSST dissert
strides
DEIRSTU studier
DEIRSTV strived
DEISSTU studies
DEISTTW twisted
DEITTTW twitted
DEKLNRU knurled
DEKLRSU skudler
DEKNNRU drunken
DEKNOSY donkeys
DEKNOTT knotted
DEKNOUY unyoked
DEKNRTU trunked
DEKOPST desktop
DEKORWY dye-work
keyword
DELLMOO modello
DELLOOW woolled
DELLOPR redpoll
DELLOSU duellos
DELLOVW △lowveld
DELMOOW elmwood
DELMORS smolder
DELMORU moulder
remould
DELMOTT mottled
DELMOUV volumed
DELNORT entrold
DELNORU lounder
roundel
roundle
DELNORY Reynold
DELNOSS oldness
DELNOTW let-down
DELNOTY notedly
DELNOUV unloved
DELNOWY dowlney
DELNPRU plunder
DELNRTU rundlet
trundle
DELNRUU unruled
DELNSSU dulness
DELNUWY unweldy
DELOOPP pleopod
DELOORW woolder

DELOOST Toledos
DELOPPP plopped
DELOPPR Doppler
dropple
DELOPPS slopped
DELOPRT droplet
DELOPRU poulder
pouldre
DELOPTT plotted
DELORRY orderly
DELORSS rodless
DELORST oldster
strodle
DELORTT dottrel
DELORUV louvred
DELOSTT slotted
DELOSZZ sozzled
DELOTUV voluted
DELPSSU plussed
DELRRSU slurred
DELRSTU strudel
DEMMRRU drummer
DEMMSTU stummed
DEMNOOR morendo
DEMNORT mordent
DEMNORY demonry
DEMNOST endmost
DEMNOTU demount
mounted
DEMNOUV unmoved
DEMNPRU rump-end
DEMOOPP popedom
DEMOOPR predoom
DEMOOTT mottoed
DEMOOTU outmode
DEMORWW dew-worm
DEMOSTY modesty
DEMSTTU smutted
DENNORT donnert
tendron
DENNORU enround
DENNOTU unnoted
untoned
DENNOTW town-end
DENNOUW unowned
DENNOUZ unzoned
DENNSTU stunned
DENNTUU untuned
DENOOST stooden
DENOOSW swooned
DENOOTU duotone
DENOOUW unwooed
DENOPPR propend
DENOPRS respond
DENOPRT drop-net
portend
protend
DENOPRU pounder
DENOPRV provend
DENOPSU unposed
DENOPUX expound

DENORRU	rondure
	rounder
	unorder
DENORRW	drowner
DENORSU	resound
	sounder
DENORSW	Wonders
DENORUW	rewound
	wounder
DENOSTU	snouted
DENOSTW	set-down
DENPRTU	prudent
	prunted
	uptrend
DENPSSU	suspend
DENRSSU	undress
DENRSSY	dryness
DENRSUU	unsured
DENSTTU	student
	stunted
DENTUVY	duvetyn
DEOOPRT	torpedo
DEOOPST	stooped
DEOORRT	redroot
DEOORRW	o'erword
DEOPPPR	propped
DEOPPRR	dropper
DEOPPST	stopped
DEOPPSW	swopped
DEOPRWY	powdery
DEOPSTT	spotted
DEOQRTU	torqued
DEORRST	rodster
DEORRSW	sworder
DEORSTW	strowed
	worsted
DEORSTY	destroy
DEORTTT	trotted
DEORTUU	outdure
DEOSSYY	△odyssey
DEOSTTU	duettos
	△testudo
DEOSTTW	swotted
DEOSTUU	duteous
DEOSTUX	tuxedos
DEPRRSU	spurred
DEPRRUY	prudery
DEPRSUU	usurped
DERRSTU	rustred
DERSSTU	trussed
DERSTUU	sutured
DFFGINU	duffing
DFFIIMR	midriff
DFFIIRT	triffid
DFFIMOR	difform
DFFLOOU	foodful
DFFOTUY	off-duty
DFGHIOS	dogfish
	fish-god
DFGIINN	finding
DFGIINY	dignify
DFGILNO	folding
DFGILOP	flip-dog
DFGINNU	funding
DFGINOU	fungoid
DFGLNUY	dung-fly
DFGLOOW	wolf-dog
DFGMOOY	fogydom
DFHILSU	dishful
DFHIMSU	mudfish
DFHINSU	dun-fish
DFILMMO	filmdom
DFILMNU	mindful
DFILNOP	pinfold
DFILOSX	sixfold
DFILOTW	twifold
DFILTUU	dutiful
DFIMNUY	mundify
DFIMOOS	foodism
DFIMORS	disform
DFIOORW	fir-wood
DFIRSTY	dry-fist
DFLMOOU	doomful
DFLOOTU	fold-out
DFLOOTW	twofold
DFLOPRY	dropfly
DFLOTWY	twyfold
DFNNOUU	unfound
DFNORUY	foundry
DFOORTY	dry-foot
DGGGIIN	digging
DGGGINO	dogging
DGGHIOS	doggish
DGGIILN	gilding
	gliding
DGGIINR	girding
	ridging
DGGIINU	△guiding
DGGIKNO	god-king
DGGILNO	godling
	lodging
DGGNORU	ungorg'd
DGHHOOO	hoghood
DGHIILN	hidling
	hilding
DGHIINS	dishing
	shindig
DGHILNO	holding
DGHILNY	hylding
DGHILOS	goldish
DGHILPY	diglyph
DGHINTU	hind-gut
	undight
DGHIOOS	goodish
DGHIOPS	dogship
	godship
DGHORTU	drought
DGHOTUY	doughty
DGIIKLN	kidling
DGIILLN	dilling
DGIILNS	sliding
DGIILNW	wilding
DGIILRY	rigidly
DGIIMMN	dimming
DGIIMNN	minding
DGIIMNS	smidgin
DGIIMOP	pigmoid
DGIIMOS	sigmoid
DGIINNN	dinning
DGIINNW	winding
DGIINOS	indigos
DGIINOV	voiding
DGIINOW	windigo
DGIINPP	dipping
DGIINPU	pinguid
DGIINRV	driving
DGIINST	tidings
DGIINTY	dignity
	tidying
DGIIORT	tigroid
DGIKMNO	kingdom
DGIKNOR	Dorking
	king-rod
DGIKNOS	dogskin
DGILLOY	godlily
DGILNOR	girlond
	lording
DGILNYY	dyingly
DGILRUY	guildry
DGIMNOO	dooming
DGIMOPY	pygmoid
DGINNNO	donning
DGINNNU	dunning
DGINNOU	undoing
DGINNUW	windgun
DGINNUY	undying
DGINOPP	dopping
DGINORV	droving
DGINORW	wording
DGINOSW	disgown
DGINOTT	dotting
DGIOPRY	prodigy
DGIORSU	Gordius
DGIQSUY	squidgy
DGISSTU	disgust
DGLNOUY	ungodly
DGLOOOW	logwood
DGLOPSY	splodgy
DGLOSYY	dyslogy
DGMNOOO	moon-god
DGMOPRU	gumdrop
DGMORUU	gurudom
DGNOOOR	godroon
DGNOOOS	good-son
DGNOOOW	good-now
DGNOORS	drongos
DGNOOTW	dogtown
DGNORSU	grounds
DGOORTT	dogtrot
DHIILNS	hidlins
DHIILOT	lithoid
DHIILSW	wildish
DHIIMMS	dimmish
DHIIMNO	hominid
DHIIMPS	midship
DHIINRU	hirudin

DHIIOPX	xiphoid
DHIIORZ	rhizoid
DHIIOST	histoid
DHIKRSU	Kurdish
DHIKSSU	duskish
DHILLOS	dollish
DHILLSU	dullish
DHILMUY	humidly
DHILNOP	△dolphin
DHILOST	doltish
DHILOSU	loudish
DHILPSU	ludship
DHILPSY	sylphid
DHILRTY	thirdly
DHIMOPR	dimorph
DHIMORU	humidor
	mid-hour
	rhodium
DHIMPSU	dumpish
DHINNOS	donnish
DHINNSU	dunnish
DHINOPS	donship
DHINOPY	hypnoid
DHINORS	dishorn
	dronish
DHINSTU	tun-dish
DHIOPTY	typhoid
DHIORSW	wordish
DHIORTY	thyroid
DHIPRSU	prudish
DHIPRSY	syrphid
DHJOPRU	jodhpur
DHKMOOU	mudhook
DHKORSY	droshky
DHLMOOU	hoodlum
DHMMRUU	humdrum
DHMNOYY	hymnody
DHNNOOU	nunhood
DHOOPRU	uphoord
DHOORSU	rhodous
DHOORTT	hot-trod
DHOPRSU	pushrod
DHORSSU	shrouds
DHORSUY	hydrous
	shroudy
DHORTUY	drouthy
DHORXYY	hydroxy
DIIIMRU	iridium
DIIIMSV	divisim
DIIINPS	insipid
DIIJNOS	disjoin
DIIKKNS	kidskin
DIIKLNS	dislink
DIIKNOT	doitkin
DIILLST	distill
DIILLVY	lividly
DIILMNS	dislimn
DIILMOS	idolism
DIILMTY	timidly
DIILNNU	indulin
DIILNWY	windily
DIILOST	idolist
DIILRSU	silurid
DIILRTY	dirtily
DIILVVY	vividly
DIILYZZ	dizzily
DIIMNOR	midiron
DIIMNOS	Odinism
DIIMORS	diorism
DIIMSSS	dismiss
DIIMSUV	vidimus
DIINNOT	tondini
DIINOQU	quinoid
DIINORS	sordini
DIINOST	Odinist
DIIOPRS	spiroid
DIIORSV	divisor
DIIPPRT	drip-tip
DIITUVY	viduity
DIJOSTU	judoist
DIKKNRU	Dunkirk
DIKLNOR	lordkin
DIKLNRY	kiln-dry
DIKLSUY	duskily
DIKNNOS	non-skid
DIKNORV	dvornik
DIKOORT	drookit
DIKORTU	droukit
DILLOSY	solidly
DILLPSY	psyllid
DILLRUY	luridly
DILMNRU	drumlin
DILMOOY	moodily
DILMORU	oil-drum
DILMOST	mistold
DILMOSU	solidum
DILMOSY	odylism
DILMTUY	tumidly
DILNNSU	dunlins
DILNOOS	oodlins
DILNOPT	diplont
DILNOQU	quodlin
DILNORT	introld
DILNOSU	unsolid
DILNOXY	indoxyl
DILNPSU	lispund
DILNPSY	spindly
DILORTU	dilutor
DILORWY	rowdily
	wordily
DILOSSU	dulosis
	solidus
DILOSTY	styloid
DILRYZZ	drizzly
DILSTUY	dustily
DIMMMOU	mim-mou'd
DIMMOST	midmost
DIMNNOO	midnoon
DIMNNOS	donnism
DIMNNOT	△dinmont
DIMNOOS	dominos
DIMNOPU	impound
DIMOPSU	spodium
DIMORSW	misword
DIMRTUU	triduum
DIMRUUV	duumvir
DINNOOR	rondino
DINNOOT	tondino
DINNOPR	non-drip
DINNOPW	pindown
DINOORS	indoors
	sordino
DINOORT	tordion
DINOOST	isodont
DINORSW	Windsor
DINORTU	turdion
DINORWW	windrow
DINOSTW	sit-down
DINOSWW	windows
DINOTUW	outwind
DINPRSY	spin-dry
DINPSTU	pin-dust
DIOORST	disroot
DIOORTT	ridotto
DIOPRST	disport
	torpids
DIOPRTY	tripody
DIOPSST	dispost
DIORRST	stridor
DIORSTT	distort
DIOSSTU	studios
DIOSUUV	viduous
DIPRSTU	disrupt
DIRSTUY	surdity
DKMOPSU	musk-pod
DKNNRUU	undrunk
DKOOOSZ	odzooks
DLLORWY	worldly
DLMMPUU	mud-lump
DLMNOOY	mylodon
DLMNOUU	unmould
DLMOSUU	modulus
DLNNOOY	Londony
DLNOOWW	low-down
DLNOPRU	puldron
DLNOPSY	spondyl
DLNORUY	roundly
DLNOSUY	soundly
DLOOPPY	polypod
DLOOPTY	tylopod
DLOOPUY	duopoly
DLOOPWY	plywood
DLOPRUY	proudly
DLOSTUW	wouldst
DMNNOOO	Monodon
DMNOOOP	monopod
DMNOOTW	towmond
DMORTUW	mudwort
DNNORUU	unround
DNNORUW	rundown
	run-down
DNNOSUU	unsound
DNNOSUW	sundown
DNNOUUW	unwound
DNNRTUU	turndun
DNOOPTW	top-down

Words marked △ may be spelled also with a capital letter

DNOORTU orotund
DNOOTUW nutwood
DNOOTWW two-down
DNOPRUU round-up
DNOPTUW put-down
DNOPUUW upwound
DNOSSUW swounds
'swounds
DNPRSUY spun-dry
DOOORSU odorous
DOOORTU outdoor
DOOPRSY prosody
DOOPRTU drop-out
DOOPSTU upstood
DOORRTU dortour
DORUVYY dyvoury

E

EEEEFRR referee
EEEEGTX exegete
EEEENTT entêtée
EEEFFFO feoffee
EEEFFOR offeree
EEEFGRU refugee
EEEFHRS shereef
EEEFLRR fleerer
EEEFMNR freemen
EEEFORS foresee
EEEFRRZ freezer
EEEGHNW wheenge
EEEGILS elegise
EEEGILZ elegize
EEEGINP epigene
EEEGINR greenie
EEEGIPR perigee
EEEGLNT genteel
EEEGMRR remerge
EEEGNNO Neogene
EEEGNOS Genoese
EEEGNPR epergne
EEEGNRR greener
reneger
EEEGNRU renegue
EEEGNRV revenge
EEEGNSS geneses
EEEGNTT genette
EEEGRRT greeter
regreet
EEEGRUX exergue
EEEHILW wheelie
EEEHLLN Hellene
EEEHLNW enwheel
EEEHLOY eye-hole
EEEHLPW wheeple
EEEHLRW wheeler
EEEHLWZ wheezle
EEEHNRW whene'er
EEEHRRW where'er
EEEHRST seether
EEEHSTT esthete
EEEILPT Peelite
EEEILRV relieve
EEEIMMS meemies
EEEIMNT emetine
EEEIMPR preemie
EEEIMRT eremite
EEEINQU queenie
EEEINSS Sienese
EEEIPSU épuisée
EEEIRRT retiree
EEEIRRV reverie
EEEIRSZ reseize
EEEISTW △sweetie
EEEJNPY jeepney
EEEJPRS jeepers
EEEKLLU ukelele
EEEKLNR kneeler
EEEKLNS sleeken
EEEKLNX Kleenex®
EEEKLPW ekpwele
EEEKLRS sleeker
EEEKNPT keepnet
EEEKRST skeeter
EEELMNT element
EEELMPX exemple
EEELNST stelene
EEELNSV elevens
EEELPRS sleeper
speeler
EEELPRT replete
EEELPST steeple
EEELRSV sleever
EEELRTV leveret
EEELSSY eyeless
EEELTTX teletex
EEEMNSS Nemeses
EEEMORT eroteme
EEEMRTX extreme
EEENNPT pentene
EEENNRT étrenne
EEENNTT entente
EEENPRT pre-teen
terpene
EEENPRV prevene
EEENPST ensteep
steepen
EEENPSW ensweep
EEENPSX expense
EEENRRS sneerer
EEENRRT enterer
re-enter
terreen
terrene
EEENRRV venerer
EEENRRW renewer
EEENRSZ sneezer
EEENRTV eventer
EEENRTX externe
EEENRUV revenue
unreeve
EEENSTW sweeten
EEENSTX extense
EEENSWY sweeney
EEEOPPT peep-toe
EEEORSV oversee
EEEORSY eyesore
EEEORVY overeye
EEEPRSS peeress
EEEPRST estrepe
steeper
EEEPRSV peevers
EEEPRSW sweeper
EEEPRSZ spreeze
EEEPRTU Euterpe
EEEQRRU requere
EEEQSUZ squeeze
EEERRRV reverer
EEERRST steerer
EEERRSV reserve
reverse
EEERSSS seeress
EEERSTV Everest
EEERSUV rêveuse
EEERSUW seruewe
EEERSVW servewe
EEERTTW tweeter
EEFFFNO enfeoff
EEFFFOR feoffer
EEFFGLU effulge
EEFFINR fen-fire
EEFFINT fifteen
EEFFNOS offense
EEFFORR offerer
EEFFSTU suffete
EEFGILN feeling
fleeing
EEFGINR feering
freeing
reefing
EEFGIRT fig-tree
EEFGLLU gleeful
EEFGLOR foreleg
EEFGLOS solfège
EEFHINW hen-wife
EEFHISY fisheye
EEFHLNS enflesh
EEFHLRS flesher
herself
EEFHNRS freshen
EEFHORT thereof
EEFHORW whereof
EEFHRRS fresher
refresh
EEFHRRU Fuehrer
EEFHRST freshet
EEFILLX flexile
EEFILNO olefine
EEFILOR forelie
EEFILRT fertile
EEFILST felsite
liefest
EEFIMRT femiter
EEFINRR refiner
EEFINRW fire-new
EEFINSS finesse

EEFIRRT	ferrite
	fir-tree
EEFISTV	festive
EEFLLRU	fueller
EEFLLTY	fleetly
EEFLMTU	teemful
EEFLNNO	enfelon
EEFLNOS	oneself
EEFLNRS	△fresnel
EEFLOOV	foveole
EEFLORS	forlese
EEFLRRU	ferrule
EEFLRTT	fettler
EEFLRTU	fleuret
EEFLRUX	flexure
EEFMNOR	foremen
EEFMNRT	ferment
EEFMOTT	mofette
EEFMPRU	perfume
EEFMSTW	fewmets
EEFMTTU	fumette
EEFNRRY	fernery
EEFNRTV	fervent
EEFNSSW	fewness
EEFORRV	forever
EEFOTTU	fouetté
EEFPRSU	perfuse
EEFRRSU	refuser
EEFRRTU	refuter
EEFRRTY	ferrety
EEFRSTT	fetters
EEGGHTU	thuggee
EEGGILN	negligé
	négligé
EEGGISV	veggies
EEGGKRS	skegger
EEGGNOR	engorge
EEGGNOY	geogeny
EEGGORR	regorge
EEGGORU	gougère
EEGGPRU	puggree
EEGHILN	heeling
EEGHINY	hygiene
EEGHIRW	reweigh
	weigher
EEGHLNU	leughen
EEGHNRT	greenth
EEGHNRY	greyhen
EEGIIRS	griesie
EEGIJNR	jeering
EEGIKLN	keeling
EEGIKNN	keening
EEGIKNP	keeping
EEGIKNR	reeking
EEGIKNT	kitenge
EEGILNP	peeling
EEGILNR	leering
	reeling
EEGILNS	seeling
EEGILNT	△gentile
EEGILRV	veliger
EEGILST	elegist
EEGIMMR	immerge
EEGIMNR	regimen
EEGIMNS	seeming
EEGIMNT	meeting
	teeming
EEGIMRS	remiges
EEGINNR	enginer
	erg-nine
	ingener
EEGINNU	genuine
	ingénue
EEGINNV	eevning
	evening
EEGINOP	epigone
EEGINOR	E-region
EEGINOS	soignée
EEGINPW	weeping
EEGINRS	greisen
EEGINRT	integer
EEGINRV	veering
EEGINSS	△genesis
EEGINSW	seewing
EEGINTV	ventige
EEGINTW	weeting
EEGINTX	exigent
EEGIOST	egotise
EEGIOTZ	egotize
EEGIRRV	griever
EEGIRTT	tergite
EEGIRTU	guérite
EEGISTV	vestige
EEGKNOR	kerogen
EEGKNRU	gerenuk
EEGLLOR	log-reel
EEGLLSS	legless
EEGLMMU	gemmule
EEGLNOR	erelong
EEGLNOU	eugenol
EEGLNOZ	lozenge
EEGLNRY	greenly
EEGLNST	lengest
EEGLORV	leg-over
EEGLRST	leg-rest
EEGLRTY	telergy
EEGMMRY	gemmery
EEGMNOS	emonges
EEGMNST	segment
EEGNORS	Negroes
EEGNPTV	vent-peg
EEGNPUX	expunge
EEGNRSS	△negress
EEGNSSU	genuses
EEGNSTU	guesten
EEGOOPY	poogyee
EEGOPRT	protégé
EEGORTV	overget
EEGORTX	Gore-Tex®
EEGOSSS	gessoes
EEGPRUX	expurge
EEGRRSS	regress
EEGRRSU	resurge
EEGRRUY	Gruyère
EEGRSSU	guesser
EEGRSTU	gesture
EEHHIMW	Heimweh
EEHHRTT	thether
EEHHRTW	whether
EEHHSTW	wheesht
EEHILLR	hellier
EEHILMN	hem-line
EEHILPS	ephelis
EEHILPV	Pehlevi
EEHILRW	whilere
EEHILST	sheltie
EEHILSX	helixes
EEHIMMS	mishmee
EEHIMNO	hemione
EEHIMPT	epithem
EEHIMST	Shemite
EEHINOR	heroine
EEHINRR	errhine
EEHINRS	henries
EEHINRT	neither
	therein
EEHINRW	wherein
EEHIORS	heroise
EEHIORZ	heroize
EEHIPRT	prithee
EEHIPSV	peevish
EEHIPTT	epithet
EEHIRSS	heiress
	hérissé
EEHIRST	heister
EEHIRSV	shrieve
EEHISTV	thieves
EEHKLOY	keyhole
EEHKLSS	shekels
EEHKOOY	eyehook
EEHLLMP	phellem
EEHLLNS	enshell
EEHLLRS	sheller
EEHLMMW	whemmle
EEHLPRT	telpher
EEHLRST	shelter
EEHLRSW	welsher
EEHLRSY	sheerly
EEHLSSU	hueless
EEHLSSV	shelves
EEHLSTT	shtetel
EEHMNOP	phoneme
EEHMNRU	enrheum
EEHMNRY	mynheer
EEHMORT	theorem
EEHMRUX	exhumer
EEHNNOS	shoneen
EEHNNRY	hennery
EEHNOPT	potheen
EEHNORT	thereon
EEHNORW	Erewhon
	nowhere
	whereon
EEHNOST	hose-net
EEHNOSW	Wheeson
EEHNRTU	Ruthene

EEHNSTU enthuse
EEHNSTV seventh
EEHOOPW whoopee
EEHOPRT hop-tree
EEHOPRU euphroe
EEHOPSS sheepos
EEHORRS Hereros
EEHORST heteros
EEHORSU rehouse
EEHORSW whereso
EEHORTT thereto
EEHORTW whereto
EEHORVW however
whoever
EEHOSTY eye-shot
EEHPRST hepster
sperthe
EEHPRTY prythee
pr'ythee
EEHRRTW wherret
EEHRTTW whetter
EEHRVWY whyever
EEHSTUY shut-eye
EEIIMPR riempie
EEIIMRT emeriti
EEIIMST itemise
EEIIMTZ itemize
EEIINRT erinite
niterie
EEIINTV invitee
EEIIRRV rivière
EEIISTV visitee
EEIKLLS skellie
EEIKLMW ewe-milk
EEIKLNY keyline
EEIKLPT pikelet
EEIKLST sleekit
EEIKNPY pink-eye
EEIKNRT kernite
EEIKNWY eye-wink
EEIKPPY pipe-key
EEIKRST keister
EEIKSTT steekit
EEIKTTT tektite
EEILLMT mellite
EEILLMY mill-eye
EEILLOR Lorelei
EEILLPS ellipse
EEILLRS leisler
EEILLRT treille
EEILLSW wellies
EEILMNR ermelin
EEILMPT implete
EEILMRV vermeil
EEILMVV Mevlevi
EEILNNO △leonine
EEILNNT lenient
EEILNNV enliven
EEILNOR eloiner
EEILNPS pensile
EEILNRT Trilene®
EEILNRV livener
EEILNSS sensile
EEILNST setline
tensile
EEILNTT entitle
EEILNTV veinlet
EEILOPT petiole
EEILORT oil-tree
troelie
EEILORV overlie
relievo
EEILOST estoile
EEILOTZ zeolite
EEILPRR replier
EEILPRS spieler
EEILPRT perlite
reptile
EEILPRU puerile
EEILPSS pelisse
EEILPST △epistle
EEILQRU relique
EEILRRV reliver
reviler
EEILRST leister
sterile
EEILRSU leisure
EEILRSV servile
EEILRTT retitle
EEILRVZ Elzevir
EEILSSS sessile
EEILSST telesis
tieless
EEILSSU ileuses
EEILSTV lievest
EEILSTX sextile
EEILSUV elusive
EEILTTX textile
EEILVWY weevily
EEIMMNS immense
EEIMMRS immerse
EEIMMSS misseem
EEIMNNO nominee
EEIMNNT eminent
EEIMNOS semeion
EEIMNOT one-time
EEIMNRV minever
EEIMNSS Meissen
△nemesis
siemens
EEIMNSW misween
EEIMNTT minette
EEIMOPS episome
EEIMOPT epitome
EEIMORS isomere
EEIMOSS meioses
EEIMOTV emotive
EEIMPRR premier
reprime
EEIMPRS emprise
imprese
premise
spireme
EEIMPRT emptier
EEIMPST empties
septime
EEIMQRU requiem
EEIMRRT trireme
EEIMRST triseme
EEIMRTT emitter
termite
EEIMSST △métisse
EEINNNP pennine
EEINNPS pennies
EEINNRT interne
EEINNRU neurine
EEINNRV enriven
innerve
nervine
EEINNST intense
EEINNTW entwine
EEINOPR pereion
pioneer
EEINOTW Owenite
EEINPPS pepsine
EEINPRR repiner
EEINPRS erepsin
EEINPRT Petrine
EEINPRZ prenzie
EEINPSS penises
EEINPST pentise
EEINPSV pensive
vespine
EEINQRU enquire
inquere
EEINQTU quieten
EEINQUY queynie
EEINRRS resiner
EEINRRT reinter
rentier
terrine
EEINRRV vernier
EEINRST trenise
EEINRSV inverse
versine
EEINRSY Erinyes
EEINRTU neurite
retinue
reunite
uterine
EEINSST sestine
EEINSTV tensive
EEINSTX sixteen
EEINSTY syenite
EEIOPPT epitope
EEIOPST poetise
EEIOPTZ poetize
EEIORRS rosiere
EEIORSV erosive
EEIOSST isoetes
EEIPPST peptise
EEIPPTT pipette
EEIPPTZ peptize
EEIPQRU perique
re-equip
repique

EEIPRRR	Perrier®
	perrier
EEIPRRS	reprise
	respire
EEIPRRV	reprive
EEIPRRZ	reprize
EEIPRSS	pressie
EEIPRST	respite
EEIPRSV	previse
EEIPRVW	preview
EEIPRZZ	prezzie
EEIQRRU	require
EEIQRSU	esquire
EEIQRTU	quieter
	requite
EEIRRRT	retirer
	terrier
EEIRRSV	reversi
	reviser
EEIRRTV	riveret
	riveter
EEIRRTW	rewrite
EEIRRVV	reviver
EEIRSSU	reissue
EEIRSSV	ivresse
EEIRSTV	restive
	Servite
	sievert
	veriest
EEIRSTX	re-exist
EEIRSUZ	seizure
EEIRTVV	vetiver
EEITUXZ	zeuxite
EEJLLMU	jumelle
EEJLRWY	jewelry
EEJNOOR	rejoneo
EEJNORS	rejones
EEJNORY	enjoyer
EEJNOSS	Joneses
EEJPRRU	perjure
EEJQRRU	jerquer
EEKKOTV	vetkoek
EEKKRRT	trekker
EEKLLNV	knevell
EEKLLSY	sleekly
EEKLLUU	ukulele
EEKLNNS	kennels
EEKLNOS	keelson
EEKLOOS	look-see
EEKLRST	kestrel
	skelter
EEKLRSZ	Szekler
EEKLSSY	keyless
EEKLSYZ	Szekely
EEKNOTY	keynote
EEKNPSU	knees-up
EEKNSST	Knesset
EEKNSTU	netsuke
EELLMOS	Moselle
EELLMRS	merells
	smeller
EELLMRV	vermell
EELLNOV	novelle
EELLORS	roselle
EELLORZ	rozelle
EELLPRS	pre-sell
	respell
	speller
EELLQRU	queller
EELLRSW	sweller
EELLSTW	well-set
EELMMOP	pommelé
EELMMPU	emplume
EELMNOO	oenomel
EELMOPR	plerome
EELMOPT	leptome
EELMORW	eelworm
EELMPST	stempel
	stemple
EELMPTT	templet
EELMRST	smelter
EELMRSU	lemures
EELMSTT	stemlet
EELNOPV	envelop
EELNOSV	Slovene
EELNOSY	esloyne
EELNOTT	notelet
EELNOTU	toluene
EELNPSY	spleeny
EELNQUY	queenly
EELNRST	slenter
EELNRTT	lettern
EELNRUV	nervule
EELNSTU	unsteel
EELNSTY	enstyle
	tensely
EELNTTU	lunette
EELOPRS	leprose
EELOPRX	explore
EELOPTU	eelpout
EELORSV	resolve
EELORTT	lorette
EELORVV	evolver
	revolve
EELOSST	osselet
	toeless
EELOSTT	teleost
EELOTUV	evolute
	velouté
EELPPRX	perplex
EELPQRU	prequel
EELPRST	Prestel®
	spelter
EELPRSU	repulse
EELPRSY	sleepry
EELPRTZ	pretzel
EELPRUX	plexure
EELPRVY	replevy
EELPSTY	steeply
EELPSUX	expulse
EELQRUY	queerly
EELRRVY	revelry
EELRSST	tressel
EELRSSU	rulesse
EELRSTT	letters
	settler
	sterlet
	trestle
EELRSTW	swelter
	wrestle
EELRSTY	restyle
	tersely
EELRSTZ	seltzer
EELSSSU	useless
EELSSSX	sexless
EELSTUY	eustyle
EELSTVW	twelves
EELSTWY	sweetly
EELTVVY	velvety
EEMMNOT	memento
EEMMOSU	mousmee
EEMMRST	stemmer
EEMNNOV	envenom
EEMNOOS	someone
EEMNOOY	mooneye
EEMNORY	moneyer
EEMNOST	temenos
EEMNPTU	umpteen
EEMOORT	me-tooer
EEMOOSW	woesome
EEMOPRR	emperor
EEMOPRT	tempore
EEMOPRV	premove
EEMOPRW	empower
EEMORRS	remorse
EEMORRU	uromere
EEMORRV	remover
EEMPPRT	pre-empt
EEMPRRT	preterm
EEMPRSS	empress
EEMPRSU	presume
	supreme
	suprême
EEMPRTT	△tempter
EEMPRTU	permute
EEMPSTT	tempest
EEMRRUU	remueur
EEMRSUX	murexes
EEMSTTU	musette
EENNORT	enteron
	tenoner
EENNORU	neurone
EENNOSS	oneness
EENNOTT	nonette
EENNOTY	neoteny
EENNPTU	Neptune
EENNQUU	unqueen
EENNRUV	unnerve
EENNSSU	unsense
EENNSSW	newness
EENOPPR	prepone
	propene
EENOPPT	peptone
EENOPST	one-step
	pentose
	posteen

EENORRV	overren
EENORTU	Euronet
EENORTV	overnet
EENOSSY	essoyne
EENOSTV	Ventôse
	ventose
EENPPRT	perpent
EENPRST	present
	△serpent
EENPRTV	prevent
EENPRTW	pew-rent
EENPSTY	stepney
EENQSTU	sequent
EENRRSU	ensurer
EENRRTY	re-entry
EENRRUV	nervure
EENRSTT	testern
EENRSTW	△western
EENRSTY	styrene
	yestern
EENRTTU	nut-tree
EENRTUV	venture
EENSSST	setness
EENSSTW	wetness
EENSTTY	teentsy
EENSTUW	unsweet
EENSTVY	seventy
EEOOPRS	operose
EEOPPRS	prepose
EEOPPTU	outpeep
EEOPRRV	reprove
EEOPRSX	exposer
EEOPRTT	treetop
EEOPRTU	outpeer
EEOPSSS	speoses
EEOPSST	poetess
EEOPSSU	espouse
	poseuse
EEOPSTT	steep-to
EEOPSTY	eye-spot
EEOPTUW	outweep
EEOQRTU	requote
EEORRST	restore
EEORRSV	reverso
EEORRTU	reroute
EEORRTV	evertor
EEORRTW	rewrote
EEORRVV	over-rev
EEORSST	osseter
	stereos
EEORSTT	rosette
EEORSTV	estover
	overset
EEORSTX	xerotes
EEORSTY	esotery
EEORSUV	oeuvres
	overuse
EEORSVW	oversew
EEORTUV	ouverte
EEPPPRY	peppery
EEPPRST	stepper
EEPPRSX	Perspex®
EEPPSUW	upsweep
EEPPSUY	eupepsy
EEPRRSS	presser
	repress
	re-press
EEPRRSU	peruser
EEPRRTV	pervert
EEPRRVY	repryve
EEPRSSU	Perseus
EEPRSSV	△vespers
EEPRSSX	express
EEPRSTT	pretest
EEPRSTU	pertuse
EEPRSTX	sexpert
EEPRTTX	pretext
EEPSTTY	typeset
EEQRRUY	equerry
EEQRSTU	quester
	request
EEQSUYZ	squeezy
EERRSTW	strewer
	wrester
EERRSVW	swerver
EERRSVY	servery
EERRTTU	reutter
	utterer
EERRTTY	rettery
EERSSTT	streets
EERSSUY	seysure
EERSTTT	strette
EERSTTU	trustee
EERSTTY	streety
EERSTUV	versute
	vesture
EERSUVW	survewe
EERTTUX	texture
EESSTTT	sestett
EESTTTX	sextett
EFFFLOT	left-off
EFFFOOR	feoffor
	off-fore
EFFGINR	reffing
EFFHILW	whiffle
EFFHIOV	hive-off
EFFHIRS	sheriff
EFFHIRW	whiffer
EFFHITW	whiffet
EFFHLSU	shuffle
EFFIIST	fifties
EFFIKLS	skiffle
EFFILLU	lifeful
EFFILNO	off-line
EFFILNS	sniffle
EFFILPR	piffler
EFFILRR	riffler
EFFILRY	firefly
EFFINRS	sniffer
EFFINST	stiffen
EFFIOPR	piffero
EFFIORT	forfeit
EFFIOST	off-site
EFFIRST	restiff
EFFLLOS	sell-off
EFFLLOW	well-off
EFFLMRU	muffler
EFFLNSU	snuffle
EFFLOSU	souffle
	soufflé
EFFLRRU	ruffler
EFFLRTU	fretful
	truffle
EFFNRSU	snuffer
EFFNRUU	unruffe
EFFOORR	offeror
EFFOPRR	proffer
EFFPRUY	puffery
EFFRSTU	stuffer
EFFSSUU	suffuse
EFGGILP	egg-flip
EFGGIRR	frigger
EFGGIRY	figgery
EFGHIMS	gemfish
EFGHIRT	fighter
	freight
EFGILMN	Fleming
EFGILNR	flinger
EFGILNS	selfing
EFGILNT	felting
EFGIMNT	figment
EFGINNP	pfennig
EFGINNR	ferning
EFGINOR	foreign
EFGINRS	fingers
EFGINRU	gunfire
EFGIORV	forgive
EFGIRRT	grifter
EFGLNTU	fulgent
EFGLORT	froglet
EFGLOSS	fogless
EFGNOOR	forgone
EFGORRU	ferrugo
EFGORRY	forgery
EFGORTU	foregut
EFHIINS	fineish
EFHIJSW	jewfish
EFHILMS	△flemish
	himself
EFHILSS	selfish
EFHILST	leftish
EFHILTY	heftily
EFHINNS	fennish
EFHINST	fish-net
	net-fish
EFHIRSS	serfish
EFHIRST	shifter
EFHIRSY	fishery
EFHISUW	huswife
EFHLLPU	helpful
EFHLLSY	fleshly
EFHLNSU	unflesh
EFHLOOX	foxhole
EFHLOPU	hopeful
EFHLOST	elf-shot
EFHLRSU	flusher

EFHLRSY freshly
EFHLSTY thyself
EFHLTTW △twelfth
EFHNORT forhent
EFHRRTU further
EFIILMS misfile
EFIILRT fitlier
EFIILRY fierily
EFIILSS fissile
EFIIMRS misfire
EFIINPR pin-fire
EFIINPV fivepin
EFIINRU unifier
EFIISSV fissive
EFIJLLY jellify
EFIJLOR frijole
EFIJLOT jetfoil
EFIKRRS frisker
EFIKRST frisket
EFILLMS misfell
EFILLOO foliole
EFILLOW low-life
EFILLUW wileful
EFILMNU fulmine
EFILMOT filemot
EFILMSS selfism
EFILMST filmset
leftism
EFILNOX flexion
EFILNSS finless
EFILOOS floosie
foliose
EFILOOZ floozie
EFILOPR profile
pro-life
EFILORT trefoil
EFILOSX sexfoil
EFILOVX fox-evil
EFILPPR flipper
EFILPPU pipeful
EFILPRY pilfery
EFILPTT felt-tip
EFILQUY liquefy
EFILRRT trifler
EFILRST stifler
EFILRTT flitter
EFILRVV flivver
EFILRZZ frizzle
EFILSST selfist
EFILSTT leftist
EFILSTU sulfite
EFILUVX fluxive
EFIMMRU fermium
EFIMNOR fermion
EFIMNTT fitment
EFIMOST fomites
EFIMTTU fumetti
EFINNOR △inferno
EFINNOS no-fines
EFINNSU funnies
EFINOPR forpine
EFINRST snifter
EFINRSU infuser
EFINRUY reunify
EFINSST fitness
EFIOOST △footsie
EFIOPRR porifer
EFIOPRT firepot
EFIORRT rotifer
EFIORRU Fourier
EFIORST foister
△forties
EFIPPRR fripper
EFIPRTY petrify
EFIRRRU furrier
EFIRRSU friseur
frisure
EFIRRTT fritter
EFIRRTU friture
fruiter
EFIRRTY terrify
EFIRSSU fissure
EFIRSTU surfeit
EFIRSTW swifter
EFIRSVY versify
EFIRTTU turfite
EFIRTUV furtive
EFIRTUX fixture
EFISTTT fittest
EFISTTY testify
EFJLSTU jestful
EFKLMNO menfolk
EFKLMOR merfolk
EFKLNUY flunkey
EFKLOPU pokeful
EFKLPSU skepful
EFLLSTU fullest
EFLMOSU fulsome
EFLMPRU frumple
EFLMSUU museful
EFLNORT forlent
EFLNORU fleuron
EFLNORW fern-owl
EFLNORY felonry
EFLNOSU sulfone
EFLNOTT fletton
fontlet
EFLNSSU fulness
EFLNSTU nestful
EFLNSUY synfuel
EFLNTTU tentful
EFLNTTY tent-fly
EFLNTUU tuneful
EFLOORR floorer
forlore
EFLOORS forsloe
EFLOORY foolery
EFLOORZ foozler
EFLORSU ourself
EFLORSW flowers
EFLORTT fortlet
EFLORTW felwort
EFLORVY flyover
overfly
EFLORWW werwolf
EFLORWY flowery
EFLOSSW self-sow
EFLPRUY preyful
EFLPSTU pestful
EFLRSTU fluster
restful
EFLRTTU flutter
EFLSTTY test-fly
EFLSTUZ zestful
EFMNOOT footmen
EFMOORZ zoeform
EFMOPRR perform
preform
EFMOPRT △pomfret
EFMOTTU fumetto
EFMPRUY perfumy
EFMRTUY furmety
EFNNORT fornent
EFNNORU Nurofen®
EFNNOTU unoften
EFNOOST festoon
EFNOOTT ten-foot
EFNORRU forerun
EFNORTU fortune
EFNORTW forwent
EFNRSTU funster
EFOOPRR reproof
EFOOPRS spoofer
EFOOPRT foretop
poofter
EFOORTW woofter
EFOPPRY foppery
EFOPRSS profess
EFOPRSU profuse
EFOPRTU poufter
EFOPRTY torpefy
EFORRSU ferrous
EFORRTY torrefy
EFORRUV fervour
EFORSSU fourses
EFPRTUY putrefy
EFPSTUY stupefy
EFRSTUU futures
EGGGILN legging
EGGGILR giggler
EGGGINP pegging
EGGGLOR goggler
EGGGLOS goggles
EGGHILR higgler
EGGHIRT thigger
EGGHLOS shoggle
EGGHORY hoggery
EGGIIPS piggies
EGGILLN gelling
EGGILMS leggism
EGGILNR niggler
EGGILNS sniggle
EGGILNU lugeing
EGGILRW wiggler
wriggle
EGGIMMN gemming

EGGINNS	ginseng
EGGINRS	snigger
EGGINRY	gingery
	greying
	niggery
EGGINTT	getting
EGGINTW	twiggen
EGGIPRR	prigger
EGGIPRY	piggery
EGGIRRT	trigger
EGGIRSW	swigger
EGGIRTW	twigger
EGGIRWY	wiggery
EGGJLRU	juggler
EGGJORS	joggers
EGGLLNO	long-leg
EGGLMPU	egg-plum
EGGLMSU	smuggle
EGGLNSU	snuggle
EGGLOOY	geology
EGGLORS	slogger
EGGLPRU	plugger
EGGLRSU	slugger
EGGNOOY	geogony
EGGNTUY	nuggety
EGGORRY	Gregory
EGGORTY	toggery
EGGPRUY	puggery
EGGSSTU	suggest
EGHHHIO	heigh-ho
EGHHIKY	high-key
EGHHIMN	highmen
EGHHIST	highest
	high-set
EGHHITX	x-height
EGHHOSW	showghe
EGHIILL	ghillie
EGHIINT	nightie
EGHIINV	inveigh
EGHIINW	weigh-in
EGHIKNR	gherkin
EGHIKRS	skreigh
	skriegh
EGHILNO	hog-line
EGHILNP	helping
EGHILNR	herling
EGHILNS	English
	shingle
EGHILNT	enlight
	lighten
EGHILPT	pightle
EGHILRT	lighter
	relight
EGHILST	sleight
EGHIMMN	hemming
EGHIMNS	meshing
EGHIMPT	empight
EGHINNU	unhinge
EGHINOS	shoeing
EGHINRR	herring
EGHINRT	righten
EGHINRW	whinger
EGHINTT	tighten
EGHIOOS	shoogie
EGHIORS	ogreish
EGHIORU	roughie
EGHIOTT	göthite
EGHIOTU	toughie
EGHIOTV	eightvo
EGHIRRT	righter
EGHIRST	sighter
EGHIRSY	greyish
EGHISTW	weights
EGHITWY	weighty
EGHLLOU	lughole
EGHLMPY	phlegmy
EGHLNOR	leghorn
EGHLNPU	engulph
EGHLNST	lengths
EGHLNTY	lengthy
EGHLOOS	shoogle
EGHLOSW	leg-show
EGHMNOU	humogen
EGHMOSU	gumshoe
EGHNOOS	hog-nose
EGHNORU	enrough
	roughen
EGHNOTU	toughen
EGHORRU	rougher
EGHOSTT	ghettos
EGHOSUU	hugeous
EGHRTUY	theurgy
EGIIKLW	wiglike
EGIILMT	legitim
EGIILNT	lignite
EGIILNV	veiling
EGIIMNP	impinge
EGIIMNS	Geminis
EGIIMRS	Isegrim
EGIIMSV	misgive
EGIINNS	insigne
	seining
EGIINNV	veining
EGIINOP	△epigoni
EGIINPS	pigsnie
EGIINRT	igniter
	tigrine
EGIINSZ	seizing
EGIINVW	viewing
EGIIPRW	periwig
EGIJKNR	jerking
EGIJLNR	jingler
EGIJLNT	jinglet
EGIJNOS	jingoes
EGIJNST	jesting
EGIJNTT	jetting
EGIKKLN	lekking
EGIKLLM	milk-leg
EGIKLNR	erl-king
EGIKLNT	kinglet
EGIKMNP	kemping
EGIKNNN	kenning
EGIKNNR	kerning
EGIKNRY	key-ring
EGILLNO	logline
EGILLNT	telling
EGILLNW	welling
EGILLNY	yelling
EGILLSU	gullies
EGILMMN	lemming
EGILMMR	glimmer
EGILMNR	gremlin
	merling
	mingler
EGILMNT	melting
EGILMNU	legumin
EGILMOR	gomeril
EGILMOS	semi-log
EGILMOU	elogium
EGILMPS	glimpse
EGILNOR	leg-iron
EGILNOS	lignose
	lingoes
EGILNOT	lentigo
EGILNPR	pingler
EGILNPS	leg-spin
	spignel
EGILNPT	pelting
EGILNPY	yelping
EGILNRS	slinger
EGILNRT	ringlet
	tingler
	tringle
EGILNRY	relying
EGILNSS	singles
EGILNST	glisten
	singlet
EGILNSW	swingle
EGILNTT	letting
EGILNTW	winglet
EGILNVY	levying
EGILOOS	goolies
EGILORR	Grolier
EGILOST	elogist
EGILPPR	gripple
EGILRST	glister
	gristle
EGILRSY	greisly
	griesly
	grisely
EGILRTT	glitter
EGILRTY	tigerly
EGILRUV	virgule
EGILRZZ	grizzle
EGILSSW	wigless
EGIMMRS	megrims
EGIMMTU	gummite
EGIMNOS	misgone
EGIMNOT	mitogen
EGIMNPR	impregn
EGIMNPT	pigment
EGIMOST	egotism
EGINNNP	penning
EGINNNR	renning
EGINNOP	opening
EGINNPU	penguin

EGINNRR grinner
EGINNRT ringent
EGINNRY ginnery
renying
EGINNSS sensing
EGINNST nesting
EGINNSU ensuing
EGINNTT netting
tenting
EGINNTV venting
EGINNVY envying
EGINOPR perigon
EGINOPS epigons
pingoes
EGINORR ignorer
EGINORS △signore
EGINORT genitor
Negrito
EGINORZ zeroing
EGINOSU igneous
EGINOSY isogeny
EGINOTT tentigo
EGINPPR repping
EGINPRS springe
EGINPSY espying
pigsney
EGINPTT petting
EGINPYY epigyny
EGINQUU queuing
EGINRRW wringer
EGINRSS ingress
EGINRST resting
stinger
EGINRSU signeur
EGINRSV serving
versing
EGINRSW swinger
EGINRSY syringe
EGINRTT gittern
retting
EGINRVV revving
EGINRVY revying
EGINSTT setting
testing
EGINSTV vesting
EGINSTW stewing
westing
EGINTTV vetting
EGINTTW wetting
EGIOPRS serpigo
EGIOPRT ego-trip
EGIOPRU groupie
pirogue
EGIORTV vertigo
EGIORTZ zorgite
EGIOSTT egotist
EGIOTUV outgive
EGIPPRR gripper
EGIPPSU guppies
EGIPRUU guipure
EGIRRTT gritter
EGIRSST Striges
tigress
EGIRTTU guttier
EGKLORW legwork
EGLLLPU leg-pull
EGLLRUY gullery
EGLLSUY gulleys
EGLMNOO engloom
EGLMNOR mongrel
EGLMOOR legroom
EGLNOOY neology
EGLNORU lounger
EGLNOST longest
EGLNOUV unglove
EGLNOXY loxygen
xylogen
EGLNOYZ lozengy
EGLNPRU plunger
EGLNRTU gruntle
EGLNSSU gunless
EGLOOSY gooleys
EGLOPSS Gospels
EGLOPTU glue-pot
EGLORRW growler
EGLORSS glosser
EGLPRSU splurge
EGLRSUU △regulus
EGLRSYY gryesly
grysely
EGLRUZZ guzzler
EGLSSTU gutless
EGLSTUU gluteus
Telugus
EGMMORT grommet
EGMMRTU grummet
EGMNORU murgeon
EGMNORY mongery
EGMNOST emongst
EGMNOYZ zymogen
EGMORSU grumose
EGMORTU gourmet
EGNNORT röntgen
EGNNPTU pungent
EGNNRUY gunnery
EGNNTUU unguent
EGNOOPS pongoes
EGNOORY orogeny
EGNOOTU outgone
EGNOOYZ zoogeny
EGNOPRS sponger
EGNOPRY progeny
pyrogen
EGNOPSU pug-nose
EGNOPSW gowpens
EGNORRW wronger
EGNORSS engross
EGNORSU surgeon
EGNORSY eryngos
EGNORUY younger
EGNOSTU tongues
EGNRRTU grunter
EGNRSTU surgent
EGNRSYY synergy
EGNRTTU grutten
turgent
EGNTTUY tent-guy
EGOORRV groover
EGOORSY goosery
EGOORTU outgoer
EGOOSTU outgoes
EGOPPST peg-tops
EGOPRRS gropers
EGOPRRU grouper
regroup
EGOPRUY guy-rope
EGORRST grosert
EGORRSU grouser
EGORRTU grouter
EGORRUY roguery
EGORTUY grey-out
EGPRSUU upsurge
EGRRSUY surgery
EGRSTTU gutters
EHHILLS hellish
EHHIMRS Rhemish
EHHINRS Rhenish
EHHIPRS hership
EHHIRTT thither
EHHIRTW whither
EHHISWY wheyish
EHHORTT thother
EHIILTT lithite
EHIINRT inherit
EHIINRZ rhizine
EHIIRST hirstie
EHIISST stishie
EHIITTT Hittite
EHIJNNO △johnnie
EHIKKSS kishkes
EHIKMNT methink
EHIKNRS kernish
EHIKNRT rethink
thinker
EHIKNST Kentish
EHIKRRS shirker
EHIKRSW whisker
EHIKSTU Kushite
EHIKSTW whisket
EHIKSWY whiskey
EHILLMN hillmen
EHILLNO hellion
EHILLNS inshell
EHILLRS rellish
EHILLRT thiller
EHILLTY lithely
EHILMPW whimple
EHILMTT meltith
EHILMUW umwhile
EHILNOP pinhole
EHILNOT hotline
neolith
EHILNPS plenish
EHILOPT hoplite

EHILOST Elohist
hostile
EHILPRT philter
philtre
EHILRRW whirler
EHILRST slither
EHILRSV shrivel
EHILRTU luthier
EHILRTW whirtle
EHILSTT Lettish
listeth
thistle
EHILSTW whistle
EHILTTU thulite
EHILTTW whittle
EHILTWY whitely
EHIMMRS shimmer
EHIMMSY shimmey
EHIMNPS shipmen
EHIMNRU inhumer
rhenium
EHIMNTY thymine
EHIMORS heroism
moreish
EHIMORT moither
EHIMORZ rhizome
EHIMOSV moshvei
EHIMPRW whimper
EHIMRST Rhemist
EHIMRSU heurism
EHIMRTT Thermit®
EHIMSTU tumshie
EHIMSTY mythise
EHIMSWY whimsey
EHIMTYZ mythize
EHINNOP phone-in
EHINNRT thinner
EHINNSW wennish
EHINOPV hop-vine
EHINOPX phoenix
EHINORS inshore
EHINOST histone
EHINOSU heinous
in-house
EHINPPS shippen
EHINPSS hipness
EHINRSV shriven
EHINRTV thriven
EHINRTW writhen
EHINRTZ zithern
EHINSSS shiness
EHINSST sithens
EHIOPPS pie-shop
EHIOPRS rosehip
EHIOPST ethiops
Peshito
EHIORRT heritor
EHIORST hoister
shortie
EHIORSY hosiery
EHIORTT thorite

EHIORTU outhire
routhie
EHIORTV overhit
EHIOSTY isohyet
EHIPPRS shipper
EHIPPRW whipper
EHIPPTW whippet
EHIPRST hipster
EHIPRSW whisper
EHIPSTT pettish
EHIRRSS sherris
EHIRRSV shriver
EHIRRTV thriver
EHIRRTW whirret
EHIRSSW swisher
EHIRSTU hirsute
EHIRSTW swither
withers
EHIRSVY shivery
EHIRTTW whitret
whitter
EHIRWZZ whizzer
EHISSTU Hussite
stushie
EHISTTW wettish
EHJMNOS Mes-John
EHKLNOR elkhorn
EHKLNOS lokshen
EHKMOOS smoke-ho
EHKNRSU hunkers
EHKRSTU tushker
EHLLNSU unshell
EHLLOOS holloes
EHLMMOW whommle
EHLMMUW whummle
EHLMNOT menthol
EHLMNOY homelyn
EHLMOOS holesom
EHLMOTT hot-melt
EHLNORT hornlet
EHLNRTU luthern
EHLNTTY tenthly
EHLOOPP hop-pole
EHLOOPT pothole
top-hole
EHLOPPS hopples
EHLOPSX phloxes
EHLOPSY spyhole
EHLORST holster
hostler
EHLORTY helotry
EHLOSTT shottle
EHLOSTY thylose
EHLPSSU plushes
EHLRSTU hustler
EHLRSUY hurleys
EHLSSTT shtetls
EHLSTTU shuttle
EHMNOOR hormone
moorhen
EHMNPTY nymphet
EHMNTTU hutment

EHMOOSS shmoose
EHMOOSW somehow
EHMOOSZ shmooze
EHMOPRW morphew
EHMORST smother
Thermos®
EHMORTU mouther
EHMORTY mothery
EHMOSWY somewhy
EHMPRTU thumper
EHMRRTU murther
EHMRSUU humerus
EHNNOOR non-hero
EHNNOPR nephron
EHNNOPY hypnone
EHNNRSU shunner
EHNNSTU unshent
EHNNSUW unshewn
EHNOOPR no-hoper
EHNOORS onshore
on-shore
sorehon
EHNOOST one-shot
EHNOPRY hyperon
EHNOPUY euphony
EHNORRT horrent
norther
EHNORRY heronry
EHNORST shorten
threnos
EHNORSU unhorse
EHNORSY noshery
EHNOSST hotness
EHNOSTT shotten
EHNOSTY honesty
EHNOSUU unhouse
EHNPRSY phrensy
EHNRSTU shunter
unherst
EHNRTWY wrythen
EHNSSSY shyness
EHOOPRW whooper
EHOOPTY oophyte
EHOORST shooter
soother
EHOPPRS shopper
EHOPPRT prophet
EHOPPRW whopper
EHOPRRY orphrey
EHOPRST strophe
EHOPRSU Orpheus
EHOPRTU pouther
EHOPRTY pothery
EHOPRUY euphory
EHORRTW thrower
EHORSTU shouter
souther
EHORSWY showery
EHORTUY outhyre
EHOSSST hostess
EHOSTTT hottest
EHOTTTW wotteth

EHPRTTU	turpeth
EHRSSTY	shyster
	thyrses
EHRSTTU	shutter
EHRSTTW	strewth
EHRSTUY	tushery
EHRTTTY	thretty
EIIILRV	rilievi
EIIILST	ileitis
EIIINPR	ripieni
EIIKLLP	liplike
EIIKLMS	mislike
EIIKLPS	pliskie
EIIKNNS	niks-nie
EIIKNSS	kinesis
EIILLMM	millime
EIILLMT	limelit
EIILLNV	villein
EIILLSW	willies
EIILLTT	tillite
EIILLTV	vitelli
EIILMNT	Minitel
EIILMNV	milvine
EIILMPR	imperil
EIILMPT	limepit
EIILMRS	milreis
EIILMRT	limiter
EIILMSS	missile
	similes
EIILMST	elitism
	élitism
	limites
EIILMSU	milieus
EIILMSV	mislive
EIILMUX	milieux
EIILNOS	elision
	isoline
	lionise
EIILNOT	etiolin
EIILNOV	olivine
EIILNOZ	lionize
EIILNRT	nitrile
EIILORV	rilievo
EIILPST	spilite
EIILQSU	silique
EIILSTT	elitist
	élitist
EIILSTU	utilise
EIILTUY	tuilyie
EIILTUZ	tuilzie
	utilize
EIILTXY	exility
EIIMMSS	mimesis
EIIMMST	mistime
EIIMNPR	primine
EIIMNRT	△interim
	termini
EIIMNRV	miniver
EIIMNTV	minivet
EIIMNTY	nimiety
EIIMOSS	meiosis
EIIMPRS	pismire
	primsie
EIIMPST	pietism
EIIMPTY	impiety
EIIMSSV	missive
EIIMSSZ	sizeism
EIINNNP	ninepin
EIINNQU	quinine
EIINNSW	insinew
EIINNTV	invenit
EIINNTW	intwine
EIINOPR	ripieno
EIINOPS	pionies
EIINORS	ioniser
	ironise
EIINORZ	ionizer
	ironize
EIINPRS	inspire
EIINQRU	inquire
EIINQTU	inquiet
EIINRTT	nitrite
EIINRTV	inviter
	vitrine
EIINRTW	write-in
EIINSST	Sistine
EIINSTT	sittine
	tiniest
EIINSTU	unities
	unitise
EIINTUV	unitive
EIINTUZ	unitize
EIIORST	riotise
EIIORSV	ivories
EIIORTZ	riotize
EIIOSTZ	zoisite
EIIPPRR	rippier
EIIPSTT	pietist
EIIPTTT	△pittite
EIIPTTU	pituite
EIIRSTV	revisit
	visiter
EIISSTX	sixties
EIISSTZ	sizeist
EIISTUV	uveitis
EIJKKSU	jukskei
EIJKNNS	Jenkins
EIJKNPR	perjink
	prejink
EIJLLNY	injelly
EIJLLOS	△jollies
EIJNORT	jointer
EIJNORY	joinery
EIJNPRU	juniper
EIJNRRU	injurer
EIJPRTU	Jupiter
EIJRSTT	jitters
EIJRTTY	jittery
EIJSSUV	jussive
EIKKLNR	klinker
EIKKNRS	skinker
EIKLLNW	inkwell
EIKLLOS	skollie
EIKLLOW	owl-like
EIKLLST	skillet
EIKLMNR	△kremlin
EIKLNRS	slinker
EIKLNRT	tinkler
EIKLNRW	winkler
	wrinkle
EIKLNSS	kinless
EIKLNST	lentisk
EIKLNSU	sunlike
EIKLNSY	skyline
EIKLNTT	knittle
EIKLNTU	nutlike
EIKLNTW	twinkle
EIKLOOP	plookie
EIKLOPU	ploukie
EIKLOTY	toylike
EIKLPRY	perkily
EIKLPSY	peskily
EIKLSTT	skittle
EIKMMRR	krimmer
EIKMMRS	skimmer
EIKMNOR	moniker
EIKMORS	irksome
EIKMOSS	Eskimos
EIKMOSY	misyoke
EIKMRSS	kirmess
EIKNNRS	skinner
EIKNOOR	rooinek
EIKNOPS	pinkoes
EIKNOSS	kenosis
EIKNPSU	spunkie
EIKNRST	stinker
EIKNRSW	winkers
EIKNRTT	knitter
	trinket
EIKNSTT	kittens
EIKNTTY	kitteny
EIKNTUZ	kunzite
EIKOPPR	pork-pie
EIKOPRS	porkies
EIKOSST	ketosis
EIKPPRS	skipper
EIKPPST	skippet
EIKPRSY	spikery
EIKPSSS	skepsis
EIKRRST	skirret
	skirter
	striker
EIKRSTT	skitter
EIKRSTU	turkies
EILLMNU	mullein
EILLMOT	melilot
EILLMOU	mouillé
EILLMST	mistell
EILLNNP	pennill
EILLNOS	niellos
EILLNSS	illness
EILLORU	rouille
EILLORZ	zorille
EILLOSV	villose
EILLPRS	spiller

EILLPSS	lipless
EILLQTU	quillet
EILLRST	stiller
	trellis
EILLRSW	swiller
EILLRSY	Sillery
EILLSTW	willest
EILMMNO	molimen
EILMMRS	slimmer
EILMNOT	molinet
EILMNSU	emulsin
EILMOPR	implore
EILMORR	lorimer
EILMORY	Lyomeri
EILMOSS	lissome
EILMPPU	plumpie
EILMPRS	prelims
	simpler
EILMPRY	primely
EILMPSU	impulse
EILMPSX	simplex
EILMPTY	emptily
EILMRRY	merrily
EILMRSS	rimless
EILMRSU	misrule
EILMRSY	miserly
EILMRTY	lymiter
EILMRVY	vermily
EILMSSY	messily
EILMSTT	smittle
EILMSUY	Elysium
EILMUUV	eluvium
EILNNPU	pinnule
EILNOOP	polonie
EILNOOV	violone
EILNOPP	plenipo
EILNOPR	proline
EILNOPS	epsilon
EILNOPT	pointel
	pontile
	topline
EILNORR	loriner
EILNORT	retinol
EILNOSS	lioness
EILNOST	Nilotes
	onliest
EILNOSU	elusion
EILNOTU	elution
	line-out
	outline
EILNOTV	violent
EILNOTW	towline
	two-line
EILNOVV	involve
EILNPRS	Pilsner
EILNPRU	purline
EILNPST	plenist
EILNPSU	spinule
EILNPTY	ineptly
EILNPUV	vulpine
EILNRST	linters
	slinter
	snirtle
EILNRSV	silvern
EILNRTY	inertly
EILNRVY	nervily
EILNSSS	sinless
EILNSSU	insulse
	silenus
EILNSTU	utensil
EILNSTW	westlin
EILNSVY	sylvine
EILNVXY	vixenly
EILOORT	troolie
EILOOST	ostiole
	stoolie
EILOOTZ	zoolite
EILOPRS	spoiler
EILOPRT	poitrel
EILOPST	pistole
EILOPSU	pileous
EILOPSV	plosive
EILOPTT	plottie
EILOPTX	exploit
EILORSS	rissole
EILORSU	soilure
EILORSW	low-rise
EILORTT	tortile
	triolet
EILORTU	outlier
EILOSTT	litotes
EILOTUV	outlive
EILPPRR	rippler
EILPPRS	ripples
	slipper
EILPPRT	ripplet
	tippler
	tripple
EILPPSS	pipless
EILPPST	stipple
EILPPSW	swipple
EILPRST	spirtle
EILPRTT	triplet
EILPRTX	Triplex®
	triplex
EILPRUU	purlieu
EILPSTT	spittle
EILPSTU	stipule
EILPSUY	spulyie
EILPSUZ	spulzie
EILPTTY	pettily
EILQRTU	quilter
EILQRUU	liqueur
EILQTUY	quietly
EILRRTW	twirler
EILRSTT	slitter
	stilter
	testril
EILRSUW	wurlies
EILRSVY	silvery
EILRSZZ	sizzler
EILRTTY	littery
	tritely
EILRTUV	rivulet
EILSSTW	witless
EILSSTY	stylise
EILSTTV	vittles
EILSTTY	stylite
	testily
EILSTVY	sylvite
EILSTYZ	stylize
EILSWZZ	swizzle
EILTWZZ	twizzle
EIMMORS	memoirs
EIMMPRR	primmer
EIMMPRU	premium
EIMMRRT	trimmer
EIMMRST	misterm
EIMMRSW	swimmer
EIMMSTZ	tzimmes
EIMNNOT	mention
EIMNNTW	mint-new
EIMNOOR	ionomer
EIMNOOS	△moonies
	noisome
EIMNOOT	emotion
EIMNOOX	exomion
EIMNOPS	peonism
	pi-meson
EIMNOPT	emption
	pimento
EIMNORS	merinos
	mersion
EIMNOST	moisten
EIMNOSW	Owenism
	winsome
EIMNOTU	Mountie
EIMNOTY	omneity
	omniety
EIMNPTU	pinetum
EIMNQSU	mesquin
EIMNRRU	murrine
EIMNRST	entrism
	minster
EIMNRSU	neurism
EIMNRTU	run-time
EIMNRVY	verminy
EIMNSSS	sensism
EIMNSST	mess-tin
	missent
EIMNSTT	mist-net
	mittens
	smitten
EIMNSTU	minutes
	mistune
EIMNSTW	miswent
EIMNUZZ	muezzin
EIMOPPR	pompier
EIMOPRR	primero
EIMOPRS	imposer
	promise
EIMOPRV	improve

EIMORST	erotism
	mortise
	trisome
EIMORSV	verismo
EIMORTT	omitter
EIMOSST	mitoses
EIMOSTT	titmose
EIMOSTU	timeous
EIMOSTZ	mestizo
EIMOTTW	two-time
EIMPRRU	primeur
EIMPRSS	impress
	Persism
	premiss
EIMPRST	imprest
EIMPRTU	imputer
EIMPSST	misstep
EIMPSTU	impetus
EIMQSTU	mesquit
EIMRSSU	misuser
	surmise
EIMRSTT	metrist
EIMRSTY	mistery
	smytrie
EIMRTTU	rut-time
EIMRTUV	vitreum
EIMRTUX	mixture
EINNOPS	pension
EINNOQU	quinone
EINNORT	intoner
	ternion
EINNORU	reunion
EINNORV	environ
EINNOST	tension
EINNOSV	venison
EINNOTT	nonetti
	tontine
EINNOVW	inwoven
EINNPRS	spinner
EINNPRT	enprint
EINNPST	spinnet
	tenpins
EINNPSY	spinney
EINNRSU	unrisen
EINNRTV	vintner
EINNRUV	unriven
EINNSSY	sinsyne
EINNSTU	Sunnite
EINNSTZ	Zennist
EINNSUW	unsinew
EINNTUW	untwine
EINOOPZ	epizoon
EINOORS	erosion
EINOOST	isotone
EINOOSZ	ozonise
EINOOTZ	zoonite
EINOOZZ	ozonize
EINOPPR	poperin
	propine
EINOPRR	roper-in
EINOPRT	pointer
	protein
	pterion
	repoint
EINOPRV	provine
EINOPSS	spinose
EINOQUX	equinox
EINORST	in-store
	tersion
	triones
EINORSU	urinose
EINORSV	version
EINORTT	tritone
EINORTU	routine
EINORTZ	trizone
EINOSSS	session
EINOSST	sonties
EINOSSU	sinuose
EINOSTT	snottie
EINOSTW	Owenist
EINOSUV	envious
	niveous
	veinous
EINOTTT	totient
EINOTTV	oven-tit
EINPPRS	nippers
	snipper
EINPPST	snippet
EINPRRT	printer
	reprint
EINPRST	Septrin®
EINPRSU	uprisen
EINPRTU	repunit
EINPRTX	Pinxter
EINPSTT	spitten
EINPSTU	puniest
EINPTTY	tintype
EINQRUY	enquiry
EINQSTU	inquest
EINQTTU	quintet
EINQTUU	unquiet
EINRRSU	insurer
EINRSSU	sunrise
EINRSTT	entrist
	stinter
EINRSTV	striven
EINRSTW	winters
EINRSTY	sintery
EINRSWY	swinery
EINRTTW	twinter
	written
EINRTUV	unrivet
	△venturi
EINRTUW	unwrite
EINRTWY	wintery
EINSSST	sensist
EINSSSU	Senussi
	sinuses
EINSSSY	synesis
EINSSTW	witness
EINSSUW	sunwise
EINSTTW	entwist
	twinset
EINSTTY	tensity
EINTTTW	twitten
EINTTUY	tenuity
EIOOPST	isotope
EIOORTV	Orvieto
EIOOSTT	tootsie
EIOPRRT	△pierrot
EIOPRST	periost
	reposit
	riposte
EIOPRSX	Siporex®
EIOPRTV	pivoter
EIOPSST	sepiost
EIOPSTU	piteous
EIOPSTY	isotype
EIOPTUW	wipeout
EIOQRTU	quoiter
EIORRRS	sorrier
EIORRRW	worrier
EIORRST	roister
EIORRSV	revisor
EIORRUV	ouvrier
EIORRVV	revivor
EIORSST	sorites
	stories
EIORSSU	serious
EIORSSX	xerosis
EIORSTT	stoiter
EIORSTV	torsive
EIORTTV	tortive
	viretot
EIORTUV	voiture
EIOSSTV	stovies
EIOSTTU	toustie
EIOSTUZ	outsize
EIPPRRT	tripper
EIPPRTT	trippet
EIPRRTY	tripery
EIPRRUV	upriver
EIPRSST	△persist
	stirpes
	stripes
EIPRSSU	suspire
EIPRSTT	spitter
	tipster
EIPRSTU	peritus
EIPRSTY	pyrites
	stripey
EIPRSUU	euripus
EIPRTTU	puttier
EIPRTUW	write-up
EIPRUVW	purview
EIQRSTU	querist
EIQRTTU	quitter
EIQRUVY	quivery
EIQRUZZ	quizzer
EIQSTUU	quietus
EIQSUZZ	quizzes
EIRRRST	stirrer
EIRRSTV	striver

Words marked △ may be spelled also with a capital letter

EIRSSTV	treviss
EIRSTTT	stretti
EIRSTTU	tertius
EIRSTTW	twister
EIRSTWZ	Switzer
EIRSUVV	survive
EIRSUVW	surview
EIRTTTW	twitter
EISSSSW	Swisses
EISSTUV	tussive
EJJMNUU	jejunum
EJJMPTU	jump-jet
EJKOORY	jookery
EJKORUY	joukery
EJLLORY	jollyer
EJLOSSY	joyless
EJMNRUY	jurymen
EJMOPTU	toe-jump
EJNORRU	rejourn
EJNORUY	journey
EJOORVY	overjoy
EJOPPRT	prop-jet
EJORSTU	jouster
EJOSTTU	outjest
EJPRRUY	perjury
EKKLOOY	olykoek
EKKLRSU	skulker
EKKOPSU	pukekos
EKLLMSU	skellum
EKLLRRU	kruller
EKLNOPR	plonker
EKLNORS	snorkel
EKLNPRU	plunker
EKLOOTW	wet-look
EKLSTTU	skuttle
EKMMORS	Kommers
EKMMRSU	skummer
EKMNORY	monkery
EKMNOSU	muskone
EKMNOSY	monkeys
EKMNPTU	unkempt
EKMNRTU	Turkmen
EKNOORS	snooker
EKNOPSU	unspoke
EKNORST	stonker
	stroken
EKNORTT	knotter
EKNORTW	network
EKNORUY	younker
EKNRTUY	turnkey
EKNSSTU	sunkets
EKOOPRV	provoke
EKOORRY	rookery
EKOORST	stooker
	strooke
EKOPPSU	upspoke
EKOPRUY	kouprey
EKORRST	stroker
EKPPSUU	seppuku
EKPSTUW	skew-put
EKRSSTU	Turkess
ELLLORR	lorrell

ELLMNOO	moellon
ELLMOOR	morello
ELLMOWY	mellowy
ELLMPUU	plumule
ELLNNOT	tonnell
ELLNOOW	woollen
ELLNOPT	pollent
ELLNOST	stollen
ELLNOSU	nousell
ELLNOSW	swollen
ELLNOWW	well-won
ELLNOXY	xylenol
ELLNPSU	unspell
ELLOOSW	woosell
ELLOOSY	loosely
ELLOPRR	proller
ELLOPTU	pollute
ELLORRT	troller
ELLORRY	rye-roll
ELLORTY	trolley
ELLORVY	loverly
ELLOSTU	outsell
	sell-out
ELLOSVY	volleys
ELLOSWY	yellows
ELLOTTU	outtell
ELLOTUW	outwell
ELLOVWY	vowelly
ELLOWYY	yellowy
ELLPSUW	upswell
ELLPSUY	pulleys
ELMMORT	trommel
ELMMPTU	plummet
ELMMRSU	slummer
ELMMSTU	stummel
ELMNOOT	moonlet
ELMNOTU	moulten
ELMNOTY	ymolten
ELMNPPU	plumpen
ELMNPUU	unplume
ELMOOPP	pompelo
ELMOOPS	pomelos
ELMOORT	tremolo
ELMOPRY	polymer
ELMOPSU	plumose
ELMORSU	emulsor
ELMOSUU	emulous
ELMOSUV	volumes
ELMPPRU	plumper
ELMPRUY	plumery
ELMRTUU	multure
ELMRTUY	elytrum
ELMRUZZ	muzzler
ELMSSSU	sumless
ELNNOPU	nonuple
ELNOOSU	unloose
ELNOOSZ	snoozle
ELNOPRU	pleuron
ELNOPRY	pronely
ELNOPST	leptons
ELNOPTU	opulent
ELNORSU	noursle

ELNORTY	elytron
ELNOSSS	sonless
ELNOSSW	lowness
ELNOSTU	lentous
ELNOSTV	solvent
ELNOTUZ	zonulet
ELNOTVY	novelty
ELNRSTY	sternly
ELNSSSU	sunless
ELNSSSY	slyness
ELNSUZZ	snuzzle
ELOOOPT	toe-loop
ELOOPRS	spooler
ELOORTT	rootlet
ELOOSTU	outsole
ELOOSWY	woolsey
ELOPPST	stopple
ELOPPSY	polypes
ELOPRRU	prouler
ELOPRRW	prowler
ELOPRRY	pyrrole
ELOPRSS	plessor
ELOPRSU	leprous
	pelorus
	perlous
	sporule
ELOPRSY	leprosy
ELOPRTT	plotter
ELOPRTU	plouter
	poulter
ELOPRTW	plowter
ELOPRTY	protyle
ELOPRVY	overply
	plovery
ELOPSST	topless
ELOPSTU	tupelos
ELORSTT	settlor
	slotter
ELORSUV	velours
ELORSUY	elusory
ELORTTY	lottery
ELORTUY	loutery
ELORTVY	overtly
ELOSSTY	systole
	toyless
	tyloses
ELOSTUU	luteous
ELOSWZZ	swozzle
ELPPRSU	purples
ELPRRSU	slurper
ELPRSTU	spurtle
ELPRTUU	pulture
ELPRUZZ	puzzler
ELPSSSU	plusses
ELPSTUU	pluteus
	pustule
ELRRSTU	rustler
ELRRTTU	turtler
ELRSSTU	lustres
ELRSTUY	sutlery
ELRSTWY	sweltry
ELRSUWY	wurleys

ELRTTUY	utterly
ELRTUUV	vulture
ELSSTYY	systyle
EMMMRUY	mummery
EMMNOOR	monomer
EMMNORY	meronym
EMMNOSU	mu-meson
EMMNOTU	omentum
EMMNOTY	metonym
EMMOPRR	prommer
EMMORSZ	momzers
EMMRSUY	summery
EMMSSUU	museums
EMNNOOR	moneron
EMNNORT	non-term
EMNNOWW	new-mown
EMNOOPT	metopon
EMNOORT	montero
EMNOOST	moonset
EMNOOSY	noysome
EMNOOTY	enomoty
EMNORRU	mourner
EMNORST	monster
EMNORTT	torment
EMNORTU	monture
	mounter
	remount
EMNOSST	stemson
EMNOSTU	unsmote
EMNOSTY	etymons
EMNRSSU	rumness
EMNRSTU	munster
	sternum
EMOOPRT	promote
EMOOPRY	pomeroy
EMOORRY	Moorery
EMOORSS	Mooress
EMOORSU	urosome
EMOOSTT	mottoes
EMOOSTW	twosome
EMOOSTY	myosote
	toysome
EMOOTUV	outmove
EMOPPTU	up-tempo
EMOPRRS	rompers
EMOPRST	stomper
EMOPRSU	supremo
EMORRSU	morsure
EMORRWY	wormery
EMORSSU	smouser
EMORSTU	oestrum
EMORSUY	mousery
EMORSUZ	zero-sum
EMOSSTT	mostest
EMOSTVZ	zemstvo
EMPRSTU	stumper
	sumpter
EMPRTTU	trumpet
EMRRSTU	△sturmer
EMRSTYY	mystery
ENNNRUY	nunnery
ENNOORT	norteño
ENNOOTT	nonetto
ENNORST	stonern
ENNORSU	non-user
ENNORTU	neutron
ENNOSSW	nowness
ENNOSTU	neuston
ENNOUVW	unwoven
ENNPSTU	unspent
ENNRSTU	stunner
ENNTTUY	untenty
ENOOPPR	propone
ENOOPPT	open-top
ENOOPRS	snooper
ENOOPST	one-stop
ENOOPSY	spooney
ENOORSU	onerous
ENOORSZ	snoozer
ENOORTT	to-torne
ENOORTW	to-worne
ENOORWW	woe-worn
ENOOSST	soonest
ENOOSTT	testoon
ENOOSTU	unsoote
ENOOTTW	two-tone
ENOOTXY	oxytone
ENOPRRU	proneur
ENOPRSS	persons
ENOPRST	postern
ENOPRTT	portent
ENOPRTY	entropy
ENOPSST	stepson
ENOPSUX	Xenopus
ENOQSTU	Quonset
ENOQTUU	unquote
ENORRST	snorter
ENORRTT	torrent
ENORRUV	overrun
ENORSSY	sensory
ENORSTT	snotter
	stentor
ENORSTU	tonsure
ENORSTW	nor'-west
ENORSTY	tyrones
ENORSUV	nervous
ENORTUY	tourney
ENOSSTT	Stetson
ENOSSTU	outness
ENOSSTW	twoness
ENOSTTU	stouten
	tenutos
ENOSTUU	tenuous
ENOSTUY	yu-stone
ENOTTUW	outwent
ENPRRSU	spurner
ENPRSTU	pre-stun
	punster
ENPRSUU	unpurse
ENPSSSU	suspens
ENPSTTU	stupent
ENPSTUW	unswept
ENRRSTU	returns
ENRRSUY	nursery
ENRRTUU	nurture
ENRRTUY	turnery
ENRSSWY	wryness
ENRSTTU	entrust
ENRSUUX	Xenurus
ENRTTUY	nuttery
EOOOPRS	oospore
EOOPPRS	opposer
	propose
EOOPPRV	popover
EOOPRRS	spoorer
EOOPRRT	protore
	trooper
EOOPRSS	poroses
EOOPRST	stooper
EOOPRTU	outrope
EOOPRTV	overtop
EOOPRTW	towrope
EOOPRVY	poovery
EOOPRYZ	zoopery
EOOPTYZ	zootype
EOORRST	rooster
	toreros
EOORSVW	oversow
EOORTUV	out-over
EOORTUW	out-owre
EOOSSSU	osseous
EOOTTUV	outvote
EOPPPRS	poppers
EOPPRRS	prosper
EOPPRSS	oppress
	porpess
EOPPRST	stopper
EOPPRSU	purpose
EOPPRSW	swopper
EOPPSSU	suppose
EOPRRSS	pressor
EOPRRST	sporter
EOPRRTU	trouper
EOPRSST	portess
	prestos
EOPRSSU	seropus
EOPRSSW	prowess
EOPRSTT	protest
	spotter
EOPRSTU	petrous
	posture
	proteus
	septuor
	spouter
EOPRSTX	exports
EOPRSUU	poursue
	uprouse
EOPRSUW	poursew
EOPRTTY	pottery
EOPRTUY	eutropy
EOPRTVY	poverty
EOPSSSS	possess
EOPSTTU	outstep
EOPSTTW	stewpot
	two-step
EOQRSTU	questor

EORRRST	△terrors
EORRSTU	rouster
	trouser
EORRSTW	strower
EORRSTY	royster
EORRTTT	trotter
EORRTTU	torture
	trouter
EORSSTU	estrous
	oestrus
	trouses
	tussore
EORSSTV	votress
EORSSTY	storeys
EORSTTT	stotter
	stretto
EORSTTW	swotter
EORSTTY	rosetty
EORSTUX	sextuor
EORTTTY	tottery
EOSTTTW	wottest
EPPRRTU	prerupt
EPPRRUU	purpure
EPPRSSU	press-up
EPPSTUW	upswept
EPRRRSU	spurrer
EPRRSUU	pursuer
	usurper
EPRRSUY	spurrey
EPRRTUU	rupture
EPRSSTY	spryest
EPRSTTU	sputter
ERRSSTU	trusser
ERRSTTU	truster
ERRSTTY	tryster
ERSSSTU	trusses
ERSSSUU	usuress
ERSSTTU	tutress
ERSSTUY	russety
ERSTTTU	stutter

F

FFFILOT	lift-off
FFGIINR	griffin
FFGIINT	tiffing
FFGILNU	luffing
FFGINOR	griffon
FFGINPU	puffing
FFGLRUY	gruffly
FFHHISU	huffish
FFHIISY	fishify
FFHIKNU	huffkin
FFHILSU	fishful
FFHILSY	fly-fish
FFHILTY	fifthly
FFHILUY	huffily
FFHIMSU	muffish
FFHIOST	toffish
FFHOOSW	show-off
FFHOPSU	push-off
FFHOSTU	shut-off
FFIILMY	miffily
FFIISUZ	ziffius
FFIKOSS	kiss-off
FFILLLU	fulfill
FFILOUZ	zuffoli
FFILPUY	puffily
FFILRTY	fritfly
FFILSTU	fistful
FFILSTY	stiffly
FFINOPS	off-spin
	spin-off
FFINOPT	pontiff
FFIORTY	fortify
FFIQSUY	squiffy
FFIRTUY	frutify
FFJMOPU	jump-off
FFKLORU	forkful
FFKLOSU	Suffolk
FFLLOOU	loofful
FFLNSUY	snuffly
FFLOOUZ	zuffolo
FFNORTU	turnoff
	turn-off
FFOOPST	stopoff
	stop-off
FGGGIIN	figging
FGGHIIS	fishgig
FGGIIZZ	fizzgig
FGGILNO	golfing
FGGILOY	foggily
FGGINOR	forging
FGHHIOS	hog-fish
FGHIINS	fishing
FGHIIPS	pig-fish
FGHILSU	sighful
FGHILTY	flighty
FGHIOSY	fogyish
FGHNOOR	foghorn
FGHORUY	froughy
FGHOTUY	foughty
FGIIKNN	knifing
FGIILLN	filling
FGIILNO	foiling
FGIILNR	rifling
FGIILNS	filings
FGIILNY	lignify
FGIINNS	finings
FGIINRR	firring
FGIINRY	nigrify
FGIINST	sifting
FGIINSX	fixings
FGIINSY	signify
FGIINTT	fitting
FGIINZZ	fizzing
FGILNOO	fooling
FGILNOP	fopling
FGILNOR	△rolfing
FGILNOW	flowing
	fowling
	wolfing
FGILNTU	fluting
FGILNTY	flyting
FGILOOY	goofily
FGILORY	glorify
FGIMNOR	forming
FGIMOSY	fogyism
FGINNNU	funning
FGINOOR	roofing
FGINOOT	footing
FGINRRU	furring
FGINRSU	surfing
FGINRTU	turfing
FGINTTU	tufting
FGIORTW	figwort
FGISTUU	fuguist
FGJLSUU	jugfuls
FGLLNUU	lungful
FGLMSUU	mugfuls
FGLNORU	furlong
FGLNOSU	songful
FGLNPUU	upflung
FGLOOUY	ufology
FGLORUU	fulgour
FGLOTUY	goutfly
FGLSTUU	gustful
	gutsful
FGNOORU	fourgon
FGNOSUU	fungous
FHIIKNS	ink-fish
FHIILMS	filmish
FHIILOS	fish-oil
FHIINNS	Finnish
FHIINPS	pinfish
FHILLSU	fullish
FHILOOS	foolish
FHILOSW	wolfish
FHILPSU	shipful
FHILPTU	pithful
FHILSUW	wishful
FHINOSU	fushion
FHINRSU	furnish
FHINSSU	sunfish
FHIOOPR	hip-roof
FHIOOST	ooftish
FHIOPPS	foppish
FHIOPSX	foxship
FHIORRY	horrify
FHIOSST	softish
FHIPPSU	pupfish
FHIRTTY	thrifty
FHIRTUY	thurify
FHKORTU	futhork
FHLLOTU	full-hot
FHLNORU	hornful
FHLNSUU	unflush
FHLOOSY	shoofly
FHLOPSU	shopful
FHLPSUU	pushful
FHLRTUU	hurtful
	ruthful
FHNOTUX	fox-hunt
FHOOORT	hoofrot
FHOOOTT	hotfoot
FIIIKNN	finikin
FIIKNYZ	zinkify

FIILLMO milfoil
FIILLSU fusilli
FIILNOT tinfoil
FIILNTY niftily
FIILPTU pitiful
FIIMMNU infimum
FIINOSS fission
FIINRTY nitrify
FIIPSTY tipsify
FIIRTVY vitrify
FIJLLOY jollify
FIJSTUY justify
FIKKLNO kinfolk
FIKLLSU skilful
FIKLNOW wolfkin
FIKLNSU skinful
FIKLRSU riskful
FIKNNOS finnsko
FIKRTUY Turkify
FILLLUW willful
FILLMOY mollify
FILLNUY nullify
FILLOTU toilful
FILLOTY loftily
FILLSTU listful
FILMNOO monofil
FILMSTU mistful
FILNNUY funnily
FILNOUX fluxion
FILNSTU tinfuls
FILNTUY unfitly
FILOOTW witloof
FILOPPT flip-top
FILORST florist
FILORTU floruit
FILORTY trifoly
FILPPUY pulpify
FILRSTY firstly
FILRYZZ frizzly
FILSSUY fussily
FILSTTU flutist
FILSTUW wistful
FILSTUY fustily
FILSTWY swiftly
FILUYZZ fuzzily
FIMMMUY mummify
FIMMORS misform
FIMNORU uniform
FIMOORV oviform
FIMORRT triform
FIMORTY mortify
FIMRTUY furmity
FIMSTYY mystify
FINOPTY pontify
FINORSS frisson
FIOORSU furioso
FIOOSTX six-foot
FIOPRST profits
FIOPRSY prosify
FIOPSTX postfix
FIORSUU furious
FIPPUYY yuppify

FIRRSTY stir-fry
FIRSSUY Russify
FKLNOOR Norfolk
FKLORUW workful
FKOOORS forsook
FLLOPTU plotful
topfull
FLLOSUU soulful
FLLOSWY fly-slow
FLLOTUU full-out
FLLOUWY wofully
FLLSTUU lustful
FLMMOUX flummox
FLMNOOU mouflon
FLMOOOT tomfool
FLMOORU roomful
FLNOORR forlorn
FLNRSUU urnfuls
FLOORSW forslow
FLOOTUW outflow
FLOPSTU potfuls
FLOSUUV fulvous
FMRSTUU frustum
FNNNUUY unfunny
FNNOORT fronton
FNOOOTT foot-ton
FNOORRW forworn
FNOORSU sunroof
FNOPRTU upfront
up-front
FNORSTY Y-fronts
FNSTTUU unstuft
FOOOPRT rooftop
FOOORTT footrot
FOOOTTU outfoot
FOOOTTW two-foot
FOOPSTT soft-top
FOORTTX foxtrot
fox-trot
FOORTUW two-four
FOPSSTU fuss-pot
FORRUWY furrowy
FORSTWY frowsty

G

GGGGIIN gigging
GGGHINO hogging
GGGHINU hugging
GGGIIJN jigging
GGGIILN ligging
GGGIINP pigging
GGGIINR rigging
GGGIINT tigging
GGGIINW wigging
GGGIINZ zigging
GGGIJNO jogging
GGGIJNU jugging
GGGILNO logging
GGGILNU lugging
GGGIMNU mugging
GGGINNO nogging
GGGINOS sogging

GGGINOT togging
GGGINPU pugging
GGGINRU rugging
GGGINSU sugging
GGGINTU tugging
GGHHIOS hoggish
GGHIIJS jiggish
GGHIINN hinging
GGHIINS sighing
GGHIIPS piggish
GGHIIRS riggish
GGHIITT thiggit
GGHIMSU muggish
GGHINSU gushing
GGHIPSU puggish
GGHLOSY shoggly
GGHOSTU thuggos
GGIIILN gingili
GGIILNP pigling
GGIILNR rigling
GGIINNN ginning
GGIINNO ingoing
GGIINNR ringing
GGIINNS signing
singing
GGIINNT tinging
GGIINPR griping
GGIINRT ringgit
GGIINSU guising
GGIIRRS grigris
GGIJNSU juggins
GGILNNO longing
GGILNNU lunging
GGILNOS gosling
GGILNOT løgting
GGILNOU △guignol
GGILNOV gloving
GGILNOW glowing
GGILNOZ glozing
GGILOOS gigolos
GGILOSY soggily
GGILRWY wriggly
GGIMMNU gumming
GGIMNSU muggins
GGINNNU gunning
GGINNOO ongoing
on-going
GGINOOP pogoing
GGINOPU upgoing
GGINORS gringos
GGINORU roguing
GGINORW growing
GGINOUV voguing
GGINPPY gypping
GGINPRU purging
GGINRST G-string
GGINRSU surging
GGINSTU gutsing
GGINTTU gutting
GGIOORS gorgios
GGIPRSY spriggy
GGNORUW rug-gown

Words marked △ may be spelled also with a capital letter

GHHHIIS	highish
GHHIKSY	sky-high
GHHILOW	high-low
GHHIOPT	high-top
GHHIORT	right-oh
GHHIRST	shright
GHHORTU	through
GHHOTTU	thought
GHIIKNT	king-hit
GHIILNR	hirling
GHIILRS	girlish
GHIINNS	shining
GHIINNT	in-thing
	nithing
GHIINNW	whining
GHIINPP	hipping
GHIINSS	hissing
GHIINST	insight
	shiting
GHIINSW	wishing
GHIINTT	hitting
	tithing
GHIINTW	whiting
GHIIRST	tigrish
GHIKLNU	hulking
GHIKNNO	honking
GHIKNOS	hog-skin
GHIKNSU	husking
GHIKRTU	tughrik
GHILLSU	gullish
GHILLTY	lightly
GHILNOS	longish
GHILNOW	howling
GHILNPU	ingulph
GHILNRU	hurling
GHILNSY	shingly
GHILNTY	nightly
GHILPTY	yplight
GHILRTY	rightly
GHILSTY	sightly
GHILTTY	tightly
GHILTWY	wightly
GHIMMNU	humming
GHIMNNY	hymning
GHIMNOS	gnomish
	moshing
GHIMNRY	rhyming
GHIMRSU	simurgh
GHIMSTT	mightst
GHINNOR	horning
GHINNOT	nothing
GHINNTU	hunting
GHINOPP	hopping
GHINOPS	ginshop
GHINORS	horsing
	shoring
GHINORT	right-on
GHINOST	hosting
GHINOSU	housing
GHINOSW	showing
GHINOTT	hotting
	tonight
GHINOTU	houting
GHINPSU	gunship
	pushing
GHINRTU	ungirth
	unright
GHINSTU	unsight
GHINTTU	hutting
GHIOPTU	hip-gout
GHIORST	rightos
GHIORSU	roguish
GHIOSUV	voguish
GHIPRST	spright
GHIPRTU	upright
GHIPTTU	uptight
GHLMOOO	homolog
GHLMOPU	hog-plum
GHLNOTY	Loghtyn
GHLOOSY	shoogly
GHLORUY	roughly
GHLOSTY	ghostly
GHLOSUY	sloughy
GHLOTUY	toughly
GHMOPTU	pug-moth
GHMORSU	sorghum
GHMOSTU	mugshot
GHNOPRY	gryphon
GHNORUU	unrough
GHNOSTU	gunshot
	noughts
	shotgun
GHNOTUY	youngth
GHOOOSW	hoosgow
GHOORSS	sorghos
GHORTUW	wrought
GHORTUY	yoghurt
GHOSTUU	outgush
GHPSTUU	push-tug
GIIJNNO	joining
GIIKKNR	kirking
GIIKLLN	killing
GIIKLMN	milking
GIIKLNN	inkling
GIIKLNT	kitling
GIIKNNP	king-pin
	pinking
GIIKNNS	sinking
GIIKNNW	winking
GIIKNNZ	zinking
GIIKNPS	pigskin
GIIKNRS	griskin
GIIKNSV	skiving
GIILLMN	milling
GIILLNO	gillion
GIILLNP	pilling
GIILLNT	tilling
GIILLNW	willing
GIILLPY	pig-lily
GIILMNN	limning
GIILMNP	limping
GIILMNS	smiling
GIILMPR	pilgrim
GIILMRY	grimily
GIILNNS	linings
GIILNNY	inlying
	lying-in
GIILNOR	ligroin
GIILNOS	soiling
GIILNOT	toiling
GIILNPP	lipping
GIILNPS	lisping
	spiling
GIILNST	listing
GIILNTT	tilting
	titling
	Tlingit
GIILNTW	witling
GIILOSS	gliosis
GIILOST	oligist
GIILRST	strigil
GIIMMNR	rimming
GIIMNPP	pimping
GIIMNPR	priming
GIIMNSS	missing
GIIMNST	misting
GIINNNP	pinning
GIINNNS	innings
	sinning
GIINNNT	tinning
GIINNNW	winning
GIINNOP	pioning
GIINNOR	ironing
GIINNPP	nipping
GIINNPS	sniping
GIINNPU	pinguin
GIINNRS	rinsing
GIINNRU	ruining
GIINNSW	inswing
GIINNTT	tinting
GIINNTU	uniting
GIINNTW	twining
GIINOPR	pig-iron
GIINORS	Signior
	signori
GIINORT	rioting
GIINPPP	pipping
GIINPPR	ripping
GIINPPS	sipping
GIINPPT	tipping
GIINPPZ	zipping
GIINPTT	pitting
GIINPTY	pitying
GIINQTU	quiting
GIINRRS	sirring
GIINRTW	△writing
GIINSTT	sitting
GIINSTU	suiting
GIINTTW	witting
GIJMPPU	pig-jump
GIJNOTT	jotting
GIJNTTU	jutting
GIKLNRU	lurking
GIKMNOS	smoking
GIKNNOW	knowing
GIKNORW	working

GIKNSTU	tusking
GILLMPU	pug-mill
GILLNNU	nulling
GILLNOO	long-oil
GILLNOP	polling
GILLNOR	rolling
GILLNOT	tolling
GILLNYY	lyingly
GILMNOR	morling
GILMNPU	lumping
GILNNOO	glonoin
	looning
GILNNSU	unsling
GILNOOP	looping
GILNOOT	looting
	tooling
GILNOPP	lopping
GILNOPS	sloping
GILNORU	louring
GILNOSW	slowing
GILNOTT	lotting
GILNOTU	tung-oil
GILNOVW	wolving
GILNOWY	yowling
GILNPRU	purling
GILNPSU	plusing
GILNPUY	uplying
GILNSTU	singult
GILNVYY	vyingly
GILOORS	girosol
GILORTT	triglot
GILORTY	trilogy
GILOSTT	glottis
GILRSTY	gristly
GILRTUY	liturgy
GILRYZZ	grizzly
GIMMMNU	mumming
GIMMNSU	summing
GIMNNOR	morning
GIMNNTU	munting
GIMNOOR	mooring
GIMNOOT	mooting
GIMNOPP	mopping
GIMNORU	rouming
GIMNOST	gnomist
GIMNOSU	mousing
	souming
GIMRSUU	guruism
GINNNOO	nooning
GINNNOR	ronning
GINNNOW	wonning
GINNNPU	punning
GINNNRU	running
GINNNSU	sunning
GINNNTU	tunning
GINNOPS	spongin
GINNORS	snoring
	sorning
GINNORU	grunion
GINNORW	ingrown
GINNOST	stoning
GINNPRU	pruning
GINNRSU	nursing
GINNRTU	turning
GINNTTU	nutting
GINNTUV	vingt-un
GINNTUY	untying
GINOOPS	sooping
GINOORT	rooting
GINOPPP	popping
GINOPPS	sopping
GINOPPT	topping
GINOPPW	wopping
GINOPRS	prosing
GINOPRU	ingroup
	pouring
GINOPRV	proving
GINOPST	posting
	stoping
GINOPTT	potting
GINOPTU	pouting
GINORSS	ingross
	signors
GINORST	sorting
GINORSU	rousing
	souring
GINORSY	signory
GINORTT	rotting
GINORTU	routing
	touring
GINOSSS	sossing
GINOSST	stingos
	tossing
GINOSSU	sousing
GINOSTT	sotting
GINOSTU	tousing
GINOSTV	stoving
GINOSTW	stowing
GINOTTT	totting
GINOTTW	wotting
GINOTUW	outwing
GINPPPU	pupping
GINPPSU	supping
GINPPTU	tupping
GINPRRU	purring
GINPRSY	springy
GINPSUW	upswing
GINPTTU	putting
GINRSST	strings
GINRSTU	rusting
GINRSTY	stringy
GINRSUU	usuring
GINRTTU	rutting
GINTTTU	tutting
GIOOPRR	porrigo
GIOPRRU	prurigo
GIOPSSY	gossipy
GIOSSYZ	zygosis
GISWWYY	wysiwyg
GJNOOSU	goujons
GJOORTT	jogtrot
GLLLOOR	log-roll
GLMOOOR	moorlog
GLMOOYY	myology
GLMORUW	lugworm
GLNNOOR	lorgnon
GLNNSUU	unslung
GLNOOOY	noology
GLNOOPR	prolong
GLNOOPY	polygon
GLNORWY	wrongly
GLNOSUW	sunglow
GLNOTTU	glutton
GLNOUYY	youngly
GLOOORY	orology
GLOOOTY	otology
GLOOOYZ	zoology
GLOORUY	urology
GLORSSY	grossly
GLPRSUY	splurgy
GMMOSUU	gummous
GMMPUUW	mugwump
GMNOORU	gunroom
GMNOORW	morwong
GMOOSTU	gomutos
GMORSUU	grumous
GMORTUW	mugwort
GMRUYYZ	zymurgy
GNNORUW	ungrown
GNNORYY	gyronny
GNNPTUU	punt-gun
GNNRUUW	unwrung
GNOOORS	gorsoon
GNOOOSS	gossoon
GNOOOYZ	zoogony
GNOPRTU	gunport
GNOPRUW	grown-up
	upgrown
GOORSTT	grottos
GOORTUW	outgrow

H

HHIIPPS	hippish
HHIISTW	whitish
HHINNSU	Hunnish
HHINORS	hornish
HHIOPST	hip-shot
HHIORSW	whorish
HHIOSTT	hottish
	shit-hot
HHKNORU	Kuh-horn
HHOOSTT	hotshot
HIIIKRS	rikishi
HIIJKNS	hijinks
HIIKMSS	Sikhism
HIIKNNT	think-in
HIIKNPS	kinship
	pinkish
HIILMTU	lithium
HIILPST	shilpit
HIILPTY	pithily
HIILRTT	trilith
HIIMPSW	wimpish
HIIMSSS	missish
HIIMSTT	shittim
HIINORS	roinish

HIINSSW swinish
HIIORST histrio
HIIPSUZ Ziphius
HIISTTT tittish
HIKLSSU luskish
HIKLSUY huskily
HIKMNOS monkish
HIKMRSU murkish
HIKNNOR inkhorn
HIKNNTU unthink
HIKNOOP hook-pin
HIKOORS rookish
HIKORSY Yorkish
HIKRSTU Turkish
HILLOPT hilltop
HILLOPY lyophil
HILLRSY shrilly
HILLRTY thrilly
HILMMOU holmium
HILMOPS lompish
△phlomis
HILMOSW wholism
HILMPSU lumpish
HILMSUY mushily
HILMTUU thulium
HILNNTY ninthly
HILOOTT otolith
HILOOTZ zoolith
HILORTU urolith
HILOSSW slowish
HILOSTU loutish
HILOSTW wholist
HILOSTY hyloist
HILOSVW wolvish
HILOSWY showily
HILOTWW whitlow
HILPRUW upwhirl
HILSSTY stylish
HILSTTY thistly
HILSTXY sixthly
HIMMMTU Thummim
HIMMOST Thomism
HIMMPSU mumpish
HIMMRSU rummish
HIMMSTY mythism
HIMNOOS moonish
HIMNSTY hymnist
HIMOORS △moorish
HIMOPRS Orphism
rompish
HIMOPSS sophism
HIMOPST photism
HIMORST rim-shot
HIMORTU thorium
HIMOSSU Suomish
HIMOSTT Thomist
HIMOTTY timothy
HIMPRSY shrimpy
HIMPRTU triumph
HIMPTUY pythium
HIMRSTY rhymist
HIMSSTU isthmus
HIMSTTY mythist
HINNNSU nunnish
HINNOOT Honiton
HINNORT tinhorn
HINNOST tonnish
HINNPSU nunship
HINOORT hornito
HINOORZ horizon
HINOOST insooth
HINOPPS shippon
HINOPSS sonship
HINORST hornist
HINORSU nourish
HINORSY roynish
HINORTW throw-in
HINOSSW snowish
HINOSTW townish
HINPPSU push-pin
HINPTUW unwhipt
HINRSTU runtish
HINSTUW Whitsun
HIOOPRS poorish
HIOPPPS poppish
HIOPPTW whip-top
HIOPRSW △worship
HIOPSST sophist
HIOPSSY physios
HIOPSTU uphoist
HIORSSU sourish
HIORSTY history
Toryish
HIOSSTT sottish
HIOTTUW outwith
without
HIQSSUY squishy
HIRSTTU ruttish
HIRSTTY thirsty
thristy
HKKLOOZ kolkhoz
HKKOOSY skyhook
HKKOSTU Sukkoth
HKNOOTU nut-hook
HKNOOWW knowhow
know-how
HKOOOPT pothook
HKORSWY workshy
HLMNOTY monthly
HLMNPYY nymphly
HLMOOTW owl-moth
HLMORRY myrrhol
HLMRTUY Lythrum
HLOOSTY soothly
HLOPRTY prothyl
HLORSTY shortly
HLOTUYY youthly
HLPRSUU sulphur
HMMNOOY homonym
HMMOOSU hoummos
HMMRTUY thrummy
HMNOPSY nymphos
HMNOPYY hyponym
HMOOPRS morphos
HMOPRSU rum-shop
HNNORSU unshorn
HNNORTU horn-nut
HNNOSTY synthon
HNNOSUW unshown
HNOOPTY typhoon
HNOORSU honours
HNOOSTU unshoot
HNORTUW unworth
HNOSTUU unshout
HNPSTUU hunt's-up
Pushtun
HNRTTUU untruth
HOOPPPS pop-shop
HOOPPST potshop
HOOPRST porthos
HOOPSTU Pushtoo
upshoot
HOOPSTY toyshop
HOORRRS horrors
HOORRST orthros
HOOSTTU outshot
HOPRSTU Hotspur
HOPRTUW upthrow
HOPSTTU shotput
HOPSTUU push-out
HOPSTUY typhous
HORSTUU outrush
HOSTTUU shut-out
HPRSSUY Syrphus
HRSSTUY thyrsus

I

IIIJJLN jinjili
IIIKMNN minikin
IIISTTW wistiti
IIJLLNO jillion
IIJMNOS misjoin
IIJNNOT injoint
IIKKNPS kip-skin
IIKLLMY milkily
IIKLLOS oil-silk
IIKLLSY silkily
IIKLMNP limpkin
IIKLMRU Krilium®
IIKLNOS oilskin
IIKLPSY spikily
IIKLRSY riskily
IIKMNOR kirimon
IIKMNPS simpkin
IIKMPRT pit-mirk
IILLLLW ill-will
IILLLMO oil-mill
IILLLSY sillily
IILLMNO million
IILLMSY slimily
IILLNOP pillion
IILLNOZ zillion
IILLNST instill
IILLNTT littlin
IILMNOS lionism
IILMORS similor

IILMOSS limosis
IILMOSZ Zoilism
IILMSTU stimuli
IILMSTY mistily
IILNNOT Nitinol
IILNNSU insulin
IILNORS sirloin
IILNOSY noisily
IILNPPY nippily
IILNPTU pili-nut
IILNPUV pulvini
IILNRSV rivlins
IILOPRT tripoli
IILOPST pilotis
IILORTV vitriol
IILOSTV violist
IILOSTZ Zoilist
IILPRVY privily
IILPSTY tipsily
IILTTUY utility
IILTTWY wittily
IIMMMNU minimum
IIMMNSU minimus
IIMNOSS mission
IIMNOSU nimious
IIMNOSZ Zionism
IIMNOTX mixtion
IIMNPRT imprint
IIMOPSU impious
IIMOSST mitosis
IIMOSSU simious
IIMOSTT Titoism
IIMPSTT Pittism
IIMRTTU tritium
IIMRTUV trivium
IIMSSTU missuit
IINNOOP opinion
IINNOTU unition
IINOPSS isospin
sinopis
IINORST ironist
IINORTT introit
IINOSTZ Zionist
IINOSUV invious
IINOTTU tuition
IINQRUY inquiry
IINRTTY △trinity
IINSTTW intwist
IIOPRSS pissoir
IIORSSV virosis
IIORSTV ivorist
visitor
IIOSTTT Titoist
IIOSTTU oustiti
IIPRSST spirits
tripsis
IIPRSTY spirity
IIPRTVY privity
IJJSTUU ju-jitsu
IJKLLOY killjoy
IJKMPSU ski-jump
IJLLLOY jollily
IJLLOTY jollity
IJLMNOR Mjölnir
IJLMPUY jumpily
IJLNOQU jonquil
IJLNOTY jointly
IJNNOTU unjoint
IKKMNOU kikumon
IKKNORT kirkton
IKLLSUY sulkily
IKLMNPU lumpkin
IKLMNRU milk-run
IKLMOOS lookism
IKLMOPS milk-sop
IKLMORS Riksmål
IKLMOSY smokily
IKLMRUY murkily
IKLMSUY muskily
IKLNOOS skolion
IKLNOOT kiloton
IKLNPSU skulpin
IKLNRWY wrinkly
IKLOOTT toolkit
IKLOSSU souslik
IKMNOOO okimono
IKMNOOS kimonos
mono-ski
IKMNORS mikrons
IKMNOSW misknow
IKMNPPU pumpkin
IKMNRTU trinkum
IKMOOST mistook
IKMOSSU koumiss
IKNNPTU unpinkt
IKNOOST isokont
IKNOPPS skin-pop
IKNOPST inkspot
IKNOSSW sow-skin
IKNPSTU sputnik
IKORSTY Yorkist
IKPRSSY krypsis
ILLLOWY lowlily
ILLMNOU mullion
ILLMNRU millrun
ILLMOOR moorill
ILLMPUY lumpily
ILLMSUU △limulus
ILLNOQU quillon
ILLNORU rullion
ILLNPUU lupulin
ILLNTUY nullity
ILLOORZ zorillo
ILLOPRY pillory
ILLOPWY pillowy
ILLOSUV villous
ILLOSUY lousily
ILLOTXY xylitol
ILLOWWY willowy
ILLPPUY pulpily
ILLQSSU squills
ILLRSUY surlily
ILLSTUY lustily
ILMMRUY rummily
ILMMSUU mimulus
ILMNOOT moonlit
ILMNOTW Miltown®
ILMOORY roomily
ILMOOSS molossi
ILMORTU turmoil
ILMOSTY moistly
ILMPSTU plumist
ILMSTUY mustily
Mytilus
ILMUYZZ muzzily
ILNNOPS non-slip
ILNNSUY sunnily
ILNOOOP poon-oil
ILNOOPS plosion
ILNOOPV volpino
ILNOOST soliton
ILNOPRU purloin
ILNOPSU upsilon
ILNOPSY ypsilon
ILNORST nostril
ILNORSU surloin
ILNORTU torulin
ILNOSTT Stilton
ILNOSTY stonily
ILNOSWY snowily
ILNOTUV volutin
ILNPSTU unspilt
ILNTTUY nuttily
ILOOORS rosolio
ILOOPST poloist
topsoil
ILOORTY olitory
ILOOSST soloist
ILOOSTY sootily
ILOOWYZ woozily
ILOPPSY soppily
ILOPRSY prosily
ILOPSUY piously
ILORRSY sorrily
ILOSSTY tossily
tylosis
ILRSSUU Silurus
ILRSTUY rustily
ILSSTTY stylist
IMMNOSU musimon
IMMNOUU muonium
IMMOPTU optimum
IMMSSTU summist
IMNNNOU munnion
IMNNOOR norimon
IMNNSSU Sunnism
IMNOOPP pompion
IMNOOPT tompion
IMNOORR morrion
IMNOORT monitor
tromino
IMNOOSS monosis
IMNOOST motions
IMNOOSU ominous
IMNOOSY isonomy
IMNOOUX oxonium

IMNOPPU pumpion
IMNORRU murrion
IMNORTY trionym
IMNOSVY visnomy
IMOOPRX proximo
IMOOSSS osmosis
IMOOSSU osmious
IMOPRST imports
tropism
IMOPRTU protium
IMOPSTU utopism
IMORSTU tourism
IMORSTY Toryism
trisomy
IMOSSYZ zymosis
IMOSTUV vomitus
IMOSTUW outswim
IMQRSUY squirmy
IMRSSTU sistrum
trismus
IMRTTUY yttrium
INNNOOR non-iron
INNNORU runnion
INNOOPS opsonin
INNOOST notions
INNOSTU nonsuit
INNQSUY squinny
INOOPRT portion
INOOPSS poisson
INOOPST options
positon
INOORST isotron
nitroso
torsion
INOORSZ zorinos
INOORTT tortoni
INOORTW tow-iron
INOOSUX noxious
INOPPST topspin
INOPPTT pint-pot
INOPPTY pit-pony
INOPSSU poussin
spinous
INOPSTU sit-upon
spinout
INORSTT Tritons
INORSTU nitrous
INORSUU ruinous
urinous
INORSUV unvisor
INOSSUU sinuous
INPRSTU unstrip
INPRSTY trypsin
INRSTTU intrust
INSSTUU sunsuit
INSTTUW untwist
INTTUWY unwitty
IOOPRSS porosis
IOOPRSV proviso
IOOPSTY isotopy
IOORSSS sorosis
IOORSTT risotto
IOORSTU riotous
IOPPPRT pitprop
IOPPRST ripstop
IOPPSST piss-pot
IOPRSSY pyrosis
IOPRSTT protist
tropist
IOPSTTU utopist
IOQRTTU quittor
IORRTTX tortrix
IORSSTU tsouris
IORSTTU tourist
IORSTTW twistor
IPRRSTU stirrup
IPRSTUU pursuit
IPSSSTY stypsis
IPTTTUY tittupy

J

JMOPTUU outjump
JNOORSU journos
sojourn

K

KLLMOSU mollusk
KLOOOTU lookout
outlook
KNNNOUW unknown
KNNORSY Nynorsk
KNOOPTT topknot
KNOPRTY krypton
KNORRTY krytron
KOOPRTW worktop
KOORTUW outwork
work-out
KOOSSUU soukous
KOOTTTY Kotytto
KORTTUW tutwork

L

LLLMMUU mulmull
LLMOOPR rollmop
LLMPPUY plumply
LLOOPRT roll-top
trollop
LLOORTU rollout
LLOPTUU pull-out
LMNOOOS Solomon
LMOOSTY toylsom
LMOPSUU plumous
LMOPSUY Olympus
LMRSTUU lustrum
LMSTUUU tumulus
LNNOPSU nonplus
LNOOPTU pultoon
LNRTUUV vulturn
LNRTUUY untruly
LOOORS oloroso
LOOORST rotolos
LOPPSUU pulpous
LOPPSUY polypus
LOPRSUY pylorus
LOPRTUY poultry
LORSTUU torulus
LOSTTUY stoutly
LPRSSUU surplus

M

MMNOSSU summons
MMOOPRS Mormops
MMOPSTY symptom
MNNOOOS monsoon
MNNOSYY synonym
MNNOTUU unmount
MNOOOPP pompoon
MNOOOYZ zoonomy
MNOOPTY toponym
MNOOSUY onymous
MNOOTTW towmont
MNOPRTU no-trump
MNORSTU nostrum
MNOSTTU muttons
MNOTTUY muttony
MOOOTYZ zootomy
MOOPPSU pompous
MOOPSSU opossum
MOOPSTT topmost
MOORTTT Tom-trot
MOOSTTU outmost
MOPSSUU spumous
MORRSTU rostrum

N

NNNSUUY unsunny
NNOOOPT pontoon
NNOOPRU pronoun
NNOOPSS sponson
NNOOPST non-stop
NNORSUW unsworn
NNOSSUY unsonsy
NNOSTYY syntony
NOOPRSS sponsor
NOORSTU unroost
NOORTUW outworn
worn-out
NOPSSTU sunspot
NOPSTUU spun-out
NORSUUZ Zonurus
NORTTUU outturn
turnout
NRSSTTU strunts
NRSSTUU sturnus
untruss
NRSTTUU untrust

O

OOOOPRT poor-oot
potoroo
OOOPRTU outroop
OOORTTU outroot
OOPRRTW row-port
OOPRSSU soursop
OOPRSTU portous
OOPRSTV provost

OOPRTTU	outport	OOPSTTU	outpost	OPPRSTY	stroppy
OOPRTUU	outpour	OORSTUU	routous	OPPRSUY	pyropus
	pour-out	OPPRRTU	purport	ORSSUUU	usurous
OOPSSTT	tosspot	OPPRSTU	support	ORSTTUU	surtout

8AAA

A

AAAACCRR	caracara	AAABHLMR	Alhambra	AAACHIPS	aphasiac
AAAACJRR	jararaca	AAABILNN	Albanian	AAACHLNR	anarchal
AAAACNRS	anasarca	AAABILTT	battalia	AAACHLSZ	chalazas
AAAADMTV	amadavat	AAABINSS	anabasis	AAACHNTY	Cathayan
AAAADTVV	avadavat	AAABINTV	Batavian	AAACIJMN	Jamaican
AAAAEMNR	Aramaean	AAABIPSS	piassaba	AAACILMN	maniacal
AAAAGGRR	agar-agar	AAABKPSS	baasskap	AAACILMR	calamari
AAAAHJMR	maharaja	AAABLMOS	abomasal	AAACILRS	Scalaria
AAAAHMNY	Mahayana	AAABLOPR	parabola	AAACILRV	calvaria
AAAAIMPR	arapaima	AAABLPRS	palabras	AAACILSY	calisaya
AAAAIRTX	ataraxia	AAABMMNR	Abram-man	AAACINRT	Craniata
AAAAJKRR	jararaka	AAACCDIN	Accadian	AAACINTV	cavatina
AAAAKKMT	takamaka	AAACCELN	calcanea	AAACIPSU	sapucaia
AAAAKKNT	katakana	AAACCEPR	carapace	AAACIRRS	sacraria
AAAAKLRZ	kala-azar	AAACCILR	calcaria	AAACIRTX	ataraxic
AAAALLVV	lava-lava	AAACCIMM	caimacam	AAACKMRT	tamarack
AAAALNTT	Atalanta	AAACCRTT	cataract	AAACLMRY	calamary
AAAAMMTT	matamata	AAACCTTU	tac-au-tac	AAACLRST	alcatras
AAAAMNRY	Ramayana	AAACDEIM	academia	AAACMRSS	macassar
AAAARRSS	sasarara	AAACDENR	Dracaena	AAACMRSU	amaracus
AAABBELT	abatable	AAACDEQU	aquacade	AAACNOSV	Casanova
AAABBHKL	kabbalah	AAACDETU	acaudate	AAACRRWY	carraway
AAABBILT	abbatial	AAACDILM	Adamical	AAACSTWY	castaway
AAABCCRT	baccarat	AAACDILR	caldaria	AAADEFWY	fade-away
AAABCHLS	calabash	AAACDINN	Canadian	AAADEGIM	Agamidae
AAABCHMU	macahuba	AAACDINR	acaridan	AAADEGNP	apanaged
AAABCINT	anabatic		Arcadian	AAADEHMV	Mahadeva
AAABCNRR	barracan	AAACDKLY	lackaday	AAADEINR	Araneida
	barranca	AAACDNNO	anaconda	AAADEKMV	Kamadeva
AAABCNRU	carnauba	AAACDNRS	sandarac	AAADEMNN	Mandaean
AAABCPRY	capybara	AAACDOTV	advocaat	AAADEMSV	Samaveda
AAABDEST	database	AAACEEFG	Fagaceae		Sama-Veda
AAABDKNT	databank	AAACEETX	Taxaceae	AAADENTV	vanadate
AAABDNNN	bandanna	AAACEGNT	agaçante	AAADEPRT	tapadera
AAABDNRS	saraband	AAACEGTU	aguacate	AAADGGHH	Haggadah
AAABDNRT	abradant	AAACEHLP	Acalepha	AAADGIMM	gammadia
AAABEGHL	galabeah	AAACEHLT	calathea	AAADGLMY	amygdala
AAABEGLL	gallabea	AAACEHLZ	chalazae	AAADHMNR	Ramadhan
AAABEHNR	habanera	AAACEHNR	Archaean	AAADHMRS	madrasah
AAABEHRT	barathea	AAACELMY	Macleaya	AAADHNRT	thanadar
AAABEILT	Labiatae	AAACELNT	analecta	AAADIILR	radialia
AAABEMPR	parabema	AAACELST	catalase	AAADIKKN	Akkadian
AAABGHIL	galabiah	AAACENNP	panacean	AAADILRU	adularia
AAABGILL	gallabia	AAACENST	Castanea	AAADIMNY	adynamia
AAABGILY	galabiya	AAACEPRV	praecava	AAADKLMN	kalamdan
AAABGLOR	algaroba	AAACGINT	caatinga	AAADKRRV	aardvark
AAABGMNQ	mbaqanga	AAACGLSW	scalawag	AAADLMNQ	qalamdan
AAABGRTU	rutabaga	AAACGMNP	campagna	AAADMNTU	tamandua
AAABHIMN	Bahamian	AAACGMNR	Armagnac	AAADMORT	matadora
		AAACHHHL	Halachah	AAADMRSS	madrassa
		AAACHINT	Cathaian	AAAEGISS	assegaai

AAAEGLMX	malaxage
AAAEGLRT	altarage
AAAEGNPP	appanage
AAAEGRST	gastraea
AAAEHMNT	anathema
AAAEHNPS	anaphase
AAAEINRR	Arenaria
AAAEKKRT	karateka
AAAEKLLV	Kalevala
AAAEKTWY	takeaway
AAAELMMN	analemma
AAAELMPT	palamate
AAAELMTX	malaxate
AAAELRTV	lavatera
AAAENNRZ	Nazarean
AAAENOPR	paranoea
AAAENPRV	paravane
AAAENPST	anapaest
AAAERTWY	tearaway
AAAFGINR	Graafian
AAAFGIRR	Fragaria
AAAFGLNO	Fanagalo
AAAFINST	fantasia
AAAFINUV	avifauna
AAAGGLLN	galangal
AAAGGLOP	galapago
AAAGHINN	Ghanaian
AAAGHINP	Panhagia
AAAGHINR	hiragana
AAAGHIPR	agraphia
AAAGHLMS	Malagash
AAAGHNTY	yataghan
AAAGILPT	patagial
AAAGILRT	aligarta
AAAGINRR	agrarian
AAAGLMSY	Malagasy
AAAGLNRS	Sangraal
AAAGLRRW	warragal
AAAGLRST	astragal
AAAGMPRR	paragram
AAAGNOPR	araponga
AAAGNPRS	parasang
AAAGNPRU	arapunga
AAAGORST	Saratoga
AAAGPRUY	Paraguay
AAAHIINW	Hawaiian
AAAHILMY	Himalaya
AAAHIMNR	maharani
AAAHIMNS	shamiana
AAAHIMRT	hamartia
AAAHINNY	Hinayana
AAAHINPR	raphania
AAAHKMNS	khansama
AAAHKRSS	rakshasa
AAAHLLLV	Valhalla
AAAHLLLW	Walhalla
AAAHMNNS	manna-ash
AAAHMNRT	amaranth
AAAHMRTT	Mahratta
AAAHNNSV	savannah
AAAHNOPR	anaphora
AAAHNSST	Sathanas
AAAHNSTY	athanasy
AAAHSWWY	wash-away
AAAHTTWY	thataway
AAAIINPR	apiarian
AAAIKKMM	kaimakam
AAAILLMR	malarial
AAAILLPT	palatial
AAAILMMM	Mammalia
AAAILMNR	malarian
AAAILMSV	malvasia
AAAILNRU	aularian
AAAILNST	Alsatian
AAAILPRV	paravail
AAAILRST	salariat
AAAILRSU	Laurasia
AAAIMMNT	Minamata
AAAIMMQQ	qaimaqam
AAAIMMRS	Aramaism
AAAIMMST	miasmata
AAAIMRST	Sarmatia
AAAIMRTT	Marattia
AAAINNRR	ranarian
AAAINOPR	paranoia
AAAINQRU	aquarian
AAAINRTT	Tatarian
AAAIPSSV	piassava
AAAKKTZZ	kazatzka
AAAKLWWY	walk-away
AAAKMNRS	namaskar
AAAKOSWY	soakaway
AAALLPRX	parallax
AAALNNPT	platanna
AAALNNTU	Annulata
AAALNPRT	rataplan
AAALNRTT	tarlatan
AAALPRST	satrapal
AAAMNOPR	panorama
AAAMNRRY	yarraman
AAAMNRST	Rastaman
AAAMNTTY	manyatta
AAAMOTTU	automata
AAAMQSTU	Squamata
AAAMRRSZ	zamarras
AAAMRTTU	traumata
AAAMRTZZ	razmataz
AAANOPRZ	parazoan
AAANORSY	sayonara
AAANPRTV	paravant
AAANQTUU	aquanaut
AAANRSTT	tarantas
AAAORSWY	soaraway
AAAPQRTU	paraquat®
AAASTWYY	stayaway
AABBCDKN	backband
AABBCDRS	scabbard
AABBCEKR	bareback
AABBCEKT	backbeat
AABBCINR	barbican
AABBCIRR	barbaric
AABBCIST	sabbatic
AABBCORS	barbasco
AABBDEIS	Abbaside
AABBDENS	baseband
AABBDERT	barbated
AABBDORS	Barbados
AABBEELR	bearable
AABBEELT	beatable
AABBEILL	bailable
AABBEKLN	bankable
AABBELLM	blamable
AABBELLS	baseball
AABBELRY	bearably
AABBEORT	bareboat
AABBHHLL	blah-blah
AABBHKSU	babushka
AABBIILL	bilabial
AABBILLL	bail-ball
AABBILRT	barbital
AABBIRSU	babirusa
AABBKLTY	baby-talk
AABBLLMY	blamably
AABBLSSU	subbasal
AABBMMOZ	zambomba
AABBNOOR	bona-roba
AABCCCHI	bacchiac
AABCCEHK	backache
AABCCELR	cable-car
AABCCELS	cascabel
AABCCERT	braccate
AABCCHIN	Bacchian
AABCCHIS	biscacha
AABCCHIZ	bizcacha
AABCCHKT	backchat
AABCCHNT	bacchant
AABCCIMR	carbamic
AABCCINN	cannabic
AABCCKKP	backpack
AABCCKLP	blackcap
AABCCKLT	black-cat
AABCCKLW	clawback
AABCCMOT	catacomb
AABCDEIN	abidance
AABCDEIT	abdicate
AABCDEKT	back-date
AABCDELL	caballed
AABCDELN	balanced
AABCDHKN	backhand
AABCDHKR	hardback
AABCDIIS	diabasic
AABCDIKL	laid-back
AABCDINT	abdicant
AABCDKLN	backland
AABCDKLO	back-load
AABCDKRW	backward
	drawback
AABCDKRY	backyard
AABCDLLN	band-call
AABCDLNR	land-crab
AABCDNRR	brancard
AABCDNST	cab-stand
AABCEEIX	Bixaceae
AABCEENY	abeyance
AABCEERS	scarabee
AABCEERT	acerbate

AABCEERV	cave-bear
AABCEGOT	cabotage
AABCEHNR	barchane
AABCEILM	amicable
AABCEIMN	ambiance
AABCEINR	carabine
AABCEIRT	bacteria
AABCEJKN	jack-bean
AABCEJNO	Jacobean
AABCEKLM	clambake
AABCEKLR	lacebark
AABCEKST	back-seat
AABCELLP	placable
AABCELLR	caballer
	race-ball
AABCELLS	scalable
AABCELNR	balancer
	barnacle
AABCELOR	albacore
AABCELRT	bracteal
AABCELWY	cableway
AABCEMRV	vambrace
AABCENYY	abeyancy
AABCEORT	△boatrace
AABCERTT	cabretta
AABCESSU	abacuses
AABCFIIL	bifacial
AABCFKLL	backfall
	fall-back
AABCFKLT	flatback
AABCFKST	fastback
AABCHIKR	back-hair
AABCHILR	brachial
AABCHINR	branchia
AABCHKKR	hark-back
AABCHKLS	backlash
AABCHKRS	shabrack
AABCHKSW	backwash
AABCHLOO	coolabah
AABCHMRY	chambray
AABCHRRT	bar-chart
AABCIILS	basilica
AABCIINR	Cabirian
AABCIJNO	Bajocian
	Jacobian
AABCIKLT	tailback
AABCILLR	bacillar
AABCILMS	balsamic
	cabalism
AABCILMY	amicably
AABCILNN	cannibal
AABCILNO	anabolic
AABCILST	basaltic
	cabalist
AABCIMNR	Cambrian
AABCINNN	cannabin
AABCINNO	Baconian
AABCINNR	cinnabar
AABCINNS	cannabis
AABCINRT	Bactrian
AABCINSU	banausic
AABCINSY	Biscayan
AABCIOSS	Scabiosa
AABCIRSS	brassica
AABCISSS	abscissa
AABCKKLT	talkback
AABCKLNO	loanback
AABCKLNY	clay-bank
AABCKLPY	playback
AABCKNRS	snack-bar
AABCKPRT	bratpack
AABCKPSS	pass-back
AABCKRRS	barracks
AABCKSWY	swayback
	sway-back
AABCLLLO	coalball
AABCLLLY	ballclay
AABCLLPY	placably
AABCLNUU	cunabula
AABCLRRY	carbaryl
AABCNORR	barranco
AABCRSTT	abstract
AABCRSWY	crab-yaws
AABDDEET	dead-beat
AABDDEHL	bald-head
AABDDEHN	headband
AABDDENR	brandade
AABDDESS	badassed
AABDDLNS	badlands
AABDDMOR	damboard
AABDEEHL	beheadal
AABDEELR	bear-lead
	readable
AABDEELT	dateable
	dealbate
AABDEELV	evadable
AABDEERY	bayadère
AABDEGIN	badinage
AABDEGIR	bigarade
AABDEGLR	gradable
AABDEGNT	T-bandage
AABDEHHI	dahabieh
AABDEHKR	hardbake
AABDEHMR	hardbeam
AABDEILN	baladine
AABDEILR	Labridae
AABDEINR	Abderian
AABDEIOU	aboideau
AABDEJLL	djellaba
AABDEKRY	daybreak
AABDELLU	laudable
AABDELMN	damnable
AABDELOR	adorable
AABDELOS	base-load
AABDELPT	baldpate
AABDELRS	baselard
AABDELRT	tradable
AABDELRW	drawable
AABDELRY	readably
AABDELSW	sawblade
AABDEMNS	beadsman
AABDEMRS	smear-dab
AABDENTU	unabated
AABDENUX	bandeaux
AABDENVW	waveband
AABDEORS	seaboard
AABDEORT	teaboard
AABDERRT	taberdar
AABDERRW	bearward
AABDERTV	vartabed
AABDERWY	waybread
AABDFHLN	fahlband
AABDFRRT	draft-bar
AABDGMOS	gambados
AABDGNOV	vagabond
AABDGORR	garboard
AABDGOTU	gadabout
AABDHINR	hair-band
AABDHLLN	hand-ball
AABDHLLR	hardball
AABDHRSU	subahdar
AABDHRSW	Bradshaw
AABDIILS	basidial
AABDILLN	balladin
AABDIMNR	madbrain
AABDINNR	rainband
AABDKNNS	sandbank
AABDLLRY	balladry
AABDLLUY	laudably
AABDLMNU	labdanum
AABDLMNY	damnably
AABDLNPT	platband
AABDLOOT	boat-load
AABDLOPR	lap-board
AABDLORR	Labrador
	larboard
AABDLORY	adorably
AABDMNNS	bandsman
AABDMNNY	bandyman
AABDNNTU	abundant
AABDNPSS	band-pass
AABDNRRY	barnyard
AABDOPRX	pax-board
AABDORSV	bravados
AABDORWY	broadway
	wayboard
AABDRRSS	brassard
AABDRSTY	bastardy
AABEEFLN	flea-bane
AABEEFLS	leaf-base
AABEEGKR	breakage
AABEEGNT	abnegate
AABEEHLL	healable
AABEEHLT	hateable
AABEEHMR	harambee
AABEEKLM	makeable
AABEEKLT	takeable
AABEEKMT	bakemeat
	makebate
AABEEKRW	bakeware
AABEELLS	leasable
	saleable
AABEELMN	amenable
	nameable
AABEELMT	tameable
AABEELPT	tapeable

Words marked △ may be spelled also with a capital letter

AABEELRS	erasable
AABEELRT	rateable
	tearable
AABEELRW	wearable
AABEELST	eatables
AABEEMPR	abampere
AABEENNW	wannabee
AABEENOR	anaerobe
AABEERRS	bear's-ear
AABEERRT	aberrate
AABEERTT	trabeate
AABEFHKL	half-beak
AABEFLMU	flambeau
AABEGHIL	galabieh
AABEGHKS	shake-bag
AABEGHLN	hangable
AABEGHNR	berghaan
AABEGHRT	earth-bag
AABEGILN	gainable
AABEGLLL	glabella
AABEGLLM	ball-game
AABEGLRT	glabrate
AABEGLRU	arguable
AABEGMNR	bargeman
AABEGMNY	mangabey
AABEGMRT	bregmata
AABEGMTT	gambetta
AABEGNOR	baronage
AABEGORT	abrogate
AABEGOST	sabotage
AABEHIRR	herbaria
AABEHITW	Wahabite
AABEHKLS	shakable
AABEHLMS	shamable
AABEHLNY	Hyblaean
AABEHLOT	oathable
AABEHLPS	shapable
AABEHLPT	alphabet
AABEHLRW	warhable
AABEHLSW	washable
AABEIKRR	air-brake
AABEILLM	mailable
AABEILLS	isabella
	sailable
AABEILNR	inarable
AABEILNS	banalise
AABEILNZ	banalize
AABEILRS	raisable
AABEILRV	variable
AABEILST	satiable
AABEILTV	ablative
AABEINOZ	zabaione
AABEINRR	Briarean
AABEINRT	rabatine
AABEINST	basanite
AABEIOTU	aboiteau
AABEIRSV	abrasive
AABEIRTU	aubretia
	aubrieta
AABEJKRW	break-jaw
AABEJMUX	jambeaux
AABEKLLT	talkable
AABEKLLW	walkable
AABEKMNR	brakeman
AABEKNPT	peat-bank
AABEKNRT	bank-rate
AABEKNRV	brake-van
AABEKPRR	parbreak
AABEKRRS	baresark
AABELLMT	meatball
AABELLNO	loanable
AABELLPP	palpable
AABELLPS	lapsable
AABELLPY	playable
AABELLSV	salvable
AABELLSY	saleably
AABELLUV	valuable
AABELMNY	amenably
AABELMOT	Metabola
AABELMST	blastema
	lambaste
AABELMSU	amusable
AABELMTT	table-mat
AABELMTU	ambulate
AABELNNT	tannable
AABELNPS	anableps
AABELNPT	pantable
AABELNRY	balneary
AABELOPR	parabole
AABELORR	arboreal
AABELOSV	lavaboes
AABELOVW	avowable
AABELPPT	tappable
AABELPRS	sparable
AABELPSS	passable
AABELRST	arbalest
AABELRTY	betrayal
	rateably
AABELSTT	statable
	tastable
AABELSTW	wastable
AABELTTU	tabulate
AABELTTX	battle-ax
AABELTUX	tableaux
AABENRRT	aberrant
AABENRST	ratsbane
AABENSTU	Antabuse®
AABEORRT	arboreta
AABEORST	rabatoes
AABFHLLL	half-ball
AABFILUX	fabliaux
AABFLLST	fastball
AABFLOTT	faltboat
	flatboat
AABGGGNN	gang-bang
AABGGNOT	taboggan
AABGGRRT	braggart
AABGHKRS	shag-bark
AABGHPRR	bar-graph
AABGILNT	bang-tail
AABGLLLO	goalball
AABGLLRY	ballyrag
AABGLMNS	slam-bang
AABGLMNU	galbanum
AABGLNPS	slap-bang
AABGLRUY	arguably
AABGMORR	barogram
AABGNORZ	garbanzo
AABHHORU	brouhaha
AABHIIMP	Amphibia
AABHIINU	bauhinia
AABHIJMY	jambiyah
AABHILLR	hair-ball
AABHILTU	habitual
AABHIMST	Baathism
	Ba'athism
AABHIMSW	Wahabism
AABHINST	habitans
AABHINTT	habitant
AABHIRST	tabashir
AABHISTT	Baathist
	Ba'athist
AABHLLSW	washball
AABHMNRS	bran-mash
AABHNOTU	△autobahn
AABHQSSU	squabash
AABHRRSU	surbahar
AABIIJLT	jail-bait
AABIILNS	Basilian
AABIITTW	wait-a-bit
AABILLLY	labially
AABILLST	ballista
AABILMNS	bailsman
AABILMNU	bimanual
AABILMOT	mail-boat
AABILNNU	biannual
AABILNOP	Polabian
AABILNOR	baronial
AABILNOT	ablation
AABILNRU	binaural
AABILNTY	banality
AABILOST	sail-boat
AABILOTT	boattail
AABILRRT	arbitral
AABILRST	arbalist
AABILRVY	variably
AABIMNNO	bonamani
AABIMNRU	manubria
AABIMORS	ambrosia
AABIMRSU	simaruba
AABINNPR	brainpan
AABINORS	abrasion
AABINRST	bartisan
AABINRTZ	bartizan
AABIORRS	sorbaria
AABIORTT	abattoir
AABIOSSY	bioassay
AABIOTVX	abat-voix
AABIRTUY	△rubaiyat
AABJLMNO	jambolan
AABJORTU	abat-jour
AABKLLPR	ballpark
AABKMNNS	banksman
AABKOPRS	soapbark
AABLLMOR	balmoral
AABLLNST	tan-balls

AABLLOPS	soap-ball
AABLLPPY	palpably
AABLLPRT	trap-ball
AABLLSTU	blastula
AABLLUVY	valuably
AABLMNOR	abnormal
AABLMNTU	ambulant
AABLNTTT	blattant
AABLOTUY	layabout
AABLPSSY	passably
AABLRRSU	saburral
AABLRSUU	subaural
AABLSTTU	abuttals
AABMMOSU	abomasum
AABMNNOO	bonamano
AABMNOTW	batwoman
AABMNRTU	rambutan
AABMORTU	marabout
	tamboura
AABMOSSU	abomasus
AABNNOST	absonant
AABORRRT	barrator
AABORSTT	barostat
AABRRRTY	barratry
AABRRSST	brassart
AACCCDIS	saccadic
AACCCHHU	cachucha
AACCCLOO	Coca-Cola®
AACCCRUY	accuracy
AACCDEFR	face-card
AACCDEIM	academic
AACCDELO	accolade
AACCDENU	caducean
AACCDERR	racecard
AACCDERS	card-case
AACCDHIL	Chaldaic
AACCDHIR	characid
AACCDORT	coat-card
AACCDOVY	advocacy
AACCEEFH	face-ache
AACCEELT	calceate
AACCEENT	cetacean
AACCEFLO	coalface
AACCEGOR	accorage
AACCEGRU	carucage
AACCEHIX	cachexia
AACCEILN	calcanei
AACCEINR	Circaean
AACCEIRR	cercaria
AACCELOR	caracole
AACCELPT	placcate
AACCELRR	carceral
AACCENRT	carcanet
AACCERTU	accurate
	carucate
AACCFGOO	cacafogo
AACCFILR	farcical
AACCFLTU	calc-tufa
AACCFOOT	cocoa-fat
AACCGILT	galactic
AACCHHIL	Halachic
AACCHILL	caillach
AACCHILP	pachalic
AACCHINR	anarchic
	characin
AACCHINS	chicanas
AACCHISV	viscacha
AACCHIVZ	vizcacha
AACCHLLT	catch-all
AACCHLOR	charcoal
AACCHLOT	cachalot
AACCHLRS	clarsach
AACCHMNO	coachman
AACCHNOR	coranach
AACCIINV	vaccinia
AACCIIST	sciatica
AACCILNU	Canicula
AACCILNV	vaccinal
AACCILRU	acicular
AACCILTT	tactical
AACCIORU	cariacou
AACCIPTY	capacity
AACCIRTY	caryatic
AACCJKRW	crackjaw
AACCJORU	carcajou
	carjacou
AACCKORT	coatrack
AACCLLRU	calcular
AACCLMNY	clamancy
AACCLPRS	calcspar
AACCLRSU	saccular
AACCORRY	Caryocar
AACCOSTT	staccato
	stoccata
AACDDEFS	sad-faced
AACDDEHI	acid-head
AACDDEIL	daedalic
AACDDENV	advanced
AACDDEOP	Decapoda
AACDDERT	dead-cart
AACDDETU	caudated
AACDDILN	candidal
AACDEEHH	headache
AACDEEHR	headrace
AACDEEHS	headcase
AACDEELS	escalade
AACDEEPS	escapade
AACDEEST	estacade
AACDEETU	ecaudate
AACDEFFT	fat-faced
AACDEFHR	hardface
AACDEFLT	falcated
AACDEGGR	aggraced
AACDEGKP	packaged
AACDEGMR	card-game
	decagram
AACDEHHY	headachy
AACDEHIN	hacienda
AACDEHLN	Chaldean
AACDEHLP	cephalad
AACDEHMR	drachmae
AACDEHPT	death-cap
AACDEHRT	cathedra
AACDEHTT	attached
AACDEILS	sidalcea
AACDEIMN	maenadic
AACDEIMS	camisade
AACDEINR	radiance
AACDEIPR	Capridae
AACDEIRS	Scaridae
AACDEIRT	radicate
AACDEJNT	adjacent
AACDELNR	calendar
	landrace
AACDELNV	valanced
AACDELOS	case-load
	escalado
AACDELTV	clavated
AACDENOT	cane-toad
AACDENPT	tap-dance
AACDENTU	aduncate
AACDENTV	tadvance
AACDEOPS	escapado
AACDEOTU	autocade
AACDEOTV	△advocate
AACDEQUY	adequacy
AACDERST	cadastre
AACDERTU	arcuated
AACDGGHI	Haggadic
AACDGINR	arcading
	carangid
	cardigan
AACDHHKR	hardhack
AACDHIIS	dichasia
AACDHILL	chillada
AACDHILR	diarchal
AACDHIMR	drachmai
AACDHINP	handicap
AACDHINR	arachnid
AACDHKRT	hardtack
AACDHLNP	handclap
AACDHLOT	cathodal
AACDHLRY	charlady
AACDHMMR	drammach
AACDHMRS	drachmas
AACDHNRT	handcart
AACDHORT	Chordata
AACDHPRS	crashpad
AACDIIMT	Adamitic
AACDIINR	Cnidaria
AACDIINS	ascidian
AACDIJLU	Judaical
AACDILLM	mail-clad
AACDILLP	palladic
AACDILMT	dalmatic
AACDILMU	caladium
AACDILNO	diaconal
AACDILNR	△cardinal
AACDILNU	Claudian
	dulciana
AACDILNV	Vandalic
AACDILOZ	zodiacal
AACDILRR	railcard
AACDIMNO	mandioca
AACDIMNY	adynamic
AACDIMOS	camisado

Words marked △ may be spelled also with a capital letter

AACDIMRS	Camisard
AACDIMRT	dramatic
AACDINNS	Scandian
AACDINOR	Orcadian
AACDINRT	radicant
	△tridacna
AACDINRY	radiancy
AACDIOTU	autacoid
AACDIRTY	caryatid
AACDITUY	audacity
AACDJQRU	△jacquard
AACDKLLN	lackland
AACDKLOP	pack-load
AACDLORT	cartload
AACDLOSS	scalados
AACDLOSV	Calvados
AACDLRTY	dactylar
AACDMMOR	cardamom
AACDMMRU	cardamum
AACDMNNO	mancando
AACDMNOR	cardamon
AACDNSST	sand-cast
AACDOOSV	avocados
AACDORRT	cartroad
AACEEEHT	Theaceae
AACEEELO	Oleaceae
AACEEFIT	facetiae
AACEEFLL	lace-leaf
AACEEFLP	paleface
AACEEGIR	acierage
	agacerie
AACEEGKU	ague-cake
AACEEGLR	clearage
AACEEGLV	cleavage
AACEEGPS	space-age
AACEEGRS	gear-case
AACEEHLP	acalephe
AACEEHLT	leachate
AACEEHRT	tracheae
AACEEILM	Limaceae
AACEEIMT	emaciate
AACEEINN	encaenia
AACEEIRT	acierate
AACEEITV	Vitaceae
AACEEKRT	caretake
AACEELMU	Ulmaceae
AACEELRT	lacerate
AACEELST	escalate
AACEELTU	aculeate
AACEEMNS	Macanese
	Maecenas
AACEEMOR	Moraceae
AACEEMRT	macerate
	racemate
AACEEMST	casemate
AACEEMSU	Musaceae
AACEENNT	catenane
AACEENRS	Canarese
	Cesarean
AACEENTT	catenate
AACEEORS	Rosaceae
AACEEPRT	caper-tea
AACEEPSS	seascape
AACEERSU	caesurae
AACEERSY	easy-care
AACEERTU	Rutaceae
AACEERTV	acervate
AACEETUV	evacuate
AACEETVX	excavate
AACEFFHL	half-face
AACEFFIN	affiance
AACEFHLP	halfpace
AACEFIST	fasciate
AACEFKLO	loaf-cake
AACEFKMS	face-mask
AACEFLRS	leaf-scar
AACEFRRU	Furcraea
AACEFRST	seacraft
AACEFRTT	artefact
AACEGHNT	chantage
AACEGILN	△angelica
AACEGILT	glaciate
AACEGINR	canaigre
AACEGIOP	apogaeic
AACEGIRR	carriage
AACEGIRV	vicarage
AACEGKPR	packager
AACEGKRT	trackage
AACEGLNY	lancegay
AACEGRSV	scavager
AACEHHLS	ash-leach
AACEHILL	achillea
	heliacal
AACEHILN	achenial
AACEHILP	△phacelia
AACEHIMR	△chimaera
AACEHIMT	haematic
AACEHIPT	Hepatica
AACEHIRS	archaise
AACEHIRT	theriaca
AACEHIRZ	archaize
AACEHISZ	Schizaea
AACEHLNT	calanthe
AACEHLNU	eulachan
AACEHLRT	tracheal
AACEHLRX	exarchal
AACEHLST	alcahest
AACEHMNP	camphane
AACEHMRS	marchesa
AACEHMST	schemata
AACEHNOP	Phocaena
AACEHNRR	Achernar
AACEHPRT	racepath
AACEHPUX	chapeaux
AACEHRRR	rear-arch
AACEHRSU	△archaeus
AACEHRTT	reattach
AACEHTUX	châteaux
AACEIILN	laciniae
AACEIINT	actiniae
AACEIIPR	Picariae
AACEIKMT	kamacite
AACEILLM	camellia
AACEILLN	alliance
	canaille
AACEILMN	analcime
	calamine
AACEILMT	calamite
AACEILNS	canalise
AACEILNT	analcite
	laitance
AACEILNU	acauline
AACEILNV	valiance
AACEILNZ	canalize
AACEILOP	alopecia
AACEILRT	tailrace
AACEILRV	△cavalier
AACEILST	saliceta
AACEIMNR	American
	Cinerama®
AACEIMNS	amnesiac
AACEIMRS	macarise
	mesaraic
AACEIMRZ	macarize
AACEIMTT	catamite
AACEIMUX	camaïeux
AACEINNO	Oceanian
AACEINPR	Caprinae
AACEINRS	canaries
AACEINRT	carinate
AACEINRV	variance
AACEINST	estancia
AACEIOPR	capoeira
AACEIPRS	airspace
AACEIPRT	apricate
AACEIPTT	apatetic
	capitate
AACEIRTV	vicarate
AACEITTV	activate
	cavitate
AACEJLTU	jaculate
AACEKKLW	cakewalk
AACEKRTT	attacker
AACELLLR	all-clear
AACELLMR	marcella
AACELLOT	allocate
AACELLTY	alleycat
AACELMNP	placeman
AACELMTU	maculate
AACELNNU	cannulae
AACELNOR	Carolean
	lecanora
AACELNPR	parlance
AACELNPT	placenta
AACELNRT	lacerant
AACELNRY	arcanely
AACELNST	analects
AACELNTU	lacunate
	tenacula
AACELOSU	acaulose
AACELPSU	scapulae
AACELRSU	caesural
AACELRWY	clearway
AACELSTY	catalyse
AACELTTY	cattleya

AACELTYZ	catalyze
AACEMNOR	amorance
AACEMNPS	spaceman
AACEMNST	camstane
AACEMRSS	massacre
AACEMSTT	cat's-meat
AACENOTU	oceanaut
AACENPRS	pancreas
AACENPST	pastance
AACENPSU	saucepan
AACENRST	canaster
AACENRTT	reactant
AACENRTU	areca-nut
AACENRTY	catenary
AACENRVZ	czarevna
AACENSTT	castanet
AACENTUV	evacuant
AACEOPRT	caproate
AACEORSU	araceous
AACEOSST	seacoast
AACEPPPR	cap-paper
AACEPPSU	pupa-case
AACERSSS	rascasse
AACERSSU	caesuras
AACERSTT	castrate
AACERTTT	tractate
AACESSTT	sceattas
AACESUWY	causeway
AACFFHLL	half-calf
AACFGRST	cragfast
AACFHMST	camshaft
AACFILLY	facially
AACFILOS	fasciola
AACFIRRT	aircraft
AACFIRTT	artifact
AACFISST	△fascista
AACFJKLP	flapjack
AACGGINO	anagogic
AACGGIOP	apagogic
AACGHIPR	agraphic
AACGHIRR	chiragra
AACGHLLO	agalloch
AACGHNOR	charango
AACGHOPZ	gazpacho
AACGHORU	guacharo
AACGIILN	Galician
AACGIIMN	magician
AACGIINR	garcinia
AACGILLN	Gallican
AACGILLO	alogical
AACGILLU	alguacil
AACGILNN	Anglican
AACGILNO	analogic
AACGILNV	galvanic
AACGILOX	coxalgia
AACGILRT	tragical
AACGIMMT	magmatic
AACGIMNN	manganic
AACGIMNP	campaign
	pangamic
AACGIMOP	apogamic
AACGIMRR	margaric
AACGIMUU	△guaiacum
AACGISTY	sagacity
AACGLMOU	glaucoma
AACGMNRS	cragsman
AACGNOSU	guanacos
AACGNRVY	vagrancy
AACHHIKR	kachahri
AACHHKNU	Chanukah
AACHHTWY	hatchway
AACHIIMR	mariachi
AACHIKNR	chinkara
AACHILLP	caliphal
AACHILLR	rachilla
AACHILMS	chamisal
AACHILMT	thalamic
AACHILNP	chaplain
AACHILPS	calipash
AACHILRV	archival
AACHIMNN	chainman
	Chinaman
AACHIMNP	chinampa
AACHIMNR	chairman
AACHIMNS	shamanic
AACHIMNT	matachin
AACHIMRR	armchair
AACHIMRS	archaism
	charisma
AACHIMSS	chiasmas
AACHIMST	cathisma
AACHINNO	Noachian
AACHINNT	acanthin
AACHINRT	canthari
AACHINSW	chainsaw
AACHIPTT	chapatti
AACHIRST	archaist
AACHIRTX	taxiarch
AACHKPSS	schapska
AACHKSTY	haystack
AACHLMNO	monachal
AACHLMOS	chloasma
AACHLORT	thoracal
AACHLSTU	calathus
AACHMMNR	marchman
AACHMNNR	ranchman
AACHMNTW	watchman
AACHMNUY	naumachy
AACHMORT	achromat
	trachoma
AACHMPRT	champart
AACHMPRY	pharmacy
AACHMRST	crash-mat
AACHNOSU	huanacos
AACHNPRS	sarpanch
AACHNRST	trashcan
AACHNRVY	navarchy
AACHNSTU	acanthus
AACHOPPR	approach
AACHORTU	racahout
AACHOTTU	tacahout
AACHRTUY	autarchy
AACIILMN	animalic
AACIILMO	maiolica
AACIILRV	vicarial
AACIIMNT	animatic
AACIINNS	Sicanian
AACIINNT	actinian
AACIINPR	picarian
AACIINPT	capitani
AACIINST	actinias
AACIJLMO	majolica
AACIJNOP	japonica
AACIKLMS	mailsack
AACIKLRR	rack-rail
AACIKMNW	mackinaw
AACIKRTU	autarkic
AACILLMR	lacrimal
AACILLMT	climatal
AACILLPY	apically
AACILLRY	racially
AACILMNT	calamint
	claimant
AACILMOR	acromial
AACILMOT	atomical
AACILMRT	mail-cart
AACILMTY	calamity
AACILNNO	Laconian
AACILNOR	Carolina
	conarial
AACILNRT	cant-rail
AACILNRV	carnival
AACILNTT	Atlantic
	△tantalic
AACILNTU	nautical
AACILNTY	analytic
AACILNUV	navicula
AACILNVY	valiancy
AACILOPR	carap-oil
AACILORV	Arvicola
AACILOTT	tail-coat
AACILPRU	piacular
AACILPST	aplastic
AACILPSZ	capsizal
AACILPTU	capitula
AACILPTY	atypical
AACILQRU	acquiral
AACILRTY	alacrity
AACILRUU	△auricula
AACILSTT	cat's-tail
	statical
AACILSTY	salacity
AACIMMNO	ammoniac
AACIMMRS	macarism
	marasmic
AACIMNOR	macaroni
	marocain
AACIMNOT	anatomic
AACIMORT	aromatic
AACIMRST	Sarmatic
AACINNOT	Catonian
AACINOPR	paranoic
AACINOPT	capitano
	pacation
AACINORT	Croatian
	raincoat

AACINORV	Racovian
AACINOTV	vacation
AACINPTY	capitayn
AACINQTU	acquaint
AACINRST	arcanist
AACINSTZ	stanzaic
AACINTTU	Tunicata
AACIPPRS	Capparis
AACIPRST	aspartic
AACIPRTY	rapacity
AACIQSTU	aquatics
AACIRRTT	△tartaric
AACIRSTT	castrati
AACIRSTZ	czaritsa
AACJKLPS	slapjack
AACJKLYZ	lazy-jack
AACJKOOR	jackaroo
AACKKNPS	knapsack
AACKLNPS	knapscal
AACKLOWY	lockaway
AACKMNRT	trackman
AACKMNST	tacksman
AACKORWY	rockaway
AACKRTWY	trackway
AACLLMMU	macallum
AACLLMRY	clay-marl
	lacrymal
AACLLNRY	carnally
AACLLRRY	carryall
	carry-all
AACLLRSY	rascally
AACLLSUU	clausula
AACLLSUY	casually
	causally
AACLLTUY	actually
AACLMNNS	clansman
AACLMNSS	classman
AACLMRRU	macrural
AACLNNOT	cantonal
AACLNNRU	cannular
AACLNNSU	cannulas
AACLNOPR	coplanar
AACLNOTT	octantal
AACLNRSU	lacunars
AACLNRUY	lacunary
AACLNTVY	vacantly
AACLOOPT	tapacolo
AACLOPTU	tapaculo
AACLORRU	oracular
AACLORSU	carousal
AACLORUV	vacuolar
AACLOSTT	cattalos
AACLPPRT	claptrap
AACLPRSU	capsular
	scapular
AACLPRTY	calyptra
AACLPSSU	scapulas
AACLPTTU	catapult
AACLRSTU	claustra
AACLRSUV	vascular
AACLSTTY	catalyst
AACLSTUY	casualty
AACMNOOR	macaroon
AACMNORS	mascaron
AACMNPRS	scrap-man
AACMNPRY	rampancy
AACMORSS	sarcomas
AACNNOSZ	canzonas
AACNPRTU	carap-nut
AACNRSTT	transact
AACOORTX	toxocara
AACOPRSU	acarpous
AACOPRTU	autocarp
AACOPSTV	postcava
AACORRTV	varactor
AACORSTT	castrato
AACORTTU	actuator
	autocrat
AADDDEEH	deadhead
	dead-head
AADDDEEL	dead-deal
AADDDEHN	dead-hand
AADDDGNR	granddad
AADDEEHT	dead-heat
AADDEELP	pale-dead
AADDEEMT	dead-meat
AADDEFHL	half-dead
AADDEFLL	dead-fall
AADDEHHR	hardhead
AADDEHLN	headland
AADDEHMN	handmade
AADDEILN	△dedalian
AADDEIRT	radiated
AADDELLW	dead-wall
AADDEMRY	daydream
AADDENRV	veranda'd
AADDGGOO	gado-gado
AADDGHLN	glad-hand
AADDGNRU	graduand
AADDGUYY	gaudy-day
AADDHHIL	lah-di-dah
AADDHHRS	shraddha
AADDHIMN	handmaid
AADDIINR	Diandria
AADDILNO	dianodal
AADDKMMO	mokaddam
AADDLLNY	landlady
AADDLNRW	landward
AADDLNRY	yardland
AADDMMQU	muqaddam
AADDNRST	sand-dart
	standard
AADDNRWY	yardwand
AADDOTYY	day-to-day
AADDRSTY	dastardy
AADEEGHR	headgear
AADEEGLT	galeated
AADEEGMN	endamage
AADEEGNR	Gadarene
AADEEHLR	hard-a-lee
AADEEHMT	meathead
AADEEILR	Airedale
AADEEIRT	eradiate
AADEEIRW	awearied
	wide-area
AADEELTV	alveated
AADEEMRR	demerara
AADEEMST	Teasmade®
AADEENPT	tapenade
AADEENTT	antedate
	Edentata
AADEEQTU	adequate
AADEFFLT	afflated
AADEFFRY	affrayed
AADEFHLT	△flathead
AADEFHST	headfast
AADEFILR	fair-lead
AADEFINT	anti-fade
AADEFIRS	faradise
AADEFIRZ	faradize
AADEFLLR	falderal
AADEFLRW	draw-leaf
AADEFLRY	defrayal
AADEFLTT	faldetta
AADEFOTU	auto-da-fé
AADEFSTY	feast-day
AADEGGRU	guardage
AADEGHLN	Danelagh
AADEGHRS	rhagades
AADEGILL	diallage
AADEGILT	gladiate
AADEGINR	drainage
	△gardenia
AADEGINT	indagate
AADEGITT	agitated
AADEGITV	divagate
AADEGJTU	adjutage
AADEGLMN	△magdalen
AADEGLMY	amygdale
AADEGLNS	seladang
AADEGRRW	draw-gear
AADEGRSV	savegard
AADEGRTU	graduate
AADEHHOR	hoarhead
AADEHILN	nail-head
AADEHILR	headrail
	railhead
AADEHIRR	diarrhea
AADEHIWY	hide-away
AADEHKMR	headmark
AADEHLLL	halalled
AADEHLMP	headlamp
AADEHLNR	anhedral
AADEHMNS	headsman
AADEHMST	masthead
AADEHNNR	near-hand
AADEHNNS	Shandean
AADEHNPS	sandheap
AADEHNRV	verandah
AADEHOPX	Hexapoda
AADEHRRW	hardware
AADEHRSS	harassed
AADEHRTY	death-ray
AADEHSTT	hastated
AADEILLR	Rallidae

AADEILMP	maid-pale
AADEILNN	Annelida
AADEILNT	dentalia
AADEILPR	praedial
AADEILPS	palisade
AADEILPT	lapidate
AADEILRS	salaried
AADEILRT	Araldite®
AADEILTV	validate
AADEIMNN	amandine
AADEIMNP	pandemia
AADEIMNR	marinade
AADEIMNT	animated
	diamanté
AADEIMPZ	diazepam
AADEIMRV	maravedi
AADEIMST	diastema
AADEINRR	darraine
AADEINRT	dentaria
	raindate
AADEIPRS	△paradise
	Sparidae
AADEIPSU	diapause
AADEIPTV	adaptive
AADEIRSV	Varidase®
AADEISST	diastase
AADEITVW	viewdata
AADEJMPY	pyjamaed
AADEJNNP	japanned
AADEKLLN	△lakeland
AADEKLNR	kalendar
AADEKLOP	peak-load
AADEKLOS	soda-lake
AADEKMNR	mandrake
AADELLPP	appalled
AADELLRT	dataller
AADELLWY	welladay
AADELMNR	alderman
	malander
AADELMNS	dalesman
	leadsman
AADELMPP	mad-apple
AADELMPT	date-palm
	palmated
AADELMYZ	amazedly
AADELNPT	peat-land
AADELNST	eastland
AADELQUU	Quaalude®
AADELRSY	saleyard
AADELRTU	radulate
AADELRTV	larvated
AADELRTY	daytaler
AADEMNNW	manna-dew
AADEMNOS	adenomas
AADEMNOT	Nematoda
AADEMNPS	spademan
AADEMNSY	dayes-man
AADEMNUZ	unamazed
AADEMORT	matadore
AADEMRRU	marauder
AADENOST	Sotadean
AADENRTT	tartaned
AADEOPRT	tapadero
AADEOPST	adespota
AADEORRT	aerodart
AADEPPRY	paper-day
AADEQRTU	quadrate
AADERRRW	rearward
AADERRST	rat-arsed
	star-read
AADERSSW	seawards
AADERSTW	eastward
	radwaste
AADERUVY	Ayurveda
AADFGLNS	sand-flag
AADFGNNO	fandango
AADFGRSU	saufgard
AADFHMNR	farm-hand
AADFHNST	handfast
AADFIINT	intifada
AADFIMRS	faradism
AADFINRU	unafraid
AADFLLLN	landfall
AADFLORW	aardwolf
AADFLOTX	toadflax
AADFLOWY	foldaway
AADFMRRY	farmyard
AADGGLNN	gangland
AADGGRST	staggard
AADGHILS	hidalgas
AADGHINN	Gandhian
AADGHIPR	diagraph
AADGHRTU	hatguard
AADGIINS	gainsaid
AADGILLR	gaillard
	galliard
AADGILMR	madrigal
	mail-drag
AADGILNO	diagonal
	gonadial
AADGILNS	salading
AADGIMNR	mridanga
AADGIMPR	paradigm
AADGIMRT	gradatim
AADGINRR	darraign
AADGINRU	guardian
AADGIQRU	quadriga
AADGLMOR	malgrado
AADGLNRS	garlands
AADGLOPR	podagral
AADGMNOR	dragoman
	Garamond
AADGMNOS	goadsman
AADGMNRS	dragsman
AADGNNOW	Gondwana
AADGNNQU	quandang
AADGNORS	Sangrado
AADGNRRU	radar-gun
AADGNRTU	guardant
AADGNRUV	vanguard
AADGRRTU	rat-guard
AADGRRUW	gurdwara
AADHHIPS	padishah
AADHIINP	aphidian
AADHILLR	halliard
AADHILNR	handrail
AADHILRV	havildar
AADHINRR	harridan
AADHLLNU	land-haul
AADHLMOY	dalmahoy
AADHLNPY	handplay
AADHLNSW	washland
AADHLPSS	slap-dash
AADHMNNY	handyman
AADHMNOU	omadhaun
AADHNSST	ash-stand
AADHNSTT	hatstand
AADHRRTW	thraward
AADHRRYZ	hazardry
AADIIMNN	Indiaman
AADIINRR	air-drain
AADIKLLO	alkaloid
AADIKLLR	killadar
AADIKLRY	△kailyard
AADIKMNS	damaskin
AADILLLO	allodial
AADILLNR	landrail
AADILLPR	palliard
AADILLRS	silladar
AADILLRY	radially
AADILMNN	mainland
AADILMNO	domainal
	domanial
AADILMNP	plaidman
AADILNOR	ordalian
AADILNPR	prandial
AADILNTT	dilatant
AADILOPS	palisado
AADILORR	railroad
AADILPRS	pardalis
AADILPRY	lapidary
AADILRRS	risaldar
AADILRSY	sail-yard
AADILRTY	trial-day
AADIMMSZ	Mazdaism
AADIMNNR	△mandarin
AADIMNRT	tamarind
AADIMNRY	dairyman
	mainyard
AADIMNRZ	zamindar
AADIMNSS	damassin
AADIMNSU	sudamina
AADIMNTU	Adiantum
AADIMNUV	vanadium
AADIMSTZ	Mazdaist
	samizdat
AADINNOT	adnation
AADINOPR	paranoid
AADINOPS	diapason
AADINOPT	adaption
AADINPRS	Spaniard
AADINPSU	Upanisad
AADINRRW	airdrawn
AADINSSS	Sassanid
AADIOPRS	△diaspora
AADIORRT	radiator

AADIPSUY	upadaisy
AADIRRSW	airwards
AADIRRSY	disarray
AADJNTTU	adjutant
AADJNTUV	adjuvant
AADKLMNR	landmark
AADKLNPR	parkland
AADKLNRS	sand-lark
AADKLRTU	talukdar
AADKMNRS	darkmans
AADKORWY	workaday
AADKPRRW	parkward
AADLLMNS	Landsmål
AADLLNSW	land-laws
AADLMNNS	landsman
AADLMNOR	mandorla
AADLMNRY	land-army
AADLMNSS	landmass
AADLMNUU	laudanum
AADLMPVY	Davy-lamp
AADLNOPR	parlando
AADLNOPS	soapland
AADLNOST	saltando
AADLORST	loadstar
AADLORTU	adulator
AADLPPRW	waldrapp
AADMMNOW	madwoman
AADMMNSU	mandamus
AADMNORS	roadsman
AADMNORT	mandator
AADMNOWY	day-woman
AADMOPPP	pappadom
AADMORRT	tramroad
AADNNPSU	Pandanus
AADNORTY	donatary
AADNOSUV	vanadous
AADNOSWY	nowadays
AADNQRSU	quadrans
AADNQRTU	quadrant
AADNQRUY	quandary
AADNRSST	sand-star
AADOPPRR	paradrop
AADOPRXY	paradoxy
AADOPSSS	passados
AADOPSTT	Datapost®
AADOPSUY	paduasoy
AADORSVY	△savoyard
AADPRSTV	star-pav'd
AADRSTUY	Saturday
AAEEEHRT	hetaerae
AAEEFRRS	seafarer
AAEEGILN	alienage
AAEEGILP	epigaeal
AAEEGINP	epigaean
AAEEGLLN	enallage
AAEEGLRY	eagle-ray
AAEEGMPR	amperage
AAEEGMTY	métayage
AAEEGNNO	Neogaean
AAEEGNPS	Pegasean
AAEEGNRS	sangaree
AAEEGPRS	sea-grape

AAEEGRST	stearage
AAEEGRSV	averages
AAEEGRTW	waterage
AAEEHIMR	haeremai
AAEEHPRT	earth-pea
	heartpea
AAEEHRRS	hare's-ear
AAEEHRTW	a-weather
	wheatear
AAEEHRWY	hereaway
AAEEILMN	Alemaine
AAEEILNT	alienate
AAEEINTT	taeniate
AAEEJMNP	jampanee
AAEEJNPS	Japanese
AAEEJNSV	Javanese
AAEEKLST	ale-stake
AAEEKLTW	latewake
AAEEKMNS	namesake
AAEEKNRS	Kanarese
AAEEKNRW	reawaken
AAEEKPRT	parakeet
AAEEKPSS	△seaspeak
AAEEKQSU	seaquake
AAEELLLM	lamellae
AAEELLMT	malleate
AAEELLPT	patellae
AAEELNNR	annealer
	lernaean
AAEELNPS	seaplane
	spelaean
AAEELORT	areolate
AAEELRTU	laureate
AAEELSST	elastase
AAEELTUV	evaluate
AAEELVWY	wayleave
AAEEMMTT	team-mate
AAEEMNPT	nametape
AAEEMNRT	man-eater
AAEEMPRS	paramese
AAEENNNT	antennae
AAEENNRZ	Nazarene
AAEENOPR	Pareoean
AAEENPRT	paranete
AAEENRRS	arrasene
AAEENRST	arsenate
	serenata
AAEENRTT	anteater
AAEENSTU	nauseate
AAEEPPRR	appearer
	rapparee
	reappear
AAEEPPRS	appeaser
AAEEPRST	asperate
	separate
AAEEPSTT	aseptate
AAEERRWW	rewarewa
AAEERSTT	stearate
AAEERSTW	seawater
AAEERSYY	yea-sayer
AAEFFGST	staffage
AAEFFILS	fail-safe

AAEFFLLL	leaf-fall
AAEFFLPR	paraffle
AAEFFSTT	taffetas
AAEFGHRW	wharfage
AAEFGITT	fatigate
AAEFGLLL	flagella
AAEFGLOT	floatage
AAEFGRTU	frautage
AAEFHLRY	half-year
AAEFILTY	fayalite
AAEFIMRR	airframe
AAEFINNT	fainéant
AAEFINTX	antefixa
AAEFLMTT	flatmate
AAEFLRTW	flatware
AAEFMRST	fermatas
AAEFMRSW	frame-saw
	saw-frame
AAEFNNOS	Ansafone®
AAEFNRRT	tara-fern
AAEFRRRW	warfarer
AAEFRRWY	wayfarer
AAEFRTTX	after-tax
AAEGGHPT	peat-hagg
AAEGGINR	grainage
AAEGGIOT	agiotage
AAEGGLNR	langrage
AAEGGLNU	language
AAEGGNOW	wagonage
AAEGGNPR	gang-rape
AAEGGNRY	garganey
AAEGGOPR	paragoge
AAEGHKRS	shake-rag
AAEGHLNP	phalange
AAEGHMRX	hexagram
AAEGHNRU	harangue
AAEGHOPY	hypogaea
AAEGHPRT	hag-taper
AAEGILLN	Galilean
AAEGILLR	galleria
AAEGILLT	alligate
AAEGILNP	△pelagian
AAEGILNR	Algerian
	regalian
AAEGILNT	agential
	alginate
AAEGILRS	gasalier
AAEGILTT	tailgate
AAEGIMNO	egomania
AAEGIMNP	pigmaean
AAEGIMNS	magnesia
AAEGIMNZ	magazine
AAEGIMRR	marriage
AAEGIMRT	gematria
	maritage
AAEGINPP	Aganippe
AAEGINPS	paganise
AAEGINPT	paginate
AAEGINPZ	paganize
AAEGINST	saginate
AAEGINTV	navigate
	vaginate

AAEGIPRU periagua
AAEGIRSV vagaries
AAEGIVWY giveaway
give-away
AAEGLLMS smallage
AAEGLLPR pellagra
AAEGLLSS galleass
AAEGLLST stallage
AAEGLLTU glutaeal
AAEGLMNV gavelman
AAEGLMST Almagest
AAEGLNOU analogue
AAEGLNPP lagnappe
AAEGLNPT plantage
AAEGLNRS Sangreal
AAEGLNRU aulnager
AAEGLNTU angulate
AAEGLOSV aasvogel
AAEGLRRS resalgar
AAEGLRRW warragle
AAEGLRST agrestal
AAEGLRTY legatary
AAEGLSVY savagely
AAEGLTUV vaultage
AAEGMMNR engramma
AAEGMNPY pygmaean
AAEGMNRV gravamen
AAEGMORR aerogram
AAEGMORS sagamore
AAEGMPRU rampauge
AAEGMRRV margrave
AAEGMRRW war-gamer
AAEGMRRY gramarye
AAEGMRTU ageratum
AAEGMTTW megawatt
AAEGNNOP neopagan
AAEGNNRU near-gaun
AAEGNOOT Notogaea
AAEGNRRR arranger
AAEGNRST staragen
AAEGNRTU runagate
AAEGNSTT stagnate
AAEGNTUV vauntage
AAEGORRT arrogate
AAEGORTT aegrotat
AAEGPPRR rag-paper
AAEGPPRW wrappage
AAEGRSTW gas-water
water-gas
AAEGRSTZ star-gaze
AAEGRSVY savagery
AAEGRVWX grave-wax
AAEGSSTW tasswage
AAEHIIRT hetairai
hetairia
AAEHILMN hielaman
AAEHILNP aphelian
AAEHILNR Harleian
AAEHILNS Sahelian
AAEHILNT anthelia
AAEHILPR parhelia
AAEHILPT Lapithae

AAEHIMNT anthemia
haematin
AAEHIMRT Mithraea
AAEHINNT Athenian
AAEHINPT aphanite
AAEHINRT Atherina
Rhaetian
AAEHINST asthenia
AAEHIRST hetairas
AAEHIRTT Hatteria
AAEHIRVW hair-wave
AAEHKLST alkahest
AAEHKMRY haymaker
AAEHLMNT methanal
AAEHLMNW whaleman
AAEHLMSY △sealyham
AAEHLMTU hamulate
AAEHLNTX exhalant
AAEHLPRS harp-seal
pearl-ash
AAEHLPRX hexaplar
AAEHLPUV upheaval
AAEHLRTT theatral
AAEHMMOT hematoma
AAEHMNPY Nymphaea
AAEHMNRS shareman
shearman
AAEHMNRT earthman
AAEHMOPR amphorae
AAEHMORT atheroma
AAEHNPST pheasant
AAEHNPSY synaphea
AAEHNTTX xanthate
AAEHOPRT opera-hat
AAEHRRSS harasser
AAEHRTWX earthwax
AAEIIKNS akinesia
AAEIIMRV viraemia
AAEIINRS Arianise
AAEIINRZ Arianize
AAEIJMNS Jamesian
AAEIJNPS Japanise
AAEIJNPZ Japanize
AAEIKKMZ kamikaze
AAEIKLLN alkaline
AAEIKLLS alkalies
alkalise
AAEIKLLZ alkalize
AAEIKMRR krameria
AAEILLLU alleluia
AAEILLMM mamillae
AAEILLMX maxillae
AAEILLPP papillae
AAEILLPT palliate
AAEILLRT arillate
AAEILLRY aerially
AAEILLTT talliate
AAEILLTV allative
AAEILMNT alaiment
laminate
AAEILMNV velamina
AAEILMRS Marsilea

AAEILMRT Armalite
material
AAEILNNN Linnaean
AAEILNNS annalise
AAEILNNZ annalize
Zelanian
AAEILNPR airplane
AAEILNPT △palatine
AAEILNRU aurelian
AAEILNRV valerian
AAEILNSS nasalise
Salesian
AAEILNSZ nasalize
AAEILNTT antliate
Latinate
AAEILNTV aventail
AAEILPPS papalise
AAEILPPZ papalize
AAEILPRT parietal
AAEILPST stapelia
AAEILRRT arterial
AAEILRSS assailer
AAEILRTV varietal
AAEILSTV aestival
salivate
AAEILSTX saxatile
AAEILTVX laxative
AAEIMNNO Maeonian
AAEIMNNR Armenian
AAEIMNOT metanoia
AAEIMNPR pearmain
AAEIMNPS spanemia
AAEIMNPT impanate
AAEIMNRR marinera
AAEIMNRT animater
marinate
AAEIMNRZ mazarine
AAEIMOPR paroemia
AAEIMOTX toxaemia
AAEIMPRS sapremia
AAEIMSUV mauvaise
AAEINNPR Naperian
AAEINNTT antenati
AAEINORT aeration
AAEINORX anorexia
AAEINPPR Priapean
AAEINPRT Patarine
Tarpeian
AAEINRRW rainwear
AAEINRST antisera
△artesian
Erastian
resinata
AAEINRSU Eurasian
AAEINRSY Aryanise
AAEINRTT reattain
AAEINRTU inaurate
AAEINRTZ atrazine
Nazarite
AAEINRYZ Aryanize

AAEINSTT astatine
sanitate
tanaiste
AAEINSTV sanative
AAEINTTT titanate
AAEIPPRS appraise
AAEIPRST aspirate
parasite
septaria
AAEIPRTT patriate
AAEIPRTZ trapezia
AAEIPRXY apyrexia
AAEIRRRT terraria
AAEIRRTT Tartarie
AAEIRSST Asterias
AAEIRSTT aristate
AAEIRTTZ zaratite
AAEITTVX taxative
AAEJLNOP jalapeño
AAEJNNPR japanner
AAEJNPSY Japanesy
AAEJNRTZ jazerant
AAEKLMRW law-maker
AAEKLMRY malarkey
AAEKLNRS larnakes
AAEKLOPP Oak-apple
AAEKMRWY way-maker
AAEKNPRT partaken
AAEKNRRR rear-rank
AAEKORTY akaryote
AAEKPRRT partaker
AAELLLMR lamellar
AAELLLPR parallel
AAELLMPU ampullae
AAELLNPU planulae
AAELLORV alveolar
AAELLPRT patellar
AAELLPST patellas
AAELLTWY alley-taw
AAELLUVV valvulae
AAELLWWY wellaway
AAELLWYY alleyway
AAELMMNO melanoma
AAELMMTU malamute
AAELMNOT malonate
AAELMNPT plateman
AAELMNRT maternal
AAELMNSS salesman
AAELMNST talesman
AAELMNSW wealsman
AAELMNSY seamanly
AAELMPRR rear-lamp
AAELMPRT malapert
AAELMPRX examplar
AAELMPRY play-mare
AAELMPSS lampasse
AAELMPST plateasm
AAELMPTV vamplate
AAELMPTY playmate
AAELMRSY lamasery
AAELMRTT maltreat
AAELNNNT antennal
AAELNNOT neonatal
AAELNNTU annulate
AAELNOSS seasonal
AAELNPPT pea-plant
AAELNPRS prenasal
AAELNPRT parental
paternal
prenatal
AAELNPRW warplane
AAELNPST pleasant
AAELNRSY analyser
AAELNRTT alterant
alternat
AAELNRTX relaxant
AAELNRYZ analyzer
AAELNSSV envassal
AAELNSSY analyses
AAELNSTT Atlantes
AAELORTY aleatory
AAELPPSU applause
AAELPRST palestra
AAELPRSY paralyse
AAELPRTT tetrapla
AAELPRYZ paralyze
AAELPSTU plateaus
AAELPSTV palstave
AAELPTUV vapulate
AAELPTUX plateaux
AAELRTUV velatura
AAELRUZZ zarzuela
AAELRWYY waylayer
AAEMMNRT armament
AAEMMSTT stemmata
AAEMNOSW seawoman
AAEMNOTZ metazoan
AAEMNPRS Parmesan
spearman
AAEMNPRT name-part
parament
AAEMNRST sarmenta
semantra
AAEMNRSY man-years
AAEMNRTT atrament
AAEMNRTW waterman
AAEMNSTU manteaus
AAEMNTUX manteaux
AAEMORTT amaretto
teratoma
AAEMORTX xeromata
AAEMOSTT steatoma
AAEMOTTU automate
AAEMPTTU amputate
AAEMQSTU squamate
AAEMRRTU armature
AAEMRTTU maturate
AAENNNST antennas
AAENNOTT annotate
AAENNSTT stannate
AAENNSTU nauseant
AAENORRU aurorean
AAENORSU araneous
AAENORTU aeronaut
AAENOSST assonate
AAENPPRT apparent
trappean
AAENPRTY prytanea
AAENPSTT antepast
AAENPSTY peasanty
AAENRSTV tsarevna
AAENRSUW unawares
AAENRTTY Tyrtaean
AAENTTTT attentat
AAEOPSTT apostate
AAEORSTT aerostat
AAEORTTV rotavate
AAEPPRRT tar-paper
AAEPPSTT appestat
AAEPRSTW pea-straw
AAEPRTXY tax-payer
AAERRSUU Saururae
AAERRTTT tartrate
AAERRTTW tar-water
AAERRWWY war-weary
AAERSTTU saturate
AAERTWWY waterway
AAFFHLLO half-loaf
AAFFILRT taffrail
AAFFINPR paraffin
AAFFINUX faux-naïf
AAFFLPST palstaff
AAFFLSTU afflatus
AAFFNNOR fanfaron
AAFGILNO golfiana
AAFGLLNU langlauf
AAFGLNRT flagrant
AAFGNRRT fragrant
AAFHHIKL khalifah
AAFHIKLT khalifat
khilafat
AAFHIRST airshaft
AAFHLMST half-mast
AAFHLSTY lay-shaft
AAFHRSUU hausfrau
AAFIILLM familial
AAFIILLR filarial
AAFIILMR familiar
AAFIINST fistiana
AAFIKLLY alkalify
AAFILLNR rainfall
AAFILLUV availful
AAFILMST fatalism
AAFILOPR parafoil
AAFILPTX pita-flax
AAFILSTT fatalist
AAFILTTY fatality
AAFIMNOR foramina
AAFINNOV Favonian
AAFINNRS safranin
AAFINORT Fanariot
AAFINRRW warfarin
AAFINSTU △faustian
AAFIRSST safarist
AAFJORZZ Afro-jazz
AAFKLSTT fast-talk

AAFLLPRT	fall-trap
	pratfall
	trap-fall
AAFLLPST	spatfall
AAFLMORV	lavaform
AAFLNORS	safronal
AAFLNOTT	floatant
AAFLSTWY	flatways
AAFMNORW	man-of-war
AAFMNRST	raftsman
AAFNPPRT	frappant
AAGGGINR	garaging
AAGGILNR	gangliar
AAGGIMNN	managing
AAGGIMNR	maraging
AAGGIRST	garagist
AAGGITTW	gigawatt
AAGGLLLY	lallygag
AAGGMNNS	gangsman
AAGHHINS	shanghai
AAGHILNN	hangnail
AAGHILPY	hypalgia
AAGHILRS	harigals
AAGHIMNS	ashaming
AAGHIMRT	taghairm
AAGHINPS	paganish
AAGHIPRR	airgraph
AAGHIRSV	vagarish
AAGHKMNY	gymkhana
AAGHLNNS	Langshan
AAGHLNOT	Loaghtan
AAGHLNPY	anaglyph
AAGHMNOY	Hogmanay
	mahogany
AAGHMRSS	marsh-gas
AAGHNOPR	agraphon
AAGHOOPZ	Zoophaga
AAGHOPPR	apograph
AAGHRRTU	arraught
AAGHSSTU	Gasthaus
AAGIILMN	imaginal
AAGIILNN	Laingian
AAGIILNS	aliasing
AAGIILNV	availing
AAGIIMST	astigmia
AAGIINNT	Ignatian
AAGIJRTU	Gujarati
AAGIKLNO	kaoliang
AAGIKLUY	Kaliyuga
AAGIKMRS	skiagram
AAGILLNU	Anguilla
AAGILLNY	allaying
AAGILLSS	galliass
AAGILLTV	gallivat
AAGILLUZ	alguazil
AAGILMMR	mailgram
AAGILMNO	magnolia
AAGILMNR	alarming
	marginal
AAGILMOT	gliomata
AAGILNOT	galtonia
AAGILNRR	larrigan

AAGILNRS	Sangrail
AAGILNUV	vaginula
AAGILOOP	apologia
AAGILPRY	plagiary
AAGILRRW	warrigal
AAGILSTT	sagittal
AAGIMMRR	marigram
AAGIMNNN	Manganin®
AAGIMNOS	angiomas
AAGIMNPS	paganism
AAGIMNRR	margarin
AAGIMNSY	gymnasia
AAGIMPTU	patagium
AAGIMSSV	savagism
AAGIMSTT	stigmata
AAGINNNY	nannygai
AAGINNOT	agnation
AAGINNTV	vaginant
AAGINNTW	awanting
AAGINPRU	pagurian
AAGINRSU	guaranis
AAGINSST	assignat
AAGINSSU	△gaussian
AAGINSSY	assaying
	gainsays
AAGIORTT	agitator
AAGIRSTV	gravitas
	stravaig
AAGKNOOR	kangaroo
AAGKNORR	Ragnarök
AAGLLMOY	allogamy
AAGLLNOO	lagoonal
AAGLLNRY	laryngal
AAGLLOPY	polygala
AAGLLOWY	Galloway
AAGLMNSS	glassman
AAGLMOPS	sago-palm
AAGLNNOO	analogon
AAGLNOPT	Plantago
AAGLNPST	gas-plant
AAGLNQUU	aqualung
AAGLNRRU	granular
AAGLNTUU	Ungulata
AAGLOPRY	paralogy
AAGLPSST	last-gasp
AAGLRRUW	warragul
AAGLRSTU	gastrula
AAGMMORT	gram-atom
AAGMNNOR	nanogram
AAGMNOPZ	zampogna
AAGMNORT	martagon
AAGMNORW	rag-woman
AAGMNRTU	armgaunt
AAGMNSSW	swagsman
AAGMNSTY	syntagma
AAGMOTUY	autogamy
AAGMOTYZ	zygomata
AAGMRSST	matgrass
AAGNNSTT	stagnant
AAGNOPRT	tragopan
AAGNORRT	arrogant
	tarragon

AAGNORTU	△argonaut
AAGNRTUY	guaranty
AAGNSTUU	Augustan
AAGOPSSS	sapsagos
AAGORSSS	sargasso
AAGORSST	oat-grass
AAGORSSU	saguaros
AAGRSSTU	sastruga
AAGRSTUZ	zastruga
AAHHIIMM	mahi-mahi
AAHHKKNU	Hanukkah
AAHHKMRS	hashmark
AAHHLLOO	holla-hoa
AAHHLLUU	hula-hula
AAHHMMSS	shammash
AAHIIKRR	hara-kiri
	hari-kari
AAHIIKRT	tarakihi
AAHIILRT	hair-tail
AAHIINTT	Tahitian
AAHIJPRS	rajaship
AAHIKLPS	pashalik
AAHILMNR	harmalin
AAHILNNT	inhalant
AAHILNOT	halation
AAHILNSS	Salishan
AAHILNST	Stahlian
AAHILNTT	Tanalith®
AAHILPSY	physalia
AAHIMNPS	pashmina
AAHINNTX	Xanthian
AAHINORT	Horatian
AAHINPRT	Parthian
AAHINRSW	rain-wash
AAHINRTU	hauriant
AAHIPSXY	asphyxia
AAHJNNOT	Jonathan
AAHKLLMR	hallmark
AAHKMOTW	tomahawk
AAHKPRSW	spar-hawk
AAHKRSSW	sawshark
AAHLLLOO	hallaloo
AAHLLOPT	allopath
AAHLMOOS	masoolah
AAHLMSTU	thalamus
AAHLNPST	ash-plant
AAHLNPTT	hat-plant
AAHMMNRS	marsh-man
AAHMMORR	Moharram
AAHMMRRU	Muharram
AAHMNORT	△marathon
AAHMNOST	hoastman
AAHMNOTX	xanthoma
AAHMNPST	phantasm
AAHMNRST	trashman
AAHMORSS	Massorah
AAHMRSST	stramash
AAHNOOTZ	Anthozoa
AAHNPRSU	Raphanus
AAHNPSTY	phantasy
AAHNRTUX	Xanthura
AAHOPRTU	autoharp

AAHRRTTW thrawart
AAHRSTTW straw-hat
AAIIILMR miliaria
AAIIIMNR niramiai
AAIIKKNN kinakina
AAIILLQU Quillaia
AAIILMNS mainsail
AAIILMNT Tamilian
AAIILMRS Marsilia
AAIILNPR Aprilian
AAIILNRZ alizarin
AAIILNSV Salvinia
AAIILNUX uniaxial
AAIILPRR Prairial
riparial
AAIILRTX triaxial
AAIILRUX auxiliar
AAIILTXY axiality
AAIIMNNR Arminian
AAIIMNNT maintain
AAIIMNPX panmixia
AAIIMNRS Arianism
AAIINNTT Titanian
AAIINOTV aviation
AAIINPRR riparian
AAIINPRS Parisian
AAIINPZZ piazzian
AAIINRST intarsia
AAIIOPST apositia
AAIIORRT air-to-air
AAIIORTZ zoiatria
AAIIPRST apiarist
AAIIRSTV aviarist
AAIIRSTW wistaria
AAIIRTVX aviatrix
AAIJLLQU Quillaja
AAIJNRYZ janizary
AAIKKNOS skokiaan
AAIKLNOR Kolarian
AAIKLNST nastalik
AAIKMNOY yakimona
AAIKMNST antimask
AAIKMRST tamarisk
AAIKNNTT antitank
AAIKSSTV svastika
AAIKSSTW swastika
AAILLLUV alluvial
AAILLMMM mammilla
AAILLMMR mamillar
AAILLMNT mantilla
AAILLMNY animally
AAILLMPT tail-lamp
AAILLNOV vallonia
AAILLPPR papillar
AAILLRRY arillary
AAILLRXY axillary
AAILMMRS alarmism
AAILMNNT lamantin
AAILMNOP palamino
AAILMNOR manorial
morainal
AAILMNOX monaxial

AAILMNPS panislam
AAILMNRU manurial
AAILMNRY laminary
AAILMNST talisman
AAILMNSV navalism
AAILMOPT lipomata
AAILMORR armorial
AAILMPPS papalism
AAILMPRT primatal
AAILMRST alarmist
alastrim
AAILMSWW Mawlawis
AAILMTTU ultimata
AAILNNOT △national
AAILNNPT plainant
plantain
AAILNNRU lunarian
AAILNNST annalist
santalin
AAILNOPS △salopian
AAILNOPT talapoin
AAILNORT notarial
rational
AAILNOST ailantos
AAILNOSV Slavonia
AAILNOTV lavation
AAILNPRT air-plant
AAILNPRU planuria
AAILNPTU Laputian
AAILNQST nasta'liq
AAILNQTU aliquant
AAILNSSY analysis
AAILNSTT Atlantis
AAILNSTY nasality
AAILNTTT latitant
AAILNTTY natality
AAILORRS rasorial
AAILORRV variolar
AAILPPRU puparial
AAILPPST papalist
AAILPRST triapsal
AAILQRSU squarial
AAILRSTT rat's-tail
AAILRSTZ Lazarist
AAILRSVY salivary
AAILSSTY staysail
AAIMMNRR arm-in-arm
AAIMMNST mainmast
AAIMMRSU samarium
AAIMNNOR Maronian
Romanian
AAIMNNRU Rumanian
AAIMNORT animator
montaria
tamanoir
AAIMNORV Moravian
AAIMNORW airwoman
AAIMNPRZ marzipan
AAIMNPTU putamina
AAIMNRRT trimaran
AAIMNRRU ranarium

AAIMNSST mantissa
satanism
AAIMNSTU amiantus
AAIMNSTY mainstay
AAIMOPRS mariposa
AAIMPRST pastrami
AAIMQRUU aquarium
AAIMRRSY misarray
AAIMRRTY martyria
AAINNOPV pavonian
AAINNOST sonatina
AAINNOSU Ausonian
AAINNOSX Saxonian
AAINNOTT natation
AAINNOTV Novatian
AAINNRTU nutarian
Turanian
AAINNSST naissant
AAINNSSY sannyasi
AAINOPSS paisanos
AAINORRS rosarian
AAINORRT Rotarian
AAINOTTX taxation
AAINPRST aspirant
partisan
AAINPRTZ partizan
AAINPSTU sapi-utan
AAINQRTU quatrain
AAINQTTU aquatint
AAINRRSS sarrasin
AAINRRST Sartrian
AAINRRSZ sarrazin
AAINRSSY Assyrian
AAINRSTU Austrian
Saturnia
AAINRSTY sanitary
AAINSSSS assassin
AAINSSTT Satanist
AAINSTTT antistat
AAINSTTY satanity
AAIOPRRT troparia
AAIOPRSU parousia
AAIOPSTU autopsia
AAIORTUZ azoturia
AAIPRSSX sparaxis
AAIQRSTU aquarist
AAIQRSUU Aquarius
AAIRSSTT tsaritsa
AAIRSTWY stairway
AAJMMORR marjoram
AAKKMMOO mako-mako
AAKLMNNS Klansman
AAKLMNSW Walkmans
AAKLMRUY yarmulka
AAKLPRTY kalyptra
AAKMMNRS marksman
AAKMNRSW swan-mark
AAKMOSSU moussaka
AAKNNSTU nunataks
AAKNPRTT tank-trap
AALLLLMP pall-mall
AALLLSTY laystall

Words marked △ may be spelled also with a capital letter

AALLMMRS	small-arm
AALLMNST	stallman
AALLMNSY	sally-man
AALLMNTY	tallyman
AALLMNUY	manually
AALLMPPY	palm-play
AALLMSST	smallsat
AALLNNUY	annually
AALLNPRU	planular
AALLNRTY	tarnally
AALLOORW	wallaroo
AALLORSU	allosaur
AALLPRST	plastral
AALLRUVV	valvular
AALMNORT	matronal
AALMNORU	monaural
AALMNOWY	laywoman
AALMNPSU	Paul's-man
AALMNPTY	tympanal
AALMNSTU	Santalum
AALMNTTU	tantalum
AALMNTUU	autumnal
AALMOOSS	massoola
AALMOPSX	axoplasm
AALMOSTT	stomatal
AALMOTXY	xylomata
AALMPPSU	paspalum
AALMPSTY	platysma
AALMQSUU	squamula
AALNNOPT	pantalon
AALNNPUU	punaluan
AALNNTUU	lunanaut
AALNOPRT	patronal
AALNOPRU	Anoplura
AALNPSTU	Platanus
AALNRRTY	arrantly
AALNSTTU	△tantalus
AALOPPRV	approval
AALOPRST	pastoral
AALORTUV	valuator
AALORTVY	lavatory
AALPRSTU	pastural
	spatular
AALRRTTY	△tartarly
AALRSSVY	vassalry
AALRSTTW	stalwart
AALRSTUY	salutary
AAMMNPRS	rampsman
AAMMOTXY	myxomata
AAMMRSSU	marasmus
AAMNNOPR	apron-man
AAMNORRS	Marranos
AAMNQSUW	squawman
AAMOPRRU	paramour
AAMORRSZ	zamarros
AAMORSTT	stromata
AAMRSSST	smartass
AANNOSST	assonant
AANNOSTT	annattos
AANNRSTY	△stannary
AANOOPPX	opopanax
AANOOPRZ	parazoon
AANOPRTY	anatropy
AANORRRT	narrator
AANORSTY	sanatory
AANORTTY	natatory
AANPPTTY	patty-pan
AANRRTTY	tartanry
AANRRTWY	warranty
AANRSTTU	saturant
AAOPSSTY	apostasy
AAORSSTT	starosta
AAORSUVV	vavasour
AAORSVVY	vavasory
AAOSTWWY	stowaway
AARRSTTU	Tartarus
AARSTTUY	statuary
ABBBDEEL	bedabble
ABBBGILN	babbling
	blabbing
ABBBHSUY	bush-baby
ABBBIRTY	Babbitry
ABBBOSTU	subabbot
ABBCCKMO	back-comb
ABBCDERS	scrabbed
ABBCDKNO	backbond
ABBCEERU	barbecue
ABBCEGIR	cribbage
ABBCEHOU	babouche
ABBCEHTU	bathcube
ABBCEIKT	backbite
ABBCEILR	barbicel
ABBCEKLU	blueback
ABBCEKNO	backbone
ABBCEKNU	buckbean
ABBCELLU	clubable
ABBCELRS	Scrabble®
	scrabble
ABBCELRU	curbable
ABBCGIOR	gabbroic
ABBCIILL	biblical
ABBCIINR	△rabbinic
ABBCIKRT	brickbat
ABBCILRY	crabbily
ABBCINOY	cabin-boy
ABBCKLOW	blow-back
ABBCKLOY	blackboy
ABBCNORY	corn-baby
ABBDDEEL	beddable
ABBDDEIL	biddable
ABBDEEER	bee-bread
ABBDEELT	bed-table
ABBDEERT	rabbeted
ABBDEILR	ad-libber
ABBDELMO	babeldom
ABBDELRR	drabbler
ABBDENRU	unbarbed
ABBDEORS	absorbed
ABBDFOOY	babyfood
ABBDGILN	dabbling
ABBDGIOR	gabbroid
ABBDHIRS	drabbish
ABBDHIRT	birdbath
ABBDHOOY	babyhood
ABBDILNO	bailbond
ABBDLLOY	baby-doll
ABBDNORW	bawd-born
	browband
ABBDRRUY	Bradbury
ABBEEIMS	Babeeism
ABBEEINR	bearbine
ABBEEJRR	jabberer
ABBEEJRS	bejabers
ABBEENOR	barebone
ABBEEQRU	barbeque
ABBEERTT	barbette
ABBEFGIR	brief-bag
ABBEGLRR	grabbler
ABBEHILS	babelish
ABBEHKRU	hub-brake
ABBEHORT	bathrobe
ABBEILMS	babelism
ABBEILNU	bubaline
ABBEILOT	bilobate
ABBEILST	bistable
ABBEINTT	tabbinet
ABBEIRRT	rabbiter
ABBEKLOO	bookable
ABBELLST	best-ball
ABBELOPP	bob-apple
ABBELOPR	probable
ABBELORU	belabour
ABBELQSU	squabble
ABBELRSY	slabbery
ABBEMOOR	aerobomb
ABBENORS	base-born
ABBEORRS	absorber
	reabsorb
ABBEORTW	browbeat
ABBERRRY	barberry
ABBERRYY	bayberry
ABBERSSW	swabbers
ABBFILLY	flabbily
ABBGGILN	gabbling
ABBGGINR	grabbing
ABBGILNR	rabbling
ABBGILNU	baubling
ABBGILNW	wabbling
ABBGINST	stabbing
ABBGINSW	swabbing
ABBGINTY	tabbying
ABBGNORW	brown-bag
ABBGORSY	Babygros
ABBHIIMS	bimbashi
ABBHILSY	shabbily
ABBHRRUY	rhubarby
ABBIINOT	bibation
ABBIKLLN	bank-bill
ABBIKNRY	kirn-baby
ABBILLOT	boatbill
ABBILLSU	sillabub
ABBILMNO	nail-bomb
ABBILOST	bioblast
ABBIMNOS	bambinos
ABBINORX	brainbox
ABBIRRTY	rabbitry

ABBIRSUU	suburbia
ABBKKNOO	bank-book
ABBLLLOW	blowball
ABBLLSUY	syllabub
ABBLOPRY	probably
ABBNRSUU	suburban
ABBOSSTY	bobstays
ABCCDEHO	caboched
ABCCDHIK	dabchick
ABCCEEHN	bechance
ABCCEELP	peccable
ABCCEEOR	caboceer
ABCCEFLU	club-face
ABCCEILY	celibacy
ABCCEIRT	bacteric
ABCCEKMO	comeback
ABCCESUU	succubae
ABCCHISU	bacchius
ABCCHNOO	cabochon
ABCCIKKK	kickback
ABCCIKKP	pickback
ABCCIKOR	abricock
ABCCILOR	carbolic
ABCCILOT	cobaltic
ABCCINOR	carbonic
ABCCIORS	ascorbic
ABCCKLLO	ballcock
ABCCKLOX	clackbox
ABCCKOOT	cockboat
ABCCOORS	baroccos
ABCCOOST	tobaccos
ABCCSSUU	succubas
ABCDDEOR	bar-coded
	brocaded
ABCDEEFK	feedback
ABCDEEHR	berdache
ABCDEELM	becalmed
ABCDEELU	educable
ABCDEEMR	embraced
ABCDEETU	abductee
ABCDEFLO	bold-face
ABCDEGIR	birdcage
	cagebird
ABCDEHIR	chair-bed
ABCDEHLU	club-head
ABCDEHNR	branched
ABCDEHOS	caboshed
ABCDEIIT	diabetic
ABCDEIKS	backside
ABCDEILR	calibred
ABCDEKLO	bale-dock
	blockade
ABCDEKLV	backveld
ABCDEKNN	neckband
ABCDEKNU	unbacked
ABCDEKOT	boat-deck
ABCDELOO	caboodle
ABCDELSU	bud-scale
ABCDEMNU	dumb-cane
ABCDEMOT	combated
ABCDENRU	unbraced
ABCDENTU	abducent
ABCDFRUY	farcy-bud
ABCDHKLO	holdback
ABCDIILO	biocidal
	diabolic
ABCDIIMY	cymbidia
ABCDIIRT	tribadic
ABCDIKLO	bail-dock
ABCDIKLR	baldrick
ABCDIKRU	baudrick
ABCDILLR	birdcall
	call-bird
ABCDILOU	cuboidal
ABCDIRSU	subacrid
ABCDKNOW	backdown
ABCDKOOR	back-door
ABCDKOPR	backdrop
ABCDKORW	backword
ABCDLLNU	clubland
ABCDLOOT	bald-coot
ABCDOORS	brood-sac
ABCDOORW	crab-wood
ABCDOPRU	cupboard
ABCDORTU	abductor
ABCDORUY	obduracy
ABCEEEFK	beefcake
ABCEEFNT	benefact
ABCEEHKL	back-heel
ABCEEHLM	bechamel
	béchamel
ABCEEHLN	alebench
ABCEEHLR	bleacher
ABCEEHLW	chewable
ABCEEHNO	bone-ache
ABCEEILT	celibate
	citeable
ABCEEIMN	ambience
ABCEEKLY	eye-black
ABCEELLO	eco-label
ABCEELNO	bone-lace
ABCEELOV	evocable
ABCEELRR	cerebral
ABCEELRT	bracelet
ABCEEMRR	embracer
ABCEEMRS	embraces
ABCEENOV	bone-cave
ABCEENRT	cabernet
ABCEERUX	berceaux
ABCEFIIT	beatific
ABCEFIKL	backfile
ABCEFIKR	backfire
	fire-back
ABCEFINO	boniface
ABCEGKLL	blackleg
ABCEGKLO	blockage
ABCEGKMU	megabuck
ABCEGKOR	brockage
ABCEGNOR	bongrace
ABCEHITT	bathetic
ABCEHKTW	bethwack
ABCEHLOR	bachelor
ABCEHLSU	chasuble
ABCEHLTU	leachtub
ABCEHMOT	hecatomb
ABCEHMRS	chambers
ABCEHNRR	brancher
ABCEHOOT	cohobate
ABCEHOPU	pabouche
ABCEHORR	broacher
ABCEHORU	barouche
ABCEHRTT	bratchet
ABCEIJNR	jib-crane
ABCEIJOT	Jacobite
ABCEIKKL	kickable
ABCEIKLR	crablike
ABCEIKRT	brick-tea
ABCEIKWZ	Zwieback
ABCEILLR	cribella
ABCEILLT	balletic
ABCEILNN	binnacle
ABCEILNU	baculine
ABCEILOR	albicore
	cabriole
ABCEILOS	sociable
ABCEILPS	B-Special
ABCEILTT	bittacle
ABCEILTU	baculite
ABCEIMST	betacism
ABCEINOO	coenobia
ABCEINTU	incubate
ABCEIORS	Aerobics®
	aerobics
ABCEIORT	boracite
ABCEIRRT	cribrate
ABCEIRSW	crabwise
ABCEIRTT	brattice
ABCEIRTY	acerbity
ABCEISSS	abscisse
ABCEISST	asbestic
ABCEJKLT	jet-black
ABCEJLTY	abjectly
ABCEKKRU	buckrake
ABCEKKSW	skewback
ABCEKLLO	lockable
ABCEKLMO	mockable
ABCEKLOO	cookable
ABCEKLPU	palebuck
ABCEKOOS	bookcase
	casebook
ABCEKOPR	back-rope
ABCELLPU	culpable
ABCELLSU	bucellas
ABCELMNY	lambency
ABCELMOS	cembalos
ABCELMRS	scambler
	scramble
ABCELNOT	balconet
ABCELNUU	nubecula
ABCELOOT	bootlace
	lace-boot
ABCELOPS	placebos
ABCELORT	brocatel
ABCELOST	obstacle
ABCELOTU	bluecoat
ABCELRSW	bescrawl

ABCELRTT	bractlet
ABCELTTU	table-cut
ABCEMNRU	cream-bun
ABCEMORS	cramboes
ABCENOUY	buoyance
ABCENTUX	excubant
ABCEOSUX	saucebox
ABCERRTU	carburet
ABCERSTU	sabre-cut
ABCERTUU	cubature
ABCESSTU	subcaste
ABCESTUU	subacute
ABCFFOTU	buff-coat
ABCFHOTW	fob-watch
ABCFIKLL	backfill
ABCFIKLT	backlift
	liftback
ABCFILOS	bifocals
ABCFKLLU	fullback
ABCFKLOX	black-fox
ABCFKOOT	back-foot
ABCFKOST	softback
ABCFLLLU	bull-calf
ABCFLMOX	flax-comb
ABCGGIMO	gambogic
ABCGHINT	batching
ABCGHKOS	hog's-back
ABCGHNPU	punch-bag
ABCGIKLN	blacking
ABCGIKNR	king-crab
ABCGILRU	Bulgaric
ABCGKLUY	lucky-bag
ABCGLNOX	clangbox
ABCHHIIS	hibachis
ABCHIIPS	biphasic
ABCHIKLS	blackish
ABCHIKRS	brackish
ABCHILMO	choliamb
ABCHILOO	coolibah
ABCHIMOR	choriamb
ABCHIMRU	brachium
ABCHINOR	bronchia
ABCHIOOR	borachio
ABCHIRRT	tribrach
ABCHKLOT	hackbolt
ABCHKMPU	humpback
	hump-back
ABCHKOOP	chapbook
ABCHKOOS	cash-book
ABCHKSUW	buck-wash
ABCHLLUU	club-haul
ABCHMOTX	matchbox
ABCHOPTX	patch-box
ABCHOTWX	watchbox
ABCIIKRR	air-brick
ABCIINOT	cibation
ABCIINSS	abscisin
ABCIIORS	isobaric
ABCIIRST	tribasic
ABCIISTY	basicity
ABCIITUX	bauxitic
ABCIKKLL	kickball
ABCIKLLL	back-lill
ABCIKLLT	back-lilt
ABCIKLST	backlist
ABCIKNPS	backspin
ABCILLNY	billy-can
ABCILLRU	lubrical
ABCILLSU	△bacillus
ABCILLSY	syllabic
ABCILMMO	cimbalom
ABCILMSU	subclaim
ABCILNPU	publican
ABCILOOR	coolibar
ABCILOSY	sociably
ABCILRRU	rubrical
ABCIMMSU	cambiums
ABCIMORR	microbar
ABCIMRTU	umbratic
ABCINORU	conurbia
ABCINPUY	panic-buy
ABCINRVY	vibrancy
ABCIORRS	barricos
ABCIOSSU	scabious
ABCIRSTT	abstrict
ABCJKOOT	boot-jack
	jackboot
ABCKKORW	backwork
ABCKLLOS	ballocks
ABCKLLPU	pull-back
ABCKLOPT	blacktop
ABCKLOSW	slowback
ABCKLOTU	blackout
ABCKMOOR	backroom
ABCKMORR	brockram
ABCKMOSS	mossback
ABCKMOST	backmost
ABCKNRTU	turnback
	turn-back
ABCKOORU	buckaroo
ABCKOPST	backstop
ABCKORUY	buckayro
ABCLLNOR	cornball
ABCLLPUY	culpably
ABCLMNOU	Columban
ABCLMOOO	coloboma
ABCLMOSY	cymbalos
ABCLMSUY	scybalum
ABCLNORY	carbonyl
ABCLORXY	carboxyl
ABCLOSUV	subvocal
ABCLPRUW	pub-crawl
ABCLSSSU	subclass
ABCLSUUU	subucula
ABCMOORT	mobocrat
ABCNNORU	conurban
ABCNNOYY	△nancy-boy
ABCNORTY	corybant
ABCNOUYY	buoyancy
ABCNRSTU	crab-nuts
ABCORRSS	crossbar
ABCORRTU	turbocar
ABCORSSU	scabrous
ABCOSSTU	subcosta
ABCOSTTU	cottabus
ABCRSTTU	subtract
ABDDDEET	addebted
ABDDEEHT	death-bed
ABDDEENR	reed-band
ABDDEERR	debarred
ABDDEEST	bedstead
	bestadde
ABDDEHMO	hebdomad
ABDDEHOY	hobdayed
ABDDEILS	disabled
ABDDEILU	buddleia
ABDDEINR	brandied
ABDDEINS	sideband
ABDDEINV	divan-bed
ABDDELOT	dead-bolt
ABDDELRY	bladdery
ABDDENNU	unbanded
ABDDENOR	dead-born
ABDDERSW	bedwards
ABDDHIOR	rhabdoid
ABDDILMO	lambdoid
ABDDILRY	ladybird
ABDDIMNO	bondmaid
ABDDIRRY	yardbird
ABDEEEFN	bedeafen
ABDEEEKR	Baedeker
ABDEEENR	Aberdeen
ABDEEERV	beavered
	bereaved
ABDEEFLM	flambéed
ABDEEGGL	bedaggle
ABDEEGHR	herbaged
ABDEEGRU	bedeguar
ABDEEHNO	bonehead
ABDEEHRT	breathed
ABDEEHST	△bethesda
ABDEEHTT	behatted
ABDEEILN	deniable
ABDEEILR	bride-ale
	rideable
ABDEEILT	delibate
ABDEEILW	bewailed
ABDEEIRT	Abderite
	ebriated
ABDEEIST	diabetes
ABDEEKMR	bedmaker
	embarked
ABDEEKNR	bedarken
ABDEELLL	labelled
ABDEELLW	weldable
ABDEELNO	Denebola
ABDEELNT	bandelet
ABDEELOR	lee-board
ABDEELPT	bed-plate
ABDEELRZ	blazered
ABDEELZZ	bedazzle
ABDEEMNS	beam-ends
	bedesman
ABDEEMRR	embarred
ABDEENNR	bannered
ABDEEPRS	bespread

ABDEEPRX	pax-brede
ABDEERRY	ryebread
ABDEERST	breasted
ABDEERTT	battered
	drabette
ABDEFFST	bed-staff
ABDEFHLR	half-bred
ABDEFLLO	foldable
ABDEFLNU	fundable
	unfabled
ABDEFLOR	fordable
ABDEFNRU	faburden
ABDEGGIL	diggable
ABDEGIIO	Gobiidae
ABDEGILN	blindage
ABDEGILU	guidable
ABDEGINO	gabioned
ABDEGINS	debasing
ABDEGIRR	abridger
ABDEGLOT	globated
ABDEGLRY	badgerly
ABDEGLSU	slug-a-bed
ABDEGNOR	bondager
ABDEGOPR	pegboard
ABDEGRSU	subgrade
ABDEHILL	billhead
ABDEHILS	dishable
ABDEHITU	habitude
ABDEHKLU	bulkhead
ABDEHLLN	handbell
ABDEHLLU	bullhead
ABDEHLOT	bolthead
ABDEHMOO	head-boom
ABDEHNTU	unbathed
ABDEHOSW	beshadow
ABDEHTTU	head-butt
ABDEIIRT	diatribe
ABDEIKMN	Medibank
ABDEIKNU	baudekin
ABDEILMN	mandible
ABDEILNR	bilander
ABDEILNT	bidental
ABDEILNY	deniably
ABDEILOV	voidable
ABDEILRV	drivable
ABDEILRY	diablery
ABDEILTU	dutiable
ABDEIMNR	brideman
ABDEIMOO	amoeboid
ABDEIMOR	amberoid
ABDEIMRU	Drambuie®
ABDEINOR	debonair
ABDEINRS	air-bends
	brandise
ABDEINSU	unbiased
ABDEINTU	unbaited
ABDEIPSS	piss-a-bed
ABDEIRTY	Darbyite
ABDEISSU	disabuse
ABDEITTU	dubitate
ABDEKLNP	plank-bed
ABDEKLSW	skewbald
ABDEKNNU	unbanked
ABDEKNRU	unbarked
ABDEKNSU	sunbaked
ABDEKORY	keyboard
ABDELLOR	bead-roll
ABDELLOT	balloted
ABDELLPU	balled-up
ABDELMNO	lemon-dab
ABDELMNU	unblamed
ABDELNOR	banderol
ABDELNRY	bylander
ABDELNSS	baldness
ABDELORU	laboured
ABDELPTY	play-debt
ABDELRSU	durables
ABDEMNOR	Doberman
ABDEMNRU	Bermudan
ABDEMOOR	rood-beam
ABDEMRSU	Bermudas
ABDEMRTU	drumbeat
	umbrated
ABDENNOS	noseband
ABDENNRW	brand-new
ABDENORW	rawboned
ABDENORY	boneyard
ABDENOTW	downbeat
ABDENRRU	unbarred
ABDENRSS	drabness
ABDENRST	bandster
ABDENRTU	breadnut
	turbaned
ABDENTTU	débutant
ABDEORRU	arboured
ABDEORRW	wardrobe
ABDEORSW	sowbread
ABDEORTU	obdurate
ABDEORUX	Bordeaux
ABDERSSU	surbased
ABDERSTU	surbated
ABDERSTW	bedstraw
ABDERTUW	draw-tube
ABDFFLOY	badly-off
ABDFFOOR	off-board
ABDFHINS	band-fish
ABDFLOOT	foldboat
ABDGGGOY	doggy-bag
ABDGHINR	hangbird
ABDGIINR	braiding
ABDGILLY	dilly-bag
ABDGILNR	bardling
ABDGILOR	gaol-bird
ABDGIMRU	guimbard
ABDGINNY	bandying
ABDGINOR	boarding
ABDGINST	dingbats
ABDGITTY	ditty-bag
ABDGLOOR	logboard
ABDHHSSU	shadbush
ABDHIIST	dishabit
ABDHILLN	handbill
ABDHILNS	blandish
ABDHINRS	brandish
ABDHIORS	broadish
ABDHIPRS	bardship
ABDHIRTY	birthday
ABDHKNOO	book-hand
	handbook
ABDHLNOS	ash-blond
ABDHLORW	blowhard
ABDHLOSW	shadblow
ABDHMOTU	badmouth
ABDHSTTU	dust-bath
ABDIIJLR	jail-bird
ABDIILLR	billiard
ABDIIMNR	midbrain
ABDIIMRS	Braidism
ABDIIMSU	basidium
ABDIINOS	obsidian
ABDIINRR	rain-bird
ABDIINTT	banditti
ABDIIRTY	rabidity
ABDIKLNR	blinkard
ABDILOST	blastoid
ABDILOTY	tabloidy
ABDILRRY	ribaldry
ABDILRZZ	blizzard
ABDILSTU	subtidal
ABDINOPR	pair-bond
ABDINOTY	antibody
ABDINRSU	Buridan's
ABDINRTY	banditry
ABDIOSUU	subaudio
ABDIRRUY	ribaudry
ABDKLNOO	bookland
ABDKOOOR	road-book
ABDLLNOS	slobland
ABDLLSTU	dust-ball
ABDLOOTX	blood-tax
ABDLRSUU	subdural
ABDLRSUY	absurdly
ABDLSTUU	subadult
ABDMNNOS	bondsman
ABDMNOOR	moor-band
ABDMNOUW	mawbound
ABDMOOPR	mopboard
ABDNNORW	own-brand
ABDNOORR	barn-door
ABDNORSU	△baudrons
ABDNORUY	boundary
ABDOORTU	outboard
ABDOOSSW	basswood
ABEEEERT	bee-eater
ABEEEFRS	freebase
ABEEEGRS	bargeese
ABEEEGRV	beverage
ABEEEHTT	hebetate
ABEEELNS	Lebanese
ABEEENRT	△tenebrae
ABEEENRV	bereaven
ABEEENST	absentee
ABEEEPRU	beau-pere
ABEEERRT	terebrae
ABEEFFNO	banoffee
ABEEFFTU	beauffet

Words marked △ may be spelled also with a capital letter

ABEEFILR	bale-fire
ABEEFILS	feasible
ABEEFILT	flea-bite
ABEEFLLL	fellable
ABEEFLLN	befallen
ABEEFLOS	beefalos
ABEEFORR	forebear
ABEEGGNR	green-bag
ABEEGHRT	berthage
ABEEGINR	baregine
	bergenia
ABEEGIRV	verbiage
ABEEGLLR	gabeller
ABEEGLTT	gettable
ABEEGMRY	emery-bag
ABEEGMTY	megabyte
ABEEGOSZ	gazeboes
ABEEGRST	absterge
ABEEGTTU	baguette
ABEEHILR	hireable
ABEEHINT	thebaine
ABEEHIRS	Hebraise
ABEEHIRZ	Hebraize
ABEEHLLL	heel-ball
ABEEHLLP	helpable
ABEEHLLR	beerhall
	harebell
ABEEHNOP	Phoebean
ABEEHNPP	behappen
ABEEHNSS	has-beens
ABEEHNTT	hebetant
ABEEHQTU	bequeath
ABEEHRRT	breather
ABEEHRST	hartbees
ABEEIIMN	bien-aimé
ABEEIKLL	likeable
ABEEIKLT	Bakelite®
ABEEIKRT	tie-break
ABEEILLR	reliable
ABEEILLV	leviable
	liveable
ABEEILNN	Biennale
ABEEILNP	plebeian
ABEEILNS	Balinese
	base-line
ABEEILNU	banlieue
ABEEILNV	enviable
ABEEILPX	expiable
ABEEILRT	liberate
ABEEILST	seablite
ABEEILSV	evasible
ABEEILSZ	seizable
	sizeable
ABEEILTV	evitable
ABEEILVW	viewable
ABEEIMRT	amberite
ABEEINSU	Eusebian
ABEEINTY	ayenbite
ABEEIPRS	bepraise
ABEEIRTT	batterie
ABEEIRTV	breviate
ABEEISSV	abessive

ABEEISTU	beauties
ABEEITUX	beauxite
ABEEJMOR	jamboree
ABEEJNPU	Punjabee
ABEEKLLW	Bakewell
ABEEKLOT	keelboat
ABEEKMNR	embanker
ABEEKMRR	re-embark
ABEEKOOP	peekaboo
ABEEKRST	bestreak
ABEELLLS	sellable
ABEELLLT	tellable
ABEELLOT	ballotee
ABEELLOV	loveable
ABEELLTT	lettable
ABEELMMR	embalmer
	emmarble
ABEELMNO	bone-meal
ABEELMOV	moveable
ABEELMPR	preamble
ABEELMRT	atremble
ABEELMSS	assemble
	assemblé
	beamless
ABEELMTT	embattle
ABEELNOP	beanpole
	openable
ABEELNRT	rentable
ABEELNTU	tuneable
ABEELOPR	operable
	ropeable
ABEELOPS	poseable
ABEELORX	exorable
ABEELRRY	ale-berry
ABEELRSU	reusable
ABEELRSV	beslaver
ABEELRTT	batteler
ABEELRTU	bateleur
	bleuâtre
ABEELSSS	baseless
ABEELSST	bateless
ABEELSSU	sublease
ABEELSTT	testable
ABEEMMNR	membrane
ABEEMMRU	bummaree
ABEEMNOR	bemoaner
ABEEMNST	basement
ABEEMNTT	abetment
	batement
ABEENNRT	banneret
ABEENNRU	eburnean
ABEENNTU	unbeaten
ABEENORS	seaborne
ABEENOTZ	benzoate
ABEENRRT	banterer
ABEENRSS	bareness
ABEENSSS	baseness
ABEEORRV	overbear
ABEEORST	rebatoes
ABEEORSZ	zero-base
ABEEORTV	overbeat
ABEEPRRY	peaberry

ABEERRRT	barterer
ABEERRST	terebras
ABEERRTT	barrette
ABEERRTV	vertebra
ABEERRTY	betrayer
	teaberry
ABEERSTU	suberate
ABEESTWY	sweet-bay
ABEFFKOR	off-break
ABEFGLLR	bergfall
ABEFHILS	fishable
ABEFHLLU	half-blue
ABEFHOOT	hoofbeat
ABEFILLL	fallible
ABEFILLM	filmable
ABEFILLR	fireball
ABEFILLT	liftable
ABEFILOT	lifeboat
ABEFILSU	fabulise
ABEFILSY	feasibly
ABEFILUZ	fabulize
ABEFIRRT	firebrat
ABEFITUY	beautify
ABEFKLNT	left-bank
ABEFLLMU	blameful
ABEFLLTU	tableful
ABEFLMOR	formable
ABEFLNRU	funebral
ABEFMORX	box-frame
ABEFMRSU	subframe
ABEFOORT	barefoot
ABEFORTU	Beaufort
ABEFRRUY	February
ABEGGHLU	huggable
ABEGGILN	beagling
ABEGGLLU	luggable
ABEGGLOS	gas-globe
ABEGGLRY	beggarly
ABEGHILP	philabeg
ABEGHILR	alberghi
ABEGHNOY	honey-bag
ABEGHORR	begorrah
ABEGHRRY	hagberry
ABEGHRST	barghest
ABEGIKNN	bean-king
ABEGIKNR	breaking
ABEGILNN	enabling
ABEGILNS	singable
ABEGILNT	bleating
	tangible
ABEGILOT	obligate
ABEGIMUX	giambeux
ABEGINOR	aborigen
ABEGINRS	bearings
ABEGINTT	abetting
ABEGINTW	wingbeat
ABEGIPPR	bagpiper
ABEGIPPS	bagpipes
ABEGIRTU	auger-bit
ABEGKORS	grosbeak
ABEGLLLU	gullable
ABEGLLOR	bargello

ABEGLORW	growable
ABEGLRUU	blagueur
ABEGLSTU	gustable
ABEGMNOS	gambeson
ABEGMNOY	bogey-man
	money-bag
ABEGMORT	bergamot
ABEGNRST	bangster
ABEGNRTU	burganet
ABEGNSTU	subagent
ABEGOORS	bargoose
ABEGORRW	row-barge
ABEGRRUV	burgrave
ABEGSSTU	substage
ABEHILLR	hairbell
ABEHILNR	hibernal
ABEHILTT	tithable
ABEHIMMS	mem-sahib
ABEHIMNO	Bohemian
ABEHIMOS	obeahism
ABEHIMRS	Hebraism
ABEHINNT	Banthine®
ABEHINST	absinthe
ABEHIOPU	euphobia
ABEHIORV	behavior
ABEHIRST	Hebraist
ABEHJORS	jobshare
ABEHKLLW	hawkbell
ABEHKNOR	hornbeak
ABEHLLRT	bethrall
ABEHLMMU	hummable
ABEHLMSS	shambles
ABEHLNOT	benthoal
ABEHLOTY	hylobate
ABEHLRST	blathers
ABEHLSSS	bashless
ABEHMNOR	hornbeam
ABEHMOOR	rehoboam
ABEHMOPT	Baphomet
ABEHNSTU	sunbathe
ABEHORRR	△abhorrer
	harborer
ABEHORST	bathorse
ABEIILMT	imitable
ABEIILNN	biennial
ABEIILNV	inviable
ABEIILPT	pitiable
ABEIILRR	libraire
ABEIILRS	biserial
ABEIILST	albitise
	sibilate
ABEIILTV	live-bait
	vitiable
ABEIILTZ	albitize
ABEIINNS	Ibsenian
ABEIJLTU	△jubilate
ABEIJMNN	△benjamin
ABEIKLLM	lamb-like
ABEIKLLN	balkline
	linkable
ABEIKLRU	buik-lear
ABEIKLSS	kissable
ABEIKMRR	rim-brake
ABEIKNOR	beak-iron
ABEIKNRS	bearskin
ABEIKRST	breaskit
ABEILLLT	tillable
ABEILLLW	willable
ABEILLMM	limbmeal
ABEILLMT	time-ball
ABEILLNT	libelant
ABEILLOS	isolable
ABEILLOV	violable
ABEILLQU	liquable
ABEILLRR	brailler
ABEILLRY	beryllia
	reliably
ABEILLST	△bastille
ABEILLTT	tiltable
ABEILMNT	bailment
ABEILMOR	bromelia
ABEILMSS	missable
ABEILNNW	winnable
ABEILNOP	opinable
ABEILNPT	pintable
ABEILNRS	rinsable
ABEILNRU	ruinable
ABEILNSS	albiness
ABEILNST	instable
ABEILNSU	sabuline
ABEILNTV	bivalent
ABEILNUV	unviable
ABEILNVY	enviably
ABEILORS	△borealis
ABEILPPT	tippable
ABEILPRT	partible
ABEILPRZ	prizable
ABEILPSS	passible
ABEILPST	epiblast
ABEILRRU	reburial
ABEILRTW	writable
ABEILRYY	bi-yearly
ABEILSSU	issuable
	suasible
ABEILSTU	suitable
ABEILSTY	beastily
ABEILSUX	bisexual
ABEIMRRU	Brumaire
ABEIMRTV	ambivert
	verbatim
ABEIMSSU	iambuses
ABEINNOS	besonian
ABEINNOZ	bezonian
ABEINNPR	brine-pan
ABEINNRU	inurbane
ABEINOOT	Boeotian
ABEINORR	airborne
ABEINORT	baritone
	obtainer
ABEINOST	botanise
	obeisant
ABEINOTZ	botanize
ABEINQSU	basquine
ABEINRST	banister
ABEINRSU	urbanise
ABEINRTU	braunite
	urbanite
ABEINRUZ	urbanize
ABEINSST	bassinet
ABEINTTU	intubate
ABEIORST	sabotier
ABEIORTT	Taborite
ABEIORTV	abortive
ABEIRRRS	barriers
ABEIRRVY	breviary
ABEIRSTY	bestiary
	△sybarite
ABEIRTTY	ytterbia
ABEITTTU	titubate
ABEJKLOU	kabeljou
ABEJLMPU	jumpable
ABEJMOOR	jeroboam
ABEJNORS	Sobranje
ABEKLMOS	smokable
ABEKLNOW	knowable
ABEKLNRY	bankerly
ABEKLNTY	blankety
ABEKLOOR	book-lear
ABEKLORW	workable
ABEKLRSS	barkless
ABEKMOOT	book-mate
ABEKNNOT	bank-note
ABEKNSSY	sneaksby
ABEKOORY	yearbook
ABEKORTU	break-out
	outbreak
ABEKORVW	break-vow
ABEKRSTY	basketry
ABELLLMU	labellum
ABELLLOR	rollable
ABELLLOT	tollable
ABELLLSY	syllable
ABELLMOR	ombrella
ABELLMRU	umbellar
	umbrella
ABELLMSS	mass-bell
ABELLNOS	bonsella
ABELLNOT	ballonet
ABELLNOW	own-label
ABELLNRU	Brunella
	rubellan
ABELLOOT	loo-table
ABELLOSV	solvable
ABELLOTU	lobulate
ABELLRVY	verbally
ABELMNNO	nobleman
ABELMNOZ	emblazon
ABELMNST	semblant
ABELMNTU	Nembutal®
ABELMOOT	mootable
ABELMOSV	movables
ABELMOVY	moveably
ABELMPTU	plumbate
ABELMRTY	Bartlemy
ABELMSSY	assembly
ABELNNOR	bannerol

ABELNNRU	lean-burn
	runnable
ABELNORZ	blazoner
ABELNOST	neoblast
	notables
ABELNQTU	blanquet
ABELNRUY	urbanely
ABELNRYZ	brazenly
ABELNSTU	unstable
ABELNSTY	absently
ABELNSUU	unusable
ABELOPRT	portable
ABELOPRU	pourable
ABELOPRV	provable
ABELOPTT	tabletop
ABELOPTX	box-pleat
ABELOQTU	quotable
ABELORRU	labourer
ABELORST	sortable
	storable
ABELORSV	absolver
ABELORWX	ox-warble
ABELOSSU	sabulose
ABELOSTU	△absolute
ABELOSTW	bestowal
ABELPRTU	pubertal
ABELQSUU	subequal
ABELRRTU	barrulet
ABELRSTU	baluster
ABELRTTU	burletta
	rebuttal
ABELSTUU	subulate
ABELTTUU	tubulate
ABEMMNOO	moonbeam
ABEMNNOR	mean-born
ABEMNORT	rent-a-mob
ABEMNOTU	umbonate
ABEMNPRU	penumbra
ABEMNSUY	sunbeamy
ABEMNTTU	abutment
ABEMORRS	embrasor
ABEMORSU	amberous
ABEMORTZ	barometz
ABENOPSU	subpoena
ABENORSS	baroness
ABENORSY	Sobranye
ABENORTT	betatron
ABENORTV	bevatron
ABENORTY	barytone
ABENOSSW	sawbones
ABENOSTY	bayonets
ABENRRTU	burnt-ear
ABENRRYZ	brazenry
ABENRSTU	unbraste
ABEOPPRY	paper-boy
ABEORRSS	braseros
ABEORSTU	saboteur
ABEORTTU	obturate
	tabouret
ABEORTUV	outbrave
ABEOSSST	asbestos
ABEOSTUV	subovate
ABEPRSSY	passer-by
ABEQRSUU	arquebus
ABERRTYY	tayberry
ABERRWXY	waxberry
ABERSSTU	abstruse
ABERTTUY	butyrate
ABESSTTU	substate
ABFFGILN	baffling
ABFFLLPU	puffball
ABFFLOST	blast-off
ABFFNOTU	bouffant
ABFGLLOO	goofball
ABFGORUU	faubourg
ABFHIIST	baitfish
ABFHILLS	fishball
ABFHIORS	boarfish
ABFHLOOT	half-boot
ABFHLSUX	flax-bush
ABFHLTTU	half-butt
ABFHOOTT	foot-bath
ABFIILLR	fibrilla
ABFILLLY	fallibly
ABFILNSU	basinful
ABFILSTU	fabulist
ABFIMORS	fibromas
ABFIRTTU	fruit-bat
ABFJORSU	frabjous
ABFKLLOR	korfball
ABFLLOOT	football
ABFLLORU	four-ball
ABFLLOST	softball
ABFLLSSU	fuss-ball
ABFLLUZZ	fuzz-ball
ABFLOSTU	boastful
ABFLOSUU	fabulous
ABFNORTU	turbofan
ABGGGINR	bragging
ABGGIJNN	jingbang
ABGGILMN	gambling
ABGGILNR	garbling
ABGGNOOT	toboggan
ABGHHIKN	bank-high
ABGHHILL	highball
ABGHHMRU	Hamburgh
ABGHINWZ	whizbang
ABGHIOPR	biograph
ABGHMORU	brougham
ABGIILNS	saibling
ABGIILOT	obligati
ABGIIMST	bigamist
ABGIINNO	bignonia
ABGIINOR	aborigin
ABGIINSS	biassing
ABGIKLNN	blanking
ABGIKNRR	ring-bark
ABGILLLR	ball-girl
ABGILLMN	lambling
ABGILMNR	marbling
	rambling
ABGILMNW	wambling
ABGILNNT	bantling
ABGILNOT	bloating
	bog-Latin
	obligant
ABGILNRT	bratling
ABGILNRW	brawling
	warbling
ABGILNST	blasting
	stabling
ABGILNTT	blatting
ABGILNTY	tangibly
ABGILOOT	obligato
ABGILORW	brigalow
ABGIMOSU	bigamous
	subimago
ABGINNOR	aborning
ABGINNRX	banxring
ABGINOOT	tabooing
ABGINOST	boasting
	bostangi
ABGINSTW	batswing
ABGINTTU	abutting
ABGIRRSS	rib-grass
ABGLLLOY	globally
ABGLLNOW	ball-gown
ABGLLORU	globular
ABGLLRUY	bullyrag
ABGLMOPU	△plumbago
ABGLMOSU	lumbagos
ABGLNOOT	longboat
ABGLNOUW	bungalow
ABGLOOTY	batology
ABGLORSU	glabrous
ABGLRRUY	burglary
ABGMNOOR	gambroon
ABGNOOST	boat-song
ABGNOOWX	box-wagon
ABGNORSU	osnaburg
ABGNOSWY	bowyangs
ABGOORST	botargos
ABHHOSTU	hush-boat
	Shabuoth
ABHHRSTU	hatbrush
ABHIINRS	brainish
ABHIIORZ	rhizobia
ABHIKLOR	kohlrabi
ABHILLPT	pithball
ABHILNOT	biathlon
ABHILOPS	basophil
ABHILRTW	whirlbat
ABHILSST	stablish
ABHIMMST	bathmism
ABHINORT	hot-brain
ABHIOSTU	hautbois
ABHIRRSU	air-brush
ABHIRSTT	brattish
ABHISTTZ	sitz-bath
ABHKLSUW	bushwalk
ABHKOOOT	boat-hook
	book-oath
ABHKORSU	kourbash
ABHLLMOT	mothball
ABHLLOOY	ballyhoo

ABHLLPSU push-ball
ABHLORTW whorlbat
ABHLOSWW washbowl
ABHLSSTU saltbush
ABHMNOTY bothyman
ABHMNSUU subhuman
ABHMOORT bathroom
ABHOORST tarboosh
ABHOOSTW showboat
ABHORSTU tarboush
ABHRRSTU tar-brush
ABIIINRY biriyani
ABIIKLSS basilisk
ABIILLMR millibar
ABIILLTY lability
ABIILMNO binomial
ABIILMNS albinism
ABIILNOT libation
ABIILNRZ brazilin
ABIILNST sibilant
ABIILPTY pitiably
ABIILRTU air-built
ABIIMNOT ambition
ABIIRSSV vibrissa
ABIJLNTU jubilant
ABIJNOOT jobation
ABIJNOST banjoist
ABIKLMNS lambskin
ABIKLNRY byrlakin
ABIKMNNR brinkman
ABIKNORR ironbark
ABIKRSTZ britzska
ABILLLPY playbill
ABILLOTT toll-bait
ABILLOVY violably
ABILLRTY tribally
ABILMNOU olibanum
ABILMOOT tail-boom
ABILMOPS bioplasm
ABILMOTU bumaloti
ABILNOOT lobation
oblation
ABILNORU unilobar
ABILNOTU ablution
abutilon
ABILNRTU tribunal
turbinal
ABILNSTU stub-nail
ABILOPST bioplast
ABILORST strobila
ABILORTY libatory
ABILOTTT tilt-boat
ABILPSSY passibly
ABILRSSY brassily
ABILRSUV subviral
ABILRTUY ruby-tail
ABILSSUY issuably
ABILSTUY suitably
ABIMMNOO mainboom
ABIMNOOW obi-woman
ABIMNOSU bimanous
ABIMNPRS snap-brim
ABIMNRTU tamburin
ABIMORSU biramous
ABIMRSST strabism
ABINNORW Brownian
ABINNRSU Burnsian
ABINOORT abortion
ABINOPTX paint-box
ABINORTU tabourin
ABINORWY rainbowy
ABINOSTT botanist
ABINRTUY urbanity
ABINTTTU titubant
ABIOPRSU biparous
ABIOPSTU subtopia
ABIORRST arborist
rib-roast
ABIORRTV vibrator
ABIORSTV vibratos
ABIORTUY obituary
ABIRRSTU airburst
ABIRSSUZ subsizar
ABJLLMPU jump-ball
ABKKMOOR bookmark
ABKLLMSU musk-ball
ABKLLNOR bankroll
ABKLOOPY playbook
ABKMOOSS mass-book
ABKNOPST stopbank
ABKNPRTU bankrupt
ABKOOPSS pass-book
ABKOORTW workboat
ABKOOSTT kottabos
ABLLMNOO moon-ball
ABLLMOOR ballroom
ABLLMOPW blowlamp
ABLLNOSW snowball
ABLLOORT root-ball
ABLLORST borstall
ABLLRTUY brutally
ABLLSSUY syllabus
ABLMNRUU alburnum
laburnum
ABLMOSTY myoblast
ABLNORYZ blazonry
ABLNOSUZ subzonal
ABLNRSUU sublunar
ABLNSUUY unusably
ABLOORTY oblatory
ABLOOSTT bootlast
ABLOOSTZ zooblast
ABLOPRSU subpolar
ABLOPRVY provably
ABLOPSUU pabulous
ABLOQTUY quotably
ABLORSSU subsolar
ABLOSSUU sabulous
ABLOSTTU subtotal
ABLPRTUY abruptly
ABMNTTUY buttyman
ABMOORTW warm-boot
ABNOORRT roborant
ABNORTUU runabout
ABNOSSSU bonassus
ABOORRSU arborous
ACCCDEIO Coccidae
ACCCDIIO △coccidia
ACCCENPY peccancy
ACCCFIIL calcific
ACCCHILO colchica
ACCCIIPR capricci
ACCCILLY cyclical
ACCDDEEN cadenced
ACCDDIIT didactic
ACCDEEEU deuce-ace
ACCDEEPT accepted
ACCDEERU cardecue
ACCDEHIL chaliced
ACCDEILO dice-coal
ACCDEILU caudicle
ACCDEILY delicacy
ACCDEINT accident
ACCDEIRT accredit
ACCDEISU caudices
ACCDELLY calycled
ACCDELSU cul-de-sac
ACCDEORR accorder
ACCDERSU accursed
ACCDESUU caduceus
ACCDGHOO coachdog
ACCDHIIR diarchic
ACCDHIIS Chasidic
ACCDHIMO dochmiac
ACCDHIOT cathodic
ACCDHLOR clochard
ACCDIIST dicastic
ACCDIITY dicacity
ACCDILOY calycoid
ACCDILTY dactylic
ACCDINOR cancroid
△draconic
ACCDIOOR coracoid
ACCDIORS sarcodic
ACCDIOST sticcado
ACCDITUY caducity
ACCDLLOY clay-cold
ACCDOOST stoccado
ACCDOOXY cacodoxy
ACCDOSUU caducous
ACCEEHIT hiccatee
ACCEEHLO cochleae
ACCEEHRT ceterach
ACCEEHST seecatch
ACCEEILR celeriac
ACCEEILS ecclesia
ACCEEIMR ice-cream
ACCEEKLN necklace
ACCEELNR clarence
ACCEELOS coalesce
ACCEELRT calcrete
ACCEENNS nascence
ACCEENPR crepance
ACCEENST acescent
ACCEEORT croceate
ACCEEPRT accepter

ACCEFFIY	efficacy
ACCEFILS	fascicle
ACCEGINO	Cocaigne
ACCEGKMO	gamecock
ACCEGNOY	co-agency
ACCEHHKO	chechako
ACCEHIKP	chickpea
	pea-chick
ACCEHILM	alchemic
	chemical
ACCEHILP	cephalic
ACCEHILT	hectical
ACCEHIMN	mechanic
ACCEHIMS	sachemic
ACCEHINO	anechoic
ACCEHINR	chicaner
ACCEHLOR	cochlear
ACCEHLOT	catechol
ACCEHNNO	chaconne
ACCEHNNY	cynanche
ACCEHNOR	charneco
	encroach
ACCEHNOT	conchate
ACCEHNRY	△chancery
ACCEHOPT	cachepot
ACCEHRST	cratches
ACCEIIST	caecitis
ACCEILLN	cancelli
ACCEILLR	clerical
ACCEILLU	caulicle
ACCEILLV	clavicle
ACCEILNS	scenical
ACCEILNT	canticle
ACCEILNV	clavecin
ACCEILNY	calycine
ACCEILOS	calicoes
ACCEILRV	cervical
ACCEIMRS	ceramics
ACCEINNR	cancrine
ACCEINRT	Nearctic
ACCEINRY	Cyrenaic
ACCEINTU	cuneatic
ACCEIOPR	cecropia
ACCEIOTV	coactive
ACCEIPRT	practice
ACCEIPSV	peccavis
ACCEIRRR	ricercar
ACCEIRTU	cruciate
ACCEISTT	ecstatic
ACCEKLNR	cracknel
ACCEKNOR	corn-cake
ACCEKNOY	Cockayne
ACCEKOPY	peacocky
ACCEKRRS	crackers
ACCELLOR	Roccella
ACCELLUY	calycule
ACCELMNY	cyclamen
ACCELNOV	conclave
ACCELNRU	caruncle
ACCELNTU	clean-cut
ACCELRSY	scarcely
ACCELRTU	clear-cut
ACCELSSU	saccules
ACCELWYY	cycleway
ACCENNSY	nascency
ACCENORR	cornacre
ACCENORT	accentor
ACCENOST	cosecant
ACCENOSU	concause
ACCEOPRT	acceptor
ACCEOPTU	occupate
ACCEORST	ectosarc
ACCEORTU	accouter
	accoutre
ACCESSTU	cactuses
ACCFFLTU	calc-tuff
ACCFHKLO	half-cock
ACCFHLTY	catchfly
ACCFIILT	lactific
ACCFLNOO	confocal
ACCFOORT	cofactor
ACCGHINO	coaching
ACCGHINT	catching
ACCGHIOR	choragic
ACCGIKMR	gimcrack
ACCGIKNR	cracking
ACCGINSU	accusing
ACCGLOOY	cacology
ACCHHITT	chitchat
ACCHHMOS	camshoch
ACCHIIRT	rachitic
ACCHIIST	chiastic
ACCHILNO	chalonic
ACCHILOR	orichalc
ACCHILOT	△catholic
ACCHINNO	cinchona
ACCHINOS	chicanos
ACCHINPU	△capuchin
ACCHIORT	thoracic
	trochaic
ACCHIPTT	catch-pit
ACCHIRRT	carritch
ACCHKLOR	charlock
ACCHKMOR	arch-mock
ACCHKORT	hock-cart
ACCHLOOT	cacholot
ACCHLOPT	cloth-cap
ACCHMORS	caschrom
ACCHNNUY	unchancy
ACCHNOOR	coronach
ACCHNOTU	couchant
ACCHORTU	cartouch
ACCHRSTY	scratchy
ACCIIIOT	oiticica
ACCIILLN	clinical
ACCIILMT	climatic
ACCIILPP	Calippic
ACCIILRT	critical
ACCIIMNN	cinnamic
ACCIINNO	aniconic
ACCIINNP	piccanin
ACCIINOT	aconitic
ACCIINPU	Puccinia
ACCIIPST	pasticci
ACCIIRTX	cicatrix
ACCIJKMR	jimcrack
ACCIKKNN	nick-nack
ACCIKKRR	rick-rack
ACCIKKTT	tick-tack
ACCIKLOT	cocktail
ACCIKNST	canstick
ACCIKOPR	apricock
ACCIKPRT	practick
ACCIKSTT	cat-stick
ACCILMOS	cosmical
ACCILMOX	cacomixl
ACCILNOT	ciclaton
ACCILNOV	volcanic
ACCILNUV	△vulcanic
ACCILORT	cortical
ACCILPRY	caprylic
ACCILRRU	circular
ACCILSSS	classics
ACCIMMOS	Occamism
ACCIMNOS	moccasin
ACCIMNTU	canticum
ACCIMORR	microcar
ACCIMORU	coumaric
ACCIMOST	Occamist
ACCIMPSU	capsicum
ACCINOOS	occasion
ACCINOOT	coaction
ACCINORT	narcotic
ACCINORV	cavicorn
ACCINOST	canticos
	Scotican
ACCINOTY	canticoy
	cyanotic
ACCIOPST	spiccato
ACCIORST	acrostic
	Socratic
ACCIORSY	isocracy
ACCIOSTT	sticcato
ACCIOSTU	acoustic
ACCIOTTT	tic-tac-to
ACCIPRST	practics
ACCIRRTT	tric-trac
ACCIRSTY	scarcity
ACCKKRSU	rucksack
ACCKMMRU	crummack
ACCKOOOT	cockatoo
ACCKOPRT	crackpot
ACCLLOSU	occlusal
ACCLLSUU	calculus
ACCLMOOP	coco-palm
ACCLSSUU	sacculus
ACCMOSTU	accustom
ACCNOOTU	cocoanut
ACCNOPRU	acorn-cup
ACCNOPTU	occupant
ACCNORTT	contract
ACCNOSTU	accounts
ACCOQSSU	squaccos
ACCORRTY	carrycot
ACDDDEIT	addicted
ACDDEEES	deceased

ACDDEEFR	red-faced
ACDDEEHT	detached
ACDDEEIT	dedicate
ACDDEEIU	deciduae
ACDDEELR	declared
ACDDEENR	credenda
ACDDEENT	decadent
ACDDEESU	Sadducee
ACDDEETU	educated
ACDDEFGO	dog-faced
ACDDEHIK	dickhead
ACDDEHKN	deck-hand
ACDDEIIL	deicidal
ACDDEIIM	△medicaid
ACDDEILU	decidual
ACDDEINR	cider-and
	riddance
ACDDEINT	dedicant
ACDDEISU	deciduas
ACDDEKLO	deadlock
	dead-lock
	deck-load
ACDDEKOR	raddocke
ACDDENTU	adducent
ACDDFOOR	food-card
ACDDGILN	cladding
ACDDHIIO	diadochi
ACDDHIMR	didrachm
ACDDHKOS	shaddock
ACDDIIOR	cardioid
ACDDILNY	candidly
ACDDILTY	didactyl
ACDDINNU	uncandid
ACDDINSY	discandy
ACDDKLNO	dockland
ACDDKORY	dockyard
ACDDORTU	adductor
ACDDOTTY	toddy-cat
ACDEEEFT	defecate
ACDEEEKS	seedcake
ACDEEEMR	reedmace
ACDEEENT	antecede
ACDEEERS	decrease
ACDEEESS	seedcase
ACDEEFFT	affected
ACDEEFIN	defiance
ACDEEFRS	frescade
ACDEEFRY	federacy
ACDEEGGN	egg-dance
ACDEEGKM	deck-game
ACDEEGLY	delegacy
ACDEEHMR	démarche
ACDEEHNR	enarched
ACDEEHNS	enchased
ACDEEIIP	epicedia
ACDEEILT	delicate
ACDEEIMN	Medicean
ACDEEIMR	△medicare
ACDEEIMT	decimate
	medicate
ACDEEINN	enneadic
ACDEEINR	déraciné
ACDEEINU	audience
ACDEEINV	deviance
	vice-dean
ACDEEIPR	Percidae
ACDEEIPS	dispeace
ACDEEJKT	jacketed
ACDEEKNR	cankered
ACDEEKRT	racketed
ACDEELNR	calender
	encradle
ACDEELNT	lanceted
ACDEELRR	declarer
ACDEELRT	△decretal
ACDEELRV	calvered
ACDEELSS	déclassé
ACDEEMNO	code-name
ACDEENNT	tendance
ACDEENNY	cayenned
ACDEENOT	anecdote
	toe-dance
ACDEENRS	ascender
	reascend
ACDEENRT	crenated
	decanter
	nectared
ACDEENRV	caverned
ACDEENRZ	credenza
ACDEENTT	dancette
	dancetté
ACDEEOPS	peasecod
ACDEEORT	decorate
ACDEEOST	seed-coat
ACDEEPRT	carpeted
ACDEERRT	terraced
ACDEESUX	caudexes
ACDEFGIP	pig-faced
ACDEFGPU	pug-faced
ACDEFHLN	flanched
ACDEFIIL	deifical
ACDEFILL	ill-faced
ACDEFILN	canfield
ACDEFILR	fricadel
ACDEFOTW	two-faced
ACDEFRSU	surfaced
ACDEFRTU	furcated
ACDEGGRS	scragged
ACDEGHIL	Gadhelic
ACDEGHOP	dog-cheap
ACDEGIIL	algicide
ACDEGIKM	magicked
ACDEGIMR	decigram
ACDEGINU	guidance
ACDEGIRS	disgrace
ACDEGLOU	cloudage
ACDEGNRS	scrag-end
ACDEGNRU	ungraced
ACDEGOTT	cottaged
ACDEHHTT	thatched
ACDEHIIP	aphicide
ACDEHILL	Helladic
ACDEHILR	Heraclid
	heraldic
ACDEHILT	dithecal
ACDEHIMS	schiedam
ACDEHIOP	Phocidae
ACDEHIRS	rachides
ACDEHIRT	thridace
	tracheid
ACDEHKLO	headlock
ACDEHKNU	unhacked
ACDEHKOV	havocked
ACDEHKRU	archduke
ACDEHLNP	planched
ACDEHLNR	chandler
ACDEHNOR	rondache
ACDEHNSU	uncashed
ACDEHORR	hard-core
ACDEHORT	chordate
ACDEHORW	cowheard
ACDEHPRU	upcheard
ACDEHPST	despatch
ACDEHPTU	death-cup
ACDEHRST	starched
ACDEIIMU	aecidium
ACDEIINR	acridine
ACDEIINS	sciaenid
ACDEIINT	actinide
	diactine
	indicate
ACDEIINU	induciae
ACDEIITV	cavitied
	vaticide
ACDEIJNU	jaundice
ACDEIKMN	main-deck
ACDEIKNP	panicked
ACDEIKNT	anticked
ACDEILLM	medallic
ACDEILLN	declinal
ACDEILLV	cavilled
ACDEILMN	med'cinal
ACDEILMO	cameloid
	melodica
ACDEILMT	maledict
ACDEILNP	panicled
ACDEILNU	Dulcinea
ACDEILNV	vine-clad
ACDEILPS	displace
ACDEILPT	plicated
ACDEILPY	dice-play
ACDEILRT	articled
ACDEILRU	auricled
	radicule
ACDEIMNO	comedian
	daemonic
	demoniac
	mid-ocean
ACDEIMNP	pandemic
ACDEIMRT	dermatic
	timecard
ACDEIMSU	Muscidae
ACDEINNR	crannied
ACDEINOP	canopied
ACDEINOS	diocesan
	oceanids

Words marked △ may be spelled also with a capital letter

ACDEINOV	voidance
ACDEINPT	pedantic
	pentadic
ACDEINRT	crinated
	dicentra
ACDEINSS	acidness
ACDEINST	distance
ACDEINTV	ci-devant
	Vedantic
ACDEINVY	deviancy
ACDEIOPS	diascope
ACDEIORS	idocrase
ACDEIORT	ceratoid
ACDEIORV	Corvidae
ACDEIOSU	edacious
ACDEIOTT	Cottidae
ACDEIPSS	spadices
ACDEIPST	spicated
ACDEIQRU	acquired
ACDEIRTT	tetracid
	tetradic
ACDEKLTW	tack-weld
ACDEKNOT	tacked-on
ACDEKNPU	unpacked
ACDEKNRU	unracked
ACDEKOST	stockade
ACDELLNU	uncalled
ACDELLOR	carolled
	collared
ACDELLOS	so-called
ACDELMOS	Damocles
ACDELMSU	muscadel
ACDELNOO	canoodle
ACDELNOR	colander
ACDELNPU	unplaced
ACDELNRY	calendry
	dry-clean
ACDELNSU	unscaled
ACDELOPT	clodpate
ACDELOPU	cupolaed
ACDELORV	overclad
ACDELOTU	oculated
ACDELRSY	sacredly
ACDELSTU	sulcated
ACDEMMRS	scrammed
ACDEMOPR	compadre
ACDEMORT	△democrat
ACDEMSTU	Muscadet
ACDENNOR	ordnance
ACDENNOT	cantoned
ACDENNST	scandent
ACDENOPR	endocarp
ACDENORS	endosarc
ACDENORY	deaconry
ACDENOSY	cyanosed
ACDENOTU	outdance
	uncoated
ACDENPST	Pandects
ACDENRTU	cedar-nut
	underact
	untraced
ACDENRVY	verdancy
ACDENSUU	uncaused
ACDENTTY	dancetty
ACDEOOPP	Copepoda
ACDEOORS	door-case
ACDEOPRU	croupade
ACDEOPRY	copyread
ACDEORRT	redactor
ACDEORSS	Sarcodes
ACDEORTU	educator
ACDEORTV	card-vote
ACDEOSTT	costated
ACDEPPRS	scrapped
ACDEQTUU	aqueduct
ACDERRSU	crusader
ACDERRTU	traducer
ACDERTUV	curvated
ACDFFHNU	handcuff
ACDFFIRT	diffract
ACDFFLOS	scaffold
ACDFIILU	fiducial
ACDFILOU	fucoidal
ACDFLRTU	turf-clad
ACDGHOTW	dog-watch
	watchdog
ACDGIILO	dialogic
ACDGILNR	cradling
ACDGILNS	scalding
ACDGIMOT	dogmatic
ACDGIOPR	podagric
ACDGKLOO	good-lack
ACDGLNOO	Golconda
ACDGNRTU	dung-cart
ACDHHNTU	unhatch'd
ACDHIINT	tachinid
ACDHIIOT	thio-acid
ACDHIISS	Hassidic
ACDHIKNP	hand-pick
ACDHIKOR	chokidar
ACDHILMN	man-child
ACDHILPR	pilchard
ACDHILPS	clapdish
ACDHINOR	hadronic
	rhodanic
ACDHINRY	dinarchy
ACDHINSW	sandwich
ACDHIOPS	scaphoid
ACDHIORY	hyracoid
ACDHIPST	dispatch
ACDHKKUW	duck-hawk
ACDHKLRU	hard-luck
ACDHKORR	hard-rock
ACDHKOSY	Hock-days
ACDHLNOR	chaldron
	chlordan
	chondral
ACDHLOPT	pad-cloth
ACDHMNTU	Dutchman
ACDHMORU	mouchard
ACDHNORW	chawdron
ACDHOOTW	woodchat
ACDHOPRY	hard-copy
ACDHORSY	dyschroa
ACDIIILN	indicial
ACDIIIPR	diapiric
ACDIIJLU	judicial
ACDIILMS	disclaim
ACDIILNO	conidial
ACDIILNS	scaldini
ACDIILSU	suicidal
ACDIILTY	calidity
	dialytic
ACDIIMNO	daimonic
ACDIIMOR	dioramic
ACDIIMOT	diatomic
	midi-coat
ACDIIMSU	ascidium
ACDIINNT	indicant
ACDIINOP	pinacoid
ACDIINOT	actinoid
	diatonic
ACDIINPR	Pindaric
ACDIIOSS	acidosis
ACDIIRST	carditis
ACDIIRTY	acridity
ACDIISST	sadistic
ACDIKLTU	duck-tail
ACDIKMOO	cookmaid
ACDIKRRY	rickyard
ACDILLOU	caudillo
	lodicula
ACDILLPY	placidly
ACDILMOR	dromical
ACDILMTU	Talmudic
ACDILNOO	conoidal
ACDILNOR	iron-clad
ACDILNOS	scaldino
ACDILNSY	syndical
ACDILNUU	nudicaul
ACDILOPY	polyacid
ACDILOUV	oviducal
ACDILPSU	cuspidal
ACDILSTY	Dactylis
ACDIMNOO	monoacid
ACDIMNSU	muscadin
	scandium
ACDIMNSY	dynamics
ACDIMOSY	docimasy
ACDINOPS	spondaic
ACDINORS	sardonic
ACDINORT	tornadic
ACDINORW	cordwain
ACDINSTY	dynastic
ACDINTUY	aduncity
ACDIOPRS	sporadic
ACDIORTT	dictator
ACDIOSTY	dystocia
ACDIPRST	adscript
ACDIPSSU	Dipsacus
ACDIRSTT	distract
ACDKMMOR	drammock
ACDLNNOR	cornland
ACDLNOPR	cropland
ACDLNORU	cauldron
ACDLNORY	condylar

ACDLNOST	Scotland
ACDLOORT	doctoral
ACDLORWY	cowardly
ACDMMNOO	commando
ACDMNORY	dormancy
	mordancy
ACDMOOPR	macropod
ACDNOORR	roncador
ACDNOORV	cordovan
ACDNOOTU	ducatoon
ACDNORRW	wardcorn
ACDNOSTW	downcast
ACDNOSUU	aduncous
ACDOOOPT	Octopoda
ACDOOPPR	podocarp
ACDOOPTY	octapody
ACDOORST	ostracod
	scordato
ACDOPRST	postcard
ACDORRWY	cowardry
ACDORSSU	crusados
ACDORSUZ	cruzados
ACDORTUY	court-day
ACDOSTTU	dust-coat
ACDRSTTU	dustcart
ACEEEFRR	carefree
ACEEEGLN	elegance
ACEEEGRS	cargeese
ACEEEIPR	earpiece
ACEEEKNT	neckatee
ACEEELMR	cameleer
ACEEENRS	encrease
ACEEENSV	evanesce
ACEEERRT	recreate
ACEEERTT	etcetera
ACEEERTX	execrate
ACEEFFIN	caffeine
ACEEFFRT	affecter
ACEEFHWY	whey-face
ACEEFILM	malefice
ACEEFKOR	ecofreak
ACEEFLPU	peaceful
ACEEFLRT	tree-calf
ACEEFLSS	faceless
ACEEFPRT	perfecta
	praefect
ACEEFPTY	type-face
ACEEFRSU	farceuse
ACEEGHNR	encharge
ACEEGHNX	exchange
ACEEGHRR	recharge
ACEEGINS	Genesiac
ACEEGIRS	Graecise
ACEEGIRZ	Graecize
ACEEGKNR	neckgear
ACEEGKRW	wreckage
ACEEGLNY	elegancy
ACEEGLPU	pucelage
ACEEGNOZ	cozenage
ACEEGNRY	reagency
ACEEGNSV	scavenge
ACEEGORR	racegoer
ACEEGORV	coverage
ACEEHIMN	Manichee
ACEEHINT	echinate
ACEEHIPT	petechia
ACEEHIRV	achiever
	chivaree
ACEEHITV	atchieve
ACEEHKNS	skeechan
ACEEHKTT	hackette
ACEEHLLN	Chellean
ACEEHLMP	empleach
ACEEHLMW	cam-wheel
ACEEHLOS	shoelace
ACEEHLSW	eschewal
ACEEHLTV	chevalet
ACEEHMNP	camphene
ACEEHMNR	menarche
ACEEHMRS	cashmere
	marchese
ACEEHNNR	enhancer
ACEEHNRV	revanche
ACEEHORT	ochreate
ACEEHPRR	preacher
ACEEHPRT	ethercap
ACEEHRRR	rere-arch
ACEEHRRS	research
	re-search
	searcher
ACEEHRRT	treacher
ACEEHRST	cheaters
ACEEHRTT	catheter
ACEEHRTY	cheatery
ACEEHSTX	cathexes
ACEEIKNP	peacenik
ACEEIKST	ice-skate
ACEEILMN	cameline
ACEEILMT	emetical
ACEEILNP	capeline
ACEEILNR	cinereal
	reliance
ACEEILNS	salience
ACEEILPS	especial
ACEEILRS	escalier
ACEEILRV	receival
ACEEIMOT	acoemeti
ACEEIMRR	rearmice
ACEEIMRS	casimere
	racemise
ACEEIMRT	cemitare
ACEEIMRZ	racemize
ACEEINNR	narceine
ACEEINPS	sapience
ACEEINPT	patience
ACEEINRS	increase
	resiance
ACEEINRT	centiare
	creatine
	increate
	iterance
ACEEINSS	Essencia
ACEEINST	cineaste
	cinéaste
ACEEINTV	enactive
ACEEINTX	exitance
ACEEIPPS	pipe-case
ACEEIPST	speciate
ACEEIPSY	say-piece
ACEEIRSU	causerie
ACEEIRSW	wiseacre
ACEEIRTV	creative
	reactive
ACEEISTV	vesicate
ACEEJKRT	jack-tree
ACEEKLMR	mackerel
ACEEKLRW	eelwrack
ACEEKMPT	empacket
ACEEKNRW	neckwear
ACEEKRRT	racketer
ACEELLNT	lancelet
ACEELLOT	ocellate
ACEELLOV	Lovelace
ACEELLPT	capellet
ACEELLRR	cellarer
ACEELLRT	cellaret
ACEELMNO	cameleon
ACEELMNP	placemen
ACEELMRS	sclerema
ACEELNPT	pentacle
ACEELNRR	larcener
ACEELNRS	cleaners
	cleanser
ACEELNRU	cerulean
ACEELNSU	nuclease
ACEELNTT	tentacle
ACEELNTU	nucleate
ACEELOPS	escalope
ACEELORS	escarole
ACEELORT	relocate
ACEELOSV	vocalese
ACEELPRR	replacer
ACEELPTU	peculate
ACEELPTY	clypeate
ACEELRSS	careless
ACEELRST	scelerat
ACEELRSV	cleavers
ACEELRTT	raclette
ACEELRTU	ulcerate
ACEELRTV	cervelat
ACEELRTX	excretal
ACEELSTT	telecast
ACEEMNNS	sceneman
ACEEMNOT	meconate
ACEEMNST	casement
ACEEMOPR	camporee
ACEEMOPT	copemate
ACEEMORS	racemose
ACEEMRRS	screamer
ACEEMRRY	creamery
ACEENNRT	entrance
ACEENORT	carotene
	one-acter
ACEENOST	notecase
ACEENPRR	parcener
ACEENPRT	perceant

ACEENRRT	recanter
	recreant
ACEENRST	reascent
	sarcenet
ACEENRTT	entr'acte
ACEENRTU	enacture
	uncreate
ACEEORST	creasote
ACEEOSTT	ecostate
ACEEPRTT	ettercap
ACEEPRTU	peracute
ACEEPRTX	excerpta
ACEEPSTT	spectate
ACEERRST	terraces
ACEERRSU	écraseur
ACEERRTU	creature
ACEERRUV	verrucae
ACEERSST	cateress
	cerastes
ACEERSSU	surcease
ACEERSSV	crevasse
ACEERTTU	eructate
ACEESSTT	cassette
ACEFFHRU	chauffer
ACEFFHRY	chaffery
ACEFFILT	face-lift
ACEFFIMS	caffeism
ACEFFLLU	full-face
ACEFGLRU	graceful
ACEFHORU	farouche
ACEFIIPR	pacifier
ACEFIIRT	artifice
ACEFILLY	facilely
ACEFILMT	calf-time
ACEFILOP	epifocal
ACEFILOS	fasciole
	focalise
ACEFILOZ	focalize
ACEFILRY	fire-clay
ACEFIMPR	campfire
ACEFINNS	finances
ACEFINRX	carnifex
ACEFIORR	air-force
ACEFIOSS	fiascoes
ACEFIRTT	trifecta
ACEFIRTY	feracity
ACEFKLRY	cly-faker
ACEFLLOV	calf-love
ACEFLLRU	leaf-curl
ACEFLLSS	calfless
ACEFLMNO	flamenco
ACEFLNOR	falconer
ACEFLNOT	conflate
	falconet
ACEFLNRY	cranefly
ACEFLORS	alfresco
ACEFLRTU	fulcrate
ACEFMNOO	moonface
ACEFNORV	conferva
ACEFNPRT	pencraft
ACEFOOPT	footpace
ACEFOORT	acre-foot
	foot-race
ACEFOPST	postface
ACEFORST	forecast
ACEFRRSU	surfacer
ACEFRRTU	fracture
ACEGGHPS	pasch-egg
ACEGGILN	cageling
	glacéing
ACEGGIOP	epagogic
ACEGHILN	leaching
ACEGHILT	lichgate
ACEGHINR	reaching
ACEGHINT	cheating
	teaching
ACEGHLRS	schläger
ACEGHLRU	rugelach
ACEGHLTY	lychgate
ACEGHMMU	chummage
ACEGHMOR	echogram
	gramoche
ACEGHNRU	uncharge
ACEGIIMP	epigamic
ACEGIINV	vicinage
ACEGILLO	collegia
ACEGILLR	allergic
ACEGILMU	mucilage
ACEGILNN	cleaning
ACEGILNR	clearing
ACEGILNV	cleaving
ACEGILNW	lacewing
ACEGILPS	Pelasgic
ACEGILRV	claviger
ACEGILRY	glyceria
ACEGILSS	glacises
ACEGILST	gelastic
ACEGIMMT	tagmemic
ACEGIMNN	menacing
ACEGIMNR	Germanic
ACEGIMNT	magnetic
ACEGIMOX	exogamic
ACEGIMRS	Graecism
ACEGIMTY	megacity
ACEGINNO	canoeing
ACEGINNT	enacting
ACEGINRT	catering
	citrange
ACEGINSS	caginess
ACEGINTX	exacting
ACEGIOTT	cogitate
ACEGIPRS	spageric
ACEGIRST	agrestic
ACEGKLOV	gavelock
ACEGKORW	cagework
ACEGKRTU	truckage
ACEGLLNO	collagen
ACEGLLSY	scaly-leg
ACEGLNOO	log-canoe
ACEGLNOS	longcase
ACEGMMPU	gemma-cup
ACEGMNOY	geomancy
ACEGMOPS	compages
ACEGMORS	scarmoge
ACEGMRRY	gramercy
ACEGNNOY	cyanogen
ACEGNNTY	tangency
ACEGNSSY	cagyness
ACEGOOPS	goose-cap
ACEGOORS	cargoose
ACEGOPRY	geocarpy
ACEGORST	escargot
ACEGORTT	cottager
ACEGORTY	category
	grey-coat
ACEGOTTY	cottagey
ACEHHIRR	hierarch
ACEHHIST	shechita
ACEHHLSU	shauchle
ACEHHMNN	henchman
ACEHHNRT	ethnarch
ACEHHNSV	Cheshvan
ACEHHPRT	heptarch
ACEHHRTT	thatcher
ACEHHRTY	hatchery
	thearchy
ACEHHTTY	hatchety
ACEHIIMS	ischemia
ACEHIINR	△reichian
ACEHIIRT	hieratic
ACEHIJKR	hijacker
ACEHIJPT	Japhetic
ACEHIKLP	kephalic
ACEHIKLW	lichwake
ACEHILLT	hellicat
ACEHILMN	inchmeal
ACEHILMO	cholemia
ACEHILMP	impleach
ACEHILMS	camelish
ACEHILNO	Chelonia
ACEHILNP	cephalin
ACEHILNT	chainlet
	chatline
	chat-line
	ethnical
ACEHILOR	halicore
	heroical
ACEHILPR	parhelic
ACEHILSS	Lachesis
ACEHILTT	athletic
	thetical
ACEHIMNP	camphine
ACEHIMNU	achenium
ACEHIMPR	camphire
ACEHIMPT	empathic
	emphatic
ACEHIMRT	rhematic
ACEHIMSS	chamises
ACEHIMST	misteach
	tachisme
ACEHIMTT	thematic
ACEHINOT	inchoate
ACEHINPT	inch-tape
ACEHINRV	vacherin
ACEHINST	asthenic

ACEHINSY	synechia
ACEHIOPS	po'chaise
ACEHIOST	toiseach
ACEHIPRS	aspheric
	parchesi
	seraphic
ACEHIPRT	chapiter
	phreatic
ACEHIPRW	pew-chair
ACEHIPST	pastiche
ACEHIPTT	pathetic
ACEHIPTW	whitecap
ACEHIRSS	rachises
ACEHIRST	Charites
ACEHIRSU	eucharis
ACEHIRSV	archives
ACEHIRSW	archwise
ACEHIRTT	theatric
ACEHISST	chastise
ACEHISTT	tachiste
ACEHISTX	cathexis
ACEHKLOV	havelock
ACEHKLPR	kreplach
ACEHKLSS	shackles
ACEHKLTY	latchkey
ACEHKMPU	muckheap
ACEHKOSW	whackoes
ACEHKOTU	tuckahoe
ACEHKRTW	thwacker
ACEHLLMO	mallecho
ACEHLLOR	orchella
ACEHLLSU	halluces
ACEHLMOT	chamelot
ACEHLMPR	carl-hemp
ACEHLNNS	channels
ACEHLNOU	eulachon
ACEHLNPT	planchet
ACEHLNRU	launcher
	relaunch
ACEHLNST	stanchel
ACEHLORT	chelator
	chlorate
	trochlea
ACEHLORU	leachour
ACEHLOST	eschalot
ACEHLPRT	chaptrel
ACEHLPRY	chapelry
ACEHLPSS	chapless
ACEHLRTU	archlute
	trauchle
ACEHLSSS	cashless
ACEHLSTT	chattels
	chattles
ACEHLSTY	chastely
ACEHMNRT	merchant
ACEHMNSS	chessman
ACEHMORT	chromate
ACEHMPRS	champers
ACEHMSTU	mustache
ACEHNNOP	pancheon
ACEHNNPT	penchant
ACEHNOPR	canephor
	chaperon
ACEHNOPT	cenotaph
ACEHNORR	ranchero
ACEHNORT	anchoret
ACEHNOSY	honey-sac
ACEHNPRT	pentarch
ACEHNPRU	unpreach
ACEHNQUU	Quechuan
ACEHNRSS	archness
ACEHNRST	snatcher
	stancher
ACEHNRTT	tranchet
ACEHNRTU	chaunter
ACEHNSTU	unchaste
ACEHNSTZ	schantze
ACEHOPRR	reproach
ACEHOPRT	arch-poet
ACEHORRS	horsecar
ACEHORRV	hover-car
	overarch
ACEHORST	charoset
	thoraces
ACEHORTT	theocrat
ACEHORTU	outreach
ACEHOSST	case-shot
ACEHOSSW	showcase
ACEHOSTU	cathouse
	soutache
ACEHOTWW	cow-wheat
ACEHPPSS	chappess
ACEHPRSU	purchase
ACEHPRTY	patchery
	petchary
ACEHRRST	starcher
ACEHRRTT	tetrarch
ACEHRSSU	chasseur
ACEHRTTY	trachyte
ACEHSSSU	chausses
ACEHSTTU	cathetus
ACEHTTUZ	zuchetta
ACEIILMN	limacine
ACEIILNR	irenical
ACEIILNS	salicine
ACEIILNT	Catiline
ACEIILST	silicate
ACEIIMRV	viraemic
ACEIIMSS	aseismic
ACEIIMTU	maieutic
ACEIINPS	piscinae
ACEIINST	canities
ACEIINTV	inactive
ACEIINTZ	anticize
ACEIIRRT	criteria
ACEIISTT	Atticise
ACEIITTZ	Atticize
ACEIJKNP	jack-pine
ACEIJMST	majestic
ACEIJNRR	jerrican
ACEIKLRY	creakily
ACEIKMNN	nickname
ACEIKMRV	△maverick
ACEIKNPS	capeskin
ACEIKPPR	pipe-rack
ACEIKRRV	vraicker
ACEILLLT	clitella
ACEILLMN	cane-mill
ACEILLMR	micellar
	millrace
ACEILLMT	metallic
ACEILLMY	mycelial
ACEILLNT	cliental
ACEILLOP	△calliope
ACEILLOR	rocaille
ACEILLOS	localise
ACEILLOT	teocalli
ACEILLOZ	localize
ACEILLPR	calliper
ACEILLPS	allspice
ACEILLPY	epically
ACEILLRV	caviller
ACEILMMO	camomile
ACEILMNN	clinamen
ACEILMNO	coalmine
ACEILMNP	manciple
ACEILMNS	mescalin
ACEILMOS	camisole
ACEILMPS	misplace
ACEILMPT	pelmatic
ACEILMRS	miracles
ACEILMRT	metrical
ACEILMST	clematis
ACEILMSU	musicale
ACEILMTU	amuletic
ACEILNNP	pannicle
	pinnacle
ACEILNNR	encrinal
ACEILNOR	acrolein
	Caroline
	creolian
	lonicera
ACEILNPT	pectinal
	planetic
ACEILNRT	clarinet
ACEILNSU	aesculin
ACEILNSY	saliency
ACEILOPR	capriole
ACEILOPT	poetical
ACEILORR	carriole
ACEILORT	erotical
	loricate
ACEILORV	arvicole
ACEILOST	societal
ACEILOSV	vocalise
ACEILOTV	locative
ACEILOVZ	vocalize
ACEILPPY	clay-pipe
	pipeclay
ACEILPRS	calipers
	spiracle
ACEILPRT	particle
	prelatic
ACEILPRU	△peculiar
ACEILPSS	slipcase

ACEILPTY etypical
ACEILPXY epicalyx
ACEILRST altrices
articles
selictar
ACEILRSV visceral
ACEILRTT tractile
ACEILRTV vertical
ACEILRTY literacy
ACEILSUV vesicula
ACEILTVY actively
ACEIMMNP pemmican
ACEIMMOS semicoma
ACEIMMRS racemism
ACEIMNOO Monoecia
ACEIMNOR coramine
ACEIMNPS spanemic
ACEIMNRU manicure
ACEIMNST semantic
ACEIMNSU semuncia
ACEIMNSY sycamine
ACEIMOPT poematic
ACEIMOTX toxaemic
ACEIMOTZ metazoic
ACEIMPRR mericarp
ACEIMPRS sapremic
ACEIMPSS escapism
ACEIMPST campsite
ACEIMPTU pumicate
ACEIMRST ceramist
matrices
ACEIMRTT trematic
ACEIMRTU muricate
ACEINNOS canonise
ACEINNOT enaction
ACEINNOZ canonize
ACEINNST ancients
instance
ACEINNSU nuisance
ACEINNTU uncinate
ACEINOPR apocrine
caponier
procaine
ACEINOPS caponise
ACEINOPZ caponize
ACEINORS scenario
ACEINORT anoretic
△creation
reaction
ACEINORV Corvinae
veronica
ACEINORX anorexic
ACEINOST canoeist
ACEINOTT taconite
ACEINOTV conative
ACEINOTX exaction
ACEINPTT pittance
ACEINPUY picayune
ACEINRRU curarine
ACEINRRY cinerary
ACEINRSS raciness

ACEINRST canister
cisterna
ACEINRTT interact
ACEINRTU Teucrian
ACEINRTV navicert
ACEINRTX xerantic
ACEINRVY vicenary
ACEINSST scanties
ACEINSSU issuance
ACEINSTV cistvaen
vesicant
ACEINTTU tunicate
ACEINTTX excitant
ACEINTTY tenacity
ACEINTUV unactive
ACEIOPRT operatic
ACEIORRV air-cover
ACEIORSV varicose
ACEIOSSU caesious
ACEIOSTT oscitate
ACEIOTVV vocative
ACEIPPRR pericarp
ACEIPRRS perisarc
ACEIPRST crispate
practise
ACEIPRTV practive
ACEIPRTY apyretic
ACEIPSST escapist
ACEIPSSU auspices
ACEIRRSU curarise
ACEIRRSW airscrew
ACEIRRTT retraict
ACEIRRTX creatrix
ACEIRRTY retiracy
ACEIRRUZ curarize
ACEIRSSV vicaress
ACEIRSTT cristate
ACEIRSTU suricate
ACEIRTTU urticate
ACEIRTTV tractive
ACEIRTUV curative
ACEIRTVY veracity
ACEISSST ecstasis
ACEISSSU saucisse
ACEISSTU sauciest
suitcase
ACEISTTU eustatic
ACEISTTW scawtite
ACEJKOOR jackeroo
ACEJLORY cajolery
ACEJMRST scramjet
ACEJNNOO joncanoe
ACEJNRRY jerrycan
ACEKKMRU muck-rake
ACEKKNRS knackers
ACEKKNRY knackery
ACEKLLOV lack-love
ACEKLMPU pack-mule
plum-cake
ACEKLNTU untackle
ACEKLORV laverock
ACEKLPRS sprackle

ACEKLSSS sackless
ACEKNNOW acknowne
ACEKNNSW swan-neck
ACEKNORT one-track
ACEKNPRU unpacker
ACEKNPSU sneak-cup
ACEKNRRT rack-rent
ACEKOORW cookware
ACEKOPRW capework
ACEKORRV overrack
ACEKORSW casework
ACEKORTU rout-cake
ACEKPSSY skyscape
ACEKQRUY quackery
ACEKRRTY racketry
ACEKRSTU ruckseat
ACEKSSUW waesucks
ACELLLRU cellular
ACELLMSU sacellum
ACELLNOT call-note
ACELLNRU nucellar
ACELLOPS collapse
escallop
ACELLORR caroller
ACELLORV coverall
overcall
ACELLOSW coleslaw
ACELLOTU loculate
ACELLPRU Lupercal
ACELLRTY rectally
ACELLSSW clawless
ACELLSTU scutella
ACELLTWY cetywall
ACELMMOU mameluco
ACELMNOR amelcorn
ACELMNRU crumenal
ACELMNSS calmness
ACELMOPT compleat
ACELMORS scleroma
ACELMORY claymore
ACELMOST molecast
ACELMOSU maculose
ACELMPSY eclampsy
ACELMSTU muscatel
ACELMSUU saeculum
ACELMTUU cumulate
ACELNNRS scrannel
ACELNORV novercal
ACELNOSU lacunose
ACELNOSZ calzones
ACELNOTT Toltecan
ACELNOTV covalent
ACELNOVY conveyal
ACELNRVY cravenly
ACELNSSU scalenus
ACELNSTY secantly
ACELOPPU populace
ACELOPRS parclose
ACELOPRT pectoral
ACELOPRU opercula
ACELOPTU copulate
ACELOPTY calotype

ACELORRT	rectoral
ACELORSS	lacrosse
ACELORST	sectoral
ACELORSU	carousel
ACELORSY	coarsely
ACELORTU	clear-out
ACELOSST	coatless
ACELOSTT	salt-cote
ACELOSTU	lacteous
	locustae
	osculate
ACELPPRS	clappers
	scrapple
ACELPRSS	claspers
ACELPRST	sceptral
	spectral
ACELPRSU	specular
ACELPTUU	cupulate
ACELPTUY	eucalypt
ACELQRUU	claqueur
ACELQSUY	lacqueys
ACELRRSW	scrawler
ACELRSSS	scarless
ACELRSTT	clatters
	scrattle
ACELRTTU	cultrate
ACELRTTY	clattery
ACELSSTT	tactless
ACELSSUU	Aesculus
ACEMMOTY	mycetoma
ACEMNORR	romancer
ACEMNOST	camstone
ACEMNPSS	campness
ACEMNRTU	cream-nut
ACEMNRUY	numeracy
ACEMNSSU	mancuses
ACEMOORS	acrosome
ACEMOOST	comatose
ACEMOPRS	mesocarp
ACEMORRT	cremator
	Mercator
ACEMORSW	case-worm
ACEMORSY	sycamore
ACEMORTY	cometary
ACEMORUX	morceaux
ACEMPSSU	campuses
ACENNNOU	announce
ACENNOSS	canoness
ACENNOTT	cotenant
ACENNOTV	covenant
ACENNOTZ	canzonet
ACENNPRY	pernancy
ACENNPTU	pecan-nut
ACENNSUY	seacunny
ACENOORT	coronate
ACENOOTZ	ectozoan
ACENOPRT	portance
ACENOPST	capstone
	open-cast
ACENOPUX	ponceaux
ACENOQTU	cotquean
ACENORRW	careworn
ACENORSS	narcoses
ACENORST	ancestor
	sortance
ACENORSU	carneous
	nacreous
ACENORTT	contrate
ACENORTU	courante
	outrance
ACENORUY	eucaryon
ACENOSST	contessa
ACENOSSV	cavesson
ACENOSTT	constate
ACENOSTV	centavos
ACENOTTU	toucanet
ACENPRSU	encarpus
ACENPTTU	punctate
ACENRSTT	transect
ACENRSTU	Etruscan
	recusant
ACENRSTY	ancestry
ACENRTTU	truncate
ACENRTUY	centaury
	cyanuret
ACENSSTW	newscast
ACEOOPSU	poaceous
ACEOORTV	evocator
	overcoat
ACEOPPRS	copperas
ACEOPRRT	recaptor
ACEOPRTT	attercop
ACEORRSU	carouser
ACEORRTT	retroact
ACEORRTU	Eurocrat
ACEORRVW	overcraw
ACEORSTT	sectator
ACEORSTV	overcast
ACEORTUY	eucaryot
ACEOSTTU	outcaste
ACEPRRTU	capturer
ACEPSTTY	typecast
ACERRSUV	verrucas
ACERSTTU	crustate
ACERSTTY	scattery
ACERTTUW	cut-water
ACFFGHIN	chaffing
ACFFHNOR	chaffron
ACFFIILO	official
ACFFILNU	fanciful
ACFFLOSW	scofflaw
ACFGHINS	Fasching
ACFGIIMN	magnific
ACFGIIPR	caprifig
ACFGIKNR	fracking
ACFGINNY	fancying
ACFGINRS	scarfing
ACFGITUY	fugacity
ACFGKNOP	packfong
ACFGLNOR	cornflag
ACFHHINW	hawfinch
ACFHILNO	falchion
ACFHILNU	faulchin
ACFHILOS	coalfish
ACFHINOU	fauchion
ACFHIRSS	scarfish
ACFHIRSW	crawfish
ACFHIRSY	crayfish
ACFHLMRU	charmful
ACFHLTUW	watchful
ACFHMNOR	chamfron
ACFHORRT	Rh-factor
ACFIILST	fistical
ACFIILSV	salvific
ACFIILTY	facility
ACFIIMPS	pacifism
ACFIIPST	pacifist
ACFIISST	Fascisti
ACFIKLNS	calfskin
ACFILLSY	fiscally
ACFILNOR	fornical
ACFILNOT	Califont®
ACFILORT	trifocal
ACFILRTY	craftily
ACFILSSY	classify
ACFIMNRU	francium
ACFIMOSS	△fascismo
ACFINORT	fraction
ACFINPRS	scarf-pin
ACFINSTY	sanctify
ACFIOSTU	factious
ACFIRTUY	furacity
ACFISSST	Fascists
ACFJKLOO	Jack-fool
ACFKLLOR	rock-fall
ACFKLORS	forslack
ACFKLOST	lockfast
ACFKLRUW	wrackful
ACFKLSSU	sackfuls
ACFKOORR	Afro-rock
	roof-rack
ACFKOPRU	four-pack
ACFKOSTT	fatstock
ACFLLMRU	cram-full
ACFLMNOO	mooncalf
ACFLNORY	falconry
ACFLOOPS	foolscap
ACFLOOTW	claw-foot
ACFLORSU	scrofula
ACFLOTUU	Foucault
ACFLRRUU	furcular
ACFMOTTU	factotum
ACFNRSTU	fructans
ACFOOSTT	cat's-foot
ACGGGILN	clagging
ACGGIINT	gigantic
ACGGIIOS	isagogic
ACGGILNN	clanging
	glancing
ACGGIOOR	coraggio
ACGGLNOU	glucagon
ACGGLRSY	scraggly
ACGHHIJK	highjack
	jack-high
ACGHHINT	hatching
ACGHIKNW	whacking

ACGHILNS	clashing
ACGHILNY	achingly
ACGHILOR	oligarch
ACGHILRT	arc-light
ACGHILRU	lug-chair
ACGHIMNR	charming
ACGHIMNT	matching
ACGHINNR	ranching
ACGHINNU	unaching
ACGHINOP	poaching
ACGHINPT	nightcap
	patching
ACGHINRR	charring
ACGHINRS	crashing
ACGHINRU	churinga
	nuraghic
ACGHINST	scathing
ACGHINTT	chatting
ACGHINTW	watching
ACGHINTY	yachting
ACGHIPRS	graphics
ACGHIQTU	acquight
ACGHLLOR	gralloch
ACGHLOOY	chaology
ACGHNTUU	uncaught
ACGHORSU	choragus
ACGHPTUU	upcaught
ACGIILNO	logician
ACGIIMOS	isogamic
ACGIIMST	sigmatic
ACGIINRT	granitic
ACGIIPRS	spagiric
ACGIJJKO	jickajog
ACGIKLNN	clanking
ACGIKLNT	tackling
	talcking
ACGIKLNU	caulking
ACGIKLRY	garlicky
ACGIKMNS	smacking
ACGIKNOR	croaking
ACGIKNRT	tracking
ACGIKNST	stacking
ACGIKPRS	gripsack
ACGILLLR	call-girl
ACGILMMN	clamming
ACGILMTU	glutamic
ACGILNOZ	Ozacling®
ACGILNPP	clapping
ACGILNPS	clasping
	scalping
ACGILNRW	crawling
ACGILRSU	surgical
ACGIMMNR	cramming
ACGIMNOS	coamings
ACGIMNPR	cramping
ACGIMNPS	scamping
ACGIMNSY	gymnasic
	syngamic
ACGIMORS	orgasmic
ACGIMRTU	Targumic
ACGINNNS	scanning
ACGINNPR	prancing
ACGINNRU	uncaring
ACGINNUV	vauncing
ACGINORY	congiary
ACGINOST	agnostic
	coasting
ACGINPRS	scarping
	scraping
ACGINRRS	scarring
ACGINRRY	carrying
ACGINSTT	scatting
ACGIOORS	gracioso
ACGIORST	orgastic
ACGIORSU	gracious
ACGIORUW	Guicowar
ACGIPRSY	spagyric
ACGJLNOU	conjugal
ACGKLMOR	glam-rock
ACGLMOUU	coagulum
ACGLNORU	clangour
ACGLOSUU	glaucous
ACGLSSTU	cutglass
ACGNNOOT	contango
ACGNORST	congrats
ACGORSSW	cowgrass
ACGPPSUU	scuppaug
ACHHHOTT	hot-hatch
ACHHILPT	phthalic
ACHHINTW	whinchat
ACHHINTY	hyacinth
ACHHIPPR	hipparch
ACHHLMOS	mashloch
ACHHLNOR	rhonchal
ACHHLPRY	phylarch
ACHHLSUY	shauchly
ACHHNTTU	nuthatch
	unthatch
ACHHPTUZ	chutzpah
ACHIILMS	chiliasm
ACHIILST	chiliast
ACHIIMNS	Mishnaic
ACHIIMRT	Mithraic
ACHIINPS	Hispanic
ACHIINPT	anti-chip
ACHIINRT	trichina
ACHIIRST	rachitis
ACHIIRSU	ischuria
ACHIJKPW	whipjack
ACHIKKNS	knackish
ACHIKKSW	kickshaw
ACHIKLLW	hickwall
ACHIKLPT	chalkpit
ACHIKNOP	pachinko
ACHIKRSW	rickshaw
ACHILLOR	orchilla
ACHILLRT	clithral
ACHILMOP	omphalic
ACHILMRS	chrismal
ACHILMTY	mythical
ACHILNNS	clannish
ACHILNOO	hoolican
ACHILNOS	lichanos
ACHILNPS	clanship
ACHILOPR	rhopalic
ACHILORT	acrolith
ACHILPSY	physical
ACHILPTY	patchily
ACHILRUY	chyluria
ACHILRVY	chivalry
ACHIMMOS	machismo
ACHIMMST	mismatch
ACHIMNNW	winchman
ACHIMNOP	champion
ACHIMNOR	choirman
	harmonic
ACHIMNPT	pitchman
ACHIMNSU	inasmuch
ACHIMOPR	amphoric
ACHIMOSS	chamisos
	isochasm
ACHIMPSS	scampish
ACHIMRST	△chartism
ACHIMSSU	chiasmus
ACHINNOP	panchion
ACHINOPR	parochin
	prochain
ACHINORT	anorthic
ACHINOTZ	hoactzin
ACHINQUU	Quichuan
ACHINSTY	Scythian
ACHIORSS	coarsish
ACHIORTV	tovarich
ACHIPPSS	sapphics
ACHIPRRT	parritch
ACHIPTTU	chupatti
ACHIRRSY	Syriarch
ACHIRRTY	triarchy
ACHIRSTT	△chartist
	straicht
ACHISTTY	chastity
ACHKKORW	hack-work
ACHKMORS	shamrock
ACHKNNUU	nunchaku
ACHKNOOT	canthook
ACHKOSSY	hassocky
ACHLLNWY	lynch-law
ACHLLORY	chorally
ACHLMSTZ	schmaltz
ACHLNOOU	oulachon
ACHLNSTY	stanchly
ACHLOPRT	calthrop
ACHLOPRY	polyarch
ACHLOPTT	potlatch
ACHLOTWX	waxcloth
ACHMNOOR	Monarcho
ACHMNORS	Romansch
ACHMNORY	monarchy
	nomarchy
ACHMNOSU	Monachus
ACHMNRSU	Rumansch
ACHMNRTU	truchman
ACHMOPST	camp-shot
ACHMORTU	outmarch
ACHMOSTY	stomachy
ACHMOTTU	outmatch

ACHMPRTU	thrum-cap
ACHNNORU	unanchor
ACHNOOOT	Ochotona
ACHNOPRU	up-anchor
ACHNPPSS	schnapps
ACHNRSTU	unstarch
ACHNRSYY	synarchy
ACHNRTUY	chauntry
ACHOORTU	co-author
ACHOORTY	chayroot
ACHOPRTY	toparchy
ACHOTTUW	outwatch
	watch-out
ACHPRSTU	push-cart
	sharp-cut
ACHRSTTU	straucht
ACIIILMN	inimical
ACIIILNS	Sicilian
ACIIILNV	civilian
ACIIINST	Sinaitic
ACIIKNNN	cannikin
ACIIKPRT	paitrick
ACIILLSU	silicula
ACIILLTV	villatic
ACIILMNR	criminal
ACIILMPT	palmitic
ACIILNOR	ironical
ACIILNOT	talionic
ACIILNPT	platinic
ACIILNSU	Siculian
ACIILNTX	Calixtin
ACIILOSV	viliacos
ACIILRTT	tritical
ACIILRTU	uralitic
ACIILSST	Silastic®
	silastic
ACIILSTV	silvatic
ACIIMNOR	morainic
ACIIMNOS	simoniac
ACIIMNOT	amniotic
ACIIMNST	actinism
ACIIMNSU	musician
ACIIMNTU	actinium
ACIIMNTY	imitancy
	intimacy
	minacity
ACIIMOTT	amitotic
ACIIMPRT	primatic
ACIIMPRV	vampiric
ACIIMRST	scimitar
ACIIMRTU	muriatic
ACIIMSTT	Atticism
ACIIMSTV	activism
ACIIMTUV	viaticum
ACIINNOP	Panionic
ACIINNOS	Socinian
ACIINNOT	inaction
	nicotian
ACIINNQU	cinquain
ACIINNTT	incitant
ACIINNTY	caninity
ACIINOOP	iopanoic
ACIINOPT	optician
ACIINORZ	zirconia
ACIINOSS	Ossianic
ACIINOSV	avionics
ACIINOTT	citation
ACIINPSS	piscinas
ACIINRSS	narcissi
ACIINRTU	uranitic
ACIIOPST	apositic
ACIIORST	aoristic
ACIIORTV	△victoria
ACIIOSTT	Taoistic
ACIIPPST	papistic
ACIIRSST	Triassic
ACIIRSTT	artistic
ACIISTTU	autistic
ACIISTTV	activist
ACIITTVY	activity
ACIITVVY	vivacity
ACIJKKPS	skipjack
ACIJKSTW	stickjaw
ACIJRSSU	Jurassic
ACIKLMST	malstick
ACIKLNOT	anti-lock
ACIKLNRY	crankily
ACIKLORY	croakily
ACIKMNTY	nicky-tam
ACIKMPST	mapstick
ACIKPRST	praktics
ACILLLOP	pollical
ACILLLPS	clap-sill
ACILLMMY	clammily
ACILLMOS	localism
ACILLNOO	colonial
ACILLNOR	carillon
ACILLNOS	scallion
ACILLOOZ	colza-oil
ACILLOQU	coquilla
ACILLORT	clitoral
ACILLORY	collyria
ACILLOST	localist
ACILLOSY	socially
ACILLOTY	locality
ACILMNNO	non-claim
ACILMNOP	complain
ACILMNOS	laconism
	no-claims
ACILMOOS	scolioma
ACILMOPR	proclaim
ACILMOPT	compital
ACILMOSV	vocalism
ACILMPTU	placitum
ACILMSSS	classism
ACILMSTY	mystical
ACILMTUY	ultimacy
ACILNOOT	location
ACILNOOV	vocalion
ACILNOPS	salpicon
ACILNOPT	△platonic
ACILNORS	clarinos
ACILNORT	contrail
ACILNORY	iron-clay
ACILNOSU	unsocial
ACILNOSV	Slavonic
	Volscian
ACILNOUV	univocal
ACILNPSS	scalpins
ACILNRSU	cislunar
ACILNRUY	culinary
	uranylic
ACILNSTU	sultanic
ACILNSTY	scantily
ACILOOPS	Scopolia
ACILOPRT	tropical
ACILORRV	corrival
ACILORST	calorist
ACILORTV	vortical
ACILORYZ	zircaloy
ACILOSTV	vocalist
ACILOTVY	vocality
ACILPRSU	spicular
ACILPRTU	pictural
ACILPSST	plastics
ACILRSTU	rustical
ACILRTUV	cultivar
	curvital
ACILSSST	classist
ACILSTUV	victuals
ACILSTVY	sylvatic
ACIMMOSS	acosmism
ACIMMTUY	cymatium
ACIMNNNO	cinnamon
ACIMNOOR	acromion
ACIMNORT	△romantic
ACIMNORU	conarium
	coumarin
ACIMNORY	acrimony
ACIMNOSS	mocassin
ACIMNOST	monastic
ACIMNOSU	un-Mosaic
ACIMNOTU	aconitum
ACIMNPTY	tympanic
ACIMNRSU	craniums
ACIMOOST	scotomia
ACIMORST	acrotism
ACIMORSY	cramoisy
ACIMOSST	acosmist
	massicot
ACIMOSTT	masticot
	stomatic
ACIMRRSY	miscarry
ACINNNOO	nonanoic
ACINNOOT	conation
	intonaco
ACINNORR	naricorn
ACINNOSS	scansion
ACINNOST	canonist
	sanction
ACINNOTU	continua
ACINNRTY	tyrannic
ACINNSTY	instancy
ACINOOPR	picaroon
ACINOOTV	vocation
ACINOPPT	panoptic

Words marked △ may be spelled also with a capital letter

ACINOPRS	parsonic
ACINORRT	contrair
ACINORSS	narcosis
ACINORST	cantoris
	cast-iron
ACINORTT	traction
ACINOSSS	cassinos
ACINOSSY	cyanosis
ACINOSTT	oscitant
ACINOSTU	anticous
ACINOSTW	wainscot
ACINOSWX	coxswain
ACINOTTX	toxicant
ACINPQUY	piquancy
ACINPSTY	synaptic
ACINRSST	Sanscrit
ACINRSTU	curtains
	saturnic
ACINRTTU	taciturn
	urticant
ACINSTTY	sanctity
	scantity
ACINSTYY	syncytia
ACIOOPST	scotopia
ACIOOTYZ	zoocytia
ACIOPRST	piscator
ACIOPRTT	protatic
ACIOPRTY	poticary
ACIOPSST	potassic
ACIOPSSU	spacious
ACIOPSTU	captious
ACIOPTTU	autoptic
ACIORSSU	scarious
ACIORSTU	Suctoria
ACIORTTY	atrocity
	citatory
ACIORTVY	voracity
ACIOSTUU	cautious
ACIPRRUU	pirarucu
ACIRRTTX	tractrix
ACIRRTUX	curatrix
ACIRSSTY	sacristy
ACISTTUY	astucity
ACJKORZZ	jazz-rock
ACKKLORR	rock-lark
ACKKMOPR	pockmark
ACKKORRW	rackwork
ACKLLPSU	skullcap
ACKLMNOS	locksman
ACKLMORU	rock-alum
ACKLOOPW	woolpack
ACKLOOSW	△woolsack
ACKMNOST	stockman
ACKMNRTU	truckman
ACKMSUVY	musk-cavy
ACKOPRRT	traprock
ACKORSTW	catworks
ACLLLLOR	roll-call
ACLLLNOY	clonally
ACLLLNUU	Lucullan
ACLLMNOU	columnal
ACLLMORU	corallum
ACLLMOSU	Mollusca
ACLLOORT	collator
ACLLOOSS	colossal
ACLLORUY	ocularly
ACLLRTUU	cultural
ACLMMNOU	communal
ACLMNOOO	coolamon
ACLMNORU	columnar
ACLMNORY	normalcy
ACLMORTU	crotalum
ACLMPRSU	scalprum
ACLMRSUU	muscular
ACLMSUUV	vasculum
ACLNOORT	colorant
ACLNOPSY	syncopal
ACLNOPTW	cow-plant
ACLNORSU	consular
ACLNORTU	calutron
ACLNOSTU	consulta
	osculant
ACLNPTUU	punctual
ACLNSSUY	unclassy
ACLOOPRR	corporal
ACLOOPRT	Coalport
ACLOOPSX	Scolopax
ACLOPRST	caltrops
ACLOPRXY	xylocarp
ACLOPSSY	calypsos
ACLOPSUU	opuscula
ACLORRTU	torcular
ACLORSTU	Crotalus
ACLORTUW	law-court
ACLOSSTU	outclass
	soul-scat
ACMMNOSY	scammony
ACMMNOYY	myomancy
ACMNOOPR	monocarp
ACMNOORR	cromorna
ACMNOORT	monocrat
ACMNOOYZ	zoomancy
ACMNOPUY	Apocynum
ACMNORTU	Turcoman
ACMNOSST	Scotsman
ACMOOPRS	coprosma
ACMOORRT	motor-car
ACMOOSST	scotomas
ACMORSTW	wormcast
ACMORSTY	costmary
ACMSUVVY	cum-savvy
ACNNNORY	cannonry
ACNNOSTT	constant
ACNOOORT	octaroon
ACNOORRY	coronary
ACNOORST	corantos
	ostracon
ACNOORSU	canorous
ACNOORTY	octonary
ACNOPSTW	snow-capt
ACNORRSY	carry-ons
ACNORRTY	contrary
ACNORSTT	contrast
ACNORTTU	turncoat
ACNORTUY	noctuary
ACNPRSUY	sprauncy
ACNPRSYY	syncarpy
ACNRRTUY	curranty
ACOOPRRS	corporas
ACOORSTU	touracos
ACOPRRTT	protract
ACORRSTT	tractors
ACORRTUY	carry-out
	curatory
ACORRTUZ	razor-cut
ACORSSUW	curassow
ACORSSWY	crossway
ACORSTTY	cryostat
ACPSSTUY	pussy-cat
ACRRSTUU	Arcturus
ADDDEEGR	degraded
ADDDEEIM	diademed
ADDDEELR	laddered
ADDDEENR	reddenda
ADDDEINW	dead-wind
ADDDEMNU	addendum
ADDDENRU	deuddarn
ADDDEOOW	dead-wood
ADDDEOPR	drop-dead
ADDDEORS	addorsed
ADDEEEFH	feed-head
ADDEEENR	deadener
	endeared
ADDEEEPR	deep-read
ADDEEFIL	defilade
ADDEEFIR	dead-fire
ADDEEFRY	defrayed
ADDEEFTT	defatted
ADDEEGLN	danegeld
ADDEEGMU	gude-dame
ADDEEGNR	deranged
ADDEEGOR	dog-eared
ADDEEGSW	saw-edged
ADDEEHLY	aldehyde
ADDEEHNR	hardened
ADDEEILN	deadline
ADDEEILP	deep-laid
ADDEEILT	detailed
ADDEEINO	one-idea'd
ADDEEISS	diseased
ADDEEIST	steadied
ADDEELLM	medalled
ADDEELLP	pedalled
ADDEELMS	alms-deed
ADDEELNU	unleaded
ADDEEMNN	demanned
ADDEEMNR	demander
ADDEENRR	reed-rand
ADDEENRW	wandered
ADDEENSS	deadness
ADDEENTT	dentated
ADDEENTU	denudate
ADDEEOPR	dead-rope
ADDEEPRT	departed
ADDEEPRV	depraved
ADDEERRT	retarded

ADDEFIIL ladified
ADDEFILT dead-lift
ADDEFILY ladyfied
ADDEFLRU dreadful
ADDEFNOW fade-down
ADDEFORW word-deaf
ADDEGIRS disgrade
ADDEGMOO good-dame
ADDEGNRU ungraded
ADDEHHIN hindhead
ADDEHHLN hand-held
ADDEHILR dihedral
ADDEHLNR land-herd
ADDEHMRU drumhead
ADDEHNNY dandy-hen
ADDEHNSU undashed
unshaded
ADDEHOPR drophead
ADDEHORW headword
ADDEHOST dead-shot
ADDEHPRU purdahed
ADDEIITV additive
ADDEILNS landside
ADDEILNT tideland
ADDEIMOS sodamide
ADDEIMRS misdread
ADDEIMTT admitted
ADDEINOS adenoids
ADDEIOPR parodied
ADDEIORS roadside
sideroad
ADDEIPPR didapper
ADDEIPRS dispread
ADDEIPSS △dipsades
ADDEIQSU squaddie
ADDEIRSW sideward
ADDEIRVZ vizarded
ADDEISSU dissuade
ADDEKNVY vandyked
ADDEKORW dead-work
ADDELLOR dollared
ADDELLPU dead-pull
ADDELMOS dolmades
ADDELNOU duodenal
unloaded
ADDELNPU pudendal
ADDELNSU unsaddle
ADDELOOR Eldorado
ADDELPRS paddlers
ADDELRST straddle
ADDELRSW swaddler
ADDELRSY saddlery
ADDELRTW twaddler
ADDEMMNU undammed
ADDEMNNU undamned
ADDEMNPU undamped
ADDENNSU sand-dune
ADDENORU unadored
ADDENPRU undraped
ADDENRST stranded
ADDENRTU untraded
ADDENRUW unwarded

ADDEOTTU outdated
ADDEPRSU superadd
ADDFFILO daffodil
ADDFFINR dandriff
ADDFFNRU dandruff
ADDGGILN gladding
ADDGIILN daidling
ADDGILNP paddling
ADDGILNW waddling
ADDGINOR daring-do
ADDGIOSY dog-daisy
ADDGMRUU mudguard
ADDGORSW godwards
ADDHHLNO handhold
ADDHIMOO maidhood
ADDHINRW hindward
ADDHINSY dandyish
ADDHIOTY hydatoid
ADDHLOOY ladyhood
ADDHOORW hardwood
ADDIIKMZ zaddikim
ADDIILUV dividual
ADDIINOT addition
ADDIINTV dividant
ADDIJMNY jim-dandy
ADDILLNW wildland
ADDILMNS △midlands
ADDILNNW landwind
ADDIMNOS diamonds
ADDIMNSY dandyism
ADDIMPSY Paddyism
ADDINNOO Dodonian
ADDINNOR ordinand
ADDINORS disadorn
ADDINQUY quiddany
ADDINRWW windward
ADDIORRT dirt-road
ADDIPTUY duty-paid
ADDKNRRU drunkard
ADDLLNOR landlord
ADDLNNOW downland
ADDLNOOW download
woodland
ADDLNORS landdros
ADDLOOSS soldados
ADDMMOOY moody-mad
ADDMOOSY doomsday
ADDNOPWY pandowdy
ADDNORWW downward
draw-down
ADDOORRY door-yard
ADDOORWW woodward
ADDOORWY woodyard
ADEEEFFR affeered
ADEEEFLR lead-free
ADEEEFLS seed-leaf
ADEEEFNY fedayeen
ADEEEFRT federate
ADEEEGLT delegate
ADEEEGNR renegade
ADEEEGNT teenaged
ADEEEGPS gapeseed

ADEEEGRS degrease
ADEEEHRX exhedrae
ADEEEHSY eyeshade
ADEEEINT detainee
ADEEEKWY weak-eyed
ADEEELPY pale-eyed
ADEEELST teaseled
ADEEELTV elevated
ADEEEMNT emendate
ADEEEMRU emeraude
ADEEENRS serenade
ADEEENTT attendee
edentate
ADEEENWZ weazened
ADEEEPRS rapeseed
ADEEEPRT repeated
ADEEERTT date-tree
ADEEFFIR effraide
ADEEFHNR freehand
ADEEFHOR forehead
ADEEFHRT earth-fed
ADEEFILN enfilade
ADEEFINR fredaine
ADEEFIOR foedarie
ADEEFIRR rarefied
ADEEFIRY reaedify
ADEEFLMS self-made
ADEEFLOR freeload
ADEEFLRR deferral
ADEEFLRT deflater
ADEEFLRW weel-far'd
ADEEFLSS fadeless
ADEEFLSX flax-seed
ADEEFMNR freedman
ADEEFMTU deaf-mute
ADEEFNOT tone-deaf
ADEEFNRU unfeared
ADEEFNSS deafness
ADEEFORR foreread
ADEEFORT foredate
ADEEFRRT raftered
ADEEFRRY defrayer
federary
ADEEGIRS disagree
ADEEGITT tide-gate
ADEEGLLT galleted
ADEEGLNR enlarged
ADEEGLNT danegelt
ADEEGMNR gendarme
ADEEGMNY Ganymede
megadyne
ADEEGMOP megapode
ADEEGMOS megadose
ADEEGNNR endanger
ADEEGNNV vendange
ADEEGNOR renegado
ADEEGNRR gardener
ADEEGNRU dungaree
under-age
ungeared
ADEEGNRV engraved
ADEEGNSS agedness

ADEEGORT	derogate
ADEEGOTW	goatweed
ADEEGPRT	pargeted
ADEEGRRR	regarder
ADEEGRRT	garreted
ADEEGRRU	redargue
ADEEGRSS	dressage
ADEEGRTT	targeted
ADEEGSWY	edgeways
ADEEGTTZ	gazetted
ADEEHHST	sheathed
ADEEHIKP	pike-head
ADEEHILN	headline
ADEEHILS	deisheal
ADEEHIPR	pier-head
ADEEHIRR	deer-hair
ADEEHIRT	head-tire
ADEEHISV	adhesive
ADEEHKWW	hawkweed
ADEEHKWY	hawk-eyed
ADEEHLLW	wellhead
ADEEHLNO	dane-hole
ADEEHLNP	hen-padle
ADEEHLNR	rehandle
ADEEHLNU	unhealed
ADEEHLSS	headless
ADEEHMMO	home-made
ADEEHMNN	menhaden
ADEEHNOT	headnote
ADEEHNRR	hardener
ADEEHNRT	adherent
	neat-herd
	threaden
ADEEHNTU	unheated
ADEEHOPR	headrope
ADEEHORS	sorehead
ADEEHORV	overhead
ADEEHRRS	redshare
ADEEHRRT	threader
ADEEHRST	headrest
ADEEHRTW	wreathed
ADEEIILS	idealise
ADEEIILZ	idealize
ADEEIINT	Tineidae
ADEEIIPR	Pieridae
ADEEIITV	ideative
ADEEIJMR	jeremiad
ADEEIKLS	lakeside
ADEEILLN	leadline
ADEEILLO	oeillade
ADEEILMN	endemial
ADEEILMR	remedial
ADEEILMT	meal-tide
ADEEILMV	medieval
ADEEILNT	date-line
	lineated
ADEEILPR	pedalier
ADEEILPS	Pleiades
ADEEILPT	depilate
	pileated
ADEEILRR	derailer
ADEEILRS	sidereal
ADEEILSV	disleave
ADEEIMNT	dementia
ADEEIMRS	maderise
ADEEIMRT	diameter
	remediat
ADEEIMRZ	maderize
ADEEIMTT	meditate
ADEEINNS	andesine
ADEEINOP	Oedipean
ADEEINPR	pindaree
ADEEINPT	diapente
ADEEINRS	arsenide
	draisene
	nearside
ADEEINRT	detainer
ADEEINST	andesite
ADEEIPRS	airspeed
ADEEIPSS	speisade
ADEEIPSV	Vespidae
ADEEIPTT	tape-tied
ADEEIRST	readiest
	siderate
	steadier
ADEEIRSV	readvise
ADEEIRTV	derivate
ADEEISST	set-aside
ADEEISSV	adessive
ADEEISTV	sedative
ADEEITVW	tidewave
ADEEKMRR	remarked
ADEEKMRT	marketed
ADEEKNPW	knapweed
ADEEKPRR	deer-park
ADEEKRST	streaked
ADEELLLP	lapelled
ADEELLMT	metalled
ADEELLMU	medullae
ADEELLMW	well-made
ADEELLNP	panelled
ADEELLNY	leadenly
ADEELLPR	pedaller
	predella
ADEELLPT	palleted
	petalled
ADEELLQU	equalled
ADEELLRS	sardelle
ADEELLRV	ravelled
ADEELLRW	well-read
ADEELLSS	leadless
ADEELLTY	elatedly
ADEELLVY	day-level
ADEELLWY	wall-eyed
ADEELMNO	lemonade
ADEELMNR	aldermen
ADEELMNS	emendals
ADEELMNT	lamented
ADEELMOS	somedeal
ADEELMRS	demersal
ADEELNNU	unaneled
ADEELNOR	oleander
ADEELNRS	Landseer
ADEELNRT	antlered
ADEELNRV	lavender
ADEELNRY	Alderney
ADEELNSU	unleased
	unsealed
ADEELNSV	enslaved
ADEELNTT	talented
ADEELNTU	unelated
ADEELOPR	lop-eared
ADEELOPS	pedaloes
ADEELORS	lease-rod
ADEELORU	aureoled
ADEELORV	overlade
ADEELOST	desolate
ADEELPPT	lappeted
ADEELPRS	relapsed
ADEELPST	pedestal
ADEELPTY	pedately
ADEELRRR	larderer
ADEELRRT	treadler
ADEELRTV	traveled
ADEELSST	dateless
	tasseled
ADEELSTY	sedately
ADEEMMSS	Mesdames
ADEEMMXY	myxedema
ADEEMNNR	mannered
ADEEMNOR	demeanor
	one-armed
ADEEMNOT	nematode
ADEEMNRS	meanders
ADEEMNSS	seedsman
ADEEMNST	stamened
ADEEMNSU	unseamed
ADEEMNTW	metewand
ADEEMNYY	many-eyed
ADEEMORS	seadrome
ADEEMORT	moderate
ADEEMPST	stampede
	stepdame
ADEEMRRY	dreamery
ADEEMRSU	measured
ADEEMRTY	meteyard
ADEENNRU	unearned
ADEENNUW	unweaned
ADEENNUY	unyeaned
ADEENOPW	weaponed
ADEENORS	reasoned
ADEENORV	endeavor
ADEENORY	aerodyne
ADEENOSS	seasoned
ADEENOTT	denotate
	detonate
ADEENPPR	end-paper
ADEENPPS	sand-peep
ADEENPRU	unreaped
ADEENPRX	expander
	re-expand
ADEENPTT	pattened
ADEENRRW	△wanderer
ADEENRSS	dearness
ADEENRSU	undersea

Words marked △ may be spelled also with a capital letter

ADEENRTT	attender
	nattered
ADEENRTU	denature
ADEENSSU	danseuse
	Sudanese
ADEENSTU	unseated
ADEENSVY	seven-day
ADEENTTV	vendetta
ADEEOPRR	paderero
ADEEORRV	overread
ADEEPPRR	prepared
ADEEPRRS	spreader
ADEEPRRT	departer
ADEEPRRU	upreared
ADEEPRST	pederast
ADEEPRSU	persuade
ADEEPRSW	perswade
ADEEPRTU	depurate
ADEEPSST	stapedes
ADEEPSWY	speedway
ADEEQRTU	détraqué
ADEERRRT	retarder
ADEERRRW	rereward
	rewarder
ADEERRST	serrated
ADEERRTW	redwater
ADEERTTT	tattered
ADEERTWW	wartweed
ADEERVYY	everyday
ADEESTTT	attested
ADEFFORT	trade-off
ADEFFOSW	sawed-off
ADEFGILO	foliaged
ADEFGILS	gasfield
ADEFGIMN	defaming
ADEFGIRS	gas-fired
ADEFGIRT	driftage
ADEFGITU	fatigued
ADEFGLLU	full-aged
ADEFGLOT	gatefold
ADEFGLRU	feldgrau
ADEFGNOR	frondage
ADEFHILS	dealfish
ADEFHILT	half-tide
ADEFHILY	hayfield
ADEFHKOR	forkhead
ADEFHLNO	half-done
ADEFHLNT	left-hand
ADEFHLTU	deathful
ADEFHNOR	forehand
ADEFHNRR	hard-fern
ADEFHOST	softhead
ADEFIIKL	fail-dike
ADEFIILR	airfield
ADEFIILS	salified
ADEFIIMR	ramified
ADEFIIRT	ratified
ADEFILLR	all-fired
ADEFILLT	ill-fated
ADEFILMN	inflamed
ADEFILNR	filander
ADEFILNT	inflated
ADEFILOT	foliated
ADEFIMPR	firedamp
ADEFINRR	infrared
ADEFINRU	Freudian
ADEFINRW	fine-draw
ADEFINYZ	denazify
ADEFIORS	foresaid
ADEFLLLU	ladleful
ADEFLLRY	alder-fly
ADEFLLST	stall-fed
ADEFLLUY	feudally
ADEFLMRU	dreamful
ADEFLNOR	foreland
ADEFLNRU	dearnful
ADEFLNRY	lady-fern
ADEFLNUU	unfeudal
ADEFLNUW	unflawed
ADEFLOPR	drop-leaf
ADEFLORT	deflator
ADEFLPRS	feldspar
ADEFLPSU	spadeful
ADEFLRTU	tradeful
ADEFLRTW	leftward
ADEFMNRU	unframed
ADEFMOSU	fumadoes
ADEFNNNU	unfanned
ADEFNOOV	Vodafone®
ADEFNSST	daftness
ADEFORRR	forrader
ADEFORRW	foreward
ADEFORUV	favoured
ADEFSSTT	stedfast
ADEGGJLY	jaggedly
ADEGGLRU	leg-guard
ADEGGLRY	raggedly
ADEGGMOY	demagogy
ADEGGNUU	ungauged
ADEGGOPY	pedagogy
ADEGGPRS	spragged
ADEGGRTY	gadgetry
ADEGHHOS	hogshead
ADEGHILT	alighted
	gilt-head
ADEGHINR	headring
ADEGHINS	sheading
ADEGHITY	eight-day
ADEGHLNO	headlong
	long-head
ADEGHMNO	hog-maned
ADEGHMOY	hey-go-mad
ADEGHNNU	unhanged
ADEGHNPU	dung-heap
ADEGHOOP	pagehood
ADEGHORT	goatherd
ADEGHOTW	dog-wheat
ADEGHRTU	daughter
ADEGHUYY	hay-de-guy
ADEGIILN	gliadine
ADEGIILP	diplegia
ADEGIINO	Ganoidei
ADEGIITT	digitate
ADEGIJSW	jigsawed
ADEGILLO	gladiole
ADEGILLR	grillade
ADEGILMN	medaling
ADEGILNO	galenoid
ADEGILNP	pedaling
	pleading
ADEGILNR	dearling
	dragline
ADEGILNS	dealings
	signaled
ADEGILNY	delaying
ADEGILOU	dialogue
ADEGILRS	Griselda
ADEGILSS	glissade
ADEGILSV	disgavel
ADEGIMNR	dreaming
	margined
ADEGIMOR	ideogram
ADEGINOR	organdie
ADEGINOS	agonised
	diagnose
ADEGINOZ	agonized
ADEGINPU	anguiped
ADEGINRR	drearing
ADEGINRT	derating
	gradient
	treading
ADEGINST	steading
ADEGINYZ	zygaenid
ADEGIORT	ergatoid
ADEGIRWY	ridgeway
ADEGISSU	disusage
ADEGKLOY	dekalogy
ADEGLLNO	Legoland
ADEGLLNU	glandule
	ungalled
ADEGLMOS	gladsome
ADEGLMPU	plumaged
ADEGLMUY	amygdule
ADEGLNOY	gondelay
ADEGLNPS	spangled
ADEGLNRS	glanders
ADEGLNSS	gladness
ADEGLNUZ	unglazed
ADEGMNOY	endogamy
ADEGMORW	wordgame
ADEGMOST	dog's-meat
ADEGNNOR	androgen
	dragonné
ADEGNNPU	unpanged
ADEGNOPU	poundage
ADEGNORT	dragonet
ADEGNPUY	pyengadu
ADEGNRRU	grandeur
ADEGNRUU	unargued
ADEGNRUZ	gazunder
	ungrazed
ADEGOORY	goodyear
ADEGOPRR	prograde
ADEGORST	goadster
ADEGORTT	garotted
ADEGORWY	dog-weary

ADEGPRRU	upgrader
ADEGRRST	dragster
ADEGTTTU	guttated
ADEHHIPR	rhaphide
ADEHHIPS	headship
ADEHHIST	shithead
ADEHHNTU	headhunt
ADEHHOST	headshot
ADEHIITZ	thiazide
ADEHIKLV	khedival
ADEHIKNS	skinhead
ADEHILLM	mill-head
ADEHILLP	phialled
	pillhead
ADEHILNP	Delphian
ADEHILNR	hardline
ADEHILNU	unhailed
ADEHIMOT	hematoid
ADEHIMRY	hydremia
ADEHINNR	rein-hand
ADEHINOP	diaphone
ADEHINOS	adhesion
ADEHINPS	deanship
ADEHINPU	dauphine
ADEHINRU	unhaired
ADEHINST	handiest
ADEHIORS	Rhodesia
ADEHIOTT	athetoid
ADEHIPRS	raphides
	Sephardi
ADEHIPSS	pisshead
ADEHIPST	sidepath
ADEHIRVW	hiveward
ADEHISSW	Swadeshi
ADEHJLOT	jolthead
ADEHKLNU	lunkhead
ADEHKNRS	redshank
ADEHKNSU	skean-dhu
	unshaked
ADEHKORW	headwork
ADEHLLOW	hallowed
ADEHLLPY	lady-help
ADEHLLRW	hellward
ADEHLMNO	homeland
ADEHLMOY	holydame
ADEHLNRW	Landwehr
ADEHLNSS	handless
ADEHLNST	△shetland
ADEHLNSU	unhalsed
ADEHLOPS	asphodel
	pholades
ADEHLRRY	heraldry
ADEHMNOS	handsome
ADEHMNOT	methadon
	thanedom
ADEHMNRS	herdsman
ADEHMNRU	unharmed
ADEHMNSU	unshamed
ADEHMOOR	headroom
ADEHMORT	mort-head
ADEHMORW	homeward
ADEHMOST	headmost
ADEHMOSU	madhouse
ADEHMPPU	pump-head
ADEHNNSW	hand-sewn
ADEHNORV	handover
	overhand
ADEHNOSS	sandshoe
ADEHNOSU	seahound
ADEHNPSU	unshaped
ADEHNPTU	unpathed
ADEHNRSS	hardness
ADEHNRSU	unshared
ADEHNRSW	swanherd
ADEHNRTU	unthread
ADEHNSSU	sunshade
	unsashed
ADEHNSUV	unshaved
ADEHNSUW	unwashed
ADEHNTTU	unhatted
ADEHNTTX	text-hand
ADEHNTUW	unthawed
ADEHOORW	harewood
ADEHOPRS	pad-horse
	rhapsode
ADEHOPXY	hexapody
ADEHORSW	shadower
ADEHORTT	throated
ADEHPSUW	washed-up
ADEHRTTW	thwarted
ADEIILMN	limnaeid
ADEIILMS	idealism
ADEIILPR	peridial
ADEIILST	idealist
ADEIILTV	dilative
ADEIILTY	ideality
ADEIIMNN	indamine
ADEIIMNR	meridian
ADEIIMPR	impaired
ADEIIMRS	semi-arid
ADEIINNS	sanidine
ADEIINOT	ideation
	taenioid
ADEIINRS	draisine
ADEIINRU	uredinia
ADEIINST	adenitis
ADEIINUV	induviae
ADEIIPRR	perradii
	prairied
ADEIIPRS	presidia
ADEIITTV	tidivate
ADEIITUV	auditive
ADEIJRSU	Judaiser
ADEIJRUZ	Judaizer
ADEIKLLO	keloidal
ADEIKLLY	ladylike
ADEIKLSW	sidewalk
ADEIKMRT	tidemark
ADEIKORT	keratoid
ADEILLMY	medially
ADEILLNN	land-line
ADEILLNU	unallied
ADEILLOR	arillode
ADEILLPS	spadille
ADEILLRT	trialled
ADEILLRV	rivalled
ADEILLSW	sidewall
ADEILMNN	land-mine
ADEILMNU	unmailed
ADEILMNY	maidenly
ADEILMOS	damoisel
ADEILMPP	palmiped
ADEILMPS	misplead
ADEILMRY	dreamily
ADEILMSS	maidless
ADEILMST	medalist
	misdealt
ADEILMSY	dysmelia
ADEILNNR	inlander
ADEILNOP	palinode
ADEILNOS	nodalise
ADEILNOT	delation
ADEILNOZ	nodalize
ADEILNPT	pantiled
ADEILNPU	paludine
ADEILNRS	islander
ADEILNST	tail-ends
ADEILNSU	unsailed
ADEILNTU	untailed
ADEILNTV	divalent
ADEILOPS	episodal
	opalised
	sepaloid
ADEILOPT	petaloid
ADEILOPZ	opalized
ADEILOQU	odalique
ADEILORS	solidare
	soredial
ADEILORT	idolater
	tailored
ADEILORV	overlaid
ADEILORX	exordial
ADEILOST	diastole
	sodalite
	solidate
ADEILOTT	datolite
ADEILOTV	dovetail
ADEILPPP	pedipalp
ADEILPRT	dipteral
	tripedal
ADEILPRU	epidural
ADEILPRV	deprival
ADEILPSS	despisal
ADEILPTU	plaudite
ADEILRRY	drearily
ADEILRSU	residual
ADEILRSY	dialyser
ADEILRTT	detrital
ADEILRTY	△dielytra
ADEILRVY	variedly
ADEILRYZ	dialyzer
ADEILSSY	dialyses
ADEILSTY	diastyle
	steadily
ADEILSUV	disvalue
ADEILSXY	dyslexia

Words marked △ may be spelled also with a capital letter

ADEILTTU altitude
latitude
ADEIMMNU unmaimed
ADEIMMST mismated
ADEIMMSZ Mazdeism
ADEIMNNO demonian
mondaine
ADEIMNOP dopamine
ADEIMNOR Armenoid
ADEIMNOS nomadise
ADEIMNOT dominate
nematoid
ADEIMNOZ nomadize
ADEIMNRR manrider
ADEIMNRZ zemindar
ADEIMNSS sidesman
ADEIMNST tidesman
ADEIMNSY dynamise
ADEIMNSZ man-sized
ADEIMNTY dynamite
ADEIMNYZ dynamize
ADEIMORR airdrome
ADEIMORT mediator
ADEIMOSS sesamoid
ADEIMPRR rampired
ADEIMPST impasted
ADEIMRRS disarmer
ADEIMRSS sidearms
ADEIMRTU muriated
ADEIMRXY ready-mix
ADEINNOT Anointed
antinode
ADEINNOV Devonian
ADEINNPT pinnated
ADEINNPU unpained
ADEINNRZ rendzina
ADEINNSU unsained
ADEINNSX disannex
ADEINNTU inundate
ADEINOPT antipode
ADEINORR ordainer
reordain
ADEINORT deration
ordinate
Rodentia
ADEINORU douanier
ADEINOST astonied
sedation
ADEINOTT antidote
tetanoid
ADEINOTV donative
ADEINPPX appendix
ADEINPRT dipteran
ADEINPRU unpaired
unrepaid
ADEINPSV spavined
ADEINRRS serranid
ADEINRSS aridness
ADEINRST strained
ADEINRSU denarius
unraised
ADEINRSV sandiver
ADEINRSY synedria
ADEINRTU daturine
indurate
ADEINRUV unvaried
ADEINRVY vineyard
ADEINSSV avidness
ADEINSTU sinuated
ADEINSTY desyatin
ADEIOPRS diaspore
ADEIOPST dioptase
ADEIOPTV adoptive
ADEIORST asteroid
ADEIORTT teratoid
ADEIORTV deviator
ADEIPRST spirated
tarsiped
ADEIPRSU upraised
ADEIPRTU eupatrid
ADEIPTTU aptitude
ADEIQRRU quarried
ADEIQSUY quayside
ADEIRRWW wiredraw
ADEIRSST disaster
ADEIRSSU radiuses
ADEIRSTT striated
ADEIRVWY driveway
ADEISSST assisted
ADEISSTT distaste
ADEISSWY sideways
ADEISTTU situated
ADEITTTU attitude
ADEJNRUW under-jaw
ADEJOPRY jeopardy
ADEJRSTU adjuster
readjust
ADEKLMRY markedly
ADEKLNSU unslaked
ADEKMNRU unmarked
ADEKMNSU unmasked
ADEKMORS darksome
ADEKNNSS dankness
ADEKNOTW take-down
ADEKNRSS darkness
ADELLMRU medullar
ADELLMSU medullas
ADELLNNU annulled
ADELLNOS Lonsdale
ADELLNPS spendall
ADELLNSS landless
ADELLNSW wallsend
ADELLNTT Lettland
ADELLNUW unwalled
ADELLOTT allotted
totalled
ADELLOVY lady-love
ADELLOWW wallowed
ADELLRWW draw-well
ADELMNOS lodesman
ADELMOOW woodmeal
ADELMOTU modulate
ADELMPTU date-plum
ADELMRRU demurral
ADELMSUY amusedly
ADELNNNU unnaneld
ADELNNOT lentando
ADELNOPR Polander
ponderal
ADELNORS Roseland
solander
ADELNORU unloader
urodelan
ADELNORV overland
rondavel
ADELNORY read-only
ADELNPRS spandrel
ADELNPRU pendular
underlap
uplander
ADELNPRY panderly
ADELNPSY dyspneal
ADELNPUY unplayed
ADELNRTY ardently
ADELNRUY underlay
ADELNSTU unsalted
ADELNSTW wetlands
ADELNTUU undulate
ADELNUUV unvalued
ADELNUZZ undazzle
ADELOORV overload
ADELOOWW woodwale
ADELOPSU paludose
ADELOPSY sepalody
ADELOPTY petalody
ADELORRV overlard
ADELORSS roadless
ADELORST lodestar
ADELOVWY avowedly
ADELPPRY dapperly
ADELPRTY dry-plate
ADELRRTU ultrared
ADELRSTT startled
ADELRTUY adultery
ADELSTTY statedly
ADEMNNNU unmanned
ADEMNNOU unmoaned
ADEMNNRU underman
ADEMNOPR name-drop
pomander
ADEMNOST stone-mad
ADEMNOWY dey-woman
ADEMNPSS dampness
ADEMNPUU unmade-up
ADEMNRRU underarm
unmarred
ADEMNRTU undreamt
ADEMNRUW unwarmed
ADEMNSUU unamused
ADEMOORT moderato
ADEMOPST stampedo
ADEMORRU armoured
ADEMORRW Romeward
ADEMORTW wardmote
ADEMOSSU Asmodeus
ADEMPRUW warmed-up

ADENNNTU	untanned
ADENNORS	Anderson
ADENNOTU	unatoned
ADENNRUW	unwarned
ADENNTUW	unwanted
ADENOOPS	epanodos
ADENOORW	wanderoo
ADENOPRR	pardoner
ADENOPRX	expandor
ADENOPSS	spadones
ADENOPSU	unsoaped
ADENOPSY	dyspnoea
ADENOPTT	not-pated
ADENORUX	rondeaux
ADENOSSY	Odyssean
ADENOTUY	autodyne
ADENOUVW	unavowed
ADENPPSU	unsapped
ADENPPTU	untapped
ADENPRSU	unspared
ADENPRTU	depurant
ADENPRTY	pedantry
ADENPRUW	unwarped
ADENPRUY	underpay
ADENQRSU	squander
ADENRRTU	untarred
ADENRRWY	wardenry
ADENRSTU	transude
ADENRSTY	dry-stane
ADENRSUY	undersay
ADENRUWY	underway
ADENSTTU	unstated
	untasted
ADENSTUW	unwasted
ADENSTUY	unstayed
	unsteady
ADENSUWY	unswayed
ADEOORRT	toreador
ADEOOTTT	tattooed
ADEOPPRR	pear-drop
ADEOPRRS	eardrops
ADEOPRRT	parroted
	predator
ADEOPRTT	tetrapod
ADEOPRUV	vapoured
ADEOPSTT	despotat
	postdate
ADEOPTTU	up-to-date
ADEORRST	roadster
ADEORRSU	road-user
ADEORRVW	overdraw
ADEORSST	assorted
ADEORSTT	road-test
ADEORSTX	extrados
ADEORSUV	savoured
ADEOSSTT	assotted
ADEPPRST	strapped
ADEPRRTU	raptured
ADEPRTTU	tarted-up
ADEQSTTU	squatted
ADERRSSW	wardress
ADERRSTT	redstart
ADERSTTU	statured
ADERSTWW	westward
ADFFGIIR	giraffid
ADFFHIRS	draffish
ADFFHNOS	hands-off
ADFFLRUU	fraudful
ADFFNNOO	off-and-on
	on-and-off
ADFFNOST	standoff
	stand-off
ADFFORSW	off-wards
ADFGINNU	unfading
ADFGLOUW	god-awful
ADFHILNS	land-fish
ADFHIOST	toadfish
ADFHIRSW	dwarfish
ADFHISTY	day-shift
ADFHLNSU	handfuls
ADFHLOOR	half-door
ADFHLOST	holdfast
ADFIILPY	lapidify
ADFIIRST	first-aid
ADFILLLN	landfill
ADFILLMN	filmland
ADFILLNW	windfall
ADFILLRU	ill-faurd
ADFILMNO	manifold
ADFIMORY	fairydom
ADFIMRSW	dwarfism
ADFIORSV	disfavor
ADFIRSTY	first-day
ADFIRTWY	drift-way
ADFKLLNO	folkland
ADFLLNOW	downfall
ADFLMNOR	landform
ADFLMNOY	manyfold
ADFLMOPR	frampold
ADFLOOWY	floodway
ADFMRSTU	studfarm
ADFORRSW	forwards
	frowards
ADGGGINR	dragging
ADGGGINS	daggings
ADGGILNN	dangling
ADGGLRSU	sluggard
ADGGORSS	dog-grass
ADGHHILN	△highland
ADGHHINN	nigh-hand
ADGHHIOR	highroad
ADGHILNN	handling
ADGHILOS	hidalgos
ADGHILPY	diaglyph
ADGHILTY	daylight
ADGHIMNS	Gandhism
ADGHINOR	hoarding
ADGHINPR	handgrip
ADGHINST	Gandhist
ADGHISTY	day-sight
ADGHITTW	tightwad
ADGHLNNO	longhand
ADGHNOTU	do-naught
ADGHNRTU	drag-hunt
ADGHOOPR	odograph
ADGHORST	drag-shot
ADGHPSYY	dysphagy
ADGHRSTU	draughts
ADGHRTUY	draughty
ADGIILLN	dialling
ADGIILLO	gladioli
ADGIILNO	gonidial
ADGIILNP	plaiding
ADGIILNR	ring-dial
ADGIILPY	pygidial
ADGIILTY	algidity
ADGIIMST	digamist
ADGIINNY	digynian
ADGIINRY	dairying
ADGIINSV	advising
ADGIJNRU	adjuring
ADGIKLNR	darkling
ADGILLNO	oil-gland
ADGILLNR	land-girl
ADGILLNW	windgall
ADGILLNY	dallying
ADGILMOR	marigold
ADGILNNS	sandling
ADGILNNU	unlading
ADGILNOT	dog-Latin
ADGILNRY	daringly
ADGILNZZ	dazzling
ADGILOOS	solidago
ADGILOPR	prodigal
ADGILORY	goliardy
	gyroidal
ADGILRSY	Ygdrasil
ADGIMNNO	Mandingo
ADGIMOSU	digamous
ADGINNST	standing
ADGINOOP	poignado
ADGINOOR	rigadoon
ADGINOTY	toadying
ADGINRSW	drawings
ADGKOOSZ	gadzooks
ADGLOOPR	drop-goal
ADGLOORY	gardyloo
ADGLOPSW	gold-wasp
ADGMNORU	gourmand
ADGNNOQU	quandong
ADGNNORS	grandson
ADGNNRYY	gynandry
ADGNOOOP	Podogona
ADGNOORU	go-around
ADGOOPRS	gospodar
ADGOPRSU	podargus
ADGORTUU	outguard
ADHHIPRS	hardship
ADHHNNOR	hand-horn
ADHHNRTY	hydranth
ADHIIMMS	Mahdiism
ADHIIMSS	Hasidism
ADHIIMST	Mahdiist
ADHIINOP	ophidian
ADHIINRW	whiniard
ADHIISST	Hasidist

Words marked △ may be spelled also with a capital letter

ADHIISTW	had-I-wist
ADHIJNNO	join-hand
ADHIKNNT	hand-knit
ADHILLMN	hand-mill
	mill-hand
ADHILLMO	hollidam
ADHILLNS	sandhill
ADHILLOP	phalloid
ADHILLOT	thalloid
ADHILMOO	homaloid
ADHILMSS	alms-dish
ADHILNPS	land-ship
ADHILNST	handlist
ADHILOPS	shipload
ADHILOPY	haploidy
ADHILOSY	holidays
ADHILPSY	ladyship
ADHIMNOS	admonish
ADHIMNOU	humanoid
ADHIMOPP	amphipod
ADHIMRTY	myriadth
ADHINRWY	whinyard
ADHINSST	standish
ADHINSTU	dianthus
ADHIOSTY	toadyish
ADHIPRSW	wardship
ADHIPRSY	shipyard
ADHIPSTY	dispathy
ADHIRSTW	wash-dirt
ADHIRTWW	withdraw
ADHKNORW	handwork
ADHLLNOS	Hollands
ADHLLOOR	hall-door
ADHLLOTY	tally-ho'd
ADHLMNOO	hand-loom
ADHLMORT	thraldom
ADHLNORW	waldhorn
ADHLNOUW	down-haul
ADHMOOPS	shampoo'd
ADHMOPRS	dram-shop
ADHMORTT	dart-moth
ADHNNOOR	honorand
ADHNOPST	hand-post
ADHNOSTU	thousand
ADHNOSUW	unshadow
ADHOOPRS	hospodar
ADHOORSW	roadshow
ADHOORYZ	△hydrozoa
ADHOPRST	potshard
ADHOPRSY	rhapsody
ADHORSTU	toadrush
ADHORSTY	short-day
ADHORSWY	showyard
ADHPSTYY	dyspathy
ADHRSTUY	Thursday
ADIIINRV	viridian
ADIIIQRU	daiquiri
ADIIKLMM	milkmaid
ADIIKLST	tailskid
ADIIKNOP	pinakoid
ADIIKNST	antiskid
ADIILLMR	milliard
ADIILLNY	idyllian
ADIILLOR	arilloid
ADIILLUV	diluvial
ADIILNOT	dilation
ADIILNSU	indusial
ADIILNSW	windsail
ADIILNTY	daintily
	Ladinity
ADIILNUV	diluvian
	induvial
ADIILOPP	diplopia
ADIILRST	distrail
ADIILSSY	dialysis
ADIILTVY	validity
ADIIMPSU	aspidium
ADIINNOT	nidation
ADIINOSY	Dionysia
ADIINOTU	audition
ADIINRST	distrain
ADIIOPRS	sporidia
ADIIOPRT	tapiroid
ADIIORST	tarsioid
ADIIPRTY	rapidity
ADIIPSTY	sapidity
ADIIPTVY	vapidity
ADIIRSTT	distrait
	triadist
ADIKKRRW	kirkward
ADIKKRRY	kirkyard
ADIKLNPS	landskip
ADIKNNNU	dunnakin
ADIKNNST	inkstand
ADIKNRST	stinkard
ADILLLPY	pallidly
ADILLMNR	mandrill
ADILLMOU	allodium
ADILLMOV	villadom
ADILLMSY	dismally
ADILLNPS	landslip
ADILLOOP	poloidal
ADILLOPS	spadillo
ADILLOSW	disallow
ADILLOSY	disloyal
ADILLRWY	willyard
ADILLSTY	distally
ADILMMOS	modalism
ADILMNNO	mandolin
ADILMNOS	salmonid
ADILMOOR	modiolar
ADILMOOW	lima-wood
ADILMOPT	diplomat
ADILMOPY	△olympiad
ADILMORU	ordalium
ADILMOST	modalist
ADILMOTY	modality
ADILMPSU	paludism
ADILNNNU	nundinal
ADILNNSU	disannul
ADILNOOR	doornail
ADILNOOV	vindaloo
ADILNOPY	palinody
ADILNOTY	nodality
ADILNPRS	spandril
ADILNPST	displant
ADILNRWY	inwardly
ADILNSSW	windlass
ADILOOPR	Polaroid®
ADILOOPZ	diplozoa
ADILOORT	toroidal
ADILOPRT	tripodal
ADILOPSS	disposal
ADILOQSU	squaloid
ADILORSY	solidary
ADILORTY	adroitly
	dilatory
	idolatry
ADILOSTY	sodality
ADILPPSY	disapply
ADILPSTU	plaudits
ADILRTTY	tilt-yard
ADILRTWY	tawdrily
ADILRWYZ	wizardly
ADIMMNOO	ammonoid
ADIMMNOS	monadism
	nomadism
ADIMMNSY	dynamism
ADIMMOOR	Maoridom
ADIMMOST	amidmost
ADIMMOTU	domatium
ADIMNNOT	dominant
ADIMNOOR	maindoor
ADIMNOST	donatism
	saintdom
ADIMNOWW	widowman
ADIMNRSY	misandry
ADIMNSTY	dynamist
ADIMOPRY	myriapod
ADIMOPST	impasto'd
ADIMOPSY	sympodia
ADIMOSTY	toadyism
ADIMOTUX	Taxodium
ADIMPRSY	pyramids
ADIMRSUU	sudarium
ADIMSSTU	stadiums
ADINNNTU	inundant
ADINNOOT	donation
	nodation
ADINNORS	iron-sand
ADINNORT	ordinant
ADINNORY	non-dairy
ADINNOTU	nudation
ADINOOPS	isopodan
ADINOOPT	adoption
ADINOORT	tandoori
ADINOOTT	dotation
ADINOPRR	raindrop
ADINOPST	pintados
ADINORRY	ordinary
ADINORST	intrados
ADINORSU	dinosaur
ADINORSV	virandos
ADINORTU	duration
ADINORWZ	Zionward
ADINOSTT	Donatist

ADINOSTU	sudation
ADINOSTY	dystonia
ADINPSSU	Sapindus
ADINRUVZ	unvizard
ADIOOPSS	apodosis
ADIOPPST	post-paid
ADIOPRST	parodist
ADIOPRSV	privados
ADIOPRTY	podiatry
ADIOPSTT	toad-spit
ADIOPSTY	dystopia
ADIORRTT	traditor
ADIORSTT	stradiot
ADIORSVY	advisory
ADIORTUY	auditory
ADIPRRTU	purtraid
ADIRRWYZ	wizardry
ADJKNRUY	junk-yard
ADJORSTU	adjustor
ADKLNOTW	talk-down
ADKLOOPT	polka-dot
ADKLOORW	woodlark
	workload
ADKMNORW	mark-down
ADKMOORR	darkroom
ADKNRSTU	stunkard
ADKORWYY	worky-day
ADKRSSWY	skywards
ADLLLNOR	land-roll
ADLLLOOY	doolally
ADLLLORY	Lollardy
ADLLNORU	all-round
ADLLNOSW	Lowlands
ADLLORSY	dorsally
ADLMMOOP	doom-palm
ADLMMOPU	doum-palm
ADLMNOOR	moorland
ADLMNORY	randomly
ADLMNOSS	mossland
ADLMOORU	malodour
ADLMOPRW	moldwarp
ADLMOPSY	psalmody
ADLMSTTU	malt-dust
ADLNNOTW	townland
ADLNNTUU	undulant
ADLNOOPR	land-poor
ADLNOPRT	△portland
ADLNOPRU	pauldron
ADLNOPWY	downplay
ADLNORWY	onwardly
ADLNOSTU	outlands
ADLOOPTY	Tylopoda
ADLOORWW	woolward
ADLOPRWY	wordplay
ADLOPSUU	paludous
ADLOQSUW	oldsquaw
ADLORSWW	sword-law
ADLORTWY	towardly
ADLPRUWY	upwardly
ADMMNOOS	doomsman
ADMMNTUU	mutandum
ADMNNORY	monandry

ADMNNOSU	soundman
ADMNNOTU	notandum
ADMNOOOT	odontoma
ADMNOORS	doorsman
	doors-man
	madroños
ADMNOOST	mastodon
ADMNOOSW	woodsman
ADMNOOSX	Saxondom
ADMNORRU	round-arm
ADMNORSW	sandworm
	swordman
ADMNPPSU	sandpump
ADMOORRW	wardroom
ADMOPPPU	poppadum
ADMORRSW	sword-arm
ADNNORTY	dynatron
ADNOOPRS	spadroon
ADNOOQRU	quadroon
ADNOORST	tornados
ADNOORTY	donatory
ADNOOSVW	advowson
ADNOQRSU	squadron
ADNORSTW	sandwort
ADNORSXY	sardonyx
ADNORTUW	untoward
ADNORWWY	wanwordy
ADNOSTTU	outstand
ADNRSSUW	sunwards
ADOOPRRT	trapdoor
ADOOPRSU	sauropod
ADOPRSSW	password
ADOPSSSU	soapsuds
ADORRSTU	dartrous
ADORSTUW	outwards
ADORSTUY	sudatory
ADORTUVY	advoutry
ADPRRTUY	purtrayd
ADRSSTTU	stardust
ADRSSUUY	Dasyurus
ADSSTUWY	sawdusty
AEEEELRS	releasee
AEEEFRTY	aftereye
AEEEGGLU	lee-gauge
AEEEGGNR	re-engage
AEEEGLLS	legalese
AEEEGLNR	generale
AEEEGLRT	eglatere
	regelate
	relegate
AEEEGLRV	leverage
AEEEGLSV	selvagee
AEEEGNPR	pea-green
AEEEGNRS	sea-green
AEEEGNRT	generate
	renegate
	teenager
AEEEGRST	steerage
AEEEGRSW	sewerage
AEEEGTTV	vegetate
AEEEHLRT	ethereal
AEEEHMPR	ephemera

AEEEHNRS	enhearse
AEEEHRRS	rehearse
AEEEHRRT	reheater
AEEEHRST	shea-tree
AEEEHSTT	aesthete
AEEEIMNX	examinee
AEEEJNTT	jeanette
AEEEKKPS	keepsake
AEEEKNRW	weakener
AEEEKPRT	peat-reek
AEEELLST	telesale
AEEELMRT	meal-tree
AEEELNPS	Nepalese
AEEELNRV	venereal
AEEELNST	selenate
AEEELPRR	△repealer
AEEELPRS	eel-spear
AEEELPRY	pearl-eye
AEEELPST	paste-eel
AEEELQSU	sequelae
AEEELRRS	releaser
AEEELRRV	revealer
AEEELRST	teaseler
AEEELRSW	weaseler
AEEELRTX	axle-tree
AEEELSSS	easeless
AEEELSTW	wet-lease
AEEELSVY	eye-salve
AEEEMMRT	metamere
AEEEMNRT	Nemertea
AEEEMNST	easement
AEEEMPRS	permease
AEEEMPRT	permeate
AEEENNRV	venerean
AEEENPTT	patentee
AEEENRST	serenate
AEEENRTT	enterate
AEEENRTV	enervate
	venerate
AEEEPPRS	Praesepe
AEEEPRRT	pear-tree
	repartee
	repeater
AEEEPSTW	sweetpea
AEEERRST	arrestee
AEEERSST	tesserae
AEEERTWY	eye-water
AEEFFKNR	frank-fee
AEEFFLLR	free-fall
AEEFFLRT	tafferel
AEEFFNRT	afferent
AEEFGILR	filagree
AEEFGINR	Faringee
AEEFGINT	gate-fine
AEEFGIRR	ferriage
AEEFGLSU	fuselage
AEEFHLLS	selfheal
AEEFHLST	self-hate
AEEFHRTY	feathery
AEEFIINR	inferiae
AEEFIKLL	leaflike
AEEFIKRW	wakerife

AEEFILMN	filename
AEEFILNR	flânerie
AEEFILNV	vine-leaf
AEEFILPR	pea-rifle
AEEFILRS	serafile
AEEFILRT	frailtee
AEEFIPSW	spaewife
AEEFKMNT	fakement
AEEFKOPR	forepeak
AEEFLLMR	femerall
AEEFLLMT	flamelet
AEEFLLNV	evenfall
AEEFLLRW	farewell
AEEFLLSS	leafless
AEEFLMNR	male-fern
AEEFLMOS	fleasome
AEEFLMSS	fameless
	self-same
AEEFLNOS	nose-leaf
AEEFLNRU	funereal
AEEFLORS	rose-leaf
AEEFLORV	overleaf
AEEFLOTV	love-feat
AEEFLRRR	referral
AEEFLRSS	fearless
AEEFLRTW	weel-far't
AEEFMNOR	foremean
	forename
AEEFMORS	fearsome
AEEFMRTY	femetary
AEEFNRST	fastener
	fenestra
AEEFNRTT	fattener
AEEFNSSS	safeness
AEEFOSTU	feateous
AEEFRSTU	features
AEEFTTUV	fauvette
AEEGGHIW	weighage
AEEGGINR	agreeing
AEEGGIRV	aggrieve
AEEGGKOR	oak-egger
AEEGGLOU	aeglogue
AEEGGLPP	egg-apple
AEEGGNNR	gangrene
AEEGGNOS	gasogene
AEEGGNOZ	gazogene
AEEGGPRU	puggaree
AEEGHILN	Hegelian
AEEGHIRT	heritage
AEEGHLLT	hell-gate
AEEGHLOT	helotage
AEEGHLRS	shearleg
AEEGHLRW	ragwheel
AEEGHMPR	grapheme
AEEGHNRS	shagreen
AEEGHRRT	gatherer
	regather
AEEGIINR	aegirine
AEEGIIRT	aegirite
AEEGILLS	legalise
AEEGILLZ	legalize
AEEGILMN	liegeman
AEEGILNR	△algerine
AEEGILNS	ensilage
AEEGILNT	galenite
	gelatine
	legatine
AEEGILNV	inveagle
AEEGILPR	perigeal
AEEGILRS	gaselier
AEEGILST	elegiast
AEEGILTV	levigate
AEEGIMNR	germaine
AEEGIMNT	geminate
AEEGIMRT	emigrate
	remigate
AEEGINPR	perigean
AEEGINRR	regainer
AEEGINRS	△gesneria
AEEGINRT	gratinée
AEEGINSS	assignee
AEEGINST	sagenite
AEEGINSV	envisage
AEEGINTV	agentive
	gate-vein
	negative
AEEGINTX	exigeant
AEEGIPQU	equipage
AEEGIRSS	greasies
AEEGIRTT	aigrette
AEEGIRTV	ergative
AEEGLLNR	allergen
AEEGLLOW	eagle-owl
AEEGLMRT	telegram
AEEGLMRY	meagrely
AEEGLNNO	Angeleno
AEEGLNNR	enlargen
AEEGLNNT	entangle
AEEGLNOS	gasolene
AEEGLNOT	elongate
AEEGLNRR	enlarger
AEEGLNST	Gnetales
AEEGLNVY	evangely
AEEGLOST	segolate
AEEGLRSS	eelgrass
	gearless
	largesse
AEEGLRTU	regulate
AEEGLRUX	exergual
AEEGLSST	gateless
AEEGLSSW	wageless
AEEGLSSY	eyeglass
AEEGLTTU	tutelage
AEEGLTUV	evulgate
AEEGMMOS	gamesome
AEEGMNOR	argemone
AEEGMNRS	agrémens
AEEGMNRT	agrément
AEEGMNSS	gameness
AEEGMNTT	tegmenta
AEEGMNTZ	gazement
AEEGMOST	somegate
AEEGMRST	gamester
AEEGMSSS	messages
AEEGMSSU	messuage
AEEGNNNO	enneagon
AEEGNNRT	generant
AEEGNNRU	enraunge
AEEGNNRV	engraven
AEEGNOST	Stone-Age
	stone-age
AEEGNPRS	sap-green
AEEGNRRT	étranger
AEEGNRRV	engraver
AEEGNRST	estrange
	segreant
	sergeant
	sternage
AEEGNRTU	gauntree
AEEGNSSS	sageness
AEEGNTTV	vegetant
AEEGOPRV	overpage
AEEGORSY	easy-goer
AEEGPRRS	asperger
	presager
AEEGPRRT	pargeter
AEEGPRSS	asperges
AEEGRRRT	regrater
AEEGRSST	Argestes
AEEGRSSW	sewer-gas
AEEGRSTW	strewage
AEEHHHNT	heath-hen
AEEHHHSS	hasheesh
AEEHHNST	ensheath
	heathens
AEEHHOOP	pahoehoe
AEEHHRTY	heathery
AEEHIJMR	Jeremiah
AEEHIKRS	shikaree
AEEHILNP	elaphine
AEEHILRS	shiralee
AEEHILRT	etherial
AEEHIMPT	epithema
AEEHIMTT	hematite
AEEHINPS	Ephesian
AEEHINRS	an-heires
	inhearse
AEEHINRT	atherine
AEEHINTT	Theatine
AEEHIPRS	Pharisee
AEEHIPST	aphetise
	hepatise
AEEHIPTT	hepatite
AEEHIPTZ	aphetize
	hepatize
AEEHIRST	hearties
AEEHIRSV	shivaree
AEEHIRTU	Eutheria
AEEHISST	esthesia
AEEHISTT	athetise
	hesitate
AEEHISTV	heaviest
AEEHITTZ	athetize
AEEHKLLR	rakehell
AEEHKLLU	keelhaul
AEEHKMOT	take-home

AEEHLLRS	ear-shell
AEEHLLSS	seashell
AEEHLMNW	wheelman
AEEHLMNY	hymeneal
AEEHLMOS	healsome
AEEHLMPT	helpmate
AEEHLNPT	elephant
AEEHLNRT	leathern
AEEHLNSS	haleness
AEEHLNTV	halve-net
AEEHLNVY	heavenly
AEEHLOPT	peat-hole
AEEHLORS	arsehole
AEEHLORV	overhale
AEEHLOSU	ale-house
AEEHLOTV	love-hate
AEEHLPST	pleaseth
AEEHLPTT	telepath
AEEHLRST	halteres
	leathers
AEEHLRTT	heartlet
AEEHLRTY	leathery
AEEHLSST	hateless
AEEHLTTY	ethylate
AEEHMMRR	hammerer
AEEHMNNY	hymenean
AEEHMNRT	three-man
AEEHMNTX	exanthem
AEEHMPSS	emphases
AEEHMRTY	erythema
AEEHMTUX	exhumate
AEEHNNSS	sneeshan
AEEHNNTX	xanthene
AEEHNOPR	earphone
AEEHNPST	stephane
AEEHNRST	hastener
AEEHNRSU	unhearse
AEEHNRTT	haterent
	threaten
AEEHNRTU	urethane
AEEHNRTW	waterhen
	wreathen
AEEHNRWY	anywhere
AEEHNSTU	uneathes
AEEHNSTW	enswathe
AEEHORRV	overhear
AEEHORSS	seahorse
	seashore
AEEHORTV	overheat
AEEHPRRS	rephrase
AEEHPRST	spreathe
AEEHPSTY	pay-sheet
AEEHRRTU	urethrae
AEEHRRTW	wreather
AEEHRTVW	whatever
AEEHRTWY	three-way
AEEIIMRT	métairie
AEEIKKLW	likewake
AEEIKLMU	leukemia
AEEIKLPT	tapelike
AEEIKLVW	wavelike
AEEIKMMR	merimake
AEEIKMNT	ketamine
AEEIKNRT	ankerite
	kreatine
AEEILLNT	tenaille
AEEILLVX	live-axle
AEEILMMN	melamine
AEEILMMT	mealtime
AEEILMNT	melanite
AEEILMRT	eremital
	matériel
	realtime
AEEILMSV	malvesie
AEEILMTZ	metalize
AEEILNNS	selenian
AEEILNPR	perineal
AEEILNPS	penalise
	sepaline
AEEILNPT	petaline
	tapeline
AEEILNPZ	penalize
AEEILNRT	elaterin
	entailer
	treenail
AEEILNSV	Vaseline®
AEEILNTV	elvanite
	ventaile
AEEILORT	aerolite
AEEILOTT	etiolate
AEEILPPP	apple-pie
AEEILPPS	seal-pipe
AEEILPRS	espalier
	pearlies
AEEILPRT	pearlite
AEEILPSW	palewise
AEEILQSU	equalise
AEEILQUX	exequial
AEEILQUZ	equalize
AEEILRRS	realiser
AEEILRRT	retailer
AEEILRRZ	realizer
AEEILRST	earliest
AEEILRSV	velarise
AEEILRTT	laterite
	literate
AEEILRTV	levirate
	relative
AEEILRVW	liveware
	reviewal
AEEILRVZ	velarize
AEEILSVW	alewives
AEEILTTV	levitate
AEEIMMNT	meantime
AEEIMNNV	Menevian
AEEIMNRX	examiner
AEEIMNST	seminate
AEEIMNUV	mauveine
AEEIMRTV	viameter
AEEIMSTT	estimate
	étatisme
AEEIMSTW	teamwise
AEEINNRS	anserine
AEEINNTV	Venetian
AEEINPRT	aperient
AEEINPRV	pea-viner
AEEINPTT	pianette
AEEINRRT	rain-tree
	retainer
AEEINRST	arsenite
	resinate
	sin-eater
	stearine
AEEINSSS	easiness
AEEINSSV	vainesse
AEEINSTT	anisette
	tetanise
AEEINTTZ	tetanize
AEEIOOPP	epopoeia
AEEIORST	etaerios
AEEIPPST	appetise
AEEIPPSU	eupepsia
AEEIPPTT	appetite
AEEIPPTZ	appetize
AEEIPRRR	rare-ripe
	repairer
AEEIPRTV	perviate
AEEIPSST	epitases
AEEIRRTT	retraite
AEEIRRVW	rear-view
AEEIRSTT	treatise
AEEIRSVV	aversive
AEEISTTT	étatiste
	steatite
AEEISTTV	estivate
AEEITTUX	eutaxite
AEEITUVX	exuviate
AEEJLNPT	jetplane
	jet-plane
AEEJLOSU	jealouse
AEEJNRST	serjeant
AEEJOPRT	pejorate
AEEJRTTW	water-jet
AEEKKLWY	lykewake
AEEKKPSY	keepsaky
AEEKLLST	skeletal
AEEKLMMU	Mameluke
AEEKLMOP	meal-poke
AEEKLMRT	telemark
AEEKLMSS	makeless
AEEKLPTY	key-plate
AEEKLSSW	wakeless
AEEKLSTY	eyestalk
AEEKMNSW	man-weeks
AEEKMORV	makeover
AEEKMOTY	yoke-mate
AEEKMRRR	remarker
AEEKMRRT	marketer
AEEKNNNS	nankeens
AEEKNPSW	△newspeak
AEEKNSSW	weakness
AEEKORRV	overrake
AEEKORST	keratose
	kreasote
AEEKORTV	overtake
	takeover

AEEKQRSU	squeaker
AEEKRRST	streaker
AEELLLTT	telltale
	tell-tale
AEELLMMS	mamselle
AEELLMRT	Tremella
AEELLNOT	let-alone
AEELLNOV	novellae
AEELLOTT	allottee
AEELLPTT	platelet
AEELLPTY	teleplay
AEELLRRT	terrella
AEELLSST	satelles
	tessella
AEELLSSZ	zealless
AEELLSTT	stellate
AEELLSWY	weaselly
AEELLTVV	valvelet
AEELMMNT	Emmental
AEELMMNU	Emmanuel
AEELMMTU	malemute
AEELMNPS	ensample
AEELMNSS	lameness
	maneless
	nameless
AEELMNST	steelman
AEELMNTT	mantelet
AEELMNTV	lavement
AEELMOTT	matelote
AEELMPRT	palm-tree
AEELMPRX	exemplar
AEELMPRY	empyreal
AEELMPTT	palmette
	template
AEELMSSS	seamless
AEELMSST	mateless
	meatless
	tameless
AEELNNRT	lanneret
AEELNNSS	leanness
AEELNOPR	peroneal
AEELNOPT	antelope
AEELNORU	aleurone
AEELNPPS	spalpeen
AEELNPSS	paleness
AEELNQSU	squalene
AEELNRSS	realness
AEELNRSV	enslaver
AEELNRTV	△levanter
	relevant
AEELNRTX	external
AEELNSST	lateness
AEELNSSV	vaneless
AEELNSWY	Wesleyan
AEELNTUV	eventual
AEELNTVY	ventayle
AEELOPRV	overleap
AEELORRS	releasor
AEELORST	oleaster
AEELORTT	tolerate
AEELORTV	elevator
AEELORTW	toleware
AEELOSTV	love-seat
AEELOTTT	teetotal
AEELPRRS	relapser
AEELPRRT	palterer
AEELPRSU	pleasure
	serpulae
AEELPRSV	vesperal
AEELPRTU	tape-lure
AEELPRTY	pterylae
AEELPSST	△spätlese
	tapeless
AEELPSTV	septleva
AEELQRSU	squealer
AEELRRSV	reversal
	slaverer
AEELRRTU	ureteral
AEELRRTV	traveler
AEELRSST	tearless
	tesseral
AEELRSSW	wareless
AEELRSTT	Letraset®
AEELRSTU	resalute
AEELRSTY	easterly
AEELRSVY	aversely
AEELSSST	sateless
	seatless
AEELSSVW	waveless
AEEMMNRS	meresman
AEEMMNTZ	mazement
AEEMMSST	messmate
AEEMNNOT	mean-tone
AEEMNNRT	remanent
AEEMNNSS	meanness
AEEMNORV	overname
AEEMNORZ	armozeen
AEEMNPRT	peterman
	peter-man
AEEMNPRY	empyrean
AEEMNPTV	pavement
AEEMNRSV	verse-man
AEEMNRSW	menswear
AEEMNRTU	numerate
AEEMNRTV	averment
AEEMNRUV	maneuver
AEEMNRVY	△everyman
AEEMNSSS	sameness
AEEMNSST	tameness
AEEMNSTU	mansuete
AEEMORST	Masorete
AEEMORSU	mouse-ear
AEEMPPRR	pamperer
AEEMPRRT	tamperer
AEEMPRSU	Serapeum
AEEMPRTT	attemper
AEEMQRRU	remarque
AEEMQTTU	maquette
AEEMRRST	remaster
	streamer
AEEMRRSU	measurer
AEEMRSST	masseter
	seamster
AEEMRSSU	measures
	reassume
AEEMRSTT	teamster
AEEMSSSU	masseuse
AEEMSSTU	meatuses
AEEMSTTU	amusette
AEENNPRY	Pyrenean
AEENNRSS	nearness
AEENNRTU	enaunter
AEENNRTV	revenant
AEENNRUX	annexure
AEENNSSS	saneness
AEENNSST	neatness
AEENNSTT	se-tenant
AEENOPRS	personae
AEENOPRU	European
AEENOPST	pea-stone
AEENORRS	reasoner
AEENORSS	seasoner
AEENORST	resonate
AEENORTV	overneat
	renovate
AEENORVW	ovenware
AEENOSTX	axe-stone
AEENPPTT	appetent
AEENPQTU	pétanque
AEENRRRW	warrener
AEENRRSS	rareness
AEENRRSW	answerer
	reanswer
AEENRRTT	natterer
AEENRRTV	taverner
AEENRSSS	searness
AEENRSST	assenter
	sarsenet
AEENRSTU	Sauterne
AEENRSVW	never-was
AEENRTTV	antevert
AEENRTTX	externat
AEENRTTY	entreaty
AEENRTUV	aventure
AEEOPRRT	paterero
	perorate
AEEOPRST	protease
AEEOPRTT	operetta
AEEORRST	ore-stare
AEEORRSU	rearouse
AEEORRSW	sowarree
AEEORRTV	overrate
AEEORRTZ	zero-rate
AEEORRVW	overwear
AEEORRVY	overyear
AEEORSSV	overseas
AEEORSTU	Euroseat
AEEPPRRR	preparer
AEEPRRRT	parterre
AEEPRRTT	patterer
AEEPRRTU	aperture
AEEPRSSS	Passeres
AEEPRSTU	superate
	upas-tree
AEEPSSWW	sweep-saw

AEEQRRUV quaverer
AEERRRST arrester
rearrest
AEERRSST asserter
reassert
AEERRSSU reassure
AEERRSTU treasure
AEERRSTV traverse
AEERRSTW sewer-rat
AEERSSSS reassess
AEERSTTT attester
AEERTTTZ terzetta
AEERVWYY everyway
AEFFGILR fire-flag
AEFFGOST off-stage
AEFFGRSU suffrage
AEFFHIKY kaffiyeh
AEFFHILL half-life
AEFFHKOS off-shake
AEFFILRT life-raft
AEFFILUV effluvia
AEFFIMRR affirmer
reaffirm
AEFFKLRU freakful
AEFFLNTU affluent
AEFFLORU four-leaf
AEFFLOSS off-sales
AEFFLSTU feastful
sufflate
AEFFMRSU earmuffs
AEFFNNSS naffness
AEFFNORT affronté
AEFFORST afforest
AEFFRTTU Tartuffe
AEFGHINR hangfire
AEFGHIST sea-fight
AEFGHMOR hog-frame
AEFGHTTU fughetta
AEFGIIRS gasifier
AEFGIMTU fumigate
AEFGINST feasting
AEFGINTU fantigue
AEFGIRRU argufier
AEFGIRTU figurate
fruitage
AEFGISTU fatigues
AEFGLLOP flagpole
AEFGLLPU full-page
AEFGLMNU fugleman
AEFGLNSS fangless
AEFGLOPR leap-frog
AEFGLORW garefowl
AEFGLRTU grateful
AEFGMNOR forgeman
AEFGMNRT fragment
AEFGNNOT fontange
AEFGNORT frontage
AEFGOOPT footpage
AEFGOORT footgear
AEFGOPRX fox-grape
AEFGORST go-faster
AEFGORTT frottage
AEFGOSSU fougasse
AEFHHLOS half-hose
AEFHIIST Shafiite
AEFHIKLP half-pike
AEFHIKRS freakish
AEFHIKSW weakfish
AEFHILLN fellahin
AEFHILLT tefillah
AEFHILMS fish-meal
AEFHILMT half-time
AEFHILNW fin-whale
AEFHILOR forhaile
AEFHILOX hexafoil
AEFHILSZ half-size
AEFHLLOS half-sole
AEFHLMRT half-term
AEFHLMSU shameful
AEFHLNOT half-note
half-tone
AEFHLPST half-step
AEFHLRTY fatherly
AEFHLTTX half-text
AEFHMMOR home-farm
AEFHMNRS freshman
AEFHNRSW fernshaw
AEFHOORT hare-foot
AEFHORTX fox-earth
AEFHRSTT farthest
AEFIILLN nail-file
AEFIILNS finalise
AEFIILNZ finalize
AEFIIMNS infamise
AEFIIMNZ infamize
AEFIIMRR Frimaire
AEFIINRS Friesian
AEFIINST fainites
AEFIIPRT aperitif
apéritif
AEFIIRRT ratifier
AEFIITVX fixative
AEFIKLRW fire-walk
AEFIKMNN knife-man
AEFIKMRR firemark
AEFIKRUW waukrife
AEFILLOS leaf-soil
AEFILLOT fellatio
AEFILLST ill-faste
AEFILLSV all-fives
AEFILMNR inflamer
rifleman
AEFILMNS misfalne
AEFILMNT filament
AEFILMTY femality
AEFILNNR infernal
AEFILNOT olefiant
AEFILNPS lifespan
AEFILNRU △fräulein
AEFILOOR aerofoil
AEFILOPR fire-opal
AEFILORS foresail
AEFILRTT filtrate
AEFILRTU filature
AEFILRUW weariful
AEFILSTU fistulae
AEFILSTV festival
AEFILSTW flatwise
AEFILTUU fauteuil
AEFIMMMR mammifer
AEFIMNRS fireman's
AEFIMNST manifest
AEFIMORR aeriform
AEFIMORT formiate
AEFIMRRS firearms
AEFIMRRW firmware
AEFINNSS fainness
AEFINOPR pinafore
AEFINORS farinose
AEFINRSS fairness
sanserif
AEFIOPRR Porifera
AEFIORRT Rotifera
AEFIORTV favorite
AEFIPRRT fire-trap
AEFIRRRY farriery
AEFIRSTW wastrife
AEFIRTUX fixature
AEFKLLOT folk-tale
AEFKLMRY flymaker
AEFKLRUW wreakful
AEFKLSTT talkfest
AEFKNORR fore-rank
AEFKNORS forsaken
AEFKOPRS forspeak
AEFKORRW workfare
AEFKORTU freak-out
AEFLLLOR leaf-roll
AEFLLMMU flammule
AEFLLNNS flannels
AEFLLNNU unfallen
AEFLLNRY fern-ally
AEFLLORV overfall
AEFLLPTU plateful
AEFLLRUX flexural
AEFLLSSW flawless
AEFLLSTY festally
AEFLMNOT matfelon
AEFLMORU formulae
fumarole
AEFLMOSS foamless
AEFLMPRR frampler
AEFLNNOT fontanel
AEFLNOPR foreplan
AEFLNOPT pantofle
AEFLNORS farnesol
AEFLNRTU flaunter
AEFLNSST flatness
AEFLNSUY unsafely
AEFLOPRT teraflop
AEFLOPRY foreplay
AEFLORRW elf-arrow
AEFLORST forestal
AEFLORSU fusarole
AEFLORTU flare-out
AEFLORTW fleawort

AEFLOSTT	falsetto
AEFLPPRY	flypaper
AEFLPSUU	pauseful
AEFLRSTT	fattrels
AEFLRTTU	aflutter
AEFLRTTY	flattery
AEFLSSTU	flatuses
AEFLSTTU	tasteful
AEFLSTUW	wasteful
AEFMNORW	men-of-war
AEFMNRRY	ferryman
AEFMORRT	reformat
AEFMORST	foremast
	mort-safe
AEFMORVW	waveform
AEFNNSTU	unfasten
AEFNOPRR	profaner
AEFNORRW	forewarn
AEFNORST	seafront
AEFNOSTW	feast-won
AEFNPRST	far-spent
AEFNRRST	transfer
AEFNRRUY	funerary
AEFNSSST	fastness
AEFNSTUY	unsafety
AEFOORTW	footwear
AEFOPRRT	forepart
	raft-rope
AEFOPRST	forepast
AEFOPTUU	pot-au-feu
AEFORRSW	forswear
AEFORRUV	favourer
AEFORRWY	forweary
AEFORSTW	forwaste
	software
AEFORSTY	forestay
AEFOSTUU	featuous
AEFOSTUV	voutsafe
AEFPRSST	pressfat
AEGGGINN	engaging
AEGGGLSS	egg-glass
AEGGHHIR	high-gear
AEGGHMSU	meshugga
AEGGHOPY	geophagy
AEGGHORU	roughage
AEGGILLR	grillage
AEGGILMN	gleaming
AEGGILNN	gleaning
AEGGILOU	oil-gauge
AEGGIMRT	gregatim
AEGGINNV	avenging
AEGGINOR	Georgian
AEGGINOS	sea-going
AEGGIOPR	arpeggio
	geropiga
AEGGIRRU	garrigue
AEGGIRWY	earwiggy
AEGGLNPT	egg-plant
AEGGLORY	gargoyle
AEGGLRST	straggle
AEGGMORR	ergogram
AEGGMORT	mortgage
AEGGNORV	overgang
AEGGNORW	△waggoner
AEGGNRST	gangster
AEGGNSST	ants'-eggs
AEGGOPRU	groupage
AEGGRSST	staggers
AEGHHORS	shear-hog
AEGHHORT	earth-hog
AEGHILLM	megillah
AEGHILLS	shigella
AEGHILMT	megalith
AEGHILNR	narghile
	nargileh
AEGHILNS	shealing
AEGHILNT	atheling
AEGHILPS	shagpile
AEGHILRT	litharge
	thirlage
AEGHIMPS	mageship
AEGHINNT	naething
AEGHINPT	night-ape
AEGHINRS	shearing
AEGHINRT	ingather
AEGHINTT	gnathite
AEGHIOPS	esophagi
AEGHIORT	eight-oar
AEGHIPPR	epigraph
AEGHIPRT	graphite
AEGHLOPY	hypogeal
AEGHLOTX	hexaglot
AEGHLRTU	laughter
AEGHLRTY	lethargy
AEGHMNOP	phenogam
AEGHMOPT	apothegm
AEGHNNOR	hanger-on
AEGHNNST	hangnest
AEGHNOPT	heptagon
	pathogen
AEGHNOPY	hypogean
AEGHNORV	hangover
	overhang
AEGHNPSW	spanghew
AEGHNRSS	gnashers
AEGHOPPR	prophage
AEGHOPPY	apophyge
AEGHOPXY	exophagy
AEGHORST	shortage
AEGHPRTU	upgather
AEGHPSUW	wage-push
AEGHRSYY	ashy-grey
AEGIILLU	aiguille
AEGIILMO	oligemia
AEGIILMR	remigial
AEGIILPS	Spigelia
AEGIILTT	litigate
AEGIIMNN	Geminian
AEGIIMNR	imaginer
	migraine
AEGIIMNS	imagines
AEGIIMTT	mitigate
AEGIINNN	nennigai
AEGIINNR	arginine
AEGIIRRT	irrigate
AEGIISTV	vestigia
AEGIJRTU	Gujerati
AEGIKLNW	weakling
AEGIKMRW	wig-maker
AEGIKNNS	sneaking
AEGIKNNW	wakening
AEGIKNPS	speaking
AEGIKNRT	retaking
AEGIKNTW	tweaking
AEGILLMS	legalism
AEGILLNV	vine-gall
AEGILLNY	genially
AEGILLPR	pillager
AEGILLPS	spillage
AEGILLRU	guerilla
AEGILLRV	all-giver
	villager
AEGILLST	legalist
	stillage
AEGILLSU	ill-usage
AEGILLTU	ligulate
AEGILLTY	legality
AEGILMMR	aglimmer
	lammiger
AEGILMNR	△germinal
	maligner
	malinger
AEGILMNS	Galenism
AEGILMNT	ligament
	metaling
AEGILMRS	regalism
AEGILMRX	lexigram
AEGILNNR	learning
AEGILNNT	gantline
AEGILNNU	ungenial
AEGILNNW	weanling
AEGILNNY	yeanling
AEGILNOR	geraniol
	regional
AEGILNOS	gasoline
AEGILNOT	gelation
	legation
AEGILNPR	pearling
AEGILNPS	pleasing
AEGILNRS	salering
	sanglier
	signaler
AEGILNRT	integral
	triangle
AEGILNRX	relaxing
AEGILNRY	layering
	yearling
AEGILNSS	gainless
	glassine
AEGILNST	eastling
	Galenist
	genitals
	stealing
AEGILNSV	leavings
	Svengali
AEGILNSW	swealing

AEGILNTV	valeting
AEGILNUV	vaginule
AEGILOPS	spoilage
AEGILOPT	pilotage
AEGILORS	gasolier
	girasole
	seraglio
AEGILPPS	slippage
AEGILPPU	pupilage
AEGILRST	regalist
AEGILRSY	greasily
AEGILRTT	aglitter
AEGILRTU	ligature
AEGILRTY	regality
AEGILRVW	law-giver
AEGILSST	Glassite
AEGIMNRT	emigrant
AEGIMNRU	geranium
AEGIMNSS	gaminess
AEGIMNST	steaming
AEGIMNSV	△veganism
AEGIMOPT	magot-pie
AEGIMORR	armigero
AEGIMORW	wagmoire
AEGIMPRU	umpirage
AEGIMQRU	quagmire
AEGIMRRT	ragtimer
AEGIMRST	magister
	sterigma
AEGIMSSU	misusage
AEGINNOT	negation
AEGINNPS	sneaping
AEGINNRS	earnings
AEGINNRV	ravening
AEGINNRY	renaying
	yearning
AEGINNST	steaning
AEGINNSU	sanguine
AEGINORR	Rogerian
AEGINORS	ignaroes
	organise
AEGINORZ	organize
AEGINPPR	papering
AEGINPRT	tapering
AEGINPRY	repaying
AEGINPTY	Egyptian
AEGINRRV	averring
AEGINRSS	reassign
AEGINRST	astringe
	ganister
AEGINRSW	swearing
AEGINRTT	treating
AEGINRTV	vintager
AEGINRTW	watering
AEGINRVW	wavering
AEGINRVY	vinegary
AEGINRWY	wearying
AEGINSST	giantess
AEGINSSY	essaying
AEGINSTU	sautéing
AEGINSTW	sweating
AEGIOPRR	progeria
AEGIORSV	viragoes
AEGIOSTX	geotaxis
AEGIPPRT	griptape
AEGIPRTY	pterygia
AEGIQRSU	squirage
AEGIRRTY	argyrite
AEGIRSTT	strigate
AEGJLTUU	jugulate
AEGKKKNO	angekkok
AEGKMNRU	gunmaker
AEGLLLMU	glumella
AEGLLLOR	l'allegro
AEGLLLSS	gall-less
AEGLLNOV	longeval
AEGLLNPS	langspel
AEGLLOPR	galloper
AEGLLORS	allegros
AEGLLORV	overgall
AEGLLORY	allegory
AEGLLOSS	goalless
AEGLLOST	log-slate
AEGLLOTT	toll-gate
AEGLLRVY	gravelly
AEGLLSSU	galluses
AEGLMNNO	mangonel
AEGLMNOW	leg-woman
AEGLMNTU	gunmetal
AEGLMOTV	megavolt
AEGLMSSU	gaumless
AEGLNNPT	plangent
AEGLNNTU	untangle
AEGLNOPT	gantlope
AEGLNORY	yearlong
AEGLNOST	tangelos
AEGLNOVW	long-wave
AEGLNPRS	spangler
	sprangle
AEGLNPSS	pangless
AEGLNPST	spanglet
AEGLNRRW	wrangler
AEGLNRST	strangle
AEGLNRSY	larynges
AEGLNRUY	gunlayer
AEGLNTTU	gauntlet
AEGLNTUU	ungulate
AEGLOOOZ	zoogloea
AEGLOOPU	apologue
AEGLOORY	aerology
AEGLOPRY	glory-pea
	play-goer
AEGLORSU	glareous
AEGLORTU	outglare
AEGLORTV	travelog
AEGLORTW	waterlog
AEGLORTY	geolatry
AEGLOSSW	galowses
AEGLOSUY	gealousy
AEGLPRSU	Spergula
AEGLPSSU	plussage
AEGLRSTU	gestural
AEGLRTUY	argutely
AEGLSTUU	glutaeus
AEGMMNOR	gammoner
AEGMMRRU	rummager
AEGMNNOT	magneton
AEGMNOOT	moon-gate
AEGMNORV	mangrove
AEGMNORY	rag-money
AEGMNOST	magnetos
AEGMNOXY	xenogamy
AEGMNRTU	argument
AEGMNSSY	gamyness
AEGMOPRW	gapeworm
AEGMORSS	gossamer
AEGMPSTU	stumpage
AEGNNOPT	△pentagon
AEGNNORT	negatron
AEGNNPRT	pregnant
AEGNNRTY	gannetry
AEGNOORS	oreganos
AEGNOPRR	parergon
AEGNORRY	orangery
AEGNORST	ragstone
	stonerag
AEGNORTT	tetragon
AEGNORTY	negatory
AEGNORUV	vargueño
AEGNOTUY	autogeny
AEGNPRYY	panegyry
AEGNRRST	stranger
AEGNRSTU	straunge
AEGNRSYY	asynergy
AEGNSSST	gastness
AEGOORSV	voragoes
AEGOOSWY	waygoose
AEGOPPST	stoppage
AEGOPPSU	suppeago
AEGOPRTU	portague
AEGOPSST	gestapos
AEGOPSSU	spousage
AEGOPSTT	gatepost
AEGORRRT	regrator
AEGORRTT	garotter
	garrotte
AEGORSTU	goat's-rue
AEGORTTU	tutorage
AEGORUVY	voyageur
AEGQRTUU	truquage
AEGRRSUV	verrugas
AEGRSTTY	strategy
AEHHHIST	shehitah
AEHHIKNS	Shekinah
AEHHIMTW	hamewith
AEHHIPSW	peishwah
AEHHISVY	yeshivah
AEHHLNTU	unhealth
AEHHNOPT	Phaethon
AEHHNRSW	hernshaw
AEHHORST	haroseth
AEHHRRST	thrasher
AEHIIKLR	hairlike
AEHIIKRT	terakihi
AEHIIKST	shiitake
AEHIILMO	hemiolia

Words marked △ may be spelled also with a capital letter

AEHIILNR hairline
AEHIIMNT thiamine
AEHIIMOP hemiopia
AEHIINNT ianthine
AEHIINTZ thiazine
AEHIIRRW wire-hair
AEHIISTV Shaivite
Shivaite
AEHIKKLW hawklike
AEHIKLLT lathlike
AEHIKLNP kephalin
AEHIKLTW what-like
AEHIKNSS sneakish
AEHILLNO nail-hole
AEHILLNT thalline
AEHILMNY hymenial
AEHILMOT halimote
AEHILMSW limewash
AEHILNOP aphelion
AEHILNRU inhauler
AEHILNTX anthelix
AEHILNTZ zenithal
AEHILOOZ Heliozoa
AEHILORT aerolith
AEHILRSS hairless
AEHILRSV shrieval
AEHILRTY heartily
AEHIMMNP Memphian
AEHIMNNU inhumane
AEHIMNRS shireman
AEHIMNSS shamisen
AEHIMNSU humanise
AEHIMNTU inhumate
AEHIMNUZ humanize
AEHIMPPT pita-hemp
AEHIMPRS samphire
seraphim
AEHIMPRT teraphim
AEHIMPRX xeraphim
AEHIMPSS emphasis
misshape
AEHIMPST mateship
shipmate
AEHIMSST mathesis
AEHINNTX xanthein
xanthine
AEHINOPU euphonia
AEHINORT anti-hero
AEHINPPY Epiphany
AEHINPRS parishen
seraphin
AEHINPRT perianth
AEHINPST △thespian
AEHINRSV enravish
vanisher
AEHINRSW sherwani
AEHINRTU haurient
AEHINRTW tarwhine
AEHINRTZ Hertzian
AEHINSST anthesis
AEHINSSZ haziness
AEHINSTT hesitant
AEHINSTW inswathe
AEHINTTT antithet
AEHIOPRS aphorise
AEHIOPRU euphoria
AEHIOPRZ aphorize
AEHIORRV overhair
AEHIORSU air-house
AEHIORTU thiourea
AEHIPPRS papisher
sapphire
AEHIPPST peatship
AEHIPRRT rathripe
AEHIPRTT threapit
AEHIPSTT Peshitta
AEHIPSWW washwipe
AEHIRRSV ravisher
AEHIRRSY Ayrshire
AEHIRSTU thesauri
AEHIRSTW waterish
AEHIRSTY hysteria
AEHISSSY essayish
AEHISSTU hiatuses
AEHISSVY yeshivas
AEHJNNOS johannes
AEHJPRSW Jews'-harp
Jew's-harp
AEHKLLRS ark-shell
AEHKMOPW mopehawk
AEHKNNSU unshaken
AEHKNSWW newshawk
AEHKOSTU shake-out
AEHLLLTY lethally
AEHLLMOP lamphole
AEHLLNRT enthrall
AEHLMMNS helmsman
AEHLMMPP hemp-palm
AEHLMNOT methanol
AEHLMNSW Welshman
AEHLMNUY humanely
AEHLMPPT pamphlet
AEHLMRSS harmless
AEHLNPRS shrapnel
AEHLNPTY enthalpy
AEHLNRTU Lutheran
AEHLNSST nathless
AEHLNSTY naythles
AEHLNTUZ hazelnut
AEHLOPRT plethora
AEHLORSY hoarsely
AEHLORUV overhaul
AEHLPPRT thrapple
AEHLPRSS splasher
AEHLPSST pathless
AEHLPSTU sulphate
AEHLRRTU urethral
AEHLSSTW thawless
AEHLSTTY stealthy
AEHMMRRU Muharrem
AEHMNNPY nymphean
AEHMNOPR morphean
AEHMNORS horseman
shoreman
AEHMNOSU houseman
AEHMNPRU prehuman
AEHMOPRT metaphor
AEHMORST Masoreth
AEHMOSTT hemostat
AEHMOSTW somewhat
AEHMPRST hampster
AEHMRRTY rat-rhyme
AEHMSSSU shamuses
AEHMSTTY amethyst
AEHMSUZZ mezuzahs
AEHNNOPT Pantheon
AEHNNOTY honey-ant
AEHNNPRU △nenuphar
AEHNNPSU unshapen
AEHNNSUV unshaven
AEHNNSUW unwashen
AEHNOOPT hanepoot
AEHNOPPY pay-phone
AEHNOPRS Orpheans
AEHNOPRT hapteron
AEHNOPST stanhope
AEHNOPTY Typhoean
AEHNOPXY xenophya
AEHNOQTU haqueton
AEHNORST Sheraton
AEHNOSTV have-nots
AEHNPRTY hen-party
AEHNRSSS rashness
AEHNRTTU earth-nut
AEHNSSTT thatness
AEHNSSTU shea-nuts
AEHNSSTW whatness
AEHNSTUW unswathe
AEHOPPRS prophase
AEHOPRST potshare
AEHOPSST pot-ashes
spathose
AEHOPSTT heatspot
AEHOPSTU tap-house
AEHOPTVY top-heavy
AEHOQRUU huaquero
AEHORRSS rose-rash
AEHORRSV overrash
AEHORRSW warhorse
AEHORRTT heart-rot
AEHORSSW sawhorse
AEHORSTT rheostat
AEHORSTU art-house
share-out
AEHORSTX thoraxes
AEHORSVW overwash
AEHORSWY horseway
AEHOSTUX house-tax
AEHPPRSU pear-push
AEHPRSST sharp-set
AEHPRSUX haruspex
AEHPRSUY euphrasy
AEHQRSSU squasher
AEHRRSTU urethras
AEHRRSTY trashery
AEHRRTTW thwarter

AEHRSTTY	shattery
AEIIINTT	initiate
AEIIKLLT	tail-like
AEIIKLNS	Sikelian
AEIIKLNT	kalinite
AEIIKNRS	kaiserin
AEIIKNSS	akinesis
AEIIKRTY	teriyaki
AEIILLMR	milliare
	Ramillie
AEIILLRV	live-rail
AEIILLTV	illative
AEIILMNN	mainline
AEIILMNS	alienism
	Milesian
AEIILMPR	imperial
AEIILMRS	Ramilies
AEIILMSS	Islamise
AEIILMST	Islamite
AEIILMSZ	Islamize
AEIILMTT	militate
AEIILNPR	plein-air
AEIILNQU	aquiline
AEIILNRR	airliner
AEIILNRT	inertial
AEIILNST	alienist
	Latinise
AEIILNSW	Lewisian
AEIILNTZ	Latinize
AEIILOTT	Italiote
AEIILPPT	tailpipe
AEIILPRT	liparite
	Reptilia
AEIILRST	listeria
AEIILRSV	rivalise
AEIILRTT	literati
AEIILRVZ	rivalize
AEIILSTV	vitalise
AEIILTVZ	vitalize
AEIIMMRT	maritime
AEIIMMSX	maximise
AEIIMMXZ	maximize
AEIIMNSZ	△simazine
AEIIMNTT	intimate
AEIIMNTU	minutiae
AEIIMNTV	vitamine
AEIIMOSS	ameiosis
AEIIMPRR	impairer
AEIIMRST	seriatim
AEIIMSSX	semi-axis
AEIINNRS	sirenian
AEIINNRT	Neritina
AEIINNTV	innative
AEIINPST	pianiste
AEIINRRV	riverain
AEIINRSS	airiness
AEIINRSY	yersinia
AEIINRTZ	Nazirite
AEIINSST	sanitise
	teniasis
AEIINSTZ	sanitize
AEIINSVV	invasive
AEIINTTT	titanite
AEIINTTU	uintaite
AEIIPRSW	pairwise
AEIIPRZZ	pizzeria
AEIIPSST	epitasis
AEIIRRTT	irritate
AEIIRSST	satirise
AEIIRSTW	wisteria
AEIIRSTZ	satirize
AEIIRTTT	tritiate
AEIIRTVZ	vizirate
AEIISTVZ	izvestia
AEIITTTV	titivate
AEIITTVV	vitative
AEIJLOSU	jalousie
AEIJORST	jarosite
AEIKKLLW	likewalk
AEIKKLPR	parklike
AEIKKMNO	kakiemon
AEIKKMRT	Kitemark
	kite-mark
AEIKLNNP	pannikel
AEIKLNOS	snake-oil
AEIKLNRS	near-silk
AEIKLNSS	sealskin
AEIKLNSW	swanlike
AEIKLNSY	sneakily
AEIKLPRT	traplike
AEIKLRST	starlike
AEIKLRTW	wartlike
AEIKLRVY	Valkyrie
AEIKLRWY	Walkyrie
AEIKLSSS	saikless
AEIKMNPR	pin-maker
AEIKMNST	mistaken
AEIKMPSS	misspeak
AEIKNPST	snake-pit
AEIKNRTW	knitwear
AEIKNSTV	kistvaen
AEIKPRSS	apres-ski
	après-ski
AEIKRSST	asterisk
AEIKRSTW	water-ski
AEILLLNY	lineally
AEILLMSY	mesially
AEILLNNO	lanoline
AEILLNNS	nainsell
AEILLNNU	uilleann
	unlineal
AEILLNOP	Apolline
AEILLNOR	allerion
AEILLNPS	splenial
AEILLNQU	quinella
AEILLNRY	linearly
AEILLNSS	nailless
	sensilla
AEILLNSW	Wellsian
AEILLNVY	venially
AEILLOTV	volatile
AEILLOVZ	Vellozia
AEILLPPR	apperill
AEILLPST	pastille
AEILLPSV	lip-salve
AEILLQTU	tequilla
AEILLRRY	raillery
AEILLRSS	railless
AEILLRSY	serially
AEILLRTT	ill-treat
AEILLRTU	tailleur
AEILLSSS	sailless
AEILLSST	tailless
AEILLSUV	allusive
AEILLSYZ	sleazily
AEILLTUZ	lazulite
AEILMMNS	melanism
AEILMMNU	Immanuel
AEILMMNY	immanely
AEILMMOR	memorial
AEILMMOT	immolate
AEILMMRT	trilemma
AEILMMSS	melismas
AEILMNNO	minneola
AEILMNNP	impannel
AEILMNNS	linesman
AEILMNOS	laminose
	semolina
AEILMNPR	Palmerin
AEILMNPW	palm-wine
AEILMNRT	terminal
	tramline
AEILMNRU	lemurian
AEILMNSS	islesman
AEILMNST	salt-mine
AEILMOPR	proemial
AEILMOPS	semi-opal
AEILMORS	moralise
AEILMORZ	moralize
AEILMPRV	primeval
AEILMPSS	pessimal
AEILMPST	petalism
	septimal
AEILMPTY	playtime
AEILMRSY	smearily
AEILMRTT	remittal
AEILMRUV	velarium
AEILMSTT	metalist
	smaltite
AEILMSTU	simulate
AEILMSTY	steamily
AEILMTTU	mutilate
	ultimate
AEILNNOS	solanine
AEILNNOT	Neo-Latin
AEILNNRT	internal
AEILNNSY	insanely
AEILNNTY	innately
AEILNOPT	Antilope
	antipole
AEILNOPU	poulaine
AEILNORT	△oriental
	relation
	taileron
AEILNORV	overlain
AEILNOST	insolate

Words marked △ may be spelled also with a capital letter

AEILNOTT	tonalite
AEILNOTV	Olivetan
AEILNPPT	pie-plant
AEILNPRS	pearlins
AEILNPRT	triplane
AEILNPSS	painless
AEILNPTT	tinplate
AEILNRSS	rainless
AEILNRST	entrails
AEILNRSY	snailery
AEILNRTT	rattline
	trail-net
AEILNRTU	retinula
	tenurial
AEILNRTV	interval
AEILNRTY	interlay
AEILNSST	eastlins
AEILNSSZ	laziness
AEILNSTT	Intelsat
AEILNSTU	insulate
AEILNSUY	uneasily
AEILNTTU	Lutetian
AEILNTVY	natively
	venality
AEILNUVV	univalve
AEILOORV	ovariole
AEILOPPR	oil-paper
AEILOPPT	oppilate
AEILOPRS	polarise
AEILOPRT	epilator
	petiolar
	tail-rope
AEILOPRZ	polarize
AEILOPST	spoliate
AEILORSS	solarise
AEILORST	soterial
AEILORSV	oversail
	valorise
AEILORSY	royalise
AEILORSZ	solarize
AEILORTT	literato
AEILORTV	violater
AEILORVZ	valorize
AEILORYZ	royalize
AEILOSTT	totalise
AEILOTTV	volitate
AEILOTTZ	totalize
AEILPPQU	appliqué
AEILPPTU	pupilate
AEILPRRS	reprisal
AEILPRST	pilaster
	plaister
AEILPRSW	slipware
AEILPRXY	pyrexial
AEILPSTY	ptyalise
AEILPSUV	plausive
AEILPTYZ	ptyalize
AEILQRSU	squailer
AEILQRTU	quartile
	requital
AEILQSUY	queasily
AEILQTUY	equality
AEILRRSU	ruralise
AEILRRTY	literary
AEILRRUZ	ruralize
AEILRSST	saltiers
	slaister
AEILRSSV	rivaless
AEILRSWY	lyra-wise
AEILRTTY	alterity
AEILRTUZ	lazurite
AEILRTVV	trivalve
AEILRTXZ	zelatrix
AEIMMMRZ	mamzerim
AEIMMNNT	immanent
AEIMMNOT	ammonite
AEIMMPST	psammite
AEIMMRTU	immature
AEIMNNOT	nominate
AEIMNNRS	reinsman
AEIMNOPP	Pompeian
AEIMNOPT	ptomaine
AEIMNORS	Romanise
AEIMNORT	Maronite
AEIMNORZ	armozine
	Romanize
AEIMNOST	somniate
AEIMNOSW	womanise
AEIMNOTZ	monazite
AEIMNOWZ	womanize
AEIMNPRT	tripeman
AEIMNPRZ	prizeman
AEIMNQRU	ramequin
AEIMNRRV	riverman
AEIMNRSU	aneurism
	Sumerian
AEIMNRSY	seminary
AEIMNRTT	martinet
AEIMNRTU	ruminate
AEIMNRTW	wariment
AEIMNRTY	tyramine
AEIMNSST	matiness
AEIMNSSZ	maziness
AEIMNTTU	matutine
AEIMNTVZ	vizament
AEIMOPTT	optimate
AEIMORST	amortise
	atomiser
AEIMORTT	amoretti
AEIMORTZ	amortize
	atomizer
AEIMOTTT	Ottamite
AEIMOTTV	motivate
AEIMPRRT	imparter
AEIMPRST	apterism
	Primates
AEIMPRTT	part-time
AEIMPRTU	apterium
AEIMQRSU	marquise
AEIMQSUU	Esquimau
AEIMRSST	asterism
AEIMRSSY	emissary
AEIMRSTT	mistreat
	teratism
AEIMRSTU	semitaur
AEIMRSTX	matrixes
AEIMRSTY	symitare
AEIMRSWW	swimwear
AEIMSSTT	misstate
AEIMSSTZ	mestizas
AEIMTTUV	mutative
AEINNNOR	Neronian
AEINNNOS	Senonian
AEINNNOX	annexion
AEINNOPV	pavonine
AEINNORS	raisonné
AEINNORT	anointer
	inornate
AEINNOST	Estonian
AEINNOTT	intonate
AEINNOTV	innovate
	venation
AEINNRRT	inerrant
AEINNRSU	unarisen
AEINNSSV	vainness
AEINNSSZ	zaniness
AEINNSTT	stannite
AEINNSUV	Venusian
AEINNTUV	unnative
	Venutian
AEINOPPT	antipope
AEINOPRT	atropine
AEINOPST	saponite
AEINOPTZ	topazine
AEINOQTU	equation
AEINORRT	anterior
AEINORRW	ironware
AEINORSS	sensoria
AEINORST	arsonite
	notarise
	rosinate
	Señorita
AEINORSV	aversion
AEINORTV	Orvietan
AEINORTZ	notarize
AEINOSST	assiento
AEINOSSX	Saxonise
AEINOSTV	stovaine
AEINOSTX	saxonite
AEINOSXZ	Saxonize
AEINOTTZ	Zantiote
AEINOTVX	vexation
AEINPPPS	Pan-pipes
AEINPPSY	Pepysian
AEINPPTX	Xantippe
AEINPPTZ	Zantippe
AEINPRRT	terrapin
AEINPRRU	unrepair
AEINPRST	pinaster
	pristane
AEINPRSU	unpraise
AEINPRTT	triptane
AEINPRTU	painture
AEINPRTX	expirant
AEINPRUV	Peruvian
AEINPSST	steapsin

AEINPSTU	supinate
AEINPSTY	epinasty
AEINPTTY	antitype
AEINQSTU	quantise
AEINQTTU	equitant
AEINQTUZ	quantize
AEINRRST	restrain
	strainer
	trainers
	transire
AEINRRTU	Etrurian
AEINRRTV	veratrin
AEINRRTW	interwar
AEINRSST	artiness
AEINRSSU	senarius
AEINRSSW	wariness
AEINRSSX	xeransis
AEINRSTT	straiten
AEINRSUZ	suzerain
AEINRTTU	tainture
AEINSSST	saintess
AEINSSTT	△titaness
AEINSSVW	waviness
AEINSSWX	waxiness
AEINSTTV	tastevin
AEINSTUV	suivante
AEINSUVV	△vesuvian
AEINTTUU	autunite
AEIOPPST	apposite
AEIOPRRT	priorate
AEIOPRRW	air-power
AEIOPRST	Isoptera
AEIOPRSV	vaporise
AEIOPRTX	expiator
AEIOPRVZ	vaporize
AEIOPTTV	optative
AEIORRRS	arrieros
AEIORTTV	rotative
AEIPPRRS	appriser
AEIPPRRZ	apprizer
AEIPQRTU	pratique
AEIPRSST	Tarsipes
AEIPRSTV	privates
AEIPRSTY	asperity
AEIPRSVY	vespiary
AEIPTTUV	putative
AEIQRRRU	quarrier
AEIQRRTU	quartier
AEIRRRTV	river-rat
AEIRRSSY	siserary
AEIRRTTT	retraitt
AEIRRTTY	△tertiary
AEIRRVWY	riverway
AEIRSSTW	waitress
AEIRSTVY	vestiary
AEIRSWWY	waywiser
AEIRTTTW	atwitter
AEISSSTY	essayist
AEJLLNPY	jelly-pan
AEJLOSUY	jealousy
AEJLOSUZ	azulejos
AEJMPSTU	jump-seat
AEJNORSZ	zanjeros
AEKKLLWY	lykewalk
AEKKMNOO	kakemono
AEKLMNOS	monk-seal
AEKLMRUW	lukewarm
AEKLMRUY	yarmulke
AEKLNNSS	lankness
AEKLNORW	walker-on
AEKLNOSY	ankylose
AEKLOPRW	rope-walk
AEKLOPTY	kalotype
AEKLORTV	overtalk
AEKLORVW	walk-over
AEKLOSST	stalkoes
AEKLPRRS	sparkler
AEKLPRST	sparklet
AEKLQRUY	Quakerly
AEKMNRSU	unmasker
AEKMOPRT	topmaker
AEKMORTW	teamwork
	workmate
AEKMPRRV	verkramp
AEKMPRTU	up-market
AEKNNRSS	rankness
AEKNORRV	overrank
AEKNORUY	eukaryon
AEKNOTTU	outtaken
AEKOPSTU	outspeak
	speakout
AEKORRWW	workwear
AEKORSTV	overtask
AEKORTUY	eukaryot
AEKOSTTU	stake-out
AEKQRSUW	squawker
AEKRRSST	starkers
AELLLRTU	tellural
AELLLSSW	wall-less
AELLLSUV	vulsella
AELLMNOZ	manzello
AELLMNTY	mentally
AELLMORR	moraller
AELLMORT	martello
AELLMOTY	tomalley
AELLMPUU	plumulae
AELLMRSY	mersalyl
AELLNOPV	volplane
AELLNORS	llaneros
AELLNOSV	novellas
AELLNOWW	enwallow
AELLNPRU	△prunella
AELLNPSS	planless
AELLNPTT	plantlet
AELLNPTU	plantule
AELLNRUY	neurally
	unreally
AELLNRVY	vernally
AELLNSST	tallness
AELLNTTY	latently
AELLNTUU	lunulate
AELLOPRS	reposall
AELLOPRW	walloper
AELLOPRY	role-play
AELLORSV	overalls
AELLORTY	alley-tor
AELLORWW	wallower
AELLOSUV	alveolus
AELLPSWW	spaw-well
AELLQRSU	squaller
AELLRRTY	retrally
AELLRTTY	latterly
AELLRTVY	trevally
AELLRWYY	lawyerly
AELLSSST	saltless
AELLSSTY	tasselly
AELLSUXY	sexually
AELMMORW	mealworm
AELMMRST	strammel
	trammels
AELMNNOT	non-metal
AELMNNOU	noumenal
AELMNNRY	mannerly
AELMNNTU	unmantle
AELMNOPS	neoplasm
	pleonasm
AELMNOST	salmonet
AELMNOSU	melanous
AELMNOYY	yeomanly
AELMNRSU	mensural
	numerals
AELMOOPT	omoplate
AELMOORS	saleroom
AELMOPRR	premolar
AELMOPRT	prometal
	temporal
AELMOPSX	exoplasm
AELMOPSY	playsome
AELMOPTT	metaplot
	palmetto
AELMORSU	ramulose
AELMORTU	emulator
AELMOSSS	molasses
AELMOSTY	atmolyse
AELMOTVZ	mazeltov
AELMOTYZ	atmolyze
AELMPRRT	trampler
AELMPRSY	lampreys
	samplery
AELMPSUX	amplexus
AELMQSUU	squamule
AELMRSTT	maltster
AELMRSTY	masterly
AELMRTUY	maturely
AELMSSST	mastless
AELNNNPU	unpannel
AELNNOOP	△napoleon
AELNNOOX	naloxone
AELNNOPP	open-plan
AELNNORU	neuronal
AELNNOSU	annulose
AELNNRTU	unlearnt
AELNOOTZ	entozoal
AELNOPRS	personal
	psoralen

AELNOPST lapstone
pleonast
AELNOPTW tow-plane
AELNORTT tetronal
tolerant
AELNORTU outlearn
AELNORTY ornately
Tyrolean
AELNPPSY spyplane
AELNPRSU purslane
supernal
AELNPRTY plenarty
AELNPSSS spanless
AELNPSSU spansule
AELNPTTU petulant
AELNPTTY patently
AELNRRTY errantly
AELNRRUV nervular
AELNRSTT slattern
AELNRSVY △sylvaner
AELNRSXY larynxes
AELNRTTW trawl-net
AELNRUWY unwarely
AELNSSST saltness
AELNSUUX unsexual
AELNTTUX exultant
AELOOPPT tape-loop
AELOOPRZ zooperal
AELOORTW Waterloo
AELOORTZ zoolater
AELOPPRS prolapse
sapropel
AELOPPSU papulose
AELOPPTU populate
AELOPPXY apoplexy
AELOPQUY opaquely
AELOPRRV reproval
AELOPRST petrosal
AELOPRSU leaprous
AELOPRVY overplay
AELOPSSS soapless
AELOPSSU espousal
sepalous
AELOPSTU petalous
AELORSTU rosulate
AELORSUU rouleaus
AELORTTV varletto
AELORTYZ zealotry
AELORUUX rouleaux
AELOSSTY asystole
AELOSTTW wastelot
AELOSTUY autolyse
AELOTUUV outvalue
AELOTUYZ autolyze
AELPRRSW sprawler
AELPRRTT prattler
AELPRSSY sparsely
AELPRSTT splatter
sprattle
AELPRSTU aplustre
AELPRSTY plastery
△psaltery

AELPSSSS passless
AELQRSUY squarely
AELQSTTU squattle
AELRRSTT startler
AELRRTVY varletry
AELRSSST starless
AELRSSTW wartless
AELRSTTU lustrate
AELRSTTY slattery
AELRSTUV vestural
AELRSUVY surveyal
AELRTTTW twattler
AELRTTUX textural
AELRTTUY tutelary
AELSSSTU saltuses
AELSSSTY stayless
AELSTTUY astutely
AEMMMOTU ommateum
AEMMMRTY mammetry
AEMMNNOY moneyman
AEMMNRRY merryman
AEMMNRTU ramentum
AEMMOORT room-mate
AEMMORST marmoset
AEMMRTUY maumetry
AEMMRTWY mawmetry
AEMNNOPW penwoman
AEMNNORS Norseman
AEMNNORT ornament
AEMNOORR marooner
AEMNOORT anteroom
AEMNOORY aeronomy
AEMNOOTZ metazoon
AEMNOPRS proseman
prose-man
AEMNOPRT empatron
AEMNOPRW manpower
AEMNORRS ransomer
AEMNORST monstera
on-stream
storeman
AEMNORSU neuromas
AEMNORSV oversman
AEMNORTU routeman
AEMNORTY monetary
AEMNORYY yeomanry
AEMNOSTU seamount
AEMNPRSS pressman
AEMNPRSU superman
AEMNPSST passment
AEMNRRUY numerary
AEMNRSSW warmness
AEMNRSTU anestrum
menstrua
transume
AEMNRSTW transmew
trewsman
AEMNRSUY aneurysm
AEMOOPRT peat-moor
AEMOOPST pomatoes
AEMOORTT amoretto
AEMOOSST maestoso

AEMOOSTT tomatoes
AEMOOSTU autosome
AEMOOTTY tomatoey
AEMOPPRS pamperos
AEMOPPRW power-amp
AEMOPRTW pomwater
tapeworm
AEMOPSST peat-moss
AEMOQSSU squamose
AEMORRRU armourer
AEMORRST rearmost
AEMORRSY rosemary
AEMORRTU Euromart
AEMORSST maestros
AEMORSSY mayoress
AEMORSTV overmast
AEMORTTU tautomer
AEMOSSTT eastmost
AEMOSSWY someways
AEMOTTZZ mozzetta
AEMPRRSY spermary
AEMPRSTU upstream
AEMQRSSU marquess
AEMRRTUV veratrum
AEMRSSTT mattress
AEMRSTTU testamur
AEMRTUUX trumeaux
AEMSTTTU testatum
AENNNTTU untenant
AENNOPRT patronne
AENNOPST pentosan
AENNOPUW unweapon
AENNORST norteñas
resonant
AENNORSU unreason
AENNORVY novenary
AENNORWY Norweyan
AENNOSSU unseason
AENNOSTU tonneaus
AENNOTUX tonneaux
AENNRSWY swannery
AENNRTTY tenantry
AENOOPST teaspoon
AENOORRT ratooner
AENOPRRY rope-yarn
AENOPRSS personas
Responsa
AENOPRTT patentor
AENOPRWY weaponry
AENOPSTT ante-post
AENORRST antrorse
AENORSST assentor
AENORSTW stoneraw
AENORSUV ravenous
AENORTTX tetraxon
AENORTTY attorney
AENOSSTW saw-tones
AENOSSTZ stanzoes
AENOSSUU nauseous
AENPRRST partners
AENPRSTT transept
AENPRSTU persaunt

AENPRSTY	Strepyan
AENPSSSY	synapses
AENPSSTW	waspnest
AENPSSTZ	△spetsnaz
AENPSTZZ	△spetznaz
AENQRRTU	quartern
AENQSTTU	questant
AENRRRTY	errantry
AENRRSSU	Serranus
AENRSSTT	tartness
AENRSSTU	anestrus
AENRSSTV	servants
AENRSTWY	sternway
AENRTUVY	vauntery
AENRTUWY	unwatery
AENSSSTV	vastness
AENSSSTW	wastness
AENSSTTU	tautness
AEOOPPPS	pappoose
AEOOPRRT	operator
AEOOPSTT	potatoes
AEOORRST	sororate
AEOORTTT	tattooer
AEOORTTV	rotovate
AEOPPRRV	approver
AEOPPSUY	pea-soupy
AEOPQRTU	paroquet
AEOPRRRT	parroter
AEOPRRST	Raptores
AEOPRRTV	overpart
AEOPRRUV	vapourer
AEOPRRVW	wrapover
AEOPRSST	espartos
	protases
AEOPRSSU	asperous
AEOPRSSV	overpass
	Passover
AEOPRSTT	prostate
AEOPRSTU	apterous
AEOPRSTV	overpast
AEOPRTWX	waterpox
AEOPTTUY	autotype
AEOQRSTU	quaestor
AEOQRSUV	vaqueros
AEOQRTTU	torquate
AEOQRTUZ	quatorze
AEORRRST	arrestor
AEORRSST	assertor
	assorter
	oratress
AEORRSTT	rostrate
AEORRTUV	avoutrer
AEORRTZZ	terrazzo
AEORSSSS	assessor
AEORSSTT	stratose
AEORSSTV	votaress
AEORSTTT	attestor
	testator
AEORSTTU	outstare
	rout-seat
AEORSTUW	outswear
AEORSTVY	overstay
AEORSUVW	waverous
AEORSVWY	oversway
AEORTUWY	outweary
AEORTVXY	vexatory
AEPPRRST	strapper
AEPRSSST	trespass
AEPRSTTU	stuprate
AEPRSTTY	tapestry
AEPRSTUX	supertax
AEPRTUVY	pyruvate
AEQRRSTU	quarters
AEQRSTTU	squatter
AEQRTTTU	quartett
AERRSSTT	starters
AERRSSTU	serratus
AERRSTUY	△treasury
AERRSTWY	rye-straw
AERSSSTY	satyress
AERSTTVY	travesty
AERTTUXY	textuary
AESSSTTU	statuses
AFFFFGGI	giff-gaff
AFFFFINN	niffnaff
AFFFFIRR	riff-raff
AFFGHIRT	affright
AFFGIIRT	graffiti
AFFGILMN	maffling
AFFGILNW	waffling
AFFGIMRS	misgraff
AFFGIORT	graffito
AFFGLNRU	far-flung
AFFHILST	flatfish
AFFHILTU	△faithful
AFFHIMRS	fish-farm
AFFHKOST	off-shakt
AFFHORRT	far-forth
AFFIINTY	affinity
AFFILLMM	flim-flam
AFFILLPP	flip-flap
AFFILNOW	Wolffian
AFFILSUX	suffixal
AFFINORR	forfairn
AFFINOSU	affusion
AFFIPSTT	tipstaff
AFFLLOOT	footfall
AFFLLTUU	faultful
AFFLOOOT	foalfoot
AFFLOOTT	flat-foot
AFFLORTU	forfault
AFFLRRUU	furfural
AFFNORSY	saffrony
AFFNRRUU	furfuran
AFGGGILN	flagging
AFGGGINR	fragging
AFGGINOT	fagoting
AFGGINRT	grafting
AFGHILLN	halfling
AFGHILNS	flashing
AFGHILNT	fanlight
AFGHILPS	flagship
AFGHINRT	farthing
AFGHINRW	wharfing
AFGHINST	shafting
AFGHIOST	goatfish
AFGHLLUU	laughful
AFGHLNSU	flashgun
AFGHLSTU	ghastful
AFGIINNT	fainting
AFGIKORT	koftgari
AFGILLNT	flatling
AFGILMNO	flamingo
AFGILNOS	sol-faing
AFGILNOT	floating
AFGILNPP	flapping
AFGILNTT	flatting
AFGILORW	gairfowl
AFGILSSY	glassify
AFGIMNTU	fumigant
AFGIMORS	gasiform
AFGIMRST	misgraft
AFGINNNS	fannings
AFGINPPR	frapping
AFGINRTU	figurant
AFGINSUY	sanguify
AFGIPRTW	gift-wrap
AFGLLNOT	flatlong
AFGLLNPU	pang-full
AFGLLRUU	fulgural
AFGLLRUY	frugally
AFGLLSSU	glassful
AFGLLSTU	gastfull
AFGLMORW	flag-worm
AFGLNNOO	gonfalon
AFGLNORU	groanful
AFGLNOUW	wagonful
AFGNNNOO	gonfanon
AFGOORTZ	zoograft
AFGORTUW	tug-of-war
AFHHIKSW	fish-hawk
AFHHLORU	half-hour
AFHIILRS	frailish
AFHIILSS	sailfish
AFHIILST	fish-tail
AFHIIMST	misfaith
AFHIINST	faintish
AFHIKLPS	hip-flask
AFHIKNRS	Frankish
AFHILLNS	halflins
AFHILLSW	wallfish
AFHILLSY	flashily
AFHILNPT	half-pint
AFHILNTT	half-tint
AFHILSST	saltfish
AFHILSTT	flattish
AFHIMNST	manshift
AFHINOSS	fashions
AFHINSTU	tuna-fish
AFHIOSSU	fashious
AFHIRSST	starfish
AFHKLNTU	thankful
AFHKMOOR	hoof-mark
AFHKORSX	foxshark
AFHLLOTU	loathful
AFHLMNOO	half-moon

AFHLOSTU outflash
AFHLRTUW wrathful
AFHNOOST fantoosh
AFHOOPTT footpath
AFIIILNP Filipina
AFIIKMRS fakirism
AFIILLLY filially
AFIILLNU unfilial
AFIILMMS △familism
AFIILMNS finalism
AFIILMST Familist
AFIILNRU unifilar
AFIILNST finalist
AFIILNTY finality
AFIIMRSY fairyism
AFIINNOS sainfoin
sinfonia
AFIINOTX fixation
AFIINSTW Swiftian
AFIIORRT triforia
AFIJMNOR Janiform
AFIKLLMO milk-loaf
AFIKLNNR franklin
AFIKLORT forktail
AFIKRSTY karstify
AFILLLMX flax-mill
AFILLLOT flotilla
AFILLLSU full-sail
AFILLLXY flax-lily
AFILLNPU plainful
AFILLTUY faultily
AFILMNOR formalin
informal
AFILMOPR paliform
AFILMOSS sol-faism
AFILNORT flatiron
inflator
AFILNPPT flippant
AFILNRUY unfairly
AFILNSTU inflatus
AFILORTY filatory
AFILOSST sol-faist
AFILRSTU fistular
AFILSSTU fistulas
AFILSTTU flautist
AFIMMNOR maniform
AFIMMORR ramiform
AFIMNOPR napiform
AFIMNORR raniform
AFIMNORT natiform
AFIMNOSU infamous
AFIMNTUU Funtumia
AFIMORRU auriform
AFIMORRV variform
AFIMORSV vasiform
AFINNOTU fountain
AFINNRTY infantry
AFINOPSY saponify
AFINQTUY quantify
AFINRSTX transfix
AFINRSUX Fraxinus
AFIORSTZ sforzati

AFIRSTTY stratify
AFJKNUZZ jazz-funk
AFJMNORU Januform
AFKLLMOS alms-folk
AFKLNOTU outflank
AFKLNPRU prankful
AFKLNSTU tankfuls
AFKMOORT footmark
AFLLLORY florally
AFLLLUWY lawfully
AFLLMNUY manfully
AFLLMORY formally
AFLLNOSW snowfall
AFLLNUUW unlawful
AFLLORSU all-fours
AFLLRTUY artfully
AFLLSTUW wastfull
AFLMNORU unformal
AFLMOPRT platform
AFLMORRU formular
AFLMORSU formulas
AFLMORTU foulmart
AFLMORTW flatworm
AFLMOSUY famously
AFLNOPRU apronful
AFLNRTUU unartful
AFLNTUUV vauntful
AFLNTUUY unfaulty
AFLOOSTT salt-foot
AFLOSTUU flatuous
AFLPRSYY fly-spray
AFLRSTTU startful
AFLRSTUY trayfuls
AFMNNORT frontman
AFMNORTU farm-toun
AFMOOPRR proforma
pro-forma
AFMORTUY fumatory
AFMOSSTU sfumatos
AFOOPRRT ratproof
AFOOPRRW war-proof
AFOOPSST soft-soap
AFOORSTT root-fast
AFOORSTZ sforzato
AFOPRRTT raft-port
AFOPRRTU four-part
AFORSTTW forswatt
AFOSSTUU fastuous
AFPPPTUY puppy-fat
AGGGGILN gaggling
AGGGHINS shagging
AGGGILNN gangling
AGGGILNS slagging
AGGGINNS snagging
AGGGINSW swagging
AGGGIYZZ zigzaggy
AGGHHINT night-hag
AGGHILNT Lagthing
AGGHILNU laughing
AGGHILST gaslight
AGGHILSY shaggily
AGGHINNS hangings

AGGHISTT gas-tight
AGGHJMNO mah-jongg
AGGHLOOT Golgotha
AGGHMOSS moss-hagg
AGGHOOTT gag-tooth
AGGIILNS silaging
AGGIILNV gingival
AGGIINNR graining
AGGIINNS gainings
AGGIJLNN jangling
AGGILMNO gloaming
AGGILMPS gig-lamps
AGGILNNO ganglion
AGGILNNS slanging
AGGILNNT gnatling
tangling
AGGILNNW wangling
AGGILNOT goatling
AGGILNPY gapingly
AGGILNRY grayling
ragingly
AGGINNOR groaning
AGGINNOT tangoing
AGGINNTW twanging
AGGINOOR Gorgonia
AGGINOWY way-going
AGGINPRS grasping
AGGINRSS grassing
AGGINRSU sugaring
AGGIRTUZ ziggurat
AGGKLNNU angklung
AGGLLLOY lollygag
AGGLLOOY algology
AGGLLOSS log-glass
AGGLMOOR logogram
AGGLOORY agrology
AGGLRSTY straggly
AGGNUWZZ zugzwang
AGHHIILT hightail
AGHHLOTU although
AGHIIPRR hairgrip
AGHIIRTT airtight
AGHIJNRT nightjar
AGHIKLRU Gurkhali
AGHIKNNT thanking
AGHIKNRS sharking
AGHILLNT allnight
all-thing
AGHILLRT all-right
AGHILMTY △almighty
AGHILNOO hooligan
AGHILNOR long-hair
AGHILNOS shoaling
AGHILNOT loathing
AGHILNPS plashing
AGHILNRS ringhals
AGHILNRY narghily
AGHILNSS lashings
slangish
slashing
AGHILNSU languish
AGHILNSW shawling

AGHILRSY	garishly
AGHILRTY	graithly
AGHILSUY	aguishly
AGHIMMNS	shamming
AGHIMMNW	whamming
AGHIMNNT	night-man
AGHIMNSS	smashing
AGHIMNTY	thingamy
AGHIMPRU	graphium
AGHINNTU	haunting
AGHINNTY	anything
AGHINPPW	whapping
AGHINPRS	harpings
	phrasing
	sharping
AGHINPRY	Phrygian
AGHINRRY	harrying
AGHINSST	hastings
AGHINSSW	swashing
	washings
AGHINUZZ	huzzaing
AGHIPRRT	trigraph
AGHIPSSW	pig's-wash
AGHIRSTT	straight
AGHIRUUW	Wahiguru
AGHLLMPU	gallumph
AGHLLNOU	long-haul
AGHLMOOR	hologram
AGHLNOSU	shogunal
AGHLNSUY	nylghaus
AGHMMOOY	homogamy
AGHMNPSU	sphagnum
AGHMOOPY	omophagy
AGHMOOTT	goat-moth
AGHMOPRY	myograph
AGHNNRUY	an-hungry
AGHNNSTU	shantung
AGHNOORS	shagroon
AGHNPRSY	syngraph
AGHNTTUU	untaught
AGHOOPYZ	zoophagy
AGHOPSSW	swagshop
AGHRSTTU	straught
AGIIINNS	insignia
AGIIINRV	Virginia
AGIIILLOV	villagio
	villiago
AGIILLTT	gilt-tail
AGIILMNS	misalign
AGIILNNP	plaining
AGIILNNU	inguinal
AGIILNNY	inlaying
AGIILNOR	original
AGIILNOT	intaglio
	ligation
	taglioni
AGIILNOX	△gloxinia
AGIILNPT	plaiting
AGIILNQU	quailing
AGIILNRS	railings
AGIILNRT	ringtail
	ring-tail
	trailing
AGIILNRV	virginal
AGIILNST	tailings
AGIILNTT	litigant
AGIILNTV	vigilant
AGIILORU	oliguria
AGIILOSV	viliagos
AGIILTVY	vagility
AGIIMNSS	amissing
AGIIMNST	giantism
AGIIMNTT	mitigant
AGIINNPT	painting
AGIINNRT	training
AGIINNST	staining
AGIINNSW	swaining
AGIINORS	signoria
AGIINORT	rigatoni
AGIINPRS	aspiring
	praising
AGIINRTT	attiring
AGIINRTY	Trigynia
AGIISSTV	visagist
AGIJNNTT	tjanting
AGIJNNTU	jaunting
AGIKKNNS	skanking
AGIKLMOR	kilogram
AGIKLNNO	Algonkin
AGIKLNNP	planking
AGIKLNRW	ring-walk
AGIKLNST	stalking
AGIKLNTY	takingly
AGIKLORY	kilogray
AGIKMNNS	king's-man
AGIKMNNU	unmaking
AGIKMNPU	upmaking
AGIKMNRR	ring-mark
AGIKMNRS	markings
AGIKMRUU	kauri-gum
AGIKNNPP	knapping
AGIKNNPR	pranking
AGIKNNPS	spanking
AGIKNNSW	swanking
AGIKNOST	goatskin
AGILLMNU	mulligan
AGILLMNY	malignly
AGILLMSU	Gaullism
AGILLNOT	long-tail
AGILLNPS	spalling
AGILLNRU	alluring
	lingular
AGILLNRW	ring-wall
AGILLNRY	nargilly
	rallying
AGILLNST	stalling
AGILLNSY	sallying
	signally
	slangily
AGILLNTY	tallying
AGILLOOR	gillaroo
AGILLOPT	gallipot
AGILLPRY	playgirl
AGILLPUY	plaguily
AGILLSSY	glassily
AGILLSTU	Gaullist
AGILMMNS	slamming
AGILMNNT	mantling
AGILMNPS	sampling
AGILMNQU	qualming
AGILMOPR	lipogram
AGILMORS	algorism
AGILNNNP	planning
AGILNNOP	pangolin
AGILNNPT	planting
AGILNNRS	snarling
AGILNNST	slanting
AGILNNUY	ungainly
AGILNOOO	oogonial
AGILNOOS	isogonal
AGILNORT	trigonal
AGILNOSS	glossina
	lassoing
AGILNOTW	wagon-lit
AGILNOTY	antilogy
AGILNPPS	slapping
AGILNPPY	applying
AGILNPRS	sparling
	springal
AGILNPTT	platting
AGILNRST	starling
AGILNRSU	singular
AGILNRTT	rattling
AGILNRTW	trawling
AGILNRVY	ravingly
AGILNRWX	wraxling
AGILNSVY	savingly
AGILNSWY	swayling
AGILNTTT	tattling
AGILNTTW	wattling
AGILNTUV	vaulting
AGILNTWZ	waltzing
AGILOORS	gloriosa
AGILOOXY	axiology
AGILORSS	grass-oil
AGILOSTU	Ustilago
AGILSYYZ	syzygial
AGIMMNRT	tramming
AGIMMNUX	Maxim-gun
AGIMMOSY	misogamy
AGIMNNRU	manuring
AGIMNOPW	pig-woman
AGIMNORS	Orangism
	organism
AGIMNORU	origanum
AGIMNORY	agrimony
AGIMNPRT	tramping
AGIMNPST	stamping
AGIMNRRY	marrying
AGIMNRSW	swarming
AGIMNSSU	assuming
AGIMORRT	migrator
AGIMQRUY	quagmiry
AGINNNNY	nannying

AGINNNOY annoying
AGINNNPS spanning
AGINNNSW swanning
AGINNOPT poignant
AGINNORT ignorant
AGINNPPS snapping
AGINNPSW spawning
wingspan
AGINNRTU naturing
AGINNSTU unsating
AGINNTTU taunting
AGINNTUV vaunting
AGINNVVY navvying
AGINOORT △rogation
AGINORRS garrison
AGINORRY iron-gray
AGINORSS assignor
AGINORST organist
roasting
AGINORTV graviton
AGINORTY gyration
organity
AGINOSTT tangoist
toasting
AGINPPRT trapping
AGINPPRW wrapping
AGINPPSW swapping
AGINPPUY appuying
AGINPRRS sparring
AGINPRRY parrying
AGINPRSS raspings
AGINQRSU squaring
AGINRRST starring
AGINRRTY tarrying
AGINRSST nit-grass
AGINRSTT starting
AGINRSTV starving
AGINRSTY sting-ray
straying
AGINSTTW swatting
AGIOORSU oragious
AGIOORSZ grazioso
AGIOORTU autogiro
AGIOPPRT △agitprop
agit-prop
AGIORRTT grattoir
AGIRSSTU sastrugi
AGIRSTUZ zastrugi
AGIRTTUY gratuity
AGJLOSUV Jugoslav
Jugo-Slav
AGJNOPST jogpants
AGKMMORY kymogram
AGKORSSW gas-works
AGLLLNOW longwall
AGLLMOPW glowlamp
AGLLOSSW Owl-glass
AGLLPRSU spur-gall
AGLLRUVY vulgarly
AGLMOOTY atmology
AGLMOOYY Mayology
AGLMOPYY polygamy
AGLNNOPS span-long
AGLNOSST glasnost
AGLNOSTY long-stay
AGLNOSWY longways
AGLNRUUV unvulgar
AGLNSSSU sunglass
AGLNSTUY yglaunst
AGLOOPST goalpost
AGLOOTUY autology
AGLOPRSS lopgrass
AGLORSSY glossary
AGLOSUVY Yugoslav
Yugo-slav
AGLPSSSY spyglass
AGLRTTUU guttural
AGLSTUUY augustly
AGMMNOOR monogram
nomogram
AGMMNOOY monogamy
AGMMOORT tomogram
AGMNNOSW gownsman
AGMNOOPR pornomag
AGMNOORS sonogram
AGMNOORY agronomy
AGMNORST Ångström
angstrom
AGMNSSTY syntagms
AGMOOOSU oogamous
AGMOOPRY porogamy
AGMOORST gas-motor
AGNNOOPT poontang
AGNNOQTU quantong
AGNNOSSW swan-song
AGNOPRST part-song
AGNORTUY nugatory
AGNPPRSU upsprang
AGNRSSTU nut-grass
AGOORRTY rogatory
AGOORTUY autogyro
AGORRSST grossart
rotgrass
AGORRTYY gyratory
AGORSTTY gyrostat
AHHHOOOW whoa-ho-ho
AHHIKLSS shashlik
AHHILNPT phthalin
AHHILOST hailshot
AHHILPSW whiplash
AHHIMMSS mishmash
AHHIMMWW whim-wham
AHHIPRSS sharpish
AHHISSWW wish-wash
AHHKMOTW hawk-moth
AHHKRSTU △kashruth
AHHLMRTY rhythmal
AHHLNOPT naphthol
AHHLOOPU hula-hoop
AHHMPRRU harrumph
AHHNORTW hawthorn
AHHOPSTU aphthous
AHHOSTUV Shavuoth
AHIIKMRS Kashmiri
AHIILNPS plainish
AHIILOST △haliotis
AHIILPRS Aprilish
AHIILPTW whiptail
AHIILRTY hilarity
AHIIMNOT himation
AHIIMNRS Irishman
AHIIMNST isthmian
AHIIMSSV Shaivism
Shivaism
AHIINOPT △photinia
AHIINPST antiship
AHIINSST saintish
AHIINSSW swainish
AHIIOPST hospitia
AHIKLNRS rinkhals
AHIKLRSY rakishly
AHIKMSST Shaktism
AHIKNPRS prankish
AHIKORRW hair-work
AHIKPRSS sparkish
AHILLMOU halloumi
AHILLMPS phallism
AHILLMSS smallish
AHILLMTU thallium
AHILLNRT inthrall
AHILLNTW wanthill
AHILLSVY lavishly
AHILMOPT philamot
AHILMOST mailshot
AHILMQSU qualmish
AHILMSST Stahlism
AHILNOPS siphonal
AHILNOPT oliphant
AHILNORT horntail
AHILOORT Lothario
AHILOPST hospital
AHILOSTT thio-salt
AHILOSTU halitous
AHILPSSY physalis
AHILRSTY trashily
AHILRTWY wrathily
AHIMMNSU humanism
AHIMMORZ mahzorim
AHIMMOSV moshavim
AHIMNORS Romanish
AHIMNOST hoistman
AHIMNOSW womanish
AHIMNRTU Mathurin
AHIMNSTU humanist
AHIMNTUX Xanthium
AHIMNTUY humanity
AHIMOPRS aphorism
AHIMOPST opsimath
AHIMORRW hair-worm
AHIMPPSS △sapphism
AHIMPRST trampish
AHIMRSST smartish
AHIMRSTY Rhytisma
AHIMSTVZ mitzvahs
AHINNNSY nannyish
AHINNOPT antiphon

AHINNORU	Huronian
AHINOPRU	ophiuran
AHINORST	trahison
AHINOSST	astonish
AHINPPSS	snappish
AHINPRST	tranship
AHINQSUV	vanquish
AHIOOPPT	photopia
AHIOORRT	root-hair
AHIOPRST	aphorist
AHIORSTV	tovarish
AHIOSTWY	hoistway
AHIPPSST	sapphist
AHIQRSSU	squarish
AHIRSSTT	startish
AHJMNOSS	Mass-John
AHJOOTTW	jaw-tooth
AHKLLOOY	holly-oak
AHKLOSTW	talkshow
AHKNOOPT	Pakhtoon
AHKNOTUY	thankyou
AHKNPSTU	Pakhtuns
AHLLMOOT	hall-moot
	moot-hall
AHLLNOOS	shalloon
AHLLNOUW	unhallow
AHLLOSSW	shallows
AHLLOSTU	thallous
AHLLOSTY	tally-hos
AHLLPRYY	phyllary
AHLMMOPY	lymphoma
AHLMNOOR	hormonal
AHLMOOPS	omphalos
AHLMOPRU	lamp-hour
AHLMOPTY	polymath
AHLMPSYY	Symphyla
AHLMSTYZ	shmaltzy
AHLNNORT	lanthorn
AHLOPSST	slapshot
AHLOPSUZ	Zalophus
AHLORRTY	harlotry
AHLRSTUY	lathyrus
AHLRTTWY	thwartly
AHMNNORT	Northman
AHMNNSTU	huntsman
AHMNOPTY	phantomy
AHMNORRS	ram's-horn
AHMNORSU	man-hours
AHMOOPSS	shampoos
AHMOORSW	washroom
AHMORRST	shortarm
AHMORSTY	harmosty
AHMORTTW	△tamworth
AHMOSTTW	mostwhat
AHMPSTYY	sympathy
AHMQSSUU	musquash
AHNNSTYY	synanthy
AHNOOPSU	aphonous
AHNOORRY	honorary
AHNOPPSW	pawnshop
AHNOPPSY	pansophy
AHNOPSST	snapshot
AHNORTWW	wanworth
AHNOSSTW	swan-shot
AHNOSTUX	xanthous
AHNOSTUZ	Zoanthus
AHNPSSTU	Pashtuns
AHOOPTYZ	zoopathy
	Zoophyta
AHOOSSTY	soothsay
AHOOSTTW	sawtooth
AHOPPRRY	Porphyra
AHOPPSSW	swap-shop
AHOPSTUW	southpaw
AHORTTUW	watt-hour
AHOSSTUY	southsay
AIIILLVX	lixivial
AIIILRVZ	vizirial
AIIIRSSS	siriasis
AIIJKMOT	komitaji
AIIJNRTX	janitrix
AIIKKSUY	sukiyaki
AIIKLLST	silktail
AIIKLNRR	larrikin
AIIKMNNN	mannikin
AIIKNNNP	pannikin
AIIKORTY	yakitori
AIIKTTZZ	tzatziki
AIILLLMT	milltail
AIILLLUV	illuvial
AIILLMRY	milliary
AIILLNNV	vanillin
AIILLNOP	pollinia
AIILLNOT	illation
AIILLNRY	Illyrian
AIILLNVY	villainy
AIILLPRS	sliprail
	spirilla
AIILLWWW	williwaw
AIILMMSS	Islamism
AIILMNOT	limation
	miltonia
AIILMNPS	alpinism
AIILMNPT	palmitin
AIILMNST	Latinism
AIILMNTT	△militant
AIILMPUV	impluvia
AIILMRST	mistrial
	trialism
AIILMRTY	limitary
	military
AIILMSTV	vitalism
AIILNOPV	pavilion
AIILNORT	train-oil
AIILNOSV	visional
AIILNPST	alpinist
	tailspin
AIILNQRU	Quirinal
AIILNRSU	Silurian
AIILNSTT	Latinist
AIILNSTY	salinity
AIILNTTY	Latinity
AIILOPPS	papilios
AIILRSTT	trialist
AIILRTTY	triality
AIILRTVY	rivality
AIILSTTV	vitalist
AIILSTTW	wait-list
AIILTTVY	vitality
AIIMMNNY	minyanim
AIIMMNRS	Marinism
AIIMMNTY	immanity
AIIMMSTX	maximist
AIIMNNOS	insomnia
AIIMNPSS	sinapism
AIIMNPSX	panmixis
AIIMNRST	Marinist
AIIMNSST	saintism
	samnitis
AIIMNSTT	△titanism
AIIMNSTV	nativism
AIIMNTTU	titanium
AIIMOPSX	apomixis
AIIMORTT	imitator
	timariot
AIIMOSST	amitosis
AIIMPPRS	priapism
AIIMPRSS	Parsiism
AIIMPRTY	imparity
AIIMRSTU	tiramisu
AIIMRUVV	vivarium
AIIMSSTT	mastitis
AIINNOPS	pianinos
AIINNORT	Tironian
AIINNOSV	invasion
AIINNQTU	quintain
AIINNSTY	insanity
AIINOOSV	avoision
AIINORTT	antiriot
	tritonia
AIINORTZ	Trizonia
AIINRRTT	irritant
AIINSTTV	nativist
	△visitant
AIINSTWX	twin-axis
AIINTTVY	△nativity
AIIORSTT	aortitis
AIIORSTV	ovaritis
AIIORTTV	vitiator
AIIPRRST	airstrip
AIIPRVVY	vivipary
AIIRSSTT	satirist
AIISSSTY	syssitia
AIJKKNOU	kinkajou
AIJLLOOR	jillaroo
AIJLLOVY	jovially
AIJLNOPT	lap-joint
AIJLNTUY	jauntily
AIJMORTY	majority
AIJNNNOU	Junonian
AIJNOPPY	popinjay
AIKKLLMW	milk-walk
AIKKLTUW	Kwakiutl
AIKKNOTY	kantikoy
AIKKRTUZ	zikkurat

AIKLLLMW	walkmill
	walk-mill
AIKLLMNT	malt-kiln
AIKLLMRR	rillmark
AIKLLMUW	waukmill
AIKLLRSS	all-risks
AIKLMMRW	milk-warm
AIKLMPTU	kalumpit
AIKLNNPS	snap-link
AIKLNPST	lantskip
AIKLNRTU	kail-runt
AIKLOSUV	souvlaki
AIKLOTTW	kilowatt
AIKMMNOO	makimono
AIKMMNRT	mint-mark
AIKMORSS	komissar
AIKNNOOS	nainsook
AIKNNSSW	swanskin
	swan-skin
AIKNORST	skiatron
AIKNORTY	karyotin
AIKNOSTT	stotinka
AIKNRSST	Sanskrit
AIKNRSSU	Russniak
AIKRSSTY	satyrisk
AILLLMMT	malt-mill
AILLLNOO	linalool
AILLMMSY	smalmily
AILLMNOT	Montilla
AILLMNQU	quillman
AILLMOST	misallot
AILLMOTY	molality
AILLMPRY	primally
AILLMUUV	alluvium
AILLNOPP	papillon
AILLNORT	anti-roll
AILLNOST	stallion
AILLNOSU	allusion
AILLNOUV	alluvion
AILLNPTY	pliantly
AILLOPPS	slop-pail
AILLOPUZ	pulza-oil
AILLOQTU	toquilla
AILLORSY	sailorly
AILLORTT	littoral
	tortilla
AILLORVY	lyra-viol
AILLOSTY	△loyalist
AILLPPRU	pupillar
AILLPPSU	supplial
AILLPRSY	spirally
AILLPRTY	paltrily
AILLPSTY	play-list
AILLPSWY	spillway
AILLRSTY	rallyist
AILLRTUY	ritually
AILLRTWY	willyart
AILLSUVY	visually
AILMMNOO	monomial
AILMMNUU	aluminum
AILMMOOR	mailroom
AILMMORS	moralism
AILMMORT	immortal
AILMMRSY	smarmily
AILMMSTU	summital
AILMNNOT	mannitol
AILMNNTU	luminant
AILMNOOP	palomino
AILMNOOR	monorail
AILMNOOS	moonsail
AILMNOOT	motional
AILMNOPR	prolamin
AILMNOPT	pilotman
AILMNOPY	Olympian
	palimony
	Polymnia
AILMNORT	torminal
AILMNPTU	platinum
AILMNRUY	luminary
AILMNSTU	simulant
AILMOORS	sailroom
AILMOORT	motorail
	motorial
AILMOPRX	proximal
AILMORSS	solarism
AILMORST	moralist
AILMORSU	solarium
AILMORSY	royalism
AILMORTY	molarity
	morality
AILMOSTU	solatium
AILMOSTV	voltaism
AILMPPSY	misapply
AILMPSST	△psalmist
AILMPSTY	ptyalism
AILMRRSU	ruralism
AILMRSSU	surmisal
AILMRSTU	altruism
	muralist
	ultraism
AILNNOOP	Polonian
AILNNOOS	Solonian
AILNNOOT	notional
AILNNOSU	unisonal
AILNNOSW	son-in-law
AILNNOTU	lunation
	Ultonian
AILNNPTU	unpliant
AILNOOPT	optional
AILNOOST	solation
AILNOPRU	unipolar
AILNOPTY	ponytail
AILNORST	tonsilar
AILNORTW	owl-train
AILNORTZ	trizonal
AILNOSSS	sassolin
AILNOSTU	Lusation
AILNOSUV	avulsion
AILNOSVY	synovial
AILNOTTV	volitant
AILNOTTY	tonality
AILNOTUX	luxation
AILNPPSY	snappily
AILNPRSU	purslain
AILNPRUV	pulvinar
AILNPSTU	nuptials
AILNPSUU	nauplius
AILNPTTU	tulipant
AILNQRTU	tranquil
AILNQTUY	quaintly
AILNRSTU	lunarist
AILNRTTU	rutilant
AILNRUWY	unwarily
AILNSSTU	stunsail
AILNSTTU	lutanist
AILNSTUU	nautilus
AILOOPRT	troopial
AILOORRS	sororial
AILOORST	isolator
AILOORTV	violator
AILOPRRV	proviral
AILOPRST	strap-oil
AILOPRSU	pliosaur
AILOPRTU	troupial
AILOPRTY	polarity
AILOPRUY	polyuria
AILORSST	solarist
AILORSTU	sutorial
AILORSTY	△royalist
	solitary
AILORTTU	tutorial
AILORTUV	outrival
AILOTTTY	totality
AILPPRUY	pupilary
AILPRRSU	spur-rial
AILPRSTU	stipular
AILPSTUY	playsuit
AILRRSTU	ruralist
AILRRSTY	starrily
AILRRTUY	rurality
AILRSTTU	altruist
	ultraist
AILRSTTY	straitly
AILRSUVV	survival
AILRTTUY	titulary
AIMMMNOU	ammonium
AIMMNORS	Romanism
AIMMNORT	mortmain
AIMMOSST	somatism
AIMMOSSU	miasmous
AIMMRRSY	mismarry
AIMMRSUU	masurium
AIMMXXYY	mixy-maxy
AIMNNOSS	mansions
AIMNNOTU	△mountain
AIMNNOTY	antimony
	antinomy
AIMNNRTU	ruminant
AIMNOOOZ	zoonomia
AIMNOOTY	myotonia
AIMNOPTV	pivot-man
AIMNOQRU	maroquin
AIMNORST	Romanist
AIMNORTU	Minotaur
AIMNORTY	minatory
AIMNOSST	stasimon

Words marked △ may be spelled also with a capital letter

AIMNOSSX	Saxonism
AIMNOSTU	manitous
AIMNOTTU	mutation
AIMNPRYY	paynimry
AIMNPSTU	sumpitan
AIMNRSTT	Tantrism
	transmit
AIMNRSTU	naturism
AIMOPRSS	prosaism
AIMOPRST	atropism
AIMOPSST	impastos
AIMOPSSY	symposia
AIMORRST	armorist
AIMORRSU	rosarium
AIMORRUV	variorum
AIMORSSU	ossarium
AIMOSSTT	somatist
AIMPPRUU	puparium
AIMPRSTY	partyism
AIMRSTTU	striatum
AIMRTTUY	maturity
AINNNOST	santonin
AINNOOTT	notation
AINNOOTV	novation
AINNOOTZ	zonation
AINNOTTU	nutation
AINNPPSS	snip-snap
AINNRSTU	insurant
AINNRSTY	tyrannis
AINNSTTY	nystatin
AINOOPTT	potation
AINOORTT	rotation
AINOOSTT	ostinato
AINOOTTV	ottavino
AINOPPRT	parpoint
AINOPPTU	pupation
AINOPRTV	proviant
AINOPSTT	postnati
AINOPSTW	swaption
AINOQRSU	narquois
AINORRSW	warrison
AINORRTU	urinator
AINORSST	arsonist
AINORSTT	strontia
AINORSTU	sutorian
AINORTVY	Vanitory®
	vanitory
AINOSSTX	Saxonist
AINOSTTU	titanous
AINPPRTT	trippant
AINPRSST	spraints
AINPRSSU	Prussian
AINPSSSY	synapsis
AINPSSTU	puissant
AINQTTUY	quantity
AINRSTTT	Tantrist
AINRSTTU	antirust
	naturist
AINRSTTY	tanistry
AIOOORRT	oratorio
AIOORSUV	ovarious
AIOPRRTT	portrait
AIOPRSST	prosaist
	protasis
AIOPRSTT	Protista
AIOPSTTU	utopiast
AIORRSTV	varistor
AIORRTWY	ryotwari
AIORSTTV	votarist
AIORSTUV	virtuosa
AIOSSSTY	isostasy
AIPPRSTT	Trappist
AIPPRSTY	papistry
AIPPTTTY	pitty-pat
AIPRRTTU	Partitur
AIPRRTTY	tray-trip
AIPRSSTU	upstairs
AIPRSSTY	sparsity
AIRRSTTY	artistry
AJKLNSTU	salt-junk
AJKNNOOU	junkanoo
AJLMPUWY	lumpy-jaw
AJMRSTUY	jurymast
AJORRTUY	juratory
AKKORSTW	task-work
AKLLMRUY	mullarky
AKLMNOOW	moonwalk
AKLNNOPT	plankton
AKLNOTTW	town-talk
AKLPRRSU	larkspur
AKMMNOOR	monomark
AKMNORTU	Turkoman
AKMOPRST	postmark
AKNOORST	ostrakon
AKNOOUYZ	yokozuna
AKNOPSTW	swankpot
AKOPRRTW	partwork
AKORSWWX	waxworks
ALLLPRUY	plurally
ALLMNORY	normally
ALLMOPSX	smallpox
ALLMORTY	mortally
ALLMOUWY	mulloway
ALLMPRUU	plumular
ALLMTUUY	mutually
ALLNOOPY	Apollyon
ALLNORSS	lasslorn
ALLOPSTY	postally
ALLORSST	allsorts
ALLORTWW	wallwort
ALLRUUVY	uvularly
ALMMNRUU	nummular
ALMMNSUU	Musulman
ALMMOOPR	lamp-room
ALMMORTW	maltworm
ALMNNOOR	non-moral
ALMNORTY	matronly
ALMOOPRY	playroom
ALMOORTU	alum-root
ALMOPPST	lamppost
ALMORSUU	ramulous
ALMOSTTU	mulattos
ALMPSSTY	symplast
ALMRTUUY	tumulary
ALNNOOPR	nonpolar
ALNNOTWY	wantonly
ALNOOPPR	propanol
ALNOOPRT	portolan
	pronotal
ALNOOPXY	polyaxon
ALNOOPYZ	polyzoan
ALNOPPTT	plant-pot
ALNOPRST	plastron
ALNOPRTU	portulan
ALNORRWY	narrowly
ALNORSVY	sovranly
ALNPPSTU	supplant
ALNRRTUU	nurtural
ALOOOPRT	Portaloo®
ALOOPPRS	proposal
ALOOPRST	postoral
ALOOPRTU	uprootal
ALOORSUV	valorous
ALOORTYZ	zoolatry
ALOPPRYY	polypary
ALOPPSSU	supposal
ALOPPSUU	papulous
ALOPRRSU	sporular
ALOPRSTT	portlast
ALOPRSTU	postural
	pulsator
ALOPRSTY	pastorly
ALOPSSSU	spousals
ALOPSTUU	patulous
ALORRSUY	surroyal
ALORSTTW	saltwort
ALORSUVY	savourly
ALORTUWY	outlawry
ALPPSTUY	platypus
ALPRRSUY	spur-ryal
ALPRSTUU	pustular
AMMNOORT	motorman
AMMNPTUY	tympanum
AMNNOOTT	montanto
AMNNORSW	mansworn
AMNNORSY	mansonry
AMNNOSTW	townsman
AMNNOTTU	mountant
AMNNOTYY	antonymy
AMNNPSTU	puntsman
AMNNSTTU	stuntman
AMNOOPPS	pompanos
AMNOORTY	many-root
AMNOOTUY	autonomy
AMNOOTWY	toywoman
AMNOOTXY	taxonomy
AMNOPRYY	paronymy
AMNOTTUY	tautonym
AMOOORSS	amorosos
AMOOPRSY	Pyrosoma
AMOORRTY	moratory
AMOORSTZ	smorzato
AMOORTWY	motorway
AMOOSSTU	astomous
AMOOTTUY	autotomy
AMOPRRST	marsport

AMOPRSTT tram-stop
AMOPRSXY paroxysm
AMOQSSUU squamous
AMORRTUY mortuary
AMORSTTU outsmart
AMORTTUY mutatory
ANNOOQTU non-quota
ANNOORST sonorant
ANNOPRTY non-party
ANNOSSTU stannous
ANNPRSUY spunyarn
ANOOPPPS pap-spoon
ANOOPRRT pronator
ANOOPRSS sopranos
ANOORSUU anourous
ANOPPPRT proppant
ANOPRSTU stroupan
ANOPRTTU trapunto
ANOQRSSU squarson
ANORSTVY sovranty
ANPRSTUU pursuant
ANRRTTUY truantry
ANRSSTYY synastry
AOOOPRST soaproot
AOOOPRSZ Sporozoa
AOOOPRTZ △protozoa
AOOPPRSY apospory
AOOPRSSU saporous
AOOPRSTT pot-roast
AOOPRSTU atropous
AOOPRSTW soapwort
AOOPRSUV vaporous
AOOPRTTY potatory
AOORRTTY rotatory
AOORSSUV savorous
AOPPRSST passport
AOPQRTTU quart-pot
AOPRRRTY parrotry
AOPRRTUY pourtray
AOPRSSTT starspot
AOPRSTTY pyrostat
AORRSTTW starwort
AORRTTWW wartwort
AORSSTTU stratous
AORSSTTY starosty
AORSTTTW two-start

B

BBBCEOWY cobwebby
BBBEINOT bobbinet
BBBEOOTU boob-tube
BBBGILNU blubbing
BBBHNOOY hobnobby
BBBHOOUU hubbuboo
BBBINOPY bobby-pin
BBBLOOXY box-lobby
BBCDEILR cribbled
BBCDERSU scrubbed
BBCDIMOY bombycid
BBCEILRS scribble
BBCEKLUU bluebuck
BBCELORS cobblers
BBCELORY cobblery
BBCEMNOU buncombe
BBCERRSU scrubber
BBCGIINR cribbing
BBCGILNO cobbling
BBCGILNU clubbing
BBCHILSU clubbish
BBCHKOOS boschbok
BBCHKSUU bush-buck
BBCILMSU clubbism
BBCILRSY scribbly
BBCILSTU clubbist
BBDDEEIR bride-bed
BBDDEEMO demobbed
BBDDEEYY beddy-bye
BBDDENUU undubbed
BBDEEMNU benumbed
BBDEENUW unwebbed
BBDEERSU subbreed
BBDEHORT throbbed
BBDEILLN bellbind
BBDEILLR bell-bird
BBDEILRR dribbler
BBDEILRT dribblet
BBDEILRU bluebird
BBDEILRY dry-bible
BBDEIMOV dive-bomb
BBDEINOR dobber-in
BBDEINRU unribbed
BBDEKOOT book-debt
BBDELLMU dumb-bell
BBDELSTU stubbled
BBDENRUU unrubbed
BBDGINRU drubbing
BBDILORT bird-bolt
BBDOSUYY busybody
BBEEEHRR herb-beer
BBEEFLLU bull-beef
BBEEHINS nebbishe
BBEEHLOW bobwheel
BBEEIIRR beriberi
BBEEIMTT bimbette
BBEEIRRS berberis
BBEELLLU bluebell
BBEFILRR fribbler
BBEFIMOR fire-bomb
BBEGIIST gibbsite
BBEGILNP pebbling
BBEGILRY glibbery
BBEHIOTW bob-white
BBEILLNO bonibell
BBEILQRU quibbler
BBEILRRY bilberry
BBEILRST stibbler
BBEIMOST bombsite
BBEIRSTU subtribe
BBEKNOOT bontebok
BBELLOUY bell-buoy
BBELLRUY lubberly
BBELORSY slobbery
BBENORSY snobbery
BBEOSTUU Subbuteo®
BBERRRUY Burberry
BBFGILNU flubbing
BBGGINRU grubbing
BBGHILNO hobbling
BBGIIJNS jibbings
BBGIILMN blimbing
BBGIILNN nibbling
BBGILMNU bumbling
BBGILNOW wobbling
BBGILNOY lobbying
BBGILNRU burbling
BBGILNSU slubbing
BBGINNSU snubbing
BBGINSTU stubbing
BBHILOSS slobbish
BBHIMOSY hobbyism
BBHINOSS snobbish
BBHINSSU snubbish
BBHIOOSY boobyish
BBHIORTY hobbitry
BBHIOSTY hobbyist
BBHIRSUY rubbishy
BBHRSSUU subshrub
BBIKLLOO billbook
BBIKLNOO bobolink
BBILLOYY billyboy
BBILOSTY lobbyist
BBILOSUU bibulous
BBIMNOSS snobbism
BBIMOOSY boobyism
BBINORRY ribbonry
BBLLNNUU buln-buln
BBLLOUYY bully-boy
BBNORSTU stubborn
BCCDHIKO dobchick
BCCDIKOR cockbird
BCCEEIRR cerebric
BCCEHIRU cherubic
BCCEIIIS cicisbei
BCCEIILO libeccio
BCCEIIOS cicisbeo
BCCEILRU crucible
BCCEMRUU cucumber
BCCIIMOR microbic
BCCIISTU cubistic
BCCILMOU columbic
BCCILOOR broccoli
BCCIMNUU Buccinum
BCCIRTUU cucurbit
BCCKLMOU bum-clock
BCCSSUUU succubus
BCDDEHIL childbed
BCDEEEHR breeched
BCDEEEMR December
BCDEEHNR bedrench
BCDEEHOU débouché
BCDEEIKN Benedick
BCDEEILR credible
BCDEEILU educible
BCDEEINT △benedict
BCDEEIRS describe
BCDEELOR corbeled

BCDEEMRU	cumbered
BCDEEORV	bedcover
BCDEEOTT	obtected
BCDEFKLO	flock-bed
BCDEHINS	disbench
BCDEHLOT	blotched
BCDEIILR	bird-lice
BCDEIIRR	rice-bird
BCDEIKRR	brick-red
	redbrick
BCDEILRY	credibly
BCDEIMNO	combined
BCDEINOU	icebound
BCDEIRSU	curbside
BCDEKOOO	codebook
BCDEKOSS	bedsocks
BCDEMNOU	uncombed
BCDENRUU	uncurbed
BCDHORSU	subchord
BCDIIMOR	bromidic
BCDIIPSU	bicuspid
BCDIKLLU	duckbill
BCDIKORR	rock-bird
BCDILMOY	molybdic
BCDILORU	colubrid
BCDIMORS	scombrid
BCDINRUU	rubicund
BCEEEFIN	benefice
BCEEEFKN	neckbeef
BCEEEHRS	breeches
BCEEEIRR	rice-beer
BCEEENRS	bescreen
BCEEEQRU	Quebecer
BCEEERSU	berceuse
BCEEFILN	fencible
BCEEFNOR	corn-beef
BCEEHKSU	buckshee
BCEEHNRU	unbreech
BCEEHPSY	by-speech
BCEEIILM	imbecile
BCEEINOT	cenobite
BCEEIRTT	brettice
BCEEKNNO	neck-bone
BCEELLOT	bellcote
BCEELOOR	borecole
BCEELRTU	tubercle
BCEEMNRU	encumber
BCEEMRRU	cerebrum
	cumberer
BCEERRSU	Cerberus
BCEERSTU	suberect
BCEFFIIR	febrific
BCEFHISU	subchief
BCEFILOR	forcible
BCEGIINO	biogenic
BCEGIMNO	becoming
BCEGLNOO	conglobe
BCEHILPU	blue-chip
BCEHIMRS	besmirch
BCEHIMRU	cherubim
BCEHINRU	cherubin
BCEHIRST	britches
BCEHIRTY	bitchery
BCEHMSTU	besmutch
BCEHNRSU	Burschen
BCEHORRU	brochure
BCEHORTY	botchery
BCEHRSTU	butcher's
BCEHRTTU	Cuthbert
BCEHRTUY	butchery
BCEIIKLN	iceblink
BCEIILMS	miscible
BCEIILNV	vincible
BCEIILST	bit-slice
BCEIIMRS	imbrices
BCEIINRS	inscribe
BCEIKLOO	booklice
BCEIKNOR	beck-iron
BCEILLNU	club-line
BCEILMRU	Mulciber
BCEILNRU	runcible
BCEILOTU	tubicole
BCEILPRU	republic
BCEIMNOU	cenobium
BCEIMOSW	combwise
BCEINOVX	biconvex
BCEIOOPS	bioscope
BCEIOOVX	voice-box
BCEIORRS	cribrose
BCEIORST	bisector
BCEJOORT	objector
BCEKLNOT	bloncket
BCEKLNUU	unbuckle
BCEKLSUY	Buckley's
BCEKMSTU	stembuck
BCEKOORU	buckeroo
BCELMOSS	combless
BCELORTU	clotebur
BCELORUV	over-club
BCELRSSU	curbless
BCEMOORS	rose-comb
BCENORRY	by-corner
BCEORRSU	obscurer
BCEORRWY	cowberry
BCFIIMOR	morbific
BCFIIORT	fibrotic
BCFILORY	forcibly
BCFIMORU	cubiform
BCFLOOTU	club-foot
BCGHINNU	bunching
BCGHINOT	botching
BCGHINTU	butching
BCGIIKNR	bricking
BCGIILMN	climbing
BCGIINRS	scribing
BCGIKLNO	blocking
BCGIKLNU	buckling
BCGIKNOR	brick-nog
BCGIMNOS	combings
BCGINNOU	bouncing
BCHIILTY	bitchily
BCHIISSU	△hibiscus
BCHIKLOS	blockish
BCHIOORY	choirboy
BCHKNORU	buckhorn
BCHKOSTU	buckshot
BCHLOOTX	box-cloth
BCHLRSUU	clubrush
BCHNOORS	bronchos
BCHNORSU	bronchus
BCHOOTUX	touch-box
BCIIKNOR	bick-iron
BCIILLSY	sibyllic
BCIIMNOO	bionomic
BCIIMORU	ciborium
BCIIMRSS	scribism
BCIINORV	vibronic
BCIIORST	sorbitic
BCIISTUY	biscuity
BCIKKNSU	buckskin
BCIKLNOT	block-tin
BCIKLOOT	bootlick
BCIKORRW	cribwork
BCILLORW	crow-bill
BCILLPUY	publicly
BCILMOSY	symbolic
BCILNOUY	bouncily
BCIMORSU	microbus
BCINOSSU	subsonic
BCINOSTU	subtonic
BCINOSUU	incubous
BCIOORST	robotics
BCIORRSS	cross-rib
BCIORRSU	cribrous
BCKKOOOO	cookbook
BCKLLOOS	bollocks
BCKLLOUY	bullocky
BCKLNOSU	sunblock
BCKOOOPY	copybook
BCLMOORU	clubroom
BCLMOSUU	Columbus
BCLOORTU	clubroot
BCMORSUU	cumbrous
BCOORSSW	crossbow
BCORSTTU	obstruct
BCRSSTUU	subcrust
BDDDEENU	unbedded
BDDDENUU	unbudded
BDDEEELL	debelled
BDDEEFLU	befuddle
BDDEEGIR	begirded
BDDEEGTU	budgeted
BDDEEIMM	bedimmed
BDDEEIMO	embodied
BDDEEINT	indebted
BDDEEINW	bindweed
BDDEEIRR	reed-bird
BDDEEIRS	birdseed
BDDEEIRY	bird-eyed
BDDEELMU	bemuddle
BDDEENNU	unbended
BDDEEORR	bordered
BDDEESSU	debussed
BDDEILNR	brindled
BDDEILOO	bloodied
BDDEINNU	unbidden

BDDEINOU unbodied
BDDEINRU underbid
BDDEIORS disorbed
BDDEIOWY widebody
BDDELOOR blood-red
BDDGINOR brodding
BDDGOOSY dogsbody
dog's-body
BDDHIIRY dihybrid
BDDHIMSU Buddhism
BDDHISTU Buddhist
BDDIMNOY mind-body
BDDINOOW woodbind
BDDINPUU pudibund
BDEEEGNO edgebone
BDEEEGRU budgeree
BDEEEHST bed-sheet
BDEEEHTU hebetude
BDEEEINS beniseed
BDEEELLR rebelled
BDEEELLV bevelled
BDEEELOS seed-lobe
BDEEELUW blueweed
BDEEELUY blue-eyed
BDEEEMMR membered
BDEEERTT bettered
BDEEERTV breveted
BDEEETTW bewetted
BDEEFFRU buffered
BDEEFILR belfried
BDEEFINN befinned
BDEEFINR befriend
BDEEFITT befitted
BDEEFOOR forebode
BDEEFOOW beef-wood
BDEEGGIW bewigged
BDEEGGNU unbegged
BDEEGGRU begrudge
BDEEGILN bleeding
BDEEGINR breeding
BDEEHLLR hell-bred
BDEEHLNO beholden
BDEEHLOR beholder
BDEEHMOR home-bred
BDEEHORV hover-bed
BDEEIILN inedible
BDEEIINY bindi-eye
BDEEIKRS kerbside
BDEEILLL libelled
BDEEILLT billeted
BDEEILLU eludible
BDEEILNN bed-linen
BDEEILNO bone-idle
BDEEILNV vendible
BDEEILOR erodible
BDEEILRW bewilder
BDEEIMRT timbered
BDEEINOT obedient
BDEEINSW bendwise
BDEEIORS osier-bed
BDEEIORU bouderie
BDEEIRRV river-bed
BDEEIRST bestride
BDEEIRSY birds-eye
bird'seye
BDEEISTU besuited
BDEEKNRU bunkered
BDEELLOW bowelled
BDEELLRW well-bred
BDEELLRY redbelly
BDEELMNO embolden
BDEELMOR rebeldom
BDEELMPU beplumed
BDEELNTU unbelted
BDEELORU redouble
BDEELOSU besouled
BDEEMNOT bodement
BDEEMORR emborder
BDEEMORY re-embody
BDEEMOSS embossed
BDEEMSSU embussed
BDEENNOT bonneted
BDEENOUY unobeyed
BDEEOPRW bepowder
BDEEORRR borderer
BDEEORST bestrode
BDEEORTU outbreed
BDEEOSSY boss-eyed
BDEEOSTT besotted
BDEEPRRU pure-bred
BDEERRTU true-bred
BDEERRWY dew-berry
BDEERTTU rebutted
BDEFIILR bird-life
BDEFIIRR fire-bird
BDEFILSU subfield
BDEFINRR fernbird
BDEFOORY fore-body
BDEGGNOU egg-bound
BDEGHHIR high-bred
BDEGHILT blighted
BDEGHIRT bedright
BDEGILNN blending
BDEGIORX Oxbridge
BDEGLLOY belly-god
BDEGLNOU bludgeon
BDEGORRY △dogberry
BDEGORSU budgeros
BDEGORUW budgerow
BDEHKOOR herd-book
BDEHLSUV bushveld
BDEIIKLR birdlike
BDEIILMR bird-lime
BDEIILTY debility
BDEIKNOR brodekin
BDEIKNSU buskined
BDEILLMU bdellium
BDEILLOW billowed
BDEILMOS semibold
BDEILMRT timbrel'd
BDEILMSU sublimed
BDEILNOU unilobed
BDEILNOY bodyline
body-line
BDEILNRS blinders
BDEILNRU unbridle
BDEILNVY vendibly
BDEILORT trilobed
BDEILORV lovebird
BDEILOSS bodiless
BDEILOSW disbowel
BDEILRRY lyre-bird
BDEILRST bristled
BDEIMNSU nimbused
BDEIMNUU unimbued
BDEIMORR imborder
BDEIMORY embryoid
BDEINOOW △woodbine
BDEINORV oven-bird
BDEINOSU Bedouins
BDEINRSU burnside
BDEINRTU turbined
BDEINRUU unburied
BDEINTTU unbitted
BDEIORRY broidery
BDEIOSUX suboxide
BDEIRSSU disburse
BDEKNOOU unbooked
BDEKOOPU booked-up
BDELLOOR bordello
doorbell
BDELLOUZ bulldoze
BDELMRUU delubrum
BDELNNUU unbundle
BDELNOSS boldness
BDELNOTU unbolted
BDELNOUU undouble
BDELNOUW unblowed
BDELOORV overbold
BDELORTU troubled
BDELPSUU subduple
BDEMNOTU untombed
BDEMNSSU dumbness
BDEMOOSY somebody
BDEMOOTT bottomed
BDENNOUY ybounden
BDENNRUU unburden
unburned
BDENOORU Eurobond
BDENOOTW bentwood
BDENORUY under-boy
BDENOSTU bone-dust
BDENRSUU unbrused
BDENRUUY underbuy
BDEOORRW borrowed
BDEOPTYY type-body
BDEORRSU suborder
BDEORRTU obtruder
BDERSTUU subtrude
BDFFIPRU puffbird
BDFGNOOU fogbound
BDFILLLO billfold
BDFINORU unforbid
BDFINRUU furibund
BDFIRRSU surfbird
BDFIRTUU fruit-bud

BDFLOTUU	doubtful
BDGGIINR	bridging
BDGHOOUY	dough-boy
BDGIIKNR	king-bird
BDGIILNN	blinding
BDGIILNU	building
BDGIINRW	birdwing
BDGILNNU	bundling
BDGILNOU	doubling
BDGILNTU	blind-gut
BDGINNOU	bounding
	unboding
BDGINOOY	boodying
BDGINORS	birdsong
	songbird
BDGINOTU	doubting
BDGNRUUY	△burgundy
BDHIIPRW	whipbird
BDHIMOOR	rhomboid
BDHIMORT	birthdom
BDHIMSUU	subhumid
BDHIORST	birdshot
BDHKOORU	Dukhobor
BDHLOOOT	blood-hot
BDHMOSUW	dumb-show
BDHNRSUU	unshrubd
BDIIINRS	brindisi
BDIILOQU	obliquid
BDIIMRUU	rubidium
BDILLOOY	bloodily
BDILMORY	morbidly
BDILNNSU	sunblind
	sun-blind
BDILNORW	wild-born
BDILNOWW	windblow
BDILNPRU	purblind
BDILOOTW	blood-wit
BDILRTUY	turbidly
BDIMNORU	moribund
BDIMOOSS	disbosom
BDIMOSTU	misdoubt
BDINNRUW	windburn
BDINORSW	snowbird
BDINRTUU	unturbid
BDIOORTY	botryoid
BDIOSTUY	bodysuit
BDIOTTXY	ditty-box
BDKNOOOR	doorknob
BDKOOORW	wordbook
BDKOORWY	bodywork
BDKOOSTU	studbook
BDLLOTUY	dolly-tub
BDLLSTUU	bulldust
BDLNOOOU	doubloon
BDLNOOUY	unbloody
BDLNOOWW	blowdown
BDLOSTUW	dust-bowl
BDMOORRS	smørbrød
BDNNOOTU	bunodont
BDNOOORW	wood-born
BDNOOPTU	pot-bound
BDNOOTUU	outbound
BDORUWZZ	buzzword
BEEEEFLN	enfeeble
BEEEENRT	terebene
BEEEENRZ	ebenezer
BEEEFLSS	feblesse
BEEEGIRS	besieger
BEEEGRTT	begetter
BEEEHIST	bheestie
BEEEHLRT	herbelet
BEEEHLWW	webwheel
BEEEHNOY	honey-bee
BEEEHOSU	bee-house
BEEEILLL	libellee
BEEEILRV	believer
BEEEINRT	bien-être
BEEEINST	ébéniste
BEEELLRR	rebeller
BEEELLRT	belleter
BEEELLRV	beveller
BEEELMNS	ensemble
BEEELMRS	resemble
BEEELMSY	beseemly
BEEELMZZ	embezzle
BEEEMMRR	remember
BEEEMNSU	unbeseem
BEEEMRSS	Bessemer
BEEENSST	sebesten
BEEEPPPR	bepepper
BEEEPRST	bepester
BEEERSST	bretesse
BEEERSTT	besetter
BEEESSST	tsessebe
BEEFFLMU	bemuffle
BEEFGHNU	hung-beef
BEEFGINR	befringe
BEEFHILS	feeblish
BEEFILLT	lifebelt
BEEFILLX	flexible
BEEFILNU	unbelief
BEEFIORT	fire-bote
BEEFIRTU	fire-tube
BEEFLORW	beflower
BEEFNORR	freeborn
BEEFNRRY	fen-berry
BEEFNRTU	unbereft
BEEGHLMR	bergmehl
BEEGIILL	eligible
BEEGIILX	exigible
BEEGILLR	gerbille
BEEGILNT	beetling
BEEGILRU	beguiler
BEEGINNR	beginner
BEEGINST	beesting
BEEGINSW	beeswing
BEEGINUU	Eugubine
BEEGKLUY	keybugle
BEEGLNOR	belonger
BEEGLRUY	blue-grey
BEEGMRSU	submerge
BEEGNOOW	wobegone
BEEGNOTT	begotten
BEEGNRSU	subgenre
BEEGNSTU	beestung
BEEHHMOT	behemoth
BEEHIJST	jib-sheet
BEEHILMN	Blenheim
BEEHLLNT	hell-bent
BEEHLOOR	borehole
BEEHLOVY	behovely
BEEHLRSS	herbless
BEEHLRST	blethers
BEEHMORW	home-brew
BEEHNOOP	neophobe
BEEHNORS	nose-herb
BEEHNRRT	△brethren
BEEIILNZ	zibeline
BEEIILST	Tebilise
BEEIILTZ	Tebilize®
BEEIINOS	ebionise
BEEIINOT	Ebionite
BEEIINOZ	ebionize
BEEIINRT	bénitier
BEEIINST	Ibsenite
BEEIJSTU	bejesuit
	Jebusite
BEEIKLTU	tubelike
BEEIKLWY	bi-weekly
BEEILLLR	libeller
BEEILLNO	lobeline
BEEILLTT	belittle
BEEILMPR	periblem
BEEILMPU	umble-pie
BEEILNSS	sensible
BEEILNST	stilbene
	tensible
BEEILNSU	nebulise
BEEILNUZ	nebulize
BEEILOTV	lovebite
BEEILRRT	terrible
BEEILRYZ	breezily
BEEIMRRU	umbriere
BEEIMRTT	embitter
BEEINNSS	beinness
BEEINORT	△tenebrio
BEEIOQSU	obsequie
BEEIORSS	soberise
BEEIORSZ	soberize
BEEIORTV	overbite
BEEIRSSU	suberise
BEEIRSUZ	suberize
BEEKMOPR	pembroke
BEEKNOPS	bespoken
BEEKNORZ	Brezonek
BEEKNOST	steenbok
BEELLNTT	bell-tent
BEELLOPR	bell-rope
BEELLORW	bellower
	rebellow
BEELLSUY	bull's-eye
BEELLTUW	tube-well
BEELMMOP	bepommel
BEELMNNO	noblemen
BEELMRRT	trembler
BEELMRRU	lumberer

BEELMRST trembles
BEELNOSS boneless
noblesse
BEELNOSU △bluenose
BEELNSSU blueness
BEELNTTU betel-nut
BEELNTUY butylene
BEELOOST obsolete
BEELOQRU breloque
BEELOSTW steelbow
BEELPRUV buplever
BEELRSSV verbless
BEELRTUU true-blue
BEELSSTU tubeless
BEEMNORV November
BEEMNRRU numberer
renumber
BEEMOPRT obtemper
BEEMORSS embosser
BEEMPPRU beer-pump
BEEMQSUU embusqué
BEEMRSSU submerse
BEEMRTTU umbrette
BEEMRTUZ zerumbet
BEENORTU bountree
BEENORTV verboten
BEENOSTU tubenose
BEENPRST besprent
BEENRSTW bestrewn
BEENRTTU brunette
BEENSSTU subtense
BEEOORRT boortree
BEEOORTT beetroot
boot-tree
BEEORRSV observer
BEEORRTU bourtree
BEEORSSU suberose
BEEORSTU tuberose
BEEORSTW bestower
BEEORSWY eyebrows
BEEPRSTY presbyte
BEERRSTW brewster
BEERRTTU rebutter
BEERSSUV subserve
subverse
BEERSTTY by-street
BEESTTTU test-tube
BEFGIILL fillibeg
BEFGIINR briefing
BEFHILSU bluefish
BEFHINOS fish-bone
BEFHIRSU bushfire
BEFIKNOX knife-box
BEFIKNOY knife-boy
BEFILLXY flexibly
BEFILMOR forelimb
BEFILOUY lifebuoy
BEFIORTT forebitt
BEFLLLUY bellyful
BEFLLORU full-bore
BEFLNORS self-born
BEFLOOOT lobe-foot
BEFLORUW furbelow
BEFLSTUU tubefuls
BEFNOORR forborne
BEFORRXY foxberry
BEGGOOOS goosegob
BEGHIILP philibeg
BEGHILRT blighter
therblig
BEGHINOR neighbor
BEGHINRT brighten
BEGHLNOU bunghole
BEGHNOTU boughten
BEGHOSTU besought
BEGHOSUU bughouse
BEGIIISS sigisbei
BEGIILLN ill-being
libeling
BEGIILLY eligibly
BEGIINRZ zingiber
BEGIIOSS sigisbeo
BEGILLLU gullible
BEGILLNU bullgine
BEGILLNY bellying
BEGILNNU Nibelung
BEGILNNY benignly
BEGILNOS Gobelins
BEGILNOV beloving
BEGILNSS blessing
glibness
BEGILNTT bletting
BEGILNUW bluewing
BEGIMNOS besoming
BEGIMOST misbegot
BEGIMOSY bogeyism
BEGINNNU unbenign
BEGINNOR ringbone
BEGINNOT not-being
BEGINOOS besognio
BEGINORS sobering
BEGINRRY berrying
BEGLLORY gor-belly
BEGLLOTU globulet
BEGLMRRU grumbler
BEGLNOUW bluegown
BEGNNTUV bung-vent
BEGNOORU bourgeon
BEGNORTU burgonet
BEGNSSUU subgenus
BEHIKLOS blokeish
BEHIKPSU push-bike
BEHILLOS shoebill
BEHILLTY blithely
BEHILMRW whimbrel
BEHILNPY biphenyl
BEHILORR horrible
BEHILRTU thurible
BEHIMNOO bonhomie
BEHINNOS shinbone
BEHINOSW wishbone
BEHIOOPR biophore
BEHIOTWY Whiteboy
BEHJNOOT on-the-job
BEHLLNOR hell-born
BEHLLOOT bolthole
BEHLLOOW blowhole
BEHLLPSU bellpush
BEHLOOPY hypobole
lyophobe
BEHLOOTT bottle-oh
BEHLOSSU sloebush
BEHMNOOR home-born
BEHMOOOX homeobox
BEHNNOUY honeybun
BEHOOOST boothose
BEHOORST theorbos
BEHOORSY horse-boy
BEHOOSUY houseboy
BEHOPRSU bush-rope
BEHORRST brothers
BEHORSSU rosebush
BEHORSUV hover-bus
BEIIIKMN minibike
BEIIKRTZ kibitzer
BEIILLMT time-bill
BEIILMMO immobile
BEIILMOS mobilise
BEIILMOZ mobilize
BEIILNNR bin-liner
BEIILNRS rinsible
BEIILOPR periboli
BEIILRST trilbies
BEIILRSX ex-libris
BEIILRTT libretti
BEIILRUZ bruilzie
BEIILSSV visibles
BEIILSTT stilbite
BEIIMNNR △renminbi
BEIIMNOS ebionism
BEIIMNSS Ibsenism
BEIIMRTT imbitter
BEIINPRT brine-pit
BEIINSTT stibnite
BEIISSTU subitise
BEIISTUZ subitize
BEIJMOSU jumboise
BEIJMOUZ jumboize
BEIJNORW bijwoner
BEIKLMOW womblike
BEIKLNRS blinkers
BEIKLOTY kilobyte
BEIKNNOR broken-in
BEIKNRRY inkberry
BEIKOORT brookite
BEILLMNO bone-mill
BEILLMSS limbless
BEILLMSU semibull
BEILLNTU bulletin
BEILLOSU libelous
BEILMMOS embolism
BEILMNOR bromelin
BEILMNOU nobelium
BEILMNRU unlimber
BEILMNUU nebulium
BEILMPTU plumbite

BEILMRSS	brimless	BELLMRUY	lumberly	BEORSUVY	overbusy
BEILNNSU	Blennius	BELLNORW	well-born	BERRSTUU	surrebut
BEILNNTU	buntline	BELLNOSU	bullnose	BERSSTTU	buttress
BEILNOPS	bonspiel	BELLNTUY	tunbelly	BERSSTUV	subverst
BEILNORV	live-born	BELLOPTY	pot-belly	BFFHORSU	brush-off
BEILNOVY	bovinely	BELLORTW	bellwort	BFFLLOUY	bully-off
BEILNSSY	sensibly	BELMNOSU	nelumbos	BFFNOSUX	snuffbox
BEILOORV	overboil	BELMOORS	bloomers	BFGHINTU	bun-fight
BEILOPPW	blowpipe	BELMOORY	bloomery	BFGIKOOT	gift-book
BEILOPSS	possible	BELMORST	temblors	BFGLLORU	bullfrog
BEILORST	strobile	BELMORSY	sombrely	BFHIILLS	bill-fish
BEILORTT	libretto	BELMORUW	rumbelow	BFHILOSW	blowfish
BEILRRTY	terribly	BELMOSST	tombless	BFHLLOOU	bull-hoof
BEILRSTY	blistery	BELMPRUY	plumbery	BFHLLSUU	blushful
BEILRTTY	bitterly	BELMRRUY	△mulberry	BFHLOSUX	flush-box
	brittley	BELMRSTU	stumbler	BFHORSUX	fox-brush
BEILSTTU	subtitle	BELMRSUY	slumbery	BFIIORSS	fibrosis
BEIMNSSU	nimbuses	BELNNOWW	new-blown	BFILLMRU	brim-full
BEIMOORS	ribosome	BELNOSUU	nebulous	BFILLSSU	blissful
BEIMORRV	overbrim	BELNSTUU	unsubtle	BFILOOST	soft-boil
BEIMORTY	biometry	BELOOPRT	bolt-rope	BFIMNORU	nubiform
BEIMORYZ	ribozyme	BELOORSW	rosebowl	BFIMORTU	tubiform
BEIMOTVY	by-motive	BELOORVW	overblow	BFINORYZ	bronzify
BEIMRSTU	resubmit	BELOOSST	bootless	BFLLNOWY	fly-blown
BEINNOSS	boniness	BELOOTUV	obvolute	BFLNOOOR	fool-born
BEINNRYZ	zebrinny	BELORRTU	troubler	BFLOORSU	subfloor
BEINORST	ribstone	BELORSSW	browless	BGGGINOR	brogging
BEINORTW	brow-tine	BELOSTUY	obtusely	BGGIILNO	obliging
BEINORTZ	bronzite	BELPRSUY	superbly	BGGIILNY	gibingly
BEINOSSX	boxiness	BELRSSSU	△brussels	BGGIINNR	bringing
BEINRRSY	nisberry	BELRSTTU	rust-belt	BGGIINRU	briguing
BEINRSTU	Burnsite	BELRSTUY	blustery	BGGILNNU	bungling
	turbines	BELSSTUY	substyle	BGGINOOT	toboggin
BEINSSSU	business	BELSTTUY	subtlety	BGHHINOR	high-born
BEIOORST	robotise	BEMNNSSU	numbness	BGHHIORW	highbrow
BEIOORTZ	robotize	BEMNOORT	trombone	BGHIINRT	birthing
BEIOQTUU	boutique	BEMNOOXY	money-box	BGHILMNU	humbling
BEIORRSU	boursier	BEMNOPRU	rump-bone	BGHILNSU	blushing
BEIORRTU	roburite	BEMNORSY	embryons	BGHILOTX	light-box
BEIORSTU	to-bruise	BEMOORRS	sombrero	BGHILRTY	brightly
BEIORSTY	sobriety	BENNNOTU	unbonnet	BGHIMOTU	bigmouth
BEIOTTZZ	bozzetti	BENNNPUY	penny-bun	BGHINRSU	brushing
BEIRRTTU	tributer	BENNOORS	Sorbonne	BGHIORSU	broguish
BEJKOOST	jestbook	BENNOOTU	boutonné	BGHNNUUY	bunny-hug
BEJORTTU	turbojet	BENORRSU	suborner	BGHNOTUU	unbought
BEKLNORY	brokenly	BENORRTU	true-born	BGHOOPTU	boughpot
BEKLOOOR	booklore	BENORRUV	overburn	BGIIKLNN	blinking
BEKLOORT	brooklet	BENORSTU	rubstone	BGIILNRS	brisling
BEKLOOSS	bookless	BENORSTW	bestrown	BGIIMMNR	brimming
BEKLORUV	overbulk	BENORSUU	burnouse	BGIINRSU	bruising
BEKMOOPS	spekboom	BENORTTU	rebutton	BGIIPRTU	Tubigrip®
BEKMOOSX	smoke-box	BENRRSUY	sunberry	BGIKLNOT	king-bolt
BEKNNORU	unbroken	BENSSSUY	busyness	BGILLNOU	globulin
BEKNOOOT	notebook	BEOORRRW	borrower	BGILLNRU	bull-ring
BEKNOORT	to-broken		reborrow	BGILLNUY	bullying
BEKOOORV	overbook	BEOORRVW	overbrow	BGILMMNU	mumbling
BEKOORST	bookrest	BEOORSTY	botryose	BGILMNOO	blooming
BEKOOTTX	textbook	BEOOTTZZ	bozzetto	BGILMNPU	plumbing
BELLLLPU	bell-pull	BEOPRRSV	Proverbs	BGILMNRU	rumbling
BELLMORT	mortbell	BEORSSSU	sorbuses	BGILMNTU	tumbling
BELLMORU	umbrello	BEORSSUU	suberous	BGILMORY	gorblimy
BELLMOSW	swell-mob	BEORSTUU	tuberous	BGILNNOS	snobling

BGILNORT	ring-bolt
BGILNORY	boringly
BGILNOTT	blotting
BGILNOTU	boulting
BGILNRRU	blurring
BGILNRTU	blurting
BGINNORW	browning
BGINNORZ	bronzing
BGINORSW	browsing
BGKLNOOU	lung-book
BGKNOOOS	songbook
BGLOORYY	bryology
BGOPRSUU	subgroup
BHIIKRSS	briskish
BHIILMPS	blimpish
BHIIMRST	misbirth
BHIIOPRT	prohibit
BHIKLLOO	billhook
BHILLNOR	hornbill
BHILLPUW	bullwhip
BHILLSTU	bullshit
BHILNSTU	bluntish
BHILORRY	horribly
BHILOSYY	boyishly
BHIMNORT	thrombin
BHIMOOPR	biomorph
BHINOPSU	unbishop
BHINORSW	brownish
BHKMNOOY	hymn-book
BHKNOOOR	hornbook
BHKOOOOT	boot-hook
BHKOOOPS	bookshop
BHLLNORU	bull-horn
BHLOOOTT	tolbooth
BHLRSUUY	bulrushy
BHMNTTUU	thumbnut
BHMOPTTU	thumbpot
BHMORSTU	thrombus
BHMPSTUU	thumbs-up
BHMPTTUU	tub-thump
BHMRRSUU	rum-shrub
BHNOSSUW	snowbush
BIIKNOOT	bootikin
BIILLMOR	morbilli
BIILLNQU	quill-nib
BIILMOTY	mobility
BIILNOOV	oblivion
BIILNOTY	nobility
BIILNTUY	nubility
BIILORST	strobili
BIILORSU	Orbilius
BIILOSSU	sibilous
BIILOSSY	biolysis
BIILSTTW	witblits
BIIMMNSY	nimbyism
BIIMMOSZ	zombiism
BIINRSTU	burinist
BIIQTUUY	ubiquity
BIIRSSTU	bursitis
BIKLNNSU	sun-blink
BIKOOUUZ	bouzouki
BILLMSUY	bullyism
BILLNOOU	bouillon
BILLSTUW	swill-tub
BILLSTUY	subtilly
BILMMPSU	plumbism
BILMOSTU	botulism
BILNOSUU	nubilous
BILOORST	sorbitol
BILOPSSY	possibly
BILORSST	bristols
BILSTTUY	subtilty
BIMNOOOR	boom-iron
BIMNORSW	Brownism
BIMNORSY	Byronism
BIMNOSTY	symbiont
BIMNRRUU	muirburn
BIMNRUUV	viburnum
BIMOSSTY	sybotism
BINNORTW	twin-born
BINOORST	isobront
BINORSTW	Brownist
BIOOPSTT	post-obit
BIOPRRSU	subprior
BIOPRSTW	bowsprit
BIORRSTU	burritos
BIORSTTY	Botrytis
BIORSTUY	bistoury
BIOSTTUY	obtusity
BIRSSTTU	subtrist
BKKOOORW	bookwork
	workbook
BKMOOORW	bookworm
BKMOORUZ	zomboruk
BKOOOPST	book-post
BLLLLOOY	loblolly
BLLMOORW	boll-worm
BLLOOPSW	slop-bowl
BLMOOOST	tombolos
BLMOOOTY	lobotomy
BLMOOSSY	blossomy
BLMOPSUU	plumbous
BLNORSUW	slow-burn
BLOOSSTY	slyboots
BLORSTUY	robustly
BLOSTUUU	tubulous
BMNORTUW	mowburnt
BMOOPTTU	bottom-up
BMOORSSU	sombrous
BMOORSTU	motor-bus
BMOORTTY	bottomry
BMORSSTU	strombus
BNNORTUW	nut-brown
BNNOTTUU	unbutton
BNNRSTUU	sunburnt
BNOOOSTW	snowboot
BNOOOSUY	sonobuoy
BNOORTUW	brownout
BNORRUUW	unburrow
BNRSSTUU	sunburst
BOOOPRSX	poor's-box
BORSTTUU	outburst

C

CCCDIILY	dicyclic
CCCEEILT	eclectic
CCCEGOSY	coccyges
CCCEIIRT	eccritic
CCCEILNY	encyclic
CCCEILUY	eucyclic
CCCHIORY	chiccory
CCCIINSU	succinic
CCCILNOY	cyclonic
CCCILOPY	cyclopic
CCCINSTU	succinct
CCCIOORS	scirocco
CCCKOORW	cock-crow
CCCLOSUU	Cocculus
CCDEEENR	credence
CCDEEHIL	clichéed
CCDEEINS	scienced
CCDEEIOP	codpiece
CCDEEKOY	cockeyed
CCDEENOR	conceder
CCDEHIPU	hiccuped
CCDEHLTU	declutch
CCDEHORS	scorched
CCDEHORT	crotched
CCDEHRTU	crutched
CCDEIILO	cleidoic
CCDEIINO	coincide
CCDEIIRT	cricetid
CCDEILOS	△scolecid
CCDEINOR	corniced
CCDEINOT	△occident
CCDEIOPU	occupied
CCDEIPRU	cider-cup
CCDELNOU	conclude
CCDELORU	occluder
CCDELOTU	occulted
CCDEORRU	occurred
CCDEOSTU	stuccoed
CCDHIIKP	dipchick
CCDHIILO	cichloid
CCDHIIOR	dichroic
CCDHINOO	conchoid
CCDIINOO	conoidic
CCDIINOS	scincoid
CCDIINST	discinct
CCDIIORT	dicrotic
CCDINOTU	conducti
CCDKOOOW	woodcock
CCDOOOOW	coco-wood
CCEEEEHH	chee-chee
CCEEGINR	recceing
CCEEHINZ	zecchine
CCEEHKKY	check-key
CCEEHKNS	schnecke
CCEEHKRS	checkers
CCEEHLOW	cow-leech
CCEEHRSY	screechy
CCEEILNR	encircle
CCEEILNT	elenctic
CCEEILPY	epicycle

Words marked △ may be spelled also with a capital letter

CCEEILRT	electric
CCEEIMNU	ecumenic
CCEEINOR	cicerone
CCEEINOV	conceive
CCEEINSS	sciences
CCEEIORV	coercive
CCEEIRSV	cervices
	crescive
CCEEITTU	eutectic
CCEEKLOR	cockerel
CCEELMNY	clemency
CCEELOSS	scoleces
CCEEMMNO	commence
CCEEMMOR	commerce
CCEEMOPS	compesce
CCEENNOS	ensconce
CCEENORT	concrete
CCEENOTY	cenocyte
CCEENRST	△crescent
CCEEOORT	coco-tree
CCEFFHKO	check-off
CCEFIIPS	specific
CCEFIRRU	crucifer
CCEFLLOU	floccule
CCEFLOOS	floccose
CCEGHIOR	choregic
CCEGIKLN	clecking
CCEGILOO	ecologic
CCEGILRY	glyceric
CCEGINNO	congenic
CCEGINRY	reccying
CCEGNOOS	cognosce
CCEHIIMR	chimeric
CCEHIIMS	ischemic
CCEHIINZ	zecchini
CCEHIKNS	chickens
CCEHIKSU	chuckies
CCEHILMO	cholemic
CCEHILNR	clincher
CCEHILOR	choleric
CCEHILOY	choicely
CCEHINOR	corniche
	enchoric
CCEHINOZ	zecchino
CCEHINST	technics
CCEHIORT	ricochet
CCEHKOTU	checkout
	check-out
CCEHLMOR	cromlech
CCEHLNNU	unclench
CCEHLRUY	cleruchy
CCEHLSTU	clutches
CCEHORRS	scorcher
CCEHORTT	crotchet
CCEHRSTU	scutcher
CCEHRTUY	cutchery
CCEIIKLN	nickelic
CCEIILNT	enclitic
CCEIILNU	culicine
CCEIILOR	licorice
CCEIILPT	ecliptic
CCEIILST	scilicet
CCEIILTU	leucitic
CCEIINNR	encrinic
CCEIINOR	ciceroni
CCEIIRRT	circiter
CCEIIRSS	eccrisis
CCEIIRTT	rectitic
CCEIIRTU	eucritic
CCEILMOO	coelomic
CCEILMOP	complice
CCEILNOR	cornicle
CCEILNUY	unicycle
CCEILOSS	scolices
CCEILRRU	curricle
CCEILRSY	cresylic
CCEILRTY	tricycle
CCEILRUU	curlicue
CCEIMNOO	economic
CCEIMOST	cosmetic
CCEIMRRU	mercuric
CCEINNOS	insconce
CCEINNOV	convince
CCEINOOR	coercion
CCEINOOZ	Cenozoic
CCEINOPT	concepti
CCEINORT	concerti
	necrotic
CCEINOST	C-section
CCEINOTT	concetti
	tectonic
CCEINOTY	conceity
CCEINPRT	precinct
CCEINRTU	cincture
CCEINSTY	synectic
CCEIOORT	crocoite
CCEIOOTX	ecotoxic
CCEIOOTZ	ectozoic
CCEIOPRT	ectropic
CCEIOPRU	occupier
CCEIORST	cortices
CCEIOSTT	Scottice
CCEIPRTU	cut-price
CCEIRSTU	Cricetus
CCEKORRY	crockery
CCEKORSU	cocksure
CCELMOPT	complect
CCELOPSY	△cyclopes
CCELOSSY	cycloses
CCENOORT	concerto
CCENOOTT	concetto
CCENORRU	corn-cure
CCENORTY	cornetcy
CCENRRUY	currency
CCEOOORR	corocore
CCEOORSU	croceous
CCEOPRUY	reoccupy
CCEORSSU	crocuses
CCEORSTU	stuccoer
CCFIINOR	cornific
CCFIIRUX	crucifix
CCFIKNOY	cocknify
CCFILLOU	flocculi
CCFILNOT	conflict
CCFKLLOU	full-cock
CCFKLOOT	cockloft
CCFLOOOO	△locofoco
CCGHHIOU	hiccough
CCGHIINN	cinching
CCGHINOU	couching
CCGIIKLN	clicking
CCGIILNR	circling
CCGIKLNO	clocking
CCGILLOY	glycolic
CCGILNOY	glyconic
CCGILOSU	glucosic
CCGINOTW	twoccing
CCHHIINN	chin-chin
CCHHIITY	ichthyic
CCHHINOT	chthonic
CCHHLRUY	churchly
CCHHNRUU	unchurch
CCHHOOOO	choo-choo
CCHHOOPP	chop-chop
CCHHOOWW	chow-chow
CCHIINUZ	zucchini
CCHIIORT	orchitic
CCHIISTU	Cushitic
CCHIKMPU	chipmuck
CCHILMOW	milch-cow
CCHINOSU	scuchion
CCHINOTY	Tychonic
CCHIPSSY	psychics
CCHKLOSY	schlocky
CCHKOOST	cockshot
CCHKOPTU	putchock
CCHKOSTU	cockshut
CCHLNTUU	unclutch
CCHNRSUY	scrunchy
CCIIKKTT	tick-tick
CCIIKNPY	picnicky
CCIILLRY	Cyrillic
CCIIMNSY	cynicism
CCIINNSU	cicinnus
CCIINORZ	zirconic
CCIIRTUY	circuity
CCIKKLOP	lockpick
	picklock
CCIKKOTT	tick-tock
CCIKNOPR	princock
CCILLLUU	Lucullic
CCILLOPP	clip-clop
CCILNSUY	succinyl
CCILOOPS	piccolos
CCILORUU	curculio
CCILOSSY	cyclosis
CCIMNRUU	curcumin
CCINOPRT	procinct
CCINOPSY	syncopic
CCINORSY	cryonics
CCIOOPST	scotopic
CCIOORSS	siroccos
CCIOOTXY	oxytocic
CCIRSSUY	circussy
CCJNNOTU	conjunct
CCKKLMUU	muckluck

CCKKOOOR	rock-cook
CCKKOORR	rock-cork
CCKMMORU	crummock
CCKMOOOR	moorcock
CCKNORTU	turncock
CCKOOPST	stopcock
CCKOPRSU	cockspur
CCLLOOPP	clop-clop
CCLLOTUY	occultly
CCLMOOPU	cocoplum
CCLNOOOR	concolor
CCLOOOSZ	zoccolos
CCLOORSU	occlusor
CCMOOORS	moroccos
CCNOORSU	concours
CCOOOORR	corocoro
CCOOSSUU	couscous
CCOOTTUU	tucotuco
CCORSSTU	crosscut
CCOTTUUU	tucutuco
CCRSUUUU	surucucu
CDDDIIOY	diddicoy
CDDEEEFN	defenced
CDDEEEJT	dejected
CDDEEENT	decedent
CDDEEHIT	cheddite
CDDEEILP	pedicled
CDDEEIRS	descried
CDDEEKNU	undecked
CDDEEKOT	docketed
CDDEEKUW	duckweed
CDDEELMO	comeddle
CDDEELSU	secluded
CDDEELUX	excluded
CDDEELUY	deucedly
CDDEERUV	decurved
CDDEFIIO	codified
CDDEIKOS	dockside
CDDEILNU	included
CDDEKNOU	undocked
CDDEKOSU	dock-dues
CDDELLOW	cold-weld
CDDEMNOU	duncedom
CDDGHILO	godchild
CDDGHIOT	ditch-dog
CDDGILNO	clodding
CDDGINSU	scudding
CDDHIIRY	dihydric
CDDHILOS	cloddish
CDDIISTY	dytiscid
CDDIKLUW	wild-duck
CDDKNOPU	duck-pond
CDDMMOUU	mocuddum
CDDOOORW	cordwood
CDEEEGIL	ice-ledge
CDEEEHST	tedesche
CDEEEINV	evidence
CDEEEIPS	epicedes
CDEEEIRV	deceiver
	received
CDEEEKNR	deer-neck
CDEEEKNW	neckweed
CDEEELLX	excelled
CDEEELOS	coleseed
CDEEELST	deselect
	selected
CDEEELUX	excludee
CDEEENNT	tendence
CDEEENOS	secondee
CDEEEPTX	expected
CDEEERRS	screeder
CDEEERSS	recessed
CDEEFFOR	coffered
	force-fed
CDEEFIIL	icefield
CDEEFIIT	feticide
CDEEFKLR	freckled
CDEEFKOR	foredeck
CDEEFNNU	unfenced
CDEEFORS	frescoed
CDEEFORT	defector
CDEEGHLO	dog-leech
CDEEGIIR	regicide
CDEEGINO	genocide
CDEEGINR	receding
CDEEGIOS	geodesic
CDEEGIOT	geodetic
CDEEHIKL	helideck
CDEEHILN	lichened
CDEEHILP	cheliped
CDEEHIPR	decipher
CDEEHIST	tedeschi
CDEEHITW	itchweed
CDEEHLMO	leechdom
CDEEHLSU	schedule
CDEEHNNU	Duchenne
CDEEHNRR	drencher
CDEEHNUW	unchewed
CDEEHRTW	wretched
CDEEHSSU	duchesse
CDEEIIMN	medicine
CDEEIIMP	epidemic
CDEEIINT	indictee
CDEEIISV	decisive
CDEEIITT	dietetic
CDEEIKLN	nickeled
CDEEIKLR	deer-lick
CDEEIKNV	invecked
CDEEIKPT	picketed
CDEEIKRW	wickered
CDEEIKTT	ticketed
CDEEILNP	pendicle
CDEEILNR	reclined
CDEEILNS	licensed
	silenced
CDEEILNT	denticle
CDEEILNU	nucleide
CDEEILRS	sclereid
CDEEILRT	derelict
CDEEILSU	Seleucid
CDEEIMNR	endermic
CDEEIMOR	mediocre
CDEEIMPR	premedic
CDEEIMRS	miscreed
CDEEIMRV	decemvir
CDEEINNT	indecent
CDEEINPS	dispence
CDEEINPT	depeinct
CDEEINTU	inductee
CDEEINTV	invected
CDEEIORV	divorcee
	divorcée
CDEEIPRS	précised
CDEEIPRT	decrepit
	depicter
CDEEIPRU	pedicure
CDEEIRRT	redirect
CDEEIRST	discreet
	discrete
CDEEIRSV	descrive
CDEEKLPS	speckled
CDEEKNRU	unrecked
CDEEKOPT	pocketed
CDEEKORW	rockweed
CDEEKOST	socketed
CDEEKRSU	suckered
CDEELLPU	cupelled
CDEELNPU	peduncle
CDEELNTY	decently
CDEELOOW	locoweed
CDEELOPU	decouple
CDEELORV	clovered
CDEELOST	closeted
CDEELPRU	preclude
CDEELRUX	excluder
CDEEMORT	ectoderm
CDEENNOS	condense
CDEENNOU	denounce
CDEENNPY	pendency
CDEENNTU	undecent
CDEENNTY	tendency
CDEENORR	cornered
CDEENORS	seconder
	seed-corn
CDEENORT	centrode
CDEENOTX	coextend
CDEENOVX	convexed
CDEENPRU	prudence
CDEENRUV	verecund
CDEENSTY	encysted
CDEEOOTV	dove-cote
CDEEOPPS	speed-cop
CDEEOPRS	proceeds
CDEEORRR	△recorder
CDEEORST	corseted
CDEEORTT	detector
CDEEOSST	cosseted
CDEEPRST	sceptred
CDEERRRU	recurred
CDEERRUV	recurved
CDEERTUV	curveted
CDEFHILL	elf-child
CDEFHIMO	chiefdom
CDEFIIIL	filicide
CDEFIIIT	citified
CDEFIIOR	codifier

CDEFIIRT	drift-ice
CDEFIITY	cityfied
CDEFINNO	confined
CDEFINNU	infecund
CDEFINOR	confider
CDEFLORY	forcedly
CDEFNORU	unforced
CDEFNOSU	confused
CDEFOSSU	focussed
CDEGIILO	Goidelic
CDEGIINO	Diogenic
CDEGINRU	reducing
CDEGINRY	decrying
CDEGINSU	seducing
CDEGINSY	dysgenic
CDEGORSW	scrowdge
CDEHIILO	helicoid
CDEHIIMO	homicide
CDEHIINO	echinoid
CDEHIKOT	Hock-tide
CDEHIKRW	herdwick
CDEHILMR	merchild
CDEHILNR	children
CDEHILOR	chloride
CDEHILRT	eldritch
CDEHIMOT	methodic
CDEHINNR	indrench
CDEHINOS	hedonics
CDEHIOOR	ochidore
CDEHIOTY	theodicy
CDEHISTT	stitched
CDEHKLSU	shelduck
CDEHLOOS	deschool
	schooled
CDEHMNTU	Dutchmen
CDEHNOOP	chenopod
CDEHOORR	rheocord
CDEHORSU	chorused
CDEHOSSU	hocussed
CDEIIILS	silicide
CDEIIIMT	miticide
CDEIIIRV	viricide
CDEIIITV	viticide
CDEIIKKS	sidekick
CDEIIKLS	sicklied
CDEIIKMM	mimicked
CDEIIKNR	ciderkin
CDEIIKRS	dricksie
CDEIILMO	domicile
CDEIILNN	inclined
CDEIILNO	indocile
CDEIILOT	idiolect
CDEIILPS	disciple
CDEIILPU	pediculi
	pulicide
CDEIILRU	ridicule
CDEIIMOS	dioecism
CDEIIMRT	dimetric
CDEIINNT	incident
CDEIINOS	decision
CDEIINRT	indirect
CDEIIOPR	periodic
CDEIIOPS	episodic
CDEIIOPT	epidotic
CDEIIPRR	cirriped
CDEIIRTU	diuretic
CDEIIRUV	virucide
CDEIKLNU	unlicked
CDEIKLOS	sidelock
CDEIKLOT	tide-lock
CDEIKLWY	wickedly
CDEIKNPU	unpicked
CDEIKNTU	tunicked
CDEIKOST	die-stock
CDEILLOR	collider
CDEILLOU	lodicule
CDEILLPU	pellucid
CDEILMOP	complied
CDEILMOS	melodics
CDEILMRU	dulcimer
CDEILMSY	dysmelic
CDEILNRY	cylinder
CDEILNSU	unsliced
CDEILOOW	woodlice
CDEILOPS	scopelid
CDEILOPU	clupeoid
CDEILORS	scleroid
CDEILORV	coverlid
CDEILOSS	disclose
CDEILPPR	crippled
CDEILRTY	directly
CDEILSXY	dyslexic
CDEIMNRU	mind-cure
CDEIMOST	Docetism
	domestic
CDEIMPRS	scrimped
CDEINNOU	uncoined
CDEINOOZ	endozoic
CDEINORR	cordiner
CDEINORS	consider
CDEINORT	centroid
	doctrine
CDEINORU	decurion
CDEINOST	deontics
CDEINOTU	eduction
CDEINOUV	unvoiced
CDEINPRS	prescind
CDEINPRU	unpriced
CDEINPSY	dyspneic
CDEINRRU	incurred
CDEINRUV	incurved
CDEINSTY	syndetic
CDEIOPRT	depictor
CDEIOPST	despotic
CDEIOPTY	copy-edit
CDEIORRT	creditor
	director
CDEIORRV	co-driver
	divorcer
CDEIORSU	discoure
CDEIORSV	discover
CDEIORSY	decisory
CDEIOSTT	Docetist
CDEIPRST	scripted
CDEIPRSY	cyprides
CDEIRSTU	crudités
CDEKLMOR	clerkdom
CDEKLMOU	duckmole
CDEKLMRU	mud-clerk
CDEKLNOU	unlocked
CDEKLOPU	uplocked
CDEKLORY	yeldrock
CDEKNOOU	uncooked
CDEKNSUU	unsucked
CDEKNTUU	untucked
CDELLNUU	unculled
CDELLOOP	clodpole
CDELLORS	scrolled
CDELLORU	colluder
CDELLOTU	cloudlet
CDELMNOO	monocled
CDELMNOU	columned
CDELMPRU	crumpled
CDELNOSS	coldness
CDELNOSU	unclosed
CDELNOSY	secondly
CDELNOUW	uncowled
CDELNRUU	uncurled
CDELOORU	△coloured
	decolour
CDELORSS	cordless
CDELRSUY	cursedly
CDELRTUU	cultured
CDELSSTU	ductless
CDEMMRSU	scrummed
CDEMNOOW	comedown
	down-come
CDEMNOTU	document
CDEMNSUU	secundum
CDEMOOPS	composed
CDEMOSTU	costumed
	customed
CDENNOUY	uncoyned
CDENOORT	creodont
CDENOOST	secodont
CDENORTU	cornuted
CDENRSUU	sun-cured
CDENRTUU	undercut
CDENRUUV	uncurved
CDEOOPST	postcode
CDEOORSU	decorous
CDEOPRRU	producer
CDEORSST	doctress
CDEORSTU	seductor
CDEOSSTU	custodes
CDEPRUUV	upcurved
CDERSTTU	destruct
CDFIILSU	fluidics
CDFIKMNU	mindfuck
CDFIKORS	disfrock
CDFNNOOU	confound
CDGHIILN	childing
CDGHINOR	chording
CDGIINOS	discoing
CDGIKLNU	duckling
CDGIKLOR	gridlock

CDGIKORT	dog-trick
CDGILNOS	scolding
CDGILNOU	clouding
CDHHIILS	childish
CDHIILTW	twichild
CDHIIOOR	chorioid
CDHIIORT	hidrotic
	trichoid
CDHIIOSZ	schizoid
CDHIISST	distichs
CDHILOOP	chilopod
CDHILOOS	△dolichos
CDHIMOSU	dochmius
CDHINNOR	chondrin
CDHIOOPW	woodchip
CDHIOORT	trochoid
CDHIOPRW	whipcord
CDHIOPRY	hydropic
CDHIOPSY	psychoid
CDHIORRT	trichord
CDHIOSUV	disvouch
CDHKOSTU	duck-shot
CDHLOOPY	copyhold
CDHNORSU	△chondrus
CDHOORRU	urochord
CDIIIMNU	indicium
CDIIIORT	dioritic
CDIIKPST	dipstick
CDIILOTY	docility
CDIILTUY	lucidity
CDIIMNOU	conidium
	oncidium
CDIIMORS	Doricism
CDIINOOS	isodicon
	oniscoid
CDIINPRY	cyprinid
CDIINSTT	distinct
CDIIOORS	soricoid
CDIIOPRT	dioptric
CDIIORSU	Dioscuri
	sciuroid
CDIIPTUY	cupidity
	pudicity
CDIIRSTT	district
CDIJNSTU	disjunct
CDIKKNOW	kickdown
CDIKKOPR	drop-kick
CDIKLOPS	slip-dock
CDIKLPUY	lucky-dip
CDIKNOSW	windsock
CDILLOTU	dulcitol
CDILLOUY	cloudily
CDILOOPS	podsolic
CDILOORS	discolor
CDILOORT	lordotic
CDILOOTY	cotyloid
CDILOPSW	cowslip'd
CDILOSST	disclost
CDILOSTY	scolytid
CDIMMOSU	modicums
CDIMOORT	microdot
CDINNQUU	quidnunc
CDINOOOR	coronoid
CDINORSW	discrown
CDINORTU	inductor
CDINOSTU	discount
CDINOSTY	dystonic
CDIOOPRS	prosodic
CDIOORRR	corridor
CDIOPRSU	cuspidor
CDISSTUY	Dytiscus
CDJLNOUY	jocundly
CDKLOOPR	droplock
CDKLOORW	cold-work
CDKMMORU	drummock
CDKOOORW	corkwood
	rock-wood
CDLLLOOP	clodpoll
CDLNOUUY	uncloudy
CDLOORSU	sour-cold
CDLOORTY	doctorly
CDLOOSTU	outscold
CDLOOSTW	Cotswold
CDMNOOPU	compound
CDMNORUU	corundum
CDNNOOOT	conodont
CDOORRUY	corduroy
CDORSSUW	cussword
CDORSTUW	sword-cut
CEEEEIPY	eye-piece
CEEEELST	selectee
CEEEEPRS	preceese
CEEEFFIR	effierce
CEEEFFRT	effecter
CEEEFINR	enfierce
CEEEFLLR	cell-free
CEEEFNOR	conferee
CEEEGINX	exigence
CEEEGITX	exegetic
CEEEGMNR	mergence
CEEEGNRV	vergence
CEEEHKOR	Cherokee
CEEEHLRV	cheverel
CEEEHNNP	penneech
CEEEHNNY	Cheyenne
CEEEHRSS	secesher
CEEEHRSW	eschewer
CEEEHRVY	cheverye
CEEEIJTV	ejective
CEEEILNN	lenience
CEEEILNS	licensee
CEEEILNT	telecine
CEEEILRT	erectile
CEEEILTV	cleveite
	elective
CEEEIMNN	eminence
CEEEIMPR	empierce
CEEEIMRR	reremice
CEEEINNT	enceinte
CEEEINOP	one-piece
CEEEINPR	piecener
CEEEINRS	ceresine
CEEEIOPT	toe-piece
CEEEIPRR	creperie
CEEEIPRV	perceive
CEEEIPST	set-piece
CEEEIRRV	receiver
CEEEIRSX	exercise
CEEEIRTV	erective
CEEEJRRT	rejecter
CEEEKNNP	penneeck
CEEELLNR	crenelle
CEEELPRT	pre-elect
CEEELRST	reselect
CEEELRTT	electret
	tercelet
CEEEMNRT	cementer
	cerement
CEEEMRTY	cemetery
CEEEMSUX	excuse-me
CEEENNPT	tenpence
CEEENNST	sentence
CEEENPRS	presence
CEEENPRT	pretence
CEEENQSU	sequence
CEEENRRS	screener
CEEENRRT	recentre
CEEENSST	centeses
CEEEPRTX	expecter
CEEERRSV	screever
CEEERRTX	excreter
CEEERSSS	recesses
CEEERSST	sesterce
CEEERTTV	crevette
CEEERTUX	executer
CEEFFORT	effector
CEEFHIKR	kerchief
CEEFHIRY	chiefery
CEEFHISS	chiefess
CEEFHIST	chiefest
CEEFHLRT	fletcher
CEEFHLRU	cheerful
CEEFIINT	inficete
CEEFILRT	telferic
CEEFILRY	fiercely
CEEFINPP	fippence
CEEFINRT	frenetic
CEEFIPRT	perfecti
CEEFIRTY	free-city
CEEFKLSS	feckless
CEEFLLLU	fuel-cell
CEEFLNOR	△florence
CEEFLNTU	feculent
CEEFLRUU	flue-cure
CEEFNORR	confrère
	enforcer
	renforce
CEEFNRVY	fervency
CEEFOPRR	perforce
CEEFOPRT	perfecto
CEEFORRS	frescoer
CEEFORSS	frescoes
CEEFORST	cost-free
	free-cost
	scot-free
CEEGGILS	egg-slice

CEEGHLOW	cogwheel
CEEGILOT	eclogite
CEEGILRT	telergic
CEEGILRU	rice-glue
CEEGIMNS	miscegen
CEEGINOR	erogenic
CEEGINPR	creeping
CEEGINRT	gentrice
CEEGINST	genetics
CEEGINSU	eugenics
CEEGINXY	exigency
CEEGIORX	exoergic
CEEGKNOS	Geckones
CEEGLLOR	colleger
CEEGMMOR	commerge
CEEGNNOO	oncogene
CEEGNNOR	congener
CEEGNNPU	pungence
CEEGNOOS	Congoese
CEEGNORT	congreet
	coregent
CEEGNORV	Congreve
	converge
CEEGNOTY	ectogeny
CEEGNRVY	vergency
CEEHHIRS	Cheshire
CEEHHMNN	henchmen
CEEHIIST	ethicise
CEEHIITZ	ethicize
CEEHIKLY	cheekily
CEEHIKNW	cheewink
CEEHILLN	chenille
	Hellenic
CEEHILLS	shell-ice
CEEHILLV	cheville
CEEHILRT	telechir
CEEHILRV	cheveril
CEEHILRW	clerihew
CEEHILRY	cheerily
CEEHILSW	swelchie
CEEHILTV	Helvetic
CEEHIMRT	hermetic
CEEHINOR	coinhere
CEEHINPR	encipher
CEEHINPT	phenetic
CEEHINST	sithence
CEEHINTT	enthetic
CEEHIORS	cheerios
CEEHIOSV	cohesive
CEEHIPRT	herpetic
CEEHIRSS	richesse
CEEHIRTU	heuretic
CEEHISTT	esthetic
CEEHKRSS	Cherkess
CEEHKRST	sketcher
CEEHKRTV	kvetcher
CEEHLLOR	Rochelle
CEEHLNOO	Holocene
CEEHLNOT	enclothe
CEEHLNPU	penuchle
CEEHLNSU	elenchus
CEEHLORT	reclothe

CEEHLOSS	echoless
CEEHLTUW	wheel-cut
CEEHMNOR	chromene
CEEHMORT	comether
CEEHMOTY	hemocyte
CEEHNNOW	nowhence
CEEHNNRT	entrench
CEEHNORT	coherent
CEEHNORV	cheveron
CEEHNQRU	quencher
CEEHNRRT	retrench
	trencher
CEEHNRST	△trenches
CEEHOPRY	coryphee
CEEHOPTT	pochette
CEEHORRS	cosherer
CEEHORRT	hectorer
	torchère
CEEHPRRY	perchery
CEEHQRSU	chequers
CEEHRTTU	teuchter
CEEIIMNP	mince-pie
CEEIIMPR	epimeric
CEEIIMRT	eremitic
CEEIINRT	icterine
CEEIINST	niceties
CEEIINVV	evincive
CEEIIPTU	cutie-pie
CEEIIRST	sericite
CEEIJNOT	ejection
CEEIJORR	rejoicer
CEEIJRUV	verjuice
CEEIKLMU	leukemic
CEEIKLNN	neckline
CEEIKLPR	pickerel
CEEIKNRS	sickener
CEEIKPRT	picketer
CEEILLLP	pellicle
CEEILLNT	lenticel
	lenticle
CEEILMPS	semplice
CEEILNNT	centinel
CEEILNNY	leniency
CEEILNOP	Pliocene
CEEILNOT	coteline
	election
CEEILNOV	violence
CEEILNPT	Pentelic
CEEILNPX	cineplex
CEEILNRR	recliner
CEEILNRS	licenser
	silencer
CEEILNRU	cerulein
CEEILNRV	vernicle
CEEILORR	recoiler
CEEILOSS	solecise
CEEILOSZ	solecize
CEEILQSU	liquesce
CEEILRST	sclerite
CEEILRSU	ciseleur
	ciselure
CEEILRSV	versicle

CEEILRTU	reticule
CEEILRTY	celerity
CEEILSSV	viceless
CEEILSTT	telestic
	testicle
CEEIMMPY	empyemic
CEEIMMRS	mesmeric
CEEIMNNY	eminency
CEEIMNPS	specimen
CEEIMORT	meteoric
CEEIMSTT	smectite
CEEINNOT	neotenic
CEEINNPZ	pince-nez
CEEINNRS	incenser
CEEINNRT	incentre
CEEINNSS	niceness
CEEINNST	nescient
CEEINORR	encierro
CEEINORT	erection
	neoteric
CEEINORV	overnice
CEEINORX	exocrine
CEEINOSS	senecios
CEEINOST	icestone
	seicento
CEEINOTV	evection
CEEINPRT	prentice
	'prentice
CEEINPST	pectines
CEEINPSX	sixpence
CEEINRST	scienter
	secretin
CEEINRSU	insecure
	sinecure
CEEINRTT	reticent
CEEINRTU	ceinture
	enuretic
CEEINSST	centesis
CEEINSTY	cysteine
CEEIOPPR	pericope
CEEIOPPS	episcope
CEEIOPTW	two-piece
CEEIORST	esoteric
CEEIORSX	exorcise
CEEIORTT	erotetic
CEEIORTX	exoteric
CEEIORXZ	exorcize
CEEIOSTV	covetise
CEEIPPRT	precepit
CEEIPPTU	eupeptic
CEEIRRTU	ureteric
CEEIRSSV	△services
CEEIRSTU	cerusite
CEEIRSTV	vertices
CEEIRSVX	cervixes
CEEISUVX	excusive
CEEJKOTT	jockette
CEEJORRT	rejector
CEEKKNPS	kenspeck
CEEKLRSS	clerkess
	reckless
CEEKNORR	reckoner

CEEKNRSU	suckener
CEEKOPRX	ox-pecker
CEEKORRT	corktree
	rocketer
CEEKOSTT	sockette
CEELLMOU	molecule
CEELLNOU	nucleole
CEELLORT	récollet
CEELLRVY	cleverly
CEELLSSU	clueless
CEELMOPT	complete
CEELMORW	welcomer
CEELMOST	telecoms
CEELMRTU	electrum
CEELNNOP	penoncel
CEELNNOT	non-elect
CEELNOPU	opulence
CEELNORS	encloser
CEELNORT	electron
CEELNORU	encolure
CEELNPTU	centuple
CEELNRTU	relucent
CEELNRTY	recently
CEELNSTU	esculent
CEELORSS	coreless
	sclerose
CEELORST	corselet
	electros
	selector
CEELORTV	coverlet
CEELOSSU	coleuses
CEELPRST	plectres
CEELRRTU	lecturer
CEELRSST	lectress
CEELRSSU	cureless
CEELRSTY	secretly
CEELRSUY	securely
CEEMMNTU	cementum
CEEMNORR	cremorne
CEEMNORW	newcomer
CEEMNORY	ceremony
CEEMNOYZ	coenzyme
CEEMOORV	overcome
CEEMOORW	owrecome
CEENNOOS	nose-cone
CEENNORT	cretonne
CEENNORU	renounce
CEENNORV	convener
CEENNOST	centones
CEENOORV	once-over
CEENOPTW	twopence
CEENORST	ten-score
CEENORSV	conserve
	converse
CEENORTT	trecento
CEENORVY	conveyer
	reconvey
CEENPPTU	tuppence
CEENPSSU	suspence
CEENRSTU	unsecret
CEENSSTU	cuteness
CEEOORRW	orecrowe
CEEOORST	creosote
CEEOPRRT	receptor
CEEOPRTX	exceptor
CEEOPRTY	cerotype
CEEOQTTU	coquette
CEEORRRS	sorcerer
CEEORRSU	recourse
	resource
CEEORRVY	recovery
CEEORSSY	cross-eye
CEEORSTX	cortexes
CEEORTTV	corvette
CEEORTUX	executor
CEEPRRSU	precurse
CEEPRSST	respects
CEERRSST	rectress
CEERRSTU	rest-cure
CEERRTUZ	creutzer
CEERSSTW	setscrew
CEERTUXY	executry
CEFFIORU	coiffeur
	coiffure
CEFFIRSU	sufficer
CEFFLORU	forceful
CEFFLRSU	scuffler
CEFFMOOR	off-comer
CEFGHINT	fetching
CEFGLNUY	fulgency
CEFHIIMS	mischief
CEFHILNR	flincher
CEFHILRT	flichter
	rich-left
CEFHINSU	fuchsine
CEFHISTU	fuchsite
CEFHLSTU	chestful
CEFHOSSU	sous-chef
CEFIILST	felsitic
CEFIILTY	felicity
CEFIIOPR	opificer
CEFIIPRT	petrific
CEFIIRRT	ferritic
	terrific
CEFIKLOR	firelock
CEFILLLO	follicle
CEFILMRU	crimeful
	merciful
CEFILNOT	flection
CEFILOUV	voiceful
CEFINNOR	confiner
CEFINNOS	confines
CEFINORS	forensic
	forinsec
CEFINORT	infector
CEFINOTT	confetti
CEFIOORT	Corfiote
CEFIOPRS	forcipes
CEFIORTY	ferocity
CEFIRSTU	frutices
CEFIRTUV	fructive
CEFKLLOS	elflocks
CEFKLOOR	forelock
CEFKLPSY	fly-speck
CEFKLRUW	wreckful
CEFLLOSU	floscule
CEFLNRUU	furuncle
CEFLNSTU	scentful
CEFOORST	soft-core
CEFORSTU	fructose
CEGGILOO	geologic
CEGGILRS	scriggle
CEGGINOO	geogonic
CEGGIORS	Georgics
	scroggie
CEGGLNOY	glycogen
CEGHHHIT	high-tech
CEGHIINY	hygienic
CEGHIKLN	heckling
CEGHILNT	letching
CEGHIMNS	scheming
CEGHINPR	perching
CEGHIRTU	theurgic
CEGHMRUY	chemurgy
CEGHNORS	groschen
CEGHOORS	hog-score
CEGHORSU	choregus
CEGIIKNV	vice-king
CEGIILNT	gentilic
CEGIILOP	epilogic
CEGIILOS	logicise
CEGIILOZ	logicize
CEGIINNT	enticing
CEGIINPR	piercing
CEGIINSS	gneissic
CEGIINTX	exciting
CEGIIOST	egoistic
CEGIJLOU	logjuice
CEGIKKLN	keckling
CEGIKLNR	reckling
CEGIKNRW	wrecking
CEGILNOO	neologic
CEGILNPU	cupeling
CEGILNRY	glycerin
CEGILNTU	cultigen
CEGILRSY	lysergic
CEGIMNOY	myogenic
CEGIMNUY	gynecium
CEGINNRT	centring
CEGINNST	scenting
CEGINNSY	ensigncy
CEGINOOP	geoponic
CEGINOOR	orogenic
CEGINOOZ	zoogenic
CEGINOPY	pyogenic
CEGINORT	gerontic
CEGINORV	covering
CEGINOTV	coveting
	Vietcong
CEGINRSU	rescuing
CEGINRSW	screwing
CEGINRSY	synergic
CEGIRSTU	scutiger
CEGLLOOU	collogue
CEGLLORY	glycerol
CEGLLRYY	glyceryl

CEGLNOTY	cogently
CEGLOOOY	oecology
CEGLOOTY	cetology
CEGMNNOO	cognomen
CEGNNPUY	pungency
CEGNOOTY	gonocyte
CEGNORSS	△congress
CEGNORSU	scrounge
CEGNORYY	cryogeny
CEGORRSU	scourger
	scrouger
CEHHHIOW	heich-how
CEHHINPY	hyphenic
CEHHNORU	hurcheon
CEHHOPTY	hypothec
CEHIILLS	chillies
CEHIILMO	hemiolic
CEHIILNN	lichenin
CEHIILNT	lecithin
CEHIILOT	eolithic
CEHIIMOP	hemiopic
CEHIIMOS	isocheim
	isochime
CEHIIMPT	mephitic
CEHIIMST	ethicism
CEHIIMTT	itch-mite
CEHIINNN	nine-inch
CEHIIOPT	Ethiopic
CEHIIRSS	Chrissie
CEHIIRST	Christie
CEHIIRTT	trichite
CEHIISTT	ethicist
	theistic
CEHIITVY	Vichyite
CEHIKLPT	klephtic
CEHIKLRS	clerkish
CEHIKLSU	suchlike
CEHIKMOS	homesick
CEHIKOST	thickoes
CEHIKSTT	thickset
CEHIKTTY	thickety
CEHILLRS	schiller
CEHILMMS	schimmel
CEHILMTY	methylic
CEHILNOP	phenolic
	pinochle
CEHILNOR	chlorine
CEHILNPY	phenylic
CEHILNSS	chinless
CEHILORT	chlorite
	clothier
CEHILORY	heroicly
CEHILPTY	phyletic
CEHILSTW	switchel
CEHILSTY	Lecythis
CEHILTTY	tetchily
CEHIMNOP	phonemic
CEHIMNOR	Nichrome®
CEHIMNSU	munchies
CEHIMOOT	homeotic
CEHIMORT	chromite
	trichome
CEHINNRT	intrench
CEHINOOS	cohesion
CEHINOPR	prochein
CEHINOPS	Echinops
CEHINOPT	phonetic
CEHINOPU	euphonic
CEHINORU	unheroic
CEHINOSY	hyoscine
CEHINOTY	onychite
CEHINPRS	pinchers
	pinscher
CEHINPRU	uncipher
CEHINRSS	richness
CEHINRST	christen
	snitcher
CEHINRTU	ruthenic
CEHIOORS	isochore
CEHIOPRS	sopheric
CEHIOPRU	euphoric
CEHIOPST	postiche
CEHIORRT	rhetoric
	torchier
CEHIORSS	orchesis
CEHIORTT	trochite
CEHIPRSS	spherics
CEHIPRST	spitcher
CEHIRSTT	stitcher
CEHIRSTY	hysteric
CEHIRTTW	twitcher
CEHIRTWY	witchery
CEHISSTT	stitches
CEHISSUW	suchwise
CEHKLLOS	skelloch
CEHKLORS	△sherlock
CEHKLOSU	suck-hole
CEHKNORW	rock-hewn
CEHKNPUY	keypunch
CEHKRSTU	huckster
CEHLLMSU	schellum
CEHLLOUY	louchely
CEHLMNOU	homuncle
CEHLNNOU	luncheon
CEHLNOTU	unclothe
CEHLORSU	sloucher
CEHLORTY	hectorly
CEHLOSTU	selcouth
CEHLPPSY	schleppy
CEHLQSUY	squelchy
CEHLSTUY	lecythus
CEHMNRTU	truchmen
CEHMNSSU	muchness
CEHMOOSZ	schmooze
CEHMORUV	overmuch
CEHNNNOU	nuncheon
CEHNNOPU	puncheon
CEHNNOSU	nonesuch
	unchosen
CEHNOORS	schooner
CEHNOPTU	putcheon
CEHNORTU	chounter
	hen-court
CEHNORVY	chevrony
CEHNSSSU	suchness
CEHNSTTU	chestnut
CEHOOORZ	zoochore
CEHOOPST	post-echo
CEHOORSU	ocherous
	ochreous
CEHOOSTU	cot-house
CEHOOSUW	cowhouse
CEHOPPRS	choppers
CEHOPPRY	prophecy
CEHORSSZ	scherzos
CEHORSTU	scouther
CEHORSTW	scowther
CEHOTTUZ	zuchetto
CEHRSTTY	stretchy
CEIIILMN	Milicien
CEIIILSV	civilise
CEIIILVZ	civilize
CEIIIMNT	ciminite
CEIIINOS	Ionicise
CEIIINOZ	Ionicize
CEIIINSS	sinicise
CEIIINSV	incisive
CEIIINSZ	sinicize
CEIIJSTU	Jesuitic
CEIIKLMR	limerick
CEIIKLNR	licker-in
CEIIKMMR	mimicker
CEIIKNSS	kinesics
CEIIKNST	kinetics
CEIIKSST	ekistics
CEIILLMT	mellitic
CEIILLNO	linoleic
CEIILLOP	pollicie
CEIILLPT	elliptic
CEIILLSU	silicule
CEIILMNT	limnetic
CEIILMOT	cimolite
CEIILNOS	isocline
	silicone
CEIILNQU	clinique
CEIILNSS	enclisis
CEIILOPP	epiploic
	epipolic
CEIILOPS	policies
CEIILORT	elicitor
CEIILOST	Siceliot
CEIILOTZ	zeolitic
CEIILPRT	perlitic
CEIILPRU	pirlicue
CEIILPTX	explicit
CEIILPTY	pyelitic
CEIILRTV	verticil
CEIILSSS	scissile
CEIIMNOT	emiction
CEIIMOPT	epitomic
CEIIMORS	isomeric
CEIIMOST	semiotic
CEIIMRRT	trimeric
CEIIMRST	meristic
	trisemic
CEIIMSST	Semitics

CEIINNOP nepionic
CEIINNOR irenicon
CEIINNOS oscinine
CEIINNOT nicotine
CEIINNRT intrince
CEIINNST inscient
CEIINOPS epinosic
CEIINOPT epitonic
CEIINORS recision
soricine
CEIINOSX excision
CEIINOTV eviction
CEIINRSU incisure
sciurine
CEIINRTU neuritic
CEIINSTU cutinise
CEIINSTY cytisine
syenitic
CEIINTUZ cutinize
CEIIOPRS iriscope
CEIIOPRT periotic
CEIIOPTT picotite
CEIIOSTV sovietic
CEIIPRSS crispies
CEIIPRST priciest
CEIIQRTU critique
CEIIRSTT rectitis
CEIIRSTV veristic
CEIISTVV vivisect
CEIJMOOU moo-juice
CEIJNORT injector
CEIJNOUV cunjevoi
CEIJRSTU justicer
CEIKKNRS knickers
CEIKKRRS skerrick
CEIKLNPS spicknel
CEIKLOSV lovesick
CEIKLRST stickler
strickle
CEIKLRSY sickerly
CEIKLRTT tricklet
CEIKMNOR monicker
CEIKMOPT impocket
CEIKMORS △ockerism
CEIKMPPU pick-me-up
CEIKMRSU musicker
CEIKNNSU insucken
CEIKNOTY cytokine
CEIKNRST stricken
CEIKNRSU unsicker
CEIKNSSS sickness
CEIKORTV tick-over
CEIKPPRU picker-up
CEIKQSTU quickset
CEIKRRTY trickery
CEIKRTTY ricketty
CEILLNOU nucleoli
CEILLOPS pollices
CEILLOQU coquille
CEILLORS orsellic
CEILLORY colliery
CEILLOTU coutille

CEILLRTU telluric
CEILMMUY mycelium
CEILMNOP compline
CEILMNOT monticle
CEILMOPR compiler
complier
CEILMOPS polemics
CEILMOSS solecism
CEILMOSU coliseum
CEILMPUU peculium
CEILMTUU lutecium
CEILNNOT contline
CEILNNSY syncline
CEILNOOS Colonies
colonise
eclosion
CEILNOOZ colonize
CEILNOPR percolin
replicon
CEILNOPT leptonic
CEILNORS incloser
licensor
CEILNPRY princely
CEILNRTU lincture
CEILNRUV culverin
CEILNSUU unsluice
CEILOPPS Popsicle®
CEILOPRT petrolic
CEILOPRV proclive
CEILOPTU epulotic
poultice
CEILOPTY epicotyl
CEILORST cloister
coistrel
creolist
CEILORTY cryolite
CEILOSST solecist
solstice
CEILOSSU △coulisse
CEILOTVY velocity
CEILPRSU surplice
CEILPRUU purlicue
CEILRRSU scurrile
CEIMMNNO mnemonic
CEIMMNOU encomium
meconium
CEIMMORT recommit
CEIMMRSY merycism
CEIMNNOO encomion
CEIMNNOY neomycin
CEIMNOPT pentomic
CEIMNOPY eponymic
CEIMNORS cremosin
sermonic
CEIMNORT intercom
CEIMNRST centrism
CEIMNSSU meniscus
CEIMOOSZ Mesozoic
CEIMOOUZ zooecium
CEIMOPRS comprise
CEIMORRT morticer
CEIMORSX exorcism

CEIMORSY isocryme
CEIMORTY emictory
CEIMOSSS cosmesis
CEIMRRSU scrimure
CEIMRRTU turmeric
CEIMSSTY systemic
CEINNNOT innocent
CEINNNOU inconnue
CEINNORS incensor
CEINNORU neuronic
CEINNORV conniver
CEINNOTU continue
CEINNOTW Newtonic
CEINOOTZ entozoic
enzootic
CEINOPPR cornpipe
CEINOPRS conspire
incorpse
CEINOPRT inceptor
CEINOPRV province
CEINOPTT entoptic
CEINOPTU unpoetic
CEINORRS resorcin
CEINORRT tricorne
CEINORSS necrosis
CEINORTT contrite
cornetti
CEINORTU neurotic
CEINORTV contrive
CEINOSSS cosiness
CEINOSSX coxiness
CEINOSTT centoist
stenotic
CEINOSTY cytosine
CEINOTTU Teutonic
CEINPRSS princess
CEINRSTT centrist
CEINRSVV crivvens
CEINRTTU intercut
tincture
CEIOOPTV co-optive
CEIOOTUV outvoice
CEIOOTXX exotoxic
CEIOPPSY episcopy
CEIOPRRU croupier
CEIOPRST persicot
CEIOPRSU precious
rice-soup
CEIOPRTU eutropic
outprice
CEIOPRTY Cypriote
CEIOPSSU specious
CEIORRTU courtier
CEIORRUZ cruzeiro
CEIORSST crosstie
CEIORSSX sixscore
CEIORSTU citreous
CEIORSTV vortices
CEIORSTX exorcist
CEIORTTU toreutic
CEIPRRST rescript

CEIPRSTU	crepitus
	pictures
	piecrust
CEIRRRSU	scurrier
CEIRRSTT	restrict
CEIRSSSU	scissure
CEIRSSTV	victress
CEIRSTUY	security
CEISSSTU	cistuses
CEJLMOUU	Leucojum
CEJLOOSY	jocosely
CEJNORRU	conjurer
CEJNRTUU	juncture
CEKKNORS	knockers
CEKLLNOR	roll-neck
CEKLLOOV	lovelock
CEKLLSSU	luckless
CEKLNOST	stenlock
CEKLOORS	cork-sole
CEKLOORV	overlock
CEKLOPST	lockstep
CEKLRRTU	truckler
CEKLRSSU	sucklers
CEKNOPST	penstock
CEKNORTU	cokernut
CEKNOSTU	unsocket
CEKOOORV	overcook
CEKOORRW	co-worker
CEKOPRST	sprocket
CEKORRTY	rocketry
CELLNSUU	nucellus
CELLNTUU	luculent
CELLOOQU	colloque
CELLOSSY	cloyless
CELLRSUY	scullery
CELMNOTY	cloyment
CELMNOUY	uncomely
CELMNTUU	muculent
CELMOOOT	locomote
CELMOOSY	cloysome
CELMOPSU	compulse
CELMOPSY	symploce
CELMOSUU	cumulose
CELMPRTU	plectrum
CELMPSUU	speculum
CELNNOTY	nocently
CELNNOUV	uncloven
CELNOORS	consoler
CELNOORT	contrôlé
CELNOORU	encolour
CELNOOSS	coolness
CELNOOVV	convolve
CELNOPRT	plectron
CELNOPUU	uncouple
CELNORTW	crownlet
CELNORWY	clownery
CELNOSUV	convulse
CELNOSVY	solvency
CELNOVXY	convexly
CELNPTUU	punctule
CELOOORV	over-cool
CELOOPSS	cesspool
CELOORRU	colourer
CELOORTW	colewort
CELOORVY	overcloy
CELOOSTU	loose-cut
CELOPSSU	Scopelus
CELOPSUU	opuscule
CELOPTTU	octuplet
CELORSST	crosslet
CELORSSU	sclerous
CELORSTY	coystrel
CELORSUU	ulcerous
	urceolus
CELORSUY	crousely
CELORTTU	courtlet
CELORTVY	covertly
CELOSTTU	culottes
CELPRRSU	scrupler
CELPRSSU	scruples
CELPRSUY	sprucely
CELRSTTU	scuttler
CELRSTUY	clustery
CEMMNOOR	commoner
CEMMNOOS	consommé
CEMMNOOY	commoney
CEMMORTU	commuter
CEMNOORR	cromorne
CEMNOOTY	monocyte
CEMNOPTT	contempt
CEMNORSU	consumer
	mucrones
CEMNRSTU	centrums
CEMOOPRS	composer
CEMOORST	Rome-scot
CEMOORSY	sycomore
CEMOOSTY	cytosome
CEMOPRSS	compress
CEMOPRTU	computer
CEMORSTU	costumer
	customer
CEMPRSTU	spectrum
CENNOORV	convenor
CENNORRT	cornrent
CENNORTU	nocturne
CENNOSTT	contents
CENOOOTZ	ectozoon
CENOOPST	scoop-net
CENOORSU	corneous
CENOORTT	cornetto
CENOORVY	conveyor
CENOPRSY	necropsy
CENOQSTU	△conquest
CENORRTU	trouncer
CENORSTU	construe
CENORSUU	cernuous
	coenurus
CENORSUY	cynosure
CENORTVY	Coventry
CENOSSTU	countess
CENPRTUU	puncture
CENRSSTU	curtness
CEOOOPST	otoscope
CEOOPRRV	overcrop
CEOORRVW	overcrow
CEOORSTW	two-score
CEOOSTUV	covetous
CEOPPRST	△prospect
CEOPRRRU	procurer
CEOPRSTW	screwtop
CEOPRSUU	cupreous
CEOQRTUY	coquetry
CEORRSTY	corsetry
CEORSTUY	courtesy
CEPPRSSU	scuppers
CEPPRTUU	uppercut
CEPRSTUU	cutpurse
CERSSUUX	excursus
CFFGIMNU	McGuffin
CFFGINOS	scoffing
CFFHINOS	chiffons
CFFIRTUY	fructify
CFGHIILN	filching
CFGIKNOR	frocking
CFGINORT	crofting
CFGINOSU	focusing
CFHIINOO	finochio
CFHIIORR	horrific
CFHIKORS	rockfish
CFHILPTY	flypitch
CFHIMOSS	scomfish
CFHIMSSU	scumfish
CFHLOPUU	pouchful
CFIIILSY	silicify
CFIIKNYZ	zinckify
CFIIKQUX	quick-fix
CFIILMNU	fulminic
CFIILOPR	prolific
CFIILPSU	pulsific
CFIIMNOS	somnific
CFIIMORT	mortific
CFIINOPT	pontific
CFIINORT	friction
CFIISSTU	Sufistic
CFIKLSTU	stickful
CFIKPSTU	puckfist
CFILMOOR	coliform
CFILRSUU	sulfuric
CFIMNOOR	coniform
CFIMNORU	unciform
CFINNOTU	function
CFIOSTTY	Scottify
CFLLOPRU	cropfull
CFLMRSUU	fulcrums
CFLNOORT	cornloft
CFLNORSU	scornful
CFLOOPSU	scoopful
CFLOPRSU	cropfuls
CFMOORST	comforts
CFNNOORT	confront
CFOOORTW	crowfoot
CFRSTUUU	usufruct
CGGGHINU	chugging
CGGHINOU	coughing
CGGIINNR	cringing
CGGILRSY	scriggly

Words marked △ may be spelled also with a capital letter

CGHIILLN	chilling
CGHIINNP	pinching
CGHIINPP	chipping
CGHIINPR	chirping
CGHIINPT	pitching
CGHIINTW	witching
CGHIKNNU	chunking
CGHIKNOS	shocking
CGHIKNSU	shucking
CGHILNOT	clothing
CGHIMNPU	chumping
CGHIMPSY	sphygmic
CGHINNOT	notching
CGHINNRU	churning
CGHINOPP	chopping
CGHINORT	torching
CGHINOSU	hocusing
CGHINOTU	touching
CGHINPTU	pinchgut
CGHINRSU	crushing
CGHLOOST	shot-clog
CGHNOOSU	souchong
CGIIILNT	lignitic
CGIIKLNN	clinking
CGIIKLNS	slicking
CGIIKLNT	tickling
CGIIKMMY	gimmicky
CGIIKNNZ	zincking
CGIIKNPR	pricking
CGIIKNPS	pickings
CGIIKNRT	tricking
CGIIKNST	sticking
CGIILMOS	logicism
CGIILNPP	clipping
CGIILOST	logicist
	logistic
CGIILRTU	liturgic
CGIIMNNO	incoming
CGIINOOS	isogonic
CGIINORT	trigonic
CGIKKNNO	knocking
CGIKLNOR	rockling
CGIKLNSU	suckling
CGIKMNOS	smocking
CGIKNORW	corkwing
	king-crow
CGIKNOST	stocking
CGIKNRTU	trucking
CGIKNSTU	gunstick
CGILLNSU	sculling
CGILLNUY	cullying
CGILMNOO	Mongolic
CGILMNPU	clumping
CGILMNSU	muscling
CGILMNUU	cingulum
	glucinum
CGILNNOW	clowning
CGILNOOY	cooingly
CGILNOPU	coupling
CGILNOSW	scowling
CGILNOTT	clotting
CGILOORU	urologic
CGILPSTY	glyptics
CGIMMNSU	scumming
CGIMNNOO	gnomonic
	oncoming
CGIMNOPU	upcoming
CGIMRRUY	micrurgy
CGINNOOR	crooning
CGINNORS	scorning
CGINNORW	crowning
CGINOOPS	scooping
CGINOOTV	cognovit
CGINOPPR	cropping
CGINORSS	crossing
CGINORSU	coursing
	scouring
	sourcing
CGINORTU	courting
CGINOSTU	scouting
CGINRRUY	currying
CGINSTTU	tungstic
CGINSTUU	Tungusic
CGKLOSTU	gust-lock
CGKNOSTU	gunstock
CGLLOSYY	glycosyl
CGLMOOYY	mycology
CGLNOOOY	oncology
CGLOOOTY	tocology
CGLOOTYY	cytology
CGMNNOOR	mongcorn
CGMNNORU	mungcorn
CGNNOOOS	coon-song
CHHIIKST	thickish
CHHIILTY	hitchily
CHHIINPT	pinch-hit
CHHIIPST	phthisic
CHHILRSU	churlish
CHHIMRTY	rhythmic
CHHIOPPS	chip-shop
CHHNORSU	rhonchus
CHHOOPTT	hotchpot
CHIIKLST	ticklish
CHIIKRST	trickish
CHIIKSTU	Kushitic
CHIILLLY	chillily
CHIILMSY	hylicism
CHIILNNP	linchpin
CHIILOST	holistic
CHIILPRY	chirpily
CHIILQSU	cliquish
CHIILSTY	hylicist
CHIIMPRU	pichurim
CHIINOPS	siphonic
CHIINORT	ornithic
CHIIORSS	chorisis
CHIIORST	historic
	orchitis
CHIIPPRU	hippuric
CHIIRSTT	tristich
CHIKLLOY	hillocky
CHIKMNNU	munchkin
CHIKMNPU	chipmunk
CHIKMNTU	mutchkin
CHIKNNOP	phinnock
CHIKOPST	tick-shop
CHIKOPTY	kyphotic
CHIKORST	trochisk
CHIKPSYY	physicky
CHILLOOT	oilcloth
CHILMOPS	complish
CHILMOSU	scholium
CHILNNPY	lynchpin
CHILNOOS	scholion
CHILNOSW	clownish
CHILNPSY	lip-synch
CHILOOOZ	holozoic
CHILOOPT	holoptic
CHILOTUY	touchily
CHILRSTY	Christly
CHIMMORU	chromium
CHIMNOOR	hormonic
CHIMNORW	inch-worm
CHIMNOSU	insomuch
CHIMNOUY	onychium
CHIMOORU	mouchoir
CHIMORST	christom
CHIMPSSY	psychism
CHINOORT	orthicon
CHINOORZ	C-horizon
CHINOPTY	hypnotic
	pythonic
	△typhonic
CHINORTU	cothurni
CHINOSSU	cushions
CHINOSTZ	schizont
CHINOSUY	cushiony
CHINSTTU	unstitch
CHIOOPPT	photopic
CHIOORSU	ichorous
CHIOORTT	orthotic
CHIOPRST	strophic
CHIOPSTY	hypocist
CHIORSSS	crossish
CHIOSSTT	Scottish
CHIPRRUY	chirrupy
CHIPRTTY	triptych
CHIPSSTY	psychist
CHIRRSSU	scirrhus
CHKMMOUY	hummocky
CHKNORSU	cornhusk
CHKOOPPR	pork-chop
CHLNOOOP	colophon
CHLNORUW	churn-owl
CHLOORSU	chlorous
CHLOPSTY	splotchy
CHLORTUY	choultry
CHMNOORT	cornmoth
CHMNORRU	crumhorn
CHMNORSU	Rumonsch
CHMNPRUU	rum-punch
CHNOOPTT	top-notch
CHNORSTU	cothurns
CHOOORTY	choy-root
CHOOORYZ	zoochory
CHOOPSTU	octopush

CHORSTTU	short-cut
CIIIKNTU	cuitikin
CIIILMPT	implicit
CIIILMSU	silicium
CIIILPST	spilitic
CIIILSTV	civilist
CIIILTVY	civility
CIIIMNSS	Sinicism
CIIIMNSV	incivism
CIIINNOS	incision
CIIINTVY	vicinity
CIIJRSTU	juristic
CIIKLLSY	sicklily
CIIKLOPT	politick
CIIKLPST	lipstick
CIIKLRTY	trickily
CIIKLSTY	stickily
CIIKMNPX	pick-'n'-mix
CIIKNOOT	cootikin
CIIKNORS	iron-sick
CIIKNPPR	pin-prick
CIILLNOP	pollinic
CIILMNOT	Miltonic
CIILMOPY	impolicy
CIILMOSS	sciolism
CIILMQSU	cliquism
CIILMRSY	lyricism
CIILNOOT	noctilio
CIILNOPS	psilocin
CIILOOPT	politico
CIILOORS	Coriolis
CIILOOTZ	zoolitic
CIILOPPT	poplitic
CIILOPST	politics
	psilotic
CIILORST	clitoris
	coistril
CIILOSST	sciolist
CIILOSTY	solicity
CIILOSVV	slivovic
CIILRSTY	lyricist
CIILRTUU	utriculi
CIIMNOOS	isonomic
CIIMNOST	monistic
	nomistic
CIIMORST	trisomic
CIIMOSST	misticos
	stoicism
CIIMRSTY	myristic
CIIMRTTU	Triticum
CIINNNOO	non-ionic
CIINNSTT	instinct
CIINOOST	isotonic
CIINOOTZ	zoonitic
CIINOPSS	psionics
CIINOPSU	opinicus
CIINORSY	incisory
CIINOSSS	scission
CIINOSTT	stiction
CIINOTTY	tonicity
CIINPSTU	sinciput
CIIOOPST	isotopic
CIIOPRST	poristic
CIIOQTUX	quixotic
CIIORRWW	wirricow
CIIOTTXY	toxicity
CIIPRRTU	pruritic
CIIPRSTU	puristic
CIIRSTTU	truistic
CIISSTTY	cystitis
CIJKOSTY	joy-stick
CIJNNOOT	conjoint
CIJNNOTU	junction
CIJOOSTY	jocosity
CIKLLMTU	tuck-mill
CIKLLOPR	killcrop
CIKLLPUY	pluckily
CIKLNOST	linstock
CIKLOSSU	soul-sick
CIKLOSTY	stockily
CIKLRSSU	kiss-curl
CIKMOORS	sickroom
CIKMOPST	mopstick
CIKNNOOS	coonskin
CIKNNOST	non-stick
CIKNORST	corn-kist
CIKOSSTT	stockist
CILLMNOR	cornmill
CILLMSUY	clumsily
	cullyism
CILLNOOT	cotillon
CILLNORS	inscroll
CILLNOSU	scullion
CILLOOOT	ocotillo
CILLOORS	criollos
CILMNOPU	pulmonic
CILMNOUU	inoculum
CILMNUUV	vinculum
CILMOORS	miscolor
CILMOPSY	△olympics
CILMPRSY	scrimply
CILMPSUU	spiculum
CILNOORU	unicolor
CILNOOST	colonist
CILNOOTU	locution
CILNOPTU	△plutonic
CILNOSUY	cousinly
CILNPSTU	insculpt
CILOOPTW	cow-pilot
CILOOPYZ	polyzoic
CILOORRT	tricolor
CILOORST	cortisol
CILOORYZ	Zircoloy®
CILOOSSU	sciolous
CILOPPRY	propylic
CILORSTY	coystril
CILOSSTY	systolic
CILOSSUU	luscious
CILPSSTU	sculpsit
CILRSTTY	strictly
CILRSTUY	crustily
CILRSUVY	scurvily
CIMNOOOZ	zoonomic
CIMNOORU	coronium
CIMNOOTY	myotonic
CIMNOPRT	comprint
CIMNORSY	cronyism
CIMNOSTU	miscount
CIMNOSUY	syconium
CIMOOOTZ	zootomic
CIMOORSS	Moriscos
CIMOSTUU	muticous
CIMOSTUY	mucosity
CINNOOSS	scoinson
CINNOOST	scontion
CINNOOTU	continuo
CINNOOTX	non-toxic
CINNOSTY	syntonic
CINNQUUX	quincunx
CINOOOPT	co-option
CINOOOTZ	zoonotic
CINOOPRS	△scorpion
CINOOPRT	protonic
CINOOSUV	covinous
CINOOTXY	oxytocin
CINOPSSY	pycnosis
CINOPSTY	synoptic
CINORSTT	contrist
CINORSTU	ructions
CINORSUY	cousinry
CINOSTUV	△viscount
CINRSTTU	instruct
CINRSTUY	scrutiny
CIOOPRSS	Scorpios
CIOOPRST	porticos
CIOOPTYZ	zootypic
CIOOQSTU	coquitos
CIOORRWW	worricow
CIOORSSU	scorious
CIOOSSTU	stocious
CIOPRSSU	Scorpius
CIORRSTU	cursitor
CIORSSSS	scissors
CIPPRRUU	purpuric
CJNOORRU	conjuror
CJRSUUUU	sucurujú
CKKNOOTU	knockout
CKKOORRW	rockwork
CKLMMOSU	slummock
CKMMORUW	muck-worm
CKMNOOOR	moonrock
CKMOOOOR	cookroom
CKNRSTUU	unstruck
CKOOPSTT	stockpot
CKOSSTUY	tussocky
CLLOOQUY	colloquy
CLMMNOOY	commonly
CLMMOOOS	Comsomol
CLMOOOTY	colotomy
CLNOOOWY	cony-wool
CLNOORTU	controul
	countrol
CLNOSTUY	uncostly
CLOOOPRT	protocol
CLOORTUY	locutory
CLOOSSSU	colossus

CLOOSSTU soul-scot
CLOPRSSY cross-ply
CLOPRSTU sculptor
CLOPSSTU cost-plus
CLOSSTUY Scolytus
CLRSSUUU surculus
CMMNNOOU uncommon
CMNOOOTY oncotomy
CMNOORRW cornworm
CMNOPSTU consumpt
CMOOPRSS moss-crop
CMOPRSUX scrumpox
CNNOOORT contorno
CNOOOORT octoroon
CNOORRTY cryotron
CNOORSTU cornutos
outscorn
CNOOTTUU count-out
CNOSTUUU unctuous
COOOPSYZ zooscopy
COOPRSUU croupous
COOPRSUY uroscopy
COORRSSW cross-row
COORRWWY worrycow
COORSSTU outcross
COORTTYZ trot-cozy

D

DDDDEEOR doddered
DDDEEEFN defended
DDDEEENU undeeded
DDDEEEPY deep-dyed
DDDEEHRS shredded
DDDEENOR reddendo
DDDEENUW unwedded
DDDEEORR dodderer
DDDEIINV dividend
DDDEILNU unlidded
DDDEIMOS dismoded
DDDEINOR dendroid
DDDEINRU underdid
DDDENORW drownded
DDDIIOOR doridoid
DDEEEFLX deflexed
DDEEEFNR defender
DDEEEFRR deferred
DDEEEGNR degender
DDEEEHNU unheeded
DDEEEIMR remedied
DDEEEIWY wide-eyed
DDEEELSS deedless
DDEEEMNT demented
DDEEEMRS demersed
DDEEENNU unneeded
DDEEENRZ Enzedder
DDEEENSU unseeded
DDEEENTX extended
DDEEENUW unweeded
DDEEEOVY dove-eyed
DDEEERRT deterred
DDEEERSV deserved
DDEEEWYY dewy-eyed
DDEEFFNO offended
DDEEFGIT fidgeted
DDEEFILW field-dew
DDEEFINR friended
DDEEFINU undefide
undefied
DDEEFIPR drip-feed
DDEEFMOR deformed
DDEEFNRU underfed
DDEEFORR fodderer
DDEEGHNU unhedged
DDEEGINR enridged
DDEEGOPS △godspeed
DDEEGOTW two-edged
DDEEHRRS shredder
DDEEIIJM Medjidie
DDEEIINT inedited
DDEEIIRV redivide
DDEEILLV devilled
DDEEILRW wildered
DDEEILWY wild-eyed
DDEEINNT indented
intended
DDEEINOS one-sided
DDEEINRT dendrite
DDEEINTU unedited
DDEEIPRV deprived
DDEELLMO modelled
DDEELLUY dull-eyed
DDEELOPX exploded
DDEEMNOR endoderm
DDEEMRRU demurred
DDEENNOR donnered
DDEENNOY endodyne
DDEENNTU untended
DDEENOPR perdendo
DDEENOPW pondweed
DDEENORR reed-rond
DDEENORS endorsed
DDEENORW wondered
DDEENPRS spredden
DDEENRSU sundered
DDEEOPRW powdered
DDEERRUV verdured
DDEFFISU diffused
DDEFIILM midfield
DDEFIIMO modified
DDEFIIMW mid-wifed
DDEFLNOU unfolded
DDEFLRUU udderful
DDEFNNUU unfunded
DDEGGLOY doggedly
DDEGGNOO doggoned
DDEGHINS shedding
DDEGILMN meddling
DDEGILNP peddling
DDEGILNS sledding
DDEGILNU ungilded
DDEGILOS dislodge
DDEGILRY gliddery
DDEGINOR der-doing
DDEGINRU ungirded
DDEGINUU unguided
DDEGIORT dog-tired
DDEGLNOS gold-ends
DDEGNORU grounded
underdog
DDEGOOOR do-gooder
DDEGOOWW Wedgwood®
DDEGRRUY drudgery
DDEHILNY hiddenly
DDEHILOO idlehood
DDEHINNU unhidden
DDEHINOR dihedron
DDEHNOOU unhooded
DDEHNRSU hundreds
DDEHOOOO hoodooed
DDEHOOSW woodshed
DDEHOOWY how-d'ye-do
DDEHORSU shrouded
DDEHRSUY shuddery
DDEIIKNY dinky-die
DDEIILNR dieldrin
DDEIIMVW mid-wived
DDEIIOPS diopside
DDEIIRSV dividers
DDEIIRUV reduviid
DDEILMOV devildom
DDEILMSU mudslide
DDEILNPS splendid
DDEILNRU unriddle
DDEILOPS displode
lopsided
DDEILOSY dysodile
DDEILQRU quiddler
DDEILRST striddle
DDEILRSY sliddery
DDEILRTW twiddler
DDEIMMNU undimmed
DDEIMNNU unminded
DDEIMNUV videndum
DDEIMOSU medusoid
DDEINNRU unridden
DDEINNTU undinted
DDEINORW wind-rode
DDEINOSW disendow
downside
DDEINOWW windowed
DDEINPPU undipped
DDEINRST stridden
DDEINRSU sun-dried
DDEINRUV dun-diver
DDEIOPRS dropsied
DDEIOPRV provided
DDEIOPSS disposed
DDEIORRS disorder
DDEIOSTW two-sided
DDEIRSSU △druidess
DDEIRSTU ruddiest
sturdied
DDELLNUU undulled
DDELNORU unlorded
DDELNSUY suddenly
DDELOORW dowel-rod

DDELOOWY wool-dyed
DDELORST stroddle
DDELOSYY dysodyle
DDEMNOOU undoomed
DDEMNOST oddments
DDEMNOUU duodenum
DDEMNPUU pudendum
DDEMOOTU outmoded
DDENNOSU unsodden
DDENOOUW unwooded
DDENORUW unworded
DDENSTUY suddenty
DDEOORWW rowdedow
DDFGIILN fiddling
DDFGILNU fuddling
DDFIIOSU fiddious
DDFMNOUU dumfound
DDGGINNO ding-dong
DDGHIINW whidding
DDGHINTU thudding
DDGIIINV dividing
DDGIIKNS skidding
DDGIILMN middling
DDGIILNP piddling
DDGIILNR riddling
DDGILNOP plodding
DDGILNOT toddling
DDGILNPU puddling
DDGIMNUY muddying
DDGIMRSU drudgism
DDGINOPR prodding
DDGINPSU puddings
spudding
DDGINPUY puddingy
DDGINRUY ruddying
DDGINSTU studding
DDGOORSY dry-goods
DDHILOSY shoddily
DDHIOSWY dowdyish
DDHLLOOO dollhood
DDIIIIVV dividivi
DDIILOPY diploidy
DDIIMMUY didymium
DDIIMRSU druidism
siddurim
DDIINOPU dupondii
DDIIQTUY quiddity
DDILOOWW wildwood
DDILORSY sordidly
DDIMOSUY didymous
DDIMOSWY dowdyism
DDINNOWW downwind
DDINOOOT odontoid
DDINOOWW woodwind
DDLLOORW Old-World
old-world
world-old
DDLMORSU doldrums
DDMNOOTY Tom-noddy
DDNOORTW down-trod
DDOORWWY rowdydow
DEEEEFRR free-reed
DEEEEFRZ defreeze
DEEEEGKR kedgeree
DEEEEKNP knee-deep
DEEEEMRR △redeemer
DEEEEMST esteemed
DEEEFGIR fire-edge
DEEEFGOR fore-edge
DEEEFILN feed-line
DEEEFINR needfire
redefine
DEEEFIPP feed-pipe
DEEEFIRW fireweed
DEEEFIRY fire-eyed
DEEEFITU Fête-Dieu
DEEEFLLR refelled
DEEEFLPT deepfelt
DEEEFLRX reflexed
DEEEFMNR freedmen
DEEEFNRS fern-seed
DEEEFNRT deferent
DEEEFNST enfested
DEEEFORV overfeed
DEEEFRRR deferrer
referred
DEEEFRRT ferreted
DEEEGIPR pedigree
DEEEGISW edgewise
DEEEGLSS edgeless
DEEEGLSV selvedge
DEEEGMRR demerger
DEEEGNNR engender
DEEEGRYY grey-eyed
DEEEHLMT helmeted
DEEEHLNO dene-hole
DEEEHLRW wheedler
DEEEHLSS heedless
DEEEHMPS hemp-seed
DEEEIKLS seedlike
DEEEILNS selenide
DEEEILTV deletive
DEEEILVW weeviled
DEEEILVY evil-eyed
DEEEIMST seed-time
DEEEINRR reindeer
DEEEINRS nereides
DEEEINTV eventide
DEEEIPPR reed-pipe
DEEEIPTX expedite
DEEEIRRR derrière
DEEEIRSS diereses
DEEEJLLW jewelled
DEEEJNRU déjeuner
DEEEKOPW pokeweed
DEEELLLV levelled
DEEELLNT dentelle
DEEELLNW newelled
DEEELLPR repelled
DEEELLPX expelled
DEEELLRV revelled
DEEELMOS somedele
DEEELMOY mole-eyed
DEEELMRU mule-deer
DEEELNPU unpeeled
DEEELNSS needless
seldseen
DEEELOPV develope
DEEELOSY sloe-eyed
DEEELPST steepled
DEEELRSS redeless
DEEELRTT lettered
DEEELRTU dule-tree
DEEELRTW tweedler
DEEELSSS seedless
DEEELSSW weedless
DEEELTVV velveted
DEEEMNNT needment
DEEEMPRT tempered
DEEEMRRU murderee
DEEEMRST deemster
DEEENNRT entender
DEEENNUW unweened
DEEENOPY open-eyed
DEEENORS endorsee
DEEENPRT repetend
DEEENPRU unpeered
DEEENPRX expender
DEEENPSS deepness
DEEENRRR renderer
DEEENRRT tenderer
DEEENRRV △reverend
DEEENRRW reed-wren
DEEENRTX extender
DEEENRUV revenued
DEEENSSS seedness
DEEENSUV vendeuse
DEEEOPRR pederero
DEEEOPRT deportee
DEEEOSTY seedy-toe
DEEERRRV verderer
DEEERRST deserter
DEEERRSV deserver
reserved
reversed
DEEERRTV reverted
DEEERSTT streeted
DEEERSTX exserted
DEEERTTV revetted
DEEESTTU suedette
DEEFFGLU effulged
DEEFFINT infefted
DEEFFNOR offender
reoffend
DEEFGINR fingered
DEEFGIUW gudewife
DEEFGLOO feelgood
feel-good
DEEFGLUW gulfweed
DEEFHISS seed-fish
DEEFHLOR freehold
DEEFHLRS feldsher
DEEFHORR Hereford
DEEFIILN fedelini
DEEFIINT definite
DEEFIIRS fireside

DEEFIIRV verified
DEEFILLT filleted
DEEFILNX inflexed
DEEFILWX flix-weed
DEEFIMTU tumefied
DEEFINRR inferred
DEEFINRZ frenzied
DEEFIORS foreside
DEEFLLNU unfelled
DEEFLLUY full-eyed
DEEFLNOR forelend
DEEFLNTU defluent
DEEFLORW deflower
flowered
DEEFLPSU speedful
DEEFMORR deformer
△reformed
re-formed
DEEFMPPU feed-pump
DEEFMPRU perfumed
DEEFNRRU refunder
DEEFNSST deftness
DEEFORST deforest
forested
DEEFRTUY duty-free
DEEGGHHO hedgehog
DEEGGHIP hedgepig
DEEGGIJR jiggered
DEEGGLOR doggerel
DEEGGNOR engorged
DEEGHHOP hedge-hop
DEEGHOPS sheepdog
DEEGHORW hedgerow
DEEGHUYY hey-de-guy
DEEGIINN indigene
DEEGIISS diegesis
DEEGILMO liegedom
DEEGILMP impledge
DEEGILNO legioned
DEEGILNR engirdle
reedling
DEEGILNS seedling
DEEGILRW weregild
DEEGILRY greedily
DEEGIMRU demiurge
DEEGINPS speeding
DEEGINRS designer
redesign
resigned
DEEGINSS edginess
DEEGINST signeted
DEEGIRST digester
Erdgeist
estridge
DEEGIRSU gudesire
DEEGJPRU prejudge
DEEGKMOR Greekdom
DEEGLNOU engouled
DEEGLNOZ lozenged
DEEGLNRU elder-gun
DEEGLNRY legendry
DEEGLOPR pledgeor
DEEGLOPS dogsleep
DEEGLORV groveled
DEEGMNRU dungmere
DEEGNNOY endogeny
DEEGOTUW goutweed
DEEHHNPY hyphened
DEEHHPRS △shepherd
DEEHILNS enshield
DEEHILRS shielder
DEEHILSV dishevel
she-devil
DEEHINRR hinderer
DEEHINRS drisheen
DEEHINST disthene
DEEHIPPS sheep-dip
DEEHIPRS hesperid
perished
shred-pie
DEEHIRRS redshire
DEEHIRRT ditherer
DEEHIRSV shrieved
DEEHIRSW shrewdie
DEEHIRTW withered
DEEHIRTY heredity
DEEHKNOS keeshond
DEEHKNSU skene-dhu
DEEHLLOV hovelled
DEEHLMNU unhelmed
DEEHLMSW Weldmesh®
weldmesh
DEEHLNPU unhelped
DEEHLORV verdelho
DEEHNORR deerhorn
deer-horn
dehorner
DEEHNORT dethrone
threnode
DEEHNOSY hony-seed
DEEHNOWY honeydew
honey-dew
DEEHORRT dehorter
DEEHORSU rose-hued
DEEHOSUY dye-house
DEEIILNS sideline
DEEIILRV liveried
DEEIIMRS dimerise
DEEIIMRZ dimerize
DEEIINSX endeixis
DEEIIPRS Pierides
DEEIIPRU prie-dieu
DEEIIRSS dieresis
DEEIIRST siderite
DEEIIRSV derisive
DEEIISSS disseise
DEEIISSW sidewise
DEEIISSZ disseize
DEEIKLLR killdeer
DEEIKLMW milk-weed
DEEIKLNN enkindle
DEEIKLNR rekindle
DEEIKLOV dovelike
DEEIKLSW silkweed
DEEIKMSY miskeyed
DEEIKNPS skin-deep
DEEIKNPY pink-eyed
DEEIKNRS deerskin
DEEIKRSU Dukeries
DEEIKSTT diskette
DEEILLMP impelled
milleped
DEEILLNO nielloed
DEEILLOR orielled
DEEILLPR perilled
DEEILLRT tredille
DEEILLRV rivelled
DEEILMNU demi-lune
DEEILMOS melodise
DEEILMOZ melodize
DEEILNOT deletion
DEEILNRU underlie
DEEILNSS idleness
DEEILNST lintseed
tinseled
DEEILNUV unveiled
DEEILOPT lepidote
petioled
DEEILORT dolerite
DEEILORV evil-doer
DEEILOTT toileted
DEEILPSY speedily
DEEILRSU leisured
DEEILRSV desilver
DEEILRTT littered
DEEILRVY delivery
DEEILSST tideless
DEEILSSV deviless
DEEILSUV delusive
DEEILTUY △yuletide
DEEIMMNS endemism
DEEIMMOS semi-dome
DEEIMMRS immersed
DEEIMNOR domineer
DEEIMNOS demonise
DEEIMNOZ demonize
DEEIMNPT pediment
DEEIMNRR reminder
DEEIMNRV vermined
DEEIMNST sediment
DEEIMNSU semi-nude
DEEIMNTT mittened
DEEIMOST tedisome
DEEIMPRR periderm
DEEIMPRS premised
DEEIMRST demister
DEEIMRTT remitted
DEEINNRT indenter
intender
DEEINNRU unreined
DEEINNST desinent
DEEINNUV unenvied
DEEINOPS disponee
DEEINOPW wide-open
DEEINORT oriented
DEEINOST sidenote

DEEINOSV	nosedive
DEEINPSS	dispense
	piedness
DEEINPSU	unespied
DEEINQSU	sequined
DEEINRRT	interred
DEEINRST	inserted
	resident
DEEINRSU	uredines
DEEINRTV	inverted
DEEINRTW	wintered
DEEINRTX	dextrine
DEEINSSW	dewiness
	wideness
DEEINSUZ	unseized
DEEINTUV	duvetine
DEEINUVW	unviewed
DEEIOPRT	peridote
DEEIOPRX	peroxide
DEEIORRV	override
DEEIORSV	overside
DEEIORTU	étourdie
DEEIOTVX	videotex
DEEIPPQU	equipped
DEEIPPRZ	zippered
DEEIPRSS	despiser
	disperse
DEEIPSST	sidestep
DEEIPSTU	deputise
DEEIPTUZ	deputize
DEEIQRRU	required
DEEIQRTU	requited
DEEIQRUV	quivered
DEEIQTUU	quietude
DEEIRRST	destrier
DEEIRRTV	verditer
DEEIRSST	dress-tie
	editress
DEEIRSSV	disserve
	dissever
DEEIRTTV	rivetted
DEEJKNTU	junketed
DEEJPRRU	perjured
DEEKKOOY	okey-doke
DEEKNNNU	unkenned
DEEKNOTW	knotweed
DEEKOOTY	yoke-toed
DEELLMOR	modeller
DEELLNOR	enrolled
DEELLNOW	well-done
DEELLORW	rowelled
	well-doer
DEELLORY	yodeller
DEELLOTW	towelled
DEELLOTX	extolled
DEELLOVW	vowelled
DEELLOVY	volleyed
DEELLSSW	weldless
DEELLSUX	duxelles
DEELMNOO	melodeon
DEELMNOW	new-model
DEELMNTU	unmelted
DEELMNTW	weldment
DEELMOOS	dolesome
DEELMOPR	empolder
DEELMOPY	employed
DEELMOSU	duelsome
DEELMRUY	demurely
DEELNNTU	tunneled
DEELNORT	redolent
DEELNORV	overlend
DEELNPRS	resplend
DEELNRTU	underlet
DEELNRTY	tenderly
DEELNSSW	lewdness
DEELNWWY	newly-wed
DEELNXYY	lynx-eyed
DEELOPRX	exploder
DEELOPRY	redeploy
DEELOPST	seed-plot
DEELORRS	solderer
DEELORSV	resolved
DEELORTT	dotterel
DEELORTV	revolted
DEELORTY	deletory
DEELORUV	louvered
DEELPRTU	drupelet
DEELPRUX	duplexer
DEELPTTY	pettedly
DEELRSTU	ulstered
DEELRSTW	lewdster
DEEMMORS	mesoderm
DEEMMRRU	dummerer
DEEMNNTU	tenendum
DEEMNOOS	moonseed
DEEMNOOY	moon-eyed
DEEMNOQU	queendom
DEEMNORT	entoderm
DEEMNOSS	demoness
	enmossed
DEEMNOUY	eudemony
DEEMOORT	odometer
DEEMOPST	deepmost
DEEMOQRU	queerdom
DEEMORSW	wormseed
DEEMORTU	udometer
DEEMPRST	dempster
DEEMRRRU	demurrer
	murderer
DEEMSSTY	systemed
DEENNNOP	pennoned
DEENNNPU	unpenned
DEENNOPT	deponent
DEENNOPU	unopened
DEENNORW	renowned
DEENNOSS	doneness
DEENNOVW	even-down
DEENNRTU	untender
DEENNRUV	unnerved
DEENNSSU	nudeness
	unsensed
DEENNTTU	unnetted
	untented
DEENNTUV	unvented
DEENOORV	overdone
DEENOPRR	ponderer
DEENORRS	endorser
DEENORRW	wonderer
DEENORTU	deuteron
DEENOSST	stenosed
DEENRRSU	sunderer
DEENRSSU	rudeness
DEENRSTU	sederunt
	underset
	undesert
DEENRSUU	underuse
DEENRSUV	unversed
DEENSTTU	untested
DEENTTUV	unvetted
DEENTTUW	unwetted
DEENTUVY	duvetyne
DEEOORRT	rood-tree
DEEOORRV	overdoer
	overrode
DEEOORSV	overdose
DEEOPPST	estopped
DEEOPRRR	preorder
DEEOPRST	reedstop
DEEOPRUZ	douzeper
DEEOPSTW	two-speed
DEEORRRV	verderor
DEEORRTT	retorted
DEEORRUV	devourer
DEEORSTT	rosetted
DEEORSTX	dextrose
DEEORSTY	storeyed
DEEORSUV	d'oeuvres
DEEORSUY	sour-eyed
DEEORTTT	tottered
DEEOSTUX	tuxedoes
DEEPRSTU	pertused
DEEPRSUY	pseudery
DEEPRUVV	revved-up
DEERRTTU	turreted
DEERRTUX	extruder
DEERSSST	stressed
DEERSSUV	suversed
DEERSTUV	vestured
DEERTTUX	textured
DEFFHILW	whiffled
DEFFILOV	fivefold
DEFFIORS	offsider
DEFFIORV	off-drive
DEFFIRSU	diffuser
DEFFLRTU	truffled
DEFFSTUY	dyestuff
DEFGHILT	flighted
DEFGIILN	fielding
DEFGIINY	deifying
	edifying
DEFGILTY	giftedly
DEFGINTU	ungifted
DEFGIOOW	goodwife
DEFGJORU	forjudge
DEFGMOOY	fogeydom
DEFGNORU	unforged

DEFHIINS	fiendish
	finished
DEFHIISV	fish-dive
DEFHILLO	lifehold
DEFHILSS	disflesh
DEFHINSU	unfished
DEFHIOOW	wifehood
DEFHLOOS	selfhood
DEFHOORS	serfhood
DEFIIILV	vilified
DEFIILLO	oilfield
DEFIILLP	filliped
DEFIILLW	wildlife
DEFIILMS	misfield
DEFIILOR	oil-fired
DEFIILPS	flip-side
DEFIILRW	wildfire
DEFIILSU	fluidise
DEFIILTY	fidelity
DEFIILUZ	fluidize
DEFIIMOR	modifier
DEFIINOT	notified
DEFIINTU	finitude
DEFIINTY	identify
DEFIIOSS	ossified
DEFIIOTV	videofit
DEFIIPRU	purified
DEFIIPSS	fissiped
DEFIIPTY	typified
DEFILLNU	unfilled
DEFILMNU	unfilmed
DEFILMOW	demi-wolf
DEFILNNO	ninefold
DEFILNOP	pond-life
DEFILNRS	flinders
DEFILNRU	unrifled
	urnfield
DEFILNRY	friendly
DEFILORU	fluoride
DEFILOTU	outfield
DEFILPRU	prideful
DEFILPTU	uplifted
DEFILRRU	flurried
DEFILRVY	fervidly
	fly-drive
DEFIMNOR	informed
DEFIMORY	remodify
DEFIMRRU	drumfire
DEFINNRU	reinfund
	unfriend
DEFINORW	forewind
DEFINRTT	drift-net
DEFINSTU	unsifted
DEFINSYY	Disneyfy
DEFINTTU	unfitted
DEFIOORW	firewood
DEFIORRV	Fervidor
DEFIOTXY	detoxify
DEFIRSSU	fissured
DEFKLORY	forkedly
DEFLLOOR	folderol
DEFLNORU	flounder
	unfolder
DEFLNRUY	fly-under
DEFLNSSU	fundless
DEFLOORT	foretold
DEFLOORV	overfold
DEFLOOSS	foodless
DEFMNORU	unformed
DEFMOOOR	foredoom
DEFNNORT	frondent
	front-end
DEFNNOSS	fondness
DEFNNOUW	new-found
DEFNOOPS	spoonfed
	spoon-fed
DEFNOORS	frondose
DEFNOORU	unroofed
DEFNOORV	overfond
DEFNOOTU	unfooted
DEFNOPRS	forspend
DEFNORRU	frondeur
DEFNORTU	fortuned
DEFNORUV	overfund
DEFNOSSW	dowfness
DEFNRRUU	underfur
	unfurred
DEFOORRW	foreword
DEGGILNS	sledging
DEGGINOV	God-given
DEGGINRU	unrigged
DEGGINUW	unwigged
DEGGIORS	disgorge
DEGGIPRS	sprigged
DEGGLMSU	smuggled
DEGGLRUY	ruggedly
DEGGNORU	ungorged
DEGHILNS	hindlegs
	shingled
DEGHILPT	plighted
DEGHILRT	red-light
DEGHINNU	unhinged
DEGHIOPS	dogeship
DEGHIPST	despight
DEGHKLOW	dog-whelk
DEGHLNOR	horngeld
DEGHLOSU	sloughed
DEGHNORT	thronged
DEGHNORY	hydrogen
DEGHOOSU	dog-house
	house-dog
DEGIIIRS	rigidise
DEGIIIRZ	rigidize
DEGIIIST	digitise
DEGIIITZ	digitize
DEGIILNR	gridelin
DEGIILNS	sideling
DEGIILNT	diligent
DEGIILNV	deviling
DEGIILNY	yielding
DEGIILTY	gelidity
DEGIIMSU	misguide
DEGIINNR	nidering
DEGIINNT	indigent
DEGIINNX	indexing
DEGIINOS	indigoes
DEGIINOV	videoing
DEGIINRS	ringside
DEGIINRT	dirigent
DEGIINST	indigest
DEGIISSU	disguise
DEGIJMSU	misjudge
DEGIKLNU	dukeling
DEGIKLOV	kid-glove
DEGIKNRY	ring-dyke
DEGILLNU	duelling
DEGILLNW	dwelling
DEGILMNO	modeling
DEGILNOP	diplogen
DEGILNOS	sidelong
DEGILNPS	spelding
DEGILNRU	indulger
DEGILNRY	yeldring
DEGILNWY	wingedly
DEGILOOR	goodlier
DEGILOOY	ideology
DEGILOSZ	goldsize
DEGILPSU	pulsidge
DEGILRZZ	grizzled
DEGIMNOS	smidgeon
DEGIMOOT	goodtime
DEGIMOOY	geomyoid
DEGINNNU	unending
DEGINNPS	spending
DEGINNRU	enduring
	unringed
DEGINNSU	unsigned
DEGINNTU	untinged
DEGINNUW	unwinged
DEGINOPS	disponge
DEGINORR	ordering
DEGINORU	guéridon
DEGINORV	ring-dove
DEGINPRS	springed
DEGINPSU	dispunge
DEGINRRY	grindery
DEGINRSS	dressing
DEGINRST	stringed
DEGINRSY	synergid
DEGINTTU	duetting
DEGIOORS	goodsire
DEGIOPRR	porridge
DEGIOPSS	gossiped
DEGIORRV	river-god
DEGIORST	grodiest
DEGJMNTU	judgment
DEGLLNOY	goldenly
DEGLLOSS	goldless
DEGLMNOT	lodgment
DEGLMOOY	demology
DEGLNOUV	ungloved
DEGLNRTU	gruntled
DEGLOOPY	pedology
DEGLOOSU	dog-louse
DEGLOOUU	duologue

DEGLORUV love-drug
DEGMMNUU ungummed
DEGNNOPY penny-dog
DEGNNORU grounden
DEGNNOUW ungowned
DEGNOORS drongoes
DEGNOOSS dog's-nose
goodness
DEGNOOST stegodon
DEGNOPSU pug-nosed
DEGNORRU grounder
DEGNORTU trudgeon
DEGNORUU unrouged
DEGNORYY gyrodyne
DEGNPRUU unpurged
DEHHILOY hidy-hole
DEHHILTW withheld
DEHHMRTY rhythmed
DEHIILLS hillside
DEHIILSV devilish
DEHIIMRU mudirieh
DEHIIMST ditheism
DEHIINNW whinnied
DEHIINSU Hinduise
DEHIINUZ Hinduize
DEHIIRST disherit
DEHIISTT ditheist
DEHIJMNO demijohn
DEHIKMOS sheikdom
DEHIKPSU dukeship
DEHILLOP phelloid
DEHILMOS demolish
DEHILMTY dimethyl
DEHILNOR inholder
DEHILNOW Whieldon
DEHILNPY diphenyl
DEHILOOR heliodor
DEHILOPS polished
DEHILPSU sulphide
DEHILPSY sylphide
DEHILRTW writhled
DEHILSTW whistled
DEHIMNOS hedonism
DEHIMPSY demyship
DEHINOPR nephroid
DEHINOPS sphenoid
DEHINOST hedonist
DEHINSUW unwished
DEHIOOVW wivehood
DEHIOPRS spheroid
DEHIOPRT trophied
DEHIORSS dishorse
DEHIORST Rhodites
DEHIORTY thyreoid
DEHIOSSU dishouse
DEHIOSSW sideshow
DEHIPSSU pseudish
DEHIRTWW withdrew
DEHKLNOU elkhound
DEHLLOPY phyllode
DEHLMORY hydromel
DEHLNOOW downhole

DEHLOOOW woodhole
DEHLOORV holdover
overhold
DEHLOOSS hoodless
DEHLOOST tool-shed
DEHLOOSW woolshed
DEHLOPRU upholder
DEHLORSU shoulder
DEHLOSTU dust-hole
DEHLRSWY shrewdly
DEHMMRTU thrummed
DEHMNOOW down-home
DEHMNOOY homodyne
DEHMNRUY unrhymed
DEHMOORW whoredom
DEHMOPRY hypoderm
DEHMORUU humoured
DEHNNTUU unhunted
DEHNOORU honoured
DEHNORSU enshroud
DEHNORSY enhydros
DEHNORTW nowt-herd
DEHNORTY threnody
DEHNOSUU unhoused
DEHNRTUY thundery
DEHOOOPP popehood
DEHOOPRT theropod
DEHOORTU out-Herod
DEHOPPPU hopped-up
DEHOPRST potsherd
DEHOPTTU hotted-up
DEHORRST redshort
DEHPPSTU shtupped
DEHRRSTU druthers
DEIIINSV divinise
DEIIINVZ divinize
DEIIIRTV viridite
DEIIISVV divisive
DEIIKLNS disliken
DEIIKLNV devilkin
DEIILLMP milliped
DEIILLMT ill-timed
tidemill
DEIILMRU delirium
DEIILMSV devilism
DEIILNNU induline
DEIILNPV vilipend
DEIILNVY divinely
DEIILORS idoliser
DEIILORZ idolizer
DEIILPSS sideslip
DEIILRST redistil
DEIILSTZ Seidlitz
DEIIMMRS dimerism
DEIIMMST mistimed
DEIIMMTT immitted
DEIIMNRT diriment
DEIIMNTU mutinied
DEIIMNUV venidium
DEIIMPRU peridium
DEIIMSVW midwives
DEIINNPP pinniped

DEIINNUV undivine
DEIINORS derision
Ironside
resinoid
DEIINORT retinoid
DEIINOST sedition
DEIINOSV visioned
DEIINPPW windpipe
DEIINPRS inspired
DEIINPRT intrepid
DEIINPRY pyridine
DEIINPTU unpitied
DEIINQSU quinsied
DEIINRST disinter
DEIINRSU disinure
DEIINSST tidiness
DEIINSTU disunite
nudities
DEIINTTU intuited
DEIINTTY identity
DEIIOPRS presidio
DEIIOPZZ pezizoid
DEIIORSX oxidiser
DEIIORTX trioxide
DEIIORTY iodyrite
DEIIORXZ oxidizer
DEIIPRST spirited
DEIIPRSZ disprize
DEIIPTTY tepidity
DEIIQSTU disquiet
DEIIRSSU diuresis
DEIJMORU demi-jour
DEIJNOPU joined-up
DEIJORRY joy-rider
DEIKKLNO △klondike
DEIKLMNU unmilked
DEIKLNNU unlinked
DEIKLNRW wrinkled
DEIKLNSS kindless
DEIKLSSS diskless
DEIKNNPU unpinked
DEIKNNSS kindness
DEIKNORV overkind
DEIKNSSU unkissed
DEIKPRSU prusiked
DEIKRSVY skydiver
DEILLMNU unmilled
DEILLNTU untilled
DEILLNUW unwilled
DEILLOOV livelood
DEILLOPW pillowed
DEILLOVW low-lived
DEILLOWW willowed
DEILLSTU duellist
DEILMNOO melodion
DEILMNSS mildness
mindless
DEILMNSU muslined
DEILMOOT dolomite
DEILMOOW lime-wood
DEILMOPR impolder
DEILMORT old-timer

DEILMORU	lemuroid
DEILMOST	melodist
DEILMOSU	emulsoid
DEILMOTV	demi-volt
DEILMPPU	plumiped
DEILMPSU	displume
DEILMPTU	multiped
DEILMSSY	demissly
DEILNNOT	indolent
DEILNNOW	down-line
DEILNOOS	solenoid
DEILNOPW	dowel-pin
DEILNORS	disenrol
DEILNOSU	delusion
	unsoiled
DEILNPRS	speldrin
DEILNPRU	underlip
DEILNRSS	rindless
DEILNRSW	swindler
DEILNRTY	trendily
DEILNSSV	vildness
DEILNSSW	wildness
	windless
DEILNSTU	unlisted
DEILNTTU	untitled
DEILNTUY	unitedly
DEILNUWY	unwieldy
DEILOOPS	poolside
DEILOOPW	woodpile
DEILOOVW	wood-evil
DEILOPPS	dip-slope
DEILOPPY	polypide
DEILOPRU	preludio
DEILOQRU	liquored
DEILORSU	souldier
DEILORSY	soldiery
DEILOSSV	dissolve
DEILOSTU	solitude
DEILPPST	stippled
DEILPPSU	supplied
DEILPPTU	pulpited
DEILPSTT	splitted
DEILPSTU	stipuled
DEILPTTU	uptilted
DEILRSVY	diversly
DEILRTVY	deviltry
DEILSTUY	sedulity
DEIMMNOS	demonism
DEIMMOST	immodest
DEIMMPST	misdempt
DEIMMRRU	mire-drum
DEIMNNOS	misdonne
DEIMNNOU	unmonied
DEIMNOOS	dominoes
DEIMNOOT	demotion
DEIMNOOX	monoxide
DEIMNOPT	piedmont
DEIMNORT	dormient
DEIMNOST	demonist
DEIMNOSW	Wodenism
DEIMNOTW	downtime
DEIMNPRU	unprimed
DEIMNPSS	misspend
DEIMNPTU	impudent
DEIMNRTU	rudiment
DEIMNSSU	unmissed
DEIMOOSS	sodomise
DEIMOOST	△sodomite
DEIMOOSZ	sodomize
DEIMORRR	mirrored
DEIMORRS	misorder
DEIMORSS	Messidor
DEIMORSU	dimerous
	soredium
DEIMORUX	exordium
DEIMOSTT	demotist
DEIMRSUU	residuum
DEINNNOT	Nintendo®
DEINNNOU	innuendo
DEINNNPU	unpinned
DEINNNTU	untinned
DEINNOOT	noontide
DEINNORU	unironed
DEINNOWW	winnowed
DEINNPRU	underpin
DEINNRUU	uninured
DEINNRUV	undriven
DEINOOPS	Poseidon
DEINOOPW	pinewood
DEINOOTV	devotion
DEINOPPW	downpipe
DEINOPRS	disponer
DEINOPRY	pyrenoid
DEINOPSS	dopiness
DEINOPSU	unpoised
DEINOPTW	dewpoint
DEINORSU	sourdine
DEINORSW	disowner
	windrose
DEINORTT	intorted
DEINORTU	diner-out
DEINORVW	overwind
DEINOSSV	voidness
DEINOSSZ	doziness
DEINOSWZ	downsize
DEINOTTU	duettino
DEINPPRU	unripped
DEINPRUZ	unprized
DEINRRTU	intruder
DEINRSSU	sundries
DEINRSTT	strident
DEINRTUW	underwit
DEINSSSY	syndesis
DEINSTUU	unsuited
DEIOPPRR	drop-ripe
DEIOPRRV	provider
DEIOPRSS	disposer
DEIOPRST	dipteros
DEIOPRSV	disprove
DEIOPRSW	dropwise
DEIOPSST	topsides
DEIORRSY	derisory
DEIORRTU	outrider
DEIORSSU	desirous
DEIORSTU	outsider
DEIORTUV	outdrive
DEIOSSTU	outsides
DEIOSTUZ	outsized
DEIPPRST	stripped
DEIPPTTU	titupped
DEIPRSSU	dispurse
DEIPRSTU	disputer
DEIPSTUV	stived-up
DEIPTTTU	tittuped
DEIRSSST	distress
DEIRSSTU	diestrus
DEIRSTTU	detritus
DEISTTTU	duettist
DEJLOOOR	jordeloo
DEJMPPUU	jumped-up
DEJNOOSW	Dow-Jones
DEKKLNOY	△klondyke
DEKKORSW	desk-work
DEKLNOOU	unlooked
DEKMORSY	smoke-dry
DEKNORUW	unworked
DEKNRSUY	undersky
DEKNSSSU	duskness
DEKORSWY	dye-works
DELLLOOP	lolloped
DELLMOOS	modellos
DELLMOSW	swelldom
DELLNOPU	unpolled
DELLNORW	rowndell
DELLNPUU	unpulled
DELLNSSU	dullness
DELLOOTW	well-to-do
DELLOPTU	polluted
DELLORRY	drollery
DELLORSS	lordless
DELLOTUW	outdwell
DELMNOOV	noveldom
DELMNORY	modernly
DELMNOSU	unseldom
DELMNOTW	meltdown
DELMNPUU	pendulum
DELMORSU	smoulder
DELMOSTY	modestly
DELNNOOR	Londoner
DELNOOSU	nodulose
DELNOOWY	woodenly
DELNOPPU	unlopped
DELNOPRS	splendor
DELNORSU	unsolder
DELNORTU	roundlet
DELNORYY	yonderly
DELNOSSU	loudness
DELNOSUU	undulose
	unsouled
DELNOSUV	unsolved
DELNRRTU	trundler
DELOOOOT	toodle-oo
DELOORRV	△overlord
DELOORRW	wordlore
DELOORSV	oversold
DELOORTY	rootedly

DELOORUV	overloud
DELOOSSW	woodless
DELOPSTU	postlude
DELOPSTW	spot-weld
DELORSSW	wordless
DELORSUY	delusory
DELOSSUU	sedulous
DELOTUVY	devoutly
DELSSSTU	dustless
DEMMNOOO	monomode
DEMMNSUU	unsummed
DEMMRSTU	strummed
DEMNOOOP	monopode
DEMNORSY	syndrome
DEMNORUW	unwormed
DEMNOSTU	mudstone
DEMNOSUU	mouse-dun
DEMOOPRR	prodrome
DEMOORST	doomster
DEMOORSU	dormouse
DEMOORTY	odometry
DENNNSUU	unsunned
DENNOOOZ	endozoon
DENNOPTU	ten-pound
DENNOTUW	unwonted
DENNPRUU	unpruned
DENNRRUU	underrun
DENNRTUU	unturned
DENOOOPR	open-door
DENOOOTW	woodnote
DENOOOVW	ovenwood
DENOOPRS	prodnose
DENOORTU	unrooted
DENOORTX	next-door
DENOOSSW	woodness
DENOPRUV	unproved
DENOPSTU	outspend
	unposted
DENOPSTW	step-down
	stewpond
DENOQTUU	unquoted
DENORRSU	rounders
DENORRUU	roundure
DENORSSU	dourness
DENORSTU	tonsured
	unsorted
DENORSTY	dry-stone
DENORSUU	unroused
	unsoured
DENORTTU	unrotted
DENORTUW	undertow
DENOSTUU	unsued-to
DENOTUUV	undevout
DENPRTUU	upturned
DENRRSUY	dry-nurse
	sur-reyn'd
DENRSSSU	sundress
DEOOORSW	rosewood
DEOOOSWW	woodwose
DEOOPPRT	pteropod
DEOOPRRS	rose-drop
DEOOPRRV	provedor
DEOOPRST	doorstep
	torpedos
DEOORRSW	sorrowed
DEOORRVW	overword
DEOORRWW	owreword
DEOPPRST	stropped
DEOPPRSU	purposed
DEOPPSSU	supposed
DEOPPSUU	souped-up
DEOPRRTU	protrude
DEOPRSST	top-dress
DEOPRSTU	sprouted
DEORRTTU	tortured
DEORSTUV	overdust
DEORSTUX	dextrous
DEORSTVY	dry-stove
DEOSSTTU	testudos
DEPPSSYY	dyspepsy
DEQRSUUY	surquedy
DERSTTTU	strutted
DFFHIOOS	food-fish
DFFIILUY	fluidify
DFFIIRTY	triffidy
DFFLMPUU	plum-duff
DFFLOORU	fourfold
DFFOORUW	woodruff
DFGGHIOT	dogfight
DFGHILOS	goldfish
DFGIIIRY	rigidify
DFGIILRY	frigidly
DFGIINNS	findings
DFGILNNO	fondling
DFGILNOO	flooding
DFGINNOU	founding
DFGINOOR	fordoing
DFGKNORU	dung-fork
DFHIIMUY	humidify
DFHIMRSU	drumfish
DFHINOOT	hindfoot
DFHINOPS	fish-pond
DFHLOOOT	foothold
DFHNOOUX	foxhound
DFIIINVY	divinify
DFIILMTU	multifid
DFIILOSY	solidify
DFIILTUY	fluidity
DFIINPRT	driftpin
DFIKNOOS	skinfood
DFILLOOT	floodlit
DFILLORY	floridly
DFILLOWW	wildfowl
DFIMOOOR	iodoform
DFINRSUW	windsurf
DFIOOPRS	disproof
DFLNOOWW	downflow
DFLOOORT	rood-loft
DFLOPRUU	proudful
DFNOOPRU	profound
DFOOOORW	woodroof
DFOOOSTW	softwood
DGGGIINS	diggings
DGGGINRU	drugging
	grudging
DGGHINOT	night-dog
DGGIILNR	ridgling
DGGIINNR	grinding
DGGIINNW	wingding
DGGILNOS	lodgings
DGGINRTU	trudging
DGGIRSTU	druggist
DGHIILNS	hidlings
DGHIIMNT	midnight
DGHIIMST	misdight
DGHIINNW	hindwing
DGHIINPS	sphingid
DGHIINRT	thirding
DGHIISST	dissight
DGHIKNOO	kinghood
DGHIKNOS	Hodgkin's
DGHILLNU	dung-hill
DGHILNOS	holdings
DGHILNRU	hurdling
DGHILOOR	girlhood
DGHIMOST	god-smith
DGHIOORS	droogish
DGHNOOTU	do-nought
DGHNOTUU	doughnut
DGHOOOTT	dogtooth
DGHORRUY	rough-dry
DGHORTUY	droughty
DGIIIMRS	dirigism
DGIIIRTY	rigidity
DGIIKLNN	kindling
DGIIKNNR	drinking
DGIILLNR	drilling
DGIILLOU	liguloid
DGIILNOS	disloign
DGIIMNOS	misdoing
DGIIMNOU	gonidium
DGIIMPUY	pygidium
DGIINNOP	poinding
DGIINNOR	Girondin
	non-rigid
DGIINNRW	windring
DGIINNSS	sindings
DGIINORR	gridiron
DGIINOSV	voidings
DGIINOTT	dittoing
DGIINPPR	dripping
DGIINRTY	dirtying
DGIINVVY	divvying
DGIINYZZ	dizzying
DGIIOTTW	two-digit
DGIKLOOY	kidology
DGIKNOOR	drooking
DGIKNOOW	kingwood
DGIKNORU	drouking
DGILLNOR	drolling
	lordling
DGILLOOW	goodwill
DGILMNOU	moulding
DGILMNPU	dumpling
DGILMSUY	smudgily

DGILNOOW woolding
DGILNORS lordings
DGILNORY yoldring
DGILNOTY dotingly
DGILOOTW giltwood
DGILOPSU solpugid
DGILOSTY stodgily
DGILRTUY turgidly
DGIMMNRU drumming
DGINNORU rounding
DGINNORW drowning
DGINNOSU sounding
DGINNOUW wounding
DGINNSSY syndings
DGINOOPS spongoid
DGINOPPR dropping
DGINOSUY digynous
DGINSTUY studying
DGLOOOPY podology
DGLOOOSY dosology
DGLOOOXY doxology
DGMOPSYY gypsydom
DGNNORUU unground
DGNOOTYZ zygodont
DGOPPPUY puppy-dog
DHHILOTW withhold
DHIIIMNS diminish
DHIIIOST histioid
idiotish
DHIILOSS solidish
DHIIMNOO hominoid
DHIIMNSU Hinduism
DHIIMPSS midships
DHIIMTUY humidity
DHIINPSW windship
DHIINSTW whinid'st
DHIINTWW withwind
DHIIOPRU ophiurid
DHIIORSS hidrosis
DHIKNOOW hoodwink
DHIKORSY hydroski
DHILLNOW downhill
DHILLOPY phylloid
DHILLORS drollish
DHILLOST tolldish
DHILMOPY lymphoid
DHILMOSY modishly
DHILOPRS lordship
DHILOPSS slipshod
DHILORRY horridly
DHIMNOST hindmost
DHIMNOSU unmodish
DHIMOOOY omohyoid
DHIMOOSS misshood
DHIMOPPY hippydom
DHINNOOR Rhinodon
DHINOORS dishonor
DHINORSU roundish
DHINOTUW who-dun-it
DHIOOPRZ rhizopod
DHIOPRSU proudish
DHIORSTY thyrsoid
DHIORSWY rowdyish
DHJOPRSU jodhpurs
DHKMNOOO monkhood
DHLLNOUW hull-down
DHLLOPYY phyllody
DHLNOSTU shouldn't
DHLOOORT roothold
DHLOOORY holy-rood
DHLORXYY hydroxyl
DHLOSSTU shouldst
DHMNOOOT homodont
DHMOOPPU pumphood
DHMORSYY Hydromys
DHMORTUY drymouth
DHNOOSWW showdown
DHNORSUU unshroud
DHNORSUW downrush
DHNOSTUW shutdown
DHOOOPRT orthopod
DHOOORTX △orthodox
DHOOPRST drop-shot
DHOORSUW woodrush
DHOPRSYY hydropsy
DHOSSTTU dust-shot
DIIIKMNS minidisk
DIIILLQU illiquid
DIIILTVY lividity
DIIIMOST idiotism
DIIIMTTY timidity
DIIINOSV division
DIIINTVY divinity
DIIIPRST dispirit
DIIIRTVY viridity
DIIITVVY vividity
DIIJNOST disjoint
DIIKLLNY kindlily
DIILLMNR millrind
DIILLMNW windmill
DIILLMPY limpidly
DIILLQUY liquidly
DIILLSTY idyllist
DIILMOSS solidism
DIILMOTY mytiloid
DIILMUUV diluvium
DIILNOTU dilution
DIILNOUV diluvion
DIILNOXY xyloidin
DIILNTUY untidily
DIILOPRT triploid
DIILOPSY ypsiloid
DIILORSU siluroid
DIILOSST solidist
DIILOSTY solidity
DIILQSUU liquidus
DIIMNNOO dominion
DIIMNNSU undinism
DIIMNOPT mid-point
DIIMNSUU indusium
DIIMOPRS prismoid
DIIMPUXY pyxidium
DIIMRUUV duumviri
DIIMTTUY tumidity
DIINNORS Dinornis
DIINNOSU disunion
DIINOORT Triodion
DIINOSSU sinusoid
DIINSTUY disunity
DIIOPRTY pityroid
DIKLMOOW milkwood
DIKLNNUY unkindly
DIKLRUUU durukuli
DIKNOOSW woodskin
DIKNORTU outdrink
DIKOOSTU ditokous
DILLMNOP millpond
DILLOORS door-sill
DILLOSTY stolidly
DILMNOOS smilodon
DILMNORW lindworm
DILMOOSU △modiolus
DILNOPSU lispound
DILNOPTW Piltdown
DILNOUWY woundily
DILOOPPY polypoid
DILOOPRY droopily
DILOORSS lordosis
DILOORSU louis-d'or
DILOOSUY odiously
DILOOTUV volutoid
DILOPRTY torpidly
DILORRTY torridly
DILORSWY drowsily
DILPRTUY putridly
DILPSTUY stupidly
DILRSTUY sturdily
DIMMNORY △myrmidon
DIMMOOSU isodomum
DIMNOOOS isodomon
DIMNOOST monodist
DIMNOSTU dismount
DIMNOSUW unwisdom
DIMNSSTU Stundism
DIMOOPRR prodromi
DIMOOPRY myriopod
DIMOORTW modiwort
DIMOPRSU misproud
DIMORSWY rowdyism
DIMOSTUY dumosity
DIMRSUUV duumvirs
DINNOORS rondinos
DINNOOST tondinos
DINOOORW ironwood
DINOOPSU dipnoous
DINOORSU nidorous
DINOOSTT odontist
DINOOSTY nodosity
DINOPRTY dry-point
DINORSTU sturnoid
DINPRTUY punditry
DINRSTUY industry
DINSSTTU Stundist
DIOOPRRT dirt-poor
proditor
DIOOPRRV providor

DIOORSTT	ridottos
DIOSSTUU	studious
DIRSSTTU	distrust
DKNNOOTW	don't-know
DKNORSUW	sow-drunk
DKOOORWW	woodwork
DKORSTUW	studwork
DLLMOOPY	dolly-mop
DLLMORSU	slumlord
DLLNOPUW	pull-down
DLLNORUY	unlordly
DLMNOOTY	mylodont
DLMORSUY	smouldry
DLNOOPRU	pouldron
DLNOOSUU	nodulous
DLNOOSWW	slow-down
DLNORTUY	rotundly
DLNOSUUU	undulous
DLOOOORS	doloroso
DLOOOOWW	wood-wool
DLOOORSU	dolorous
DLOOPPUW	pulpwood
DLOOPPYY	polypody
DMNNOOOT	monodont
DMNOOSTW	downmost
DMOOORWW	woodworm
	wormwood
DMOPPPUU	puppodum
DMOPPPUY	puppydom
DMPPPUUY	mudpuppy
DNNOOPRU	pundonor
DNNOORTW	torn-down
DNNOOSSU	od's-nouns
DNNOOTWW	down-town
DNNORTUW	downturn
	turn-down
DNOOOOPW	poon-wood
DNOOPPRU	propound
DNOOPRSW	snowdrop
DNOOPRTU	round-top
DNOOPRUW	downpour
DNOORSUW	wondrous
DNOOSTWW	stowdown
DNOPRSSU	sundrops
DNORRSUU	surround
DNORSSUY	undrossy
DOOOPRST	doorpost
	doorstop
DOOORSTU	outdoors
DOOPPRTU	top-proud
DOOPRRSY	rosy-drop
DOOPRRTW	drop-wort
DOOPSWWY	powsowdy
DOORRSUU	ordurous
DOORRTTU	trout-rod
DOORSSUU	sudorous

E

EEEEFNRZ	enfreeze
EEEEFRRZ	refreeze
EEEEGGRR	greegree
EEEEGMRR	re-emerge
EEEEGNSV	Genevese
EEEEGQSU	squeegee
EEEELLPX	expellee
EEEELLVY	eye-level
EEEELMST	teleseme
EEEELNSV	sleeveen
EEEENRRV	veneerer
EEEEPPSW	peesweep
EEEEPRRV	repreeve
EEEEPTTW	peetweet
EEEFFGIR	fee-grief
EEEFFLOR	forefeel
EEEFFLTY	effetely
EEEFFNOR	Freefone®
EEEFFNRT	efferent
EEEFFORT	forefeet
EEEFFRVW	feverfew
EEEFIPRR	repriefe
EEEFLSST	feetless
EEEFNNPY	penny-fee
EEEFNORS	foreseen
EEEFNRRT	referent
	rent-free
EEEFNRSS	freeness
EEEFNRTT	enfetter
EEEFNRUZ	unfreeze
EEEFORRV	overfree
EEEFPRUZ	freeze-up
EEEFRRRT	ferreter
EEEGGILN	negligee
	negligée
EEEGHINT	eighteen
EEEGHLRS	sheerleg
EEEGHORV	hog-reeve
EEEGILNV	enveigle
EEEGILPS	espiègle
EEEGIMTV	Vegemite®
EEEGINNR	engineer
EEEGINRS	energise
	greenies
EEEGINRV	engrieve
EEEGINRZ	energize
EEEGIRTY	tiger-eye
EEEGISSX	exegesis
EEEGISTV	egestive
EEEGITVV	vegetive
EEEGLMOS	gleesome
EEEGLNRT	greenlet
EEEGMNRT	emergent
EEEGMNRU	merengue
EEEGMORT	geometer
EEEGNNRS	sengreen
EEEGNOSV	Genovese
EEEGNRRU	reneguer
EEEGNRRV	revenger
EEEGNRRY	greenery
EEEGNRSV	revenges
EEEGOPRT	protégée
EEEGRRST	regreets
EEEHILRW	erewhile
	while-ere
	wire-heel
EEEHIRST	etherise
EEEHIRTZ	etherize
EEEHITWY	white-eye
EEEHKLNO	kneehole
EEEHLMPT	helpmeet
EEEHLNTV	eleventh
EEEHLNTY	ethylene
EEEHLNXY	hexylene
EEEHLOPP	peep-hole
EEEHLOPW	weephole
EEEHLORS	hose-reel
EEEHMNTV	vehement
EEEHMRYY	eye-rhyme
EEEHNNPT	nepenthe
EEEHNNQU	henequen
EEEHNPPS	sheep-pen
EEEHNPRS	ensphere
EEEHNRSS	hereness
EEEHNRVW	whenever
EEEHORRS	Hereroes
EEEHORST	shoetree
EEEHPRST	spreethe
EEEHRRVW	wherever
EEEIKLMS	misleeke
EEEIKNPS	Pekinese
EEEILLRV	reveille
EEEILMRS	seemlier
EEEILMRT	lime-tree
EEEILNNO	éolienne
EEEILNPR	pelerine
EEEILNRY	eyeliner
EEEILNST	selenite
EEEILRRV	reliever
EEEILSSW	elsewise
EEEILSTV	televise
EEEILTVW	teleview
EEEIMNRS	Ménière's
EEEIMNRU	meunière
EEEIMPRR	premiere
	première
EEEIMPRS	emperise
EEEIMPRZ	emperize
EEEIMRRS	△miserere
EEEIMRTT	remittee
EEEINNNT	nineteen
EEEINNRT	internee
EEEINNSS	Siennese
EEEINNSV	Viennese
EEEINNSY	nine-eyes
EEEINQTU	queenite
EEEINRSS	eeriness
EEEINRST	eternise
EEEINRTT	reinette
EEEINRTZ	eternize
EEEINTUX	euxenite
EEEIPPRT	pipe-tree
EEEIPRRV	reprieve
EEEIQSUX	exequies
EEEIRRSV	rerevise
EEEIRRTV	retrieve
EEEIRRVW	reviewer
EEEIRTVX	exertive

EEEJKKNR	knee-jerk
EEEJLLRW	jeweller
EEEKLNNR	enkernel
EEEKLPSW	ekpweles
EEEKMNSS	meekness
EEEKMRSS	kermesse
EEEKNNSS	keenness
EEEKNORS	kerosene
EEEKNORV	overknee
EEEKOPRV	overkeep
EEELLLRV	△leveller
EEELLLSW	sewellel
EEELLNQU	quenelle
EEELLNSW	well-seen
EEELLPRR	repeller
EEELLRRT	reteller
EEELLRRV	reveller
EEELLVWY	wye-level
EEELMNST	elements
	steelmen
EEELMOPP	empeople
EEELMOPY	employee
EEELMORT	telomere
EEELMOTT	omelette
EEELMRTU	muleteer
EEELMSSS	seemless
EEELMSST	teemless
EEELNOPV	envelope
EEELNOSV	novelese
EEELNQTU	queenlet
EEELNRSW	newsreel
EEELNRSY	serenely
EEELNRTV	nervelet
EEELNRTY	Terylene®
EEELOPPR	repeople
EEELORST	sloetree
EEELPRSS	peerless
EEELPRSY	sleepery
EEELPTTY	Teletype®
EEELRRTT	letterer
EEELRSST	treeless
EEELRSTT	resettle
EEELRSTV	verselet
EEELRSVY	severely
EEELRTVV	velveret
EEELSSTW	weetless
EEELSTVY	steevely
EEELTTTX	teletext
EEEMMRUZ	mezereum
EEEMNNTT	tenement
EEEMNORZ	mezereon
EEEMNRST	entremes
EEEMNSST	meetness
EEEMORRV	evermore
EEEMORST	stereome
EEEMORTV	overteem
EEEMPRRT	temperer
EEEMPRSS	empressé
EEEMRRTX	extremer
EEEMRSST	semester
EEEMRSTX	extremes
EEENNOPR	neoprene
EEENNRST	étrennes
EEENNSSV	evenness
EEENOPRR	reopener
EEENORSV	overseen
EEENORVW	overween
EEENORVY	everyone
EEENPPRS	prepense
EEENPRRT	repenter
EEENPRST	pre-teens
	pretense
EEENPSSX	expenses
EEENPSTW	sweep-net
EEENRRST	resenter
EEENRRSV	renverse
EEENRRTU	returnee
EEENRRTV	reverent
EEENRSTV	Serevent®
EEENRSTY	yestreen
EEENSSTW	tweeness
EEEOPRRV	overpeer
EEEORRST	rose-tree
EEEORRSV	overseer
EEEPPPRR	pepperer
EEEPRRST	pesterer
EEEPRRSU	reperuse
EEEPRRSV	perverse
	preserve
EEEPRRTW	pewterer
EEEPSTTT	septette
EEEQRRUV	verquere
EEEQRSUZ	squeezer
EEERRRSV	reverser
EEERRSSV	reserves
EEERRSTT	resetter
EEERSTVX	vertexes
EEERSTWZ	tweezers
EEESSTTT	sestette
EEESTTTX	sextette
EEFFFGLU	gefuffle
EEFFFKLU	kefuffle
EEFFGIIS	effigies
EEFFGIRR	greffier
EEFFHIKY	keffiyeh
EEFFILLS	self-life
EEFFISUV	effusive
EEFFKLOR	folk-free
EEFFLLST	self-left
EEFFLNTU	effluent
EEFFLORT	forefelt
EEFFRRSU	sufferer
EEFGIILR	filigree
EEFGILNR	fleering
EEFGILNS	feelings
EEFGILNT	fleeting
EEFGINRR	refringe
EEFGINRZ	freezing
EEFGIRRU	refigure
EEFGLNRY	greenfly
EEFGLNUV	vengeful
EEFGNOOR	foregone
EEFGOORR	foregoer
EEFHHLNS	hen-flesh
EEFHILLR	hellfire
	hell-fire
EEFHILMO	home-life
EEFHIMOR	home-fire
EEFHIRSV	feverish
EEFHIRTY	etherify
EEFHLLPS	self-help
EEFHLLWY	flywheel
EEFHLMOT	homefelt
EEFHLMST	themself
EEFHLSTY	fly-sheet
EEFHMORR	herefrom
EEFHNORT	forehent
EEFHNRSW	fresh-new
EEFHORRT	therefor
EEFHORRW	wherefor
EEFHORST	free-shot
	shot-free
EEFHORSW	foreshew
EEFIIKLL	lifelike
EEFIIKLW	wifelike
EEFIILLN	lifeline
EEFIILMT	lifetime
EEFIILNV	five-line
EEFIILSZ	life-size
EEFIIMNN	feminine
EEFIIMNS	feminise
EEFIIMNZ	feminize
EEFIIRRV	verifier
EEFIKLLS	self-like
EEFIKLRS	serflike
EEFIKNNP	penknife
EEFILLMT	telefilm
EEFILLRW	free-will
EEFILLSS	lifeless
EEFILMOS	lifesome
EEFILMST	fistmele
EEFILMTX	Flextime®
EEFILNRT	life-rent
EEFILNSS	fineless
EEFILNUV	nieveful
EEFILORS	free-soil
EEFILPRR	pilferer
EEFILRSS	fireless
EEFILRSU	fusileer
EEFILSSW	wifeless
EEFIMORT	foretime
EEFINNSS	fineness
EEFINNTU	fine-tune
EEFINORV	overfine
EEFINRRY	refinery
EEFINRSS	finesser
	rifeness
EEFINRSU	reinfuse
EEFIPRST	fire-step
EEFIRRSU	sure-fire
EEFIRSTT	frisette
EEFIRSTY	esterify
EEFISSSW	fess-wise
EEFKNORT	reef-knot
EEFLLNSS	fellness

Words marked △ may be spelled also with a capital letter

EEFLLORT	foretell
	toll-free
EEFLLOSV	self-love
EEFLLRSU	self-rule
EEFLLRXY	reflexly
EEFLLSSS	selfless
EEFLMNSU	menseful
EEFLMORU	fumerole
EEFLNORT	forelent
EEFLNORW	enflower
EEFLNOST	felstone
EEFLNRTU	refluent
EEFLNSSS	selfness
EEFLNSSU	senseful
EEFLNTUV	eventful
EEFLORRW	flowerer
	reflower
EEFLORTV	leftover
EEFLORTW	floweret
EEFLORWW	werewolf
EEFLOSUX	flexuose
EEFMNORT	fomenter
EEFMORRR	△reformer
EEFMPRRU	perfumer
EEFNNORS	enfrosen
EEFNORST	enforest
	softener
EEFNORTU	fourteen
EEFNORTW	forewent
EEFNQRTU	frequent
EEFNRTTU	unfetter
EEFOORRT	rooftree
EEFOPRRT	free-port
EEFOPRST	Freepost®
	post-free
EEFORRST	△forester
	fosterer
	reforest
EEFORRSU	ferreous
EEFORRTY	feretory
EEFORSUV	feverous
EEFORSUY	four-eyes
EEFOSSTT	fossette
EEGGGOOS	goose-egg
EEGGHLLS	eggshell
EEGGHLOR	hoggerel
EEGGHMSU	meshugge
EEGGIJRR	rejigger
EEGGIKNR	△greeking
EEGGILNR	legering
EEGGIMNR	emerging
EEGGIMRT	egg-timer
EEGGINNR	greening
EEGGINRS	greesing
EEGGINRT	greeting
EEGGINSU	segueing
	siege-gun
EEGGLOOR	geologer
EEGGORTT	go-getter
EEGGPRRS	preggers
EEGGPRSU	egg-purse
EEGGQRSU	squegger
EEGHHIKN	knee-high
EEGHHINT	heighten
EEGHIIST	eighties
EEGHIKRS	Greekish
EEGHILNS	sheeling
EEGHILNW	wheeling
EEGHILRS	sleigher
EEGHILTW	white-leg
EEGHINPT	phengite
EEGHINRS	greenish
EEGHINST	seething
	sheeting
EEGHINTT	teething
EEGHINWZ	wheezing
EEGHIOTT	goethite
EEGHISST	sightsee
EEGHISTY	eyesight
EEGHLNNT	lengthen
EEGHMNOY	hegemony
EEGHMPSU	mug-sheep
EEGHNNRU	enhunger
EEGHNOOP	geophone
EEGHNOPS	phosgene
EEGHNOPY	hypogene
EEGHNSSU	hugeness
EEGHOPTY	geophyte
EEGHORTT	together
EEGHOSTT	ghettoes
EEGIIKTW	Ewigkeit
EEGIILNR	lingerie
EEGIILNV	inveigle
EEGIINRT	re-ignite
EEGIINTV	genitive
EEGIKLNS	sleeking
EEGIKLOT	eklogite
EEGILNOR	eloigner
EEGILNPS	sleeping
EEGILNRR	lingerer
EEGILNRU	reguline
EEGILNST	steeling
EEGILNSV	sleeving
EEGILOPU	epilogue
EEGILOSU	eulogies
	eulogise
EEGILOUZ	eulogize
EEGILQSU	squilgee
EEGILRSU	regulise
EEGILRTV	verligte
EEGILRTY	legerity
EEGILRUZ	regulize
EEGIMNNS	meninges
EEGIMNRT	regiment
EEGIMNRU	meringue
EEGIMNSU	eugenism
EEGINNQU	queening
EEGINNRS	sneering
EEGINNRT	entering
EEGINNRW	renewing
EEGINNRY	enginery
EEGINNST	steening
EEGINNSU	unseeing
EEGINNSV	evenings
EEGINNSZ	sneezing
EEGINNTV	eventing
EEGINOPR	perigone
EEGINOPS	epigones
EEGINORR	erigeron
EEGINORV	virogene
EEGINOST	egestion
EEGINPSW	sweeping
EEGINQUU	queueing
EEGINRRS	resigner
EEGINRST	steering
	streigne
EEGINRSU	seigneur
EEGINRSW	sewering
EEGINRTU	geniture
EEGINRTX	genetrix
EEGINRUZ	Zigeuner
EEGINSSU	geniuses
EEGINSTU	eugenist
EEGINSTV	steeving
EEGINSTW	sweeting
EEGINTTV	vignette
EEGINTUX	teguexin
EEGIOPSU	epigeous
EEGIORST	ergotise
EEGIORTZ	ergotize
EEGIORVV	overgive
EEGIPRST	prestige
EEGIRRST	register
EEGIRSTT	grisette
EEGJORSU	goujeers
EEGLMNOP	emplonge
EEGLMNTU	emulgent
EEGLMOSS	glosseme
EEGLNNTU	ungentle
EEGLNOPY	polygene
EEGLNOTY	telegony
EEGLOOST	Togolese
EEGLORRV	groveler
EEGMMOSU	gemmeous
EEGMNOST	emongest
	gemstone
EEGMNTTU	tegument
EEGMORSU	gruesome
EEGMORTY	geometry
EEGNNORT	△roentgen
EEGNNOSS	goneness
EEGNNOSV	evensong
EEGNOORV	engroove
EEGNOOST	osteogen
EEGNOPTY	genotype
EEGNORST	estrogen
EEGNORSU	generous
EEGNORSY	eryngoes
EEGNPRUX	expunger
EEGNRSSY	greyness
EEGNRSUY	△guernsey
EEGNRTTU	tung-tree
EEGOPRSU	superego
EEGOPRTU	Portugee
EEGORRST	ostreger
EEGORSTU	urostege

EEHHIPSS	sheepish
EEHHIRTW	herewith
EEHHLLLO	hell-hole
EEHHLRST	threshel
EEHHNOSU	hen-house
EEHHRRST	thresher
EEHIIKLV	hivelike
EEHIITTW	white-tie
EEHIKLLT	hell-kite
EEHIKLMO	homelike
EEHIKRRS	shrieker
EEHILLMS	shlemiel
EEHILLNP	helpline
EEHILMNU	helenium
EEHILNNO	nine-hole
EEHILNOP	neophile
EEHILNPW	pin-wheel
EEHILORT	hotelier
EEHILRSS	heirless
EEHILSSV	hiveless
EEHILWYZ	wheezily
EEHIMMPT	Memphite
EEHIMPRS	emperish
EEHIMPST	epithems
EEHIMQUV	△vehmique
EEHIMRST	erethism
	etherism
EEHIMRTT	thermite
EEHINNQU	henequin
EEHINNRS	enshrine
EEHINNRT	inherent
EEHINNSS	sneeshin
EEHINORT	etherion
EEHINPRS	insphere
EEHINPRT	nephrite
	prehnite
	trephine
EEHINRTT	thirteen
EEHINRTW	whitener
EEHINSTT	sheet-tin
EEHINSTV	hive-nest
EEHIOPPS	hosepipe
EEHIORST	isothere
	theorise
EEHIORTZ	theorize
EEHIPPST	psephite
EEHIPPTY	epiphyte
EEHIPRRS	perisher
EEHIPRSS	Hesperis
EEHIPRST	treeship
EEHIPRTT	perthite
	pith-tree
	tephrite
	threepit
EEHIPSST	steepish
EEHIPSUU	euphuise
EEHIPUUZ	euphuize
EEHIQRSU	queerish
EEHIRRSV	shiverer
EEHIRRSW	wherries
EEHIRSTT	etherist
EEHIRTVY	thievery
EEHISSTW	sweetish
EEHJLOWY	joy-wheel
EEHLLMSS	helmless
EEHLLORV	hoveller
EEHLLPSS	helpless
EEHLMOOS	holesome
EEHLMOSS	homeless
EEHLNOTT	telethon
EEHLNOTV	vent-hole
EEHLOPSS	hopeless
EEHLORST	hosteler
EEHLORSV	shoveler
EEHLOSSS	shoeless
EEHLPPRS	shlepper
EEHLPRSU	spherule
EEHLPRTY	three-ply
EEHLRSTY	sheltery
EEHLSSTW	thewless
EEHMMOPR	morpheme
EEHMMORT	ohmmeter
EEHMNOOS	moonshee
EEHMNOSW	somewhen
EEHMOORT	rheotome
EEHMORST	rest-home
EEHMORVW	whomever
EEHNNORT	enthrone
EEHNNPPU	unheppen
EEHNNSSS	neshness
EEHNNSTU	unnethes
EEHNOORS	one-horse
EEHNOPRU	hereupon
EEHNOPST	poshteen
EEHNOPTY	hypnotee
	neophyte
EEHNORSW	heronsew
EEHNORTU	hereunto
EEHNORTV	overhent
EEHNPRSU	sheep-run
	unsphere
EEHNRRTY	Tyrrhene
EEHNRTTU	untether
EEHOOPRS	oosphere
EEHOORSV	overshoe
	over-shoe
EEHOOTTY	eye-tooth
EEHOPPSW	peep-show
EEHOPPSX	sheep-pox
EEHOPRST	sheep-rot
EEHOPRVY	overhype
EEHORRTX	exhorter
EEHORSVW	whosever
EEHORTTU	thereout
EEHORTUW	whereout
EEHPRSSU	Hesperus
EEHPRSTY	physeter
EEHRSSSU	usheress
EEIIKLPP	pipelike
EEIIKLSW	likewise
	wise-like
EEIILLMM	millième
EEIILLMT	melilite
EEIILLOP	eolipile
EEIILMNN	nine-mile
EEIILMNT	ilmenite
	melinite
EEIILMSS	emissile
EEIILNNT	Leninite
EEIILNPP	pipeline
EEIILNTV	lenitive
EEIILSTW	lewisite
EEIIMMTT	mimetite
EEIIMNOT	meionite
EEIIMSST	Semitise
EEIIMSSV	emissive
EEIIMSTZ	Semitize
EEIINNST	nineties
EEIINORT	erionite
EEIINPPR	piperine
EEIINPPW	pipe-wine
EEIINPRV	viperine
EEIINRRV	riverine
EEIINRSS	resinise
	sirenise
EEIINRSZ	resinize
	sirenize
EEIINRTT	intertie
	retinite
EEIINSSV	inessive
EEIIPRTT	epitrite
EEIIQSTU	equities
EEIIQTUV	quietive
EEIIRRTV	tirrivee
EEIIRSTV	verities
EEIJKRST	jet-skier
EEIJLNNU	julienne
EEIJLNRT	jetliner
EEIJLNUV	juvenile
EEIJNNOR	enjoiner
EEIJNOTV	vee-joint
EEIKLLRY	kyrielle
EEIKLMRT	milk-tree
EEIKLNSS	likeness
EEIKLNST	nestlike
EEIKLORS	roselike
EEIKLORT	lorikeet
EEIKLPST	spikelet
EEIKLRST	triskele
EEIKNORS	kerosine
EEIKNRRT	tinkerer
EEIKOQUV	equivoke
EEIKPPRR	kipperer
EEILLLVW	live-well
EEILLMPR	impeller
EEILLMRU	reillume
EEILLNSY	senilely
EEILLNVV	venville
EEILLORS	orseille
EEILLPSS	ellipses
EEILLPSY	sleepily
EEILLSSV	veilless
EEILLTVY	velleity
EEILLVWY	weevilly
EEILMNNU	enlumine
EEILMNOP	pemoline

EEILMNOS	Seminole
EEILMNRU	lemurine
	relumine
EEILMNSU	selenium
	semilune
EEILMOPS	polemise
EEILMOPZ	polemize
EEILMORT	motelier
EEILMOST	mesolite
	misletoe
EEILMSST	timeless
EEILMSUV	emulsive
EEILMSVV	Mevlevis
EEILNNOR	one-liner
EEILNNST	sentinel
EEILNOPR	leporine
EEILNOST	noselite
EEILNOSV	novelise
EEILNOVZ	novelize
EEILNPPZ	zeppelin
EEILNPRS	△pilsener
EEILNPRU	perilune
EEILNPRV	replevin
EEILNRSS	reinless
EEILNRST	listener
	re-enlist
EEILNRTY	entirely
	lientery
EEILNRUV	unveiler
EEILNSSV	evilness
	vileness
EEILORRT	loiterer
EEILORRV	overlier
EEILORST	literose
EEILORSV	relievos
EEILORVV	overlive
	overveil
EEILOSTW	sweet-oil
EEILOSVW	vowelise
EEILOTTT	toilette
EEILOVWZ	vowelize
EEILPPSS	pipeless
EEILPPSY	epilepsy
EEILPRST	epistler
EEILPSSV	pelvises
EEILPSTY	epistyle
EEILRSST	riteless
	tireless
EEILRSSW	wireless
EEILSSTW	witeless
EEILSSVW	viewless
EEILSTVY	stievely
EEIMMORS	memorise
EEIMMORZ	memorize
EEIMMOST	sometime
EEIMMRST	meristem
	mimester
	mismetre
EEIMMRSU	eumerism
EEIMMRTT	term-time
EEIMMSTU	semi-mute
EEIMNOPS	episemon

EEIMNORS	emersion
EEIMNORT	timoneer
EEIMNORV	vomerine
EEIMNOST	monetise
	semitone
EEIMNOTX	xenotime
EEIMNOTZ	monetize
	time-zone
EEIMNPRU	perineum
EEIMNPST	sepiment
EEIMNQSU	mesquine
EEIMNRRT	terminer
EEIMNRTU	mutineer
EEIMNRTV	virement
EEIMNSSS	Essenism
EEIMOPRS	promisee
	reimpose
EEIMOPST	epsomite
EEIMORST	tiresome
EEIMORTV	overtime
EEIMORTX	oximeter
EEIMOSSW	somewise
EEIMPPRS	episperm
EEIMPPST	pipe-stem
EEIMPRRS	simperer
EEIMPRSS	impresse
	mesprise
	premises
EEIMPRSZ	mesprize
EEIMPSSY	empyesis
EEIMQSTU	mesquite
EEIMRRTT	remitter
	trimeter
EEIMRSTU	emeritus
EEIMRTTY	temerity
EEINNPTT	penitent
EEINNRSW	new-risen
EEINNRTT	internet
	renitent
EEINNRTV	re-invent
EEINNRUX	xenurine
EEINNSTT	sentient
EEINOPPR	peperino
	peperoni
EEINOPRS	isoprene
EEINORRT	reorient
EEINORSS	essoiner
EEINORST	serotine
EEINORSV	eversion
EEINORTT	tenorite
EEINORTX	exertion
EEINOSST	essonite
EEINOSTT	noisette
	teosinte
EEINPPRW	pen-wiper
EEINPPTV	vent-pipe
EEINPPTZ	Zentippe
EEINPRSS	ripeness
EEINPRSU	resupine
EEINPRTX	inexpert
EEINPSTT	spinette
EEINQRRU	enquirer

EEINQRSU	squireen
EEINRRST	inserter
	reinsert
EEINRRSU	reinsure
EEINRRTV	inverter
EEINRRTX	interrex
EEINRSST	interess
EEINRSSU	enuresis
EEINRSTT	interest
	sternite
EEINRSTU	esurient
EEINRSTV	reinvest
	servient
	sirvente
EEINRSTX	intersex
EEINRSTY	serenity
EEINRSUV	universe
EEINRSWW	newswire
	wire-sewn
EEINRTTY	entirety
	eternity
	trey-tine
EEINSSSW	wiseness
EEINSSSX	sexiness
EEINSTTW	tentwise
	twenties
EEINSTTX	existent
EEIOPPRR	rope-ripe
EEIOPPRS	epispore
EEIOPRRT	portière
EEIOPRRV	overripe
EEIOPRST	poetries
EEIORRTV	overtire
EEIORRTX	exterior
EEIORRUV	ouvrière
EEIORSST	erotesis
EEIORSVW	overwise
EEIORSVZ	oversize
EEIORVVW	overview
EEIORVWW	wirewove
EEIPPRRS	perspire
EEIPPRTY	peripety
EEIPRRTT	preterit
EEIPRSTT	pretties
EEIPRSTX	pre-exist
EEIPRSTY	perseity
EEIPRTUV	eruptive
EEIPSSTW	stepwise
EEIPSTUY	Puseyite
EEIQRRRU	requirer
EEIQRRTU	requiter
EEIQRRUV	verquire
EEIQRTUY	queerity
EEIQSSSU	esquisse
EEIRRSSV	reversis
EEIRRSTV	reverist
EEIRRTTT	titterer
EEIRSTVY	severity
EEIRTTTZ	terzetti
EEJJLNUY	jejunely
EEJKMOOS	jokesome
EEJLLORY	jolleyer

EEJLPSTU	pulsejet
EEJPRRRU	perjurer
EEJPRSTU	superjet
EEKKORWW	workweek
EEKLLNRY	kernelly
EEKLLPTW	well-kept
EEKLNNNU	unkennel
EEKLNOST	skeleton
EEKLNOSV	velskoen
EEKNOPST	knee-stop
EEKNOSTY	keystone
EEKNSSSW	skewness
EEKOORST	kreosote
EEKORSTV	overkest
EEKRRTUZ	kreutzer
EELLLLMP	pell-mell
EELLLOVW	low-level
EELLMPTU	plumelet
EELLNORR	enroller
EELLNOUV	nouvelle
EELLNPRU	prunelle
EELLNSSW	wellness
EELLNSTU	entellus
EELLOPTV	top-level
EELLORST	solleret
EELLORSV	oversell
EELLORTX	extoller
EELLORVY	volleyer
EELLOSSV	loveless
EELLOSUV	levulose
EELLRSSU	ruleless
EELMMPUX	exemplum
EELMNOOS	lonesome
EELMNSUY	unseemly
EELMNTTU	temulent
EELMNTUY	unmeetly
EELMOOSV	lovesome
EELMOPRY	employer
EELMOPSY	polyseme
EELMORST	molester
EELMORTY	remotely
EELMOSSV	moveless
EELMOTVW	twelvemo
EELMPPRU	empurple
EELMPRTU	plum-tree
EELMRRTU	murrelet
EELMRSST	termless
EELMRSTY	smeltery
EELMRTUX	luxmeter
EELMSSST	stemless
EELNNOSS	loneness
EELNNRTU	tunneler
EELNNUVY	unevenly
EELNOORS	loosener
EELNOPPU	unpeople
EELNOPRT	petronel
EELNOPTY	polytene
EELNOQTU	eloquent
EELNORST	entresol
EELNORTT	teletron
EELNORTV	overlent
EELNOSSS	noseless
	soleness
EELNOSST	noteless
	toneless
EELNOSSU	selenous
EELNOSSZ	zoneless
EELNOSTV	love-nest
EELNOTVV	evolvent
EELNSSSW	newsless
EELNSSTT	tentless
EELNSSTU	tuneless
EELNSTTU	unsettle
EELOOPRT	Peterloo
EELOPPST	estoppel
EELOPRRX	△explorer
EELOPRTT	teleport
EELOPSTU	outsleep
	sleep-out
EELOQRUY	requoyle
EELORRSV	resolver
EELORRTV	revolter
EELORRUV	overrule
EELORRVV	revolver
EELORSSS	roseless
EELORSTU	resolute
EELORSTY	Tyrolese
EELORTTU	roulette
EELORTUV	revolute
	true-love
EELOSSTU	setulose
EELOSSTV	voteless
EELOSTTX	sextolet
EELPPSTU	septuple
EELPRTXY	expertly
EELPSSUX	plexuses
EELPSTUX	sextuple
EELRRSTW	wrestler
EELRSSST	restless
EELRSSTY	tyreless
EELRSTWY	westerly
EELSSTTX	textless
EEMMNOOP	menopome
EEMMNOST	mementos
EEMMNOTV	movement
EEMMOORS	merosome
EEMNNRSU	Mensuren
EEMNORRS	sermoner
EEMNORST	sermonet
EEMNORSU	mounseer
EEMNPRTU	erumpent
	untemper
EEMNRSTU	muenster
EEMNSSTU	muteness
	tenesmus
EEMNSTTV	vestment
EEMOORRV	moreover
EEMOORTT	roomette
EEMOOSSX	exosmose
EEMOPRRS	premorse
EEMOQRSU	Moresque
EEMOQTTU	moquette
EEMORRTU	mouterer
	outremer
EEMORSST	somerset
EEMORSTU	temerous
EEMOTTTU	teetotum
EEMPRRSU	presumer
EEMPRSST	sempster
EEMRRSTU	musterer
EEMRRTTU	mutterer
EENNNOOO	one-on-one
EENNNOSS	nonsense
EENNNOTV	non-event
EENNNPTY	tenpenny
EENNOOOT	one-to-one
EENNOORT	rotenone
EENNOPSS	openness
EENNOPTX	exponent
EENNORRW	renowner
EENNSSTX	nextness
EENOORST	roestone
EENOORTV	overtone
EENOPPRS	propense
EENOPRSS	response
EENOPRST	protense
EENOPRSU	peroneus
EENOPRTT	entrepot
	entrepôt
EENOPRXY	pyroxene
EENORSSS	soreness
EENORSSU	neuroses
EENORSTT	onsetter
	setter-on
EENORSTX	extensor
EENORTVW	overwent
EENOSSST	stenoses
EENOSSWY	snow-eyes
EENPRSST	pertness
	presents
EENPRSSU	pureness
EENPRSTT	strepent
EENPRSTU	purse-net
EENPSSSU	suspense
EENPSTTU	petuntse
EENPTTUZ	petuntze
EENRRRTU	returner
EENRRSTV	renverst
EENRRTUV	venturer
EENRSSSU	sureness
EENRSSTU	trueness
EENRSTUW	wet-nurse
EEOOOTTT	toe-to-toe
EEOOPRST	proteose
EEOOPRSX	exospore
EEOOPRTZ	zoetrope
EEOORRVV	rove-over
EEOORRVW	overwore
EEOORRZZ	zero-zero
EEOPPRSS	porpesse
EEOPRRRT	reporter
EEOPRRRV	reprover
EEOPRRSU	reposure
EEOPRRTT	potterer

EEOPRRTX	exporter
	re-export
EEOPRSSS	espresso
EEOPRSST	portesse
EEOPRSSU	espouser
	repoussé
EEOPRSSX	expresso
EEOPRSTV	overstep
EEOPRSTY	serotype
EEOPRSUX	exposure
EEOPSSTW	sweetsop
EEOQRTTU	roquette
EEORRRST	resorter
	restorer
	retrorse
EEORRRTT	retorter
EEORRSSV	reversos
EEORRSTX	extrorse
EEORRTTT	totterer
EEORRTTU	teru-tero
EEORRTUV	overture
	trouvère
EEORSTVX	vortexes
EEORTTTZ	terzetto
EEOSSTTT	sestetto
EEPQRRUU	perruque
EEPRRSSU	pressure
EEPRSTTU	setter-up
	upsetter
EERRSSTU	tressure
EERRSTUV	vesturer
EERRSTVY	revestry
EERRSUVY	resurvey
EERSTTTU	utterest
EFFGILRU	grieful
EFFGINOR	offering
EFFHIILS	file-fish
EFFHIISW	fishwife
EFFHIITT	fiftieth
EFFHILRW	whiffler
EFFHIOTW	off-white
EFFHLLSU	shelf-ful
EFFHLLSY	flesh-fly
EFFHLRSU	shuffler
EFFHOORS	offshore
EFFIINSS	iffiness
EFFILNRS	sniffler
EFFILNSS	sniffles
EFFILORT	forelift
EFFILRSU	siffleur
EFFINOSU	effusion
EFFIOPRS	pifferos
EFFIOPST	off-piste
EFFIORST	forfeits
EFFIORTW	write-off
EFFIQRSU	squiffer
EFFLMNUU	unmuffle
EFFLNRSU	snuffler
EFFLNRUU	unruffle
EFFLNSSU	snuffles
EFFNRSSU	snuffers
EFFOOORT	forefoot

EFFORRUV	overruff
EFGGIINN	feigning
EFGGILOS	solfeggi
EFGGIRTU	egg-fruit
EFGGORRY	froggery
EFGHHIIV	high-five
EFGHIINR	Feringhi
EFGHILSU	fish-glue
EFGHINOT	night-foe
EFGHINRT	frighten
EFGHIOSY	fogeyish
EFGHIRSY	grey-fish
EFGHNOTU	foughten
EFGIILNU	figuline
EFGIIMNS	misfeign
EFGIINNR	infringe
	refining
EFGIINRU	figurine
EFGIITUV	fugitive
EFGIKNOR	foreking
EFGILLNO	lifelong
	long-life
EFGILLNU	fuelling
EFGILLUU	guileful
EFGILMOR	filmgoer
EFGILNOR	florigen
EFGILNTT	fettling
EFGILNTW	left-wing
EFGILPRU	fire-plug
EFGIMOSY	fogeyism
EFGIMRUU	refugium
EFGINNNP	pfenning
EFGINORV	forgiven
EFGINORW	forewing
EFGINPUY	pinguefy
EFGINRRY	ferrying
EFGINRTT	fretting
EFGINRTY	gentrify
EFGIOPTT	pettifog
EFGKMOOS	fog-smoke
EFGLOOVX	foxglove
EFGLRSUU	surgeful
EFGLSSTU	slugfest
EFGNOSST	songfest
EFGNSSUU	funguses
EFHHIRSS	freshish
EFHIILMN	Niflheim
EFHIILNS	line-fish
EFHIILST	tilefish
EFHIINRS	finisher
EFHIIPPS	pipefish
EFHIIPRS	fireship
EFHIIRSS	Friesish
EFHIIRSW	fish-weir
EFHIKOOR	fire-hook
EFHILTWY	whitefly
EFHIOOOR	forhooie
EFHIOPRS	foreship
EFHIORSS	rosefish
EFHIORSV	overfish
EFHIORTT	fortieth
EFHIPRSS	serfship

EFHIRRTU	thurifer
EFHISSTW	fish-stew
EFHKLNOU	funkhole
EFHLLLSU	shellful
EFHLNORS	hornfels
EFHLOOSS	hoofless
EFHLOOST	elf-shoot
EFHLOPST	top-shelf
EFHLORSY	horsefly
EFHLORVY	hover-fly
EFHLOSUU	houseful
EFHLOSUY	housefly
EFHNRRSU	fresh-run
EFHOORSW	foreshow
EFHOOSST	soft-shoe
EFHORRTY	frothery
EFHRSTTU	furthest
EFIIILRV	vilifier
EFIIINNT	infinite
EFIIIRVV	vivifier
EFIIKRRS	fire-risk
EFIILLNT	tefillin
EFIILLRS	frillies
EFIILNTY	felinity
	finitely
EFIILOQU	filioque
EFIILPRT	rifle-pit
EFIILRSU	fusilier
EFIILSTT	fitliest
EFIIMMNS	feminism
EFIIMNOS	fisnomie
EFIIMNST	feminist
EFIIMNTY	feminity
EFIINORR	inferior
EFIINORT	notifier
EFIINPSV	fivepins
EFIINPSX	spinifex
EFIINRRT	ferritin
EFIINRSY	resinify
EFIINSUV	infusive
EFIIPRRU	purifier
EFIIPRST	△spitfire
EFIIPRTY	typifier
EFIIRTUV	fruitive
EFIIRVVY	revivify
EFIJLORS	frijoles
EFIKLOOR	rooflike
EFIKLORW	life-work
EFIKNNOS	finnesko
EFIKNORS	foreskin
EFIKNRSU	refusnik
EFIKORRW	firework
EFIKRTUY	key-fruit
EFILLLNU	fluellin
EFILLLSW	self-will
EFILLMSU	smileful
EFILLMTU	full-time
EFILLORV	overfill
EFILLOSU	fusel-oil
EFILLRUY	irefully
EFILLSTY	stellify
EFILLTUY	futilely

EFILMRSS firmless
EFILMSUY emulsify
EFILNNTU influent
EFILNORU fluorine
EFILNOSU noiseful
EFILNRTT flittern
EFILNUWY unwifely
EFILOPRR profiler
pro-lifer
EFILOPRW fire-plow
EFILOPST sept-foil
EFILORTU fluorite
EFILPPSU pipefuls
EFILPRTU uplifter
EFILPSTU spiteful
EFILPSTY self-pity
EFILRSST riftless
EFILRSTT flitters
EFILRSTW fewtrils
EFILRTTU fruitlet
EFILSTTW swiftlet
EFIMNORR informer
reinform
reniform
EFIMNORS ensiform
EFIMNRSS firmness
EFIMORRT retiform
EFIMORRW fireworm
EFIMORST setiform
EFIMOSST semi-soft
EFIMOSTT ofttimes
EFIMRSTU fremitus
EFINNOOT nine-foot
EFINNORS infernos
EFINNPSU fine-spun
EFINOPTX pontifex
EFINORRT frontier
EFINORSU refusion
EFINOSSX foxiness
EFINOSSZ foziness
EFINRSST snifters
EFIOPRRT port-fire
profiter
EFIORRTT retrofit
EFIPPRRY frippery
EFIPRRUY repurify
EFIPRTTY prettify
EFIRRRUY furriery
EFIRRTUY fruitery
EFKLLOOR folklore
EFKLMNOS menfolks
EFKLNOTU folk-tune
EFKLORUW fluework
EFKNOORW foreknow
EFKORRTW fretwork
EFLLLOOW woolfell
EFLLLOWY fellowly
EFLLLPSU spellful
EFLLLPTU full-pelt
EFLLNSSU fullness
EFLLNTUY fluently
EFLLOORW follower
EFLLOOTW footwell
EFLLORUV overfull
EFLLOSST self-lost
soft-sell
EFLLOUWY woefully
EFLLRUUY ruefully
EFLLSUUY usefully
EFLMMRUY flummery
EFLMNRUU frenulum
EFLMORRY formerly
EFLMORSS formless
EFLNOOSU felonous
EFLNORTT frontlet
EFLNOSSU foulness
EFLNOSSW self-sown
EFLNOSTY stonefly
EFLNSUUU unuseful
EFLOORSS roofless
EFLOORSW foreslow
EFLOORTU footrule
EFLOORVW overflow
EFLOOSST footless
EFLOPRUW powerful
EFLOPSTW fowl-pest
EFLORRUY ryeflour
EFLORSUY yourself
EFLORTWY fly-tower
EFLOSUUX flexuous
EFLPRSSU pressful
EFLPRSUU purseful
EFLRSTUU frustule
EFLRSTUY flustery
EFMNORTY fromenty
EFMNRTUY frumenty
furmenty
EFMOORST foremost
EFMOORSU foursome
EFNNOOOR forenoon
EFNNORST fornenst
EFNNORUZ unfrozen
EFNOOOTT footnote
EFNOOPRT pentroof
EFNOOSST eftsoons
EFNOPRST forspent
EFNORRST renforst
re'nforst
EFNOSSST softness
EFOOOPRT foot-rope
EFOOORST footsore
EFOOPRSY spoofery
EFOOPSTT footstep
EFOORRSW forswore
EFOORSTT footrest
EFOPRRSU profuser
EFORRSST fortress
EFORRSTW frowster
EFORRSTY forestry
EFORRTTU frotteur
EFORSSST fostress
EGGGILNS leggings
EGGGNNOR ronggeng
EGGGOOOS goosegog
EGGGORRY groggery
EGGHIINW weighing
EGGHIKSW egg-whisk
EGGHIRWY Whiggery
EGGHOOTT egg-tooth
EGGHRTUY thuggery
EGGIINNS singeing
EGGIINNT tingeing
EGGIKNOS gingkoes
ginkgoes
EGGILLNY gingelly
EGGILNNU lungeing
EGGILNRS sniggler
EGGILNRU grueling
EGGILNRY gingerly
EGGILQSU squiggle
EGGILRRW wriggler
EGGINORR gorgerin
rogering
EGGINOUV vogueing
EGGINRSS gressing
EGGINSSU guessing
EGGIPRRY priggery
EGGJLRUY jugglery
EGGLLNOS long-legs
EGGLMOOY gemology
EGGLMRSU smuggler
EGGLORUY gurgoyle
EGGLRSTU struggle
EGGMNTUY nutmeggy
EGGNOOPS egg-spoon
EGGNOOST geognost
EGGNOOSY geognosy
EGGNORST gongster
EGGNRSUY snuggery
EGGOORSU gorgeous
EGHHIIRS high-rise
EGHHILNO high-lone
EGHHILTY eighthly
EGHHINSS △highness
EGHHIPRU higher-up
EGHHIPTY type-high
EGHHISTT high-test
EGHHLOOW whole-hog
EGHHORUW rough-hew
EGHIILNR hireling
EGHIILNS sheiling
shieling
EGHIINTV thieving
EGHIIPTT tithe-pig
EGHIIRST tigerish
EGHILLNS shelling
EGHILLNW well-nigh
EGHILNPT penlight
EGHILNRS shingler
EGHILNSS shingles
EGHILNSV shelving
EGHILNSY Yenglish
EGHILNTU tile-hung
EGHILNUW △glühwein
EGHILORT regolith
EGHILPRT plighter

EGHIMPRU	grumphie
EGHIMSTT	mightest
EGHINNOT	one-night
EGHINNOY	honeying
EGHINNSS	nighness
EGHINNST	sennight
	se'nnight
EGHINOST	histogen
EGHINOSU	ginhouse
EGHINPSS	sphinges
EGHINRSU	ushering
EGHINTTW	whetting
EGHIOPSU	pishogue
EGHIORRV	river-hog
EGHIOSTV	eightvos
EGHIOTUW	outweigh
	weigh-out
EGHIQRTU	requight
EGHIRRUY	hierurgy
EGHIRSTT	streight
EGHLLNUW	well-hung
EGHLMNOP	phlegmon
EGHLNRUY	hungerly
EGHLOOOR	horologe
EGHLOORY	rheology
EGHLOOSU	log-house
EGHLOOTY	ethology
	theology
EGHLOPRU	plougher
EGHMNOOY	homogeny
EGHMNORS	gemshorn
EGHMOPUY	hypogeum
EGHMOSUU	mug-house
EGHNNNYY	gynny-hen
EGHNOOPR	prong-hoe
EGHNOOPT	photogen
EGHNOOTY	theogony
EGHNORUV	overhung
EGHNOSUU	gunhouse
EGHNOTUU	Huguenot
EGHNRSTT	strength
EGHOOOSW	hoosegow
EGHORRTW	regrowth
EGIIKKLN	king-like
EGIIKLLO	killogie
EGIIKNSZ	king-size
EGIILMMN	immingle
EGIILMTW	lime-twig
EGIILNNU	linguine
EGIILNOR	religion
EGIILNRS	Riesling
EGIILNRT	girtline
	tireling
EGIILNRV	reviling
EGIILNSW	wiseling
EGIILRTZ	glitzier
EGIIMNNU	ingenium
EGIIMNRS	Isengrim
	semi-ring
EGIIMNRT	ring-time
EGIIMNSV	misgiven
EGIIMNTT	emitting
EGIIMOPT	impetigo
EGIIMORR	grimoire
EGIIMRST	tigerism
EGIINNPR	repining
EGIINNST	steining
EGIINOPR	peignoir
EGIINORS	seignior
EGIINPRX	expiring
EGIINQTU	quieting
EGIINRRT	retiring
EGIINRST	strigine
EGIINRSU	signieur
EGIINRSW	ringwise
EGIINRTU	intrigue
EGIINRTV	riveting
EGIINRTX	genitrix
EGIINRVV	reviving
EGIITUXY	exiguity
EGIJMMNY	jemmying
EGIJNQRU	jerquing
EGIKKNRT	trekking
EGIKLNOS	songlike
EGIKLNPS	skelping
EGIKLNSS	kingless
EGIKNORV	overking
EGIKNPPS	skepping
EGILLMNS	smelling
EGILLNNO	long-line
EGILLNOR	Negrillo
EGILLNOV	livelong
EGILLNPS	spelling
EGILLNSW	swelling
EGILLNTU	glutelin
EGILLOOR	gloriole
EGILMMRY	glimmery
EGILMNOT	long-time
EGILMNPU	implunge
EGILMNST	smelting
EGILMOUU	eulogium
EGILNNNO	long-nine
EGILNNST	nestling
EGILNOPP	popeling
EGILNORW	lowering
EGILNOSU	ligneous
EGILNOSW	longwise
EGILNOTW	toweling
EGILNPRS	sperling
	springle
EGILNPRY	replying
EGILNRRY	erringly
EGILNRSS	ringless
EGILNRST	lingster
	△sterling
EGILNRSW	newsgirl
EGILNSSS	signless
EGILNSSU	ugliness
EGILNSSW	wingless
EGILNSTT	settling
EGILNVXY	vexingly
EGILOOSU	isologue
EGILOOTY	etiology
EGILORTY	gyrolite
EGILOSTU	eulogist
EGILRRZZ	grizzler
EGILRTTY	glittery
EGIMMNST	stemming
EGIMNNNO	mignonne
EGIMNOOR	Geronimo
EGIMNORS	negroism
EGIMNOSU	geminous
EGIMNPRU	impugner
EGIMNPTT	tempting
EGIMNPTY	emptying
EGIMNRSS	grimness
EGIMNRUY	eryngium
EGIMORST	ergotism
EGIMOSTW	twigsome
EGINNNUY	ennuying
EGINNORS	nose-ring
EGINNORT	nitrogen
EGINNORV	vigneron
EGINNPPY	penny-pig
EGINNRRU	unerring
EGINNRTV	ventring
EGINOORV	ingroove
EGINOPRY	pigeonry
EGINORRY	iron-grey
EGINORSS	goriness
EGINORST	Negritos
EGINORSY	seignory
EGINORTU	outreign
	routeing
EGINORTW	towering
EGINORVW	overwing
EGINPPPR	prepping
EGINPPST	stepping
EGINPRRS	springer
EGINPRSS	pressing
EGINPRTU	reputing
EGINPRYY	perigyny
EGINQRUY	querying
EGINQSTU	questing
EGINRRST	restring
	ringster
	stringer
EGINRRTY	retrying
EGINRSST	trigness
EGINRSSY	syringes
EGINRSTW	strewing
EGINRSVW	swerving
EGINRTTU	uttering
EGINSTTT	stetting
EGIOPRTU	portigue
EGIORSST	strigose
EGIORSSU	griseous
EGIORSTV	vertigos
EGIORSTY	oystrige
EGIORSUV	grievous
EGIOSUUX	exiguous
EGIRRSTY	registry
EGIRSTTT	grittest
EGISSYYZ	syzygies
EGISTTTU	guttiest
EGJLNORU	jongleur

EGJLNOTU jelutong
EGLLMORW gromwell
EGLLOOPY pelology
EGLMNOOS longsome
EGLMNOOY menology
EGLMNORT long-term
EGLMNSSU glumness
EGLMOPRU promulge
EGLMORSS gormless
EGLNNOOR longeron
EGLNNOSS longness
EGLNNTUY ungently
EGLNOOOY oenology
EGLNOOPR prolonge
EGLNOOPY penology
EGLNOORS slogorne
EGLNOORV overlong
EGLNOOSV love-song
EGLNOPYY polygeny
EGLNORSU longeurs
EGLNORUU longueur
EGLNOSSS songless
EGLNPTUV vent-plug
EGLNRTUY urgently
EGLOOORY oreology
EGLOOPRU prologue
EGLOOPTY logotype
EGLOORSY serology
EGLOOSXY sexology
EGLOPRTU grouplet
EGLORRWY growlery
EGLORSUU rugulose
EGLORSUY rugosely
EGMNNOOY monogeny
nomogeny
EGMNOOOS mongoose
EGMNOORY merogony
EGMNOOSU mungoose
EGMNRSSU grumness
EGMNSSSU smugness
EGNNOOTY ontogeny
EGNNOSTU gunstone
EGNNOTTU ungotten
EGNNSSSU snugness
EGNNSTTU tungsten
EGNOORRV governor
EGNOOTUX ox-tongue
EGNOPPRU oppugner
EGNORRST stronger
EGNORSST songster
EGNORSTT tongster
EGNORSTU sturgeon
EGNORSTY sentry-go
EGNOSTTT tong-test
EGNOSTUY youngest
EGNPRSUU supergun
EGNSSTUU Tunguses
EGOOPRRU prorogue
EGOORRVW overgrow
EGOORSTT grottoes
EGOPRRSS progress
EGOPRRSU groupers
EGOPSSUY gypseous
EHHIIPRS heirship
EHHIISTV thievish
EHHILMNT helminth
EHHILOST shithole
EHHINOPT thiophen
EHHIOPRS heroship
EHHIORTT hitherto
EHHIOTTW white-hot
EHHIRSSW shrewish
EHHLOOST shothole
EHHNOORS shoehorn
EHHNOOSS Shoshone
EHHNSSUY hen-hussy
EHHOOPST theosoph
EHHOOSTU hothouse
EHHORSTU shouther
EHHOSTUV Shevuoth
EHIIKLPT pithlike
EHIIKLPW whiplike
EHIILOSS heliosis
EHIILRSV liverish
EHIIMNNT Nethinim
EHIIMPST mephitis
EHIINNOS inhesion
EHIINNQU heniquin
EHIINNRS inshrine
EHIINRRT hirrient
EHIINSVX vixenish
EHIIPRST ship-tire
EHIIPRSV viperish
EHIIRRTX heritrix
EHIIRSSU huissier
EHIIRSTT thirties
EHIISTTX sixtieth
EHIJLSWY Jewishly
EHIJOSTV Jehovist
EHIKLLNO kiln-hole
EHIKLNOS sinkhole
EHIKLOSY yokelish
EHIKLRSU rushlike
EHIKMNST methinks
EHIKNRRS shrinker
EHIKOPRS pokerish
EHIKRSSW whiskers
EHIKRSWY whiskery
EHILLLMO molehill
EHILLMOP Philomel
EHILLMOT mote-hill
EHILLMOY homelily
EHILLOPY lyophile
EHILLPTY phyllite
EHILLRRT thriller
EHILLRTY litherly
EHILLSSW swellish
EHILLSWW well-wish
EHILMOOR heirloom
EHILMOST helotism
EHILMPSY symphile
EHILMQUU umquhile
EHILNOOP oenophil
EHILNOSS △holiness
EHILNOST Holstein
EHILNOSV novelish
EHILNOTX xenolith
EHILNSWY newishly
EHILOOPZ zoophile
EHILOOST Holostei
EHILOPRS pilhorse
polisher
EHILOPRT heliport
EHILOPSS slip-shoe
EHILOPST helistop
isopleth
EHILORTY rhyolite
EHILPSSS shipless
EHILPSST pithless
EHILPSTU sulphite
EHILRSST thrissel
EHILRSTT thristle
EHILRSTW whistler
EHILRSTY slithery
EHILRTTW whittler
EHILRTTY triethyl
EHIMMNUY hymenium
EHIMMRSY shimmery
EHIMNOPR morphine
EHIMNORT thermion
EHIMNOSU hemionus
EHIMNOTT monteith
EHIMNPRS phrenism
EHIMNPST shipment
EHIMNRRU murrhine
EHIMNRRY myrrhine
EHIMOOSS homeosis
EHIMOOST smoothie
EHIMOPRS sopherim
EHIMOPST Mephisto
EHIMORST isotherm
EHIMPPSS psephism
EHIMPRRS shrimper
EHIMPRSU murphies
EHIMPSUU △euphuism
EHIMPTTU umptieth
EHIMRSST smithers
EHIMRSTY smithery
EHIMSSTY methysis
EHINNOPR phoner-in
EHINNOTW non-white
EHINNRST thinners
EHINNSST thinness
EHINNSSU sunshine
EHINNSTT thinnest
EHINOPPR hornpipe
EHINOPRT triphone
EHINOPRY Hyperion
EHINOPST siphonet
EHINORSS herisson
EHINOSTU outshine
EHINPRSU punisher
EHINPSSX sphinxes
EHINSSST thisness
EHIOOPSW whoopsie

EHIOOSST	stooshie
EHIOPPPS	popeship
EHIOPPST	poetship
EHIOPPSU	Eohippus
EHIOPSTT	Peshitto
EHIOPTTW	whitepot
EHIORSTT	theorist
EHIORSTW	worthies
EHIORTWZ	howitzer
EHIOSSTU	house-sit
EHIOSTVY	yeshivot
EHIOTTUW	white-out
EHIPQSUY	physique
EHIPRSST	hipsters
	thripses
EHIPRSSW	whispers
EHIPRSTW	whipster
EHIPRSWY	whispery
EHIPSTUU	euphuist
EHIRRSTT	thirster
EHIRSTTW	whitster
EHIRTTTW	whittret
EHISSTUW	thuswise
EHJMNOSS	Mess-John
EHKLNOOT	knot-hole
EHKLOSTY	lekythos
EHKMMNOR	Mon-Khmer
EHKMOORW	homework
EHKMORSU	humoresk
EHKMORSW	mesh-work
EHKNNRSU	shrunken
EHLLMOPY	phyllome
EHLLNSTU	nutshell
EHLLOOOP	loophole
EHLLOPST	top-shell
EHLMNOTU	molehunt
EHLMNOUY	unhomely
EHLMOORW	wormhole
EHLMORTY	motherly
EHLNNOPU	unholpen
EHLNOOSW	snow-hole
EHLNOPSU	sulphone
EHLNORSS	hornless
EHLNOSTY	honestly
EHLNSSSU	lushness
	shunless
EHLOOPRT	porthole
	potholer
EHLOOPTY	holotype
EHLOPPRT	thropple
EHLORSTT	throstle
EHLORSTY	hostelry
EHLORTTT	throttle
EHLOSSTW	thowless
EHLOSSTY	thyloses
EHLRSSTU	hurtless
	ruthless
EHMMRRTU	thrummer
EHMNOOST	smoothen
EHMNOOTW	home-town
EHMNOOTY	theonomy
EHMNOPSU	homespun
EHMNPRYY	hypernym
EHMOOOTZ	zoothome
EHMOOPTY	homotype
EHMOORST	smoother
EHMOPRSU	Morpheus
EHMORSTY	smothery
EHMORTUV	vermouth
EHMOTUZZ	mezuzoth
EHMRTUYY	△eurythmy
EHNNOPRT	penn'orth
EHNNORRT	northern
EHNNORTU	unthrone
EHNNOSTU	unhonest
EHNOOPTY	honeypot
EHNOORRU	honourer
EHNOORST	hen-roost
EHNOORSW	whoreson
EHNOORTW	honewort
EHNOOSSW	snowshoe
EHNOPRST	Strephon
EHNOPSSS	poshness
EHNORSTT	thornset
EHNORSTU	△southern
EHNOSTUU	nuthouse
EHNRSSTU	huntress
EHNSSSTU	thusness
EHOOPRTY	orthoepy
EHOOPSTU	housetop
	pothouse
EHOOPTYZ	zoophyte
EHOORSST	orthoses
EHOORSTV	overshot
EHOORSTW	two-horse
EHOOSTUU	outhouse
EHOPPRSY	prophesy
EHOPRSST	hot-press
EHOPRSTY	trophesy
EHOPRSUV	push-over
EHOPRTUY	eutrophy
EHOPSTUY	Typhoeus
EHORSTUY	try-house
EHRRSTTU	thruster
EIIILMSS	similise
EIIILMSZ	similize
EIIILPPR	liripipe
EIIIMMNS	minimise
EIIIMMNZ	minimize
EIIIRRTV	tirrivie
EIIJKNRT	jirkinet
EIIKKLLM	milklike
EIIKLLMN	limekiln
EIIKLLMT	kill-time
EIIKLLNO	lionlike
EIIKLMRS	misliker
EIIKLOST	Sikeliot
EIIKNNSS	inkiness
EIIKNNSW	wineskin
EIILLLVY	livelily
EIILLMMR	millirem
EIILLMNR	milliner
EIILLMNS	slimline
EIILLMNU	illumine
EIILLNST	niellist
EIILLNSU	suilline
EIILLNTV	vitellin
EIILLOOV	olive-oil
EIILLPSS	ellipsis
EIILLSUV	illusive
EIILMNNS	Leninism
EIILMNNT	liniment
EIILMNOT	limonite
EIILMNSS	liminess
EIILMOPT	impolite
EIILMSTT	mistitle
EIILMSTY	myelitis
EIILNNOT	lenition
EIILNNST	Leninist
EIILNOSS	oiliness
EIILNOTT	toilinet
EIILNQTU	quintile
EIILNSSW	wiliness
EIILNSTY	senility
EIILNSVY	sylviine
EIILNTTU	intitule
EIILNTUV	vituline
EIILNTVY	Vinylite
EIILOPST	pisolite
EIILORTT	troilite
EIILOTVV	volitive
EIILPRSU	plurisie
EIILPSST	pitiless
EIILPSTY	pyelitis
EIILPSUZ	spuilzie
EIILRSTU	utiliser
EIILRTUZ	utilizer
EIIMMNNO	△menomini
EIIMMNNT	imminent
	miniment
EIIMMNSU	immunise
EIIMMNTU	imminute
EIIMMNUZ	immunize
EIIMMPRU	imperium
EIIMMSSS	seismism
EIIMMSST	Semitism
EIIMNNOR	iron-mine
EIIMNOPT	pimiento
EIIMNORT	Minorite
EIIMNOSS	emission
EIIMNOST	Timonise
EIIMNOSV	visnomie
EIIMNOTV	monitive
EIIMNOTZ	Timonize
EIIMNRSS	miriness
EIIMNRST	minister
EIIMNRTT	intermit
EIIMNRTX	intermix
EIIMOPRX	mirepoix
EIIMOPST	optimise
EIIMOPTZ	optimize
EIIMOSSV	omissive
EIIMOSUX	eximious
EIIMOTVV	vomitive
EIIMPRSS	misprise
EIIMPRSZ	misprize

EIIMQSTU quietism
EIIMRSTT metritis
EIIMRSTW miswrite
EIIMSSSV missives
EIIMSSTT Semitist
EIINNNPS ninepins
EIINNOSU unionise
EIINNOSV envision
EIINNOUZ unionize
EIINNPSS spinnies
EIINNRTV invertin
EIINNSST tininess
EIINOPRS ripienos
EIINOPST sinopite
EIINOPTT petition
EIINORRT interior
EIINORSV revision
visioner
EIINPRRS inspirer
EIINPRST pristine
EIINPSTZ pint-size
EIINPTUV punitive
EIINQRRU inquirer
EIINQTUY equinity
inequity
EIINRSST sinister
EIINRSSW wiriness
EIINRSTT sitter-in
EIINRSTU neuritis
EIINSSSZ siziness
EIIOPSTV positive
EIIOSSTT osteitis
EIIOTTTV totitive
EIIPRRTW tripwire
EIIPRSTT rispetti
EIIPRSTY pyritise
EIIPRTYZ pyritize
EIIPSSTT stipites
EIIQRSTU Quirites
EIIQSTTU quietist
EIIRSTTU uteritis
EIJJNTUY jejunity
EIJMNPSS jimpness
EIJNORTU jointure
EIJNOSTT jettison
EIJRSTUY Jesuitry
EIKLLMSS milkless
EIKLLNTW well-knit
EIKLLNUY unlikely
EIKLLORV overkill
EIKLLSSS skilless
EIKLMNOS moleskin
EIKLNOOR looker-in
△oerlikon
EIKLNOSW snowlike
EIKLNPRS sprinkle
EIKLNRST linkster
strinkle
EIKLNRTW twinkler
EIKLNSSS skinless
EIKLNSTT knittles
EIKLOORT rootlike
EIKLOPRW pilework
EIKLSSTT skittles
EIKMMORS mirksome
EIKMNOST tokenism
EIKMNOSU mousekin
EIKNNOST inkstone
EIKNNPSS pinkness
EIKNOPRS rose-pink
EIKNPRST Pinkster
EIKNPRTU turnpike
EIKNRRTU returnik
EIKOPPRW pipework
EIKOPRSV overskip
EIKORRWW wirework
EIKPRRSU spruiker
EIKPSTYY tipsy-key
EILLLNTY lent-lily
EILLLOVY lovelily
EILLLPUV pulville
EILLLSSW will-less
EILLMNOS Sémillon
EILLMNOU linoleum
EILLMOPS plimsole
EILLMPSS misspell
psellism
EILLMPTU multiple
EILLMUVX vexillum
EILLNOOP loop-line
EILLNOPY epyllion
EILLNOST stellion
EILLNOTU luteolin
EILLNPQU quill-pen
EILLNPST ill-spent
EILLNPUU lupuline
EILLNSTY silently
tinselly
EILLNSVY snivelly
EILLNUVY unlively
EILLOOSW woollies
EILLOPTY politely
EILLORST trilloes
trollies
EILLOSSS soilless
EILLOSST toilless
EILLRSTT testrill
EILLRSVY silverly
EILLSSST listless
EILLSTUV vitellus
EILMMSST slimmest
EILMNOSS solemnis
EILMNOSU emulsion
EILMNOSV novelism
EILMNOTU moulinet
EILMNOTY mylonite
EILMNPSS limpness
EILMNPSU splenium
EILMNPTU tump-line
EILMNRST minstrel
EILMNSSS slimness
EILMNSTU muslinet
EILMNTUY minutely
untimely
EILMOOPS liposome
EILMOOST toilsome
EILMOPRR implorer
EILMOPRS pelorism
EILMOPRW pile-worm
EILMOPST mile-post
polemist
EILMPPRU impurple
EILMPRUY impurely
EILMPSST misspelt
EILMRSSY remissly
EILMRSUU Merulius
EILMTTUU lutetium
EILMTTUY multeity
EILNNOST insolent
EILNNOSW snowline
EILNNOTV vinolent
EILNNTTY intently
EILNOOPP epiploon
EILNOOPS polonise
EILNOOPW pine-wool
EILNOOPZ polonize
EILNOOST oilstone
EILNOOSW low-noise
EILNOPPS plenipos
EILNOPPY polypine
EILNOPRT Interpol
topliner
EILNOPRU neuropil
EILNOPTU unpolite
EILNOPTY Linotype®
EILNORRT ritornel
EILNORTT trotline
EILNOSSW lewisson
EILNOSTV novelist
EILNOSUV evulsion
EILNOTUV involute
EILNOTXY Xylonite®
xylonite
EILNOTYZ zylonite
EILNPRST splinter
EILNPSSU splenius
EILNPSTW split-new
EILNPSUY supinely
EILNQUUY uniquely
EILNRSTU insulter
lustrine
EILNRSTY tinselry
EILNRSUU Ursuline
EILNRTUV virulent
EILNRTWY winterly
EILNSSTT tintless
EILNSSTW westlins
EILNSTTU lutenist
EILNSUWY unwisely
EILOOPTZ zopilote
EILOORTV overtoil
EILOPPTY polypite
EILOPRSS oil-press
EILOPRSU perilous
EILOPRSV overslip
slip-over

EILOPRTW	pilewort
EILOPSTT	pistolet
EILOPSUV	Pluviôse
	pluviose
EILORRTU	ulterior
EILORRTV	liver-rot
EILORTTY	toiletry
EILOSTTT	stiletto
EILOSTUV	love-suit
	solutive
EILPPPRY	preppily
EILPPRRT	trippler
EILPPRST	stippler
EILPPRSU	periplus
	supplier
EILPPRSY	slippery
EILPPRTU	pulpiter
EILPPSSU	supplies
EILPRSTT	splitter
EILPRSTY	priestly
	spritely
EILPRSUU	purlieus
EILPRSUY	pleurisy
EILPRTTY	prettily
EILQRRSU	squirrel
EILQRSUY	squirely
EILQSTUU	lustique
EILRRTWY	writerly
EILRSSST	stirless
EILRSSTY	sisterly
EILRSTTU	surtitle
EILRSTTW	wristlet
EILRSTTZ	strelitz
EIMMMNOT	immoment
EIMMMORZ	momzerim
EIMMNNOT	moniment
EIMMNNTU	muniment
EIMMNORS	misnomer
EIMMOOST	me-tooism
EIMMOPRU	emporium
EIMMOPST	metopism
EIMMOSTT	totemism
EIMMPRSU	premiums
EIMMPSSU	pessimum
EIMMRRST	Strimmer®
EIMMRSUY	Erysimum
EIMNNOOT	noontime
EIMNNOPT	imponent
EIMNNOPY	pin-money
EIMNNOTT	ointment
EIMNNOUY	euonymin
EIMNOOPS	empoison
EIMNOORS	moonrise
EIMNOORT	remotion
EIMNOORV	omnivore
EIMNOPRS	Peronism
EIMNOPRT	orpiment
EIMNOPST	nepotism
	pimentos
EIMNOPTT	impotent
EIMNORSS	Minoress
EIMNORSU	inermous
	△monsieur
EIMNORTW	time-worn
EIMNORTY	enormity
EIMNPRSS	primness
EIMNPSST	misspent
EIMNRSST	trimness
EIMNRSTU	△terminus
EIMNRSTY	entryism
	misentry
EIMOORST	motorise
EIMOORTZ	motorize
EIMOOTTT	Ottomite
EIMOPPRR	improper
EIMOPRRS	primrose
	promiser
EIMOPRRT	importer
	reimport
EIMOPRRV	improver
EIMOPRST	imposter
EIMOPRUU	europium
EIMOPSTY	peyotism
EIMOQSTU	misquote
EIMORRST	mortiser
EIMORRTT	remittor
EIMORRWW	wireworm
EIMORSTU	misroute
	moisture
EIMORSTY	isometry
EIMORSVW	overswim
EIMORTTW	two-timer
EIMOSSTZ	mestizos
EIMOSTTT	totemist
EIMOSTTU	titmouse
EIMPSSTY	emptysis
EIMPSSUY	Puseyism
EIMQSTUY	mystique
EIMRRSSU	surmiser
EIMRSSST	△mistress
EINNOOTX	neotoxin
EINNORSV	environs
EINNORTT	tontiner
EINNORTU	neutrino
EINNORTV	inventor
	noverint
EINNORWW	winnower
EINNOSSS	nosiness
EINNOSTT	tinstone
EINNPRSY	spinnery
EINNPSSU	puniness
EINNPSSY	spinneys
EINNPSXY	sixpenny
EINNRSTU	sturnine
EINNRTTU	nutrient
EINOOPRS	poisoner
EINOORSZ	ozoniser
EINOORZZ	ozonizer
EINOOSSZ	ooziness
EINOOTXX	exotoxin
EINOPPRV	vine-prop
EINOPRRS	prisoner
EINOPRSS	poriness
	pression
	ropiness
EINOPRST	Peronist
	pointers
EINOPRSU	pruinose
EINOPRSV	overspin
EINOPRSY	Epyornis
EINOPRTU	eruption
EINOPRTW	port-wine
EINOPSTT	nepotist
EINOPSWX	swine-pox
EINOQSTU	question
EINOQTTU	quotient
EINORRST	introrse
EINORRTV	invertor
EINORSSS	rosiness
EINORSSU	neurosis
	resinous
EINORSTT	tenorist
EINORSTV	investor
EINORSTY	tyrosine
EINORSUV	souvenir
EINORTTU	ritenuto
EINOSSSS	sessions
EINOSSST	stenosis
EINOSSSU	Senoussi
EINOSTUU	tenuious
EINOSTVY	venosity
EINPPRRT	pre-print
EINPPSTY	snippety
EINPRRST	sprinter
EINPRRTU	prurient
EINPRSST	spinster
EINPRSTU	unpriest
EINPRTTU	inputter
EINPSTTX	spintext
	spin-text
EINQRSTU	squinter
EINQRTTU	quit-rent
EINQTTTU	quintett
EINRSSST	instress
EINRSSXY	syrinxes
EINRSTTY	entryist
EINRTUUV	unvirtue
EINSSSSU	Senussis
EINSSTUX	unsexist
EINSSTWY	swine-sty
EINSSTXY	syntexis
EIOOPPRS	porpoise
EIOOPPST	opposite
EIOOPRST	portoise
EIOORRSS	sororise
EIOORRSZ	sororize
EIOORSTT	tortoise
EIOPPRTW	pipewort
EIOPRRSS	prioress
EIOPRRSU	superior
EIOPRRTV	overtrip
EIOPRSTT	rispetto
EIOPRSTV	sportive

EIOPRSUV	pervious
	previous
	viperous
EIOPRTTT	triptote
EIOPRTTY	petitory
EIOPRTUZ	outprize
EIOPSTTY	peyotist
EIORRRST	errorist
EIORRRTU	roturier
EIORRSST	resistor
	sorriest
EIORRSTV	servitor
EIORRSVY	revisory
EIORSSTY	serosity
EIORSTTU	tutorise
EIORSTUV	virtuose
	vitreous
EIORTTUZ	tutorize
EIPPRRST	stripper
EIPPRRTY	trippery
EIPQRSTU	quipster
EIPRRRSU	spurrier
EIPRRSSU	surprise
EIPRRSTZ	spritzer
EIPRSVVY	spivvery
EIQRRSTU	squirter
EIQRSSSU	squiress
EIQRUYZZ	quizzery
EIRRSTTU	trustier
EIRSSSTU	suitress
EIRTTTUY	tityre-tu
EIRTTTWY	twittery
EIRTTUWZ	wurtzite
EJLOPSTU	pulsojet
EJMOORTT	motor-jet
EJMOPPRU	jump-rope
EJMOPRUV	overjump
EJNORSUY	journeys
EJNSSSTU	justness
EKKMORSY	kromesky
EKLNOOOR	looker-on
	onlooker
EKLNOOTV	love-knot
EKLNOSST	knotless
EKLOOORV	overlook
EKLOOPSW	slowpoke
EKLORSSW	workless
EKLSSSTU	tuskless
EKMMORSU	murksome
EKMOOPRR	morepork
EKMOORSW	worksome
EKMRSTUY	musketry
EKNNOPSU	unspoken
EKNOOPRW	openwork
EKNOORST	rose-knot
	strooken
EKNORTTW	tent-work
EKOOPRRV	provoker
EKOOPRRW	ropework
EKOOPRSY	spookery
EKOORRVW	overwork
	work-over
EKOPPRST	Prospekt
EKOPRSTU	upstroke
EKORRUVY	kurveyor
ELLLMOWY	mellowly
ELLLNSUY	sullenly
ELLMNOSY	solemnly
ELLMNOTY	moltenly
ELLMNPUY	lumpenly
ELLMOORS	morellos
ELLMPPUW	pump-well
ELLNNSSU	nullness
ELLNOORV	lovelorn
ELLNOPRU	prunello
ELLNORWW	well-worn
ELLNOSVY	slovenly
ELLNOUVY	unlovely
ELLOORRV	roll-over
ELLOPRST	pollster
ELLOPRTU	polluter
ELLOPRUV	pullover
ELLOPSST	plotless
ELLORRST	stroller
ELLORSTY	trolleys
ELLOSSSU	soulless
ELLOSTUW	outswell
ELLPPSUY	supplely
ELLSSSTU	lustless
ELMMNOTU	lomentum
ELMMNOTY	momently
ELMMRSTU	strummel
ELMMRSUY	summerly
ELMNNOSU	unsolemn
ELMNOOOP	monopole
ELMNOOSS	moonless
ELMNOPSU	pulmones
ELMNUUZZ	unmuzzle
ELMOOPPS	pompelos
ELMOOPSY	polysome
ELMOORST	tremolos
ELMOORSY	morosely
ELMOOSSY	lysosome
ELMOPRTY	metopryl
ELMOPRYY	polymery
ELMOPSYY	polysemy
ELMOSYYZ	lysozyme
ELMPRSSU	rumpless
ELMRRTUU	multurer
ELNNOOSU	unloosen
ELNNOPTU	nonuplet
ELNOOSST	solonets
ELNOOSTZ	solonetz
ELNOPPTU	punt-pole
ELNOPTTY	potently
ELNORSTU	turnsole
ELNORSVY	slovenry
ELNORTTY	rottenly
ELNOSSSW	slowness
	snowless
ELNOSSTW	townless
	wontless
ELNPPSUU	unsupple
ELNPRTUU	purulent
ELOOPRSU	superloo
ELOOPRUW	owerloup
ELOOPSSS	sesspool
ELOORSST	rootless
ELOORSTU	torulose
ELOORSUV	oversoul
ELOOSSST	sootless
ELOPPRRY	properly
ELOPRRTY	porterly
ELOPRSTY	prostyle
ELOPRSUV	overplus
ELOPRSYY	pyrolyse
ELOPRXYY	pyroxyle
ELOPRYYZ	pyrolyze
ELOPSSST	spotless
	stopless
ELORSTUY	souterly
	urostyle
ELORTTTU	troutlet
ELOSSTUU	setulous
ELPRSSSU	spurless
ELPRSTTU	splutter
ELRSSSTU	rustless
ELRSTTUY	sluttery
ELSSSTUY	styluses
EMMMNOTU	momentum
EMMNNOTU	monument
EMMNORSU	summoner
EMMNORYY	meronymy
EMMNOTTU	tomentum
EMMNOTYY	metonymy
EMMOOORS	roomsome
EMMOORSS	mess-room
EMMOPTTY	pommetty
EMMRRRUU	murmurer
	remurmur
EMMRSTYY	symmetry
EMNNNOOU	noumenon
EMNNOOOT	monotone
EMNOOPTY	△monotype
EMNOORST	mesotron
	monteros
EMNOORSU	enormous
	nemorous
EMNOORSW	newsroom
EMNOORTY	noometry
EMNOOSUV	venomous
EMNOOTTY	tenotomy
EMNOOTUV	outvenom
EMNOPSYY	spy-money
EMNORSTT	sortment
EMNORSUU	numerous
EMNOSUUY	euonymus
EMOOPRRT	promoter
EMOOPRSY	pyrosome
EMOOPRSZ	zoosperm
EMOOPSSU	espumoso
EMOORSSS	moss-rose
EMOORTYZ	zoometry
EMOPPRRT	prompter
EMOPRSSU	spermous
	supremos

EMORRRUU rumourer
EMORSSTU strumose
EMOSSTTW westmost
EMOSSTVZ zemstvos
EMPRRTUY trumpery
EMPRSTTU strumpet
ENNNORTY non-entry
ENNOOORT tenoroon
ENNOOOTZ entozoon
ENNOOPPT opponent
ENNOORST norteños
ENNOORTV non-voter
ENNOOSTT nonettos
ENNOPRSU unperson
ENNOPRUV unproven
ENNOPTWY twopenny
ENNORSST sternson
ENNORTTU unrotten
ENNOSSTU sunstone
ENNPPTUY tuppenny
ENNPRRUU runner-up
ENOOOSSZ zoonoses
ENOOPPST postpone
ENOOPRSS poorness
ENOOPSTT potstone
top-stone
ENOORRVW overworn
ENOORSTT rot-stone
ENOPPRRU unproper
ENOPRTTU putter-on
ENOPRTUW uptowner
ENOPSSSY synopses
ENOPSTTU outspent
ENORRTUU tournure
ENORRTUV overturn
turnover
ENORSSSU sourness
ENORSTTU stentour
ENORSTTY snottery
ENORSTUV ventrous
vent'rous
ENOSSSUU sensuous
ENPRSSSY spryness
ENPRTTUY unpretty
ENRRRTUU nurturer
EOOOPRRT proto-ore
EOOOPRSS soporose
EOOOPRSZ zoospore
EOOOPRTZ zootrope
EOOORRST rose-root
EOOPPRRS proposer
EOOPPSST postpose
EOOPPTTY topotype
EOOPRRTU outroper
uprooter
EOOPRSTU porteous
EOOPRSTV overpost
stopover
EOOPRTUW outpower
EOOPRTWW two-power
EOORRRSW sorrower
EOORSSTU oestrous
EOORTTUV outvoter
EOPPRRTY property
EOPPRSSU purposes
supposer
EOPPSSSU supposes
EOPRRSST portress
EOPRRSTU posturer
EOPRRUVY purveyor
EORRRTTU torturer
EORRSSST stressor
trossers
EORRSSTU trousers
EORRSSTW trowsers
EORRSUVY surveyor
EORRTUUV trouveur
EORSSTTU tutoress
EORSTTUW outwrest
EORSTUUV vertuous
EPPPRTUY puppetry
EPPRSSSU suppress
EPPRSSUY superspy
EPRSTTUY sputtery
EQRRTUUU truqueur
ERRSTTTU strutter

F

FFFFPPUU puff-puff
FFFMOOTU footmuff
FFGGIILN gliffing
FFGHIINW whiffing
FFGHIORS frog-fish
FFGHIRSU gruffish
FFGIILNP piffling
FFGIINNS sniffing
FFGIINPS spiffing
FFGILNRU ruffling
FFGINNSU snuffing
FFGINSTU stuffing
FFHIISST stiffish
FFHIISTY fiftyish
FFHILOSU foul-fish
FFHILOSW wolf-fish
FFHIOPSS spoffish
FFHIRSSU surffish
FFHLORTY froth-fly
FFHOOOST offshoot
FFIILMOR filiform
FFIILNSY sniffily
FFIILNTY flintify
FFIINOOS soffioni
FFIKLORT fork-lift
FFIKLRSU friskful
FFILLOPP flip-flop
FFILLTUY fitfully
FFILOPST split-off
FFILRTUU fruitful
FFILRTUY fruit-fly
FFILSTUY stuffily
FFIMORSU fusiform
FFINOPRT offprint
FFKLORSU forkfuls
FFLMNOOU moufflon
FFLNOTUU fountful
FFLORRUU furfurol
FFNSTUUY unstuffy
FFOOORTU four-foot
FFOORRUU frou-frou
FFOORSST off-sorts
FGGGIINR frigging
FGGGILNO flogging
FGGGINOR frogging
FGGHIINT fighting
FGGHINTU gunfight
FGGIILNN flinging
FGGILNOR frogling
FGGINOOR forgoing
FGHIIKNS kingfish
FGHIILNT in-flight
FGHIINST shifting
FGHILLTU lightful
FGHILMTU mightful
FGHILNSU flushing
lung-fish
FGHILNTY night-fly
FGHILRTU rightful
FGHIOPST giftshop
FGHIOTTU outfight
FGHISSTU fish-guts
FGHLORUU furlough
FGHNOTUU unfought
FGIIKNRS frisking
FGIILLNR frilling
FGIILLNS fillings
FGIILLRT lift-girl
FGIILNOO folioing
FGIILNPP flipping
FGIILNRT flirting
trifling
FGIILNST stifling
FGIILNTT flitting
FGIINNUY unifying
FGIINRTT fritting
FGIINRTU fruiting
FGIINSST siftings
FGIINSTT fittings
FGIIRSTU figurist
FGILLNOW wolfling
FGILMNOR long-firm
FGILNNTU gunflint
FGILNOOR flooring
FGILNOOT footling
FGILNOOZ foozling
FGILNOSS flossing
FGILNOST softling
FGILNOTU outfling
FGILNPRU purfling
FGILNTYY fly-tying
FGINNORW frowning
FGINOOPR proofing
FGINORST frosting
FGIOPRST frog-spit
FGKLNOOS folk-song
FGLLMOOU gloomful
FGLNORUW wrongful

FGLOOOST footslog
FGNOORTU unforgot
FHHIKOOS fish-hook
FHHOORST shofroth
FHIIKLMS milkfish
FHIIKNSS fishskin
FHIILLTY filthily
FHIILRST flirtish
FHIILSTY shiftily
FHIKLLLO hillfolk
FHIKMNOS monkfish
FHIKNORT forthink
FHILLOOT foothill
FHILLORT hill-fort
FHILMPSU lumpfish
FHILMRTU mirthful
FHILORSU flourish
FHILORTY frothily
FHIMNOOS moon-fish
FHIMPRSU frumpish
FHINRTTU unthrift
FHIOOPTT Photofit®
photofit
FHIORSTY fortyish
FHLLLOTU lothfull
FHLLOSTU slothful
FHLMOTUU mouthful
FHLOOSTU soothful
FHLOOTTU toothful
FHLORTTU trothful
FHLORTUW worthful
FHLORTUY fourthly
FHLOSTUU outflush
FHLOTUUY youthful
FHLRTTUU truthful
FHOOORST forsooth
FIIILNOP Filipino
FIIINNTY infinity
FIIJNORT joint-fir
FIIKLRSY friskily
FIILLMSY flimsily
FIILLMTU multifil
FIILLNTY flintily
FIILMNRY infirmly
FIILMOPR piliform
FIILMPSY simplify
FIILTTUY futility
FIIMOPRS pisiform
FIIMOSTY moistify
FIINNOSU infusion
FIINORTU fruition
FIINTUXY unfixity
FIIQUYZZ quizzify
FIKKLNOS kinsfolk
FIKLLLSU skillful
FIKLNOSW wolfskin
FIKNORSW forswink
FILLLTTU full-tilt
FILLLUWY wilfully
FILLNORS no-frills
FILLNSUY sinfully
sulfinyl
FILLNUUW unwilful
FILLOPPY floppily
FILLOPSU spoilful
FILMOPRS slipform
FILMORRY lyriform
FILMOSSU mofussil
FILMPPTU lift-pump
FILNOSUX fluxions
FILORSTY frostily
FILRSTTU tristful
FILSTTUY stultify
FIMMNOOR omniform
FIMMORRU muriform
FIMOPRRY pyriform
FIMORTUY fumitory
FIMOSTUY fumosity
FIMRSTUU futurism
FINOPRTZ zip-front
FINORSUY infusory
FIOORSSU furiosos
FIORTTUY fortuity
FIPRSSUY Prussify
FIRSTTUU futurist
FIRTTUUY futurity
FJLLOUYY joyfully
FJLNOUUY unjoyful
FKKLOORW workfolk
FKKOORTW koftwork
FKLMOOOT folkmoot
FKLNRTUU trunkful
FKMOORRW formwork
FKNORSUW forswunk
FKOOORTW footwork
FLLNOOOW follow-on
FLLOOPUW follow-up
upfollow
FLMNORUU mournful
FLMOOORW moorfowl
FLMOORSU roomfuls
FLMOOSSW moss-flow
FLMORSTU stormful
FLNOOPSU spoonful
FLNOOSTU snootful
FLOOOPTT poltfoot
FLOOPTTY toplofty
FLOOSSTW soft-slow
FLOPRSTU sportful
FLORTTUU troutful
FLRSTTUU trustful
FMNOOOOR moonroof
FMOOPPTU foot-pump
FMRSSTUU frustums
FNNOOORT frontoon
FNOOORTW footworn
FNOOPRSU sunproof
FNOORRSW forsworn
FNOORRTW front-row
FNOORTUW outfrown
FOOOPSTT footpost

G

GGGGIILN giggling
GGGGILNO goggling
GGGGILNU glugging
GGGHIILN higgling
GGGHIINT thigging
GGGHIINW whigging
GGGHINOS shogging
GGGIILNN niggling
GGGIINPR prigging
GGGIINSW swigging
GGGIJLNO joggling
GGGIJLNU juggling
GGGILNOS slogging
GGGILNPU plugging
GGGINNSU snugging
GGGINORT trogging
GGHHIISW Whiggish
GGHIILNT lighting
GGHIIMSW Whiggism
GGHIINRT righting
GGHIINST sighting
GGHIIPRS priggish
GGHILSSU sluggish
GGHIMSTU thuggism
GGHINOST ghosting
GGHOOPRS grog-shop
GGIIKLNN kingling
GGIILLNR grilling
GGIILMNN mingling
GGIILMNY ginglymi
GGIILNNP pingling
GGIILNNS singling
GGIILNNT tingling
GGIIMPRS priggism
GGIINNNR grinning
GGIINNOR groining
GGIINNRW wringing
GGIINNSS sing-sing
GGIINNST stinging
GGIINNSW swinging
GGIINNUV ungiving
GGIINPPR gripping
GGIIRRSS grisgris
gris-gris
GGILLNUW gull-wing
GGILLOOW golliwog
GGILMMNO glomming
GGILMNOO glooming
GGILNNOU lounging
GGILNNPU plunging
GGILNORW growling
GGILNORY glorying
GGILNTTU glutting
GGILQSUY squiggly
GGINNOOS goings-on
ongoings
GGINNOPP Ping-Pong®
ping-pong
GGINNOSS singsong
GGINNOTU tonguing
GGINNRTU grunting
GGINOOTU outgoing
GGINOPRS proggins

GGINOPRU	grouping
GGINORTU	grouting
GGLLOOWY	gollywog
GGLLPUUY	plug-ugly
GGLNOOST	long-togs
GGOOOORR	groo-groo
GHHIIKRS	high-risk
GHHIILST	lightish
GHHIIPSW	Whigship
GHHIIRST	rightish
GHHIISTT	tightish
GHHILOSU	ghoulish
GHHIMOST	highmost
GHHIORSU	roughish
GHHIOSTU	toughish
GHHOORTU	△thorough
GHHOSTTU	thoughts
GHIIJNOS	jingoish
GHIIKNNT	thinking
GHIIKNPS	kingship
GHIIKNSW	whisking
GHIILLNS	shilling
GHIILMST	mislight
GHIILMTY	mightily
GHIILNRW	whirling
GHIILNST	tinglish
GHIILNSY	Yinglish
GHIILNTW	whitling
GHIILTTW	twilight
GHIIMMNW	whimming
GHIINNNT	thinning
GHIINOST	hoisting
GHIINPPS	shipping
GHIINPPW	whipping
GHIINRRS	shirring
GHIINRRW	whirring
GHIINRST	shirting
GHIINRSV	shriving
GHIINRTV	thriving
GHIINRTW	writhing
GHIINSSW	swishing
GHIINSTT	shitting
GHIINTTW	twi-night
GHIINWZZ	whizzing
GHIIORSV	vigorish
GHIIOSTV	Visigoth
GHIIRSTT	rightist
GHIKLNTY	knightly
GHIKLSTY	skylight
GHIKMRUU	Gurmukhi
GHIKNNTU	unknight
GHILLOTW	lowlight
	owl-light
GHILLSTY	slightly
GHILMPSU	glumpish
GHILNOPS	longship
GHILNOPY	hopingly
GHILNOSS	sloshing
GHILNOSU	housling
GHILNOTW	night-owl
GHILNRUY	hungrily
GHILNSTU	hustling
	sunlight
GHILOPRS	shop-girl
GHILORSW	showgirl
GHILPRTY	triglyph
GHIMNOPR	morphing
GHIMNOPU	gumphion
GHIMNPTU	thumping
GHIMNSTU	gunsmith
GHINNNOT	non-thing
GHINNNSU	shunning
GHINNORT	northing
GHINNOST	nothings
GHINNSTU	shunting
GHINOOPW	whooping
GHINOOST	shooting
	soothing
GHINOPPS	shopping
GHINOPPW	whopping
GHINORTW	ingrowth
	throwing
GHINOSSU	housings
GHINOSTT	shotting
GHINOSTU	shouting
	southing
GHINOSTW	wing-shot
GHINOSUY	youngish
GHINOTTU	outnight
GHINRRSU	rush-ring
GHINRRUY	hurrying
GHINSSTU	hustings
GHINSTTU	shutting
GHIORTTU	outright
GHIOSTTU	outsight
GHIPRSUU	guruship
GHLMOOOY	homology
GHLNNOOR	longhorn
GHLNOORU	hourlong
GHLNORSU	slughorn
GHLNOTYY	yongthly
GHLOOORY	horology
GHLORTUU	turlough
GHMPSSUY	sphygmus
GHNOPYYY	hypogyny
GHNOSTUU	unsought
GHOORTUU	rough-out
GHOORTUY	yoghourt
GHOPRTUW	upgrowth
GIIILMNT	limiting
GIIILNNU	linguini
GIIILOTV	vitiligo
GIIINNOS	ionising
GIIINNOT	ignition
GIIINNOZ	ionizing
GIIINNTV	inviting
GIIINSTV	visiting
GIIJMNOS	jingoism
GIIJNNOW	jowing-in
GIIJNOST	jingoist
GIIKKLNP	kingklip
GIIKKNNS	skinking
GIIKLLNS	skilling
GIIKLNNT	tinkling
GIIKLNRS	skirling
GIIKMMNS	skimming
GIIKMNPS	skimping
GIIKNNNS	skinning
GIIKNNST	stinking
GIIKNNTT	knitting
GIIKNPPS	skipping
GIIKNRST	skirting
	striking
GIILLLMR	mill-girl
GIILLNPS	spilling
GIILLNQU	quilling
GIILLNRT	trilling
GIILLNST	stilling
GIILLNSW	swilling
GIILLNTT	littling
GIILLOPW	polliwig
GIILLPSW	pigswill
GIILLTUY	guiltily
GIILLTYZ	glitzily
GIILMMNS	slimming
GIILMNPS	simpling
GIILMNPY	implying
GIILMNZZ	mizzling
GIILMPSU	pugilism
GIILNNSY	lyings-in
GIILNNTW	twinling
GIILNNUV	unliving
GIILNPPR	rippling
GIILNPPS	slipping
GIILNPRS	spirling
GIILNPRT	tripling
GIILNQSU	quisling
GIILNQTU	quilting
GIILNRVY	virginly
GIILNSTT	slitting
	stilting
GIILNSTU	linguist
GIILNSTY	stingily
GIILNSZZ	sizzling
GIILPSTU	pugilist
GIIMMNPR	primming
GIIMMNRT	trimming
GIIMMNSW	swimming
GIIMNNOY	ignominy
GIIMNOPS	imposing
GIIMNOTT	omitting
GIIMNOTV	vomiting
GIIMNSSW	swingism
GIIMORRS	rigorism
GIINNNOT	intoning
GIINNNPS	spinning
GIINNNSW	winnings
GIINNNTW	twinning
GIINNOPT	pointing
GIINNORS	nigrosin
GIINNORT	ignitron
GIINNPPS	snipping
GIINNPRT	printing
GIINNRSS	rinsings
GIINNRTU	untiring

GIINNSTT stinting
GIINOPST positing
GIINOPTV pivoting
GIINORST roisting
GIINPPRT tripping
GIINPRSS rispings
GIINPRST striping
GIINPRSU uprising
GIINPRXY pixy-ring
GIINPSTT spitting
GIINPTTU tituping
GIINQTTU quitting
GIINQUZZ quizzing
GIINRRST stirring
GIINRSTV striving
GIINRSTW △writings
GIINSSSW swissing
GIINSSTU suitings
GIINSTTW twisting
GIINTTTW twitting
GIIORRST rigorist
GIIPRSTZ spritzig
GIJKLNOY jokingly
GIJKNNRU junk-ring
GIJLLNOY jollying
GIJLNOST jostling
GIKKLNSU skulking
GIKLNNOP plonking
GIKLNNRU knurling
GIKLNNUY unkingly
GIKLNOPR porkling
GIKLORRW workgirl
GIKNNOST stonking
GIKNNOTT knotting
GIKNNRTU trunking
GIKNOPST kingpost
GIKNORRW ringwork
GIKNORST stroking
GIKNORSW workings
GILLMOOY gloomily
GILLNORT trolling
GILLNOSY losingly
GILLNOVY lovingly
GILLNPRU ring-pull
GILLNPUY pulingly
GILLNSUY sullying
GILLOOPW polliwog
GILLOPSS lip-gloss
GILLOPWY pollywig
GILLORVY gillyvor
GILLOSSY glossily
GILMMNSU slumming
GILMMTUY multigym
GILMNOPY mopingly
GILMNORT mortling
GILMNOSS moslings
GILMNOTT mottling
GILMNOTU moulting
GILMNOVY movingly
GILMNSUY musingly
GILMOOSY misology
GILMPRUY grumpily

GILNNOTW townling
GILNNOUV unloving
GILNNRSU nursling
GILNOOSY Sinology
GILNOOVY vinology
GILNOOWY wooingly
GILNOPPP plopping
GILNOPPS slopping
GILNOPRW prowling
GILNOPSY posingly
spongily
GILNOPTT plotting
GILNORVY rovingly
GILNOSTT slotting
GILNOTUY outlying
GILNPRSU spurling
GILNPRYY pryingly
GILNPSSU plussing
GILNPUZZ puzzling
GILNRRSU slurring
GILNRSTU lustring
rustling
GILNRTTU turtling
GILNRTYY tryingly
GILNTUUY unguilty
GILOOORS rosoglio
GILOOOST oologist
GILOORSU glorious
GILOORVY virology
GILOOSSS isogloss
GILOOSTY sitology
GILOSTUY gulosity
GIMMMNUY mummying
GIMMNSTU stumming
GIMMOSSU gummosis
GIMNNORS mornings
GIMNNORU mourning
GIMNNOTU mounting
GIMNNOUV unmoving
GIMNOOOU oogonium
GIMNOOPS spooming
GIMNOORS moorings
GIMNOPTU gumption
GIMNORRW ringworm
GIMNORST storming
GIMNOSYY misogyny
GIMNPRTU trumping
GIMPSSYY gypsyism
GINNNSTU stunning
GINNOOSW swooning
GINNOPSS sponsing
GINNOPSY pyonings
GINNOPTU gunpoint
GINNORST snorting
GINNPRSU spurning
GINNRSTU turnings
unstring
GINOOPPS opposing
GINOOPST stooping
GINOPPPR propping
GINOPPST stopping
toppings

GINOPPSW swopping
GINOPRST sporting
GINOPSST signpost
GINOPSTT spotting
GINOPSTU spouting
GINORRWY worrying
GINORSTT Storting
GINORSTW strowing
GINORSTY roysting
storying
GINORTTT tott'ring
trotting
GINORTTU trouting
tutoring
GINOSTTW swotting
GINOSTUW outswing
GINPPRSU upspring
GINPRRSU spurring
GINPRSUU pursuing
usurping
GINPTTUY puttying
GINRSSTU trussing
GINRSTTU trusting
GIOOPRRS porrigos
GIOORRSU rigorous
GIOORSTU goitrous
GIOORSUV vigorous
GIOPRRSU prurigos
GIOPRSST Strigops
GIOPRSSY gossipry
GIOPRSTU groupist
GIORSTUY rugosity
GKLOOOTY tokology
GLLNOSUW low-slung
GLLOOPTY polyglot
GLLOOPWY pollywog
GLLOOXYY xylology
GLMNOOOT monoglot
GLMNOOOY monology
nomology
GLMNRTUU ngultrum
GLMOOOPY pomology
GLMOORWW glow-worm
GLMOOYYZ zymology
GLNNOPSU long-spun
GLNOOOSY nosology
GLNOOOTY ontology
GLNOOPYY polygony
GLNOPYYY polygyny
GLNORSTY strongly
strongyl
GLNORTUW lungwort
GLNOSSUV Volsungs
GLNOTTUY gluttony
GLOOOPSY posology
GLOOOPTY optology
topology
GLOOORUY ourology
GLOOPSSY gossypol
GLOOPTYY typology
GLOORSUU orgulous
GMMNOTUY tommy-gun

GMNNOOOY monogony
GMNNOOYY monogyny
GNNPRSUU unsprung
GNNRSTUU unstrung
GNOORSUW wrongous
GNPPRSUU upsprung
GOORSSTU gross-out
GOORTTUW goutwort

H

HHHHSSUU hush-hush
HHIIKKOO Khoikhoi
HHIILOPT thiophil
HHIINNST thinnish
HHIIPSST phthisis
HHILPSSY sylphish
HHIMNPSY nymphish
HHIMPSSU sumphish
HHINOOSS Shoshoni
HHINOOSW nohowish
HHIORSST shortish
HHKKSSUU khuskhus
HHMRSTUY rhythmus
HHOOOOPP pooh-pooh
HHOOPPRS △phosphor
HHOORSTT hot-short
HIIILMNS △nihilism
HIIILNST nihilist
HIIILNTY nihility
HIIIMRSS Irishism
HIIINRST rhinitis
HIIJNOPT hip-joint
HIIKMNST misthink
HIIKMRSS skirmish
HIIKOPRS piroshki
HIIKOPRZ pirozhki
HIIKQRSU quirkish
HIIKSSTT skittish
HIILMMSS slimmish
HIILMOST homilist
HIILMPSU △silphium
HIILMPSY impishly
HIILMSWY whimsily
HIILMTUY humility
HIILNOPS Sinophil
HIILPSST thlipsis
HIILPSSY syphilis
HIILRSTY shirtily
HIILSSTT stiltish
HIIMNSTT tinsmith
HIIMOPSS phimosis
HIIMOPST Ophitism
HIINORST histrion
HIINPSTW twinship
HIIORSST histrios
HIIPPQSU quippish
HIIPPRSU Hippuris
HIKKNOST kink-host
HIKMNSUU minshuku
HIKNOTTU outthink
HIKOOPRT trip-hook
HIKOOPSS spookish
HIKOORSU Kuroshio
HIKOPSSY kyphosis
HILLMOOT moot-hill
HILLMSUY mulishly
HILLNOUY unholily
HILLOSWY silly-how
HILMNOOT monolith
HILMOOPT philomot
HILMOPSY mopishly
HILMPPSU plumpish
HILMPSYY symphily
HILNOPSU unpolish
HILNOSTY tonishly
HILOOPYZ zoophily
HILOORST short-oil
HILOOTTY toothily
HILOPPSY popishly
HILORTUX Ulothrix
HILORTWY worthily
HILOSSTY thylosis
HILOSTYY toyishly
HILPPRSU purplish
HILPPSUY uppishly
HILSSTTU sluttish
HIMMOPRU △phormium
HIMNOPRX phorminx
HIMNOPSY phisnomy
HIMNORRS horn-rims
HIMOOPRS isomorph
HIMOPRSW shipworm
HIMOPRWW whipworm
HIMORSTU humorist
HIMOTTVZ mitzvoth
HINNOSTW thin-sown
HINNPSTU thin-spun
HINNSSUY sunshiny
HINOORST hornitos
HINOPSSY hypnosis
HINOPSTW township
HINORTXY thyroxin
HIOOPRTT poortith
HIOORSST orthosis
HIOOSSTT shootist
HIOPRSUZ rhizopus
HIOPSSTY phytosis
HIORRSSY sorryish
HIORSTTU struthio
HIOSSTTU stoutish
HIPPPSUY puppyish
HIPSUYZZ zizyphus
HJKNOPSU junk-shop
HJMOPSTU jump-shot
HJNOOOPR poor-John
HKKOOPYY hoky-poky
HKMNORRU krumhorn
HKMOOORW hook-worm
HKNOORRW hornwork
HKOOPRSW workshop
HLLLOOWY hollowly
HLLMNOOU monohull
HLLOPPRY prophyll
HLLPPSUU push-pull
HLMOOSTY smoothly
HLMOPTUY Plymouth
HLNOOPPY polyphon
HLOOPPSS slop-shop
HLOOPRRY lorry-hop
HLOOSSTU soul-shot
HLPRSUUY sulphury
HMMNOOYY homonymy
HMMOORSU mushroom
HMMRSTUU humstrum
HMNOOOST moonshot
HMNOOOTY homotony
HMNOORRW hornworm
HMNOOSTU unsmooth
HMNOPSYY symphony
HMNOPYYY hyponymy
HMOOOPRZ zoomorph
HMOOORSW showroom
HMOOPTYY homotypy
HMOORSUU humorous
HMOPSSTU puss-moth
HNOOOOPR oophoron
HNOOPRSW shopworn
HNOOPRTU horn-pout
HNOORRTW hornwort
HNOORSTU △southron
HNORTUWY unworthy
HNPSSTUU Pushtuns
HOOOOTTT hoot-toot
HOOOSTTU outshoot
shoot-out
HOOPPSTY photopsy
HOOPRRST porthors
HOORTTUW outworth
throw-out
HOOTTTUU hout-tout
HOPPRRYY porphyry
HOPRRSUY pyrrhous
HPRSTTUU upthrust

I

IIIIPPRR piri-piri
IIIKLNPS spilikin
IIIKMNSS mini-skis
IIILLMNP minipill
IIILLMNU illinium
IIILLNOS illision
IIILMRSV virilism
IIILMUVX lixivium
IIILNOPP Pilipino
IIILRTVY virility
IIIMMMNS minimism
IIIMMNST intimism
minimist
IIIMMPRS imprimis
IIIMNSTT intimist
IIIMNTTY intimity
IIINORRS irrision
IIINPRST inspirit
IIINQTUY △iniquity
IIINSSTU sinuitis
IIIOSTTU ouistiti

IIJJSTUU	jiu-jitsu
IIJLNOOT	joint-oil
IIJNNSTU	ninjitsu
IIKKLMNR	kirn-milk
IIKLLNOS	skillion
IIKLMPSY	skimpily
IIKLQRUY	quirkily
IIKNOSTT	stotinki
IILLLPTU	Lilliput
IILLLPUV	pulvilli
IILLMNOS	millions
IILLMRTU	trillium
IILLMUUV	illuvium
IILLNOOR	orillion
IILLNORT	trillion
IILLNOST	stillion
IILLNOSU	illusion
IILLOPUV	pulvilio
IILMMNOS	Molinism
IILMMPSS	simplism
IILMMSUU	simulium
IILMNORT	mirliton
IILMNOST	Molinist
IILMNOSU	Limousin
IILMNSTU	luminist
IILMORST	troilism
IILMOTTY	motility
IILMPSST	simplist
IILMRSSY	missilry
IILNNOOT	nolition
IILNOORS	rosin-oil
IILNOOST	inositol
IILNOOTV	volition
IILOOPPR	liripoop
IILOPSSS	psilosis
IILOPSST	ptilosis
IILOPSTY	pilosity
IILORSTT	troilist
IILRSSTU	△silurist
IILSTUUV	uvulitis
IILSTUVV	vulvitis
IIMMNOST	Timonism
IIMMNTUY	immunity
IIMMOPST	optimism
IIMMOPSU	opiumism
IIMMSTTU	mittimus
IIMNNOOT	monition
IIMNNOSU	△unionism
IIMNNOTU	munition
IIMNOOSS	omission
IIMNOPRS	imprison
IIMNOPST	mispoint
IIMNORTT	intromit
IIMNORTY	minority
IIMNOSST	simonist
IIMNOSTT	Timonist
IIMNPRST	misprint
IIMNPTUY	impunity
IIMNRSTY	ministry
IIMOPSTT	optimist
IIMOSSTY	myositis
IIMOTTVY	motivity
IIMPRTUY	impurity
IIMRRTTU	Trimurti
IIMRRTUV	triumvir
IIMSSTUW	swimsuit
IINNOPPT	pinpoint
IINNOPTU	punition
IINNOSTU	inustion
	△unionist
IINNPSST	tinsnips
IINNSTTU	tinnitus
IINOOPST	position
IINOSTVY	vinosity
IINQRSUU	Quirinus
IINRTTUY	triunity
IIOOPPUU	piou-piou
IIOOPSTV	oviposit
IIOOSTTY	otiosity
IIOPPSTV	pop-visit
IIOPRRTY	priority
IIORRRSY	irrisory
IIORSTUV	virtuosi
IIPRSSTU	spiritus
IJLLMNOR	Mjöllnir
IJNNSTUU	ninjutsu
IKKLNORW	linkwork
IKKLNOSY	kolinsky
IKKORSSY	△sikorsky
IKLLMORW	mill-work
IKLLOOTV	kilovolt
IKLLOSSY	kyllosis
IKLMORSW	silkworm
IKLMORTW	milkwort
IKLNOPST	slipknot
IKLOOPSY	spookily
IKNNOPSY	ponyskin
IKNNRSTU	turnskin
IKNOOPRT	pinkroot
IKNOORRW	ironwork
IKNOPSTW	townskip
IKORSSTU	kurtosis
IKORSTTU	outskirt
ILLLMOPS	△plimsoll
ILLLMPPU	pulpmill
ILLLOOPP	lollipop
ILLMOPRW	pillworm
ILLMOSSY	lissomly
ILLMPTUY	multiply
	multi-ply
ILLOOPRW	poorwill
ILLOORSZ	zorillos
ILLOPPSS	slipslop
ILLOPPSY	sloppily
ILLOPRTW	pillwort
ILLOPRXY	prolixly
ILLOPSTT	pot-still
ILLORSTU	trollius
ILLORSUY	illusory
ILLOTTWY	wittolly
ILLRSTUY	sultrily
ILMNOOPS	polonism
ILMNOOPU	polonium
ILMNOSUU	luminous
ILMOPPSU	populism
ILMOPSTU	Psilotum
ILMORSTY	stormily
ILMOSTUV	volumist
ILMOSTUY	timously
ILMPPTUU	pulpitum
ILMPSTUY	stumpily
ILMSSTUU	stimulus
ILMSTTUY	smuttily
ILNOOPSV	volpinos
ILNOOPSY	spoonily
ILNOORTW	toil-worn
ILNOOSTU	solution
ILNOOSTY	snootily
ILNOOTTT	tint-tool
ILNOOTUV	volution
ILNOPSSW	snowslip
ILNOPSTU	unspoilt
ILNORSTY	nitrosyl
ILNORTXY	nitroxyl
ILNOSSTW	stowlins
ILNOSTTY	snottily
ILNPSUUV	pulvinus
ILOOPPPY	poppy-oil
ILOOPPRS	propolis
ILOORSTU	risoluto
ILOPPSTU	populist
ILOPRSTY	sportily
ILOPSTTY	spottily
ILOPSUUV	pluvious
ILOQRTUU	loquitur
ILPPRTUY	pulpitry
ILRSTTUY	trustily
ILRSTUUX	luxurist
IMMOORTU	motorium
IMMRSTUY	summitry
IMMRTTUU	rum-ti-tum
IMNNOOTT	monotint
IMNNOSUU	numinous
IMNOOPSU	opsonium
IMNOORST	trominos
IMNOORTY	monitory
IMNOORVY	omnivory
IMNOSTUU	mutinous
IMNRSTUU	untruism
IMOOPRRS	promisor
IMOOPRST	impostor
IMOOPRTU	muir-poot
IMOOQSTU	mosquito
IMOORSTT	motorist
IMOORSTU	sumotori
	timorous
IMOORSTY	morosity
IMOORTVY	vomitory
IMOOSSTY	myosotis
IMOPRRSY	primrosy
IMOPRTUU	muir-pout
IMORSTTU	tutorism
IMPPPSUY	puppyism
IMRSSTTU	mistrust
IMRSSTTY	mistryst
INNNNOOU	non-union

INNNORTU trunnion
INNNOSTY syntonin
INNOOPSS sponsion
INNOOPSU unpoison
INNOORST notornis
INNOPRSU unprison
INOOOSSZ zoonosis
INOOOTXZ zootoxin
INOOPRST positron
sorption
INOOPSTT spittoon
INOOPTTU outpoint
INOORSTY sonority
INOPRTTU print-out
INOPRTUY punitory
INOPRTWY port-winy
INOPSSSY synopsis
INORTUVY ivory-nut
INPPRRUU purpurin
INPRSTTU turnspit
IOOPRRSV provisor
IOOPRSSV provisos
IOOPRSSY isospory
IOOPRSTY isotropy
porosity
IOORRSTY sorority
IOORRTTT trottoir
IOORSSTT risottos
IOORSSUV voussoir
IOORSTTU tortious
IOORSTUV virtuoso
IOORSUUX uxorious
IOOSSTTU stotious
IOPRRSUV provirus
IOPRSSUU spurious
IOPRSTTU outstrip
IOPRSTUU poursuit
IOPRSTUY pyritous
IOPRSUVX poxvirus
IOQRTUXY quixotry
IORRSUVV survivor
IORSSUUU usurious
IORSTTUY touristy
yttrious
IORSTUUV virtuous
IPRRSTUU pruritus

J

JLNSTUUY unjustly
JLOOSUYY joyously
JNNOORRU △nonjuror
JNOOSUUY unjoyous

K

KKNOORTW knotwork
KKOOSSUU kouskous
KLLMNSUU numskull
KLMMOOOS Komsomol
KLMMPSUU musk-plum
KLNORSTY klystron
KLOOORWW woolwork
KLOOPRSW slopwork
KMOOORRW workroom
KNOOORTT root-knot
KOORSTUW outworks

L

LLOOPRTY trollopy
LLOOPRYY roly-poly
LLOSUUVV volvulus
LMNOOOPY △monopoly
LMNOOPYY polyonym
LMOOOORT tool-room
LMOOPRTU Pulmotor®
LMOOPSYY polysomy
LMOORSWW slowworm
LMOOSSSU molossus
LMOPPRTY promptly
LMRSSTUU lustrums
LNOOOPRT poltroon
LNOOOPYZ polyzoon
LNOOPPRY propylon
LOOOORSS olorosos
LOOPPSUU populous
LOOPPSUY polypous
LOOPSSST stop-loss
LOPSSTUW plus-twos
LORSSTUU lustrous

M

MMOOPPRU pump-room
MMOORTTY tommy-rot
MNNOOOTY monotony
MNNOSYYY synonymy
MNOOORTW moonwort
MNOOORXY oxymoron
MNOOPRTU pronotum
MNOOPTYY toponymy
MNOPRSTU no-trumps
MNORSTUU surmount
MOOOOPRT moor-poot
MOOOPRRT promotor
MOOOPRTU moor-pout
MOOORRTW tomorrow
MOORRSUU rumorous
MOORSTUU tumorous
MOORSTUY urostomy
MOPPRSTU rump-post
MORSSTUU strumous
MSSTTUUU tsutsumu

N

NNOOOPST spontoon
NOOOPPRS prosopon
NOOORSSU sonorous
NRSTTUUY untrusty

O

OOOPPRRT prop-root
OOOPRSSU soporous
OOPRSTTU outsport
OORSTTUU tortuous
OPRSSSUU sourpuss

R

RRSSSUUU susurrus

9 AAA

A

AAAABCLLV △balaclava
AAAABCLMN balmacaan
AAAABENNT Nabataean
AAAABIKLL balalaika
AAAABJLMY jambalaya
AAAACCHMT tacamahac
AAAACCHRR arracacha
AAAACDIMM macadamia
AAAACDJNR jacaranda
AAAACDKLY alack-a-day
AAAACEHNP panachaea
AAAACGILT agalactia
AAAACIRRU araucaria
AAAACLRRZ alcarraza
AAAACMNRT catamaran
AAAAGLPRT alpargata
AAAAHHJMR maharajah
AAAAHMNRT maranatha
AAAAILLPR paralalia
AAAALLMMY Malayalam
AAAAMNPRY pranayama
AAAAMPRTT paramatta
AAAANRRTT tantarara
tarantara

AAAANRRTV Navaratra
AAAARRSSS sassarara
AAABBDINR Barbadian
AAABBINRR barbarian
AAABBLMOX Balaam-box
AAABCCEMN Maccabean
AAABCCHHR bacharach
AAABCCHLN bacchanal
AAABCCHNR charabanc
char-à-banc
AAABCDEIR Carabidae
AAABCDIIT adiabatic
AAABCDRRU barracuda
AAABCEIRS scarabaei
AAABCELTT cabaletta
AAABCELTU acetabula
AAABCEMRT carbamate
AAABCENRS sarbacane
AAABCHIRT △batrachia
AAABCHNNR anabranch
AAABCHNRU carnahuba
AAABCIKTT katabatic
AAABCILNT abactinal
AAABCINPR Pan-Arabic
AAABCIQTU aquabatic
AAABCISST catabasis
AAABCKNNT cantabank
AAABCLMOR carambola
AAABCLMRU ambulacra
AAABCLNOT canal-boat
AAABDEEHH dahabeeah
AAABDEGRV bavardage
AAABDEINT Tabanidae
AAABDELNR Aldebaran
AAABDELPT adaptable
AAABDENRS sarabande
AAABDHHIY dahabiyah
AAABDILLS sabadilla
AAABDOQRU aquaboard
AAABEEMNO amoebaean
AAABEGHLL gallabeah
AAABEGMSS ambassage
AAABEILLV available
AAABEILMN alabamine
AAABEILMT Balaamite
AAABEKPRR parabrake
AAABEKRWY breakaway
AAABELLPT palatable
AAABELMOT Ametabola
AAABELMSS amassable
AAABELRST alabaster
AAABELSSY assayable
AAABGHILL gallabiah
AAABGHILY galabiyah
AAABGILLY gallabiya
AAABGINRS barasinga
AAABGLORR algarroba
AAABHLRST △balthasar
AAABHLRTZ △balthazar
AAABIKSST katabasis
AAABILLTV ablatival
AAABILLVY availably
AAABILMNS Balsamina
AAABINNSU banausian
AAABIPRSS parabasis
AAABJLMNO jambolana
AAABKNOTT tanka-boat
AAABLLPTY palatably
AAABLOPRS parabolas
AAACCCEET Cactaceae
AAACCCHHH cha-cha-cha
AAACCDELV cavalcade
AAACCDHMN camanachd
AAACCDILR cardiacal
AAACCDRSU cascadura
AAACCEEER Aceraceae
AAACCEEHR Characeae
AAACCEHIM cachaemia
AAACCELLN calcaneal
AAACCELNN calcanean
AAACCELNV calavance
AAACCELPR palace-car
AAACCENRV caravance
AAACCFLOT catafalco
AAACCHKMT tacmahack
AAACCINSU Caucasian
AAACCIRTT ataractic
AAACCLMNO calamanco
AAACCLMST cataclasm
AAACDDILN dandiacal
AAACDEHLN Chaldaean
AAACDEINR acaridean
AAACDEIRS Ascaridae
AAACDENRV caravaned
AAACDHINR Arachnida
AAACDHNRS sandarach
AAACDIINR acaridian
AAACDILNR calandria
AAACDLMRU dulcamara
AAACDLRST cadastral
AAACDNRSS Cassandra
AAACEEHLP Acalephae
AAACEEIOZ Aizoaceae
AAACEELMV Malvaceae
AAACEELRU Lauraceae
AAACEENNO Anonaceae
AAACEENRS Caesarean
AAACEGORT Arctogaea
AAACEHLNP acalephan
AAACEHLNV avalanche
AAACEHRTT Tracheata
AAACEIMNR Americana
AAACEIMNT catamenia
AAACEIMPR paramecia
AAACEIMTT atacamite
AAACEINRS Caesarian
AAACEMMNR cameraman
AAACENRRV caravaner
AAACFILNT fanatical
AAACGILNT agnatical
AAACGILRS sacralgia
AAACGLLSW scallawag
AAACHILNR anarchial
AAACHILNW Walachian

AAACHIMNT matachina
AAACHIMNU naumachia
AAACHIMST chiasmata
AAACHINRS anacharis
AAACHLMNT nachtmaal
AAACHLNRT charlatan
AAACHLPRR chaparral
AAACHLRRT catarrhal
AAACHNPTY panchayat
AAACHOSUY ayahuasco
AAACIIRSS acariasis
AAACILLMR camarilla
AAACILNOR Aaronical
AAACILNPT aplanatic
AAACILNRT lactarian
AAACILNRU lacunaria
AAACILNST Castalian
satanical
AAACILRTU actuarial
AAACINOPR paranoiac
AAACINOTT catatonia
AAACINRSU casuarina
AAACINSTT anastatic
AAACLMMPW macaw-palm
AAACLMNPU campanula
AAACLMPST cataplasm
AAACLNRSY canal-rays
AAACLRSUV avascular
AAACMORST sarcomata
AAACMRSST camass-rat
AAACMRTUX taraxacum
AAADDEILN △daedalian
AAADDHMRY hamadryad
AAADDILNR Dalradian
AAADDINNR Dardanian
AAADEEINR Araneidae
AAADEFFNR fanfarade
AAADEFGMR megafarad
AAADEFIST asafetida
AAADEGNPP appanaged
AAADEGNTV advantage
AAADEHRTV Theravada
AAADEINRV Varanidae
AAADELMMR marmalade
AAADEMNOT adenomata
AAADEOPTZ zapateado
AAADEPRST tapaderas
AAADGLRVX gravadlax
AAADGMMNR grandmama
AAADGNPPR grandpapa
AAADHHPRZ haphazard
AAADHIOPR adiaphora
AAADHLMRS dharmsala
AAADHMRSS madrassah
AAADILLNP Palladian
AAADILMNT Dalmatian
AAADILPRS paradisal
AAADINNOS Adansonia
AAADIOPPR parapodia
AAADLLMNS Landsmaal
AAADLMMNN landamman
AAADLMNTY adamantly
AAADLMPRY lampadary
AAADLNNSY analysand
AAADLOPRX paradoxal
AAADMNRTY mandatary
AAADORSVY Sarvodaya
AAAEEGLOP paleogaea
AAAEEGRRR arrearage
AAAEEGRTW agateware
AAAEEHMNR maharanee
AAAEEKNRS area-sneak
AAAEFGMNU megafauna
AAAEGGLRV galravage
AAAEGGRTV aggravate
AAAEGILNS analgesia
AAAEGLLLT talegalla
AAAEGLLPR paralegal
AAAEGLMNU malagueña
AAAEGLNNS salangane
AAAEGLSSV vassalage
AAAEGMNNT manganate
AAAEHMMOT haematoma
AAAEHMNST anathemas
AAAEHMNTT Matthaean
AAAEILMRS lamaserai
AAAEILPRX paralexia
AAAEILQRU laquearia
AAAEIMNPS spanaemia
AAAEIMNRS Amerasian
AAAEIMPRS sapraemia
AAAELLNPT panatella
AAAELNNTT antenatal
Atlantean
Tantalean
AAAELNPQU aquaplane
AAAELNTTT tantalate
AAAELPRST palaestra
AAAEMPRST aspartame
AAAEMRRRT terramara
AAAENRRTT Tartarean
AAAEPRSSS apsarases
AAAFFNNOR fanfarona
AAAFGIRSX Saxifraga
AAAFIKNRS Afrikaans
AAAFINORS Afro-Asian
AAAFIRRST △rastafari
AAAFLORST solfatara
AAAFRSSSS sassafras
AAAGGLOPS galapagos
AAAGHJNNT Jagannath
AAAGHLLNP phalangal
AAAGHPPRR paragraph
AAAGILLRT alligarta
AAAGILOPR paralogia
AAAGILRST tarsalgia
AAAGIMNOT angiomata
AAAGIMNRV gravamina
AAAGIMRRT margarita
AAAGINNRV Varangian
AAAGINRRT rangatira
AAAGLLMOS alalagmos
AAAGLNPTY Anaglypta®
AAAGLRSST astragals

AAAGMNPTY pantagamy
AAAGNORRT Tarragona
AAAGPRSSU asparagus
AAAHHIMNS shamianah
AAAHHKMNS khansamah
AAAHHLLMS mashallah
AAAHIKKLT kathakali
AAAHILMNY Himalayan
AAAHIMNRU marihuana
AAAHINSVV Vaishnava
AAAHKNRST astrakhan
AAAHLLOTY △ayatollah
AAAHMNNTT Manhattan
AAAHMNPST phantasma
AAAHMNRTT harmattan
AAAHNOPTT apathaton
AAAIILLLP palilalia
AAAIILMNR Laminaria
AAAIINRST sanitaria
AAAIJMNRU marijuana
AAAIKKLMR kalamkari
AAAILMMMN mammalian
AAAILMNPR palmarian
AAAILMNSY Malaysian
AAAILMORT amatorial
AAAILNNOT Anatolian
AAAILNNPR planarian
AAAILNNTT Tantalian
AAAILNPPT antipapal
AAAILNRST artisanal
AAAILNRSU Laurasian
AAAILNSST assailant
AAAILPPRS appraisal
AAAIMNNOZ △amazonian
AAAIMNNRT amarantin
AAAIMNNST Tasmanian
AAAIMNNTZ manzanita
AAAIMNORT amatorian
inamorata
AAAIMNRST Samaritan
Sarmatian
AAAINNSSS Sassanian
AAAINOPRS saponaria
AAAINORST sanatoria
AAAINORTT natatoria
AAAINQTTU aquatinta
AAAINRRTT Tartarian
AAAINRRTV Navaratri
AAAINRSTT astrantia
AAAINSSST anastasis
AAAIPPRZZ paparazzi
AAAIPRSTX parataxis
AAAKLMOOZ Kalamazoo®
AAAKMRSTU Kamasutra
AAALMNRSY salaryman
AAALMORTX malaxator
AAALNPSTY anaplasty
AAALNRSSV salvarsan
AAALNRTTU △tarantula
AAALOOPPS Appaloosa
AAAMMNRST man-at-arms
AAAMNNOTZ amazon-ant
AAAMNRSTU Amarantus
AAANPRTUV paravaunt
AAANRSSTT tarantass
AAAOPPRZZ paparazzo
AAAPPRSTU apparatus
AAARRSSSU sussarara
AABBCCIRR bricabrac
bric-à-brac
AABBCDEIL abdicable
AABBCDKLN blackband
AABBCDKOR back-board
AABBCEHLL beach-ball
AABBCEINR Caribbean
AABBCEKKR breakback
AABBCEOOT babacoote
AABBCILMS cabbalism
AABBCILST cabbalist
AABBCKLLL blackball
AABBCKMRR barmbrack
AABBCORSS barbascos
AABBDDNOR broadband
AABBDEELT debatable
AABBDEKNR bandbrake
AABBDEKOR bakeboard
AABBDEORS Barbadoes
baseboard
AABBDLLNY bandy-ball
AABBDNOST bandobast
AABBEEKLR breakable
AABBEELLM blameable
AABBEFFGL bafflegab
AABBEHILL habilable
AABBEHILT habitable
AABBEIILT bilabiate
AABBEILLL ballabile
AABBEINRT Barnabite
rabbinate
AABBEINST sabbatine
AABBEIRRS barbarise
AABBEIRRZ barbarize
AABBEISST sabbatise
AABBEISTZ sabbatize
AABBELLMY blameably
AABBELRST barbastel
AABBEORST absorbate
AABBHILTY habitably
AABBIILLL ballabili
AABBIMRRS barbarism
AABBIMSST sabbatism
AABBIRRTY barbarity
AABBIRSSU babirussa
AABBORRSU barbarous
AABCCCCEI beccaccia
AABCCDEFR crab-faced
AABCCEEMS Maccabees
AABCCEFKL blackface
AABCCEHLT catchable
AABCCEHNT bacchante
AABCCEKLM camelback
AABCCEKPS backspace
AABCCELSU accusable
AABCCHHKT hatchback

AABCCHIKN back-chain
AABCCHKKU huckaback
AABCCHLOR carbachol
AABCCHNOW chawbacon
AABCCHNST bacchants
AABCCIKKP pickaback
AABCCILOT catabolic
AABCCIORT acrobatic
AABCCJKKL blackjack
AABCCKKRT backtrack
AABCCKLLO coal-black
AABCCKLRW back-crawl
AABCCKRRY carry-back
AABCDDEFL bald-faced
AABCDDENN dance-band
AABCDDORR cardboard
AABCDEEFR barefaced
AABCDEEHH beachhead
AABCDEELN danceable
AABCDEHKL blackhead
AABCDEILL cable-laid
cebadilla
AABCDEIMR carbamide
AABCDEIRR barricade
AABCDEKLL blacklead
AABCDEKLP back-pedal
AABCDEKLR lack-beard
AABCDELNR barnacled
AABCDELPR clapbread
AABCDELRT card-table
AABCDEMRV vambraced
AABCDEMSU ambuscade
AABCDENNO abondance
AABCDENNU abundance
AABCDENOR carbonade
AABCDFRRT bard-craft
AABCDHILN baldachin
AABCDHILR Archibald
AABCDILMS labdacism
AABCDIMNO Cambodian
AABCDIORR barricado
AABCDIORS scaraboid
AABCDIORT abdicator
AABCDKRSW backwards
AABCDLNSS scablands
AABCDLOPR clapboard
AABCDLSUU subcaudal
AABCDMOSU ambuscado
AABCDNNUY abundancy
AABCDNOOR carbonado
AABCDNORT cant-board
AABCDORST broadcast
AABCEEEEN Ebenaceae
AABCEEELP peaceable
AABCEEHLR reachable
AABCEEHLT teachable
AABCEEIRU Rubiaceae
AABCEEKLS leaseback
AABCEEKNR canebrake
AABCEELLR lacerable
AABCEELLV cleavable
AABCEELPS escapable
AABCEELPY peaceably
AABCEELRS calabrese
AABCEELRT traceable
AABCEELTT cabalette
AABCEELTX exactable
AABCEENRR aberrance
AABCEERTT bracteate
AABCEFILN fanciable
AABCEFIRT fabricate
AABCEFOSU fabaceous
AABCEFOTU about-face
AABCEGILR algebraic
AABCEGKLM blackgame
AABCEGKST backstage
AABCEGLMR cablegram
AABCEGPRT carpetbag
carpet-bag
AABCEHILR Hebraical
AABCEHINR branchiae
AABCEHIRT brachiate
AABCEHITZ chabazite
AABCEHKLW whaleback
AABCEHLMT matchable
AABCEHLNY chalybean
AABCEHLPT patchable
AABCEHLTW watchable
AABCEILLM claimable
AABCEILLN caballine
AABCEILMN imbalance
AABCEILMP impacable
AABCEILMR bicameral
AABCEILNP incapable
AABCEILNT cantabile
AABCEILRT bacterial
calibrate
AABCEIMNR mainbrace
AABCEIMTT metabatic
AABCEINOR anaerobic
AABCEINRR carabiner
AABCEINRS braincase
AABCEINRT bacterian
AABCEISSS abscissae
AABCEJKMR amberjack
AABCEKKLS slack-bake
AABCEKLPT back-plate
AABCEKLRT trackable
AABCEKPPR paperback
AABCEKRRR barracker
AABCEKRTW backwater
AABCELLLO allocable
AABCELLOR caballero
AABCELLOT locatable
AABCELLSS classable
AABCELMMR crammable
AABCELMNU ambulance
AABCELMOR carambole
AABCELNNU unbalance
AABCELNPU uncapable
AABCELNRS barnacles
AABCELNTU unactable
AABCELOOS calaboose
AABCELORR barcarole

AABCELORZ carbazole
AABCELPPR crab-apple
AABCELRTT tractable
AABCELRTU trabecula
AABCELRTY traceably
AABCEMORX box-camera
AABCEMOST emboscata
AABCENORT carbonate
AABCENRRY aberrancy
AABCENRTV vantbrace
AABCEORST ascorbate
AABCEPRRT barret-cap
AABCERRTU carburate
AABCFHKLS flashback
AABCFINRT fabricant
AABCGILLN caballing
AABCGKLNS back-slang
AABCGLRSS glass-crab
AABCGNORS gas-carbon
AABCHILNR branchial
AABCHIMNR Brahmanic
AABCHKLSW blackwash
AABCHRRUY Brachyura
AABCIILLS basilical
AABCIILNS basilican
AABCIILRS albricias
AABCIINOT anabiotic
AABCIKLLM blackmail
AABCIKLNR lack-brain
AABCIKLOT katabolic
AABCILLRY bacillary
AABCILLSY basically
AABCILMNO cobalamin
AABCILNOT botanical
AABCILNPY incapably
AABCILOPR parabolic
AABCILPSU subapical
AABCILRUV vibracula
AABCIMNOR macrobian
AABCIMORZ Mozarabic
AABCINNOR carbanion
AABCINORR Carbonari
AABCIOQRU aquarobic
AABCISSSS abscissas
AABCKLLMP lamp-black
AABCKLLRT trackball
AABCKLLST backstall
AABCKLPSU back-spaul
AABCKLRSY scaly-bark
AABCKMPRR crampbark
AABCKORRZ razor-back
AABCKORTT track-boat
AABCKRSTW swart-back
AABCKSSTY backstays
AABCLORSS coal-brass
AABCLORUV vocabular
AABCLRSSU subsacral
AABCLRTTY tractably
AABCMNOTT combatant
AABCNOORR barracoon
AABCNORRS barrancos
AABDDEEHR breadhead
AABDDEGLS saddlebag
AABDDEHOR headboard
AABDDEIKR dika-bread
AABDDEINR brain-dead
AABDDELPT baldpated
AABDDENNO abandoned
AABDDHORR hardboard
AABDDHORS dashboard
AABDDNNST bandstand
AABDDORRT dartboard
AABDEEFKR brake-fade
AABDEEGLL bald-eagle
AABDEEILU beau-ideal
AABDEELLP pleadable
AABDEELLR balladeer
AABDEELMN amendable
AABDEELNS lease-band
AABDEELRT tradeable
AABDEEMNO endamoeba
AABDEEMSS embassade
AABDEENNO abandonee
AABDEERTT trabeated
AABDEFGLR fardel-bag
AABDEFHKL half-baked
AABDEFLNU unfadable
AABDEFLOR broad-leaf
loaf-bread
AABDEGINO gabionade
AABDEGINR gabardine
AABDEGLRU guardable
AABDEGMOR board-game
AABDEGMOS gambadoes
AABDEGNRR bargander
AABDEHHIY dahabiyeh
AABDEHJLL djellabah
AABDEHKNR handbrake
AABDEHLNR handlebar
AABDEHLSY abashedly
AABDEHNSU unabashed
AABDEIILN inaidable
AABDEIINO Anobiidae
AABDEILLN balladine
AABDEILLT dilatable
AABDEILMR admirable
AABDEILMT table-maid
AABDEILNR bird-alane
drainable
AABDEILNU unaidable
AABDEILOV avoidable
AABDEILRV adverbial
AABDEILSV advisable
AABDEINST bastinade
AABDELLNT tableland
AABDELLST ballasted
AABDELNOR bandalore
AABDELNRU burd-alane
AABDELPPY dapple-bay
AABDELRTW Bretwalda
draw-table
AABDELTWY tway-blade
AABDEMNNR brand-name
AABDEMORT dreamboat

AABDEMRTU adumbrate
AABDEORST adsorbate
AABDEORSV bravadoes
AABDERRSS debarrass
AABDGGNOR gangboard
AABDGIILR garibaldi
AABDGLNOR Langobard
AABDGNNOW bandwagon
AABDHIORZ biohazard
AABDHORSW washboard
AABDHRSUY subahdary
AABDIJNOR jaborandi
AABDILLST balladist
AABDILMNO abdominal
AABDILMRY admirably
AABDILNQU baldaquin
AABDILORS sailboard
AABDILORT broadtail
tailboard
AABDILSVY advisably
AABDINNRT trainband
AABDINOST bastinado
AABDINSTW waistband
AABDKLORW boardwalk
AABDLLORW wallboard
AABDLNSST sandblast
AABDLOOSW balsawood
AABDLORUY day-labour
AABDLRSTY bastardly
AABDORRST starboard
AABDORSWY broadways
AABEEEGLR agreeable
AABEEENST sea-beaten
AABEEFLLT table-leaf
AABEEFNST beanfeast
AABEEGGLU gaugeable
AABEEGILM imageable
AABEEGLLL glabellae
AABEEGLLT bagatelle
AABEEGLRR barrelage
AABEEGLRY agreeably
AABEEGLSZ sleazebag
AABEEGLTT get-at-able
AABEEGMSS embassage
AABEEHKLS shakeable
AABEEHLLX exhalable
AABEEHLMS shameable
AABEEHLPS shapeable
AABEEHNSU hause-bane
AABEEHRST sea-bather
tabasheer
AABEEHRTT heartbeat
AABEEILLN alienable
AABEEILRS raiseable
AABEEINRS △béarnaise
AABEEKLPP bakeapple
AABEEKLPS speakable
AABEELLLM malleable
AABEELLNR learnable
AABEELLRT alterable
AABEELMMT emblemata
AABEELMPR praeamble
AABEELMRS laser-beam
AABEELNTU uneatable
AABEELORT elaborate
AABEELPRR reparable
AABEELPRS separable
AABEELPRY repayable
AABEELPST baseplate
AABEELRTT treatable
AABEELRTV avertable
AABEELRTW tableware
AABEELTTX battle-axe
AABEEMNOT entamoeba
AABEEMNST abasement
AABEEMNTT abatement
AABEEQRSU arabesque
AABEFGILT fatigable
AABEFKRST breakfast
AABEFLLMM flammable
AABEFLLMU album-leaf
AABEFLLOT floatable
AABEFLLPP flappable
AABEFLMSU flambeaus
AABEFLMUX flambeaux
AABEFLORV favorable
AABEGGINO gabionage
AABEGGMNR beggar-man
AABEGHILL gallabieh
AABEGHILY galabiyeh
AABEGHLLU laughable
AABEGHORR harborage
AABEGIILL bailliage
AABEGILNV navigable
AABEGINRR bargainer
AABEGIRRT arbitrage
AABEGKLOR gaol-break
AABEGKMRS △bergamask
AABEGKNNT bank-agent
AABEGLLLR glabellar
AABEGLNRT grantable
AABEGLPRS graspable
AABEGLRTT rattlebag
AABEGMNRT bar-magnet
AABEGNNOT tonga-bean
AABEGNORT abnegator
AABEGPSSY by-passage
AABEHHRTT earth-bath
AABEHIITW Wahabiite
AABEHINRR herbarian
AABEHITTU habituate
AABEHLOTW whaleboat
AABEHLSSS abashless
AABEHMNST abashment
AABEHOPQU aquaphobe
AABEHRTTW bathwater
AABEIILLS labialise
AABEIILLZ labialize
AABEIIMNR bain-marie
AABEIIMNS baisemain
AABEIIRTU aubrietia
AABEIIRTV bivariate
AABEIJKLR jail-break
AABEIJMNS semi-bajan

Words marked △ may be spelled also with a capital letter

AABEIKLNS △balkanise
lake-basin
AABEIKLNZ △balkanize
AABEIKNRR karabiner
AABEILLLR albarelli
AABEILLLT talliable
AABEILLMN laminable
AABEILLNR ballerina
AABEILLNS Sabellian
AABEILLPP appliable
AABEILLRT bilateral
trailable
AABEILLSW Wallabies
AABEILMNU unamiable
AABEILNOT anabolite
AABEILNPT paintable
AABEILNRT trainable
AABEILNRZ balzarine
AABEILPST basipetal
AABEILRSU subaerial
AABEILSTT stabilate
AABEIMNOT abominate
AABEIMNRT bairn-team
AABEIMSST metabasis
AABEINORS arabinose
AABEINRRV verbarian
AABEINRST abstainer
AABEINRVW brain-wave
AABEIRRTT arbitrate
AABEKLLTT table-talk
AABEKLMNU unmakable
AABEKLNST beanstalk
AABEKMNRS brakes-man
AABEKNNOT tonka-bean
AABEKNPPR bank-paper
AABELLLMR alarm-bell
AABELLLOR albarello
AABELLLOW allowable
AABELLNNR bannerall
AABELLNPT plantable
AABELLNSU unsalable
AABELLPPR palpebral
AABELLSUV valuables
AABELMNNU unnamable
AABELMNST stableman
AABELMNTU untamable
AABELMRTU maturable
AABELMSSU assumable
AABELNPST pantables
AABELNPUY unpayable
AABELNRTY bay-antler
AABELNSTU unsatable
AABELNSUY unsayable
AABELOPRV vaporable
AABELORRZ razorable
AABELORST astrolabe
AABELORTT rotatable
AABELPRRY reparably
AABELPRSY separably
AABELRRST arblaster
AABELRSSU assurable
AABELRSTU saturable
AABELRTTU tablature
AABEMNRTT rabatment
AABEMOSTT steamboat
AABEMRRSS embarrass
AABEOPPRT approbate
AABEOPRRS boar-spear
AABFGILSU basifugal
AABFIIMNS Fabianism
AABFIINST Fabianist
AABFIMORT fibromata
AABFLORVY favorably
AABGGIMNO gambogian
AABGGRRYY argy-bargy
AABGHIRST barghaist
AABGHLLUY laughably
AABGHOPRR barograph
AABGILNRU Bulgarian
AABGILNVY navigably
AABGIMOSU ambagious
AABGINNOR born-again
AABGINORU baragouin
AABGINRTT rabatting
AABGLOORR algarrobo
AABGNORSZ garbanzos
AABGNRRUW burrawang
AABGOORRT abrogator
AABHHIKSU hibakusha
AABHIILRZ △bilharzia
AABHIIMNP amphibian
AABHIIMSW Wahabiism
AABHIIRSW waribashi
AABHIMRVZ △barmizvah
AABHIMSSW bashawism
AABHIMSVZ △basmizvah
AABHIMTVZ △batmizvah
AABHINNOT Bathonian
AABHINRSW brainwash
AABHINSSW washbasin
AABHIPRRV vibraharp
AABHLLOWX boxwallah
AABHLSSTT bath-salts
AABHMRRTU barathrum
AABIIILMR mirabilia
AABIILLMS labialism
AABIILNOT notabilia
AABIILNRR librarian
AABIILNRZ Brazilian
AABIILNST balanitis
AABIIMNSS Sabianism
AABIINNRT Britannia
AABIINOSS anabiosis
AABIINRTV bivariant
AABIINRZZ Zanzibari
AABIJNOTW jawbation
AABILLNPT △paintball
AABILLORS isallobar
AABILMNOS anabolism
AABILMNRU manubrial
AABILMOPY amblyopia
AABILMORS ambrosial
AABILMPST baptismal
AABILNOTT battalion

AABILRRSU	bursarial
AABILRTUU	Tubularia
AABIMNNOU	buonamani
AABIMNORS	△ambrosian
AABIMORSU	simarouba
AABINORTT	boat-train
AABINOSTW	boatswain
AABIOSTTW	waistboat
AABIRRRTY	arbitrary
AABIRTTTU	ribattuta
AABKLOTUW	walkabout
AABKMOORZ	zamboorak
AABLLLOWY	allowably
AABLLMSYY	abysmally
AABLLNTTY	blatantly
AABLLORSY	aryballos
AABLLOSTV	Baltoslav
AABLLRSTU	blastular
AABLLRSYY	syllabary
AABLLRTUY	tabularly
AABLMNORY	myrobalan
AABLMNRWY	byrlaw-man
AABLMNTUY	untamably
AABLMOOPS	opobalsam
AABLMORTT	altar-tomb
AABLMORTU	ambulator
AABLMSSUY	assumably
AABLORSST	albatross
AABLORTTU	tabulator
AABLRSSTU	subastral
AABLSSSUV	subvassal
AABMMOSTY	Ambystoma
AABMNNOOU	buonamano
AABMNOSTW	batswoman
AABNNSTTU	Bantustan
AABNRSSTV	vant-brass
AABORRTUY	abortuary
AABRSSTTU	substrata
AACCCEHIM	cachaemic
AACCCHIOP	capocchia
AACCCHIRS	saccharic
AACCDDINY	candidacy
AACCDEELT	calceated
AACCDEHKR	crackhead
AACCDEIIR	acaricide
AACCDEIMS	academics
AACCDEIRV	cadaveric
AACCDEJNY	adjacency
AACCDHLOO	coachload
AACCDHLRU	archducal
AACCDIINR	circadian
AACCDIMNO	mandiocca
AACCDIOSU	Caucasoid
AACCDNORT	accordant
AACCEEEIR	Ericaceae
AACCEEFMR	face-cream
AACCEEIRR	cercariae
AACCEEIST	Cistaceae
AACCEEJNU	Juncaceae
AACCEEKMR	cream-cake
AACCEELNR	clearance
AACCEENOR	Cornaceae

AACCEENRT	cancerate
	reactance
AACCEFGOU	cacafuego
AACCEFHKL	chalkface
AACCEGHPR	charge-cap
AACCEGORU	accourage
AACCEHHQU	chechaqua
AACCEHILL	cailleach
AACCEHINR	cane-chair
AACCEHJKP	cheap-jack
AACCEHMPY	campeachy
AACCEHMRU	cauchemar
AACCEHRRT	character
AACCEHSTW	watchcase
AACCEIILN	caecilian
AACCEILMT	acclimate
AACCEILNR	calcarine
AACCEILNT	analectic
AACCEILST	ascetical
AACCEILTU	aciculate
AACCEINNR	Cancerian
AACCEINRR	cercarian
AACCEINRS	Saracenic
AACCEINTV	vaccinate
AACCEIRRT	ricercata
AACCEJKLN	lance-jack
AACCEJKSU	Jack-sauce
AACCEKNRS	crankcase
AACCEKRRT	racetrack
AACCELLLN	canal-cell
AACCELLTU	calculate
AACCELMNU	calcaneum
AACCELMTY	cyclamate
AACCELNSU	calcaneus
AACCELNTU	accentual
AACCELSTU	sacculate
AACCENPTT	acceptant
AACCEORTT	coarctate
AACCERSSY	accessary
AACCERSTU	Crustacea
AACCFGOOS	cacafogos
AACCFIILP	pacifical
AACCHIILL	cailliach
AACCHILMO	mail-coach
AACCHIMPR	camp-chair
AACCHIMSY	sciamachy
AACCHINRS	saccharin
AACCHINRT	anthracic
AACCHIRTT	cathartic
AACCHIRTU	autarchic
AACCHMRSU	△saccharum
AACCHNNWY	wanchancy
AACCHORTU	raccahout
AACCIILNV	vaccinial
AACCIILST	ascitical
	sciatical
AACCIINPS	capsaicin
AACCIINTT	tactician
AACCIKKPP	pickapack
AACCILLNO	cloacalin
	cloacinal
	laconical

AACCILLNY calycinal
AACCILLSS classical
AACCILLUV clavicula
AACCILMNU cacuminal
AACCILNNO canonical
AACCILNOR acronical
AACCILNRU canicular
AACCILOOS Colocasia
AACCILPRT practical
AACCILSTT stalactic
AACCILTTY catalytic
AACCIMNOR carcinoma
macaronic
AACCINOTT catatonic
toccatina
AACCINPRT pancratic
AACCINPTY captaincy
AACCINRTT Antarctic
AACCIOOPT cacotopia
AACCIOPRT capacitor
AACCIOPSU capacious
AACCIRSST sarcastic
AACCKMNRS cracksman
AACCKRRTT cart-track
AACCLLRUY calculary
AACCLMORY cyclorama
AACCLMSTY cataclysm
AACCLNORY acronycal
AACCLORRV carvacrol
AACCMNOPY accompany
AACCOPRRS sarcocarp
AACCORTUY autocracy
AACCOSSTT staccatos
stoccatas
AACDDEETU decaudate
AACDDEHLS scaldhead
AACDDEHMR dead-march
AACDDEINR Decandria
AACDDEINT candidate
AACDDEIRT radicated
AACDDELOP decapodal
AACDDENOP decapodan
AACDDENSU Sadducean
AACDDENTU aduncated
AACDDEOPT coadapted
AACDDGNOT cat-and-dog
AACDDHIMR didrachma
AACDDIIST Dadaistic
AACDDMORU docudrama
AACDDNRTY dandy-cart
AACDEEEFT defaecate
AACDEEEHP headpeace
AACDEEFLN lean-faced
AACDEEFLT defalcate
AACDEEHHR headreach
AACDEEHRS scare-head
AACDEEIIR Iridaceae
AACDEEILM Camelidae
AACDEEIMT acetamide
emaciated
AACDEEIRT eradicate
AACDEELRT lacerated
AACDEELTU aculeated
AACDEEMNS △damascene
AACDEEMRT camerated
demarcate
AACDEEMST casemated
AACDEENRV readvance
AACDEENTT decantate
AACDEETUX excaudate
AACDEFFHL half-faced
AACDEFFIN affianced
AACDEFFIR fair-faced
AACDEFGRU face-guard
AACDEFHRS headscarf
AACDEFIKR acidfreak
AACDEFIST fasciated
AACDEFLRS false-card
AACDEGINY Decagynia
AACDEGIOT dacoitage
AACDEGLNO decagonal
AACDEGNOS gasconade
AACDEGNST stag-dance
AACDEHHIR headchair
AACDEHHRS head-crash
AACDEHILN enchilada
AACDEHLLN dance-hall
AACDEHLRT cathedral
AACDEHMMT cat-hammed
AACDEHORT octahedra
AACDEIINU audiencia
AACDEIIRS Sciaridae
AACDEIIRT Arctiidae
AACDEILLN dalliance
AACDEILLT dialectal
AACDEILLV cevadilla
AACDEILMR creamlaid
AACDEILNO Laodicean
AACDEILNT cadential
AACDEILPS asclepiad
AACDEILTU acidulate
AACDEIMMS academism
AACDEIMNR admirance
cardamine
AACDEIMNY cyanamide
AACDEIMPR paramedic
pre-adamic
AACDEIMSS camisades
AACDEIMST academist
steadicam®
AACDEINOT diaconate
AACDEINOV avoidance
AACDEINPS cispadane
AACDEIRSS ascarides
AACDEJKLL jackalled
AACDEJKMP jam-packed
AACDEKLRY lardy-cake
AACDEKMRT tarmacked
AACDELLNU calendula
AACDELMNO Damoclean
AACDELMNS Candlemas
AACDELNOT anecdotal
AACDELNPS landscape
AACDELNRT declarant

AACDEMNTU manducate
AACDEMOPR campeador
AACDENNNO cannonade
AACDENNST adnascent
ascendant
AACDENORR carronade
AACDENOSS cassonade
AACDENOTU coadunate
AACDENPRT tap-dancer
AACDERSTT castrated
AACDFHNRT handcraft
AACDFIILT fatidical
AACDFORRT roadcraft
AACDGHINR drag-chain
AACDGIILL diallagic
AACDGILRY cardialgy
AACDGINOR carangoid
AACDGLMOR cladogram
AACDHIILR rachidial
AACDHIILS dichasial
AACDHIINR rachidian
AACDHIIRR Richardia
AACDHILMS chaldaism
AACDHILMY chlamydia
AACDHILOP phacoidal
AACDHINOR arachnoid
AACDHINOT acanthoid
AACDHINRT cantharid
AACDHLNPS handclasp
AACDHLNRS crashland
AACDHLNTY land-yacht
AACDHNSTY sand-yacht
AACDHPRRS card-sharp
AACDIILNT diactinal
AACDIINNR cnidarian
AACDIINRR Ricardian
AACDIIPRS paradisic
AACDIISST diastasic
AACDIISTT diastatic
AACDILLRU cuadrilla
AACDILLRY radically
AACDILMNO monadical
AACDILMNY dynamical
AACDILMRU caldarium
AACDILNTY dilatancy
AACDILOPR parodical
AACDILRRU radicular
AACDIMOSS camisados
AACDIMRST dramatics
AACDINNOR △draconian
AACDINNOT contadina
AACDINORS Sarcodina
AACDINORT Octandria
AACDINRTU Traducian
AACDIOSUU audacious
AACDIPRTY cryptadia
AACDIQRTU quadratic
AACDIRSSY dyscrasia
AACDIRSTY caryatids
AACDJNTUY adjutancy
AACDJNUVY adjuvancy
AACDKORRT trackroad
AACDKRSTY stackyard
AACDLMORS rascaldom
AACDLNORS corn-salad
AACDMMOST datacomms
AACDNOSTT coatstand
AACDOOPRW carap-wood
AACDOORST Ostracoda
AACDOORTV advocator
AACDORSTW coastward
AACDPRRSY scrapyard
AACEEEGNR careenage
AACEEEGNT Gnetaceae
AACEEEILM Meliaceae
AACEEEKMP make-peace
AACEEELMN Lemnaceae
AACEEFINN fainéance
AACEEFIRT cafeteria
AACEEFLMR lace-frame
AACEEFLPT face-plate
AACEEFLRT leaf-trace
AACEEFRRT aftercare
AACEEFRSV face-saver
AACEEGILL elegiacal
AACEEGKLN angel-cake
AACEEGKPR repackage
AACEEGLLR cellarage
AACEEGNRR carrageen
AACEEHHRT heartache
AACEEHIPT Hepaticae
AACEEHLNR Heraclean
AACEEHLNU Acheulean
AACEEHLPT cephalate
AACEEHPRT eparchate
AACEEHPTY Typhaceae
AACEEHRTT tracheate
AACEEHRTV cave-earth
AACEEHRTX exarchate
AACEEIILL Liliaceae
AACEEIILT Tiliaceae
AACEEILMU leucaemia
AACEEILOV Violaceae
AACEEJKPT pea-jacket
AACEEJLTU ejaculate
AACEEKLRY layer-cake
AACEEKMPR pacemaker
AACEEKMRS casemaker
AACEEKRRT caretaker
AACEELNPS pleasance
AACEELNPT placentae
AACEELNRT nectareal
AACEELNRU caerulean
AACEELNST elastance
AACEELNTU anucleate
AACEELPPR lace-paper
AACEELPRT △paraclete
AACEELRRY relay-race
AACEELRTT altercate
AACEEMNNU amenaunce
AACEEMNNY Mycenaean
AACEEMRRW creamware
AACEEMRTW macaw-tree
AACEEMRTY Myrtaceae

AACEENNRT	nectarean
AACEENRSV	cesarevna
AACEENRTU	centaurea
AACEENRTX	excarnate
AACEEOPRS	aerospace
AACEEPPRS	paper-case
AACEEPRSS	cassareep
AACEEPRSV	parasceve
AACEERTTU	reactuate
AACEFFIRT	affricate
AACEFGLNR	flagrance
AACEFGNRR	fragrance
AACEFGOPR	forage-cap
AACEFGORT	factorage
AACEFGOSU	fagaceous
AACEFHLST	half-caste
AACEFILPR	prefacial
AACEFINNY	faineancy
AACEFINRR	Africaner
AACEFINST	fascinate
AACEFLLTU	falculate
AACEFLMPR	farm-place
AACEFLPRT	after-clap
AACEGHIMR	archimage
AACEGHINR	chain-gear
AACEGHLNR	archangel
AACEGHLTT	Gaeltacht
AACEGHMNP	champagne
AACEGHMNR	charge-man
AACEGHNOR	anchorage
AACEGHRST	gatecrash
AACEGILLN	angelical
	Galenical
AACEGILNS	analgesic
AACEGILRT	cartilage
AACEGILST	agelastic
AACEGIMNO	egomaniac
AACEGISTT	castigate
AACEGKRWY	graywacke
AACEGLMOU	guacamole
AACEGLORT	cataloger
AACEGLOST	galactose
AACEGLOSU	coagulase
AACEGLOTU	catalogue
	coagulate
AACEGNORR	arrogance
AACEGNORT	cartonage
AACEGNRSU	cane-sugar
	sugarcane
AACEGOPST	scapegoat
AACEGORTT	greatcoat
AACEHHINS	shanachie
AACEHIIMS	ischaemia
AACEHIIRT	hieratica
AACEHILLN	Achillean
AACEHILLO	echolalia
AACEHILMO	cholaemia
AACEHILMT	malachite
AACEHILNS	selachian
AACEHILNT	châtelain
AACEHILNU	Acheulian
AACEHILPT	caliphate
	hepatical
AACEHILRT	theriacal
AACEHIMNN	Manichean
AACEHIMNT	machinate
AACEHIMNU	achaenium
AACEHIMTT	athematic
AACEHINNT	acanthine
AACEHINRR	rancheria
AACEHINRS	anarchise
AACEHINRT	catarhine
AACEHINRW	△chinaware
AACEHINRZ	anarchize
AACEHINST	Hanseatic
AACEHIOPT	apothecia
AACEHIOST	taoiseach
AACEHIPRS	praiseach
AACEHIPTT	apathetic
AACEHIRRS	archaiser
AACEHIRRZ	archaizer
AACEHIRST	catharise
AACEHIRSY	easy-chair
AACEHIRTZ	catharize
AACEHIRZZ	chiarezza
AACEHKLNO	kalanchoe
AACEHKMOR	hackamore
AACEHKRSV	haversack
AACEHLMPP	peach-palm
AACEHLMRS	mareschal
AACEHLMUU	chalumeau
AACEHLRTT	clathrate
AACEHMNPR	marchpane
AACEHMRSY	camera-shy
AACEHNNPS	snaphance
AACEHNNSY	seannachy
AACEHNOPR	canephora
AACEHNOTV	anchoveta
AACEHNPTY	tachypnea
AACEHNRST	cane-trash
AACEHNSSS	Sassenach
AACEHPPRS	scrapheap
AACEHPRTU	parachute
AACEHRRTY	tracheary
AACEHRSST	catharses
AACEIILNT	laciniate
AACEIINRR	cineraria
AACEIIRTV	vicariate
AACEIJKRT	air-jacket
AACEIKNPS	sink-a-pace
AACEILLPT	capitella
AACEILLRS	rascaille
AACEILLRV	varicella
AACEILLTV	laticlave
	vacillate
AACEILMMN	immanacle
AACEILMNN	Alemannic
AACEILMNP	campanile
AACEILMPS	eclampsia
AACEILMST	mica-slate
AACEILMTV	calmative
AACEILNNR	carnelian

AACEILNNT cantilena
lancinate
AACEILNPP appliance
AACEILNPT analeptic
AACEILNRS arsenical
carnalise
AACEILNRT lacertian
nectarial
AACEILNRZ carnalize
AACEILNSU saliaunce
AACEILNTV venatical
AACEILORT aleatoric
AACEILPPT applicate
AACEILPSS asclepias
AACEILPTU apiculate
AACEILRRT erratical
AACEILRSS sacralise
AACEILRST sectarial
AACEILRSZ sacralize
AACEILSSU casualise
AACEILSTU actualise
AACEILSTX catalexis
AACEILSUZ casualize
AACEILTUZ actualize
AACEIMNPS spanaemic
AACEIMNPT mancipate
AACEIMNTU acuminate
AACEIMOPR paroemiac
AACEIMPRS sapraemic
AACEIMRSS Caesarism
AACEIMRST marcasite
AACEIMSTT masticate
AACEINNRT incarnate
AACEINOPR paranoeic
AACEINOPT copataine
AACEINOST caseation
AACEINRRT tarriance
AACEINRRV arrivance
AACEINRST ascertain
Cartesian
sectarian
AACEIORRT acroteria
AACEIOSST associate
AACEIPRSS cassaripe
AACEIPSTU auspicate
AACEIPTTV captivate
AACEIRSST Caesarist
staircase
AACEISTUV causative
AACEJKKLN ankle-jack
AACEJKLNP jack-plane
AACEJKLNT Jack-a-Lent
AACEJKLPP apple-jack
AACEJKLSV Jack-slave
AACEJKMOT Mao-jacket
AACEKLPSW space-walk
AACEKMRST caste-mark
AACEKNRRS ransacker
AACEKPPTY pay-packet
AACEKPSTT peat-stack
AACELLLRU acellular
AACELLLUV vallecula
AACELLMNR cellarman
AACELLNOR lanceolar
olecranal
AACELLNOW allowance
AACELLNPT placental
AACELLNRY Carlylean
AACELLNST castellan
AACELLSTY clay-slate
AACELLSUU clausulae
AACELLTUV clavulate
AACELMNNU unmanacle
AACELMNTT cattleman
AACELMOOT Coelomata
AACELMRST smart-alec
AACELMSST classmate
AACELNNTU antelucan
cannulate
AACELNORT anorectal
AACELNPST placentas
AACELNRST ancestral
AACELNTTU tentacula
AACELOPPR paper-coal
AACELOPRT acropetal
AACELORST escalator
AACELOSTT cattaloes
AACELOTUV autoclave
vacuolate
AACELPPRT apple-cart
AACELPRTY calyptera
caprylate
AACELPSTU aspectual
capsulate
AACELPSTY catalepsy
AACELPTXY cataplexy
AACELRRTU creatural
AACELRRTY carrytale
AACELRSTY catalyser
AACELRTUW caterwaul
AACELRTUX curtalaxe
AACELRTYZ catalyzer
AACEMNNRU manurance
AACEMNOPR campanero
AACEMNORY aeromancy
AACEMNPRT mercaptan
AACEMNRST sacrament
AACEMOPRT cameo-part
AACEMORRT macerator
AACEMORST stoma-care
AACEMRSTY camsteary
AACENNNOY annoyance
AACENNOSS assonance
AACENOPRS Scorpaena
AACENORST ostracean
AACENPPRY apparency
AACENPRRY parcenary
AACENRSSU anacruses
assurance
AACENRSSV canvasser
AACENRTTU cauterant
AACENSSTT castanets
AACEOOPPT apocopate
AACEORTUV evacuator

AACEORTVX	excavator
AACEOSTUX	taxaceous
AACFFFFRS	scaff-raff
AACFFJKST	jack-staff
AACFFKPST	packstaff
AACFGLNRY	flagrancy
AACFGNRRY	fragrancy
AACFHIMNR	chamfrain
AACFHJKST	jackshaft
AACFHKLRT	half-track
AACFIILNN	financial
AACFIILRT	trifacial
AACFILNOT	factional
	falcation
AACFILORT	factorial
AACFINSTT	fantastic
AACFKLPRT	flaptrack
AACFKRSTT	fast-track
AACFMNRST	craftsman
AACGGIKNP	packaging
AACGGIOPR	paragogic
AACGHHIRY	hagiarchy
AACGHILPR	graphical
AACGHIMNP	champaign
AACGHMORT	tachogram
AACGHMPRY	cymagraph
AACGHOPSZ	gazpachos
AACGHORSU	guacharos
AACGILLMR	calligram
AACGILLMY	magically
AACGILLOS	scagliola
AACGILLRT	Largactil®
AACGILNNR	ring-canal
AACGILNOR	organical
AACGILOST	costalgia
AACGIMMRT	grammatic
AACGIMOTU	autogamic
AACGIMPRT	pragmatic
AACGIOSSU	sagacious
AACGLLSWY	scallywag
AACGLNOOT	octagonal
AACGLNOTU	coagulant
AACGLOORY	acarology
AACGMORRT	cartogram
AACGNNSTY	stagnancy
AACHHHIUU	chihuahua
AACHHKKNU	Chanukkah
AACHHLNOO	hoolachan
AACHIILPT	aliphatic
AACHIIMNT	matachini
AACHIIMRS	mariachis
AACHIIPRS	pharisaic
AACHIIRRV	charivari
AACHIKMSY	skiamachy
AACHILMRS	marischal
AACHILNOZ	chalazion
AACHILOPR	parochial
AACHILOPT	chipolata
AACHILORS	Charolais
AACHILPST	asphaltic
AACHILSST	thalassic
AACHIMNOR	harmonica
AACHIMNRS	anarchism
AACHIMRRT	matriarch
AACHIMRST	Catharism
AACHIMSTT	asthmatic
AACHINOPR	anaphoric
	pharaonic
AACHINORT	Tocharian
AACHINPRS	parischan
AACHINRST	anarchist
	cantharis
AACHIOPPT	apophatic
AACHIPRRT	patriarch
AACHIPRSS	chaprassi
AACHIRRST	Aristarch
AACHIRSST	catharsis
AACHIRSTT	Catharist
AACHLLMRY	lachrymal
AACHLLPTY	cataphyll
AACHLMNOR	monarchal
AACHLMOST	stomachal
AACHLMPTY	match-play
AACHLMRSY	marshalcy
AACHMNNOR	anchor-man
AACHMNORW	charwoman
AACHMNSTY	yachtsman
AACHNNOTY	anthocyan
AACHNOPRT	anthocarp
AACHNOSTU	acanthous
AACHNOTTY	chatoyant
AACHNPRTY	pyracanth
AACHNRSTU	cantharus
AACHOPPRY	△apocrypha
AACHPRSSY	chaprassy
AACHQSSTU	sasquatch
AACIIILNS	siciliana
AACIILLRT	altricial
AACIILMNP	campanili
AACIILMRS	racialism
AACIILMST	ismatical
	lamaistic
AACIILNPT	ancipital
AACIILNPU	Paulician
AACIILNST	Castilian
AACIILNTV	vaticinal
AACIILPRT	piratical
AACIILRST	racialist
	satirical
AACIILSTV	viaticals
AACIIMMST	miasmatic
AACIIMOTX	axiomatic
AACIINNOP	poinciana
AACIINNOT	nicotiana
AACIINNST	antiscian
AACIINORT	raciation
AACIINPRT	△patrician
AACIINRTZ	Nazaritic
AACIIPRRY	air-piracy
AACIIPRST	parasitic
AACIIRRTU	urticaria
AACIIRTVY	air-cavity
AACIISTTV	atavistic
AACIJNOTT	jactation

AACIKLLNT lack-Latin
AACIKNPRT pack-train
AACILLLQU quail-call
AACILLMNY manically
AACILLMRS lacrimals
AACILLNOR Corallian
AACILLNOT allantoic
AACILLNRY ancillary
AACILLNTV vacillant
AACILLNTY actinally
AACILLOXY coaxially
AACILLPRY capillary
AACILLPTY capitally
AACILMNRS carnalism
AACILMPST plasmatic
AACILMRRY lacrimary
AACILMRSS rascalism
AACILMRSU simulacra
AACILMRTU matricula
AACILMSSU casualism
AACILNNOR non-racial
AACILNNOV volcanian
AACILNNUV △vulcanian
AACILNOPT pactional
placation
AACILNORT cantorial
AACILNOTT lactation
AACILNOTV clavation
AACILNOTY claytonia
AACILNPPT applicant
AACILNPSV Pan-Slavic
AACILNQTU quantical
AACILNRST carnalist
AACILNRTY carnality
AACILNRUV navicular
AACILNRUY caulinary
AACILNTTY latitancy
AACILOPRS prosaical
AACILORTU auctorial
caliatour
AACILOSSU salacious
AACILPRSU spiracula
AACILPRTU capitular
AACILPRTY paralytic
AACILQTTU acquittal
AACILRRTU articular
AACILRRUU auricular
AACILRSTT cart's-tail
AACILRSTY rascality
satyrical
AACILSSTY catalysis
AACILSTTU actualist
AACILSTUY causality
AACILTTUY actuality
AACIMNNNU Mancunian
AACIMNOPR panoramic
AACIMNORR Armorican
AACIMNORS macaronis
AACIMNORT manticora
AACIMNOTT mactation
AACIMNPST campanist
AACIMORSX macro-axis
AACIMORTU amaurotic
AACIMOTTU automatic
AACIMPSST spasmatic
AACIMRRSU sacrarium
AACIMRSTY camstairy
AACIMRTTU traumatic
AACINNOPT pontianac
AACINNORT carnation
AACINNOST santonica
AACINOOTV avocation
AACINOOTZ Actinozoa
AACINOPRS caparison
AACINOPRT paratonic
AACINOPST capitanos
AACINORRV Carnivora
AACINORTU arcuation
AACINORTV covariant
AACINOSST cassation
AACINOSTU causation
AACINOTTU actuation
AACINOTUV vacuation
AACINPRTY captainry
AACINRRVY arrivancy
AACINRSST sacristan
AACINRSSU anacrusis
AACIOPRSU rapacious
AACIOPSTT apostatic
AACIORTTV activator
AACIOSTTW waistcoat
AACIPRSSU paracusis
AACJKRSTW △jack-straw
AACJKSSTY jack-stays
AACJLORTU jaculator
AACLLLMOS small-coal
AACLLMNTY clamantly
AACLLOPRS collapsar
AACLLOPRY allocarpy
AACLLPRTY party-call
AACLLRSTU claustral
AACLLRSUU clausular
AACLLTTUY tactually
AACLMORRZ razor-clam
AACLMRRYY lacrymary
AACLNOPTU cantaloup
AACLNRUUV avuncular
AACLOOPST tapacolos
AACLOPRRR parlor-car
AACLOPRTU portulaca
AACLOPRTY placatory
play-actor
AACLOPSTU tapaculos
AACLORSTV slavocrat
AACLPRSUY capsulary
scapulary
AACLRRTUY cartulary
AACMMOORS cosmorama
AACMNORST stramaçon
AACMNOTTU catamount
AACMOOSTT scotomata
AACNRSTUY sanctuary
AACOOPSTT capotasto

AACORRTTT attractor
tractator
AACORSSWY cassowary
AADDDELPS pad-saddle
AADDDGNRY grandaddy
AADDEEFHT fat-headed
AADDEEHPS sapheaded
AADDEEILV dead-alive
AADDEEMRY ready-made
AADDEERTW dead-water
AADDEFHLR half-adder
AADDEGMNU undamaged
AADDEGRTU graduated
AADDEHHIR hardihead
AADDEHHMN ham-handed
AADDEHMNR hermandad
AADDEHMPT death-damp
AADDEHRTW deathward
AADDEILNO adenoidal
AADDEINRW Edwardian
AADDEIOPZ Zapodidae
AADDELLNS sandalled
AADDELLPS saddle-lap
AADDELMNN landdamne
AADDELMNR dream-land
raddleman
AADDELRST astraddle
AADDEMNNT demandant
AADDEMNOR △andromeda
AADDENNOO Dodonaean
AADDENPTU unadapted
AADDEORST roadstead
AADDGMNNO man-and-dog
AADDHNNST handstand
AADDHNRRW hard-drawn
AADDIIMNY Didynamia
AADDIIMRY dairymaid
AADDIINRV Dravidian
AADDILMSY lady's-maid
AADDINPRT dandiprat
AADDLLRUW auld-warld
AADDLNRSW landwards
AADDLRSTY dastardly
AADDNPRTY dandyprat
AADDNRSST standards
AADEEEHLS headlease
AADEEELRT tea-dealer
AADEEFHMR headframe
AADEEFLPR flap-eared
AADEEGHMT megadeath
AADEEGHNP phagedena
AADEEGHRS shag-eared
AADEEGLMN △magdalene
AADEEGNOR orangeade
AADEEGNPP appendage
AADEEHHKS headshake
AADEEHHLW whale-head
AADEEHHRX hexahedra
AADEEHINY Hyaenidae
AADEEHLSW alewashed
AADEEHPRS spearhead
AADEEHPST heapstead
AADEEHRRT heart-dear
AADEEHRTT death-rate
AADEEHRTW head-water
AADEEIKWW wideawake
AADEEILMV mediaeval
AADEEIRRT reradiate
AADEEKMNS damaskeen
AADEEKMRY make-ready
AADEELLMN allemande
AADEELLSW sea-walled
AADEELNPS esplanade
AADEELORT areolated
AADEELPRR ale-draper
AADEELTUV devaluate
AADEEMNRT tradename
AADEEMRSU admeasure
AADEEMRTW medaewart
AADEEORTT toad-eater
AADEEPPRT parapeted
AADEEPPST peat-spade
AADEEPRST estrapade
paederast
AADEERRTT retardate
AADEESTTV devastate
AADEFGLNN fandangle
AADEFGRSU safeguard
AADEFHNOR aforehand
AADEFHNPS fan-shaped
AADEFILNT fantailed
AADEFILTT fat-tailed
AADEFINNR farandine
AADEFINST fantasied
AADEFIORS aforesaid
AADEFLNOR farandole
AADEFMPRT after-damp
AADEFMRST farmstead
AADEFOSTU autos-da-fé
AADEFRRTW afterward
AADEFSSTT steadfast
AADEGGLNU languaged
AADEGHNRU harangued
AADEGHNRY hydrangea
AADEGIINU Iguanidae
AADEGILLR gaillarde
AADEGILRT taligrade
AADEGIMNT diamagnet
AADEGINRR darraigne
AADEGINRT tragedian
AADEGINTV vaginated
AADEGIPRS disparage
AADEGIQRU quadrigae
AADEGLLOP gallopade
AADEGLNNR engarland
rangeland
AADEGLNNT land-agent
AADEGLNRV landgrave
AADEGLNST standgale
AADEGLNTU angulated
AADEGLRSS gala-dress
AADEGLRUX axle-guard
AADEGLRVW waldgrave
AADEGMNNU unmanaged

AADEGMOSV	savagedom
AADEGMSUU	gaudeamus
AADEGNORT	road-agent
AADEGNRRT	regardant
AADEGNTUZ	ungazed-at
AADEGORSS	dogaressa
AADEGRRRT	rag-trader
AADEGRRRU	rearguard
AADEGRRVY	graveyard
AADEGRSTU	date-sugar
AADEHHKNS	handshake
AADEHILRR	diarrheal
AADEHIMOT	haematoid
AADEHIMPS	Phasmidae
AADEHIMRY	hydraemia
AADEHINNO	anhedonia
AADEHINRX	Hexandria
AADEHIORR	diarrhoea
AADEHIPRT	apartheid
	hit-parade
AADEHIRST	stairhead
AADEHIRZZ	hazardize
AADEHKMST	death-mask
AADEHLLLL	hallalled
AADEHLLST	headstall
AADEHLMNN	manhandle
AADEHLMPS	lampshade
AADEHLMRT	hard-metal
AADEHLMSY	ashamedly
AADEHLNNP	panhandle
AADEHLNRT	heartland
AADEHMNOW	head-woman
AADEHMNST	deathsman
AADEHMNSU	unashamed
AADEHNORT	rhodanate
AADEHNPPR	hand-paper
AADEHNRSY	anhydrase
AADEHORRW	arrow-head
AADEHPRST	hard-paste
AADEHPRTT	death-trap
AADEHRRTW	earthward
AADEHRSWY	ready-wash
AADEIILRS	radialise
AADEIILRZ	radialize
AADEIINRT	dietarian
AADEIIPRS	praesidia
AADEIIPTU	Tupaiidae
AADEIIRRT	irradiate
AADEIIRTV	radiative
AADEIJNPS	jaspidean
AADEIKNRS	sneak-raid
AADEILLPT	dial-plate
AADEILLRT	arillated
	lardalite
AADEILMNN	almandine
AADEILMNT	laminated
AADEILMRT	diametral
AADEILNNR	Adrenalin®
	adrenalin
AADEILNPT	lead-paint
AADEILNSS	sea-island
AADEILNST	tanalised
AADEILNSV	vandalise
AADEILNTZ	tanalized
AADEILNVZ	vandalize
AADEILPRR	perradial
AADEILPRU	praeludia
AADEILPRY	Pyralidae
AADEILPST	stapedial
AADEILRTT	rat-tailed
AADEILRTV	travailed
AADEILRTY	radiately
AADEILTUV	laudative
AADEIMMNR	Dramamine®
AADEIMNNP	pandemian
AADEIMNNR	mandarine
	meandrian
AADEIMRRR	ram-raider
AADEIMRST	dramatise
AADEIMRTZ	dramatize
AADEINPTT	patinated
AADEINRST	steradian
AADEINRTT	antitrade
	attainder
AADEIOPTU	audiotape
AADEIPPRS	disappear
AADEIPRST	disparate
AADEIPRTY	paediatry
AADEJRUVY	Yajurveda
AADEKMORR	road-maker
AADEKMRRT	trademark
AADEKMRTY	market-day
AADEKNNSS	sand-snake
AADELLMNR	mallander
AADELLMRY	alarmedly
AADELLNNP	land-plane
AADELLNPR	Laplander
AADELLNTU	landaulet
AADELLNUV	land-value
AADELLNUY	unallayed
AADELLQRU	quadrella
AADELMMOR	melodrama
AADELMNOR	ealdorman
AADELMNRS	malanders
AADELMORT	road-metal
AADELNNTU	annulated
AADELNRSU	Ausländer
AADELNSTW	wasteland
AADELPPRU	applauder
AADELPRTW	draw-plate
AADELRRSS	ressaldar
AADELRSTT	trade-last
AADELRSWY	seawardly
AADELRTTY	latter-day
AADEMMNOR	memoranda
AADEMNOOR	enamorado
AADEMNOPT	tamponade
AADEMNPRS	ampersand
AADEMNPRZ	amperzand
AADEMNPSS	spadesman
AADEMNRST	tradesman
AADEMOQRU	aquadrome
AADEMORTT	Trematoda
AADEMPSTT	date-stamp

AADENNPPT	appendant
AADENNTTT	attendant
AADENPPRS	sandpaper
AADENPRTU	pandurate
AADENRRTT	retardant
AADENRRTW	warranted
AADENSSUY	unassayed
AADEOPRRS	paradores
AADEOPRRX	paradoxer
AADEOPRST	tapaderos
AADEOPSSS	passadoes
AADERRSVY	adversary
AADERSSTW	eastwards
AADERSTTU	saturated
AADERSTWW	war-wasted
AADFFHNST	handstaff
AADFFIITV	affidavit
AADFGNNOS	fandangos
AADFHHLRY	half-hardy
AADFILNRY	fairyland
AADFIMRRY	dairy-farm
AADFMNRST	draftsman
AADFMNRSU	fraudsman
AADFNRRST	transfard
AADGGHIST	Haggadist
AADGGHLRY	haggardly
AADGGLNOR	galdragon
AADGHHINS	shanghai'd
AADGHIJRR	jaghirdar
AADGHILNP	phalangid
AADGHILRS	harigalds
AADGHIMPR	diaphragm
AADGHINRT	Adi-Granth
AADGHIPSY	dysphagia
AADGHLNSS	hand-glass
AADGHRRSS	hardgrass
AADGILMNY	amygdalin
AADGILNOR	girandola
AADGILORT	gladiator
AADGILRRU	guardrail
AADGIMMMR	mridamgam
AADGIMMNO	gammadion
AADGIMMNR	mridangam
AADGIMNRU	marauding
AADGIMORR	radiogram
AADGIMORU	audiogram
AADGINORT	gradation
	indagator
AADGLLNRU	glandular
AADGLLRUY	gradually
AADGLLRWY	wallydrag
AADGLMSUY	Amygdalus
AADGLNOOW	wagonload
AADGLNRRY	garlandry
AADGLNRSS	grassland
AADGLNSSS	sandglass
AADGMNORS	dragomans
AADGMNRSU	guardsman
AADGMRRTU	dramaturg
AADGNNRTU	grand-aunt
AADGOORSV	Avogadro's
AADGORRTU	graduator

AADGORRTY	gradatory
AADGORSST	toadgrass
AADHILRST	tahsildar
AADHIMOPP	Amphipoda
AADHINOTT	thanatoid
AADHINPSU	Upanishad
AADHIPSSY	dysphasia
AADHKLNRS	land-shark
AADHLLMNS	small-hand
AADHLLNST	hallstand
AADHLMNRS	marshland
AADHNSSTW	washstand
AADHORRSU	hadrosaur
AADHORSUZ	hazardous
AADHPRRST	hardparts
AADIIKLRY	kailyaird
AADIILRRT	triradial
AADIILRTY	radiality
AADIIMMOT	ommatidia
AADIIMMST	Adamitism
AADIIMNRY	dimyarian
AADIIMNRZ	zamindari
AADIINNNT	Dinantian
AADIINNRS	Sardinian
AADIINNRW	Darwinian
AADIINORT	radiation
AADIINRRT	irradiant
	Triandria
AADIIORTU	auditoria
AADIISSST	diastasis
AADIJNNOR	Jordanian
AADILLMOR	armadillo
AADILLMOY	amyloidal
AADILLMPU	△palladium
AADILLMRY	amaryllid
AADILLNOT	allantoid
AADILLNPU	paludinal
AADILLOPS	sapodilla
AADILLPRY	radial-ply
AADILMNNO	adnominal
AADILMNOR	Maoriland
AADILMNSU	sudaminal
AADILMNSV	vandalism
AADILMOPS	plasmodia
AADILMORT	maladroit
AADILMOST	mastoidal
AADILMPRY	pyramidal
AADILMPST	lampadist
AADILMRTY	Admiralty
AADILNNOT	antinodal
	Daltonian
AADILNNPR	plain-darn
AADILNOPT	antipodal
AADILNOTT	antidotal
AADILNOTU	adulation
	laudation
AADILNRTY	radiantly
AADILORSY	day-sailor
AADILORTT	dilatator
AADILOSVW	disavowal
AADILPSSY	dysplasia
AADIMNNOR	Monandria

AADIMNNOT damnation
AADIMNQSU damasquin
AADIMNRYZ zamindary
AADIMNSUV avisandum
AADIMNUVZ avizandum
AADIMOPRY Myriapoda
AADIMORSS madarosis
AADIMQRSU maquisard
AADIMRSTT dramatist
AADINNNOT andantino
AADINNOPT pandation
AADINNORS sardonian
AADINOORT adoration
AADINORRT road-train
AADINPRRT drain-trap
AADINPSSS spadassin
AADIORRTY radiatory
AADIPRSXY dyspraxia
AADIPSSUY ups-a-daisy
AADISSTUY tayassuid
AADKLNPRS parklands
AADKLORSV △volksraad
AADKLRWWY awkwardly
AADKPRRSW parkwards
AADLLOPSU palladous
AADLMMPSU plumdamas
AADLMNPSW swampland
AADLORTUY adulatory
laudatory
AADLRWWYY waywardly
AADMMNOOR monodrama
AADMNORTY damnatory
mandatory
AADMNQRUU quadruman
AADNNORSU anandrous
AADNOOPSW sapanwood
AADOOPRSU Sauropoda
AADOPPRST strappado
AADQRSTUU quadratus
AAEEEKLTV take-leave
AAEEELMPS pease-meal
AAEEEMRTT meat-eater
AAEEFFLLM flame-leaf
AAEEFGMRT aftergame
AAEEFHRTT afterheat
AAEEFINNS feiseanna
AAEEFLLMT leaf-metal
AAEEFLOTV faveolate
AAEEFLRSW self-aware
AAEEGGGRT aggregate
AAEEGGLLN galengale
AAEEGHKLW eagle-hawk
AAEEGIJMR jigamaree
AAEEGILNR generalia
AAEEGILTV laevigate
AAEEGIMNR Gramineae
AAEEGINRT Reaganite
AAEEGINTV evaginate
AAEEGIRTV variegate
AAEEGIRTW waiterage
AAEEGLNSU Elaeagnus
AAEEGMMNX Gammexane®
AAEEGMNNS manganese
AAEEGMNOP Agapemone
AAEEGMNST stage-name
AAEEGNPRT parentage
AAEEGNRRR rearrange
AAEEGNRRT ergataner
AAEEGNRTU guarantee
AAEEGPRSS repassage
AAEEGPRSU gaspereau
AAEEGRTTW Watergate
AAEEHIMTT haematite
AAEEHISST aesthesia
AAEEHKMRS rakeshame
AAEEHLMNY hymenaeal
AAEEHLMTW wheatmeal
AAEEHLRRS rehearsal
AAEEHMNNY hymenaean
AAEEHMNTT hetmanate
AAEEHMNTU Athenaeum
AAEEHMNTX exanthema
AAEEHMPST metaphase
AAEEHNRST hare-stane
AAEEHPSVW waveshape
AAEEHRRRT rare-earth
AAEEHRRSW shareware
AAEEHRTWY thereaway
AAEEIKLMU leukaemia
AAEEILLRV lavaliere
AAEEILLTV alleviate
AAEEILMMN melanemia
AAEEILNPR perinaeal
AAEEILNTV aventaile
AAEEILRTT retaliate
AAEEIMNRT reanimate
AAEEIMNTV emanative
AAEEIMNTX examinate
exanimate
AAEEINRST arseniate
AAEEIPTTX expatiate
AAEEISTTV aestivate
AAEEJNPSS Japaneses
AAEEKLNNP palankeen
AAEEKNPTW wapentake
AAEEKPRRT parrakeet
AAEEKPSSY speakeasy
AAEELLLMT lamellate
AAEELLMNS sallee-man
AAEELLNRW wellanear
AAEELLOTV alveolate
AAEELLPPT appellate
AAEELLPTT patellate
AAEELLQRU aquarelle
AAEELMNPS pleaseman
AAEELMNPT name-plate
AAEELMSST matelasse
matelassé
AAEELMSTT stalemate
AAEELNOPR aeroplane
AAEELNRTT alternate
AAEELNRTV ervalenta
revalenta
AAEELPPRR reapparel

AAEELPRRV palaverer
AAEEMMNTZ amazement
AAEEMMPTZ △temazepam
AAEEMNNSS anamneses
AAEEMPRRT parameter
AAEEMRRRT terramare
AAEEMRSTT masterate
AAEEMRTTX taxameter
AAEENNPRY Pyrenaean
AAEENRRTW warrantee
AAEENRSSW awareness
AAEENTTTU attenuate
AAEEOPRTV evaporate
AAEEPPRRW paperware
AAEEPRRTY ratepayer
AAEEPRSST separates
AAEERSTTT tea-taster
AAEERTVWW water-wave
AAEFFHLMR half-frame
AAEFFIILT affiliate
AAEFFILRS Rafflesia
AAEFFINPR paraffine
AAEFFINRT raffinate
AAEFGILTT flagitate
AAEFGINRS seafaring
AAEFGIRSX saxifrage
AAEFGLMOR megaflora
AAEFGLRVW flag-waver
AAEFGORRS farragoes
AAEFHIKLT khalifate
AAEFHLLPT half-plate
AAEFHLLRT All-father
earthfall
AAEFHLPRT flare-path
AAEFHLRTX earthflax
AAEFHMRTT aftermath
hamfatter
AAEFHMSST shamefast
AAEFHRSTT earthfast
AAEFIKNNR Frankenia
AAEFIKNRR Afrikaner
AAEFILMRR fire-alarm
AAEFILNNR Falernian
AAEFILNTX antefixal
AAEFILPTT palafitte
AAEFILRTY fairytale
AAEFIMMNR mainframe
AAEFIMNOU meiofauna
AAEFINNRS safranine
AAEFINSST fantasise
AAEFINSTZ fantasize
AAEFINTTU infatuate
AAEFJLLNW jaw-fallen
AAEFKLLST leaf-stalk
AAEFLLLRY fallalery
AAEFLLRTW waterfall
AAEFLNRRT fraternal
AAEFLORTU autoflare
AAEFLSSTU sulfatase
AAEFMNSTY safetyman
AAEFMRRTX tax-farmer
AAEFNQSTU fantasque
AAEGGILLN galingale
AAEGGILNT gangliate
AAEGGILNW Galwegian
AAEGGILRV gilravage
AAEGGINNT gigantean
AAEGGINRR gregarian
Gregarina
AAEGGINRU rain-gauge
AAEGGIRRS gargarise
AAEGGIRRZ gargarize
AAEGGIRST garagiste
AAEGGLLNO gallonage
AAEGGMSSU megagauss
AAEGGOPRU paragogue
AAEGHIILM hemialgia
AAEGHILRT Thargelia
AAEGHIMSS mishegaas
AAEGHINXY Hexagynia
AAEGHLLPY hypallage
AAEGHLNOX hexagonal
AAEGHLNPR phalanger
AAEGHLNPS phalanges
AAEGHLOPY hypogaeal
AAEGHLPRT tragelaph
AAEGHLRTW waghalter
AAEGHMNOP phaenogam
AAEGHMSSU meshugaas
AAEGHNOPR orphanage
AAEGHNOPY hypogaean
AAEGHNRRU haranguer
AAEGHOPRR aerograph
AAEGIILMO oligaemia
AAEGIILNT genitalia
AAEGIILQU aquilegia
AAEGIITTV agitative
AAEGIKNNW awakening
AAEGILLNT allegiant
AAEGILLNV villanage
AAEGILMRR armigeral
AAEGILNNN annealing
AAEGILNNT galantine
AAEGILNOS analogise
AAEGILNOZ analogize
AAEGILNPP appealing
lagniappe
AAEGILNPS Pelasgian
AAEGILNRU neuralgia
AAEGILNSV galvanise
AAEGILNUV vaginulae
AAEGILNVZ galvanize
AAEGILRST agrestial
AAEGILRTT tailgater
AAEGIMMNS mismanage
AAEGIMNNS magnesian
AAEGIMNNT manganite
AAEGIMNOR ergomania
AAEGIMNRR margarine
AAEGIMNRS Reaganism
AAEGIMNRT marginate
AAEGIMRRT margarite
AAEGIMRSY Magyarise
AAEGIMRYZ Magyarize

AAEGINNRT tanagrine
AAEGINNRW Wagnerian
AAEGINORT aragonite
AAEGINOTV evagation
AAEGINRRR arraigner
AAEGINRSU guaranies
AAEGINRSY asynergia
gainsayer
AAEGINRTT gratinate
AAEGIPRST pargasite
AAEGIRTTV gravitate
AAEGISTTT sagittate
AAEGLLNOV longaeval
AAEGLLNRY laryngeal
AAEGLLSTZ salt-glaze
AAEGLMORT gremolata
AAEGLMTTU glutamate
AAEGLNRTU granulate
AAEGLOPRS pearl-sago
AAEGLPRRY pearl-gray
AAEGLPRSV palsgrave
AAEGLPRVY pay-gravel
AAEGLRSSW glassware
AAEGLRSTY slate-gray
AAEGLRTTU gratulate
AAEGMMNNO Agamemnon
AAEGMMNOR anemogram
AAEGMNNOR Orangeman
AAEGMNNPR Pan-German
AAEGMNOPT tamponage
AAEGMNORT matronage
AAEGMNPRT pentagram
AAEGMNPSU sagapenum
AAEGMNRTT termagant
AAEGMPRST strap-game
AAEGMRRTT △tetragram
AAEGMRSTT stratagem
AAEGMRSTU gastraeum
AAEGNNOOT Notogaean
AAEGNOPRS parsonage
AAEGNOPRT patronage
AAEGNPRTY pageantry
AAEGNRTTU great-aunt
AAEGOPPRT propagate
AAEGOPRSU Areopagus
AAEGPRSTU pasturage
AAEGRRSTZ stargazer
AAEGRSTYZ stargazey
AAEHHIMTV have-at-him
AAEHHLNOT halothane
AAEHHLPTT phthalate
AAEHHRTTX hearth-tax
AAEHILLLU alleluiah
AAEHILMMS △hamamelis
AAEHILMNR harmaline
AAEHILNTV △leviathan
AAEHILORT hariolate
AAEHILRTW heir-at-law
AAEHIMNOT theomania
AAEHIMRST ashramite
AAEHIMRTU hematuria
AAEHINPSY synapheia
AAEHIPRRS parrhesia
AAEHIPSUU Euphausia
AAEHIRRVW hair-waver
AAEHJNNNO Johannean
AAEHKLNRS ranshakle
AAEHKMRSY haymakers
AAEHKNOSW oakenshaw
AAEHLLMSU alum-shale
AAEHLLPUY Up-Helly-Aa
AAEHLLSTU haustella
AAEHLMNOY hyalonema
AAEHLMSTU steam-haul
AAEHLNPPT pentalpha
AAEHLNPSX phalanxes
AAEHLOPPR phalarope
AAEHLPRST asphalter
AAEHMMMNR hammerman
AAEHMMNOT Mahometan
AAEHMNPRS phraseman
AAEHMNRSS sharesman
AAEHMNRSW washerman
AAEHMOSTT haemostat
AAEHMPRRY pararhyme
AAEHMRSTU shamateur
AAEHNOOPT haanepoot
AAEHNPSST pheasants
AAEHNPSWW wapenshaw
AAEHNRRTX Xenarthra
AAEHNRSTT attrahens
AAEHNRTTT attrahent
AAEHNSTUY euthanasy
AAEHPPRTY parhypate
AAEHRRSTT earth-star
AAEIIKNRT air-intake
AAEIILMNS animalise
AAEIILMNZ animalize
AAEIILMRT marialite
AAEIILNRZ alizarine
AAEIILNST Salientia
AAEIILPTX epitaxial
AAEIILRST aerialist
AAEIILRTY aeriality
AAEIIMNNT inanimate
AAEIIMNRS semi-Arian
AAEIIMRST artemisia
AAEIINNPR Napierian
AAEIINNRT Aretinian
AAEIINSST taeniasis
AAEIINSTT insatiate
AAEIIRTVV variative
AAEIJLNNP plain-Jane
AAEIKLLRZ lazar-like
AAEIKLMRS sail-maker
AAEIKLTTV talkative
AAEIKMNRR rainmaker
AAEIKNRSU Euskarian
AAEIKPRRY perikarya
AAEIKRSTT karateist
AAEILLMMM mammillae
AAEILLMMT mamillate
AAEILLMNP mail-plane
AAEILLMNT alimental

AAEILLNPS sailplane
AAEILLNPT tailplane
AAEILLPPT papillate
AAEILLPRR arpillera
AAEILLPRT prelatial
AAEILLPSS paillasse
palliasse
AAEILLRTV relatival
AAEILMMNO melomania
AAEILMMST melismata
AAEILMNRU melanuria
AAEILMNTU aluminate
AAEILMOPR paroemial
AAEILMPRV primaeval
AAEILMPTT palmitate
AAEILMRST mare's-tail
materials
AAEILMRTU tularemia
AAEILNNSU annualise
AAEILNNUZ annualize
AAEILNORT alienator
rationale
AAEILNPRT perinatal
AAEILNSTT tantalise
AAEILNTTT tantalite
AAEILNTTZ tantalize
AAEILORTV variolate
AAEILPPTT palpitate
AAEILPRST psalteria
AAEILPRTZ trapezial
AAEILRSSW wassailer
AAEILRSTU estuarial
AAEILRSTW altarwise
AAEIMMRRS marmarise
AAEIMMRRZ marmarize
AAEIMNNOO oenomania
AAEIMNNOT emanation
AAEIMNNOX xenomania
AAEIMNNSS anamnesis
AAEIMNNTX examinant
AAEIMNOST anatomise
AAEIMNOTZ amazonite
anatomize
AAEIMNPRR repairman
AAEIMNSTT emanatist
staminate
AAEIMORST aromatise
AAEIMORTZ aromatize
AAEIMPRRS spermaria
AAEIMPRST spermatia
AAEIMRRST airstream
AAEINNORT arenation
AAEINORRT aerotrain
AAEINORTX exaration
AAEINPPRT appertain
AAEINPRST septarian
AAEINQTTU antiquate
AAEINRRTV narrative
AAEINRRTW rainwater
AAEINRSST star-anise
AAEINRSTU estuarian
AAEINRSTY Satyrinae
AAEINSTTT satinetta
AAEINSTTU unsatiate
AAEIORSTX aerotaxis
AAEIPPRRS appraiser
AAEIPSSTV passivate
AAEIRRSTT tartarise
AAEIRRTTZ tartarize
AAEIRSSTV aviatress
AAEISSSUV assuasive
AAEJKLRWY jaywalker
AAEJMORTT état-major
AAEJPPRWW wapper-jaw
AAEJRTTTU jettatura
AAEKKPRST skatepark
AAEKKTYYY yakety-yak
AAEKLMPRT platemark
AAEKLPRST lapstrake
lapstreak
AAEKMMNRT market-man
AAEKMRRTW watermark
AAEKMRSTY staymaker
AAEKNNRTU nunataker
AAELLLMOR malleolar
AAELLLNRY allenarly
AAELLLRTY laterally
AAELLMNTT maltalent
AAELLMNTY allayment
AAELLMPTY palmately
AAELLMQSU squamella
AAELLMSTU alum-slate
AAELLNPPT appellant
AAELLNSTT neat-stall
AAELLPPRW wallpaper
AAELLPRST palestral
AAELLSUXY asexually
AAELMMNOS melanomas
AAELMMORR marmoreal
AAELMMOST Melastoma
AAELMMPST metaplasm
AAELMMRST Martlemas
AAELMNNRZ ranzelman
AAELMNOSU mausolean
AAELMNRSY man-slayer
AAELMOPPR palampore
AAELMOPRZ lorazepam
AAELNNOPT pantaleon
AAELNNPTU pennatula
AAELNNRTT alternant
AAELNOPRT rotaplane
AAELNORZZ lazzarone
AAELNPPRU unapparel
AAELNPPSS sans-appel
AAELNPRTY planetary
AAELNPSTT pantalets
AAELNPSUX pansexual
AAELNRSTT translate
AAELNRSTX transaxle
AAELNSTTU sultanate
AAELNSTTX sextantal
AAELOPPRY propylaea
AAELOPRST pastorale
AAELOPSSU asepalous

AAELOPSTU	apetalous
AAELORRSU	rearousal
AAELORTTZ	lazaretto
AAELPPRRS	pearl-spar
AAELPPRST	star-apple
AAELPPRTT	apple-tart
AAELPRRSY	paralyser
AAELPRRYZ	paralyzer
AAELPSTTU	spatulate
AAELRRSTV	traversal
AAELRSSTU	assaulter
	australes
	saleratus
AAELRSTTW	saltwater
AAELSSSSV	vassaless
AAELSSTWY	leastways
AAEMMNSST	amassment
AAEMMORTT	mattamore
AAEMNORST	manor-seat
AAEMNORTU	neuromata
AAEMNORTY	emanatory
AAEMNORTZ	Mozartean
AAEMNPRTT	apartment
AAEMNPSST	passament
AAEMNRRTY	arrayment
AAEMNRSST	stearsman
AAEMNRSSW	wasserman
AAEMNSSTT	statesman
AAEMORSTT	amarettos
	roast-meat
AAEMPRSTU	separatum
AAEMPRSTY	paymaster
AAEMRRSST	smartarse
AAEMRSSTY	say-master
AAENNNRST	transenna
AAENNNRTY	antennary
AAENNTTTU	attenuant
AAENPRSST	apartness
AAENPRSTY	peasantry
AAENPSSTY	synaptase
AAENRRRTW	warranter
AAEOPRRST	separator
AAEOPRRVW	vaporware
AAEOPRSTT	pastorate
AAEPPRRST	spare-part
AAFFFGLST	flagstaff
AAFFGNRSU	suffragan
AAFFILNOT	afflation
AAFFIMNRT	affirmant
AAFFINPRY	paraffiny
AAFGILMNS	△falangism
AAFGILNRS	Franglais
AAFGILNST	△falangist
AAFGINRRW	warfaring
AAFGINRWY	wayfaring
AAFGIORSS	ossifraga
AAFGLLORT	allograft
AAFGLORSU	sugarloaf
AAFGORTTU	autograft
AAFHILNST	anti-flash
AAFHLLORY	half-royal
AAFHLMOTU	Fomalhaut
AAFIIRRYY	airy-fairy
AAFILLNOP	Fallopian
AAFILMNOR	foraminal
AAFILNOTX	aflatoxin
AAFILORUW	Rauwolfia
AAFIMORTU	fumatoria
AAFINRTTU	Tartufian
AAFINSSTT	fantasist
AAFMORRTW	marrowfat
AAFNRSTTY	fantastry
AAFRRTTYY	arty-farty
AAGGIMNOR	angiogram
AAGGIMNPR	rampaging
AAGGIMRRS	gargarism
AAGGINOWY	going-away
AAGGINSSU	assuaging
AAGGKLNNP	gangplank
AAGGLLLSS	glass-gall
AAGGLNOSY	synagogal
AAGHIILMP	Malpighia
AAGHIJRTU	Gujarathi
AAGHIKMNY	haymaking
AAGHIKPRS	skiagraph
AAGHILLLN	halalling
AAGHILNRS	ashlaring
	Shangri-la
AAGHILORS	Haloragis
AAGHIMOOP	omophagia
AAGHIMPRR	marigraph
AAGHINNNY	nannyghai
AAGHINNRU	Hungarian
AAGHINPRS	phansigar
AAGHINRSS	harassing
AAGHIORST	goat's-hair
AAGHIRRSS	hair-grass
AAGHJNNTU	Jugannath
AAGHLLOPR	allograph
AAGHLNPRY	pharyngal
AAGHLOPXY	Xylophaga
AAGHNOOPR	angophora
AAGHNOOPZ	zoophagan
AAGHNPRST	strap-hang
AAGHOPRTU	autograph
AAGHOPTUY	autophagy
AAGIIMMNS	magianism
AAGIIMNNT	animating
AAGIIMNRY	imaginary
AAGIINOTT	agitation
AAGIINRTT	antitragi
AAGIJNNNP	japanning
AAGIKLNNO	Algonkian
AAGIKMRSS	kissagram
AAGIKNPRT	partaking
AAGILLNOZ	gallinazo
AAGILLNPP	appalling
AAGILLNTV	gallivant
AAGILLNVY	vaginally
AAGILLORT	alligator
AAGILLPSW	galliwasp
AAGILMMNU	magnalium
AAGILMNNO	agnominal
AAGILMNNS	signalman

Words marked △ may be spelled also with a capital letter

AAGILMNNT △malignant
AAGILMNSV galvanism
AAGILMNSY gymnasial
AAGILMNYZ amazingly
AAGILMOPY Polygamia
AAGILMORS sialogram
AAGILMRST magistral
AAGILNORU urolagnia
AAGILNOST analogist
nostalgia
AAGILNRUU inaugural
AAGILNRUV vulgarian
AAGILNSTV galvanist
AAGILNWYY waylaying
AAGIMMNOT gammation
AAGIMMRSY Magyarism
AAGIMNPRT ptarmigan
AAGIMSSST massagist
AAGINNRTU turnagain
AAGINOPRS sporangia
AAGINORTV navigator
AAGINPTXY tax-paying
AAGINSTTU sitatunga
AAGIORSUV vagarious
AAGIPSSTY paysagist
AAGIRSTTY sagittary
AAGKMORYY karyogamy
AAGKNNOTW tank-wagon
AAGKNOORS △kangaroos
AAGLLLNTY gallantly
AAGLLMPSS lamp-glass
AAGLLNNTU ungallant
AAGLLNRSU slangular
AAGLLNRTY gallantry
AAGLLOPSS opal-glass
AAGLLRSUY sugarally
AAGLMMMOY mammalogy
AAGLMNORU granuloma
AAGLMPRSU palm-sugar
AAGLNNNOO nonagonal
AAGLNOOSU analogous
AAGLNOOUZ guanazolo
AAGLNRRUY granulary
AAGLNRTTU gratulant
AAGMMMMOR mammogram
AAGMNNOST mangostan
AAGMNNOSU manganous
AAGMOOPSU apogamous
AAGMRSSSU sargassum
AAGNNNOTY nanny-goat
AAGNNORTU orang-utan
AAGNORRTU guarantor
AAGNORSTU Angostura
AAGNOTTUV avant-goût
AAGORSSSS sargassos
AAHHHOOOW whoa-ho-hoa
AAHHIIMRS maharishi
AAHHIJPRS rajahship
AAHHILLLS shillalah
AAHHILLNS inshallah
AAHHIMRTY arhythmia
AAHHORSTT Ashtaroth
AAHIKNORT Tokharian
AAHIKRSST katharsis
AAHIKRSTY Kshatriya
AAHILMNOT Malathion®
AAHILMTUZ azimuthal
AAHILNORT inhalator
AAHILNSTU ailanthus
AAHILORTU authorial
AAHILPSXY asphyxial
AAHIMMNSS △shamanism
AAHIMNOPY hypomania
AAHIMNPST phantasim
AAHIMNSST shamanist
AAHIMNSTT thanatism
AAHIMNSTU amianthus
AAHIMNTTU thaumatin
AAHINOORR honoraria
AAHINOPRT Phanariot
AAHINORRV Harrovian
AAHINPSWW wapinshaw
AAHINPTTY antipathy
AAHINRRTU Arthurian
AAHINSTTT thanatist
AAHIOPPSS apophasis
AAHIORSTU haustoria
AAHIPRRSY hairspray
AAHKLNOTT talkathon
AAHKLNOTW walkathon
AAHLLMOSW Hallowmas
AAHLLOPTY allopathy
AAHLLSTTT Hallstatt
AAHLMNNTU lanthanum
AAHLMPSTU asphaltum
AAHLOPRST alphasort
AAHLPPPSY slap-happy
AAHMNNSTY shantyman
AAHMNOSTX xanthomas
AAHMNPPRY paranymph
AAHMNPSST phantasms
AAHMOPPRR paramorph
AAHNNOSTU ananthous
AAHNORTUX Xanthoura
AAHNRSTUY Thysanura
AAHORTWWY throwaway
AAIIILMNS Ismailian
AAIIILMRT militaria
AAIIKNNRU Ukrainian
AAIIKNPST Pakistani
AAIIKPRTT △tripitaka
AAIILMMNS animalism
AAIILMNRT mail-train
AAIILMNST animalist
AAIILMNTY animality
AAIILMPRT impartial
primatial
AAIILNNPU Paulinian
AAIILNPPZ Lippizana
AAIILNRTV antiviral
AAIILOPZZ pizzaiola
AAIILORTV viatorial
AAIILRUXY auxiliary
AAIIMMNST animatism

AAIIMNNOT animation
AAIIMPPRR primipara
AAIINNRTU △unitarian
AAIINNRTV invariant
AAIINOPRT topiarian
AAIINORTV variation
AAIINOSTT satiation
AAIINPRRU Ripuarian
AAIINRRTU Ruritania
AAIIQRSTU aquariist
AAIJMRSSW swarajism
AAIJNRSSY janissary
AAIJRSSTW swarajist
AAIKKTYYY yakity-yak
AAIKLLOSS alkalosis
AAIKLMMNS slammakin
AAIKLNOSV Slovakian
AAIKLOSUV souvlakia
AAIKNNOPT pontianak
AAIKNQRTU antiquark
AAIKRSTTU autarkist
AAILLLMUX maxillula
AAILLLNOT lallation
AAILLMMRY mamillary
AAILLMMXY maximally
AAILLMOPP papilloma
AAILLMORT tamarillo
AAILLMRRY armillary
AAILLMRSY amaryllis
AAILLMRTY maritally
martially
AAILLMRXY maxillary
AAILLNOPT Altiplano
AAILLNOST allantois
AAILLNPRU nullipara
AAILLNTVY valiantly
AAILLOPTZ zapotilla
AAILLOPXY polyaxial
AAILLPPRY papillary
AAILLPRTY partially
AAILLPSTY spatially
AAILMMORS amoralism
AAILMNNPS plainsman
AAILMNOPT palmation
AAILMNORS sailor-man
AAILMNORT laminator
AAILMNORW railwoman
AAILMNOST atonalism
AAILMNPRU manipular
AAILMNSST talismans
AAILMNSTT tantalism
AAILMNTTU matutinal
AAILMORST amoralist
AAILMORSU malarious
AAILMPRSU marsupial
AAILMPRTU multipara
AAILNNOPT planation
AAILNNOST santolina
AAILNNOSV Slavonian
AAILNNOTW Waltonian
AAILNNPQU palanquin
AAILNNPRU uniplanar
AAILNOPPT palpation
AAILNOPSS passional
sponsalia
AAILNOPUW paulownia
AAILNOPVV Pavlovian
AAILNORST rationals
AAILNORTT latration
AAILNORZZ lazzaroni
AAILNOSTT atonalist
saltation
stational
AAILNOSTV △salvation
AAILNOTTY atonality
AAILNOTUV valuation
AAILNPPTT palpitant
AAILNPRTU tarpaulin
unpartial
AAILNPTTY antitypal
AAILOORRT oratorial
AAILOORTZ zoolatria
AAILOPRRT raptorial
AAILOPRRY pair-royal
AAILORRST sartorial
AAILPPRRU pluripara
AAILPRSSY paralysis
AAILRRRTY tirra-lyra
AAILRSSWY wassailry
AAIMMNNOO monomania
AAIMMNRST Martinmas
AAIMMORRY myriorama
AAIMMRSSU Marasmius
AAIMNNORU Roumanian
AAIMNOOPS opsomania
AAIMNOORT inamorato
AAIMNOPRY pyromania
AAIMNOPTY typomania
AAIMNORTZ Mozartian
AAIMNOSTT anatomist
AAIMNRSTT tarantism
AAIMNRSTX marxisant
AAIMOORRT moratoria
AAIMORSSU amaurosis
AAIMQRSUU aquariums
AAINNNSSY sannyasin
AAINNNTTU annuitant
AAINNORRT narration
AAINNORTT tarnation
AAINNRSTU Saturnian
AAINOORRT △oratorian
AAINOPSTT antipasto
AAINOPSTU sapi-outan
AAINORRST sartorian
AAINPSSTT antispast
AAINPSTXY anaptyxis
AAINQRTUY antiquary
AAINSSSTT assistant
AAIOPPRRT apparitor
AAIOPQRTU paraquito
AAIOPRRST aspirator
AAIOPSTTU autopista
AAIORRTTT trattoria
AAIPRRSTT trap-stair

AAIPRRTTU partitura
AAJOPRRTW parrot-jaw
AAKKMMOOS mako-makos
AAKNOOSST saskatoon
AALLLMOPS alloplasm
AALLMMRSS small-arms
AALLNNOPY △pollyanna
AALLNRTUY naturally
AALLORRUY aurorally
AALLPRSTU palustral
plaustral
AALMMNOSW alms-woman
AALMNNPST plantsman
AALMNOOSU anomalous
AALMNOPRT patrolman
AALMNOPTU Pulmonata
AALMNORST Monastral
AALMNPRTY rampantly
AALMOOSTU autosomal
AALMOQSSU squamosal
AALMORTYY mayoralty
AALNNOOPT △pantaloon
AALNNRTUU lunarnaut
unnatural
AALNOOPZZ pozzolana
AALNOPSST postnasal
AALNOPSTT postnatal
AALNOPUZZ puzzolana
AALNOSTTU tantalous
AALNPRTWY lawn-party
AALNSSTWY slantways
AALOPRRTY portrayal
AALORSSVV valvassor
AALORSTTY saltatory
AALORSTVY salvatory
AALORTTUY autolatry
AAMMNNOWX Manxwoman
AAMNNPRTY pantryman
AAMNOORSW oarswoman
AAMNOOTTU automaton
AAMNOPRTU paramount
AAMNORSTZ stramazon
AAMNQRRUY quarryman
AAMOPRTTU amputator
AANNOORTT annotator
AANNORSTT stannator
AANOOPVZZ pavonazzo
AANORRRTW warrantor
AANORRRTY narratory
AANORSTTU astronaut
AANPRSSSU Parnassus
AAOORRTTV Rotavator®
AAOPRRSTY raspatory
AAORRSTTU saturator
AAPQRRSUY quarry-sap
ABBBCELLU clubbable
ABBBCELRU bubble-car
ABBBEILRU air-bubble
ABBBIRTTY Babbittry
ABBCCEHKN back-bench
ABBCCKKLO back-block
ABBCCKKLU blackbuck
ABBCDEKNO backboned
ABBCDEKOW bow-backed
ABBCDELRY crabbedly
ABBCDIKLR blackbird
ABBCDKORU buckboard
ABBCDLOOY clabby-doo
ABBCEIKRT backbiter
ABBCEILLM climbable
ABBCEILRS scribable
ABBCEKLLU blue-black
ABBCEKLNO bone-black
ABBCELRRS scrabbler
ABBCGINRS scrabbing
ABBCHIKRT bath-brick
ABBCHNRSU subbranch
ABBCIIOSU bibacious
ABBCIMOST bombastic
ABBCKLLUY buckyball
ABBCKLOOT bootblack
ABBDEEERT breed-bate
ABBDEELNO blade-bone
ABBDEELRU △bluebeard
ABBDEGILR bridgable
ABBDEGLNU bugle-band
ABBDEILOT bobtailed
ABBDEILRT bird-table
ABBDEILTU dubitable
ABBDELLNY belly-band
ABBDELORU double-bar
ABBDELOTU doubtable
ABBDELSUU subduable
ABBDGIILN ad-libbing
ABBDGILNR drabbling
ABBDHLOOT blood-bath
ABBDHNNOO hob-and-nob
ABBDHOOTY tabbyhood
ABBDILLOR billboard
broadbill
ABBDILTUY dubitably
ABBDIMORR broad-brim
ABBDKNORU bark-bound
ABBDLLORU bull-board
ABBDMNOOR bombardon
ABBDMOQSU bomb-squad
ABBDRRSUY Bradburys
Bradbury's
ABBEEELRT table-beer
ABBEEKLRU rebukable
ABBEELLMS semblable
ABBEELOPR probeable
ABBEELRRS slabberer
ABBEELRRY blaeberry
ABBEENRRY baneberry
ABBEERRRY bear-berry
ABBEGIJNR jabbering
ABBEGINRT rabbeting
ABBEHINOS Hobbesian
ABBEHLOTU tabbouleh
ABBEIINRT rabbinite
ABBEILMOT bombilate
ABBEILMUY bum-baylie
ABBEILOST biostable

ABBEIMNOS	bombasine
ABBEIMNOT	bombinate
ABBEIMNOZ	bombazine
ABBEINORT	barbitone
	barbotine
ABBEKLOOT	table-book
ABBELLMSY	semblably
ABBELLNSU	bull-beans
ABBELMOOZ	bamboozle
ABBELOSTY	stableboy
ABBELQRSU	squabbler
ABBEMORTU	obumbrate
ABBENOORY	baboonery
ABBENORRT	Barberton
ABBENORST	absorbent
ABBERSUUU	subbureau
ABBFHLLSU	flashbulb
ABBGIILOT	obbligati
ABBGIINNO	Gibbonian
ABBGILLNO	billabong
ABBGILMNR	brambling
ABBGILOOT	obbligato
ABBGINORS	absorbing
ABBHINOOS	baboonish
ABBHIOPST	abbotship
ABBHIQSSU	squabbish
ABBHISTUY	bathybius
ABBHMOPPY	bomb-happy
ABBHOOTTY	baby-tooth
ABBIIMNRS	rabbinism
ABBIINRST	rabbinist
ABBILLORU	bilobular
ABBIMNNOR	Ribbon-man
ABBLLMOOR	broomball
ABBLLOOTX	ballot-box
ABBOOPRTY	booby-trap
ABBOORRWY	barrow-boy
ABCCCEFIO	beccafico
ABCCCKKLO	blackcock
ABCCEEIKP	backpiece
ABCCEENRU	buccaneer
ABCCEINOV	biconcave
ABCCEINRU	buccanier
ABCCELNRU	carbuncle
ABCCEMNRU	cumbrance
ABCCEMNTU	accumbent
ABCCEOOST	tobaccoes
ABCCFHIKS	backfisch
ABCCFIINO	Fibonacci
ABCCFIMOR	bacciform
ABCCHHKNU	hunchback
ABCCHKLOT	back-cloth
ABCCHKNOT	notchback
ABCCHKOTU	touchback
ABCCHLTUY	yacht-club
ABCCIIJNO	Jacobinic
ABCCIIJOT	Jacobitic
ABCCIKLLO	acock-bill
ABCCIKLRY	brickclay
ABCCIKRST	crabstick
ABCCILLOU	bucolical
ABCCILLUY	cubically

ABCCILNOO	obconical
ABCCILORU	corbicula
ABCCIRSTU	subarctic
ABCCJKKLO	jack-block
ABCCKKKNO	knock-back
ABCCKKOOR	crookback
ABCCKLLOO	block-coal
ABCCKORSS	back-cross
ABCCKORTU	backcourt
ABCCMOORY	mobocracy
ABCDDEEHU	debauched
ABCDDEEIL	decidable
ABCDDEFLO	bold-faced
ABCDDEILU	adducible
ABCDDEIRR	cedar-bird
ABCDDKORU	duck-board
ABCDEEEHU	debauchee
ABCDEEGRR	berg-cedar
ABCDEEHMR	chambered
ABCDEEHPT	bepatched
ABCDEEHRU	debaucher
ABCDEEIKR	bridecake
ABCDEEILM	medicable
ABCDEEILR	calibered
ABCDEEIMR	Barmecide
ABCDEEJKT	bed-jacket
ABCDEEPRT	carpet-bed
ABCDEESSS	abscessed
ABCDEFIKL	backfield
ABCDEFOOT	boot-faced
ABCDEGIKR	ridgeback
ABCDEGIMR	Cambridge
ABCDEHIPS	chip-based
ABCDEHIRU	Bruchidae
ABCDEHKLO	blockhead
ABCDEIJLU	judicable
ABCDEIKLS	backslide
ABCDEIKRU	baudricke
	rudbeckia
ABCDEILNO	balconied
ABCDEILRV	devil-crab
ABCDEIORT	bacteroid
ABCDEIORZ	bezoardic
ABCDEIRRV	cab-driver
ABCDELLNO	blond-lace
ABCDELLNU	bull-dance
ABCDENORR	bread-corn
	cornbread
ABCDENORS	absconder
ABCDENOSU	case-bound
	subdeacon
ABCDEOORT	obcordate
ABCDFLNOU	calf-bound
ABCDHINRS	disbranch
ABCDHIOPR	chipboard
ABCDHIRSY	Charybdis
ABCDIKRRY	brickyard
ABCDILLNO	blind-coal
ABCDILMOR	Lombardic
ABCDILOOT	baldicoot
ABCDILOPR	clipboard
ABCDILSUY	subacidly

ABCDINOOT bandicoot
ABCDINOTU abduction
ABCDINTUY dubitancy
ABCDKLOOR roadblock
ABCDKLOOW blackwood
ABCDKOORR corkboard
ABCDKOOSW backwoods
ABCDKORSW backsword
ABCDLNRSU scrubland
ABCDNORSS crossband
ABCEEELLR cerebella
ABCEEELLT electable
ABCEEELPR perceable
ABCEEELRT celebrate
ABCEEELRX execrable
ABCEEENRR cerberean
ABCEEERRR rerebrace
ABCEEERRT cerebrate
ABCEEFIRS brief-case
ABCEEFKLT Blackfeet
ABCEEFLTU flûte-à-bec
ABCEEFORR fore-brace
ABCEEGHRR herb-grace
ABCEEGKNR greenback
ABCEEHIOT cohabitee
ABCEEHIRT Rechabite
ABCEEHLLY belly-ache
ABCEEHLRS bleachers
ABCEEHLRY bleachery
ABCEEHMRR chamberer
ABCEEHMST beech-mast
ABCEEHRST bretasche
ABCEEILMR merciable
ABCEEILNV bivalence
ABCEEILSX excisable
ABCEEILTX excitable
ABCEEIMRV embracive
ABCEEINOS obeisance
ABCEEINRR carbineer
cerberian
ABCEEIRST bacterise
ABCEEIRTZ bacterize
ABCEEKKNR breakneck
ABCEEKPRS backspeer
ABCEEKPSW sweepback
ABCEELMNS semblance
ABCEELNRT celebrant
ABCEELNST albescent
ABCEELNUU nubeculae
ABCEELORT bracteole
ABCEELORV revocable
ABCEELOSU leuco-base
ABCEELOTV covetable
ABCEELRSU rescuable
securable
ABCEELRXY execrably
ABCEELSUX excusable
ABCEEMMRT Camembert
ABCEEMORR embraceor
ABCEEMORT embrocate
ABCEEMRRY embracery
ABCEENRTY cybernate
ABCEENSTT tabescent
ABCEEORST obsecrate
ABCEEOSSU sebaceous
ABCEEPRRU cupbearer
ABCEERSSY crab's-eyes
ABCEERSTT bescatter
ABCEFHLSU flashcube
ABCEFILRU febricula
ABCEFINOR forecabin
ABCEFIRTU bifurcate
ABCEFOSTU obfuscate
ABCEGHILN bleaching
ABCEGILOT cogitable
ABCEGIMNR cambering
embracing
ABCEGIMRT bregmatic
ABCEGKMSU megabucks
ABCEGKRTU tuckerbag
ABCEGLLLU bugle-call
ABCEGNSUY subagency
ABCEGRSUU sugar-cube
ABCEHILTY chalybite
ABCEHINOT aitchbone
ABCEHINRT Brechtian
ABCEHIOOP ecophobia
ABCEHKLLL hell-black
ABCEHKLLS shellback
ABCEHKLOS shockable
shoeblack
ABCEHKMNR benchmark
ABCEHKORS horseback
ABCEHKRRY hackberry
ABCEHKSTU ash-bucket
ABCEHKTUW buckwheat
ABCEHLNRT branchlet
ABCEHLOPW peach-blow
ABCEHLOTU touchable
ABCEHLRSU crushable
ABCEHMSSU subschema
ABCEHNOOR Orobanche
ABCEHNRRY branchery
ABCEHOQRU quebracho
ABCEHPRSU caper-bush
ABCEIILNS sibilance
ABCEIILRS irascible
ABCEIIMRT imbricate
ABCEIINRR carbinier
ABCEIJLNU jubilance
ABCEIJNOT abjection
ABCEIKLOV olive-back
ABCEIKMQU quickbeam
ABCEIKPRS backspeir
ABCEIKRTW write-back
ABCEILLOS obeliscal
ABCEILLRR cribellar
ABCEILLSS classible
ABCEILMOT metabolic
ABCEILMST cembalist
ABCEILNNU incunable
ABCEILNOT balection
ABCEILNRU incurable
ABCEILNVY bivalency

ABCEILORT	cabriolet
ABCEILOTT	cobaltite
ABCEILRTU	lubricate
ABCEILRUX	Excalibur
ABCEILSTU	Baculites
	bisulcate
ABCEIMMUX	excambium
ABCEIMNOT	combinate
ABCEIMNOX	excambion
ABCEIMOTV	combative
ABCEIMRTU	bacterium
ABCEINORS	carbonise
	escribano
ABCEINORZ	carbonize
ABCEIORRS	barricoes
ABCEIRRSU	carburise
ABCEIRRTU	rubricate
ABCEIRRUZ	carburize
ABCEISSSS	abscisses
ABCEJNSTU	subjacent
ABCEKKORR	rock-brake
ABCEKLNSS	blackness
ABCEKLPRU	parbuckle
ABCEKNORR	cornbrake
ABCEKORTU	outbacker
ABCEKPSTW	sweptback
ABCELLRSU	subcellar
ABCELLRSW	screwball
ABCELMNOY	belomancy
ABCELMOOR	rocambole
ABCELMOPT	comptable
ABCELMORU	calembour
ABCELMOSY	cymbaloes
ABCELMOTU	columbate
ABCELMRRS	scrambler
ABCELMRTU	tumble-car
ABCELNOST	constable
ABCELNOTU	countable
ABCELNRUU	uncurable
ABCELORSU	crab-louse
ABCELORVY	revocably
ABCELOSTT	ectoblast
ABCELRSST	bractless
ABCELRSTU	scrutable
ABCELRTTY	battle-cry
ABCELRTUU	lucubrate
ABCELSSUU	subclause
ABCELSUXY	excusably
ABCEMNOPR	cramp-bone
ABCEMORSS	crossbeam
ABCEMORSY	embryo-sac
ABCEMRSUV	Verbascum
ABCENNRRU	cab-runner
ABCENORTY	baronetcy
ABCENRRRY	cranberry
ABCENRTUU	Bucentaur
ABCENSSTU	substance
ABCEOOPRS	baroscope
ABCEOPRRY	reprobacy
ABCEORSTU	base-court
ABCEOSTUV	suboctave
ABCFGHIKT	fightback
ABCFHIKLS	blackfish
ABCFHIKST	back-shift
ABCFHIKSY	fishyback
ABCFHRSTU	bushcraft
ABCFIMMOR	cambiform
ABCFKLOOT	Blackfoot
ABCGGIKPY	piggyback
ABCGHIKLT	back-light
ABCGHIKST	backsight
ABCGHINNR	branching
ABCGHLOOS	schoolbag
ABCGIKLNS	slingback
ABCGIKNOR	king-cobra
ABCGIKNSW	backswing
	swing-back
ABCGILMNS	scambling
ABCGIMNOT	combating
ABCGKNOUW	buck-wagon
ABCHHIKSS	backshish
ABCHHKSUW	bushwhack
ABCHIILLN	chilblain
ABCHIIMNR	Brahminic
ABCHIIOST	isobathic
ABCHIKRST	britschka
ABCHILMOS	shambolic
ABCHILNOR	bronchial
ABCHILTUV	Lubavitch
ABCHIOORS	borachios
ABCHIOORT	cohabitor
ABCHKLLUW	bullwhack
ABCHKLORT	bark-cloth
ABCHKMTTU	thumbtack
ABCHKNORT	thornback
ABCHKORTW	throwback
ABCHLLNPU	punch-ball
ABCHLMORT	barm-cloth
ABCHNORRS	cornbrash
ABCIIIKLW	bailiwick
ABCIIILPT	bicipital
ABCIIKNRS	brainsick
ABCIILLMU	umbilical
ABCIILLST	ballistic
ABCIILMOR	microbial
ABCIILNOS	basilicon
ABCIILNOT	albinotic
ABCIILNSY	sibilancy
ABCIILRSY	irascibly
ABCIIMNOR	microbian
ABCIINNRT	Britannic
ABCIINRRU	rubrician
ABCIINSSS	abscissin
ABCIIRSTY	△sybaritic
ABCIJLNUY	jubilancy
ABCIKLLRW	brickwall
ABCIKLLST	blacklist
ABCIKNORS	rock-basin
ABCILLMRU	lumbrical
ABCILLORU	bilocular
ABCILLSSY	syllabics
ABCILMNOU	Columbian
ABCILMSTY	cymbalist
ABCILMSUX	subclimax

ABCILNNOU	connubial
ABCILNOPT	panic-bolt
ABCILNORU	binocular
ABCILNRTU	lubricant
ABCILNRUY	incurably
ABCILOPSY	polybasic
ABCILORRU	courbaril
	orbicular
ABCILORTU	tubicolar
ABCIMNOOS	monobasic
ABCIMOSTU	subatomic
ABCIMRSTY	cambistry
ABCINORTU	incubator
ABCINOSTU	subaction
ABCINOSTY	obstinacy
ABCINTTUY	titubancy
ABCISTUVY	subcavity
ABCKKNOST	bank-stock
ABCKLOOSS	class-book
ABCKNORRW	crown-bark
ABCKOOPRS	scrapbook
ABCKORSUY	buckayros
ABCKRSTUY	rusty-back
ABCLLSUZZ	scuzzball
ABCLMNOUW	clubwoman
ABCLMORUY	columbary
ABCLORSUU	subocular
ABCLOSSTU	subcostal
ABCLOSSUY	scybalous
ABCMOSSUU	submucosa
ABCMRRTUY	crumb-tray
ABCNORSTU	obscurant
	subcantor
ABCNORSTY	corybants
ABCRSSTTU	substract
ABDDDEELR	bladdered
ABDDDIPRY	paddy-bird
ABDDEEEST	besteaded
ABDDEEGHI	bigheaded
ABDDEEGRR	berg-adder
ABDDEEIRT	diet-bread
ABDDEELLU	deludable
ABDDEELMO	beadledom
ABDDEELZZ	bedazzled
ABDDEENRR	brandered
ABDDEENRU	unbearded
ABDDEENSU	undebased
ABDDEEPRS	bedspread
ABDDEGGOR	badger-dog
ABDDEHMNO	mob-handed
ABDDEIILV	dividable
ABDDEIIMR	bridemaid
ABDDEILSS	slab-sided
ABDDEINRU	unbraided
ABDDEIORS	broadside
	sideboard
ABDDEIRRU	ribaudred
ABDDELOPX	paddle-box
ABDDELOSW	saddlebow
ABDDFILOR	forbiddal
ABDDGORUY	bodyguard
ABDDHINTW	bandwidth
ABDDILNNS	sand-blind
ABDDJMNOO	odd-jobman
ABDDNRSTU	dust-brand
ABDEEEFLR	deferable
ABDEEEGLL	delegable
ABDEEELMN	emendable
ABDEEELRY	bleareyed
ABDEEFHLR	half-breed
ABDEEFILN	definable
ABDEEFLTU	debateful
ABDEEFORR	free-board
ABDEEFRST	breast-fed
ABDEEGGLR	bedraggle
ABDEEGHIN	beheading
ABDEEGINR	gaberdine
ABDEEGMOR	embargoed
ABDEEGNRR	bergander
ABDEEGORR	garderobe
ABDEEGRRY	greybeard
ABDEEHINR	haberdine
	Hebridean
ABDEEHLLT	death-bell
ABDEEHLNW	band-wheel
ABDEEHMOS	besom-head
ABDEEHOSU	bead-house
ABDEEHRRT	earth-bred
ABDEEHRSW	shewbread
ABDEEIILR	diablerie
ABDEEILLR	ébrillade
ABDEEILLW	wieldable
ABDEEILLY	yieldable
ABDEEILMS	demisable
ABDEEILMT	bedlamite
ABDEEILNO	Belonidae
ABDEEILNR	bandelier
	breadline
ABDEEILNS	disenable
ABDEEILRS	desirable
ABDEEILRV	derivable
	driveable
ABDEEILSV	devisable
ABDEEINST	besainted
ABDEEINTT	bidentate
ABDEEINTU	butadiene
ABDEEITTU	beatitude
ABDEELLPS	speedball
ABDEELLRR	barrelled
ABDEELLRV	verballed
ABDEELLTY	belatedly
ABDEELMTT	embattled
ABDEELNOP	pedal-bone
ABDEELNOR	banderole
	bandoleer
ABDEELNOT	denotable
ABDEELNPR	prebendal
ABDEELNPS	spendable
ABDEELNRU	endurable
ABDEELOPS	deposable
ABDEELOUX	double-axe
ABDEELRSS	beardless
ABDEEMNOT	abodement
ABDEEMNRT	debarment

ABDEEMNSU	sunbeamed
ABDEEMRSY	Ember-days
ABDEENOTY	bayoneted
ABDEENQTU	banqueted
ABDEENRRT	bartender
ABDEENRRU	underbear
ABDEENRTU	unrebated
ABDEENTTU	débutante
ABDEEOPST	speedboat
ABDEEORRU	bordereau
ABDEERRST	redbreast
ABDEFFLNU	unbaffled
ABDEFIISX	basifixed
ABDEFILNY	definably
ABDEFINRR	firebrand
ABDEFOOPR	bead-proof
ABDEGGGIN	debagging
ABDEGGLSU	sluggabed
ABDEGGMOR	beggardom
ABDEGIINN	Big-endian
ABDEGIINU	biguanide
ABDEGIIRR	air-bridge
	brigadier
ABDEGINRR	debarring
ABDEGLLMO	gambolled
ABDEGLNRU	ungarbled
ABDEGNNOR	dannebrog
ABDEGNSTU	Bundestag
ABDEGRTUY	budgetary
ABDEHHIRT	heathbird
ABDEHIINR	Hebridian
ABDEHILNO	hobnailed
ABDEHLNOS	ash-blonde
ABDEHLOOT	bloodheat
ABDEHLORT	holderbat
ABDEHLOTW	death-blow
ABDEHLRSU	subhedral
ABDEHNORT	heart-bond
ABDEHNRRT	brandreth
ABDEHOOST	beasthood
ABDEHORSW	showbread
ABDEHRRSY	shadberry
ABDEIILNU	inaudible
ABDEIILOS	diabolise
ABDEIILOZ	diabolize
ABDEIINSW	basin-wide
ABDEIKLNR	drinkable
ABDEIKMRS	disembark
ABDEIKNRS	snakebird
ABDEIKNRW	break-wind
	windbreak
ABDEIKRST	Dekabrist
ABDEILLLO	labelloid
ABDEILLTU	dilutable
ABDEILMMS	bedlamism
ABDEILMOR	bromeliad
ABDEILNNO	bandoline
ABDEILNOR	bandolier
	bird-alone
ABDEILNRU	unridable
ABDEILRSY	desirably
ABDEILRVY	derivably
ABDEIMNRS	bridesman
	bride's-man
ABDEIMNRU	Bermudian
ABDEIMPPT	bit-mapped
ABDEINORW	rainbowed
ABDEINOST	bastioned
ABDEINRSS	rabidness
ABDEINSSU	unbiassed
ABDEINSSW	bawdiness
ABDEIOORT	boodie-rat
ABDEIORSW	broadwise
ABDEIPRRU	upbraider
ABDEKLORW	bladework
ABDEKNORW	breakdown
ABDEKORRW	wordbreak
ABDELLLSY	syllabled
ABDELLMOU	mouldable
ABDELLMRU	umbrella'd
ABDELLOTU	lobulated
ABDELLPSU	ballsed-up
ABDELLRSS	ball-dress
ABDELMNOY	baldmoney
ABDELMOTY	molybdate
ABDELMRSU	subdermal
ABDELNNOO	bandoleon
ABDELNNSS	blandness
ABDELNOOR	bandolero
ABDELNOST	endoblast
ABDELNOSV	bond-slave
ABDELNOUW	woundable
ABDELNRUY	endurably
ABDELNSTU	Dunstable
ABDELORUV	boulevard
ABDELTTUU	tubulated
ABDEMNNOR	Dobermann
ABDEMOORR	breadroom
ABDENNNOO	bandoneon
ABDENNOST	band-stone
ABDENOORR	road-borne
ABDENOPSU	subpoena'd
ABDENORRY	errand-boy
ABDENORSS	broadness
ABDENORST	adsorbent
ABDENORSW	sword-bean
ABDENOSTU	eastbound
ABDENRSTU	Bundesrat
ABDENRSTY	bystander
	stander-by
ABDENRSUW	subwarden
ABDEOORRT	breadroot
ABDEOORRV	overboard
ABDEOORWZ	zebra-wood
ABDEORRRW	wardrober
ABDERRUYY	rybaudrye
ABDFHLLOO	half-blood
ABDFHLNOU	half-bound
ABDFIIRRR	friarbird
ABDFOOORR	roof-board
ABDFOOORT	board-foot
	footboard
ABDFORRSU	surfboard
ABDGHINSU	sgian-dubh

ABDGHLLOU dough-ball
ABDGIILNY abidingly
ABDGILNNR brandling
ABDGILNOU bungaloid
ABDGILOOY diabology
ABDGINNOU abounding
ABDGINORR organ-bird
ABDGINORS signboard
ABDGINRRY brigandry
ABDGKOORU guard-book
ABDGLNOOR Longobard
ABDHIINNR hindbrain
ABDHIMORY hybridoma
ABDHIMRTY dithyramb
ABDHINRST shirtband
ABDHIOPRS shipboard
ABDHLNSUY husbandly
ABDHNOORU boar-hound
ABDHNRSUY husbandry
ABDHOOPRS shopboard
ABDIIILLN libidinal
ABDIILLRS billiards
ABDIILMOS diabolism
ABDIILNUY inaudibly
ABDIILOST diabolist
idioblast
ABDIIMPRY bipyramid
ABDIIMRST tribadism
ABDILLMOR millboard
ABDILNOOR blood-rain
ABDILOPRS slip-board
ABDILRSSU disbursal
ABDILRYZZ blizzardy
ABDIMNNOT badminton
ABDIMNOPU dumb-piano
ABDIMRSSU absurdism
ABDINNNOO bandonion
ABDINNORR brand-iron
ABDINNORU rain-bound
ABDINORRY by-ordinar
ABDINRSTW wristband
ABDIRSSTU absurdist
ABDIRSTUY absurdity
ABDKNOOST bookstand
ABDLMOOOR broadloom
ABDLMOORW △warmblood
ABDLOPPRU pulpboard
ABDLORSSU subdorsal
ABDMMNOSU △ombudsman
ABDMNNOOW bondwoman
ABDMNOOWY woman-body
ABDMOOORR boardroom
ABDNOORSW snowboard
ABEEEEFRT beefeater
ABEEEFKST beefsteak
ABEEEFLOS beefaloes
ABEEEFLRR referable
ABEEEFLRZ freezable
ABEEEGGRT egg-beater
ABEEEGLLR relegable
ABEEEGLNR generable
ABEEEGLNS Bengalese
ABEEEGLNV vengeable
ABEEEGLRU beleaguer
ABEEEGLRV bevel-gear
ABEEEGLTV vegetable
ABEEEHLSW wheelbase
ABEEEHMRT embreathe
ABEEEKLST eel-basket
ABEEEKNRV break-even
ABEEEKPRR barkeeper
ABEEELLSV base-level
ABEEELMPR permeable
ABEEELNRT enterable
ABEEELNRV venerable
ABEEELNRW renewable
ABEEELNSU unseeable
ABEEELRRV reverable
ABEEELRST steerable
ABEEELRSV severable
ABEEEMRST bee-master
ABEEERRTT terebrate
ABEEERRTV verberate
vertebrae
ABEEERTUX exuberate
ABEEERWYZ breezeway
ABEEFFILN ineffable
ABEEFFLOR offerable
ABEEFGLOR forgeable
ABEEFIKRR fire-break
ABEEFILLT life-table
ABEEFILNR inferable
ABEEFILRS bas-relief
ABEEFLRSU refusable
ABEEFLRTU refutable
ABEEFLSSU self-abuse
ABEEFORST roast-beef
ABEEGGINU béguinage
ABEEGGLMR Lambegger
ABEEGHILW weighable
ABEEGHNOR habergeon
ABEEGILLV levigable
ABEEGILNN bengaline
ABEEGINRU aubergine
ABEEGKORR brokerage
ABEEGLLMO Malebolge
ABEEGLMNR embrangle
ABEEGLNPR pregnable
ABEEGLNPS bespangle
ABEEGLNVY vengeably
ABEEGLOPR bargepole
porbeagle
ABEEGLRTU butlerage
ABEEGLSSU guessable
ABEEGLTVY vegetably
ABEEGMNRW wambenger
ABEEGMORS embargoes
ABEEGNNRT rennet-bag
ABEEGNORS Boanerges
ABEEGNRSU subgenera
ABEEHHKSS baksheesh
ABEEHHSTT bath-sheet
ABEEHILRT heritable
ABEEHILTT biathlete

ABEEHIMNR	Brahminee
ABEEHIMSV	misbehave
ABEEHIMTW	whitebeam
ABEEHINRT	hibernate
	inbreathe
ABEEHIRRS	Hebraiser
ABEEHIRRZ	Hebraizer
ABEEHKORS	brake-shoe
ABEEHKOSU	bakehouse
ABEEHLMPS	blaspheme
ABEEHLNOW	whalebone
ABEEHLRRT	blatherer
ABEEHNORT	bone-earth
ABEEHNORY	honey-bear
ABEEHNRTY	Abernethy
ABEEHOOPR	aerophobe
ABEEHORTU	hereabout
ABEEIINRT	inebriate
ABEEIKLST	beastlike
ABEEIKMRT	breaktime
ABEEIKNST	snakebite
ABEEILLMR	mirabelle
ABEEILLNR	ballerine
ABEEILMNO	Meliboean
ABEEILMRS	miserable
ABEEILMST	estimable
ABEEILMTT	timetable
ABEEILNNT	intenable
ABEEILNPS	albespine
ABEEILNQU	inequable
ABEEILNRR	inerrable
ABEEILNRS	baseliner
	rinseable
ABEEILPPT	appetible
ABEEILPRT	pier-table
ABEEILPRX	expirable
ABEEILQTU	equitable
ABEEILRSV	revisable
	verbalise
ABEEILRTT	albertite
ABEEILRTV	avertible
	veritable
ABEEILRVV	revivable
ABEEILRVZ	verbalize
ABEEILSTW	tablewise
ABEEIMNSS	beaminess
ABEEINRTV	binervate
ABEEINSST	asbestine
ABEEIPRST	rebaptise
ABEEIPRTZ	rebaptize
ABEEIRRSS	brasserie
	brassiere
	brassière
ABEEIRRST	biserrate
ABEEJLLNU	banjulele
ABEEJLLNY	jellybean
ABEEJLNOY	enjoyable
ABEEJNPUU	Punjaubee
ABEEKLNSS	bleakness
ABEEKLORV	revokable
ABEEKLOSU	leuko-base
ABEEKLRSS	brakeless
ABEEKLSTW	skew-table
ABEEKMORR	robe-maker
ABEEKNOST	bakestone
ABEEKNPSU	unbespeak
ABEELLLMT	bell-metal
ABEELLLPS	spellable
ABEELLMSS	blameless
ABEELLMTU	umbellate
ABEELLORT	tolerable
ABEELLOVV	evolvable
ABEELMMOR	memorable
ABEELMNRU	numerable
ABEELMORU	belamoure
ABEELMORV	removable
ABEELMOSV	moveables
ABEELMPRY	permeably
ABEELMPTT	temptable
ABEELMRSS	assembler
ABEELMRSU	resumable
ABEELMRTW	Bartlemew
ABEELNNTU	untenable
ABEELNPSU	spulebane
ABEELNPSY	albespyne
ABEELNQUU	unequable
ABEELNRTU	tenurable
ABEELNRTZ	bez-antler
ABEELNRVY	venerably
ABEELOPRV	proveable
ABEELOPSX	exposable
ABEELOSTT	seabottle
ABEELPRRV	preverbal
ABEELPRST	beplaster
ABEELPRSU	superable
ABEELPRTU	reputable
ABEELRRTV	vertebral
ABEELRSSZ	brazeless
ABEELRTTU	utterable
ABEEMMNTY	embayment
ABEEMNTTT	battement
ABEEMORRT	barometer
ABEEMRRSU	embrasure
ABEEMRRUZ	embrazure
ABEENNORV	raven-bone
ABEENNSTU	sunbeaten
ABEENORWY	bone-weary
ABEENQRTU	banqueter
ABEENQTTU	banquette
ABEENRRST	sternebra
ABEENRRSY	naseberry
ABEENRRTT	terebrant
ABEENRSST	steenbras
ABEENRTUX	exuberant
ABEEOPRRT	reprobate
ABEEOPRTT	peter-boat
ABEEOSTUU	beauteous
ABEEPRSTT	bespatter
ABEERRRTT	barretter
ABEFFILNY	ineffably
ABEFFLOSU	buffaloes
ABEFGHILT	fightable
ABEFGILLN	befalling
ABEFGILNR	frangible

ABEFGILRU figurable
ABEFHIMRS amber-fish
ABEFHLRTU breathful
ABEFIILLR fibrillae
ABEFIILNU unifiable
ABEFIILOT bifoliate
ABEFIIMRT fimbriate
ABEFILLRT filtrable
ABEFILNRU funebrial
ABEFILRST fire-blast
ABEFILTUU beautiful
ABEFINORR forebrain
ABEFKLSTU basketful
ABEFLLLMU flabellum
ABEFLLLUY balefully
ABEFLLNUY banefully
ABEFLLRRU barrefull
barrelful
ABEFLNOSW wolfsbane
ABEFLRTUY refutably
ABEFOORST bear's-foot
ABEFORRTY ferry-boat
ABEFRTTTU butter-fat
ABEGGINSS bagginess
ABEGGLLRU bugger-all
ABEGGNOPS spongebag
ABEGHIKUW weigh-bauk
ABEGHILLP phillabeg
ABEGHILRT rightable
ABEGHILST sightable
ABEGHINRR harbinger
ABEGHINRT breathing
ABEGHMRRU hamburger
ABEGHRSSU sagebrush
ABEGIILLT litigable
ABEGIILMT mitigable
ABEGIILNS abseiling
ABEGIILNT ignitable
ABEGIILNW bewailing
ABEGIILRR irrigable
ABEGIINOR △aborigine
baignoire
ABEGIKMNR embarking
ABEGILLLN labelling
ABEGILLMN emballing
ABEGILLOS globalise
ABEGILLOZ globalize
ABEGILMMN embalming
ABEGILMNR imbrangle
ABEGILMNY beamingly
ABEGILNOR ignorable
ABEGILRSU Bulgarise
ABEGILRUZ Bulgarize
ABEGIMNNO bemoaning
ABEGIMNRR embarring
ABEGIMRRS ambergris
gris-amber
ABEGINNNT benignant
ABEGINNRT bantering
ABEGINNRU unbearing
ABEGINNTT battening
ABEGINOST obsignate
ABEGINRSW sabre-wing
ABEGINSST beastings
ABEGJORTU objurgate
ABEGJSTUU subjugate
ABEGKMNOY monkey-bag
ABEGKMORS bergomask
ABEGKRSTU grubstake
ABEGLLLSS bell-glass
ABEGLLORS bargellos
ABEGLLSWY swag-belly
ABEGLMORU beglamour
ABEGLMUZZ muzzle-bag
ABEGLNORU lounge-bar
ABEGLOPRU groupable
ABEGLOSTT bottle-gas
gas-bottle
ABEGLRSSU bluegrass
ABEGMMMRU △brummagem
ABEGMNOOR boomerang
ABEGMNOOW wagenboom
ABEGMNOSY moneybags
ABEGNRRSU gas-burner
ABEGNRSST bent-grass
ABEGOORST botargoes
ABEGORSTU subrogate
ABEHHLOOP halophobe
ABEHHOSTU bathhouse
bath-house
ABEHIINNR Hibernian
ABEHIINRT inhabiter
reinhabit
ABEHIITTW whitebait
ABEHIKLNT thinkable
ABEHIKNTT bethankit
ABEHILLRS shillaber
ABEHILMOP amphibole
ABEHILMRS herbalism
ABEHILOTT batholite
ABEHILRST herbalist
ABEHILRSY bearishly
ABEHILRTY breathily
heritably
ABEHILSST establish
ABEHILTTY bathylite
ABEHIMRRU herbarium
ABEHINOOP neophobia
ABEHIOPRU euphorbia
ABEHIORRV herbivora
ABEHIORUV behaviour
ABEHIPRRS herb-Paris
ABEHIRRTT birth-rate
ABEHISSTW whitebass
ABEHKLLRS shellbark
ABEHKNNOS shankbone
ABEHLLOST blast-hole
ABEHLLSTU sublethal
ABEHLMNSU bushelman
ABEHLMORT alembroth
ABEHLMOTU mouthable
ABEHLMPSY blasphemy
ABEHLMSTU bush-metal
ABEHLNNSU shunnable

ABEHLOOST shootable
ABEHLOOTT tholobate
ABEHLOPRY hyperbola
ABEHLORTT betrothal
ABEHLORTW bowler-hat
ABEHLOSTY Hylobates
ABEHLOTTW bath-towel
ABEHMOORT Theobroma
ABEHNORRT abhorrent
earthborn
ABEHNOTTU thenabout
ABEHNRRTU heartburn
ABEHNRSTU sunbather
ABEHOOSTU boathouse
houseboat
ABEHORRRU harbourer
ABEHQRSUU harquebus
ABEIIILRR librairie
ABEIIKLNR bairnlike
ABEIIKMNR minibreak
ABEIILLLR illiberal
ABEIILLMT limitable
ABEIILLRT biliteral
ABEIILMNR birlieman
ABEIILMSS amissible
ABEIILMTV lambitive
ABEIILNRT nail-biter
ABEIILNRZ brazilein
ABEIILRRT irritable
ABEIILRTV vibratile
ABEIILSST stabilise
ABEIILSTV visitable
ABEIILSTZ stabilize
ABEIIMNRT bairn-time
ABEIINNPT bipinnate
ABEIINNRT inebriant
ABEIIPRTT bipartite
ABEIIRSSV vibrissae
ABEIIRTVV vibrative
ABEIKLLNU unlikable
ABEIKLNSS balkiness
ABEIKNNRT interbank
ABEIKNORW wake-robin
ABEIKNRRV riverbank
ABEILLLMS slimeball
ABEILLLNT libellant
ABEILLLRY liberally
ABEILLNOT tabellion
ABEILLNPU unpliable
ABEILLNUV unlivable
ABEILLPSU plausible
ABEILLRTX Bellatrix
ABEILLSSU subsellia
ABEILLSSY syllabise
ABEILLSYZ syllabize
ABEILMMOV immovable
ABEILMMSW swimmable
ABEILMMTU immutable
ABEILMNNO nominable
ABEILMNOR bromelain
ABEILMNSS balminess
ABEILMOPS imposable
ABEILMORT Baltimore
ABEILMPTU imputable
ABEILMRSV verbalism
ABEILMRSY miserably
ABEILMRTU umbratile
ABEILMSTU sublimate
ABEILMSTY estimably
ABEILNORR rail-borne
ABEILNOSS bonilasse
ABEILNPRT printable
ABEILNPSU subalpine
ABEILNRRY inerrably
ABEILNRSS brainless
ABEILNRSU insurable
sublinear
ABEILNRTU untirable
ABEILNSUV subniveal
ABEILNSUZ unsizable
ABEILOQSU obsequial
ABEILORRT liberator
ABEILORST strobilae
ABEILORTT trilobate
ABEILORTU Labourite
ABEILPPST blast-pipe
ABEILPRST periblast
ABEILQTUY equitably
ABEILRSTU brutalise
ABEILRSTV verbalist
ABEILRTUZ brutalize
ABEILRTVY verbality
veritably
ABEILRVVY revivably
ABEILSTTW twistable
waistbelt
ABEILSUVY abusively
ABEILTTTT tittlebat
ABEIMMNRT timber-man
ABEIMNRSS barminess
ABEIMNRST tribesman
ABEIMNRSU submarine
ABEIMNRTU inumbrate
ABEIMPRST rebaptism
ABEINNORS Serbonian
ABEINNOST sanbenito
ABEINNRST bannister
ABEINNSTT abstinent
ABEINNSUV subnivean
ABEINNTYZ Byzantine
ABEINOORT aerobiont
reboation
ABEINOPRT bioparent
ABEINORTT torbanite
ABEINOSTT obstinate
ABEINPRST breastpin
stepbairn
ABEINPSTU unbaptise
ABEINPTUZ unbaptize
ABEINRSST banisters
ABEINRTTU tribunate
turbinate
ABEIOPRTV probative
ABEIORRTV river-boat

ABEIPSSTT se-baptist
ABEIRRRST barrister
ABEIRRSST arbitress
ABEIRRTTW wart-biter
ABEIRTTTU attribute
ABEJKLOUW kabeljouw
ABEJLNOYY enjoyably
ABEJMORST job-master
ABEKKMOOR bookmaker
ABEKLLMOS smoke-ball
ABEKLNNSS blankness
ABEKLNOOT ankle-boot
ABEKLOOPT bookplate
ABEKLORSU bark-louse
ABEKLORTW table-work
worktable
ABEKMOORT bootmaker
ABEKNNNPY penny-bank
ABELLLMRU larum-bell
ABELLMNTY lambently
ABELLMORS small-bore
ABELLNOSU unlosable
ABELLNOUV unlovable
ABELLORTY tolerably
ABELLOVVW blow-valve
ABELMMNRU lumberman
ABELMMORY memorably
ABELMNORY embryonal
ABELMNOUV unmovable
ABELMNPRU penumbral
ABELMNRTT tremblant
ABELMNRUY numerably
ABELMNSTT blastment
ABELMNSTU submental
ABELMOORT motorable
ABELMORVY removably
ABELMOSST mesoblast
ABELMPSSU subsample
ABELNNORV non-verbal
ABELNNTUU untunable
ABELNOPTU unpotable
ABELNOSST slabstone
ABELNOSTT entoblast
ABELNOSYZ lazy-bones
ABELNPTUY untypable
ABELNRSTU subaltern
ABELNRSUU subneural
ABELNRTTU turntable
ABELNSTUU sublunate
ABELOOPPS opposable
ABELOOTVY obovately
ABELOPPRS sorb-apple
ABELOPRST sportable
ABELOPRVY proveably
ABELOPTTY talbotype
ABELOSSST boastless
ABELOSTTY stylobate
ABELPRSUU pursuable
ABELPRSUY superably
ABELPRTUY reputably
ABELRSSUV subversal
ABELRSUYY Aylesbury
ABEMNORWY byrewoman
ABEMOOPRR broomrape
ABEMOPRTY ambrotype
ABEMORRTU arboretum
ABEMORRTY barometry
ABEMORSSU Mössbauer
ABEMRSSTU truss-beam
ABENNSTTU subtenant
ABENOOSTT stoneboat
ABENOPRRS barperson
ABENORSTV △observant
ABEOOPRTW powerboat
ABEOORRSU arboreous
ABEOPRRSY soapberry
ABEOQRSUU bourasque
ABEOSSSTU asbestous
ABEOSTTUW west-about
ABEPRRRSY raspberry
ABEPRRSTU superbrat
ABEPRSSSY passers-by
ABEPRTTTU butter-pat
ABERSSTTU substrate
ABFHLLSUY bashfully
ABFHLNSUU unbashful
ABFHSTTTU butt-shaft
ABFIILLRR fibrillar
ABFIIORSU bifarious
ABFILLSYY syllabify
ABFILMSUY subfamily
ABFILNSSU basinfuls
ABFLLLSTU full-blast
ABFLLOOPR ball-proof
ABGGIINPP bagpiping
ABGGIKNPY piggy-bank
ABGGILNNR brangling
ABGGINNRS bangsring
ABGGINORT tarboggin
ABGGINRST string-bag
ABGGLOORY garbology
ABGGNTTUY butty-gang
ABGHIKNRT right-bank
ABGHILLLT light-ball
ABGHILMNS shambling
ABGHINORR abhorring
ABGHINWZZ whizz-bang
ABGHIOPRY biography
ABGIILLNU bilingual
ABGIIMTUY ambiguity
ABGIJNNOW jawboning
ABGIKLLNY balkingly
ABGILLMOS globalism
ABGILLNOT balloting
ABGILLOTY billy-goat
ABGILNRTT brattling
ABGILOOST obligatos
ABGIMOSSU subimagos
ABGIMOSUU ambiguous
ABGINOSTW swingboat
ABGLMNOOS boomslang
ABGLMOPSU plumbagos
ABGLOOTTY battology
ABHHHIKSS bakhshish

ABHHIIRUV	bahuvrihi
ABHHILLOZ	Hizbollah
ABHHILLUZ	Hizbullah
ABHHILOTT	batholith
ABHHILTTY	bathylith
ABHHIPSSU	subahship
ABHHIRRSU	hair-brush
ABHIILLMS	bismillah
ABHIKLLSW	hawksbill
ABHIKMRRT	birthmark
ABHILMNTU	thumbnail
ABHILMOPY	amphiboly
ABHILNOOT	halobiont
ABHILNRSU	nail-brush
ABHILNRTY	labyrinth
ABHIOOOPZ	zoophobia
ABHIOPSTU	about-ship
ABHKMMRTU	thumb-mark
ABHLMPRSU	lampbrush
ABHLOPSTY	hypoblast
ABHMNOSUW	bushwoman
ABHNORRUU	unharbour
ABHOOPTUY	autophoby
ABHOPRTYY	Bryophyta
ABIIILLTY	liability
ABIIILMRS	△mirabilis
ABIIILNTY	inability
ABIIILTVY	viability
ABIIILLNRT	brilliant
ABIIILLRST	Braillist
ABIIILMNNO	binominal
ABIIILMNOS	albinoism
ABIIILMRST	tribalism
ABIIILNOOT	abolition
ABIIILNOOV	boliviano
ABIIILNORT	libration
ABIIILNORY	nobiliary
ABIIILORST	sibilator
ABIIILORTT	Trilobita
ABIIILRRTY	irritably
ABIIILRSTT	tribalist
ABIIILSTTY	stability
ABIIILSTUY	suability
	usability
ABIIMOSTU	ambitious
ABIIMRRTU	arbitrium
ABIINOOTV	obviation
ABIINORTV	vibration
ABIJNRRRY	brinjarry
ABIKMNRUU	Burakumin
ABILLMSSY	syllabism
ABILLNOPT	ballpoint
ABILLNPUY	unpliably
ABILLOPRX	pillar-box
ABILLORRZ	razor-bill
ABILLPSUY	plausibly
ABILMMOTU	bummaloti
ABILMMOVY	immovably
ABILMMTUY	immutably
ABILMNOUV	ovalbumin
ABILMOORS	ribosomal
ABILMORSU	labourism
ABILMORXY	xylorimba
ABILMPTUY	imputably
ABILMRSTU	brutalism
ABILNOPRS	Planorbis
ABILNOPSS	slop-basin
ABILNOSTU	ablutions
	sublation
ABILNRTVY	vibrantly
ABILOOPTT	pilot-boat
ABILOORSU	laborious
ABILORRTY	libratory
ABILORSTU	labourist
ABILRSTTU	brutalist
ABILRSTUY	salubrity
ABILRTTUY	brutality
ABIMMNRUU	manubrium
ABIMNORTU	tambourin
ABIMNORTY	abnormity
ABIMRSTUX	submatrix
ABINNNORU	Brunonian
ABINOOPRT	probation
ABINOOPST	spoonbait
ABINOPRTU	abruption
ABINOPSTU	subtopian
ABINRRTTU	turribant
ABIORRTVY	vibratory
ABIORSTTU	stirabout
ABIPRSTTY	baptistry
ABIRRTTUY	tributary
ABJLLOOTY	jollyboat
ABKLLOOST	bookstall
ABKLMOOPS	psalm-book
ABLLLOOST	stoolball
ABLLMOOSW	lamb's-wool
ABLLOORTU	roll-about
ABLMNORSU	subnormal
ABLMNOUVY	unmovably
ABLNNTUUY	untunably
ABLNORSUU	alburnous
ABLNRSUUY	sublunary
ABLRSSTUY	substylar
ABMNNOORW	woman-born
ABMNOORSU	abnormous
ABMNORRST	barnstorm
ABMOOORTT	motor-boat
ABMPRSTTU	bump-start
ABNORTTUU	about-turn
	turnabout
ABOOPRRTY	probatory
ABOOPRSTT	bootstrap
ABOORRTTU	obturator
ABRRSTTUW	bratwurst
ACCCCEHIT	cachectic
ACCCDEEEN	accedence
ACCCDEEIN	accidence
ACCCDILOY	cacodylic
ACCCEEENS	acescence
ACCCEENSY	acescency
ACCCEGLOY	coccygeal
ACCCEHITT	cathectic
ACCCEIIPV	cevapcici
ACCCEIIRT	cicatrice

ACCCEILLO	calcicole
ACCCEIOPT	copacetic
ACCCENOPU	occupance
ACCCGINOY	coccygian
ACCCHIKNP	pack-cinch
ACCCHKMOT	cockmatch
ACCCHKOOR	cockroach
ACCCHNOTY	cony-catch
ACCCHOPRT	catch-crop
ACCCIILLY	alicyclic
ACCCIILMT	climactic
ACCCIIOPR	capriccio
ACCCNOPUY	occupancy
ACCDDEEEN	decadence
ACCDDEENY	decadency
ACCDDEHOR	decachord
ACCDDEILS	discalced
ACCDDIIST	didactics
ACCDDIORS	disaccord
ACCDDKNOY	dandy-cock
ACCDEEEHN	déchéance
ACCDEEHIK	chickadee
ACCDEEHTW	catchweed
ACCDEEIST	desiccate
ACCDEELLN	cancelled
ACCDEFILS	fascicled
ACCDEFILY	decalcify
ACCDEGKOR	deck-cargo
ACCDEGLNO	clogdance
ACCDEHIIL	Cichlidae
ACCDEHIKR	deckchair
ACCDEHIST	decastich
ACCDEIIIM	Cimicidae
ACCDEIILN	Icelandic
ACCDEIILT	dialectic
ACCDEIILU	Culicidae
ACCDEILLP	piccadell
ACCDEILNR	calendric
ACCDEINST	desiccant
ACCDEIORW	cowardice
ACCDEKLOP	cock-padle
ACCDEKOSS	cassocked
ACCDELNOY	calcedony
ACCDEMNOO	cacodemon
ACCDEMOOR	macrocode
ACCDEMOPT	compacted
ACCDEMORR	camcorder
ACCDEMORY	△democracy
ACCDENORS	arcsecond
ACCDENSUU	unaccused
ACCDEORRS	scorecard
ACCDEORTU	accoutred
ACCDFILLY	flaccidly
ACCDGINOR	according
ACCDHHRUY	archduchy
ACCDHIIIS	ischiadic
ACCDHIIOR	radicchio
ACCDHIISS	Chassidic
ACCDHIKLS	clackdish
ACCDHINOR	chancroid
ACCDHMORT	match-cord
ACCDHNPRU	cardpunch
	punch-card
ACCDHOOOW	coachwood
ACCDHOORT	octachord
ACCDHORTW	catchword
ACCDIIINT	diactinic
ACCDIIIRT	diacritic
ACCDIILLP	piccadill
ACCDIILST	cladistic
ACCDIIOPT	apodictic
ACCDIIOSU	dicacious
ACCDIKLOR	cocklaird
ACCDILLOY	cycloidal
ACCDIMORR	microcard
ACCDINOOR	accordion
ACCDINORT	△dracontic
ACCDIOOPT	octapodic
ACCDIOSST	sticcados
ACCDKNORW	crackdown
ACCDLOPTU	cloud-capt
ACCDLORSW	scald-crow
ACCDLORUY	dulocracy
ACCDNOORT	concordat
ACCDOOOOW	cocoa-wood
ACCDOOSST	stoccados
ACCDORRTU	court-card
ACCEEEHSX	cache-sexe
ACCEEELNR	canceleer
ACCEEELRS	recalesce
ACCEEENRR	recreance
ACCEEGLMY	megacycle
ACCEEHHKO	cheechako
ACCEEHIKR	chickaree
ACCEEHILR	chelicera
ACCEEHIST	catechise
ACCEEHITY	haecceity
ACCEEHITZ	catechize
ACCEEHKMT	checkmate
ACCEEHLOT	cochleate
ACCEEHNPR	perchance
ACCEEHOST	cacoëthes
ACCEEILLS	ecclesial
ACCEEILMU	leucaemic
ACCEEILNR	arc-en-ciel
	cancelier
ACCEEILRT	clericate
ACCEEIPTV	acceptive
ACCEEIQSU	acquiesce
ACCEEIRRR	ricercare
ACCEEIRTV	accretive
ACCEEISTX	exsiccate
ACCEEKLOR	ear-cockle
ACCEEKLOT	cockateel
ACCEELLOR	clearcole
ACCEELNOR	concealer
ACCEELNPR	pre-cancel
ACCEELPST	spectacle
ACCEENNST	canescent
ACCEENORT	concreate
ACCEENRRY	recreancy
ACCEENRSU	recusance
	securance

ACCEEOPRS	praecoces
ACCEEOPSU	cepaceous
ACCEEORSU	ceraceous
ACCEEOSTU	cetaceous
ACCEFFFIL	cliff-face
ACCEFFHNO	off-chance
ACCEFGILU	calcifuge
ACCEFHLNU	chanceful
ACCEFHLOT	face-cloth
ACCEFIIRS	sacrifice
ACCEFILSU	fascicule
ACCEGHOSU	gauchesco
ACCEGIKNO	Cockaigne
ACCEGINOR	acrogenic
ACCEGIOPR	geocarpic
ACCEGIORT	categoric
ACCEGIOTT	geotactic
ACCEHHIOR	coach-hire
ACCEHHIRT	thearchic
ACCEHHIST	schechita
ACCEHHKOT	heathcock
ACCEHHLRU	church-ale
ACCEHHOQU	chechaquo
ACCEHIIMS	ischaemic
ACCEHIIRV	vice-chair
ACCEHIKLR	checkrail
ACCEHIKNR	raincheck
ACCEHILMO	cholaemic
ACCEHILNO	coachline
	cochineal
ACCEHILNT	technical
ACCEHILOR	choleraic
	oricalche
ACCEHILRU	cleruchia
ACCEHIMNS	mechanics
	mischance
ACCEHIMST	catechism
	schematic
ACCEHINOR	anchor-ice
ACCEHINRY	chicanery
ACCEHIRTT	architect
ACCEHIRVZ	czarevich
ACCEHISTT	catechist
ACCEHKOPT	patchocke
ACCEHKPSS	pass-check
ACCEHLNOR	chloracne
ACCEHLOOT	chocolate
ACCEHLOPT	catchpole
ACCEHMMNU	mumchance
ACCEHMNTT	catchment
ACCEHNRRU	cranreuch
ACCEHORRT	torch-race
ACCEHORTU	cartouche
ACCEHORTV	overcatch
ACCEHORTY	theocracy
ACCEHRRST	scratcher
ACCEHRSST	scratches
ACCEIILMN	calcimine
ACCEIILRT	icterical
ACCEIIMNR	cineramic
ACCEIIMNT	cinematic
ACCEIIMTV	cevitamic
ACCEIINOS	cocainise
ACCEIINOT	ice-action
ACCEIINOZ	cocainize
ACCEIINRT	circinate
ACCEIIPRT	accipiter
ACCEIIRST	cicatrise
ACCEIIRTZ	cicatrize
ACCEIISTV	siccative
ACCEIKLOT	cockatiel
ACCEIKOSX	△coxsackie
ACCEIKRSW	wisecrack
ACCEILLOT	laccolite
ACCEILLRS	clericals
ACCEILMOT	celomatic
ACCEILMPT	eclamptic
ACCEILNRT	centrical
ACCEILNST	△canticles
ACCEILNTU	inculcate
ACCEILOPR	precocial
ACCEILPST	sceptical
ACCEILRTU	circulate
ACCEIMNPT	impeccant
ACCEIMOSU	micaceous
ACCEINNOS	accension
ACCEINOOZ	Caenozoic
ACCEINORT	accretion
	anorectic
ACCEINOSS	accession
ACCEINSTU	encaustic
	succinate
ACCEINSTX	exsiccant
ACCEINTXY	excitancy
ACCEIORTT	corticate
ACCEIPRVY	pervicacy
ACCEIPSTY	cityscape
ACCEKLMNO	cockleman
ACCEKLNRS	cracknels
ACCEKMORS	smock-race
ACCEKNORR	corncrake
ACCELLOOT	collocate
ACCELLOSU	calculose
ACCELLTUU	cucullate
ACCELNOPY	cyclopean
ACCELNOVY	concavely
	covalency
ACCELNPTY	peccantly
ACCELOTUY	autocycle
ACCELPRTU	claret-cup
ACCEMNORY	ceromancy
ACCEMOPRR	cremocarp
ACCEMOPRT	recompact
ACCEMORTY	macrocyte
ACCENNOSS	non-access
ACCENNOTY	co-tenancy
ACCENOORS	coenosarc
ACCENOOTV	convocate
ACCENORSU	cancerous
ACCENRSUY	recusancy
ACCEORRSW	scarecrow
ACCEORRUY	Eurocracy
ACCEORSSY	accessory
ACCEORSTU	coruscate

ACCFFHHIN chaffinch
ACCFIILOR calorific
ACCFIILSS classific
ACCFIILSU fasciculi
ACCFIISST fascistic
ACCFIITTY facticity
ACCFIKNSY fancy-sick
ACCFIMORS sacciform
ACCFIMORT cactiform
ACCFINNOU Confucian
ACCFKOORT frock-coat
ACCFLLORU floccular
ACCGHIIKN chiacking
ACCGHIINN chicaning
ACCGHIIRR chiragric
ACCGHLNOO cacholong
ACCGIKLNR crackling
ACCGNORYY gynocracy
ACCHHIILR chiliarch
ACCHHIIOP chipochia
ACCHHIOPW coachwhip
ACCHHLORS scholarch
ACCHHMNRU churchman
ACCHHNOOR coach-horn
ACCHHORRS Rorschach
ACCHHRUWY churchway
ACCHIIIST ischiatic
ACCHIILRV chivalric
ACCHIINNP chincapin
ACCHIKLNO lock-chain
ACCHIKPST chapstick
ACCHILLOO alcoholic
ACCHILLOT laccolith
ACCHILNOR chronical
ACCHILOPS slip-coach
ACCHILORT Holarctic
ACCHILOTU acoluthic
ACCHILPSY psychical
ACCHIMNOR monarchic
ACCHIMNSY mischancy
ACCHIMOPR camphoric
ACCHIMORT chromatic
ACCHIMOST stomachic
ACCHINORT archontic
ACCHIOSTT octastich
ACCHIRTTY trachytic
ACCHKLMOT matchlock
ACCHKLOPT pack-cloth
ACCHKLOST sackcloth
ACCHKLSTU saltchuck
ACCHKNPRU rack-punch
ACCHKOOOP cock-a-hoop
ACCHKOORW coachwork
ACCHLLOPT catchpoll
ACCHLOORT colcothar
ochlocrat
ACCHLOOSW slowcoach
ACCHLOOTY chocolaty
ACCHMNOST Scotchman
ACCHNOOPY cacophony
ACCHNOPYY phycocyan
ACCHNORSU chancrous
ACCHOSSTU succotash
ACCIIILNN clinician
ACCIIINTV anticivic
ACCIILLPP Callippic
ACCIILLSY salicylic
ACCIILLVY civically
ACCIILNOR conciliar
ACCIILOPT occipital
ACCIILTVY acclivity
ACCIIMNOS cocainism
ACCIIMNPT panmictic
ACCIIMNUV vaccinium
ACCIIMOPT apomictic
ACCIIMQSU caciquism
ACCIINOOZ Cainozoic
ACCIINOST cocainist
ACCIINRTY intricacy
ACCIIOPST pasticcio
ACCIIORST isocratic
ACCIIOSTT isotactic
ACCIISSTU casuistic
ACCIITTTY tacticity
ACCIKKNNY nick-nacky
ACCIKMRSU music-rack
ACCIKNOSW cockswain
ACCILLMOY comically
ACCILLNOY conically
ACCILLNYY cynically
ACCILNOPY cyclopian
ACCILNORV clavicorn
ACCILNOTU ciclatoun
noctiluca
ACCILORTU coticular
ACCILORVY acyclovir
ACCILOSUV acclivous
ACCILPRTY cryptical
ACCILRRUU curricula
ACCILRTUU cuticular
ACCIMNOPS pancosmic
ACCIMNORY acronymic
ACCIMOORS crocosmia
ACCIMORTY timocracy
ACCIMPRTU practicum
ACCINNNOU uncanonic
ACCINOOSS occasions
ACCINOPRR Capricorn
ACCINOSTY oscitancy
ACCINOSTZ scazontic
ACCINOTVY concavity
ACCINSTTY syntactic
ACCIOPRST sarcoptic
ACCIOPRTT catoptric
ACCIOPRTY procacity
ACCIOPSST spiccatos
ACCIOSSTT sticcatos
ACCIOSSTU acoustics
ACCJKORSS crossjack
ACCKLOORR coral-rock
ACCLLOSUU calculous
ACCLLSUUY calyculus
ACCLMOPTY compactly
ACCLNNNOO colcannon

ACCLRSSUU	succursal
ACCMMOORS	macrocosm
ACCMNOORY	monocracy
	nomocracy
ACCMNOTUY	contumacy
ACCMOOPRT	compactor
ACCMOOPRY	macrocopy
ACCMOORST	cosmocrat
ACCNNOOTU	no-account
ACCNNOSTY	constancy
ACCNOORTT	contactor
ACCNORSTU	coruscant
ACCNORTTU	cunctator
ACCOPRRUY	procuracy
ACCOPRSTY	cystocarp
ACDDDEEIT	dedicated
ACDDEEEIT	dedicatee
ACDDEEFNU	undefaced
ACDDEEIMT	medicated
ACDDEEITU	deciduate
ACDDEEMNO	code-named
ACDDEENUY	undecayed
ACDDEEORT	decorated
ACDDEFGOO	goodfaced
ACDDEFHIS	dish-faced
ACDDEFIII	acidified
ACDDEFLPU	fuddle-cap
ACDDEFORY	fore-caddy
ACDDEGLLO	gold-laced
ACDDEGNOO	dodecagon
ACDDEHRRU	hard-cured
ACDDEIINS	discandie
ACDDEIITV	addictive
ACDDEIJNU	jaundiced
ACDDEIKLU	luckie-dad
ACDDEIMOP	campodeid
ACDDEINRX	card-index
ACDDEIORT	dedicator
ACDDEITUV	adductive
ACDDEKOST	deadstock
ACDDELNRU	underclad
ACDDELOPT	clodpated
ACDDELRSU	scuddaler
ACDDENRRU	undercard
ACDDEOORW	cedarwood
ACDDFILSY	caddis-fly
ACDDHHNSU	dachshund
ACDDHIILM	maid-child
ACDDHIRRU	arch-druid
ACDDIILOS	discoidal
ACDDIILRU	druidical
ACDDIIMOU	diacodium
ACDDIINOO	diacodion
ACDDIINOT	addiction
ACDDILNPU	duplicand
ACDDIMSSU	Sadducism
ACDDINOTU	adduction
ACDDLLNOU	cloudland
ACDDLNORW	cold-drawn
ACDDMOORT	mad-doctor
ACDDNOORT	doctorand
ACDEEEHIP	headpiece
ACDEEEHNR	adherence
ACDEEELRY	clear-eyed
ACDEEELSS	déclassée
ACDEEEMRT	decametre
ACDEEENTT	dancettee
ACDEEEPRT	deprecate
ACDEEERST	decastere
	desecrate
ACDEEERTU	re-educate
ACDEEFFLS	self-faced
ACDEEFFNU	uneffaced
ACDEEFHMR	chamfered
ACDEEFHWY	whey-faced
ACDEEFIKR	friedcake
ACDEEFKRT	afterdeck
ACDEEFNTU	fecundate
ACDEEFORT	defecator
ACDEEFRRT	redecraft
	refracted
ACDEEGLOU	decalogue
ACDEEGNNO	endecagon
ACDEEGOPU	decoupage
	découpage
ACDEEHIIL	Helicidae
ACDEEHINT	echinated
ACDEEHIOR	Orchideae
ACDEEHIPP	epedaphic
ACDEEHIRT	tracheide
ACDEEHKNY	hackneyed
ACDEEHLLN	chandelle
ACDEEHLLT	death-cell
ACDEEHLOS	closehead
ACDEEHLPT	chapleted
ACDEEHNNT	enchanted
ACDEEHNRU	unreached
ACDEEHNRV	chavender
ACDEEHNST	chastened
ACDEEHRRT	chartered
	three-card
ACDEEIILP	epicedial
ACDEEIINP	epicedian
ACDEEIIRT	Icteridae
ACDEEIJTV	adjective
ACDEEILMN	demi-lance
	endemical
ACDEEILMR	declaimer
ACDEEILNN	celandine
	decennial
ACDEEILNR	Icelander
ACDEEILNT	declinate
ACDEEILNU	Euclidean
ACDEEILPU	Clupeidae
ACDEEILRS	d'escalier
ACDEEILRT	decalitre
ACDEEILTU	elucidate
ACDEEIMNO	macédoine
ACDEEIMNP	impedance
ACDEEINOS	oceanides
ACDEEINRS	Ecardines
ACDEEIOPR	adipocere
ACDEEIPRT	predicate
ACDEEIPTU	paedeutic

ACDEEIRRT traceried
ACDEEIRST c'est-à-dire
ACDEEISST ecstasied
ACDEEITUV educative
ACDEEKKNR knackered
ACDEEKPPR prepacked
ACDEELLMR marcelled
ACDEELLOT decollate
ocellated
ACDEELLPR parcelled
ACDEELLST steel-clad
ACDEELNNU uncleaned
ACDEELNRR calendrer
ACDEELNRS esclandre
ACDEELNRU uncleared
ACDEELNTT tentacled
ACDEELNTU nucleated
ACDEELORS seed-coral
ACDEELRST △decretals
ACDEELSTY decastyle
ACDEELTUV cut-leaved
ACDEEMMUV vade-mecum
ACDEEMNOR Decameron
ACDEEMNRU unamerced
ACDEENNRU endurance
ACDEENNRY decennary
ACDEENNST ascendent
ACDEENNTU dance-tune
ACDEENOPR rope-dance
ACDEENOSS deaconess
ACDEENRTU uncreated
ACDEEOPRR crop-eared
ACDEEORRW cowardree
ACDEEPRRT red-carpet
ACDEERRTT retracted
ACDEERSTT scattered
ACDEERSTU reductase
ACDEESSTU decussate
ACDEFFILT afflicted
ACDEFFIST disaffect
ACDEFFLLU full-faced
ACDEFFMOR cofferdam
ACDEFGLNO long-faced
ACDEFGMSU smug-faced
ACDEFHINR arch-fiend
ACDEFHINT thin-faced
ACDEFIIIL edificial
ACDEFIIIR acidifier
ACDEFIILR clarified
ACDEFIILT feticidal
ACDEFIIRS sacrifide
scarified
ACDEFILLO coalfield
ACDEFILOR coal-fired
ACDEFILRU cauldrife
ACDEFILUV adviceful
ACDEFINRT infracted
ACDEFKLNO folk-dance
ACDEFLLOR called-for
ACDEFLNOR force-land
landforce
ACDEFLORZ calfdozer
ACDEFMNOO moon-faced
ACDEFORSS cross-fade
ACDEGGIMO demagogic
ACDEGGIOP pedagogic
ACDEGGIRT cat-rigged
ACDEGHINR chagrined
ACDEGHIRS discharge
ACDEGHNNU unchanged
ACDEGHNRU uncharged
ACDEGHOOP good-cheap
ACDEGIILR regicidal
ACDEGIIRT citigrade
ACDEGILNO genocidal
ACDEGILOO logaoedic
ACDEGIMNO endogamic
ACDEGINNR ring-dance
ACDEGINNS ascending
ACDEGINOY gynaecoid
ACDEGIRRS disgracer
ACDEGIRRT cartridge
ACDEGLOOS gas-cooled
ACDEGMNOO come-and-go
ACDEGMORY God-a-mercy
ACDEGNOOP pogo-dance
ACDEHHIKT thickhead
ACDEHHIRS rhachides
ACDEHHKOS shock-head
ACDEHHLOT headcloth
ACDEHHNTU unhatched
ACDEHHORX hexachord
ACDEHIIMR chimaerid
ACDEHIIRR diarrheic
ACDEHIITT diathetic
ACDEHIKLN kneidlach
ACDEHIKMR march-dike
ACDEHIKST headstick
ACDEHILLO cheloidal
ACDEHILMN name-child
ACDEHINNO anhedonic
ACDEHINNR hindrance
ACDEHINNU unchained
ACDEHINRT theandric
ACDEHINSV cavendish
ACDEHIORT Trochidae
ACDEHIPRS Sephardic
ACDEHIPRT dirt-cheap
ACDEHIPST cadetship
ACDEHKMOP chokedamp
ACDEHKMRY march-dyke
ACDEHKOST headstock
ACDEHLLRT dratchell
ACDEHLMSY chlamydes
ACDEHLNOR chlordane
ACDEHLNOT decathlon
ACDEHLNRS Chandler's
ACDEHLNRY chandlery
ACDEHLPRY parchedly
ACDEHLRWY wych-alder
ACDEHMMOS sachemdom
ACDEHMNRU uncharmed
ACDEHMNTU unmatched
ACDEHMOST stomached

ACDEHMPRY pachyderm
ACDEHNNRT trenchand
ACDEHNOOT chaetodon
ACDEHNOPR cardphone
phonecard
ACDEHNORW crown-head
ACDEHNRRT trenchard
ACDEHNRSW hand-screw
ACDEHNRTU uncharted
ACDEHNSTU unscathed
ACDEHNTUW unwatched
ACDEHOOPT chaetopod
ACDEHOOPW peach-wood
ACDEHORSS crosshead
ACDEIIINT dietician
ACDEIILMN adminicle
medicinal
ACDEIILNO lidocaine
ACDEIILNT identical
ACDEIILNX indexical
ACDEIILPU Pulicidae
ACDEIILRV larvicide
veridical
ACDEIILST deistical
ACDEIILTW twice-laid
ACDEIIMMY immediacy
ACDEIIMNR Amerindic
ACDEIIMRT diametric
matricide
ACDEIINOR Crinoidea
ACDEIINOS sciaenoid
ACDEIINOT dianoetic
ACDEIINRS inside-car
ACDEIINST andesitic
dianetics®
ACDEIINTV vindicate
ACDEIIOPR aperiodic
ACDEIIORS Soricidae
ACDEIIPRR parricide
ACDEIIPRT patricide
ACDEIIPTU paideutic
ACDEIIPTY diapyetic
ACDEIIRSU Sciuridae
ACDEIKLLP pickadell
ACDEIKMPR rampicked
ACDEIKRST sidetrack
ACDEILLMY decimally
medically
ACDEILLOU lodiculae
ACDEILLTY edictally
ACDEILMNU unclaimed
undecimal
ACDEILNNP pinnacled
ACDEILNNT declinant
ACDEILNTU acidulent
ACDEILNVY divalency
ACDEILOOP alopecoid
ACDEILOOR air-cooled
ACDEILOST dislocate
ACDEILOSY Lycosidae
ACDEILOTY Dicotylae
ACDEILPRU pedicular
ACDEILPTU duplicate
ACDEIMNNO dominance
ACDEIMNNT mendicant
ACDEIMNOP companied
compendia
ACDEIMNSU muscadine
ACDEIMNTY mendacity
ACDEIMORT decimator
ACDEIMOSY Samoyedic
ACDEIMRTU muricated
ACDEINNOR ordinance
ACDEINNOT contadine
ACDEINNTU uncinated
ACDEINORR coriander
ACDEINORS Dinoceras
iron-cased
ACDEINORT redaction
ACDEINOTU education
Noctuidae
ACDEINOTV advection
ACDEINPRT predicant
tap-cinder
ACDEINRTY Antrycide®
ACDEINSTY asyndetic
cystidean
syndicate
ACDEINTTU tunicated
ACDEIOORS Dioscorea
ACDEIORST Cordaites
ACDEIOSTY Cystoidea
ACDEIPRST practised
ACDEIPRTY predacity
ACDEIPSTU cuspidate
ACDEIQTTU acquitted
ACDEIRSTY dicastery
ACDEIRTTU dictature
ACDEIRUVY △ayurvedic
ACDEISSTY ecdysiast
ACDEITTTW cat-witted
ACDEKMOOS mockadoes
ACDEKMSTU duck's-meat
ACDEKNRTU untracked
ACDEKNRUV raven-duck
ACDELLOPS scalloped
ACDELLORR corralled
ACDELMOPR placoderm
ACDELMORY comradely
ACDELMTUU cumulated
ACDELNNOO colonnade
ACDELNNOR clarendon
ACDELNNTU candlenut
ACDELNOOW lance-wood
ACDELNOSU unsolaced
ACDELNOTU unlocated
ACDELNRSU sclaunder
ACDELNRTY trancedly
ACDELNRUY underclay
ACDELNSSU unclassed
ACDELOPSW slow-paced
ACDELOPTU cupolated
ACDELPRSY clepsydra
ACDELRTTU cultrated

ACDEMMMNO	commendam
ACDEMMNOR	commander
ACDEMMOOR	macrodome
ACDEMNOPR	compander
ACDEMOORT	motorcade
ACDEMORTY	democraty
ACDENNNSU	unscanned
ACDENNRST	transcend
ACDENOORT	coronated
ACDENOOTT	cottonade
ACDENORSW	sword-cane
ACDENORSY	△secondary
ACDENORTU	undercoat
ACDENPTTU	punctated
ACDENRRSU	unscarred
ACDENRRTU	undercart
ACDENRSSW	sand-screw
ACDENRSTU	undercast
ACDENRTTU	reductant
	truncated
ACDEOORRT	decorator
ACDEOORTT	doctorate
ACDEOPRRT	carpet-rod
ACDEORRST	co-starred
ACDEORRTT	detractor
ACDEORSST	coat-dress
	dress-coat
ACDEORSTU	ceratodus
	croustade
ACDEORSUZ	cruzadoes
ACDEORTUY	educatory
ACDERSTTU	crustated
ACDESSTUY	case-study
ACDFFHNSU	handcuffs
ACDFHILSS	scaldfish
ACDFIIILP	lapidific
ACDFIIRUY	fiduciary
ACDFINNOT	confidant
ACDFINTUY	facundity
ACDFNTTUY	candytuft
ACDFOORTW	woodcraft
ACDGHIMOY	dichogamy
ACDGHIPSY	dysphagic
ACDGIILOR	goliardic
ACDGIINNR	dining-car
ACDGIINNY	cyaniding
ACDGIIRST	digastric
ACDGILNSS	scaldings
ACDGIMOST	dogmatics
ACDGINRTU	traducing
ACDGLLOOR	dog-collar
ACDHIIIST	stichidia
ACDHIILMO	homicidal
ACDHIILST	distichal
ACDHIIMOR	chromidia
ACDHIIMSS	Chasidism
ACDHIIMSU	dichasium
ACDHIKLNO	knaidloch
ACDHIKORW	chowkidar
ACDHIKPRT	pitch-dark
ACDHILMUY	diachylum
ACDHILNOY	diachylon

ACDHILOOP	Chilopoda
ACDHILPSS	scaldship
ACDHILRSY	chrysalid
ACDHILRUY	hydraulic
ACDHILSTT	last-ditch
ACDHIMNOR	man-orchid
ACDHIMORT	chromatid
	dichromat
ACDHINORS	disanchor
ACDHIOPRS	rhapsodic
ACDHIORSY	dyschroia
ACDHIORYZ	hydrazoic
ACDHIOSUV	disavouch
ACDHIRRSU	churidars
ACDHLOOSY	day-school
	schoolday
ACDHLORTY	cloth-yard
ACDHMOOTW	doomwatch
	matchwood
ACDHNORRU	roundarch
ACDHOOPPS	scaphopod
ACDHOORRU	Urochorda
ACDHORTWW	watchword
ACDIIILMT	miticidal
ACDIIILOT	idiotical
ACDIIILRV	viricidal
ACDIIIMOT	idiomatic
ACDIIJLRU	juridical
ACDIIJMOT	comitadji
ACDIIJRUY	judiciary
ACDIIJSTU	Judaistic
ACDIIKLLP	pickadill
ACDIIKNOS	Dicksonia
ACDIILLTY	callidity
ACDIILMNO	dominical
ACDIILNOR	crinoidal
ACDIILOSS	dissocial
ACDIILOST	diastolic
ACDIILPTY	placidity
ACDIILRUV	virucidal
ACDIILSTU	dualistic
ACDIIMNNO	Dominican
ACDIIMPRY	pyramidic
ACDIIMRTY	mydriatic
ACDIINNOT	contadini
ACDIINORS	radionics
ACDIINORT	△indicator
ACDIINOSY	Dionysiac
ACDIINOTT	dictation
ACDIINRTY	rancidity
ACDIIOPRT	diatropic
ACDIIRTTX	dictatrix
ACDIJORTU	judicator
ACDIKKNST	kickstand
ACDIKLLPR	pack-drill
ACDIKNQSU	quicksand
ACDIKNRST	rickstand
ACDIKRRTT	dirt-track
ACDIKRSTY	yardstick
ACDILLLOO	colloidal
ACDILLLUY	ludically
ACDILLOOR	coralloid

Words marked △ may be spelled also with a capital letter

ACDILLORY cordially
ACDILLOSU caudillos
ACDILMNOO monodical
ACDILMOPS psalmodic
ACDILMOPY diplomacy
ACDILMOTU comatulid
ACDILNOOR coordinal
co-ordinal
ACDILNORT doctrinal
ACDILNORU rain-cloud
uncordial
ACDILNOSY synodical
ACDILNPRS landscrip
ACDILOOPT octaploid
ACDILOORT doctorial
ACDILOPRS dropsical
ACDILORSY corydalis
ACDILOSTU custodial
ACDILOSUU acidulous
ACDILOTUV oviductal
ACDILRTTY tridactyl
ACDILSTTY dactylist
ACDIMNNOY dominancy
ACDIMNORS △draconism
ACDIMOPSS △spasmodic
ACDIMORTY mordacity
ACDINNOOT contadino
ACDINOSTU custodian
ACDIORTTY dictatory
ACDJLNTUY adjunctly
ACDJOORTU coadjutor
ACDKLMOSY lady-smock
ACDKLORTU truck-load
ACDKMNNOO monadnock
ACDKORRSW sword-rack
ACDKORSTY stockyard
ACDLMNOOY condyloma
ACDLMNOPW clampdown
ACDLNNUUY undulancy
ACDLNSTYY syndactyl
ACDLOOPPY clappy-doo
ACDMMNOOS commandos
ACDMMNORU △communard
ACDMNOOPR compandor
ACDMOOPRR comprador
ACDMOOSUV muscovado
ACDMPRRTU trump-card
ACDNNORUU uncandour
ACDOORRSS crossroad
ACDORRTUY courtyard
ACEEEFIRS cease-fire
ACEEEFLNR freelance
ACEEEFPRS free-space
ACEEEGHPR repechage
ACEEEGLNY eye-glance
ACEEEGNNV vengeance
ACEEEGRST secretage
ACEEEHHRW eachwhere
ACEEEHIPT petechiae
ACEEEHIRV echeveria
ACEEEHNPR cheapener
ACEEEHPRT peach-tree
ACEEEHSTV cheesevat
ACEEEILMP piecemeal
ACEEEIMPT peacetime
ACEEEINPT epaenetic
ACEEEIPPP peace-pipe
ACEEEIPRT piece-rate
ACEEEJLSW jewel-case
ACEEEKNQU queen-cake
ACEEEKRRT racketeer
ACEEELNOP Paleocene
ACEEELNRT crenelate
ACEEELNRV relevance
ACEEELNTU enucleate
ACEEELNTY acetylene
ACEEELPRT peat-creel
ACEEELPSS peaceless
ACEEELRST scelerate
ACEEELSSS ceaseless
ACEEEMNNR remanence
ACEEEMNPR permeance
ACEEENPPT appetence
ACEEENPRS esperance
ACEEENPRT pecan-tree
ACEEENRSV severance
ACEEENRTW new-create
ACEEFFHRR chafferer
ACEEFFHRU réchauffé
ACEEFFITV affective
ACEEFFLMT maleffect
ACEEFFLNU affluence
ACEEFFLTU effectual
ACEEFFNRY fancy-free
ACEEFHHKL half-cheek
ACEEFHITW white-face
ACEEFHLNP halfpence
ACEEFHLPR parfleche
ACEEFHORR forereach
ACEEFHORT foreteach
ACEEFIKNS case-knife
ACEEFILNR rail-fence
ACEEFILNV venefical
ACEEFILPR fireplace
ACEEFINOR Coniferae
ACEEFINRT interface
ACEEFIRSS fricassee
ACEEFLORR coral-reef
ACEEFLOTV volte-face
ACEEFMORT forcemeat
ACEEFMPRV camp-fever
ACEEFNORV confervae
ACEEFRRST scart-free
ACEEGHIRU gaucherie
ACEEGHLLN challenge
ACEEGHNRX exchanger
ACEEGHNSX sex-change
ACEEGIILS gaelicise
ACEEGIILZ gaelicize
ACEEGILNR generical
ACEEGILNS Cingalese
ACEEGILNT clientage
genetical
ACEEGILNV evangelic

ACEEGILRS sacrilege
ACEEGILRV vice-regal
ACEEGIMNR Germanice
ACEEGIMRU megacurie
ACEEGINOR recoinage
ACEEGINRV grievance
ACEEGIRTT cigarette
ACEEGKRWY greywacke
ACEEGLLOU colleague
ACEEGLNRT rectangle
ACEEGLRSS graceless
ACEEGMNOR geomancer
ACEEGMNUY gynaeceum
ACEEGMOPS megascope
ACEEGNNPR pregnance
ACEEGNORU encourage
ACEEGNRSV scavenger
ACEEGNRSY sergeancy
ACEEGNSSY cageyness
ACEEGOOPR cooperage
ACEEGORST escortage
ACEEGRTTU curettage
ACEEHHTUX Hexateuch
ACEEHIIPR hairpiece
ACEEHILMS alchemise
ACEEHILMZ alchemize
ACEEHILPT petechial
ACEEHILRT cheralite
ethereal
heretical
ACEEHILRV chevalier
ACEEHIMNS achimenes
mechanise
ACEEHIMNZ mechanize
ACEEHIMPR impeacher
ACEEHIMPS hemispace
ACEEHINNS sennachie
ACEEHINNV enhancive
ACEEHINPT phenacite
ACEEHINRR rancherie
ACEEHINST hesitance
ACEEHIPRS Parcheesi®
ACEEHIRRS cashierer
ACEEHISTT aesthetic
ACEEHKOPR choke-pear
ACEEHKPST packsheet
ACEEHLMNO chameleon
ACEEHLMOO haemocoel
ACEEHLMPV champlevé
ACEEHLNNR channeler
ACEEHLNRU △herculean
ACEEHLNSS seneschal
ACEEHLPSS chapeless
ACEEHLRSS reachless
ACEEHLRTW cartwheel
ACEEHLRTY teacherly
ACEEHLSST teachless
ACEEHMMRT machmeter
ACEEHMNRY arch-enemy
ACEEHMOTY haemocyte
ACEEHMRSU charmeuse
ACEEHMTTU humectate
ACEEHNNOS encheason
ACEEHNNRT enchanter
ACEEHNOPR canephore
chaperone
ACEEHNPSS cheapness
ACEEHNRST chastener
ACEEHNRTT entrechat
ACEEHNRTY Cytherean
ACEEHNSTU chanteuse
ACEEHOPRR orepearch
ACEEHORRS racehorse
ACEEHORRV overreach
ACEEHORST escheator
ACEEHOSTU theaceous
ACEEHPRTY archetype
ACEEHRRRT charterer
recharter
ACEEHRRSS archeress
ACEEHRRTT chatterer
ACEEHRRTY treachery
ACEEIILPT tailpiece
ACEEIINPT epainetic
ACEEIJQRU Jacquerie
ACEEIKLLS scalelike
ACEEIKRST ice-skater
ACEEILLNP capelline
ACEEILLRT reticella
ACEEILLST celestial
ACEEILLTV vellicate
ACEEILMRR reclaimer
ACEEILMRT △carmelite
ACEEILMST timescale
ACEEILMTT telematic
ACEEILNPR percaline
Periclean
ACEEILNPT pectineal
ACEEILNPW wipe-clean
ACEEILNRS scare-line
ACEEILNRT interlace
lacertine
reclinate
ACEEILNTY ceylanite
ACEEILOPV piacevole
ACEEILPRS periclase
ACEEILPRT replicate
ACEEILPTX explicate
ACEEILRST cartelise
ACEEILRTZ cartelize
zelatrice
ACEEILSUV vesiculae
ACEEIMMNN immanence
ACEEIMMNT mincemeat
ACEEIMMRT metameric
ACEEIMNPR mepacrine
ACEEIMNRT incremate
ACEEIMNSX exciseman
ACEEIMPRT imprecate
ACEEIMPST empaestic
space-time
ACEEIMRRS careerism
ACEEIMRSS cassimere

ACEEIMRST	miscreate
	stream-ice
ACEEIMRTT	metricate
ACEEINNPS	spinacene
ACEEINNRT	nectarine
ACEEINNTU	enunciate
ACEEINOPR	caponiere
ACEEINPRU	△epicurean
ACEEINPTT	pectinate
ACEEINRRS	increaser
ACEEINRSS	scenarise
ACEEINRST	cisternae
ACEEINRSZ	scenarize
ACEEINRTT	Encratite
ACEEINSSV	ascensive
ACEEIORST	esoterica
ACEEIORTX	excoriate
ACEEIOSSS	écossaise
ACEEIOTVV	evocative
ACEEIPRTT	crepitate
ACEEIPRTV	precative
ACEEIPSTX	expiscate
ACEEIQRRU	reacquire
ACEEIRRST	careerist
ACEEIRRTW	rice-water
ACEEIRSSV	caressive
ACEEIRSTU	cauterise
ACEEIRSTV	viscerate
ACEEIRTTX	extricate
ACEEIRTUZ	cauterize
ACEEISSST	ecstasise
ACEEISSTZ	ecstasize
ACEEJNRSY	serjeancy
ACEEKLNNR	enranckle
ACEEKORST	sea-rocket
ACEELLLOT	locellate
ACEELLLSU	cellulase
ACEELLORT	electoral
ACEELLPSS	placeless
ACEELLRSY	Carlylese
ACEELLSSS	scaleless
ACEELMNPT	placement
ACEELMNRT	recalment
ACEELMNST	select-man
ACEELMOOR	cameo-rôle
ACEELMOOT	coelomate
ACEELMOPS	someplace
ACEELMORT	late-comer
ACEELNNOR	ale-conner
ACEELNNRU	cannelure
ACEELNNSS	cleanness
ACEELNORT	coeternal
	tolerance
ACEELNPRT	percental
ACEELNPTU	petulance
ACEELNRSS	clearness
ACEELNRTU	calenture
	crenulate
ACEELNRVY	relevancy
ACEELNSTT	latescent
ACEELNTUX	exultance
ACEELOOSU	oleaceous
ACEELOPRT	percolate
ACEELORRT	correlate
ACEELORSS	casserole
ACEELORSW	lower-case
ACEELORTT	lectorate
ACEELORTU	urceolate
ACEELPSSS	scapeless
	spaceless
ACEELPSTU	speculate
ACEELPTUX	exculpate
ACEELQRRU	lacquerer
ACEELRRTT	clatterer
ACEELRSST	traceless
ACEELRTTU	reluctate
ACEELRTUY	electuary
ACEELSSST	casteless
ACEELSSSU	causeless
ACEELSSTT	cast-steel
ACEEMNNRY	remanency
ACEEMNNTT	enactment
ACEEMNPST	scapement
ACEEMNRRY	mercenary
ACEEMNTTX	exactment
ACEEMOPRT	Mecoptera
ACEEMOPST	copes-mate
ACEEMORRS	sarcomere
ACEEMORTT	octameter
ACEEMORVW	creamwove
ACEEMRRST	cremaster
ACEEMRRTU	mercurate
ACEEMRSTY	mercy-seat
ACEENNNOR	cannoneer
ACEENNNTT	annectent
ACEENNOPR	can-opener
ACEENNORS	resonance
ACEENNOST	caen-stone
	Cantonese
ACEENNOSV	sovenance
ACEENNOTT	centonate
ACEENNRST	renascent
ACEENNRTY	centenary
ACEENPPTY	appetency
ACEENPRRT	carpenter
ACEENPTTX	exceptant
	expectant
ACEENRRTU	crenature
ACEENRSSY	necessary
ACEENRTTU	utterance
ACEENSSTU	acuteness
ACEENSSTX	exactness
ACEENTTUX	executant
ACEEOOPRT	cooperate
	co-operate
ACEEOPRRT	procreate
ACEEOPRTV	patercove
ACEEORRTT	rectorate
ACEEORRTV	overreact
ACEEORRTW	water-core
ACEEORTUY	eucaryote
ACEEORTVX	over-exact
ACEEOSSTU	setaceous
ACEEPPRSU	upper-case

ACEEPRRTU	recapture
ACEERRSST	creatress
ACEERRSTT	scatterer
	streetcar
ACEERRSTY	secretary
ACEERSSTT	tesseract
ACEERSSTU	secateurs
ACEERSSTX	exactress
ACEFFFLRU	carfuffle
ACEFFGINT	affecting
ACEFFHRUU	chauffeur
ACEFFIIOT	officiate
ACEFFIKMR	mafficker
ACEFFINOT	affection
ACEFFIOPY	pay-office
ACEFFIORT	forficate
ACEFFOSTU	suffocate
ACEFGHLNU	changeful
ACEFGHLRU	chargeful
ACEFGIRTU	fruit-cage
ACEFGLNOR	gerfalcon
ACEFHIINT	chieftain
ACEFHILPR	half-price
ACEFHINRS	franchise
ACEFHIPRY	preachify
ACEFHIRRU	fraîcheur
ACEFHIRTU	faithcure
ACEFHLLOS	half-close
ACEFHLNOR	arch-felon
ACEFHLNWX	flax-wench
ACEFHLSTU	scatheful
ACEFHMNNR	Frenchman
ACEFHMORT	homecraft
ACEFHOSUV	vouchsafe
ACEFHRTTY	fratchety
ACEFIILLS	Filicales
ACEFIILMS	facsimile
ACEFIILRR	clarifier
ACEFIINNR	financier
ACEFIIRRS	scarifier
ACEFIIRRT	△artificer
ACEFIIRTV	fricative
ACEFIISST	satisfice
ACEFIITTV	factitive
ACEFIJKKN	jackknife
ACEFIKRTU	fruitcake
ACEFILNNO	falconine
ACEFILNRZ	frenzical
ACEFILNSS	fanciless
ACEFILOPR	caprifole
ACEFILORT	fortalice
ACEFILOSU	filaceous
ACEFILOTV	olfactive
ACEFIMORT	formicate
ACEFINORT	fornicate
ACEFINRTU	canefruit
ACEFINSTT	fatiscent
ACEFINSTU	infuscate
ACEFINTTV	ventifact
ACEFIOPRT	forcipate
ACEFIORST	factorise
ACEFIORSU	feracious
ACEFIORTZ	factorize
ACEFIOSTU	facetious
ACEFIRSSW	scarfwise
ACEFJLNOR	jerfalcon
ACEFKLNOR	cornflake
ACEFKLORS	foreslack
ACEFKORST	task-force
ACEFLLLSU	full-scale
ACEFLLMRU	full-cream
ACEFLLRUY	carefully
ACEFLMNOS	flamencos
ACEFLMOPY	pomace-fly
ACEFLMOTU	camouflet
ACEFLNRUU	uncareful
ACEFLPTUU	teacupful
ACEFLRRUY	curry-leaf
ACEFLRSST	craftless
ACEFLRSUU	saucerful
ACEFLTTUU	fluctuate
ACEFNORSV	confervas
ACEFNRRTU	runecraft
ACEFNRSTT	transfect
ACEFOOPRS	roofscape
ACEFOPRRT	after-crop
ACEFORRRT	refractor
ACEFOSTUU	tufaceous
ACEFRTTUU	fructuate
ACEGGHLRU	ruggelach
ACEGGINOR	racegoing
ACEGHHILP	high-place
ACEGHHMSU	camsheugh
ACEGHILRT	lethargic
ACEGHILSU	Ausgleich
ACEGHILTT	tight-lace
ACEGHIMPR	graphemic
ACEGHIMRS	mischarge
ACEGHINPR	preaching
ACEGHINRS	searching
ACEGHIRST	Reichstag
ACEGHLOOS	school-age
ACEGHMNNT	McNaghten
ACEGHMNOS	cheongsam
ACEGHMORT	hectogram
ACEGHMORY	hercogamy
ACEGHNRRU	grauncher
ACEGHOPRR	cerograph
ACEGHOPTY	phagocyte
ACEGHRRSU	surcharge
ACEGIILLS	△gallicise
ACEGIILLZ	△gallicize
ACEGIILMS	gaelicism
ACEGIILNS	anglicise
ACEGIILNT	genitalic
ACEGIILNV	vigilance
ACEGIILNZ	anglicize
ACEGIIMNT	enigmatic
ACEGIINNT	antigenic
ACEGIINRR	ricegrain
ACEGIINST	sagenitic
ACEGIIRRT	geriatric
ACEGIKNRT	racketing
ACEGIKPRR	rag-picker

ACEGIKRST	gear-stick
ACEGILLLO	collegial
ACEGILLNO	collegian
ACEGILLOR	allegoric
ACEGILLOT	colligate
ACEGILNNO	congenial
ACEGILNNS	cleansing
ACEGILNRU	neuralgic
ACEGILNRW	clearwing
ACEGILNSS	cassingle
ACEGILRTU	curtilage
	graticule
ACEGIMMRS	scrimmage
ACEGIMMST	tagmemics
ACEGIMNOT	geomantic
ACEGIMNRS	screaming
ACEGIMNRT	centigram
ACEGIMNST	magnetics
ACEGIMNTU	mutagenic
ACEGIMNUY	gynaecium
ACEGIMTUZ	zeugmatic
ACEGINNOR	ignorance
ACEGINNOT	négociant
ACEGINNSU	unceasing
ACEGINOOT	Notogaeic
ACEGINOSU	cousinage
ACEGINOTU	autogenic
ACEGINPRT	carpeting
ACEGINPRY	panegyric
ACEGINRRT	terracing
ACEGINRSS	caressing
ACEGIOPRR	paregoric
ACEGIOSTT	geostatic
ACEGIPPRS	scrippage
ACEGIRRSS	rice-grass
ACEGIRSTT	strategic
ACEGJNOTU	conjugate
ACEGLMNRY	clergyman
ACEGLNNOU	uncongeal
ACEGLNNPY	plangency
ACEGLNOSU	consulage
ACEGMMNOO	commonage
ACEGMMRSU	scrummage
ACEGNNOTT	cotangent
ACEGNNPRY	pregnancy
ACEGORRTU	corrugate
ACEGPRSTU	scrapegut
ACEHHHINS	Shechinah
ACEHHHIST	shechitah
ACEHHILPS	chelaship
ACEHHIRRY	hierarchy
ACEHHIRSS	rhachises
ACEHHISTX	hexastich
ACEHHLSTT	shtetlach
ACEHHLWYZ	wych-hazel
ACEHHMNTT	hatchment
ACEHHMOTY	theomachy
ACEHHMRTW	Wehrmacht
ACEHHMSSY	Hesychasm
ACEHHNRTY	ethnarchy
ACEHHOOTT	toothache
ACEHHORST	charoseth
ACEHHPRTY	heptarchy
ACEHHSSTY	Hesychast
ACEHIILTU	halieutic
ACEHIIMNT	hematinic
ACEHIIMRU	hieracium
ACEHIINNP	Phenician
ACEHIINPP	epiphanic
ACEHIINRT	trichinae
ACEHIIPPT	epitaphic
ACEHIIRST	charities
ACEHIISTT	atheistic
ACEHIKNOV	Chekovian
ACEHIKORT	artichoke
ACEHIKRST	heart-sick
ACEHILLLY	helically
ACEHILLRT	cleithral
ACEHILLTY	ethically
ACEHILMMO	chamomile
ACEHILMRT	thermical
ACEHILMST	alchemist
ACEHILMTW	witchmeal
ACEHILNNO	chelonian
ACEHILNOR	enchorial
ACEHILNOT	chelation
ACEHILNSS	chainless
ACEHILNTU	unethical
ACEHILNTY	thylacine
ACEHILOPT	phacolite
ACEHILORW	archilowe
ACEHILPRS	spherical
ACEHILPRY	preachily
ACEHILRUV	vehicular
ACEHILSTT	athletics
ACEHILTTY	tachylite
ACEHIMMNS	mechanism
ACEHIMNOO	hemoconia
ACEHIMNRY	machinery
ACEHIMNST	mechanist
ACEHIMOPT	omphacite
ACEHIMORY	cherimoya
ACEHIMRTU	rheumatic
ACEHINNOP	open-chain
ACEHINNOT	oenanthic
ACEHINNRY	Hercynian
ACEHINNST	encanthis
ACEHINOPR	parochine
ACEHINORT	anchorite
	antechoir
ACEHINORX	chronaxie
ACEHINOSV	schiavone
ACEHINRRU	△hurricane
ACEHINRSS	chariness
ACEHINSTY	hesitancy
ACEHINTTU	authentic
ACEHINTUY	Eutychian
ACEHIOOTZ	zoothecia
ACEHIOPRY	coryphaei
ACEHIORRT	hierocrat
ACEHIORST	rhotacise
ACEHIORTZ	rhotacize
ACEHIOSTT	athetosic
ACEHIOTTT	athetotic

ACEHIOTTW	whitecoat
ACEHIPPSS	spaceship
ACEHIPRTY	architype
ACEHIPSTT	pathetics
ACEHIRRRT	trierarch
ACEHIRRST	Reichsrat
ACEHIRSTT	theatrics
ACEHIRSTU	Eucharist
ACEHIRSTV	tsarevich
ACEHIRSTX	exarchist
ACEHKLNSU	unshackle
ACEHKLOSU	hause-lock
ACEHKMORY	chromakey
ACEHKOPRS	pack-horse
ACEHKORST	shortcake
ACEHLLLMS	clamshell
ACEHLLLOR	chlorella
ACEHLMOPR	polemarch
ACEHLMORV	love-charm
ACEHLMOST	moschatel
ACEHLMOTV	love-match
ACEHLMRSS	charmless
ACEHLMSST	matchless
ACEHLMSSY	chlamyses
ACEHLNNPU	up-Channel
ACEHLNNRU	uncharnel
ACEHLNOSY	anchylose
ACEHLNPSU	spleuchan
ACEHLNPTY	phlyctena
ACEHLOOSU	coalhouse
ACEHLOPSU	cephalous
ACEHLOPSW	showplace
ACEHLORRT	trochlear
ACEHLORSU	house-carl
ACEHLORTT	charlotte
ACEHLPRSU	sprauchle
ACEHLPSSU	sphacelus
ACEHLRSST	chartless
ACEHLTTYY	tachylyte
ACEHMNOPY	cymophane
ACEHMNOTY	theomancy
ACEHMNPRT	parchment
ACEHMNSTY	scytheman
ACEHMNTTU	humectant
ACEHMORST	stomacher
ACEHMORTV	overmatch
ACEHMOSTT	chemostat
ACEHMOSTU	moustache
ACEHMPRTY	champerty
ACEHNNRTT	trenchant
ACEHNOQTU	hacqueton
ACEHNORRS	rancheros
ACEHNORSS	anchoress
ACEHNORST	arch-stone
ACEHNORTY	honey-cart
ACEHNOSTT	stonechat
ACEHNOSTU	ceanothus
ACEHNPPRS	schnapper
ACEHNPRTY	pentarchy
ACEHNRSST	chantress
ACEHNRSTU	stauncher
ACEHNRSUZ	schnauzer
ACEHOOSTU	housecoat
ACEHOPRRS	sharecrop
ACEHOPRST	chaseport
ACEHOPRSU	proseucha
ACEHOPRTY	pothecary
ACEHOPSST	chassepot
ACEHORRST	cart-horse
	orchestra
ACEHORRTU	treachour
ACEHORSTU	cart-house
ACEHORSTY	theocrasy
ACEHORSXY	xerochasy
ACEHORTTY	athrocyte
ACEHORTVW	overwatch
ACEHPRRSU	purchaser
ACEHRRTTY	tetrarchy
ACEHRSSTT	crash-test
ACEHSTTUZ	zuchettas
ACEIIILNS	siciliane
ACEIIILST	italicise
ACEIIILTZ	italicize
ACEIIINNP	epinician
ACEIIKLMS	sicklemia
ACEIIKLNT	kinetical
ACEIIKMNT	kinematic
ACEIILLNN	canellini
ACEIILLOT	ciliolate
ACEIILLTV	levitical
ACEIILMMT	mimetical
ACEIILMOV	voice-mail
ACEIILMPR	empirical
ACEIILMPT	implicate
ACEIILMSS	seismical
ACEIILMST	climatise
ACEIILMSV	vicesimal
ACEIILMTZ	climatize
ACEIILNNT	anticline
ACEIILNNV	vicennial
ACEIILNPS	cisalpine
ACEIILNST	inelastic
	sciential
ACEIILNTX	Calixtine
ACEIILORT	aerolitic
ACEIILOSS	socialise
ACEIILOST	socialite
ACEIILOSV	viliacoes
ACEIILOSZ	socialize
ACEIILPRT	pearlitic
ACEIILRST	eristical
	realistic
ACEIILRTT	lateritic
	triticale
ACEIILSTV	calvities
ACEIIMMNR	Cimmerian
ACEIIMMRU	americium
ACEIIMNOT	emication
ACEIIMNRT	criminate
	metrician
ACEIIMNSS	△messianic
ACEIIMPTT	impactite
ACEIIMPTV	impactive
ACEIIMRST	△armistice

ACEIIMSTU	maieutics
ACEIINNOT	aconitine
ACEIINNRT	incertain
ACEIINOTV	noviciate
ACEIINPRS	periscian
	precisian
ACEIINPRT	pictarnie
ACEIINPST	epinastic
ACEIINRTT	intricate
	triactine
ACEIINRTY	itineracy
ACEIINTTT	nictitate
ACEIIOSTV	sociative
ACEIIPRST	peirastic
ACEIIPSTT	epistatic
ACEIIRSTT	ceratitis
ACEIIRSTV	variscite
ACEIISTTT	steatitic
ACEIITTUX	eutaxitic
ACEIJKNPS	jack-snipe
ACEIJKRRV	river-jack
ACEIJNOSU	jouisance
ACEIKLLNN	lack-linen
ACEIKLMNS	sickleman
ACEIKLNNS	cleanskin
ACEIKLNPT	tan-pickle
ACEIKLNRS	clearskin
ACEIKLPRS	spraickle
ACEIKLPST	skeptical
ACEIKNPTW	pack-twine
ACEIKNSST	tackiness
ACEIKNSSW	wackiness
ACEIKOPRT	air-pocket
ACEIKOPST	kopasetic
ACEIKPPRT	pipe-track
ACEIKSSTT	seat-stick
ACEILLLMS	millscale
ACEILLLRT	clitellar
ACEILLLXY	lexically
ACEILLMOP	polemical
ACEILLMOT	collimate
ACEILLNOR	collinear
	△coralline
ACEILLNPS	spellican
ACEILLNPT	plant-lice
ACEILLORS	localiser
ACEILLORT	corallite
ACEILLORZ	localizer
ACEILLOST	oscillate
ACEILLOTV	collative
ACEILLPRS	callipers
ACEILLPSY	specially
ACEILLPTY	plicately
ACEILLRST	cellarist
ACEILLSSU	sulcalise
ACEILLSUZ	sulcalize
ACEILMMNO	Commelina
	melomanic
ACEILMMSS	mescalism
ACEILMNNU	luminance
ACEILMNOP	policeman
ACEILMNOR	coalminer
ACEILMNOT	melanotic
ACEILMNRU	melanuric
	numerical
ACEILMNSU	masculine
	semuncial
ACEILMNTU	culminate
ACEILMOPT	Ptolemaic
ACEILMORS	lacrimose
ACEILMOSS	coseismal
ACEILMOSU	limaceous
ACEILMPST	emplastic
ACEILMPTV	palm-civet
ACEILMRRU	△mercurial
ACEILMRST	cartelism
ACEILMRSU	simulacre
ACEILMRTU	climature
	tularemic
ACEILMSTU	salicetum
ACEILNNOR	cornelian
ACEILNNOT	octennial
ACEILNNTY	anciently
ACEILNOPR	porcelain
ACEILNOPT	point-lace
ACEILNORS	censorial
ACEILNORT	clarionet
	crotaline
ACEILNOST	coastline
	sectional
ACEILNOSV	volcanise
ACEILNOTU	inoculate
ACEILNOVZ	volcanize
ACEILNPTU	inculpate
ACEILNRST	larcenist
ACEILNRTU	centurial
ACEILNRTY	certainly
ACEILNSSS	scaliness
ACEILNSUV	vulcanise
ACEILNTUV	vulcanite
ACEILNTXY	inexactly
ACEILNUVZ	vulcanize
ACEILOOPZ	Paleozoic
ACEILOPPS	episcopal
ACEILOPRT	precoital
ACEILOPSS	Asclepios
ACEILOPST	scapolite
ACEILOQUV	equivocal
ACEILORRT	rectorial
ACEILORST	sclerotia
	sectorial
ACEILORSV	vocaliser
ACEILORTT	tectorial
ACEILORTV	vectorial
ACEILORVZ	vocalizer
ACEILOTTU	autotelic
ACEILOTWY	wyliecoat
ACEILPPPR	paper-clip
ACEILPRST	palestric
ACEILPRTU	plicature
ACEILPRTX	X-particle
ACEILPSSU	Asclepius
	capsulise
ACEILPSTU	spiculate

ACEILPSTY	specialty
ACEILPSUZ	capsulize
ACEILPTUY	eucalypti
ACEILRRTU	recruital
	reticular
ACEILRSTT	cartelist
ACEILRSTU	sterculia
ACEILRSTV	cat-silver
ACEILRSUV	vesicular
ACEILRTUV	lucrative
	revictual
ACEILTTUV	cultivate
ACEIMMNNY	immanency
ACEIMMNOT	comminate
ACEIMNNOO	Neocomian
ACEIMNNOT	monactine
ACEIMNOPS	campesino
ACEIMNORT	cremation
	manticore
ACEIMNOST	encomiast
ACEIMNOTT	omittance
ACEIMNPTU	pneumatic
ACEIMNRST	Encratism
	miscreant
ACEIMNRSU	muscarine
ACEIMNSST	semantics
ACEIMNSTU	mint-sauce
ACEIMNTYZ	enzymatic
ACEIMOPRS	premosaic
ACEIMORST	Masoretic
ACEIMORTU	autocrime
ACEIMORVW	microwave
ACEIMPRST	spermatic
ACEIMRSTU	cauterism
	cerastium
ACEIMRTTU	micturate
ACEINNNOR	cannonier
ACEINNNSS	canniness
ACEINNOOV	Novocaine®
ACEINNORS	censorian
ACEINNORT	container
	crenation
	narcotine
ACEINNOSS	△ascension
ACEINNOST	cantonise
ACEINNOTZ	cantonize
ACEINNRRY	inerrancy
ACEINNRSU	insurance
	nuisancer
ACEINNRTU	encurtain
	runcinate
	uncertain
ACEINNRTY	ancientry
ACEINNSST	cantiness
	incessant
ACEINOOST	iso-octane
ACEINOOTV	evocation
ACEINOPRT	recaption
ACEINOPST	stenopaic
ACEINOPTY	cytopenia
ACEINORRT	cinerator
ACEINORRV	carnivore
ACEINORSS	scenarios
ACEINORST	narcotise
ACEINORTT	carnotite
ACEINORTU	cautioner
	Cointreau®
ACEINORTZ	narcotize
ACEINOSST	cessation
ACEINOSTU	tenacious
ACEINOSUV	vinaceous
ACEINPRRY	pericrany
ACEINPRSS	scarpines
ACEINPRTT	crepitant
ACEINPRUY	pecuniary
ACEINPSSU	puissance
ACEINQTTU	quittance
ACEINRSST	scenarist
ACEINRSSZ	craziness
ACEINRSTU	securitan
ACEINRSTY	insectary
ACEINRTTY	certainty
ACEINRTUV	incurvate
ACEINSSSU	sauciness
ACEINSSTT	cattiness
	tacitness
ACEINSTTY	intestacy
ACEIOPRRS	acrospire
ACEIOPRST	patricoes
ACEIOPRSU	auriscope
	parecious
ACEIOPRTV	proactive
ACEIOPSTV	vitascope
ACEIOPTTT	petticoat
ACEIORSST	ostracise
	Socratise
ACEIORSTZ	ostracize
	Socratize
ACEIORSUV	veracious
ACEIOSSTW	coastwise
ACEIPQRTU	practique
ACEIPRRST	practiser
ACEIPRSTT	scarpetti
ACEIPSSTU	spacesuit
ACEIQSTUY	sequacity
ACEIRSTTU	rusticate
ACEIRSUWY	cruiseway
ACEIRTUVV	curvative
ACEISSTTU	suscitate
ACEJKKMOS	smoke-jack
ACEJKKRSY	skyjacker
ACEJLMSUU	majuscule
ACEKKMRRU	muck-raker
ACEKKOSTT	stocktake
ACEKLLMMU	mallemuck
ACEKLLPSS	plackless
ACEKLNSSS	slackness
ACEKLOPRW	workplace
ACEKLORSW	scalework
ACEKLORTW	towel-rack
ACEKLRSST	trackless
ACEKMSTUW	mucksweat
ACEKNNRSS	crankness
ACEKNORSU	cankerous

ACEKORRTW rockwater
ACEKPRSSU sapsucker
ACEKRSTUW awestruck
ACELLLMOU columella
ACELLLNUU Lucullean
ACELLMNOY call-money
ACELLMORS allcomers
ACELLMORU molecular
ACELLMRSW swarm-cell
ACELLMSTU castellum
ACELLNNUY uncleanly
ACELLNOPS pollen-sac
ACELLNORU nucleolar
ACELLNRTY centrally
ACELLNRUY unclearly
ACELLOQUY coequally
ACELLORSS sclerosal
ACELLORST sclerotal
ACELLORSU cellarous
ACELLORSV coveralls
ACELLPSSS scalpless
ACELLRSTU scutellar
ACELLRSUY secularly
ACELLSSSS classless
ACELMMNOS commensal
ACELMMNSU muscleman
ACELMMOSU mamelucos
ACELMNOST calmstone
ACELMNTUU tenaculum
ACELMOPST ectoplasm
ACELMORRU clamourer
ACELMORSS scleromas
ACELMORSU Mucorales
ACELMORSY lacrymose
ACELMOSUU ulmaceous
ACELNNOOR olecranon
ACELNOOSV volcanoes
ACELNOPRV Provençal
ACELNORSU larcenous
ACELNORTU nucleator
recountal
ACELNORTY alectryon
ACELNORUV rounceval
ACELNOSSV vocalness
ACELNOSTU consulate
ACELNOTUU outlaunce
ACELNPRTU crapulent
ACELNPTUY petulancy
ACELNRSUU unsecular
ACELNRTTU reluctant
ACELNTUXY exultancy
ACELOOPRR corporeal
ACELOORTW water-cool
ACELOOSTT coelostat
ACELOPRRU opercular
preocular
ACELOPRTU peculator
ACELOPSTU scopulate
ACELORRST stercoral
ACELORRSU carrousel
ACELORSSU caroluses
ACELOSSTU cassoulet
ACELOSTTY octastyle
ACELOSTUU cautelous
ACELPPRRU curlpaper
ACEMMMSUY mummy-case
ACEMMOTTU commutate
ACEMNNOOY oenomancy
ACEMNNORR corner-man
ACEMNOOPS moonscape
ACEMNOPSS encompass
ACEMNORTU mucronate
ACEMNOSTU caumstone
ACEMOOPSS somascope
ACEMOOPSU pomaceous
ACEMOORSU moraceous
ACEMOOTYZ Mycetozoa
ACEMOPSSS compasses
ACEMORRTY crematory
ACEMORSTU castoreum
ACEMOSSUU musaceous
ACEMOSTVY vasectomy
ACEMPRSUY supremacy
ACENNNORU announcer
ACENNOOPR cornopean
ACENNOOTT connotate
Notonecta
ACENNPTUU nuncupate
ACENNSSST scantness
ACENNSSTU uncessant
ACENOOPRT co-operant
ACENOORST corantoes
ACENOOTTY tycoonate
ACENOPRRT copartner
procreant
ACENOPRST sportance
ACENOPSSW snowscape
ACENOPSTW townscape
ACENOPSTY syncopate
ACENOPTYY cyanotype
ACENOQRTU croquante
ACENORRTU raconteur
ACENORSTU courtesan
nectarous
ACENORSUV cavernous
ACENORTUZ courtezan
ACENOSSST contessas
ACENOSSTT stonecast
ACENOSSTZ scazontes
ACENOSTTU En-Tout-Cas®
ACENOSTUU cutaneous
ACENPRRTY carpentry
ACENPRSUU pursuance
ACENPTTUU punctuate
ACENRRSUY cursenary
ACENRSSSS crassness
ACENRSTUU Centaurus
ACEOOPRRT corporate
ACEOOPRSS ascospore
ACEOORSSU rosaceous
ACEOORTVY evocatory
ACEOPRRTY precatory
ACEOPRSST Sarcoptes
ACEOPRSSY caryopses

ACEOPRSTT	scarpetto
	spectator
ACEORRRTT	retractor
ACEORRRVY	overcarry
ACEORRSTU	craterous
ACEORRTTX	extractor
ACEORSSTW	worst-case
ACEORSTTY	astrocyte
ACEORSTUU	rutaceous
ACEQRSTUU	square-cut
ACERRTUUV	curvature
ACFFGHILN	cliffhang
ACFFGIMNU	MacGuffin
ACFFIILNO	officinal
ACFFIINOT	officiant
ACFFILMOR	falciform
ACFFILORU	Forficula
ACFFIMNPU	muffin-cap
ACFFLOOST	calf's-foot
ACFFLOSTW	cowl-staff
ACFGHILNN	flanching
ACFGHINRT	fratching
ACFGHMORR	frogmarch
ACFGIIMNO	magnifico
ACFGIKLNY	cly-faking
ACFGIKLST	flagstick
ACFGIKNRT	kingcraft
ACFGINORT	factoring
ACFGINRRS	scarf-ring
ACFGINRSU	surfacing
ACFGIOSUU	fugacious
ACFGLNORY	gyrfalcon
ACFGNORST	songcraft
ACFHHHILT	half-hitch
ACFHIILRT	chairlift
ACFHILNOU	faulchion
ACFHILORS	coral-fish
ACFHILPRT	flip-chart
ACFHIMPRS	cramp-fish
ACFHIPRSS	fish-scrap
ACFHKORST	rock-shaft
ACFHLNORW	half-crown
ACFHLORTW	flowchart
ACFHMORSU	forasmuch
ACFIIILMR	mirifical
ACFIIILOR	orificial
ACFIILLNY	finically
ACFIILNOT	fictional
ACFIILOPR	caprifoil
ACFIILRSU	surficial
ACFIILTUV	fluviatic
ACFIIMNOR	aciniform
ACFIINSTU	faunistic
ACFIIOPRV	vaporific
ACFIJKRTU	jack-fruit
ACFIKNRSS	scarfskin
ACFILMNOR	lanciform
ACFILMORU	cauliform
	formulaic
	fumarolic
ACFILMORV	claviform
ACFILNNOR	francolin
ACFILNOOT	olfaction
ACFILNPPY	flippancy
ACFILNRTY	franticly
ACFILNRUU	funicular
ACFILORST	trifocals
ACFIMNORT	formicant
ACFIMOOST	motoscafi
ACFIMOPRR	capriform
ACFIMORRY	formicary
ACFINORRT	infractor
ACFINORTU	furcation
ACFIORSTU	fractious
ACFIORSUU	furacious
ACFKMRRTU	truck-farm
ACFKNORWY	fancywork
ACFKORRTW	craftwork
ACFLLORSS	crossfall
ACFLLORSU	floscular
ACFLLTTUY	tactfully
ACFLMNOOR	conformal
ACFLNTTUU	fluctuant
ACFLOORTY	olfactory
ACFLOSTUU	Foucault's
ACFMOOOST	motoscafo
ACFMOSTTU	factotums
ACFOORRUY	Fourcroya
ACFOOSTUU	autofocus
ACFORTTUY	outcrafty
ACFRRTUUY	fructuary
ACGGGINRS	scragging
ACGGHNNPU	gang-punch
ACGGIIKMN	magicking
ACGGIIOSS	isagogics
ACGGILRSY	scraggily
ACGGINOTT	cottaging
ACGGIOORS	coraggios
ACGHHHIIR	highchair
ACGHHILNT	hatchling
ACGHHILSS	high-class
ACGHHINTT	thatching
ACGHIILNO	chiliagon
ACGHIIMOY	chiyogami
ACGHIIPRT	graphitic
ACGHIKNOV	havocking
ACGHIKNTW	thwacking
ACGHILNNO	long-chain
ACGHILORY	oligarchy
ACGHILPRY	graphicly
ACGHIMMOO	homogamic
ACGHIMOOP	omophagic
ACGHINNOT	gnathonic
ACGHINNST	stanching
ACGHINRTT	night-cart
ACGHLMOOY	logomachy
ACGHLOORY	archology
ACGHMOPRY	cymograph
ACGHMOPYY	mycophagy
ACGHOPSSY	psychogas
ACGHORSTU	roughcast
ACGIIIMST	imagistic
ACGIIKNNP	panicking
ACGIIKNNT	anticking

ACGIIKNRV vraicking
ACGIILLLO illogical
ACGIILLMS △gallicism
ACGIILLNV cavilling
ACGIILLOR cigarillo
ACGIILMNS anglicism
ACGIILNST anglicist
ACGIILRTY gracility
ACGIIMSTT stigmatic
ACGIINNOR inorganic
ACGIINNRT nigricant
ACGIINOST agonistic
ACGIIORST orgiastic
ACGIKNNPU unpacking
ACGILLLOY logically
ACGILLNOR carolling
ACGILLNOU unlogical
ACGILLOOY caliology
ACGILLOST collagist
ACGILMOPY polygamic
ACGILNNST scantling
ACGILNOST gnostical
nostalgic
ACGILNOXY coaxingly
ACGILNPRY carpingly
ACGILNRSW scrawling
ACGIMMNOO monogamic
ACGIMMNRS scramming
ACGIMMORR microgram
ACGIMNNOO cognomina
ACGIMNNOP companing
ACGIMNNOR romancing
ACGIMNOOR agronomic
ACGIMNORR cairngorm
ACGIMNOSS gasconism
ACGIMNOTU contagium
ACGIMNPRR cramp-ring
ACGIMNSTY gymnastic
nystagmic
ACGIMOOPR porogamic
ACGIMOORS sociogram
ACGIMOPRT pictogram
ACGIMOTYZ zygomatic
ACGINNNOT cantoning
ACGINNOOT cognation
contagion
ACGINNOPY canopying
poignancy
ACGINNOST cognisant
ACGINNOTZ cognizant
ACGINOOTY Octogynia
ACGINOPSW coping-saw
ACGINPPRS scrapping
ACGINPTUY pugnacity
ACGIOORSS graciosos
ACGJNNOTU conjugant
ACGJNORRU currajong
ACGKLNORT long-track
ACGKNOORU rock-guano
ACGLLORWY gally-crow
ACGLMOORU colour-mag
ACGLMOORY macrology
ACGLNOOST long-coats
ACGLOOPRY carpology
ACGLOORSY sarcology
ACGLOORTY cartology
ACGLOOSTY scatology
ACGMNNOOR Cro-Magnon
ACGMNORYY gyromancy
ACGMOPRTY cryptogam
ACGNNOOST contangos
ACGNORRUW currawong
ACGORRSUY surrogacy
ACHHIIRST rhachitis
ACHHIKLSS shashlick
ACHHILNOR rhonchial
ACHHILOPT phacolith
ACHHILORT haircloth
ACHHIMRTY arhythmic
ACHHINNOT chthonian
ACHHINOST chainshot
ACHHIORST Tocharish
ACHHIPRSU push-chair
ACHHLLLOT cloth-hall
ACHHLOSTW washcloth
ACHHLPRYY phylarchy
ACHHNORTY Rhynchota
ACHHNRSTY chrysanth
ACHIIKNNP chinkapin
ACHIILMOS isochimal
ACHIILMSW whimsical
ACHIILOTT halitotic
ACHIILRTY chirality
ACHIIMNST machinist
ACHIIMORY chirimoya
ACHIINPSY physician
ACHIINRST Christian
trichinas
ACHIIOPST pistachio
ACHIIPRSV vicarship
ACHIIPRTU upaithric
ACHIIRRTT arthritic
ACHIIRSTT citharist
trachitis
ACHIIRSTV archivist
ACHIJKMST jacksmith
ACHIKKNPT pick-thank
ACHIKKSSW kickshaws
ACHIKLMST mahlstick
ACHIKMMOS Ockhamism
ACHIKMOST Ockhamist
ACHIKNORW chainwork
ACHIKPRUY Puck-hairy
ACHILLLOY allicholy
ACHILLNTY Chantilly
ACHILLOST sailcloth
ACHILMNPY nymphical
ACHILMPTY lymphatic
ACHILNOPT piña-cloth
ACHILNORT antichlor
ACHILNRUY raunchily
ACHILNSTU clianthus
ACHILNSTY snatchily
ACHILOPRT arctophil

ACHILOPTU	patchouli
ACHILORST	choralist
ACHILORTV	archivolt
ACHILORUZ	rhizocaul
ACHILOSST	scholiast
ACHILPSTU	sulphatic
ACHILRSSY	chrysalis
ACHILRSTY	starchily
ACHILSTTY	cattishly
ACHIMMNOS	monachism
ACHIMMORZ	machzorim
ACHIMMOSS	masochism
ACHIMNOPY	hypomanic
ACHIMNORS	harmonics
ACHIMNORT	chromatin
ACHIMNOST	macintosh
	monachist
ACHIMNSTW	switchman
ACHIMOOTX	homotaxic
ACHIMORST	rhotacism
ACHIMORYZ	mycorhiza
ACHIMOSST	masochist
ACHIMOSTU	mustachio
ACHIMRSST	Christmas
ACHIMRSSW	scrimshaw
ACHINNOST	stanchion
ACHINNOTW	Chinatown
ACHINNSTY	synanthic
ACHINOORT	chinaroot
ACHINOPPS	pansophic
ACHINOPRT	anthropic
	rhapontic
ACHINORRU	hurricano
ACHINORST	thrasonic
ACHINPRST	chinstrap
ACHINRSTU	trachinus
ACHINRSTY	strychnia
ACHINRTUY	uncharity
ACHIOOPST	sociopath
ACHIOPPRS	hippocras
ACHIOPRRZ	rhizocarp
ACHIORSTV	tovarisch
ACHIOSSTU	astichous
ACHIPRSUY	haruspicy
ACHIQRRSU	squirarch
ACHKLMNOO	kloochman
ACHKLNOOS	solonchak
ACHKMORTU	touchmark
ACHKNORRW	hornwrack
ACHKOPRTW	patchwork
ACHLLORSY	scholarly
ACHLMNOOS	schoolman
ACHLMORSW	slow-march
ACHLMSTYZ	schmaltzy
ACHLNOTUU	outlaunch
ACHLNSSSU	Anschluss
ACHLNSTUY	staunchly
ACHLOOSTU	△holocaust
ACHLOPRYY	polyarchy
ACHLOPTUY	patchouly
ACHLORTTY	tray-cloth
ACHMMNOOY	monomachy
ACHMNORSU	Roumansch
ACHMNRSTU	truchmans
ACHMOOPRS	promachos
ACHMOORRT	chart-room
ACHNOOPRY	acrophony
ACHNOPSTY	sycophant
ACHOOPSYZ	Scyphozoa
ACHOORSTT	short-coat
ACHOPRSTU	stroupach
ACHOPSTTW	stopwatch
ACHOPSTUY	hypocaust
ACHORTTTU	cut-throat
ACHPRSSUY	chuprassy
ACIIILMST	Islamitic
	Italicism
ACIIILNOS	siciliano
ACIIILNTT	latticini
ACIIIMNST	animistic
ACIIINPPR	principia
ACIIINPST	pianistic
	sincipita
ACIIISSTV	Sivaistic
ACIIJRSTU	justiciar
ACIIKMNRT	Minitrack®
ACIIKNOOZ	Kainozoic
ACIIKPRRT	Prakritic
ACIILLNOS	isoclinal
ACIILLNST	scintilla
ACIILLOPT	political
ACIILMNPU	municipal
ACIILMNSV	Calvinism
ACIILMNTY	militancy
ACIILMOSS	△socialism
ACIILMOSU	malicious
ACIILMQTU	quitclaim
ACIILMRSU	curialism
ACIILNOOT	coalition
ACIILNOPT	plication
ACIILNOSX	clinoaxis
ACIILNOTT	latticino
ACIILNOVV	convivial
ACIILNPPR	principal
ACIILNPST	cisplatin
ACIILNSTV	Calvinist
ACIILOPRT	pictorial
ACIILORST	soritical
ACIILOSST	△socialist
ACIILOSTY	sociality
ACIILOSVV	slivovica
ACIILPRTY	pyritical
ACIILQUZZ	quizzical
ACIILRSTU	curialist
	rusticial
ACIILSTTT	tactilist
ACIILTTTY	tactility
ACIIMMOSS	mosaicism
ACIIMMPST	psammitic
ACIIMNNOS	aniconism
	insomniac
ACIIMNNOT	antimonic
	antinomic
ACIIMNOPT	impaction

ACIIMNORT	mortician
ACIIMNOSU	minacious
ACIIMOPRS	micropsia
ACIIMOPST	simpatico
ACIIMORTT	triatomic
ACIIMOSST	mosaicist
ACIIMOSTT	atomistic
ACIIMOTTY	atomicity
ACIIMPRST	prismatic
ACIIMRSSY	Syriacism
ACIIMRSTY	Myristica
ACIIMSTUV	viaticums
ACIINNORU	Uriconian
ACIINNOST	aniconist
	onanistic
ACIINNOTT	nictation
ACIINNOTU	incaution
ACIINOORT	octonarii
ACIINOOST	sociation
ACIINOPST	panoistic
ACIINORTV	Victorian
ACIINOSTT	actionist
ACIINOTTX	antitoxic
ACIINOTTY	atonicity
ACIINPRTU	puritanic
ACIINPTTY	antitypic
ACIINRRTY	irritancy
ACIIOPRST	psoriatic
ACIIOPRTT	patriotic
ACIIOPTZZ	pizzicato
ACIIORSTZ	zoiatrics
ACIIORSUV	vicarious
ACIIOSSTT	isostatic
ACIIOSUVV	vivacious
ACIIPRSTT	patristic
ACIIPRSTX	piscatrix
ACIIPTTVY	captivity
ACIISSTTT	statistic
ACIJKLOPT	pilot-jack
ACIKKNNOT	antiknock
ACIKKRSTT	kick-start
ACIKLMSTU	maulstick
ACIKLNOOP	plain-cook
ACIKLOSTT	tailstock
ACIKLPSST	slapstick
ACIKNRTTW	twin-track
ACIKOPSSY	skiascopy
ACIKPRSTT	trap-stick
ACILLLNUU	Lucullian
ACILLLRYY	lyrically
ACILLMORT	millocrat
ACILLMRSY	Carlylism
ACILLMSUY	musically
ACILLNNSY	synclinal
ACILLNOOT	collation
ACILLNOTU	clout-nail
ACILLOOQU	colloquia
ACILLOPTY	optically
	topically
ACILLORST	cloistral
ACILLORTV	Victrolla®
	victrolla
ACILLOSTY	callosity
	stoically
ACILLOTXY	toxically
ACILLPTYY	typically
ACILMMOTT	committal
ACILMNNTU	culminant
ACILMNOOS	Salomonic
ACILMNOPT	complaint
	compliant
ACILMNOSV	△volcanism
ACILMNOUY	Alcyonium
ACILMNSUU	unmusical
ACILMNSUV	△vulcanism
ACILMOORS	lacrimoso
ACILMOPRS	comprisal
ACILMORST	crotalism
ACILMORSY	isocrymal
ACILMPTUU	capitulum
ACILMSSTU	simulcast
ACILNNNUY	uncannily
ACILNNOTU	continual
ACILNNQTU	clinquant
ACILNNRUU	ranunculi
ACILNOPRT	prolactin
ACILNOPST	△platonics
ACILNORTT	contralti
ACILNORTY	latrociny
ACILNOSTU	sulcation
ACILNOSTV	△volcanist
ACILNOTTU	luctation
ACILNPTUY	untypical
ACILNRSTU	lincrusta
ACILNSTUV	△vulcanist
ACILNSTYY	syncytial
ACILOOPRS	acropolis
ACILOOPST	△apostolic
ACILOORST	castor-oil
ACILOOSSU	solacious
ACILOPRTY	placitory
ACILOQTUY	loquacity
ACILORRSU	cursorial
ACILORRVY	corivalry
ACILORSSU	ossicular
ACILORSTU	ocularist
	suctorial
ACILOTTUY	autolytic
ACILPPRSY	scrappily
ACILPPSTU	supplicat
ACILPSTTY	styptical
ACILRRTUU	utricular
ACILSSTTY	systaltic
ACIMMNOOT	monatomic
ACIMMNOTY	myomantic
ACIMMORRS	Camorrism
ACIMMORSS	commissar
ACIMNNOOP	companion
ACIMNNOOX	monaxonic
ACIMNNOTY	antonymic
ACIMNOOST	onomastic
ACIMNOOTU	autonomic
ACIMNOOTX	taxonomic
ACIMNOOTZ	zoomantic

ACIMNOPRR	cramp-iron
ACIMNOPRY	parcimony
ACIMNORST	narcotism
ACIMNOSUU	acuminous
ACIMNOSUV	Muscovian
ACIMOPSSY	symposiac
ACIMORRST	Camorrist
ACIMORSST	ostracism
ACIMORSTT	stromatic
ACIMOSTTU	comitatus
ACIMPRSTY	sympatric
ACIMRSTTU	strumatic
ACINNNOOT	connation
ACINNORST	constrain
	transonic
ACINNQSUY	squinancy
ACINNRTUU	uncurtain
ACINOORRS	corrasion
ACINOORST	consortia
	Ostracion
ACINOOSST	iconostas
ACINOPSTU	acupoints
ACINOPSUU	usucapion
ACINORSST	croissant
ACINORSTT	narcotist
	Nostratic
	stratonic
ACINORSTU	suctorian
ACINORSTY	carnosity
ACINORTTU	curtation
	ructation
ACINORTUV	curvation
ACINORTUY	cautionry
ACINOSSSU	saucisson
ACINRSSSU	narcissus
ACINRSSUU	uraniscus
ACIOOPRSU	paroicous
ACIOOPRSZ	saprozoic
ACIOOPRTT	copatriot
ACIOORSTU	atrocious
ACIOORSUV	voracious
ACIOPRSSY	caryopsis
ACIOPRSTT	prostatic
ACIOPRSTY	piscatory
ACIOSSTUU	astucious
ACIPSSTTU	Psittacus
ACIRRSTYZ	stir-crazy
ACIRSSTUY	casuistry
ACJKOPRST	jockstrap
ACJLLORUY	jocularly
ACJLOORTU	joculator
ACKKMNOPY	pockmanky
ACKLLNPSU	knapscull
ACKLLNRTU	trunk-call
ACKLMOOOR	cloakroom
ACKLNORST	cornstalk
ACKLORRWY	warlockry
ACKLORSST	cross-talk
ACKLORSSW	crosswalk
ACKMOORST	stackroom
ACKMOPRRS	crop-marks
ACKMOPRSW	scamp-work
ACKRSTTUY	cutty-sark
ACLLLOSUY	callously
ACLLMNOSU	molluscan
ACLLNOOPT	locoplant
ACLLOOPRT	practolol
ACLLOORRY	corollary
ACLMMNOOW	common-law
ACLMMOTUU	commutual
ACLMNOORU	colourman
	monocular
ACLMOOPST	camp-stool
ACLMOORSS	classroom
ACLMOORSU	clamorous
ACLMOPRTU	palm-court
ACLMOPSTY	cytoplasm
ACLMRSTUU	claustrum
ACLMSSUUV	vasculums
ACLNNORTU	nocturnal
ACLNOORTT	contralto
ACLNOORTU	colourant
ACLNOPSTY	nyctalops
ACLOOORRT	coralroot
ACLOORRTW	coralwort
ACLOORSUU	oraculous
ACLOORUWY	colourway
ACLOPRSTY	pyroclast
ACLOPRSUU	crapulous
ACLOPRTTU	plutocrat
ACLOPRTUY	culpatory
ACLORSUUY	raucously
ACLOSTUUY	Autolycus
ACLOSUUVY	vacuously
ACMMNOORT	commorant
ACMNNOOST	oncostman
ACMNOORRT	cormorant
ACMNOOSTU	cosmonaut
ACMNOPRYY	pyromancy
ACMNOPTTU	computant
ACMORRSUU	macrurous
ACMORSTUY	customary
ACMRSTUUY	custumary
ACNNNOOST	consonant
ACNOOPRRY	procaryon
ACNOOPRST	corposant
ACNOOPRTV	provocant
ACNOORRSU	rancorous
ACNOPRTTU	punctator
ACNORSTTY	contrasty
ACOOPPRRS	sporocarp
ACOOPRRTY	procaryot
ACOOPSTUY	autoscopy
ACOORSSTU	autocross
ACOPRRRTY	parrot-cry
ACORRRSUY	cursorary
ACORRSSTT	star-crost
ACORRSTTU	scrutator
ACOSSTTTY	statocyst
ADDDEEEHR	red-headed
ADDDEEHNR	redhanded
ADDDEEKLS	skedaddle
ADDDEENRU	undreaded
ADDDEERSS	addressed

ADDDEFIIN	dandified
ADDDEGINO	dead-doing
ADDDEGLOP	dog-paddle
ADDDEGMNO	goddamned
ADDDEIINS	disdained
ADDDEIIOP	Dipodidae
ADDDEIIOR	Dorididae
ADDDEIMNO	diamonded
ADDDELNSU	unsaddled
ADDDHMNOO	hodmandod
ADDEEEGRY	degree-day
ADDEEEHRT	hederated
ADDEEELLV	dead-level
ADDEEEMNR	meandered
ADDEEENRR	end-reader
ADDEEEPRT	depredate
ADDEEERRT	retreaded
ADDEEERSS	addressee
ADDEEFFNR	affrended
ADDEEFNNT	defendant
ADDEEFNSS	fadedness
ADDEEFRRU	defrauder
ADDEEGHIP	pigheaded
ADDEEGHRU	rug-headed
ADDEEGILM	middle-age
ADDEEGINN	deadening
ADDEEGJMU	judge-made
ADDEEGLNR	glandered
ADDEEGLNS	sedgeland
ADDEEHHOT	hotheaded
ADDEEHILL	ill-headed
ADDEEHIRR	drerihead
	red-haired
ADDEEHLNP	hen-paddle
ADDEEHMOP	mop-headed
ADDEEHNNO	one-handed
ADDEEHNOT	not-headed
ADDEEHOSU	deadhouse
ADDEEHOTW	tow-headed
	two-headed
ADDEEHRSS	headdress
ADDEEHRTY	dehydrate
ADDEEILRV	dare-devil
ADDEEIMTT	meditated
ADDEEINTY	tie-and-dye
ADDEEIOTX	deoxidate
ADDEEIPRR	draperied
ADDEELMNR	reddleman
ADDEELMNT	addlement
ADDEELNUY	undelayed
ADDEELPPW	dewlapped
ADDEELRSS	dreadless
ADDEEMNNU	unamended
ADDEEMNRU	undreamed
ADDEEMORR	dromedare
ADDEENNPT	dependant
ADDEENORU	Oudenarde
ADDEENOST	stone-dead
ADDEENPRW	deep-drawn
ADDEENSWY	Wednesday
ADDEEOPRS	desperado
ADDEEORTV	overdated
ADDEEPRSS	adpressed
ADDEERRSS	addresser
	readdress
ADDEERSSS	addresses
ADDEFFHNO	offhanded
ADDEFFLOS	offsaddle
ADDEFFPRU	puff-adder
ADDEFIIPT	pedatifid
ADDEFIKLR	darkfield
ADDEFILRW	fieldward
ADDEFINSS	faddiness
ADDEGGINR	degrading
ADDEGGOOT	dog-eat-dog
ADDEGHINR	hag-ridden
ADDEGIITT	digitated
ADDEGIMNN	demanding
	maddening
ADDEGIRRS	disregard
ADDEGLNOT	long-dated
ADDEGLRUY	guardedly
ADDEGNOOR	gadrooned
ADDEGNORW	downgrade
ADDEGNRRU	undergrad
ADDEGNRUU	unguarded
ADDEHHOTY	hydathode
ADDEHIILP	Didelphia
ADDEHINRY	anhydride
ADDEHINSY	hendiadys
ADDEHIRRW	hard-wired
ADDEHIRTW	deid-thraw
ADDEHLNNU	unhandled
ADDEHLRRU	hard-ruled
ADDEHNNRU	underhand
ADDEHNORS	hardnosed
ADDEHNORU	Roundhead
ADDEHNOTW	two-handed
ADDEHTTUY	death-duty
ADDEIIIMT	dimidiate
ADDEIILNX	Dixieland
ADDEIIMNR	air-minded
ADDEIKNPP	kidnapped
ADDEILLNS	landslide
ADDEILMMN	middleman
ADDEILMNO	Domdaniel
ADDEILNNO	dandelion
ADDEILNRU	underlaid
ADDEILNSV	sand-devil
ADDEILPSY	displayed
ADDEILSVY	advisedly
ADDEIMMNN	man-minded
ADDEIMNRU	unadmired
ADDEIMNSY	many-sided
ADDEIMORT	dermatoid
ADDEINNRU	undrained
ADDEINOUV	unavoided
ADDEINPRU	underpaid
ADDEINRTT	dittander
ADDEINRTU	indurated
ADDEINSUV	unadvised
ADDEIRSSU	dissuader
ADDEIRSSW	sidewards
ADDELMMOU	mould-made

ADDELMNRU ruddleman
ADDELNOTU nodulated
ADDELNSUW unswaddle
ADDELNTUU undulated
ADDELNUZZ undazzled
ADDEMORRY dromedary
ADDENNORU unadorned
ADDENNRTU redundant
ADDENNTUU undaunted
ADDENOORT deodorant
ADDENOPTU unadopted
ADDENORUY duodenary
ADDENORVW dove-drawn
ADDENOSTU astounded
ADDENRRUW underdraw
ADDENRRUY Dundreary
ADDENRTWY wet-and-dry
ADDEOORRV drove-road
ADDEOORST door-stead
ADDEORRSS addressor
ADDEORRTW adderwort
ADDEPQRUU quadruped
ADDFIIQRU quadrifid
ADDFILNRT drift-land
ADDFKNNUY dandyfunk
ADDFLLNOO land-flood
ADDGGINRR Gradgrind
ADDGHNORU draghound
ADDGILMNY maddingly
ADDGILNTW twaddling
ADDHHINRT third-hand
ADDHHIOOR hardihood
ADDHIKNSW wind-shak'd
ADDHLOOTU adulthood
ADDHNNORU roundhand
ADDHNORSW sword-hand
ADDIIIOPS aspidioid
ADDIIKMST tsaddikim
ADDIIKMTZ tzaddikim
ADDIIMQST tsaddiqim
ADDIIMQTZ tzaddiqim
ADDINNNOU Dundonian
ADDINORSU diandrous
ADDINRSWW windwards
ADDLLNORY dandy-roll
ADDLMOPTY toddy-palm
ADDLNORST landdrost
ADDNNOPUW up-and-down
ADDNORSWW downwards
ADDRSSTUY Dryasdust
ADEEEEGLY eagle-eyed
ADEEEFHRT feathered
ADEEEFIRR federarie
ADEEEFIRY reaedifye
ADEEEFLLT leafleted
ADEEEFNRR referenda
ADEEEFRTU defeature
ADEEEFRTW feed-water
ADEEEGGRT gadgeteer
ADEEEGLPR pearl-edge
ADEEEGLRV △everglade
leveraged
ADEEEGPRS grapeseed
ADEEEGTTV vegetated
ADEEEHLST sheet-lead
ADEEEHRST heartseed
ADEEEHRTW weathered
ADEEEIIPR Epeiridae
ADEEEILMN madeleine
ADEEEILNT delineate
ADEEEIMRT remediate
ADEEEINRU Uredineae
ADEEEIRSS diaereses
ADEEEKKNW weak-kneed
ADEEEKNSW snakeweed
ADEEELLMN enamelled
ADEEELLNS lease-lend
lend-lease
ADEEELLST teaselled
ADEEELNRV land-reeve
ADEEELNTT dae-nettle
ADEEELPRS seed-pearl
ADEEELPRY pearl-eyed
ADEEELRUV rue-leaved
ADEEEMNTT dementate
ADEEEMOST edematose
ADEEENRRS serenader
ADEEENRST East-ender
ADEEEPPRR paper-reed
ADEEEPRST desperate
ADEEEQRTU détraquée
ADEEERTTU deuterate
ADEEERTWW waterweed
ADEEFFILR fieldfare
ADEEFGGLR reflagged
ADEEFGINN deafening
ADEEFHIRT death-fire
ADEEFHNRS hands-free
ADEEFIISV five-a-side
ADEEFIKRR fire-drake
ADEEFILOR Florideae
ADEEFILOT defoliate
ADEEFILRS feralised
ADEEFILRW weel-faird
ADEEFILRZ feralized
ADEEFILSU feudalise
ADEEFILUZ feudalize
ADEEFIMST defeatism
ADEEFIORT foederati
ADEEFISTT defeatist
ADEEFLLMW well-famed
ADEEFLLST stall-feed
ADEEFLNOS leaf-nosed
ADEEFLORT deflorate
floreated
ADEEFLOTW two-leafed
ADEEFLPRY palfreyed
ADEEFLRTU defaulter
ADEEFLRTW Delftware
ADEEFLRUW weel-faur'd
ADEEFMNOR forenamed
ADEEFMORR reformade
ADEEFNOST stone-deaf
ADEEGGINR gingerade

ADEEGGINS	disengage
ADEEGGIRV	aggrieved
ADEEGGITU	tide-gauge
ADEEGGJLT	jet-lagged
ADEEGGLOT	lodge-gate
ADEEGGMOU	demagogue
ADEEGGNNU	unengaged
ADEEGGOPU	pedagogue
ADEEGGRST	staggered
ADEEGHNNR	greenhand
ADEEGHNOR	negrohead
ADEEGHNRU	ahungered
ADEEGILLR	galleried
ADEEGILNW	wide-angle
ADEEGILOU	idealogue
ADEEGIMOY	Geomyidae
ADEEGINNR	endearing
	engrained
	grenadine
ADEEGINPU	anguipede
ADEEGINRR	grenadier
ADEEGINRT	denigrate
ADEEGINST	designate
ADEEGIUVW	waveguide
ADEEGLLLY	allegedly
ADEEGLLRV	gravelled
ADEEGLNNR	Englander
ADEEGLNOR	long-eared
ADEEGLNOT	elongated
ADEEGLNRY	legendary
ADEEGLOOW	eaglewood
ADEEGLPRU	red-plague
ADEEGLTTU	tegulated
ADEEGMNRR	germander
ADEEGMNRS	gendarmes
ADEEGMNRT	garmented
ADEEGMNTU	augmented
ADEEGMRRU	demurrage
ADEEGNNRS	△greensand
ADEEGNNUV	unavenged
ADEEGNORR	reed-organ
ADEEGNORS	renegados
ADEEGNQRU	drag-queen
ADEEGNRST	estranged
ADEEGNRSU	dungarees
ADEEGORRZ	razor-edge
ADEEGRRSS	reed-grass
ADEEGRSUY	Argus-eyed
ADEEGSTTU	degustate
ADEEHHITW	whitehead
ADEEHHLLT	hell-hated
ADEEHHLSW	dash-wheel
ADEEHHMRY	head-rhyme
ADEEHHNOP	headphone
ADEEHHNPY	hedyphane
ADEEHIKLT	deathlike
ADEEHIKTV	khedivate
ADEEHILNP	hen-paidle
ADEEHILNR	headliner
ADEEHILNS	headlines
ADEEHIMNV	mid-heaven
ADEEHIMOR	Homeridae
ADEEHINOR	rhoeadine
ADEEHINRT	herniated
ADEEHINSS	headiness
ADEEHIRRV	river-head
ADEEHIRTV	rivet-head
ADEEHKLRS	sheldrake
ADEEHLLNS	hanselled
ADEEHLLOS	leasehold
ADEEHLLST	date-shell
ADEEHLMOR	dreamhole
ADEEHLOOS	loosehead
ADEEHLORW	rowel-head
ADEEHLSSS	shadeless
ADEEHLSST	deathless
ADEEHMNOT	methadone
ADEEHMOST	homestead
ADEEHNOST	headstone
ADEEHNPPR	apprehend
ADEEHNRSU	unhearsed
ADEEHNRTU	unearthed
ADEEHORSU	eard-house
ADEEHORSV	overheads
	overshade
ADEEHOSWY	eyeshadow
ADEEHPRSY	sharp-eyed
ADEEHRRTY	rehydrate
ADEEHRSTT	shattered
ADEEHRSTW	draw-sheet
	watershed
ADEEHSTUX	exhausted
ADEEIILRS	idealiser
ADEEIILRZ	idealizer
ADEEIIMMT	immediate
ADEEIIMST	mediatise
ADEEIIMTV	mediative
ADEEIIMTZ	mediatize
ADEEIINRT	Neritidae
ADEEIIPRV	Viperidae
ADEEIIRSS	diaeresis
ADEEIKLPS	spadelike
ADEEILLMW	well-aimed
ADEEILLNT	niellated
ADEEILLSS	idealless
ADEEILMNN	Mendelian
ADEEILMPP	palmipede
ADEEILMPR	epidermal
	impleader
ADEEILMRS	misleader
	misleared
ADEEILMTY	mediately
ADEEILNRT	interdeal
	tail-ender
ADEEILOTT	etiolated
ADEEILPRR	lip-reader
ADEEILPRS	pearlised
ADEEILPRZ	pearlized
ADEEILPSS	displease
ADEEILRRT	irrelated
ADEEILRSV	velarised
ADEEILRVZ	velarized
ADEEILTUY	eudialyte
ADEEILVVY	ivy-leaved

ADEEIMMNR mermaiden
ADEEIMMNS misdemean
ADEEIMMRT dreamtime
ADEEIMNNO menadione
ADEEIMNOS Maeonides
ADEEIMNOU eudemonia
ADEEIMNRR remainder
ADEEIMNST semantide
ADEEIMOPR Meropidae
ADEEIMSST demitasse
ADEEINNOS adenosine
ADEEINNPR panniered
ADEEINPST pedantise
ADEEINPTZ pedantize
ADEEINRSS readiness
ADEEINRTT denitrate
ADEEINRUW unwearied
ADEEINSTT destinate
ADEEINTVV adventive
ADEEIOPRT periodate
ADEEIOPTV videotape
ADEEIORST sorediate
ADEEIPPSS passepied
ADEEIPPST peptidase
ADEEIPRRS draperies
ADEEIPRSV eavesdrip
ADEEIPRTU repudiate
ADEEIPRTV predative
ADEEIPSTW waist-deep
ADEEIRRTW read-write
ADEEIRSTV advertise
ADEEIRSTW waterside
ADEEIRTTT tetradite
ADEEIRTTW tidewater
ADEEIRTTX extradite
ADEEIRTVZ advertize
ADEEISSTT △stateside
steadiest
ADEEISTTW statewide
ADEEITUVX exudative
ADEEJMRSU △mudéjares
ADEEJOPRR jeoparder
ADEEJRSTU Judas-tree
ADEEKLSST seed-stalk
ADEEKLSTY stalk-eyed
ADEEKMNOY Yankeedom
ADEEKMRSS dressmake
ADEEKNNSS nakedness
ADEEKNNUW unwakened
ADEEKNRTU undertake
ADEEKNRUW unwreaked
ADEEKRRST redstreak
ADEELLLRU laurelled
ADEELLMNR mallender
ADEELLMRT martelled
ADEELLMRV marvelled
ADEELLMTU medullate
ADEELLNNP pannelled
ADEELLNRY learnedly
ADEELLORV overalled
ADEELLPPR rappelled
ADEELLRTV travelled
ADEELLRVV varvelled
ADEELLSST tasselled
ADEELLSTT stellated
ADEELLTXY exaltedly
ADEELMMOP melampode
ADEELMMOR melodrame
ADEELMNOP pademelon
ADEELMOPS mole-spade
ADEELMORU remoulade
rémoulade
ADEELMORX exodermal
ADEELMRSS dreamless
ADEELNNRU unlearned
ADEELNORV overladen
ADEELNOST endosteal
ADEELNPST seed-plant
ADEELNPSU unpleased
ADEELNPTU pendulate
unpleated
ADEELNRRS slanderer
ADEELNRRU launderer
ADEELNRSU underseal
ADEELNRTU unaltered
unrelated
ADEELNRUX unrelaxed
ADEELNSSV Valdenses
ADEELNSSW Waldenses
ADEELNSTY slant-eyed
ADEELNTTY day-nettle
ADEELNTUX unexalted
ADEELOPRV overpedal
ADEELORST desolater
ADEELOTVW two-leaved
ADEELPRST plastered
ADEELRRTT red-rattle
ADEELRRTU adulterer
ADEELRSST tradeless
ADEELRSTY steelyard
ADEELRSVY adversely
ADEELRTVY avertedly
ADEEMMNNT amendment
ADEEMMORT dermatome
ADEEMMOXY myxoedema
ADEEMNOPR open-armed
promenade
ADEEMNORT emendator
Notre-Dame
ADEEMNORU demeanour
enamoured
ADEEMNOUY eudaemony
ADEEMNRRU maunderer
ADEEMOORR aerodrome
ADEEMOPRR madrepore
ADEEMORRX xeroderma
ADEEMORTT trematode
ADEEMORUW meadow-rue
ADEEMOSTU edematous
ADEEMPSTU despumate
ADEEMQRRU remarqued
ADEEMRSTW smartweed
ADEENNORR non-reader
ADEENNPRT trepanned

ADEENNQRU	quarenden
ADEENNRTU	underta'en
	undertane
ADEENNTTX	extendant
ADEENOPRT	ponderate
ADEENORSS	road-sense
ADEENORUV	endeavour
ADEENORVY	oven-ready
ADEENOSSU	Soudanese
ADEENPPRU	unpapered
ADEENPRSS	panderess
ADEENPSST	adeptness
ADEENQRRU	quarender
ADEENQSTU	Dantesque
ADEENRRTU	underrate
ADEENRRUW	underwear
ADEENRSTW	newstrade
ADEENRSTY	sedentary
ADEENRSUY	undersaye
ADEENRTTU	untreated
ADEENRTTV	advertent
ADEENRTUV	adventure
ADEENRTUW	unwatered
ADEENSSST	satedness
ADEENSSUY	unessayed
ADEEOOPPR	peraeopod
ADEEOPRSV	eavesdrop
ADEEOPSTT	despotate
ADEEORRRS	rear-dorse
ADEEORRTV	over-trade
ADEEORRTZ	zero-rated
ADEEPQRTU	parqueted
ADEEPRRSU	persuader
ADEEPRRTU	departure
ADEEPRSTU	depasture
ADEEPRSTY	pederasty
ADEEQRRTU	quartered
ADEERRSTV	traversed
ADEERSTTW	wadsetter
ADEERSTYY	yesterday
ADEESSTUU	assuetude
ADEFFIILS	falsified
ADEFFNORS	saffroned
ADEFFNORT	affronted
ADEFGHORT	godfather
ADEFGIIMN	magnified
ADEFGIIRT	gratified
ADEFGILLS	gas-filled
ADEFGILRU	lifeguard
ADEFGINRY	defraying
ADEFGINTT	defatting
ADEFGIRRU	fireguard
ADEFGLNOO	angel-food
ADEFGLOOT	floodgate
ADEFGLRRU	regardful
ADEFHIMST	ham-fisted
ADEFHINRT	threadfin
ADEFHIPSS	spadefish
ADEFHLNOZ	half-dozen
ADEFHLOOR	floorhead
ADEFHLOOS	falsehood
ADEFHLPST	feldspath
ADEFHNORU	unheard-of
ADEFIILMP	amplified
ADEFIILQU	qualified
ADEFIIPRR	rapid-fire
ADEFIISST	satisfied
ADEFIKKLR	frikkadel
ADEFILLSU	fusillade
ADEFILMNS	fieldsman
ADEFILMSU	feudalism
ADEFILNNR	Finlander
ADEFILNNZ	△zinfandel
ADEFILNOR	floridean
ADEFILNOT	deflation
	defoliant
ADEFILNRS	filanders
ADEFILNTY	defiantly
ADEFILORT	floriated
ADEFILSTU	feudalist
ADEFILTUY	feudality
ADEFINNRW	fine-drawn
ADEFINOPR	pinafored
ADEFITTTW	fat-witted
ADEFKNNRU	unfranked
ADEFLLLSU	ladlefuls
ADEFLLMOU	leaf-mould
ADEFLLMSY	damselfly
ADEFLLTUW	waldflute
ADEFLMMOR	malformed
ADEFLOPST	soft-pedal
ADEFLOTTW	twa-lofted
ADEFLPSSU	spadefuls
ADEFLRRUW	rewardful
ADEFLRSTW	leftwards
ADEFMNNTU	fundament
ADEFMOORR	reformado
ADEFMORTT	formatted
ADEFNNOSU	nefandous
ADEFNORRW	forwander
ADEFOOORT	oar-footed
ADEFOOPRR	proofread
ADEFOOTTU	out-of-date
ADEFORRRW	forwarder
ADEFORRTV	overdraft
ADEFORRTW	afterword
ADEFORTUY	feudatory
ADEFPRSTU	turf-spade
ADEFRRSTU	fraudster
ADEGGGIZZ	zigzagged
ADEGGHHIR	high-grade
ADEGGHILN	hang-glide
ADEGGIITZ	dziggetai
ADEGGILNR	langridge
ADEGGINNR	gardening
ADEGGINRR	regarding
ADEGGMNOR	doggerman
ADEGGNORU	groundage
ADEGHHILT	headlight
ADEGHHITT	tight-head
ADEGHINNR	hardening
ADEGHINRS	degarnish
ADEGHINSU	anguished

ADEGHIOPR eidograph
ideograph
ADEGHIRRT Third-Ager
ADEGHIRST sight-read
ADEGHLNOO angelhood
ADEGHLNTY day-length
ADEGHLORS gasholder
ADEGHMORU home-guard
ADEGHNNRU anhungred
ADEGHNOPR hop-garden
ADEGHNOPY endophagy
ADEGHNOST death-song
ADEGHNOUZ gaze-hound
ADEGHRRTU draughter
ADEGIILOS dialogise
ADEGIILOT dialogite
ADEGIILOZ dialogize
ADEGIINNR ingrained
ADEGIINPR diapering
ADEGIKLNV gavelkind
ADEGILLMM gimmalled
ADEGILLMN medalling
ADEGILLNN all-ending
ADEGILLNO glenoidal
ADEGILLNP pedalling
ADEGILLNS signalled
ADEGILLOS gladioles
ADEGILNNU unaligned
ADEGILNOR girandole
negroidal
ADEGILNOS alongside
ADEGILNPS pleadings
ADEGILNRT treadling
triangled
ADEGILNRU gerundial
ADEGILNST desalting
ADEGILNTW delta-wing
ADEGILRVW wildgrave
ADEGILTUV divulgate
ADEGIMNNN demanning
ADEGIMNRS ganderism
semi-grand
ADEGIMNTU magnitude
ADEGIMORV videogram
ADEGIMOST dogmatise
ADEGIMOTZ dogmatize
ADEGIMRRS misregard
ADEGINNRT integrand
ADEGINNRW wandering
ADEGINORS dragonise
grandiose
organised
ADEGINORZ dragonize
organized
ADEGINOSS diagnoses
ADEGINOYZ zygaenoid
ADEGINPRS spreading
ADEGINPRT departing
ADEGINRRS grandsire
ADEGINRRW rewarding
ADEGINSSU gaudiness
ADEGINSTY steadying
ADEGIOPRS posigrade
ADEGIORRS rodgersia
ADEGIORUX aigre-doux
ADEGIOTUU autoguide
ADEGIPRRT partridge
ADEGIRTTU gratitude
ADEGLLNOO gallooned
ADEGLLOPT gold-plate
ADEGLMNOO moon-glade
ADEGLNNTU untangled
ADEGLNOST Gladstone
ADEGLNPUU unplagued
ADEGLOOPY paedology
ADEGLRSSU guardless
ADEGMOPRR deprogram
ADEGNNOPR pendragon
ADEGNNORY androgyne
ADEGNNRSS grandness
ADEGNOORS goosander
ADEGNOPRT godparent
ADEGNORSS dragoness
ADEGNORSU dangerous
ADEGNORTU nature-god
ADEGNOSTW downstage
ADEGNRSSU ungrassed
ADEGOORSY goodyears
ADEGORRTT garrotted
ADEHHIPRS rhaphides
ADEHHLLRS hardshell
ADEHHNOOT thanehood
ADEHHNORY hornyhead
ADEHHORST short-head
ADEHHOTUY youthhead
ADEHIIIPX Xiphiidae
ADEHIIIPZ Ziphiidae
ADEHIIKLV khedivial
ADEHIILLR ill-haired
ADEHIILNP delphinia
ADEHIIMNO Hominidae
ADEHIIMNS maidenish
ADEHIINRU Hirudinea
ADEHIIPRT rhipidate
ADEHIIRRR hairdrier
ADEHIISST diathesis
ADEHIJMNU mujahedin
ADEHIKNPS handspike
ADEHIKNSW windshake
ADEHILLOW lowlihead
ADEHILLST still-head
ADEHILMNS mishandle
ADEHILMOT ethmoidal
ADEHILMRS shield-arm
ADEHILMSY shield-may
ADEHILNOR hodiernal
ADEHILNPR △philander
ADEHILNRR hardliner
ADEHILNST Nithsdale
ADEHILOPX hexaploid
ADEHILOXY oxy-halide
ADEHILRRT trihedral
ADEHILSTU lustihead
ADEHIMNOR rhodamine

ADEHIMNRS	Sanhedrim
ADEHIMNRT	hardiment
ADEHIMOPP	hippodame
ADEHIMOSU	housemaid
ADEHIMPRS	Sephardim
ADEHIMPSS	misshaped
ADEHIMRTY	diathermy
ADEHINNRS	Sanhedrin
ADEHINNSS	handiness
ADEHINOPU	audiphone
ADEHINORS	rhodanise
	Rhodesian
ADEHINORZ	rhodanize
ADEHINOSS	adhesions
ADEHINPRS	insphear'd
ADEHINPRT	printhead
ADEHINRSS	hardiness
ADEHINRST	interdash
	tarnished
ADEHINRTY	anhydrite
ADEHINRYZ	hydrazine
ADEHINSSS	shadiness
ADEHIOPRT	atrophied
ADEHIPPRS	sapphired
ADEHIPRST	therapsid
ADEHIPRSY	Syrphidae
ADEHIPSUU	euphausid
ADEHIRRRY	hairdryer
ADEHIRRTT	third-rate
ADEHIRSTW	dishwater
ADEHIRSVW	hivewards
ADEHIRSVY	yravished
ADEHISSTY	dysthesia
ADEHJLLOY	jollyhead
ADEHJLOSU	Judas-hole
ADEHKNNTU	unthanked
ADEHKNOSW	hawk-nosed
	shakedown
ADEHKORSU	dark-house
ADEHLLNOR	Hollander
ADEHLLNSS	shell-sand
ADEHLLORT	death-roll
ADEHLLOTY	tally-hoed
ADEHLLRSW	hellwards
ADEHLNOTW	handtowel
ADEHLOPRY	polyhedra
ADEHMMOTU	mouth-made
ADEHMOOPS	shampooed
ADEHMOPRY	hypoderma
ADEHMORSW	homewards
ADEHNNOST	stonehand
ADEHNNTUU	unhaunted
ADEHNOOPV	Vodaphone
ADEHNORST	stone-hard
ADEHNORTW	two-hander
ADEHNORVY	hydrovane
ADEHNPRSS	hand-press
ADEHNPRSU	urn-shaped
ADEHOOPRT	Theropoda
ADEHOORSU	roadhouse
ADEHOORTW	heartwood
ADEHOOSTT	statehood
ADEHOPPPY	poppy-head
ADEHOPPTY	heptapody
ADEHORRSW	shoreward
ADEHORRSY	dray-horse
ADEHORSUY	dayr'house
ADEHOSTUW	washed-out
ADEHTUVYY	heavy-duty
ADEIIILNT	initialed
ADEIIINNS	Indianise
ADEIIINNZ	Indianize
ADEIIINPR	peridinia
ADEIIINTT	dietitian
ADEIILLMS	misallied
ADEIILMNN	Mindelian
ADEIILMNV	vindemial
ADEIILMOZ	imidazole
ADEIILMTY	Mytilidae
ADEIILNPT	pintailed
ADEIILNRT	deliriant
	drain-tile
ADEIILNRU	uredinial
ADEIILNST	disentail
ADEIILOOR	Oriolidae
ADEIILOPS	apsidiole
	episodial
ADEIILORT	editorial
ADEIILPPP	Pedipalpi
ADEIILPRS	presidial
ADEIILPTU	Tipulidae
ADEIILPTX	pixilated
ADEIILQTU	liquidate
	qualitied
ADEIILRSU	Siluridae
ADEIILSVY	Sylviidae
ADEIIMNOT	mediation
ADEIIMNRZ	zemindari
ADEIIMOTT	diatomite
ADEIIMRTX	mediatrix
ADEIIMSSV	admissive
	misadvise
	misavised
ADEIINNOU	Unionidae
ADEIINORR	ordinaire
ADEIINOTV	deviation
ADEIINPPR	drainpipe
ADEIINPRS	Pindarise
ADEIINPRZ	Pindarize
ADEIINRVV	vivandier
ADEIINSTU	indusiate
ADEIINTUV	induviate
ADEIIPRRS	disrepair
ADEIIPRSS	dispraise
ADEIIPSST	dissipate
ADEIIPSSY	diapyesis
ADEIIRSST	Aristides
ADEIIRSTT	disattire
	distraite
ADEIIRTTV	traditive
ADEIISUXZ	diazeuxis
ADEIJLOSU	jalousied
ADEIKKSST	kidstakes
ADEIKLNPU	plaid-neuk

ADEIKMORS kaiserdom
ADEIKNNNP pen-and-ink
ADEIKNPPR kidnapper
ADEIKNPRS spikenard
ADEIKNPRT predikant
ADEIKNRRR rank-rider
ADEIKRSTW water-ski'd
ADEILLLMO lamelloid
ADEILLMNN ill-manned
ADEILLMNO medallion
ADEILLMOT metalloid
ADEILLMRT treadmill
ADEILLMST medallist
ADEILLNST installed
ADEILLPRU preludial
ADEILLPSY Psyllidae
ADEILLQRU quadrille
ADEILLRTW dill-water
ADEILMNNO mandoline
ADEILMNOV movieland
ADEILMNRT tramlined
ADEILMNST dismantle
ADEILMNTU datum-line
dentalium
ADEILMOPT diplomate
ADEILMOPY polyamide
ADEILMORR mail-order
ADEILMPTU amplitude
ADEILMSTU simulated
ADEILMTTU mutilated
ADEILNNPU unplained
ADEILNNRU underlain
ADEILNOPP panoplied
ADEILNOPS delapsion
ADEILNOPT planetoid
ADEILNOPU aneuploid
ADEILNPPU unapplied
ADEILNPRU Paludrine®
ADEILNPSU unpalsied
ADEILNPTU unplaited
ADEILNRRT interlard
ADEILNRSY synedrial
ADEILNRTT tridental
ADEILNRTU uitlander
ADEILNRUY unreadily
ADEILNSSV validness
ADEILOPRS polarised
ADEILOPRT depilator
ADEILOPRZ polarized
ADEILOPSU lapideous
ADEILOQSU odalisque
ADEILORST estradiol
ADEILORVY olive-yard
ADEILPRSS dispersal
ADEILPRSY displayer
ADEILPSSS sapidless
ADEILPTTU platitude
ADEILRSXY Xyridales
ADEILRTTU rutilated
ADEILRTVV trivalved
ADEILSSTU lassitude
ADEILSTTU altitudes
ADEIMMRST midstream
ADEIMNNTU indumenta
ADEIMNOPR meropidan
ADEIMNOPT ademption
ADEIMNORS masonried
randomise
ADEIMNORZ randomize
ADEIMNOSS mid-season
ADEIMNOST staminode
ADEIMNPRR reprimand
ADEIMNPRS panderism
spiderman
ADEIMNPRU drepanium
ADEIMNPST pedantism
ADEIMNRRU murrained
unmarried
ADEIMNRSU nursemaid
ADEIMNRTY dynamiter
ADEIMNRYZ zemindary
ADEIMOPST impastoed
ADEIMORTT trematoid
ADEIMORTY mediatory
ADEIMPRST red-tapism
spermatid
ADEIMPRSY pyramides
ADEIMRTTU diatretum
ADEIMRTUX admixture
ADEIMRTXY taxidermy
ADEINNNPS inspanned
ADEINNNTT intendant
ADEINNOTT dentation
ADEINNPTU unpainted
ADEINNRTU untrained
ADEINNSSS sandiness
ADEINNSTU unstained
ADEINNTTU untainted
ADEINOOPS poinadoes
ADEINOPPT appointed
ADEINOPRR preordain
ADEINOPRT predation
ADEINOPSS passioned
ADEINOPST △antipodes
ADEINORRS serranoid
ADEINORSU deinosaur
ADEINORTY arytenoid
ADEINORUZ Zonuridae
ADEINOTUX exudation
ADEINPPRS sandpiper
ADEINPPST standpipe
ADEINPRSS rapidness
ADEINPRSU unpraised
ADEINPRTT trepidant
ADEINPSSS sapidness
ADEINPSSV vapidness
ADEINRRSV river-sand
ADEINRRWW wiredrawn
ADEINRSST tardiness
ADEINRSTU Sturnidae
ADEINRTTU unattired
ADEINSSST staidness
ADEINSSTU sustained
ADEINSTTU disattune

ADEINSTTV Adventist
ADEIOPRSU deiparous
ADEIOPRSV privadoes
ADEIOPRTT dioptrate
ADEIOPRTZ trapezoid
ADEIORSTT storiated
ADEIORTVY deviatory
ADEIPPRSU dispauper
ADEIPPSSY dyspepsia
ADEIPRRSU perradius
ADEIPRSTT red-tapist
ADEIPRTVY depravity
ADEIPSSTU stapedius
ADEIPSSUX pseudaxis
ADEIRRSUY residuary
ADEIRSSTU auditress
ADEIRSTVY adversity
ADEISTTUV vastitude
vedutista
ADEKLNNPU unplanked
ADEKLNOSY ankylosed
ADEKMNNOY donkey-man
ADEKMOQRU Quakerdom
ADEKNOOSW snakewood
ADEKNSTUU eduskunta
ADEKOPRSW spadework
ADELLLOWY allowedly
ADELLMRUY medullary
ADELLNOPR landloper
land-loper
ADELLNORW △lowlander
ADELLNOUY unalloyed
ADELLNTUU lunulated
ADELLOORW low-loader
ADELLOPRT patrolled
ADELLRRWY dry-waller
ADELLRTXY dextrally
ADELMNNUY mundanely
ADELMNOPS endoplasm
ADELMNOPY padymelon
ADELMORSU asmoulder
ADELMSSUY assumedly
ADELNNNPU unplanned
ADELNNNPY pennyland
ADELNNORW landowner
ADELNNPTU unplanted
ADELNOOST loadstone
ADELNOPSY dyspnoeal
ADELNORRV Land-Rover®
ADELNORTU outlander
ADELNORUY roundelay
ADELNPRUY underplay
ADELNRSSU laundress
ADELNRTVY verdantly
ADELNSSTU dauntless
ADELNSTUU unsaluted
ADELOOOSW aloes-wood
ADELOOPRT door-plate
ADELOORST desolator
ADELOPTUY played-out
ADELOSTUY autolysed
ADELOTUYZ autolyzed
ADELPQRUU quadruple
ADELPRSSY sparsedly
ADELRRSTY drysalter
ADELRSSUY assuredly
ADELSTTTW Weltstadt
ADEMMNOPP mappemond
ADEMMORST masterdom
ADEMNNORT adornment
ADEMNNRUU unmanured
ADEMNORSU meandrous
ADEMNPSTU unstamped
ADEMNRRSU snare-drum
ADEMNRTUU unmatured
ADEMNSSUU unassumed
ADEMOORRT moderator
ADEMOORST astrodome
ADEMOORSY doomsayer
mooseyard
ADEMORRSW Romewards
ADEMOSTTW two-masted
ADENNNSTU suntanned
ADENNOSST △sandstone
ADENNOSTY asyndeton
ADENNSSTW news-stand
ADENOORST tornadoes
ADENOORTT detonator
ADENOOSTT toadstone
ADENOOTWZ zante-wood
ADENOOWWX woodwaxen
ADENOPPTY pentapody
ADENOPRSU panderous
ADENOPRTV davenport
ADENOPRUV up-and-over
ADENOPSTW paste-down
ADENOQRSU squadrone
ADENORRUY year-round
ADENORRUZ unrazored
ADENORSTV overstand
ADENORTTU rotundate
ADENOTTWY wyandotte
ADENPRRTU underpart
ADENPRSSU underpass
ADENQRSUU unsquared
ADENRRSTW sternward
ADENRRTUY day-return
ADENRSSUU unassured
ADEOOPPRT Pteropoda
ADEOPPRTT tappet-rod
ADEOPRRTU depurator
ADEOPRRTW top-drawer
ADEOPRRTY predatory
ADEOPRSTU outspread
ADEOPRTTW two-parted
ADEOPRTTY tetrapody
ADEOQRTTU torquated
ADEORRSTT rostrated
ADEORRSWW swear-word
ADEORRTUV advoutrer
ADERRSTWY stewardry
ADERSSTWW westwards
ADFFFFRUU ruff-a-duff
ADFFGIIOR giraffoid

ADFFIIMRS	disaffirm
ADFFILNTU	find-fault
ADFGILNOU	fungoidal
ADFGINORS	sangfroid
ADFGLNORY	dragonfly
ADFGOORRU	roof-guard
ADFHINRST	first-hand
ADFHIOORY	fairyhood
ADFHLNOPU	half-pound
ADFHLNORU	half-round
ADFHLOORY	foolhardy
ADFHLORSW	half-sword
ADFIILNOT	latifondi
ADFIILOOP	filopodia
ADFIILRST	drift-sail
ADFILMNOS	manifolds
ADFILMSUY	dismayful
ADFINOORX	Oxfordian
ADFINORSZ	sforzandi
ADFINRRTU	turf-drain
ADFIORSUV	disfavour
ADFIRRSTT	stardrift
ADFKLMOOR	floodmark
ADFLLLOOW	floodwall
ADFLLOOST	faldstool
ADFLORRWY	forwardly
	frowardly
ADFMOOPPR	damp-proof
ADFNOORSZ	sforzando
ADFNORRTW	frontward
ADGGGHOSY	shaggy-dog
ADGGILNRY	niggardly
ADGGILRSY	Yggdrasil
ADGHHILNS	Highlands
ADGHHINRT	right-hand
ADGHHOOPR	hodograph
ADGHIIMNS	Gandhi-ism
ADGHIIOPR	idiograph
ADGHIKOOW	gawkihood
ADGHILLLU	guildhall
ADGHILNSY	dashingly
ADGHIMNOR	harmdoing
ADGHINOOT	gianthood
ADGHINORS	dragonish
ADGHINOSW	shadowing
ADGHINPRS	handgrips
ADGHINRTU	indraught
ADGHINRTW	nightward
ADGHIPRSU	guardship
	guard-ship
ADGHIRRTW	rightward
ADGHNORSU	ground-ash
ADGHNOSTU	staghound
ADGHORRUW	rough-draw
ADGHORTUX	draught-ox
ADGHPRTUU	up-draught
ADGIIILNT	digitalin
ADGIIILST	digitalis
ADGIIJNNO	adjoining
ADGIILMOS	sigmoidal
ADGIILNSS	glissandi
ADGIILOST	dialogist
ADGIIMNNR	manriding
ADGIIMNRS	disarming
ADGIIMNSY	dismaying
ADGIIMNTT	admitting
ADGIINNNT	indignant
ADGIINORT	granitoid
ADGIINOSS	diagnosis
ADGIINRTY	dignitary
ADGIINSSV	dissaving
ADGIIRTVY	gravidity
ADGIKLLMN	milk-gland
ADGIKLNRS	darklings
ADGILLNUY	languidly
ADGILLOSU	gladiolus
ADGILMNSU	guildsman
ADGILNNOU	unloading
ADGILNNST	Landsting
ADGILNORY	adoringly
ADGILNOSS	glissando
ADGILNPRS	springald
ADGILNRTY	dartingly
ADGILOORY	radiology
ADGILOOUY	audiology
ADGIMMOST	dogmatism
ADGIMNNOS	Mandingos
ADGIMNORS	dragonism
ADGIMOSTT	dogmatist
ADGINNNUW	undawning
ADGINNOOU	iguanodon
ADGINNOPR	pardoning
ADGINNRST	ringstand
ADGINOPRY	parodying
ADGINPRSY	dayspring
ADGLMNOOS	dog-salmon
ADGLNOORY	andrology
ADGLNOOTY	odontalgy
ADGMNNORU	groundman
ADGMOOPRS	spodogram
ADGMOORRU	guardroom
ADGMOORTY	dogmatory
ADGNNORYY	androgyny
ADGOOPRST	gastropod
ADGOOPRSU	podagrous
ADHHIMOPR	rhamphoid
ADHHNOORU	hoarhound
ADHHNOOTT	hot-and-hot
ADHHNORST	shorthand
ADHHOPRSS	sharp-shod
ADHIIJMNU	mujahidin
ADHIIKLNR	drink-hail
ADHIILLOT	lithoidal
ADHIILOPU	audiophil
ADHIILOPX	xiphoidal
ADHIILORZ	rhizoidal
ADHIILPRS	lairdship
ADHIIMMRS	Midrashim
ADHIIMPSS	amidships
ADHIIMSSS	Hassidism
ADHIIOPSU	aphidious
ADHIIPSSY	diaphysis
ADHIKLPSS	skaldship
ADHIKMNNU	humankind

ADHIKNORW	handiwork
ADHILLOSW	dishallow
ADHILMNPY	nymphalid
ADHILMOOP	omphaloid
ADHILNNUY	unhandily
ADHILNOPY	hypnoidal
ADHILNPSU	uplandish
ADHILOPTY	typhoidal
ADHIMNOSY	Mondayish
ADHIMNRST	thirdsman
ADHIMSTYY	dysthymia
ADHINNRTU	hit-and-run
ADHINOORT	radiothon
ADHINOOST	sainthood
ADHINOPSY	dysphonia
ADHINORTY	hydration
ADHINRTWW	withdrawn
ADHINSTTW	withstand
ADHIOOPRZ	Rhizopoda
ADHIOPRSY	dysphoria
ADHISTWWY	widthways
ADHKNORWY	handywork
ADHLLMORT	thralldom
ADHLMNOUY	lyam-hound
ADHLNNORT	northland
ADHLNOSTU	southland
ADHMNOOOW	womanhood
ADHMOORSY	hydrosoma
ADHNNRSTU	handsturn
ADHNOORYZ	hydrozoan
ADHNORRTW	northward
ADHNORSUY	anhydrous
ADHNORTUY	hydronaut
ADHNOSSTU	thousands
ADHOOPRRT	arthropod
ADHORSTTY	hydrostat
ADHORSTUW	southward
ADIIIMPRS	diapirism
ADIIINNST	Indianist
ADIIINORS	Isidorian
ADIIINOSZ	isoniazid
ADIIIOSSX	ixodiasis
ADIIJKSST	disjaskit
ADIIKKRRY	kirkyaird
ADIILLNTU	lunitidal
ADIILLNVY	invalidly
ADIILLOPS	spadillio
ADIILLPTY	pallidity
ADIILMNNO	mandilion
ADIILMOPS	idioplasm
ADIILMPVY	impavidly
ADIILMSSS	dismissal
ADIILMSTY	dismality
ADIILNOPT	platinoid
ADIILNOPU	nauplioid
ADIILNOQU	quinoidal
ADIILOORV	varioloid
ADIILOPRS	sporidial
ADIIMNOSS	admission
ADIIMNOST	staminoid
ADIIMNOUZ	diazonium
ADIIMNPRS	Pindarism
ADIIMNRSW	Darwinism
ADIIMOSTT	diatomist
ADIIMRSSY	mydriasis
ADIINNOST	disanoint
ADIINNOSY	Dionysian
ADIINOOTX	oxidation
ADIINOQTU	quotidian
ADIINORTT	△tradition
ADIINORTV	divinator
ADIINOSST	soi-disant
	stasidion
ADIINPRST	Pindarist
ADIINRSTT	distraint
ADIINRSTU	saturniid
ADIINRSTW	Darwinist
ADIIOPSTY	adiposity
ADIIPRSTY	disparity
ADIISSTUY	assiduity
ADIISTTVY	vastidity
ADIJKSSSU	Judas-kiss
ADIJMOPSU	Poujadism
ADIJOPSTU	Poujadist
ADIKLMNRS	alms-drink
ADIKMNNOW	womankind
ADILLLPSU	spauld-ill
ADILLMNOO	almond-oil
ADILLNOPT	land-pilot
ADILLNOPU	planuloid
ADILLNRUY	diurnally
ADILLOPTW	tallow-dip
ADILLORRX	rix-dollar
ADILLQSUY	squalidly
ADILMNNOY	△mandylion
ADILMNOOS	salmonoid
ADILMNOST	△daltonism
ADILMNRUU	Duralumin®
	duralumin
ADILMOPSY	sympodial
ADILMRUUV	duumviral
ADILMSTTU	Talmudist
ADILNNNOO	Londonian
ADILNOOST	isodontal
ADILNRTUU	diuturnal
ADILNSTTY	distantly
ADILOOPRS	prosodial
ADILOPRSV	disproval
ADILORSTW	sword-tail
ADIMNNTUY	mundanity
ADIMNOORT	admonitor
	dominator
ADIMNOPRY	pyramidon
ADIMNOSTY	staminody
ADIMOOQSU	Quasimodo
ADIMORTTX	dot-matrix
ADIMORTUW	moudiwart
ADIMORTWW	mowdiwart
ADINNORTW	down-train
ADINNOSST	dissonant
ADINNPRTU	tip-and-run
ADINOOPRS	prosodian
ADINOOSTT	odonatist
ADINOOSTW	satinwood

ADINOPSTY	dystopian
ADINORSTW	downstair
ADINPSTTU	disputant
ADIOOPSTU	adoptious
ADIORRSTT	traditors
ADIOSSSUU	assiduous
ADIPSSUYY	upsy-daisy
ADJMMOOOR	major-domo
ADJMMORRU	drum-major
ADKNORRTU	trunk-road
ADKOORRSW	roadworks
ADLLLORRY	Lollardry
ADLLNOSTU	Lotus-land
ADLLOPRWY	play-world
ADLMNORTY	mordantly
ADLMNRSTU	Landsturm
ADLMOOPRR	prodromal
ADLMOORTU	modulator
ADLMOPRUW	mouldwarp
ADLNOPRYY	polyandry
ADLOOOSTT	toadstool
ADLOPRSWY	swordplay
ADLORSUUY	arduously
ADLORTUWY	outwardly
ADLPQRUUY	quadruply
ADMMORRTY	martyrdom
ADMNNORSU	roundsman
ADMNNOSSY	synodsman
ADMNOOOST	odontomas
ADMNOORSZ	smorzando
ADMNOORTY	dynamotor
ADMNOOSUV	novodamus
ADMNORSST	sandstorm
ADMNORSSW	swordsman
ADMOOPPRU	pompadour
ADNNOOOTT	Notodonta
ADNNORRUU	runaround
ADNNOSSWW	swansdown
	swans-down
ADNOOTTUU	out-and-out
ADNOPRRTY	protandry
ADNOPRRUW	wrapround
ADNOPSSTU	sandspout
ADOOORRWW	arrowwood
ADOPRRTUY	pourtrayd
AEEEEHMPR	ephemerae
AEEEELRTV	re-elevate
AEEEEPPSW	peaseweep
AEEEETTTT	tête-à-tête
AEEEFGLNR	leaf-green
AEEEFGLRT	telferage
AEEEFGNRR	free-range
AEEEFHLLN	fellaheen
AEEEFHRRT	heart-free
	hereafter
AEEEFHRTV	fever-heat
AEEEFIRRT	fire-eater
AEEEFLMRT	flame-tree
AEEEFLMRZ	ramfeezle
AEEEFNNST	Fasten-e'en
AEEEFSTTT	estafette
AEEEGGGNR	greengage
AEEEGGILR	gier-eagle
AEEEGGNNR	engrenage
AEEEGGNPR	pre-engage
AEEEGGNRS	sage-green
AEEEGGRST	segregate
AEEEGHLRW	gearwheel
AEEEGHPRT	page-three
AEEEGIMNR	menagerie
AEEEGINTX	exigeante
AEEEGLLNV	vellenage
AEEEGLNOP	Paleogene
AEEEGLRRV	gear-lever
AEEEGLRTT	letter-gae
AEEEGLSTW	sweet-gale
AEEEGMNNP	empennage
AEEEGMNRT	agreement
	égarement
AEEEGNRRT	étrangère
AEEEGNRSS	eagerness
AEEEGPRRT	grapetree
AEEEGRRRT	garreteer
AEEEGRRTT	targeteer
AEEEGRSTT	streetage
AEEEGRTTZ	gazetteer
AEEEGRTUZ	gauze-tree
AEEEHHNST	ensheathe
AEEEHKNRR	hearkener
AEEEHLLMN	mallee-hen
AEEEHLMPR	ephemeral
AEEEHMNST	mane-sheet
AEEEHMPRS	ephemeras
AEEEHMRTX	hexameter
AEEEHNNRT	enhearten
AEEEHNRTW	enwreathe
AEEEHRRRS	rehearser
AEEEHRSTT	tearsheet
AEEEILLOT	elaeolite
AEEEILRTT	elaterite
AEEEIMNRX	re-examine
AEEEIPPRT	papeterie
AEEEIRRTT	reiterate
AEEEKMRRT	△marketeer
	tee-marker
AEEEKNRST	tree-snake
AEEEKNRTT	entertake
AEEELLMNR	enameller
AEEELLMNT	elemental
AEEELLRST	teaseller
AEEELLRSW	weaseller
AEEELLSST	tessellae
AEEELMPTT	metapelet
AEEELMSTW	sweetmeal
AEEELNNPP	peneplane
AEEELNPRT	plane-tree
AEEELPPRT	apple-tree
AEEELPTTU	epaulette
AEEEMMNST	semanteme
AEEEMNNRT	nemertean
AEEEMNRST	erasement
AEEEMNRTU	enumerate
AEEEMORRT	aerometer
	areometer

AEEEMPRTT	temperate
AEEEMRRSU	remeasure
AEEEMRTVW	wavemeter
AEEEMSTTW	sweetmeat
AEEENNPRT	perennate
AEEENOPVW	open-weave
AEEENORTX	exonerate
AEEENPRTT	penetrate
AEEENPRTU	Euterpean
AEEENRRST	easterner
AEEENRRTW	treenware
AEEENRTTV	eventrate
AEEENTTUV	eventuate
AEEENTTUX	extenuate
AEEEQRSTU	tee-square
AEEERSTTW	Teeswater
AEEESSTTY	essayette
AEEFFFMUW	fee-faw-fum
AEEFFILRT	after-life
AEEFFNORT	affrontee
	affrontée
AEEFFRSTT	staff-tree
AEEFGILMS	self-image
AEEFGILPR	pilferage
AEEFGINRS	far-seeing
AEEFGIRRT	fire-grate
AEEFGLLOT	flageolet
AEEFGLMOR	foregleam
AEEFGLNUV	avengeful
AEEFGLORV	gaol-fever
AEEFGLORW	flowerage
AEEFGLSTW	sweet-flag
AEEFGORRT	frog-eater
AEEFGORST	forestage
	fosterage
AEEFGRRSU	sugar-free
AEEFHIRSS	sea-fisher
AEEFHLMST	flesh-meat
AEEFHLRTT	heartfelt
AEEFIJLRV	jail-fever
AEEFILNRT	interleaf
AEEFILNSS	leafiness
AEEFILOTX	exfoliate
AEEFILPPR	paper-file
AEEFILPPW	apple-wife
AEEFILRST	reistafel
AEEFILRSV	life-saver
AEEFILRWY	life-weary
AEEFIMMRT	timeframe
AEEFIMORT	aforetime
AEEFIMRTT	aftertime
AEEFINSTT	festinate
AEEFINSTX	antefixes
AEEFIRRTW	fire-water
AEEFIRSTT	feast-rite
AEEFIRSTW	wasterife
AEEFKLOVW	folk-weave
AEEFKOPRS	forespeak
AEEFLLMSS	flameless
AEEFLLNNW	new-fallen
AEEFLLOOS	loose-leaf
AEEFLNRST	fenestral
AEEFLNSSS	falseness
AEEFLORST	foresteal
AEEFLOSTV	love-feast
AEEFLRRTT	flatterer
AEEFLRTUW	weel-faurt
AEEFLRTUY	featurely
AEEFMNNRU	unfreeman
AEEFMNORS	△freemason
AEEFMNORW	freewoman
AEEFMRRSS	farmeress
AEEFNNORT	foreanent
AEEFOPRRT	perforate
AEEFORSTT	foretaste
AEEFPRSSU	supersafe
AEEFPRSTU	perfusate
AEEGGILNO	galiongee
AEEGGINRR	gregarine
AEEGGLNOY	genealogy
AEEGGMORT	mortgagee
AEEGGORRT	toeragger
AEEGGRRST	staggerer
AEEGGRRSW	swaggerer
AEEGHIMRT	hermitage
AEEGHINRR	rehearing
AEEGHINRS	garnishee
AEEGHLORU	auger-hole
AEEGHLOST	segholate
AEEGHLPRT	telegraph
AEEGHMNOP	megaphone
AEEGHMRTZ	megahertz
AEEGHNRSW	greenwash
AEEGHNRSY	ashen-grey
AEEGHOSTU	gatehouse
AEEGIILNS	genialise
AEEGIILNZ	genialize
AEEGIIMNR	gaminerie
AEEGIINNR	air-engine
AEEGILLMS	misallege
AEEGILLNS	all-seeing
AEEGILLNV	villenage
AEEGILLRT	treillage
AEEGILLRV	villagree
AEEGILLST	legislate
AEEGILMMR	mailmerge
AEEGILMNN	malengine
	meningeal
AEEGILMNR	greenmail
AEEGILMNS	semiangle
AEEGILMSS	imageless
AEEGILNNT	eglantine
	inelegant
AEEGILNNV	leavening
AEEGILNRV	revealing
AEEGILNST	anglesite
	teaseling
AEEGILNSW	anglewise
AEEGILRTU	gauleiter
AEEGIMMTV	gemmative
AEEGIMNNN	engine-man
AEEGIMNRS	Germanise
AEEGIMNRT	germinate
AEEGIMNRZ	Germanize

AEEGIMNSS gessamine
AEEGIMNST magnesite
magnetise
AEEGIMNTT magnetite
AEEGIMNTZ magnetize
AEEGIMOST isogamete
AEEGIMPTT pegmatite
AEEGIMRRT remigrate
AEEGIMRTU mugearite
AEEGINNRR engrainer
AEEGINNRT △argentine
△tangerine
AEEGINNYZ zygaenine
AEEGINOPP pigeon-pea
AEEGINOPS espionage
AEEGINOTT negotiate
AEEGINPRT interpage
pignerate
repeating
AEEGINPRV grapevine
AEEGINRST stingaree
AEEGINRTT argentite
integrate
AEEGINRTW Wagnerite
AEEGINSTU sautéeing
AEEGIOPSU epigaeous
AEEGIQRSU squireage
AEEGISTTV gestative
AEEGJLMOU megajoule
AEEGJNORR jargoneer
AEEGLLNOR organelle
AEEGLLNRY generally
AEEGLLNTY elegantly
AEEGLMNNT gentleman
AEEGLMNRY germanely
AEEGLMNST segmental
AEEGLMNTT tegmental
AEEGLMOOS mesogloea
AEEGLMORT glomerate
AEEGLNNOS Angelenos
AEEGLNNPT pentangle
AEEGLNOPS espagnole
AEEGLNORS sloganeer
AEEGLNRSS angerless
largeness
AEEGLNTTU languette
AEEGLOPRT petrolage
AEEGLORVZ overglaze
AEEGLPRRY pearl-grey
AEEGLPRSS grapeless
AEEGLRSSV graveless
AEEGLRSTY slate-grey
steel-gray
AEEGMNNRU ungermane
AEEGMNOTY gate-money
AEEGMNRRS merganser
AEEGMNRST agréments
AEEGMNRTU augmenter
AEEGMOOTZ zoogamete
AEEGMOPRS megaspore
AEEGMORST gasometer
megastore
AEEGNNSTW newsagent
AEEGNOPRS personage
AEEGNORRT generator
AEEGNORTT teratogen
AEEGNORTU entourage
AEEGNOTTW wagonette
AEEGNOTXY oxygenate
AEEGNPRSS passenger
AEEGNRRST estranger
AEEGNRRVY engravery
AEEGNRSST greatness
AEEGNRSSV graveness
AEEGNSSST gastnesse
AEEGNSSUV vagueness
AEEGOOSSW wasegoose
AEEGOPPST estoppage
AEEGOPRRT porterage
reportage
AEEGORRTV overgreat
AEEGORRVZ overgraze
AEEGORTTW gate-tower
AEEGPRTUX expurgate
AEEHHINST insheathe
AEEHHJLRR △lehrjahre
AEEHHLOSW hawsehole
AEEHHNNPT naphthene
AEEHHNPTY hyphenate
AEEHHNRTY heathenry
AEEHHNSTU unsheathe
AEEHHOOVY yo-heave-ho
AEEHHPSSW sheep-wash
AEEHIKNPT phenakite
AEEHILLTW tailwheel
AEEHILMNW meanwhile
AEEHILNSS Sinhalese
AEEHILNTV Helvetian
AEEHILORV overhaile
AEEHILPST ephialtes
AEEHILRRS shirralee
AEEHILRTT theralite
AEEHIMNST mainsheet
AEEHIMPRR epirrhema
AEEHIMPRT Hemiptera
AEEHIMPRY hyperemia
AEEHIMPSS emphasise
AEEHIMPST empathise
AEEHIMPSZ emphasize
AEEHIMPTZ empathize
AEEHIMRST hetaerism
time-share
AEEHIMSTW white-seam
AEEHINPRS Hesperian
seraphine
AEEHINRSV haversine
AEEHINRTU eutherian
AEEHINRTW inwreathe
near-white
AEEHINSSV heaviness
AEEHIPPRT epitapher
AEEHIPPSW hawsepipe
AEEHIPRRT ratheripe
three-pair

AEEHIPRSS	apheresis
AEEHIPRST	sphaerite
AEEHIRSTT	hetaerist
AEEHIRTWW	whiteware
AEEHISSST	aesthesis
AEEHISSTT	athetesis
AEEHKLLRS	lark's-heel
AEEHKLLRY	rakehelly
AEEHKLPSW	sheepwalk
AEEHKMMOR	homemaker
AEEHKMORS	shoemaker
AEEHLLMOW	wholemeal
AEEHLLNOW	Hallowe'en
AEEHLLORS	aeroshell
AEEHLLOSW	wholesale
AEEHLMMNT	Emmenthal
AEEHLMNSY	hymeneals
AEEHLMPRY	melaphyre
AEEHLMRTY	erythemal
AEEHLMSSS	shameless
AEEHLMTTY	methylate
AEEHLNOPS	anopheles
AEEHLNOPT	phenolate
AEEHLNRST	hesternal
AEEHLNSST	natheless
AEEHLOPST	telophase
AEEHLPSSS	phaseless
	shapeless
AEEHLPTTY	telepathy
AEEHLRSST	hartlesse
	heartless
AEEHLRTWY	weatherly
AEEHLSTTW	whet-slate
AEEHLSTXY	hexastyle
AEEHMMORT	hammer-toe
AEEHMMPSY	emphysema
AEEHMNNOP	phenomena
AEEHMNORR	menorrhea
AEEHMNORT	nathemore
AEEHMNOTT	moth-eaten
AEEHMNSTX	exanthems
AEEHMOPRS	semaphore
AEEHMORST	heartsome
	horsemeat
AEEHMOSTU	house-mate
AEEHMPRST	petersham
AEEHNOOPR	aerophone
AEEHNOORT	Oenothera
AEEHNOPRT	open-heart
AEEHNOPTX	toxaphene
AEEHNORTT	earth-tone
AEEHNOSTU	neat-house
AEEHNPRRS	sharpener
AEEHNRTTT	tenth-rate
AEEHNRTUW	unwreathe
AEEHNSTTY	Thyestean
AEEHOPRTY	aerophyte
AEEHORRRS	rearhorse
AEEHORRST	heart-sore
AEEHORRSW	raree-show
AEEHORSTV	overhaste
AEEHORSTW	whatsoe'er
AEEHORSUW	warehouse
AEEHPRRTT	three-part
AEEHPRSTU	superheat
AEEHRRSTT	ratherest
	three-star
AEEHRRSTV	harvester
AEEHRSTUX	exhauster
AEEIIINRS	niaiserie
AEEIILLOP	aeolipile
AEEIILMNT	eliminate
AEEIILQRU	reliquiae
AEEIILRSS	serialise
AEEIILRST	Israelite
AEEIILRSZ	serialize
AEEIILSTV	Leavisite
AEEIIMNRR	marinière
AEEIIMNST	amenities
AEEIINNOT	neoteinia
AEEIINRSY	yersiniae
AEEIINRTT	itinerate
AEEIIPPRT	peripetia
AEEIIPRTV	aperitive
AEEIIRSTV	varieties
AEEIIRTTV	iterative
AEEIIRTVZ	vizierate
AEEIJLRSS	jaileress
AEEIJMNSS	jessamine
AEEIJPRSS	jasperise
AEEIJPRSZ	jasperize
AEEIKKLNS	snakelike
AEEIKLLPT	plate-like
AEEIKLNPR	Keplerian
AEEIKLNPS	aspen-like
AEEIKLNSS	leakiness
AEEIKLSTY	yeastlike
AEEIKMNSY	Yankeeism
AEEIKNNSY	Keynesian
AEEIKNPPW	wink-a-peep
AEEIKNRRS	ink-eraser
AEEIKNSSW	snakewise
AEEIKRRSS	seraskier
AEEIKRSTW	awestrike
AEEILLMNT	metalline
AEEILLMOT	emolliate
AEEILLMST	metallise
AEEILLMTZ	metallize
AEEILLNOT	lineolate
AEEILLNTT	littleane
AEEILLOPY	aeolipyle
AEEILLPST	palletise
AEEILLPTT	paillette
AEEILLPTZ	palletize
AEEILLSTT	satellite
AEEILLTVW	wavellite
AEEILMMRS	marmelise
AEEILMMRZ	marmelize
AEEILMMST	lemmatise
	semi-metal
AEEILMMTZ	lemmatize
AEEILMNNT	alinement
	lineament
AEEILMNNU	eumelanin

AEEILMNRY mine-layer
AEEILMNSS mealiness
AEEILMORT meliorate
AEEILMPSS misplease
AEEILMPST time-lapse
AEEILMRST misrelate
salimeter
AEEILMRTT altimeter
AEEILMRTU elaterium
AEEILMRTW limewater
AEEILMTUV emulative
AEEILNNPP peneplain
AEEILNNPR perennial
AEEILNNSX sexennial
AEEILNNTV △levantine
△valentine
AEEILNOPX pleonexia
AEEILNOTV elevation
AEEILNPPP pineapple
AEEILNPRU epineural
AEEILNPRX explainer
AEEILNPSX expansile
AEEILNRSS earliness
AEEILNRSU unrealise
AEEILNRSV vernalise
AEEILNRTU retinulae
AEEILNRTV eviternal
intervale
AEEILNRTW waterline
AEEILNRUZ unrealize
AEEILNRVZ vernalize
AEEILNSST essential
AEEILNSSV aliveness
AEEILNTTV ventilate
AEEILOPTT petiolate
AEEILORRT arteriole
AEEILPPRY pipe-layer
AEEILPRRV reprieval
AEEILPRST prelatise
AEEILPRTZ prelatize
AEEILQRSU equaliser
AEEILQRUZ equalizer
AEEILQUVV equivalve
AEEILRRTV retrieval
AEEILRSSW weariless
AEEILRSTU Aleurites
AEEILRSTV versatile
AEEILRSTY seriately
AEEILRTTU elutriate
AEEILSSTW leastwise
AEEILSSUX sexualise
AEEILSUXZ sexualize
AEEILSVVY evasively
AEEIMNNOX xenomenia
AEEIMNNPP Menippean
AEEIMNNPT impennate
AEEIMNNRT nemertian
AEEIMNNRV venireman
AEEIMNNZZ mezzanine
AEEIMNPRU perinaeum
AEEIMNRRU numeraire
numéraire
AEEIMNRTT terminate
AEEIMNRTV verminate
AEEIMNSSS seaminess
AEEIMNSST meatiness
AEEIMNSTT estaminet
AEEIMNSTV avisement
AEEIMNTVV vivamente
AEEIMOPPR peperomia
AEEIMORSS isomerase
AEEIMORST osmeteria
AEEIMORSW wearisome
AEEIMPRSS Parseeism
AEEIMPRST spare-time
AEEIMPRTT impetrate
AEEIMRSTT tasimeter
AEEIMRTTX taximeter
AEEINNNSS inaneness
AEEINNPST septennia
AEEINNRRW innerwear
Wernerian
AEEINNRTT entertain
Terentian
AEEINNRTV innervate
AEEINNSST insensate
AEEINNSSV naiveness
naïveness
AEEINNSTT intensate
AEEINOPPT appointee
AEEINORTT orientate
AEEINPPST pepsinate
AEEINPRSS parenesis
passerine
AEEINPRST pistareen
sparteine
AEEINPRTU petaurine
AEEINPSVX expansive
AEEINRRTT reiterant
AEEINRRTV veratrine
AEEINRSSW weariness
AEEINRSTT reinstate
AEEINRSTU estuarine
AEEINRSTV invertase
AEEINRSTY eyestrain
AEEINSSTV assentive
AEEINSTTT enstatite
intestate
satinette
AEEINSTTU austenite
AEEINTTTV attentive
tentative
AEEIOPRTV evaporite
operative
AEEIPPRST appetiser
AEEIPPRSU pauperise
AEEIPPRTZ appetizer
AEEIPPRUZ pauperize
AEEIPRRST sparterie
AEEIPRRTV privateer
AEEIPRSSV aspersive
AEEIPRSTW taperwise
AEEIPRSVV pervasive
AEEIPRTTX extirpate

AEEIPSSST	epistases
AEEIRRSTV	arrestive
AEEIRSSTT	sestertia
AEEIRSSTV	assertive
AEEJKRRTW	jerkwater
AEEJLMRSU	Jerusalem
AEEJMORTT	majorette
AEEJMRSTT	jetstream
	jet-stream
AEEJNRSST	jesserant
AEEJNRSTY	serjeanty
AEEKLLSSS	slakeless
AEEKLMNNN	kennel-man
AEEKLMORV	lovemaker
AEEKLRSSW	wreakless
AEEKLSTTW	sweet-talk
AEEKMMRRY	merry-make
AEEKMNRTT	tent-maker
AEEKMNRTW	newmarket
AEEKMOPRR	rope-maker
AEEKMOPST	peat-smoke
AEEKMRSTY	master-key
AEEKNORTV	overtaken
AEEKOPRSU	Eurospeak
AEEKORSST	keratoses
AEEKORTUY	eukaryote
AEEKQRSSU	Quakeress
AEEKQRSUY	squeakery
AEELLLMOS	lamellose
AEELLLSUV	vulsellae
AEELLMMSS	mamselles
AEELLMNTW	well-meant
AEELLMRSS	realmless
AEELLNPRT	repellant
AEELLNPTX	expellant
AEELLNRRT	rentaller
AEELLNRST	entralles
AEELLNRTY	eternally
AEELLOPPV	love-apple
AEELLOPST	Sellotape®
	sellotape
	soleplate
AEELLOSUV	laevulose
AEELLRRTV	traveller
AEELLRSST	tessellar
AEELLRSVY	severally
AEELLRTTU	tellurate
AEELLSSUV	valueless
AEELLSSVV	valveless
AEELMMNRT	entrammel
AEELMNOPR	melon-pear
AEELMNOST	telamones
AEELMNPSS	ampleness
AEELMNRTV	ravelment
AEELMOPPR	palempore
AEELMORST	elastomer
AEELMOSWY	awesomely
AEELMPRST	emplaster
AEELMPRXY	exemplary
AEELMPSSY	esemplasy
AEELMPTTY	type-metal
AEELMRSST	semestral
AEELMRSTT	streamlet
AEELMRTTU	tremulate
AEELMRTTW	melt-water
AEELNNNTU	antennule
AEELNNOSS	aloneness
AEELNNPRY	arle-penny
AEELNOPST	pleonaste
AEELNOSUV	leavenous
AEELNPRRV	pre-vernal
AEELNPRTV	prevalent
AEELNPRTY	net-player
AEELNQSSU	equalness
AEELNRSST	alertness
AEELNRSTX	externals
AEELNRSTY	earnestly
AEELNRTTV	tervalent
AEELNRTTY	ternately
AEELNRTUV	vulnerate
AEELNSSST	staleness
AEELNSTVX	sexvalent
AEELNSUVW	news-value
AEELOPPRS	rose-apple
AEELOPPTY	paleotype
AEELOPRSU	leaperous
AEELOPRTY	epeolatry
AEELORRTV	revelator
AEELORSTU	teleosaur
AEELORSTY	areostyle
AEELORTVY	elevatory
AEELORUVV	overvalue
AEELPPRRU	puerperal
AEELPPRSS	paperless
AEELPPRTU	perpetual
AEELPQTTU	plaquette
AEELPRRST	plasterer
AEELPRRSU	pleasurer
	reperusal
AEELPRRTU	prelature
AEELPRSSS	spareless
AEELPRSST	prelatess
AEELPRSTT	saltpeter
	saltpetre
AEELPRSTU	pulse-rate
AEELPRTUY	eutrapely
AEELPSSSU	pauseless
AEELPSUVW	pulse-wave
AEELQSTUZ	quetzales
AEELRRSTU	serrulate
AEELRSSTV	varletess
AEELRSSTW	waterless
AEELRSTUY	austerely
AEELRSTVY	severalty
AEELSSSTT	stateless
	tasteless
AEEMMNORT	manometer
AEEMMNSTU	amusement
AEEMMORTT	atmometer
AEEMMPRUY	empyreuma
AEEMMRRST	stammerer
AEEMNNNTX	annexment
AEEMNNOPR	praenomen
AEEMNNORT	nanometre

AEEMNNOTT △atonement
AEEMNNPRT permanent
AEEMNOPRT treponema
AEEMNOPSU menopause
AEEMNOPYZ apoenzyme
AEEMNORTW worm-eaten
AEEMNORUV manoeuvre
AEEMNPRTY pentamery
repayment
AEEMNPSST passement
AEEMNQRSU queen's-arm
AEEMNRSST mare's-nest
steersman
AEEMNRTTT treatment
AEEMNSSTT means-test
AEEMNSSTY mateyness
AEEMNSTTT statement
△testament
AEEMOPRTW pome-water
AEEMORRSU rearmouse
AEEMORRTT Rotameter®
AEEMORRTY aerometry
AEEMORSST Massorete
AEEMORTTU amourette
AEEMORTUX auxometer
AEEMPRRTU premature
AEEMPRTTT attempter
reattempt
trampette
AEEMPRTTU permutate
AEEMPTTXX tax-exempt
AEEMRRSTT smatterer
AEEMRTTTW wattmeter
AEENNOPRT one-parent
AEENNOPST pentosane
AEENNOPTT panettone
AEENNPRRT trepanner
AEENNPRSY Pyreneans
AEENNPRTT penetrant
repentant
AEENNRRTT re-entrant
AEENOPPRT notepaper
AEENOPRST Esperanto
personate
AEENOPTTT potentate
AEENORRST nor'-easter
AEENORRTV venerator
AEENORRTW rowan-tree
AEENORSTW stoneware
AEENPPRRT entrapper
AEENPPRRU unprepare
AEENPPRSW newspaper
AEENPRRTU enrapture
AEENPRSSS spareness
AEENPRSST apertness
taperness
AEENPRSTY septenary
AEENPRTTY Pernettya
AEENRRSTU saunterer
AEENRRTUV nervature
AEENRSSTU Sauternes
AEENRSTUV rune-stave
AEENSSSTW wasteness
AEEOOPRTZ azeotrope
AEEOORRTT root-eater
AEEOPPRSU pea-souper
AEEOPPSSU pease-soup
AEEOPRRST patereros
AEEOPRSTT poetaster
AEEOPRSTX extrapose
AEEORRSTT erostrate
AEEORRSTV overstare
AEEORRSTW rosewater
AEEORRSVW overswear
AEEORRTUV avouterer
AEEORRTUW outerwear
AEEORRVWY overweary
AEEORSTTV overstate
AEEORSTTW twoseater
AEEPPRSSU pauperess
AEEPRRSTU repasture
AEEPRSTTU pertusate
AEEPRSTXY apteryxes
AEEQRSSTU sequestra
AEEQRTTTU quartette
AEEQRTUUX exequatur
AEERRRSSU reassurer
AEERRRSTT restarter
AEERRRSTU serrature
treasurer
AEERRRSTV traverser
AEERRTTVX extravert
AEESTTTTU statuette
AEFFFLTUW Luftwaffe
AEFFGHORS shroffage
AEFFGIINR giraffine
AEFFIILRS falsifier
AEFFIIPRR pifferari
AEFFIJMOR fife-major
AEFFIKPST pikestaff
AEFFILLUV effluvial
AEFFILORT firefloat
AEFFINORS raffinose
AEFFIOPRR pifferaro
AEFFIORRT forfaiter
AEFFIRSTW stiffware
AEFFLLRUY fearfully
AEFFLLTUY fatefully
AEFFLNOPT pantoffle
AEFFLNRUU unfearful
AEFFLORSW safflower
AEFFMORST off-stream
AEFFNOOSS offseason
AEFFORSTV overstaff
AEFGHILNS angel-fish
AEFGHIRST gearshift
AEFGHLRTU flaughter
AEFGHORRT forgather
AEFGIILNR filigrane
AEFGIIMNR magnifier
AEFGIIRRT gratifier
AEFGILLRY fragilely
AEFGILNRT faltering
AEFGILORT fortilage

AEFGILOSU	Solifugae
AEFGILRUY	lay-figure
AEFGIMORT	fogramite
AEFGINNRU	unfearing
AEFGINNST	fastening
AEFGINNTT	fattening
AEFGINRRT	raftering
AEFGINRRY	rarefying
AEFGINRST	afterings
AEFGINRTU	figurante
AEFGIORSS	ossifrage
AEFGIRSTT	gas-fitter
AEFGISTTU	fustigate
AEFGLLLMU	flagellum
AEFGLLMNU	flugelman
AEFGLNOST	flagstone
AEFGLORTW	afterglow
AEFGLRTUU	fulgurate
AEFGMORRR	ferrogram
AEFGNOPRT	front-page
AEFGNORRT	frontager
AEFGNORTX	xenograft
AEFGOOPPR	page-proof
AEFGOOPRU	ague-proof
AEFHHISST	sheatfish
AEFHHLLLS	half-shell
AEFHHLLTU	healthful
AEFHHLOTW	heath-fowl
AEFHIINRS	sherifian
AEFHIKMST	makeshift
AEFHILLMR	half-miler
AEFHILLTT	half-title
AEFHILMRT	half-timer
AEFHILORS	loaferish
AEFHILPST	fish-plate
AEFHILSST	faithless
AEFHIMNRS	fisherman
AEFHINORS	fashioner
	refashion
AEFHINTTT	antitheft
AEFHIPRSS	fish-spear
	spearfish
AEFHKLMRS	shelf-mark
AEFHLLTUY	hatefully
AEFHLNNPY	halfpenny
AEFHLNOTU	Fluothane®
AEFHLNSSW	newsflash
AEFHLORSV	flash-over
AEFHLORTW	earthwolf
AEFHLOSTV	love-shaft
AEFHLRTTU	threatful
AEFHLSSST	shaftless
AEFHMORSU	farmhouse
AEFHOORST	hare's-foot
AEFIIKLRY	fairylike
AEFIILMNS	semifinal
AEFIILMPR	amplifier
AEFIILNNT	infantile
AEFIILNTV	inflative
AEFIILQRU	qualifier
AEFIILRRT	trial-fire
AEFIIMNNS	Fenianism
AEFIINNNT	infantine
AEFIINRTU	infuriate
AEFIIRSST	satisfier
AEFIJLRST	rijstafel
AEFIKLNSS	flakiness
AEFILLMNS	misfallen
AEFILLNOT	fellation
AEFILLNSS	self-slain
AEFILLOOT	foliolate
AEFILLOST	fellatios
AEFILLUVZ	avizefull
AEFILMMOR	oriflamme
AEFILMNTU	fulminate
AEFILMORS	formalise
AEFILMORZ	formalize
AEFILMRSW	welfarism
AEFILNNUZ	influenza
AEFILNORT	reflation
AEFILNRSS	frailness
AEFILOPRR	poriferal
AEFILORRT	rotiferal
AEFILORTU	foliature
AEFILPRST	strip-leaf
AEFILPRSU	praiseful
AEFILRRTV	river-flat
AEFILRSTW	welfarist
AEFIMMNRT	firmament
AEFIMNORW	firewoman
AEFIMNOSS	foaminess
AEFIMNOST	manifesto
AEFIMNOTX	tamoxifen
AEFIMORSS	misfeasor
AEFIMORTV	formative
AEFINNSST	faintness
AEFINOPRR	poriferan
AEFINORSS	Sanforise
AEFINORSU	nefarious
AEFINORSZ	Sanforize
AEFINRTZZ	frizzante
AEFINSSTT	fattiness
AEFIORRRW	fire-arrow
AEFIORRST	forestair
AEFIORTUV	favourite
AEFIRRSTT	first-rate
AEFKLLUWY	wakefully
AEFKLNOSW	snowflake
AEFKLOOST	sootflake
AEFKLORSV	slave-fork
AEFKLORSW	falsework
AEFKMORRW	framework
AEFKNNRSS	frankness
AEFKOORST	forest-oak
AEFLLLNNY	flannelly
AEFLLMNOW	fellow-man
AEFLLNTTU	flatulent
AEFLLORST	astrofell
	forestall
AEFLLRTUW	well-faurt
AEFLLRTUY	tearfully
AEFLLSSTU	faultless
AEFLMORTU	formulate
AEFLMORWY	mayflower

AEFLMRSTU	masterful
AEFLMRTTU	matterful
AEFLNOOSS	aloofness
AEFLNOPRY	profanely
AEFLNOPTU	pantoufle
AEFLNOSTU	sulfonate
AEFLNSSUW	awfulness
AEFLOOPRT	roof-plate
AEFLOOPTT	footplate
AEFLORSSV	favorless
AEFLORTWW	waterfowl
AEFLOSSTT	falsettos
AEFLOSSTU	fossulate
AEFLPRRUY	prayerful
AEFLRSTTU	flustrate
AEFLRSTUU	sulfurate
AEFLRSTUW	wasterful
AEFMNOORW	forewoman
AEFMOPRST	stop-frame
AEFMORRRT	terraform
AEFMORRTT	formatter
AEFMORSTT	aftermost
AEFNNOORT	afternoon
AEFNOOSTT	neat's-foot
AEFNOPRRS	perforans
AEFNOPRRT	perforant
AEFNORTTU	fortunate
AEFNORTVW	wavefront
AEFNRSSTT	sternfast
AEFNRSSTU	transfuse
AEFOPRRTY	prefatory
AEFOPSSTT	softpaste
AEFPRSSTU	superfast
AEFRRSTTU	frustrate
AEGGGINRU	ring-gauge
AEGGHIKNT	knightage
AEGGHINRT	gathering
	nightgear
AEGGHIRTZ	gigahertz
AEGGHOPRR	ergograph
AEGGHOPRY	geography
AEGGIILNS	silageing
AEGGIINPU	guinea-pig
AEGGILLNT	galleting
AEGGILNOO	geologian
AEGGIMNSS	messaging
AEGGIMOPT	maggot-pie
AEGGINNRV	engraving
AEGGINOOR	gorgoneia
AEGGINORR	Gregorian
AEGGINOSY	easy-going
AEGGINPRT	pargeting
AEGGINRRT	regrating
AEGGINRTT	targeting
AEGGINTTZ	gazetting
AEGGIOPRS	arpeggios
AEGGLNNOR	long-range
AEGGLNRRY	glengarry
AEGGLRRST	straggler
AEGGMORRT	mortgager
AEGGNOSUY	synagogue
AEGGNPRSS	press-gang
AEGGORRSS	aggressor
AEGGORUVY	gyrovague
AEGHHINST	sheathing
AEGHHIPRT	high-taper
AEGHHOPTY	theophagy
AEGHHRRTU	hearth-rug
AEGHIJRTU	Gujerathi
AEGHIKNNR	hankering
AEGHIKNRS	ring-shake
	shrinkage
AEGHILLMS	megillahs
AEGHILLNY	healingly
AEGHILNOX	holing-axe
AEGHILNRS	ashlering
	shearling
AEGHILNRT	earthling
	heartling
AEGHILNSV	shaveling
AEGHILRRT	rear-light
AEGHILRTY	light-year
AEGHIMMNR	hammering
AEGHIMNRS	Germanish
AEGHIMNRT	nightmare
AEGHIMNST	eightsman
AEGHIMORR	hierogram
AEGHIMOTT	Gothamite
AEGHIMPPR	epiphragm
AEGHIMPRT	tephigram
AEGHINNPP	happening
AEGHINOPS	siphonage
AEGHINPPU	upheaping
AEGHINRRS	garnisher
AEGHINRSV	haverings
AEGHINRTW	nightwear
AEGHIOOPS	oesophagi
AEGHIOPST	hospitage
AEGHIPPRY	epigraphy
AEGHIPRRS	serigraph
AEGHIPSTT	spaghetti
AEGHKMORY	herkogamy
AEGHLMOSU	laughsome
AEGHLMOSY	Moygashel®
	moygashel
AEGHLMPRU	galumpher
AEGHLNORU	hour-angle
AEGHLNPRY	nephralgy
AEGHLOOPR	oleograph
AEGHLOORR	logorrhea
AEGHLOOTY	atheology
AEGHLOPTT	heptaglot
AEGHLOPXY	xylophage
AEGHLORTT	larghetto
AEGHLRSTU	slaughter
AEGHMNOPR	nephogram
AEGHMOPUY	hypogaeum
AEGHMPRYY	hypergamy
AEGHNNPRU	pergunnah
AEGHNOORR	gonorrhea
AEGHNOPRT	pot-hanger
AEGHNOPTY	pathogeny
AEGHNOSTU	shogunate
AEGHNPRSY	pharynges

AEGHNSSST	ghastness
AEGHOPRST	grapeshot
AEGHOPRXY	xerophagy
AEGHOPSSU	esophagus
AEGHORRTU	ore-raught
AEGHRTTUX	extraught
AEGIILLNN	lilangeni
AEGIILLRS	grisaille
AEGIILLRT	argillite
AEGIILLSS	gallisise
AEGIILLST	sigillate
AEGIILLSZ	gallisize
AEGIILMNR	regiminal
AEGIILMSV	vigesimal
AEGIILNPS	Spigelian
AEGIILNRS	realising
AEGIILNRV	Vergilian
AEGIILNRZ	realizing
AEGIILNSS	signalise
AEGIILNSZ	signalize
AEGIILNTV	genitival
	vigilante
AEGIILNTY	geniality
AEGIILOSV	viliagoes
AEGIILSTV	vestigial
AEGIIMMRT	immigrate
AEGIIMNNX	examining
AEGIINNRT	retaining
AEGIINNST	sin-eating
AEGIINORT	originate
AEGIINOSV	voisinage
AEGIINOTT	goniatite
AEGIINRST	granitise
AEGIINRTT	granitite
AEGIINRTW	waitering
AEGIINRTZ	granitize
AEGIINSTT	instigate
AEGIINTTU	tinguaite
AEGIIRSTT	Stagirite
AEGIISSTV	visagiste
AEGIJNNTU	juneating
AEGIJNORS	jargonise
AEGIJNORZ	jargonize
AEGIKKMNR	kingmaker
AEGIKLLSS	glasslike
AEGIKLNPP	king-apple
AEGIKMMRS	skrimmage
AEGIKMNRT	marketing
AEGIKNNRS	ring-snake
AEGIKNQSU	squeaking
AEGIKNRST	streaking
AEGIKNSSW	gawkiness
AEGILLLLY	illegally
AEGILLLNU	gallinule
AEGILLMNT	metalling
AEGILLNNP	panelling
AEGILLNOS	lignaloes
	lign-aloes
AEGILLNPR	pellagrin
AEGILLNPS	langspiel
AEGILLNQU	equalling
AEGILLNRS	signaller
AEGILLNRV	ravelling
AEGILLNTU	lingulate
AEGILLPPU	pupillage
AEGILLPRS	aspergill
AEGILLRRU	guerrilla
AEGILLRST	allergist
AEGILLRVY	villagery
AEGILMNNT	alignment
	lamenting
AEGILMNNY	meaningly
AEGILMNPT	pigmental
AEGILMNRY	malingery
AEGILMNTU	glutamine
AEGILMORR	rigmarole
AEGILMORS	glamorise
AEGILMORZ	glamorize
AEGILNNOO	neologian
AEGILNORS	seignoral
AEGILNORU	neuroglia
AEGILNORY	legionary
AEGILNOSS	sloganise
AEGILNOSZ	sloganize
AEGILNPRS	pearlings
	relapsing
AEGILNQSU	squealing
AEGILNRST	triangles
AEGILNRSV	slavering
AEGILNRSY	syringeal
AEGILNRTU	granulite
	traguline
AEGILNRTV	traveling
AEGILNRTY	ingrately
AEGILNRWY	wearingly
AEGILNSST	eastlings
	tasseling
AEGILNSSW	wineglass
AEGILNSTY	teasingly
AEGILOOPS	apologise
AEGILOOPZ	apologize
AEGILOOTY	aetiology
AEGILORSS	seraglios
AEGILORST	goslarite
AEGILORSU	glaireous
AEGILORTU	trialogue
AEGILPPRR	paper-girl
AEGILPPTU	plague-pit
AEGILPRSS	pier-glass
AEGILPRTV	gravel-pit
AEGILPRTY	pterygial
AEGILRRRU	irregular
AEGILRSUV	vulgarise
AEGILRTUV	virgulate
AEGILRUVZ	vulgarize
AEGIMMNOT	gemmation
AEGIMMNRS	Germanism
AEGIMMNRU	germanium
AEGIMMNRY	yammering
AEGIMMNST	magnetism
AEGIMMNSU	magnesium
AEGIMNNNO	no-meaning
AEGIMNNNS	Minnesang
AEGIMNNNU	unmeaning

AEGIMNNRT germinant
AEGIMNNSS manginess
AEGIMNNSY gymnasien
AEGIMNNTU Augmentin®
AEGIMNOPS panegoism
AEGIMNORS Orangeism
AEGIMNORT morganite
AEGIMNPRT tampering
AEGIMNRST Germanist
mastering
streaming
AEGIMNRSU measuring
AEGIMNRSW Wagnerism
AEGIMNSTT agistment
magnetist
AEGIMPRST mag-stripe
AEGIMRSTY magistery
AEGINNOPS sapogenin
AEGINNORS reasoning
AEGINNORT Argentino
AEGINNORW Norwegian
AEGINNORZ organzine
AEGINNOSS seasoning
AEGINNOTT negotiant
AEGINNPRT parenting
AEGINNRSS angriness
ranginess
AEGINNRST gannister
AEGINNRTT integrant
rattening
AEGINOPPR organ-pipe
AEGINOPRT operating
orange-tip
pignorate
AEGINORRS organiser
AEGINORRV granivore
overgrain
AEGINORRY regionary
AEGINORRZ organizer
AEGINORSV sea-roving
AEGINORTU outraigne
AEGINORTY iatrogeny
AEGINOSST agonistes
AEGINOSTT gestation
AEGINPRST trapesing
AEGINPSSS gaspiness
AEGINQRUV quavering
AEGINRRST astringer
AEGINRRTU garniture
AEGINRSTU signature
AEGINRSTW Wagnerist
AEGINRTTY yattering
AEGINRWZZ Zwanziger
AEGINSSSS gassiness
AEGINSSST staginess
AEGINSSUZ gauziness
AEGINSTUU Augustine
AEGIPRSST spagerist
AEGIPRTUV purgative
AEGIRRRST registrar
AEGIRSTTY Stagyrite
AEGISTTUV gustative
AEGKOPRRW parge-work
AEGLLNORV governall
AEGLLNOST gallstone
AEGLLOPRS gallopers
AEGLLOSSW gallowses
Owle-glass
AEGLLRRUY regularly
AEGLLRTUY tegularly
AEGLMNOOY anemology
AEGLMNORW angleworm
lawmonger
AEGLMOPRY pyelogram
AEGLMRSSY lyme-grass
AEGLNOPRY gyroplane
AEGLNOPTY pentalogy
AEGLNORSU granulose
AEGLNOSTU langouste
AEGLNRRST strangler
AEGLNRSST strangles
AEGLNRSTY strangely
AEGLNRUVY ungravely
AEGLOOSUV volageous
AEGLOPPRU propagule
AEGLOPRSS glass-rope
AEGLORRTU regulator
AEGLORTTY tetralogy
AEGLPRSSS graspless
AEGLRSSSU sugarless
AEGMMOPRR programme
AEGMNNORT magnetron
AEGMNOORW woomerang
AEGMNORRU neurogram
AEGMNORRW warmonger
AEGMNORTU augmentor
AEGMNOSTU mangouste
AEGMNOTTU mangetout
AEGMNRTTU gutter-man
AEGMOOSUX exogamous
AEGMOPRRR reprogram
AEGMOPRRT petrogram
AEGMORRUW auger-worm
AEGMORSSY gossamery
AEGMORSTY gasometry
AEGNNORSU non-usager
AEGNNPRTU repugnant
AEGNNSSTU gauntness
AEGNOOSSW swan-goose
AEGNORRWY garryowen
AEGNORSUV vargueños
AEGNRSSTU assurgent
AEGNSTTTU tungstate
AEGOOPRRT prorogate
AEGOOSWYZ wayzgoose
AEGOPRSTU après-goût
AEGORRRTT garrotter
AEGORRSSV overgrass
AEGORRSTT gas-retort
AEGORRSTU surrogate
AEGORSSTU stegosaur
AEGORSTTY gestatory
AEHHILLOP halophile
AEHHILLPT tephillah

AEHHILLTW	Whitehall
AEHHILLTY	healthily
AEHHILNPT	phthalein
AEHHINPST	thaneship
AEHHIORRS	horsehair
AEHHIPPSS	shipshape
AEHHIRRST	ratherish
AEHHISSVY	yeshivahs
AEHHISTWW	whitewash
AEHHKLRSU	shear-hulk
AEHHLLMST	Stahlhelm
AEHHLLPRS	harp-shell
AEHHLNTUY	unhealthy
AEHHLOPTY	halophyte
AEHHMOOPT	homeopath
AEHHNOPTY	theophany
AEHHNORSW	heronshaw
AEHHNRSSS	harshness
AEHHOPPST	phosphate
AEHHOPTTY	theopathy
AEHHORSTT	Ashtoreth
AEHHOSSUW	washhouse
AEHIIKNRT	heartikin
AEHIILMTU	humiliate
AEHIILNOP	neophilia
AEHIILNSY	hyalinise
AEHIILNTX	antihelix
AEHIILNYZ	hyalinize
AEHIIMNST	histamine
AEHIIMOPS	hemiopsia
AEHIIMRST	hetairism
AEHIIMRTY	Himyarite
AEHIINOPT	Ethiopian
AEHIINRSS	hairiness
AEHIINTTU	uintahite
AEHIIPSTT	hepatitis
AEHIIRSTT	hetairist
AEHIJLOSU	jailhouse
AEHIJNNNO	Johannine
AEHIKKLMS	milk-shake
AEHIKLMNU	humanlike
AEHIKMNPS	phenakism
AEHIKMRSS	Shakerism
AEHIKMRTW	mark-white
AEHIKNPSV	knaveship
AEHIKNSSS	shakiness
AEHIKPRSS	ekphrasis
AEHIKQRSU	Quakerish
AEHILLMOP	Philomela
AEHILLMSZ	shlimazel
AEHILLOPT	paleolith
AEHILLPRY	Phillyrea
AEHILLPTY	philately
AEHILLTTY	lethality
AEHILLTWW	whitewall
AEHILLTWY	wealthily
AEHILMNOP	nemophila
AEHILMNOS	Holmesian
AEHILMNPS	nephalism
AEHILMPSS	sisal-hemp
AEHILMRTY	tail-rhyme
AEHILNNOT	anthelion
AEHILNOOZ	heliozoan
AEHILNOPP	philopena
AEHILNOPR	parhelion
AEHILNOPS	phaseolin
AEHILNORT	lion-heart
AEHILNOST	hailstone
AEHILNPRS	planisher
AEHILNPST	nephalist
AEHILNQRU	harlequin
AEHILOPST	hospitale
AEHILORST	horsetail
	isotheral
AEHILOSSW	shoalwise
AEHILOSTT	heliostat
AEHILOSTY	isohyetal
AEHILPPST	plate-ship
AEHILPPTY	epiphytal
AEHILPRST	prelatish
AEHILRSTY	hairstyle
AEHIMMRTU	Mithraeum
AEHIMNNOT	anthemion
AEHIMNORS	harmonise
AEHIMNORT	Harmonite
AEHIMNORZ	harmonize
AEHIMNPPS	mishappen
AEHIMNPSS	misshapen
AEHIMNPST	pantheism
AEHIMNRST	mishanter
AEHIMNRTU	Mathurine
AEHIMOPXY	hypoxemia
AEHIMOSST	hematosis
AEHIMPRSS	seraphims
AEHIMPSST	steamship
AEHIMQSSU	squeamish
AEHIMRTUZ	rheumatiz
AEHINNOST	Esthonian
AEHINNRTU	Hunterian
	Ruthenian
AEHINOPST	pantihose
	siphonate
AEHINORSS	hoariness
AEHINORST	Senhorita
AEHINORTT	anorthite
AEHINPPSS	happiness
AEHINPPTT	tappit-hen
AEHINPPTX	Xanthippe
AEHINPRSS	seraphins
AEHINPSSS	apishness
AEHINPSSY	Sisyphean
AEHINPSTT	pantheist
AEHINRRST	tarnisher
AEHINRRSV	varnisher
AEHINRRTY	erythrina
AEHINRSST	starshine
AEHINRSSW	sherwanis
AEHINSSST	hastiness
AEHINSSSW	washiness
AEHINSTTY	Thyestian
AEHIOPPRY	hyperopia
AEHIOPRRS	aphoriser
	pair-horse
AEHIOPRRZ	aphorizer

AEHIORSTT hesitator
AEHIORSTU authorise
AEHIORSTX rheotaxis
AEHIORTTV hortative
AEHIORTUZ authorize
AEHIOSSTT athetosis
AEHIPRSTT therapist
AEHIRRSTT trashtrie
AEHIRTTWW whittawer
AEHJLNOPP apple-John
John-apple
AEHKLNSST thankless
AEHKMMOPR hammerkop
AEHKMNORR horn-maker
AEHKMORST shotmaker
AEHKNOOPS hoop-snake
AEHKORRTW earthwork
AEHLLLMPS lamp-shell
AEHLLLMRS shell-marl
AEHLLMOST homestall
AEHLLMRTY thermally
AEHLLNNOT non-lethal
AEHLLNOOP allophone
AEHLLOORW holloware
AEHLLPRUX prehallux
AEHLLPSSU phalluses
AEHLLPSSY haplessly
AEHLLSSSW shawlless
AEHLLSSTU thalluses
AEHLMNOPY palm-honey
AEHLMOOST loathsome
AEHLMOPSU palmhouse
AEHLMOPTY ampholyte
AEHLMORST malt-horse
AEHLMOSSU alms-house
AEHLMOSTU malt-house
AEHLNNOPR alpenhorn
AEHLNNOPT panthenol
AEHLNOPTT Pentothal®
AEHLNOSSS shoalness
AEHLNPSUY unshapely
AEHLNRTUY unearthly
AEHLNSTUV slave-hunt
AEHLOPPSY polyphase
AEHLOPRST astrophel
AEHLOPRSY horseplay
AEHLOPRTU hourplate
AEHLOPRTY ephoralty
AEHLOPSUY playhouse
AEHLORSST salt-horse
AEHLORTUU outhauler
AEHLPRRSU spherular
AEHLRSSTW wrathless
AEHMMNOTY mythomane
AEHMMNPUY nymphaeum
AEHMMOORT harmotome
AEHMNNSSU humanness
AEHMNOOPS monophase
moonphase
AEHMNOPST phantosme
AEHMNORSS shoresman
AEHMNRRWY wherryman
AEHMNRSTU transhume
AEHMOOPRS shampooer
AEHMOOPRT Homoptera
AEHMOORSS smasheroo
AEHMOPPRT top-hamper
AEHMORRTW earthworm
AEHMORTWW wheatworm
AEHMOSSTU masthouse
AEHMPRRTY hypermart
AEHNNOPRT Parthenon
AEHNNRSSU unharness
AEHNNSTUW whunstane
AEHNOOPRR harpooner
AEHNOOPSX saxophone
AEHNOORST hoar-stone
AEHNOPRTU neuropath
AEHNOPRTY honey-trap
AEHNOPSSU saphenous
AEHNORSTT north-east
AEHNPRSSS sharpness
AEHNPRSXY pharynxes
AEHOOORRT otorrhoea
AEHOOPRRY pyorrhoea
AEHOOPSTT osteopath
AEHOORSTX orthoaxes
AEHOPPRVY overhappy
AEHOPPSSY apophyses
AEHOPRSSU rasp-house
AEHOPSSTT posthaste
AEHORSSTU authoress
AEHORSTTW water-shot
AEHORSTVW short-wave
AEHORSTVY overhasty
AEHORSTWY seaworthy
AEHOSSTTU south-east
AEHRSSTUU thesaurus
AEIIIKNNP epinikian
AEIIILRVZ vizierial
AEIIILTVX lixiviate
AEIIIMPRT primitiae
AEIIIMTTV imitative
AEIIINTVV vivianite
AEIIJLNUV juvenilia
AEIIKKTTW kittiwake
AEIIKLLNS snail-like
AEIIKLNOS kaolinise
AEIIKLNOT kaolinite
AEIIKLNOZ kaolinize
AEIIKLNPS spike-nail
AEIIKLNST saintlike
AEIIKLRST triskelia
AEIIKLRTV larvikite
AEIIKMRSS kaiserism
AEIIKNPRU kauri-pine
AEIIKRRST air-strike
AEIIKRSTT keratitis
AEIILLMNN millennia
AEIILLMNR Millerian
AEIILLMRS Ramillies
AEIILLMRT mitraille
AEIILLNTY lineality
AEIILLTTT titillate

AEIILMNNR	mainliner
AEIILMNNT	eliminant
AEIILMNPS	maniplies
AEIILMNRU	luminaire
AEIILMNSU	aluminise
AEIILMNUZ	aluminize
AEIILMOSV	malvoisie
AEIILMRSS	serialism
AEIILMRTT	literatim
AEIILNNOP	neopilina
AEIILNNOT	lineation
AEIILNNRT	triennial
AEIILNOPT	epilation
	polianite
AEIILNORV	Oliverian
AEIILNOTV	inviolate
AEIILNPRT	reptilian
AEIILNPST	platinise
AEIILNPTV	plaintive
AEIILNPTZ	platinize
AEIILNRRT	trilinear
AEIILNRST	Listerian
AEIILNRSU	uniserial
AEIILNRTY	linearity
AEIILNSTW	waistline
AEIILNSVY	Sylviinae
AEIILNTVY	veniality
AEIILORST	solitaire
AEIILORTV	variolite
AEIILOSSZ	assoilzie
AEIILOSTV	isolative
AEIILOTVV	violative
AEIILPPQU	quail-pipe
AEIILQSTU	qualities
AEIILRRTY	irreality
AEIILRSST	serialist
AEIILRSTU	ritualise
	uralitise
AEIILRSTV	vitaliser
AEIILRSTY	seriality
AEIILRTUZ	ritualize
	uralitize
AEIILRTVZ	vitalizer
AEIILSSUV	visualise
AEIILSUVZ	visualize
AEIIMNPRS	mainprise
AEIIMNPST	impatiens
AEIIMNPTT	impatient
AEIIMNRTU	miniature
AEIIMPRRS	impresari
AEIIMPRSS	mispraise
AEIIMPRSV	vampirise
AEIIMPRVZ	vampirize
AEIIMPSSV	impassive
AEIIMRRSV	arrivisme
AEIINNNTV	antivenin
AEIINNOPT	inopinate
AEIINNOST	antinoise
AEIINNOTV	evanition
AEIINNPTT	in-patient
AEIINNQTU	inquinate
AEIINNRSS	raininess
AEIINNRTT	itinerant
	nitratine
AEIINNRTU	uraninite
AEIINNSTU	insinuate
AEIINOPRW	piano-wire
AEIINOPTX	expiation
AEIINORST	seriation
AEIINORTT	iteration
AEIINOTTV	evitation
	novitiate
AEIINRRTY	itinerary
AEIINRSSY	yersinias
AEIINRTUV	urinative
AEIINSTTU	inusitate
AEIINSTTY	insatiety
AEIIPRSTV	privatise
AEIIPRTTV	partitive
AEIIPRTVV	privative
AEIIPRTVZ	privatize
AEIIPSSST	epistasis
AEIIPSSTX	epistaxis
AEIIPSTTT	stipitate
AEIIRRSTT	arteritis
AEIIRRSTU	retiarius
AEIIRRSTV	arriviste
AEIIRSSTW	stairwise
AEIIRTTVW	writative
AEIISTVYZ	izvestiya
AEIITTTTV	tittivate
AEIITTTUV	attuitive
AEIJKLNSU	Seljukian
AEIJMNNSS	Jansenism
AEIJNNSST	Jansenist
AEIJNRSST	janitress
AEIJNSSZZ	jazziness
AEIKKLLOO	look-alike
AEIKKNNSS	snakeskin
AEIKLLNNP	pannikell
AEIKLLNPT	plant-like
AEIKLLPTY	kallitype
AEIKLMNNU	unmanlike
AEIKLMNOS	kalsomine®
AEIKLMNOW	womanlike
AEIKLMNWY	milken-way
AEIKLMOSS	smoke-sail
AEIKLNNSS	lankiness
AEIKLNORT	oil-tanker
AEIKLNRSS	larkiness
AEIKLNRUW	unwarlike
AEIKLPRSS	sparklies
AEIKLQSUY	squeakily
AEIKLRSTW	strawlike
AEIKLRSTY	streakily
AEIKLRSVY	Valkyries
AEIKMQRSU	Quakerism
AEIKNNPRS	spinnaker
AEIKNNSSS	snakiness
AEIKNOOST	Isokontae
AEIKNORSU	urokinase
AEIKNPSSW	pawkiness
AEIKNQSSU	quakiness
AEIKOPRST	periaktos

AEIKOPRSV perovskia
AEIKORSST keratosis
AEIKPPQSU pipsqueak
AEIKPRSST piss-taker
AEILLLPPU papillule
AEILLLRTY literally
AEILLMMST small-time
AEILLMNRY millenary
AEILLMNSY seminally
AEILLMPPR paper-mill
AEILLMSSY aimlessly
AEILLMSTT metallist
AEILLNNOT tenaillon
AEILLNOPT pollinate
AEILLNORW Orwellian
AEILLNPRY plenarily
AEILLNPST panellist
AEILLNPTT pétillant
AEILLNRST reinstall
AEILLNRTU tellurian
AEILLNRTW trawl-line
AEILLNSTY saliently
AEILLOPPS papillose
AEILLOPPT papillote
popliteal
AEILLOPST apostille
AEILLORTW towel-rail
AEILLPPTU pupillate
AEILLPRSU pluralise
AEILLPRUZ pluralize
AEILLPSTU pulsatile
AEILLRRTY artillery
AEILLRRVW river-wall
AEILLRSST trail-less
AEILLRSSV rivalless
AEILLRSTW stairwell
AEILLRTVY vitellary
AEILLRTWY waterlily
AEILLRVXY vexillary
AEILLSTTY statelily
AEILMMMNN Immelmann
AEILMMNPS △pelmanism
AEILMMNST mentalism
Simmental
AEILMMORS memorials
AEILMNNOT melatonin
AEILMNNPS pennalism
plainsmen
AEILMNNSS manliness
AEILMNOOT emotional
AEILMNOPR prolamine
AEILMNOPT emptional
AEILMNORS normalise
Orleanism
AEILMNORT lion-tamer
mentorial
AEILMNORZ normalize
AEILMNOSS loaminess
melanosis
AEILMNOTU emulation
AEILMNPRT reimplant
AEILMNPSU asplenium
AEILMNPSY manyplies
AEILMNPTU penultima
AEILMNRST tramlines
AEILMNRSU semilunar
unrealism
AEILMNRVY liveryman
AEILMNSTT mentalist
AEILMNTTY mentality
AEILMORRS moraliser
AEILMORRZ moralizer
AEILMORST mortalise
AEILMORTZ mortalize
AEILMOSTU mouse-tail
AEILMOSTZ zealotism
AEILMPRST prelatism
AEILMRTTY altimetry
AEILMSSUX sexualism
AEILMSSVY massively
AEILMSTTU stimulate
AEILMSTUU mutualise
AEILMTUUZ mutualize
AEILNNNOR non-linear
AEILNNNOV novennial
AEILNNOPR nonpareil
AEILNNOST tensional
AEILNNOSV Slovenian
AEILNNOSY △lyonnaise
AEILNNOTV anti-novel
AEILNNPSS plainness
AEILNNPSU peninsula
AEILNNPTU pinnulate
AEILNNPTW twin-plane
AEILNNPTY pinnately
AEILNNRST internals
AEILNNTUV univalent
AEILNOOPS polonaise
AEILNOPPR piperonal
AEILNOPRT prelation
rantipole
AEILNOPST Platonise
sealpoint
AEILNOPTT potential
AEILNOPTU epulation
AEILNOPTZ Platonize
AEILNORSS sensorial
AEILNORST Orleanist
relations
serotinal
AEILNORSV versional
AEILNORTT natrolite
tentorial
AEILNORTU outlinear
AEILNOSSS sessional
AEILNOSSV Slavonise
AEILNOSVZ Slavonize
AEILNPRST strapline
AEILNPRTY interplay
painterly
AEILNPSTU spinulate
AEILNPSTY sapiently
AEILNPTTY patiently
AEILNPTUV pulvinate

AEILNQTUY antiquely
AEILNRRTU retinular
AEILNRSST trainless
AEILNRSTT sterilant
AEILNRSUV universal
AEILNRTTV trivalent
AEILNRTUY unreality
AEILNRTVY vernality
AEILNSSST saltiness
slatiness
stainless
AEILNSSTT taintless
AEILNSSTW slantwise
AEILNSTUY sinuately
AEILNSTVY sylvanite
AEILNSUUX unisexual
AEILOOSTT ostiolate
AEILOPRRS polariser
AEILOPRRZ polarizer
AEILOPRST saprolite
AEILOPRTT portatile
AEILOPRTV prolative
AEILOPTYZ zelotypia
AEILOQRUU Euraquilo
AEILORRTT literator
AEILORSST tailoress
AEILORSTT totaliser
AEILORTTX textorial
AEILORTTZ totalizer
AEILOSSST sassolite
AEILPPRST periplast
AEILPPRTU preputial
AEILPQRSU pasquiler
AEILPQSTU plastique
AEILPRSTT prelatist
AEILPRTVY privately
AEILPSSVY passively
AEILPSTTU stipulate
AEILPSTUV pulsative
AEILQRRUY reliquary
AEILRRTWW law-writer
AEILRSSTY slaistery
AEILRSTTU literatus
AEILRTTTW latter-wit
AEILRTUUX luxuriate
AEILSSSTV vistaless
AEILSSTUX sexualist
AEILSSUVY suasively
AEILSTUXY sexuality
AEIMMMNOT mammonite
AEIMMNNNO Memnonian
AEIMMNNOO monoamine
AEIMMNNRS △mannerism
AEIMMNNTU △minuteman
AEIMMNOPT pantomime
AEIMMRSSU summarise
AEIMMRSUZ summarize
AEIMMSTUV summative
AEIMNNNOO neonomian
AEIMNNNQU mannequin
AEIMNNOPU pneumonia
AEIMNNORS Normanise
AEIMNNORZ Normanize
AEIMNNOSY anonymise
AEIMNNOSZ neo-Nazism
AEIMNNOTT mentation
AEIMNNOYZ anonymize
AEIMNNPTY inpayment
AEIMNNRST △mannerist
AEIMNOPRT protamine
AEIMNORRS Romaniser
rosmarine
AEIMNORRZ Romanizer
AEIMNORST matronise
AEIMNORSW womaniser
AEIMNORTV normative
AEIMNORTW tire-woman
AEIMNORTZ matronize
AEIMNORWZ womanizer
AEIMNOSST Samsonite®
AEIMNOSSX Semi-Saxon
AEIMNPRST spearmint
AEIMNRRST ranterism
AEIMNRSTT stream-tin
AEIMNRSTU antiserum
misaunter
AEIMNRSTX Axminster
AEIMNRTTY maternity
AEIMNSSSS massiness
AEIMOPRRT imperator
AEIMOPRTX proximate
AEIMOPSTT optimates
AEIMORRSV Averroism
AEIMORSTT estimator
AEIMORTTU autotimer
AEIMPPRSU pauperism
AEIMPRRTT part-timer
AEIMPRSSY pyramises
AEIMPRSTU septarium
AEIMPRTUZ trapezium
AEIMQSTUU quaesitum
AEIMQSUUX Esquimaux
AEIMRRRTU terrarium
AEIMRRSTY martyrise
AEIMRRTTY termitary
AEIMRRTYZ martyrize
AEIMSSTTU mussitate
AEINNNOTW Newtonian
AEINNNPTU Neptunian
AEINNOPSX expansion
AEINNOPTT panettoni
AEINNORST Nestorian
rain-stone
Rosinante
AEINNORTU neuration
AEINNORTV nervation
vernation
AEINNORTZ Rozinante
AEINNOSST sensation
AEINNOSTW wantonise
AEINNOTTT attention
tentation
AEINNOTWZ wantonize
AEINNPPSS nappiness

AEINNPSST	inaptness
AEINNRRTU	Turnerian
AEINNRSTT	transient
AEINNRSTU	saturnine
AEINNRSTY	tyrannise
AEINNRTYZ	tyrannize
AEINNSSST	nastiness
AEINNSSTT	nattiness
AEINNSSTW	tawniness
AEINOOPRT	operation
AEINOOPSU	ionopause
AEINOORTX	exoration
AEINOPPPR	Popperian
AEINOPPRT	reappoint
AEINOPRSS	aspersion
AEINOPRST	patronise
	Peronista
AEINOPRSV	pervasion
AEINOPRSY	Aepyornis
AEINOPRTT	reptation
AEINOPRTU	epuration
	épuration
AEINOPRTV	overpaint
AEINOPRTZ	patronize
AEINOPSSS	soapiness
AEINOPSTT	septation
AEINOQRTU	inquorate
	ortanique
AEINOQTTU	totaquine
AEINORRST	serration
AEINORRTV	overtrain
AEINORSST	assertion
AEINORSSU	arsenious
AEINORSTT	stationer
AEINORSTV	overstain
AEINOSSST	assientos
AEINOSTTT	testation
AEINPPSSS	sappiness
AEINPRRST	transpire
AEINPRSST	paintress
AEINPRTTY	paternity
AEINPSSST	pastiness
AEINRRSST	tarriness
AEINRRSTT	inter-arts
	restraint
AEINRRTTV	travertin
AEINRSSTT	resistant
	tartiness
AEINRSSTU	sustainer
AEINSSSTT	tastiness
AEINSSTTT	tattiness
AEIOPRRSS	aspersoir
AEIOPRRSV	vaporiser
AEIOPRRVZ	vaporizer
AEIOPRTTV	portative
	vaporetti
AEIOPRTXY	expiatory
AEIOQTTUV	quotative
AEIORRSTV	Averroist
AEIORRTTT	trattorie
AEIORTUVV	uvarovite
AEIOSSSTT	steatosis
AEIOSTUVX	vexatious
AEIPPRSTU	△peripatus
AEIPRRSST	spiraster
AEIPRRSTT	tear-strip
AEIPRRSTU	rapturise
AEIPRRTUZ	rapturize
AEIPRRTVY	Varityper®
AEIPRSSTU	prussiate
AEIPRSTTU	petaurist
AEIPRSTUZ	trapezius
AEIPRSTWY	pit-sawyer
AEIPRSTYZ	party-size
AEIPSSTTV	tipstaves
AEIQRRTTU	triquetra
AEIQRRTUU	quaeritur
AEIQRTTTU	quartetti
AEIQRTTUZ	quartzite
AEIRRSSSY	sisserary
AEIRRSSTT	traitress
AEIRRSTTU	striature
AEIRRTTTU	triturate
AEIRSSTTU	tessitura
AEIRSTTTX	testatrix
AEIRSTTUY	austerity
AEISSTTUW	sweatsuit
AEJKMNORY	monkey-jar
AEJLLOSUY	jealously
AEJLNOSUU	unjealous
AEJOPRSSU	jasperous
AEJOPSTUX	juxtapose
AEKKLRRSY	skylarker
AEKKMNOOS	kakemonos
AEKLLSSST	stalkless
AEKLMOORT	toolmaker
AEKLMORSS	lossmaker
AEKLMORTW	metalwork
AEKLPRSSS	sparkless
AEKMMNOSS	monk's-seam
AEKMNOOQU	moonquake
AEKMNOORR	moonraker
AEKMNOPRS	pranksome
AEKMNOPSS	spokesman
AEKMNORSY	sokemanry
AEKMOORSY	karyosome
AEKMPRRSS	pressmark
AEKNOORST	snakeroot
AEKNPRRST	prankster
AEKNRSSST	starkness
AEKOOPSST	soopstake
AEKOPPRRW	paperwork
AEKOPRTYY	karyotype
AEKORRTWW	waterwork
AEKORRWWX	waxworker
AELLLMOSU	malleolus
AELLLOPRR	lap-roller
AELLLPPSY	play-spell
AELLLPTUU	pullulate
AELLLRSTU	stellular
AELLLSSWY	lawlessly
AELLMMOPY	polylemma
AELLMNOSZ	manzellos
AELLMNOTT	allotment

AELLMNOWW	well-woman
AELLMNRUY	numerally
AELLMNSSS	smallness
AELLMOPRY	permalloy
AELLMORST	martellos
AELLMORTY	allometry
AELLMPRST	smell-trap
AELLMPTUU	plumulate
AELLMQSSU	qualmless
AELLNOORT	lanterloo
AELLNOPRT	plant-lore
AELLNOSTT	attollens
AELLNOSTW	stonewall
AELLNOTTT	attollent
AELLNPSST	plantless
AELLNQUUY	unequally
AELLNRTUY	neutrally
AELLNRTVY	ventrally
AELLNSSUY	sensually
AELLOOPRT	allotrope
AELLOPRRT	patroller
AELLOPRTW	pot-waller
AELLOPRTY	prolately
AELLOPTUV	pole-vault
AELLORRST	rostellar
AELLORSTY	allostery
AELLORSWW	swallower
AELLORTTY	allottery
AELLOSUYZ	zealously
AELLRSSTY	artlessly
AELLTTUXY	textually
AELMMNOST	malmstone
AELMMOOPS	amplosome
AELMMORST	△maelstrom
AELMMOSUU	mausoleum
AELMMRSTY	symmetral
AELMNNNTU	annulment
AELMNNOOP	monoplane
AELMNOOPR	lampooner
AELMNOORT	monolater
AELMNOORY	monolayer
AELMNOPPY	empanoply
AELMNOPTU	pulmonate
AELMNORST	marlstone
AELMNORTT	tremolant
AELMNORWW	lawnmower
AELMNOSSW	womanless
AELMNOSTU	alum-stone
AELMNOSTY	salt-money
AELMNOTTU	outmantle
AELMNPSTU	psalm-tune
AELMNRSTU	menstrual
	Ulsterman
AELMNRTTU	tremulant
AELMOOPRT	plate-room
AELMOORSS	salesroom
AELMOPSTT	palmettos
AELMOSTTU	mulattoes
AELMRTWXY	myrtle-wax
AELNNPTWY	twalpenny
AELNOPRSY	layperson
AELNORSTU	Solutrean
AELNORTVW	navelwort
AELNOSUUZ	unzealous
AELNOTUVV	vol-au-vent
AELNRRSSU	ruralness
AELNRRUVY	vulnerary
AELNRSTTU	resultant
AELNSSSTU	sultaness
AELNSSSUU	usualness
AELOOPRSU	leaporous
AELOOPRSX	exosporal
AELOOPRVY	parleyvoo
AELOORRTT	tolerator
AELOORRVW	love-arrow
AELOPPRWY	powerplay
AELOPRRTW	pearlwort
AELOPRRTY	proletary
	pyrolater
AELOPRSTU	sporulate
AELOPRSTV	overplast
AELOPRTWY	polywater
AELOPSSSU	espousals
AELOPSTTU	postulate
AELORRSTW	laserwort
AELORRSTX	extrorsal
AELORTTUV	outtravel
AELPPPPRU	paper-pulp
AELPPRRUU	purpureal
AELPRSSST	psaltress
	strapless
AELPRSSTU	pertussal
	supersalt
AELPSTTUU	pustulate
AELQRRTUY	quarterly
AEMMNNOTY	momentany
AEMMNORRW	marrow-men
AEMMNORTY	manometry
	momentary
AEMMNRSTU	sarmentum
AEMMORSSY	massymore
AEMMRSTYY	asymmetry
AEMNNORST	ornaments
	semantron
AEMNNORTT	remontant
AEMNNOSWW	newswoman
AEMNOOPRT	protonema
AEMNOORTT	Nototrema
AEMNOORTX	taxonomer
AEMNORRTU	numerator
AEMNORSTU	anoestrum
AEMNORSTV	transmove
AEMNORSTY	monastery
AEMNPPRSY	panspermy
AEMNPRTUY	prytaneum
AEMNRSSST	smartness
AEMNRSTTU	transmute
AEMNRSTVY	vestryman
AEMOOORRT	aeromotor
AEMOORSTT	stateroom
AEMOORSTX	xerostoma
AEMOPRRTY	temporary
AEMOPRSTU	mouse-trap
AEMOPSTTY	asymptote

AEMORSTTW	two-master
AEMPPRTUW	pump-water
AEMPRRSTU	supermart
AEMPRSSTY	spymaster
AEMQRRTUY	marquetry
AEMRRSSTU	surmaster
AEMRSSTTW	straw-stem
AENNORRST	resnatron
AENNORSTY	sonnetary
AENNPSSTU	unaptness
AENNRSSTY	tyranness
AENNRSTTU	transeunt
AENOOPPRT	protanope
AENOOPSST	soapstone
AENOORRST	resonator
AENOORRTV	renovator
AENOPRRTW	part-owner
AENOPRSST	patroness
	transpose
AENOPRSUV	supernova
AENORRTWW	water-worn
AENORSSTT	starstone
AENORSSTU	anestrous
	anoestrus
AENORSTTY	attorneys
AENORSTWW	snow-water
AENPRTTTU	perttaunt
AENQSSSTU	squatness
AENRRSTVY	servantry
AENRSSSTW	swartness
AENRSSTTV	transvest
AEOOPPRRT	porporate
AEOOPRSTZ	rose-topaz
AEOOPRTTV	vaporetto
AEOORRSTV	overroast
AEOORTTUU	autoroute
AEOPQRRTU	parroquet
AEOPRRRTY	portrayer
AEOPRRSSY	aspersory
AEOPRRSTT	prostrate
AEOPRRSTU	prosateur
	pterosaur
AEOPRRSTW	spearwort
AEOPRSTTY	poetastry
AEOPRSTWY	top-sawyer
AEOQRRSSU	squarrose
AEOQRSTUZ	quartzose
AEOQRTTTU	quartetto
AEORRSSTY	assertory
AEORRSTZZ	terrazzos
AEORSSTUU	trousseau
AEPPRSTUU	suppurate
AEPQRRTUY	parquetry
AEPRRSSTU	superstar
AEQRRSTUY	try-square
AERRSSTUU	susurrate
AERRSSVYY	arsy-versy
AERRSTTWY	stewartry
AFFFFINNY	niff-naffy
AFFGIIRST	sgraffiti
AFFGIKNOT	taking-off
AFFGIORST	sgraffito
AFFHHILST	half-shift
AFFHILRSY	raffishly
AFFHIPSTW	whipstaff
AFFIILNPT	plaintiff
AFFILLNTY	flay-flint
AFFILNOUX	affluxion
AFFILNRUY	ruffianly
AFFIMNNPU	muffin-pan
AFFIPSSTT	tipstaffs
AFFLOOTTU	footfault
AFFMOORST	staffroom
AFGGGINOT	faggoting
AFGGIINTU	fatiguing
AFGGILNOS	fog-signal
AFGHHILLT	half-light
AFGHHIRST	fish-garth
AFGHILLNS	halflings
AFGHILLNT	nightfall
AFGHILSTT	light-fast
AFGHINOSU	fish-guano
AFGHIPRTW	whip-graft
AFGHLLSTU	ghastfull
AFGHMOORT	homograft
AFGHNRTUU	unfraught
AFGHORSTU	far-sought
AFGIIILNR	filigrain
AFGIILNNU	unfailing
AFGIILNSY	salifying
AFGIILRTY	fragility
AFGIIMNRS	misfaring
AFGIIMNRY	ramifying
AFGIIMSTU	fastigium
AFGIINRRY	fairy-ring
AFGIINRTY	ratifying
AFGIKNORS	forsaking
AFGILLMNY	flamingly
AFGILLNRY	flaringly
AFGILLNST	flatlings
AFGILLNUY	gainfully
AFGILLOPT	pilot-flag
AFGILMNOS	flamingos
AFGILMNOY	foamingly
AFGILNNTU	flaunting
AFGILNNUU	ungainful
AFGILNNWY	fawningly
AFGILNORV	flavoring
AFGILRSTU	frugalist
AFGILRTUY	frugality
AFGIMNORU	anguiform
AFGIMORTU	fumigator
AFGIMORTY	fogramity
AFGINNPRY	frying-pan
AFGINOORT	frigatoon
AFGIOSTTT	fagottist
AFGLLSSSU	glassfuls
AFGLNRTUU	fulgurant
AFGNRSUUY	ray-fungus
AFGORSSST	soft-grass
AFHHLRTTU	half-truth
AFHIIKNOP	kniphofia
AFHIILNSS	snail-fish
AFHIILPRS	April-fish

AFHILRSTW trawl-fish
AFHIMNOSW fish-woman
AFHIORRSZ razor-fish
AFHIORSTY forsythia
AFHIRSTTU Tartufish
AFHLLMRUY harmfully
AFHLLORST shortfall
AFHLMNRUU unharmful
AFHLOOPPY fool-happy
AFHOORRST hoar-frost
AFHOOSSTT soothfast
AFIIILNOT filiation
AFIILNNOT inflation
AFIILNOOT foliation
AFIILRSTT stairlift
AFIIMNRRY infirmary
AFIINNOST saintfoin
AFIINORSU △infusoria
AFIIORRTU fioritura
AFIJKORST forjaskit
AFIKLLMOT milk-float
AFIKLORTY forky-tail
AFILLNOUX fluxional
AFILLNPTU plaintful
AFILLNPUY painfully
AFILMMORS formalism
AFILMNNTU fulminant
AFILMOPRS salpiform
AFILMORRV larviform
AFILMORST formalist
AFILMORTY formality
AFILNNPUU unpainful
AFILNOOTT flotation
AFILNORST frost-nail
AFILNOSTU sulfation
AFILNQUUY unqualify
AFILOORSS fossorial
AFIMMMMOR mammiform
AFIMNNORT informant
AFIMNOORT formation
AFIMORRTU tauriform
AFIMRSTTU Tartufism
AFINOOPRR rainproof
AFINOPRTY profanity
AFIOORSTT stairfoot
AFIORTTTT tit-for-tat
AFIOSTTUU fatuitous
AFKLOOSTT footstalk
AFKMOOPRR proof-mark
AFKNNORRT front-rank
AFLLLPUYY playfully
AFLLMNOUY moanfully
AFLLMOORT malt-floor
AFLLOOSTT foot-stall
AFLMORRUY formulary
AFLNOOPTU puftaloon
AFLOOPSTY splay-foot
AFLOORSUV flavorous
AFLOPRRSU fluorspar
AFMNORRST transform
AFMOORSTY Styrofoam®
styrofoam
AFMORRTTU trout-farm
AFNORSTWY frontways
AFOOPRRST star-proof
AFOORSSTZ sforzatos
AFORRSTTU Astroturf®
AGGGILLNY laggingly
AGGGINPRS spragging
AGGHHILSY haggishly
AGGHILOOY hagiology
AGGHILSWY waggishly
AGGHLOOPR logograph
AGGIIIMNN imagining
AGGIILNNS signaling
AGGIILNNT ting-a-ling
AGGIILNVW law-giving
AGGIIMNST gigantism
AGGIIMNTY gigmanity
AGGIINNOS agonising
AGGIINNOZ agonizing
AGGIINNTV vintaging
AGGILLLNY gallingly
AGGILLNOP galloping
AGGILLNRY glaringly
AGGILNNOS ganglions
singalong
AGGILNNPS spangling
AGGILNNRW wrangling
AGGILNNTW twangling
AGGILNOPY play-going
AGGILNPSY gaspingly
AGGILNRTY gratingly
AGGILOORY agriology
AGGIMMNNO gammoning
AGGINNOOR gorgonian
AGGINORRS grosgrain
AGGINORTT garotting
AGGMOORRT mortgagor
AGGMOSTYY mystagogy
AGHHIISTW waist-high
AGHHIKNTW nighthawk
AGHHILRTU ultra-high
AGHHILTUY haughtily
AGHHINRST thrashing
AGHHLOOPR holograph
AGHHMOOPR homograph
AGHIILLNP phialling
AGHIILLTT tail-light
AGHIILNRT night-rail
AGHIINNNT tanghinin
AGHIINNSV vanishing
AGHIINPST giantship
AGHIINRSV ravishing
AGHIINRTT raintight
AGHIIORSV viragoish
AGHIIRRST hairst-rig
AGHIKLNTW night-walk
AGHIKNNST thankings
AGHILLLOP Gallophil
AGHILLMPT lamplight
AGHILLNOP △anglophil
AGHILLNRY narghilly
AGHILLNTY haltingly

AGHILMORT algorithm
logarithm
AGHILNPSS splashing
AGHILNPTY plaything
AGHILNTUY naughtily
AGHILOOPT Lotophagi
AGHILRSTT starlight
AGHIMNNRU unharming
AGHIMNRST hamstring
AGHIMNRTY nightmary
AGHIMNSST sightsman
AGHIMOPRY amphigory
AGHIMORST histogram
AGHIMOSTT Gothamist
AGHIMSTTU mistaught
AGHINNSTU unhasting
AGHINNTTU unhatting
AGHINOQSU qinghaosu
AGHINORRW harrowing
AGHINORTU authoring
AGHINPSUW washing-up
AGHINRRSY garnishry
AGHINRTTW thwarting
AGHIPRSUU augurship
AGHKKOSYZ kok-saghyz
AGHKMOPRY kymograph
AGHKOORSS grasshook
AGHLLOOPY haplology
AGHLMNOPU ploughman
AGHLMOOPR lagomorph
AGHLMOOTU goalmouth
AGHLNOOTY anthology
AGHLNOSTU onslaught
AGHLOOPTY pathology
AGHLOPPRY polygraph
AGHLOPPYY polyphagy
AGHLOPRXY xylograph
AGHLORSSU hour-glass
AGHMNOOPR monograph
nomograph
phonogram
AGHMNOOPY monophagy
AGHMNRSTU hamstrung
AGHMOOPRT photogram
tomograph
AGHMOPRYY myography
AGHNOOPRS sonograph
AGHNOPSSU sphagnous
AGHNPRSUW spur-whang
AGHOOPRRT rotograph
AGHOOPRRY orography
AGHOOPRYZ zoography
AGHOPRRUY urography
AGHORSTTY hygrostat
AGIIILNRV Virgilian
AGIIIMNPR impairing
AGIIIMNST imaginist
AGIIINNNS sinningia
AGIIINNRT Nigritian
AGIIINNRV Virginian
AGIIINSTV vaginitis
AGIIKLMNR grimalkin
AGIIKMNNP pin-making
AGIIKMNST mistaking
AGIILLNOR gorillian
AGIILLNRT trialling
AGIILLNRV rivalling
AGIILLNRY railingly
AGIILLNUV ingluvial
AGIILLNWY wailingly
AGIILLOSV villagios
villiagos
AGIILLRSY sigillary
AGIILMNTY malignity
AGIILNNPT pantiling
AGIILNNST saintling
AGIILNNWZ Zwinglian
AGIILNORS originals
sailoring
signorial
AGIILNORT largition
tailoring
AGIILNORU Liguorian
AGIILNOST intaglios
AGIILNQSU squailing
AGIILNRSV virginals
AGIILNSSS isinglass
AGIILNSTW swingtail
AGIILNTWY waitingly
AGIIMMNRT immigrant
AGIIMMSST sigmatism
AGIIMNORT migration
AGIIMNOST sigmation
AGIIMNRST maistring
AGIIMNSSS misassign
AGIIMNSSY missaying
AGIIMORTT mitigator
AGIIMRSTT trigamist
AGIINNORS △signorina
AGIINNRST straining
AGIINNRTT intrigant
AGIINNRTY trigynian
AGIINORST trisagion
AGIINPPRS apprising
AGIINPPRZ apprizing
AGIINPRST traipsing
AGIIORRRT irrigator
AGIIPRSST spagirist
AGIIRSSTT gastritis
AGIIRSTTU guitarist
AGIJLNRRY jarringly
AGIJNORST jargonist
AGIKLMRSU milk-sugar
AGIKLNOSY soakingly
AGIKLNOTT talking-to
AGIKLNPRS sparkling
AGIKLNQUY quakingly
AGIKLRSSS silk-grass
AGIKMNNSU unmasking
AGIKMNOPT topmaking
AGIKMORSS kissogram
AGIKNQSUW squawking
AGILLLNRU all-ruling
AGILLLNUY lingually

AGILLLOPY	palillogy
AGILLMNRS	ring-small
AGILLNNNU	annulling
AGILLNNPT	plantling
AGILLNOPW	walloping
AGILLNOTT	allotting
	totalling
AGILLNOWW	wallowing
AGILLNQSU	squalling
AGILLNSTY	lastingly
AGILMNNOO	Mongolian
AGILMNNOT	lamington
AGILMNOPS	panlogism
AGILMNPRT	trampling
AGILMNSUY	amusingly
AGILMOORS	lagrimoso
AGILMOORY	Mariology
AGILMRSUV	vulgarism
AGILNNOPS	plainsong
AGILNNOQU	Algonquin
AGILNNOTY	atoningly
AGILNNPTY	pantingly
AGILNNRTY	rantingly
AGILNNRWY	warningly
AGILNNWYY	yawningly
AGILNOPYY	Polygynia
AGILNORRY	roaringly
AGILNORSY	soaringly
AGILNORVY	vainglory
AGILNOSTW	wagon-lits
	wagons-lit
AGILNPRSW	sprawling
AGILNPRSY	raspingly
	sparingly
AGILNPRTY	pratingly
AGILNPRYY	prayingly
AGILNPSTT	splatting
AGILNPSUY	pausingly
AGILNRSTT	startling
AGILNRSTY	staringly
	strayling
AGILNTTTW	twattling
AGILOOPST	apologist
AGILOPRUY	uropygial
AGILOQRSU	gas-liquor
AGILPRSUW	Walpurgis
AGILRRTUY	garrulity
AGILRTUVY	vulgarity
AGIMMNSUY	gymnasium
AGIMNNOOR	marooning
AGIMNNOOY	Monogynia
AGIMNNORS	amornings
AGIMNNSUU	unamusing
AGIMNNSUY	synangium
AGIMNORST	sigmatron
AGIMNORSU	ignoramus
AGIMOOSSU	isogamous
AGIMOPRRS	spirogram
AGIMORRTY	migratory
AGIMORSTU	trigamous
AGIMRSTTU	Targumist
AGINNORRW	narrowing
AGINNOSUV	△sauvignon
AGINNPRSU	unsparing
AGINNRUVY	unvarying
AGINNSTUU	Tungusian
AGINNSTUW	unwasting
AGINNSTUY	unstaying
AGINOOPSS	poison-gas
AGINOPRTT	pottingar
AGINOPRTU	purgation
AGINOPRUV	vapouring
AGINORSTY	signatory
AGINOSTTU	gustation
AGINOTTTU	guttation
AGINPPRST	strapping
	trappings
AGINPPRSW	wrappings
AGINPRSTU	upstaring
AGINQRRUY	quarrying
AGINQSTTU	squatting
AGINSTTUU	situtunga
AGIOORSTU	autogiros
AGIOPRRSY	spirogyra
AGIPRSSTY	spagyrist
AGJKNORRU	kurrajong
AGKLMNOOY	golomynka
AGKLOORYY	karyology
AGKLORSSW	glasswork
AGKNORSST	knotgrass
AGKOPRSTU	task-group
AGLLNOOPY	polygonal
AGLMOORSU	glamorous
AGLMOORYY	Maryology
AGLMPRSUU	lump-sugar
	sugar-lump
	sugarplum
AGLNOORUY	uranology
AGLNORSUU	granulous
AGLNOSTYZ	lazy-tongs
AGLOOPRTY	patrology
AGLOORSST	glossator
AGLOORSTY	astrology
AGLOOTTUY	tautology
AGLOPPRUY	playgroup
AGLOPRSST	grass-plot
AGLORRSSU	grossular
AGLORRSUU	garrulous
AGLORSSTW	glasswort
AGMMNOORS	groomsman
AGMMOSTUU	gummatous
AGMNNORST	strongman
AGMNORRST	strongarm
AGMNOSSUY	syngamous
AGMNRTUYZ	zygantrum
AGMNSSTUY	nystagmus
AGMOOOSUZ	zoogamous
AGNNOPPTU	oppugnant
AGNPSSTUW	wasp-stung
AGNRRSTUY	strangury
AGOORSTUY	autogyros
AGOPRRTUY	purgatory
AGOPRSUVY	gravy-soup
AGORSTTUY	gustatory

AHHIKLSWY	hawkishly
AHHIKORST	Tokharish
AHHILLOPY	halophily
AHHILLWWY	whillywha
AHHILMOPT	philomath
AHHILTTUW	withhault
AHHIORSTU	authorish
AHHLORSTU	short-haul
AHHMOPRTU	mouth-harp
AHHMOSTUW	mouthwash
AHHNORRST	hartshorn
AHHOOSTTW	toothwash
AHIIILSST	lithiasis
AHIILLOST	sialolith
AHIILMNTU	humiliant
AHIILOOPZ	zoophilia
AHIILORSU	hilarious
AHIILOSST	halitosis
AHIILPRSV	rivalship
AHIIMMRST	Mithraism
AHIIMRSTT	Mithraist
AHIINOPPR	Hipparion
AHIINORST	historian
AHIINPSST	saintship
AHIIPPRTY	hippiatry
AHIIPRSSZ	sizarship
AHIIRRSTT	arthritis
AHIJMOPRS	majorship
AHIKKNNTT	think-tank
AHIKKNRSS	sharkskin
AHIKLMSWY	mawkishly
AHIKLNSVY	knavishly
AHILLNRTT	thrillant
AHILLOPRT	prothalli
AHILLOPSV	Slavophil
AHILLOSSW	sallowish
AHILLOSTW	tallowish
AHILLPSSY	splashily
AHILLPSTW	whipstall
AHILLSSTY	saltishly
AHILLSSVY	slavishly
AHILMNNUY	inhumanly
AHILMOPRS	rhopalism
AHILMOPSY	syphiloma
AHILMORST	hail-storm
AHILMPRTU	triumphal
AHILMRSTY	lathyrism
AHILNOPTY	notaphily
AHILNORTT	triathlon
AHILNPPUY	unhappily
AHILOORST	Lotharios
AHILORTTY	throatily
AHILOSTTT	statolith
AHILPSSWY	waspishly
AHILQSSUY	squashily
AHILRSSTT	startlish
AHIMMMNOS	mammonish
AHIMMMOSS	shammosim
AHIMMNORU	harmonium
AHIMMOPRS	amorphism
AHIMNNORY	inharmony
AHIMNOOSU	homousian
AHIMNOPRS	orphanism
AHIMNORST	△harmonist
AHIMNPPSU	upmanship
AHIMNPSTY	sympathin
AHIMNRTUU	anthurium
AHIMOOSTX	homotaxis
AHIMOPRSY	mayorship
AHIMOPSTY	opsimathy
AHIMOPSUX	amphioxus
AHIMORRSW	marrowish
AHIMORSTU	authorism
AHINNOOPT	phonation
AHINNOPTY	antiphony
	△typhonian
AHINNOTTU	Huttonian
AHINOOPRR	orpharion
AHINOOPTY	hypotonia
AHINOORTT	hortation
AHINOPRSS	parsonish
AHINPRSST	transship
	trans-ship
AHIOOPPST	photopsia
AHIOORSTX	orthoaxis
AHIOPPRRY	porphyria
AHIOPPSSY	apophysis
AHIOPRSTU	out-parish
AHIOPRSUV	vapourish
AHIOPRSUX	Xiphosura
AHIOPSTXY	hypotaxis
AHIORRSST	arthrosis
AHIORRTWY	airworthy
AHIORTTUY	authority
AHJNNORWY	Johnny-raw
AHKLOOSTU	akoluthos
AHKNOOPST	Pakhtoons
AHKORSSWW	swashwork
AHLLLOSWY	shallowly
AHLLMOOPR	allomorph
AHLLMORUY	humorally
AHLLOPSTY	tallyshop
AHLLOPSUY	aphyllous
AHLMNOSWY	showmanly
AHLMOOOPR	homopolar
AHLMOOPSY	homoplasy
AHLMOOPTY	homotypal
AHLMOPTYY	polymathy
AHLNOTXXY	xanthoxyl
AHLNOTXYZ	zanthoxyl
AHLORSTTW	stalworth
AHLORSTUW	twalhours
AHMMNOTTU	mutton-ham
AHMNOOPTY	taphonomy
AHMOOPRSU	amorphous
AHMORRSTW	marshwort
AHNNNOOTY	hootnanny
AHNOOPRTY	phonatory
AHNOOPTUY	autophony
AHNOPSTYY	hyponasty
AHNORRTTY	thyratron
AHOOPRRTX	prothorax
AHOOPRTTU	autotroph
AHOOPSTTT	Photostat®

AHOORRSTW	arrow-shot
AHOORRTTY	hortatory
AHOORTWWX	thorow-wax
AHPRSSTTU	push-start
AIIILLNTY	initially
AIIILMMSS	Ismailism
AIIILMNST	laminitis
AIIILMPRT	primitial
AIIIMNNOT	miniation
AIIIMNOTT	imitation
AIIIMPRST	primitias
AIIINNNOT	inanition
AIIINNSTY	asininity
AIIINORST	irisation
AIIINORTT	initiator
AIIINOTTV	vitiation
AIIJLOTVY	joviality
AIILLMRSY	similarly
AIILLPRRS	spirillar
AIILLPRST	pillarist
AIILLRSTT	triallist
AIILLRTVY	trivially
AIILMMNUU	aluminium
AIILMNNOT	Miltonian
AIILMNORT	trinomial
AIILMNPSU	Paulinism
AIILMNRTY	matriliny
AIILMNSST	Stalinism
AIILMOSST	altissimo
AIILMPRRY	primarily
AIILMPRSS	spiralism
AIILMPRTY	primality
AIILMRSTU	ritualism
AIILNOOST	isolation
AIILNOOTV	violation
AIILNOPST	pianolist
AIILNOQTU	liquation
AIILNORSV	livraison
AIILNOSTT	siltation
AIILNOTTU	tuitional
AIILNPRST	air-splint
AIILNPRTY	patriliny
AIILNPSTU	Paulinist
AIILNRSST	sinistral
AIILNSSTT	Stalinist
AIILPRSST	spiralist
	spritsail
AIILPRSTU	spiritual
AIILPRSTY	spirality
AIILRSTTU	ritualist
AIILSSTUV	visualist
AIILSTUVY	visuality
AIIMMPRSV	vampirism
AIIMNNORS	Rosminian
AIIMNNTUY	unanimity
AIIMNOPRS	prosimian
AIIMNOPSS	impassion
AIIMNOSTY	animosity
AIIMNPSTT	timpanist
AIIMNRSSY	Syrianism
AIIMOPRRS	apriorism
AIIMPSSSV	passivism
AIIMRSTUU	Mauritius
AIIMRSUVV	vivariums
AIINNOPRS	sopranini
AIINNORTT	nitration
AIINNORTU	ruination
	urination
AIINNOSTU	sinuation
AIINNOTTX	antitoxin
AIINNPRRT	rain-print
AIINNQQUU	quinquina
AIINOOQRU	Iroquoian
AIINOPRST	spiration
AIINOPRTT	partition
AIINOPRTV	privation
AIINORSTT	striation
AIINORSVY	visionary
AIINORTTT	attrition
	titration
AIINOSTTU	situation
AIINOSTXX	saxitoxin
AIINOTTTU	attuition
AIINQTTUY	antiquity
AIINRSTUV	antivirus
AIINRTUVV	Vitruvian
AIIOPRRST	apriorist
AIIOPRRTY	apriority
AIIOPRSSS	psoriasis
AIIOPRSTT	parotitis
	topiarist
AIIOPRTVY	oviparity
AIIORRRTT	irritator
AIIORSTTV	visitator
AIIPRTTUY	pituitary
AIIPSSSTV	passivist
AIIPSSTVY	passivity
AIJNNNOOS	Jonsonian
AIKKLNORS	Raskolnik
AIKLLLMUW	waulkmill
AIKLLMMOR	milk-molar
AIKLMNRTU	trunk-mail
AIKLNOPRW	plainwork
AIKLNOSSY	ankylosis
AIKLNOSTT	klinostat
AIKLRRUVY	Valkyriur
AIKMMNOOS	makimonos
AIKMNNOSW	kinswoman
AIKMORSSV	visor-mask
AIKNNOOST	isokontan
AIKNOOOPS	poison-oak
AIKORRSTW	stairwork
AILLLMTUW	multi-wall
AILLLPRUV	pulvillar
AILLMMORY	immorally
AILLMNNOY	nominally
AILLMNOUV	voluminal
AILLMOOPS	liposomal
AILLMOOTT	tomatillo
AILLMOPTY	optimally
AILLMPRSU	pluralism
AILLNORST	tonsillar
AILLNORSU	lunisolar
AILLNOSSW	snail-slow

AILLNOSUV villanous
AILLNOTUU ululation
AILLNRSUY insularly
AILLOPPSU papillous
AILLOPSST plastisol
AILLOPTVY pivotally
AILLORUXY uxorially
AILLPPRUY pupillary
AILLPRSTU pluralist
AILLPRTUY plurality
AILLRTTUY titularly
AILLRTUVY virtually
AILMMOORT immolator
AILMMORST △immortals
AILMMRSUY summarily
AILMMSTUU mutualism
AILMMTTUU ultimatum
AILMNOOPS palominos
AILMNOOSS Molossian
AILMNOPRT trampolin
AILMNOPSS spoilsman
AILMNOPST Platonism
AILMNOPSY amylopsin
AILMNORTY normality
trionymal
AILMNORUV mournival
AILMNOSUU aluminous
AILMNSTTU stimulant
AILMOORRT rail-motor
AILMOPRVY ivory-palm
AILMOPSSY symposial
AILMORSTU simulator
AILMORTTU mutilator
AILMORTTY mortality
AILMOSSTY atmolysis
AILMPRSTY palmistry
AILMTTUUY mutuality
AILNNOPTU Plutonian
AILNNOSSW sons-in-law
AILNNSTTU insultant
AILNNSTTY instantly
AILNNSTUY unsaintly
AILNOOPRT portolani
prolation
AILNOORST tonsorial
torsional
AILNOOSTV solvation
AILNOOTUV ovulation
AILNOPSTT Platonist
AILNOPSTU platinous
pulsation
AILNOQRTU tan-liquor
AILNORSTU insulator
Solutrian
AILNOSUXY anxiously
AILNPPSTU suppliant
AILNPQTUY piquantly
AILNRTUUX luxuriant
AILOOPRST spoliator
AILOOPTTU autopilot
AILOORSSS rosa-solis
AILOORSUV variolous
AILOPRSTV post-viral
AILORRTTY traitorly
AILORSUVY savourily
variously
AILOSSTUY autolysis
AILPRRSSU surprisal
AILPRSTUY stipulary
AILQRSTUY squiralty
AIMMMMNOS mammonism
AIMMMNOST mammonist
AIMMNNOOT motion-man
AIMMNNORS Normanism
AIMMNNOST Montanism
AIMMNOOTY amniotomy
AIMMNORTY matrimony
AIMMNOSTU summation
AIMMPRSUU marsupium
AIMMRRTUY martyrium
AIMMRSSTU summarist
AIMNNOORT nominator
AIMNNOPST pointsman
AIMNNOSTT Montanist
AIMNNOSUU unanimous
AIMNNOTYY anonymity
AIMNOPRSY parsimony
AIMNOPRTT important
AIMNOPRTY patrimony
AIMNORRST rainstorm
AIMNORRTU ruminator
AIMNORSUU uniramous
AIMNORTTW taint-worm
AIMNPSTTY tympanist
AIMNRSSTU saturnism
AIMOORSTY amorosity
AIMOORTTV motivator
AIMOPSSTU potassium
AIMPSSSTU assumpsit
AIMQRSTUU Utraquism
AINNNNOTU nunnation
AINNNOSTU unisonant
AINNOOOTZ ozonation
AINNOOPRS sopranino
AINNOOPRT pronation
AINNOORTT intonator
AINNOORTV innovator
AINNORSTT strontian
AINNOSUUX unanxious
AINNOTTWW witwanton
AINOOPPRT appointor
apportion
AINOOPRRT proration
troparion
AINOOPRST rat-poison
AINOOPTTU autopoint
AINOOQTTU quotation
AINOORSTT sortation
AINOOSSTT ostinatos
AINOOSTTV ottavinos
AINOOTTUX autotoxin
AINOPRSST sopranist
AINOPRSTU Proustian
supinator

AINOPRSUU uniparous
AINORSTTU outstrain
AINORSTUU souari-nut
AINPSSTUU puissaunt
AINRSSTTU saturnist
AINRSTTTU antitrust
AIOOORRST oratorios
AIOOPRSTV protoavis
AIOOPRSUV apivorous
oviparous
AIOOSTTTT tattooist
AIORRSSTU sartorius
AIORRSTUV rotavirus
AIPRRSTTU rapturist
AIQRSTTUU Utraquist
AJMNORUWY jurywoman
AJMPRSTTU jump-start
AJPRRTUYY party-jury
AKKLLNPSU knapskull
AKKLLOSTY yolk-stalk
AKLLMMOWY mollymawk
AKLLMNOSU molluskan
AKLMNORWY workmanly
AKLMNPSTU musk-plant
AKLORSSTW saltworks
AKMNOORWW workwoman
AKMNORSTU Turkomans
AKMORRSWY marrowsky
AKNNORSYY synkaryon
AKNOOPRRY prokaryon
AKOOPRRTY prokaryot
AKOOPRSSW soap-works
ALLMNOSTW small-town
ALLNOOPTY polytonal
ALLNOOPYZ polyzonal
ALLNOPTTU pollutant
ALLNORUYY unroyally
ALLNSUUUY unusually
ALLOOPRTY allotropy
ALLOPPRUY popularly
ALLOPRSTY sallyport
ALLRSTUUY suturally
ALMMNRUUY nummulary
ALMMNSSUU Mussulman
ALMNNOOOS monsoonal
ALMNNOUWY unwomanly
ALMNOOPTY toponymal
ALMNOORTY monolatry
ALMNOPRUY pulmonary
ALMNOPSST mossplant
ALMOORSUY amorously
ALMOPSTYY polymasty
ALNNOOPST loon-pants
ALNOOOPRT portolano
ALNOPPRUU unpopular
ALNOPSTTU postulant
ALNORTUVY voluntary
ALNPSTTUU pustulant
ALOOOPRTZ protozoal
ALOOPRRTW owl-parrot
ALOOPRYYZ polyzoary
ALOOPSTYZ zooplasty
ALOPPRSSU prolapsus
ALOPRRSUY spur-royal
ALOPRRTYY pyrolatry
ALOPRSTUY pulsatory
AMNNOOSUY anonymous
AMNOOOPRT Monotropa
AMNOOPSTW postwoman
AMNOORSTY astronomy
AMNOPRSST sportsman
AMNPRSTTU transumpt
AMOOORSTV vasomotor
AMORRSTWW strawworm
AMPRSTUUY sumptuary
ANNOOPRSU nonparous
ANNORSTUY tyrannous
ANNRRTTUU nurturant
ANOOOPRSZ sporozoan
ANOOOPRTZ protozoan
ANOOPSSWY spoonways
ANOPRRSTT transport
ANORSUUVY unsavoury
ANRRSSTUU susurrant
AOOORRRTW arrowroot
AOOORRTTV Rotovator®
rotovator
AOOPRRSTT protostar
AOPRRSTTW strapwort
AOPRRSTUU rapturous
AORRRTWWY worrywart
AORSTTTUY statutory

B

BBBCKOOSY bobbysock
BBBDEEELP pebble-bed
BBBDEELRU blubbered
BBBEEELMU bumble-bee
BBBEEELUZ Beelzebub
BBBEELORS beslobber
BBBEELRSU beslubber
BBBEGLMUU bubble-gum
BBBEHJOOR hobjobber
BBBEINNOT bobbin-net
BBCCHKLOU chubb-lock
BBCEHKMOT bomb-ketch
BBCEHLOUY cubby-hole
BBCEHORRY bob-cherry
cherry-bob
BBCEILRRS scribbler
BBCEIRSSU subscribe
BBCGINRSU scrubbing
BBCIIILMS biblicism
BBCIIILST biblicist
BBCKKLOOO block-book
BBDDEESYY beddy-byes
BBDDEJOOR odd-jobber
BBDDILOOR blood-bird
BBDEEHMTU bethumbed
BBDEELMTU betumbled
BBDEELOTT bed-bottle
BBDEGIMNO demobbing
BBDEHMOPT depth-bomb
BBDEIMRRU umber-bird

BBDEIORRW bower-bird
BBDELMMOU Bumbledom
BBDNOORUW brow-bound
BBDNOSTUU bundobust
BBEEEEINR bebeerine
BBEEEGGLR beglerbeg
BBEEEHLMU humble-bee
BBEEEINRR berberine
BBEEFLLUY bully-beef
BBEEGILNO gobbeline
BBEEHINRS nebbisher
BBEEILLNO bellibone
BBEEINRTZ rebbetzin
BBEEIRRSU rubberise
BBEEIRRUZ rubberize
BBEELRRUY blueberry
BBEFLORRY robber-fly
BBEGGNOOW wobbegong
BBEGHIIRS gibberish
BBEGHILOS bobsleigh
BBEGINSSU gubbinses
BBEGLMTUU tumble-bug
BBEGORTTU bog-butter
BBEHLLMOS bombshell
BBEHLNOOY honey-blob
BBEHLOSSY hobbyless
BBEHRRSUY shrubbery
BBEILLNNO bonnibell
BBEINNOSS nobbiness
BBEINSSTU tubbiness
BBEJNORTU nutjobber
BBEKMMOOS smoke-bomb
BBEORTTUX butter-box
BBERRTTUU butterbur
BBFGIILNR fribbling
BBFHIILRS fribblish
BBFMOOOPR bomb-proof
BBGGIJMOU jiggumbob
BBGHILNOO hobgoblin
BBGHIMOST bomb-sight
BBGHINORT throbbing
BBGIIILMN bilimbing
BBGIILNQU quibbling
BBGIINQSU squibbing
BBGIIOSTY gibbosity
BBGILNOSY sobbingly
BBGILOSUY gibbously
BBHILLNOO Hobbinoll
BBHILOSYY yobbishly
BBHILRSUY rubbishly
BBIIILNRU bilirubin
BBIIKMTUZ kibbutzim
BBIIMNORS Ribbonism
BBILOSTUY bulbosity
BBLLOSUUY bulbously
BCCCIMOOX coxcombic
BCCCKMOOS cockscomb
cock's-comb
BCCDEHKOY body-check
BCCDKLMUU dumb-cluck
BCCEEILOR coercible
BCCEHIILO libecchio
BCCEHIKNP pinchbeck
BCCEHKKOO checkbook
BCCEIIILM imbecilic
BCCEIILOS libeccios
BCCEIINOT cenobitic
BCCEILORY coercibly
BCCEINNOU concubine
BCCEINORS conscribe
BCCEINSUU succubine
BCCEKLORU cocklebur
BCCHKOORT cock-broth
BCCIILSTY bicyclist
BCCIKLLOY billycock
BCCIKNOOR cock-robin
BCCIORSTU scorbutic
BCCKORSSU crossbuck
BCCMOORXY coxcombry
BCCMORRUY currycomb
BCCOSSUUU succubous
BCDDEEILU deducible
BCDDIIKRY dicky-bird
BCDDLLOOO coldblood
BCDEEEEHS beseeched
BCDEEEFIN beneficed
BCDEEEINO obedience
BCDEEHIIR herbicide
BCDEEHOOW beech-wood
BCDEEIIRV verbicide
BCDEEILRU reducible
BCDEEINOT Cobdenite
BCDEEIRRS describer
BCDEEJSTU subjected
BCDEELLOR corbelled
BCDEELOST bed-closet
BCDEELRTU tubercled
BCDEEMNTU decumbent
BCDEHLOSV boschveld
BCDEIILNO indocible
BCDEIILNU inducible
BCDEILSTU bile-ducts
BCDEIMNOS Cobdenism
BCDEIMRSU discumber
BCDEISTUU decubitus
BCDELNRUU underclub
BCDEORRSS crossbred
BCDEORRUY body-curer
BCDGIKLOR gold-brick
BCDHKNOUU buckhound
BCDIIMMUY cymbidium
BCDIKRSTU brick-dust
BCDILMNOW climb-down
BCDIMOORS scombroid
BCDKLOOOW woodblock
BCDKNOOOS boondocks
BCDKNOORU rock-bound
BCDNOOPRU cropbound
BCDOPRTUY by-product
BCEEEEHRS beseecher
BCEEEEHTT tête-bêche
BCEEEFHNR beech-fern
free-bench
BCEEEHKNO cheekbone

BCEEEKLPS	bespeckle
BCEEEKQRU	Quebecker
BCEEELQRU	becquerel
BCEEFILRU	febricule
BCEEGHINR	breeching
BCEEGIINR	bigeneric
BCEEGINRS	big-screen
BCEEHHLNO	bench-hole
BCEEHILOS	cohesible
BCEEHIORS	bee-orchis
BCEEHKOOR	chokebore
BCEEHORTT	brochette
BCEEHPRUY	hypercube
BCEEHRTTU	trebuchet
BCEEIIKNN	Nickie-ben
BCEEIILNV	evincible
BCEEIJOTV	objective
BCEEILLOR	corbeille
BCEEILLOS	bellicose
BCEEILLRU	rubicelle
BCEEILRTY	celebrity
BCEEIMMOS	misbecome
BCEEIMNOR	recombine
BCEEINOOT	coenobite
BCEEIOQSU	Québecois
BCEEIPRRS	prescribe
BCEEISSUV	subsecive
BCEEJNORT	△jobcentre
BCEEKNORZ	Zernebock
BCEELNOSY	obscenely
BCEELOOSS	obsolesce
BCEELRTUU	tubercule
BCEEMNRTU	recumbent
BCEEMRRSU	cerebrums
BCEENPSTU	pubescent
BCEENRSTU	rubescent
BCEEORTTU	courbette
BCEFFIOOX	box-office
BCEFFIOOY	office-boy
BCEFFIOSU	suboffice
BCEFIIKRR	firebrick
BCEFIIRTY	febricity
BCEFIJOTY	objectify
BCEFIORTY	fibrocyte
BCEFKLTUU	bucketful
BCEGIIKTT	big-ticket
BCEGIKNTU	bucketing
BCEGILNOR	corbeling
BCEGKTTUU	gutbucket
BCEGLOOSU	goose-club
BCEHIIOST	bioethics
BCEHIMRSU	cherubims
BCEHINNOT	benthonic
BCEHINOOP	neophobic
BCEHIOQUU	chibouque
BCEHIPSSU	spicebush
BCEHKLLOO	blockhole
BCEHKNORW	workbench
BCEHLLNPU	bell-punch
BCEHLOSUU	clubhouse
BCEHLRTUY	butcherly
BCEHMNOOY	honeycomb
BCEIIINOT	ebionitic
BCEIIIRST	Briticise
BCEIIIRTZ	Briticize
BCEIIJNOT	bijection
BCEIIJSTU	Jebusitic
BCEIILNVY	evincibly
BCEIILPSU	publicise
BCEIILPUZ	publicize
BCEIIMORT	biometric
BCEIINOST	bisection
BCEIINRRS	inscriber
BCEIINSSU	subincise
BCEIIOPRT	prebiotic
BCEIJNOOT	objection
BCEIKLPUY	public-key
BCEIKNOST	steinbock
BCEILLMRU	cribellum
BCEILMNOU	△columbine
BCEILMOPT	comptible
BCEILMOTU	columbite
BCEILMRSU	crumblies
BCEILNOOT	bolection
BCEILNORU	colubrine
BCEILPSTU	spec-built
BCEIMNNOU	uncombine
BCEIMNNTU	incumbent
BCEIMNOOU	coenobium
BCEIMNORY	embryonic
BCEIMORRW	micro-brew
BCEIMORTY	embryotic
BCEINORTW	twice-born
BCEINOSTY	obscenity
BCEINSSUU	incubuses
BCEIOPRRS	proscribe
BCEIORSST	crossbite
BCEIORSTT	obstetric
BCEIPRSTY	presbytic
BCEJNSTUU	unsubject
BCEKMRSUU	bumsucker
BCEKNPRUY	cyberpunk
BCEKOORRR	corkborer
	rock-borer
BCEKORTUX	tuckerbox
BCELMOOTY	lobectomy
BCELOOSSU	colobuses
	lobscouse
BCELORSUY	obscurely
BCEMMORTU	combretum
BCEMOORSY	corymbose
BCEMOTTUY	tubectomy
BCENOOPUX	pounce-box
BCENOORRR	cornborer
BCENOORRY	corner-boy
BCENORSTU	curbstone
BCEOOPRRY	cryoprobe
BCEOORTTY	boycotter
BCEORRRWY	crowberry
BCEORSTUX	subcortex
BCEPRTTUU	buttercup
BCFFIKSTU	buff-stick
BCFHILLNU	bullfinch
BCFIMMORY	cymbiform

BCFIMOORR cobriform
BCGHILNOT blotching
BCGHILNTU nightclub
BCGHORSSU scrog-bush
BCGIIMNNO combining
BCGILMNSU scumbling
BCGKNOPRU prongbuck
BCGNOOOTT bog-cotton
BCGORSSSU scrog-buss
BCHHIIISU shibuichi
BCHHIKSSU buckshish
BCHIIOPRS bishopric
BCHIIRSTU hubristic
BCHIKLOPS block-ship
BCHIKLSUY buckishly
BCHILOOPY lyophobic
BCHINORTY Brythonic
BCHKNORSU buck's-horn
BCHKNORTU buckthorn
BCHKOOTTU bucktooth
BCHLNOPUW punch-bowl
BCHLOOOSY schoolboy
BCHLOORTW blowtorch
BCHMOOOTT toothcomb
BCIIIMRST Briticism
BCIIKKLNR brick-kiln
BCIILMSUU umbilicus
BCIILPSTU publicist
BCIILPTUY publicity
BCIILRTUY lubricity
BCIIMNOOS bionomics
BCIIMOSTY symbiotic
BCIINORTT Brittonic
BCIIOOOTZ zoobiotic
BCIKKNOST knob-stick
BCIKKNSSU buckskins
BCIKKORRW brickwork
BCIKLNOTT tint-block
BCIKNOQRU quick-born
BCILLORSS crossbill
BCILLORSW crow's-bill
BCILMMOUU columbium
BCILMNOOZ zinc-bloom
BCILMOSSY symbolics
BCILMRSUU lumbricus
BCILORSUU lubricous
BCIMNORSU submicron
BCIMOOTTU Timbuctoo
BCIOOPRSS proboscis
BCIOORSTT Octobrist
BCIOPRSTU subtropic
BCIORSTUY obscurity
BCIPRSSTU subscript
BCJKLOOSS joss-block
BCKKLOORW blockwork
BCKNORRTU burnt-cork
BCMNOOORR brcom-corn
BCMOORSTU combustor
BCMOSSUUU submucous
BCRSSTTUU substruct
BDDDEEINR bedridden
BDDDEIIOS disbodied
BDDEEEINZ bedizened
BDDEEGIMN embedding
BDDEEGORX dredge-box
BDDEEIRSU debruised
BDDEELNNU unblended
BDDEELRRU de-blurred
BDDEENORT betrodden
BDDEENRRU underbred
BDDEEOPPR bedropped
BDDEEORTU redoubted
BDDEFILOW fiddle-bow
BDDEFINOR forbidden
BDDEFIORR forbidder
BDDEFLOOU blood-feud
BDDEGINRU unbridged
BDDEGLOOU doodlebug
BDDEHINOU hide-bound
BDDEHLOOS bloodshed
BDDEIILNS blind-side
BDDEIISUV subdivide
BDDEILNNU unblinded
BDDEILNRU unbridled
BDDEIMOSY disembody
BDDEINRSU disburden
BDDEIRSTU disturbed
BDDEKNOSU deskbound
desk-bound
BDDELNOOU unblooded
BDDELSUUY subduedly
BDDENNOUU unbounded
BDDENOTUU undoubted
BDDENSUUU unsubdued
BDDFILLNO blindfold
BDDFMNOUU dumbfound
BDDILNORW word-blind
BDDIMNORU mound-bird
BDDINNOUW windbound
BDDLOOOOW bloodwood
BDDLOOSTU blood-dust
BDDNOORUW wordbound
BDDNOTUUY duty-bound
BDEEEELRV belvedere
BDEEEENNS benne-seed
BDEEEESTT bed-settee
BDEEEFINT benefited
BDEEEGHOT hedge-bote
BDEEEGLUW bugle-weed
BDEEEINNS benni-seed
BDEEELNOS nosebleed
BDEEELORT dor-beetle
BDEEELSTT settle-bed
BDEEEMMNT embedment
BDEEENRTU debenture
BDEEERRRY deerberry
BDEEERSTW bestrewed
BDEEERTTV brevetted
BDEEFIILS disbelief
BDEEFILRT filter-bed
BDEEFIORR fire-robed
BDEEFLLOW bedfellow
BDEEFLORW flower-bed
BDEEFOORR foreboder

BDEEFOOTW webfooted
BDEEGGLOW bow-legged
BDEEGHILL hedgebill
BDEEGHINT benedight
benighted
BDEEGHNOR hedge-born
BDEEGILLN debelling
BDEEGINOR ridge-bone
BDEEGMRSU submerged
BDEEGOORU bodeguero
BDEEHILPS bedelship
BDEEHORTT betrothed
BDEEIILLN indelible
BDEEIILRS derisible
BDEEIINNZ benzidine
BDEEIKLNR blinkered
BDEEILLRW bridewell
BDEEILMSS dissemble
BDEEIMMRS dismember
BDEEIMORR embroider
BDEEINOSS sidebones
BDEEINRRT interbred
BDEEINRTU underbite
BDEEIORRR broiderer
BDEEIRSTT bed-sitter
BDEEKNRUU unrebuked
BDEEKOORW brookweed
BDEELLSSY blessedly
BDEELNOUV unbeloved
BDEELNRRU blunderer
BDEELNSSU unblessed
BDEELORST bolstered
BDEEMRSSU submersed
BDEEMSTTU besmutted
BDEEOPSTT bespotted
BDEEORSTY oyster-bed
BDEEORVYY everybody
BDEEPRRTU perturbed
BDEFIILRR rifle-bird
BDEFIIRTU brutified
BDEFILLOO life-blood
BDEFILLSU self-build
BDEFILNOO blood-fine
BDEFILRTU flute-bird
BDEFINORY boyfriend
BDEFLLORU full-orbed
BDEFLORUW flower-bud
BDEFLOSTU self-doubt
BDEGGHMUU humbugged
BDEGGINTU budgeting
BDEGGNUUY dune-buggy
BDEGHILNO beholding
BDEGIIILR dirigible
BDEGIILOS disoblige
BDEGIIMMN bedimming
BDEGIKOOU guidebook
BDEGILNNY bendingly
BDEGIMNOY embodying
BDEGINNNU unbending
BDEGINSSU debussing
BDEGIORRX box-girder
BDEGLOOOR gore-blood
BDEGMMTUU mum-budget
BDEHIIRSY hybridise
BDEHIIRYZ hybridize
BDEHINORY honey-bird
BDEHINRRY hindberry
BDEHIORRS shorebird
BDEHIORSU bird-house
BDEHLLOSY bodyshell
BDEHLMNUU unhumbled
BDEHLOOWY whole-body
BDEHMNOOU homebound
BDEHNOTUY bountyhed
BDEHNRSUU unbrushed
underbush
BDEHORTWY bed-worthy
BDEIIILSV divisible
BDEIIILTY edibility
BDEIILLNY indelibly
BDEIILSTV devil's-bit
BDEIIRTTU turbidite
BDEIISSSU subsidise
BDEIISSUZ subsidize
BDEILLNOO blood-line
BDEILLNPS spellbind
BDEILLNSS blindless
BDEILMOOR Dormobile®
BDEILMPRU plume-bird
BDEILMSSY dissembly
BDEILNNSS blindness
BDEILOOTW blood-wite
BDEILOQTU quodlibet
BDEILORRV bird-lover
BDEILORSU bird-louse
BDEILORUV overbuild
BDEIMNOST disentomb
BDEIMSTTU submitted
BDEINNORW windborne
BDEINORTX tinderbox
BDEINOSST dib-stones
BDEINOSTU soundbite
sound-bite
BDEINRSST bird's-nest
BDEINRSSU sideburns
BDEINRSUU unbruised
BDEINRUZZ unbrizzed
BDEIOORRW brier-wood
BDEIORSTU subeditor
BDEIPRSTU buprestid
BDEIRRSTU disturber
BDEIRRSUV bus-driver
BDEKOOORR order-book
BDEKOOOTU booked-out
BDELLMOSY symbolled
BDELLMRUY drum-belly
BDELLNOSU bull-nosed
BDELLOORS bordellos
BDELLOOSS bloodless
BDELLORUZ bulldozer
BDELMNPUU unplumbed
BDELMNTUU untumbled
BDELMRTUY tumble-dry
BDELNNTUU unblunted

BDELNOOTU doubleton
BDELNOSSU boundless
BDELNOTTU unblotted
BDELOOPRU pure-blood
BDELOOTUV obvoluted
BDELOOUUY double-you
BDELOPRSU superbold
BDELORSTW sword-belt
BDELOSSTU doubtless
BDEMMNOSU Ombudsmen
BDENNOOST bondstone
BDENNOPUU upbounden
BDENNOSSU snub-nosed
BDENNOTTU obtundent
BDENNRSUU sunburned
BDENOORUV overbound
BDENORSUU burdenous
BDENOSTUW westbound
BDEOOOPTT top-booted
BDEOOORRW wood-borer
BDEORSSTU sodbuster
BDFHIILNS blindfish
BDFHNOOOU hoof-bound
BDFILORTT drift-bolt
BDFIOORST bird's-foot
BDFLLLOOU full-blood
BDFLLNOUU full-bound
BDFLOOORU foul-brood
BDFOOOTUY out-of-body
BDGHIINRT nightbird
BDGIILLNO ill-boding
BDGIINNNU unbinding
BDGILNOOY bloodying
BDGINNOOR boning-rod
BDGINORTU obtruding
BDHIIMRSY hybridism
BDHIIRRTY trihybrid
BDHIIRTYY hybridity
BDHIMOOPS bishopdom
BDHIORSUY hybridous
BDHKOOORU Doukhobor
BDHKOORSU Dukhobors
BDHLOOOST bloodshot
BDHOORSUW brushwood
BDHRSSTUU dust-brush
BDIIILSVY divisibly
BDIIINNRU indirubin
BDIIKNOSS 'sbodikins
BDIIKNRST stink-bird
BDIILRSTT stiltbird
BDIIMORTY morbidity
BDIINOSUU indubious
BDIIOSTUY dubiosity
BDIIRTTUY turbidity
BDIKKNRSU skunkbird
BDILLORSW sword-bill
BDILMNNOO moonblind
BDILMNORW blindworm
BDILNNOSW snow-blind
BDILNNOWW windblown
BDILNOOSU soil-bound
BDILOSUUY dubiously
BDIMORRST stormbird
BDINNOORU iron-bound
BDINOOWWW bow-window
BDIORRSTU subtorrid
BDLLOOSTU bloodlust
BDLMOOORW blood-worm
BDLMOOSUY molybdous
BDLOOOORT bloodroot
BDLOOSSUU subdolous
BDMNOOOOR doorn-boom
BDNNOORRY brondyron
BDNNOOSUW snowbound
BDNOOORTU root-bound
BDNOOSTUU outbounds
BDNORSTUW downburst
BEEEEEKPR beekeeper
BEEEEHNRS shebeener
BEEEEKMRW Ember-week
BEEEELLMR belle-mère
BEEEFLORW bee-flower
BEEEGIKLL bilge-keel
BEEEGIMNS beseeming
BEEEGLNRU blue-green
BEEEGLTUZ Betelgeuz
BEEEGNNOR green-bone
BEEEGNOOW woebegone
BEEEGNOTW go-between
BEEEHLLOR hellebore
BEEEHLRRT bletherer
BEEEHORSU beer-house
BEEEHPRRT herb-Peter
BEEEHRSSW Hebrewess
BEEEIKLLR rebel-like
BEEEILLOT oil-beetle
BEEEILMMS emblemise
BEEEILMMZ emblemize
BEEEILMNT belemnite
BEEEILNUV unbelieve
BEEEILRSV eversible
BEEEIMMSS misbeseem
BEEEIMRSV semibreve
BEEEINNTW in-between
BEEEINRSS beeriness
BEEEKOPRX boxkeeper
BEEEKRRRS berserker
BEEELLSTU steel-blue
BEEELMNTV bevelment
BEEELMRRS resembler
BEEELMRZZ embezzler
BEEELSSSU sublessee
BEEEMNORY beer-money
BEEEMNSTT besetment
BEEEMPRST September
BEEENORST tenebrose
BEEENOSSS obeseness
BEEENRRSY neesberry
BEEFFGIRU febrifuge
BEEFFHLUW buff-wheel
BEEFGIILR Félibrige
BEEFGLOST self-begot
BEEFHLOUV behoveful
BEEFHOTTT theft-bote

BEEFIILMS	misbelief
BEEFILRSS	briefless
	fiberless
	fibreless
BEEFINRSS	briefness
BEEFKLRUU	rebukeful
BEEFLNNUW	funnel-web
BEEFNNRUU	unberufen
BEEFNORTU	befortune
BEEFOORTY	freebooty
BEEGGIINS	besieging
BEEGGINTT	begetting
BEEGHIILN	Ghibeline
BEEGHINNT	benighten
BEEGHINRT	benighter
BEEGHIRTY	eyebright
BEEGIILLL	illegible
BEEGIILNV	believing
BEEGIINOT	Gibeonite
BEEGILLNR	rebelling
BEEGILLNV	bevelling
BEEGILLNW	wellbeing
BEEGILNRS	inselberg
BEEGILNSS	beingless
BEEGILNUU	unbeguile
BEEGINNSS	beingness
BEEGINRTT	bettering
BEEGINRTV	breveting
BEEGINSST	beestings
BEEGINSTT	besetting
BEEGKLNTU	kent-bugle
BEEGLNOOS	△bolognese
BEEHIINRS	hibernise
BEEHIINRZ	hibernize
BEEHIIRTX	exhibiter
BEEHILLMS	embellish
BEEHILMPU	humble-pie
BEEHILNOR	heliborne
BEEHIMRSW	Hebrewism
BEEHINRTT	terebinth
BEEHIOPRS	biosphere
BEEHIORRS	herborise
BEEHIORRV	herbivore
BEEHIORRZ	herborize
BEEHIPSST	sheep's-bit
BEEHLLRSU	busheller
BEEHLMSSU	humblesse
BEEHLOPRY	hyperbole
BEEHMORUY	homebuyer
BEEHNOOPX	xenophobe
BEEHOOSTU	house-bote
BEEHORSUW	brew-house
BEEIILLNZ	zibelline
BEEIILNNT	intenible
BEEIILNRT	libertine
BEEIILRST	liberties
BEEIINRTY	inebriety
BEEIKLMRU	berkelium
BEEIKLRTU	brutelike
BEEILLNOR	rebellion
BEEILLNTU	ebullient
BEEILLORT	bolletrie
BEEILLRTU	bulletrie
	rubellite
BEEILMNPU	numble-pie
BEEILMNSS	nimblesse
BEEILMPRU	lumber-pie
BEEILMRTT	embrittle
BEEILNNOZ	benzoline
BEEILNOPX	exponible
BEEILNOSS	nobilesse
BEEILNPRU	prenubile
BEEILNRSU	blue-rinse
	nebuliser
BEEILNRUZ	nebulizer
BEEILOTTU	oubliette
BEEILRSST	tribeless
BEEILSTUV	vestibule
BEEIMNRST	tenebrism
BEEIMRRSU	reimburse
BEEINNOTT	bentonite
BEEINORST	tenebrios
BEEINRRWY	wineberry
BEEINRSTT	tenebrist
BEEINRSTU	subentire
	Trubenise
BEEINRTTU	butterine
BEEINRTTY	tenebrity
BEEINRTUZ	Trubenize®
BEEIOQSSU	obsequies
BEEIOSSSV	obsessive
BEEIQRTTU	briquette
BEEIRRTTU	retribute
BEEIRSSSU	subseries
BEEJNRRUY	Juneberry
BEEKLRRSY	berserkly
BEEKNOPSU	unbespoke
BEEKNORST	kerbstone
BEEKOPRRY	pokeberry
BEELLLMUU	umbellule
BEELLORRW	well-borer
BEELLORSU	resoluble
BEELLORTW	bell-tower
BEELLRTUY	bully-tree
BEELMOORT	bolometer
BEELMORST	temblores
BEELMRRSU	slumberer
BEELNNOSS	nobleness
BEELNOPSU	spulebone
BEELNOSTU	bluestone
BEELORSVY	obversely
	verbosely
BEELORTTX	letterbox
BEELOSSTU	boletuses
BEELQRSUU	burlesque
BEELRRSTU	blusterer
BEELRSTTU	subletter
BEEMMNNOR	non-member
BEEMNORST	bemonster
BEEMNRTTU	rebutment
BEEMOPRRY	pre-embryo
BEENNOOTU	boutonnée
BEENOQSTU	obsequent
BEENORRST	resorbent

BEENORSSS soberness
BEENORSTU tenebrous
BEENORSUU eburneous
BEENRSSTU bruteness
BEENRSTUU subtenure
BEEOORRSW boerewors
BEEOPPPRX pepper-box
BEEOPPRSY presbyope
BEEORSSUU subereous
BEEORSTTU soubrette
BEEORSTTY streetboy
BEEPRRRTU perturber
BEEPRRSTY presbyter
BEERRSTUV subverter
BEFFGINTU buffeting
BEFFLNSSU bluffness
BEFGIINTT befitting
BEFGILNSU fungibles
BEFHIRRSU brush-fire
furbisher
refurbish
BEFHKLOOS bookshelf
BEFHOOTTT theftboot
BEFIILNOR fibroline
BEFIILNSU infusible
BEFIILORT fibrolite
BEFIILRTY febrility
BEFILLSTU self-built
BEFILNOOR foilborne
BEFILNTTY fly-bitten
BEFILRWYY fly-by-wire
BEFINOPRU ibuprofen
BEFIORSTT frostbite
BEFLLLOPY belly-flop
BEFLLOTTU bottleful
BEFLORRWY wolfberry
BEFLRTTUY butterfly
BEGGGILNY beggingly
BEGGGLOOX goggle-box
BEGGHMRUU humbugger
BEGGIINNN beginning
BEGGIINOO boogieing
BEGGINOSS bogginess
BEGHHILST high-blest
BEGHHINOT thighbone
BEGHHOTTU bethought
BEGHIILLP phillibeg
BEGHILLNT night-bell
BEGHINORT night-robe
BEGHINORU neighbour
BEGHIORSU brogueish
BEGHLNORU bugle-horn
BEGHNRTUU bug-hunter
BEGHOORTT borghetto
BEGHORRUX Roxburghe
BEGIIILNT ignitible
BEGIILLLN libelling
BEGIILLLY illegibly
BEGIILLNT billeting
BEGIIMNRT timbering
BEGIINNTY benignity
BEGIINSST biestings
BEGIINSTT besitting
BEGIJRTTU jitterbug
BEGILLNOW bowelling
BEGILLOTU globulite
BEGILMNRT trembling
BEGILMNRU lumbering
BEGILMOOR embroglio
BEGILMORY gorblimey
BEGILMPPU bilge-pump
BEGILMRRU Limburger
BEGILNNNO ennobling
BEGILNSSU bulginess
BEGILRTTU litter-bug
BEGIMNSSU embussing
BEGINOOSS besognios
BEGINOOSU biogenous
BEGINORSU subregion
BEGINORSV observing
BEGINOSTT besotting
BEGINRTTU rebutting
BEGIOORSU bourgeois
BEGLMORTY bog-myrtle
BEGLOORTT globe-trot
BEHHLLORT hell-broth
BEHHLMOTU thumb-hole
BEHHMOOOP homophobe
BEHHOSSUU bush-house
BEHIIINRT inhibiter
BEHIILPST phlebitis
BEHIIMNOY yohimbine
BEHIIORTX exhibitor
BEHIIRRST Britisher
BEHIIRSTT bitterish
BEHIKLMTU thumblike
BEHIKLOSV △bolshevik
BEHIKLRSU shrublike
BEHILLNTY thin-belly
BEHILMNRU rhumb-line
BEHILPRSU publisher
republish
BEHIMMNOO bonhommie
BEHIMRRWY whimberry
BEHINRRSU burnisher
BEHINRRWY whinberry
BEHINSSSU bushiness
BEHIOPSSS bishopess
BEHIORRST herborist
BEHIORRVY herbivory
BEHIORSTT theorbist
BEHKMOSSU smokebush
BEHKNOSUU bunkhouse
BEHLLSSSU blushless
BEHLMSSTU thumbless
BEHLORRTY brotherly
BEHLORSST throbless
BEHLORSSU blush-rose
BEHLRSSSU shrubless
BEHMOOOOX homoeobox
BEHMOORST thrombose
BEHMORSSU rhombuses
BEHNNRTUU unburthen
BEHNOOPXY xenophoby

BEHNORSTU	buhrstone
BEHOPRTYY	bryophyte
BEIIILNSV	invisible
BEIILLNSY	△sibylline
BEIILMOPU	epilobium
BEIILMORS	mobiliser
BEIILMORZ	mobilizer
BEIILMOSS	omissible
BEIILMRSX	ex-librism
BEIILMSSU	sublimise
BEIILMSUZ	sublimize
BEIILOOPR	periboloi
BEIILORTT	trilobite
BEIILRSTX	ex-librist
BEIILSSTU	subtilise
BEIILSTUZ	subtilize
BEIINNRSS	brininess
BEIINOOVV	ovibovine
BEIINORSU	inebrious
BEIINRTTU	Tribunite
BEIIORSST	sorbitise
BEIIORSTY	ebriosity
BEIIORSTZ	sorbitize
BEIIPRTTT	bitter-pit
BEIKLMOOR	brooklime
BEIKLNOTT	ink-bottle
BEIKLNSSU	bulkiness
BEIKMOORT	motor-bike
BEIKNOSSS	boskiness
BEIKNRSSS	briskness
BEILLLOSU	libellous
BEILLLTUW	well-built
BEILLMNOY	money-bill
BEILLMRUY	beryllium
BEILLMSUY	sublimely
BEILLNOSU	insoluble
BEILLOQUY	obliquely
BEILLRTTY	brittlely
BEILLSSSS	blissless
BEILLSTUY	subtilely
BEILMMNUU	nelumbium
BEILMOPTT	bottle-imp
BEILMOSSY	symbolise
BEILMOSYZ	symbolize
BEILNOPSS	sponsible
BEILNORRU	oil-burner
BEILNPRTU	blueprint
BEILNRSSU	burliness
BEILOOPRS	peribolos
BEILOOPRT	pot-boiler
BEILOPRSU	peribolus
BEILOPSSS	possibles
BEILORSSU	subsoiler
BEILORSTT	librettos
BEILSSTTU	subtitles
BEILSTTUY	subtilety
BEIMNORST	brimstone
BEIMNOSSU	omnibuses
BEIMNPSSU	bumpiness
BEIMOSSTW	misbestow
BEIMRSTTU	submitter
BEIMRTTUY	ytterbium
BEINNNOSS	bonniness
BEINNOOTT	obtention
BEINNOOTV	obvention
BEINOOPRT	obreption
BEINOORSV	obversion
BEINOOSSS	obsession
BEINOOSSZ	booziness
BEINORSST	Britoness
BEINORSUU	rubineous
BEINOSSSS	bossiness
BEINOTTWY	bytownite
BEINRSSUU	subursine
BEIOOPRRU	pourboire
BEIOORRRT	brier-root
BEIOQRSTU	sobriquet
BEIORSTUV	obtrusive
BEIORSTVY	verbosity
BEIPRSSTU	Buprestis
BEIPRSTUY	superbity
BEJLNOORW	jobernowl
BEKKNOOOT	book-token
BEKLOOOSU	booklouse
BEKLOOSTY	stylebook
BEKNNNOUW	unbeknown
BEKOOORST	bookstore
BELLMOOSS	bloomless
BELLMORSU	umbrellos
BELLMPSSU	plumbless
BELLOOTWY	welly-boot
BELLOOWYY	yellow-boy
BELMMOOSS	emblossom
BELMOOORW	elbow-room
BELMOORSS	reblossom
BELMOORTY	bolometry
BELMOPSUU	plumbeous
BELNNSSTU	bluntness
BELNOORVW	overblown
BELNOOTVV	obvolvent
BELNRTTUU	turbulent
BELOOTTTW	two-bottle
BELORSSSU	sublessor
BELQRSUUY	brusquely
BEMMNSTUU	submentum
BEMNOORSU	unbosomer
BEMNOOSTT	tombstone
BEMNORTUU	outnumber
BEMNOSSUX	buxomness
BEMOOPRRY	proembryo
BEMOORRSS	sombreros
BEMRRTTUU	rum-butter
BEMSSSTUY	subsystem
BENNOORSW	brown-nose
BENNORSSW	brownness
BENOOSTUU	bounteous
BENOPSTTU	subpotent
BENORRSTU	burrstone
BENORRSWY	snowberry
BENORSTTU	obstruent
BENRTTTUU	butternut
	nutbutter
BEOPPRSYY	presbyopy
BFFIIMORR	fibriform

Words marked △ may be spelled also with a capital letter

BFGHILLTU bullfight
BFHHIORRT frithborh
BFHIRSTUU bush-fruit
BFIIILLNR fibrillin
BFIILMORY myofibril
BFIINORSU fibrinous
BFILNOTUU △bountiful
BFIMORRSU bursiform
BFINORRST first-born
BFLLLNOUW full-blown
BFMMOOORR bromoform
BFOORTUWY four-by-two
two-by-four
BGGHIILNT blighting
BGGILLNUY bulgingly
BGGILMNRU grumbling
BGHHILNOW high-blown
BGHILMNTU thumbling
BGHILOPRU rib-plough
BGHIMNRTU thumb-ring
BGHINORTU inbrought
BGHINRSTU sunbright
BGHLOOPUY ploughboy
BGHOPRTUU upbrought
BGIIIKPRR Kirbigrip®
kirbigrip
BGIIIMNNO biomining
BGIIKPRRY kirby-grip
BGIILLNOW billowing
BGIILMNSU subliming
BGIILMOOR imbroglio
BGIILNRST bristling
BGIILOOST biologist
BGIIMNRUY minirugby
BGIINNNRU inburning
BGIKNOPRS △springbok
BGILLNSTU stingbull
BGILMNNUY numbingly
BGILMNOOY myoglobin
BGILNNRUY △bunny-girl
burningly
BGILNORTU troubling
BGILNUYZZ buzzingly
BGILOORTY tribology
BGILOOSTY globosity
BGINNORTU binturong
BGINNPRUU upburning
BGINOORRW borrowing
BGINOPRSX box-spring
BGINORSTW bowstring
BGLLOOSUU globulous
BGLMOOPUY bumpology
BGLMOOSYY symbology
BGNOORSTX strongbox
BGNORSTUW bowstrung
BHHNORSTU thornbush
BHIIINORT inhibitor
BHIILLLLY hill-billy
BHIILLNOT billionth
BHIIMORUZ △rhizobium
BHIINRSTU un-British
BHIINRTTW twin-birth
BHIKMNSTU thumbkins
BHIKNNSUU shubunkin
BHIKNOOSU unbookish
BHILLLSUY bullishly
BHILLNORT thornbill
BHILMNOTY bimonthly
BHILMOOPR ombrophil
BHILOORSY boorishly
BHILRSTUY brutishly
BHIMOOSTY tomboyish
BHIORRTTW birthwort
BHIOSWYZZ showbizzy
BHJOORSTW jobsworth
BHKORRSUW brushwork
BHLLLOORS loll-shrob
BHLLOOOTT tollbooth
BHLMPSUUY subphylum
BHMNOOOSU bonhomous
BHNOORSTW snow-broth
BIIILNSVY invisibly
BIIIORSSV vibriosis
BIIKNNRSY skinny-rib
BIILLOSUY biliously
BIILLSSTY Sibyllist
BIILMSTUY sublimity
BIILNOOVW violin-bow
BIILOOSUV oblivious
BIILOQTUY obliquity
BIILSTTUY subtility
BIIMMNORS brominism
BIIMOPRTY improbity
BIIMOSSSY symbiosis
BIISSTTYY itsy-bitsy
BIKLNNOSW snowblink
BILLNOOPS spoonbill
BILLNORST stillborn
BILLNOSUY insolubly
BILLOPSTU slop-built
BILMMOSSY △symbolism
BILMOSSTY symbolist
BILMSSSUY submissly
BILNNOTUU unbuilt-on
BILOOPRTU Politburo
BILOOSUVY obviously
BILORSSTU strobilus
BIMNORSTY brimstony
BIMOPSTUU bumptious
BINOOOSUX obnoxious
BINOORSST Sorbonist
BINOORSTU obtrusion
BINOOSUUV unobvious
BKLLMNSUU numbskull
BKLLOORUY bully-rook
BKMOORUUZ zumbooruk
BKOOORSTY storybook
BLLORTTUU bull-trout
BLMORSSUU slumbrous
BLOORSTUU troublous
BLORSSTUU blustrous
BLRSTTUUW blutwurst
BLSSSTUUU subsultus
BMOOPPRTX prompt-box

Words marked △ may be spelled also with a capital letter

BOOOORRSU ouroboros
BOOPPRRTU turboprop

C

CCCCILNOY concyclic
CCCDIIMOU coccidium
CCCEEILST eclectics
CCCEEINRT eccentric
CCCEIILPY epicyclic
CCCEIINOR Ciceronic
CCCEILOOT coccolite
CCCENOORT concocter
CCCGINOOO gonococci
CCCHIINNO cinchonic
CCCHIKNOP pinchcock
CCCHILMOU colchicum
CCCHILOOT coccolith
CCCIILMSY cyclicism
CCCIILOSY isocyclic
CCCIILRTY tricyclic
CCCIILTYY cyclicity
CCCIOORSS sciroccos
CCCNOOORT concoctor
CCDDEKOUY decoy-duck
CCDDELNOU concluded
CCDEEEHKR checkered
CCDEEEINS decencies
CCDEEERSU succeeder
CCDEEHIKM chemicked
CCDEEHIKW chickweed
CCDEEHKNU unchecked
CCDEEHORT crocheted
CCDEEIINN incidence
CCDEEIINT endeictic
CCDEEINNY indecency
CCDEEINOT conceited
CCDEEIOTV decoctive
CCDEELLOT collected
CCDEEMOOR coco-de-mer
CCDEENNOR concerned
CCDEENNOT connected
CCDEENORS crescendo
CCDEENORT concerted
CCDEEORTU decocture
CCDEFIIRU crucified
CCDEIIKNP picnicked
CCDEIILPR dip-circle
CCDEILOOR crocodile
CCDEILOOS scolecoid
CCDEILSTY dyslectic
CCDEIMOOR microcode
CCDEINOOT decoction
CCDEINOUV conducive
CCDEINRTU cinctured
CCDEISTTY dystectic
CCDEKORSS dock-cress
CCDELNOTU occludent
CCDHHIRSU dischurch
CCDHIIMOR dichromic
CCDHKOOUW woodchuck
CCDIILNRY cylindric
CCDIIOORT corticoid
CCDKLMOOU cuckoldom
CCDKLORUY cuckoldry
CCDNOORTU conductor
CCDNOSTUU conductus
CCDOOOSUW cocuswood
CCEEEFLNU feculence
CCEEEHHRR recherché
CCEEEHNOR coherence
CCEEEHRRS screecher
CCEEEIKNP neckpiece
CCEEEINNS nescience
CCEEEINRT reticence
CCEEELLOR clerecole
CCEEFHHRT cherchef't
CCEEFILLY life-cycle
CCEEFLNUY feculency
CCEEGINOR concierge
CCEEGINOT ectogenic
CCEEGINTY cynegetic
CCEEHIKNR checkrein
CCEEHILMY hemicycle
CCEEHKNNS schnecken
CCEEHKORV overcheck
CCEEHLORT cerecloth
CCEEHNORY coherency
CCEEHOTTU couchette
CCEEIINNS inscience
CCEEIIPPR precipice
CCEEIKRRT cricketer
CCEEILNNO on-licence
CCEEILNOR reconcile
CCEEILOST scolecite
CCEEILPRY pericycle
CCEEIMNOU oecumenic
CCEEIMNSU ecumenics
CCEEINNNO innocence
CCEEINORS cicerones
CCEEINORT ectocrine
CCEEINRTX excentric
CCEEINRTY reticency
CCEEIRRST rectrices
CCEEIRSTT tectrices
CCEELLORT recollect
re-collect
CCEELOSTY cystocele
CCEELOTUY leucocyte
CCEELPRSU crepuscle
CCEENNORT concenter
concentre
connecter
reconnect
CCEENOOTY coenocyte
CCEFFIIIL felicific
CCEFHILOU choiceful
CCEFIIRRU crucifier
CCEFKNOYY cockneyfy
CCEGHIMRU chemurgic
CCEGINNOO oncogenic
CCEGINOPS pigsconce
CCEGINORY cryogenic
CCEHHKLOU chuckhole
CCEHIKLLT check-till

CCEHIKLOO chokecoil
CCEHIKLST checklist
CCEHILNOR chronicle
CCEHILORU euchloric
CCEHILRTU hut-circle
CCEHINOSZ zecchinos
CCEHIOOPR pro-choice
CCEHIORST orchestic
CCEHKLNOT neckcloth
CCEHKLORS schlocker
CCEHKMOOR checkroom
CCEHKOORS cockhorse
CCEHKOPRR rock-perch
CCEHKOPST spot-check
CCEHLOSTY cholecyst
CCEHLPSUY push-cycle
CCEHNNOOS sconcheon
CCEHNNOSU scuncheon
CCEHNOSTU scutcheon
CCEHORTTY crotchety
CCEHOTTUZ zucchetto
CCEHRRTUY cutcherry
CCEIIIPRT epicritic
CCEIIIRST criticise
sericitic
CCEIIIRTZ criticize
CCEIIKNPR picnicker
CCEIILMST Celticism
CCEIILNOT niccolite
CCEIILNYZ cyclizine
CCEIILRTY clericity
CCEIILSTT Celticist
CCEIIMOSS coseismic
CCEIINSTU succinite
CCEIIOPRU picocurie
CCEIKLLOY kilocycle
CCEIKLOSW clockwise
CCEIKNOSS cockiness
CCEILNOSY concisely
CCEILNOTY cyclonite
CCEILOOST sociolect
CCEILORST sclerotic
CCEILOSUV occlusive
CCEILRRTY tricycler
CCEILRSTY recyclist
CCEILSSUU Leuciscus
CCEIMNOOS economics
CCEIMNRUU curcumine
CCEIMORTY microcyte
CCEIMOSST cosmetics
CCEINNNOY innocency
CCEINNOST conscient
CCEINNOTT conticent
CCEINOOSS consocies
CCEINORRT incorrect
CCEINOSTT tectonics
CCEINPRST precincts
CCEINRSTY syncretic
CCEINSSTY synectics
CCEINSTTY syntectic
CCEIOPPRS porcpisce
CCEIOPRTY precocity
CCEKLOOUZ ouzel-cock
CCEKORRSS rockcress
CCEKORRSW corkscrew
CCELLNOOY colonelcy
CCELLOORT collector
CCELMOOTY colectomy
CCELNSTUU succulent
CCELOPRSU corpuscle
CCELOPSSY △cyclopses
CCELORRTY correctly
CCELORTUU coculture
CCENNNORU unconcern
CCENNOORT connector
CCENNOSTU concentus
CCENOOORY cocoonery
CCENOORST concertos
CCENOORSU concourse
CCENOORTV convector
CCENOPSTU conceptus
CCENORRTU occurrent
CCENORSTU succentor
CCENSSSUU unsuccess
CCEOOORSS Socceroos
CCEOOPRSY cryoscope
CCEOORRRT corrector
CCEOPPRUY preoccupy
CCEORRSUU succourer
CCEORSSSU successor
CCEOSSUUX exsuccous
CCFGHIKOT cockfight
CCFGKLLOO clock-golf
CCFHIINOO finocchio
CCFHKKORU fork-chuck
CCFHKLLOU chock-full
CCFHKLLUU chuck-full
CCFIIILOOR colorific
CCFIMORRU cruciform
CCFKOOOST cocksfoot
CCFLLOSUU flocculus
CCFLOOOOS locofocos
CCGHHINOU chincough
CCGHHINRU churching
CCGHIIKLN chickling
CCGHIINPU hiccuping
CCGHIKLNU chuckling
CCGHILOOP choplogic
CCGHINORS scorching
CCGHINSTU scutching
CCGIINOPP coppicing
CCGILLLOY glycollic
CCGILMOOY mycologic
CCGILNOTU occulting
CCGINNOOO cocooning
CCGINOPUY occupying
CCGINORRU occurring
CCGLLLOOY glycocoll
CCHHIMRSU churchism
CCHHOOPST hopscotch
CCHIIIRTT trichitic
CCHIILORT chloritic
trochilic
CCHIIMOPR microchip

CCHIINOOR	chorionic
CCHIINOST	conchitis
CCHIINSUZ	zucchinis
CCHIIOORS	isochoric
CCHIIORRT	cirrhotic
	trichroic
CCHIKLLOO	cook-chill
CCHIKOPST	chopstick
CCHILLOTY	cyclolith
CCHILOORT	chlorotic
CCHINRSTY	strychnic
CCHIOPSTY	psychotic
CCHLNOOTY	colocynth
CCHOORRSU	Corchorus
CCIIILNOS	isoclinic
CCIIILNRT	triclinic
CCIIILOST	silicotic
CCIIILOSU	cilicious
CCIIIMRST	criticism
CCIIINNOT	nicotinic
CCIIKKNST	nickstick
CCIIKKRST	rickstick
CCIIKLLOP	pillicock
CCIILNOTY	clonicity
CCIILOOST	scoliotic
CCIILOPRT	proclitic
CCIIMOSST	Scoticism
CCIINNNSU	cincinnus
CCIIORRTT	tricrotic
CCIIOSSTT	Scotistic
CCIIRRTUY	circuitry
CCIKKORSS	cross-kick
CCILMOSTU	occultism
CCILNOOPY	polyconic
CCILNOORU	councilor
CCILNOOSU	occlusion
CCILNOOTY	oncolytic
CCILOORST	colostric
CCILORSUU	curculios
CCILOSTTU	occultist
CCIMMOORS	microcosm
CCIMOOPRY	microcopy
CCINOOSSU	conscious
CCINOPRST	conscript
CCINOPSTY	syncoptic
CCINORSTT	constrict
CCIOOOPRZ	coprozoic
CCIOOOPSZ	zooscopic
CCIOOPRSU	uroscopic
CCIOOTTXY	cytotoxic
CCKKLOORW	clockwork
CCKKOORSS	rock-socks
CCKMOORST	storm-cock
CCKOOPPPY	poppycock
CCLNOORTY	cyclotron
CCNORSTTU	construct
CCOOOORRS	corocoros
CCOOPRSYY	cryoscopy
CCOOSTTUU	tucotucos
CCOSTTUUU	tucutucos
CDDDEEENS	descended
CDDDEEILY	decidedly
CDDDEEINU	undecided
CDDDEILNO	condiddle
CDDDELORS	scroddled
CDDDENRUU	uncrudded
CDDEEEFLT	deflected
CDDEEEIIW	weedicide
CDDEEENRS	descender
	redescend
CDDEEGLLU	cudgelled
CDDEEHHIU	cuddeehih
CDDEEHLSU	scheduled
CDDEEIKRU	eider-duck
CDDEEILSY	Clydeside
CDDEEISST	dissected
CDDEEITUV	deductive
CDDEEKNRU	underdeck
CDDEEMNNO	condemned
CDDEEMNRU	credendum
CDDEENRUU	unreduced
CDDEENSUU	unseduced
CDDEHIILP	didelphic
CDDEHKLSU	sheldduck
CDDEIILMO	domiciled
CDDEIINRT	dendritic
CDDEIIOSV	videodisc
CDDEIIRST	discredit
CDDEILTUU	dulcitude
CDDEIMOOU	duodecimo
CDDEINOTU	deduction
CDDEIOSUU	deciduous
CDDELNOUU	unclouded
CDDELNRUU	uncurdled
CDDELOOOP	opodeldoc
CDDENORUW	uncrowded
CDDHHILOO	childhood
CDDHIIORY	hydriodic
CDDHINOOR	chondroid
CDDILNOOY	condyloid
CDEEEEFNR	deer-fence
	deference
CDEEEEKNW	ewe-necked
CDEEEEPRR	creepered
CDEEEFFOR	force-feed
CDEEEFITV	defective
CDEEEFLRT	reflected
CDEEEFORW	cowfeeder
CDEEEGINR	decreeing
CDEEEGINX	exceeding
CDEEEHKNP	henpecked
CDEEEHKRT	three-deck
CDEEEHNRU	uncheered
CDEEEHORR	decoherer
CDEEEHPRU	upcheered
CDEEEHQRU	chequered
CDEEEILRS	sclereide
CDEEEIMRR	remercied
CDEEEIMRT	decimeter
	decimetre
CDEEEINNS	desinence
CDEEEINPT	centipede
CDEEEINRS	residence
CDEEEINRT	intercede

CDEEEINUV	undeceive
CDEEEIPTV	deceptive
CDEEEIRST	decistere
CDEEEIRTV	decretive
CDEEEITTV	detective
CDEEEKNTW	'tween-deck
CDEEELLNR	crenelled
CDEEELLOT	décolleté
CDEEELNOR	redolence
CDEEELNTU	unelected
CDEEELORT	electrode
CDEEEMNRT	decrement
CDEEEMNTU	educement
CDEEENPRT	precedent
CDEEEOPRR	proceeder
CDEEEOPRU	doucepere
CDEEEORRT	retrocede
CDEEEPRST	sceptered
CDEEFIILR	rice-field
CDEEFIIMR	mercifide
CDEEFIINT	deficient
CDEEFIIOT	foeticide
CDEEFIIPS	specified
CDEEFIIRT	certified
	rectified
CDEEFILTU	deceitful
CDEEFILUV	deviceful
CDEEFINOT	defection
CDEEFIORT	fore-cited
CDEEFKLOT	fetlocked
CDEEFKNSU	fen-sucked
CDEEFKOST	feedstock
CDEEFLORT	deflector
CDEEFLRUU	flue-cured
CDEEFNORR	conferred
CDEEFNOSS	confessed
CDEEGIILN	ceilinged
	diligence
CDEEGIIMR	germicide
CDEEGIINN	indigence
CDEEGILRY	glyceride
CDEEGINNO	endogenic
CDEEGINPR	preceding
CDEEGINRS	screeding
CDEEGIOST	geodetics
CDEEGLLRU	cudgeller
CDEEGNOST	congested
	decongest
CDEEHHIRS	cherished
CDEEHIINN	echidnine
CDEEHIKRS	shickered
CDEEHIKTT	thicketed
CDEEHIKTY	thick-eyed
CDEEHILLS	chiselled
CDEEHINOT	ethnocide
CDEEHINST	dehiscent
CDEEHIORT	ditrochee
CDEEHKOOR	door-cheek
CDEEHKOSU	deckhouse
CDEEHLORY	hydrocele
CDEEHLPPS	schlepped
CDEEHLRSU	scheduler
CDEEHNORV	chevroned
CDEEHOPRS	cosphered
CDEEHPPRU	up-perched
CDEEHRSTT	stretched
CDEEIILRT	deciliter
	decilitre
CDEEIILTV	videlicet
CDEEIIMNR	mediciner
CDEEIIMNT	menticide
CDEEIIMPR	epidermic
CDEEIIMPU	epicedium
CDEEIIMRV	decemviri
	vermicide
CDEEIIPRR	cirripede
CDEEIIPST	pesticide
CDEEIIPTV	depictive
CDEEIIRTV	directive
CDEEIISTT	dietetics
CDEEIJNOT	dejection
CDEEIJPRU	prejudice
CDEEIJRUV	verjuiced
CDEEIKKNR	knickered
CDEEIKLLN	nickelled
CDEEIKLRS	slickered
CDEEIKQUY	quick-eyed
CDEEILLNP	pencilled
CDEEILNNO	indolence
CDEEILNPR	pendicler
CDEEILNST	stenciled
CDEEILORR	Cordelier
CDEEILORS	creolised
CDEEILORZ	creolized
CDEEILPRT	predilect
CDEEILSTU	celsitude
CDEEILTXY	excitedly
CDEEIMMXY	myxedemic
CDEEIMNNU	decennium
CDEEIMNOU	eudemonic
CDEEIMNPU	impudence
CDEEIMRSV	decemvirs
CDEEINNOR	endocrine
CDEEINNSU	secundine
CDEEINOPT	deception
CDEEINORT	recondite
CDEEINOSS	decession
CDEEINOTT	detection
CDEEINPRU	unpierced
CDEEINRRS	discerner
CDEEINRST	stridence
CDEEINRSY	residency
CDEEINTTX	extincted
CDEEINTUX	unexcited
CDEEIORRS	crosiered
CDEEIOTTU	eutectoid
CDEEIPRRT	predicter
CDEEIPRTU	depicture
CDEEIRSTT	decretist
CDEEIRSUV	decursive
CDEEIRTTU	certitude
	rectitude
CDEEIRTUV	reductive
CDEEISTUV	seductive

CDEEJORTY dejectory
CDEEKLNOW low-necked
CDEEKLORW lower-deck
CDEEKLPRS spreckled
CDEEKMNRU muckender
CDEEKNORS knee-cords
CDEEKNRWY wry-necked
CDEEKORTW two-decker
CDEELLMOP compelled
CDEELLNRU cullender
CDEELMNTU demulcent
CDEELMOPT completed
CDEELMOPX decomplex
CDEELNORY redolency
CDEELORSS sclerosed
CDEELORST corsleted
CDEELRSTU clustered
CDEEMMNOR recommend
CDEEMNNOT contemned
CDEEMOOPS decompose
CDEENNORS condenser
CDEENNORT contender
CDEENNORU denouncer
CDEENNOTT contented
CDEENNSTU unscented
CDEENOOPS endoscope
CDEENOORT coroneted
CDEENOPRS drop-scene
CDEENORUV uncovered
CDEENOSSU douceness
CDEENOSTT contested
CDEENPRTY encrypted
CDEENRRTU decurrent
CDEENRSSU crudeness
CDEENRSUU unsecured
CDEEOPRRR prerecord
CDEEOPRRU procedure
reproduce
CDEEOPRSS processed
CDEEOPRTT protected
CDEEOPRTY deceptory
CDEEOQTTU coquetted
CDEEORRTY decretory
CDEEORSSY cross-eyed
CDEEPRSSU percussed
CDEEPSSTU suspected
CDEERTTUV curvetted
CDEFFIIIL difficile
CDEFGIINU fungicide
CDEFHIILW child-wife
CDEFHIORS cod-fisher
CDEFIIIST fideistic
CDEFIINST disinfect
CDEFIIOST △scotified
CDEFIKLOR frolicked
CDEFILNOR cornfield
CDEFIMNOR confirmed
CDEFINNOT confident
CDEFINTUY fecundity
CDEFKNORU unfrocked
CDEFLORUU cul-de-four
CDEFNOORW downforce
CDEFNOSUU unfocused
CDEGGLNOU unclogged
CDEGHHIIV high-viced
CDEGIILOO ideologic
CDEGIIMRU demiurgic
CDEGIINNY indigency
CDEGIKNOT docketing
CDEGILOOP logopedic
CDEGILOSU glucoside
CDEGILOSY glycoside
CDEGIMOUW cowdie-gum
CDEGINNOS consigned
CDEGINORR recording
CDEGINOTY dictyogen
CDEGINRSY descrying
CDEGINSSY dysgenics
CDEGLORST goldcrest
CDEHHOORR rheochord
CDEHIIKLL childlike
CDEHIILNO lichenoid
CDEHIIOPT pithecoid
CDEHIIORT dichroite
CDEHIKLSU shielduck
CDEHIKPSY physicked
CDEHILLOV love-child
CDEHILLSS childless
CDEHILNSS childness
CDEHILPST stepchild
CDEHINORT chondrite
threnodic
CDEHINOSU cushioned
CDEHINOUU eunuchoid
CDEHIORSV dish-cover
CDEHIORTW dowitcher
CDEHIOSTU dithecous
CDEHISTTY dysthetic
CDEHKLLSU shellduck
CDEHKMMOU hummocked
CDEHKNOSU unshocked
CDEHKOSUV duckshove
CDEHLNORU chondrule
CDEHLNOTU unclothed
CDEHNOOTT thecodont
CDEHNOTUU untouched
CDEHNSTUY unscythed
CDEHOOOPS hodoscope
CDEIIILSV civilised
CDEIIILVZ civilized
CDEIIIRST sideritic
CDEIIKMTW mid-wicket
CDEIIKRST sick-tired
CDEIILLNO decillion
CDEIILNTU inductile
CDEIILOPR prolicide
CDEIILORT doleritic
CDEIILOSU delicious
CDEIILPUV vulpicide
CDEIILRRU ridiculer
CDEIILTVY declivity
CDEIIMNOS meniscoid
CDEIIMNTY mendicity

CDEIIMRST	miscredit
	misdirect
CDEIINNOT	incondite
	nicotined
CDEIINNTU	unincited
CDEIINOPT	depiction
CDEIINORT	cretinoid
	direction
CDEIINRTT	interdict
CDEIINTUV	inductive
CDEIIOOSU	dioecious
CDEIIOPRT	peridotic
CDEIIORUX	uxoricide
CDEIIORVV	divorcive
CDEIIRRTX	directrix
CDEIJNNOO	conjoined
CDEIKLNSU	klendusic
	unsickled
CDEIKPPRU	up-pricked
CDEILLLOU	△celluloid®
CDEILNNOY	indolency
CDEILNOPU	unpoliced
CDEILNORY	cordyline
CDEILNOTU	Dulcitone®
CDEILNPPU	unclipped
CDEILNSSU	lucidness
CDEILOOPS	scopeloid
CDEILOSUV	declivous
CDEILOTTW	twice-told
CDEILPRSU	surpliced
CDEILPSUU	△pediculus
CDEILRTUY	credulity
CDEIMMNOO	incommode
CDEIMMORY	myrmecoid
CDEIMMOTT	committed
CDEIMMSUY	music-demy
CDEIMNNOT	condiment
CDEIMNOPR	princedom
CDEIMNORU	indecorum
CDEIMNRRU	mind-curer
CDEIMORTU	udometric
CDEIMOSST	domestics
CDEINNOTU	continued
	unnoticed
CDEINOPRT	procident
CDEINOPSY	dyspnoeic
CDEINORSU	decursion
CDEINORTU	introduce
	reduction
CDEINORTV	contrived
CDEINOSTU	seduction
CDEINPRTU	unpredict
CDEINRSSU	curdiness
CDEINRSTY	stridency
CDEINTTUV	ventiduct
CDEIOOPRT	porticoed
CDEIOORST	scorodite
CDEIOPRRT	predictor
CDEIOPRST	dip-sector
CDEIOPRSU	cuspidore
CDEIORRST	recordist
CDEIORRTY	△directory
CDEIORSST	dissector
CDEIORSSU	discourse
CDEIORSTU	custodier
CDEIORSTV	discovert
CDEIORSVY	discovery
CDEIOSSTT	Docetists
CDEIPPSTY	dyspeptic
CDEKLNPUU	unplucked
CDEKLOORY	crookedly
CDEKNOORU	undercook
CDEKNOSTU	unstocked
CDELLOSSU	cloudless
CDELMOOPU	coupledom
CDELNNOOT	condolent
CDELNOORT	decontrol
CDELNOORU	undercool
CDELNOOST	stone-cold
CDELNOOSW	closedown
CDELNOOTY	cotyledon
CDELNOPUU	uncoupled
CDELNORSU	scoundrel
CDELOORSU	coloureds
CDELOORUV	overcloud
CDELOPRSU	supercold
CDELORSUU	credulous
CDEMMOOOR	commodore
CDENNORUW	uncrowned
CDENNOTUU	uncounted
CDENOOPRS	drop-scone
CDENOOPSY	endoscopy
CDENOORRS	scorrendo
CDENOORRT	corrodent
CDENOORST	consorted
CDENOORTT	contorted
CDENOORTU	contoured
CDENOPPRU	uncropped
CDENORSSU	uncrossed
CDENORSUU	unscoured
	unsourced
CDENORSWW	screw-down
CDENPRTUU	punctured
CDEOOOPST	octopodes
CDEOOOPSW	copsewood
CDEOORRVW	overcrowd
CDEOORSST	doctoress
CDEOORSWW	woodscrew
CDFFIILTU	difficult
CDFGHILNO	goldfinch
CDFGIINNO	confiding
CDFGIINOY	codifying
CDFHINORY	chondrify
CDFIILOOR	dolorific
CDFIIMOST	discomfit
CDFIIORSU	sudorific
CDFIMOORR	cordiform
CDFIORRTU	Fructidor
CDFKOOSTU	duck's-foot
CDGHIILNS	chidlings
CDGHLLOOT	gold-cloth
CDGIILNNU	including
CDGIIOTYZ	dizygotic

CDGIKLOST	goldstick
CDGILNNOY	condignly
CDHHIIOTY	ichthyoid
CDHHILOST	dish-cloth
CDHIIINOT	chitinoid
	dithionic
CDHIILLNW	wind-chill
CDHIIMOPR	dimorphic
CDHIIMORS	dichroism
CDHIIORRS	scirrhoid
CDHIIORST	orchidist
CDHIIPSTW	dip-switch
CDHIIRRTY	trihydric
CDHILOSTU	dish-clout
CDHIMNOOR	monorchid
CDHIMOOTY	dichotomy
CDHIMSTYY	dysthymic
CDHINOPSY	dysphonic
CDHIOOPRR	cirrhopod
CDHIOOPRY	chiropody
CDHIOOPSZ	schizopod
CDHIOPRSY	dysphoric
CDHIOPRTY	hydroptic
CDHIOPRWY	whipcordy
CDHLOORST	cold-short
CDHMNOOOR	monochord
CDHNNOOOU	coonhound
CDHNOOORT	notochord
CDHNOOTUW	touchdown
CDHOOORTW	torchwood
CDHOOOTUW	touchwood
CDHOORRST	short-cord
CDIIILMNS	diclinism
CDIIINNOT	indiction
CDIIINOOT	idioticon
CDIIIORST	dioristic
CDIIISTVY	viscidity
CDIIJOSUU	judicious
CDIILMOOT	dolomitic
CDIILNOSU	diclinous
CDIILPTUY	duplicity
CDIILTTUY	ductility
CDIIMMORU	cormidium
CDIIMNPUY	pycnidium
CDIIMOOST	sodomitic
CDIIMORST	dicrotism
CDIINNOOT	condition
CDIINNOTU	induction
CDIINOPRY	cyprinoid
CDIIOOPRS	scorpioid
CDIIOPRST	dioptrics
CDIIORRTT	tortricid
CDIIPRSTU	tricuspid
CDIJNOTUY	jocundity
CDIKLOORS	rock-solid
CDIKMRSTU	drumstick
CDIKOOPRW	prickwood
CDILLNOOO	collodion
CDILOOOPT	octoploid
CDILOORSU	discolour
CDILOOSTY	scolytoid
CDILORSUU	ludicrous
CDIMMNOOS	discommon
CDIMMOOTY	commodity
CDIMNOORU	doronicum
CDIMNORSY	syndromic
CDIMOOPRR	prodromic
CDINORSSW	crosswind
CDIOORRRS	corridors
CDIOORSTU	dicrotous
CDIRSSSUU	discursus
CDKKNNOOW	knock-down
CDKKNOOOR	doorknock
CDMNNORUU	conundrum
CDMNORSUW	scrumdown
CDMOOORTY	cordotomy
CDNNOOTUW	count-down
CDOORRSSW	crossword
CDOORRSUY	corduroys
CEEEEEHSW	ewe-cheese
CEEEEFFNR	efference
CEEEEFNRR	reference
CEEEEGMNR	emergence
CEEEEHILP	heel-piece
CEEEEHMNV	vehemence
CEEEENRRV	reverence
CEEEEORRV	recoveree
CEEEFFITV	effective
CEEEFFLNU	effluence
CEEEFHLTT	flechette
	fléchette
CEEEFILNN	line-fence
CEEEFINNR	inference
CEEEFINPV	fivepence
CEEEFLNRU	refluence
CEEEFLNSS	fenceless
CEEEFLRRT	reflecter
CEEEFNORR	re-enforce
CEEEFNQRU	frequence
CEEEFPRRT	perfecter
CEEEGILNT	telegenic
CEEEGIMNS	miscegene
CEEEGINRT	energetic
CEEEGISTX	exegetics
CEEEGLMNU	emulgence
CEEEGLNOR	conger-eel
CEEEGLNRT	neglecter
CEEEGMNRY	emergency
CEEEHILPS	sheep-lice
CEEEHILST	scheelite
CEEEHINNR	inherence
CEEEHINPS	nipcheese
CEEEHIPST	tip-cheese
CEEEHLNTY	entelechy
CEEEHLOPR	creep-hole
CEEEHLRSS	cheerless
	rechlesse
CEEEHLRUV	chevelure
CEEEHMNVY	vehemency
CEEEHNRVW	whencever
CEEEHOPRS	ecosphere
	pre-echoes
CEEEHOPST	sheepcote
CEEEHQRUX	△exchequer

CEEEHRTTV chevrette
CEEEIIMPT timepiece
CEEEIINRV vicereine
CEEEIJRTV rejective
CEEEIKPRR pickeerer
CEEEILLNT clientele
clientèle
CEEEILNOP Pleiocene
CEEEILNST △celestine
CEEEILPSS epicleses
pieceless
CEEEILPSY eye-splice
CEEEILRST electrise
Leicester
CEEEILRTT tiercelet
CEEEILRTZ electrize
CEEEILSTT celestite
CEEEILSTV selective
CEEEIMNTT cementite
CEEEIMRRS mercerise
CEEEIMRRZ mercerize
CEEEINNNP ninepence
CEEEINNPT penitence
CEEEINNRT centenier
CEEEINNST sentience
CEEEINOPS nose-piece
CEEEINPRT epicenter
epicentre
CEEEINQUV vice-queen
CEEEINRSU esurience
CEEEINSTX existence
CEEEIPRRV perceiver
CEEEIPRSU précieuse
CEEEIPRTV receptive
CEEEIPTVX exceptive
CEEEIRRSX exerciser
CEEEIRSSV recessive
CEEEIRSSX exercises
CEEEIRSTV secretive
CEEEIRSVX ex-service
CEEEIRTVX excretive
CEEEISSVX excessive
CEEEITUVX executive
CEEEJMNTT ejectment
CEEEKNRSV neckverse
CEEEKORRT rocketeer
CEEELLNTX excellent
CEEELMNTU temulence
CEEELNOQU eloquence
CEEELNOSY Ceylonese
CEEELOPST telescope
CEEELORTV clove-tree
CEEELOTTT côtelette
CEEELPRST preselect
CEEELRSST electress
CEEEMNRRT recrement
CEEEMNRTX excrement
CEEEMSTUY Eumycetes
CEEENNORV reconvene
CEEENNRST secernent
sentencer
CEEENNSST senescent
CEEENNSSU unessence
CEEENORTT entrecôte
CEEENOSTY synoecete
CEEENQRSU sequencer
CEEENRSST erectness
CEEEOPSTT escopette
CEEEORRRV recoverer
CEEEPRRST respecter
CEEEPRSTU persecute
CEEFFIINT efficient
CEEFFILOR life-force
CEEFFIOOR o're-office
CEEFFIOSU coiffeuse
CEEFFNORT off-centre
CEEFGHILN fleeching
CEEFGIKPR fig-pecker
CEEFGINNR ring-fence
CEEFGLNTU genuflect
CEEFHIIST fetichise
CEEFHIITZ fetichize
CEEFHILRS fish-creel
CEEFHILSS chiefless
CEEFHIPSY speechify
CEEFHLPSU speechful
CEEFHMNNR Frenchmen
CEEFIILRT feliciter
CEEFIINTV infective
CEEFIIRRT certifier
rectifier
CEEFILNNU influence
CEEFILNRT fernticle
CEEFILRTY electrify
CEEFIMNOR confirmee
CEEFIMORT focimeter
CEEFIMPRT imperfect
CEEFINORR confrérie
reinforce
CEEFINORT refection
CEEFINTTU fettucine
CEEFIRRST firecrest
CEEFKLLSS fleckless
CEEFLOORS foreclose
CEEFLORRT reflector
CEEFLORSS forceless
CEEFLORSU fluoresce
CEEFLPRTY perfectly
CEEFNOPRU fourpence
CEEFNORRR conferrer
CEEFNPRTU unperfect
CEEFNQRUY frequency
CEEFNRSTU rufescent
CEEFOPRRT perfector
CEEFOPRSS forcepses
CEEFOPRST perfectos
CEEFORRTY refectory
CEEGHIMNO hegemonic
CEEGHINNO hecogenin
CEEGHINRW Greenwich
CEEGIILPS spicilege
CEEGIIMNS miscegine
CEEGIINRS isenergic
CEEGIINRV receiving

CEEGIINST Genesitic
CEEGILLNX excelling
CEEGILNOO Oligocene
CEEGILNOT telegonic
CEEGILNRY glycerine
CEEGIMORT geometric
CEEGINNOS consignee
CEEGINNRS screening
CEEGINNRT centering
centreing
CEEGINNST ignescent
CEEGINNSY syngeneic
CEEGINOOT oogenetic
CEEGINOPS engiscope
CEEGINORS congeries
recognise
CEEGINORX exergonic
CEEGINORZ recognize
CEEGINPRS cee-spring
CEEGINPTX excepting
expecting
CEEGINRSV screeving
CEEGIORRS groceries
CEEGJKLOT jockteleg
CEEGKNOOS goose-neck
CEEGLNOOS Congolese
CEEGNOPSY engyscope
CEEGORTTU courgette
CEEHHIRVW whichever
CEEHHOPST hope-chest
CEEHIILTT helictite
CEEHIIPTT epithetic
CEEHIIRTT erethitic
CEEHIKKNT thick-knee
CEEHIKNRT kitchener
thickener
CEEHIKPPR pike-perch
CEEHILLMS schlemiel
CEEHILLRS chiseller
CEEHILNOS lichenose
CEEHILNRS schlieren
CEEHILPRT telpheric
CEEHILRSV cleverish
CEEHILSTT telestich
CEEHIMPRY hyperemic
CEEHIMPTY chemitype
CEEHIMRST hermetics
CEEHIMRSW shrewmice
CEEHIMTUV humective
CEEHINNRY inherency
CEEHINPRT phrenetic
CEEHINPST phenetics
CEEHINPSU euphenics
CEEHINQTU technique
CEEHINRTT threnetic
CEEHINRTY hercynite
CEEHINSST techiness
CEEHINSTU euthenics
CEEHINSTZ Zechstein
CEEHINSUU eunuchise
CEEHINUUZ eunuchize
CEEHIOPSW showpiece
CEEHIORRT torchière
CEEHIORSS coheiress
CEEHIORTT heterotic
theoretic
CEEHIPRRY cherry-pie
CEEHIPRTT pitch-tree
CEEHLLNOP cellphone
CEEHLORSU lecherous
CEEHLPPRS schlepper
CEEHLPRSU sepulcher
sepulchre
CEEHLQRSU squelcher
CEEHLRSST retchless
CEEHMMOOR home-comer
CEEHMNORZ chernozem
CEEHMOORZ zoechrome
CEEHMORTT ectotherm
CEEHNOPRR percheron
CEEHNOPRY coryphene
CEEHNOSTT chest-note
CEEHOPRRV overperch
CEEHOPRSU proseuche
CEEHOPTTY ectophyte
CEEHORRTU retoucher
CEEHPRRSY sprechery
CEEHRRSTT stretcher
CEEIIKLNN nickeline
CEEIIKLNS nickelise
CEEIIKLNZ nickelize
CEEIILNPR pericline
CEEIILNRT lienteric
CEEIILNST insectile
selenitic
CEEIILPPT epileptic
CEEIILPRX pre-exilic
CEEIILPSS epiclesis
CEEIIMMNN imminence
CEEIIMNRS reminisce
CEEIIMOST semeiotic
CEEIIMPRS imprecise
CEEIIMPST epistemic
CEEIIMRST metricise
CEEIIMRTZ metricize
CEEIINNOR eirenicon
CEEIINNRS insincere
CEEIINNRT encrinite
CEEIINNTV incentive
CEEIINPRT recipient
CEEIINPTV inceptive
CEEIINPTX excipient
CEEIINRST cretinise
CEEIINRSV in-service
CEEIINRTZ cretinize
CEEIINSST scientise
CEEIINSTZ scientize
CEEIINTVV invective
CEEIIOPST poeticise
CEEIIOPTZ poeticize
CEEIIORRT écritoire
CEEIIORST eroticise
CEEIIORTZ eroticize
CEEIIPRSS Persicise

CEEIIPRSU	epicurise
CEEIIPRSV	precisive
CEEIIPRSZ	Persicize
CEEIIPRUZ	epicurize
CEEIIQSTU	equisetic
CEEIIRRTT	trieteric
CEEIJLOUV	love-juice
CEEIJLSSU	juiceless
CEEIJNORT	rejection
CEEIJNRTT	interject
CEEIKKSSS	skeesicks
CEEIKMSTT	metestick
CEEIKNOPS	kinescope
CEEIKNQRU	quickener
	requicken
CEEIKOPRW	piece-work
	workpiece
CEEILLLNO	lioncelle
CEEILLLOV	level-coil
CEEILLLTU	cellulite
CEEILLNNT	centinell
CEEILLNPR	penciller
CEEILLNSW	clew-lines
CEEILLNTT	intellect
CEEILLOTV	covellite
CEEILMNNT	inclement
CEEILMNPR	Crimplene®
CEEILMNSU	luminesce
CEEILMORS	misoclere
CEEILMRSS	crimeless
	merciless
CEEILMRUV	vermicule
CEEILNNOS	insolence
CEEILNOPR	crepoline
	pencil-ore
CEEILNORS	scoreline
CEEILNORT	centriole
CEEILNOST	selection
CEEILNOTY	ceylonite
CEEILNPRT	princelet
CEEILNPST	splenetic
CEEILNRSU	licensure
CEEILNRSY	sincerely
CEEILNRTV	ventricle
CEEILNRUV	virulence
CEEILOPTT	pectolite
CEEILOPTU	poeticule
CEEILORRT	terricole
CEEILORSX	△excelsior
CEEILOSSS	isosceles
CEEILOSSV	voiceless
CEEILPRSS	priceless
CEEILPRSW	screw-pile
CEEILPRSY	precisely
CEEILRSTW	crewelist
CEEILRSUV	reclusive
CEEILSSUV	seclusive
CEEILSUVX	exclusive
CEEIMMNSU	ecumenism
CEEIMMOTT	committee
CEEIMNNRT	increment
CEEIMNOOS	economise
CEEIMNOOZ	economize
CEEIMNOPT	impotence
CEEIMNOST	centesimo
CEEIMNSTU	intumesce
CEEIMRRSU	mercurise
CEEIMRRUZ	mercurize
CEEINNORS	ninescore
	recension
CEEINNPTY	penitency
CEEINNRTY	renitency
CEEINNSTY	sentiency
CEEINOPRS	pericones
	preconise
CEEINOPRT	reception
CEEINOPRZ	preconize
CEEINOPTX	exception
CEEINORRS	encierros
CEEINORRT	tierceron
CEEINORSS	recession
CEEINORST	necrotise
	resection
	secretion
CEEINORSU	cinereous
CEEINORTV	covin-tree
CEEINORTX	excretion
CEEINORTZ	necrotize
CEEINOSSS	△secession
CEEINOSSY	synoecise
CEEINOSTX	exsection
CEEINOSYZ	synoecize
CEEINOTUX	execution
CEEINPRRU	prurience
CEEINPRSS	crepiness
	princesse
CEEINPRST	prescient
	reinspect
CEEINPRSU	unprecise
CEEINPRTT	intercept
CEEINQRTU	quercetin
CEEINQSTU	quiescent
CEEINRRSV	scrivener
CEEINRSTT	intersect
CEEINRSTV	virescent
CEEINRSUY	esuriency
CEEINSSTY	necessity
CEEIOORTZ	ozocerite
CEEIOORVV	voice-over
CEEIOPPRS	periscope
CEEIOPRRV	overprice
CEEIOPSST	cespitose
CEEIORRST	corsetier
CEEIORRSX	exorciser
CEEIORRXZ	exorcizer
CEEIORSST	sectorise
CEEIORSSU	sericeous
CEEIORSTV	vectorise
CEEIORSTZ	sectorize
CEEIORTVZ	vectorize
CEEIRRRTU	recruiter
CEEIRRSUV	recursive
CEEIRSSTU	cerussite
CEEIRSUVX	excursive

CEEIRTUXX executrix
CEEJORRTT retroject
CEEKKKNNO knock-knee
CEEKLOTUY leukocyte
CEEKLPSSS speckless
CEEKLRUVY culver-key
CEEKNPRTU nutpecker
CEELLLOSU cellulose
CEELLMNTY clemently
CEELLMOPR compeller
CEELLNORS ensorcell
CEELLOPTU locuplete
CEELLORTU Courtelle®
CEELLRSUY reclusely
CEELMMPTU emplectum
CEELMNOPT emplecton
CEELMNOUW unwelcome
CEELMNTUY temulency
CEELMOOTU leucotome
CEELMOPRT completer
CEELNNNOP pennoncel
CEELNOORT contrôlée
CEELNORSU enclosure
CEELNOSSS closeness
CEELNOSTU consultee
CEELNPRUU purulence
CEELNRSSU cruelness
CEELNSSST scentless
CEELNSTTU lutescent
CEELOPRRT prelector
CEELOPSTY telescopy
CEELORSSS scleroses
CEELORSUU ceruleous
CEELORSUX exclosure
CEELORTTU court-leet
CEELRSSST crestless
CEELRSSTU truceless
CEEMMNORT commenter
CEEMNNORT contemner
CEEMNOORT oncometer
CEEMNOPRT contemper
CEEMNOPTT competent
CEEMNORSU cornemuse
CEEMNSTTU tumescent
CEEMOOPRS recompose
CEEMOORSS Morescoes
CEEMORRTY cryometer
CEEMORSUV curvesome
CEEMORTTY cytometer
CEEMOSSTY ecosystem
CEEMPRTUX excerptum
CEEMQRTUU quercetum
CEENNORRT rencontre
CEENNORRU renouncer
CEENNORTU encounter
CEENNRSSU sunscreen
CEENOOPST copestone
CEENOPRRT precentor
CEENOPRST copresent
CEENOPSTT Pentecost
CEENOQRRU reconquer
CEENORRSV conserver
CEENORRTV converter
reconvert
CEENORSTT contester
CEENORSTW sweetcorn
CEENRRRTU recurrent
CEENRRTUX excurrent
CEEOORRRV recoveror
CEEOORRSV overscore
CEEOORRVV overcover
CEEOPPRRT preceptor
CEEOPRRSS reprocess
CEEOPRRTX excerptor
CEEOPRSTU prosecute
CEEOQRTTU croquette
CEEORRSSS sorceress
CEEORRSST crosstree
rectoress
CEEORRSSU resources
CEEORRSTW worcester
CEEORRSTY secretory
CEEORRSUV verrucose
CEEORRTUV coverture
CEEORRTXY excretory
CEEORSSTT crossette
CEEORTUXY executory
CEEPRRRRU precurrer
CEEPRRSSU repercuss
CEERRRSTU resurrect
CEFFFFLUU cuffuffle
CEFFFLRUU curfuffle
CEFFHINRY Frenchify
CEFFIINOT coffinite
CEFFORTTU off-cutter
CEFGHIILN chiefling
CEFGIKLNR freckling
CEFGINORS frescoing
CEFGINORU configure
CEFHHIIPS chiefship
CEFHIILSS fish-slice
CEFHIIMST fetichism
CEFHIINNP pine-finch
CEFHIISTT fetichist
CEFHIITWW witch-wife
CEFHIKRSW wreckfish
CEFHILMOR cheliform
CEFHINORS rosefinch
CEFHKLLOU choke-full
CEFHKOORS foreshock
CEFHLOORT forecloth
CEFHMOORT forthcome
home-croft
CEFHOORSU corfhouse
CEFHPRRSU surfperch
CEFIIKNTY finickety
CEFIIKQRU quick-fire
CEFIIKRST fire-stick
CEFIILNRT inflicter
CEFIILNRU luciferin
CEFIILTWY Wyclifite
CEFIINNOT infection
CEFIINOPT pontifice
CEFIINTTU fettucini

CEFIIORRS	scorifier
CEFIKORSS	fossicker
CEFIMNORR	confirmer
	reconfirm
CEFIMNORT	cteniform
CEFIMNORU	cuneiform
CEFIMOPRR	perciform
CEFIMORRU	eruciform
CEFIMORTT	tectiform
CEFIMORTU	comfiture
CEFINNNOU	unconfine
CEFINOORT	△confiteor
CEFINORSS	forensics
CEFINORSU	confiseur
CEFINORTU	confiture
CEFIOORSU	ferocious
CEFIORRSS	crossfire
CEFIORSST	frescoist
CEFIORSTU	fruticose
CEFKLNOSW	snowfleck
CEFKLOPTU	pocketful
CEFKLORSS	frockless
CEFKOORRW	workforce
CEFLNNOTU	confluent
CEFLNOSTY	confestly
CEFLOORSU	soul-force
CEFMNOORR	conformer
CEFMOORRT	△comforter
	recomfort
CEFMOPPRU	force-pump
CEFNNOORT	confronté
CEFNOORSS	confessor
CEFOOPSTY	fetoscopy
CEFOORRSU	fourscore
CEFOORRTU	forecourt
CEFOORSTV	softcover
CEGHIILOP	geophilic
CEGHIINPR	ciphering
CEGHIINSY	hygienics
CEGHIIOST	gothicise
CEGHIIOTZ	gothicize
CEGHILLOU	guilloche
CEGHILMTU	gemütlich
CEGHILNTV	vetchling
CEGHILOOR	rheologic
CEGHILOOT	ethologic
	theologic
CEGHINNQU	quenching
CEGHINNRW	wrenching
CEGHINOOT	Neo-Gothic
	theogonic
CEGHINORS	coshering
CEGHINORT	hectoring
CEGHIOPTY	geophytic
CEGHKNORU	roughneck
CEGHLOOUY	euchology
CEGHMNOOR	chromogen
CEGIIJNOR	rejoicing
CEGIIKLNN	nickeling
CEGIIKNNS	sickening
CEGIIKNPT	picketing
CEGIIKNTT	ticketing
CEGIILNNR	reclining
CEGIILNSY	lysigenic
CEGIIMNOT	mitogenic
CEGIINOTV	cognitive
CEGIINPRS	précising
CEGIIOSTT	egotistic
CEGIKNNOR	reckoning
CEGIKNOPT	pocketing
CEGIKNOST	socketing
CEGILLMOU	collegium
CEGILLNPU	cupelling
CEGILMMNO	commingle
CEGILMNOW	welcoming
CEGILNOPY	polygenic
CEGILNOST	closeting
CEGILNRSU	surcingle
CEGILOOOZ	zoogloeic
CEGILOOST	ecologist
CEGIMNNOO	monogenic
CEGIMNOOR	ergonomic
CEGIMNOUY	gynoecium
CEGIMNOYZ	zymogenic
CEGINNOOT	ontogenic
CEGINNORS	consigner
CEGINOOPR	coopering
CEGINOOPS	geoponics
CEGINOPPR	coppering
CEGINOPRY	pyrogenic
CEGINOPTY	genotypic
CEGINORRT	corrigent
CEGINORST	corseting
CEGINORTV	vectoring
CEGINOSST	cosseting
CEGINOSTT	stegnotic
CEGINRRRU	recurring
CEGINRTUV	curveting
CEGIOOPRT	geotropic
CEGLNOORY	necrology
CEGMNNOOS	cognomens
CEGMNOOSY	cosmogeny
CEGNNOORR	negro-corn
CEGNNORTU	congruent
CEGNOORSU	Coregonus
CEGNORRSU	scrounger
CEGNORSUY	surgeoncy
CEGOOPRSY	gyroscope
CEHHHIIKT	hitch-hike
CEHHIIMST	hemistich
CEHHILLMS	schlemihl
CEHHILLOT	cholelith
CEHHIMOST	shochetim
CEHHIMSTT	hem-stitch
CEHHLOOTU	touch-hole
CEHHOOPSU	chophouse
	chop-house
CEHIIILST	cheilitis
CEHIIKLRS	lickerish
CEHIIKLTW	witchlike
CEHIILMNS	lichenism
CEHIILMOT	homiletic
CEHIILNOT	ichnolite
	Neolithic

CEHIILNST	lichenist
CEHIILOOZ	heliozoic
CEHIILOST	Elohistic
CEHIIMMPT	Memphitic
CEHIIMMRS	chimerism
CEHIIMNST	ethnicism
CEHIIMSTY	mythicise
CEHIIMTYZ	mythicize
CEHIINPPT	pitchpine
CEHIINPRT	nephritic
	phrenitic
CEHIINSST	itchiness
CEHIINTTY	ethnicity
CEHIIPPPT	pitchpipe
CEHIIPPST	psephitic
CEHIIPPTY	epiphytic
CEHIIPRRT	peritrich
CEHIIPRTT	perthitic
	tephritic
CEHIIRSTT	Thersitic
CEHIIRSTU	heuristic
CEHIJPSTW	Jew's-pitch
CEHIKLMTV	milk-vetch
CEHIKLPRS	clerkship
CEHIKLSTY	sketchily
CEHIKNPRT	phrentick
CEHIKNSST	thickness
CEHIKOPPR	hop-picker
CEHIKOPPT	hip-pocket
CEHIKPRSW	shipwreck
CEHILLNSS	chillness
CEHILMNTU	lunch-time
CEHILMOOS	molochise
CEHILMOOZ	molochize
CEHILMOTY	hemolytic
CEHILNOOR	holocrine
CEHILNOPR	necrophil
CEHILNOSU	lichenous
CEHILNOTU	touchline
CEHILNPSU	siphuncle
	uncleship
CEHILNSTZ	schnitzel
CEHILOOPS	heliscoop
CEHILOPPT	pitch-pole
CEHILOPRT	plethoric
CEHIMMOPR	morphemic
CEHIMMORS	micromesh
CEHIMNNOU	ichneumon
CEHIMNOPS	phonemics
CEHIMNOSS	mochiness
CEHIMNSUU	eunuchism
CEHIMOOOT	homoeotic
CEHIMOPRT	morphetic
CEHIMOPXY	hypoxemic
CEHIMORRT	trichrome
CEHIMORST	hectorism
CEHIMORTT	thermotic
CEHIMPRUY	Hypericum
CEHIMPTYY	chemitypy
CEHIMRSTY	chemistry
CEHIMSTTY	methystic
CEHINOORS	isochrone
CEHINOPRT	nephrotic
CEHINOPRU	neurochip
CEHINOPST	Ctesiphon
	phonetics
CEHINOPTY	neophytic
CEHINORST	sticheron
CEHINOSTU	cushionet
CEHINPRST	sphincter
CEHINRSST	snitchers
CEHINSTTY	synthetic
CEHIOOPRT	orthoepic
CEHIOORRT	coheritor
CEHIOPPRS	copperish
CEHIOPPRT	prophetic
CEHIOPRTT	prothetic
CEHIOPRTU	eutrophic
CEHIOPRTV	overpitch
CEHIOPRTY	hypocrite
CEHIORRST	chorister
CEHIOSSST	schistose
CEHIPRRSU	superrich
CEHIPRRTY	cherry-pit
CEHIRSSTY	hysterics
CEHIRSTTY	stitchery
CEHITTTWY	witchetty
CEHKLMNOO	kloochmen
CEHKLNORS	schnorkel
CEHKLOOSU	lockhouse
CEHKLORSU	suck-holer
CEHKOOOSU	cookhouse
CEHKOOPPT	hop-pocket
CEHKRSTUY	huckstery
CEHLLOOPT	photocell
CEHLLORUY	holy-cruel
CEHLMNOUU	homuncule
CEHLNOSZZ	schnozzle
CEHLNOTTT	tent-cloth
CEHLOOOSU	coolhouse
CEHLOOPRS	preschool
CEHLOORSY	schoolery
CEHLOOSTU	clout-shoe
CEHLOPSST	slop-chest
CEHLOSSTU	touchless
CEHMOOPRT	ectomorph
CEHMOORRU	urochrome
CEHMOTTYY	thymocyte
CEHMRSTTU	schmutter
CEHNNORTU	truncheon
CEHNNRTUW	nut-wrench
CEHNOOTTU	Touchtone®
	touchtone
CEHNOOTYZ	zootechny
CEHNORRRS	schnorrer
CEHOOOPRS	horoscope
CEHOPSSSY	psychoses
CEHOPTTUY	touch-type
CEHORSTUY	scouthery
CEHOSTTUZ	zuchettos
CEIIIILMNS	Miliciens
CEIIILNRU	Ricinulei
CEIIILRSV	civiliser
CEIIILRVZ	civilizer

CEIIIMNRS	irenicism
CEIIIMSTV	victimise
CEIIIMTVZ	victimize
CEIIINNOP	epinicion
CEIIINNPT	incipient
CEIIINRSU	cuisinier
CEIIIPSTT	pietistic
CEIIJNNOT	injection
CEIIJNSSU	juiciness
CEIIJNSTU	injustice
CEIIKLMPS	mispickel
CEIIKLMQU	quicklime
CEIIKLMST	Kelticism
CEIIKLRTY	ricketily
CEIIKNNPR	princekin
CEIIKNPRT	nit-picker
CEIIKRSTU	Turkicise
CEIIKRTUZ	Turkicize
CEIILLNNO	linolenic
CEIILMNSU	miniscule
CEIILMORT	microlite
CEIILMPSS	simplices
CEIILNNOR	crinoline
CEIILNPPR	principle
CEIILNSUV	inclusive
CEIILOPST	epistolic
CEIILOQRU	liquorice
CEIILOSSU	siliceous
CEIILPRTU	pleuritic
CEIILRSST	scleritis
CEIILSTTY	sectility
CEIILSTUV	Leviticus
CEIIMMNNY	imminency
CEIIMNOST	semitonic
CEIIMNRST	cretinism
CEIIMNSST	scientism
CEIIMOPST	impeticos
	poeticism
CEIIMORRW	microwire
CEIIMORST	eroticism
	isometric
	meroistic
CEIIMOSST	semiotics
CEIIMOSTX	exoticism
CEIIMPRSU	epicurism
CEIIMRRTT	trimetric
CEIIMRSTT	metricist
CEIIMTTUV	viticetum
CEIINNOPT	inception
CEIINNORT	incretion
CEIINNOST	insection
CEIINOPPW	wincopipe
CEIINOPRS	precision
CEIINOPRT	proteinic
CEIINORRT	criterion
	tricerion
CEIINORTV	victorine
CEIINPRSS	priciness
CEIINPSSS	spiciness
CEIINRSTT	sternitic
CEIINRSTX	extrinsic
CEIINRSTY	sincerity
CEIINRSUV	incursive
CEIINRTTY	intercity
CEIINRTYZ	citizenry
CEIINSSTT	scientist
CEIIOOPTZ	epizootic
CEIIORSST	isosteric
CEIIORSTT	eroticist
CEIIORSTU	triecious
CEIIPPTTY	pepticity
CEIIPSTTY	septicity
CEIIRSSTU	rusticise
CEIIRSTUZ	rusticize
CEIIRTTVY	verticity
CEIJKMOSY	jockeyism
CEIJNORTT	introject
CEIKLNNPY	lickpenny
CEIKLNOPV	clovepink
CEIKLNORT	interlock
CEIKLNOST	close-knit
CEIKLNOSU	nickelous
CEIKLNSSS	slickness
CEIKLNSSU	luckiness
CEIKLOPST	stockpile
CEIKLORTU	courtlike
CEIKLOSTV	livestock
CEIKLRSST	trickless
CEIKMNORS	misreckon
CEIKMNSSU	muckiness
CEIKMORST	tricksome
CEIKMRSTU	semi-truck
CEIKNOOPS	koniscope
CEIKNORSS	corkiness
	rockiness
CEIKNOSTT	stockinet
CEIKNOSTV	vine-stock
CEIKNQSSU	quickness
CEIKNRSSU	sicknurse
CEIKOPRRT	rope-trick
CEIKORRTV	overtrick
CEIKPPRSU	pick-purse
CEIKPQSTU	quickstep
CEIKRRSTT	trickster
CEILLLMTU	clitellum
CEILLMOOW	come-o'-will
CEILLNOOR	corolline
CEILLNOUV	involucel
CEILLOPPT	pole-clipt
CEILLOQSU	coquilles
CEILLOSUV	collusive
	colluvies
CEILLPSTY	sylleptic
CEILMNNOO	monocline
CEILMNOOS	semicolon
CEILMNOPU	encolpium
CEILMNOTU	monticule
CEILMNSUU	minuscule
CEILMOPRY	micropyle
	polymeric
CEILMOPTY	lipectomy
CEILMRTUU	△reticulum
CEILNNOOP	encolpion
CEILNNOOS	cloisonné

CEILNNOTU	countline
CEILNOOTU	elocution
CEILNOPRU	pronuclei
CEILNORST	sclerotin
CEILNORSU	inclosure
	reclusion
CEILNORUV	involucre
	volucrine
CEILNOSSU	seclusion
CEILNOSUX	exclusion
CEILNRSSU	curliness
CEILNRUVY	virulency
CEILNSSTU	linctuses
CEILOOPRT	coprolite
CEILOORSU	colourise
CEILOORUZ	colourize
CEILOPPRT	proleptic
CEILOPRSU	supercoil
CEILOPRSV	coverslip
CEILORSSS	sclerosis
CEILOSSSU	coulisses
CEILOSTVY	costively
CEILRSUVY	cursively
CEIMMNNOS	mnemonics
CEIMMNOOR	monomeric
CEIMMNOOS	economism
	monoecism
CEIMMNOSU	communise
	encomiums
CEIMMNOTU	comminute
CEIMMNOTY	metonymic
CEIMMNOUZ	communize
CEIMMOORS	microsome
CEIMMOORT	microtome
CEIMMRSTY	symmetric
CEIMNNOPU	pneumonic
CEIMNNORS	encrimson
CEIMNNORT	Comintern
CEIMNNOTU	emunction
CEIMNOOPT	coemption
CEIMNOORT	microtone
CEIMNOOST	economist
CEIMNOOSU	monecious
CEIMNOPTY	impotency
CEIMNOSSY	synoecism
CEIMNRTUV	centumvir
CEIMOOPRR	micropore
	poromeric
CEIMOOPRT	compotier
CEIMOOPST	△composite
CEIMOORSS	Moriscoes
CEIMOORTZ	zoometric
CEIMOOSTX	exosmotic
CEIMOPRTU	ectropium
CEIMOPSUU	pumiceous
CEIMORSTU	costumier
CEIMOSSTU	customise
CEIMOSTUV	△muscovite
CEIMOSTUZ	customize
CEINNNOOX	connexion
CEINNNOTT	△continent
CEINNNOTV	connivent
CEINNOOTV	connotive
CEINNORSY	incensory
CEINNORTU	centurion
	continuer
CEINNOSTT	centonist
CEINNRRTU	incurrent
CEINNTTUX	unextinct
CEINOOPRT	ectropion
CEINOORST	cortisone
CEINOORTU	co-routine
CEINOPPRU	porcupine
CEINOPRRS	conspirer
CEINOPRRT	intercrop
CEINOPRST	inspector
CEINOPRSV	provinces
CEINOPRTT	cotter-pin
CEINOPRXY	pyroxenic
CEINOPSTT	entoptics
CEINOPSUU	pecunious
CEINORRRS	serricorn
CEINORRSU	recursion
CEINORRTV	contriver
CEINORSTT	cornetist
CEINORSTU	cretinous
CEINORSUX	excursion
CEINOSTUV	contusive
CEINOTVXY	convexity
CEINPRRUY	pruriency
CEINPRSSS	crispness
CEINRSTWW	twin-screw
CEIOOPRSS	coreopsis
CEIOOPRST	porticoes
CEIOOPRTZ	zoetropic
CEIOORRSV	corrosive
CEIOORSTV	vorticose
CEIOPPRRT	periproct
CEIOPRRTY	procerity
CEIOPRSSU	prescious
CEIORRSSS	scissorer
CEIORRSTT	tortrices
	trisector
CEIORRSTU	scrutoire
CEIORRSUZ	cruzeiros
CEIORRTUU	couturier
CEIORSSSW	crosswise
CEIORSSTV	victoress
CEIORSTTU	toreutics
CEIPPRRST	prescript
CEIPRRSTU	△scripture
CEIRRSTTU	stricture
CEJKOOTUY	outjockey
CEJOOPRRT	projector
CEKKNOPRU	knocker-up
CEKKORSTY	skyrocket
CEKLNNPUY	luck-penny
CEKLOSSST	stockless
CEKMNORTU	mockernut
CEKNORSTU	orestunck
CEKOORSTV	overstock
CELLMOPXY	complexly
CELLMSTUU	scutellum
CELLNOSUU	nucleolus

CELLOOPTY collotype
CELMNOOOT melocoton
CELMNOSUU lucumones
CELMNOTUY contumely
CELMNPRUU uncrumple
CELMOOPRY copolymer
co-polymer
CELMOOSSU colosseum
CELMOOTUY leucotomy
CELMOPRUU operculum
CELMOPSUX complexus
CELMOTTYY tylectomy
CELMPRSTU plectrums
CELNOORSU counselor
CELNOOSTU consolute
CELNOOTUV convolute
CELNOPRST plectrons
CELNOPRTU corpulent
CELNORSSW crownless
CELNORSTU consulter
CELNOSSTU countless
CELNPRUUY purulency
CELNRRTUY currently
CELNRTTUU truculent
CELOOPRSU supercool
CELOOPRTU turcopole
CELOORTUY elocutory
CELOOSTTY octostyle
CELORRSUU soul-curer
CELORRSUY reclusory
CELORSSUU surculose
CELORSUXY exclusory
CELPRSTUU sculpture
CELRSSSTU crustless
CEMMNOORT commentor
CEMNNOOPT component
CEMNNOORT contemnor
CEMNOOOQU monocoque
CEMNOOORS monoceros
CEMNOOOSU oncomouse
CEMNOORTY necrotomy
CEMNORTUY emunctory
CEMOOPRST composter
CEMOOPRSU composure
CEMOOPSTU mutoscope
CEMOOPTTY topectomy
CEMORRSUU mercurous
CEMORRSWW screw-worm
CEMORTTYY cytometry
CEMPRSTUU prescutum
CENNOOPPY opponency
CENNOOPRU pronounce
CENNOORST cornstone
CENNOSSSU consensus
CENNRRTUU uncurrent
CENOOPRST stonecrop
CENOOQRRU △conqueror
CENOORRST consorter
CENOORRTV convertor
CENOORSUU coenourus
CENOORTUV overcount
CENOORTYY tycoonery
CENORRSTU construer
CENORSSSS crossness
CENORSSTW crow's-nest
CENORSTXY xenocryst
CENPRRTUU puncturer
up-current
CENPSSTUU unsuspect
CENRRSTUW turn-screw
CENRSSSTU curstness
CEOOOPPRS poroscope
CEOOPPRSY pyroscope
CEOOPRRRT prorector
CEOOPRRSS processor
CEOOPRRST prosector
CEOOPRRTT △protector
CEOOPSSTU octopuses
CEOORRSSS rose-cross
CEOORRSSU sorcerous
CEOORRSSV crossover
CEOORSTTY trot-cosey
CEOORSTUU courteous
CEOPRRRSU precursor
CEOPRRRTU corrupter
CEOPRRRUU procureur
CEOPRRSSU percussor
procuress
CEOPRSSTU susceptor
CEOPRSSTW crow-steps
CEORRSUUV verrucous
CEPRSSSUU Cupressus
CERRSTTUU structure
CFFFIISTU fisticuff
CFFGIINSU sufficing
CFFIIOOSU officious
CFFLOOORU off-colour
CFFORRSSU cross-ruff
CFGHIILNN flinching
CFGIIIKNN finicking
CFGIIINSS significs
CFGIILLMN clingfilm
CFGIINNNO confining
CFGILNNOU flouncing
CFGINOSSU focussing
CFHIINNOO finnochio
CFHIINOOR honorific
CFHIINPST pinchfist
CFHIKOPRT pitchfork
CFHIKOSST stockfish
CFHIORSSS crossfish
CFHLOOOTT footcloth
CFHLOPSUU pouchfuls
CFIIKKLNS skinflick
CFIILMMOR microfilm
CFIILNORT inflictor
CFIILORST floristic
CFIIMOPRS pisciform
CFIIMORRR cirriform
CFIIOOPRS soporific
CFIKLLNOT flintlock
CFIKLLOOR folkloric
CFIKLNOSW snowflick
CFILNSUUU funiculus

Words marked △ may be spelled also with a capital letter

CFIMMNOOR	Cominform
CFIMMOORR	microform
CFIMNOORR	confirmor
	corniform
CFIMORRUV	curviform
CFIMORSTU	scutiform
CFIMORSTY	cystiform
CFINNOOSU	confusion
CFIOOPRRY	corporify
CFKLOORRU	rock-flour
CFKNOORSW	forswonck
CFLLOORUU	colourful
CFLNOORRU	cornflour
CFLOOOSTT	coltsfoot
CFLOOPSSU	scoopfuls
CFMNNOORU	unconform
CFOOORSTW	crowfoots
	crow's-foot
CFORSTUUU	fructuous
CGGIKNOST	gong-stick
CGHIILLNS	schilling
CGHIILNST	chitlings
CGHIILORR	choir-girl
CGHIIMOST	Gothicism
CGHIINSTT	stitching
CGHIINSTW	switching
CGHIINTTW	twitching
CGHIIOSTT	Gothicist
CGHIKKNOU	kink-cough
CGHILNOOS	schooling
CGHILNOOY	ichnology
CGHILNOSU	slouching
CGHILOOOR	horologic
CGHILOORY	chirology
CGHILORUY	grouchily
CGHINNOPU	pounching
CGHINORSU	chorusing
CGHINORTW	night-crow
CGHINOSSU	hocussing
CGHIOPRTY	copyright
CGHLLNOOT	longcloth
CGHLOOORY	chorology
CGHLOOPYY	phycology
CGHNOORST	torch-song
CGIIIKMMN	mimicking
CGIIILNNN	inclining
CGIIKLNPR	prickling
CGIIKLNRT	trickling
CGIIKMMRY	gimmickry
CGIIKMNSU	musicking
CGIILMNNY	mincingly
CGIILMNUU	glucinium
CGIILNPPR	crippling
CGIILOSST	logistics
CGIILRSTU	liturgics
CGIINNOOT	cognition
	incognito
CGIINNOUV	unvoicing
CGIINNRRU	incurring
CGIJNNORU	conjuring
CGIKLMNOY	mockingly
CGIKLNRTU	truckling
CGIKNOPRS	prick-song
CGIKNOSST	stockings
CGILLNORS	scrolling
CGILMNOOO	monologic
CGILMNOPY	complying
CGILMNPRU	crumpling
CGILMOORY	micrology
CGILMOOYZ	zymologic
CGILNNNUY	cunningly
CGILNNOOR	longicorn
CGILNNRUU	uncurling
CGILNOOOT	ontologic
CGILNOOOY	iconology
CGILNOORU	colouring
CGILNOPUV	loving-cup
CGILNORTU	courtling
CGILOOOPT	topologic
CGILOOOSY	sociology
CGIMMNNOO	commoning
CGIMMNNOU	communing
CGIMMNRSU	scrumming
CGIMMNSSU	scummings
CGIMNNOOS	gnomonics
CGIMNNOSU	consuming
CGINNOORS	consignor
CGINNOOTT	cotton-gin
CGINNORTU	trouncing
CGINORRSS	ring-cross
CGINORSSU	scourings
CGINORTUY	congruity
CGLMOOOSY	cosmology
CGLMOOSUY	muscology
CGLOOOPRY	coprology
CGMNOOOSY	cosmogony
CGNNOOTTU	guncotton
CGNOORSUU	congruous
CHHILOOST	soothlich
CHHIMRSTY	rhythmics
CHHIOPSUU	Ophiuchus
CHHKLLOOY	hollyhock
CHHLNORUU	lunch-hour
CHIIILPPP	△philippic
CHIIILRTT	trilithic
CHIIKKNST	thickskin
CHIIKLPST	thick-lips
CHIIKLSSY	sickishly
CHIIKLSTY	kitschily
CHIIKNNOV	chinovnik
CHIILLOPY	lyophilic
CHIILMORT	microlith
CHIILOOTZ	zoolithic
CHIILORTU	urolithic
CHIILORTY	rhyolitic
CHIILOSTW	wholistic
CHIILPTTY	typhlitic
CHIIMMNSU	Munichism
CHIIMMSTY	mythicism
CHIIMOSTT	Thomistic
CHIIMPSSY	physicism
CHIIMSTTY	mythicist
CHIINOSTU	chitinous
CHIINOSTY	onychitis

Words marked △ may be spelled also with a capital letter

CHIIOPSST	sophistic
CHIIORRSS	cirrhosis
CHIIORSST	trichosis
CHIIORSTY	hircosity
CHIIPSSTY	physicist
CHIIRSSTT	strictish
	tristichs
CHIKLMNPU	milk-punch
CHIKLMNRU	churnmilk
CHIKLMOST	locksmith
CHIKNOSTW	thick-sown
CHIKNOTTW	witchknot
CHIKOOPTT	pick-tooth
	toothpick
CHIKOPSTW	whipstock
CHILLNOOT	loincloth
CHILLOPPT	pitch-poll
CHILLORTY	torch-lily
CHILMNOUU	homunculi
CHILNOPSU	sulphonic
CHILOOPRT	coprolith
CHILOOPTY	holotypic
CHILOORSS	chlorosis
CHILOPRTU	Turcophil
CHILORSTU	trochilus
CHILORTUY	ulotrichy
CHILOSTTY	cystolith
	lithocyst
CHILPRSUU	sulphuric
CHILRRSUY	currishly
CHIMMNOOY	homonymic
CHIMNOOOT	homotonic
CHIMNOOPT	monopitch
CHIMNOORY	chironomy
CHIMNOOST	monostich
CHIMNOPSY	symphonic
CHIMNORSU	unchrisom
CHIMOOPRT	morphotic
CHIMOOPTY	homotypic
CHIMPSTYY	symphytic
CHIMRSTYY	chymistry
CHINOOPST	photonics
CHINOOPTY	hypotonic
CHINOORTZ	chorizont
CHINOPRRY	Pyrrhonic
CHINOPSTU	countship
CHINSSSYY	synchysis
CHIOOOPRZ	zoophoric
CHIOOPRTT	orthoptic
CHIOOPSSY	sciosophy
CHIOOPTYZ	zoophytic
CHIOORSTT	orthotics
CHIOPRSTU	courtship
CHIOPRSYY	hypocrisy
CHIOPSSSY	psychosis
CHIORRSSU	scirrhous
CHIOSSSTU	schistous
CHIPSSTTU	putschist
CHKMOPSUU	musk-pouch
CHKNOORST	stockhorn
CHKOPRSTU	truck-shop
CHLMOORTT	mortcloth
CHLNOOOPY	colophony
CHLNOTUUY	uncouthly
CHLOOPPSU	slop-pouch
CHLOOPTYY	hypocotyl
CHLOPPTYY	polyptych
CHMNOOORT	monotroch
CHMNOOPYY	cohyponym
CHMORRRUW	churr-worm
CHNNORSYY	synchrony
CHNOPPPRU	punch-prop
CHNOPSSTY	post-synch
CHNORSTUU	cothurnus
CHOOOPPTY	photocopy
CHOOOPRSY	horoscopy
CIIILLLTY	illicitly
CIIILMNOT	limonitic
CIIILMOPT	impolitic
CIIILOPST	pisolitic
CIIILORTV	vitriolic
CIIILOSSS	silicosis
CIIILOSSU	silicious
CIIIMMNOR	micro-mini
CIIIMRSTT	triticism
CIIIMSTTW	witticism
CIIINNRST	intrinsic
CIIIOSTVY	viciosity
CIIKNNOPT	nickpoint
CIIKNNOTY	cytokinin
CIIKOPPRT	rock-pipit
CIILLNOOP	cipollino
CIILLNOOS	collision
CIILLNOOT	cotillion
	octillion
CIILLNPUU	lupulinic
CIILLNUVY	uncivilly
CIILLOPTY	politicly
CIILMNOTY	mylonitic
CIILMPRSY	scrimpily
CIILNNOSU	inclusion
CIILNOOST	colonitis
CIILNOPTU	punctilio
	unpolitic
CIILOOPST	politicos
CIILOORST	solicitor
CIILOOSSS	scoliosis
CIILOPRSS	proclisis
CIILOSUVY	viciously
CIILSSTTY	stylistic
CIIMMSSTY	mysticism
CIIMNORSU	criminous
CIIMNORUZ	zirconium
CIIMORSTV	vorticism
CIIMRSSTU	rusticism
CIINNNOTU	inunction
CIINNORSU	incursion
CIINNOTUY	innocuity
CIINOOPRT	inotropic
CIINOPSSU	suspicion
CIINORSUU	incurious
CIINOSTVY	synovitic
CIINPSSTU	sinciputs
CIINRTUVY	incurvity

CIIOOPRST	isotropic
CIIOPRSTT	proctitis
	protistic
	tropistic
CIIORSTTU	touristic
CIIORSTTV	vorticist
CIIORSTUV	virtuosic
CIIORSTUY	curiosity
CIIORTTVY	vorticity
CIIOSSTVY	viscosity
CIIRSTTUY	rusticity
CIJKOSSST	joss-stick
CIJNNOTTU	T-junction
CIKKORSTW	stickwork
CIKLLNUUY	unluckily
CIKLNOSTT	lintstock
CIKLOSSTT	stocklist
CIKOPSSST	poss-stick
CILLLNOUY	cullionly
CILLMORUY	collyrium
CILLNOOSU	collusion
CILLOOORU	oil-colour
CILLOOOST	ocotillos
CILLOOOTY	coyotillo
CILLOPPUW	pillow-cup
CILLOQRUW	crow-quill
CILLORSSS	cross-sill
CILMNOOOS	Solomonic
CILMNOSTU	columnist
CILMOORSU	miscolour
CILMOTYYZ	zymolytic
CILNOORUU	unicolour
CILNOOSSY	oncolysis
CILOOPSUY	copiously
CILOORRTU	tricolour
CILOORSTU	colourist
CILOPPTYY	polytypic
CILOPRTYY	pyrolytic
CILOPRXYY	pyroxylic
CILORRSUY	cursorily
CILORSUUY	curiously
CILOSSTYY	cytolysis
CILRSTTUU	culturist
CILRSTUUU	utriculus
CIMMMNOSU	△communism
CIMMNNOOU	△communion
CIMMNOOOT	commotion
CIMMNOSTU	△communist
CIMMNOTUY	△community
CIMMOORTY	microtomy
CIMMOPPRU	micropump
CIMNNOOOT	monotonic
CIMNNOSYY	synonymic
CIMNNOTUU	continuum
CIMNOOOPP	nicompoop
CIMNOOPTY	monotypic
	toponymic
CIMNOOTXY	mycotoxin
CIMNSTUYY	syncytium
CIMOOTUYZ	zoocytium
CIMOPRSSU	promuscis
CIMOPSTTU	computist
CIMOPSTTY	symptotic
CINNOOPRU	pronuncio
CINNOOSTU	continuos
	contusion
CINNOOSUU	innocuous
CINOOOPRT	co-portion
CINOOORRS	corrosion
CINOOPRST	optronics
CINOOSSUY	synoicous
CINOOTTXY	cytotoxin
CINOPRRTU	incorrupt
CINORSUUU	uncurious
CINOSTUVY	viscounty
CIOOOPRSZ	zoosporic
CIOOOPRTZ	protozoic
CIOOPSSTU	posticous
CIOPPRRST	proscript
CIOPRRSTY	scriptory
CIORRRSUU	scurriour
CIORRSTUY	cursitory
CKKOORSTW	stockwork
CKLLNOORR	rock-'n'-roll
CKMOOORST	stockroom
CKNOORRWW	crownwork
CKNRSSTUU	sunstruck
CKOOORSTT	rootstock
CLLMOOPRT	comptroll
CLLOORRTU	court-roll
CLMOOOORT	locomotor
CLMOOOSTY	colostomy
CLMOORSTU	colostrum
CLMOPSUUU	opusculum
CLMOSSUUU	musculous
CLNOOPRSU	proconsul
CLNOORSTU	consultor
CLNOOSUUY	nocuously
CLNORTUUY	uncourtly
CLOOPRSUU	colour-sup
CLOPRRTUY	corruptly
CMNOOORST	cosmotron
CMNOPRTYY	cryptonym
CMOOORRTU	courtroom
CMOOORSST	motocross
CMOOORTTU	moot-court
CMOOSTTYY	cystotomy
CNNOOORST	contornos
CNNOOOSSU	consonous
CNOOOPRSS	cosponsor
CNOOPRSTW	crown-post
CNOORSSTW	crosstown
CNOPRRTUU	uncorrupt
CNOPRTUUY	up-country
COOOPPRSY	poroscopy
COOOPRSUY	ouroscopy
COOPRSSTY	sporocyst
COORRSTUU	sour-crout

D

DDDDEGIOS	disgodded
DDDEEHILL	ill-hedded
DDDEELNUU	undeluded
DDDEEMNRU	reddendum

DDDEENORS	reddendos
DDDEGINOR	doddering
DDDEHIILP	didelphid
DDDEIILVY	dividedly
DDDEIINUV	undivided
DDDILLOOP	doddipoll
DDDLLOOPY	doddypoll
DDEEEEHLR	red-heeled
DDEEEEHLY	heddle-eye
DDEEEFILS	seed-field
DDEEEFNRS	Defenders
DDEEEFNRU	underfeed
DDEEEGGLR	red-legged
DDEEEGIPR	pedigreed
DDEEEHNPR	deprehend
DDEEEIMMS	misdeemed
DDEEEINRX	Dexedrine®
DDEEEIRTU	deuteride
DDEEELOPV	developed
DDEEENNOP	open-ended
DDEEENNPT	dependent
DDEEENOPT	deep-toned
DDEEENPRT	pretended
DDEEEPRSS	depressed
DDEEERSWY	dyer's-weed
DDEEESTUU	desuetude
DDEEFGLNU	unfledged
DDEEFIIMY	demi-deify
DDEEFILNU	undefiled
DDEEFINNU	undefined
DDEEFINOP	dope-fiend
DDEEFIRTW	drift-weed
DDEEGGGLO	dog-legged
DDEEGGILT	gilt-edged
DDEEGHILT	delighted
DDEEGINNP	depending
DDEEGLNPU	unpledged
DDEEGOOPS	good-speed
DDEEHIINT	hiddenite
DDEEHINNR	hinder-end
DDEEHNOOY	needy-hood
DDEEHNORU	deer-hound
DDEEHNRRU	hundreder
DDEEIILMV	demi-devil
DDEEIILNS	sidelined
DDEEIIOSX	deoxidise
DDEEIIOXZ	deoxidize
DDEEIIPPT	dipeptide
DDEEIKLNN	enkindled
DDEEILLLY	ill-deedly
DDEEILLPS	dispelled
DDEEILLRS	seed-drill
DDEEILLRV	drivelled
DDEEIMMNO	demi-monde
DDEEIMNPU	unimpeded
DDEEINNUX	unindexed
DDEEINOPS	dispondee
DDEEINORW	eiderdown
DDEEINPSS	dispensed
DDEEINRSU	underside
	undesired
DDEEINRTT	tridented
DDEEIOORS	deodorise
DDEEIOORZ	deodorize
DDEEIRSSS	side-dress
DDEEKLOOR	red-looked
DDEELLOPR	red-polled
DDEELOTVY	devotedly
DDEELRSSU	udderless
DDEELRSWY	dyer's-weld
DDEENNORU	underdone
DDEENNOUW	unendowed
DDEENORRT	retrodden
DDEENORRU	underdoer
	unordered
DDEENORTU	outredden
DDEENORUY	round-eyed
DDEENPSSU	suspended
DDEENRSSU	undressed
DDEEORSTY	destroyed
DDEFFIINT	diffident
DDEFFMORU	dufferdom
DDEFGGIOT	God-gifted
DDEFGIIIN	dignified
DDEFGILLO	goldfield
DDEFGINOR	foddering
DDEFGINRU	drug-fiend
DDEFILOOT	floodtide
DDEFIRSTY	dry-fisted
DDEFLLOOW	Oddfellow
DDEFNNOUU	unfounded
DDEFNNRUU	underfund
DDEGGNRUU	ungrudged
DDEGHHIIR	high-dried
DDEGHINRS	shredding
DDEGIIIRW	rigwiddie
DDEGIIMSU	misguided
DDEGIINNR	niddering
DDEGIINSS	giddiness
DDEGIISSU	disguised
DDEGIJLLU	ill-judged
DDEGIKMNO	kingdomed
DDEGINNPU	puddening
DDEGINORR	derring-do
DDEGINPRU	redding-up
DDEGINRRU	undergird
DDEGIOOSZ	good-sized
DDEGISSTU	disgusted
DDEGLNNUU	delundung
DDEGLNOOR	goldenrod
DDEGLOOOP	poodle-dog
DDEGNOOOR	godrooned
DDEGNOVWY	down-gyved
DDEGOOORY	do-goodery
DDEHHNRTU	hundredth
DDEHIILPS	Didelphis
DDEHIIRSY	Yiddisher
DDEHILPSY	Didelphys
DDEHIORSW	drowsihed
DDEHIORXY	hydroxide
DDEHNORRU	hundredor
DDEIIKLNR	kiln-dried
DDEIIKNRT	diet-drink
DDEIILLST	distilled

DDEIILLSU	disillude
DDEIILRST	estrildid
DDEIINORS	iron-sided
DDEIINPRS	spin-dried
DDEIINSST	dissident
DDEIIOOXY	oxy-iodide
DDEIKLNNU	unkindled
DDEILLNRU	undrilled
DDEILMNOW	low-minded
DDEILNRRU	unriddler
DDEILNTUU	undiluted
DDEILORWW	worldwide
DDEILSTUV	dust-devil
DDEILSTUY	studiedly
DDEIMMOSU	desmodium
DDEIMNSSU	muddiness
DDEINOSSW	dowdiness
DDEINRSSU	dissunder
	ruddiness
DDEINSTUU	unstudied
DDEIOPPRU	proud-pied
DDEIOPRSV	disproved
DDEIORSTT	distorted
DDELMNOOO	noodledom
DDELMNOUU	unmoulded
DDELOORTT	odd-lotter
DDENNORTU	untrodden
DDENNORTW	downtrend
DDENNORUU	unrounded
DDENNORUW	undrowned
DDENNOSUU	unsounded
DDENNOUUW	unwounded
DDENOORUW	underwood
DDENOPSUU	pudendous
DDEOOPPSU	pseudopod
DDFIOORTW	driftwood
DDGGINOOO	do-gooding
DDGIILMNS	middlings
DDGIILNRS	riddlings
DDGIILNTW	twiddling
DDGIINORR	riding-rod
DDGILNNOY	noddingly
DDGIMOOOS	do-goodism
DDHIOOOWW	widowhood
DDHLMOOOU	hood-mould
DDIIKKNWY	kiddywink
DDIIOSUUV	dividuous
DDILLOPRR	drop-drill
DDIMPTUYY	iddy-umpty
DDINOPSUU	dupondius
DDNNOORUW	round-down
DDOOORWWW	row-dow-dow
DEEEEFHST	sheet-feed
DEEEEGNRW	greenweed
DEEEEGNRY	green-eyed
DEEEEJLWW	jewel-weed
DEEEEKNRW	weekender
DEEEFGIKN	knife-edge
DEEEFIIRR	re-edifier
DEEEFIKNR	reed-knife
DEEEFINPR	predefine
DEEEFINSV	defensive
DEEEFIRRR	free-rider
DEEEFIRRV	free-diver
DEEEFLLNU	needleful
DEEEFLRUX	deflexure
DEEEFMNOR	enfreedom
DEEEFMNRT	deferment
	fermented
DEEEFPRRR	preferred
DEEEFRRYZ	freeze-dry
DEEEGGLNO	one-legged
DEEEGIMNR	redeeming
DEEEGISWW	wedgewise
DEEEGKLNT	kentledge
DEEEGLNNU	needle-gun
DEEEGLNOY	golden-eye
DEEEGMNST	segmented
DEEEGNNRU	engendure
DEEEGNRTT	detergent
DEEEGRRTT	regretted
DEEEHILMS	seemlihed
DEEEHILPS	ephelides
DEEEHILSW	side-wheel
DEEEHILTT	△dithelete
DEEEHIMPR	ephemerid
DEEEHINPR	ephedrine
DEEEHINSS	heediness
DEEEHLMSY	seemlyhed
DEEEHLRST	sheltered
DEEEHMNRU	enrheumed
DEEEHMRSS	medresseh
DEEEHNOSY	honey-seed
DEEEHNPRR	reprehend
DEEEHNRRU	hereunder
DEEEHORSW	shoreweed
DEEEIILSS	dieselise
DEEEIILSZ	dieselize
DEEEILLMP	millepede
DEEEILLVW	weevilled
DEEEILNNT	needle-tin
DEEEILNRT	tree-lined
DEEEILPTV	depletive
DEEEILRRV	deliverer
	redeliver
DEEEILSSW	edelweiss
DEEEIMNRT	determine
DEEEIMNSU	Eumenides
DEEEIMSST	disesteem
DEEEINNNZ	endenizen
DEEEINNSS	neediness
DEEEINNTV	net-veined
DEEEINPTX	expedient
DEEEINRRS	reindeers
DEEEINRSS	reediness
DEEEINRST	tenderise
	teredines
DEEEINRTZ	tenderize
DEEEINSSS	seediness
DEEEINSSW	weediness
DEEEIPRTX	expediter
DEEEIRRVW	riverweed
DEEEIRSTV	detersive
DEEEKLLNN	kennelled

DEEEKNPRU underkeep
DEEELLPSW speedwell
DEEELLRVV vervelled
DEEELMNOW lemon-weed
DEEELNOPV enveloped
DEEELOPRV developer
redevelop
DEEELORRS rose-elder
DEEELPSSS speedless
DEEELRRTT red-letter
DEEELRSTW sweltered
DEEEMNNOV envenomed
DEEEMNRTT determent
DEEEMOPRT pedometer
DEEEMORST dose-meter
DEEEMORSU deer-mouse
mouse-deer
DEEEMPRST destemper
DEEENNQUU unqueened
DEEENNRTU unentered
DEEENNRUW unrenewed
DEEENNSSS denseness
DEEENORRS re-endorse
DEEENPPRU underpeep
DEEENPRRT △pretender
DEEENRRSV renversed
DEEENRRTT deterrent
DEEENRSUV undeserve
unsevered
DEEENSSVX vexedness
DEEEOORVW woodreeve
DEEEOPRRS pedereros
DEEEOPRTV predevote
DEEEORRRS reredorse
DEEEORRSS reredosse
DEEEORRST ore-rested
DEEEORSTV stevedore
DEEEORSUV désoeuvré
DEEEORSVX oversexed
over-sexed
DEEEPRRSS repressed
DEEEPRSST speedster
DEEEPRSSU supersede
DEEERRRSS redresser
DEEFFFSTU feedstuff
DEEFFILLT left-field
DEEFFINRT different
DEEFFNORU unoffered
DEEFFOPRR proffered
DEEFGIILN Englified
DEEFGIILR filigreed
DEEFGILNY feignedly
DEEFGINNR finger-end
DEEFGINNU unfeigned
DEEFGINRR deferring
DEEFGIRRU red-figure
DEEFGJORU forejudge
DEEFGLORV gold-fever
DEEFHLLUY heedfully
DEEFHLNSU unfleshed
DEEFHLNUU unheedful
DEEFHLOPS sheepfold
DEEFHLORT threefold
DEEFIIKLN fiend-like
DEEFIILMN minefield
DEEFIILNR infielder
DEEFIILQU liquefied
DEEFIILSZ life-sized
DEEFIINNS definiens
DEEFIINRS densifier
DEEFIIPRT petrified
DEEFIIPSS fissipede
DEEFIIRRT terrified
DEEFIIRSV versified
DEEFIISTT testified
DEEFILLOV fieldvole
DEEFILNOP open-field
DEEFILNOX deflexion
DEEFILNRY refinedly
DEEFILORT trefoiled
DEEFILPRS self-pride
DEEFILRSV self-drive
DEEFIMPST septemfid
DEEFINNPR pen-friend
DEEFINNRU unrefined
DEEFINRRU underfire
DEEFINRUV under-five
DEEFINSST fetidness
DEEFINSSX fixedness
DEEFIORRT torrefied
DEEFIPRRV perfervid
DEEFIPRTU putrefied
DEEFIPSTU stupefied
DEEFIRSTU surfeited
DEEFLLNNU funnelled
DEEFLLNUU unfuelled
DEEFLLNUY needfully
DEEFLLPSU full-speed
DEEFLNNUU unneedful
DEEFLNOSV sevenfold
DEEFLNRSU underself
DEEFLNRTU underfelt
DEEFNOOPS spoon-feed
DEEFNOPRS forespend
DEEFNORRU refounder
DEEFNRTTU unfretted
DEEFNRTUU unrefuted
DEEFOPRSS professed
DEEFORRST defroster
DEEGGIMOR demi-gorge
DEEGGIRSU ruggedise
DEEGGIRUZ ruggedize
DEEGGLOTW two-legged
DEEGGMNTU nutmegged
DEEGGOPRW egg-powder
DEEGHHIPS high-speed
DEEGHILNW wheedling
DEEGHINNU unheeding
DEEGHINUW unweighed
DEEGHOORS gooseherd
DEEGIILNS ingle-side
DEEGIILNU guideline
DEEGIILRT ridge-tile
DEEGIINTY tie-dyeing

DEEGIISTV digestive
DEEGIKLNT kintledge
DEEGILLOR liege-lord
DEEGILNNS single-end
DEEGILNRT ringleted
DEEGILNSS gelidness
DEEGILNST legendist
DEEGILOOU ideologue
DEEGILOPR ridge-pole
DEEGILRSY lysergide
DEEGILSSU guideless
DEEGIMNPT pigmented
DEEGIMNRY remedying
DEEGIMORT geometrid
DEEGINNRR rendering
DEEGINNRT tendering
DEEGINNTW net-winged
DEEGINORT redingote
DEEGINPRS predesign
DEEGINRRR derringer
DEEGINRRT deterring
DEEGINRSV deserving
DEEGINRTU negritude
négritude
DEEGINRTV divergent
DEEGINRUV gerundive
DEEGIOPRR ridge-rope
DEEGIOSST geodesist
DEEGIPRST predigest
DEEGJMNTU judgement
DEEGKLNNO dog-kennel
DEEGKLNOW knowledge
DEEGLLOOP lodgepole
DEEGLLORV grovelled
DEEGLMNOT lodgement
DEEGLNTTU englutted
DEEGLORTT dog-letter
DEEGNNNOU endungeon
DEEGNNORU dungeoner
DEEGNOORW greenwood
DEEGNORRU reguerdon
DEEGNORSS engrossed
DEEGNORWW weed-grown
DEEGNOUYY young-eyed
DEEGNSSUU unguessed
DEEHHILNW hind-wheel
DEEHHILOY hidey-hole
DEEHHIMRY hemihedry
DEEHHIORS horsehide
DEEHIINPT pethidine
DEEHIKRSW whiskered
DEEHILMOR helidrome
DEEHILNUY unheedily
DEEHILORU hierodule
DEEHILOTU hôtel-Dieu
DEEHILPRS eldership
DEEHILRSV shriveled
DEEHIMOST methodise
DEEHIMOTZ methodize
DEEHINOOP ideophone
DEEHINORT dinothere
DEEHINRRV hen-driver
DEEHINRSW swineherd
DEEHINRTY enhydrite
DEEHINTTW hen-witted
DEEHIOPRT herpetoid
DEEHIORSS shore-side
DEEHLLOSU houselled
DEEHLLOSV shovelled
DEEHLNOPR penholder
DEEHLOPRW pew-holder
DEEHLORST holstered
DEEHLPSST depthless
DEEHLRSSS shredless
DEEHMOORT hodometer
DEEHMORST smothered
DEEHMRTUY thrum-eyed
DEEHNNOPS sphendone
DEEHNOOQU queenhood
DEEHNOPTY endophyte
DEEHNORRT dethroner
DEEHNRRTU thunderer
DEEHNRSUU unushered
DEEHOOPRT heteropod
DEEHOORTX heterodox
DEEHOOSUV dove-house
DEEHRSTTU shuttered
DEEHSSTTU dustsheet
DEEIIINPR pieridine
DEEIIKNRS die-sinker
DEEIILLMP millipede
DEEIILNSS sidelines
DEEIIMNTT midinette
DEEIIMPQU demipique
DEEIIMPRS epidermis
DEEIIMSSV demissive
DEEIINNPP pinnipede
DEEIINNRT interdine
DEEIINPST desipient
DEEIINRTU inerudite
DEEIIOPST epidosite
DEEIIPSSW sideswipe
DEEIIRRSV riverside
DEEIIRRTV river-tide
DEEIIRTVV divertive
DEEIJNORR rejoinder
DEEIJNRTV jet-driven
DEEIJPRUZ prejudize
DEEIKLLNR knee-drill
DEEIKLLRS killdeers
DEEIKLNSW slinkweed
DEEIKLNSX sex-linked
DEEIKLOVY yoke-devil
DEEIKNORV overinked
DEEIKNORY kidney-ore
DEEILLLNT lintelled
DEEILLLNW well-lined
DEEILLLOW well-oiled
DEEILLMNO ill-omened
DEEILLMTW well-timed
DEEILLNRW indweller
DEEILLNST tinselled
DEEILLNSV snivelled
DEEILLNSW Willesden

DEEILLNTV divellent
DEEILLRRT tredrille
DEEILLRRV driveller
DEEILLRST stellerid
trellised
DEEILLRSV ill-versed
DEEILLRTU telluride
DEEILLRTW well-tried
DEEILLRVY deliverly
DEEILLSSW wieldless
DEEILLSVW swivelled
DEEILMMNS Mendelism
DEEILMNTV devilment
DEEILMOTV demi-volte
DEEILMPTU multipede
DEEILNNPU penduline
DEEILNNRU underline
DEEILNOPT depletion
DEEILNPTU plenitude
DEEILNRTU interlude
DEEILNSSX indexless
DEEILNTVY evidently
DEEILOPPS dispeople
DEEILOPRS despoiler
pelorised
DEEILOPRZ pelorized
DEEILPPRS slippered
DEEILPRSS prideless
DEEILRRSS riderless
DEEILRRTY retiredly
DEEILRSVY diversely
DEEILRTUY eruditely
DEEIMNNPT impendent
DEEIMNNRU undermine
DEEIMNORS demersion
modernise
DEEIMNORZ modernize
DEEIMNPTU unemptied
DEEIMNRTT detriment
DEEIMNRTU undertime
unmerited
DEEIMNSSX mixedness
DEEIMOORT meteoroid
DEEIMOPRR peridrome
DEEIMORST dosimeter
DEEIMORSX exodermis
DEEIMPRST distemper
DEEIMPRTT permitted
DEEIMRSST misdesert
DEEIMRTUU deuterium
DEEINNNPU unpennied
DEEINNOOY onion-eyed
DEEINNORT internode
DEEINNOTT detention
DEEINNPRU unripened
DEEINNQSU sequinned
DEEINNRTU indenture
DEEINNSSS snideness
DEEINNSUW unsinewed
DEEINOPPR drone-pipe
DEEINOPRT terpenoid
DEEINOPTX pentoxide
DEEINORST desertion
detersion
DEEINORSW rosin-weed
DEEINPRRU under-ripe
DEEINPRRV pen-driver
DEEINPRSS dispenser
DEEINPRST president
DEEINPRUX unexpired
DEEINPSST tepidness
DEEINRRSU surreined
DEEINRSST △dissenter
tiredness
DEEINRSSW weirdness
DEEINRSUV unrevised
DEEIOOPPR pereiopod
DEEIOOPTX exopodite
DEEIOPPRW △piepowder
DEEIOPRTX expeditor
DEEIOPRVW power-dive
DEEIORRRV overrider
DEEIORRVV overdrive
DEEIORSVZ oversized
DEEIORTTX tetroxide
DEEIOTTVX videotext
DEEIPRRSS disperser
DEEIPRSTU disrepute
DEEIQRTTU requitted
DEEIRSTTV test-drive
DEEIRSTUV divesture
servitude
DEEIRTTXY dexterity
DEEISTTTU destitute
DEEJNORUY journeyed
DEEJOORVY overjoyed
DEEKKOOYY okey-dokey
DEEKLLNNU unknelled
DEEKLNOSV veldskoen
DEEKNORUV unrevoked
DEELLMMOP pommelled
DEELLMMPU pummelled
DEELLMSSU musselled
DEELLNNTU tunnelled
DEELLNQUU unquelled
DEELLNRSU undersell
DEELLNRSY slenderly
DEELLNSSY endlessly
DEELLOPPR propelled
DEELLOPRT petrolled
DEELLORTW trowelled
DEELMOORV velodrome
DEELNNOOS Londonese
DEELNNPST splendent
DEELNNPTY pendently
DEELNOOST lodestone
DEELNOPPU unpeopled
DEELNPRRU plunderer
DEELNSTTU unsettled
DEELOOPRS rope-soled
DEELOPRSY reposedly
DEELOPRTY depletory
DEELORRSS orderless
DEELORSSW dowerless

DEELPRTUY reputedly
DEEMMOOSS desmosome
DEEMNNOTW endowment
DEEMNNOUY unmoneyed
DEEMNOOSS endosmose
DEEMNOPRS endosperm
DEEMNOPSU spodumene
DEEMNORTT tormented
DEEMNORUV unremoved
DEEMNOSTU endosteum
DEEMNPTTU untempted
DEEMOORST osteoderm
DEEMPRTTU trumpeted
DEEMRRSSU murderess
DEENNORTU undernote
undertone
DEENNOSST notedness
DEENNRSTU nurse-tend
DEENOOPRS endospore
DEENOPRRS responder
DEENOPRRV provender
DEENOPRSV overspend
DEENOPRUX expounder
DEENOPSUX unexposed
DEENPRSSU suspender
unpressed
DEENRRRSU surrender
DEENRRSTU unredrest
DEENRSSTU untressed
DEENRSTUV undervest
DEENRSTYY dysentery
DEENRTTUU unuttered
DEEOOPRRT torpedoer
DEEOOPRRV provedore
DEEOOPRST torpedoes
DEEOOSTWW sweetwood
DEEOPRRSS depressor
DEEOPRSSW prowessed
DEEOPRSUZ douzepers
DEEOPSSSS possessed
DEEORRSSV overdress
DEEORRSTU trousered
DEEORRSTX dextrorse
DEEORRSTY destroyer
DEEORSTUX dexterous
DEERRSSTU tressured
DEFFGINNO offending
DEFFIIORT fortified
DEFFIISUV diffusive
DEFFILLLU fulfilled
DEFFILNTU diffluent
DEFFILSUY diffusely
DEFFIMRSU dufferism
DEFFINOOT fin-footed
DEFFLNRUU unruffled
DEFFLORTU toruffled
DEFFNNSUU unsnuffed
DEFFNSTUU unstuffed
DEFGGIINT fidgeting
DEFGGILLN fledgling
DEFGGLRUU grudgeful
DEFGHILOT eightfold
DEFGIIILN lignified
DEFGIIINS signified
DEFGIILOR glorified
DEFGIINNR friending
DEFGIINWX fixed-wing
DEFGIIRSU disfigure
DEFGILNSU designful
DEFGINRUU unfigured
DEFGNNORU underfong
DEFGOOPRR drop-forge
DEFHHLOOS fleshhood
DEFHIILSV devil-fish
DEFHIIORR horrified
DEFHINRSU furnished
underfish
DEFHIORRS rodfisher
DEFHLOOOW wholefood
DEFIIINRT nitrified
DEFIIIRTV vitrified
DEFIIISSS sissified
DEFIIJSTU justified
DEFIILLLO oil-filled
DEFIILLMO mollified
DEFIILLNU nullified
DEFIILMSU semifluid
DEFIIMMMU mummified
DEFIIMNNY indemnify
DEFIIMORT mortified
DEFIIMRWY midwifery
DEFIIMSTY mystified
DEFIINRTY denitrify
DEFIINSST disinfest
DEFIIRSVY diversify
DEFIIRTVY devitrify
fervidity
DEFIKLORW fieldwork
DEFIKORTW twiforked
DEFILLNNO linen-fold
DEFILLRUY direfully
DEFILMNRU remindful
DEFILMSUY demulsify
DEFILNORT interfold
DEFILNOSW snowfield
DEFILNOUX defluxion
DEFILNSSU fluidness
DEFILNSTU disfluent
unstifled
DEFILORSX dorsiflex
DEFILRSST driftless
DEFIMNORT dentiform
DEFIMNORU uniformed
DEFIMORRT triformed
DEFIMORTW twiformed
DEFIMORTY deformity
DEFIMSTYY demystify
DEFIORSST disforest
DEFIORTTU fortitude
DEFIOSTTW two-fisted
DEFKOORTW two-forked
DEFKORTWY twyforked
DEFLLLOUY dolefully
DEFLLNOUW well-found

DEFLLORSW self-rowld
DEFLLRSSU full-dress
DEFLNOORU unfloored
DEFLNORUW underflow
wonderful
DEFLSSTUY self-study
DEFMORTWY twyformed
DEFNOORRU under-roof
DEFNOORTU underfoot
DEFNOOSST soft-nosed
DEFNORSSU foundress
DEFNORSUU unsued-for
DEFOOOSTV dove's-foot
DEFOOOTTW two-footed
DEGGGIMRU gum-digger
DEGGHOORT hot-dogger
DEGGIINNS designing
DEGGIINRV diverging
DEGGIMNOR niggerdom
DEGGINOSS dogginess
DEGGLMORU mudlogger
DEGGLNPUU unplugged
DEGHHINOT high-toned
DEGHHOTTU thoughted
DEGHIILNS shielding
DEGHIILPR hip-girdle
DEGHIILST sidelight
DEGHIINST night-side
DEGHIINTT night-tide
DEGHIIPSU guideship
DEGHIJPSU judgeship
DEGHIKORY hygrodeik
DEGHILMSU gumshield
DEGHILNTU undelight
unlighted
DEGHILPTU uplighted
DEGHILSTU light-dues
DEGHIMNRU humdinger
DEGHINRTU ungirthed
DEGHINSTU unsighted
DEGHIORTV overdight
DEGHMOORR herd-groom
DEGHMOORT godmother
DEGHNNRUU underhung
DEGHNORUW grewhound
DEGHNORUY greyhound
DEGHOORSS dogshores
DEGIIIMRS dirigisme
semi-rigid
DEGIIIRST digitiser
dirigiste
DEGIIIRTZ digitizer
DEGIIKNSZ king-sized
DEGIILLNV devilling
DEGIILNNR niderling
red-lining
DEGIILNRW wildering
DEGIIMNNP impending
DEGIIMRSU misguider
DEGIINNOS diosgenin
DEGIINNSS dinginess
DEGIINOSS gneissoid
DEGIINOST digestion
DEGIINRRS ringsider
DEGIINRSS rigidness
DEGIINRTU nigritude
DEGIINRTV diverting
DEGIINSTU distingué
DEGIIOORW rigwoodie
DEGIIRRSV verdigris
DEGIIRSSU disguiser
DEGIKLNOU ungodlike
DEGIKNNRU underking
DEGILLMNO modelling
DEGILLNOV long-lived
DEGILLNOW dowelling
well-doing
DEGILMNNU unmingled
DEGILMNOR goldminer
DEGILNNRU underling
DEGILNNTU indulgent
DEGILNNYY denyingly
DEGILNOOR gondolier
DEGILNORS soldering
DEGILNOSS godliness
DEGILNOST Odelsting
DEGILNOTU longitude
DEGILNPRS speldring
DEGILOOST goodliest
DEGILOOSW wild-goose
DEGILOOTV dog-violet
DEGILOSTT glottides
DEGIMNRRU demurring
DEGIMRSUU demiurgus
DEGINNORW wondering
DEGINNRRU under-ring
DEGINNRSU sundering
undersign
DEGINNRUW underwing
DEGINNSSY dyingness
DEGINOOSS goodiness
DEGINOPSS podginess
DEGINORUV devouring
DEGINPSSU pudginess
DEGIOORTW tiger-wood
DEGIOPRTY pterygoid
DEGIOPSTU guidepost
DEGLLOSSY godlessly
DEGLNOOST goldstone
DEGLNOOUZ Zeuglodon
DEGLNORSU groundsel
DEGLNOSSU unglossed
DEGMNOORU ungroomed
DEGNNORSU undersong
DEGNNORUW undergown
DEGNOORRW wrongdoer
DEGNOOSTT stegodont
DEGNOPRUW gunpowder
DEGORRSTU drug-store
DEHHIKMOS sheikhdom
DEHHINOSY hoydenish
DEHHIOPPS phosphide
DEHHLLNOU hellhound
DEHHLOOSU household

DEHHLORST threshold
DEHHNOORU horehound
DEHIIINST histidine
DEHIILMST △dithelism
DEHIILOOP iodophile
DEHIILPSV devilship
DEHIILRSS disrelish
DEHIIMNSU disinhume
DEHIIMNTY thymidine
DEHIIMOPP hippiedom
DEHIINNRU hirundine
DEHIINOOP idiophone
DEHIIOSTY hideosity
DEHIIPSTY △diphysite
DEHIIRSSV disshiver
DEHIISTWW widthwise
DEHIKLNOR inkholder
DEHILLLOR drill-hole
DEHILMNOU lime-hound
DEHILNOPT dolphinet
DEHILNPSU Delphinus
DEHILOORT rhodolite
DEHILOSTW dishtowel
DEHILOSUY hideously
DEHILRRUY hurriedly
DEHIMMOST Methodism
DEHIMNOSY hoydenism
DEHIMNSSU humidness
DEHIMORRT △thermidor
DEHIMOSTT △methodist
DEHINNOOR Rhineodon
DEHINNOPR endorphin
DEHINOORT rhodonite
DEHINOOSW swinehood
DEHINORRT trihedron
DEHINORST disthrone
DEHINORVW windhover
DEHINOSST dishonest
DEHINPPUW unwhipped
DEHINRRUU unhurried
DEHINRSUV unshrived
DEHIOOSST sideshoot
DEHIOOTWW howtowdie
whitewood
DEHIORSTY hysteroid
DEHIORSUY yird-house
DEHKLOOST stokehold
DEHKMOOOS smokehood
DEHKNOOOS hook-nosed
DEHLLOOSU doll-house
DEHLMNOPY endolymph
DEHLMNOUY lyme-hound
DEHLMOORU hordeolum
DEHLMOORW wormholed
DEHLNOSSW seldshown
DEHLORSYY hydrolyse
DEHLORTYY hydrolyte
DEHLORYYZ hydrolyze
DEHLOSSTU shouldest
DEHLPRSUU desulphur
DEHMMOPRU prud'homme
DEHMNOOPR endomorph
DEHMOORSY hydrosome
DEHMOORTY hodometry
DEHMORRWY rhyme-word
DEHNNNSUU unshunned
DEHNNOOPS △sphenodon
DEHNNOSUW newshound
DEHNOOPRS horsepond
DEHNORSTU undershot
DEHNORSUY enhydrous
DEHNPRTUU upthunder
DEHOOOPPT hooped-pot
DEHOOORSW woodhorse
DEHOOOSUW woodhouse
DEHOOPRTY orthopedy
DEHOOSSSU dosshouse
DEHOSTUUY house-duty
DEIIIKNTT identikit
Identi-Kit
DEIIILLMT illimited
DEIIILMSS dissimile
DEIIILQSU liquidise
DEIIILQUZ liquidize
DEIIILRSV virilised
DEIIILRVZ virilized
DEIIINNQU quinidine
DEIIINSSS disseisin
DEIIINSSZ disseizin
DEIIKKLNR kilderkin
DEIIKLNNX index-link
DEIIKNRSV skin-diver
DEIILLMPY impliedly
DEIILLMTY limitedly
DEIILLNOT tellinoid
DEIILLNST instilled
DEIILLOPR pilloried
DEIILLOPS ellipsoid
DEIILLRST distiller
DEIILMNTU unlimited
DEIILMOSS semisolid
DEIILMQUU deliquium
DEIILMRSU deliriums
DEIILNNUV unlived-in
DEIILNOPR iprindole
DEIILNOTU toluidine
DEIILNOXY xyloidine
DEIILNSSV lividness
DEIILOPRT reptiloid
DEIILORSU delirious
DEIILPPTU lippitude
DEIILPTTT tip-tilted
DEIILSUVV divulsive
DEIIMMRSU disimmure
DEIIMNNOS dimension
DEIIMNNST misintend
DEIIMNNTY indemnity
DEIIMNOSS demission
DEIIMNOSX endomixis
DEIIMNRSS mini-dress
DEIIMNRTW mid-winter
DEIIMNRUU uredinium
DEIIMNSST timidness
DEIIMORTV dormitive

DEIIMPRSS	misprised
DEIIMPRSU	presidium
DEIIMPRTU	Pteridium
DEIIMRTTY	tridymite
DEIINNNOT	indention
DEIINNOOP	opinioned
DEIINNORS	Deinornis
DEIINNORT	rendition
DEIINNOSU	unionised
DEIINNOTT	dentition
DEIINNOTV	vendition
DEIINNOUZ	unionized
DEIINNRTW	interwind
DEIINNSSW	windiness
DEIINNTUV	uninvited
DEIINOPRT	perdition
DEIINOPSS	indispose
DEIINORSS	Ironsides
DEIINORST	disorient
DEIINORSV	diversion
DEIINORTT	detrition
DEIINORTU	erudition
DEIINPRRS	spin-drier
DEIINPSTZ	pint-sized
DEIINRSST	dirtiness
DEIINSSTV	disinvest
DEIINSSVV	vividness
DEIINSSZZ	dizziness
DEIINSTUV	unvisited
DEIINTTTW	nitwitted
DEIIOPRSS	presidios
DEIIORSSS	disseisor
	siderosis
DEIIORSSZ	disseizor
DEIIOSSTU	seditious
DEIIOSTTY	tediosity
DEIIPRRST	priest-rid
DEIIPRSTT	dipterist
DEIIRSTVY	diversity
DEIIRSUVV	redivivus
DEIISTTUV	vedutisti
DEIJNNOTU	unjointed
DEIJNNRUU	uninjured
DEIKKLNOR	klondiker
DEIKKNOOP	pondokkie
DEIKLLNSU	unskilled
DEIKLLOSV	Volkslied
DEIKLNSTU	Kunstlied
DEIKLORSW	swordlike
DEIKMMNSU	unskimmed
DEIKMNNOW	womenkind
DEIKNNNSU	unskinned
DEIKNSSSU	duskiness
DEILLLPUV	pulvilled
DEILLMNOU	mullioned
DEILLMNUU	unillumed
DEILLNOSS	dolliness
DEILLNPSU	unspilled
DEILLNSTU	unstilled
DEILLNSUU	unsullied
DEILLOPST	pistolled
DEILLORSY	soldierly
DEILLPRTU	uptrilled
DEILLSTTY	stiltedly
DEILMMOTU	multimode
DEILMNOPT	implodent
DEILMNUXY	unmixedly
DEILMOOSU	melodious
DEILMOPSY	disemploy
DEILMTTUU	multitude
DEILNNOOS	Londonise
DEILNNOOZ	Londonize
DEILNOPSU	unspoiled
DEILNOPTU	unpiloted
DEILNOPTY	pointedly
DEILNORSU	undersoil
DEILNOSSS	solidness
DEILNOSSU	delusions
DEILNOTUV	involuted
DEILNRSSU	luridness
DEILNSTTY	stintedly
DEILOOPPT	toodle-pip
DEILOORTW	Lowrie-tod
	Tod-lowrie
DEILOPPTW	two-lipped
DEILORRWY	worriedly
DEILORVWW	world-view
DEILOSSTU	dissolute
DEILOSTUY	tediously
DEILOSUVY	deviously
DEILRSSTU	dislustre
DEIMMMRSU	midsummer
DEIMMNORS	△modernism
DEIMMNOUY	neodymium
DEIMMNRTU	untrimmed
DEIMMNSSU	dumminess
DEIMMOSTY	immodesty
DEIMNOOSS	moodiness
DEIMNOPRU	impounder
DEIMNOPSU	unimposed
DEIMNORST	△modernist
DEIMNORTY	modernity
DEIMNOTUV	unmotived
DEIMNPRTU	imprudent
DEIMNPSSU	dumpiness
DEIMNRSTU	rudiments
DEIMNRSTY	trendyism
DEIMNRSUY	synedrium
DEIMNSSTU	tumidness
DEIMOOORT	ideomotor
DEIMOPPUY	yuppiedom
DEIMOPRRS	primrosed
DEIMOPRSS	sporidesm
DEIMOPSST	despotism
DEIMOQRSU	squiredom
DEIMORSTY	dosimetry
DEIMORSUX	exordiums
DEINNNOSU	innuendos
DEINNOPTU	unpointed
DEINNORRV	non-driver
DEINNORSU	unrosined
DEINNORSY	synedrion
DEINNOSSW	downiness
DEINNOSTU	tendinous

DEINNPRTU	unprinted
DEINNRSUU	uninsured
DEINNRTTU	undertint
DEINNSTTU	unstinted
DEINOOPRT	portioned
DEINOORST	detorsion
DEINOORTT	detortion
DEINOOSSW	woodiness
DEINOOSTV	devotions
DEINOPPRR	properdin
DEINOPRST	drip-stone
DEINOPRSV	disproven
DEINOPRTV	provident
DEINOPRUV	unprovide
DEINORRUW	unworried
DEINORSSW	rowdiness
	wordiness
DEINORSTU	detrusion
DEINORSUU	uredinous
DEINORTWW	write-down
DEINOSSTT	dottiness
DEINOSTTU	duettinos
DEINPRRSY	spin-dryer
DEINPRSTU	unstriped
DEINPSTWW	windswept
DEINRRSTU	unstirred
DEINRSTTY	dentistry
DEINSSSTU	dustiness
DEINSTTUW	untwisted
DEIOOPRST	depositor
DEIOOPRSV	disproove
DEIOOPRTX	protoxide
DEIOOPSTW	woodspite
DEIOOPSUW	pousowdie
DEIOPRRST	postrider
DEIOPRSSU	disposure
DEIOPRSTU	dipterous
DEIOPRTTU	torpitude
DEIORSSTU	dioestrus
	outsiders
DEIORSSUU	residuous
DEIOTTTUW	outwitted
DEIPPTTTU	tittupped
DEIPRRSSU	surprised
DEIPRRSTU	disrupter
DEIPRSUVY	dispurvey
DEIPRTTUU	turpitude
DEIRSSSTU	dress-suit
DEJKMNORU	Junkerdom
DEKKLNORY	klondyker
DEKLNNRUY	drunkenly
DEKNOORTU	undertook
DEKNORRUW	underwork
DELLMOSWY	Lymeswold®
DELLNOPSW	spelldown
DELLNORSS	drollness
DELMNOOOV	moon-loved
DELMNOUVY	unmovedly
DELMNPRUU	unrumpled
DELMNPSUU	pendulums
DELMNUUZZ	unmuzzled
DELMOOORX	loxodrome
DELMOPUZZ	puzzledom
DELNNOOOS	solenodon
DELNNOPSU	nonplused
DELNOORWW	low-downer
DELNOPRSU	splendour
DELNOPRTU	underplot
DELNOPSUU	pendulous
DELNORRUY	unorderly
DELNOSSSU	soundless
DELNOSSUW	woundless
DELNPRTUY	prudently
DELOOOSUW	woodlouse
DELOORSSU	odourless
DELOORSUU	urodelous
DELORSSSW	swordless
DELORSTUY	desultory
DELOSTUUY	duteously
DELPRSUUY	usurpedly
DEMNNORUU	unmourned
DEMNNOTUU	unmounted
DEMNOPSUY	pseudonym
DEMNORSTU	undermost
DEMOOORTW	two-roomed
DEMOOOSUW	woodmouse
DEMOOPPRU	propodeum
DEMORRSUU	murderous
DEMPPRTUU	trumped-up
DENNORSSU	roundness
DENNORSUW	sundowner
DENNOSSSU	soundness
DENOOOPPR	propodeon
DENOOOPTW	woodentop
DENOOORST	doorstone
DENOOOSTW	woodstone
DENOOPPSU	unopposed
DENOOPRST	dropstone
DENOOPRSU	ponderous
DENOOPRTV	devonport
DENOORSTU	tournedos
DENOORSUW	wonderous
DENOORUVW	overwound
DENOPPPRU	unpropped
DENOPPRRU	underprop
DENOPPSTU	unstopped
DENOPRSSU	proudness
DENOPSTTU	unspotted
DENORTTUU	untutored
DENOSTUUU	unduteous
DENPRSUUU	unpursued
DENRRRSUY	surrendry
DENRSSTUU	untrussed
DENRSTTUY	studentry
DEOOORRTW	rood-tower
DEOOPRRUV	overproud
DEOPPRRSS	drop-press
DEORRSUUV	verdurous
DEORSTUVY	overstudy
DEPPTTTUU	put-putted
DEQRRSUUY	surquedry
DFFFOOSTU	foodstuff
DFFGINPUU	duffing-up
DFFHINSSU	snuff-dish

DFFIINOSU diffusion
DFGHIILRT frithgild
DFGIIIMNW midwifing
DFGIIINNY indignify
DFGIIIRTY frigidity
DFGIIMNOY modifying
DFGIINNUY undignify
DFGILNNOU foundling
unfolding
DFGILNNOY goldfinny
DFGOOOSST soft-goods
DFHHINOSU hound-fish
DFHILOORY hydrofoil
DFHINORSU round-fish
DFHIORSSW swordfish
DFHLNOOUW wolfhound
DFIILORTY floridity
DFIINPRST spindrift
DFIINSTWW wind-swift
DFIIOPRST disprofit
DFIKOOPRS skidproof
DFILLMNUY mindfully
DFILLTUUY dutifully
DFILMNNUU unmindful
DFILNTUUU undutiful
DFINOOPRW windproof
DFINORSTW snowdrift
DFIOORTUW fruitwood
DFLLMOOTU mould-loft
DFNOOOPTU foot-pound
DFOOOORTU out-of-door
DFOOPRSTU dustproof
DFOOSTTUY dusty-foot
DGGHILOSY doggishly
DGGHINOOT goodnight
DGGHNOORU groundhog
DGGIILLNY glidingly
DGGINNOOW down-going
DGGINNORU grounding
DGHHIINST hindsight
DGHHINOOT thinghood
DGHHINOPT diphthong
DGHHOORSU roughshod
DGHIINTTW windtight
DGHIKNOOS king's-hood
DGHILMOST goldsmith
DGHILNOPU upholding
DGHILOTUY doughtily
DGHIMOPSY sphygmoid
DGHINNOOT do-nothing
DGHINOOOO hoodooing
DGHINORSU shrouding
DGHINORTW downright
right-down
DGHLOORYY hydrology
DGHOOOSTT dog's-tooth
DGHOORSUU sourdough
DGIIIMNVW midwiving
DGIIINNOT indigotin
DGIIINNRT nitriding
DGIIINNTY indignity
DGIIJNORY joy-riding
DGIIKNSVY sky-diving
DGIILLNSY slidingly
DGIILLOOR gorilloid
DGIILNNPS spindling
DGIILNNSW swindling
DGIILNNWY windingly
DGIILNRST stridling
DGIILOORY iridology
DGIIMNORS Girondism
DGIINNNUW unwinding
DGIINNOWW windowing
DGIINOPRV providing
DGIINOPSS disposing
DGIINORST Girondist
DGIIRTTUY turgidity
DGIKLNOPS goldspink
DGIKNOPSW gowdspink
DGILLNORW worldling
DGILLNOUY ungodlily
DGILLOOWY good-willy
DGILLOPSY splodgily
DGILMNOOO △mongoloid
DGILNNORY droningly
DGILNNOSY goldsinny
DGILNNOWY down-lying
DGILNNUYY undyingly
DGILOOOSY dosiology
DGILOOTTY dittology
DGIMNRSUY Grundyism
DGINNOSSU soundings
DGINNOSWW downswing
DGINOORSW swing-door
DGINOPPRS droppings
DGINORSTU strouding
DGINORUVY ground-ivy
DGLNOOPTY Glyptodon
DGMNNSUUU mundungus
DGMOORRUW gourd-worm
DGNNORTUU groundnut
DGOORRSUU sour-gourd
DHHLOORST shorthold
DHHOOOTUY youthhood
DHIIILSTT lithistid
DHIIIMPRU rhipidium
DHIIINOPR rhipidion
DHIIIPSTY hispidity
DHIILLPRS drillship
DHIILNRWW whirlwind
DHIILOPSY syphiloid
DHIINOORT ornithoid
DHIINTWWY withywind
DHIIOOPRU ophiuroid
DHIKLSSUY duskishly
DHILLOSTY doltishly
DHILMOOYY mylohyoid
DHILMPSUY dumpishly
DHILNNOOS Londonish
DHILNORSY dronishly
DHILOOSTU lustihood
DHILPRSUY prudishly
DHIMNOSTY hymnodist
DHIMORSTW wordsmith

DHIMORSUU dishumour
DHINNOTUW whodunnit
DHINOOPRS rhodopsin
DHINOOPTY hypnotoid
DHINOORSU dishonour
DHINOPPSU shippound
DHINOPRUW whip-round
DHINORTWW windthrow
DHIOOSTTW withstood
DHKMNOOOS monkshood
DHKNORUYY hunky-dory
DHLLOOOWY Hollywood
DHLLOOPPY phyllopod
DHLLOOPSY dolly-shop
DHLMOOTUU loudmouth
DHLNOOOPT lophodont
DHLNOOSUW slow-hound
DHLOPRTUY hydropult
DHNOOORYZ hydrozoon
DHNOORTWW down-throw
throw-down
DHNOOSTUW Southdown
DHNORSTUU thundrous
DHOOORTXY orthodoxy
DHOOPPPUY puppyhood
DHOPRSTYY dystrophy
DIIIKMRST midi-skirt
DIIILMPTY limpidity
DIIILNPSY insipidly
DIIILQTUY liquidity
DIIINOSSU insidious
DIIINOSUV invidious
DIIKKNNRY rinky-dink
DIIKNNPSY skinny-dip
DIILLMNOO modillion
DIILNOSUV divulsion
DIILOPRTY triploidy
DIILOSTTY stolidity
DIIMNNOOS dominions
DIIMNOORT dormition
DIIMOORTY iridotomy
DIIMOPRSU sporidium
DIIMORSSY dimissory
DIIMPRTUU tripudium
DIINNOOQU quinonoid
DIINOPRSS disprison
DIINOPRXY pyridoxin
DIIOPRTTY torpidity
DIIORRTTY torridity
DIIPRTTUY putridity
DIIPSTTUY stupidity
DIJNOTUWW jut-window
DIKNOOSTW stinkwood
DILLNOSUY unsolidly
DILLOOPPY polyploid
DILLOOPTT dottipoll
DILMNNOOS Londonism
DILMNPUUU impundulu
DILMOOPPY polypidom
DILNOOOPZ diplozoon
DILNOPSUX spondulix
DILNOQTUW down-quilt
DILOOOPYZ polyzooid
DILOOPTUW tulipwood
DIMMOPSUY sympodium
DIMNOPRUU purdonium
DIMNORSTW windstorm
DIMOOOOSV voodooism
DIMOOOSSU isodomous
DIMOORRTY dormitory
DIMOORTUW moudiwort
DIMOORTWW mowdiwort
DINOOORSU inodorous
DINOPRRTU round-trip
DINOPTTUY point-duty
DINORTTUY rotundity
DIOOOOSTV voodooist
DIOOOPSSU isopodous
DIOOPRRTY proditory
DIOOPRSST prosodist
DIOPRRSTU disruptor
DKLNOOORU look-round
DKNOORSTW sword-knot
DLLNORUWY unworldly
DLMOOORXY loxodromy
DLNNOSUUY unsoundly
DLOOORSUY odorously
DMNOORRUW roundworm
DMOOPRRSU prodromus
DMORSSTTU dust-storm
DNNORRTUU turnround
DNOOORRTU ororotund
DNOOPSTUW downspout
DNOORTUWW woundwort
DOOORSTUY outdoorsy

E

EEEEELRTY eyeleteer
EEEEFHLRW freewheel
EEEEFHRST freesheet
EEEEFRRTV fever-tree
EEEEGGRRS greegrees
EEEEGHINT tee-heeing
EEEEGNRRV evergreen
EEEEHLMPT telepheme
EEEEHLRSW elsewhere
EEEELMRTT telemeter
EEEELNSSV elevenses
EEEELNTVV velveteen
EEEEMNNTV événement
EEEENNSTV seventeen
EEEENOPRY eye-opener
EEEENPRST presentee
EEEENRSTW sweetener
EEEEPRRSV persevere
EEEERSTVY yestereve
EEEFFINRT fifteener
EEEFFMTTU muffettee
EEEFGHINR Feringhee
EEEFGKNRU fenugreek
EEEFHIRTT tithe-free
EEEFHLORW fore-wheel
EEEFHNOPR freephone

EEEFHNRRS freshener
refreshen
EEEFHORRT therefore
EEEFHORRW wherefore
EEEFHORTT foreteeth
EEEFHRRRS refresher
EEEFILLTU feuilleté
EEEFILRRS serrefile
EEEFILRRV free-liver
EEEFILRVX reflexive
EEEFINRRT interfere
EEEFISSSW fesse-wise
EEEFLLNRU fullerene
EEEFLNSST fleetness
EEEFLORRV △free-lover
EEEFLRSTY freestyle
EEEFLRTTU fleurette
EEEFMNORW freewomen
EEEFNORST freestone
EEEFORTUZ freeze-out
EEEFPRRRR preferrer
EEEGGORTT georgette
EEEGHLRSS sheerlegs
EEEGHOPRS geosphere
EEEGIKNPS Pekingese
EEEGILLNR leger-line
EEEGILLSS liegeless
EEEGILMNR lime-green
EEEGILMNS gelsemine
EEEGINNOT eigentone
EEEGINNRV veneering
EEEGINPRR peregrine
EEEGINRVV revengive
EEEGIRSTY geyserite
tiger's-eye
EEEGISTTX exegetist
EEEGKLNRU Kerguelen
EEEGKLRSS Greekless
EEEGLLNTY genteelly
EEEGLMNNT gentlemen
EEEGLNNTU ungenteel
EEEGLRSTY steel-grey
EEEGMNNRU energumen
EEEGMNNTV vengement
EEEGMNRSS messenger
EEEGMORRT ergometer
EEEGNNRSS greenness
EEEGNORRV overgreen
EEEGNPRSU supergene
EEEGRTTUV vee-gutter
EEEHILLNS △hellenise
EEEHILLNZ △hellenize
EEEHILMTT Thelemite
EEEHILNNP nepheline
EEEHILNPT nephelite
EEEHILNRT three-line
EEEHILPRT three-pile
EEEHILRTU eleutheri
EEEHIMPRS ephemeris
EEEHIMPSU euphemise
EEEHIMPUZ euphemize
EEEHKLOSU house-leek
EEEHLMNTY methylene
EEEHLMSST themeless
EEEHLNOPT telephone
EEEHLNOSW nose-wheel
EEEHLNRST enshelter
EEEHLNSST netheless
EEEHLOPSU △peel-house
△pele-house
EEEHLRRST shelterer
EEEHMMNTY enthymeme
EEEHMNOPR ephemeron
EEEHMORRT rheometer
EEEHMORST threesome
EEEHMORSW somewhere
EEEHNNPST Nepenthes
EEEHNORSW whensoe'er
EEEHNRSST thereness
threeness
EEEHNRSSW whereness
EEEHNRVWY everywhen
EEEHNSSTW news-sheet
EEEHOPRSX exosphere
EEEHORSTU ethereous
tree-house
EEEHPRSST Herpestes
EEEHRSTTU usherette
EEEIIKLNV keelivine
EEEIIKRST kieserite
EEEIKLNQU queen-like
EEEIKLNVY keelyvine
EEEIKMRST kermesite
EEEIKNNPR innkeeper
EEEILLMRV vermeille
EEEILLPST pelletise
EEEILLPTZ pelletize
EEEILLSUV veilleuse
EEEILMNRV envermeil
EEEILMNTX exilement
EEEILMSST seemliest
EEEILNNRV enlivener
EEEILNPRS perseline
pre-senile
EEEILNSTX extensile
EEEILOSTT Teleostei
EEEILPTVX expletive
EEEILRSTV televiser
EEEILRSTX exsertile
EEEILSVWY swivel-eye
EEEIMMNNO △menominee
EEEIMMRSS mesmerise
EEEIMMRSZ mesmerize
EEEIMMSST misesteem
EEEIMNNRT nemertine
nine-metre
EEEIMNRTX extermine
EEEIMORRT eriometer
EEEIMORTT meteorite
EEEIMPRRT perimeter
EEEINNPRS persienne
EEEINNRTV intervene
EEEINORRT orienteer
EEEINORST neoterise

EEEINORTZ neoterize
EEEINPRRS reserpine
EEEINPRTY pyreneite
EEEINPSVX expensive
EEEINQSUZ queen-size
EEEINRRTW wernerite
EEEINRSST interesse
EEEINRSTT serinette
EEEINRSTV resentive
EEEINRSTX sixteener
EEEINRTTV retentive
EEEINSSTV seventies
EEEINSTVX extensive
EEEIPRRTT pierrette
preterite
EEEIPRSTX expertise
EEEIPRTXZ expertize
EEEIQTTTU etiquette
EEEIRRRTV retriever
EEEIRRTVV revertive
EEEIRSTTV serviette
EEEJKNRTU junketeer
EEEJLLRWY jewellery
EEEJRSTTT jet-setter
EEEKLLNSW knee-swell
EEEKLNSSS sleekness
EEEKMMORT mekometer
EEEKMORST smoketree
EEEKMRSTU musketeer
EEEKNOPST open-steek
EEEKNOSTY synoekete
EEEKOOPRZ zoo-keeper
EEELLNPRT repellent
EEELLNPTX expellent
EEELLPSSS sleepless
EEELMMNOP Melpomene
EEELMNOPT elopement
EEELMNSSS menseless
EEELMOPPR merpeople
EEELMRTTY telemetry
EEELMRTXY extremely
EEELNNPTY pentylene
EEELNOPTT leptotene
EEELNORVW wolverene
EEELNOSTT solenette
EEELNOTTV novelette
EEELNQSSU queenless
EEELNRRTY terrenely
EEELNRSSV nerveless
EEELNSSSS senseless
EEELNSSST tenseless
EEELOPRSV oversleep
EEELOPRTW △peel-tower
△pele-tower
EEELRRSVY reversely
EEEMMNOST mementoes
EEEMMOPRT emmetrope
EEEMNNRTU enurement
EEEMNOORT oenometer
EEEMNOPRT treponeme
EEEMNORRS sermoneer
EEEMNORRV nevermore
EEEMNORST merestone
EEEMNOXYZ exoenzyme
EEEMNRSTT entremets
EEEMNRSTY mesentery
EEEMNRTTV revetment
EEEMNRTUX unextreme
EEEMOPRTX extempore
EEEMORRSU reremouse
EEEMRSTTX extremest
EEENNORST sonneteer
EEENNSSST tenseness
EEENOPPRW pew-opener
EEENORSUV venereous
EEENPRRST presenter
represent
re-present
EEENPRRTV preventer
EEENPRSUV supervene
EEENPSSST steepness
EEENQRSSU queerness
EEENRRSTW △westerner
EEENRRSUV unreserve
EEENRSSST terseness
EEENSSSTW sweetness
EEEOPRRTV portreeve
EEEOPRSST poetresse
EEEORRSTV oversteer
EEEORRTVX over-exert
EEEPPPRTU puppeteer
EEEPRRRSV preserver
EEEPRRRTV perverter
EEEPRRSSV preserves
EEEPRSTTU superette
EEEQRRSTU requester
EEEQRSSTU sequester
EEERRTTUX retexture
EEFFFKLRU kerfuffle
EEFFFMNOT feoffment
EEFFGHOPT off-the-peg
EEFFGINOT teeing-off
EEFFGLNTU effulgent
EEFFHILLS shelf-life
EEFFHINTT fifteenth
EEFFHLRSU reshuffle
EEFFILSSU siffleuse
EEFFIMNRU muffineer
EEFFINOSV offensive
EEFFINRST stiffener
EEFFIORRT forfeiter
EEFFLOOTT fleet-foot
EEFFOPRRR profferer
EEFFORSTT off-street
setter-off
EEFGHIORW foreweigh
EEFGHIRRT freighter
EEFGILLNR refelling
EEFGILLNY feelingly
EEFGILNNU unfeeling
EEFGILRSS griefless
EEFGIMRUV vermifuge
EEFGINORR foreigner
EEFGINRRR referring

EEFGINRRT	ferreting
EEFGIORTV	forgetive
EEFGIPRRU	prefigure
EEFGLNRTU	refulgent
EEFGLRRTU	regretful
EEFGORRTT	forgetter
EEFHIIKLT	thief-like
EEFHIISST	fetishise
EEFHIISTZ	fetishize
EEFHIJLSW	jewelfish
EEFHIKLLS	shelflike
EEFHILLOW	whole-life
EEFHILLRS	shellfire
EEFHINPRY	hyperfine
EEFHINQSU	queen-fish
EEFHINSST	heftiness
EEFHIORSU	firehouse
EEFHIOSUW	housewife
EEFHISSTW	sweetfish
EEFHLLSSS	fleshless
EEFHLMNST	fleshment
EEFHLMOTU	mouthfeel
EEFHLORUW	four-wheel
EEFHMORRT	therefrom
EEFHMORRW	wherefrom
EEFHNORSW	foreshewn
EEFHNRSSS	freshness
EEFHOORRS	fore-horse
	foreshore
EEFHOORTT	three-foot
EEFHORRTU	three-four
EEFHRRRTU	furtherer
EEFIILLNP	fillipeen
EEFIILMTX	flexitime
EEFIILNRT	infertile
EEFIILQRU	liquefier
EEFIILRST	fertilise
EEFIILRTZ	fertilize
EEFIIMNTY	femineity
EEFIIMRRT	metrifier
EEFIINRSS	fieriness
EEFIIPRTW	tripe-wife
EEFIIRRRT	terrifier
EEFIIRRSV	versifier
EEFIIRSTT	testifier
EEFIKLMRV	milk-fever
EEFIKLNSS	knifeless
EEFIKLRTY	kite-flyer
EEFIKNRST	knife-rest
EEFIKNRSU	refusenik
EEFILLLOS	filoselle
EEFILLPTY	pelletify
EEFILLRTY	fertilely
EEFILLSTY	lifestyle
EEFILMPXY	exemplify
EEFILNORX	reflexion
EEFILNRUX	inflexure
EEFILNTUW	wulfenite
EEFILORTU	outrelief
EEFILSTVY	festively
EEFIMNRTT	refitment
EEFINNPVY	fivepenny
EEFINORST	firestone
	forestine
EEFINPRSU	superfine
EEFINRRST	renfierst
EEFINRSTU	interfuse
EEFIOPRRT	profiteer
EEFIOPRRW	fire-power
EEFIPPRRR	fripperer
EEFIPRSTU	stupefier
EEFIPRSUV	perfusive
EEFIRRRTT	fritterer
EEFIRRRTU	fruiterer
EEFIRRSTU	surfeiter
EEFIRRTTU	fruit-tree
EEFKLLTTU	kettleful
EEFKNOORT	foretoken
EEFLLNPSU	spleenful
EEFLLOPWW	pew-fellow
EEFLMORTW	flowmeter
EEFLNNNTU	funnel-net
EEFLNOSTU	nose-flute
EEFLNRSTU	resentful
EEFLNRTVY	fervently
EEFLOPRSU	reposeful
EEFLORRTX	retroflex
EEFLORSTV	leftovers
EEFLRSTTU	streetful
EEFMNOORW	forewomen
EEFMOPRRR	performer
EEFMPRRUY	perfumery
EEFNNOSST	oftenness
EEFNOPRST	forespent
EEFOPRRRV	perfervor
EEFOPRRTY	ferrotype
EEFPRSSUU	superfuse
EEGGIILNT	gelignite
EEGGIKLNR	Greekling
EEGGILMNR	gemel-ring
EEGGILNNT	negligent
EEGGILNSS	legginess
EEGGILOOS	geologise
EEGGILOOZ	geologize
EEGGINNPU	pug-engine
EEGGINNRV	revenging
EEGGINRRS	sniggerer
EEGGINRST	gee-string
EEGGINRTT	gettering
EEGGIORSU	egregious
EEGGOORRV	overgorge
EEGGRSSTU	suggester
EEGHHIITT	eightieth
EEGHHILLV	high-level
EEGHHIRTT	thegither
EEGHIKNTW	weeknight
EEGHILMNT	metheglin
EEGHILNNT	enlighten
EEGHILNRS	Englisher
EEGHIMOST	egotheism
	eightsome
EEGHINNSS	sneeshing
EEGHINPST	phengites
EEGHINRRR	herringer

EEGHINRTT	tightener
EEGHIORVW	overweigh
EEGHIOSTT	ghettoise
EEGHIOTTZ	ghettoize
EEGHIPPST	peep-sight
EEGHIRSST	sightseer
EEGHLLNOP	phellogen
EEGHLOORT	theologer
EEGHLOOTT	logothete
EEGHLOOTU	theologue
EEGHNNNYY	gynney-hen
EEGHNNORR	greenhorn
EEGHNOOPS	geophones
EEGHNOOPT	photogene
EEGHNORTU	toughener
EEGIILMNT	gmelinite
EEGIILNNO	oil-engine
EEGIILNRV	inveigler
	relieving
EEGIILNST	gentilise
EEGIILNTZ	gentilize
EEGIILOPS	epilogise
EEGIILOPZ	epilogize
EEGIILORS	religiose
EEGIILPRV	privilege
EEGIILRUX	religieux
EEGIINRSU	signeurie
EEGIINSTV	ingestive
EEGIISTTZ	△zeitgeist
EEGIJLLNW	jewelling
EEGIJLNRY	jeeringly
EEGIJNNNT	jenneting
EEGIKLNNU	ingleneuk
EEGILLLNV	levelling
EEGILLNPR	repelling
EEGILLNPX	expelling
EEGILLNRV	revelling
EEGILLNRY	leeringly
	reelingly
EEGILLNTV	Glenlivet®
EEGILLNVW	well-given
EEGILLSSU	guileless
EEGILMMSU	gelsemium
EEGILMNSY	seemingly
EEGILNNRT	relenting
EEGILNNUY	genuinely
EEGILNOOS	neologise
EEGILNOOZ	neologize
EEGILNORV	line-grove
EEGILNPWY	weepingly
EEGILNRST	steerling
EEGILNRTT	lettering
EEGILNRTW	weltering
EEGILNRVY	veeringly
EEGILNSSX	single-sex
EEGILNTVV	velveting
EEGILNTWY	weetingly
EEGILNTXY	exigently
EEGILOPSS	gospelise
EEGILOPSZ	gospelize
EEGILORST	sortilege
EEGILSTTW	Weltgeist
EEGIMNNSU	unseeming
EEGIMNPRT	tempering
EEGIMOORV	moviegoer
EEGINNNUU	ungenuine
EEGINNSSV	givenness
EEGINNTUW	unweeting
EEGINOOSS	oogenesis
EEGINORSS	egression
EEGINORSV	sovereign
EEGINOSSS	gneissose
EEGINOSXY	oxygenise
EEGINOTTU	tongue-tie
EEGINOXYZ	oxygenize
EEGINPPPR	peppering
EEGINPRSS	speerings
EEGINPSSW	sweepings
EEGINQSUZ	squeezing
EEGINRRST	restringe
EEGINRRSV	reversing
EEGINRSSY	synergise
EEGINRSTW	swingtree
	westering
EEGINRSTY	eye-string
EEGINRSYZ	synergize
EEGINRTTV	revetting
	vignetter
EEGIOPRSS	serpigoes
EEGIORSTV	vertigoes
EEGIRRSSU	régisseur
EEGISSTUW	guestwise
EEGLLLPRU	leg-puller
EEGLLMORU	glomerule
EEGLLOOTY	teleology
EEGLLOPRS	gospeller
EEGLLORRV	groveller
EEGLNORTT	lorgnette
EEGLNOTTU	tonguelet
EEGLNSSUY	glueyness
EEGLPPUZZ	puzzle-peg
EEGLPRSUU	superglue
EEGLRSSSU	surgeless
EEGMMNTTU	tegmentum
EEGMNNOTU	engoûment
EEGMNOORR	greenroom
EEGNOORST	oestrogen
EEGNOORSU	erogenous
EEGNOOSTY	osteogeny
EEGNOOSUX	exogenous
EEGNOPRRR	porrenger
EEGNORRSS	engrosser
EEGNORSSV	governess
EEGNORSTY	greystone
EEGNPSTUY	type-genus
EEGNRRSTU	resurgent
EEGOOPSST	goose-step
EEGOPRTUU	Portuguee
EEGOQRSTU	grotesque
EEGORRTTU	tregetour
EEHHINOPT	thiophene
EEHHINOSS	shoeshine
EEHHINOVY	hive-honey
EEHHINPSY	hyphenise

EEHHINPYZ hyphenize
EEHHIORTT thio-ether
EEHHIOSTW white-shoe
EEHHIRTTW therewith
EEHHIRTWW wherewith
EEHHKLRSU sheer-hulk
EEHHKOOPS sheep-hook
EEHHLLLOS shell-hole
EEHHNOPPS phosphene
EEHHOORSS horseshoe
EEHIIKLRS heli-skier
EEHIILRTT Hitlerite
EEHIINNTT ninetieth
EEHIIPSST epithesis
EEHIIRTTW witherite
EEHIKLLLS shell-like
EEHIKMNSV Menshevik
EEHIKNPSS sheepskin
EEHILLLMS shell-lime
EEHILLLMW mill-wheel
EEHILLMNS Hellenism
EEHILLNST Hellenist
EEHILMNOP Philomene
EEHILMOST lithesome
EEHILMOSW somewhile
EEHILMTUV helvetium
EEHILNNOS nineholes
EEHILNOOP oenophile
EEHILNOPX xenophile
EEHILNORS shoreline
EEHILNOSU house-line
EEHILNPRS replenish
EEHILNPSS spleenish
EEHILNRST inshelter
EEHILNSSS shineless
EEHILNSST litheness
EEHILOPRU Europhile
EEHILOPTY heliotype
EEHILORTV rivet-hole
EEHILPSVY peevishly
EEHILRSTW erstwhile
EEHIMMPSU euphemism
EEHIMNRRT herriment
EEHIMOPRT hemitrope
EEHIMPRRW whimperer
EEHIMRSST hermitess
EEHINNORT threonine
EEHINOPST phonetise
EEHINOPSU euphonise
pine-house
EEHINOPTT epitheton
EEHINOPTZ phonetize
EEHINOPUZ euphonize
EEHINOPVW viewphone
EEHINORST sheet-iron
EEHINORSV overshine
EEHINORTT thereinto
EEHINORTW whereinto
EEHINOSST hessonite
EEHINPQSU queenship
EEHINPRRT trephiner
EEHINPRSS phrenesis
EEHINSSTW whiteness
EEHINSTTU euthenist
EEHINSTTX sixteenth
EEHINTTTW twentieth
EEHIOPRTT tephroite
EEHIOQRTU theorique
EEHIORRST rhetorise
theoriser
EEHIORRTZ rhetorize
theorizer
EEHIORSST heterosis
EEHIORSTW otherwise
EEHIPPRRY periphery
EEHIPPSSY epiphyses
EEHIPRRSW whisperer
EEHIPRSUV superhive
EEHIRRSST heritress
EEHIRRTTY erythrite
EEHKLLNOY knee-holly
EEHKLOOST stokehole
EEHKLORWW wheelwork
EEHKMPSSU musk-sheep
EEHKNRTUY turkey-hen
EEHKORSTW worksheet
EEHLLLSSS shell-less
EEHLLMMRU hummeller
EEHLLORST hosteller
EEHLLORSV shoveller
EEHLLOSUW wellhouse
EEHLMOOSU mouse-hole
EEHLMOOSW wholesome
EEHLMORRU home-ruler
EEHLMORTY mother-lye
EEHLMORVW overwhelm
EEHLMOSZZ shemozzle
EEHLMPSSY emphlyses
EEHLMRSSY rhymeless
EEHLNOPTY polythene
telephony
EEHLNOSSW wholeness
EEHLNOSSY honeyless
EEHLNSTVY seventhly
EEHLOOPTT telephoto
EEHLORSSS horseless
shoreless
EEHLOSSST hostlesse
EEHLOSSSU houseless
EEHMMOORY homeomery
EEHMNOOPR pheromone
EEHMNOORW homeowner
EEHMNOOTT nomothete
EEHMNOPRT phonmeter
EEHMNORTY heteronym
EEHMNPTTU umpteenth
EEHMNRRTY herryment
EEHMOPSTY mesophyte
EEHMORRST smotherer
EEHMRRRTU murtherer
EEHMRRSTY rhymester
EEHMRRTUY eurytherm
EEHNNOOST hone-stone
EEHNOOPRS noosphere

EEHNOPPTY	phenotype
EEHNOPRRS	prehensor
EEHNOPRTU	thereupon
EEHNOPRUW	whereupon
EEHNOPSTU	penthouse
EEHNOPTTX	textphone
EEHNOPTTY	entophyte
EEHNORRST	shortener
EEHNORRTT	thorntree
EEHNORSST	otherness
EEHNORTTU	thereunto
EEHNORTUW	whereunto
EEHNOSTTW	whetstone
EEHNPPRSU	pen-pusher
EEHNSSSTY	syntheses
EEHOOPRRT	rheotrope
EEHOOPRSU	rope-house
EEHOORSSV	over-shoes
EEHOORSVW	howsoever
	whosoever
EEHOPRRSU	superhero
EEHOPRSTY	hey-presto
EEHOPRTXY	xerophyte
EEHOPSSTU	pesthouse
EEHORSSTU	rest-house
EEHPRTTXY	hypertext
EEIIKLRRV	riverlike
EEIIKNNTZ	zinkenite
EEIILLMRT	millerite
EEIILLMTW	willemite
EEIILLNTV	vitelline
EEIILNNRT	interline
EEIILNOTV	olivenite
EEIILNRST	resilient
EEIILNSTU	luteinise
EEIILNTUZ	luteinize
EEIILOPST	sepiolite
EEIILRSST	Listerise
	sterilise
EEIILRSSV	silverise
EEIILRSTZ	Listerize
	sterilize
EEIILRSVZ	silverize
EEIIMMPRT	prime-time
EEIIMMRST	eremitism
EEIIMNOST	Simeonite
EEIIMNPRS	mire-snipe
EEIIMNRSU	menuisier
EEIIMOPST	epitomise
EEIIMOPTZ	epitomize
EEIIMORSS	isomerise
EEIIMORSZ	isomerize
EEIIMRSSV	remissive
EEIINNNPT	penninite
EEIINNRTV	intervein
EEIINNSTT	intestine
EEIINNSTV	intensive
EEIINNTTV	intentive
EEIINNTVV	inventive
EEIINPRRS	reinspire
EEIINRRVV	viverrine
EEIINRSTT	enteritis
EEIINRSTW	winterise
EEIINRSVV	inversive
EEIINRTVW	interview
EEIINRTWZ	winterize
EEIINSSST	sensitise
EEIINSSTV	sensitive
EEIINSSTZ	sensitize
EEIINSSVW	viewiness
EEIIOPQSU	equipoise
EEIIOSSTV	sovietise
EEIIOSTVZ	sovietize
EEIIPRSSW	spirewise
EEIIPSUXZ	epizeuxis
EEIIQRSTU	requisite
EEIIQSTUX	exquisite
EEIIRSSTV	resistive
EEIJKKNRR	ink-jerker
EEIJKNNOT	knee-joint
EEIJKNRSS	jerkiness
EEIJMMNSS	jemminess
EEIJNSSTT	jettiness
EEIKKNRST	steenkirk
EEIKLMORT	kilometre
EEIKLNRSU	nurselike
EEIKLRTWY	tri-weekly
EEIKMNORT	konimeter
EEIKNPRSS	perkiness
EEIKNRRTT	trinketer
EEIKOORTZ	ozokerite
EEIKOPSSW	spokewise
EEILLMNOT	emollient
EEILLMNPT	impellent
EEILLMOPR	millepore
EEILLMSSS	smileless
EEILLNNPU	plenilune
EEILLNNTY	leniently
EEILLNRSV	sniveller
EEILLOPSW	powellise
EEILLOPTU	petiolule
EEILLOPTW	△powellite
EEILLOPWZ	powellize
EEILLRSTT	rillettes
EEILLRSTU	tellurise
EEILLRSUV	surveille
EEILLRSUY	leisurely
EEILLRSVY	servilely
EEILLRTTU	tellurite
EEILLRTUZ	tellurize
EEILLSSTT	titleless
EEILLSUVY	elusively
EEILLTTTU	tuillette
EEILMMNPT	implement
EEILMMNSY	immensely
EEILMMORS	sommelier
EEILMMORT	milometer
EEILMMPSU	semiplume
EEILMNNOT	eloinment
EEILMNNTY	eminently
EEILMNORT	Nilometer
EEILMNOSS	solemnise
EEILMNOST	△limestone
	milestone

EEILMNOSZ	solemnize
EEILMNPPR	pimpernel
EEILMNSTU	musteline
EEILMOPRY	pleiomery
EEILMOPST	septimole
EEILMORTT	tremolite
EEILMOSTT	mistletoe
EEILMOSVW	semivowel
EEILMPSSS	simplesse
EEILMRSTY	lysimeter
EEILNNPSS	penniless
EEILNNSTY	intensely
EEILNOORS	oleo-resin
EEILNOPPS	plenipoes
EEILNOPRT	interlope
	repletion
	terpineol
EEILNOPRV	polverine
EEILNOPTT	telepoint
EEILNORSV	noveliser
EEILNORVV	reinvolve
EEILNORVW	wolverine
EEILNORVZ	novelizer
EEILNOSSS	noiseless
EEILNOSSU	selenious
EEILNOSTT	tile-stone
EEILNOSTV	novelties
EEILNOTUV	veloutine
EEILNPRUV	pulverine
EEILNPSSS	spineless
EEILNPSTT	pestilent
EEILNPSVY	pensively
EEILNRSTU	unsterile
EEILNRSVY	inversely
EEILNSSSW	sinewless
EEILNTUVW	nut-weevil
EEILOPRST	epistoler
	pistoleer
EEILOPRTX	exploiter
EEILOPSST	politesse
EEILOPSSW	slopewise
EEILOPSTT	epistolet
EEILOPSVX	explosive
EEILORSTV	televisor
EEILORTTT	ottrelite
EEILOSTTT	toilet-set
EEILOTUVV	evolutive
EEILPPRTU	pulpiteer
EEILPRSSS	spireless
EEILPRSTU	serpulite
EEILPRSTY	peristyle
EEILPRSUV	prelusive
	pulverise
	repulsive
EEILPRTTU	tulip-tree
EEILPRUVZ	pulverize
EEILPSSTU	sleepsuit
EEILPSUVX	expulsive
EEILRRSSV	riverless
EEILRSTVY	restively
EEILRSUVV	revulsive
EEILSSSSU	issueless
EEILSTTTU	suttletie
EEIMMMRSS	mesmerism
EEIMMNRRT	merriment
EEIMMNRTT	remitment
EEIMMORRT	memoriter
EEIMMORST	meteorism
EEIMMOSST	sometimes
EEIMMPRST	mistemper
EEIMMRSST	mesmerist
EEIMMRSTU	summiteer
EEIMMRSTW	swimmeret
EEIMMRSTX	extremism
EEIMNNNOT	Mennonite
EEIMNNORW	mine-owner
EEIMNNOST	minestone
EEIMNNRTT	interment
EEIMNNRTU	inurement
EEIMNNSTT	sentiment
EEIMNOPTX	exemption
EEIMNORSS	sermonise
EEIMNORST	neoterism
EEIMNORSZ	sermonize
EEIMNOSTX	sixteenmo
EEIMNPQTU	equipment
EEIMNPRSS	primeness
EEIMNPSST	emptiness
EEIMNRRSS	merriness
EEIMNRRTU	intermure
EEIMNRTTT	remittent
EEIMNSSSS	messiness
EEIMNSTTV	vestiment
EEIMOORTZ	merozoite
EEIMOPRST	peristome
	temporise
EEIMOPRTZ	temporize
EEIMOQSTU	quietsome
EEIMORRTV	overtimer
EEIMORSST	esoterism
EEIMORSTT	meteorist
EEIMPPRRS	perisperm
EEIMPRRTT	permitter
	pretermit
EEIMPRRTY	perimetry
EEIMPRSTV	septemvir
EEIMPSSTU	impetuses
EEIMQSTUU	equisetum
EEIMRRSTT	trimester
EEIMRSSSU	△messieurs
EEIMRSSTY	mysteries
EEIMRSTTX	extremist
EEIMRTTXY	extremity
EEIMSSSTY	systemise
EEIMSSTTU	sutteeism
EEIMSSTYZ	systemize
EEINNNNPY	ninepenny
EEINNNRSU	nunneries
EEINNOPPS	Nipponese
EEINNOPRS	pensioner
EEINNOPRT	interpone
	tin-opener
EEINNOPST	penistone
	stone-pine

Words marked △ may be spelled also with a capital letter

EEINNORTT retention
EEINNORTZ interzone
EEINNOSST sonnetise
EEINNOSTV veinstone
EEINNOSTW wine-stone
EEINNOSTX extension
EEINNOSTZ sonnetize
EEINNPRST spinneret
EEINNPRTT pertinent
EEINNPRTY perennity
EEINNPSST ineptness
EEINNPSWY penny-wise
EEINNRSST inertness
EEINNRSSV Inverness
nerviness
EEINNSSSW newsiness
EEINOPPPR pepperoni
EEINOPPST peptonise
pipestone
EEINOPPTZ peptonize
EEINOPRRV overripen
EEINOPRSS personise
EEINOPRST interpose
EEINOPRSZ personize
EEINOPSTT potentise
EEINOPTTZ potentize
EEINOQRUV véronique
EEINORRSV reversion
versioner
EEINORRTU routineer
EEINORSTT neoterist
EEINORSTX exsertion
EEINOSSTV ostensive
EEINOSTTU Teutonise
EEINOTTUZ Teutonize
EEINPRRTT interpret
EEINPRSSW winepress
EEINPSSSW spewiness
EEINPSSTT pettiness
EEINQSSTU quietness
EEINQSTUY squint-eye
EEINQTTTU quintette
EEINRRRSU reinsurer
EEINRRSTT intersert
EEINRRTTW rewritten
EEINRSSSW sweirness
EEINRSSSY syneresis
EEINRSSTT interests
resistent
triteness
EEINRSSTW witnesser
EEINSSSTT testiness
EEINSTTXY extensity
EEIOOPRSV overpoise
EEIOPPSTV stovepipe
EEIOPRRVZ overprize
EEIOPRTTU pirouette
EEIOPSTTT pettitoes
EEIOQQUUV equivoque
EEIORRRST roisterer
terrorise
EEIORRRSV reservoir
EEIORRRTZ terrorize
EEIORRSTX exteriors
EEIORRTTV retortive
EEIORRTVW overwrite
EEIORRTVY ivory-tree
EEIORSSUV overissue
EEIORSTTT storiette
EEIORSTVX extorsive
EEIORTTVX extortive
EEIPPRRTY periptery
EEIPRRSTT preterist
EEIPRSSST priestess
EEIPRSSUV supervise
EEIPRSTTT pet-sitter
EEIPRTTWY typewrite
EEIQRSSSU esquiress
EEIRRSSTV reservist
EEIRRSSTW writeress
EEIRRTTTW twitterer
EEIRSSSTT tristesse
EEIRSTTTU restitute
EEIRSTTUV vestiture
EEIRSTTUX texturise
EEIRSTUVX extrusive
EEIRTTUXZ texturize
EEJMNNOTY enjoyment
EEJMPQUUU queue-jump
EEJNNNRWY Jenny-wren
EEJNOQSUU Junoesque
EEJNORRUY journeyer
EEJNOSSTW Jew's-stone
EEKKORSTY keystroke
EEKLMOOTU leukotome
EEKLMOSSS smokeless
EEKLNOOTV love-token
EEKLNORRS snorkeler
EEKLNPRSU spelunker
EEKLORSTW steelwork
EEKMNOPSS spokesmen
EEKMORRTY kryometer
EEKNORRTW networker
EEKNRRTTU tree-trunk
EELLLMSSS smell-less
EELLLNOSU Olenellus
EELLMNOOS lemon-sole
EELLMPSSU plumeless
EELLNNRTU tunneller
EELLNORRS norseller
EELLNPSTW well-spent
EELLOOPRT trollopee
EELLOPPRR propeller
EELLOPPRX prepollex
EELLORRTW troweller
EELLORSSV loverless
EELLORSVW overswell
EELLOSSVW vowelless
EELLPRSSU supersell
EELLPSSSU pulseless
EELLPSSSY syllepses
EELLPSTUW well-set-up
EELLSSSTY styleless
EELLSSSUY uselessly

EELMMNOTU	emolument
EELMMRSUW	Welsummer
EELMNNORT	enrolment
EELMNOOTY	teleonomy
EELMNOSSS	solemness
EELMNOSSY	moneyless
EELMNOTTX	extolment
EELMOOPST	leptosome
EELMOOSTY	toylesome
EELMOPPRY	pre-employ
EELMOPRTU	petroleum
EELMOPRTX	metroplex
EELMORTTV	voltmeter
EELMORTUV	volumeter
EELMORTXY	xylometer
EELMOSTVW	twelvemos
EELMPRSUY	supremely
EELNNNTTU	tunnel-net
EELNNOPRS	personnel
EELNNQUUY	unqueenly
EELNOOSSS	looseness
EELNOPPRY	propylene
EELNOPSTU	plenteous
EELNORSSW	ownerless
EELNORSTV	resolvent
EELNORTUV	volunteer
EELNOSSST	stoneless
EELNPPRUX	unperplex
EELNPRSTY	presently
EELOOPRSY	operosely
EELOPPRSS	prolepses
EELOPRRSY	leprosery
EELOPRRTU	pétroleur
	poulterer
EELOPRSSW	powerless
EELOPRSTY	polyester
	proselyte
EELOPRTXY	expletory
EELORRRUV	overruler
EELORRTUV	revel-rout
EELORSSST	ostleress
EELORSSTW	towerless
EELORSSUV	ourselves
EELPPSTTU	septuplet
EELPRSSXY	expressly
EELPRSTUU	sepulture
EELPSTTUX	sextuplet
EELRSSTTU	utterless
EEMMNNOSY	Mnemosyne
EEMMNOORT	metronome
	monometer
	monotreme
EEMMOORST	osmometer
EEMMORTYZ	zymometer
EEMMRSSTU	summerset
EEMNNOPRY	Rome-penny
EEMNNOPST	penstemon
EEMNOORTT	tonometer
EEMNOOSTT	tomentose
EEMNOPRYZ	proenzyme
EEMNORRTT	tormenter
EEMNORSTU	rousement
EEMNRSTTW	strewment
EEMOOOSTT	osteotome
EEMOOPRTT	optometer
	potometer
EEMOORSTU	meteorous
EEMOPPRRT	pre-emptor
EEMOPRRTY	pyrometer
EEMORRRVY	overmerry
EEMOSTTTU	teetotums
EEMPRRTTU	trumpeter
EEMPRSSTT	temptress
EEMPRSTTU	tree-stump
EENNNPRTY	penny-rent
EENNOOPRT	pontoneer
EENNOOSTU	neotenous
EENNOPRSS	proneness
EENNPRTUY	truepenny
EENNRSSST	sternness
EENOORRSU	erroneous
EENOORSTV	overtones
EENOPPRTT	prepotent
EENOPQSTU	queen-post
EENOPRRSS	responser
EENOPRSTV	overspent
EENOPSTTY	Stenotype®
EENORRSTW	nor'wester
	nor'-wester
EENORRTUY	tourneyer
EENORSSSW	worseness
EENORSSUY	Norueyses
EENORSTUU	souteneur
EENORTTTU	neutretto
EENOSSSTX	sextoness
EENPRRSTY	serpentry
EENPRRTUV	unpervert
EENPRSSSU	suspenser
EENRSSTTU	utterness
EEOOPRRVW	overpower
EEOORRTVW	overtower
EEOOSSSTX	exostoses
EEOOSSTTV	ovotestes
EEOPPPPRT	pepper-pot
EEOPPRSSU	superpose
EEOPRRRSS	repressor
EEOPRRRTY	repertory
EEOPRRSST	porteress
EEOPRRSSV	overpress
EEOPRRSTT	protester
EEOPRSSSS	espressos
	repossess
EEOPRSSTU	pesterous
	proteuses
EEOPRSTTU	route-step
EEOPRSTUX	exposture
EEOPSSTTU	poussette
EEORRRSTY	roysterer
EEORRRTTV	retrovert
EEORRSSTU	retroussé
EEORRSTTU	teru-teros
EEORRSTUV	overtures
EEORRSTVW	overstrew
	overwrest

EEORRTTVX	extrovert
EEORSSTTU	roussette
EEORSSTUW	sou'-wester
EEORSTTTU	setter-out
	tetterous
EEORSTTTY	storyette
EEORSTTTZ	terzettos
EEORSTTWW	sweet-wort
EEOSSSTTT	sestettos
EEPRRSSSU	pressures
EEPRRSTTU	sputterer
EERRSTTTU	stutterer
EFFFLORTU	effortful
EFFGGILNU	effulging
EFFGGINOR	goffering
EFFGINORS	offerings
EFFGINRSU	suffering
EFFGLOOSV	gloves-off
EFFGLORTU	forgetful
EFFGNRSSU	gruffness
EFFHIIKNS	fish-knife
EFFHIKSWW	skew-whiff
EFFHILRSY	fly-fisher
EFFHILRWY	whifflery
EFFHINSSU	huffiness
EFFHLLSSU	shelf-fuls
EFFIIMNSS	miffiness
EFFIIORRT	fortifier
EFFILLLRU	fulfiller
EFFILMUUV	effluvium
EFFILNOUX	effluxion
EFFILRSTU	strifeful
EFFINPSSU	puffiness
EFFINSSST	stiffness
EFFINSTUV	veinstuff
EFFIOOPRR	fireproof
EFFIORRTY	refortify
EFFIORTVY	△forty-five
EFFISSUUV	suffusive
EFFLLRTUY	fretfully
EFFLORRUU	furfurole
EFFLORSTY	forest-fly
EFFNOORRT	forefront
EFFOORRTY	offertory
EFFOPRTTU	off-putter
EFFORSTUV	overstuff
EFGGIINNR	fingering
EFGGILOOS	solfeggio
EFGGINOOR	foregoing
EFGGINOSS	fogginess
EFGHHIILR	△high-flier
EFGHHILRY	△high-flyer
EFGHIILNT	nightlife
EFGHIILOT	eightfoil
EFGHIILRT	firelight
EFGHIINRT	nightfire
EFGHILLNS	fleshling
EFGHILNSS	fleshings
EFGHILPRT	preflight
EFGHILTWY	flyweight
EFGHINORT	forenight
EFGHIOOSS	goose-fish
EFGHIOOTT	eightfoot
	eight-foot
EFGHIORST	foresight
	grief-shot
EFGHLLNTU	lengthful
EFGHLNRUU	hungerful
EFGIIINRS	signifier
EFGIILLNT	filleting
EFGIILNPR	pilfering
EFGIINNRR	inferring
EFGIINNSS	finessing
EFGIINPRT	fingertip
EFGIINRTT	refitting
EFGIINRVY	verifying
EFGIKLNOT	Folketing
EFGILNORW	flowering
	reflowing
EFGILOSTY	festilogy
EFGILRTUU	fulgurite
EFGIMNTUY	tumefying
EFGINNOST	softening
EFGINOOSS	goofiness
EFGINORST	fostering
EFGLLNORU	gronefull
EFGLLNTUY	fulgently
EFGLNOPUW	gowpenful
EFGLNORSW	self-wrong
EFGLOOSTY	festology
EFGLOOTUV	tug-of-love
EFGNOORTT	forgotten
EFGOOOST	goosefoot
EFHHILLSS	shellfish
EFHHKLOOS	flesh-hook
EFHIIKPSS	spikefish
EFHIIMSST	fetishism
EFHIINPSS	snipefish
EFHIINSSS	fishiness
EFHIINSSW	swine-fish
EFHIIRRTT	thriftier
EFHIISSTT	fetishist
EFHIJLLSY	jellyfish
EFHIKNORT	forethink
EFHILLORS	fill-horse
EFHILLSSY	selfishly
EFHILMNOS	lemonfish
EFHILNSSU	unselfish
EFHILNSTT	flesh-tint
EFHILORST	rifle-shot
	short-life
EFHILOSSU	fish-louse
EFHILSSST	shiftless
EFHINOOTT	fine-tooth
EFHINORRT	firethorn
EFHINOSST	stonefish
EFHINRRSU	furnisher
	refurnish
EFHIORRST	shotfirer
EFHLLLOTU	lothefull
EFHLLNORY	holly-fern
EFHLLNPUU	unhelpful
EFHLLNSUY	unfleshly
EFHLLOPUY	hopefully

EFHLLOSST soft-shell
EFHLLOSUV shovelful
EFHLLTTWY twelfthly
EFHLMOORS shelfroom
EFHLMORSW fleshworm
EFHLNNSSU nun's-flesh
EFHLNOPUU unhopeful
EFHLNSSSU flushness
EFHLOOPSU flophouse
EFHLORSST frothless
EFHLORSTW self-worth
EFHLORSUV overflush
EFHLORSUW showerful
EFHLOSSUU housefuls
EFHNOORSW foreshown
EFHNORTUX fox-hunter
EFHOOORST horse-foot
EFHOOORTT foretooth
EFHOORRSU four-horse
EFHOSTTUU theftuous
EFIIJRSTU justifier
EFIILLLST still-life
EFIILLMOR mollifier
EFIILLNRU nullifier
EFIILLRST fillister
EFIILMNSS filminess
EFIILMOTT leitmotif
EFIILNNOX inflexion
EFIILOPSV spoilfive
EFIILOSSS fossilise
EFIILOSSZ fossilize
EFIILPRTT filter-tip
EFIILRTTY fertility
EFIIMORRT mortifier
EFIIMRSTT first-time
EFIIMRSTY mystifier
EFIINNSST niftiness
EFIINNSTY intensify
EFIINOPRX prefixion
EFIINORRS fire-irons
EFIIORRTU fioriture
EFIISTTVY festivity
EFIJKORST forjeskit
EFIJLLMOR jelliform
EFIKLORST frostlike
EFIKMNNOO moon-knife
EFIKNNSSU funkiness
EFIKNORSS forkiness
EFIKORRST foreskirt
EFIKORRSW fireworks
EFILLMOPU filoplume
EFILLMRTU full-timer
EFILLNPTU plentiful
EFILLOOOS foliolose
EFILMNORT lentiform
EFILMNOSY solemnify
EFILMOPRV pelviform
EFILMOPRX plexiform
EFILMORSU formulise
EFILMORUZ formulize
EFILNNORT front-line
EFILNOORS solferino
EFILNOOSU felonious
EFILNORTW interflow
EFILNOSST loftiness
EFILOPSSU self-pious
EFILOSSTU fistulose
EFILPRSTU spriteful
EFILQRUUV quiverful
EFILRSSTU fruitless
EFILRTUVY furtively
EFIMMORRS reformism
EFIMMORRV vermiform
EFIMNNOPR penniform
EFIMNNRTU furniment
EFIMOPRST septiform
EFIMORRST fire-storm
reformist
restiform
EFIMORRSV versiform
EFINNNSSU funniness
EFINNORTU infortune
EFINNSSTU unfitness
EFINOOPRT forepoint
EFINOPRSU perfusion
EFINOPRSY personify
EFINOPRTY prenotify
EFINORRST frontiers
EFINORSTW frontwise
EFINORTUZ fortunize
EFINRRSSU furriness
EFINRRTUU furniture
EFINRSSTU turfiness
EFINSSSSU fussiness
EFINSSSTU fustiness
EFINSSSTW swiftness
EFINSSUZZ fuzziness
EFIOORSTX six-footer
EFIOORSUV oviferous
EFIORTTTU outfitter
EFIOSSTUV festivous
EFKLMNOOW womenfolk
EFKLMORUW fluke-worm
EFKNNOORW foreknown
EFLLMOSTU molestful
EFLLMOSUY fulsomely
EFLLMSUUY musefully
EFLLNTUUY tunefully
EFLLOOVWW vow-fellow
EFLLRSTUU resultful
EFLLRSTUY restfully
EFLLSTUYZ zestfully
EFLNNTUUU untuneful
EFLNOORVW overflown
EFLNOPRTU profluent
EFLNORSST frontless
EFLNORSUW sunflower
EFLNOSSUW wofulness
EFLNRSTUU unrestful
EFLOOOOST footloose
EFLOOPRSS proofless
EFLOOPRTW flowerpot
EFLOPRSUY profusely
EFLORRRTU terrorful

EFLORSSST	frostless
EFLPRSUUX	superflux
EFLRSSSTU	stressful
EFLRSSTTU	self-trust
EFNNOOSTT	font-stone
EFNNOPRUY	fourpenny
EFNNORTUU	unfortune
EFNOORSST	foster-son
EFOOOPRRV	overproof
EFOOPRRSS	professor
EFOOPSSTT	footsteps
EFOOQRRTU	Roquefort
EFOORRSUV	fervorous
EFOPRSSTU	supersoft
EGGGILMSU	misguggle
EGGGINOTT	go-getting
EGGGINQSU	squegging
EGGHIILNS	sleighing
EGGHIINNW	whingeing
EGGHIINRS	niggerish
EGGHIINTW	weighting
EGGHINORR	hog-ringer
EGGIILNNR	lingering
EGGIIMNRS	niggerism
EGGIINNSW	swingeing
EGGILLNRU	gruelling
EGGILNORV	groveling
EGGILOORS	goose-girl
EGGILOOST	geologist
EGGILOPRW	porwiggle
EGGIMNNOR	mongering
EGGIMNSSU	mugginess
EGGINNORV	governing
EGGINNPTU	tuning-peg
EGGINOORS	gorgonise
EGGINOORV	going-over
	overgoing
EGGINOORZ	gorgonize
EGGINOOSS	geognosis
EGGINOOSW	goose-wing
EGGINORSU	gingerous
EGGINOSSS	sogginess
EGGINRTTU	guttering
EGGIORRTU	outrigger
EGGLMMOOY	gemmology
EGGLNOORS	sloggorne
EGGLRRSTU	struggler
EGHHILOST	sight-hole
EGHHINRST	threshing
EGHHIORTU	eight-hour
EGHHMOTTU	methought
EGHHNORUW	rough-hewn
EGHHNOTTU	thoughten
EGHIIKNRS	shrieking
EGHIILLMT	limelight
EGHIILNNT	night-line
EGHIILNRT	girthline
EGHIILNST	gentilish
	sightline
EGHIILPPT	pipe-light
EGHIILTWY	weightily
EGHIIMNTT	night-time
EGHIINNTW	whitening
EGHIINPRS	perishing
EGHIINRSV	shivering
EGHIINRTW	withering
EGHIINSTY	hygienist
EGHIINTWW	whitewing
EGHIKLOST	ghostlike
EGHILLMOT	megilloth
EGHILLNTY	lengthily
EGHILLOOP	logophile
EGHILLOOY	heliology
EGHILLOSU	gill-house
EGHILLOTV	lovelight
EGHILLSST	lightless
EGHILMOST	lightsome
EGHILNNSU	un-English
EGHILNOPR	negrophil
EGHILNRSY	Englishry
EGHILNRTU	night-rule
EGHILNSST	lightness
	nightless
EGHILOORY	hierology
EGHILPRTU	uplighter
EGHILRSST	rightless
EGHILSSST	sightless
EGHIMNORT	△mothering
EGHIMNOST	something
EGHIMPPSU	pemphigus
EGHINNSST	thingness
EGHINORSU	rehousing
EGHINORSW	showering
EGHINORTV	overnight
EGHINOSTY	histogeny
EGHINRSST	rightness
EGHINRSTT	night-rest
EGHINRTUW	wuthering
EGHINSSTT	tightness
EGHIOPRSU	rogueship
EGHIOPRTT	tightrope
EGHIORSTU	righteous
EGHIORSTV	oversight
EGHIRSTTU	theurgist
EGHLLLOUY	gully-hole
EGHLMNOPU	ploughmen
EGHLMOOOU	homologue
EGHLNOOPY	nephology
	phenology
EGHLNOORS	longshore
	sloghorne
EGHLNOOSU	longhouse
EGHLNOOTY	ethnology
EGHLNOPYY	phylogeny
EGHLNORSU	slughorne
EGHLOOORR	horologer
EGHLOOOSS	goloshoes
EGHLOORTY	therology
EGHLOOTYY	hyetology
EGHLOSUUY	hugeously
EGHMNOORW	home-grown
EGHMNRTUU	mug-hunter
EGHMOOPSS	gomphoses
EGHNNOPYY	hypnogeny

EGHNOOOPR gonophore
EGHNOOPRY gynophore
EGHNOOPTY photogeny
EGHNOPTYY phytogeny
EGHNORSSU roughness
EGHNOSSTU oughtness
toughness
EGHOOPSUY hypogeous
EGHOPTYYZ zygophyte
EGIIINRTV Irvingite
EGIIKLNSV king's-evil
EGIIKNNRT tinkering
EGIIKRSTZ sitzkrieg
EGIILLMNP impelling
EGIILLNNO nielloing
EGIILLNOR gorilline
EGIILLNPR perilling
EGIILMNST gentilism
EGIILMORS mirligoes
EGIILMPRR pilgrimer
EGIILNNPP lippening
EGIILNNST tinseling
EGIILNNUV unveiling
EGIILNORT loitering
EGIILNOST gilsonite
EGIILNOSU uliginose
EGIILNPSS singspiel
EGIILNRSV silvering
EGIILNRVW liver-wing
EGIILNSUV ingluvies
EGIILNTTY gentility
EGIILOORS religioso
EGIILOPST epilogist
EGIILORSU religious
EGIILSTTZ glitziest
EGIIMNNPT impingent
EGIIMNNSS minginess
EGIIMNORS Origenism
EGIIMNPRS simpering
EGIIMNRSS griminess
EGIIMNRTT remitting
EGIIMOPST impetigos
EGIIMSTUV vestigium
EGIINNORS nigrosine
signorine
EGIINNOST ingestion
EGIINNOSU ingenious
EGIINNRRT interring
EGIINNRSW inswinger
EGIINNTUY ingenuity
EGIINOPTT tiptoeing
EGIINORST Origenist
EGIINORSY seigniory
EGIINPPQU equipping
EGIINPRSS speirings
EGIINQRRU requiring
EGIINQRUV quivering
EGIINRRTU intriguer
EGIINRSST sistering
EGIINRTTT tittering
EGIINRTTV rivetting
EGIINRTTY integrity
EGIJKNNTU junketing
EGIJLLNOY jolleying
EGIJLNSTY jestingly
EGIKLNNOO inglenook
EGIKNNTUY tuning-key
EGIKNOOSS goose-skin
EGILLLNTY tellingly
EGILLMNTY meltingly
EGILLMORU glomeruli
EGILLMOTU guillemot
EGILLNNOR enrolling
EGILLNORS Negrillos
EGILLNORW rowelling
EGILLNOTT ill-gotten
EGILLNOTW towelling
EGILLNOTX extolling
EGILLNPTY peltingly
EGILLNPUW upwelling
EGILLOSSY syllogise
EGILLOSYZ syllogize
EGILLSSTU guiltless
EGILMNOOS Mongolise
neologism
EGILMNOOZ Mongolize
EGILMOOSY semiology
EGILMOSUU eulogiums
EGILNNNTU tunneling
EGILNNOSS lessoning
EGILNNOST singleton
EGILNNRSU nurseling
EGILNOORY irenology
EGILNOOST neologist
EGILNOOSU Sinologue
EGILNOPRX exploring
EGILNORTV revolting
EGILNORVV revolving
EGILNORVY overlying
EGILNOSSX long-sixes
EGILNOTVY longevity
EGILNPRST springlet
EGILNRSTU resulting
EGILNRSTW wrestling
EGILNSSST stingless
EGILNSUVW swivel-gun
EGILOOPRS prologise
EGILOOPRZ prologize
EGILORSTY sortilegy
EGILORTUV voltigeur
EGILOSSTT glottises
EGIMMNNOU immunogen
EGIMMNORS monergism
EGIMMNRSU summering
EGIMMNSSU gumminess
EGIMNNORS sermoning
EGIMNNORT mentoring
EGIMNNORY ring-money
EGIMNNTUU minute-gun
EGIMNORSV misgovern
EGIMNORTW wit-monger
EGIMNOSTT misgotten
EGIMNOTUY timenoguy
EGIMNPRSU presuming

EGIMNRSSY	synergism
EGIMNRTTU	muttering
EGIMPRTUY	pterygium
EGINNNRUV	unnerving
EGINNNUVY	unenvying
EGINNOSTT	onsetting
EGINNOSUU	ingenuous
EGINNOTTW	towing-net
EGINNPRUY	penguinry
EGINNRSTT	stringent
EGINNRSTU	insurgent
	unresting
EGINNRTUV	venturing
EGINNTTUV	vingt-et-un
EGINOOPRT	protogine
EGINOOPSS	spongiose
EGINOOSSU	isogenous
EGINOPPPR	poppering
EGINOPPST	estopping
EGINOPRRR	porringer
EGINOPRRT	reporting
EGINOPRRV	reproving
EGINOPRST	progestin
EGINOPRTT	pottering
	pottinger
	repotting
EGINOPSSY	gossypine
EGINOPSUY	epigynous
EGINORRST	rostering
EGINORRTW	intergrow
EGINORSTT	gritstone
EGINORTTT	tottering
EGINOSSST	stegnosis
EGINOSSTU	goutiness
EGINPSTTU	upsetting
EGINPSTWW	sweptwing
EGINRSSTU	russeting
EGINRSSTY	synergist
EGINRSUVY	surveying
EGINSSSTU	gustiness
	gutsiness
EGIOORSUV	ovigerous
EGIPPRTTU	gruppetti
EGKORSSUW	guesswork
EGLLLOORR	log-roller
EGLLMNORY	mongrelly
EGLMNOOOU	monologue
EGLMOOORV	overgloom
EGLMOORTY	metrology
EGLMOOSUY	museology
EGLMOOTYY	etymology
EGLNNPTUY	pungently
EGLNOOOPY	poenology
EGLNOOPRR	prolonger
EGLNOORUY	neurology
EGLNOOSUV	longevous
EGLNORSTY	strongyle
EGLNOSTUU	glutenous
EGLNRTTUY	turgently
EGLOOOSTY	osteology
EGLOOPRTY	petrology
EGLOOPSTY	pestology
EGLOPSTYY	pygostyle
EGMNOOOSS	mongooses
EGMOORSTU	guest-room
EGMOPRSYZ	zygosperm
EGNNNRRUU	gunrunner
EGNNORSSW	wrongness
EGNNOSSUY	youngness
EGNOOOSUZ	zoogenous
EGNOOPRSS	prognoses
EGNOOPRSY	sporogeny
EGNOOPSSU	spongeous
EGNOORRVW	overgrown
EGNOORSUU	urogenous
EGNOOSUXY	oxygenous
EGNOOTTUU	outtongue
EGNORSSSS	grossness
EGNORSSTT	strongest
EGNORSTUY	youngster
EGNRRTTUU	turret-gun
EGOOPRSYZ	zygospore
EGOPPRTTU	gruppetto
EHHIIRTTT	thirtieth
EHHILLLSY	hellishly
EHHILMOOP	homophile
EHHILOPRS	philhorse
EHHIMNPSY	hyphenism
EHHIMRSTY	rhythmise
EHHIMRTYZ	rhythmize
EHHINOPPS	phosphine
EHHINORTW	nowhither
EHHIOPPST	phosphite
EHHIOPRSW	horsewhip
EHHIOSTVY	yeshivoth
EHHIPRSSU	ushership
EHHLOOOPT	holophote
EHHLOOPTY	holophyte
EHHLOPTYY	hylophyte
EHHLOSSUU	lush-house
EHHMNOOOP	homophone
EHHMORTTU	home-truth
EHHMRTUYY	△eurhythmy
EHHNOSTUU	house-hunt
EHHOOPSTY	theosophy
EHHORSTTU	thrust-hoe
EHIIJNORT	joint-heir
EHIIKLMTW	milk-white
EHIIKNSTT	kittenish
EHIILLNPT	tephillin
EHIILLNSS	hilliness
EHIILLOPT	helipilot
EHIILLRSW	ill-wisher
EHIILLTWY	lily-white
EHIILMRST	Hitlerism
EHIILNOPS	Sinophile
EHIILNTTW	lintwhite
EHIILOOPT	ophiolite
EHIILPRST	Philister
EHIILPSSY	syphilise
EHIILPSYZ	syphilize
EHIILRSTT	Hitlerist
EHIIMMPST	mephitism
EHIIMRSTT	tritheism

Words marked △ may be spelled also with a capital letter

EHIINNSSS shininess
EHIINNSSW whininess
EHIINOPST Tisiphone
EHIINORRT inheritor
EHIINPPRW whipper-in
EHIINPRST nephritis
phrenitis
EHIINPSST pithiness
EHIINRSSS Irishness
EHIINSTUV Vishnuite
EHIIPPRTU hippurite
EHIIPPSSY epiphysis
EHIIQRSUV quiverish
EHIIRSTTT tritheist
EHIJKMOST jokesmith
EHIKLLNPS shell-pink
EHIKLLPSY sylph-like
EHIKLMNPY nymphlike
EHIKLMOSU milk-house
EHIKLMPST klephtism
EHIKLNPRY hyperlink
EHIKLOOTT toothlike
EHIKLORSW shriek-owl
EHIKLORTZ kilohertz
EHIKLRTTU truthlike
EHIKMNOSY monkeyish
EHIKNOOPR pinhooker
EHIKNPRRS pre-shrink
EHIKNSSSU huskiness
EHIKORRSY Yorkshire
EHIKPRSSU spike-rush
EHILLMORS mill-horse
EHILLOPSU Lusophile
EHILLOSTY hostilely
EHILLOSWY yellowish
EHILMOOTT lithotome
EHILMOSSY hemolysis
EHILMOSZZ shimozzle
EHILMPPRY perilymph
EHILMPSSY emphlysis
EHILMRSST mirthless
EHILMRSTU Lutherism
EHILMRTTY trimethyl
EHILNNOOP phelonion
EHILNOOPT lithopone
phonolite
EHILNOOPY oenophily
EHILNOSTU shoutline
EHILNOSUY heinously
EHILOPRXY xerophily
EHILOPTYY heliotypy
EHILPRRSU rulership
EHILPSTTY pettishly
EHILRSSST shirtless
EHILRSTTU Lutherist
EHIMNNOOR monorhine
EHIMNNOOS moonshine
EHIMNOPRS premonish
EHIMNOPST phonetism
EHIMNOPSU euphonism
EHIMNOPUU euphonium
EHIMNORST horsemint
EHIMNRTUU ruthenium
EHIMNSSSU mushiness
EHIMNSTTU tunesmith
EHIMOOOSS homoeosis
EHIMOORST shire-moot
EHIMOOSTZ zootheism
EHIMOPPRR perimorph
EHIMORSTT short-time
EHIMPRRTU triumpher
EHIMRRSTY erythrism
EHINNOPSS phoniness
EHINNORSS horniness
EHINNOSTW whinstone
EHINNRSUV unshriven
EHINOOOPR ionophore
EHINOPRSS nephrosis
EHINOPRSW ownership
ship-owner
EHINOPSTT phonetist
EHINOPSTY hypnotise
EHINOPSVY envoyship
EHINOPTYZ hypnotize
EHINORRSU nourisher
EHINORSSS horsiness
EHINORTXY thyroxine
EHINOSSSW showiness
EHINOSTWW snow-white
EHINOTTUW withouten
EHINPRRTY pyrethrin
EHINPRSTU superthin
EHINPSSSU pushiness
EHINRSSSU rushiness
EHINSSSTY synthesis
EHINSTTWY twentyish
EHIOOPRTW wirephoto
EHIOPPRST tripe-shop
EHIOPRSST prothesis
sophister
EHIORRSTV overshirt
EHIORSTTU stouthrie
EHIPRSTTY prettyish
EHJOOSSSU joss-house
EHJOPRRSY jerry-shop
EHKLLORSW shellwork
EHKLLSSTU tusk-shell
EHKLOOOST tokoloshe
EHKLOTTYY thelytoky
EHKMRSSUW musk-shrew
EHKNORSTU trunk-hose
EHKOOOSTT theotokos
EHKOORRSW workhorse
EHKOORSUW housework
workhouse
EHLLMOPSY mesophyll
EHLLOOSTU tollhouse
EHLMMOPTU plume-moth
EHLMORSSU humorless
EHLMOSSTU mouthless
EHLNOOPPY polyphone
EHLNOOPXY xylophone
EHLNOORST sloethorn
EHLNOOSTY holystone

EHLNORRTY	northerly
EHLNORSST	thornless
EHLOOOSTU	toolhouse
EHLOOPSTU	spout-hole
EHLOOPSTV	hovel-post
EHLOOPSTY	photolyse
EHLOOSSTT	toothless
EHLOPRSTU	upholster
EHLOPSTYY	hypostyle
EHLORRTTT	throttler
EHLORSSTT	trothless
EHLORSSTW	worthless
EHLORSTUY	southerly
EHLPRSTUU	sulphuret
EHLRSSTTU	truthless
EHMMNOORY	monorhyme
EHMMOOPRS	mesomorph
EHMNNOOOY	honeymoon
EHMNOSTUU	mouse-hunt
EHMNPRYYY	hypernymy
EHMOOOPRS	sophomore
EHMOOORSU	houseroom
EHMOOOSTT	toothsome
EHMOOOSTU	moot-house
EHMOOPRRX	xeromorph
EHMOOPSTU	shoot-'em-up
EHMOOPTTY	mythopoet
EHMOORRTY	horometry
EHMOOSTUY	youthsome
EHMORRSTT	short-term
EHMPRRTUY	△pyrethrum
EHNNOORST	hornstone
EHNOOOPPR	phonopore
EHNOOOPPT	optophone
EHNOOORTT	orthotone
EHNOOPPRY	pyrophone
EHNOOPPTY	phonotype
EHNOOPSTT	on-the-spot
EHNOOPSTY	honeypots
EHNOOSSTT	stoneshot
EHNOOSTUW	townhouse
EHNOOTTTT	△hottentot
EHNOPRTTU	pot-hunter
EHNOPSSTY	△pythoness
EHNORSSST	shortness
EHNORSTTW	north-west
	west-north
EHNRSTTUU	unshutter
EHOOOPRSU	poorhouse
EHOOORSTU	root-house
EHOOORSTV	overshoot
EHOOPPTTY	phototype
EHOOPRRTV	hoverport
EHOOPRSST	posthorse
EHOOPRSTU	porthouse
EHOOPSSTU	posthouse
EHOORRTVW	overthrow
EHORRSTTW	throwster
EHOSSTTUW	south-west
EIIIKNNOP	epinikion
EIIILNNQU	inquiline
EIIILSTTU	utilities
EIIIMNSTT	intimiste
EIIIMPRTV	△primitive
EIIINNPST	insipient
EIIINPRST	ripienist
EIIINRSTT	retinitis
EIIINTTUV	intuitive
EIIJMSSTU	Jesuitism
EIIJNNORT	interjoin
EIIJQRTUY	jequirity
EIIKKNRST	steinkirk
EIIKLMNSS	milkiness
EIIKLNNRT	interlink
EIIKLNRSW	wrinklies
EIIKLNSSS	silkiness
EIIKNNPPR	nipperkin
EIIKNNPSS	pinkiness
EIIKNNRTT	interknit
EIIKNPSSS	spikiness
EIIKNRSSS	riskiness
EIILLLMMO	millimole
EIILLMNRU	illuminer
EIILLMNRY	millinery
EIILLMOST	mollities
EIILLMSST	limitless
EIILLNNOP	penillion
EIILLNOPT	pointillé
EIILLNSSS	silliness
EIILLOPRS	pillorise
EIILLOPRZ	pillorize
EIILMMORS	meliorism
EIILMNOPS	moniplies
EIILMNOPT	impletion
EIILMNOPX	implexion
EIILMNORV	vermilion
EIILMNOSU	limousine
EIILMNPPS	mislippen
EIILMNPRU	primuline
EIILMNSSS	sliminess
EIILMOPPS	epipolism
EIILMOPSV	implosive
EIILMORST	meliorist
EIILMORTY	meliority
EIILMOTTV	leitmotiv
EIILMPRSU	puerilism
EIILMPSST	simpliste
EIILMPSUV	impulsive
EIILMRSST	Listerism
EIILMRSSV	servilism
EIILMRSSY	missilery
EIILNNOQU	quinoline
EIILNOSSS	soiliness
EIILNOTTV	volitient
EIILNPSST	splenitis
EIILNPSTY	pensility
EIILNPTUV	vulpinite
EIILNQTUY	inquietly
EIILNRTUY	neurility
EIILNSTTY	tensility
EIILNSTVY	sylvinite
EIILNTUVY	unitively
EIILOPQTU	politique
EIILOPSST	spilosite

EIILOQSSU	siliquose
EIILORSTV	Vitreosil®
EIILORTTV	Vitrolite®
EIILPRSTU	pleuritis
	spirituel
EIILPRTUY	puerility
EIILRSTTY	sterility
EIILRSTTZ	strelitzi
EIILRSTVY	servility
EIIMMMORS	memoirism
EIIMMNORS	immersion
EIIMMNOSS	misoneism
EIIMMNRST	terminism
EIIMMNSTY	immensity
EIIMMORSS	isomerism
EIIMMORST	memoirist
EIIMMOSTV	emotivism
EIIMMPSSS	pessimism
EIIMMRTUX	immixture
EIIMNNORR	iron-miner
EIIMNOPST	impsonite
	pimientos
EIIMNORSS	missioner
	remission
EIIMNOSST	misoneist
EIIMNOSTU	minutiose
EIIMNOSUV	vimineous
EIIMNOTZZ	mizzonite
EIIMNPRST	Petrinism
EIIMNPRSU	supermini
EIIMNRSTT	terminist
EIIMNSSST	mistiness
EIIMOPRSU	imperious
EIIMOPRSV	improvise
EIIMOPSTT	epitomist
EIIMOSSTV	sovietism
EIIMPSSST	pessimist
EIINNNOST	intension
EIINNNOTT	intention
EIINNNOTV	invention
EIINNORST	insertion
EIINNORSV	inversion
EIINNOSSS	noisiness
EIINNPPSS	nippiness
EIINNPSSS	spininess
EIINNRSTT	internist
EIINNSSTT	insistent
	tintiness
EIINNSTTY	intensity
EIINOPRSV	prevision
EIINOPTVW	viewpoint
EIINORSSS	resinosis
EIINORSTU	routinise
EIINORSTY	seniority
EIINORTUZ	routinize
EIINPPRST	pin-stripe
EIINPSSST	tipsiness
EIINQTTTU	quintetti
EIINRSTUV	intrusive
EIINRTTUV	nutritive
	vetturini
EIINSSSYZ	synizesis
EIINSSTTW	wittiness
EIINSTTTU	institute
EIIORRTUV	voiturier
EIIORSSTT	sottisier
EIIPRRTUV	irruptive
EIIQRRSTU	quirister
EIIRSSSTV	visitress
EIJJKNOTU	juke-joint
EIJKLLOOU	kilojoule
EIJKMNRSU	Junkerism
EIJKMPRSU	ski-jumper
EIJKNNSSU	junkiness
EIJLLMNOT	jolliment
EIJLLNOSS	jolliness
EIJLMNPTU	mint-julep
EIJLNOSST	jointless
EIJMNPSSU	jumpiness
EIJNNOSST	jointness
EIJNORRSU	surrejoin
EIJNORSST	jointress
EIJNPRSUU	Juniperus
EIKLLLSSS	skill-less
EIKLMNOSS	moleskins
EIKLMORSY	irksomely
EIKLNNRTU	trunk-line
EIKLNNRUW	unwrinkle
EIKLNPRRS	sprinkler
EIKLNSSSU	sulkiness
EIKLRSSST	skirtless
EIKMMNOSY	monkeyism
EIKMNNORT	Komintern
EIKMNNOST	Minkstone
EIKMNOORS	mono-skier
EIKMNORSY	risk-money
EIKMNOSSS	smokiness
EIKMNRSSU	murkiness
EIKMNSSSU	muskiness
EIKNNOPRT	△pinkerton
EIKNNPSSU	punkiness
EIKNOORST	sooterkin
EIKNORRTW	interwork
EIKNORSTV	overstink
EIKNRRTTY	trinketry
EIKORRSTV	overskirt
EIKORRSTW	workerist
EIKORSTTU	outstrike
	strikeout
EILLMNORW	mill-owner
EILLMNOST	millstone
EILLMNSSU	sensillum
EILLMOPSW	Powellism
EILLMOSSY	lissomely
EILLMPTTU	multiplet
EILLMPTUX	multiplex
EILLMRTUU	tellurium
EILLNOPRU	nullipore
EILLNORRT	ritornell
EILLNORST	stornelli
EILLNORTU	tellurion
EILLNOSSW	lowliness
EILLNOSTY	stone-lily
EILLNOTVY	violently

EILLNPUUV pulvinule
EILLNSSST stillness
EILLNSSSY sinlessly
EILLOPRST postiller
EILLOPRSV overspill
spillover
EILLOPRTY pellitory
EILLOPRWW willpower
EILLOPSST pilotless
EILLOPTUV pollutive
EILLOSTTY stylolite
EILLPSSSY syllepsis
EILLSSTWY witlessly
EILMMMOSS Moslemism
EILMMNNUU nummuline
EILMMNTUU nummulite
EILMMOPSY misemploy
EILMNOOSY noisomely
EILMNOPST simpleton
EILMNOPSY monyplies
EILMNORST line-storm
EILMNORTT tormentil
EILMNOSTY solemnity
EILMNOSWY winsomely
EILMNPSSU lumpiness
EILMOOSTY ileostomy
EILMOSTUY timeously
EILMRSTUU multiuser
EILNNOOQU quinolone
EILNNOOSS looniness
EILNNOSTV insolvent
EILNNPSTU unslept-in
EILNOOPSX explosion
EILNOOTUV evolution
EILNOPRRU purloiner
EILNOPRSU repulsion
EILNOPSST pointless
EILNOPSSU spinulose
EILNOPSTV pontlevis
EILNOPSUX expulsion
EILNORSSY sensorily
EILNORSTY storyline
EILNORSUV revulsion
EILNORTUY routinely
EILNOSSSU lousiness
EILNOSSTT siltstone
EILNOSUVY enviously
EILNPPSSU pulpiness
EILNPQTUU quintuple
EILNPRSST printless
EILNPRSTY splintery
EILNQTUUY unquietly
EILNRSSSU surliness
EILNRSTTU turnstile
EILNRTUUV vulturine
EILNSSSTT stintless
EILNSSSTU lustiness
EILOPPRSS prolepsis
EILOPPRTY propylite
EILOPRSTY leprosity
EILOPSTUY piteously
EILORRTVW liverwort
EILORSSUY seriously
EILOSSTTT stilettos
EILQRRSUY squirrely
EIMMNNOST mnemonist
EIMMNNSTU muniments
EIMMNOORS Monroeism
EIMMNOORT Mormonite
EIMMNOPRS persimmon
EIMMNRSSU rumminess
EIMMOOPRU pomoerium
prooemium
EIMMOORST timorsome
EIMMOPRSU emporiums
EIMMOPSTU impostume
EIMNNOOTZ monzonite
EIMNNOPRT prominent
EIMNNORST innermost
EIMNNPTUU neptunium
EIMNNRTTU nutriment
EIMNNSTTU unsmitten
EIMNOOOPR prooemion
EIMNOOPRS Peronismo
EIMNOOPRT premotion
EIMNOORSS roominess
EIMNOORST Monroeist
trominoes
EIMNOPRSU simon-pure
EIMNOPRTU entropium
importune
EIMNOQRUY querimony
EIMNORRTW worriment
EIMNORSST monitress
EIMNORSSU sensorium
EIMNORSUV verminous
EIMNORTTU tentorium
EIMNOSSSS mossiness
EIMNOSSST moistness
EIMNOSTTU Teutonism
EIMNOSTTY testimony
EIMNOSTUU untimeous
EIMNOTTZZ mezzotint
EIMNSSSSU mussiness
EIMNSSSTU mustiness
EIMNSSUZZ muzziness
EIMOOPRST Pooterism
EIMOOPRTV promotive
EIMOORRSW worrisome
EIMOORSSU isomerous
EIMOOSSSX exosmosis
EIMOPRRST misreport
EIMOPRSTU imposture
EIMOPRTYZ prozymite
EIMOPSTUU impetuous
EIMORRRST terrorism
EIMORRSSY remissory
EIMORRSTU trimerous
EIMORRTTW mitre-wort
EIMORSUVY voyeurism
EIMOSTTTT motettist
EIMPRSTTY prettyism
EIMPRSTUY supremity
EINNNOTTY nonentity

EINNNSSSU	sunniness
EINNOOPRT	entropion
	pontonier
	prenotion
EINNOORST	ironstone
	serotonin
EINNORSTU	neutrinos
EINNORTVY	inventory
EINNOSSST	stoniness
EINNOSSSW	snowiness
EINNOSSTX	non-sexist
EINNOSSTY	syntonise
EINNOSTYZ	syntonize
EINNOSUUV	unenvious
EINNPRSTW	newsprint
EINNPSTTU	Neptunist
EINNRTTUW	unwritten
EINNSSTTU	nuttiness
	sustinent
EINOOPPRT	preoption
EINOOPRRS	prerosion
EINOOPRRT	portioner
EINOOPSSW	spoonwise
EINOORRST	retorsion
EINOORRTT	retortion
EINOORTTX	extortion
EINOORTTY	notoriety
EINOOSSST	sootiness
EINOOSSWZ	wooziness
EINOPPSSS	soppiness
EINOPRRTV	overprint
EINOPRSSS	prosiness
EINOPRSTU	pertusion
EINOPRSUU	penurious
EINOPSSSY	synopsise
EINOPSSTT	pottiness
EINOPSSYZ	synopsize
EINOQTTTU	quintetto
EINORRSSS	sorriness
EINORRTTV	introvert
EINORRTUU	nouriture
EINORSSUU	unserious
EINORSTTU	ritenutos
EINORSTUX	extrusion
EINORTTUV	vetturino
EINOSTTTU	Teutonist
EINOSTTVY	ventosity
EINPRRTTU	interrupt
EINPRSSSU	pursiness
EINRRSSTU	run-resist
EINRSSSTU	rustiness
EINRSTTUY	strenuity
EIOOPRRST	posterior
	repositor
EIOOPRSSV	provisoes
EIOOPRSTX	expositor
EIOOPRSTY	operosity
EIOOPRSTZ	zooperist
EIOOSSSTX	exostosis
EIOOSSTTV	ovotestis
EIOPPRRTY	propriety
EIOPPRSUV	purposive
EIOPRRTTV	vertiport
EIOPRSTTU	proustite
EIOPRSTTY	posterity
EIOQRSTUU	turquoise
EIORRRSTT	terrorist
EIORRRTTY	△territory
EIPQRTTUY	triptyque
EIPRRRSSU	surpriser
EIPRSSSTU	pertussis
EIQRSSTTU	questrist
	squitters
EIRSSTTTU	trustiest
EJLLOSSYY	joylessly
EJMNORUWY	jurywomen
EJMPRSTUW	△jews'-trump
EJNOORRSU	sojourner
EJOPRRSUU	perjurous
EKKOOPRRW	poker-work
EKLLNNOWW	well-known
EKLMOOTUY	leukotomy
EKLNOOORS	lookers-on
EKMMOOORS	smoke-room
EKMNNOORS	non-smoker
EKMNNORUY	monkey-run
EKMNNOTUY	monkey-nut
EKMNNOTYY	teknonymy
EKMNOOPSY	pyknosome
EKMNOOPTY	monkey-pot
EKMNOOSTU	musketoon
EKNOOPRUV	unprovoke
EKNOOPSTU	outspoken
EKNOORSTW	stonework
EKNORSSTU	sunstroke
EKNORSTUV	overstunk
EKOOPRRSW	ropeworks
EKOORRTUW	outworker
EKOORSTTW	twostroke
EKOPRRSSW	presswork
EKORRTTUW	tutworker
ELLLMSUUV	vulsellum
ELLMNOOPY	poll-money
ELLMOPSUU	plumulose
ELLMORSTU	rostellum
ELLMOSUUY	emulously
ELLMRSTUU	surmullet
ELLNOORST	stornello
ELLNOPRSU	prunellos
ELLNOPTUY	opulently
ELLOOSTUU	luteolous
ELLOPSTYY	polystyle
ELLORSTUU	tellurous
ELMMNSSUU	Mussulmen
ELMNNOOST	somnolent
ELMNOOPSU	monopulse
ELMNOOSTY	monostyle
ELMNOPSTU	plum-stone
ELMNPPSSU	plumpness
ELMOORSTW	lowermost
ELMOORSUY	lyomerous
ELMORSSST	stormless
ELMORSTUU	tremulous
ELNOORSUY	onerously

ELNOPPSTU	pulpstone
ELNORSUVY	nervously
ELNOSTUUY	tenuously
ELOOPPTTT	pottle-pot
ELOORSTUW	louse-wort
ELOORSTVY	love-story
ELOPPRSUY	purposely
ELOPRRSUW	rowel-spur
ELOPRRSUY	prelusory
ELOPRSSST	sportless
ELOPRSUUV	pulverous
ELOPSSSTU	spoutless
ELOQRSUUU	querulous
ELORSSTTU	troutless
ELORSTTUU	outlustre
ELORSTUVY	overlusty
ELPPRSSUU	superplus
ELPRSTTUY	spluttery
ELRSSSTTU	trustless
EMMNOOSTU	momentous
EMMNORTTU	tormentum
EMMNOSSSU	summonses
EMMNRSTUU	menstruum
EMMOORSTY	osmometry
EMNNOOOST	moonstone
EMNNRRRUU	rum-runner
EMNOOOPTT	monoptote
EMNOOPSUY	eponymous
EMNOORRTT	tormentor
EMNOORSTT	mort-stone
EMNOORTTY	tonometry
EMNOORTUV	overmount
EMNOORTUY	neurotomy
EMNOORTWY	moneywort
EMNOOSTTU	tomentous
EMNOPRRTU	no-trumper
EMNOPRSSU	responsum
EMNORSSTT	sternmost
EMOOORRST	storeroom
EMOOOSTTY	osteotomy
EMOOPRRSS	pressroom
EMOOPRTTY	optometry
EMOOPSSSU	espumosos
EMOORSTTU	outermost
EMOORTTUY	uterotomy
EMOPPRRTU	prompture
EMOPPRSTU	uppermost
EMOPRRTUV	overtrump
EMOPRRTYY	pyrometry
EMORSTTTU	uttermost
ENNNOOPRS	non-person
ENNNPRTUY	turn-penny
ENNOOOPRT	pontooner
ENNOOPPRT	proponent
ENNOPPSTY	penny-post
ENNOPRTWY	penny-wort
ENNORRTUU	outrunner
ENNORSTTU	turnstone
ENNPRRSUU	runners-up
ENOOPPRST	postponer
ENOOPPRTU	opportune
ENOOPRRSS	responsor
ENOOPRRTU	root-prune
ENOORSSTY	ostensory
ENOORSTTW	stonewort
ENOOSSTTU	sostenuto
ENOPPRSTU	unstopper
ENOPRRSTT	sternport
ENOPRSSSU	suspensor
ENOPRSSTT	sternpost
ENOPRSTTY	post-entry
ENOPSTTYY	stenotypy
ENORSSTUU	strenuous
ENORSTTUY	out-sentry
ENORSTUUV	venturous
ENOSSSTTU	stoutness
ENOTTTWWY	twenty-two
ENRRSSTUU	untrusser
EOOOPRRTU	outrooper
EOOPPRRSS	oppressor
EOOPPRRST	prepostor
EOOPPRTTY	prototype
EOOPRRSTT	protestor
EOOPRRTTU	out-porter
EOOPRRTUU	outpourer
EOOPRSSSS	possessor
EOOPRSTUU	eutropous
EOORSTTWY	two-storey
EOPPRRSTU	supporter
EOPPRSSST	stop-press
EOPRRSSTU	pro-estrus
EOPRTTTUU	putter-out
EORRSSSST	strossers
EORRSTTUV	overtrust
EORRSTUXY	extrusory

F

FFGHIILNW	whiffling
FFGHILNSU	shuffling
FFGHILRTU	frightful
FFGILNNSU	snuffling
FFGILNPUY	puffingly
FFGILNRTU	truffling
FFGIMNORU	fungiform
FFGINOPRS	offspring
FFHHILSUY	huffishly
FFHLORSUU	four-flush
FFHMOORTY	froth-fomy
FFIILMOST	off-limits
FFIINOSUX	suffixion
FFILMOORR	floriform
FFINOSSUU	suffusion
FFIOORSTT	first-foot
FFIOOSTTW	swift-foot
FFLLMNSUU	snuff-mull
FFLLNORTU	full-front
FFLMNOOSU	moufflons
FFLOOOOPR	foolproof
FFORRSUUU	furfurous
FGGIINORV	forgiving
FGHHILNOW	high-flown
FGHHIOOPR	high-proof
FGHIIINNS	finishing
FGHIILLTY	flightily

FGHIINSST stingfish
FGHIKLORT folk-right
FGHILLPTU plightful
FGHILNOTW night-fowl
FGHILOOTT footlight
light-foot
FGHILOPTT top-flight
FGHINORTT fortnight
FGHLNORTU throngful
FGHMOORTU frogmouth
FGIIILLNN infilling
FGIIILLNP filliping
FGIIILNVY vilifying
FGIIINVVY vivifying
FGIIKLNSY ski-flying
FGIILLLRT flirt-gill
gillflirt
FGIILLNPU upfilling
FGIILMNOR ligniform
FGIILNNOW inflowing
FGIILNNOY foiningly
FGIILNPTU uplifting
FGIILNRST firstling
FGIILNSTY siftingly
FGIILNTTY fittingly
FGIINNOPT fining-pot
FGIINNOTY notifying
FGIINNTTU unfitting
FGIINOPRT profiting
FGIINOSSY ossifying
FGIINPRUY purifying
FGIINPTYY typifying
FGILLNOOW following
FGILLNOWY flowingly
FGILNRRUY flurrying
FGILOOSTU ufologist
FGILSSTUU fustilugs
FGIMNORUU unguiform
FGINOSTUY fungosity
FGLLNORUW full-grown
FGLLNOSUY songfully
FGLOORSUU fulgorous
FGLORSUUU fulgurous
FGNOOORTW wrong-foot
FHHIORTTW forthwith
FHIIIKLLS killifish
FHIIJNOST fish-joint
FHIILOPST pilot-fish
FHIILRTTY thriftily
FHIIORSTY historify
FHIKNRSTU trunkfish
FHILLOOST foothills
FHILLOOSY foolishly
FHILLOSWY wolfishly
FHILLSUWY wishfully
FHILNSUUW unwishful
FHILOPPSY foppishly
FHILORSUY flourishy
FHILRSTTU thirstful
FHINNRSUU unfurnish
FHINNSTUY tunny-fish
FHINOOPRT hoofprint
FHINRTTUY unthrifty
FHLLPSUUY pushfully
FHLLRTUUY hurtfully
ruthfully
FHLMOSTUU mouthfuls
FHLNRTUUU unhurtful
FHLOOOPRS shop-floor
FHMOOOPRT mothproof
FHNOOPRST shopfront
FHOOOPRST shotproof
FHOORRSUU four-hours
FIIILNOPS Filipinos
FIIILSSTY fissility
FIIIMNRTY infirmity
FIIJLLLRT jillflirt
FIIKLNNST skinflint
FIILLMORV villiform
FIILLMOTU multifoil
FIILLPTUY pitifully
FIILMORTU trifolium
FIILMPRST film-strip
FIILNNOUX influxion
FIILNPTUU unpitiful
FIILOPRST profilist
FIILORTVY frivolity
FIILPRSTU spiritful
FIIMMNORS misinform
FIIMMORRT mitriform
FIIMNOPRS spiniform
FIIMNOSSU fusionism
FIIMORRTU triforium
FIIMORRTV vitriform
FIINOSSTU fusionist
FIIORSTUY furiosity
FIKKLNOSS kinsfolks
FIKLLLSUY skilfully
FIKLLNSUU unskilful
FIKMMNOOR Kominform
FILLLPSTU full-split
FILLSTUWY wistfully
FILMMORSU formulism
FILMMORTU multiform
FILMNORUY uniformly
FILMNOSUU fulminous
sulfonium
FILMORSTU formulist
FILMORSTY styliform
FILMORUVV vulviform
FILNPRTUY turnip-fly
FILOOOPRT portfolio
FILOORSSU fluorosis
FILOORSUV frivolous
FILORRSTY floristry
FILORSUUY furiously
FILOSSTUU fistulous
FIMMMORU mummiform
FINOOPRSU profusion
FINOOPRTT footprint
FKKLOORSW workfolks
FKLNOOSTW townsfolk
FKLNRSTUU trunkfuls
FKMNOOSTY moskonfyt

FKOOORTUW out-of-work
FKOORRSTW frostwork
FLLLOSUUY soulfully
FLLLSTUUY lustfully
FLLNOORRY forlornly
FLNOOPSSU spoonfuls
FLOOOOSTT footstool
FLOOOPPRT plot-proof
FLOOOPTTU poultfoot
FLOORRSUW sorrowful
FLOPRSSUU plus-fours
FOOPRRSTU rust-proof
FOOPSSTUY pussyfoot

G

GGGHINRSU shrugging
GGGIILNNS sniggling
GGGIILNRW wriggling
GGGIINPRS sprigging
GGGIINRST strigging
GGGILMNSU smuggling
GGGILNTUY tuggingly
GGHHHIILT highlight
GGHHILOSY hoggishly
GGHHINORW high-grown
GGHIIILRW whirligig
GGHIILNNS shingling
GGHIILNNT lightning
GGHIILNST slighting
GGHIILNSY sighingly
GGHIILPSY piggishly
GGHIINNSU unsighing
GGHIINRTW right-wing
GGHIINSST sight-sing
GGHILNNOT nightlong
GGHILNOPU ploughing
GGHILNSUY gushingly
GGHILOOPR logogriph
GGHINNORT thronging
GGHINNOTW nightgown
GGHINPSUU upgushing
GGHLOORYY hygrology
GGIIIMNNP impinging
GGIIIMNSV misgiving
GGIIJNNOR jingo-ring
GGIILNNRY ringingly
GGIILNNSW swingling
GGIILNNSY singingly
GGIILNPRY gripingly
GGIINNORW ingrowing
GGIINNPRS springing
GGIINNRST stringing
GGIINNSWW swing-wing
GGIINOPSS gossiping
GGIINOTUV outgiving
GGILLNNOY longingly
GGILLNOWY glowingly
GGILMNSUY ginglymus
GGILMOOSY gismology
GGILMOOYZ gizmology
GGILNNOUY youngling
GGILNOPRY gropingly
GGIMNOORS Gongorism
GGINOORST Gongorist
GGINOOSTU goings-out
outgoings
GGINOPRUW upgrowing
GGLNNORUW lung-grown
GHHIILPST lightship
GHHIILSST slightish
GHHILOPRY hygrophil
GHHILRSTU rushlight
GHHLORTUY throughly
GHIIKNNRS shrinking
GHIIKNSTT skin-tight
GHIIKNTTT tight-knit
GHIILLLMT light-mill
GHIILLNRS shrilling
GHIILLNRT thrilling
GHIILLRSY girlishly
GHIILNNSY shiningly
GHIILNNTY hintingly
GHIILNNWY whiningly
GHIILNOST night-soil
GHIILNSSY hissingly
GHIILNSTW whistling
GHIILNTTW whittling
GHIILRSTY tigrishly
GHIIMNPRS shrimping
GHIINNNWY whinnying
GHIINNPSU punishing
GHIINNRSU inrushing
GHIINNSUW unwishing
GHIKNORTW night-work
GHILLOOPT loop-light
GHILLOOPY philology
GHILLOOTY lithology
GHILLOSTW lowlights
GHILMNNOT monthling
GHILMNOOT moonlight
GHILNOOPT potholing
GHILNOORY rhinology
GHILNOPYY philogyny
GHILNOSST slingshot
GHILNPSUY pushingly
GHILNSTUY unsightly
GHILOOOPY ophiology
GHILOOPPY hippology
GHILOOSTY histology
GHILOPSTT spotlight
stoplight
GHILORSUY roguishly
GHILPRSTY sprightly
GHILPRTUY uprightly
GHIMMNRTU thrumming
GHIMMNTUY thingummy
GHIMNOOST smoothing
GHIMNOSST songsmith
GHIMOOPSS gomphosis
GHIMORSTW misgrowth
GHINOPSTT nightspot
GHINORRTT troth-ring
GHINORSST strongish
GHINORSTT Storthing

GHINORTUW inwrought
GHINPPSTU shtupping
GHINRSTTU thrusting
GHIORRSTY hygristor
GHIORSTTW growthist
GHLLOOOPY hoplology
GHLMNOOYY hymnology
GHLMOOTYY mythology
GHLNOOOPY phonology
GHLNOOPYY hypnology
GHLNOSSTU slung-shot
GHLNOSTUY unghostly
GHLNOTUYY youngthly
GHLOOPTYY phytology
GHMNOOPSY gymnosoph
GHMNOOSUU humongous
GHMNOSUUU humungous
GHNNOOPRR pronghorn
GHNOORSTW shortgown
GHNORRSUW rush-grown
GHNORTUUW unwrought
GHOOORSTT Ostrogoth
GHOORTTUW outgrowth
GHOPRTUUW upwrought
wrought-up
GIIIKKNST ski-kiting
GIIIKLMNS misliking
GIIIKMNSV vikingism
GIIILOSTU litigious
GIIIMMNTT immitting
GIIIMNRSV Irvingism
GIIIMNRUV virginium
GIIIMRSST mistigris
GIIINNORS signorini
GIIINNOSV visioning
GIIINNQRU inquiring
GIIINPRST spiriting
GIIINRTVY virginity
GIIJKNORS skijoring
GIIKLNNPU uplinking
GIIKLNNTW twinkling
GIIKLNNWY winkingly
GIIKNNNUW unwinking
GIIKNNORW inworking
GIIKNPRSU prusiking
GIIKNRSST skirtings
GIILLLNWY willingly
GIILLMNPY limpingly
GIILLMNSY smilingly
GIILLMRST grist-mill
GIILLNNUW unwilling
GIILLNPSY lispingly
GIILMNNSU unsmiling
GIILMNSSY missingly
GIILNNNWY winningly
GIILNNOTU untoiling
GIILNNPPY nippingly
GIILNNSTU insulting
GIILNNTWY twiningly
GIILNOSUU uliginous
GIILNPPRY rippingly
GIILNPPST stippling
GIILNPRST stripling
GIILNPRSY springily
GIILNPSTT splitting
GIILNPTYY pityingly
GIILNRSTY stringily
GIILNTTWY wittingly
GIILOOSTY sitiology
GIILOSSST glossitis
GIILRSTTU liturgist
GIIMMNRST trimmings
GIIMNNOOR rooming-in
GIIMNNTUY mutinying
GIIMNOPRS promising
GIIMNOPRV improving
GIIMNORRR mirroring
GIIMNOTTW two-timing
GIIMNRSSU surmising
GIINNNOWW winnowing
GIINNNPTU tuning-pin
GIINNOORS △signorino
GIINNOPRU inpouring
GIINNPPRU unripping
GIINNPRST sprinting
GIINNPTTU inputting
GIINNPTUY unpitying
GIINNQSTU squinting
GIINNRSSU sunrising
GIINNRTUW unwriting
GIINNSSTU unsisting
GIINNSTUU unsuiting
GIINNTTUW unwitting
GIINPPRST stripping
GIINPPTTU titupping
GIINPSTTU upsitting
GIINPTTTU tittuping
GIINQRSTU squirting
GIINRSUVV surviving
GIIORRSUU irriguous
GIJLLNOTY joltingly
GIJLNTTUY juttingly
GIJNNNORU nonjuring
GIKLLORRW grillwork
GIKLNNOOO onlooking
GIKLNNOWY knowingly
GIKLNOOOY koniology
GIKNNNOUW unknowing
GIKNNORUW unworking
GIKNOOPRV provoking
GILLLLNOY lollingly
GILLLNOOP lolloping
GILLMNOOY limnology
GILLMOSSY syllogism
GILLNOPSY slopingly
GILLNORST strolling
GILLNORUY louringly
GILLOOOPY oligopoly
GILLOORSU orgillous
GILMMNOOS △mongolism
GILMNOPRY rompingly
GILMOOSTY myologist
GILNNNPUY punningly
GILNNNRUY runningly

GILNOOORY onirology
GILNOORUY urinology
GILNOPPTY toppingly
GILNOPTUY poutingly
GILNORSUY rousingly
GILNORTTU troutling
GILNOSTUU glutinous
GILNPPSUY supplying
GILNPRRUY purringly
GILNSSTUU singultus
GILOOORST orologist
GILOOOSSU isologous
GILOOOSTT otologist
GILOOOSTZ zoologist
GILOORSTU urologist
GIMMNPSUU summing-up
GIMMNRRUU murmuring
GIMMNRSTU strumming
GIMMOSTUY gummosity
GIMNNOORS Monsignor
GIMNNORSU mournings
GIMNOORSU ginormous
GIMNOPPRT prompting
GIMOPRUUY uropygium
GIMOPSSUY Gossypium
GIMOPSTUU gumptious
GINNNOOTV non-voting
GINNNRTUU unturning
GINNOOPRT Orpington
GINNORSST no-strings
GINNPRTUU upturning
GINOOPRSS prognosis
GINOOPRTU uprooting
GINOOPSSU spongious
GINOORRSW sorrowing
GINOORSTU trigonous
GINOPPPTU topping-up
GINOPPRST stropping
GINOPPSSU supposing
GINOPRSST Stringops
GINOPRSTU outspring
sprouting
GINOPTTTU totting-up
GINOPTTUW tuptowing
GINORRTTU torturing
GINORSTUY trigynous
GINPPTTUU up-putting
GINRSTTTU strutting
GLLOOPTTY polyglott
GLLOOPTUY plutology
GLMNOOPUY polygonum
GLNOOOSTY nostology
GLOOOPRTY tropology
GMNOORSSW moss-grown
GNOOOOSUZ zoogonous
GNOOPRTYY protogyny
GOORSSTUU goustrous
GOPRSTWYY gypsywort
GORRSTUWY worryguts

H

HHHMNNOUY Houyhnhnm
HHHOOPRST shophroth
HHIILNORT rhinolith
HHIIRSTTY thirtyish
HHILOOPPT photophil
HHILORSWY whorishly
HHIMOOSST smoothish
HHIMRSTTY rhythmist
HHIORTTWW Whitworth
HHLMOOPYY homophyly
HHMMOOOPR homomorph
HHMMOSTUU mushmouth
HHMNOOOPY homophony
HHNOORRST shorthorn
HIIIPRSVZ vizirship
HIIKMSTWY tim-whisky
HIILLMNOT millionth
HIILLNOTZ zillionth
HIILLOSWW willowish
HIILMPSSU silphiums
HIILMPSWY wimpishly
HIILNOPSY Sinophily
HIILNORTT trilithon
HIILNSSWY swinishly
HIILOQRSU liquorish
HIILOSTTY hostility
HIILPPPSU pupilship
HIILPSTTY typhlitis
HIILRSTTY thirstily
HIIMNOPRS minorship
HIIMNORST ironsmith
HIIMNOSST Shintoism
HIIMNSSUV Vishnuism
HIIMOPSTU hospitium
HIIMORSST historism
hit-or-miss
HIIMRSSTU hirsutism
HIINOPSSY hypinosis
HIINOSSTT Shintoist
HIIOPPRRS priorship
HIKLMOOTT milk-tooth
HIKNNORST stinkhorn
HIKNNOSSY hyson-skin
HIKOOPSTT skip-tooth
HILLLMTUU multihull
HILLLOOST tol-lolish
HILLMOOTT mill-tooth
HILLMORUU ill-humour
HILLMPSUY lumpishly
HILLNPSUY sulphinyl
HILLNSTTU still-hunt
HILLOOPRW whirlpool
HILLOSTUY loutishly
HILLOSVWY wolvishly
HILLSSTYY stylishly
HILMMPSUY mumpishly
HILMOOSYZ hylozoism
HILMOOTTY lithotomy
HILMOPRSY rompishly
HILNNOSTY tonnishly
HILOOPTXY toxophily
HILOOSTYZ hylozoist
HILOPRSSU Russophil

HILORSSTT	short-list
HILORSSUY	sourishly
HILOSSTTY	sottishly
HILRSTUUV	vulturish
HIMNNOOSY	moonshiny
HIMNOPSTY	hypnotism
HIMOOPRSS	morphosis
HIMOOPRST	motor-ship
HIMPSSSYY	symphysis
HINOPPRRY	porphyrin
HINOPSTTY	hypnotist
HIOOPPRRY	porphyrio
HIOOPPRST	troop-ship
HIOORSTTT	orthotist
HIOPRSSTY	sophistry
HIOPRSTTU	tutorship
HIORRSTTY	thyristor
HKKNNOOTY	honky-tonk
HKMMNORRU	krummhorn
HKNOOOOPS	spoonhook
HLMOOPPRY	polymorph
HLMOOPPXY	pompholyx
HLNOOPPYY	polyphony
HLOOPPRSY	sporophyl
HMMOOPSTY	tommy-shop
HMMPSTUYY	Symphytum
HMNNOOOPY	monophony
HMNOORSTT	northmost
HMOOOPRTU	poor-mouth
HMOOOPRYZ	zoomorphy
HMOOPTTYY	phytotomy
HMOOSSTTU	southmost
HNOOPPTYY	phonotypy
HNOOPRTTY	phytotron
HNOORSTUU	Southroun
HOOOPRSUZ	zoophorus
HOOOPRTYZ	zootrophy
HOOORTTTW	toothwort
HOOPPTTYY	phototypy
HOOPRSSTT	shortstop

I

IIIKLLNPS	spillikin
IIIKMNRST	miniskirt
IIILNOSTV	violinist
IIILNTTUY	inutility
IIILOSUVX	lixivious
IIIMMNOSS	immission
IIIMPRSST	spiritism
IIIMRRTUV	triumviri
IIINNOTTU	intuition
IIINNRRTT	trinitrin
IIINOSSTV	visionist
IIINPRTTU	pituitrin
IIINSSSTU	sinusitis
IIIOSTTVY	vitiosity
IIIPRSSTT	spiritist
IIJNORSUU	injurious
IIJNORTUY	juniority
IIKKLNNSS	slinkskin
IIKLNORST	nitro-silk
IIKNNNOOS	onion-skin
IIKNTTTUU	Inuktitut
IILLLOPUV	pulvillio
IILLMNOPU	pollinium
IILLMPRSU	spirillum
IILLNNNOO	nonillion
IILLNORST	trillions
IILLOSTVY	villosity
IILMMMSSU	Muslimism
IILMMNOST	Miltonism
IILMMPUUV	impluvium
IILMNOOPS	implosion
IILMNOPSU	impulsion
IILMNOSTV	voltinism
IILMNPSUV	vulpinism
IILMOPSSS	solipsism
IILMOPSUY	impiously
IILNOOPST	postilion
IILNSSTUY	insulsity
IILNTTUWY	unwittily
IILOOPSTY	isopolity
IILOPRTXY	prolixity
IILOPSSST	solipsist
IILORTTTY	tortility
IILOSTVVZ	slivovitz
IILOSTVWZ	slivowitz
IIMNNOSTU	munitions
IIMNOOSSU	simonious
IIMNOOSTT	motionist
IIMNOPSSZ	Spinozism
IIMNORSTU	routinism
IIMOPRTXY	proximity
IIMOQSTUX	quixotism
IIMORSTTU	tutiorism
IIMRRSTUV	triumvirs
IIMRRTUVY	triumviry
IIMRSSTTU	strumitis
IINNOORST	intorsion
IINNOORTT	intortion
IINNOOSTT	notionist
IINNOOSUX	innoxious
IINNORSTU	intrusion
IINNORTTU	nutrition
IINOOPRSV	provision
IINOOPSVY	poison-ivy
IINOOQTTU	quotition
IINOORSTT	sortition
IINOPRRTU	irruption
IINOPSSTY	spinosity
IINOPSSTZ	Spinozist
IINORSTTU	introitus
	routinist
IINOSSTUY	sinuosity
IINOSSTVY	synovitis
IIOOPRSST	spiritoso
IIOPRSSTU	spiritous
IIORSTTTU	tutiorist
IJMNOORTW	jointworm
	joint-worm
IKNOORRSW	ironworks
IKORSSTTU	outskirts
ILLLOOPPS	lollipops
ILLLPSUUV	pulvillus

ILLMOORST stillroom
ILLNOOPSU pollusion
ILLNOOPTU pollution
ILLNOPVYY polyvinyl
ILLOOQSUY soliloquy
ILLOQRTUW quillwort
ILMNOOOPY polyomino
ILMNOOSUY ominously
ILMNOPSTU Plutonism
ILMNOPTUU plutonium
ILMOSSYYZ zymolysis
ILMRSTUUV vulturism
ILNNOSSTW stownlins
ILNOOPRST Prontosil®
ILNOOPRSU prolusion
ILNOOSUXY noxiously
ILNOPRXYY pyroxylin
ILNOPSSUU spinulous
ILNOPSTTU Plutonist
ILNORSUUY ruinously
ILNOSSUUY sinuously
ILOOPPRSY isopropyl
ILOOPPSSY polyposis
ILOOPRTTU tulip-root
ILOOPSTXY pixy-stool
ILOORSSTU torulosis
ILOORSTUY riotously
ILOPRSSYY pyrolysis
ILORSUUUX luxurious
IMMMNOORS Mormonism
IMMMPSSUU mumpsimus
IMMOPPRTU impromptu
IMMOPSSUY symposium
IMMPSSSUU sumpsimus
IMNNOOPTW topminnow
IMNOOOPRT promotion
IMNOOOSSU isonomous
IMNOOOSTZ zoonomist
IMNOORSTU torminous
IMNORSTTU strontium
IMOOOSTTZ zootomist
IMOOPPSTY pomposity
IMOOPRRSS promissor
IMOOQSSTU mosquitos
IMOORSSTU sumotoris
IMOPSSSTY symptosis
IMORSUVXY myxovirus
INNOOPSTU poison-nut
INNOOQRTU quintroon
INNOOSSUU unisonous
INOOOPSSU poisonous
INOOORSTU notorious
INOOPPRTU pourpoint
INOOPRSSU prisonous
INOPPRTTU turnip-top
INOPPSTTU pint-stoup
INOPSSTTY synoptist
IOOORRRST orris-root
IOOPPRRTU potpourri
IOOPPRSST proptosis
IOOPRRSVY provisory
IOORSSTUV virtuosos
IOPRSSTTU posturist
IOPRSTTUU poursuitt

K

KKNORRTUW trunk-work

L

LLOOOPRRS poor's-roll
LMNNOOOXY monoxylon
LMNOOPTUY plutonomy
LMNOOPYYY polyonymy
LMOOPPSUY pompously
LOOPPRRSU propulsor
LOOPPRSUY Polyporus
LOOPRRSUY prolusory
LOORSTUUY routously
LOPSSTUUU pustulous
LORSTUUUV vulturous

M

MMORRSUUU murmurous
MNNOOOPSY monopsony
MNOORSSTU monstrous
MNOORSSTW snowstorm
MOPSSTUUU sumptuous

N

NNOOSSTUY syntonous
NOOOOPRTZ protozoon
NOOOPPSSU soupspoon

O

OOPRRSTVY provostry
OOPRSSTUU stuporous
OORRSTTUU torturous

10AAA

A

AAAAABCCRS asarabacca
AAAAALLMMY Malayalaam
AAAABCCEMN Maccabaean
AAAABCENRS scarabaean
AAAABDLNNN Bananaland
AAAABEHNNT Nabathaean
AAAABEMPRT parabemata
AAAABHMMNR Abraham-man
AAAABILMRV Ambarvalia
AAAABLMRRT Malabar-rat

AAAACCILPR	carapacial
AAAACDEEIN	Naiadaceae
AAAACDMMRT	tarmacadam
AAAACEEILR	Araliaceae
AAAACLMNRT	almacantar
AAAADEMNNT	adamantean
AAAADGLNNR	Angaraland
AAAAEEGLOP	palaeogaea
AAAAEGLMMT	amalgamate
AAAAELMNQU	aquamanale
AAAAGGLLNN	alang-alang
AAAAGHRSTY	satyagraha
AAAAHINNST	Athanasian
AAAAHIPPRS	paraphasia
AAAAILNRTT	tartanalia
AAAAIMNNNP	Panamanian
AAAALMNRSZ	△salmanazar
AAAALPRSTT	parastatal
AAAAMPRRTT	parramatta
AAABBCILST	sabbatical
AAABBDHSTY	Sabbath-day
AAABBDRRST	bastard-bar
AAABCCHLNS	bacchanals
AAABCCHNRS	charabancs
	char-à-bancs
AAABCCKNSV	canvasback
AAABCCLMTU	catacumbal
AAABCDEIRS	scarabaeid
AAABCDELNR	candelabra
AAABCEGGGR	baggage-car
AAABCEHLMR	beach-la-mar
AAABCEHLTT	attachable
AAABCEKLTT	attackable
AAABCELLLR	clarabella
AAABCELRTU	acetabular
AAABCELSTT	cabalettas
AAABCERSSU	scarabaeus
AAABCHILNR	abranchial
AAABCHINRT	batrachian
AAABCIKRSS	cassia-bark
AAABCIQSTU	aquabatics
AAABCLLMRU	ambulacral
AAABCOORRT	barracoota
AAABCORRTU	barracouta
AAABDEEGLM	damageable
AAABDEHLRZ	hazardable
AAABDEILNN	alabandine
AAABDEILNT	alabandite
AAABDMNRRU	barramunda
AAABDMORSS	ambassador
AAABDORRST	astarboard
AAABEEGLMN	manageable
AAABEELLPP	appealable
AAABEELPPS	appeasable
AAABEGGMNR	garbageman
AAABEGIMNR	mangabeira
AAABEGLMNY	manageably
AAABEHLNPT	analphabet
AAABEILLSS	assailable
AAABEILNTT	attainable
AAABEINPST	anabaptise
AAABEINPTZ	anabaptize
AAABELLNSY	analysable
AAABELLNYZ	analyzable
AAABELLRST	alablaster
AAABELNRRT	narratable
AAABGHILLY	gallabiyah
AAABGHINRS	barasingha
AAABHIOPQU	aquaphobia
AAABHNRSSU	sub-Saharan
AAABIMNPRS	Pan-Arabism
AAABIMNPST	anabaptism
AAABINPSTT	△anabaptist
AAABKNOSTT	tanka-boats
AAACCCEEIR	Caricaceae
AAACCCIORT	cacciatora
AAACCCJKKR	crackajack
AAACCDEHIR	Characidae
AAACCDEILM	academical
AAACCEEILS	Salicaceae
AAACCEHRSS	saccharase
AAACCEHRST	saccharate
AAACCEIILR	alcaicería
AAACCEIPTT	capacitate
AAACCENOSU	acanaceous
AAACCHILNR	anarchical
AAACCHKKMT	hackmatack
AAACCHPRTT	cataphract
AAACCILLPR	Callicarpa
AAACCILLRS	cascarilla
AAACCILNST	anaclastic
AAACCIMORT	acroamatic
AAACCIPRTT	paratactic
AAACCLMNOS	calamancos
AAACCMOPRR	macrocarpa
AAACDDENSU	Sadducaean
AAACDDJKNY	Jack-a-dandy
AAACDEGINR	Carangidae
AAACDEIMMS	macadamise
AAACDEIMMZ	macadamize
AAACDELMNR	calamander
AAACDENNRV	caravanned
AAACDGIILR	cardialgia
AAACDHINNR	arachnidan
AAACDIILMT	Adamitical
AAACDIIPRS	paradisaic
	paradisiac
AAACDIKLSY	lackadaisy
AAACDILMRT	dramatical
AAACDILRTY	caryatidal
AAACDIMNRU	anacardium
AAACEEGNOR	Onagraceae
AAACEEHMNR	Rhamnaceae
AAACEEILMS	Alismaceae
AAACEELNOS	Solanaceae
AAACEENPPR	appearance
AAACEENRRV	caravaneer
AAACEEOPST	Sapotaceae
AAACEFLQTU	catafalque
AAACEGHLPR	cephalagra
AAACEGNORT	Arctogaean
AAACEHIMNN	Manichaean
AAACEHIMNU	naumachiae
AAACEHIRRT	Trachearia

Words marked △ may be spelled also with a capital letter

AAACEILMNT	catamenial
AAACEINNRT	catenarian
AAACEINPRS	parascenia
AAACEINPST	anapaestic
AAACEINRRS	sarracenia
AAACEJKNPS	jackanapes
AAACELLNPT	aplacental
AAACELMPRT	metacarpal
AAACELPSTY	acatalepsy
AAACENNRRV	caravanner
AAACFINNPR	Pan-African
AAACFMNORU	macrofauna
AAACGGILNO	anagogical
AAACGGILOP	apagogical
AAACGHNRTT	tragacanth
AAACGHOPRS	Sarcophaga
AAACGILLNO	analogical
AAACGILMRT	ragmatical
AAACGIMRRV	Marcgravia
AAACGINNRV	caravaning
AAACHILLNW	Wallachian
AAACHIMNRT	marchantia
AAACHIMNSU	naumachias
AAACHIPPRS	paraphasic
AAACHJOPRS	chaparajos
AAACHLMNNR	manna-larch
AAACHLNOTU	anacolutha
AAACHNPRTY	pyracantha
AAACHOSSUY	ayahuascos
AAACHQTUUU	△chautauqua
AAACIILRUV	Avicularia
AAACIINNPR	Incaparina
AAACIIRSSS	ascariasis
AAACIKLMNP	pack-animal
AAACIKLMNR	Lamarckian
AAACIKLRTU	autarkical
AAACILLMNU	animalcula
AAACILLMNY	maniacally
AAACILLNTY	analytical
AAACILLNUV	Vulcanalia
AAACILLRTU	Ural-Altaic
AAACILMMNO	ammoniacal
AAACILMNOT	anatomical
AAACILNORY	Alcyonaria
AAACILNPST	anaplastic
AAACILNRSS	carnassial
AAACILNRST	scarlatina
AAACILORRT	crotalaria
AAACILRTTU	Articulata
AAACIMMORZ	△macrozamia
AAACINNPRT	pancratian
AAACINRRTT	△tractarian
AAACISSSTT	catastasis
AAACLMNPRU	campanular
AAACLMNRTU	almucantar
AAACLMNRVY	cavalryman
AAACLPRRSW	wrap-rascal
AAACMNNRTT	marcantant
AAACNRTTTT	attractant
AAADDEINRW	Edwardiana
AAADDELMPT	maladapted
AAADDELNOT	adelantado
AAADDGIRRT	Tardigrada
AAADDHMRSY	hamadryads
AAADEEGHNP	phagedaena
AAADEFIOST	asafoetida
AAADEFISST	assafetida
AAADEGGLNR	garlandage
AAADEGGRTV	aggravated
AAADEGINRV	△devanagari
AAADEGNRTV	avant-garde
AAADEIMNNT	adamantine
AAADEIMNRZ	mazarinade
AAADEIMSTT	diastemata
AAADEINPRS	paradisean
AAADEIPTTV	adaptative
AAADEIRRSV	adversaria
AAADELMNRS	salamander
AAADEOPSTZ	zapateados
AAADGHIRSW	sharawadgi
AAADGILLNR	granadilla
AAADGLLNOR	allargando
AAADGMMMNR	grandmamma
AAADGMNORR	mandragora
AAADGNOPPR	△propaganda
AAADHHLMRS	dharmshala
AAADHMMMNU	Muhammadan
AAADIILNPR	lapidarian
AAADIILORR	Radiolaria
AAADIILPRS	paradisial
AAADIINPRS	paradisian
AAADILMORR	alarm-radio
AAADILNNSU	Andalusian
AAADILNOPR	paranoidal
AAADILOPPR	parapodial
AAADIMNOTT	datamation
AAADINOPTT	adaptation
AAADLMMNNN	landammann
AAADLNQRTU	quadrantal
AAADMNQRUU	Quadrumana
AAADORSTTU	autostrada
AAADQRRTUU	quadratura
AAAEEILMMN	melanaemia
AAAEFGLLLT	Flagellata
AAAEFLMNST	malfeasant
AAAEGGIMNT	gametangia
AAAEGHLLNP	phalangeal
AAAEGHTTWW	wag-at-the-wa'
AAAEGILMNR	managerial
AAAEGILPPR	paraplegia
AAAEGINPRS	asparagine
AAAEGIPRSS	air-passage
AAAEGLMTTU	malaguetta
AAAEGLMTXY	metagalaxy
AAAEGMRRTV	margravate
AAAEGPSSWY	passageway
AAAEHIMRTU	haematuria
AAAEHINSTU	euthanasia
AAAEHIRSTW	washateria
AAAEHJNPRT	japan-earth
AAAEHLMRSS	Marshalsea
AAAEHNOPPR	epanaphora
AAAEHPPRRS	paraphrase
AAAEIILNTT	Italianate

Words marked △ may be spelled also with a capital letter

AAAEILLPST palatalise
AAAEILLPTZ palatalize
AAAEILMNQU aquamanile
AAAEILMPST metaplasia
AAAEILMRTU tularaemia
AAAEILNPPR parapineal
AAAEILNPRT planetaria
AAAEILNPTT palatinate
AAAEIMNNRT amarantine
AAAEIMNPRS paramnesia
AAAEIMNQRU aquamarine
AAAEIMNRTU Mauretania
AAAEKLPRRW parawalker
AAAELLNRRZ Ranzellaar
AAAELLNRTT tarantella
AAAELLPRST palaestral
AAAELMMNOT melanomata
AAAELMNRSS △salmanaser
AAAELMNRTT atramental
AAAELMPRRT parametral
AAAELMRSTT metatarsal
AAAELNPQRU aquaplaner
AAAELSSTWY leastaways
AAAEMORTTT teratomata
AAAFGINNUU anguifauna
AAAFLORSST solfataras
AAAGGHIRSW sharawaggi
AAAGGILLNO algolagnia
AAAGGILRST gastralgia
AAAGGNNRTU △gargantuan
AAAGHILRRT arthralgia
AAAGHIOPTU autophagia
AAAGHLLMOP Mallophaga
AAAGHNPPRT pantagraph
AAAGHNPSTU agapanthus
AAAGIIILMNR marginalia
AAAGIILMST galimatias
AAAGIIRSTT Sagittaria
AAAGILLMNO Gallomania
AAAGILMNNO △anglomania
AAAGIMMNRR grammarian
AAAGIMNORT Maoritanga
AAAGIMNSTT anastigmat
AAAGINNOPT Patagonian
AAAGLOPRSS paraglossa
AAAGLRSSTU △astragalus
AAAGMNNRSS manna-grass
AAAGMNSTTY syntagmata
AAAGPRRSSS sparagrass
AAAHHHOOOW whoa-hoa-hoa
AAAHHIMNSY shamiyanah
AAAHIIJMRY jamahiriya
AAAHIILPPR paraphilia
AAAHIKMNRT Karmathian
AAAHILMRRS air-marshal
AAAHILNSST thalassian
AAAHIMNNOT anthomania
AAAHIMNSTY Mahayanist
AAAHINOPPR paraphonia
AAAHINORTZ Zoantharia
AAAHINRRTU Arthuriana
AAAHIPRRRT pararthria
AAAHLMNPST phantasmal
AAAHLNPXYY anaphylaxy
AAAHMNOTTX xanthomata
AAAHMNRSTU Amaranthus
AAAHPPRRST paraphrast
AAAIIJNNRZ janizarian
AAAIILLMRR armillaria
AAAIILLNTT natalitial
AAAIILMNNR laminarian
AAAIIMNPRS Arimaspian
AAAIINNRST sanitarian
AAAIIRRTWY raiyatwari
AAAILLMNNZ manzanilla
AAAILLMNPR rampallian
AAAILLORTV lavatorial
AAAILLRRST altar-rails
AAAILMNOTX malaxation
AAAILMNPST aplanatism
AAAILMNRWY railwayman
AAAILNORTT natatorial
AAAILNRSTU Australian
△saturnalia
AAAIMNORST inamoratas
AAAIMRTTTV amritattva
AAAINNPRSS Parnassian
AAALLLLLPY all-play-all
AAALMNOPRR paranormal
AAALNNOSST assonantal
AAAMNNORTT tramontana
AAAMRTZZZZ razzmatazz
AABBBEILTV babblative
AABBBELORS absorbable
AABBCCKKOT back-to-back
AABBCDEEKR barebacked
AABBCDKLOR blackboard
AABBCDNRSU unscabbard
AABBCEFGLY cabbage-fly
AABBCEILRS ascribable
AABBCELMOT combatable
AABBCIILNR rabbinical
AABBCIJKRT jack-rabbit
AABBDDEORR breadboard
AABBDDEORS broad-based
AABBDEEELT debateable
AABBDEGILR abridgable
AABBDEGORR barge-board
AABBDEILRY abbey-laird
AABBDELORS adsorbable
AABBDEOORV above-board
AABBDLLNRY brandy-ball
AABBEEGLRU Aberglaube
AABBEEHLRT breathable
AABBEEIRTV abbreviate
AABBEEKLRS breakables
AABBEELLRS baseballer
AABBEELLRT barbellate
AABBEELNRU unbearable
AABBEELNTU unbeatable
AABBEIISSS babesiasis
AABBEILLLS ballabiles
AABBEILLNU unbailable
AABBEILMNO abominable

AABBEILNOT	obtainable
AABBEILRRT	arbitrable
AABBEIMNWZ	Zimbabwean
AABBEKLLST	basketball
AABBEKLRWY	baby-walker
AABBELLMNU	unblamable
AABBELNRUY	unbearably
AABBGGILNR	Balbriggan
AABBHORRRU	harbour-bar
AABBILLNTU	balibuntal
AABBILMNOY	abominably
AABBILNNOY	Babylonian
AABBIORSSU	babiroussa
AABBLLMNUY	unblamably
AABBLLORRW	ball-barrow
AABBMMNPYY	namby-pamby
AABBNNUUYY	bunya-bunya
AABCCDEFKL	blackfaced
AABCCDELOR	accordable
AABCCEELPT	acceptable
AABCCEHNST	bacchantes
AABCCEILLN	calcinable
AABCCEKKPR	backpacker
AABCCEKPRS	backspacer
AABCCELLLU	calculable
AABCCELOST	accostable
AABCCELPTY	acceptably
AABCCENOOS	cocoa-beans
AABCCHINST	catch-basin
AABCCIILST	cabalistic
AABCCIINNR	cinnabaric
AABCCIINRT	bacitracin
AABCCIKNRR	crackbrain
AABCCIMORT	imbroccata
AABCCINOTU	accubation
AABCCIORST	acrobatics
AABCCLLLUY	calculably
AABCDDEHKN	back-handed
AABCDDEHKR	hardbacked
AABCDDEKLR	ladder-back
AABCDDEKLS	saddleback
AABCDDORRY	cardboardy
AABCDEEHLT	detachable
AABCDEEILR	eradicable
AABCDEEKNR	breakdance
AABCDEELLR	declarable
AABCDEELNS	ascendable
AABCDEFRSS	brass-faced
AABCDEHKNR	back-hander
AABCDEIILT	diabetical
AABCDEILMR	Barmecidal
AABCDEIOTV	advice-boat
AABCDELMNU	manducable
AABCDELNNU	unbalanced
AABCDELNSU	subdecanal
AABCDELPRW	parcel-bawd
AABCDENNOR	carbonnade
AABCDERSTT	abstracted
AABCDGKLRU	blackguard
AABCDHIINR	Dibranchia
AABCDHINRY	Charybdian
AABCDHKLOR	chalkboard
AABCDHMORT	matchboard
AABCDHOPRT	patchboard
AABCDIILLO	diabolical
AABCDIINOT	abdication
AABCDILMMS	lambdacism
AABCDINRRY	canary-bird
AABCDIORRS	barricados
AABCDKLPSU	back-spauld
AABCDKLRWY	backwardly
AABCDLLNPU	cup-and-ball
AABCDMOSSU	ambuscados
AABCDNNORT	contraband
AABCDNOORS	carbonados
AABCEEEFFL	effaceable
AABCEEELMR	amerceable
AABCEEELTU	Betulaceae
AABCEEEMRR	mace-bearer
AABCEEERTT	ebracteate
AABCEEERTU	Tuberaceae
AABCEEERTX	exacerbate
AABCEEFNRZ	brazen-face
AABCEEGHLN	changeable
AABCEEGHLR	chargeable
AABCEEGKRT	age-bracket
AABCEEHILV	achievable
AABCEEHLRS	searchable
AABCEEHLTY	chalybeate
AABCEEHRST	sabretache
AABCEEILMR	amerciable
AABCEEIMRT	bacteremia
AABCEEINRR	carabineer
AABCEEIRTU	eubacteria
AABCEEIRTV	abreactive
AABCEEKSST	basket-case
AABCEELLLR	recallable
AABCEELLNS	cleansable
AABCEELLOT	locateable
AABCEELMOT	come-at-able
AABCEELNRT	tabernacle
AABCEELPST	aspectable
AABCEELRTU	trabeculae
AABCEESTTU	subacetate
AABCEFIILP	pacifiable
AABCEFIILT	beatifical
AABCEFLORT	factorable
AABCEGHLNY	changeably
AABCEGHLRY	chargeably
AABCEGKRST	gas-bracket
AABCEGLLOU	coagulable
AABCEGLMNN	blancmange
AABCEHIKNR	chainbrake
AABCEHILPT	alphabetic
AABCEHILRT	charitable
AABCEHINRT	branchiate
AABCEHINTU	habitaunce
AABCEHJNOT	Jacobethan
AABCEHKLRT	blackheart
AABCEHKMNR	harman-beck
AABCEHKORS	ahorseback
AABCEHLMNR	chambranle
AABCEHLNST	stanchable
AABCEHLOUV	avouchable

AABCEHPSTY	bathyscape
AABCEHQRSU	shabracque
AABCEIILLM	bacillemia
AABCEIINRR	carabinier
AABCEIINTU	beautician
AABCEILLMP	implacable
AABCEILLPP	applicable
AABCEILMOT	ametabolic
AABCEILMST	masticable
AABCEILNOT	actionable
AABCEILOSS	associable
AABCEILPSZ	capsizable
AABCEILQRU	acquirable
AABCEINNOS	ocean-basin
AABCEINORT	abreaction
AABCEIORST	aerobatics
AABCEIRSTT	tetrabasic
AABCEKKMRR	backmarker
AABCEKLRTW	blackwater
AABCEKNORS	rackabones
AABCEKOPTT	packet-boat
AABCELLLOT	collatable
AABCELLNSU	unscalable
AABCELLORR	barcarolle
AABCELLORS	caballeros
AABCELMOPR	comparable
AABCELMTUU	acetabulum
AABCELNOTU	outbalance
AABCELRRTU	trabecular
AABCERRSTT	abstracter
AABCERRTUU	bureaucrat
AABCERSTUU	subarcuate
AABCFIORRT	fabricator
AABCFLNORU	confabular
AABCGIILLM	galliambic
AABCGIKNRR	barracking
AABCGILLSU	subglacial
AABCGINORT	boat-racing
AABCGKMMNO	backgammon
AABCGLRRTU	cat-burglar
AABCHHIMPR	amphibrach
AABCHILRTY	charitably
AABCHINOOP	canophobia
AABCHINOTT	cohabitant
AABCHIOOPR	acrophobia
AABCHIOPQU	aquaphobic
AABCHIRSXY	brachyaxis
AABCHKLMOR	Bramah-lock
AABCHKLPSS	splash-back
AABCHLMNPR	palm-branch
AABCHLNOOR	halocarbon
AABCHLRRUY	brachyural
AABCHMORUY	moucharaby
AABCIILLMY	iambically
AABCIILNOT	anabolitic
AABCIILPTY	capability
AABCIILTTY	actability
AABCIIOPRT	parabiotic
AABCIKRSST	backstairs
AABCILLLSY	syllabical
AABCILLMPY	implacably
AABCILLNNY	cannibally
AABCILLPPY	applicably
AABCILMORU	columbaria
AABCILMOST	catabolism
AABCILMRTU	umbratical
AABCILNNNO	cannabinol
AABCILNNUU	incunabula
AABCILNOTY	actionably
AABCILNRSU	subcranial
AABCILNSUV	subclavian
AABCILORRT	calibrator
AABCILRSTU	arcubalist
	ultrabasic
AABCIMOORT	macrobiota
AABCIMORST	acrobatism
AABCINRSST	cat's-brains
AABCIOQRSU	aquarobics
AABCIQSTUU	subaquatic
AABCKLMOOR	blackamoor
AABCLLNNNO	cannonball
AABCLMMRUU	ambulacrum
AABCLMOPRY	comparably
AABCLORUVY	vocabulary
AABCLRSTTY	abstractly
AABCNORSST	contrabass
AABCORRSTT	abstractor
AABDDDEEHL	bald-headed
AABDDEEEHR	bareheaded
AABDDEEGLR	degradable
AABDDEEHNR	barehanded
AABDDEELMN	demandable
AABDDEGGNS	sandbagged
AABDDEHLMO	hebdomadal
AABDDEHLRS	balderdash
AABDDEHMOR	hebdomadar
AABDDEILRR	air-bladder
AABDDEIMNR	madbrained
AABDDEINST	bastinaded
AABDDELOPR	pedal-board
AABDDELOPT	paddle-boat
AABDDEORRY	day-boarder
AABDDILLMO	lambdoidal
AABDEEELMS	sealed-beam
AABDEEEMNO	endamoebae
AABDEEFLRY	defrayable
AABDEEGHNR	head-banger
AABDEEGLRR	regardable
AABDEEGNRS	greaseband
AABDEEHKKW	hawk-beaked
AABDEEHRRT	threadbare
AABDEEILNT	detainable
AABDEEKPRR	parbreaked
AABDEELNPX	expandable
AABDEELNRU	unreadable
AABDEELRRV	laverbread
AABDEELRRW	rewardable
AABDEEMNOV	above-named
AABDEEQRSU	arabesqued
AABDEFFLOR	affordable
AABDEFINRT	fatbrained
AABDEFIRSY	fairy-beads
AABDEGGINR	brigandage
AABDEGGNRS	sandbagger

AABDEGGORU	broad-gauge
AABDEGHNSU	husbandage
AABDEGIMNR	brand-image
AABDEGIMRR	Bridgerama
AABDEGIMRS	bragadisme
AABDEGLPRU	upgradable
AABDEGORST	goat's-beard
AABDEGORSW	board-wages
AABDEGRRSS	beard-grass
AABDEHKNST	hand-basket
AABDEHKRSW	hawksbeard
AABDEHNSTW	sweath-band
AABDEHORRT	earth-board
AABDEILLLU	illaudable
AABDEILLNR	banderilla
AABDEILLSY	dialysable
AABDEILLYZ	dialyzable
AABDEILMTT	admittable
AABDEILNOR	ordainable
AABDEILNOT	dealbation
AABDEILOST	Blastoidea
AABDEINNOR	Aberdonian
AABDEINRTZ	bartizaned
AABDEIRSST	bastardise
AABDEIRSTZ	bastardize
AABDEJLSTU	adjustable
AABDEKLLNR	randle-balk
AABDEKORST	skateboard
AABDELLNNO	belladonna
AABDELNOPR	pardonable
AABDELORRZ	razor-blade
AABDELRSTU	balustrade
AABDEMNOSW	beadswoman
AABDEMNRST	bandmaster
AABDEMORSS	embassador
AABDEOPPRR	paperboard
AABDEOPRST	pasteboard
AABDFHLORS	flash-board
AABDFLOORT	float-board
AABDGHRRTU	draught-bar
AABDGIILNW	law-abiding
AABDGIKNOS	baking-soda
AABDHMNNSU	husbandman
AABDHNORRW	hand-barrow
AABDHNORTT	throat-band
AABDILLLUY	illaudably
AABDILLORY	aryballoid
AABDILMNRU	mandibular
AABDILOOPR	paraboloid
AABDIMNRRU	barramundi
AABDIMRSST	bastardism
AABDJLSTUY	adjustably
AABDLNNTUY	abundantly
AABDLNOPRY	pardonably
AABDLORRTY	bardolatry
AABDNNPRSY	brandy-snap
AABDOORRRW	broad-arrow
AABDORRSTW	strawboard
AABEEEKRRX	axe-breaker
AABEEELLPR	repealable
AABEEELLRS	releasable
	resealable
AABEEELLRV	revealable
AABEEELPRT	repeatable
AABEEELRRT	talebearer
AABEEEMNOT	entamoebae
AABEEFILRR	rarefiable
AABEEFLLLT	flabellate
AABEEGILNR	regainable
AABEEGLLRS	greaseball
AABEEGLMSS	assemblage
AABEEGLOVY	voyageable
AABEEGLRTT	targetable
AABEEGNNRU	near-begaun
AABEEGNORT	baronetage
AABEEGRSUV	subaverage
AABEEHKRRT	heartbreak
AABEEHLLNU	unhealable
AABEEHLQTU	bequeathal
AABEEHLRTT	earth-table
AABEEILLRS	realisable
AABEEILLRZ	realizable
AABEEILMNX	examinable
AABEEILNRS	inerasable
AABEEILNRT	retainable
AABEEILPRR	repairable
AABEEINRRR	arrière-ban
AABEEJKRRW	jaw-breaker
AABEEKLMRR	remarkable
AABEEKLMRT	marketable
AABEEKLRRW	law-breaker
AABEEKRRTW	breakwater
AABEELLLSZ	sleazeball
AABEELLMNT	lamentable
AABEELLNPT	plane-table
AABEELLNSU	unsaleable
AABEELLPRR	pall-bearer
AABEELMNNU	unamenable
	unnameable
AABEELMNTU	untameable
AABEELMRSU	measurable
AABEELMSTT	metastable
	stablemate
AABEELNNTT	tenantable
AABEELNORS	reasonable
AABEELNOSS	seasonable
AABEELNPTT	patentable
AABEELNRSU	unerasable
AABEELNRSW	answerable
AABEELNRTU	untearable
AABEELNRUW	unwearable
AABEELNTTT	tablanette
AABEELOPRV	evaporable
AABEELPPRY	prepayable
AABEELRRST	arbalester
	arrestable
AABEELRSST	assertable
AABEELSSSS	assessable
AABEELSTTT	attestable
AABEERRTTV	Vertebrata
AABEFFIILL	affiliable
AABEFFILMR	affirmable
AABEFGILTU	fatiguable
AABEFGKLNR	klangfarbe

AABEFGKLST flag-basket
AABEFHLMOT fathomable
AABEFIILLS salifiable
AABEFILLNT inflatable
AABEFIMORS framboesia
AABEFLORUV favourable
AABEFNORRT forbearant
AABEGHILLY gallabiyeh
AABEGHINST sea-bathing
AABEGHORRU harbourage
AABEGIILMN imaginable
AABEGILNOZ zabaglione
AABEGILNRV Belgravian
AABEGILNSS assignable
AABEGILRST algebraist
AABEGINNOT abnegation
AABEGINRRU rue-bargain
AABEGIORTV abrogative
AABEGIRRRT arbitrager
AABEGKRRSU sugar-baker
AABEGLNRUU unarguable
AABEGLOPPR propagable
AABEGMNRSU submanager
AABEHIILTT habilitate
AABEHIKMRT habit-maker
AABEHILORV behavioral
AABEHINRRT Herbartian
AABEHIOOPR aerophobia
AABEHKLNSU unshakable
AABEHLQSSU squashable
AABEHLRSZZ △belshazzar
AABEHQRSSU squabasher
AABEIILNRV invariable
AABEIILNST insatiable
AABEIILNTU unilabiate
AABEIILRSV braaivleis
AABEIILSST assibilate
AABEIIMNSS baisemains
AABEIIMOSS amoebiasis
AABEIJLOSU Beaujolais
AABEIKLMST mistakable
AABEIKNNRV knave-bairn
AABEILLMNU unmailable
AABEILLMPP impalpable
AABEILLNRS ballerinas
AABEILLNUV invaluable
AABEILMNTU albuminate
AABEILMNTV ambivalent
AABEILMPRT impartable
AABEILMPSS impassable
AABEILMSUX ambisexual
AABEILNNOT balneation
AABEILNRSY inerasably
AABEILNRUV unvariable
AABEILNSTU unsatiable
AABEILNTTT batteilant
AABEILOPRS parabolise
AABEILOPRZ parabolize
AABEILQRRU quarriable
AABEILRRST arbalister
breastrail
AABEILRSTU tabularise
AABEILRTUZ tabularize
AABEIMPRTV vampire-bat
AABEINORRT aberration
AABEINORTT trabeation
AABEINRRTW water-brain
AABEINSSTT bastnäsite
AABEKKMNRR banker-mark
AABEKLLNNR rannel-balk
rannle-balk
AABEKLLNRT rantle-balk
AABEKLMRRY remarkably
AABEKLRTTW wattlebark
AABEKOPRRT parrot-beak
AABELLLORS albarellos
AABELLLPRY ball-player
AABELLMNTY lamentably
AABELLNPUY unplayable
AABELLNUUV unvaluable
AABELMNORS ransomable
AABELMNOTU ablutomane
AABELMNSUU unamusable
AABELMNTUY untameably
AABELMRSUY measurably
AABELNNOTU unatonable
AABELNORSY reasonably
AABELNOSSY seasonably
AABELNPSSU unpassable
AABELNRSWY answerably
AABELNSUWY unswayable
AABELOORRT elaborator
AABELOPPRV approvable
AABELOPRRT proratable
AABELPPRSY parablepsy
AABELPRSTU pasturable
AABELSTTTU statutable
AABEMRSTTU masturbate
AABFFIILTY affability
AABFLMNOTY flamboyant
AABFLORUVY favourably
AABGGHINSY gay-bashing
AABGGLRRTY braggartly
AABGHILOOP algophobia
AABGIILMNY imaginably
AABGIILNOR △aboriginal
AABGIMNORY Gorbymania
AABGIMNPTW gambit-pawn
AABGIMORTY ambagitory
AABGINNOOT Tobagonian
AABGINNOTW angwantibo
AABGINOORT abrogation
AABGINORTU outbargain
AABGIOSSSS bagassosis
AABGLNRSUU subangular
AABGLNRUUY unarguably
AABGLOORRS algarrobos
AABHHIMTVZ △bathmizvah
AABHHIPSSW bashawship
AABHIINNTT inhabitant
AABHIINOTT habitation
AABHILLTUY habitually
AABHILORTY habilatory
AABHIMMNRS Brahmanism

AABHIMRSTV	△barmitsvah
AABHIMRTVZ	△barmitzvah
AABHIMSSTV	△basmitsvah
AABHIMSTTV	△batmitsvah
AABHIMSTVZ	△basmitzvah
AABHIMTTVZ	△batmitzvah
AABHINOOPP	panophobia
AABHIOOPTU	autophobia
AABHKLNSUY	unshakably
AABHLLLOOU	hullabaloo
AABHLPSSYY	hypabyssal
AABHOPRTUV	vapour-bath
AABHOSTTUW	whatabouts
AABIIILMTY	amiability
AABIIINNPR	bipinnaria
AABIILLSTY	salability
AABIILMTTY	tamability
AABIILNRVY	invariably
AABIILNSTY	insatiably
AABIILRTTY	ratability
AABIILTTXY	taxability
AABIIMNOSS	bonamiasis
AABIINNSSY	Abyssinian
AABIINPRST	bipartisan
AABIINQRUU	ubiquarian
AABIIOPRSS	parabiosis
AABIJNORTU	abjuration
AABIKLMOST	katabolism
AABIKNOPRT	Portakabin®
AABILLMNUY	bimanually
AABILLMPPY	impalpably
AABILLMSST	lamb's-tails
AABILLNNUY	biannually
AABILLNOOT	oblational
AABILLNRUY	binaurally
AABILLNUVY	invaluably
AABILLRUVV	bivalvular
AABILMNOTU	ambulation
AABILMPSSY	impassably
AABILMRSST	strabismal
AABILNOORT	abortional
AABILNOTTU	tabulation
AABILNRTUU	tubularian
AABILOPRST	parabolist
AABILOSTTU	battailous
AABILPRTUY	patibulary
AABIMNOORT	abominator
AABINPRRST	bairn's-part
AABIORRRTT	arbitrator
AABKKOORRU	kookaburra
AABLLMNORY	abnormally
AABLLMOSTU	salbutamol
AABLLNOPST	planoblast
AABLMMOSTY	Amblystoma
AABLMORTUY	ambulatory
AABLNRSTUU	subnatural
AABLOORRTY	laboratory
AABLOPRRRU	bar-parlour
AABLORTTUY	tabulatory
AABLRSSTTU	substratal
AABLSTTTUY	statutably
AABMORRRTW	barrow-tram
AABNOORRTW	narrow-boat
AABORRRSTU	barratrous
AACCCDENOR	accordance
AACCCDNORY	accordancy
AACCCEENPT	acceptance
AACCCEILTT	catalectic
AACCCEIORT	cacciatore
AACCCEKRRT	cat-cracker
AACCCENPTY	acceptancy
AACCCEOSTU	cactaceous
AACCCINRUY	inaccuracy
AACCDDEHKN	cack-handed
AACCDDEISS	caddis-case
AACCDDIILS	didascalic
AACCDDIILT	didactical
AACCDEENNS	ascendance
AACCDEENSU	succedanea
AACCDEERRZ	care-crazed
AACCDEGHRR	charge-card
AACCDEHIRS	saccharide
AACCDEHNOR	archdeacon
AACCDEILNT	accidental
AACCDEILTU	aciculated
AACCDEIMNU	unacademic
AACCDEIORT	coradicate
	co-radicate
AACCDEJNOT	coadjacent
AACCDELLNO	candle-coal
AACCDELLTU	calculated
AACCDELRST	cardcastle
	cat's-cradle
AACCDELSTU	sacculated
AACCDEMNOO	cacodaemon
AACCDENNSY	ascendancy
AACCDERSTY	scaredy-cat
AACCDHIILN	Chalcidian
AACCDHILMO	dochmiacal
AACCDHINRT	catch-drain
AACCDHIORS	saccharoid
AACCDIIRTY	caryatidic
AACCDIISTU	diacaustic
AACCEEELRT	accelerate
AACCEEEPRY	Cyperaceae
AACCEEFFOT	face-to-face
AACCEEFHSS	chasse-café
AACCEEGPRS	scapegrace
AACCEEIMRY	Myricaceae
AACCEEINPU	Punicaceae
AACCEEIRTU	Urticaceae
AACCEELLNT	cancellate
AACCEELLOT	calceolate
AACCEELNRT	accelerant
AACCEENTTU	accentuate
AACCEEORSU	aceraceous
AACCEEORTV	coacervate
AACCEEPRSU	caper-sauce
AACCEFGOSU	cacafuegos
AACCEFIIPT	pacificate
AACCEFLORT	calefactor
AACCEFPRST	spacecraft
AACCEGHOST	stagecoach
AACCEGIORT	Arctogaeic

AACCEGLLNO glance-coal
AACCEHILLM alchemical
AACCEHILMN mechanical
AACCEHINNT cachinnate
AACCEHINNW wanchancie
AACCEHINRS saccharine
AACCEHINRU Chaucerian
AACCEHIRSS saccharise
AACCEHIRSV viscachera
AACCEHIRSZ saccharize
AACCEHLNOT coelacanth
AACCEHNOTY chatoyance
AACCEHORSS saccharose
AACCEHRRTT rat-catcher
AACCEHRRTY charactery
AACCEILLNO cloacaline
AACCEILOPR praecocial
AACCEILPRT Palearctic
AACCEILPTT cataleptic
AACCEINNOT canonicate
AACCEINORV covariance
AACCEINOSU acinaceous
AACCEINPRT pancreatic
AACCEINPTV captivance
AACCEINRTT cantatrice
AACCEINRTU inaccurate
AACCEIORTT aerotactic
AACCEIRRTU caricature
AACCEISTUV accusative
AACCELLNNO cannel-coal
AACCELLOTT toccatella
AACCELLTUY calyculate
AACCELMTUU accumulate
AACCELORSU calcareous
AACCELRTUY accurately
AACCENRSTU crustacean
AACCFHIRSY saccharify
AACCFILLRY farcically
AACCFILRSU fascicular
AACCFINNRS Franciscan
AACCGHHLNS Nachschlag
AACCGHIORY hagiocracy
AACCGHIPRY graphicacy
AACCGHLOSS glass-coach
AACCGHOPRY cacography
AACCHHIINN chinachina
AACCHIIMRS archaicism
AACCHIIRST archaistic
AACCHILNPY chaplaincy
AACCHIMORT achromatic
AACCHINNOR anachronic
AACCHINOPT cataphonic
AACCHLNORY acronychal
AACCHLOPTY Phytolacca
AACCHMORSU Scaramouch
AACCHNOTYY chatoyancy
AACCIILLMT climatical
AACCIILLNU canaliculi
AACCIILORS sacroiliac
AACCIINORV Cavicornia
AACCIINPRT practician
AACCIINPTY incapacity
AACCIINRSS △circassian
AACCIIOSTT stiacciato
AACCILLMOT malo-lactic
AACCILLRUV clavicular
AACCILLTTY tactically
AACCILMMUY immaculacy
AACCILMNOR romancical
AACCILNNOS canonicals
AACCILNNOT Clactonian
AACCILNOOS occasional
AACCILOSTU acoustical
AACCILPRST practicals
AACCILPTTU catapultic
AACCILRTUY articulacy
AACCIMNORS carcinomas
macaronics
AACCINNRSZ cancrizans
AACCINOOPT cacotopian
AACCINORTV vaccinator
AACCINOSTU accusation
anacoustic
AACCINPTTY anaptyctic
AACCINRSTU anacrustic
AACCINSTTY asyntactic
AACCIORTTU autocratic
AACCJJKKYY Jacky-Jacky
AACCKLLMOR alarm-clock
AACCLLOORS sarcocolla
AACCLLORTU calculator
AACCLLRTUU accultural
AACCLNOTTU contactual
AACCLNRRUU caruncular
AACCLORSVY slavocracy
AACCMNNOPY capnomancy
AACCMNOPTT accomptant
AACCMNORTY cartomancy
AACCNNOTTU accountant
AACCNORSST sacrosanct
AACCORSTUY accusatory
AACDDEEHLR decahedral
AACDDEEIMP aide-de-camp
AACDDEEIRT eradicated
AACDDEGINR cardiganed
AACDDEHKKN kack-handed
AACDDEIJTU adjudicate
AACDDEINNR decandrian
AACDDEINSV disadvance
AACDDEKLPS pack-saddle
AACDDELLNS scandalled
AACDDGLNRU grand-ducal
AACDDHKPWY paddy-whack
AACDDIOTTU autodidact
AACDEEEERS △resedaceae
AACDEEEFNS defeasance
AACDEEEMNS damasceene
AACDEEFFLS false-faced
AACDEEFHMS shamefaced
AACDEEFHNR face-harden
AACDEEFPPR paper-faced
AACDEEGMMR decagramme
AACDEEGNOT anecdotage
AACDEEHLRT thread-lace

AACDEEHNRS	case-harden
AACDEEHRTT	tracheated
AACDEEHRTX	ex-cathedra
AACDEEIINS	Sciaenidae
AACDEEIINT	taeniacide
AACDEEILNY	Lycaenidae
AACDEEILRT	dilacerate
AACDEEINRT	deracinate
	ecardinate
AACDEEIPTT	decapitate
AACDEEIRXY	Xyridaceae
AACDEEITTV	deactivate
AACDEELNRR	calendarer
AACDEELNTU	anucleated
AACDEELOSS	escaladoes
AACDEENNRR	ance-errand
AACDEENNTT	attendance
AACDEENRSY	canary-seed
AACDEEOPSS	escapadoes
AACDEESUWY	causewayed
AACDEFFIRT	affricated
AACDEFGLSS	glass-faced
AACDEFINRR	Africander
AACDEFINRU	fricandeau
AACDEFJNSU	Janus-faced
AACDEFLNNO	flanconade
AACDEFLORT	defalcator
AACDEFPSTY	pasty-faced
AACDEFRRTT	tradecraft
AACDEGGIOP	paedagogic
AACDEGHHNR	charge-hand
AACDEGHINS	casinghead
AACDEGINNY	decagynian
AACDEGNORS	gasconader
AACDEHHTTW	deathwatch
AACDEHILNR	Heraclidan
AACDEHIORS	icosahedra
AACDEHIORY	△hyracoidea
AACDEHKPRT	pack-thread
AACDEHLMTY	chlamydate
AACDEHLORT	octahedral
AACDEHNTTU	unattached
AACDEHOOPT	Chaetopoda
AACDEHORTY	cathode-ray
AACDEIILNT	laciniated
AACDEIILRS	radicalise
AACDEIILRZ	radicalize
AACDEIILUV	Aviculidae
AACDEIINRR	irradiance
AACDEIIPRT	paediatric
AACDEIIRRT	irradicate
AACDEIIRTV	divaricate
AACDEIJLTV	adjectival
AACDEILLLN	candelilla
AACDEILMNO	demoniacal
AACDEILMNR	aldermanic
AACDEILMNT	declaimant
AACDEILMRY	acrylamide
AACDEILNNO	Caledonian
AACDEILNOR	androecial
AACDEILNPS	snail-paced
AACDEILNPT	pedantical
AACDEILNSS	scandalise
AACDEILNSZ	scandalize
AACDEILORT	Crotalidae
AACDEIMNRU	admiraunce
AACDEIMNTT	admittance
AACDEIMNTU	acuminated
AACDEIMOPR	paramedico
AACDEINQTU	acquainted
AACDEINQUY	inadequacy
AACDEINRRW	warrandice
AACDEINRST	discarnate
AACDEINSUV	disavaunce
AACDEIORRT	Cortaderia
	eradicator
AACDEIRSTY	caryatides
AACDEJLNTY	adjacently
AACDELMNNU	unmanacled
AACDELMOPR	camelopard
AACDELNSST	sandcastle
AACDELOPRT	leopard-cat
AACDELORRT	declarator
AACDELORST	sacerdotal
AACDELORSU	lardaceous
AACDELOTUV	vacuolated
AACDELPSTU	scapulated
AACDELRTWY	tawdry-lace
AACDEMRRST	master-card
AACDENNTTY	attendancy
AACDENTTUU	unactuated
AACDEOPRRS	radarscope
AACDEORSUV	cadaverous
AACDFHINRT	handicraft
AACDFIILLS	falsidical
AACDFIINOO	aficionado
AACDFIINOR	Africanoid
AACDFIMNRT	frantic-mad
AACDFIMORR	microfarad
AACDGGINRR	drag-racing
AACDGHIIPR	diagraphic
AACDGHRTUW	watchguard
AACDGILMOT	dogmatical
AACDGILOPR	podagrical
AACDGIMORR	cardiogram
AACDGINNPT	tap-dancing
AACDGNRSUY	sugar-candy
AACDGORSTU	coastguard
AACDHIINSY	daisy-chain
AACDHILLMY	chlamydial
AACDHINORT	anthracoid
AACDHIRRSU	Charadrius
AACDHLMNRS	marchlands
AACDHLORSY	day-scholar
AACDHMNORR	orchardman
AACDHNNORY	chardonnay
AACDHOOPPS	Scaphopoda
AACDHOSSTW	shadowcast
AACDIILLRV	larvicidal
AACDIILMRS	Radicalism
AACDIILMRT	matricidal
AACDIILNOP	pinacoidal
AACDIILPRR	parricidal
AACDIILPRT	patricidal

AACDIILRTY radicality
AACDIILSTT diastaltic
AACDIIMNRY △adriamycin®
AACDIINORS Icosandria
AACDIINORT radication
AACDIINRRY irradiancy
AACDIJLLUY Judaically
AACDILLMTU Talmudical
AACDILLNRY cardinally
AACDILMORY myocardial
AACDILNOPS spondaical
AACDILNORS sardonical
AACDILNSTY dynastical
AACDILOPRS sporadical
AACDIMNRTU undramatic
AACDINNORT octandrian
AACDINNOST contadinas
AACDINOOTV advocation
AACDINORRT ration-card
AACDINRRSW Drawcansir
AACDIQRSTU quadratics
AACDJNOTTU coadjutant
AACDLMORRU armour-clad
AACDLNOSSU scandalous
AACDLOSTUY adactylous
AACDMMNNOT commandant
AACDNOORST ostracodan
AACDNOORWY canary-wood
AACDNORRSS crossandra
AACDOOPRRT paradoctor
AACDOOPRST capodastro
AACDOORTVY advocatory
AACDORRSTU scordatura
AACDORSSTW coastwards
AACEEEGHST escheatage
AACEEEGLLN allegeance
AACEEEIOST Isoetaceae
AACEEEIPPR Piperaceae
AACEEEKMPR peacemaker
AACEEELMNP elecampane
AACEEELMRT telecamera
AACEEELNOP Palaeocene
AACEEEOPRT Proteaceae
AACEEFLMSU acesulfame
AACEEFQRSU square-face
AACEEGGHNR gearchange
gear-change
AACEEGHNRR carragheen
AACEEGILLN allegiance
AACEEGILNS Genesiacal
AACEEGLLRS large-scale
AACEEGLNUY launcegaye
AACEEGMOST escamotage
AACEEGMPRS megaparsec
AACEEHHLRT healthcare
AACEEHILMU leuchaemia
AACEEHILNR Heracleian
AACEEHILNT châtelaine
AACEEHINNS seannachie
AACEEHINRY Rhyniaceae
AACEEHKPST cheapskate
AACEEHLMNO chamaeleon
AACEEHLNPT antechapel
AACEEHLPST sphacelate
AACEEHLRTT trachelate
AACEEHLRTY Lythraceae
AACEEHMNRY aerenchyma
AACEEHMPPR paper-mâché
AACEEHNNRT anthracene
AACEEHPPRS paper-chase
AACEEHPRTW peach-water
AACEEIKNPS sinke-a-pace
AACEEILMRS caramelise
AACEEILMRZ caramelize
AACEEILPRT altarpiece
AACEEILRTV lacerative
AACEEILSTT elasticate
AACEEIMMOS Mimosaceae
AACEEIMNPT emancipate
AACEEINPRT Capernaite
paraenetic
AACEEIPPRT appreciate
AACEEIPSSY assay-piece
AACEEIRTTV reactivate
AACEEITUVV evacuative
AACEEKLRRW race-walker
AACEELLLUV valleculae
AACEELLNOT lanceolate
AACEELLORT reallocate
AACEELLPRT carpellate
AACEELMSTU emasculate
AACEELNNRT alternance
AACEELNOSU sauce-alone
AACEELNPPS spaceplane
AACEELNTTT neat-cattle
AACEELOPRT capreolate
AACEELOPRY Pyrolaceae
AACEELOPSU paleaceous
AACEELRTVY acervately
AACEENNRSS arcaneness
AACEENORSU arenaceous
AACEENOSUV avenaceous
AACEEPPRTY peace-party
AACEEPRSTT peat-caster
AACEERSSTV stavesacre
AACEFFGINY faying-face
AACEFFGLOS scaffolage
AACEFFIMNR affirmance
AACEFGINSV face-saving
AACEFGLMOU camouflage
AACEFGNRSU gas-furnace
AACEFGRSTT stagecraft
AACEFHLLNP chapfallen
AACEFHLMNR arch-flamen
AACEFIILLM maleficial
AACEFIILTT facilitate
AACEFIINRS Africanise
AACEFIINRZ Africanize
AACEFIINST fanaticise
AACEFIINTZ fanaticize
AACEFILMOS leaf-mosaic
AACEFINORT arefaction
AACEFINRRU Eurafrican
AACEFJKRRT jack-rafter

AACEFLLLPR cellar-flap
AACEFLLOTW tallow-face
AACEFLMORT malefactor
AACEFLRRTU Fratercula
AACEFLRSTU sucralfate
AACEFMNRSU surfaceman
AACEFRRRTY refractary
AACEFRRTTW watercraft
AACEFRSTTT statecraft
AACEGHILNR alcheringa
AACEGHILNW ca'ing-whale
AACEGHINOR archegonia
AACEGHLRSW scrag-whale
AACEGHMOPR macrophage
AACEGILLMN △magellanic
AACEGILLPR pre-glacial
AACEGILMNN malignance
AACEGILMNT magnetical
AACEGILORT categorial
AACEGILOTZ catalogize
AACEGILPPR paraplegic
AACEGILPRS spagerical
AACEGIMNOR ergomaniac
AACEGIMNPR campaigner
AACEGINRSS Cassegrain
AACEGIPPRR paper-cigar
AACEGJNOTU Conjugatae
AACEGLMNOR carmagnole
AACEGLMORY acromegaly
AACEGLORTU cataloguer
AACEGMNNNO cannon-game
AACEGMNRTY termagancy
AACEGNNORT cartonnage
AACEHHILRR hierarchal
AACEHHKLMS hamshackle
AACEHIIMNR hemicrania
AACEHIIMNT haematinic
AACEHIIPRR hiera-picra
AACEHIKLNN ankle-chain
AACEHILLLY heliacally
AACEHILMMS Michaelmas
AACEHILMPR alphameric
AACEHILMPT alphametic
emphatical
AACEHILNRS Lancashire
AACEHILNTX hexactinal
AACEHILOPT apothecial
AACEHILPRS seraphical
AACEHILPRX hexaplaric
AACEHILPST chaptalise
AACEHILPTT pathetical
AACEHILPTZ chaptalize
AACEHILRTT theatrical
AACEHIMMNN machineman
man-machine
AACEHIMMPR amphimacer
AACEHIMMTT mathematic
AACEHIMNOO haemoconia
AACEHIMNOT theomaniac
AACEHIMNRT carthamine
Rachmanite
AACEHIMNSU naumachies
AACEHINPRS parischane
AACEHINRRT catarrhine
AACEHINRST Charentais
AACEHINRTT anthracite
AACEHINSTU Eustachian
AACEHIOPRX echopraxia
AACEHIORST Oireachtas
AACEHIPRRT arch-pirate
AACEHIPRSS Caesarship
AACEHIRRTV architrave
AACEHJKMMR jackhammer
AACEHJOPRS chaparejos
AACEHKLMRS ramshackle
AACEHKLNRS ranshackle
AACEHKMMRT matchmaker
match-maker
AACEHKMNNY hackneyman
AACEHKMRTW watchmaker
AACEHLLPSU Alcelaphus
AACEHLMUUX chalumeaux
AACEHLNPTY phlyctaena
AACEHLOPSU acephalous
AACEHLOPTY Polychaeta
AACEHLPRRT Petrarchal
AACEHLPRTY archetypal
AACEHMNPRY parenchyma
AACEHMNRTY athermancy
AACEHMNTTT attachment
AACEHMOPRT camphorate
AACEHNNPSU snaphaunce
AACEHNOPTY tachypnoea
AACEHNORTT archontate
AACEHNPRRT Petrarchan
AACEHNPSWW wapenschaw
AACEHOPPRS approaches
AACEHOPRTY apothecary
AACEIILLPR capillaire
AACEIILLRT Lacertilia
AACEIILNRV valerianic
AACEIILPST capitalise
AACEIILPTZ capitalize
AACEIIMNOT emaciation
AACEIIMPRT parmacitie
AACEIINNRV invariance
AACEIINORT acieration
AACEIINPTT anticipate
AACEIINTTV inactivate
vaticinate
AACEIIOPSS Cassiopeia
AACEIIPRRS persicaria
AACEIIPRTT patriciate
AACEIJLMST majestical
AACEIKLLRS rascal-like
AACEIKLRTT racket-tail
AACEILLMNU animalcule
AACEILLNOS escallonia
AACEILLNPT planetical
AACEILLNRT carnallite
AACEILLNTT cantillate
AACEILLOSU alliaceous
AACEILLPRT prelatical
AACEILLPRU Lupercalia

AACEILLRRV varicellar
AACEILLRTU calliature
AACEILLRVY cavalierly
AACEILLSTY salicylate
AACEILMMNO melomaniac
AACEILMMTU △immaculate
AACEILMNOT Celtomania
noematical
AACEILMNPR imparlance
AACEILMNPS campaniles
AACEILMNRT reclaimant
AACEILMNRU unicameral
AACEILMNTU calumniate
AACEILMRRT tricameral
AACEILMRTU tularaemic
AACEILNORT creational
laceration
reactional
AACEILNOST escalation
AACEILNPSU Esculapian
AACEILNPTU paniculate
AACEILNRRT intercalar
AACEILNRTU retinacula
AACEILOOPZ Palaeozoic
AACEILORRT acroterial
AACEILPRST palaestric
AACEILPTTU capitulate
AACEILRTTU articulate
AACEILRTUU auriculate
AACEILSTTT stalactite
AACEILSTTU actualités
AACEILTTTW tattie-claw
AACEIMMPRU △paramecium
AACEIMNNOR Cameronian
AACEIMNNRU un-American
AACEIMNNST anamnestic
AACEIMNORS macaronies
AACEIMNORT cameration
maceration
racemation
AACEIMNORU oceanarium
AACEIMNRSS Saracenism
AACEIMOPST aposematic
AACEIMPRRT parametric
AACEIMSTTT metastatic
AACEINNNTU annunciate
AACEINNOTT catenation
AACEINNPRT pancreatin
AACEINNRTU centaurian
AACEINORTU aeronautic
AACEINORTV acervation
vacationer
AACEINOTUV evacuation
AACEINOTVX excavation
AACEINQRTU reacquaint
AACEINRSST incrassate
AACEINSSST assistance
AACEIORSTT aerostatic
AACEIRTTTV attractive
AACEJKNRTT natterjack
AACEKKTYYY yackety-yak
AACEKLOOPR opera-cloak
AACEKLRRTY tracklayer
AACEKMORRW camerawork
AACELLLORT collateral
AACELLLRST saltcellar
AACELLLRUV vallecular
AACELLNOSW allowances
AACELLPRRY carpellary
AACELMMORS sarcolemma
AACELMNOPT complanate
AACELMNOPZ clonazepam
AACELMOPSU palmaceous
AACELMORST coalmaster
scleromata
AACELMOSUV malvaceous
AACELMOSUY amylaceous
AACELMPRST campestral
AACELMRTUU maculature
AACELNOPTU cantaloupe
AACELNPSTU pulsatance
AACELNRRUV vernacular
AACELNRTTU tentacular
AACELNSSSU casualness
AACELOPPSY △apocalypse
AACELOPRSU acarpelous
AACELORSTY escalatory
AACELORSUU lauraceous
AACELPRTTY calyptrate
AACELSTTUU auscultate
AACEMNOPRS campaneros
mascarpone
AACEMNOPRT compearant
AACEMNOPSW spacewoman
AACEMPRSTU metacarpus
AACENNOOSU anonaceous
AACENNOTTZ canzonetta
AACENNSSTV vacantness
AACENOPPRV approvance
AACENOTTUZ Uto-Aztecan
AACENRTTTX extractant
AACEORRTTT terracotta
AACFFIINPR paraffinic
AACFFIIRRT air-traffic
AACFGIILMN magnifical
AACFGIIMNT Magnificat
AACFGILLNW wall-facing
AACFHKNRST crankshaft
AACFHLLOTW fallow-chat
AACFHLNORW half-a-crown
AACFIIILRT artificial
AACFIILLMN flaminical
AACFIILLSV salvifical
AACFIILNRV acriflavin
AACFIILSTT fatalistic
AACFIIMNRS Africanism
AACFIIMNST fanaticism
AACFIIMORR formicaria
AACFIINOST fasciation
AACFIINPSU piscifauna
AACFIINRST Africanist
AACFILLOSU fallacious
AACFILMORT matrifocal
AACFILNORT fractional

AACFILOPRT	patrifocal
AACFILORST	solfataric
AACFILRTTY	fractality
AACFILTTUY	factuality
AACFIMNORU	microfauna
AACFINORST	fascinator
AACFINORTY	factionary
AACFINOSTT	fantastico
AACFJLMMRY	clamjamfry
AACFLMOORR	macroflora
AACFNRSTTU	surfactant
AACFRRTTYY	arty-crafty
AACGGIILOS	sialagogic
AACGHHINPR	Chinagraph®
AACGHHOPRT	tachograph
AACGHHPRTY	tachygraph
AACGHILLOR	oligarchal
AACGHILNPY	anaglyphic
AACGHILPRY	caligraphy
AACGHILRRT	arthralgic
AACGHILRTV	galravitch
AACGHINORR	chair-organ
AACGHIOPRS	sarcophagi
AACGHLMRUU	chaulmugra
AACGHLSSTW	watchglass
AACGHMMOSY	chasmogamy
AACGHNNSUU	Anschauung
AACGHOPSTY	scatophagy
AACGIILLST	glacialist
AACGIILNOT	glaciation
AACGIILPRS	spagirical
AACGIIMRRT	margaritic
AACGIIMSTT	astigmatic
AACGIKMNRT	tarmacking
AACGILLRTY	tragically
AACGILMNNY	malignancy
AACGILMRTU	Targumical
AACGILNPTY	anaglyptic
	play-acting
AACGILOPRT	proctalgia
AACGILPRSY	spagyrical
AACGIMNORT	morganatic
AACGIMPRST	pragmatics
AACGIMRSTY	magistracy
AACGINORTU	argonautic
AACGINPRSS	panic-grass
AACGINRTTT	attracting
AACGIORSTT	castigator
AACGKRRSSW	grasswrack
AACGLLMOOY	malacology
AACGLNORTU	octangular
AACGLOORTU	coagulator
AACGLOOSTY	astacology
AACHHHIKSU	shakuhachi
AACHHILNPT	naphthalic
AACHHNNPSU	snaphaunch
AACHHOPRTY	Charophyta
AACHIILLOR	allochiria
AACHIILNOP	canophilia
AACHIIMNPS	amphiscian
AACHIINNOT	Antiochian
AACHIINPTT	antipathic
AACHIIRSSU	Saurischia
AACHILLOPT	allopathic
AACHILLORS	Charollais
AACHILMNOR	harmonical
	monarchial
AACHILNNPT	plainchant
AACHILNPRY	chaplainry
AACHILNPSY	Lychnapsia
AACHILOPRY	acarophily
AACHILPRSU	haruspical
AACHIMMNOO	monomachia
AACHIMMNRS	Rachmanism
AACHIMNNOR	anharmonic
	Monarchian
AACHIMNNRU	Manchurian
AACHIMNOOS	monochasia
AACHIMNOPR	anamorphic
AACHIMNORS	maraschino
AACHIMNORT	achromatin
	machinator
AACHIMNORW	chairwoman
AACHIMNPST	phantasmic
AACHIMPRST	pharmacist
AACHIMRRTY	matriarchy
AACHINOPPR	paraphonic
AACHINOPRY	△paronychia
AACHINPSTT	phantastic
AACHINPSWW	wapinschaw
AACHINRSTU	Carthusian
AACHIPRRTY	patriarchy
AACHIPRSTY	parastichy
AACHIRSTTU	autarchist
AACHLLMRSY	lachrymals
AACHLLOPRT	phallocrat
AACHLLORTT	altar-cloth
AACHLMMOOS	school-ma'am
AACHLMRRYY	lachrymary
AACHLNNNOT	nonchalant
AACHLOPPRY	apocryphal
AACHLRRTUY	chartulary
AACHMOOPRT	apochromat
AACHMORTUY	tauromachy
AACHORRSTU	catarrhous
AACHPRSTTW	watchstrap
AACIIIMSST	Asiaticism
AACIILLNNT	anticlinal
AACIILLNOS	salicional
AACIILLOPT	apolitical
AACIILMNOS	simoniacal
AACIILMNPS	panislamic
AACIILMNST	talismanic
AACIILMNTX	anticlimax
AACIILMPRT	primatical
AACIILMPST	capitalism
AACIILNNOR	Carolinian
AACIILNNST	annalistic
AACIILNOPT	capitolian
AACIILNORS	salicornia
AACIILNOST	antisocial
AACIILNRTT	triactinal
AACIILPPST	papistical
AACIILPSTT	capitalist

AACIILRRTU urticarial
AACIILRSTT artistical
AACIIMNRST anti-racism
AACIIMNSTV Vaticanism
AACIIMOSTX axiomatics
AACIINNPTT anticipant
AACIINNRRT △trinacrian
AACIINOPRT aprication
AACIINOPTT capitation
AACIINORTV △victoriana
AACIINOTTV activation
cavitation
AACIINRSTT anti-racist
AACIINSTTT antistatic
AACIINSTTV Vaticanist
AACIIORSUV avaricious
AACIJLNOTU jaculation
AACIKLMMRS Lamarckism
AACILLMORT matrilocal
AACILLMOSY mosaically
AACILLNOOT allocation
AACILLNOPT Platonical
AACILLNORS rascallion
AACILLNTUY nautically
AACILLOOPR coprolalia
AACILLOPRT allopatric
patrilocal
AACILLSTTY statically
AACILMNNOT monactinal
AACILMNORT romantical
AACILMNOST monastical
AACILMNOTU maculation
AACILMNOTY claymation
AACILMORRT lacrimator
AACILMOSTU calamitous
AACILMPPRY paralympic
AACILMRRTU matricular
AACILNNOSV Sclavonian
AACILNNRTY tyrannical
AACILNNTUY unanalytic
AACILNOOTV vocational
AACILNOPPT panoptical
AACILNOPRS parsonical
AACILNOPTY nyctalopia
AACILNORSS scansorial
AACILNORTT tractional
AACILNPTTU capitulant
AACILOORRT oratorical
AACILOPPRT applicator
AACILOPSTU apolaustic
AACILOPTTU autoptical
AACILORRTU curatorial
AACILPRRSU spiracular
AACILPRRTU particular
AACILPRTUY capitulary
AACILTTTUY tactuality
AACIMMMNOU ammoniacum
AACIMMNNOO monomaniac
AACIMNNOXY axinomancy
AACIMNOOPS opsomaniac
AACIMNOPRY pyromaniac
AACIMNPRTU pancratium
AACIMOPRSU rampacious
AACIMORRST Camorrista
AACIMORSTT masticator
AACIMRRTUU atracurium
AACINNOORT octonarian
AACINNORTT incantator
AACINNOSTT Constantia
AACINNQTUU unacquaint
AACINOOPTT coaptation
AACINORSTT castration
AACINORTTT attraction
AACINORTUY auctionary
cautionary
AACINPRSTT pancratist
practisant
AACIOOPPRT apotropaic
AACIORRSTT aristocrat
AACIOSSUVX saxicavous
AACIPRSSTT Spartacist
AACJKRSSTW jack-straws
AACJLMRSUU majuscular
AACJLORTUY jaculatory
AACKNORSVW canvas-work
AACLLORRUY oracularly
AACLLRSUVY vascularly
AACLMMOPSY mycoplasma
AACLMNNOSW clanswoman
AACLMOPRSS sarcoplasm
AACLMORRTY lacrymator
AACLNNORTU connatural
AACLOOPRRT parrot-coal
AACLOORRTU coloratura
AACLOPRRRU parlour-car
AACMNNOPRU manna-croup
AACMNOPRUY paramouncy
AACMNRSSUU cassumunar
AACMOOPRRT comparator
AACMOORRTU coat-armour
AACNNNOSTT constantan
AACNORRSTT transactor
AACNORRSTW narrowcast
AACOOPPRSU apocarpous
AACOOPSSTT capotastos
AACOPRRSTU artocarpus
AACORRSTTT stratocrat
AADDDDGNRY granddaddy
AADDDEEHHR hard-headed
AADDDEEHRT death-adder
AADDDEELLR all-dreaded
AADDDEELPT addle-pated
AADDDEELUV value-added
AADDDEHHNR hard-handed
AADDDEILPR paradiddle
AADDDEILRT taradiddle
AADDDHNNYY handy-dandy
AADDEEEHKW weak-headed
AADDEEFHIR fair-headed
AADDEEGHST stag-headed
AADDEEHHOR hoar-headed
AADDEEHHOT head-to-head
AADDEEHHST death's-head
AADDEEHILN nail-headed

AADDEEHIMN maidenhead
AADDEEHIRR drearihead
AADDEEHKNW weak-handed
AADDEEHMNY many-headed
AADDEEHNNT neat-handed
AADDEEHNRR hard-earned
AADDEEHNRV verandahed
AADDEEHORR roadheader
AADDEEHRST sad-hearted
AADDEEIRST desiderata
AADDEEIRWY day-wearied
AADDEEISTT state-aided
AADDEEKLMR madder-lake
AADDEEMRRY daydreamer
AADDEEPPRT preadapted
AADDEFHNST fast-handed
AADDEFLSST saddle-fast
AADDEGGLRY ragged-lady
AADDEGGNRT egg-and-dart
AADDEGHLNR glad-hander
AADDEGHNOR dragonhead
AADDEGIILT digladiate
AADDEGIRRT tardigrade
AADDEGMNOR Armageddon
AADDEGNNOR dragonnade
AADDEHIILP Diadelphia
AADDEHIMNN handmaiden
AADDEHNRUZ unhazarded
AADDEHRSTW deathwards
AADDEIILPT dilapidate
AADDEIIMNP indapamide
AADDEIMNTT additament
AADDEIRSUY Dasyuridae
AADDELMRSS maladdress
AADDELPRRT trap-ladder
AADDENPRTU pandurated
AADDGIILLO diallagoid
AADDGILMOY amygdaloid
AADDGNNRST grandstand
AADDHHINNN hand-in-hand
AADDHHNNOT hand-to-hand
AADDHNNRSY shandrydan
AADDIILNOT additional
AADDIIMNNY didynamian
AADDIMNRTY dynamitard
AADDINORRT ritardando
AADDLNOOSW sandalwood
AADEEEGLMR game-dealer
AADEEELNPT peel-and-eat
AADEEELRSY day-release
AADEEFGLRT deflagrate
AADEEFILRR fair-leader
AADEEFLNRT trade-falne
AADEEGGOPU paedagogue
AADEEGINYZ Zygaenidae
AADEEGIRTV variegated
AADEEGNRRU daguerrean
AADEEGNRST degreasant
AADEEGNRTU guaranteed
AADEEGOPRT pagoda-tree
AADEEHHLRX hexahedral
AADEEHHMMR hammerhead
AADEEHKNSS snake's-head
AADEEHLNVY heavy-laden
AADEEHLORS Rhoeadales
AADEEHLPPT lappet-head
AADEEHLRTT rattle-head
AADEEHMRST headmaster
head-stream
AADEEHMRVY heavy-armed
AADEEHNPRT pentahedra
AADEEHNRVW heavenward
AADEEHPPRS pear-shaped
AADEEHQRSU headsquare
squarehead
AADEEHRRTT tetrahedra
AADEEIILMN Limnaeidae
AADEEILMNN Madelenian
AADEEILMNT delaminate
AADEEILNNR adrenaline
AADEEILNST desalinate
AADEEILRSW ladieswear
AADEEILRTV revalidate
AADEEIMNOT Nematoidea
AADEEIMNOU eudaemonia
AADEEIMNRU Muraenidae
AADEEIMPRS emparadise
AADEEIMPRT pre-Adamite
AADEEINNNR Enneandria
AADEEINQTU inadequate
AADEEINRRS Serranidae
AADEEIORST Asteroidea
AADEEIPRST deaspirate
AADEEIQTUV adequative
AADEEIRRWW war-wearied
AADEEIRSTT asteriated
AADEEKNNUW unawakened
AADEELLLMT lamellated
AADEELLLPR paralleled
AADEELLPPR apparelled
AADEELLPRY playleader
AADEELLRRS serradella
AADEELNNNU unannealed
AADEELNNRT △neandertal
AADEELNRSX alexanders
AADEELQTUY adequately
AADEELRSSW easselward
AADEELRTTU adulterate
AADEEMNNOY anadyomene
AADEEMNSSZ amazedness
AADEEMPRRT Dermaptera
AADEEMQRSU masquerade
AADEEMQSTU desquamate
AADEENPPSU suppedanea
unappeased
AADEENSTVZ Zend-Avesta
AADEENTTTU attenuated
AADEEORTTY ready-to-eat
AADEEPRSTY paederasty
AADEFFNORT fore-and-aft
AADEFGRRTU after-guard
AADEFHIIRR fair-haired
AADEFHLNOZ half-a-dozen
AADEFHLNRT fatherland

Words marked △ may be spelled also with a capital letter

AADEFIKNRR Afrikander
AADEFIMNOT defamation
AADEFINNRR farrandine
AADEFINTTU infatuated
AADEFKLRSW △dewar-flask
AADEFMORTY defamatory
AADEFRRSTW afterwards
AADEGGILLT daggle-tail
AADEGGILNT gangliated
AADEGGINRS aggrandise
AADEGGINRZ aggrandize
AADEGHHINS shanghaied
AADEGHHIRS shag-haired
AADEGHIINR hearing-aid
AADEGHNNRT Ndrangheta
'Ndrangheta
AADEGHNOTY death-agony
AADEGIINTV indagative
AADEGILLNR grenadilla
AADEGILMNR lead-arming
AADEGILPRR paraglider
AADEGILRST saltigrade
AADEGILTTY agitatedly
AADEGIMNPR map-reading
AADEGIMNRS smaragdine
AADEGIMNRT marginated
AADEGIMRST smaragdite
AADEGINOTT toad-eating
AADEGINRRS disarrange
AADEGIOPRR radiopager
AADEGIPRRS disparager
AADEGKNPRT peg-tankard
AADEGLLNRU eglandular
AADEGLNNRS rangelands
AADEGLNOPR pedal-organ
AADEGLNQRU quadrangle
AADEGLNRTU granulated
AADEGMRRTU dramaturge
AADEGNNRRU unarranged
AADEGNORSS Sangradoes
AADEGNSSUU unassuaged
AADEGOORVV avvogadore
AADEHIILOT Haliotidae
AADEHIIMNR maidenhair
AADEHIINRT antheridia
AADEHIIPRS sphaeridia
AADEHILMRT diathermal
AADEHILNRT Thailander
AADEHILORR diarrhoeal
AADEHILRSW hawser-laid
AADEHINNRX hexandrian
AADEHINOTZ Zoanthidae
AADEHINPRT Heptandria
AADEHINRSS hansardise
AADEHINRSZ hansardize
AADEHINRTV Theravadin
AADEHIOPST Hitopadesa
AADEHJNRRW Wanderjahr
AADEHLLMRS marshalled
AADEHLNNPR panhandler
AADEHLRSSY harassedly
AADEHMMMNO Mahommedan
Mohammedan
AADEHMMMNU Muhammedan
AADEHMNRST master-hand
AADEHNSSTV handstaves
AADEHPRSST star-shaped
AADEHRRSTW earthwards
AADEIILNOT ideational
AADEIILNTV invalidate
AADEIIMNNR Amerindian
AADEIIMNNT diamantine
maintained
AADEIIMNST disanimate
mediastina
AADEIIMPRS imparadise
AADEIIMRTV admirative
AADEIINNTV vanadinite
AADEIINORT eradiation
AADEIINPTV inadaptive
AADEIINRST asteridian
AADEIIRRTT triradiate
AADEIKSSTU diaskeuast
AADEILLMMT mamillated
AADEILLMTU Adullamite
AADEILLPPT papillated
AADEILLQSU quesadilla
AADEILLRRS serradilla
AADEILLRTU laurdalite
AADEILMMST Lammas-tide
AADEILMNNR mainlander
AADEILMNNT nidamental
AADEILMNOS Salmonidae
AADEILMNTY animatedly
AADEILMORT tailor-made
AADEILMRTX taxidermal
AADEILNNSW Waldensian
AADEILNPRS palisander
AADEILNPRT land-pirate
AADEILNRSU unsalaried
AADEILNRTW land-waiter
AADEILNSSU unassailed
AADEILNSTU andalusite
AADEILOPSS palisadoes
AADEILORRR railroader
AADEILORST asteroidal
AADEILPPRS disapparel
AADEILPTVY adaptively
AADEIMMNOT ammoniated
AADEIMNNSW swan-maiden
AADEIMNNTU unanimated
AADEIMNRTV animadvert
AADEINNOPT △antipodean
AADEINNPRT Pentandria
AADEINNQRU quadrennia
AADEINNRTY Tyrannidae
AADEINORTY arytaenoid
AADEINPQSU pasquinade
AADEINPRSU unparadise
AADEINPTTY day-patient
AADEINQTTU antiquated
AADEINRRTT Tetrandria
AADEINSTTU unsatiated

AADEIOPQRU radiopaque
AADEIORSTV advisorate
AADEIPPTTT pit-a-patted
AADEIPRSST disparates
AADEISTTVV devastavit
AADEKKNRST stark-naked
AADEKNPTTU put-and-take
AADEKNRSTT start-naked
AADELLMNRS mallanders
AADELLMNRY aldermanly
AADELLNPPU unappalled
AADELLNPTT platteland
AADELLNSUV land-values
AADELLRTTY tally-trade
AADELMNPTU datum-plane
paludament
AADELMNRRY aldermanry
AADELMORST loadmaster
AADELNNOST stand-alone
AADELNNSUY unanalysed
AADELNNUYZ unanalyzed
AADELNRTTU adulterant
AADELNRTUY day-neutral
AADELORTTX extradotal
AADEMMNSSU mandamuses
AADEMMORTU trou-madame
AADEMNOORS enamorados
AADEMNORTY amendatory
AADEMNQRUU quadrumane
AADEMRRSTY yard-master
AADENNRTTU denaturant
AADENQRSTU quadrantes
AADENRSTTU transudate
AADEOPRRUX paradoxure
AADEORSTTV devastator
AADEQRRTUU quadrature
AADEQRRTUY quarter-day
AADFFGHNSY shandygaff
AADFFHNSST handstaffs
AADFGLNOPR flap-dragon
AADFHLLLOR half-dollar
AADFIILMPT palmatifid
AADFIILNTU latifundia
AADFLNRSTT strandflat
AADGGILMNY damagingly
AADGHINSWY washing-day
AADGHIOPRR radiograph
AADGHIOPRU audiograph
AADGHIPRSY dysgraphia
AADGHLLNOP hand-gallop
AADGHMNRTU draughtman
AADGIIIRSS giardiasis
AADGIIMNRR ram-raiding
AADGIINNOT indagation
AADGIINNRT grant-in-aid
AADGIINNSU ungainsaid
AADGIINOTV divagation
AADGIJNORU jaguarondi
AADGIJNRUU jaguarundi
AADGIKMNOR road-making
AADGILLNOY diagonally
AADGILMNSU salmagundi
AADGILMRSU gradualism
AADGILNOOT odontalgia
AADGILNOSY disanalogy
AADGILNPPU applauding
AADGILORTY gladiatory
AADGILRSTU gradualist
AADGILRTUY graduality
AADGIMNRST magistrand
AADGINOPST spatangoid
AADGINORTU graduation
AADGINORTY indagatory
AADGLMNSUY salmagundy
AADGMNNORT Montagnard
AADGMRRTUY dramaturgy
AADGNNOPRS snapdragon
AADGOOPRST Gastropoda
AADHIIOPRS aphrodisia
AADHIKRSWW awkwardish
AADHILLMOO homaloidal
AADHILLNPS Laplandish
AADHILRTWW withdrawal
AADHIMNNOS madonnaish
AADHIMNORY hydromania
AADHINOOPR adiaphoron
AADHINOPSU diaphanous
AADHINORSW rain-shadow
AADHIRRSTY dysarthria
AADHLLLLNO allhallond
AADHOOPRRT Arthropoda
AADIIINSTT antiaditis
AADIIKLNOP pinakoidal
AADIILLNST tillandsia
AADIILNOPT lapidation
AADIILNOTT dilatation
AADIILNOTV validation
AADIILPRST lapidarist
triapsidal
AADIILQRUV quadrivial
AADIIMNOPS dipsomania
AADIIMNORT admiration
AADIINNRRT triandrian
AADIINNSST Sandinista
AADIINORSU Dinosauria
AADIIOPRST parasitoid
AADIIPRSST aspidistra
AADIIRRSTV Stradivari
AADIJNORTU adjuration
AADIKMRSVZ vizard-mask
AADILLMOPS plasmodial
AADILLMORS armadillos
AADILLOPSU palladious
AADILNOPRY Polyandria
AADILNORTU durational
AADILNSSUW duniwassal
AADILPRRTU ultra-rapid
AADIMNNOOX Monaxonida
AADIMNOSTY mastodynia
AADIMNPRTY pantrymaid
AADIMOPPRU parapodium
AADINNNOST andantinos
AADINORRUV ouvirandra
AADIOPRSSU Sauropsida

AADIOPRSTX	paradoxist
AADIORSTVY	advisatory
AADIQRRTUX	quadratrix
AADJMNNPRU	panjandrum
AADJORRTUY	adjuratory
AADKLNORUW	walk-around
AADLMNNNOS	no-man's-land
AADLMNNRUY	laundry-man
AADLMNORTU	Laundromat®
AADLNOQRSU	squadronal
AADMNOOOTT	odontomata
AADMNOORSU	anadromous
AADMNPSSUY	ampussy-and
AADNOOPPSW	sappanwood
AADNOPRRUW	wraparound
AADOPPRSST	strappados
AAEEEGGRTX	exaggerate
AAEEEGLNOP	Palaeogene
AAEEEGLNRT	generalate
AAEEEGLSST	easselgate
AAEEEGNRRW	wage-earner
AAEEEHRSST	heartsease
	heart's-ease
AAEEELNPRS	paraselene
AAEEELRSTT	real-estate
AAEEEMORRT	araeometer
AAEEEPRSTX	exasperate
AAEEERSSTV	asseverate
AAEEFGIMRT	after-image
AAEEFGINTU	taeniafuge
AAEEFGLLLT	flagellate
AAEEFGMRSW	sewage-farm
AAEEFHHLST	leaf-sheath
AAEEFHHSTW	wheatsheaf
AAEEFHRSTV	aftershave
AAEEFKKQSU	Kafkaesque
AAEEFKMMRR	frame-maker
AAEEFLRSST	aftersales
AAEEFRSTTT	aftertaste
AAEEGGIPRT	arpeggiate
AAEEGGPPRU	paper-gauge
AAEEGHLNOT	halogenate
AAEEGHLOPS	esophageal
AAEEGHLPRY	harpy-eagle
AAEEGHMNOP	Phenogamae
AAEEGILMNN	emalangeni
AAEEGILNRV	evangeliar
AAEEGILNTT	gelatinate
AAEEGIMNRT	emarginate
AAEEGIMRRR	remarriage
AAEEGIMSSX	Sexagesima
AAEEGINPRT	repaginate
AAEEGINRTV	vegetarian
AAEEGIOPRT	Areopagite
AAEEGKMRRV	grave-maker
AAEEGLMNOP	epagomenal
AAEEGLMPRS	palm-grease
AAEEGLNNNO	enneagonal
AAEEGLNRTW	angel-water
AAEEGMMNNT	management
AAEEGMMORR	aerogramme
	aérogramme
AAEEGMNRSS	manageress
AAEEGNPRRR	prearrange
AAEEGNRSXY	sexagenary
AAEEGNSSSV	savageness
AAEEGQRRTU	quarterage
AAEEHHILRT	hartie-hale
AAEEHILRTX	exhilarate
AAEEHIMPRY	hyperaemia
AAEEHIMPTT	epithemata
AAEEHIMRTT	Metatheria
AAEEHINSST	anesthesia
AAEEHIPRSS	aphaeresis
AAEEHIRSTW	washeteria
AAEEHKLORT	oak-leather
AAEEHKQRTU	earthquake
	heart-quake
AAEEHLLRTW	all-weather
AAEEHLPRTT	earth-plate
AAEEHMNORR	amenorrhea
AAEEHMNRTW	weatherman
AAEEHMPRST	metaphrase
AAEEHRRSTW	shearwater
AAEEHRRTTW	heartwater
AAEEIKLMNS	seamanlike
AAEEILLLRV	lavallière
AAEEILLQTU	illaqueate
AAEEILLRTT	alliterate
AAEEILMNNS	Melanesian
AAEEILMORT	ameliorate
AAEEILNPRT	penetralia
AAEEILPRTU	eutrapelia
AAEEILRTTV	alterative
AAEEILRTVX	relaxative
AAEEILTUVV	evaluative
AAEEIMNRRW	Weimaraner
AAEEINPPRV	papaverine
AAEEINPRRT	pea-trainer
AAEEINPRSS	paraenesis
AAEEINPRST	inseparate
AAEEINSTUV	nauseative
AAEEIPPRRS	reappraise
AAEEIPQRTU	equiparate
AAEEIPRRTT	repatriate
AAEEIPRRTV	reparative
AAEEIPRSTV	separative
AAEEIPRTTX	expatriate
AAEEJNPQSU	Japanesque
AAEEJNPRSY	Japanesery
AAEEJPRRSW	jasperware
AAEEKLLRWY	lake-lawyer
AAEEKLPRSV	parkleaves
AAEEKMPPRR	paper-maker
AAEEKQRTUW	waterquake
AAEELLMSST	matellasse
AAEELLPRTY	plate-layer
AAEELLTTTT	tattle-tale
AAEELMNOPT	Ptolemaean
AAEELMNRST	man-stealer
AAEELMPRRT	marprelate
AAEELMPSTY	Sympetalae
AAEELMRRTT	tetrameral
AAEELNNPTU	pennatulae

AAEELNPRRT	parenteral
AAEELNPRTT	tea-planter
AAEELOPPTY	palaeotype
AAEELORSTY	araeostyle
AAEELPRSTY	separately
AAEELPRTTT	rattle-pate
AAEEMMNRRT	rearmament
AAEEMNNSSU	amanuenses
AAEEMNSSTT	estatesman
AAEEMORRTY	araeometry
AAEEMRSSTT	stearsmate
AAEEMSSSTT	metastases
AAEENNPRSY	Pyrenaeans
AAEENORRYY	year-on-year
AAEENQRTTU	quaternate
AAEENRRTTT	retreatant
AAEENRSSTV	tsesarevna
AAEENRSTTY	asynartete
AAEEPPRSTW	wastepaper
AAEEPRSSTW	pease-straw
AAEFFFTTTU	tuftaffeta
AAEFFGILNY	yaffingale
AAEFFHRSTT	aftershaft
AAEFGGHRTU	fraughtage
AAEFGIISTT	fastigiate
AAEFGINNPR	frangipane
AAEFGKLMRR	marker-flag
AAEFGLLLNT	flagellant
AAEFGLMNRT	fragmental
AAEFGRRSST	aftergrass
AAEFHINRTT	faint-heart
AAEFHLLRYY	half-yearly
AAEFHPRSST	spear-shaft
AAEFILLNRX	fraxinella
AAEFILMNOU	meiofaunal
AAEFINPRST	afterpains
AAEFKMNRRT	tank-farmer
AAEFLLNSTU	fustanella
AAEFMRRSTW	afterswarm
AAEGGGLNUV	luggage-van
AAEGGILLRV	gillravage
AAEGGILNSW	Glaswegian
AAEGGILOSU	sialagogue
AAEGGILRRV	gilravager
AAEGGINORT	agrégation
AAEGHHINRS	shanghaier
AAEGHILMPS	phlegmasia
AAEGHILNPR	nephralgia
AAEGHILORT	hagiolater
AAEGHILPSY	hypalgesia
AAEGHILRTU	gaultheria
AAEGHIMMNO	hemangioma
AAEGHINNNS	shenanigan
AAEGHINNXY	hexagynian
AAEGHINPTY	Heptagynia
AAEGHLNNRS	Langerhans
AAEGHLNOPT	heptagonal
AAEGHLNPRY	pharyngeal
AAEGHMNOPR	anemograph
	phanerogam
AAEGHNPPRT	pentagraph
AAEGHOPRRY	aerography
	areography
AAEGHRSSSV	shave-grass
AAEGIILLNT	genitalial
AAEGIILLNV	villainage
AAEGIILPRS	plagiarise
AAEGIILPRZ	plagiarize
AAEGIIMNRR	inmarriage
AAEGIINNTV	invaginate
AAEGIINRTT	ingratiate
AAEGIKMMRR	magi-marker
AAEGILLMNT	ligamental
AAEGILLMQU	maquillage
AAEGILLNOT	allegation
AAEGILLPRS	aspergilla
AAEGILLRSU	sugarallie
AAEGILMNRT	martingale
AAEGILMSTT	stalagmite
AAEGILNNTT	tangential
AAEGILNOPT	palagonite
AAEGILNRST	sternalgia
AAEGILNRSV	galvaniser
AAEGILNRVZ	galvanizer
AAEGILNSWX	sealing-wax
AAEGILOPRS	paralogise
AAEGILOPRZ	paralogize
AAEGILPRTY	apterygial
AAEGIMNRRS	misarrange
AAEGIMNRRV	margravine
AAEGIMPRST	pragmatise
	Sparagmite
AAEGIMPRTZ	pragmatize
AAEGIMRSTT	magistrate
	sterigmata
AAEGINNOST	antagonise
AAEGINNOTZ	antagonize
AAEGINNPTY	Pentagynia
AAEGINNSTU	nauseating
AAEGINOPRT	paragonite
AAEGINORRT	arragonite
AAEGINPRST	paste-grain
AAEGINRTTV	Gravettian
AAEGINRTTY	Tetragynia
AAEGINRTUU	inaugurate
AAEGINSTTT	tea-tasting
AAEGIORRTV	variegator
AAEGIRRSTV	stravaiger
AAEGKLLRVW	gravel-walk
AAEGKLMNOS	maskalonge
AAEGKMNNOS	maskanonge
AAEGLLPSST	plate-glass
AAEGLMORSU	megalosaur
AAEGLNNOPT	pentagonal
AAEGLNORTT	tetragonal
AAEGLNRRTU	granulater
AAEGLOPRSS	opera-glass
AAEGLRSSTW	waterglass
AAEGMMPPUW	wampumpeag
AAEGMOPRSU	rampageous
AAEGNOPRST	apron-stage
AAEGOPPRRT	rapportage
AAEGOPRTTY	Apterygota

AAEHHILLLU halleluiah
AAEHHJLLLU hallelujah
AAEHHLNOPY hyalophane
AAEHHLPRTY hypaethral
AAEHHMNSTU Haemanthus
AAEHIILMNS leishmania
AAEHIILNNT annihilate
AAEHIILTWW wait-a-while
AAEHIIMNOP hemianopia
AAEHIINOPT Aethiopian
AAEHIINPPT epitaphian
AAEHIIRRRS hair-raiser
AAEHIKMNSZ Ashkenazim
AAEHIKRRST hairstreak
AAEHILLOPT palaeolith
AAEHILNNOT anhelation
AAEHILNOTX exhalation
AAEHILNRTX exhilarant
AAEHIMMNOT methomania
AAEHIMNPRU Amphineura
AAEHIMNPRY hypermania
AAEHIMNPSS seamanship
AAEHIMNPST phantasime
AAEHIMNSTY myasthenia
AAEHIMOPXY hypoxaemia
AAEHIMOSST haematosis
AAEHIMRSTU amateurish
AAEHIMSTTU thaumasite
AAEHINNORV Hanoverian
AAEHIPRSST parathesis
AAEHIPSTXY asphyxiate
AAEHISTTTW tattie-shaw
AAEHISTTUW Watteauish
AAEHKLLMRT market-hall
AAEHLLMNOY hyalomelan
AAEHLLMRRS marshaller
AAEHLLRSWW wall-washer
AAEHLMRTTT lattermath
AAEHLNOPSY synaloepha
AAEHLNRRTX xenarthral
AAEHLPSSTU sulphatase
AAEHLPSTTU spathulate
AAEHMNORRT marathoner
AAEHMNORTW earthwoman
woman-hater
AAEHMNRSST harassment
AAEHMNRSTV harvestman
AAEHMORTTX metathorax
AAEHMOSTTY stay-at-home
AAEHMPRSTT metaphrast
AAEHNOPRST anastrophe
AAEHNOPSWW weapon-shaw
AAEHNPPSWW wappenshaw
AAEHNPRSST trans-shape
AAEHNPRSTY pheasantry
AAEHPPRSSY paraphyses
AAEIIILNST Italianise
AAEIIILNTZ Italianize
AAEIIKLLNS alkalinise
AAEIIKLLNZ alkalinize
AAEIILLPTV palliative
AAEIILMMRT immaterial
AAEIILMNRS laminarise
seminarial
AAEIILMNRT Terminalia
AAEIILMNRZ laminarize
AAEIILMPTV ampliative
AAEIILMSST assimilate
AAEIILNNOT alienation
alineation
AAEIILNNST salientian
AAEIILNPST sapiential
AAEIILNSTV insalivate
AAEIILPRST partialise
patrialise
AAEIILPRTZ partialize
patrialize
AAEIIMNNNR Riemannian
AAEIIMNNRS seminarian
AAEIIMNNRT maintainer
AAEIIMPPRR primiparae
AAEIINRTUV univariate
AAEIIPPRSV appraisive
AAEIIPRSST parasitise
AAEIIPRSTZ parasitize
AAEIJLMNNV javelin-man
AAEIJLNNUV Juvenalian
AAEIKLMNOT Keltomania
AAEIKLMNOZ Amazon-like
AAEIKLMORT tailormake
AAEIKMRSST samarskite
AAEIKNNNOT Neo-Kantian
AAEIKNPRST painstaker
AAEILLLMUX maxillulae
AAEILLLRST saltarelli
AAEILLMNOT malleation
AAEILLMNPT palliament
AAEILLMPRX premaxilla
AAEILLMRTY materially
AAEILLNORT relational
AAEILLNRTU unilateral
AAEILLNSTW Eatanswill
AAEILLORTV alleviator
AAEILLRRTT trilateral
AAEILLRTTY laterality
AAEILLRTVY varietally
AAEILMMNNT immanental
AAEILMNNSU semi-annual
AAEILMNPRT △parliament
AAEILMNPTU manipulate
AAEILMNRRT interramal
AAEILMNRSU aneurismal
AAEILMNRTT alternatim
AAEILMNRTU unmaterial
AAEILMNRTY alimentary
AAEILMNRUV Verulamian
AAEILMNSST assailment
AAEILMORRT Mariolater
AAEILMPRRT premarital
AAEILMPSST metaplasis
AAEILMRSST mare's-tails
AAEILNNOPT △neapolitan
AAEILNNOTV venational
AAEILNNRTU Laurentian

AAEILNNRTW Lawrentian
AAEILNOORT areolation
AAEILNOPRS personalia
AAEILNOPST spaniolate
AAEILNORST senatorial
AAEILNORTT alteration
AAEILNORTU laureation
AAEILNORTV venatorial
Voltairean
AAEILNORTX relaxation
AAEILNOTTX exaltation
AAEILNOTUV evaluation
AAEILNPRST psalterian
AAEILNRSTT tantaliser
AAEILNRSTU naturalise
AAEILNRTTZ tantalizer
AAEILNRTUZ naturalize
AAEILOPRRT praetorial
AAEILOQRTU equatorial
AAEILORRTT retaliator
AAEILPPRSS paralipses
AAEILPPRST epiplastra
AAEILPPSUV applausive
AAEILQRSSU square-sail
AAEILRRSTU Sertularia
AAEILRSTTU australite
AAEILSTUXY asexuality
AAEIMMNORT metromania
AAEIMMNRST mainstream
AAEIMMNTTY Tammanyite
AAEIMMRSTU amateurism
AAEIMNNOPR Pomeranian
praenomina
AAEIMNNOSY mayonnaise
AAEIMNNOTT antimonate
AAEIMNNSSU amanuensis
AAEIMNNTTT attainment
AAEIMNOORT erotomania
AAEIMNOPPT Papiamento
AAEIMNORTX examinator
AAEIMNPPRS panspermia
AAEIMNPRTZ nitrazepam
AAEIMNQSTU antimasque
AAEIMNRTTT antimatter
AAEIMPRSST separatism
AAEIMQRSTU marquisate
AAEIMQRSUU seaquarium
AAEIMRSTTU traumatise
AAEIMRTTUZ traumatize
AAEIMSSSTT metastasis
AAEINNNOTX annexation
AAEINNNTTU annuntiate
AAEINNORRT enarration
AAEINNQRTU quarantine
AAEINNRSST Stannaries
AAEINNRTUV avanturine
AAEINOPRRT praetorian
reparation
AAEINOPRST separation
AAEINOPSST passionate
AAEINPRSTU Pasteurian
AAEINRRSTW warrantise
AAEINRRTTZ tartrazine
AAEINRTTTU attainture
AAEIOPRTTX expatiator
AAEIOPSSTT apostatise
AAEIOPSTTZ apostatize
AAEIPRRSTX separatrix
AAEIPRSSTT separatist
AAEKMMRSST mass-market
AAEKMRSSTT taskmaster
AAEKRRSTUU sauerkraut
AAELLLLPRY parallelly
AAELLLMNOS salmonella
AAELLLNPRU unparallel
AAELLLORST saltarello
AAELLMNRTY maternally
AAELLMORTT martellato
AAELLMORZZ mozzarella
AAELLMPRTY malapertly
AAELLNOSSY seasonally
AAELLNPPRW parpen-wall
AAELLNPRTY parentally
paternally
AAELLNPSTY pleasantly
AAELLRSTTT Tattersall
AAELMNNORT ornamental
AAELMNNRTU unmaternal
AAELMNOPPW apple-woman
AAELMNOPSU menopausal
AAELMNOSSW saleswoman
AAELMNRRTW trawlerman
AAELMNRSUY aneurysmal
AAELMOOPTZ Pelmatozoa
AAELMORRSS serrasalmo
AAELMORRTY Maryolater
AAELMRRTUX extramural
AAELNNNPRU penannular
AAELNNPRTU unparental
AAELNNPSTU pennatulas
unpleasant
AAELNORRTT alternator
AAELNORSTT altar-stone
AAELNPPRTY apparently
AAELNPRRSU suprarenal
AAELNPRSTT transeptal
AAELNPRSTY pleasantry
AAELNRSTUV transvalue
AAELOOPSTT apostolate
AAELORRSTX extra-solar
AAELORRTTV travelator
AAELORSTTZ lazarettos
AAELPRRSTU superaltar
AAELPRRTTT rattle-trap
AAEMNNORTT tramontane
AAEMNNRRTY rent-an-army
AAEMNNRSTV man-servant
servant-man
AAEMNOOSST anastomose
AAEMNPRSTT apartments
AAEMOPSSZZ passamezzo
AAEMPRSSTT pastmaster
AAEMRSSTTU metatarsus
AAENNPPRTU unapparent

AAENORSSTT	assentator
AAENORTTTU	attenuator
AAENPSSTTW	sweatpants
AAENQRRTUY	△quaternary
AAENRRSTTU	restaurant
AAEOOPRRTV	evaporator
AAEOPPRRRT	preparator
AAEOPPRSUV	papaverous
AAEOPRRRTY	reparatory
AAEOPRRSTY	separatory
AAEORRRSST	terra-rossa
AAEORRSTTU	tartareous
AAEQRRSTUW	quarter-saw
AAEQRSTUUY	quaestuary
AAFFGIMNRU	△ragamuffin
AAFFINRTTU	Tartuffian
AAFGGILNVW	flag-waving
AAFGIINNPR	frangipani
AAFGILMNNT	Flamingant
AAFGINNRRT	infragrant
AAFGKLNRUU	Aufklärung
AAFGLLNRTY	flagrantly
AAFGLNRRTY	fragrantly
AAFHIMNNRU	infrahuman
AAFIIILRSS	filariasis
AAFIILLMRY	familiarly
AAFIILMNRU	unfamiliar
AAFIINRRTU	fruitarian
AAFILNOOTT	floatation
AAFILOPRSS	passiflora
AAFIMMORRS	samariform
AAFIMOORRS	afrormosia
AAFIOQRSTU	aquafortis
AAGGHINNRU	haranguing
AAGGHLNNSW	slang-whang
AAGGIILLNN	ilang-ilang
AAGGIINNRR	arraigning
AAGGIINNSY	gainsaying
AAGGIINRRT	air-grating
AAGGINRSTZ	stargazing
AAGGLLLOSS	galloglass
AAGGLLNNYY	ylang-ylang
AAGGMNOORR	organogram
AAGGNNOOWW	wonga-wonga
AAGHHIMNWY	highwayman
AAGHIILMNP	Malpighian
AAGHIINRVW	hair-waving
AAGHILLLLN	hallalling
AAGHILMNPU	gnaphalium
AAGHILNPPR	planigraph
AAGHILNPST	phalangist
AAGHILOPPY	polyphagia
AAGHILORTY	hagiolatry
AAGHINPRSS	springhaas
AAGHIPPRSY	pasigraphy
AAGHLNOPXY	xylophagan
AAGHMMMOPR	mammograph
AAGHNOPPRT	pantograph
AAGHNOPPTY	pantophagy
AAGHOPRSTY	Pythagoras
AAGHOPRTUY	autography
AAGIIILLRS	Sigillaria
AAGIIILNRT	tagliarini
AAGIIINNRV	viraginian
AAGIIKMNNR	rainmaking
AAGIIKNPRT	parakiting
AAGIIILLNOT	alligation
AAGIIILLNVY	availingly
AAGIIILMPRS	plagiarism
AAGIIILNNPS	salpingian
AAGIIILNNUV	unavailing
AAGIIILNSSW	wassailing
AAGIIILPRST	plagiarist
AAGIIMNRST	stigmarian
AAGIINNOPT	pagination
AAGIINNOST	sagination
AAGIINNOTV	navigation
AAGIJKLNWY	jaywalking
AAGIKMNRST	king-at-arms
AAGILLLNUU	Anguillula
AAGILLMNRY	alarmingly
	marginally
AAGILLNOSZ	gallinazos
AAGILLORSS	glossarial
AAGILLSTTY	sagittally
AAGILMNNSU	sign-manual
AAGILMNOOR	agronomial
AAGILMNORS	organismal
AAGILMOPRS	paralogism
AAGILNNOQU	Algonquian
AAGILNNOTU	angulation
AAGILNOPRS	sporangial
AAGILNORTY	gyrational
AAGILNOSTV	solivagant
AAGILNPRTU	tarpauling
AAGILNRRTU	triangular
AAGILNRTUY	angularity
AAGILRSSSS	sisal-grass
AAGIMMPRST	pragmatism
AAGIMMRSTT	grammatist
AAGIMNNOST	antagonism
AAGIMNNPRW	warming-pan
AAGIMNPRSU	sparganium
AAGIMNSSTY	gymnasiast
AAGIMPRSTT	pragmatist
AAGINNOOPR	piano-organ
AAGINNOSTT	antagonist
	stagnation
AAGINNRRTW	warranting
AAGINNRSUY	sanguinary
AAGINOOPRZ	Zaporogian
AAGINOORRT	arrogation
AAGINOPRSS	paragnosis
AAGINRSTTU	antitragus
AAGLLMOOSU	allogamous
AAGLLNOPTT	topgallant
AAGLLNRRUY	granularly
AAGLLOOSTW	goat-sallow
AAGLMMOPSY	plasmogamy
AAGLMNORSU	granulomas
AAGLMOPSTY	plastogamy
AAGLNNOOSX	Anglo-Saxon
AAGLNNSTTY	stagnantly
AAGLNOOSTY	satanology

AAGLNORRTU	granulator
AAGLNORRTY	arrogantly
AAGMMMNOWY	mammy-wagon
AAGMOOSTUU	autogamous
AAGOOPPRRT	propagator
AAGORRRSSW	arrow-grass
AAHHILMOPT	ophthalmia
AAHHIMMMSS	shammashim
AAHHIMRRTY	arrhythmia
AAHHLORSTT	throat-lash
AAHIILLNOR	rhinolalia
AAHIILNNOT	inhalation
AAHIILNNTU	Lithuanian
AAHIIMNPRS	airmanship
AAHIIMPRSS	pharisaism
AAHILLOPRT	prothallia
AAHILLOPTW	topi-wallah
AAHILMNSTU	Malthusian
AAHILMOOTX	homotaxial
AAHILMTTUZ	altazimuth
AAHILNNOPT	antiphonal
AAHILOPPSY	hypoplasia
AAHIMMNOTY	mythomania
AAHIMOOPPR	apomorphia
AAHINOPSTX	xanthopsia
AAHINOSSTT	thanatosis
AAHINPSTXY	asphyxiant
AAHIPPRSSY	paraphysis
AAHJKMPRRU	rajpramukh
AAHKKNNPYY	hanky-panky
AAHKLORRSW	ashlar-work
AAHKMORSTY	matryoshka
AAHKOPTUUW	pohutukawa
AAHLLLLNOW	allhallown
AAHLLLLOSW	All-Hallows
AAHLLMOPSY	hyaloplasm
AAHLMOPSTY	staphyloma
AAHLOPRSTY	hyoplastra
AAHMOPRSST	Ramphastos
AAHNNNOOTY	hootananny
AAHNNRSTUY	thysanuran
AAHNOPRTTU	naturopath
AAHNORRSTU	anarthrous
AAHNPRSTTY	phantastry
AAHPRSTTUU	tatpurusha
AAHRSTTWWY	thwartways
AAIIILMMNT	militiaman
AAIIILMNRT	limitarian
AAIIILMNST	Italianism
AAIIILNQRU	Quirinalia
AAIIILNSTT	Italianist
AAIIJJPPPP	jippi-jappa
AAIIJLNORT	janitorial
AAIIKLLNTY	alkalinity
AAIIKMNNST	Kantianism
AAIILLNOPT	palliation
AAIILLNPST	plastilina
AAIILLNUXY	uniaxially
AAIILMMRST	martialism
AAIILMMSTX	maximalist
AAIILMNNOT	antimonial
	lamination
AAIILMNOPT	ampliation
AAIILMPRST	partialism
	patrialism
AAIILMRSTT	martialist
AAIILNNSTT	instantial
AAIILNNSTU	Lusitanian
AAIILNORRT	irrational
AAIILNORST	solitarian
AAIILNORTV	Voltairian
AAIILNOSTV	salivation
AAIILNOTTT	latitation
AAIILNPPZZ	Lippizzana
AAIILNPSTU	Paulianist
AAIILNRSTY	sanitarily
AAIILPPRSS	paralipsis
AAIILPRSTT	partialist
AAIILPRTTY	partiality
	patriality
AAIILPSTTY	spatiality
AAIILRRRRT	tirra-lirra
AAIIMMNNOT	immanation
AAIIMMNRSX	Marxianism
AAIIMNNNOT	antinomian
AAIIMNNOPT	impanation
AAIIMNNRTU	Ruminantia
AAIIMNPRTU	panaritium
AAIIMNRSTU	sanitarium
AAIIMNRSTZ	Nazaritism
AAIIMPPRRS	primiparas
AAIIMPRSST	parasitism
AAIINNNOST	nanisation
AAIINNNOTZ	nanization
AAIINNOPTT	patination
AAIINNOSTT	sanitation
AAIINNQQUU	quinaquina
AAIINNRRTU	Ruritanian
AAIINNRSTY	insanitary
AAIINNRTUV	univariant
AAIINOPPRT	apparition
AAIINOPRST	aspiration
AAIINOPRTT	patriation
	tritanopia
AAIINPTTVY	Patavinity
AAIINRSSTT	sanitarist
AAIIRSSSTY	satyriasis
AAIKKMORSV	maskirovka
AAIKORRSTW	tarsia-work
AAILLLOPVW	pillow-lava
AAILLLPSTU	Pulsatilla
AAILLMPRUU	Plumularia
AAILLNNOOP	Apollonian
AAILLNNOTY	nationally
AAILLNNOVV	Villanovan
AAILLNNSTT	installant
AAILLNOPST	spallation
AAILLNORTY	notarially
	rationally
AAILLOPRTY	palliatory
AAILLRSTUY	salutarily
AAILMNOPRU	Pulmonaria
AAILMNOTTU	mutational
AAILMNPSSV	Pan-Slavism

AAILMNRRTU	intramural
AAILMNRSTU	naturalism
AAILMOPPRX	approximal
AAILMOPSTY	polymastia
AAILMORRTY	Mariolatry
AAILNNNOTU	annulation
AAILNNOOTT	notational
AAILNNOPTT	plantation
AAILNNORRV	non-arrival
AAILNNOSTT	altisonant
AAILNNOTTT	altitonant
AAILNNOTTU	nutational
AAILNNRTUY	annularity
AAILNOORTT	rotational
AAILNOPPTU	papulation
AAILNOPTTV	pot-valiant
AAILNOPTUV	vapulation
AAILNOSTTU	salutation
AAILNPQSTU	pasquilant
AAILNPRSTU	palustrian
AAILNPSSTV	Pan-Slavist
AAILNRSSUY	uranalysis
AAILNRSTTU	naturalist
AAILNRSTUY	insalutary
AAILOORRTV	variolator
AAILORSTTT	altostrati
AAIMMMNSTY	Tammanyism
AAIMMORRSS	marmarosis
AAIMMOSSTU	miasmatous
AAIMMOSTTU	automatism
AAIMMRSTTU	traumatism
AAIMNNOOST	nostomania
AAIMNNORSY	mansionary
AAIMNOORST	inamoratos
AAIMNOOTTU	automation
AAIMNOPTTU	amputation
AAIMNOQSTU	squamation
AAIMNORSTU	sanatorium
AAIMNORTTU	maturation
	natatorium
AAIMOORSTU	amatorious
AAIMOSTTTU	automatist
AAINNNOOTT	annotation
AAINNORSXY	synaxarion
AAINNRSTUY	unsanitary
AAINOOPPRT	protanopia
AAINOPRSSY	passionary
AAINOPSTTY	pay-station
AAINOQRTTU	quartation
AAINOQRTUZ	quatorzain
AAINORSTTU	saturation
AAINORSTTV	starvation
AAINORSTTY	stationary
AAINORSTUU	saouari-nut
AAINPPRSTY	spray-paint
AAINPSTTWY	panty-waist
AAIOPQRSTU	paraquitos
AAIOPRRSTY	aspiratory
AAIORRSTTT	trattorias
AAKKLLTTYY	talky-talky
AAKKLLTWYY	walky-talky
AAKLMOPRSY	karyoplasm

AAKLNORSUY	ankylosaur
AAKMMNORSW	markswoman
AAKORRTTTU	Turko-Tatar
AALLLLNNUU	nulla-nulla
AALLLLOTWW	wall-to-wall
AALLMNOTWY	tallywoman
AALLMNTUUY	autumnally
AALLOPRSTY	pastorally
AALLORSSUU	Allosaurus
AALLPSSWYY	palsy-walsy
AALLRSTTWY	stalwartly
AALMMOOPSS	plasmosoma
AALMNORSTY	Lyon-at-arms
AALMOOPPRS	malapropos
AALMOOPRTY	laparotomy
AALMOPRSXY	paroxysmal
AALMORRTYY	Maryolatry
AALNNNORTU	non-natural
AALNNOOPST	pantaloons
AALNNPRSTT	transplant
AALNNRRSTU	translunar
AALNOOPUZZ	pozzuolana
AALNOPRSST	transposal
AALNOPRSTU	unpastoral
AALNORRSTT	translator
AALNPRRSUU	supralunar
AALOORRTTV	travolator
AALOPRRSTU	Australorp
AALOPSTTUY	autoplasty
AALORRSTTY	astrolatry
AALORSTTUY	salutatory
AAMNNOTTTU	tantamount
AAMNOOPRSY	paronomasy
AAMNOOSTTU	automatons
AAMNOPRTTU	portmantua
AAMOORSSSU	Mosasauros
AAMOOSSTTU	astomatous
AANOOPRSTU	anatropous
AAOOPPRRST	paratroops
ABBBBINORY	baby-ribbon
ABBBCEILNO	bobbin-lace
ABBBCEORRR	robber-crab
ABBBCIKRTU	buck-rabbit
ABBBDDRUUU	rub-a-dub-dub
ABBBEELMNT	babblement
ABBBEILNRU	unbribable
ABBBIIMSTT	Babbittism
ABBCCKKLOS	back-blocks
ABBCDEEHMR	bedchamber
ABBCDEIMOY	Bombycidae
ABBCDEMRRU	breadcrumb
ABBCDKLOOR	blockboard
ABBCEEEIPY	abbey-piece
ABBCEILMNO	combinable
ABBCEILRSU	subcaliber
	subcalibre
ABBCEINRSS	crabbiness
ABBCEINSSS	scabbiness
ABBCEINSTU	subcabinet
ABBCEJKORW	jabberwock
ABBCEJLLOT	object-ball
ABBCEKKLOR	brake-block

ABBCEKKSTU buck-basket
ABBCEKLRRY blackberry
ABBCEKMNRU back-number
ABBCELLNUU unclubable
ABBCELLOTU cobalt-blue
ABBCELNRUU uncurbable
ABBCENORSY absorbency
ABBCGIIKNT backbiting
ABBCGIIORT gabbroitic
ABBCIILLLY biblically
ABBCIILLNU unbiblical
ABBCIIRRTU barbituric
ABBCIKORRT rock-rabbit
ABBCKLLLUY black-bully
ABBCKNOTTU button-back
ABBDDEEILO able-bodied
ABBDEEGILR bridgeable
ABBDEEHLPS pebbledash
ABBDEEIRRW barbed-wire
ABBDEELNNU unbendable
ABBDEENRRU unbarbered
ABBDEERRRY breadberry
ABBDEFIORR fiberboard
fibreboard
ABBDEILSUU subaudible
ABBDEIMNRY baby-minder
ABBDEIMORR bombardier
ABBDEINRSS drabbiness
ABBDEJLNOR land-jobber
ABBDEKLNOU double-bank
ABBDEKNNSU Bundesbank
ABBDELLNRU land-lubber
ABBDELORSY absorbedly
ABBDELOSSU double-bass
ABBDGGINOR Brobdignag
ABBDGILLNY dabblingly
ABBDHORRSU broadbrush
ABBEEEILLV believable
ABBEEEKLRT bark-beetle
ABBEEELPRW pebble-ware
ABBEEELQSU babelesque
ABBEEELRRR beer-barrel
ABBEEELRRY barley-bree
ABBEEGILLR Gibberella
ABBEEGLMNT gabblement
ABBEEGNRTT Battenberg
ABBEEKRTTU butter-bake
ABBEELLRTT better-ball
ABBEELMNRT rabblement
ABBEELORSV observable
ABBEELRSTU bluebreast
ABBEELRTTU rebuttable
ABBEENORST breastbone
ABBEENRRSU base-burner
ABBEENRTTU butter-bean
ABBEEORRTW browbeater
ABBEERRRUW rubberwear
ABBEFILNSS flabbiness
ABBEGGLLRU bull-beggar
ABBEGNORTT Battonberg
ABBEGNRTTU Battenburg
ABBEHILORT rabbit-hole
ABBEHINSSS shabbiness
ABBEHOPRRS barbershop
barber-shop
ABBEIILMNO bibliomane
ABBEIIOSSS babesiosis
ABBEILLMSU sublimable
ABBEILMOPR improbable
ABBEILNORS ribbon-seal
ABBEILNOTU obnubilate
ABBEILNSSS slabbiness
ABBEILNSSW wabbliness
ABBEILNTTU balbutient
ABBEIRSTTY baby-sitter
ABBEJMPRUY baby-jumper
ABBEKLLRRU barrel-bulk
ABBEKMMORR marker-bomb
ABBELLRSTU ball-buster
ABBELLRTTU butter-ball
ABBELMSSUU subsumable
ABBELOORRY barley-broo
ABBELOPRTW pot-wabbler
ABBELORSVY observably
ABBEORTTTU butter-boat
ABBERRTTUY buttery-bar
ABBFFIILMU bumbailiff
ABBFHIIRST rabbitfish
ABBFILORST fibroblast
ABBGHINOTX bathing-box
ABBGHINRRU rhubarbing
ABBGILNSTY stabbingly
ABBGILOOST obbligatos
ABBHIIMNOS Hobbianism
ABBHILNOSY Babylonish
ABBILMOPRY improbably
ABBILORSTU suborbital
ABBLLNOTTU button-ball
ABCCCEFIOS beccaficos
ABCCCEMNUY accumbency
ABCCDEEIRT brecciated
ABCCDELNRU carbuncled
ABCCDHLNTU band-clutch
ABCCDKNOOY cock-a-bondy
ABCCEEEIRT Rebeccaite
ABCCEEELNS albescence
ABCCEEENST tabescence
ABCCEEILMP impeccable
ABCCEEILSS accessible
ABCCEEIMRS Rebeccaism
ABCCEEKNRT centre-back
ABCCEELLOY bel-accoyle
ABCCEELLRY recyclable
ABCCEEPRSY cyberspace
ABCCEFFIKO back-office
ABCCEHILRU cherubical
ABCCEHIMOR cibachrome
ABCCEILLRU circulable
ABCCEILMPY impeccably
ABCCEILORU corbiculae
ABCCEILSSY accessibly
ABCCEINOSU suboceanic
ABCCEKNORR cornerback
ABCCHIILMO choliambic

ABCCHIIMOR	choriambic
ABCCHIIRRT	tribrachic
ABCCHIKLNO	block-chain
ABCCHIKLPT	pitch-black
ABCCHIKSTT	backstitch
ABCCHIKSTW	switchback
ABCCHILOSU	calico-bush
ABCCHILOTU	coachbuilt
ABCCILORXY	carboxylic
ABCCILRTUU	cucurbital
ABCCIMOORT	mobocratic
ABCCINORTU	buccinator
ABCCINORTY	corybantic
ABCCKLLOUY	cockabully
ABCCMOPSTU	subcompact
ABCCNOOPRY	carbon-copy
ABCCNOORSY	snobocracy
ABCDDEEHLU	club-headed
ABCDDEFIKL	fiddleback
	fiddle-back
ABCDDEKLOR	badderlock
ABCDEEEELR	decreeable
ABCDEEEILV	deceivable
ABCDEEELLT	delectable
ABCDEEELPR	deprecable
ABCDEEELRT	celebrated
ABCDEEELTT	detectable
ABCDEEHLNU	unbleached
ABCDEEHNRU	unbreached
ABCDEEHRUY	debauchery
ABCDEEIKRS	bride's-cake
ABCDEEILLN	declinable
ABCDEEILNS	ascendible
ABCDEEILNU	ineducable
ABCDEEILPR	predicable
ABCDEEILPS	despicable
ABCDEEILRT	creditable
ABCDEEILVY	deceivably
ABCDEEIOPR	broadpiece
ABCDEEKLRV	backvelder
ABCDEEKNOT	boat-necked
ABCDEELLNO	blonde-lace
ABCDEELLNY	belly-dance
ABCDEELLTY	delectably
ABCDEELLUX	excludable
ABCDEELMRS	descramble
ABCDEELNUU	uneducable
ABCDEELORR	recordable
ABCDEENRTY	cybernated
ABCDEFIKNR	back-friend
ABCDEFIRTU	bifurcated
ABCDEFOSTU	obfuscated
ABCDEGKMOS	gobsmacked
ABCDEGKORR	rock-badger
ABCDEHIILR	herbicidal
ABCDEHKMPU	hump-backed
ABCDEHMORY	brachydome
ABCDEHNNRU	unbranched
ABCDEHORSS	chessboard
ABCDEIILMO	biomedical
ABCDEIILNT	indictable
ABCDEIILNV	vindicable
ABCDEIIORT	aborticide
	bacterioid
ABCDEIKLRS	backslider
ABCDEIKOUV	bivouacked
ABCDEIKRST	bread-stick
ABCDEILLNU	includable
ABCDEILORU	Colubridae
ABCDEILPSY	despicably
ABCDEILRTU	traducible
ABCDEILRTY	creditably
ABCDEILSTU	subdialect
ABCDEIMORS	Scombridae
ABCDEIPRRS	crispbread
ABCDEIRRRS	bird-scarer
ABCDEJKOOT	jackbooted
ABCDELNNOO	condonable
ABCDELRRSY	scaldberry
ABCDEOORRS	scoreboard
ABCDEORSTU	subcordate
ABCDERRRTU	curbtrader
ABCDGKNORU	background
ABCDHIILNR	brainchild
ABCDHINNRU	nudibranch
ABCDHINORU	chairbound
ABCDHIOOPR	brachiopod
ABCDHLOORT	broadcloth
ABCDHNOORT	notch-board
ABCDIILLSY	disyllabic
ABCDIIMNOY	biodynamic
ABCDIIRSTY	scabridity
ABCDIISTUY	subacidity
ABCDILNOST	cnidoblast
ABCDIOTVYY	body-cavity
ABCDNNORRY	cornbrandy
ABCEEEIKRR	icebreaker
ABCEEEILNT	enticeable
ABCEEEILPR	pierceable
ABCEEEILRV	receivable
ABCEEEINNS	bienséance
ABCEEEJLRT	rejectable
ABCEEELLRR	cerebellar
ABCEEELPTX	expectable
ABCEEELTUX	executable
ABCEEENRUX	exuberance
ABCEEFIILN	beneficial
ABCEEFNORT	benefactor
ABCEEGILLR	clergiable
ABCEEGLLRY	clergyable
ABCEEHHKSS	backsheesh
ABCEEHILNR	hibernacle
ABCEEHKLST	sketchable
ABCEEHKNQU	bank-cheque
ABCEEHKRTU	hackbuteer
ABCEEHLMRY	chamber-lye
ABCEEHLNQU	quenchable
ABCEEHLSTU	subchelate
ABCEEHNORR	abhorrence
ABCEEHORSU	herbaceous
ABCEEIJLNT	injectable
ABCEEIKLNR	linebacker
ABCEEILLNR	reclinable
ABCEEILLNS	licensable

ABCEEILLPX explicable
ABCEEILMMT emblematic
ABCEEILNNU enunciable
ABCEEILNOT noticeable
ABCEEILRTX extricable
ABCEEINNOZ benzocaine
ABCEEINNST abstinence
ABCEEJKLTU bluejacket
ABCEEJNSST abjectness
ABCEEKRRRY crakeberry
ABCEEKRSTT back-street
ABCEELLMRW Camberwell
ABCEELLORT brocatelle
ABCEELLPUX exculpable
ABCEELNNOV convenable
ABCEELNOTT balconette
ABCEELNOVY conveyable
ABCEELNRRU uncerebral
ABCEELNRSU censurable
ABCEELOPRW pace-bowler
ABCEELORRT celebrator
ABCEELORTV table-cover
ABCEELOSTT case-bottle
ABCEELPTXY expectably
ABCEELRTVV velvet-crab
ABCEENOPRR reprobance
ABCEENOPRS spaceborne
ABCEENORSV observance
ABCEENRUXY exuberancy
ABCEERRRTU carbureter
ABCEFHINOR chief-baron
ABCEFHNORT beachfront
ABCEFILLOT olfactible
ABCEFILNNO confinable
ABCEFILORT clofibrate
ABCEFLNOSU confusable
ABCEFLNOTU confutable
ABCEFRSSUU subsurface
ABCEGHIMNR chambering
ABCEGILNOS cognisable
ABCEGILNOZ cognizable
ABCEGINNNY benignancy
ABCEGLNOOT conglobate
ABCEHIIMRS Hebraicism
ABCEHIIRST Hebraistic
ABCEHIKNRS Reichsbank
ABCEHIKRRT brick-earth
ABCEHILNNR branch-line
ABCEHILORW elbow-chair
ABCEHILPRT birthplace
ABCEHIMNRT Chambertin
ABCEHIMNTU Buchmanite
ABCEHIMOPT baphometic
ABCEHIMORT bichromate
ABCEHIMRRT hermit-crab
ABCEHINNRV vine-branch
ABCEHINORR chairborne
ABCEHIOOPR aerophobic
ABCEHIPPRR paper-birch
ABCEHIPRRY hyperbaric
ABCEHIPRTY hyperbatic
ABCEHKLORT heart-block
ABCEHLLNTU lunch-table
ABCEHLLOTT tablecloth
ABCEHLMOOP peach-bloom
ABCEHLNRSS branchless
ABCEHLPSUU Bucephalus
ABCEHMOPRT chamberpot
ABCEHNORRY abhorrency
ABCEHNRSTU subchanter
ABCEHOQRSU quebrachos
ABCEHORTTX chatterbox
ABCEHPRSTU subchapter
ABCEHRRSTU subcharter
ABCEIIJNOS Jacobinise
ABCEIIJNOZ Jacobinize
ABCEIILLMT bimetallic
ABCEIILLNN inclinable
ABCEIILLNR brilliance
ABCEIILMTU umbilicate
ABCEIILNOS insociable
ABCEIILPST epiblastic
ABCEIINTUV incubative
ABCEIIOORT aerobiotic
ABCEIKKMRR brickmaker
ABCEIKKSTY stickybeak
ABCEIKLNPU unpickable
ABCEIKLRRY bricklayer
ABCEIKLRSV silverback
ABCEIKNPRU Purbeckian
ABCEILLMOP compliable
ABCEILLNOU inoculable
ABCEILLNPU inculpable
ABCEILLNRS cranesbill
crane's-bill
ABCEILLTUV cultivable
ABCEILMOPT compatible
ABCEILMRUY embryulcia
ABCEILMSTU table-music
ABCEILNNSU incunables
ABCEILNOSU unsociable
ABCEILNOTY noticeably
ABCEILNPRU △republican
ABCEILNRRU incurrable
ABCEILRSTU subarticle
ABCEIMNRTT mitten-crab
ABCEIMOORT macrobiote
ABCEIMORRT barometric
ABCEINNSTY abstinency
ABCEINORSS escribanos
ABCEINRRST transcribe
ABCEIORSUU rubiaceous
ABCEIRRRSU subcarrier
ABCEJKLMRU lumberjack
ABCEKKLMOS smoke-black
ABCEKKORRW backworker
ABCEKKORST back-stroke
ABCEKLLNOU unlockable
ABCEKLLOOR cellar-book
ABCEKLLOWY yellowback
ABCEKLRTTU turtleback
ABCEKMRRTU curbmarket
ABCELLLMOO Collembola
ABCELLLORU blue-collar

ABCELLNOOS consolable
ABCELLOORU colourable
ABCELLOOST blastocoel
ABCELLOSTU leucoblast
ABCELLRTUU culturable
ABCELMMNOO commonable
ABCELMMOTU commutable
ABCELMMPRU lumber-camp
ABCELMNOSU consumable
ABCELMNRSU unscramble
ABCELMOPTU computable
ABCELMOSTU customable
ABCELMRSTU clubmaster
ABCELMRTTU tumble-cart
ABCELNORRY △barleycorn
ABCELNRSTU subcentral
ABCELNRSUU subnuclear
ABCELNRSUY censurably
ABCELOOPRV provocable
ABCELOPPRY clapperboy
ABCELOPRRU procurable
ABCELRRTUU tubercular
ABCELSTUUY subacutely
ABCEMOOPRT amboceptor
ABCEMOSSUU submucosae
ABCENNSSTU subnascent
ABCENNSTUY subtenancy
ABCENOPUUY upbuoyance
ABCENORSST crab-stones
ABCENORSTY corybantes
ABCENORSVY observancy
ABCENORTTU obtruncate
ABCENRRTUY △canterbury
ABCEOORRST Serbo-Croat
ABCEORRRTU carburetor
ABCEOSSSUY byssaceous
ABCERRSTTU subtracter
ABCFILMORU baculiform
ABCGHIIOPR biographic
ABCGHLORYY brachylogy
ABCGHNORYZ zygobranch
ABCGHNRSSU bunch-grass
ABCGIILLOO biological
ABCGIINRTT bratticing
ABCGIKNOPX packing-box
ABCGILMNRS scrambling
ABCGILNOSY cognisably
ABCGILNOYZ cognizably
ABCHHILOTT habit-cloth
ABCHHIOPRS archbishop
ABCHIILMOP amphibolic
ABCHIILOOT halobiotic
ABCHIILOPS basophilic
ABCHIILOTT batholitic
ABCHIILTTY bathylitic
ABCHIINOTU tibouchina
ABCHIKLMST blacksmith
ABCHIKLRST Blackshirt
ABCHILTTUY yacht-built
ABCHIMMNSU Buchmanism
ABCHIMORSU choriambus
ABCHINOOPY cynophobia
ABCHIORTYY charity-boy
ABCHKLLOTU tchoukball
ABCHKLNORT blackthorn
ABCHKNORRW branch-work
ABCHKOOSTW swatchbook
ABCHNORRTU turnbroach
ABCIIILNST albinistic
ABCIIINOTT antibiotic
ABCIIJMNOS Jacobinism
ABCIIJMOST Jacobitism
ABCIILLNRY brilliancy
ABCIILLOTY biotically
ABCIILLSST ballistics
ABCIILMOPS bioplasmic
ABCIILNOOT bilocation
ABCIILRTUY curability
ABCIIMNOSS Ambisonics®
ambisonics
ABCIIMOORT microbiota
ABCIIMRSST strabismic
ABCIINNOTU incubation
ABCIINORRT cribration
ABCIINOSSS abscission
ABCIINRSTU urbanistic
ABCIJNNOTU abjunction
ABCIKLLORY rockabilly
ABCIKLORVY ivory-black
ABCIKNORRT rick-barton
ABCILLMOSY symbolical
ABCILLNPUY inculpably
ABCILLRRUY rubrically
ABCILLRTUU bicultural
ABCILMOPTY compatibly
ABCILMOSTY myoblastic
ABCILMRUUV vibraculum
ABCILNOORS Sorbonical
ABCILNORSU binoculars
ABCILNOSUY unsociably
ABCILORRTU lubricator
ABCILOSTUV vocabulist
ABCIMOSSTU subatomics
ABCINORTUY incubatory
ABCIORRRTU rubricator
ABCIPPRSUU suprapubic
ABCKKNOOTU knockabout
ABCKLLOOWY woollyback
ABCKNPRTUY bankruptcy
ABCLLOORUY colourably
ABCLMMRUUU umbraculum
ABCLMOSSUU submucosal
ABCLORRTUU lucubrator
ABCLORSSUY scabrously
ABCLOSSTTY blastocyst
ABCLRSSTUU subcrustal
ABCNNRRTUU currant-bun
ABCNOORRTU court-baron
ABCORRSTTU subtractor
ABDDEEEFLN defendable
ABDDEEEHNO bone-headed
ABDDEEELNP dependable
ABDDEEGGLR bedraggled
ABDDEEGHIR bridgehead

ABDDEEHLLU	bull-headed
ABDDEEHLOO	beadlehood
ABDDEEHMOR	hebdomader
ABDDEEIMNS	base-minded
ABDDEEINTT	bidentated
ABDDEELNPY	dependably
ABDDEELRST	bestraddle
ABDDEENRRU	undebarred
ABDDEGHKOU	dough-baked
ABDDEGILNR	land-bridge
ABDDEGINRU	unabridged
ABDDEGIORR	road-bridge
ABDDEGIRRW	drawbridge
ABDDEHHINN	behindhand
ABDDEHILLR	hard-billed
ABDDEHILNR	bridle-hand
ABDDEHILOR	hard-boiled
ABDDEIIMRS	bridesmaid
	bride's-maid
ABDDEILLLS	saddlebill
ABDDEILORR	bridle-road
ABDDEINNRS	sand-binder
ABDDEIORSS	sideboards
ABDDELNORR	borderland
ABDDELNRTU	bladder-nut
ABDDELORSW	sword-blade
ABDDENORRU	under-board
ABDDGGINPU	pudding-bag
ABDDHNRSUY	dandy-brush
ABDDLMOORU	mouldboard
ABDDOORRSW	broadsword
ABDEEEEHLT	beetlehead
ABDEEEELMR	redeemable
ABDEEEFHRT	featherbed
ABDEEEFILS	defeasible
ABDEEEFLRR	deferrable
ABDEEEFRST	breast-feed
ABDEEEGGLR	barelegged
ABDEEEGLLP	pledgeable
ABDEEEGNRR	beer-garden
ABDEEEHLNT	needle-bath
ABDEEEHNRV	heaven-bred
ABDEEEILLN	delineable
ABDEEEILMR	remediable
ABDEEEILRT	deliberate
ABDEEEINRV	aberdevine
ABDEEELLPT	depletable
ABDEEELMRY	redeemably
ABDEEELNPX	expendable
ABDEEELNRR	renderable
ABDEEELNRZ	land-breeze
ABDEEELNTX	extendable
ABDEEELRYY	bleary-eyed
ABDEEELSTT	detestable
ABDEEEMNST	debasement
ABDEEEMNTT	debatement
ABDEEENRUV	unbeavered
ABDEEEPRST	breast-deep
ABDEEERSTW	sweetbread
ABDEEFFHLU	bufflehead
ABDEEFGILR	leaf-bridge
ABDEEFHNOR	beforehand
ABDEEFLMOR	deformable
ABDEEFLNRU	refundable
ABDEEFOORT	barefooted
ABDEEGHIRT	big-hearted
ABDEEGHNRR	herb-garden
ABDEEGILNS	designable
ABDEEGILRT	ledger-bait
ABDEEGLNUW	unwedgable
ABDEEGLOPU	double-page
ABDEEGLORT	gold-beater
ABDEEGORRV	verge-board
ABDEEHILLS	déshabillé
ABDEEHILLT	billet-head
ABDEEHILLV	ill-behaved
ABDEEHILPS	beadleship
ABDEEHILRR	halberdier
ABDEEHIMRT	timber-head
ABDEEHIMSV	misbehaved
ABDEEHIRTW	whitebeard
ABDEEHLLPS	bell-shaped
ABDEEHLLTU	bullet-head
ABDEEHLOTT	bottle-head
	table-d'hôte
ABDEEHLTTY	hye-battel'd
ABDEEHMMRU	head-bummer
ABDEEHNRTU	unbreathed
ABDEEHORRS	horse-bread
ABDEEHORST	broadsheet
ABDEEHRTTU	butterhead
ABDEEIILTT	debilitate
ABDEEIKNNY	kidney-bean
ABDEEILLMR	mallee-bird
ABDEEILMRY	remediably
ABDEEILNNU	undeniable
ABDEEILNRU	unrideable
ABDEEILNUW	unbewailed
ABDEEILORR	rear-boiled
ABDEEILPRU	repudiable
ABDEEILPRV	deprivable
ABDEEILPSS	despisable
ABDEEIMRRT	time-barred
ABDEEIMRTX	ambidexter
ABDEEINNOR	debonnaire
ABDEEINNRR	Bernardine
ABDEEIOPRT	paedotribe
ABDEEISTTU	beatitudes
ABDEEKLOTU	double-take
ABDEEKORRY	keyboarder
ABDEEKRRRT	kerb-trader
ABDEELLLNU	unlabelled
ABDEELLMRU	umbrellaed
ABDEELLMTU	umbellated
ABDEELLOPR	deplorable
ABDEELLPSU	spuleblade
ABDEELMRRU	demurrable
ABDEELNOPR	ponderable
ABDEELNORS	endorsable
ABDEELOPTX	box-pleated
ABDEELORTT	battledore
ABDEELPRRU	perdurable
ABDEELRSTU	balustered
ABDEELSTTY	detestably

ABDEEMORRY	emery-board
ABDEENOPSU	subpoenaed
ABDEENPRRY	prebendary
ABDEENRSUY	subdeanery
ABDEENRTTU	unbattered
ABDEENRTUY	unbetrayed
ABDEEOORVW	beaver-wood
ABDEFFRSTU	breadstuff
ABDEFGIRRT	raft-bridge
ABDEFIILMO	modifiable
ABDEFIIMRT	fimbriated
ABDEFIKNOR	knife-board
ABDEFILMOR	formidable
ABDEFIRRRT	rafter-bird
ABDEFIRRTU	breadfruit
ABDEFLLOTU	double-flat
ABDEFLNORU	unfordable
ABDEGGIRRU	budgerigar
ABDEGGNOOT	tobogganed
ABDEGHINSU	subheading
ABDEGHIORW	weighboard
ABDEGHORTU	dearbought
ABDEGIINNR	brigandine
ABDEGILNSY	debasingly
ABDEGILNTY	debatingly
ABDEGIMNRT	abridgment
ABDEGINORY	reading-boy
ABDEHIILLS	dishabille
ABDEHIKLLW	hawk-billed
ABDEHILPRT	bridle-path
ABDEHINORT	hot-brained
ABDEHINRTT	hard-bitten
ABDEHIRRSU	air-brushed
ABDEHLLOOY	ballyhooed
ABDEHLOORT	heart-blood
ABDEHNORRS	shard-borne
ABDEHNORTU	earthbound
ABDEHNRSTU	Bundesrath
	subtrahend
ABDEHORRST	shortbread
ABDEHORTTU	outbreath'd
ABDEHOSUWY	bawdy-house
ABDEIIKLLS	dislikable
ABDEIILMPS	bipedalism
ABDEIILMSS	admissible
ABDEIILNOT	delibation
ABDEIILOSX	oxidisable
ABDEIILOXZ	oxidizable
ABDEIILPSS	dissipable
ABDEIITTUV	dubitative
ABDEIKQRRU	Quaker-bird
ABDEIKRTTU	dika-butter
ABDEILLLNY	blind-alley
ABDEILLLSY	disyllable
ABDEILMNRT	timberland
ABDEILMSTU	sublimated
ABDEILNNUY	undeniably
ABDEILNORY	debonairly
ABDEILNSUY	unbiasedly
ABDEILOPRV	providable
ABDEILOPSS	disposable
ABDEILORTT	trilobated
ABDEILPSTU	disputable
ABDEILRTTW	wattlebird
ABDEIMNRST	disbarment
ABDEIMNSTU	submediant
ABDEIMORZZ	morbidezza
ABDEIMRRTY	timberyard
ABDEIMRSSY	bradyseism
ABDEIMRTUW	dumb-waiter
ABDEINNOTU	unobtained
ABDEINPSTU	unbaptised
ABDEINPTUZ	unbaptized
ABDEINRTTU	turbinated
ABDEKLLOTU	double-talk
ABDEKLOPRU	double-park
ABDEKMOORS	smokeboard
ABDELLOOPT	blood-plate
ABDELLOPRY	deplorably
ABDELMORST	blastoderm
ABDELMRRUY	lumber-yard
ABDELNOORS	bandoleros
ABDELNOPSU	spauld-bone
ABDELNORTU	round-table
ABDELNORUU	unlaboured
ABDELNOSUV	unabsolved
ABDELOORTT	battledoor
ABDELORTUY	obdurately
ABDELPRRUY	perdurably
ABDEMNORRS	roberdsman
ABDEMORRWY	body-warmer
ABDENOORUV	overabound
ABDENOPPRU	paperbound
ABDENORRST	sternboard
ABDENORTUW	water-bound
ABDENRSSSU	absurdness
ABDENRSSTY	standers-by
ABDEOORRTT	otter-board
ABDEOPRRST	spot-barred
ABDFGIINOR	fair-boding
ABDFILMORY	formidably
ABDFILNORU	floribunda
ABDFLOOORR	floorboard
ABDGGINORR	bordraging
ABDGIINPRU	upbraiding
ABDGINNRST	band-string
ABDGINORTU	groundbait
ABDGLNOOOW	blood-wagon
ABDGNORSSU	ground-bass
ABDHHILORT	rhabdolith
ABDHIIINOT	adhibition
ABDHILMOOR	rhomboidal
ABDHINRTUY	unbirthday
ABDIIILRTY	ridability
ABDIIILSTY	disability
ABDIIILTUY	audibility
ABDIIIRSTT	diatribist
ABDIILMNOU	albuminoid
ABDIILMOTY	bimodality
ABDIILNOOS	obsidional
ABDIILORRT	tailor-bird
ABDIILPTUY	dupability
ABDIILRTUY	durability
ABDIINOTTU	dubitation

ABDIIRSSUY	subsidiary
ABDILLNOST	Bollandist
ABDILLRYZZ	blizzardly
ABDILNOOST	bloodstain
ABDILNORSU	subordinal
ABDILOORTY	botryoidal
ABDILOORWZ	brazil-wood
ABDILPSTUY	disputably
ABDIMNOOSU	abdominous
ABDIMNRRUU	burramundi
ABDINOORTU	obduration
ABDINOPRRS	parson-bird
ABDINRRTTY	tyrant-bird
ABDINRSTTU	disturbant
ABDLLOOORY	blood-royal
ABDLMNOOTT	bottom-land
ABDMNNOOSW	bondswoman
ABDNOORTUU	roundabout
ABDOORRSTY	storyboard
ABDOORRTUU	troubadour
ABEEEEFLLT	flea-beetle
ABEEEERRTV	beaver-tree
ABEEEFIKLM	make-belief
ABEEEFLLRU	refuelable
ABEEEFLPRR	preferable
ABEEEFLRRR	referrable
ABEEEGGLRS	segregable
ABEEEGIMNN	beam-engine
ABEEEHKLRW	brake-wheel
ABEEEHRSTT	hartebeest
ABEEEIKLNR	Berkeleian
ABEEEIKRRT	tie-breaker
ABEEEILLRV	relievable
ABEEEILMRR	irremeable
ABEEEILRVW	reviewable
ABEEELLSTT	settleable
ABEEELMPRT	temperable
ABEEELMRSS	reassemble
ABEEELNPRT	penetrable
ABEEELNPRU	unpeerable
ABEEELNRSW	renewables
ABEEELQSUZ	squeezable
ABEEELRRSV	reservable
ABEEEMMNST	embasement
ABEEEMNRTT	rebatement
ABEEEMRSTT	beetmaster
ABEEENNOZZ	azobenzene
ABEEENQRTU	banqueteer
ABEEEOPRSS	pease-brose
ABEEEORSTT	stereobate
ABEEERRTTV	vertebrate
ABEEFFLMNT	bafflement
ABEEFFLOST	offsetable
ABEEFFLRSU	sufferable
ABEEFHLRST	self-breath
ABEEFIILNS	infeasible
ABEEFIILRV	verifiable
ABEEFIIRTU	beautifier
ABEEFIKRST	fire-basket
ABEEFILLRT	filterable
ABEEFILNOR	Froebelian
ABEEFILNRR	inferrable
ABEEFILNSU	unfeasible
ABEEFILNTT	flea-bitten
ABEEFLLNSU	self-unable
ABEEFLMORR	reformable
ABEEFLOPRR	perforable
ABEEFLORRU	free-labour
ABEEFLORSW	safe-blower
ABEEFLPRRY	preferably
ABEEFLRSSU	self-abuser
ABEEGHIOPR	biographee
ABEEGHLLNR	bellhanger
ABEEGIINRS	raising-bee
ABEEGILMNR	germinable
ABEEGILNOT	negotiable
ABEEGILNRT	integrable
ABEEGILNSS	Albigenses
ABEEGILRTU	glauberite
ABEEGILRTW	bilge-water
ABEEGIRSTU	aubergiste
ABEEGLNOPS	spongeable
ABEEGLNORV	governable
ABEEGLNPUX	expugnable
ABEEGLNRRY	angleberry
ABEEGMMNNO	gombeen-man
ABEEGMOSSY	message-boy
ABEEGNRSTT	abstergent
ABEEHILLRS	relishable
ABEEHILORT	heriotable
ABEEHILPRS	perishable
ABEEHIMNTT	Benthamite
ABEEHINOTT	hebetation
ABEEHKNORS	boneshaker
ABEEHLLNPU	unhelpable
ABEEHLMPRS	blasphemer
ABEEHLRSST	breathless
ABEEHMORTT	bathometer
ABEEHMRTTY	bathymeter
ABEEHNNORV	heaven-born
ABEEHOORRS	seborrhoea
ABEEHORSTU	hereabouts
ABEEHORTTU	outbreathe
	thereabout
ABEEHORTUW	whereabout
ABEEHPRRSY	barysphere
ABEEHQRSUU	harquebuse
ABEEHRSTTT	breath-test
ABEEHRSTTU	shea-butter
ABEEIILLMN	eliminable
ABEEIILLNS	isabelline
ABEEIILLRS	liberalise
ABEEIILLRZ	liberalize
ABEEIILNPX	inexpiable
ABEEIILNRS	inerasible
ABEEIILNTV	inevitable
ABEEIILSST	bestialise
ABEEIILSTZ	bestialize
ABEEIIRRRZ	bizarrerie
ABEEIKLLLS	klebsiella
ABEEIKLLNU	unlikeable
ABEEIKLNRT	ankle-biter
ABEEIKNNRT	barkentine
ABEEILLMNR	bellarmine

ABEEILLNRU unreliable
ABEEILLNST listenable
ABEEILLNTV ventilable
ABEEILLNUV unliveable
ABEEILLRSU leisurable
ABEEILMMOV immoveable
ABEEILMNRT terminable
ABEEILMNSU albumenise
ABEEILMNUZ albumenize
ABEEILMOST metabolise
ABEEILMOTT metabolite
ABEEILMOTZ metabolize
ABEEILMRRY irremeably
ABEEILMSTV semblative
ABEEILNNTV inventable
ABEEILNNUV unenviable
ABEEILNOPR inoperable
ABEEILNORV verbena-oil
ABEEILNORX inexorable
ABEEILNPSX expansible
ABEEILNRSS bleariness
ABEEILNRST insertable
ABEEILNSUZ unseizable
unsizeable
ABEEILORTT obliterate
ABEEILPRRS respirable
ABEEILPRTX extirpable
ABEEILQRRU requirable
ABEEILQRTU requitable
ABEEILRRTU tree-burial
ABEEILRSSU reissuable
ABEEIMMRRT timber-mare
ABEEINNPRR pine-barren
ABEEINPTUY pine-beauty
ABEEINRTUX exurbanite
ABEEIORTTX exorbitate
ABEEIRRSTW sweet-briar
ABEEIRSSTV abstersive
ABEEJMMNNT enjambment
ABEEKKMRRT kerb-market
ABEEKLLMRT market-bell
ABEEKMMNNT embankment
ABEEKMMNRT embarkment
ABEEKNORST stonebreak
ABEEKNRSTW West-Banker
ABEELLLNSU unsellable
ABEELLLNTU untellable
ABEELLMNTU ante-bellum
ABEELLMOPY employable
ABEELLMORU bellamoure
ABEELLNOUV unloveable
ABEELLNRUV vulnerable
ABEELLNTTU unlettable
ABEELLORSV resolvable
ABEELLPRUV pulverable
ABEELMMMNT embalmment
ABEELMNORZ emblazoner
ABEELMNOUV unmoveable
ABEELMNPRU rumple-bane
ABEELMNRST resemblant
ABEELMNRSU Lebensraum
mensurable
ABEELMNTTT battlement
ABEELMORST blastomere
ABEELMPRSU presumable
ABEELMPRTU permutable
ABEELMRSSY reassembly
ABEELNNTUU untuneable
ABEELNOPRS personable
ABEELNOSST oblateness
ABEELNPRTY penetrably
ABEELNQTTU blanquette
ABEELNRRTU returnable
ABEELNRTUY untyreable
ABEELNSSST stableness
ABEELNSSSU usableness
ABEELOPRRR beer-parlor
ABEELOPRRT reportable
ABEELOPRTX exportable
ABEELORRST restorable
ABEEMNNNOT abonnement
ABEEMNORTY embryonate
ABEEMRRSTW brewmaster
ABEENNNRRU runner-bean
ABEENNORSV raven's-bone
ABEENNRRSS barrenness
ABEENNRRSU baserunner
ABEENNRSSU urbaneness
ABEENNRSSZ brazenness
ABEENORRTW waterborne
water-borne
ABEENORSST baronetess
ABEENRRSTU subterrane
ABEEOPRRRT reprobater
ABEEOPRRTX exprobrate
ABEEPRRTTU perturbate
ABEFFGILRU febrifugal
ABEFFILNST snaffle-bit
ABEFFLNRUU unruffable
ABEFFLRSUY sufferably
ABEFGILORV forgivable
ABEFGILRSS fiberglass
fibreglass
ABEFGINORR forbearing
ABEFHIRRTT afterbirth
ABEFHRRSTU surf-bather
ABEFIILLLN infallible
ABEFIILLRT fibrillate
ABEFIILNOT notifiable
ABEFIILNTU infibulate
ABEFILLLNU unfallible
unfillable
ABEFILOPRT profitable
ABEFIMMOOR amoebiform
ABEFKLSSTU basketfuls
ABEFKNORRT break-front
ABEFLLLMUY blamefully
ABEFLLLORW ball-flower
ABEFLLOORT footballer
ABEFLLRRSU barrelfuls
ABEGGIMNOR embargoing
ABEGGNOORT tobogganer
ABEGGNOPSS spongebags
ABEGGNRSTU gangbuster

ABEGHHIRST	breast-high
ABEGHHMRRU	hamburgher
ABEGHIKSUW	weigh-bauks
ABEGHILLTT	light-table
ABEGHINOOP	genophobia
ABEGHINRTU	thunbergia
ABEGHIOOPR	ergophobia
ABEGHIOPRR	biographer
ABEGHLLLUY	belly-laugh
ABEGHLLOOP	Gallophobe
ABEGHLLOPU	ploughable
ABEGHLNOOP	△anglophobe
ABEGHNRRSU	bushranger
ABEGHQSUUU	usquebaugh
ABEGHRSTTU	bestraught
ABEGHRSTUV	harvest-bug
ABEGIIJNTW	Jew-baiting
ABEGIILNNT	intangible
ABEGIILNRT	Gilbertian
ABEGIIMNRT	reaming-bit
ABEGIINNRT	brigantine
ABEGIINOST	abiogenist
ABEGIKLNNT	blanketing
ABEGILLLRT	ballet-girl
ABEGILLNOY	all-obeying
ABEGILLNRV	verballing
ABEGILMNPU	impugnable
ABEGILNNTU	untangible
ABEGILNRSW	swingle-bar
ABEGILRRSU	burglarise
ABEGILRRUZ	burglarize
ABEGINNORS	Bergsonian
ABEGINNQTU	banqueting
ABEGINRSSU	ear-bussing
ABEGLLNOOY	balneology
ABEGLNORRY	loganberry
ABEGMORRSS	brome-grass
ABEGMORSUU	umbrageous
ABEGNNSTTU	subtangent
ABEGNOORST	brant-goose
ABEGNORRTU	gubernator
ABEHHILLST	sheathbill
ABEHHIOOPT	theophobia
ABEHHORRTT	heart-throb
ABEHIIILPS	bailieship
ABEHIILMNT	habiliment
ABEHIKLNRS	shrinkable
ABEHIKLSTT	basket-hilt
ABEHIKNOOP	kenophobia
ABEHIKNRRS	shin-barker
ABEHILLOPS	polishable
ABEHILMPRS	blepharism
ABEHILNPSU	punishable
ABEHILOOPZ	zelophobia
ABEHILOPST	hospitable
ABEHILPRSY	perishably
ABEHILPSTT	battleship
ABEHILPSTU	bisulphate
ABEHILRSTV	silver-bath
ABEHIMMNST	Benthamism
ABEHIMNNST	banishment
ABEHIMRRSU	herbariums
ABEHINOOPX	xenophobia
ABEHINOPRV	vibraphone
ABEHKLRSUW	bushwalker
ABEHLMORTW	Bartholmew
ABEHLMOTTU	ethambutol
ABEHLNOORU	△honourable
ABEHLOOPSV	Slavophobe
ABEHLOPRSY	hyperbolas
ABEHLORTTU	bluethroat
ABEHLOSTTW	wash-bottle
ABEHLRSUWY	bush-lawyer
ABEHMMNSTU	ambushment
ABEHMNORRT	brother-man
ABEHMRSSTU	bushmaster
ABEHMRTTYY	bathymetry
ABEHNOPRTY	hyperbaton
ABEHNORSST	stonebrash
ABEHNOSTTU	thenabouts
ABEHOORSTT	sabre-tooth
ABEHOORSTW	showboater
ABEHQRSSUU	harquebuss
ABEIIILLMN	bimillenia
ABEIIILMNT	inimitable
ABEIIILNNZ	Leibnizian
ABEIIILNSS	sensibilia
ABEIILLMRS	liberalism
ABEIILLNNY	biennially
ABEIILLNOV	inviolable
ABEIILLRST	liberalist
ABEIILLRTY	liberality
ABEIILLSTT	ballistite
ABEIILLSTU	utilisable
ABEIILLTUZ	utilizable
ABEIILMNSS	lesbianism
ABEIILMNSU	albuminise
ABEIILMNUZ	albuminize
ABEIILMPRT	impartible
ABEIILMPSS	impassible
ABEIILMRST	bimestrial
ABEIILMSST	bestialism
ABEIILNORT	liberation
ABEIILNOTT	nobilitate
ABEIILNPRS	inspirable
ABEIILNPXY	inexpiably
ABEIILNRSY	inerasibly
ABEIILNTTY	tenability
ABEIILNTVY	inevitably
ABEIILQTUY	equability
ABEIILRSST	stabiliser
ABEIILRSTZ	stabilizer
ABEIILSTTY	bestiality
ABEIILSTUY	sueability
ABEIIMNTTU	bituminate
ABEIINNRRT	interbrain
ABEIINNRSS	braininess
ABEIINRSTU	urbanities
ABEIINRTTU	abiturient
ABEIIOORSS	aerobiosis
ABEIKLNNSU	unsinkable
ABEIKNOPRT	breakpoint
ABEILLLNTU	untillable
ABEILLMMOS	embolismal

ABEILLMSTU	stimulable
ABEILLNNST	tennis-ball
ABEILLNOSV	insolvable
ABEILLNOSW	Boswellian
ABEILLNSSS	ballsiness
ABEILLNSTU	insultable
ABEILLRSUY	leisurably
ABEILLSUXY	bisexually
ABEILMMOST	metabolism
ABEILMMOSV	immovables
ABEILMNQRU	lambrequin
ABEILMNRTY	liberty-man
	terminably
ABEILMNSSW	wambliness
ABEILMOOTU	automobile
ABEILMOPRT	importable
ABEILMOPRV	improvable
ABEILMORTY	traymobile
ABEILMRSSU	surmisable
ABEILNNORS	Selbornian
ABEILNNOSS	bonnilasse
ABEILNNRUY	inurbanely
ABEILNNUVY	unenviably
ABEILNOOPS	poisonable
ABEILNOPRY	inoperably
ABEILNORXY	inexorably
ABEILNPRUZ	unprizable
ABEILNPSXY	expansibly
ABEILNSTUU	unsuitable
ABEILOPRRV	proverbial
ABEILOPSTU	bipetalous
ABEILORRTY	liberatory
ABEILORSTT	strobilate
ABEILORTVY	abortively
ABEILRSTUV	vestibular
ABEILRSUVV	survivable
ABEIMNNOTT	obtainment
ABEIMNORTT	montbretia
ABEIMNORTU	tambourine
ABEIMNRRSU	submariner
ABEIMOSSTU	abstemious
ABEINNORTU	eburnation
ABEINNORTV	native-born
ABEINNOSST	sanbenitos
ABEINNOSTT	abstention
ABEINNRRTU	interurban
ABEINNRSST	bannisters
ABEINNRSSW	brawniness
ABEINOPRRW	brainpower
ABEINORSST	abstersion
ABEINORTTX	exorbitant
ABEINPRRSU	superbrain
ABEINRRSTU	subterrain
ABEINRSSSS	brassiness
ABEIOPPRSY	presbyopia
ABEIOPRSTV	absorptive
ABEIORRRST	rib-roaster
ABEIORRSTT	birostrate
ABEIOSSSST	asbestosis
ABEIPRRSTT	bitter-spar
ABEIPRSTTY	baptistery
ABEIRSTUVY	subvariety
ABEKKMOORR	bookmarker
ABEKKORSTW	basketwork
	workbasket
ABEKLLOSTU	leukoblast
ABEKLNNOUW	unknowable
ABEKLNOPTT	knap-bottle
ABEKLNORUW	unworkable
ABEKLOOPRV	provokable
ABEKMNNOTU	mountebank
ABEKMNOOTY	monkey-boat
ABEKNOPRRW	pawnbroker
ABEKNORSTT	breast-knot
ABEKNORSTY	oyster-bank
ABEKNRSTTU	tankbuster
ABEKORRSTW	breastwork
ABELLLLOVY	volleyball
ABELLMOSTY	myeloblast
ABELLNOSUV	unsolvable
ABELLORRRU	bull-roarer
ABELLOSTUY	absolutely
ABELLRSSTU	substellar
ABELLSSSUY	syllabuses
ABELMMNOSU	somnambule
	summonable
ABELMNNOOW	noblewoman
ABELMNORXY	onyx-marble
ABELMNORYZ	emblazonry
ABELMNOUVY	unmoveably
ABELMNPRRU	lamp-burner
ABELMOOPRT	promotable
ABELMOORSU	laboursome
ABELMPRSUY	presumably
ABELMPRTTU	palm-butter
ABELNNRTUU	unturnable
ABELNOOPST	tablespoon
ABELNOPRUV	unprovable
ABELNOQTUU	unquotable
ABELNORRTT	latter-born
ABELNORRTW	brow-antler
ABELNORSTU	neuroblast
ABELNRRTUU	nurturable
ABELNRSSTU	substernal
ABELOOPPRS	proposable
ABELOOPRST	blastopore
ABELOORRUV	overlabour
ABELOOSSTT	osteoblast
ABELOPPSSU	supposable
ABELOPRSTT	table-sport
ABELOPRTTX	prattlebox
ABELRSSTUY	abstrusely
ABELRSTTTU	salt-butter
ABELRTTUUU	tubulature
ABEMMNORSU	membranous
ABEMNNOSTU	submontane
ABEMNOORRW	marrow-bone
ABEMNOORWW	bowerwoman
ABEMNORRST	robertsman
ABEMPPRSTU	breast-pump
ABENNOPRSX	box-spanner
ABENORRRTW	barrenwort
ABENORRRWY	rowan-berry
ABENPRRTTU	perturbant

ABENPRSSTU	abruptness
ABEOOPRRRT	reprobator
ABEOORRSTV	observator
ABEOORSTUU	rouseabout
ABEOQRRTUY	quarter-boy
ABEOQSSUUU	subaqueous
ABERRRSTWY	strawberry
ABFFGILLNY	bafflingly
ABFFIKMOOR	kaffir-boom
ABFFLNOTUU	buffalo-nut
ABFFMOORST	broomstaff
ABFGHOORRU	farborough
ABFGILNOTW	batfowling
ABFIIILRTY	friability
ABFIILLLNY	infallibly
ABFIILLRRY	fibrillary
ABFIILNORV	riboflavin
ABFILOPRTY	profitably
ABFILOSTUY	fabulosity
ABFJLORSUY	frabjously
ABFLLOSTUY	boastfully
ABFLLOSUUY	fabulously
ABFLNOSTUU	unboastful
ABGGGILNRY	braggingly
ABGGGINORW	growing-bag
ABGGILLMNO	gambolling
ABGHHINTTU	bathing-hut
ABGHHMORTU	Homburg-hat
ABGHIMNSTU	mashing-tub
ABGHINNSTU	sunbathing
ABGHINOOPY	gynophobia
ABGHIOPRRV	vibrograph
ABGHIRRSTT	star-bright
ABGHOORRUY	Yarborough
ABGIIILNNT	nail-biting
ABGIILNNTY	intangibly
ABGIILNOOT	obligation
ABGIIMNNOO	Mabinogion
ABGIIMNNST	bantingism
ABGIIMNORS	Grobianism
ABGIIMNPPT	bit-mapping
ABGIINNORU	Bourignian
ABGIKKMNOO	bookmaking
ABGIKMNOOT	bootmaking
ABGILLMNOU	lumbang-oil
ABGILLMNRY	ramblingly
ABGILLMNWY	wamblingly
ABGILLNNOO	ballooning
ABGILLNRWY	warblingly
ABGILLNSUU	sublingual
ABGILMOSUY	bigamously
ABGILOORTY	obligatory
ABGILOOSTT	batologist
ABGIMOOTTW	witgatboom
ABGINNRRSU	nursing-bra
ABGINOORRT	roborating
ABGINOORTW	rowing-boat
ABGINORRTU	barring-out
ABGJORSTUU	subjugator
ABGLLLORUY	globularly
ABGLNOORUY	urbanology
ABGMOPRRSU	subprogram
ABHHIMOOOP	homophobia
ABHHORRSUW	bush-harrow
ABHIIMMNRS	Brahminism
ABHIIMNSST	absinthism
ABHIIMOPSU	amphibious
ABHIIOOPST	sitophobia
ABHIIOOPTX	toxiphobia
ABHIIRSSTY	△sybaritish
ABHILLRSTW	whirlblast
ABHILOPSTY	hospitably
ABHILORTUW	whirl-about
ABHILOSSTT	histoblast
ABHIMNOOOP	monophobia
ABHIMNORRS	marsh-robin
ABHIMOOPSY	mysophobia
ABHINOOOPS	nosophobia
ABHINPRSTU	paint-brush
ABHIOOPPRY	pyrophobia
ABHIPRRSSU	bursarship
ABHLLLORSU	loll-shraub
ABHLLMSTTU	thumbstall
ABHLMOOSTY	homoblasty
ABHLNOORUY	honourably
ABHLORRRUW	hurlbarrow
ABHORRTTUY	ruby-throat
ABIIILLPTY	pliability
ABIIILLTVY	livability
ABIIILMNTY	inimitably
ABIIILMSST	stibialism
ABIIILNOST	sibilation
ABIIINOSST	antibiosis
ABIIIORSTT	tibiotarsi
ABIIJLNOTU	jubilation
ABIILLMNSU	subliminal
ABIILLNOVY	inviolably
ABIILLNSTY	sibilantly
ABIILMOTVY	movability
ABIILMPRTY	impartibly
ABIILMPSSY	impassibly
ABIILMTTUY	mutability
ABIILNNOTY	non-ability
ABIILNOOSV	bolivianos
ABIILNOTTY	bitonality
	notability
ABIILNPRST	split-brain
ABIILOPRTY	bipolarity
ABIILORSTY	sibilatory
ABIIMRSSTY	△sybaritism
ABIINNOTTU	intubation
ABIINNRTUY	inurbanity
ABIINORSTV	vibrations
ABIINOTTTU	titubation
ABIIORSTTU	obituarist
ABIIQRTUUY	ubiquitary
ABIJLLNTUY	jubilantly
ABIJNOORTU	objuration
ABIKLNNOPT	point-blank
ABIKNOOORT	ration-book
ABILLNOOST	balloonist
ABILLNOOTU	lobulation
ABILLNORUU	unilobular
ABILLNOSVY	insolvably

ABILLOPRRT	parrot-bill
ABILMNOSUU	albuminous
ABILMNOTUW	woman-built
ABILMOPRVY	improvably
ABILMOPSSY	Amblyopsis
ABILMOSSTU	absolutism
ABILNOOSTU	absolution
ABILNOTTUU	tubulation
ABILNSTUUY	unsuitably
ABILOORSTV	absolvitor
ABILORSSUU	salubrious
ABILOSSTTU	absolutist
ABILRTTUUY	tubularity
ABIMNNOOTU	umbonation
ABIMNORRST	brainstorm
ABIMRSSSTU	strabismus
ABINNORSTW	town's-bairn
ABINNRSTTU	subintrant
ABINOOPRST	absorption
ABINOORTTU	obturation
ABINOOSSST	bassoonist
ABINOSSTTU	substation
ABJLNOORUX	journal-box
ABLNRRTUUW	burr-walnut
ABLOORSTUY	absolutory
ABLOPPSSUY	supposably
ABLOPSTTUY	tuboplasty
ABLORRSUWW	law-burrows
ABLORRTTUU	turbulator
ABMOORSTTY	strabotomy
ABMRSSTTUU	substratum
ABNOORRSTU	brontosaur
ABOOPRSSTT	bootstraps
ABOORSTTUU	roustabout
ACCCCIKKLL	click-clack
ACCCEEELNS	calescence
ACCCEEENNS	canescence
ACCCEEHITT	catechetic
ACCCEENRST	accrescent
ACCCEFHKOR	cockchafer
ACCCEGINOS	cacogenics
ACCCEHILOT	chalcocite
ACCCEHIPRT	ecphractic
ACCCEHKOPT	patchcocke
ACCCEHORTW	cowcatcher
ACCCEHORUU	accoucheur
ACCCEIILRT	cicatricle
ACCCEIIRST	cicatrices
ACCCEIKORT	cockatrice
ACCCEILLNY	encyclical
ACCCEILMOP	accomplice
ACCCEIMNPY	impeccancy
ACCCELMORY	macrocycle
ACCCGLNOOO	gonococcal
ACCCHHIIMR	arch-chimic
ACCCHHILOO	chocaholic
ACCCHINOOP	cacophonic
ACCCHKOPST	spatchcock
ACCCHLOORY	ochlocracy
ACCCHOOTUU	caoutchouc
ACCCIILLOT	laccolitic
ACCCIIOPRS	capriccios
ACCCIKMORR	microcrack
ACCCILLLYY	cyclically
ACCCILMOOX	coxcomical
ACCCILMOPY	complicacy
ACCCILMORY	cycloramic
ACCCINOPPU	cappuccino
ACCDDEEINT	accidented
ACCDDEEIRT	accredited
ACCDDEIILL	cicadellid
ACCDDEKLOP	cock-paddle
ACCDEEENNS	ascendence
ACCDEEHLOT	cochleated
ACCDEEINNS	incandesce
ACCDEELPST	spectacled
ACCDEELPTY	acceptedly
ACCDEENNST	candescent
ACCDEENNSY	ascendency
ACCDEENNTU	unaccented
ACCDEEORTU	accoutered
ACCDEFHKLO	half-cocked
ACCDEFKMOS	smock-faced
ACCDEHIRST	cash-credit
ACCDEHLNOY	chalcedony
ACCDEHNORT	torch-dance
ACCDEIILNY	indelicacy
ACCDEIILST	dialectics
ACCDEIIMOY	Cecidomyia
ACCDEIIOPT	apodeictic
ACCDEIITUZ	diazeuctic
ACCDEIKLNW	candlewick
ACCDEIKLOT	cocktailed
ACCDEILLOP	peccadillo
ACCDEILNOO	calcedonio
ACCDEILNOT	△occidental
ACCDEILOPY	cyclopedia
ACCDEIMNNY	mendicancy
ACCDEIMNSU	dance-music
ACCDEIMORT	democratic
ACCDEINNTU	inductance
ACCDEIORST	desiccator
ACCDEIORTT	corticated
ACCDEIOSST	sticcadoes
ACCDELLTUU	cucullated
ACCDELOPSU	cloudscape
ACCDELRSUY	accursedly
ACCDEMOSTU	accustomed
ACCDENORTT	contracted
ACCDFIILTY	flaccidity
ACCDGNOOOR	raccoon-dog
ACCDHHRRUW	churchward
ACCDHHRRUY	churchyard
ACCDHIINOR	diachronic
ACCDHILNOO	conchoidal
ACCDHILORR	clarichord
ACCDHILORV	clavichord
ACCDIILLOP	piccadillo
ACCDIILLPY	piccadilly
ACCDIILNOO	conoidical
ACCDIILNOY	cycloidian
ACCDIILOOR	Crocodilia
ACCDIILSST	cladistics
ACCDIIMOST	docimastic

ACCDIINNOO diaconicon
ACCDIIOSTU diacoustic
ACCDIKLOOR clock-radio
ACCDILNOOR concordial
ACCDILOOOW calico-wood
ACCDILORSU sdrucciola
ACCDINORTT contradict
ACCDLOORUY doulocracy
ACCDNNOORT concordant
ACCEEEEHKS cheesecake
ACCEEEHILR chelicerae
ACCEEEHIST seecatchie
ACCEEEHRTY eye-catcher
ACCEEELNST latescence
ACCEEELPRT receptacle
ACCEEENNRS △renascence
ACCEEENPTX expectance
ACCEEFHLRT leechcraft
ACCEEFINST fatiscence
ACCEEFIRRU Cruciferae
ACCEEHHKLO cheechalko
ACCEEHHKOS cheechakos
ACCEEHILNP encephalic
ACCEEHINSV chevisance
ACCEEHIRST catechiser
ACCEEHIRSV cesarevich
ACCEEHIRTZ catechizer
ACCEEHISST catechesis
ACCEEHLNSS chanceless
ACCEEHMNNY cenenchyma
ACCEEHMNTU catechumen
ACCEEHNORR encroacher
ACCEEILLRT electrical
ACCEEILMNU ecumenical
ACCEEILMRS cream-slice
ACCEEILNPS pencil-case
ACCEEILNTY acetylenic
ACCEEILORT calico-tree
ACCEEILORV varicocele
ACCEEILSST ecclesiast
ACCEEIMNRS miscreance
ACCEEINPQU cinquepace
ACCEEIORSU ericaceous
ACCEEIRTUX excruciate
ACCEEKOOPR peacock-ore
ACCEEKOPRY peacockery
ACCEEKORST cockteaser
ACCEELNOST coalescent
ACCEELNOSV convalesce
ACCEELNPRU crapulence
ACCEELNRTU reluctance
ACCEELNRUX Clarenceux
ACCEELNSTT lactescent
ACCEELNSTU caulescent
ACCEELPSST spectacles
ACCEEMNRST marcescent
scarcement
ACCEEMNSTU accusement
ACCEEMOSTY ascomycete
ACCEENNNOV convenance
ACCEENNOVY conveyance
ACCEENOPRR coparcener
ACCEENORST consecrate
ACCEENPTXY expectancy
ACCEENRSSS scarceness
ACCEENTUXY executancy
ACCEEORRSU racecourse
ACCEEORSTU △cretaceous
ACCEFFIINY inefficacy
ACCEFFIITY efficacity
ACCEFHLRTY flycatcher
ACCEFIILPS specifical
ACCEFIIRRS sacrificer
ACCEFIKNRT fan-cricket
ACCEFILLOR calciferol
ACCEFILMOR calceiform
ACCEFILRYY fairy-cycle
ACCEFINOST confiscate
ACCEFLLOTU flocculate
ACCEGIINOR cariogenic
ACCEGIKLNN necklacing
ACCEGILLNN cancelling
ACCEGILLNO collagenic
ACCEGILLOO ecological
ACCEGILNOT lactogenic
ACCEGIMOPS megascopic
ACCEGINNOR carcinogen
ACCEGINNOS cognisance
ACCEGINNOZ cognizance
ACCEHHIIRR hierarchic
ACCEHHIPRT heptarchic
ACCEHHOORS coach-horse
ACCEHHRRTU church-rate
ACCEHIILMR chimerical
ACCEHIIMRT chemiatric
ACCEHIINNT technician
ACCEHIINPT epicanthic
ACCEHIKOPS peacockish
ACCEHILLMY chemically
ACCEHILLTY hectically
ACCEHIMNNU unmechanic
ACCEHIMNOO maconochie
ACCEHIMPRT emphractic
ACCEHIMRSU Chaucerism
ACCEHINORT Acherontic
anchoretic
ACCEHIORRY hierocracy
ACCEHIORST escharotic
ACCEHIORTT theocratic
ACCEHIRRTT tetrarchic
ACCEHIRTVZ czarevitch
ACCEHKLNOT checklaton
ACCEHKOORS a-cockhorse
ACCEHLLNOR chancellor
ACCEHLMOOR homocercal
ACCEHLOOTY chocolatey
ACCEHLORRY cherry-coal
ACCEHLOSUY chylaceous
ACCEHMNOOR comanchero
ACCEHNNPTY catchpenny
ACCEHNNRTY trenchancy
ACCEHNOOTY choanocyte
ACCEHNORTT technocrat
trench-coat

ACCEHOORSU	ochraceous
ACCEHORRUW	crouch-ware
ACCEIILNOT	conciliate
ACCEIILNRS	circensial
ACCEIILRRT	rectricial
ACCEIILRTT	tectricial
ACCEIILSSS	classicise
ACCEIILSSZ	classicize
ACCEIIMRST	ceramicist
ACCEIIMSST	asceticism
ACCEIINNNT	cincinnate
ACCEIINNOR	Ciceronian
ACCEIINNRS	circensian
ACCEIINRST	Cistercian
ACCEIIRSTX	cicatrixes
ACCEIKKNNT	nick-nacket
ACCEIKRRTW	wit-cracker
ACCEILLLOR	claircolle
ACCEILLNRU	unclerical
ACCEILLNSY	scenically
ACCEILMMOR	commercial
ACCEILMNOO	economical
ACCEILMNOP	compliance
ACCEILMOOT	coelomatic
ACCEILMOPT	complicate
ACCEILMORS	microscale
ACCEILMOST	cacomistle
	cosmetical
ACCEILNOSS	neoclassic
ACCEILNOTU	noctilucae
ACCEILNRST	calc-sinter
ACCEILOPPT	apoplectic
ACCEILOPRR	reciprocal
ACCEIMNORS	conacreism
ACCEIMNRSY	miscreancy
ACCEINNNOV	connivance
ACCEINNOOR	cancionero
ACCEINNOPR	Copernican
ACCEINNORT	concertina
ACCEINNSSY	incessancy
ACCEINOORS	occasioner
ACCEINOOST	consociate
ACCEINORST	Cestracion
ACCEINTTUV	cunctative
ACCEIOORSU	coriaceous
ACCEIOPPSY	episcopacy
ACCEIOPRTY	pyro-acetic
ACCEIOPTUV	occupative
ACCEIORRTU	Eurocratic
ACCEIORSTX	exsiccator
ACCEIORTUY	eucaryotic
ACCEIOSSTT	sticcatoes
ACCEIOSSTU	cistaceous
ACCEIRRSTT	tractrices
ACCEJNOSUU	juncaceous
ACCEKKLMOR	clockmaker
ACCEKNRRTU	nutcracker
ACCELLNOSU	cancellous
ACCELLOORT	colorectal
ACCELLSSUU	calculuses
ACCELMNOPT	complacent
ACCELMOPRS	camel-corps
ACCELNOPTU	conceptual
ACCELNOTXY	nectocalyx
ACCELNRTUY	reluctancy
ACCELOOPST	lactoscope
ACCELORTTU	coal-cutter
ACCEMNNORY	necromancy
ACCEMORSTU	reaccustom
ACCENNNOOS	consonance
ACCENOORSU	cornaceous
ACCENORSTY	consectary
ACCENORTTU	counteract
ACCEORSUUV	curvaceous
ACCFFFFHHI	chiffchaff
ACCFHIRTTW	witchcraft
ACCFIIIMPS	pacificism
ACCFIIIPST	pacificist
ACCFIINNOT	fantoccini
ACCFILMORY	calyciform
ACCFILSSUU	fasciculus
ACCFIMNORR	cancriform
ACCFIMOPTY	compactify
ACCFNOORRT	corn-factor
ACCFORRTTU	courtcraft
ACCFORSTTU	scoutcraft
ACCGGHILOO	cholagogic
ACCGHIIIOP	pichiciago
ACCGHIILOR	oligarchic
ACCGHINRST	scratching
ACCGHIOPTY	phagocytic
ACCGHIRSTW	scratch-wig
ACCGHLOPRY	cyclograph
ACCGIIMORT	tragicomic
ACCGIKLNRS	cracklings
ACCGILNSUY	accusingly
ACCGINNOTU	accounting
ACCGINORTU	accoutring
ACCGINORTY	gynocratic
ACCGOSTUYZ	zygocactus
ACCHHIILLN	△chinchilla
ACCHHIILRY	chiliarchy
ACCHHILLSS	clish-clash
ACCHIIILST	chiliastic
ACCHIILORT	acrolithic
ACCHIILTTY	tachylitic
ACCHIIMOSS	isochasmic
ACCHIIMSST	mica-schist
	schismatic
ACCHIINORT	anchoritic
ACCHIINOTY	thiocyanic
ACCHIINRST	stracchini
ACCHIKMQTU	quick-match
ACCHIKMSTT	matchstick
ACCHILMOPS	accomplish
ACCHILNNPS	splanchnic
ACCHILNOOT	△catholicon
ACCHILOOST	Catholicos
ACCHILOOTU	acolouthic
ACCHILOSST	scholastic
ACCHILRSTY	scratchily
ACCHILTTYY	tachylytic
ACCHIMNOOY	iconomachy
ACCHIMNORY	chiromancy

ACCHIMORST	chromatics
ACCHINOOPR	acrophonic
ACCHINORST	stracchino
ACCHIOPRSZ	schizocarp
ACCHIOPTTY	hypotactic
ACCHIOSSTT	stochastic
ACCHMOOORT	motor-coach
ACCHMORSST	cross-match
ACCHNOPSYY	sycophancy
ACCHNORRST	cornstarch
ACCHOOPRTY	cacotrophy
ACCHOPRSST	crosspatch
ACCIIILLLP	piccalilli
ACCIILLLNY	clinically
ACCIILLNOY	iconically
ACCIILLRTY	critically
ACCIILMNOS	laconicism
ACCIILMORU	coumarilic
ACCIILMOTY	comicality
ACCIILMSSS	classicism
ACCIILNNOT	calcitonin
ACCIILNORY	conciliary
ACCIILNRTU	uncritical
ACCIILOPRT	pictorical
ACCIILORTY	caloricity
ACCIILSSST	classicist
ACCIIMNNNO	cinnamonic
ACCIIMNOOT	iconomatic
ACCIIMNOPS	misocapnic
ACCIIMNRSU	muscarinic
ACCIIMORTT	timocratic
ACCIINNNPY	piccaninny
ACCIINNOST	canonistic
ACCIINNOTY	canonicity
ACCIINNSST	scintiscan
ACCIINORSS	carcinosis
ACCIIOPRSU	capricious
ACCIIOTTVY	coactivity
ACCIISTTUY	causticity
ACCIKKKKNN	knick-knack
ACCIKKRRTT	trick-track
ACCILLMORY	millocracy
ACCILLMOSY	cosmically
ACCILLRRUY	circularly
ACCILLSUUU	cauliculus
ACCILMNNOU	councilman
ACCILMNOOS	iconoclasm
ACCILMNOPT	complicant
ACCILMNOPY	compliancy
ACCILMORSS	crossclaim
ACCILNOOST	iconoclast
ACCILNOPTY	nyctalopic
ACCILNORTU	inculcator
ACCILNOSTV	conclavist
ACCILNSSTY	synclastic
ACCILOPPRY	polycarpic
ACCILORRTU	circulator
ACCILRRRUU	curricular
ACCIMMOORS	cosmoramic
ACCIMNOOPR	monocarpic
ACCIMNOOPT	compaction
ACCIMNOORT	monocratic
ACCINNOTTU	cunctation
ACCINOOPRU	cornucopia
ACCINOOPTU	occupation
ACCINOPRSY	conspiracy
ACCIOOPRSU	procacious
ACCIOOPSTU	autoscopic
ACCIOPRSTT	catoptrics
ACCIORSUUV	curvacious
ACCKLMOORU	cockalorum
ACCKORSTTU	track-scout
ACCLOPRTUY	plutocracy
ACCNNNOOSY	consonancy
ACCNOOPRRY	pornocracy
ACCNOORRTT	contractor
ACCNORTTUY	cunctatory
ACDDDEGIPY	giddy-paced
ACDDDGIRTU	drug-addict
ACDDEEEINP	dependacie
ACDDEEEIRT	rededicate
ACDDEEENNP	dependance
ACDDEEENRT	dead-centre
ACDDEEHLOO	coolheaded
ACDDEEHLTY	detachedly
ACDDEEHNOR	decahedron
ACDDEEIIPT	diapedetic
ACDDEEIITV	dedicative
ACDDEELLOT	decollated
ACDDEELLRY	declaredly
ACDDEELLSY	Clydesdale
ACDDEELNRU	undeclared
ACDDEELNTY	decadently
ACDDEENNRU	redundance
ACDDEENNST	descendant
ACDDEENNSU	unascended
ACDDEENTUU	uneducated
ACDDEESSTU	decussated
ACDDEFGHOU	doughfaced
ACDDEFNORU	round-faced
ACDDEGHNNY	cynghanedd
ACDDEGILNO	Iceland-dog
ACDDEGINOT	date-coding
ACDDEHIIIP	aphidicide
ACDDEHKLRU	herald-duck
ACDDEHLORR	card-holder
ACDDEHNNOS	second-hand
ACDDEHNOOO	deaconhood
ACDDEIIJTU	dijudicate
ACDDEIILTU	dilucidate
ACDDEIINOT	dedication
ACDDEIKNRS	crank-sided
ACDDEILMOU	duodecimal
ACDDEINNSS	candidness
ACDDEIOPSU	pseudoacid
ACDDEIORTY	dedicatory
ACDDEIPSTU	cuspidated
ACDDEIRSTT	distracted
ACDDEKLLNO	land-locked
ACDDEKLORS	dreadlocks
ACDDELNNOO	colonnaded
ACDDELNOOW	candlewood
ACDDELNOPU	candle-doup
ACDDENNRUY	redundancy

ACDDENORSU decandrous
ACDDENORSW sword-dance
ACDDEOOPSU decapodous
ACDDFHIORU chaudfroid
ACDDGHILNR grandchild
ACDDIINOPS dispondaic
ACDDILNNUY uncandidly
ACDDIMORSW caddis-worm
ACDDINORST discordant
ACDEEEEHHS cheese-head
headcheese
ACDEEEELNS needle-case
ACDEEEELRT decelerate
ACDEEEEPRS predecease
ACDEEEFHPS sheep-faced
ACDEEEFLNR fer-de-lance
ACDEEEFMNN defenceman
ACDEEEFMNT defacement
ACDEEEGNRY degeneracy
ACDEEEHLTT decathlete
ACDEEEHNRT head-centre
ACDEEEILSU Seleucidae
ACDEEEIPRT depreciate
ACDEEELNRT candle-tree
ACDEEELSTT telecasted
ACDEEEMNST casemented
ACDEEENNTT antecedent
ACDEEENRTV advertence
ACDEEEORRT redecorate
ACDEEERRST desecrater
ACDEEERSUY saucer-eyed
ACDEEFFHRT far-fetched
ACDEEFFLTY affectedly
ACDEEFFNTU unaffected
ACDEEFHITW white-faced
ACDEEFHORS horse-faced
ACDEEFINOT defecation
ACDEEFINWZ wizen-faced
ACDEEFIRSS fricasseed
ACDEEFKOPR poker-faced
ACDEEFLNOR confederal
ACDEEFLNOY falcon-eyed
ACDEEFOPRW face-powder
ACDEEFORST forecasted
ACDEEGHINP phagedenic
ACDEEGHLLN challenged
ACDEEGHNNO hendecagon
ACDEEGIIMN mediagenic
ACDEEGIINT diagenetic
ACDEEGILMO geomedical
ACDEEGILOS geodesical
ACDEEGILOT geodetical
ACDEEGIMMR decigramme
ACDEEGINNR grand-niece
ACDEEGINRR adrenergic
ACDEEGINRT centigrade
ACDEEGIORU aigre-douce
ACDEEGLLOU colleagued
ACDEEGLLRW well-graced
ACDEEGLNRT rectangled
ACDEEGORTY grey-coated
ACDEEHIINO Echinoidea
ACDEEHILNR chandelier
ACDEEHIMRS Archimedes
ACDEEHINNR hinderance
ACDEEHINOT theodicean
ACDEEHIORT cote-hardie
ACDEEHKLLS shellacked
ACDEEHLLMU chaud-mellé
ACDEEHLLNN channelled
ACDEEHLLRT thread-cell
ACDEEHLLST satchelled
ACDEEHLORT cloth-eared
ACDEEHLRRU hurdle-race
ACDEEHMNTT detachment
ACDEEHNNRS hand-screen
ACDEEHNRSU unsearched
ACDEEHOPPR copperhead
ACDEEHPSST despatches
ACDEEIILMP epidemical
ACDEEIILMS decimalise
medicalise
ACDEEIILMZ decimalize
medicalize
ACDEEIILNT indelicate
ACDEEIILTT dietetical
ACDEEIIMRT acidimeter
ACDEEIIMTV medicative
ACDEEIKPRR prick-eared
ACDEEILLNP lead-pencil
pencil-lead
ACDEEILLNR Cinderella
ACDEEILLRS escadrille
ACDEEILLTY delicately
ACDEEILMNR endermical
ACDEEILMNT maledicent
ACDEEILMPR premedical
ACDEEILMRV decemviral
ACDEEILNRS calendries
ACDEEILNRT credential
interlaced
ACDEEILNSU Seleucidan
ACDEEILOPS Scopelidae
ACDEEILOSV devocalise
ACDEEILOVZ devocalize
ACDEEILPRY dice-player
ACDEEILPTU pediculate
ACDEEILRTT red-lattice
ACDEEIMMNT medicament
ACDEEIMNNO encomienda
ACDEEIMNOU eudaemonic
ACDEEIMNRT endermatic
ACDEEIMOTT comedietta
ACDEEIMPRT mercaptide
ACDEEIMRST medicaster
miscreated
ACDEEINNNT intendance
ACDEEINNTU denunciate
ACDEEINORS Deinoceras
ACDEEINOST cestoidean
ACDEEINPPS appendices
ACDEEINPTT pectinated
ACDEEINRRW wire-dancer
ACDEEINSST desistance

ACDEEIORTV decorative
ACDEEIOTTX detoxicate
ACDEEIPRST pederastic
ACDEEIPSTU paedeutics
ACDEEIRTTV detractive
ACDEEITTUX exactitude
ACDEEKLNRY cankeredly
ACDEELLLPW well-placed
ACDEELLLTU cellulated
ACDEELLMPU cul-de-lampe
ACDEELLNPS spancelled
ACDEELLNRU unrecalled
ACDEELLOPS escalloped
ACDEELMORT ectodermal
ACDEELMORU leucoderma
ACDEELMRTU emerald-cut
ACDEELNNOV decennoval
ACDEELNNSU uncleansed
ACDEELNORR corn-dealer
ACDEELNOST adolescent
ACDEELNRTU crenulated
ACDEELOORT decolorate
ACDEELOPPY Pelecypoda
ACDEELOPRV overplaced
ACDEELORTU edulcorate
ACDEELRRTT letter-card
ACDEEMMNOR commandeer
ACDEEMMNPT decampment
ACDEEMNOTY adenectomy
ACDEEMORSU decamerous
ACDEENNOPR ponderance
ACDEENNORR once-errand
ACDEENNOST condensate
ACDEENNOTV covenanted
ACDEENNRSU sunderance
ACDEENOPRR rope-dancer
ACDEENORST second-rate
ACDEENPRRU perdurance
ACDEENPRST stepdancer
ACDEENPRTU uncarpeted
ACDEENRSSS sacredness
ACDEENRTTU detruncate
ACDEENRTVY advertency
ACDEEOPRRT deprecator
tape-record
ACDEEOPRSU predaceous
ACDEEORRST desecrator
stereocard
ACDEFFIKRT trafficked
ACDEFFLORS scaffolder
ACDEFGHILT light-faced
ACDEFGILNY defacingly
ACDEFGINOR dog-fancier
ACDEFHILNS candlefish
ACDEFHOSUV vouchsafed
ACDEFIIINT nidificate
ACDEFIILMS facsimiled
ACDEFIILOT foeticidal
ACDEFIILSS classified
ACDEFIINPU unpacified
ACDEFIINST sanctified
ACDEFIIRRT fratricide
ACDEFILMTU multifaced
ACDEFILSSY declassify
ACDEFINNOT confidante
ACDEFINORT deforciant
ACDEFIOPRT forcipated
ACDEFIRSSY decrassify
ACDEFLNOOT foot-candle
ACDEFNORRU uncared-for
ACDEFNRRTU under-craft
ACDEFNRSUU unsurfaced
ACDEFPTTUY putty-faced
ACDEGGIOPS pedagogics
ACDEGHHILP high-placed
ACDEGHILTT tight-laced
ACDEGHIRRS discharger
ACDEGHRRSU surcharged
ACDEGIILMN declaiming
ACDEGIILMR germicidal
ACDEGIINNN indignance
ACDEGIINOR radiogenic
ACDEGIINOT Cotingidae
ACDEGIINST die-casting
ACDEGIIRRR cirrigrade
ACDEGILNRW arc-welding
ACDEGILOOP logopaedic
ACDEGILOOR Coolgardie
ACDEGILOST decalogist
ACDEGIMNOY geodynamic
ACDEGINNOR androgenic
ACDEGINORR corrigenda
ACDEGINRTT detracting
ACDEGIORSU discourage
ACDEGJNOTU conjugated
ACDEGLLOPR placer-gold
ACDEGLNNRU grand-uncle
ACDEGLNORS cradlesong
ACDEGLOORS socdolager
ACDEGNOSUY decagynous
ACDEGOOPRS scrapegood
ACDEGORRTU corrugated
ACDEHHIMOR Hemichorda
ACDEHHNTTU unthatched
ACDEHHOPRT heptachord
ACDEHHORTY hydrotheca
ACDEHIILLO helicoidal
ACDEHIIMRT diathermic
ACDEHIINNS disenchain
ACDEHIIORR diarrhoeic
ACDEHILLMT ill-matched
ACDEHILMOT methodical
ACDEHILMRS Childermas
ACDEHILNRS Reichsland
ACDEHILNST Shetlandic
ACDEHILORT chloridate
ACDEHIMORT dichromate
ACDEHINNST disenchant
ACDEHINOPS deaconship
ACDEHINOPT Dictaphone®
ACDEHINORT ditrochean
ACDEHINRSZ scherzandi
ACDEHIOPPT heptapodic
ACDEHIPRST dispatcher

ACDEHIPSST dispatches
ACDEHIRTTW ditch-water
ACDEHKLNSU unshackled
ACDEHLLNPU punch-ladle
ACDEHLLNRY chandlerly
ACDEHLMOOS dame-school
ACDEHLNOSY anchylosed
ACDEHLNRSU rush-candle
ACDEHLOOPP cephalopod
ACDEHLRSTY starchedly
ACDEHMOSTU moustached
ACDEHNNORU unanchored
ACDEHNNSTU unstanched
ACDEHNOORT octahedron
ACDEHNOPRT pentachord
ACDEHNORSZ scherzando
ACDEHNRSTU unstarched
ACDEHOPRSY hydrospace
ACDEHORRTT tetrachord
ACDEIIILST idealistic
ACDEIIINTV indicative
ACDEIIIPRR Cirripedia
ACDEIIJTUV judicative
ACDEIIKNNS Dickensian
ACDEIILLOT idiolectal
ACDEIILMMS decimalism
ACDEIILMMT dilemmatic
ACDEIILMRS disclaimer
ACDEIILMRV vermicidal
ACDEIILMST decimalist
ACDEIILNNT incidental
ACDEIILOPR periodical
ACDEIILOPS episodical
ACDEIILORS cordialise
ACDEIILORZ cordialize
ACDEIILPST pesticidal
septicidal
ACDEIILPTU Pediculati
ACDEIIMNOT decimation
medication
ACDEIIMRTX taxidermic
ACDEIIMRTY acidimetry
ACDEIINNRY incendiary
ACDEIINOSY isocyanide
ACDEIINPRY Cyprinidae
ACDEIIORSU iridaceous
ACDEIIOSST dissociate
ACDEIIPPRY cypripedia
ACDEIIPRST pediatrics
ACDEIIPSTU paideutics
ACDEIJNTUV adjunctive
ACDEIJRTUU judicature
ACDEILLORR cordillera
ACDEILLTUV victualled
ACDEILMNOR decinormal
ACDEILMOST domestical
ACDEILNNOR endocrinal
ACDEILNORT centroidal
declinator
ACDEILNORY corydaline
ACDEILNOSV volcanised
ACDEILNOVZ volcanized
ACDEILNPSS placidness
ACDEILNRTW winter-clad
ACDEILNSTY syndetical
ACDEILOPRR precordial
ACDEILOPST despotical
ACDEILORSU radiculose
ACDEILORTU elucidator
ACDEILOSTU Locustidae
ACDEILOSTY Scolytidae
ACDEILOSUY edaciously
ACDEILOTTU colatitude
ACDEILPSTU disculpate
ACDEILRTTW wildcatter
ACDEIMMORY immoderacy
ACDEIMNNNO demi-cannon
ACDEIMNNOP △pandemonic
ACDEIMNNOR corn-maiden
ACDEIMNOPR incompared
ACDEIMNORU androecium
ACDEIMNOSU mendacious
ACDEIMNRSU muscardine
ACDEIMOPRR madreporic
ACDEINNNTY intendancy
ACDEINNOSS dissonance
ACDEINNRSS rancidness
ACDEINOORT carotenoid
co-ordinate
decoration
ACDEINOPPT pentapodic
ACDEINOPRS scorpaenid
ACDEINOQRU quadricone
ACDEINORRW cordwainer
ACDEINORST draconites
ACDEINORTT detraction
ACDEINOSTT anecdotist
ACDEINOSTW wainscoted
ACDEINOTTX detoxicant
ACDEINPRST discrepant
ACDEINPSTT pandectist
ACDEINRTUV incurvated
ACDEINSTTU sanctitude
ACDEIOOPRS radioscope
ACDEIOPRST ceratopsid
ACDEIOPRSU predacious
ACDEIOPRTT tetrapodic
ACDEIOPSSU spadiceous
ACDEIORSTU outside-car
ACDEIOSSTT tossicated
ACDEIOSTTT tosticated
ACDEIPQRSU quadriceps
ACDEIQRSTU quadrisect
ACDEIRSSTT dictatress
ACDEIRSSTU crassitude
ACDEIRSSTY dyscrasite
ACDEIRSTTU rusticated
ACDEIRTTUV traductive
ACDEKKMOPR pockmarked
ACDEKMORST dock-master
ACDEKMPRSU muckspread
ACDEKNRSSU sandsucker
ACDEKNRSUV raven's-duck

ACDEKORSTY	rocksteady
	rock-steady
ACDELLOORT	decollator
ACDELLORSW	worldscale
ACDELMNOOR	△coromandel
ACDELMNOTU	columnated
	documental
ACDELNOORT	decolorant
ACDELNOOTY	acotyledon
ACDELNORTU	edulcorant
ACDELNPRUU	peduncular
ACDELNRSSU	underclass
ACDELOORRW	wool-carder
ACDELOPPTU	clapped-out
ACDELOPRRU	procedural
ACDELOSSTU	outclassed
ACDEMMNORY	commandery
ACDEMMOSTU	custom-made
ACDEMNORTU	mucronated
ACDEMOOPRR	compradore
ACDEMOPRSU	damp-course
ACDEMORRSS	cross-armed
ACDEMPRSTU	spermaduct
ACDENNNOOR	ordonnance
ACDENNNOOS	nanosecond
ACDENNOPRY	ponderancy
ACDENOPPSW	snow-capped
ACDENOPSTY	syncopated
ACDENORRTU	underactor
ACDENORRTW	rent-a-crowd
ACDENRRRTU	redcurrant
ACDENRRSTU	transducer
ACDENRSTTU	cruet-stand
ACDEOORRVW	woodcarver
ACDEOPPRSU	pseudocarp
ACDEOPRRTT	protracted
ACDEOPRSUU	drupaceous
ACDEORRTTY	detractory
ACDFFHINSU	handicuffs
ACDFGIIINY	acidifying
ACDFGIILNU	fungicidal
ACDFGLNORU	calf-ground
ACDFIILLUY	fiducially
ACDFIIMORR	radiciform
ACDFIMNNOR	confirmand
ACDFORRSTW	swordcraft
ACDGHINORR	orcharding
ACDGHIOPRT	Dictograph®
ACDGHIPRSY	dysgraphic
ACDGHNOOTU	touch-and-go
ACDGIIIMNR	gramicidin
ACDGIILOOR	radiologic
ACDGIINORS	disorganic
ACDGIINORT	riding-coat
ACDGIINOST	diagnostic
ACDGILNOOT	odontalgic
ACDGILOORY	cardiology
ACDGIMMNNO	commanding
ACDGINNPRU	cup-and-ring
ACDGLOTYYZ	zygodactyl
ACDGMNOPRU	campground
ACDHHLNOOR	anchor-hold
ACDHIIILRT	crithidial
ACDHIIIOPT	idiopathic
ACDHIILOSZ	schizoidal
ACDHIIMSSS	Chassidism
ACDHILLRYY	hydrically
ACDHILMNOW	woman-child
ACDHILMOOS	schoolmaid
ACDHILNOOP	chilopodan
ACDHILOORT	trochoidal
ACDHILRSST	third-class
ACDHILRSSY	chrysalids
ACDHILRSUY	hydraulics
ACDHIMSTYY	dysthymiac
ACDHINOOOX	chionodoxa
ACDHIOOPRR	Cirrhopoda
ACDHIOOPRS	Discophora
ACDHIOOPSZ	Schizopoda
ACDHIOPRSW	cowardship
ACDHIORRST	orchardist
ACDHIORTTY	trachytoid
ACDHLOORRU	urochordal
ACDHLOORSW	schoolward
ACDHLOOSSY	schooldays
ACDHMNOORS	chondromas
ACDHMNORYY	hydromancy
ACDHMNOTUW	Dutchwoman
ACDIIIJLNU	injudicial
ACDIIIMMRU	miracidium
ACDIIINNOT	indication
ACDIIJLLUY	judicially
ACDIIJNOTU	judication
ACDIILLOPR	prolicidal
ACDIILLSUY	suicidally
ACDIILMOPT	diplomatic
ACDIILMOST	modalistic
ACDIILOPRT	dioptrical
ACDIILORST	clostridia
ACDIILORTY	cordiality
	radiolytic
ACDIILORUX	uxoricidal
ACDIIMNOOT	coati-mondi
ACDIIMNORT	antidromic
ACDIIMNOSY	isodynamic
ACDIIMNOTU	coati-mundi
ACDIIMNSTY	dynamicist
	dynamistic
ACDIINNORY	inordinacy
ACDIINOORT	carotinoid
ACDIINOORV	Ordovician
ACDIINOOST	scotodinia
ACDIINORSU	dinosauric
ACDIINORTV	vindicator
ACDIINORTY	dictionary
	indicatory
ACDIINOSTT	donatistic
ACDIINRTUY	iracundity
ACDIIOORTX	radiotoxic
ACDIIOPRST	parodistic
ACDIJNNOTU	adjunction
ACDIJORTUX	coadjutrix
ACDIJORTUY	judicatory
ACDIKLORRZ	rock-lizard

ACDIKNQSUY quick-sandy
ACDILLMNOU calmodulin
ACDILLOOST idoloclast
ACDILNRSTU translucid
ACDILOOPRS prosodical
ACDILOOPTY octaploidy
ACDILOPRTU duplicator
ACDILORSSU discoursal
ACDILPSSTY dysplastic
ACDIMMORUY myocardium
ACDIMNORTU Dracontium
ACDIMOORSU mordacious
ACDINNOSSY dissonancy
ACDINOORRT rain-doctor
ACDINORSTY syndicator
ACDINORTTU traduction
ACDIOOPRSY radioscopy
ACDIOOSTUU outdacious
ACDKLMOSSY lady's-smock
ACDKNORSTU soundtrack
ACDLLOOPSW codswallop
cod's-wallop
ACDLLOPTYY polydactyl
ACDLLORSSW world-class
ACDLMNOOSY condylomas
ACDLNSTYYY syndactyly
ACDMNOOPSY spodomancy
ACDMOOSSUV muscovados
ACDNOORSTU octandrous
ACDOORRSSS crossroads
ACEEEEGNPR Greenpeace
ACEEEFFMNT effacement
ACEEEFFTTU effectuate
ACEEEFIPRT afterpiece
ACEEEFLNRR freelancer
ACEEEFMNNT enfacement
ACEEEGILNN inelegance
ACEEEGILTX exegetical
ACEEEGINRT great-niece
ACEEEGNPRT percentage
ACEEEGNRRY regeneracy
ACEEEHILSV chevesaile
ACEEEHIRTT hereticate
ACEEEHKPRS cash-keeper
ACEEEHLMOT hematocele
ACEEEHLPSW scape-wheel
ACEEEHORRT Heterocera
ACEEEHRRRS researcher
ACEEEHRRRT treacherer
ACEEEIMRST camsteerie
ACEEEINNNT ante-Nicene
ACEEEINRRS reincrease
ACEEEINRRT reiterance
ACEEEINRSS nécessaire
ACEEEIPPRV apperceive
ACEEEIRRST secretaire
ACEEEIRRTV recreative
ACEEEIRSTV eviscerate
ACEEEIRTVX execrative
ACEEEKPPPR pepper-cake
ACEEELLNPR repellance
ACEEELLNRT crenellate
ACEEELMNNT enlacement
ACEEELNPRV prevalence
ACEEELORTT electorate
ACEEELOSTT steatocele
ACEEELPRVY everyplace
ACEEELPSSS escapeless
ACEEELRSTT telecaster
ACEEELRTUX exulcerate
ACEEEMMNRT amercement
ACEEEMNNPR permanence
ACEEEMNNST encasement
ACEEEMNPRT temperance
ACEEEMNPST escapement
ACEEEMNRST meatscreen
ACEEEMNRTT metacentre
ACEEEMNRTX excrementa
ACEEENNOTV covenantee
ACEEENNPRT penetrance
repentance
ACEEENNRRT re-entrance
ACEEENNSTV evanescent
ACEEEPRRTU recuperate
ACEEEPRSTT pace-setter
ACEEERRTTT terracette
ACEEFFHLRS schefflera
ACEEFFHSUU chauffeuse
ACEEFFIMNY effeminacy
ACEEFFLSST affectless
ACEEFFNRSU sufferance
ACEEFGIRST siegecraft
ACEEFHINPR pine-chafer
ACEEFHINRS franchisee
ACEEFHLNRT centre-half
ACEEFHNORT technofear
ACEEFHORRS rose-chafer
ACEEFIIILN Filicineae
ACEEFIILTT felicitate
ACEEFIJKLT life-jacket
ACEEFILMNT maleficent
ACEEFILNRT frenetical
ACEEFILNSS facileness
ACEEFILNST leaf-insect
ACEEFILRSU luciferase
ACEEFIORTV vociferate
ACEEFIRRTV refractive
ACEEFKORRW faceworker
ACEEFLLNTU flatulence
ACEEFLLORV cloverleaf
ACEEFLLPUY peacefully
ACEEFLNPUU unpeaceful
ACEEFLNSTV flavescent
ACEEFLORST forecastle
ACEEFLRTTU leaf-cutter
ACEEFNQRTU queencraft
ACEEFOPSSU pousse-café
ACEEFORRST forecaster
ACEEFPRSTU superfecta
ACEEFRRRTU refracture
ACEEGGGINP pace-egging
ACEEGGILNO genealogic
ACEEGGLPSU egg-capsule
ACEEGGNORT congregate

ACEEGHILNT	genethliac
ACEEGHLLNR	challenger
ACEEGHLNRT	acre-length
ACEEGHLNSS	changeless
ACEEGHLRSS	chargeless
ACEEGHNORV	changeover
ACEEGHNRRT	rent-charge
ACEEGHORRV	overcharge
ACEEGILLNR	allergenic
ACEEGILLOT	collegiate
ACEEGILLPR	peelgarlic
ACEEGILNNY	inelegancy
ACEEGILNTU	geniculate
ACEEGILSTU	sluicegate
ACEEGIMNOR	cinema-goer
ACEEGINNPT	pangenetic
ACEEGIORRT	groceteria
ACEEGIORST	categories
	categorise
ACEEGIORTZ	categorize
ACEEGIOTTX	excogitate
ACEEGLMNOR	camerlengo
ACEEGLNORV	overglance
ACEEGLNRTU	great-uncle
ACEEGLNRTW	clew-garnet
ACEEGLRTUV	culvertage
ACEEGMMOSU	gemmaceous
ACEEGNNORV	governance
ACEEGNNPRU	repugnance
ACEEGNORRU	encourager
ACEEGNRSVY	scavengery
ACEEGOPRST	corpse-gate
ACEEHHILNW	chainwheel
ACEEHHILRW	wheelchair
ACEEHHIRRS	heresiarch
ACEEHHPTTU	Heptateuch
ACEEHIIPRT	perithecia
ACEEHILMNN	manchineel
ACEEHILMRT	hermetical
ACEEHILNNP	encephalin
ACEEHILNNS	channelise
ACEEHILNNZ	channelize
ACEEHILNST	anthelices
ACEEHILPTT	telepathic
ACEEHIMNPZ	chimpanzee
ACEEHIMPRY	hyperaemic
ACEEHIMPTT	empathetic
ACEEHIMRTX	hexametric
ACEEHIMSST	schematise
ACEEHIMSTZ	schematize
ACEEHIMTTT	metathetic
ACEEHINNOT	Antiochene
ACEEHINNPT	phenacetin
ACEEHINOPR	peacherino
ACEEHINPRS	phrenesiac
ACEEHIORRT	charioteer
ACEEHISSTT	aesthetics
ACEEHKMNSU	hamesucken
ACEEHLLMOS	cameo-shell
ACEEHLLMPW	wheel-clamp
ACEEHLLNOP	cellophane®
ACEEHLNNOP	encephalon
ACEEHLNPRU	leprechaun
ACEEHLNPRW	leprechawn
ACEEHLNPTT	planchette
ACEEHLNPTY	phlyctenae
ACEEHLOPTY	polychaete
ACEEHLRSSS	searchless
ACEEHLRSST	thale-cress
ACEEHLRTVW	lever-watch
ACEEHLSSST	scatheless
ACEEHMMRSU	meerschaum
ACEEHMNNST	encashment
ACEEHMNPRT	preachment
ACEEHMNRST	Manchester
ACEEHMOPSS	mesoscaphe
ACEEHMORTT	tachometer
ACEEHMPRTY	pachymeter
ACEEHMRTTY	tachymeter
ACEEHNOPST	peach-stone
ACEEHNPTTU	Pentateuch
ACEEHNRSST	stern-chase
ACEEHNSSST	chasteness
ACEEHOPRRR	reproacher
ACEEHOPRSU	proseuchae
ACEEHORRST	trace-horse
ACEEHPPRSY	hyperspace
ACEEHPRRSU	repurchase
ACEEHPRTUY	hyperacute
ACEEHRRSTU	△chartreuse
ACEEIILMRT	eremitical
ACEEIILNTT	licentiate
ACEEIILPSS	specialise
ACEEIILPSZ	specialize
ACEEIILSST	elasticise
ACEEIILSTZ	elasticize
ACEEIIMNPT	impatience
ACEEIIMPST	episematic
	septicemia
ACEEIINNRT	creatinine
	incinerate
ACEEIINRSU	Cuisenaire
ACEEIIPSST	asepticise
ACEEIIPSTZ	asepticize
ACEEIIRRST	sericteria
ACEEIIRTTV	recitative
ACEEIITTVX	excitative
ACEEIKLMNS	simnel-cake
ACEEIKLRRS	arse-licker
ACEEIKNNSS	snick-a-snee
ACEEIKPRTT	ticker-tape
ACEEILLMST	mile-castle
ACEEILLMTY	emetically
ACEEILLORT	electorial
ACEEILLPSY	especially
ACEEILMMRS	mesmerical
ACEEILMNOR	ceremonial
ACEEILMNOT	colemanite
	melaconite
ACEEILMNRT	mercantile
ACEEILMNST	centesimal
	lemniscate
ACEEILMOSU	meliaceous
ACEEILMPTT	metaleptic

ACEEILMSTT telematics
telesmatic
ACEEILNNNT centennial
ACEEILNNPT Pentelican
ACEEILNNUV univalence
ACEEILNOPU leucopenia
ACEEILNORT neoterical
ACEEILNPRT epicentral
ACEEILNRRT centre-rail
ACEEILNRST centralise
ACEEILNRSU nuclearise
ACEEILNRTV cantilever
trivalence
ACEEILNRTZ centralize
ACEEILNRUZ nuclearize
ACEEILORTV corelative
ACEEILORTX exoterical
ACEEILPPRT preceptial
ACEEILPRSW parcelwise
ACEEILRRSU curselarie
ACEEILRRTT retractile
ACEEILRSSU secularise
ACEEILRSUZ secularize
ACEEILRTTU reticulate
ACEEILRTUV ulcerative
ACEEILRTVY creatively
reactively
ACEEILSTUV vesiculate
ACEEIMNNRS Emi-Scanner®
ACEEIMNNST incasement
ACEEIMNORU Mucorineae
ACEEIMNRSS creaminess
ACEEIMNRSV serviceman
ACEEIMNRTT remittance
ACEEIMORRT aerometric
ACEEIMPRST spermaceti
ACEEIMRSTT tetrasemic
ACEEINNPRS Spencerian
ACEEINNRST transience
ACEEINOPST stenopaeic
ACEEINORRT recreation
ACEEINORST estanciero
ACEEINORTU auctioneer
ACEEINORTX execration
ACEEINPPRT apprentice
pine-carpet
ACEEINPRST interspace
ACEEINRSST △resistance
ACEEINRTTT tetractine
ACEEINRTUV unreactive
ACEEINRTVY inveteracy
ACEEINSSTV activeness
ACEEIOOPRS aeciospore
ACEEIOPPST episcopate
ACEEIOPSST caespitose
ACEEIOQTUV equivocate
ACEEIPQRSU picaresque
ACEEIPRRSV riverscape
ACEEIQRSTU requiescat
ACEEIRRSUW cruisewear
ACEEIRRTTV retractive
ACEEIRSTTU Securitate
ACEEIRTTVX extractive
ACEEJLMNOT cajolement
ACEEKLLNNO kennel-coal
ACEEKLLOWY yellowcake
ACEEKLLRSS salesclerk
ACEEKNOPTT packet-note
ACEEKNRRRT rack-renter
ACEEKORRRW careworker
ACEEKORRSW caseworker
ACEELLLMOU columellae
ACEELLMNRT recallment
ACEELLNOTU nucleolate
ACEELLNPRY repellancy
ACEELLNPST pallescent
ACEELLORTT collarette
ACEELLRSSY carelessly
ACEELLSTTU scutellate
ACEELMNOST solacement
ACEELMNOTY melanocyte
ACEELMOPRT clapometer
ACEELMORTT lactometer
ACEELNOPRV Provençale
ACEELNOPST opalescent
ACEELNORRT necrolater
ACEELNPRSU superclean
ACEELNPRSY screenplay
ACEELNPRVY prevalency
ACEELNRRTY recreantly
ACEELOOPRT Coleoptera
ACEELOORSU oleraceous
ACEELOPPRT Plecoptera
ACEELOPRTU operculate
ACEELOSSTT cassolette
ACEELPPRTU perceptual
ACEELQRRUU craquelure
ACEELRRTUY creaturely
ACEEMMNNPT encampment
ACEEMMNOTT commentate
ACEEMMORSU commeasure
ACEEMNNPRY permanency
ACEEMNOPST compensate
ACEEMNORTY cyanometer
ACEEMNPRST escarpment
ACEEMOSTUZ eczematous
ACEENNOPRV provenance
ACEENNOPSU pennaceous
ACEENNORTV contravene
covenanter
ACEENNOTTZ canzonette
ACEENNPRTU purtenance
ACEENNPRTY penetrancy
ACEENNPRVY prevenancy
ACEENNRRTY re-entrancy
ACEENNRSSV cravenness
ACEENNSSTU sustenance
ACEENOOSTU coetaneous
ACEENOPRTT pernoctate
ACEENORSSS coarseness
ACEENORSST antecessor
ACEENORSTU nectareous
raconteuse
ACEENPRSTT respectant

ACEENPRUVY	purveyance
ACEENRRTUU	nature-cure
ACEENRSSST	ancestress
ACEENRSSTW	newscaster
ACEENRSUVY	surveyance
ACEEORRSTT	stercorate
ACEEORRTXY	execratory
ACEEOSSTTU	testaceous
ACEEPRRRTU	recapturer
ACEEPRSTUU	superacute
ACEERRSSTW	watercress
ACEFFGINSU	suffigance
ACEFFGNSUU	face-fungus
ACEFFHLPSU	shuffle-cap
ACEFFIILTV	afflictive
ACEFFIIMNS	caffeinism
ACEFFIIORR	air-officer
ACEFFIKRRT	trafficker
ACEFFILNOO	loan-office
ACEFFILORW	law-officer
ACEFFINSSU	suffisance
ACEFFOSTUU	tuffaceous
ACEFGHIRRT	freight-car
ACEFGIKLRU	craigfluke
ACEFGILNST	self-acting
ACEFGINRRT	refracting
ACEFGLLRUY	gracefully
ACEFGLNRUU	ungraceful
ACEFHHIRRS	archerfish
ACEFHIINTT	fianchetti
ACEFHILPST	felspathic
ACEFHILRTU	ultrafiche
ACEFHINOTT	fianchetto
ACEFHINRRS	franchiser
ACEFHIRRSV	fish-carver
ACEFHKORST	aftershock
ACEFHLLNOP	chopfallen
ACEFHLOPRY	hyperfocal
ACEFHORRTV	hovercraft
ACEFHORSTU	housecraft
ACEFIIIILNN	filicinean
ACEFIIILST	facilities
ACEFIILMSS	facsimiles
ACEFIILNRU	Luciferian
ACEFIILORR	calorifier
ACEFIILPST	spiflicate
ACEFIILRSS	classifier
ACEFIINRST	△sanctifier
ACEFIKLLNS	sick-fallen
ACEFILNORS	forinsecal
ACEFILNOST	self-action
ACEFILNTUU	funiculate
ACEFILOOSU	foliaceous
ACEFILRSSY	reclassify
ACEFIMNOSS	Neofascism
ACEFINORRT	refraction
ACEFINORTV	vociferant
ACEFINOSST	Neofascist
ACEFINRSST	craftiness
ACEFIRRRTV	rivercraft
ACEFIRRTTU	trifurcate
ACEFKLNORS	cornflakes
ACEFKLOPPR	flock-paper
ACEFLLNOOR	once-for-all
ACEFLLNTUY	flatulency
ACEFLMORUU	camoufleur
ACEFLOOSTV	calves'-foot
ACEFLPSTUU	teacupfuls
ACEFLRSSUU	saucerfuls
ACEFNNOSST	confessant
ACEFNOPRTT	Pontefract
ACEFORRRTY	refractory
ACEFRRSSTU	surfcaster
ACEGGHILNN	changeling
ACEGGHIOPR	geographic
ACEGGHLOOU	cholagogue
ACEGGILLOO	geological
ACEGGINNOO	ocean-going
ACEGGINNSV	scavenging
ACEGGINRSS	cragginess
ACEGGNNORT	congregant
ACEGHHIJKR	highjacker
ACEGHHINOT	high-octane
ACEGHHLOOR	hog-cholera
ACEGHHOPRR	choregraph
ACEGHHOPRT	hectograph
ACEGHIILMT	megalithic
ACEGHIINRS	cashiering
ACEGHIIPPR	epigraphic
ACEGHILMPT	phlegmatic
ACEGHILPSY	hypalgesic
ACEGHILRTT	tight-lacer
ACEGHILRTU	theurgical
ACEGHIMNNU	machinegun
ACEGHIMNOP	megaphonic
	phenogamic
ACEGHIMPRS	graphemics
ACEGHINNNT	enchanting
ACEGHINOPT	pathogenic
ACEGHINRTT	chattering
ACEGHIOOPS	hagioscope
ACEGHIRSTW	switchgear
ACEGHLOORY	archeology
ACEGHOPRRY	cerography
ACEGHOPRTV	vectograph
ACEGHORTUV	overcaught
ACEGHRRRSU	surcharger
ACEGIIKNST	ice-skating
ACEGIILLST	legalistic
ACEGIILMTY	legitimacy
ACEGIILNNO	lignocaine
ACEGIILOST	egoistical
ACEGIIMOST	isogametic
ACEGIIMPTT	pegmatitic
ACEGIINNRS	increasing
ACEGIINORT	iatrogenic
ACEGIIOTTV	cogitative
ACEGIIPRST	epigastric
ACEGIIRRST	geriatrics
ACEGIKKLOR	goalkicker
ACEGIKLNNS	slackening
ACEGIKMRTY	kerygmatic
ACEGILLNOO	neological
ACEGILLNPR	parcelling

ACEGILLOOS oligoclase
ACEGILLPRT parcel-gilt
ACEGILMNNY menacingly
ACEGILMNOR camerlingo
ACEGILMRSS melic-grass
ACEGILNNOR iron-glance
ACEGILNNOT congenital
ACEGILNOOP geoponical
ACEGILNOPR pelargonic
ACEGILNOTU glauconite
ACEGILNPPR clappering
ACEGILNQRU lacquering
ACEGILNRST sternalgic
ACEGILNTXY exactingly
ACEGILOOPT apologetic
ACEGIMMMNO mammogenic
ACEGIMMRRS scrimmager
ACEGIMORST gasometric
ACEGINNNRT entrancing
ACEGINNOST costeaning
ACEGINNRST transgenic
ACEGINNRTU uncreating
ACEGINNSTT casting-net
ACEGINNTUX unexacting
ACEGINOPRS saprogenic
ACEGINOSTU autogenics
ACEGINRSTT scattering
ACEGIORSTT categorist
ACEGIOSSTT geostatics
ACEGIRSSTT strategics
ACEGKMNOOR mock-orange
ACEGKNORRT garnet-rock
ACEGKORSTU goatsucker
ACEGLMOSUU glumaceous
ACEGLNOOOY oceanology
ACEGLOOPRT colportage
ACEGLOOPSY escapology
ACEGLOOTUY autecology
ACEGLOPPRS scrog-apple
ACEGMMRRSU scrummager
ACEGMNOORR Greco-Roman
ACEGNNPRUY repugnancy
ACEGNOORSU acrogenous
ACEGNOORTY octogenary
ACEGNRSSUY assurgency
ACEGNRSTTU scatter-gun
ACEGOOPRRT proctorage
ACEGOORSUU courageous
ACEGOPRRSU supercargo
ACEGPRRSTU gut-scraper
ACEHHIKNOV Chekhovian
ACEHHILOPT Achitophel
ACEHHILTWZ witch-hazel
ACEHHIMPSS sachemship
ACEHHINNPT naphthenic
ACEHHINOPT theophanic
ACEHHINORT rhinotheca
ACEHHIRRST Reichsrath
ACEHHKLLNS chank-shell
ACEHHLOPRT heptachlor
ACEHHLSSTT thatchless
ACEHHMNNOW henchwoman
ACEHHORSTU charthouse
ACEHIILLPT philatelic
ACEHIILMOS isocheimal
ACEHIILMPT mephitical
ACEHIILMRT hermitical
ACEHIILNNO Heliconian
ACEHIILNOP neophiliac
ACEHIILNPR hair-pencil
ACEHIILPST cephalitis
ACEHIILSTT theistical
ACEHIILSTU halieutics
ACEHIILTTY ethicality
ACEHIIMMNS Manicheism
ACEHIIMRTT arithmetic
ACEHIINNOP Phoenician
ACEHIINNRT Cerinthian
interchain
ACEHIINORT anti-heroic
ACEHIINOTV inchoative
ACEHIINTTT antithetic
ACEHIIOPST teichopsia
ACEHIIPRRT peritricha
ACEHIIRSTT tracheitis
ACEHIKLNSS chalkiness
ACEHIKMNOS chain-smoke
ACEHIKMRRS reichsmark
ACEHIKPPST packet-ship
ACEHILLMSZ schlimazel
ACEHILLNTY ethnically
ACEHILLOOS alcoholise
ACEHILLOOZ alcoholize
ACEHILLORY heroically
ACEHILLPRY Caerphilly
ACEHILLTTY thetically
ACEHILMMST mischmetal
ACEHILMOOP phocomelia
ACEHILMOTY haemolytic
ACEHILNOPT phonetical
ACEHILNOPU euphonical
ACEHILNORT chlorinate
ACEHILNORU unheroical
ACEHILNOTY inchoately
ACEHILNPRS phrensical
ACEHILNSST schalstein
ACEHILOORZ coleorhiza
ACEHILOOTZ zoothecial
ACEHILOPRT arctophile
cartophile
ACEHILOPST telophasic
ACEHILORRT rhetorical
ACEHILRSTY hysterical
ACEHILSSST scaithless
ACEHIMMSST schematism
ACEHIMNNOR enharmonic
ACEHIMNNOY hemocyanin
ACEHIMNOPT phonematic
ACEHIMNORS monarchise
ACEHIMNORU euharmonic
ACEHIMNORY hieromancy
ACEHIMNORZ monarchize
ACEHIMNOTT theomantic
ACEHIMNPRY hypermanic

ACEHIMNPTU	unemphatic
ACEHIMNRST	mischanter
ACEHIMNRSV	revanchism
ACEHIMNSTY	myasthenic
ACEHIMOPRT	amphoteric
	metaphoric
ACEHIMOPTU	apothecium
ACEHIMOPXY	hypoxaemic
ACEHIMORTT	hematocrit
ACEHIMOSTT	hemostatic
ACEHIMOSTX	chemotaxis
ACEHIMPSTY	metaphysic
ACEHIMRSTT	chrematist
ACEHIMRSTU	rheumatics
ACEHIMSSTT	schematist
ACEHINOORT	orthocaine
ACEHINOPSS	poachiness
ACEHINOPTT	heptatonic
ACEHINORRT	chitarrone
ACEHINORTV	chevrotain
ACEHINPSTT	pentastich
ACEHINPSTU	epicanthus
ACEHINPTTU	unpathetic
ACEHINRSTV	revanchist
ACEHINSSTT	chattiness
ACEHIOPRRT	Chiroptera
ACEHIOPRSX	echopraxis
ACEHIOPSST	post-chaise
ACEHIPPSTT	pettichaps
ACEHIPRRST	arch-priest
ACEHIPRSSU	haruspices
ACEHIPRSTU	curateship
	pasticheur
ACEHIPRSTW	pear-switch
ACEHIPRSTY	psychiater
ACEHIPRTTU	picture-hat
ACEHIQRRSU	squirearch
ACEHIRRRTY	trierarchy
ACEHIRSTTT	tetrastich
ACEHIRSTTV	tsarevitch
ACEHJKNNOY	Johnny-cake
ACEHJRRSUW	jaw-crusher
ACEHKLMMOR	hammerlock
ACEHKLNNTZ	lanzknecht
ACEHKLNOST	chalkstone
	shecklaton
ACEHLLMNOY	melancholy
ACEHLLNORS	acorn-shell
ACEHLLOORS	chloralose
ACEHLLOSTY	shellycoat
ACEHLLPRSU	sepulchral
ACEHLMNOOT	monothecal
ACEHLMOOST	school-mate
ACEHLMORSY	lachrymose
ACEHLNOOPS	Sophoclean
ACEHLNORSS	anchorless
ACEHLNORST	charleston
ACEHLNORUV	overlaunch
ACEHLNSSST	stanchless
ACEHLNSTUY	unchastely
ACEHLOORST	orthoclase
ACEHLOPPRT	paper-cloth
ACEHLOPTTU	touch-plate
ACEHLORRST	orchestral
ACEHLPRTYY	phylactery
ACEHMNNSUU	Munchausen
ACEHMNORST	march-stone
ACEHMNOSTY	chemonasty
ACEHMNOTUV	avouchment
ACEHMNPRTY	parchmenty
ACEHMNRRTY	merchantry
ACEHMOPRTT	carpet-moth
ACEHMOPRTY	chromatype
ACEHMORRTU	route-march
ACEHMORTTY	tachometry
ACEHMOSSTU	moustaches
ACEHMRTTYY	tachymetry
ACEHNNORTT	contrahent
ACEHNNSSST	stanchness
ACEHNOOPRT	Ctenophora
ACEHNOPRSU	canephorus
ACEHNOPTYY	cyanophyte
ACEHNORRTT	trochanter
ACEHNRSSTU	chauntress
ACEHNSSTUW	cashew-nuts
ACEHOOPPRR	carpophore
ACEHOOPSTU	tophaceous
ACEHOORRST	Orthoceras
ACEHOPPRTU	touch-paper
ACEHOPRSUY	coryphaeus
ACEHOPSTUY	typhaceous
ACEHORTTWW	watchtower
ACEHPPSTTY	petty-chaps
ACEHRSSSUU	chaussures
ACEIIIKNST	ekistician
ACEIIILMSS	Islamicise
ACEIIILMSZ	Islamicize
ACEIIILRST	Israelitic
ACEIIINTTV	incitative
ACEIIIRTTV	recitativi
ACEIIISTTV	activities
ACEIIJLSTU	Jesuitical
ACEIIKMNST	kinematics
ACEIIKRSTT	rickettsia
ACEIILLLPT	elliptical
ACEIILLNNN	cannellini
ACEIILLNPR	periclinal
ACEIILLNRY	irenically
ACEIILLOSU	liliaceous
ACEIILLRTY	illiteracy
ACEIILLSTT	satellitic
ACEIILMMST	melismatic
ACEIILMNST	melanistic
ACEIILMNSU	semi-uncial
ACEIILMOPT	epitomical
ACEIILMPSS	specialism
ACEIILNNRT	encrinital
ACEIILNOPT	capitoline
ACEIILNORV	arvicoline
ACEIILNOSX	saxicoline
ACEIILNOTT	actinolite
ACEIILNPST	Plasticine®
ACEIILNTVY	inactively
ACEIILOSTU	tiliaceous

ACEIILPPRT	participle
ACEIILPRTT	triplicate
ACEIILPSST	plasticise
	specialist
ACEIILPSTY	speciality
ACEIILPSTZ	plasticize
ACEIILRSSS	scleriasis
ACEIILSTTY	elasticity
ACEIIMNNRU	neuraminic
ACEIIMNORT	Marcionite
ACEIIMNPST	emancipist
ACEIIMNRRU	cinerarium
ACEIIMNRSU	musicianer
ACEIIMOTTV	comitative
ACEIIMPSST	asepticism
ACEIIMRSTT	tasimetric
ACEIINNNTV	Vincentian
ACEIINNORT	cineration
ACEIINNQRU	quinacrine
ACEIINNRTY	itinerancy
ACEIINOPST	speciation
ACEIINORTT	recitation
ACEIINOSTV	vesication
ACEIINOTTX	excitation
	intoxicate
ACEIINPPRT	principate
ACEIINPSTT	antiseptic
	psittacine
ACEIINRTVY	inveracity
ACEIINSSTT	sanctities
ACEIINSTTU	austenitic
ACEIIORRRT	certiorari
ACEIIORTTV	recitativo
ACEIIPPSST	epispastic
ACEIIRRSSU	cuirassier
ACEIIRSTTV	astrictive
ACEIIRTTVY	creativity
	reactivity
ACEIISSSTY	essayistic
ACEIJKMNTU	minute-jack
ACEIJKPRST	Jack-priest
ACEIJNORTT	trajection
ACEIKKNNSS	knackiness
ACEIKLRSTV	travel-sick
ACEIKMNOPT	pockmantie
ACEIKMRRST	arsmetrick
ACEIKNNRSS	crankiness
ACEIKNPTTW	pawnticket
ACEIKORTUY	eukaryotic
ACEIKQRTUW	quick-water
ACEILLLOPW	lace-pillow
	pillow-lace
ACEILLLPRU	pellicular
ACEILLMNSY	miscellany
ACEILLMORT	allometric
ACEILLMPTU	capitellum
ACEILLMRTY	metrically
ACEILLNNNO	cannelloni
ACEILLNOOT	ocellation
ACEILLNORT	citronella
ACEILLNRTU	lenticular
ACEILLOPSW	pillowcase

ACEILLOPTY	poetically
ACEILLOQTU	colliquate
ACEILLORST	allosteric
	sclerotial
ACEILLORTV	vorticella
ACEILLOSTY	societally
ACEILLOTXY	exotically
ACEILLPRUY	peculiarly
ACEILLPSTY	septically
ACEILLRTUV	victualler
ACEILLRTVY	vertically
ACEILMMNNO	mnemonical
ACEILMMNSS	clamminess
ACEILMNOPR	complainer
ACEILMNORS	sermonical
ACEILMNRST	centralism
ACEILMNRTU	unmetrical
ACEILMNRUW	lawrencium
ACEILMOPRR	proclaimer
ACEILMOPRT	pleromatic
ACEILMRRUV	vermicular
ACEILMRSSU	secularism
ACEILMSSTU	salicetums
ACEILMTUUV	cumulative
ACEILNNOOP	Napoleonic
ACEILNNOTU	nucleation
ACEILNNRTU	unicentral
ACEILNNRUU	uninuclear
ACEILNNUVY	univalency
ACEILNOORT	corelation
	iconolater
	relocation
ACEILNOORU	Eriocaulon
ACEILNOPRT	pratincole
ACEILNOPST	neoplastic
	pleonastic
ACEILNOPTU	peculation
	unpoetical
ACEILNOPTY	polyactine
ACEILNORTU	ulceration
ACEILNORTY	lectionary
ACEILNOSSS	socialness
ACEILNOSTU	inosculate
ACEILNOTUV	novaculite
ACEILNPPSU	suppliance
ACEILNRSTT	centralist
ACEILNRSTU	lacustrine
ACEILNRTTY	centrality
ACEILNRTVY	trivalency
ACEILNRUUX	luxuriance
ACEILNSSSS	classiness
ACEILOOPRT	laeotropic
ACEILOOSUV	olivaceous
	violaceous
ACEILOPPRS	sapropelic
ACEILOPPTY	paleotypic
ACEILOPRRT	replicator
ACEILOPRTX	explicator
ACEILOPTUV	copulative
ACEILOQTUY	coequality
ACEILPPSTU	supplicate
ACEILPRTUU	apiculture

ACEILRRSUV versicular
ACEILRRTUY reticulary
ACEILRSSTU secularist
ACEILRSTTU testicular
trisulcate
ACEILRSTUY secularity
ACEILRTUUV aviculture
ACEIMMNORT manometric
ACEIMMRSTY asymmetric
ACEIMNNOST cismontane
ACEIMNNRUY innumeracy
ACEIMNOPRT importance
ACEIMNOPSS campesinos
ACEIMNOPTT Camptonite
pentatomic
ACEIMNORUY Aureomycin®
ACEIMNPPRS panspermic
ACEIMNPSTU pneumatics
ACEIMNQTTU acquitment
ACEIMNRRTY Terramycin®
ACEIMOOPST Compositae
ACEIMOPPPT apopemptic
ACEIMORRST miscreator
ACEIMORRTT meritocrat
ACEIMORRTU acroterium
ACEIMORSST Massoretic
ACEIMORTTT tetratomic
ACEIMORTTU tautomeric
ACEIMSSTTY systematic
ACEINNNOSU uncanonise
unisonance
ACEINNNOUZ uncanonize
ACEINNOORT incoronate
nero-antico
ACEINNOPTT pentatonic
ACEINNORTU enunciator
ACEINNOTTU continuate
ACEINNRRSU insurancer
ACEINNRSTY transiency
ACEINNRTUU nunciature
ACEINNSSST scantiness
ACEINNSSTT intactness
ACEINOORRT acroterion
ACEINOORTV revocation
ACEINOPPST episcopant
ACEINOPRTU precaution
ACEINOPRTY capernoity
ACEINOPSSU spinaceous
ACEINOPSTT constipate
costean-pit
ACEINORRTT retraction
triaconter
ACEINORSSY cessionary
ACEINORSTU recusation
ACEINORTTU eructation
ACEINORTTX extraction
ACEINOSTTU unicostate
ACEINOSTTV constative
ACEINPSSUU puissaunce
ACEINPSTUU usucapient
ACEINRSTTU scaturient
ACEINRSUVV survivance
ACEINRTUVY unveracity
ACEINSSSTT scattiness
ACEIOOPRRT aerotropic
ACEIOOPRSU paroecious
ACEIOOPRTZ azeotropic
ACEIOOPTTV co-optative
ACEIOORTTU autoerotic
ACEIOPRRSU precarious
ACEIOQSSUU sequacious
ACEIORSTTT tricostate
ACEIORSTVY vesicatory
ACEIORTTXY excitatory
ACEIPPRSTT tapescript
ACEIPQRSTU practiques
ACEIPRSTTX spectatrix
ACEIRRSTUW rustic-ware
ACEJKLPPSU supplejack
ACEJNOSUUY jouysaunce
ACEJNOSUVY jovysaunce
ACEJORRTTY trajectory
ACEKKMOSST smokestack
ACEKLLORTW wall-rocket
ACEKLLRSTU lackluster
lacklustre
ACEKLNOPST alpenstock
ACEKLOOPRW wool-packer
ACEKMNORRW cankerworm
ACEKOPSSST sack-posset
ACEKPRRSSY skyscraper
ACELLMNOTU loculament
ACELLOOOST osteocolla
ACELLOPRTY pectorally
ACELLOPSTU leucoplast
ACELLOPTUY eucalyptol
ACELLORRTY trolley-car
ACELLORSSW lower-class
ACELLORSUX sexlocular
ACELLPRSTY spectrally
ACELLSSTTY tactlessly
ACELMMNOOW commonweal
ACELMNNOTT malcontent
ACELMNTTUU tentaculum
ACELNNOOTT notonectal
ACELNNOSSU consensual
ACELNNOTUV △conventual
ACELNOPRRU pronuclear
ACELNOPRSY narcolepsy
ACELNOPRTX contraplex
ACELNOPSTY nyctalopes
ACELNORRTY necrolatry
ACELNOTTUX contextual
ACELNPTTUU punctulate
ACELNRTTUY truncately
ACELOOPRRT coal-porter
percolator
ACELOORRTW watercolor
ACELOOSSTT osteoclast
ACELOPRSSU processual
ACELOPRSTU speculator
ACELOPRSWY cow-parsley
ACELOPSTUU pultaceous
ACELORRSTY clearstory

ACELPPRSSU	upper-class
ACELPRSSSU	superclass
ACELPSTUUY	eucalyptus
ACEMMMMOTY	mammectomy
ACEMMNORTY	commentary
ACEMMNOSTU	consummate
ACEMMOSTTY	mastectomy
ACEMNNNOTT	cantonment
ACEMNNORST	monstrance
ACEMNOOPRT	montero-cap
ACEMNOOTYZ	mycetozoan
ACEMNOSTTY	nematocyst
ACEMOOPRRS	macrospore
ACEMOORSTU	octamerous
ACEMORSTUY	myrtaceous
ACENNOORTU	onocentaur
ACENNOORTV	covenantor
ACENNORSTV	conservant
	conversant
ACENNOSTTT	contestant
ACENOOPPST	pantoscope
ACENOOPRVY	overcanopy
ACENOORRSZ	scorzonera
ACENOPPRRY	pyrenocarp
ACENOPRRTY	copartnery
ACENORRSWY	cornerways
ACENORSTYZ	stone-crazy
ACENOSSSTT	stone's-cast
ACENPRSSTU	percussant
ACENRSSTTU	tersanctus
ACEOOOPRRT	co-operator
ACEOOPPRST	Psocoptera
ACEOOPRRRT	procreator
ACEOOPRRSU	porraceous
ACEOOPRRTY	procaryote
ACEOOPSSTT	statoscope
ACEOORRTVY	revocatory
ACEOORSSTU	ostraceous
ACEORRRSTY	stercorary
ACEORSTUXY	excusatory
ACFFGHILNY	chaffingly
ACFFGIIKMN	mafficking
ACFFGIILNT	afflicting
ACFFHNRSTU	churn-staff
ACFFHORSTT	torch-staff
ACFFIILLOY	officially
ACFFIILNOT	affliction
ACFFIILNOU	unofficial
ACFFIILOTY	officialty
ACFFIIOORT	officiator
ACFFILLNUY	fancifully
ACFFORSSST	cross-staff
ACFGHILNNU	flaunching
ACFGHMORRS	frog's-march
ACFGIILNRY	clarifying
ACFGIINRSY	scarifying
ACFGILOPRY	profligacy
ACFGINOORT	foot-racing
ACFHILNOPR	Francophil
ACFHIMRSTT	smithcraft
ACFHIOPRST	factorship
ACFHLLTUWY	watchfully
ACFHLMOSTU	stomachful
ACFHLNTUUW	unwatchful
ACFHOOPRRS	crash-proof
ACFIIILMST	familistic
ACFIIILNTY	finicality
ACFIILLOPR	prolifical
ACFIILMMOR	limaciform
ACFIILNOPT	pontifical
ACFIILNORT	frictional
ACFIINNORS	infrasonic
ACFIINNORT	infarction
	infraction
ACFIINOSTT	factionist
ACFIIOSTTU	factitious
ACFIJNORST	scarf-joint
ACFILLLORU	follicular
ACFILLORUY	cauliflory
ACFILMOORR	microflora
ACFILNNOOT	conflation
ACFILNNOTU	functional
ACFILOSTUY	factiously
ACFILRSSST	first-class
ACFINNSTUY	unsanctify
ACFINOORRT	fornicator
ACFINOORSU	facinorous
ACFLNOORTW	contraflow
ACFLNRRUUU	furuncular
ACFLOORSTU	colourfast
ACFOORRRTT	rotorcraft
ACGGGILNRS	scraggling
ACGGHHIRWY	Whiggarchy
ACGGHIILOO	hagiologic
ACGGHINNNU	unchanging
ACGGHINOPY	hypnagogic
ACGGHINOTT	chittagong
ACGGIILLOT	Glagolitic
ACGGIILNNO	ganglionic
ACGGIILOOS	sialogogic
ACGGILLNNY	glancingly
ACGGILLOOY	glaciology
ACGGIMOSTY	mystagogic
ACGHHIINRT	night-chair
ACGHHILNTT	night-latch
ACGHHIMUUV	high-vacuum
ACGHHINTTW	night-watch
	watch-night
ACGHHIOPRR	chirograph
ACGHHORSYY	hygrochasy
ACGHIIKNRS	king's-chair
ACGHIILRTV	gilravitch
ACGHIINPSW	wishing-cap
ACGHIIOPPX	xiphopagic
ACGHIKNNOR	king-archon
ACGHIKNOPS	hop-sacking
ACGHILMNRY	charmingly
ACGHILNSST	nightclass
ACGHILNSTY	scathingly
ACGHILOOPT	pathologic
ACGHIMNNOP	champignon
ACGHIMNNRU	uncharming
ACGHIMOPRR	micrograph
ACGHIMOPRY	myographic

ACGHINNORR	anchor-ring
ACGHINNPTU	hunting-cap
ACGHINNSTU	staunching
ACGHINNTTU	hunting-cat
ACGHINOPRT	prognathic
ACGHINOPRZ	zincograph
ACGHIOOPRR	orographic
ACGHIOOPRZ	zoographic
ACGHIOPPRT	pictograph
ACGHIOPRRU	urographic
ACGHIRRTTW	cartwright
ACGHLLOSST	glass-cloth
ACGHLOOPRY	carphology
ACGHMMOORR	chromogram
ACGHMNOORR	chronogram
ACGHMOPRSY	psychogram
ACGHOOPPRY	coprophagy
ACGIIKKMNS	sick-making
ACGIIKLLPR	pilgarlick
ACGIILLMSU	Caligulism
ACGIILLORS	cigarillos
ACGIILLOST	logistical
ACGIILLOTY	logicality
ACGIILLRTU	liturgical
ACGIILMNTU	glutaminic
ACGIILNOOR	air-cooling
ACGIILNOSU	caliginous
ACGIILNPUU	Pinguicula
ACGIILNRTU	granulitic
ACGIILNRTY	laryngitic
ACGIILNSST	anglistics
ACGIIMMRRT	trigrammic
ACGIIMNORS	organicism
	organismic
ACGIIMNRST	scintigram
ACGIINNOTT	incogitant
ACGIINOOTT	cogitation
ACGIINORST	organicist
ACGIINOSST	agonistics
ACGIINPRST	practising
ACGIINQTTU	acquitting
ACGIIORSTY	graciosity
ACGIJKKNSY	skyjacking
ACGIKKMNRU	muck-raking
ACGILLMOOY	limacology
	myological
ACGILLNORR	corralling
ACGILLOOOR	orological
ACGILLOOOZ	zoological
ACGILLOORU	urological
ACGILLOPRY	pyrogallic
ACGILLRSUY	surgically
ACGILMNNOO	cognominal
	gnomonical
ACGILMOSTY	clistogamy
ACGILNNPRY	prancingly
ACGILNOORY	craniology
ACGILNOPSS	Panglossic
ACGILNOSST	glasnostic
ACGILOORST	astrologic
ACGILOOTTU	tautologic
ACGILORSUU	glucosuria
ACGILORSUY	glycosuria
	graciously
ACGILOSUVY	Yugoslavic
ACGIMNNOPY	companying
ACGIMNNORY	nigromancy
ACGIMNOORS	agronomics
ACGIMNOPSS	compassing
ACGIMNSSTY	gymnastics
ACGIMOOPRT	gamotropic
ACGINNORRY	carrying-on
ACGINNOSTW	nowcasting
ACGINOOSTU	contagious
ACGINOPSUU	pugnacious
ACGINORRST	co-starring
ACGINORSUU	ungracious
ACGINPPRTU	parting-cup
ACGINPRRST	spring-cart
ACGIORSTTY	gyrostatic
ACGJLLNOUY	conjugally
ACGJLNNOUU	unconjugal
ACGLNOORSU	clangorous
ACGMOPRRTY	cryptogram
ACGMOPRTYY	cryptogamy
ACGNNOPPUY	oppugnancy
ACGOORRRTU	corrugator
ACHHIILPST	phthisical
ACHHIIPRTU	hupaithric
ACHHILMOPT	ophthalmic
ACHHILMRTY	rhythmical
ACHHILOOPS	shopaholic
ACHHILOPTY	halophytic
ACHHIMRRTY	arrhythmic
ACHHINNOTT	Antichthon
ACHHINOPRS	archonship
ACHHIOPPST	phosphatic
ACHHNOOTTU	autochthon
ACHHNOPRSY	chrysophan
ACHHOPPSTY	psychopath
ACHIIIMRTY	Himyaritic
ACHIIIPPRT	hippiatric
ACHIIIRSST	trichiasis
ACHIIISSTV	Shivaistic
ACHIIJKNRS	jinricksha
ACHIIKLNNY	kinchin-lay
ACHIIKNPSU	puschkinia
ACHIILLMPS	phallicism
ACHIILNOPT	notaphilic
ACHIILNOPY	cynophilia
ACHIILOOPR	Ciliophora
ACHIILORST	historical
ACHIILORTU	thiouracil
ACHIIMNNOR	inharmonic
ACHIIMNRSS	△sinarchism
ACHIIMNSTU	humanistic
ACHIIMNSUV	chauvinism
ACHIIMOPPP	hippocampi
ACHIINNOOT	inchoation
ACHIINNOPT	antiphonic
ACHIINNORT	Corinthian
ACHIINNPQU	chinquapin
ACHIINORST	sticharion
ACHIINORSU	air-cushion

ACHIINORTT chittaroni
ACHIINPSUY picayunish
ACHIINRSST sinarchist
ACHIINRSTT Antichrist
ACHIINSTUV chauvinist
ACHIIOPRST aphoristic
ACHIIOPSST pistachios
ACHIJMNOTT match-joint
ACHIKKNPRS shrinkpack
ACHIKLOORW workaholic
ACHIKMNOST mackintosh
ACHIKMNOUU makunouchi
ACHIKMNRSS scrimshank
ACHILLMOOS alcoholism
ACHILLMORS chloralism
ACHILLMTYY mythically
ACHILLNNSY clannishly
ACHILLNOOP allophonic
ACHILLNOPY phonically
ACHILLOOYZ hylozoical
ACHILLOPRT prothallic
ACHILLOSTT lithoclast
ACHILLPSYY physically
ACHILMNOTY lithomancy
ACHILMOPTY polymathic
ACHILMORYZ mycorhizal
ACHILMPSSY scampishly
ACHILMRTTU thalictrum
ACHILNOORS isochronal
ACHILNOSSY anchylosis
ACHILOPPSY polyphasic
ACHILOPRTY arctophily
cartophily
ACHILORSUV chivalrous
ACHILOSTTW waistcloth
ACHIMMNORS monarchism
ACHIMMOOPR Commiphora
ACHIMNNOOR harmonicon
ACHIMNOOPS monophasic
ACHIMNOOPT taphonomic
ACHIMNOPTW pitchwoman
ACHIMNOPTY amphictyon
ACHIMNORST monarchist
ACHIMNSSTU miscanthus
ACHIMORRTT trichromat
ACHIMORRYZ mycorrhiza
ACHIMOSSTU mustachios
ACHIMRSSTY Christmasy
ACHINOORST cartoonish
ACHINSTTUY unchastity
ACHIOOPSTY sociopathy
ACHIOPRSTY physiocrat
ACHIOPRTTY potty-chair
ACHIOPSTTY hypostatic
ACHIPRSTYY psychiatry
ACHIQRRSUY squirarchy
ACHIRSTTWW wristwatch
ACHKLLOSST shockstall
ACHKLMNOOT klootchman
ACHKLMORSS marshlocks
ACHKORRSTT short-track
ACHLLLLOYY allycholly
ACHLLOOPSY playschool
ACHLMMOORS school-marm
ACHLMNORUU homuncular
ACHLNNORSY synchronal
ACHLOOOSTU acolouthos
ACHLOORSUW colourwash
ACHLORSTWZ schwarzlot
ACHMOOSSTU stomachous
ACHMOSSUYY Hyoscyamus
ACHNNNOOST cannon-shot
ACHNNORSYY asynchrony
ACHNOOPPRY apocryphon
ACHNOOPSYZ scyphozoan
ACIIIILMST Ismailitic
ACIIIKLNOT kaolinitic
ACIIILLMNP Ampicillin®
ACIIILLMNY inimically
ACIIILMORT miarolitic
ACIIILMSST Islamicist
ACIIILNOPT politician
ACIIILNORS incisorial
ACIIILNOSS sicilianos
ACIIILNOTT latticinio
ACIIILNPPR principial
ACIIILNPST sincipital
ACIIILORTV variolitic
ACIIILSTTV vitalistic
ACIIIMNSTV anticivism
ACIIINNOTT incitation
ACIIINRSTT inartistic
ACIIINSTTV nativistic
ACIIINTTVY inactivity
ACIIJLRSTU juristical
ACIIJRSTUY justiciary
ACIIKNNNPY pickaninny
ACIIKNRSST Sanskritic
ACIILLMNRY criminally
ACIILLMSSY salicylism
ACIILLNNOS Scillonian
ACIILLNORS nicrosilal
ACIILLNORY ironically
ACIILLRTTY tritically
ACIILMNORS consimilar
ACIILMNOST monistical
ACIILMNRTY matricliny
ACIILMNSUY musicianly
ACIILMORST moralistic
ACIILMSTUY musicality
ACIILNOORT lorication
ACIILNOPPR pilocarpin
ACIILNOPRV provincial
ACIILNORTT tinctorial
ACIILNOSTT solicitant
ACIILNOTXY anxiolytic
ACIILNPRTY patricliny
ACIILOPRST poristical
ACIILOPTTY topicality
ACIILOSSUV lascivious
ACIILPRSTU puristical
ACIILPSTTY plasticity
ACIILPTTYY typicality
ACIILRSTTU altruistic

ACIILRTTTY tractility
ACIIMMNOPT pantomimic
ACIIMMNSTU numismatic
ACIIMNORST Marcionist
Romanistic
ACIIMNPTTY tympanitic
ACIIMNRSSS narcissism
ACIIMNRSTU manicurist
ACIIMOPRSS prosaicism
ACIIMOPRST porismatic
ACIINNOOTV invocation
ACIINNOSTU insouciant
ACIINNOTTX intoxicant
ACIINOOSTT oscitation
ACIINOOTTX toxication
ACIINOPRST ascription
crispation
ACIINOPRTT tritanopic
ACIINOPSTU ancipitous
ACIINORSTT astriction
ACIINORTTU urtication
ACIINOSTUU incautious
ACIINRSSST narcissist
ACIINRSTTU naturistic
unartistic
ACIINRSTUY cystinuria
ACIIOPRRST scriptoria
ACIIOPSSUU auspicious
ACIIOPSTZZ pizzicatos
ACIIORSTVY varicosity
ACIIPRSSTT patristics
ACIIPSSTTY spasticity
ACIIQRTTUZ quartzitic
ACIISSSTTT statistics
ACIJLORTUY jocularity
ACIKKLMNOR Kilmarnock
ACIKLMRTTU multi-track
ACIKLNNOPT planktonic
ACIKOPRTYY karyotypic
ACILLLNOOY colonially
ACILLLOOQU colloquial
ACILLMNNOO monoclinal
ACILLMOORT collimator
ACILLMOTUU altocumuli
ACILLMOTUV multivocal
ACILLMSTYY mystically
ACILLNOOTU allocution
ACILLNOQTU colliquant
ACILLNORUU unilocular
ACILLNORUV involucral
ACILLNOSUY unsocially
ACILLNOUVY univocally
ACILLOOPRT allotropic
ACILLOORST oscillator
ACILLOORUX uxorilocal
ACILLOPRTY tropically
ACILLORRTU trilocular
ACILLORTVY vortically
ACILLRSTUY rustically
ACILMMOORS microsomal
ACILMMRSUU simulacrum
ACILMNOOOS nosocomial
ACILMNOORT microtonal
ACILMNORTY matrocliny
ACILMNOSUU calumnious
ACILMNOTUU cumulation
ACILMNRSUU minuscular
ACILMNSTUY stimulancy
ACILMOOOTZ zootomical
ACILMOOPRT compilator
ACILMOOPTY polyatomic
ACILMOPRRY micropylar
ACILMOPSTY polymastic
ACILMORSUU miraculous
ACILMPRSUU spiraculum
ACILNNPSUU panniculus
ACILNOOORT coloration
ACILNOOPRR incorporal
ACILNOOPTU copulation
ACILNOOPXY polyaxonic
ACILNOOPZZ pozzolanic
ACILNOORTU inoculator
ACILNOORTY iconolatry
ACILNOOSTU osculation
ACILNOOTTT cottontail
ACILNOPRTY patrocliny
ACILNOPSTY synoptical
ACILNORRTY contrarily
ACILNORSTU ultrasonic
ACILNOSTTY oscitantly
ACILNPPSTU supplicant
ACILNRTTUY taciturnly
ACILNRUUXY luxuriancy
ACILOOPRRT proctorial
ACILOOPSTT postcoital
ACILOOPSTZ zooplastic
ACILOOQSUU loquacious
ACILOOSSUX saxicolous
ACILOPPRSU Pilocarpus
ACILOPSSUY spaciously
ACILOPSTTY calotypist
ACILOPSTUY captiously
ACILORRRVY corrivalry
ACILORRTUV vorticular
ACILORTTUV cultivator
ACILOSTUUY cautiously
ACILPPTUVY pulp-cavity
ACILPRRSTU scriptural
ACIMMNOPSS pancosmism
ACIMMNORTY matronymic
ACIMMOPRRS macroprism
ACIMMORSSY commissary
ACIMNNOORY oniromancy
ACIMNNORTU unromantic
ACIMNNOSTY sanctimony
ACIMNOOPRS comparison
ACIMNOOPSS compassion
ACIMNOORST astronomic
ACIMNOORTY craniotomy
ACIMNOOSST onomastics
ACIMNOOSTU autonomics
ACIMNOPPTU pump-action

ACIMNOPRTY	importancy
	patronymic
	pyromantic
ACIMNPRSTU	manuscript
ACIMOOPRTT	compatriot
ACIMOORTVY	varicotomy
ACIMOPSTTY	asymptotic
ACINNNOSTT	inconstant
ACINNNOTTU	continuant
ACINNOOORT	coronation
ACINNOOPPT	panopticon
ACINNOPRST	conspirant
ACINNOPTTU	punctation
ACINNORSST	transonics
	trans-sonic
ACINNORSTT	constraint
ACINNORTTU	truncation
ACINNSTTYY	nyctinasty
ACINOOOPTT	co-optation
ACINOOPPRT	protanopic
ACINOORSTT	cartoonist
ACINOORSTU	octonarius
ACINOORTVY	invocatory
ACINOPSTUU	usucaption
ACINORSTTU	crustation
ACINPRRSTT	transcript
ACIOPRRTTU	pourtraict
ACIOPRSTTY	pyrostatic
ACIORRSTTU	rusticator
ACJNOORRTU	conjurator
ACKKNRSTUW	knackwurst
ACKLLOORRW	collar-work
ACKLMNOORS	rock-salmon
ACKOOPRSTY	pastrycook
ACKOQRRTUZ	quartz-rock
ACLLLLOORR	rollcollar
ACLLLRTUUY	culturally
ACLLMMNOUY	communally
ACLLMNNOOO	monoclonal
ACLLMORTUU	multocular
ACLLMRSUUY	muscularly
ACLLNPTUUY	punctually
ACLLOOPRRY	corporally
ACLLORRSSY	rally-cross
ACLLPRSTUU	sculptural
ACLMMNOOTY	commonalty
ACLMOORSTY	cosmolatry
ACLNNOSTTU	consultant
ACLNNOSTTY	constantly
ACLNNOSTUV	convulsant
ACLNNPTUUU	unpunctual
ACLNNRSUUU	Ranunculus
ACLNOORSTT	contraltos
ACLNOORSUY	canorously
ACLNOPSTUY	postulancy
ACLOOPRSTU	postocular
ACLOOPRTUY	copulatory
ACLOORSTUY	osculatory
ACLRRSTTUU	structural
ACMMOORTTU	commutator
ACMNNORTUY	countryman
ACMNOORSUY	acronymous
ACMNOOSSTW	Scotswoman
ACMOOOPRTT	compotator
ACMOOPRTTU	computator
ACNNNOSTTU	unconstant
ACNOOPPRRT	contraprop
ACNOOPRRTY	port-crayon
ACNOOPRSTY	syncopator
ACNOPRSSUY	syncarpous
ACNOPRTTUU	punctuator
ACOOOPRRRT	corporator
ACOOOPRRTV	provocator
ACOOPRRRTT	protractor
ACOOPRRRTU	procurator
ACOPRRSSTY	cross-party
ADDDEEEHNW	hand-weeded
ADDDEEFHIL	fiddlehead
ADDDEEGILM	middle-aged
ADDDEEHLMU	muddlehead
ADDDEEHNRU	dunderhead
ADDDEEILSS	sidesaddle
ADDDEEKLRS	skedaddler
ADDDEELLPW	well-padded
ADDDEFILPY	paddy-field
ADDDEGNORU	dead-ground
ADDDEILNOR	dendroidal
ADDDELLOTY	toddy-ladle
ADDDELOOPW	paddle-wood
ADDEEEEPST	deep-seated
ADDEEEFHNR	free-handed
ADDEEEFNTU	undefeated
ADDEEEGHRY	grey-headed
ADDEEEHNNV	even-handed
ADDEEEHORS	soreheaded
ADDEEEIMNS	dense-media
ADDEEEIMNW	maidenweed
ADDEEEIRST	desiderate
ADDEEELNTT	dead-nettle
ADDEEELRST	saddletree
ADDEEELRTT	dead-letter
ADDEEENNRU	unendeared
ADDEEENRTV	denervated
ADDEEFHLNT	left-handed
ADDEEFHNOR	forehanded
ADDEEFHOST	soft-headed
ADDEEFIINN	definienda
ADDEEFILOT	defoliated
ADDEEFMNOR	fore-damned
ADDEEFNRVY	dandy-fever
ADDEEGGHLU	head-lugged
ADDEEGGINS	disengaged
ADDEEGHITW	dead-weight
ADDEEGHLNO	long-headed
ADDEEGHPRS	sharp-edged
ADDEEGNRRU	unregarded
ADDEEHLLNS	handselled
ADDEEHLNRU	unheralded
ADDEEHNNOP	open-handed
ADDEEHNNRU	unhardened
ADDEEHNNSS	handedness
ADDEEHNOOW	woodenhead
ADDEEHNORV	overhanded
ADDEEHNRTU	unthreaded

ADDEEHRRTY	dehydrater
ADDEEIIMMX	mixed-media
ADDEEIINNR	△dinanderie
ADDEEIINRT	ride-and-tie
ADDEEIIPSS	diapedesis
ADDEEIKMNW	weak-minded
ADDEEILNSS	deadliness
ADDEEILPSS	displeased
ADDEEIMNRR	mind-reader
ADDEEIMRXY	ready-mixed
ADDEEINNRU	unindeared
ADDEEIPPRV	dive-dapper
ADDEEIPRSW	widespread
ADDEEJNRUW	underjawed
ADDEEKORST	deadstroke
ADDEELLMTU	medullated
ADDEELLSSS	saddleless
ADDEELMNOR	endodermal
ADDEELMNOY	almond-eyed
ADDEELMOTU	demodulate
ADDEELNOSS	saddle-nose
ADDEELOPRR	rope-ladder
ADDEELORSS	saddle-sore
ADDEELPRST	stepladder
ADDEELPRVY	depravedly
ADDEEMNNRU	undernamed
ADDEEMNORR	road-mender
ADDEENNPUX	unexpanded
ADDEENNTTU	unattended
ADDEENORRU	round-eared
ADDEENORST	adderstone
ADDEENPRTU	dunderpate
ADDEENPRUV	undepraved
ADDEENQRSU	squandered
ADDEENRRTU	unretarded
ADDEENRRUW	unrewarded
ADDEEOPRRT	depredator
ADDEEOPRSS	desperados
ADDEFHIINS	dead-finish
ADDEFHILRS	fish-ladder
ADDEFHIRST	hard-fisted
ADDEFHLLNU	full-handed
ADDEFHNORU	four-handed
ADDEFIIILP	lapidified
ADDEFIIMNR	fair-minded
ADDEFIKNTY	fat-kidney'd
ADDEFILRSW	fieldwards
ADDEFLLOOP	flapdoodle
ADDEFLLRUY	dreadfully
ADDEFLMNOY	many-folded
ADDEGHHHIN	high-handed
ADDEGHILOO	goodlihead
ADDEGHILST	dead-lights
ADDEGHLNOR	dog-handler
ADDEGHLOOY	goodlyhead
ADDEGIKNNP	padding-ken
ADDEGINNRU	undreading
ADDEGIORRS	dorsigrade
ADDEGJMNTU	adjudgment
ADDEGLMNNO	gold-end-man
ADDEGMNORR	dendrogram
ADDEGRRSSU	dressguard
ADDEHHILNS	shield-hand
ADDEHHPRSU	hard-pushed
ADDEHIILMS	shield-maid
ADDEHIILNP	didelphian
ADDEHIJMNU	mujaheddin
ADDEHILNNR	hinderland
ADDEHIMNOO	maidenhood
ADDEHINNOR	iron-handed
ADDEHIOORR	drearihood
ADDEHIORSW	drowsihead
ADDEHIRSYZ	hydrazides
ADDEHKNORW	handworked
ADDEHLLNOR	landholder
ADDEHLORST	stadholder
ADDEHMNNOW	hand-me-down
ADDEHNORSY	dandy-horse
ADDEHNOSUW	unshadowed
ADDEHNOTUW	death-wound
ADDEHORRTY	dehydrator
ADDEHORSTT	short-dated
ADDEIILLSV	ill-advised
ADDEIIMSSV	misadvised
ADDEIIPSST	dissipated
ADDEILMTTY	admittedly
ADDEIMNRSW	miswandred
ADDEIMNSUY	undismayed
ADDEIMNTTU	unadmitted
ADDEINNORU	unordained
ADDEINNOTU	denudation
ADDEINNRRU	underdrain
ADDEINOORS	radiosonde
ADDEINRSTU	disnatured
ADDEIPRRSY	spray-dried
ADDEJNSTUU	unadjusted
ADDELMNOPY	paddymelon
ADDELMOORS	saddleroom
ADDELMORRW	dream-world
ADDELNNORW	wonderland
ADDELNOORW	woodlander
ADDENNOPRU	unpardoned
ADDENNPRUU	up-and-under
ADDENNRSTU	understand
ADDENOQRSU	squadroned
ADDEORRSTW	adder's-wort
ADDFFILLOY	daffodilly
ADDFIILNSU	disdainful
ADDFILMORY	myriadfold
ADDGHIINRR	hard-riding
ADDGILLNWY	dawdlingly
ADDGILLOSS	dildo-glass
ADDGKNORRU	dark-ground
ADDGORRSUW	sword-guard
ADDHIILMOS	old-maidish
ADDHILORSU	shroud-laid
ADDIIILNUV	individual
ADDIILLNST	distilland
ADDIILMMOS	old-maidism
ADDILLLLYY	dilly-dally
ADDIMNOSUY	didynamous
ADDLNORWWY	downwardly
ADDNNOOTUW	down-and-out
ADEEEEFHRT	feed-heater

ADEEEEGNRT	degenerate
ADEEEEHRTX	exheredate
ADEEEELNRT	enterdeale
ADEEEELRTT	leaderette
ADEEEFIKNY	Yankeefied
ADEEEFILLR	file-leader
ADEEEFILRS	federalise
ADEEEFILRZ	federalize
ADEEEFIRTV	federative
ADEEEFLLTT	leafletted
ADEEEFLORR	freeloader
ADEEEFMNNS	defenseman
ADEEEFRRRT	free-trader
ADEEEGGGLT	gate-legged
ADEEEGGLNR	near-legged
ADEEEGHNRS	shagreened
ADEEEGILMN	gleemaiden
ADEEEGKNRR	green-drake
ADEEEGLLNR	generalled
ADEEEGLNTW	tangleweed
ADEEEGLRSV	Everglades
ADEEEGLRTU	deregulate
ADEEEGNNRR	endangerer
ADEEEHHNRT	hen-hearted
ADEEEHHPSS	sheep's-head
ADEEEHHSST	headsheets
ADEEEHILMS	seemlihead
ADEEEHKLLR	lark-heeled
ADEEEHLNSV	sleevehand
ADEEEHLPSY	sleepy-head
ADEEEHLRTT	letterhead
ADEEEHLRTW	tread-wheel
ADEEEHNRTT	threatened
ADEEEIKMMN	maiden-meek
ADEEEINNTV	Venetianed
ADEEEINSSV	seven-a-side
ADEEEIORWW	woe-wearied
ADEEEIPRRT	pied-à-terre
ADEEEIPTTX	expeditate
ADEEEIRRTT	reiterated
ADEEEIRSTT	Eastertide
ADEEEJKMRT	jerked-meat
ADEEEKNNUW	unweakened
ADEEELLMNP	empanelled
ADEEELLNRW	well-earned
ADEEELNNSS	leadenness
ADEEELNNUV	unleavened
ADEEELNPRU	unrepealed
ADEEELNRRT	randle-tree
ADEEELNRSU	underlease
ADEEELNRSW	newsdealer
ADEEELNRUV	unrevealed
ADEEELNSST	elatedness
ADEEELPRTY	repeatedly
ADEEEMNNRT	endearment
	man-entered
ADEEEMNRSU	demeasnure
ADEEEMOOST	oedematose
ADEEEMPRTT	attempered
ADEEEMRRST	streamered
ADEEENPRTT	predentate
ADEEENPRTU	unrepeated
ADEEENRRSW	newsreader
ADEEENRSSS	searedness
ADEEENSSST	sedateness
ADEEEPPRWY	wapper-eyed
ADEEFFLORU	four-leafed
ADEEFGHIRU	figurehead
ADEEFGLLSZ	self-glazed
ADEEFGLNNW	newfangled
ADEEFGLNRS	self-danger
ADEEFGLRRS	self-regard
ADEEFGMNRT	fragmented
ADEEFHILTW	wheatfield
ADEEFHLNRT	left-hander
ADEEFHLORW	flower-head
ADEEFHLRST	self-hatred
ADEEFHNRTU	unfathered
ADEEFILLNS	self-denial
ADEEFILMRS	federalism
ADEEFILRSS	self-raised
ADEEFILRST	federalist
ADEEFILSSU	diseaseful
ADEEFINNRR	ferrandine
ADEEFINORT	federation
ADEEFINORZ	fazendeiro
ADEEFINRRW	fire-warden
ADEEFIORSV	fore-advise
ADEEFIPRTV	five-parted
ADEEFIRSTU	disfeature
ADEEFLLLNN	flannelled
ADEEFLLSSY	fadelessly
ADEEFLORUV	four-leaved
ADEEFMNORW	freedwoman
ADEEFMNRTY	defrayment
ADEEFNNSTU	unfastened
ADEEFNRTUU	unfeatured
ADEEFOPRRT	perforated
ADEEFORSTU	foederatus
ADEEGGHHRU	head-hugger
ADEEGGHINR	niggerhead
ADEEGGHLOR	loggerhead
ADEEGGJNSS	jaggedness
ADEEGGNRSS	raggedness
ADEEGGNRUY	gaudy-green
ADEEGHHIRR	high-reared
ADEEGHIKNW	weak-hinged
ADEEGHILRT	lethargied
ADEEGHIRRY	grey-haired
ADEEGHISUY	hay-de-guise
ADEEGHNNRU	anhungered
ADEEGHNRRU	eard-hunger
ADEEGHNRTU	ungathered
ADEEGHSUYY	hay-de-guyes
ADEEGIINSS	diagenesis
ADEEGILLRT	treillaged
ADEEGILNOT	delegation
ADEEGILNRR	ringleader
ADEEGIMNNR	meandering
ADEEGIMORT	diagometer
ADEEGINNOT	denegation
ADEEGINRRT	gradienter
	intergrade
ADEEGINRTW	dewatering

ADEEGIORTV	derogative
ADEEGLLNRY	enlargedly
ADEEGLNORT	goal-tender
ADEEGLNORZ	angledozer
ADEEGLNPRU	plunderage
ADEEGLNRUZ	underglaze
ADEEGLNTTU	gauntleted
ADEEGLORTY	derogately
ADEEGLPPRY	dapple-grey
ADEEGLRRSS	regardless
ADEEGMNORT	dermatogen
ADEEGMNRSS	gensdarmes
ADEEGNNRRU	ungarnered
ADEEGNNRTU	underagent
ADEEGNORRS	rose-garden
ADEEGNORRT	dragon-tree
ADEEGNRRSW	greensward
ADEEGNRRTU	ungartered
ADEEGOORSV	overdosage
ADEEGOORSW	greasewood
ADEEGORRRT	retrograde
ADEEGORSTU	uredo-stage
ADEEHHILMR	hemihedral
ADEEHHISST	dissheathe
ADEEHHLOSV	shovelhead
ADEEHHMNOT	heathendom
ADEEHHNOPS	headphones
ADEEHHNORX	hexahedron
ADEEHHNPTY	hyphenated
ADEEHHNRTU	headhunter
ADEEHHNSTU	unsheathed
ADEEHHORTT	death-throe
ADEEHHRRTW	hetherward
ADEEHIIKTV	khediviate
ADEEHIILLV	livelihead
ADEEHIILPS	aedileship
ADEEHIIRRW	wire-haired
ADEEHIJKNR	jerkinhead
ADEEHIKLRS	shieldrake
ADEEHILLOV	lovelihead
ADEEHILMNR	mind-healer
ADEEHILMRW	dreamwhile
ADEEHILNOT	endothelia
ADEEHILNTU	heulandite
ADEEHILOPP	paedophile
ADEEHILPPR	hare-lipped
ADEEHILPRS	dealership
	leadership
ADEEHILSVY	adhesively
ADEEHILSWY	daisy-wheel
ADEEHIMNSU	dehumanise
ADEEHIMNUZ	dehumanize
ADEEHINRST	dishearten
ADEEHIPRRS	readership
ADEEHIRRSS	sherardise
ADEEHIRRSZ	sherardize
ADEEHIRRTY	hereditary
ADEEHJLORT	jolterhead
ADEEHKLLNT	death-knell
ADEEHKLLRS	shelldrake
ADEEHKNOTT	death-token
ADEEHKORRW	headworker
ADEEHLLNRT	enthralled
ADEEHLLOWY	yellowhead
ADEEHLMTTY	methylated
ADEEHLNOTW	down-at-heel
ADEEHLNRST	Shetlander
ADEEHLOOSX	aldohexose
ADEEHLPUZZ	puzzle-head
ADEEHMNPRU	unhampered
ADEEHNNRTU	underneath
ADEEHNRRTU	underearth
ADEEHNRRTW	netherward
ADEEHNSTVY	△seventh-day
ADEEHOOPRT	Heteropoda
ADEEIIJNRR	jardinière
ADEEIIKLMN	maidenlike
ADEEIILMTT	delimitate
ADEEIILNSS	desalinise
ADEEIILNSZ	desalinize
ADEEIILNTV	delineavit
	evidential
ADEEIILSTV	devitalise
ADEEIILTVZ	devitalize
ADEEIIMNRU	minauderie
ADEEIIMNTV	vindemiate
ADEEIIMTTV	meditative
ADEEIINORV	Vireonidae
ADEEIINRST	distrainee
ADEEIINRVV	vivandière
ADEEIINSST	dessiatine
ADEEIIRRVV	Viverridae
ADEEIIRTTW	tide-waiter
ADEEIIRTVV	derivative
ADEEIJOPRS	jeopardise
ADEEIJOPRZ	jeopardize
ADEEIKKMRT	kite-marked
ADEEIKLLWW	weak-willed
ADEEIKLMNN	kennel-maid
ADEEIKNRRT	dreikanter
	tea-drinker
ADEEIKRSST	asterisked
ADEEIKRSTW	water-skied
ADEEILLMRY	remedially
ADEEILLMVY	medievally
ADEEILLPRS	espadrille
ADEEILLRRU	dérailleur
ADEEILLUVV	vaudeville
ADEEILMNPT	pedimental
ADEEILMNRT	derailment
ADEEILMORS	demoralise
ADEEILMORU	Lemuroidea
ADEEILMORZ	demoralize
ADEEILMPRR	peridermal
ADEEILMSTU	Mustelidae
ADEEILNNTT	tendential
ADEEILNNTU	unentailed
ADEEILNORT	delineator
ADEEILNPRT	interplead
ADEEILNRSU	unrealised
	Uredinales
ADEEILNRTU	adulterine
ADEEILNRUZ	unrealized
ADEEILNSSV	disenslave

ADEEILNTTT dilettante
ADEEILNTTW lean-witted
ADEEILOPPT deoppilate
ADEEILOPRS depolarise
ADEEILOPRZ depolarize
ADEEILOPTT petiolated
ADEEILORSV devalorise
ADEEILORVZ devalorize
ADEEILPRRV pearl-diver
ADEEILPRST pilastered
ADEEILPRTU tulip-eared
ADEEILRSSU Aussiedler
ADEEILRSTU adulterise
ADEEILRTUZ adulterize
ADEEIMMNSS maimedness
ADEEIMMORT immoderate
ADEEIMMRSU immeasured
ADEEIMNNOT denominate
emendation
ADEEIMNNTT detainment
ADEEIMNNUX unexamined
ADEEIMNPRT pandermite
ADEEIMNRRT dreariment
ADEEIMNRRW new-married
ADEEIMNRSS dreaminess
ADEEIMNSTV advisement
ADEEIMNSTW tandemwise
ADEEIMORRS drearisome
ADEEIMORRT radiometer
ADEEIMORRX xerodermia
ADEEIMORTU audiometer
ADEEIMOTTV demotivate
ADEEIMQRRU quadrireme
ADEEIMRSST mediatress
sidestream
ADEEINOPRT Pontederia
ADEEINORTT orientated
ADEEINOTTV denotative
ADEEINPPSX appendixes
ADEEINPRRU unrepaired
ADEEINPRST pedestrian
ADEEINPTUX unexpiated
ADEEINRRSS dreariness
ADEEINRRST restrained
ADEEINRSTT straitened
ADEEINRSTU denaturise
ADEEINRTTT tridentate
ADEEINRTUZ denaturize
ADEEINSSST steadiness
ADEEINSSTY dessyatine
ADEEIOPRSX peroxidase
ADEEIPRSTT tapestried
ADEEIPRTUV depurative
ADEEIRRRWW wiredrawer
ADEEIRRSTV advertiser
ADEEIRRTVW waterdrive
ADEEIRSSTT dissertate
ADEEJKLNRU junk-dealer
ADEEJNOORR rejoneador
ADEEKLLMRW well-marked
ADEEKLMORU leukoderma
ADEEKMNRRU unremarked
ADEEKMRRSS dressmaker
ADEEKNNRTU undertaken
ADEEKNORST drakestone
ADEEKNRRTU undertaker
ADEELLMMRT trammelled
ADEELLMNRS mallenders
ADEELLMNTU unmetalled
ADEELLMTUV datum-level
ADEELLNNPU unpanelled
ADEELLNQUU unequalled
ADEELLNRSS sallenders
ADEELLNRUV unravelled
ADEELLORSS loss-leader
ADEELLOSTY desolately
ADEELLQRRU quarrelled
ADEELMNNTU malentendu
unlamented
ADEELMNORT almond-tree
ADEELMNPUX unexampled
ADEELMNTZZ dazzlement
ADEELMORTY moderately
ADEELMRSUY measuredly
ADEELNNQSU Queensland
ADEELNNSUV unenslaved
ADEELNNTTU untalented
ADEELNOPRU endopleura
ADEELNORRV overlander
ADEELNRRUY underlayer
ADEELNRTTU laundrette
ADEELNRUUV undervalue
ADEELOPPTU depopulate
ADEELOPRSS leopardess
ADEELPPRRY preparedly
ADEELRRSSW rewardless
ADEELRRSTU serrulated
ADEELRSSTU adulteress
ADEEMNNNRU unmannered
ADEEMNNTTT attendment
ADEEMNOPRR promenader
ADEEMNORST sordamente
ADEEMNORTY emendatory
ADEEMNORYY ready-money
ADEEMNPPRU unpampered
ADEEMNPRTT department
ADEEMNRRTT retardment
ADEEMNRSTU unmastered
unstreamed
ADEEMNRSUU unmeasured
ADEEMNSTUU mansuetude
ADEEMOOSTU oedematous
ADEEMOPRRT Dermoptera
ADEEMORRVW warmed-over
ADEEMORSST dermatoses
ADEENNNTTU untenanted
ADEENNOPUW unweaponed
ADEENNORSU unreasoned
ADEENNOSSU unseasoned
ADEENNPRTT pretendant
ADEENNPRTU unparented
ADEENNPTTU unpatented
ADEENNRSUW unanswered
ADEENOPRST personated

ADEENORSTW down-easter
ADEENPPRRU unprepared
ADEENPPRSS dapperness
ADEENPRRTU enraptured
ADEENPRSST depressant
ADEENPRSTY present-day
ADEENQRRRU quarrender
ADEENQRRSU squanderer
ADEENRRTUV adventurer
ADEENRRTUW underwater
ADEENRSTTU understate
ADEENSTTTU unattested
ADEEOOPSTT seed-potato
ADEEOPRRSV overspread
spread-over
ADEEOQRSTU square-toed
ADEEORRRRT rear-dorter
ADEEORSTWY ready-to-sew
ADEEPQRTTU parquetted
ADEERRSTTW streetward
ADEERRSTYY starry-eyed
ADEERSSSTW stewardess
ADEERSSTVX sex-starved
ADEERSSTYY yesterdays
ADEFFGGGIR gaff-rigged
ADEFFGHIRT affrighted
ADEFFLOOTT flat-footed
ADEFGGINOR God-fearing
ADEFGHIRST far-sighted
ADEFGHOORT good-father
ADEFGIINOR Indigofera
ADEFGIRTVY gravity-fed
ADEFHHOORT fatherhood
ADEFHILMSS damselfish
ADEFHILTTW halfwitted
ADEFHINPRT pathfinder
ADEFHLLPUX half-duplex
ADEFHLTTWY Twelfth-day
ADEFHMNOTU unfathomed
ADEFHOORSW foreshadow
ADEFHORRST draft-horse
ADEFIILNRS flindersia
ADEFIINOPS saponified
ADEFIINRTU unratified
ADEFIIRRST first-aider
ADEFIIRSTT stratified
ADEFIKLORT fork-tailed
ADEFILLLRY all-firedly
ADEFILLLSU full-sailed
ADEFILLNNW windfallen
ADEFILMNNU uninflamed
ADEFILMNOR manifolder
ADEFILNNTU uninflated
ADEFILOORT defoliator
ADEFILORTU fluoridate
ADEFILPRSU despairful
ADEFIMMSTU deaf-mutism
ADEFINOORR foreordain
ADEFINOPRS infraposed
ADEFINRSST draftiness
ADEFKLNOTU untalked-of
ADEFKLORST tradesfolk
ADEFLLMNNU full-manned
ADEFLLNNOW downfallen
ADEFLLRTWY leftwardly
ADEFLNRTUU fraudulent
ADEFLOORTW floodwater
waterflood
ADEFLOPRSY self-parody
ADEFLORRTW afterworld
ADEFMOORRS reformados
ADEFNNOPRU unprofaned
ADEFOOPRWX wax-proofed
ADEFOPRRTU four-parted
ADEFRRSTTU frustrated
ADEGGGILNR laggen-gird
ADEGGHILNR hang-glider
ADEGGHOOTT gag-toothed
ADEGGHORUY hydragogue
ADEGGIINRS niggardise
ADEGGIINRZ niggardize
ADEGGIMMOS demagogism
ADEGGIMOPS pedagogism
ADEGGIPRSW digger-wasp
ADEGGLOORS sogdolager
ADEGGNOPTU get-up-and-go
ADEGHHIIRS high-raised
ADEGHHILNR △highlander
ADEGHHINST nightshade
ADEGHHISTT high-tasted
ADEGHIINPS Sphingidae
ADEGHILMRT light-armed
ADEGHILNNR rehandling
ADEGHILNOR long-haired
ADEGHILNSU languished
ADEGHINNSW hand-sewing
ADEGHINPRS springhead
ADEGHIOPRY ideography
ADEGHLNNRU land-hunger
ADEGHLOOPY edaphology
ADEGHLORSW gold-washer
ADEGHLRTUY daughterly
ADEGHMOPRY demography
ADEGHNORST headstrong
ADEGHNORTT hard-gotten
ADEGHNRRUY eard-hungry
ADEGHNRTTU draught-net
ADEGHOOPTT gap-toothed
ADEGHORSUU guardhouse
ADEGIIILST digitalise
ADEGIIILTZ digitalize
ADEGIIIMNS disimagine
ADEGIILLSU seguidilla
ADEGIILMNS misleading
ADEGIILNOT deligation
gadolinite
gelatinoid
ADEGIILNPR lip-reading
ADEGIILNRT ring-tailed
ADEGIILTTY digitately
ADEGIIMNNU unimagined
ADEGIIMNRS misreading
ADEGIINPRS despairing
spinigrade

ADEGIINRTT dirt-eating
ADEGIKLNOR dragonlike
ADEGILLNPY pleadingly
ADEGILLNYY delayingly
ADEGILMNRY dreamingly
ADEGILMRTU multigrade
ADEGILNNNO non-aligned
ADEGILNNNT landing-net
ADEGILNNRS sanderling
ADEGILNNUY undelaying
ADEGILNOSY agonisedly
ADEGILNOTT glottidean
ADEGILNOYZ agonizedly
ADEGILNPPR dapperling
ADEGILNRRR errand-girl
ADEGILNRTT glitterand
ADEGILNRUV gerundival
ADEGILORRY goliardery
ADEGILOSTW slow-gaited
ADEGIMNNOS Mandingoes
ADEGIMNNRU maundering
undreaming
ADEGIMNOPU impoundage
ADEGIMNORS gormandise
ADEGIMNORZ gormandize
ADEGIMOPSU pseudimago
ADEGIMORST dogmatiser
ADEGIMORTZ dogmatizer
ADEGINNPRW drawing-pen
ADEGINNSSU unassigned
ADEGINOOPS poignadoes
ADEGINOORT derogation
Trogonidae
ADEGINORRT denigrator
ADEGINORRV overdaring
ADEGINORST designator
ADEGINPRSW wingspread
ADEGIORRTY argyrodite
ADEGIPRRST partridges
ADEGJLMNTU judgmental
ADEGKNRRRU △krugerrand
ADEGLLMOSY gladsomely
ADEGLMORST stream-gold
ADEGLNORSU glanderous
ADEGLOPRSY dog-parsley
ADEGMMOPRR programmed
ADEGMNNOOR gander-moon
ADEGMNNOYY dynamogeny
ADEGMNOOSU endogamous
ADEGNOOORW orange-wood
ADEGNOOPST steganopod
ADEGNOORTU good-nature
ADEGNOPRRS sandgroper
ADEGOOPRST gasteropod
ADEGOORRTY derogatory
ADEHHIIPRT diphtheria
ADEHHILPRS heraldship
ADEHHIRRTW hitherward
ADEHHIRSSW dishwasher
ADEHHLLOOR holohedral
ADEHHNOOPR rhodophane
ADEHHNOPRY hydrophane
ADEHIILOPU audiophile
ADEHIILPTW whiptailed
ADEHIIMRTT mithridate
ADEHIINNRU hirudinean
ADEHIINOTT dithionate
ADEHIIOPRU Ophiuridae
ADEHIIPSUU euphausiid
ADEHIKNNSW wind-shaken
ADEHILLLSW shieldwall
ADEHILLNTW thin-walled
ADEHILLORU loudhailer
ADEHILNNRS hinderlans
ADEHILNNRT hinterland
ADEHILNOPS sphenoidal
ADEHILNORT threnodial
ADEHILNORZ endorhizal
ADEHILNRST disenthral
ADEHILOPRS spheroidal
ADEHILPRUY hyperdulia
ADEHILPSTU disulphate
ADEHIMNNTU minute-hand
ADEHIMNORY Rhodymenia
ADEHIMORTU rheumatoid
ADEHIMSSSW Swadeshism
ADEHINOOPR radiophone
ADEHINOSST astonished
ADEHINPRSW wardenship
ADEHINPSSU dauphiness
ADEHINRSST Sanhedrist
ADEHINRSUV unravished
ADEHIOOPRT orthopedia
ADEHIOORTW waiterhood
ADEHIOPRRW hair-powder
ADEHIOPRSS rhapsodise
ADEHIOPRSZ rhapsodize
ADEHIORTUZ Authorized
ADEHIRRTWW withdrawer
ADEHKNORRW work-harden
ADEHLLMOPR lampholder
ADEHLLNOOR loan-holder
ADEHLLNOUW unhallowed
ADEHLLOPRY polyhedral
ADEHLMNORT enthraldom
motherland
ADEHLMNOSY handsomely
ADEHLMNPPU pump-handle
ADEHLMOPRY hypodermal
ADEHLMOPTY methyldopa
ADEHLNOPRY hydroplane
ADEHLOSSSW shadowless
ADEHLRTTWY thwartedly
ADEHMMNOPR hammer-pond
ADEHMMOPRR drop-hammer
ADEHMNNOSU unhandsome
ADEHMNOTTU muttonhead
ADEHMOORST masterhood
ADEHMORRTW threadworm
ADEHNOOPRR androphore
ADEHNOOPRT parenthood
ADEHNOPPRS sand-hopper
ADEHNOPRSS sharp-nosed
ADEHNORSUX hexandrous

Words marked △ may be spelled also with a capital letter

ADEHOOPRTY	orthopaedy
ADEHOORSVW	overshadow
ADEHOOSTTW	saw-toothed
ADEHOPRRTU	pourtrahed
ADEHORRSSW	shorewards
ADEIIILLNT	initialled
ADEIIILMSU	Simuliidae
ADEIIIMNTT	intimidate
ADEIIINNPP	Pinnipedia
ADEIIINNPR	peridinian
ADEIIINOSZ	isoniazide
ADEIIKNNST	ink-stained
ADEIIKNSSY	dyskinesia
ADEIILLMPX	maxilliped
ADEIILLPTX	pixillated
ADEIILLRTV	vitrailled
ADEIILLSTT	distillate
ADEIILMMTU	multimedia
ADEIILMNOR	meridional
ADEIILMNSU	unidealism
ADEIILNNPR	dinner-pail
ADEIILNOPT	depilation
ADEIILNORT	deliration
ADEIILNOTV	inviolated
ADEIILNRST	disentrail
ADEIILNRTT	intertidal
ADEIILNTTT	dilettanti
ADEIILORST	idolatrise
ADEIILORTZ	idolatrize
ADEIIMNNOT	antimonide
ADEIIMNOTT	meditation
ADEIIMNOTV	admonitive
	dominative
ADEIIMNPRU	unimpaired
ADEIIMNRST	administer
ADEIIMNSTY	disamenity
ADEIIMPRSU	praesidium
ADEIIMPRTU	tepidarium
ADEIIMRSTT	dermatitis
ADEIINNNOS	Indonesian
ADEIINNORT	inordinate
ADEIINNOTW	nationwide
ADEIINNOTX	indexation
ADEIINNOTZ	denization
ADEIINNPPT	pinnatiped
ADEIINNRST	disentrain
ADEIINNSST	daintiness
ADEIINORST	sideration
ADEIINORTV	derivation
ADEIINPPRS	drainpipes
ADEIINPTTU	inaptitude
ADEIINRRST	distrainer
ADEIINRTUV	indurative
ADEIINTTUV	unvitiated
ADEIIPRRSS	dispraiser
ADEIIPRRSY	presidiary
ADEIIPRTTU	tripudiate
ADEIIPRTTW	pittie-ward
ADEIIRRTVX	taxi-driver
ADEIISSSUV	dissuasive
ADEIJLNOPT	lap-jointed
ADEIJMMNRW	windjammer
ADEIJOPSSU	jaspideous
ADEIKLLLRY	lady-killer
ADEIKLLNUY	unladylike
ADEIKLNSTY	litany-desk
ADEILLNOOS	solenoidal
ADEILLNOSU	delusional
ADEILLNPRU	unpillared
ADEILLNPSS	pallidness
ADEILLNRRT	tendrillar
ADEILLNRTU	ill-natured
ADEILLNRUV	unrivalled
ADEILLPSTU	plastidule
ADEILLQRRU	quadriller
ADEILLRRST	ill-starred
ADEILMNNOR	molendinar
ADEILMNNUY	unmaidenly
ADEILMNOPR	palindrome
ADEILMNORT	intermodal
	tremolandi
ADEILMNRST	dismantler
ADEILMNRTU	rudimental
ADEILMNSSS	dismalness
ADEILMNSTU	dentaliums
ADEILMNTVY	ivy-mantled
ADEILMOPSS	psalmodise
ADEILMOPSZ	psalmodize
ADEILMPRUU	praeludium
ADEILNNORT	internodal
ADEILNNPTU	pinnulated
ADEILNOOST	desolation
ADEILNOOTV	devotional
ADEILNOPPT	pedal-point
	pentaploid
ADEILNORTY	ordinately
ADEILNOTUV	unviolated
ADEILNPRTU	prudential
ADEILNPTUV	pulvinated
ADEILNQTUU	unqualited
ADEILNRSTY	strainedly
ADEILNSTTU	testudinal
ADEILNSTUY	unsteadily
ADEILOORST	oestradiol
ADEILOPQRU	quadripole
ADEILOPRTT	tetraploid
ADEILOPRTY	depilatory
ADEILOPSSU	disepalous
ADEILOPSTU	dipetalous
ADEILORSST	idolatress
ADEILOSSTT	solid-state
ADEILPPPSU	pedipalpus
ADEILRSTTU	stridulate
ADEILRTTXY	dextrality
ADEIMMNNTU	nidamentum
ADEIMMNRST	mastermind
ADEIMMNTTU	manumitted
ADEIMMORST	moderatism
ADEIMNNORT	ordainment
ADEIMNNOTU	mountained
ADEIMNNRSU	unseminar'd
ADEIMNOORS	moon-raised
ADEIMNOORT	moderation
ADEIMNORRS	randomiser

ADEIMNORRZ	randomizer
ADEIMNORSW	randomwise
ADEIMNORTW	woman-tired
ADEIMNPRTU	unimparted
ADEIMNRRRU	red-murrain
ADEIMNRSTY	mistrayned
ADEIMORRTX	moderatrix
ADEIMORSST	dermatosis
ADEIMORTUW	moudiewart
ADEIMORTWW	mowdiewart
ADEIMRTUUV	duumvirate
ADEINNOOTT	denotation
	detonation
ADEINNOPWW	windowpane
ADEINNRSSW	inwardness
ADEINNRSTU	unstrained
ADEINOOPRT	readoption
ADEINOPRTU	depuration
ADEINOPTTU	deputation
ADEINORSST	adroitness
	intradoses
ADEINORSUV	adenovirus
ADEINPPRSU	unapprised
ADEINPRSST	dispersant
ADEINPRSSY	dispensary
ADEINPRUUV	unpurvaide
ADEINQRRUU	unquarried
ADEINRSSTW	tawdriness
ADEINRSTTU	unstriated
ADEINRTTUW	twi-natured
ADEINSSSTU	unassisted
ADEIOPPRSV	disapprove
ADEIOPRRTU	repudiator
ADEIOPRSTY	depositary
ADEIORRSTT	traditores
ADEIORSSTT	siderostat
ADEIPPRRTY	day-tripper
ADEIRSSTWY	strideways
ADEJMNSTTU	adjustment
ADEJOOPRSU	jeopardous
ADEKMNORTW	down-market
ADELLLORSS	dollarless
ADELLNOPRU	land-louper
ADELLNORRU	all-rounder
ADELLNOTTU	unallotted
ADELLNTUUY	undulately
ADELLOORRR	road-roller
ADELMMNTUU	nummulated
ADELMMOOSS	desmosomal
ADELMMOPSS	plasmodesm
ADELMNOORT	tremolando
ADELMNPRTU	untrampled
ADELMOPSTU	deutoplasm
ADELNNPRTU	underplant
ADELNOPRSS	pardonless
ADELNORSSU	slanderous
ADELNOUVWY	unavowedly
ADELNRSTTU	delustrant
ADELNRSTUW	wanderlust
ADELOORSTY	desolatory
ADELOORTWY	two-year-old
ADELORRWWY	world-weary
ADELORSTUU	adulterous
ADELPQRTUU	quadruplet
ADELPQRUUX	quadruplex
ADELRRSTYY	drysaltery
ADELRSTWWY	westwardly
ADEMMMNORU	memorandum
ADEMNNORSU	unransomed
ADEMNOPRST	pond-master
ADEMNORRUU	unarmoured
ADEMNORSTW	downstream
ADENNOOPRT	pteranodon
ADENNORRRU	roadrunner
ADENNPRSTU	underpants
ADENOPPRUV	unapproved
ADENORSSTW	towardness
ADENPPRSTU	unstrapped
ADENPRSSUW	upwardness
ADENPRSTUU	unpastured
ADENRRSSTW	sternwards
ADENRRSUYY	day-nursery
ADENRTTUWY	twy-natured
ADEOPRRTUY	depuratory
ADFFGIMNOP	damping-off
ADFFIIINRT	triffidian
ADFFLLRUUY	fraudfully
ADFGHHORTU	hard-fought
ADFGHINORS	dragon-fish
ADFGHORRTU	rough-draft
ADFGILMNOR	glandiform
ADFGILNNUY	unfadingly
ADFGINORRU	fairground
ADFGINORRW	forwarding
ADFGOORSTU	footguards
ADFHILRSWY	dwarfishly
ADFHINNOOT	infanthood
ADFHINNORU	four-in-hand
ADFIIILNOS	solifidian
ADFIIINNPT	pinnatifid
ADFIILMRSU	disulfiram
ADFIILQSUY	disqualify
ADFIIOSSTU	fastidious
ADFIISSSTY	dissatisfy
ADFILLMNOY	manifoldly
ADFILLNOOP	flood-plain
ADFILMORRU	raduliform
ADFILORSTY	faldistory
ADFIMMNOOR	monadiform
ADFIMOQRRU	quadriform
ADFINNOOTU	foundation
ADFINNORSU	infrasound
ADFLNORSTW	strandwolf
ADFNOORSSZ	sforzandos
ADFNOORTUY	foudroyant
ADFNORRSTW	frontwards
ADGGGINORU	gauging-rod
ADGGHINTUY	gaudy-night
ADGGILLRSY	Yggdrasill
ADGGINNOOR	gadrooning
ADGHHIILOS	hidalgoish
ADGHHOPRRY	hydrograph
ADGHIILLNN	dining-hall
ADGHIILMOS	hidalgoism

ADGHIINRSS disgarnish
ADGHIIOPRT graphitoid
ADGHIKMRTU khidmutgar
ADGHILNNST Landsthing
ADGHIMNOPP hopping-mad
ADGHINNPRS handspring
ADGHINNSTT nightstand
ADGHINRRTW right-drawn
ADGHIRRSTW rightwards
ADGHIRSTTU distraught
ADGHLLNOPU ploughland
ADGHLOPRUY dray-plough
ADGHNOORRU honor-guard
ADGHOOPRXY doxography
ADGIIILLRS sigillarid
ADGIIILNNV invaliding
ADGIIINOTT digitation
ADGIIKNNPP kidnapping
ADGIIKNNRR rank-riding
ADGIILMNNN land-mining
ADGIILMNOU gadolinium
ADGIILMNRY admiringly
ADGIIMNNRU unadmiring
ADGIIMNRSW misdrawing
ADGIINNPRW drawing-pin
ADGIINOOOZ zoogonidia
ADGIINPRTW writing-pad
ADGIINRSST distringas
ADGIKNORWY working-day
ADGILLNRWY drawlingly
ADGILLNYZZ dazzlingly
ADGILLOPRY prodigally
ADGILNNNOW land-owning
ADGILNNPRS land-spring
ADGILNNTUU undulating
ADGILNOSSS glissandos
ADGIMMNORS gormandism
ADGIMMNPUY mumping-day
ADGIMNNRSY gynandrism
ADGIMNOOSY doomsaying
ADGIMNOSTY nystagmoid
ADGIMOOPRU amido-group
ADGINNOSTU astounding
ADGINNPSTU upstanding
ADGINRRSTW drawstring
draw-string
ADGLLNOSUU glandulous
ADGLMNOOOY monadology
ADGLNOPRUY playground
ADGMNNORSU groundsman
ADGMNORSSU groundmass
ADGNNORSUY gynandrous
ADGNOOORRT dragon-root
ADGNOPSTUW wasp-tongu'd
ADGORRSSSW sword-grass
ADHHILLNOS Hollandish
ADHHNOOOPR orphanhood
ADHHNOSTTU thousandth
ADHHOPRTYY hydropathy
ADHIIILSTT Lithistida
ADHIILLNOP phalloidin
ADHIILNRST disinthral
ADHIIMMNPS midshipman
ADHIIMNSST hit-and-miss
ADHIIMSTTU humidistat
ADHIINNSTU Hindustani
ADHILLOPRS dollarship
ADHILLPRUW uphillward
ADHILNNOOT hand-lotion
ADHILNOPYY hypolydian
ADHILNOSTU outlandish
ADHILOOPRS drosophila
ADHILORSTY thyrsoidal
ADHIMNORSY disharmony
ADHINNOOOT nationhood
ADHINOOPRT anthropoid
ADHINOOPRY hypodorian
radiophony
ADHINOOPSS soda-siphon
ADHINSTUWY Whitsunday
ADHIOPRSST rhapsodist
ADHIOPRSTY dystrophia
ADHIORSTXY hydrotaxis
ADHIPRRTTY third-party
ADHLLOOPPY Phyllopoda
ADHLMOORSY hydrosomal
ADHLNOPSSW splashdown
ADHMNOOORT matronhood
ADHNORRSTW northwards
ADHOORRTWY roadworthy
ADHORSSTUW southwards
ADIIILMNSV invalidism
ADIIILMRSS dissimilar
ADIIILNOSV divisional
ADIIILNTVY invalidity
ADIIINNOTV divination
ADIIINOTTV tidivation
ADIILLORTY dilatorily
ADIILMMNSU maudlinism
ADIILMMPSU impaludism
ADIILMNOXY △mixolydian
ADIILMOPRR primordial
ADIILMOPRS prismoidal
ADIILMORSS solidarism
ADIILNNOTU nidulation
ADIILNORRY ordinarily
ADIILNOSSU sinusoidal
ADIILNRSTU diurnalist
industrial
ADIILOPPSY polydipsia
ADIILOQRTU liquidator
ADIILORSST solidarist
ADIILORSSY radiolysis
ADIILORSTY solidarity
ADIILQSTUY squalidity
ADIIMMMOTU ommatidium
ADIIMNNOOT admonition
domination
ADIIMNNOSS Sandinismo
ADIIMNOPRY pyramidion
ADIIMNRSST misandrist
ADIIMOPRST diatropism
ADIIMORTUU auditorium
ADIIMPRSTY pyramidist

ADIIMQRUUV quadrivium
ADIINNNOTU inundation
ADIINNOORT ordination
ADIINNOORY onirodynia
ADIINNORTU induration
ADIINOPPST disappoint
ADIINOPSSS dispassion
ADIINORRST distrainor
ADIINORTVY divinatory
ADIINOSSSU dissuasion
ADIIOPRSTT podiatrist
ADIIPRRTUY tripudiary
ADILLLMORS Lollardism
ADILLLOSYY disloyally
ADILLNSSTT standstill
still-stand
ADILLOSTYY disloyalty
ADILMMOPSU plasmodium
ADILMNNOTY dominantly
ADILMNOOOP monopodial
ADILMNOOTU modulation
ADILMOPSST psalmodist
ADILMORSTU mustard-oil
ADILMORTUY modularity
ADILNNOOTU nodulation
ADILNNOTUU undulation
ADILNOPSUU paludinous
ADILNRSTTU stridulant
ADILOORSTU idolatrous
ADILOPRTUY plauditory
ADIMNNRSUY synandrium
ADIMNOORTY admonitory
ADIMNORSSU misandrous
ADIMOPSSST spasmodist
ADIMORSTUU sudatorium
ADIMQRRUUV quadrumvir
ADINNOPSTT standpoint
ADINNORRUY unordinary
ADINOOPRST adsorption
ADINORRSTU triandrous
ADINORSSTW downstairs
ADIORSSSTU disastrous
ADIORSSSUY dissuasory
ADLLOORRTY lordolatry
ADLMOOORSU malodorous
ADLNOOTUWW walnutwood
ADLNORSTUU ultrasound
ADLNORTUUY undulatory
ADLNORTUWY untowardly
ADMNNOORSU monandrous
ADMOOOPSTT stomatopod
ADNNORRTUU turnaround
ADNNORSSUY synandrous
AEEEEFLLRT leafleteer
AEEEEGKMPR gamekeeper
AEEEEGKPRT gate-keeper
AEEEEGNRRT regenerate
AEEEEKPRRT peat-reeker
AEEEELPRRS prerelease
AEEEENRTTX exenterate
AEEEESTTTT tête-à-têtes
AEEEFFGLRU effleurage
AEEEFFIMNT effeminate
AEEEFFMNRT affeerment
AEEEFHINRS shereefian
AEEEFHLRST flesh-eater
AEEEFHNPRT pen-feather
AEEEFHRRTT thereafter
AEEEFHRRTW whereafter
AEEEFILSTT life-estate
AEEEFINRTZ antifreeze
AEEEFKMRRT free-market
AEEEFLLNST △fenestella
AEEEFLLPTT plate-fleet
AEEEFLLTVV velvet-leaf
AEEEFLMNSS femaleness
AEEEFNRRST transferee
AEEEFNRSTT fenestrate
AEEEFNSSTV Fastens-eve
AEEEGGMNNT engagement
AEEEGHLPRT telpherage
AEEEGHNRRT greenheart
AEEEGIKNPS sea-keeping
AEEEGILNRS generalise
AEEEGILNRV vinegar-eel
AEEEGILNRZ generalize
AEEEGILNSV evangelise
AEEEGILNUV eigenvalue
AEEEGILNVZ evangelize
AEEEGINNOR aero-engine
AEEEGINNRT ingenerate
AEEEGINRTV generative
AEEEGITTVV vegetative
AEEEGKLOPR goalkeeper
AEEEGKNPRS greenspeak
AEEEGLLNSU Euglenales
AEEEGLMNRT regalement
AEEEGLNOPR orange-peel
AEEEGLNOST eagle-stone
AEEEGLRRTU reregulate
AEEEGMNNRT enragement
AEEEGMNNTV avengement
AEEEGMNRSS meagreness
AEEEGMNSTT segmentate
AEEEGNORRT orange-tree
AEEEGNRSSV avengeress
AEEEGPRSSX expressage
AEEEGQSTUU squeteague
AEEEHHINST heathenise
AEEEHHINTZ heathenize
AEEEHHPRST three-phase
AEEEHIKLRS hearse-like
AEEEHIRSTW weatherise
AEEEHIRTWZ weatherize
AEEEHLLRTY ethereally
AEEEHLMSTT sheet-metal
AEEEHLNSST nathelesse
AEEEHLRSST shear-steel
AEEEHMNORX hexaëmeron
AEEEHMPRTT heptameter
AEEEHMSSTT metatheses
AEEEHNNNPT nepenthean
AEEEHNNRTT thereanent
AEEEHNNSTV heaven-sent

AEEEHNORTY	honey-eater
AEEEHNRRTT	threatener
AEEEHRSTTW	sweetheart
AEEEIILRRS	earlierise
AEEEIILRRZ	earlierize
AEEEIIPPRT	peripeteia
AEEEIKNPRS	speakerine
AEEEILLSTT	little-ease
AEEEILNRST	eternalise
AEEEILNRTV	interleave
AEEEILNRTZ	eternalize
AEEEILRTVV	revelative
AEEEIMNNRT	Nemertinea
AEEEIMNRTT	intemerate
AEEEIMNSTV	Vietnamese
AEEEIMPRTV	permeative
AEEEIMRSTT	Eastertime
AEEEINNNTV	antivenene
AEEEINNRTT	intenerate
AEEEINRTTV	entreative
	inveterate
AEEEINRTVV	enervative
AEEEINRTVW	interweave
AEEEJKRRRT	tear-jerker
AEEEJNRTUV	rejuvenate
AEEEKKPPRR	park-keeper
AEEEKMRRSV	verse-maker
AEEEKPSSTW	sweepstake
AEEELLLRTT	tale-teller
AEEELLSSTT	tessellate
AEEELMMNPT	empalement
AEEELMMNRT	Emmentaler
AEEELMNNTT	lentamente
	tenemental
AEEELMNPTU	epaulement
AEEELMNRTT	manteltree
AEEELMNRTV	revealment
AEEELMNRTY	elementary
AEEELNNSTY	enneastyle
AEEELNORVV	overleaven
AEEELNOSTT	teleostean
AEEEMMNORT	anemometer
AEEEMNPRTT	pentameter
AEEEMNRRTU	remunerate
AEEEMORSTT	taseometer
AEEEMPPRRY	emery-paper
AEEEMRRTTT	tetrameter
AEEEMRSSTT	steersmate
AEEEMRSTTW	watersmeet
AEEENNPSTT	septennate
AEEENORSTT	stone-eater
AEEENRRSTU	entreasure
AEEENRSSSV	averseness
AEEENRSTVY	eye-servant
AEEEOPRRST	patereroes
AEEEPPRRTT	perpetrate
AEEEPPRTTU	perpetuate
AEEERRSTYY	yesteryear
AEEERSTTWW	sweetwater
	sweet-water
AEEFFGIRTU	effigurate
AEEFFHORRT	forefather
AEEFFLLORR	free-for-all
AEEFFLSTUX	exsufflate
AEEFFORRST	reafforest
AEEFGGHIRT	freightage
AEEFGHINRT	feathering
AEEFGHIRRT	heart-grief
AEEFGHORRT	foregather
AEEFGILLNT	leafleting
AEEFGILPRS	persiflage
AEEFGINORW	orange-wife
AEEFGIRTTU	Guttiferae
AEEFGLPRSU	presageful
AEEFHHINRT	Fahrenheit
AEEFHIKLRT	fatherlike
AEEFHIKLTW	flake-white
AEEFHIKNST	sneak-thief
AEEFHIKRTT	thief-taker
AEEFHILRSS	seal-fisher
AEEFHINPRT	pin-feather
AEEFHLOPPR	leaf-hopper
AEEFHLRSST	fatherless
AEEFHMMORR	fore-hammer
AEEFHMORSU	frame-house
AEEFHMORTT	fathometer
AEEFHMRRSV	marsh-fever
AEEFHPRSTT	stepfather
AEEFHRRSTW	freshwater
AEEFIIRRRS	fire-raiser
AEEFIKLRRW	fire-walker
AEEFIKNPPR	paper-knife
AEEFIKNRSS	freakiness
AEEFILNNTT	life-tenant
AEEFILNPRR	palfrenier
AEEFILOPRT	perfoliate
AEEFILPRSS	self-praise
AEEFIMNRRT	freemartin
AEEFIMRRST	fire-master
AEEFIMRSTU	misfeature
AEEFINRRST	fraternise
AEEFINRRTZ	fraternize
AEEFIQRSUV	five-square
AEEFKLLLRW	fell-walker
AEEFLLLMOW	mallee-fowl
AEEFLLMSST	smell-feast
AEEFLLNNOT	fontanelle
AEEFLLRSSY	fearlessly
	self-slayer
AEEFLMORSY	fearsomely
AEEFLOSTUY	feateously
AEEFNNSSSU	unsafeness
AEEFNRRRST	retransfer
AEEFORRSTU	four-seater
AEEGGHILRT	lighterage
AEEGGHOPRR	geographer
AEEGGIINSV	ease-giving
AEEGGINOPR	arpeggione
AEEGGINORS	seignorage
AEEGGINRRS	grangerise
AEEGGINRRZ	grangerize
AEEGGINTTV	vegetating
AEEGGIRSSV	aggressive
AEEGGIRTTU	egurgitate

AEEGGMORRT	remortgage
AEEGGNORTV	voetganger
AEEGGNORTY	ergatogyne
AEEGGNRRSS	grass-green
AEEGHHMORR	hemorrhage
AEEGHIILMP	hemiplegia
AEEGHIKMTW	make-weight
AEEGHILMNO	hegemonial
AEEGHILNRT	leathering
AEEGHILNSS	Singhalese
AEEGHILPST	legateship
AEEGHILRST	lethargise
AEEGHILRTZ	lethargize
AEEGHINRRS	rehearsing
AEEGHINRRV	Rhinegrave
AEEGHINRTV	Rh-negative
AEEGHINRTW	weathering
AEEGHIPPRR	epigrapher
AEEGHKNNRS	greenshank
AEEGHLLRSU	auger-shell
AEEGHLMORT	geothermal
AEEGHLNTVW	wavelength
AEEGHLOOTT	theologate
AEEGHLORTT	altogether
AEEGHLPRTY	telegraphy
AEEGHLSSST	sheet-glass
AEEGHMNOOT	homogenate
AEEGHMNORT	hate-monger
	thereamong
AEEGHMORTY	heterogamy
AEEGHORSTT	othergates
AEEGHPRRSY	spreaghery
AEEGIILLLS	illegalise
AEEGIILLLZ	illegalize
AEEGIILLNV	villeinage
AEEGIILMTT	legitimate
AEEGIILNST	gelatinise
AEEGIILNTZ	gelatinize
AEEGIIMNNT	ingeminate
AEEGIIMNST	enigmatise
AEEGIIMNTZ	enigmatize
AEEGIINRRT	garnierite
AEEGILLMNN	enamelling
AEEGILLNST	teaselling
AEEGILLORS	allegorise
AEEGILLORZ	allegorize
AEEGILLRTY	galleryite
AEEGILMNRR	malingerer
AEEGILMNRT	regimental
AEEGILMNSV	evangelism
AEEGILNNSS	genialness
AEEGILNORT	regelation
	relegation
AEEGILNRRT	interregal
AEEGILNRST	easterling
	generalist
AEEGILNRTY	generality
AEEGILNSTV	△evangelist
AEEGILNTVY	negatively
AEEGILOPTX	exploitage
AEEGILRRSU	regularise
AEEGILRRUZ	regularize
AEEGILRTUV	regulative
AEEGIMNNRT	regainment
AEEGIMNNSV	Genevanism
AEEGIMNPRT	impregnate
AEEGIMNQSU	gaminesque
AEEGIMNRST	magnetiser
AEEGIMNRTZ	magnetizer
AEEGIMNSTU	mutagenise
AEEGIMNTUZ	mutagenize
AEEGIMORRT	morigerate
AEEGIMRRTU	marguerite
AEEGIMRRTV	gravimeter
AEEGINNNSU	ensanguine
AEEGINNORT	generation
	renegation
AEEGINNPSS	pangenesis
AEEGINNRRT	interregna
AEEGINNRTT	entreating
AEEGINNRTV	enervating
AEEGINNSSY	Syngenesia
AEEGINNSUX	exsanguine
AEEGINORRS	reorganise
AEEGINORRZ	reorganize
AEEGINOTTV	vegetation
AEEGINPRSY	panegyrise
AEEGINPRYZ	panegyrize
AEEGINRRTX	generatrix
AEEGINRSSS	greasiness
AEEGINRSSV	vernissage
AEEGIPRRTW	gripe-water
AEEGIPRSST	petrissage
AEEGJLLNOR	jargonelle
AEEGLLLOSW	gallows-lee
AEEGLLNRST	stallenger
AEEGLLORTT	allegretto
AEEGLLSTWY	galley-west
AEEGLMMNOR	meal-monger
AEEGLMNNTT	tanglement
AEEGLMNOST	tanglesome
AEEGLMNPRT	graplement
AEEGLMNTTU	tegumental
AEEGLMOPSU	plaguesome
AEEGLNORST	estrangelo
AEEGLNORTU	outgeneral
AEEGLNORTV	graveolent
	lovat-green
AEEGLNSSTT	tassel-gent
AEEGLOPRSU	grape-louse
	plague-sore
AEEGLORTUV	travelogue
AEEGMNNOST	mangosteen
AEEGMNNOTW	meganewton
AEEGMNOPRR	pearmonger
AEEGMNOQSU	Monegasque
AEEGMNRRTU	garmenture
AEEGMNRSTY	segmentary
AEEGMORRST	stereogram
AEEGNNORTV	governante
AEEGNOPRST	grapestone
AEEGNOPRSW	spongeware
AEEGNORSTV	gravestone
AEEGNORTTY	teratogeny

AEEGNPRRTU	page-turner
AEEGNRSSTU	arguteness
AEEGOPRSSU	repoussage
AEEHHHINST	heathenish
AEEHHIMNST	heathenism
AEEHHINRRR	hen-harrier
AEEHHINRST	earth-shine
AEEHHIRTTW	white-heart
AEEHHKNPSS	sheepshank
AEEHHLLSST	healthless
AEEHHLMOST	healthsome
AEEHHLMSTU	Methuselah
AEEHHLORTW	heart-whole
AEEHHLOTWW	wholewheat
AEEHHLSSST	sheathless
AEEHHNOPRT	open-hearth
AEEHHORSTU	earth-house
AEEHIILLPT	epithelial
AEEHIILMST	Ishmaelite
AEEHIISTTV	hesitative
AEEHIKLNNP	enkephalin
AEEHILLORT	heliolater
AEEHILMNRS	shale-miner
AEEHILMNTY	ethylamine
AEEHILMPRT	epithermal
	hemipteral
AEEHILMRST	thermalise
AEEHILMRSZ	Alzheimer's
AEEHILMRTT	Thermalite®
AEEHILMRTZ	thermalize
AEEHILNNOP	anopheline
AEEHILPPRR	peripheral
AEEHILPRST	sphalerite
AEEHILPRTW	pearl-white
AEEHILRTTT	triathlete
AEEHILSTVW	white-slave
AEEHIMNOPP	epiphonema
AEEHIMNPRT	hemipteran
AEEHIMNSTW	anthemwise
AEEHIMRRST	time-sharer
AEEHIMRSTU	rheumatise
AEEHIMRTUZ	rheumatize
AEEHIMSSTT	metathesis
AEEHINNORW	Erewhonian
AEEHINNPRT	pantherine
AEEHINPRST	interphase
AEEHINPSTT	stephanite
AEEHINRRTW	Wertherian
AEEHINRSST	earthiness
	heartiness
AEEHINRTTU	uintathere
AEEHINSSTT	antitheses
AEEHIPPRRS	periphrase
AEEHIRTTWW	white-water
AEEHISTUVX	exhaustive
AEEHKKNRUZ	Hakenkreuz
AEEHKMORST	earth-smoke
AEEHKNOSSU	snake-house
AEEHKOPSSV	spokeshave
AEEHKORSTT	heatstroke
AEEHKOSSTU	steakhouse
AEEHLLLPRS	pearl-shell
AEEHLLOPTW	whole-plate
AEEHLLORSW	wholesaler
AEEHLMMRSS	hammerless
AEEHLMNNOP	phenomenal
AEEHLMNPRT	telpherman
AEEHLMORTX	exothermal
AEEHLMPRSW	sperm-whale
AEEHLNPPST	sheep-plant
AEEHLNRSTT	nettle-rash
AEEHLPRSSS	phraseless
AEEHLPRTWY	telpherway
AEEHLRSSTW	wreathless
AEEHLRTTTY	tetraethyl
AEEHMNNSSU	humaneness
AEEHMNOORR	menorrhoea
AEEHMNOPRT	Heptameron
	Promethean
AEEHMOOSTT	Etheostoma
AEEHMOPRST	atmosphere
AEEHMORRRT	arthromere
AEEHMORRST	horse-tamer
AEEHMORRTV	earthmover
AEEHMORSUX	hexamerous
AEEHNOOPRR	harpooneer
AEEHNOPPTY	phaenotype
AEEHNORSSS	hoarseness
AEEHNORSTV	note-shaver
AEEHNOSTTW	Wheatstone
AEEHNPRSST	pantheress
AEEHNRTUUY	Euthyneura
AEEHOOPRST	peashooter
AEEHOOPSST	apotheoses
AEEHORSTVW	whatsoever
AEEHORTTXY	heterotaxy
AEEHPRRSTT	three-parts
AEEHPRSUVY	superheavy
AEEIIKNRST	keratinise
AEEIIKNRTZ	keratinize
AEEIILLRST	literalise
AEEIILLRTT	illiterate
AEEIILLRTZ	literalize
AEEIILMNNT	eminential
AEEIILMNRS	mineralise
AEEIILMNRZ	mineralize
AEEIILNNSU	Eleusinian
AEEIILNPRX	pre-exilian
AEEIILNRTT	retinalite
	trilineate
AEEIILOSST	ateleiosis
AEEIILQRRU	reliquaire
AEEIILRRTV	irrelative
AEEIILRSTV	relativise
	revitalise
AEEIILRTVZ	relativize
	revitalize
AEEIIMNNST	inseminate
AEEIIMNSTT	anti-Semite
AEEIIMPRTV	imperative
AEEIIMSTTV	estimative
AEEIINNPRS	Parisienne
AEEIINPPRT	peripetian
AEEIINPPRZ	piperazine

AEEIINPRSS	Persianise
AEEIINPRSZ	Persianize
AEEIINRRVV	△viverrinae
AEEIINRSTU	uniseriate
AEEIINTTTV	entitative
AEEIIPPTTV	appetitive
AEEIIPRSST	asperities
	patisserie
	pâtisserie
AEEIJMNOST	Jamesonite
AEEIJOPRTV	pejorative
AEEIKLNOPU	leukopenia
AEEIKLNSSW	weakliness
AEEIKLRRWW	wire-walker
AEEIKMMORV	movie-maker
AEEIKMNNRR	reim-kennar
AEEIKMNORS	noisemaker
AEEIKNNSSS	sneakiness
AEEIKNRSTT	kersantite
AEEIKRRSTW	water-skier
AEEILLLLNV	villanelle
AEEILLMNST	enamellist
AEEILLNPRT	Parnellite
AEEILLPRST	palletiser
AEEILLPRTZ	palletizer
AEEILLPSTT	stipellate
AEEILLRTVY	relatively
AEEILLSSTT	satellites
AEEILLSTUV	televisual
AEEILMMNPT	impalement
AEEILMMNRU	neurilemma
AEEILMNNTT	entailment
AEEILMNORS	neorealism
AEEILMNPRT	planimeter
AEEILMNRST	streamline
AEEILMNRTT	retailment
AEEILMNSSS	measliness
AEEILMNSTU	Mustelinae
	semilunate
AEEILMORRS	remoralise
AEEILMORRZ	remoralize
AEEILMORTT	meteorital
AEEILMPRRT	perimetral
AEEILMPSST	metalepsis
AEEILMRSST	semestrial
AEEILMRTTT	littermate
AEEILNNNPY	penny-a-line
AEEILNNPST	septennial
AEEILNNSTT	sentential
AEEILNNTTU	lieutenant
AEEILNOPRT	peritoneal
AEEILNORST	neorealist
AEEILNORTV	△revelation
AEEILNPRRU	perineural
AEEILNPRSS	pearliness
AEEILNPRST	episternal
	presential
AEEILNPSTV	splenative
AEEILNQSTU	sequential
AEEILNQTUV	equivalent
AEEILNRRTV	irrelevant
AEEILNRSTT	eternalist
AEEILNRSTU	neutralise
AEEILNRTUV	unrelative
AEEILNRTUZ	neutralize
AEEILNSSSU	sensualise
AEEILNSSSZ	sleaziness
AEEILNSSUZ	sensualize
AEEILNSTVX	sexivalent
AEEILOPRST	periosteal
AEEILORRSV	revalorise
AEEILORRVZ	revalorize
AEEILPPRRT	peripteral
AEEILPRRSV	reap-silver
AEEILPRSSS	praiseless
AEEILPRSSY	erysipelas
AEEILPSTTU	estipulate
AEEILRRTTU	literature
AEEIMMMRST	metamerism
AEEIMMOPRT	emmetropia
AEEIMMORTV	memorative
AEEIMMRSSU	mismeasure
AEEIMNNORT	enantiomer
AEEIMNNRTT	retainment
AEEIMNNRTU	innumerate
AEEIMNOPRT	permeation
AEEIMNORTT	marionette
AEEIMNOSTT	maisonette
AEEIMNPRRU	praemunire
AEEIMNRSSS	smeariness
AEEIMNRSTT	martensite
	misentreat
AEEIMNRTTT	attirement
AEEIMNRTTV	avertiment
AEEIMNSSST	steaminess
AEEIMOPQSU	semi-opaque
AEEIMOPRTU	opium-eater
AEEIMORRTV	variometer
AEEIMPRSST	passimeter
AEEIMQRSUV	semiquaver
AEEINNNSSS	insaneness
AEEINNNSST	innateness
AEEINNNTTT	tennantite
AEEINNORST	santioneer
AEEINNORTV	enervation
	veneration
AEEINNPPTT	inappetent
AEEINNPRSS	Spenserian
AEEINNRTUV	aventurine
AEEINNSSSU	uneasiness
AEEINNSSTT	assentient
AEEINNSSTV	nativeness
AEEINOPTTT	potentiate
AEEINPRSTU	resupinate
AEEINQRSTU	equestrian
AEEINQSSSU	queasiness
AEEINQSTTU	Titanesque
AEEINRRRST	restrainer
AEEINRRTTT	triternate
AEEINRRTTV	travertine
AEEINRRTVY	veterinary
AEEINRSSST	reastiness
AEEINRSSSY	synaeresis

AEEINRSSTW	ear-witness
	wateriness
AEEINRSTTT	interstate
AEEINRSTTW	wine-taster
AEEINRTTXY	extraneity
AEEINSSSTW	sweatiness
AEEINSSSTY	yeastiness
AEEIOPRRSV	overpraise
AEEIPPRRST	perspirate
AEEIPRSSTT	striptease
AEEIPRSSTU	pasteurise
AEEIPRSSUV	persuasive
AEEIPRSTTX	sexpartite
AEEIPRSTUZ	pasteurize
AEEIPRTTUV	reputative
	vituperate
AEEIQRSSUW	squarewise
AEEIRRRTVW	river-water
AEEIRRSTVY	revestiary
AEEJLNORSU	journalese
AEEJNRRSTY	serjeantry
AEEKLLMNPR	palm-kernel
AEEKLOPRRW	rope-walker
AEEKMMNORY	money-maker
AEEKMMNPRY	kempery-man
AEEKMMRRRY	merrymaker
AEEKMNORTY	money-taker
AEEKMORRTU	Euromarket
AEEKMPRRTV	verkrampte
AEEKMRSTTT	test-market
AEEKMSSTUY	eyas-musket
AEEKNNOSST	snakestone
AEELLLSTTU	stellulate
AEELLLSTTY	stellately
AEELLMMRRT	trammeller
AEELLMNOTV	malevolent
AEELLMNQRU	man-queller
AEELLMNRTU	allurement
AEELLMNSSY	namelessly
AEELLNOPRT	petronella
AEELLNRRUV	unraveller
AEELLNRTVY	relevantly
AEELLNRTXY	externally
AEELLNSSTT	talentless
AEELLNTUVY	eventually
AEELLORRSU	rose-laurel
AEELLORSTT	rostellate
AEELLORTTU	autoteller
AEELLOTTTY	teetotally
AEELLQRRRU	quarreller
AEELMMNORU	neurolemma
AEELMMNRTT	trammel-net
AEELMNOPRT	planometer
AEELMNORTV	overmantel
AEELMNORTW	watermelon
AEELMNSTTV	vestmental
AEELMOPPSS	ampelopses
AEELMOPRSY	polymerase
AEELMOPRTX	extemporal
AEELMOPSTT	palmettoes
AEELMORTTV	voltameter
AEELMPRSTT	streetlamp
AEELMRSSST	masterless
	streamless
AEELMRSSTT	matterless
AEELMRSSTU	emulatress
AEELNNPRSY	arles-penny
AEELNNPTTU	antepenult
AEELNNQSTU	lansquenet
AEELNNSSTT	tenantless
AEELNOOPTX	ox-antelope
AEELNOPRST	pearl-stone
AEELNOPSSW	weaponless
AEELNORSSS	reasonless
AEELNORTVZ	zero-valent
AEELNOSSSS	seasonless
AEELNOSTUV	suaveolent
AEELNPRSST	parentless
AEELNPRTTW	wentletrap
AEELNPSTTY	pentastyle
AEELNRRTTY	trey-antler
AEELNRSSSW	answerless
AEELOPPRTU	repopulate
AEELOPSSTT	salopettes
AEELOQRRUU	roquelaure
AEELORRTVY	revelatory
AEELORSTTU	lotus-eater
AEELPPRRRU	paper-ruler
AEELPRRSSY	prayerless
AEELPRSTUX	superexalt
AEELRRSTUW	lustreware
AEELRSTTTY	tetrastyle
AEEMMNORTT	ante-mortem
AEEMMNORTY	anemometry
AEEMNNOPRS	praenomens
AEEMNNOPRT	Pentameron
AEEMNNORRT	ornamenter
AEEMNNORUV	mavourneen
AEEMNNPRTT	entrapment
AEEMNNPRTW	enwrapment
AEEMNNTTTU	attunement
AEEMNOPRST	treponemas
AEEMNOPTTT	tapotement
AEEMNOQRSU	Romanesque
AEEMNORRTU	enumerator
AEEMNORRUV	manoeuvrer
AEEMNORSST	sarmentose
AEEMNORSUV	manoeuvres
AEEMNORSWW	womenswear
AEEMNPPRST	sapperment
AEEMNPPRTY	prepayment
AEEMNPRSSX	expressman
AEEMNRRSTT	arrestment
AEEMNRSSTU	matureness
AEEMNRSTTU	menstruate
AEEMNSSSST	assessment
AEEMORRSTV	overmaster
AEEMORRTTV	overmatter
AEEMORSSTT	eastermost
AEEMORSTUU	outmeasure
AEEMPRRTTU	ear-trumpet
AEEMRSSSST	seamstress
AEENNNPSTY	penny-stane
AEENNORSST	ornateness

AEENNRSSUW unwareness
AEENOORRTX exonerator
AEENOPQSSU opaqueness
AEENOPRRTT penetrator
AEENOPRRTU △neuroptera
AEENOPRSUV supernovae
AEENORSTUX extraneous
AEENORTTUX extenuator
AEENPPRSTT step-parent
AEENPRSSSS sparseness
AEENQRSSSU squareness
AEENRRSSTV transverse
AEENRRSTUU untreasure
AEENSSSTTU astuteness
AEENSSTTTU sustentate
AEEOPRRSTT tetraspore
AEEOPRSTTY poetastery
AEEOPRTTTT tetraptote
AEEOQRSSTU square-toes
AEEORRSTVY overstayer
AEEPPRRTUW Tupperware®
AEEPRRSSST trespasser
AEEPRRSSUV supersaver
AEEPRSSTTU superstate
AEEPRSSWXY expressway
AEEQRSSTUY satyresque
AEEQSSTTUU statuesque
AEFFFTTTUY tuftaffety
AEFFGGINRU gauffering
AEFFGHINRT affrighten
AEFFGKMNOY monkey-gaff
AEFFHIMRRS fish-farmer
AEFFIIINTV affinitive
AEFFILNSTU insufflate
AEFFILRSST tariffless
AEFFINORTV affrontive
AEFFKNRSTU snuff-taker
AEFFLLNTUY affluently
AEFFLLPPRY fly-flapper
AEFFNPPRSU snuff-paper
AEFFOOSTTU affettuoso
AEFGGGILNR reflagging
AEFGGILNSS flagginess
AEFGHHLLNT half-length
AEFGHIINSS sea-fishing
AEFGHILRTT after-light
AEFGHINRRW wharfinger
AEFGHLSTTU self-taught
AEFGHNORTU fearnought
AEFGHORTTU foretaught
AEFGIILLOR florilegia
AEFGIILMST smifligate
AEFGIILNNR fingernail
AEFGIILNSV life-saving
AEFGIIRTUV figurative
AEFGIKMNRR fingermark
AEFGILLLMR flame-grill
AEFGILMNNU meaningful
AEFGILMNOR lageniform
AEFGILMNOS flamingoes
AEFGILMNRY ley-farming
AEFGILMRUV vermifugal
AEFGILNPRS leaf-spring
AEFGILNRTT flattering
AEFGILNRTU ingrateful
AEFGILNRVY vinegar-fly
AEFGILOPRT profligate
AEFGIPRRTU grapefruit
AEFGLLOPUW fowl-plague
AEFGLLRTUY gratefully
AEFGLNOOTT tanglefoot
AEFGLNRTUU ungrateful
AEFGMORRRS ferrograms
AEFHHHISST sheathfish
AEFHHIMMRS hammer-fish
AEFHHIPRST fathership
AEFHHLNRTU half-hunter
AEFHHLORSY halfe-horsy
AEFHHLOSSU flash-house
AEFHHORSST shaft-horse
AEFHIINRTT interfaith
AEFHIKLLRT half-kirtle
AEFHIKLRSY freakishly
AEFHILLLOW hail-fellow
AEFHILMNOT fathom-line
AEFHILNRTT flint-heart
AEFHILNSSS flashiness
AEFHILPPRS flapperish
AEFHILRSST half-sister
AEFHIMMNST famishment
AEFHIMNRSU fish-manure
AEFHLLLOVY half-volley
AEFHLLMSUY shamefully
AEFHLMOSST fathomless
AEFHLNRTUY unfatherly
AEFHLRSTVY harvest-fly
AEFHMOOPRS shame-proof
AEFHORRTTU fourth-rate
AEFIIINNTT infinitate
AEFIILLTUV fluviatile
AEFIILMNTY feminality
AEFIILNOTU unifoliate
AEFIILNRTT infiltrate
AEFIILORTT trifoliate
AEFIIMNNOS infamonise
AEFIIMNNOZ infamonize
AEFIIMNRRR infirmarer
AEFIINQRTU quantifier
AEFIINSSTU fustianise
AEFIINSTUZ fustianize
AEFIJLRSTT rijsttafel
AEFIKNOPRS fair-spoken
AEFILLMMOR malleiform
AEFILLNNRY infernally
AEFILLNNUZ influenzal
AEFILLRUWY wearifully
AEFILMNSTY manifestly
AEFILMORRT formaliter
life-mortar
AEFILMORTW wolframite
AEFILNORSU laniferous
AEFILNORTU fluorinate
AEFILNSSTU faultiness
AEFILOORTX exfoliator

AEFILOQRTU	quatrefoil
AEFILORSSU	saliferous
AEFILPQRUY	pre-qualify
AEFIMNORYY	fairy-money
AEFIMNOSST	manifestos
AEFIMRSSTU	mutessarif
AEFINNRSSU	unfairness
AEFINOOPRT	fortepiano
	pianoforte
AEFINORRST	rainforest
AEFINORSTY	fairy-stone
AEFINORTTU	refutation
AEFINRRTTY	fraternity
AEFIORRSUU	auriferous
AEFKLNORSY	forsakenly
AEFKNNORSU	unforsaken
AEFLLLOPWY	playfellow
AEFLLLORWW	wallflower
AEFLLNOORT	root-fallen
AEFLLNOSSW	fallowness
AEFLLNSSUW	lawfulness
AEFLLOORRY	ferro-alloy
AEFLLORSSV	flavorless
AEFLLPSUUY	pausefully
AEFLLSTTUY	tastefully
AEFLLSTUWY	wastefully
AEFLMNNSSU	manfulness
AEFLMOORSV	flavorsome
AEFLMORRSV	salverform
AEFLNOOSTT	float-stone
AEFLNOPRRT	prefrontal
AEFLNRSSTU	artfulness
AEFLNRSTUW	wanrestful
AEFLNSTTUU	untasteful
AEFLOOPPRT	plate-proof
AEFLOORUVV	love-favour
AEFLORSSUV	favourless
AEFLORSTTU	flatterous
AEFMNOSSSU	famousness
AEFMOORRTW	foot-warmer
AEFMOPRRST	permafrost
AEFMORRSTY	oyster-farm
AEFNORRRST	transferor
AEFNORRTTW	waterfront
AEFNRRSSTU	transfuser
AEFOOPRRRT	perforator
AEFOOPRRTW	waterproof
AEFOORRSTT	tortfeasor
AEFOPRRSTU	perforatus
AEFOQRRSUU	four-square
AEGGGILNNY	engagingly
AEGGGINRST	staggering
AEGGGINRSW	swaggering
AEGGGIRYZZ	zigzaggery
AEGGHIMOPS	geophagism
AEGGHIMORW	whiggamore
AEGGHINSSS	shagginess
AEGGHIOPST	geophagist
AEGGHLOPTU	ploughgate
AEGGHOOPSU	geophagous
AEGGIILMPR	pilgrimage
AEGGIJMRST	jigger-mast
AEGGIKLNOS	Ginkgoales
AEGGIKNNSS	knagginess
AEGGILLNRV	gravelling
AEGGILOOSU	sialogogue
AEGGIMNRRS	Grangerism
AEGGIMNRRT	triggerman
AEGGINNPRS	gingersnap
AEGGINORSS	aggression
AEGGINPRTT	pargetting
AEGGINQSSU	quagginess
AEGGIORRSU	gregarious
AEGGJNRTUU	△juggernaut
AEGGLLNOOY	angelology
AEGGLRSUZZ	gas-guzzler
AEGGMOSTUY	mystagogue
AEGGNNOORY	organogeny
AEGGNNORSU	gangrenous
AEGGOORSSS	goose-grass
AEGHHIKNRR	high-ranker
AEGHHILLLS	shillelagh
AEGHHILOPR	heliograph
AEGHHILRTT	earth-light
AEGHHIOPRR	hierograph
AEGHHLORSU	horselaugh
AEGHHMOPPT	apophthegm
AEGHHNOPPR	nephograph
AEGHHOPRTY	hyetograph
AEGHIILOST	goliathise
AEGHIILOTZ	goliathize
AEGHIINRSV	vinegarish
AEGHIIPRST	graphitise
AEGHIIPRTZ	graphitize
AEGHIKMNOS	shoemaking
AEGHIKNRST	Kentish-rag
AEGHILLLOP	Gallophile
AEGHILLNNS	hanselling
AEGHILLNOP	△anglophile
AEGHILLNRT	allnighter
AEGHILMNNS	Englishman
AEGHILMNOS	home-signal
AEGHILMNRT	lighterman
AEGHILMORT	lithomarge
AEGHILNOOT	theologian
AEGHILNORW	wholegrain
AEGHILNRSU	languisher
AEGHILNSSS	gashliness
AEGHILNSTT	stealthing
AEGHILPRXY	lexigraphy
AEGHIMMOPR	mimeograph
AEGHIMNPST	stamp-hinge
AEGHIMSTTT	steamtight
AEGHINNRTV	night-raven
AEGHINPRRS	rangership
AEGHINPRSS	springhase
AEGHINPRTT	night-taper
AEGHINRSSS	garishness
AEGHINRSTT	straighten
AEGHIPRRSY	serigraphy
AEGHIRTTTW	watertight
AEGHJLLPRY	jellygraph
AEGHLLOSSW	Howleglass
AEGHLMNNST	lengthsman

AEGHLMNRST arms-length
AEGHLMOOOT homologate
AEGHLMOOTY hematology
AEGHLMOPTU plough-team
AEGHLNNOOP △anglophone
AEGHLNOOPY phaenology
AEGHLNOORR gonorrheal
AEGHLNOORS alongshore
AEGHLNOOSU halogenous
AEGHLNSTWY lengthways
AEGHLOOORR logorrhoea
AEGHLOOPRY oleography
AEGHLOOPTY hepatology
AEGHLORSTT larghettos
AEGHLORSUV overslaugh
AEGHLOSSSU glasshouse
AEGHLRSTUY slaughtery
AEGHMMORRT thermogram
AEGHMNOOPR △gramophone
AEGHMNOPRS sphenogram
AEGHNNOOWY honey-wagon
AEGHNOOORR gonorrhoea
AEGHNOORSW horse-gowan
AEGHNOPRRY granophyre
AEGHNOPRST stenograph
AEGHNOPRVY venography
AEGHNORRST short-range
AEGHNOSUXY hexagynous
AEGHOOPRRY oreography
AEGHOOPRRZ zoographer
AEGHOOPSSU oesophagus
AEGHOOPSUX exophagous
AEGHOOPSUY hypogaeous
AEGHOORSTV shove-groat
AEGHOPRRXY xerography
AEGHORRTUV overraught
AEGHORSSUU sugarhouse
AEGIIILNTV invigilate
AEGIIIMTTV mitigative
AEGIIIRRTV irrigative
AEGIIKNRSS ear-kissing
AEGIILLLTY illegality
AEGIILLOSV villagioes
villiagoes
AEGIILLPTV pit-village
AEGIILMNRT trigeminal
AEGIILMNSX maxi-single
AEGIILMPST split-image
AEGIILNOPR perigonial
AEGIILNOTV levigation
AEGIILNPPY pipe-laying
AEGIILNPRV prevailing
AEGIILRTTT glitterati
AEGIIMMNNO meningioma
AEGIIMNNOT gemination
AEGIIMNORT emigration
remigation
AEGIIMNRRU migraineur
AEGIIMNSTT enigmatist
AEGIIMNSTV negativism
time-saving
AEGIIMSSTT stigmatise
AEGIIMSTTZ stigmatize
AEGIINNOST isoantigen
AEGIINNPRT repainting
AEGIINNRTT intrigante
AEGIINOPPR pigeon-pair
AEGIINORTV invigorate
AEGIINPPST appetising
AEGIINPPTZ appetizing
AEGIINRSTV gainstrive
AEGIINSTTV negativist
AEGIINTTVY agentivity
negativity
AEGIIRRSTT geriatrist
AEGIIRTTVY ergativity
AEGIKLLRST grillsteak
AEGIKLMMOR kilogramme
AEGIKLMNOV lovemaking
AEGIKLNNSY sneakingly
AEGIKLNPSY speakingly
AEGIKLNRWW wing-walker
AEGIKMNNOS maskinonge
AEGIKMNOPR rope-making
AEGIKNNPSU unspeaking
AEGIKNNSST takingness
AEGIKNPRSS king's-spear
AEGILLLLNT all-telling
AEGILLLLNU Lingulella
AEGILLMNRV marvelling
AEGILLNORY orange-lily
regionally
AEGILLNOXY glyoxaline
AEGILLNPPR rappelling
AEGILLNPRU prelingual
AEGILLNPSY pleasingly
AEGILLNRST stallinger
AEGILLNRTV travelling
AEGILLNRTY integrally
AEGILLNSST tasselling
AEGILLNSTY stealingly
AEGILLORST allegorist
legislator
AEGILLPSSX △plexiglass
AEGILMMNNT malignment
AEGILMNNNR Ringelmann
AEGILMNNOR non-gremial
AEGILMNOOP monoplegia
AEGILMNORY mineralogy
AEGILMNRST streamling
AEGILMSSTT gestaltism
AEGILMSTTU multi-stage
AEGILNNOOT elongation
AEGILNNOSU lanuginose
AEGILNNPSU unpleasing
AEGILNNRTU unaltering
AEGILNNRYY yearningly
AEGILNNSSS slanginess
AEGILNNSUY sanguinely
AEGILNOOSU oleaginous
AEGILNORSU lanigerous
AEGILNORTU regulation
urogenital
AEGILNORVY overlaying

AEGILNOSTU gelatinous
AEGILNPRST plastering
AEGILNPRTY taperingly
AEGILNRSTV starveling
AEGILNRVWY waveringly
AEGILNRWYY wearyingly
AEGILNSSSS glassiness
AEGILOORST aerologist
AEGILOPRTT graptolite
AEGILORRSS gressorial
AEGILRRTUY regularity
AEGILSSTTT Gestaltist
AEGIMMNRST stammering
AEGIMMORSS seismogram
AEGIMNNORU enamouring
AEGIMNNPRT impregnant
AEGIMNNRSV serving-man
AEGIMNNSST assignment
AEGIMNOPRS angiosperm
AEGIMNORSU gramineous
AEGIMNORTW worm-eating
AEGIMNPRTY pigmentary
AEGIMNRRST ringmaster
AEGIMNRSTT smattering
AEGIMORRSU armigerous
AEGIMORRTY emigratory
AEGIMOSSTT stigmatose
AEGIMRRTVY gravimetry
AEGINNNOTV non-vintage
AEGINNNPRT trepanning
AEGINNORRS engarrison
AEGINNPPRW enwrapping
AEGINNRSTT astringent
AEGINNRSTU sauntering
AEGINNRSUW unswearing
AEGINNRUVW unwavering
AEGINNRUWY unwearying
AEGINNSSSV savingness
AEGINOORTT negotiator
AEGINORRTT integrator
AEGINORRTZ zero-rating
AEGINORSUU aeruginous
AEGINPPRTT tappet-ring
AEGINPRSTU supergiant
AEGINPRSTY panegyrist
AEGINPSTTU Septuagint
AEGINQRRTU quartering
AEGINRRSSU reassuring
AEGINRRSTT registrant
AEGINRRSTU austringer
AEGINRRSTV traversing
AEGINRSSSS grassiness
AEGINRSSSU sugariness
AEGIOPRSTU Portugaise
AEGIRRRSTY registrary
AEGIRSSTTT strategist
AEGKLLRRUY gully-raker
AEGLLMORRU glomerular
AEGLLMORWY galley-worm
AEGLLMRTUY metallurgy
AEGLLNNPTY plangently
AEGLLNOPST long-staple
AEGLLOPRSU pellagrous
AEGLMNOOOV avgolemono
AEGLMNOOTY nematology
AEGLMNORSS lemon-grass
AEGLMOPRTU promulgate
AEGLMPRSSU plume-grass
AEGLNNOOST logan-stone
AEGLNNPRTY pregnantly
AEGLNOOPRT prolongate
AEGLNOOSUV longaevous
AEGLNSSSSU sunglasses
AEGLOORRST astrologer
AEGLOORTTY teratology
AEGLOPPSTU plague-spot
AEGLORRTUY regulatory
AEGLPRSSUU surplusage
AEGMMNRTUU argumentum
AEGMMOPRRR programmer
AEGMNOORST gastronome
AEGMNORRST starmonger
AEGNNNPRTU unpregnant
AEGNNRTUUY unguentary
AEGNOOORRT orange-root
AEGNOORTXY oxygenator
AEGNOOSTUU autogenous
AEGNOPRSTT patter-song
AEGNOPSTUW wasp-tongue
AEGNRRSSST transgress
AEGNSSSTUU augustness
AEGOORSTUU outrageous
AEGOPRRTUX expurgator
AEGPRRSSSU supergrass
AEHHHILOPT Ahithophel
AEHHIILMOP hemophilia
AEHHILNOPT lithophane
AEHHILNSTU Helianthus
AEHHIMNPST hetmanship
AEHHINOPRT hierophant
AEHHINPRST pantherish
AEHHINRTWY anywhither
AEHHLNOPTT heptathlon
AEHHLOOPRS holophrase
AEHHLOPTTU heath-poult
AEHHMOOOPT homoeopath
AEHHMOOPTY homeopathy
AEHHNOOPRT anthophore
AEHHNOPRTY hypaethron
AEHHORTTWY hateworthy
AEHIIKNPST kinesipath
AEHIIKPRSS kaisership
AEHIILNOPX philoxenia
AEHIILNPST Philistean
AEHIILOPRZ pileorhiza
AEHIILOSTX heliotaxis
AEHIIMNSTT antitheism
AEHIIMNSTU humanities
AEHIINOSTT hesitation
AEHIINPPRS sapphirine
AEHIINSSTT antithesis
AEHIINSTTT antitheist
AEHIIPPRRT Rhipiptera
AEHIIPPSTT epitaphist

AEHIKKNOPT	pinakothek
AEHIKLLLRW	hillwalker
AEHIKLNSSY	sneakishly
AEHIKLSSST	skaithless
AEHIKMNNST	Kentish-man
AEHIKMSTWY	Wykehamist
AEHIKNRSSS	rakishness
AEHILLLNSS	snail-shell
AEHILLMOST	allotheism
AEHILLOOVW	view-halloo
AEHILLOPSV	Slavophile
AEHILLOPTW	pilot-whale
AEHILLOPTY	polyhalite
AEHILLORSV	all-overish
AEHILLORTY	heliolatry
AEHILLOSTY	halloysite
AEHILLSTTY	stealthily
AEHILMMNST	Simmenthal
AEHILMMRTT	tilt-hammer
AEHILMNNUY	inhumanely
AEHILMNOPY	anemophily
AEHILMNSTV	lavishment
AEHILMOPRT	hemitropal
AEHILMORST	isothermal
	thimerosal
AEHILMOSSY	haemolysis
AEHILMPSTU	multiphase
AEHILNNOOP	phaelonion
AEHILNNOPS	Alphonsine
AEHILNOOPP	philopoena
AEHILNOPRZ	rhizoplane
AEHILNOPST	Polianthes
AEHILNOPTT	thiopental
AEHILNPSTY	staphyline
AEHILNSSSV	lavishness
AEHILNSTTY	hesitantly
AEHILOOPRT	ophiolater
AEHILOPRST	hospitaler
	trophesial
AEHILORRTY	hierolatry
AEHILRSTVY	shrievalty
AEHIMMRSTU	rheumatism
AEHIMNNPPS	penmanship
AEHIMNNSTV	vanishment
AEHIMNNSUU	unhumanise
AEHIMNNUUZ	unhumanize
AEHIMNOPPS	hippomanes
AEHIMNORRS	harmoniser
AEHIMNORRZ	harmonizer
AEHIMNOTUX	exhumation
AEHIMNRSSS	marshiness
AEHIMNRSTV	ravishment
AEHIMNSSTU	enthusiasm
AEHIMOOPTY	mythopoeia
AEHIMORRSV	Averrhoism
AEHIMOSSST	hemostasis
AEHIMOSTTU	autotheism
AEHIMPRSST	mastership
	shipmaster
AEHIMPSSTY	sympathies
	sympathise
AEHIMPSTYZ	sympathize

AEHINNNOOT	hootnannie
AEHINNOPRT	antiphoner
AEHINNPSTT	tenantship
AEHINNRRTY	Tyrrhenian
AEHINNRTVW	wanthriven
AEHINOPRTU	euphoriant
AEHINORRTV	hovertrain
AEHINOSTUX	exhaustion
AEHINQRSUV	vanquisher
AEHINRSSST	trashiness
AEHINRSSTW	wrathiness
AEHINSSTTU	enthusiast
AEHIOOPSST	apotheosis
AEHIOPPRRS	repair-shop
AEHIORRSTV	Averrhoist
AEHIORSSST	air-hostess
AEHIORSTTY	hesitatory
AEHIOSTTTU	autotheist
AEHIRSSTTW	sweatshirt
	sweat-shirt
AEHIRSTTWW	thwartwise
AEHKLMRTUW	lukewarmth
AEHKLNNSUY	unshakenly
AEHKLNOSTY	honey-stalk
AEHLLMRSSY	harmlessly
AEHLLMSTUU	haustellum
AEHLLOORWW	hollow-ware
AEHLLOPRXY	phylloxera
AEHLLORRSZ	razor-shell
AEHLMNORTT	antler-moth
AEHLMNOSWW	Welshwoman
AEHLMNPTTU	pentathlum
AEHLMOOPRS	Homorelaps
AEHLMOOSUX	homosexual
AEHLMORRYY	rhyme-royal
AEHLMPSSYY	symphyseal
AEHLNNOPTT	pentathlon
AEHLNOPSTU	plant-house
	sulphonate
AEHLNOPTTY	entophytal
AEHLNORTTT	tetrathlon
AEHLOOPRRY	pyorrhoeal
AEHLORRSVY	overrashly
AEHLORSSTU	authorless
AEHLPRSTUU	sulphurate
AEHLRTTUUV	truth-value
AEHMMMTUWY	mummy-wheat
AEHMNOORSU	manor-house
AEHMNOORSW	horse-woman
AEHMNORTWY	nameworthy
AEHMNPRSUU	superhuman
AEHMNRSTTU	anthersmut
AEHMNRTTUY	nature-myth
AEHMNSSTTY	assythment
AEHMOOPSTT	smoothpate
AEHMOORSTX	mesothorax
AEHMOPRRTT	Tetramorph
AEHMORSTTT	thermostat
AEHNNNOOTY	hootenanny
AEHNNOOPST	panton-shoe
AEHNOOOPRT	orthopnoea
AEHNOOPRST	heart-spoon

AEHNOOPSSU sousaphone
AEHNOPRTUY neuropathy
AEHNORSTWW snow-wreath
AEHOOPPRST apostrophe
AEHOOPPRTY opotherapy
AEHOOPRRTT △orthoptera
AEHOOPRTYZ zootherapy
AEHOOPSSTZ zoothapses
AEHOOPSTTT toothpaste
AEHOOPSTTY osteopathy
AEHOORSSTY soothsayer
AEHOPPRSTY saprophyte
AEHOPRSTUY house-party
AEHOPSSSTY hypostases
AEHORRRSTW rest-harrow
AEHORRTTVW overthwart
AEHPPRRSSU supersharp
AEHPRSSTTY strathspey
AEIIIILNST initialise
AEIIIILNTZ initialize
AEIIIINTTV initiative
AEIIILLMTW Williamite
AEIIILMNOS isoaminile
AEIIILMRST militarise
AEIIILMRTZ militarize
AEIIILMSTV similative
AEIIILMTTV limitative
AEIIILRSTV trivialise
AEIIILRTVZ trivialize
AEIIILSTTV vitalities
AEIIIMMNPR imipramine
AEIIIMNRST ministeria
AEIIIMNSTV vitaminise
AEIIIMNTVZ vitaminize
AEIIIRRTTV irritative
AEIIISTTVV visitative
AEIIKLLNPR pain-killer
AEIIKLLORS sailorlike
AEIIKLRTUV laurvikite
AEIILLLMMS millesimal
AEIILLLMNN millennial
AEIILLLTVY illatively
AEIILLMNPP Pimpinella
AEIILLMNSS sinsemilla
AEIILLMNTU illuminate
AEIILLMPRY imperially
AEIILLMRST literalism
AEIILLNRTU uniliteral
AEIILLNSSV villainess
AEIILLOSTV alveolitis
volatilise
AEIILLOTVZ volatilize
AEIILLPSTT pistillate
AEIILLRRTT triliteral
AEIILLRRTU tirailleur
AEIILLRRTY literarily
AEIILLRSTT literalist
AEIILLRSTV silvertail
AEIILLRTTY literality
AEIILMMMOR immemorial
AEIILMNNOS nominalise
AEIILMNNOZ nominalize
AEIILMNORT eliminator
AEIILMNRST mineralist
AEIILMNSTY seminality
AEIILMNSZZ mizzen-sail
AEIILMNTTY intimately
AEIILMOPST optimalise
AEIILMOPTZ optimalize
AEIILMOSSS isoseismal
AEIILMRSTV relativism
AEIILMRSVV revivalism
AEIILMSTUV simulative
AEIILNNOPT antilopine
AEIILNNORS rosaniline
AEIILNNSSU insulinase
AEIILNNSTT intestinal
AEIILNOOTT etiolation
AEIILNOPSS spaniolise
AEIILNOPSZ spaniolize
AEIILNORRT irrelation
AEIILNORSV revisional
AEIILNORTT literation
AEIILNORTV leviration
AEIILNOSST leontiasis
AEIILNOTTV levitation
tonalitive
velitation
AEIILNPPRZ Lippizaner
AEIILNPRZZ Lipizzaner
AEIILNQTUY inequality
AEIILNRSTY silentiary
AEIILNRTTV intervital
AEIILOPPTV oppilative
AEIILOPSTV spoliative
AEIILORTTV vitriolate
AEIILRSSUV visualiser
AEIILRSTTV relativist
AEIILRSTTZ strelitzia
AEIILRSTVV revivalist
AEIILRSUVZ visualizer
AEIILRTTVY △relativity
AEIIMMNPRT impairment
AEIIMMNSSS Messianism
AEIIMNNNOT innominate
AEIIMNNOST Noetianism
semination
AEIIMNNOTT antimonite
AEIIMNNOTV nominative
AEIIMNOSTT estimation
AEIIMNOSTV somniative
AEIIMNQTUY equanimity
AEIIMNRSST seminarist
AEIIMNRTUV ruminative
AEIIMNSSST Messianist
AEIIMOPRRS impresario
AEIIMPTTUV imputative
AEIINNOQTU inequation
AEIINNOSST enantiosis
AEIINNOTVV innovative
AEIINNPRTT tripinnate
AEIINNPSST paintiness
AEIINNSTTX inexistant
AEIINOPPST inapposite

AEIINOPPTT appetition
AEIINOPPTV appointive
AEIINOPRTX expiration
AEIINOPSTT poinsettia
AEIINOPSTU utopianise
AEIINOPTUZ utopianize
AEIINOQTTU equitation
AEIINOSTTV estivation
AEIINOTUVX exuviation
AEIINPRSTU puritanise
AEIINPRTTU unipartite
AEIINPRTUZ puritanize
AEIINPSSST antisepsis
inspissate
AEIINQTTUV quantitive
AEIINRRTTT trinitrate
AEIINRSSSU Russianise
AEIINRSSUZ Russianize
AEIINRSTTV revisitant
transitive
AEIIOPPRTT propitiate
AEIIOPPSTV appositive
AEIIOPRRSS proairesis
AEIIPRRSTV privatiser
AEIIPRRTTT tripartite
AEIIPRRTVZ privatizer
AEIJLNORSU journalise
AEIJLNORUZ journalize
AEIJLNOSSV jovialness
AEIJNNSSTU jauntiness
AEIJNOOPRT pejoration
AEIJRSTTWW jaw-twister
AEIKLLMNSU muslin-kale
AEIKLLMPPR lapper-milk
AEIKLMMNRS slammerkin
AEIKLMNORT matron-like
AEIKLMNORY monkey-rail
AEIKLMNOTY monkey-tail
AEIKLMNSTY mistakenly
AEIKLMPPRR ripple-mark
AEIKMNNRTU Turkmenian
AEIKNOPRRY perikaryon
AEIKNORSTU keratinous
AEILLLNQSU line-squall
AEILLLSUVY allusively
AEILLMMRST mill-stream
AEILLMNPRS Parnellism
AEILLMNPTU multiplane
AEILLMNRTY terminally
AEILLMPPSS small-pipes
AEILLMPRVY primevally
AEILLMTTUY ultimately
AEILLNNPRU plenilunar
AEILLNNRTY internally
AEILLNOPTT potentilla
AEILLNORTY orientally
AEILLNPSST plaintless
AEILLNPSSY painlessly
AEILLNRTUY tenurially
AEILLOPSTT postillate
AEILLORSSS sailorless
AEILLORTUV trouvaille

AEILLPSSTT pastellist
AEILLQRRTU quarter-ill
AEILLRRTTU Turritella
AEILLRSTTU illustrate
AEILMMNORT montelimar
AEILMMNSSS smalminess
AEILMMRTUY immaturely
AEILMNNOTY nominately
AEILMNNSTT instalment
AEILMNOPRS impersonal
AEILMNOPRT trampoline
AEILMNORTU tourmaline
AEILMNOSST assoilment
AEILMNPRTY planimetry
AEILMNRSTU neutralism
AEILMNRTTT latter-mint
AEILMNSSSU sensualism
AEILMNSTTU last-minute
AEILMOORRT meliorator
AEILMOPPSS ampelopsis
AEILMOPRST peristomal
AEILMOPSST semipostal
AEILMOPSTT Ptolemaist
AEILMPPSST palimpsest
AEILMPRSST slipstream
AEILMPRSSU plumassier
AEILMPRSTU psalterium
AEILMPRTUU pari-mutuel
AEILMRRSSU surrealism
AEILMSTTUX textualism
AEILNNNPPY penny-plain
AEILNNOPSY Polynesian
AEILNNORTT intolerant
AEILNNORTZ interzonal
AEILNNOSST nationless
AEILNNPRSU △peninsular
AEILNNPRTT interplant
AEILNNPSST pliantness
AEILNNRRTU interlunar
AEILNNRSTT lanternist
AEILNOOPRT tropaeolin
AEILNOORTT toleration
AEILNOPPST pentapolis
AEILNOPRRT interpolar
AEILNOPRRV rain-plover
AEILNOPRST interposal
AEILNOPRTU eruptional
AEILNORRTT torrential
AEILNORRTY anteriorly
AEILNORTTV ventilator
AEILNOTTUX exultation
AEILNPPRTU prenuptial
AEILNPRSST paltriness
AEILNPRSTU palustrine
AEILNPSUUV unplausive
AEILNRRTUY unliterary
AEILNRSTTU neutralist
AEILNRSTUU laurustine
AEILNRTTUY neutrality
AEILNSSSTU sensualist
AEILNSSTUU nautiluses
AEILNSSTUY sensuality

AEILOOPSST	apostolise
AEILOOPSTZ	apostolize
AEILOOPTTZ	topazolite
AEILOPPRST	Leptospira
AEILOPPRSU	popularise
AEILOPPRUZ	popularize
AEILOPPSTY	appositely
AEILOPRSSU	plesiosaur
AEILOPRSTT	tetrapolis
AEILOPRSTY	epistolary
AEILOPTTVY	optatively
AEILORRTTU	elutriator
AEILORSTTU	staurolite
AEILPRRSTY	peristylar
AEILPRRTWY	play-writer
AEILPRSSUV	supervisal
AEILQRRTTU	triquetral
AEILRRSSTU	surrealist
AEILSTTTUX	textualist
AEIMMNNRSS	mismanners
AEIMMNORST	monetarism
AEIMMNOTUU	auto-immune
AEIMMNPRTT	impartment
AEIMMNRSSS	smarminess
AEIMMNRSTT	mint-master
AEIMMNRSTY	symmetrian
AEIMMNSTZZ	mizzen-mast
AEIMMPRRSU	spermarium
AEIMMPRSTU	spermatium
AEIMNNNOTT	anointment
AEIMNNOPRR	mainpernor
AEIMNNORTU	numeration
AEIMNOOPZZ	mezzo-piano
AEIMNOORST	aeronomist
AEIMNOPRTT	armipotent
	portamenti
AEIMNOPRTW	tripe-woman
AEIMNOPRWZ	prizewoman
AEIMNOPTTT	temptation
AEIMNOQSUU	equanimous
AEIMNORRST	ironmaster
AEIMNORRTT	terminator
AEIMNORSTT	monetarist
AEIMNORSTU	Mousterian
AEIMNPPRST	pentaprism
AEIMNPSSSW	swampiness
AEIMNPSTTY	tympanites
AEIMNRRRTY	intermarry
AEIMNRRSTT	retransmit
AEIMNRSSTU	antiserums
AEIMOORSTX	xerostomia
AEIMOOTTUV	automotive
AEIMOPRRTU	praetorium
AEIMPRSSST	masspriest
AEIMPRSSTU	pasteurism
AEIMPRSTUZ	trapeziums
AEIMPSSTUV	assumptive
AEIMQRSTUZ	quizmaster
AEIMRRRSTU	terrariums
AEIMRRSTTT	ritt-master
AEINNNOPST	pensionnat
AEINNOORTV	renovation
AEINNOPRSY	pensionary
AEINNOQRTU	quaternion
AEINNORRSU	raisonneur
AEINNORSTT	stentorian
AEINNOSTTT	attentions
AEINNQSSTU	quaintness
AEINNRSSUW	unwariness
AEINOOPPRT	propionate
AEINOOPRRT	peroration
AEINOORRTT	orientator
AEINOPPPRT	preappoint
AEINOPPRST	spear-point
AEINOPRRST	patroniser
	periastron
AEINOPRRTW	powertrain
AEINOPRRTZ	patronizer
AEINOPRSSU	persuasion
AEINOPRSTT	prestation
AEINOPRSTU	superation
AEINOPRSTW	waitperson
AEINOPRTTU	reputation
AEINOPRTTY	potentiary
AEINOPTTTU	out-patient
AEINORRSST	serrations
AEINORRSTU	souterrain
AEINORRSTV	overstrain
AEINORSSTY	tyrosinase
AEINORSTTY	stationery
AEINPPRSST	trappiness
AEINPPRSTW	wit-snapper
AEINPRRSTU	rupestrian
AEINPRRTTU	parturient
AEINPRSTTT	strepitant
AEINQRTTUY	quaternity
AEINRRSSST	starriness
AEINRSSSTT	straitness
AEINRSTUYZ	suzerainty
AEIOPRRRST	respirator
AEIOPRRTTX	extirpator
AEIOPRRTXY	expiratory
AEIORRRSSW	warrioress
AEIPRSTUUV	usurpative
AEIRSSSTUU	saussurite
AEJMNNORUY	journeyman
AEKKMNRRTU	trunk-maker
AEKLLMRUWY	lukewarmly
AEKLLOPSTU	leukoplast
AEKLORTTWW	wattlework
AEKMNORTTW	market-town
AEKMOORTTY	keratotomy
AEKMORRSTW	masterwork
	workmaster
AEKOOPRRTY	prokaryote
AEKOPRRSTY	oyster-park
AEKORRSTWW	waterworks
AELLMNNOUY	noumenally
AELLMNORTY	trolley-man
AELLMOPRTY	temporally
AELLMOPSSY	plasmolyse
AELLMOPSYZ	plasmolyze
AELLMORSUV	marvellous
AELLNOOPRT	Trollopean

AELLNOPPRT propellant
AELLNOPRSY personally
AELLNOPSTU plant-louse
AELLNOPTVY polyvalent
AELLNORTTY tolerantly
AELLNOSSSW sallowness
AELLNPRSUY supernally
AELLNPTTUY petulantly
AELLNRSTTY slatternly
AELLNTTUXY exultantly
AELLOPPRSU all-purpose
AELLOPRSUY superalloy
AELLPRSTUU sepultural
AELLRTTUXY texturally
AELMMNNOTU monumental
AELMMOOPSS plasmosome
AELMMOPRRW palmer-worm
AELMMPRSTU emplastrum
AELMNNNRUY unmannerly
AELMNNOOTV monovalent
AELMNOOPRT monopteral
protonemal
AELMNOOPRY lampoonery
AELMNOPRST emplastron
AELMNOPRSU neuroplasm
AELMNOPRTT portmantle
AELMNOPSTY polysemant
AELMNORSSS ransomless
AELMNSSSUW swan-mussel
AELMOOPPTT tappet-loom
AELMOOPRTU tropaeolum
AELMOPPRUY propylaeum
AELMOPRTTU petrolatum
AELMOPRTTY temporalty
AELMOQSSUU squamulose
AELMORRSSU armourless
AELMORRSSW marrowless
AELMORSSTU somersault
AELMORSTTT lattermost
AELMRSSTTU mulattress
AELMTTTUUU tumultuate
AELNNOPRYY pennyroyal
AELNNORSTY resonantly
AELNOPRSST patronless
AELNOPRSTY personalty
AELNOPSTTT talent-spot
AELNORSUVY ravenously
AELNOSSUUY nauseously
AELNPPRSTU supplanter
AELNPRRSUU superlunar
AELOOOPRTY aeolotropy
AELOPPRRRU pourparler
AELOPRRSUY super-royal
AELOPSSTTU postulates
AELORRTTTW otter-trawl
AELORSSSUV savourless
AELPPPPTUY puppet-play
AELPPSSTUY platypuses
AEMMNOPRTU map-mounter
AEMMNORSTY Asymmetron
AEMMNOSTUZ Montezuma's
AEMMNRSTYY mystery-man
AEMMOSSTTU stemmatous
AEMNNNOPTY non-payment
AEMNNOOSST stonemason
AEMNNORTTT attornment
AEMNNORTTU tournament
AEMNNRRSUY nurseryman
AEMNOOPRTT portamento
AEMNOORRST astronomer
AEMNOPRSSW presswoman
AEMNOPRSUW superwoman
AEMNORRTUY uranometry
AEMNORSSTT assortment
AEMNORSSTU sarmentous
AEMNRRSTTU transmuter
AEMOOPSTTY somatotype
AEMOPRRSSW swarm-spore
AEMOPRSSTT postmaster
AEMORRSTTW masterwort
AEMORRSTTY astrometry
AENNNOSSTW wantonness
AENNOPSTTY stannotype
AENNORRSSW narrowness
AENNORRSTT non-starter
AENOOPRRST personator
AENOOPRTXY paroxytone
AENOOQRRTU quarteroon
AENOORSSTU anoestrous
treasonous
AENOPRRSST transposer
AENOPRSSUV supernovas
AENOPRSTTT △protestant
AENPRRSTTU transputer
AEOOPPRRRT propraetor
AEOOPPRRST praepostor
AEOOPPRSTU tropopause
AEOOPRSTTV vaporettos
AEOPPRRRTU rapporteur
AEOPRRSSTW sportswear
AEOPRRSSUY persuasory
AEOPRSTTUW waterspout
AEORSSSTUU trousseaus
AEORSSTUUX trousseaux
AEPRRSTUUU usurpature
AFFFFINNYY niffy-naffy
AFFFGILLNO falling-off
AFFGIILNSY falsifying
AFFGIINORT forfaiting
AFFGIIRSTT graffitist
AFFGIMRSSU suffragism
AFFGINNORT affronting
AFFGIRSSTU suffragist
AFFGNOORST stroganoff
AFFHIINRSU ruffianish
AFFHILLTUY faithfully
AFFHILNTUU unfaithful
AFFHIRSTTU Tartuffish
AFFIIMNRSU ruffianism
AFFILNOSTU sufflation
AFFIMRSTTU Tartuffism
AFGGGILNNU unflagging
AFGGIIMNNY magnifying
AFGGIINRTY gratifying

AFGGILMNOR	gangliform
AFGGLLNSUU	fungus-gall
AFGHHILLST	flashlight
AFGHILNPSU	upflashing
AFGHIORTWY	right-of-way
AFGHLLSTUY	ghastfully
AFGHNOOSTU	Nothofagus
AFGIILLNSY	sail-flying
AFGIILMNPY	amplifying
AFGIILNQUY	qualifying
AFGIILOSTU	flagitious
AFGIIMNOTU	fumigation
AFGIINORTU	figuration
AFGIINOTTU	fugitation
AFGIINSSTY	satisfying
AFGIKMNORS	king-of-arms
AFGILLNOTY	floatingly
AFGILNORUV	flavouring
AFGIMNORTT	formatting
AFGIMORTUY	fumigatory
AFGINNOOPS	poison-fang
AFHHLLORUY	half-hourly
AFHIILMOPR	phialiform
AFHIINOSST	fashionist
AFHILLMORT	thalliform
AFHILNOPST	flash-point
AFHIOPRRST	parrot-fish
AFHKLLNTUY	thankfully
AFHKLNNTUU	unthankful
AFHLLORTTU	throat-full
AFHLLRTUWY	wrathfully
AFIIINNNTT	infinitant
AFIIINNRTY	infinitary
AFIIKLORTT	forkit-tail
AFIILLLNUY	unfilially
AFIILLRRTY	fritillary
AFIILLSTUV	fluvialist
AFIILMNOSW	Wolfianism
AFIILNNOST	fontinalis
AFIILNORSU	infusorial
AFIILNORTT	filtration
	flirtation
AFIIMORSTV	favoritism
AFIINNORSU	infusorian
AFIINSSTTU	fustianist
AFIIORRSTU	trifarious
AFILLLLTYY	tilly-fally
AFILLMNORY	informally
AFILLNPPTY	flippantly
AFILMNOSUY	infamously
AFILNORUXY	fluxionary
AFIMMOQRSU	squamiform
AFIMMORTUU	fumatorium
AFIMNOORSU	foraminous
AFIMNRSTUU	rumfustian
AFIMOOPRRV	vaporiform
AFIMORRSTT	stratiform
AFLLLNUUWY	unlawfully
AFLLMNNUUY	unmanfully
AFLLMNOUWY	womanfully
AFLLNRTUUY	unartfully
AFLOOOPRSW	sloop-of-war
AFLOOOPRTT	foot-patrol
AGGGGIINZZ	zigzagging
AGGGIIINNV	gaingiving
AGGGILNRST	straggling
AGGHHOPRRY	hygrograph
AGGHIINNRS	garnishing
AGGHILLNUY	laughingly
AGGHILNNSY	gnashingly
AGGHILNNUW	whaling-gun
AGGHILNORT	light-organ
AGGHILNSST	night-glass
AGGHLOOPRY	graphology
	logography
AGGIIIMNNS	imaginings
AGGIILLNNS	signalling
AGGIILNNTU	agglutinin
AGGIIMNNNS	singing-man
AGGILLNNSY	slangingly
AGGILLNNTY	tanglingly
AGGILLNORR	rag-rolling
AGGILLNOTY	gloatingly
AGGILLOOST	algologist
AGGILMORSY	gargoylism
AGGILNNTWY	twangingly
AGGILNPRSY	graspingly
AGGILOORST	agrologist
AGGINNSSWW	swing-swang
AGGINORRTT	garrotting
AGGINOSSTU	outgassing
AGGLNOOORZ	Gorgonzola
AGGLOORSTY	gastrology
AGGMOSSTUY	mystagogus
AGGNORRSSW	grass-grown
AGHHILOPRT	lithograph
AGHHIOPPPY	hippophagy
AGHHLOOPRY	holography
AGHHNOOPPR	phonograph
AGHHOOPPRT	photograph
AGHHOOPRRT	orthograph
AGHHOOPRRY	horography
AGHHORTUWY	throughway
AGHIILNORS	Anglo-Irish
AGHIIMNNTT	tithingman
AGHIINNRSV	varnishing
AGHIINPRRS	hairspring
AGHIINRTWW	wainwright
AGHIKMNOST	shotmaking
AGHIKMRTTU	khitmutgar
AGHILLNOSW	shallowing
AGHILLNOTY	loathingly
	tally-hoing
AGHILLOPTU	plough-tail
AGHILMORST	logarithms
AGHILNNTUY	hauntingly
AGHILNPRST	springhalt
AGHILNPSTY	night-palsy
AGHILNRSTT	stringhalt
AGHILOPPRY	lipography
AGHILOPPSY	gypsophila
AGHILPRTWY	playwright
AGHILRSTTY	straightly
AGHIMMOPRY	mimography

AGHIMNOOPS	siphonogam
AGHIMNPRTU	upright-man
AGHINNRTTU	rat-hunting
AGHINOPTTW	towing-path
AGHIOPPRRS	spirograph
AGHIOPPSUX	xiphopagus
AGHKMOPRYY	kymography
AGHLMMOPRY	lymphogram
AGHLMNOPSU	ploughman's
AGHLNOOORT	orthogonal
AGHLOPPRYY	polygraphy
AGHLOPRSTY	stylograph
AGHLOPRXYY	xylography
AGHMMOOOSU	homogamous
AGHMNOOPRY	gramophony
	monography
	nomography
AGHMNOOPTY	pathognomy
AGHMNOORTU	mouth-organ
AGHMOOOPSU	omophagous
AGHMOOPRTY	tomography
AGHNNOOPRU	harpoon-gun
AGHNOOPRSY	nosography
	sonography
AGHNOORSTT	goat's-thorn
AGHOOOPSUZ	zoophagous
AGHOOPPRTY	topography
AGHOOPRSST	gastrosoph
AGHOPPRRYY	pyrography
AGHOPPRTYY	typography
AGIIIILNNT	initialing
AGIIILMNNN	mainlining
AGIIILNOTT	litigation
AGIIILNSTV	vitalising
AGIIILNTVZ	vitalizing
AGIIIMNOTT	mitigation
AGIIINORRT	irrigation
AGIIKKMNNR	marking-ink
AGIIKNNNPR	napkin-ring
AGIIKNPSST	piss-taking
AGIILLMNSY	misallying
AGIILLNNST	installing
AGIILLNNUU	unilingual
AGIILLNORY	originally
AGIILLNRTU	trilingual
AGIILLNRTY	trailingly
AGIILLNRVY	virginally
AGIILLNTVY	vigilantly
AGIILLRTTY	gratillity
AGIILNNORU	unoriginal
AGIILNPRST	springtail
AGIILNPRSY	aspiringly
	praisingly
AGIILNRSTY	laryngitis
AGIILOOSTX	axiologist
AGIIMMOSST	misogamist
AGIIMMSSTT	stigmatism
AGIIMNNPRS	mainspring
AGIIMNOPTU	impugation
AGIIMNORSU	migrainous
AGIIMNSSUV	vaginismus
AGIIMORTTY	mitigatory
AGIIMSSTTT	stigmatist
AGIINNNNPS	inspanning
AGIINNNTTU	untainting
AGIINNOORT	ignoration
AGIINNORTV	invigorant
AGIINNPRSU	unaspiring
AGIINNRTTU	intriguant
AGIINNSSTU	sustaining
AGIINNSTUY	sanguinity
AGIINOORRT	originator
AGIINOPRRR	rip-roaring
AGIINORSTT	instigator
AGIINORSUV	viraginous
AGIINPPRSW	ripping-saw
AGIKKLNRSY	skylarking
AGIKLMNOOT	toolmaking
AGIKLNNPRY	prankingly
AGIKLNNPSY	spankingly
AGIKMNNOOR	moonraking
AGIKMNNOTU	Kuomintang
AGIKMNNRTU	marking-nut
AGILLLNRUY	alluringly
AGILLLNRYY	rallyingly
AGILLNNRSY	snarlingly
AGILLNNSTY	slantingly
AGILLNOPRT	patrolling
AGILLNRSUY	singularly
AGILLNTTTY	tattlingly
AGILLOOSSS	isoglossal
AGILLOOSTT	isoglottal
AGILLOOTWW	goat-willow
AGILMNSSUY	assumingly
AGILMOOSTT	atmologist
AGILMOOSTU	gliomatous
AGILMOOSTY	Mayologist
AGILMOPSTY	polygamist
AGILNNNOPY	non-playing
AGILNNNOYY	annoyingly
AGILNNOPTY	poignantly
AGILNNOPYY	polygynian
AGILNNORTY	ignorantly
AGILNNOSUU	lanuginous
AGILNNPPSY	snappingly
AGILNNTTUY	tauntingly
AGILNNTUVY	vauntingly
AGILNOOSTU	antilogous
AGILNORTYY	gyniolatry
AGILNRSTTY	startingly
AGILOORSTY	aristology
AGILORSSST	glossarist
AGIMMNNORY	May-morning
AGIMMNOOST	monogamist
AGIMMNSSUY	gymnasiums
AGIMNNNOOY	monogynian
AGIMNNSSUU	unassuming
AGIMNOOPRU	amino-group
AGIMNOORST	agronomist
AGIMNOPRSU	sporangium
AGINNOOPRT	organ-point
AGINNPPSUW	swan-upping
AGINNPRSUW	pruning-saw
AGINNRSTUW	turning-saw

AGINOOOPRS sporogonia
AGINOORSUV voraginous
AGINPRSSSU surpassing
AGINSTYYYZ antisyzygy
AGIORSTTUU gratuitous
AGKLORSSSW glassworks
AGLLLOOPRY pyrogallol
AGLLNOOPYY palynology
AGLLRTTUUY gutturally
AGLMOOOPTY potamology
AGLMOOOSTY somatology
AGLMOOPSUY polygamous
AGLMOPPRUU propagulum
AGLNOORSUU languorous
AGLOOOSTUU autologous
AGLOOPPRYY papyrology
AGMMNOOOSU monogamous
AGMNNOORWW woman-grown
AGMNOORSTY gastronomy
AGMOORSTTY gastrotomy
AGMORRSTUU surrogatum
AGOORRSSST grass-roots
AHHILLWWWY whillywhaw
AHHILMOPTY philomathy
AHHILOPSTY lithophysa
AHHIMNOPRY rhinophyma
AHHIMNOPST phantomish
AHHIMNOSTY Mishnayoth
AHHIMNPTUY hypanthium
AHHIOOPRRZ Rhizophora
AHHIOPRSTU authorship
AHHIPRSTTW thwartship
AHHISSWWYY wishy-washy
AHHLLMOOTY homothally
AHHLLOOOPT holophotal
AHIIIJKNRS jinrikisha
AHIIILNPPP Philippian
philippina
AHIIILNPST Philistian
AHIIIMMPSX amphimixis
AHIIKMNRSS Krishnaism
AHIILMORTU humiliator
AHIILOOPPT topophilia
AHIIMNNOTU inhumation
AHIIMNNTUY inhumanity
AHIIMNORSW Irishwoman
AHIIRSSTTW shirtwaist
AHIJMORUUY jumhouriya
AHIJNNNOOS Johnsonian
AHIKKMNRSS skrimshank
AHIKLPRSSY sparkishly
AHIKNPRRSW shrink-wrap
AHIKNPSSTU Skupshtina
AHILLMQSUY qualmishly
AHILLORTTY litholatry
AHILMMOPPS psammophil
AHILMMORSU humoralism
AHILMNNOOR monorhinal
AHILMNOPYY Polyhymnia
AHILMNOSWY womanishly
AHILMORSTU humoralist
AHILMPSSYY symphysial
AHILNOORTZ horizontal
AHILNOPSTU sulphation
AHILNPPSSY snappishly
AHILNPSSTU sultanship
AHILOOPRTY ophiolatry
AHIMNOOOSU homoousian
AHIMNOORRU honorarium
AHIMNOORSU harmonious
AHIMNOPPSS pansophism
AHIMNOPRST matronship
AHIMNOPRTY Amphitryon
AHIMNPRTTU triumphant
AHIMORSTUU haustorium
AHINNOOPRT Trophonian
AHINNOPRRY Pyrrhonian
AHINOPPSST pansophist
AHINOPRSTY notaryship
AHINOPRSUX xiphosuran
AHINPRSTTU truantship
AHIOOPSSTZ zoothapsis
AHIOOPSTTX phototaxis
AHIOPPRSST pastorship
AHIOPSSSTY hypostasis
AHKLMOPRYY karyolymph
AHKLOOOSTU akolouthos
AHLLLLNOOW allhollown
AHLLMOOSTT small-tooth
AHLLOPRSTU prothallus
AHLLOPTXYY phyllotaxy
AHLMMOOPSY homoplasmy
AHLNOPSTUY polyanthus
AHLOOPRSTU south-polar
AHLORRSTTU ultrashort
AHMNNOORSU honours-man
AHMNNOOSTU Anthonomus
AHMNOOPRTU protohuman
AHMNPSTUYY unsympathy
AHMOOPRTYY amyotrophy
AHMOPRSTTU mouthparts
AHNNOSSTUY synanthous
AHNNOSTTWY shantytown
AHNOOPRRXY oropharynx
AHNOOPRTYZ zoanthropy
AHNOOPSTTY nostopathy
photonasty
AHNOOPTTUY tautophony
AHNOPPRTTY tryptophan
AHOOPPRTTY protopathy
Protophyta
AHOOPRRTXY orthopraxy
AHOORRTTTW throatwort
AIIIINNOTT initiation
AIIILLMNTU △illuminati
AIIILLMRTY militarily
AIIILLPPST papillitis
AIIILMMMNS minimalism
AIIILMMNST minimalist
AIIILMMRST militarism
AIIILMNOSS moniliasis
AIIILMNOTT limitation
AIIILMRSTT militarist
AIIILMRSTV trivialism

AIIILMRSTY	similarity
AIIILNOPTX	pixilation
AIIILORSTV	visitorial
AIIILRTTVY	triviality
AIIIMNNOTT	intimation
AIIIMNOPSS	pianissimo
AIIIMPRSVV	viviparism
AIIINNOOST	ionisation
AIIINNOOTZ	ionization
AIIINNOTTV	invitation
AIIINORRTT	irritation
AIIINORTTT	tritiation
AIIINORTTY	initiatory
AIIINOSTTV	△visitation
AIIINOTTTV	titivation
AIIIPRSSTY	pityriasis
AIIIPRTVVY	viviparity
AIIKLNOOSS	kaolinosis
AIILLMNNTU	illuminant
AIILLMNORY	millionary
AIILLMNTTY	militantly
AIILLNOOTV	volitional
AIILLNOSUV	villainous
AIILLNOSVY	visionally
AIILLNOTUV	outvillain
AIILLOORTV	volitorial
AIILLORSTY	solitarily
AIILLORTTT	titillator
AIILLOSSTT	solstitial
AIILLOTTVY	volatility
AIILLPRSTY	pistillary
AIILLSTUVV	valvulitis
AIILMMMORS	immoralism
AIILMMNNOS	nominalism
AIILMMNOOT	immolation
AIILMMNRSU	luminarism
AIILMMORST	immoralist
AIILMMORTY	immorality
AIILMNNOST	nominalist
AIILMNNOTU	lumination
AIILMNOORT	monitorial
AIILMNOSTU	simulation
AIILMNOTTU	mutilation
AIILMNRSSU	insularism
AIILMNRSTU	luminarist
AIILMNRTUY	unmilitary
AIILMORSTV	Voltairism
AIILMRRTUV	triumviral
AIILMRSTUV	virtualism
AIILNNOOST	insolation
AIILNNOSTU	insulation
AIILNOOPPT	oppilation
AIILNOOPST	positional
	spoliation
AIILNOOTTV	volitation
AIILNPTTUY	nuptiality
AIILNRSSUY	urinalysis
AIILNRSTUY	insularity
AIILQRSTUY	squirality
AIILRSTTUV	virtualist
AIILRTTTUY	titularity
AIILRTTUVY	virtuality
AIIMMNNOTU	ammunition
AIIMMPRRTU	imprimatur
AIIMMRTTUY	immaturity
AIIMNNNOOT	nomination
AIIMNNOORS	Morisonian
AIIMNNORTU	rumination
AIIMNNRSTT	ministrant
AIIMNOOTTV	motivation
AIIMNOPRTV	provitamin
AIIMNOPRTY	omniparity
AIIMNOPSTU	utopianism
AIIMNOPTTU	imputation
AIIMNORSSY	missionary
AIIMNPRSTU	puritanism
AIIMNPSSTU	impuissant
AIIMNPSTTY	tympanitis
AIIMNQRSSU	△sinarquism
AIIMNRSSSU	Russianism
AIIMOPRSTT	patriotism
AIIMORRSTT	traitorism
AIIMOSSTTT	stomatitis
AIIMPRRSTT	tripartism
AIINNNOOTT	intonation
AIINNNOOTV	innovation
AIINNOPSTU	supination
AIINNORSTT	transition
AIINNORSTU	insinuator
AIINOOPPST	apposition
AIINOPRRST	inspirator
AIINOPSSST	Passionist
AIINORTTUY	tuitionary
AIINORTTVY	invitatory
AIINQRSSTU	sinarquist
AIINRSSSTU	Russianist
AIIOPRSUVV	viviparous
AIIPPRSSTU	Aristippus
AIIPRSTTVY	varitypist
AIJLMNORSU	journalism
AIJLNORSTU	journalist
AIKLMNNOPS	salmon-pink
AIKLOPSTUV	Volapükist
AIKLORSSYY	karyolysis
AIKNNOPRSS	Parkinson's
AIKNOPRSTW	paintworks
AILLLLTVYY	tilly-vally
AILLMMORTY	immortally
AILLMNOOPY	polynomial
AILLMOOSTT	tomatillos
AILLMOPRTU	multipolar
AILLMOPRXY	proximally
AILLMQRTUZ	quartz-mill
AILLNNOOTY	notionally
AILLNNOSUY	unisonally
AILLNOOPRT	pollinator
	Trollopian
AILLNOOPTY	optionally
AILLNOOSTU	solutional
AILLNOPPTT	pilot-plant
AILLNORSTY	tonsillary
AILLNQRTUY	tranquilly
AILLOOPRRT	pillar-root
AILLOORRSY	sororially

AILLORSTTY	stillatory
AILLORTTUY	tutorially
AILMMNORTU	unimmortal
AILMNNOOOS	Solomonian
AILMNNOOPR	pronominal
AILMNNORSU	surnominal
AILMNNRTUY	ruminantly
AILMNOOPST	lampoonist
AILMNORTUY	unmorality
AILMOOPRRT	imploratOR
AILMOOPRST	prostomial
AILMOOPSTU	lipomatous
AILMORSTTU	stimulator
AILMORSTUY	simulatory
AILMOSSSTY	asystolism
AILNNOOPSS	sponsional
AILNNOPRST	rosin-plant
AILNNQRTUU	untranquil
AILNOOOPST	piano-stool
AILNOOPPTU	population
AILNOOPRSS	sponsorial
AILNOOTTUV	volutation
AILNORSTTU	lustration
AILNOSTTUU	ustulation
AILNPSSTUY	puissantly
AILOOPRSTY	spoliatory
AILOPPRTUY	popularity
AILOPRSTTU	stipulator
AIMMNORSTU	stramonium
AIMMOORRTU	moratorium
AIMMTTXXYY	mixty-maxty
AIMNOOPRSU	omniparous
AIMNOORSTY	somniatory
AIMNOOSTTU	autonomist
AIMNOOSTTX	taxonomist
AIMNOPSSTU	△assumption
AIMNRSTTUU	△nasturtium
AIMOOORTVY	ovariotomy
AIMOPRSSTT	prostatism
AIMOPSSSTY	symposiast
AIMOQSSTUY	squamosity
AINNOOPRSS	sopraninos
AINNOOPRTT	antiproton
AINNOORTVY	innovatory
AINNOPRSTT	strapontin
AINOOOPPRT	pornotopia
AINOOPRSTY	anisotropy
AINOOPSSTU	outpassion
AINOORRSUV	ranivorous
AINOOSTTTU	outstation
AINOPRSTTU	stupration
AINOPRSTUU	usurpation
AINORRSSTT	transistor
AINORRSTTY	transitory
AINORSTTUU	suturation
AINPRSTUUV	pursuivant
AIOOPRRSUU	uproarious
AIOOPRSTVY	vaporosity
AIOOQSTTUU	quotatious
AIOORRSTTU	traitorous
AIOPPPRSUU	pupiparous
AIOPRRSUVV	parvovirus
AIORRRTTTU	triturator
AKLLMMOSUW	musk-mallow
AKMNORTTUW	tutworkman
ALLMNOOSUY	allonymous
ALLOOPPRRT	poll-parrot
ALLOORSUVY	valorously
ALLOPRSTYY	polystylar
ALLOPRTTUY	plutolatry
ALMMNSSSUU	Mussulmans
ALMNOORSTY	monostylar
ALMOOPPRST	protoplasm
ALMOPSTTUU	postulatum
ALMRTTUUUY	tumultuary
ALNOOOPRST	portolanos
ALNPRSTUUY	pursuantly
ALOOORSTUZ	zoolatrous
ALOOPPRSTT	protoplast
ALOOPPRTTY	prototypal
ALOOPRSTTU	postulator
ALOOPRSUVY	vaporously
ALOPRTUUVY	voluptuary
AMMOOSTUXY	myxomatous
AMNNOOSTUY	antonymous
AMNNOOSTWW	townswoman
AMNOOOSTUU	autonomous
AMNOOPRSUY	paronymous
AMOORSSTTU	stromatous
AMOPPRRTUY	promptuary
AMOPPRSTTU	postpartum
	post-partum
ANNOOPRSST	transposon
ANOOOPRSTZ	protozoans
AOOOPPRSSU	aposporous
AOOOPPRSTU	apotropous
AOOPRRRSTZ	razor-strop
AOPRRSTUUY	usurpatory

B

BBBCEEILRS	bescribble
BBBCEEORWY	cobwebbery
BBBCJKLOUY	bubbly-jock
BBBDEEINOR	beribboned
BBBEEIINRW	wine-bibber
BBBEHHLOSU	hobble-bush
BBBEOORSXY	bobbysoxer
BBBGHIJNOO	hobjobbing
BBBGHINNOO	hobnobbing
BBBGIIKNOS	skibobbing
BBBHRSSUUY	subshrubby
BBBLLOOWWY	blow-by-blow
BBCDEIKORR	rock-ribbed
BBCDEIRSSU	subscribed
BBCEEKNRRU	rubberneck
BBCEELNOOU	bubonocele
BBCEHINSSU	chubbiness
BBCEIRRSSU	subscriber
BBCGIIINRT	crib-biting
BBCGIILNRS	scribbling
BBDDDDUUYY	buddy-buddy
BBDEEFLSTU	stubble-fed
BBDEEGIILL	big-bellied
BBDEEIMORV	dive-bomber

BBDEEINORW	ribbon-weed
BBDEHNRSUU	unshrubbed
BBDEIKNOOR	bookbinder
BBDEIMNORT	bond-timber
BBDEIRRTTU	butter-bird
BBDELOPSUU	pseudobulb
BBDHIIOPRS	bishop-bird
BBEEEFGRRU	beefburger
BBEEEFIRSW	beef-brewis
BBEEEFORST	best-before
BBEEEHNNRT	herb-bennet
BBEEELLSUV	bull-beeves
BBEEELORTT	beer-bottle
BBEEHORRRT	herb-Robert
BBEELLOTTU	bluebottle
BBEELMORTT	letter-bomb
BBEELMOSSV	bomb-vessel
BBEELNNOTU	blue-bonnet
BBEEMMNNTU	benumbment
BBEFLMOOTU	bumble-foot
BBEGIILOPY	bibliopegy
BBEGILNRSU	slubbering
BBEGLOOSSU	subglobose
BBEHHILOST	shibboleth
BBEHHOORSY	hobby-horse
BBEHMOOOPR	ombrophobe
BBEIILLOOP	bibliopole
BBEIKLLORR	bill-broker
BBEIKLMOOO	bookmobile
BBEIKNNOSS	knobbiness
BBEILNOSSW	wobbliness
BBEINSSSTU	stubbiness
BBEIOOPRYZ	booby-prize
BBEKLORRUW	rubble-work
BBELMMSTUU	stumblebum
BBELOOPRTW	pot-wobbler
BBEMOORRRU	rubber-room
BBEMPRTTUU	butter-bump
BBEOORRRTU	root-rubber
BBFHIINORS	ribbonfish
BBGHIINRSU	rubbishing
BBGHILLNOY	hobblingly
BBGHIMNOTU	thingumbob
BBGIILLNNY	nibblingly
BBGIILLOOY	bibliology
BBGILNNSUY	snubbingly
BBHIIILLOP	bibliophil
BBHILNOSSY	snobbishly
BBHNOSTTUU	button-bush
BBIIIIMNOT	imbibition
BBIIKKNTUZ	kibbutznik
BBIILLOOPY	bibliopoly
BBILLOSUUY	bibulously
BBIMNOORRW	ribbon-worm
BBIMNOORSU	Bourbonism
BBINOORSTU	Bourbonist
BBJMMMOOUU	Mumbo-Jumbo
	mumbo-jumbo
BBLMOORSUY	Bloomsbury
BBLNORSTUY	stubbornly
BBOOOSSSTY	bossyboots
BCCDEEEMNU	decumbence
BCCDEEILOT	decoctible
BCCDEEMNUY	decumbency
BCCDEILNOU	conducible
BCCEEEILLR	cerebellic
BCCEEEMNRU	recumbence
BCCEEENPSU	pubescence
BCCEEIINOS	bioscience
BCCEEINRTY	cybernetic
BCCEEMNRUY	recumbency
BCCEHIILOS	libecchios
BCCEHIIMRU	cherubimic
BCCEHNORSS	crossbench
BCCEIIIMSS	cicisbeism
BCCEIINOOT	coenobitic
BCCEILORSU	scrobicule
BCCEIMNNUY	incumbency
BCCEKMOOPT	pocket-comb
BCCESSSUUU	succubuses
BCCHIINORT	bronchitic
BCCIIRSTUU	subcircuit
BCDDEEGIKR	deck-bridge
BCDDEEILTU	deductible
BCDDEIKLLU	duck-billed
BCDDHIISTU	Buddhistic
BCDEEEEHMR	béche-de-mer
BCDEEEFILT	defectible
BCDEEEHNRU	unbreeched
BCDEEEIINT	△benedicite
BCDEEEILPT	deceptible
BCDEEEILTT	detectible
BCDEEEIRRS	redescribe
BCDEEEKLPS	bespeckled
BCDEEELMRY	Decemberly
BCDEEHLNNU	unblenched
BCDEEHLOST	bedclothes
BCDEEHOPRS	beech-drops
BCDEEHORUU	debouchure
BCDEEIILNR	incredible
BCDEEIIPRR	bride-price
BCDEEILNNZ	zinc-blende
BCDEEILNRU	uncredible
BCDEEIMRST	Decembrist
BCDEEINSSU	subsidence
BCDEEINSTU	Benedictus
BCDEEKLLNU	bull-necked
BCDEEKLRTU	truckle-bed
BCDEEMNORU	code-number
BCDEEMNRUU	uncumbered
BCDEEMOORS	rose-combed
BCDEENOSST	second-best
BCDEEORRSS	crossbreed
BCDEFIIKLR	brickfield
BCDEFLOOTU	club-footed
BCDEHIRRRY	bird-cherry
BCDEHLOORS	school-bred
BCDEIILLNU	includible
BCDEIILNRY	incredibly
BCDEIILOOS	obeliscoid
BCDEILOORR	corrodible
BCDEILOPRU	producible
BCDEINORTU	counterbid
BCDEINSSUY	subsidency

BCDEKORTTU	butterdock
BCDELORRUY	cloudberry
BCDEMMNRUU	cummerbund
BCDENORRUV	curbvendor
BCDENORSUU	unobscured
BCDENRRSUU	underscrub
BCDGIIOSTU	dog-biscuit
BCDHHIILRT	childbirth
BCDHOOOPRU	brood-pouch
BCDIIILOTY	docibility
BCDIILMORU	lumbricoid
BCDIIMMSUY	cymbidiums
BCDILLOTUU	cloud-built
BCDILOOSSU	discobolus
BCDINOSTUU	subduction
BCDKLOOOST	bloodstock
BCDKMRSTUU	dumbstruck
BCDKORRUUW	burrow-duck
BCDLORSTUU	cloudburst
BCEEEEHLSU	blue-cheese
BCEEEFFILT	effectible
BCEEEFINNT	beneficent
BCEEEGHINS	beseeching
BCEEEHLRSS	breechless
BCEEEIIKRT	riebeckite
BCEEEIJLRT	rejectible
BCEEEILLNU	ebullience
BCEEEILPRT	receptible
BCEEEIRSTU	erubescite
BCEEELLMRU	cerebellum
BCEEENORRS	resorbence
BCEEENRSTU	erubescent
BCEEFIINRT	tenebrific
BCEEFIOPRS	fiberscope
	fibrescope
BCEEFLLRUW	curfew-bell
BCEEFPRSTU	subprefect
BCEEGIINOT	biogenetic
BCEEGINRSU	subgeneric
BCEEHIMPTU	thumbpiece
BCEEHIRTWY	bewitchery
BCEEHKLNOU	huckle-bone
BCEEHKOOQU	cheque-book
BCEEHKORRY	chokeberry
BCEEHMNRSU	Übermensch
BCEEHMORUU	embouchure
BCEEHNOOPR	necrophobe
BCEEIILPST	plebiscite
BCEEIIRRST	cerebritis
BCEEIJSTUV	subjective
BCEEIKLMNR	limber-neck
BCEEILLMRU	Illecebrum
BCEEILLNPU	blue-pencil
BCEEILLNUY	ebulliency
BCEEILLOOS	cellobiose
BCEEILMOST	comestible
BCEEILNORT	Colbertine
BCEEILNOTY	by-election
BCEEIPRRRS	prescriber
BCEEIPRRSY	spiceberry
BCEEIPSSSU	subspecies
BCEEJLOSST	objectless
BCEEKLNOTT	bottle-neck
BCEEKLORSW	skew-corbel
BCEEKLORTU	blue-rocket
BCEELMRSSU	cumberless
BCEELNOTTU	cuttle-bone
BCEELNRTUU	turbulence
BCEEMMNRTU	cumberment
BCEEMMORSU	cumbersome
BCEEOOORRR	corroboree
BCEFFIKOOO	office-book
BCEFFIORSU	subofficer
BCEFHNNORT	front-bench
BCEFIJSTUY	subjectify
BCEFILNORU	unforcible
BCEFILNOSU	confusible
BCEFKLSTUU	bucketfuls
BCEGHIINTW	bewitching
BCEGHINRTU	butchering
BCEGIILNSU	subceiling
BCEGIILORR	corrigible
BCEGILLNOR	corbelling
BCEGILMNOY	becomingly
BCEGILOOOY	bioecology
BCEGIMNNOU	unbecoming
BCEGMORSSU	comburgess
BCEHHNNOUY	honeybunch
BCEHIIIOTV	cohibitive
BCEHIIMOST	biochemist
BCEHIINSST	bitchiness
BCEHIIOPRS	biospheric
BCEHILNOOR	bronchiole
BCEHILOOPZ	zelophobic
BCEHILOPRY	hyperbolic
BCEHINNSSU	bunchiness
BCEHINPRSU	subphrenic
BCEHKKOOST	sketchbook
BCEHKLOOSU	blockhouse
BCEHMRSTUW	thumbscrew
BCEHOOOPST	Scotophobe
BCEHOOPRTU	Turcophobe
BCEIIILMMS	immiscible
BCEIIILMTY	imbecility
BCEIIILNNV	invincible
BCEIIKLLLS	sicklebill
BCEIIKLRRT	rib-tickler
BCEIILMMOS	embolismic
BCEIIMNOST	cenobitism
BCEIIMOQTU	coquimbite
BCEIIMORST	biometrics
BCEIINOOTX	xenobiotic
BCEIJNOSTU	subjection
BCEIKLOORT	bootlicker
BCEIKNRRRU	rickburner
BCEIKOOTTY	tickety-boo
BCEILLMOOO	locomobile
BCEILMOORT	bolometric
BCEILNPSSU	publicness
BCEILNRTUU	tuberculin
BCEILOORRS	corrosible
BCEIMOOPRR	microprobe
BCEIMOSTUV	combustive
BCEINNOSSU	bounciness

BCEINOPSTU subception
BCEINORTTU contribute
BCEINOSSTU subsection
BCEIOPPRSY presbyopic
BCEIOPRRRS proscriber
BCEIORSSTT obstetrics
BCEJKMPRUU buck-jumper
BCEJLOOSTU object-soul
BCEKKLNOUW knuckle-bow
BCEKKOOOPT pocket-book
BCEKLNRTUU turnbuckle
BCEKLOPSTU slop-bucket
BCEKOOORSU sourcebook
BCEKORRTTU rock-butter
BCEKRSTTUU rust-bucket
BCELMOOORW wool-comber
BCELMRTUUU tuberculum
BCELNRTUUY turbulency
BCELOPSTUU suboctuple
BCELRSTUUU subculture
BCEMNOPRTU procumbent
BCEMOORSSX Scombresox
BCENOOPTUX pouncet-box
BCENOORSSS crossbones
BCEOORRSSW crossbower
BCEORRSTTU obstructer
BCFIIMORRR cribriform
BCFOSSSUUU subfuscous
BCGHINNTUU cub-hunting
BCGHINOOPY gynophobic
BCGIKLLNOO bollocking
BCGIKMNSUU bumsucking
BCGIKNPRSU springbuck
BCHHIMOOOP homophobic
BCHIIINOOT cohibition
BCHIIMOOPR biomorphic
BCHIINORST bronchitis
BCHIIOPSSY biophysics
BCHIMNOOOP monophobic
BCHIMOORTT thrombotic
BCHIOOORRT orthoboric
BCHIOOPPRY pyrophobic
BCIIILNNVY invincibly
BCIIILORTT trilobitic
BCIILNOPSY psilocybin
BCIILORSUU lubricious
BCIKKORRSW brickworks
BCIKMOORST broomstick
BCIKNOPTTU pin-buttock
BCILOOSTUU tubicolous
BCIMNOOSTU combustion
BCIMORRSTU microburst
BCINOSSSTU consubsist
BCIOPRSSTU subtropics
BCKMOORUUZ zumbooruck
BCKOORRTTU rock-turbot
BCLLNOOOTT cotton-boll
BCLMORSUUY cumbrously
BCNOORRUWY cony-burrow
BCOORRSTTU obstructor
BDDDEEIIOW wide-bodied
BDDDEELOOR red-blooded
BDDDEELOUY double-dyed
BDDEEEILLV bedevilled
BDDEEEILRW bewildered
BDDEEELOUY double-eyed
BDDEEENRTU debentured
BDDEEEOPRW deep-browed
BDDEEGNTUU unbudgeted
BDDEEIMMNU unbedimmed
BDDEEIMNNR mind-bender
BDDEEIMNOU unembodied
BDDEEINNNU unbedinned
BDDEEINRST bestridden
BDDEEIORRV overbidder
BDDEELMORU dumbledore
BDDEELNRTU trundle-bed
BDDEELOOYY bloody-eyed
BDDEENNRUU unburdened
BDDEFILLOU full-bodied
BDDEFIOOST soft-bodied
BDDEGILLOU double-gild
BDDEHIIPPR bird-hipped
BDDEHINOOR behind-door
BDDEHLNOOR bond-holder
BDDEHLOOOT hot-blooded
BDDEIIPRRS bird-spider
BDDEIIRSUV subdivider
BDDEIIRTTW bird-witted
BDDEILMORW middlebrow
BDDEILNOOU unbloodied
BDDEILNRUU underbuild
BDDEILOOSZ blood-sized
BDDEIMNORU dendrobium
BDDELLORUW dull-browed
BDDELMORRU drumbledor
BDDFGIINOR forbidding
BDDHLNOOOU bloodhound
BDDIIKNSSU 'sbuddikins
BDDIKLNNRU blind-drunk
BDEEEEELTY beetle-eyed
BDEEEEJLLW bejewelled
BDEEEELRTW beweltered
BDEEEFILNS defensible
BDEEEFINRR befriender
BDEEEFINTT benefitted
BDEEEFITTW beef-witted
BDEEEFLOTT bottle-feed
BDEEEGILRT telebridge
BDEEEGINSW beeswinged
BDEEEGLNTU dung-beetle
BDEEEHLLNR hellbender
BDEEEHMORW home-brewed
BDEEEIILSV disbelieve
BDEEEILNSS edibleness
BDEEEILNTX extendible
BDEEEILNUV unbelieved
BDEEEILSTW wildebeest
BDEEEIMRTT embittered
BDEEEINNRZ Benzedrine®
BDEEEINRRT interbreed
BDEEEKLNOO needle-book
BDEEELLMOW embowelled
BDEEELMNOR emboldener

BDEEELMTUW	tumbleweed
BDEEELORTU	doubletree
BDEEELRRRY	elderberry
BDEEENRTTU	unbettered
BDEEEPRRSS	bedpresser
BDEEERRSVW	bed-swerver
BDEEFGGLOO	foolbegged
BDEEFGIINR	debriefing
BDEEFIINST	disbenefit
BDEEFILNRS	self-binder
BDEEFILNSY	defensibly
BDEEFLOOOT	lobe-footed
BDEEFORRST	forest-bred
BDEEGHIRTY	bright-eyed
BDEEGIILST	digestible
BDEEGIINNR	inbreeding
BDEEGILLOR	gor-bellied
BDEEGILNUU	unbeguiled
BDEEGILRSS	bridgeless
BDEEGIMOSU	disembogue
BDEEGINRRT	regent-bird
BDEEGINTTW	bed-wetting
BDEEGIORRV	overbridge
BDEEGOORSU	bodegueros
BDEEHILLPS	bedellship
BDEEHIOPSW	bishopweed
BDEEHLNNOR	hornblende
BDEEHLNNOU	unbeholden
BDEEHNRSUW	Bundeswehr
BDEEIILMOS	demobilise
BDEEIILMOZ	demobilize
BDEEIILNNV	invendible
BDEEIILNRR	bridle-rein
BDEEIILRSW	bridle-wise
BDEEIILRTV	divertible
BDEEIILSTV	divestible
BDEEIINNOT	inobedient
BDEEILLNTU	tunbellied
BDEEILLOPT	pot-bellied
BDEEILMOSU	semi-double
BDEEILMOSW	disembowel
BDEEILMRSS	dissembler
BDEEILNNOS	disennoble
BDEEILNNUV	unvendible
BDEEILNORR	borderline
BDEEILNOTY	obediently
BDEEILNRSU	blue-rinsed
BDEEILORSW	bowdlerise
BDEEILORWZ	bowdlerize
BDEEIMMNOT	embodiment
BDEEIMNRTU	untimbered
BDEEIMOOSS	somebodies
BDEEIMORRS	besom-rider
BDEEIMORRY	embroidery
BDEEINNOTU	unobedient
BDEEIORSSS	sobersides
BDEEIPPPRR	bird-pepper
BDEEIRRSSU	redisburse
BDEEKNORRV	kerb-vendor
BDEELLNRUY	underbelly
BDEELNOSSU	doubleness
BDEELORRSS	borderless
BDEELOSTTY	besottedly
BDEEMNNRUU	unnumbered
BDEEMNORSU	burdensome
BDEEMNSTUU	subduement
BDEENNNOTU	unbonneted
BDEENNORRU	underborne
BDEENORRUV	overburden
BDEENORSUV	unobserved
BDEENOSTUW	unbestowed
BDEENRTTUU	unbuttered
BDEFFIILSU	diffusible
BDEFGINOOR	foreboding
BDEFGIOORT	footbridge
BDEFGSSTUU	fuss-budget
BDEFILLOST	soft-billed
BDEFILNORW	brownfield
BDEFILOOST	fieldboots
	soft-boiled
BDEFNOORTW	bow-fronted
BDEGGGIINN	egg-binding
BDEGGLNOOO	boondoggle
BDEGHHIINR	highbinder
BDEGHIMOTU	bigmouthed
BDEGHINNOU	hinge-bound
BDEGHLNOUU	double-hung
BDEGHNORUU	underbough
BDEGIILLMR	limb-girdle
BDEGIILLNV	diving-bell
BDEGIIMNTU	minibudget
	mini-budget
BDEGIINORR	broidering
	riding-robe
BDEGIKORRW	bridge-work
BDEGILLORT	tollbridge
BDEGILNNOT	Bedlington
BDEGILNNRU	blundering
BDEGILNRRU	de-blurring
BDEGIMOORR	bridegroom
BDEGINOORY	gooneybird
BDEGLMNTUU	tumble-dung
BDEHIILPSU	bisulphide
BDEHIIRRSY	hybridiser
BDEHIIRRYZ	hybridizer
BDEHIMNTUX	thumb-index
BDEHIMOORS	rhomboides
BDEHINRSTU	disburthen
BDEHIRSTTU	butter-dish
BDEHKLOOOR	book-holder
BDEHLLNOSU	shellbound
BDEHLOOORS	blood-horse
BDEHNOOSUU	housebound
BDEHNORTUX	thunderbox
BDEHNRRSUU	underbrush
	undershrub
BDEIIILNRV	biliverdin
BDEIILLNOV	bidonville
BDEIILMORS	disembroil
BDEIILMRSS	missel-bird
BDEIIRSTTU	distribute
BDEIJNORSU	subjoinder
BDEIKLNOTU	double-knit
BDEIKNNORW	wind-broken

BDEILLMOTU multilobed
BDEILLORWY yellowbird
BDEILLOSSU dissoluble
BDEILLOTUX billet-doux
BDEILMNSUU unsublimed
BDEILMOOSS disselboom
BDEILMORSW bowdlerism
BDEILNNOST stone-blind
BDEILNOOSS bloodiness
BDEILNOOWW window-bole
BDEILORSTU distrouble
BDEIMMOOSS disembosom
BDEIMNORSS morbidness
BDEIMOORXY oxy-bromide
BDEINOORSS broodiness
BDEINRSSTU turbidness
BDEIOORTTW bitterwood
BDEKNNOORW broken-down
BDELLNOPSU spellbound
BDELLOORVY overboldly
BDELLORTUY troubledly
BDELMMNOUY molybdenum
BDELMNOOOY blood-money
BDELMNOTUW tumbledown
BDELNOOOST bloodstone
BDELNORTUU untroubled
BDEMNNOOUY money-bound
BDEMNOOTTU unbottomed
BDEMOORRRS smørrebrød
BDEMOORRSY dyer's-broom
BDENNOTTUU unbuttoned
BDENNRRTUU underburnt
BDENOORRUW unborrowed
BDENOPTTUU buttoned-up
BDEOOPPPRY body-popper
BDFLLOTUUY doubtfully
BDFLNOTUUU undoubtful
BDFNOORSTU frostbound
BDGHIILNNT night-blind
BDGIIIKNRS bird-skiing
BDGIIKNNRY by-drinking
BDGIILNPUU upbuilding
BDGIINOORT riding-boot
BDGIINORVX driving-box
BDGIINRSTU disturbing
BDGIKMNOSU subkingdom
BDGILLOOTU blood-guilt
BDGILNNNUU unbundling
BDGILNOORY broodingly
BDGILNOTUY doubtingly
BDGINNOTUU undoubting
BDGINOOORW wood-boring
BDGLOOOPRU blood-group
BDGLRRSTUU Struldbrug
BDHIIIINST disinhibit
BDHIILRRWY whirlybird
BDHILOPRYY polyhybrid
BDHIMNOORY monohybrid
BDHKOOORSU Doukhobors
BDHLNOOTTU buttonhold
BDHMNOSTUW thumbs-down
BDHNNOORTU northbound
BDHNOOSTUU southbound
BDIIIILNST libidinist
BDIIIILNOSU libidinous
BDIILOORST strobiloid
BDILLNPRUY purblindly
BDILMOOSSY molybdosis
BDKNNOOORY △donnybrook
BDMNOORSTU stormbound
BDNOOOTTUW button-wood
BEEEEFLNSS feebleness
BEEEEGIKNP beekeeping
BEEEEGILLY eye-legible
BEEEEGINNR beer-engine
BEEEEGLSTU Betelgeuse
BEEEEILNPT pine-beetle
BEEEELLNSW well-beseen
BEEEELORST rose-beetle
BEEEELORTV rove-beetle
BEEEELRSSZ breezeless
BEEEEMMRRR rememberer
BEEEFILLRX reflexible
BEEEFILLSS beliefless
BEEEFILRRR referrible
BEEEFIMORT beforetime
BEEEFMRRUZ bumfreezer
BEEEFOORRT freebooter
BEEEGGRRUV vegeburger
BEEEGHINNS shebeening
BEEEGHLOSU glebe-house
BEEEGIILLR re-eligible
BEEEGILNRS inselberge
BEEEGLNRUY bluey-green
BEEEGMOORS ember-goose
BEEEHIPRST sheep-biter
BEEEHLLRTW bell-wether
BEEEIILMSV misbelieve
BEEEIKLLRR bierkeller
BEEEIKMNRT knee-timber
BEEEILNRUV unbeliever
BEEEILNSTX extensible
BEEEILRRSV reversible
BEEEILRRTV revertible
BEEEIMRRTT embitterer
timber-tree
BEEEIMRSTT beetmister
BEEEINRSSZ breeziness
BEEEINTTWY betweenity
BEEEIRRSTW sweet-brier
BEEEKKOOPR bookkeeper
BEEEKLMSTU musk-beetle
BEEELLPRSV vesper-bell
BEEELLRSST bestseller
BEEELLRTTU bullet-tree
BEEELMMNST emblements
BEEELMNOTU éboulement
BEEELNNOTV benevolent
BEEELNRSST trebleness
BEEELORTTT bottle-tree
BEEEMMNRTU embruement
BEEEMNRTTT betterment
BEEENNPRYZ benzpyrene
BEEENORSTT bonesetter

Words marked △ may be spelled also with a capital letter

BEEENRRSTU	subterrene
BEEENRSSTT	betterness
BEEEOQSUXZ	squeeze-box
BEEERRTTTU	butter-tree
BEEFGIINNT	benefiting
BEEFGRSTUU	subterfuge
BEEFIILLNX	inflexible
BEEFIILNRR	inferrible
BEEFILLMRU	umbellifer
BEEFILMORS	Froebelism
BEEFILRSTU	subfertile
BEEFINNOTU	bufotenine
BEEFIORRTT	forebitter
BEEFIORSSU	sebiferous
BEEFIRTTUW	butter-wife
BEEFLLLORW	bell-flower
	flower-bell
BEEGGIILLN	negligible
BEEGGLOORT	bootlegger
BEEGHIILLN	Ghibelline
BEEGHIKNSU	husking-bee
BEEGHILNRT	blethering
BEEGHNOOPR	negrophobe
BEEGIIILLN	ineligible
BEEGIILNRT	Gilbertine
BEEGIILNST	ingestible
BEEGIINOSS	biogenesis
BEEGILLNRR	bell-ringer
BEEGILMNOT	obligement
BEEGILMNRS	resembling
BEEGILNNNU	Nibelungen
BEEGINRTTV	brevetting
BEEGIOORSU	bourgeoise
BEEGLNOTUU	blue-tongue
BEEGMNORYY	embryogeny
BEEGNNOTTU	unbegotten
BEEGNOORST	brent-goose
BEEGNSSSUU	subgenuses
BEEGOORRSY	gooseberry
BEEGRRSTTU	Grubstreet
BEEHHLRSUW	brushwheel
BEEHIIITVX	exhibitive
BEEHILLOPT	phlebolite
BEEHILMOST	blithesome
BEEHILNSST	blitheness
BEEHILOSSV	bolshevise
BEEHILOSVZ	bolshevize
BEEHIMMPRS	membership
BEEHINRRRY	Rheinberry
	Rhineberry
BEEHLMNSSU	humbleness
BEEHMOORST	bothersome
BEEHMOORTT	mother-to-be
BEEIIJORTU	bijouterie
BEEIIKLMRT	kimberlite
BEEIILMNRT	timberline
BEEIILMRSS	remissible
BEEIILNNSS	insensible
BEEIILNNTV	inventible
BEEIILRSST	resistible
BEEIILSSTX	bissextile
BEEIKKNORR	knobkerrie
BEEIKLNPRS	besprinkle
BEEILLLLRS	bell-siller
BEEILLLOVW	boll-weevil
BEEILLMNTU	minute-bell
BEEILLOOTW	wellie-boot
BEEILLOPRW	pillow-beer
	pillow-bere
BEEILLOPSX	explosible
BEEILLORSU	rebellious
BEEILLOSSW	Boswellise
BEEILLOSWZ	Boswellize
BEEILLRSTT	belletrist
BEEILMNNSS	nimbleness
BEEILMNRRU	lime-burner
BEEILNNSSU	unsensible
BEEILNOSST	ostensible
BEEILRSTUX	extrusible
BEEILSSSSU	subsessile
BEEIMMNRTU	imbruement
BEEIMORRST	sombrerite
BEEIMORRTT	tribometer
BEEIMORRTV	vibrometer
BEEIMORSSV	misobserve
BEEIMORSTT	timber-toes
BEEINNORRT	Norbertine
BEEINORRTT	torbernite
BEEINORSTU	tenebrious
BEEINRSSTT	bitterness
BEEINRSTTU	burnettise
BEEINRTTUZ	burnettize
BEEIPRSTUV	subreptive
BEEIQRRSUU	brusquerie
BEEIRSSUVV	subversive
BEEKLLOORS	bookseller
BEEKLOORRV	love-broker
BEEKLOORTT	letter-book
BEEKNNOOPT	poke-bonnet
BEEKNNOPSU	unbespoken
BEEKNNORSS	brokenness
BEEKNOORST	stone-broke
BEELLMORSU	umbrelloes
BEELLNOPTU	pollen-tube
BEELLOOSTY	obsoletely
BEELLRRTTU	bell-turret
BEELMMMNTU	mumblement
BEELMMNSUW	mumble-news
BEELMMORSU	lumbersome
BEELMNNOOW	noblewomen
BEELMNRSSU	numberless
BEELNOOSTT	bottle-nose
BEELNPRTUU	puberulent
BEELNSSSTU	subtleness
BEELOQSTTU	blottesque
BEELORSTUV	oversubtle
BEEMMNNOTT	entombment
BEEMMNOSST	embossment
BEEMMOORRT	ombrometer
BEEMMRRSSU	bressummer
BEEMNORSSS	sombreness
BEEMNOSTTW	bestowment
BEEMOPRRSY	pre-embryos
BEEMORSTTT	bettermost

BEENOORRST	stoneborer
BEENOSSSTU	obtuseness
BEENPRSSSU	superbness
BEENQSSTUU	subsequent
BEENRRTTUY	Tyburn-tree
BEEPPRRTUY	prepuberty
BEEPRRSTYY	presbytery
BEFFIIMNTU	mini-buffet
BEFFIJKNRU	buff-jerkin
BEFFILLMNU	muffin-bell
BEFFNOORUY	buffoonery
BEFGHIILRT	fire-blight
BEFGHIRRSU	fishburger
BEFGIINNOR	fibrinogen
BEFGILNORW	fingerbowl
BEFHHLORST	flesh-broth
BEFHHLRSSU	flesh-brush
BEFHILLMTU	thimbleful
BEFHILOSTT	bottle-fish
BEFHIRSTTU	butter-fish
BEFHLNORSW	fresh-blown
BEFIILLNXY	inflexibly
BEFIILLORS	fibrillose
BEFIILRSTU	filibuster
BEFILLRSTY	blister-fly
BEFIMORRTU	tuberiform
BEFINORSUU	nubiferous
BEFLLMRSUU	slumberful
BEFLLMRTUU	tumblerful
BEFLLOSTTU	bottlefuls
BEFLNOSTUY	self-bounty
BEFNOORRST	forest-born
BEGGHIINNT	benighting
BEGGHMRUUY	humbuggery
BEGGIILLNY	negligibly
BEGGILNNOS	belongings
BEGHHOOPRY	hygrophobe
BEGHIILMRT	thimblerig
BEGHIILNRT	blithering
BEGHIINRRT	rebirthing
BEGHILLNSU	bushelling
BEGHILMNOO	hemoglobin
BEGHILNORY	neighborly
BEGHIMORST	brightsome
BEGHINRSST	brightness
BEGHNOSTUU	unbesought
BEGHOORSTT	borghettos
BEGHOORTUV	overbought
BEGHRSTTUU	shutterbug
BEGIIILLNY	ineligibly
BEGIIILLTY	legibility
BEGIIIMNRT	ignimbrite
BEGIIKLRTZ	blitzkrieg
BEGIIKNRTT	bitter-king
BEGIILLNTT	belittling
BEGIILMRTU	limburgite
BEGIILNRST	blistering
BEGIILNRTT	bitterling
BEGIINORSU	rubiginose
BEGIKLNRUY	rebukingly
BEGIKNNOSU	bousingken
BEGILLNORW	well-boring
BEGILMNRSU	slumbering
BEGILMOORS	embroglios
BEGILNNNUY	unbenignly
BEGILNORST	bolstering
BEGILNORSY	soberingly
BEGILNRSTU	blustering
BEGILNSTTU	subletting
BEGILOOOXY	exobiology
BEGILPSTTU	spittlebug
BEGIMNNORW	embrowning
BEGIMNORSS	Bergsonism
BEGINNORWZ	bronze-wing
BEGINNOSTX	nesting-box
BEGINNOSUU	nubigenous
BEGINOOOTT	gnotobiote
BEGLMOORYY	embryology
BEGNORRUYY	youngberry
BEGOOPPRST	gobstopper
BEGOORRTTT	bogtrotter
BEHHIKRSSU	bush-shrike
BEHHIOOPPP	hippophobe
BEHHOOOPPT	photophobe
BEHHOOPPSY	hypsophobe
BEHIIIINTV	inhibitive
BEHIIINOTX	exhibition
BEHIIOPRRT	prohibiter
BEHIIORTXY	exhibitory
BEHIKOPRRS	shipbroker
BEHILLORWW	willowherb
BEHILMOOPR	ombrophile
BEHILMOSSV	bolshevism
BEHILOSSTV	bolshevist
BEHILPRSTU	butlership
BEHILRSTTU	bur-thistle
BEHIMOPRUU	euphorbium
BEHINORSTT	birthstone
BEHINOSSSY	boyishness
BEHIOPRSTT	hop-bitters
BEHLMOOPTY	phlebotomy
BEHLNOOTTU	buttonhole
BEHMOOORST	smooth-bore
BEHMOORSST	thromboses
BEHMPRTTUU	tub-thumper
BEHOOPRSSU	Russophobe
BEIIILMMOS	immobilise
BEIIILMMOZ	immobilize
BEIIILNQTU	biquintile
BEIIILNSSV	invisibles
BEIIIMNOST	ebionitism
BEIIIMNSTU	bituminise
BEIIIMNTUZ	bituminize
BEIIIOOPSS	biopoiesis
BEIILLLRSV	silverbill
BEIILLNOTU	ebullition
BEIILLOSSU	solubilise
BEIILLOSUZ	solubilize
BEIILMOPSS	impossible
BEIILMRTUY	muliebrity
BEIILNNSSY	insensibly
BEIILNORST	strobiline
BEIILPRSTU	spirit-blue
BEIILRSSTY	resistibly

BEIILRSTTT librettist
BEIIMSSSUV submissive
BEIINNOQUU ubiquinone
BEIINORSTY insobriety
BEIJLRRTUY jerry-built
BEIKLMRTTU butter-milk
BEIKMNOOTU minute-book
BEILLLMMRU lumber-mill
BEILLMOSSW Boswellism
BEILLMSSUU subsellium
BEILLOOTTU bouillotte
BEILLOPRST billposter
BEILMMNSUU nelumbiums
BEILMNOOSW snowmobile
BEILMOOOST lobotomise
BEILMOOOTZ lobotomize
BEILMOOSST obsoletism
BEILMOPRST problemist
BEILMORSSY symboliser
BEILMORSYZ symbolizer
BEILMSTUUV vestibulum
BEILNNSSUY unsensibly
BEILNOOOST obsoletion
BEILNOPRSW spin-bowler
BEILNOPSSU unpossible
BEILNOSSTY ostensibly
BEILNOSTUY nebulosity
BEILNSSSTU subtilness
BEILSSTUUV subsultive
BEIMNNOOPT embonpoint
BEIMNORSSU submersion
BEIMORRSTU Morris-tube
BEIMPRSSTY presbytism
BEINNOSTUV subvention
BEINOPRSTU subreption
BEINORSSUV subversion
BEINORSTUU subroutine
BEINSSSTTU subsistent
BEIOOQSSUU obsequious
BEIOORRTTT bitter-root
BEIOORSSTU boisterous
BEIOQRSTUU soubriquet
BEIORRRTTU retributor
BEIORSTTUY tuberosity
BEISSTTTUU substitute
BEJKLNOTTU junk-bottle
BEKLNNORUY unbrokenly
BEKMNORSSU mossbunker
BEKMOORSTU muster-book
BEKNOORSTY stony-broke
BELLMOPSTU post-bellum
BELLNNOOSU non-soluble
BELLNOSUUY nebulously
BELLOOSSTY bootlessly
BELLORSTUY trolleybus
BELMMOORRU lumber-room
BELMOOSSTT bottomless
BELMORSSUU slumberous
BELNOORSWW snowblower
BELNOPPRRU purple-born
BELOOPRSTT lobster-pot
BELOPRSUUU puberulous
BELORSSTUU blusterous
BELORSTTUU outbluster
BEMMOORTYY embryotomy
BEMNOOSSTT bottomness
BEMNOPRSUU penumbrous
BEMOOPRRSY proembryos
BENNOORRSW brown-noser
BENNOORSTW brownstone
BENOORRTTW torrent-bow
BENORSSSTU robustness
BEORRTTTUW butterwort
BFFGIIJLNU luffing-jib
BFFNNORSUW snuff-brown
BFFOORRUUY four-by-four
BFGHILNTYY fly-by-night
BFGIINRTUY brutifying
BFGILLMNUY fumblingly
BFHIMOOSTT bottom-fish
BFIIILSTUY fusibility
BFIIIORSST fibrositis
BFIILLORSU fibrillous
BFILLLSSUY blissfully
BFILLNSSUU unblissful
BFLLMOOTTU full-bottom
BGGGHIMNUU humbugging
BGGIIINNNR inbringing
BGGIILLNOY obligingly
BGGIINNPRU upbringing
BGGILLNNUY bunglingly
BGHHIINRTT birthnight
BGHHIIRRTT birthright
BGHIINNRSU burnishing
BGHIJNOOPP job-hopping
BGHIKORRTW bright-work
BGHILLMNUY humblingly
BGHILLNSUY blushingly
BGHILNNSUU unblushing
BGHINNOTUX hunting-box
BGIIILNOTY ignobility
BGIIILNSTU bilinguist
BGIIKLNNNU unblinking
BGIILMOORS imbroglios
BGIILNOOPT pot-boiling
BGIILNOSSU subsoiling
BGIIMNSTTU submitting
BGIINNORRV virgin-born
BGIINORSUU rubiginous
BGIJLLMNUY jumblingly
BGILLMMNUY mumblingly
BGILLMNRUY rumblingly
BGILLMRSUU mulligrubs
BGILMNOOSS blossoming
BGILMOORTY timbrology
BGILOORSTY bryologist
BGILORSUUU lugubrious
BGIMNOOORR robing-room
BGINPRSTUU upbursting
BHHIMORSTY biorhythms
BHHOORSTTU toothbrush
BHIIIINNOT inhibition
BHIIIMRSST Britishism
BHIIINORTY inhibitory

BHIIKMNPSU bumpkinish
BHIIKMNSTU thumbikins
BHIILLRSTT stillbirth
BHIIOOPRRT prohibitor
BHIMNPRTTU thumbprint
BHIMOORSST thrombosis
BHINORRSTW Brownshirt
BHINORTWWY whity-brown
BHKNOOOTTU button-hook
BHLLOOSSUU holus-bolus
BHLLRRUUYY hurly-burly
BHNOPSTTUU push-button
BHOOOOPSUZ zoophobous
BIIIILRSTY risibility
BIIIILSTVY visibility
BIIILMMMOS immobilism
BIIILMMOTY immobility
BIILLLLSYY silly-billy
BIILLNOSTU bullionist
BIILLOSTUY solubility
BIILLOTUVY volubility
BIIMNOSSSU submission
BIIMNOSTUU bituminous
BIINOSSSSY byssinosis
BIIOQSTUUU ubiquitous
BIKLLORSST stork'sbill
BIKLMNOOSU book-muslin
BILLMNORUU rumbullion
BILLMOORSU morbillous
BILLNOORTU tourbillon
BILMMNOOTU immunoblot
BILMMOOOSV Oblomovism
BIMNOORSTT trombonist
BIMOOPPRRU opprobrium
BINNOORSST Sorbonnist
BINOPSSSUU subspinous
BIOORSSTUU robustious
BKMOOOPPRT prompt-book
BLLOOTTUWY woollybutt
BLMMOORSSU rum-blossom
BLORSSTUUY subsultory
BMMOOOSTTT bottommost

C

CCCCGINOOO gonococcic
CCCCIIMOOR micrococci
CCCDEILOPY cyclopedic
CCCDEIMRUU circumduce
CCCDIMRTUU circumduct
CCCEEHKKLR checkclerk
CCCEEINNOS conscience
CCCEEINRST crescentic
CCCEEINTUY cecutiency
CCCEELNSUU succulence
CCCEENORRU occurrence
CCCEHIILMY hemicyclic
CCCEHIILNO colchicine
CCCEHIMOTY ecchymotic
CCCEHKORSS crosscheck
CCCEIILPRY pericyclic
CCCEIIMRSU circumcise
CCCEIIRSTY cysticerci
CCCEILOTUY leucocytic
CCCEINNORT concentric
CCCEINOOSU coccineous
CCCEINOOTV concoctive
CCCEIOOPRT eccoprotic
CCCEKKORSU cocksucker
CCCEKLNOOR corncockle
CCCELNSUUY succulency
CCCGNOOOSU gonococcus
CCCHHILOOO chocoholic
CCCHIKOPST spitchcock
CCCHILMOOY homocyclic
CCCHILMOSU colchicums
CCCILLOPYY polycyclic
CCCILMNOOY monocyclic
CCCILNSTUY succinctly
CCCINNOOOT concoction
CCCIOOPRSY cryoscopic
CCCLOORSSY cyclo-cross
CCDDEENNOS condescend
CCDDEIKMNO midden-cock
CCDEEEENPR precedence
CCDEEEFIIN deficience
CCDEEEHINS dehiscence
CCDEEEKNRW crew-necked
CCDEEENPRY precedency
CCDEEENRST crescented
decrescent
CCDEEERRSU recrudesce
CCDEEFIINY deficiency
CCDEEFINNO confidence
CCDEEGINSU succeeding
CCDEEHIORT ricocheted
CCDEEHMOSY ecchymosed
CCDEEHNOSY synecdoche
CCDEEIIIPT epideictic
CCDEEIILRT dielectric
CCDEEIIOPS speciocide
CCDEEIIPPR precipiced
CCDEEILMOO coomceiled
CCDEEIMORT ectodermic
CCDEEINOPR procidence
CCDEEKLNOW cowl-necked
CCDEELMOPT complected
CCDEELNNOO condolence
CCDEENNORT concentred
CCDEENORSS crescendos
CCDEENRRUY decurrency
CCDEFINNOY confidency
CCDEFKLLOU full-cocked
CCDEHNORSU unscorched
CCDEIIILOT idiolectic
CCDEIIKLSS dickcissel
CCDEIILOPY epicycloid
CCDEIINNOR endocrinic
CCDEIINNOT coincident
CCDEIINORT endocritic
CCDEIIOSTT Docetistic
CCDEIKLOSU cuckoldise
CCDEIKLOUZ cuckoldize
CCDEIMOOOT octodecimo
CCDEINNOST disconnect

CCDEINOOPS	endoscopic
	picosecond
CCDEINOPUU	unoccupied
CCDEINORST	disconcert
CCDEINOTUV	conductive
CCDEKMNOOY	cockneydom
CCDELOOORU	colour-code
CCDEMOORTY	cordectomy
CCDGIILOSY	glycosidic
CCDGILNNOU	concluding
CCDGILOOOY	codicology
CCDHIIIORT	dichroitic
CCDHIIMOOT	dichotomic
CCDHIINORT	chondritic
CCDILOORSU	Crocodilus
CCDIMNOSTU	misconduct
CCDINNOOTU	conduction
CCEEEEHIKP	cheekpiece
CCEEEELLNX	excellence
CCEEEENNSS	senescence
CCEEEFFIIN	efficience
CCEEEFNNOR	△conference
	conférence
CCEEEGINOS	geoscience
CCEEEHIKPS	pick-cheese
CCEEEIINPR	recipience
CCEEEINPRS	prescience
CCEEEINQSU	quiescence
CCEEEINRSV	virescence
CCEEEIOPSS	ecospecies
CCEEEKLNOS	skene-occle
CCEEELLNXY	△excellency
CCEEEMMNOR	recommence
CCEEEMNOPR	recompence
CCEEEMNOPT	competence
CCEEEMNSTU	tumescence
CCEEENOPRS	copresence
	co-presence
CCEEENRRRU	recurrence
CCEEENRSTX	excrescent
CCEEEORRUV	crève-coeur
CCEEFFIINY	efficiency
CCEEFFILNO	off-licence
CCEEFIKNRT	fen-cricket
CCEEFINTTU	fettuccine
CCEEFKLORS	self-cocker
CCEEFLNNOU	confluence
CCEEGHINOT	geotechnic
CCEEGINNOR	congeneric
CCEEGINNOT	congenetic
CCEEGINORT	egocentric
	geocentric
CCEEGNNORU	congruence
CCEEHHKOPU	cheekpouch
CCEEHIILRT	telechiric
CCEEHIINST	technicise
CCEEHIINTZ	technicize
CCEEHINOSS	choiceness
CCEEHIOPTU	touch-piece
CCEEHKLLPS	spellcheck
CCEEHLORSW	screech-owl
CCEEHNOSTU	escutcheon
CCEEIIINNP	incipience
CCEEIIILMRS	semicircle
CCEEIILPTU	epicuticle
CCEEIINPRY	recipiency
CCEEIIPRTT	peritectic
CCEEIIRRTU	circuiteer
CCEEIKLLLS	sickle-cell
CCEEIKLPUY	lucky-piece
CCEEILLOTV	collective
CCEEILMNNY	inclemency
CCEEILNOPT	pleonectic
CCEEILNORR	reconciler
CCEEILNORT	electronic
CCEEILOPST	telescopic
CCEEILORVY	coercively
CCEEINNNOT	continence
CCEEINNNOV	connivence
CCEEINNOTV	connective
CCEEINNRRU	incurrence
CCEEINNRST	increscent
CCEEINNRTU	encincture
CCEEINOPRT	preconceit
CCEEINOPTV	conceptive
CCEEINORST	concretise
CCEEINORTV	concretive
CCEEINORTZ	concretize
CCEEINOSSV	concessive
CCEEINOTVV	convective
CCEEINQSUY	quiescency
CCEEIOPRSS	crosspiece
CCEEIOPSTT	copesettic
CCEEIORRTV	corrective
CCEEISSSUV	successive
CCEEJNORTU	conjecture
CCEEKKLOYY	cockyleeky
CCEELNOPRU	corpulence
CCEELNORTY	concretely
CCEELNRTUU	truculence
CCEELPRSUU	crepuscule
CCEEMNOPTY	competency
CCEENOPRRT	preconcert
CCEENRRRUY	recurrency
CCEFHIIMOR	microfiche
CCEFIIINST	scientific
CCEFIINPSU	unspecific
CCEFIKLOOV	five-o'clock
CCEFILLLRU	full-circle
CCEFILMRUX	circumflex
CCEFILNOTU	conceitful
CCEFIMRSUU	circumfuse
CCEFINNOOT	confection
CCEFLLNOTU	flocculent
CCEFLSSSUU	successful
CCEGGILNOY	glycogenic
CCEGHHORRU	churchgoer
CCEGHIIKMN	chemicking
CCEGHIILNO	conchiglie
CCEGHINORT	crocheting
CCEGIIKNRT	cricketing
CCEGIILNNR	encircling
CCEGILLNOT	collecting
CCEGILNOOR	necrologic

CCEGIMNOOS	cosmogenic
CCEGINNNOR	concerning
CCEGINORSY	cryogenics
CCEGNNORUY	congruency
CCEHHILOTV	clove-hitch
CCEHHLRSSU	churchless
CCEHIIIMOS	isocheimic
CCEHIIMNST	technicism
CCEHIIMOOR	heroi-comic
CCEHIINNNO	cinchonine
CCEHIINNOS	cinchonise
CCEHIINNOZ	cinchonize
CCEHIINSTT	technicist
CCEHIIRSTU	ischuretic
CCEHIKMOOR	mock-heroic
CCEHIKNOPT	checkpoint
CCEHIKNOPX	chickenpox
CCEHIKNOSY	cockneyish
CCEHILNORR	chronicler
CCEHILNORS	Chronicles
CCEHILOOPR	pleochroic
CCEHILOPRR	perchloric
CCEHILORRU	hour-circle
CCEHILORVW	cow-chervil
CCEHIMOSSY	ecchymosis
CCEHIOPTTY	ectophytic
CCEHIORRST	orchestric
CCEHIORSST	orchestics
CCEHKLOOST	hot-cockles
CCEHKNOORY	honey-crock
CCEHKNOOST	chockstone
CCEHKORTUU	chucker-out
CCEHLMOTYY	cyclothyme
CCEHMOORTY	cytochrome
CCEHNOPRUW	cowpuncher
CCEHNOSSST	Scotchness
CCEHOSTTUZ	zucchettos
CCEIIILNOR	ricinoleic
CCEIIINNPY	incipiency
CCEIIINNRT	encrinitic
CCEIIIRSTV	cervicitis
CCEIILMNOR	microcline
CCEIILOSST	solecistic
CCEIIMNOST	misconceit
CCEIIMOORS	seriocomic
CCEIIMPSST	scepticism
CCEIINNOPT	concipient
CCEIINOTVV	convictive
CCEIINRTTY	centricity
CCEIIOORST	crocoisite
CCEIIOPPRS	periscopic
CCEIIORTVY	coercivity
CCEIIOSSTT	Scotticise
CCEIIOSTTZ	Scotticize
CCEIKKOPPT	pick-pocket
CCEIKLOTUY	leukocytic
CCEIKMNOSY	cockneyism
CCEIKNOSSS	cocksiness
CCEILLLOSU	cellulosic
CCEILLMTUY	multicycle
CCEILLNOOT	collection
CCEILNNOSU	nucleonics
CCEILNOSUV	conclusive
	vice-consul
CCEILOOQTU	coquelicot
CCEIMMRRUU	circummure
CCEIMNNOOU	uneconomic
CCEIMNORST	concretism
CCEIMNOSTT	concettism
CCEIMNRTUV	circumvent
CCEIMOOPRS	microscope
CCEIMOPRSU	circumpose
CCEIMORRST	miscorrect
CCEIMORRTY	cryometric
CCEIMORTTY	cytometric
CCEINNNOOT	connection
CCEINNNOTY	continency
CCEINNNOVY	connivency
CCEINNOOPT	△conception
CCEINNOORT	concertino
	concretion
CCEINNOOSS	concession
CCEINNOOTV	convection
CCEINOOOPS	iconoscope
CCEINOORRT	correction
CCEINOORTY	cryoconite
CCEINORSTT	concretist
CCEINOSSSU	succession
CCEINOSSUV	concussive
CCEINOSTTT	concettist
CCEINOTUVY	vice-county
CCEIOOPRSU	precocious
CCEISSSUUV	successive
CCEKKORTUY	turkey-cock
CCEKMOORST	comstocker
CCEKNNOORY	cockernony
CCEKORRTTU	cork-cutter
CCELLOSTYY	cyclostyle
CCELMOORTY	motor-cycle
CCELMOOSTY	cyclostome
CCELNOPRUY	corpulency
CCELNOSSTU	occultness
CCELNRTUUY	truculency
CCELOOOPPS	colposcope
CCELOPRSUU	corpuscule
CCELPRSTUU	cluster-cup
CCEMNNOOPY	componency
CCEMOSTTYY	cystectomy
CCENNORRTU	concurrent
CCENOOPRSY	necroscopy
CCENOOPRTU	contrecoup
CCENOPSSTU	conspectus
CCENORRTTU	corn-cutter
CCEOOPSSTY	cystoscope
CCEOORRRTY	correctory
CCFFFFHHUU	chuff-chuff
CCFGIINRUY	crucifying
CCFHIMNOOR	conchiform
CCFIILMORU	culiciform
CCFIMMORUU	cucumiform
CCFKKMOORS	smock-frock
CCFKLOOORU	four-o'clock
CCGHHIKOTT	chock-tight
CCGHLNOOOY	conchology

CCGIIIKNNP	picnicking
CCGIILMOOR	micrologic
CCGIILNRTY	tricycling
CCGIILOOOS	sociologic
CCGIINNNOV	convincing
CCGILLOTYY	glycolytic
CCGILORSUU	glucosuric
CCGILORSUY	glycosuric
CCGIMNOOOS	cosmogonic
CCGINNORRU	concurring
CCGIOOPRSY	gyroscopic
CCHHHOOPTT	hotchpotch
CCHHIIOTTY	ichthyotic
CCHIIIRSTT	tristichic
CCHIILNNOO	conchiolin
CCHIILOPRY	cryophilic
CCHIIMNNOS	cinchonism
CCHIIMNOOR	chironomic
CCHIIMORRT	trichromic
CCHIIMPSSY	psychicism
CCHIINORTY	chronicity
CCHIIOPRTY	hypocritic
CCHIIPSSTY	psychicist
CCHIKLNQUU	quick-lunch
CCHIKLOSTT	lockstitch
CCHIKOPSST	chopsticks
CCHILOOPRY	polychroic
CCHILORSTW	scritch-owl
CCHIMNOOOR	monochroic
CCHIMORTYY	cymotrichy
CCHINNORSY	synchronic
CCHIOOOPRS	horoscopic
CCHIORSSTU	trochiscus
CCHKLOORRS	schorl-rock
CCHNOOSTUY	coconut-shy
CCHOOPSSUU	hocus-pocus
CCIIILMORT	microlitic
CCIIILOSST	sciolistic
CCIIKKQRTU	quicktrick
CCIIKKQSTU	quick-stick
CCIIILLNOPY	polyclinic
CCIILMNNOO	monoclinic
CCIILMNNOY	lincomycin
CCIILMOPTY	complicity
CCIILOOPRT	coprolitic
CCIILRSTTY	tricyclist
CCIIMMOORT	microtomic
CCIIMNOSTV	convictism
CCIIMOSSTT	Scotticism
CCIIMOSTUV	Muscovitic
CCIINNNOTY	concinnity
CCIINNOOTV	conviction
CCIINOOPRS	scorpionic
CCIIORSTUU	circuitous
CCIKOOPSTU	cuckoo-spit
CCILLLOSUU	colliculus
CCILLNOORU	councillor
CCILLOOPTY	collotypic
CCILMNORUU	corniculum
CCILMRRUUU	curriculum
CCILNNOOSU	conclusion
CCILNOOOTU	coconut-oil
CCILOOOPRT	protocolic
CCILOOPRTY	polycrotic
CCIMOOPRSY	microscopy
CCINNNOOSU	concinnous
CCINNOOSSU	concussion
CCINOSSSUU	succussion
CCINOSTUVY	viscountcy
CCIOOOPPRS	poroscopic
CCIOPPRRTY	procryptic
CCIORRSSSS	criss-cross
CCJLNNOTUY	conjunctly
CCLLOOORTU	collocutor
CCLNOORSUY	conclusory
CCLOOOPPSY	colposcopy
CCOOPSSTYY	cystoscopy
CDDDLRSUUY	sculduddry
CDDEEEEGKL	deckle-edge
CDDEEEENNP	dependence
CDDEEEINUV	undeceived
CDDEEEJLTY	dejectedly
CDDEEELNOR	needlecord
CDDEEEMNTU	deducement
CDDEEENNPY	dependency
CDDEEENNST	descendent
CDDEEENTTU	undetected
CDDEEFFIIN	diffidence
CDDEEGGKLU	duck-legged
CDDEEGINNS	descending
CDDEEIINSS	dissidence
CDDEEIJPRU	prejudiced
CDDEEILRSY	Clydesider
CDDEEIMNOR	endodermic
CDDEEINORS	considered
CDDEEINRSU	undescried
CDDEEINRTU	undirected
CDDEELLSUY	secludedly
CDDEELMOSU	cuddlesome
CDDEELNUUX	unexcluded
CDDEENNOSU	unseconded
CDDEENORRU	unrecorded
CDDEEOOPSU	pseudocode
CDDEFFHISU	dischuffed
CDDEFKOOTU	duck-footed
CDDEFNNOOU	confounded
CDDEGIKLOR	gridlocked
CDDEIINPRS	disprinced
CDDEIKMMNU	muck-midden
CDDEILOOUV	loud-voiced
CDDEIMMNOS	discommend
CDDEIMMOOS	discommode
CDDEIMOOSU	duodecimos
CDDEINORUV	undivorced
CDDELLLOOR	cold-rolled
CDDELOOORS	closed-door
CDDEMNOOPU	decompound
CDDENOORTU	undoctored
CDDENOPRTU	end-product
CDDENOPRUU	unproduced
CDDFILORSU	discordful
CDDHILSTUY	child-study
CDDIILNORY	cylindroid
CDDIKOSTTY	toddy-stick

CDDILNSUUU Didunculus
CDDILOOPSU diplodocus
CDDINNOOTY dicynodont
CDEEEEGNRT detergence
CDEEEEINPX expedience
CDEEEENRRT deterrence
CDEEEFFINR difference
CDEEEFFNTU uneffected
CDEEEFHIKR kerchiefed
CDEEEFIILP fieldpiece
CDEEEFILST self-deceit
CDEEEFILTV deflective
CDEEEGIIPR ridge-piece
CDEEEGINRV divergence
CDEEEGNRTY detergency
CDEEEHIPRR decipherer
CDEEEHKLOR cork-heeled
CDEEEHLNSU enschedule
CDEEEHLRSU reschedule
CDEEEHOOSW cheesewood
CDEEEIINPS desipience
CDEEEILOPV velocipede
CDEEEILQSU deliquesce
CDEEEIMNNO comedienne
comédienne
CDEEEIMNNP impendence
CDEEEINNPZ pince-nezed
CDEEEINPXY expediency
CDEEEINRRT interceder
CDEEEINRSW widescreen
CDEEEINRUV unreceived
CDEEEINSST desistence
CDEEEKNSTW 'tweendecks
CDEEELLNUX unexcelled
CDEEELMNOT dolcemente
CDEEELOPRS crêpe-soled
CDEEELORRT telerecord
CDEEELPTXY expectedly
CDEEEMNSTU seducement
CDEEENNORS recondense
CDEEENNRSU unscreened
CDEEENPTUX unexpected
CDEEENTUUX unexecuted
CDEEERRSTT street-cred
CDEEFFINRY differency
CDEEFIINRT dentifrice
CDEEFIIPRX fixed-price
CDEEFILNOT deflection
CDEEFILNRT fernticled
CDEEFINNTU uninfected
CDEEFINTUV defunctive
CDEEFLNORT centrefold
CDEEFLNORY enforcedly
CDEEFNNORU unenforced
CDEEFNORSS forcedness
CDEEGHHIKN high-necked
CDEEGHIKQU quick-hedge
CDEEGIKNNR ring-necked
CDEEGILNNU indulgence
CDEEGILNUV divulgence
CDEEGINOPR proceeding
CDEEGINRVY divergency
CDEEGIOOPS piece-goods
CDEEHIILOP ophicleide
CDEEHIILTT △ditheletic
CDEEHIIPRR cirrhipede
CDEEHIMNOR echinoderm
CDEEHINNRU unenriched
CDEEHLNOSV veldschoen
CDEEHLOORS deschooler
CDEEHLRTWY wretchedly
CDEEHMNOPR comprehend
CDEEHNNQUU unquenched
CDEEHNNRTU untrenched
CDEEHNORTU untochered
CDEEIIILSV decivilise
CDEEIIILVZ decivilize
CDEEIIIMNT cimetidine
CDEEIIINSV indecisive
CDEEIILSVY decisively
CDEEIIMNTY endemicity
CDEEIIMPRS spermicide
CDEEIINOPW cowdie-pine
CDEEIINRST indiscreet
indiscrete
iridescent
CDEEIINSUV undecisive
CDEEIIORRT cordierite
Directoire
CDEEIIPRTV predictive
CDEEIIRSSV disservice
CDEEIIRSTV discretive
CDEEIISSTV dissective
CDEEIJNORU unrejoiced
CDEEIJNOST dejections
CDEEIKNNST deck-tennis
CDEEIKNPSS pickedness
CDEEIKNSSW wickedness
CDEEILLNST stencilled
CDEEILMNOU undecimole
CDEEILNNOS declension
CDEEILNNSU unlicensed
CDEEILNNTY indecently
CDEEILNOOS decolonise
CDEEILNOOZ decolonize
CDEEILNOPY epicondyle
CDEEILNOSS disenclose
CDEEILNOSU nucleoside
CDEEILNOTU nucleotide
CDEEILNPSU uneclipsed
CDEEILNRTU interclude
CDEEILOORS decolorise
CDEEILOORZ decolorize
CDEEILORRS Cordeliers
CDEEILORST cloistered
CDEEILRSTY discreetly
discretely
CDEEIMMOXY myxoedemic
CDEEIMNNPY impendency
CDEEIMNNTU inducement
CDEEIMNOSU eudemonics
CDEEIMNPRU imprudence
CDEEIMORRX xerodermic
CDEEINNOSS descension

CDEEINNRSW windscreen
CDEEINNSSU secundines
CDEEINOPRV △providence
CDEEINORRS reconsider
CDEEINORUV undervoice
CDEEINPRSY presidency
CDEEINRSST directness
CDEEINRSTY dysenteric
CDEEIOPRRV overpriced
CDEEIOPSTU deceptious
CDEEIORRSV discoverer
rediscover
CDEEIORSTU courtesied
CDEEIPRRSS cider-press
CDEEIPRSST disrespect
CDEEIRRSST directress
CDEEIRRSTT derestrict
restricted
CDEEKKKNNO knock-kneed
CDEEKLNRRU under-clerk
CDEEKLTUVV velvet-duck
CDEEKNNORU unreckoned
CDEEKNPRUU unpuckered
CDEEKNRTUU untuckered
CDEEKOOPRW peckerwood
woodpecker
CDEELLNOSU counselled
CDEELMNOUW unwelcomed
CDEELMORRS scleroderm
CDEELNNOSU unenclosed
CDEELNOVXY convexedly
CDEEMNNOPR precondemn
CDEEMNNOST secondment
CDEEMOOPRS decomposer
CDEEMOPRSS compressed
decompress
CDEENNNOTT contendent
CDEENNORSU uncensored
CDEENNORSY condensery
CDEENNORTV convertend
CDEENNRSUU uncensured
CDEENOOOTT odontocete
CDEENOORRS rood-screen
CDEENOOSTT cottonseed
CDEENOOTTW cottonweed
CDEENORRSU underscore
CDEENORRUV undercover
CDEENORSTU uncorseted
unescorted
CDEENOSTUU consuetude
CDEENPRSTU unsceptred
CDEENRRSTU undercrest
CDEENRSSSU cursedness
CDEENSSSSU cussedness
CDEEOPRRRU reproducer
CDEERSSSTU seductress
CDEFFILNRU undercliff
CDEFFINNOU uncoffined
CDEFGHIKLT flight-deck
CDEFHINORU four-inched
CDEFHIORSY cod-fishery
CDEFIIIILS silicified
CDEFIIINPR princified
CDEFIIOSTT Scottified
CDEFILLOUV full-voiced
CDEFILNSUY disfluency
CDEFILORSS crossfield
CDEFILORST disc-floret
CDEFILORSW disc-flower
CDEFINNNOU unconfined
CDEFINNORU uninforced
CDEFINNOTU defunction
CDEFINOORV confervoid
CDEFLNORUY unforcedly
CDEFLNOSUY confusedly
CDEFNNOSUU unconfused
CDEFNORRTU undercroft
CDEFNOSSUU unfocussed
CDEGGILLNU cudgelling
CDEGHHIIPR high-priced
CDEGHJOTUU touch-judge
CDEGHOOORT tocher-good
CDEGIILNNY incedingly
CDEGIINNRS discerning
CDEGIINOTU digoneutic
CDEGIINSST dissecting
CDEGIIORTY ergodicity
CDEGIKNOST stockinged
CDEGILMMNO commingled
CDEGILNNUY indulgency
CDEGILNOPU decoupling
CDEGILNSUY seducingly
CDEGILOOPS logopedics
CDEGILOORS socdoliger
CDEGINNNOT contending
CDEGINORSW scowdering
CDEGIOORRR corregidor
CDEGLOOORS socdologer
CDEGMNORUU curmudgeon
CDEHHIIPRT diphtheric
CDEHHOORRY hydrochore
CDEHIIISTT ditheistic
CDEHIILOPS discophile
CDEHIILORS chloridise
CDEHIILORZ chloridize
CDEHIILPTY diphyletic
CDEHIINOST hedonistic
CDEHIINRTY enhydritic
CDEHIKMNOT kitchendom
CDEHILNRSU nurse-child
CDEHILOOST schooltide
CDEHILOPRY polyhedric
CDEHILOPTW low-pitched
CDEHIMNRSU unsmirched
CDEHIMOPRY hypodermic
CDEHINOOOV novicehood
CDEHINOOPR princehood
CDEHINOPTY endophytic
CDEHIOOORW hoodie-crow
CDEHIOOPRT orthopedic
CDEHIOORSU orchideous
CDEHISSTTT set-stitch'd
CDEHKORSUV duckshover
CDEHLNOORY chlorodyne

CDEHLNOOSU unschooled
CDEHLOOPPR clodhopper
CDEHLOOPRY copyholder
CDEHMNOTUW Dutchwomen
CDEHNOOORT octohedron
CDEHNORSUU chunderous
CDEHOOPRSY hydroscope
CDEIIILLST stillicide
CDEIIILNNS disincline
CDEIIILNOT indicolite
CDEIIILNPS discipline
CDEIIIMRSV recidivism
CDEIIINNOS indecision
CDEIIINTVV vindictive
CDEIIIRSTV recidivist
CDEIIJNOST disjection
CDEIIKLSST sick-listed
CDEIILNNOR crinolined
CDEIILNOPU unpolicied
CDEIILNOSS disinclose
CDEIILNPPR principled
CDEIILNRTY cylindrite
indirectly
CDEIILOSTU solicitude
CDEIIMNNTT indictment
CDEIIMOORT iodometric
CDEIIMORRS misericord
CDEIIMORTY iridectomy
mediocrity
CDEIIMOSTT demoticist
CDEIIMPRTU impictured
CDEIINOPRT prediction
CDEIINORST discretion
soricident
CDEIINOSST dissection
CDEIINSTTU discutient
CDEIIOOPTX exopoditic
CDEIIOORRS sororicide
CDEIIORSUV veridicous
CDEIIPRSTU pedicurist
CDEIIRSSUV discursive
CDEIISSSUV discussive
CDEIKNRRTU under-trick
CDEIKNRSUW wind-sucker
CDEIKOPPRT cork-tipped
CDEIKOPPTT pockpitted
CDEIKOQSTU deck-quoits
CDEIKPTTUY picket-duty
CDEILLLPUY pellucidly
CDEILLNOOR corn-dollie
CDEILNNOSU uninclosed
CDEILNOSSU cloudiness
discounsel
CDEILOPRTU productile
CDEILOPSUU pediculous
CDEILORSSU disclosure
CDEIMMNOPU compendium
CDEIMMNOTU comminuted
CDEIMNOOPS incomposed
CDEIMNOOST endosmotic
CDEIMNOOSY diseconomy
CDEIMNOSTU undomestic
CDEIMNOSUU mucedinous
CDEIMOOPSS discompose
CDEIMOSSTU customised
CDEIMOSTUZ customized
CDEIMPRSTU spermiduct
CDEINNOSST disconsent
CDEINNOSTT discontent
CDEINNRTUU under-tunic
CDEINOORSU indecorous
CDEINOPRTY decryption
CDEINORRTU introducer
CDEINORSTU discounter
rediscount
CDEINPRSTU unscripted
CDEIOPRRST descriptor
CDEIOPRRTU picture-rod
CDEIOPRTUV productive
CDEIORRSSU discourser
CDEIRRSTTU strictured
CDEJNNOSSU jocundness
CDEKMMOOST mock-modest
CDEKNORSTU understock
CDELLNOORT controlled
CDELMNOSUY consumedly
CDELMOOPSY composedly
CDELMOOPTT complotted
CDELNNOOSU unconsoled
CDELNOORUU uncoloured
CDELNOORUY Euroclydon
CDELNOOTUV convoluted
CDELNPRSUU unscrupled
CDELNRTUUU uncultured
CDELOOORUV dove-colour
CDELOORSUY decorously
CDELORRSSU russel-cord
CDELPRSTUU sculptured
CDEMMNOTUU uncommuted
CDEMMOOORS cosmodrome
CDEMNNOSUU unconsumed
CDEMNOOPRU compounder
CDEMNOSTUU uncustomed
CDENNOOPRU pronounced
CDENOOPRRS correspond
CDEOOOPSTU scooped-out
CDEOORTTUW wood-cutter
CDEOPRRSTU cropduster
CDEORRSTTU destructor
CDERRSTTUU structured
CDFFIILTUY difficulty
CDFGHIINOS cod-fishing
CDFHILOOPR childproof
CDFHIOORST doctor-fish
CDFIMOORST discomfort
CDGHILNOTU night-cloud
CDGHILOORY hydrologic
CDGIINOPRR riding-crop
CDGIKLLOOS goldilocks
CDGILLNOSY scoldingly
CDGILMOOOY docimology
CDGINNOOPY pycnogonid
CDGINPPRUY dry-cupping
CDHHIILLSY childishly

CDHHIOORST Christhood
CDHIIIMSTU stichidium
CDHIILOOST Dolichotis
CDHIIMMORS dichromism
CDHIIMMORU chromidium
CDHIIMNOOR chironomid
CDHIINORST chondritis
CDHIIOORTT diorthotic
CDHIIOSSTU distichous
CDHILLNRRU churn-drill
CDHILOORSV dichlorvos
CDHILOOSSU holodiscus
CDHILOPRYY polyhydric
CDHILORSUU dolichurus
CDHILORTYY hydrolytic
CDHIMNOORY monohydric
CDHINOOOSU cousinhood
CDHINOOPRY hydroponic
CDHIOOPRST doctorship
CDHIOPRSTY dystrophic
CDHKNNPRUU punch-drunk
CDHLMMNOOO commonhold
CDHMOOORTY chordotomy
CDIIILNOTY indocility
CDIIIMPTUY impudicity
CDIIINNSTT indistinct
CDIIINOSSS discission
CDIILNOOSU nidicolous
CDIILNPSUU sipunculid
CDIILNSTTY distinctly
CDIILORSUU ridiculous
CDIINNOOST conditions
CDIINOPSUU cupidinous
CDIINORSSU discursion
CDIINOSSSU discussion
CDIIRSSSTU discursist
CDIJNORSTU disjunctor
CDIKORSSTW sword-stick
CDILLMOOSU molluscoid
CDILLOQUUY dulciloquy
CDILMOOORX loxodromic
CDILMOOPUY △lycopodium
CDILOOOPTY octoploidy
CDIMMOOOSU commodious
CDINOOPRST spin-doctor
CDINOOPRTU production
CDIORRSSUY discursory
CDNOOOOTTW cottonwood
CDOOOPSTU octopodous
CEEEEFFRSV effervesce
CEEEEFLLSS fleeceless
CEEEEFLRST free-select
CEEEEFNPRR preference
CEEEEGIPTX epexegetic
CEEEEHIMST cheesemite
CEEEEHIPRT three-piece
CEEEEHIRSW cheesewire
CEEEEHNPRT threepence
CEEEEINPRX experience
CEEEEIRSVY eye-service
CEEEELLNPR repellence
CEEEELNORT enterocele
CEEEELNRST telescreen
CEEEENNPSV sevenpence
CEEEENNRST resentence
CEEEENRRRV reverencer
CEEEFFGLNU effulgence
CEEEFFLORS effloresce
CEEEFFLSST effectless
CEEEFGLNRU refulgence
CEEEFHIKNT kitchen-fee
CEEEFHLMNT fleechment
CEEEFHLRTT three-cleft
CEEEFHNRTT trench-feet
CEEEFILRTV reflective
CEEEFINNNS Fescennine
CEEEFINORU nourice-fee
CEEEFINRRS firescreen
CEEEFINRRT centre-fire
CEEEFINRSS fierceness
CEEEFIPRTV perfective
CEEEFLLOOW fleece-wool
CEEEFMNRST fremescent
CEEEFNRSTV fervescent
CEEEFPRRTU prefecture
CEEEGGILNN negligence
CEEEGHIKLN ingle-cheek
CEEEGHINPT eightpence
CEEEGIINPT epigenetic
CEEEGILNTV neglective
CEEEGINNOT neogenetic
CEEEGINOTX exogenetic
CEEEGINRST energetics
CEEEGINRTV vicegerent
viceregent
CEEEGINSTU eugenecist
CEEEGLNORT electrogen
CEEEGNRRSU resurgence
CEEEHHLORS horse-leech
CEEEHIKNSS cheekiness
CEEEHIMSTT chemisette
CEEEHINPTT epenthetic
CEEEHINRSS cheeriness
CEEEHINSSS cheesiness
CEEEHINSTT teschenite
CEEEHKNPRY henpeckery
CEEEHKRSSS Cherkesses
CEEEHLPSSS speechless
CEEEHMMNSY mesenchyme
CEEEHMNOSW somewhence
CEEEHMORTT hectometre
CEEEHNOPSS ecphoneses
CEEEHNORSS chersonese
CEEEHOQRUU Eurocheque
CEEEHORRST threescore
CEEEHORSST scoresheet
CEEEHORSTT hectostere
CEEEIILMPT epimeletic
CEEEIILNRS resilience
CEEEILLTVY electively
CEEEILMNNT △clementine
CEEEILMORT ceilometer
CEEEILMRTT telemetric
CEEEILNNRT centreline

CEEEILNORT re-election
CEEEILNPRT percentile
CEEEILNPST pestilence
CEEEIMNNTT enticement
CEEEIMNNTV evincement
CEEEIMNORS ceremonies
CEEEIMNRST mesenteric
CEEEIMNRTT centimeter
centimetre
CEEEIMNTTX excitement
CEEEIMOPSU mousepiece
CEEEIMRRRS merceriser
CEEEIMRRRZ mercerizer
CEEEINNPPY penny-piece
CEEEINNPRT pertinence
CEEEINORRT re-erection
CEEEINPRTT penteteric
CEEEINTTWY winceyette
CEEEIORRST corsetière
CEEEIORTVX overexcite
CEEEIPPRTV perceptive
preceptive
CEEEIPRSTV respective
CEEEKKLNPS kenspeckle
CEEEKKLOPR lock-keeper
CEEEKRRSSU seersucker
CEEELLLNTT nettle-cell
CEEELLNNOP penoncelle
CEEELLNPRY repellency
CEEELLRRWY crewellery
CEEELMORRT electromer
CEEELNRSSV cleverness
CEEELNSSST selectness
CEEELORSST electoress
CEEELORSTT corselette
CEEELPSSTX exceptless
CEEELRRSSU recureless
CEEEMNNRST secernment
CEEEMNOPRS recompense
CEEEMNORRT centromere
CEEEMNOTYZ ectoenzyme
CEEEMNRSTU securement
CEEEMOPRSU creepmouse
CEEENNRSST recentness
CEEENOPPRT prepotence
CEEENORSSV seven-score
CEEENRRSTT rest-centre
CEEENRSSST secretness
CEEENRSSSU secureness
CEEERSSTUX executress
CEEFFFIIOR fire-office
CEEFFFLNOU offenceful
CEEFFHNORU forfeuchen
CEEFFINPTY fifty-pence
CEEFFIOORV overoffice
CEEFGHINNR greenfinch
CEEFGILNRT reflecting
CEEFGINRTU centrifuge
CEEFGLLNTU neglectful
CEEFGLNRUY refulgency
CEEFHHNORT henceforth
CEEFHKLOPS folk-speech
CEEFHLLRUY cheerfully
CEEFHLNRUU uncheerful
CEEFHLOORS free-school
CEEFHNOORS forechosen
CEEFHORTTU fourchette
CEEFIILNRT ferniticle
CEEFIILNTV inflective
CEEFIIMNNU munifience
CEEFIINORS confiserie
CEEFIINPRT perficient
CEEFIJLNST self-inject
CEEFIJLORU rejoiceful
CEEFIKLNRT ferntickle
CEEFIKLNSS fickleness
CEEFIKLORT life-rocket
CEEFILNORT reflection
CEEFILNRTY fernyticle
CEEFILORVX flexi-cover
CEEFILRTTU file-cutter
CEEFINOORT fore-notice
CEEFINOPRT perfection
CEEFINOSUV veneficous
CEEFIORRSU ceriferous
CEEFKLLSSY fecklessly
CEEFKLORTT fetterlock
CEEFLNOPRU profluence
CEEFLNORST florescent
CEEFLPPRTU pluperfect
CEEFLPRSTU respectful
CEEFMNNORT conferment
CEEFOORRSU forecourse
CEEFORRRSS cross-refer
CEEGHIILMP hemiplegic
CEEGHIINPT nightpiece
CEEGHIMORT geothermic
CEEGHIMOST geochemist
CEEGHIORST eightscore
CEEGHLNORT greencloth
CEEGHLOPST clothes-peg
CEEGHNOPSS speech-song
CEEGIINOST isogenetic
CEEGIINPRV perceiving
CEEGIINSTT geneticist
CEEGIINSTU eugenicist
CEEGIKNRST greenstick
CEEGILLOOT teleologic
CEEGILNNOT neglection
CEEGILNPRY creepingly
CEEGINNOOR coregonine
CEEGINNORU encoignure
neurogenic
CEEGINNQSU sequencing
CEEGINNRSS screenings
CEEGINNRST nigrescent
CEEGINNRSU insurgence
CEEGINNSTY syngenetic
CEEGINOORT erotogenic
orogenetic
CEEGINOOST osteogenic
CEEGINOPRZ precognize
CEEGINORRS recogniser
CEEGINORRZ recognizer

CEEGINORST	estrogenic
CEEGINOSTV	congestive
CEEGINPRST	respecting
CEEGINPRTX	excerpting
CEEGINRSTY	synergetic
CEEGMOTYYZ	zygomycete
CEEGNNORTV	convergent
CEEGNOOSTU	ectogenous
CEEGNPRSUU	upsurgence
CEEGNRSTTU	turgescent
CEEHHILNOY	honey-chile
CEEHHILPTW	pitch-wheel
CEEHHIMORT	come-hither
CEEHHKOOTT	cheektooth
CEEHHMNNOW	henchwomen
CEEHHNOTTY	theotechny
CEEHIIMRST	erethismic
CEEHIIPPRR	peripheric
CEEHIIRRST	heritrices
CEEHIIRSTT	erethistic
CEEHIKPPRS	schipperke
CEEHILMNOP	clomiphene
CEEHILNOPR	necrophile
CEEHILNOPT	telephonic
CEEHILNORU	euchlorine
CEEHILOOPS	helioscope
CEEHILOPRT	helicopter
CEEHILORTT	hectolitre
CEEHILOSVY	cohesively
CEEHILPSST	ecthlipses
CEEHILSSTY	chessylite
CEEHIMMOOR	homeomeric
CEEHIMMPSY	emphysemic
CEEHIMNNRT	enrichment
CEEHIMNTTU	technetium
CEEHIMOPTU	mouthpiece
CEEHIMORRY	cherimoyer
CEEHIMORTX	exothermic
CEEHINNORT	incoherent
CEEHINOPPR	Hippocrene
CEEHINOPSS	ecphonesis
CEEHINORSS	heroicness
CEEHINPPRW	pipe-wrench
CEEHINRRST	rechristen
CEEHINRSTW	Winchester
	Winchester®
CEEHINSSTT	tetchiness
CEEHIOPRSX	exospheric
CEEHIORSTT	theoretics
CEEHIRSTTY	hysteretic
CEEHKLOOPT	pocket-hole
CEEHLLMORT	mother-cell
CEEHLLNOSW	well-chosen
CEEHLMORTY	emery-cloth
CEEHLMOSZZ	schemozzle
CEEHLNOOPT	technopole
CEEHLNORTY	coherently
CEEHLNORWW	crown-wheel
CEEHLNQSSU	quenchless
CEEHLORSST	tocherless
CEEHMMOORR	chromomere
CEEHNOOPPS	nephoscope
CEEHNOOPRT	ctenophore
CEEHNOORTT	heterocont
CEEHNOPRTY	hypocentre
CEEHNPPRTU	thruppence
CEEHOOPRRS	horse-coper
CEEHOOPSST	post-echoes
CEEHOPRSTY	spherocyte
CEEIIILNNS	sicilienne
CEEIIINNPS	insipience
CEEIIINSTZ	citizenise
CEEIIINTZZ	citizenize
CEEIIJORST	jeistiecor
CEEIIKLNPR	princelike
CEEIIKLNPT	picket-line
CEEIILLLTV	vitellicle
CEEIILLMRV	vermicelli
CEEIILNOSU	isoleucine
CEEIILNRSY	resiliency
CEEIILNRTT	centiliter
	centilitre
CEEIILPRSV	lip-service
CEEIILRTTY	erectility
CEEIILTTVY	electivity
CEEIIMMPRT	metempiric
CEEIIMNNTT	incitement
CEEIIMORTT	meteoritic
CEEIIMOSST	semeiotics
CEEIIMPRRT	perimetric
CEEIIMPSSS	speciesism
CEEIIMPSST	epistemics
CEEIIMQRSU	semicirque
CEEIINNSST	insistence
CEEIINOPRW	cowrie-pine
CEEIINOSST	sectionise
CEEIINOSTZ	sectionize
CEEIINPPRT	percipient
CEEIINPSTV	inspective
CEEIINRSTT	interstice
CEEIINSSTZ	citizeness
CEEIINTTVX	extinctive
CEEIIOPPSS	episcopise
CEEIIOPPSZ	episcopize
CEEIIORRST	escritoire
CEEIIPSSST	speciesist
CEEIIRSSTU	securities
	securitise
CEEIIRSTUZ	securitize
CEEIJLOPRT	projectile
CEEIJOPRTV	projective
CEEIKLNRSS	silkscreen
CEEIKNOTTZ	zone-ticket
CEEIKNPRTY	pernickety
CEEIKNRSSS	sickerness
CEEILLNRST	stenciller
CEEILLOOPT	coleoptile
CEEILLORSS	recoilless
CEEILLPRTT	letter-clip
CEEILMNOOT	teleonomic
CEEILMNOPT	incomplete
CEEILMNORT	clinometer
CEEILMNOSS	comeliness
CEEILMNSTU	semilucent

CEEILMOPTV completive
CEEILNNSTU inesculent
CEEILNOORS recolonise
CEEILNOORW wine-cooler
CEEILNOORZ recolonize
CEEILNOPRT prelection
CEEILNORST encloister
CEEILNORTT crinolette
CEEILNORVY overnicely
CEEILNQSTU liquescent
CEEILNRSUY insecurely
CEEILNRTUV ventricule
CEEILORRST cloisterer
CEEILORSST sclerotise
CEEILORSTZ sclerotize
CEEILOSSUV vesiculose
CEEILPRSUV preclusive
CEEIMMNOSU oecumenism
CEEIMMOPRT emmetropic
CEEIMMORRT micrometer
micrometre
CEEIMNNOPR prominence
CEEIMNOORS economiser
CEEIMNOORT iconometer
CEEIMNOORZ economizer
CEEIMNSSSU meniscuses
CEEIMORSTV viscometer
CEEIMOSSTV vicomtesse
CEEINNNOTV convenient
CEEINNOPST post-Nicene
CEEINNORTU recontinue
CEEINNOSTT cosentient
CEEINNPRTY pertinency
CEEINNPSST spinescent
CEEINOOPST teinoscope
CEEINOPPRT perception
CEEINOPRSS precession
CEEINOPRTU pie-counter
CEEINOPRTX excerption
CEEINORRSW cornerwise
CEEINORSTV ventricose
CEEINORTTV convertite
CEEINORTTY coeternity
CEEINOSSTX exoticness
CEEINOSTTX coexistent
CEEINPRRTX precentrix
CEEINPRSTU putrescine
CEEINPRTTU percutient
CEEINRRSTU scrutineer
CEEINRSSTY syncretise
CEEINRSTTT trecentist
CEEINRSTTV vitrescent
CEEINRSTYZ syncretize
CEEINRTTUX extincture
CEEIOPRTTV protective
CEEIOPSTUX exceptious
CEEIORRTUU couturière
CEEIORSTTU tricoteuse
CEEIPRRSUV precursive
CEEIPRSSUV percussive
CEEIPSSTUV susceptive
CEEJNOOSSS jocoseness
CEEJOPRRTU projecture
CEEKLLRSSY recklessly
CEEKLMOPRT rock-temple
CEEKLNRTTU turtleneck
CEEKLOORRV overlocker
CEEKLOPSST pocketless
CEEKLOPSTU outspeckle
CEEKLORRWW crewelwork
CEEKLRSUVY culver-keys
CEEKNOORRV overreckon
CEEKOPSTTV vest-pocket
CEELLMOPTY completely
CEELMMNOPT complement
CEELMNNOOS somnolence
CEELMNOOSU nucleosome
CEELMNOPTU couplement
CEELMOORTU coulometer
CEELNORSVY conversely
CEELNORVVY revolvency
CEELORRSTY clerestory
CEEMMOTXYY myxomycete
CEEMNNSTTY encystment
CEEMNOOPSS meconopses
CEEMNOORST centrosome
CEEMNOORUV unovercome
CEEMNOOSTU coenosteum
CEEMNOPRSU preconsume
CEEMNOPRTU recoupment
CEEMNOPRTY pycnometer
CEEMNORTUY neurectomy
CEEMNPSSTU spumescent
CEEMOOPPRS precompose
CEEMOOPTTU outcompete
CEEMOORSTT scotometer
CEEMOPRRSS recompress
CEEMORTTUY uterectomy
CEENNOQSTU consequent
CEENNORRTU rencounter
CEENNOSSVX convexness
CEENNPRSSY pennycress
CEENOPPPRR peppercorn
CEENOPPRTY prepotency
CEENOPRSTT torpescent
CEENOQRSSU conqueress
CEENOQRSTU reconquest
CEENORSTUU countersue
CEENORTTUX contexture
CEENPRRRTU percurrent
CEENPRSSSU spruceness
CEENPRSTTU putrescent
CEEOOPRSTV Vertoscope®
CEEOPPRRTY preceptory
CEEOPRRSTT retrospect
CEEOPRRSTU persecutor
CEEPRTTTUY type-cutter
CEERSSSUUX excursuses
CEFFFHIORS coffer-fish
CEFFGIILOR office-girl
CEFFHIINOR chiffonier
CEFFHINSSU chuffiness
CEFFIIKKLN flick-knife
CEFFIILTWY Wycliffite

CEFFIINSTU	sufficient
CEFFIOOPST	post-office
CEFFLLORUY	forcefully
CEFGIINPSY	specifying
CEFGIINRTY	certifying
	rectifying
CEFGINNORR	conferring
CEFHILPRTU	pitcherful
CEFHILPRTY	flypitcher
CEFHILSTTU	cuttlefish
CEFHNOORTT	trench-foot
CEFIIILNTV	inflictive
CEFIIILNTY	infelicity
CEFIIIMNST	feministic
CEFIIKLRRT	rick-lifter
CEFIIKQRRU	quick-firer
CEFIILNNOT	inflection
CEFIILNOQU	cinquefoil
CEFIILOPRY	fire-policy
CEFIILOSTU	felicitous
CEFIIMNNTU	munificent
CEFIINOPRT	proficient
CEFIINOPST	pontifices
CEFIINOSTU	infectious
CEFIKLOORT	foot-licker
CEFILLMRUY	mercifully
CEFILMNRUU	unmerciful
CEFILMOORS	frolicsome
CEFILMOPRY	clypeiform
CEFILMOPXY	complexify
CEFILOPRRS	rifle-corps
CEFILORSUU	luciferous
CEFIMORRSU	securiform
CEFIMORSUU	muciferous
CEFINNOOSS	confession
CEFINOORSU	coniferous
CEFINORSUU	nuciferous
CEFINRSSSU	scurfiness
CEFIOORSUV	vociferous
CEFKLOPSTU	pocketfuls
CEFLLOORSU	self-colour
CEFLLSTTUU	scuttleful
CEFLNOORRW	cornflower
CEFLOORRWW	crow-flower
CEFLPSSTUU	suspectful
CEFOOOPSTY	foetoscopy
CEGGHIMNUW	chewing-gum
CEGGHIORST	ostrich-egg
CEGGIILNNR	cringeling
CEGGILNOSS	clogginess
CEGGIMNTTU	gem-cutting
CEGGINNORV	converging
CEGGINOOST	geognostic
CEGHIIKNNT	thickening
CEGHIILLNS	chiselling
CEGHIILOOR	hierologic
CEGHIINNUY	unhygienic
CEGHIINORZ	rhizogenic
CEGHIINOST	histogenic
CEGHIINRTT	chittering
CEGHILMNOP	phlegmonic
CEGHILNOOP	nephologic

CEGHILNPPS	schlepping
CEGHILNQSU	squelching
CEGHILOORY	cheirology
CEGHILOPRY	hypergolic
CEGHIMMNOO	home-coming
CEGHINNOPY	hypnogenic
CEGHINOOPT	photogenic
CEGHINOORR	gonorrheic
CEGHINOORT	orthogenic
CEGHINOPTY	phytogenic
	pythogenic
CEGHINORRU	chirurgeon
CEGHINORTY	trichogyne
CEGHIOPSSY	geophysics
CEGHIRRRUY	chirurgery
CEGHLNOOTY	technology
CEGHOOPRSY	hygroscope
CEGIIINOSV	visiogenic
CEGIIINSST	gneissitic
CEGIIJNORS	rejoicings
CEGIIKLLNN	nickelling
CEGIIKMNRS	smickering
CEGIIKNNQU	quickening
CEGIIKPRST	pig-sticker
CEGIILLNNP	pencilling
CEGIILNNPR	princeling
CEGIILNNSS	clinginess
CEGIILNNST	stenciling
CEGIILNNTY	enticingly
CEGIILNPRY	piercingly
CEGIILNTXY	excitingly
CEGIILOPTT	epiglottic
CEGIILOSTU	eulogistic
CEGIINNRSV	scrivening
CEGIINNTUX	unexciting
CEGIINOSST	Gnosticise
CEGIINOSTZ	Gnosticize
CEGIINRRTU	recruiting
CEGIJNOPRT	projecting
CEGIKNORST	stockinger
CEGILLMNOP	compelling
CEGILLMOSU	collegiums
CEGILLOOXY	lexicology
CEGILMOORT	metrologic
CEGILNNOST	clingstone
CEGILNORWY	coweringly
CEGILNOTVY	covetingly
CEGILNRSTU	clustering
CEGILORSSS	scissor-leg
CEGIMNNNOT	contemning
CEGIMNOORS	ergonomics
CEGIMNORTU	tumorgenic
CEGINNNOTT	contingent
CEGINNOOST	congestion
CEGINNOQRU	conquering
CEGINNORST	constringe
CEGINNOSTT	contesting
CEGINNRRUU	unrecuring
CEGINNRSTY	stringency
CEGINNRSUY	insurgency
CEGINOPRTT	protecting
CEGINOQTTU	coquetting

CEGINRTTUV curvetting
CEGLMOOOTY cometology
CEGLMOOTYY mycetology
CEGLNOOSYY synecology
CEGOOPRRTY gyrocopter
CEHHHIIKRT hitch-hiker
CEHHIILMNT helminthic
CEHHILORSW shriche-owl
shriech-owl
CEHHIMRTUY eurhythmic
CEHHIOOPRT theophoric
CEHHIOOPST theosophic
CEHHIOPRST hectorship
CEHHIOPTTY hypothetic
CEHHKLLOSS shellshock
CEHHLOORST horse-cloth
CEHIIINRST trichinise
CEHIIINRTZ trichinize
CEHIIJOSTV Jehovistic
CEHIIKLRST Christlike
CEHIIKRTTW whitterick
CEHIILLNSS chilliness
CEHIILLOOP oleophilic
CEHIILMOST homiletics
Mesolithic
CEHIILNORS chlorinise
CEHIILNORZ chlorinize
CEHIILNPST clientship
CEHIILOPTY heliotypic
CEHIILORTY leiotrichy
CEHIILPSST ecthlipsis
CEHIIMNORT thermionic
CEHIIMNORY Hieronymic
CEHIIMOPRT hemitropic
CEHIIMRSTY mythiciser
CEHIIMRTYZ mythicizer
CEHIINOPPR periphonic
CEHIINOPSV noviceship
CEHIINORST trichinose
CEHIINPRSS chirpiness
CEHIINPSST pitchiness
CEHIIOSTTY histiocyte
CEHIIPRSTY sphericity
CEHIIPSTUU euphuistic
CEHIIRRTTU urethritic
CEHIIRRTTY erythritic
CEHIIRSSTU heuristics
CEHIJKOPSY jockeyship
CEHIKRSTTU trekschuit
CEHIKRSTYY hystericky
CEHILLMSSU music-shell
CEHILMOOPR lipochrome
CEHILMOOST schooltime
CEHILMOPPY Polyphemic
CEHILNOPRY necrophily
CEHILNOPST clothes-pin
CEHILOOPST Scotophile
CEHILOORST holosteric
CEHILOPRST lectorship
CEHILOPRTU Turcophile
CEHILORSTY chrysolite
chrysotile
CEHILRSSST Christless
CEHIMMOPRS morphemics
CEHIMNOOPR microphone
CEHIMNOORR chironomer
CEHIMNOORY cheironomy
CEHIMNOOTT nomothetic
CEHIMNOPTY chimneypot
CEHIMNOPUY eponychium
CEHIMOOORT homoerotic
CEHIMOOPTY mythopoeic
CEHIMOOTUZ zoothecium
CEHIMOPRTY microphyte
CEHIMOPSTY mesophytic
CEHIMORSSU semichorus
CEHIMORSTT thermotics
CEHIMORTTY mother-city
CEHIMOSSUU music-house
CEHINNNPPY penny-pinch
pinchpenny
CEHINNOPTU unphonetic
CEHINNRSTU unchristen
CEHINNRSTY strychnine
CEHINOOPRS rhinoscope
CEHINOORRS rhinoceros
CEHINOORRT rhinocerot
CEHINOPPRR pronephric
CEHINOPPTY phenotypic
CEHINOPRSS censorship
CEHINOPRSY hypersonic
CEHINOPRTY hypertonic
CEHINOPSTT open-stitch
pitchstone
CEHINOPTTY entophytic
CEHINORSTU urosthenic
CEHINOSSTU touchiness
CEHIOOPRRT rheotropic
CEHIOOPRRY pyorrhoeic
CEHIOOPRSY hieroscopy
CEHIOORRRT retrochoir
CEHIOPRRST rectorship
CEHIOPRSTT prosthetic
CEHIOPRTXY xerophytic
CEHIOQSTTU coquettish
CEHIORSTVW switch-over
CEHKLNOSUY hony-suckle
CEHKNORRSU cornhusker
CEHKOOPPRR rock-hopper
CEHKOORSST stockhorse
CEHKRSSSTU huckstress
CEHLMOOPRY polychrome
CEHLMOORXY xylochrome
CEHLMOPTYY lymphocyte
CEHLOOOPRT tocopherol
CEHLOPRSTY polychrest
CEHMMNOOOR monochrome
CEHMMOOORS chromosome
CEHMMOTTYY thymectomy
CEHMNOOTTU touch-me-not
CEHMOOPRTY chromotype
cormophyte
ectomorphy
CEHNOOPRTT top-notcher

CEHNOOSTTU	touchstone
CEHNOPRSTY	phenocryst
CEHNOPRTYY	pyrotechny
CEHOOPRSTU	octopusher
CEHOORSTUU	courthouse
CEHORSTTTU	outstretch
CEIIIILSTV	civilities
CEIIIKNOST	isokinetic
CEIIILLNNP	penicillin
CEIIILNPTX	inexplicit
CEIIILNSVY	incisively
CEIIILOPST	politicise
CEIIILOPTZ	politicize
CEIIIMMPRS	empiricism
CEIIIMOSSS	isoseismic
CEIIIMPRST	empiricist
CEIIIMRSTV	victimiser
CEIIIMRTVZ	victimizer
CEIIIMSSTY	seismicity
CEIIINPPRT	precipitin
CEIIIQSTTU	quietistic
CEIIJNNTUV	injunctive
CEIIKLNSSS	sickliness
CEIIKLOPRT	politicker
CEIIKMPSST	skepticism
CEIIKNOSTT	kenoticist
	tokenistic
CEIIKNRSST	trickiness
CEIIKNSSST	stickiness
CEIILLLSTU	cellulitis
CEIILLNNOT	centillion
CEIILLNRTU	citrulline
CEIILLOSSU	siliculose
CEIILLPTXY	explicitly
CEIILMNNOU	lenocinium
CEIILMOPST	polemicist
CEIILMORTT	tremolitic
CEIILMSSTV	victimless
CEIILNNOST	consilient
CEIILNOPRU	rupicoline
CEIILNOSTU	licentious
CEIILNOSTV	novelistic
CEIILNPPRS	principles
CEIILNQSSU	cliquiness
CEIILNRTUV	ventriculi
CEIILOOPST	politicoes
CEIILOPSTX	post-exilic
CEIIMMORSS	microseism
CEIIMNNOST	omniscient
CEIIMNRSSU	sinecurism
CEIIMNRTUV	centumviri
CEIIMORSST	isometrics
CEIIMORSTT	cottierism
CEIIMOSTTT	totemistic
CEIINNOPST	cispontine
	inspection
CEIINNORSV	environics
CEIINNOTTX	extinction
CEIINNSSTY	insistency
CEIINOPRST	isentropic
	triniscope
CEIINOPRSU	pernicious
CEIINOPRTV	voiceprint
CEIINOPSTT	nepotistic
CEIINORSSS	rescission
CEIINORSTT	trisection
CEIINPSSTU	suscipient
CEIINRSSTU	scrutinise
	sinecurist
CEIINRSTUY	insecurity
CEIINRSTUZ	scrutinize
CEIIOOPSTZ	epizootics
CEIIOORSTU	trioecious
CEIIOPRSTY	preciosity
CEIIOPSSTY	speciosity
CEIIORSTTU	triticeous
CEIIORSTVV	vivisector
CEIIPSSTUY	Puseyistic
CEIIRRSTTX	trisectrix
CEIJNOOPRT	projection
CEIJNORSTU	surjection
CEIKKORRST	kicksorter
CEIKKORRWW	wickerwork
CEIKLNNOST	clinkstone
CEIKLNOSST	slickstone
CEIKLNPSSU	pluckiness
CEIKLOOPRW	wool-picker
CEIKLOORTV	rock-violet
CEIKLOPRSU	prick-louse
CEIKMOPRTV	mock-privet
CEIKNORRWZ	zinc-worker
CEIKNOSSST	stockiness
CEIKOPSTTU	soup-ticket
CEILLMNORR	corn-miller
CEILLNOOPT	ponticello
CEILLOOQSU	colloquise
CEILLOOQUZ	colloquize
CEILLORSSW	scrollwise
CEILMMNOPT	compliment
CEILMNOOPT	completion
CEILMNOOPX	complexion
CEILMNOOTT	melicotton
CEILMNORTY	clinometry
CEILMNOSSU	miscounsel
CEILMNPSSU	clumpiness
CEILMNSSSU	clumsiness
CEILMOOOTV	locomotive
CEILMOOPST	leptosomic
CEILMOPSUV	compulsive
CEILMOPTXY	complexity
CEILMORSTU	sclerotium
CEILMORTUV	volumetric
CEILMOSTUU	meticulous
CEILNNNOTY	innocently
CEILNNOSVY	insolvency
CEILNNPRUY	unprincely
CEILNOOPRS	necropolis
CEILNOORRS	resorcinol
CEILNOOSTZ	solonetzic
CEILNOPRSU	preclusion
CEILNORSTU	uncloister
CEILNORTTY	contritely
CEILNOSSST	costliness
CEILNOSSTT	clottiness

CEILNOSTUV	consultive
CEILNOSUVV	convulsive
CEILNPRSSY	princessly
CEILOORTTT	troctolite
CEILOPRSUU	periculous
CEILOPRSUY	preciously
CEILOPSSUY	speciously
CEILORRTUY	courtierly
CEILORSSST	cloistress
CEIMMMNOTT	commitment
CEIMMNOORT	metronomic
CEIMMNOQUU	communique
	communiqué
CEIMMNORTY	metronymic
CEIMMOOPRS	compromise
CEIMMOPSTU	miscompute
CEIMMORRTY	micrometry
CEIMMORSSU	commissure
CEIMMORTUX	commixture
CEIMNNOPRY	prominency
CEIMNNOSTT	miscontent
CEIMNOOOSU	monoecious
CEIMNOOPRT	pome-citron
CEIMNOOPSS	meconopsis
CEIMNOORTY	iconometry
CEIMNOPRSU	proscenium
CEIMNORSST	misconster
CEIMNORSUU	ceruminous
CEIMNPRSSS	scrimpness
CEIMNRSSTY	syncretism
CEIMOOPRRS	microspore
CEIMOOPRSY	myrioscope
CEIMOOPRTT	competitor
CEIMOORSTU	eco-tourism
CEIMOORSTY	sociometry
CEIMOPRRTY	pyrometric
CEIMORSTVY	viscometry
CEINNNOOSS	consension
CEINNNOOTT	contention
CEINNNOOTV	convention
CEINNOORSV	conversion
CEINNOORTT	cornettino
CEINNOOSTY	non-society
CEINNOPRTY	encryption
CEINNOPTUX	expunction
CEINNOSSTT	consistent
CEINOOPRRT	correption
	porrection
CEINOOPRSS	procession
CEINOOPRTT	protection
CEINOOPRTV	provection
CEINOOPSTT	stenotopic
CEINOORSSU	censorious
CEINOORTTV	contortive
CEINOORTUX	neurotoxic
CEINOOSSUY	synoecious
CEINOPRSSU	croupiness
	percussion
	supersonic
CEINOPRSTT	introspect
CEINOPRSTU	supertonic
CEINOQRRTU	quercitron
CEINORRSST	intercross
CEINORSSUX	excursions
CEINORSTTT	cornettist
CEINORSTUV	ventricous
CEINOSSTUU	incestuous
CEINOSTTTU	constitute
CEINRSSSTT	strictness
CEINRSSSTU	crustiness
CEINRSSSUV	scurviness
CEINRSSTTY	syncretist
CEIOOPRRST	proctorise
CEIOOPRRTY	corporeity
CEIOOPRRTZ	proctorize
CEIOOSSTXY	exocytosis
CEIOPPRRTT	protreptic
CEIOPRRTTX	protectrix
CEIOPRRTUV	corruptive
CEIOPRRTWY	copywriter
CEIORRSSSY	rescissory
CEIPPRSTTY	typescript
CEJJKMOPUY	jump-jockey
CEJNOORRTU	contre-jour
CEKLLLSSUY	lucklessly
CEKLMPRSUU	lumpsucker
CEKOOPPRRW	copperwork
CEKOORRSUW	coursework
CEKORRSTUV	overstruck
CELLLNTUUY	luculently
CELLNOORRT	controller
CELLNOORSU	counsellor
CELLOOOSST	close-stool
CELLOORRSY	Rolls-Royce®
CELLOORSSU	colourless
CELLORSUUY	ulcerously
CELMMOPTUY	lumpectomy
CELMNNOOSY	somnolency
CELMNOOOOT	melocotoon
CELMOOPRTY	completory
CELMOORSTY	sclerotomy
CELMOORTUY	coulometry
CELNOPRSUU	pronucleus
CELNOPSTYY	pycnostyle
CELOOOPRSU	procoelous
CELOOORRSU	rose-colour
CELOOORRUV	overcolour
CELOOPRRTU	colporteur
CELOORTUUZ	zooculture
CELOOSSSSU	colossuses
CELOOSTUVY	covetously
CELPRSSSTU	sculptress
CEMMNNOOSS	commonness
CEMNOOORSU	monocerous
CEMOOPPRRW	copperworm
CEMOOPRRSS	compressor
CEMOOPRSTU	composture
CENNNNOOTT	non-content
CENNNORRTU	non-current
CENNOOPRRU	pronouncer
CENOOOPRUZ	zero-coupon
CENOOPPRSY	pycnospore
CENOORRTTV	controvert
CENOORSSST	cross-stone

CENOORSTTY	Notoryctes
CENOPRSTUY	counterspy
CEOOPPRRST	prospector
CEOOPRRSTU	prosecutor
CEOOPRRTTY	protectory
CEOPPRSSTU	prospectus
CEOPRRRSUY	percursory
	precursory
CEPPRRSTUU	upper-crust
CFFFIISSTU	fisticuffs
CFFGIIIORR	frigorific
CFFGIIKNOT	ticking-off
CFFGILNOOO	cooling-off
CFFGILNOSY	scoffingly
CFGHIILLNY	filchingly
CFGIIKLNOR	frolicking
CFGIIKNOSS	fossicking
CFGIIMNNOR	confirming
CFGIINNORU	Finno-Ugric
	Ugro-Finnic
CFGIINNOSY	consignify
CFGIINOPRT	forcing-pit
CFGIINOSTY	Scotifying
CFGILOSUUU	lucifugous
CFHIMOPRSY	scyphiform
CFHKOOOPRS	shock-proof
CFHLLOOORT	floorcloth
CFHLMOOORR	chloroform
CFHOORRSTU	fourscorth
CFIIILNNOT	infliction
CFIIIMNORS	incisiform
CFIIINOSTT	fictionist
CFIIIOSTTU	fictitious
CFIILMOOSU	fimicolous
CFIILNOPRU	unprolific
CFIILORSST	floristics
CFIIMORRST	cristiform
CFIINNNOOT	non-fiction
CFIIOOPRRT	torporific
CFIIRSTTUU	futuristic
CFILMMORUU	cumuliform
CFILMOOPRU	poculiform
CFILMOORTY	cotyliform
CFILMORRTU	cultriform
CFILNOSTUU	fonticulus
CFIMNOORST	conformist
CFIMNOORTY	conformity
CFLLNORSUY	scornfully
CFLLOOSSUU	flosculous
CFLOOORRUU	four-colour
CFLOORSSUU	scrofulous
CGGHINNOTU	hunting-cog
CGGHINOOPY	hypnogogic
CGGIIKNPSU	sucking-pig
CGGIILNNRY	cringingly
CGGINNORSU	scrounging
CGHHILORTT	torchlight
CGHHINRRTU	night-churr
CGHIIIOSTV	Visigothic
CGHIIKLNOP	holing-pick
CGHIIKNPSY	physicking
CGHIIKNSTT	nightstick
CGHIILLOOP	philologic
CGHIILLOOT	lithologic
CGHIILMORT	microlight
CGHIILNNPY	pinchingly
CGHIILNTWY	witchingly
CGHIILOOOP	ophiologic
CGHIILOOST	histologic
CGHIILOPST	phlogistic
CGHIILPRTY	triglyphic
CGHIKLNOSY	shockingly
CGHIKNORTW	thick-grown
CGHILLOORS	schoolgirl
CGHILMOOTY	mythologic
CGHILNOTUY	touchingly
CGHILNRSUY	crushingly
CGHILOORTY	trichology
CGHILOOSTY	stichology
CGHILORSST	crosslight
CGHIMNOORY	chirognomy
CGHINOOSYZ	schizogony
CGHLNOOORY	chronology
CGHLOOPSYY	psychology
CGHNOOPSYY	psychogony
CGIIIJNOST	jingoistic
CGIIIKNNPT	nit-picking
CGIIILNNTY	incitingly
CGIIILNOST	soliciting
CGIIILNSTU	linguistic
CGIIILPSTU	pugilistic
CGIIKLLNOR	rollicking
CGIILMNOOV	moving-coil
CGIILOOSTT	isoglottic
CGIIMMNOTT	committing
CGIIMNOSST	Gnosticism
CGIIMNSSUW	swing-music
CGIINNNOTU	unnoticing
CGIINNOOST	incognitos
CGIINOTTUY	contiguity
CGIKLLNOOR	rollocking
CGIKLNNOTU	locking-nut
CGIKLNOOPR	porlocking
CGIKNOSSTW	swing-stock
CGILLNOSWY	scowlingly
CGILLOSSYY	glycolysis
CGILMOOSTY	mycologist
CGILMOOSUY	musicology
CGILNNOSTU	consulting
CGILNOOOST	nostologic
	oncologist
CGILOOOPRT	tropologic
CGILOOOTXY	toxicology
CGILOOSTTY	cytologist
CGIMNRRRUU	curmurring
CGINOOPRST	prognostic
CGINOOSTUU	contiguous
CGINOPPTYY	copy-typing
CGLOOOPRTY	proctology
CGLOOORTYY	oryctology
CGLOOPRTYY	cryptology
CGNOOOSTUY	octogynous
CHHIIKPSTY	phthisicky
CHHIIOSSTY	ichthyosis

CHHIIPSTTW	whip-stitch
CHHILLRSUY	churlishly
CHHILMOOPR	chromophil
CHHILOOPTY	holophytic
CHHILORSTW	shritch-owl
CHHIMNOOOP	homophonic
CHHIOOPPRS	phosphoric
CHHLLOOPRY	chlorophyl
CHHMMOOORY	homochromy
CHIIIILNST	nihilistic
CHIIILOOPT	ophiolitic
CHIIILPSTY	syphilitic
CHIIINORST	histrionic
CHIIINORTT	trithionic
CHIIIPPRTU	hippuritic
CHIIKLLSTY	ticklishly
CHIIKLRSTY	trickishly
CHIILMNOOT	monolithic
CHIILMOOTT	lithotomic
CHIILNOOPT	phonolitic
CHIILNORTY	chlorinity
CHIILOSTTY	histolytic
CHIIMOOPRS	isomorphic
CHIIMOPRRT	trimorphic
CHIIMORRST	trichroism
CHIIMORSST	ostrichism
CHIIMORSTU	humoristic
CHIINNOPPT	pinchpoint
CHIINNOPSU	pin-cushion
CHIINOPRSX	crio-sphinx
CHIINOPSSU	cousinship
CHIINORSTU	trichinous
	unhistoric
CHIIORSSSU	rhoicissus
CHIIOSSSVY	vichyssois
CHIIPRRSTY	pyrrhicist
CHIIRRSTUU	Trichiurus
CHIKKLLSTU	thick-skull
CHIKNOQRTU	quickthorn
CHIKORSTTW	stitchwork
	throw-stick
CHILLNOSWY	clownishly
CHILLOPSTY	splotchily
CHILNOOPPY	polyphonic
CHILNOOPXY	xylophonic
CHILNOOQRU	chloroquin
CHILNOPSSU	consulship
CHILOOPPSY	policy-shop
CHILOOPTTY	photolytic
CHIMMNOORS	monorchism
CHIMNNOOOP	monophonic
CHIMNOORSU	Chironomus
CHIMNRSSTY	strychnism
CHIMOOOPRS	sophomoric
CHIMOOOPRZ	zoomorphic
CHIMOOPRSY	hypocorism
CHIMOORTTY	trichotomy
CHINOOORTT	orthotonic
CHINOOPPTY	phonotypic
CHINOOPRSY	rhinoscopy
CHIOOOPRTT	orthotopic
CHIOOOPRTZ	zootrophic
CHIOOPPRRY	pyrophoric
CHIOOPPTTY	phototypic
CHIOOPRSTT	orthoptics
CHIOOPTTXY	phytotoxic
CHIORSTTTW	stitchwort
CHKLOOORSW	schoolwork
CHLMMMOTUY	mummy-cloth
CHLMNOSUUU	homunculus
CHLMOOOORS	schoolroom
CHLMOOPRYY	polychromy
CHMMNOOORY	monochromy
CHMNOOPTTU	mutton-chop
CHMOOPPPSY	psychopomp
CHNNOOORRT	chronotron
CHNOOORRTT	trochotron
CHOOOORSUZ	zoochorous
CHOOPRRSUY	cryophorus
CIIIIKLOPT	poikilitic
CIIIILNNQU	inquilinic
CIIIILNTVY	incivility
CIIILLMPTY	implicitly
CIIILMNRTU	triclinium
CIIILMPSST	simplistic
CIIILMPSTY	simplicity
CIIILNOSTT	tonsilitic
CIIILPRTTY	triplicity
CIIIMNNOST	nicotinism
CIIIMNORTU	tirocinium
CIIIMNPPRU	principium
CIIIMOPSTT	optimistic
CIIINNNOTT	intinction
CIIJNNNOTU	injunction
CIIKKNNOPT	knickpoint
CIIKMORRST	microskirt
CIILLMOOSU	limicolous
CIILLNOOPS	cipollinos
CIILLNOOTU	illocution
CIILLOSTTY	stylolitic
CIILMMNTUU	nummulitic
CIILMOOPRS	micropolis
CIILNOPSTU	punctilios
CIILNOSSYZ	zincolysis
CIILOOSSTU	solicitous
CIILOOSTUV	viticolous
CIILOPRTVY	proclivity
CIILRRSTUY	scurrility
CIILSSSTTY	stylistics
CIIMMNOOSS	commission
CIIMMNOOTX	commixtion
CIIMMOPRRS	microprism
CIIMNNOOTZ	monzonitic
CIIMNOPRRT	microprint
CIIMORRSTT	tricrotism
CIINNNOOPT	conniption
CIINNOORTT	contrition
CIINNOTTUY	continuity
CIINOOPRTX	picrotoxin
CIINOPRRST	corn-spirit
CIINOSSSTY	cystinosis
CIIOORSTUV	victorious
CIIOPRSTTU	prosciutti
CIIOPSSSUU	suspicious

CIIPSTTTYY stypticity
CIJKNOOSTT joint-stock
CIJLNNOOTY conjointly
CIKLLOSSTT stock-still
CIKMNOOPPU nickumpoop
CIKORRSTUW rustic-work
CILLMNOOTT cotton-mill
CILLMOOQUU colloquium
CILLMORSUY collyriums
CILLOOQSTU colloquist
CILLOPRSTU portcullis
CILLOSSUUY lusciously
CILMMOPUUV compluvium
CILMNOOOOT locomotion
CILMNOOPSU compulsion
CILMNOOPYY polyonymic
CILMNORUUV involucrum
CILMNOSTUU monticulus
CILNNOOSUV convulsion
CILOOPRSSY corylopsis
CILOOPRSUU rupicolous
CILORRSSUU scurrilous
CIMNNOOOPP nincompoop
CIMNNOSTUU continuums
CIMNOOORXY oxymoronic
CIMNOOPRSU compursion
CIMNOOPSTY toponymics
CIMNOORSST consortism
CIMNOORSTU consortium
CIMOOOPRST compositor
CINNOOORTT contortion
CINNOOPRSU pronuncios
CINNOOSTUU continuous
CINOOOPRST nootropics
CINOOOPRSY oniroscopy
CINOOPRRTU corruption
CINOOPRSUY urinoscopy
CINOORSSTY consistory
CINOORSUUV nucivorous
CINORRSTTU instructor
CINORSSTUU scrutinous
CINOSTTUUY unctuosity
CIOOPRSSTU uroscopist
CIOOPRSTTU prosciutto
CIOORRSTTU tricrotous
CIOPPRRSSY procrypsis
CIOPPRSSTT PostScript®
postscript
CKKNORSTUW knockwurst
CKLLOORRSW scrollwork
CKMNOORSTU moonstruck
CLLMOOPRUU plum-colour
CLLMOOSSUU molluscous
CLMMNNOOUY uncommonly
CLMNOOOSUU monoculous
CLMOOOORTU oculomotor
CLMOOOORTY locomotory
CLMOOPRSUY compulsory
CLNOOOPTTY polycotton
CLNOORSTUY consultory
CLNOORTUWY low-country
CLNOSTUUUY unctuously
CLOOOPPSTY coppy-stool
CLOOOPRRTU prolocutor
CLOOOPSTUY polytocous
CLOOORSSTU colostrous
CLOOPPRSUU colour-supp
CLOOSTTTUY cutty-stool
CLOPRSSUUU scrupulous
CMNOOOOSTU monotocous
CMNOOORTTW cotton-worm
CMOOPPPRTY prompt-copy
CMOOSSTTYY cystostomy
COOOPPRRRT proproctor
COOORSSTTU costus-root

D

DDDDDFUUYY fuddy-duddy
DDDDDHOOYY hoddy-doddy
DDDEEEFNNU undefended
DDDEEFIOST △eisteddfod
DDDEEINOSW disendowed
DDDEEINPRS dispredden
DDDEEIORRS disordered
DDDEFILOOW fiddlewood
DDDEGIIOOR didgeridoo
DDDOORWWYY rowdy-dowdy
DDEEEEELTW △tweedledee
DDEEEEMNRU unredeemed
DDEEEFGLNW new-fledged
DDEEEFIMNR free-minded
DDEEEHIRST three-sided
DDEEEHLNUY unheededly
DDEEEIMNNV even-minded
DDEEEIMNPT pedimented
DDEEEIMNRT determined
DDEEEIMNRU unremedied
DDEEEINNTX inextended
DDEEEIRSSV dissevered
DDEEELMMOS meddlesome
DDEEELMNTY dementedly
DDEEELMTUW Tweedledum
DDEEELNTXY extendedly
DDEEELRSVY deservedly
DDEEENNRRU unrendered
DDEEENNRTU untendered
DDEEENNTUX unextended
DDEEENRRTU undeterred
DDEEENRSUV undeserved
DDEEENRSUX undersexed
DDEEEOOPRT deep-rooted
DDEEFFLNOY offendedly
DDEEFFNNOU unoffended
DDEEFGIRRU red-figured
DDEEFHIRST redshifted
DDEEFIIINT identified
DDEEFIILLN ill-defined
DDEEFIILMR midfielder
DDEEFIINSY Disneyfied
DDEEFIINTU definitude
DDEEFINNRU unfriended
DDEEFLMORY deformedly
DDEEGGHOOP hodgepodge
DDEEGGNNUU nudge-nudge

DDEEGGNOSS doggedness
DDEEGHNORY hodden-grey
DDEEGIINST indigested
DDEEGILNSY designedly
DDEEGILSTY digestedly
DDEEGINNSU undesigned
DDEEGINSTU undigested
DDEEGJLLUW well-judged
DDEEHIILNP didelphine
DDEEHILNSU unshielded
DDEEHINNRU unhindered
DDEEHINNSS hiddenness
DDEEHLORSU shouldered
DDEEHNRTUY ythundered
DDEEIIKLLR riddle-like
DDEEIIKLMN like-minded
DDEEIILMNV evil-minded
DDEEIIMNOT demi-ditone
DDEEIIMOPR epidermoid
DDEEIIMRSU desiderium
DDEEIINRSW sidewinder
DDEEIIOPST epidotised
DDEEIIOPTZ epidotized
DDEEIIORSX deoxidiser
DDEEIIORXZ deoxidizer
DDEEIKMORS smoke-dried
DDEEILLMNW well-minded
DDEEILLNRT tendrilled
DDEEILNNTY intendedly
DDEEILNOSY one-sidedly
DDEEILSTTU lust-dieted
DDEEIMMOPR demirepdom
DDEEIMNNOP open-minded
DDEEIMNNRU underminde
DDEEIMNORS endodermis
DDEEIMNPRU epidendrum
DDEEIMNRTU undertimed
DDEEINNNTU unintended
DDEEINOOPT endopodite
DDEEINOPRS perdendosi
DDEEINORRV overridden
DDEEINPRUV undeprived
DDEEINRRUV underdrive
DDEEINRRUW underwired
DDEEINRSUZ undersized
DDEEINRTUV undiverted
DDEEINSTUV undivested
DDEEIOORRS deodoriser
DDEEIOORRZ deodorizer
DDEEIRSSST distressed
DDEELLOORW olde-worlde
DDEELNOPRU undeplored
DDEELRRSSU rudderless
DDEENNOPST despondent
DDEENNORTU undernoted
undertoned
DDEENNOSSS soddenness
DDEENNPRSU underspend
DDEENNSSSU suddenness
DDEENOPPST end-stopped
DDEENOPRUW unpowdered
DDEENRRSSU underdress
DDEEOORRSW o'er-drowsed
DDEFFILSUY diffusedly
DDEFGIIIIR rigidified
DDEFHIIMUY dehumidify
DDEFHIRRSU rudder-fish
DDEFHLNORU fund-holder
DDEFIIILOS solidified
DDEFIIMNOU unmodified
DDEFIIORSX dorsifixed
DDEFILLNOU ill-founded
DDEFILNNSU nun's-fiddle
DDEFIMNORR dendriform
DDEFINORRW word-finder
DDEFKNNRUU dunderfunk
DDEFMNORUU dumfounder
DDEGGGILOR gold-digger
DDEGHHIIMN high-minded
DDEGHINRSU shuddering
DDEGHMNOUU humdudgeon
DDEGHNORTU thunder-god
DDEGIILNNR nidderling
DDEGIILNRY deridingly
DDEGIINPPU pudding-pie
DDEGILNNOW long-winded
DDEGILNUUV undivulged
DDEGILOORS dog-soldier
DDEGINNOPS desponding
DDEGINNORU redounding
DDEGLLNOUU loud-lunged
DDEGLNOORY dendrology
DDEGLNORUY groundedly
DDEGNNORUU ungrounded
DDEGNOORUV ground-dove
DDEGOORSSS dress-goods
DDEHHNOOOY hoydenhood
DDEHIIIMNS diminished
DDEHIILNOP delphinoid
DDEHIILNSW windshield
DDEHIILPSU disulphide
DDEHILOPSU didelphous
DDEHIMNOST hiddenmost
DDEHINOPRS dendrophis
DDEHINOSSS shoddiness
DDEHIOOOPT photodiode
DDEIIIKKNW kiddiewink
DDEIIIMPSY epididymis
DDEIIIPRST dispirited
DDEIIJNOST disjointed
DDEIIKNRRV drink-drive
DDEIIMNNOU diminuendo
DDEIINOPSS indisposed
DDEIINOSTU duodenitis
DDEIINOSUX unoxidised
DDEIINOUVZ zidovudine
DDEIINOUXZ unoxidized
DDEIIOPRSS dispersoid
DDEIIOPRSV disprovide
DDEIKNNRUW wunderkind
DDEILLNPSY splendidly
DDEILLTTUW dull-witted
DDEILMMOST middlemost
DDEILOPSSY disposedly

DDEILORRSY	disorderly
DDEIMMOSSU	desmodiums
DDEIMNOORR	room-ridden
DDEINOORRW	iron-worded
DDEINOPRUV	unprovided
DDEINOPSSU	undisposed
DDEINOPSUW	upside-down
DDEINORSSS	sordidness
DDEINPSTUU	undisputed
DDEJRRRUUY	jury-rudder
DDEKLNOOOW	downlooked
DDELNORRUW	underworld
DDENNOORSU	round-nosed
DDENNORTUW	downturned
DDENOORSTU	understood
DDENRSTUUY	understudy
DDGGILNRUY	drudgingly
DDGGOOOOYY	goody-goody
DDGHIINOOR	riding-hood
DDGHIIRRYY	hirdy-girdy
DDGHILNTUY	thuddingly
DDGHLNOORU	ground-hold
DDGHRRUUYY	hurdy-gurdy
DDGIILLNRY	riddlingly
DDGIINNPSU	spudding-in
DDGIKLNOOO	odd-looking
DDGILLNOPY	ploddingly
DDHIIMSSY	Yiddishism
DDHIIINORU	hirudinoid
DDHINOOPTY	diphyodont
DDHOOOOUWY	how-do-you-do
DDIIIMNUUV	individuum
DDIIKLNTWY	tiddlywink
DDINNOOOTT	notodontid
DDINOOOPRT	diprotodon
DDOOOOORRT	door-to-door
DEEEEEFPRZ	deep-freeze
DEEEEENSWZ	sneezeweed
DEEEEFFLRS	self-feeder
DEEEEFLRSS	self-seeder
DEEEEFNRST	enfestered
DEEEEFNRTT	tenderfeet
DEEEEGNNRR	engenderer
DEEEEHLLLW	well-heeled
DEEEEHPRST	three-speed
DEEEELLSSW	weeldlesse
DEEEELMRSS	redeemless
DEEEELNORW	ne'er-do-weel
DEEEELSSSV	seed-vessel
DEEEEOPRRS	pedereroes
DEEEFFOORR	free-fooder
DEEEFFOORT	free-footed
DEEEFGILNR	greenfield
DEEEFHILNS	needlefish
DEEEFHILWX	fixed-wheel
DEEEFHLORR	freeholder
DEEEFHORSW	foreshewed
DEEEFILLSX	self-exiled
DEEEFILMNT	defilement
DEEEFIMNNT	definement
DEEEFLORRW	deflowerer
DEEEFMNORW	freedwomen
DEEEFMNRRU	referendum
DEEEFNRTTU	unfettered
DEEEFORRST	deer-forest
DEEEGGGLOY	goggle-eyed
DEEEGHHHIL	high-heeled
DEEEGHISUY	hey-de-guise
DEEEGHSUYY	hey-de-guyes
DEEEGIKNNW	weekending
DEEEGILLNR	ledger-line
DEEEGILMTY	gimlet-eyed
DEEEGILNSY	single-eyed
DEEEGIMORT	Geodimeter®
DEEEGINRSS	greediness
DEEEGIRRST	deregister
	registered
DEEEGIRSSV	degressive
DEEEGLLOPR	poll-degree
DEEEGLNORV	glendoveer
DEEEGLNRSS	genderless
DEEEGLORRS	gelder-rose
DEEEGNNRRU	engendrure
DEEEGNNRUV	unrevenged
DEEEGNORSU	degenerous
DEEEGORRVY	overgreedy
DEEEHILOTT	△diothelete
DEEEHILPRT	three-piled
DEEEHIMNRT	Methedrine®
DEEEHINORT	deinothere
DEEEHIPRSS	Hesperides
DEEEHJNTUZ	Judenhetze
DEEEHLLSSY	heedlessly
DEEEHLLTWW	well-thewed
DEEEHLMNTU	unhelmeted
DEEEHLNORS	lederhosen
DEEEHLOTTY	△dyothelete
DEEEHLOTWW	two-wheeled
DEEEHLPRSU	spur-heeled
DEEEHNORTY	heterodyne
DEEEHNRRTU	thereunder
DEEEHNRRUW	whereunder
DEEEHNRTTU	untethered
DEEEIIMNPR	meperidine
DEEEIIPTVX	expeditive
DEEEIKLLRW	weedkiller
DEEEIKNPRS	deep-sinker
DEEEILLMOS	demoiselle
DEEEILLMST	millet-seed
DEEEILMRSS	remediless
DEEEILNRSS	slenderise
DEEEILNRSZ	slenderize
DEEEILNRUV	unrelieved
DEEEILPTXY	expeditely
DEEEILRRVY	redelivery
DEEEILRSSS	desireless
DEEEILRSVW	silverweed
DEEEIMNOST	demonetise
DEEEIMNOTZ	demonetize
DEEEIMNRRT	determiner
DEEEIMNRST	densimeter
DEEEIMORTU	eudiometer
DEEEIMPRTV	redemptive
DEEEIMRSTV	time-served

DEEEINNPTV pendentive
DEEEINORST désorienté
DEEEINPRST predestine
DEEEINPSSS speediness
DEEEINRRST residenter
tenderiser
DEEEINRRTZ tenderizer
DEEEINRSTT interested
DEEEINSSTW tweediness
DEEEIORRTU étourderie
DEEEIPRSSV depressive
DEEEIRRSSV redressive
DEEEIRSSTT sidestreet
DEEEIRSTWX dexterwise
DEEEKLLSYY skelly-eyed
DEEEKLNORW needlework
DEEEKOOPRR door-keeper
DEEELLNORW ne'er-do-well
DEEELLNPRU unrepelled
DEEELLNSSY needlessly
DEEELLOWWY yellow-weed
DEEELNRTTU unlettered
DEEELOPPRV predevelop
DEEELOPPTT pottle-deep
DEEELRRSVY reservedly
reversedly
DEEELRSSST desertless
DEEEMNNOTT denotement
DEEEMNNOTU denouement
dénouement
DEEEMNOTTV devotement
DEEEMNPRTU untempered
DEEEMNRSSU demureness
DEEEMNSTTV vestmented
DEEENNPRTT pretendent
DEEENNPRTU unrepented
DEEENNRRUV unreverend
DEEENNRSST tenderness
DEEENNRSSU enuredness
undersense
DEEENNRSTU unresented
DEEENOOSWZ sneezewood
DEEENOPTTT tête-de-pont
DEEENPPPRU unpeppered
DEEENPRSSU superdense
DEEENPSSTT pettedness
DEEENRRSTU understeer
DEEENRRSUV undeserver
unreserved
unreversed
DEEENRRTUV unreverted
DEEEOPSTTY eye-spotted
DEEEORRRRT reredorter
DEEEORSSTY seed-oyster
DEEEPPRSSU superspeed
DEEEPRRSSU superseder
DEEFFLOOTT left-footed
DEEFFNORSS offendress
DEEFGGILLN fledgeling
DEEFGGLORU four-legged
DEEFGHINRT frightened
DEEFGIINRV free-diving
DEEFGINNRS finger's-end
DEEFGINSST giftedness
DEEFGLNNOS dog's-fennel
DEEFHMORRS fresherdom
DEEFHOORSW foreshowed
DEEFIIINNT indefinite
DEEFIIINRT identifier
DEEFIIINTV definitive
DEEFIIIRVV revivified
DEEFIILLST stellified
DEEFIILNRS friendlies
DEEFIILNTY definitely
DEEFIINRUV unverified
DEEFIINRVW viewfinder
DEEFIKLLLS self-killed
DEEFILLLSW self-willed
DEEFILLNTU unfilleted
DEEFILLRSU fleur-de-lis
DEEFILMMSU misdeemful
DEEFILMOSU fieldmouse
DEEFILNOST fieldstone
DEEFILNRSS friendless
DEEFILNRSV self-driven
DEEFILNRTU unfiltered
DEEFILOPSS self-poised
DEEFILORTU outfielder
DEEFILPPTT felt-tipped
DEEFILPSTU despiteful
DEEFINOSST foetidness
DEEFINRSSV fervidness
DEEFKNORSS forkedness
DEEFLLLORS self-rolled
DEEFLLMORW well-formed
DEEFLLNOUW unfellowed
DEEFLLOTVW twelvefold
DEEFLLPSUY speedfully
DEEFLLRSUY fleur-de-lys
DEEFLLSSTY self-styled
DEEFLMNNOT enfoldment
DEEFLMRRSU self-murder
DEEFLOORVW overflowed
DEEFMNNRTU refundment
DEEFMNORRU unreformed
DEEFMNPRUU unperfumed
DEEFNNOSTU unsoftened
DEEFNOORTT tenderfoot
DEEFNORSTU unforested
unfostered
DEEFOOQRTU fore-quoted
DEEFOORSTU surefooted
DEEFORRUWW furrow-weed
DEEGGGLLNO long-legged
DEEGGHNRTU thunder-egg
DEEGGIIPRW periwigged
DEEGGINRSS dregginess
DEEGGNRSSU ruggedness
DEEGHHNORT thornhedge
DEEGHINOUY honey-guide
DEEGHINSTT night-steed
DEEGHINSTU Gesundheit
DEEGHLNOOT gentlehood
DEEGHNRRUY yerd-hunger

DEEGIIINNS	indigenise
DEEGIIINNZ	indigenize
DEEGIILPRV	privileged
DEEGIIMMNS	misdeeming
DEEGIINNRT	ingredient
DEEGIINSTU	distinguée
DEEGIIRSSV	digressive
DEEGILNNRT	tenderling
DEEGILNOPV	developing
DEEGILNRSY	resignedly
DEEGILNSSS	designless
DEEGILRSST	stridelegs
DEEGIMNNST	designment
DEEGINOOPT	pigeon-toed
DEEGINORSS	degression
DEEGINOTTU	tongue-tied
DEEGINPRSS	depressing
DEEGINRTTW	dew-retting
DEEGNNOOSU	endogenous
DEEGNNORUV	ungoverned
DEEGNORRUV	undergrove
DEEGORRTXY	dextrogyre
DEEHHIIRST	hitherside
DEEHHIMNOR	hemihedron
DEEHHRRSTU	reed-thrush
DEEHIIKLLS	shieldlike
DEEHIIRSTT	hereditist
DEEHILLRSV	shrivelled
DEEHILLSSS	shieldless
DEEHILLSWW	well-wished
DEEHILMORS	demolisher
DEEHILNRSU	unrelished
DEEHILOOTT	theodolite
DEEHILORTV	hot-livered
DEEHILOTTY	△dyothelite
DEEHINOOPV	videophone
DEEHINPRSU	unperished
DEEHINRTUW	unwithered
DEEHIOPPRS	prophesied
DEEHIORRRS	horse-rider
DEEHIORSTV	Shrovetide
DEEHIRRTTU	redruthite
DEEHKNOOSS	hookedness
DEEHLLMOPR	phelloderm
DEEHLLOOWY	hollow-eyed
DEEHLMNRUW	underwhelm
DEEHLNOSUU	unhouseled
DEEHLOPRTY	type-holder
DEEHLPPRUU	purple-hued
DEEHMORRTY	hydrometer
DEEHNOORTT	heterodont
DEEHNOPRTU	three-pound
DEEHNORSUW	unshowered
DEEHNRSSSW	shrewdness
DEEHOORSUW	dower-house
DEEHOORTXY	heterodoxy
DEEIIIMNSV	semi-divine
DEEIIIMPTV	impeditive
DEEIIINPPR	piperidine
DEEIIIOPRT	epidiorite
DEEIIKLNRT	tinder-like
DEEIIKLPRS	spiderlike
DEEIILLMPR	imperilled
DEEIILLNOS	linseed-oil
DEEIILLOPT	lepidolite
DEEIILMNVW	vine-mildew
DEEIILMSTX	sex-limited
DEEIILNNVY	vinylidene
DEEIILNSST	distensile
DEEIILNSSW	wieldiness
DEEIILNSTT	disentitle
DEEIILORST	siderolite
DEEIILPRRV	pile-driver
DEEIILRSSV	silverside
DEEIILRSVY	derisively
DEEIIMMNPT	impediment
DEEIIMNNRT	dinner-time
DEEIIMNNTT	inditement
DEEIINNRTT	Tridentine
DEEIINNSSV	divineness
DEEIINNSTW	disentwine
DEEIINOPTX	expedition
DEEIINPTTU	ineptitude
DEEIINQSTU	disquieten
DEEIINQTUU	inquietude
DEEIINRSSV	divineress
DEEIINRTTW	wintertide
DEEIINSSST	sensitised
DEEIINSSSY	syneidesis
DEEIINSSTV	distensive
DEEIINSSTZ	sensitized
DEEIIOPRSX	peroxidise
DEEIIOPRTT	peridotite
DEEIIOPRXZ	peroxidize
DEEIIOPSTV	depositive
DEEIIPRSSV	dispersive
DEEIIPRSSW	sideswiper
DEEIJMNOSW	jimson-weed
DEEIJNORRU	rejoindure
DEEIKKNPRU	dukkeripen
DEEIKLNORT	rodent-like
DEEIKLOPRU	dike-louper
DEEIKORSST	sidestroke
DEEILLMPSS	misspelled
DEEILLSUVY	delusively
DEEILMMNPT	dimplement
DEEILMNRTW	wilderment
DEEILMOPRY	polymeride
DEEILNNNRU	underlinen
DEEILNNORT	tenderloin
DEEILNNQTU	delinquent
DEEILNNRSS	dinnerless
DEEILNNSTU	unlistened
DEEILNNTTU	unentitled
DEEILNOPSV	disenvelop
DEEILNORSU	sourdeline
DEEILNPTTU	plentitude
DEEILNRSSW	wilderness
DEEILNRSUU	unleisured
DEEILNRTVY	invertedly
DEEILNSSTU	diluteness
DEEILOPPRS	rose-lipped
DEEILOPPRT	dopplerite
DEEILORSSV	redissolve

DEEILOSTTT	stilettoed
DEEILRRSSV	driverless
DEEIMMMRTU	medium-term
DEEIMMNOSU	eudemonism
DEEIMMRSTU	summertide
DEEIMNNNTT	intendment
DEEIMNNRRU	underminer
DEEIMNNRTU	underntime
DEEIMNNRUV	menu-driven
DEEIMNOOPS	empoisoned
DEEIMNOPRT	redemption
DEEIMNOPTT	idempotent
DEEIMNORRS	moderniser
DEEIMNORRZ	modernizer
DEEIMNRSTW	Midwestern
	stemwinder
DEEIMNRSTY	densimetry
DEEIMNRTTU	unremitted
DEEIMNSTTV	divestment
DEEIMOOSTU	tediousome
DEEIMOPRRY	pyromeride
DEEINNNOSU	innuendoes
DEEINNOPRS	prednisone
DEEINNORRW	irrenowned
DEEINNRSST	trendiness
DEEINNRSSU	inuredness
DEEINNRSTU	indentures
DEEINNSSTU	unitedness
DEEINNSTUV	uninvested
DEEINOPRSS	depression
DEEINOPSUW	upsideowne
DEEINORRUY	reioyndure
DEEINORSTT	rose-tinted
DEEINPRRST	rinderpest
DEEINPRRSU	underprise
DEEINPRRUZ	underprize
DEEINPRSTU	unrespited
DEEINPRSTY	predestiny
DEEINQRRUU	unrequired
DEEINQRTUU	unrequited
DEEINQSTUY	squint-eyed
DEEINRRTUW	underwrite
DEEINRSSSY	synderesis
DEEINRSSTU	unresisted
	unsistered
DEEINSSTTU	testudines
DEEIOPPRRT	propertied
DEEIOPPRSS	predispose
DEEIOPPRSW	Piepowders
DEEIOPRSUX	superoxide
DEEIOPSSSU	disespouse
DEEIOPSSTU	despiteous
DEEIORRSTV	overstride
DEEIORTTTX	text-editor
DEEIPPRRSU	purse-pride
DEEIPRRTUY	eurypterid
DEEIRRSSST	distresser
DEEJNPRRUU	unperjured
DEEKLMRTTU	kettledrum
DEEKOORRVW	overworked
DEELLMNOUW	unmellowed
DEELLMOOSY	dolesomely
DEELLMPUVY	dumpy-level
DEELLNORTY	redolently
DEELLNRTUW	well-turned
DEELLORSVY	resolvedly
DEELLORTUW	out-dweller
DEELMNOPTY	deployment
DEELMNOPUY	unemployed
DEELMNOSSS	seldomness
DEELMNOSTU	unmolested
DEELNNOOST	selenodont
DEELNNOSSU	unlessoned
DEELNNRTUY	untenderly
DEELNOORRW	one-worlder
DEELNOPRUX	unexplored
DEELNORSUV	unresolved
DEELNOSTUU	edentulous
DEELOORTTW	letter-wood
DEELOOVVYY	lovey-dovey
DEELOPRRTT	drop-letter
DEELOPRRTY	reportedly
DEELOPRSTW	spot-welder
DEELORTTUV	turtledove
DEEMMNRSUU	unsummered
DEEMNNOPRT	ponderment
DEEMNNORSS	modernness
DEEMNNORTW	wonderment
DEEMNNRSTU	sunderment
DEEMNOORRY	money-order
DEEMNOPRTT	deportment
DEEMNORSTU	tremendous
DEEMNORTUV	devourment
DEEMOOPRRT	petrodrome
DEEMOORRST	drosometer
DEEMOPRRTY	redemptory
DEENNNORUW	unrenowned
DEENNOOSSW	woodenness
DEENNOPPRT	propendent
DEENNOPRST	respondent
DEENNOPRTU	ten-pounder
DEENNORSVW	news-vendor
DEENNOSSTW	wontedness
DEENNRRTUU	unreturned
DEENOOPRTT	torpedo-net
DEENOORSST	rootedness
DEENOPRRTU	unreported
DEENOPRRUV	unreproved
DEENOPRRUW	under-power
DEENOQRTUU	underquote
DEENORRSTU	unrestored
DEENORSUVZ	rendezvous
DEENOSSTUV	devoutness
DEENPRSSSU	suspenders
DEENPRUUVY	unpurveyed
DEENRSSSTU	unstressed
DEENRSUUVY	unsurveyed
DEEOOPRRSU	uredospore
DEEOPPRSSU	superposed
DEEOPRRRSU	superorder
DEEOQRSTUU	Tudoresque
DEEPPRRSUU	super-duper
DEEPPRSSSU	suppressed
DEFFGLORTU	truffle-dog

DEFFHIMORS sheriffdom
DEFFINNOST soft-finned
DEFFLNORTY fly-fronted
DEFFOOORTU four-footed
DEFFOOOSTT soft-footed
DEFGGILLRU full-rigged
DEFGHILLTU delightful
DEFGHILNOR fingerhold
DEFGHINRTU unfrighted
DEFGIILNRR girlfriend
DEFGIILNYY edifyingly
DEFGIINNUY unedifying
DEFGIINRSS frigidness
DEFGILLNSU sdeignfull
DEFGILLNUW full-winged
DEFGIMNNPU Empfindung
DEFGINOOTW wing-footed
DEFGLLOOOW goodfellow
DEFGNOORRU foreground
DEFHIIIKSW whiskified
DEFHIIIMRU humidifier
DEFHIILNSY fiendishly
DEFHIINNSU unfinished
DEFHIINPRS friendship
DEFHILORSU flourished
DEFHLOPRSU proud-flesh
DEFHNOOORT horn-footed
DEFHNOOPRU unhoped-for
DEFHORRRTU rutherford
DEFIIILMPS simplified
DEFIIILNTY infidelity
DEFIIINNOT definition
DEFIIINNTU infinitude
DEFIIKLLSU dislikeful
DEFIILLNRY friendlily
DEFIILORSU fluoridise
DEFIILORUZ fluoridize
DEFIILSTTU stultified
DEFIINORST iron-fisted
DEFIINOSSU unossified
DEFIINPRUU unpurified
DEFIIOPRSU perfidious
DEFIIRRRTV river-drift
DEFIKLORSW fieldworks
DEFILLORWW wildfowler
DEFILLPRUY pridefully
DEFILNNRUY unfriendly
DEFILNORSS floridness
DEFILNORWW windflower
DEFILNPTUU unuplifted
DEFILOORSU florideous
DEFILPRSUU superfluid
DEFIMMORSU medusiform
DEFIMNNORU uninformed
DEFINOPRTU unprofited
DEFINRRSUW windsurfer
DEFIOPRSSS disprofess
DEFKLMNOUY flunkeydom
DEFLLMMSUU full-summed
DEFLNOORRU underfloor
DEFLNOORTU unforetold
DEFLNOORVY overfondly
DEFLNOTTWY twentyfold
DEFLOOOPTT polt-footed
DEFLOOOSTW slow-footed
DEFNNORTUU unfortuned
DEFNOOPRRU underproof
DEFNOORSUU founderous
DEFNORRUUW unfurrowed
DEFOOORSTY rosy-footed
DEFOORTTTX foxtrotted
DEGGHIILLR hill-digger
DEGGHIIPRS ship-rigged
DEGGIJRRUY jury-rigged
DEGGILOORS sogdoliger
DEGGINNORU undergoing
DEGGLOOORS sogdologer
DEGGMNOOOR Demogorgon
DEGGNOOSTU dog's-tongue
DEGHHIIKLT high-kilted
DEGHHILOSU high-souled
DEGHIILLNS shieldling
DEGHIILNRT right-lined
DEGHIILTTW twilighted
DEGHIIMOPP pemphigoid
DEGHIINRRT nightrider
DEGHIKNNTU unknighted
DEGHILNNSU unshingled
DEGHILNOOS singlehood
DEGHILNOST Odelsthing
DEGHINNORT dethroning
DEGHINNRTU thundering
DEGHINOSSU doughiness
DEGHINRRUY yird-hunger
DEGHINRSST nightdress
DEGHIORRRU rough-rider
DEGHLNOPUU unploughed
DEGHMOOORT good-mother
DEGHNNRTUU dung-hunter
DEGHNRRUYY yerd-hungry
DEGHPRRSUU drug-pusher
DEGIIIKNNS die-sinking
DEGIIILNOT indigolite
DEGIILLNNW indwelling
DEGIILLNPS dispelling
DEGIILLNRV drivelling
DEGIILLNTY diligently
DEGIILLNYY yieldingly
DEGIILNNTY indigently
DEGIILNNUY unyielding
DEGIILNORS soldiering
DEGIILOOST ideologist
DEGIIMNRSY semi-drying
DEGIINNOSU indigenous
DEGIINNRSU undesiring
DEGIINNSST dissenting
DEGIINORRV overriding
DEGIINORSS digression
DEGIINOSST disgestion
DEGIINPRST springtide
DEGIINPTUU pinguitude
DEGIJLNSTU Jugendstil
DEGIKLMOOR grimlooked
DEGILLOOTY deltiology

DEGILMNRSU mudslinger
DEGILNNNUY unendingly
DEGILNNORU loundering
DEGILNNRUY enduringly
underlying
DEGILNOOSS goodliness
DEGILNRSTU disgruntle
DEGILOOOOZ zoogloeoid
DEGILOOPST pedologist
DEGIMNORTW wrong-timed
DEGIMNSSSU smudginess
DEGINNNORW dinner-gown
DEGINNORST grindstone
stringendo
DEGINNORSU resounding
DEGINNRSSU undressing
DEGINNRSTU unstringed
DEGINOOOPW woodpigeon
DEGINORSSU gourdiness
DEGINORSTY destroying
DEGINOSSST stodginess
DEGINPRSUW spur-winged
DEGINRSSTU turgidness
DEGIOORSST good-sister
DEGKLOOOOR good-looker
DEGLLNORSU groundsell
DEGLMNOOOY demonology
DEGLNNRSUU underslung
DEGLNOOOTY deontology
DEGLNOOTUZ zeuglodont
DEGLNORSSU groundless
DEGLOOPSUY pseudology
DEGLOORTTY troglodyte
DEGLOORTUW towel-gourd
DEGNNOOOTY odontogeny
DEGNNOOPSW sponge-down
DEGNNORRUW undergrown
DEGNNRRRUU drug-runner
DEGNOOOPSW spongewood
DEGNOORRUV overground
DEGOOORSUW woodgrouse
DEHHILNOTW withholden
DEHHILNTUW unwithheld
DEHHILOPRS ship-holder
DEHHILORTW withholder
DEHHIMOORR hemorrhoid
DEHHLNOOOR holohedron
DEHHLORRSU rush-holder
DEHHMOOORT motherhood
DEHHMOOTTU hot-mouthed
DEHHNOOPRY hydrophone
DEHHOPRTYY hydrophyte
DEHIIINRST disinherit
DEHIIKLLOO likelihood
DEHIILLOOV livelihood
DEHIILLSVY devilishly
DEHIILMNPU delphinium
DEHIILMOST △diothelism
DEHIILNNRS hinderlins
DEHIILNPSS displenish
DEHIILNPSY sylphidine
DEHIIMNPRU nephridium
DEHIINOPSY hypnoidise
DEHIINOPYZ hypnoidize
DEHIINORSS disherison
DEHIINRSSW widershins
DEHIIOPRST editorship
DEHIIOPSTY △diophysite
DEHIIORRST disheritor
DEHIKOORSW woodshrike
DEHILMOSTY △dyothelism
DEHILNOPSU unpolished
DEHILNORTU unitholder
DEHILOOPSS shopsoiled
DEHILORSTV short-lived
DEHIMMNORR horn-rimmed
DEHIMMPSSY dysphemism
DEHIMNORST hindermost
DEHIMNOSSS modishness
DEHIMOOPPR hippodrome
DEHIMOPRSY hypodermis
DEHINNPSUU unpunished
DEHINOORRS dishonorer
DEHINOPRTU tripehound
DEHINORRSS horridness
DEHINORSTT threnodist
DEHINOSSTY dishonesty
DEHINRRSTU undershirt
DEHIOOPRST priesthood
DEHIOOQRSU squirehood
DEHIOORSST sisterhood
DEHIOPPRSW worshipped
DEHIOPRRTY pyrethroid
DEHIOPSTYY △dyophysite
DEHIRRSSST dress-shirt
DEHLLOOSSU doll's-house
DEHLNOOPRY polyhedron
DEHLNOUUZZ unhouzzled
DEHLOORRTW otherworld
DEHLORSSSU shroudless
DEHMMNOORY monorhymed
DEHMNOOPRY endomorphy
DEHMNOOSTU unsmoothed
DEHMOORSSY hydrosomes
DEHMORRTYY hydrometry
DEHMORTUWY wry-mouthed
DEHNNOORUU unhonoured
DEHNNORSUU nursehound
DEHNOOOPRS personhood
DEHNOOPRTU horned-pout
DEHNOORRSU horrendous
DEHNOORSTU undershoot
DEHNOORSUU roundhouse
DEHNOORTTU otter-hound
DEHNORSTUU thunderous
DEHOOPRRWY hydropower
DEHOOPRSUU house-proud
DEHOORRRST short-order
DEIIILMQSU semi-liquid
DEIIILMSTU similitude
DEIIILNSST dissilient
DEIIILOPRT ripidolite
DEIIILQRSU liquidiser
DEIIILQRUZ liquidizer

DEIIILSVVY divisively
DEIIIMNORS iridosmine
DEIIIMNPRU △peridinium
DEIIIMNPRY pyrimidine
DEIIIMNTUV diminutive
DEIIIMSSSV dismissive
DEIIINNSTT tendinitis
DEIIINORSV redivision
DEIIJMNORS misjoinder
DEIIKLLNOR kirn-dollie
DEIIKLNNSS kindliness
DEIILLMPTU multiplied
DEIILLNORW iron-willed
DEIILLNUWY unwieldily
DEIILLOPST pistillode
DEIILLOSTV still-video
DEIILLPSUV pulvilised
DEIILLPUVZ pulvilized
DEIILLRSTY distillery
DEIILMNOOT demolition
DEIILMNPSS limpidness
DEIILMNSTT distilment
DEIILMOOST dolomitise
DEIILMOOTZ dolomitize
DEIILNOSVV disinvolve
DEIILNPRTY intrepidly
DEIILNQSSU liquidness
DEIILNSTUU unutilised
DEIILNTUUZ unutilized
DEIILPRSTY spiritedly
DEIILQSTUY disquietly
DEIIMMSSTY midi-system
DEIIMNOPRT diremption
DEIIMOPRSV disimprove
DEIIMPRSSU presidiums
DEIINNOQRU inquirendo
DEIINNORSV disenviron
DEIINNOSSS dissension
DEIINNOSST distension
DEIINNOSTT distention
tendonitis
DEIINNPRSU uninspired
DEIINNSSTU untidiness
DEIINOOPST deposition
positioned
DEIINOPRSS dispersion
DEIINOPRXY pyridoxine
DEIINORTTW iron-witted
DEIINPPRST pin-striped
DEIINPRSTU unspirited
DEIIOPSSTU dispiteous
DEIIORSTTV distortive
DEIIPRSTUV disruptive
DEIIPSSSTU spissitude
DEIJLNOOTW dowel-joint
DEIJNNNOOR non-joinder
DEIKKNNOPS kind-spoken
DEIKLMNOPS mild-spoken
DEIKLNNRUW unwrinkled
DEIKLNSTUY klendusity
DEIKMNNORY drink-money
DEIKNNNORR non-drinker
DEIKNNNSSU unkindness
DEIKNNRSUW swine-drunk
DEIKNRRSTU underskirt
DEIKOPRRSW spiderwork
DEILLMNSSY mindlessly
DEILLNNOTY indolently
DEILLNOPUW unpillowed
DEILLNORSS lordliness
DEILLPRRSS drill-press
DEILMMOSTY immodestly
DEILMNNOSU unsmiled-on
DEILMNOPRU unimplored
DEILMNOSSU mouldiness
DEILMNPTUY impudently
DEILNNOUVV uninvolved
DEILNOOOTT odontolite
DEILNOORWW wool-winder
DEILNOOTUV devolution
DEILNOQRUU unliquored
DEILNOSSST stolidness
DEILNOSSTV dissolvent
DEILNOSSWW windowless
DEILNPPSUU unsupplied
DEILNRSTTY stridently
DEILOOPSSU solipedous
DEILOORRVW wool-driver
DEILOPRSUU preludious
DEILOPSSTY stylopised
DEILOPSTYZ stylopized
DEILORSSUY desirously
DEILPPSSUY supply-side
DEIMMNNTUU indumentum
DEIMMOPSTU impostumed
DEIMNNOSTW disownment
DEIMNOOSSS endosmosis
DEIMNOPRSU unpromised
DEIMNOPRTU minute-drop
DEIMNOPRUV unimproved
DEIMNORSTU unmortised
DEIMNRSSUU unsurmised
DEIMOORRTY odorimetry
DEIMOORTUW moudiewort
DEIMOORTWW mowdiewort
DEIMOPRSSU dispermous
DEIMRSSTTY mistrysted
DEINNNORTU trunnioned
DEINNNOSUW unsinnowed
DEINNNOUWW unwinnowed
DEINNOOPSU unpoisoned
DEINNOPRSU unprisoned
DEINNORTUW interwound
DEINOOPRSS droopiness
DEINOOPRST desorption
DEINOORSWW rose-window
DEINOOSSSU odiousness
DEINOPRSST torpidness
DEINOPSSSU suspensoid
DEINORRSST torridness
DEINORRTTT dirt-rotten
DEINORSSSS drossiness
DEINORSSSW drowsiness
DEINORSSUU undesirous

DEINPPRSTU unstripped
DEINPRSSTU putridness
DEINPSSSTU stupidness
DEINRSSSTU sturdiness
DEIOOPRRTV proveditor
DEIOOPRSTT torpedoist
DEIOOPRSTY depository
DEIOPRRSTW spiderwort
DEIOPSSSSS dispossess
DEIRRSSTTU distruster
DEKKNOORWY donkey-work
DEKLLMNSUU numskulled
DEKMNOPPUY donkey-pump
DEKNOOPRUV unprovoked
DEKNOOPTTT topknotted
DEKNOORRWW wonderwork
DEKNOORSTW downstroke
DEKOOORRWW woodworker
DELLLOPTUY pollutedly
DELLNOPTUU unpolluted
DELLOOOWWY yellow-wood
DELLOSSUUY sedulously
DELNNOPSSU nonplussed
DELNNOTUWY unwontedly
DELNOOORTT rondoletto
DELNOOPRTU pleurodont
DELNOPRSSU splendrous
DELNOPRSUU plunderous
DELOOORRUV louver-door
louvre-door
DELOOPRTUU trou-de-loup
DELOORUUUX douloureux
DELOPPSSUY supposedly
DELORRTTUY torturedly
DELORSTUXY dextrously
DEMMNNOSUU unsummoned
DEMMOORSUW summerwood
DEMNOOOPST Podostemon
DEMNOOPRST post-modern
DEMNOPPRTU unprompted
DEMNORSTUU surmounted
DENNOOPRSU pundonores
DENNRRTUUU unnurtured
DENOOPPRRU propounder
DENOOPPRSU unproposed
DENOPPRSUU unpurposed
DENOPRRTTU protrudent
DENOPRSSUU supersound
DENOPSSTUU stupendous
DENORRSTUY understory
DENORRTTUU untortured
DEOORRSSUU uredosorus
DEOPPRRSUU purse-proud
DFFIIMORTY difformity
DFGGIIINNY dignifying
DFGHIINORS fishing-rod
rodfishing
DFGHILLOOT floodlight
DFGHILOOSY old-fogyish
DFGIIILLNR fringillid
DFGIIIMORT digitiform
DFGIILORSY disglorify
DFGIINOSUU nidifugous
DFGIINRRSU surf-riding
DFGILMNPUY fly-dumping
DFGILSSTUU disgustful
DFHIINRSSU disfurnish
DFHILLNOPY dolphin-fly
DFHILORTTY thirtyfold
DFHLLRSUYY sulfhydryl
DFHLOOOOPT photoflood
DFHNOOOSTU hounds-foot
DFIILMOOPU filopodium
DFIIOOOPRT idiot-proof
DFINOOPRST spoondrift
DFINOPRTUY profundity
DFLNOOPRUY profoundly
DFNOOOPRSU soundproof
DFOOOORSTU out-of-doors
DFOOOPRRSW swordproof
DGGGHINOOT hot-dogging
DGGGILMNOU mudlogging
DGGGILNRUY grudgingly
DGGGINNRUU ungrudging
DGGHINORRU rough-grind
DGGIIILMNO ginglimoid
DGGIIINSSU disguising
DGGIIKLNOO good-liking
DGGIILNNRY grindingly
DGGIINSSTU disgusting
DGGILNNORU groundling
DGGILNOOTU outlodging
DGGINNOOOR godrooning
DGGINNOORW wrongdoing
DGHHIKNOOT knighthood
DGHHNOORUU rough-hound
DGHIIINPRW riding-whip
DGHIIKLNOO kinglihood
DGHIILMNTY midnightly
DGHIILPRTY ditriglyph
DGHIINOORV virginhood
DGHINRRUYY yird-hungry
DGHLNOORST stronghold
DGHMOOORUU good-humour
DGHNOORSUW showground
DGIIIJNNOS disjoining
DGIIIKNNSV skin-diving
DGIIILLNST distilling
DGIIIMORTU digitorium
DGIIINPTUY pinguidity
DGIIINRSTU riding-suit
DGIIINSTUV diving-suit
DGIIKLOOST kidologist
DGIIKNNPRU drinking-up
DGIILNOSSV dissolving
DGIILNYYZZ dizzyingly
DGIIMMNNOR mid-morning
DGIIMNNOOR dining-room
DGIIMNORSW miswording
DGIINNOPRU pundigrion
DGIIOOPRSU prodigious
DGILLNORSU groundsill
DGILNNOSUY soundingly
DGILNNOUWY woundingly

DGILNOOPRY droopingly
DGILOOOPST podologist
DGINNOOPRU undrooping
DGINNOOPRW roping-down
DGINOOPRSW springwood
DGKNOORRUW groundwork
DGLNOOOOTY odontology
DGLNOOPRTU groundplot
DGLNOOPTTY glyptodont
DGMOOOORRW good-morrow
DGNOOPRRUX groundprox
DHHILOPRYY hydrophily
DHHMOOOSST smooth-shod
DHHOORSTUW woodthrush
DHIILOOPSS pholidosis
DHIIMMOPRS dimorphism
DHIINORSUU hirudinous
DHIIOORSST diorthosis
DHIIOPRSSW disworship
DHIIORSTTU struthioid
DHILMOOSTU Lithodomus
DHILORSSYY hydrolysis
DHIMOOPRSU dimorphous
DHINOOOPRT ornithopod
DHINOOPSWW window-shop
DHINOPRSTY dystrophin
DHINORTUWY whodunitry
DHIOOOPTYZ zoophytoid
DHLOOPPRYY hydropolyp
DHMNOORTUU round-mouth
DHMOOORRTY orthodromy
DHNNOSTUUW shunt-wound
DHNOOORTUX unorthodox
DHOORRSSTW shortsword
DIIIINPSTY insipidity
DIIILNOSTY insolidity
DIIILSTTUY disutility
DIIIMMORSU iridosmium
osmiridium
DIIIMNNOTU diminution
DIIIMNOSSS dismission
DIILLNOSWW windowsill
DIILNOOPSS displosion
DIILNOSTUY unsolidity
DIIMMOPRRU primordium
DIIMOORSSS osmidrosis
DIIMORSSSY dismissory
DIINOORSTT distortion
DIINOPRSTU △disruption
DIINRTTUUY diuturnity
DIIOOPRSST dispositor
DILLOOPPYY polyploidy
DILMOOPPUY Polypodium
DILNOOPSTW splintwood
DILORSSTUU stridulous
DILOSSTUUY studiously
DIMMNOOOPU monopodium
DIMOPRSSUY dysprosium
DINOORTTUY orotundity
DLLOOORSUY dolorously
DLNOOPSSUY spondylous
DLNOORSUWY wondrously

E

EEEEEGPSSX epexegeses
EEEEELMSSS seemelesse
EEEEEMPRST Peter-see-me
EEEEFFNSST effeteness
EEEEFKLRSS self-seeker
EEEEFLMSST self-esteem
EEEEFLRSSV self-severe
EEEEFRRRSV free-verser
EEEEGILNST genteelise
EEEEGILNTZ genteelize
EEEEGIPSSX epexegesis
EEEEGNRTTV genevrette
EEEEHIMRSU euhemerise
EEEEHIMRUZ euhemerize
EEEEHIRRSV shire-reeve
EEEEHLLOTY eyelet-hole
EEEEHLMRWY emery-wheel
EEEEHNPSST epentheses
EEEEHORRSW wheresoe'er
EEEEHPSSSY sheep's-eyes
EEEEHRRVWY everywhere
EEEEIIPSTW sweetie-pie
EEEEIKKPPR pike-keeper
EEEEIKMPRT timekeeper
EEEEILRTTV televérité
EEEEILRTVW televiewer
EEEEIMRSTT semiterete
EEEEINPSSW sweep-seine
EEEEKLPRSS keeperless
EEEEKMRRSY kerseymere
EEEELLORRT reel-to-reel
EEEELLSSSV sleeveless
EEEELMNNTV enlevement
enlèvement
EEEELNRTTT nettle-tree
EEEELORSVV oversleeve
EEEEMNRSST entremesse
EEEENNRRVV Never-Never
never-never
EEEENNRSSS sereneness
EEEENNTWYY teeny-weeny
EEEENRSSSV severeness
EEEENRSTVY yestereven
EEEETTTTWW tweet-tweet
EEEFFHIRRS free-fisher
EEEFFIIMNS effeminise
EEEFFIIMNZ effeminize
EEEFFNOOST toffee-nose
EEEFGILNRR rifle-green
EEEFGINORS foreseeing
EEEFGLNRUV revengeful
EEEFHOORRT heretofore
EEEFILLRSS reliefless
EEEFILLRTT letter-file
EEEFILNRRT life-renter
EEEFILORRS free-soiler
EEEFIMNNRT refinement
EEEFIMNRTV fermentive
EEEFINORRR ferronière
EEEFINORRV over-refine

EEEFINRRRT	interferer
EEEFKNOPRS	free-spoken
EEEFLLMSTT	self-mettle
EEEFLLORRT	foreteller
EEEFLOPRSS	self-repose
EEEFLORRVY	overfreely
EEEFLRRSTY	freestyler
EEEFLRSSTT	fetterless
EEEFMNPRRT	preferment
EEEFNNORSU	unforeseen
EEEFNORRTU	fourteener
EEEFNQRRTU	frequenter
EEEFORRSTT	forest-tree
EEEGHHINTT	eighteenth
EEEGHILNST	genteelish
EEEGHIMNOT	eighteenmo
EEEGHKLNNT	knee-length
EEEGHNORSU	greenhouse
EEEGHNORTY	heterogeny
EEEGHRRTWY	grey-wether
EEEGIILLNS	selegiline
EEEGIILRSU	religieuse
EEEGIINPSS	epigenesis
EEEGIINRSS	greisenise
EEEGIINRSU	seigneurie
EEEGIINRSZ	greisenize
EEEGIIPRSS	periegesis
EEEGILMNST	genteelism
EEEGILNRST	singletree
EEEGILNSST	gentilesse
EEEGIMNNRT	enregiment
EEEGIMORST	geometrise
EEEGIMORTZ	geometrize
EEEGINNORS	rose-engine
EEEGINNOSS	neogenesis
EEEGINNRRT	re-entering
EEEGINNSTW	sweetening
EEEGINOPRY	epeirogeny
EEEGINRRST	enregister
	interreges
EEEGIRRRST	reregister
EEEGIRRSSV	regressive
EEEGKLMNOU	leukemogen
EEEGLMNRTY	emergently
EEEGLNNSST	gentleness
EEEGLNOSTZ	seltzogene
EEEGMNNOTU	engouement
EEEGNNORST	greenstone
EEEHHIMPRS	hemisphere
EEEHHLORSW	wheelhorse
EEEHHLOSUW	wheelhouse
EEEHHORRTW	otherwhere
EEEHIKLPRS	spherelike
EEEHIKPPRS	keepership
EEEHILLTWW	whewellite
EEEHILMORT	heliometer
EEEHILMRTW	mitre-wheel
EEEHILNPRS	prehensile
EEEHIMMRSU	Euhemerism
EEEHIMNRST	smithereen
EEEHIMPRST	ephemerist
EEEHIMRSTU	euhemerist
EEEHINNNTT	nineteenth
EEEHINPRSV	prehensive
EEEHINPSST	epenthesis
EEEHINSSWZ	wheeziness
EEEHINSTTV	seventieth
EEEHJLOSUW	jewel-house
EEEHKOPPRS	shopkeeper
EEEHLLNTVY	eleventhly
EEEHLMNPTT	hemp-nettle
EEEHLMNTVY	vehemently
EEEHLMOPST	speleothem
EEEHLMSSTV	themselves
EEEHLNOPRT	telephoner
EEEHLOPSSU	sheep-louse
EEEHLORTWW	two-wheeler
EEEHLPRSSS	sphereless
EEEHMNORRT	nethermore
EEEHMNORTV	veneer-moth
EEEHMOPRSS	mesosphere
EEEHMOPRSU	ephemerous
EEEHMORTTY	hyetometer
EEEHNNPRTY	threepenny
EEEHNORSVW	whensoever
EEEHNOSTWY	honey-sweet
EEEHNRSSTT	sternsheet
EEEIIPRTTV	repetitive
EEEIJNRSUV	rejuvenise
EEEIJNRUVZ	rejuvenize
EEEIKLLNTT	nettlelike
EEEIKLMSWY	semi-weekly
EEEILLPTVV	velvet-pile
EEEILMMORT	mileometer
EEEILMNRTV	revilement
EEEILMNSSS	seemliness
EEEILMPRTV	pelvimeter
EEEILMPRTX	pleximeter
EEEILMRSST	missel-tree
EEEILNOPPS	penelopise
EEEILNOPPZ	penelopize
EEEILNPRRT	terreplein
EEEILNPSSS	sleepiness
EEEILNRRST	re-enlister
EEEILNSSST	sleetiness
	steeliness
EEEILOPRRS	leproserie
EEEILRRTTW	telewriter
EEEIMMNNOS	Menominees
EEEIMMRRSS	mesmeriser
EEEIMMRRSZ	mesmerizer
EEEIMNNPRT	pre-eminent
	repinement
EEEIMNOPST	Piemontese
EEEIMNORST	remonetise
EEEIMNORTZ	remonetize
EEEIMNPRTX	experiment
EEEIMNRRTT	retirement
EEEIMNRSTT	tensimeter
EEEIMNRTVV	revivement
EEEIMOPRTZ	piezometer
EEEIMPPRTV	pre-emptive
EEEIMPSTTV	tempestive
EEEIMRRSTV	time-server

EEEINNPRSS	persiennes
EEEINNPRST	serpentine
EEEINNPRTV	prevenient
EEEINNRRTV	intervener
EEEINNRSST	entireness
EEEINOPPPR	pipe-opener
EEEINOQSTU	questionee
EEEINPPRSV	prepensive
EEEINPRRST	enterprise
EEEINPRSST	serpentise
EEEINPRSSU	purse-seine
EEEINPRSTV	presentive
	vespertine
EEEINPRSTZ	serpentize
EEEINPRTVV	preventive
EEEINPSSST	steepiness
EEEINRRRTV	irreverent
EEEINRSSTW	westernise
EEEINRSTWZ	westernize
EEEINSSTWY	eye-witness
EEEIOPRRRT	repertoire
EEEIPRRSSV	repressive
EEEIPRRSVV	perversive
EEEIPRRTTU	répétiteur
EEEIPRSSUV	supervisee
EEEIPRSSVX	expressive
EEEIRSSTTW	streetwise
EEEJJNNSSU	jejuneness
EEEKLNOSST	sleekstone
EEEKLORRTW	teleworker
EEEKMNORTV	revokement
EEELLNPSSS	spleenless
EEELLNPSUV	eleven-plus
EEELLNRSST	relentless
EEELLORTTV	love-letter
EEELLPRSSY	peerlessly
EEELLRSSTT	letterless
EEELMMOSTT	mettlesome
EEELMNNRTT	relentment
EEELMNOSTT	nettlesome
EEELMNOTVV	evolvement
EEELMNSTTT	settlement
EEELMOOSTT	teleostome
EEELNOTTVW	twelve-note
	twelve-tone
EEELNPPRSY	prepensely
EEELNRRTVY	reverently
EEELNRSTTW	newsletter
EEELOOPPRV	overpeople
EEELOPRSTU	pétroleuse
EEELORSVWW	werewolves
EEELPRRSVY	perversely
EEELPRSSTU	reputeless
EEELRSSSVW	swerveless
EEELRSTTTU	ulsterette
EEEMMNOTUV	mouvementé
EEEMNNORST	mesenteron
EEEMNNRSTT	resentment
EEEMNNSSTU	unmeetness
EEEMNOPRST	treponemes
EEEMNORSST	remoteness
EEEMNORSTT	sermonette
EEEMNPRSTT	pesterment
EEENNNPSVY	sevenpenny
EEENNNSSUV	unevenness
EEENNRRTUV	unreverent
EEENORSTWZ	sneezewort
EEENOSTTUW	outsweeten
EEENPRSSTX	expertness
EEEOOPRSVX	overexpose
EEEOPRSTTY	stereotype
EEEOPRTTUV	éprouvette
EEEPPRRRSU	rere-supper
EEEPRRSSUX	expressure
EEEPRSSTUW	supersweet
EEEPRSTTTY	typesetter
EEFFGIINRV	fivefinger
	five-finger
EEFFGINORR	forefinger
EEFFGNRSTU	greenstuff
EEFFHLRRSU	refreshful
EEFFILLLRS	self-filler
EEFFILSUVY	effusively
EEFFIMNNTT	infeftment
EEFFIORRTU	forfeiture
EEFFLOORTT	left-footer
EEFFLORSST	effortless
EEFFNORRTY	effrontery
EEFFSSTTUW	sweet-stuff
EEFGHHIITV	five-eighth
EEFGHILNOR	fingerhole
EEFGHINRRS	refreshing
EEFGHLOOSS	gooseflesh
EEFGIINRRT	gentrifier
EEFGILLNRY	fleeringly
EEFGILLNTY	fleetingly
EEFGILNRSS	fingerless
	fringeless
EEFGILNRTW	left-winger
EEFGINNRRT	refringent
EEFGINPRRR	preferring
EEFGKLLNOT	gentlefolk
EEFGLLMNOR	fellmonger
EEFGLLNUVY	vengefully
EEFGLMNNTU	engulfment
EEFGLNPRTU	prefulgent
EEFGORRTTY	forgettery
EEFHHIORST	horse-thief
EEFHHLORSS	horseflesh
EEFHIILNRS	line-fisher
EEFHIKLSTT	fish-kettle
EEFHILLORW	fellow-heir
EEFHILNSSS	fleshiness
EEFHILNSTT	nettle-fish
EEFHILORSV	fire-shovel
EEFHILRSVY	feverishly
EEFHINRSTY	net-fishery
EEFHLNORTW	front-wheel
EEFHMOORST	foster-home
EEFHNORTTU	fourteenth
EEFHOOPRST	proof-sheet
EEFHOOPSST	sheep's-foot
EEFHORRSUY	ferry-house
EEFIIKLLNU	unlifelike

EEFIIKLNUW unwifelike
EEFIILMNNY femininely
EEFIILMRSU emulsifier
EEFIILNSSW wifeliness
EEFIILRRST fertiliser
EEFIILRRTZ fertilizer
EEFIIMNNNU unfeminine
EEFIINNSST finiteness
EEFIINSSST feistiness
EEFIKLLLRS self-killer
EEFIKMNNOY knife-money
EEFIKNNOPS fine-spoken
EEFILLLSSY lifelessly
EEFILLNOTU feuilleton
EEFILMNOQU mefloquine
EEFILMRSTU muster-file
EEFILNNORT △florentine
EEFILNRSSU irefulness
EEFILNSSZZ fizzenless
EEFILOOPRR poor-relief
EEFILOORSU oleiferous
EEFILPRRSU persifleur
EEFILQRTUU requiteful
EEFILRSSST strifeless
EEFIMNOSTT oftentimes
EEFINNORRT interferon
EEFINNQRTU infrequent
EEFINOPSST fesse-point
EEFINOSSTV five-stones
EEFINTTVWY twenty-five
EEFIORRRTX fox-terrier
EEFIORSSTU setiferous
EEFIORSTWY oyster-wife
EEFIPRRTUX prefixture
EEFIRRSSTU fruiteress
EEFKLLOOWY yoke-fellow
EEFLLNNRRU fellrunner
EEFLLORSSW flowerless
EEFLMORRSU remorseful
EEFLNNSSTU fluentness
EEFLNNTUUV uneventful
EEFLNOSSUW woefulness
EEFLNQRTUY frequently
EEFLNRSSUU ruefulness
EEFLNSSSUU usefulness
EEFLORRTTU four-letter
EEFLRSSTTU streetfuls
EEFLRSSTUU futureless
EEFMOORTZZ mezzo-forte
EEFNNORRRU forerunner
EEFNNQRTUU unfrequent
EEFNOORSTY festoonery
EEFOPRRRUV perfervour
EEGGGILMOS gigglesome
EEGGHHINRY high-energy
EEGGHMNNOO hogen-mogen
EEGGINRRTT regretting
EEGGISSTUV suggestive
EEGHHIOSUW weigh-house
EEGHHIRSTT high-street
EEGHHORRUW rough-hewer
EEGHHORSTU see-through
EEGHIKLRSU kieselguhr
EEGHILNOOP pigeonhole
EEGHILNOPR negrophile
EEGHILNRST sheltering
EEGHILNSTW lengthwise
EEGHILNSWW swing-wheel
EEGHILOOST theologise
EEGHILOOTZ theologize
EEGHILSSTW weightless
EEGHIMMNOS hegemonism
EEGHIMNOOS homogenise
EEGHIMNOOZ homogenize
EEGHIMNOST hegemonist
EEGHINNORT one-nighter
EEGHINNPTY eightpenny
EEGHINPRST regentship
EEGHINRTVY everything
EEGHIORTVW overweight
EEGHIPRRSV vergership
EEGHLOORTY heterology
EEGHLOPRTU plough-tree
EEGHMORRTY hygrometer
EEGHNNRSTT strengthen
EEGHNOORTY heterogony
EEGHNOPSYZ zygosphene
EEGHNORSUU sure-enough
EEGHORSSTU otherguess
EEGHOSSTUU guest-house
EEGIIILMST legitimise
EEGIIILMTZ legitimize
EEGIIKLPRS kriegspiel
EEGIILNNST lentigines
EEGIILNORR religioner
EEGIILNRVV ever-living
EEGIILNTVY genitively
EEGIILOPSU epiloguise
EEGIILOPUZ epiloguize
EEGIIMMNSS misseeming
EEGIINNQTU quietening
EEGIINPRSS serpigines
EEGIINRRTV retrieving
EEGIINRSSV ingressive
EEGIINRSTV vertigines
EEGIJNSTTT jet-setting
EEGIKLLNNN kennelling
EEGIKLNOTU tonguelike
EEGIKORSSW siegeworks
EEGILLOPSS gospellise
EEGILLOPSW Owlspiegle
EEGILLOPSZ gospellize
EEGILMMNNT minglement
EEGILMNNOT eloignment
EEGILMNORS mongrelise
EEGILMNORZ mongrelize
EEGILMOOSY semeiology
EEGILNNPPU pulp-engine
EEGILNNPSU unsleeping
EEGILNNRSY sneeringly
EEGILNNSSS singleness
EEGILNOSST telegnosis
EEGILNPPRX perplexing
EEGILNPSST single-step

EEGILNPSWY sweepingly
EEGILNRSTW sweltering
EEGILORRST sortileger
EEGIMNNOOR engine-room
EEGIMNNOTT mignonette
EEGIMNNRST resignment
EEGIMNNTTU integument
EEGIMNOORT goniometer
EEGIMORSTT geometrist
EEGINNOOSS noogenesis
EEGINNOPPS pepsinogen
EEGINNORST röntgenise
EEGINNORTZ röntgenize
EEGINNPRUY penguinery
EEGINNRRSU rune-singer
EEGINNSSSY syngenesis
EEGINNSSVX vexingness
EEGINOORSS orogenesis
EEGINOPSSY pyogenesis
EEGINORRSS regression
EEGINORRWW wine-grower
EEGINORSTY generosity
EEGINPRRST perstringe
EEGINPRSTT presetting
EEGIOPPRRT ego-tripper
EEGIORSSTU setigerous
EEGIORSTTU urostegite
EEGLLNOOSY selenology
EEGLLNOTTW well-gotten
EEGLLOOPSY speleology
EEGLMMNOOY emmenology
EEGLMNOORV love-monger
EEGLMNOOVY glove-money
EEGLMNOPRT peltmonger
EEGLMNORRT long-termer
EEGLMORSUY gruesomely
EEGLNOOSTU telegonous
EEGLNORSUY generously
EEGLNOSSTU tongueless
EEGLOORRST ergosterol
EEGLORRSTU trouser-leg
EEGMNNORSW newsmonger
EEGMNNORTV △government
EEGMNOOPRS spermogone
EEGMNOSSSU ugsomeness
EEGNNOOSUX xenogenous
EEGNNORSUU ungenerous
EEGNORSSVY governessy
EEGNORSTTU tonguester
EEGOPRSTUU Portuguese
EEGORRRSST retrogress
EEHHIKMNTT methinketh
EEHHILOPTY heliophyte
EEHHILORTW otherwhile
EEHHILPSSY sheepishly
EEHHIMNOST henotheism
EEHHINOSTT henotheist
EEHHINRTTT thirteenth
EEHHNRRRTU Herrnhuter
EEHHNRSTUY heresy-hunt
EEHHOOPRST theosopher
EEHHOORRSS horseshoer
EEHHOORSUW whorehouse
EEHHOPSSTY hypotheses
EEHIIKLNRS shrinelike
EEHIILLMNW Wilhelmine
EEHIILMPTU epithelium
EEHIILNOPR perihelion
EEHIIMNNOT methionine
EEHIIPRSVW viewership
EEHIIRRSTX heritrixes
EEHIJNSSSW Jewishness
EEHIKLMNOU unhomelike
EEHILLLOSV olive-shell
EEHILLMRST mitre-shell
EEHILLNSSS shelliness
EEHILLORTZ lherzolite
EEHILLPRST tellership
EEHILLRSWW well-wisher
EEHILMNOSS homeliness
EEHILMOPRT thermopile
EEHILMOSSW somewhiles
EEHILNNRTY inherently
EEHILNORTT enterolith
EEHILNRTUW whereuntil
EEHILOOPRT heliotrope
EEHILOSTTU silhouette
EEHILPRSTU spherulite
EEHILRSSTV thriveless
EEHIMNNRTU mine-hunter
EEHIMNPRRT permethrin
EEHIMNPRST reshipment
EEHIMOPRSV empoverish
EEHIMRRSTW Wertherism
EEHIMRSSTV verse-smith
EEHINNOPRS prehension
EEHINNOPRT interphone
EEHINNORST enthronise
△rhinestone
EEHINNORTZ enthronize
EEHINNOSST tennis-shoe
EEHINNSSSW newishness
EEHINOOPRS ionosphere
EEHINOPRTT three-point
EEHINSSSTY synthesise
EEHINSSTTY synthetise
EEHINSSTYZ synthesize
EEHINSTTYZ synthetize
EEHIOPPRRS prophesier
EEHIOPPRST epistrophe
EEHIORRRSV river-horse
EEHIORSTTU stoutherie
EEHIRSSSTY hysteresis
EEHJNNOOSS Johnsonese
EEHKKOOPYY hokey-pokey
EEHKLNORRV Herrenvolk
EEHKMOORRW homeworker
EEHKMOOSSU smokehouse
EEHKNOORTT heterokont
tenterhook
EEHLLLPSSY helplessly
EEHLLMNOOP mellophone
EEHLLMNOSY shell-money
EEHLLMOSZZ shlemozzle

EEHLLNSSUV Venus-shell
EEHLLOPSSY hopelessly
EEHLLORSTW tower-shell
EEHLMNOOYZ holoenzyme
EEHLMNORTU molehunter
EEHLMORSST motherless
EEHLMORVWY vowel-rhyme
EEHLNOOSSV shovelnose
EEHLNORSST throneless
EEHLOORSTW towel-horse
EEHLORSSSW showerless
EEHMMOOORY homoeomery
EEHMMOPRTU prometheum
EEHMNNNOOP phenomenon
EEHMNOOPRT phonometer
EEHMNOORTY heteronomy
EEHMNOOSTT nomothetes
EEHMNOOSUY honey-mouse
EEHMNORSTT nethermost
EEHMOOPRTT photometer
EEHMOORRVW hover-mower
EEHMOORSVW howsomever
whomsoever
EEHMOPRSTT stepmother
EEHMOPRSTY hypsometer
EEHMOQRSUU humoresque
EEHMORSSUW shrewmouse
EEHNNOOSTY honey-stone
EEHNNOPRTY Entryphone®
EEHNNOPSSY phoneyness
EEHNNORRRT northerner
EEHNOOOPRR orpheoreon
EEHNOORSST stonehorse
EEHNOPPRXY nephropexy
EEHNOPRRSY prehensory
EEHNOPRSUY Euphrosyne
EEHNOPSSTU penthouses
EEHNOPSTTU theopneust
EEHNOPSTUY hypotenuse
EEHNORRSTU △southerner
EEHOOPRRSW horsepower
EEHOOPRSUW powerhouse
EEHOOPRTTV over-the-top
EEHOOPSTTY osteophyte
EEHOORRSVW overshower
EEHOORSSTU storehouse
EEHOPPRSST prophetess
EEHOPRSSST prostheses
EEHORRSTTW otter-shrew
EEIIIMMRSS immiserise
EEIIIMMRSZ immiserize
EEIIIMNRSS miniseries
EEIIKLLMRT time-killer
EEIIKLLNSS likeliness
EEIIKLNPRW periwinkle
EEIIKLPRST priest-like
EEIIKLQRSU squirelike
EEIIKLRSST sisterlike
EEIILLMMRT millimetre
EEIILLMNRU reillumine
EEIILLNSSV liveliness
EEIILMNSST timeliness
EEIILNNRST listener-in
EEIILNOSTV television
EEIILNOTTT toilinette
EEIILOPSST epistolise
EEIILOPSTZ epistolize
EEIILOPTVX exploitive
EEIILORSTT toiletries
EEIILOSSUZ Louis-Seize
EEIILRRSST steriliser
EEIILRRSTZ sterilizer
EEIIMNNPTT impenitent
pentimenti
EEIIMNNTTV invitement
EEIIMNRTTW wintertime
EEIIMNRTZZ intermezzi
EEIIMOPRST epitomiser
EEIIMOPRTZ epitomizer
EEIIMPRSSV impressive
permissive
EEIIMPRSTV septemviri
EEIINNNSTT insentient
EEIINNRTTW intertwine
EEIINNSSTT intestines
EEIINNSTTX inexistent
EEIINOPRTT △petitioner
repetition
EEIINRSSST sensitiser
EEIINRSSTZ sensitizer
EEIINRTTVY eviternity
EEIIOPSTVX expositive
EEIIORRSST rotisserie
rôtisserie
EEIIPQRSTU perquisite
EEIIPRSSTV persistive
EEIIRRSTTU ureteritis
EEIJKNPRTY perjinkety
EEIJLLNUVY juvenilely
EEIJMNNNOT enjoinment
EEIKKLNNPS skip-kennel
EEIKLLNOSV slovenlike
EEIKLLNRSW well-sinker
EEIKLMMRSU summerlike
EEIKLNNSSU unlikeness
EEIKLNPSTT kettle-pins
EEIKLORRVW evil-worker
EEIKMNORRW mine-worker
EEIKOPRSTV perovskite
EEIKORRRWW wireworker
EEIKORRSTV overstrike
EEILLLLRWW well-willer
EEILLLOTVW well-to-live
EEILLLPSTV split-level
EEILLLRSST tillerless
EEILLMMORT immortelle
EEILLMNSSS smelliness
EEILLMPPPR peppermill
EEILLMPRTW pewter-mill
EEILLMSSTY timelessly
EEILLNNOSS loneliness
EEILLNORRT ritornelle
EEILLNORVZ Zollverein
EEILLNOSSV loveliness

EEILLNSSTT littleness
EEILLOPRRT tiller-rope
EEILLOTWYY yellow-yite
EEILLPRRUW wire-puller
EEILLRSSTU Russellite
EEILLRSSTY tirelessly
EEILLSSVWY viewlessly
EEILMNNOTT entoilment
EEILMNNSTT enlistment
EEILMNORSS solemniser
EEILMNORSZ solemnizer
EEILMNOSSU mousseline
EEILMNOTTU Moulinette®
EEILMNPSSS simpleness
EEILMOOSTT Teleostomi
EEILMOPRSY polymerise
EEILMOPRYZ polymerize
EEILMORSTY tiresomely
EEILMORTVY overtimely
EEILMOSSTV motiveless
EEILMPRSTU pulsimeter
EEILMPRTVY pelvimetry
EEILMPRTXY pleximetry
EEILNNOQTU ineloquent
EEILNNORTY Tyrolienne
EEILNNPRSU spinnerule
EEILNNPTTY penitently
EEILNNSSST silentness
EEILNOPPTT poplinette
EEILNOPRRT interloper
EEILNOPSST politeness
EEILNORTVV intervolve
EEILNOSSTW stolenwise
EEILNPRSST tripleness
EEILNRSTUY esuriently
EEILOOPRST teliospore
EEILOOPSST Osteolepis
EEILORRSTU irresolute
EEILORRTTW △rottweiler
EEILORRTXY exteriorly
EEILORSTUV resolutive
EEILORSVWY overwisely
EEILPPRTXY perplexity
EEILPPSTUV suppletive
EEILPRRSTY sperrylite
EEILPRRSUV pulveriser
EEILPRRUVZ pulverizer
EEILPRSSST stripeless
EEILPRSTTU supertitle
EEILRSSSST resistless
sisterless
EEILRSSTTZ strelitzes
EEILRSSTUV virtueless
EEIMMMNRTU immurement
EEIMMMORSS mesomerism
EEIMMMRSTU summertime
EEIMMORSTU osmeterium
EEIMMPRSTT stimpmeter
EEIMMRSSTY symmetrise
EEIMMRSTYZ symmetrize
EEIMNNNRTT internment
EEIMNNOPTT pentimento
EEIMNNORST minestrone
EEIMNNPSTU Pennisetum
septennium
EEIMNNSSTU minuteness
EEIMNNSTTV investment
EEIMNOPPRT pre-emption
EEIMNOPRTU peritoneum
EEIMNOPSTU pumie-stone
EEIMNORRSS sermoniser
EEIMNORRSZ sermonizer
EEIMNORRTT nitrometer
EEIMNORRTU urinometer
EEIMNORTTT Tintometer®
EEIMNORTZZ intermezzo
EEIMNOSSTX sixteenmos
EEIMNPPPRT peppermint
EEIMNPRSSU impureness
EEIMNPRSTU episternum
EEIMNRSSSS remissness
EEIMNRSSTU terminuses
EEIMNRSSTW westernism
EEIMNRSTUV misventure
EEIMOOPRST opisometer
opsiometer
EEIMOPRRST spirometer
temporiser
EEIMOPRRTZ temporizer
EEIMOPRSTU periosteum
EEIMPPRRUU puerperium
EEIMPPRSTU suppertime
EEIMPRRSSU impressure
presurmise
EEIMPRSSTV septemvirs
EEIMPRSTUV resumptive
EEIMRSSTTU sestertium
EEINNNSSTT intentness
EEINNOPPRT porpentine
EEINNOPRSS presension
EEINNOPRST pretension
pre-tension
EEINNOPRTT ten-pointer
EEINNOPRTV prevention
EEINNORRTV intervenor
EEINNOSSTW swinestone
EEINNPRSSU unripeness
EEINNPRTTU turpentine
EEINNPSSSU supineness
EEINNQSSUU uniqueness
EEINNRSSTV inventress
EEINNSSSUW unwiseness
EEINOOPRSS pensieroso
EEINOOSSST otioseness
EEINOPPRSV propensive
EEINOPQTTU equipotent
EEINOPRRSS repression
EEINOPRRST interposer
EEINOPRRSV perversion
EEINOPRSSV responsive
EEINOPRSSX expression
EEINOPRSTV protensive
EEINOPRTXY pyroxenite
EEINOQRSTU questioner

EEINORRSUV overinsure
EEINORRTVW overwinter
EEINPPPRSS preppiness
EEINPRSSTT persistent
prettiness
EEINPSSSUV suspensive
EEINQSSTUY squint-eyes
EEINRRSTWW news-writer
EEINRSSSTY synteresis
EEINSSTTUV sustentive
EEIOPPRSSV oppressive
EEIOPRRSTV resorptive
EEIOPRRTTU pirouetter
EEIOPRSSST stereopsis
EEIOPRSTTT operettist
EEIOPSSSSV possessive
EEIORRRRST terroriser
EEIORRRRTZ terrorizer
EEIPPRTTUY perpetuity
EEIPQRRRUU perruquier
EEIPRRSSSU pressurise
EEIPRRSSUZ pressurize
EEIPRRSTVY perversity
EEIPRRTTWY typewriter
EEIPRSSSTT step-sister
EEIRRSSSTV servitress
EEJLMNOSTT jostlement
EEJLMRSTWY Jew's-myrtle
EEKLLNOPSW well-spoken
EEKLOOORRV overlooker
EEKLOOPPRW workpeople
EEKLORSSTW steelworks
EEKMNOOPRY monkey-rope
EEKMNOPRTY pyknometer
EEKMRSSTTU musket-rest
EELLLOPRSS slop-seller
EELLMNNORT enrollment
EELLMNOOSY lonesomely
EELLMNOSSW mellowness
EELLMNTTUY temulently
EELLMOSSVY movelessly
EELLNNSSSU sullenness
EELLNNSSUW unwellness
EELLNOPPRT prepollent
propellent
EELLNOQTUY eloquently
EELLNOSSTY tonelessly
EELLNOSSWY yellowness
EELLORSTUY resolutely
EELLRSSSTU lustreless
resultless
EELLRSSSTY restlessly
EELMMNOPTY employment
EELMMNOSTU emoluments
EELMNNOSSS solemnness
EELMNNOSTU ensoulment
EELMNOPPRT propelment
EELMNOPPSU pumple-nose
EELMNPPSTU supplement
EELMNPTUZZ puzzlement
EELMOPRSTU pulsometer
EELMORRSST tremorless
EELMORSTTY metrostyle
EELMORSTUY temerously
EELMSSSSTY systemless
EELNNORRTU unrelentor
EELNNORTUU Eurotunnel
EELNOPPRSY propensely
EELNOPRSTW spleenwort
EELNPPSSSU suppleness
EELNRRSSTU returnless
EELOOPPSSS opposeless
EELOOPRSTT protostele
EELOOPRSTU petroleous
EELOOPRSTY proteolyse
EELOPSSSSU spouseless
EELORRRSST terrorless
EELORRRSTY retrorsely
EELORSSUVY yourselves
EELPPRSSSU supperless
EELPRRSTTU splutterer
EELRSSSSST stressless
EEMMOORRTT tromometer
EEMNNOPSTT pentstemon
EEMNNORRRU Rome-runner
EEMNOOPRTY petromoney
EEMNOORSSS moroseness
EEMNOORTTY enterotomy
EEMNORRSTY yestermorn
EEMNPRRSTU presternum
EEMOORRSTT streetroom
EEMOORSTTY stereotomy
EEMOPPRRTY peremptory
EEMPRSSSST sempstress
EEMQRSSTUU sequestrum
EENNNNOOSS no-nonsense
EENNNOPSTY penny-stone
EENNOQRSTU quernstone
EENNORRRUV overrunner
EENNORSSTT rottenness
EENNOSSSTY syntenoses
EENNRSSTUU untrueness
EENOPPRRSS properness
EENORRRTUV overturner
EENORSTTTU neutrettos
EEOPPPRRTW pepperwort
EEOPPPRSSU presuppose
EEOPPRRSUW superpower
EEOPPRSSSS prepossess
EEOPRRSSTU streperous
superstore
EEOPRSTTYY stereotypy
EEORRSSSTV overstress
EEORRSTTTW setterwort
EEPRRSTUUY Eurypterus
EFFFILNSSU fluffiness
EFFGHIINRS fish-finger
EFFGHNOORU forfoughen
EFFGIINNST stiffening
EFFGILLNOT telling-off
EFFGILPRTU truffle-pig
EFFGINOPRR proffering
EFFGIORRUU four-figure
EFFIIKNRTU fruit-knife

EFFIINNSSS	sniffiness
EFFILLMNTU	fulfilment
EFFILNSSTU	fitfulness
EFFILOPRST	self-profit
EFFINNOPRS	off-spinner
EFFINNPTYY	fifty-penny
EFFINNSSSU	snuffiness
EFFINSSSTU	stuffiness
EFGGHILOTV	glove-fight
EFGGHINRTU	gunfighter
EFGGIIILNV	life-giving
EFGGIILNNR	fingerling
EFGGIILNSV	self-giving
EFGGIINNNU	unfeigning
EFGGIINNRR	ring-finger
EFGGILOOSS	solfeggios
EFGGINORTT	forgetting
EFGHIIKNRS	kingfisher
EFGHIINNST	net-fishing
EFGHIIPRTZ	prizefight
EFGHILLSST	flightless
EFGHILNSSW	swing-shelf
EFGHILOPRU	fire-plough
EFGHILORTV	overflight
EFGHIMNORS	fishmonger
EFGHIMORST	frightsome
EFGHIRSTTU	fish-gutter
EFGHLLLNTU	full-length
EFGHLLNORU	flugelhorn
	flügelhorn
EFGHNNOTUU	unfoughten
EFGHOOPPRR	frog-hopper
EFGIIKLNTY	kite-flying
EFGIILNQUY	liquefying
EFGIILNRSS	self-rising
EFGIILTUVY	fugitively
EFGIIMNORS	foreignism
EFGIINNNTU	fine-tuning
EFGIINPRST	firing-step
EFGIINPRSY	presignify
EFGIINPRTY	petrifying
EFGIINRRTY	terrifying
EFGIINRSTU	surfeiting
EFGIINRSVY	versifying
EFGIINSTTY	testifying
EFGIKLNORS	folk-singer
EFGIKORRUW	figurework
EFGILLLUUY	guilefully
EFGILLNOSV	self-loving
EFGILLNRSU	self-ruling
EFGILLORRW	flower-girl
EFGILMNOSV	self-moving
EFGILNNOTW	fowling-net
EFGILNOOST	single-foot
EFGILNORST	fosterling
EFGIMNOPRR	performing
EFGINNORUV	unforgiven
EFGINOPRSS	professing
EFGINOPRST	fingerpost
EFGINORRTY	torrefying
EFGINPRTUY	putrefying
EFGINPSTUY	stupefying
EFGLNOPRTU	profulgent
EFGOOOOSST	goosefoots
EFHIILNSST	filthiness
EFHIILRSSV	silverfish
EFHIINSSST	shiftiness
EFHIIRSTTT	thriftiest
EFHIKLNSUY	flunkeyish
EFHIKNORST	frithsoken
EFHILLOPSW	fellowship
EFHILOOPRT	hop-trefoil
EFHILOPRST	shop-lifter
EFHILORSTW	fish-trowel
EFHILORSUX	flexihours
EFHILORSWW	werwolfish
EFHILRSSTT	thriftless
EFHINORSST	frothiness
EFHIORSTTU	stouthrief
EFHLLOOPRS	shellproof
EFHLLOSSUV	shovelfuls
EFHLMOORTW	moth-flower
EFHLMORSTY	smother-fly
EFHLMOTTUU	flutemouth
EFHLOORSWW	flower-show
EFHMMOORRT	thermoform
EFHNRTTTUU	tuft-hunter
EFHOOOPRSU	proof-house
EFIIIINNTV	infinitive
EFIIILLMOR	millefiori
EFIIILMNTY	feminility
EFIIILMPRS	simplifier
EFIIILNNTY	infinitely
EFIIIMMNNS	femininism
EFIIIMNNTY	femininity
EFIIKNNOPT	knife-point
EFIIKNRSSS	friskiness
EFIILMNSSS	flimsiness
EFIILNNSST	flintiness
EFIILNORRY	inferiorly
EFIILOPRSU	piliferous
EFIILRSTTU	stultifier
EFIIMNNRSS	infirmness
EFIIMOPRRV	viperiform
EFIIMORRSU	Fourierism
EFIIORSTUV	vitiferous
EFIKLMNSUY	flunkeyism
EFIKLNOSSS	folksiness
EFIKNPTTUY	putty-knife
EFILLMORST	stelliform
EFILLNSSUW	wilfulness
EFILLOOPRW	low-profile
EFILLPSTUY	spitefully
EFILMNOOST	self-motion
EFILMNOSUU	fulmineous
EFILMOPRSU	promiseful
EFILMORRTY	elytriform
EFILMORSTW	mist-flower
EFILNNSSSU	sinfulness
EFILNOORSS	solferinos
EFILNOOSSS	foisonless
EFILNOPPSS	floppiness
EFILNORTWW	twinflower
EFILNOSSSU	fusionless

EFILOPRSST	profitless
EFIMNOORRV	overinform
EFIMNOORSU	omniferous
EFIMNORSTU	misfortune
EFIMOOPRRT	proteiform
EFIMOOPRSU	pomiferous
EFINNORRTY	forty-niner
EFINOOPRSS	profession
EFINOPRRRT	ferro-print
EFINORRRTV	riverfront
EFINORRSTT	strife-torn
EFINORSSST	frostiness
EFIOOPRRSU	poriferous
EFIOORRSTU	rotiferous
EFIOORSSSU	ossiferous
EFJLLORUWY	July-flower
EFJLNOSSUY	joyfulness
EFKLLOORWW	workfellow
EFKLMMOORY	folk-memory
EFKLMNOOSW	womenfolks
EFKLNOOPSU	foul-spoken
EFKMOOOPRS	smokeproof
EFKMOORSST	frost-smoke
EFKNOOPSST	soft-spoken
EFKOORRSTU	four-stroke
EFLLLOPSUY	spoylefull
EFLLMOOORW	room-fellow
EFLLMORSSY	formlessly
EFLLNSUUUY	unusefully
EFLLOPRUWY	powerfully
EFLMNOOORW	moon-flower
EFLMOOORTY	tomfoolery
EFLOOPRTUY	fluorotype
EFLOPPRSUU	purposeful
EFMOOPRRTU	outperform
EFNNOORRSU	non-ferrous
EFNOORRSTT	storefront
EFNORTTUWY	twenty-four
EFOOPRRSTU	four-poster
EGGGHILMSU	mishguggle
EGGGIILNNR	niggerling
EGGGIINNRS	sniggering
EGGGIJJOTY	jiggety-jog
EGGGIMNNTU	nutmegging
EGGGINORSS	grogginess
EGGHHIMTTU	hug-me-tight
EGGHHIPRSU	hip-huggers
EGGHIILNNT	lightening
EGGHIINNUW	unweighing
EGGHINNOTU	toughening
EGGHINOORS	shore-going
EGGHINSTTU	guest-night
EGGIILMMNR	glimmering
EGGIILNRST	glistering
EGGIILNRTT	glittering
EGGIILNRVY	grievingly
EGGIINNOPW	pigeon-wing
EGGILLLNPU	leg-pulling
EGGILLNORV	grovelling
EGGILMOOST	gemologist
EGGILNNRSU	gunslinger
EGGILNNTTU	englutting
EGGILNOORT	toggleiron
EGGILNSSUY	guessingly
EGGINNOOOR	gorgoneion
EGGINNORSS	engrossing
EGGINOSSTU	suggestion
EGGLLOOOPX	googolplex
EGGLNOOOSY	gnoseology
EGGLOOPTYY	Egyptology
EGGLOORSUY	gorgeously
EGHHILLORR	high-roller
EGHHILOPRY	hieroglyph
EGHHILOSTU	lighthouse
EGHHIMORST	highermost
EGHHINNORT	night-heron
EGHHINOSTU	night-house
EGHHOORSUU	rough-house
EGHHOPRTYY	hygrophyte
EGHIIIKLNS	heli-skiing
EGHIIJNNOT	hinge-joint
EGHIILMNSS	Englishism
EGHIILNNPS	plenishing
EGHIILNRSV	shriveling
EGHIILNSST	sightlines
EGHIILRSTY	tigerishly
EGHIIMMNRS	shimmering
EGHIIMNPRW	whimpering
EGHIIMNSST	mightiness
EGHIINNPRT	trephining
EGHIINNPSS	ensignship
EGHIINNSST	thinginess
EGHIINPPTW	whippeting
EGHIINPRSW	whispering
EGHIINRTTW	twi-nighter
EGHIINSTUX	extinguish
EGHIKLNSST	knightless
EGHIKMOSTT	smoketight
EGHIKNOTUW	huntiegowk
EGHILLNOST	hostelling
EGHILLNOSU	houselling
EGHILLNOSV	shovelling
EGHILLNPST	night-spell
EGHILLOOPR	philologer
EGHILLOOPU	philologue
EGHILLOOTV	light-o'-love
EGHILMOOOS	homologise
EGHILMOOOZ	homologize
EGHILNORVY	hoveringly
EGHILNSSST	slightness
EGHILOOPPT	phlogopite
EGHILOOPSU	geophilous
EGHILOORST	rheologist
EGHILOOSTT	ethologist
	theologist
EGHILOPSUW	ploughwise
EGHILORTTW	light-tower
EGHIMNOPRS	phorminges
EGHIMNORST	smothering
EGHIMNRRTY	merry-night
EGHIMOPPSU	pemphigous
EGHIMOSSTU	mouse-sight
EGHIMOSUYZ	hemizygous
EGHINNORST	shortening

EGHINOOSTT	theogonist
EGHINORSST	shoestring
EGHINORSTU	southering
EGHINRSTTU	shuttering
EGHIORSTTW	ghost-write
EGHLMOORTY	mythologer
	thermology
EGHLNOOPRY	nephrology
	phrenology
EGHLOOORTY	heortology
EGHLOOPPSY	psephology
EGHLOPPRTY	petroglyph
EGHMNOOOSU	homogenous
EGHMNOOPRY	morphogeny
EGHMOOOTYZ	homozygote
EGHMORRTYY	hygrometry
EGHOORRTUW	ore-wrought
EGHOORRTVW	overgrowth
EGIIILMMST	legitimism
EGIIILMPRS	pilgrimise
EGIIILMPRZ	pilgrimize
EGIIILMSTT	legitimist
EGIIILNNPP	pipelining
EGIIILNORR	irreligion
EGIIIMNNST	meningitis
EGIIKKLNNU	unkinglike
EGIIKLLLNW	well-liking
EGIIKLLTUY	guilty-like
EGIIKLNNRS	ink-slinger
EGIIKLNNSS	kingliness
EGIIKLNPRS	springlike
EGIIKNNRTT	trinketing
EGIIKNPPRS	skippering
EGIIKNPRST	priest-king
EGIILLNNST	tinselling
EGIILLNNSV	snivelling
EGIILLNOTU	guillotine
EGIILLNRSV	silverling
EGIILLNRVY	revilingly
EGIILLNSVW	swivelling
EGIILLRSTV	silver-gilt
EGIILNNPRY	repiningly
EGIILNPRST	priestling
EGIILNQRSU	squireling
EGIILNRRTY	retiringly
EGIILNRSSS	grisliness
EGIILNRSTU	linguister
EGIILNRVVY	revivingly
EGIILNSSTU	guiltiness
EGIILNSSTZ	glitziness
EGIILOPSTT	epiglottis
EGIIMNNRTU	unmeriting
EGIIMNOPRT	primogenit
EGIIMNOPRU	perigonium
EGIIMNPRST	springtime
EGIIMNPRTT	permitting
EGIINNNPRU	unrepining
EGIINNOPTT	ignipotent
EGIINNORSS	ingression
EGIINNSSST	stinginess
EGIINNSTUU	Unigenitus
EGIINORRST	roistering

EGIINORRTT	intertrigo
EGIINRRSTW	sign-writer
EGIINRSSTT	grittiness
EGIINRTTTW	twittering
EGIINSTTTV	vignettist
EGIJKNNSTU	junketings
EGIJNNORUY	journeying
EGIJNOTTTU	outjetting
EGIKLLORRW	grille-work
EGIKLNNPSU	spelunking
EGIKLORRSW	silkgrower
EGIKNNNOST	Kensington
EGIKNNORTW	networking
EGIKNOOQSU	quink-goose
EGILLLNPSY	spellingly
EGILLLNSWY	swellingly
EGILLLORWY	yellow-girl
EGILLMMNPU	pummelling
EGILLNNNTU	tunnelling
EGILLNNOTW	wellington
EGILLNOPPR	propelling
EGILLNOPRT	petrolling
EGILLNORTW	trowelling
EGILLNORWY	loweringly
EGILLNPRSW	wellspring
EGILLNTUXY	exultingly
EGILLOOQSU	goose-quill
EGILLORSSY	syllogiser
EGILLORSYZ	syllogizer
EGILMMNORS	mongrelism
EGILMNOOOS	monologise
EGILMNOOOZ	monologize
EGILMNOOSS	gloominess
EGILMNOPRR	longprimer
EGILMNOPSY	polygenism
EGILMNOPTT	melting-pot
EGILMNOSUU	leguminous
EGILMNPTTY	temptingly
EGILMOOSSY	seismology
EGILNNOSST	slingstone
EGILNNOSSV	lovingness
EGILNNRRUY	unerringly
EGILNNSTTU	unsettling
EGILNOOORY	oneirology
EGILNOOOST	oenologist
EGILNOOPST	penologist
EGILNOPSTY	polygenist
EGILNORRUV	overruling
EGILNORRVW	liver-grown
EGILNORTWY	toweringly
EGILNOSSSS	glossiness
EGILNOSSUY	lysigenous
EGILNOSTTU	gluttonise
EGILNOTTUZ	gluttonize
EGILNPRSSS	springless
EGILNPRSSY	pressingly
EGILNQRUYY	queryingly
EGILNQSTUY	questingly
EGILNRSSST	stringless
EGILNRSTTU	lutestring
EGILOOORST	oreologist
EGILOOPRSU	prologuise

EGILOOPRUZ prologuize
EGILOORSST serologist
EGILOOSSTX sexologist
EGILORSUVY grievously
EGILOSUUXY exiguously
EGIMMNNOOS monogenism
EGIMMNNPTU impugnment
EGIMNNOORR ironmonger
EGIMNNOORS Monsignore
EGIMNNOOST monogenist
EGIMNNOOSU omnigenous
EGIMNNORTT tormenting
EGIMNOORST ergonomist
EGIMNOORTY goniometry
EGIMNPRSSU grumpiness
EGIMNPRTTU trumpeting
EGIMOOPRST geotropism
EGIMOORRSU morigerous
EGINNOPRSU unreposing
EGINNOPSSS sponginess
EGINNORRTW intergrown
EGINNRSUVW unswerving
EGINNSSTTU sunsetting
EGINOOPPST pigeon-post
EGINOOPRRT progenitor
EGINOPRSTY serotyping
EGINOPRSUY perigynous
EGINORRSTU trousering
EGINORRSTW songwriter
EGINORSTUW outswinger
EGINOSTTTU outsetting
EGINPRSTTU sputtering
EGINRSTTTU stuttering
EGIOPPRSUU pupigerous
EGKNOORTUW tongue-work
EGLLMORSUU glomerulus
EGLMNOOOTY entomology
EGLMNOORUY numerology
EGLMNOOYYZ enzymology
EGLNNORSUU sunlounger
EGLNOOOPRY ponerology
EGLNOOPSUY polygenous
EGLNOOSUXY xylogenous
EGLOOORRWW wool-grower
EGLOOPRTYY pyretology
EGMMNOPRSY gymnosperm
EGMMPRUUWY mugwumpery
EGMNNOOOSU monogenous
EGNOOPRSUY pyrogenous
EGNOORRSTV overstrong
EGNORRSTUV overstrung
EGNORSSSST songstress
EGNPQRRSUU quersprung
EGOPPRRSUU supergroup
EGOPRSTTUY Pterygotus
EHHIILOPPP hippophile
EHHIILSTVY thievishly
EHHIIMSTTW whitesmith
EHHILLORST thill-horse
EHHILMOPRT thermophil
EHHILMOSTY hylotheism
EHHILOOPPS philosophe
EHHILOPSTY lithophyse
EHHILOPTTY lithophyte
EHHILORTWW worthwhile
EHHILOSTTY hylotheist
EHHILRSSWY shrewishly
EHHIMORSTT hithermost
EHHINORTTW whitethorn
EHHIOOPRRZ rhizophore
EHHIOPPPTY hippety-hop
EHHIOPSSTY hypothesis
EHHLLOOSTT toothshell
EHHLMRSSTY rhythmless
EHHLOOOPPR lophophore
EHHMMOOOPR homeomorph
EHHMNNOOTY honeymonth
EHHMNORTTU moth-hunter
EHHMORSTTU home-thrust
EHHNOOOPPR phonophore
EHHNOOOPPT photophone
EHHOOOPPRT photophore
EHHOOPPRST phosphoret
EHHOOPRRTY orthophyre
EHHOPPRSTU phosphuret
EHHOPPSSYY hypophyses
EHIIILNPPP philippine
EHIIILNPST △philistine
EHIIILPPPS Philippise
EHIIILPPPZ Philippize
EHIIINRRTX inheritrix
EHIIIPRSVZ viziership
EHIIKLNPSX sphinxlike
EHIIKMRRSS skirmisher
EHIIKMSTWY tim-whiskey
EHIILLOPSY lyophilise
EHIILLOPYZ lyophilize
EHIILMOPRT limitrophe
EHIILNOOPS eosinophil
EHIILNQRSU relinquish
EHIILORTTT lithotrite
EHIIMNOPSX phoenixism
EHIIMNPSSS impishness
EHIIMNSSSW whimsiness
EHIIMOPRSV impoverish
EHIIMPPRSU umpireship
EHIIMPPSTY epiphytism
EHIINNPRST internship
EHIINNRTTY Thirty-nine
EHIINOOPSV visiophone
EHIINPPSSW whippiness
EHIINRSSST shirtiness
EHIINSSSTT shittiness
EHIIOPRSTV Rh-positive
EHIIPPRRST tripperish
EHIIPPRSST priestship
EHIIPQRSSU squireship
EHIIPRRSTW writership
EHIIPRSTTY Triphysite
EHIIRRSTTU urethritis
EHIIRSSTTY hysteritis
EHIKLMNOPY lymphokine
EHIKLOOSVW swivel-hook
EHIKLOPRSY pokerishly

EHIKMNOTTT	kitten-moth
EHILLMNPUY	phillumeny
EHILLNRSSS	shrillness
EHILLOSSTU	stillhouse
EHILMNOPST	polishment
EHILMNSSSU	mulishness
EHILMOPSTY	polytheism
EHILNNORTU	lion-hunter
EHILNNOSSU	unholiness
EHILNOPRTU	neutrophil
EHILNOSSSW	owlishness
EHILOOPRST	strophiole
EHILOOPRTY	heliotropy
EHILOOPSTU	pilot-house
EHILOPRSSU	Russophile
EHILOPSTTY	polytheist
EHILPRSSUU	sulphurise
EHILPRSUUZ	sulphurize
EHILRSSSTT	thirstless
EHIMMNOOST	monotheism
EHIMMOPRTU	promethium
EHIMMOPSTU	imposthume
EHIMNNOORS	moonshiner
EHIMNNPSTU	punishment
EHIMNOORTY	herniotomy
EHIMNOOSTT	monotheist
EHIMNOPRST	mentorship
EHIMNOPSSS	mopishness
EHIMOOPRRU	eriophorum
EHIMOPPRST	prophetism
EHIMOPPSSU	mesohippus
EHIMOPSSTY	hemoptysis
EHIMORRSTT	thermistor
EHIMORRTUV	river-mouth
EHIMPRRTUY	triumphery
EHIMRSTTTU	time-thrust
EHINNORSST	thorniness
EHINNOSSST	tonishness
EHINOOPSUU	euphonious
EHINOOSSTT	toothiness
EHINOPPRTY	periphyton
EHINOPRRTY	pyrrhotine
EHINOPRSTY	hypnotiser
EHINOPRTYZ	hypnotizer
EHINOPSSTX	sextonship
EHINORSSTW	worthiness
EHINORSTUU	ruthenious
EHINOSSSTY	toyishness
EHINPPSSSU	uppishness
EHINSSSTTY	synthesist
EHINSSTTTY	synthetist
EHIOOPPRRS	spirophore
EHIOOPRSSU	puir's-hoose
EHIOOPRSTT	orthoepist
EHIOOPRTTX	thixotrope
EHIOORSSTX	six-shooter
EHIOPPRRSW	worshipper
EHIOPPRRTY	porphyrite
EHIOPRRSTY	prehistory
EHIOPRRTTY	pyrrhotite
EHIOPRSSST	prosthesis
EHIOPRSSUU	puir's-house
EHIPPRRSSU	pursership
EHIPRRSTTU	turret-ship
EHIPRSSTUY	suretyship
EHJMOPRSUW	showjumper
EHKMOOPRSU	skeuomorph
EHKMOSSTTU	musket-shot
EHKOPRSSTU	push-stroke
EHLLNOOSSW	hollowness
EHLLRSSTUY	hurtlessly
	ruthlessly
EHLMNOPPTY	nympholept
EHLMNORTUY	unmotherly
EHLMOOPPRY	pleomorphy
EHLMOPPSUY	Polyphemus
EHLMORSSUU	humourless
EHLNOORSSU	honourless
EHLNORSTUY	southernly
EHLOOPPRRY	plerophory
EHLOOPRSTU	toolpusher
EHLOORTVWY	loveworthy
EHLOPRSTUY	upholstery
EHMMOOPRSY	mesomorphy
EHMMOORRSU	mushroomer
EHMMOORSUU	humoursome
EHMNOOORRT	throne-room
EHMNOOOSTU	theonomous
EHMNOOPRTY	nephrotomy
EHMNOOSSST	smoothness
EHMOOPRSTT	mother-spot
EHMOOPRTTY	photometry
EHMOORRTTW	motherwort
EHMOPRSTYY	hypsometry
EHNNOPRTWY	pennyworth
EHNNPPRTUY	thruppenny
EHNOOPPRRS	pronephros
EHNOORTTWY	noteworthy
EHNORSTWWY	newsworthy
EHOOOPPRRS	sporophore
EHOOOPPRTT	phototrope
EHOOOPRRST	troop-horse
EHOOOPRSSU	poor's-house
EHOOPPRSTY	sporophyte
EHOOPPRTTY	protophyte
	tropophyte
EHOPPPSTUW	puppet-show
EHOPRSSSTY	hypostress
EHORRSTTUV	overthrust
EHORSSTTUU	trust-house
EIIILLLMRT	millilitre
EIIILMNNOP	epilimnion
EIIILORSTV	vitriolise
EIIILORTVZ	vitriolize
EIIIMNOSSS	missionise
EIIIMNOSSZ	missionize
EIIIMSSTVY	emissivity
EIIINPRRST	reinspirit
EIIIOPRRST	priorities
	prioritise
EIIIOPRRTZ	prioritize
EIIJKNPRTY	perjinkity
EIIJLNTUVY	juvenility
EIIJMNORTT	mitre-joint

EIIJMNSTTU	just-in-time
EIIKLLNRTW	winterkill
EIIKLNORST	triskelion
EIIKLNPSTT	kittle-pins
EIIKLNRSSV	silverskin
EIIKMOPRRS	morris-pike
EIIKNNNSSS	skinniness
EIIKNQRSSU	quirkiness
EIILLLSUVY	illusively
EIILLMMNNU	millennium
EIILLMNOOT	emollition
EIILLMNOVY	minivolley
EIILLMOPTY	impolitely
EIILLMPRTU	multiplier
EIILLNOPST	septillion
EIILLNORRT	ritornelli
EIILLNORTT	tortellini
EIILLNOSTX	sextillion
EIILLPPRSY	slipperily
EIILLPSSTY	pitilessly
EIILMMNNTY	imminently
EIILMNNSTT	instilment
EIILMNOSST	lentissimo
EIILMNOSTY	mylonitise
EIILMNOTYZ	mylonitize
EIILMOSUXY	eximiously
EIILNNOTUV	univoltine
EIILNOPRST	prosilient
EIILNORRTY	interiorly
EIILNOSSSV	visionless
EIILNPPSSS	slippiness
EIILNRSSTY	sinisterly
EIILNRSTUV	lentivirus
EIILNSSSTT	stiltiness
EIILOPRSTU	reptilious
EIILOPSSTT	epistolist
EIILOPSTVY	positively
EIILORSTTY	literosity
EIILPRSSST	spiritless
EIIMMOPRSV	misimprove
EIIMMORSTU	immeritous
EIIMMPRSUY	perimysium
EIIMNNORSU	reunionism
EIIMNOPRSS	impression
	permission
EIIMNRSSST	ministress
EIIMOOPSTY	episiotomy
EIIMOPRRSV	improviser
EIIMOPRSSV	promissive
EIIMOPRSUV	impervious
EIIMORRRSW	mirrorwise
EIIMORSSTU	moisturise
EIIMORSTUZ	moisturize
EIINNNORTU	interunion
EIINNNOSTT	intentions
EIINNNRTTU	innutrient
EIINNORSTU	reunionist
EIINNRSSTW	wintriness
EIINOOPRST	reposition
	re-position
EIINOOPSTX	exposition
EIINOORSUV	Eurovision
EIINORSSTV	versionist
EIINORTTWZ	zwitterion
EIINPRSSST	stripiness
EIINQSSUZZ	quizziness
EIINRSSTTW	twin-sister
EIINRSTTTU	instituter
EIINRSTTTW	intertwist
EIINRSTUVY	university
EIINRTTTWY	nitwittery
EIINSSTTTU	institutes
EIIOOPPSTV	oppositive
EIIOOPRSSU	uropoiesis
EIIOQRRSTU	requisitor
EIIORSTTVY	vitreosity
EIIPRTTUVY	eruptivity
EIJNORSSTU	jointuress
EIJOPRRSUU	perjurious
EIKLMNOSSY	Lysenkoism
EIKLRSSSTU	tusser-silk
EIKMNOORST	moonstrike
EIKMNOSTUY	monkey-suit
EIKNNOSSTT	knottiness
	stinkstone
EIKNNPSSSU	spunkiness
EIKNOOPSSS	spookiness
EIKOPPRRST	strip-poker
EIKORSTTTY	Trotskyite
EILLLLSSWY	will-lessly
EILLLSSSTY	listlessly
EILLMOOSTY	toilsomely
EILLMPSSSU	psellismus
EILLNNOSTY	insolently
EILLNOOPSS	pollenosis
EILLNOORRT	ritornello
EILLNOPTUY	unpolitely
EILLNOSSTT	stone-still
EILLNRTUVY	virulently
EILLOPPPPR	pill-popper
EILLOPRSUY	perilously
EILLORRTUY	ulteriorly
EILLORTTTU	litter-lout
EILLQRRSUY	squirrelly
EILMMNOOPU	polemonium
EILMMOPRSY	polymerism
EILMMSSSTU	summitless
EILMNNOSTU	insoulment
EILMNNRTUU	unruliment
EILMNNSTTU	insultment
EILMNOOOPS	monopolise
EILMNOOOPZ	monopolize
EILMNOOSST	motionless
EILMNOPTTY	impotently
EILMNOSSSS	lissomness
EILMNRSSTY	minstrelsy
EILMOOPRST	metropolis
EILMOPPRRY	improperly
EILMOPSUUX	implexuous
EILMORSSTT	moss-litter
EILMRSSSTY	mistressly
EILNNNOOTV	non-violent
EILNNOOSTW	low-tension
EILNNOSTTW	Tinseltown

EILNNRSSUU	unruliness
EILNOOOPTV	love-potion
EILNOORSTU	resolution
	re-solution
EILNOORTUV	revolution
EILNOOSTUV	evolutions
EILNOPPRTW	nipplewort
EILNOPPSSS	sloppiness
EILNOPPSTU	suppletion
EILNOPRSST	portliness
EILNOPRSSX	prolixness
EILNOPRSUU	unperilous
EILNOPRXYY	pyroxyline
EILNORRSTY	introrsely
EILNORSSUY	neurolysis
	resinously
EILNOSTUUV	velutinous
EILNPQTTUU	quintuplet
EILNPRRTUY	pruriently
EILNPRSSTY	spinsterly
EILNPRSTUY	unpriestly
EILNRSSSTU	sultriness
EILNRSSTUY	unsisterly
EILOOPPSTY	oppositely
EILOPPRSUV	propulsive
EILOPRRSTU	protrusile
EILOPRRSUY	superiorly
EILOPRSSTY	pterylosis
EILOPRSTUY	pyrolusite
EILOPRSTVY	sportively
EILOPRSUVY	perviously
	previously
	viperously
EILRRSTUVW	liverwurst
EIMMNNORSW	non-swimmer
EIMNNOOPTT	omnipotent
EIMNNOPRST	prisonment
EIMNNORSUU	innumerous
EIMNNOSSYY	synonymise
EIMNNOSYYZ	synonymize
EIMNNRSTTU	instrument
EIMNOOPRRT	premonitor
EIMNOOPRSS	spoonerism
EIMNOOSTTT	tenotomist
EIMNOOTTZZ	mezzotinto
EIMNOPRRTU	importuner
EIMNOPRSTU	resumption
EIMNORSSST	storminess
EIMNORSSSU	sensoriums
EIMNORSTUY	numerosity
EIMNPSSSTU	stumpiness
EIMNSSSTTU	smuttiness
EIMOOQSSTU	mosquitoes
EIMOPRRSTU	romper-suit
EIMOPRRSTY	spirometry
EIMORSSTUY	mysterious
EIMQRRTTUU	triquetrum
EINNNOOPRT	pontonnier
EINNOOPPRS	propension
EINNOOPRST	protension
EINNOOPSTU	out-pension
EINNOORTUX	neurotoxin
EINNOOSSST	snootiness
EINNOPSSSU	suspension
EINNOSSSTT	snottiness
EINNOSSSTY	syntenosis
EINNOSSSUU	insensuous
EINNOSSTTU	sustention
EINNPRTTUY	turpentiny
EINOOPPRSS	oppression
EINOOPRRST	resorption
EINOOPRSTU	proteinous
EINOOPSSSS	possession
EINOOPTTTT	totipotent
EINOORSSST	rootsiness
EINOORSSTU	serotinous
EINOORTTTX	tetrotoxin
EINOPPRSTY	propensity
EINOPRRRST	ripsnorter
EINOPRSSST	sportiness
EINOPRSTTY	protensity
EINOPSSSTT	spottiness
EINOQRTTUU	tourniquet
EINORRRTUU	nourriture
EINPRSSSST	spinstress
EINRSSSTTU	trustiness
EIOOOPRSTZ	sporozoite
EIOOPPRRRT	proprietor
EIOOPPRRST	prepositor
EIOOPRRSST	posteriors
EIOOPRRSSU	repoussoir
EIOOPRRSTY	repository
EIOOPRSSTT	strepitoso
EIOOPRSSTU	isopterous
EIOOPRSTXY	expository
EIOORRSSTU	roisterous
EIOORSTTUZ	zootsuiter
EIOPPRRSTY	prosperity
EIOPPRSTUV	supportive
EIOPRRSSUV	supervisor
EIOPRRSTTU	tripterous
EIOPRRSTUV	protrusive
EIOPRRTTVY	protervity
EIOPRSSTTU	strepitous
EIOPRSTTTU	prostitute
EIORRRSTUV	retrovirus
EIORRSTTTU	restitutor
EJNNSSSTUU	unjustness
EJNOOSSSUY	joyousness
EKLNOORSTV	lover's-knot
EKLOORRTUW	work-to-rule
EKMMNOPPUY	monkey-pump
EKNORRSSTW	sternworks
EKOPPRRSUW	upperworks
EKORRTTTUY	turkey-trot
ELLLOSSSUY	soullessly
ELLMMPSSUU	mussel-plum
ELLMORRSTU	muster-roll
ELLNNOPTUY	polytunnel
ELLNPRTUUY	purulently
ELLOOORTWY	yellow-root
ELLOORTWWY	yellow-wort
ELLOPSSSTY	spotlessly
ELMMOOPPSU	pompelmous

ELMNOORSUY	enormously
ELMNOOSUVY	venomously
ELMNORSUUY	numerously
ELMNPPSTUY	supplyment
ELMOOPRSUY	polymerous
ELMOOPRTUY	pleurotomy
ELMOOPRTXY	protoxylem
ELMORSTTYY	stylometry
ELNOOOPRTU	poultroone
ELNOORSTUU	ultroneous
ELNOPPRRUY	unproperly
ELNOSSSUUY	sensuously
ELOOORRSTW	woolsorter
ELOORRSSSW	sorrowless
ELOPPRSTUY	Polypterus
	suppletory
ELOPPRSUVY	oversupply
ELOPRSTTUU	turtle-soup
EMMNRSSTUU	menstruums
EMMNRSTUYY	unsymmetry
EMMOOPRSTT	post-mortem
EMNNOOOPRT	monopteron
EMNOOOPRST	monopteros
EMNOOPPRTT	prompt-note
EMNOOQSTUU	musquetoon
EMNOPPRSST	promptness
EMNORRSTUU	surmounter
EMNORSSTUU	menstruous
EMNOSTTTUU	mutton-suet
EMOOORRSTV	servomotor
EMOORRSTVY	vestry-room
ENOOPPRSST	postperson
ENOOPRRSSY	responsory
ENOOPRSSSU	porousness
ENOOPRSTTU	portentous
ENOORSTTTU	troutstone
ENOOSSSSTY	synostoses
ENOPRSSSUY	suspensory
EOOOPRSSUX	exosporous
EOOOSSTTTV	voetstoots
EOOPPRRSSU	prosperous
EOOPRRSSTU	pro-oestrus
EOOPRSSSSY	possessory
EOORRSSTTU	stertorous
EOORRSSTUY	roysterous
EOPPRRSSSU	suppressor
EOPPRRSTUU	supporture

F

FFFFIITTYY	fifty-fifty
FFGHIIINRS	griffinish
FFGHIILNSY	fly-fishing
FFGHIIOPPR	hippogriff
FFGHIMNRUU	humgruffin
FFGHORSTUU	rough-stuff
FFGIIIMNRS	griffinism
FFGIILLLNU	fulfilling
FFGIILNNSY	sniffingly
FFGIINORTY	fortifying
FFGIJMNOPU	jumping-off
FFGINOPTTU	off-putting
FFIIRRSTTU	first-fruit
FFILLRTUUY	fruitfully
FFILNRTUUU	unfruitful
FFILOORRST	first-floor
FGGHHIILNY	high-flying
FGGHIIINNT	infighting
	in-fighting
FGGHINOORT	forthgoing
FGGIIILNNY	lignifying
FGGIIINNSY	signifying
FGGIILNORY	glorifying
FGHHIORRTT	forthright
FGHHLOTTUU	thoughtful
FGHIILNSTU	insightful
FGHIINNSTU	unshifting
FGHIINORRY	horrifying
FGHILLRTUY	rightfully
FGHILNRTUU	unrightful
FGHILOOPRT	light-proof
FGHILOOSTT	footlights
FGHILPRSTU	sprightful
FGHINNOTUX	fox-hunting
FGHMOORSTU	frog's-mouth
FGIIINNRTY	nitrifying
FGIIJNSTUY	justifying
FGIIKLNRSY	friskingly
FGIILLMNOY	mollifying
FGIILLNNUY	nullifying
FGIILLNRTY	flirtingly
	triflingly
FGIILLNSTY	stiflingly
FGIILMNORU	linguiform
FGIILNOSUU	fuliginous
FGIILNPPTY	fly-tipping
FGIIMMMNUY	mummifying
FGIIMNORTY	mortifying
FGIIMNSTYY	mystifying
FGIIMORRST	strigiform
FGIINOTTTU	fitting-out
	outfitting
FGIKLNOOOR	looking-for
FGIKNNORTU	tuning-fork
FGIKNRSSUY	sky-surfing
FGILLNOTUY	floutingly
FGILNNORWY	frowningly
FGILNOOTUW	outflowing
FGILNOPSTY	flyposting
FGIMNOOPRS	spongiform
FGLLNORUWY	wrongfully
FGLOORTUUY	futurology
FHILLMRTUY	mirthfully
FHILOORSTT	frithstool
FHILOPRSUW	worshipful
FHLLLOSTUY	slothfully
FHLLOTUUYY	youthfully
FHLLRTTUUY	truthfully
FHLNRTTUUU	untruthful
FIILMMNOOR	moniliform
FIILMMORTY	mytiliform
FIILMNOPPY	mini-floppy
FIILMOPRSY	ypsiliform
FIILNOSTUX	fluxionist
FIIMNORTUY	uniformity

FIIMOORSST	fortissimo
FIIMORSTTU	fortuitism
FIINORTTUU	futurition
FIIORSTTTU	fortuitist
FIKLLLLSUY	skillfully
FIKLLOORST	folklorist
FILLOOPTTY	toploftily
FILNOORSUU	uniflorous
FILOOOPRST	portfolios
FIMNOSTTTU	mutton-fist
FIOORSTTUU	fortuitous
FLLMNORUUY	mournfully
FLLMORSTUY	stormfully
FLLOPRSTUY	sportfully
FLLRSTTUUY	trustfully
FLNRSTTUUU	untrustful
FMOOOPRRST	stormproof
FUUWYYZZZZ	fuzzy-wuzzy

G

GGGIILLNNY	nigglingly
GGGIJLLNUY	jugglingly
GGGILNRSTU	struggling
GGHHHIILST	highlights
GGHHIILNTT	night-light
GGHHIILSWY	Whiggishly
GGHHIILTTT	light-tight
GGHHIINNTT	night-night
GGHHIINSTT	night-sight
GGHHINRSTU	high-strung
GGHIILNPTU	lighting-up
GGHIILPRSY	priggishly
GGHIIPRRYY	higry-pigry
GGHILLSSUY	sluggishly
GGHILNOSTU	oughtlings
GGIIIINSTV	gingivitis
GGIIINNRTU	intriguing
GGIILLMNNY	minglingly
GGIILNNSTY	stingingly
GGIILNNSWY	swingingly
GGILLLNOOR	log-rolling
GGILLNNOUY	loungingly
GGILLNORWY	growlingly
GGILNNRTUY	gruntingly
GGILNOOOSY	gnosiology
GGINNNNRUU	gunrunning
GGLLOOOSSY	glossology
GGLLOOOTTY	glottology
GGLNOOOPSY	spongology
GHHIILSTTY	tightishly
GHHIINRSTT	nightshirt
GHHIIPRSTW	shipwright
GHHILLOPTY	lithoglyph
GHHILLOSUY	ghoulishly
GHHIMOSTTU	misthought
GHHINOPRTT	triphthong
GHHIOPPPRY	hippogryph
GHHLOOPPTY	photoglyph
GHHLOORTUY	thoroughly
GHHNOORTUU	unthorough
GHHNORRTUU	run-through
GHHOORTTUU	throughout
GHHOPRTTUU	put-through
	throughput
GHIIKLNNTY	thinkingly
GHIIKNNNTU	unthinking
GHIIKNSSTT	skin-tights
GHIILLMRTW	millwright
GHIILNOPSS	polishings
GHIILNRTVY	thrivingly
GHIILNRTWY	writhingly
GHIILNWYZZ	whizzingly
GHIILOOSTY	histiology
GHIIMNNOST	nothingism
GHIIMNPRTU	triumphing
GHIINNORSU	nourishing
GHIKLNNTUY	unknightly
GHIKNOORTW	hot-working
GHILMNPTUY	thumpingly
GHILMOOORU	△horologium
GHILNOOPRU	plough-iron
GHILNOOPST	phlogiston
GHILNOOSTT	night-stool
GHILNOOSTY	soothingly
GHILNORTTT	throttling
GHILNOSTTU	gluttonish
GHILNOSTUY	shoutingly
GHILNRRUYY	hurryingly
GHILOOORST	horologist
GHILOOPSYY	physiology
GHILOORSTT	grith-stool
GHIMMNOPTU	humming-top
GHINNOPTTU	pot-hunting
GHINNRRUUY	unhurrying
GHLLOOPTYY	typhlology
GHLMOOOOSU	homologous
GHLMOOOPRY	morphology
GHLNOOPSUW	snowplough
GHLOOOPRTY	trophology
GHMNOOPSYY	gymnosophy
GHMOOOSUYZ	homozygous
GHMOOPRYYZ	zygomorphy
GHNOOPSUYY	hypogynous
GHOORTTUUW	outwrought
GIIIILNRSV	virilising
GIIIILNRVZ	virilizing
GIIIIMMNNS	minimising
GIIIIMMNNZ	minimizing
GIIIKNNRTW	writing-ink
GIIILLNNST	instilling
GIIILNNPRT	tirling-pin
GIIILNNTVY	invitingly
GIIIMNNNOR	iron-mining
GIIIMNNPRT	imprinting
GIIIMNRSTY	myringitis
GIIINNNTUV	uninviting
GIIINRSSTY	syringitis
GIIJKKNORS	skikjöring
GIIJKMNPSU	ski-jumping
GIIKLLLNOO	ill-looking
GIIKLLNNTY	tinklingly
GIIKLMMNSY	skimmingly
GIIKLMNPSY	skimpingly
GIIKLMNRSY	smirkingly

GIIKLNNPRS sprinkling
GIIKLNNRST strinkling
GIIKLNNSTY stinkingly
GIIKLNPPSY skippingly
GIIKLNRSTY strikingly
GIIKNORSTU ski-touring
GIIKNRSTWY sky-writing
GIILLLNOPU louping-ill
GIILLLNPUV pulvilling
GIILLNNOPR rolling-pin
GIILLNOPRY pillorying
GIILLNOPST pistolling
GIILLNPPRY ripplingly
GIILLNSYZZ sizzlingly
GIILMMNRTY trimmingly
GIILMMNSWY swimmingly
GIILMNOORV living-room
GIILMNOPSY imposingly
GIILMOOSST misologist
GIILNNNOTY intoningly
GIILNNPPSU unslipping
GIILNNRTUY untiringly
GIILNNSTTY stintingly
GIILNOOPST topsoiling
GIILNOORSU inglorious
GIILNOOSST Sinologist
GIILNOOSTV vinologist
GIILNPPRTY trippingly
GIILNPRSST slip-string
GIILNRRSTY stirringly
GIILNRSTUY linguistry
GIILNRSTVY strivingly
GIILNTTTWY twittingly
GIILOORSTV virologist
GIIMNNOORS Monsignori
GIIMNNOPSU unimposing
GIIMNOORRT tiring-room
GIIMNOSSTY misogynist
GIINNNSTTU unstinting
GIINNSTTUW untwisting
GIINOTTTUW outwitting
GIINPPRSST strippings
GIINPPTTTU tittupping
GIINPRRSSU surprising
GIJKMNPSUY sky-jumping
GIJNNOORSU sojourning
GIJNOTTTUU outjutting
GIKKLLNSUY skulkingly
GIKMNNNOOS non-smoking
GIKNNORSTT strong-knit
GILLNNOUVY unlovingly
GILLNOOPRT trolloping
GILLNOPRWY prowlingly
GILLNOPTTY plottingly
GILLNPUYZZ puzzlingly
GILLNRSTUY rustlingly
GILLOORSUY gloriously
GILMMNOOUY immunology
GILMNNORUY mourningly
GILMNNUUZZ unmuzzling
GILMNOOOST monologist
nomologist
GILMNOOSVW slow-moving
GILMOOOPST pomologist
GILMOOSTYZ zymologist
GILNNNOPSU nonplusing
GILNNNSTUY stunningly
GILNNOOSWY swooningly
GILNNORSTY snortingly
GILNOOOPSY oligopsony
GILNOOOSST nosologist
GILNOOOSTT ontologist
GILNOOPSTY stoopingly
GILNOPRSTY sportingly
GILNORRWYY worryingly
GILNPRSUUY pursuingly
usurpingly
GILNRSTTUY trustingly
GILOOOPSTT optologist
topologist
GILOOOPSTU goloptious
GILOOORSTY storiology
GILOOPRSTT proglottis
GILOOPSTTY typologist
GILOOPSTUU goluptious
GILOORRSUY rigorously
GILOORSUVY vigorously
GIMNNNRRUU rum-running
GIMNNOORSS Monsignors
GIMNOOSSUY misogynous
GINNOOPSTU unstooping
GINNOPRSTU unsporting
GINNRSSTUU untrussing
GINOOPPTTU topping-out
GINOOPRRSU ring-porous
GINOOPRRTU nitro-group
GINOOPRTUU outpouring
GINOPPRSTU supporting
GINOPRRSTW springwort
GINPPTTTUU put-putting
GINTTTTTUU tut-tutting
GKOOORRTTW grotto-work
GLNOOPSUYY polygynous
GLNOORSUWY wrongously
GLNOOSTTUU gluttonous
GMNNOOOSUY monogynous
GMNOOOOPTY pogonotomy
GMNOOORRST strongroom

H

HHILOOPPSY philosophy
HHILOOPPTY photophily
HHIMOOOPPR ophiomorph
HHIMOOPRRZ rhizomorph
HHINOOPPSS shop-in-shop
HHIOPPSSYY hypophysis
HHLLOPPSYY hypsophyll
HHLMOPRTYY polyrhythm
HHNOOOPPTY photophony
HHOOPPRSSU phosphorus
HIIKLSSTTY skittishly
HIILLNORTT trillionth
HIILMMPSSY symphilism
HIILMOOPSZ zoophilism

HIILNOPRTT lithoprint
HIILOOPSTZ zoophilist
HIILOPPPSU Pliohippus
HIILOPPSTW pistol-whip
HIILORTTTY lithotrity
HIILOSSSTY histolysis
HIIMMNOPRS morphinism
HIIMOPRSSW misworship
HIIMSSTTYY hitty-missy
HIINOORSST ornithosis
HIINORRSUV rhinovirus
HIIOOOPRST oophoritis
HIIOOTTTYY hoity-toity
HIJMNNOOSS Johnsonism
HIKLNORSTW thrown-silk
HILLOOPRST trollopish
HILLSSTTUY sluttishly
HILMNOPSUU sulphonium
HILMNORTTY trimonthly
HILMOPSSUY symphilous
HILNORTUWY unworthily
HILOOOPSUZ zoophilous
HILOOPRSTY polyhistor
HILOOPSSTY photolysis
HIMMNOOTYY homonymity
HIMNNOOPSY symphonion
HIMNOOOOPR omophorion
HIMNOPRRSY Pyrrhonism
HIMNOPSSTY symphonist
HIMOOPRRST orthoprism
HINOOPTTXY phytotoxin
HINOPRRSTY Pyrrhonist
HIOOPPRRSY porphyrios
HIOOPRSTTT orthoptist
HIOOPRTTXY thixotropy
HIORSSTTUU struthious
HKNOOOUWWY you-know-who
HLLOOPPRSY sporophyll
HLMOOOSTUY hylotomous
HLMOORSUUY humorously
HLMOPSSUYY symphylous
HLOPRSSUUU sulphurous
HMMNOOOSUY homonymous
HMMOOORTTU motormouth
HMNOOOOSTU homotonous
HMOOPSSTUU posthumous
HNNORSSTUY synthronus
HOOOOSSTTT hoots-toots
HOOOPPRTTY phototropy
HOOOPRRTTY orthotropy
HOOPPRRSUY porphyrous
△pyrophorus
HOOSSTTTUU houts-touts

I

IIIKLLNPSS spillikins
IIIKLLNPSW pilliwinks
IIILLMMMSU simillimum
IIILLMMNSU illuminism
IIILLMNSTU illuminist
IIILLNOPST pillionist
IIILNOSSTT tonsilitis
IIIMMNNOTU imminution
IIIMNOOPST imposition
IIIMNOPRSS misprision
IIIMOPSSTV positivism
IIINNOOPST opinionist
IIINOQRSTU inquisitor
IIINOQSTUU iniquitous
IIIOPSSTTV positivist
IIIOPSTTVY positivity
IIKLMNNOOT link-motion
IIKLOOPSTT Ostpolitik
IILLLLNWYY willy-nilly
IILLLLWWYY willy-willy
IILLLOPPSW pillowslip
IILLLOPSUV pulvillios
IILLMOOSTU mollitious
IILLNOOPST postillion
IILMMNOOSU moliminous
IILMNOPSTY postliminy
IILMNOSTUY luminosity
IILMOSTUUV multivious
IILNNOOTUV involution
IILNNOTTUY non-utility
IILNOOQRRU iron-liquor
IILOOPRSUX prolixious
IIMMOORTUV vomitorium
IIMNNOOSSU insomnious
IIMOOPRSST isotropism
IINOOOPPST opposition
IINOOPRSSV provisions
IINOOPRSTT portionist
IINORSSSTU sinistrous
IINORSTTTU institutor
IINORSTTUU nutritious
IIOOOPRSTV ovipositor
IIOOPPRSTU propitious
IIOPRSSSUU suspirious
IIOPRSSTUU spirituous
IIOPRSSTUY spuriosity
IIORSTTUVY virtuosity
IJLNOOOSTT joint-stool
IKMORSSTTY Trotskyism
IKNOPRRSTW printworks
IKORSSTTTY Trotskyist
ILLMNOSUUY luminously
ILLMOQTUUY multiloquy
ILLOPPPSSY slipsloppy
ILMNOOOPST monopolist
ILMNOOOPSY polyominos
ILMNOOOSTW slow-motion
ILMNOOQSUY somniloquy
ILMNOOSUUV voluminous
ILMNOSTUUY mutinously
ILMOORSTUY timorously
ILMORSTTUY multistory
ILNOOPPRSU propulsion
ILNOPRSTUU pultrusion
ILOOPPRSST spoilsport
ILOORSTTUY tortiously
ILOORSUUXY uxoriously
ILOPRSSUUY spuriously
ILORSSUUUY usuriously

ILORSTUUVY	virtuously
IMMOOPRSTU	prostomium
IMNNOSSTYY	synonymist
IMNNOSTYYY	synonymity
IMNOOORSUV	omnivorous
IMOOPRRSSY	promissory
IMTUUYZZZZ	tuzzi-muzzy
INOOOPPRRT	proportion
INOOPRRSTU	protrusion
INOOSSSSTY	synostosis
INOQRSTUWY	quinsy-wort
INORSTUUUV	unvirtuous
IOOOPRSSSU	isosporous
IOOOPRSSTU	isotropous
IOOORSSSUV	ossivorous
IOORSTTTUY	tortuosity

L

LLOOPPSUUY	populously
LLORSSTUUY	lustrously
LMNOOOSUXY	monoxylous
LMOOORRRTY	motor-lorry
LMOOOSTUXY	xylotomous
LMOSTTUUUU	tumultuous
LNOOORSSUY	sonorously
LNOOPPSUUU	unpopulous
LOOPPRRSUY	propulsory
LOOPSTUUUV	voluptuous
LOORSTTUUY	tortuously

M

MMPPPRUUYY	rumpy-pumpy
MNNOOOOSTU	monotonous
MNNOOSSUYY	synonymous
MNOOOPRRTY	promontory
MNOORSSTUU	monstruous
MTUUYYZZZZ	tuzzy-muzzy

N

NOOOPRSTTU	trout-spoon

O

OOOOPRSSUZ	zoosporous
OOPPPSSWYY	popsy-wopsy
OPRSTTUVYY	topsy-turvy

11AAA

A

AAAAABBCDRR	abracadabra
AAAAABHHMRT	Mahabharata
AAAAANRRTTT	taratantara
AAAABBCELNR	Calabar-bean
AAAABBINRST	△sabbatarian
AAAABCCHILN	bacchanalia
AAAACCCELMN	Malacca-cane
AAAACCEEHNT	Acanthaceae
AAAACDEENNP	Pandanaceae
AAAACEELNPT	Platanaceae
AAAACEELNST	Santalaceae
AAAACEEMNRT	Marantaceae
AAAACGILPSS	passacaglia
AAAACNRRSVY	caravansary
AAAADEHRTVV	Atharvaveda
AAAAEEHNNPT	Panathenaea
AAAAFINRRST	△rastafarian
AAAAGHIPPRR	paragraphia
AAAAHIPPRRX	paraphraxia
AAAAHMNPSTT	phantasmata
AAAALLLOOPZ	lalapalooza
AAAAMRTZZZZ	razzamatazz
AAABBCCEEMO	Bombacaceae
AAABBCEGLMP	cabbage-palm
	palm-cabbage
AAABBEINRSS	Bessarabian
AAABCCDLRRY	Barclaycard
AAABCCEEILL	Bacillaceae
AAABCCHNRSS	chars-à-bancs
AAABCDDIRRY	bradycardia
AAABCDEEINR	abecedarian
AAABCDEIORS	scarabaeoid
AAABCDELNRS	candelabras
AAABCDEMNRU	maceranduba
AAABCDFIORS	fascia-board
AAABCDKLNNT	Black-and-Tan
	black-and-tan
AAABCDLLLNW	ball-and-claw
	claw-and-ball
AAABCEEIMRT	bacteraemia
AAABCEGILLR	algebraical
AAABCEHINRT	abranchiate
AAABCEHPRSU	chapeau-bras
AAABCEIILLM	bacillaemia
AAABCEIMPRT	parabematic
AAABCEIRSST	scarabaeist
AAABCELLLOT	allocatable
AAABCELRTTT	attractable
AAABCHILMNR	Brahmanical
AAABCHLLMPS	paschal-lamb
AAABCILLNTY	abactinally
AAABCILLOPR	parabolical
AAABCILNOTT	ablactation
AAABDEGGNOV	vagabondage
AAABDEILNPT	inadaptable
AAABDELNPTU	unadaptable
AAABEEGLLSV	salvageable
AAABEEHLNPT	analphabete
AAABEGILNPR	plea-bargain
AAABEGKMNNR	bank-manager
AAABEGOPSST	passage-boat
AAABEHIMNPS	△amphisbaena

AAABEIIJNRZ Azerbaijani
AAABEIILNRS Rabelaisian
AAABEILLMRT ambilateral
AAABEILLNUV unavailable
AAABEILNRST alabastrine
AAABEILPPRS appraisable
AAABELLNPTU unpalatable
AAABELNRRTW warrantable
AAABENNOPRT Bonapartean
AAABFINNORT Fontarabian
AAABGHIOOPR agoraphobia
AAABHIKRSTV svarabhakti
AAABHIOPRST astraphobia
AAABIINORST arabisation
AAABIINORTZ arabization
AAABILLNUVY unavailably
AAABIMPPRST parabaptism
AAABLLNPTUY unpalatably
AAABLNOPRSU parabolanus
AAABLNRRTWY warrantably
AAACCCEILTT acatalectic
AAACCCEINPT capacitance
AAACCCILLTT catallactic
AAACCCILMST cataclasmic
AAACCCILSTT cataclastic
AAACCCISTTU catacaustic
AAACCDEEIPS Dipsacaceae
AAACCDEHRST saccharated
AAACCDEIIMN academician
AAACCDEILMS academicals
AAACCDHIRTY tachycardia
AAACCEEELLN Canellaceae
AAACCEEHSTT attaché-case
AAACCEENOPY Apocynaceae
AAACCEERSTY Styracaceae
AAACCEFLOST catafalcoes
AAACCEHINPU ipecacuanha
AAACCEHNOPR achaenocarp
AAACCEILLOR calceolaria
AAACCEILNRS Saracenical
AAACCEILPRT Palaearctic
AAACCEILPTT acataleptic
AAACCELMNOS calamancoes
AAACCGILNPT pan-galactic
AAACCGLLMNO clog-almanac
AAACCHILLRY archaically
AAACCHILNRT charlatanic
AAACCHILRTT cathartical
AAACCHILRTU autarchical
AAACCILLNRU canalicular
AAACCILLPRT parallactic
AAACCILLSTT stalactical
AAACCILLTTY catalytical
AAACCILMNOT acclamation
AAACCILRRTU caricatural
AAACCILSTUV accusatival
AAACCIMNORT carcinomata
AAACCLMOPRT caprolactam
AAACCLMORTY acclamatory
AAACDEEEILP Pedaliaceae
AAACDEEILOX Oxalidaceae
AAACDEEIMRR camaraderie
AAACDEEMRRY camera-ready
AAACDEFIJNN Janian-faced
AAACDEHINRT acidanthera
AAACDEILMPR paramedical
pre-adamical
AAACDEILNRT cardinalate
AAACDEINRTY caryatidean
AAACDGILNRT crag-and-tail
AAACDHILNOR arachnoidal
AAACDHILNRT cantharidal
AAACDIIMNRS Arcadianism
AAACDILOPRX paradoxical
AAACDILQRTU quadratical
AAACEEEGINR Geraniaceae
AAACEEFIMRU Fumariaceae
AAACEEFLMNS malfeasance
AAACEEGILNO Loganiaceae
AAACEEGNNRR carrageenan
AAACEEILNOV Valoniaceae
AAACEENPPRS appearances
AAACEENRTTV caravanette
AAACEFLMNRS MacFarlane's
AAACEFLRTTU artefactual
AAACEGHILLP cephalalgia
AAACEGHILNW caaing-whale
AAACEGILMNO egomaniacal
AAACEGIRRWY carriageway
AAACEGLLLRT call-at-large
AAACEHILLPR parheliacal
AAACEHILPTT apathetical
AAACEHINNPT Panathenaic
AAACEHINRRT trachearian
AAACEILLMNR all-American
AAACEILLNPT Placentalia
AAACEILNPRS Paracelsian
AAACEILNPSU Aesculapian
AAACEILORSU araliaceous
AAACEIMMPRU paramaecium
AAACEIMNNPR Pan-American
AAACEINPRRT carpentaria
AAACEIPPRRT paraparetic
AAACELMNPTU campanulate
AAACELMNRST sacramental
AAACELMOPRT paracetamol
AAACFGILNPT flag-captain
AAACFILLNTY fanatically
AAACFILNSTT fantastical
AAACFIMNNOR Francomania
AAACFIMNRRT aircraftman
AAACFJLMNRY clanjamfray
AAACGGILOPR paragogical
AAACGHIPPRR paragraphic
AAACGHLMOYZ chalazogamy
AAACGHLOPRS sarcophagal
AAACGIINNRU Aurignacian
AAACGILLNTY agnatically
AAACGILMMRT grammatical
AAACGILMNNO △anglomaniac
AAACGILMPRT pragmatical
AAACGILNNNP Pan-Anglican
AAACGIMPRST sparagmatic
AAACGINNNRV caravanning

AAACGNRRSSY canary-grass
AAACHHIPSTY tachyphasia
AAACHIILPPR paraphiliac
AAACHIILPRS pharisaical
AAACHIKPPRT apparatchik
AAACHILMRRT matriarchal
AAACHILMSTT asthmatical
AAACHILNOPR anaphorical
AAACHILNOTU anacoluthia
AAACHILPRRT patriarchal
AAACHILRSWY cash-railway
AAACHIMNNOT anthomaniac
AAACHLNRRTY charlatanry
AAACHNQTUUU Chautauquan
AAACIILMOTX axiomatical
AAACIILNOTT Taliacotian
AAACIILPRST parasitical
AAACIKLRRWY rack-railway
AAACILLMNRU animalcular
AAACILLMPST plasmatical
AAACILLNORV Convallaria
AAACILLNSTY satanically
AAACILLRTUY actuarially
AAACILLSTTT stalactital
AAACILMOTTU automatical
AAACILMPSST spasmatical
AAACILNNORY alcyonarian
AAACILNNRST Lancastrian
AAACILOPSTT apostatical
AAACIMNNORY acronymania
AAACINPRSTT pancratiast
AAACINPSTUU sapucaia-nut
AAACINQSTUU aquanautics
AAADDEHMRSY hamadryades
AAADDELNOST adelantados
AAADDFHNRST hard-and-fast
AAADEFFNNOR fanfaronade
AAADEFIOSST assafoetida
AAADEGILMNN Magdalenian
AAADEGIMRUV marivaudage
AAADEGLNRTV landgravate
AAADEHIMPST Phasmatidae
AAADEHMNOWY home-and-away
AAADEHMNRRW hardwareman
AAADEHMOPST Phasmatodea
AAADEHNRSWW wash-and-wear
AAADEILMPTV maladaptive
AAADEILNNRX Alexandrian
AAADEILRRSV adversarial
AAADEIMNNNS Sandemanian
AAADEIMNNRT mandarinate
AAADENNNRST transandean
AAADENNPRST transpadane
AAADFFHHLLN half-and-half
AAADFLNRRTU auld-farrant
AAADGGINORT aggradation
AAADGHILMPR diaphragmal
AAADGIILMNR madrigalian
AAADGILNORT gradational
AAADHHLPRYZ haphazardly
AAADIILNORR radiolarian
AAADILMOQRU maquiladora
AAADIMOPRST paramastoid
AAADJMNNPRU panjandarum
AAAEEELNPRS paraselenae
AAAEEGGMNST stage-manage
AAAEEGHMNOP Phaenogamae
AAAEEGINPRS paragenesia
AAAEEGRTTVX extravagate
AAAEEHINSST anaesthesia
AAAEEHMNTTX exanthemata
AAAEERSTTVX extravasate
AAAEFNRSSWY farawayness
AAAEGHILNRT Argathelian
AAAEGHIMMNO haemangioma
AAAEGHPPRRR paragrapher
AAAEGIILNRT egalitarian
AAAEGILMMNO megalomania
AAAEGIMRRTV margraviate
AAAEGLOPRSS paraglossae
AAAEGNRTTVX extravagant
AAAEHIILMPT epithalamia
AAAEHILMSST thalassemia
AAAEHILNPRT paranthelia
AAAEHILNPRX hexaplarian
AAAEHIMNNRT amaranthine
AAAEHINPPRR paraphrenia
AAAEHINPPRT Aphaniptera
AAAEHMNNOPP panomphaean
AAAEHPPRRRS paraphraser
AAAEIIMPRST parasitemia
AAAEILMNNOT emanational
AAAEILMNOPT petalomania
AAAEILPPRRS reappraisal
AAAEIMNNRTU Mauretanian
AAAEINSSSST assassinate
AAAEIPPRRSS paraparesis
AAAEKLMNOOT malakatoone
AAAEKMMNRTU mantua-maker
AAAELMNPRTT apartmental
AAAEMRSSSTY assay-master
AAAEPPRSSTU apparatuses
AAAFFFILNST Falstaffian
AAAFFINPRWX paraffin-wax
AAAGGGINRTV aggravating
AAAGGHHIOPR Hagiographa
AAAGGINORTV aggravation
AAAGHIMNOPR graphomania
AAAGIILNPRS parasailing
AAAGIIMNRRS agrarianism
AAAGIINNRSU sanguinaria
AAAGIINRSTT sagittarian
AAAGILNNPQU aquaplaning
AAAGILNPRTV travail-pang
AAAGKNOORRT kangaroo-rat
rat-kangaroo
AAAGLLOPRSS paraglossal
AAAGLMNORTU granulomata
AAAGLMNRSTU mangalsutra
AAAGMNNORST manna-groats
AAAHIIILNNTT antithalian
AAAHILMOPRT prothalamia
AAAHILNPSXY anaphylaxis
AAAHIMNNORT Marathonian

AAAHINNORTZ	zoantharian
AAAHINPSSTT	phantasiast
AAAHIPPRRSX	paraphraxis
AAAHNNOPSTY	satanophany
AAAIILLMMMR	mammillaria
AAAIILMPRSU	Marsupialia
AAAIILNORTV	variational
AAAIILNPRTV	travail-pain
AAAIILNPSTU	saintpaulia
AAAIINNQRTU	antiquarian
AAAILLMORTY	amatorially
AAAILLNOTUV	valuational
AAAILLORSTT	saltatorial
AAAILNNRSTU	saturnalian
AAAILOPRRTT	raptatorial
AAAIMNNOOST	antonomasia
AAAIMNOOPRS	paronomasia
AAAOPRSSTUU	Apatosaurus
AABBCCIILST	cabbalistic
AABBCDEINRT	brace-and-bit
AABBCEEEGRT	cabbage-tree
AABBCEEGORS	cabbage-rose
AABBCEEKKRR	backbreaker
AABBCEGHMOT	cabbage-moth
AABBCEGMORW	cabbage-worm
AABBCEGNOTW	cabbagetown
AABBCEGOORT	cabbage-root
AABBCEINORT	bicarbonate
AABBCKLLNOO	balloon-back
AABBDEEGILR	abridgeable
AABBDEEKRST	bread-basket
AABBDEEORRV	△beaverboard
AABBDEFFLOR	baffle-board
AABBDEGLNRR	land-grabber
AABBDEILLOR	Della-Robbia
AABBEEIRRTV	rebarbative
AABBEEKLLRR	ball-breaker
AABBEEKLNRU	unbreakable
AABBEEKLRRY	barley-brake
	barley-break
AABBEELLMNU	unblameable
AABBEELLRST	barbastelle
AABBEEQRRSU	barbaresque
AABBEFGLRST	flabbergast
AABBEGIINRT	bear-baiting
AABBEGILLNR	ball-bearing
AABBEHIILNT	inhabitable
AABBEHILLOS	abolishable
AABBEHILMNO	abhominable
AABBEHILNTU	unhabitable
AABBEHLSSST	Sabbathless
AABBEIORRTV	abbreviator
AABBEIRRTTU	barbiturate
AABBELLMNUY	unblameably
AABBELORRSU	subarboreal
AABBFGIMNRY	baby-farming
AABBHHIOOPT	bathophobia
AABBHIKOSUZ	Bashi-Bazouk
AABBIIILMNO	bibliomania
AABBIIKLNTY	bankability
AABBLORRSUY	barbarously
AABCCCHKRST	backscratch
	scratchback
AABCCDEEKLM	camel-backed
AABCCDEKLOT	black-coated
AABCCEELLNO	concealable
AABCCEILPRT	practicable
AABCCEKRSTT	backscatter
AABCCELMOPT	accomptable
AABCCELNOTT	contactable
AABCCELNOTU	accountable
AABCCELNSUU	unaccusable
AABCCERRUUY	bureaucracy
AABCCGIKKNP	backpacking
AABCCGILLNR	calling-crab
AABCCIIJLNO	Jacobinical
AABCCIIJLOT	Jacobitical
AABCCILMOST	saltimbocca
AABCCILPRTY	practicably
AABCCLNOTUY	accountably
AABCCLNRRUU	carbuncular
AABCCLNSUUY	unaccusably
AABCDDEEHKL	blackheaded
AABCDDEORST	broadcasted
AABCDDIKMNO	diamond-back
AABCDEEELLR	leader-cable
AABCDEEFLRY	barefacedly
AABCDEEFNRZ	brazen-faced
AABCDEEHRRT	acre-breadth
AABCDEEILMT	alembicated
AABCDEEKNRR	breakdancer
AABCDEELNRT	tabernacled
AABCDEENORT	decarbonate
AABCDEFIIIL	acidifiable
AABCDEFNOSU	bauson-faced
AABCDEHIMMR	chambermaid
AABCDEHNPRY	peach-brandy
AABCDEIKLSV	black-a-vised
AABCDEILNRY	clay-brained
AABCDEINORT	debarcation
AABCDEINRRU	unbarricade
AABCDEIORRS	barricadoes
AABCDELMNRU	candelabrum
AABCDEMOSSU	ambuscadoes
AABCDENOORS	carbonadoes
AABCDEORRST	broadcaster
	rebroadcast
AABCDGGIOOR	△braggadocio
AABCDGHKRTU	back-draught
AABCDGIKLNO	back-loading
AABCDHHORTT	thatch-board
AABCDHIOOPR	Brachiopoda
AABCDHMNORY	rhabdomancy
AABCDIINNNO	cannabinoid
AABCDIIQRTU	biquadratic
AABCDILNOSU	subdiaconal
AABCDILNRSU	subcardinal
AABCDINOORR	radiocarbon
AABCEEEENRV	Verbenaceae
AABCEEEGINO	Begoniaceae
AABCEEEHLST	escheatable
AABCEEEIIRS	Ribesiaceae
AABCEEEILLO	Lobeliaceae

AABCEEELLPR replaceable
AABCEEELNPU unpeaceable
AABCEEELRRT retraceable
AABCEEERRSU Burseraceae
AABCEEFLRRT refractable
AABCEEFNORR forbearance
AABCEEGLLNO congealable
AABCEEHILMP impeachable
AABCEEHKLRT leather-back
AABCEEHLNRU unreachable
AABCEEHLNTU unteachable
AABCEEHLORX Lochaber-axe
AABCEEHMMRR hammer-brace
AABCEEHMNRT antechamber
AABCEEHMRST beach-master
AABCEEIINRR carabiniere
AABCEEILLMR reclaimable
AABCEEILMNV ambivalence
AABCEEILNPS inescapable
AABCEEILNQU equibalance
AABCEEILNRS increasable
AABCEEILPPR appreciable
AABCEELMNSS assemblance
AABCEELNORV overbalance
AABCEELNPSS capableness
AABCEELNPSU unescapable
AABCEELNRST scarlet-bean
AABCEELNRTU untraceable
AABCEELORTT bracteolate
AABCEELRRTT retractable
AABCEELRSTT scatterable
AABCEELRTTU trabeculate
AABCEELRTTX extractable
AABCEFIIRTV fabricative
AABCEFILNOT labefaction
AABCEFINOTT tabefaction
AABCEFLMNOY flamboyance
AABCEFLNOTU confabulate
AABCEGHNORT baton-charge
AABCEHHPSTY bathyscaphe
AABCEHIINNT inhabitance
AABCEHIKRST basket-chair
AABCEHILLRY Hebraically
AABCEHILMNR chamberlain
AABCEHILNRU hibernacula
AABCEHILSST chastisable
AABCEHIMNRR rain-chamber
AABCEHLMNTU unmatchable
AABCEHLNSTU staunchable
AABCEHLPRSU purchasable
AABCEHMSSTU subschemata
AABCEIIINRR carabinieri
AABCEIILNNS cannibalise
AABCEIILNNZ cannibalize
AABCEIINNNR cinnabarine
AABCEIKLLMR blackmailer
AABCEILLMRY reclaimably
AABCEILLNSU suballiance
AABCEILLORY aerobically
AABCEILLPRU burial-place
AABCEILLRTU articulable
AABCEILLSTY syllabicate
AABCEILMNVY ambivalency
AABCEILNNOT containable
AABCEILNORT baronetical
carbonalite
AABCEILNRTT intractable
AABCEILPPRT parableptic
AABCEILPPRY appreciably
AABCEIMNORT embarcation
AABCEIMNPRR Pre-Cambrian
AABCEIRSTTV abstractive
AABCEKKLMRT black-market
AABCEKLLRRT trackerball
AABCEKQRRTU quarterback
AABCELLLOPS collapsable
AABCELLOORT collaborate
AABCELMNOTU uncomatable
AABCELMOPSS compassable
AABCELMRTUU umbraculate
AABCELNORTY carbonylate
AABCELNRTTU untractable
AABCEOORRSU arboraceous
AABCEOORTTZ Azotobacter
AABCFIINORT fabrication
AABCFLMNOYY flamboyancy
AABCGGGIKNN back-ganging
AABCGHILLNS balls-aching
AABCGHIOOPR agoraphobic
AABCGIILLMS galliambics
AABCGILLNRR call-barring
AABCGILLOOT batological
AABCHIILMNR Brahminical
AABCHIINNTY inhabitancy
AABCHIINORT brachiation
AABCHNOPPRW Cappah-brown
AABCIIILMTY amicability
AABCIIJNNOT △antijacobin
△anti-Jacobin
AABCIILLPTY placability
AABCIILMNNS cannibalism
AABCIILNORT calibration
AABCIILRSTY △sybaritical
AABCIIMNNOS Baconianism
AABCILLNOTY botanically
AABCILLOSTV Baltoslavic
AABCILMNOST saltimbanco
AABCILNNRUU incunabular
AABCILNRTTY intractably
AABCILOSTTY biocatalyst
AABCIMNORRS Carbonarism
AABCINNOORT carbonation
AABCINORRTU carburation
AABCINORSTT abstraction
AABCKMNSSTU subtacksman
AABCKMOORRR barrack-room
AABCLPRSSUU subcapsular
subscapular
AABCMNNOOTY botanomancy
AABCNOORSST contrabasso
AABDDDEFMNU deaf-and-dumb
AABDDDELOPR paddle-board
AABDDEELORV broad-leaved
AABDDEELRSS addressable

AABDDEGGORR	daggerboard
AABDDEHHNRT	hand-breadth
AABDDEHMORY	hebdomadary
AABDDEINOST	bastinadoed
AABDDELNNOY	abandonedly
AABDDHLNNSU	husbandland
AABDDNRSSTU	substandard
AABDEEFGLLR	deflagrable
AABDEEGIMRR	marriage-bed
AABDEEGLPRU	upgradeable
AABDEEHHRRS	haberdasher
AABDEEHINRR	hare-brained
AABDEEHLSTY	beastly-head
AABDEEINNRT	bandeirante
AABDEELMNNU	unamendable
AABDEELPRSU	persuadable
AABDEEMRRSS	embarrassed
AABDEEQRSUU	arquebusade
AABDEGGHINN	head-banging
AABDEGILMNN	landing-beam
AABDEGILNOR	load-bearing
AABDEGILNOS	diagnosable
AABDEGINOSV	vagabondise
AABDEGINOVZ	vagabondize
AABDEGNORTU	unabrogated
AABDEHHIRRT	hairbreadth
AABDEHIINRR	hair-brained
AABDEHRSTWY	breadthways
AABDEIILNSV	inadvisable
AABDEIILRTY	readability
AABDEIKNORT	debarkation
AABDEILLNOT	labiodental
AABDEILLRVY	adverbially
AABDEILMNTU	mandibulate
AABDEILNNRU	undrainable
AABDEILNOUV	unavoidable
AABDEILNSUV	unadvisable
AABDEILORRS	sailboarder
AABDEILORRT	labradorite
AABDEIMRTUV	adumbrative
AABDEINOSST	bastinadoes
AABDELLNNRY	blarney-land
AABDELLNSTU	unballasted
AABDELNNTUU	undauntable
AABDELORRUY	day-labourer
AABDEMNNNOT	abandonment
AABDFFOORWY	off-Broadway
AABDGGGHINN	handbagging
AABDGHINOSV	vagabondish
AABDGIINNST	bastinading
AABDGIINRSW	bias-drawing
AABDGIMNOSV	vagabondism
AABDGINRSTW	bastard-wing
AABDGLNRSSY	brandy-glass
AABDHHOOPRR	Rhabdophora
AABDHIILNTU	habitudinal
AABDHIKLNOY	bank-holiday
AABDHIOSTTV	Bodhisattva
AABDHLOPRSS	splashboard
AABDHMMOORY	rhabdomyoma
AABDIILLTUY	laudability
AABDIILMNTY	damnability

AABDIILMQRU	Liquidambar
AABDILLMNOY	abdominally
AABDILNOUVY	unavoidably
AABDILNSUVY	unadvisably
AABDILOORRS	boardsailor
AABDIMNOOOW	Amboina-wood
AABDIMNORTU	adumbration
AABDIMPSSUY	bumpsadaisy
AABDMNOOOWY	Amboyna-wood
AABDMOORRRT	mortarboard
AABDNRRRSTU	surtarbrand
AABEEEFKRRS	safe-breaker
AABEEEGLNRU	unagreeable
AABEEEHLRTW	weatherable
AABEEEKSTVW	basketweave
AABEEELNRTT	entreatable
AABEEERRRTW	Water-bearer
AABEEFFLLPT	baffle-plate
AABEEFGIRRR	barrage-fire
AABEEGGIIRR	argie-bargie
AABEEGGLLRR	argle-bargle
AABEEGILNRT	talebearing
AABEEGINNRT	annabergite
AABEEGLMNTU	augmentable
AABEEGLNTTU	ungetatable
	unget-at-able
AABEEGMNOTU	beaumontage
AABEEGMRRST	bargemaster
AABEEHILNTZ	Elizabethan
AABEEHILPST	alphabetise
AABEEHILPTZ	alphabetize
AABEEHKLNSU	unshakeable
AABEEHLRSTY	breathalyse
AABEEHLRTYZ	breathalyze
AABEEIILLNN	inalienable
AABEEILLLQU	illaqueable
AABEEILLNNU	unalienable
AABEEILLNPX	explainable
AABEEILLNRT	inalterable
AABEEILMNSS	amiableness
AABEEILNNRR	inenarrable
AABEEILNORT	inelaborate
AABEEILNPRS	inseparable
AABEEILNRUW	unweariable
AABEEILORTV	elaborative
AABEEILPRRR	irreparable
AABEEINRRRT	train-bearer
AABEEINRRST	brain-teaser
AABEEINSSTT	bastnaesite
AABEEKKMORR	make-or-break
AABEEKKMRST	△basket-maker
AABEEKLNPSU	unspeakable
AABEEKLPSTT	plate-basket
AABEELLLMNU	unmalleable
AABEELLMNOT	balletomane
AABEELLNPTT	battleplane
AABEELLNRTU	unalterable
AABEELLNSSS	salableness
AABEELLORTY	elaborately
AABEELLPRRY	pearl-barley
AABEELLPRSU	pleasurable
AABEELMNSST	tamableness

Words marked △ may be spelled also with a capital letter

AABEELMPPRR marble-paper
AABEELMPRTU perambulate
preambulate
AABEELMPTTT attemptable
AABEELNORST treasonable
AABEELNORTU unelaborate
AABEELNPRSU unseparable
AABEELNRTTU entablature
untreatable
AABEELNRTUV unavertable
AABEELNSSSV savableness
AABEELPRSTT breastplate
AABEELRRSTT sabre-rattle
AABEELRRSTV traversable
AABEELRRTTU terebratula
AABEEMMOPRT meprobamate
AABEEMNRTTT rabattement
AABEENRRSTU sauerbraten
AABEFFIILLS falsifiable
AABEFGIILMN magnifiable
AABEFHILNOS fashionable
AABEFHILPST half-baptise
AABEFHILPTZ half-baptize
AABEFIILLQU qualifiable
AABEFIILSST satisfiable
AABEFILLMMN inflammable
AABEFLLNPPU unflappable
AABEFLMNOTY flamboyante
AABEFLMNTUU funambulate
AABEGGGLLRY gally-bagger
gally-beggar
AABEGGILMNT gaming-table
AABEGGLNSUU sublanguage
AABEGIILNNS Albigensian
AABEGIILNNV innavigable
AABEGIIMNRT time-bargain
AABEGIJKNRW jawbreaking
AABEGIKLMNW walking-beam
AABEGIKNORR aerobraking
AABEGILNNUV unnavigable
AABEGILNORS organisable
AABEGILNORZ organizable
AABEGIRRRTU arbitrageur
AABEGJSSTUU assubjugate
AABEGLLMOST megaloblast
AABEGLNORRR barrel-organ
AABEGLRRSUY barley-sugar
AABEHHIOPPT taphephobia
AABEHILNRST tarnishable
AABEHILORUV behavioural
AABEHIMNOOP anemophobia
AABEHKLNSUY unshakeably
AABEHKLRRST Halbstarker
AABEHLMOSTT hematoblast
AABEHMPRRSS Bramah-press
AABEIILLMSS assimilable
AABEIILLNNY inalienably
AABEIILLSTY saleability
AABEIILMMOR memorabilia
AABEIILMNTY amenability
AABEIILMORT biomaterial
AABEIILMTTY tameability
AABEIILNRRT libertarian
AABEIILRTTY rateability
AABEIILRTWY wearability
AABEIKMNORT embarkation
AABEILLLRTY bilaterally
AABEILLMNPU manipulable
AABEILLMRRU air-umbrella
AABEILLNNUY unalienably
AABEILLNRTY inalterably
AABEILLRRTU Turbellaria
AABEILLRRTZ trail-blazer
AABEILLRSUY subaerially
AABEILMMOST ametabolism
AABEILMNRRU unmarriable
AABEILNNPTU unpaintable
AABEILNNSTU unstainable
AABEILNOORT elaboration
AABEILNORTT anteorbital
AABEILNPRSY inseparably
AABEILNRRTT rattle-brain
AABEILNRSTT transitable
AABEILNRUWY unweariably
AABEILNSSTU sustainable
AABEILOPRSV vaporisable
AABEILOPRVZ vaporizable
AABEILPPRSS parablepsis
AABEILPRRRY irreparably
AABEIMNRRTT arbitrament
AABEINNOORT anaerobiont
AABEINNORSV non-abrasive
AABEIOPPRTV approbative
AABEIOPRSST taboparesis
AABEKLLLNNR rannell-balk
AABEKLNPSUY unspeakably
AABELLLNOUW unallowable
AABELLLPRSU subparallel
AABELLMNRTU umbrella-ant
AABELLNRTUY unalterably
AABELLOPPRT ballot-paper
AABELLPRSUY pleasurably
AABELMMNSSY assemblyman
AABELMNOSTT nematoblast
AABELMOOSTU ametabolous
AABELMPRRUY preambulary
AABELNOOPTY paleobotany
AABELNORSTY treasonably
AABELOORRTY elaboratory
AABELPRSSSU surpassable
AABFHILNOSY fashionably
AABFILLMMNY inflammably
AABFLLNPPUY unflappably
AABGGIMRRST braggartism
AABGHHIOOPP phagophobia
AABGHIILNTY hangability
AABGHILNOOP △anglophobia
AABGIILMNSU subimaginal
AABGIILNNVY innavigably
AABGILMNRSU submarginal
AABGINNOSTW angwantibos
AABGINORSSU Sanguisorba
AABGLNSTUUU Subungulata

AABHHIMSTTV	△bathmitsvah
AABHHIMTTVZ	△bathmitzvah
AABHHIOOPPT	pathophobia
	taphophobia
AABHIILORTT	habilitator
AABHIINOTTU	habituation
AABHILLNRTY	labyrinthal
AABHIMNPSST	batsmanship
AABHINOOPPT	pantophobia
AABHKNOORTT	katabothron
AABIIILRTVY	variability
AABIIILSTTY	satiability
AABIIKLLTTY	talkability
AABIILLNOOT	abolitional
AABIILLNORT	librational
AABIILLPPTY	palpability
AABIILLSTVY	salvability
AABIILMNRUU	albuminuria
AABIILMOOTU	automobilia
AABIILNORTV	vibrational
AABIILORSTU	atrabilious
AABIILOSTTU	ablatitious
AABIILRRRTY	arbitrarily
AABIIMMNORT	timbromania
AABIIMNNOOT	abomination
AABIINORRTT	arbitration
AABIIRRRTTX	arbitratrix
AABILLMORSY	ambrosially
AABILLMORTY	△balmorality
AABILLMPSTY	baptismally
AABILLMRSUY	syllabarium
AABILLRSUXY	subaxillary
AABILMMNORS	abnormalism
AABILMNORTY	abnormality
AABILNOOPRT	probational
AABILNORSTT	trailbaston
AABILNORTUY	ablutionary
AABILNSSTTU	substantial
AABIMNOPRST	Bonapartism
AABINNOPSTU	subpanation
AABINOOPPRT	approbation
AABINOPRSTT	Bonapartist
AABINORRSTU	saburration
	subarration
AABLMMNORSU	somnambular
AABLNNORRTU	natural-born
AABMORRSTTU	masturbator
AABOOPPRRTY	approbatory
AACCCCEHILT	cachectical
AACCCDEJNOY	coadjacency
AACCCDEOSUY	cycadaceous
AACCCEILPTT	cataplectic
AACCCEJKKRR	crackerjack
AACCCGHIOPR	cacographic
AACCCGIKNRT	cat-cracking
AACCCGIORST	cacogastric
AACCCHHILRS	clairschach
AACCCHNOSTU	cash-account
AACCCHORSTT	scratch-coat
AACCCIILLMT	climactical
AACCCIILRTU	cicatricula
AACCCILMSTY	cataclysmic
AACCCNNOTUY	accountancy
AACCDDEINOR	endocardiac
AACCDEEHIOR	Orchidaceae
AACCDEEILST	discalceate
AACCDEELLNT	cancellated
AACCDEELNOR	accelerando
AACCDEHIRTT	cathedratic
AACCDEIILLT	dialectical
AACCDEIILPS	Asclepiadic
AACCDEIIMMS	academicism
AACCDEIIPRR	pericardiac
AACCDEILLNR	calendrical
AACCDEILNOT	anecdotical
AACCDEILNST	accidentals
AACCDEILOPY	cyclopaedia
AACCDEIMNNO	non-academic
AACCDEMMOOT	accommodate
AACCDENNORT	contradance
AACCDGIORYZ	zygocardiac
AACCDHIINOR	characinoid
AACCDHIINRT	cantharidic
AACCDHILNOR	chancroidal
AACCDHLOORT	octachordal
AACCDHLPTYY	pachydactyl
AACCDIIILRT	diacritical
AACCDIILOPT	apodictical
AACCDLMORTY	macrodactyl
AACCDLNORTY	accordantly
AACCEEFILNT	calefacient
AACCEEFILTV	calefactive
AACCEEFKRRS	safe-cracker
AACCEEILTTT	atelectatic
AACCEEINPRS	parascience
AACCEEINRRT	incarcerate
AACCEEINRTV	revaccinate
AACCEEKLRRW	crackleware
AACCEELLNOT	collectanea
AACCEELLRTU	recalculate
AACCEELNSTU	acaulescent
AACCEELORRT	accelerator
AACCEELPRTU	receptacula
AACCEEMNOPR	compearance
AACCEENNOTT	concatenate
AACCEFHSTTY	safety-catch
AACCEFILNOT	calefaction
AACCEFILSTU	fasciculate
AACCEFLORTY	calefactory
AACCEGHILLP	cephalalgic
AACCEGHILNR	archangelic
AACCEGHNRTT	gnatcatcher
AACCEGHOPRR	cacographer
AACCEGIKNPS	packing-case
AACCEGILMOR	acromegalic
AACCEGILORT	categorical
AACCEGILOTT	geotactical
AACCEGNORST	scant-o'-grace
AACCEGORRTY	ergatocracy
AACCEHHMOST	stomachache
AACCEHHPRST	catch-phrase
AACCEHIIMNN	mechanician
AACCEHIIMNR	air-mechanic
AACCEHILMNS	mechanicals

AACCEHILMOT machicolate
AACCEHILMRT mail-catcher
AACCEHILMST catechismal
schematical
AACCEHINOPT pinacotheca
AACCEHIRSST catachresis
AACCEHLNNNO nonchalance
AACCEHMORSU △scaramouche
AACCEHNRTTW want-catcher
AACCEHORSTU chartaceous
AACCEIILMST acclimatise
AACCEIILMTZ acclimatize
AACCEIIMNOT amino-acetic
AACCEIINPRT Capernaitic
AACCEILLSTY ascetically
AACCEILLTUU cauliculate
AACCEILLTUV calculative
AACCEILMPRT malpractice
AACCEILNORS anisocercal
AACCEILORSS accessorial
AACCEILOSSU salicaceous
AACCEIMNOPR accompanier
AACCEINNORT Anacreontic
canceration
AACCEINOPTT acceptation
AACCEINPTUV captivaunce
AACCEINQTTU acquittance
AACCEKKTYYY yackety-yack
AACCEKNRRTU currant-cake
AACCELLNTUY accentually
AACCELLPPRW clapperclaw
AACCELMNUUV vacuum-clean
AACCELNRTUU caruncculate
AACCELPRSTU spectacular
AACCELRTTUU acculturate
AACCENOPRRY coparcenary
AACCENORSUY sauce-crayon
AACCFIIILNR carnificial
AACCFIIILRS sacrificial
AACCFIILLPY pacifically
AACCFIILRTY farcicality
AACCFIIMNOR acinaciform
AACCFIIOPRT pacificator
AACCFILMORR calcariform
AACCGHIILRR chiragrical
AACCGHIKNOT hacking-coat
AACCGHIMMOS chasmogamic
AACCGHIMNNR arm-chancing
AACCGHINRTT rat-catching
AACCGILLNTU calculating
AACCHIIMRST charismatic
AACCHIINRST anarchistic
AACCHIINRTT anthracitic
AACCHILLOTY chaotically
AACCHILLPTY hypallactic
AACCHILMNOR monarchical
AACCHILMOST stomachical
AACCHILORRV vicar-choral
AACCHINOPST cataphonics
AACCHIPPRSY parapsychic
AACCHLLOTTW tallow-catch
AACCHLNSTUY calycanthus
AACCIIILRST racialistic
AACCIILLNTY actinically
AACCIILMNOT acclimation
AACCIILMOPT apomictical
AACCIILMPRT impractical
AACCIILNNOT calcination
AACCIILNORV Clavicornia
AACCIILSSTU casuistical
AACCIILSTTT stalactitic
AACCIINNOTV vaccination
AACCIINOPSU incapacious
AACCIINOSTU acoustician
AACCILLLNOY laconically
AACCILLLSSY classically
AACCILLNNOY canonically
AACCILLNOTU calculation
AACCILLNSSU unclassical
AACCILLNSUU canaliculus
AACCILLOOPR coprolaliac
AACCILLPRTY practically
AACCILLSTUY caustically
AACCILNNNOU uncanonical
AACCILNOSTU sacculation
AACCILNPRTU unpractical
AACCILNSTTY syntactical
AACCILOPPTY apocalyptic
AACCILOPSUY capaciously
AACCIMNOPST accompanist
AACCINOORTT coarctation
AACCINORTVY vaccinatory
AACCIOPRRST paracrostic
AACCIORRSTY aristocracy
AACCLMORTUU accumulator
AACCLNOPRTY plantocracy
AACCLNORTTU contractual
AACCLOORSST sacrocostal
AACCMORSTUY accustomary
AACCORRSTTY stratocracy
AACDDDEINOR Dodecandria
AACDDEEEFNS defeasanced
AACDDEEEHLR clear-headed
AACDDEEHNRT dendrachate
AACDDEEIMOP Campodeidae
AACDDEEIMPS aides-de-camp
AACDDEGINOY Dodecagynia
AACDDEHINPP handicapped
AACDDEHKLNS slack-handed
AACDDEILNOR endocardial
AACDDEINRTU candidature
AACDDEINTUU nudicaudate
AACDDIIINSS candidiasis
AACDDIJORTU adjudicator
AACDEEEFLSW weasel-faced
AACDEEEORRS Droseraceae
AACDEEEPPRT peace-parted
AACDEEFFINT caffeinated
AACDEEGHINP phagedaenic
AACDEEGKPSS deck-passage
AACDEEHIIMR Chimaeridae
AACDEEHILMX hexadecimal
AACDEEHILNR Heracleidan
AACDEEHIMMN machine-made

AACDEEHIMNR	Archimedean
AACDEEHLPST	sphacelated
AACDEEHRSSV	headscarves
AACDEEIILRS	deracialise
AACDEEIILRZ	deracialize
AACDEEIIRTV	eradicative
AACDEEILNRS	calendarise
AACDEEILNRZ	calendarize
AACDEEILRSS	desacralise
AACDEEILRSZ	desacralize
AACDEEILRTV	declarative
AACDEEILSTT	elasticated
AACDEEIPRST	paederastic
AACDEELLMOS	Camaldolese
AACDEELLNOT	lanceolated
AACDEELLRSS	class-leader
AACDEELLSTT	castellated
AACDEELMOPR	cameleopard
AACDEEMNNTV	advancement
AACDEEMNOSU	Osmundaceae
AACDEENOPRR	opera-dancer
AACDEENPRRS	parascender
AACDEENQRSU	square-dance
AACDEENTUVX	unexcavated
AACDEFFGLOS	scaffoldage
AACDEFILNOT	defalcation
AACDEFIMNOT	madefaction
AACDEFINRUX	fricandeaux
AACDEFLLOTW	tallow-faced
AACDEGGILMO	demagogical
AACDEGGILOP	pedagogical
AACDEGHIPRS	cigar-shaped
AACDEGIIMNT	diamagnetic
AACDEGIMNNS	damascening
AACDEGLRSTU	castle-guard
AACDEGORSTU	sugar-coated
AACDEHIIMRT	adiathermic
AACDEHIINRT	Trachinidae
AACDEHILORS	icosahedral
AACDEHIMPRY	pachydermia
AACDEHIMRTY	diathermacy
AACDEHINOTT	anticathode
AACDEHINPPR	handicapper
AACDEHINRST	cantharides
AACDEHIPPRT	crappit-head
AACDEHIRRTV	architraved
AACDEHKLNNR	crankhandle
AACDEHLMPRY	pachydermal
AACDEHLNRWX	wax-chandler
AACDEHLOOPP	Cephalopoda
AACDEHMOPRT	camphorated
AACDEHMORSU	Machaerodus
AACDEHMRRTT	tetradrachm
AACDEHPRRRS	card-sharper
AACDEIILMRT	diametrical
AACDEIILMRV	vice-admiral
AACDEIILPRR	pericardial
AACDEIIMPRT	pre-adamitic
AACDEIIMSTT	diastematic
AACDEIINNNR	incarnadine
AACDEIINNRT	incardinate
AACDEIINORT	eradication
AACDEIINPRR	pericardian
AACDEIIORTV	radioactive
AACDEIIPRST	paediatrics
AACDEIIPRSU	parasuicide
AACDEILLLTY	dialectally
AACDEILLMOT	Camaldolite
AACDEILMNOT	declamation
AACDEILNOPT	pedal-action
AACDEILNORT	declaration
AACDEILNOTU	educational
AACDEILNPTU	paniculated
AACDEILNRRU	ruridecanal
AACDEILNRSS	radicalness
	scandaliser
AACDEILNRST	calendarist
AACDEILNRSZ	scandalizer
AACDEILOPRR	praecordial
AACDEILORRT	redactorial
AACDEILRSTT	strait-laced
AACDEILRTTU	articulated
AACDEILRTUU	auriculated
AACDEILSTTT	stalactited
AACDEIMNNOP	△pandemoniac
AACDEIMNORT	demarcation
AACDEIMNORY	aerodynamic
AACDEIMOPRS	paramedicos
AACDEINNORT	carnationed
AACDEINNOTT	decantation
AACDEINOPRS	caparisoned
AACDEINORST	stenocardia
AACDEINOTUV	coadunative
AACDEINRSST	incrassated
AACDEIOPRTT	parti-coated
AACDELLNOTY	anecdotally
AACDELMORTY	declamatory
AACDELNPTTY	pentadactyl
AACDELOOPRT	proctodaeal
AACDELORRTY	declaratory
AACDELRTTTY	tetradactyl
AACDEMNOSTU	cat-and-mouse
AACDEMORRRU	armoured-car
AACDENOPRTT	pedantocrat
AACDEOPRRRS	road-scraper
AACDEOPRTTY	party-coated
AACDFFIINOO	afficionado
AACDFIILLTY	fatidically
AACDFIILRRT	fratricidal
AACDFIINOOS	aficionados
AACDGGHIIST	Haggadistic
AACDGHIOPRR	cardiograph
AACDGHOPRSU	cardophagus
AACDGILNNPS	landscaping
AACDGILNPRY	playing-card
AACDGIMRRTU	dramaturgic
AACDGINNSST	sand-casting
AACDGLMORTY	dactylogram
AACDGNNOOTY	contango-day
AACDHIIMRTT	△mithradatic
AACDHIIOPRS	aphrodisiac
AACDHILOPRS	rhapsodical
AACDHIMORSU	Machairodus
AACDHMOPRSY	psychodrama

AACDHOORRTU Urochordata
AACDIILMNRU adminicular
AACDIILMNTT mid-Atlantic
AACDIILMPRY pyramidical
AACDIILORTT dictatorial
AACDIIMMRST dramaticism
AACDIIMNOPS dipsomaniac
AACDIINNORS icosandrian
AACDILLLOOR coralloidal
AACDILLMNOY nomadically
AACDILLMNYY dynamically
AACDILLMOPS psalmodical
AACDILLRSTY drastically
AACDILMOPSS spasmodical
AACDILNPSST landscapist
AACDILORTTY artiodactyl
AACDILOSUUY audaciously
AACDIMMOOTY mycodomatia
AACDIMNNOOR monocardian
AACDIMNNOTU manducation
AACDIMNORST nostradamic
AACDINNOOTU coadunation
AACDKLNOORT cool-tankard
AACDKNORRTW dock-warrant
AACDLMNOOTY condylomata
AACDMNORTUY manducatory
AACDMOORSTU catadromous
AACDOOPRSST capodastros
AACEEEGGLNU aleggeaunce
AACEEEHLMOT haematocele
AACEEEJMNTT ejectamenta
AACEEFFLLNN face-flannel
AACEEFILLTT lattice-leaf
AACEEFIMNSS misfeasance
AACEEFIRRTV rarefactive
AACEEFNNNOS non-feasance
AACEEFNORRT confarreate
AACEEGGNRSW swagger-cane
AACEEGHNOPR chaperonage
AACEEGHNPRR crapehanger
AACEEGHRRST gatecrasher
AACEEGIKMNP peacemaking
AACEEGILLLY elegiacally
AACEEGILLNV evangelical
AACEEGIMNOR Moringaceae
AACEEGINNRR carrageenin
AACEEGINPRT paragenetic
AACEEGLLNOS collagenase
AACEEGMMORT macrogamete
AACEEHHLTUX hexateuchal
AACEEHHMPTY chamaephyte
AACEEHILMNR Amelanchier
AACEEHILNRT Heraclitean
AACEEHILSTT aesthetical
AACEEHIMPPR papier-mâché
AACEEHINSTT anaesthetic
AACEEHLLNRT chantarelle
AACEEHLNNPY anencephaly
AACEEHLNNSV clean-shaven
AACEEHLNPTY phlyctaenae
AACEEHLORTT leather-coat
AACEEHLPRRT arch-prelate
AACEEHMNPPT appeachment
AACEEHMPRST spermatheca
AACEEHRRTTT tetrarchate
AACEEIIMNRS Americanise
AACEEIIMNRZ Americanize
AACEEIIMNST Scitamineae
AACEEIIMPST septicaemia
AACEEIJLTUV ejaculative
AACEEILLMNS mésalliance
miscellanea
AACEEILMPRU Primulaceae
AACEEILMTVX exclamative
AACEEILNNRS encarnalise
AACEEILNNRZ encarnalize
AACEEILNRTT intercalate
AACEEILOPST Psilotaceae
AACEEILORST aeroelastic
AACEEILRRST secretarial
AACEEILRTTV altercative
AACEEILSSTT atelectasis
AACEEIMMNRT amerciament
AACEEIMMORS Mesoamerica
AACEEIMNNNT maintenance
AACEEIMORRT araeometric
AACEEIMRSSU eremacausis
AACEEINNNRT centenarian
AACEEINNRRT reincarnate
AACEEINNRSS necessarian
△renaissance
AACEEIPRRTV prevaricate
AACEEIRRSST tracasserie
AACEEIRRSTT secretariat
AACEEKLLNST alkalescent
AACEEKLMPRT market-place
AACEEKNPRST carpet-snake
AACEELLLTUV valleculate
AACEELMNPRU emparlaunce
AACEELNPSTU encapsulate
AACEELNSSTT sclate-stane
AACEELNTTTU tentaculate
AACEEMNORST ocean-stream
AACEEMNOSTU amentaceous
AACEENRRSSU reassurance
AACEENRRTUV averruncate
AACEFFHINRS affranchise
AACEFFIIRTV affricative
AACEFFILNOT affectional
AACEFFINOTT affectation
AACEFGGHINR chafing-gear
AACEFGHINRR far-reaching
AACEFGINPRS spacefaring
AACEFGLNORT conflagrate
AACEFGORTTY factory-gate
AACEFIILLNS fiançailles
AACEFIILNRT interfacial
AACEFIILNRV acriflavine
AACEFILLLMY malefically
AACEFILMNOT malefaction
AACEFILTTUV facultative
AACEFINORRT rarefaction
AACEFINORRV vicar-forane
AACEFINORSU farinaceous

AACEFINORTT fractionate
AACEFLMORTY malefactory
AACEFLNSSTU factualness
AACEFMNRTUU manufacture
AACEFNPRRTT parent-craft
AACEGHHNOTT chaetognath
AACEGHILLRT lethargical
AACEGHILNOR archegonial
AACEGHILOOT Oligochaeta
AACEGHILOPR △archipelago
AACEGHIMNOP phaenogamic
AACEGHIOPRR areographic
AACEGHLLSSV cheval-glass
AACEGHLOORY archaeology
AACEGHNORTU autochanger
AACEGHPRTTU gutta-percha
AACEGIILLPR periglacial
AACEGIILMNT enigmatical
AACEGIIMNNT magnetician
AACEGIIMRRS miscarriage
AACEGIIOPRT Areopagitic
AACEGIKLNNW walking-cane
AACEGIKLNRW race-walking
AACEGILLLNY angelically
AACEGILLLOR allegorical
AACEGILLMMR calligramme
AACEGILLMNN name-calling
AACEGILLNPY callipygean
AACEGILLOOR aerological
AACEGILLOPS plagioclase
AACEGILLTUV victuallage
AACEGILNPRY panegyrical
AACEGILOSTU cataloguise
AACEGILOTUV coagulative
AACEGILOTUZ cataloguize
AACEGILRSTT strategical
AACEGIMMNRT engrammatic
AACEGIMNNOR cinema-organ
AACEGIMNNPR permanganic
AACEGIMNOPT compaginate
AACEGIMNORS Reaganomics
AACEGINNRTW watering-can
AACEGINPPRT rate-capping
AACEGINPRTW watering-cap
AACEGINPSTT peat-casting
AACEGLNRRTU rectangular
AACEGMNOORR Graeco-Roman
AACEGMNOSTY gynaecomast
AACEGNOORSU onagraceous
AACEHHILSTX hexastichal
AACEHIILLOR allocheiria
AACEHIILMPT epithalamic
AACEHIILRSV cavalierish
AACEHIILSTT atheistical
AACEHIIMMNS Manichaeism
AACEHILLMNO melancholia
AACEHILLNTU hallucinate
AACEHILMNNN manna-lichen
AACEHILMRSV vice-marshal
AACEHILMRTU rheumatical
AACEHILMSST thalassemic
AACEHILNPST chainplates
AACEHILNRTT intrathecal
AACEHILNTTU authentical
AACEHILPPSS Cephalaspis
AACEHILRRRT trierarchal
AACEHILRSTT theatricals
AACEHIMMSTT mathematics
AACEHIMNNOT technomania
AACEHIMNNOY haemocyanin
AACEHIMORST achromatise
AACEHIMORTT haematocrit
AACEHIMORTZ achromatize
AACEHIMOSTT haemostatic
AACEHINOTTY thiocyanate
AACEHINPPRR paranephric
AACEHINPRRT Petrarchian
AACEHIOPRST Spirochaeta
AACEHIPRSTU haruspicate
AACEHKNRSSS harness-cask
AACEHLMNRTW law-merchant
AACEHLOOPRR Rhopalocera
AACEHLOPTUY autocephaly
AACEHMMNNRT merchantman
AACEHMNNRST transmanche
AACEHMNORSU rhamnaceous
AACEHNNORST anthracnose
AACEHNOPRVY anchovy-pear
AACEHNOPSWW weapon-schaw
AACEHNPPSWW wappenschaw
AACEHOPRSTT catastrophe
AACEHOPSSTU spathaceous
AACEIIKLMNT kinematical
AACEIILLMNS misalliance
AACEIILLNRT lacertilian
AACEIILLNRV incarvillea
AACEIILLRTV leviratical
AACEIILMRRR mail-carrier
AACEIILMRSV cavalierism
AACEIILNPRR pericranial
AACEIILNRRT interracial
AACEIILPPRR pericarpial
AACEIILPPTV applicative
AACEIIMMNRS Americanism
AACEIIMNNPT mine-captain
AACEIIMNRST Americanist
creatianism
AACEIIMNRTV carminative
AACEIIMQSTU semi-aquatic
AACEIINORTT ratiocinate
AACEIIOSSTV associative
AACEIIPPRTT participate
AACEIJLNOTU ejaculation
AACEIKLLOPU leucoplakia
AACEILLLSTY elastically
AACEILLMNPT implacental
AACEILLMNSU animalcules
AACEILLMPUX amplexicaul
AACEILLNTTY tetanically
AACEILLNTVY venatically
AACEILLOPRR Procellaria
AACEILLPRRT Caterpillar®
caterpillar
AACEILLPRST palestrical

AACEILLRRTY	erratically
AACEILLRSST	rascalliest
AACEILMNOPY	alycompaine
AACEILMNORT	reclamation
AACEILMNOTX	exclamation
AACEILMNPTU	pneumatical
AACEILMORRT	crematorial
AACEILMOSSU	alismaceous
AACEILMPRST	spermatical
AACEILMPSTT	metaplastic
	palmatisect
AACEILMRTTU	matriculate
AACEILNNOSS	ascensional
AACEILNNPTT	pentactinal
AACEILNOPRT	anaplerotic
AACEILNORST	ancestorial
AACEILNORTT	altercation
AACEILNPSTU	incapsulate
AACEILNRRTU	retinacular
AACEILNRRTY	intercalary
AACEILNRTTT	tetractinal
AACEILOPPTY	palaeotypic
AACEILPRSTU	spiraculate
AACEILPRTTU	catapultier
	particulate
AACEILRSSUV	vascularise
AACEILRSUVZ	vascularize
AACEILSTUVY	causatively
AACEIMMOPRU	paramoecium
AACEIMMOSTT	metasomatic
AACEIMNNOTT	contaminate
AACEIMNOORT	erotomaniac
AACEIMNOPRT	emancipator
AACEIMNPRST	campestrian
AACEIMNPRSU	parascenium
AACEIMOPRTV	comparative
AACEINNORTT	recantation
AACEINNORTX	excarnation
AACEINNRSTU	unsectarian
AACEINNRTTT	interactant
AACEINOPRST	ceratopsian
AACEINORRTY	reactionary
AACEINORSTU	aeronautics
AACEINPQRTU	preacquaint
AACEINRSSTU	sanctuarise
AACEINRSTTY	asynartetic
AACEINRSTUZ	sanctuarize
AACEIOPPRRT	appreciator
AACEIORSSTT	aerostatics
AACEJKQRRTU	quarter-jack
AACEJLORTUY	ejaculatory
AACEKKLRRTW	track-walker
AACEKLQRSUV	quacksalver
AACELLNRSTY	ancestrally
AACELLOPRSU	acarpellous
AACELLOPRTY	acropetally
AACELMNNNOT	cannon-metal
AACELMORRSU	scale-armour
AACELMORSTU	emasculator
AACELMORTXY	exclamatory
AACELMRSSST	master-class
AACELMRTTTX	malt-extract
AACELNNRSTT	transcalent
AACELNOOSSU	solanaceous
AACELNORSTT	translocate
AACELOOPPRS	laparoscope
AACELPRSSTY	play-actress
AACELQRTUUU	aquaculture
AACELRSTUUV	vasculature
AACENOOPSSU	saponaceous
AACENORRTVY	contrayerva
AACEOOPSSTU	sapotaceous
AACEOPPRSUY	papyraceous
AACFFIINORT	affrication
AACFFIORRTT	trafficator
AACFGIINNST	fascinating
AACFGLNNORT	conflagrant
AACFHORRTTU	authorcraft
AACFHPSSTTU	upcast-shaft
AACFIILLNNY	financially
AACFIILORTT	facilitator
AACFIINNOST	fascination
AACFIKRSTTT	first-attack
AACFILLNOTV	lactoflavin
AACFILLNRTY	frantically
AACFILMORRS	scalariform
AACFILNORST	infracostal
AACFIMMNOPR	campaniform
AACFINORRTY	fractionary
AACFLNORRTU	currant-loaf
AACFMNORSTW	craftswoman
AACFMNORTUY	manufactory
AACFNORSTUU	anfractuous
AACGGILLLOO	algological
AACGGILLOOR	agrological
AACGGILNOSY	synagogical
AACGGILOPTY	ptyalagogic
AACGHHILNOT	Chilognatha
AACGHHPRTYY	tachygraphy
AACGHIIPPRS	pasigraphic
AACGHIKMMNT	matchmaking
AACGHIKMNTW	watchmaking
AACGHILLPRY	calligraphy
	graphically
AACGHILNNOT	gnathonical
AACGHIMNNTW	man-watching
AACGHIMNRSY	gymnasiarch
AACGHINRRST	starch-grain
AACGHIOPRTU	autographic
AACGHLMOORU	chaulmoogra
AACGHLNOORY	arachnology
AACGHNOOPPR	coprophagan
AACGHNOOPRR	coronagraph
AACGHOPRRTY	cartography
AACGHOPRSSU	sarcophagus
AACGIILLMNS	Gallicanism
AACGIILLNTV	vacillating
AACGIILLOOX	axiological
AACGIILMNNS	Anglicanism
AACGIILMSTT	stalagmitic
	stigmatical
AACGIILNNNT	lancinating
AACGIILNNOR	Carolingian
AACGIILNOST	agonistical

AACGIIMRSTT	magistratic
AACGIINOSTT	castigation
AACGIINPTTV	captivating
AACGIINRSST	staircasing
AACGIJNNRTU	jaunting-car
AACGIKLNRTY	tracklaying
AACGILLNORY	organically
AACGILLOPST	post-glacial
AACGILMNOOR	agronomical
AACGILMNSTY	gymnastical
AACGILNOOTU	coagulation
AACGILOORST	acarologist
AACGILOSSUY	sagaciously
AACGIMMNORR	marconigram
AACGIMMNRTU	ungrammatic
AACGIMNSTTY	syntagmatic
AACGIMOPRTY	Cryptogamia
AACGINNOTTV	noctivagant
AACGINORSST	nasogastric
AACGIORSTTY	castigatory
AACGLLNOOTY	octagonally
AACGLMNOOPY	campanology
AACGLOORTUY	coagulatory
AACGMNORSTY	gastromancy
AACGRSSSSTU	tussac-grass
AACHHIIMPPT	amphipathic
AACHHLORTTT	throat-latch
AACHIIINRST	△christiania
AACHIILLNRV	arch-villain
AACHIILOPRT	arctophilia
AACHIILORST	ahistorical
AACHIIMNNOT	machination
AACHIIMNSST	shamanistic
AACHIINPPST	captainship
AACHIINRSSU	saurischian
AACHILLMOPY	malacophily
AACHILLOPRY	parochially
AACHILMNOOS	monochasial
AACHILMOPPP	hippocampal
AACHILMOSTU	moustachial
AACHILNOPPS	pansophical
AACHILNOPRT	anthropical
AACHILNOPRY	paronychial
AACHILNORST	thrasonical
AACHILQRRSU	squirarchal
AACHIMMNOTY	mythomaniac
AACHIMMORST	achromatism
AACHIMNNORS	anachronism
AACHIMNOPTT	phantomatic
AACHIMNORSS	maraschinos
AACHIMNOTTY	Titanomachy
AACHIMOPPRR	paramorphic
AACHINNNOTY	anthocyanin
AACHINORSST	anthracosis
AACHIORRRTT	arch-traitor
AACHIPPSSTY	pataphysics
	'pataphysics
AACHIPRSTTU	parachutist
AACHLLOOSTU	holocaustal
AACHLMORRTY	lachrymator
AACHLNNOOTU	anacoluthon
AACHMMRRSUU	harum-scarum
AACHMNOSTWY	yachtswoman
AACHMOORSTU	achromatous
AACHNNOORSU	anachronous
AACHORRSTTY	Thyrostraca
AACIIILNNOT	laciniation
AACIIILNOST	laicisation
AACIIILNOTZ	laicization
AACIIILPPRT	participial
AACIIJNOTTT	jactitation
AACIILLMRTU	multiracial
AACIILLNOOT	coalitional
AACIILLNOTV	cavillation
	vacillation
AACIILLNTTY	△titanically
AACIILLPRTY	capillarity
	piratically
AACIILLRSTY	satirically
AACIILMNNOT	antinomical
AACIILMNOST	anomalistic
AACIILMNSTT	Atlanticism
AACIILMPRST	prismatical
AACIILNNNOT	lancination
AACIILNOPPT	application
AACIILNPRTU	puritanical
AACIILNPRTY	patricianly
AACIILNPTTY	antitypical
AACIILNRSTU	unsatirical
AACIILNSTTT	Atlanticist
AACIILNTTYY	analyticity
AACIILOPRST	piscatorial
AACIILPRSTT	patristical
AACIILPRTUY	piacularity
AACIILRRTUU	utricularia
AACIILSSTTT	statistical
AACIIMNNOPT	mancipation
AACIIMNNORT	animatronic
AACIIMNNOTU	acumination
AACIIMNOOTX	toxicomania
AACIIMNOSTT	mastication
AACIINNNORT	△incarnation
AACIINNNOTT	incantation
AACIINOOSST	association
AACIINOPRTT	anticipator
AACIINORTTV	vaticinator
AACIINOSTTV	vacationist
AACIINPPRTT	participant
AACIINPSSTT	antispastic
AACILLLOPST	alloplastic
AACILLMOSTY	somatically
AACILLNOPRS	rapscallion
AACILLNOPTY	polyactinal
AACILLOOPST	apostolical
AACILLOPRSY	prosaically
AACILLORTVY	vacillatory
AACILLOSSUY	salaciously
AACILLPRTUY	capitularly
AACILLPSSTY	spastically
AACILLRRUUY	auricularly
AACILMNNOPT	complainant
AACILMNOOTU	autonomical
AACILMNOOTX	taxonomical
AACILMNOPRT	proclaimant

AACILMNOPST	complaisant
AACILMNORTU	calumniator
AACILMORRTY	lacrimatory
AACILMPPRSY	paralympics
AACILNNOPSV	Pan-Slavonic
AACILNNOPSY	calypsonian
AACILNOOTUV	vacuolation
AACILNOPRTY	coplanarity
AACILNORTVY	clairvoyant
AACILOPPRTY	applicatory
AACILOPRSUY	rapaciously
AACILOPSTTU	autoplastic
AACILORRTTU	articulator
AACILORRTUY	oracularity
AACILRSTUVY	vascularity
AACIMNNNOTT	contaminant
AACIMNOOSTT	anastomotic
AACIMNOPRTY	mancipatory
AACIMORSTTY	masticatory
AACINNNORTU	annunciator
AACINNORSTT	transaction
AACINNORTTY	incantatory
AACINNRRSTU	transuranic
AACINOOOPPT	apocopation
AACINOPRSTT	pantisocrat
AACINOPRSTU	carnaptious
AACLMMOPSSY	mycoplasmas
AACLMORRTYY	lacrymatory
AACLNNNOOST	consonantal
AACLNPSTTUU	Tantalus-cup
AACLOOPPRSY	laparoscopy
AACLOPRSSTU	supracostal
AACLORSTTUU	auscultator
AACMNOPRTUY	paramountcy
AACMOORSSTU	sarcomatous
AACMOORSTTY	astrocytoma
AACNOOPRRTT	Pantocrator
AADDDDEEEHL	addle-headed
AADDDEEHHRY	hydra-headed
AADDDEIILPT	dilapidated
AADDDEIIOPS	Dasipodidae
AADDDEILRRT	tarradiddle
AADDEEEHHVY	heavy-headed
AADDEEELLRV	alder-leaved
AADDEEGHLNR	large-handed
AADDEEHHNVY	heavy-handed
AADDEEHHRRT	hard-hearted
AADDEEHKMRT	death-marked
AADDEEHLPRY	paraldehyde
AADDEEHORRW	arrow-headed
AADDEEILRST	AIDS-related
AADDEEIMRST	dedramatise
AADDEEIMRTZ	dedramatize
AADDEEMMQUZ	queez-maddam
AADDEFFLPST	paddle-staff
AADDEFHLPST	paddle-shaft
AADDEGHINRR	hard-grained
AADDEGHIRSV	hard-visaged
AADDEGHNORS	dragon's-head
AADDEGHNRTU	dreadnaught
AADDEGINORT	degradation
	gradationed
AADDEGIRTTY	tardy-gaited
AADDEGLLOOY	logodaedaly
AADDEGNNORS	dragonnades
AADDEHINNPT	hand-painted
AADDEHNRRTW	drawn-thread
AADDEIILPPP	Pedipalpida
AADDEIKNPRR	park-and-ride
AADDEINRSST	standardise
AADDEINRSTZ	standardize
AADDEIOPRSX	Paradoxides
AADDEJLMSTU	maladjusted
AADDELLNNSU	unsandalled
AADDELNRSTW	land-steward
AADDELPQRUU	quadrupedal
AADDENRSSST	dastardness
AADDGHINRRY	daring-hardy
AADDGIILORT	digladiator
AADDIIINNRT	Trinidadian
AADDIILOPRT	dilapidator
AADDILLOOPR	olla-podrida
AADDILMNRUY	laundry-maid
AADDINORRST	ritardandos
AADDNNNORST	non-standard
AADEEEFHHRT	feather-head
AADEEEFHLLN	halfendeale
AADEEEFNRSY	free-and-easy
AADEEEGGHRS	shagge-eared
AADEEEGGRTX	exaggerated
AADEEEGLPRS	spread-eagle
AADEEEHHLRT	leather-head
AADEEEHKRTW	weak-hearted
AADEEEHLNNR	enneahedral
AADEEEHLPRT	pale-hearted
AADEEEPPRTU	depauperate
AADEEFGLLLT	flagellated
AADEEFHHLRT	half-hearted
AADEEFILNRT	anti-federal
AADEEFINNTT	anti-feedant
AADEEFLLNRT	trade-fallen
AADEEGILPSV	pale-visaged
AADEEGILRRT	laterigrade
AADEEGINRTU	aguardiente
AADEEGLLRUY	leaguer-lady
AADEEGNORRT	anterograde
AADEEHHPRST	heart-shaped
AADEEHIINRT	Atherinidae
AADEEHJNRRW	Wanderjahre
AADEEHKMRRT	threadmaker
AADEEHKQRTU	earthquaked
AADEEHLNNRT	△neanderthal
AADEEHLNPPT	pad-elephant
AADEEHLNPRT	pentahedral
AADEEHLRRTT	tetrahedral
AADEEHLRTTT	death-rattle
AADEEHMNSSS	ashamedness
AADEEHMRRTW	warm-hearted
AADEEHNRSVW	heavenwards
AADEEHPPRRT	thread-paper
AADEEILLMVY	mediaevally
AADEEILNNRX	△alexandrine
AADEEILNRTX	alexandrite
AADEEINNNNR	enneandrian

AADEEINPPSW	weasand-pipe
AADEEINRSTT	tear-stained
AADEEIPPRTV	preadaptive
AADEEIRRTTV	retardative
AADEEIRSTVV	adversative
AADEEISTTVV	devastative
AADEEJNOORR	rejoneadora
AADEEJPPRWW	wapper-jawed
AADEEKLMSST	damask-steel
AADEELLNTTU	landaulette
AADEELMNRSU	land-measure
AADEELNPTTT	pantaletted
AADEELPRTTT	rattle-pated
AADEELRRSTV	slave-trader
AADEEMNNNTU	antemundane
AADEEMQRRSU	masquerader
AADEENPRSTU	unseparated
AADEEORRRST	rear-roasted
AADEEORRTWY	ready-to-wear
AADEESSTTTY	steady-state
AADEFGHNRRT	grandfather
AADEFGIILNR	fair-dealing
AADEFGIISTT	fastigiated
AADEFGLORRT	deflagrator
AADEFHLRSTV	half-starved
AADEFIMNORT	foraminated
AADEFLLMMTU	flammulated
AADEFLMNNTU	fundamental
AADEFLSSTTY	steadfastly
AADEFNSSTTU	unsteadfast
AADEGGHNRSS	haggardness
AADEGGIINRR	Gregarinida
AADEGGILLRT	draggle-tail
AADEGGILNNR	landing-gear
AADEGGLNRSS	garden-glass
AADEGHINRRW	hard-wearing
AADEGIILLRS	galliardise
AADEGIILNTT	intagliated
AADEGILMNPR	reading-lamp
AADEGILNNRV	landgravine
AADEGILNPRT	plantigrade
AADEGILNRVW	waldgravine
AADEGINNTUV	unnavigated
AADEGINSTTV	devastating
AADEGLLNRSS	garlandless
AADEGMNRRST	grandmaster
AADEGMORSSW	meadow-grass
AADEGNNOPRU	unparagoned
AADEGNNPRRT	grandparent
AADEGOOPRST	Gasteropoda
AADEGOPPRTT	targa-topped
AADEHIILOPP	paedophilia
AADEHIINPTY	diaphaneity
AADEHILLNOS	hollandaise
AADEHILMNOP	Monadelphia
AADEHILMNPY	Nymphalidae
AADEHILNNST	lanthanides
AADEHINOPPY	hypnopaedia
AADEHINOSTT	head-station
AADEHIPSTXY	asphyxiated
AADEHJMNORS	John-a-dreams
AADEHLMNRRS	marshlander
AADEHLMNSUY	unashamedly
AADEHNPTUWY	unpathwayed
AADEHPPRSST	strap-shaped
AADEHPRSSTT	spatterdash
AADEIIIRRTV	irradiative
AADEIILMNST	mediastinal
AADEIILMORT	mediatorial
AADEIILNRRT	interradial
AADEIINNQRU	quadriennia
AADEIINORRT	reradiation
AADEIIPRSTT	paediatrist
AADEIKMNORT	demarkation
AADEILLLMOT	metalloidal
AADEILLMRTY	diametrally
AADEILLNOPT	planetoidal
AADEILMNRRT	intradermal
AADEILMNRTY	aldermanity
AADEILNNQRU	quadrennial
AADEILNORST	desalinator
AADEILNOTUV	devaluation
AADEILNPSST	displeasant
AADEILNSSUW	duniewassal
AADEILOPRTZ	trapezoidal
AADEILORRTV	advertorial
AADEILPRSTY	disparately
AADEIMMNNOO	demonomania
AADEIMMNRST	disarmament
AADEIMNNNOP	△pandemonian
AADEIMNNOSW	madonnawise
AADEIMNRSTV	maidservant
	servant-maid
AADEINNNPRT	pentandrian
AADEINNNRST	transandine
AADEINNRRTT	tetrandrian
AADEINNTTTU	unattainted
AADEINOPRTV	depravation
AADEINORRTT	retardation
AADEINORSST	diatessaron
AADEINOSTTV	devastation
AADEINPQRSU	pasquinader
AADEINPRSTU	unaspirated
AADEINPRSUY	dyspareunia
AADEIPSSTWW	wasp-waisted
AADEKLNNRRT	dark-lantern
AADEKNRSSWW	awkwardness
AADELLMNSTY	lady's-mantle
AADELLNNORT	rallentando
AADELMNOOSY	loadsamoney
AADELNNOOPT	pantalooned
AADELNPRSTU	pasture-land
AADELORRTTU	adulterator
AADEMNOOSTU	adenomatous
AADEMNORSTW	tradeswoman
AADENNNOTTU	unannotated
AADENNRRTUW	unwarranted
AADENPRSTTT	standpatter
AADENRRSTTU	understrata
AADENRSSWWY	waywardness
AADENRSTTUU	unsaturated
AADEOQRRRTU	quarter-road
AADEORRRTTY	retardatory
AADFFIINOPR	paraffinoid

AADFFORRSTW fast-forward
AADFGHILLNN half-landing
AADFGHIMORR rhagadiform
AADFGHINNST handfasting
AADFHHILLOY half-holiday
AADFMNOORRS mansard-roof
AADGGIILNPR paragliding
AADGGIINOPR radiopaging
AADGHHIKNNS handshaking
AADGHHILMNN Highlandman
AADGHHOPRSW shadowgraph
AADGHINOSSW washing-soda
AADGHIOPRRY radiography
AADGHLRRRYY hydrargyral
AADGHMNOPRY dynamograph
AADGHMNRSTU draughtsman
AADGIIIMNTW waiting-maid
AADGIILLNOV Gallovidian
AADGIILMRST madrigalist
AADGIILNNNO Anglo-Indian
AADGILNNOST Gladstonian
AADGIMNRSUV vanguardism
AADGINOPRTU upgradation
AADGLLLNRUY glandularly
AADHIIIKNRS kaisar-i-Hind
AADHIILMPRS admiralship
AADHIILNOPR dolphinaria
AADHIIMOPRS adiaphorism
AADHIINOPRS Aphrodisian
AADHIIOPRST adiaphorist
AADHIOOPRSU adiaphorous
AADHIOPPRTY paratyphoid
AADHIOPRRTY parathyroid
AADHLOOPRRT arthropodal
AADHLORSUYZ hazardously
AADHMOORSTY hydrosomata
AADHNOPQRUY quadraphony
AADHNORSUUZ unhazardous
AADIIINNNOR Indo-Iranian
AADIIINORRT irradiation
AADIIJNOSTU Judaisation
AADIIJNOTUZ Judaization
AADIILLNTTU altitudinal
latitudinal
AADIILNOPSS anadiplosis
AADIILNORTT traditional
AADIILNTTTU attitudinal
AADIILOSUUV audiovisual
AADIIMNOPST △adoptianism
AADIINNOTTX antioxidant
AADIINOPSTT adoptianist
AADILLMNNOY Madonna-lily
AADILLMNOOT amontillado
AADILLMORTY maladroitly
AADILLMPRYY pyramidally
AADILMOPRRU parlour-maid
AADILNNOPRT Portlandian
AADILOORSTV vasodilator
AADILOPPRSV disapproval
AADIMNNSSYY syndyasmian
AADINOPRSSU sauropsidan
AADKMOORSTU katadromous
AADLMOOPRWY palmyra-wood
AADMNORSSTU Nostradamus
AADMOOOPSTT Stomatopoda
AAEEEFHPRTT feather-pate
AAEEEHNRRTW earthenware
AAEEEHPRTTU Therapeutae
AAEEEHRRTTW water-heater
AAEEEIJMNNR Marie-Jeanne
AAEEELMNPPR paper-enamel
AAEEELNPPSS epanalepses
AAEEEMNPPST appeasement
AAEEFHHILRT faith-healer
AAEEFHHLLRT half-leather
AAEEFHILRTT tail-feather
AAEEFHIRRTW fair-weather
AAEEFHLMRSU half-measure
AAEEFHLRRTT flat-earther
AAEEFHMRRRS sharefarmer
AAEEFHRRSTT feather-star
AAEEFIINNST fainéantise
AAEEFNRRSST transferase
AAEEGGGIRTV aggregative
AAEEGGGLRTY aggregately
AAEEGGINNRW wage-earning
AAEEGGLMORT agglomerate
AAEEGGMNNOT megatonnage
AAEEGGORRTX exaggerator
AAEEGHHMORR haemorrhage
AAEEGHINRST heart-easing
AAEEGHLOOPS oesophageal
AAEEGHNPPRR paper-hanger
AAEEGHRRTTX tax-gatherer
AAEEGIKLNTV leave-taking
AAEEGIKNNRW reawakening
AAEEGILLLNS selaginella
AAEEGILLLTT tagliatelle
AAEEGILLNNT gentianella
AAEEGILMSSX sexagesimal
AAEEGILNPPT eating-apple
AAEEGILNRVY evangeliary
AAEEGILPRTT tetraplegia
AAEEGINNOPS neopaganise
AAEEGINNOPZ neopaganize
AAEEGINPRSS paragenesis
AAEEGINRRTW graniteware
AAEEGKNRRST garter-snake
AAEEGLLRSSU leaguer-lass
AAEEGLMNOPT planogamete
AAEEGLNNORV navel-orange
AAEEGLNSSTV vantageless
AAEEGLPRSTY stage-player
AAEEGMNNRRT arrangement
AAEEGMNOPRT pomegranate
AAEEGMNSSTU assuagement
AAEEGNPPRRT garnet-paper
AAEEHHKRRST Earthshaker
AAEEHHLNNPT naphthalene
AAEEHHLRSTW wash-leather
AAEEHIILMNS leishmaniae
AAEEHILMOPR hemeralopia
AAEEHIMMNPT amphetamine
AAEEHIMMSTT mathematise

AAEEHIMMTTZ mathematize
AAEEHIMNORT etheromania
AAEEHINPSST panesthesia
AAEEHINRSTT Anthesteria
AAEEHINSSST anaesthesis
AAEEHIPRSST paresthesia
AAEEHKMPRRS phrasemaker
AAEEHLLMNOY hyalomelane
AAEEHLLSTTU haustellate
AAEEHMNOORR amenorrhoea
AAEEHORRSTT steatorrhea
AAEEHPRSTTT shatter-pate
AAEEIILLTVV alleviative
AAEEIILMRST materialise
AAEEIILMRTZ materialize
AAEEIILRRST arterialise
AAEEIILRRTZ arterialize
AAEEIILRTTV retaliative
AAEEIINRSSV sansevieria
AAEEIIPTTVX expatiative
AAEEIKLLMRT alkalimeter
AAEEILLLPRS parallelise
AAEEILLLPRZ parallelize
AAEEILLMPRX premaxillae
AAEEILLPPTV appellative
AAEEILLPRST ipselateral
AAEEILLQRTU equilateral
AAEEILMMPST semipalmate
AAEEILNNPRT penetralian
AAEEILNOPRT peritonaeal
AAEEILNPPSS epanalepsis
AAEEILNPRTX Praxitelean
AAEEILNPTVX explanative
AAEEILNRTTV alternative
AAEEILPPRSS paraleipses
AAEEILPSTTT latiseptate
AAEEIMNSSTV amativeness
AAEEIMOQSTU metasequoia
AAEEIMSSSTT metastasise
AAEEIMSSTTZ metastasize
AAEEINRRSTT tea-strainer
AAEEIOPRTVV evaporative
AAEEIORSTTX stereotaxia
AAEEIPPRRRS reappraiser
AAEEIPPRRTV preparative
AAEEISTTTTV attestative
AAEEKLMRTUV market-value
AAEEKLNRSTT rattlesnake
AAEELLLMNOS salmonellae
AAEELLNRTTY alternately
AAEELLPRSTU △pasteurella
AAEELLRRTUW laurel-water
AAEELMNPPRT apparelment
AAEELMNSTTT testamental
AAEELMPRRTW plate-warmer
AAEELNNPTTV pentavalent
AAEELNPQRRU quarrel-pane
AAEELNPSTTT pantalettes
AAEELNRRSTT retranslate
AAEELNRTTTV tetravalent
AAEELOPRTTX extrapolate
AAEELQRRSTU quarter-seal
AAEELRRSTTU serratulate
AAEEMMPRRSU map-measurer
AAEEMMPRTUY empyreumata
AAEEMNOPRTT treponemata
AAEEMNORSTZ estramazone
AAEEMNORTUX auxanometer
AAEEMNPPRTT appartement
AAEEMNRSTTT testamentar
AAEEMQRSSTU marquessate
AAEENNOPPRU pan-European
AAEENNRSSUW unawareness
AAEENPRRTTT tetrapteran
AAEENPRSTTT transeptate
AAEEOPRRSTX exasperator
AAEEPPRSTTU pâte-sur-pâte
AAEFFFFTTTU tufftaffeta
AAEFFFILRSS self-affairs
AAEFFIIMRTV affirmative
AAEFGHILNRT farthingale
AAEFGILLNRT tear-falling
AAEFGILPRST septifragal
AAEFGLLLORT flagellator
AAEFGMNRRTY fragmentary
AAEFHILLLNT hälleflinta
AAEFHILMRRS fire-marshal
AAEFHILNRTW father-in-law
AAEFIIILMRS familiarise
AAEFIIILMRZ familiarize
AAEFIIORRSV savoir-faire
AAEFILMMNRT firmamental
AAEFILMNRTY filamentary
AAEFILOPRRT prefatorial
AAEFLLNRRTY fraternally
AAEFLLORRTX extrafloral
AAEFLNRRRST transferral
AAEFMMNORST foremastman
AAEGGGINORT aggregation
AAEGGILLNOW Gallowegian
AAEGGILNNVZ navel-gazing
AAEGGILNTTU agglutinate
AAEGGIMMNTU gametangium
AAEGGIMNNUZ magazine-gun
AAEGGLMMORU grammalogue
AAEGGLOPTUY ptyalagogue
AAEGGMMNRST gammerstang
AAEGGMNORST steganogram
AAEGGNORRSS orange-grass
AAEGGNORRUW narrow-gauge
AAEGHHIPPRY hyperphagia
AAEGHIMNORR menorrhagia
AAEGHIMNPRS managership
AAEGHINNNSS shenanigans
AAEGHINOORT Ornithogaea
AAEGHLLNOXY hexagonally
AAEGHLMOOTY haematology
AAEGHLNNOPY angelophany
AAEGHLOPPRY paleography
AAEGHLPRSTU Tragelaphus
AAEGHMNOPRY anemography
AAEGHMOPRRS phraseogram
AAEGHMRTTUU thaumaturge
AAEGHNOPRTY Pythagorean

AAEGHNPRRST	strap-hanger
AAEGIIIMNTV	imaginative
AAEGIILMNPS	Pelagianism
AAEGIILMNRS	marginalise
AAEGIILMNRZ	marginalize
AAEGIILMRST	magisterial
AAEGIIMMNRT	immarginate
AAEGIIMMNTV	megavitamin
AAEGIIMMRRS	mismarriage
AAEGIINNNRT	Argentinian
AAEGIINNOTV	evagination
AAEGIINORTV	variegation
AAEGIIRTTVV	gravitative
AAEGIKMNPPR	paper-making
AAEGIKNNNUW	unawakening
AAEGILLLNPR	paralleling
AAEGILLNPPR	apparelling
AAEGILLNPPY	appealingly
AAEGILMMNOS	Maglemosian
AAEGILMNNOS	nonagesimal
AAEGILMNRTY	ligamentary
AAEGILMNSTU	glutaminase
AAEGILNNPPU	unappealing
AAEGILNNRTT	alternating
AAEGILNOPRS	saprolegnia
AAEGILNOSTT	gestational
AAEGILNPPSY	appeasingly
AAEGILNPRSV	palsgravine
AAEGILNQRUU	equiangular
AAEGILNRTTU	triangulate
AAEGILNRTUV	granulative
AAEGILORSTT	gestatorial
AAEGILPRRSU	Spergularia
AAEGIMNNOPS	neopaganism
AAEGIMNNRRT	arraignment
AAEGIMNNTTU	antimutagen
AAEGIMORRTU	outmarriage
AAEGIMPRRST	pragmatiser
AAEGIMPRRTZ	pragmatizer
AAEGINNNPTY	pentagynian
AAEGINNPPRT	parapenting
AAEGINNRTTY	tetragynian
AAEGINOPRST	aspergation
AAEGIOPPRTV	propagative
AAEGIOPSTTY	steatopygia
AAEGKLLMNOS	maskallonge
AAEGLLNNSST	gallantness
AAEGLLNNTTY	tangentally
AAEGLLNORTY	angelolatry
AAEGLLORRST	Grallatores
AAEGLMNRTTY	termagantly
AAEGLNNPRTU	pentangular
AAEGLNRSTTU	strangulate
AAEGLORSSTT	tessaraglot
AAEGNNORTWY	orange-tawny
AAEGNOQRSSU	squarsonage
AAEGORRTUUV	autogravure
AAEHHIILMOP	haemophilia
AAEHHILNPST	naphthalise
AAEHHILNPTZ	naphthalize
AAEHIILMNSS	leishmanias
AAEHIIMNOPS	hemianopsia
AAEHIIMNSST	histaminase
AAEHIJLNOPP	Japanophile
AAEHILLPRRT	earth-pillar
AAEHILNOOPY	hypoaeolian
AAEHILNPSTW	Westphalian
AAEHILNSSTU	ailanthuses
AAEHILOORRS	sialorrhoea
AAEHILORRTX	exhilarator
AAEHILPPRSY	hyperplasia
AAEHIMOSSST	haemostasis
AAEHIMPRSST	metaphrasis
AAEHIMPRSTU	amateurship
AAEHINNNOOT	hootanannie
AAEHLLLLNOW	allhallowen
AAEHLLLOPTY	allelopathy
AAEHLNPRSTY	phalanstery
AAEHMMORSST	atom-smasher
AAEHMNORSTU	athermanous
AAEHMNORSWW	washerwoman
AAEHMOPRTTU	thaumatrope
AAEHNOPPRRS	paranephros
AAEIIILRSUX	auxiliaries
AAEIIJMORRT	majoritaire
AAEIILLMNNR	millenarian
AAEIILLMNRT	matrilineal
AAEIILLNNOT	allineation
AAEIILLNOTV	alleviation
AAEIILLNPRT	patrilineal
AAEIILLNRSV	Vallisneria
AAEIILLPRST	ipsilateral
AAEIILLPTXY	epitaxially
AAEIILMMRST	materialism
AAEIILMNNTY	inanimately
AAEIILMNRRT	matrilinear
AAEIILMRSTT	materialist
AAEIILMRTTY	materiality
AAEIILNNNTV	Valentinian
AAEIILNNOST	nationalise
AAEIILNNOTZ	nationalize
AAEIILNNPST	Palestinian
AAEIILNORST	rationalise
	realisation
AAEIILNORTT	retaliation
AAEIILNORTZ	rationalize
	realization
AAEIILNPRRT	patrilinear
AAEIILNRTTV	tire-valiant
AAEIILNSTTY	insatiately
AAEIILPPRSS	paraleipsis
AAEIILQTTUV	qualitative
AAEIIMNNORT	reanimation
AAEIIMNNOTT	antimoniate
AAEIIMNNOTX	examination
	exanimation
AAEIIMNRSST	Erastianism
AAEIINNPPRT	paripinnate
AAEIINNSTTT	instantiate
AAEIINOPTTX	expatiation
AAEIINOSTTV	aestivation
AAEIKKLLOPU	leukoplakia
AAEIKKLMNOU	kamelaukion
AAEIKLLMRTY	alkalimetry

AAEIKLLTTVY	talkatively
AAEIKLMNOPT	kleptomania
AAEILLLMPRS	parallelism
AAEILLLPPTU	papillulate
AAEILLLPRST	parallelist
AAEILLMPRVY	primaevally
AAEILLNOPPT	appellation
AAEILLORTTU	ratatouille
AAEILLORTVY	alleviatory
AAEILLPPRST	epiplastral
AAEILLQRSTU	aquarellist
AAEILMNNOTT	lamentation
AAEILMNNRSU	semi-annular
AAEILMNORST	monasterial
AAEILMNPRST	paternalism
AAEILMNPRTU	planetarium
AAEILMNRRTU	ultramarine
AAEILMNRSST	martialness
AAEILMOPTTT	totipalmate
AAEILNNOPSX	expansional
AAEILNNOPTX	explanation
AAEILNNORTT	alternation
AAEILNNOSST	sensational
AAEILNNOTTT	attentional
AAEILNNPRST	transalpine
AAEILNNPSST	plainstanes
AAEILNNPTTU	antenuptial
AAEILNOOPRT	operational
AAEILNOPPRY	piano-player
	player-piano
AAEILNOPRRT	proletarian
AAEILNOPRSS	anaplerosis
AAEILNORTUV	revaluation
AAEILNOSSTY	seasonality
AAEILNRRSTT	intertarsal
AAEILNRRSTU	sertularian
AAEILNRRTVY	narratively
AAEILNRSTTV	translative
AAEILNRSTUX	intrasexual
AAEILOPPRRS	paper-sailor
AAEILOPRRTT	proletariat
AAEILOQRSTU	quaestorial
AAEILORRTTY	retaliatory
AAEILORSSSS	assessorial
AAEILQRRRTU	quarter-rail
AAEIMNNRRST	transmarine
AAEIMNNSTTT	attainments
AAEIMNNTTTT	attaintment
AAEIMOPPRTX	approximate
AAEINNOPRTT	trepanation
AAEINNOSSTT	assentation
AAEINNOTTTU	attenuation
AAEINNRRSVY	anniversary
AAEINOOPRTV	evaporation
AAEINOORSTT	aerostation
AAEINOPPRRT	preparation
AAEINOPRRST	reparations
AAEINORRSTT	arrestation
AAEINOSTTTT	attestation
AAEIOPPPRRT	appropriate
AAEIOPPRRSS	appressoria
AAEIOPRRRTT	repatriator
AAEIOPRRSTU	Pterosauria
AAEIOPRTTXY	expatiatory
AAEIORSSTTV	assortative
AAEKMMNORTW	market-woman
AAELLLMNOSS	salmonellas
AAELLLORSST	saltarellos
AAELLMRSSTT	stallmaster
AAELLOPSSTT	Elastoplast®
AAELLORRSTT	stellarator
AAELLRSSTTT	Tattersall's
AAELMNOORSV	vomeronasal
AAELMNSSTTY	statesmanly
AAELMOPRRTU	armour-plate
	plate-armour
AAELMORRSSS	serrasalmos
AAELNNRSSTU	naturalness
AAELNOOPPRS	aplanospore
AAELNOPRTXY	explanatory
AAELNRRSSTV	transversal
AAELNRRSTUV	transvaluer
AAELNRSSSTV	servant-lass
AAELNRSSTUX	transsexual
	trans-sexual
AAEMMNOORTT	Monotremata
AAEMMNORSST	master-mason
AAEMNNOOSTZ	amazon-stone
AAEMNNORTUV	verumontana
AAEMNOOPRTT	protonemata
AAEMNOOSSST	anastomoses
AAEMNOPRTTU	portmanteau
AAEMNORSTTU	atramentous
AAEMNOSSTTW	stateswoman
AAEMNPPRTTY	part-payment
AAEMOOPRSTZ	spermatozoa
AAEMOPSSSZZ	passamezzos
AAEMORSSTTT	toastmaster
AAENNPPRTTU	appurtenant
AAENNPRRSTT	transparent
AAENNPRSTTU	supernatant
AAENQRRSTUW	quarter-sawn
AAEOOPPRRRT	paratrooper
AAEOPPRRRTY	preparatory
AAEOPRSSTTU	stratopause
AAEQRRRTUWY	quarry-water
AAFFGHHIINS	haaf-fishing
AAFFGILOPST	gaff-topsail
AAFFIIILNOT	affiliation
AAFFIILNOPR	paraffin-oil
AAFFIIMNORT	affirmation
AAFFIMORRTY	affirmatory
AAFGGGGILNW	flag-wagging
AAFGIILNOTT	flagitation
AAFGIKLNSTT	fast-talking
AAFGIKMNNRT	tank-farming
AAFGILLMRUY	gallimaufry
AAFGILNOSTT	stagflation
AAFGINORRSU	farraginous
AAFHILLLLSY	fallalishly
AAFIIILMRTY	familiarity
AAFIIIMNNRR	infirmarian
AAFIILNRSTU	fustilarian
AAFIINNOTTU	infatuation

AAFILMNOORT formational
AAFIMNNNRTY infantryman
AAFINNOOPRT profanation
AAFIOQRSTTU aquafortist
AAFLNNOORST nasofrontal
AAFNOOPRRTY profanatory
AAGGGHILNSU laughing-gas
AAGGGILNSSZ glass-gazing
AAGGHHIINNS shanghaiing
AAGGHHIOPRY hagiography
AAGGHINOPRY angiography
AAGGILLNSTZ salt-glazing
AAGGILNNTTU agglutinant
AAGGIMNRSTU Gargantuism
AAGGINRSTTU Gargantuist
AAGGLLLOSSW gallowglass
AAGGNNOORTU orang-outang
AAGHHIILMNU high-alumina
AAGHHLOPPRY haplography
AAGHHOPPRTY pathography
AAGHIIINRRS hair-raising
AAGHIILLNOP △anglophilia
AAGHIILNRTV rival-hating
AAGHILLMNPY lymphangial
AAGHILLMNRS marshalling
AAGHILNRSSY harassingly
AAGHILOPRSY sialography
AAGHILPPRSY psaligraphy
AAGHIMRRSTT straight-arm
AAGHINOPSSV shaving-soap
AAGHIOPPRTY typographia
AAGHIRSTTWY straightway
AAGHKNOOOPR kangaroo-hop
AAGHLNOOTTY thanatology
AAGHMMMOPRY mammography
AAGHMMNOORR harmonogram
AAGHMRTTUUY thaumaturgy
AAGHNOPPRTY pantography
AAGHNOPRRUY uranography
AAGHOOPSTUU autophagous
AAGIIILLNRS sigillarian
AAGIIIMNNOT imagination
AAGIIJMMNNT antijamming
AAGIIKNNPST painstaking
AAGIILMMNRS marginalism
AAGIILMNNTY animatingly
AAGIILMNRST marginalist
AAGIILMNRTY marginality
AAGIILNNSTT tantalising
AAGIILNNTTZ tantalizing
AAGIIMMNNTY magnanimity
AAGIIMMSSTT astigmatism
AAGIINNORSS anagnorisis
AAGIINNOSST assignation
AAGIINNSTTU unsatiating
AAGIINNSTUU Augustinian
AAGIINORTTV gravitation
AAGIINPPTTT pit-a-patting
AAGIIRSSTTU Sagittarius
AAGILLLNPPY appallingly
AAGILLLOOSS glossolalia
AAGILLMNNTY malignantly
AAGILLMOORY malariology
AAGILMMMOST mammalogist
AAGILMNNOOR Anglo-Romani
AAGILNNOPSS Panglossian
AAGILNNORTU granulation
AAGILNNOSST glasnostian
AAGILNOOPRS sporangiola
AAGILNOPSTY angioplasty
AAGILNORSSU agranulosis
AAGILNORTTU gratulation
AAGILNOSUVY Yugoslavian
AAGILNRRTUY granularity
AAGILOPRRTU purgatorial
AAGIMMNNOSU magnanimous
AAGINOOPPRT propagation
AAGINOPRRTU purgatorian
AAGINORRTUU inaugurator
AAGLLLNNTUY ungallantly
AAGLLMNRTUU multangular
AAGLLNOOSUY analogously
AAGLMNNNOOR Anglo-Norman
AAGLMOOPSUY apogamously
AAGLNOOPRTW patrol-wagon
AAGLOOPRTXY protogalaxy
AAGLORRTTUY gratulatory
AAHHILMPRSS marshalship
AAHHLLOPTTY Thallophyta
AAHHMOPRSST Rhamphastos
AAHHOPRRTTY arthropathy
AAHIILMMPXY maximaphily
AAHIILMNNOT Hamiltonian
AAHIILMNSST Stahlianism
AAHIILNNORT annihilator
AAHIILNOORT hariolation
AAHIINPRSST antiphrasis
AAHIINPSTTT antipathist
AAHIJNNNOOS Johnsoniana
AAHIKKLNOSV kalashnikov
AAHILLLOPRT prothallial
AAHILLMNOPY phyllomania
AAHILLOPSTT allopathist
AAHILLOPTXY litholapaxy
AAHILPPSSST pissasphalt
AAHIMMNNOPY nymphomania
AAHIMNOPRSS oarsmanship
AAHINNOPRTY antiphonary
AAHINOPSSTT thanatopsis
AAHIOPRSTXY asphyxiator
AAHKNOORTTV katavothron
AAHKOPRRSWW sparrow-hawk
AAHLLMMORSW marshmallow
marsh-mallow
AAHLLOPRSTY hyoplastral
AAHMNNRSTTU transhumant
AAHMNOOPRSU anamorphous
AAHNNOPRSXY nasopharynx
AAHNOOPSTUU autophanous
AAHNOPRTTUY naturopathy
AAHOPRRSTTT throat-strap
AAIIILNRTTU utilitarian
AAIIIMMNNRS Arminianism
AAIIIMNNNOT inanimation

AAIIIMNNTTV	antivitamin
AAIIINNRRTT	Trinitarian
AAIIKMNOPRT	imparkation
AAIILLLNPSU	sinupallial
AAIILLMMNOT	mamillation
AAIILLMPRTY	impartially
AAIILLNOPRS	Apollinaris
AAIILLNPRST	pillar-saint
AAIILMMNORT	matrimonial
AAIILMMNPSS	panislamism
AAIILMNNOST	nationalism
AAIILMNNOTV	nominatival
AAIILMNOPRT	patrimonial
AAIILMNOPST	maintopsail
AAIILMNOPTU	tulipomania
AAIILMNORST	rationalism
AAIILMNPSST	panislamist
AAIILNNOSTT	nationalist
AAIILNNOTTY	nationality
AAIILNOORTV	variolation
AAIILNOPPTT	palpitation
AAIILNORSTT	rationalist
AAIILNORTTT	attritional
AAIILNORTTY	rationality
AAIILNOSTTU	situational
AAIILNOTTTU	attuitional
AAIIMMNORSV	Moravianism
AAIIMNNOSTV	Novatianism
AAIIMNOOSTT	atomisation
AAIIMNOOTTZ	atomization
AAIIMNOPRTT	impartation
AAIIMNOPSTT	impastation
AAIIMNORRST	Rotarianism
AAIIMNPRTVY	parvanimity
AAIIMNRSSTU	sanitariums
AAIINNOQTTU	antiquation
AAIINNOSTTV	Novatianist
AAIINOPRSST	aspirations
AAIIOPRSSST	parasitosis
AAILLLOSTWW	swallow-tail
AAILLMNPRUU	plumularian
AAILLNRUUVV	univalvular
AAILLOOPRYZ	polyzoarial
AAILLORRSTT	latirostral
AAILLORRSTY	sartorially
AAILLRRTUVV	trivalvular
AAILMMNOSTU	summational
AAILMMOPPRS	malapropism
AAILMNOPRTU	manipulator
AAILMNRSTTT	transmittal
AAILMOPRSST	pastoralism
AAILNNORSTT	translation
AAILNOPTUUV	upvaluation
AAILOORSTTT	totalisator
AAILOORTTTZ	totalizator
AAILOPRRSUV	larviparous
AAILOPRSSTT	pastoralist
AAIMMNNOORY	monomyarian
AAIMMNOPSTT	maintopmast
AAIMMNOSSUY	immunoassay
AAIMNOOOSTT	somatotonia
AAIMNOOSSST	anastomosis
AAIMNORSSTU	sanatoriums
AAIMNORSTTU	natatoriums
AAIMOOPPRST	apotropaism
AAINNNOPRST	non-partisan
AAINOOPRSTT	asportation
AAINOORRSTZ	Zoroastrian
AAINORRSTTU	instaurator
AAINORRSTUU	saourari-nut
AAIOPPRSUVV	papovavirus
AALLNNRTUUY	unnaturally
AALMMMOPSTY	mammoplasty
AALMMOOPSST	somatoplasm
AALMNNOPSTW	plantswoman
AALMNOOPRTW	patrolwoman
AALMNOOPRTY	protanomaly
AALMNOPRTUY	paramountly
AALMNPRSTUY	palmyra-nuts
AALNNNORSTU	non-naturals
AALNNRRSTUY	translunary
AALNOPRRSTT	transportal
AALNOPRSTUY	uranoplasty
AALNORRSTTY	translatory
AALORSSTTTU	altostratus
AAMNOOPRSTY	Trypanosoma
AAMNPRSSTTY	smartypants
AAMOOPRRTUU	out-paramour
AANNORRSTUY	tyrannosaur
AANOOPPRSTV	avant-propos
ABBBBEELRUY	abbey-lubber
ABBBCELLNUU	unclubbable
ABBBCENORUY	baby-bouncer
ABBBEELMNRT	brabblement
ABBBEHLMRSU	bramble-bush
ABBBERRRSSU	brass-rubber
ABBCCDEHKNU	bunch-backed
ABBCCEEHKNR	backbencher
ABBCCEEHMOR	beachcomber
ABBCCEEINOR	bone-breccia
ABBCCEKKLOR	back-blocker
ABBCCNOORSY	snobbocracy
ABBCDEEFIKO	biofeedback
ABBCDEEILRS	describable
ABBCDEENRSS	crabbedness
ABBCDEENSSS	scabbedness
ABBCDEIKLRR	blackbirder
ABBCDEKLORW	black-browed
ABBCDEMRRSU	breadcrumbs
ABBCDGIKLNO	black-boding
ABBCEEEHRRS	bear's-breech
ABBCEEEKLLT	black-beetle
ABBCEEKLORT	beta-blocker
ABBCEHIIKLN	kibble-chain
ABBCEHIILOT	bibliotheca
ABBCEHILLMR	bill-chamber
ABBCEHIOPRY	cyberphobia
ABBCEIILNRS	inscribable
ABBCEJKORWY	jabberwocky
ABBCGIIIMNN	minicabbing
ABBCHIILOST	Hobbistical
ABBCIILLTUY	clubability
ABBCIILMNOY	bibliomancy
ABBDDEGIORR	bridgeboard

ABBDDEIINRR	bird-brained
ABBDEEEFINR	beef-brained
ABBDEEILRST	bestridable
ABBDEELORTU	redoubtable
ABBDEGILNOT	bold-beating
ABBDEIILNTU	indubitable
ABBDEIINRRU	india-rubber
ABBDEILORTU	boat-builder
ABBDELNOTUU	undoubtable
ABBDELNSUUU	unsubduable
ABBDEMMNORT	bombardment
ABBDFFILORU	buffalo-bird
ABBDGGINNOR	Brobdingnag
ABBDGIJLNNO	land-jobbing
ABBDIILNTUY	indubitably
ABBEEEILNRT	beetlebrain
ABBEELMSSSU	subassemble
ABBEELORRSU	rabble-rouse
ABBEELPRRTU	perturbable
ABBEEMNSSTU	subbasement
ABBEFFLOORU	buffalo-robe
ABBEGGHLMUU	humbuggable
ABBEGIJLNRY	jabberingly
ABBEGINORTW	browbeating
ABBEHHIPRSU	rubbish-heap
ABBEHILLPSU	publishable
ABBEHIORRTY	bribery-oath
ABBEHLORRTY	barley-broth
ABBEHNOORTT	Berthon-boat
ABBEIILLORT	bibliolater
ABBEIJNORTT	rabbet-joint
ABBEILORTTY	liberty-boat
ABBEINRSSUU	suburbanise
ABBEINRSTUU	suburbanite
ABBEINRSUUZ	suburbanize
ABBELLMRSUU	subumbrella
ABBELMSSSUY	subassembly
ABBELORRRTU	retrobulbar
ABBEMPRRSTU	rubber-stamp
ABBGHIMNOTU	thingumabob
ABBGHIMNOTY	thingamybob
ABBGIILLNTU	bull-baiting
ABBGIINSTTY	baby-sitting
ABBGILLNSTU	ball-busting
ABBGILNORSY	absorbingly
ABBGINORRSS	ribbon-grass
ABBGLLORSUU	subglobular
ABBIILLORTY	bibliolatry
ABBIILMNOOT	bombilation
ABBIILMOPRS	probabilism
ABBIILOPRST	probabilist
ABBIILOPRTY	probability
ABBIIMNNOOT	bombination
ABBIMNOORTU	obumbration
ABBIMNRSSUU	suburbanism
ABBINRSTUUY	suburbanity
ABBLLLLOOYY	loblolly-bay
ABCCCILORY	carbocyclic
ABCCCHKKLOO	chock-a-block
ABCCCILMOOX	coxcombical
ABCCDDHIIKY	chick-a-biddy
ABCCDEEIIRT	bactericide
ABCCDEENNOS	abscondence
ABCCDEFHIKN	finch-backed
ABCCDEHHKNU	hunchbacked
ABCCDEHIRRT	bird-catcher
ABCCDEIIILL	bacillicide
ABCCDEKKOOR	crookbacked
ABCCDHHORRU	broad-church
ABCCDKLLNOU	cock-and-bull
ABCCEEHKLNU	uncheckable
ABCCEEILMRS	marcescible
ABCCEEILNOO	eccaleobion
ABCCEEILNOV	conceivable
ABCCEEKLOPU	peacock-blue
ABCCEELLLOT	collectable
ABCCEELNNOT	connectable
ABCCEELORRT	correctable
ABCCEEMNNRU	encumbrance
ABCCEFILNOS	confiscable
ABCCEFIORSU	bacciferous
ABCCEGINNOU	concubinage
ABCCEHIILMO	biochemical
ABCCEHILSTT	cable-stitch
ABCCEHINRTT	tectibranch
ABCCEHOORTT	boot-catcher
ABCCEIILLNO	conciliable
ABCCEIILNOT	cenobitical
ABCCEIILPTY	peccability
ABCCEIKKLPR	prickle-back
ABCCEIKKLST	stickleback
ABCCEIKLMRT	balm-cricket
ABCCEILNOVY	conceivably
ABCCEILNSSU	cubicalness
ABCCEILORTU	corbiculate
ABCCEILOSTT	ectoblastic
ABCCEILRRUV	cruciverbal
ABCCEINORRT	centrobaric
ABCCEINRRTY	barycentric
ABCCEIOOPPT	tobacco-pipe
ABCCELORSUU	succourable
ABCCELRRRUW	curb-crawler
ABCCEOORTTU	cocoa-butter
ABCCIILLNSU	subclinical
ABCCIILRSTU	subcritical
ABCCIIMOORT	macrobiotic
ABCCIIORSSU	scribacious
ABCCIKLMNOR	cramboclink
ABCCILLLOUY	bucolically
ABCCILORRSU	scrobicular
ABCCILORSTU	subcortical
ABCCINNORUY	concubinary
ABCCINNOTTU	concubitant
ABCCINOOSTT	tobacconist
ABCCINORTUY	buccinatory
ABCCIOORSUV	baccivorous
ABCCKNOOOTU	account-book
	book-account
ABCCKNORTUY	back-country
ABCCNORSTTU	subcontract
ABCDDEEELNS	descendable
ABCDDEEFLOU	double-faced
ABCDDEEHLUY	debauchedly
ABCDDEEHNUU	undebauched

ABCDDEEILNU	undecidable
ABCDDEELNOS	close-banded
ABCDDEFINOR	forbiddance
ABCDDEFLOOY	bloody-faced
ABCDDEKNORU	round-backed
ABCDDENORSS	crossbanded
ABCDEEEERRT	decerebrate
ABCDEEEHORS	cheeseboard
ABCDEEEKORR	code-breaker
ABCDEEEMMRY	May-December
ABCDEEFHILL	bleach-field
ABCDEEHMNTU	debauchment
ABCDEEIILMM	immedicable
ABCDEEIILMN	medicinable
ABCDEEILLMN	clean-limbed
ABCDEEILORV	divorceable
ABCDEEILPRT	predictable
ABCDEEINORS	decarbonise
ABCDEEINORZ	decarbonize
ABCDEEIRRSU	decarburise
ABCDEEIRRUZ	decarburize
ABCDEELLNRY	belly-dancer
ABCDEELMMNO	commendable
ABCDEELMNNO	condemnable
ABCDEELNNOS	condensable
ABCDEELNRRY	candleberry
ABCDEELOPSU	double-space
ABCDEELORRS	close-barred
ABCDEENORRT	centreboard
ABCDEERRTTU	carburetted
ABCDEFIINRR	bird-fancier
ABCDEHIKPRS	brickshaped
ABCDEHILSTW	switchblade
ABCDEHIRRTW	birdwatcher
ABCDEHLMOOR	bachelordom
ABCDEIILLRU	billiard-cue
ABCDEIILMRU	Lumbricidae
ABCDEIILOSS	dissociable
ABCDEIILTUY	educability
ABCDEIINSTU	subindicate
ABCDEIIPSTU	bicuspidate
ABCDEILPRTY	predictably
ABCDEILSSSU	discussable
ABCDEINOORT	notice-board
ABCDEINRSTU	disturbance
ABCDEINSSSU	subacidness
ABCDEIOOPRS	Proboscidea
ABCDEIORRSV	scriveboard
ABCDEIPPRTY	bradypeptic
ABCDEKLLORS	balderlocks
ABCDELLORUY	boulder-clay
ABCDELMMNOY	commendably
ABCDENORSUY	subdeaconry
ABCDEORRRSS	crossbarred
ABCDGIIKLNS	backsliding
ABCDGIKNNOW	backing-down
ABCDHIIMRTY	dithyrambic
ABCDHIIRSTU	Hudibrastic
ABCDHINOOPR	branchiopod
ABCDHIORSTW	switchboard
ABCDHLOOORS	board-school
ABCDHNOORRY	hydrocarbon
ABCDIIILOST	idioblastic
ABCDIILOSSY	dissociably
ABCDIIMNOSY	biodynamics
ABCDMNORRUU	Carborundum®
ABCEEEFFLOT	coffee-table
ABCEEEFIINT	beneficiate
ABCEEEFLNOR	enforceable
ABCEEEGLLNT	neglectable
ABCEEEHMNRT	beech-marten
ABCEEEILMPR	imperceable
ABCEEEILNRX	inexecrable
ABCEEEILPRV	perceivable
ABCEEEILPTT	battle-piece
ABCEEEILRSV	serviceable
ABCEEEILRSX	exercisable
ABCEEEINNSS	bienséances
ABCEEELMNRS	resemblance
ABCEEELORRV	recoverable
ABCEEELPRRU	recuperable
ABCEEELPRST	respectable
ABCEEEMMNRR	remembrance
ABCEEEMMNRT	embracement
ABCEEFGHORR	herb-of-grace
ABCEEFHMMRU	fume-chamber
ABCEEFIILPS	specifiable
ABCEEFIILRT	certifiable
	rectifiable
ABCEEFIINRY	beneficiary
ABCEEFILLMR	leaf-climber
ABCEEFINNOT	benefaction
ABCEEFINRTU	rubefacient
ABCEEFLNORR	conferrable
ABCEEFNORTY	benefactory
ABCEEGHLLNT	cable-length
ABCEEGIIKNR	icebreaking
ABCEEGIIMPT	gambit-piece
ABCEEGIINOT	abiogenetic
ABCEEHIKLPU	pickelhaube
ABCEEHILMST	thimble-case
ABCEEHINPST	spinach-beet
ABCEEHKLNOS	shackle-bone
ABCEEHORRRT	torchbearer
ABCEEIILNTX	inexcitable
ABCEEIJOTTV	objectivate
ABCEEILLMPT	Campbellite
ABCEEILLNTU	ineluctable
ABCEEILMRRS	cerebralism
ABCEEILNOPT	beneplacito
ABCEEILNORT	celebration
ABCEEILNSUX	inexcusable
ABCEEILNTUX	unexcitable
ABCEEILORRV	irrevocable
ABCEEILPRVY	perceivably
ABCEEILRRST	cerebralist
ABCEEILRRSU	irrecusable
ABCEEILRSVY	serviceably
ABCEEILRTTX	extractible
ABCEEILSSST	ecblastesis
ABCEEIMRTUU	eubacterium
ABCEEINNOST	incense-boat
ABCEEINNRTY	bicentenary
ABCEEINORRT	cerebration

ABCEEINORTX	exorbitance
ABCEEIORSTT	stereobatic
ABCEEKKLNRU	bare-knuckle
ABCEEKKORRR	rock-breaker
ABCEEKLRRRW	kerb-crawler
ABCEELLLMOP	compellable
ABCEELLMOPT	completable
ABCEELLOOST	blastocoele
ABCEELNOQRU	conquerable
ABCEELNORSV	conservable
	conversable
ABCEELNOSTT	contestable
ABCEELNRSSU	curableness
ABCEELNRSTU	cluster-bean
ABCEELOPRRR	procerebral
ABCEELORRTY	celebratory
ABCEELPRSTY	respectably
ABCEELPSSTU	suspectable
ABCEELRTTUU	tuberculate
ABCEENORRST	arborescent
ABCEENORSTU	counterbase
ABCEENPRRTU	perturbance
ABCEEORRRSS	crossbearer
ABCEEORSTUU	tuberaceous
ABCEERRRTTU	carburetter
ABCEFGIKLRU	black-figure
ABCEFHIKLRS	black-fisher
ABCEFHNOOPR	Francophobe
ABCEFIILRTY	certifiably
ABCEFILMNOR	confirmable
ABCEFINORTU	rubefaction
ABCEFKLLLOW	black-fellow
ABCEFLMNOOR	conformable
ABCEFLMOORT	comfortable
ABCEGIILNOT	incogitable
ABCEGILMNRY	embracingly
ABCEGILNNOS	consignable
ABCEGILNOPW	pace-bowling
ABCEGILNOST	blastogenic
ABCEGJLOSST	object-glass
ABCEGORSTUY	subcategory
ABCEHHIOOPT	theophobiac
ABCEHHKRSUW	bushwhacker
ABCEHIIMRST	Rechabitism
ABCEHIIMRSW	Micawberish
ABCEHILMORS	bachelorism
ABCEHILRTUV	Lubavitcher
ABCEHIMRTTY	bathymetric
ABCEHINOOPR	necrophobia
ABCEHIOPRRS	broach-spire
ABCEHKLLOST	shackle-bolt
ABCEHKLNOSU	unshockable
ABCEHLNNORU	luncheon-bar
ABCEHLNOTUU	untouchable
ABCEHLNRSUU	uncrushable
ABCEHLORTTT	bottle-chart
ABCEHNOORRW	bower-anchor
ABCEHRRSTTU	chart-buster
ABCEIIILLSV	civilisable
ABCEIIILLVZ	civilizable
ABCEIIIOSTV	bisociative
ABCEIIJLSTU	justiciable
ABCEIIKLNRT	tickle-brain
ABCEIILMNRU	Mulciberian
ABCEIILMRTY	imbricately
ABCEIILNOSV	cablevision
ABCEIILRTUV	lubricative
ABCEIIMMRSW	Micawberism
ABCEIIMNOTV	combinative
ABCEIIORSST	bacteriosis
ABCEIKNORTW	cabinetwork
ABCEILLLMRW	wallclimber
ABCEILLLOPS	collapsible
ABCEILLLOQU	colliquable
ABCEILLMORU	bimolecular
ABCEILLRTUV	carvel-built
ABCEILMOPRS	comprisable
ABCEILMOPRT	problematic
ABCEILMORST	meroblastic
ABCEILMOSST	mesoblastic
ABCEILNNOTU	continuable
ABCEILNORTV	contrivable
ABCEILNRSTU	inscrutable
ABCEILNSUXY	inexcusably
ABCEILORRSU	orbiculares
ABCEILORRVY	irrevocably
ABCEILORSTT	obstetrical
ABCEILPSTUU	usucaptible
ABCEILRRSUY	irrecusably
ABCEILRSTUU	bursiculate
ABCEILRSTUV	subvertical
ABCEIMNNORT	recombinant
ABCEIMNOORT	embrocation
ABCEINNORTY	cybernation
ABCEINOORST	obsecration
ABCEINORRTU	carburetion
ABCEINORTXY	exorbitancy
ABCEINRRRST	transcriber
ABCEIOOPRRT	bicorporate
ABCEIRSTTUV	subtractive
ABCELLLMNOO	collembolan
ABCELLLRSUU	subcellular
ABCELMORTUU	tuberculoma
ABCELNNORTU	contubernal
ABCELNNOTUU	uncountable
ABCELNORSTU	construable
ABCELNORSVY	conversably
ABCELORSSUU	scaberulous
ABCENRRSTUY	canterburys
ABCEOOORRRT	corroborate
ABCEORRRTTU	carburettor
ABCEORSTUUY	butyraceous
ABCFGIIKNTT	backfitting
ABCFHINOOST	sonofabitch
ABCFIILLMOR	bacilliform
ABCFIINORTU	bifurcation
ABCFINOOSTU	obfuscation
ABCFLMNOORY	conformably
ABCFLMOORTY	comfortably
ABCFOORSTUY	obfuscatory
ABCGGHINNPU	punching-bag
ABCGHIKNSUW	buck-washing
ABCGHILNOOP	△anglophobic
ABCGIIKKMNR	brickmaking

ABCGIIKLNRY bricklaying
ABCGIIKNOUV bivouacking
ABCGIINNPUY panic-buying
ABCGIKNPSSU buck-passing
ABCGILLMNSY scamblingly
ABCGILLOORY bryological
ABCHHIILOTT batholithic
ABCHHIILTTY bathylithic
ABCHHILOOOP ochlophobia
ABCHHLNOOPR lophobranch
ABCHIILNOOT halobiontic
ABCHIILNRTY labyrinthic
ABCHIILOPSY biophysical
ABCHIIOOPTX toxiphobiac
ABCHILLOOST holoblastic
ABCHILMNPSU clubmanship
ABCHILMOOST homoblastic
ABCHILNOPRT branch-pilot
ABCHILOPSTY hypoblastic
ABCHIMNORSU subharmonic
ABCHIMPRRSY brachyprism
ABCHINOOPTY nyctophobia
ABCHINORRSY chrysarobin
ABCHIOOOPPS scopophobia
ABCHIOOOPST Scotophobia
ABCHIOOPRTU Turcophobia
ABCHLMNOPRU pulmobranch
ABCHORRSUUY brachyurous
ABCIIILNRTU tribunicial
ABCIIILOSTY sociability
ABCIIILRSTT tribalistic
ABCIIIMNORT imbrication
ABCIIINNRTU tribunician
ABCIIINOOST bisociation
ABCIIKLNRSY brainsickly
ABCIILLMRSU lumbricalis
ABCIILLPTUY culpability
ABCIILLRSTY trisyllabic
ABCIILLSTYY syllabicity
ABCIILNOPTU publication
ABCIILNORTU lubrication
ABCIILORRSU orbicularis
ABCIIMNNOOT combination
ABCIINORRTU rubrication
ABCIINORSTT abstriction
ABCIIOOPRST saprobiotic
ABCIKLMOTTU buttock-mail
ABCILLNNOUY connubially
ABCILLNORUY binocularly
ABCILLNORYY Byronically
ABCILLORRUY orbicularly
ABCILMMNOSU somnambulic
ABCILMMORUU columbarium
ABCILMNNUUU incunabulum
ABCILMRSTUU rumbustical
ABCILNNOORS Sorbonnical
ABCILNORTUU lucubration
ABCILNRSTUY inscrutably
ABCILOPRSTU subtropical
ABCILORSUUV baculovirus
ABCIMNOORTY combinatory
ABCIMNORSTY corybantism
ABCINNOORTU conurbation
ABCINOORSTU obscuration
ABCINORSTTU subtraction
ABCLLRSTUUU subcultural
ABCMNOORSSW crossbowman
ABCNOOORRRT corroborant
ABCNORRSTUY subcontrary
ABCORRSSTTU substractor
ABDDDEEEFLS false-bedded
ABDDDEIMNOR broadminded
ABDDEEEGLMR marble-edged
ABDDEEEILTY baddeleyite
ABDDEEELNOR bandoleered
ABDDEEELRTT treble-dated
ABDDEEEMPRT bad-tempered
ABDDEEENSSS debasedness
ABDDEEGGLNY bandy-legged
ABDDEEHILLS shad-bellied
ABDDEEHLOSU double-shade
ABDDEEIIMNR bridemaiden
ABDDEEILNOR bandoliered
ABDDEEPRRRY drap-de-Berry
ABDDEFHLLOO half-blooded
ABDDEFLNORU fardel-bound
ABDDEHNNSUU unhusbanded
ABDDEIIILNV individable
ABDDEIILNUV undividable
ABDDEILLNRU dull-brained
ABDDEILMRSW swim-bladder
ABDDEIMNNST disbandment
ABDDEINOWWY bay-windowed
ABDDELMOORW warm-blooded
ABDDELMORRW bladder-worm
ABDDELORRTW bladderwort
ABDDGIINNRV driving-band
ABDDGIINORV diving-board
ABDDGINOORR dragoon-bird
ABDEEEFRRST fast-breeder
ABDEEEGLLOU double-eagle
ABDEEEGLNUW unwedgeable
ABDEEEHILRT hereditable
ABDEEEHLLVW well-behaved
ABDEEEILLRV deliverable
ABDEEEIMNTW between-maid
ABDEEEKLNTW blanketweed
ABDEEELLOPV developable
ABDEEELMNRU denumerable
ABDEEELNSST belatedness
ABDEEENRRRU underbearer
ABDEEEORRTT teeter-board
ABDEEEOTTTV vedette-boat
ABDEEEPRSTT bespattered
ABDEEERRTTV vertebrated
ABDEEFGNOSU sang-de-boeuf
ABDEEFIILNN indefinable
ABDEEFIINRT defibrinate
ABDEEFILLTT battlefield
ABDEEFILNNU undefinable
ABDEEGGINRR △gingerbread
ABDEEGHNORY honey-badger
ABDEEGILLSW swag-bellied
ABDEEGIMNRT abridgement

ABDEEGINPRS	bespreading
ABDEEGLNOTU	double-agent
ABDEEGLOSTU	about-sledge
ABDEEHILRTW	bridewealth
ABDEEHILSST	established
ABDEEHIRSTW	breadthwise
ABDEEHLOSTT	tables-d'hôte
ABDEEHNRRTU	underbreath
ABDEEIIKLLS	dislikeable
ABDEEIILNOT	obediential
ABDEEIILRST	detribalise
ABDEEIILRTZ	detribalize
ABDEEIILSST	destabilise
ABDEEIILSTZ	destabilize
ABDEEIKNRRW	Windbreaker®
ABDEEILMNNO	denominable
ABDEEILMNRS	simnel-bread
ABDEEILMNST	disablement
ABDEEILMSSS	disassemble
ABDEEILNPSS	dispensable
ABDEEILNRSU	undesirable
ABDEEILNRUV	undriveable
ABDEEILNSSU	audibleness
ABDEEILORRT	deliberator
ABDEEILORTT	obliterated
ABDEEINNRRW	breadwinner
ABDEEIPRSTU	Buprestidae
ABDEEKLNOOR	book-learned
ABDEEKLOPSU	double-speak
ABDEEKMNORY	monkey-bread
ABDEELLLORR	Rollerblade®
	rollerblade
ABDEELMNOTU	demountable
ABDEELMNRUY	denumerably
ABDEELNNRUU	unendurable
ABDEELNOSST	bloatedness
ABDEELNRSSU	durableness
ABDEELNRSTW	△waldsterben
ABDEELOPPTT	tabletopped
ABDEELORRTT	letter-board
ABDEELORRTW	world-beater
ABDEELORSTY	destroyable
ABDEELRSSTT	battledress
ABDEEMNORTY	embryonated
ABDEEORRRSW	sword-bearer
ABDEEQRRRTU	quarter-bred
ABDEFFLORRU	luffer-board
ABDEFGINORR	fingerboard
ABDEFHOORTT	footbreadth
ABDEFIILLRT	fibrillated
ABDEFIILNNY	indefinably
ABDEFLLOTUU	double-fault
ABDEGGILNOR	Goldbergian
ABDEGGILNOT	gold-beating
ABDEGGINORR	ragged-Robin
ABDEGGINRWY	windbaggery
ABDEGHHILTT	high-battled
ABDEGHHOORU	headborough
ABDEGHLOOPS	bog-asphodel
ABDEGIILNNT	dining-table
ABDEGIILSSU	disguisable
ABDEGIINPRT	paint-bridge
ABDEGIKNOOR	reading-book
ABDEGILLNRV	gravel-blind
ABDEGINNPSW	spawning-bed
ABDEGLMOOTT	bottom-glade
ABDEGNOORUV	above-ground
ABDEHHMOORR	rhombohedra
ABDEHIINNTU	uninhabited
ABDEHIKLNSU	husbandlike
ABDEHILNOSU	unabolished
ABDEHILSTUY	bushy-tailed
ABDEHKMMRTU	thumb-marked
ABDEHLLMOOR	hall-bedroom
ABDEHLNSSSU	husbandless
ABDEHLOORST	heart's-blood
ABDEHLOORSV	shovelboard
ABDEHLOPRSU	double-sharp
ABDEHMOORRT	motherboard
ABDEHNORRUU	unharboured
ABDEHNORTTU	Tudorbethan
ABDEHNOSSTU	basset-hound
ABDEHORRSUU	harbour-dues
ABDEIIILNTY	deniability
ABDEIILLLST	distillable
ABDEIILLTWY	weldability
ABDEIILMNOT	indomitable
ABDEIIMNOST	demi-bastion
ABDEIINRTTU	inturbidate
ABDEIKLNNRU	undrinkable
ABDEILLLSSY	dissyllable
ABDEILLOSSV	dissolvable
ABDEILMNOPU	impoundable
ABDEILMOTTU	tolbutamide
ABDEILMSSSY	disassembly
ABDEILNPSSY	dispensably
ABDEILNRSUY	undesirably
ABDEILNSSUY	unbiassedly
ABDEILOPRSV	disprovable
ABDEINNORWW	window-barne
ABDEINORSTU	subordinate
ABDEKMNOORY	monkey-board
ABDELLLNSUY	unsyllabled
ABDELLMNRSU	slumberland
ABDELLNOORS	ob-and-soller
ABDELMOORST	bloodstream
ABDELNNOSUU	unsoundable
ABDELNNOUUW	unwoundable
ABDELNNRUUY	unendurably
ABDELOORRUV	louver-board
	louvre-board
ABDELOOSTWY	bloody-sweat
ABDELOPRRTU	protrudable
ABDEMNOORWW	meadow-brown
ABDENNORSTV	bondservant
ABDENOPRSUU	superabound
ABDFGHIILNN	half-binding
ABDFIILLSYY	disyllabify
ABDFIILNNUU	infundibula
ABDFILMOORR	dolabriform
ABDFLLOOORW	follow-board
ABDFNOORUUX	fauxbourdon
ABDGGHIKNOO	badging-hook
ABDGHIIINRT	riding-habit

ABDGHINNOSW	bond-washing
ABDGHINPSSU	spud-bashing
ABDGIILLLNU	all-building
ABDGIINNOPR	pair-bonding
ABDGILLOOOY	diabolology
ABDGILLORSW	gallows-bird
ABDGILMORRU	bur-marigold
ABDGILNOPTT	blotting-pad
ABDGINOPRRS	springboard
ABDGINORRST	stringboard
ABDGMOORRSS	smörgåsbord
ABDHHIOOPRY	hydrophobia
ABDHIMNNOPS	bondmanship
ABDHIMOOOPR	dromophobia
ABDIIILRTVY	drivability
ABDIILLMSSY	disyllabism
ABDIILMNOTY	indomitably
ABDIILNOTUZ	Butazolidin®
ABDIINOORSY	obsidionary
ABDIINOOSTY	isoantibody
ABDIINOSTUU	subaudition
ABDILLORRRW	drill-barrow
ABDILNOOPSV	blood-spavin
ABDIMNNOSTU	subdominant
ABDIMNOORTT	motor-bandit
ABDINORRSUY	subordinary
ABDLMOORRSU	dorsolumbar
ABDLNOOOSTT	odontoblast
ABDMOORRUZZ	moorbuzzard
ABDNRRRSTUU	surturbrand
ABEEEEFLORS	foreseeable
ABEEEEGLNRR	regenerable
ABEEEEIKLMV	make-believe
ABEEEEMNRTV	bereavement
ABEEEERRRTV	reverberate
ABEEEFLLLRU	refuellable
ABEEEFLMNRT	fermentable
ABEEEFLPRRR	preferrable
ABEEEGGILLN	negligeable
ABEEEGIRRTV	verbigerate
ABEEEGLORSW	elbow-grease
ABEEEGLRRTT	regrettable
ABEEEHHINPR	hebephrenia
ABEEEHHLLRT	bell-heather
ABEEEHORRTV	over-breathe
ABEEEHQRRSU	queer-basher
ABEEEIILNPS	plebeianise
ABEEEIILNPZ	plebeianize
ABEEEILLPRV	repleviable
ABEEEILMMPR	impermeable
ABEEEILMMST	emblematise
ABEEEILMMTZ	emblematize
ABEEEILNRSV	inseverable
ABEEEILRRTV	retrievable
ABEEEIMNSST	absenteeism
ABEEEJMMNNT	enjambement
ABEEELMNNTT	entablement
ABEEELMNRRU	remunerable
ABEEELNNRUV	unvenerable
ABEEELNNSST	tenableness
ABEEELNPRST	presentable
ABEEELNPRTV	preventable
ABEEELNQSSU	equableness
ABEEELPPRRT	perpetrable
ABEEELPPRTU	perpetuable
ABEEELPRRSV	preservable
ABEEEMOPRTT	obtemperate
ABEEENRRRTV	reverberant
ABEEEPRRRSU	purse-bearer
ABEEFFHLRTU	buff-leather
ABEEFFILORT	forfeitable
ABEEFGILNRR	refrangible
ABEEFGLORTT	forgettable
ABEEFIILLQU	liquefiable
ABEEFILNRSS	friableness
ABEEFILPRTU	putrefiable
ABEEFILRRTU	irrefutable
ABEEFLLNSSU	balefulness
ABEEFLMOPRR	performable
ABEEFLNNSSU	banefulness
ABEEFNRRRTU	afterburner
ABEEGIIJNTW	wag-'n-bietjie
ABEEGIILNRT	libertinage
ABEEGIILRRS	bersaglieri
ABEEGIINOSS	abiogenesis
ABEEGILMNPR	impregnable
ABEEGILNRUZ	gaberlunzie
ABEEGILOTTT	tattie-bogle
ABEEGILRRST	registrable
ABEEGINORRV	overbearing
ABEEGLRRTTY	regrettably
ABEEGNORSST	barge-stones
ABEEHHPRSTY	bathysphere
ABEEHIILNRT	inheritable
ABEEHIKPRRS	ship-breaker
ABEEHILLSTW	whistleable
ABEEHILPRSS	perishables
ABEEHILRSST	establisher
	re-establish
ABEEHILSTUX	exhaustible
ABEEHIMOOPT	emetophobia
ABEEHINPRSS	spine-basher
ABEEHINRSSS	bearishness
ABEEHINRSST	breathiness
ABEEHIRRTTT	bitter-earth
ABEEHKNORRT	heartbroken
ABEEHKOPRRS	shopbreaker
ABEEHLORRSU	barrel-house
ABEEHLORRWW	wheelbarrow
ABEEHLOSSTU	bastel-house
	bastle-house
ABEEHNOPRRY	hyperborean
ABEEHORRSTT	rother-beast
ABEEHORSTTU	thereabouts
ABEEHORSTUW	whereabouts
ABEEIILMNPS	plebeianism
ABEEIILMNST	inestimable
ABEEIILMPRV	imperviable
ABEEIILNQTU	inequitable
ABEEIILQRTU	equilibrate
ABEEIKLLRSV	Baskerville
ABEEIKLMORR	boiler-maker
ABEEILLMOPT	tempolabile
ABEEILLNORT	intolerable

ABEEILLNPSS	pliableness
ABEEILLNRSS	liberalness
ABEEILLOPTX	exploitable
ABEEILLOTTT	toilet-table
ABEEILMMOSV	immoveables
ABEEILMMPRY	impermeably
ABEEILMMSTT	emblematist
ABEEILMNNOT	mentionable
ABEEILMNNRU	innumerable
ABEEILMNOOT	emotionable
ABEEILMNRTU	unmeritable
ABEEILMORRV	irremovable
ABEEILNNOPS	pensionable
ABEEILNPRSU	insuperable
ABEEILNQTUU	unequitable
ABEEILNRTTU	inutterable
ABEEILNRTUV	unavertible
ABEEILNSSST	beastliness
ABEEILPPRRS	perspirable
ABEEILPPRTT	bitter-apple
ABEEILPRSSU	persuasible
ABEEILPRTUV	vituperable
ABEEILRRTVY	retrievably
ABEEIMNNOTU	aminobutene
ABEEIMNRRTT	arbitrement
ABEEINNQRTU	barquentine
ABEEINORRTT	terebration
ABEEINORRTV	verberation
ABEEINPRRST	Epstein-Barr
ABEEINSSSUV	abusiveness
ABEEIOPRRTV	reprobative
ABEEIORSTVV	observative
ABEEIQRRSUU	arquebusier
ABEEIRRTTTU	reattribute
ABEEJLNNOUY	unenjoyable
ABEEKLNORTV	overblanket
ABEEKRRRSTY	tarry-breeks
ABEELLLMSSY	blamelessly
ABEELLLMTUY	umbellately
ABEELLRRTVY	vertebrally
ABEELMMNORU	unmemorable
ABEELMNORUV	unremovable
ABEELMNOSSV	movableness
ABEELMNSSTU	mutableness
ABEELNNOSST	notableness
ABEELNNSSTU	tunableness
ABEELNPRSTY	presentably
ABEELNRTTUU	unutterable
ABEELNRTUXY	exuberantly
ABEELOPRRRU	beer-parlour
ABEELOPSSSS	possessable
ABEELORUVYY	by-your-leave
ABEELOSTUUY	beauteously
ABEELPPRRTU	prepubertal
ABEELPRRSTY	presbyteral
ABEELPRTTTU	butter-plate
ABEEMMNORSU	membraneous
ABEEMNORSTT	storm-beaten
ABEEMNRSSTU	surbasement
ABEEMORRSTT	strabometer
ABEEOPRRTTU	protuberate
ABEEPPRRTTU	butter-paper
ABEFFIILORT	fortifiable
ABEFFLNSTUU	subaffluent
ABEFGIIILNS	signifiable
ABEFGIILNNR	infrangible
ABEFGILNOSW	safe-blowing
ABEFGILNSST	self-basting
ABEFHHLORRT	half-brother
ABEFHLNSSSU	bashfulness
ABEFIIILRTV	vitrifiable
ABEFIIILSTY	feasibility
ABEFIIJLSTU	justifiable
ABEFIILLOOT	bifoliolate
ABEFIILNOSS	fissionable
ABEFILLMRRU	umbrella-fir
ABEFILLNOOR	fire-balloon
ABEFILLNRTU	unfiltrable
ABEFILLTUUY	beautifully
ABEFILNTUUU	unbeautiful
ABEFILRRTUY	irrefutably
ABEFIMORSST	asbestiform
ABEFIRRTTUY	fairy-butter
ABEFLMOORTT	foot-lambert
ABEFLNNRSSU	branfulness
ABEGGIILNOR	Globerigina
	globigerina
ABEGGMNORRU	Munro-bagger
ABEGHILLPPT	apple-blight
ABEGHILMNOO	haemoglobin
ABEGHILNSUW	washing-blue
ABEGHINNRTU	unbreathing
ABEGHINOOPR	negrophobia
ABEGHINRRSU	rush-bearing
ABEGHINRRTU	Antiburgher
ABEGIIILMMT	immitigable
ABEGIIKLNNT	inking-table
ABEGIILMNTU	unmitigable
ABEGIIMNSSU	subimagines
ABEGIIRRSTU	subirrigate
ABEGIJMNNPU	jumping-bean
ABEGIJORTUV	objurgative
ABEGIKMNORW	working-beam
ABEGILLNPSS	passing-bell
ABEGILLOOPY	palebiology
ABEGILMNOSW	womb-leasing
ABEGILMNPRY	impregnably
ABEGILNNNTY	benignantly
ABEGILNNRTY	banteringly
ABEGILNOORW	wool-bearing
ABEGILNORSU	subregional
ABEGILNOSUU	albugineous
ABEGILOOORY	aerobiology
ABEGINNNNTU	unbenignant
ABEGINNORTU	gubernation
ABEGLLNOOPR	prolongable
ABEGLLORSSW	glass-blower
ABEGLLOSSTT	bottle-glass
ABEGLNSTUUU	subungulate
ABEGLOOOPTT	potato-bogle
ABEGMORRSTU	burgomaster
ABEHHHRRSTU	hearth-brush
ABEHHIIOOPR	hierophobia
ABEHIIILLPS	baillieship

ABEHIILMNST	habiliments
ABEHIILMOPT	amphibolite
ABEHIILPRST	blepharitis
ABEHIIMMNOS	△bohemianism
ABEHIIMORSV	behaviorism
ABEHIINNORT	hibernation
ABEHIINRSST	inhabitress
ABEHIIORSTV	behaviorist
ABEHIKLNNTU	unthinkable
ABEHILMNOST	abolishment
ABEHILNORSU	nourishable
ABEHILOOPRU	ailurophobe
ABEHILOPRSW	worshipable
ABEHINOORTT	botheration
ABEHIOOOPRT	erotophobia
ABEHLMNOSUW	bushelwoman
ABEHLMOORTW	Bartholomew
ABEHLMOPSSU	blasphemous
ABEHLMORTWY	blameworthy
ABEHLNNNSUU	unshunnable
ABEHLNORRTY	abhorrently
ABEHLORRSSU	harbourless
ABEHMNRSTUU	subterhuman
ABEHMOOTTVY	bottom-heavy
ABEHNNOOTTY	ethnobotany
ABEHNORSTTY	east-by-north
ABEHOOORRTT	orthoborate
ABEHOORRRVW	hover-barrow
ABEHOSSTTUY	east-by-south
ABEIIIILLST	liabilities
ABEIIILLLMT	illimitable
ABEIIILLNOR	billionaire
ABEIIILLRTY	reliability
ABEIIILLTVY	liveability
ABEIIILNNTZ	Leibnitzian
ABEIIINNORT	inebriation
ABEIILLLLRY	illiberally
ABEIILLLMNU	illuminable
ABEIILLMMST	bimetallism
ABEIILLMNRY	bimillenary
ABEIILLMPSU	implausible
ABEIILLMSTT	bimetallist
ABEIILLRSTT	bristle-tail
ABEIILMNNNO	innominable
ABEIILMNSTY	inestimably
ABEIILMOTVY	moveability
ABEIILNNSTV	vinblastine
ABEIILNOPRT	prelibation
ABEIILNQTUY	inequitably
ABEIILNRRTT	intertribal
ABEIILNRTTY	rentability
ABEIILNSTUV	unvisitable
ABEIILOPPRT	propitiable
ABEIILORTXY	exorability
ABEIILRSSST	stabilisers
ABEIILRSSTZ	stabilizers
ABEIILRSTVY	versability
ABEIILSTUXY	bisexuality
ABEIIMNORSV	ambiversion
ABEIINRRSST	bar-sinister
ABEIIRTTTUV	attributive
ABEIKLLLSTT	skittle-ball
ABEIKLLNOOT	kite-balloon
ABEIKNNRRSU	brankursine
ABEILLLRSTY	trisyllable
ABEILLMOTTU	multilobate
ABEILLNNOOV	balloon-vine
ABEILLNORTY	intolerably
ABEILLNPSUU	unplausible
ABEILLNRSSY	brainlessly
ABEILMNNRUY	innumerably
ABEILMNRSTU	subterminal
ABEILMORRVY	irremovably
ABEILMOSSTW	misbestowal
ABEILMRSTUU	semi-tubular
ABEILNNOSSU	non-issuable
ABEILNNPRTU	unprintable
ABEILNNSTTY	abstinently
ABEILNOOSSS	obsessional
ABEILNORSSU	Belorussian
ABEILNOSTTY	obstinately
ABEILNPRSUY	insuperably
ABEILOORRTT	obliterator
ABEILOPRTUU	Politbureau
ABEILORSSTW	belowstairs
ABEILQRSTUU	square-built
ABEILRRSTTT	brittle-star
ABEIMNNSSSU	businessman
ABEIMNORRRY	marionberry
ABEIMNORSTW	tribeswoman
ABEINNNOQTU	tonquin-bean
ABEINNNRSTU	burnt-sienna
ABEINNORSTV	inobservant
ABEINOOPRRT	probationer
	reprobation
ABEINOORSTV	observation
ABEINOOSTTT	obtestation
ABEINOSSTTU	abstentious
ABEINOSSTUU	subitaneous
ABEINSSTTUV	substantive
ABEIRSSTTUV	substrative
ABEJMORRTTU	turbo-ram-jet
ABEKORSTTTU	trout-basket
ABELMNORRSY	salmonberry
ABELNOPPSTU	unstoppable
ABELNOPRTTU	pearl-button
ABELNORSTVY	observantly
ABELNRTTUUY	unutterably
ABELOPPRSTU	supportable
ABELOPRTTTY	bottle-party
ABELRRSTTUU	surrebuttal
ABEMNOORRSW	marrow-bones
ABEMNORRRST	barnstormer
ABEMNORTTUW	butter-woman
ABENNORSTUV	unobservant
ABENNOSSTUY	buoyantness
ABENOPRRTTU	protuberant
ABEOOPRRRTY	reprobatory
ABEOORRSTVY	observatory
ABEOPRRRTTU	perturbator
ABERRSSTUUY	subtreasury
ABFFILLMSTU	bull-mastiff
ABFGHINRSTU	surf-bathing
ABFGIILNNRY	infrangibly

ABFGILLNOOT	footballing
ABFIIILLLMS	fallibilism
ABFIIILLLST	fallibilist
ABFIIILLLTY	fallibility
ABFIIIMNORT	fimbriation
ABFIIJLSTUY	justifiably
ABFIILORSUY	bifariously
ABFILLOOSTT	footballist
ABFILMNSTUU	funambulist
ABGGGHIKNOO	bagging-hook
ABGGGINNOOT	tobogganing
ABGGGINNSTU	gangbusting
ABGGILOOORY	agrobiology
ABGGILOORST	garbologist
ABGGINOOSTT	tobogganist
ABGHHOORRTU	tharborough
ABGHIINRSTT	brattishing
ABGHIINSTTU	bathing-suit
ABGHIKLLNOO	booking-hall
ABGHIKLNSUW	bushwalking
ABGHILLNOOY	ballyhooing
ABGHILMOOPY	amphibology
ABGHNOOPRSY	snobography
ABGIIILMMTY	immitigably
ABGIIILNTTY	tangibility
ABGIILLLNUY	bilingually
ABGIILMNTUY	unmitigably
ABGIILNRTUV	rib-vaulting
ABGIINNOOST	obsignation
ABGIINORRST	rib-roasting
ABGIJNOORTU	objurgation
ABGIJNOSTUU	subjugation
ABGIKNNOPRW	pawnbroking
ABGIKNNSTTU	tankbusting
ABGIKNRRSTY	stringy-bark
ABGILLORTUY	globularity
ABGILMNOOST	gonimoblast
ABGILMNOSUU	lumbaginous
ABGILMOSUUY	ambiguously
ABGILNNORUU	unlabouring
ABGILORRSUU	burglarious
ABGIMNOSUUU	unambiguous
ABGINOORSTU	subrogation
ABGINOORSTY	obsignatory
ABGJOORRTUY	objurgatory
ABGLLOOPRYY	pyroballogy
ABGMOORSSTT	bottom-grass
ABHHIMNPSSU	bushmanship
ABHHINOOOPP	phonophobia
ABHHIOOOPPT	photophobia
ABHHIOOPPSY	hypsophobia
ABHIIIOOPST	sitiophobia
ABHILMOOPSU	amphibolous
ABHIOOPRSSU	Russophobia
ABHLOOPRSTT	trophoblast
ABIIIILMTTY	imitability
ABIIIILNTVY	inviability
ABIIILLLMTY	illimitably
ABIIILLOSTY	isolability
ABIIILNNTWY	winnability
ABIIILNOSTU	antibilious
ABIIILNRTTU	tribunitial
ABIIILNSTTY	instability
ABIIILPRTTY	partibility
ABIIILPSSTY	passibility
ABIIILRTTVY	vibratility
ABIIILSTTUY	suitability
ABIIINNRTTU	tribunitian
ABIIINOPRTT	bipartition
ABIIKLORTWY	workability
ABIILLLNRTY	brilliantly
ABIILLMPSUY	implausibly
ABIILLOSTVY	solvability
ABIILMNOSTU	sublimation
ABIILMOSTUY	ambitiously
ABIILNOOQTU	obliquation
ABIILNORTTU	tribulation
ABIILNRSTUY	insalubrity
ABIILOPRTTY	portability
ABIILOQTTUY	quotability
ABIILRRTTUY	tributarily
ABIIMNNOORT	bromination
ABIIMNNSTYZ	Byzantinism
ABIIMNOOPRT	improbation
ABIIMNORSTT	nimbostrati
ABIIMNOSTUU	unambitious
ABIINNSTTYZ	Byzantinist
ABIINOOPSTT	obstipation
ABIINOORSTT	abortionist
ABIINORTTTU	attribution
ABIIORSSTTU	tibiotarsus
ABILLNPSUUY	unplausibly
ABILLOORSUY	laboriously
ABILLOPRRSW	sparrow-bill
ABILLORSTTU	sublittoral
ABILMOORTUU	taurobolium
ABILMORSTUU	umbratilous
ABILNOORSUU	unlaborious
ABILNOSTUUX	subluxation
ABINNOORSTU	subornation
ABLNOPPSTUY	unstoppably
ABLOPPRSTUY	supportably
ABMOORSSTTY	smarty-boots
ACCCCEEENRS	accrescence
ACCCCILMOOR	micrococcal
ACCCCILMORY	macrocyclic
ACCCDEEENNS	candescence
ACCCDEHILNO	chalcedonic
ACCCDEILOPY	cyclopaedic
ACCCDENNOOR	concordance
ACCCDENNOTU	conductance
ACCCEEELNOS	coalescence
ACCCEEELNST	lactescence
ACCCEEFNORT	café-concert
ACCCEEHILRS	ecclesiarch
ACCCEEHISTT	catechetics
ACCCEEHMNOR	chance-comer
ACCCEEHOSUU	accoucheuse
ACCCEEILNRT	eccentrical
ACCCEELMNOP	complacence
ACCCEELNOPT	conceptacle
ACCCEHIISTT	catechistic
ACCCEHIMOTT	chemotactic

ACCCEHNORTY	cony-catcher
	technocracy
ACCCEIILMRT	climacteric
ACCCEILNPTY	pentacyclic
ACCCEILORTU	leucocratic
ACCCEILRTTY	tetracyclic
ACCCEINORRT	acrocentric
ACCCEKNORRR	corn-cracker
ACCCELMNOPY	complacency
ACCCENNNORY	concernancy
ACCCHHIINNO	Cochin-China
ACCCHIILLOT	laccolithic
ACCCHILOORT	ochlocratic
ACCCHOOPRTY	ptochocracy
ACCCHORRSYY	chrysocracy
ACCCIILLTYY	cyclicality
ACCCIIOOPRS	capriccioso
ACCCILLOOSU	calcicolous
ACCCIMMOORS	macrocosmic
ACCCIMOOPRS	macroscopic
ACCCIMOORST	cosmocratic
ACCCINOPPSU	cappuccinos
ACCCLOOOPRT	protococcal
ACCCNOOSTTU	cost-account
ACCDDEINORS	discordance
ACCDDIIIMST	didacticism
ACCDDINORSY	discordancy
ACCDEEEENNT	antecedence
ACCDEEEKNNR	crane-necked
ACCDEEELNOS	adolescence
ACCDEEENRST	crescentade
ACCDEEFHHKL	half-checked
ACCDEEFHLNT	fetch-candle
ACCDEEFNORY	△confederacy
ACCDEEFOPPR	copper-faced
ACCDEEHHKLU	chuckle-head
ACCDEEHIORS	archdiocese
ACCDEEIISTV	desiccative
ACCDEEILNPR	pencil-cedar
ACCDEEIMNOR	decameronic
ACCDEEINPRS	discrepance
ACCDEEIORTT	decorticate
ACCDEELNNOU	unconcealed
ACCDEEMNSUU	succedaneum
ACCDEENNORT	contredance
ACCDEFHITTY	chitty-faced
ACCDEFILNSS	flaccidness
ACCDEFNOSTU	safe-conduct
ACCDEHHRSSU	archduchess
ACCDEHILPRY	diphycercal
ACCDEHIMPRY	pachydermic
ACCDEHINORW	choice-drawn
ACCDEHLMORW	clam-chowder
ACCDEHLNOXY	chalcedonyx
ACCDEHNRSTU	unscratched
ACCDEIILLTY	deictically
ACCDEIINOST	desiccation
ACCDEIKLNST	candlestick
ACCDEILLOPS	peccadillos
ACCDEILMOPT	complicated
ACCDEINOOST	consociated
ACCDEINOOTU	coeducation
ACCDEINPRSY	discrepancy
ACCDEIPRRTU	picture-card
ACCDELMOPTY	compactedly
ACCDELNOSSS	second-class
ACCDEMNOORY	demonocracy
ACCDEMNOPTU	uncompacted
ACCDGILNORY	accordingly
ACCDGILNOST	cold-casting
ACCDGINORRS	scoring-card
ACCDHHLRTUU	Durchlaucht
ACCDHHNSSUU	such-and-such
ACCDHHRRSUW	churchwards
ACCDHIIMORT	dichromatic
ACCDHINORYY	hydrocyanic
ACCDHIORTTY	hydrotactic
ACCDIIINNOS	scincoidian
ACCDIIKKNPP	pick-and-pick
ACCDIILLLOU	loculicidal
ACCDIILLNRY	cylindrical
ACCDIILLORY	codicillary
ACCDIILMNNY	clindamycin
ACCDIILNOOR	crocodilian
ACCDIIOSSTU	diacoustics
ACCDIMOSSTU	disaccustom
ACCDLNRSUUU	△dracunculus
ACCEEEEHMRS	cream-cheese
ACCEEEENNSV	evanescence
ACCEEEFILMN	maleficence
ACCEEEFLNRT	reflectance
ACCEEEHHKOS	cheechakoes
ACCEEEHILRT	chelicerate
ACCEEEHLLOP	cephalocele
ACCEEEIKKLO	cockaleekie
	cock-a-leekie
ACCEEELLNPS	pallescence
ACCEEELNOPS	opalescence
ACCEEELNRST	recalescent
ACCEEFHPRST	speechcraft
ACCEEFIIPST	specificate
ACCEEFIIRTT	certificate
ACCEEFIKRRR	firecracker
ACCEEFINORV	vociferance
ACCEEFNRRST	screencraft
ACCEEGHIKMN	game-chicken
ACCEEGHILMO	geochemical
ACCEEGHINTY	eye-catching
ACCEEGLNSTU	glaucescent
ACCEEHHIIRS	Escherichia
ACCEEHHIRRT	arch-heretic
ACCEEHHKRSW	screech-hawk
ACCEEHHNTTT	catch-the-ten
ACCEEHILMNO	chameleonic
ACCEEHILNRT	chanticleer
ACCEEHILRST	telearchics
ACCEEHIPRRT	Pherecratic
ACCEEHIRRTU	charcuterie
ACCEEHIRSTV	cesarevitch
ACCEEHIRSTW	cesarewitch
ACCEEHKLNNT	lance-knecht
ACCEEHKORTW	weathercock
ACCEEHLLNRY	chancellery
ACCEEHLMORT	molecatcher

ACCEEHLNOXY	cyclohexane
ACCEEHMNNOY	coenenchyma
ACCEEHMNRSY	sarcenchyme
ACCEEHMORSU	escarmouche
ACCEEIILNRT	electrician
ACCEEIISTVX	exsiccative
ACCEEIKKLOP	peacock-like
ACCEEIKKLPR	place-kicker
ACCEEILLLRT	all-electric
ACCEEILMNOU	oecumenical
ACCEEILNNST	incalescent
ACCEEILNRUX	Clarencieux
ACCEEILRRTU	recirculate
ACCEEIMNOPS	CinemaScope®
ACCEEIMNRSU	miscreaunce
ACCEEIMNRTT	metacentric
ACCEEINPRTT	net-practice
ACCEEINQSTU	acquiescent
ACCEEIOPRRT	reciprocate
ACCEEIORSSS	accessorise
ACCEEIORSSZ	accessorize
ACCEEIORTTX	excorticate
ACCEELLOPRT	leptocercal
ACCEELMNNOT	concealment
ACCEEMNNORR	necromancer
ACCEEMNOPPU	comeuppance
ACCEEMOSSTY	Ascomycetes
ACCEENNNOSV	convenances
ACCEENNNOTU	countenance
ACCEENNORSV	conversance
ACCEENNORTT	concentrate
	concertante
ACCEENNORVY	conveyancer
ACCEENOPRRY	coparcenery
ACCEENOPRTU	counterpace
ACCEENORRRT	catercorner
ACCEENPSSTU	susceptance
ACCEEOPPRTU	preoccupate
ACCEEOPRSUY	cyperaceous
ACCEFFHRTTU	chaff-cutter
ACCEFFIIOSU	efficacious
ACCEFHIINTY	chieftaincy
ACCEFHIKOPS	peacock-fish
ACCEFILORSU	calciferous
ACCEFINORRT	Afrocentric
	Afro-centric
ACCEGHIINST	catechising
ACCEGHIINTZ	catechizing
ACCEGHIKNQU	quick-change
ACCEGHILMRU	chemurgical
ACCEGHIOPRR	cerographic
ACCEGHLLRTU	gull-catcher
ACCEGHOPRRS	crescograph
ACCEGIKMRRY	gimcrackery
ACCEGILLOPY	cycloplegia
ACCEGILOOTU	autecologic
ACCEGINORTU	accoutering
ACCEGKLNOPS	spang-cockle
ACCEHHISSTY	Hesychastic
ACCEHHRSTUV	stave-church
ACCEHIILLRT	Callitriche
ACCEHIILNST	calisthenic
ACCEHIILOPT	ophicalcite
ACCEHIILOST	△catholicise
ACCEHIILOTZ	△catholicize
ACCEHIIMNST	mechanistic
ACCEHIIORRT	hierocratic
ACCEHIIRSTU	Eucharistic
ACCEHILLMNO	melancholic
ACCEHILLNTY	technically
ACCEHILMOOZ	zoochemical
ACCEHILMOPR	microcephal
ACCEHILNNTU	untechnical
ACCEHILNOOT	Neo-Catholic
ACCEHILOOPZ	zoocephalic
ACCEHILOORT	chocolatier
ACCEHILOPPR	procephalic
ACCEHILPRTY	phylacteric
ACCEHIMNNOR	chrominance
ACCEHIMNORT	mechatronic
ACCEHIMNORY	cheiromancy
ACCEHIMORTT	tachometric
ACCEHIMPSTY	metapsychic
ACCEHIMRTTY	McCarthyite
	tachymetric
ACCEHKLNOST	schecklaton
ACCEHKOPPTT	patch-pocket
ACCEHLLMNOY	collenchyma
ACCEHLLNORY	chancellory
ACCEHLRSSST	scratchless
ACCEHMNOORS	comancheros
ACCEIIILMST	metasilicic
ACCEIIINPRT	accipitrine
ACCEIILLMRS	clericalism
ACCEIILLNPR	preclinical
ACCEIILLRST	clericalist
ACCEIILNORR	cornice-rail
ACCEIILNSTV	clavecinist
ACCEIILNTUV	inculcative
ACCEIILPRRT	precritical
ACCEIILRRSU	circularise
ACCEIILRRUZ	circularize
ACCEIILRTUV	circulative
ACCEIIMNOST	cosmetician
	encomiastic
ACCEIINNOSU	insouciance
ACCEIINOSTX	exsiccation
ACCEIIPRTVY	pervicacity
ACCEIIPTTVY	acceptivity
ACCEIIRRSTT	criticaster
ACCEIKKNNRY	nick-nackery
ACCEIKKOTTT	tick-tack-toe
ACCEIKLORTU	leukocratic
ACCEIKNRSSS	car-sickness
ACCEILLNRTY	centrically
ACCEILLPSTY	sceptically
ACCEILMNOSS	comicalness
ACCEILMOPST	ectoplasmic
ACCEILMSSTU	multi-access
ACCEILNNOTY	anticyclone
ACCEILNNSSY	cynicalness
ACCEILNOPRT	narcoleptic
ACCEILNORTT	contractile
ACCEILNORTU	corniculate

Words marked △ may be spelled also with a capital letter

ACCEILNSTTY	syntectical
ACCEILOPRST	ceroplastic
ACCEILOPSTT	ectoplastic
ACCEILOPTTU	octuplicate
ACCEILORSSY	accessorily
ACCEIMMNOTU	communicate
ACCEIMNNORT	necromantic
ACCEIMNORTY	craniectomy
ACCEIMNOSTY	Actinomyces
ACCEIMORRTY	meritocracy
ACCEINNNOTU	continuance
ACCEINNOORS	cancioneros
ACCEINNORSU	coinsurance
ACCEINNORTV	contrivance
ACCEINOPRRT	reciprocant
ACCEINOPSUU	punicaceous
ACCEINORSTU	cater-cousin
ACCEINORTTV	contractive
ACCEINSSSTU	causticness
ACCEIOORSSU	scoriaceous
ACCEIORSTUU	urticaceous
ACCEJLNORTU	conjectural
ACCEKLMORST	master-clock
ACCEKLOPRTY	kleptocracy
ACCEKORRTTU	racket-court
ACCELLORSUY	sclerocauly
ACCELMMNOOP	commonplace
ACCELNOOORT	concolorate
ACCELPRRSUU	crepuscular
ACCEMNOPSST	compactness
ACCENNORSVY	conservancy
	conversancy
ACCENOOPRTU	pococurante
ACCENOORRST	consecrator
ACCENOPPRTU	preoccupant
ACCENOPRRTT	precontract
ACCENORRTTU	contracture
ACCENPRTUUU	acupuncture
ACCEORSSTUU	crustaceous
ACCFGILOSUU	calcifugous
ACCFHIRSTTT	stitchcraft
ACCFHLOORST	schoolcraft
ACCFIILOPRY	prolificacy
ACCFIIMOORR	coraciiform
ACCFILMORSU	sacculiform
ACCFINOORST	confiscator
ACCFLNORTUY	calf-country
ACCGHIIIOPS	pichiciagos
ACCGHIILRRU	chirurgical
ACCGHIIOOPS	hagioscopic
ACCGHIOOPPR	coprophagic
ACCGIILNOTU	glauconitic
ACCGIILNRTU	circulating
ACCGIINNNOT	canting-coin
ACCGIINNOTY	incogitancy
ACCGILLMOOY	mycological
ACCGILLOOTY	cytological
ACCGILNOORY	carcinology
ACCGIMOPRTY	cryptogamic
ACCGINORSTU	coruscating
ACCHHIINSTT	chainstitch
ACCHHMNORUW	churchwoman
ACCHIIIMMPT	amphimictic
ACCHIIIRSTT	citharistic
ACCHIILMOST	△catholicism
ACCHIILOPRT	cartophilic
ACCHIILOSST	scholiastic
ACCHIILOTTY	catholicity
ACCHIIMNORT	chiromantic
ACCHIIMOSST	masochistic
ACCHIINPSYY	physiciancy
ACCHIIOOPST	sociopathic
ACCHIIOPPRT	Hippocratic
ACCHIIOPRRZ	rhizocarpic
ACCHIIPRSTY	psychiatric
ACCHILLNORY	chronically
ACCHILLPSYY	psychically
ACCHILMOTYY	cyclothymia
ACCHILOOSTU	holocaustic
ACCHIMMRSTY	McCarthyism
ACCHIMNORTY	crithomancy
ACCHINNOPYY	phycocyanin
ACCHINOOSTT	octastichon
ACCHINOPSTY	sycophantic
ACCHIOOPRRT	prothoracic
ACCHIOOPTTT	phototactic
ACCHIOORRSU	chiaroscuro
ACCHIOPRSYY	physiocracy
ACCHKNOORST	anchor-stock
ACCHKORRSTW	scratch-work
ACCHLLOORSY	chrysocolla
ACCHMNNOOYY	onychomancy
ACCHMNOOSTW	Scotchwoman
ACCHNOOOPSU	cacophonous
ACCIIIKKNPW	Pickwickian
ACCIIILMNRT	matriclinic
ACCIIILNPRT	patriclinic
ACCIIILNSTV	Calvinistic
ACCIIILOSST	socialistic
ACCIIILRSTU	curialistic
ACCIIILRTTY	criticality
ACCIILLLNOX	cloxacillin
ACCIILLNNNO	non-clinical
ACCIILLOPTY	occipitally
ACCIILMNORT	matroclinic
ACCIILNNOTU	inculcation
ACCIILNNQUU	quincuncial
ACCIILNOORT	conciliator
ACCIILNOPRT	patroclinic
ACCIILNORTU	circulation
ACCIILNOTVY	volcanicity
ACCIILNTUVY	vulcanicity
ACCIILOSTUV	acclivitous
ACCIILRRTUY	circularity
ACCIINNSTTY	nyctinastic
ACCIINORRSU	Rosicrucian
ACCIJNNOTUV	conjunctiva
ACCIKKKKNNY	knick-knacky
ACCIKKOOTTT	tick-tack-too
ACCIKNPRSTU	panic-struck
ACCILLNOOOT	collocation
ACCILLOOSUU	caulicolous
ACCILLPRTYY	cryptically
ACCILMNRRUU	circumlunar

Words marked △ may be spelled also with a capital letter

ACCILMOPRRU	circumpolar
ACCILMOPSTY	cytoplasmic
ACCILMORRSU	circumsolar
ACCILNOOTTU	occultation
ACCILNORTUY	inculcatory
ACCILOOPSTV	post-vocalic
ACCILOPRSTY	pyroclastic
ACCILOPRTTU	plutocratic
ACCILORRTUY	circulatory
ACCIMMNNOTU	communicant
ACCIMNNOOTT	concomitant
ACCIMNOTTUY	contumacity
ACCINNNOSTY	inconstancy
ACCINNOOOTV	convocation
ACCINNOOPRU	cornucopian
ACCINNOORTT	contraction
ACCINOOPPST	pantoscopic
ACCINOOPRSY	cranioscopy
ACCINOORRRW	carrion-crow
ACCINOORSTU	coruscation
ACCINOSTTUU	cunctatious
ACCIOOPRRTY	procaryotic
ACCIORSSSTY	sarcocystis
ACCKOOPRRSW	cock-sparrow
ACCLMNOOPTU	coconut-palm
ACCLNNOSTUY	consultancy
ACCLNOOORTU	octonocular
ACCLNORSUUU	caruncúlous
ACCLOPRRSUU	corpuscular
ACDDEEEEPRS	predeceased
ACDDEEFFIST	disaffected
ACDDEEGIKLR	griddle-cake
ACDDEEHHIKT	thick-headed
ACDDEEHHKOS	shock-headed
ACDDEEHIPPW	widechapped
ACDDEEHLNOS	close-handed
ACDDEEHLORT	cold-hearted
ACDDEEHLOST	dead-clothes
ACDDEEHLRUY	curly-headed
ACDDEEIINTU	indeciduate
ACDDEEILPTU	pediculated
ACDDEEIMSSU	Sadduceeism
ACDDEEINNNR	dinner-dance
ACDDEELOSTY	dodecastyle
ACDDEENNOPT	co-dependant
ACDDEHINSSS	caddishness
ACDDEHKMORU	archdukedom
ACDDEHLLOST	saddlecloth
ACDDEHNOOPY	dodecaphony
ACDDEHNORRU	roundarched
ACDDEIILNRT	dendritical
ACDDEIJNNUU	unjaundiced
ACDDEILLMSS	middle-class
ACDDEILMOSU	duodecimals
ACDDEIMNORU	endocardium
ACDDEIMNRST	discardment
ACDDEINOOPT	paedodontic
ACDDELLMNOU	mould-candle
ACDDGIJKNPU	Jack-pudding
ACDDHINOORS	doch-an-doris
ACDDIIMORSU	diascordium
ACDDILOSTUY	didactylous
ACDEEEEHLRR	cheerleader
ACDEEEFLNRT	needlecraft
ACDEEEFLRST	self-created
ACDEEEFNORT	△confederate
ACDEEEGLLOT	décolletage
ACDEEEHORRV	overreached
ACDEEEIKLNS	linseed-cake
ACDEEEILLPT	pedicellate
ACDEEEILNRV	deliverance
ACDEEEIMPRT	premedicate
ACDEEEIMRTV	decemvirate
ACDEEEINPRU	preaudience
ACDEEEINRTV	revendicate
ACDEEEIPRTT	decrepitate
ACDEEEIPRTV	deprecative
ACDEEELLNRT	crenellated
ACDEEELLRVW	cave-dweller
ACDEEELORRT	decelerator
ACDEEENNSTT	antecedents
ACDEEFFILLT	ill-affected
ACDEEFFINOT	affectioned
ACDEEFGINRU	figure-dance
ACDEEFILNRZ	fence-lizard
ACDEEFLMOTT	mottle-faced
ACDEEFLNRUU	fraudulence
ACDEEFNRRTU	unrefracted
ACDEEGGNORT	congregated
ACDEEGGNRSS	craggedness
ACDEEGHHPRT	depth-charge
ACDEEGHILRS	sledge-chair
ACDEEGHNRRU	undercharge
ACDEEGILLMO	medico-legal
ACDEEGILNNR	calendering
ACDEEGILNTU	geniculated
ACDEEGINPRT	deprecating
ACDEEGINRTU	nectar-guide
ACDEEGKLNOW	acknowledge
ACDEEHHKNRR	handkercher
ACDEEHILNOP	encephaloid
ACDEEHILNPP	Chippendale
ACDEEHILPSY	psychedelia
ACDEEHIMNOR	Echinoderma
ACDEEHIMNPU	unimpeached
ACDEEHIMNRS	merchandise
ACDEEHIMNRZ	merchandize
ACDEEHINRTW	windcheater
ACDEEHIORTT	octahedrite
ACDEEHKKLNU	knuckle-head
ACDEEHKNNUY	unhackneyed
ACDEEHLLOSU	close-hauled
ACDEEHLNPRR	randle-perch
ACDEEHLRRRU	hurdle-racer
ACDEEHMNORW	reach-me-down
ACDEEHNNNTU	unenchanted
ACDEEHNNSTU	unchastened
ACDEEHNPRSS	parchedness
ACDEEHNRRTU	unchartered
ACDEEIILLTV	divellicate
ACDEEIILLTY	eidetically
ACDEEIILMTV	maledictive
ACDEEIILTUV	elucidative
ACDEEIIMRST	mediatrices

ACDEEIINPST	pedanticise
ACDEEIINPTZ	pedanticize
ACDEEIINRTV	revindicate
ACDEEIIOPPS	epidiascope
ACDEEIIPRTV	predicative
ACDEEIIRRRV	arrivederci
ACDEEIJLTVY	adjectively
ACDEEIJPRTU	prejudicate
ACDEEIKLRST	stickleader
ACDEEILLMNY	endemically
ACDEEILLORS	radicellose
ACDEEILMNRU	unreclaimed
ACDEEILMORU	leucodermia
ACDEEILNNST	clandestine
ACDEEILNOTT	delectation
ACDEEILNPST	lapidescent
ACDEEILNRST	credentials
ACDEEILNRTU	declinature
ACDEEILNTTU	denticulate
ACDEEILPRTU	reduplicate
ACDEEILRTTU	reticulated
ACDEEILSTUV	vesiculated
ACDEEIMNOSU	eudaemonics
ACDEEIMNPRT	predicament
ACDEEIMNRTY	determinacy
ACDEEIMORST	democratise
ACDEEIMORTZ	democratize
ACDEEIMOSTT	domesticate
ACDEEINNRRY	yince-errand
ACDEEINNRST	disentrance
ACDEEINOPRT	capernoited
	deprecation
ACDEEINORST	considerate
	desecration
ACDEEINORTU	decurionate
	re-education
ACDEEINORTV	verde-antico
ACDEEIOPRRT	depreciator
ACDEEIOPTTT	petticoated
ACDEEIORRTT	△directorate
ACDEEIPPRRT	paper-credit
ACDEEKLLSTW	well-stacked
ACDEEKQRRTU	quarterdeck
ACDEELLMORU	leucodermal
ACDEELLNOTU	nucleolated
ACDEELMMNOT	telecommand
ACDEELMORRS	scleroderma
ACDEELNOPRW	candle-power
ACDEELNPTUU	pedunculate
ACDEELOORTW	water-cooled
ACDEELOPRTU	operculated
ACDEELORSSV	cross-leaved
ACDEELRSTTY	scatteredly
ACDEELSSTUY	decussately
ACDEEMNRTTU	traducement
ACDEENORRST	second-rater
ACDEEOPRRTY	deprecatory
ACDEERRSSTT	detractress
ACDEFFIIRTV	diffractive
ACDEFGHLLRU	full-charged
ACDEFGILRSU	disgraceful
ACDEFHILPST	feldspathic
ACDEFHMOOST	smooth-faced
ACDEFIIINNT	infanticide
ACDEFIIINOT	deification
	edification
ACDEFIILSTU	feudalistic
ACDEFIIORTY	edificatory
ACDEFINNOTU	fecundation
ACDEFIRRTTU	trifurcated
ACDEFLLNORU	full-acorned
	uncalled-for
ACDEFLMMNOS	self-command
ACDEFLNRUUY	fraudulency
ACDEGGIIINT	giganticide
ACDEGHIILNP	hiding-place
ACDEGHIIOPR	ideographic
ACDEGHILLNT	candlelight
ACDEGHILNNR	chandlering
ACDEGHILORR	cigar-holder
ACDEGHIMOPR	demographic
ACDEGHOORTU	rough-coated
ACDEGIILLOO	ideological
ACDEGIILMRU	demiurgical
ACDEGIILSST	Distalgesic®
ACDEGIIMNSU	misguidance
ACDEGIINNRW	wire-dancing
ACDEGIKLNTW	tack-welding
ACDEGIKPRTU	picket-guard
ACDEGILLOOP	pedological
ACDEGILOOPS	logopaedics
ACDEGIMNOSY	geodynamics
ACDEGIMORTY	tragicomedy
ACDEGINNPST	stepdancing
ACDEGINOPRY	copyreading
ACDEGINRRTT	direct-grant
ACDEGKLOORS	sockdolager
ACDEGOORSTT	scattergood
ACDEHIIIPRR	Cirrhipedia
ACDEHIIKMNT	kitchen-maid
ACDEHIILOPP	paedophilic
ACDEHIILORT	Trochilidae
ACDEHIINNRV	chain-driven
ACDEHIIOPRT	diaphoretic
ACDEHIIPPRT	crappit-heid
ACDEHILLLPY	delphically
ACDEHILMPTY	itchy-palmed
ACDEHILOPSU	dicephalous
ACDEHILOPSY	psychodelia
ACDEHILRSSY	chrysalides
ACDEHIMOPRS	comradeship
ACDEHIMOSTU	mustachioed
ACDEHINNNTU	uninchanted
ACDEHINNOST	stanchioned
ACDEHINOORS	icosahedron
ACDEHINSSTU	unchastised
ACDEHINSTUZ	unchastized
ACDEHIOOPRT	orthopaedic
ACDEHIPSTTY	dyspathetic
ACDEHKLNNST	landsknecht
ACDEHKMRSTU	Deutschmark
ACDEHLLLOPY	phylloclade
ACDEHLMOSUY	chlamydeous
ACDEHLNPRTU	thunderclap

Words marked △ may be spelled also with a capital letter

ACDEHLPRTYY	hyperdactyl
ACDEHMNNOOR	enchondroma
ACDEHMOOPST	smooth-paced
ACDEHMOORTW	doomwatcher
ACDEHNNSTUU	unstaunched
ACDEHNOOPRS	sancho-pedro
ACDEHNOORST	octahedrons
ACDEHNORSSZ	scherzandos
ACDEHNPRSUU	unpurchased
ACDEHOORRTU	urochordate
ACDEIIILMOT	domiciliate
ACDEIIINTVV	vindicative
ACDEIIJLPRU	prejudicial
	pre-judicial
ACDEIILLMNY	medicinally
ACDEIILLNTY	identically
ACDEIILLORV	varicelloid
ACDEIILLRVY	veridically
ACDEIILLSTY	deistically
ACDEIILMNOT	malediction
ACDEIILMPRS	spermicidal
ACDEIILNNOT	declination
ACDEIILNORT	directional
ACDEIILNOTU	elucidation
ACDEIILNOTV	valediction
ACDEIILNPTU	induplicate
ACDEIILORRT	directorial
ACDEIILPRSU	Pedicularis
ACDEIILPTUV	duplicative
ACDEIILRTUV	diverticula
ACDEIIMMNOS	demoniacism
ACDEIIMNPST	pedanticism
ACDEIIMORRT	radiometric
ACDEIIMORTU	audiometric
ACDEIIMPRRU	pericardium
ACDEIINNRTY	tyrannicide
ACDEIINOPRT	predication
ACDEIINORRT	doctrinaire
ACDEIIORRTT	Tortricidae
ACDEIIRSTTV	distractive
ACDEIJNPRTU	prejudicant
ACDEILLNOOT	decollation
ACDEILMNOPS	endoplasmic
ACDEILMNOTU	columniated
ACDEILMORTY	maledictory
ACDEILNOOPY	Lycopodinae
ACDEILNOOST	consolidate
ACDEILNOOSW	wood-sanicle
ACDEILNOPST	endoplastic
ACDEILNORSS	cordialness
ACDEILNORSY	secondarily
ACDEILNORTY	declinatory
ACDEILNOSTT	Scotlandite
ACDEILNOSUV	unvocalised
ACDEILNOTTU	tentaculoid
ACDEILNOUVZ	unvocalized
ACDEILNRTUU	uncurtailed
ACDEILORTUY	elucidatory
ACDEILORTVY	valedictory
ACDEILPPSTY	dyspeptical
ACDEILPRTUU	duplicature
ACDEIMNNOOP	companioned
ACDEIMNNOPU	uncompanied
ACDEIMORSTT	democratist
ACDEINNNOSU	uncanonised
ACDEINNNOUZ	uncanonized
ACDEINNOORT	incoronated
ACDEINNORST	constrained
ACDEINNORTU	denunciator
	underaction
ACDEINNRTUU	uncurtained
ACDEINOOPRS	scorpaenoid
ACDEINOOPRY	Procyonidae
ACDEINOORRT	Corrodentia
	recordation
ACDEINOORST	co-ordinates
	decorations
ACDEINOPRTY	trypanocide
ACDEINOPSTT	constipated
ACDEINORRWY	cordwainery
ACDEINORTUV	decurvation
ACDEINOSSTU	decussation
ACDEINOSTTU	outdistance
ACDEINOSTTW	wainscotted
ACDEINPRSTU	unpractised
ACDEIOPPRRT	dipterocarp
ACDEIOPRRTY	predicatory
ACDEIOPRSSY	caryopsides
ACDEIOPRSTT	disceptator
ACDEIORSUXY	xyridaceous
ACDEIRSTTUY	daisy-cutter
ACDEJORSSTU	coadjutress
ACDEKOPRSTT	spatterdock
ACDELLOPTTY	leptodactyl
ACDELNOOPRS	scolopendra
ACDELNOORTU	tan-coloured
ACDELNPTTUU	punctulated
ACDELOORRTU	edulcorator
ACDELOPRTTY	pterodactyl
ACDEMMMNNOT	commandment
ACDEMMNOORT	commendator
ACDEMNNORTU	countermand
ACDEMNORTUY	documentary
ACDEMOOPRTU	proctodaeum
ACDEMOORRST	ostracoderm
ACDEMOPRSSU	mass-produce
ACDENNNNOUU	unannounced
ACDENORRTUW	counterdraw
ACDEORRSSST	star-crossed
ACDFFGIINNT	fact-finding
ACDFFGILNOS	scaffolding
ACDFFIILMOO	officialdom
ACDFFIINORT	diffraction
ACDFGHHIINS	chafing-dish
ACDFGILMNOU	mould-facing
ACDFHILPSTU	dispatchful
ACDFHINORRT	drift-anchor
ACDFKLOORRW	lock-forward
ACDGGIILNNR	dancing-girl
ACDGHIIIOPR	idiographic
ACDGHIMOOSU	dichogamous
ACDGHIOPRSY	discography
ACDGIIILOST	dialogistic
ACDGIIKLNOR	riding-cloak

ACDGIINOSST diagnostics
ACDGIINRSTT distracting
ACDGIIORSSU disgracious
ACDGILNOORW wool-carding
ACDGILNRTUY traducingly
ACDGIMNNOPU up-and-coming
ACDGINNOOPY Pycnogonida
ACDGINOORVW woodcarving
ACDGINORSST cross-dating
ACDGIOPRRTU agriproduct
ACDGLLOOTYY dactylology
ACDHHIILOTY ichthyoidal
ACDHHIOPRRS harpsichord
ACDHHIOPRTY hydropathic
ACDHHIORRSY Hydrocharis
ACDHIIIMRTT △mithridatic
ACDHIILOOPR chiropodial
ACDHIIMNORS diachronism
disharmonic
ACDHIINOOPR radiophonic
ACDHIIOPRST diastrophic
ACDHILOOPSZ schizopodal
ACDHIMNOORT trichomonad
ACDHIMNORSY dysharmonic
ACDHIMNORTY hydromantic
ACDHIMNRSSY scrimshandy
ACDHINOOPRS discophoran
ACDHINOORSU diachronous
ACDHIORSTTY hydrostatic
ACDHLNOOORT notochordal
ACDHLOORSSW schoolwards
ACDHNOPRSUY Hydnocarpus
ACDIIILLNPS disciplinal
ACDIIILLOTY idiotically
ACDIIILMORY domiciliary
ACDIIILORST dioristical
ACDIIIMNOTU unidiomatic
ACDIIINNOTV vindication
ACDIIJLLRUY juridically
ACDIIKNOOST dockisation
ACDIIKNOOTZ dockization
ACDIILLLLYY idyllically
ACDIILLORST clostridial
ACDIILMNOPR palindromic
ACDIILMNSSY syndicalism
ACDIILMOOST sodomitical
ACDIILMOPST diplomatics
ACDIILMSTTU Talmudistic
ACDIILNNOOT conditional
ACDIILNNOTU inductional
ACDIILNOOST dislocation
ACDIILNOPTU duplication
ACDIILNSSTY syndicalist
ACDIIMORSTY myocarditis
ACDIINNOSTY syndication
ACDIINOOPRS Scorpionida
ACDIINOPRST adscription
ACDIINORSTT distraction
ACDIINORTVY vindicatory
ACDIIOORRRR air-corridor
ACDIIOORSSS sarcoidosis
ACDILLNORTY doctrinally
ACDILLNOSYY synodically
ACDILLORSTY crystalloid
ACDILNOSUUU nudicaulous
ACDIMNOOPST spodomantic
ACDIMNOOSTT mastodontic
ACDIMOOORRT cardiomotor
ACDINNNOOOT condonation
ACDINOOORRT co-ordinator
ACDINOORSSU icosandrous
ACDINOPRRTU drop-curtain
ACDKLLNOORR rock-and-roll
ACDLLNOORTU dual-control
ACDLLOPTYYY polydactyly
ACDLNOOORTY condolatory
ACDMNOOOPUZ azo-compound
ACDNORRSTTU transductor
ACDOOORSSTU ostracodous
ACEEEEEKPPR peace-keeper
ACEEEEHPRRS cheeseparer
ACEEEERSTWZ tweezer-case
ACEEEFFFRTT after-effect
ACEEEFFKMOR coffee-maker
ACEEEFLNRRU nuclear-free
ACEEEGHHRST chargesheet
ACEEEGHNPRR crepehanger
ACEEEGILNRT energetical
ACEEEGIMNST miscegenate
ACEEEGIMNTT metagenetic
ACEEEGLMNOU leucaemogen
ACEEEGLOTTT telecottage
ACEEEGMNOPR peace-monger
ACEEEGNORRU re-encourage
ACEEEHIIMPR epicheirema
ACEEEHILNNP encephaline
ACEEEHIMNTV achievement
ACEEEHINSST cenesthesia
ACEEEHIORVV overachieve
ACEEEHKLNRT leather-neck
ACEEEHKMPRS speechmaker
ACEEEHLLNRT chanterelle
ACEEEHLMNOS chaenomeles
ACEEEHLRSST teacherless
ACEEEHMNNNT enhancement
ACEEEHMNSTT escheatment
ACEEEHMORTT tacheometer
ACEEEILLMRR crémaillère
ACEEEILMNPT mantelpiece
ACEEEILNPPR pipe-cleaner
ACEEEILNQUV equivalence
ACEEEILNRRV irrelevance
ACEEEIMPRST masterpiece
ACEEEINNPPT inappetence
ACEEEINRSSS necessaries
ACEEEINSSTT necessitate
ACEEEIPTTVX expectative
ACEEEJKLPST steeplejack
ACEEEJORSTT ejector-seat
ACEEELLMNOV malevolence
ACEEELLSSSY ceaselessly
ACEEELMMNPT emplacement
ACEEELMNPRT replacement
ACEEELMNRRT recremental

ACEEELMNRTX excremental
ACEEELQRRTU lacquer-tree
ACEEEMNNRTT re-enactment
ACEEEMNRTTW cement-water
ACEEENPPRTU perpetuance
ACEEEOPRTTX expectorate
ACEEEPRSSTT streetscape
ACEEFFGHINN chaff-engine
ACEEFFIILOS officialese
ACEEFFILNTU ineffectual
ACEEFFILTVY affectively
ACEEFFIOPPR paper-office
ACEEFFLLTUY effectually
ACEEFFMNORT afforcement
ACEEFHINNRS enfranchise
ACEEFHIRRTW fire-watcher
ACEEFHKLTTW Twelfth-cake
ACEEFHLRRSU researchful
ACEEFHNRRTU furtherance
ACEEFIISTTT testificate
ACEEFILLNVY venefically
ACEEFILLORT refocillate
ACEEFILNRSU increaseful
ACEEFILPRUU Cupuliferae
ACEEFIMNORS freemasonic
ACEEFIMNTTU tumefacient
ACEEFINOPTT tepefaction
ACEEFINORRT refectorian
ACEEFLLNRST crestfallen
ACEEFLNRSSU carefulness
ACEEFLORRUV overcareful
ACEEFLORSUU ferulaceous
ACEEFLOTTUV octave-flute
ACEEFLPRRTU prefectural
ACEEFMNOPRR performance
ACEEGGIMMNO emmenagogic
ACEEGGIMNOT geomagnetic
ACEEGHHNOSU change-house
ACEEGHHORSU charge-house
ACEEGHHPRRY hypercharge
ACEEGHILLNR all-cheering
ACEEGHILMNO hegemonical
ACEEGHILOOT oligochaete
ACEEGHILPRT telegraphic
ACEEGHINNOX ion-exchange
ACEEGHINNRT interchange
ACEEGHKRSTU hucksterage
ACEEGHMMORT hectogramme
ACEEGHNRRSU chargenurse
ACEEGHPRRSU supercharge
ACEEGIILNNT geanticline
ACEEGIINPRR ear-piercing
ACEEGIKNNPP kneecapping
knee-capping
ACEEGILLNOR collegianer
ACEEGILLNRY generically
ACEEGILLNTY genetically
ACEEGILLNUY eugenically
ACEEGILMMRT telegrammic
ACEEGILMORT geometrical
ACEEGILNRRY gyre-carline
ACEEGILNSTT telecasting
ACEEGILOPSU specialogue
ACEEGILPRTT tetraplegic
ACEEGILSTTU gesticulate
ACEEGIMMNPT camp-meeting
ACEEGIMMNRT centigramme
ACEEGIMMORT microgamete
ACEEGINORTT teratogenic
ACEEGIRRRTY cerargyrite
ACEEGKLNOOR cook-general
ACEEGLLRSSY gracelessly
ACEEGLMNNOT congealment
ACEEGLMNOPR place-monger
ACEEGLMNORS camerlengos
ACEEGLNNSTU languescent
ACEEGMNORRS scaremonger
ACEEGNNORRS organ-screen
ACEEGNNOSST cognateness
ACEEGPPRRSU caper-spurge
ACEEGRRSSSU rescue-grass
ACEEHHILPTW Whitechapel
ACEEHHIPRST teachership
ACEEHHIRTTT Thatcherite
ACEEHHITTTT hatchettite
ACEEHHLMRST crash-helmet
ACEEHHLORST hearse-cloth
ACEEHHNORST sheet-anchor
ACEEHHOPTTY hypothecate
ACEEHIILNOT Aeneolithic
ACEEHIILNST antihelices
ACEEHIILPRT perithecial
ACEEHIIMRST hetaerismic
ACEEHIINNRT inheritance
ACEEHIIPPRT perihepatic
ACEEHIIRSTT theatricise
ACEEHIIRTTZ theatricize
ACEEHIKNRTW kitchenware
ACEEHILLNNP △panhellenic
ACEEHILLRTY heretically
ACEEHILNPRT phrenetical
ACEEHILNRTT threnetical
ACEEHILNSST ethicalness
ACEEHILORTT theoretical
ACEEHIMMNPT impeachment
ACEEHIMNNNT enchainment
ACEEHIMNNSU unmechanise
ACEEHIMNNUZ unmechanize
ACEEHIMNOPR rope-machine
ACEEHIMNRST cashierment
ACEEHIMORTT theorematic
ACEEHIMRRSW schwärmerei
ACEEHIMRSTT catheterism
ACEEHIMRTTY erythematic
ACEEHINNSTZ Nietzschean
ACEEHINOPRS peacherinos
ACEEHINORST heteroscian
ACEEHINORTT Theocritean
ACEEHINPRSS preachiness
ACEEHINPRTT parenthetic
ACEEHIOPRRT Cheiroptera
ACEEHIOPRST spirochaete
ACEEHIPRRST Petrarchise
ACEEHIPRRTZ Petrarchize

ACEEHIPRTTU therapeutic
ACEEHIPRTVY hyperactive
ACEEHIRSSTV tsesarevich
ACEEHIRSSTW tsesarewich
ACEEHJKLLST shell-jacket
ACEEHKLLOPT placket-hole
ACEEHKLORRT rock-leather
ACEEHLLRRST shell-crater
ACEEHLMOPSY mesocephaly
ACEEHLNOPSU encephalous
ACEEHLNPRTU place-hunter
ACEEHLOORRU leucorrhoea
ACEEHLOPRRT perchlorate
ACEEHLORSTT earth-closet
ACEEHMMNNRT merchantmen
ACEEHMNNNTT enchantment
ACEEHMNNRRT trencherman
ACEEHMNNSTT chastenment
ACEEHMOPTTY hepatectomy
ACEEHMOPXYY Myxophyceae
ACEEHMORRTY archeometry
ACEEHMORTTY tacheometry
ACEEHNNORRT archenteron
ACEEHNNOSTT chansonette
ACEEHNNRSST enchantress
ACEEHNRRSST stern-chaser
ACEEHORRSTT orchestrate
Sachertorte
ACEEHORRSTU treacherous
ACEEHORRTTU treachetour
ACEEIIKRSTT rickettsiae
ACEEIILLNPT penicillate
ACEEIILLNRT rectilineal
ACEEIILLPPT epileptical
ACEEIILMNRS criminalese
ACEEIILNRRT rectilinear
ACEEIILPRSS specialiser
ACEEIILPRSU peculiarise
ACEEIILPRSZ specializer
ACEEIILPRTT periclitate
ACEEIILPRUZ peculiarize
ACEEIILPTVX explicative
ACEEIILRRST rectiserial
ACEEIIMNRRT recriminate
ACEEIIMRSTV miscreative
ACEEIINNTUV enunciative
ACEEIINOPRT capernoitie
ACEEIINRSST canisterise
ACEEIINRSTZ canisterize
ACEEIINRTTV interactive
ACEEIIPPRTT peripatetic
precipitate
ACEEIIPRTTV crepitative
ACEEIIRSSTT cassiterite
ACEEIJNNRTT interjacent
ACEEIKMPRRT market-price
ACEEIKNRSTW awe-stricken
ACEEIKNSSSS seasickness
ACEEILLLSTY celestially
ACEEILLNNSS cleanliness
ACEEILLNPST splenetical
ACEEILLORST selectorial
ACEEILLORTV vorticellae
ACEEILLRTVY cleverality
ACEEILMNNRT incremental
ACEEILMNRRY mercenarily
ACEEILMORRT calorimeter
ACEEILMORST elastomeric
ACEEILMPSST esemplastic
ACEEILMRTUV vermiculate
ACEEILNNORT intolerance
ACEEILNNOTU enucleation
ACEEILNNRST intercensal
ACEEILNNTUU uninucleate
ACEEILNNTUY lieutenancy
ACEEILNOPTX exceptional
ACEEILNORSS recessional
ACEEILNORST secretional
ACEEILNOSSS secessional
ACEEILNOSST coessential
ACEEILNPRRT pericentral
ACEEILNPRTT centripetal
ACEEILNPTTY pectinately
ACEEILNQUVY equivalency
ACEEILNRRVY irrelevancy
ACEEILNRSST treacliness
ACEEILNRSSY necessarily
ACEEILNSSST elasticness
ACEEILNTTTU tentaculite
ACEEILORRTV correlative
ACEEILORTUX executorial
ACEEILOTVVY evocatively
ACEEILPRTTY rectipetaly
ACEEILPSTUV speculative
ACEEILSTTTU testiculate
ACEEIMMNORT anemometric
ACEEIMMNRRS mercenarism
ACEEIMMOPRR microampere
ACEEIMMORST commiserate
ACEEIMNNOTT cementation
ACEEIMNORRT craniometer
ACEEIMNORTT actinometer
ACEEIMNPRTT permittance
ACEEIMNQRTU acquirement
ACEEINNNSST ancientness
ACEEINNOPTZ pentazocine
ACEEINNORSS reascension
ACEEINNPPTY inappetency
ACEEINNPTTX inexpectant
ACEEINNRRSU reinsurance
ACEEINNSSTX inexactness
ACEEINOPTTX expectation
ACEEINORSST estancieros
ACEEINPRRST transpierce
ACEEINRRSTV transceiver
ACEEIOOPRTV co-operative
ACEEIOPPRSU piperaceous
ACEEIOPRRTV procreative
ACEEIORRSTV eviscerator
ACEEIORRTTV retroactive
ACEEIORSTTX stereotaxic
ACEEIPRSTUV superactive
ACEEIRSSTTU resuscitate
ACEEJNPRSTU superjacent

ACEEKLMNRTT	tracklement
ACEEKMRRSTW	wreckmaster
ACEEKPRRSST	racket-press
ACEELLMNRSS	small-screen
ACEELLNORTY	coeternally
ACEELLNOSTT	constellate
ACEELLOOPRT	coleopteral
ACEELLOPTUY	eucalyptole
ACEELLQRSUY	Carlylesque
ACEELLRSSTY	tracelessly
ACEELLSSSUY	causelessly
ACEELMNNOOV	monovalence
ACEELMNOPTT	contemplate
ACEELNNNSSU	uncleanness
ACEELNNRSSU	unclearness
ACEELNOOPRT	coleopteran
ACEELNOPRTU	counterplea
ACEELNOPSTT	Pentecostal
ACEELNORSTU	counterseal
ACEELNPTTXY	expectantly
ACEELOORRTW	water-cooler
ACEELOPPPRT	copperplate
ACEELOPPRTT	Plectoptera
ACEEMMMOORT	commemorate
ACEEMNNNOTU	mountenance
ACEEMNNORTU	connumerate
ACEEMNNRRUY	unmercenary
ACEEMNORTTY	cementatory
ACEEMOPRTTU	computerate
ACEEMORSTTT	stactometer
ACEENNNOPRU	preannounce
ACEENNOPRTU	counterpane
ACEENNORSTT	consternate
ACEENNPPRSY	scrapepenny
ACEENNPTTUX	unexpectant
ACEENNRSSUY	unnecessary
ACEENOORSTT	cotoneaster
ACEENOPRTTX	expectorant
ACEEOOPRSTU	proteaceous
ACEEOORSSTU	ostreaceous
ACEEOPRRRTU	recuperator
ACEEOPRSTUV	superoctave
ACEEORRSTUW	watercourse
ACEEPPRRTTU	paper-cutter
ACEEPRRSSUU	acupressure
ACEEPRSSSTT	spectatress
ACEFFFGILOR	flag-officer
ACEFFFIMORS	farm-offices
ACEFFGHILNR	cliffhanger
ACEFFGILNTY	affectingly
ACEFFGINNTU	unaffecting
ACEFFIILPST	spifflicate
ACEFFIITTVY	affectivity
ACEFFIKOPRR	park-officer
ACEFFILORTU	forficulate
ACEFFILRSST	trafficless
ACEFFIOSTUV	suffocative
ACEFGHLLNUY	changefully
ACEFGHLNNOR	Anglo-French
ACEFGHOOPRR	proof-charge
ACEFGIIINST	significate
ACEFGIIMNNT	magnificent
ACEFGIIMNOS	magnificoes
ACEFGIINNNR	refinancing
ACEFGIINNRT	interfacing
ACEFGILNRTU	centrifugal
ACEFGILNTTU	leaf-cutting
ACEFGINORTU	configurate
ACEFHHINSTT	snatch-thief
ACEFHIILNPS	pelican-fish
ACEFHIINRTY	chieftainry
ACEFHILNOPR	Francophile
ACEFHILNOSU	leaf-cushion
ACEFHILRSTY	self-charity
ACEFHLNRTUY	half-century
ACEFHLOPRRU	reproachful
ACEFHMNNORW	Frenchwoman
ACEFHMORRTT	mothercraft
ACEFHNNOOPR	△francophone
ACEFHOORSTU	house-factor
ACEFIIILNRT	fairniticle
ACEFIIIMNRT	rifacimenti
ACEFIIINORT	reification
ACEFIIKLLRT	flickertail
ACEFIILMNOR	infomercial
ACEFIILNNSS	finicalness
ACEFIILNRTY	fairnyticle
ACEFIILPRSU	superficial
ACEFIILRSTW	welfaristic
ACEFIIMNORT	rifacimento
ACEFIIMNOTT	metafiction
ACEFIINOPTT	pontificate
ACEFIINORST	fractionise
ACEFIINORSU	facinerious
ACEFIINORTZ	fractionize
ACEFIINRRTU	curtain-fire
ACEFILLORUW	cauliflower
ACEFILNORTT	fractionlet
ACEFILORSTU	lactiferous
ACEFILOSTUY	facetiously
ACEFIMNOTTU	tumefaction
ACEFIMORRRT	crateriform
ACEFINNOTTU	functionate
ACEFINNRSST	franticness
ACEFINOTTUV	confutative
ACEFINPRSTY	presanctify
ACEFINRRRTU	franc-tireur
ACEFIOORRTV	vociferator
ACEFIPRRSTT	priestcraft
ACEFKLMORST	flock-master
ACEFKMORRST	stock-farmer
ACEFKMRRRTU	truck-farmer
ACEFLLLOSSW	class-fellow
ACEFLNSSTTU	tactfulness
ACEGGHILLNN	challenging
ACEGGHOPSUY	psychagogue
ACEGGILLMOO	gemological
ACEGGILLNOU	colleaguing
ACEGGINNORU	encouraging
ACEGGINRSSS	scragginess
ACEGGLNOOYY	gynaecology
ACEGHHILOPR	helicograph
ACEGHHILRST	searchlight
ACEGHHIMORR	hemorrhagic

ACEGHHLORTU	leach-trough
ACEGHHNORST	short-change
ACEGHHOOPRR	choreograph
ACEGHHOPRRY	choregraphy
ACEGHIILPRX	lexigraphic
ACEGHIILRRU	hierurgical
ACEGHIIPRRS	serigraphic
ACEGHIKLLNS	shellacking
ACEGHIKLNNT	lance-knight
ACEGHIKMNOP	epoch-making
ACEGHILLNNN	channelling
ACEGHILLNRT	night-cellar
ACEGHILLOOR	rheological
ACEGHILLOOT	ethological
	theological
ACEGHILNOOT	theogonical
ACEGHILNRSY	searchingly
ACEGHILOPSY	geophysical
ACEGHIMNNRT	merchanting
ACEGHIMNORU	archegonium
ACEGHINNPRU	unpreaching
ACEGHINOPRV	venographic
ACEGHINORRS	horse-racing
ACEGHINPRSS	graphicness
ACEGHIOOPRR	oreographic
ACEGHIOPRRX	xerographic
ACEGHLOOSTY	eschatology
ACEGHLOPTTY	glyptotheca
ACEGHMOORSU	hercogamous
ACEGHNOPRSY	scenography
ACEGHOOPRSU	creophagous
ACEGHOOPSTY	phagocytose
ACEGIIKLNRS	arse-licking
ACEGIILLNNV	clean-living
ACEGIILLOTV	colligative
ACEGIILOSTT	egotistical
ACEGIILRSST	sacrilegist
ACEGIIMNOST	isomagnetic
ACEGIIMNRST	Germanistic
ACEGIIMRRTV	gravimetric
ACEGIINRRRR	ring-carrier
ACEGIINRSTU	cauterising
ACEGIINRSTW	writing-case
ACEGIINRTUZ	cauterizing
ACEGIIPRRST	perigastric
ACEGIJNOTUV	conjugative
ACEGIKNORST	orange-stick
ACEGILLMRTU	metallurgic
ACEGILLNNOR	non-allergic
ACEGILLNNOY	congenially
ACEGILLNNRU	unrecalling
ACEGILLNOOO	oenological
ACEGILLNOOP	penological
ACEGILLNOSS	logicalness
ACEGILLOOOR	oreological
ACEGILLOORS	serological
ACEGILLOOSX	sexological
ACEGILMNORS	camerlingos
ACEGILMNRSY	screamingly
ACEGILMOSTY	cleistogamy
ACEGILNNNOU	uncongenial
ACEGILNNOOS	cloisonnage
ACEGILNNOOT	congelation
ACEGILNNPRS	spring-clean
ACEGILNNSUY	unceasingly
ACEGILNOSUU	cauligenous
ACEGILNRSSY	caressingly
ACEGILNRSTT	scatterling
ACEGILNTUUU	unguiculate
ACEGILOOPST	apologetics
ACEGILOORTT	teratologic
ACEGILORSUV	clavigerous
ACEGILRRTUU	agriculture
ACEGIMNNOOT	cognominate
ACEGIMNNOPR	panic-monger
ACEGIMNNORT	centimorgan
ACEGIMNOOST	somatogenic
ACEGIMNOOTZ	zoomagnetic
ACEGINNNOSU	consanguine
ACEGINNOPRY	panegyricon
ACEGINNORTY	octingenary
ACEGINNRSTY	astringency
ACEGINNSSTW	newscasting
ACEGINOOPRT	co-operating
ACEGINOORTV	overcoating
ACEGINORSTV	overcasting
ACEGINOSTTV	casting-vote
ACEGINRTTTU	rate-cutting
ACEGIOORTTX	excogitator
ACEGIOPRSSU	scapigerous
ACEGKLNNOUW	luckengowan
ACEGKLOPSST	pocket-glass
ACEGKRSSTTU	stage-struck
ACEGLLNOOSU	collagenous
ACEGLLOSTYY	glycosylate
ACEGLMNORWY	clergywoman
ACEGLNOPRTY	calyptrogen
ACEGLNORTUY	granulocyte
ACEGLORRSSV	clovergrass
ACEGLRSSTTU	glass-cutter
ACEGMNNORSS	Congressman
ACEGMOPRRST	spectrogram
ACEGMORSTTY	gastrectomy
ACEGNORRSST	cross-garnet
ACEGOOPRSST	gastroscope
ACEGRRSSTTU	grass-cutter
ACEHHIILMOP	hemophiliac
ACEHHIILMST	hemistichal
ACEHHIIMRRS	hierarchism
ACEHHIINNTY	hyacinthine
ACEHHILNOTT	chloanthite
ACEHHIMNOPS	machine-shop
ACEHHIMOOPT	homeopathic
ACEHHIMOSTT	theomachist
ACEHHIMRSTT	Thatcherism
ACEHHINOPPY	phycophaein
ACEHHINOPTT	Phaethontic
ACEHHINRRTU	heart-urchin
ACEHHIPRSTT	heptarchist
ACEHHKLRTUY	hurly-hacket
ACEHHLMMORT	hammercloth
ACEHHLNOORT	anthochlore
ACEHHMNNSUU	Munchhausen
ACEHHOPRTYY	hypothecary

ACEHIIIMRST hetairismic
ACEHIIINPSS △hispanicise
ACEHIIINPSZ △hispanicize
ACEHIILLMOT homiletical
ACEHIILLNRT tiller-chain
trichinella
ACEHIILLOPT Paleolithic
ACEHIILLOST isolecithal
ACEHIILMSTT athleticism
ACEHIILNOPR necrophilia
ACEHIILNPRT nephritical
ACEHIILOSTT chiastolite
ACEHIILPPTY epiphytical
ACEHIILRSTT Thersitical
ACEHIILRSVW swivel-chair
ACEHIILSTWW Welwitschia
ACEHIIMNOPT hemianoptic
ACEHIIMRSTT theatricism
ACEHIIMSSST schismatise
ACEHIIMSSTZ schismatize
ACEHIINNOPT phonetician
ACEHIINNTTU inauthentic
ACEHIINORRT rhetorician
ACEHIINPRSY physicianer
ACEHIINPSTT pantheistic
ACEHIKLLORS scholar-like
ACEHIKMNORS chain-smoker
ACEHIKMNORW machine-work
ACEHIKMRTUY rheumaticky
ACEHIKRRSSS sherris-sack
ACEHIKRSSTW cat's-whisker
ACEHIKRSTTV harvest-tick
ACEHILLMRTY thermically
ACEHILLOPRT plethorical
ACEHILLORTW white-collar
ACEHILLPRSY spherically
ACEHILMMNPY lamp-chimney
ACEHILMNOOR melanochroi
ACEHILMOPTU plaice-mouth
ACEHILMORTT thermotical
ACEHILNPRST sphincteral
ACEHILNSTTY synthetical
ACEHILOOPRT orthoepical
ACEHILOOTTU acolouthite
ACEHILOPPRT prophetical
ACEHILOSSST cholestasis
ACEHILRSSSY chrysalises
ACEHIMMOPRT metamorphic
ACEHIMNNSTT tennis-match
ACEHIMNOPSS championess
ACEHIMNORSS marchioness
ACEHIMNOSYY hyoscyamine
ACEHIMNOTTU humectation
ACEHIMNTTUW minute-watch
ACEHIMOOSTT homeostatic
ACEHIMOPRST atmospheric
ACEHIMORRST choirmaster
ACEHIMORSST metachrosis
ACEHIMORTTX thermotaxic
ACEHIMPRRST Petrarchism
ACEHIMPSSTY metaphysics
ACEHIMPSTTY sympathetic
ACEHINNNORS chansonnier
ACEHINNNRTT intrenchant
ACEHINNOPTT pantothenic
ACEHINNRSSU raunchiness
ACEHINNSTTY synanthetic
ACEHINNTTUU unauthentic
ACEHINOOPRZ Phanerozoic
ACEHINOPRRS chairperson
ACEHINOPRRT chiropteran
ACEHINOPRTU neuropathic
ACEHINORRST orchestrina
ACEHINORRSU hurricanoes
ACEHINPSSTT pentastichs
ACEHINRSSST starchiness
ACEHINSSSTT cattishness
ACEHIOOPSTT osteopathic
ACEHIOOPTTV photoactive
ACEHIOORTTV cohortative
ACEHIOPRRST creatorship
ACEHIOPRRTT Trichoptera
ACEHIPRRSTT Petrarchist
ACEHIPRSSUY hyperacusis
ACEHIQRRSUY squirearchy
ACEHKKLLMSU Muschelkalk
ACEHKKRRSSU sharksucker
ACEHKORRTWW workwatcher
ACEHKRRSTTU heart-struck
ACEHLLMRSSY charmlessly
ACEHLLMSSTY matchlessly
ACEHLLOORRS horse-collar
ACEHLMOOPTY cephalotomy
ACEHLMOSSST stomachless
ACEHLNNRTTY trenchantly
ACEHLNOPRTY lycanthrope
ACEHLNSSSTU staunchless
ACEHLOPSUXY sceuophylax
ACEHLORSTUY lythraceous
ACEHMNOPRSY prosenchyma
ACEHMNOPRTY tephromancy
ACEHMOORTTY tracheotomy
ACEHMOPRSTU champertous
ACEHNNOOPRT ctenophoran
ACEHNNSSSTU staunchness
ACEHNOORTTU tautochrone
ACEHNPRSSTU snatch-purse
ACEHOOPPSTY hepatoscopy
ACEHOOPRRST prothoraces
ACEHOPRRSSY chrysoprase
ACEHOPRRTYY cryotherapy
ACEHORSSTTT scattershot
ACEHORSSTTV torch-staves
ACEIIIILNSV civilianise
ACEIIIILNVZ civilianize
ACEIIIKNRST kinesiatric
ACEIIILMNRS criminalise
ACEIIILMNRZ criminalize
ACEIIILMPTV implicative
ACEIIILNOTT elicitation
ACEIIILPSTT pietistical
ACEIIIMNNRT incriminate
ACEIIIMNOST semiotician
ACEIIIMNRTV criminative

ACEIIIMNSTT	anti-Semitic
ACEIIINNNRZ	cinnarizine
ACEIIIQSTUV	acquisitive
ACEIIKLLOOR	kilocalorie
ACEIIKLRSTT	rickettsial
ACEIIKNOTTU	autokinetic
ACEIIKNRSSS	air-sickness
ACEIIKRSSTT	rickettsias
ACEIILLLTVY	levitically
ACEIILLMMTY	mimetically
ACEIILLMNNU	illuminance
ACEIILLMPRY	empirically
ACEIILLNOTV	vellication
ACEIILLNRTV	intervallic
ACEIILLNRUV	curvilineal
ACEIILLNSTT	scintillate
ACEIILLOPST	epistolical
ACEIILLOSTV	oscillative
ACEIILLPRTU	pleuritical
ACEIILMNPRT	planimetric
ACEIILMNSSU	masculinise
ACEIILMNSUZ	masculinize
ACEIILMORST	isometrical
ACEIILMOTTU	itacolumite
ACEIILMPRSU	Laserpicium
ACEIILMRRTT	trimetrical
ACEIILNNORT	reclination
ACEIILNOORT	coalitioner
ACEIILNOPPR	pilocarpine
ACEIILNOPRT	replication
ACEIILNOPTX	explication
ACEIILNOQTU	equinoctial
ACEIILNOSSV	Slavonicise
ACEIILNOSVZ	Slavonicize
ACEIILNOTUV	inoculative
ACEIILNPRUY	pecuniarily
ACEIILNRRUV	curvilinear
ACEIILNRSTU	unrealistic
ACEIILNRSTX	extrinsical
ACEIILNRTTY	intricately
ACEIILOORVV	cavo-rilievo
ACEIILORRST	escritorial
ACEIILPRRTU	picture-rail
ACEIILPRSST	plasticiser
ACEIILPRSTT	peristaltic
ACEIILPRSTZ	plasticizer
ACEIILPRTUY	peculiarity
ACEIILRTTVY	verticality
ACEIIMMNOTV	comminative
ACEIIMNNORS	Micronesian
ACEIIMNNORT	incremation
ACEIIMNNRST	manneristic
ACEIIMNOPRT	imprecation
ACEIIMNORST	creationism
	miscreation
	romanticise
ACEIIMNORTT	interatomic
	metrication
ACEIIMNORTZ	romanticize
ACEIIMNPRRU	pericranium
ACEIIMNPSSU	impuissance
ACEIIMNRSTT	martensitic
ACEIIMNRSTU	insectarium
ACEIIMNSSTT	semanticist
ACEIIMOPSSU	cassiopeium
ACEIINNNOST	incensation
ACEIINNNOTU	enunciation
ACEIINNOPTT	pectination
ACEIINNORRT	incinerator
ACEIINNORTT	interaction
ACEIINNPSTT	pinnatisect
ACEIINNRTTY	incertainty
ACEIINOORTX	excoriation
ACEIINOPRTT	crepitation
ACEIINOPSTT	pectisation
ACEIINOPSTX	expiscation
ACEIINOPTTZ	pectization
ACEIINORSTT	creationist
	reactionist
ACEIINORSTV	Insectivora
ACEIINORTTX	extrication
ACEIINPPRTT	precipitant
ACEIINPRTTY	antipyretic
	pertinacity
ACEIIOOPPST	aposiopetic
ACEIIORSTTV	recitativos
ACEIJKLOPTT	pilot-jacket
ACEIJLMMPRU	claim-jumper
ACEIJMNOQTU	Jacqueminot
ACEIKLLPRTT	lick-platter
ACEIKLLPSTY	skeptically
ACEIKLORTTW	lattice-work
ACEIKLPPRRY	prickly-pear
ACEIKMRSTTT	smart-ticket
ACEILLLMNOR	lamellicorn
ACEILLLMOPY	polemically
ACEILLLNORT	citronellal
ACEILLLNRUU	unicellular
ACEILLLPSTY	sylleptical
ACEILLMMSTY	symmetallic
ACEILLMNNOT	non-metallic
ACEILLMNORW	Cromwellian
ACEILLMNOST	Callistemon
ACEILLMNRUY	numerically
ACEILLMNSUY	masculinely
ACEILLMORSY	lacrimosely
ACEILLMRRUY	mercurially
ACEILLNNOTY	octennially
ACEILLNOOPR	precolonial
ACEILLNOPTU	cupellation
ACEILLNOSTY	sectionally
ACEILLNOTTY	tonetically
ACEILLNRSTY	crystalline
ACEILLOPPRT	proleptical
ACEILLOPPSY	episcopally
ACEILLOQUVY	equivocally
ACEILLORSUV	varicellous
ACEILLORTVY	vectorially
ACEILLRRTUY	reticularly
ACEILLRSSTY	crystallise
ACEILLRSTTY	crystallite
ACEILLRSTYZ	crystallize
ACEILLRTUVY	lucratively
ACEILLSSTUV	victualless

ACEILMMNOSU	communalise
ACEILMMNOTY	metonymical
ACEILMMNOUZ	communalize
ACEILMMORTT	recommittal
ACEILMMRSTY	symmetrical
ACEILMNNORT	conterminal
ACEILMNNSUU	unmasculine
ACEILMNOOPS	scopolamine
ACEILMNOOPW	policewoman
ACEILMNOTTU	monticulate
ACEILMNRTTU	curtailment
ACEILMNRTUU	retinaculum
ACEILMNSSSU	musicalness
ACEILMORRTY	calorimetry
ACEILMRRTUU	mariculture
ACEILNNNOSS	nonsensical
ACEILNNNOTT	continental
ACEILNNOOPT	Neoplatonic
ACEILNNRTUY	uncertainly
ACEILNNSSTY	incessantly
ACEILNOOPRR	incorporeal
ACEILNOOPRT	Neotropical
	percolation
ACEILNOORRT	correlation
ACEILNOORSU	arenicolous
ACEILNOORTU	unicolorate
ACEILNOOSTY	loan-society
ACEILNOPSTU	speculation
ACEILNOPSTX	xenoplastic
ACEILNOPTUX	exculpation
ACEILNOQUUV	unequivocal
ACEILNORRTU	interocular
ACEILNORSTT	intercostal
ACEILNORTTU	reluctation
ACEILNORTUV	countervail
	involucrate
ACEILNOSSST	stoicalness
ACEILNOSTUY	tenaciously
ACEILNPSSTY	typicalness
ACEILNRRRTU	intercrural
ACEILNRRTUV	ventricular
ACEILOOOPRT	aeolotropic
ACEILOOPPRS	polariscope
ACEILOOSSST	osteoclasis
ACEILOPRRTT	protractile
ACEILOPRTXY	explicatory
ACEILORSUVY	veraciously
ACEILORTVYY	viceroyalty
ACEILPPRTUY	picture-play
ACEILPRSTTU	curtail-step
ACEILPRSTTY	spectrality
ACEILPRSTUX	speculatrix
ACEILPSSTTU	speculatist
ACEILQRTUUU	aquiculture
ACEILRRTTUU	turriculate
ACEIMMOOSSU	mimosaceous
ACEIMMORRTU	crematorium
ACEIMMOTTUV	commutative
ACEIMMPRSSU	supremacism
ACEIMNNNOTT	containment
ACEIMNNOORY	oneiromancy
ACEIMNOOPRS	rose-campion
ACEIMNOORTX	axonometric
ACEIMNORRTU	mercuration
ACEIMNORRTY	craniometry
ACEIMOPRRTY	cryptomeria
	imprecatory
ACEIMOPTTUV	computative
ACEIMORTTTU	tautometric
ACEIMPRSSTU	supremacist
ACEIMSSSTTY	systematics
ACEINNNNSSU	uncanniness
ACEINNOORTT	contorniate
ACEINNOOTTV	connotative
ACEINNORSTT	transection
ACEINNORTUY	enunciatory
ACEINNOSTTY	encystation
ACEINNPRSTU	Pentacrinus
ACEINNPTUUV	nuncupative
ACEINNRRTUW	currant-wine
ACEINNRTTUY	uncertainty
ACEINOOOPRT	co-operation
ACEINOOPRRT	incorporate
	procreation
ACEINOOPRTU	aponeurotic
ACEINOORRTT	retroaction
ACEINOPPRTY	cappernoity
ACEINOPRSSS	prosaicness
ACEINOPRSTU	precautions
ACEINORRTTU	centuriator
ACEINORRTTY	contrariety
ACEINORSTTV	contrastive
ACEINORSUUV	unveracious
ACEINPPRSSS	scrappiness
ACEINPTTUUV	punctuative
ACEINRRTUUV	incurvature
ACEINRSSSSU	narcissuses
ACEINRSSTTU	resuscitant
ACEINRSSTTV	transvestic
ACEIOOPRRTV	corporative
ACEIOOPRTVV	provocative
ACEIOOQRTUV	equivocator
ACEIOPRRSTT	tetrasporic
	triceratops
ACEIOPRRSTY	caryopteris
ACEIOPRRTTV	protractive
ACEIOPRSTUU	precautious
ACEIOPRSTXY	expiscatory
ACEKLLRSSTY	tracklessly
ACEKMNORRTU	countermark
ACELLLMORUY	molecularly
ACELLMMNOSY	commensally
ACELLMNOPSU	nucleoplasm
ACELLMORSYY	lacrymosely
ACELLMPRTTU	trumpet-call
ACELLMPSSSU	mussel-scalp
ACELLNORSUY	larcenously
ACELLNOSSSU	callousness
ACELLNRTTUY	reluctantly
ACELLOOPRRY	corporeally
ACELMNNOOPT	componental
ACELMNNOORT	nomenclator
ACELMNNOORU	mononuclear
ACELMNNOOVY	monovalency

ACELMNNOPTT	contemplant
ACELMNOOOTY	Monocotylae
ACELMPSSSUU	mussel-scaup
ACELMRSTUUU	musculature
ACELNNOOPVX	plano-convex
ACELNNRSTTU	translucent
ACELNNRTTUU	unreluctant
ACELNORSUUV	cavernulous
ACELNORSUVY	cavernously
ACELNOSSTTU	sansculotte
ACELNPPRTUU	prepunctual
ACELOOPPRSS	pop-lacrosse
ACELOOPRRTT	protectoral
ACELOOPRRTY	corporately
ACELOORRSUU	coelurosaur
ACELOORRTUW	watercolour
ACELOPRSTUY	speculatory
ACELOPRTUXY	exculpatory
ACELORSSTUY	locust-years
ACEMMNOORTT	commentator
ACEMMNOPRTT	compartment
ACEMNOOPRST	compensator
ACEMORSSTTU	scoutmaster
ACENNOORRTT	contra-tenor
ACENNOPRSTU	span-counter
ACENNPRTTYY	Nancy-pretty
ACENOOPRRTY	porte-crayon
ACENOORRSTV	conservator
ACENOPPRSTU	supportance
ACENOPRRSTU	Procrustean
ACENOPRRTTU	counterpart
ACENOPRSTTU	constuprate
ACENORSSSUU	raucousness
ACENORSTTUY	country-seat
ACENOSSSUUV	vacuousness
ACEOOPPRRSS	carpospores
ACEOOPRRTUV	provocateur
ACEOOPRSSTU	stauroscope
ACEOPRRSSTT	sportcaster
ACEORSSSSSY	syssarcoses
ACFFGIIKNRT	trafficking
ACFFGINOSTU	suffocating
ACFFHILLNOW	fallow-finch
ACFFIIILMOS	officialism
ACFFIIILOTY	officiality
ACFFINOOSTU	suffocation
ACFGHIIKNPS	fish-packing
ACFGHINOSUV	vouchsafing
ACFGIIINNST	significant
ACFGIIINSST	satisficing
ACFGIILNSSY	classifying
ACFGIINNSTY	sanctifying
ACFGILNTTUU	fluctuating
ACFGINRSSTU	surfcasting
ACFGLLOOOTY	olfactology
ACFHIILNOOR	honorifical
ACFHIMORRST	ostrich-farm
ACFHIOPRSTY	factory-ship
ACFHLMOSSTU	stomachfuls
ACFIIILLMRY	mirifically
ACFIIILMSST	facsimilist
ACFIIINNOTU	unification
ACFIIINORTV	vinificator
ACFIILMNORU	californium
ACFIILMORST	formalistic
ACFIILMSSSY	misclassify
ACFIILNOPST	pontificals
ACFIIMMORRU	formicarium
ACFIIMNOORT	formication
ACFIIMNORST	informatics
ACFIINNOORT	fornication
ACFIINOOPRT	forcipation
ACFIIOPRRTU	purificator
ACFILLMOORR	coralliform
ACFILLOOPTT	toploftical
ACFILLOSTUU	lactifluous
ACFILMNNOTU	malfunction
ACFILMOORSS	macrofossil
ACFILMOPRRS	scalpriform
ACFILMORSUV	vasculiform
ACFILNOTTUU	fluctuation
ACFILORSTUY	fractiously
ACFIMNOORRT	confirmator
ACFINNOOTTU	confutation
ACFINNORTUY	functionary
ACFINORTTUU	fructuation
ACFNNNOOOPR	cannon-proof
ACGGHIILNTT	tight-lacing
ACGGHILOOPR	graphologic
	logographic
ACGGIIKKLNO	goalkicking
ACGGIJNNOTU	conjugating
ACGGIKNOSTZ	gazing-stock
ACGHHIILLMN	Chillingham
ACGHHILOOPR	holographic
ACGHHINOPRY	ichnography
ACGHHIOPPTY	phytophagic
ACGHHIOPRRY	chirography
ACGHHMNORSU	ramgunshoch
ACGHHNOOPRR	chronograph
ACGHHNOOPYY	onychophagy
ACGHHOOPRRY	chorography
ACGHHOPPRSY	psychograph
ACGHHOSTTTU	thoughtcast
ACGHIIKNNPT	thinking-cap
ACGHIILLNOP	△anglophilic
ACGHIILLRTV	gillravitch
ACGHIILMORT	algorithmic
	logarithmic
ACGHIILNORT	granolithic
ACGHIILRRTY	charity-girl
ACGHIINPRTY	pharyngitic
ACGHIIPRSST	sphragistic
ACGHIKMOPRY	kymographic
ACGHILLMOOO	homological
ACGHILLOOOR	horological
ACGHILMOOPR	lagomorphic
ACGHILMOORT	cologarithm
ACGHILMOOST	logomachist
ACGHILNNOOP	△anglophonic
ACGHILNNSTY	snatchingly
ACGHILNOOTU	touch-in-goal
ACGHILNRSTT	latch-string
ACGHILNRSTU	nautch-girls

ACGHILOPPRY	polygraphic
ACGHILOPRXY	xylographic
ACGHIMNOOPR	gramophonic
	monographic
	nomographic
ACGHIMOOPRT	tomographic
ACGHIMOPRRY	micrography
ACGHIMOPSTY	mycophagist
	phagocytism
ACGHIMORRST	Christogram
ACGHINOOPRS	nosographic
ACGHINOOPRY	iconography
ACGHINOPRRY	granophyric
ACGHINOPRYZ	zincography
ACGHINPRSTW	watchspring
ACGHIOOPPRT	topographic
ACGHIOPPRTY	pictography
	typographic
ACGHIOPRSTY	hypogastric
ACGHIRSTTTU	straight-cut
ACGHMOOPRSY	cosmography
ACGHNOOOPRR	coronograph
ACGHOPPRRTY	cryptograph
ACGIIILNOST	logistician
ACGIIILNPST	salpingitic
ACGIIINNTTT	nictitating
ACGIIKLLPRY	pilgarlicky
ACGIIKLMNPS	lip-smacking
ACGIILLLLOY	illogically
ACGIILLNOOS	Sinological
ACGIILLNOOT	colligation
ACGIILLNOST	oscillating
ACGIILLNTUV	victualling
ACGIILLOORV	virological
ACGIILMNNOP	complaining
ACGIILNNOOT	cognitional
ACGIILOPRTT	graptolitic
ACGIIMNOSST	agnosticism
ACGIIMRSTTU	Targumistic
ACGIINNNOST	incognisant
ACGIINNNOTZ	incognizant
ACGIINNOSTW	wainscoting
ACGIJJKMNPU	jumping-jack
ACGIJLNOTUY	conjugality
ACGIJNNOOTU	conjugation
ACGIKKNNORT	knock-rating
ACGIKKNOSTT	stocktaking
ACGILLMNOOO	monological
	nomological
ACGILLMOOOP	pomological
ACGILLMOORS	oscillogram
ACGILLMOOTY	climatology
ACGILLMOOYZ	zymological
ACGILLNOOOS	nosological
ACGILLNOOOT	ontological
ACGILLNOSTY	gnostically
ACGILLNRRYY	rallying-cry
ACGILLNRSWY	scrawlingly
ACGILLOOOPS	posological
ACGILLOOOPT	topological
ACGILLOOPTY	typological
ACGILLOPSUY	callipygous
ACGILMOOOST	somatologic
ACGILNORSUY	carousingly
ACGIMNNOORY	craniognomy
ACGIMNOOPRU	carpogonium
ACGIMNOORST	gastronomic
ACGINNOPSTW	townscaping
ACGINNORRSY	carryings-on
ACGINOORRTU	corrugation
ACGINOORSTY	cosignatory
ACGINOOSTUV	noctivagous
ACGIORSSTTY	gyrostatics
ACGLLNOOOVY	volcanology
ACGLLNOOUVY	vulcanology
ACGMOOPRRTU	compurgator
ACGMOOPRSSY	gyrocompass
ACHHIILLPTY	ithyphallic
ACHHIILMOPT	philomathic
ACHHILLMOOT	homothallic
ACHHILLOOOT	thio-alcohol
ACHHILOPRSS	scholarship
ACHHINOORTX	Xanthochroi
ACHHINSSTUZ	schizanthus
ACHHIOPSTYZ	Schizophyta
ACHHIORSTUY	ichthyosaur
ACHHNOOOPRY	Onychophora
ACHHNOOSTTU	autochthons
ACHHNOOTTUY	autochthony
ACHHOPPSTYY	psychopathy
ACHIIIMMRST	Mithraicism
ACHIIIMNPSS	hispanicism
ACHIIIPPRST	hippiatrics
ACHIIJKNRSW	jinrickshaw
ACHIILLMSWY	whimsically
ACHIILMOSTT	Thomistical
ACHIILMPSSY	physicalism
ACHIILNOPST	canophilist
ACHIILNRSTY	Christianly
ACHIILOOPPR	coprophilia
ACHIILOOPPS	scopophilia
ACHIILOOPST	Scotophilia
ACHIILOPRSV	corivalship
ACHIILOPSST	sophistical
ACHIILPSSTY	physicalist
ACHIILPSTYY	physicality
ACHIIMNORST	harmonistic
ACHIIMOPPRT	amphiprotic
ACHIINNRSTU	unchristian
ACHIINOORST	chorisation
ACHIINOORTZ	chorization
	Zonotrichia
ACHILLORSST	choirstalls
ACHILMOOPST	homoplastic
ACHILMORRYZ	mycorrhizal
ACHILNOOOPS	piano-school
ACHILNOORRT	chlorinator
ACHILNPSTTW	switch-plant
ACHILOOPTYZ	zoophytical
ACHILOPPSTY	hypoplastic
ACHILOSSTTW	waistcloths
ACHIMMNOOSU	monochasium
ACHIMNNNOOR	non-harmonic
ACHIMNOORST	Trichomonas

ACHIMNOPTYY amphictyony
ACHIMNPPSSY panpsychism
ACHIMOOPRSY hypocorisma
ACHIMOOPRTU automorphic
ACHIMOOPRTY amyotrophic
ACHIMOOSSST Schistosoma
ACHIMOPPPSU hippocampus
ACHIMOPRSSY symposiarch
ACHIMOPSSTY scyphistoma
ACHIMORRSTY chrismatory
ACHIMRSSSTY Christmassy
ACHINOOPRTZ zoanthropic
ACHINOOPSTT photonastic
ACHINOOPTTU tautophonic
ACHINPPSSTY panpsychist
ACHIOOPPRST apostrophic
ACHIOOPPRTT haptotropic
protopathic
ACHIOOPRTTU autotrophic
ACHIOORSTTT orthostatic
ACHIOPPRSTY saprophytic
ACHIOPRRSTU curatorship
ACHKLMNOOST klootchmans
ACHLLNORSUY unscholarly
ACHLLOOPRST chloroplast
ACHLMMOOORS chromosomal
ACHLMNOORTU motor-launch
ACHLMOOPRST chromoplast
ACHLNOPRTYY lycanthropy
ACHMMNOOORT monochromat
ACHMNOOPSUY cymophanous
ACHMOOORTTY thoracotomy
ACHNNOSTTUY nyctanthous
ACHNOPRSTYY sycophantry
ACHOOPRRSTY arthroscopy
ACIIIILMNTY inimicality
ACIIILLMOPT impolitical
ACIIILLMPTU capillitium
ACIIILLNOTV villication
ACIIILMNOPT implication
ACIIILMNRST criminalist
ACIIILMNRTY criminality
ACIIILMOPST apoliticism
ACIIILNNNOT inclination
ACIIILNNRST intrinsical
ACIIILNPSTU Paulinistic
ACIIILRSTTU ritualistic
ACIIIMNNORT crimination
ACIIIMNNOSS Socinianism
ACIIIMOSSVV vivacissimo
ACIIINNOTTT nictitation
ACIIINOQSTU acquisition
ACIIINPRSST Priscianist
ACIIIOSSTTU ascititious
ACIILLLOPTY politically
ACIILLMNOOS colonialism
ACIILLMNOOT collimation
ACIILLMNPUY municipally
ACIILLMOSUY maliciously
ACIILLMOTTY mitotically
ACIILLNNSTT scintillant
ACIILLNOOST colonialist
oscillation
ACIILLNOPTU unpolitical
ACIILLNORST carillonist
ACIILLNOVVY convivially
ACIILLNPPRY principally
ACIILLOPRTY pictorially
ACIILLPRSTU pluralistic
ACIILLQUYZZ quizzically
ACIILMNNOPT incompliant
ACIILMNNOTU culmination
ACIILMNOOPT compilation
ACIILMNOPST Platonicism
ACIILMNORTU latrocinium
ACIILMNOSSU unsocialism
ACIILMNOSUU unmalicious
ACIILMNSSTU masculinist
ACIILMNSTUY masculinity
ACIILNNOOTU inoculation
ACIILNNOPTU inculpation
ACIILNNORSY synclinoria
ACIILNNORTY inclinatory
ACIILNNSTTU instinctual
ACIILNOSTUY unsociality
ACIILNOTTUV cultivation
ACIILOOPSST isapostolic
ACIILOPRRST scriptorial
ACIILORSSST scissortail
ACIILORSTTU staurolitic
ACIILORSUVY vicariously
ACIILOSUVVY vivaciously
ACIILPPSTUV supplicavit
ACIIMMMNOST mammonistic
ACIIMMNNOOT commination
ACIIMMNORST romanticism
ACIIMMNOSST monasticism
ACIIMMNSSTU numismatics
ACIIMMOOPRR comprimario
ACIIMNNOSTT Montanistic
ACIIMNOORSU acrimonious
ACIIMNORRTY criminatory
ACIIMNORSTT romanticist
ACIINNORTUV incurvation
ACIINOOPRST anisotropic
ACIINOOSSST iconostasis
ACIINOOSTTT tostication
ACIINOPRTTU unpatriotic
ACIINORSTTU rustication
ACIINOSSTTU suscitation
ACIINRTTTUY taciturnity
ACIIOPSSSTT psittacosis
ACIIORRSTUU urticarious
ACIIRSSSTUU saussuritic
ACIJNNOORTU conjuration
ACIKOOPRRTY prokaryotic
ACILLMNOPTY compliantly
ACILLMNSUUY unmusically
ACILLMOOSTY osmotically
ACILLMOPSTY plasmolytic
ACILLMOTYYZ zymotically
ACILLNNOOOP apollonicon
ACILLNNOTUY continually

ACILLNOOPRR	incorporall
ACILLOORSTY	oscillatory
ACILMMMNOSU	communalism
ACILMMNOOOT	commotional
ACILMMNOOTY	commonality
ACILMMNOSTU	communalist
ACILMMORSSU	commissural
ACILMMRSSUU	simulacrums
ACILMNNOPTU	uncompliant
ACILMNNOSYY	synonymical
ACILMNOOPTY	toponymical
ACILMNORTUY	columnarity
ACILMNOSTUU	musculation
ACILMOOPRTY	compilatory
ACILMOOPSTX	toxoplasmic
ACILMORSTUY	customarily
ACILMRSTUUY	muscularity
ACILNNOOOST	consolation
ACILNOOORTU	colouration
ACILNOOPSTU	unapostolic
ACILNOORRST	conirostral
ACILNOORSTX	consolatrix
ACILNOORTUY	inoculatory
	locutionary
ACILNOPRTUY	inculpatory
ACILNORSSTU	ultrasonics
ACILNPSTTUU	punctualist
ACILNPTTUUY	punctuality
ACILOOPRRTY	corporality
ACILOORSTUY	atrociously
ACILOORSUVY	voraciously
ACILOPRSTUY	crapulosity
ACILOSSTUUY	astuciously
ACIMMNOORTY	comminatory
ACIMMNOOTTU	commutation
ACIMMOPSTTY	symptomatic
ACIMMORSTUU	muscatorium
ACIMNNOOOST	onomasticon
ACIMNNOOPRY	Cypro-Minoan
ACIMNNOSTYY	synonymatic
ACIMNOOOPTT	compotation
ACIMNOOOSTT	somatotonic
ACIMNOOPSSU	poison-sumac
ACIMNOOPTTU	computation
ACIMNOPRTUY	importunacy
ACIMOOPRRST	corporatism
ACINNNNOOST	inconsonant
ACINNNOOOTT	connotation
ACINNNOPTUU	nuncupation
ACINNOOPRTT	contraption
ACINNOOPSTY	syncopation
ACINNOORTTU	continuator
ACINNOPTTUU	punctuation
ACINNORSSST	trans-sonics
ACINOOOPRRT	corporation
ACINOOOPRTV	provocation
ACINOOPRRST	conspirator
ACINOOPRRTT	protraction
ACINOOPRRTU	procuration
ACINOORRSTU	contrarious
ACINOORRSUV	carnivorous
ACINOPRSTUU	curnaptious
ACIOOPRRSTT	corporatist
ACIORSSSSSY	syssarcosis
ACKOOPRRRSW	rock-sparrow
ACLLMOORSUY	clamorously
ACLLMOSTUUU	altocumulus
ACLLNNORTUY	nocturnally
ACLLOORSUUY	oraculously
ACLLOPRSTYY	polycrystal
ACLMNOORSTY	monocrystal
ACLNNNOOSTY	consonantly
ACLNOOORSTY	consolatory
ACLNOOPRRSU	proconsular
ACLNOORRSUY	rancorously
ACLOOPPRSUY	polycarpous
ACLOOPRSUXY	xylocarpous
ACLOORRSTUW	straw-colour
ACMMNOORSTU	consummator
ACMNOOOPRSU	monocarpous
ACMOOOPRTTY	compotatory
ACMOOOSSTTU	scotomatous
ACNNOPRTUUY	nuncupatory
ACNOOPRSSUU	Uranoscopus
ACOOOPRRTVY	provocatory
ACOOPRRRTUY	procuratory
ADDDDEEGHIY	giddy-headed
ADDDDEEHMUY	muddy-headed
ADDDEEHIILP	Didelphidae
ADDDEEHNNRU	underhanded
ADDDEEHNORU	round-headed
ADDDEEIMMTU	medium-dated
ADDDEEIMNST	middenstead
ADDDEELNOSS	saddle-nosed
ADDDEENRSSU	unaddressed
ADDDEFGORRT	draft-dodger
ADDDEGGINRY	dandy-rigged
ADDDEGGLOPY	doggy-paddle
ADDDERSSTTU	star-studded
ADDDHILMOOO	old-maidhood
ADDDIMNOSTU	diamond-dust
ADDEEEEHKLS	sleek-headed
ADDEEEEHLLV	level-headed
ADDEEEEHLST	steel-headed
ADDEEEFILSU	defeudalise
ADDEEEFILUZ	defeudalize
ADDEEEGHPSW	wedge-shaped
ADDEEEGILTW	wedge-tailed
ADDEEEGLNTU	undelegated
ADDEEEHHITW	white-headed
ADDEEEHHNRT	three-handed
ADDEEEHIKNS	hide-and-seek
ADDEEEHLLPW	paddle-wheel
ADDEEEHLLSW	swell-headed
ADDEEEHLMTY	metaldehyde
ADDEEEHMPTY	empty-headed
ADDEEEIRTWW	wide-watered
ADDEEELLPST	pedestalled
ADDEEEOPRSS	desperadoes
ADDEEFGHINN	hand-feeding
ADDEEFGHIRT	dead-freight
ADDEEFMNRTU	defraudment
ADDEEFNORRW	forwandered
ADDEEGHHILT	light-headed

ADDEEGHILPY pigheadedly
ADDEEGHNORW wrong-headed
ADDEEGIISTT sedigitated
ADDEEGIKMNR redding-kame
ADDEEGIKNRS reading-desk
ADDEEGILMNR large-minded
ADDEEGILRST girdlestead
ADDEEGINPRW deep-drawing
ADDEEGINRRW reed-drawing
ADDEEGJMNTU adjudgement
ADDEEGNRSSU guardedness
ADDEEHHINTW white-handed
ADDEEHHNRTU thunderhead
ADDEEHIILNP Delphinidae
ADDEEHIKNRT kind-hearted
ADDEEHILMRT middle-earth
ADDEEHISTTU death-duties
ADDEEHLNNSU unhandseled
ADDEEHLNORV overhandled
ADDEEHMNPTY empty-handed
ADDEEHNORTW down-hearted
ADDEEHPPPUY puppy-headed
ADDEEHPRRSS hard-pressed
ADDEEIILRST Estrildidae
ADDEEILLSVW well-advised
ADDEEILRRVY dare-devilry
ADDEEIMNORY ready-monied
ADDEEIMNTTU unmeditated
ADDEEIMRSTU desideratum
ADDEEINOPRT depredation
ADDEEINSSSV advisedness
ADDEEIRTTWY ready-witted
ADDEELLRSSY dreadlessly
ADDEELNORUV round-leaved
ADDEEMNNNRU undermanned
ADDEEMNPRRU underdamper
ADDEEMNRSTU undermasted
ADDEENORTWW watered-down
ADDEENPRSUU unpersuaded
ADDEENRSTTU understated
ADDEEOPRRTY depredatory
ADDEFFHLNOY offhandedly
ADDEFHINSSS faddishness
ADDEFLNOORT front-loaded
ADDEGGHORTU goddaughter
ADDEGGIIIRT digitigrade
ADDEGHHILNT light-handed
ADDEGHHINRT right-handed
ADDEGHILRST saddleg-irth
ADDEGHNORTU dreadnought
ADDEGIIMNNR mind-reading
ADDEGILMNNY maddeningly
ADDEGIMNNNU undemanding
ADDEGIMNNOR road-mending
ADDEGINNOSU undiagnosed
ADDEGINNRST △angst-ridden
ADDEGJMNTUY judgment-day
ADDEGLNRUUY unguardedly
ADDEGNOORTU good-natured
ADDEHHIOPRY Hydrophidae
ADDEHHMORTU hardmouthed
ADDEHHNNORY horny-handed
ADDEHHNOOPR rhododaphne
ADDEHHNORST short-handed
ADDEHIILMOT thalidomide
ADDEHILNNRS hinderlands
ADDEHILOPSU diadelphous
ADDEHINORTY dehydration
ADDEHLORSTT stadtholder
ADDEHMORSUY hydromedusa
ADDEHNRRTTU thunder-dart
ADDEHOPRSSW sword-shaped
ADDEIIINTUV individuate
ADDEIINOOTX deoxidation
ADDEIINORST disordinate
ADDEIKMNRRR dram-drinker
ADDEILLMMNS small-minded
ADDEILMORSU modularised
ADDEILMORUZ modularized
ADDEILNSTUY dual-density
ADDEILNSUVY unadvisedly
ADDEIMNOORS rose-diamond
ADDEIOOPPSU pseudopodia
ADDELMNOTUU unmodulated
ADDELMOORTU demodulator
ADDELNNRTUY redundantly
ADDELNNTUUY undauntedly
ADDELNORRTY dendrolatry
ADDELOOOPRW leopard-wood
ADDEMNOOORT rodomontade
ADDEMNOOPSU pseudomonad
ADDENOORSSW sanderswood
ADDEOOPSTTT toad-spotted
ADDGHILLNNO landholding
ADDGHILNOOR roadholding
ADDGHNORTUW down-draught
ADDGIMNNOPW damping-down
ADDHIILNOOV invalidhood
ADDIIIIMNOT dimidiation
ADDIIIOSTTU addititious
ADDIINORSTU suraddition
ADDIJNOSUWW △judas-window
ADDILLMNORS landlordism
ADDLLOORRSW sword-dollar
ADEEEEFGHRT feather-edge
ADEEEEFHLRT three-leafed
ADEEEEFHRRT free-hearted
ADEEEEFPPRR paper-feeder
ADEEEEGGRST desegregate
ADEEEEHIMPR Ephemeridae
ADEEEEHLRTV three-leaved
ADEEEFHNRTU unfeathered
ADEEEFHNRTW weather-fend
ADEEEFILNRT deferential
ADEEEFINSTV defensative
ADEEEFNRRRY referendary
ADEEEFNRSTT fenestrated
ADEEEGGILNW eagle-winged
ADEEEGHLMPT dephlegmate
ADEEEGILMNR legerdemain
ADEEEGIMNRR gendarmerie
ADEEEGIMNST demagnetise
ADEEEGIMNTZ demagnetize
ADEEEGIMORT Geometridae

ADEEEGINNRT	tragedienne
	tragédienne
ADEEEGKLNNR	Kendal-green
ADEEEGMNNRT	derangement
ADEEEGMNRST	désagrément
ADEEEGNOTXY	deoxygenate
ADEEEHIIPRS	Hesperiidae
ADEEEHIMPSS	de-emphasise
ADEEEHIMPSZ	de-emphasize
ADEEEHIRSTW	wise-hearted
ADEEEHLLORS	leaseholder
ADEEEHLORRS	horse-dealer
ADEEEHMORST	homesteader
ADEEEHMRSTT	three-masted
ADEEEHNNNOR	enneahedron
ADEEEHNOPRT	open-hearted
ADEEEHNRRSU	unrehearsed
ADEEEHNRTUW	unweathered
ADEEEHPRRTT	three-parted
ADEEEHPRSST	spreadsheet
ADEEEHRRTTU	true-hearted
ADEEEIILNTV	delineative
ADEEEIIMMOR	aide-mémoire
ADEEEIIMNRV	Vendémiaire
ADEEEIINSSV	vine-disease
ADEEEILLMNS	linseed-meal
ADEEEILMNTY	demyelinate
ADEEEILNRRT	interdealer
ADEEEILSSUX	desexualise
ADEEEILSUXZ	desexualize
ADEEEIMNRTT	determinate
ADEEEIMNSST	mediateness
ADEEEIMPPRR	pipe-dreamer
ADEEEIMPRTT	premeditate
ADEEEIORRTT	deteriorate
ADEEEIPPRSU	depauperise
ADEEEIPPRUZ	depauperize
ADEEEIPRRST	pieds-à-terre
ADEEEIRRSTV	readvertise
ADEEEKKLNWY	weak-kneedly
ADEEEKLLLRW	lake-dweller
ADEEEKLRRST	deerstalker
ADEEELLNSWY	Wensleydale
ADEEELLPSTT	steel-plated
ADEEELLSSTT	tessellated
ADEEELMNNOW	needlewoman
ADEEELMNSST	délassement
ADEEELNNRSS	learnedness
ADEEELNRSST	relatedness
ADEEELNRTTU	launderette
ADEEELNSSTX	exaltedness
ADEEELPRSTY	desperately
ADEEEMMNNRT	reamendment
ADEEEMNNTTT	attendement
ADEEEMNPRTT	département
ADEEEMNPRTV	depravement
ADEEEMNSTTT	statemented
ADEEEMOSTWW	meadowsweet
ADEEENOPRTU	deuteranope
ADEEENRSSSV	adverseness
ADEEEPRSSSU	supersedeas
ADEEFFIINRT	differentia
ADEEFGGLOPR	leap-frogged
ADEEFGILNOR	freeloading
ADEEFGINNRR	rangefinder
ADEEFGINNRV	never-fading
ADEEFGINORR	forereading
ADEEFGIRTVY	gravity-feed
ADEEFGKLNPR	frank-pledge
ADEEFHLLRTU	full-hearted
ADEEFHORSTT	soft-hearted
ADEEFIIINNT	definientia
ADEEFILLNOX	deflexional
ADEEFILNRST	self-trained
ADEEFILNSUU	unfeudalise
ADEEFILNUUZ	unfeudalize
ADEEFILPRSS	self-despair
ADEEFIMRSTU	misfeatured
ADEEFINNRRT	after-dinner
ADEEFINNSST	defiantness
ADEEFINORSZ	fazendeiros
ADEEFINRRTW	water-finder
ADEEFIOPSST	safe-deposit
ADEEFKLOOPR	poodle-faker
ADEEFLLNPST	self-planted
ADEEFLLORSV	severalfold
ADEEFLMSSSU	self-assumed
ADEEFLOPPRR	paper-folder
ADEEFLRRSSX	flax-dresser
ADEEFLRSSSU	self-assured
ADEEFMOORRS	reformadoes
ADEEFNORSSV	favoredness
ADEEFNRRRST	transferred
ADEEFOOPRRR	proofreader
ADEEFPRSTTU	superfatted
ADEEGGGIRRV	grave-digger
ADEEGGHLORS	loggerheads
ADEEGGHNSSS	shaggedness
ADEEGGINUWZ	gauze-winged
ADEEGGLORTW	waterlogged
ADEEGGMORUY	demagoguery
ADEEGGOPRUY	pedagoguery
ADEEGHHHIRT	high-hearted
ADEEGHIKSTW	weak-sighted
ADEEGHINPRS	grandeeship
ADEEGHINRST	near-sighted
ADEEGHIRRST	sight-reader
ADEEGHMOPRR	demographer
ADEEGHNNPRW	grand-nephew
ADEEGHNOPRS	hedge-parson
ADEEGHNORSU	garden-house
ADEEGHNORTY	hydrogenate
ADEEGHNRRUY	yeard-hunger
ADEEGIINNST	indesignate
ADEEGIINSTV	designative
ADEEGILNNRY	endearingly
ADEEGILNNST	disentangle
ADEEGILNTTU	deglutinate
ADEEGIMORRT	gradiometer
ADEEGINNNSU	ensanguined
ADEEGINNSUX	exsanguined
ADEEGJLMNTU	judgemental
ADEEGLLNOSU	eglandulose
ADEEGLNRTUU	unregulated

ADEEGMMOPRR	deprogramme
ADEEGMNNRTU	ungarmented
ADEEGMNNTUU	unaugmented
ADEEGMNRRRY	gerrymander
ADEEGMORTUY	deuterogamy
ADEEHHIIRTW	white-haired
ADEEHHIMSST	missheathed
ADEEHHLORRS	shareholder
ADEEHHMMNOO	home-and-home
ADEEHHNORSX	hexahedrons
ADEEHIIKMNT	nikethamide
ADEEHIILTTW	white-tailed
ADEEHIIOPRS	isodiaphere
ADEEHIKNPPS	snake-hipped
ADEEHILLNOT	endothelial
ADEEHILNOPT	elephantoid
ADEEHILNORT	lion-hearted
ADEEHILNPRR	philanderer
ADEEHILNSST	deathliness
ADEEHINORRT	iron-hearted
ADEEHINRSST	threadiness
ADEEHINSTUX	inexhausted
ADEEHIORTTV	dehortative
ADEEHIRRRSS	hairdresser
ADEEHKMNORT	mother-naked
ADEEHKORSTT	death-stroke
ADEEHLLORSV	slaveholder
ADEEHLMNOTT	mentholated
ADEEHLNOSST	loathedness
ADEEHLNPRTU	thunder-peal
ADEEHMNOPTU	pneumathode
ADEEHNNOPRT	pentahedron
ADEEHNNPRSU	undershapen
	unsharpened
ADEEHNNRSSU	unharnessed
ADEEHNOOSWW	shawnee-wood
ADEEHNORRTT	tetrahedron
ADEEHNOSSTW	stonewashed
ADEEHNRRSTW	netherwards
ADEEHNRSTUV	unharvested
ADEEHNSTUUX	unexhausted
ADEEIILLMPX	maxillipede
ADEEIILLNRT	interallied
ADEEIILMMSV	medievalism
ADEEIILMMTY	immediately
ADEEIILMNRT	intermedial
ADEEIILMSTV	medievalist
ADEEIILNNOT	delineation
ADEEIILNNST	desinential
ADEEIILNRST	residential
ADEEIILNSST	de-Stalinise
ADEEIILNSTZ	de-Stalinize
ADEEIIMMNPT	impedimenta
ADEEIIMNNPT	pentamidine
ADEEIIMNORT	remediation
ADEEIIMNSST	disseminate
ADEEIIMRSTX	taxidermise
ADEEIIMRTXZ	taxidermize
ADEEIINOPRS	sideropenia
ADEEIINPSTT	stipendiate
ADEEIINRTVY	evidentiary
ADEEIIPRTUV	repudiative
ADEEIIPRTVV	deprivative
ADEEIIRSTVV	derivatives
ADEEIKLMORU	leukodermia
ADEEIKNRRST	dreikanters
ADEEILLMNNR	ill-mannered
ADEEILLNRST	stelleridan
ADEEILLNRTT	trendle-tail
ADEEILMNORT	endometrial
ADEEILMNRST	streamlined
ADEEILMNRTT	detrimental
ADEEILMNRVY	delivery-man
ADEEILMOPST	diplomatese
ADEEILMOSTV	dame's-violet
ADEEILNNPRR	linen-draper
ADEEILNNPTT	pentlandite
ADEEILNNPUX	unexplained
ADEEILNNRTT	interdental
ADEEILNPRSU	under-espial
ADEEILNRSTW	windlestrae
ADEEILNRSTY	disentrayle
	sedentarily
ADEEILNRUWY	unweariedly
ADEEILNRVVY	delivery-van
ADEEILOPPRT	Lepidoptera
ADEEILPQSSU	sesquipedal
ADEEILPRSSU	displeasure
ADEEILRRSTV	evil-starred
ADEEILRRSVV	slave-driver
ADEEILRRTTU	literatured
ADEEIMMNORS	misdemeanor
ADEEIMMNOSU	eudaemonism
ADEEIMMORST	maisterdome
ADEEIMNNPTU	antependium
ADEEIMNNRTT	determinant
	detrainment
ADEEIMNOPPR	Pompeian-red
ADEEIMNOPRT	predominate
ADEEIMNOPSS	empassioned
ADEEIMNOSTU	eudaemonist
ADEEIMNRSTV	steam-driven
ADEEIMNRSTY	sedimentary
ADEEIMOPRRT	madreporite
ADEEIMPRSSU	mispersuade
ADEEIMRTTTY	tetradymite
ADEEINNRSSU	unreadiness
ADEEINNRTTV	inadvertent
ADEEINOPRST	desperation
ADEEINOPTTT	potentiated
ADEEINORTTU	deuteration
ADEEINOSTTT	detestation
ADEEINPRRSU	underpraise
ADEEINQRTUV	verd-antique
ADEEINRSTUV	disaventure
ADEEIPRRTUY	Eurypterida
ADEEJMNRRRY	jerrymander
ADEEKLLMORU	leukodermal
ADEEKLOPRSU	loudspeaker
ADEELLMRSSY	dreamlessly
ADEELLNNRUY	unlearnedly
ADEELLNRTUV	untravelled
ADEELMNOORT	demonolater
ADEELMOORST	osteodermal

ADEELNOOPST	aldopentose
ADEELNPRSTU	unplastered
ADEELNRRUUV	undervaluer
ADEELNRTTVY	advertently
ADEELOPPRRW	pearl-powder
ADEELOPPRTW	plate-powder
ADEELOQSSTU	soldatesque
ADEEMMNORTY	dynamometer
ADEEMMORSTY	maysterdome
ADEEMNNSSTU	untamedness
ADEEMNOPPRR	name-dropper
ADEEMNORSTT	demonstrate
ADEEMNOSTVW	woman-vested
ADEEMNPPSUU	suppedaneum
ADEEMNPTTTU	unattempted
ADEEMNRRRWY	merry-andrew
ADEEMRRSTTU	mustard-tree
ADEENNNORSU	enneandrous
ADEENNNRTTU	undertenant
ADEENNPRTTU	unpatterned
ADEENRRSTUV	untraversed
ADEENRRSUWY	under-sawyer
ADEENRSSSSU	assuredness
ADEENRSSTUV	adventuress
ADEEOOPPRRV	Depo-Provera®
ADEEOPRRRSW	reed-sparrow
ADEERRSSTTW	streetwards
ADEFFILNRTU	fault-finder
ADEFFIORSST	disafforest
ADEFFLLORTU	altoruffled
ADEFGGINRRU	fingerguard
ADEFGIINRTU	ungratified
ADEFGILLNOS	self-loading
ADEFGILMNNS	self-damning
ADEFGITTUUY	fatigue-duty
ADEFGKNOORS	△god-forsaken
ADEFGLLNSSU	gladfulness
ADEFGLLRRUY	regardfully
ADEFHILOORS	foolhardise
ADEFHILOORZ	foolhardize
ADEFHILOPST	felspathoid
ADEFHINNOSU	unfashioned
ADEFHIRUYZZ	fuzzy-haired
ADEFHLMOPTU	flap-mouthed
ADEFHLNOPRU	half-pounder
ADEFHLOOPPR	flapperhood
ADEFIIILNOT	defiliation
ADEFIILLQUY	qualifiedly
ADEFIILNOOT	defoliation
ADEFIILNQUU	unqualified
ADEFIINNOTU	infeudation
ADEFIINSSTU	unsatisfied
ADEFILLORUV	ill-favoured
ADEFILLRSTY	lady-trifles
ADEFILMNOSU	sulfonamide
ADEFILNOORT	defloration
ADEFILNOSUX	sulfadoxine
ADEFILSSTTU	distasteful
ADEFIMNOORT	deformation
ADEFIORRSUV	disfavourer
ADEFLNOORRT	front-loader
ADEFLNORUUV	unflavoured
ADEFLOOPSTY	splay-footed
ADEFMNORRST	transformed
ADEFMNORTTU	unformatted
ADEFNORRSSW	forwardness
	frowardness
ADEFNRRRSTY	dry-transfer
ADEFOORRRVW	overforward
ADEGGHILNRT	right-angled
ADEGGHIOPSU	pedagoguish
ADEGGIINNRW	wide-ranging
ADEGGIINRRV	driving-gear
ADEGGILNNOT	goal-tending
ADEGGILNOSV	long-visaged
ADEGGILNRUU	unguligrade
ADEGGILRSSU	sluggardise
ADEGGILRSUZ	sluggardize
ADEGGIMMOSU	demagoguism
ADEGGIMOPSU	pedagoguism
ADEGGINNRRU	unregarding
ADEGGINOSTY	steady-going
ADEGGMNORST	gangsterdom
ADEGGMNORTU	unmortgaged
ADEGGNNOOPS	egg-and-spoon
ADEGHHINNTU	headhunting
ADEGHHINRRT	right-hander
ADEGHHLNORU	rough-handle
ADEGHIILMNN	mind-healing
ADEGHILLNNS	handselling
ADEGHILNNSW	swing-handle
	swingle-hand
ADEGHIMNRST	hamstringed
ADEGHINNRSU	ungarnished
ADEGHMNNORT	gander-month
ADEGHMNORRT	grandmother
ADEGHMOPRRY	dermography
ADEGHNOOPSU	endophagous
ADEGHNRRUYY	yeard-hungry
ADEGHOOPRRX	doxographer
ADEGHOPPRSU	pseudograph
ADEGHORRTUV	overdraught
ADEGIIIKMNR	Kimeridgian
ADEGIILLMNT	metalliding
ADEGIILMNPS	mispleading
ADEGIILNOTV	dovetailing
ADEGIILNPSS	displeasing
ADEGIILOPRS	prodigalise
ADEGIILOPRZ	prodigalize
ADEGIIMNORT	demigration
ADEGIIMNOSS	misdiagnose
ADEGIIMNRST	mistreading
ADEGIIMNTTU	unmitigated
ADEGIINNORS	inorganised
ADEGIINNORT	denigration
ADEGIINNORZ	inorganized
ADEGIINNOST	designation
ADEGIINNTUV	undeviating
ADEGIINOPRR	Perigordian
ADEGIINORSS	disorganise
ADEGIINORSZ	disorganize
ADEGIINRRWW	wiredrawing
ADEGIINRSTV	advertising
ADEGIINRTTU	ingratitude

ADEGIIPRSTV	tripe-visag'd
ADEGIKMNRSS	dressmaking
ADEGIKNNRTU	undertaking
ADEGIKNRRST	ring-straked
ADEGILLOSSU	gladioluses
ADEGILNNRWY	wanderingly
ADEGILNNSSU	languidness
ADEGILNORSY	grandiosely
ADEGILNOSTW	long-waisted
ADEGILNPRSY	spreadingly
ADEGILNPRVY	depravingly
ADEGILOOPST	paedologist
ADEGILOOPSU	pseudologia
ADEGIMNOORR	reading-room
ADEGIMNORRS	gormandiser
ADEGIMNORRZ	gormandizer
ADEGIMNORSU	gourmandise
ADEGINNNORW	dinner-wagon
ADEGINNNRUW	unwandering
ADEGINNNTTU	unattending
ADEGINNORSU	unorganised
ADEGINNORUZ	unorganized
ADEGINNQRSU	squandering
ADEGINNRRUW	unrewarding
ADEGINORRRV	river-dragon
ADEGINORRTV	over-trading
ADEGINORSTY	designatory
ADEGINOSTTU	degustation
ADEGINPRSST	tap-dressing
ADEGKLMNNOY	monkey-gland
ADEGLMOORTY	dermatology
ADEGLNORSUY	dangerously
ADEGMNNOTUY	many-tongued
ADEGNNOORSU	androgenous
ADEGNNOPUUZ	ungazed-upon
ADEGORSTTUY	degustatory
ADEHHIMOORR	haemorrhoid
ADEHHIOPPST	phosphatide
ADEHHIORRSS	horseradish
ADEHHIRRSTW	hitherwards
ADEHHIRRTTW	thitherward
ADEHHIRRTWW	whitherward
ADEHIIMMPST	midshipmate
ADEHIIMNOPR	diamorphine
ADEHIIMNRTU	antheridium
ADEHIIMPRSU	sphaeridium
ADEHIINNOPT	Diophantine
ADEHIIOOPRU	Ophiuroidea
ADEHIIOPRSS	diaphoresis
ADEHIIOPSVV	vaivodeship
ADEHIIOPSVW	waivodeship
ADEHIIORSTT	historiated
ADEHIIPRSSV	advisership
ADEHIKNORSW	whiskerando
ADEHILLMOSW	mishallowed
ADEHILLNRST	disenthrall
ADEHILMNOOP	Monodelphia
ADEHILNPRYY	hyperlydian
ADEHILORSTY	hysteroidal
ADEHIMMMMOS	Mohammedism
ADEHIMNOPRS	hand-promise
	preadmonish
ADEHIMNPSSS	dampishness
ADEHIMORSTU	diathermous
ADEHIMRRSTT	third-stream
ADEHINNNSSU	unhandiness
ADEHINNRSTU	untarnished
ADEHINNRSUV	unvarnished
ADEHINNRTTW	handwritten
ADEHINOORTT	dehortation
ADEHINOORTZ	antherozoid
ADEHINOPRRY	hyperdorian
ADEHINORRTY	rehydration
ADEHINOSSSW	shadowiness
ADEHINRSTTW	withstander
ADEHIOPPSSY	diapophyses
ADEHIOPRRTY	pyritohedra
ADEHIORRSST	arthrodesis
ADEHIPRSSTW	stewardship
ADEHIPRSTTW	sharp-witted
ADEHISTTTWY	hasty-witted
ADEHJLOOOSU	jealoushood
ADEHLLLMORS	smallholder
ADEHLMOOPRT	leopard-moth
ADEHLNORSTU	southlander
ADEHLORSTYY	hydrolysate
ADEHMNNORSS	horn-madness
ADEHNNOPSTU	open-and-shut
ADEHNOORTTW	down-to-earth
ADEHNOPRSTU	heptandrous
ADEHNORRSTW	sand-thrower
ADEHOOPPRTY	paedotrophy
ADEHOORRTTW	tooth-drawer
ADEHOORRTTY	dehortatory
ADEIIILMSST	dissimilate
ADEIIIMMMST	immediatism
ADEIIINNTTU	uninitiated
ADEIIIOPSTV	diapositive
ADEIIIPSSTV	dissipative
ADEIIISSSTU	assiduities
ADEIILLLOPS	ellipsoidal
ADEIILLNRTT	trindle-tail
ADEIILLNRTU	interludial
ADEIILLORTY	editorially
ADEIILMNNOS	dimensional
ADEIILMNRSU	semi-diurnal
ADEIILMOPST	diplomatise
ADEIILMOPTZ	diplomatize
ADEIILMSSTU	dissimulate
ADEIILNNORT	internodial
ADEIILNNSSV	invalidness
ADEIILNQTUU	unqualitied
ADEIIMMNNOS	demonianism
ADEIIMMNSTU	mediastinum
ADEIIMNOPSS	impassioned
ADEIIMNORSS	readmission
ADEIIMRSTTX	taxidermist
ADEIINNNOTT	indentation
ADEIINNOOPS	Poseidonian
ADEIINNOOPT	opinionated
ADEIINNOORY	oneirodynia
ADEIINNORTT	denitration
ADEIINNOSTT	destination
ADEIINNOTTV	vendidation

ADEIINOOPRT periodontia
ADEIINOPRTT trepidation
ADEIINOPRTU repudiation
ADEIINOPRTV deprivation
ADEIINOPSST Passiontide
ADEIINORRTT traditioner
ADEIINORSTY seditionary
ADEIINORTTX extradition
ADEIINPRSTY stipendiary
ADEIINPSSST inspissated
ADEIINQSTTU equidistant
ADEIINRRSTU interradius
ADEIIOPRSTX ideopraxist
ADEIIPSTTUV disputative
ADEIKLLNSST kiss-and-tell
ADEIKNPPRSS sand-skipper
ADEILLMRRST drill-master
ADEILLNNRSU disannuller
ADEILLNRTTU trundle-tail
ADEILLORSST ill-assorted
ADEILLOSVWW swallow-dive
ADEILLRSTTU illustrated
ADEILMNNORY molendinary
ADEILMNOPTU deplumation
ADEILMNORSU unmoralised
ADEILMNORUZ unmoralized
ADEILMNTTUU unmutilated
ADEILNNTTUY untaintedly
ADEILNOOPRT deploration
periodontal
ADEILNOPPTY pentaploidy
ADEILNOPRSU unpolarised
ADEILNOPRUY pleurodynia
ADEILNOPRUZ unpolarized
ADEILNPRSTU prudentials
ADEILNQSSSU squalidness
ADEILNRSTWW windlestraw
ADEILNSSTUY sustainedly
ADEILOPRRTY predatorily
ADEILOPRTTY tetraploidy
ADEILOPSTTT toad-spittle
ADEIMMNNOPU △pandemonium
ADEIMMNSSTT dismastment
ADEIMNNOORT denominator
ADEIMNNOPRT predominant
ADEIMNNORSU unromanised
ADEIMNNORUZ unromanized
ADEIMNNQRUU quadrennium
ADEIMNOORST moderations
ADEIMNOPSTU despumation
ADEIMNORSTU nematodirus
ADEIMNOTTUV unmotivated
ADEIMNRRSUY nurserymaid
ADEIMNRRTUY rudimentary
ADEIMNRSTTT transmitted
ADEIMNRSTUV adventurism
ADEIMOPRTUY apodyterium
ADEINNOOPRT ponderation
ADEINNOPPTU unappointed
ADEINNOPSSU unpassioned
ADEINNOQRTU quaternion'd
ADEINNQSTUU unquantised
ADEINNQTUUZ unquantized
ADEINNSSSTT distantness
ADEINNSSSTU unstaidness
ADEINNSSTUU unsustained
ADEINOOPRTT deportation
ADEINOPRRTU perduration
ADEINOPRRTW word-painter
ADEINOPRSST dispensator
ADEINPRSTUY superdainty
ADEINQRRTUW quarter-wind
ADEINRSTTUV adventurist
ADEINRSTTUY testudinary
ADEIOPRRTTY trepidatory
ADEIORRSSTT dissertator
ADEJMNNORTU adjournment
ADEJMNORRTY Tom-and-Jerry
ADELLMMORTY troll-my-dame
ADELLNOSUWW unswallowed
ADELLNSSTUY dauntlessly
ADELLOORRSU Euro-dollars
ADELMNOORST tremolandos
ADELMNOORTY demonolatry
ADELMNORRTU ultra-modern
ADELNOPPTUU unpopulated
ADELOOPPRTU depopulator
ADELOPPRSUU dual-purpose
ADELOPRRSWY swordplayer
ADEMMMNORSU memorandums
ADEMMNNOOSS moon-madness
ADEMMNORTYY dynamometry
ADEMNNOSTTU astoundment
ADEMNOOPSSU pseudomonas
ADEMNOORTTY attorneydom
ADEMNOPRSTU pound-master
ADEMORSSTTY storm-stayed
ADENNOPPSTT pendant-post
ADENNOPRRST transponder
ADENNOPRSTU pentandrous
ADENOORTTUU out-and-outer
ADENOPPPRSY Podsnappery
ADENOPRRRTY proterandry
ADENOPRRSTT transported
ADENORRSTTU tetrandrous
ADENORSSSUU arduousness
ADENORSSTUW outwardness
ADENORSTUUV adventurous
ADENPRSSSUU unsurpassed
ADEOOPRSTTU tetrapodous
ADFFHINOSST standoffish
ADFGIIILNPY lapidifying
ADFGIIIMRRU frigidarium
ADFGIILLLNN landfilling
ADFGIINNRSU fund-raising
ADFIIILLNNU nullifidian
ADFIILMNTUU latifundium
ADFILLMSUYY dismayfully
ADFIMNOPRRU panduriform
ADFINNOORRZ rinforzando
ADFINNOOSTU foundations
ADFLMOORSUW world-famous
ADGGGHIILNN hang-gliding
ADGGHHIOORS road-hoggish

ADGGHIILNSW wash-gilding
ADGGHILMOTY God-almighty
ADGGIINNNWW wing-and-wing
ADGGLMOOOTY dogmatology
ADGHHIINRTT hard-hitting
ADGHHILNOPT diphthongal
ADGHHNORTUW handwrought
ADGHHOPRRYY hydrography
ADGHIILNNPS landing-ship
ADGHIINNRTW handwriting
ADGHIKNORRW hardworking
ADGHINNNNRU hand-running
running-hand
ADGHIOPRTTY dittography
ADGHMRRRUYY hydrargyrum
ADGHNOOOPRT odontograph
ADGHNOPRRSU sharp-ground
ADGIIIILOOSS idioglossia
ADGIIINNNOT indignation
ADGIIINOOTT goniatitoid
ADGIIINSTVY visiting-day
ADGIILLMOSY sigmoidally
ADGIILNNNTY indignantly
ADGIILNOTUV divulgation
ADGIILOORST radiologist
ADGIILOOSTU audiologist
ADGIILOPRTY prodigality
ADGIINNPPPR dripping-pan
ADGIINOPTUY audiotyping
ADGIINORRSS disgarrison
ADGIINORSTY grandiosity
ADGILMNNNOR morning-land
ADGILMNOSUW guildswoman
ADGILNNOOPS poison-gland
ADGILNOOSSY glossodynia
ADGIMMNORSU gourmandism
ADGIMNOORRW drawing-room
ADGINNNOPRU unpardoning
ADGINNOSTTU outstanding
ADGINOORRTU ground-to-air
ADGINRSTTYY trysting-day
ADGLNOOOOTY odonatology
ADGNNNOQTUU quandong-nut
ADGNNOORSUY androgynous
ADHHIMRSTYY dysrhythmia
ADHHMNOOTTU hand-to-mouth
ADHHOORRTXY hydrothorax
ADHIIIMOPRU ophidiarium
ADHIIMOPPST hippodamist
ADHIIOPPSSY diapophysis
ADHIIOPRSTU auditorship
ADHIIORRSST diarthrosis
ADHILLOOPRT prothalloid
ADHILLORRRW drill-harrow
ADHILMNOOSW old-womanish
ADHIMOOPPSU amphipodous
hippodamous
ADHINOOOPRT Ornithopoda
ADHINOOORTT orthodontia
ADHINOORRSY dishonorary
ADHIOOORRTT traitorhood
ADHLNORRTWY northwardly
ADHLORSTUWY southwardly
ADHNOOPQRUY quadrophony
ADIIIINORST iridisation
ADIIIINORTZ iridization
ADIIILLMSUV diluvialism
ADIIILLSTUV diluvialist
ADIIILNOQTU liquidation
ADIIIMOSSTT mastoiditis
ADIIINOPSST dissipation
ADIIINORSVY divisionary
ADIIIOPRSTT parotiditis
ADIIILLMORTT midlittoral
ADIILLNOQRU quadrillion
ADIILMOOSSY amyloidosis
ADIILMOPSTT diplomatist
ADIILNORTUY dilutionary
ADIILNRSSTU industrials
ADIIMMNNORY myrmidonian
ADIIMMNOSTU staminodium
ADIIMNNOOST dominations
ADIIMNOOPST △adoptionism
ADIIMNOSTTU dismutation
ADIIMORSTUU auditoriums
ADIINNOORRT Torridonian
ADIINOOPSTT adoptionist
ADIINOPSTTU disputation
ADIIOOPRSUV avoirdupois
ADIIOPSTTUY audiotypist
ADILLMOPSYY sympodially
ADILNNOSSTY dissonantly
ADILORRSTTU stridulator
ADILOSSSUUY assiduously
ADINRSTTTUY transit-duty
ADKLNOOTUWY talk-you-down
ADLNOOPRSUY polyandrous
ADNOOPRRSTU protandrous
ADOOOPPRRSU prosauropod
ADOOOPRSSUU sauropodous
AEEEEFFMRRZ freeze-frame
AEEEEGHLRSS grease-heels
AEEEEGLMSST Telemessage®
AEEEEGLNSUV seven-league
AEEEEHHNSST heathenesse
AEEEEHILRST etherealise
AEEEEHILRTZ etherealize
AEEEEHLRTTT leatherette®
AEEEEHMRSTU rheumateese
AEEEEILMRST time-release
AEEEEJLMSST lese-majesté
AEEEELLMNOS leesome-lane
AEEEELMNRST releasement
AEEEELNPPQU queene-apple
AEEEEMMPRRT permeameter
AEEEEPRRSTV perseverate
AEEEESSTTTT têtes-à-têtes
AEEEFFLOPPT toffee-apple
AEEEFGIKNPS safe-keeping
AEEEFGIRRRT refrigerate
AEEEFHINRRT hereinafter
AEEEFHMPRRS sheep-farmer
AEEEFILNRRT referential
AEEEFLLMPSX self-example

AEEEFLLNNTT flannelette
AEEEFLRSSTU featureless
AEEEFNNRSST Fastern's-e'en
AEEEFPRSTTU superfetate
AEEEGGILNOS genealogise
AEEEGGILNOZ genealogize
AEEEGGIRSTV segregative
AEEEGGMMNOU emmenagogue
AEEEGHLPRRT telegrapher
AEEEGHNPRTW great-nephew
AEEEGHORRTT theatre-goer
AEEEGILMMRR lammergeier
AEEEGIMNSST metagenesis
AEEEGINORTT renegotiate
AEEEGINPRRT peregrinate
AEEEGINRRTT reintegrate
AEEEGLMMRRY lammergeyer
AEEEGLMNNRT enlargement
AEEEGMNNRSS germaneness
AEEEGMNPRST presagement
AEEEGMNQRSU Germanesque
AEEEGNORRRT regenerator
AEEEGNQRSUW Wagneresque
AEEEHHLMMRV helve-hammer
AEEEHIKLNNP enkephaline
AEEEHILNNPT elephantine
AEEEHILNRTU eleutherian
AEEEHILPSTT telepathise
AEEEHILPTTZ telepathize
AEEEHILRTTY ethereality
AEEEHILSSTT telesthesia
AEEEHIMMSST hematemesis
AEEEHIMPRSS re-emphasise
AEEEHIMPRSZ re-emphasize
AEEEHIMRSTX hexametrise
AEEEHIMRTXZ hexametrize
AEEEHIMSSTT metathesise
AEEEHIMSTTZ metathesize
AEEEHIPRSST aspheterise
AEEEHIPRSTZ aspheterize
AEEEHIRSTWW weather-wise
AEEEHLMMNRT Emmenthaler
AEEEHLMOPST spelaeothem
AEEEHLMPPRT pamphleteer
AEEEHLMRSTW master-wheel
AEEEHLNPTTT pentathlete
AEEEHLORRTV overleather
AEEEHMPRSST sheep-master
AEEEHMRRSTT three-master
AEEEHNOSSTU senate-house
AEEEHNPRSST parentheses
AEEEHNRSTTW news-theatre
AEEEHOPRRTT Heteroptera
AEEEHORRTVW overweather
AEEEHPRRSTU superheater
AEEEHPRSSWW sweep-washer
AEEEHQRRSTU three-square
AEEEIILNRRT inertia-reel
AEEEIINPPRT peripeteian
AEEEIINQSTU Equisetinae
AEEEIIRRTTV reiterative
AEEEILLLPWY peelie-wally
AEEEILMNRST mesenterial
AEEEILMNRTT melanterite
AEEEILMPRST time-pleaser
AEEEILNORTV re-elevation
AEEEILNRRTV reverential
AEEEILNRSTV interleaves
AEEEILNRSTX externalise
AEEEILNRTXZ externalize
AEEEILNSTUV eventualise
AEEEILNTUVZ eventualize
AEEEILQSSTU Equisetales
AEEEIMNPRTT impenetrate
intemperate
AEEEIMNRTTX exterminate
AEEEIMNRTUV enumerative
AEEEIMPRTTV temperative
AEEEIMQRRTU marqueterie
AEEEINNRRTT entertainer
AEEEINOPRSU europeanise
AEEEINOPRUZ europeanize
AEEEINORRTT reorientate
AEEEINORTVX exonerative
AEEEINPRTTV penetrative
AEEEINSSSVV evasiveness
AEEEINTTUVX extenuative
AEEEJLMSSTY lese-majesty
AEEEJLMSTYZ leze-majesty
AEEEKLLOSTX exoskeletal
AEEEKLLPRSW sleepwalker
AEEEKMORRTT keratometer
AEEEKPSSSTW sweepstakes
AEEELLLMNTY elementally
AEEELLORRSV sallee-rover
AEEELLORSSW slow-release
AEEELLORTTT teetotaller
AEEELMMNNPT empanelment
AEEELMNNSTV enslavement
AEEELMPRTTY temperately
AEEELMRSSSU measureless
AEEELNSSSSW awelessness
AEEELPPRTVV velvet-paper
AEEELPQRSTU plateresque
AEEELRRSSVX sex-reversal
AEEEMMNPRTT temperament
AEEEMMNRSTU measurement
AEEEMNNRTTT entreatment
AEEEMNNRTTY tenementary
AEEEMNOSSSW awesomeness
AEEEMNRSTTT restatement
AEEEMORRSUV overmeasure
AEEEMPRRTTU temperature
AEEENNRSSST earnestness
AEEENORRSTV overearnest
AEEENPRRSTV perseverant
AEEENRSSSTU austereness
AEEEOPPRRRV overprepare
AEEEORRSTUV auto-reverse
AEEEQRSSTTU sequestrate
AEEFFFFIMUW fee-fi-faw-fum
AEEFFGILLNR free-falling
AEEFFGRSTTU suffragette
AEEFFILNNRS snaffle-rein

AEEFFLNRSSU fearfulness
AEEFFLNSSTU fatefulness
AEEFGGGLLTU left-luggage
AEEFGHILLNS self-healing
AEEFGHILNRT half-integer
AEEFGHORRTT heterograft
AEEFGIIMNRS fair-seeming
AEEFGILLNSS self-sealing
AEEFGILLNTT leafletting
AEEFGILNPRT fingerplate
AEEFGILNRSS fragileness
AEEFGINRRRT refrigerant
AEEFGIPRRTU prefigurate
AEEFGLLORSW gallows-free
AEEFGMNNRTT engraftment
AEEFGOOPRRS greaseproof
AEEFHHILRSW whale-fisher
AEEFHHORSTU house-father
AEEFHILNNPS halfpennies
AEEFHILPRRS pearl-fisher
AEEFHKLLRST shelftalker
AEEFHKLMRST flesh-market
AEEFHLLMNST mantelshelf
AEEFHLNSSTU hatefulness
AEEFHMORRRT farthermore
AEEFHORRSTU frater-house
AEEFIILNNRT inferential
AEEFIILOTVX exfoliative
AEEFILLNRST self-reliant
AEEFILNSTTY festinately
AEEFILOPRRT proliferate
AEEFILPPRRT filter-paper
AEEFIMNOSST manifestoes
AEEFIMOPRRT imperforate
AEEFIMORRTV reformative
AEEFINPRSTZ zip-fastener
AEEFINRRRST fraterniser
AEEFINRRRTZ fraternizer
AEEFIOPRRTV perforative
AEEFKLNSSUW wakefulness
AEEFLLNRRUY funerreally
AEEFLLORRST forestaller
AEEFLLPRSUU pleasureful
AEEFLMORRTU reformulate
AEEFLMRSSTY self-mastery
AEEFLNRSSTU tearfulness
AEEFLOPPRRS proper-false
AEEFLRRSSTT self-starter
AEEFMNOPRTY forepayment
AEEFMNORRSY △freemasonry
AEEFNNOPRSS profaneness
AEEFNOPPRST pop-fastener
AEEFNRRRRST transferrer
AEEFOQRRRTU forequarter
AEEFPPRRSTU aftersupper
AEEFPRSSTUY supersafety
AEEGGGNNRRZ Grenzgänger
AEEGGHHMNSU meshuggenah
AEEGGIINORS seigniorage
AEEGGILLNNR generalling
AEEGGILMRSS message-girl
AEEGGILNOST genealogist
AEEGGIMNOSS gamogenesis
AEEGGINORST segregation
AEEGGINQSTU gigantesque
AEEGGIRRTTU regurgitate
AEEGGORSTTY geostrategy
AEEGHHITVWY heavyweight
AEEGHHNRRTU earth-hunger
AEEGHIILMNS Hegelianism
AEEGHIKLLNU keelhauling
AEEGHILLMRT hellgramite
AEEGHILMRWY whigmaleery
AEEGHILNPRS generalship
AEEGHILNPSS single-phase
AEEGHIMMRTU Megatherium
AEEGHINNRTT threatening
AEEGHINORTV overheating
AEEGHINOSTU eating-house
AEEGHIPPRTW paper-weight
AEEGHIPRRRS serigrapher
AEEGHIQRSTU eight-square
AEEGHLNOPRS selenograph
AEEGHLNORST estranghelo
AEEGHLRRSTU slaughterer
AEEGHMOPTTY gametophyte
AEEGHNOOSTT agonothetes
AEEGHNPRSTV stevengraph
AEEGHOOPRST ostreophage
AEEGHOPRRST stereograph
AEEGIIKLLLS skilligalee
AEEGIILLSTV legislative
AEEGIILLTTU aiguillette
AEEGIILMNPT leaping-time
AEEGIILNNOR legionnaire
AEEGIILNORS regionalise
AEEGIILNORZ regionalize
AEEGIILNPPR appleringie
AEEGIILNRST gelatiniser
AEEGIILNRSU seigneurial
AEEGIILNRTZ gelatinizer
AEEGIIMNRTV germinative
AEEGIINRTTV integrative
vinaigrette
AEEGIINSTTV investigate
AEEGIJKNRRT tear-jerking
AEEGIKMNRSV verse-making
AEEGILLMNNP empanelling
AEEGILLMNNW well-meaning
AEEGILLNNTY inelegantly
AEEGILLORRS allegoriser
AEEGILLORRZ allegorizer
AEEGILLRSTU legislature
AEEGILMNNRT engrailment
realignment
AEEGILMNNSS meaningless
AEEGILMNOSU Leguminosae
AEEGILMNRST regimentals
AEEGILNNPRS Spenglerian
AEEGILNNPSY palingenesy
AEEGILNNRTT intertangle
AEEGILNNRUV unrevealing
AEEGILNRSTV △everlasting
AEEGILRRSTW sweater-girl

Words marked △ may be spelled also with a capital letter

AEEGIMMNSTY	May-meetings
AEEGIMNOTTW	witenagemot
AEEGIMNSSTU	mutagenesis
AEEGIMSSTTU	guesstimate
AEEGINNORST	generations
	nitrogenase
AEEGINNPRTT	penetrating
AEEGINNRSTV	evening-star
AEEGINNTTUX	extenuating
AEEGINOPPRT	oppignerate
AEEGINORRRV	overgrainer
AEEGINORRTT	interrogate
AEEGINOSSTU	autogenesis
AEEGIOPRRTV	prerogative
AEEGKORSSWW	sewage-works
AEEGLLMNNTY	gentlemanly
AEEGLLMNOTY	metallogeny
AEEGLLMNSTY	segmentally
AEEGLLMORTU	glomerulate
AEEGLLNSSTT	tassell-gent
AEEGLLOOPSY	spelaeology
AEEGLLORSTT	allegrettos
AEEGLLORSTW	gallows-tree
AEEGLMNNOTW	gentlewoman
AEEGLMNOOPR	prolegomena
AEEGLMNORSU	long-measure
AEEGLMNORSW	wranglesome
AEEGLMNRSST	garmentless
AEEGMMOORRT	meteorogram
AEEGMMOPRRR	reprogramme
AEEGMNNOSST	magnesstone
AEEGMNORRTV	overgarment
AEEGMNRTTUY	tegumentary
AEEGNNORTUV	gouvernante
AEEGNNRSSST	strangeness
AEEGNOSSSSU	gaseousness
AEEGORRSSTU	retroussage
AEEGPPPRRSS	pepper-grass
AEEHHILNSST	healthiness
AEEHHILRTTW	therewithal
	whitleather
AEEHHILRTWW	wherewithal
AEEHHIRRTTV	rivet-hearth
AEEHHIRSTWW	whitewasher
AEEHHLLMRST	Stahlhelmer
AEEHHMNORTY	hearth-money
AEEHHMORSTV	harvest-home
AEEHHNNPRTY	hearth-penny
AEEHHNORSTT	hearth-stone
AEEHHPRRSSU	share-pusher
AEEHIIKNSST	kinesthesia
AEEHIILMOPT	epithelioma
AEEHIIMPRSS	phariseeism
AEEHIINNORT	anti-heroine
AEEHIINPRST	traineeship
AEEHIKLMRRS	sharemilker
AEEHIKPPRSS	speakership
AEEHIKRRSTT	heart-strike
AEEHILLMOST	mesothelial
AEEHILMMNTY	methylamine
AEEHILNPPRS	planisphere
AEEHILNPSSS	shapeliness
AEEHILNRSST	earthliness
AEEHILNSSTW	wealthiness
AEEHILPPRST	prelateship
AEEHILPSTTT	telepathist
AEEHILRSSTY	hysteresial
AEEHIMNNPST	panentheism
AEEHIMNNSTV	evanishment
AEEHIMNSTTY	amethystine
AEEHIMPPRSS	pre-emphasis
AEEHIMPRSST	aspheterism
AEEHIMRSTTT	tetratheism
AEEHIMRSTTV	harvest-mite
AEEHIMRSTTX	hexametrist
AEEHINNNOOT	hootenannie
AEEHINNPSTT	panentheist
AEEHINORSTU	△heterousian
AEEHINPRSST	parenthesis
AEEHINRRSTV	varnish-tree
AEEHIOOPRTT	heterotopia
AEEHIOOPSST	apotheosise
AEEHIOOPSTZ	apotheosize
AEEHIORSTTX	heterotaxis
AEEHIORTTVX	exhortative
AEEHIPPRRSS	periphrases
AEEHKLOORRU	leukorrhoea
AEEHKMORSTU	market-house
AEEHKMPRRTY	hypermarket
AEEHKOPRRTY	keratophyre
AEEHLLMSSSY	shamelessly
AEEHLLNORTY	lonely-heart
AEEHLLRSSTY	heartlessly
AEEHLMNNRTT	enthralment
AEEHLMNOOPR	melanophore
AEEHLMRRTUY	eurythermal
AEEHLNPSSSS	haplessness
AEEHLNSSSST	hatlessness
AEEHLOPPRTY	pelotherapy
AEEHLPPRSTU	persulphate
AEEHLSSSTUX	exhaustless
AEEHMMMORTT	mammoth-tree
AEEHMMNRTUX	xeranthemum
AEEHMNNNOOP	phaenomenon
AEEHMNOOPRT	nematophore
AEEHMNOPRTY	Hymenoptera
AEEHMNPRRTU	preterhuman
AEEHMOPRSTU	heptamerous
AEEHMORRRTT	earth-tremor
AEEHMORRSTW	whoremaster
AEEHMORRTTW	mother-water
AEEHMORSSTU	housemaster
AEEHMORSTTW	weathermost
AEEHMORSTVW	whatsomever
AEEHMPPRSTY	spermaphyte
AEEHNNOPRSW	answerphone
AEEHNOPRSTU	houseparent
AEEHNORRSTT	north-easter
AEEHNORRTWW	weather-worn
AEEHOPRRSTY	serotherapy
AEEHORSSTTU	south-easter
AEEHRSSSTUU	thesauruses
AEEIIILMNTV	eliminative
AEEIIILMPRS	imperialise

AEEIIILMPRZ	imperialize
AEEIIINNNST	Einsteinian
AEEIIKLLNPS	spaniel-like
AEEIILLMMPR	milliampere
AEEIILLRRST	literaliser
AEEIILLRRTZ	literalizer
AEEIILLSSTT	satellitise
AEEIILLSTTZ	satellitize
AEEIILMMORS	memorialise
AEEIILMMORZ	memorialize
AEEIILMNRRS	mineraliser
AEEIILMNRRZ	mineralizer
AEEIILMORTV	meliorative
AEEIILMRRST	semi-trailer
AEEIILNNPTT	penitential
AEEIILNNRRT	interlinear
AEEIILNNRST	internalise
AEEIILNNRTZ	internalize
AEEIILNNSST	inessential
AEEIILNORST	orientalise
AEEIILNORTZ	orientalize
AEEIILNSTTX	existential
AEEIILNTTVV	ventilative
AEEIILRSSTW	saltierwise
	saltirewise
AEEIILRTTVY	iteratively
AEEIIMMSSTT	misestimate
AEEIIMNNRTT	interminate
AEEIIMNRTTV	terminative
AEEIIMPRTTV	impetrative
AEEIINNSTTV	intensative
AEEIINNTTTV	inattentive
AEEIINOPRTV	inoperative
AEEIINORRTT	reiteration
AEEIINQSTTU	Titianesque
AEEIINSTUVV	vesuvianite
AEEIIOPRSST	sepiostaire
AEEIIPRRSTV	reprivatise
AEEIIPRRTVZ	reprivatize
AEEIIPRTTVX	extirpative
AEEIKLNRSSW	warlikeness
AEEIKNQSSSU	squeakiness
AEEIKNRSSST	streakiness
AEEIKOPRRST	perestroika
AEEILLLMPRT	pearl-millet
AEEILLMMNPT	implemental
AEEILLMNOPS	psilomelane
AEEILLMPRXY	exemplarily
AEEILLNNPRY	perennially
AEEILLNNSXY	sexennially
AEEILLNOSTT	stellionate
AEEILLNRSST	literalness
AEEILLNRTVY	eviternally
AEEILLNSSTY	essentially
AEEILLOORTV	alto-relievo
AEEILLRSSWY	wearilessly
AEEILLRSTVY	versatilely
AEEILMNNSTT	sentimental
AEEILMNORRS	renormalise
AEEILMNORRZ	renormalize
AEEILMNORST	salinometer
AEEILMNPRST	sempiternal
AEEILMNPRTV	prevailment
AEEILMNPTTU	penultimate
AEEILMNRSTX	externalism
AEEILMNSSSS	aimlessness
AEEILMNSSWY	Wesleyanism
AEEILMNSTTV	vestimental
AEEILMOPRRT	polarimeter
AEEILMORRST	solarimeter
AEEILMORSWY	wearisomely
AEEILMOSTTT	teetotalism
AEEILMPPRRS	perispermal
AEEILMPRTXY	exemplarity
AEEILNNNPRY	penny-a-liner
AEEILNNOOPT	napoleonite
AEEILNNOPTX	exponential
AEEILNNOSTX	extensional
AEEILNNPSTU	peninsulate
AEEILNNPSTW	twalpennies
AEEILNNRRTU	interneural
AEEILNNSSTU	unessential
AEEILNNSSTY	insensately
AEEILNOPRSS	personalise
AEEILNOPRSZ	personalize
AEEILNOPRTT	interpolate
AEEILNORRSV	reversional
AEEILNORSST	interosseal
AEEILNORSTV	Revelations
AEEILNPRSTT	interseptal
	septentrial
AEEILNPRSTV	vespertinal
AEEILNPSVXY	expansively
AEEILNRRSTT	intersertal
AEEILNRRSTU	neutraliser
AEEILNRRTUZ	neutralizer
AEEILNRSSSS	airlessness
AEEILNRSTTX	externalist
AEEILNRSTUX	intersexual
AEEILNRTTXY	externality
AEEILNSSSTT	stateliness
AEEILNTTTVY	attentively
	tentatively
AEEILNTTUVY	eventuality
AEEILOPPRST	sapropelite
AEEILOPPSSU	episepalous
AEEILOPPSTU	epipetalous
AEEILOPRTVX	explorative
AEEILOPRTVY	operatively
AEEILORSSTY	areosystile
AEEILPPPPST	pipe-stapple
AEEILPPQRSU	apple-squire
AEEILPRSTUV	superlative
AEEILPRSVVY	pervasively
AEEILPSTTUX	exstipulate
AEEILQRRTUV	quarter-evil
AEEILQRSSTU	sesquialter
AEEILRRRSTT	terrestrial
AEEILRRSTTW	slate-writer
AEEILRRTTTU	littérateur
AEEILRSSTVY	assertively
AEEILRSTTUV	resultative
AEEIMMNNPRT	impermanent
AEEIMMNPRST	pentamerism

AEEIMMRRSTT tetramerism
AEEIMNNNRTT entrainment
AEEIMNNOPRT prenominate
AEEIMNNORTU enumeration
mountaineer
AEEIMNNOSTT maisonnette
AEEIMNNPRTT intemperant
AEEIMNNSTTT instatement
AEEIMNOPRST impersonate
AEEIMNOPRSU Europeanism
AEEIMNOPRTU peritonaeum
AEEIMNRRSTT tin-streamer
AEEIMNRSSST streaminess
AEEIMNRSTUV mensurative
AEEIMNSSSSV massiveness
AEEIMNSSSUV amusiveness
AEEIMOPRRST temporaries
AEEIMOPRRTV vaporimeter
AEEIMORRSTU temerarious
AEEIMQRSTTU marquisette
AEEIMSSSTTY systematise
AEEIMSSTTYZ systematize
AEEINNNOPRT perennation
AEEINNOORTX exoneration
AEEINNOPRSX re-expansion
AEEINNOPRTT penetration
AEEINNORSTV anteversion
AEEINNORSVV varsovienne
AEEINNORTTV eventration
AEEINNOTTUX extenuation
AEEINNPPRTT appertinent
AEEINNQSSTU antiqueness
AEEINNTTTUV unattentive
AEEINOPRSTU Europeanist
AEEINOPRSTV personative
AEEINOPRTUV unoperative
AEEINOQSSSU Ossianesque
AEEINORRSST reassertion
AEEINORRSTV reservation
AEEINORTVXY over-anxiety
AEEINPRSSST spessartine
AEEINPRSSTT Esperantist
AEEINPRSSTU septenarius
AEEINPRSSTV privateness
AEEINPSSSSV passiveness
AEEINRSSTUV unassertive
AEEINSSSSUV suasiveness
AEEIOPPRRTX expropriate
AEEIORRSTTV restorative
AEEIORSSTTX stereotaxis
AEEIPPRRSSU superpraise
AEEIPRRSSTU pasteuriser
AEEIPRRSTUZ pasteurizer
AEEIPRSSSTT spessartite
AEEJLNOSSSU jealousness
AEEJNORRTUV rejuvenator
AEEKLLORRST roller-skate
AEEKLMORRTW metalworker
AEEKMMNORTY money-market
AEEKMMRSSTY system-maker
AEEKMORSTTT staktometer
AEEKMPRRSTU supermarket
AEEKNPRRSTU supertanker
AEELLLNPRTY repellantly
AEELLMMNOTU emolumental
AEELLMMORWY yellow-ammer
AEELLMNORTT reallotment
AEELLMORRST steam-roller
AEELLMPRSSU pearl-mussel
AEELLNORRTT retrolental
AEELLNORSTW stonewaller
AEELLNOSUVZ allez-vous-en
AEELLNPRTVY prevalently
AEELLNSSSSW lawlessness
AEELLOPRSTU pastourelle
AEELLOPRTUV pole-vaulter
AEELLPPRRUY puerperally
AEELLPPRTUY perpetually
AEELLPSSSUY pauselessly
AEELLSSSTTY tastelessly
AEELMMOOPPS pampelmoose
AEELMMOPPSU pampelmouse
AEELMNNPRTY permanently
AEELMNNRTUV unravelment
AEELMNPRTTT prattlement
AEELMOPRSTV volt-amperes
AEELMOQRRSU quarrelsome
AEELMPRRTUY prematurely
AEELMPRSTTT letter-stamp
AEELNNPRTTY repentantly
AEELNNSSSSU sensualness
AEELNOPRSSS salesperson
AEELNOPRSST prolateness
AEELNOSSSUZ zealousness
AEELNPSSSSS saplessness
AEELNRSSSST artlessness
AEELNRSSSTV servantless
AEELOORSUVZ over-zealous
AEELOPPPTVV poppet-valve
AEELOPRRSTY pearl-oyster
AEELOPSTTUX expostulate
AEELORSSTTU Lotus-eaters
AEELORSSTUU Teleosaurus
AEELPPPTUVV puppet-valve
AEELPPRRSTY parsley-pert
AEELPRRSSTU raptureless
AEELPRRSTTU perlustrate
AEELPRSSSTU pastureless
AEEMNNOQRSU Nornamesque
AEEMNNRSSTV men-servants
AEEMNOPRSTU pentamerous
AEEMNOPRTVY overpayment
AEEMNOQRTTU Quantometer®
quantometer
AEEMNORRRTU remunerator
AEEMNORRSTT remonstrate
AEEMNORSSTT easternmost
AEEMNRSSTTT stentmaster
AEEMOPRRTXY extemporary
AEEMORRSTTU tetramerous
AEEMRRSSTTT streetsmart
AEEMRSSSSTY seamstressy
AEENNNPRTTU unrepentant
AEENNOPPRST parpen-stone

AEENNOPRRTU neuropteran
AEENNORSSST sarsen-stone
AEENOOPRSSU aponeuroses
AEENOPPRSUW superweapon
AEENOPRRSTT △paternoster
AEENOQRRTTU quarter-note
quarter-tone
AEENORTTUXY extenuatory
AEENPRRSSTT serpent-star
AEENPRRSTUU supernature
AEENQRSSTTU sequestrant
AEEOPPRRRTT perpetrator
prêt-à-porter
AEEOPPRRTTU perpetuator
AEEOQRRSTUU terraqueous
AEEORRRSTVY reservatory
AEFFFFTTTUY tufftaffety
AEFFGHIINNT infangthief
AEFFGHILRTU fire-flaught
AEFFGIMSTUU suffumigate
AEFFHILRSTY sheriffalty
AEFFHINRSSS raffishness
AEFFIIKLNRU ruffian-like
AEFFIIMNORR foraminifer
AEFFKNRRRTU frankfurter
AEFFLLNRUUY unfearfully
AEFFMSSSTTY staff-system
AEFGGILNRSS fingerglass
AEFGGINRRSS finger-grass
AEFGHHORRTU throughfare
AEFGHIILNSS seal-fishing
AEFGHILLORT fothergilla
AEFGHILMNRS self-harming
AEFGHLOPRXY flexography
AEFGHOPRRRY ferrography
AEFGHORRTTW aftergrowth
AEFGHORRTUV overfraught
AEFGIIINRRS fire-raising
AEFGIIKLNRW fire-walking
AEFGIILNRSS self-raising
AEFGIINNPRT finger-paint
AEFGIKLLLNW fell-walking
AEFGILLMORU Glumiflorae
AEFGILLNRST fingerstall
AEFGILLNRTY falteringly
AEFGILLOSTY galley-foist
AEFGILNNOOR gonfalonier
AEFGILNNRTU unfaltering
AEFGILNNSSU gainfulness
AEFGILNORSU soul-fearing
AEFGILNPPST self-tapping
AEFGINNNSSW fawningness
AEFGINNORRW forewarning
AEFGINORSUU guaniferous
AEFGINRRSTU transfigure
AEFHHIIRSTT hatti-sherif
AEFHHLLLTUY healthfully
AEFHHLLNTUU unhealthful
AEFHIILMNPS lifemanship
AEFHILLSSTY faithlessly
AEFHLMNRSSU harmfulness
AEFHMORRSTT farthermost
AEFHOOTTUWY out-of-the-way
AEFIIKLNNRT franklinite
AEFIILLNNOX inflexional
AEFIILLNNTU influential
AEFIILNNORT reinflation
AEFIILNNRTY infernality
AEFIILNOOTX exfoliation
AEFIIMNORTV informative
AEFIINNOSTT festination
infestation
sinfonietta
AEFIINNRSTT transfinite
AEFIKOPRRTT profit-taker
AEFILLLMMOR lamelliform
AEFILLMOPRT patelliform
AEFILLNRTTU intreatfull
AEFILLRRTTU ultrafilter
AEFILMNOSTU filamentous
AEFILMORRSU formularise
AEFILMORRUZ formularize
AEFILMPRSUY superfamily
AEFILNNPSSU painfulness
AEFILNOOPST point-of-sale
AEFILNORSUY nefariously
AEFILOPRRTY prefatorily
AEFIMMMORSU mammiferous
AEFIMNNNORT antenniform
AEFIMNNNRTY infantrymen
AEFIMNNOOTT fomentation
AEFIMNNORSU manniferous
AEFIMNOORRT △reformation
re-formation
AEFIMOPRRTZ trapeziform
AEFINNNOPTU fountain-pen
AEFINNRRRST transferrin
AEFINOOPRRT perforation
AEFINOOPRST pianofortes
AEFINOORSTT forestation
AEFINRSSTUV transfusive
AEFKLLOORRW floorwalker
AEFKLLORSTW flower-stalk
AEFKNNORRRT front-ranker
AEFLLLNTTUY flatulently
AEFLLLOPRUW all-powerful
AEFLLLSSTUY faultlessly
AEFLLMRSTUY masterfully
AEFLLNPSSUY playfulness
AEFLLORSSUV flavourless
AEFLLPRRUYY prayerfully
AEFLLRSTUWY wasterfully
AEFLMOORSUV flavoursome
AEFLNOOPSTU teaspoonful
AEFLNORTTUY fortunately
AEFLORRSTWW strawflower
AEFMNORRRST transformer
AEFMOOPPRRT tamper-proof
AEFMOOPRSTT foretopmast
AEFMOORRRTY reformatory
AEFNNORTTUU unfortunate
AEFNOSSSTUU fatuousness
AEGGHHILOTV high-voltage
AEGGHIILNNT nightingale

AEGGHIINNRT ingathering
AEGGHIIRRRT hair-trigger
AEGGHIMNOSU gaming-house
AEGGHINOOPT photo-ageing
AEGGHINSSSW waggishness
AEGGHKLNRSU Enghalskrug
AEGGHLOOPRR logographer
AEGGHNNOOWY honey-waggon
AEGGIILMPRR pilgrimager
AEGGIINRTTU ingurgitate
AEGGILNNORW longwearing
AEGGILNNRSS glaringness
AEGGIMNOOTY geitonogamy
AEGGIMNRSST gangsterism
AEGGINNNRRU running-gear
AEGGINORRVZ overgrazing
AEGGINORRZZ zero-grazing
AEGGINRRTTU regurgitant
AEGGLNNOOST loggan-stone
AEGGLOORRST gastrologer
AEGHHILOPRY heliography
AEGHHINSSTU haughtiness
AEGHHIOPRRY hierography
AEGHHLOPRSU ploughshare
AEGHHMOPRRT thermograph
AEGHHNOPRTY ethnography
AEGHHOOPRRR horographer
AEGHHOOPSTU theophagous
AEGHHOPRTYY hyetography
AEGHHOTTUVW thought-wave
AEGHIILNNSW washing-line
AEGHIIMNRST time-sharing
AEGHIINPTTY tithe-paying
AEGHIINRTTT night-attire
AEGHIINRTTW weight-train
AEGHIIPPRST epigraphist
AEGHIJMNPRU jumping-hare
AEGHIKLNRTW night-walker
AEGHIKNOOPR reaping-hook
AEGHIKNOPRT kinetograph
AEGHIKNRSTV thanksgiver
AEGHILLMPRT lamplighter
AEGHILLNNRT enthralling
AEGHILMNOPR Germanophil
AEGHILMOPSU meliphagous
AEGHILNOOST anthologise
AEGHILNOOTZ anthologize
AEGHILNOPSV leaving-shop
AEGHILNSSST ghastliness
AEGHILPRSTY sight-player
AEGHIMMOPRR mimographer
AEGHIMNNRST garnishment
AEGHIMNORTV earthmoving
AEGHIMOPRSS seismograph
AEGHINNOSST night-season
AEGHINNSSTU naughtiness
AEGHINNSTTU hunting-seat
AEGHINORSUW warehousing
AEGHINOSSST goatishness
AEGHINPRTTT patent-right
AEGHINRRSTT heart-string
AEGHLNOOORR gonorrhoeal
AEGHLNOOPTY pantheology
AEGHLOOPRSY phraseology
AEGHLOPPRYY pyelography
AEGHLOPRRXY xylographer
AEGHMNOOPRR monographer
nomographer
AEGHMNOOPSU phenogamous
AEGHMNOOPTY entomophagy
AEGHMOOPRRT ergatomorph
AEGHMOPRSUY hypergamous
AEGHNOOPRRS nosographer
sonographer
AEGHNOOPSTU pathogenous
AEGHNOPRSTY stenography
AEGHNOPSTUY heptagynous
AEGHNORSTTU hart's-tongue
AEGHOOPPRRT topographer
AEGHOOPRSTY osteography
ostreophagy
AEGHOPPRRRY reprography
AEGHOPPRRSS grasshopper
AEGHOPPRRTY petrography
typographer
AEGIIILLNTT gentilitial
AEGIIILMNPR primigenial
AEGIIILNNTT gentilitian
AEGIIILNORS seigniorial
AEGIIIMNPRT pairing-time
AEGIIINORTV originative
AEGIIINSTTV instigative
AEGIIKLLNRT giant-killer
AEGIIKLNSST glaikitness
AEGIIKNRSTW water-skiing
AEGIILLNOST legislation
AEGIILLNTVY genitivally
AEGIILMNOPR primogenial
AEGIILMNORS regionalism
AEGIILMOSST legatissimo
AEGIILNNRTU △interlingua
AEGIILNORRY religionary
AEGIILNORST regionalist
AEGIILNRRSV silver-grain
AEGIILNRSSU singularise
AEGIILNRSUZ singularize
AEGIILNRTTY integrality
AEGIIMMORRR mirror-image
AEGIIMMRSTU magisterium
AEGIIMNNNRU unremaining
AEGIIMNNORT germination
AEGIIMNNORV Merovingian
AEGIIMNNRST instreaming
AEGIIMNOPRT impignorate
AEGIIMNORRT remigration
AEGIIMPRSTU epigastrium
AEGIINNNORT Ignorantine
AEGIINNOOTT negotiation
AEGIINNORRS searing-iron
AEGIINNORST resignation
AEGIINNORTT integration
AEGIINNORTU unoriginate
AEGIINNOSTT negationist
AEGIINNPRST sign-painter

AEGIINNRRST	restraining
AEGIINNRTTU	intriguante
AEGIINNSTTW	wine-tasting
AEGIINORTTX	negotiatrix
AEGIINRRTVX	extra-virgin
AEGIINRSSTW	waitressing
AEGIJLMTTUU	multijugate
AEGIJMNORTT	majoretting
AEGIKLLNNST	stalling-ken
AEGIKLNQSUY	squeakingly
AEGIKMMNNOY	money-making
AEGIKMMNRRY	merrymaking
AEGIKNPRSTU	purse-taking
AEGILLMMNRT	trammelling
AEGILLMNNTY	lamentingly
AEGILLMOOPS	megalopolis
AEGILLMPRSU	△aspergillum
AEGILLMRSST	millet-grass
AEGILLNNOPR	pollen-grain
AEGILLNNRUV	unravelling
AEGILLNOPRY	role-playing
AEGILLNQRRU	quarrelling
AEGILLNRSVY	slaveringly
AEGILLOPRSW	gallows-ripe
AEGILLOSSTT	toilet-glass
AEGILLPRSSU	Aspergillus
AEGILLRRRUY	irregularly
AEGILMMNOTU	gemmulation
AEGILMNNNUY	unmeaningly
AEGILMNNOPS	plasminogen
AEGILMNOORT	glomeration
AEGILMNOPRU	pelargonium
AEGILMNOSTU	ligamentous
AEGILMNRSTY	streamingly
AEGILMNSSTU	minute-glass
AEGILMOOPST	plagiostome
AEGILMOOSSY	semasiology
AEGILNNOSTU	langoustine
AEGILNNRSTV	navel-string
AEGILNNSSST	lastingness
AEGILNNSSTY	assentingly
AEGILNOOPRS	sporangiole
AEGILNOOSSX	xenoglossia
AEGILNORSST	Interglossa
AEGILNOSTTU	lotus-eating
AEGILNQRUVY	quaveringly
AEGILNRRSTV	servant-girl
AEGILNRSUUV	unvulgarise
AEGILNRTTYY	yatteringly
AEGILNRUUVZ	unvulgarize
AEGILOOSTTU	tautologise
AEGILOOTTUZ	tautologize
AEGILPRTUVY	purgatively
AEGILRSTTUU	gutturalise
AEGILRTTUUZ	gutturalize
AEGIMMMNORX	maxim-monger
AEGIMMOPRSU	gemmiparous
AEGIMNOOPRS	spermogonia
AEGIMNORSSU	ignoramuses
AEGINNNOPRS	none-sparing
AEGINNNORSU	unreasoning
AEGINNOOTXY	oxygenation
AEGINNOPRST	personating
AEGINNOPSST	passing-note
AEGINNOPSTV	paving-stone
AEGINNOPTUX	expugnation
AEGINNORRTT	interrogant
AEGINNOSSUU	sanguineous
AEGINNPRSSS	sparingness
AEGINOOPPRT	oppignorate
AEGINOPRTTW	watering-pot
AEGINOPRTUX	expurgation
AEGINOPSTTV	post-vintage
AEGINPRRSTW	springwater
AEGIPRRRTYY	pyrargyrite
AEGKLORRSSW	glassworker
AEGKMNORSSY	monkey-grass
AEGLLNOOPTY	planetology
AEGLLNOSSSW	gallowsness
AEGLLOPRUYZ	zygopleural
AEGLNNOOOTY	neonatology
AEGLNNOTTUU	notungulate
AEGMNOOOPTT	potamogeton
AEGMNOORRST	gastronomer
AEGNNNPRTUU	unrepugnant
AEGNNOPSTUY	pentagynous
AEGNOOPRSSU	saprogenous
AEGNOORSTTU	tetragonous
AEGNORSTTUY	tetragynous
AEGOORRRSST	grass-rooter
AEGOORRRTUV	rotogravure
AEGOPRRRUVY	pyrogravure
AEGOPRRTUXY	expurgatory
AEGORSSSTUU	△stegosaurus
AEHHIIMPSSS	Messiahship
AEHHIKMMSSY	shimmy-shake
AEHHIKNSSSW	hawkishness
AEHHILLNTUY	unhealthily
AEHHILOPSTY	lithophysae
AEHHIMOPRTY	hypothermia
AEHHINNOPTY	hyphenation
AEHHINOORRR	rhinorrhoea
AEHHIOPPSST	phosphatise
AEHHIOPPSTZ	phosphatize
AEHHIORTTTW	whitethroat
AEHHLLOPTTY	thallophyte
AEHHLMMOORT	homothermal
AEHHLMOPRTY	hypothermal
AEHHLOOPRTX	axerophthol
AEHHLOPPSYY	hypophyseal
AEHHMOOOPTY	homoeopathy
AEHHMOOPRRT	Theromorpha
AEHHMORSTWY	shameworthy
AEHHNOPPRTY	nephropathy
AEHHNOPRRTY	tenorrhaphy
AEHHNOPRTTY	theanthropy
AEHHOOPPRST	phosphorate
AEHIIILMTUV	humiliative
AEHIIILRSST	Israelitish
AEHIIKMRSTT	Mekhitarist
AEHIIKNPSTY	kinesipathy
AEHIILLOPRU	ailurophile
AEHIILLPSTT	philatelist

AEHIILOPRRT	horripilate
	retrophilia
AEHIILOPSST	hospitalise
AEHIILOPSTZ	hospitalize
AEHIILPRSTT	peristalith
AEHIIMNNORY	Hieronymian
AEHIIMPPRST	primateship
AEHIIMRSTUV	Sivatherium
AEHIINOPRRS	parishioner
AEHIINORSTU	isothenuria
AEHIINORTTT	trithionate
AEHIIPPRRSS	periphrasis
AEHIKLMRSUW	lukewarmish
AEHIKMNNORT	ink-horn-mate
AEHIKMNSSSW	mawkishness
AEHIKNNSSSS	snakishness
AEHIKNNSSSV	knavishness
AEHILLNOSST	loathliness
AEHILLOPPTY	apophyllite
AEHILLOPRST	hospitaller
AEHILLPRSTU	hill-pasture
AEHILMMOPPS	psammophile
AEHILMNOPPY	Polyphemian
AEHILMNORTW	mother-in-law
AEHILMNOTTY	methylation
AEHILMNOTXY	hematoxylin
AEHILMNRSTU	Lutheranism
AEHILMOSSTY	hematolysis
AEHILMQSSUY	squeamishly
AEHILNOPTXY	phytoalexin
AEHILNPRRTY	platyrrhine
AEHILNPRSST	shinplaster
AEHILNSSSST	saltishness
AEHILNSSSSV	slavishness
AEHILOOPPRR	plerophoria
AEHILOPPSST	apostleship
AEHILOPRSTY	physiolater
AEHILORRTTY	theriolatry
AEHILORSTVY	overhastily
AEHILORTTVY	hortatively
AEHILPRSTWY	whist-player
AEHIMMNNNRY	ninny-hammer
AEHIMNNNSSS	mannishness
AEHIMNOOPPR	apomorphine
AEHIMNOPRST	misanthrope
AEHIMNOPRSY	hypersomnia
AEHIMOOSSST	homeostasis
AEHIMOPRSTT	metaphorist
AEHIMOPSSTY	haemoptysis
AEHIMORSTTX	thermotaxis
AEHIMPPRSTU	hippeastrum
AEHIMPQSTUY	sympathique
AEHIMPRSSTY	sympathiser
AEHIMPRSTYZ	sympathizer
AEHINNPPSSU	unhappiness
AEHINNSSSTY	synanthesis
AEHINOORSTT	anorthosite
AEHINOORTTX	exhortation
AEHINOPRSST	senatorship
AEHINOPRSTT	antistrophe
AEHINOPSSTT	stephanotis
AEHINORRSST	enarthrosis
AEHINORSSTT	throatiness
AEHINPPRRST	partnership
	transhipper
AEHINPRSSTV	servantship
AEHINPSSSSW	waspishness
AEHINQSSSSU	squashiness
AEHINRSSSTW	swarthiness
AEHIOOPRRTT	Prototheria
AEHIOPPRRST	praetorship
AEHIOPSSSTY	hypostasise
AEHIOPSSTTY	hypostatise
AEHIOPSSTYZ	hypostasize
AEHIOPSTTYZ	hypostatize
AEHKLLNSSTY	thanklessly
AEHKMMORRST	mother's-mark
AEHKNOORRTY	arrhenotoky
AEHKOORRSTT	heart-strook
AEHLLLMOOPR	allelomorph
AEHLLMOOSTY	loathsomely
AEHLLNOSSSW	shallowness
AEHLMNOOTXY	Hematoxylon
AEHLMOPPRRY	lamprophyre
AEHLOPRSSTT	short-staple
AEHMMOOOPRT	ommatophore
AEHMMOPPSTY	psammophyte
AEHMNOORRSS	harness-room
AEHMNORSTTY	thermonasty
AEHNOOPRRTT	orthopteran
AEHNOOPRSST	snapshooter
AEHNOOPRSTU	Eoanthropus
AEHNOPPRSTT	pattern-shop
AEHNOPPRTTY	tryptophane
AEHNORSTUWY	unseaworthy
AEHNPRRUXYY	Eurypharynx
AEHOOPRRRST	arthrospore
AEHOOPRRSTT	trapshooter
AEHOOPRRSTX	prothoraxes
AEHOORRTTXY	exhortatory
AEIIILLMNOR	millionaire
AEIIILLMNST	sillimanite
AEIIILLTTTV	titillative
AEIIILMMPRS	imperialism
AEIIILMNNOT	elimination
AEIIILMNRST	ministerial
AEIIILMPRST	imperialist
AEIIILMPRTY	imperiality
AEIIILMRRSV	verisimilar
AEIIILMTTVY	imitatively
AEIIILNNNRT	nitraniline
AEIIILNPRST	plein-airist
AEIIIMNORRT	minoritaire
AEIIIMNRSTU	miniaturise
AEIIIMNRTUZ	miniaturize
AEIIINNSTUV	insinuative
AEIIINPRSTV	inspirative
AEIIINQSTTU	antiquities
AEIIKLLOPRT	realpolitik
AEIIKLMNPRS	marlinspike
AEIIKNOSSTU	autokinesis
AEIILLLMNTU	multilineal
AEIILLMMNNR	man-milliner
AEIILLMMNRS	millenarism

AEIILLMNRTU	multilinear
AEIILLMRRTU	mitrailleur
AEIILLMRSTU	multiserial
AEIILLNNRTY	triennially
AEIILLNOPST	pillion-seat
AEIILLNOTVX	vexillation
AEIILLNOTVY	inviolately
AEIILLNPRTY	reptilianly
AEIILLNPTVY	plaintively
AEIILLNRSUY	uniserially
AEIILLNTUUX	luxulianite
AEIILLOORTV	alto-rilievo
AEIILLPRRSU	pluriserial
AEIILLRRSTT	artillerist
AEIILMMORST	immortalise
	memorialist
AEIILMMORTZ	immortalize
AEIILMNOORT	melioration
AEIILMNORST	misrelation
	Orientalism
	relationism
AEIILMNORTY	eliminatory
AEIILMNOSTT	testimonial
AEIILMNOSTV	love-in-a-mist
	neovitalism
AEIILMNPRRY	preliminary
AEIILMNPTTY	impatiently
AEIILMOPRST	peristomial
AEIILMPRSTU	Laserpitium
AEIILMPSSVY	impassively
AEIILMRRSTT	trimestrial
AEIILMRRSTY	literaryism
AEIILMSTTUV	stimulative
AEIILNNNOST	intensional
AEIILNNNOTT	intentional
AEIILNNORST	insertional
AEIILNNORTV	inventorial
AEIILNNOTTV	ventilation
AEIILNNPRST	interspinal
AEIILNNRSTT	transilient
AEIILNNRTTY	internality
	itinerantly
AEIILNNSSST	saintliness
AEIILNOPRSV	previsional
AEIILNOPSTX	post-exilian
AEIILNORSSS	insessorial
AEIILNORSTT	Orientalist
	relationist
AEIILNORTTU	elutriation
AEIILNORTTY	orientality
AEIILNOSTTV	neovitalist
AEIILNPPRZZ	Lippizzaner
AEIILNPRSST	spinsterial
AEIILNQRTUZ	tranquilize
AEIILNRSSTV	silvestrian
	trivialness
AEIILNRSSTW	sister-in-law
AEIILORRRTT	territorial
AEIILORRSTV	servitorial
AEIILORSTTU	lateritious
AEIILPRSSST	peristalsis
AEIILPRTTVY	partitively
AEIILPRTVVY	privatively
AEIILRSTTVY	versatility
AEIILTTTUVY	attuitively
AEIIMMMNNST	immanentism
AEIIMMNNSSW	Weismannism
AEIIMMNNSTT	immanentist
AEIIMMNRSTT	martinetism
AEIIMMRRTTU	termitarium
AEIIMNNOPTT	omnipatient
AEIIMNNORST	inseminator
	nitrosamine
AEIIMNNORTT	termination
AEIIMNNORTV	vermination
AEIIMNOPRTT	impetration
AEIIMNPRRSS	primariness
AEIIMOPPRRT	impropriate
AEIIMOPRRSS	impresarios
AEIIMOPRSTV	improvisate
AEIIMRRTTUV	triumvirate
AEIINNNORST	Tironensian
AEIINNNORTV	innervation
AEIINNNOSVV	non-invasive
AEIINNNOTTT	inattention
AEIINNNQQUU	quinquennia
AEIINNOORTT	orientation
AEIINNOQRTU	enquiration
AEIINNORSTT	reinstation
AEIINNPRSST	spinsterian
AEIINOPPSTT	peptisation
AEIINOPPTTZ	peptization
AEIINOPRRST	respiration
	retinispora
AEIINOPRRTT	partitioner
	repartition
AEIINOPRSTU	utopianiser
AEIINOPRTTX	extirpation
AEIINOPRTTY	petitionary
AEIINOPRTUZ	utopianizer
AEIINORRSVY	revisionary
AEIINORRTTY	anteriority
AEIINPPRSTT	Trappistine
AEIINPRSSSU	Prussianise
AEIINPRSSUZ	Prussianize
AEIINPSTVXY	expansivity
AEIINSSTTUV	antitussive
AEIIOOPPSSS	aposiopesis
AEIIORRSVVV	savoir-vivre
AEIJMNORSTT	master-joint
AEIJNNNOTTT	joint-tenant
AEIKKLMNORW	workmanlike
AEIKLLRSTTW	stilt-walker
AEIKLMORSTW	sea-milkwort
AEIKLNNOPPS	plain-spoken
AEIKMNNPRTU	turnpike-man
AEILLMNNSTT	installment
AEILLMNOOTY	emotionally
AEILLMNRTUV	intervallum
AEILLMNTTUV	multivalent
AEILLMOOSTT	tomatilloes
AEILLMPRSST	spill-stream
AEILLNNOOTV	non-volatile
AEILLNNOSTY	tensionally

AEILLNOOTUV	evolutional
AEILLNOPTTY	potentially
AEILLNOSSSY	sessionally
AEILLNRSTUV	surveillant
AEILLNRSUVY	universally
AEILLNSSSTY	stainlessly
AEILLNSSTTY	taintlessly
AEILLNSUUXY	unisexually
AEILLNTUUXY	luxulyanite
AEILLORTTUV	ultraviolet
AEILMMMSSTY	symmetalism
AEILMMNORTY	momentarily
AEILMNNNSSU	unmanliness
AEILMNNOOPS	Napoleonism
AEILMNNOOTU	unemotional
AEILMNNOSSW	womanliness
AEILMNNRTTU	nutrimental
AEILMNOOSTT	molestation
AEILMNOPPRY	propylamine
AEILMNOPRRT	trampoliner
AEILMNOPRSS	personalism
AEILMNORTVY	normatively
AEILMNPPRSU	paper-muslin
AEILMOPRRSU	leprosarium
AEILMOPRRTY	polarimetry
	temporarily
AEILMOPRTTY	temporality
AEILMOPRTXY	proximately
AEILMOQSTTU	△milquetoast
AEILNNOOPST	Napoleonist
AEILNNOPRSU	unipersonal
AEILNNOPSST	plainstones
AEILNNORTUV	vulneration
AEILNNRRTUY	interlunary
AEILNNRSTTY	transiently
AEILNOOPRTX	exploration
AEILNOPPRST	epiplastron
AEILNOPPTTY	△platinotype
AEILNOPRRST	tripersonal
AEILNOPRSST	personalist
AEILNOPRSTY	personality
AEILNOPRTUV	pulveration
AEILNOPSSSS	passionless
AEILNORRSTU	serrulation
AEILNOTTUVV	voluntative
AEILNRSSTVY	sylvestrian
AEILOOPRRRT	reportorial
AEILOPPRRSU	populariser
AEILOPPRRUZ	popularizer
AEILOPRSTTU	tripetalous
AEILOSTUVXY	vexatiously
AEIMMNPPRSS	panspermism
AEIMMNRSSSU	summariness
AEIMMOPSTTU	impostumate
AEIMMORSTTU	tautomerism
AEIMMPRSSTU	△suprematism
AEIMMSSSTTY	systematism
AEIMNNOORTY	ration-money
AEIMNNOPPTT	appointment
AEIMNNORSTT	ornamentist
AEIMNNORSTU	mensuration
AEIMNNSSTTU	sustainment
AEIMNOORSST	astronomise
AEIMNOORSSU	anisomerous
AEIMNOORSTZ	astronomize
AEIMNOPRTTU	importunate
	permutation
AEIMNORRTTY	terminatory
AEIMNORSSTU	stramineous
AEIMNORSTTY	attorneyism
AEIMNORTTTU	mutteration
AEIMNOSSSTY	seismonasty
AEIMNPPRSST	panspermist
AEIMNRRSTTT	transmitter
AEIMOOPRRST	aerotropism
AEIMOORRTTY	arteriotomy
AEIMOORSTTU	autoerotism
AEIMOPRRSSU	aspersorium
AEIMOPRRTTY	impetratory
AEIMOPSTTTU	temptatious
AEIMPRRTTUY	prematurity
AEIMPRSSTTU	△suprematist
AEIMSSSTTTY	systematist
AEINNNORSTY	Tyronensian
AEINNNORTTU	antineutron
AEINNOOPRST	personation
AEINNOOSTTT	ostentation
AEINNOPSTTY	spontaneity
AEINNOQRSTU	quaternions
AEINNORRTUV	nervuration
AEINNORSTUV	intravenous
AEINNOSSSUX	anxiousness
AEINNRRSTTU	unrestraint
AEINNRSSSSU	Russianness
AEINOOPPRRT	reapportion
AEINOOPRRST	retinospora
AEINOOPRSSU	aponeurosis
AEINOOPRTTX	exportation
AEINOORRSTT	△restoration
AEINOORSUVX	over-anxious
AEINOPPPQRU	appropinque
AEINOPRSSSV	vasopressin
AEINOQRSTUY	questionary
AEINORSSSUV	savouriness
	variousness
AEINQSSSTTU	squattiness
AEIOOOPPPRS	prosopopeia
AEIOPPRRRTY	proprietary
AEIOPRRRSTY	respiratory
AEIOPRRRTTU	portraiture
AEIOPRRTTUV	vituperator
AEIOPRRTTXY	extirpatory
AEIPPRSTUUV	suppurative
AEKKLMMORSV	Volkskammer
AEKLLPRSSSY	sparklessly
AEKLMOPRRSW	sampler-work
AEKLOPRRSTW	plasterwork
AEKLPPPRUWY	puppy-walker
AEKMNOOPSSW	spokeswoman
AEKOPRRSTTW	spatterwork
AELLMSSTTYY	tally-system
AELLNOOPRTW	pot-walloner
AELLNOPRSTT	patent-rolls
AELLOOPPRTW	pot-walloper

AELLOOPRSTW	wool-stapler
AELLOQRRSUU	quarrellous
AELMMRSSTUU	summersault
AELMNOPRRSU	supernormal
AELMNORSTUW	Ulsterwoman
AELMOPSSTUY	sympetalous
AELNNNOPRTW	town-planner
AELNNSSSUUU	unusualness
AELNOPRSTTY	oyster-plant
AELNPRRSUUY	superlunary
AELOOPRRTXY	exploratory
AELOOPSSTTY	osteoplasty
AELOPPRRRSU	pourparlers
AEMNNORRSTT	△remonstrant
AEMNOOPRSTY	trypanosome
AEMNOORSSSU	amorousness
AEMNOORSTWY	oyster-woman
AEMOOPPRRRU	amour-propre
AEMORRSTTTU	trout-stream
AENNOOPSSTU	spontaneous
AENOPRRRSTT	transporter
AENORRSTTTU	sternutator
AENORSSTTTU	sustentator
AENPPRSSSTU	suppressant
AEOOPPPRRTY	party-pooper
AEOOPRRSSSV	vasopressor
AEOPRSTTTYY	oyster-patty
AEOQRRSTTUU	outquarters
AFFFGHILRTU	affrightful
AFFGHIIMNRS	fish-farming
AFFGHIMNRUU	humgruffian
AFFGHLLRTUU	full-fraught
AFFGHLOPSTU	plough-staff
AFFGIILMNRY	affirmingly
AFFGIKNNSTU	snuff-taking
AFFIINOSTUX	suffixation
AFFILNORSTU	insufflator
AFFLLLNORTU	full-frontal
AFGGHIINNRT	nightfaring
AFGGIILNTUY	fatiguingly
AFGGIINSSTT	gas-fittings
AFGGINOORTZ	zoografting
AFGHHIILNTU	highfalutin
AFGHILMOPRY	filmography
AFGHIORSTWY	right-of-ways
	rights-of-way
AFGHLORTTUU	trough-fault
AFGIIINNRTU	infuriating
AFGIILLNNTY	inflatingly
AFGIILLNNUY	unfailingly
AFGIILMNNTU	fulminating
AFGIILNNOTU	antifouling
AFGIIMNORRT	granitiform
AFGIIMORSTT	sagittiform
AFGIINNNORU	Finno-Ugrian
AFGIINNOPSY	saponifying
AFGIINOSTTU	fustigation
AFGIINRSTTY	stratifying
AFGILLNNTUY	flauntingly
AFGILMNOPRT	platforming
AFGILMNORRU	granuliform
AFGILNORTUU	fulguration
AFGINOOPPTT	foot-tapping
AFGINRRSTTU	frustrating
AFGLLOOOSTW	gallows-foot
AFHHIORTTWY	faithworthy
AFHLLMNRUUY	unharmfully
AFHLOOPPRSS	splashproof
AFHLOOSSTTY	soothfastly
AFIIIILNNTV	infinitival
AFIIILMNNST	infantilism
AFIIILNRSTU	fustilirian
AFIIIMPRSSS	fissiparism
AFIIINNORTU	infuriation
AFIIIPRSSTY	fissiparity
AFIILLLMOPR	lapilliform
AFIILLMMMOR	mamilliform
AFIILLMOPPR	papilliform
AFIILLNOSTU	fusillation
AFIILMNNOTU	fulmination
AFIILMNOPRU	naupliiform
AFIILMNORTY	informality
AFIILMOPRRS	spiraliform
AFIILNORRTT	infiltrator
AFIILORSTTU	flirtatious
AFIIMNNOORT	information
AFIIMNOORSU	omnifarious
AFIIMORSTUV	favouritism
AFIINNORSTX	transfixion
AFIIOPRSSSU	fissiparous
AFILLMNOPRU	planuliform
AFILMNOORTU	formulation
AFILMNORTUY	fulminatory
AFILNNOOSTU	sulfonation
AFILNORSTTU	flustration
AFIMMNOPRTY	tympaniform
AFIMMORSTUU	fumatoriums
AFIMNOORRTY	informatory
AFINNORSSTU	transfusion
AFINORRSTTU	frustration
AFKKLMPRTUU	Kulturkampf
AFLMOPRRTUY	poultry-farm
AGGGIIJNNOR	jagging-iron
AGGGILNOOTY	gigantology
AGGGILNSUZZ	gas-guzzling
AGGHHIIKNNR	high-ranking
AGGHHLOPPRY	glyphograph
AGGHHNORTUU	throughgaun
AGGHIIJMNTU	thingumajig
AGGHIIJMNTY	thingamyjig
AGGHIIKNNTW	night-waking
AGGHIILNNSU	languishing
AGGHIILOOST	hagiologist
AGGHINORTWW	wagonwright
AGGHLNOOPSY	sphagnology
AGGHMMOPRSY	sphygmogram
AGGIIKLNNWW	wing-walking
AGGIILNNOSS	sloganising
AGGIILNNOSY	agonisingly
AGGIILNNOSZ	sloganizing
AGGIILNNOYZ	agonizingly
AGGIILNRSST	tiring-glass
AGGIINNOPRT	pig-ignorant
AGGIINNPRST	part-singing

Words marked △ may be spelled also with a capital letter

AGGIINORTTU	gurgitation
AGGIKLNNOSW	walking-song
AGGIKNNOSUW	wauking-song
AGGILLNNOPY	long-playing
AGGILLNNTWY	twanglingly
AGGIMMNOPRR	programming
AGGIMMOORTU	maggotorium
AGGLLNOORYY	laryngology
AGGLOOORSTY	agrostology
AGHHIIMNRST	nightmarish
AGHHIIRSSTT	straightish
AGHHILOPRTY	lithography
AGHHLOOPSUY	hylophagous
AGHHLORTUWY	laughworthy
AGHHMNOPRYY	hymnography
AGHHMOPRTYY	mythography
AGHHNOOPPRY	phonography
AGHHOOPPRTY	photography
AGHHOOPRRTY	orthography
AGHHOORTUWX	thoroughwax
AGHHOPPRSYY	hypsography
AGHHOPPRTYY	phytography
AGHIIILMNTU	humiliating
AGHIIKLLLNW	hillwalking
AGHIILLNOOP	philologian
AGHIILMNOOS	hooliganism
AGHIILNNSVY	vanishingly
AGHIILNRSVY	ravishingly
AGHIIMOSTTX	thigmotaxis
AGHIINNOSST	astonishing
AGHIINPRSTY	pharyngitis
AGHIKNORRSW	work-sharing
AGHILMNNORY	gymnorhinal
AGHILMNOOTY	mythologian
AGHILNOOSTT	anthologist
AGHILNOPRTW	whaling-port
AGHILNORRWY	harrowingly
AGHILNRTTWY	thwartingly
AGHILOOPSTT	pathologist
AGHIMNNSSTU	hunting-mass
AGHIMNOOPSY	siphonogamy
AGHIMNOPRST	prognathism
AGHIMOPRSTY	myographist
	Pythagorism
AGHINNOPPSW	swan-hopping
AGHINOOSSTY	soothsaying
AGHIOOPPSUX	xiphopagous
AGHIOOPRRST	torsiograph
AGHIOOPRSTZ	zoographist
AGHIOOPSTUX	toxiphagous
AGHIOPPRRSY	spirography
AGHIORSTTTU	straight-out
AGHLLOOPSSY	hypoglossal
AGHLOOPPSUY	polyphagous
AGHLOOPSUXY	xylophagous
AGHLOPRSTYY	stylography
AGHMNOOOPSU	monophagous
AGHNNOSSTUY	syngnathous
AGHNOOPPRRY	pornography
AGHNOOPRSTU	prognathous
AGHOOPRSSTY	gastrosophy
AGHOORRSTTW	groatsworth
AGIIIILLNNT	initialling
AGIIIILLNOST	sigillation
AGIIIILLNTTT	titillating
AGIIIILMNSTV	vigilantism
AGIIIILNORTV	invigilator
AGIIIILNORTY	originality
AGIIIILNPSST	salpingitis
AGIIIILNSTTW	waiting-list
AGIIIIMMNORT	immigration
AGIIIINNNSTU	insinuating
AGIIIINNOORT	origination
AGIIIINNOSTT	instigation
AGIIKKNNRST	skating-rink
AGIIKNPRSSY	sky-aspiring
AGIILMNNOTY	longanimity
AGIILMNRSSU	singularism
AGIILMNSTTU	stimulating
AGIILMOOPST	Plagiostomi
AGIILMOORST	Mariologist
AGIILMOOSST	gliomatosis
AGIILNRSSTU	singularist
AGIILNRSTUY	singularity
AGIIMMNNTTU	manumitting
AGIIMNNORTW	tiring-woman
AGIIMNOORTW	waiting-room
AGIINNOOPRT	pignoration
AGIINNOPRST	patronising
AGIINNOPRTZ	patronizing
AGIINNSSSTU	unassisting
AGIINOORRTV	invigorator
AGIINORSTTT	tritagonist
AGIINPRRTTW	part-writing
AGIKLLNPRSY	sparklingly
AGILLMNNOOU	monolingual
AGILLNOPSTU	post-lingual
AGILLNRSTTY	startlingly
AGILMMNPSUW	lignum-swamp
AGILMNNOOSU	longanimous
AGILMNNSUUY	unamusingly
AGILMNRSSUY	laryngismus
AGILMOOPRTY	primatology
AGILMOORSTY	Maryologist
AGILMOOSTTU	tautologism
AGILMORRRSS	mirror-glass
AGILNNPRSUY	unsparingly
AGILNOPPRVY	approvingly
AGILNOPRUVY	vapouringly
AGILNOSSSUU	salsuginous
AGILOORSSYY	Assyriology
AGILOOSTTTU	tautologist
AGIMMNOORST	mooring-mast
AGIMMOOPRST	gamotropism
AGIMNNNORRY	non-marrying
AGIMNORRSTU	organistrum
AGINNOPPRUV	unapproving
AGINNOPRRST	apron-string
AGINNOPRSST	transposing
AGINNOQRRTU	quarrington
AGINOOOPRRT	prorogation
AGINOOPRSTT	protagonist
AGINOORRSTU	surrogation
AGINOORRSUV	granivorous

AGLLLNOOPYY polygonally
AGLLLOOPTTY polyglottal
AGLLMOORSUY glamorously
AGLLORRSUUY garrulously
AGLMNOOPTUY polygonatum
AGLMNOORTYY laryngotomy
AGLMOOOSTTY stomatology
AGLMOOPRRTU promulgator
AGLMOORRTYY martyrology
AGLMOPRSSUU glamourpuss
AGLOOOSTTUU tautologous
AGMOORSSTTY gastrostomy
AHHIIIPRSST phthiriasis
AHHILLOOPSU halophilous
AHHILLPSTUY △ithyphallus
AHHILMOPSTT ophthalmist
AHHILMOPSTY hylopathism
AHHILNOORTU holothurian
AHHILOPPSYY hypophysial
AHHILOPSTTY hylopathist
AHHIMNNOOPR harmoniphon
AHHIMNOPSSW showmanship
AHHINORSTUZ rhizanthous
AHHIPRSSTTW thwartships
AHHKNORTTWY thankworthy
AHHLLNOPTXY xanthophyll
AHIIILMNOTU humiliation
AHIIIPPRSTT hippiatrist
AHIIJNOPRST janitorship
AHIILLORSUY hilariously
AHIILMNOPST notaphilism
AHIILMORTUY humiliatory
AHIILNOPRRT horripilant
AHIILNOPSTT notaphilist
AHIILOPSTTY hospitality
AHIILPSSTTY staphylitis
AHIILRSSTTY hairstylist
AHIIMMNSSTU shunamitism
AHIIMNNOSST Smithsonian
AHIIMNNRRTU antirrhinum
AHIIMNOOOSU homoiousian
AHIIMOOPPPT hippopotami
AHIIOPRRSTT traitorship
AHIKKOORRSW kwashiorkor
AHIKLMOORSW workaholism
AHIKMNOPRSW workmanship
AHILLMOPRTU prothallium
AHILLNNOPSY pollyannish
AHILLOPSTXY phyllotaxis
AHILMMOOPSU ammophilous
AHILMORTTUU multi-author
AHILNOPRSTY rhinoplasty
AHILOORRTTY hortatorily
AHILOPPRSXY prophylaxis
AHILOPRSTYY physiolatry
AHIMNOOPSTT taphonomist
AHIMNOORRSU honorariums
AHIMNOPRSTY misanthropy
AHIMOORSTUZ rhizomatous
AHIMOPRSSTY stasimorphy
AHINNOORRST horrisonant
AHINOOPPRST patroonship
AHINOOPSSTX saxophonist
AHINOORRSTU ornithosaur
AHIOOPRRSTX orthopraxis
AHIOOPRSTTX trophotaxis
AHKNOOTUWWY you-know-what
AHLLNOORSTW sallow-thorn
AHLMNOTUXXY Xanthoxylum
AHLMNOTUXYZ Zanthoxylum
AHLMOOPPRST trophoplasm
AHLMOOPRSUY amorphously
AHLNOOPRSTY hyoplastron
AHLOPRRSTUU sulphurator
AHNORSSTUUY thysanurous
AHOOPPRSSTU apostrophus
AIIIILNOTVX lixiviation
AIIIKLMNRRS larrikinism
AIIILLLNPTU △lilliputian
AIIILLNOPTX pixillation
AIIILLNOQTU illiquation
AIIILLNOTTT titillation
AIIILLNOTUV illuviation
AIIILLRSTTV vitraillist
AIIILMNOSTT limitations
AIIILNNOTTU intuitional
AIIILNORSTT institorial
AIIILNOSTTU utilisation
AIIILNOTTUZ utilization
AIIIMNRSTTU miniaturist
AIIIMPPRRTY primiparity
AIIIMPSSTVY impassivity
AIIINNNOQTU inquination
AIIINNNOSTU insinuation
AIIINNOPRST inspiration
AIIINNOQRTU inquiration
AIIINNOSTTU inusitation
unitisation
AIIINNOTTUZ unitization
AIIINOTTTTV tittivation
AIIKNRSSSTT Sanskritist
AIILLMMNOTU multinomial
AIILLMNORTU illuminator
AIILLMPRSTU multispiral
AIILLNNOOPT pollination
AIILLNPRTUY nulliparity
AIILLNRSSTY sinistrally
AIILLPPRTUY pupillarity
AIILLPRSTUY spiritually
AIILMMORTTY immortality
AIILMNOOPRT imploration
AIILMNOOPST malposition
AIILMNOOSST solmisation
AIILMNOOSTZ solmization
AIILMNOSTTU stimulation
AIILMOOPSST lipomatosis
AIILMPRTTUY multiparity
AIILMRSSUVV survivalism
AIILNNOOSTT notionalist
AIILNNORTTU nutritional
AIILNOOPRSV △provisional
AIILNOORTVY volitionary
AIILNOPRTUY unipolarity
AIILNOPSTTU stipulation

AIILNORTUUX luxuriation
AIILNOSSTTY stylisation
AIILNOSTTYZ stylization
AIILNPRSTUU unspiritual
AIILNQRTTUY tranquility
AIILPRSTTUY spiritualty
AIILRSSTUVV survivalist
AIIMMNNOSSU manumission
AIIMMNOPSTT pantomimist
AIIMMNSSTTU numismatist
AIIMNNOOSTU antimonious
AIIMNOOPRTT importation
AIIMNOOPRTX proximation
AIIMNOSSTTU mussitation
AIIMNOSTTTU mutationist
AIIMNPRSSSU Prussianism
AIIMOPPRRSU primiparous
AIIMOPPRRTU ipratropium
AIINNOOOPRT opinionator
AIINNOOOSTZ ozonisation
AIINNOOOTZZ ozonization
AIINNOORSTT nitrosation
AIINNORSTUY insinuatory
AIINOPRRSTY inspiratory
AIINOPRRSUU uriniparous
AIINOPRRTTU parturition
AIINOPRSSST inspissator
AIINOPRSSTU suspiration
AIINORRTTTU trituration
AIIOOPPRRTT propitiator
AIIOPRRSTTT portraitist
AIIOPRSSTTT prostatitis
AILLLNOOPRU allopurinol
AILLLNOPTUU pullulation
AILLLNOSUVY villanously
AILLMOOPRST allotropism
AILLMOPSSSY plasmolysis
AILLMOPSTUY ampullosity
AILLNOOSTTY litany-stool
AILLNOPRSUU nulliparous
AILLNORTUVY voluntarily
AILLNPPSTUY suppliantly
AILLNRTUUXY luxuriantly
AILLOOPRSTT postillator
AILLOPPPRTU tulip-poplar
AILLORRSTTU illustrator
AILMMNNOTUU nummulation
AILMMNOSTUU multanimous
AILMMOPSSTY polymastism
AILMNNOSTTU multisonant
AILMNNOSUUY unanimously
AILMNOOOPRT promotional
AILMNOPRTTY importantly
AILMNORSTUV voluntarism
AILMOOPRRTY imploratory
AILMOOPRUYZ polyzoarium
AILMOPRSTUU multiparous
AILNNORTUVY involuntary
AILNNRTUUUX unluxuriant
AILNOOPRSTU sporulation
AILNOOPSTTU postulation
AILNOPPSTTU post-nuptial
AILNOPSTTUU pustulation
AILNORSTTUV voluntarist
AILNORSUUVY unsavourily
AILNRSSTUUU laurustinus
AILOOPRSUVY oviparously
AILOPRSTTUY stipulatory
AILORSTTTUY statutorily
AIMMNORRTUU murmuration
AIMMOORRSTU moratoriums
AIMMOOSSTXY myxomatosis
AIMNNOOPTTU mountain-top
AIMNNOOSTUU mountainous
AIMNNOPRTTU unimportant
AIMOPPRRSTY post-primary
AINNOOOPPRT pornotopian
AINOOOPRRSW arrow-poison
AINOOPRRSTT prostration
AINOPPRSTUU suppuration
AINORRSSTUU susurration
AKLNNOOOPTZ zooplankton
ALLNOOOPPRR △propranolol
ALLNOPPRUUY unpopularly
ALLOOOPRSTU allotropous
ALLOORSTWWW swallow-wort
ALMMNOSSUUW Mussulwoman
ALMNNOOSUYY anonymously
ALMNOOORSTU monolatrous
ALNNORSTUYY tyrannously
ALOOOPRSTUV pot-valorous
ALOOPRSTTUY postulatory
ALOPRRSTUUY rapturously
AMNOOPRSSTW sportswoman
AMNOOSTTUUY tautonymous
AMOOPRRRTTY protomartyr
ANOOOPRRTTY protonotary

B

BBBBDEEELRU beblubbered
BBBEEHLLLSU bubble-shell
BBBEELMMORY lobby-member
BBBEGIIINNW wine-bibbing
BBCDEEORRRU rubber-cored
BBCDEHIIKRT thick-ribbed
BBCDEHIRRTU butcher-bird
BBCEEGIILLR gibberellic
BBCEEHNNOOU bonne-bouche
BBCEELNOOST cobblestone
BBCEGIIILOP bibliopegic
BBCEGINNOUV nubbing-cove
BBCEILMOSTU combustible
BBCEJKOORST stockjobber
BBCEKLORSTU blockbuster
BBCGIINRSSU subscribing
BBCGIMOORRY borborygmic
BBCIIILLOOP bibliopolic
BBDDEELLOOU blue-blooded
BBDDEENOORR Broederbond
BBDDEILLNOU double-blind
BBDDEILORUY body-builder
BBDEEHHLOOY hobbledehoy
BBDEEHIRRSU shrubberied
BBDEGIIMNOV dive-bombing

BBDEIKNOORY bookbindery
BBDELLNOOTT bottle-blond
BBDELNOOOSY bloody-bones
BBDELNRSSUU blunderbuss
BBDGHLOOOTU blood-bought
BBDGIIKNNOO bookbinding
BBEEEHRRSTU sheet-rubber
BBEEELNOPST pebble-stone
BBEEGIILLNR gibberellin
BBEEGILMRSU submergible
BBEEILLMRTY belly-timber
BBEEILMRSSU submersible
BBEEILNSSSU subsensible
BBEEINNNOOR bonbonnière
BBEELNORSTU rubble-stone
BBEENORRSYY boysenberry
BBEFGIIMNOR fire-bombing
BBEFILORSUU bulbiferous
BBEGGGILNOW begging-bowl
BBEGINOSSSU gibbousness
BBEHIIILLOP bibliophile
BBEHINRSSSU shrubbiness
BBEHLORSTTU bottle-brush
BBEHMOORSTU bumbershoot
BBEIILMSSSU submissible
BBELLNOTTUY belly-button
BBELMPPPUUY bumble-puppy
BBELNOSSSUU bulbousness
BBGHILNOORY hobgoblinry
BBGHILNORTY throbbingly
BBGIILLNQUY quibblingly
BBGILMNOTUX tumbling-box
BBGINOPRSTU rubbing-post
BBGMOORRSUY borborygmus
BBHIIILLOPY bibliophily
BBJMMMOOSUU mumbo-jumbos
BBLLLLOOOYY loblolly-boy
BCCDEEHKLOU double-check
BCCDEILNOTU conductible
BCCDEIOPSUU pseudocubic
BCCEEEEFINN beneficence
BCCEEEENRSU erubescence
BCCEEEHOPPR copper-beech
BCCEEENRSUY erubescency
BCCEEIILNOR incoercible
BCCEEILLLOT collectible
BCCEEILNNOT connectible
BCCEEILNOSS concessible
BCCEEILORRT correctible
BCCEEINRSTY cybernetics
BCCEFFIKLOO office-block
BCCEFIIPSSU subspecific
BCCEGILNOOS cognoscible
BCCEHILLNTU clench-built
BCCEHILPSUY push-bicycle
BCCEHINOOPR necrophobic
BCCEIIIRSTU rice-biscuit
BCCEIILNNOV convincible
BCCEIILNORU ribonucleic
BCCEIINOOOT biocoenotic
BCCEIINOORT necrobiotic
BCCEIKLMORR rock-climber
BCCEIKLORSS brissel-cock
BCCEIMNOOSU subeconomic
BCCHHILOOOP ochlophobic
BCCHIOOOPST Scotophobic
BCDDDELLOOO cold-blooded
BCDDEEEILNS descendible
BCDDEEILOOS close-bodied
BCDDEEINRSU undescribed
BCDDEGIMNOR redding-comb
BCDDEHLOTUU double-Dutch
BCDEEEEIRRS decerebrise
BCDEEEEIRRZ decerebrize
BCDEEEFINNU unbeneficed
BCDEEEHIMRS Decemberish
BCDEEEIINNO inobedience
BCDEEEIINNT Benedictine
BCDEEEIINTV benedictive
BCDEEEIORRS cerebroside
BCDEEHILNPT pitchblende
BCDEEHMNOOY honeycombed
BCDEEHMNOTU debouchment
BCDEEIIILRT liberticide
BCDEEIIIMNO biomedicine
BCDEEIILNRS discernible
BCDEEIILPRS discerpible
BCDEEIILRRU irreducible
BCDEEIILSST dissectible
BCDEEIIMRSS misdescribe
BCDEEIINNOT benediction
BCDEEILNOSS docibleness
BCDEEILNRUU unreducible
BCDEEIMNRSU disencumber
BCDEEIMRTUU decumbiture
BCDEEINORSV bond-service
BCDEEINORTY benedictory
BCDEEJNSTUU unsubjected
BCDEELMNTUY decumbently
BCDEGHNRRSU bergschrund
BCDEHILNNOR hornblendic
BCDEHILORSU subchloride
BCDEIIILRTY credibility
BCDEIILNRSY discernibly
BCDEIILOQTU quodlibetic
BCDEIILRRUY irreducibly
BCDEIILSSSU discussible
BCDEIINNRSU uninscribed
BCDEIKLOQUU double-quick
BCDEINORRSS incrossbred
BCDEIOOPRSS proboscides
BCDEKLOORSU bloodsucker
BCDELMNOSUU muscle-bound
BCDELOORSSU double-cross
BCDENNOORTU counterbond
BCDGIIKMNOR mockingbird
BCDHHIOOPRY hydrophobic
BCDHIMOORRY hydrobromic
BCDIILMORTU trombiculid
BCDIINRTUUY rubicundity
BCDIIRSSTTU subdistrict
BCDILLNOORU colour-blind
BCEEEELNNOV benevolence
BCEEEFILPRT perfectible

BCEEEGMNRSU submergence
BCEEEHHINPR hebephrenic
BCEEEHKLTUW bucket-wheel
BCEEEILPPRT perceptible
BCEEEILPRTX excerptible
BCEEEINNOPT bonnet-piece
BCEEELLMRSU cerebellums
BCEEELLORSU cerebellous
BCEEENNOSSS obsceneness
BCEEENQSSUU subsequence
BCEEFIMNORT fibrocement
fibrocement®
BCEEFIMORRR cerebriform
BCEEFINOSTT cost-benefit
BCEEGHMOOSU gobe-mouches
BCEEGILNOST congestible
BCEEHHINPRS benchership
BCEEHHNOOPT technophobe
BCEEHIIINRS △hibernicise
BCEEHIIINRZ △hibernicize
BCEEHIMNTTW bewitchment
BCEEHIOORRS seborrhoeic
BCEEHKLRRUY huckleberry
BCEEHNOOPST benthoscope
BCEEIIJOSTV objectivise
BCEEIIJOTVZ objectivize
BCEEIILRSTV vitrescible
BCEEIINRRST interscribe
BCEEIJLOTVY objectively
BCEEILLLOSY bellicosely
BCEEILMNNOT contemnible
BCEEILMOSST comestibles
BCEEILNORST bristlecone
BCEEILNORTV convertible
BCEEILPPRTY perceptibly
BCEEILPRSTU putrescible
BCEEILPSSTU susceptible
BCEEILRSTUU tuberculise
BCEEILRTUUZ tuberculize
BCEEINOOOSS biocoenoses
BCEEINSSSTU subsistence
BCEEIOPRSST corbie-steps
BCEEIPRRSSU superscribe
BCEEIRRSSTT bitter-cress
BCEEJLSSSTU subjectless
BCEEKKLNNOU knuckle-bone
BCEELLMOSUU submolecule
BCEELLNORTU clenbuterol
BCEELMNRTUY recumbently
BCEELNOOSST obsolescent
BCEELORSTUU tuberculose
BCEELRRRUWY curlew-berry
BCEEMNORSTU obscurement
BCEEMNOSTTU obmutescent
BCEEMOPRRRU procerebrum
BCEENOORRTU counterbore
BCEENORSSSU obscureness
BCEFFNORTUU counterbuff
BCEGHILNNNU unblenching
BCEGIIILNOOY cine-biology
ciné-biology
BCEGIIMMNOS misbecoming
BCEGILMOORY embryologic
BCEHHIILOOP heliophobic
BCEHHIIMRTT timber-hitch
BCEHHIIOOPR hierophobic
BCEHHILNOOT holobenthic
BCEHIIIMNRS Hibernicism
BCEHIJPSSTU subjectship
BCEHIKLMOOR hook-climber
BCEHILNOSST blotchiness
BCEHIMNRSSU Burschenism
BCEHIMOORRS chrisom-robe
BCEHKLNOOTU luckenbooth
BCEHKMMORSU Kommersbuch
BCEHKOPRRTU pork-butcher
BCEHLORRSYY chrysoberyl
BCEHLORTTTU butter-cloth
BCEHMOORTTY thrombocyte
BCEHMORRSUU rhumb-course
BCEIIJMOSTV objectivism
BCEIIJOSTTV objectivist
BCEIIJOTTVY objectivity
BCEIIKLLRST billsticker
BCEIILLOSTY bellicosity
BCEIIMNOOST coenobitism
BCEIINOOOSS biocoenosis
BCEIINOORSS necrobiosis
BCEIJNSTUUV subjunctive
BCEIKLLMNOO nickel-bloom
BCEIKLLOSVW swivelblock
BCEIKOOPRTU picture-book
BCEIKOOTTTY tickettyboo
BCEILLNOSUV convulsible
BCEILLORSSU brucellosis
BCEILMNNTUY incumbently
BCEILMOOPSS compossible
BCEILMOORRT root-climber
BCEILMORTUU microtubule
BCEILNORTVY convertibly
BCEILOPRRTU corruptible
BCEILPSSTUY susceptibly
BCEIOOPRSSS proboscises
BCEIORSTTUV obstructive
BCEIPRSSSUY presbycusis
BCEKKLMNOOY monkey-block
BCEKKOOOORY cookery-book
BCEKKOORRST stockbroker
BCEKLMOSSTY block-system
BCELNOORTUW counterblow
BCELORSTUUU tuberculous
BCELSTTTTUU scuttlebutt
BCEOOOPRSST stroboscope
BCFIIILORTY forcibility
BCFILMOORRU colubriform
BCGIIIKLNRT rib-tickling
BCGIIKLNOOT bootlicking
BCGIINOOOTT gnotobiotic
BCGIKLNOPPU upping-block
BCGILMNOOOW wool-combing
BCGILMNRSUU lignum-scrub
BCGILNOOPUX coupling-box
BCGILOOORYY cryobiology
BCHHIOOOPPT photophobic

BCHIOOPRSSU	Russophobic
BCIIIILMSTY	miscibility
BCIIIILNTVY	vincibility
BCIIILLORUU	cuir-bouilli
BCIIINNOSSU	subincision
BCIILLORSSS	scissor-bill
BCIILLORUUY	cuir-bouilly
BCIILMOSSTY	symbolistic
BCIINOORSTT	obstriction
BCIIOORSTTU	biscuit-root
BCIJNNOSTUU	subjunction
BCIKLLLOOPW	pillow-block
BCILMOSTTUU	custom-built
BCILOPRRTUY	corruptibly
BCIMOOSSTUU	combustious
BCINOORRTTU	contributor
BCINOORSTTU	obstruction
BDDDEEEGLOU	double-edged
BDDDEEEINRT	interbedded
BDDDEEIIMOS	disembodied
BDDDEEINRRU	underbidder
BDDEEEIMMRS	dismembered
BDDEEEIMNRT	débridement
BDDEEELNORU	double-ender
BDDEEFILLLN	blind-felled
BDDEEFILLNS	self-blinded
BDDEEFLSSUU	self-subdued
BDDEEGIIRRV	bridge-drive
BDDEEGINRRU	underbridge
BDDEEGNRTUU	underbudget
BDDEEIINOST	disobedient
BDDEEILLOSW	disbowelled
BDDEEILLOUV	double-lived
BDDEEILMNNO	noble-minded
BDDEEILOOOS	loose-bodied
BDDEEIMNORS	sober-minded
BDDEEIMNRSU	disemburden
BDDEELOOPRU	pure-blooded
BDDEENSSSUU	subduedness
BDDEFILNORY	forbiddenly
BDDEFINNORU	unforbidden
BDDEFLLLOOU	full-blooded
BDDEFMNORUU	dumbfounder
BDDEGGINORX	dredging-box
BDDEGHHILOO	highblooded
BDDEGIILOTU	double-digit
BDDEGIIMNNN	mind-bending
BDDEGIINORV	overbidding
BDDEGMOORRY	Dogberrydom
BDDEHINNOUU	unhidebound
BDDEHINRRTU	thunderbird
BDDEIINRSTU	distribuend
BDDEINOOWWW	bow-windowed
BDDEINRSTUU	undisturbed
BDDELNNOUUY	unboundedly
BDDELNOTUUY	undoubtedly
BDDFILLNNOU	unblindfold
BDDIIKNOOSS	od's-bodikins
BDDIINPTUUY	pudibundity
BDEEEEHIRST	therebeside
BDEEEEIIMRR	Biedermeier
BDEEEFGINRW	web-fingered
BDEEEFILOOU	oeil-de-boeuf
BDEEEFILRRU	reef-builder
BDEEEFINNTU	unbenefited
BDEEEHIKRSW	bewhiskered
BDEEEHILMTW	thimbleweed
BDEEEIILRSV	disbeliever
BDEEEILLNTU	belle-de-nuit
BDEEEILMNTV	bedevilment
BDEEEILMPRT	redemptible
BDEEEILPRSS	depressible
BDEEEIMMRRS	disremember
BDEEEIMNNTZ	bedizenment
BDEEEIMORRR	embroiderer
BDEEELLLOVW	well-beloved
BDEEELNSSSS	blessedness
BDEEELORTTX	letterboxed
BDEEFHIILLS	fish-bellied
BDEEFIIINRS	defibrinise
BDEEFIIINRZ	defibrinize
BDEEFLLNORU	bell-founder
BDEEGGHIIRW	weighbridge
BDEEGHINNTU	unbenighted
BDEEGHIORSU	bridge-house
BDEEGIILLNV	bedevilling
BDEEGIILNRW	bewildering
BDEEGINORTU	outbreeding
BDEEGLNORRY	goldenberry
BDEEGMNRSUU	unsubmerged
BDEEHIILLTW	white-billed
BDEEHILMNSU	unblemished
BDEEHLLMTUW	well-thumbed
BDEEHNNRTUU	unburthened
BDEEIILNNYZ	benzylidine
BDEEIILNSST	distensible
BDEEIIMRSTT	disembitter
BDEEIIRSTTU	distributee
BDEEILLMOOS	loose-limbed
BDEEILLNPRS	spellbinder
BDEEILMNOTY	molybdenite
BDEEILMRRTU	tumble-drier
BDEEILNORST	stereoblind
BDEEILORRSW	bowdleriser
BDEEILORRWZ	bowdlerizer
BDEEIMMORRV	overbrimmed
BDEEINNRTTU	underbitten
BDEEIOORSXY	deoxyribose
BDEEIORSSTU	sober-suited
BDEELLOORTT	bloodletter
BDEELNOOSTT	bottle-nosed
BDEELNORTUY	double-entry
BDEELPRRTUY	perturbedly
BDEENNNORTU	under-bonnet
BDEENORSTTU	deobstruent
BDEENPRRTUU	unperturbed
BDEFGHIILRT	bright-field
BDEFLLNORTU	bull-fronted
BDEFLLNORUY	bell-foundry
BDEFLLOOORW	blood-flower
BDEFLNOOORZ	blood-frozen
BDEGGHIILLN	hedging-bill
BDEGGIINRSW	swing-bridge
BDEGHOOORRT	good-brother

BDEGIILMNSS dissembling
BDEGIINNRST bird-nesting
BDEGILNNNUY unbendingly
BDEGIMORRSY Dogberryism
BDEGINORSTW bowstringed
BDEGLOORTTU bottle-gourd
gutterblood
BDEHHOOORRT brotherhood
BDEHIIINNTU uninhibited
BDEHIILPRSU shipbuilder
BDEHIKLNOTU doublethink
BDEHILNPSUU unpublished
BDEHILOOPRY hyperboloid
BDEHINNRSUU unburnished
BDEHINNRTUW burn-the-wind
BDEHLNORTTU thunderbolt
BDEHMOOORST smooth-bored
BDEHNORRSUY hounds-berry
BDEIIIILNSV indivisible
BDEIIIILNTY inedibility
BDEIIILMSSS dismissible
BDEIIILNTVY vendibility
BDEIIISSUVV subdivisive
BDEIILMRSUU subdelirium
BDEIIRRSTTU distributer
BDEIKNORSTU strikebound
BDEILLOSTUX billets-doux
BDEILNORSTY blind-storey
BDEILNTTTUW blunt-witted
BDEINORSTTU Brotstudien
BDEINOSSSUU dubiousness
BDEISSTTTUU substituted
BDELLOSSTUY doubtlessly
BDELNOOPRST bloodsprent
BDELOOSTTUU double-stout
BDEMOOORSSY rosy-bosomed
BDFILMOSTUU misdoubtful
BDGGIIILNOS disobliging
BDGGIIINNRS singing-bird
BDGHIIMMNRU humming-bird
BDGIILMNNOW mind-blowing
BDGIILNOTUU outbuilding
BDGIIMMNNNU mind-numbing
BDGILLOOTUY blood-guilty
BDGILNOOPTY blood-typing
BDGINNOORRU ground-robin
BDGINOOPPPY body-popping
BDGNORRSTUU groundburst
BDHKOORSTUY Dukhobortsy
BDHNNOOORUU honour-bound
BDIIIILNSVY indivisibly
BDIIINOSSUV subdivision
BDIIMNORTUY moribundity
BDIIMOORRSS bromidrosis
BDIIORRSTTU distributor
BDINRSSTUUY subindustry
BDLMNOOTTUU button-mould
BEEEEGIMNST besiegement
BEEEEHLLSVW bevel-wheels
BEEEEIMNTTW betweentime
BEEEELPPPRT betel-pepper
BEEEENNSSTW betweenness
BEEEFLORRTU troublefree
BEEEFOORRTY freebootery
BEEEGIINNOR bioengineer
BEEEGILLNRT belligerent
BEEEGILLNSS legibleness
BEEEGILMNSY beseemingly
BEEEGILMNTU beguilement
BEEEGIMNNSU unbeseeming
BEEEGINRRST Steinberger
BEEEGLNORTT bottle-green
greenbottle
BEEEHILLMRS embellisher
BEEEHILLNOR helleborine
BEEEHILNPRS prehensible
BEEEHLORTTT three-bottle
BEEEHLPSSTU steeplebush
BEEEIIJLMSU semi-jubilee
BEEEIILMRSV misbeliever
BEEEIKNRTTU knee-tribute
BEEEILLRTYZ leze-liberty
BEEEILMPPRT pre-emptible
BEEEILNNORV non-believer
BEEEILNPRTV preventible
BEEEILPRRSS repressible
BEEEILPRRTV pervertible
BEEEILPRSSX expressible
BEEEIMMMRRS misremember
BEEEIMMNOTT emboîtement
BEEEIOQRTUU bouquetière
BEEEIRSTTTW bittersweet
BEEELMMNOTW embowelment
BEEELMMNRTT tremblement
BEEELMNNNOT ennoblement
BEEELORSSWY eyebrowless
BEEEMMNORTW embowerment
BEEENOPPRTY teeny-bopper
BEEENOPPRWY weeny-bopper
BEEENORSSSV verboseness
BEEENQRRSUY Queensberry
BEEFGIINNTT benefitting
BEEFGINOORT freebooting
BEEFGINRSUZ subfreezing
BEEFGLLOORW globeflower
BEEFHLLRRSU fuller's-herb
BEEFIKNRTTU butter-knife
BEEFILNRRST bristle-fern
BEEFILRSTTU butterflies
BEEFKLLRUUY rebukefully
BEEGGIILNSY besiegingly
BEEGGILSSTU suggestible
BEEGHIINPST sheep-biting
BEEGHIMNNTT benightment
BEEGHINNORR herring-bone
BEEGIILLNVY believingly
BEEGIILNNUV unbelieving
BEEGIILNQTU quilting-bee
BEEGIIMNRTT embittering
BEEGIIOORSU bourgeoisie
BEEGIKKNOOP bookkeeping
BEEGILLMNOW embowelling
BEEGILLNSST bestselling
BEEGILNNOSS ignobleness

BEEGILNSSSU	leg-business
BEEGIMNOSTT	misbegotten
BEEGINOPRRY	pigeon-berry
BEEGNNOORTU	bonnet-rouge
BEEGNORRTUU	bourtree-gun
BEEHIKLORRT	brotherlike
BEEHILMMNST	blemishment
BEEHILOPRSY	hyperbolise
BEEHILOPRYZ	hyperbolize
BEEHILPRRSU	republisher
BEEHIMNOORT	theobromine
BEEHKNOORSU	house-broken
BEEHLRRRTUY	hurtleberry
BEEHMNORTTT	betrothment
BEEHNORRTUV	overburthen
BEEHOPRRSTT	stepbrother
BEEIIILPSTT	epistilbite
BEEIILLORSS	brise-soleil
BEEIILMPRSS	impressible
	permissible
BEEIILNSSSV	visibleness
BEEIIRRTTUV	retributive
BEEILLLNTUY	ebulliently
BEEILLORRSU	irresoluble
BEEILLRRRTU	bull-terrier
BEEILLRSTTT	bellettrist
BEEILMMNORT	embroilment
BEEILMNSSSU	sublimeness
BEEILNOPRSS	responsible
BEEILNOQSSU	obliqueness
BEEILNPSSSU	suspensible
BEEILNRSSTT	brittleness
BEEILNSSSTU	subtileness
BEEILPRRSSY	repressibly
BEEIMPRSSTT	Septembrist
BEEINNOORTU	boutonnière
BEEINORRSTT	sternotribe
BEEINORSTTY	tenebrosity
BEEINORTTTW	twitter-bone
BEEINRRRTWY	winterberry
BEEINRSSTTU	butteriness
BEEINRSSTUV	subservient
BEEJLNOSSSS	joblessness
BEEKMNOORRY	money-broker
BEELLLLOWYY	yellow-belly
BEELLMRSSSU	slumberless
BEELLNOSSUV	volubleness
BEELMMORSSU	slumbersome
BEELMOORSTU	troublesome
BEELPRSSTUU	supersubtle
BEENQRSSSUU	brusqueness
BEERRRSTTUU	surrebutter
BEFGHILLRTU	bullfighter
BEFGIILNTTY	befittingly
BEFGIINNTTU	unbefitting
BEFGILMRRUY	mulberry-fig
BEFHILLMSTU	thimblefuls
BEFHILLOSSW	bellows-fish
BEFHLMORTUU	rule-of-thumb
BEFHLOORRTW	froth-blower
BEFIIILLTXY	flexibility
BEFIILNORRU	neurofibril
BEFILMNRSSU	brimfulness
BEFIMOORRSU	morbiferous
BEFIMORRSUU	umbriferous
BEFINORSTTT	frostbitten
BEFLLMRSTUU	tumblerfuls
BEFLLOOPRTU	bullet-proof
BEGGGILNOOT	bootlegging
BEGGHIINNOR	neighboring
BEGGIILLNNR	bell-ringing
BEGGIILLNUY	beguilingly
BEGGIINNNNU	unbeginning
BEGGILNOOVX	boxing-glove
BEGHHIIRTTW	birth-weight
BEGHIINNOSW	wishing-bone
BEGHILLNOSU	bell-housing
BEGHILNORUY	neighbourly
BEGHINRRSSU	herring-buss
BEGHIPRRSTU	superbright
BEGIIIILLTY	eligibility
BEGIIILNOSTU	biting-louse
BEGIKLLNOOS	bookselling
BEGILLMNRTY	tremblingly
BEGILMNNRTU	untrembling
BEGILNORSVY	observingly
BEGINNORSUV	unobserving
BEHHIOOPSTT	theophobist
BEHIIIOPRTV	prohibitive
BEHIIMNPRRS	brine-shrimp
BEHIIMOSTWY	△whiteboyism
BEHIINPRSTU	tribuneship
BEHIINRRTTY	herb-trinity
BEHIINRSSST	Britishness
BEHIKNOOSSS	bookishness
BEHIKOOSTTX	textbookish
BEHILLNSSSU	bullishness
BEHILLRSTTU	bullshitter
BEHILMNPSTU	publishment
BEHILMOPRSY	hyperbolism
BEHIMNNRSTU	burnishment
BEHINOORSSS	boorishness
BEHINORRTTW	twin-brother
BEHINRSSSTU	brutishness
BEHIOORRSUV	herbivorous
BEHLLLSSSUY	blushlessly
BEHLNOORTTU	buttonholer
BEHLNORRTUY	unbrotherly
BEHNORSTTWY	west-by-north
BEHOSSTTUWY	west-by-south
BEIIILMNRST	libertinism
BEIIILMQRUU	equilibrium
BEIIILNSSTY	sensibility
BEIIILNSTTY	tensibility
BEIIILQRSTU	equilibrist
BEIIILQRTUY	equilibrity
BEIIILRRTTY	terribility
BEIILLORSSY	berylliosis
BEIILMPRSSY	permissibly
BEIILNOSSSU	biliousness
BEIILNRSSST	bristliness
BEIILRRSSTV	verslibrist
BEIINORRTTU	retribution
BEIINORSTUV	inobtrusive

BEILLLLOSUY libellously
BEILLMPSTUU submultiple
BEILLORRSUY irresolubly
BEILLORSSTT stilbestrol
BEILMNOOPSS monoblepsis
BEILMNOORTW winter-bloom
BEILMORRSTW bristle-worm
BEILMORSSTU mossbluiter
BEILMSSTTUY system-built
BEILNOPRSSY responsibly
BEILOPRRSTU protrusible
BEILORSTUVY obtrusively
BEIMNPPRTUU turbine-pump
BEIMNSSSSSU submissness
BEIMOORRTTV river-bottom
BEIMPSSTUUV subsumptive
BEINOOSSSUV obviousness
BEINORSTUUV unobtrusive
BEINPRRTTTU butter-print
BEINQRRSUYY quinsy-berry
BEINSSTTTUU substituent
BEIOPRRSSSU subprioress
BEIORRRTTUY retributory
BEIORSSTUUV subvitreous
BEKLMOPRRUW plumber-work
BEKNNNOSTUW unbeknownst
BELLNRTTUUY turbulently
BELNOORTTUW trouble-town
BELNOOSTUUY bounteously
BENOPRSSTTU press-button
BERRSSTTTUU trustbuster
BFILLNOTUUY bountifully
BFILOORSTUU tubiflorous
BGGHIILLNTY blightingly
BGGILLMNRUY grumblingly
BGGINNOORUU bourguignon
BGGINOORTTT bogtrotting
BGGLMOOORSS grog-blossom
BGHHIIMORSW highbrowism
BGHHLOORTTU through-bolt
BGHIINOPPWY whipping-boy
BGHIMNPTTUU tub-thumping
BGIIILLLTUY gullibility
BGIIKNOORTW writing-book
BGIILLNNPRU pruning-bill
BGIILNNOPSW spin-bowling
BGIILNNORRU burling-iron
BGIILOORSTT tribologist
BGIINOOOSST gnotobiosis
BGIINOSTTTW towing-bitts
BGILLMNSTUY stumblingly
BGINOOOPPTT boot-topping
BGLLMOOOSYY symbolology
BHHMMOOPTUY hop-o'-my-thumb
BHIIINOOPRT △prohibition
BHIIIOPRSTU triphibious
BHIILMOPRTY timbrophily
BHIIOOPRRTY prohibitory
BHILMOOSTYY tomboyishly
BHIMNOOPRRT prothrombin
BIIILMOPSSS possibilism
BIIILOPSSST possibilist
BIIILOPSSTY possibility
BIIILORSTTY torsibility
BIIKLLMORST Bristol-milk
BIILLNOORTU tourbillion
BIILLOOSUVY obliviously
BIILMORRTUU lubritorium
BIILOOQSTUU obliquitous
BIIMNOOSTUX moxibustion
BILMOPSTUUY bumptiously
BILNOOOSUXY obnoxiously
BIMNOPSSTUU subsumption
BIMORSSTUUU rumbustious
BINNOOOSUUX unobnoxious
BIOOOPPRRSU opprobrious
BLLMMOOPSSU plum-blossom
BLLMORSSUUY slumbrously
BLLOORSTUUY troublously
BLMNORSSUUU unslumbrous
BMMNOTTTUUY tummy-button
BNOORRSTUWW burrowstown

C

CCCCIMOORSU micrococcus
CCCDEEIINNO coincidence
CCCDEHINOSY synecdochic
CCCDEIINNOY coincidency
CCCDENNOOTU unconcocted
CCCDGINOOOO gonococcoid
CCCDIIIOOSS coccidiosis
CCCDILOOPSU diplococcus
CCCEEEENRSX excrescence
CCCEEENRSXY excrescency
CCCEEFLLNOU flocculence
CCCEEIILMST eclecticism
CCCEENNORRU concurrence
CCCEENNORST concrescent
CCCEFIINOPS conspecific
CCCEFILMRTU circumflect
CCCEHHIKLRS schrecklich
CCCEIIMRRSU circumciser
CCCEIINNOPY concipiency
CCCEIMPRSTU circumspect
CCCEINOOPRS necroscopic
CCCEIRSSTUY cysticercus
CCCENNORRUY concurrency
CCCHIIINNNO cinchoninic
CCCHILMOTYY cyclothymic
CCCIIMMOORS microcosmic
CCCIIMOOPRS microscopic
CCCINOOOSSU coconscious
CCCINORSTUY succinctory
CCCOOOPRSTU Protococcus
CCDDEEENORS decrescendo
CCDDEEENSUU unsucceeded
CCDDEKLNOUU uncuckolded
CCDEEEFHIKN chicken-feed
CCDEEEIINRS iridescence
CCDEEELLORT recollected
CCDEEENNORT concentered
CCDEEGIMNOO comedogenic
CCDEEHILPSY psychedelic
CCDEEHIORTT ricochetted

CCDEEIIINST	insecticide
CCDEEIILMRS	semicircled
CCDEEIILRRR	circle-rider
CCDEEIIRRST	directrices
CCDEEILMORU	leucodermic
CCDEEILNOTY	conceitedly
CCDEEILRRSS	dress-circle
CCDEEIMOSTY	discomycete
CCDEEINNOUV	unconceived
CCDEEIOPPRU	preoccupied
CCDEELLLOTY	collectedly
CCDEELLNOTU	uncollected
CCDEELNNOOS	condolences
CCDEELNNORY	concernedly
CCDEELNNOTY	connectedly
CCDEEMNNOTU	conducement
CCDEENNNORU	unconcerned
CCDEENNNOTU	unconnected
CCDEENNORTU	unconcerted
CCDEENORRTU	uncorrected
CCDEFIMRSUU	circumfused
CCDEHILOPSY	psychodelic
CCDEHIOOPRS	dichroscope
CCDEIILNOPS	condisciple
CCDEIILOORT	crocidolite
CCDEIMOOOST	octodecimos
CCDEINNNOUV	unconvinced
CCDEINNOTUV	unconvicted
CCDEINORSTT	constricted
CCDEIOPRRTU	picture-cord
CCDENORSSTU	conductress
CCDENORSTTU	deconstruct
CCDENORSUUU	unsuccoured
CCDGILNNOUY	conducingly
CCDHHILLOOS	schoolchild
CCDHHIOORRY	hydrochoric
CCDHILOOPYY	hypocycloid
CCDHIOPRRTY	cryptorchid
CCEEEEFMNRS	fremescence
CCEEEEILNST	telescience
CCEEEEINPRT	centrepiece
CCEEEFHIKNR	neckerchief
CCEEEFIKNPT	picket-fence
CCEEEFLNORS	florescence
CCEEEGINNRS	nigrescence
CCEEEGINOTT	ectogenetic
CCEEEGINRVY	vicegerency
CCEEEGNNORV	convergence
CCEEEGNRSTU	turgescence
CCEEEHHLOST	cheesecloth
CCEEEHINNOR	coinherence
	incoherence
CCEEEHIPRRS	speech-crier
CCEEEHORRTT	crotcheteer
CCEEEHORRTY	heterocercy
CCEEEIINPPR	percipience
CCEEEIKOPPT	pocket-piece
CCEEEILNQSU	liquescence
CCEEEIMORRT	coercimeter
CCEEEINNNOV	convenience
CCEEEINNPSS	spinescence
CCEEEINOPRV	preconceive
CCEEEINOPSS	cenospecies
CCEEEINOSTX	coexistence
CCEEEINRSTV	vitrescence
CCEEEIRSTUX	executrices
CCEEELORTTU	electrocute
CCEEEMNPSSU	spumescence
CCEEENNOQSU	consequence
CCEEENOPRST	torpescence
CCEEENPRSTU	putrescence
CCEEFFIINOT	coefficient
CCEEFFIINSU	sufficience
CCEEFIIMNNU	munificence
CCEEFIINOPR	proficience
CCEEFILNOST	self-conceit
CCEEFLNNORS	self-concern
CCEEFLNOPST	self-concept
CCEEFNORTTU	counterfect
CCEEGHINOST	geotechnics
CCEEGINNNOT	contingence
CCEEGINOOTT	geotectonic
CCEEGINOTTY	cytogenetic
CCEEGNNOOST	cognoscente
CCEEGNNORVY	convergency
CCEEGNOOPRS	precognosce
CCEEGNOORRT	concert-goer
CCEEGNRSTUY	turgescency
CCEEHHINOTT	theotechnic
CCEEHHKORRY	chokecherry
CCEEHHLORSW	schreech-owl
CCEEHIKLNOR	nickel-ochre
CCEEHILORST	cholesteric
CCEEHIMORTT	ectothermic
CCEEHINNORY	incoherency
CCEEHINORRS	choirscreen
CCEEHINORTT	theocentric
CCEEHKLLLOS	cockleshell
CCEEHMOPTYY	phycomycete
CCEEHNORSTU	touch-screen
CCEEHNRRSWW	screw-wrench
CCEEIILNNOS	consilience
CCEEIILORST	isoelectric
CCEEIILRTTY	electricity
CCEEIIMMNSU	ecumenicism
CCEEIIMNNOS	omniscience
CCEEIIMNOSV	misconceive
CCEEIIMNRTT	centimetric
CCEEIIMOSST	cosmeticise
CCEEIIMOSTZ	cosmeticize
CCEEIINOPTV	nociceptive
CCEEIINPPRY	percipiency
CCEEIINPRRT	pericentric
CCEEIKLMORT	mole-cricket
CCEEILMORTY	myoelectric
CCEEILNNORT	non-electric
CCEEILNNOTV	conventicle
CCEEILNOOPR	cornice-pole
CCEEILNORST	electronics
CCEEILNORSY	cycloserine
CCEEILNORTT	telocentric
CCEEILNOSST	conceitless
CCEEILNQSUY	liquescency
CCEEIMNOORT	econometric

CCEEINNNOVY	conveniency
CCEEINNOQTU	cinquecento
CCEEINNOSSS	conciseness
CCEEINNOSST	consistence
CCEEINORRTU	Eurocentric
CCEEINOSTUV	consecutive
CCEEIOPRSTU	Euro-sceptic
CCEEJNORRTU	conjecturer
CCEELSSSSSU	successless
CCEEMNNNORT	concernment
CCEENOPSSTU	conceptuses
CCEENORRSST	correctness
CCEEOOPRSTV	vectorscope
CCEEOORRRTV	overcorrect
CCEFFIINSUY	sufficiency
CCEFGIKLNOS	self-cocking
CCEFHIIISTT	fetichistic
CCEFHIIMORS	microfiches
CCEFIIIPSTY	specificity
CCEFIILNOTV	conflictive
CCEFIINNOPS	non-specific
CCEFIINOPRY	proficiency
CCEFILMOORS	scoleciform
CCEFINORSST	cross-infect
CCEFIORRSUU	cruciferous
CCEFKLLOORW	flower-clock
CCEGHIILNOR	cholinergic
CCEGHIINORT	ricocheting
CCEGHIINOSZ	schizogenic
CCEGHIKNRST	check-string
CCEGHINOPSY	psychogenic
CCEGIINOOTX	toxicogenic
CCEGILNOORY	eccrinology
CCEGILNOOSY	synecologic
CCEGINNNORT	concentring
CCEGINNNOTY	contingency
CCEGINNOOST	cognoscenti
CCEGINOPRTY	cryptogenic
CCEHHIOSSTT	schottische
CCEHHLNOORY	rhynchocoel
CCEHIIKNNOV	kinchin-cove
CCEHIILNOPR	necrophilic
CCEHIILOOPS	helioscopic
CCEHIIMNOOR	cheironomic
CCEHIINPRST	sphincteric
CCEHIIPRRTY	hypercritic
CCEHIKMOORS	mock-heroics
CCEHIKNOOOR	cornice-hook
CCEHIKNPTTU	ticket-punch
CCEHILLNOOR	clinochlore
CCEHILNOORT	Technicolor®
CCEHILNOPTY	polytechnic
CCEHIMNOORT	homocentric
CCEHIMNOSTU	technomusic
CCEHIMNOTYZ	zymotechnic
CCEHIMOOPRT	chemotropic
	ectomorphic
CCEHIMOORTY	orchiectomy
CCEHIMOOSTT	cosmothetic
CCEHINNRSSU	crunchiness
CCEHINOOSTZ	zootechnics
CCEHINOPRTY	pyrotechnic
CCEHIOOPRTT	ectotrophic
CCEHIORRSUV	hircocervus
CCEHKLOSTTU	shuttlecock
CCEHKNPRSUU	sucker-punch
CCEHLNOOPSY	lychnoscope
CCEHMOOOPRS	chromoscope
CCEHNOOOPRS	chronoscope
CCEIIIMPRTU	empiricutic
CCEIIINSSTT	scientistic
CCEIIJMNORT	microinject
CCEIILMNORT	clinometric
CCEIILMORST	cliometrics
CCEIILOOPRT	poliorcetic
CCEIIMMORRT	micrometric
CCEIIMMOSST	cosmeticism
CCEIIMOORST	sociometric
CCEIIMORSTV	viscometric
CCEIINNNOST	inconscient
CCEIINOORST	coercionist
CCEIIOPRRTY	reciprocity
CCEIJNNOTUV	conjunctive
CCEIKLMOORT	mortice-lock
CCEIKLNOPRU	cupro-nickel
CCEILLNOOST	collections
CCEILMOORTU	coulometric
CCEILMORUVV	circumvolve
CCEILNNOTTU	noctilucent
CCEILNOPRTY	polycentric
CCEILNORRTY	incorrectly
CCEILOOPRTU	police-court
CCEINNNOOST	connections
CCEINNOORST	concertinos
CCEINNOOSTU	consecution
CCEINNOSSTY	consistency
CCEINOOPSTU	conceptious
CCEJNNORTUU	conjuncture
CCEKLORRTTU	turret-clock
CCEKMOORSTY	comstockery
CCELLNSTUUY	succulently
CCELNOOOOPS	colonoscope
CCELNOOPPRW	copple-crown
CCELORSSSUU	succourless
CCENORRSTTU	constructer
	current-cost
	reconstruct
CCEOOOPPRST	proctoscope
CCFGIILNNOT	conflicting
CCFIIINORUX	crucifixion
CCFIILNNOOT	confliction
CCGGHHINORU	churchgoing
CCGHIIKMNOT	thick-coming
CCGHILNOOOR	chronologic
CCGHILNORSY	scorchingly
CCGHILOOPSY	psychologic
CCGHIOOPRSY	hygroscopic
CCGIILOOOTX	toxicologic
CCHHIIORSST	Scotch-Irish
CCHIIILMORT	microlithic
CCHIIINORTT	trichinotic
CCHIIIOSTTY	histiocytic
CCHIILOOPPS	scopophilic
CCHIIMNOOPR	microphonic

CCHIIMOOORV	Mohorovicic
CCHIIMOPRTY	microphytic
CCHIIMORSTW	microswitch
CCHIINOOPRS	rhinoscopic
CCHILMNOORY	chylomicron
CCHILMOOPRY	polychromic
CCHIMMNOOOR	monochromic
CCHIMNOOPSY	psychonomic
CCHIMOOPRTY	cormophytic
	mycotrophic
CCHIOOOPRST	orthoscopic
CCHIOOPSTXY	psychotoxic
CCHIOPRSSYY	cryophysics
CCHIORRSSST	Christ-cross
CCHIORSSSTT	cross-stitch
CCIIINNOTVY	convicinity
CCIIINOORRT	onirocritic
CCIIKKQSSTU	quick-sticks
CCIILOOPSSU	piscicolous
CCIIMMNOSTU	communistic
CCIINNOOSSU	inconscious
CCIINNOOSTV	convictions
CCIINOPRTTY	nyctitropic
CCIINOPSTUY	conspicuity
CCIJNNNOOTU	conjunction
CCIKLMNOOTU	coconut-milk
CCIKMMOOSST	comstockism
CCILMRRSUUU	curriculums
CCILNNOOSSU	conclusions
CCILNOOPRSY	cyclosporin
CCILNOOSSUY	consciously
CCILNOOSTUU	noctilucous
CCILOOORSTU	corticolous
CCIMNNOOPTU	compunction
CCINNOOSSUU	unconscious
CCINOOPSSUU	conspicuous
CCINOORRSTT	constrictor
CCIOOPRSSTY	sporocystic
CCKNOORRTUY	country-rock
CCLLOOORTUY	collocutory
CCLNOOOOPSY	colonoscopy
CCLNOOOORSU	concolorous
CCNOORRSTTU	constructor
CCOOOPPRSTY	proctoscopy
CDDDEEEEGKL	deckle-edged
CDDDEEENNSU	undescended
CDDDEEILNUY	undecidedly
CDDDELRSUUY	sculduddery
CDDEEEENPRT	precedented
CDDEEEFFOPR	pedder-coffe
CDDEEEILPRT	predilected
CDDEEEINNUV	unevidenced
CDDEEEIPRTU	decrepitude
CDDEEENNOPS	despondence
CDDEEENNOPT	co-dependent
CDDEEEOPRRR	prerecorded
CDDEEFILNSU	self-induced
CDDEEHLNSUU	unscheduled
CDDEEHNNRSU	sundrenched
CDDEEIINORT	rodenticide
CDDEEILTUVY	deductively
CDDEEINNRSU	undiscerned
	unrescinded
CDDEEINPRRU	underpriced
CDDEEMMNNOU	uncommended
CDDEENNOPSY	despondency
CDDEEOORRVW	overcrowded
CDDEFIIKLST	fiddlestick
CDDEFIIMOST	discomfited
CDDEGILLNOW	cold-welding
CDDEHIILMNR	childminder
CDDEHIINRTW	witch-ridden
CDDEIIILNNS	disinclined
CDDEIINNOOT	conditioned
CDDEIINOSUU	indeciduous
CDDEILNOOTY	dicotyledon
CDDEILNOSSU	undisclosed
CDDEILOORSU	discoloured
CDDEIMMOORS	desmodromic
CDDEINSSSUU	undiscussed
CDDEKKNNOOW	knocked-down
CDDELLLMOOY	mollycoddle
CDDELOOPPTU	cloud-topped
CDDGIKNNOPU	ducking-pond
CDDGIKNOPPU	pock-pudding
CDEEEEFFLNS	self-defence
CDEEEEFHMNO	home-defence
CDEEEEFLLST	self-elected
CDEEEEFLNSS	defenceless
CDEEEEFLORS	close-reefed
CDEEEEGINRR	regredience
CDEEEEHKORS	rose-cheeked
CDEEEEHKRRT	three-decker
CDEEEEINPRX	experienced
CDEEEFHNRRT	trencher-fed
CDEEEFIILRT	electrified
CDEEEFILSTX	self-excited
CDEEEFILTVY	defectively
CDEEEFIORRT	fore-recited
CDEEEFIRRST	fire-crested
CDEEEFLNRST	self-centred
CDEEEFLNRTU	unreflected
CDEEEFLORSV	self-covered
CDEEEFMNORT	deforcement
CDEEEGIIMNO	geomedicine
CDEEEGILNXY	exceedingly
CDEEEGINORS	derecognise
CDEEEGINORZ	derecognize
CDEEEHKORSY	rosy-cheeked
CDEEEIINSST	necessitied
CDEEEIKLNST	needlestick
CDEEEILLNTT	intellected
CDEEEILMNOR	microneedle
CDEEEILNOST	deselection
CDEEEILNSTT	delitescent
CDEEEILOPRV	velocipeder
CDEEEILPTVY	deceptively
CDEEEINNRTT	intercedent
CDEEEINPRTU	unreceipted
CDEEEINPRUV	unperceived
CDEEEINRSUX	unexercised
CDEEEINSSTX	excitedness
CDEEEINSSTY	needcessity

CDEEELLORVW	well-covered
CDEEELNPRTY	precedently
CDEEEMMNORR	recommender
CDEEEMNNOOR	encomendero
CDEEENNNSTU	unsentenced
CDEEENNOPRS	respondence
CDEEENORRTT	retrocedent
CDEEENORRUV	unrecovered
CDEEENPRSTU	unrespected
CDEEEOPRRSS	predecessor
CDEEFFIKNST	stiff-necked
CDEEFFINORU	unofficered
CDEEFHOORUV	forevouched
CDEEFIILNTY	deficiently
CDEEFIINPSU	unspecified
CDEEFIINRTU	uncertified
	unrectified
CDEEFIKLNRT	ferntickled
CDEEFILLTUY	deceitfully
CDEEFILNNTU	uninflected
CDEEFILNORT	field-cornet
CDEEFILNORY	ecofriendly
CDEEFILOSST	close-fisted
CDEEFIMNORT	comet-finder
CDEEFLNOSSY	confessedly
CDEEFNNORST	frondescent
CDEEFNNOSSU	unconfessed
CDEEFNORSTT	soft-centred
CDEEFOPRRTW	word-perfect
CDEEGGLORSS	cross-legged
CDEEGHHLOOS	hedge-school
CDEEGIINOPT	doting-piece
CDEEGIJLOPU	police-judge
CDEEGINOPRS	proceedings
CDEEGNOSSSU	second-guess
CDEEHHNORRS	horse-drench
CDEEHIILOTT	△diotheletic
CDEEHIINNOS	Indo-Chinese
CDEEHIINNST	indehiscent
CDEEHIKNNTU	unthickened
CDEEHILMNNR	men-children
CDEEHILOTTY	△dyotheletic
CDEEHIMNORT	endothermic
CDEEHIMNOST	Demosthenic
CDEEHIOPRTV	overpitched
CDEEHIOQSTU	discotheque
	discothèque
CDEEHLNORTU	underclothe
CDEEHNNORTU	truncheoned
CDEEHNOORSU	echo-sounder
CDEEHNORTUU	unretouched
CDEEIIILNSS	dissilience
CDEEIIIMPTY	epidemicity
CDEEIIKLNSS	slickenside
CDEEIILNORT	dereliction
CDEEIIMNRST	densimetric
CDEEIIMORRS	misericorde
CDEEIIMOSST	domesticise
CDEEIIMOSTZ	domesticize
CDEEIINOPTV	point-device
CDEEIINORRT	redirection
CDEEIINRSTV	viridescent
CDEEIINRTTU	incertitude
CDEEIIPRSTV	descriptive
	discerptive
CDEEIISTTTV	detectivist
CDEEIKLMORU	leukodermic
CDEEIKLNNOO	nickelodeon
CDEEIKNNQUU	unquickened
CDEEIKOPSTZ	pocket-sized
CDEEILLOPPS	close-lipped
CDEEILNNQUY	delinquency
CDEEILNOORT	intercooled
CDEEILNSSTU	ductileness
CDEEILOORSU	decolourise
CDEEILOORUZ	decolourize
CDEEILOPRSU	supercoiled
CDEEILRSUVY	decursively
CDEEILRTUVY	reductively
CDEEILSTUVY	seductively
CDEEIMNNORS	encrimsoned
CDEEIMNNRST	discernment
CDEEIMNOPRS	endospermic
CDEEIMNOPTY	idempotency
CDEEIMNORTV	divorcement
CDEEIMOOPST	decomposite
CDEEIMOORST	osteodermic
CDEEIMOOSTX	sextodecimo
CDEEINNOSTU	tendencious
CDEEINNPRST	prescindent
CDEEINOORTT	condottiere
CDEEINORRTU	reintroduce
CDEEINPRSUU	superinduce
CDEEIOOOPPS	opeidoscope
CDEEIORRSVY	rediscovery
CDEEIORRTXY	ex-directory
CDEEIRRRSVW	screwdriver
CDEEIRSTTUV	destructive
CDEEJNOPRTU	unprojected
CDEEKNNRSSU	druckenness
CDEEKNOORSS	crookedness
CDEEKORRSTY	dyer's-rocket
CDEELLMNOPU	uncompelled
CDEELMNNOOT	condolement
CDEELMNOPTU	uncompleted
CDEELNNOTTY	contentedly
CDEELNRRTUY	decurrently
CDEELNRTTUU	uncluttered
CDEELPSSTUY	suspectedly
CDEEMNNNOTU	uncontemned
CDEEMNOPRTU	producement
CDEENNOPRSY	respondency
CDEENNOQRUU	unconquered
CDEENNORTUU	unrecounted
CDEENNORTUV	unconverted
CDEENNOSTTU	uncontested
CDEENOPRSSU	unprocessed
CDEENOPRTTU	unprotected
CDEENORRTUV	undercovert
CDEENPSSTUU	unsuspected
CDEEOOPPSSU	pseudoscope
CDEEOOPRRUV	overproduce
CDEFFLOOORU	off-coloured
CDEFHIINRTW	witch-finder

CDEFHILORST foster-child
CDEFHIOOPRT pitch-roofed
CDEFIINNTUY infecundity
CDEFIINORST disinfector
CDEFIINORTU countrified
CDEFILNNOTY confidently
CDEFIMNNORU unconfirmed
CDEFINORTUY countryfied
CDEFLNOOORS second-floor
CDEFMNOORTU uncomforted
CDEGGLRSUUY sculduggery
CDEGHHHIIPT high-pitched
CDEGHILNOOS deschooling
CDEGIILNNNU undeclining
CDEGIINNORS considering
CDEGIINOPTY copy-editing
CDEGIKLOORS sockdoliger
CDEGILMNOOO demonologic
CDEGIMNORRU corrigendum
CDEGINNNOSS condignness
CDEGINNOOOT odontogenic
CDEGKLOOORS sockdologer
CDEGMORRSUY dog's-mercury
CDEHHIOORSU orchid-house
CDEHHNOOOPR chordophone
CDEHIIINNOR enchiridion
CDEHIIKLLNU unchildlike
CDEHIIKLPPT thick-lipped
CDEHIIKTTTW thick-witted
CDEHIILLNOT decillionth
CDEHIILOOTT theodolitic
CDEHIILOTTY △dyothelitic
CDEHIIMOOST dichotomise
CDEHIIMOOTZ dichotomize
CDEHIIMOSTT Methodistic
CDEHIIOOPRT epitrochoid
CDEHILMNOOP monodelphic
CDEHILMORSU music-holder
CDEHILOORXY oxy-chloride
CDEHILPRTUU pulchritude
CDEHIMNOOPR endomorphic
CDEHIMNOOUX xenodochium
CDEHIMNORST Christendom
CDEHIMORRTU thermoduric
CDEHIMORRTY hydrometric
CDEHINOOPRT endotrophic
CDEHINOORST Chondrostei
CDEHIOOPRST orthopedics
CDEHIOPRRST short-priced
CDEHKLOORST stockholder
CDEHLNOORSU under-school
CDEHLNOOSUY endochylous
CDEHOOORRST horse-doctor
CDEIIILNPRS discipliner
CDEIIILNSUV uncivilised
CDEIIILNUVZ uncivilized
CDEIIIMMSTU mediumistic
CDEIIINNORT indirection
CDEIIINNTVY incendivity
CDEIIINSTTV distinctive
CDEIIIOPRTY periodicity
CDEIIIRTTVY directivity
CDEIIISSTUV vicissitude
CDEIIJNSTUV disjunctive
CDEIIKQTTUW quick-witted
CDEIILLMNOS millisecond
CDEIILLOSUY deliciously
CDEIILLPTUY pellucidity
CDEIILNOSTU unsolicited
CDEIILNRTUY incredulity
CDEIILNTUVY inductively
CDEIILOORST sclerotioid
CDEIILOPSSU pediculosis
CDEIILOSTUV declivitous
CDEIIMMOOST commodities
CDEIIMNORST modernistic
CDEIIMOSTTY domesticity
CDEIIMPPRUY cypripedium
CDEIINNOORT conditioner
recondition
CDEIINNOSTU discontinue
CDEIINOORTT condottieri
CDEIINOPRST description
discerption
CDEIINORRTU irreduction
CDEIINRSTTU distincture
CDEIIOOPRTX dexiotropic
CDEIIORSSUV discoursive
CDEIJNRSTUU disjuncture
CDEIKLNORTW trickle-down
CDEILNNOTUY continuedly
CDEILNOORUU unicoloured
CDEILNOPSST split-second
CDEILNORSUU incredulous
CDEILOORRTU tricoloured
CDEIMMNOPSU compendiums
CDEIMMNOTTU uncommitted
CDEIMNOOPSU compendious
CDEIMNOSSTY syndesmotic
CDEINNOPRST nondescript
CDEINNORTUV uncontrived
CDEINNRTTUU untinctured
CDEINORSSSU unscissored
CDEINORSTTU destruction
CDEINORSTUY countryside
CDEINORTUWY countrywide
CDEIORSSTUY discourtesy
CDEKKNOOORR doorknocker
CDEKLOORSUY sky-coloured
CDEKMMOOSTY mock-modesty
CDELLLOSSUY cloudlessly
CDELLNORSUY scoundrelly
CDELLOOOPRT protocolled
CDELLOPRRUW crowd-puller
CDELLORSUUY credulously
CDELOOORTUW tow-coloured
CDENOPRRTUU uncorrupted
CDFFIILLTUY difficultly
CDFGGILNOOR cold-forging
CDFGIILNNOY confidingly
CDFILLOSUUU dulcifluous
CDFINNOSTUY dysfunction
CDGHHIINOPT diphthongic
CDGHILNOOPP clodhopping

CDGHILOOORY	orchidology
CDGIIKNNSUW	wind-sucking
CDGIILOOSUY	suicidology
CDGIILOSSTY	dyslogistic
CDGILNNOPRU	curling-pond
CDGILNOOOOT	odontologic
CDGILOORTTY	troglodytic
CDGINNOOOPY	pycnogonoid
CDGINOOTTUW	woodcutting
CDGINOPRSTU	crop-dusting
CDHHIILOPRY	hydrophilic
CDHHIOPRTYY	hydrophytic
CDHHNNOORTY	rhynchodont
CDHIIIMOOPR	idiomorphic
CDHIIIOORST	choroiditis
CDHIILPRSUU	disulphuric
CDHIIMOOPPR	hippodromic
CDHIIMOOSTT	dichotomist
CDHIIOOPRST	chiropodist
CDHIMOOORRT	orthodromic
CDHIMOOOSTU	dichotomous
CDHINOOORTT	orthodontic
CDHINOOPRSY	hydroponics
CDHIOOPRRTY	hydrotropic
CDIIIJNOSUU	injudicious
CDIIILNTTUY	inductility
CDIIINNOSTT	distinction
CDIIINTTUVY	inductivity
CDIIJLOSUUY	judiciously
CDIIJNNOSTU	disjunction
CDIILMORSTU	clostridium
CDIILMPSTUU	multicuspid
CDIILNOPSTY	spondylitic
CDIILNOPSUU	sipunculoid
CDIILOPSTUU	duplicitous
CDIIMMNNOOU	condominium
CDIIMMNOOTY	incommodity
CDIIOOOOSTV	voodooistic
CDIKLNOPSSU	spondulicks
CDILLORSUUY	ludicrously
CDILMOOORSX	loxodromics
CDILOOORUUU	douroucouli
CDINNOOPRTY	Cyprinodont
CDMNOOOPUXY	oxy-compound
CEEEEEGMNRR	re-emergence
CEEEEEPRRRT	treecreeper
CEEEEHNRVWY	everywhence
CEEEEHPRSSS	cheesepress
CEEEEILNORT	electioneer
CEEEEIMMNPT	empiecement
CEEEEIMNNPR	pre-eminence
CEEEEINNPRV	prevenience
CEEEEINRRRV	irreverence
CEEEEINRSTX	re-existence
CEEEEJNRSUV	rejuvenesce
CEEEFFFLNOS	self-offence
CEEEFFIINTV	ineffective
CEEEFFILTVY	effectively
CEEEFFLNOSS	offenceless
CEEEFGLLNST	self-neglect
CEEEFHIIPRS	speechifier
CEEEFIKQRUZ	quick-freeze
CEEEFILRSSV	self-service
CEEEFINNQRU	infrequence
CEEEFINORRT	refectioner
CEEEFLPRSST	self-respect
CEEEFMNNORT	enforcement
CEEEFNPRSST	perfectness
CEEEGGHINNS	gegenschein
CEEEGGNORRR	greengrocer
CEEEGHINRSW	cheesewring
CEEEGIINOPR	epeirogenic
CEEEGIINPST	epigenetics
CEEEGIKNORT	greenockite
CEEEGILMNNO	meningocele
CEEEGIMNORT	merogenetic
CEEEGINNOSS	cenogenesis
CEEEGINNOTX	xenogenetic
CEEEGINOSST	ectogenesis
CEEEHHKLNOP	heckelphone
CEEEHHMMRSY	rhyme-scheme
CEEEHHMOPRS	chemosphere
CEEEHIKNTTT	kitchenette
CEEEHILORTT	heteroclite
CEEEHILSTTT	telesthetic
CEEEHIMNRTU	hermeneutic
CEEEHIMORST	heteroecism
CEEEHIMPRTY	hyperemetic
CEEEHINSSST	cenesthesis
CEEEHIPRRSU	supercherie
CEEEHIQRSUW	chequerwise
CEEEHLNPRSU	ensepulchre
CEEEHLRTTUW	wheel-cutter
CEEEHMOPRSS	moss-cheeper
CEEEHOPPRST	sheet-copper
CEEEIIKLNTT	telekinetic
CEEEIIMNNPT	impenitence
CEEEIIMPRSV	misperceive
CEEEIIMRSTV	time-service
CEEEIINNNRT	internecine
CEEEIINNNST	insentience
CEEEIINNRTV	internecive
CEEEIINNSTX	inexistence
CEEEIIPRRTV	irreceptive
CEEEIJMNORT	rejoicement
CEEEIKLLNST	nickel-steel
CEEEIKNNRSS	snickersnee
CEEEIKNQRTU	quicken-tree
CEEEILLORRT	electrolier
CEEEILLSTVY	selectively
CEEEILMORTV	velocimeter
CEEEILNNOQU	ineloquence
CEEEILNNOTV	non-elective
CEEEILNOPRT	pre-election
CEEEILNOPST	Pleistocene
CEEEILNORST	reselection
CEEEILNRRUV	culverineer
CEEEILRSSSV	serviceless
CEEEILRSSVY	recessively
CEEEILRSTVY	secretively
CEEEILSSVXY	excessively
CEEEILTUVXY	executively
CEEEIMNNNST	incensement
CEEEINNOPRV	provenience

CEEEINNOSTV	venesection
CEEEINNRSSS	sincereness
CEEEINORTUX	executioner
CEEEINOSTVX	coextensive
CEEEINPRRSW	screen-wiper
CEEEINPRRTT	intercepter
CEEEINPRSSS	preciseness
CEEEINPRSST	persistence
CEEEINPRTUV	unreceptive
CEEEINRSTVV	revivescent
CEEEIOPRRSV	over-precise
CEEEIPPRSTV	perspective
CEEEIPPSSTY	type-species
CEEEIPRSTUV	persecutive
CEEEIRSTUXX	executrixes
CEEEJNNSTUV	juvenescent
CEEEKMNORSS	smokescreen
CEEELLLNTXY	excellently
CEEELLNNNOP	pennoncelle
CEEELLNOPPR	prepollence
CEEELLORSTY	electrolyse
CEEELLORTTY	electrolyte
CEEELLORTYZ	electrolyze
CEEELMMOTTU	telecommute
CEEELMNOSSW	welcomeness
CEEELMORRST	sclerometer
CEEELNRSSSU	recluseness
CEEELOPRRST	preselector
CEEELOPRTTY	electrotype
CEEELPRSSST	respectless
	scepterless
	sceptreless
CEEEMMNRTUX	excrementum
CEEEMNNNOTT	contenement
CEEEMNNOSTT	cement-stone
CEEEMNORTTY	enterectomy
CEEEMNRTTTU	curettement
CEEEMOPRSTU	computerese
CEEENNNOQSU	non-sequence
CEEENNOPRTT	penteconter
CEEENPRRSST	precentress
CEEENPRRSSU	superscreen
CEEEOOPRSST	stereoscope
CEEEPPRRSST	preceptress
CEEFFIIINNT	inefficient
CEEFFIILNTY	efficiently
CEEFGHHIMRT	Fehmgericht
CEEFGIINSTU	insectifuge
CEEFGINNRRY	refringency
CEEFHHNORTT	thenceforth
CEEFHHNORTW	whenceforth
CEEFHIKNNRT	trench-knife
CEEFHILORSU	cheliferous
CEEFHINNRSS	Frenchiness
CEEFHIPPRST	prefectship
CEEFHMNNORW	Frenchwomen
CEEFHMOORRR	ferro-chrome
CEEFHMOORRT	home-crofter
CEEFIIKLNRT	fernitickle
CEEFIINOSUV	veneficious
CEEFIIPRSSU	superficies
CEEFIKLNORR	ferro-nickel
CEEFIKLNRTY	fernytickle
CEEFILLORSU	celliferous
CEEFILMPRTY	imperfectly
CEEFILNNOSS	confineless
CEEFILNORSU	fluorescein
CEEFIMNNNOT	confinement
CEEFINNQRUY	infrequency
CEEFINORTTU	counterfeit
CEEFINPRSTU	superinfect
CEEFKLMORSY	self-mockery
CEEFLLRSTUU	self-culture
CEEFLNNOSTT	self-content
CEEFLNORSTU	fluorescent
CEEFLNPRTUY	unperfectly
CEEFLOORRSU	foreclosure
CEEFLORRSUU	resourceful
CEEFMNNOTTU	confutement
CEEGHHIMRTV	Vehmgericht
CEEGHIKNNRR	neck-herring
CEEGHIMNOOT	homogenetic
CEEGHIMNORT	thermogenic
CEEGHINOPST	pigeon-chest
CEEGIILNSTY	lysigenetic
CEEGIIMNOTT	mitogenetic
CEEGIIMNSST	miscegenist
CEEGIINORTV	recognitive
CEEGILMNORR	relic-monger
CEEGILNNOSY	geosyncline
CEEGILNOPTY	polygenetic
CEEGILNOSTT	telegnostic
CEEGILNPTXY	expectingly
CEEGILOOOSS	sociologese
CEEGIMNNOOT	monogenetic
CEEGINNOOSS	oncogenesis
CEEGINNOOTT	ontogenetic
CEEGINOORST	oestrogenic
CEEGINOPRTY	pyrogenetic
CEEGINOSSTY	cytogenesis
CEEGIOPRRTU	picture-goer
CEEGLLOORTY	electrology
CEEGLNRRSUY	curly-greens
CEEGMOSTYYZ	Zygomycetes
CEEGNNOORSU	congenerous
CEEHHIILPRS	helispheric
CEEHHIIMPRS	hemispheric
CEEHHILMOOR	heliochrome
CEEHHILNOPT	technophile
CEEHHIMNRST	cherishment
CEEHHIORSVW	whichsoever
CEEHHMORSTT	home-stretch
CEEHHNNOPRS	henchperson
CEEHIIINORS	chinoiserie
CEEHIIKNOOS	cookie-shine
CEEHIIKNSTT	kinesthetic
CEEHIILLNST	Hellenistic
CEEHIILLRSS	schillerise
CEEHIILLRSZ	schillerize
CEEHIILMORT	heliometric
CEEHIIMNOPS	phonemicise
CEEHIIMNOPZ	phonemicize
CEEHIIMPRTU	perithecium
CEEHIIMPSTU	euphemistic

CEEHIIMPTTY	epithymetic
CEEHIIMRTTY	hermeticity
CEEHIINOPST	phoneticise
CEEHIINOPTZ	phoneticize
CEEHIINPPRR	perinephric
CEEHIKNOORT	kinetochore
CEEHIKNPSSS	peckishness
CEEHIKNSSST	sketchiness
CEEHILLNOST	clothes-line
CEEHILMNORT	thermocline
CEEHILMORRT	chlorimeter
CEEHILNORST	cholesterin
CEEHILOPRST	electorship
CEEHILPRSTU	lectureship
CEEHIMMOOOR	homoeomeric
CEEHIMNOORR	cheironomer
CEEHIMPTTUY	emphyteutic
CEEHIMRRTUY	eurythermic
CEEHINOORRT	rhinocerote
CEEHINQSTTU	queen-stitch
CEEHIOOPRTT	heterotopic
CEEHIOPRRST	Terpsichore
CEEHIOPRTTY	heterotypic
CEEHKLNOSUY	honeysuckle
	honey-suckle
CEEHKNOOPPT	pocketphone
CEEHKNORSTT	netherstock
CEEHKNORSUY	honey-sucker
CEEHKOQRRUW	chequerwork
CEEHKRSSSTU	hucksteress
CEEHLLNOTTT	nettle-cloth
CEEHLLOOPST	clothes-pole
CEEHLLOORST	cholesterol
CEEHLLORSUY	lecherously
CEEHLMOORRT	chlorometer
CEEHLMRSTWZ	Weltschmerz
CEEHLNOOPRR	chloroprene
CEEHLOOPRRS	preschooler
CEEHLOORRTU	three-colour
CEEHLRSSSTT	stretchless
CEEHMNOORRT	chronometer
CEEHMNOORST	stenochrome
CEEHMNOPRTY	nephrectomy
CEEHMNORSST	tschernosem
CEEHMOOPRSS	cosmosphere
CEEHMOOPRST	thermoscope
CEEHMOORRTT	trochometer
CEEHMOPRSTY	psychometer
CEEHNNORRTU	truncheoner
CEEHNOORRTT	orthocentre
CEEHNORRSTY	cherry-stone
CEEHNORSTWY	oyster-wench
CEEHNOSSTTY	scythe-stone
CEEHOOPRRSU	horse-couper
CEEHOOPSSTT	stethoscope
CEEHORRSTTV	overstretch
CEEHORRTTYY	erythrocyte
CEEIIINNSTV	incentivise
CEEIIINNTVZ	incentivize
CEEIIISTVVV	vivisective
CEEIIKNRSST	ricketiness
CEEIILMPRSY	imprecisely
CEEIILMPRTX	pleximetric
CEEIILMRTUV	vermiculite
CEEIILNNRSY	insincerely
CEEIILNRSTV	virilescent
CEEIILSTTVY	selectivity
CEEIIMMPRST	metempirics
CEEIIMNNPTY	impenitency
CEEIIMNNRST	reminiscent
CEEIIMOPTTV	competitive
CEEIIMORSST	esotericism
CEEIIMORSTT	meteoritics
CEEIIMORSTX	exotericism
CEEIIMPPRRS	perispermic
CEEIIMRRSTU	sericterium
CEEIINNNSTY	insentiency
CEEIINNOSTV	venisection
CEEIINNOTUX	inexecution
CEEIINNPRST	serpentinic
CEEIINORSTV	insectivore
CEEIINPRSST	resipiscent
CEEIINRSTVV	reviviscent
CEEIIORSSTT	esotericist
CEEIIPPTTUY	eupepticity
CEEIIPRRTUW	picture-wire
CEEIIPRTTVY	receptivity
CEEIIRRSTTV	restrictive
CEEIJNORRTT	interjector
CEEIKLLNRST	skillcentre
CEEIKNOOPST	kinetoscope
CEEIKNOSTTT	stockinette
CEEIKNRRSTU	kernicterus
CEEILLMNNTY	inclemently
CEEILLMRSSU	music-seller
CEEILLMRSSY	mercilessly
CEEILLPRSSY	pricelessly
CEEILLSUVXY	exclusively
CEEILMMNOPT	compilement
CEEILMNNSTU	luminescent
CEEILMNRSTU	multiscreen
CEEILMOORRT	colorimeter
CEEILMOPSTU	Telescopium
CEEILMORTVY	velocimetry
CEEILNNNOOT	non-election
CEEILNNNOOV	non-violence
CEEILNNOPST	pencil-stone
CEEILNOOPRS	necropoleis
CEEILNOORRT	intercooler
CEEILNOPRTU	neuroleptic
CEEILNORTTT	electrotint
CEEILNPRSST	split-screen
CEEILNPRSTY	presciently
CEEILNQSTUY	quiescently
CEEILNSUUVX	unexclusive
CEEILOORSTV	locorestive
CEEILOORTTV	toilet-cover
CEEILOPSSTT	telescopist
CEEILPPRSTY	clyster-pipe
CEEILRRSTUU	sericulture
CEEILRSUVXY	excursively
CEEIMNNOOPT	omnipotence
CEEIMNNOPTT	incompetent
CEEIMNNORTU	countermine

CEEIMNNSTTU	intumescent	CEENOPPPRRY	peppercorny
CEEIMNOORSU	ceremonious	CEENOPQRSTU	pre-conquest
CEEIMNORTTU	counter-time	CEENORSTTTU	stonecutter
CEEIMNRRTTU	recruitment	CEEOOPRSSTY	stereoscopy
CEEIMOOPSSS	seismoscope	CEEOPRRSSTT	protectress
CEEIMOPRSSV	compressive	CEEOPRRSTUY	persecutory
CEEIMOPRSTU	computerise	CEEORRRRSTU	resurrector
CEEIMOPRTUZ	computerize	CEERRRSTTUU	restructure
CEEINNNOSTT	consentient	CEFFHIINNOR	chiffonnier
CEEINNOORRT	reconnoiter	CEFFHIRSSTT	festschrift
	reconnoitre	CEFFINRSSSU	scruffiness
CEEINNOOSTX	coextension	CEFFIORRSUU	furciferous
CEEINOOPRST	retinoscope	CEFGGIINNNR	ring-fencing
CEEINOORSST	stereosonic	CEFGIIINPRX	price-fixing
CEEINOPRRTT	interceptor	CEFGIKLLNOS	self-locking
CEEINOPRSTU	persecution	CEFGILLNOSS	self-closing
CEEINORRSST	intercessor	CEFHIIISSTT	fetishistic
CEEINORRSTU	intercourse	CEFHIIKNSTW	knife-switch
CEEINORTUVW	counter-view	CEFHILORSUY	chyliferous
CEEINOSSSTU	necessitous	CEFHIMORSUY	chymiferous
CEEINOSSSTV	costiveness	CEFHLLOORSU	flesh-colour
CEEINPRSSTY	persistency	CEFIIMNORST	insectiform
CEEIOPPRSTV	prospective	CEFIINORSUZ	zinciferous
CEEIOPRRTUV	overpicture	CEFIKNOQRUZ	quick-frozen
CEEIOPRSSTT	stereoptics	CEFILLLOOSU	folliculose
CEEIOPRSTTY	stereotypic	CEFILMORSUU	culmiferous
CEEIORRTTTY	yttro-cerite	CEFILNOORRT	fire-control
CEEIPQRSTUU	picturesque	CEFILNOORTU	counterfoil
CEEJMNOPRTT	projectment	CEFILOORSUY	ferociously
CEEKLRRSTVY	vestry-clerk	CEFIMORRRUV	verruciform
CEEKOORRRTT	retro-rocket	CEFINOORRSU	corniferous
CEELLMNOUWY	unwelcomely	CEFIOPRRSUU	cupriferous
CEELLNOORTT	telecontrol	CEFKOOOPTTU	out-of-pocket
CEELLNOPPRY	prepollency	CEFLLNNOTUY	confluently
CEELLRSSTUU	cultureless	CEFLLNOORST	self-control
CEELMNNOOST	consolement	CEFLMOORSST	comfortless
CEELMNOPSSX	complexness	CEFLOOOPRSU	fluoroscope
CEELMNOPSTY	splenectomy	CEFNOORRTTU	counterfort
CEELMNOPTTY	competently	CEFNOPRRTUY	perfunctory
CEELNNOSSTT	contentless	CEGHIIILNRST	christingle
CEELNOOOPRT	coleopteron	CEGHIIILNRTT	chitterling
CEELNOOPPST	copple-stone	CEGHIINNRST	christening
CEELNRRRTUY	recurrently	CEGHILLNOOY	lichenology
CEELOPRTTYY	electrotypy	CEGHILMOOOR	oligochrome
CEELPSSSSTU	suspectless	CEGHILNOOOU	euchologion
CEEMMNNOOSS	commonsense	CEGHILNOOPR	phrenologic
CEEMMOOPRTT	Comptometer®	CEGHIMNOORY	cheirognomy
CEEMMOSTXYY	Myxomycetes	CEGHIMOOOST	Moeso-gothic
CEEMNNNOTTT	contentment	CEGHIMORRTY	hygrometric
CEEMNNORTTU	recountment	CEGHINOOORR	gonorrhoeic
CEEMNNRSTTU	encrustment	CEGHINOORST	orthogenics
CEEMNOORTUV	countermove	CEGHINORRST	torch-singer
CEEMNOPRRTU	procurement	CEGHINORSSU	grouchiness
CEEMNOPRSTT	contretemps	CEGHINORSTU	scouthering
CEEMNORRTUU	countermure	CEGHINSUWZZ	zwischenzug
CEEMOPRRSSU	compressure	CEGHIOOPRST	geostrophic
CEENNOOPPST	postponence	CEGHLLNOOST	long-clothes
CEENNOORRST	cornerstone	CEGHLNOOORR	chronologer
CEENNRRSSTU	currentness	CEGIIILOPST	epilogistic
CEENOORRSTV	controverse	CEGIIINORST	Origenistic
	seroconvert	CEGIIJLNORY	rejoicingly
CEENOORTTUV	counter-vote	CEGIIJNNORU	unrejoicing

CEGIIKLNNSY	sickeningly
CEGIIKLNSST	singlestick
CEGIILLNNST	stencilling
CEGIILMOOSS	seismologic
CEGIILNOOST	neologistic
CEGIILNOTVY	cognitively
CEGIILOOPST	geopolitics
CEGIIMMNNOU	immunogenic
CEGIIMNOORT	goniometric
CEGIIMNORTU	tumorigenic
CEGIINNOORT	recognition
CEGIINORRSU	crinigerous
CEGIINRSSTY	synergistic
CEGIKLNOORV	overlocking
CEGILLLNNOO	colonelling
CEGILLMNOWY	welcomingly
CEGILLNNOSU	counselling
CEGILNOORST	necrologist
CEGILNOOSTY	insectology
	Scientology®
CEGILNORSSS	single-cross
CEGIMNNNOST	consignment
CEGIMOOORRV	microgroove
CEGINNNNSSU	cunningness
CEGINNNORTU	incongruent
CEGINNOOPST	coping-stone
CEGINNORSTU	countersign
CEGINOORRSU	cornigerous
CEGINOORRTY	recognitory
CEGINOPPRST	prospecting
CEGINORSTUY	courtesying
CEGLMMOORYY	myrmecology
CEGLMOOOSTY	cosmetology
CEGLMOOSSTY	glossectomy
CEGLNOOOSYY	synoecology
CEGLNOORTUW	counter-glow
CEGLOOPRSTY	spectrology
CEGLOORSTUY	Etruscology
CEGLOPRSUUU	groupuscule
CEGNNOPPRSU	scuppernong
CEGORRRSUYY	cryosurgery
CEHHIILOTTY	ichthyolite
CEHHIIMMOPR	hemimorphic
CEHHIINORRT	tichorrhine
CEHHIINPRTT	pinch-hitter
CEHHILMOORY	heliochromy
CEHHILMRSUY	△helichrysum
CEHHILOSTTW	wholestitch
CEHHIMMOORT	homothermic
CEHHIMOOPRT	theomorphic
CEHHIMRSTUY	eurhythmics
CEHHIOPSTYZ	schizophyte
CEHHIPRSTTY	Pterichthys
CEHHLOOOSSU	schoolhouse
CEHHMNORSSY	synchromesh
CEHHMOOOPRR	chromophore
CEHHMOOPRTY	phytochrome
CEHHOOOPRRT	trochophore
CEHIIINPSTZ	citizenship
CEHIIIORSST	historicise
CEHIIIORSTZ	historicize
CEHIIIRSTTT	tritheistic
CEHIIJPSSTU	justiceship
CEHIIKKNNST	kitchen-sink
CEHIIKLLRSY	lickerishly
CEHIIKLORST	ostrich-like
CEHIIKMNNUY	chimney-nuik
CEHIIKNSSSS	sickishness
CEHIILMNTTU	multiethnic
CEHIILOOPRT	heliotropic
CEHIILOPPRS	scripophile
CEHIILPRSTU	spherulitic
CEHIIMNOPST	phonemicist
	phoneticism
CEHIIMNOQTU	monchiquite
CEHIIMNORST	thermionics
CEHIIMOPPRR	perimorphic
CEHIIMOSSUV	mischievous
CEHIINOOPRS	ionospheric
CEHIINOORRT	coinheritor
CEHIINOORSS	isochronise
CEHIINOORSZ	isochronize
CEHIINOPRTY	hyperinotic
CEHIINOPSTT	phoneticist
CEHIINORSTU	cushion-tire
CEHIIOOSTTZ	zootheistic
CEHIIOPRRST	prehistoric
CEHIIOPRSVY	viceroyship
CEHIIOSSSVY	vichyssoise
CEHIKMNNOOY	chimney-nook
CEHIKOOPRTT	tooth-picker
CEHILLNNOPU	Punchinello
CEHILLNOOPS	colonelship
CEHILLOOTTT	toilet-cloth
CEHILMOOPPR	pleomorphic
CEHILMOOPRS	pleochroism
CEHILMOORST	schorlomite
CEHILMORRTY	chlorimetry
CEHILMORTTY	thermolytic
CEHILNOOPST	technopolis
CEHILNOOQRU	chloroquine
CEHILOPRSUY	perichylous
CEHIMMOOPRS	mesomorphic
CEHIMMOOSST	cosmotheism
CEHIMNOOPRX	xenomorphic
CEHIMNORRSS	scrimshoner
CEHIMOOPRRX	xeromorphic
CEHIMOOPRTT	photometric
CEHIMOOPTTY	mythopoetic
CEHIMOOSSST	schistosome
CEHIMOPPRST	coppersmith
CEHIMOPRSTY	hypsometric
CEHIMORSTTY	stichometry
CEHINNORSSY	synchronise
CEHINNORSYZ	synchronize
CEHINOORRST	orchestrion
CEHINOPPRST	pitchperson
CEHINOPPRTU	unprophetic
CEHINOPRSSY	hypersonics
CEHINORSSSY	synchoresis
CEHINORSTUY	cushion-tyre
CEHINRRSSSU	currishness
CEHIOOOPPRT	photocopier
CEHIOOPSTTY	osteophytic

CEHIOPRSSTT	prosthetics
CEHLLLOPRSY	sclerophyll
CEHLMOORRTY	chlorometry
CEHLMOPTTYY	T-lymphocyte
CEHLNOOSTUY	honey-locust
CEHLOOPPRST	clothes-prop
CEHLOPRSSUU	sepulchrous
CEHMMNOOORS	common-shore
CEHMMOOORSX	X-chromosome
CEHMMOOORSY	Y-chromosome
CEHMNOOOSTU	monothecous
CEHMNOORRTY	chronometry
CEHMNOORSTY	stenochromy
CEHMOPRSTYY	psychometry
CEHNNORTTUU	hunt-counter
CEHNNOSSTUU	uncouthness
CEHOOPSSTTY	stethoscopy
CEIIILLMNPU	Penicillium
CEIIILLNSST	illicitness
CEIIILLPTTY	ellipticity
CEIIILMORST	melioristic
CEIIILMPRST	simpliciter
CEIIILNNPTY	incipiently
CEIIIMNOPRS	imprecision
CEIIIMNOSST	misoneistic
CEIIIMPSSST	pessimistic
CEIIINNRSTV	vincristine
CEIIINNRSTY	insincerity
CEIIINNSTTV	instinctive
CEIIINOPRTT	peritonitic
CEIIINORSTU	cineritious
CEIIINOSTVV	vivisection
CEIIINPRSTV	inscriptive
CEIIIOPRSTT	periostitic
CEIIIORSTTU	icteritious
CEIIKKMQSSU	kiss-me-quick
CEIIKLLPSTT	lickspittle
CEIIKLNOORV	olivine-rock
CEIIKLNPRSS	prickliness
CEIIKLOOPTY	poikilocyte
CEIIKLQRSUV	quicksilver
CEIIKLRSSTV	silver-stick
CEIIKNRSSST	tricksiness
CEIILLNSUVY	inclusively
CEIILMSSUVX	exclusivism
CEIILNOPRSY	prosiliency
CEIILNRTUUV	viniculture
CEIILOOPPRT	pleiotropic
CEIILORSSTT	sclerotitis
CEIILRTTUUV	viticulture
CEIILSSTUVX	exclusivist
CEIILSTUVXY	exclusivity
CEIIMNOOPST	incomposite
CEIIMNOOPTT	competition
CEIIMNOPSUU	impecunious
CEIIMNORRTT	nitrometric
CEIIMNORSTU	neuroticism
CEIIMNOSTTU	Teutonicism
CEIIMNPRSSS	scrimpiness
CEIIMOOPSTV	compositive
CEIIMOPRRST	spirometric
CEIIMORRRTW	microwriter
CEIIMORRSTU	courtierism
CEIINNNNOTT	incontinent
CEIINNNORTU	internuncio
CEIINOOSSSY	synoeciosis
CEIINOPRSSS	prescission
CEIINORRSTT	restriction
CEIINOSSSUV	viciousness
CEIINRRSSTU	scrutiniser
CEIINRRSTUZ	scrutinizer
CEIINRSTTUV	instructive
CEIIOPPRSTU	precipitous
CEIIORRRSTT	terroristic
CEIIORSSSSW	scissorwise
CEIIORSTUVY	voyeuristic
CEIIPPRSTUY	perspicuity
CEIJOOORSSU	jocoserious
CEIKLMOORST	mortise-lock
CEIKLNNSSUU	unluckiness
CEIKNNORSTU	countersink
CEILLLNNORS	linen-scroll
CEILLLNOOOV	violoncello
CEILLLOSUVY	collusively
CEILLNOOPST	ponticellos
CEILLOORRUV	liver-colour
CEILMMNOPST	compliments
CEILMMOORSU	Coulommiers
CEILMMOPRUY	promycelium
CEILMOOOPST	cosmopolite
CEILMOORRTY	colorimetry
CEILMOPRTUU	pomiculture
CEILMORSUUV	vermiculous
CEILNNNOTTY	continently
CEILNOOOTUV	coevolution
CEILNOOPRTU	perlocution
CEILNORSSTU	courtliness
CEILNPRSTUU	insculpture
CEILNRSTUUV	ventriculus
CEILOOOPRST	protocolise
CEILOOOPRTZ	protocolize
CEILOOPRRSS	cross-or-pile
CEILOOPRRTU	turcopolier
CEILOOPRTTY	proteolytic
CEILOORRSTU	terricolous
CEILOORRSVY	corrosively
CEILOPRRSTU	trouser-clip
CEILORSSTVY	victoryless
CEIMMNNOOUX	excommunion
CEIMMNORSSU	consumerism
CEIMMOORRTT	tromometric
CEIMNNOOPTY	omnipotency
CEIMNOOPRSS	compression
CEIMNOORSTU	coterminous
CEIMNOPSSTU	postscenium
CEIMNOPSTUV	consumptive
CEIMNORSSTU	consumerist
	misconstrue
CEINNOORSSU	connoisseur
CEINNOOSTTU	contentious
CEINNORSTTU	tennis-court
CEINNOSTTTU	constituent
CEINOOOPRSY	oneiroscopy
CEINOOPPRST	prospection

CEINOOPRRTU	neurotropic
CEINOOPRSTT	stenotropic
CEINOOPRSTU	point-source
	prosecution
CEINOOPRSTY	retinoscopy
CEINOOPSSSU	copiousness
CEINOOPTTTY	totipotency
CEINOPRSSSU	supersonics
CEINORRSSSU	cursoriness
CEINORSSSUU	curiousness
CEINOSSSSUV	viscousness
CEINOSSSTUV	viscountess
CEIOOOPRRTZ	Proterozoic
CEIOPPRSSUU	perspicuous
CEIOPRRSTUX	prosecutrix
CEIPPRRSSTU	superscript
CEJOPRRSSUY	jury-process
CEKLLMPPTUU	plume-pluckt
CEKNNORSTUU	countersunk
CEKNOORRTUW	counterwork
	counter-work
CEKOOPPRRSW	copperworks
CELLMOOPRRT	comptroller
CELLNOORRTU	counter-roll
CELLNOPRTUY	corpulently
CELLNRTTUUY	truculently
CELLOPRTUUY	polyculture
CELMNNOORTT	controlment
CELMNOORTUU	monoculture
CELMOOORSUU	mouse-colour
CELNOOORSTU	stone-colour
CELNOOPRTTU	counter-plot
CELOOOPRRST	coprosterol
CELOORSTUUY	courteously
CEMMNOOPRTT	comportment
CEMOOOPPSTY	metoposcopy
CENNOOSSSUU	nocuousness
CENNORRTTUU	counter-turn
CENOORRSTVY	controversy
CENOORSTUUU	uncourteous
CENOPRRSSTU	corruptness
CEPRRSSTTUU	superstruct
CFFGIIIOORR	frigorifico
CFFGINOORSU	offscouring
CFFIIINOOSU	inofficious
CFFIILOOSUY	officiously
CFFIINOOSUU	unofficious
CFFLNOORSUU	snuff-colour
CFGHIIKNSSU	sucking-fish
CFGHIILLNNY	flinchingly
CFGHIILNNNU	unflinching
CFGHIMNOORT	forthcoming
CFGHIMNORTU	furthcoming
CFGIIIKNQRU	quick-firing
CFGIIILMNOR	microfiling
CFGIINOSTTY	Scottifying
CFGIKMNOORR	rock-forming
CFGIMNOPPRU	forcing-pump
CFIIILOPRTY	prolificity
CFIILMOORSS	microfossil
CFILLLOOSUU	folliculous
CFILLMOOORR	corolliform
CFILMOOPPRY	microfloppy
CFINORSTUUU	infructuous
CFKLNOORTUY	country-folk
CFLNORSUUUU	furunculous
CFLOOOPRSUY	fluoroscopy
CFNORSTUUUU	unfructuous
CGGHILNOOOS	schoolgoing
CGGIIIKNPST	pig-sticking
CGGIINOORST	Gongoristic
CGGILNOOOTT	glottogonic
CGHHIKOSTTU	thought-sick
CGHHILOOTYY	ichthyology
CGHHIOPRTYY	hygrophytic
CGHIILOOPSY	physiologic
CGHIILOORST	chirologist
CGHIKNNORSU	cornhusking
CGHILMOOOPR	morphologic
CGHILOOORST	chorologist
CGHILOOPSTY	phycologist
CGHILOORSTY	Christology
CGHIMNOORST	shortcoming
CGHIMOOOTYZ	homozygotic
CGHIMOOPRYZ	zygomorphic
CGHINNOPRTU	hunting-crop
CGHIOOORSTT	Ostrogothic
CGIIIKLNOPT	politicking
CGIIILNSSTU	linguistics
CGIIINNPRTU	unit-pricing
CGIIINOTTVY	cognitivity
CGIIKKNOPST	poking-stick
CGIIKLLMNTU	tucking-mill
CGIIKLNOPST	stockpiling
CGIIKNNRSSU	sicknursing
CGIIKNOPSTT	poting-stick
CGIILLOSSTY	syllogistic
CGIILMNOORY	criminology
CGIILMOOOSS	sociologism
CGIILMOORST	micrologist
CGIILMOOTVY	victimology
CGIILNNNSUU	cunnilingus
CGIILNOOOST	iconologist
CGIILOOOSST	sociologist
CGIINNNNOUV	unconniving
CGIINNORSST	cross-tining
CGIINNORTUY	incongruity
CGIKLNOOORT	rocking-tool
CGIKNOPPSTU	upping-stock
CGILLNNOORT	controlling
CGILLOOPTTY	polyglottic
CGILMNNOPUY	uncomplying
CGILMNOOPTT	complotting
CGILMOOOSST	cosmologist
CGILNPRSTUU	sculpturing
CGIMNOOOSST	cosmogonist
CGIMNOOOTYZ	monozygotic
CGINNNOOPRU	pronouncing
CGINNOORSUU	incongruous
CGINOOPRSTY	pyrognostic
CGINOORSSTU	outcrossing
CGLNOORSUUY	congruously
CHHIILOOPPS	philosophic
CHHIILOOPPT	photophilic

CHHIILOPTTY lithophytic
CHHIIMORSTY isorhythmic
CHHIIMRTTYY rhythmicity
CHHIINORSTY ichthyornis
CHHILMOOPRY hylomorphic
CHHILMOORTY lithochromy
CHHILOPPSYY psychophily
CHHIMMOOOPR homomorphic
CHHINOOOPPT photophonic
CHHINORSSUW urchin-shows
CHHIOOPRRTY orthophyric
CHHIOORSTTY orthostichy
CHHKOOORRRS shock-horror
CHHLLLOOPRY chlorophyll
CHHMOOOPRTY photochromy
CHHNORSUXYY oxyrhynchus
CHIIILORTTT lithotritic
CHIIIMMNRSU Michurinism
CHIIIMORSST historicism
CHIIINORSST histrionics
trichinosis
CHIIIORSSTT historicist
CHIIIORSTTY historicity
CHIIKMNNORT kinchin-mort
CHIIKNSSTTY shinty-stick
CHIILLNOOTT octillionth
CHIILNOPSTY cynophilist
CHIILOOPRTT protolithic
CHIILOOSTYZ hylozoistic
CHIILOPPRSY scripophily
CHIIMNOORSS isochronism
CHIIMOOPRTX mixotrophic
CHIINOPSTTY hypnotistic
CHIIOOPRTTX thixotropic
CHIIOPPRRTY porphyritic
CHIIORSSTTU tristichous
CHIIOSSSTTY schistosity
CHILMOOPPRY polymorphic
CHILMOOPRSY polychroism
CHILMOPRTUY Polytrichum
CHILMOPSTUY Polystichum
CHILOORSTUU ulotrichous
CHIMMNOOOPR monomorphic
CHIMNNOORTU unicorn-moth
CHIMNNORSSY synchronism
CHIMNOOPPPY hypnopompic
CHIMNOOPRRS prochronism
CHINOOORSSU isochronous
CHINOORRSTU trichronous
CHIOOOPPRRS sporophoric
CHIOOOPPRTT phototropic
CHIOOOPRRTT orthotropic
CHIOOOPRSST horoscopist
CHIOOPPRRST proctorship
CHIOOPPRSTY sporophytic
CHIOOPPRTTY protophytic
tropophytic
CHIOPSTTTUY touch-typist
CHKMOOSSTTU tussock-moth
CHMNOOOTTTU cottonmouth
CHMOOOPRSTY psychomotor
CHNNOORRSTY synchrotron
CHNNOORSSUY synchronous
CHRRRRSUUYY hurry-scurry
CIIIIKKKLLN killikinick
CIIIIKKKNNN kinnikinick
CIIIILNOSTV violinistic
CIIIIPRSSTT spiritistic
CIIILLMOPTY impoliticly
CIIILLNOSTT tonsillitic
CIIILMNOSTY consimility
CIIILOPSSST solipsistic
CIIIMNORTTU micturition
CIIINNOPRST inscription
CIIINOOSTTY isotonicity
CIIINOPSSTZ Spinozistic
CIIINORSTUY incuriosity
CIILLOORSTT torticollis
CIILNOOPSTU liposuction
CIILNOPSTUU punctilious
CIILNORSUUY incuriously
CIIMMNNOOTU comminution
CIIMMNOOTUX immunotoxic
CIIMMOORSTT microtomist
CIIMNOOOPST composition
CIIMNRSSTTU misinstruct
CIIMOPRRSTU scriptorium
CIIMOPRSTUY promiscuity
CIIMPRRSSTU scripturism
CIINNOPSSUU unsuspicion
CIINNORSTTU instruction
CIINOOPSSTY pinocytosis
CIINOPSSTTY synoptistic
CIIOOPRSSUV piscivorous
CIIPRRSSTTU scripturist
CIKNOOPRUWY pick-your-own
CILLMOOQSUU colloquiums
CILLMOORTUU multicolour
CILMNNOOOSU monoclinous
CILMNOOOSTU monticolous
CILMNOOSTUU monticulous
CILMOOPRSTU compulsitor
CILMOOPRSTY polycrotism
CILNNOOOTUV convolution
CILNNOOSSUV convulsions
CILNNOOSUUY innocuously
CILNOOOPRTU prolocution
CILNOOORSUU unicolorous
CILNOPRRTUY incorruptly
CILOOOPRSTT protocolist
CILOOPRRTUX prolocutrix
CIMNNNOOSYY synonymicon
CIMNNOOPSTU consumption
CIMNOORSSTU consortiums
CIMOOOPRRSU microporous
CIMOOOPSSTU compositous
CIMOOPRSSUU promiscuous
CIMOPRSSTUU scrumptious
CINNOOORTTT nitrocotton
CINOORSTTTU constitutor
CIOOPRSSTTU prosciuttos
CLLNOOSUUVV convolvulus

D

DDDDEEEEFIL	fiddle-de-dee
DDDEEFIOSST	eisteddfods
DDDEEGILORV	devil-dodger
DDDEEGIMOSS	demigoddess
DDDEEIILMSZ	middle-sized
DDDEEOPRWXY	proxy-wedded
DDDEFHLNORU	hundredfold
DDDEHLOOORT	toddlerhood
DDDEIILNUVY	undividedly
DDDEILLMORW	middle-world
DDDEIMNOPRU	proud-minded
DDDEKLRSUUY	skulduddery
DDDENNOORTW	down-trodden
DDEEEEEGHLW	wedge-heeled
DDEEEEILMRR	riddle-me-ree
DDEEEFILLNW	well-defined
DDEEEFIMNRS	Defenderism
DDEEEFLNORU	enfouldered
DDEEEFLOSTV	self-devoted
DDEEEGINPRU	unpedigreed
DDEEEHILLSV	dishevelled
DDEEEHMOPTU	deep-mouthed
DDEEEIINPRS	deserpidine
DDEEEILLRSW	well-desired
DDEEEILLRVW	well-derived
DDEEEILMNRT	intermeddle
DDEEEILNRUV	undelivered
DDEEEIMPRST	distempered
DDEEEINNNPT	△independent
DDEEEINNOPR	epidendrone
DDEEEINNPRT	interdepend
DDEEELLNOWW	well-endowed
DDEEELLORRW	well-ordered
DDEEELLRSSW	well-dressed
DDEEELNOPUV	undeveloped
DDEEELNPRTY	pretendedly
DDEEEMNORRT	dendrometer
DDEEENOSSTV	devotedness
DDEEENPRSSU	undepressed
DDEEENRRSSU	unredressed
DDEEEORTTUV	true-devoted
DDEEFFGLLLU	full-fledged
DDEEFIIIMNN	indemnified
DDEEFIIIRSV	diversified
DDEEFIIMNNU	definiendum
DDEEFLLNOUW	well-founded
DDEEGHILLTY	delightedly
DDEEGHILNTU	undelighted
DDEEGILNNPY	dependingly
DDEEGINNNPU	undepending
DDEEGINNRSU	undersigned
DDEEGINNRTY	tender-dying
DDEEGNNORUU	unguerdoned
DDEEGNOPRSU	groundspeed
DDEEHILRSSS	dress-shield
DDEEHINRSSS	reddishness
DDEEHMORSSU	shuddersome
DDEEIIKLNNX	index-linked
DDEEIIMNNOS	dimensioned
DDEEIINRRST	disinterred
DDEEIIQSTUU	disquietude
DDEEIKNNRSS	kindredness
DDEEILMNNTW	dwindlement
DDEEILMNPUY	unimpededly
DDEEILMOPSY	disemployed
DDEEILNOPSU	undespoiled
DDEEILPRSSY	dispersedly
DDEEINNOORR	Eriodendron
DDEEINNPSSU	undispensed
DDEEINNRRUV	under-driven
DDEEINRSSYY	Sydneysider
DDEEINSSSTU	studiedness
DDEELLNORTW	well-trodden
DDEELLNORUW	well-rounded
DDEENNORSSU	roundedness
DDEENNPSSUU	unsuspended
DDEENORSTUY	undestroyed
DDEEOOPPRST	doorstepped
DDEEOORRSVW	over-drowsed
DDEFFIILNTY	diffidently
DDEFGIIINNU	undignified
DDEFHILNOOP	phonofiddle
DDEFHILOOOS	solid-hoofed
DDEFLNNOUUY	unfoundedly
DDEGHIILMNT	light-minded
DDEGHIIMNRT	right-minded
DDEGHILLSTU	dull-sighted
DDEGHIMNOTU	tough-minded
DDEGHIOPSSS	goddess-ship
DDEGHLNOPRY	dendroglyph
DDEGIILMSUY	misguidedly
DDEGIILSSUY	disguisedly
DDEGIIMNPTU	pudding-time
DDEGIINPPPU	pudding-pipe
DDEGIINRSSV	diving-dress
DDEGIINSSUU	undisguised
DDEGILMNOST	dislodgment
DDEGILNRSTU	disgruntled
DDEGILSSTUY	disgustedly
DDEGIMNNORW	wrong-minded
DDEGINNORUW	round-winged
DDEGMNOOOSS	moon-goddess
DDEGNNORRUU	underground
DDEHHIIOPRT	diphtheroid
DDEHIIKNPRS	kindredship
DDEHIINRSSW	widdershins
DDEHINORSSU	disenshroud
DDEHINORSTW	short-winded
DDEHIOOORWW	widowerhood
DDEHLMOOTUU	loudmouthed
DDEIIINORUX	idoxuridine
DDEIIKNRRRV	drink-driver
DDEIILLNSTU	undistilled
DDEIILLOPSS	ill-disposed
DDEIIMNNOSU	diminuendos
DDEIIMOORRV	room-divider
DDEILMMNOSW	slimmed-down
DDEILNOPSSU	splendidous
DDEILNOSSUV	undissolved
DDEIMNOORUZ	zoodendrium
DDEINNOOPRV	non-provided
DDEINORSTTU	undistorted

DDGGGGIILNO gold-digging
DDGIIINNNOV non-dividing
DDGIIKLMNPU milk-pudding
DDGILMNPPUU plum-pudding
DDHIMOOORUW rhodium-wood
DDIIIMRTTUY rumti-iddity
DDIIKLNSTWY tiddlywinks
DDINOOOPRTT diprotodont
DEEEEEFHRST sheet-feeder
DEEEEFLNRUZ needle-furze
DEEEEGGHLRT three-legged
DEEEEGGLLPV level-pegged
DEEEEGKLOPR lodge-keeper
DEEEEHILRSW side-wheeler
DEEEEHIMPRS ephemerides
DEEEEHLMOSW wheedlesome
DEEEEHNPRRR reprehender
DEEEEILRRRV redeliverer
DEEEEILSSSY sessile-eyed
DEEEEIMNRRT redetermine
DEEEEKNPRRU underkeeper
DEEEELLNRTW well-entered
DEEEELNRSUV undersleeve
DEEEEMOPRST speedometer
DEEEENNRSSW renewedness
DEEEENNSTUW unsweetened
DEEEENRRRSU surrenderee
DEEEEPRRSSU supersedere
DEEEEQRSSTU sequestered
DEEEFFGILNS self-feeding
DEEEFFNOOST toffee-nosed
DEEEFGINNSS feignedness
DEEEFGNORTU free-tongued
DEEEFHLNSSU heedfulness
DEEEFHLORUW four-wheeled
DEEEFHNRRSU unrefreshed
DEEEFIILMPX exemplified
DEEEFILNSTV self-evident
DEEEFILNSVY defensively
DEEEFINNRSS refinedness
DEEEFLLORRW elder-flower
DEEEFLLOSVV self-evolved
DEEEFLMPSTT self-tempted
DEEEFLNNSSU needfulness
DEEEFLOPRSW self-powered
DEEEFLORRTX retroflexed
DEEEFMNNRTU unfermented
DEEEFMNRRSU referendums
DEEEFMOORRV overfreedom
DEEEFNPRRRU unpreferred
DEEEGHHILLT light-heeled
DEEEGHIPRST hedge-priest
DEEEGHIRRTW hedge-writer
DEEEGIMNRTV divergement
DEEEGINNNRV never-ending
DEEEGINOSXY deoxygenise
DEEEGINOXYZ deoxygenize
DEEEGMNNSTU unsegmented
DEEEHHPRSSS shepherdess
DEEEHILNPRS replenished
DEEEHIMRRSU Rudesheimer
Rüdesheimer
DEEEHIRSTTU three-suited
DEEEHKNOORT three-nooked
DEEEHLNNORT Heldentenor
DEEEHLNRSTU unsheltered
DEEEHMOPRTT hot-tempered
DEEEIILRSSV desilverise
DEEEIILRSVZ desilverize
DEEEIIMPRTX time-expired
DEEEIINNPTX inexpedient
DEEEIINSSST desensitise
DEEEIINSSTZ desensitize
DEEEILLMPRT ill-tempered
DEEEILLNNST sentinelled
DEEEILLNRSS elderliness
DEEEILMMNUV mendelevium
DEEEILNNOPT needlepoint
DEEEILNPTXY expediently
DEEEILORSTU deleterious
DEEEIMMPRST mistempered
DEEEIMNOPTT mont-de-piété
DEEEIMNPRTV deprivement
DEEEINPRRUV unreprieved
DEEEINPRTUX expenditure
DEEEINQSSUY Disneyesque
DEEEINRRSST retiredness
DEEEINRRSSV vine-dresser
DEEEINRRUVW underviewer
DEEEKNOPPRU pound-keeper
DEEELLNRRSU underseller
DEEELLPPRXY perplexedly
DEEELLRTTTU telluretted
DEEELMNNORY moneylender
DEEELMNOPTV development
DEEELMNOTVV devolvement
DEEELNNPRST resplendent
DEEELNNRSSS slenderness
DEEELNNSSSS endlessness
DEEELNPPRUX unperplexed
DEEELNRRTTU underletter
DEEELNSSSTT settledness
DEEELOOPRST rood-steeple
DEEELOOPRVV overdevelop
DEEELRRSSUV verdureless
DEEEMNNORST endorsement
DEEEMNNORTW re-endowment
DEEEMNORSSV removedness
DEEEMOPRRWY emery-powder
DEEENNPRTUV unprevented
DEEENNRRSTU nurse-tender
DEEENOPRSSS reposedness
DEEENOPRSUX underexpose
DEEENOPSSSX exposedness
DEEENOPSTTU pedetentous
DEEENPRRTUV unperverted
DEEENPRSSUX unexpressed
DEEENRRRRSU surrenderer
DEEENRRSTTT trendsetter
DEEEOPRSTTY stereotyped
DEEEPRRSSST pre-stressed
DEEEPRRSSUU supersedure
DEEFFGILRSU self-figured
DEEFFIINNRT indifferent

DEEFFILNRTY differently
DEEFFINORTU unforfeited
DEEFFINSSSU diffuseness
DEEFFORSTUV overstuffed
DEEFGGHHIIN high-feeding
DEEFGHILLST self-delight
DEEFGHIORST foresighted
DEEFGIINNRX index-finger
DEEFGIINSST fidgetiness
DEEFGIKNORW weeding-fork
DEEFGILNNSY self-denying
DEEFGILNNUY unfeignedly
DEEFGIOORTT tiger-footed
DEEFHHLOOOW whole-hoofed
DEEFHIIKSWY whiskeyfied
DEEFHILTTTW Twelfth-tide
DEEFHINOOTT fine-toothed
DEEFHLLNUUY unheedfully
DEEFHLLOSST soft-shelled
DEEFHLOOOTW whole-footed
DEEFIIINNST intensified
DEEFIILLMST self-limited
DEEFIILMRSU demulsifier
DEEFIILNQUU unliquefied
DEEFIILNSTV self-invited
DEEFIINOPRS personified
DEEFIINRRTU unterrified
DEEFIKLORRW fieldworker
DEEFILLRSSU fleurs-de-lis
DEEFILMOPSS self-imposed
DEEFILMSSSU self-misused
DEEFILNRSSU direfulness
DEEFILORSTY oyster-field
DEEFINNSSUX unfixedness
DEEFIORRTTT retrofitted
DEEFLLNNUUY unneedfully
DEEFLLNOSSU dolefulness
DEEFLLRSSUY fleurs-de-lys
DEEFLNOORST fender-stool
DEEFLNRSTUU unflustered
DEEFLOPRSSY professedly
DEEFMNOPRRU unperformed
DEEFMORRRSS dress-reform
DEEFNOORSTT tenderfoots
DEEFNOPRSSU unprofessed
DEEFNOPRTUY type-founder
DEEFOORRTTW wood-fretter
DEEGGGHILLT light-legged
DEEGGGHLORU rough-legged
DEEGGILNORR dégringoler
DEEGGINNOOV good-evening
DEEGGINOOSW goose-winged
DEEGHHILMTT high-mettled
DEEGHHILSXY highly-sexed
DEEGHHIOPRW high-powered
DEEGHHOPSSY hedge-hyssop
DEEGHIILLMT limelighted
DEEGHIINTWW white-winged
DEEGHIKNOOW weeding-hook
DEEGHILLOSV glove-shield
DEEGHILLSST delightless
DEEGHILMOST delightsome
DEEGHILNNSU un-Englished
DEEGHILNNTU unlightened
DEEGHILNNUY unheedingly
DEEGHINORSY hydrogenise
DEEGHINORYZ hydrogenize
DEEGHINRTUW underweight
DEEGHLNRSST dress-length
DEEGHNORSTU groundsheet
DEEGIIINSTV indigestive
DEEGIILSTVY digestively
DEEGIILTTUV deglutitive
DEEGIIMNNOR domineering
DEEGIJMNPRU jumping-deer
DEEGILLNOSS single-soled
DEEGILLNPSS spindle-legs
DEEGILMNOOY endemiology
DEEGILMNTUV divulgement
DEEGILNORUV overindulge
DEEGILNRSVY deservingly
DEEGILNRTVY divergently
DEEGIMNNSST dessignment
DEEGIMORSUU demiurgeous
DEEGINNRSUV undeserving
DEEGINNRTUU ungenitured
DEEGINORSTU dentigerous
DEEGJMNPRTU prejudgment
DEEGLLMOORW well-groomed
DEEGLNOSSSS godlessness
DEEGLOOPSUU pseudologue
DEEHHIIMMRS hemihedrism
DEEHHLOORSU householder
DEEHHOPRRSY hydrosphere
DEEHIILMSTT △ditheletism
DEEHIILOPRS siderophile
DEEHIILSTTW white-listed
DEEHIIMPRSU hesperidium
DEEHIINNPSZ denizenship
DEEHIIOPRSS spheroidise
DEEHIIOPRSZ spheroidize
DEEHIKLNRTU thunder-like
DEEHILLORTT title-holder
DEEHILMNOTU endothelium
DEEHILNNOTW down-the-line
DEEHIMPRTUW white-rumped
DEEHINNORST disenthrone
DEEHINOPSTY dehypnotise
DEEHINOPTYZ dehypnotize
DEEHINOSSSU hideousness
DEEHINOSSSV doveishness
DEEHINRRSSU hurriedness
DEEHKLOPTUY loup-the-dyke
DEEHLLOOSUW whole-souled
DEEHLNORRTW netherworld
DEEHLNRSSTU thunderless
DEEHLPRSTUU sulphureted
DEEHMNOOPTU open-mouthed
DEEHMOORRTY hydrometeor
DEEHMOORSVW howsomdever
DEEHNNORSTU underhonest
DEEIIIQSTUV disquietive
DEEIIKLLMRV milk-livered
DEEIIKLLMSS semi-skilled

DEEIIKLLORS	soldierlike
DEEIIKLNPRS	kinderspiel
DEEIIKLNSSS	dislikeness
DEEIILLLRVY	lily-livered
DEEIILMNSST	limitedness
DEEIILMNSSU	disseminule
DEEIILMORTV	limited-over
DEEIILNOPRS	Lepidosiren
DEEIILRSSSV	silversides
DEEIIMMNRST	determinism
DEEIIMMNRTU	intermedium
DEEIIMMPRSU	peridesmium
DEEIIMNNOPS	demi-pension
DEEIIMNOPTT	piedmontite
DEEIIMNPSST	dissepiment
DEEIIMNRRST	△irredentism
DEEIIMNRSTT	determinist
DEEIIMORRST	deteriorism
DEEIINNNOTT	intentioned
DEEIINNSSTT	dissentient
DEEIINOPSTV	point-devise
DEEIINPRSTY	serendipity
DEEIINRRSTT	△irredentist
DEEIINRSSTT	disinterest
DEEIINRTTXY	indexterity
DEEIIOPSTUX	expeditious
DEEIIOQSSUX	sesquioxide
DEEIIORRRTT	territoried
DEEIIORRTTY	deteriority
DEEIIRRRRVV	river-driver
DEEIIRSTTUV	divestiture
DEEIJMNOPSW	jimpson-weed
DEEIKLLORSV	Volkslieder
DEEIKNNOSTY	kidney-stone
DEEILLNOPRU	perduellion
DEEILMMOSST	seldom-times
DEEILMNOPST	despoilment
DEEILMNRTUY	unmeritedly
DEEILNNORVY	non-delivery
DEEILNOPTUX	unexploited
DEEILNORRSS	orderliness
DEEILNSSSTT	stiltedness
DEEILOPPPTY	polypeptide
DEEILOPSSTU	Lepidosteus
DEEIMMNORTU	endometrium
DEEIMNNOOTU	unemotioned
DEEIMNNOSTU	unmoistened
DEEIMNOPRSY	money-spider
DEEIMNPRSSU	unimpressed
DEEINNNOPSU	unpensioned
DEEINNNORST	non-resident
DEEINNOPSST	pointedness
DEEINNOSTTU	tendentious
DEEINNPRSTU	superintend
DEEINNSSSTT	stintedness
DEEINNSSTUW	unwitnessed
DEEINOPRRVW	power-driven
DEEINORRRVW	owner-driver
DEEINORSSUW	series-wound
DEEINOSSSTU	tediousness
DEEINOSSSUV	deviousness
DEEINPRRTTU	interrupted
DEEINRRRTUW	underwriter
DEEIOOPRRSU	urediospore
DEEIOOPRRTV	proveditore
DEEIOORSTUV	overtedious
DEEIOPRRTUY	eurypteroid
DEEKLNOORRU	underlooker
DEEKNNNRSSU	drunkenness
DEEKNORRRUW	underworker
DEELLLMRSUW	slum-dweller
DEELLNORTWW	town-dweller
DEELLNSTTUY	unsettledly
DEELMNORTTY	tormentedly
DEELORSTUXY	dexterously
DEEMNNORTTU	untormented
DEEMNOORTUY	Deuteronomy
DEEMNOSSSSY	syndesmoses
DEENNSSSTTU	stuntedness
DEENOPRSTTU	unprotested
DEENOPSSSSU	unpossessed
DEENOPSSSTT	spottedness
DEENORRRRSU	surrenderor
DEENORRSTUY	understorey
DEENOSSSTUU	duteousness
DEEOOPPRRST	doorstepper
DEEOORSTTWY	two-storeyed
DEEORSSSTTU	stressed-out
DEFFGINNNOU	unoffending
DEFFGINORUV	duffing-over
DEFFIILORSS	fossil-fired
DEFFIILSUVY	diffusively
DEFFIINORSU	Rediffusion®
DEFFIINORTU	unfortified
DEFFILLLNUU	unfulfilled
DEFFILLNRUU	underfulfil
DEFFINPPRSU	snuff-dipper
DEFFIOOSTTW	swift-footed
DEFGHIISTTT	tight-fisted
DEFGHILOOSY	old-fogeyish
DEFGHILOOTT	light-footed
DEFGHINORSU	unsighed-for
DEFGHOOORTU	rough-footed
DEFGIIINNTY	identifying
DEFGIILNNSW	self-winding
DEFGIINNSYY	Disneyfying
DEFGIINSTWW	swift-winged
DEFGILLNSUY	sdeignfully
DEFGILNRSSY	fly-dressing
DEFHIMNORTU	mouth-friend
DEFHINNRSUU	unfurnished
DEFHINORSUW	unwished-for
DEFHINPRSTT	spendthrift
DEFHIOOPRST	fish-torpedo
DEFHLLMOTUU	full-mouthed
DEFHLMOOTUU	foul-mouthed
DEFIIIMNSTY	misidentify
DEFIIINRTUV	unvitrified
DEFIIJNSTUU	unjustified
DEFIILLMNOR	ill-informed
DEFIILQSTUU	disquietful
DEFIIMNORTU	unmortified
DEFILMNNSSU	mindfulness
DEFILNSSTUU	dutifulness

DEFILOOORST	foot-soldier
DEFILOORUXY	oxy-fluoride
DEFILRSSSTU	distressful
DEFIMNORSTU	misfortuned
DEFINNOORRU	iron-founder
DEFIOOORRSU	odoriferous
DEFIOORRSSU	dorsiferous
DEFKLNOOORU	unlooked-for
DEFLLNORUWY	wonderfully
DEFLNOOSSTW	twofoldness
DEFLOOOOSTT	footstooled
DEFNOOPRRUU	four-pounder
DEFNOPRTUYY	type-foundry
DEGGHHHIILT	highlighted
DEGGHHHIIST	high-sighted
DEGGHIILNTW	light-winged
DEGGHILNOST	long-sighted
DEGGHINOSSS	doggishness
DEGGIIILNST	single-digit
DEGGIILNNSY	designingly
DEGGIILNORV	riding-glove
DEGGIILNRVY	divergingly
DEGGIINNNSU	undesigning
DEGGIJLLNUW	well-judging
DEGGKLRSUUY	skulduggery
DEGGLNNOOTU	long-tongued
DEGHHIINSTY	high-density
DEGHIILNNRS	hinderlings
DEGHIILNNRY	hinderingly
DEGHIILPPTT	tight-lipped
DEGHIIMNRRY	riding-rhyme
DEGHIINNTTU	hunting-tide
DEGHIINORRS	horse-riding
	riding-horse
DEGHILMNOOP	phlegmonoid
DEGHILNORSU	shouldering
DEGHILNORTW	downlighter
DEGHILOSSTW	slow-sighted
DEGHINNOPRR	herring-pond
DEGHINOSSTU	doughtiness
DEGHLMOOOTY	methodology
DEGHNNOOPRR	prong-horned
DEGHNOOOSTT	honest-to-God
DEGHNOORSUY	hydrogenous
DEGHNOORXYY	oxy-hydrogen
DEGHNORRTUW	undergrowth
DEGIIINNOST	indigestion
DEGIIINQSTU	disquieting
DEGIIKNRSTW	writing-desk
DEGIIILLNPTW	pit-dwelling
DEGIIILLNRSU	sliding-rule
DEGIIILNOTTU	deglutition
DEGIIILNRTVY	divertingly
DEGIIMNNNRU	undermining
DEGIIMNNORT	morning-tide
DEGIINNRRUW	underwiring
DEGIINNRTUV	undiverting
DEGIINOPRVW	power-diving
DEGIINRSSST	distressing
DEGIJMMNSTU	misjudgment
DEGIKLMNOSS	kingdomless
DEGILLNNTUY	indulgently
DEGILLNOPRY	deploringly
DEGILMNORSU	smouldering
DEGILNNOPRY	ponderingly
DEGILNNORWY	wonderingly
DEGILNNOSSU	ungodliness
DEGILNOPSSS	splodginess
DEGILNORUVY	devouringly
DEGILOOPRTY	pteridology
DEGILORTTUY	deglutitory
DEGINNNSSUY	undyingness
DEGINNOSTTW	down-setting
DEGINOPRSST	top-dressing
DEGLLNORSUW	groundswell
DEGLOORSTTY	Troglodytes
DEGNNOORSTU	stoneground
DEGNOOOTUWY	woody-tongue
DEHHIILMNOT	helminthoid
DEHHILMOORS	holohedrism
DEHHLNOSTUU	sleuth-hound
DEHHMMOSTUU	mush-mouthed
DEHHOOOPPRT	prophethood
DEHIIILMSTT	△dithelitism
DEHIIKNNNST	thin-skinned
DEHIILMNPSU	delphiniums
DEHIILOPRSS	soldiership
DEHIILPRSTU	trisulphide
DEHIIMNORTU	dinotherium
DEHIINORSTZ	disthronize
DEHIINSTTUW	Whitsuntide
DEHIIOOPSVV	voivodeship
DEHIIOPRSTT	hot-spirited
DEHIKNSSSSU	duskishness
DEHILLMORUU	ill-humoured
DEHILLNOSSS	dollishness
DEHILNOSSST	doltishness
DEHILNOSSTY	dishonestly
DEHILNOSTTW	thistledown
DEHILNRRUUY	unhurriedly
DEHILPRSTUU	disulphuret
DEHIMMOPSTU	imposthumed
DEHIMNPSSSU	dumpishness
DEHINNORSSS	dronishness
DEHINNORSUU	unnourished
DEHINOORRSU	dishonourer
DEHINORSSSW	wordishness
DEHINORSSTU	drouthiness
DEHINPRSSSU	prudishness
DEHINPSSTTU	studentship
DEHINRRSTTU	underthirst
DEHIOOOPPRT	photoperiod
DEHIOOPRSTT	orthopedist
DEHLLNOOWWY	wholly-owned
DEHLNOOPRSY	polyhedrons
DEHMOOPPRSU	pseudomorph
DEHNOOOOPRT	odontophore
DEHNORRSSTU	undershorts
DEHNRRSTTUU	underthrust
DEIIILLSSUV	disillusive
DEIIIMNPRSU	peridiniums
DEIIINNPSSS	insipidness
DEIIINPRTTY	intrepidity
DEIIIOPSSTV	dispositive

DEIILLMNNUU unillumined
DEIILLMNTUY unlimitedly
DEIILLORSUY deliriously
DEIILLQRRUV quill-driver
DEIILMPRSTW limp-wristed
DEIILNOORWW oriel-window
DEIILNOPRRY pyrrolidine
DEIILNOSSTU delusionist
DEIILOPRSTW low-spirited
DEIILOSSTUV dissolutive
DEIILOSSTUY seditiously
DEIIMNOOSST endomitosis
DEIIMNOOSTV misdevotion
DEIIMNOPRTV improvident
DEIIMNORTTT intromitted
DEIINNOQRSU inquirendos
DEIINOOSTTV devotionist
DEIINOSSSTU dissentious
DEIINOSTTTU destitution
DEIIOQSSTUU disquietous
DEIKLNNPRSU unsprinkled
DEILLMOOSUY melodiously
DEILLMRSTUY dusty-miller
DEILLNORSSW worldliness
DEILLNORSTU tendrillous
DEILLNORSUY unsoldierly
DEILLORSTUY desultorily
DEILLORSWWY worldly-wise
DEILLOSSTUY dissolutely
DEILMNOORSW one-worldism
DEILMNOOSUU unmelodious
DEILMNPRTUY imprudently
DEILNOPRTVY providently
DEILNOPSTUY pendulosity
DEILOOOORSW rosewood-oil
DEILPPRSSUY supply-sider
DEILPRRSSUY surprisedly
DEIMMNNOPTU impoundment
DEIMMNNSTUU indumentums
DEIMMRSSTYY dissymmetry
DEIMNNOPSWY penny-wisdom
DEIMNOOPRSU imponderous
DEIMNOORRTV motor-driven
DEIMNOPRSST spinsterdom
DEIMNOPRSTT disportment
DEIMNOSSSSY syndesmosis
DEIMOORRSUV merdivorous
DEIMOPPRTTU promptitude
DEINNOOPRTU unportioned
DEINNOPRTUV unprovident
DEINOOPRSTU torpedinous
DEINOOPRSTY ponderosity
DEINPRRSSUU unsurprised
DEIOPPRRSTY disproperty
DEKOORRSTWW worsted-work
DELLNOPSUUY pendulously
DELLNOSSSUY soundlessly
DELMORRSUUY murderously
DELNOOORSTT rondolettos
DELNOOPRSSU splendorous
DELNOOPRSUY ponderously
DELNPPRSUUY undersupply
DELOOPRSTUU trous-de-loup
DELOPPRRTUY purportedly
DELOPRRUWZZ word-puzzler
DEMOOPRRSTU Petrodromus
DEMOOPRTTUW trumpet-wood
DEMOORSSSTT storm-tossed
DENNNOSSSUU unsoundness
DENNOOSSTTY snotty-nosed
DENNORRSSUU Sensurround®
DENOOORSSSU odorousness
DENOOPPRRSW snow-dropper
DENOOPPRSTU petropounds
DENOPPRSTUU unsupported
DEOPPRTTUWY putty-powder
DFFIIISTUVY diffusivity
DFGGIIIINRY rigidifying
DFGGINOOPRR drop-forging
DFGIIILNOSY solidifying
DFGIIIMNNRT drift-mining
DFGIILLNOWW wildfowling
DFGIINNRSUW windsurfing
DFHHIILNOPS dolphin-fish
DFHMOOORTUW word-of-mouth
DFIILLLMNOO millionfold
DFIILMOSTUU multifidous
DFILLMNNUUY unmindfully
DFILLNTUUUY undutifully
DFILRSSTTUU distrustful
DFINNOORRUY iron-foundry
DGGHIIILNRT riding-light
DGGIIINNNRW ring-winding
DGGIILMNNSU mudslinging
DGGIKLNOOOO good-looking
DGGIMNNOOOR good-morning
DGGINNNRRUU drug-running
DGHIIIIMNNS diminishing
DGHIIINSSTU distinguish
DGHILLLOPRU drill-plough
DGHILMORSTY goldsmithry
DGHILOORSTY hydrologist
DGHILOPRTYY tyroglyphid
DGHLNOORSTU ground-sloth
DGIIIINPRST dispiriting
DGIIIKNRRST riding-skirt
DGIIILOORST iridologist
DGIILNNOPRU lip-rounding
DGIILNOPSSY disposingly
DGIIMNOOOUZ zoogonidium
DGIINNOSTTW down-sitting
DGILNNOOOSY sindonology
DGILNOORSTY strongyloid
DGINNORRSUU surrounding
DHHIOOPRTYY hypothyroid
DHHLLPRSUYY sulphhydryl
DHHNOOOSTTU hound's-tooth
DHHNOOPRTYY hydrophyton
DHIIIMPSSTY △diphysitism
DHIIIORSTTY thyroiditis
DHILLNOOPPY podophyllin
DHILMOOOSTU lithodomous
DHINNORTUWY whodunnitry
DHINOOSTTUW unwithstood

DHIOOORTTUW without-door
DHLLMOOPPUY Podophyllum
DHLOOPRXYYY polyhydroxy
DHNOOORTUXY unorthodoxy
DIIIILLQTUY illiquidity
DIIIIMNOSSV △divisionism
DIIIINOSSTV divisionist
DIIIKNOPSST od's-pitikins
DIIILLNOSSU disillusion
DIIILNOSSUY insidiously
DIIILNOSUVY invidiously
DIIIMMNORTU tridominium
DIIIMNOPRSS disimprison
DIIINNOSSTU disunionist
DIIINNOSUUV uninvidious
DIIINOOPSST disposition
DIILNOOSSTU dissolution
DIILNOPSSTY spondylitis
DIINORSSTUU industrious
DILMOOPSTUY stylopodium
DILNOOORSUY inodorously
DILNOOPSSSY spondylosis

E

EEEEEGKNPRR green-keeper
EEEEENPRRST representee
EEEEFHNRRRS refreshener
EEEEFIISTWW sweetie-wife
EEEEFILQRTU téléférique
EEEEGIILPRS espièglerie
EEEEGILLNRW green-wellie
EEEEGLNNSST genteelness
gentlenesse
EEEEGLNRSSV revengeless
EEEEGMNNRTV revengement
EEEEGNNQRTU queen-regent
EEEEHKLOPRT hotel-keeper
EEEEHKOPRSU housekeeper
EEEEHNNSTTV seventeenth
EEEEHORRSVW wheresoever
EEEEIINRTVW interviewee
EEEEIMNPRSW minesweeper
EEEEKOPRRST storekeeper
EEEELLRSTTV street-level
EEEELNPRSST repleteness
EEEELRRSSSV reverseless
EEEEMNPRSTT estrepement
EEEEMNRSSTX extremeness
EEEEMORRSTT stereometer
EEEENPRRRST representer
EEEFFFMNNOT enfeoffment
EEEFFGILLNS self-feeling
EEEFFHILRTW whiffletree
EEEFFILLRST self-fertile
EEEFGIKLNSS self-seeking
EEEFGILLNSS feelingless
EEEFHIKNRRT freethinker
EEEFHLORRUW four-wheeler
EEEFHMNRRST △refreshment
EEEFHOORRTT theretofore
EEEFIILMPRX exemplifier
EEEFILLRSST self-sterile
EEEFILLRVXY reflexively
EEEFIMNNRRW Minenwerfer
EEEFINNORRR ferronnière
EEEFINPRRSU superrefine
EEEFINRRTTV vine-fretter
EEEFLMPRSSU perfumeless
EEEFLORRWWY werewolfery
EEEFLPRSSSX self-express
EEEFMOORRRV forevermore
EEEGGHHMNSU meshuggeneh
EEEGGHORTTT get-together
EEEGGIINNNR engineering
EEEGGJLNNRU jungle-green
EEEGGMNNORT engorgement
EEEGHIKMNOP home-keeping
EEEGHIMNOST eighteenmos
EEEGHINOSST esthesiogen
EEEGIILMNNS gelseminine
EEEGIINPPRW weeping-ripe
EEEGIINPRSS perigenesis
EEEGIINPSST epigenesist
EEEGILLLNST teleselling
EEEGILLNORU genouillère
EEEGILNRSTW swingletree
EEEGIMNNSSS seemingness
EEEGIMNORSS merogenesis
EEEGIMNRSTU true-seeming
EEEGINNNSSU genuineness
EEEGINNORVW overweening
EEEGINNOSSX xenogenesis
EEEGINNRRTW wintergreen
EEEGINPRRSV persevering
EEEGIORRSST grossièreté
EEEGLLNNTUY ungenteelly
EEEGLLNSSSS leglessness
EEEGLMNNOTW gentlewomen
EEEGLNOORVY venereology
EEEGMNORRSV verse-monger
EEEHHILLLNP philhellene
EEEHHILPPTW Hepplewhite
EEEHHILRSTW elsewhither
EEEHHLLLMST helmet-shell
EEEHHMOSTTT thesmothete
EEEHHNPRSTY hypersthene
EEEHIILNNPT nephelinite
EEEHIINNPPR epinephrine
EEEHILLNPRT telpherline
EEEHILNPRRS replenisher
EEEHILPPRTW whippletree
EEEHILPRSSV sheep-silver
EEEHILRSSTV shirt-sleeve
EEEHIMMNPRT penthemimer
EEEHIMNNOPS phenomenise
EEEHIMNNOPZ phenomenize
EEEHIMNRSST smithereens
EEEHIMPRSSY hyperemesis
EEEHINPSSSV peevishness
EEEHKLMNOWY monkey-wheel
EEEHLLNOPTW Pelton-wheel
EEEHLLRSSST shelterless
EEEHLMNOOTT △monothelete
EEEHLMORTUV three-volume

EEEHLMRRTTY	rhyme-letter
EEEHLNNOSST	nonetheless
EEEHMMORRTT	thermometer
EEEHMOPRRST	spherometer
EEEHNRSSSTT	sternsheets
EEEHOORSSVW	whosesoever
EEEIIKLNSST	telekinesis
EEEIILLMPSS	semi-ellipse
EEEIIMNQRSU	mesquinerie
EEEIINNPSVX	inexpensive
EEEIINNRRST	Niersteiner
EEEIINRRTTV	irretentive
EEEIINRRTVW	interviewer
EEEIIORRSTX	exteriorise
EEEIIORRTXZ	exteriorize
EEEIIPRRSTT	peristerite
EEEIIPRRTTV	preteritive
EEEIKLNNQUU	unqueenlike
EEEIKLNOSST	skeletonise
EEEIKLNOSTZ	skeletonize
EEEIKLNPRST	serpentlike
EEEILLMRUVX	merveilleux
EEEILMNNNTV	enlivenment
EEEILMNNTTT	entitlement
EEEILMOORTT	meteorolite
EEEILMPRSST	plessimeter
EEEILNNPSSS	pensileness
EEEILNNQSSU	queenliness
EEEILNPRRTT	teleprinter
EEEILNPSVXY	expensively
EEEILNRTTVY	retentively
EEEILNSSTVV	velvetiness
EEEILNSTVXY	extensively
EEEILQRSSTU	requiteless
EEEIMMNNSSS	immenseness
EEEIMMORSST	seismometer
EEEIMNNNORT	mentonnière
EEEIMNNRRTT	reinterment
EEEIMNORSTT	tensiometer
EEEIMNQQRUU	quinquereme
EEEIMNQRRTU	requirement
EEEIMNQRTTU	requitement
EEEIMOPRSTX	extemporise
EEEIMOPRTXZ	extemporize
EEEIMORRTTV	terremotive
EEEINNNSSST	intenseness
EEEINNPRSTT	presentient
	spinnerette
EEEINNPRTUX	unexperient
EEEINNPSSSV	pensiveness
EEEINNPSUVX	unexpensive
EEEINNRTTUV	unretentive
EEEINORRRSV	reversioner
EEEINPPPRSS	pepperiness
EEEINPQRSTU	Pinteresque
EEEINPRRRST	enterpriser
EEEINPRRRTT	interpreter
	reinterpret
EEEINPRRSST	intersperse
EEEINPRRSSU	purse-seiner
EEEINPRSTTX	pre-existent
EEEINRSSSTV	restiveness
EEEINRSTTWW	winter-sweet
EEEKLNOOSTX	exoskeleton
EEEKLNRSTUV	trunksleeve
EEEKLORRSTW	steelworker
EEELLLNPRTY	repellently
EEELLLPSSSY	sleeplessly
EEELLNRSSVY	nervelessly
EEELLNSSSSY	senselessly
EEELLOPRSSU	soul-sleeper
EEELMNNOPTV	envelopment
EEELMORRSSS	remorseless
EEELNNOPSST	spleenstone
EEELNNPTVWY	twelve-penny
EEELNOPQTUV	Pont-l'évêque
EEELNSSSSSU	uselessness
EEELNSSSSSX	sexlessness
EEELORRSTVW	overwrestle
EEELPRRSSTT	letterpress
EEELRSSTTUX	textureless
EEEMMNOPRTV	premovement
EEEMMNOPRTW	empowerment
EEEMNNPRSTT	presentment
EEEMNORSTUV	venturesome
EEEMNPRSSSU	supremeness
EEEMNPRSTTY	empty-nester
EEEMOQRRTTU	torque-meter
EEEMORRSTTY	stereometry
EEEMPRRTTTU	trumpet-tree
EEENNPRSSST	presentness
EEENOOPRSSS	operoseness
EEENOPRRRST	representor
EEENPRSSSSX	expressness
EEENQRRSTUU	Turneresque
EEEOPRRSTTY	stereotyper
EEFFFHHLOST	off-the-shelf
EEFFGHIIRRT	fire-fighter
EEFFGIINRSV	fivefingers
EEFFGILNRSU	glue-sniffer
EEFFGLLNTUY	effulgently
EEFFHILNTTY	fifteenthly
EEFFIINNOSV	inoffensive
EEFFILLPPTU	fipple-flute
EEFFILNOSVY	offensively
EEFFINNOSUV	unoffensive
EEFFIORRRSU	ferriferous
EEFFLNRSSTU	fretfulness
EEFFLOOPRRS	self-reproof
EEFGGIOPRTT	pettifogger
EEFGHHORTTU	free-thought
EEFGHIILRRT	firelighter
EEFGHINRRST	frighteners
EEFGHIORRTV	overfreight
EEFGHLMNORS	fleshmonger
EEFGIILNOPR	pigeon-flier
EEFGILLLORW	gelliflowre
EEFGILLNNUY	unfeelingly
EEFGILLNRSY	self-relying
EEFGILNNOPS	self-opening
EEFGILNNOUX	genuflexion
EEFGILNOPRY	pigeon-flyer
EEFGILNORRW	reflowering
EEFGILNRSSV	self-serving

EEFGILORRTW tiger-flower
EEFGIMMORSU gemmiferous
EEFGINNORSS foreignness
EEFGINORSSV forgiveness
EEFGLLOORXY reflexology
EEFGLLRRTUY regretfully
EEFGLOOORSW goose-flower
EEFGMNOORTT forget-me-not
EEFHIKNORRT forethinker
EEFHILLNSSS fleshliness
EEFHILNSSSS selfishness
EEFHILOOPRT photo-relief
EEFHILORSTU lethiferous
EEFHILORSWW werewolfish
EEFHILOSUWY housewifely
EEFHIORSUWY housewifery
EEFHLLNPSSU helpfulness
EEFHLNOPSSU hopefulness
EEFHMORRRTU furthermore
EEFHMORRSTU furthersome
EEFHNOORRST foreshorten
EEFHORRSTTT setter-forth
EEFIIINNRST intensifier
EEFIIISSTTV festivities
EEFIILNORRX irreflexion
EEFIILNRRTX life-rentrix
EEFIILRTVXY reflexivity
EEFIINNOPRR friponnerie
EEFIINOPRRS personifier
EEFIKNORSTY oyster-knife
EEFILLLMNTU mellifluent
EEFILLLMRSU millefleurs
EEFILLMORSU melliferous
EEFILMORRTU fluorimeter
EEFILMORSWW werewolfism
EEFILNNRTTU interfluent
EEFILNORSSW floweriness
EEFILOOPRRT profiterole
EEFILOORSST loosestrife
EEFINRSSTUV furtiveness
EEFIOPRSSTU pestiferous
septiferous
EEFLLNORTTU fortune-tell
EEFLLNRSTUY resentfully
EEFLLOPRSUY reposefully
EEFLMNORSTT self-torment
EEFLMNOSSSU fulsomeness
EEFLMNRSTTU flusterment
EEFLMOORRTU fluorometer
EEFLNNRSTUU unresentful
EEFLNNSSTUU tunefulness
EEFLNOPRSUU unreposeful
EEFLNORSSTU fortuneless
EEFLNORSSUV overfulness
EEFLNPSSSUU suspenseful
EEFLNRSSSTU restfulness
EEFLNSSSTUZ zestfulness
EEFLORRSTTU self-torture
EEFNOPRSSSU profuseness
EEFNORRSSTU foster-nurse
EEFOPRRRRSU fore-spurrer
EEGGGIINRRT rigging-tree
EEGGGINNPTT tent-pegging
EEGGHHLOORW whole-hogger
EEGGHIINSST sightseeing
EEGGHMNNOOS hogen-mogens
EEGGILLNNTY negligently
EEGGILNNRVY revengingly
EEGGILORSUY egregiously
EEGGIMNOOTT go-to-meeting
EEGGNOOPRST progestogen
EEGHHILRTWW wheelwright
EEGHHIPPRST high-stepper
EEGHHLLNOTW whole-length
EEGHHOPPRTU peep-through
EEGHIILPPRT pipe-lighter
EEGHIINRSTW wishing-tree
EEGHIINSSTW weightiness
EEGHIKNOPPS shopkeeping
EEGHILMMNOT gentilhomme
EEGHILNNRST netherlings
EEGHILNNSST lengthiness
EEGHILNOOPR pigeonholer
EEGHILNOOPS pigeonholes
EEGHILNOSSY hylogenesis
EEGHILOORST theologiser
EEGHILOORSY heresiology
EEGHILOORTZ theologizer
EEGHILRSTTT streetlight
EEGHIMNNNTU unhingement
EEGHIMNOORS homogeniser
EEGHIMNOORZ homogenizer
EEGHIMNOOSS homogenesis
EEGHIMNOOTY homogeneity
EEGHIMOORST isogeotherm
EEGHINNPTWY pennyweight
EEGHINOOPSU pigeon-house
EEGHINORRTV overnighter
EEGHINRSTTY yesternight
EEGHLMMORTU grummet-hole
EEGHLOOPRTY herpetology
EEGHMNOOOSU homogeneous
EEGHMNOORRW whoremonger
EEGHNORSTYY hysterogeny
EEGHNOSSSUU hugeousness
EEGIIILNORS religionise
EEGIIILNORZ religionize
EEGIIIMNPST impetigines
EEGIIKLLLOS skilligolee
EEGIIKLPRSS kriegsspiel
EEGIILLNNTT intelligent
EEGIILMNNRT intermingle
EEGIILNNOST lentiginose
EEGIIMMNNPT impingement
EEGIIMNNNRS Minnesinger
EEGIIMNRSTV time-serving
EEGIINNNRTV intervening
EEGIINNORST nitrogenise
EEGIINNORTZ nitrogenize
EEGIINNRSTT interesting
EEGIINNRTUU unigeniture
EEGIINPRRTY peregrinity
EEGIKLNORTW teleworking
EEGIKMNOOPR keeping-room

EEGILLLNPRY	repellingly
EEGILLLSSUY	guilelessly
EEGILLMOOST	teleologism
EEGILLOOSTT	teleologist
EEGILLORRRU	guerrillero
EEGILMNNSST	meltingness
EEGILMOOSTY	etymologise
EEGILMOOTYZ	etymologize
EEGILNNNRTU	unrelenting
EEGILNNPRTY	repentingly
EEGILNNRSTY	resentingly
	single-entry
EEGILNNTUWY	unweetingly
EEGILNOPSSY	polygenesis
EEGILNORSVY	sovereignly
EEGILNPRSTY	pesteringly
EEGILOPRSTT	poltergeist
EEGIMNNNORT	Montenegrin
EEGIMNNOOSS	monogenesis
EEGIMNNORSU	Monseigneur
EEGIMNNOTTW	town-meeting
EEGIMNNPRTU	untempering
EEGIMNNRRTU	interregnum
EEGIMNORSTW	swingometer
EEGIMNPRSST	sempstering
EEGINNNPRTU	unrepenting
EEGINNNRSTU	unresenting
EEGINNOOSST	ontogenesis
EEGINNRRSTT	restringent
EEGINOORRTU	rouge-et-noir
EEGINOPRRTU	progeniture
EEGINORRSTU	terrigenous
EEGINORSTVY	sovereignty
EEGINPRSTTU	guttersnipe
EEGINPSTTTY	typesetting
EEGIOPRRSSV	△progressive
EEGKLLMNSUU	muskellunge
EEGLMOOORTY	meteorology
EEGLOQRSTUY	grotesquely
EEGMNNORRST	morgenstern
EEGMNNORSST	engrossment
EEGNOOORSTU	erotogenous
EEGNOOOSSTU	osteogenous
EEGOQRRSTUY	grotesquery
EEHHIINRTTW	therewithin
EEHHILLNSSS	hellishness
EEHHILMOPRT	thermophile
EEHHILOPRST	lithosphere
EEHHILORSTW	otherwhiles
EEHHIMORSTW	somewhither
EEHHINSSSWY	wheyishness
EEHHIOOPSST	theosophise
EEHHIOOPSTZ	theosophize
EEHHIOPRRSZ	rhizosphere
EEHHIOPSSTY	hypothesise
EEHHIOPSTTY	hypothetise
EEHHIOPSTYZ	hypothesize
EEHHIOPTTYZ	hypothetize
EEHHLORSUUY	hurley-house
EEHHMOORSTU	house-mother
EEHHNOPSTUY	hypothenuse
EEHHNORSTUU	house-hunter
EEHHOOPPRST	photosphere
EEHHOOPRRTT	heterotroph
EEHIIJNOPST	josephinite
EEHIIKNSSST	kinesthesis
EEHIILMNTUW	minute-while
EEHIILRSTVW	silver-white
EEHIIMNORTY	Hieronymite
EEHIIMPPRRS	premiership
EEHIINRRSST	inheritress
EEHIIORSTTT	historiette
EEHIKMNNOSY	monkey-shine
EEHILMMOSTU	mesothelium
EEHILMNOOTT	△monothelite
EEHILMOPPRS	spermophile
EEHILNOORST	line-shooter
EEHILNOPPRS	nephrolepis
EEHILNOPRRT	leptorrhine
EEHILNOPSTT	telephonist
EEHILNOSTTV	novelettish
EEHILNSTTXY	sixteenthly
EEHILORRSTT	horse-litter
EEHILSSTTUW	shuttlewise
EEHIMMNNOPS	phenomenism
EEHIMNNOPST	phenomenist
EEHIMNORRTW	mine-thrower
EEHIMOPPRRS	emperorship
EEHIMOPRSTU	hemipterous
EEHIMPSSTUY	emphyteusis
EEHINNOOPTT	thiopentone
EEHINNORRST	northernise
EEHINNORRTZ	northernize
EEHINNOSSSU	heinousness
EEHINOPSTVY	hypotensive
EEHINORRTTU	rinthereout
EEHINORSSSW	showeriness
EEHINORSSTU	southernise
EEHINORSTUZ	southernize
EEHINPSSSTT	pettishness
EEHINRSSSTU	hirsuteness
EEHINRSSSTY	synthesiser
EEHINRSSTTY	synthetiser
EEHINRSSTYZ	synthesizer
EEHINRSTTYZ	synthetizer
EEHIOPRRSTW	tree-worship
EEHIPRSSTTU	trusteeship
EEHKNOORSTT	tenterhooks
EEHLLLMSSSU	mussel-shell
EEHLLLRSTTU	turtle-shell
EEHLLMOOSWY	wholesomely
EEHLLORSSTY	oyster-shell
EEHLLRRTTTU	truth-teller
EEHLMNOOSUW	unwholesome
EEHLMNOTTVW	twelvemonth
EEHLOPRRSTU	reupholster
	upholsterer
EEHLORSTTYY	heterostyly
EEHLPRSSTUU	supersleuth
EEHMMOOORSU	homeomerous
EEHMMORRTTY	thermometry
EEHMMORSSUU	summerhouse
EEHMNNOOORY	honeymooner
EEHMOPPRSTY	spermophyte

EEHMORRRSTT	short-termer
EEHNOOOPRSZ	ozonosphere
EEHNOOPRSTY	stereophony
EEHNOPQSTUY	Pythonesque
EEHNOPSTTUY	theopneusty
EEHNORRSTTW	north-wester
EEHOOPPRRST	troposphere
EEHOOPRRSTU	porterhouse
	porter-house
EEHOOPRRSTY	heterospory
EEHOORRRTVW	overthrower
EEHORSSTTUW	south-wester
EEHPRRSSSTY	hyperstress
EEIIIMNNSTU	einsteinium
EEIIIMRRSSV	irremissive
EEIIINNSSTV	insensitive
EEIIINNSTTV	intensitive
EEIIINSTTVV	investitive
EEIIKLNNRTU	interleukin
EEIILLNRSTY	resiliently
EEIILLPPRST	pipistrelle
EEIILLPRSTU	spirituelle
EEIILMMNPRT	imperilment
EEIILMNOSSU	emulsionise
EEIILMNOSUZ	emulsionize
EEIILMNRSSS	miserliness
EEIILNNPRRT	line-printer
EEIILNNRSST	listeners-in
EEIILNNSTVY	intensively
EEIILNNTVVY	inventively
EEIILNRSSSV	silveriness
EEIILNSSTVY	sensitively
EEIILORSTUZ	Louis-Treize
EEIILQSTUXY	exquisitely
EEIILRSSTVY	resistively
EEIIMNNORTU	munitioneer
EEIIMNNPRTT	impertinent
EEIIMNOPRTV	premonitive
EEIIMNORTTX	Intoximeter®
	intoximeter
EEIIMNPRRUU	perineurium
EEIINNNORTV	re-invention
EEIINNNOSTX	inextension
EEIINNNTUVV	uninventive
EEIINNORRST	reinsertion
EEIINNORRTT	irretention
EEIINNPRRWZ	prize-winner
EEIINNSSTUV	unsensitive
EEIINOPRRTT	preterition
EEIINQRSTUU	unrequisite
EEIINRSTTUV	investiture
EEIINRTTTVY	retentivity
EEIIOPPRSTV	prepositive
EEIIOPRSTTU	repetitious
EEIIORRTTXY	exteriority
EEIIRSTTTUV	restitutive
EEIKLLNORUV	unloverlike
EEIKLNNNPWY	pennywinkle
EEIKLOPPRSU	purpose-like
EEIKMNORSSS	irksomeness
EEILLMMSTUV	summit-level
EEILLMPRTUX	multiplexer
EEILLNOPQTU	equipollent
EEILLNORRTU	ritournelle
EEILLNOSSSY	noiselessly
EEILLNPRRST	print-seller
EEILLNPSSSY	spinelessly
EEILLNPSTTY	pestilently
EEILLNRSUUY	unleisurely
EEILLOPSVXY	explosively
EEILLPRSUVY	prelusively
	repulsively
EEILMNNOTVV	involvement
EEILMNOOSST	emotionless
EEILMNOSSSS	lissomeness
EEILMNRTTTY	remittently
EEILMOOPRSU	pleiomerous
EEILMOPRSSS	promiseless
EEILMOPRTUV	pluviometer
EEILMPRSSTY	plessimetry
EEILMRRSSUV	river-mussel
EEILNNOPPTT	plenipotent
EEILNNOSSST	tensionless
EEILNNPRTTY	pertinently
EEILNNSSSSS	sinlessness
EEILNOORTVV	overviolent
EEILNORSSSU	elusoriness
EEILNOSSTVY	ostensively
EEILNOSTTTV	novelettist
EEILNSSSSTW	witlessness
EEILOPPPPST	pipe-stopple
EEILOPRSSTY	proselytise
EEILOPRSTYZ	proselytize
EEILORSTVXY	extorsively
EEIMMMNPRSU	menispermum
EEIMMNOPRTV	improvement
EEIMMNPRSST	impressment
EEIMMNPRSTU	sempiternum
EEIMMORSSTY	seismometry
EEIMMORSTYZ	zymosimeter
EEIMMPRSUVV	sempervivum
EEIMNNNORTV	environment
EEIMNNOOSSS	noisomeness
EEIMNNOPRST	omnipresent
EEIMNNOSSSW	winsomeness
EEIMNNRTTTU	unremittent
EEIMNNSSTTV	investments
EEIMNORSTTY	tensiometry
EEIMNORSTZZ	intermezzos
EEIMNRSSTTW	Westminster
EEIMOPPRSSU	superimpose
EEIMPPRSTUV	presumptive
EEINNNOSTTX	non-existent
EEINNOORTTX	enterotoxin
EEINNOPPRSS	nose-nippers
EEINNOPRSTT	septentrion
EEINNORRTTV	interventor
EEINNOSSSUV	enviousness
EEINNOSSTTU	sententious
EEINNQSSTUU	unquietness
EEINOORRTTX	extortioner
EEINOPRSTTU	pretentious
EEINOPSSSTU	piteousness
EEINORRSTUV	enterovirus

EEINORSSSSU seriousness
EEINPRRRTTU interrupter
EEINPRTTTWY typewritten
EEINRRSTUWW Wienerwurst
EEIOPRRRSTW prose-writer
EEIOPRRSSSU superioress
EEIOPRSSSTX expositress
EEIPPRSSSUV suppressive
EEJLNOSSSSY joylessness
EEKKOORRRTV △voortrekker
EEKLLMOSSSY smokelessly
EEKLORRSTTW trestlework
EEKMNOOPRTV provokement
EEKMNOOPSSW spokeswomen
EEKOOORRSTV overstrooke
EELLLMNOOWY lemon-yellow
EELLLOORRTW roller-towel
EELLMPPRSTU pullet-sperm
EELLNOPSTUY plenteously
EELLNPRTUUV pulverulent
EELLOPRSSWY powerlessly
EELLORRSTTY storyteller
EELMMOOOPPS pompelmoose
EELMMOOPPSU pompelmouse
EELMMOORTUV volumometer
EELMNOSSSUU emulousness
EELNNSSSSSU sunlessness
EELNOOPPSTW townspeople
EELNOORRSUY erroneously
EELNOPRSTYY polystyrene
EELNOPSSSST toplessness
EELNORSTTTU turtle-stone
EELOPPRSSSU purposeless
EELOPRRSSUW low-pressure
EELOPRSTUUV supervolute
EEMNNRSTTTU entrustment
EEMNOORSTTY enterostomy
EEMNOPRTTTU trumpet-tone
EEMNORSSTTW westernmost
EEMOORRSTTU torturesome
EEMOPSSTTTT tempest-tost
EEMOPSSTTUU tempestuous
EENNOORSSSU onerousness
EENNOORSTTT rottenstone
EENNOQRSUUY Runyonesque
EENNORSSSUV nervousness
EENNOSSSTUU tenuousness
EENOOPPRRSW personpower
EEOOPRRSSSS repossessor
EEPPRRRSTUU purpresture
EFFGHNOORTU forfoughten
EFFGIINNORS sin-offering
EFFGIINORSY foresignify
EFFGIORRSUU frugiferous
EFFGLLORTUY forgetfully
EFFHHIIPRSS sheriffship
EFFHHINSSSU huffishness
EFFHILOOSTT offset-litho
EFFHINOSSST toffishness
EFFHLORRSUU four-flusher
EFFILOORRSU floriferous
EFFIOORRSTT first-footer
EFGGHIINNRT frightening
EFGGHIIRRST triggerfish
trigger-fish
EFGGLOOORST footslogger
EFGHHIILOPR high-profile
EFGHHOORTTU forethought
EFGHIIILNNS fishing-line
line-fishing
EFGHIILNSST flightiness
EFGHIILORTT right-to-life
EFGHILNORTW night-flower
EFGHINORSSU surgeonfish
EFGHLNRSTTU strengthful
EFGIIILLNNR fringilline
EFGIIINRVVY revivifying
EFGIILLMORU florilegium
EFGIILLNPRY pilferingly
EFGIILLNSTY stellifying
EFGIILMNSTT filmsetting
EFGIINNPRRT fingerprint
EFGIINOPRUW rouping-wife
EFGIKLLLNRU fell-lurking
EFGIKLNNOSW self-knowing
EFGIKNNOORW foreknowing
EFGILLLORWY gillyflower
EFGILLNNNRU fell-running
EFGILMNOORT montgolfier
EFGILMORSUU glumiferous
EFGILNNOSSW flowingness
EFGILNNPRSU self-pruning
EFGILNOORVW overflowing
EFGIMMORSUU gummiferous
EFGINNNOSTU unsoftening
EFGINORRSUU ferruginous
EFGIOPRSSUY gypsiferous
EFGIORSTTUU guttiferous
EFGLMNOOTTU leg-of-mutton
EFGLNNOSSSU songfulness
EFGNNOORTTU unforgotten
EFHHOOPPRRT froth-hopper
EFHIILORSTY life-history
EFHIILRRSTT shirtlifter
EFHIINRSSTT thriftiness
EFHIIOPRRSW fire-worship
EFHILLNSSUY unselfishly
EFHILLSSSTY shiftlessly
EFHILNOOSSS foolishness
EFHILNOSSSU fushionless
EFHILNSSSUW wishfulness
EFHILOPRSSW self-worship
EFHIMNNRSTU furnishment
EFHIMPRSTTU trumpet-fish
EFHINOPPSSS foppishness
EFHIORRSTUU thuriferous
EFHLLNOPUUY unhopefully
EFHLNPSSSUU pushfulness
EFHLNRSSTUU hurtfulness
EFHLOSTTUUY theftuously
EFHMORRSTTU furthermost
EFHOOOPRRSW showerproof
EFIIILNRTTY infertility
EFIIINORRTY inferiority

EFIIJLNOSTT	stifle-joint
EFIIKNORSUZ	zinkiferous
EFIIKRRSSTT	first-strike
EFIILMOORTZ	zeolitiform
EFIILNNOOPS	self-opinion
EFIILNPSSTU	pitifulness
EFIIMMNORRS	misinformer
EFIINNORSTU	interfusion
EFIINOPRSSU	spiniferous
EFIINORRSUU	uriniferous
EFIKLLNSSSU	skilfulness
EFILLLMOSUU	mellifluous
EFILLLNPTUY	plentifully
EFILLNOOSUY	feloniously
EFILLRSSTUY	fruitlessly
EFILNORSTUU	interfluous
EFILNSSSTUW	wistfulness
EFILOOPRRSU	proliferous
EFILOORSUUV	ovuliferous
EFILOPPRSTU	life-support
EFILORSSTUY	styliferous
EFILPRSTUUY	superfluity
EFIMNNORSSU	uniformness
EFIMNOORSSU	somniferous
EFIMOORRSTU	mortiferous
EFINOOORSUZ	ozoniferous
EFINOPRRSST	first-person
EFINOPRSSUU	superfusion
EFINORSSSTW	frowstiness
EFINORSSSUU	furiousness
EFIOOPRRTUV	virtue-proof
EFIORRSTTUY	yttriferous
EFKMOOPRSTU	musket-proof
EFKNNNOORUW	unforeknown
EFLLNNTUUUY	untunefully
EFLLNORSSTY	frontlessly
EFLLNOSSSUU	soulfulness
EFLLNSSSTUU	lustfulness
EFLLOOPPRRU	proof-puller
EFLNNOORRSS	forlornness
EFLOPPRSSTU	self-support
EFLOPRSSUUU	superfluous
EFNNNORRRTU	front-runner
EFOOPRSSTUY	pussyfooter
EGGGIIINPRW	periwigging
EGGGLNOOSSW	snow-goggles
EGGHHHIILRT	highlighter
EGGHHIILTTW	lightweight
EGGHHINOSSS	hoggishness
EGGHIINPSSS	piggishness
EGGHIINRRTW	right-winger
EGGHIINRSST	sight-singer
EGGHILLNRRU	herring-gull
EGGHLNOORSW	hornswoggle
EGGIIKLNTWY	tiggywinkle
EGGIILLNNRY	lingeringly
EGGIILNNSWY	swingeingly
EGGIINNORWW	wine-growing
EGGIKLMMORW	glimmer-gowk
EGGILMMOOST	gemmologist
EGGLMMNOOOR	gloom-monger
EGGLNOOORTY	gerontology

EGHHHOORSTU	hog-shouther
EGHHIIKNRST	night-shriek
EGHHIINNOST	high-tension
EGHHIMORRTT	mother-right
EGHHINNRTTU	night-hunter
EGHHKNOTTUW	hunt-the-gowk
EGHHLLORSTU	trough-shell
EGHHLOSSTTU	thoughtless
EGHIIIMNTTW	whiting-time
EGHIIKLNRSY	shriekingly
EGHIILLNRSV	shrivelling
EGHIILLNSWW	well-wishing
	wishing-well
EGHIILLOSSS	shigellosis
EGHIILNNSST	thingliness
EGHIILNPRSY	perishingly
EGHIILNRSSS	girlishness
EGHIILNRSVY	shiveringly
EGHIILNRTWY	witheringly
EGHIILNSSST	sightliness
EGHIILOORST	hierologist
EGHIINNNSSS	shiningness
EGHIINNOPSS	sphingosine
EGHIINNPRSU	unperishing
EGHIINNRTUW	unwithering
EGHIINORSTU	tiring-house
EGHIINRSSST	tigrishness
EGHIKMNOORW	homeworking
EGHIKNORRTW	night-worker
EGHILLSSSTY	sightlessly
EGHILMNOORT	moonlighter
EGHILMNOSTU	unlightsome
EGHILMOOSTY	mythologise
EGHILMOOTYZ	mythologize
EGHILNOOPRT	gerontophil
EGHILNOOPST	nephologist
	phenologist
EGHILNOOSTT	ethnologist
EGHILNOOSTU	lithogenous
EGHILNOSSST	ghostliness
EGHILORSTUY	righteously
EGHILPRSSST	sprightless
EGHINNNOSST	nothingness
EGHINOORSUZ	rhizogenous
EGHINOPPRSY	prophesying
EGHINOPRRTT	night-porter
EGHINOPRSSU	springhouse
	surgeonship
EGHINORRTTW	intergrowth
EGHINORSSSU	roguishness
EGHINORSTUU	unrighteous
EGHINPRSSTU	uprightness
EGHINRRTUWW	wither-wrung
EGHIORRSTTW	ghost-writer
EGHKNOOPRSU	rough-spoken
EGHLLNRTUUY	gully-hunter
EGHLMNOOPSU	phlegmonous
EGHLOPPRTYY	petroglyphy
EGHNNOOPSUY	hypnogenous
EGHOORRTUVW	overwrought
EGIIIKLLMNT	time-killing
EGIIIKLMMNT	milking-time

EGIIILMNORS	religionism
EGIIILNNNRT	interlining
EGIIILNNNST	listening-in
EGIIILNORST	religionist
EGIIILORRSU	irreligious
EGIIILORSTY	religiosity
EGIIIMNNRST	ministering
EGIIIMNPRRW	priming-wire
EGIIINNOPRT	pre-ignition
EGIIINNOPTT	petitioning
EGIIKLLNNSW	well-sinking
EGIIKLNOOSY	kinesiology
EGIIKNORRWW	wireworking
EGIILLMNPSS	misspelling
EGIILLNNSSW	willingness
EGIILLNORTY	loiteringly
EGIILLNPRUW	wire-pulling
EGIILLNRSTW	ill-wresting
EGIILLORSUY	religiously
EGIILMNNSSS	smilingness
EGIILMNPRSY	simperingly
EGIILMOOSST	semiologist
EGIILNNNSTU	unlistening
EGIILNNNSUV	nun's-veiling
EGIILNNOSTU	lentiginous
EGIILNNOSTV	Livingstone
EGIILNNOSUY	ingeniously
EGIILNNTTUY	ungentility
EGIILNORSUU	unreligious
EGIILNOSTTT	stilettoing
EGIILNQRUVY	quiveringly
EGIILNRSSST	gristliness
EGIILNRSSTY	resistingly
EGIIMNNRTTU	unremitting
EGIIMNOPRST	temporising
EGIIMNOPRTZ	temporizing
EGIINNNNSSW	winningness
EGIINNNQRUU	unenquiring
EGIINNOQSTU	questioning
EGIINNOSTTU	tentiginous
EGIINNPRSSS	springiness
EGIINNRSSST	stringiness
EGIINNRSSTU	unresisting
EGIINOPRRTX	progenitrix
EGIINOPRSSU	serpiginous
	spinigerous
EGIINORRSTT	intertrigos
EGIINORSTUV	vertiginous
EGIINPRTTWY	typewriting
EGIIOPRSSTU	prestigious
EGIKKNORSTY	keystroking
EGIKLLLNOOW	well-looking
EGIKLLNNORS	snorkelling
EGIKLLNOSWY	king's-yellow
EGIKLNRTUUV	king-vulture
EGIKNNNOSSW	knowingness
EGIKNOORRVW	working-over
EGILLLOOVXY	vexillology
EGILLLSSTUY	guiltlessly
EGILLNNOSTW	wellingtons
EGILLNORTVY	revoltingly
EGILMNOOOSU	monologuise
EGILMNOOOUZ	monologuize
EGILMNOORTY	terminology
EGILMNPRSUY	presumingly
EGILMNRTTUY	mutteringly
EGILMOOORSU	oligomerous
EGILMOORSTT	metrologist
EGILMOOSSTU	museologist
EGILMOOSTTY	etymologist
EGILMOPRSUU	plumigerous
EGILNNOSUUY	ingenuously
EGILNNRSTTY	stringently
EGILNNRSTUY	unrestingly
EGILNNRTUVY	venturingly
EGILNOOOPST	poenologist
EGILNOORSTU	neurologist
EGILNOPRRTY	reportingly
EGILNOPRRVY	reprovingly
EGILNOPRTTY	potteringly
EGILNORTTTY	totteringly
EGILNPRSTTU	spluttering
EGILOOORSTY	soteriology
EGILOOOSSTT	osteologist
EGILOOPRSSY	perissology
EGILOOPRSTT	petrologist
EGILOOPSSTT	pestologist
EGIMMNOSTUY	gynostemium
EGIMNNOORRY	ironmongery
EGIMNNPRSUU	unpresuming
EGIMNOOORZZ	Mezzogiorno
EGIMNOORRSV	misgovernor
EGIMNOORRTT	Trimetrogon
EGIMOPRRSSS	progressism
EGINNNORRUV	overrunning
EGINNNRRTUU	unreturning
EGINNOORSTU	nitrogenous
EGINNOPPSTU	upping-stone
EGINNOPRRUV	unreproving
EGINOOPRRSS	progression
EGINOPPRRST	ring-stopper
EGINORRSSTU	trouserings
EGINPRRSSTU	superstring
EGIOORRSSSU	gressorious
EGIOPRRSSST	progressist
EGLLNOPPRSU	long-purples
EGNOOOPRSSU	sporogenous
EGNOOPRRTYY	proterogyny
EGNOORSSTTY	oyster-tongs
EHHIIMPSSTY	physitheism
EHHIINRSSTW	withershins
EHHIINSSSTW	whitishness
EHHILMNOSTU	helminthous
EHHILOOPPRS	philosopher
EHHIMOOPRRT	theriomorph
EHHIMOOPSST	theosophism
EHHIMRSTTUY	eurhythmist
EHHINORSSSW	whorishness
EHHIOOPPRSS	phosphorise
EHHIOOPPRST	phosphorite
EHHIOOPPRSZ	phosphorize
EHHIOOPRRSW	hero-worship
EHHIOOPSSTT	theosophist
EHHIOPPPRST	prophetship

EHHIOPSSSST	hostess-ship
EHHMMOOOOPR	homoeomorph
EHHMMOOOPRY	homeomorphy
EHHOOPPRSTY	hypostrophe
EHHOPPRRTYY	hypertrophy
EHIIILLPPST	phillipsite
EHIIILOSSTT	hostilities
EHIIKLLMSTT	milk-thistle
EHIIKLRSVWY	whisky-liver
EHIIKNNPSSS	pinkishness
EHIILMRSSTV	silversmith
EHIILNOOPRT	heliotropin
EHIILNOOPST	oenophilist
EHIILOOPTTX	toxophilite
EHIIMNOSSTT	smithsonite
EHIIMNPSSSW	wimpishness
EHIIMNSSSSS	missishness
EHIINNSSSSW	swinishness
EHIINOPRSSY	hyperinosis
EHIINOPRTTY	hyponitrite
EHIINPRSSST	spinsterish
EHIINRSSSTT	thirstiness
EHIIRRRSSTT	shit-stirrer
EHIKLMSSTTU	musk-thistle
EHIKLNSSSSU	luskishness
EHIKLORRSTW	silk-thrower
EHILLMRSSTY	mirthlessly
EHILLNRSTTU	still-hunter
EHILLOPPSUY	epiphyllous
EHILLORTTTW	littleworth
EHILMMNOOST	△monothelism
EHILMMNOSTY	semi-monthly
EHILMNOOPTY	entomophily
EHILMNPSSSU	lumpishness
EHILMOPTTUY	Plymouthite
EHILMORSSTY	thermolysis
EHILNOSSSTU	loutishness
EHILNSSSSTY	stylishness
EHILOOPRSUX	xerophilous
EHILOPRSSSW	worshipless
EHILOPSSTTW	whistle-stop
EHIMMNPSSSU	mumpishness
EHIMMOOORST	homoerotism
EHIMNNORRST	northernism
EHIMNNORSTU	nourishment
EHIMNOOPSTY	△monophysite
EHIMNOORTTU	Nototherium
EHIMNOPRSSS	rompishness
EHIMNORSSTU	southernism
EHIMOOPRRST	rheotropism
EHIMOOPRSTU	hemitropous
EHIMOOPSTTY	mythopoeist
EHINNNNSSSU	nunnishness
EHINNNOSSST	tonnishness
EHINNOOPSTY	hypotension
EHINOOPRRTT	ornithopter
EHINORSSTTU	Struthiones
EHINOSSSSTT	sottishness
EHIOOOPRRSU	eriophorous
EHIOOOPRTTZ	trophozoite
EHIOOPRSSTT	photoresist
EHIOPRSSTTT	prosthetist
EHIORRRTVWY	riverworthy
EHKLOOSTTUY	thelytokous
EHKNNOOOSTT	nook-shotten
EHKNOOPRSST	short-spoken
EHKOORSTTUY	turkey-shoot
EHLLORSSTWY	worthlessly
EHLMMOOOPRY	homopolymer
EHLMNOPPSYY	nympholepsy
EHLMOOOSTTY	toothsomely
EHLMPPRSUUY	superphylum
EHLOOPRSTTY	phytosterol
EHLOPRSSSTU	upholstress
EHLOPRSSUUU	sulphureous
EHMNNOORSTU	hunter's-moon
EHMNOORRSTT	northermost
EHMNOORSTWY	money's-worth
EHMOOOPRSTU	homopterous
EHMOORSSTTU	southermost
EHMOORSTTYY	hysterotomy
EHNNOOPRTTW	two-penn'orth
EHNOOOPRRTT	orthopteron
EHNOOPRRTUY	neurotrophy
EHNOOPSTTUY	entophytous
EHNOORSSTTW	stone's-throw
EHOOPPRSSTW	show-stopper
EHOOQRTTUWY	quoteworthy
EIIIINQSTUV	inquisitive
EIIIKLNNPSW	pilniewinks
EIIILMPRTVY	primitively
EIIILNNPSTY	insipiently
EIIILNTTUVY	intuitively
EIIILORSSST	listeriosis
EIIIMMNRSTU	ministerium
EIIIMNORRSS	irremission
EIIIMNORSSV	revisionism
EIIINOPRSTT	peritonitis
EIIINOPSTTT	petitionist
EIIINOQRSTU	requisition
EIIINORRTTY	interiority
EIIINORSSSY	yersiniosis
EIIINORSSTV	revisionist
EIIINRSSTTY	sinisterity
EIIINSSTTVY	sensitivity
EIIINSTTTUV	institutive
EIIIOPRSSTT	periostitis
EIIIRSSTTVY	resistivity
EIIKLLOPTTW	Weltpolitik
EIIKLMRSTTU	multistrike
EIIKLNNNPWY	pinnywinkle
EIIKNOPRSSY	pyrokinesis
EIILLLMSSTY	limitlessly
EIILLMMNNSU	millenniums
EIILLMPSUVY	impulsively
EIILLOOQSSU	soliloquise
EIILLOOQSUZ	soliloquize
EIILMOPRSUY	imperiously
EIILNNSSTTY	insistently
EIILNOOPPRT	lipoprotein
EIILNOPRSTV	silver-point
EIILNOQSUUZ	Louis-Quinze
EIILNRSTUVY	intrusively
EIILNRTTUVY	nutritively

EIILOPPRSTY	propylitise
EIILOPPRTYZ	propylitize
EIILPRRTUVY	irruptively
EIIMMNNNOST	Mennonitism
EIIMNNOOPRT	premonition
EIIMNNOPSTU	pneumonitis
EIIMNORRTTT	intromitter
EIIMOORRSTU	meritorious
EIIMOPPRRTY	impropriety
EIIMOPRSSST	prestissimo
EIIMOPSTTUY	impetuosity
EIIMORRSSTU	moisturiser
EIIMORRSTUZ	moisturizer
EIINOOPPRST	preposition
	pre-position
EIINOPRSSUV	supervision
EIINOPRSSUX	isoxsuprine
EIINOQSSTTU	questionist
EIINORRSSST	sinistrorse
EIINORSTTTU	restitution
EIIOPPRRRTX	proprietrix
EIIOPPSSTUV	suppositive
EIIOPQRRSTU	perquisitor
EIIOPRRSSTX	xerotripsis
EIIOPRRSTUY	superiority
EIIOQRRSTUY	requisitory
EIKKLRRSTUU	Kulturkreis
EIKLLORRSTW	trellis-work
EIKMMOOPRSU	opium-smoker
EILLMOORSUV	mellivorous
EILLMOPRTUX	multiplexor
EILLNOORRST	ritornellos
EILLNOPSSTY	pointlessly
EILLOPRRSUY	prelusorily
EILLOPRSTTV	stilt-plover
EILMNNOPRTY	prominently
EILMNOOOPRS	monopoliser
EILMNOOOPRZ	monopolizer
EILMNOPRTUY	importunely
EILMNOPTTTU	multipotent
EILMNOSTUUY	untimeously
EILMOOSSSTU	tous-les-mois
EILMOPRSSTY	proselytism
EILMOPSTUUY	impetuously
EILMORSTTUY	multistorey
EILNOOPRSST	portionless
EILNOPRSUUY	penuriously
EILNOQRTUVY	ventriloquy
EILOOPRRSTY	posteriorly
EILOOPRSSTY	proteolysis
EILOPPRRSTW	slipperwort
EIMMMNOOSTU	immomentous
EIMMOOPRSUZ	zoospermium
EIMNNOOSSSU	ominousness
EIMNOOPRRTY	premonitory
EIMNOORSTTU	neurotomist
EIMNOOSTTZZ	mezzotintos
EIMNOPPRSTU	presumption
EIMOOPRRSSX	expromissor
EIMOOPRSTTT	optometrist
EIMOORRSUVV	vermivorous
EIMRRSSSSTU	surmistress
EINNOOPPRTU	inopportune
EINNOOPRSSS	responsions
EINNOOPSSTT	post-tension
EINNOOSSSUX	noxiousness
EINNORSSSUU	ruinousness
EINNOSSSSUU	sinuousness
EINOORSSSTU	riotousness
EINOPPRSSSU	suppression
EINOPRRRTTU	interruptor
EINOPSSTTTY	stenotypist
EINORSSTTUY	strenuosity
EIOPRRSSUVY	supervisory
EIOQRRSTTUU	triquetrous
EIORRSTTTUY	restitutory
EJKNOORRUWY	journey-work
EJMNNOORSTU	sojournment
EKMNNOOSTUY	teknonymous
EKNNNNOSSUW	unknownness
ELLMNNOOSTY	somnolently
ELLMORSTUUY	tremulously
ELLOQRSUUUY	querulously
ELMMNOOSTUY	momentously
ELMNORSTUUU	untremulous
ELNOOOPRRTY	poltroonery
ELNOOPPRTUY	opportunely
ELNORSSTUUY	strenuously
ELNORSTUUVY	venturously
ELOPPRRSSTU	purportless
ELOPPRSSSTU	supportless
EMNOOPPSSSU	pompousness
EMNOPPRSTTU	supportment
EMOOOPRRSST	moss-trooper
ENOORRSTTUU	torrentuous
EOPPRRSSSTU	supportress
EOPRRRTTUUW	rupturewort

F

FFFGHIIMNTU	muffin-fight
FFGGHIINORS	fishing-frog
FFGHILLNSUY	shufflingly
FFGHILLRTUY	frightfully
FFIIRRSSTTU	first-fruits
FFIMNORRUWY	muffin-worry
FGGGIILNORT	rigging-loft
FGGHIILNNTY	night-flying
FGGHIINNOTT	nothing-gift
FGGHIINSTTU	fish-gutting
FGGIIMNNORT	morning-gift
FGGIINNORUV	unforgiving
FGHHNOOTTUU	unthought-of
FGHIIINNNSU	unfinishing
FGHIILLOPTW	pillow-fight
FGHIILNOPST	shop-lifting
FGHIILNORSU	flourishing
FGHIINNPSTU	punt-fishing
FGHIINNRSSU	furnishings
FGHIINOPSTT	fitting-shop
FGHILNORTTY	fortnightly
FGHINNTTTUU	tuft-hunting
FGIIILMNPSY	simplifying
FGIILLLLMNU	fulling-mill
FGIILLNPTUY	upliftingly

FGIILNNTTUY	unfittingly
FGIILNSTTUY	stultifying
FGIIMNNNORU	uninforming
FGIINNOPRTU	unprofiting
FGIINNOPSTU	fusing-point
FGIINNORRTU	turfing-iron
FGINNORSSUW	snowsurfing
FGINOORTTTX	foxtrotting
FGIOORRSUUV	frugivorous
FHHIINOOPST	photo-finish
FHIILNRTTUY	unthriftily
FHIKNOOPRRS	shrink-proof
FHLLNRTUUUY	unhurtfully
FHNOOOPRRST	thornproofs
FIILLNOOSUX	solifluxion
FIILLNPTUUY	unpitifully
FIIMMNOORTY	omniformity
FIIRTTTTTUU	tutti-frutti
FIKLLLNSUUY	unskilfully
FILLOORSUVY	frivolously
FILMRSSTTUU	mistrustful
FILNOORSSTY	frontolysis
FLLOORRSUWY	sorrowfully

G

GGHHIORTUW	highwrought
GGHHIILLNOR	high-rolling
GGHIILLNSTY	slightingly
GGHILNOPSUW	swing-plough
GGHINNNOSTU	hunting-song
GGHINORRSTU	rough-string
GGHLMOOPSYY	sphygmology
GGIIINNRSTW	sign-writing
GGILNOOORWW	wool-growing
GGIMNNNOORW	morning-gown
GGLMNNOOOOY	gnomonology
GHHIINNPTUW	hunting-whip
GHHILOPRTTT	troth-plight
GHHINNNORTU	hunting-horn
GHHINOOPRTU	thorough-pin
GHHIORSTTWY	sightworthy
GHHLLOPRTUU	pull-through
GHHLOOPPTYY	photoglyphy
GHHMNNOOOPT	monophthong
GHIIIKMNRSS	skirmishing
GHIIKLNNRSY	shrinkingly
GHIIKLNTTTY	tightly-knit
GHIIKNNNRSU	unshrinking
GHIILLLNRTY	thrillingly
GHIILLNSTWY	whistlingly
GHIILLOOPST	philologist
GHIILLOOSTT	lithologist
GHIILNNPSUY	punishingly
GHIILNOORST	rhinologist
GHIILNOPSTY	philogynist
GHIILOOOPST	ophiologist
GHIILOOPPST	hippologist
GHIILOOSSTT	histologist
GHIINOPPPTW	whipping-top
GHIINOPPRSW	worshipping
GHIJMNOPSUW	showjumping
GHIKNNNOOTW	know-nothing
GHIKNNOOPRU	pruning-hook
GHILLOOOPST	hoplologist
GHILLOOPSYY	syphilology
GHILLOPSTTU	plough-stilt
GHILMMNRTUY	thrummingly
GHILMNOOSTY	hymnologist
GHILMOOSTTY	mythologist
GHILNOOOPST	phonologist
GHILNOOORTY	ornithology
GHILNOOPSUY	philogynous
GHILOOPSSUY	physiologus
GHILOOPSTTY	phytologist
GHIMNNOORRS	morsing-horn
GHIMNOOPSYY	physiognomy
GHIMOOOSSYZ	homozygosis
GHINNNOSTTU	Huntington's
GHINOORRTUW	wrought-iron
GHLLMOPUYYZ	Zygophyllum
GHLOPRSTUYY	Tyroglyphus
GIIIINNPRST	inspiriting
GIIIKNNNOPR	pinking-iron
GIIIKNNNPRT	printing-ink
GIIILLOSTUY	litigiously
GIIILNNPRSY	inspiringly
GIIILNNQRUY	inquiringly
GIIIMNNOOSU	ignominious
GIIIMNNOPRR	priming-iron
GIIINNNPRSU	uninspiring
GIIINNNQRUU	uninquiring
GIIKLLLNOSU	soul-killing
GIIKLNNNUWY	unwinkingly
GIIKMMNNOST	skimmington
GIIKNNOPPPS	skin-popping
GIILLLLMNOR	rolling-mill
GIILLLNNUWY	unwillingly
GIILLMNNSUY	unsmilingly
GIILLMNOOST	limnologist
GIILLMNOPRY	imploringly
GIILLMNPTUY	multiplying
GIILLNNSTUY	insultingly
GIILMNOPRSY	promisingly
GIILMNOPRVY	improvingly
GIILNNOQTUY	longinquity
GIILNNPTUYY	unpityingly
GIILNNQSTUY	squintingly
GIILNNTTUWY	unwittingly
GIILNOORSUV	lignivorous
GIIMMNPPPRU	pump-priming
GIIMNNOPRSU	unpromising
GIIMNNOPRTU	importuning
GIIMNOORSTT	sitting-room
GIINNNOPSTW	winning-post
GIINNOPRRST	ripsnorting
GIINOOPRRSU	porriginous
GIINOORSTUV	vortiginous
GIINOPRRSUU	pruriginous
GIINRTTTTYY	nitty-gritty
GIJLMOSTUUU	multijugous
GIKLMORSTUW	silkworm-gut
GIKLNNNOUWY	unknowingly
GIKLNOOPRVY	provokingly
GIKNNOOPRUV	unprovoking

GILLNOSTUUY glutinously
GILLOOPSTTU plutologist
GILMMNRRUUY murmuringly
GILMNOOOSTU monologuist
GILNNNOPSSU nonplussing
GILNORRTTUY torturingly
GILNRSTTTUY struttingly
GIMMNNOOORR morning-room
GIMMNNRRUUU unmurmuring
GIMMNOORTYY myringotomy
GIMMNOPRTUU rumgumption
GIMNNORSTUU surmounting
GIMNOOOPRSU sporogonium
GIMNOORSTYY syringotomy
GINNOOPRRTU root-pruning
GINNOOPRSTT strongpoint
GINOOPPSTTU stopping-out
GNOOOPRSTUY protogynous

H

HHIINOSSTWW wishtonwish
HHILMOOPSTY holophytism
HHIMNOOPPSU phosphonium
HHIMOOPPRSS phosphorism
HHMNOOOOPSU homophonous
HHMNOOORTUU mouth-honour
HHOOOPPRSSU phosphorous
HIIIKKLMNPS milk-kinship
HIIILMNOPSS Sinophilism
HIIIMNORSST histrionism
HIILLNNNOOT nonillionth
HIILLOPRSWW will-worship
HIILMNNOOPY hypolimnion
HIILMOOSTTT lithotomist
HIILOORRTTT lithotritor
HIILOPRSTTY lithotripsy
HIIMMOOPRSS isomorphism
HIIMMOPRRST trimorphism
HIIMNOOPRST monitorship
HIIOOPRSSTU Istiophorus
HILLOOPSUXY xylophilous
HILLOPRSTUY triphyllous
HILMMOPSTUY Plymouthism
HILMOOOSTTU lithotomous
HILMOPSTTUY Plymouthist
HILNOOPPSTY polyphonist
Psilophyton
HILNOOPSTXY xylophonist
HILOOPRSTYY polyhistory
HILOORTTWWW whitlow-wort
HIMMOOOPRSZ zoomorphism
HIMNOOPSSUY symphonious
HIMOOOPRSSU isomorphous
HIMOOPRRSTU trimorphous
HIMOOPSTTTY phytotomist
HIMOORTTTWY thirty-twomo
HINNOOOPRTU honour-point
HINOOORRSSU horrisonous
HINOOPPRSSS sponsorship
HINOOPPSTTY phonotypist
HINOOPRRTTY thyrotropin
HINOOPRSTUY hyponitrous
HIOOPPRSSTV provostship
HIOOPPSSTYY hypotyposis
HKRRRRSUUYY hurry-skurry
HMOOOOPRSSU homosporous
HMOOOPPRRTY morphotropy
HOOOPPRRSUY pyrophorous
HORRSTTTUWY trustworthy

I

IIIILMNNQSU inquilinism
IIIILNNQTUY inquilinity
IIIIMMPRSTV primitivism
IIIIMNSTTUV intuitivism
IIIIMPRSTTV primitivist
IIIINNOQSTU △inquisition
IIILLMNOPST pointillism
IIILLMNOSSU illusionism
IIILLNNOQTU quintillion
IIILLNOPSTT pointillist
IIILLNOSSTT tonsillitis
IIILLNOSSTU illusionist
IIILLOPRSSS spirillosis
IIILNNOQSUU inquilinous
IIINNNORTTU innutrition
IIINNOSTTTU institution
IIINOOOPSTV oviposition
IIINSSTTTTU institutist
IIJLNORSUUY injuriously
IILLOOQSSTU soliloquist
IILLORSSTUU illustrious
IILNNOOSUXY innoxiously
IILNOOSSTTU solutionist
IILOOPRRSVY provisorily
IIMMNNOOTUX immunotoxin
IIMNOOPRSTU positronium
IIMNOPRTTUY importunity
IIMOOPRSSTT Soroptimist
IINNNNOOSTU non-unionist
IINNOOPRRTY non-priority
IINOOOPPRST proposition
IINOOPPSSTU supposition
IINOPPQRTUY propinquity
IIOOPPRRTTY top-priority
ILLOPSSUWWY pussy-willow
ILLORSUUUXY luxuriously
ILMNOOPSTTU plutonomist
ILNOOOPSSUY poisonously
ILNOOORSTUY notoriously
ILNORSUUUUX unluxurious
IMNNOOOPSST monopsonist
IMNOOOPRSTY tropomyosin
IMNOOPPRSTU opportunism
IMNOORSSTTY monstrosity
IMOOPPRSTTU pittosporum
IMOPSSTTUUY sumptuosity
INOOOPPRRST proportions
INOOPPRSTTU opportunist
INOOPPRTTUY opportunity
INOPPTTTUUU input-output
IOOPPRSSTUY suppository
IOOPRRSTTTU prostitutor

L

LMMORRSUUUY murmurously
LMNOOOPSUYY polyonymous
LMNOORSSTUY monstrously
LMOPSSTUUUY sumptuously

M

MOOOPRRSSTT stormtroops

12AAA

A

AAAAAALMRSTT taramasalata
AAAAACEEMNRT Amarantaceae
AAAAACINRRSV caravansarai
AAAABBEKLMST Balaam-basket
AAAABCCELNRU baccalaurean
AAAABCCHILNN bacchanalian
AAAABCDEEIRS Scarabaeidae
AAAABCIILLMT Balaamitical
AAAABDELNNNR Bananalander
AAAABDMNRSSU massaranduba
AAAACCCCIRTU acciaccatura
AAAACCEEIMRT Tamaricaceae
AAAACCHINRTT anacathartic
AAAACCILMORT acroamatical
AAAACCILPRTT paratactical
AAAACCLMORST Malacostraca
AAAACDIILPRS paradisaical
paradisiacal
AAAACDIIMORT acaridomatia
AAAACDIMOORT acarodomatia
AAAACEEEEGLN Elaeagnaceae
AAAACEEEPPRV Papaveraceae
AAAACEEIMRTT Marattiaceae
AAAACEILNPST anapaestical
AAAACEINRRSV caravanserai
AAAACGIMMNRT anagrammatic
AAAACHINRSST anacatharsis
AAAACHNNPRTT Panchatantra
AAAACILMNPRU Campanularia
AAAACIMNRSST antimacassar
AAAADEPQRRTU paraquadrate
AAAADILMNNRS salamandrian
AAAAEEHNNNPT Panathenaean
AAAAEGGLNPRU paralanguage
AAAAEGILMMTV amalgamative
AAAAEGINPRSS asparaginase
AAAAEGNRTVXZ extravaganza
AAAAEHILMSST thalassaemia
AAAAEIIMPRST parasitaemia
AAAAEIMMNRRT armamentaria
AAAAGILMMNOT amalgamation
AAAAIILLMNRT antimalarial
AAAAILLPRRSS sarsaparilla
AAAAILNRSSTU Australasian
AAAALLLLOOPZ lallapalooza
AAABBDEENNNR banana-bender
AAABBEIILLOV bioavailable
AAABBINRRSTU antibarbarus
AAABCCIILLST cabalistical
AAABCDEELLNW weal-balanced
AAABCDHIINRT Dibranchiata
AAABCEEGILRR carriageable
AAABCEEGINOR Boraginaceae
AAABCEEIMRSU Simarubaceae
AAABCEERSSSU scarabaeuses
AAABCEHILLPT alphabetical
AAABCEHILNPT analphabetic
AAABCEHLOPPR approachable
AAABCEIILNRT celibatarian
AAABCEILLRWY cable-railway
AAABCEILMNRU air-ambulance
AAABCELMMNNU ambulanceman
AAABCELMRTWY cable-tramway
AAABCELNRRTU tabernacular
AAABCGILLOTV Volga-Baltaic
AAABCIILRRUV vibracularia
AAABCIINPSTT anabaptistic
AAABCILNORUV vocabularian
AAABDEEKKMNR make-and-break
AAABDEILMRST dramatisable
AAABDEILMRTZ dramatizable
AAABDEMNRSSU masseranduba
AAABDEMRSSSS ambassadress
AAABDGHMNRSS smash-and-grab
AAABDIILPTTY adaptability
AAABDILLOOPR paraboloidal
AAABEEGILMRR marriageable
AAABEEGLMNNU unmanageable
AAABEEILNPPS inappeasable
AAABEELLNPPU unappealable
AAABEELNPPSU unappeasable
AAABEGGGINRT baggage-train
AAABEGLMNNUY unmanageably
AAABEHLMOSTT haematoblast
AAABEIIJNRSZ Azerbaijanis
AAABEIILMNNT maintainable
AAABEILLMNOT balletomania
AAABEILLNSSU unassailable
AAABEILNNTTU unattainable
AAABEILNORRT aberrational
AAABELLNNSUY unanalysable
AAABELLNNUYZ unanalyzable
AAABELLNRSSW ballanwrasse
AAABELLNRSTT translatable
AAABELNOOPTY palaeobotany
AAABELQSTTUU absquatulate
AAABGIILNRRT Gibraltarian
AAABHIILNOTT habitational

AAABHINOOPST satanophobia
AAABIIILLTVY availability
AAABIILLPTTY palatability
AAABIILNNOST banalisation
AAABIILNNOTZ banalization
AAABILNNOOTT labanotation
AAABILNNTTUY unattainably
AAABILNPRSSU △sublapsarian
AAACCCDILLSY saccadically
AAACCCEEIINV Vacciniaceae
AAACCCHIPRTT cataphractic
AAACCCILLSTT catallactics
AAACCDEEEIPR Epacridaceae
AAACCDEEIORT Cordaitaceae
AAACCDEILLMY academically
AAACCDEILMNO decalcomania
AAACCDHILORS saccharoidal
AAACCDHNRRSY cash-and-carry
AAACCDIINRRT intracardiac
AAACCEEEHISZ Schizaeaceae
AAACCEELRSSU Crassulaceae
AAACCEFHNNTT café-chantant
AAACCEGILMTT metagalactic
AAACCEHNOSTU acanthaceous
AAACCEIINPTT incapacitate
AAACCEILLLNR cancellarial
AAACCEILLNNR cancellarian
AAACCEILLNTU canaliculate
AAACCEINNQTU acquaintance
AAACCELNRSSU crassulacean
AAACCGHILMOZ chalazogamic
AAACCHILLNRY anarchically
AAACCHILNPTY anaphylactic
AAACCHILPSTY cataphysical
AAACCIINOPTT capacitation
AAACCILORSTU accusatorial
AAACDDEHIIRR Charadriidae
AAACDEEGJLNU Juglandaceae
AAACDEEILNPS Asclepiadean
AAACDEGIIPRR carriage-paid
AAACDEHMPRTY Pachydermata
AAACDEINRSTT tradescantia
AAACDENNOPSU pandanaceous
AAACDGIIMMRT diagrammatic
AAACDGIIMPRT paradigmatic
AAACDHIINNRT cantharidian
AAACDIINNNSV Scandinavian
AAACDILLMRTY dramatically
AAACDILORTTY Artiodactyla
AAACDINOOPTT coadaptation
AAACDLMMNOPY lampadomancy
AAACEEEGINNT Gentianaceae
AAACEEEHMNPY Nymphaeaceae
AAACEEEILMRS Marsileaceae
AAACEEENPPRR reappearance
AAACEEGILMNO Magnoliaceae
AAACEEGLLOPY Polygalaceae
AAACEEGNRTVX extravagance
AAACEEHILNNP anencephalia
AAACEEHIPSUU Euphausiacea
AAACEEIILNSV Salviniaceae
AAACEEILNPRT paraenetical
AAACEENPRRTW peace-warrant
AAACEFIMNORR Afro-American
AAACEFINSTTT fantasticate
AAACEGGGLOTU galactagogue
AAACEGIILMRR mail-carriage
AAACEGILMMNO megalomaniac
AAACEGILMOST galactosemia
AAACEGIMNPRT paramagnetic
AAACEGNNOPRY paracyanogen
AAACEGNRTVXY extravagancy
AAACEHILLMPR alphamerical
AAACEHILMMTT mathematical
AAACEHILMSST thalassaemic
AAACEHILPRST share-capital
AAACEHIMRRTT matriarchate
AAACEHIPRRTT patriarchate
AAACEIJLMORW majolicaware
AAACEILLPRST palaestrical
AAACEILMOOST osteomalacia
AAACEILMPRRT parametrical
AAACEILNNRST Lancasterian
AAACEILNORTU aeronautical
AAACEILOPPRT pearl-tapioca
AAACEILORSTT aerostatical
AAACEJKLNNRT Jack-a-lantern
AAACELNOPSTU platanaceous
AAACELNOSSTU santalaceous
AAACELOSTTUY autocatalyse
AAACELOTTUYZ autocatalyze
AAACEMNRRSTY sacramentary
AAACFIINRRTT anti-aircraft
AAACFIMNRRST aircraftsman
AAACFLMNRTUU manufactural
AAACGGILLNOY anagogically
AAACGGILLOPY apagogically
AAACGIILLNNT anti-Gallican
AAACGIILNOTT Tagliacotian
AAACGIIMNSTT anastigmatic
AAACGILLLNOY analogically
AAACGILLLNVY galvanically
AAACGILLMMMO mammalogical
AAACGIMNOORS angiosarcoma
AAACHHIPRSTY tachyphrasia
AAACHIIKPPRT apparatchiki
AAACHIKPPRST apparatchiks
AAACHILMNPST phantasmical
AAACHILMNRST charlatanism
AAACHIMNORTU tauromachian
AAACHIMNSTTT antasthmatic
AAACHIPPRRST paraphrastic
AAACHLLPRTYY cataphyllary
AAACHMNNOPPR panpharmacon
AAACIIIILNNRT catilinarian
AAACIILLMNST talismanical
AAACIILNNOST canalisation
AAACIILNNOTZ canalization
AAACIILNNRRT intracranial
AAACILLLNTYY analytically
AAACILLMNOTY anatomically
AAACILLNNTUY unanalytical
AAACILMMNNOO monomaniacal
AAACILMNOPRY pyromaniacal

AAACILNOOPPU Papanicolaou
AAACILPPRTTY party-capital
AAACIMNNOTTU catamountain
AAACLLMNORSY nasolacrymal
AAACLMMOPSTY mycoplasmata
AAACNNNORTTT contranatant
AAADDDEEILNV dead-and-alive
AAADDEEIIPRS Paradiseidae
AAADDEGINSTV disadvantage
AAADDGILLMOY amygdaloidal
AAADDGLNNNOW Gondwanaland
AAADDIINOPRX paradoxidian
AAADDILMNORS salamandroid
AAADDLMNPRST lamp-standard
AAADEGILNRTV landgraviate
AAADEGILPQRU quadraplegia
AAADEGIMQRSU Quadragesima
AAADEGNOSTUV advantageous
AAADEHILNPRS nail-head-spar
AAADEHNRRTTW death-warrant
AAADEIIMNNST East-Indiaman
AAADEILMNNRS salamandrine
AAADEILNNPRT anteprandial
AAADEIMNRTTY Tetradynamia
AAADEINOPRTT readaptation
AAADFIINORST faradisation
AAADFIINORTZ faradization
AAADGHIMNOOT agathodaimon
AAADGIILLORT gladiatorial
AAADGIILNORT gladiatorian
AAADGIMNRSTV avant-gardism
AAADGINRSTTV avant-gardist
AAADGLNQRRUU quadrangular
AAADIILLMNPS Palladianism
AAADIINNOPTT inadaptation
AAADILMOQRSU maquiladoras
AAAEEGGLMNTU metalanguage
AAAEEGGMNRST stage-manager
AAAEEGHMNOPR Phanerogamae
AAAEEGINNRSX sexagenarian
AAAEEGLMNOPT aplanogamete
AAAEEGMNNPRT permanganate
AAAEEHIMNSTT anathematise
AAAEEHIMNTTZ anathematize
AAAEEHINPSST panaesthesia
AAAEEHIPRSST paraesthesia
AAAEELMMNSST meat-salesman
AAAEEMMMOPST mammee-sapota
AAAEGGPPRSTU egg-apparatus
AAAEGHIMNOPR Phanerogamia
AAAEGHLLTTWW wag-at-the-wall
AAAEGHLOPPRY palaeography
AAAEGILLMOTT agalmatolite
AAAEGINNNNOR nonagenarian
AAAEGLOPRSST paraglossate
AAAEHHKLLNRS hallan-shaker
AAAEHIMNORTT theatromania
AAAEHINSSTTU euthanasiast
AAAEHKORSTUV katharevousa
AAAEHMOPRRTY aromatherapy
AAAEHNPRSTTY parasyntheta
AAAEIIILNQRTU equalitarian
AAAEILLLNPRT antiparallel
AAAEILMNOPPR paralipomena
AAAEILMRRTTX extramarital
AAAEILNPPRRS prelapsarian
AAAEIMNNRSST transaminase
AAAELQQRSUUV quaquaversal
AAAEMMRRSSTT master-at-arms
AAAENOPRSUYY pay-as-you-earn
AAAFHHLMNORT half-marathon
AAAFMMNNORSW man-of-war's-man
AAAGGIOPPRTU appoggiatura
AAAGHIIMPRST amphigastria
AAAGHIMNPRST paragnathism
AAAGHIPPRRST paragraphist
AAAGHIRSTTWY straightaway
AAAGHNOPRSTU paragnathous
AAAGIILNNOTV navigational
AAAGILLLORRT grallatorial
AAAHIILNNOTT antihalation
AAAHIIMMNORT arithmomania
AAAHIIMNNRTU humanitarian
AAAHKMMNOTUY thank-you-ma'am
AAAHLLMNPSTY phantasmally
AAAIILLMMMRS mammillarias
AAAIILLNNOPR Apollinarian
AAAIILMPRRTY paramilitary
AAAIILNNNOTT anti-national
AAAIILNNOSST nasalisation
AAAIILNNOSTZ nasalization
AAAIILNOPPRT apparitional
AAAIILNOPRST aspirational
AAAIILNORTTT totalitarian
AAAIIMMNRSST Samaritanism
AAAIINPPRSST Patripassian
AAAIKLNORSUY Ankylosauria
AAAILLNOSTTU salutational
AAAILMNORTTU maturational
AAAILNORSTTU salutatorian
AAAINNNRRSTU transuranian
AAAINORSSSST assassinator
AAALLLLOOPZ lollapalooza
AAALMMOOPSST plasmosomata
AABBBEERRTTY baby-batterer
AABBCCEMOOSU bombacaceous
AABBCDEEEHRR bare-breached
AABBCDEKLLNU black-and-blue
AABBCDELRSSS scabbardless
AABBCEEGHITW cabbage-white
AABBCEEHLNRU unbreachable
AABBCEGIKKNR backbreaking
AABBCEHNRSTY baby-snatcher
AABBCGIKLLLN blackballing
AABBCIIILMNO bibliomaniac
AABBCIILLNRY rabbinically
AABBCIIMORRX mixobarbaric
AABBCNOORSST contrabbasso
AABBDEIMNRRY barmy-brained
AABBDGGILNNR land-grabbing
AABBDIILLLLR billiard-ball
AABBDILMNOSU subabdominal
AABBEEEHLQTU bequeathable
AABBEEELNRSS bearableness

AABBEEHLNRTU	unbreathable
AABBEEIRRTUV	abbreviature
AABBEEKLNNOR	non-breakable
AABBEELLMNSS	blamableness
AABBEGIKLLNR	ball-breaking
AABBEGILLNRS	ball-bearings
AABBEGINRSTW	rabbeting-saw
AABBEIINORTV	abbreviation
AABBEILNNOTU	unobtainable
AABBEILRTTTU	attributable
AABBEIMMNPSY	namby-pambies
AABBEINRRRTW	rabbit-warren
AABBEIORRTVY	abbreviatory
AABBHIIILTTY	habitability
AABBIILNRRSU	sublibrarian
AABCCDEIILRT	bactericidal
AABCCDEIKNRR	crackbrained
AABCCDEILLSY	decasyllabic
AABCCDELMMOO	accommodable
AABCCDHLRTYY	brachydactyl
AABCCEEEMORT	Combretaceae
AABCCEEHLNRT	carte-blanche
AABCCEELNPTU	unacceptable
AABCCEHHLPRY	brachycephal
AABCCEHINOPR	cancerphobia
AABCCEHOORTT	tobacco-heart
AABCCEILLLNU	incalculable
AABCCEILLMOV	clavicembalo
AABCCEILMNOR	microbalance
AABCCEIRRTUU	bureaucratic
AABCCELNORTT	contractable
AABCCENOORSU	carbonaceous
AABCCGIKKNRT	backtracking
AABCCHHIIMPR	amphibrachic
AABCCHIINSTU	antibacchius
AABCCILLLNUY	incalculably
AABCCINRSTTU	subantarctic
AABCCKLNRRTU	blackcurrant
AABCDDDEEKLS	saddlebacked
AABCDDEKLRRW	bladderwrack
AABCDDIILNRR	cardinal-bird
AABCDEEHKLRT	black-hearted
AABCDEEIILNR	ineradicable
AABCDEEILLPS	displaceable
AABCDEELLLNW	well-balanced
AABCDEELLLSY	decasyllable
AABCDEELLNRT	ballet-dancer
AABCDEELNNSU	unascendable
AABCDEELRTTU	trabeculated
AABCDEGIKLSV	black-visaged
AABCDEGIKNNR	breakdancing
AABCDEHIINRT	dibranchiate
AABCDEHNNRST	bandersnatch
AABCDEHORRTY	carbohydrate
AABCDEIILNRY	ineradicably
AABCDEILORUV	vocabularied
AABCDEINOSTU	subdiaconate
AABCDEKNRSSW	backwardness
AABCDELOPPRR	clapperboard
AABCDELRSTTY	abstractedly
AABCDENRRRTU	currant-bread
AABCDEOPRRRS	scraperboard
AABCDGGIOORS	△braggadocios
AABCDGINORST	broadcasting
AABCDGKLLRUY	blackguardly
AABCDHINOOPR	Branchiopoda
AABCDHINORSU	subarachnoid
AABCDHIOPSTT	dispatch-boat
AABCDIILLLOY	diabolically
AABCDIMNORSY	barodynamics
AABCDKMNOOSW	backwoodsman
AABCDKMNORSW	backswordman
AABCEEEEKPRR	peace-breaker
AABCEEEFFILN	ineffaceable
AABCEEEGHLNX	exchangeable
AABCEEEHLLNW	balance-wheel
AABCEEEHLNST	balance-sheet
AABCEEEILMOR	Bromeliaceae
AABCEEELORTT	ebracteolate
AABCEEEMQRSU	macaberesque
AABCEEENORTT	beta-carotene
AABCEEFFILNY	ineffaceably
AABCEEFIPRRT	prefabricate
AABCEEGGPRRT	carpetbagger
AABCEEGHLNNU	unchangeable
AABCEEGHLNXY	exchangeably
AABCEEGIINNO	Bignoniaceae
AABCEEHIKNRR	chain-breaker
AABCEEHILNUV	unachievable
AABCEEHLMNRT	merchantable
AABCEEHLNRSU	unsearchable
AABCEEHLOPRR	reproachable
AABCEEIKMNRT	cabinetmaker
AABCEEILLMMT	emblematical
AABCEEILMNSS	amicableness
AABCEEINORTX	exacerbation
AABCEEKMNORR	marker-beacon
AABCEEKNNOPS	pease-bannock
AABCEELLLNRU	unrecallable
AABCEELLNOOT	oblanceolate
AABCEELLNPSS	placableness
AABCEELLORRT	correlatable
AABCEELMNOTU	uncomeatable
AABCEELMNSSU	assemblaunce
AABCEFIILLSS	classifiable
AABCEFIILLTY	beatifically
AABCEFIILNST	sanctifiable
AABCEFLNRSTU	blast-furnace
AABCEGHILPTY	bathypelagic
AABCEGHLNNUY	unchangeably
AABCEGILLNOU	incoagulable
AABCEGLNRRUU	gubernacular
AABCEHHNOOPR	arachnophobe
AABCEHIILNRT	incharitable
AABCEHIILRST	Hebraistical
AABCEHIILTTY	teachability
AABCEHIIMNPS	amphisbaenic
AABCEHILNRTU	uncharitable
AABCEHKLLOPR	alpha-blocker
AABCEHLMNORS	elasmobranch
AABCEHLNNSTU	unstanchable
AABCEHLNRSUY	unsearchably
AABCEHNNRRTW	bench-warrant
AABCEIIILPST	capabilities

AABCEIILLNPP	inapplicable
AABCEIILMMRS	bicameralism
AABCEIILMNOT	alembication
AABCEIILMRST	bicameralist
AABCEIILPPRT	participable
AABCEIILRTTY	traceability
AABCEIINOORT	anaerobiotic
AABCEILLLLTY	balletically
AABCEILLNPPU	unapplicable
AABCEILLNSUV	vulcanisable
AABCEILLNUVZ	vulcanizable
AABCEILLTTUV	cultivatable
AABCEILMNNOT	contaminable
AABCEILMNOPR	incomparable
AABCEILMORRT	barometrical
AABCEILMORVW	microwavable
AABCEILNOOPT	paleobotanic
AABCEILNPSUZ	uncapsizable
AABCEINRRSTT	scatterbrain
AABCEIORSTTT	bacteriostat
AABCEKLQRRTU	black-quarter
AABCEKNORTTU	back-to-nature
AABCENRSSSTT	abstractness
AABCFHINOOPR	△francophobia
AABCFILORSTU	subfactorial
AABCFLNOORTU	confabulator
AABCGHHPRRYY	brachygraphy
AABCGHIILOPR	biographical
AABCGHILNOOP	△anglophobiac
AABCGHNOPPRW	Cappagh-brown
AABCGIKLNPPS	back-slapping
AABCGIKNRSTT	backstarting
AABCGILLLSUY	subglacially
AABCGILLOOTT	battological
AABCHHIIMOOP	aichmophobia
AABCHIIMORTT	microhabitat
AABCHIINOOTT	cohabitation
AABCHILNRTUY	uncharitably
AABCIIILNPTY	incapability
AABCIILLNPPY	inapplicably
AABCIILLPRSY	parisyllabic
AABCIILMRSST	strabismical
AABCIIMMNORT	timbromaniac
AABCIKMNOTTU	back-mutation
AABCILLLLSYY	syllabically
AABCILMNOPRY	incomparably
AABCILMNOSST	saltimbancos
AABCILRRSUUU	subauricular
AABCINORSTUU	subarcuation
AABCLLOOORRT	collaborator
AABCLNORSTUY	constabulary
AABCMNNNOOTT	non-combatant
AABDDDEEILNR	addle-brained
AABDDDENRRST	△standardbred
AABDDEHLLMOY	hebdomadally
AABDDEILMNTU	mandibulated
AABDDGHORRTU	draughtboard
AABDDLMNOOTZ	zalambdodont
AABDEEEGILRS	disagreeable
AABDEEELNRSS	readableness
AABDEEGILRSY	disagreeably
AABDEEGINRTU	drainage-tube
AABDEEHHRRSY	haberdashery
AABDEEHORRTW	weatherboard
AABDEEIILRSV	adverbialise
AABDEEIILRVZ	adverbialize
AABDEEILRTTX	extraditable
AABDEEKLNRTU	undertakable
AABDEEKORRST	skateboarder
AABDEELLNSSU	laudableness
AABDEELMNNSS	damnableness
AABDEELNOPRS	leopard's-bane
AABDEELNORSS	adorableness
AABDEELNORTU	unelaborated
AABDEEMORRSU	board-measure
AABDEENNPRWY	brandy-pawnee
AABDEFLLNNOR	flannelboard
AABDEGIIMSTU	disambiguate
AABDEGIJMORR	brigade-major
AABDEGILNRTW	drawing-table
AABDEGLLMNOR	balladmonger
AABDEHHIRRST	hair's-breadth
AABDEHIINSTT	absinthiated
AABDEHINTTUU	unhabituated
AABDEHLNOSUW	unshadowable
AABDEHRRSTTW	straw-breadth
AABDEIILNRST	distrainable
AABDEILLLOSW	disallowable
AABDEIMNORRS	dermabrasion
AABDEIMOPPST	paedobaptism
AABDEIMRRSSS	disembarrass
AABDEIOPPSTT	paedobaptist
AABDELMORTUY	deambulatory
AABDELNNOPRU	unpardonable
AABDELOPRRST	plasterboard
AABDGHINORSW	washing-board
AABDGIILNORS	boardsailing
	sailboarding
AABDGIINNOST	bastinadoing
AABDGILNNSST	sandblasting
AABDHLNNRSSU	slash-and-burn
AABDIIILLTTY	dilatability
AABDIIILSTVY	advisability
AABDIMOOPSSY	boomps-a-daisy
AABDINOOTTUY	autoantibody
AABDLNNOPRUY	unpardonably
AABDLOORRSTU	bardolatrous
AABEEEFKMRRR	frame-breaker
AABEEEGLMPRS	gas-permeable
AABEEEGLMRSS	reassemblage
AABEEEHHLRTT	heather-bleat
AABEEEHKRRRT	heartbreaker
AABEEEILLPRR	irrepealable
AABEEELLNPRU	unrepealable
AABEEELLNRUV	unrevealable
AABEEELLNSSS	saleableness
AABEEELMNNSS	amenableness
AABEEELMNSST	tameableness
AABEEELNPRTU	unrepeatable
AABEEELRRTTU	terebratulae
AABEEFFLORST	afforestable
AABEEFGIKNRS	safe-breaking
AABEEFGILRRR	irrefragable
AABEEFHINRRT	feather-brain

AABEEFILMNST manifestable
AABEEFKRSSTT breakfast-set
AABEEFLLRSTY self-betrayal
AABEEFLNRRST transferable
AABEEGGGRSTU subaggregate
AABEEGIILRTY agreeability
AABEEGILMNST magnetisable
AABEEGILMNTZ magnetizable
AABEEGIMNORR marriage-bone
AABEEGIRRSTT Gastarbeiter
AABEEGLNOUVY unvoyageable
AABEEGMNOTUU beaumontague
AABEEHIILRTT rehabilitate
AABEEHLMQRSU Alhambresque
AABEEHLRRSTY breathalyser
AABEEHLRRTYZ breathalyzer
AABEEIILLRRS irrealisable
AABEEIILLRRZ irrealizable
AABEEIILPRRR irrepairable
AABEEILLLNPP inappellable
AABEEILLPRRY irrepealably
AABEEILMMRSU immeasurable
AABEEILMNOTT antimetabole
AABEEILNPRRU unrepairable
AABEEILNPRSS inseparables
AABEEILNRRST restrainable
AABEEILNRSSV variableness
AABEEINRRTTV Invertebrata
AABEEKLMNRRU unremarkable
AABEEKLMNRTU unmarketable
AABEELLMRSTT ballet-master
AABEELLNPPSS palpableness
AABEELLNSSUV valuableness
AABEELMNORUV manoeuvrable
AABEELMNRSUU unmeasurable
AABEELMPPRRR paper-marbler
AABEELNNNTTU untenantable
AABEELNNORSU unreasonable
AABEELNNOSSU unseasonable
AABEELNNRSUW unanswerable
AABEELNOSSVW avowableness
AABEELNPSSSS passableness
AABEELNRSTTU subalternate
AABEELRRSTTU terebratulas
AABEEMORRRRU armour-bearer
AABEENNRRSTU subterranean
AABEFGILRRRY irrefragably
AABEFHLMNOTU unfathomable
AABEFIILNOPS saponifiable
AABEFIILNQTU quantifiable
AABEFILLLNOT flabellation
AABEFLLMMNNO non-flammable
AABEFLMORRRU farm-labourer
AABEFLNORUUV unfavourable
AABEFLNRSSTU transfusable
AABEGGILLNTU agglutinable
AABEGGINORRS organiser-bag
AABEGGINORRZ organizer-bag
AABEGHIINRRT air-breathing
AABEGHIKNORT oath-breaking
AABEGHIKNRTT breathtaking
AABEGHIMNTTW bantamweight
AABEGHLLTWWY wag-by-the-wall
AABEGIILMNNU unimaginable
AABEGIKKMNST basket-making
AABEGILLOOPY palaebiology
AABEGILNNSSU unassignable
AABEGILNPPRT table-rapping
AABEGIMNRRTT battering-ram
AABEGLMMOPRR programmable
AABEHILLORVY behaviorally
AABEHILNQSUV vanquishable
AABEHILNSSTU habitualness
AABEHILORSTU authorisable
AABEHILORTUZ authorizable
AABEHIMMNOPR marimbaphone
AABEHINRRSTT shatter-brain
AABEIIILLNTY alienability
AABEIIILLLMTY malleability
AABEIIILLMNSS Sabellianism
AABEIIILLMRST bilateralism
AABEIIILLNRTY learnability
AABEIIILLORST isobilateral
AABEIIILLRTTY alterability
AABEIIILPRRTY reparability
AABEIIILPRSTY separability
AABEIIILRRRST barristerial
AABEIINOORSS anaerobiosis
AABEIKLMNSTU unmistakable
AABEILLNRRTU turbellarian
AABEILMMRSUY immeasurably
AABEILNPRRST transpirable
AABEINSSTTTU substantiate
AABELMMNOSTU somnambulate
AABELMNRSTTU transmutable
AABELMNRSUUY unmeasurably
AABELMOPRRTU perambulator
AABELNNORSUY unreasonably
AABELNNOSSUY unseasonably
AABELNNRSTTU subalternant
AABELNNRSUWY unanswerably
AABELNOPRSST transposable
AABELNSTTTUU unstatutable
AABFFGLORSSU buffalo-grass
AABFHLMNOTUY unfathomably
AABFIILLMMTY flammability
AABFIILNORRT infraorbital
AABFLLMNOTYY flamboyantly
AABFLMNORTUU funambulator
AABFLNORUUVY unfavourably
AABGHHIOOPPR graphophobia
AABGHIINNRSW brainwashing
AABGIIILNOUV bougainvilia
AABGIIILNTVY navigability
AABGIILLNOOT obligational
AABGIILLNORY aboriginally
AABGIILLNRTZ trail-blazing
AABGIILMNNUY unimaginably
AABGILLMOOST glioblastoma
AABGILNORSUV labour-saving
AABHIIILNOTT habilitation
AABHIIILRSSZ bilharziasis
AABHIIINNOTT inhabitation
AABHIILNNRTY labyrinthian

AABHIILOOPRU	ailurophobia
AABHINORRSTU	subarrhation
AABHINOSSTTU	subhastation
AABIIILMNTUY	unamiability
AABIIILNOSST	assibilation
AABIIILNRTTY	trainability
AABIIINQRTUU	ubiquitarian
AABIILLOTWY	allowability
AABIILLNSTUY	unsalability
AABIILNNNTTU	tintinnabula
AABIILNOORTY	abolitionary
AABIILORSSTT	stabilisator
AABIILORSTTZ	stabilizator
AABIINNOORTT	anti-abortion
AABIINNORSTU	urbanisation
AABIINNORTUZ	urbanization
AABIINOORRST	arborisation
AABIINOORRTZ	arborization
AABIKLMNSTUY	unmistakably
AABILLMRSUXY	submaxillary
AABILLNOSTTU	blastulation
AABILNSSTTUV	substantival
AABILOPRRSTU	supraorbital
AABIMNORSTTU	masturbation
AABINOOPRRTY	probationary
AABLLMMOSUXY	xylobalsamum
AABLMMNNOSTU	somnambulant
AABLMMNORSUY	somnambulary
AABLMNRSTTUY	transmutably
AABLNSTTTUUY	unstatutably
AABLORRRSTUY	barratrously
AABMNNOOTTUW	man-about-town
AABMORRSTTUY	masturbatory
AACCCEEHILTT	catechetical
AACCCEENNPTU	unacceptance
AACCCEGNORYY	gynaecocracy
AACCCEHILNOT	coelacanthic
AACCCEHIRSTT	catachrestic
AACCCHILNOOP	cacophonical
AACCCIOSSTTU	catacoustics
AACCDDEHIIRS	disaccharide
AACCDDHHNOOR	doch-an-dorach
AACCDDIILLTY	didactically
AACCDDIIOTTU	autodidactic
AACCDDINORST	disaccordant
AACCDEEFHHTT	hatchet-faced
AACCDEELLNTY	cyclandelate
AACCDEFILSTU	fasciculated
AACCDEFLOSVY	self-advocacy
AACCDEHHPRRU	church-parade
AACCDEHILMOT	machicolated
AACCDEHILTXY	hexadactylic
AACCDEHNORRY	archdeaconry
AACCDEIIILNT	dialectician
AACCDEIILOPT	apodeictical
AACCDEILLNTY	accidentally
AACCDEILMORT	democratical
AACCDEILOOPS	Scolopacidae
AACCDEINNTUV	unvaccinated
AACCDEIRTUUV	curvicaudate
AACCDEKMPUUV	vacuum-packed
AACCDELLNRSU	Della-Cruscan
AACCDELLNTUU	uncalculated
AACCDENOPRTY	pedantocracy
AACCDGINRRRY	card-carrying
AACCDIILNOTU	claudication
AACCDIIOPRTT	catadioptric
AACCDILLLTYY	dactylically
AACCDLLOORRY	dollarocracy
AACCDLMORTYY	macrodactyly
AACCDMMOOORT	accommodator
AACCEEEHIPRY	Hypericaceae
AACCEEEILRTV	accelerative
AACCEEEKLLNS	alkalescence
AACCEEHILNNP	anencephalic
AACCEEHIRRST	characterise
AACCEEHIRRTZ	characterize
AACCEEHMPPRR	camp-preacher
AACCEEIILLPR	capercaillie
AACCEEIILPRZ	capercailzie
AACCEEILNORT	acceleration
AACCEEILRRTT	recalcitrate
AACCEEKLLNSY	alkalescency
AACCEELMMNTU	calceamentum
AACCEELORRTY	acceleratory
AACCEELPRRTU	receptacular
AACCEENRSSTU	accurateness
AACCEFFRRSTU	surface-craft
AACCEFGIKNRS	safe-cracking
AACCEFHLRRTU	characterful
AACCEFILLORY	Calyciflorae
AACCEGHIILPR	archipelagic
AACCEGHILMOR	agrochemical
AACCEHHIILRR	hierarchical
AACCEHHILNTT	chalcanthite
AACCEHIIMNRV	vice-chairman
AACCEHILLMNO	melancholiac
AACCEHILLMNY	mechanically
AACCEHILMNNU	unmechanical
AACCEHILNORT	anchoretical
AACCEHILORTT	theocratical
AACCEHILPRTY	archetypical
AACCEHILRRTT	tetrarchical
AACCEHIMNNOT	technomaniac
AACCEHIMORTT	metathoracic
AACCEHIMPRTU	pharmaceutic
AACCEHIMRRST	characterism
AACCEHLMNTYY	calycanthemy
AACCEHLMOPRY	macrocephaly
AACCEIILLNRT	anticlerical
AACCEIILMRST	acclimatiser
AACCEIILMRTZ	acclimatizer
AACCEILLMSTU	miscalculate
AACCEILLNNOT	cancellation
AACCEILLNOSS	neoclassical
AACCEILLOPPT	apoplectical
AACCEILLOPSU	capillaceous
AACCEILLPRSS	preclassical
AACCEILLSTTY	ecstatically
AACCEILMNOPS	complaisance
AACCEILMTUUV	accumulative
AACCEILNORVY	clairvoyance
AACCEILNPSUU	Sipunculacea
AACCEILNRRTT	recalcitrant

AACCEILNRTUY	inaccurately
AACCEILNTTUY	accentuality
AACCEILSTUVY	accusatively
AACCEINNORST	transoceanic
AACCEINNOTTU	accentuation
AACCEINOORTV	coacervation
AACCEIOPRTVY	overcapacity
AACCELLOORSU	corallaceous
AACCELLRRSTY	crystal-clear
AACCELNNOOPV	plano-concave
AACCELNNRSTY	transcalency
AACCENOOPSUY	apocynaceous
AACCEORSSTUY	styracaceous
AACCFIIINOPT	pacification
AACCFIINPRST	transpacific
AACCFIIOPRTY	pacificatory
AACCFIIORRST	scarificator
AACCGHHIPRTY	tachygraphic
AACCGHHLOPRY	chalcography
AACCGHIILLOR	oligarchical
AACCGHIILLPR	calligraphic
AACCGHILOPTY	phagocytical
AACCGHIOPRRT	cartographic
AACCGIILMORT	tragicomical
AACCGILLOORT	cartological
AACCGILLOOST	scatological
AACCHHIILNOR	Archilochian
AACCHIIINRTT	antirachitic
AACCHIILMSST	schismatical
AACCHIILNORT	anchoritical
AACCHIILNOTT	anticatholic
AACCHIINNNOT	cachinnation
AACCHIINRSTY	saccharinity
AACCHILLOPRT	phallocratic
AACCHILLOSST	scholastical
AACCHIMNOPRT	panchromatic
AACCHIMOOPRT	apochromatic
AACCHINNORTY	cachinnatory
AACCHIOPRSTT	catastrophic
AACCHLLNORYY	acronychally
AACCHOPPRSUY	pachycarpous
AACCIIILPSTT	capitalistic
AACCIILLMSSS	classicalism
AACCIILLSSST	classicalist
AACCIILLSSTY	classicality
AACCIILMORTT	timocratical
AACCIILMPRST	practicalism
AACCIILNRTUY	inarticulacy
AACCIILOPPRT	paroccipital
AACCIILPRSTT	practicalist
AACCIILPRTTY	practicality
AACCIINNOPRR	Capricornian
AACCIIORRSTT	aristocratic
AACCIIRRSTTU	caricaturist
AACCIKKORSTY	kakistocracy
AACCILLLNOVY	volcanically
AACCILLNNOOP	plano-conical
AACCILLNOOSY	occasionally
AACCILLNORTY	narcotically
AACCILLORSTY	acrostically
	Socratically
AACCILLOSTUY	acoustically
AACCILMNNOOT	conclamation
AACCILMNOTUU	accumulation
AACCILMNPSUY	scapulimancy
AACCILMOPRSS	sarcoplasmic
AACCILNOOPTU	occupational
AACCILNORVYY	clairvoyancy
AACCIMNOPSTY	accompanyist
AACCINOPRSTY	pantisocracy
AACCIORRSTTT	stratocratic
AACCLMNOPSUY	scapulomancy
AACCLMOOSTTY	Cyclostomata
AACCLNORRTTU	contractural
AACCOOOSSTTT	coast-to-coast
AACCOQRSTTUY	squattocracy
AACDDDEEHLOR	dodecahedral
AACDDEEEHLTY	acetaldehyde
AACDDEGILLOO	logodaedalic
AACDDEGINNOY	dodecagynian
AACDDEIIJTUV	adjudicative
AACDDEIILNOT	dedicational
AACDDEIILORT	dedicatorial
AACDDEILMNNR	carnal-minded
AACDDEIMOOPR	Macropodidae
AACDDEIORRTX	dextrocardia
AACDDIIJNOTU	adjudication
AACDEEEFFINT	decaffeinate
AACDEEEHRRTT	earth-created
AACDEEFHLMSY	shamefacedly
AACDEEGHINRS	scare-heading
AACDEEGHLNNO	hendecagonal
AACDEEHIMSTT	semi-attached
AACDEEHINSTZ	zantedeschia
AACDEEIILLPR	pedicellaria
AACDEEIILPST	decapitalise
AACDEEIILPTZ	decapitalize
AACDEEIKLRTT	racket-tailed
AACDEEILLNNR	calendar-line
AACDEEILLPRV	pedal-clavier
AACDEEILMMNT	medicamental
AACDEEILMRVY	devil-may-care
AACDEEILNPSS	displeasance
AACDEEILNRTT	intercalated
AACDEEILRTTU	dearticulate
AACDEEIMMSSU	cuisse-madame
AACDEEIMNRTT	readmittance
AACDEEINOPRS	Scorpaenidae
AACDEELNPTTY	pentadactyle
AACDEELNRSTW	candle-waster
AACDEGGHIRSS	gas-discharge
AACDEGGHNNOR	egg-and-anchor
AACDEGILLNNP	landing-place
AACDEGILLOOP	paedological
AACDEGILMNOY	geodynamical
AACDEGILNNOU	Languedocian
AACDEGILNNPR	candle-paring
AACDEGILNOTU	longicaudate
AACDEGILPQRU	quadraplegic
AACDEGINNPRS	parascending
AACDEGLNOTUU	uncatalogued
AACDEHHIMORT	Hemichordata
AACDEHIILOPP	paedophiliac
AACDEHIINNRT	cantharidine

AACDEHILLLRY heraldically
AACDEHIMNRTY diathermancy
AACDEHLMOSUY achlamydeous
AACDEHLOPRRT procathedral
AACDEHLORRTT tetrachordal
AACDEHNOPPRU unapproached
AACDEIIIPRST parasiticide
AACDEIILLMSY salicylamide
AACDEIILMNOS Laodiceanism
AACDEIILMNTU adminiculate
AACDEIILNORT dilaceration
AACDEIILNRTU clairaudient
AACDEIINNORT deracination
AACDEIINOPTT decapitation
AACDEIINOTTV deactivation
AACDEIIOSSST disassociate
AACDEIJLLTVY adjectivally
AACDEILLMNOY demoniacally
AACDEILLNOSW disallowance
AACDEILLNPTY pedantically
AACDEILLPRRY dicarpellary
AACDEILMMORT melodramatic
AACDEILNOSTT anecdotalist
AACDEIMNORSY aerodynamics
AACDEIMOOSTU diatomaceous
AACDEINNOSSY Ascension-day
AACDEINNQTUU unacquainted
AACDEINOPSSU sapindaceous
AACDEINOSSTU unassociated
AACDELLLNOTW tallow-candle
AACDELLORSTY sacerdotally
AACDELNPTTYY pentadactyly
AACDELRTTTYY tetradactyly
AACDFFIINOOS afficionados
AACDFGILNNRT landing-craft
AACDFGIMNPRT camp-drafting
AACDFIIILNNT infanticidal
AACDGHHOOPRT cathodograph
AACDGHIIOPRR radiographic
AACDGHILNNPU launching-pad
AACDGHILNNRS crash-landing
AACDGHILNNTY land-yachting
AACDGHINNSTY sand-yachting
AACDGHIOPRRY cardiography
AACDGHORRRSS orchard-grass
AACDGIILLOOR radiological
AACDGIILLOOU audiological
AACDGIILRSTU gradualistic
AACDGILLMOTY dogmatically
AACDHIILNPRS cardinalship
AACDHIIMNOOR orchidomania
AACDHIMNOORT machairodont
AACDHINOPQRU quadraphonic
AACDIIINORTV divarication
AACDIILLMOPT diplomatical
AACDIILLNOTY diatonically
AACDIILMNOST disclamation
AACDIILNNRTY tyrannicidal
AACDIILNOSTT donatistical
AACDIIMNRSTU Traducianism
AACDIINNORRT doctrinarian
AACDIINORSST dracontiasis
AACDIINRSTTU Traducianist
AACDILLNORSY sardonically
AACDILLNSTYY dynastically
AACDILLOPRSY sporadically
AACDILNOPRTY trypanocidal
AACDIMMNOORT monodramatic
AACDJLMOOQRU Jacquard-loom
AACDLLNOSSUY scandalously
AACDMNOOPPRU para-compound
AACEEEEGINRS Gesneriaceae
AACEEEEHNNPT Nepenthaceae
AACEEEEIQSTU Equisetaceae
AACEEEFGIRRR carriage-free
AACEEEGILNRT angelica-tree
AACEEEHHOPPY Phaeophyceae
AACEEEHILNRT Heracleitean
AACEEEILLOVZ Velloziaceae
AACEEEIRRSTT secretariate
AACEEEJMNRTT rejectamenta
AACEEELNORTT Coelenterata
AACEEFFINOTT affectionate
AACEEFGIORRR forecarriage
AACEEGGILLNO genealogical
AACEEGHILLNT genethliacal
AACEEGHINNRR carragheenin
AACEEGHINORT archegoniate
AACEEGHINPST space-heating
AACEEGHNPRTX part-exchange
AACEEGILNRRV vicar-general
AACEEGLLPTTU cattle-plague
AACEEGLMORTT galactometer
AACEEGLNOOPY Polygonaceae
AACEEHIILPRT perichaetial
AACEEHIINSTT aesthetician
AACEEHILMRTX hexametrical
AACEEHILMTTT metathetical
AACEEHILOPRT Choripetalae
AACEEHIMNORT etheromaniac
AACEEHIMNTTX exanthematic
AACEEHINSSTT anaesthetics
AACEEHINTTTU authenticate
AACEEHKMNRRS snake-charmer
AACEEHLMPRST spermathecal
AACEEHLNPTTU pentateuchal
AACEEHLPPSSW cashew-apples
AACEEHMNRTTT reattachment
AACEEHMORRTY archaeometry
AACEEHNNPPST happenstance
AACEEIILMSTT metasilicate
AACEEIILPRST recapitalise
AACEEIILPRTZ recapitalize
AACEEIINRSST sectarianise
AACEEIINRSTZ sectarianize
AACEEIIPPRTV appreciative
AACEEILLMOPT paleoclimate
AACEEILLMPTT metaleptical
AACEEILLMSTT telesmatical
AACEEILMPPRS pre-eclampsia
AACEEILNORRT recreational
AACEEILPRSTX extra-special
AACEEILPRTTU recapitulate
AACEEIMMNORS △mesoamerican

Words marked △ may be spelled also with a capital letter

AACEEIMNORRU	Euro-American
AACEEINPRSST	paracentesis
AACEEIOPRSTT	ectoparasite
AACEEIORSTTW	waistcoateer
AACEEIRRRRTW	Water-carrier
AACEEKLNQSUY	squeaky-clean
AACEELLLNOTY	lanceolately
AACEELNRRTUX	extranuclear
AACEENNPPRTU	appurtenance
AACEENNPRRST	transparence
AACEENNPRRTT	carpenter-ant
AACEENPRRSSU	preassurance
AACEFFMORTTT	matter-of-fact
AACEFGMNNORR	Franco-German
AACEFHINPSSU	saucepan-fish
AACEFIIILTTV	facilitative
AACEFINOSSTT	fantasticoes
AACEFINOSSTU	assuefaction
AACEFIORRSTU	surface-to-air
AACEFMNRRTUU	manufacturer
AACEGGHIINNR	chain-gearing
AACEGGHILOPR	geographical
AACEGGHINNPR	crapehanging
AACEGGINOPST	scapegoating
AACEGHHIMORR	haemorrhagic
AACEGHHPRRTY	tachygrapher
AACEGHILLMPT	phlegmatical
AACEGHILLOOT	atheological
AACEGHILLPRR	calligrapher
AACEGHILOPPR	paleographic
AACEGHILOPRS	archipelagos
AACEGHIMNOPR	anemographic
	phanerogamic
AACEGHIMOPTT	apothegmatic
AACEGHMMOPRY	Myrmecophaga
AACEGHMOPRRY	ceramography
AACEGHNOOPRY	oceanography
AACEGHOPRRRT	cartographer
AACEGIIINRRT	geriatrician
AACEGIILLNNT	geanticlinal
AACEGIILLNRT	interglacial
AACEGIILLOOT	aetiological
AACEGIILPRRS	slip-carriage
AACEGIIMMPRT	epigrammatic
AACEGIIMMRST	grammaticise
AACEGIIMMRTZ	grammaticize
AACEGIKLNPPR	parking-place
AACEGIKNPPPR	packing-paper
AACEGILLMNRY	Germanically
AACEGILLMNTY	magnetically
AACEGILLNOSU	gallinaceous
AACEGILLNRTW	watering-call
AACEGILLOOPT	apologetical
AACEGILLORSU	argillaceous
AACEGILLORTY	categorially
AACEGILLPRSU	superglacial
AACEGILMORST	gasometrical
AACEGILNRSST	tragicalness
AACEGILNRTUW	caterwauling
AACEGIMNORSU	graminaceous
AACEGINNOORT	octogenarian
AACEGLLOPSSW	scapegallows
AACEGLNOOPSV	galvanoscope
AACEGLNORTTU	congratulate
AACEGLOPRSSV	salvage-corps
AACEGLRRSTYZ	crystal-gazer
AACEGMNOSTYY	gynaecomasty
AACEHHHMOPRT	rhamphotheca
AACEHHIILMOP	haemophiliac
AACEHHILOPRZ	Rhizocephala
AACEHIILLOPT	Palaeolithic
AACEHIILMPRX	alexipharmic
AACEHIILMRTT	arithmetical
AACEHIILNTTT	antithetical
AACEHIILOPRS	parochialise
AACEHIILOPRZ	parochialize
AACEHIIMMNNS	Manicheanism
AACEHIINPTTT	antipathetic
AACEHIJLMMPR	clamjamphrie
AACEHILLLTTY	athletically
AACEHILLMPTY	emphatically
AACEHILLMTTY	thematically
AACEHILLPRSY	seraphically
AACEHILLPTTY	pathetically
AACEHILLRTTY	theatrically
AACEHILMNNOR	enharmonical
AACEHILMNPRU	alphanumeric
AACEHILMOPRT	metaphorical
AACEHILMPSTY	metaphysical
AACEHILNOPST	sphacelation
AACEHILQRRSU	squirearchal
AACEHILRSTTT	tetrastichal
AACEHIMPRSTT	metaphrastic
AACEHIMPRSTU	Ramapithecus
AACEHIOPRSST	cataphoresis
AACEHLLOOPRR	rhopaloceral
AACEHMNNRSTU	transhumance
AACEHMNORRST	march-treason
AACEHMOPRRSY	hypersarcoma
AACEHNOPRRTY	narco-therapy
AACEHPRRRTTY	charterparty
AACEIIINPTTV	anticipative
AACEIILLMMNT	Macmillanite
AACEIILLMRTT	altimetrical
AACEIILNOPPS	episcopalian
AACEIILNPRTT	antiparticle
AACEIILNRTTU	inarticulate
AACEIIMNNOPT	emancipation
AACEIIMNORST	racemisation
AACEIIMNORTZ	racemization
AACEIIMNRSST	Cartesianism
	sectarianism
AACEIINNNOTT	incatenation
AACEIINNNTUV	annunciative
AACEIINOPPRT	appreciation
AACEIINORTTV	reactivation
AACEIINPRSTT	pancreatitis
AACEIINRSSTV	incrassative
AACEIJKRSTTT	straitjacket
AACEIJLLMSTY	majestically
AACEIKLMNOPT	kleptomaniac
AACEILLLLMTY	metallically
AACEILLLPRTY	prelatically
AACEILLMMTUY	immaculately

AACEILLMNOTY	noematically
AACEILLMNSTY	semantically
AACEILLNOORT	reallocation
AACEILLNOPRR	procellarian
AACEILLNOPST	pleonastical
AACEILLNPRTU	unprelatical
AACEILLNPTUY	paniculately
AACEILLOPRTY	operatically
AACEILLRTTUY	articulately
AACEILMMNORT	manometrical
AACEILMMRSTY	asymmetrical
AACEILMNOSTU	emasculation
AACEILMSSTTY	systematical
AACEILNNOPTT	placentation
AACEILNOPRTU	precautional
AACEILNOSSTV	vacationless
AACEILNRTTUU	unarticulate
AACEILOPRSTT	spectatorial
AACEILRSTTTU	straticulate
AACEILRTTTVY	attractively
AACEIMNNOOPT	companionate
AACEIMNOPRTY	emancipatory
AACEIMNPPRST	panspermatic
AACEINORRTTT	retractation
AACEINORRTUV	avant-courier
AACEINRTTTUV	unattractive
AACEIOPPRRTY	appreciatory
AACEIOPRRRTV	prevaricator
AACEJKLNNORT	Jack-o'-lantern
AACEKNNORSTU	cantankerous
AACELLLLORTY	collaterally
AACELLNRRUVY	vernacularly
AACELLOOSSSU	salsolaceous
AACELLORRSST	cross-lateral
AACELMORSTUY	emasculatory
AACELNORRSSU	oracularness
AACELNPRRSUU	supernacular
AACELPPPRRTY	claptrappery
AACEMMNRSSTU	crassamentum
AACEMNOORSTT	Entomostraca
AACEMOOORSST	osteosarcoma
AACENNPRRSTY	transparency
AACENORRRTUV	averruncator
AACEORRSSTUU	Ceratosaurus
AACFGHOPRRTY	fractography
AACFGIIINOST	gasification
AACFGIILLMNY	magnifically
AACFHIMNPRST	craftmanship
AACFIIIILNRT	inartificial
AACFIIILLRTY	artificially
AACFIIILMORR	microfilaria
AACFIIILNNST	financialist
AACFIIILNOPT	palification
AACFIIILNOST	salification
AACFIIILNOTT	facilitation
AACFIIILNRTU	unartificial
AACFIIIMNORT	ramification
AACFIIINNOPT	panification
AACFIIINNOTZ	Nazification
AACFIIINORTT	ratification
AACFIILLLSVY	salvifically
AACFIILMNOST	factionalism
AACFIILNOOST	focalisation
AACFIILNOOTZ	focalization
AACFIILNOSTT	factionalist
AACFIILOQRTU	qualificator
AACFIIMNSSTT	fantasticism
AACFIINOSSTT	satisfaction
AACFILLLOSUY	fallaciously
AACFILLNORTY	fractionally
AACFILMORSTT	stalactiform
AACFINOORRTT	fractionator
AACFIORSSTTY	satisfactory
AACGGHHIIOPR	hagiographic
AACGGHIILLOO	hagiological
AACGGHIMNOTY	gigantomachy
AACGGIILLNTY	gigantically
AACGGILMOSTY	mystagogical
AACGHHOPRRTY	chartography
AACGHILLOOPT	pathological
AACGHILMOPRY	myographical
AACGHILOOPRR	orographical
AACGHILOOPRZ	zoographical
AACGHIMNOPRR	marconigraph
AACGHIMNRSTT	crash-matting
AACGHIMRTTUU	thaumaturgic
AACGHINOPPRT	pantographic
AACGHINOPRRU	uranographic
AACGHLMOOPRY	pharmacology
AACGHMMOORRT	chromatogram
AACGHOOPPRSU	carpophagous
AACGHOOPRSSU	sarcophagous
AACGHOOPSSTU	scatophagous
AACGIIKNNOTT	action-taking
AACGIIILNNORV	Carlovingian
AACGIIILNORTT	coat-trailing
AACGIIMMMRST	grammaticism
AACGIIMMRRTT	trigrammatic
AACGIINNOSTT	antagonistic
AACGIINOSTTW	waistcoating
AACGIJKNORST	roasting-jack
AACGIKLNQSUV	quacksalving
AACGILLMOOST	malacologist
AACGILLOORST	astrological
AACGILLOOTTU	tautological
AACGILLRRTUU	agricultural
AACGILNRTTTY	attractingly
AACGILOOSSTT	astacologist
AACGIMMOPRRT	programmatic
AACGIMNOPRTY	cryptogamian
AACGINOOPRSU	angiocarpous
AACGINOPPRTU	group-captain
AACGLMOOSTUU	glaucomatous
AACGLNNORTTU	congratulant
AACHHIILNPPS	chaplainship
AACHHIIMNPRS	chairmanship
AACHHILMOPTY	hypothalamic
AACHHINOORTX	xanthochroia
AACHHOOPPRST	approach-shot
AACHIILLNPSY	Hispanically
AACHIILMNNOR	inharmonical
AACHIILMOPRS	parochialism
AACHIILNNOPT	antiphonical
AACHIILOORST	aristolochia

AACHIILOPRTY	parochiality
AACHIIMNNOST	machinations
AACHIIMNOOPT	potichomania
AACHIIMPRRST	patriarchism
AACHIINOPRST	Aristophanic
AACHIINPRSTT	antiphrastic
AACHIINRRTTT	antarthritic
AACHIKORSTUW	autorickshaw
AACHILLMNORY	harmonically
AACHILMMNOOT	monothalamic
AACHILMNOOPT	taphonomical
AACHILMNORTY	lachrymation
AACHILOPRRSU	scrophularia
AACHILOPSTTY	hypostatical
AACHIMMNNOPY	nymphomaniac
AACHIMNOPRRS	parachronism
AACHIMOOPRST	chromatopsia
AACHIMPPRSSY	parapsychism
AACHINOPRTTU	naturopathic
AACHIRRSTTUZ	Zarathustric
AACHLLNNNOTY	nonchalantly
AACHLMMNOOPY	omphalomancy
AACHLMOPPRYY	polypharmacy
AACHLMORRTYY	lachrymatory
AACHMOORSTTU	trachomatous
AACHNOOPRSTU	anthocarpous
AACIIINNOPTT	anticipation
AACIIINNOTTV	inactivation
	vaticination
AACIIINSSTTT	statistician
AACIILLLOPTY	apolitically
AACIILLMMNSU	animalculism
AACIILLMNOSY	simoniacally
AACIILLMNSTU	animalculist
AACIILLMOTTY	amitotically
AACIILLNNOTT	cantillation
AACIILLNOOST	localisation
AACIILLNOOTZ	localization
AACIILLNOSTY	antisocially
AACIILLPPSTY	papistically
AACIILLRSTTY	artistically
AACIILLSTTUY	autistically
AACIILMMNOPT	pantomimical
AACIILMMORSS	commissarial
AACIILMNNOTU	calumniation
AACIILMOPRST	porismatical
AACIILNOOSTV	vocalisation
AACIILNOOTVZ	vocalization
AACIILNOPTTU	capitulation
AACIILNORTTU	articulation
AACIILNRSTTU	naturalistic
AACIILORSTTU	tralaticious
AACIILORSUVY	avariciously
AACIILPRRSUY	supraciliary
AACIIMMORSST	commissariat
	marcatissimo
AACIIMNNORST	animatronics
AACIIMNOSSTU	causationism
AACIIMOTTTUY	automaticity
AACIINNNNOTU	△annunciation
AACIINNNOOST	canonisation
AACIINNNOOTZ	canonization
AACIINNORSST	incrassation
AACIINOOSSST	associations
AACIINOPRTTY	anticipatory
AACIINOSSTTU	causationist
AACIIOORSSTX	toxocariasis
AACIIOPPRRTT	participator
AACILLLNOPTY	platonically
AACILLMNORTY	romantically
AACILLMNOSTY	monastically
AACILLMOSTUY	calamitously
AACILLNNRTYY	tyrannically
AACILLNOOTVY	vocationally
AACILLNORTTY	cantillatory
AACILLOORRTY	oratorically
AACILLOPTTUY	autoptically
AACILLPRRTUY	particularly
AACILMNNOOPT	complanation
AACILMNNORTU	unromantical
AACILMNOOPRT	proclamation
AACILMNOORST	astronomical
AACILMNORTUY	calumniatory
AACILMOPSTTY	asymptotical
AACILMORRTTU	court-martial
	matriculator
AACILNORSTTU	claustration
AACILNOSTTUU	auscultation
AACILOPRTTUY	capitulatory
AACILORRTTUY	articulatory
AACIMMNOORTY	microanatomy
AACIMMOPSTTY	asymptomatic
AACIMNNOOPWY	companionway
AACIMNNOOTTU	non-automatic
AACIMNOOPRST	paronomastic
AACIMOORSSST	sarcomatosis
AACINNOOSTTT	constatation
AACINNORSSTT	transactions
AACINOORRTTT	tractoration
AACINORSSTTU	astronautics
AACIOPRRRTTY	pyrotartaric
AACLLNNORTUY	connaturally
AACLMOOPRRTY	proclamatory
AACLNNOPRTTU	contrapuntal
AACLNPRSTTYY	cryptanalyst
AACLORSTTUUY	auscultatory
AACLPRRSSTUU	supracrustal
AACMOORSSTTY	astrocytomas
AADDDEEHLPSS	saddle-shaped
AADDEEEHHMMR	hammer-headed
AADDEEEHLRTT	rattle-headed
AADDEEFHILNT	life-and-death
AADDEEFHRRTU	hard-featured
AADDEEGHILNT	death-dealing
AADDEEGHLSSY	glassyheaded
AADDEFHORRUV	hard-favoured
AADDEFINORTU	defraudation
AADDEGLLOOSU	logodaedalus
AADDEGNOPRRU	parade-ground
AADDEIIMNRSW	Edwardianism
AADDEIINPRRV	Pre-Dravidian
AADDEINRRSST	standardiser
AADDEINRRSTZ	standardizer
AADDELMMOPRY	lampadedromy

AADDGHINNRST hard-standing
AADDGIIILNOT digladiation
AADDGIINORST disgradation
AADDIIILNOPT dilapidation
AADDIILLNOTY additionally
AADEEEFHLRST false-hearted
AADEEEGHLRRT large-hearted
AADEEEGHRRTT great-hearted
AADEEEGIRRRR arrière-garde
AADEEEGMMNNT endamagement
AADEEEHHRTVY heavy-hearted
AADEEEHNPRST reed-pheasant
AADEEELNNRRT △neandertaler
AADEEEMNPRTW deepwaterman
AADEEENQSSTU adequateness
AADEEFFNORRT fore-and-after
AADEEFHINRTT faint-hearted
AADEEGGGIRST disaggregate
AADEEGGLMORT agglomerated
AADEEGINRTUV unvariegated
AADEEGKMNRRT market-garden
AADEEHIINRRT hereditarian
AADEEHIIPSUU Euphausiidae
AADEEHIIRSST radiesthesia
AADEEHILNPRT plain-hearted
AADEEHILNQRU harlequinade
AADEEHIMMSTT mathematised
AADEEHIMMTTZ mathematized
AADEEHISSSTY dysaesthesia
AADEEHLPRSSV salver-shaped
AADEEHOPRRTZ trapezohedra
AADEEHQRRSTU headquarters
AADEEIILMMSV mediaevalism
AADEEIILMSTV mediaevalist
AADEEIIMNNRT antemeridian
AADEEIKLLMNR aldermanlike
AADEEILLNUVV vaudevillean
AADEEILMMPST semipalmated
AADEEILNQTUY inadequately
AADEEILNRSTU denaturalise
AADEEILNRTUZ denaturalize
AADEEIMMNNRR remainder-man
AADEEIMMNNST misdemeanant
AADEEIMNRRTV animadverter
AADEEIMQSTUV desquamative
AADEEINOPRST endoparasite
AADEEINOPRTU deuteranopia
AADEEINPSSTV adaptiveness
AADEEJLNNRTW lantern-jawed
AADEELLLNPRU unparalleled
AADEELLNPPRU unapparelled
AADEELLRZZZZ razzle-dazzle
AADEELMNPRTT departmental
AADEELNRTTUU unadulterate
AADEEMNNRTUX extramundane
AADEEQRRSTUW quarter-sawed
AADEFFIIILST disaffiliate
AADEFFIILNTU unaffiliated
AADEFGILNORT deflagration
AADEFGIMNRRW drawing-frame
AADEFHIIPRSS paradise-fish
AADEFHINNOTU fountain-head
AADEFIILNSUZ sulfadiazine
AADEFIKMNORR Afrikanerdom
AADEFILMORTY defamatorily
AADEFILNORTY deflationary
AADEFLNOOSST fast-and-loose
AADEGGILNNST landing-stage
AADEGGLNNRST gangsterland
AADEGHINNSTY Syngnathidae
AADEGHIOPRRR radiographer
AADEGHIPRSTU graduateship
AADEGHMNNNRU under-hangman
AADEGIILLNNP plain-dealing
AADEGIILPQRU quadriplegia
AADEGIIMMNST diamagnetism
AADEGILLLRWY wallydraigle
AADEGINOPPRS propagandise
AADEGINOPPRZ propagandize
AADEGINPPRRW drawing-paper
AADEGLNPRSST △star-spangled
AADEGLNRSTTU strangulated
AADEGOPRSTTU postgraduate
AADEGQRRRTUU quarter-guard
AADEHIKLMORY holidaymaker
AADEHILLOPPY Polyadelphia
AADEHILMNPRS aldermanship
AADEHILNORRT enarthrodial
AADEHINOPPRS parasphenoid
AADEHIOPRRTY radio-therapy
AADEHNORSTUY thousand-year
AADEIIILNOPP Papilionidae
AADEIIILNOST idealisation
AADEIIILNOTZ idealization
AADEIILLNNPR Pirandellian
AADEIILLNOTY ideationally
AADEIILLNTUV antediluvial
AADEIILLNUVV vaudevillian
AADEIILMNNOT delamination
AADEIILMNRTY Lymantriidae
AADEIILNNOST desalination
AADEIILNNQRU quadriennial
AADEIILNNTUV antediluvian
AADEIILNORTV derivational
revalidation
AADEIILNRSTT interstadial
AADEIIMNNNTU unmaintained
AADEIIMNOPRT pteridomania
AADEIIMNORST maderisation
AADEIIMNORTZ maderization
AADEIIMNRSTT administrate
AADEIINNNORW Neo-Darwinian
AADEIINNORST Tardenoisian
AADEIINOPRST deaspiration
AADEIKLMNRTW milk-and-water
AADEILNNNORR noradrenalin
AADEILNNSSUW dunniewassal
AADEILNORTTU adulteration
AADEILNQRTUV quadrivalent
AADEILNRTUVY valetudinary
AADEIMMNNOPU △pandaemonium
AADEIMNNNRTU intramundane
AADEIMNOQSTU desquamation
AADEINOPRRTT anti-predator

AADEINOPRRUX	paradoxurine
AADEINORSTTU	desaturation
AADEINRRSTTT	transit-trade
AADELLNNORST	rallentandos
AADELMMNPTUU	paludamentum
AADELMNNRTUU	ultramundane
AADELMOPRRTU	armour-plated
AADELNNNPSTU	sun-and-planet
AADELNNRSTTU	untranslated
AADEMMOOSTTU	stomatodaeum
AADEMNNNRSTU	transmundane
AADEMNNPRSUU	supramundane
AADEMOQRSTUY	desquamatory
AADFFHLORRSW	flashforward
AADFGHILNNRT	farthingland
AADFILNNOOTU	foundational
AADGHIINPRSU	guardianship
AADGIIIMPRRV	primigravida
AADGIILMRTUV	multigravida
AADGIILNNORT	Darlingtonia
AADGIINNNORS	Grandisonian
AADGILLNPPUY	applaudingly
AADGILNOOSSU	disanalogous
AADGIMNOPPRS	propagandism
AADGIMRRSTTU	dramaturgist
AADGINOOPRRT	progradation
AADGINOPPRST	propagandist
AADGLOOOPRXY	paradoxology
AADHIILOPPSY	diapophysial
AADHILNOOPRT	anthropoidal
AADHILNOPSUY	diaphanously
AADIIILNNOTV	invalidation
AADIIILNORTV	divinatorial
AADIILMNOQRU	quadrinomial
AADIIMNNOOST	nomadisation
AADIIMNNOOTZ	nomadization
AADIIMNNRSTT	administrant
AADIINORRTTY	traditionary
AADIIRRSSTUV	Stradivarius
AADILLMNOOST	amontillados
AADILNOPPRST	postprandial
AADILOORSTVY	vasodilatory
AADIMNPSSTTT	standpattism
AADINNORSTTU	transudation
AADLMNNORUWY	laundry-woman
AADMNOQRSUUU	quadrumanous
AADNORRSTTUY	transudatory
AAEEEEKKLLTT	talkee-talkee
AAEEEFHLLNNV	heaven-fallen
AAEEEGGIRTVX	exaggerative
AAEEEGGLNNRT	agent-general
AAEEEHILSSTT	telaesthesia
AAEEEHIMMSST	haematemesis
AAEEEHINSSTT	anaesthetise
AAEEEHINSTTZ	anaesthetize
AAEEEHLLPRTT	plate-leather
AAEEEHLNPRST	elephant's-ear
AAEEEHNPSSTY	pheasant's-eye
AAEEEIKRRSST	seraskierate
AAEEEILPRSTT	tapsalteerie
AAEEEIPRSTVX	exasperative
AAEEELLPRSTU	Pasteurellae
AAEEEMPRSSSU	passemeasure
AAEEENPRSSST	separateness
AAEEFGHRRSST	feather-grass
AAEEFHHLRRST	father-lasher
AAEEFHILRRTU	heart-failure
AAEEFHLMRSSU	half-measures
AAEEFHLORSSV	half-seas-over
AAEEFHNOPRTU	herpetofauna
AAEEFHRSSTTV	harvest-feast
AAEEFIILRRSS	laisser-faire
AAEEFIILRSSZ	laissez-faire
AAEEFLLPPSSU	self-applause
AAEEFNNPRSST	snap-fastener
AAEEGGGGLLRT	raggle-taggle
AAEEGGGGPRRW	wagger-pagger
AAEEGGIMNOSS	agamogenesis
AAEEGGIMNRTV	Gram-negative
AAEEGGINNRTU	guaranteeing
AAEEGGINORTX	exaggeration
AAEEGGLLNSSU	languageless
AAEEGGORRTXY	exaggeratory
AAEEGHHRRSST	sage-thrasher
AAEEGHILNPRT	tragelaphine
AAEEGHILPRSY	hyperalgesia
AAEEGHINRSTT	thereagainst
AAEEGHINRSTW	whereagainst
AAEEGHLMOPTY	hepatomegaly
AAEEGHLOPPRR	paleographer
AAEEGIILMNPS	Semi-Pelagian
AAEEGIILNNPS	palingenesia
AAEEGIILNPRT	patrilineage
AAEEGIILNSTU	Ustilagineae
AAEEGIIMNNRY	aye-remaining
AAEEGIKLMNRS	leasing-maker
AAEEGILMNNOT	△antilegomena
AAEEGIMNNSWZ	newsmagazine
AAEEGIMNOPRS	Angiospermae
AAEEGIMNTTUV	augmentative
AAEEGIMPSSTU	Septuagesima
AAEEGIMRSSTW	semi-water-gas
AAEEGINNSTUX	exsanguinate
AAEEGINPRSTX	exasperating
AAEEGINRSSTV	asseverating
AAEEGJLMNORR	major-general
AAEEGLMNORTV	galvanometer
AAEEGLNNPRWY	Penang-lawyer
AAEEGLNOOPTT	goat-antelope
AAEEGLOPRSSS	opera-glasses
AAEEGLRRRTUX	extra-regular
AAEEGMNOPSSY	passage-money
AAEEGMRRRSTT	garret-master
AAEEGNPRSTUY	septuagenary
AAEEHHIMPRTT	amphitheatre
AAEEHHMNRSTW	what's-her-name
AAEEHHORRTTT	heart-to-heart
AAEEHIIKNSST	kinaesthesia
AAEEHIILRTVX	exhilarative
AAEEHIIMPRST	hemiparasite
AAEEHILMNNOP	phaeomelanin
AAEEHILOPRST	heteroplasia
AAEEHILPRSTU	laureateship
AAEEHIMNNPRS	arsphenamine

AAEEHINNRSTU	neurasthenia
AAEEHINPPRRT	heir-apparent
AAEEHINSSSTY	synaesthesia
AAEEHINSSTTT	anaesthetist
AAEEHKMNRRSS	harness-maker
AAEEHKMORRTT	katharometer
AAEEHLMNOQTU	methaqualone
AAEEHLOPPTXY	heat-apoplexy
AAEEHMNORSUW	warehouseman
AAEEHMOORSTT	Heterosomata
AAEEHOORRSTT	steatorrhoea
AAEEHPRRSTTW	sprat-weather
AAEEIIJNOPRS	japonaiserie
AAEEIIKKLLTW	walkie-talkie
AAEEIILLMRSS	Marseillaise
AAEEIILLRTTV	alliterative
AAEEIILMNTTV	alimentative
AAEEIILMORTV	ameliorative
AAEEIIMPRSST	semiparasite
AAEEIINNRRTV	veterinarian
AAEEILLLPRSW	parallelwise
AAEEILLLRRSS	laisser-aller
AAEEILLLRSSZ	laissez-aller
AAEEILLMNPST	planetesimal
AAEEILLNORTV	revelational
AAEEILLPRSTT	septilateral
AAEEILMNRSST	materialness
AAEEILMORRST	alstroemeria
AAEEILNORRTT	re-alteration
AAEEILNORSTT	Aristotelean
AAEEILNORSTU	teleosaurian
AAEEILNPPRSU	pleasure-pain
AAEEILNPRSST	pleasantries
AAEEILNPRSTW	water-spaniel
AAEEILNSSTVX	laxativeness
AAEEILOPRRTT	proletariate
AAEEILQRSSTU	sesquialtera
AAEEIMNOPSST	empassionate
AAEEIMNPPRST	appraisement
AAEEINNNORTX	reannexation
AAEEINOPRSTX	exasperation
AAEEINORSSTV	asseveration
AAEEINPPRRST	paper-stainer
AAEEJKMMNRTZ	katzenjammer
AAEEKMNPRRTT	pattern-maker
AAEELLNPRRTY	parenterally
AAEELLPRSSTU	Pasteurellas
AAEELMMNRTTT	maltreatment
AAEELMNPRSST	malapertness
AAEELMNPRSTT	saltpetreman
AAEELNNPSSST	pleasantness
AAEELORSSTYY	araeosystyle
AAEELPQRRTTU	quarter-plate
AAEEMNNPPRSW	newspaperman
AAEEMNRSTTTY	testamentary
AAEEMPRSSSUY	passy-measure
AAEENNOSSSTU	assentaneous
AAEENNPPRSST	apparentness
AAEENNPRSTUU	superannuate
AAEERRRSTTUU	restaurateur
AAEFFIIMNORR	Foraminifera
AAEFFQRRSTTU	quarterstaff
AAEFGHHIILNT	faith-healing
AAEFGHILLNRT	half-integral
AAEFGHLLNNPR	flannelgraph
AAEFGIKLMNRW	walking-frame
AAEFGILLLNOT	flagellation
AAEFGINNORTT	engraftation
AAEFGINRRTUW	fugie-warrant
AAEFGIPRTTUY	fatigue-party
AAEFGLLLORTY	flagellatory
AAEFGNNRRSST	fragrantness
AAEFHILMNSSS	fish-salesman
AAEFHILNRSTW	fathers-in-law
AAEFILLNSSSY	self-analysis
AAEFILNORRTY	reflationary
AAEFILNPRTVY	trypaflavine
AAEFILNQRRTU	quarter-final
AAEFIMRSSTTU	mutessarifat
AAEFLLOPPRSV	self-approval
AAEFLMNOOPTT	footplateman
AAEFLNOQRRTU	quartern-loaf
AAEGGHHIOPRR	hagiographer
AAEGGHLNNRSW	slang-whanger
AAEGGHMNOPRT	magnetograph
AAEGGHNOPRST	steganograph
AAEGGIIMNRRR	marriage-ring
AAEGGIIMNRRS	gregarianism
AAEGGIINOPRT	arpeggiation
AAEGGLLNORRY	organ-gallery
AAEGHHIKNRST	earthshaking
AAEGHHOPPRRS	phraseograph
AAEGHIILNRTX	exhilarating
AAEGHIKNQRTU	earthquaking
AAEGHIMMNPSS	gamesmanship
AAEGHIMMORRT	hierogrammat
AAEGHIMNRRTW	heartwarming
AAEGHIMORRRT	metrorrhagia
AAEGHINPPRSW	paper-washing
AAEGHKNOPRRU	keraunograph
AAEGHLMNRSTU	manslaughter
	slaughterman
AAEGHLMOPPRY	ampelography
AAEGHLOPRTTU	Telautograph®
AAEGHMNOOPSU	phaenogamous
AAEGHMNOSTTU	metagnathous
AAEGHMNOTTUY	thaumatogeny
AAEGHNOPPRRT	pantographer
AAEGHNOPRRRU	uranographer
AAEGHOOPPRRV	evaporograph
AAEGIILLNOST	legalisation
AAEGIILLNOTZ	legalization
AAEGIILMNORT	emigrational
AAEGIILNNOTT	gelatination
AAEGIIMNNORT	emargination
AAEGIIMNNRSW	Wagnerianism
AAEGIINNOPRT	repagination
AAEGIINNPPRT	appertaining
AAEGIINNPSTV	vase-painting
AAEGIKKMMNRT	market-making
AAEGILLNNTTY	tangentially
AAEGILMNOPRS	angiospermal
AAEGILNNPRTV	vinegar-plant
AAEGILNNRRWY	early-warning

AAEGILNNSTUY nauseatingly
AAEGILNPSTTU Septuagintal
AAEGIMMNNPRS Pan-Germanism
AAEGIMNNOTTU augmentation
AAEGIMNRRRTU ring-armature
AAEGIMNRRSTT transmigrate
AAEGIMNRSTTX taxing-master
AAEGIMNSTTTY syntagmatite
AAEGIMRRSTTU magistrature
AAEGINORSSTU stegosaurian
AAEGINPRRTTW water-parting
AAEGKLLMORSW gallows-maker
AAEGLLNNOPTY pentagonally
AAEGLLNORTTY tetragonally
AAEGLLNPPPRT grapple-plant
AAEGLMNORTVY galvanometry
AAEGLMOOPSSU gamosepalous
AAEGLMOOPSTU gamopetalous
AAEGLMORSSUU megalosaurus
AAEHHILMOPTX exophthalmia
AAEHHIMNSSTW what's-his-name
AAEHHIMRRRRS marsh-harrier
AAEHHINNOPST phonasthenia
AAEHIIILNNTV annihilative
AAEHIILMMPTU epithalamium
AAEHIILMNOPT epithalamion
AAEHIILNORTX exhilaration
AAEHIINOPRTZ azathioprine
AAEHIINOPSTT hepatisation
AAEHIINOPTTZ hepatization
AAEHIKNOSTTV stakhanovite
AAEHILLNNNPY phenylalanin
AAEHILMMRSTU rheumatismal
AAEHILMNOTXY haematoxylin
AAEHILMNPSSS salesmanship
AAEHILMOSSTY haematolysis
AAEHILMRSTUY amateurishly
AAEHILNNOPRT paranthelion
AAEHILNNRSTT transleithan
AAEHILNOPPSS Phalaenopsis
AAEHILORRTXY exhilaratory
AAEHIMMRSSTU shamateurism
AAEHIMNNSSSU haussmannise
AAEHIMNNSSUZ haussmannize
AAEHIMNORSTY hysteromania
AAEHIMNPRSTW watermanship
AAEHIMNSSTTW what's-its-name
AAEHINNOPTTY enantiopathy
AAEHINOPPRST Siphonaptera
AAEHINOPSSTY enhypostasia
AAEHLMNOOTXY Haematoxylon
AAEHMMNOOPRT Nematomorpha
AAEHMNOOPRSS anamorphoses
AAEHMOORSTTU atheromatous
AAEHNOPRRSTT prostanthera
AAEHNOPRSTTY Thysanoptera
AAEHOPPPRSSY parapophyses
AAEIIILMSSTV assimilative
AAEIIIMMNRSS semi-Arianism
AAEIILLMMRTY immaterially
AAEIILLMNRTX intermaxilla
AAEIILLMRTTX extralimital
AAEIILLNOQTU illaqueation
AAEIILLNORTT alliteration
AAEIILLNPSTU sinupalliate
AAEIILLNPSTY sapientially
AAEIILMNNOTT alimentation
AAEIILMNNRRT interlaminar
AAEIILMNOORT amelioration
AAEIILMNPTUV manipulative
AAEIILMOPRRT imperatorial
AAEIILMRTTUV multivariate
AAEIILNNOPST penalisation
AAEIILNNOPTZ penalization
AAEIILNOPRST epistolarian
AAEIILNOQSTU equalisation
AAEIILNOQTUZ equalization
AAEIILNORSTT Aristotelian
laterisation
AAEIILNORSTV velarisation
AAEIILNORTTZ laterization
AAEIILNORTVZ velarization
AAEIILNPRSTT interspatial
AAEIILPPRSVY appraisively
AAEIIMNOPSST impassionate
AAEIINNOSTTT tetanisation
AAEIINNOTTTZ tetanization
AAEIINOPQRTU equiparation
AAEIINOPRRTT repatriation
AAEIINOPRTTX expatriation
AAEIINQTTTUV quantitative
AAEILLLMRTTU multilateral
AAEILLLNORTY relationally
AAEILLLNRTUY unilaterally
AAEILLLRRTTY trilaterally
AAEILLMNNSUY semi-annually
AAEILLMNRRTY artilleryman
AAEILLMPRRXY premaxillary
AAEILLNNTTTW tenant-at-will
AAEILLNORSTY senatorially
AAEILLOQRTUY equatorially
AAEILLPPSUVY applausively
AAEILLQRSSTU quasi-stellar
AAEILMNNOSTT Lamentations
AAEILMNORSTV malversation
AAEILMNPSSUX pansexualism
AAEILMNRSSTT mistranslate
AAEILNNOPPTT pentapolitan
AAEILNNOPRTT replantation
AAEILNNOPTTX explantation
AAEILNNQTTUV quantivalent
AAEILNNRSTUU unnaturalise
AAEILNNRTUUZ unnaturalize
AAEILNOPRTTT tetrapolitan
AAEILNOPSSTU antisepalous
AAEILNOPSSTY passionately
AAEILNOPSTTU antipetalous
AAEILNOPSTZZ Pestalozzian
AAEILNORSTTW law-stationer
AAEILNPPSUUV unapplausive
AAEILNPSSTUX pansexualist
AAEILNRSSSTU salutariness
AAEILORRSTTT latirostrate
AAEIMMMOSSTT metasomatism

AAEIMNNOTTUY ayuntamiento
AAEIMNOOOOPT onomatopoeia
AAEINNOPRSXY expansionary
AAEINNOPSSTU unpassionate
AAEINNORSSTU Austronesian
AAEINOPRRSTU pterosaurian
AAEINOQRSTUY quaestionary
AAEINORRSTTU restauration
AAEKLMNNORTU nomenklatura
AAEKLMORRTWW low-watermark
AAEKLNNOOPRT aeroplankton
AAEKLOPRSTTY keratoplasty
AAEKNORRSTTT stratotanker
AAELLMNNORTY ornamentally
AAELLNNPSTUY unpleasantly
AAELLNOPRSTT entoplastral
AAELLNRSSTUU ultrasensual
AAELMNNNORTU unornamental
AAELMNNORTTU ultramontane
AAELMNOOPRTT protonematal
AAELMOOPRSTZ spermatozoal
AAELNNOOPRTY pantaloonery
AAELNNPRRSTT transplanter
AAELNNPRSTUY unpleasantry
AAELNPRRSTUU supernatural
AAELNRSSSTTW stalwartness
AAELOOPRRTTX extrapolator
AAEMNNNORSTT transmontane
AAEMNNOORTUY neuroanatomy
AAEMNOOPRSTZ spermatozoan
AAEMNOPRSTTU portmanteaus
AAEMNOPRTTUX portmanteaux
AAEMOORSTTTU teratomatous
AAEMOOSSTTTU steatomatous
AAEMQRRRSTUY quarrymaster
AAEOPPRSSTTU passe-partout
AAEOPRRRSSTW parrot-wrasse
AAEOPRRRTTTY pyrotartrate
AAFFGIKLNSTW walking-staff
AAFFGILLNNSY snaffling-lay
AAFFLNOOPSTU pufftaloonas
AAFGHINNPRST span-farthing
AAFGIKLMNNOR frankalmoign
AAFIIILNRTTU futilitarian
AAFIILLMNRUY unfamiliarly
AAFIILMMNNOT inflammation
AAFIILNNORTY inflationary
AAFILLMMNOTU flammulation
AAFILMMNOORT malformation
AAFILMMNORTY inflammatory
AAGGHNOOPRRY organography
AAGGIIINNRTT ingratiating
AAGGIIKLLNSS galligaskins
AAGGIKLLNRSS larking-glass
AAGGIKNQRSSU quaking-grass
AAGGLMMOORTY grammatology
AAGGNNOORTUU ourang-outang
AAGHHIINORRR rhinorrhagia
AAGHHMNOOPRR harmonograph
AAGHIINNNORT nothingarian
AAGHIINNOSTW △washingtonia
AAGHIKLNNORS loan-sharking
AAGHILMOORTY hamartiology
AAGHIMOOPRST Mastigophora
AAGHINOPPSTT pantophagist
AAGHIPRRSTTY stratigraphy
AAGHIRSSTTWY straightways
AAGHLLMOOPSU mallophagous
AAGHLMOOTTUY thaumatology
AAGHLOOPPRRY polarography
AAGHMRSTTUUU thaumaturgus
AAGHNOOPPSTU pantophagous
AAGHOOPPRSSU saprophagous
AAGIIILNORRT irrigational
AAGIIINNNOTV invagination
AAGIIINNORTT ingratiation
AAGIIILMNNRTU marginal-unit
AAGIIILNNRSUY sanguinarily
AAGIIMNNOTWW waiting-woman
AAGIINNOORST organisation
AAGIINNOORTZ organization
AAGIINNORTUU inauguration
AAGILLLORSSY glossarially
AAGILLMNTUWY mulligatawny
AAGILLNRRTUY triangularly
AAGILNNORSTU granulations
AAGILNNSSTWY slantingways
AAGILNORSTTU gastrulation
AAGILOOPRSTY parasitology
AAGIMNNRRSTT transmigrant
AAGINORRTUUY inauguratory
AAGLMNOPRSSY laryngospasm
AAGLMOORTTUY traumatology
AAGOPRRRSSSW sparrow-grass
AAHHIIMRRSTT hamarthritis
AAHHINNNOTTX anthoxanthin
AAHHIOPPRSTU phosphaturia
AAHHLMOPSTUY hypothalamus
AAHIIILLOPRU ailurophilia
AAHIIILNNNOT annihilation
AAHIIMNNOSTU humanisation
AAHIIMNNOTUZ humanization
AAHIIMOPPRSS paraphimosis
AAHIINOPSTXY asphyxiation
AAHIINPPRSST partisanship
AAHIINPRRSTT panarthritis
AAHIKMMNPRSS marksmanship
AAHIKMNOSSTV stakhanovism
AAHILLMOPRSX morphallaxis
AAHILLNNOPSY pollyannaish
AAHILLNNOPTY antiphonally
AAHILLOPRSTX trophallaxis
AAHILMMOPRTU prothalamium
AAHILMNOOPRT prothalamion
AAHIMMOPPRRS paramorphism
AAHIMNOOPRSS anamorphosis
AAHIOPPPRSSY parapophysis
AAHLMNOPRSUY orphan-asylum
AAHLNORRSTUY anarthrously
AAHLOPRRSTTY arthroplasty
AAHMNOOSTTUX xanthomatous
AAHMOQRRSSUW marrow-squash
AAHNOPPRRSTU paranthropus

AAIIILMNOSST	assimilation
	Islamisation
AAIIILMNOSTZ	Islamization
AAIIILMPRTTY	impartiality
AAIIILNNOSTV	insalivation
AAIIILNOSTTV	visitational
	vitalisation
AAIIILNOTTVZ	vitalization
AAIIILORSTTV	visitatorial
AAIIIMNNRSTU	△unitarianism
AAIIIMNOSSTV	avitaminosis
AAIIINNNOSTT	insanitation
AAIIINNOSSTT	sanitisation
AAIIINNOSTTZ	sanitization
AAIIINORSTTV	variationist
AAIIKLNSSSTV	Stanislavski
AAIILLMOSSTT	altaltissimo
AAIILLNNOSTT	installation
AAIILLNOOTTV	volitational
AAIILLNORRTY	irrationally
AAIILMNNOPTT	implantation
AAIILMNNOPTU	manipulation
AAIILMNOORST	moralisation
AAIILMNOORTZ	moralization
AAIILMNOOTTV	motivational
AAIILMNOSSTT	saltationism
AAIILMNOSSTV	Salvationism
AAIILNNORSTT	transitional
AAIILNOOPPST	appositional
AAIILNOOPRST	polarisation
AAIILNOOPRTZ	polarization
AAIILNOORSST	solarisation
AAIILNOORSTV	valorisation
AAIILNOORSTZ	solarization
AAIILNOORTVZ	valorization
AAIILNOOSTTT	totalisation
AAIILNOOTTTZ	totalization
AAIILNORRSTU	ruralisation
AAIILNORRTUZ	ruralization
AAIILNOSSTTT	saltationist
AAIILNOSSTTV	Salvationist
AAIILORSTTTU	tralatitious
AAIIMNNOORST	Romanisation
AAIIMNNOORTZ	Romanization
AAIIMNOORSTT	amortisation
AAIIMNOORTTZ	amortization
AAIINNNNOSTU	antoninianus
AAIINNOQSTTU	quantisation
AAIINNOQTTUZ	quantization
AAIINNORSTTU	instauration
AAIINOOPRSTV	vaporisation
AAIINOOPRTVZ	vaporization
AAILLMNNOPSY	pollyannaism
AAILLMNOPRTT	all-important
AAILLMNOTTUY	mutationally
AAILLMOPRTYY	morality-play
AAILLORSTTUY	salutatorily
AAILMNOPRTUY	manipulatory
AAILMOORRSTU	Mariolatrous
AAILOORSSTTU	saltatorious
AAIMNNRRSTUU	transuranium
AAIMNOOSSTTT	somatostatin
AAINNORSTTUU	unsaturation
AAINORSSTTUU	Titanosaurus
AAIOOPPPRRRT	appropriator
AAKLNNNNOOPT	nanoplankton
AAKLNORSSUUY	Ankylosaurus
AALLMOOPPRST	protoplasmal
AALMOORRSTUY	Maryolatrous
ABBBBBBEEILL	bibble-babble
ABBBBEEGGILL	gibble-gabble
ABBBBEEILLRR	ribble-rabble
ABBBCEEHLNOT	technobabble
ABBBCEHLOPSY	psychobabble
ABBBCEILRSSU	subscribable
ABBBCELNNORY	bonny-clabber
ABBBCIILLTUY	clubbability
ABBBDDEEEHLU	bubble-headed
ABBBDELORYZZ	bobby-dazzler
ABBBEELMRRRY	bramble-berry
ABBBEHLMORTU	blabbermouth
ABBBGINRRSSU	brass-rubbing
ABBBHIIILOOP	bibliophobia
ABBCCEGHIMNO	beachcombing
ABBCDEEHIMRR	bride-chamber
ABBCDEEKKNOR	broken-backed
ABBCDGIIKLNR	blackbirding
ABBCEEGGKLRU	buckle-beggar
ABBCEEKLNOSS	backboneless
ABBCEENORTUY	abbey-counter
ABBCEFHILMNR	bramble-finch
ABBCEGHINNTU	nubbing-cheat
ABBCEIKRRSTU	rabbit-sucker
ABBCELOOORRR	corroborable
ABBCFIILORST	fibroblastic
ABBDDEEKLNOU	double-banked
ABBDEEEGINRT	bate-breeding
ABBDEEFLORSS	self-absorbed
ABBDEHIILRSY	hybridisable
ABBDEHIILRYZ	hybridizable
ABBDEILLMRRU	umbrella-bird
ABBDELLLNRUY	land-lubberly
ABBDELNORTTY	brandy-bottle
ABBDENORRSSU	brass-bounder
ABBDFFIILNOU	bound-bailiff
ABBDHIKOORTY	birthday-book
ABBDILMOOPSS	bomb-disposal
ABBEEEELMMRR	rememberable
ABBEEEILLNUV	unbelievable
ABBEEELMMRRY	rememberably
ABBEEELNRTTU	unbetterable
ABBEEGMNORRR	barber-monger
ABBEEILLNUVY	unbelievably
ABBEEILMRRSU	reimbursable
ABBEEILNORSV	inobservable
ABBEEILOPQRU	equiprobable
ABBEEILRRTTU	irrebuttable
ABBEELNORSUV	unobservable
ABBEELORRRSU	rabble-rouser
ABBEELRRSTUV	subvertebral
ABBEFFLORRUY	buffalo-berry
ABBEGIINNOTT	babingtonite
ABBEHIIMNOSS	Hobbesianism
ABBELLMRRSUU	subumbrellar

ABBENNNOORST non-absorbent
ABBGHIILOPRY bibliography
ABBIIIILMNOT imbibitional
ABBIILNNOOTU obnubilation
ABCCCEEHMNOY come-by-chance
ABCCHOOOPTU tobacco-pouch
ABCCCINNOTUY concubitancy
ABCCDEEELPST bespectacled
ABCCDEEHILNN blanc-de-Chine
ABCCDEEHKKLU huckle-backed
ABCCDEEHKORR checkerboard
ABCCDEHILORU coachbuilder
ABCCDGHIINRT bird-catching
ABCCDHILRSTU scratchbuild
ABCCDKLORUZZ buzzard-clock
ABCCEEEKPRRT bracket-creep
ABCCEEELNORT concelebrate
ABCCEEENORRS arborescence
ABCCEEGINNRU buccaneering
ABCCEEHINRSU buccaneerish
ABCCEEIILNSS inaccessible
ABCCEEILLNOR reconcilable
ABCCEELNNORT concelebrant
ABCCEELORRSU clare-obscure
clear-obscure
ABCCEEMNNRRU encumbrancer
ABCCEENNOSTT contabescent
ABCCEENORRTU counterbrace
ABCCEHIIMNOS biomechanics
ABCCEHILLRUY cherubically
ABCCEHLOOOTX chocolate-box
ABCCEHMNRRTU curb-merchant
ABCCEIIILRST criticisable
ABCCEIIILRTZ criticizable
ABCCEIIILNOOT coenobitical
ABCCEIILNSSY inaccessibly
ABCCEILLNORY reconcilably
ABCCEILMMNOU communicable
ABCCEILNNOOS conscionable
ABCCEILNORTT contractible
ABCCEILORRSU clair-obscure
ABCCEILORSTU scrobiculate
ABCCENOORRRY raccoon-berry
ABCCGILNRRUW curb-crawling
ABCCHHILOOOP ochlophobiac
ABCCHILLMORU chlorambucil
ABCCHILRSTTU scratchbuilt
ABCCHIOOORRT orthoboracic
ABCCIILLSTUY cubistically
ABCCIILOPSTU suboccipital
ABCCIIMOORST macrobiotics
ABCCILLOOSTY octosyllabic
ABCCILMMNOUY communicably
ABCCILNNOOSY conscionably
ABCDDEHIILNR Hildebrandic
ABCDDGIKLNPU black-pudding
ABCDEEEHILPR decipherable
ABCDEEEHLORR breech-loader
ABCDEEEILNTT indetectable
ABCDEEEILNUV undeceivable
ABCDEEELLNTU undelectable
ABCDEEELNRTU uncelebrated
ABCDEEELNTTU undetectable
ABCDEEGHLORU double-charge
ABCDEEGIKNOR code-breaking
ABCDEEHIPPRR bread-chipper
ABCDEEIILLNN indeclinable
ABCDEEILMNSS dissemblance
ABCDEEILMOST domesticable
ABCDEEILNNSU unascendible
ABCDEEILNORS considerable
ABCDEEILNRTU uncreditable
ABCDEEILORSV discoverable
ABCDEEIORRSV scrieveboard
ABCDEEKKLNRU bare-knuckled
ABCDEELMOOPS decomposable
ABCDEELRTTUU tuberculated
ABCDEEMNOOTT cane-bottomed
ABCDEFGIKLRU black-figured
ABCDEFMOPRUU fume-cupboard
ABCDEGHIILNR childbearing
child-bearing
ABCDEGHORRTU turbocharged
ABCDEGILNOTU double-acting
ABCDEHHLOOOR bachelorhood
ABCDEHNORSTY body-snatcher
ABCDEIIILLRT liberticidal
ABCDEIILLNNY indeclinably
ABCDEIILRSTT distractible
ABCDEILNORSY considerably
ABCDEILNOSTU discountable
ABCDEILPSTUU subduplicate
ABCDEINOOPRS proboscidean
ABCDEKKLLNOO bollock-naked
ABCDEKLOORRU dock-labourer
ABCDELOOPRUV cupboard-love
ABCDGHIINRTW bird-watching
ABCDGIKNNOUW back-wounding
ABCDGINNORSS crossbanding
ABCDGINOORRS scoring-board
ABCDHIIRSSTU Hudibrastics
ABCDHLNOORST chondroblast
ABCDIILMNOPU public-domain
ABCDIINOOPRS proboscidian
ABCDINNORSUY subordinancy
ABCEEEENPRRT carpenter-bee
ABCEEEFFIORR office-bearer
ABCEEEFNRSST benefactress
ABCEEEHHINPR hebephreniac
ABCEEEIILMPR impierceable
ABCEEEILNTUX inexecutable
ABCEEEKRRRTU truce-breaker
ABCEEELNNORU renounceable
ABCEEEMMNRRR remembrancer
ABCEEEMMNRRS remembrances
ABCEEENORSUV verbenaceous
ABCEEFFIINRT febrifacient
ABCEEFIILLNY beneficially
ABCEEFIILNNU unbeneficial
ABCEEFINORST sorbefacient
ABCEEFLLOORS foreclosable
ABCEEGHLLNST cable's-length
ABCEEGHMRSTU guest-chamber
ABCEEGILLLNO eco-labelling

ABCEEGILNORS recognisable
ABCEEGILNORZ recognizable
ABCEEGLOPRSU barge-couples
ABCEEHKMNRRT kerb-merchant
ABCEEHLNNQUU unquenchable
ABCEEHMMNNRT embranchment
ABCEEIILLNPX inexplicable
ABCEEIILLTTY electability
ABCEEIILNNNT bicentennial
ABCEEIILNRTX inextricable
ABCEEIINNNST inabstinence
ABCEEILLSSTU subcelestial
ABCEEILMMORS commiserable
ABCEEILNNOTU unnoticeable
ABCEEILNORSU ribonuclease
ABCEEILNOSSS sociableness
ABCEEILRSSTU resuscitable
ABCEEINNORSV inobservance
ABCEEINOORRT cerebrotonia
ABCEEINRRSTU canterburies
ABCEEJKLMRTU lumber-jacket
ABCEEJNRSTTU subterjacent
ABCEEKLNNORU unreckonable
ABCEEKLORRTW lower-bracket
ABCEEKPPRRTU upper-bracket
ABCEELLLNOSU counsellable
ABCEELLMNOPT contemplable
ABCEELLMSTTU lamb's-lettuce
ABCEELLNPSSU culpableness
ABCEELMMMOOR commemorable
ABCEELMRRTTU marble-cutter
ABCEELOPRRSV procès-verbal
ABCEELOPRSTU prosecutable
ABCEENNOORSX resonance-box
ABCEENNORSUV unobservance
ABCEENOPRRTU protuberance
ABCEEOOPRRRT baroreceptor
ABCEEORRSSUU burseraceous
ABCEFFINOORR baron-officer
ABCEFILNNNOU unconfinable
ABCEGHILLORR bachelor-girl
ABCEGHLNOOST hog-constable
ABCEGHORRRTU turbocharger
ABCEGIILNNOS incognisable
ABCEGIILNNOZ incognizable
ABCEGIJLMNOR crambo-jingle
ABCEGIKLNRRW kerb-crawling
ABCEGILNORSY recognisably
ABCEGILNORYZ recognizably
ABCEGILNPRUY burying-place
ABCEGILOORTY bacteriology
ABCEGLLNOOTU conglobulate
ABCEGLMNRUUU gubernaculum
ABCEHHILOPRS bachelorship
ABCEHHINOOPT technophobia
ABCEHHRTTTUY buttery-hatch
ABCEHIILLNRY Hibernically
ABCEHIJKNOTX △jack-in-the-box
ABCEHIKNRSSS brackishness
ABCEHIKSSTTT basket-stitch
ABCEHILLOPRY hyperbolical
ABCEHILMNRUU hibernaculum
ABCEHKLRSSUW swashbuckler
ABCEHLMOOPSS peach-blossom
ABCEHLNNQUUY unquenchably
ABCEIIILLRST liberalistic
ABCEIIILTTXY excitability
ABCEIIIMNORT biometrician
ABCEIIILNPXY inexplicably
ABCEIIILMNOPT incompatible
ABCEIIILNRTUV vibratiuncle
ABCEIIILNRTXY inextricably
ABCEIIILOORST borosilicate
ABCEIIILORSTT cristobalite
ABCEIIILORTVY revocability
ABCEIIILPRSTY plebiscitary
ABCEIINORSTT obstetrician
ABCEILLNNOOS inconsolable
ABCEILLNTUUV uncultivable
ABCEILMMNOTU incommutable
ABCEILMNNOSU inconsumable
ABCEILMNOPRU pre-Columbian
ABCEILMNOPTU incomputable
ABCEILMOPRST problematics
ABCEILNORTUU elucubration
ABCEILOPRRTT protractible
ABCEIPRSSSUY presbyacusis
ABCELLLNOORT controllable
ABCELLLOOSTY octosyllable
ABCELMNOOPSU uncomposable
ABCELNNORTUY contubernyal
ABCELNOPRRUU unprocurable
ABCELNORSTTU counterblast
ABCELOPRRSUU subopercular
ABCEMNNORRRU Marcobrunner
ABCEMOOPSSSW bow-compasses
ABCENORSSSSU scabrousness
ABCENOSSTUUU subcutaneous
ABCFGHIIKLNS black-fishing
ABCFLNOOORRU fluorocarbon
ABCGGHIIKLNT back-lighting
ABCGHHIKNSUW bushwhacking
ABCGHINRSTTU chart-busting
ABCGIIKLLNST blacklisting
ABCGIILLLOOY biologically
ABCGILLMNRSY scramblingly
ABCGILNNOOOT conglobation
ABCHIIKLOSTY shockability
ABCHIILLOSTU thiobacillus
ABCHIILOOPRU ailurophobic
ABCHIIOOOPTX toxicophobia
ABCHIOOOPPST scoptophobia
ABCIIIILRSTY irascibility
ABCIIIKLSTTY stickability
ABCIIILMNOTU umbilication
ABCIIILNRTUY incurability
ABCIIILRTTTY tractibility
ABCIILLNRTTU brilliant-cut
ABCIILMNOPTY incompatibly
ABCIILNNOTUY connubiality
ABCIILNNSTUU incunabulist
ABCIILNPPRSU subprincipal
ABCIIMNNOOST combinations
ABCIINORSTUU turbinacious

ABCILLLMOSYY symbolically
ABCILLLOPSYY polysyllabic
ABCILLMNOOSY monosyllabic
ABCILLNNOOSY inconsolably
ABCILMMNOSTU noctambulism
ABCILMMNOTUY incommutably
ABCILMNNOSUY inconsumably
ABCILMNOSTTU noctambulist
ABCILMORRTUU microtubular
ABCILOOPSSTU subapostolic
ABCIMNORSSTU obscurantism
ABCIMNORSTUU rambunctious
ABCINORRTTUY contributary
ABCINORSSTTU obscurantist
substraction
ABCOOOORRRRT corroborator
ABDDDEEEHLOU double-headed
ABDDDEEHLNOU double-handed
ABDDEEEEEHLT beetleheaded
ABDDEEEGGGLR badger-legged
ABDDEEEHIRTW white-bearded
ABDDEEEHLLTU bullet-headed
ABDDEEEHLNYZ benzaldehyde
ABDDEEEHLORU double-header
ABDDEEELLORU double-dealer
ABDDEEELNNPU undependable
ABDDEEGGLORU double-dagger
ABDDEEGLLOUZ double-glazed
ABDDEEILLNRU unriddleable
ABDDEEIMNNST absent-minded
ABDDEELMNNOU double-manned
ABDDEGILNPRS spring-bladed
ABDDEILMNPST blind-stamped
ABDDEILNNSSY day-blindness
ABDDEILNOOST bloodstained
ABDDEKMOOOSY Domesday-book
ABDDGLNOOORS dragon's-blood
ABDDHILMNNOO hoodman-blind
ABDDKMOOOOSY Doomsday-book
ABDDNOORTUUW outward-bound
ABDEEEEILMRR irredeemable
ABDEEEELLLSV base-levelled
ABDEEEELMNRU unredeemable
ABDEEEFIILNS indefeasible
ABDEEEGHLRRW hedge-warbler
ABDEEEGILLRT great-bellied
ABDEEEHILRRS shield-bearer
ABDEEEHLLRTW well-breathed
ABDEEEIILMRR irremediable
ABDEEEIILRTV deliberative
ABDEEEILLRTY deliberately
ABDEEEILMNRT determinable
ABDEEEILMRRY irredeemably
ABDEEEILNRTU undeliberate
ABDEEEIMSTTW time-bewasted
ABDEEEKLORRR broker-dealer
ABDEEELMNTTT battlemented
ABDEEELMNTZZ bedazzlement
ABDEEFHILMRT half-timbered
ABDEEFIIILNT identifiable
ABDEEFIILNSY indefeasibly
ABDEEFINSTUU subinfeudate
ABDEEGHLNORT long-breathed
ABDEEGILLNPS speedballing
ABDEEGILMNRS disembrangle
ABDEEGINNRRU underbearing
ABDEEGINOPST speedboating
ABDEEGKLLNOW knowledgable
ABDEEGLNOSTU obtuse-angled
ABDEEHHOPRRS rhabdosphere
ABDEEHILMRTW marbled-white
ABDEEHLRSTTU lust-breathed
ABDEEHNNORTU unbreathed-on
ABDEEHNORTUW weather-bound
ABDEEHOORSTT sabre-toothed
ABDEEIIILTTV debilitative
ABDEEIILMRRY irremediably
ABDEEIILNORT deliberation
ABDEEIILRSST destabiliser
ABDEEIILRSTZ destabilizer
ABDEEIINORTY obedientiary
ABDEEIIPRSST base-spirited
ABDEEILLMRTT reimbattell'd
ABDEEILLNORR banderillero
ABDEEILMNOPR imponderable
ABDEEILMNRTY determinably
ABDEEILMRSSS disassembler
ABDEEILORRUV boulevardier
ABDEEILPRSTU disreputable
ABDEEINNORSS debonairness
ABDEEINNSSSU unbiasedness
ABDEEJNORTUY journey-bated
ABDEEKLNNRTU underblanket
ABDEEKORRRSW sword-breaker
ABDEELLLORRR rollerblader
ABDEELLPRSTU spurtle-blade
ABDEELMNORST demonstrable
ABDEENORSSTU obdurateness
ABDEFFGIILNR diffrangible
ABDEFFHLORSU shuffle-board
ABDEFIIILLOS solidifiable
ABDEFIIILNTY definability
identifiably
ABDEFIILMNOR informidable
ABDEFIILMNOU unmodifiable
ABDEFIILMNRR rifleman-bird
ABDEFILMNORU unformidable
ABDEFINOSTUU subfeudation
ABDEFNORRSSU brassfounder
ABDEFORSTUUY subfeudatory
ABDEGHINRSST bathing-dress
ABDEGIIILNTT debilitating
ABDEGIIKNOPR boarding-pike
ABDEGIKNOPRW baking-powder
ABDEGILLLNNY belly-landing
ABDEGILNORRU organ-builder
ABDEGILNORTW world-beating
ABDEGKLLNOWY knowledgably
ABDEGLNORTTU battleground
ABDEHHLMOORR rhombohedral
ABDEHHNOSSUU house-husband
ABDEHIIILMNS diminishable
ABDEHIILNSUV devil-in-a-bush
ABDEHIILSSST disestablish

ABDEHILMNNST	blandishment
ABDEHILNOORS	dishonorable
ABDEHIMNRRST	Rembrandtish
ABDEHNORUYZZ	honey-buzzard
ABDEHORRTTUY	ruby-throated
ABDEIIILMNSS	inadmissible
ABDEIIILMTXY	mixed-ability
ABDEIIILNOTT	debilitation
ABDEIIILRSTY	desirability
ABDEIIILRTVY	driveability
ABDEIIILNPSTU	indisputable
ABDEIILORSTU	subeditorial
ABDEIILTTUVY	dubitatively
ABDEIIOOPRSS	basidiospore
ABDEIIRSTTUV	disturbative
ABDEILMNSTUU	unsublimated
ABDEILPRSTUY	disreputably
ABDEIMMNRRST	Rembrandtism
ABDEIMORSTUX	ambidextrous
ABDELMNORSTY	demonstrably
ABDELOOQRRTU	quarter-blood
ABDENOORSTWY	sword-bayonet
ABDENOQRRTUU	quarter-bound
ABDFGINORRSU	surfboarding
ABDFIILNNRUU	infundibular
ABDFIILNOOOV	bioflavonoid
ABDGHINOOSWX	shadow-boxing
ABDGIILOOORY	radiobiology
ABDGIINNNORR	branding-iron
ABDGIINNOORR	ironing-board
ABDGILNORRUU	burial-ground
ABDGIMNNNORU	mourning-band
ABDGINNNORRU	running-board
ABDGINNOORSW	snowboarding
ABDHIIMRSTTY	dithyrambist
ABDHIIRSTTUY	birthday-suit
ABDHILNOORSY	dishonorably
ABDHINOOOOPT	odontophobia
ABDIIIILNTUY	inaudibility
ABDIIILMNSSY	inadmissibly
ABDIIILRSSUY	subsidiarily
ABDIIIRSSTUY	subsidiarity
ABDIILLMOTUY	modulability
ABDIILNPSTUY	indisputably
ABDIIRRSTTUY	distributary
ABDLNOORTUUY	roundaboutly
ABEEEFILLMRU	Umbelliferae
ABEEEFILNSSS	feasibleness
ABEEEGILNORT	renegotiable
ABEEEHILNOTV	above-the-line
ABEEEHKLRSTT	bletherskate
ABEEEHKORRRS	horse-breaker
ABEEEHKORRSU	house-breaker
ABEEEHMNQTTU	bequeathment
ABEEEIJMNNRT	benjamin-tree
ABEEEILLNRSS	reliableness
ABEEEILLNRUV	unrelievable
ABEEEILLPRSV	replevisable
ABEEEILMNPRT	impenetrable
ABEEEILMNRTX	exterminable
ABEEEILNNSSV	enviableness
ABEEEILRRSTV	silver-beater
ABEEEINNPRTV	brevipennate
ABEEEINNRTTW	winter-beaten
ABEEEINRRTTV	invertebrate
ABEEEKNORRST	stone-breaker
ABEEELLMRRTU	umbrella-tree
ABEEELLRSTTT	trestle-table
ABEEELMMNTTT	embattlement
ABEEELMNOSSV	moveableness
ABEEELNSSSSS	baselessness
ABEEELQRSSTU	sequestrable
ABEEEMMNQRTU	embarquement
ABEEEMMPRSTY	May-September
ABEEEMPRSTTU	subtemperate
ABEEEOPRRSTT	obstreperate
ABEEEORRRRTV	reverberator
ABEEEPRRSTTY	presbyterate
ABEEFFILNRSU	insufferable
ABEEFFLNRSUU	unsufferable
ABEEFIILMNST	manifestible
ABEEFIILNRUV	unverifiable
ABEEFILLNRTU	unfilterable
ABEEFILMOPRR	imperforable
ABEEFILMORRR	irreformable
ABEEFKLNOORW	foreknowable
ABEEFLLMNSSU	blamefulness
ABEEFLLMSSSY	self-assembly
ABEEFLMNORRU	unreformable
ABEEGGIILNOR	globigerinae
ABEEGGILNRSS	beggarliness
ABEEGHINQRSU	queer-bashing
ABEEGHMNOOPR	Germanophobe
ABEEGIILNSTV	investigable
ABEEGIKNPSTU	speaking-tube
ABEEGILLNORT	bertillonage
ABEEGILNNPUX	inexpugnable
ABEEGILNNSSS	singableness
ABEEGILNNSST	tangibleness
ABEEGILNORRT	interrogable
ABEEGLNNORUV	ungovernable
ABEEGLNNPUUX	unexpugnable
ABEEHHIILOPP	ephebophilia
ABEEHIILMPRS	imperishable
ABEEHIKLRSTT	blatherskite
ABEEHILLMORT	thermolabile
ABEEHILLORTT	Bertholletia
ABEEHILNORTT	bletheration
ABEEHILNPRSU	unperishable
ABEEHILPRSST	pre-establish
ABEEHLLRSSTY	breathlessly
ABEEHLMORSTT	thermostable
ABEEHLNNOORR	blennorrhoea
ABEEHLOPRSST	blastosphere
ABEEHLORSTTW	bottle-washer
ABEEHLORSTTY	heteroblasty
ABEEIIILLLRS	illiberalise
ABEEIIILLLRZ	illiberalize
ABEEIILLOSTT	biosatellite
ABEEIILMNNRT	interminable
ABEEIILMNSST	imitableness
ABEEIILMPRTY	permeability
ABEEIILNNPSX	inexpansible
ABEEIILNPRTX	inextirpable

ABEEIILNPSST	pitiableness
ABEEIILORTTV	obliterative
ABEEIILPRRRS	irrespirable
ABEEIKMOPRRS	break-promise
ABEEILLNNRUV	invulnerable
ABEEILLNOPRT	interpolable
ABEEILLORRSV	irresolvable
ABEEILLPRSUV	pulverisable
ABEEILLPRUVZ	pulverizable
ABEEILMMNRSU	immensurable
ABEEILMMOORS	aeroembolism
ABEEILMNPRTY	impenetrably
ABEEILNOQSTU	questionable
ABEEILNPSSSS	passibleness
ABEEILNSSSTU	suitableness
ABEEILOORSSV	basso-relievo
ABEEILOPPRRX	expropriable
ABEEILOPRRRV	irreprovable
ABEEILPRRSTY	presbyterial
ABEEINNORSTV	Observantine
ABEEINORRTTV	vertebration
ABEEINORSSTV	abortiveness
ABEEINPRRSTY	△presbyterian
ABEEIOPRRTVX	exprobrative
ABEEIPRRTTUV	perturbative
ABEEKLLNOPST	pollen-basket
ABEEKLMORRTU	troublemaker
ABEEKLNNOSSW	knowableness
ABEEKLNORSSW	workableness
ABEEKORRSSTT	breaststroke
ABEELLLORTTY	trolley-table
ABEELLMNOPUY	unemployable
ABEELLNNRUUV	unvulnerable
ABEELLNORSUV	unresolvable
ABEELLNPRSUU	unrepulsable
ABEELLORSTUW	water-soluble
ABEELMMNNOTZ	emblazonment
ABEELMOOPSSS	pease-blossom
ABEELNNRRTUU	unreturnable
ABEELNNSSSTU	unstableness
ABEELNOPRRTU	unreportable
ABEELNOPRRUV	unreprovable
ABEELNOQSSTU	quotableness
ABEELNOSSSTU	absoluteness
ABEELNRSTTUU	unutterables
ABEELOPPRSSU	superposable
ABEELORSTTTU	trouble-state
ABEEMMRRSSTU	breastsummer
ABEENRSSSSTU	abstruseness
ABEERRRSSTUU	subtreasurer
ABEFFIIILNTY	ineffability
ABEFFILLLMOR	flabelliform
ABEFFILNRSUY	insufferably
ABEFGILNORRY	forbearingly
ABEFGILNORUV	unforgivable
ABEFGINNRRTU	afterburning
ABEFIIMNNORS	Febronianism
ABEFILLORTUU	Tubuliflorae
ABEFILMORRRY	irreformably
ABEFILNOPRTU	unprofitable
ABEFILNRSSTU	transfusible
ABEFIMNOORRU	neurofibroma
ABEFLNOSSSTU	boastfulness
ABEFLNOSSSUU	fabulousness
ABEGGHILLLMN	gambling-hell
ABEGGHIOOPRY	biogeography
ABEGGIILLNST	billingsgate
ABEGHHINOOPP	phengophobia
ABEGHHKORRTU	breakthrough
ABEGHIINNPSS	spine-bashing
ABEGHIKNOPRS	shopbreaking
ABEGHILNRRTW	night-brawler
ABEGHINNRRTU	heartburning
ABEGHLOPRSTU	breastplough
ABEGHNOOPRRS	snobographer
ABEGIILNRTTW	writing-table
ABEGIINRSSSU	agribusiness
ABEGIKLNNOOR	book-learning
ABEGILLLNOWY	bowling-alley
ABEGILLMORSU	semiglobular
ABEGILLNOOST	balneologist
ABEGILLOOOPY	paleobiology
ABEGILMNNPUU	unimpugnable
ABEGILNNPUXY	inexpugnably
ABEGILNNRTTU	table-turning
ABEGILRRSSST	bristle-grass
ABEGINNOSSTU	seasoning-tub
ABEGINORSSSU	agrobusiness
ABEGLMORSUUY	umbrageously
ABEGLNNORUVY	ungovernably
ABEHIIILRTTY	heritability
ABEHIIIMNNRS	Hibernianism
ABEHIILMPRSY	imperishably
ABEHIILNNRTY	labyrinthine
ABEHIILNOPST	inhospitable
ABEHIIMORSUV	behaviourism
	misbehaviour
ABEHIIORSTUV	behaviourist
ABEHIKLNNRSU	unshrinkable
ABEHILLNOPSU	unpolishable
ABEHILMNSSTT	stablishment
ABEHILNNPSUU	unpunishable
ABEHILNOPSTU	unhospitable
ABEHILNOPSTY	hypnotisable
ABEHILNOPTYZ	hypnotizable
ABEHILNORRTW	brother-in-law
ABEHILOOOPRU	ailourophobe
ABEHLORRSTTY	erythroblast
ABEIIILLLRTY	illiberality
ABEIIILLNNRT	brilliantine
ABEIIILRTVVY	revivability
ABEIILLLMPTU	multipliable
ABEIILLORTTY	tolerability
ABEIILMMORTY	memorability
ABEIILMNNNOS	innominables
ABEIILMNNRTY	interminably
ABEIILMNOPRS	imprisonable
ABEIILMNOSST	ambitionless
ABEIILMNRTUY	numerability
ABEIILMORTVY	removability
ABEIILMPTTTY	temptability
ABEIILNNOSTU	nebulisation
	sublineation
ABEIILNNOTUZ	nebulization

ABEIILNNTTUY	untenability
ABEIILNOORTT	obliteration
ABEIILNORRTT	interorbital
ABEIILOORSSV	basso-rilievo
ABEIILOQRRTU	equilibrator
ABEIIMNRSTUU	subminiature
ABEIINORSSTU	suberisation
ABEIINORSTUZ	suberization
ABEILLNNRUVY	invulnerably
ABEILLNOPPRT	bipropellant
ABEILLNORRTU	interlobular
ABEILLOPRRVY	proverbially
ABEILLORRSVY	irresolvably
ABEILMNOSUUX	exalbuminous
ABEILMOSSTUY	abstemiously
ABEILNOQSTUY	questionably
ABEILNORSSUY	Byelorussian
ABEILNORTTXY	exorbitantly
ABEILNRSTTUY	subalternity
ABEILOPRRRVY	irreprovably
ABEINOOPRRST	reabsorption
ABEINOOPRRTX	exprobration
ABEINOPRRTTU	perturbation
ABELLLLOPSYY	polysyllable
ABELLLMNOOSY	monosyllable
ABELLMMNOSSW	swell-mobsman
ABELLMOOPPSS	apple-blossom
ABELMNORSTUU	surmountable
ABELNOPPSSUU	unsupposable
ABEMOORSTTWY	bottom-sawyer
ABEOOPRRRTXY	exprobratory
ABEOPRRRTTUY	perturbatory
ABFGHIIMNORT	habit-forming
ABFGIIILNRTY	frangibility
ABFGIIILRTUY	figurability
ABFIIILLNORT	fibrillation
ABFIIILLRTTY	filtrability
ABFIIILNNOTU	infibulation
ABFILLLORTUU	tubulifloral
ABFILNOPRTUY	unprofitably
ABGGGIMNNORU	Munro-bagging
ABGGILLNOSSW	glass-blowing
ABGGILNNRSSU	burning-glass
ABGHHILORRTU	harbour-light
ABGHHINRSSUV	shaving-brush
ABGHHOORSSTU	thorough-bass
ABGHIILMNRSU	rhumb-sailing
ABGHIIMMNSTW	swimming-bath
ABGHILNOSSTT	shot-blasting
ABGIIIILNTTY	ignitability
ABGIIILLMNSU	bilingualism
ABGIILLNORTT	trolling-bait
ABGIILLOORTY	obligatorily
ABGILMNOPSUU	plumbaginous
ABGILNOORSTU	urbanologist
ABGIMNNORRST	barnstorming
ABHIIILORSSZ	bilharziosis
ABHIIKMNNPRS	brinkmanship
ABHIILNOPSTY	inhospitably
ABHIIMNNORTT	antithrombin
ABHIINOPRSTV	vibraphonist
ABHILNNPSUUY	unpunishably
ABHIMNNORRTU	Northumbrian
ABIIIILMSSTY	amissibility
ABIIIILRRTTY	irritability
ABIIILLPPTUY	pupilability
ABIIILLPSTUY	plausibility
ABIIILMMOTVY	immovability
ABIIILMMTTUY	immutability
ABIIILMNOOST	abolitionism
	mobilisation
ABIIILMNOOTZ	mobilization
ABIIILMPTTUY	imputability
ABIIILNNOOTT	nobilitation
ABIIILNOOSTT	abolitionist
ABIIILNRSTUY	insurability
ABIILLLMNSUY	subliminally
ABIILMMOOSTU	automobilism
ABIILMOOSTTU	automobilist
ABIILNOORSTT	strobilation
ABIILNORSSUU	insalubrious
ABIILOOPPSTY	opposability
ABIILOPRSTTY	sportability
ABIIMNORSTTU	tambourinist
ABIIOPRSTTVY	absorptivity
ABILLLMORTUU	multilobular
ABILLLNOOOPT	pilot-balloon
ABILLORSSUUY	salubriously
ABILMMMNOSSU	somnambulism
ABILMMNOSSTU	somnambulist
ABILMNORSTUY	subnormality
ABIMNORSSTTU	nimbostratus
ABIOPRRSTTTU	portrait-bust
ABLLMOORSTYY	symbololatry
ABLOOOPRSSTU	obstropalous
ABNOORRSSTUU	brontosaurus
ACCCDEEEELNS	decalescence
ACCCDEEENNOT	once-accented
ACCCDIIOOSTT	coccidiostat
ACCCEEEELNRS	recalescence
ACCCEEEGLNSU	glaucescence
ACCCEEEILNNS	incalescence
ACCCEEEINQSU	acquiescence
ACCCEEHMNOTU	accouchement
ACCCEEIILSST	ecclesiastic
ACCCEEILLLTY	eclectically
ACCCEELNOSTY	nectocalyces
ACCCEGIINNOR	carcinogenic
ACCCEHIILRTU	cicatrichule
ACCCEHINORTT	technocratic
ACCCEHINOSTU	Echinocactus
ACCCEHIOORSU	cichoraceous
ACCCEHKLORTW	clock-watcher
ACCCEIJMNRTU	circumjacent
ACCCEILNNORT	concentrical
ACCCEIMNNOOT	concomitance
ACCCEIMNRSTU	circumstance
ACCCENOPPRUY	preoccupancy
ACCCGHILOPRY	cyclographic
ACCCHHIILLOT	Chalcolithic
ACCCHIIOPRRT	chiropractic
ACCCHIIOPRSZ	schizocarpic
ACCCIILNNOTY	anticyclonic
ACCCIILNOOST	iconoclastic

ACCCIMNNOOSY	coscinomancy
ACCCIMNNOOTY	concomitancy
ACCCNOOORTTY	cottonocracy
ACCDDDEHIIKL	chick-a-diddle
ACCDDEEIIILN	Cicindelidae
ACCDDEEINRTU	unaccredited
ACCDDEHINOOP	dodecaphonic
ACCDEEEHLMNY	chance-medley
ACCDEEEILNPS	lapidescence
ACCDEEELORSU	cedrelaceous
ACCDEEENORST	deconsecrate
ACCDEEFIIRTT	certificated
ACCDEEHLRSTY	cradle-scythe
ACCDEEIIILPT	epideictical
ACCDEEIILNOT	indoleacetic
ACCDEEIKNOPT	patience-dock
ACCDEEILLOPS	peccadilloes
ACCDEEILNOPY	encyclopedia
ACCDEEINNNST	incandescent
ACCDEEINNORS	considerance
ACCDEEINNORT	concertinaed
ACCDEELNPSTU	unspectacled
ACCDEENOSSUU	succedaneous
ACCDEENRSSSU	accursedness
ACCDEHHNRRUW	churchwarden
ACCDEHILMOPS	accomplished
ACCDEHIOORSU	orchidaceous
ACCDEHLNNORR	corn-chandler
ACCDEIIILMST	dialecticism
ACCDEIILLOPS	piccadilloes
ACCDEIILLOPY	epicycloidal
ACCDEIILNNOT	coincidental
ACCDEILLNOTY	occidentally
ACCDEILNOORU	Cain-coloured
ACCDEILNOPTU	conduplicate
ACCDEILOOSUY	calycoideous
ACCDEIMNORTU	undemocratic
ACCDEINNORRT	androcentric
ACCDELNORTTY	contractedly
ACCDEMNOSTUU	unaccustomed
ACCDEOOPRSTY	despotocracy
ACCDFIIINOOT	codification
ACCDGIINNNSS	scanning-disc
ACCDGILOTYYZ	zygodactylic
ACCDIILOORSU	radicicolous
ACCDIIMNNOOU	incomunicado
ACCDIINOORST	accordionist
ACCDINOORRTT	contradictor
ACCDLNNOORTY	concordantly
ACCDLOOPSTYY	dactyloscopy
ACCEEEFFIOPR	peace-officer
ACCEEEHILNPP	epencephalic
ACCEEEHLORRT	heterocercal
ACCEEEILSSST	Ecclesiastes
ACCEEENNORVY	reconveyance
ACCEEENORRST	reconsecrate
ACCEEFGIIMNN	magnificence
ACCEEFHHIRTT	thief-catcher
ACCEEGHILNOT	geotechnical
ACCEEGILNNOR	congenerical
ACCEEGILNORT	geocentrical
ACCEEGINNORS	recognisance
ACCEEGINNORZ	recognizance
ACCEEHHILORT	chalicothere
ACCEEHHRRSTT	charter-chest
ACCEEHIILNPT	encephalitic
ACCEEHIKNSTU	chuckie-stane
ACCEEHILMOPS	mesocephalic
ACCEEHIMORTT	tacheometric
ACCEEHIORSSS	chassé-croisé
ACCEEHIORTTT	heterotactic
ACCEEHIRRTTU	architecture
ACCEEHLMNRSY	sclerenchyma
ACCEEHMNNORT	encroachment
ACCEEIINNORT	interoceanic
ACCEEIINNRSS	circassienne
ACCEEIINPPRT	precipitance
ACCEEIJNNRTY	interjacency
ACCEEILLLRTY	electrically
ACCEEILLMNUY	ecumenically
ACCEEILLOPST	telescopical
ACCEEILNPTTU	centuplicate
ACCEEILNRTTY	tetracycline
ACCEEINNPTXY	inexpectancy
ACCEEINOPSTU	pectinaceous
ACCEEINORSTV	consecrative
ACCEEIORSTTT	stereotactic
ACCEEKNOOPST	peacock-stone
ACCEELLOORTT	collectorate
ACCEELMPRTUU	receptaculum
ACCEELNNOSTV	convalescent
ACCEELNNRSTU	translucence
ACCEELPRRWYY	creepy-crawly
ACCEEMNORTTU	accouterment
	accoutrement
ACCEEMNRSTTU	accustrement
ACCEENNNORTU	countenancer
ACCEENNORSTU	unconsecrate
ACCEENOPRRSU	pre-cancerous
ACCEFFIIJKNO	△jack-in-office
ACCEFGIIINNS	significance
ACCEFHILMNSU	mischanceful
ACCEFHILMRTU	lucifer-match
ACCEFIIILNST	scientifical
ACCEFIILLPSY	specifically
ACCEFIILLRST	self-critical
ACCEFILLOORW	calico-flower
ACCEGGILNOOY	gynaecologic
ACCEGHHIOPRT	hectographic
ACCEGHILOOST	eschatologic
ACCEGHINOPRS	scenographic
ACCEGIIKNRSW	wisecracking
ACCEGIILMOST	cleistogamic
ACCEGIINNNOS	incognisance
ACCEGIINNNOZ	incognizance
ACCEGIINRTUX	excruciating
ACCEGILLLOOY	ecologically
ACCEGILLNOOR	necrological
ACCEGILNNNOU	unconcealing
ACCEGILNNORT	Anglocentric
ACCEGIMRRTUY	circumgyrate
ACCEGINNNOVY	conveyancing
ACCEGNOORRTY	gerontocracy
ACCEHHILOSSZ	eschscholzia

ACCEHIILLMRY	chimerically
ACCEHIILLNST	callisthenic
ACCEHIILMOOR	heroi-comical
ACCEHIILNOPR	necrophiliac
ACCEHIILNORR	rhinocerical
ACCEHIILNSST	calisthenics
ACCEHIILNTTY	technicality
ACCEHIIMNORT	cheiromantic
ACCEHIIMRSTT	chrematistic
ACCEHIIRRTTW	carriwitchet
ACCEHIIRSTTT	tetrastichic
ACCEHIKLMOOR	mock-heroical
ACCEHILLLORY	cholerically
ACCEHILMNOOR	melanochroic
ACCEHILMOPRS	accomplisher
ACCEHILMOPRY	microcephaly
	pyrochemical
ACCEHILNNNOT	non-technical
ACCEHILOORSU	orichalceous
ACCEHILOPRTY	chalcopyrite
ACCEHIMNORST	mechatronics
ACCEHIMOORST	mesothoracic
ACCEHIMORTTT	thermotactic
ACCEHIMPSSTY	metapsychics
ACCEHINNNOPT	pantechnicon
ACCEHINOOPRT	acrophonetic
ACCEHINORRTT	trochanteric
ACCEHINRSSST	scratchiness
ACCEHIOPSTVY	psychoactive
ACCEHKLOOSVZ	Czechoslovak
ACCEHLOORSSU	schorlaceous
ACCEHMNNORRT	corn-merchant
ACCEHMNORRTU	countercharm
	countermarch
ACCEHMOPSTUU	moustache-cup
ACCEHMORSTTU	scattermouch
ACCEHOOOPRST	thoracoscope
ACCEHOOPRSTY	tracheoscopy
ACCEIIILNOTV	conciliative
ACCEIIILPSST	specialistic
ACCEIIKKMNRS	camiknickers
ACCEIILLLNTY	enclitically
ACCEIILLOSST	solecistical
ACCEIILMMORT	microclimate
ACCEIILMNNOP	incompliance
ACCEIILMOORS	seriocomical
ACCEIILMOPTV	complicative
ACCEIILMRRSU	semicircular
ACCEIILNORTV	intervocalic
ACCEIILNRSST	criticalness
ACCEIILOPRRR	irreciprocal
ACCEIILOSSTV	viscoelastic
ACCEIILPRTUU	epicuticular
ACCEIILRSSTU	secularistic
ACCEIIMNOPRR	picrocarmine
ACCEIIMORRTT	meritocratic
ACCEIINORTUX	excruciation
ACCEIINPPRTY	precipitancy
ACCEIIOPRSUV	pervicacious
ACCEIIPPRSTY	perspicacity
ACCEIKKKKNNT	knick-knacket
ACCEIKKNNRSS	snicker-snack
ACCEIKLOPRTT	kleptocratic
ACCEILLMMORY	commercially
ACCEILLMNOOY	economically
ACCEILLMOSTY	cosmetically
ACCEILLNNORT	centroclinal
ACCEILLNOTTY	tectonically
ACCEILLNSTYY	synectically
ACCEILLOPRRY	reciprocally
ACCEILMMNORU	uncommercial
ACCEILMNNOOU	uneconomical
ACCEILMNORTU	counter-claim
ACCEILMOPRSU	microcapsule
ACCEILNNOOTV	convectional
ACCEILNOORRT	correctional
ACCEILNOSSSU	successional
ACCEILOPRSST	ceroplastics
ACCEILOPRSTY	paleocrystic
ACCEIMNNOORT	concremation
ACCEIMNOSTTY	nematocystic
ACCEIMNRTTUU	circumnutate
ACCEINNNNOOS	inconsonance
ACCEINNOORST	consecration
ACCEINOOPRTU	reoccupation
ACCEIOOPRRRT	reciprocator
ACCEIORSTTUV	curvicostate
ACCEKNNORSTU	snack-counter
ACCELLMNOPTY	complacently
ACCELLOOORSU	corollaceous
ACCELLOORTTX	tax-collector
ACCELNNRSTUY	translucency
ACCELNOOPPRY	cyclopropane
ACCELNSSSTUY	successantly
ACCELOOOPSSU	scolopaceous
ACCENNOORRTT	concentrator
ACCENOOOPRRT	concorporate
ACCENOORRSTY	consecratory
ACCENOPRRSTU	counterscarp
ACCFGIIINNSY	significancy
ACCFIIIINOTT	citification
ACCFIIINOTTY	cityfication
ACCFIIMNNOSU	Confucianism
ACCFIINNOOST	confiscation
ACCFIINNOSTU	Confucianist
ACCFILLNOOTU	flocculation
ACCFILNOORST	olfactronics
ACCFINOORSTY	confiscatory
ACCGHHIINOPR	ichnographic
ACCGHHIOOPRR	chorographic
ACCGHHIORSTY	hygrochastic
ACCGHIIKNORR	rocking-chair
ACCGHIIMOPRR	micrographic
ACCGHIIMOTTT	thigmotactic
ACCGHIINOPRZ	zincographic
ACCGHIIOPPRT	pictographic
ACCGHILLOOOR	chorological
ACCGHILLOOPY	phycological
ACCGHILNRSTY	scratchingly
ACCGHIMOOPRS	cosmographic
ACCGIILLMOOR	micrological
ACCGIILLOOOS	sociological
ACCGILLMOOOS	cosmological
ACCGILMNOOOS	cosmogonical

ACCGILNORTUY	granulocytic
ACCHHIIIRSSS	rachischisis
ACCHHIILLNRU	Churchillian
ACCHHIINRTUY	churchianity
ACCHHILLOOTY	ichthyocolla
ACCHHINOORTX	xanthochroic
ACCHHIOPPSTY	psychopathic
ACCHHLMNORUW	Low-Churchman
ACCHIIINSTUV	chauvinistic
ACCHIILOOPPS	scopophiliac
ACCHIILOPRTY	hypocritical
ACCHIIMMORST	chromaticism
ACCHIIMNOOST	iconomachist
ACCHIIMNOPTY	amphictyonic
ACCHIIMNORST	monarchistic
ACCHIIMOORST	isochromatic
ACCHIIMORRTT	trichromatic
ACCHIIMORTTY	chromaticity
ACCHIIOPRSTY	physiocratic
ACCHILLNNOOO	non-alcoholic
ACCHILLOPTTY	phyllotactic
ACCHILNNORSY	synchronical
ACCHILNOPRTY	lycanthropic
ACCHILOOPSSY	psychosocial
ACCHILOPPRTY	prophylactic
ACCHIMNOOPPT	phonocamptic
ACCHINOOOPSU	cacophonious
ACCHINOOPSTT	phonotactics
ACCHIOOPRRRT	chiropractor
ACCHIOOPRSTT	octastrophic
ACCHIOOPRTTT	trophotactic
ACCHIOORRSSU	chiaroscuros
ACCHIOOSSTTU	octastichous
ACCIIILNNOOT	conciliation
ACCIIINRSSST	narcissistic
ACCIILLNRTUY	uncritically
ACCIILLOPRTY	pictorically
ACCIILMMOORT	microtomical
ACCIILMNOOPT	complication
ACCIILNOORTY	conciliatory
ACCIILOPRSUY	capriciously
ACCIIMOOPRTT	compatriotic
ACCIINNOOOST	consociation
ACCIINNOOPTU	inoccupation
ACCIJLNNOTUV	conjunctival
ACCILLNOOTTU	colluctation
ACCILLORTUUV	vocicultural
ACCILMOOPSST	cosmoplastic
ACCILNOPRSTY	prostacyclin
ACCILNOSSTTU	sansculottic
ACCILOPRSSTY	pyroclastics
ACCIMMNOORTU	communicator
ACCIMNOOSSTU	cosmonautics
ACCIMNOOSTUU	contumacious
ACCINOSSSTUU	succussation
ACCIOOOPSTTU	optoacoustic
ACCIOOPRSSTU	stauroscopic
ACDDDEEHNOOR	dodecahedron
ACDDDEEINSST	addictedness
ACDDDEFGINPU	pudding-faced
ACDDDENOORSU	dodecandrous
ACDDEEEFLSTU	self-educated
ACDDEEEHIMST	semi-detached
ACDDEEEHNSST	detachedness
ACDDEEELLTUW	well-educated
ACDDEEHLLNOR	candle-holder
ACDDEEHORRST	hard-sectored
ACDDEEIIMNST	demi-distance
ACDDEEILNNOU	duodecennial
ACDDEEILNTTU	denticulated
ACDDEEIMOSSU	Discomedusae
ACDDEEIMOSTT	domesticated
ACDDEELNPTUU	pedunculated
ACDDEFNNNOOR	cannon-fodder
ACDDEGHIMNPS	camp-shedding
ACDDEGHINRSU	undischarged
ACDDEGIINNRS	discandering
ACDDEGNOOSUY	dodecagynous
ACDDEHIKLRUY	hydraulicked
ACDDEHINORSU	deuch-an-doris
ACDDEHINPSTU	undispatched
ACDDEIIIPRSV	disprivacied
ACDDEIILNORU	radionuclide
ACDDEIILNPTU	induplicated
ACDDEIINNOTV	non-addictive
ACDDEIINORST	endocarditis
ACDDEILLOSTY	dislocatedly
ACDDEILNOOST	consolidated
ACDDEILRSTTY	distractedly
ACDDEIMNOSSU	discomedusan
ACDDEINNNSSU	uncandidness
ACDDEINOOPST	paedodontics
ACDDEINRSTTU	undistracted
ACDDEMOPRSSU	mass-produced
ACDDENNNOOPR	pro-and-conned
ACDDGIKLNOSU	sack-doudling
ACDDHHIIMNOT	diamond-hitch
ACDDHIMNORYY	hydrodynamic
ACDDIIIJNOTU	dijudication
ACDDIIILNOTU	dilucidation
ACDDILNORSTY	discordantly
ACDDINNORSTU	undiscordant
ACDDKLOOOPST	paddock-stool
ACDEEEFFFLST	self-affected
ACDEEEFFLLTW	well-affected
ACDEEEFFNSST	affectedness
ACDEEEGINOPT	paedogenetic
ACDEEEGKLLRT	ledger-tackle
ACDEEEHINRUV	underachieve
ACDEEEHKLNRT	halter-necked
ACDEEEIIPRTV	depreciative
ACDEEEILNOPV	velocipedean
ACDEEEILNORT	deceleration
ACDEEEILNPRT	precedential
ACDEEEILNRST	decentralise
ACDEEEILNRTV	cantilevered
ACDEEEILNRTZ	decentralize
ACDEEEILNRUZ	denuclearize
ACDEEEILNSST	delicateness
	delicatessen
ACDEEEINNRTV	inadvertence
ACDEEEINRSSV	disseverance
ACDEEEKNNRSS	cankeredness
ACDEEELNNOSU	endonuclease

ACDEEELNNTTY	antecedently
ACDEEFFLNTUY	unaffectedly
ACDEEFHHIKNR	handkerchief
ACDEEFHNORRW	henceforward
ACDEEFIINRRY	ferricyanide
ACDEEFILLNOT	deflectional
ACDEEFILMTTU	multifaceted
ACDEEFINORRY	ferrocyanide
ACDEEFNRRSUU	undersurface
ACDEEGGNRSSS	scraggedness
ACDEEGHILRST	clear-sighted
ACDEEGHLLNNU	unchallenged
ACDEEGIINOPT	doating-piece
ACDEEGILLOTY	geodetically
ACDEEGILNORS	close-grained
ACDEEGILNOSS	cladogenesis
ACDEEGILNRSY	decreasingly
ACDEEGILORVV	gravel-voiced
ACDEEGINRSSS	dressing-case
ACDEEGKNOTTU	tongue-tacked
ACDEEGNNORSS	gas-condenser
ACDEEGNNOSTT	decongestant
ACDEEHHILORX	hexachloride
ACDEEHHOOPRY	Rhodophyceae
ACDEEHIILLTT	△ditheletical
ACDEEHIINNRS	Schneiderian
ACDEEHIKLPSS	sickle-shaped
ACDEEHILLOOS	de-alcoholise
ACDEEHILLOOZ	de-alcoholize
ACDEEHILLORW	orchilla-weed
ACDEEHILMNOR	echinodermal
ACDEEHILNNOP	diencephalon
ACDEEHILNNRT	Netherlandic
ACDEEHIMNNSU	unmechanised
ACDEEHIMNNUZ	unmechanized
ACDEEHIMNRRS	merchandiser
ACDEEHIMNRRZ	merchandizer
ACDEEHINNRST	disenchanter
ACDEEHISSTTY	dysaesthetic
ACDEEHLORTTY	heterodactyl
ACDEEHMNORSW	reach-me-downs
ACDEEHNNOPRU	unchaperoned
ACDEEHNOPRRU	unreproached
ACDEEHNRSSST	starchedness
ACDEEIILLMPY	epidemically
ACDEEIILLNTY	indelicately
ACDEEIILLTTY	dietetically
ACDEEIILNOPV	velocipedian
ACDEEIIMNRTY	intermediacy
ACDEEIINOPRT	depreciation
ACDEEIINQSTU	equidistance
ACDEEIINTTUX	inexactitude
ACDEEIIOOPRS	aecidiospore
ACDEEIKLOOPS	kaleidoscope
ACDEEILLNNOS	declensional
ACDEEILLRTUV	culvertailed
	revictualled
ACDEEILMNPST	displacement
ACDEEILMORRS	sclerodermia
ACDEEILMRTUV	vermiculated
ACDEEILNNNOU	non-Euclidean
ACDEEILNNOSS	descensional
ACDEEILNOOPY	Lycopodineae
ACDEEILNSSST	distanceless
ACDEEILORTUV	edulcorative
ACDEEILORTVY	decoratively
ACDEEILRTTVY	detractively
ACDEEILSTTTU	testiculated
ACDEEIMNNOPR	predominance
ACDEEIMORRTX	xerodermatic
ACDEEINNOOTT	Notonectidae
ACDEEINNOPRR	preordinance
ACDEEINNRTVY	inadvertency
ACDEEINOOPRT	coin-operated
ACDEEINOOPRV	overcanopied
ACDEEINOORRT	redecoration
ACDEEINOPRTU	deuteranopic
ACDEEINOSSSU	edaciousness
ACDEEIOPPRTU	propaedeutic
ACDEEIOPRRTY	depreciatory
ACDEEKMPRRSU	muckspreader
ACDEELMNNOTT	malcontented
ACDEELNNNOTU	non-nucleated
ACDEELNOPRTU	counter-paled
	counterplead
ACDEELOPRRRY	record-player
ACDEELOPRTTY	pterodactyle
ACDEEMNOPPTY	appendectomy
ACDEEMOPSTTY	stapedectomy
ACDEENNNOTUV	uncovenanted
ACDEENNNRSTT	transcendent
ACDEENNNRTUY	undertenancy
ACDEENNOOPRV	over-cannoped
ACDEENOORSTU	Neoceratodus
ACDEEOORRSSU	droseraceous
ACDEFFIINOST	disaffection
ACDEFHIINRSS	disfranchise
ACDEFHINNRSU	unfranchised
ACDEFIIIMOTV	modificative
ACDEFIILNNOT	confidential
ACDEFIILNSSU	unclassified
ACDEFIILNSTY	sanctifiedly
ACDEFIINNSTT	disinfectant
ACDEFIINNSTU	unsanctified
ACDEFIINOORT	deforciation
ACDEFILLLOTU	folliculated
ACDEFIMMOOPR	campodeiform
ACDEGHILNRRU	hurdle-racing
ACDEGHIOPRRS	discographer
ACDEGIILPQRU	quadriplegic
ACDEGIIMNNOR	Indo-Germanic
ACDEGIIOOPRT	diageotropic
ACDEGIKNNRSW	sneck-drawing
ACDEGIKNRSSS	dressing-sack
ACDEGILLOOTY	dialectology
ACDEGILNNOST	long-distance
ACDEGILNRTTY	detractingly
ACDEGILNTUUU	unguiculated
ACDEGINORRSS	cross-grained
ACDEGKLLOORS	slockdolager
ACDEGKNORRTU	racket-ground
ACDEGNORRTUU	counter-guard
ACDEHHIILNOR	chiliahedron
ACDEHHLOSTTU	slouch-hatted

ACDEHHOORRSU orchard-house
ACDEHIIILSTT ditheistical
ACDEHIIIRRTU Trichiuridae
ACDEHIILMMOT immethodical
ACDEHIIMNNOT indomethacin
ACDEHIIMNOOR Chironomidae
ACDEHIIPRTYY hyperacidity
ACDEHILLMOTY methodically
ACDEHILMNOTU unmethodical
ACDEHILOOPRT orthopedical
ACDEHILORSTY hydroelastic
ACDEHIMNRRSS scrimshander
ACDEHIMOOPPR paedomorphic
ACDEHIOOPRST orthopaedics
ACDEHLPRTYYY hyperdactyly
ACDEHLPSTTTU Platt-Deutsch
ACDEHMMNOORT doom-merchant
ACDEHMNNOORS enchondromas
ACDEHMOOOSTT smooth-coated
ACDEHMOPRSUY pachydermous
ACDEIIILNSTU unidealistic
ACDEIIILNTVY indicatively
ACDEIIILOSSS dissocialise
ACDEIIILOSSZ dissocialize
ACDEIIILRTVY veridicality
ACDEIIIMMORT radiomimetic
ACDEIIIMNNOT nicotinamide
ACDEIIIMNNRS incendiarism
ACDEIIIMNRST discriminate
ACDEIIIMORST isodiametric
ACDEIIINOPRT antiperiodic
ACDEIIINPPST appendicitis
ACDEIIINRSTT disintricate
ACDEIIINRTTU antidiuretic
ACDEIIIOPRTY aperiodicity
ACDEIIIOSSTV dissociative
ACDEIIIPRRST pericarditis
ACDEIILLNNTY incidentally
ACDEIILLOPRY periodically
ACDEIILLOPSY episodically
ACDEIILNOPTU pediculation
ACDEIILNORST discretional
ACDEIILNOSSU unsocialised
ACDEIILNOSUZ unsocialized
ACDEIILRRTUV diverticular
ACDEIIMNOSTU miseducation
ACDEIIMOPRRT madreporitic
ACDEIINNNOTU denunciation
ACDEIINNOORT inco-ordinate
ACDEIINNOOTT conditionate
ACDEIINNOPRT pentacrinoid
ACDEIINNORTT indoctrinate
ACDEIINOORTV co-ordinative
ACDEIINOOTTX detoxication
ACDEIINOPSTT disceptation
ACDEIINOSTTU educationist
ACDEIINRSSTV vindicatress
ACDEIIPRSTTU tricuspidate
ACDEIJLNTUVY adjunctively
ACDEIKNORSTT stock-in-trade
ACDEILLMOOSU Molluscoidea
ACDEILLMOSTY domestically
ACDEILLMRSUY scullery-maid
ACDEILLNSTYY syndetically
ACDEILLOOPSY Lycopodiales
ACDEILLOPSTU leucoplastid
ACDEILLOPSTY despotically
ACDEILMNOPRU unproclaimed
ACDEILMNOSUY mendaciously
ACDEILMOPSTU deutoplasmic
ACDEILNOOORT decoloration
ACDEILNOORTU edulcoration
ACDEILNOORTY co-ordinately
ACDEILNOOSST disconsolate
ACDEILNOPRSS cross-and-pile
ACDEILNORSSW cowardliness
ACDEILNTTUUV uncultivated
ACDEILOORRUV varicoloured
ACDEILRRTTUU turriculated
ACDEIMMNNOOT commendation
ACDEIMMNORTY dynamometric
ACDEIMMOOORR air-commodore
ACDEIMNNNOOT condemnation
ACDEIMNNOPRY predominancy
ACDEIMNORRRS morris-dancer
ACDEIMOORSTT domesticator
ACDEIMOPRSTU promuscidate
ACDEINNNOOST condensation
ACDEINNNOSTU unsanctioned
ACDEINNORRTU counter-drain
ACDEINNORTTU detruncation
ACDEINNORTUY denunciatory
ACDEINOOPRRT incorporated
ACDEINOPRTTV privat-docent
ACDEINORRRSU sound-carrier
ACDEINORRTUV turacoverdin
ACDEINORSTTU decrustation
ACDEIOOPRRST discorporate
ACDEIPRRTTVY party-verdict
ACDELMNOORUY many-coloured
ACDELNOORTYY cotyledonary
ACDELNOPRRUU unprocedural
ACDELOPRRTTY protractedly
ACDEMMMNNOST Commandments
ACDEMMNOORTY commendatory
ACDEMNNOORTY condemnatory
ACDENNPTTUUU unpunctuated
ACDEORSTTTUU autodestruct
ACDFIIIINNOT nidification
ACDFIIIMNOOT modification
ACDFIIMOORTY modificatory
ACDGGHIINNNW wind-changing
ACDGGIINORSU discouraging
ACDGHHIOPRRY hydrographic
ACDGHILLOORY hydrological
ACDGHIMNOOTW doomwatching
ACDGIIINRSTV visiting-card
ACDGIIKNNRST skirt-dancing
ACDGIILOORST cardiologist
ACDGILLOOTYY dactyliology
ACDGILMMNNOY commandingly
ACDGINOOOPRT gonadotropic
ACDHHIIKNNTT thick-and-thin
ACDHHIMNOORR harmonichord

ACDHHINOOPRY	hypochondria
ACDHHINOORTX	xanthochroid
ACDHIIMMORST	dichromatism
ACDHIIMNOORT	mitochondria
ACDHIINOOPRS	radiophonics
ACDHIIOPRSTT	dictatorship
ACDHILNOSSUY	lady's-cushion
ACDHINNOORST	chondrostian
ACDHINOOPQRU	quadrophonic
ACDHINOPSSTT	pitch-and-toss
ACDHIORSSTTY	hydrostatics
ACDHNRSTTTUU	cut-and-thrust
ACDIIIJLLNUY	injudicially
ACDIIILNNPST	disciplinant
ACDIIILNPRSY	disciplinary
ACDIIILOSSTY	dissociality
ACDIIIMNNRST	discriminant
ACDIIIMNORTV	mid-Victorian
ACDIIINNOORT	air-condition
ACDIIINOOSST	dissociation
ACDIIIOSSTTU	adscititious
ACDIILLMNPTU	multiplicand
ACDIILLOOPSU	lapidicolous
ACDIILMNOPTU	undiplomatic
ACDIILNOOQTU	coloquintida
ACDIINNOOORT	co-ordination
ACDIINORSSYY	idiosyncrasy
ACDIIOORRSUV	radicivorous
ACDILLMOOORX	loxodromical
ACDILLOOPRSY	prosodically
ACDILLOOPSUU	paludicolous
ACDILMNSSTYY	syndactylism
ACDILMOOPRSU	cladosporium
ACDILMOORSUY	mordaciously
ACDILNNOOSTU	non-custodial
ACDILNOOORST	consolidator
ACDILNOOPRTU	productional
ACDILNORSUUU	iracundulous
ACDILORSTTUY	tridactylous
ACDIMMMOOTUY	mycodomatium
ACDIMOORRRTY	dormitory-car
ACDINNORSTTU	transduction
ACDINOOQRSTU	conquistador
ACDLNOSSTUYY	syndactylous
ACDLOOOPRSTT	post-doctoral
ACEEEEFJKRRT	reefer-jacket
ACEEEEGIKNPP	peace-keeping
ACEEEEGILPTX	epexegetical
ACEEEEHLPSST	steeplechase
ACEEEEHRSSTT	cheesetaster
ACEEEELNORTT	coelenterate
ACEEEELNPRSS	pearl-essence
ACEEEENPRRSV	perseverance
ACEEEFILLNRS	self-reliance
ACEEEFLNPSSU	peacefulness
ACEEEFNNRRST	transference
ACEEEGHINPRS	cheeseparing
ACEEEGHNNRTU	enterchaunge
ACEEEGIKNRRT	racketeering
ACEEEGILLTXY	exegetically
ACEEEGINNOSS	caenogenesis
ACEEEGINRRST	generatrices
ACEEEGNNRRUY	unregeneracy
ACEEEHHLRRTU	eleutherarch
ACEEEHHLRTTW	ratchet-wheel
ACEEEHIISSTT	aestheticise
ACEEEHIISTTZ	aestheticize
ACEEEHILSTTT	telaesthetic
ACEEEHIMNQTU	cinematheque
	cinemathèque
ACEEEHINOSST	coenesthesia
ACEEEHIRRSTV	heart-service
ACEEEHLNNOPP	epencephalon
ACEEEHMORRTT	trocheameter
ACEEEHMORTTT	cathetometer
ACEEEHNOORTT	Heterocontae
ACEEEILLLNTT	lenticellate
ACEEEILNNNSV	Valenciennes
ACEEEILRTVXY	execratively
ACEEEIMMNNPR	impermanence
ACEEEIMNNPRT	intemperance
ACEEEIMNRSVX	ex-serviceman
ACEEEINNPRST	scene-painter
ACEEEINRSSTV	creativeness
	reactiveness
ACEEEIPPPRTV	apperceptive
ACEEEIPRRTUV	recuperative
ACEEEIRRRRTV	river-terrace
ACEEELLOPRTT	electroplate
ACEEELMOPRST	spermatocele
ACEEELNNSTVY	evanescently
ACEEELNOTXYY	oxy-acetylene
ACEEELNRSSSS	carelessness
ACEEEMNNNRTT	entrancement
ACEEENNNPRTU	unrepentance
ACEEENNRRTTY	tercentenary
ACEEENNRSTXY	sexcentenary
ACEEEPPPRRST	pepper-caster
ACEEERRSSSTW	watercresses
ACEEFFFGILNS	self-effacing
ACEEFFIKLRTT	raffle-ticket
ACEEFFILSTUX	exsufflicate
ACEEFFILTTUY	effectuality
ACEEFFINOTTU	effectuation
ACEEFGHIMNST	Gemeinschaft
ACEEFGHLLSST	Gesellschaft
ACEEFGIINRSS	fricasseeing
ACEEFGILLNNS	self-cleaning
ACEEFGILNRST	self-catering
ACEEFGIRRSTU	figure-caster
ACEEFGLLNNOT	falcon-gentle
ACEEFGLMORRT	reflectogram
ACEEFGLNRSSU	gracefulness
ACEEFHIINSST	chieftainess
ACEEFHIORSTU	chaetiferous
ACEEFHLOPRRS	self-reproach
ACEEFHMNNRTT	fent-merchant
ACEEFIILNQTU	liquefacient
ACEEFIIPRTTV	petrifactive
ACEEFIKNNNRS	frankincense
ACEEFILLNRTY	frenetically
ACEEFILLRTTT	cattle-lifter
ACEEFILNNORT	conferential
ACEEFILNORST	self-creation

ACEEFILOPRRT	prefectorial
ACEEFIMPRRTU	picture-frame
ACEEFINOPRTT	perfectation
ACEEFINPRTTU	putrefacient
ACEEFINPSTTU	stupefacient
ACEEFIPRTTUV	putrefactive
ACEEFIPSTTUV	stupefactive
ACEEFLLNPUUY	unpeacefully
ACEEFLOPPRST	craftspeople
ACEEFNOPPRST	copper-fasten
ACEEGGHINNPR	crepehanging
ACEEGGHNPRSS	sprechgesang
ACEEGGINNRSV	scavengering
ACEEGGIORSTT	geostrategic
ACEEGGNORTUU	counter-gauge
ACEEGHIKMNPS	speechmaking
ACEEGHIKNNRT	kitchen-range
ACEEGHIKNPST	packing-sheet
ACEEGHILLMNS	mischallenge
ACEEGHILNNOT	genethliacon
ACEEGHILNNTW	canting-wheel
ACEEGHILNOSU	chaise-longue
ACEEGHILPRSY	hyperalgesic
ACEEGHIMNPST	camp-sheeting
ACEEGHINNRRT	interchanger
ACEEGHINOPTT	pathogenetic
ACEEGHIRRSST	cash-register
ACEEGHLNRTUY	legacy-hunter
ACEEGHLOPRRT	electrograph
ACEEGHLORSTV	grave-clothes
ACEEGHMNNORY	money-changer
ACEEGHNOPRRR	necrographer
ACEEGHPRRRSU	supercharger
ACEEGIILMNSV	evangelicism
ACEEGIILNSTV	evangelistic
ACEEGIIMNORT	geometrician
ACEEGIIOTTVX	excogitative
ACEEGIKLNPRT	tangle-picker
ACEEGIKMSSST	message-stick
ACEEGIKNNRRV	nerve-racking
ACEEGILLLOOT	teleological
ACEEGILLLRTY	telergically
ACEEGILLMNOT	metallogenic
ACEEGILLNRSV	silver-glance
ACEEGILLNTUY	geniculately
ACEEGILNNPST	nesting-place
ACEEGILNPRST	resting-place
ACEEGILQRRSU	squirrel-cage
ACEEGIMNORST	miscegenator
ACEEGINNOSSY	cyanogenesis
ACEEGINNRSTV	ingravescent
ACEEGLLMMORU	gram-molecule
ACEEGLLOOOPY	paleoecology
ACEEGLMNOORT	conglomerate
ACEEGMNOPRRT	carpetmonger
ACEEGNNORTTU	counter-agent
ACEEGOPRRSSU	supercargoes
ACEEHHILPRTT	terephthalic
ACEEHHIOPSTT	Theopaschite
ACEEHHIOPTTT	theopathetic
ACEEHHIPPRRS	preachership
ACEEHHIPRRSU	hire-purchase
ACEEHHLLORTT	leather-cloth
ACEEHHLMNRTY	nychthemeral
ACEEHHLORTTW	weathercloth
ACEEHHMOPRTY	chemotherapy
ACEEHHOPRSTU	chapterhouse
ACEEHHOPRTTY	tracheophyte
ACEEHHORRSTU	Charterhouse
ACEEHIIKNSTT	kinaesthetic
ACEEHIILLNRT	trichinellae
ACEEHIILMNOS	isocheimenal
ACEEHIILNPST	encephalitis
ACEEHIILPPRR	peripherical
ACEEHIIMPRRT	epirrhematic
ACEEHIIMPRTU	perichaetium
ACEEHIIMSSTT	aestheticism
ACEEHIINORTT	theoretician
ACEEHIISSTTT	aestheticist
ACEEHIKKNNTV	kitchen-knave
ACEEHIKLMNRT	merchantlike
ACEEHILLMORS	Hemerocallis
ACEEHILLMRTY	hermetically
ACEEHILMNRRU	machine-ruler
ACEEHILMORRT	rheometrical
ACEEHILNORSS	heroicalness
ACEEHILNPQSU	Chaplinesque
ACEEHILOPRSX	exospherical
ACEEHIMNPRST	parchmentise
ACEEHIMNPRTZ	parchmentize
ACEEHIMNSSTT	chastisement
ACEEHINNRSTU	neurasthenic
ACEEHINOPRRT	cheiropteran
ACEEHINPRRTT	interchapter
ACEEHINSSTTY	synaesthetic
ACEEHIOOPRST	aethrioscope
ACEEHIPRRSTU	creatureship
ACEEHIPRRTUY	curietherapy
ACEEHIPRSTTU	therapeutics
ACEEHIRSSTTV	tsesarevitch
ACEEHIRSSTTW	tsesarewitch
ACEEHKKNORRS	horse-knacker
ACEEHLLLORST	Rochelle-salt
ACEEHLLOORSV	school-leaver
ACEEHLLOPSWY	peach-yellows
ACEEHLLRRRUY	cherry-laurel
ACEEHLMNNOTU	luncheon-meat
ACEEHLMOPRTY	cephalometry
ACEEHLOPRRSS	reproachless
ACEEHNNSSSTU	unchasteness
ACEEHOPPRRRS	sharecropper
ACEEIIIMNOST	semeiotician
ACEEIILLRTTV	verticillate
ACEEIILMMPRT	metempirical
ACEEIILMORTT	meteoritical
ACEEIILMPRRT	perimetrical
ACEEIILMRRSU	mercurialise
ACEEIILMRRUZ	mercurialize
ACEEIILNOPRS	porcelainise
ACEEIILNOPRZ	porcelainize
ACEEIILNORST	neorealistic
ACEEIILNOSST	sectionalise
ACEEIILNOSTZ	sectionalize
ACEEIIMMRSTT	meristematic

ACEEIIMNNORT	enantiomeric
ACEEIIMNPRSU	Epicureanism
ACEEIINNORST	containerise
ACEEIINNORTZ	containerize
ACEEIINNRTUV	renunciative
ACEEIINORSTV	evisceration
ACEEIINORTTX	exercitation
ACEEIINPPPRT	appercipient
ACEEIINRRSST	irresistance
ACEEIJMNSSST	majesticness
ACEEIKNNRSTT	tennis-racket
ACEEILLLNTTU	intellectual
ACEEILLMNORY	ceremonially
ACEEILLMNSTY	centesimally
ACEEILLMNTUV	multivalence
ACEEILLMOPTV	compellative
ACEEILLMORTY	meteorically
ACEEILLNNORT	crenellation
ACEEILLNOPRS	porcellanise
ACEEILLNOPRT	porcellanite
ACEEILLNOPRZ	porcellanize
ACEEILLNORTY	neoterically
ACEEILLNRSUV	surveillance
ACEEILLORSTY	esoterically
ACEEILLORTXY	exoterically
ACEEILLRTTUY	reticulately
ACEEILMMNPST	misplacement
ACEEILMNNOTV	nomenclative
ACEEILMNOPRU	police-manure
ACEEILMNOPTY	pinealectomy
ACEEILNOPPRT	perceptional
ACEEILNOPRSS	precessional
ACEEILNOPRTU	inoperculate
ACEEILNORTUX	exulceration
ACEEILNRSSTV	verticalness
ACEEILOOPRRS	corporealise
ACEEILOOPRRZ	corporealize
ACEEILOPPRRT	preceptorial
ACEEILPPRSTV	perspectival
ACEEILRRTTVY	retractively
ACEEIMMMNOTT	committeeman
ACEEIMMNNPRY	impermanency
ACEEIMMOOSST	semicomatose
ACEEIMMPRTUY	empyreumatic
ACEEIMNNOORR	oneiromancer
ACEEIMNNORTT	conterminate
ACEEIMNOPSTV	compensative
ACEEIMNORSSX	cross-examine
ACEEIMNORSVW	servicewoman
ACEEIMNRTTUV	centumvirate
ACEEINNRRTTY	tricentenary
ACEEINOORRTV	overreaction
ACEEINOPPPRT	apperception
ACEEINOPRRRT	carton-pierre
ACEEINOPRRTU	recuperation
ACEEINOPRSTT	inspectorate
ACEEINOPSTTX	expectations
ACEEINORSTVV	△conservative
	conversative
ACEEIORSTTUY	stereoacuity
ACEEIRRSTTUY	treasure-city
ACEEJKKMNOTY	monkey-jacket
ACEEKLLOSTTY	cytoskeletal
ACEELLMMNOPT	complemental
ACEELLMOPTTY	patellectomy
ACEELLOOPRRT	electropolar
ACEELMNNORTU	nomenclature
ACEELMNOOSTU	lomentaceous
ACEELMNOPTTU	outplacement
ACEELMPRRTUU	permaculture
ACEELNOPSSTT	Pentecostals
ACEELNSSSSTT	tactlessness
ACEELPSSTUUY	eucalyptuses
ACEEMMNORSTU	commensurate
ACEEMNNNNOTU	announcement
ACEEMNNNOTUU	mountenaunce
ACEEMNNORRST	remonstrance
ACEEMOPRSTTY	spermatocyte
ACEENOPRSTUU	percutaneous
ACEEOOPRRTTT	△protectorate
ACEEOOPRRTTX	expectorator
ACEEOPPPRRST	pepper-castor
ACEEOPRRRTUY	recuperatory
ACEFFIIILMOS	semi-official
ACEFFIIKNNPS	Pecksniffian
ACEFFIINRRTT	intertraffic
ACEFFILNNSSU	fancifulness
ACEFFORRSUUU	furfuraceous
ACEFGHHLPRSU	sprachgefühl
ACEFGHIINRTW	fire-watching
ACEFGIIILMNS	facsimileing
ACEFGIIKNNRV	carving-knife
ACEFGILLNNOT	falcon-gentil
ACEFGILORSSU	self-gracious
ACEFGLLNRUUY	ungracefully
ACEFHHHIRSTY	fish-hatchery
ACEFHIIMNRTU	fruit-machine
ACEFHLNSSTUW	watchfulness
ACEFHNORSTTU	countershaft
ACEFIIIKLNRT	fairnitickle
ACEFIIILNOST	fictionalise
ACEFIIILNOTT	felicitation
ACEFIIILNOTZ	fictionalize
ACEFIIINORTV	verification
ACEFIIIPRTUV	purificative
ACEFIIKLNRTY	fairnytickle
ACEFIILLNNOT	inflectional
ACEFIILLRRTY	terrifically
ACEFIILNOQTU	liquefaction
ACEFIILORSTU	laticiferous
ACEFIILORTUV	curvifoliate
ACEFIILPRSSU	superficials
ACEFIILSTTVY	self-activity
ACEFIIMNNOST	somnifacient
ACEFIIMNORTV	confirmative
ACEFIINOORTV	vociferation
ACEFIINOPRTT	petrifaction
ACEFIIORRSTV	versificator
ACEFIIORRTVY	verificatory
ACEFIIORSTTT	testificator
ACEFIIOSSSTT	fissicostate
ACEFIIRRTTUV	vitrifacture
ACEFIIRRTTVY	refractivity
ACEFILLNORSY	forensically

ACEFILMNOPRT	placentiform
ACEFILNNOOSS	confessional
ACEFILNOOPST	pelican's-foot
ACEFILORRRTY	refractorily
ACEFIMNORRST	Afrocentrism
ACEFINNORSTT	transfection
ACEFINOORRTT	torrefaction
ACEFINOPRTTU	putrefaction
ACEFINOPSTTU	stupefaction
ACEFINORRSST	fornicatress
ACEFINOSSSTU	factiousness
ACEFKLOPTTTU	futtock-plate
ACEFLLMOOPRW	camp-follower
ACEFLMOORTTY	olfactometry
ACEFNOPRRSST	craftsperson
ACEGGGHILMOP	phlegmagogic
ACEGGHHHIINR	high-reaching
ACEGGHINRRTY	gathering-cry
ACEGGIIKMNNR	cringe-making
ACEGGIILNNST	single-acting
ACEGGIKNNOOR	cooking-range
ACEGGIKRSSTW	swagger-stick
ACEGGILLLOOY	geologically
ACEGGILLMMOO	gemmological
ACEGGILNOOST	geognostical
ACEGGIMNORTY	gyromagnetic
ACEGGINNOORT	congregation
ACEGHHIILOPR	heliographic
ACEGHHIIOPRR	hierographic
ACEGHHINOPRT	ethnographic
ACEGHHIOPRRR	chirographer
ACEGHHIOPRRY	cheirography
ACEGHHIOPRTY	hyetographic
ACEGHHNOPRTY	technography
ACEGHHNORRST	short-changer
ACEGHHOOPRRR	chorographer
ACEGHHOOPRRY	choreography
ACEGHIILLNYY	hygienically
ACEGHIILLOOR	hierological
ACEGHIKMNOPR	epoch-marking
ACEGHIKNPRTT	carpet-knight
ACEGHILLNNOU	hallucinogen
ACEGHILLNOOP	nephological
	phenological
ACEGHILLNOOT	ethnological
ACEGHILMOPYY	hypoglycemia
ACEGHILNNNTY	enchantingly
ACEGHILNOPTT	Plectognathi
ACEGHILNRRTW	night-crawler
ACEGHILOOPRS	phraseologic
ACEGHILOOPTY	hepaticology
ACEGHILOPRXY	lexicography
ACEGHIMOPRRR	micrographer
ACEGHINOPRRZ	zincographer
ACEGHINOPRST	stenographic
ACEGHIOPPRRR	reprographic
ACEGHIOPPRRT	petrographic
ACEGHIOPRRST	cerographist
ACEGHIORRSST	rags-to-riches
ACEGHIRRSTTT	garter-stitch
ACEGHMOOPRRS	cosmographer
ACEGHMOOPRTY	cometography
ACEGHNOOPRSU	necrophagous
ACEGHOPPRRST	spectrograph
ACEGHOPPRTYY	ectypography
ACEGIIILLMTY	illegitimacy
ACEGIIILNNOV	vaginicoline
ACEGIIINOTTV	incogitative
ACEGIIINSTTV	negativistic
ACEGIIKKMNTY	mickey-taking
ACEGIILLLMOS	collegialism
ACEGIILLLOTY	collegiality
ACEGIILLMOOS	semiological
ACEGIILLOOPT	geopolitical
ACEGIILLOSTU	eulogistical
ACEGIILLOSTY	egoistically
ACEGIILNNOST	single-action
ACEGIILNNOTU	geniculation
ACEGIILNNOTY	congeniality
ACEGIILNNRSY	increasingly
ACEGIILORSSU	sacrilegious
ACEGIIMNORRT	microgranite
ACEGIIMNORST	Gastrocnemii
ACEGIIMNTTUY	mutagenicity
ACEGIINOOTTX	excogitation
ACEGIKLLNPRU	lurking-place
ACEGIKLLNSSS	gallsickness
	gall-sickness
ACEGIKLNOOPP	cooking-apple
ACEGIKNPPRSS	packing-press
ACEGILLLNOOY	neologically
ACEGILLMOORT	metrological
ACEGILLMOOTY	etymological
ACEGILLNNOSY	geosynclinal
ACEGILLNNOTY	congenitally
ACEGILLNOOOP	poenological
ACEGILLNOORU	neurological
ACEGILLNORSY	early-closing
ACEGILLNORVW	wallcovering
ACEGILLNRTTY	clatteringly
ACEGILLOOOST	osteological
ACEGILLOOPRT	petrological
ACEGILLOOPST	pestological
ACEGILNNOTTU	conglutinate
ACEGILNOOOST	oceanologist
ACEGILNOOPRT	organoleptic
ACEGILNOOPTU	unapologetic
ACEGILNOORTW	water-cooling
ACEGILNRSTTY	scatteringly
ACEGILOOPSST	escapologist
ACEGILORSTTU	gesticulator
ACEGIMNNORSU	cousin-german
ACEGINNOPRTZ	precognizant
ACEGINNORRTU	raconteuring
ACEGINOPRRSU	superorganic
ACEGINORSSSU	graciousness
ACEGIOOOPPRT	apogeotropic
ACEGLLNOOPTY	placentology
ACEGLMNORTYY	laryngectomy
ACEGLNOOPRSY	laryngoscope
ACEGLNOOPRTY	proteoglycan
ACEGLNOORSUY	acrogenously
ACEGLOORSUUY	courageously
ACEGOOPRSSTU	stegocarpous

ACEHHIIMRSTT	Mechitharist
ACEHHIINOPRT	hierophantic
ACEHHILMOPTX	exophthalmic
ACEHHILMRTUY	eurhythmical
ACEHHILOOPST	theosophical
ACEHHILOPTTY	hypothetical
ACEHHIMOOOPT	homoeopathic
ACEHHINNOSTT	antichthones
ACEHHINOPRTT	theanthropic
ACEHHLLNNORY	Rhynchonella
ACEHHMORSTTY	chrestomathy
ACEHHNOOSTTU	autochthones
ACEHHOOPRTTY	hypothecator
ACEHIIIKNPST	kinesipathic
ACEHIIINRSST	christianise
ACEHIIINRSTZ	christianize
ACEHIIINSTTT	antitheistic
ACEHIILLNRST	trichinellas
ACEHIILMNNTT	anthelmintic
ACEHIILMOPSU	pleiochasium
ACEHIILNOTUV	cheluviation
ACEHIILNPPRS	planispheric
ACEHIILNPRST	sphincterial
ACEHIILOPRRT	retrophiliac
ACEHIILPRSTY	sphericality
ACEHIIMORSTT	iatrochemist
ACEHIINNORST	Neo-Christian
ACEHIINOPPPR	hippocrepian
ACEHIINPRRST	prechristian
	pre-Christian
ACEHIINSSTTU	enthusiastic
ACEHIINTTTUY	authenticity
ACEHIIOPPRST	Hippocratise
ACEHIIOPPRTZ	Hippocratize
ACEHIIOPSSTT	sophisticate
ACEHIIPPRRST	periphrastic
ACEHIIPSSTUV	Sivapithecus
ACEHIKRRSSSW	kirschwasser
ACEHILLMNNTU	multichannel
ACEHILLMNOPY	phonemically
ACEHILLNOPST	plainclothes
ACEHILLNOPTY	phonetically
ACEHILLNORUY	unheroically
ACEHILLORRTY	rhetorically
ACEHILLORSTU	Ulotrichales
ACEHILLRSTYY	hysterically
ACEHILMNOOTT	nomothetical
ACEHILMOORRT	horometrical
ACEHILMOPTYY	polycythemia
ACEHILNNNSSS	clannishness
ACEHILNNORUW	unicorn-whale
ACEHILNOPPTY	phenotypical
ACEHILNPPRTT	pitcher-plant
ACEHILOOPSTT	photoelastic
ACEHILOPRSTU	tricephalous
ACEHILPPRSTY	hyperplastic
ACEHIMMMNSTT	mismatchment
ACEHIMMNORST	metachronism
ACEHIMNPSSSS	scampishness
ACEHIMOOOSTT	homoeostatic
ACEHIMOPRRTT	tetramorphic
ACEHIMOPRSST	atmospherics
ACEHIMOPSSTY	scyphistomae
ACEHIMORSTTT	thermostatic
ACEHIMPPRSTY	spermaphytic
ACEHIMRSSTTW	master-switch
ACEHINOPPRTU	hippocentaur
ACEHINOPSSTY	sycophantise
ACEHINOPSTTY	enhypostatic
ACEHINOPSTYZ	sycophantize
ACEHLLLMOSST	small-clothes
ACEHLLMORSYY	lachrymosely
ACEHLMMNOOTW	△commonwealth
ACEHLMOORSST	schoolmaster
ACEHLOPSSUXY	psychosexual
ACEHMMNOOORT	monochromate
ACEHMOORSTTY	tracheostomy
ACEHMOORTTTY	tetrachotomy
ACEHMOPRRTYY	crymotherapy
ACEHOORRRSTT	orchestrator
ACEHOORSSTTY	athrocytoses
ACEHPRRSTTUY	trachypterus
ACEIIIKNRSST	kinesiatrics
ACEIIILLRSTT	literalistic
ACEIIILMNNSS	inimicalness
ACEIIILMNPSU	municipalise
ACEIIILMNPUZ	municipalize
ACEIIILNSTTY	inelasticity
ACEIIILRSTTV	relativistic
ACEIIILRSTVV	revivalistic
ACEIIIMNPRSS	precisianism
ACEIIINNNORT	incineration
ACEIIINNRSTT	intrinsicate
ACEIIINPRSST	precisianist
ACEIIJLLSTUY	Jesuitically
ACEIILLLLPTY	elliptically
ACEIILLLNSUV	all-inclusive
ACEIILLMNSST	miscellanist
ACEIILLMNTUU	multicauline
ACEIILLMPTTU	multiplicate
ACEIILLNORRT	Torricellian
ACEIILLNORTY	collinearity
ACEIILLOQTUV	colliquative
ACEIILMMNRST	mercantilism
ACEIILMMRRSU	mercurialism
ACEIILMNORSS	mini-lacrosse
ACEIILMNOSST	sectionalism
ACEIILMNRSTT	mercantilist
ACEIILMOPPSS	episcopalism
ACEIILMOPRRT	polarimetric
ACEIILMOPRST	semi-tropical
ACEIILMRRSTU	mercurialist
ACEIILNNNRTU	internuncial
ACEIILNNOPST	inspectional
ACEIILNNRSTY	transiliency
ACEIILNOORST	creolisation
ACEIILNOORTZ	creolization
ACEIILNOPRST	inspectorial
ACEIILNORTTU	reticulation
ACEIILNOSSTT	sectionalist
ACEIILNOSTUV	vesiculation
ACEIILNRSSTT	triticalness
ACEIILNRSTTT	clarinettist
ACEIILNRSTTU	neutralistic

ACEIILNSSSTU	sensualistic
ACEIILOPRSTT	politicaster
ACEIILOQTUVY	equivocality
ACEIILPRRSUY	superciliary
ACEIILPSSTUY	Puseyistical
ACEIILRRSSTU	surrealistic
ACEIILRRTTTY	retractility
ACEIIMMNNNOT	antimnemonic
ACEIIMMNORTU	communitaire
ACEIIMNORRRT	recriminator
ACEIIMNORSTT	cremationist
ACEIIMNOSSST	seismonastic
ACEIIMNOSSTU	scitamineous
ACEIIMNPTTUY	pneumaticity
ACEIIMOPRSTT	peristomatic
ACEIINNNORTU	renunciation
ACEIINNORTTU	centuriation
ACEIINNOTTUV	continuative
ACEIINOOQTUV	equivocation
ACEIINOORSTV	viscerotonia
ACEIINOPRRTT	practitioner
ACEIINOPRSTU	pertinacious
ACEIINORRSTW	contrariwise
ACEIIOPPRRTT	precipitator
ACEIIOQRTTUU	autocritique
ACEIJLNOOPRT	projectional
ACEIJNNNOTTY	joint-tenancy
ACEILLLNRTUY	lenticularly
ACEILLMMNOOT	monometallic
ACEILLMMNOPT	complimental
ACEILLMNOOPT	compellation
ACEILLMNOOPX	complexional
ACEILLMNORUU	unimolecular
ACEILLMNRTTU	multicentral
ACEILLMNRTUU	multinuclear
ACEILLMNTUVY	multivalency
ACEILLMORTUV	volumetrical
ACEILLMORTUY	molecularity
ACEILLMSTTUU	multisulcate
ACEILLMTUUVY	cumulatively
ACEILLNNORRU	carillonneur
ACEILLNOPTUY	unpoetically
ACEILLNORTUY	neurotically
ACEILLNOSTTU	scutellation
ACEILLNOTTUY	Teutonically
ACEILMMMNOSS	commensalism
ACEILMMNOSTY	commensality
ACEILMNNOOPT	componential
ACEILMNSSSTY	mysticalness
ACEILMOOPRRS	corporealism
ACEILMOOPRTT	optometrical
ACEILMOOPSTT	leptosomatic
ACEILMOPRRTY	pyrometrical
ACEILMOPRSUU	primulaceous
ACEILMOPSTUV	compulsative
ACEILMOSTTTU	multicostate
ACEILNNNOOTV	conventional
ACEILNOOPRSS	processional
ACEILNOOPRSU	porcelainous
ACEILNOOPRTT	lactoprotein
ACEILNOORTUY	elocutionary
ACEILNOPQTUU	pauciloquent
ACEILNOPRSSU	percussional
ACEILNORSUXY	exclusionary
ACEILNOSTTUV	consultative
ACEILOOPRRST	corporealist
	prosectorial
ACEILOOPRRTT	protectorial
ACEILOOPRRTY	corporeality
ACEILOOPSSTT	osteoplastic
ACEILOPPRRTT	protreptical
ACEILOPRRSUY	precariously
ACEILOPSSTUU	stipulaceous
ACEILORRRSTT	rectirostral
ACEILPPRSSTU	superplastic
ACEIMMNNOOTT	commentation
ACEIMMNOSTUV	consummative
ACEIMMOORRST	commiserator
ACEIMNNNORTT	conterminant
ACEIMNNOOPST	compensation
ACEIMNNOPRTU	unimportance
ACEIMNOOOOPT	onomatopoeic
ACEIMNOOSSTT	somatotensic
ACEIMNOPRSTY	cryptomnesia
ACEIMNORRSST	stercoranism
ACEIMNORSSTV	△conservatism
ACEIMNPSTTUU	mispunctuate
ACEIMNSSTTUY	unsystematic
ACEIMOOPRSTZ	spermatozoic
	zoospermatic
ACEIMOPRRSTU	periostracum
ACEINNNOOTTT	contentation
ACEINNNORSTV	inconversant
ACEINNOOPRTT	pernoctation
ACEINNOORSTV	conservation
	conversation
ACEINNOOSTTT	contestation
ACEINNORRSST	contrariness
ACEINNORRTUY	renunciatory
ACEINNORSTTU	encrustation
ACEINOOPPRSX	praxinoscope
ACEINOPSSSSU	spaciousness
ACEINOPSSSTU	captiousness
ACEINORRSSTT	stercoranist
ACEINORRSTVX	conservatrix
ACEINORRTTTU	contriturate
ACEINORRTUUV	vaunt-courier
ACEINOSSSTUU	cautiousness
ACEIOOPRRRRT	troop-carrier
ACEIOOPRRRTT	tricorporate
ACEIOOQRTUVY	equivocatory
ACEIORRSSTTU	resuscitator
ACEJLLNRRTUY	currant-jelly
ACEKLNPRSTTU	planet-struck
ACEKLOOQRRUU	Quaker-colour
ACELLMOPSUUU	plumulaceous
ACELLNNOSSUY	consensually
ACELLNOOPRSU	porcellanous
ACELLNOTTUXY	contextually
ACELMMNOSTUY	consummately
ACELMNOOPRTT	contemplator
ACELMNPRSUUU	supernaculum
ACELNNRSSUUU	ranunculuses
ACELNOOPRSTU	proconsulate

Words marked △ may be spelled also with a capital letter

ACELOOOPSSTU	octosepalous
ACELOOOPSTTU	octopetalous
ACEMMMOOORRT	commemorator
ACEMNOOPRRTY	contemporary
ACEMNOOPRSTY	compensatory
ACEMOOPRRSTU	macropterous
ACENNNORSTUV	unconversant
ACENNOORSSSU	canorousness
ACENOOQRTTTU	quattrocento
ACENOORRSTVY	conservatory
ACEOOPRRSTTT	troposcatter
ACEOPRRSSSTT	sportscaster
ACFFGGHIILNN	cliffhanging
ACFFIILLNOUY	unofficially
ACFGIIILNOTU	uglification
ACFGIIINORST	significator
ACFGIKMNRRTU	truck-farming
ACFGILNPSTTU	scalping-tuft
ACFHHLNORSSY	synchroflash
ACFHIIIMNOTU	humification
ACFHIILLORRY	horrifically
ACFHLLNTUUWY	unwatchfully
ACFIIIILNOTV	vilification
ACFIIIIMNNOT	minification
ACFIIIINNOTV	vinification
ACFIIIINOTVV	vivification
ACFIIILNOPST	spiflication
ACFIIINNOOTT	notification
ACFIIINNORTT	antifriction
ACFIIINOOSST	ossification
ACFIIINOPRTU	△purification
ACFIIINOPTTY	typification
ACFIIINORTTV	vitrifaction
ACFIIJORSTTU	justificator
ACFIILLLOPRY	prolifically
ACFIILLNOPTY	pontifically
ACFIILNNNOOT	non-fictional
ACFIILOSTTUY	factitiously
ACFIIMNNOORT	confirmation
ACFIIMNORRRT	trinacriform
ACFIINORRTTU	trifurcation
ACFIIOPRRTUY	purificatory
ACFILLNNOTUY	functionally
ACFIMNNOOORT	conformation
ACFIMNOORRTY	confirmatory
ACFRRSTUUUUY	usufructuary
ACGGHHIOPRRY	hygrographic
ACGGHILNNNUY	unchangingly
ACGGIILLOOST	glaciologist
ACGGILNPPSSU	cupping-glass
ACGGILNSSTTU	glass-cutting
ACGHHHIOPTYY	ichthyophagy
ACGHHIILOPRT	lithographic
ACGHHINOOPPR	phonographic
ACGHHINOORTT	orthognathic
ACGHHIOOPPRT	photographic
ACGHHIOOPRRT	orthographic
ACGHHIOPPRTY	phytographic
ACGHHLOOSTTU	school-taught
ACGHHNOOPRRY	chronography
ACGHHOPPRSYY	psychography
ACGHIIKNSSTV	shaving-stick
ACGHIILLLOOP	philological
ACGHIILLLOOT	lithological
ACGHIILLNOOR	rhinological
ACGHIILLOOOP	ophiological
ACGHIILLOOST	histological
ACGHIINNRRSU	nursing-chair
ACGHIINPRSTY	scintigraphy
ACGHIIPRSSST	sphragistics
ACGHILLMOOTY	mythological
ACGHILLNOOOP	phonological
ACGHILLOOPRS	oscillograph
ACGHILLOOPTY	phytological
ACGHILOPRSTY	stylographic
ACGHINOOPPRR	pornographic
ACGHIOOPPRST	coprophagist
ACGHIOOPSSTY	phagocytosis
ACGHKLOPPUYY	happy-go-lucky
ACGHOOOPPRSU	coprophagous
ACGHOPPRRTYY	cryptography
ACGIIILLLOTY	illogicality
ACGIIILLNSTU	linguistical
ACGIIILLPSTU	pugilistical
ACGIIILNOSTY	caliginosity
ACGIIINNOTTX	intoxicating
ACGIIKKLNSTW	walking-stick
ACGIIKKNPRST	kicking-strap
ACGIIKLNNORU	caulking-iron
ACGIILLLMNOO	limnological
ACGIILLLRTUY	liturgically
ACGIILLMOOST	limacologist
ACGIILMNOSUU	mucilaginous
ACGIILNOORST	craniologist
ACGIILNOOSUV	vaginicolous
ACGIILNPPSTU	supplicating
ACGIILOOPPRT	plagiotropic
ACGIIMORRTVY	microgravity
ACGIINNNOOST	consignation
ACGIINNNOOTT	contignation
ACGIINNOOSTT	contagionist
ACGIINNOSTTW	wainscotting
ACGIKLNORSSW	working-class
ACGILLLOOOYZ	zoologically
ACGILLMNNOOY	gnomonically
ACGILLNOOOST	nostological
ACGILLOOOPRT	tropological
ACGILNNNOTTU	conglutinant
ACGILNOOSTUY	contagiously
ACGILNOPSUUY	pugnaciously
ACGILNORSUUY	ungraciously
ACGIMNOOPRTU	compurgation
ACGIMOPRSTTY	cryptogamist
ACGINNOORSTY	consignatory
ACGKORSSSSTU	tussock-grass
ACGLLNOORSUY	clangorously
ACGLNOOPRSYY	laryngoscopy
ACGMOOPRRTUY	compurgatory
ACGMOOPRSTUY	cryptogamous
ACHHHNOOPRRY	Rhynchophora
ACHHIIINORST	Ornithischia
ACHHIILMNOPR	philharmonic
ACHHIIMNOPPS	championship
ACHHIIMOSTTY	stichomythia

ACHHIIMOSTYZ	schizothymia
ACHHILLMRTYY	rhythmically
ACHHILLOPTTY	thallophytic
ACHHILMNRTUY	unrhythmical
ACHHILOOPRST	holophrastic
ACHHILORTTYY	ichthyolatry
ACHHIMNNOSTU	Chimonanthus
ACHHINNOPTXY	phycoxanthin
ACHHINOPRSTY	christophany
ACHHINOPSSTY	sycophantish
ACHIIIINRSST	trichiniasis
ACHIIILLOPRU	ailurophilic
ACHIIILMSTWY	whimsicality
ACHIIILNORST	histrionical
ACHIIIMNPSSU	musicianship
ACHIIIMNRSST	Christianism
ACHIIINRSTTY	Christianity
ACHIIKLMOPTT	Machtpolitik
ACHIILLLOSTY	holistically
ACHIILLMOOTT	lithotomical
ACHIILLNOSSU	hallucinosis
ACHIILLORSTY	historically
ACHIILNNOORT	chlorination
ACHIILNOPRST	rhinoplastic
ACHIILNORSTU	unhistorical
ACHIILOOPPST	scoptophilia
ACHIILOPRRSV	corrivalship
ACHIILOPRSTT	arctophilist
	cartophilist
ACHIIMNOPRST	misanthropic
ACHIIMOOPPPT	hippopotamic
ACHIIMOPPRST	Hippocratism
ACHIINNNORST	non-Christian
ACHIINOPRSTT	antistrophic
ACHIIPRSSTTY	psychiatrist
ACHIKLLOOPST	lock-hospital
ACHIKMORTUUV	kurchatovium
ACHILLNOORSY	isochronally
ACHILLNOPTYY	hypnotically
ACHILLORSUVY	chivalrously
ACHILMOOOPRS	sophomorical
ACHILMOPPRRY	lamprophyric
ACHILMORSTYY	lachrymosity
ACHILNNOPSTU	cushion-plant
ACHILNOOPPTY	phonotypical
ACHILNORSUUV	unchivalrous
ACHILOOOPTTV	photovoltaic
ACHILOOPPRRS	corporalship
ACHILORRSTTY	Christolatry
ACHIMMOPPSTY	psammophytic
ACHIMNNOORTY	ornithomancy
ACHIMNNORSSY	asynchronism
ACHIMNOOPSSU	poison-sumach
ACHIMOPSSSTY	scyphistomas
ACHINOOSTTTU	Southcottian
ACHIOOPRRSUZ	rhizocarpous
ACHIOORSSTTY	athrocytosis
ACHIOPRSSSTY	astrophysics
ACHIQRSSTTUZ	quartz-schist
ACHMMNOOORSY	monochromasy
ACHMOOORSTTY	thoracostomy
ACHNNOORSSUY	asynchronous
ACIIIILMRSTT	militaristic
ACIIIILNOSTV	civilisation
ACIIIILNOTVZ	civilization
ACIIIILORSST	sacroiliitis
ACIIIJLMSSTU	△justicialism
ACIIILLMPTTU	multicipital
ACIIILMMNPSU	municipalism
ACIIILMNNOST	nominalistic
ACIIILMNOOST	coalitionism
ACIIILMNPTUY	municipality
ACIIILNOOSTT	coalitionist
	solicitation
ACIIILNOPRTT	triplication
ACIIILNOSTVV	convivialist
ACIIILNOTVVY	conviviality
ACIIILNPPRTY	△principality
ACIIILQTUYZZ	quizzicality
ACIIIMMNORST	Marcionitism
ACIIIMNORSTV	Victorianism
ACIIIMPRSSTT	patristicism
ACIIINNOOTTX	intoxication
ACIIINNOSTTU	cutinisation
ACIIINNOTTUZ	cutinization
ACIIINOPSSUU	inauspicious
ACIIINPRRTTU	antipruritic
ACIIIPRSSSTY	scissiparity
ACIIJLLRSTUY	juristically
ACIIJLNORSTU	journalistic
ACIILLNOOQTU	colliquation
ACIILLNOPRVY	provincially
ACIILLNORSTT	scintillator
ACIILLNRTUUV	vinicultural
ACIILLOQTUXY	quixotically
ACIILLOSSUVY	lasciviously
ACIILLPRSTUY	puristically
ACIILLRSSTTY	crystallitis
ACIILMNNOOTU	columniation
ACIILMNORSTU	matriclinous
ACIILMOOPSST	apostolicism
ACIILNNOOOST	colonisation
ACIILNNOOOTZ	colonization
ACIILNNOOSTU	inosculation
ACIILNNOSTUY	insouciantly
ACIILNOORSST	consistorial
ACIILNOPPSTU	supplication
ACIILNOPRSTU	patriclinous
ACIILNORSSSS	nail-scissors
ACIILNOSTUUY	incautiously
ACIILOOPSTTY	apostolicity
ACIILOPSSUUY	auspiciously
ACIILPRSTTUU	apiculturist
ACIIMMOOPRRS	comprimarios
ACIIMNOPRTTU	protactinium
ACIIMNOPSSSU	Passion-music
ACIINNNOOORT	incoronation
ACIINNNOOTTU	continuation
ACIINNOOPSTT	constipation
ACIINNOORSST	consistorian
ACIINNORSTTU	incrustation
ACIINOPRRSUV	picornavirus
ACIINOPSSUUU	unauspicious
ACILLLLOOQUY	colloquially

ACILLLMORTUU	multilocular
ACILLLOPRRUU	plurilocular
ACILLMNOSUUY	calumniously
ACILLMOOOTYZ	zootomically
ACILLMORSUUY	miraculously
ACILLNNOOSUV	convulsional
ACILLNOPSTYY	synoptically
ACILLOOPRRTY	proctorially
ACILLOOQSUUY	loquaciously
ACILLPRRSTUY	scripturally
ACILMMNNOOTT	non-committal
ACILMNOOOPST	cosmopolitan
ACILMNOORSTU	matroclinous
ACILMNORSUUU	unmiraculous
ACILMOOPPRST	protoplasmic
ACILNNNOSTTY	inconstantly
ACILNNOOORTT	contortional
ACILNNOOSTTU	consultation
ACILNNOPTTUU	punctulation
ACILNOOPRSTU	patroclinous
ACILNPRRSTUU	unscriptural
ACILOOPPRSTT	protoplastic
ACILOOPPRTTY	prototypical
ACILOPPRSTUY	supplicatory
ACILORRRSTUV	curvirostral
ACIMMMNOPRUU	cuprammonium
ACIMMNNOOSTU	consummation
ACIMOOOPRSTT	somatotropic
ACINNNORSTTU	unconstraint
ACINNOORRSUV	oncornavirus
ACINNOPRTTUU	puncturation
ACINOOOPRRRT	incorporator
ACINOPRSSTUU	transpicuous
ACIORRRSSTTU	cirro-stratus
ACLLLPRSTUUY	sculpturally
ACLLMNOOORSU	salmon-colour
ACLLMNOORTUU	monocultural
ACLLRRSTTUUY	structurally
ACLMOOPRSTUY	compulsatory
ACLNOORSTTUY	consultatory
ACMMNOORSTUY	consummatory
ACMNNOORTUWY	countrywoman
ACMOOORRRTTT	motor-tractor
ACNOOOPPRSTT	contrapposto
ADDDDEEEHLMU	muddleheaded
ADDDDEEEHNRU	dunderheaded
ADDDDEEFFILL	fiddle-faddle
ADDDEEEHNOOW	woodenheaded
ADDDEEFIOSTU	eisteddfodau
ADDDEEGHKNOU	dough-kneaded
ADDDEEGHNRTU	hundred-gated
ADDDEEHIILPY	Didelphyidae
ADDDEENNRSTU	understanded
ADDDEFIILMNO	diamond-field
ADDDFGGINORT	draft-dodging
ADDDIILLMNOR	diamond-drill
ADDEEEEFLNRS	self-endeared
ADDEEEEHLNRT	Threadneedle
ADDEEEGGHLOR	loggerheaded
ADDEEEGNNNRU	unendangered
ADDEEEHILPRT	triple-headed
ADDEEEHINRST	disheartened
ADDEEEHLPUZZ	puzzle-headed
ADDEEEIIRSTV	desiderative
ADDEEEIMPRTT	premeditated
ADDEEEINSSSS	diseasedness
ADDEEEKLNOOY	Yankee-Doodle
ADDEEEMNORYY	ready-moneyed
ADDEEENPRSSV	depravedness
ADDEEEOPPRSV	eavesdropped
ADDEEFFNRSTU	understaffed
ADDEEFHLLNTY	left-handedly
ADDEEFHLMORY	formaldehyde
ADDEEFILNORS	self-ordained
ADDEEFLNRSSU	dreadfulness
ADDEEFNORSSW	word-deafness
ADDEEGGILLNN	dingle-dangle
ADDEEGGILNOR	dégringolade
ADDEEGHHLOUY	oughly-headed
ADDEEGHILNNS	single-handed
ADDEEGHMRSTU	hedge-mustard
ADDEEGHNORTY	hydrogenated
ADDEEGILNNPS	landing-speed
ADDEEGINPPSU	pease-pudding
ADDEEGJMNTUY	judgement-day
ADDEEGNORSTU	adder's-tongue
ADDEEHHILPSS	shield-shaped
ADDEEHIILMNS	shield-maiden
ADDEEHILMNOW	diamond-wheel
ADDEEHLLOOWY	woolly-headed
ADDEEHMNOTTU	mutton-headed
ADDEEHMORSUY	Hydromedusae
ADDEEHOPRRTU	proud-hearted
ADDEEIIMMNNO	demi-mondaine
ADDEEIIMNSST	disseminated
ADDEEIINOPRT	Torpedinidae
ADDEEIINORST	desideration
ADDEEIKLMNWY	weak-mindedly
ADDEEILLPSSY	displeasedly
ADDEEILORRWW	world-wearied
ADDEEIMNSSSY	dismayedness
ADDEEINOPRST	depredations
ADDEEINRSTUV	disadventure
	unadvertised
ADDEELNRRUWY	unrewardedly
ADDEENNORRUV	over-and-under
	under-and-over
ADDEENNRRSTU	understander
ADDEFGIILLNN	landing-field
ADDEFGILRRSU	disregardful
ADDEFHILNOOS	old-fashioned
ADDEFHILOPST	feldspathoid
ADDEFIIILQSU	disqualified
ADDEFIIISSST	dissatisfied
ADDEFLNNNOUW	Newfoundland
ADDEGGINRRRY	Gradgrindery
ADDEGIINORSS	disorganised
ADDEGIINORSZ	disorganized
ADDEGILNOPRS	spring-loaded
ADDEGILNPPTU	pudding-plate
ADDEGINNRRUW	underdrawing
ADDEHIILPPRZ	lizard-hipped
ADDEHIMNNOSU	unadmonished
ADDEHINPRRWY	whip-and-derry

ADDEHMNOOORT rhodomontade
ADDEHMNORSUY hydromedusan
ADDEIIIQTTUV quidditative
ADDEIILMSSVY misadvisedly
ADDEIILNQTUU unliquidated
ADDEIILPSSTY dissipatedly
ADDEIINOPPST disappointed
ADDEILMNNSTU undismantled
ADDEILMNOOTU demodulation
ADDEIMNNORRW narrow-minded
ADDEINNOOOTT Notodontidae
ADDEMNOOORRT rodomontader
ADDEMNOOPRSU pseudorandom
ADDEMNOOPSSU pseudomonads
ADDENNOORTUW down-and-outer
ADDENNORSSWW downwardness
ADDFHIIMORTY hydatidiform
ADDFHLNOOSTU thousandfold
ADDFIILLNSUY disdainfully
ADDFLNNOOSTU lost-and-found
ADDGIILNSSTU studdingsail
studding-sail
ADDIIIINNOPR diprionidian
ADDIIILLNUVY individually
ADEEEEFHNPRT pen-feathered
ADEEEEGINRTV degenerative
ADEEEEGLNRTY degenerately
ADEEEEILMRST timed-release
ADEEEEMNPRTW deepwatermen
ADEEEFFIINRT differentiae
ADEEEFGHINTV heaven-gifted
ADEEEFGILNRR rifle-grenade
ADEEEFHILSSV self-adhesive
ADEEEFHINPRT pin-feathered
ADEEEFILLRST alder-liefest
ADEEEFLPPRRS self-prepared
ADEEEFNNOSST tone-deafness
ADEEEGGHILST eagle-sighted
ADEEEGGINNRT degenerating
ADEEEGGNRSTU unsegregated
ADEEEGHLMMRS sledgehammer
ADEEEGHLPRSY hedge-parsley
ADEEEGILOPRS grapeseed-oil
ADEEEGIMNRST demagnetiser
disagreement
ADEEEGIMNRTZ demagnetizer
ADEEEGINNORT degeneration
ADEEEGINOPSS paedogenesis
ADEEEGINPRST predesignate
ADEEEGINRRTT redintegrate
ADEEEGLNNRSS enlargedness
ADEEEGLNRSTW strangle-weed
ADEEEGMNNNRT endangerment
ADEEEGNOQRUW queen-dowager
ADEEEHHILRST heater-shield
ADEEEHHLORTW whole-hearted
ADEEEHIIMNPR ephemeridian
ADEEEHIMNRTT hereditament
ADEEEHINORTX exheredation
ADEEEHINSSSV adhesiveness
ADEEEHIRRTTT tetrahedrite
ADEEEHLNNRRT Netherlander
ADEEEHLRSTTX tax-sheltered
ADEEEHNNRTTU unthreatened
ADEEEIILMNRS demineralise
ADEEEIILMNRZ demineralize
ADEEEIILNPTX expediential
ADEEEIIMMRST semi-diameter
ADEEEIIMNRTT intermediate
ADEEEIIORRST aerosiderite
ADEEEILLMMOS △mademoiselle
ADEEEILLMNOP lepidomelane
ADEEEILMNORT radioelement
ADEEEILNPRRT interpleader
ADEEEILRRTTY reiteratedly
ADEEEIMPRSTT distemperate
ADEEEINPRSTT predestinate
ADEEEJNOORRS rejoneadores
ADEEEKLLNOST endoskeletal
ADEEELLMNNRW well-mannered
ADEEELNNQRSU Queenslander
ADEEELNOSSST desolateness
ADEEELOPPRST tradespeople
ADEEEMNOQSUW queen-meadows
ADEEEMNORSST moderateness
ADEEEMNPPRSS pamperedness
ADEEENNTTUUX unextenuated
ADEEENOPPRRT preponderate
ADEEENPPRRSS preparedness
ADEEENPRRTUV peradventure
ADEEENRSSVYY everydayness
ADEEEOPPRRRV overprepared
ADEEEOPPRRSV eavesdropper
ADEEEOPRRSUV overpersuade
ADEEFFGHINRT affrightened
ADEEFFHIRSTT stiff-hearted
ADEEFFIILNRT differential
ADEEFGILLLMR flame-grilled
ADEEFGINNORT finger-and-toe
ADEEFGINNRST free-standing
ADEEFGIRSSTU fatigue-dress
ADEEFGLLNNWY newfangledly
ADEEFGLNORRW flower-garden
ADEEFHILNRTT flint-hearted
ADEEFHILORUX hexafluoride
ADEEFHILRSTV harvest-field
ADEEFHINNOSW new-fashioned
ADEEFIILLNPS field-spaniel
ADEEFILNNOST self-anointed
ADEEFILNPTXY fixed-penalty
ADEEFILORUVV evil-favoured
ADEEFIMOPRRT imperforated
ADEEFINNRSTU Frauendienst
ADEEFINORSTV arfvedsonite
ADEEFLLORUVW well-favoured
ADEEFLLPRSTU apfelstrudel
ADEEFNNORRUW unforewarned
ADEEFNOPRRTU unperforated
ADEEFNORSSUV favouredness
ADEEGGGNNOTU egg-and-tongue
ADEEGGHIRSTT straightedge
ADEEGGIQRRSU square-rigged
ADEEGGLNOPPR doppelganger
doppelgänger

ADEEGHHILRTT	light-hearted
ADEEGHHINOSS	high-seasoned
ADEEGHHINSTW	sheath-winged
ADEEGHILNORS	horse-dealing
ADEEGHIMNOST	homesteading
ADEEGHINNRRT	heart-rending
ADEEGHLMOPRT	dephlegmator
ADEEGHLOORST	leathergoods
ADEEGHOPRRSW	hedge-sparrow
ADEEGHPRSTTU	stepdaughter
ADEEGIILNNOU	Euglenoidina
ADEEGIINRSTT	disintegrate
ADEEGIIPPRTW	periwig-pated
ADEEGIKLLLNW	lake-dwelling
ADEEGIKLNRST	deerstalking
ADEEGIKNNRRT	kindergarten
ADEEGIKNPSST	speedskating
ADEEGIKNRRST	ring-streaked
ADEEGILLORVY	gaol-delivery
ADEEGILNNRSU	undersealing
ADEEGILNORTU	deregulation
ADEEGILORTVY	derogatively
ADEEGIMNNNRU	undermeaning
ADEEGINNRTTU	unintegrated
ADEEGIOPRRTV	prerogatived
ADEEGJMNSTTU	judgment-seat
ADEEGLLRRSSY	regardlessly
ADEEGLMNOSSS	gladsomeness
ADEEGLRSTUVV	velvet-guards
ADEEGMNNOORR	gander-mooner
ADEEGMNNRRTU	undergarment
ADEEGNOOPSST	Steganopodes
ADEEGNOORRVW	wood-engraver
ADEEGNPRTUUX	unexpurgated
ADEEGORRTTXY	dextrogyrate
ADEEHHIKNRRS	headshrinker
ADEEHHNNPTUY	unhyphenated
ADEEHIILMNTY	diethylamine
ADEEHIILRRTY	hereditarily
ADEEHIKLNOOP	kaleidophone
ADEEHILNPSTY	synadelphite
ADEEHIMNPPRS	misapprehend
ADEEHIMRSSST	headmistress
ADEEHINNOOST	Hindoostanee
ADEEHINORSTU	house-trained
ADEEHLLNNRTU	unenthralled
ADEEHLMMOTUY	mealy-mouthed
ADEEHLMOOSTV	smooth-leaved
ADEEHLPPRSSU	pedal-pushers
ADEEHLPRSTUU	desulphurate
ADEEHMNNOSSS	handsomeness
ADEEHMNORRSY	dysmenorrhea
ADEEHMOPRTTY	dermatophyte
ADEEHNNOPRST	pentahedrons
ADEEHNORRSTT	tetrahedrons
ADEEHNORSTTY	stony-hearted
ADEEHORSSTUW	house-steward
ADEEHORSTTTU	stout-hearted
ADEEIIILMRST	demilitarise
ADEEIIILMRTZ	demilitarize
ADEEIIILMTTV	delimitative
ADEEIIILORST	editorialise
ADEEIIILORTZ	editorialize
ADEEIIJLLRVY	jail-delivery
ADEEIIKPRSTW	weak-spirited
ADEEIILLNNTT	Little-endian
ADEEIILLNTVY	evidentially
ADEEIILMMNPT	impedimental
ADEEIILMNNSS	maidenliness
ADEEIILMTTVY	meditatively
ADEEIILNNRST	internalised
ADEEIILNNRTZ	internalized
ADEEIILNPRST	presidential
ADEEIILOPPTV	deoppilative
ADEEIILRTVVY	derivatively
ADEEIIMNNOTV	denominative
ADEEIIMNNRSU	unseminaried
ADEEIIMNPRST	mean-spirited
ADEEIIMNRRTY	intermediary
ADEEIINOPTTX	expeditation
ADEEIINORSTT	disorientate
ADEEIINPSSTV	dispensative
ADEEIINRRSTY	residentiary
ADEEIINRRTVW	water-diviner
ADEEIIPPRSSU	dispauperise
ADEEIIPPRSUZ	dispauperize
ADEEIIRSSTTV	dissertative
ADEEIKLLMPPR	lappered-milk
ADEEIKLMPPRR	ripple-marked
ADEEIKNRRRTW	water-drinker
ADEEILLNOTTU	andouillette
ADEEILLORSTV	travel-soiled
ADEEILLPRSTV	silver-plated
ADEEILMMORTY	immoderately
ADEEILMNTTTU	multidentate
ADEEILMPRTTY	timely-parted
ADEEILNNTTUV	unventilated
ADEEILNOTTVY	denotatively
ADEEILNRRSTY	restrainedly
ADEEIMMNORSU	misdemeanour
ADEEIMNNNRTU	intermundane
ADEEIMNNRTTU	unterminated
ADEEIMNRSTUV	misadventure
ADEEINNOOPRU	Indo-European
ADEEINNOPRST	respondentia
ADEEINNRRSTU	unrestrained
ADEEINNSSSTU	unsteadiness
ADEEINORRSTV	overstrained
ADEEIRRRSTTW	water-strider
ADEEJMNRSTTU	readjustment
ADEELLMMNRTU	untrammelled
ADEELLMORUZZ	muzzle-loader
ADEELMOPRSTU	deuteroplasm
ADEELNPPRRUY	unpreparedly
ADEELOOPRRSW	solar-powered
ADEEMMOSTUXY	myxedematous
ADEEMNNNORTU	unornamented
ADEEMNNPRSUU	supermundane
ADEEMNNPRTUY	underpayment
ADEEMNOPPRSW	newspaperdom
ADEENNOORRST	androsterone
ADEENNOPPRRT	preponderant
ADEENORSSSST	assortedness
ADEENORSSTUW	sweet-and-sour

ADEFFGHILRTY	affrightedly
ADEFFHORSSTT	short-staffed
ADEFFIKKNNOR	knife-and-fork
ADEFGGIINNNR	rangefinding
ADEFGHILNRTT	right-and-left
ADEFGIIILLNR	Fringillidae
ADEFGIIKNNRW	drawing-knife
ADEFGIILLNPY	playing-field
ADEFGILNNSST	self-standing
ADEFGILNORSU	glandiferous
ADEFGINNNSSU	unfadingness
ADEFGINOOPRR	proofreading
ADEFHHLNRSTU	thunderflash
ADEFHIMNOORS	fore-admonish
ADEFHINRSSSW	dwarfishness
ADEFHLLORTTU	full-throated
ADEFIIILNNOT	definitional
ADEFIIILQRSU	disqualifier
ADEFIILNOSTT	deflationist
ADEFIINNQTUU	unquantified
ADEFIINRSTTU	unstratified
ADEFILMNNOSS	manifoldness
ADEFILMNORSU	unformalised
ADEFILMNORUZ	unformalized
ADEFINNOORTU	foundationer
	refoundation
ADEFLLNRTUUY	fraudulently
ADEFLMNORTUU	unformulated
ADEGGHIINRST	sight-reading
ADEGGHILNRTU	daughterling
ADEGGHINORRU	rough-grained
ADEGGIILNRTW	water-gilding
ADEGGIINORST	disgregation
ADEGGINNORRR	organ-grinder
ADEGHHILNORS	shareholding
ADEGHHIPRSST	sharp-sighted
ADEGHHOPRRRY	hydrographer
ADEGHHORRSTU	draught-horse
ADEGHHORSTUU	draught-house
ADEGHIINNPRT	printing-head
ADEGHIINRRSS	hairdressing
ADEGHILLNOSV	slaveholding
ADEGHINORRST	horse-trading
ADEGHINRSSTU	draughtiness
ADEGHJLLMNTU	judgment-hall
ADEGHLLNORST	stranglehold
ADEGHLNOSSTU	thousand-legs
ADEGHNOPRSTU	sharp-tongued
ADEGHOPPRSUY	pseudography
ADEGIIIKMMNR	Kimmeridgian
ADEGIIILNRTT	interdigital
ADEGIILLMNSY	misleadingly
ADEGIILLNNTU	dentilingual
ADEGIILMNNRT	mind-altering
ADEGIILMNORS	demoralising
ADEGIILMNORZ	demoralizing
ADEGIILNORSS	digressional
ADEGIILNPRSY	despairingly
ADEGIIMNRRST	riding-master
ADEGIINNORTU	unoriginated
ADEGIINNPRSU	undespairing
ADEGIINOORRT	granodiorite
ADEGILLNORUZ	lounge-lizard
ADEGILNNRSSW	drawlingness
ADEGILNOOTUZ	Zeuglodontia
ADEGILOORRTY	derogatorily
ADEGIMNNOPPR	name-dropping
ADEGIMNORRSU	measuring-rod
ADEGINOPRSTU	outspreading
ADEGIORRSSWW	grass-widower
ADEHHILLPPSU	△philadelphus
ADEHHILMOORR	hemorrhoidal
ADEHHIMOORRS	haemorrhoids
ADEHHIRRSTTW	thitherwards
ADEHHIRRSTWW	whitherwards
ADEHHLMORRTY	hydrothermal
ADEHHOOPRSTT	sharp-toothed
ADEHHOPRRTYY	hydrotherapy
ADEHIIIMRSTT	mithridatise
ADEHIIIMRTTZ	mithridatize
ADEHIILMOSSY	hemodialysis
ADEHIILNSTTT	dilettantish
ADEHIIMNORRT	Thermidorian
ADEHIIMNORSS	disharmonise
ADEHIIMNORSZ	disharmonize
ADEHIIMOPRST	mediatorship
ADEHIINOORTT	Theriodontia
ADEHIIOPPRRT	Rhipidoptera
ADEHIIORSSTU	disauthorise
ADEHIIORSTUZ	disauthorize
ADEHIKNORSSW	whiskerandos
ADEHILLOORWY	woolly-haired
ADEHILLSSTTY	lady's-thistle
ADEHILMNNOOP	monodelphian
ADEHILMNOPSU	sulphonamide
ADEHILOPRRTY	pyritohedral
ADEHILOPRSTU	triadelphous
ADEHIMMNNOST	admonishment
ADEHIMNRTTWW	withdrawment
ADEHINNOOPTY	phytonadione
ADEHINNORTTY	one-and-thirty
ADEHINNQSUUV	unvanquished
ADEHINOOORTZ	antherozooid
ADEHINOPPRST	sharp-pointed
ADEHINORSTUU	unauthorised
ADEHINORTUUZ	unauthorized
ADEHINQRRSTU	hindquarters
ADEHIOOPRSTT	orthopaedist
ADEHIOPPRTTY	Pteridophyta
ADEHLMNNOSUY	unhandsomely
ADEHLMNOOPSU	monadelphous
ADEHLMOPSTUY	splay-mouthed
ADEHOOPSTTTT	Photostatted
ADEIIILMNOTT	delimitation
ADEIIIMNORST	dimerisation
ADEIIIMNORTZ	dimerization
ADEIIIMNOSTV	deviationism
ADEIIINOSTTV	deviationist
ADEIIINSTTTU	attitudinise
ADEIIINTTTUZ	attitudinize
ADEIILLMNORY	meridionally
ADEIILLNPRUV	Liverpudlian
ADEIILLSTUVV	vaudevillist
ADEIILMNSTTT	dilettantism

ADEIILNNOPUV	unpavilioned
ADEIILNNORTY	inordinately
ADEIILNOOPPT	deoppilation
ADEIILNOOPST	depositional
	despoliation
ADEIILNOPRTV	providential
ADEIILNORSST	dilatoriness
ADEIILSSSUVY	dissuasively
ADEIIMMNOORT	immoderation
ADEIIMNNNOOT	denomination
ADEIIMNNORSW	Neo-Darwinism
ADEIIMNNOSTU	mountainside
ADEIIMNNQRUU	quadriennium
ADEIIMNNRSTT	distrainment
ADEIIMNOPRST	postmeridian
ADEIIMNORSST	disseminator
ADEIINNNQQUU	quinquenniad
ADEIINNOORRT	reordination
ADEIINNOPSST	dispensation
ADEIINNORRSS	ordinariness
ADEIINNORSTW	Neo-Darwinist
ADEIINOOPRST	disoperation
ADEIINOOPRTX	peroxidation
ADEIINOOPSTT	depositation
ADEIINOQRTUZ	quartz-iodine
ADEIINORRSVY	diversionary
ADEIINORSSTT	dissertation
ADEIINOSTTUV	adventitious
ADEIIOOOPRST	radio-isotope
ADEIIOPPRRST	dispropriate
ADEIKLLOPSTU	leukoplastid
ADEIKNOOPTTY	kidney-potato
ADEIKNOPRRTU	turnpike-road
ADEILLLNOOSY	solenoidally
ADEILLLNRTUY	ill-naturedly
ADEILLNOOTVY	devotionally
ADEILLNPRTUY	prudentially
ADEILLPPRSSY	lady's-slipper
ADEILMNNNSTU	disannulment
ADEILMNSTTUU	unstimulated
ADEILNOOPPTU	depopulation
ADEILNOPRRSU	superordinal
ADEILNORRSTT	dentirostral
ADEILNORRSTV	dorsiventral
ADEILNORSSTW	towardliness
ADEILNSSSTUY	unassistedly
ADEIMMOPRSUY	praseodymium
ADEIMOOPRSTZ	spermatozoid
ADEINNOPRSSU	underpassion
ADEINNOPRSTU	unpatronised
ADEINNOPRTUZ	unpatronized
ADEINOPRSSTY	dispensatory
ADEINOPRTTVZ	privat-dozent
ADEINORSSTUV	disaventrous
ADEJLOOPRSUY	jeopardously
ADEKMNNORRUW	under-workman
ADELLMMORSTY	troll-my-dames
ADELLNNORSSU	all-roundness
ADELLNORSSUY	slanderously
ADELLOOPRRST	petrodollars
ADELLORSTUUY	adulterously
ADELNORRSUVY	land-surveyor
ADEMNNRSTTUU	untransmuted
ADEMNOORRSTT	demonstrator
ADEMNRRSTTUU	understratum
ADEMOPRRSSTU	superstardom
ADEMOPRRSTUY	pseudomartyr
ADENNORSSTUW	untowardness
ADENNORSTUUV	unadventrous
ADENOPQRRTUU	quarter-pound
ADENOQRRRTUU	quarter-round
ADEOORRRSUVY	road-surveyor
ADFFGIILNNTU	fault-finding
ADFGGGINOORT	foot-dragging
ADFGHIINRSTV	driving-shaft
ADFGHOOPRRTU	draught-proof
ADFGILNNOORT	front-loading
ADFHMNOOOTTU	foot-and-mouth
ADFIIILNNOST	disinflation
ADFIIILNOSTU	fluidisation
ADFIIILNOTUZ	fluidization
ADFIILNOORTU	fluoridation
ADFIILOSSTUY	fastidiously
ADFIINOSSTUU	unfastidious
ADGGIIMNNORS	gormandising
ADGGIIMNNORZ	gormandizing
ADGGILNNNOST	long-standing
ADGHHKOORSTU	draught-hooks
ADGHIKLNORSW	world-shaking
ADGHILLLMNOS	smallholding
ADGHIMRRRSYY	hydrargyrism
ADGHINOORTTW	tooth-drawing
ADGHNOOOPRTY	odontography
ADGHOOOPRSTT	dogtooth-spar
ADGIIIINOSTT	digitisation
ADGIIIINOTTZ	digitization
ADGIIIMNOSSS	misdiagnosis
ADGIILLNNNSU	disannulling
ADGIILLNNOTU	longitudinal
ADGIILNNPRST	landing-strip
ADGIINNOPRTW	word-painting
ADGILLNNTUUY	undulatingly
ADGILMOOPRYY	pyramidology
ADGILNNOSTUY	astoundingly
ADGIMNNOORST	standing-room
ADGINNOOOPRT	gonadotropin
ADGINOPPRRWW	word-wrapping
ADGINORRSTUY	agroindustry
ADGLLLNOSUUY	glandulously
ADGLNNOORTUW	long-drawn-out
ADGOOOPRSSTU	gastropodous
ADHHIOPRSTTY	hydropathist
ADHHNOOPRSUY	hydrophanous
ADHIIIMMRSTT	mithridatism
ADHIILMNOPRU	dolphinarium
ADHIILNOPSTT	Dantophilist
ADHIIMOORRTU	radio-thorium
ADHIIMOPRSST	diastrophism
ADHIINOOPRST	radiophonist
ADHILLNOSTUY	outlandishly
ADHINNNOOPSY	sindonophany
ADHLLOPSSUYY	dasyphyllous
ADHLNOOOOPRT	odontophoral
ADHNNOOOOPRT	odontophoran

ADIIIIMNNOTT	intimidation
ADIIILLMRSSY	dissimilarly
ADIIILLNOSTT	distillation
ADIIIMNORTTY	intimidatory
ADIIINNNOORT	inordination
ADIIINOPRTTU	tripudiation
ADIIINORRTTV	vitro-di-trina
ADIIINORSTTT	traditionist
ADIILLMOPRRY	primordially
ADIILLNOSSUY	sinusoidally
ADIILLNRSTUY	industrially
ADIILLOPSTUV	post-diluvial
ADIILLORSTTY	distillatory
ADIILMMNRUUU	duraluminium
ADIILMNOPRST	palindromist
ADIILMORSSTU	dissimulator
ADIILNOPSTUV	post-diluvian
ADIILNORSTTU	stridulation
ADIILNOSTTUU	altitudinous
	latitudinous
ADIIMNNNOOSS	non-admission
ADIIOPSSTTUU	disputatious
ADILLMNOOOPY	monopodially
ADILLNRSTTUY	stridulantly
ADILLOORSTUY	idolatrously
ADILORRSTTUY	stridulatory
ADILORSSSTUY	disastrously
ADIOOPRRSSUU	sudoriparous
ADMNOOOOSTTU	odontomatous
AEEEEGGMNNRT	re-engagement
AEEEEGHLPRST	telegraphese
AEEEEGINRRTV	regenerative
AEEEEGNNRRTU	unregenerate
AEEEEHHPRRSS	sheepshearer
AEEEEHLPRSST	sheep-stealer
AEEEEIIPRSTT	tapsieteerie
AEEEENPRRSTT	serpent-eater
AEEEFFILMNTY	effeminately
AEEEFGIKMNRT	feeing-market
AEEEFHIKLNRT	leather-knife
AEEEFHILRSTV	live-feathers
AEEEFHINRRTT	thereinafter
AEEEFHINRSST	featheriness
AEEEFIKLNPTT	palette-knife
AEEEFILNPRRT	preferential
AEEEFIMNRTTV	fermentative
AEEEFLMNSSSS	self-sameness
AEEEFLNRSSSS	fearlessness
AEEEFLORSTTW	telesoftware
AEEEGGHLNSTT	snaggleteeth
AEEEGHIILMRW	whigmaleerie
AEEEGHINOSST	aesthesiogen
AEEEGHIRSTTZ	gazetteerish
AEEEGILNNPSS	palingeneses
AEEEGILNNRRV	line-engraver
AEEEGILNRSST	single-seater
AEEEGILTTVVY	vegetatively
AEEEGIMNNSTV	envisagement
AEEEGINNORRT	regeneration
AEEEGINNSSTV	negativeness
AEEEGINOPRTT	prenegotiate
AEEEGINORRTT	interrogatee
AEEEGINORSTV	seronegative
AEEEGINRRTTV	vinegarrette
AEEEGIRRSTTV	tergiversate
AEEEGLLNSSTT	tassel-gentle
AEEEGLMNNNTT	entanglement
AEEEGLNNRTTT	tangle-netter
AEEEGLNOPSTT	espagnolette
AEEEGMMNORTT	magnetometer
AEEEGMMNOSSS	gamesomeness
AEEEGMNNRSTT	estrangement
AEEEGMNOPRSU	pergameneous
AEEEGNNNQRTU	queen-regnant
AEEEGNORRRTY	regeneratory
AEEEGOPRRSTU	supererogate
AEEEHILMPRTY	ephemerality
AEEEHILNNSSV	heavenliness
AEEEHIMNNOPP	epiphenomena
AEEEHINPPRSV	apprehensive
AEEEHINPRSST	parenthesise
AEEEHINPRSTZ	parenthesize
AEEEHINRRTTW	interwreathe
AEEEHIRSSTUX	heterauxesis
AEEEHKNOPPRS	speakerphone
AEEEHLLLPRRS	pearl-sheller
AEEEHLLNNRTW	lantern-wheel
AEEEHLNPRTTW	pattern-wheel
AEEEHLNSSSST	hatelessness
AEEEHLORSTUX	heterosexual
AEEEHMMNORTT	methanometer
AEEEHMNNSTTW	enswathement
AEEEHMORTTTX	methotrexate
AEEEHQRRRTTU	three-quarter
AEEEIILMNRRS	remineralise
AEEEIILMNRRZ	remineralize
AEEEIILMPRTT	temperalitie
AEEEIILMRSTT	semiliterate
AEEEIILNPRTX	experiential
AEEEILLMMNST	elementalism
AEEEILLNPRTT	interpellate
AEEEILMNPRTX	experimental
AEEEILMNRTTY	intemerately
AEEEILNRSSTV	relativeness
AEEEILNRTTVY	inveterately
AEEEIMNNNRTT	entraînement
AEEEIMNPPSTT	appetisement
AEEEIMNRRTUV	remunerative
AEEEIMOPRRTV	evaporimeter
AEEEIMORSTTV	overestimate
AEEEIMPRSTTV	septemvirate
AEEEINNORTTX	exenteration
AEEEINPRRTTT	interpretate
AEEEINPRSTTV	presentative
AEEEINPRTTVV	preventative
AEEEINRRTTUX	extra-uterine
AEEEIOPPRRTV	preoperative
AEEEIPRRSTVV	preservative
AEEEIRRSTVVX	extraversive
AEEEKLNOOPRS	saloon-keeper
AEEEKLRRSTTW	streetwalker
AEEEKMOPRRRT	pro-marketeer
AEEELLPRSSSU	pleasureless
AEEELLRRSTTW	Wall-Streeter

AEEELMNNSSSS	namelessness	AEEGGILLMMNN	mingle-mangle
AEEELMNORSYY	eleemosynary	AEEGGILNNORS	sloganeering
AEEELMNSSSST	tamelessness	AEEGGILRSSVY	aggressively
AEEEMNNORSTY	earnest-money	AEEGGIMMNOST	geomagnetism
AEEEMNRSSSST	reassessment	AEEGGIMNOSTT	geomagnetist
AEEEMOOPRRTV	evaporometer	AEEGGINRSSTT	resting-stage
AEEENNNPRSTY	earnest-penny	AEEGGIQRRRSU	square-rigger
AEEENNPRRSTT	representant	AEEGHHILOPRR	heliographer
AEEEOPRRRSTV	perseverator	AEEGHHIOPRRR	hierographer
AEEFFGHIRRTU	father-figure	AEEGHHNOPRRT	ethnographer
AEEFFGIMNORT	meat-offering	AEEGHIINNRRV	Rhinegravine
AEEFFHORRSTT	foster-father	AEEGHILLMMRT	hellgrammite
AEEFFIJNNORS	Jeffersonian	AEEGHILMNOPR	Germanophile
AEEFFLLRSTTY	self-flattery	AEEGHILNOPSU	leaping-house
AEEFFLNNSSTU	affluentness	AEEGHILNORTW	watering-hole
AEEFGHINRSST	sergeant-fish	AEEGHILORRUV	heliogravure
AEEFGIILNNRV	never-failing	AEEGHILPRSTT	telegraphist
AEEFGILLNPSS	self-pleasing	AEEGHINOPSST	pathogenesis
AEEFGINRRRSU	sugar-refiner	AEEGHINPRSST	sergeantship
AEEFGIORRRRT	refrigerator	AEEGHINRRSTT	straightener
AEEFGLNOORRW	orange-flower	AEEGHLLORRTT	toll-gatherer
AEEFGLNRSSTU	gratefulness	AEEGHLNOPRSY	selenography
AEEFHHILRSWY	whale-fishery	AEEGHLOORSTT	theologaster
AEEFHIKNRSSS	freakishness	AEEGHMNOOSTU	hematogenous
AEEFHILLQRTU	quill-feather	AEEGHMNOPRRS	phrasemonger
AEEFHILNRSST	fatherliness	AEEGHMOOPRRT	meteorograph
AEEFHILPRRSY	pearl-fishery	AEEGHMOORSTU	heterogamous
AEEFHLMNSSSU	shamefulness	AEEGHNOPRRST	stenographer
AEEFHLMORRTW	flame-thrower	AEEGHNORRSTW	snow-gatherer
AEEFHOOPRRTW	weatherproof	AEEGHNORSSTU	anotherguess
AEEFIILMPPRR	preamplifier	AEEGHOORSSTV	harvest-goose
AEEFIILNORTT	interfoliate	AEEGHOPPRRRR	reprographer
AEEFIKNNNRST	Frankenstein	AEEGHOPPRRRT	petrographer
AEEFILMNORRT	interfemoral	AEEGHOPRRSTY	stereography
AEEFILNRSTVV	snifter-valve	AEEGIIILLMTT	illegitimate
AEEFILOPRSTU	petaliferous	AEEGIIKLNPSV	evil-speaking
AEEFILPRRSST	filter-passer	AEEGIILLMTTY	legitimately
AEEFIMNNORTT	fermentation	AEEGIILMNORS	mineralogise
AEEFIMNNSSST	manifestness	AEEGIILMNORZ	mineralogize
AEEFIMNORSTU	amentiferous	AEEGIILNNORS	Legionnaire's
AEEFIMOPRRTV	performative		Legionnaires'
	preformative	AEEGIILNNPSS	palingenesis
AEEFINNORSTT	fenestration	AEEGIINNNRTT	entertaining
AEEFINNOSTUX	soixante-neuf	AEEGIINORRTV	reinvigorate
AEEFKNNORSSS	forsakenness	AEEGIINPRRTV	privateering
AEEFLMNOOPTT	footplatemen	AEEGIKLLNPSW	sleepwalking
AEEFLMNORSTT	forestalment	AEEGIKLNSTTT	giant's-kettle
AEEFLNSSSTTU	tastefulness	AEEGIKNRRSTT	street-raking
AEEFLNSSSTUW	wastefulness	AEEGILLLNPSW	well-pleasing
AEEFLOPQRSUW	pasque-flower	AEEGILLRSSST	legislatress
AEEFNOPRRSTT	foster-parent	AEEGILNNNOPT	longipennate
AEEFOOPRRSST	professorate	AEEGILNNPRST	single-parent
AEEFOQRRRSTU	forequarters	AEEGILNNPSSS	pleasingness
AEEGGGGHHILL	higgle-haggle	AEEGILNNRTTY	entreatingly
AEEGGGGILLWW	wiggle-waggle	AEEGILNNSSSS	gainlessness
AEEGGGHLMOPU	phlegmagogue	AEEGILNORRTU	reregulation
AEEGGGIMNNRV	gem-engraving	AEEGIMNNOSTT	segmentation
AEEGGGINNNSS	engagingness	AEEGIMNNRSST	reassignment
AEEGGHNORTTU	gang-there-out	AEEGIMNNSTTT	statementing
AEEGGIINNOSS	angiogenesis	AEEGIMNRRSST	mastersinger
AEEGGIJJLLNN	jingle-jangle	AEEGIMORRTTV	gravitometer
AEEGGIKKLNSS	keeking-glass	AEEGINNNSSSU	sanguineness

AEEGINNRSSST	transgenesis
AEEGINNRSSVW	waveringness
AEEGINOPRRRT	peregrinator
AEEGINOPRSTT	poetastering
AEEGINORSSTT	negotiatress
AEEGKNOORSTU	keratogenous
AEEGLLMNOPSY	splenomegaly
AEEGLLMNRUWZ	mangel-wurzel
AEEGLLPRRSUU	spurge-laurel
AEEGLMNNORTV	governmental
AEEGLMNNRSTT	stranglement
AEEGMMNORTTY	magnetometry
AEEGMNOPRRRY	prayer-monger
AEEGMNOPRSTY	spermatogeny
AEEGNOPRRSTU	supererogant
AEEHHHILNSTY	heathenishly
AEEHHHOPRRTT	threeha'porth
AEEHHILMMNTU	Helianthemum
AEEHHILOPRTY	heliotherapy
AEEHHIMPRRTY	hyperthermia
AEEHHINPRSTY	hypersthenia
AEEHHLLORTTY	heterothally
AEEHHLMMOORT	homeothermal
AEEHHLMPRRTY	hyperthermal
AEEHHNOOPRTT	theatrophone
AEEHHNOPPRTY	phanerophyte
AEEHHOPPRTTY	phreatophyte
AEEHIIKNSSST	kinaesthesis
AEEHIILMOPST	epitheliomas
AEEHIIMNPRSX	examinership
AEEHIINORSTT	etherisation
AEEHIINORTTZ	etherization
AEEHIINPRRST	retainership
AEEHIINSTUVX	inexhaustive
AEEHIJNPRSST	serjeantship
AEEHIKNNSSSS	sneakishness
AEEHILLMNNPS	Panhellenism
AEEHILLMNNPU	panhellenium
AEEHILLNNNOP	panhellenion
AEEHILLNNPST	Panhellenist
AEEHILMMNRST	Simmenthaler
AEEHILMMOOST	mesothelioma
AEEHILMNSTUY	lese-humanity
AEEHILNOPRRS	prehensorial
AEEHILNRSSSS	hairlessness
AEEHILNSSSTT	stealthiness
AEEHILSTUVXY	exhaustively
AEEHIMMORRTT	arithmometer
AEEHIMNNORTT	nitromethane
AEEHIMNOPRTZ	promethazine
AEEHIMORSTTT	theorematist
AEEHINNOPPRS	apprehension
AEEHINOORSTU	△heteroousian
AEEHINOPRRTY	erythrope-nia
AEEHINORRRST	horse-trainer
AEEHINRSSSTW	waterishness
AEEHIPPRRXYY	hyperpyrexia
AEEHIPRSTTTU	therapeutist
AEEHKMMMNORY	monkey-hammer
AEEHKNNOORTT	heterokontan
AEEHLLMMORWY	yellowhammer
AEEHLLMNNOPY	phenomenally
AEEHLLMNNRTT	enthrallment
AEEHLLMNOOPT	metallophone
AEEHLLMORTXY	exothermally
AEEHLMNRSSSS	harmlessness
AEEHLMPRRSUU	superhumeral
AEEHLNOPRTUY	polyurethane
AEEHLNPRSSUY	hypersensual
AEEHLOPRSTTY	heteroplasty
AEEHLORSSTUV	harvest-louse
AEEHMMNOORRT	harmonometer
AEEHMMOOPRST	metamorphose
AEEHMNNOPRTY	hymenopteran
AEEHMNOOPRRT	Enteromorpha
AEEHMORSTTUY	erythematous
AEEHNNORRSTT	north-eastern
AEEHNOOPRSST	epanorthoses
AEEHNORRSSSV	overrashness
AEEHNORSSTTU	south-eastern
AEEHOPRRRSTW	spear-thrower
AEEHOPRRSSTT	stratosphere
AEEHOQRRRSTU	quarter-horse
AEEIIILRSTTV	relativities
AEEIIIMMTTXX	mixtie-maxtie
AEEIIKLMNPRS	marline-spike
AEEIIKMNNSSY	Keynesianism
AEEIILLLRTTY	illiterately
AEEIILLMRSTU	mitrailleuse
AEEIILLNOSTV	televisional
AEEIILLNPSTT	pestilential
AEEIILLRRTVY	irrelatively
AEEIILMNSSST	essentialism
AEEIILMPRTVY	imperatively
AEEIILMRSTTU	multiseriate
AEEIILNNOPRS	isoprenaline
AEEIILNNPRTY	perenniality
AEEIILNNPSTT	penitentials
AEEIILNOPRTT	repetitional
AEEIILNRRSST	literariness
AEEIILNRSSUV	universalise
AEEIILNRSTUY	uniseriately
AEEIILNRSUVZ	universalize
AEEIILNSSSTT	essentialist
AEEIILNSSTTY	essentiality
AEEIILOPTTVX	exploitative
AEEIILPRRSTU	pluriseriate
AEEIINNNORTT	inteneration
AEEIINNORSTT	eternisation
AEEIINNORTTZ	eternization
AEEIINNPRTTY	penitentiary
AEEIINNRRTTU	intrauterine
AEEIINSSTTVV	vitativeness
AEEIIPRTTUVV	vituperative
AEEIIQRSSTTU	sesquitertia
AEEIJLNNOPRT	jointer-plane
AEEIJLOPRTVY	pejoratively
AEEIJNNORTUV	rejuvenation
AEEIKLLLSTTY	skittle-alley
AEEIKMNNSSST	mistakenness
AEEILLLLTVYY	tilley-valley
AEEILLLSTUVY	televisually
AEEILLMNRTTT	ill-treatment
AEEILLNNPRTT	interpellant

AEEILLNNPSTY	septennially
AEEILLNNSTTY	sententially
AEEILLNORSST	relationless
AEEILLNOSSTT	tessellation
AEEILLNOSSTV	volatileness
AEEILLNPRRTU	interpleural
AEEILLNPRSTY	presentially
AEEILLNQSTUY	sequentially
AEEILLNQTUVY	equivalently
AEEILLNRRSTT	interstellar
AEEILLNRRTVY	irrelevantly
AEEILLNSSSUV	allusiveness
AEEILLTTTTTT	tittle-tattle
AEEILMNNNRSS	mannerliness
AEEILMNNRSTT	reinstalment
AEEILMNORRTU	euroterminal
AEEILMNRSSST	masterliness
AEEILMOPRTTU	Mitteleuropa
	Mittel-Europa
AEEILMPPRSTU	perpetualism
AEEILMPRRSSU	superrealism
AEEILMPSTTTU	multiseptate
AEEILMQRRRTU	quarter-miler
AEEILNNNOSST	non-essential
AEEILNNPRSTY	tennis-player
AEEILNNPSSSS	painlessness
AEEILNNRTTUY	lieutenantry
AEEILNNSSSUU	unsensualise
AEEILNNSSUUZ	unsensualize
AEEILNOPRRTT	interpolater
AEEILNOPRSSX	expressional
AEEILNPRRSST	interspersal
AEEILNPRSSST	plasteriness
AEEILPPRRSTY	parsley-piert
AEEILPPRSTTU	perpetualist
AEEILPPRTTUY	perpetuality
AEEILPRRSSTU	superrealist
AEEILPRSSUVY	persuasively
AEEILPRTTUVY	reputatively
AEEIMMNORSTT	amortisement
AEEIMMNORTTZ	amortizement
AEEIMMNRSSTU	immatureness
AEEIMMNRSTTT	mistreatment
AEEIMMNSSTTT	misstatement
AEEIMMRRTTXX	mixter-maxter
AEEIMNNNORTT	intermontane
AEEIMNNOOPRT	porte-monnaie
AEEIMNNORRTU	remuneration
AEEIMNORRTTX	exterminator
AEEIMNPPRSSW	newspaperism
AEEIMNRSTTVY	vestimentary
AEEIMOQRSTUU	mousquetaire
AEEIMPRSSSUV	supermassive
AEEIMRSSSTTY	systematiser
AEEIMRSSTTYZ	systematizer
AEEINNOPRSTT	presentation
AEEINNPRRRTU	intrapreneur
AEEINOORRSSU	aeroneurosis
AEEINOORTTTX	extortionate
AEEINOPPRRTT	perpetration
AEEINOPPRTTU	perpetuation
AEEINOPPSSST	appositeness
AEEINOPRRSTV	preservation
AEEINORRRSVY	reversionary
AEEINORRSTVX	extraversion
AEEINPRSSUUV	unpersuasive
AEEINRSSTTTV	transvestite
AEEINRSTTTUV	sternutative
AEEINSSTTTUV	sustentative
AEEIPPRRSSTT	Strepsiptera
AEEIPPRRTTTT	pitter-patter
AEEKLLORRRST	roller-skater
AEEKLMNRSSUW	lukewarmness
AEEKMOPRRSTU	posture-maker
AEEKMORRSSTT	masterstroke
AEELLLMNOTVY	malevolently
AEELLLNOPSWY	Naples-yellow
AEELLLORTTWY	yellow-rattle
AEELLMNOQRUW	woman-queller
AEELLMNPPSTU	supplemental
AEELLPRRSSYY	prayerlessly
AEELMMNORTUY	emolumentary
AEELMNOPRSST	temporalness
AEELMNPRRSTU	premenstrual
AEELMOOPRSTU	somatopleure
AEELNOPRSSTT	plasterstone
AEELNORSTUXY	extraneously
AEELNPRSSSUU	supersensual
AEELNRRSSTVY	transversely
AEELOOPPRTUV	overpopulate
AEELOPRSTUUV	superovulate
AEELQSSTTUUY	statuesquely
AEEMMNNOOSTU	momentaneous
AEEMMRRSSTTU	muster-master
AEEMNOOPRSTU	temporaneous
AEEMNOORTUUV	outmanoeuvre
AEEMNORRRTUY	remuneratory
AEENNOPRRSTU	neuropterans
AEENNORSSSUV	ravenousness
AEENNOSSSSUU	nauseousness
AEENOPRSSSTT	statesperson
AEENORRSSTXY	extrasensory
AEEOOPRSTUUX	autoexposure
AEEOPRRRSTVY	preservatory
AEEOPRRSTTTU	tetrapterous
AEEOQRRSSTTU	sequestrator
AEFFGHIMNRTT	affrightment
AEFFGHINOTTU	outfangthief
AEFFGIINORTU	effiguration
AEFFGILLLMOR	flagelliform
AEFFHILNSSTU	faithfulness
AEFFILMMORSU	flammiferous
AEFFILNOSTUX	exsufflation
AEFGGGILNOPR	leap-frogging
AEFGHHIILNSW	whale-fishing
AEFGHHOORRTU	thoroughfare
AEFGHHOORTTU	aforethought
AEFGHHORTTTU	afterthought
AEFGHIILNPRS	pearl-fishing
AEFGHIINRRTT	freight-train
AEFGHILNRSST	farthingless
AEFGIILLLORU	Liguliflorae
AEFGIILRTUVY	figuratively
AEFGIIMNRSTU	misfeaturing

AEFGIINPPSWW	wife-swapping
AEFGILLNORST	forestalling
AEFGILLNRTTY	flatteringly
AEFGILLNSSUW	wineglassful
AEFGILLOPRTY	profligately
AEFGILNNRTTU	unflattering
AEFGILNORTWW	water-flowing
AEFGIMNNORRT	morning-after
AEFGIMNORRRT	terraforming
AEFGINNRRRST	transferring
AEFGINORSSUU	sanguiferous
AEFGLLNRTUUY	ungratefully
AEFGOORRRSTY	agroforestry
AEFHHIMNPRSS	freshmanship
AEFHIINNSSST	faintishness
AEFHIINRRSST	fish-strainer
AEFHILMNORSS	salmon-fisher
AEFHINOSSSSU	fashiousness
AEFHKLNNSSTU	thankfulness
AEFHLLLNOTWY	fly-on-the-wall
AEFHLLNOSSTU	loathfulness
AEFHLNRSSTUW	wrathfulness
AEFHOOPRRSTT	shatterproof
AEFIIILMNSST	semifinalist
AEFIIILNRTTV	infiltrative
AEFIIIMNNOST	feminisation
AEFIIIMNNOTZ	feminization
AEFIILLMOTTU	multifoliate
AEFIILLNOOTU	unifoliolate
AEFIILNOOPRT	perfoliation
	prefoliation
AEFIIMNNNOTT	infotainment
AEFIINOPRSTT	fortepianist
AEFIINORSTTU	titaniferous
AEFIKLNNPPRT	flint-knapper
AEFILMMNNOOT	monofilament
AEFILNNORRTT	interfrontal
AEFILNNOSSTU	fountainless
AEFILNNPPSST	flippantness
AEFILNOOPRRT	prefloration
AEFILNOOPRSS	professional
AEFILNOOPSTU	puftaloonies
AEFILOOPRRSS	professorial
AEFILOPPRSUU	papuliferous
AEFILOPRRSTT	self-portrait
AEFILORSSTUU	salutiferous
AEFIMNNORRST	frontiersman
AEFIMNNORTTU	frumentation
AEFIMNOOPRRT	preformation
AEFINNORSSTU	stanniferous
AEFLLNNSSUUW	unlawfulness
AEFLLORSTTUY	flatterously
AEFLNOOPSSTU	teaspoonfuls
AEFLNOPRRSTU	superfrontal
AEGGGILNNOTU	agglutinogen
AEGGGILNRSTY	staggeringly
AEGGGILNRSWY	swaggeringly
AEGGHIPPRRTY	trigger-happy
AEGGHLNOOSTT	snaggletooth
AEGGHOOOPRYZ	zoogeography
AEGGILMNNOTU	Muggletonian
AEGGILORRSUY	gregariously
AEGGIMNNORRW	warmongering
AEGGINNPRSSS	graspingness
AEGGLOOORSTY	astrogeology
AEGGMNNOORRT	röntgenogram
AEGHHIILLLNS	shealing-hill
AEGHHILOPRRT	lithographer
AEGHHIMORSTT	home-straight
AEGHHINOSSUW	washing-house
AEGHHIPRSUWY	superhighway
AEGHHMNOPRRY	hymnographer
AEGHHMOPRRTY	mythographer
	thermography
AEGHHNOOPPRR	phonographer
AEGHHNORSTTU	through-stane
AEGHHOOPPRRT	photographer
AEGHHOOPRRRT	orthographer
AEGHHOPPRRTY	phytographer
AEGHIILLTUWW	williewaught
AEGHIILNSTTY	hesitatingly
AEGHIIMOPRSW	image-worship
AEGHIINNSTTU	unhesitating
AEGHIINPPRSW	sapphire-wing
AEGHIIOOPSST	oesophagitis
AEGHIKNNRRTT	knight-errant
AEGHILLOPPRS	ellipsograph
AEGHILMNNOSW	Englishwoman
AEGHILMNNSTU	languishment
AEGHILMOOSTT	hematologist
AEGHILNNRTTU	turning-lathe
AEGHILNPRRSW	wranglership
AEGHILOOPSTT	hepatologist
AEGHILQRRTTU	quarterlight
AEGHIMMNNRTU	tuning-hammer
AEGHIMMNOPRY	hemp-agrimony
AEGHIMNORSUW	house-warming
AEGHIMOPRSSY	seismography
AEGHINOPRRSW	power-sharing
AEGHINPRRSSU	purse-sharing
AEGHINRRSSTT	heart-strings
AEGHINRSSSTT	straightness
AEGHLMMNOOOU	homologumena
AEGHLMNNOORS	longshoreman
AEGHLMOORTUY	rheumatology
AEGHLORSSTUU	slaughterous
AEGHMNOOOPTT	photomontage
AEGHNNOOPRTY	anthropogeny
AEGHNOOPPRRR	pornographer
AEGHOOPRRSST	gastrosopher
AEGHOOPRRTUV	photogravure
AEGHOPPSSYYZ	zygapophyses
AEGIIIILTTTV	vitilitigate
AEGIIILMNOTT	legitimation
AEGIIIMNNNOT	ingemination
AEGIIINNPRSW	awe-inspiring
AEGIILLNNOTW	△wellingtonia
AEGIILLNNRTU	interlingual
AEGIILLNPRVY	prevailingly
AEGIILMNOPRT	primogenital
AEGIILMNORST	mineralogist
AEGIILNNNSSU	ungainliness
AEGIILNNORTU	urinogenital
AEGIILNNPRUV	unprevailing

AEGIILNORSTY seignioralty
AEGIILNPPSTY appetisingly
AEGIILNPPTYZ appetizingly
AEGIILNPRSTT ear-splitting
AEGIILNRSTTW slate-writing
AEGIILRRRTUY irregularity
AEGIIMNNOPRT impregnation
AEGIIMNNOPTT pigmentation
AEGIIMNNRSTT tin-streaming
AEGIIMNOORRT morigeration
AEGIIMOPRSTV Gram-positive
AEGIINNNOPST nose-painting
AEGIINNNRSTT intransigent
AEGIINNPPSTU unappetising
AEGIINNPPTUZ unappetizing
AEGIINNPRSSS aspiringness
AEGIINNSTUXY exsanguinity
AEGIINORRSTT registration
AEGIINORSTTV investigator
AEGIINPPRRTW writing-paper
AEGIIOPRRSTT prestigiator
AEGIKLMNORTW metalworking
AEGILLMPRSSU aspergillums
AEGILLMRSTTU metallurgist
AEGILLNNOSTW stonewalling
AEGILLNNPSUY unpleasingly
AEGILLQRSSUU liqueur-glass
AEGILMMNRSTY stammeringly
AEGILMNNNNOT non-alignment
AEGILMNNOQTU magniloquent
AEGILMNOOSTT nematologist
AEGILMNRSTTY smatteringly
AEGILMOOOPRY paroemiology
AEGILNNNOSTU sanguinolent
AEGILNNRSTTY astringently
AEGILNNRSTUY saunteringly
AEGILNNRUVWY unwaveringly
AEGILNNRUWYY unwearyingly
AEGILNOOPRST antigropelos
AEGILNRRSSUY reassuringly
AEGILOORSTTT teratologist
AEGILORRSSTU grossularite
AEGIMMNOOSTZ zoomagnetism
AEGIMNNRTUUU unguentarium
AEGINNNPRRSU spear-running
AEGINNORSSTU nugatoriness
AEGINNOSSUUX exsanguinous
AEGINOORRRTT interrogator
AEGINOPRSTTU pregustation
AEGIPRRSTUVY supergravity
AEGLLMNTTUUU multungulate
AEGLLNOOOPTY paleontology
AEGLLOOOOPYZ paleozoology
AEGLMNOOPTUY pneumatology
AEGLNNOOTTUU notoungulate
AEGLOORSTUUY outrageously
AEGNORRRSSST transgressor
AEGOOPSSTTUY steatopygous
AEHHIIILMSST Ishmaelitish
AEHHILLMSSTT Stahlhelmist
AEHHILNOORRR rhinorrhoeal
AEHHILNOPPRT philanthrope
AEHHILOPSTTU thiosulphate
AEHHIMNNOOPR harmoniphone
AEHHIMNOPRSS horsemanship
AEHHIMOOPRRT Theriomorpha
AEHHIMOOPRST Thesmophoria
AEHHIMOOPRTY rhythmopoeia
AEHHIMOOPSTT homeopathist
AEHHIOPPRSTT triphosphate
AEHHLMOOPSTX exophthalmos
AEHHLMOPSTUX exophthalmus
AEHHLOPPSTUY hyposulphate
AEHHNOPPRTYY hypnotherapy
AEHHOOPPRTTY phototherapy
AEHHOOPRRSST sharpshooter
AEHIIIKPRSST sphairistike
AEHIIILNOOPS eosinophilia
AEHIIILNOPSS hispaniolise
AEHIIILNOPSZ hispaniolize
AEHIIIMNPRTY pyrithiamine
AEHIILLOOPRU ailourophile
AEHIILNOPRST relationship
AEHIILPRRSTT hair-splitter
AEHIIMNNRRTY Martini-Henry
AEHIIMNRTTUU Uintatherium
AEHIINNSSSSW swainishness
AEHIINOPRRST prehistorian
AEHIIRRSSTTW shirtwaister
AEHIKKMNRRSS skrimshanker
AEHILLMORSTY isothermally
AEHILLOORSTU heliolatrous
AEHILLPRSTTT lath-splitter
AEHILMNOOPSU anemophilous
AEHILMNORSTW mothers-in-law
AEHILMNQSSSU qualmishness
AEHILMOOPRST photorealism
AEHILOOPRSTT strophiolate
AEHIMMMOPRST metamorphism
AEHIMMOPRSTT metamorphist
AEHIMMOPSTTU imposthumate
AEHIMNNOOPRT enantiomorph
AEHIMNNOOSSU mansion-house
AEHIMNNOPPSU one-upmanship
AEHIMNNOSSSW womanishness
AEHIMNNOSSTT astonishment
AEHIMNNPRSTT transhipment
AEHIMNNQSTUV vanquishment
AEHIMOOOSSST homoeostasis
AEHINNOPRTTX xanthopterin
AEHINNPPSSSS snappishness
AEHINOOPRRTT prototherian
AEHINOOPRSST epanorthosis
AEHINOPRSTTU neuropathist
AEHINOPRSTTY attorneyship
AEHINPPRRSST transshipper
AEHIOOPPRSST apostrophise
AEHIOOPPRSTZ apostrophize
AEHIOOPSSTTT osteopathist
AEHIOPQRSSTU quaestorship
AEHIOPRRSTWY praiseworthy
AEHIOPRSSSSS assessorship
AEHLMNPRSUUY superhumanly
AEHLNOPSSTUY polyanthuses

AEHLOPPRSTUY	pyrosulphate
AEHMNOOPRTUX	pneumothorax
AEHNNORSSTUY	synantherous
AEHNOOPRRSSU	sarrusophone
AEHNORRSSSTY	synarthroses
AEIIILLMNTUV	illuminative
AEIIILNNNORT	nitro-aniline
AEIIILNRSTTT	interstitial
AEIIILPRSSTU	spiritualise
AEIIILPRSTUZ	spiritualize
AEIIILRSTTTV	relativitist
AEIIIMMNORST	immiseration
AEIIIMMNSSTT	anti-Semitism
AEIIIMNNNOST	insemination
AEIIIMNORSSS	missionarise
AEIIIMNORSSZ	missionarize
AEIIIMNOSSTT	Semitisation
AEIIIMNOSTTZ	Semitization
AEIIIMNRSTTV	ministrative
AEIIINNOOPTV	opinionative
AEIIINNRSTTV	intransitive
AEIIINORSTTV	revisitation
AEIIIOPPRTTV	propitiative
AEIIKKNORSSY	karyokinesis
AEIIKLLNORSU	unsailorlike
AEIIKLNRSTTU	unartistlike
AEIILLLLMMSY	millesimally
AEIILLLNTUUX	luxullianite
AEIILLLPRRTU	pluriliteral
AEIILLMMMORY	immemorially
AEIILLNQRSTU	tranquillise
AEIILLNQRTUZ	tranquillize
AEIILLPRRSTT	rail-splitter
AEIILLQRRSTU	squirrel-tail
AEIILLRSTTUV	illustrative
AEIILMMNOOST	emotionalism
AEIILMNNOTVY	nominatively
AEIILMNOOTTY	emotionality
AEIILMNRSSUV	Universalism
AEIILMNRTUVY	ruminatively
AEIILMNSTTUY	simultaneity
AEIILMORSSTT	Aristotelism
AEIILMPRTTTU	multipartite
AEIILMPTTUVY	imputatively
AEIILNNNQQUU	quinquennial
AEIILNNOOPTY	opinionately
AEIILNNOORTT	intoleration
AEIILNNOOSTV	novelisation
AEIILNNOOTVZ	novelization
AEIILNNOPSST	splenisation
AEIILNNOPSTZ	splenization
AEIILNOOPSTX	expositional
AEIILNOOPTTX	exploitation
AEIILNOPPSTY	inappositely
AEIILNOPTTTY	potentiality
AEIILNORSSST	solitariness
AEIILNQRRTUZ	tranquilizer
AEIILNQTTUVY	quantitively
AEIILNRSSSTW	sisters-in-law
AEIILNRSSTUV	Universalist
AEIILNRSTTVY	transitively
AEIILNRSTUVY	universality
AEIILNSTUUXY	unisexuality
AEIIMMNNNOOS	neonomianism
AEIIMMNOORST	memorisation
AEIIMMNOORTZ	memorization
AEIIMNNOOSTT	monetisation
AEIIMNNOOTTZ	monetization
AEIIMNNOPSSX	expansionism
AEIIMNNORSST	Nestorianism
AEIIMNNOSSST	sensationism
AEIIMNRSSSTV	transmissive
AEIINNNORTTU	antineutrino
AEIINNOOPTTT	potentiation
AEIINNOPRSTU	resupination
AEIINNOPSSTX	expansionist
AEIINNORSTTT	strontianite
AEIINNOSSSTT	sensationist
AEIINOPPRRST	perspiration
AEIINOPRSTTT	strepitation
AEIINOPRTTUV	vituperation
AEIINPRRSSSU	Prussianiser
AEIINPRRSSUZ	Prussianizer
AEIKMNOQRSTU	question-mark
AEIKMRSSSSTT	taskmistress
AEILLLLPRRRT	Pralltriller
AEILLMMMSSTY	symmetallism
AEILLMMNOSTT	misallotment
AEILLMNOPRSY	impersonally
AEILLMNPRSUU	superluminal
AEILLNNORTTY	intolerantly
AEILLNOOPSXY	polysiloxane
AEILLNOORTUV	revolutional
AEILLNOOSTTW	wollastonite
AEILLNOQRTUV	ventriloqual
AEILLNORRTTY	torrentially
AEILMNNOOPRT	melanotropin
AEILMNNOOPST	Neoplatonism
AEILMNNRSTTU	instrumental
AEILMNOOPRTT	metropolitan
AEILMNOQSUUY	equanimously
AEILMNOSSTUU	simultaneous
AEILMOORSTTT	stromatolite
AEILNNOOPSTT	Neoplatonist
AEILNNOSTTYY	enantiostyly
AEILNNQRSSTU	tranquilness
AEILNOOPRRSS	responsorial
AEILNOOPRRTT	interpolator
AEILNOOPSSSS	possessional
AEILNOORTUVY	evolutionary
AEILNOPRSSSU	suspensorial
AEILNORRSTTU	tenuirostral
AEILNORRSUVY	revulsionary
AEILOOOPPPRS	prosopopeial
AEILOOPRSTTY	epistolatory
AEILOPRSSSUU	Plesiosaurus
AEIMMOPSSTTY	symptomatise
AEIMMOPSTTYZ	symptomatize
AEIMNNOORSST	Montessorian
AEIMNNOPPSTT	appointments
AEIMNNORSTTU	menstruation
AEIMNOOPPTTT	tappet-motion
AEIMNOOPRRST	impersonator
AEIMNOPRSSTU	reassumption

AEIMNPRSTTUV transumptive
AEIMNRSSSTTV transvestism
AEIMOPPRRSSU appressorium
AEINNNNOOTTT non-attention
AEINNNOPRSTT transpontine
AEINNNORSSTT non-resistant
AEINNOOPRTTY enantiotropy
AEINNORRSSTV transversion
AEINNORSTTTU sternutation
AEINNOSSTTTU sustentation
AEINOOPRSTTT protestation
AEINOORRTTXY extortionary
AEINOOSSTTTU ostentatious
AEINOPRRSTTT train-spotter
AEINOPRRSTTV transportive
AEINRSSSTTTV transvestist
AEIOOOOPPPRS prosopopoeia
AEIOOPPRRRTX expropriator
AEIOPPRRRSTY perspiratory
AEIOPPRRSTTU superpatriot
AEIOPRRSTTTY Post-Tertiary
AEIOPRRTTUVY vituperatory
AEJMMOPRRTTU trumpet-major
AELLLMORSUVY marvellously
AELLMMNNOTUY monumentally
AELLOOPPSSUY polysepalous
AELLOOPPSTUY polypetalous
AELMNOOOPSSU monosepalous
AELMNOOOPSTU monopetalous
AELNNOOPRSTT entoplastron
AELOOORRTTVY levorotatory
AELOOPRSTTUX expostulator
AEMMNNORTUUV verumontanum
AEMNNOORSSTY stonemasonry
AEMNNOPRRSTT Premonstrant
AEMNOOOPRSTZ spermatozoon
AEMNOOOPRSZZ mezzo-soprano
AEMNOOORSTXY serotaxonomy
AEMNOORRRSTT remonstrator
AEMPRRSSTTUU superstratum
AENOOPRSSSUV vaporousness
AENORRSTTTUY sternutatory
AEOOPPRRSSTU Euro-passport
AEOOPRRSSTTU tetrasporous
AFFGILNNORTY affrontingly
AFFHILLNTUUY unfaithfully
AFFIILNNOSTU insufflation
AFGGGILLNNUY unflaggingly
AFGGHHIILNTU highfaluting
AFGGHIINPRTW whip-grafting
AFGGIILNRTYY gratifyingly
AFGHILMNNORU half-mourning
AFGIIILLNSSU fissilingual
AFGIIKNOPRTT profit-taking
AFGIILLLLORU liguliflorал
AFGIILLMNORU anguilliform
AFGIILLOSTUY flagitiously
AFGIILNSSTYY satisfyingly
AFGIINNNNOWW winnowing-fan
AFGIINNSSTUY unsatisfying
AFGIKNOORSTT toasting-fork
AFGIMNNORRST transforming
AFGIMNORRSTY transmogrify
AFHKLLNNTUUY unthankfully
AFIIILLNRSTU fustillirian
AFIIILMNNOST inflationism
AFIIILNNORTT infiltration
AFIIILNNOSTT inflationist
AFIILMORSTUU multifarious
AFIILNNOORTU fluorination
AFIILNOOOPRV pavilion-roof
AFIILORRSSST fissirostral
AFIIMMNNORST misinformant
AFIIMMNOORST misformation
AFILLMNOPSTU slumpflation
AFIMMNORRSST transformism
AFIMNORRSSTT transformist
AGGGILLNRSTY stragglingly
AGGHHLOPPRYY glyphography
AGGHHMOPPRSY sphygmograph
AGGHIIKNNSTV △thanksgiving
AGGHIILNPSTY sight-playing
AGGHILOOPRST graphologist
AGGHLNOOPRYY pharyngology
AGGHLOOPRSSY glossography
AGGHLOPPRTYY glyptography
AGGIIIKLLNNT giant-killing
AGGIINNOPRSW growing-pains
AGGIKLLNOOSS looking-glass
AGGIKLNNOSUW waulking-song
AGGIKLNPPRSU sparking-plug
AGHHIIMNNOTU mountain-high
AGHHIIOPPPST hippophagist
AGHHILNOPRTT triphthongal
AGHHILOOPSTU lithophagous
AGHHIMNOPSTY hypognathism
AGHHINOPPRYY hypophrygian
AGHHIOOOPPSU ophiophagous
AGHHIOOPPPSU hippophagous
AGHHIOOPPRST opisthograph
AGHHIOOPRSUZ rhizophagous
AGHHIOPPRSYY physiography
AGHHLMOPPRYY lymphography
AGHHMOOPPRRY morphography
AGHHNOOPSTUY hypognathous
AGHHOOPPSTUY phytophagous
AGHIIINNPRST training-ship
AGHIILMNPSTY lymphangitis
AGHIINNPPRST transhipping
AGHIKLNOOPRS sharp-looking
AGHILLNNOORT all-or-nothing
AGHILMNOOOOT homologation
AGHILMNOORTU ornithogalum
AGHIMNOOPRST gramophonist
monographist
AGHIMOPRSTUY hypogastrium
AGHINNOOPSST snapshooting
AGHINOOPRSTT trapshooting
AGHIOPPRSTTY typographist
AGHIOPPSSYYZ zygapophysis
AGHLLMOOPSUY gamophyllous
AGHLLNOOORTY orthogonally
AGHLMOOOPRSU lagomorphous
AGHLNNOOPRYY laryngophony

AGHLNOOOPRTY anthropology
AGHLOOOOPTYZ zoopathology
AGHMNOOPRTYY pharyngotomy
AGHNNOOOPRTY anthropogony
AGIIIILNNOTV invigilation
AGIIILLMNNTU illuminating
AGIIILMNNSWZ Zwinglianism
AGIIILNNSTWZ Zwinglianist
AGIIIMNORSTT migrationist
AGIIINNOORTV invigoration
AGIIKLMNSTTU multitasking
AGIIKLNNOPTT talking-point
AGIILLLMNTUU multilingual
AGIILLOPSSSS salpiglossis
AGIILMNNORSU unmoralising
AGIILMNNORUZ unmoralizing
AGIILMNNRTUY ruminatingly
AGIILNNNORRS snarling-iron
AGIILNNPRSUY unaspiringly
AGIILNOORSUV vainglorious
AGIILNOSSTUU ustilaginous
AGIIMNNRSTTT transmitting
AGIINNNSSTUU unsustaining
AGIINNOORSTT toasting-iron
AGILLNNOORST snarling-tool
AGILLNOOPPTW pot-walloping
AGILLNOOPSTY palynologist
AGILMNNSSUUY unassumingly
AGILMNOOPRSU sporangiolum
AGILMNOOPRTU promulgation
AGILMOOOPSTT potamologist
AGILNNNNOPTW town-planning
AGILNNOOOPRT prolongation
AGILNPRSSSUY surpassingly
AGILOOPPRSTY papyrologist
AGILORSTTUUY gratuitously
AGIMMNOPRSUY progymnasium
AGIMNOOOSSTU angiostomous
AGIMNOORSSTT gastronomist
AGINNOOPPRTU propugnation
AGINNOPRRSST apron-strings
AGINNOPRRSTT transporting
AGINOOPRSSTT protagonists
AGINOORSSUUV sanguivorous
AGLLMOOPSUYY polygamously
AGLLNOORSUUY languorously
AHHHHIIPPRRU hip-hip-hurrah
AHHHIIOOPPRY hip-hip-hooray
AHHIILMOPSTT ophthalmitis
AHHIILOPPSST hospital-ship
AHHILLLLSSYY shilly-shally
AHHILLMMOOST homothallism
AHHILNOOPSTU anthophilous
AHHILNOPPRTY philanthropy
AHHIMNNPSSTU huntsmanship
AHHINNOPRSTT strophanthin
AHHINOOOPPRS Siphonophora
AHHNOPRSSTTU strophanthus
AHIIILORSSTU urolithiasis
AHIILMMPRSTU triumphalism
AHIILMPRSTTU triumphalist
AHIIMMNORSTU harmoniumist
AHIIMNNOORSU inharmonious
AHILLNOORTYZ horizontally
AHILLOORSTTU litholatrous
AHILMNOORSUY harmoniously
AHILMNPRTTUY triumphantly
AHILMOOOPRTY homopolarity
AHILNNOOPSTU sulphonation
AHILNOPPRSTY psilanthropy
AHILNOPRSTUU sulphuration
AHILOOOPRSTU ophiolatrous
AHIMMOOPRSTU automorphism
AHIMMOOPSSTU amphistomous
AHIMNNOORSUU unharmonious
AHIMNOOPRSST misanthropos
AHIMOOPPPSTU hippopotamus
AHIMOOPPRSTT haptotropism
AHIMOOPPRSTU amphitropous
AHIMOPPRSSTY saprophytism
AHINNOOPRSTT antistrophon
AHINNOPRSSTU Sinanthropus
AHINOOPSSTUY autohypnosis
AHINORRSSSTY synarthrosis
AHKLLNNOOOPT holoplankton
AHLNOOPPRSTY hypoplastron
AHMNOOOPRTTY anthropotomy
AHNOOOPRRTTY prothonotary
AIIIILLMNOTT illimitation
AIIIILNORSTV virilisation
AIIIILNORTVZ virilization
AIIIIMMNNOST minimisation
AIIIIMMNNOTZ minimization
AIIILLMNNOTU illumination
AIIILLNNOSTT instillation
AIIILMMNORST trinomialism
AIIILMMNTTUV multivitamin
AIIILMNOOSST isolationism
AIIILMNORSTT trinomialist
AIIILMPRSSTU spiritualism
AIIILNOORTTV vitriolation
AIIILNOOSSTT isolationist
AIIILNRSSTTY sinistrality
AIIILPRSSTTU △spiritualist
AIIILPRSTTUY spirituality
AIIIMMNNORSS Rosminianism
AIIIMMNNOSTU immunisation
AIIIMMNNOTUZ immunization
AIIIMNNORSTT ministration
AIIIMNOOPSTT optimisation
AIIIMNOOPTTZ optimization
AIIINNNOOSTU unionisation
AIIINNNOOTUZ unionization
AIIINNOPSSST inspissation
AIIINOOPPRTT propitiation
AIIINOPRRTTT tripartition
AIIINOPRSTTT partitionist
AIIINRSTTTVY transitivity
AIIKMNNOPRSS Parkinsonism
AIILLLNOOTVY volitionally
AIILLLNOSUVY villainously
AIILLLOSSTTY solstitially
AIILLMMNNOTU mill-mountain
multinominal

AIILLMNOORTY	monitorially
AIILLNNOOTUV	involutional
AIILLNOOPSTT	postillation
AIILLNORSTTU	illustration
AIILLNQRTTUY	tranquillity
AIILMNNORTTU	malnutrition
AIILMNOPRSTT	trampolinist
AIILMNOPRSTY	postliminary
AIILMORSTUUV	multivarious
AIILNNOOOPST	Polonisation
AIILNNOOOPTZ	Polonization
AIILNNOOOSST	solonisation
AIILNNOOOSTZ	solonization
AIILNNOTTUUV	invultuation
AIILNOOOPPST	oppositional
AIILNORRSSST	sinistrorsal
AIILNORRSTTY	transitorily
AIILOPRSUVVY	viviparously
AIIMMMNOSSTU	missummation
AIIMMNOORTWY	mini-motorway
AIIMMNOTTUUY	auto-immunity
AIIMNNORSSST	transmission
AIIMNOOORSTT	motorisation
AIIMNOOORTTZ	motorization
AIIMNOOPRSSU	parsimonious
AIIMNOOQSTTU	misquotation
AIIMOOORSTTV	ovariotomist
AIIMOOPPRRRT	impropriator
AIIMOOPRRSTV	improvisator
AIINOOPRRSVY	provisionary
AIIOOPPRRTTY	propitiatory
AILLMNNOOPRY	pronominally
AILLNOOPTTYY	polytonality
AILLORRSTTUY	illustratory
AILMNORSTUVY	voluntaryism
AILMNOTTTUUU	tumultuation
AILNOOOPPRRT	proportional
AILNOPPRTUUY	unpopularity
AILNORSTTUVY	voluntaryist
AILOOPRRSUUY	uproariously
AILOORRSTTUY	traitorously
AIMNNOPRSTTU	transumption
AIMNOOOPRSTT	somatotropin
AINOOORRSTTT	rotor-station

B

BBBBBEEHLLUU	hubble-bubble
BBBBDEELLOUU	double-bubble
BBCDEINRSSUU	unsubscribed
BBCEEEHORSUY	breeches-buoy
BBCEEILMNRST	scribblement
BBCEEKORRRUY	roebuck-berry
BBCEGHILNRTU	nightclubber
BBCEJKOORSTY	stockjobbery
BBCEKLLMOPRU	plumber-block
BBCELLLOOSWY	collywobbles
BBCENOORRSTU	bronco-buster
BBCGIILLNRSY	scribblingly
BBCGIJKNOOST	stockjobbing
BBCGIKLNOSTU	blockbusting
BBCIIKLORRST	Bristol-brick
BBDDGIILNOUY	body-building
BBDEEEELORTW	beetle-browed
BBDEEELOPPRW	pebble-powder
BBDEEEMNNSSU	benumbedness
BBDEEGGKLOOO	gobbledegook
BBDEEILNOPRU	Bible-pounder
BBDEELLMOOTT	bell-bottomed
BBDEELLNOOTT	bottle-blonde
BBDEGGKLOOOY	gobbledygook
BBDEGIILNOTU	double-biting
BBDEHLOOORRT	blood-brother
BBDEIIILSSUV	subdivisible
BBDELMOOOTTU	double-bottom
BBDGIILNOOVY	voiding-lobby
BBEEEEEHIJSY	heeby-jeebies
BBEEFORRSTUV	Berufsverbot
BBEEGMNORRUY	money-grubber
BBEEHILMPRTU	Bible-thumper
BBEELLMMRTUU	rumble-tumble
BBEFGHLLOOTU	bull-of-the-bog
BBEFLORTTUWY	butterfly-bow
BBEGIIILOPST	bibliopegist
BBEGILLNRSUY	slubberingly
BBEGINNORSTU	rubbing-stone
BBEHILNOSSSS	slobbishness
BBEHINNOSSSS	snobbishness
BBEILNOSSSUU	bibulousness
BBENNORSSSTU	stubbornness
BBGHIILMNOOS	hobgoblinism
BBGHIMMNOTUY	thingummybob
BBGIIILLOOST	bibliologist
BBHJNNOOOOSS	Hobson-Jobson
BBHMOOOOPRSU	ombrophobous
BBIIILLOOPST	bibliopolist
BCCCEIIMRRSU	circumscribe
BCCDEGHIKNOY	body-checking
BCCDNOORSTUU	bus-conductor
BCCEEEHKRRRY	checkerberry
BCCEEELNOOSS	obsolescence
BCCEEEMNOSTU	obmutescence
BCCEEHNORRSS	crossbencher
BCCEEIILNOSV	obliviscence
BCCEEINOORRT	cerebrotonic
BCCEHHINOOPT	technophobic
BCCEHNOOOPRS	bronchoscope
BCCEHORSTTTU	butterscotch
BCCEILMOORTY	motor-bicycle
BCCGIIKLMNOR	rock-climbing
BCCHILLOOPSU	public-school
BCCHNOOOPRSY	bronchoscopy
BCCINOOSSSUU	subconscious
BCCIOOOPRSST	stroboscopic
BCCKOORSSTTU	cross-buttock
BCDDDEEEKLOU	double-decked
BCDDEEEIINOS	disobedience
BCDDEEEKLORU	double-decker
BCDDEEKLLOOU	double-locked
BCDDEIIILTUY	deducibility
BCDEEEEKNSTW	between-decks
BCDEEEFIILNT	indefectible
BCDEEEIILNTT	indetectible
BCDEEEILNRSS	credibleness
BCDEEEKORRST	stockbreeder

BCDEEEMNNRUU	unencumbered
BCDEEFIIKLRR	brickfielder
BCDEEFIJNORT	object-finder
BCDEEGIIINPR	birding-piece
BCDEEIILPRST	discerptible
BCDEEIIOPPRR	bodice-ripper
BCDEEILOPRRU	reproducible
BCDEEILRSTTU	destructible
BCDEEIMNNRUU	unincumbered
BCDEEINORRSS	incrossbreed
BCDEEINPRRSU	unprescribed
BCDEELORSTUU	tuberculosed
BCDEEMOOPRSS	obcompressed
BCDEIIILRTUY	reducibility
BCDEIIILSSUV	subcivilised
BCDEIIILSUVZ	subcivilized
BCDEIILNOORR	incorrodible
BCDEIILNORTU	introducible
BCDEINORSTUU	subintroduce
BCDELOORRUUY	ruby-coloured
BCDENORSTTUU	unobstructed
BCDGIIIKLNSU	sick-building
BCDGIKLNOOSU	bloodsucking
BCEEEEEHKNRS	knee-breeches
BCEEEEFNRRSU	subreference
BCEEEEGHRRSU	cheeseburger
BCEEEEGILLNR	belligerence
BCEEEFILNNTY	beneficently
BCEEEGHILNSY	beseechingly
BCEEEGILLNRY	belligerency
BCEEEIIILMMS	semi-imbecile
BCEEEIKOORSX	exercise-book
BCEEEINRSSUV	subservience
BCEEEIRRRSVY	serviceberry
BCEEEMMNNRTU	encumberment
BCEEENPPRSTU	prepubescent
BCEEFHNNORRT	front-bencher
BCEEFILNORSS	forcibleness
BCEEGILLMNOW	well-becoming
BCEEGIMNNOSS	becomingness
BCEEHLLNOSST	Stellenbosch
BCEEIIJSSTUV	subjectivise
BCEEIIJSTUVZ	subjectivize
BCEEIILLRSTT	belletristic
BCEEIJLSTUVY	subjectively
BCEEIJNNOOTV	non-objective
BCEEILLOOPSU	ebullioscope
BCEEILMNOPTT	contemptible
BCEEILMOPRSS	compressible
BCEEILOPRRTY	pro-celebrity
BCEEIMMOSTTU	subcommittee
BCEEIMNOPRRY	pre-embryonic
BCEEIMORRRWY	micro-brewery
BCEEINRSSUVY	subserviency
BCEEJLNOOSST	object-lesson
BCEEKKLNNOSU	knuckle-bones
BCEELMMOORTU	coulombmeter
BCEELNOORTVY	conveyor-belt
BCEELOORRTTU	butter-cooler
BCEFFLNORTUU	counterbluff
BCEGHIILNTWY	bewitchingly
BCEGHIMNNOOY	honeycombing
BCEGIIILNORR	incorrigible
BCEGIKKLNOOR	booking-clerk
BCEGIKLNOSTU	bluestocking
BCEGILMNNOUY	unbecomingly
BCEGILNOOOOY	biocoenology
BCEHHLORSSTU	clothes-brush
BCEHIIILOSTY	cohesibility
BCEHIIMORSTY	biochemistry
BCEHIINOPPRS	prince-bishop
BCEHIINOSTTY	biosynthetic
BCEHIMORSTUY	heir-by-custom
BCEIIINOSSTT	bioscientist
BCEIIJMSSTUV	subjectivism
BCEIIJNNOSTU	insubjection
BCEIIJSSTTUV	subjectivist
BCEIIJSTTUVY	subjectivity
BCEIIKLLNRTU	clinker-built
BCEIIILNOORRS	incorrosible
BCEIIILNRSTTU	instructible
BCEIINORTTUV	contributive
BCEIIPRSSTUV	subscriptive
BCEIKNRTTTUY	Tyburn-ticket
BCEILLOOPSUY	ebullioscopy
BCEILLORTTUY	butty-collier
BCEILMNOPTTY	contemptibly
BCEILOOPRTUU	probouleutic
BCEILORSSTUU	tuberculosis
BCEILRRTTUUY	trituberculy
BCEINNNOSTTU	subcontinent
BCEINOPRSSTU	subinspector
BCEIOPRSSSUY	presbycousis
BCEKLLMMOPRU	plummer-block
BCEKMOOSTTUU	mouse-buttock
BCELMOPRSUUU	suboperculum
BCEMNORSSSUU	cumbrousness
BCEMOOOPPRTT	copper-bottom
BCERRSSTTUUU	substructure
BCFIILMMORRU	lumbriciform
BCGGGIIKNNOR	brick-nogging
BCGHHILNOTTU	bolting-hutch
BCGIIILNORRY	incorrigibly
BCGIIILMOOORY	microbiology
BCGIIILOOOOSY	sociobiology
BCGIINOOOSTT	gnotobiotics
BCGIKKNOORST	stockbroking
BCGILLNOORUY	cryoglobulin
BCHHIIMORSTY	biorhythmics
BCHHILOOOSSY	schoolboyish
BCHHIMOOORRT	orthorhombic
BCHIIIOPSSTY	biophysicist
BCHIIOOOPRTT	trophobiotic
BCHILMOORTTY	thrombolytic
BCIILLMOOOTY	locomobility
BCIINNOORTTU	contribution
BCIINOPRSSTU	subscription
BCIKNOOOOPRS	book-scorpion
BCILMMNOSUUU	cumulonimbus
BCIMMNOSTUUY	subcommunity
BCINOORRTTUY	contributory
BCINORSSTTUU	substruction
BDDDEEILMNOU	double-minded
BDDDEELOOTTU	double-dotted

BDDDEILMNOOY	bloody-minded
BDDDGILNOOPU	blood-pudding
BDDEEEEFILMN	feeble-minded
BDDEEEFINNRU	unbefriended
BDDEEEINNSST	indebtedness
BDDEEFLMOORU	double-formed
BDDEEGGINOOR	good-breeding
BDDEEGIINNRT	interbedding
BDDEEGJMNTTU	judgment-debt
BDDEEIKNNORW	broken-winded
BDDEEILMNSSU	undissembled
BDDEEILNRRUU	underbuilder
BDDEEILOOPTT	pottle-bodied
BDDEIINSSSUU	unsubsidised
BDDEIINSSUUZ	unsubsidized
BDDEILMNORUU	mound-builder
BDDFGIILNORY	forbiddingly
BDDGIILNORUW	word-building
BDEEEEMMNRRU	unremembered
BDEEEFIILNNS	indefensible
BDEEEFILOOSU	oeils-de-boeuf
BDEEEFMNOORT	forebodement
BDEEEGILNNOS	nosebleeding
BDEEEGLNORTU	ground-beetle
BDEEEHIILLTW	white-bellied
BDEEEHMORRTU	mouth-breeder
BDEEEILLMRTW	well-timbered
BDEEEILMNRTW	bewilderment
BDEEEILNNSSV	vendibleness
BDEEEILRTUVY	delivery-tube
BDEEEIMMNORT	re-embodiment
BDEEEIMNRTTU	unembittered
BDEEELMNORTU	redoublement
BDEEENOSSSTT	besottedness
BDEEFGILORUU	double-figure
BDEEFIILNNSY	indefensibly
BDEEFILMNOOT	nimble-footed
BDEEGIIILNST	indigestible
BDEEGLNOOTUU	double-tongue
BDEEHIILLMSS	disembellish
BDEEHINOSTUU	hebetudinous
BDEEHLLOORTT	bottle-holder
BDEEIIILNRTV	indivertible
BDEEIILMNTTW	nimble-witted
BDEEIILNNOTY	inobediently
BDEEIIMRRTTU	turbidimeter
BDEEIINNRSST	bend-sinister
BDEEIIRRSTTU	redistribute
BDEEIJLRRRUY	jerry-builder
BDEEILLORSTT	bottle-slider
BDEEILMRRRTU	tumbler-drier
BDEEIMNRSSTU	disbursement
BDEEINORTTTW	twitter-boned
BDEELNORSUVY	unobservedly
BDEELOORSTUY	double-storey
BDEFGILNOORY	forebodingly
BDEFGINNOORU	unforeboding
BDEFHOOOTTUY	out-of-the-body
BDEFLLMOOTTU	full-bottomed
BDEFLNOSSTUU	doubtfulness
BDEGHHINOOOR	neighborhood
BDEGHHOORRTU	△thoroughbred
BDEGHILORRTU	guild-brother
BDEGIIILNSTY	indigestibly
BDEGIILLNOSW	disbowelling
BDEGIINNRSST	bird's-nesting
BDEGILLNNRUY	blunderingly
BDEGILLNOOTT	bloodletting
BDEGILNOOOPS	pigeon's-blood
BDEGINOPRTUW	powdering-tub
BDEHHLORSSTU	subthreshold
BDEHHMNOOORR	rhombohedron
BDEHIINOPRTU	unprohibited
BDEHMOOORSTW	smooth-browed
BDEHMOORSTTU	rush-bottomed
BDEIIIILLNTY	indelibility
BDEIIIORSTVY	biodiversity
BDEIIIRSTTUV	distributive
BDEIIILLNOSSU	indissoluble
BDEIIILORSSUU	subdelirious
BDEILMNOOSSY	molybdenosis
BDEILNNPRSSU	purblindness
BDEIMNNOOSTY	endosymbiont
BDELLNORTUUY	untroubledly
BDELLOORRTUW	trouble-world
BDEOOPRTUWYY	woodburytype
BDFIILMNNUUU	infundibulum
BDGGGIILMNNO	mind-boggling
BDGHHIOORRTU	thirdborough
BDGHIIILNPSU	shipbuilding
BDGHILOOORYY	hydrobiology
BDGIIKNNORTU	drinking-bout
BDGIINNRSTUU	undisturbing
BDGILLMNOOUW	blow-moulding
BDGILNNOTUUY	undoubtingly
BDHHOOOPRSUY	hydrophobous
BDHIIMOORRSS	bromhidrosis
BDHILOORSTTY	bloodthirsty
BDIIIIILSTVY	divisibility
BDIIIILNOSTY	libidinosity
BDIIILLNOSUY	libidinously
BDIIILNNOSUU	unlibidinous
BDIIINORSTTU	distribution
BDIILLNOSSUY	indissolubly
BEEEEEFLMNNT	enfeeblement
BEEEEFHINORR	hereinbefore
BEEEEIMNSTTW	betweentimes
BEEEEKLMNRRT	knee-trembler
BEEEELMMNTZZ	embezzlement
BEEEFGLNOSTT	self-begotten
BEEEFILLNSSX	flexibleness
BEEEFLLMMORW	fellow-member
BEEEGGGIRRUV	veggie-burger
BEEEGHOORRUV	borough-reeve
BEEEGIILLMNS	ill-beseeming
BEEEGIMOORSU	embourgeoise
BEEEGMMNRSTU	submergement
BEEEHIINNRTT	terebinthine
BEEEHILLNOTW	below-the-line
BEEEHIMPRSST	Septemberish
BEEEHQRRSTUU	Thurberesque
BEEEIILNNSTX	inextensible
BEEEIILRRRSV	irreversible
BEEEIIRRTTVZ	Zeitvertreib

Words marked △ may be spelled also with a capital letter

BEEEILLMNTTT	belittlement
BEEEILLRSSTT	blister-steel
BEEEILNNSSSS	sensibleness
BEEEILNRRSST	terribleness
BEEEILOPPRST	tribespeople
BEEEIMMNRTTT	embitterment
BEEEIMPRRSST	Septembriser
BEEEIMPRRSTZ	Septembrizer
BEEEINNNORTZ	nitrobenzene
BEEEIRRSSSSW	Besserwisser
BEEEKNORRSTU	bunko-steerer
BEEELLNNOTVY	benevolently
BEEELNOOPRTT	bottle-opener
BEEELNOOSSST	obsoleteness
BEEFFGHILNUW	buffing-wheel
BEEFGIINNRRT	birefringent
BEEFIILRRSTU	filibusterer
BEEFIORRSTUU	tuberiferous
BEEGGHIINNNT	benightening
BEEGGIIOOOOW	boogie-woogie
BEEGGILNNORW	bowling-green
BEEGHILNORSS	neighborless
BEEGHINNRTTU	hunger-bitten
BEEGHNOOOPRT	gerontophobe
BEEGIIILLLNT	intelligible
BEEGIIILMNSV	misbelieving
BEEGIILNNPUX	inexpungible
BEEGILMORSTY	boy-meets-girl
BEEGLOORRTTT	globetrotter
BEEHIIILTVXY	exhibitively
BEEHIIINORTX	exhibitioner
BEEHILLMOSTY	blithesomely
BEEHILMOOPST	phlebotomise
BEEHILMOOPTZ	phlebotomize
BEEHILNORRSS	horribleness
BEEHLOORSTUU	trouble-house
BEEHLORRRTWY	whortleberry
BEEHNOOPRRTU	porte-bonheur
BEEIIILMRRSS	irremissible
BEEIIILRRSST	irresistible
BEEIIKLNSSSU	businesslike
BEEIILNRSSTU	unresistible
BEEIILRRRSVY	irreversibly
BEEIILRRSSTV	verslibriste
BEEIJLLMOOST	mosbolletjie
BEEILLLORSUY	rebelliously
BEEILPPRSSSU	suppressible
BEEILPRSSTUU	supersubtile
BEEIMNORTTUY	tribute-money
BEEINNORRTUW	winterbourne
BEEKMNNNOOTY	bonnet-monkey
BEEKNNNORSSU	unbrokenness
BEELLLLOORTY	loblolly-tree
BEELLMNRSSUY	numberlessly
BEELNNOSSSUU	nebulousness
BEELNOOSSSST	bootlessness
BEELNQSSTUUY	subsequently
BEELORSTTUVY	oversubtlety
BEEOOPRRSSTU	obstreperous
BEFGIILNORTU	foreign-built
BEFGIIOORSUY	bourgeoisify
BEFIILRSTTUY	subfertility
BEFILLMNRSSU	brimfullness
BEFILLNSSSSU	blissfulness
BEFILMOPRSUU	plumbiferous
BEFILOOORSSU	soboliferous
BEFLNRTTTUUY	butterfly-nut
BEGGHIINNORU	neighbouring
BEGGIILNNOSS	obligingness
BEGHINNORSUU	burning-house
BEGIIIILLLTY	illegibility
BEGIIILLLNTY	intelligibly
BEGIILLMMNSW	swimming-bell
BEGIILOOOSTX	exobiologist
BEGIINORRSVW	virgin's-bower
BEGILLMNRSUY	slumberingly
BEGILLNRSTUY	blusteringly
BEGILMNNRSUU	unslumbering
BEGILMOORSTY	embryologist
BEGILNOOORUY	neurobiology
BEHHNOOPSTTY	phytobenthos
BEHIILMNPSSS	blimpishness
BEHIINOSSSTY	biosynthesis
BEHILLMMRSTU	miller's-thumb
BEHILMOOPSTT	phlebotomist
BEHILMORRTTU	trouble-mirth
BEHLOOORSTTU	troubleshoot
BEIIIIILSSTV	visibilities
BEIIILLMMNNU	bimillennium
BEIIILLMMNSU	bimilleniums
BEIIILLNOSSU	insolubilise
BEIIILLNOSUZ	insolubilize
BEIIILRRSSTY	irresistibly
BEIIILSSTTUV	vestibulitis
BEIILLLLLORU	Lillibullero
BEIILLLLORRU	Lilliburlero
BEIILMSSSUVY	submissively
BEIIMNSSSUUV	unsubmissive
BEIINOOSSSST	obsessionist
BEIIOOPRSTTU	obreptitious
BEIISSTTTUUV	substitutive
BEILLOORSSTT	stilboestrol
BEILMNRSTTUU	butter-muslin
BEILOOQSSUUY	obsequiously
BEILOORSSTUY	boisterously
BEILOPPRSTUU	purpose-built
BEINPPRTTTUY	Tyburn-tippet
BELLMORSSUUY	slumberously
BELMNOOPRYYY	polyembryony
BEOORRSSTTTU	buttress-root
BFGGHIILLNTU	bullfighting
BFIIIILNSTUY	infusibility
BFIIILNNORSY	fibrinolysin
BFIILLMMOORR	morbilliform
BFIILMOORRST	strobiliform
BGGGHIILNNTU	lightning-bug
BGGIIMNNOOSW	swinging-boom
BGGILNOOOOTY	gnotobiology
BGHIILLNSTTU	bullshitting
BGHILLNNSUUY	unblushingly
BGHILLNOOOPT	polling-booth
BGHILOOOOPTY	photobiology
BGIIIIILNTTY	ignitibility
BGIIIKNOOSTV	visiting-book

BGIIILNNOOPT boiling-point
BGIIJLMMNOOY Jimmy-o'Goblin
jimmy-o'goblin
BGIIKLLNNNUY unblinkingly
BGIILMOORSTT timbrologist
BGIIMNNSTTUU unsubmitting
BGIINNNOPRTU burning-point
BGILLORSUUUY lugubriously
BGILNOORRUWW burrowing-owl
BHIIOOOPRSST trophobiosis
BHILMOOOPRSU ombrophilous
BHIOOPRSSSTU Russophobist
BIIIIILNSTVY invisibility
BIIILLNOSTUY insolubility
BIILOQSTUUUY ubiquitously
BIINOSSTTTUU substitution
BILLORSSTUUY subsultorily
BILOORSSTUUY robustiously
BLOOOPRSSTUU obstropulous

C

CCCCEEENNORS concrescence
CCCCEHINOOSU echinococcus
CCCDEEILNOPY encyclopedic
CCCDHIIOOPRS dichroscopic
CCCEEHILORTY heterocyclic
CCCEEHKNORTU countercheck
CCCEEIINRTTY eccentricity
CCCEEILNNOTU noctilucence
CCCEEIMNRRTU circumcentre
CCCEILMORTUU circumlocute
CCCEINNOPSTU concupiscent
CCCEINNSSSTU succinctness
CCCEIOOPRSTT streptococci
CCCEMNOOPSUU pneumococcus
CCCIIIMNORSU circumcision
CCCIIIMORRTU microcircuit
CCDDEEENNOPY co-dependency
CCDDEEENORSS decrescendos
CCDDEEHIILNR cliché-ridden
CCDDEEINNOST disconnected
CCDEEEEHINPR crêpe-de-chine
CCDEEEEILNST delitescence
CCDEEEEMNSTU detumescence
CCDEEEFNNORS frondescence
CCDEEEHIINNS indehiscence
CCDEEEHNOSTU escutcheoned
CCDEEEIINRSV viridescence
CCDEEEIKLLLS sickle-celled
CCDEEENRRSTU recrudescent
CCDEEFILOPSU self-occupied
CCDEEHORSTUV overscutched
CCDEEIILNORR irreconciled
CCDEEIKNQSTU quick-scented
CCDEEILMORRS sclerodermic
CCDEEILNNORU unreconciled
CCDEEIMOSSTY Discomycetes
CCDEEIORRTTU correctitude
CCDEELOOPPRS close-cropped
CCDEGIIILNRR circle-riding
CCDEHIILNSTY schindyletic
CCDEHILNNORU unchronicled
CCDEHIMNOSSY synecdochism
CCDEHIMOORTY orchidectomy
CCDEHIOOOPRS dichrooscope
CCDEIILLMOSU molluscicide
CCDEIILNNOTY coincidently
CCDENOPRSTUU superconduct
CCDGHIILNORW childcrowing
CCDGKNOOOORU drongo-cuckoo
CCDGKNOOORUU ground-cuckoo
CCDHHILOORRY hydrochloric
CCDHHINOOOPR chordophonic
CCDIIILNRTYY cylindricity
CCDIINOTTUVY conductivity
CCDNNNOOORTU non-conductor
CCEEEEHRSTTU cheesecutter
CCEEEEIIKKLO cockieleekie
CCEEEEINRSVV revivescence
CCEEEEJNNSUV juvenescence
CCEEEELLMNOS emollescence
CCEEEELLRRVV clever-clever
CCEEEFIMNORS scene-of-crime
CCEEEFINNORR conférencier
CCEEEFLNORSU fluorescence
CCEEEGHHIKRW checkweigher
CCEEEGILNORT electrogenic
CCEEEHINNOST ethnoscience
CCEEEHOOPRRT porte-cochère
CCEEEIILNRSV virilescence
CCEEEIIMNNRS reminiscence
CCEEEIINNRST inter-science
CCEEEIINPRSS resipiscence
CCEEEIINRSVV reviviscence
CCEEEILLORTV recollective
CCEEEILMNNRT encirclement
CCEEEILMNNSU luminescence
CCEEEILMORRT electromeric
CCEEEIMNNOPT incompetence
CCEEEIMNNSTU intumescence
CCEEEINNNOST consentience
CCEEEINNORSU neuroscience
CCEEEINOOPSS coenospecies
CCEEEINORSSV coerciveness
CCEEEINRSVVY revivescency
CCEEELOOPRST electroscope
CCEEEMMMNNOT commencement
CCEEEMNOPPRT cement-copper
CCEEENNOQSSU consequences
CCEEENNORSST concreteness
CCEEFFIIINNY inefficiency
CCEEFFIIKOTT ticket-office
CCEEFGINNNOR conferencing
CCEEFIIIPSST site-specific
CCEEFINNOORT confectioner
CCEEFNOORRTU counter-force
CCEEGGILNOTY glycogenetic
CCEEGILLOOSY ecclesiology
CCEEGINNNORT concentering
CCEEGINOOSTT geotectonics
CCEEGINOSTTY cytogenetics
CCEEHHIKNNTW kitchen-wench
CCEEHHLOPPRU churchpeople
CCEEHIILNORT heliocentric

CCEEHIILORTT	heteroclitic
CCEEHIKLNPST	pencil-sketch
CCEEHIKLNRRT	lick-trencher
CCEEHIKNOSTU	chuckie-stone
CCEEHIMMNNOT	mnemotechnic
CCEEHIMOSTYZ	schizomycete
CCEEHINNORTT	ethnocentric
CCEEHINNOSTU	inescutcheon
CCEEHIOPTTUY	hypoeutectic
CCEEHKLOORST	electroshock
CCEEHMOPSTYY	Phycomycetes
CCEEHOPRRRTY	hypercorrect
CCEEIIIIKKKW	kickie-wickie
CCEEIILLOSTV	collectivise
CCEEIILLOTVZ	collectivize
CCEEIILMNSTU	multiscience
CCEEIIMMNOSU	oecumenicism
CCEEIINNNNOT	incontinence
CCEEIINPRSSY	resipiscency
CCEEIINRSVVY	reviviscency
CCEEILLLOTVY	collectively
CCEEILLNOORT	recollection
CCEEILLORTTY	electrolytic
CCEEILMORRST	sclerometric
CCEEILNNORTV	conventicler
CCEEILNNOTVY	connectively
CCEEILNOORTT	electrotonic
CCEEILOOPRTT	electro-optic
CCEEILOPRRTY	pyro-electric
CCEEILOPRTTY	electrotypic
CCEEILSSSUVY	successively
CCEEIMMNOSTY	meniscectomy
CCEEIMNNNOTV	convincement
CCEEIMNNOPTY	incompetency
CCEEIMNOORST	econometrics
CCEEINNNORTT	interconnect
CCEEINOORRRT	correctioner
CCEEINSSSUUV	unsuccessive
CCEEIOOPRSST	stereoscopic
CCEELMNNOTUY	locum-tenency
CCEENORRRUUY	Eurocurrency
CCEEOOPPRSST	spectroscope
CCEFHINOORSU	conchiferous
CCEFIIINNSTU	unscientific
CCEFIILMRSUU	circumfusile
CCEFILMNRTUU	circumfluent
CCEFLLSSSUUY	successfully
CCEFLNSSSUUU	unsuccessful
CCEFOOOPRRRT	proof-correct
CCEGHIIKQRTU	get-rich-quick
CCEGHIINORTT	ricochetting
CCEGHIKMNOOR	checking-room
CCEGHILMOPYY	hypoglycemic
CCEGIIIMNNOR	criminogenic
CCEGIINPRTTU	price-cutting
CCEGILMMOORY	myrmecologic
CCEGINNNNORU	unconcerning
CCEHHIILMOOR	heliochromic
CCEHHORSTTUV	overschutcht
CCEHIILLNOPU	nucleophilic
CCEHIILMORRT	chlorimetric
CCEHIIMORSTT	stichometric
CCEHIINOORRT	rhinocerotic
CCEHIKLNORRW	clincher-work
CCEHILMOORRT	chlorometric
CCEHILNOORTU	technicolour
CCEHIMNOORRT	chronometric
CCEHIMNOSTYZ	zymotechnics
CCEHIMOOPRST	thermoscopic
CCEHIMOPRSTY	psychometric
CCEHINOPRSTY	pyrotechnics
CCEHIOOPSSTT	stethoscopic
CCEHKLOORSTT	throstle-cock
CCEHLOOORSUU	ochroleucous
CCEHNNOPRTUU	counter-punch
CCEHNOOPRSSY	synchroscope
CCEIIIMMORSS	microseismic
CCEIIINOORRT	oneirocritic
CCEIILLMOSTV	collectivism
CCEIILLOSTTV	collectivist
CCEIILLOTTVY	collectivity
CCEIILMNRTTU	multicentric
CCEIILNNOSUV	inconclusive
CCEIILOOPRST	poliorcetics
CCEIILPRSTUU	pisciculture
CCEIIMOOPSSS	seismoscopic
CCEIINNNNOTY	incontinency
CCEIINNOTTVY	connectivity
CCEIINOORSTV	viscerotonic
CCEIINORSTTV	constrictive
CCEIINRSSTTY	syncretistic
CCEILLNOSUVY	conclusively
CCEILLOOOPSS	oscilloscope
CCEILNNOSUUV	unconclusive
CCEILOOPRSUY	precociously
CCEILOOSSTUY	leucocytosis
CCEIMNOPRSTY	cryptomnesic
CCEIMOOOPPST	metoposcopic
CCEINNOSTTUY	constituency
CCEINOOPRSSU	preconscious
CCEINOORSSST	cross-section
CCEINOPSTTUY	conspectuity
CCEINORRSSTU	Russocentric
CCEINORSTTUV	constructive
CCELNNORRTUY	concurrently
CCELOPRSSUUU	crepusculous
CCENOPRRSTTU	preconstruct
CCENORRRSSTU	cross-current
CCEOOPPRSSTY	spectroscopy
CCFGGHIIKNOT	cockfighting
CCFIIMNORSUU	circumfusion
CCFILMORSUUU	circumfluous
CCFILOOOPRSU	fluoroscopic
CCGHIKNNORSU	corn-shucking
CCGHILNOOOST	conchologist
CCGIILNNNOVY	convincingly
CCGIIMNOOPRY	microcopying
CCGIINNNNOUV	unconvincing
CCGILMNOORTY	motorcycling
CCGINORSSTTU	crosscutting
CCHHIIIIQQUU	chiquichiqui
CCHHIIILOTTY	ichthyolitic
CCHHIILMOOPR	chromophilic
CCHHIIMOSTTY	stichomythic

CCHHIIMOSTYZ	schizothymic
CCHHIIOPSTYZ	schizophytic
CCHHILMOORST	chrisom-cloth
CCHHILMORSUW	Low-Churchism
CCHHIMNOOOPR	chromophonic
CCHHIMOOOPRT	photochromic
CCHHNNOORSUY	Oncorhynchus
CCHIIILOORST	orthosilicic
CCHIIMOPRSSY	microphysics
CCHIIMOPSSTY	psychoticism
CCHIIOOPRSTY	hypocoristic
CCHIIORRSTTU	short-circuit
CCHIMMNNOOPS	pinchcommons
CCHIMNOOPSSY	psychonomics
CCHIMOORSTUY	cymotrichous
CCHIOOOSSTTU	octostichous
CCHIOOPPRSTY	psychotropic
CCIIILLOOSSU	silicicolous
CCIIINNNNOTY	inconcinnity
CCIIKKKSSWYY	kicksy-wicksy
CCIILMOOOPST	cosmopolitic
CCIILNNNOOSU	inconclusion
CCIILNNNSTUU	cunnilinctus
CCIILORSTUUY	circuitously
CCIIMOOPRSST	microscopist
CCIINNNNOOSU	inconcinnous
CCIINNOOPRST	conscription
CCIINNOORSTT	constriction
CCIIOOTTTXYY	cytotoxicity
CCIKNOOOPRRS	rock-scorpion
CCILMOORSTTY	motorcyclist
CCILMORRSUUU	cirro-cumulus
	cumulocirrus
CCIMMNNOOPUU	communion-cup
CCIMNOOPSTUU	compunctious
CCIMNORSSTTU	misconstruct
CCINNOORSTTU	construction
CCLMOOOSSTUY	cyclostomous
CCNOORRSSTUY	cross-country
CDDDEEFIIOST	eisteddfodic
CDDEEEEFILSV	self-deceived
CDDEEEEINNNP	△independence
CDDEEEEJNSST	dejectedness
CDDEEEFILRST	self-directed
CDDEEEILLRTW	well-directed
CDDEEEINNNPY	△independency
CDDEEFLOPRSU	self-produced
CDDEEGILNOSU	cloud-seeding
CDDEEHLNNOSU	non-scheduled
CDDEEHLNORTU	underclothed
CDDEEHMOOPRU	home-produced
CDDEEIIKLNSS	slickensided
CDDEEIILMMNO	middle-income
CDDEEIJNPRUU	unprejudiced
CDDEEINNORSU	unconsidered
CDDEEINNOSTT	discontented
CDDEEINORSUV	undiscovered
CDDEEMNNOTUU	undocumented
CDDEEMNOOPSU	undecomposed
CDDEEMNOOTUY	duodenectomy
CDDEENOOPPRS	dropped-scone
CDDEENOPRRUU	under-produce
CDDEFIIKLSST	fiddlesticks
CDDEFLNNOOUY	confoundedly
CDDEHILNOSSS	cloddishness
CDDEHLLOORSU	cold-shoulder
CDDEHLNORTUU	thundercloud
CDDEHMOOORST	odd-come-short
CDDEILNOOPRS	scolopendrid
CDDEINNORTUU	unintroduced
CDDEMNNOOPUU	uncompounded
CDDGIINNORSU	undiscording
CDDGILLMNOOU	cold-moulding
CDDIIMMOOSTY	discommodity
CDEEEEEGHPRR	hedge-creeper
CDEEEEFILNSV	self-evidence
CDEEEEFILRSV	self-deceiver
CDEEEEHNRRTT	three-centred
CDEEEEIINNPX	inexpedience
CDEEEEIKLPRW	pickerel-weed
CDEEEELNNPRS	resplendence
CDEEEELORRSV	record-sleeve
CDEEEENPRSSU	supersedence
CDEEEENSSTTW	sweet-scented
CDEEEFFGINOR	force-feeding
CDEEEFFIINNR	indifference
CDEEEFGIMNNN	fence-mending
CDEEEFHILRST	chesterfield
CDEEEFIJLNTU	fuel-injected
CDEEEFILLORW	flower-delice
CDEEEFLLORUW	flower-de-luce
	flower-deluce
CDEEEFLORRTT	retroflected
CDEEEGIKLNRS	single-decker
CDEEEGINOSTV	decongestive
CDEEEHIMNPRT	decipherment
CDEEEHIRSTTW	white-crested
CDEEEHNOOPTT	detectophone
CDEEEHNRSSTW	wretchedness
CDEEEIIINSTZ	decitizenise
CDEEEIIINTZZ	decitizenize
CDEEEIINNPXY	inexpediency
CDEEEIINSSSV	decisiveness
CDEEEILMNORT	declinometer
CDEEEILNQSTU	deliquescent
CDEEEIMNORTT	mine-detector
CDEEEINNNORS	non-residence
CDEEEINPRSST	decrepitness
CDEEEINRSSST	discreetness
	discreteness
CDEEEIORRRSV	rediscoverer
CDEEEKLNPSSS	speckledness
CDEEEKLNRTTU	turtle-necked
CDEEELNNPRSY	resplendency
CDEEELNOORST	electrosonde
CDEEELNPTUXY	unexpectedly
CDEEEMNNNOTU	denouncement
CDEEEMNNOORS	encomenderos
CDEEENPRSTUU	unpersecuted
CDEEFFHILOOR	office-holder
CDEEFFHOORRT	off-the-record
CDEEFFIINNRY	indifferency
CDEEFHLLOOSS	self-schooled
CDEEFHLNOOOV	cloven-hoofed

Words marked △ may be spelled also with a capital letter

CDEEFIINOSTT defectionist
CDEEFIIORRST corrie-fisted
CDEEFILNNNUU uninfluenced
CDEEFILORRST self-director
CDEEFLLOORSU self-coloured
CDEEFLMNOSSU self-consumed
CDEEFLNOOOTV cloven-footed
CDEEFLRSSTTU self-destruct
CDEEFNNOSSSU confusedness
CDEEFOORSSTT soft-sectored
CDEEGHILNRSU rescheduling
CDEEGIILRRTY triglyceride
CDEEGINNOOST decongestion
CDEEGINNORSU unrecognised
CDEEGINNORUZ unrecognized
CDEEGLNOOSTU close-tongued
CDEEHHKLLOSS shellshocked
CDEEHIIINNOR encheiridion
CDEEHIIRSTTW wire-stitched
CDEEHIKLORTT ticket-holder
CDEEHINNRSTU unchristened
CDEEHINORTWW white-crowned
CDEEHIOPRRRS recordership
CDEEHLMOOSTU close-mouthed
CDEEHLNORSTU underclothes
CDEEHLNPRSUU unsepulchred
CDEEHORSTTTU outstretched
CDEEIIILNSVY indecisively
CDEEIIILOPST depoliticise
CDEEIIILOPTZ depoliticize
CDEEIIINNSTV disincentive
CDEEIIINRTTV interdictive
CDEEIILLMPSU semipellucid
CDEEIILMNRSY semicylinder
CDEEIILMNRUV demi-culverin
CDEEIILNNORV overinclined
CDEEIILNOPRT predilection
CDEEIILNRSTY indiscreetly
indiscretely
iridescently
CDEEIILOPSTV velocipedist
CDEEIILORSVV silver-voiced
CDEEIILPRTVY predictively
CDEEIILRSTVY discretively
CDEEIIMNOPRV improvidence
CDEEIINNRSST indirectness
CDEEIIORSSTU discourteise
CDEEIKNORSST second-strike
CDEEILLNPSSU pellucidness
CDEEILMNOOPX complexioned
CDEEILNOORUW wine-coloured
CDEEILNORSTU uncloistered
CDEEILNPRTYY type-cylinder
CDEEILRRSTTY restrictedly
CDEEIMNNOSTT miscontented
CDEEIMNOORTU Deuteronomic
CDEEIMOOSSTX sextodecimos
CDEEIMPRSTUW wide-spectrum
CDEEINOPPRRT intercropped
CDEEINRRSTTU unrestricted
CDEEIOPRRTUV reproductive
CDEEIOPSSSUY pseudocyesis
CDEEIORRSTUV discoverture
CDEELLNNOSUU uncounselled
CDEELOOORRSU rose-coloured
CDEEMNOOPSSS composedness
CDEEMOOPRRSS decompressor
CDEENNNOOOST second-to-none
CDEENNOOPRST corespondent
CDEENNRRRTUU undercurrent
CDEENOORSSSU decorousness
CDEENRRSTTUU enstructured
CDEEOOPRSTUY deuteroscopy
CDEFFIIILSTU difficulties
CDEFHILNOORS school-friend
CDEFIIINNOST disinfection
CDEFIIMORSTU discomfiture
CDEFIINOSTTU unscottified
CDEFILNNNOUY unconfinedly
CDEFLNNOSUUY unconfusedly
CDEGHHIIKSTT thick-sighted
CDEGHHILOORU high-coloured
CDEGHIIKQSTU quick-sighted
CDEGHILORSST cross-lighted
CDEGHINNOOSU echo-sounding
CDEGHIOOPSTU pseudo-Gothic
CDEGIIMNOOSY gynodioecism
CDEGIINNNRSU undiscerning
CDEGIKLMNNOU neck-moulding
CDEGIKNNOSTU unstockinged
CDEGINOORRVW overcrowding
CDEGLMNORUUY curmudgeonly
CDEHHIIIPRTT diphtheritic
CDEHHIILNSSS childishness
CDEHIIILOPRS siderophilic
CDEHIIILPPSS discipleship
CDEHIIKKNNST thick-skinned
CDEHIIKNORTY hydrokinetic
CDEHIILLORSV shrill-voiced
CDEHIILNOOSV school-divine
CDEHIILNSSSY schindylesis
CDEHIIMNOSUU eunuchoidism
CDEHIIMPSSTY dysphemistic
CDEHIINOOOPR conidiophore
CDEHIINORTYZ hydrozincite
CDEHIIOPRRST directorship
CDEHIKKLLSTU thick-skulled
CDEHILLOOPRY policy-holder
CDEHIMNOOORS chondriosome
CDEHIMORTTYY rhytidectomy
CDEHINORSTTY thirty-second
CDEHIORRTTWY creditworthy
CDEIIIILNNPS indiscipline
CDEIIIJRSTUV jurisdictive
CDEIIILNNPSU undiscipline
CDEIIILNTVVY vindictively
CDEIIIMNORST misdirection
CDEIIINNORST indiscretion
CDEIIINNORTT interdiction
CDEIILMRTUUV diverticulum
CDEIILNNPPRU unprincipled
CDEIILRSSUVY discursively
CDEIIMMNOOSS commissioned
decommission

CDEIIMMRSSTY	dissymmetric
CDEIIMNOPRRT	microprinted
CDEIIMNORSTU	reductionism
CDEIINNNOOSX	disconnexion
CDEIINNOOPRT	precondition
CDEIINNSSSTT	distinctness
CDEIINOOOPRS	conidiospore
CDEIINOOPRST	periodontics
CDEIINORRTTY	interdictory
CDEIINORSTTU	reductionist
CDEIINORTTUV	introductive
CDEIKNRSTTUY	sky-tinctured
CDEILNOORSUY	indecorously
CDEILOPRTUVY	productively
CDEIMOOPRSSU	discomposure
CDEINNRSTTUU	uninstructed
CDEINOOPRRTU	reproduction
CDEINOPRTUUV	unproductive
CDEIOORSSTUU	discourteous
CDEKNORRSTUW	wonder-struck
CDELLNNOORTU	uncontrolled
CDELNNOOPRUY	pronouncedly
CDELNOOOSTUY	cotyledonous
CDELNPRSTUUU	unsculptured
CDELOOORRSUY	rosy-coloured
CDELOORRSTUU	rust-coloured
CDENNNOOPRUU	unpronounced
CDENRRSTTUUU	unstructured
CDFGIIIMNOST	discomfiting
CDFHILOORRUY	hydrofluoric
CDFIILMNORRY	cylindriform
CDGHIIILPRTY	ditriglyphic
CDGHIILLOOTY	thiodiglycol
CDGHIILNOORS	riding-school
CDGIIINNNOOT	conditioning
CDGIIKLNOSSU	cloud-kissing
CDGIIMMNNOOR	common-riding
CDGIKLNOOSTU	ducking-stool
CDGIMNNOOPRU	ring-compound
CDHHIIIMORTY	idiorhythmic
CDHHIOOOPRTY	hypotrochoid
CDHIIIMOOPRS	isodimorphic
CDHIMOOORRST	orthodromics
CDHINOOORSTT	orthodontics
CDHIOOOPRSSU	discophorous
CDHIOOOPSSUZ	schizopodous
CDIIIJNORSTU	jurisdiction
CDIIILNNSTTY	indistinctly
CDIILLORSUUY	ridiculously
CDIIMMNOOOSU	incommodious
CDIIMMNOSTUY	discommunity
CDIINNOORTTU	introduction
CDIINOOOOPSS	podoconiosis
CDIIOPRTTUVY	productivity
CDIKLNOOOPSS	spondoolicks
CDILMMOOOSUY	commodiously
CDINOORRTTUY	introductory
CDMMNNOOOOPU	mono-compound
CEEEEEHNNRST	cheese-rennet
CEEEEFFIKORS	office-seeker
CEEEEFFNRSTV	effervescent
CEEEEFILLSTV	self-elective
CEEEEFINNRRT	interference
CEEEEFLORRST	free-selector
CEEEEGHMNORS	cheesemonger
CEEEEGLLNRTT	tercel-gentle
CEEEEHHOPPRS	cheesehopper
CEEEEHIMNNPR	preheminence
CEEEEHNORSVW	whencesoever
CEEEEIILMPTT	etepimeletic
CEEEEIINNPRX	inexperience
CEEEEIKKPRTW	wicket-keeper
CEEEEILRSSTV	teleservices
CEEEEINPRSTX	pre-existence
CEEEEINRRRSV	sir-reverence
CEEEELMORRTT	electrometer
CEEEELNPRSST	pretenceless
CEEEFFINNOTV	non-effective
CEEEFFLNORST	efflorescent
CEEEFFLNORTT	left-of-centre
CEEEFGHHIMRT	Fehmgerichte
CEEEFGILLNST	self-electing
CEEEFHINRSST	scene-shifter
CEEEFHLNRSSU	cheerfulness
CEEEFIILRRTV	irreflective
CEEEFIIMPRTV	imperfective
CEEEFILLLMNU	mellifluence
CEEEFILLNOST	self-election
CEEEFILLNOSV	self-violence
CEEEFILLRTVY	reflectively
CEEEFILNNRTU	interfluence
CEEEFILNRTUV	unreflective
CEEEFILPRTVY	perfectively
CEEEFKLNSSSS	fecklessness
CEEEGGNORRRY	greengrocery
CEEEGHHIMRTV	Vehmgerichte
CEEEGIILLNNT	intelligence
CEEEGIINRSTV	receiving-set
CEEEGIKLMNOU	leukemogenic
CEEEGINOOSTT	osteogenetic
CEEEGINOPRTT	petrogenetic
CEEEHHINRSSS	cheerishness
CEEEHIIMRSTU	euhemeristic
CEEEHIIPRRSV	receivership
CEEEHIKPRRRT	three-pricker
CEEEHILLOPRT	electrophile
CEEEHIMNPSWY	chimney-sweep
CEEEHIMNRSTU	hermeneutics
CEEEHINOSSSV	cohesiveness
CEEEHIOORSTU	heteroecious
CEEEHLLPSSSY	speechlessly
CEEEHLNNOTTU	luncheonette
CEEEHLNORTUW	counter-wheel
CEEEHLNOSSST	clothes-sense
CEEEHMNNNRTT	entrenchment
CEEEHMNNRRTT	retrenchment
CEEEHMOORRST	stereochrome
CEEEHNOPRRST	centrosphere
CEEEHPPPRRRY	cherry-pepper
CEEEIILLNTTV	intellective
CEEEIIMNNPRT	impertinence
CEEEIIMPPRTV	imperceptive
CEEEIINPRTTV	interceptive
CEEEIINRRSTV	interservice

CEEEIIPRRSTV	irrespective
CEEEIJKLNRRT	tercel-jerkin
CEEEIKNOPRSS	specksioneer
CEEEIKNOPRST	specktioneer
CEEEILLNOPQU	equipollence
CEEEILNNOPPT	plenipotence
CEEEILNOPRST	preselection
CEEEILPRSTVY	respectively
CEEEIMNNOPRS	omnipresence
CEEEIMORRSTT	stereometric
CEEEINNNOSTX	non-existence
CEEEINNORSSV	overniceness
CEEEINNOTUVX	non-executive
CEEEINNQSSTU	quintessence
CEEEINOPRSTU	counterpeise
CEEEINOSSTVV	covetiveness
CEEEINPPRTUV	unperceptive
CEEEINPRSTUV	unrespective
CEEEINRRRSTW	screenwriter
CEEEIORRSSTV	retrocessive
CEEEIPPRSSSU	superspecies
CEEEIPRRSSUV	repercussive
CEEEIRRRSTUV	resurrective
CEEEKLNRSSSS	recklessness
CEEELLNPRUUV	pulverulence
CEEELMMORTTU	telecommuter
CEEELMNOPSST	completeness
CEEELMORRTTY	electrometry
CEEELNOPRSTU	Pleuronectes
CEEELNOPRSTW	steeple-crown
CEEELOPRRTTY	electrotyper
CEEELORRSSSU	resourceless
CEEELORSTTVV	velvet-scoter
CEEEMNNNORTU	renouncement
CEEEMOPRRSTT	spectrometer
CEEENNORSSTU	counter-sense
CEEENNPRTUUV	venepuncture
CEEENOOPRRSV	Provence-rose
CEEEOOPRRTTX	exteroceptor
CEEFFHINORTU	office-hunter
CEEFFIINNNOT	non-efficient
CEEFFLNORSSU	forcefulness
CEEFFNOORRTU	counteroffer
CEEFGHOPRRTU	rough-perfect
CEEFGIILNOPW	fowling-piece
CEEFGIILNRTY	electrifying
CEEFGIILNSTX	self-exciting
CEEFGIKNOSTT	stocking-feet
CEEFGILLNRTY	reflectingly
CEEFGILNNOTU	genuflection
CEEFGILNNRTU	unreflecting
CEEFGLLLNTUY	neglectfully
CEEFHKMORRTU	motherfucker
CEEFHLLNRUUY	uncheerfully
CEEFIILNORRT	irreflection
CEEFIILRTTVY	reflectivity
CEEFIIMNOPRT	imperfection
CEEFIINOPRST	frontispiece
CEEFILMNRSSU	mercifulness
CEEFILNOSSUV	voicefulness
CEEFILNOSUVY	veneficously
CEEFINNOPRTU	unperfection
CEEFLLPRSTUY	respectfully
CEEFLMNOPSTT	self-contempt
CEEFMOORRRTU	recomforture
CEEFNOORSSSS	confessoress
CEEGGILLNNTY	neglectingly
CEEGGILNOSSY	glycogenesis
CEEGHIINORTZ	rhizogenetic
CEEGHIINOSTT	histogenetic
CEEGHILNOPTY	phylogenetic
CEEGHILOOPRT	herpetologic
CEEGHIMORSTY	geochemistry
CEEGHINNOPTY	hypnogenetic
CEEGHINOORTT	orthogenetic
CEEGHINOPRSS	sheep-scoring
CEEGHINOPTTY	phytogenetic
CEEGHINORSTY	hysterogenic
CEEGHINORTUW	counter-weigh
CEEGIIKLNSTW	single-wicket
CEEGIILLNPRS	selling-price
CEEGIINNORTT	reciting-note
CEEGIINNPRSS	piercingness
CEEGIINOPRTV	precognitive
CEEGIKKNNOOR	knee-crooking
CEEGIKLLNOPS	glockenspiel
CEEGIKLNPTTU	putting-cleek
CEEGILMOOORT	meteorologic
CEEGINOORRVV	vice-governor
CEEGINOPRRSS	reprocessing
CEEGINOPRSSW	weeping-cross
CEEGMNOORRST	costermonger
CEEHHIILLLNP	philhellenic
CEEHHIINOSTT	henotheistic
CEEHHIMMOORT	homeothermic
CEEHHINOPRSZ	schizophrene
CEEHHINPRSTY	hypersthenic
CEEHHLOORSST	clothes-horse
CEEHHMNNORTY	nychthemeron
CEEHHMOOPRRS	chromosphere
CEEHHNOORRTY	heterochrony
CEEHHOOPPRSS	phosphoresce
CEEHHOOPRRST	trochosphere
CEEHIILLNPRS	spine-chiller
CEEHIINPPRST	prenticeship
	'prenticeship
CEEHIIOPRRSS	perichoresis
CEEHIIPPRRST	peristrephic
CEEHIKKLNTUW	white-knuckle
CEEHIKLSTTTT	kettlestitch
CEEHIKMNOSSS	homesickness
CEEHIKOOPRSU	cookie-pusher
CEEHILMMOPRY	myrmecophile
CEEHILMNOOTT	△monotheletic
CEEHILNNORTY	incoherently
CEEHIMMORRTT	thermometric
CEEHIMMPRSST	sprechstimme
CEEHIMNNNRTT	intrenchment
CEEHINOOPRST	stereophonic
CEEHINOORRSS	rhinoceroses
CEEHINOORRST	rhinocerotes
CEEHINOPPRTU	Picturephone®
CEEHINOPSTTU	theopneustic
CEEHIOOPRSTU	Oreopithecus

CEEHIOPRSTUU	picture-house
CEEHIOPRSTUX	executorship
CEEHIPPRRTYY	hyperpyretic
CEEHKLLOORRY	roller-hockey
CEEHKMNNORWY	monkey-wrench
CEEHLLNQSSUY	quenchlessly
CEEHLMOOPRTU	thermocouple
CEEHLOPRSSST	clothes-press
CEEHMOORRSTY	stereochromy
CEEHMOPRRSTY	psychrometer
CEEHMORSTTYY	hysterectomy
CEEHNORSSSTT	technostress
CEEHOOPRRSTU	urethroscope
CEEHOORRRSSU	horse-courser
CEEIIIMNPPRT	impercipient
CEEIIINNPRTT	intercipient
CEEIIINNSSSV	incisiveness
CEEIIJNNORTT	interjection
CEEIIJNORSTT	rejectionist
CEEIIKKLLRST	stickler-like
CEEIIKLLNRSV	nickel-silver
CEEIIKLORRTU	courtierlike
CEEIIKRRTTTW	ticket-writer
CEEIILLMNOTT	monticellite
CEEIILLMNPSX	mill-sixpence
CEEIILLNNORT	intercolline
CEEIILLNNOTT	intellection
CEEIILLRRUUW	curliewurlie
CEEIILMNNORT	inclinometer
CEEIILMPRSST	plessimetric
CEEIILNNPRSS	princeliness
CEEIILNPSSTX	explicitness
CEEIILOOPSSU	leucopoiesis
CEEIIMMORSST	seismometric
CEEIIMNNPRTY	impertinency
CEEIIMNOSSSS	secessionism
CEEIIMNOSTTU	cementitious
CEEIIMOPPRTT	micropipette
CEEIIMOPRSSU	semi-precious
CEEIIMORRSTU	meretricious
CEEIIMORSSTV	viscosimeter
CEEIINNNNOTV	inconvenient
CEEIINNOPRST	reinspection
CEEIINNOPRTT	interception
CEEIINNORSST	intercession
CEEIINNORSTT	intersection
CEEIINOPRRST	peristeronic
CEEIINOPRSTT	receptionist
CEEIINORSSUX	excursionise
CEEIINORSUXZ	excursionize
CEEIINOSSSST	secessionist
CEEIINPSSTUV	insusceptive
CEEIIPPRRSTV	prescriptive
CEEIIPPRTTVY	perceptivity
CEEIJNOORRTT	retrojection
CEEIKLMNPPRU	pumpernickel
CEEIKLNORSSS	session-clerk
CEEIKOPRRTTT	ticket-porter
CEEILLMNOPTY	incompletely
CEEILLNOPQUY	equipollency
CEEILLORSSTY	electrolysis
CEEILLPRSUVY	preclusively
CEEILMMNOPRT	complimenter
CEEILMNNNOOS	insomnolence
CEEILMNNOSSU	uncomeliness
CEEILMOOPRSY	co-polymerise
CEEILMOOPRYZ	co-polymerize
CEEILMOOSTTU	coletitmouse
CEEILMRRTUUV	vermiculture
CEEILNNNOTVY	conveniently
CEEILNNOPPTY	plenipotency
CEEILNNPSSTU	spinulescent
CEEILNOOPRSS	necropolises
CEEILOOPRSTT	coleopterist
CEEILOPRTTVY	protectively
CEEILPRSSUVY	percussively
CEEIMMMNORTT	recommitment
CEEIMMNNORTU	intercommune
CEEIMMNOORST	commorientes
CEEIMNNORTTV	contrivement
CEEIMNOOPRST	contemporise
CEEIMNOOPRTZ	contemporize
CEEIMNOORSTT	econometrist
CEEIMNORRSTU	Eurocentrism
CEEIMNORSUZZ	mizzen-course
CEEINNNOORTV	conventioner
CEEINNNOQSTU	inconsequent
CEEINNOORRRT	reconnoitrer
CEEINNOORRSV	reconversion
CEEINNORRTTV	interconvert
CEEINNORSSTT	contriteness
CEEINNPRTUUV	venipuncture
CEEINNRRRTTU	intercurrent
CEEINOOPRRSS	processioner
CEEINOOPRRTT	interoceptor
CEEINOOPRSTT	stereopticon
CEEINOOPRSTU	counterpoise
CEEINOORRSST	retrocession
CEEINOPRRSSU	repercussion
CEEINOPRSSSU	preciousness
CEEINOPSSSSU	speciousness
CEEINORRRSTU	△resurrection
CEEINORRSSTY	intercessory
CEEINORSTTTU	reconstitute
CEEIOOPRRSTT	stereotropic
CEEIOPRRTTTW	write-protect
CEEKLLNSSSSU	lucklessness
CEEKLLOORTWY	yellow-rocket
CEEKLNOOSTTY	cytoskeleton
CEEKOOPRRSSU	pressure-cook
CEELLNOORTTV	electron-volt
CEELMNNOOSST	somnolescent
CEELMOOORRTT	electromotor
CEELNNOQSTUY	consequently
CEELNOOPPTUY	county-people
CEELNOORSTTU	electrotonus
CEELNORSSSUU	ulcerousness
CEELOOOPRSTU	coleopterous
CEELOOPPRSTU	plecopterous
CEELPRRSSTUU	supercluster
CEEMOPRRSTTY	spectrometry
CEENNOOQRSTU	queen-consort
CEENNOORRTTU	counter-tenor
CEENOOOPPRSS	snooperscope

CEENOOSSSTUV	covetousness
CEEOPPRSSSTU	prospectuses
CEFFGIKNNOOR	off-reckoning
CEFFGILNOSSU	self-focusing
CEFFHIKNSTTU	kitchen-stuff
CEFFIIINNSTU	insufficient
CEFFIILNSTUY	sufficiently
CEFFIINNSTUU	unsufficient
CEFFIORRSTUU	fructiferous
CEFFIORSSTUU	suffruticose
CEFGHIMNOORT	home-crofting
CEFGHINOORSU	forcing-house
CEFGIIIKLNNR	fingerlickin'
CEFGIIKLLNRY	flickeringly
CEFGIILNOSTT	close-fitting
CEFHHILNOPRS	French-polish
CEFHIMOORSSU	moschiferous
CEFHLLLOOOSW	schoolfellow
CEFHLMOOORRR	chloroformer
CEFHLMOOORRU	fluorochrome
CEFIIILNOSTU	infelicitous
CEFIIILORSSU	siliciferous
CEFIIIORRSTU	Fourieristic
CEFIILLOSTUY	felicitously
CEFIILMNNTUY	munificently
CEFIILMORRTU	fluorimetric
CEFIILNOPRSS	prolificness
CEFIILNOPRTY	proficiently
CEFIILNORSST	frictionless
CEFIILNOSTUY	infectiously
CEFIIOORSTVY	vociferosity
CEFILLMNRUUY	unmercifully
CEFILLMOORSY	frolicsomely
CEFILLORRTUU	floriculture
CEFILMOORRTU	fluorometric
CEFILNNOSSTU	functionless
CEFILOORSUVY	vociferously
CEFILOPRSUUU	cupuliferous
CEFLNNORSSSU	scornfulness
CEFLNOORRTUY	counter-flory
CEFMNNNOORTT	confrontment
CEFNOOOPRRTU	counterproof
CEGGIIMNOTVY	gingivectomy
CEGHHIILOPRY	hieroglyphic
CEGHHIILOTVY	high-velocity
CEGHHILNOSTT	nightclothes
CEGHHINOOPTT	photo-etching
CEGHHLNOPRTU	trench-plough
CEGHIILNRSTT	chitterlings
CEGHIILOORST	cheirologist
CEGHIIOPSSTY	geophysicist
CEGHIKNNOSSS	shockingness
CEGHIKNOORRS	rocking-horse
CEGHILNOOORS	chronologise
CEGHILNOOORZ	chronologize
CEGHILNOOSTT	technologist
CEGHILNORRUY	chirurgeonly
CEGHILNORTTU	counterlight
CEGHILOOOSTY	stoechiology
CEGHILOOPSSY	psychologise
CEGHILOOPSYZ	psychologize
CEGHILOPPRTY	petroglyphic
CEGHINNOSSTU	touchingness
CEGHMOOPPSSY	sphygmoscope
CEGIIKLLNQSU	quick-selling
CEGIIKMNNORS	misreckoning
CEGIIKNRRSTT	trickstering
CEGIILLOOSTX	lexicologist
CEGIILNNPSTY	inspectingly
CEGIIMNNOOST	monogenistic
CEGIINNOOPRT	precognition
CEGIINOPTTYY	genotypicity
CEGIJKNOSSTT	jesting-stock
CEGIKLNOOSST	stocking-sole
CEGIKLNOSSST	stockingless
CEGIKNNOORST	rocking-stone
CEGILLNORSSS	cross-selling
CEGILMMOOTUY	etymologicum
CEGILMNOOOTY	etymologicon
CEGILNNNOSTY	consentingly
CEGILNNNOTTY	contingently
CEGILNNOQRUY	conqueringly
CEGILNNORSTU	curling-stone
CEGILNNOSTTY	contestingly
CEGILNOOPRTU	glucoprotein
CEGILNOOPRTY	glycoprotein
CEGILNOOSSTY	synecologist
CEGILNOPRTTY	protectingly
CEGIMNOOPRSY	myringoscope
CEGIMNOORRSU	microsurgeon
CEGIMORRRSUY	microsurgery
CEGINNNNOSTU	unconsenting
CEGINNNOORTW	conning-tower
CEGINNNORSTT	constringent
CEGINNOSTTTU	stonecutting
CEGINNPSSTUU	unsuspecting
CEGMOOSTUYYZ	zygomycetous
CEHHIILMOPRT	thermophilic
CEHHIILOPRST	lithospheric
CEHHIIMOSSTT	histochemist
CEHHILNRSSSU	churlishness
CEHHILOOPRTY	hypochlorite
CEHHILORSTTT	torch-thistle
CEHHIMMOOOPR	homeomorphic
CEHHIMOOPSTT	photochemist
CEHHIOOPPRST	photospheric
CEHHIOPPRRTY	hypertrophic
CEHIIIKLSTTT	Sittlichkeit
CEHIIILNOOPS	eosinophilic
CEHIIKLNSSST	ticklishness
CEHIIKNRSSST	trickishness
CEHIILLNNOTT	centillionth
CEHIILMNOPRS	necrophilism
CEHIILNQSSSU	cliquishness
CEHIILNRSSST	Christliness
CEHIILOORSTU	leiotrichous
CEHIILOPSTTY	polytheistic
CEHIIMNOOSTT	monotheistic
CEHIIMNOPRUY	perionychium
CEHIIMNSSTTY	syntheticism
CEHIIMOORSTT	trichotomise
CEHIIMOORTTZ	trichotomize
CEHIIMOPPRST	propheticism
CEHIINNOPRTY	pericynthion

CEHIIOPRRSTU	peritrichous
CEHIKMOOPRSU	skeuomorphic
CEHILLNNOPSU	Punchinellos
CEHILLNNORSU	unicorn-shell
CEHILLOPPTYY	polyphyletic
CEHILMMOPRYY	myrmecophily
CEHILMNOOPTY	monophyletic
CEHILMNOPPTY	nympholeptic
CEHILNNOSSSW	clownishness
CEHILNOOPRSU	necrophilous
CEHILNOPSSST	splotchiness
CEHILOQSTTUY	coquettishly
CEHILORRTTUU	horticulture
CEHILPPRRSUU	persulphuric
CEHIMMOOPRST	chemotropism
CEHIMNORRTYY	erythromycin
CEHIMOOPRRTT	thermotropic
CEHIMOORSTYZ	zoochemistry
CEHIMOPPRSTY	spermophytic
CEHINNORRSSY	synchroniser
CEHINNORRSYZ	synchronizer
CEHINOOPRRTU	neurotrophic
CEHINOPRSTTY	pyrotechnist
CEHINOQSTTUU	uncoquettish
CEHINOSSSSTT	Scottishness
CEHIOOPPRRST	tropospheric
CEHIOOPRRSTU	chiropterous
CEHIOOPRRTTT	tithe-proctor
CEHIOPPRSSTY	petrophysics
CEHLLLOPRSYY	sclerophylly
CEHMOOOOPRTY	oophorectomy
CEHMOOSSSTUU	customs-house
CEHMOPRRSTYY	psychrometry
CEHNOOOPRRSU	necrophorous
CEHNOORSTUUY	country-house
CEHOOOPPRSST	photo-process
CEHOOPRRSTUY	urethroscopy
CEIIIIILNSTV	incivilities
CEIIILLMRTUV	verticillium
CEIIILMNPSST	implicitness
CEIIINNORSTU	reunionistic
CEIIINOPRSST	precisionist
CEIIJLNNTUVY	injunctively
CEIIJNNOORTT	introjection
CEIIJOPRTTVY	projectivity
CEIIKLLPSTTY	lickety-split
CEIIKLQRSUVY	quicksilvery
CEIIKLSSTWZZ	swizzle-stick
CEIILLNOSTUY	licentiously
CEIILLRSTUUV	silviculture
CEIILMNNOOPT	incompletion
CEIILMNNOSTY	omnisciently
CEIILMNOSSUX	exclusionism
CEIILMOPRTUV	pluviometric
CEIILNNORSTU	interclusion
CEIILNOOSTTU	elocutionist
CEIILNOPRSUY	perniciously
CEIILNOSSSTU	seclusionist
CEIILNOSSTUX	exclusionist
CEIILOPRSSUU	supercilious
CEIIMMNOORSS	commissioner
	recommission
CEIIMMNOPRTU	minicomputer
CEIIMOORSSTT	sociometrist
CEIIMORSSTVY	viscosimetry
CEIINNNORSTU	internuncios
CEIINNNOSSTT	inconsistent
CEIINNORRSTU	insurrection
CEIINOOPRRTY	incorporeity
CEIINOPPRRST	prescription
CEIINOPRRSTT	prestriction
CEIINOPRRTUV	incorruptive
CEIINORSSTUX	excursionist
CEIINOSTTTUV	constitutive
CEIIOPPRRSTV	proscriptive
CEIIPRRRSTTW	scriptwriter
CEIIPSSTTUVY	susceptivity
CEIJKKLNNOTU	knuckle-joint
CEIKKMNORSTY	monkey-tricks
CEIKLLORSTUY	kill-courtesy
CEIKLOOPPSTT	pocket-pistol
CEIKLOOSSTUY	leukocytosis
CEIKMNNOORST	moon-stricken
CEILLLNOOOSV	violoncellos
CEILLMOPSUVY	compulsively
CEILLMOSTUUY	meticulously
CEILLNOSUVVY	convulsively
CEILLRSTUUVY	sylviculture
CEILMNOOSTTY	tonsilectomy
CEILMNOOSTUU	contumelious
CEILNNOSSTTY	consistently
CEILNOORRTTU	interlocutor
CEILNOORSSUY	censoriously
CEILNOSSSSUU	lusciousness
CEILNOSSTUUY	incestuously
CEILOOORSSST	otosclerosis
CEILOOPQRTUY	pectoriloquy
CEILOOSSSSUW	colossus-wise
CEIMNNOOPRSU	mispronounce
CEIMNNOORSTU	conterminous
CEIMNOPRSTTY	streptomycin
CEIMOOPRRSTU	micropterous
CEINNOOPRTTU	counterpoint
CEINNOORSSUU	uncensorious
CEINPSSSTTUU	intussuscept
CEINRRSSSTTU	instructress
CEKORRRRSTTU	terror-struck
CELMNOPRTUUU	mucopurulent
CELMNOTTTTUU	mutton-cutlet
CELNOOORRSTV	servocontrol
CEMMNNNOOSSU	uncommonness
CEMNOOPSTTUU	contemptuous
CEMOOOORRSTT	motor-scooter
CENNOSSSTUUU	unctuousness
CEOOPPRRSSSU	cross-purpose
CFFGIIIOORRS	frigorificos
CFFGINOORSSU	offscourings
CFGIKNOOOSTT	stocking-foot
CFGIMNNNOORU	unconforming
CFIIILOSTTUY	fictitiously
CFIILLNOOSTU	solifluction
CFIIMMNOORST	Cominformist
CFILNORSSUUU	furunculosis
CFIMNNOORTUY	unconformity

CFIOORRSTUUV	fructivorous
CGHHILOOPPTY	photoglyphic
CGHIIKNNOSSU	king's-cushion
CGHIILOOOPRT	oligotrophic
CGHIILOOOSTY	stoichiology
CGHIILOORSTT	trichologist
CGHIIMNOOPSY	physiognomic
CGHIIMOOPRTT	thigmotropic
CGHIKKNNOOPS	knocking-shop
CGHILLNOOPST	slop-clothing
CGHILMOOPSSY	psychologism
CGHILNOOORST	chronologist
CGHILOOPSSTY	psychologist
CGHINNOPSSTY	post-synching
CGHINOOOPPTY	photocopying
CGHINOOOSSUZ	schizogonous
CGIIIMNNOPRR	crimping-iron
CGIIIMNOSSTY	misogynistic
CGIIINNRSSTU	scrutinising
CGIIINNRSTUZ	scrutinizing
CGIIKLNNORSS	cross-linking
CGIIKNRSSSTU	kissing-crust
CGIILMOOSSTU	musicologist
CGIILNNOPRSY	conspiringly
CGIILOOOSTTX	toxicologist
CGIINNOOSTUU	incontiguous
CGIKLLNOORST	rolling-stock
CGILLNOOOPRT	protocolling
CGILMNNNOOPY	non-complying
CGILNOOOPSSU	spongicolous
CGILNOOSTUUY	contiguously
CGILOOOPRSTT	proctologist
CGILOOPRSTTY	cryptologist
CGIMNNOOORTU	counting-room
CGINOOPRSSTY	pyrognostics
CHHIIMOOOPPR	ophiomorphic
CHHILMOPRTYY	polyrhythmic
CHHINOOPRTTY	trichophyton
CHHINORRSSTT	Christ's-thorn
CHHLOOOPRSUY	hypochlorous
CHHMMOOOORSU	homochromous
CHIIILMNOOPS	iconophilism
CHIIILNOOPST	iconophilist
CHIIILOOPTTX	toxophilitic
CHIIILOPRTTT	lithotriptic
CHIILMOPRSTU	Turcophilism
CHIILOOPRSTY	polyhistoric
CHIIMNNRSSTY	strychninism
CHIIMNOOPSTY	△monophysitic
CHIINOOOPSTT	opisthotonic
CHIINOORSTTZ	chorizontist
CHIINOPSSTUV	viscountship
CHILOOOPPRSU	coprophilous
CHIMMNOOORST	monochromist
CHIMNOOOPRST	monostrophic
CHIMNOOOSSTU	monostichous
CHIMNOPRSTYY	chymotrypsin
CHIMOOOPPRRT	morphotropic
	protomorphic
CHIMOOORSTTU	trichotomous
CHINOOOPRSTY	ornithoscopy
CHINOOORSSTU	orthocousins
CHINOOPPSTTY	post-hypnotic
CHIOOOPPRRTT	prototrophic
	trophotropic
CHIOOORSSSTT	scissor-tooth
CHKOORRRRSTU	horror-struck
CHNNOORRTTUY	north-country
CIIIIIMNOSTU	inimicitious
CIIIIOPSSTTV	positivistic
CIIILLMPTTUY	multiplicity
CIILLOOSSTUY	solicitously
CIILMNNORSUY	synclinorium
CIILMNOOOPST	monopolistic
CIILMOOOTTVY	locomotivity
CIILNOOSSTUU	unsolicitous
CIILOORSTUVY	victoriously
CIILOPSSSUUY	suspiciously
CIIMNOPRSTTY	nyctitropism
CIINNOOPRRTU	incorruption
CIINNOOSTTTU	constitution
CIINNORSSTTU	instructions
CIINOOOPRSST	oniroscopist
CIINOOPPRRST	proscription
CIINOPSSSUUU	unsuspicious
CIJLNORSSTUU	jurisconsult
CILLMOOPRSUY	compulsorily
CILLORRSSUUY	scurrilously
CILNNOOSTUUY	continuously
CILNORSSTUUY	scrutinously
CILOPRSSTUUY	scrupulosity
CIMMNNNNOOOU	non-communion
CLLOPRSSUUUY	scrupulously
CLNOPRSSUUUU	unscrupulous
CMNOOPRSTUYY	cryptonymous

D

DDDDEEILLNNO	niddle-noddle
DDDEEENRRSSU	underdressed
DDDEEIIIMPSY	epididymides
DDDEEIINORVZ	zero-dividend
DDDEEINORRSU	undisordered
DDDEEINOSTTW	sodden-witted
DDDEELMMTTUY	muddy-mettled
DDDEGGHINOPU	hodge-pudding
DDDEGHINOOSW	woodshedding
DDDEHNNOOORR	rhododendron
DDDEIIKLNTWY	tiddledywink
DDEEEEFHNRTT	tender-hefted
DDEEEELLRSVW	well-deserved
DDEEEEMNNSST	dementedness
DDEEEENRSSSV	deservedness
DDEEEFGNORRU	ground-feeder
DDEEEFMNORSS	deformedness
DDEEEGGILPRS	spider-legged
DDEEEGGILRST	stridelegged
DDEEEGMOOPRT	good-tempered
DDEEEIIMNNRT	indetermined
DDEEEILMNRRT	intermeddler
DDEEEILMNRTY	determinedly
DDEEEIMNNRTU	undetermined
DDEEEINNOSSS	one-sidedness
DDEEEINPSSSS	despisedness
DDEEELNOPPRU	underpeopled

DDEEELNOPRUV underdevelop
DDEEELNRSUVY undeservedly
DDEEENOPRRUW underpowered
DDEEENORSUVZ rendezvoused
DDEEEOPRRSSW power-dressed
DDEEFFGLLLUY fully-fledged
DDEEFFINSSSU diffusedness
DDEEFHIIIMRU dehumidifier
DDEEFIIINNTU unidentified
DDEEFIIKLLSS self-disliked
DDEEGHIILMTW middleweight
DDEEGIILMNNS single-minded
DDEEGILMNOST dislodgement
DDEEGILNNSUY undesignedly
DDEEGINNNPWY penny-wedding
DDEEGLLNORUW well-grounded
DDEEHIMNOSTU unmethodised
DDEEHIMNOTUZ unmethodized
DDEEHINRRTUV thunder-drive
DDEEIIIIKKNW kiddiewinkie
DDEEIILLMNVY evil-mindedly
DDEEIILMMNPS simple-minded
DDEEIIMNNOSU diminuendoes
DDEEIINPRRST priest-ridden
DDEEIKNNRRUW wunderkinder
DDEEILLOPSSW well-disposed
DDEEILMMNOTY motley-minded
DDEEILNNPSSS splendidness
DDEEILNSTUVY undivestedly
DDEEIMNNORSU unmodernised
DDEEIMNNORUZ unmodernized
DDEEIMNNOSTW disendowment
DDEEINOSSSTW two-sidedness
DDEEIOPSSSSS dispossessed
DDEELNNOPSTY despondently
DDEFGHILLOOT floodlighted
DDEFGIILNRST fiddle-string
DDEFGINNNRUU underfunding
DDEGHILNRSUY shudderingly
DDEGHMOOORUU good-humoured
DDEGIKMNNORU underkingdom
DDEGILNNOPSY despondingly
DDEGILNOORST dendrologist
DDEGIMNNORST strong-minded
DDEGINNOPSTU pudding-stone
DDEGINNORSSW dressing-down
DDEGLNNORUUY ungroundedly
DDEGLNOOORSU dendrologous
DDEHIIIMNNSU undiminished
DDEHILNNOOPR △philodendron
DDEHILORRRTW Third-Worlder
DDEHMMNOOTUV venom'd-mouth'd
DDEHMNOORTUU round-mouthed
DDEIIILPRSTY dispiritedly
DDEIIJLNOSTY disjointedly
DDEIILNNOORR liriodendron
DDEIILNOPSSU splendidious
DDEILLMNOOWY woolly-minded
DDEILNOPRUVY unprovidedly
DDEILNPSTUUY undisputedly
DDEIMNOORRWW dormer-window
DDEIMOOPPSUU pseudopodium
DDGHILMNOOOU hood-moulding
DDGIIIKNNRRV drink-driving
DDIIIMPRTTUY rumpti-iddity
DEEEEEMNPRTV even-tempered
DEEEEGMNNNRT engenderment
DEEEEHLNNORT Heldentenöre
DEEEEHLNSSSS heedlessness
DEEEEILMPRTV evil-tempered
DEEEEIMNPRRT predetermine
DEEEEIMNPRTX experimented
DEEEELLMPRTW well-tempered
DEEEELNNSSSS needlessness
DEEEENRRSSSV reservedness
DEEEFGINRRYZ freeze-drying
DEEEFIINNSST definiteness
DEEEFINPRRSU superrefined
DEEEFINRRTTT interfretted
DEEEFLLMOPSY self-employed
DEEEFLMRRRSU self-murderer
DEEEFNNQRTUU unfrequented
DEEEGHILNPRS spring-heeled
DEEEGHIORTVW over-weighted
DEEEGIINNRRV engine-driver
DEEEGIKNNNOY donkey-engine
DEEEGIMNNRTU unregimented
DEEEGINNNRTU engine-turned
DEEEGINNRSSS resignedness
DEEEGINNRSSV evening-dress
DEEEGINRRSTU unregistered
DEEEGJMNPRTU prejudgement
DEEEHHLPRSSS shepherdless
DEEEHHNRSTTU thunder-sheet
DEEEHIILRTVW white-livered
DEEEHILMNSTV dishevelment
DEEEHILNSSTW swindle-sheet
DEEEHINRSSTW witheredness
DEEEHKLLORTT kettle-holder
DEEEHLNNORST Heldentenors
DEEEHLORSTTY heterostyled
DEEEHMNNORTT dethronement
DEEEHNOPRRTU three-pounder
DEEEHOOSTTTW sweet-toothed
DEEEIILPPRVY delivery-pipe
DEEEIINRSSST desensitiser
DEEEIINRSSSV derisiveness
DEEEIINRSSTZ desensitizer
DEEEILLMRSSY remedilessly
DEEEILLNRUVY unrelievedly
DEEEILMOPRSY depolymerise
DEEEILMOPRYZ depolymerize
DEEEILNRSTTY interestedly
DEEEILNSSSUV delusiveness
DEEEIMNNOPST semideponent
DEEEIMNOPRRT redemptioner
DEEEIMNOPSTT monts-de-piété
DEEEIMNORSTT densitometer
DEEEIMNRRSTW Midwesterner
DEEEIMNRSSTV disseverment
DEEEIMPRRTTT pretermitted
DEEEINNOPRST pre-tensioned
DEEEINNRSTTU uninterested
DEEEINOPPRTU neuropeptide

DEEEINPRSSST	presidentess
DEEEINPRSTUV	superevident
DEEEINRSSTTU	entertissued
DEEEIPRRSSSU	depressurise
DEEEIPRRSSUZ	depressurize
DEEEJLLOPPRT	jet-propelled
DEEEKLNNOOST	endoskeleton
DEEELMNOPRTY	redeployment
DEEELNORSSSV	resolvedness
DEEELNRRSUVY	unreservedly
DEEEMMNOORST	endosmometer
DEEENNORRTTW	Donnerwetter
DEEENORSSUVZ	rendezvouses
DEEEOPPRSSSS	prepossessed
DEEFFHINRRSU	undersheriff
	under-sheriff
DEEFGHINNRTU	unfrightened
DEEFGIIKNNRR	knife-grinder
DEEFGINNORWZ	freezing-down
DEEFGINORRSY	rosy-fingered
DEEFGJLMNSTU	self-judgment
DEEFGJMNORTU	forejudgment
DEEFHIIIMNSS	semi-finished
DEEFHIINNSSS	fiendishness
DEEFHIINORSV	overfinished
DEEFHINORTTW	white-fronted
DEEFIIILNNTY	indefinitely
DEEFIIILNTVY	definitively
DEEFIIINNORT	redefinition
DEEFIILNNRSS	friendliness
DEEFIILNRSTU	unfertilised
DEEFIILNRTUZ	unfertilized
DEEFIILNSTTY	self-identity
DEEFIIPRRTVY	perfervidity
DEEFILLMNORW	well-informed
DEEFILLNOSSU	self-delusion
DEEFILLNOSVV	self-involved
DEEFILLPSTUY	despitefully
DEEFILNOOSTV	self-devotion
DEEFILNPRSSU	pridefulness
DEEFILNRRSUY	user-friendly
DEEFINNSSTTU	unfittedness
DEEFLOORSTUY	surefootedly
DEEFMNOPRRRU	underperform
DEEFNNOORSSV	overfondness
DEEGGIMNORST	disgorgement
DEEGGINNORTU	teeing-ground
DEEGGINNOSTW	weeding-tongs
DEEGHHILNPRS	shepherdling
DEEGHIILLNSV	dishevelling
DEEGHIILNRVW	driving-wheel
DEEGHIINNSTW	winding-sheet
DEEGHILLLPTW	well-plighted
DEEGHNNOOTUY	honey-tongued
DEEGIIILPRSV	disprivilege
DEEGIILLLNPW	pile-dwelling
DEEGIILMOOPY	epidemiology
DEEGIILNNSSY	yieldingness
DEEGIILNOPSS	diplogenesis
DEEGIILNPRUV	unprivileged
DEEGIILRSSVY	digressively
DEEGIILSSSSU	disguiseless
DEEGIIMNSSTU	disguisement
DEEGIINOPRST	predigestion
DEEGIINPRSTW	Speedwriting®
DEEGIINRRSTW	wire-stringed
DEEGIJMMNSTU	misjudgement
DEEGIKLMNOSW	misknowledge
DEEGILLLNORV	levelling-rod
DEEGILLNRSSW	well-dressing
DEEGILMNNNOY	moneylending
DEEGILNNPRTY	pretendingly
DEEGILNNRTTU	underletting
DEEGILNOPRRV	ringed-plover
DEEGILNORRTT	ring-dotterel
DEEGILNPRSSY	depressingly
DEEGINNNNSSU	unendingness
DEEGINNNPRTU	unpretending
DEEGINNNRSTU	nurse-tending
DEEGINNRSTTT	trendsetting
DEEGLLOOSTYY	dysteleology
DEEGMNNOORRW	wondermonger
DEEHHIIMOPRS	hemispheroid
DEEHHMNOOTUY	honey-mouthed
DEEHIILLNPPS	nipple-shield
DEEHIIMNORTU	deinotherium
DEEHIINPRSST	residentship
DEEHIINRSSST	dissenterish
DEEHIKLNNOSW	whole-skinned
DEEHILMOSTTY	△dyotheletism
DEEHILPRSSUU	desulphurise
DEEHILPRSUUZ	desulphurize
DEEHIMNOORTU	time-honoured
DEEHIOPPRTTY	pteridophyte
DEEHLPRSTTUU	sulphuretted
DEEHNNORSTTU	thunder-stone
DEEIIIMNRTTV	divertimenti
DEEIIINSSSVV	divisiveness
DEEIILNNSSUW	unwieldiness
DEEIILNRSSTU	unsterilised
DEEIILNRSTUU	underutilise
DEEIILNRSTUZ	unsterilized
DEEIILNRTUUZ	underutilize
DEEIIMNNRSTT	disinterment
DEEIIMNORSTT	endometritis
DEEIIMNORTTV	divertimento
DEEIIMNRSSST	dissenterism
DEEIIMORRTTU	dumortierite
DEEIINNSSSTU	unsensitised
DEEIINNSSTUZ	unsensitized
DEEIINPRSSST	spiritedness
DEEIINQSSSTU	disquietness
DEEIINRSSTTU	intertissued
DEEIJLNOOOST	loose-jointed
DEEIJNORRRSU	surrejoinder
DEEIKKNNRRSU	underskinker
DEEIKNNORSSV	overkindness
DEEIKRSTTTUU	skutterudite
DEEILLNNQTUY	delinquently
DEEILMNNSSSS	mindlessness
DEEILMNRTTUY	unremittedly
DEEILNNOSTTU	unlistened-to
DEEILNPRRTTU	triple-turned
DEEILNQRTUUY	unrequitedly

DEEIMNNRSTTU instrumented
DEEIMNORSTTY densitometry
DEEIMOPPRRST pteridosperm
DEEIMOPPRSSU superimposed
DEEIMOPRRSTT Redemptorist
DEEINNOQSTUU unquestioned
DEEINOOPSSSS possessioned
DEEINOPPRRTU unpropertied
DEEINORSSSSU desirousness
DEEINOSSTTUU testudineous
DEEINPRSSUUV unsupervised
DEEIOORRTVWY ivory-towered
DEEKNNRRTUUY under-turnkey
DEEKNOORRRWW wonder-worker
DEELLNOPSSTU pollutedness
DEELMNORSTUY tremendously
DEELNOOSSSSW woodlessness
DEELNOSSSSUU sedulousness
DEELPPRSSSUY suppressedly
DEEMNNORSTUU untremendous
DEEMOOORSSTU osteodermous
DEENNNOSSTUW unwontedness
DEENOOPRSSST dessertspoon
DEENORSSSTUX dextrousness
DEENPPRSSSUU unsuppressed
DEFFGINOOORW wood-offering
DEFFINOORRSU frondiferous
DEFFLNOORSSU fourfoldness
DEFGGNOOORTT god-forgotten
DEFGHHIIILTY high-fidelity
DEFGHIILNNTU hunting-field
DEFGHILLLTUY delightfully
DEFGHILLNTUU undelightful
DEFGHINRRSUY rushy-fringed
DEFGIIIMNNNY indemnifying
DEFGIIINRSVY diversifying
DEFGINNOPTUY type-founding
DEFHHINRTTUY unthriftyhed
DEFHIINNPRSU unfriendship
DEFHIMNOORST hindforemost
DEFIILLNNRUY unfriendlily
DEFIILNOORSX dorsiflexion
DEFIILNOSSSU unfossilised
DEFIILNOSSUZ unfossilized
DEFIILOPRSUY perfidiously
DEFILOOORRSU doloriferous
DEFILOORSTUY do-it-yourself
DEFILRSSSTTU self-distrust
DEFIOORRSSUU sudoriferous
DEFNNOOPRSSU profoundness
DEGGHILLORRS shrill-gorged
DEGGHILNNOTU hunting-lodge
DEGGHLOOORYY hydrogeology
DEGGINNOOPRU ground-pigeon
DEGGINNORSSW dressing-gown
DEGGKLLRSUUY skullduggery
DEGHHHILORSU shoulder-high
DEGHHIIIPRST high-spirited
DEGHHIINOPST diphthongise
DEGHHIINOPTZ diphthongize
DEGHHIORSSTT short-sighted
DEGHHLOOTTUW low-thoughted
DEGHIIILNRSS disrelishing
DEGHIKNOORRS drongo-shrike
DEGHILMORSTY goldsmithery
DEGHILNNRTUY thunderingly
DEGHINORSSTU droughtiness
DEGHNNOOSTUU hound's-tongue
DEGHNORRTUUW underwrought
DEGIIIKLNNNX index-linking
DEGIIINNRRST disinterring
DEGIIINNSTUY disingenuity
DEGIIKLMOPRR milk-porridge
DEGIIKNOPRSW powder-skiing
DEGIILLNNUYY unyieldingly
DEGIILLNOPRR rope-drilling
DEGIILLOOSTT deltiologist
DEGIILNNOSUY indigenously
DEGIILNNSSTY dissentingly
DEGIILNOPRSU ligniperdous
DEGIINNNNPRU underpinning
DEGIINNOSSUU disingenuous
DEGIINNRRTUW underwriting
DEGIINOPPRSS predisposing
DEGILLNOPPRW dropping-well
DEGILMNOOOST demonologist
DEGILMOPPRRU plum-porridge
DEGILNNORSUY resoundingly
DEGILNOOOSTT deontologist
DEGILOOPRSTT proglottides
DEGIMNNOORUV mourning-dove
DEGIMNOORRSS dressing-room
DEGINNNNRRUU underrunning
DEGINNORRTUW winter-ground
DEGINOOPPRST doorstepping
DEGLLNORSSUY groundlessly
DEGMNOORRRUY merry-go-round
DEHHIIIPRSTT diphtheritis
DEHHIILOPRTY hydrophilite
DEHHILMNOTTW withholdment
DEHHILNNOTUW unwithholden
DEHIIIMMNNST diminishment
DEHIIINNORSS disinherison
DEHIIKLLNOOU unlikelihood
DEHIILOPRSVW devil-worship
DEHIIMOORSTU idiothermous
DEHIIOPRRSSY hyperidrosis
DEHIKLNRSTUW whistle-drunk
DEHILLOOOSWY Hollywoodise
DEHILLOOOWYZ Hollywoodize
DEHILOOPRRSV overlordship
DEHIMORRSTWY wordsmithery
DEHINNOOQRUY hydroquinone
DEHINOOPRRTY pyritohedron
DEHINOOPRSST spinsterhood
DEHINOPPRSUW unworshipped
DEHIOOOPRRTT orthopteroid
DEHLLNOOPSUY endophyllous
DEHLLOORRTWY otherworldly
DEHLMNOOOPSU monodelphous
DEHLMNPPRTUU thunder-plump
DEHLNOORRSUY horrendously
DEHLNORSTUUY thunderously
DEHMNORRSTTU thunderstorm

DEHNOOORSTUW	southernwood
DEIIIIQSSTUV	disquisitive
DEIIILLNOPRR	pillion-rider
DEIIILMNTUVY	diminutively
DEIIIMNPRSTT	dispiritment
DEIIINNNOSTT	Nintendoitis
DEIIINORSSTV	diversionist
DEIIKLNNNSSU	unkindliness
DEIIKNNPPRSY	skinny-dipper
DEIILOPSSTUY	dispiteously
DEIILPRSTUVY	disruptively
DEIIMNNNOTUU	unmunitioned
DEIIMNNOPRSU	unimprisoned
DEIINOOPRSTT	periodontist
DEIIOOPPRRST	poor-spirited
DEIJNPRRSTUU	jurisprudent
DEILLMORTUXY	dolly-mixture
DEILMMNOOPSY	polydemonism
DEILNOORUVWW	louver-window
	louvre-window
DEILOOPRRRSU	lord-superior
DEILRSSSSTTU	distrustless
DEIMNNOPRTUU	unimportuned
DEIMNOPSTUYY	pseudonymity
DEINOOOPPRRT	proportioned
DEINOOORTTTX	tetrodotoxin
DEINOSSSSTUU	studiousness
DEIOOPRSSSSS	dispossessor
DEIOPRSTTUVY	topside-turvy
DEKLNOOPRUVY	unprovokedly
DELNNOOPSTYY	polysyndeton
DELNOOORSSSU	dolorousness
DELNOPSSTUUY	stupendously
DEMNOOPSSUUY	pseudonymous
DENNOORSSSUW	wondrousness
DFFGIINNPPSU	snuff-dipping
DFFIIIMNOSSU	diffusionism
DFFIIINOSSTU	diffusionist
DFGIIKKLNOUY	kilfud-yoking
DFGILLSSTUUY	disgustfully
DFHILNOOOPSU	pound-foolish
DGGGILNNRUUY	ungrudgingly
DGGHHIINNOSU	high-sounding
DGGHIILNNORT	lightning-rod
DGGHINNOTTUU	doughnutting
DGGIILNSSTUY	disgustingly
DGGIINNOPPRR	ring-dropping
DGHIIKNNNORR	drinking-horn
DGHIIMNNOOST	do-nothingism
DGHIINNNSTUW	shunt-winding
DGHINNORSTUW	hunting-sword
DGHLLNOOORUW	hollow-ground
DGIIILLNQRUV	quill-driving
DGIIIOOPRSTY	prodigiosity
DGIILNNOSSUV	undissolving
DGIILOOPRSUY	prodigiously
DGIIMMNNOPSW	swimming-pond
DGILMOORSTTY	troglodytism
DGILNOOOOSTT	odontologist
DGINNORRSSUU	surroundings
DHHIILOOPPPS	phospholipid
DHHILOOPRSUY	hydrophilous
DHHOOPRSTUYY	hydrophytous
DHIMOOOOPSST	opisthodomos
DHIMOOPRRSTY	hydrotropism
DHINOOORSTTT	orthodontist
DHLNOOOPPTYY	polyphyodont
DHLNOOORTUXY	unorthodoxly
DHMMPPTTUUYY	Humpty-dumpty
DHMNNOOOOPTY	monophyodont
DHNOOOOPRSTU	Odontophorus
DIIIINOQSSTU	disquisition
DIIIOQRSSTUY	disquisitory
DIILNOOSSTUU	solitudinous
DIIOOOPRRSTU	proditorious
DINOOORRTTUY	ororotundity

E

EEEEEHHLRRTW	three-wheeler
EEEEEKPRRSTT	streetkeeper
EEEEFGHILNRW	freewheeling
EEEEFLNRRSTV	self-reverent
EEEEGHHILNOT	eighteen-hole
EEEEGIILNPSS	spiegeleisen
EEEEHILPQRTU	téléphérique
EEEEHINPRRSV	reprehensive
EEEEHLMNOPRT	nephelometer
EEEEHLNRRSTW	stern-wheeler
EEEEHLNRSSTV	nevertheless
EEEEHMNORRTV	neverthemore
EEEEILLMRSUV	merveilleuse
EEEEILPPRSST	spire-steeple
EEEEIMNPRRTX	experimenter
EEEEIMNRRTTV	retrievement
EEEEIMNRSTTX	extensimeter
EEEEINNQRSTU	equestrienne
EEEELMNRSTTT	resettlement
EEEELNPRSSSS	peerlessness
EEEELNRSSSST	treelessness
EEEEMMNPRSST	empressement
EEEEMNNRRSTV	renversement
EEEEMNORSTTX	extensometer
EEEENNPRRRTU	entrepreneur
EEEENNSSTWYY	teensy-weensy
EEEENPRRSSSV	perverseness
EEEEORRTTTTT	teeter-totter
EEEFFIMORSTU	effusiometer
EEEFFINSSSUV	effusiveness
EEEFFLLNNORW	fennel-flower
EEEFGIINNRTT	engine-fitter
EEEFGILNORSY	foreseeingly
EEEFGINNORSU	unforeseeing
EEEFGLLNRUVY	revengefully
EEEFGLNNRUUV	unrevengeful
EEEFGLNNSSUV	vengefulness
EEEFGNNOORSS	foregoneness
EEEFHINRSSSV	feverishness
EEEFHMNRRSST	refreshments
EEEFIILLLLMU	millefeuille
EEEFIILNRRTT	interfertile
EEEFIILNRSTT	life-interest
EEEFIIMNNNSS	feminineness
EEEFILLNSSSS	lifelessness
EEEFILNORSTX	self-exertion

EEEFILNRSSTT	self-interest
EEEFILNSSTTX	self-existent
EEEFINNORSSV	overfineness
EEEFLLNSSSSS	selflessness
EEEFLLORRSST	forset-seller
EEEFLLORSSST	fosset-seller
EEEFNNQRSSTU	frequentness
EEEGGGILLNPV	level-pegging
EEEGGILLMRRU	Geiger-Müller
EEEGHHILNTTY	eighteenthly
EEEGHIKNOPSU	housekeeping
EEEGHILRTTTW	letter-weight
EEEGHILRTTWW	welterweight
EEEGHIMNOSTU	meeting-house
EEEGHINNRSSS	greenishness
EEEGHINSTTVY	seventy-eight
EEEGHNNRRSTT	strengthener
EEEGHNORSSTT	togetherness
EEEGHOORTTYZ	heterozygote
EEEGIIKNNPSW	swine-keeping
EEEGIILMNNTV	inveiglement
EEEGIINNORRT	orienteering
EEEGIKMNNNOY	monkey-engine
EEEGIKNOPRST	storekeeping
EEEGIKNPPRRS	springkeeper
EEEGILOQRRSU	Grolieresque
EEEGILRRSSVY	regressively
EEEGIMNRSSSU	Messeigneurs
EEEGINNORSSU	neurogenesis
EEEGINNPSSSW	sweepingness
EEEGINOOSSST	osteogenesis
EEEGINOPRSST	petrogenesis
EEEGIOQRRSTU	grotesquerie
EEEGLNNNSSTU	ungentleness
EEEGMNORSSSU	gruesomeness
EEEGNNORSSSU	generousness
EEEGNOOPRRST	progesterone
EEEHHHIMMPRT	hephthemimer
EEEHHINPSSSS	sheepishness
EEEHHIRRTVWY	everywhither
EEEHHLNORTUV	eleventh-hour
EEEHHMOPRRST	thermosphere
EEEHHNRRSTUY	heresy-hunter
EEEHILLMNNOS	Neohellenism
EEEHILMNRTTY	trimethylene
EEEHILNNNTTY	nineteenthly
EEEHILRSSSTV	shirtsleeves
EEEHIMNNNRST	enshrinement
EEEHIMNOOSTT	etheostomine
EEEHIMNRSTTU	hermeneutist
EEEHIMORSSTX	heterosexism
EEEHINNOPRRS	reprehension
EEEHINOPRRSU	superheroine
EEEHINPRSTVY	hypertensive
EEEHINSSSSTW	sweetishness
EEEHIORSSTTX	heterosexist
EEEHLLLORTWY	trolley-wheel
EEEHLLNOPTYY	polyethylene
EEEHLLNPSSSS	helplessness
EEEHLMNOPRTY	nephelometry
EEEHLMNOSSSS	homelessness
EEEHLNOPSSSS	hopelessness
EEEHMNNNORTT	enthronement
EEEHMOORRSTU	heteromerous
EEEHNOPRRRSY	reprehensory
EEEIILMNPRSU	periselenium
EEEIILPRTTVY	repetitively
EEEIIMNPSTTV	intempestive
EEEIIMOPRRST	isoperimeter
EEEIINNNRTTV	intervenient
EEEIINNPRSST	serpentinise
EEEIINNPRSTT	serpentinite
EEEIINNPRSTZ	serpentinize
EEEIINPRRTTV	interpretive
EEEIINPRSSVX	inexpressive
EEEIIPQRRSTU	prerequisite
EEEIJLNNSSUV	juvenileness
EEEILMNNPRTY	pre-eminently
EEEILMNNRSTT	re-enlistment
EEEILMNNSSSU	unseemliness
EEEILMNSSSST	timelessness
EEEILMOORVZZ	mezzo-relievo
EEEILNNPRSTY	serpentinely
EEEILNPRTVVY	preventively
EEEILNRRRTVY	irreverently
EEEILNRSSSST	tirelessness
EEEILPRRSSVY	repressively
EEEILPRSSVXY	expressively
EEEILRRRTTTW	letter-writer
EEEIMNNPRSTT	presentiment
EEEIMNNPRSTU	supereminent
EEEIMNNRSTTV	reinvestment
EEEIMNORSSST	tiresomeness
EEEIMNORSSTT	sensitometer
EEEIMNPRRSST	misrepresent
EEEIMOORRSST	stereoisomer
EEEIMOPRRRST	respirometer
EEEIMOPRSTUX	time-exposure
EEEINNPRSSTX	inexpertness
EEEINNPRSTUV	supervenient
EEEINOORRTVX	overexertion
EEEINOPRRSSV	overripeness
EEEINPRRSSTT	interpretess
EEEINPRSSTUV	eruptiveness
EEEINPRSSUVX	unexpressive
EEEINRRTTTUX	intertexture
EEEIORRSTVVX	extroversive
EEEKLOOPPPSS	spokespeople
EEELLLNRSSTY	relentlessly
EEELLMORRTTU	tellurometer
EEELMNNOOSSS	lonesomeness
EEELMNNSTTTU	unsettlement
EEELMNOSSSSV	movelessness
EEELMNPPRSTU	supplementer
EEELMOPPRRTT	teleprompter
EEELNNOSSSST	tonelessness
EEELNOPRSSSS	responseless
EEELNORSSSTU	resoluteness
EEELNRSSSSST	restlessness
EEELOOPRSTTU	teleutospore
EEENNOPPRSSS	propenseness
EEENNOPRSSTT	serpent-stone
EEENNOPRSTTU	enteropneust
EEENOORSSTTT	testosterone

EEEOOPRRSUVX overexposure
EEEOPRRRSSUV overpressure
EEFFHLLRRSUY refreshfully
EEFGGIILNRSU single-figure
EEFGGIOPRTTY pettifoggery
EEFGHIIKNNRT free-thinking
EEFGHIILNRRT Freightliner®
freightliner
EEFGHIILRTTW weight-lifter
EEFGHIIPRRTZ prizefighter
EEFGHILNRRSY refreshingly
EEFGHINNRRSU unrefreshing
EEFGIILMNPXY exemplifying
EEFGIIMMNRSW free-swimming
EEFGIIMNNNRT infringement
EEFGIINOPRRT profiteering
EEFGIINSSTUV fugitiveness
EEFGIKNNOORT foretokening
EEFGILLNSSUU guilefulness
EEFGINORRSUU ferrugineous
EEFHLNORTTUY fourteenthly
EEFHLOPRSTTY flesh-pottery
EEFHMOORRSTT foster-mother
EEFIIINNNSST infiniteness
EEFIIMNORSSU seminiferous
EEFIIMOQRSTU equisetiform
EEFIINORRSSU resiniferous
EEFILLORSSTU stelliferous
EEFILMORSTTU flitter-mouse
EEFILNNQRTUY infrequently
EEFILNOORRTX retroflexion
EEFILNPSSSTU spitefulness
EEFIMNOPRRST serpentiform
EEFIORRSSSTT foster-sister
EEFKLMNOORWY monkey-flower
EEFLLMORRSUY remorsefully
EEFLLNNTUUVY uneventfully
EEFLLNORSSUV overfullness
EEFLMNORRSUU unremorseful
EEFLMNORSSSS formlessness
EEFLNNQRTUUY unfrequently
EEFLNNSSSUUU unusefulness
EEFLNOORSSSS rooflessness
EEFLNOPRSSUW powerfulness
EEFOOPRRSSSS professoress
EEGGGHMRRUU hugger-mugger
EEGGILSSTUVY suggestively
EEGGINNPRTTU putting-green
EEGGNOORSSSU gorgeousness
EEGHHHORRTTU therethrough
EEGHHHORRTUW wherethrough
EEGHHIILLLNS sheeling-hill
EEGHHINOORSS horseshoeing
EEGHHIPRRSSU high-pressure
EEGHIINOSSST histogenesis
EEGHIINRSSST tigerishness
EEGHIINRSTUX extinguisher
EEGHIINRTTWW winter-weight
EEGHIKNNORST north-seeking
EEGHIKNOSSTU south-seeking
EEGHIKNRRSTU hunger-strike
EEGHILMNORVW overwhelming
EEGHILNOOPRS phrenologise
EEGHILNOOPRT gerontophile
EEGHILNOOPRZ phrenologize
EEGHILNOPSSY phylogenesis
EEGHIMMRSTUW summer-weight
EEGHIMNOSSTY mythogenesis
EEGHINNOPSSY hypnogenesis
EEGHINOORSST orthogenesis
EEGHINOPSSTY phytogenesis
EEGHLNRSSSTT strengthless
EEGHLOOORSTU heterologous
EEGHMMOPRSTY sphygmometer
EEGHNOOORSTU heterogonous
EEGHOORSTUYZ heterozygous
EEGIILLNNNST sentinelling
EEGIILLNORSS religionless
EEGIILLNPRST still-peering
EEGIILNPSSTU sleeping-suit
EEGIINNNPRST serpentining
EEGIINNNRTTT internetting
EEGIINNPRRST enterprising
EEGIINNRRSST retiringness
EEGIIRRSSTVY regressivity
EEGIJMNPQUUU queue-jumping
EEGIKLNORSTW steelworking
EEGILLNNPSUX sun-expelling
EEGILLNOOSST selenologist
EEGILLNPPRXY perplexingly
EEGILLOOPSST speleologist
EEGILLORRRSU guerrilleros
EEGILMNOOOST entomologise
EEGILMNOOOTZ entomologize
EEGILMOOPPSS goose-pimples
EEGILMOOPSTY epistemology
EEGILNOPRTTU triple-tongue
EEGILNORRSTU Eurosterling
EEGILORRSTUY elytrigerous
EEGIMNNORRTT retromingent
EEGIMNNPSSTT temptingness
EEGIMNNRRSTU interregnums
EEGIMNOORRTT trigonometer
EEGINNNRRSSU unerringness
EEGINNOSSSUY syngenesious
EEGINOOPRRVW overpowering
EEGINOOPRSSS sporogenesis
EEGINOPRRSST progenitress
resting-spore
EEGINOPRSTTY stereotyping
EEGINORSSSUV grievousness
EEGINOSSSUUX exiguousness
EEGINRRSTTTY trysting-tree
EEGLMNNOOOPR prolegomenon
EEGLNNORSUUY ungenerously
EEGMMNORSSTY system-monger
EEGNNOORRSUU neurosurgeon
EEGNORRRSUUY neurosurgery
EEHHIIMMOPRT hemimorphite
EEHHIINSSSTV thievishness
EEHHILLNOPTY theophylline
EEHHILNRTTTY thirteenthly
EEHHINRSSSSW shrewishness
EEHHLLOPRTYY heterophylly

EEHHLMNORTTY	three-monthly
EEHHMMORRTTY	rhythmometer
EEHHMOOPRRTY	heteromorphy
EEHHOOOSSTUU	house-to-house
EEHHOOPRRTTY	heterotrophy
EEHHOOSSUUYY	housey-housey
EEHIILNPRSST	listenership
EEHIILNPRSTY	prehensility
EEHIIMNPPRRU	perinephrium
EEHIKLLNRRTU	hunter-killer
EEHILLMNNSSU	sneeshin-mull
EEHILMNORSST	motherliness
EEHILNNPSTWY	penny-whistle
EEHILNOOPSST	siphonostele
EEHILOPPRTTT	throttle-pipe
EEHILOPSSTTU	spittle-house
EEHIMNORSSST	smotheriness
EEHINNOPRSTY	hypertension
EEHINOOSSSSU	session-house
EEHLLMPRSTTU	trumpet-shell
EEHLNRSSSSTU	hurtlessness
	ruthlessness
EEHMMOOOORSU	homoeomerous
EEHMNNOOORRU	neurohormone
EEHMNOOORSTU	heteronomous
EEHMORRSTUUY	eurythermous
EEHNNORRSTTW	north-western
EEHNORSSTTUW	south-western
EEIIIILLRRTW	tirlie-wirlie
EEIIIJLNSTUV	juvenilities
EEIIIKLNNNPW	pinniewinkle
EEIIIKNNRSST	interkinesis
EEIIILLMRSTV	millisievert
EEIIIMNRSSTV	intermissive
EEIIINPRRSTU	perineuritis
EEIIINRSSSTW	sinisterwise
EEIIKLLMNRRV	vermin-killer
EEIIKLLNNSSU	unlikeliness
EEIIKLOOPSSU	leukopoiesis
EEIILLMPQTUU	equimultiple
EEIILLNNSSUV	unliveliness
EEIILLNSSSUV	illusiveness
EEIILMNNPTTY	impenitently
EEIILMNNSSTU	untimeliness
EEIILMNOPSST	impoliteness
EEIILMOORVZZ	mezzo-rilievo
EEIILMPRSSVY	impressively
	permissively
EEIILNPPRSSS	slipperiness
EEIILNPRSSST	priestliness
EEIILNPSSSST	pitilessness
EEIILNRSSSST	sisterliness
EEIILOPSTVXY	expositively
EEIIMNNOTTTU	munitionette
EEIIMNNRTTTT	intermittent
EEIIMNOPRRSS	reimpression
EEIIMNOSSSSV	omissiveness
EEIIMNPRRSTT	misinterpret
EEIIMNPRSSTT	impersistent
EEIIMNPRSSUV	unimpressive
EEIIMNPRSTTY	sempiternity
EEIIMNRRTTUX	intermixture
EEIIMOPRRSTY	isoperimetry
EEIINNNORTTV	intervention
EEIINNOPQTTU	inequipotent
EEIINNORSTTT	retentionist
EEIINNOSSTTX	extensionist
EEIINNPPSSST	snippetiness
EEIINOPRRSSV	irresponsive
EEIINOPSSSTV	positiveness
EEIINORRSTVV	introversive
EEIINORRTTVV	introvertive
EEIINPRRTTUV	interruptive
EEIIOOPRSSTV	seropositive
EEIIPRSSTVXY	expressivity
EEIJNNNNPRSY	Jenny-spinner
EEILLLNSSSSW	will-lessness
EEILLNNOQTUY	ineloquently
EEILLNNOSSSV	slovenliness
EEILLNNOSSUV	unloveliness
EEILLNSSSSST	listlessness
EEILLORRSTUY	irresolutely
EEILLRSSSSTY	resistlessly
EEILMNOOSSST	toilsomeness
EEILMNPRSTTU	multipresent
EEILMOOPRSST	metropolises
EEILMOPPRRTY	peremptorily
EEILMORSSSTU	moistureless
EEILMPRSTUVY	resumptively
EEILMRSSSSST	mistressless
EEILNNOORTTU	nitrotoluene
EEILNNOPSSTU	unpoliteness
EEILNOOPPRSY	polyisoprene
EEILNOORRSTU	△resolutioner
EEILNOORRTUV	revolutioner
EEILNOPRSSSU	perilousness
EEILNOPRSSVY	responsively
EEILNOQSSSTU	questionless
EEILNORTUUVV	vulvo-uterine
EEILNPRSSTTY	persistently
EEILNPSSSUVY	suspensively
EEILOPPRSSVY	oppressively
EEILOPRRSSTY	proselytiser
EEILOPRRSTUV	retropulsive
EEILOPRRSTYZ	proselytizer
EEILOPSSSSVY	possessively
EEIMMNNOOPST	empoisonment
EEIMNNNOPRSY	money-spinner
EEIMNNOOPPRS	perispomenon
EEINNOOPRSTU	out-pensioner
EEINNOPRSSTT	septentrions
EEINNOPRSSTU	serpentinous
EEINNOPRSSUV	unresponsive
EEINNOPRSTUV	supervention
EEINNOPRTTTV	ventripotent
EEINNPRSSTTU	unprettiness
EEINOOPPSSST	oppositeness
EEINOOPRSSSS	repossession
EEINOOPRSSTT	enteroptosis
EEINOORRRSTV	retroversion
EEINOORRSTVX	extroversion
EEINOORSSSTU	interosseous
EEINOPPRSSUV	unoppressive
EEINOPRRSTTU	neuropterist

Words marked △ may be spelled also with a capital letter

EEINOPRSSSSU supersession
EEINOPRSSSTV sportiveness
EEINOPRSSSUV perviousness
previousness
EEINORSSSTUV vitreousness
EEIOPPRRRSST proprietress
EEKLMNOPUYZZ monkey-puzzle
puzzle-monkey
EEKNOOPPRSSS spokesperson
EEKNOPPRSTTY pretty-spoken
EELLLOOWWYYY yellow-yowley
EELLNNOORSSV lovelornness
EELLNOSSSSSU soullessness
EELMMNNOPTUY unemployment
EELMOOOSSTTU teleostomous
EELMOPPRRSUY superpolymer
EELNNPPSSSUU unsuppleness
EELNOOPRSSTT streptosolen
EELNOPRRSTUU seropurulent
EELNOPSSSSST spotlessness
EEMNNOOPPSTT postponement
EEMNNOORSSSU enormousness
EEMNNOOSSSUV venomousness
EEMNNORSSSUU numerousness
EENNOOPRSTTY none-so-pretty
EENNOSSSSSUU sensuousness
EENNTTTTWWYY twenty-twenty
EENOOPRRSTUU neuropterous
EENOPRRSSSUY supersensory
EEOOPPRRSSTU preposterous
EEPPRRTTTTYY pretty-pretty
EFFGGHIIINRT fire-fighting
EFFGGIIILNNSU glue-sniffing
EFFGHILORSTU foresightful
EFFGIINOOPRR fireproofing
EFFHNOOORSTU front-of-house
EFFILNRSSTUU fruitfulness
EFGGGIINOPTT pettifogging
EFGGHHIIINSV high-five-sign
EFGGHIILLNST self-lighting
EFGGHIILNRST self-righting
EFGGIILNNOPY pigeon-flying
EFGGILNORTTY forgettingly
EFGHHIINRSTY night-fishery
EFGHHILNTTTW Twelfth-night
EFGHIIKLNNST self-thinking
EFGHIIKNNNTU hunting-knife
EFGHIILORRTT right-to-lifer
EFGHIINRRSTT first-nighter
EFGHILNRSSTU rightfulness
EFGIIINNNSTY intensifying
EFGIIKNNNPRU pruning-knife
EFGIILNNRSST triflingness
EFGIILNOPRTW powerlifting
EFGIILNORSUV griseofulvin
EFGIILNRRTYY terrifyingly
EFGIIMORRSST Strigiformes
EFGIINNOPRSY personifying
EFGIINNRRTUY unterrifying
EFGIINORRTTT retrofitting
EFGILLOORSSU self-glorious
EFGILNNNOORW non-flowering
EFGILOORRSSU self-rigorous
EFGIMNNOPRRU unperforming
EFGLNNORSSUW wrongfulness
EFHILLMNORTU run-of-the-mill
EFHILLRSSTTY thriftlessly
EFHILMNRSSTU mirthfulness
EFHILNOPSSSY self-hypnosis
EFHILOORRSUV overflourish
EFHLLNOSSSTU slothfulness
EFHLNOSSTUUY youthfulness
EFHLNRSSTTUU truthfulness
EFIIIILNNTVY infinitively
EFIILMNORSUU luminiferous
EFIILMOPRSVY oversimplify
EFIINOPRSSTU perfusionist
EFIIOPRRSTUY pyritiferous
EFIKLLLNSSSU skillfulness
EFILLMNOSSUU self-luminous
EFILLOPRSSTY profitlessly
EFILNOOPSSTT toploftiness
EFIOOOPRRSSU soporiferous
EFLLOPPRSUUY purposefully
EFLMNNORSSUU mournfulness
EFLMNORSSSTU stormfulness
EFLNOPRSSSTU sportfulness
EFLNRSSSTTUU trustfulness
EFMNOORTTUWY twenty-fourmo
EFNNOORRSSSW forswornness
EGGGHJLOOPRU plough-jogger
EGGGIILNNRSY sniggeringly
EGGGILNNOOST logging-stone
EGGHHIINPPST high-stepping
EGGHHIINSSSW Whiggishness
EGGHIILNOSTU soughing-tile
EGGHIINPRSSS priggishness
EGGHILNSSSSU sluggishness
EGGHLOOOOPTY photogeology
EGGIILLMMNRY glimmeringly
EGGIILLNRSTY glisteringly
EGGIILLNRTTY glitteringly
EGGILOOPSTTY Egyptologist
EGGIMNOOPRSS gossip-monger
EGGLNNOOORTY röntgenology
EGHHHOORRTTU through-other
EGHHIIILLLNS sheiling-hill
shieling-hill
EGHHIILPRSTY high-priestly
EGHHILNOSSSU ghoulishness
EGHHINNOSTUU house-hunting
EGHHMNOOPPSY sphygmophone
EGHHMORRTTUY merrythought
EGHHNOORSSTU thoroughness
EGHHNOORSTTU through-stone
EGHIIIMNRSTV shriving-time
EGHIIINOPRSS seigniorship
EGHIIKLNNSST knightliness
EGHIILLLNSSS shillingless
EGHIILMNOPRS negrophilism
EGHIILMNPRWY whimperingly
EGHIILNOPRST negrophilist
EGHIILNPRSWY whisperingly
EGHIILOPSSTT stegophilist

EGHIINNOSSTW	wishing-stone
EGHIINNRSSTV	thrivingness
EGHIINOSSTTU	house-sitting
EGHILLNRTTTU	truth-telling
EGHILMNORSTY	smotheringly
EGHILMOORSTY	mythologiser
EGHILMOORTYZ	mythologizer
EGHILNOOPRST	nephrologist
	phrenologist
EGHILNPRSTUU	sulphureting
EGHILOOORSTT	heortologist
EGHILOOPPSST	psephologist
EGHIMNOOORSU	rooming-house
EGHINNORTTTU	otter-hunting
EGHINOOPRRSV	governorship
EGHINOOPSTTT	photosetting
EGHINORRTTUW	interwrought
EGIIILNOSTTU	gentilitious
EGIIIMNOPSTU	impetiginous
EGIIINNNRTTW	intertwining
EGIIINNNSSTV	invitingness
EGIIJLNNORTU	jointing-rule
EGIIKLLNNORR	inking-roller
EGIIKLMMNOSU	mouse-milking
EGIIKLNPPRRS	klipspringer
EGIIKNNRSSST	strikingness
EGIIKNOPPPRS	skipping-rope
EGIILMNNOPTT	melting-point
EGIILMOOSSST	seismologist
EGIILNNNPRUY	unrepiningly
EGIILNPRSSTY	persistingly
EGIILNRTTTWY	twitteringly
EGIIMMNNSSSW	swimmingness
EGIIMNNOPSSS	imposingness
EGIIMNOOPRRT	primogenitor
EGIIMNOORRST	△risorgimento
EGIIMRSSSTTU	Trismegistus
EGIINNNORSST	non-resisting
EGIINPSSTTUY	tissue-typing
EGIIOPRRSSTW	gossip-writer
EGIJMMNOPSUU	jumping-mouse
EGIKKNNOPRTY	pony-trekking
EGIKLLMNOORY	Kremlinology
EGILLNORSTTY	storytelling
EGILMNNORTTY	tormentingly
EGILMNOOOSTT	entomologist
EGILMNOORSTU	numerologist
EGILMNOOSTYZ	enzymologist
EGILNNNOSSUV	unlovingness
EGILNNRSUVWY	unswervingly
EGILNOOPRSUY	pyroligneous
EGILNOORSSSU	gloriousness
EGILNOPRSTTY	protestingly
EGILNPRSTTUY	sputteringly
EGILNRSTTTUY	stutteringly
EGIMMNOOPRSU	spermogonium
EGIMNOORRTTY	trigonometry
EGINNOPRSTTU	unprotesting
EGINNOPSSSSU	unpossessing
EGINNOPSTTTU	putting-stone
EGINOORRSSSU	rigorousness
EGINOORSSSUV	vigorousness
EGINPRRSSSTU	purse-strings
EGLNNOOPRUYY	neurypnology
EHHIILLOOPSU	heliophilous
EHHIILOOPPSS	philosophise
EHHIILOOPPSZ	philosophize
EHHIIMMMOPRS	hemimorphism
EHHILMRSSSTU	missel-thrush
EHHILMRSSTTU	mistle-thrush
EHHILOOPPSSS	philosophess
EHHILOPPSTUY	hyposulphite
EHHIMMOOPRST	theomorphism
EHHIMNOOPRST	thermosiphon
EHHIMNPSSSSU	sumphishness
EHHINOOOPPRS	siphonophore
EHHMMOOOOPRY	homoeomorphy
EHHMMOOORSTU	homothermous
EHHMNOOOPRTY	phytohormone
EHIIIILNPSST	Philistinise
EHIIIILNPSTZ	Philistinize
EHIIILORSTTT	lithotritise
EHIIILORTTTZ	lithotritize
EHIIKLMOOPRT	poikilotherm
EHIIKNOOPSST	photokinesis
EHIIKNSSSSTT	skittishness
EHIILLMNPSTU	phillumenist
EHIILLOPSTWW	will-o'-the-wisp
EHIILMOOPRST	heliotropism
EHIILOPRRTTT	lithotripter
EHIIMNPRSTUX	xiphisternum
EHIIMPRSSSST	mistress-ship
EHIINOOOPRSS	ionophoresis
EHIINPPRSSST	spinstership
EHIIOPPRRSSU	superiorship
EHIIOPRRSSTV	servitorship
EHILLOPPRTYY	pyrophyllite
EHILMMOOPPRS	pleomorphism
EHILMMOPRSTU	lithospermum
EHILMOOQRRTU	mother-liquor
EHILNOOPSUUY	euphoniously
EHILNOORTTWY	noteworthily
EHILNSSSSTTU	sluttishness
EHILOPRSSUWY	whisperously
EHIMMOOOORSU	homoiomerous
EHIMMORRSSTT	short-termism
EHIMOOPPRRSU	perimorphous
EHIMOOPPRRTY	pyromorphite
EHIMORRSSTTT	short-termist
EHINNORSSTUW	unworthiness
EHINOOORSSTT	orthotonesis
EHINOOPPRSST	nephroptosis
EHINOPRRSTTY	phrontistery
EHIOOPRRSTTT	orthopterist
EHIOPRRSSUVY	surveyorship
EHKMNOOOPSST	smooth-spoken
EHLMOOOPPRSU	pleomorphous
EHMMOOOPRSSU	mesomorphous
EHMNNOORRSTT	northernmost
EHMNOORSSSUU	humorousness
EHMNOORSSTTU	southernmost
EHMOOOPRRSUX	xeromorphous
EHNNOORRTUVW	unoverthrown
EHOOOPRRSTTU	orthopterous

EIIIILMRSTVY	verisimility
EIIILLMNOPST	pointillisme
EIIILLNOPSTT	pointilliste
EIIILMORSSUV	verisimilous
EIIIMMMNORSS	immersionism
EIIIMMNORSST	immersionist
EIIIMNNORSST	intermission
EIIIMNOOPRST	reimposition
EIIIMNORSSTV	intromissive
EIIIMPRTTTVY	permittivity
EIIINNOORSTT	isotretinoin
EIIINOPQRSTU	perquisition
EIIINQRSSSTU	inquisitress
EIILLMNOTTUV	multivoltine
EIILLNOOSSTV	volitionless
EIILLOOQRSSU	soliloquiser
EIILLOOQRSUZ	soliloquizer
EIILLPRSSSTY	spiritlessly
EIILMNOOQSSU	somniloquise
EIILMNOOQSUZ	somniloquize
EIILMNOOSTUV	evolutionism
EIILMOOPPRST	pleiotropism
EIILMOPRSUVY	imperviously
EIILMRSTTUVY	multiversity
EIILNOORRSTU	irresolution
EIILNOOSTTUV	evolutionist
EIILNOPRSTUY	polyneuritis
EIIMMNNOPRST	imprisonment
EIIMNNNQQUUU	quinquennium
EIIMNNORTTTT	intromittent
EIIMNOOPRSSX	expromission
EIIMNOOQRSUU	querimonious
EIIMOPRSSSST	prestissimos
EIIMORRRRRTW	mirror-writer
EIINNOORRSTV	introversion
EIINNOPRRTTU	interruption
EIINNOPRSSTU	interspinous
EIINOORSTTTX	extortionist
EIINOPRSSTTU	superstition
EIIOOPPSSTTV	postpositive
EIIOOPRRSTTY	posteriority
EIKMORRSSSTW	workmistress
EILLMNOQTTUU	multiloquent
EILLMOPRTUVY	overmultiply
EILMNNOOPTTY	omnipotently
EILMNNOSSSUU	luminousness
EILMOPPRSTUU	multipurpose
EILMORSSTUYY	mysteriously
EILMRSSSSTTU	mistrustless
EILNOOPRRSTU	retropulsion
EILOOPRRSTUY	pleurisy-root
EILOPRRSTUVY	protrusively
EIMMNNORSSUW	snow-in-summer
EIMNNNOSSSUU	numinousness
EIMNNOSSSTUU	mutinousness
EIMNOOORRSST	sensorimotor
EIMNOOOSSSTU	isostemonous
EIMNOORSSSTU	timorousness
EIMNOPRSSSUU	suspensorium
EIMNORSSTUUV	misventurous
EIMOPRSSSSTT	postmistress
EINNRSSSTTUU	untrustiness
EINOORSSSUUX	uxoriousness
EINOPRSSSSUU	spuriousness
EINORSSSSUUU	usuriousness
EINORSSSTUUV	virtuousness
EIOOOOPRSSST	osteoporosis
EIOPRRRSSTTW	sportswriter
ELLNOORSTUUY	ultroneously
ELNOOPPSSSUU	populousness
ELNOOPRSTTUY	portentously
ELOOPPRRSSUY	prosperously
ELOORRSSTTUY	stertorously
EMOPPRSSTUUU	presumptuous
ENNOOORSSSSU	sonorousness
ENOOPPRRSSST	sportsperson
ENOOPPRRSSUU	unprosperous
ENOORSSSTTUU	tortuousness

F

FFILLNRTUUUY	unfruitfully
FFLLOOSSTTYY	softly-softly
FGGGILNOOOST	footslogging
FGHHILORRTTY	forthrightly
FGHHLLOTTUUY	thoughtfully
FGHHLNOTTUUU	unthoughtful
FGHIILLMNOTU	mouth-filling
FGHIILNORRYY	horrifyingly
FGHILLNRTUUY	unrightfully
FGHILLPRSTUY	sprightfully
FGHINOPRTTTU	forth-putting
FGIIILNOSTUY	fuliginosity
FGIIILLNOSUUY	fuliginously
FGILOORSTTUU	futurologist
FHIIKKRSSWYY	whisky-frisky
FHIILOOSTTWY	foolish-witty
FHIINOOOPSST	photofission
FHILLOPRSUWY	worshipfully
FHILNOPRSUUW	unworshipful
FHLLNRTTUUUY	untruthfully
FIILLLMOPRUV	pulvilliform
FIILMMORTTUY	multiformity
FILLMOORSTUU	multiflorous
FILOORSTTUUY	fortuitously

G

GGGHHINOORTU	through-going
GGGHIIINNSST	sight-singing
GGGILLNRSTUY	strugglingly
GGHHHIITTTYY	highty-tighty
GGHHILNRSTUY	highly-strung
GGHHILOPRTUW	ploughwright
GGHHOORRTUUW	rough-wrought
GGHIIINNNNSY	singing-hinny
GGHIIJMMNTUY	thingummyjig
GGHIILMNNOOT	moonlighting
GGHIINNOOSTW	wing-shooting
GGIIILNNRTUY	intriguingly
GGIILLOORTUY	liturgiology
GGIIMNNNORRU	mourning-ring
GGIINNOOPRTW	growing-point
GGIINNOPSSTW	swinging-post
GGILLOOOSSST	glossologist
GGILMNNOORRY	morning-glory

GGILNOOOPSST spongologist
GHHIIILLLLNS shilling-hill
GHHILOOPRSUY hygrophilous
GHHINOPRRTTU print-through
GHIIKLNNNTUY unthinkingly
GHIILNNORSUY nourishingly
GHIILOOORSTY historiology
GHIILOOPSSTY physiologist
GHIINNNORSUU unnourishing
GHIINOPPPSTW whipping-post
GHILMOOOPRST morphologist
GHILMOOOPSSU Ophioglossum
GHILNOOPPRRY lorry-hopping
GHIMMOOPRSYZ zygomorphism
GHIMNOOPSSTY gymnosophist
GHLMOOOPPSUY pompholygous
GHLOOOOPTYYZ zoophytology
GHMOOOPRSUYZ zygomorphous
GIIILLMNNNPS spinning-mill
GIIILNNORSTV violin-string
GIIIMNNORTTT intromitting
GIIKLLMNOOST milking-stool
GIILLNOORSUY ingloriously
GIILMMNOOPSW swimming-pool
GIILMMNOOSTU immunologist
GIILMNNOOSTU monolinguist
GIILNORRSSTU soul-stirring
GIILNPRRSSUY surprisingly
GIILOOORSSTT storiologist
GIINNNOPRTTU turning-point
GILLMOOPRSSY prosyllogism
GILNOORSSSTY strongylosis
GILOOOPRSTTY protistology
GIMNOOOPRSST moss-trooping
GINOOOPRRSTU nitroso-group
GLLNOOSTTUUY gluttonously
GLLOOOPSTTUY polyglottous
GLOOOOOPRTYZ protozoology

H

HHIIILOOPPST ophiophilist
HHIILLOOPSTU lithophilous
HHIILMOOPPSS philosophism
HHIILNOOPRTY ornithophily
HHIILOOPPSST philosophist
HHIILOOPRSUZ rhizophilous
HHIIOOPRSSTU Histiophorus
HHILMMOOPRSY hylomorphism
HHILOOOPPSTU photophilous
HHIMMMOOOPRS homomorphism
HHIMNOOOPRRT ornithomorph
HHINOOPRRTTY thyrotrophin
HHMMOOOOPRSU homomorphous
HHMMOOOTTTUU mouth-to-mouth
HHMNOOOPPRTY pythonomorph
HIIIILMNPSST △philistinism
HIIILORSTTTT lithotritist
HIILLMNOOPSU limnophilous
HIILLOOPPRWW whippoorwill
HIILMOPRSSSU Russophilism
HIILNOOPRSTU nitrophilous
HIILOOPRRTTT lithotriptor
HIILOPRSSSTU Russophilist
HIIOOPRSSTUV virtuosoship
HIIOPRRSSUVV survivorship
HILMMOOPPRSY polymorphism
HILOOOPPRSTU tropophilous
HIMOOOPPRSTT phototropism
HIMOOOPRRSTT orthotropism
HIMOORSTTTWY thirty-twomos
HINOOOOPSSTT opisthotonos
HIOOOPRRSTTY proto-history
HLLLOOPPSUYY polyphyllous
HLMMNOOOSUYY homonymously
HLMOOOPPRSUY polymorphous
HLMOOPSSTUUY posthumously
HMMNOOOOPRSU monomorphous
HOOOOPPRRSSU sporophorous
HOOOOPRRSTTU orthotropous

I

IIIIMMMNNPYY miminy-piminy
IIIIMMNNNPYY niminy-piminy
IIIIMNNOSTTU intuitionism
IIIINNOSTTTU intuitionist
IIILMNOOPSSU posliminious
IIILNOQSTUUY iniquitously
IIIMNNOORSST intromission
IIIMNOORTTUV vomiturition
IIINNORSSTTU intrusionist
IIINNORSTTTU nutritionist
IIINNORSTTUU innutritious
IIIOPRSSTTUY spirituosity
IILMMNOOQSSU somniloquism
IILMNOOPSSTU postliminous
IILMNOOQSSTU somniloquist
IILMNOOSTUVY voluminosity
IILMOOPRRSSY promissorily
IILMOOPSSTYY polymyositis
IILNORSSSTUY sinistrously
IILNORSTTUUY nutritiously
IILOOPPRSTUY propitiously
IINNNNOORSTU non-intrusion
IINNOOOPPTTT point-to-point
IINOOOPPSSTT postposition
IINOOPPRSTUU unpropitious
IINOOPRSTTTU prostitution
IIOOPPSSSTUU suppositious
ILLMNOOOSTTY tonsillotomy
ILLMNOOSUUVY voluminously
ILLMOOQSTUUU multiloquous
ILNORSTUUUVY unvirtuously
ILOOPSTTUUVY voluptuosity
ILOPRSTTUVYY topsy-turvily
IMNOORSSTTUY monstruosity
IMOOPPRRSTUY pityrosporum
INNNOOOOPSSU non-poisonous

L

LLMOSTTUUUUY tumultuously
LLOOPSTUUUVY voluptuously
LMNNOOOOSTUY monotonously
LMNNOOSSUYYY synonymously
LMNOSTTUUUUU untumultuous

O

OOOOSSTTTWYY tootsy-wootsy

13AAA

A

AAAAACCDEEINR Anacardiaceae
AAAAACEEHMNRT Amaranthaceae
AAAAACEHIMSTT acatamathesia
AAAABCCEELRTU △baccalaureate
AAAABCCILNNOT tobaccanalian
AAAABCDIILLTY adiabatically
AAAABCEEILMNS Balsaminaceae
AAAABDEEGLNTV advantageable
AAAABDILMORSS ambassadorial
AAAABEGGGILMN baggage-animal
AAAABEHILNPRT alphabetarian
AAAACCCEEORRY Caryocaraceae
AAAACCDEEIPPR Capparidaceae
AAAACCDIIKLLS lackadaisical
AAAACCEEINRSU Casuarinaceae
AAAACCEELMNPU Campanulaceae
AAAACCHILLNRT charlatanical
AAAACCILLLPRT parallactical
AAAACCLMNORST malacostracan
AAAACDIILLNRT cardinalatial
AAAACEEEILNRV Valerianaceae
AAAACEEFGIRSX Saxifragaceae
AAAACEGILMOST galactosaemia
AAAACEHILMNTT anathematical
AAAACEMNORSTU amarantaceous
AAAACGHILPPRR paragraphical
AAAACIOPSSSTT apocatastasis
AAAADILMNOPTT maladaptation
AAAAEGIMMNRST anagrammatise
AAAAEGIMMNRTZ anagrammatize
AAAAEHILNPPRR paraphernalia
AAAAELNNSTTVW savanna-wattle
AAAAGIMMMNRST anagrammatism
AAAAGIMMNRSTT anagrammatist
AAAAHILMNNPST phantasmalian
AAABBCCIILLST cabbalistical
AAABBCEFINORR Afro-Caribbean
AAABBCILMMNPY namby-pambical
AAABBEIIMNRRS semi-barbarian
AAABBIINORRST barbarisation
AAABBIINORRTZ barbarization
AAABCCCEKLLTU back-calculate
AAABCCEEHNOOR Orobanchaceae
AAABCCELNNORR acorn-barnacle
AAABCCILLORTY acrobatically
AAABCDEELNRRS scandal-bearer
AAABCDEHINRTU △chateaubriand
AAABCDIKNORTW backwardation
AAABCEEILNRST ascertainable
AAABCEENPPRSU subappearance
AAABCEFILNOTT labefactation
AAABCEGILLLRY algebraically
AAABCEHINRRTT Tetrabranchia
AAABCEIILNRTT antibacterial
AAABCEILLNORY anaerobically
AAABCEILNOOPT palaeobotanic
AAABCHHINOOPR arachnophobia
AAABCILLLOPRY parabolically
AAABCILNORSTT abstractional
AAABDEELNPSST adaptableness
AAABDEGIILMTY damageability
AAABDEGIINNRS drainage-basin
AAABDEGMNNNOR rag-and-bone-man
AAABEEGLLNSUV unsalvageable
AAABEEGLNSSUU unassuageable
AAABEEHLLRSTV ballast-heaver
AAABEEILLNSSV availableness
AAABEELLNPSST palatableness
AAABEGIILMNTY manageability
AAABEGILNNSUY ungainsayable
AAABEILLMNPTU manipulatable
AAABELNNRRTUW unwarrantable
AAABHHINOOPTT thanatophobia
AAABHIOOPPRST astrapophobia
AAABIIILLNOST labialisation
AAABIIILLNOTZ labialization
AAABIIILNTTTY attainability
AAABIIKLNNOST △balkanisation
AAABIIKLNNOTZ △balkanization
AAABLNNRRTUWY unwarrantably
AAACCCEEHLNTY Cyclanthaceae
AAACCCGHILOPR cacographical
AAACCDEHLLNPS paschal-candle
AAACCDEIILMMS academicalism
AAACCDEIIPSTT discapacitate
AAACCDEILLNTU canaliculated
AAACCDHIILNOR archidiaconal
AAACCEEEILORU Eriocaulaceae
AAACCEEGINNTY Nyctaginaceae
AAACCEEILLNRT cancellariate
AAACCEELNNRUU Ranunculaceae
AAACCEELOPRTU Portulacaceae
AAACCEGHMNOST stagecoachman
AAACCEGILRTTX extragalactic
AAACCEILLMORS scleromalacia
AAACCELNORTYY cyanoacrylate
AAACCGILLLMOO malacological
AAACCGILLOOST astacological
AAACCHILPPRSY parapsychical
AAACCHLORSSTY thalassocracy
AAACCHLORTTTY thalattocracy
AAACCIILLSTTT stalactitical

AAACCIILMNOTT	acclimatation
AAACCILLLNOTU	calculational
AAACCILLLTTYY	catalytically
AAACCILLMNORY	macaronically
AAACCILLOPPTY	apocalyptical
AAACCILLRSSTY	sarcastically
AAACCILOTTTUY	autocatalytic
AAACDDEGHHILT	Gaidhealtachd
AAACDDEIMMNSU	unmacadamised
AAACDDEIMMNUZ	unmacadamized
AAACDEEEGHNRY	Hydrangeaceae
AAACDEEINPPRS	disappearance
AAACDEGHPRRTU	drag-parachute
AAACDEGLMOSUY	amygdalaceous
AAACDEHIMNRTY	adiathermancy
AAACDEIIILRUV	Aviculariidae
AAACDEIIINPRT	paediatrician
AAACDEIILMOPS	Lasiocampidae
AAACDEIILMPRT	pre-adamitical
AAACDEILMNNOP	△pandemoniacal
AAACDEILMNORY	aerodynamical
AAACDGHIIMPRT	diaphragmatic
AAACDGILMNOOR	macrodiagonal
AAACDGILMRRTU	dramaturgical
AAACDHIINOPRS	anaphrodisiac
AAACDHILNOPTY	anaphylactoid
AAACDIIILLNRT	cardinalitial
AAACDIIMMORTU	acaridomatium
AAACDILLOPRXY	paradoxically
AAACDIMMOORTU	acarodomatium
AAACEEEEHLMTY	Thymelaeaceae
AAACEEEFFILRS	Rafflesiaceae
AAACEEEFIKNNR	Frankeniaceae
AAACEEEHNPRRT	Pherecrataean
AAACEEELMMOST	Melastomaceae
AAACEEELOOPRT	Tropaeolaceae
AAACEEFIILOQU	Aquifoliaceae
AAACEEGHIILMP	Malpighiaceae
AAACEEGHINORT	Archegoniatae
AAACEEGIRRRTW	water-carriage
AAACEEGLLOSTU	sale-catalogue
AAACEEHINPSUU	euphausiacean
AAACEEIILNOPP	Papilionaceae
AAACEEILLMOPT	palaeoclimate
AAACEEILMORRT	araeometrical
AAACEEINNPPRT	appertainance
AAACEENNNOPPR	non-appearance
AAACEEOPPRSUV	papaveraceous
AAACEFFILNPRS	paraffin-scale
AAACEGHILOPPR	palaeographic
AAACEGHLOORRT	galactorrhoea
AAACEGIINNRSS	Cassegrainian
AAACEGILMNNOR	Anglo-American
AAACEGIMNOSTY	gynaecomastia
AAACEHIILLMNV	Machiavellian
AAACEHIIMMNNS	Manichaeanism
AAACEHIIMMNTT	mathematician
AAACEHILLMTTY	athematically
AAACEHILLPTTY	apathetically
AAACEHIMOOPPR	pharmacopoeia
AAACEIILMNNRT	Latin-American
AAACEIJNOPRRT	terra-japonica
AAACEIKLMNNOR	Neo-Lamarckian
AAACEILLMNOTX	exclamational
AAACEILNNSSST	satanicalness
AAACEIMOPPRSS	△caesaropapism
AAACELLMNRSTY	sacramentally
AAACELLNORRTT	contralateral
AAACELRRSTUVW	water-vascular
AAACELRRSTUVX	extravascular
AAACENRRRSTTU	restaurant-car
AAACFIILLLMOX	maxillofacial
AAACFIIMNNPRS	Pan-Africanism
AAACFILLNSTTY	fantastically
AAACFIMNORRTW	aircraftwoman
AAACGGHIIMNOT	gigantomachia
AAACGHIILPPRS	pasigraphical
AAACGIILLMSTT	stalagmitical
AAACGILLMMRTY	grammatically
AAACGILLMNSTY	synallagmatic
AAACGILLMPRTY	pragmatically
AAACGILMMNRTU	ungrammatical
AAACGILNNOTTU	anticoagulant
AAACHHINNNTTX	canthaxanthin
AAACHIILLPRSY	pharisaically
AAACHIIMNSTTT	antiasthmatic
AAACHILLMSTTY	asthmatically
AAACHILLNOPRY	anaphorically
AAACHIMOOPRST	achromatopsia
AAACIIKLMMNRS	Lamarckianism
AAACIILLMNOST	anomalistical
AAACIILLMOTXY	axiomatically
AAACIILLPRSTY	parasitically
AAACIILNNNOTT	incantational
AAACIILNORSST	sacralisation
AAACIILNORSTZ	sacralization
AAACIILNOSSTU	casualisation
AAACIILNOSTTU	actualisation
AAACIILNOSTUZ	casualization
AAACIILNOTTUZ	actualization
AAACIIMNRRSTT	Tractarianism
AAACIINRRTTVY	intracavitary
AAACIIORSSTTU	Austroasiatic
AAACILLMOTTUY	automatically
AAACILLMRTTUY	traumatically
AAACILNNORSSY	narco-analysis
AAACILNNORSTT	transactional
AAACILNNRSTTT	transatlantic
AAACILNPRRSTU	intracapsular
AAACILNRRSTUV	intravascular
AAACILOSSTTUY	autocatalysis
AAACMOORSTTTY	astrocytomata
AAADDDEGINSTV	disadvantaged
AAADEFINQRRSU	fair-and-square
AAADEGILMQRSU	quadragesimal
AAADEGINRSTTV	avant-gardiste
AAADEHHIMNNRT	Rhadamanthine
AAADEHHNPRSSZ	haphazardness
AAADEHILMOPPR	lampadephoria
AAADEILLQRRTU	quadrilateral
AAADEIMNNQRSU	squandermania
AAADEINOPPRTT	preadaptation
AAADELLLMNRSY	small-and-early
AAADELMMOPSST	plasmodesmata

AAADGHILMNRTU	draught-animal
AAADGILLNORTY	gradationally
AAADIIILNORST	radialisation
AAADIIILNORTZ	radialization
AAADIIMNORSTT	dramatisation
AAADIIMNORTTZ	dramatization
AAAEEEHKNPRSS	Shakespearean
AAAEEGHLOPPRR	palaeographer
AAAEEGMMMNNNT	man-management
AAAEEHIKNPRSS	Shakespearian
AAAEEHKLMRSWZ	shalwar-kameez
AAAEEILMNOPPR	paraleipomena
AAAEEILNNPRTT	plantain-eater
AAAEEJLNRSTTW	serjeant-at-law
AAAEFGILLLMNO	flagellomania
AAAEFHILLMORT	Thalamiflorae
AAAEFIILMMRST	materfamilias
AAAEFIILMPRST	paterfamilias
AAAEFNNORSSTV	savanna-forest
AAAEGGIMNOPRS	megasporangia
AAAEGIIILNNRT	inegalitarian
AAAEGIILMMNRS	managerialism
AAAEGIILMNRST	managerialist
AAAEGILLOPRRT	alligator-pear
AAAEGILMNORSU	megalosaurian
AAAEGILNNPRTU	Pantagruelian
AAAEGIMMNNORR	neogrammarian
AAAEGIMMNPRST	paramagnetism
AAAEGINORTTVX	extravagation
AAAEGKLNOOPPR	kangaroo-apple
AAAEGLLLMOPRR	parallelogram
AAAEGLNRTTVXY	extravagantly
AAAEHHILMPRTT	amphitheatral
AAAEHILNNPRST	phalansterian
AAAEIILMNNOTX	examinational
AAAEIILNPRRTT	intraparietal
AAAEIILNRRRTT	intra-arterial
AAAEILLLNOPPT	appellational
AAAEILLRRTXXY	extra-axillary
AAAEILMMNNPRT	parliament-man
AAAEILMNPRRTY	parliamentary
AAAEILPPPRSTT	papaprelatist
AAAEIMMMNRRTU	armamentarium
AAAEINORSTTVX	extravasation
AAAFHILLLMORT	thalamifloral
AAAGGGILNRTVY	aggravatingly
AAAGGKNOORRSS	kangaroo-grass
AAAGHHNOPRTTY	thanatography
AAAGHIINNNRTY	anythingarian
AAAGIILNNOSTV	galvanisation
AAAGIILNNOTVZ	galvanization
AAAGIILNORTTV	gravitational
AAAGIILNSSTVW	waiting-vassal
AAAGIIMMNSSTT	anastigmatism
AAAGILMOOPSTT	Plagiostomata
AAAGIMMNPRSTT	pangrammatist
AAAGLLNOPSTVY	galvanoplasty
AAAHHILMNOPPT	panophthalmia
AAAHIINORRTTU	authoritarian
AAAHILMNPSTTY	phantasmality
AAAHILOPPPRSY	parapophysial
AAAHINRRSTTUZ	Zarathustrian
AAAHLLLLMOSSW	All-hallowmass
AAAHLMORTTTUY	thaumatolatry
AAAIIILMNNOST	animalisation
AAAIIILMNNOTZ	animalization
AAAIIIMNNRSST	sanitarianism
AAAIIINNQRTTU	antiquitarian
AAAIILMNRSSTU	Australianism
AAAIILNNNORTT	intranational
AAAIILNNOSTTT	tantalisation
AAAIILNNOTTTZ	tantalization
AAAIIMNNPRSSS	Parnassianism
AAAIINNORSTTV	intravasation
AAAIINNOSSSST	assassination
AAAIINORRSTTT	tartarisation
AAAIINORRTTTZ	tartarization
AAAILLNNORSTT	translational
AAAILLNORRSTT	translatorial
AAAILLPRRSUXY	supra-axillary
AAAILNNNORSTT	transnational
AAAILNNOPRSTU	supranational
AAALNORSSTTUU	Atlantosaurus
AAAMNORSTTTUY	traumatonasty
AABBBCDEGIORR	cribbage-board
AABBBEGINRTTY	baby-battering
AABBBIILORSTY	absorbability
AABBCDEEEEIRR	Berberidaceae
AABBCDEELNRST	belt-and-braces
AABBCEILNRRST	transcribable
AABBCGHINNSTY	baby-snatching
AABBCIINRRSUU	suburbicarian
AABBCILLMOSTY	bombastically
AABBDDEEGILOR	biodegradable
AABBDEEINRTUV	unabbreviated
AABBDEGGIINRT	badger-baiting
AABBDEIILLLRT	billiard-table
AABBDGGIINNOR	Brobdignagian
AABBDIILORSTY	adsorbability
AABBDIINORSTW	boatswain-bird
AABBDILMNRSUU	submandibular
AABBEEEKLNRSS	breakableness
AABBEEELLMNSS	blameableness
AABBEEHILNSST	habitableness
AABBEGIKNNRRS	barnsbreaking
AABBEHIILNNTU	uninhabitable
AABBEIILLOSSU	bouillabaisse
AABBEIIMMRRSS	semi-barbarism
AABBEILNOPRTT	pentobarbital
AABBEKKLLNNTY	blankety-blank
AABBENORRSSSU	barbarousness
AABBHIMMNPSYY	namby-pambyish
AABBIMMMNPSYY	namby-pambyism
AABCCCEEIRTUU	Cucurbitaceae
AABCCCEHKRRST	backscratcher
AABCCDHLRTYYY	brachydactyly
AABCCEEEEILLR	Illecebraceae
AABCCEEEEKRRU	rebecca-eureka
AABCCEEKLRRRR	cracker-barrel
AABCCEELLNNOU	unconcealable
AABCCEGIMMRSU	circumambages
AABCCEHHLPRYY	brachycephaly
AABCCEHINOOPR	cancerophobia
AABCCEIILMPRT	impracticable

AABCCEIILPTTY	acceptability
AABCCEILLMOSV	clavicembalos
AABCCEILMNRSV	canvas-climber
AABCCEILNPRTU	unpracticable
AABCCELMOPRTY	campylobacter
AABCCELNNOTUU	unaccountable
AABCCIIILLNOT	actinobacilli
AABCCIIILNNST	cannibalistic
AABCCIIJLLNOY	Jacobinically
AABCCIILMPRTY	impracticably
AABCCILLLOSTU	lactobacillus
AABCCILLRSUUV	subclavicular
AABCCLNNOTUUY	unaccountably
AABCDEEEFNRSS	barefacedness
AABCDEEFIPRRT	prefabricated
AABCDEEIIMRSZ	semicarbazide
AABCDEELORSXY	decarboxylase
AABCDEELRRSTT	battle-scarred
AABCDEENNORUV	overabundance
AABCDEGIKLLNP	back-pedalling
AABCDEGILLNNT	ballet-dancing
AABCDEGILLRRT	ball-cartridge
AABCDEHIIMORT	thiocarbamide
AABCDEHIKLNTW	black-and-white
AABCDEIILTTUY	educatability
AABCDEINNOORT	decarbonation
AABCDELOPPRRS	clapperboards
AABCDGHIMNORT	matchboarding
AABCDGIKLMRSU	blackguardism
AABCDGILMNSSY	scambling-days
AABCDHNNOORRT	root-and-branch
AABCDIMNNORST	contrabandism
AABCDINNORSTT	contrabandist
AABCEEEELNPSS	peaceableness
AABCEEEGHLLLN	challengeable
AABCEEEGIINRZ	Zingiberaceae
AABCEEEHIOPRU	Euphorbiaceae
AABCEEEHLNSST	teachableness
AABCEEEILLPRR	irreplaceable
AABCEEEILRSTU	Eubacteriales
AABCEEELLNPRU	unreplaceable
AABCEEELLNSSV	cleavableness
AABCEEELNRSST	traceableness
AABCEEGHIOPRT	bacteriophage
AABCEEGLNOORS	barnacle-goose
	goose-barnacle
AABCEEHILMNPU	unimpeachable
AABCEEHLMNORT	thermobalance
AABCEEIILLMRR	irreclaimable
AABCEEIILNPPR	inappreciable
AABCEEILLMNRU	unreclaimable
AABCEEILLPRRY	irreplaceably
AABCEEILMNRSV	vraisemblance
AABCEEILMORVW	microwaveable
AABCEEIRRSTUU	bureaucratise
AABCEEIRRTUUZ	bureaucratize
AABCEELLNOSTU	sublanceolate
AABCEELMMORSU	commeasurable
AABCEELNRSSTT	tractableness
AABCEEMMNORSU	membranaceous
AABCEFGILLNNS	self-balancing
AABCEFIIINOTT	beatification
AABCEFIINORTT	abortifacient
AABCEFIOPRRRT	prefabricator
AABCEGHIILNTY	changeability
AABCEGIIKMNNT	cabinetmaking
AABCEGILLMOST	megaloblastic
AABCEGILOPSSY	abyssopelagic
AABCEGINOORSU	boraginaceous
AABCEGLLNORTU	congratulable
AABCEHIILPRTV	variable-pitch
AABCEHILLLMNR	lamellibranch
AABCEHILLPSTY	heptasyllabic
AABCEHILMRTTY	bathymetrical
AABCEHILNSSTU	unchastisable
AABCEHILNSTUZ	unchastizable
AABCEHINORRSW	rainbow-chaser
AABCEHLNNSTUU	unstaunchable
AABCEHLNPRSUU	unpurchasable
AABCEIILLMRRY	irreclaimably
AABCEIINORRTT	nitrobacteria
AABCEIIRSTTTY	tetrabasicity
AABCEILLMNRUY	unreclaimably
AABCEILLMOPRT	problematical
AABCEILLNPSTY	pentasyllabic
AABCEILLOORTV	collaborative
AABCEILLRSTTY	tetrasyllabic
AABCEILMNNOOP	companionable
AABCEILNNNOTU	uncontainable
AABCEILNNORST	constrainable
AABCEILRSTTVY	abstractively
AABCEIMORSSUU	simarubaceous
AABCEINOORRST	Serbo-Croatian
AABCEIRRSTTUU	bureaucratist
AABCEKNOORSSV	book-canvasser
AABCELMMNNOSU	somnambulance
AABCELNOOPRTY	polycarbonate
AABCFIILORTTY	factorability
AABCFIKMNOORT	back-formation
AABCFILNNOOTU	confabulation
AABCFILORRSUV	fibrovascular
AABCFLNOORTUY	confabulatory
AABCGIILLOTUY	coagulability
AABCHIILLNRTY	labyrinthical
AABCHIMNOPRRS	marsipobranch
AABCHIORRSSUU	△brachiosaurus
AABCIIILLMPTY	implacability
AABCIIILLNSTT	antiballistic
AABCIIILLPPTY	applicability
AABCIIILMNORT	antimicrobial
AABCIIILOSSTY	associability
AABCIIILQRTUY	acquirability
AABCIILLLRSTY	trisyllabical
AABCIILLNOSTY	syllabication
AABCIILMNOORT	combinatorial
AABCIILMOPRTY	comparability
AABCIILMRRUUV	vibracularium
AABCIINNOORST	carbonisation
AABCIINNOORTZ	carbonization
AABCIINORRSTU	carburisation
AABCIINORRTUZ	carburization
AABCILLNOOORT	collaboration
AABCILLNOOSTU	suballocation
AABCILLNOOSTV	Baltoslavonic

AABCILMNNOOPY	companionably
AABCILNNOORTY	carbonylation
AABCNNOOORSST	contrabassoon
AABDDDGILNNSW	swaddling-band
AABDDEEILLLOR	radiolabelled
AABDDEGGINRRW	badger-drawing
AABDDEIILNSSU	indissuadable
AABDDGIINNORR	draining-board
AABDDIILNSSUY	indissuadably
AABDEEEGILRSS	disagreeables
AABDEEEHLMRRT	marble-hearted
AABDEEFGIILNT	indefatigable
AABDEEGLLNORR	roller-bandage
AABDEEILMNRSS	admirableness
AABDEEILNRRTT	rattle-brained
AABDEEILNSSSV	advisableness
AABDEELLRRTUV	barrel-vaulted
AABDEELNPRSUU	unpersuadable
AABDEEMNRRSSU	unembarrassed
AABDEERRSTTTU	statute-barred
AABDEFGIILNTY	indefatigably
AABDEGIKNORST	skateboarding
AABDEHIIILSTT	dishabilitate
AABDEIILMNRST	administrable
AABDEIILNPTXY	expandability
AABDEILMNPRRU	premandibular
AABDEILMRTUVY	adumbratively
AABDELLMNRSTU	umbrella-stand
AABDELNORRUYY	boundary-layer
AABDENNPRSTUU	superabundant
AABDFFIILORTY	affordability
AABDHIMNORSTT	rhabdomantist
AABEEEEGLNRSS	agreeableness
AABEEEEHNRTTW	weather-beaten
AABEEEFLMNSST	self-abasement
AABEEEGILLNRS	generalisable
AABEEEGILLNRZ	generalizable
AABEEEHRRRTTW	water-breather
AABEEEILPRSVW	variable-sweep
AABEEELLLMNSS	malleableness
AABEEELNNSSTU	uneatableness
AABEEELNORSST	elaborateness
AABEEELNPRSSS	separableness
AABEEFGILNSST	fatigableness
AABEEFLNORSSV	favorableness
AABEEFLNRRRST	transferrable
AABEEGHIKNRRT	heartbreaking
AABEEGHLLNSSU	laughableness
AABEEGHLLRSTU	slaughterable
AABEEGILMORST	metagrabolise
AABEEGILMORTZ	metagrabolize
AABEEGILNNSSV	navigableness
AABEEHLNOPRTY	balneotherapy
AABEEIILLNNPX	inexplainable
AABEEIKLMNSTU	unmistakeable
AABEEIKMNORRT	re-embarkation
AABEEILLNNPUX	unexplainable
AABEEILLNORTY	inelaborately
AABEEILMNNSSU	unamiableness
AABEELLLNOSSW	allowableness
AABEELLLRSTTY	tetrasyllable
AABEELLNPRSUU	unpleasurable

AABEELMNNSSTU	untamableness
AABEELNNPRSUU	superannuable
AABEELNRRSTUV	untraversable
AABEEMMNRRSST	embarrassment
AABEFHILMOPRT	alphabetiform
AABEFHILNNOSU	unfashionable
AABEFIILLNQUU	unqualifiable
AABEFIILNSSTU	unsatisfiable
AABEFILLMMNNU	uninflammable
AABEFILMORSSU	balsamiferous
AABEFKMOORRST	breakfast-room
AABEFLMNORRST	transformable
AABEGHINNRRTU	bargain-hunter
AABEGHINQRSSU	square-bashing
AABEGIILLNOUV	bougainvillea
AABEGIJKLNRWY	jawbreakingly
AABEGILLOOOPY	palaeobiology
AABEGILNORRTU	gubernatorial
AABEGILNRRSTT	sabrerattling
	sabre-rattling
AABEGLLOPPRSS	palpable-gross
AABEGLNORSTUU	obtuse-angular
AABEHIILORRTT	rehabilitator
AABEHILLORUVY	behaviourally
AABEHLMOPPRSS	blepharospasm
AABEHMORRRSTU	harbour-master
AABEIIILLRSTY	realisability
AABEIIILLRTYZ	realizability
AABEIIILMNTXY	examinability
AABEIIKLMRTTY	marketability
AABEIILLLOSTV	volatilisable
AABEIILLLOTVZ	volatilizable
AABEIILLMNSSU	unassimilable
AABEIILLNSTUY	unsaleability
AABEIILMSTTTY	metastability
AABEIILNORSTV	verbalisation
AABEIILNORTVZ	verbalization
AABEIILNRSTWY	answerability
AABEIILOPRTVY	evaporability
AABEIIMNNRSTU	antisubmarine
AABEIINRRRSST	arbitrariness
AABEIKLMNSTUY	unmistakeably
AABEILLNOPRSU	unpolarisable
AABEILLNOPRUZ	unpolarizable
AABEILMNOPRTU	perambulation
AABEILMNRSTTT	transmittable
AABEILNNSSTUU	unsustainable
AABEILNOOPSTT	paleobotanist
AABEILNOORSTV	observational
AABEILOQRSTUU	subequatorial
AABELLLMNPRTU	umbrella-plant
AABELLNPRSUUY	unpleasurably
AABELMMNOSSWY	assemblywoman
AABELMNOORSTU	neuroblastoma
AABELMOPRRTUY	perambulatory
	preambulatory
AABELMOPRSSTT	spermatoblast
AABELNOPRRSTT	transportable
AABELNPRSSSUU	unsurpassable
AABELNRRSTTUU	subternatural
AABFHILNNOSUY	unfashionably
AABFILMNNOTUU	funambulation

AABFLMNORTUUY	funambulatory
AABGHIOOPRTUY	autobiography
AABGIIILMNORS	aboriginalism
AABGIIILNORTY	△aboriginality
AABGIILLNOOST	globalisation
AABGIILLNOOTZ	globalization
AABGILNRRSTUU	subtriangular
AABGLLNOOSSSU	Balanoglossus
AABHHIIMOOPRT	arithmophobia
AABHIIILNPRRS	librarianship
AABHIILOOOPRU	ailourophobia
AABIIIILNRTVY	invariability
AABIIIILNSTTY	insatiability
AABIIILLMPPTY	impalpability
AABIIILMPSSTY	impassability
AABIIILNOSSTT	stabilisation
AABIIILNOSTTZ	stabilization
AABIILNNNRTTU	tintinnabular
AABIILNNSSTTU	insubstantial
AABIILNORSTTU	brutalisation
AABIILNORTTUZ	brutalization
AABILLNSSTTUY	substantially
AABILNNSSTTUU	unsubstantial
AABLMMNOORSTU	somnambulator
AABLNPRSSSUUY	unsurpassably
AACCCDILMORTY	macrodactylic
AACCCEEILNRRT	recalcitrance
AACCCEENNNOPT	non-acceptance
AACCCEGINORTY	gynaecocratic
AACCCEHIILSTT	catechistical
AACCCEHILMOPR	macrocephalic
AACCCEHMORSSY	Saccharomyces
AACCCEIILLMRT	climacterical
AACCCFIIILNOT	calcification
AACCCGHHILOPR	chalcographic
AACCCHILLOORT	ochlocratical
AACCCIIILMNTT	anticlimactic
AACCCIILLLMTY	climactically
AACCDDEIORRTX	dextrocardiac
AACCDEEEHILTY	Lecythidaceae
AACCDEEEIMRRT	demi-caractère
AACCDEEEIOORS	Dioscoreaceae
AACCDEEIIINOV	Vaccinioideae
AACCDEEIILNRU	clairaudience
AACCDEEILNOPY	△encyclopaedia
AACCDEEILOOPY	Lycopodiaceae
AACCDEENNTTUU	unaccentuated
AACCDEHHIKNRZ	chicken-hazard
AACCDEHIIRRST	trisaccharide
AACCDEHIOPRSU	pseudo-archaic
AACCDEIILLLTY	dialectically
AACCDEIILMNST	accidentalism
AACCDEIILNTTY	accidentality
AACCDEIINNSTT	antidesiccant
AACCDEIINORTT	accreditation
AACCDEILNNNOT	non-accidental
AACCDEILNOOTU	coeducational
AACCDEILNPTTY	pentadactylic
AACCDEIMMOOTV	accommodative
AACCDEIMNNOPU	unaccompanied
AACCDEINOPRTT	pedantocratic
AACCDFIIIINOT	acidification
AACCDGIILLOOR	cardiological
AACCDGIMMNOOT	accommodating
AACCDHIILNOOT	diacatholicon
AACCDHIIMNOOR	orchidomaniac
AACCDIILLOPTY	apodictically
AACCDILMNOTYY	dactyliomancy
AACCDIMMNOOOT	accommodation
AACCEEEHMNTTU	catechumenate
AACCEEEILMMNO	Commelinaceae
AACCEEEILRSTU	Sterculiaceae
AACCEEENPRRRY	canary-creeper
AACCEEFILORST	calefactories
AACCEEFIRSTUV	surface-active
AACCEEGIMORTT	categorematic
AACCEEHILMNOT	catecholamine
AACCEEHILMPRY	hypercalcemia
AACCEEHIMORRT	archaeometric
AACCEEHIMRRST	saccharimeter
AACCEEHIOSSUZ	schizaeaceous
AACCEEHLRRSST	characterless
AACCEEHMORRST	saccharometer
AACCEEIILMRST	reacclimatise
AACCEEIILMRTZ	reacclimatize
AACCEEIIMRSTY	Myristicaceae
AACCEEILPPRTU	picture-palace
AACCEELLPPRRW	clapperclawer
AACCEFIIINOTT	acetification
AACCEFILORRSU	calcariferous
AACCEGGHINOST	stagecoaching
AACCEGGHINPPR	charge-capping
AACCEGHHLOPRR	chalcographer
AACCEGHIJKKNT	hacking-jacket
AACCEGHILOPRR	cerographical
AACCEGHINOOPR	oceanographic
AACCEGIILNRTT	intergalactic
AACCEGILLNOOO	oceanological
AACCEGILLOOTU	autecological
AACCEGILLORTY	categorically
AACCEGILLOTTY	geotactically
AACCEHHLOPPSY	scaphocephaly
AACCEHIILMORT	iatrochemical
AACCEHIILRSTU	△eucharistical
AACCEHILLMRSV	clishmaclaver
AACCEHILLMSTY	schematically
AACCEHILLPPTY	platycephalic
AACCEHILLPRTY	phylacterical
AACCEHILMORTT	tachometrical
AACCEHILMPSTY	metapsychical
AACCEHILMRTTY	tachymetrical
AACCEHILRRTTU	architectural
AACCEHIMPRSTU	pharmaceutics
AACCEHIMRRSTY	saccharimetry
AACCEHMOOPRSU	camphoraceous
AACCEIILLMOPT	paleoclimatic
AACCEIILMNOST	encomiastical
AACCEIILNOPTT	acceptilation
AACCEIINNORRT	incarceration
AACCEIINNORTV	revaccination
AACCEILLMRTUV	circumvallate
AACCEILLNSSSS	classicalness
AACCEILMNNORT	necromantical
AACCEILNPRSST	practicalness

Words marked △ may be spelled also with a capital letter

AACCEILOPRSTY	palaeocrystic
AACCEIMMNNOPT	accompaniment
AACCEINNNOOTT	concatenation
AACCEINOPPPRT	copper-captain
AACCEINOPSSSU	capaciousness
AACCEKNORTTTU	counter-attack
AACCELLNOOPRR	lance-corporal
AACCELLPRSTUY	spectacularly
AACCELNPRSTUU	unspectacular
AACCELORSSSUU	crassulaceous
AACCFIIILLRSY	sacrificially
AACCFIIILNORT	clarification
AACCFIIINNORT	carnification
AACCFIIINOPRT	caprification
AACCFIIINORST	scarification
AACCFIILNOSTU	fasciculation
AACCGGIILLLOO	glaciological
AACCGHILLNOOT	Anglo-Catholic
AACCGIILLNOOR	craniological
AACCGILLNNTUU	uncalculating
AACCHIILMNOOT	machicolation
AACCHIILMNORT	chiromantical
AACCHIILPRSTY	psychiatrical
AACCHIILQRRSU	squirarchical
AACCHIIMORTTY	achromaticity
AACCHIIMPRSSU	suprachiasmic
AACCHIINNORST	anachronistic
AACCHILLMORTY	chromatically
AACCHILLOPRTT	trophallactic
AACCHILNOPSTY	sycophantical
AACCIIILLNSTV	Calvinistical
AACCIIINNOOST	cocainisation
AACCIIINNOOTZ	cocainization
AACCIIINORSTT	cicatrisation
AACCIIINORTTZ	cicatrization
AACCIILLMOPTY	apomictically
AACCIILLMPRTY	impractically
AACCIILLSSTUY	casuistically
AACCIILMNOOSS	occasionalism
AACCIILMNPSTU	scapulimantic
AACCIILNOOSST	occasionalist
AACCIILNOOSTY	occasionality
AACCIIMOSSSTT	staccatissimo
AACCIINOPRSTT	pantisocratic
AACCIKKNNORTY	nick-nackatory
AACCILLNPRTUY	unpractically
AACCILLNSTTYY	syntactically
AACCILLOPSSST	postclassical
AACCILMNOPSTU	scapulomantic
AACCILNNOOOTV	convocational
AACCILNNOORTT	contractional
AACCILNORTTUU	acculturation
AACCIMNOORSTU	carcinomatous
AACCINOQRSTTU	quasi-contract
AACCINORSSTTY	sacrosanctity
AACDDEEELLNVV	advanced-level
AACDDEEGJOTUV	judge-advocate
AACDDEGILLNRS	scaling-ladder
AACDDEHIINPST	candidateship
AACDDELMNORSU	Dendrocalamus
AACDDKLNOORSW	cloak-and-sword
AACDEEEIILLPR	pedicellariae
AACDEEEMOOPST	Podostemaceae
AACDEEFILMSTU	sulfacetamide
AACDEEGHINNRS	case-hardening
AACDEEGIIRRRV	carriage-drive
AACDEEGINORRS	coarse-grained
AACDEEGINRRRU	undercarriage
AACDEEGNNNORR	non-regardance
AACDEEHIMNORT	Echinodermata
AACDEEHIOSTUZ	autoschediaze
AACDEEHLLMTWY	what-d'ye-call-'em
AACDEEHNRSSVZ	ranz-des-vaches
AACDEEILLRTVY	declaratively
AACDEEILMNPRT	predicamental
AACDEEILNPPTU	appendiculate
AACDEEILNQRUV	quadrivalence
AACDEEILOOPPY	Polypodiaceae
AACDEEILORSST	sacerdotalise
AACDEEILORSTZ	sacerdotalize
AACDEEIMMNRTY	medicamentary
AACDEEIMNNOTT	decontaminate
AACDEEINNRSTU	unascertained
AACDEEINPPRTU	unappreciated
AACDEENNNNOTT	non-attendance
AACDEFFIIMNRS	disaffirmance
AACDEGGILLOPY	pedagogically
AACDEGHIILOPR	ideographical
AACDEGHIOPRRR	cardiographer
AACDEGIMNNRST	dancing-master
AACDEGINNQRSU	square-dancing
AACDEGJLNOSUU	juglandaceous
AACDEGLMNNORS	scandalmonger
AACDEHIIMNRRT	archimandrite
AACDEHILLTTWY	what-d'ye-call-it
AACDEHILOOPRT	orthopaedical
AACDEHIMOSSTU	autoschediasm
AACDEHIORRSTT	trisoctahedra
AACDEHLOSTUXY	hexadactylous
AACDEHMNNOORT	enchondromata
AACDEHNOPRSST	stop-and-search
AACDEIIJLRTUX	extrajudicial
AACDEIILLMRTY	diametrically
AACDEIILMRTVY	vice-admiralty
AACDEIILNORTV	valedictorian
AACDEIILRSTTU	disarticulate
AACDEIINNPTTU	unanticipated
AACDEIINNRSTT	transactinide
AACDEILLMORTY	declamatorily
AACDEILLNOTUY	educationally
AACDEILLORRTY	declaratorily
AACDEILMORSST	sacerdotalism
AACDEILNRSTTU	ultra-distance
AACDEILNRTTUU	unarticulated
AACDEILOORTUW	caliature-wood
AACDEILORSSTT	sacerdotalist
AACDEILPQRTUU	quadruplicate
AACDEIMNNNOTT	decontaminant
AACDEIMNOQRTU	quartodeciman
AACDEINNORSUU	arundinaceous
AACDEINOSSSUU	audaciousness
AACDEKLNORSVY	sandy-laverock
AACDELMNNRSSU	underclassman
AACDFHNOSSTTW	downcast-shaft

AACDFIIIMNNOT	damnification
AACDFIILLOPRS	spadicifloral
AACDGHHOOPRTY	cathodography
AACDGHINOSSTW	shadowcasting
AACDGHLOPRTYY	dactylography
AACDGIIILLOST	dialogistical
AACDGIIINNOST	diagnostician
AACDGIILLNNOO	clinodiagonal
AACDGILMRRSTU	garlic-mustard
AACDHHILOPRTY	hydropathical
AACDHIIINORST	arachnoiditis
AACDHIIIOPRST	adiaphoristic
AACDHIILOORSU	Dolichosauria
AACDHILLLRUYY	hydraulically
AACDHILLOPRSY	rhapsodically
AACDHILORSTTY	hydrostatical
AACDHIMMOOSSS	sadomasochism
AACDHIMOOSSST	sadomasochist
AACDHINOPQRSU	quadraphonics
AACDHLMMNOOSY	chlamydomonas
AACDHOOOPRRTT	Protochordata
AACDIIILLMOTY	idiomatically
AACDIIILPQRTU	quadricipital
AACDIIIMNORTU	radio-actinium
AACDIIINNNORT	incardination
AACDIIIORTTVY	radioactivity
AACDIIJLLSTUY	Judaistically
AACDIIKMNOOPR	macropinakoid
AACDIILLLSTUY	dualistically
AACDIILLMNOPR	palindromical
AACDIILLMPRYY	pyramidically
AACDIILLORTTY	dictatorially
AACDIILNNOPTU	pandiculation
AACDIILNOOORT	radiolocation
AACDIILNOOOTU	audio-location
AACDIIMNOPSST	antispasmodic
AACDILLMOPSSY	spasmodically
AACDILLOQRRUU	quadrilocular
AACDIMNORSSTY	astrodynamics
AACEEEGLNNRST	lance-sergeant
AACEEEHJKLRTT	leather-jacket
AACEEEILMNOOP	Polemoniaceae
AACEEFLNRSSSU	self-assurance
AACEEGHILOPRS	archipelagoes
AACEEGHILOPST	Stegocephalia
AACEEGHLMNOPR	encephalogram
AACEEGHLMOPSU	megacephalous
AACEEGHNOOPRR	oceanographer
AACEEGILLLNVY	evangelically
AACEEGILLNNUV	unevangelical
AACEEGILMMRTT	telegrammatic
AACEEGILNPRTW	watering-place
AACEEGINNOSTU	gentianaceous
AACEEGLLOOOPY	palaeoecology
AACEEHIILRSTT	theatricalise
AACEEHIILRTTZ	theatricalize
AACEEHIIMMSTT	mathematicise
AACEEHIIMMTTZ	mathematicize
AACEEHIIMNPRT	ramapithecine
AACEEHIJNNOPS	Japano-Chinese
AACEEHILLSTTY	aesthetically
AACEEHILMORTT	theorematical
AACEEHILMPSTY	mesaticephaly
AACEEHILNPRTT	parenthetical
AACEEHINNRSTU	neurastheniac
AACEEHLLMRSTV	velt-mareschal
AACEEHLNNOPPR	parencephalon
AACEEHLNOPRST	Encephalartos
AACEEHMNOORRT	Rhaeto-Romance
AACEEHMNOPSUY	nymphaeaceous
AACEEHMOPRSTT	spermatotheca
AACEEHOPRRTXY	archaeopteryx
AACEEIILNRTTV	intercalative
AACEEIILPPRTT	peripatetical
AACEEIIMNNRSU	un-Americanise
AACEEIIMNNRUZ	un-Americanize
AACEEIIMPPRST	misappreciate
AACEEIINNRSST	necessitarian
AACEEIJLNRTTU	interjaculate
AACEEILMMNORT	anemometrical
AACEEILMMRTTU	multicamerate
AACEEILMRRTTX	extrametrical
AACEEILNNOPPU	panleucopenia
AACEEILNNQTUV	quantivalence
AACEEILNQRSUV	carnivalesque
AACEEILNRRSUV	vernacularise
AACEEILNRRUVZ	vernacularize
AACEEIMMNNRTT	remittance-man
AACEEIMNNRSTT	ascertainment
AACEELLLRRTUX	extracellular
AACEEMNORSSTU	sarmentaceous
AACEENNORSSST	Saracen's-stone
AACEFHLLOPRSW	paschal-flower
AACEFIIIILRST	artificialise
AACEFIIIILRTZ	artificialize
AACEFIIILQTUV	qualificative
AACEFIILMNOTT	metafictional
AACEFIILNORST	fractionalise
AACEFIILNORTZ	fractionalize
AACEFILLTTUVY	facultatively
AACEFINNOORRT	confarreation
AACEGGHILNORT	gathering-coal
AACEGHHIMNPST	camp-sheathing
AACEGHHINOPRT	ethnographica
AACEGHIILLPRX	lexigraphical
AACEGHILLLRTY	lethargically
AACEGHILLNOOP	phaenological
AACEGHILLOPPY	plagiocephaly
AACEGHILMOPPT	apophlegmatic
AACEGHILMOPYY	hypoglycaemia
AACEGHILNOPRV	venographical
AACEGHILOOPRR	oreographical
AACEGHILOORST	archaeologist
AACEGHIMNOPRT	cinematograph
AACEGHOPRSSSU	sarcophaguses
AACEGIILLMNOR	mineralogical
AACEGIILLMNTY	enigmatically
AACEGIILLNNTY	antigenically
AACEGIILMRRTV	gravimetrical
AACEGILLLLORY	allegorically
AACEGILLLMRTU	metallurgical
AACEGILLNPRYY	panegyrically
AACEGILLOORTT	teratological
AACEGILLRSTTY	strategically

AACEGILMNOOSU magnoliaceous
AACEGILMNORTV galvanometric
AACEGINOSSSSU sagaciousness
AACEGLLNRRTUY rectangularly
AACEGLLOOPSUY polygalaceous
AACEHHIIMPRTT amphitheatric
AACEHHINPSSTY psychasthenia
AACEHHLOOPRTX cephalothorax
AACEHIIIMNRTT arithmetician
AACEHIIIMPRST hemiparasitic
AACEHIILLMMSV Machiavellism
AACEHIILLNTUV hallucinative
AACEHIILLSTTY atheistically
AACEHIILMRSTT theatricalism
AACEHIILNOPST cephalisation
AACEHIILNOPTZ cephalization
AACEHIILNPSTT pantheistical
AACEHIILRTTTY theatricality
AACEHIIMMMSTT mathematicism
AACEHIIMNNOST mechanisation
AACEHIIMNNOTZ mechanization
AACEHIIMNPSTY metaphysician
AACEHIIOPSSST associateship
AACEHILLMRTUY rheumatically
AACEHILLNTTUY authentically
AACEHILMNPRRU hurricane-lamp
AACEHILMOPRST atmospherical
AACEHILMOPTYY polycythaemia
AACEHILMPSTTY sympathetical
AACEHILNOPPRT paleanthropic
AACEHILNOPRTU neuropathical
AACEHILPRSTXY extra-physical
AACEHIMNOORRT Rhaeto-Romanic
AACEHIMPRSTTU pharmaceutist
AACEHINOPRTTY actinotherapy
AACEHINORTTTU authenticator
AACEHINPRSTTY parasynthetic
AACEHLNOPSSYY psychoanalyse
AACEHLNOPSYYZ psychoanalyze
AACEHLOOPSTUU autocephalous
AACEHNOPPRRTY parthenocarpy
AACEHNOPRSSTT phase-contrast
AACEIIILMRSTT materialistic
AACEIIIMPRSST semiparasitic
AACEIIINORTTV ratiocinative
AACEIIIPPRTTV participative
AACEIILLLMNOR Lamellicornia
AACEIILLLPRST parallelistic
AACEIILLLRSTY realistically
AACEIILLMNPRT planimetrical
AACEIILLNPSTY epinastically
AACEIILLPRSTY peirastically
AACEIILMMNRSU unicameralism
AACEIILMNRSTU unicameralist
AACEIILMNSSST ismaticalness
AACEIILMPTTTU multicapitate
AACEIILNNORTT intercalation
AACEIILNNOSTT cat-o'-nine-tails
AACEIILNOPPRT reapplication
AACEIILNORSTT cartelisation
AACEIILNORTTZ cartelization
AACEIILNOSSUV salviniaceous
AACEIILNPRSTT paternalistic
AACEIILNRSSST satiricalness
AACEIILPRRSTU particularise
AACEIILPRRTUZ particularize
AACEIIMMOSTTU semi-automatic
AACEIIMNNOTTV contaminative
AACEIIMNORRST reactionarism
AACEIIMNSSTTY systematician
AACEIINNNORRT reincarnation
AACEIINNORSST scenarisation
AACEIINNORSTZ scenarization
AACEIINOPRRTV prevarication
AACEIINORRSTT reactionarist
AACEIINORSTTU cauterisation
AACEIINORTTUZ cauterization
AACEIINRRRSTU curtain-raiser
AACEIKLMMNORS Neo-Lamarckism
AACEILLLNRRTU intracellular
AACEILLMNPTUY pneumatically
AACEILLPRRRTY tricarpellary
AACEILMNRRSUV vernacularism
AACEILMOPRTVY comparatively
AACEILMORTTTU tautometrical
AACEILNNOPSTU encapsulation
AACEILNOOPRRT procreational
AACEILNOPRSSS prosaicalness
AACEILNOSSSSU salaciousness
AACEILNPRRSTU interscapular
AACEILNRRSTUV vernacularist
AACEILNRRTUVY vernacularity
AACEILOPRRTTX extratropical
AACEIMMNORTUU communautaire
AACEIMNNRSTTT transmittance
AACEIMNOOPSST compassionate
AACEIMNOPSSTY synaposematic
AACEINNORRTUV averruncation
AACEINOPRRSTT procrastinate
AACEINOPRRTUY precautionary
AACEINOPRSSSU rapaciousness
AACEINORRSTUV avant-couriers
AACEINPRRSSTT transcriptase
AACELLMNNORTU nomenclatural
AACELNORRSUUV neurovascular
AACELNRSSTTUU sustentacular
AACEMNNOORSTT entomostracan
AACENNOPRRSTT transportance
AACFFIIILNOST falsification
AACFFIIINORTT tariffication
AACFGIIIMNNOT magnification
AACFGIIINORTT gratification
AACFGIILLLOUV fluvio-glacial
AACFGILNNOORT conflagration
AACFGIMNNRTUU manufacturing
AACFGNOOORTTT contrafagotto
AACFHIMNPRSST craftsmanship
AACFIIIILRTTY artificiality
AACFIIILMNOPT amplification
palmification
AACFIIILNOQTU qualification
AACFIIIMNNORT informatician
AACFIILMNORST fractionalism
AACFIILMORTTY matrifocality

AACFIILNORSTT	fractionalist
AACFIILOPRTTY	patrifocality
AACFIILOQRTUY	qualificatory
AACFIINNOORTT	fractionation
AACFIINOORSTT	factorisation
AACFIINOORTTZ	factorization
AACFINNORRSSU	Franco-Russian
AACFINORSTTUY	anfractuosity
AACGGHILLOOPR	graphological
	logographical
AACGGIIKNNPTU	unit-packaging
AACGGILLLLOOY	algologically
AACGGILLOORST	gastrological
AACGGILNRSTYZ	crystal-gazing
AACGHHIMNNTTW	night-watchman
AACGHHIPRSTTY	tachygraphist
AACGHHMOOPRRT	chromatograph
AACGHIILLMORT	logarithmical
AACGHIILLPRST	calligraphist
AACGHIIPRRSTT	stratigraphic
AACGHILLNNOTY	gnathonically
AACGHILLOPRXY	xylographical
AACGHILMNOOPR	monographical
	nomographical
AACGHILMOPRTY	climatography
AACGHILNNSUWY	launching-ways
AACGHILNOORST	arachnologist
AACGHILOOPPRT	topographical
AACGHILOPPRTY	typographical
AACGHIMRSTTUU	thaumaturgics
AACGHMNOOPRSY	pharmacognosy
AACGIIILNNOST	anglicisation
AACGIIILNNOTZ	anglicization
AACGIIINPPRTT	participating
AACGIILLLNTVY	vacillatingly
AACGIILLMSTTY	stigmatically
AACGIILLNNORY	inorganically
AACGIILLNOSTY	agonistically
AACGIILMMOPRT	lipogrammatic
AACGIILNORSTU	cartilaginous
AACGIILNORTTU	graticulation
AACGIIMNNOOPT	compagination
AACGIINNOOTTV	noctivagation
AACGIJLNNOOTU	conjugational
AACGILLLNOOPY	palynological
AACGILLLNOSTY	nostalgically
AACGILLMNSTYY	gymnastically
AACGILLMOOOPT	potamological
AACGILLMOOOST	somatological
AACGILMNOOPST	campanologist
AACGILMNOORST	gastronomical
AACGIMMMNOORT	monogrammatic
AACGINNORRSTW	narrowcasting
AACGLNOORRTTU	congratulator
AACHHIILLMOPT	philomathical
AACHHIIORSTUY	Ichthyosauria
AACHHILNNOPTY	phthalocyanin
AACHHIMNOORTX	xanthochromia
AACHHIMNOPRSY	physharmonica
AACHHIMNPSSTY	yachtsmanship
AACHIIIMNNOST	Antiochianism
AACHIIINNRSTT	antichristian
AACHIIINRRTTT	antiarthritic
AACHIILLNNOTU	hallucination
AACHIILRSTTWY	railway-stitch
AACHIIMMNNORS	Monarchianism
AACHIINOPRSTU	haruspication
AACHILLLMPTYY	lymphatically
AACHILLMOOPSU	malacophilous
AACHILLNORSTY	thrasonically
AACHILLNORTUY	hallucinatory
AACHILNOOPTTU	tautophonical
AACHILOPRSSTY	astrophysical
AACHIMMNOPRST	panchromatism
AACHIMMOOPRST	apochromatism
AACHIMNNNOOPR	panharmonicon
AACHIMOPRSSTT	catastrophism
AACHIOPPRSSSY	parapsychosis
AACHIOPRSSTTT	catastrophist
AACHLLLOOPRST	chloroplastal
AACHLNNOORSUY	anachronously
AACHLNOPSSTYY	psychoanalyst
AACHLOOPRSTTY	thoracoplasty
AACIIIILNOSTT	italicisation
AACIIIILNOTTZ	italicization
AACIIILLNNNOT	inclinational
AACIIILLNPSTY	pianistically
AACIIILLOPTTY	apoliticality
AACIIILLPPRTY	participially
AACIIILMNOSST	antisocialism
AACIIILNNOSTT	nationalistic
AACIIILNOOSST	socialisation
AACIIILNOOSTZ	socialization
AACIIILNORSTT	rationalistic
AACIIILNOSSTT	antisocialist
AACIIILNOSTTY	antisociality
AACIIINNOORTT	ratiocination
AACIIINNOTTVX	X-inactivation
AACIIINOPPRTT	participation
AACIIIOSSTTVY	associativity
AACIILLMORTTY	triatomically
AACIILLMOSTTY	atomistically
AACIILLMPRSTY	prismatically
AACIILLNPRTUY	puritanically
AACIILLOPRTTY	patriotically
AACIILLOSSTTY	isostatically
AACIILLSSTTTY	statistically
AACIILMNOOSTV	vocationalism
AACIILMNORSSY	microanalysis
AACIILMNORTTU	matriculation
AACIILMNORTTY	romanticality
AACIILMPRRSTU	particularism
AACIILNNOOSTV	volcanisation
AACIILNNOOTVZ	volcanization
AACIILNNOSTUV	vulcanisation
AACIILNNOTUVZ	vulcanization
AACIILNOOSTUV	vacuolisation
AACIILNOOTUVZ	vacuolization
AACIILNPPRTTY	participantly
AACIILOSSTTTU	stalactitious
AACIILPRRSTTU	particularist
AACIILPRRTTUY	particularity
AACIIMMNNORTU	communitarian
AACIIMNNNOOTT	contamination

AACIIMORRSSTT aristocratism
AACIINNNNOSTT Constantinian
AACIINNNOOSTT cantonisation
AACIINNNOOTTZ cantonization
AACIINNOORSTT narcotisation
AACIINNOORTTZ narcotization
AACIINOORRTTY ratiocinatory
AACIIOPPRRTTY participatory
AACILLLOOPSTY apostolically
AACILLMNOOSTY onomastically
AACILLMNOOTXY taxonomically
AACILLMNOPSTY complaisantly
AACILLNOOPSTU unapostolical
AACILLOPRRTTU ultra-tropical
AACILMMOPSTTY symptomatical
AACILMNNOPSTU uncomplaisant
AACILMNOOPTTU computational
AACILMNRRSTUU intramuscular
AACILMORRTTUY matriculatory
AACILNNOORSTT translocation
AACILNPRSSTYY cryptanalysis
AACILOOPRRRTU procuratorial
AACIMOPRSTTTU post-traumatic
AACLQRRSTTUYZ quartz-crystal
AADDEEEEHHRTW weather-headed
AADDEEEHQRRTU headquartered
AADDEEELMPRST paddle-steamer
AADDEEGGILLRT draggle-tailed
AADDEEGNRRTUU undergraduate
AADDEEHHIPSSW waspish-headed
AADDEEHHLRRTY hard-heartedly
AADDEELNRTTUU unadulterated
AADDEGGHNRRTU granddaughter
AADDEGHNORRUY rough-and-ready
AADDEGHOPRRSS Addressograph®
AADDEHHNNORSU hare-and-hounds
AADDEILNRSSST dastardliness
AADDIIILNOPST dilapidations
AADEEEGGHIMRR hedge-marriage
AADEEEGGLRTXY exaggeratedly
AADEEEGGNRTUX unexaggerated
AADEEEHLNNRRT △neanderthaler
AADEEEIILMRST dematerialise
AADEEEIILMRTZ dematerialize
AADEEEIKNSSWW wide-awakeness
AADEEEIMNNRRT △mediterranean
AADEEELNRRTVW lavender-water
AADEEEMMNRSTU admeasurement
AADEEFHHLLRTY half-heartedly
AADEEFNSSSSTT steadfastness
AADEEGILMORRT radiotelegram
AADEEGIMNPRST disparagement
AADEEGINNNSTU ensanguinated
AADEEHIMMMNOS Mohammedanise
AADEEHIMMMNOZ Mohammedanize
AADEEHIMNOPRT diaphanometer
AADEEHLLRRTTY tetrahedrally
AADEEHLOPRRTZ trapezohedral
AADEEHLORRTTT tetartohedral
AADEEIIILNNOST denationalise
AADEEIIILNNOTZ denationalize
AADEEIIMNNRSU neuraminidase
AADEEIKLMNRST tradesmanlike
AADEEILMMORST melodramatise
AADEEILMMORTZ melodramatize
AADEEILNNNORR noradrenaline
AADEEILNOPPSS epanadiploses
AADEEILNRSTTV travel-stained
AADEEILNRTTTV travel-tainted
AADEEINPRSSST disparateness
AADEEIOPRRSST parrot-disease
AADEELLNRRTWW well-warranted
AADEELNPPPRST pepper-and-salt
AADEENNPRSTUU superannuated
AADEFFIINORRT diffarreation
AADEFGHLNRRTY grandfatherly
AADEFIIILLMNSU sulfanilamide
AADEFIIILNOSTU feudalisation
AADEFIIILNOTUZ feudalization
AADEFIIILOQRTU quadrifoliate
AADEFILMNOPPR manifold-paper
AADEFKLNOORRT foot-land-raker
AADEFLLMNNTUY fundamentally
AADEFLNSSTTUY unsteadfastly
AADEGGLNRTTUU gauntlet-guard
AADEGGNNORRST great-grandson
AADEGHILNRTUW daughter-in-law
AADEGHMOPRRTY dermatography
AADEGIIIMPRRV primigravidae
AADEGIIILMNQRU quadrigeminal
AADEGIIILMRTUV multigravidae
AADEGILLMNORT road-metalling
AADEGILMNNRSU land-measuring
AADEGILNSTTVY devastatingly
AADEGIMNRRSTW drawing-master
AADEGINNQRRUY quadringenary
AADEGINNRSTTW water-standing
AADEGINNRTUUU uninaugurated
AADEHHIILLNPP Philadelphian
AADEHHILMOORR haemorrhoidal
AADEHIILMOSSY haemodialysis
AADEHIILNPSUZ sulphadiazine
AADEHILLLLOTW All-hallowtide
AADEHILNOPRRY hydro-airplane
AADEHIMMMMNOS Mohammedanism
AADEHIMNORSTU diathermanous
AADEHNORRSTTW north-eastward
AADEHNORSSSUZ hazardousness
AADEHORSSTTUW south-eastward
AADEIIILMSSST disassimilate
AADEIIIMNOSTT mediatisation
AADEIIIMNOTTZ mediatization
AADEIIILLMORTY mediatorially
AADEIIILLNRRTY interradially
AADEIIILLQRRTU quadriliteral
AADEIIILMMNRST maladminister
AADEIIILMNSSTU unassimilated
AADEIIILNOPPSS epanadiplosis
AADEIIILNRSSTU disnaturalise
AADEIIILNRSTUZ disnaturalize
AADEIIMNNOORT enantiodromia
AADEIIMNNORSV animadversion
AADEIINOPSSST dispassionate
AADEIIPQRRTTU quadripartite

AADEIKKMNPSSU	kiss-and-make-up
AADEILLLOSTWW	swallow-tailed
AADEILLNNQRUY	quadrennially
AADEILLOPSTUY	dialypetalous
AADEILMMORSTT	melodramatist
AADEILMNORSST	maladroitness
AADEILNNRSTUU	unnaturalised
AADEILNNRTUUZ	unnaturalized
AADEIMNORRRTU	armoured-train
AADEIMQRRTUUV	quadrumvirate
AADEINORRRTXY	extraordinary
AADEJLMMNSTTU	maladjustment
AADELMOPRSTTY	dermatoplasty
AADELNNRRTUWY	unwarrantedly
AADEMNORSTTUY	tetradynamous
AADFHIMNPRSST	draftsmanship
AADFIIOQRRSUU	quadrifarious
AADFIKLLMOORW	maid-of-all-work
AADGGIILNPRSY	disparagingly
AADGGILORSSST	dog's-tail-grass
AADGHIILOPRST	gladiatorship
AADGHIINNRSVY	varnishing-day
AADGHILNOOORT	orthodiagonal
AADGIIILNNTWY	lady-in-waiting
AADGIIIMPRRSV	primigravidas
AADGIILLNQRUU	quadrilingual
AADGIILMRSTUV	multigravidas
AADGIILNNSSTT	distant-signal
AADGILNNOPRST	prostaglandin
AADGLMNNOOOSX	Anglo-Saxondom
AADHILNORRSTY	synarthrodial
AADIIIINNNOST	Indianisation
AADIIIINNNOTZ	Indianization
AADIILLNOORST	dollarisation
AADIILLNOORTZ	dollarization
AADIILLNORTTY	traditionally
AADIILLOSUUVY	audiovisually
AADIILNNOPSTT	displantation
AADIIMNNOORST	randomisation
AADIIMNNOORTZ	randomization
AADIIMNORRSTT	administrator
AAEEEFLNRSSSW	self-awareness
AAEEEFNPPRRST	paper-fastener
AAEEEGGLNNRST	agents-general
AAEEEGMNNRRRT	rearrangement
AAEEEGNOORRRT	aerogenerator
AAEEEGNRSTTUX	États-Généraux
AAEEEHILPPRRT	Pre-Raphaelite
AAEEEHLNPRSST	elephant's-ears
AAEEEIKMNRRTT	anti-marketeer
AAEEEILMNNNOS	Neo-Melanesian
AAEEELMMNPRTT	temperamental
AAEEFGIILMNRZ	magazine-rifle
AAEEFGILLNNNS	self-annealing
AAEEFGINRRTWY	wayfaring-tree
AAEEFHMNSSSST	shamefastness
AAEEFHORSTTTT	state-of-the-art
AAEEFIIMNSTTV	manifestative
AAEEFNPPRRRST	transfer-paper
AAEEGGHINPRTT	gathering-peat
AAEEGGILMORTV	agglomerative
AAEEGGILNNRSV	seal-engraving
AAEEGHIMMORRT	hierogrammate
AAEEGHIMOPSTT	apothegmatise
AAEEGHIMOPTTZ	apothegmatize
AAEEGHMNOOSTU	haematogenous
AAEEGIILMNRRS	marriage-lines
AAEEGIILMNRUV	evangeliarium
AAEEGIILNNORV	evangeliarion
AAEEGIIMMPRST	epigrammatise
AAEEGIIMMPRTZ	epigrammatize
AAEEGIIMNRRRT	intermarriage
AAEEGIIMNRSTV	vegetarianism
AAEEGIIMSSTTT	semi-sagittate
AAEEGILLMSSXY	sexagesimally
AAEEGILMNOORR	oleomargarine
AAEEGILNNPPSS	appealingness
AAEEGILNRSTVY	evangelistary
AAEEGIMMMNNST	mismanagement
AAEEGIMNPRSTU	measuring-tape
AAEEGIMNRTTUV	argumentative
AAEEGINOPRSTU	eusporangiate
AAEEGJMNORRST	sergeant-major
AAEEGLMMORSTT	stalagmometer
AAEEGLOOPSSUY	go-as-you-please
AAEEHHMOPPSTT	metaphosphate
AAEEHIILMNSSS	leishmaniases
AAEEHIILMOPTT	epitheliomata
AAEEHIILNPSST	elephantiasis
AAEEHIKLMMRRV	Hammerklavier
AAEEHILLNNNPY	phenylalanine
AAEEHILMNNOST	ethanolamines
AAEEHILMOPRTU	Palaeotherium
AAEEHILMPPRRS	Pre-Raphaelism
AAEEHIMNPRRTY	hypernatremia
AAEEHIMNPSSTT	panaesthetism
AAEEHINRSSTTT	heat-resistant
AAEEHIPPRRSTY	hyperparasite
AAEEHMNOSTTUX	exanthematous
AAEEHMOPRRRST	spermatorrhea
AAEEHNORSSTTT	east-north-east
AAEEHOSSSTTTU	east-south-east
AAEEIIILMMRST	immaterialise
AAEEIIILMMRTZ	immaterialize
AAEEIILMNNRTT	interlaminate
AAEEIILNPRRTT	interparietal
AAEEIIMNNNSST	inanimateness
AAEEIIMNNORTX	re-examination
AAEEIINNSSSTT	insatiateness
AAEEIKLMNSSTT	statesmanlike
AAEEIKLNSSTTV	talkativeness
AAEEILLLPPTVY	appellatively
AAEEILLNRTTVY	alternatively
AAEEILNRRSTTT	transliterate
AAEEILOPRTTVX	extrapolative
AAEEILPPRRTVY	preparatively
AAEEILPRSSSSZ	laissez-passer
AAEEIMMNRRRST	master-mariner
AAEEIMNNPPRTT	appertainment
AAEEIMNPRRSTV	privateersman
AAEELMNPRSSSU	supersalesman
AAEELNPRRRTTU	preternatural
AAEEMQRRRSTTU	quartermaster
AAEEPRRSSTTUU	supersaturate

AAEFFGMNORSUW	woman-suffrage
AAEFFIILMNORR	foraminiferal
AAEFFIILMRTVY	affirmatively
AAEFFIIMNORRT	reaffirmation
AAEFFINOORSTT	afforestation
AAEFGILLLMNST	flagellantism
AAEFGILMNRRTY	fragmentarily
AAEFGIMNNORSU	manganiferous
AAEFGIMNNORTT	fragmentation
AAEFHILLOSTUZ	sulfathiazole
AAEFIIMNNOSTT	manifestation
AAEFILLOPRRTY	prefatorially
AAEFILLRRTTTU	ultrafiltrate
AAEFILMMMORSU	mammaliferous
AAEGGHINNPPRS	paper-hangings
AAEGGHNOPRSTY	steganography
AAEGGIIKLMNNS	leasing-making
AAEGGIILLRTUV	villeggiatura
AAEGGIILNTTUV	agglutinative
AAEGGILMNOORT	agglomeration
AAEGGIMNNOORT	aggiornamento
AAEGGLNOOPRTU	protolanguage
AAEGHHIKMRRTW	high-watermark
AAEGHIILMNOPR	Germanophilia
AAEGHIKMNOPRT	kinematograph
AAEGHILMNRSTW	whaling-master
AAEGHILMOOSTT	haematologist
AAEGHIMOPSTTT	apothegmatist
AAEGHINNPPSWW	wappenshawing
AAEGHIOPRRRTY	arteriography
AAEGHIPRRRSTT	stratigrapher
AAEGHLLMOPRTY	metallography
AAEGHLMNNOORS	alongshoreman
AAEGHLNOQRTUZ	quartz-halogen
AAEGHLOPPSYYZ	zygapophyseal
AAEGHLOPRTTUY	telautography
AAEGHMNOOPRSU	phanerogamous
AAEGHNOOPRRTY	organotherapy
AAEGIIILMNTVY	imaginatively
AAEGIIIMNNRSS	imaginariness
AAEGIIIMNNTUV	unimaginative
AAEGIILLLORST	legislatorial
AAEGIILLMRSTY	magisterially
AAEGIILLNSSTU	Ustilaginales
AAEGIILMNNPRT	parliamenting
AAEGIILMNRSST	sailing-master
AAEGIILNNTTTY	tangentiality
AAEGIIMMPRSTT	epigrammatist
AAEGIIMNNORST	Germanisation
AAEGIIMNNORTZ	Germanization
AAEGIIMNNOSTT	magnetisation
AAEGIIMNNOTTZ	magnetization
AAEGIIMNQQSUU	Quinquagesima
AAEGIINNNRSTT	intransigeant
AAEGIKLLMMNOR	mallemaroking
AAEGIKLNPPRSW	walking-papers
AAEGIKMMNRSST	mass-marketing
AAEGILLMNOOPT	megalopolitan
AAEGILLNRTTUY	triangulately
AAEGILMNPRSTU	Pantagruelism
AAEGILNNOPRTU	Pantagruelion
AAEGILNPRSTTU	Pantagruelist
AAEGILOPRRTUX	expurgatorial
AAEGIMNNORTTU	argumentation
AAEGINOORSTTY	geostationary
AAEGINPPPPRRW	wrapping-paper
AAEGIOPRRSTUY	Sauropterygia
AAEGLLNOOOPTY	palaeontology
AAEGLLOOOOPYZ	palaeozoology
AAEGLMMORSTTY	stalagmometry
AAEGLNNOOSSSU	analogousness
AAEHHILMNNPTY	naphthylamine
AAEHHILMOPRTX	xerophthalmia
AAEHHIMMPRRSS	marsh-samphire
AAEHIIILMNSSS	leishmaniasis
AAEHIIIMNNSTT	antihistamine
AAEHIIORTTTUV	authoritative
AAEHILMNPRSST	phalansterism
AAEHILNPRSSTT	phalansterist
AAEHIMNPSSSTT	statesmanship
AAEHINOPPRSTU	aphanipterous
AAEHINPRSSSTY	parasynthesis
AAEHLNOPPRSTU	Paleanthropus
AAEHMOPPRSTTY	Spermatophyta
AAEHNNOPRSTTY	parasyntheton
AAEIIILMMMRST	immaterialism
AAEIIILMMRSTT	immaterialist
AAEIIILMMRTTY	immateriality
AAEIIILNORRST	irrationalise
AAEIIILNORRTZ	irrationalize
AAEIIILNORSST	serialisation
AAEIIILNORSTZ	serialization
AAEIIIMNNPPRT	imparipinnate
AAEIIKMNNNOST	Neo-Kantianism
AAEIIKMNORTTZ	marketization
AAEIIILLLMNRTY	matrilineally
AAEIIILLLNPRTY	patrilineally
AAEIIILLMNOSTT	metallisation
AAEIIILLMNOTTZ	metallization
AAEIIILLMNRSTU	unilateralism
AAEIIILLMRRSTT	trilateralism
AAEIIILLNOPSTT	palletisation
AAEIIILLNOPTTZ	palletization
AAEIIILLNRSTTU	unilateralist
AAEIIILLNRTTUY	unilaterality
AAEIIILLQTTUVY	qualitatively
AAEIIILLRRSTTT	trilateralist
AAEIIILMMNOPST	semipalmation
AAEIIILMNNORTT	terminational
AAEIIILMNORSTV	Voltaireanism
AAEIIILMNPRSST	impartialness
AAEIIILMRRTTXY	extralimitary
AAEIIILNNNORTT	△international
AAEIIILNNORSTV	vernalisation
AAEIIILNNORTVZ	vernalization
AAEIIILNOPRRTT	intrapetiolar
AAEIIILNOPRSSU	plesiosaurian
AAEIIILNORRTTT	trilateration
AAEIIILORSTUUV	suovetaurilia
AAEIIMNOPRSST	separationism
AAEIIMOPPRTVX	approximative
AAEIINNNOSTTX	annexationist
AAEIINNNSTTTY	instantaneity
AAEIINOPPPRRT	inappropriate

AAEIINOPPRSTU	pauperisation
AAEIINOPPRTUZ	pauperization
AAEIINOPRSSTT	separationist
AAEIIOPPPRRTV	appropriative
AAEILLNNOSSTY	sensationally
AAEILLNOPRTXY	explanatorily
AAEILMNNOOPPR	paralipomenon
AAEILMOPPRTXY	approximately
AAEILNNNOSSTU	unsensational
AAEILNNOPRSTU	supernational
AAEILNNORRSTT	retranslation
AAEILNOOORTTV	laevorotation
AAEILNOOPRTTX	extrapolation
AAEILNOORTUVV	overvaluation
AAEILOOPPRRRT	propraetorial
AAEILOPPPRRTY	appropriately
AAEILOPPRRRTY	preparatorily
AAEIMMNPPRSST	panspermatism
AAEIMNNNOORTT	ornamentation
AAEIMNNOSTTUY	ayuntamientos
AAEIMNOPRSSST	master-passion
AAEIMNORSSTTT	station-master
AAEIMNPPRSSTT	panspermatist
AAEIMNRSTTTUV	transmutative
AAEINNNOSSTTU	instantaneous
AAEINOOPPRRRT	propraetorian
AAEINOPPPQRTU	appropinquate
AAEINOPPPRRTU	unappropriate
AAEIOOPPRRSTT	protospataire
AAELLNRRSSTVY	transversally
AAELMOPPRRSTU	supratemporal
AAELNNNRSSTUU	unnaturalness
AAELNNOPRRSST	transpersonal
AAELNNPRRSTTY	transparently
AAELOOORRTTVY	laevorotatory
AAELOOPRRTTXY	extrapolatory
AAEMMNPRRSTUU	paramenstruum
AAENNNPRRSTTU	untransparent
AAFFGHINPRSSU	suffraganship
AAFFIINNOPRRT	nitroparaffin
AAFHINOOPRRST	parrot-fashion
AAFIIILMNRTUY	unfamiliarity
AAFIILMNNOORT	informational
AAFIILMNOORST	formalisation
AAFIILMNOORTZ	formalization
AAGGGIILNNTTU	agglutinating
AAGGHHIIOPRST	hagiographist
AAGGIILNNOTTU	agglutination
AAGGIILNNPSST	glass-painting
AAGHHIKLMNRST	knight-marshal
AAGHHINOOPPRT	anthropophagi
AAGHHNOOPPRTU	phonautograph
AAGHHNOOPPRTY	anthropophagy
AAGHHOPPRRRYY	rhyparography
AAGHIILMNORTT	antilogarithm
AAGHIIMMPRSTU	amphigastrium
AAGHILOPPSYYZ	zygapophysial
AAGHIMMRSTTUU	thaumaturgism
AAGHIMNOOPRST	mastigophoran
AAGHIMRSTTTUU	thaumaturgist
AAGHINOPRRSTU	uranographist
AAGHKNNOOORRT	kangaroo-thorn
AAGHNOORSSTUU	saurognathous
AAGIIIKMRRSUU	maurikigusari
AAGIIILLNOSTV	villagisation
AAGIIILLNOTVZ	villagization
AAGIIINNORSTT	granitisation
AAGIIINNORTTZ	granitization
AAGIIJNNOORST	jargonisation
AAGIIJNNOORTZ	jargonization
AAGIIILMOORST	malariologist
AAGIILLNNSTTY	tantalisingly
AAGIILLNNTTYZ	tantalizingly
AAGIILMNOORST	glamorisation
AAGIILMNOORTZ	glamorization
AAGIILNNORTTU	triangulation
AAGIILNORSTUV	vulgarisation
AAGIILNORTUVZ	vulgarization
AAGIILNRRTTUY	triangularity
AAGIINNPPRSTY	spray-painting
AAGILMMNNOSUY	magnanimously
AAGILMNORRSTT	mortal-staring
AAGILNNNPRSTT	transplanting
AAGILNNORSTTU	strangulation
AAGIMNORRRSTT	transmigrator
AAGINOOOPPRSS	prosopagnosia
AAGLMNOORSTUU	granulomatous
AAHHNOOPPRTTY	anthropopathy
AAHIIILLOOPRU	ailourophilia
AAHIIILNNOSTY	hyalinisation
AAHIIILNNOTYZ	hyalinization
AAHIILLPPRSTX	xiphiplastral
AAHIILMMNSSTU	Malthusianism
AAHIILMNOPRSW	animal-worship
AAHIILNNPRRTY	platyrrhinian
AAHIIMMNNOOPR	morphinomania
AAHIIMNNOORST	harmonisation
AAHIIMNNOORTZ	harmonization
AAHIIMNNRSSTT	transisthmian
AAHIIMNOOPPPT	hippopotamian
AAHIINOORSTTU	authorisation
AAHIINOORTTUZ	authorization
AAHIINPSSSSTT	assistantship
AAHILNNOPSSYY	hypno-analysis
AAHIMRRSSTTUZ	Zarathustrism
AAHLLMOOPSTUY	polythalamous
AAHLLOPPSSTYY	staphyloplasy
AAHLMMNOOOSTU	monothalamous
AAHLNOOPRRTTY	anthropolatry
AAIIILMNORRST	irrationalism
AAIIILMNORSTV	Voltairianism
AAIIILNNOPRST	inspirational
AAIIILNORRSTT	irrationalist
AAIIILNORRTTY	irrationality
AAIIILNORSTTU	ritualisation
	uralitisation
AAIIILNORTTUZ	ritualization
	uralitization
AAIIILNOSSTUV	visualisation
AAIIILNOSTUVZ	visualization
AAIIIMMNNNOST	antinomianism
AAIIIMNNNOSST	Saint-Simonian
AAIIINNNOSTTT	instantiation
AAIIINNOSSTTT	sanitationist

AAIIINOPRSTTV	privatisation
AAIIINOPRTTVZ	privatization
AAIILLMMNORTY	matrimonially
AAIILLMNNOTTU	multinational
AAIILLMNNOTVY	nominatively
AAIILLMNOPRTY	patrimonially
AAIILLNOPRSTU	pluralisation
AAIILLNOPRTTW	partition-wall
AAIILLNOPRTUZ	pluralization
AAIILMNNOORST	normalisation
AAIILMNNOORTZ	normalization
AAIILMNOOPTTT	totipalmation
AAIILMNOSTTUU	mutualisation
AAIILMNOTTUUZ	mutualization
AAIIMNNNORSTT	transmination
AAIIMNOOPPRTX	approximation
AAIIMNRSSTTTV	Vansittartism
AAIINNOPRRSTT	transpiration
AAIINNORRSTTY	transitionary
AAIINOOPPPRRT	appropriation
AAIKMNOOQRTTU	quotation-mark
AAILLMOOPPSTU	papillomatous
AAILLNOOPSTTU	postulational
AAILNNOPPSTTU	supplantation
AAILNOOOPRRTT	protonotarial
AAIMNNORSTTTU	transmutation
AAIMOPRRSUVXY	paramyxovirus
AAINOOOPRRTTT	protonotariat
AAINOPRRRSTTY	transpiratory
AAKLNNNNNOOPT	nannoplankton
AALMNOOOPRSTU	protanomalous
AALMOOPSSTTTY	stomatoplasty
AANNORRSSTUUY	tyrannosaurus
ABBBBCEEHLMRU	bubble-chamber
ABBCDEEEHMORR	robe-de-chambre
ABBCDEEIILNRS	indescribable
ABBCDEEILNRSU	undescribable
ABBCDEIILNRSY	indescribably
ABBCDGIILNPRS	scribbling-pad
ABBCEEIJLNOOT	objectionable
ABBCEEKLORRRY	roe-blackberry
ABBCEGIKLNRRY	blackberrying
ABBCEGIMNOPRT	carpet-bombing
ABBCEHIILORTY	bibliothecary
ABBCEHKOORRSS	shock-absorber
ABBCEIJLNOOTY	objectionably
ABBCEILNORTTU	contributable
ABBCGHIIILOPR	bibliographic
ABBCGIIILLLOO	bibliological
ABBCHHILOORSY	hobby-horsical
ABBCIIILLLOOP	bibliopolical
ABBCIIILMNOTY	combinability
ABBCIIILOPRST	probabilistic
ABBDDELNRTUWY	wet-and-dry-bulb
ABBDDGIILNORU	building-board
ABBDEEEEILNRT	beetlebrained
ABBDEGIKLNNOU	double-banking
ABBDEIILRSTTU	distributable
ABBDFFILMNNSU	blindman's-buff
ABBEEEGHLNSTY	shabby-genteel
ABBEEEGLLPSSS	pebble-glasses
ABBEEGNORRRSU	barber-surgeon
ABBEEHINOORTX	hexobarbitone
ABBEEILMPRRTU	imperturbable
ABBEELMMNOOTZ	bamboozlement
ABBEGHIILOPRR	bibliographer
ABBEGILNORRSU	rabble-rousing
ABBEHLLORRTUU	bulbourethral
ABBEIIILOPRST	probabilities
ABBEILMPRRTUY	imperturbably
ABBEILSSTTTUU	substitutable
ABBGHIIILOPST	bibliophagist
ABBIIILLORSTT	bibliolatrist
ABBIIILMOPRTY	improbability
ABBIILLOORSTU	bibliolatrous
ABCCCEEENNOST	contabescence
ABCCCILLMOOXY	coxcombically
ABCCDEELNOOUV	double-concave
ABCCDEILORSTU	scrobiculated
ABCCDGHIILNOU	coachbuilding
ABCCDHHIIOPRW	coachwhip-bird
ABCCEEIILMMRS	immarcescible
ABCCEEIILNNOV	inconceivable
ABCCEEILNNOSS	non-accessible
ABCCEEILNNOUV	unconceivable
ABCCEEJLNORTU	conjecturable
ABCCEFFHINORR	branch-officer
ABCCEHIILLMOY	biochemically
ABCCEHILORTTT	brattice-cloth
ABCCEIIILMPTY	impeccability
ABCCEIIILSSTY	accessibility
ABCCEIIILNNOVY	inconceivably
ABCCEIILORTTY	bacteriolytic
ABCCEIIMMNRTU	circumambient
ABCCEIKLNOSTW	constablewick
ABCCEILNNOUVY	unconceivably
ABCCEIMMORTUY	mycobacterium
ABCCELNORSTTU	constructable
ABCCHHIIOPRRS	archbishopric
ABCCHKOQTTTUU	quatch-buttock
ABCCIILORRTXY	tricarboxylic
ABCCIIMNOORST	combinatorics
ABCCIINORSTTU	antiscorbutic
ABCCNOORRSTTU	subcontractor
ABCDDEEEHNSSU	debauchedness
ABCDDEEELNNSU	undescendable
ABCDDEEGINPRT	carpet-bedding
ABCDDEEHLRRRY	bladder-cherry
ABCDDEEIILRST	discreditable
ABCDDEEIKLMRT	middle-bracket
ABCDDEEILTTUX	tax-deductible
ABCDDEIILRSTY	discreditably
ABCDEEEHLRRST	barrel-chested
ABCDEEEILMNRT	clean-timbered
ABCDEEEINORRT	decerebration
ABCDEEELMMNOR	recommendable
ABCDEEFLMRRUY	mulberry-faced
ABCDEEGHILNOR	breech-loading
ABCDEEGIILRTT	lattice-bridge
ABCDEEGILRRTT	cartridge-belt
ABCDEEIIILTVY	deceivability
ABCDEEIILLTY	delectability
ABCDEEIILMNNU	unmedicinable
ABCDEEIILNNOT	benedictional

ABCDEEILNNNOS incondensable
ABCDEEILNPRTU unpredictable
ABCDEELLOORSU sable-coloured
ABCDEELMMNNOU uncommendable
ABCDEELMMNORY recommendably
ABCDEELMOPPRW wamble-cropped
ABCDEGILLMNOU cable-moulding
ABCDEHIILNNRR brainchildren
ABCDEHINOPSSU subdeaconship
ABCDEIIILLNPS disciplinable
ABCDEIIILNORT bidirectional
ABCDEIIILNOSS indissociable
ABCDEIIILNTUY ineducability
ABCDEIIILPRTY predicability
ABCDEIIILPSTY despicability
ABCDEIIINSTUV subindicative
ABCDEIILLOQTU quodlibetical
ABCDEILNPRTUY unpredictably
ABCDEILNSSSUU undiscussable
ABCDELMMNNOUY uncommendably
ABCDEMOPRRSTU broad-spectrum
ABCDGHINOOPPR chopping-board
ABCDHIILLLORT billiard-cloth
ABCDIIIILNTVY vindicability
ABCDIIINNOSTU subindication
ABCEEEELNRSSX execrableness
ABCEEEFIILLRT electrifiable
ABCEEEFIILNNT beneficential
ABCEEEFLNNORU unenforceable
ABCEEEILNOPTX exceptionable
ABCEEEILNPRUV unperceivable
ABCEEEILNRSUV unserviceable
ABCEEEILNSSTX excitableness
ABCEEEILORRRV irrecoverable
ABCEEEILORTVX overexcitable
ABCEEELNORRUV unrecoverable
ABCEEELNORSSV revocableness
ABCEEELNSSSUX excusableness
ABCEEFIIINNOT beneficiation
ABCEEFILNNORU uninforceable
ABCEEGHILMNRS single-chamber
ABCEEGHILNOPT benthopelagic
ABCEEGILNORSW bowling-crease
ABCEEGIMNNRSS embracingness
ABCEEHILNSSSU blanchisseuse
ABCEEHILORSTT heteroblastic
ABCEEHIMNRSTY chimneybreast
ABCEEHIMOPRRS promise-breach
ABCEEHINNNPRR perennibranch
ABCEEHKLOSSTT clothes-basket
ABCEEHLNOSSTU touchableness
ABCEEIIILRTVY receivability
ABCEEIILNPRSU republicanise
ABCEEIILNPRUZ republicanize
ABCEEILMOORSU bromeliaceous
ABCEEILNNORSV inconversable
ABCEEILNNOSTT incontestable
ABCEEILNNRSSU incurableness
ABCEEILNOPRRS cerebrospinal
ABCEEILNOPTXY exceptionably
ABCEEILNPRUVY unperceivably
ABCEEILORRRVY irrecoverably
ABCEEILRRSTTU battle-cruiser
ABCEEIMNORSSV misobservance
ABCEEIMNOSSTV combativeness
ABCEELMMNORSU commensurable
ABCEELNNOOPRU pronounceable
ABCEELNNOQRUU unconquerable
ABCEELNNORSUV unconversable
ABCEELNNOSTTU uncontestable
ABCEELNORRUVY unrecoverably
ABCEELOORSTTT bottle-coaster
ABCEENNNOORSV non-observance
ABCEEOPRRSUVX procès-verbaux
ABCEFGIILMMNR climbing-frame
ABCEFHIILLMRU Liebfraumilch
ABCEFIIILNOPT plebification
ABCEFIIINORTV verbification
ABCEFILOORSTU cobaltiferous
ABCEFINOORRSU △carboniferous
ABCEFLMNNOORU unconformable
ABCEFLMNOORTU uncomfortable
ABCEGHHOORRTU thoroughbrace
ABCEGHILOPRTY copyrightable
ABCEGHIMNNSUU submachine-gun
ABCEGIIILLOOOP paleobiologic
ABCEGIILLOOOX exobiological
ABCEGIINNOOSU bignoniaceous
ABCEGILLMOORY embryological
ABCEGILNNNOOZ non-cognizable
ABCEHIIIKLMNS mashie-niblick
ABCEHIIKLSTTY sketchability
ABCEHILLMOOOT holometabolic
ABCEHILNOPSST constableship
ABCEHILOOOPPT photocopiable
ABCEHKLLORSTU bullock's-heart
ABCEHLOOPRSTU claustrophobe
ABCEHOPRRSTUY brachypterous
ABCEIIJNOOTTV objectivation
ABCEIIKNNRSSS brainsickness
ABCEIILLLMPTU multiplicable
ABCEIILMNOPST incompatibles
ABCEIILMNPRSU republicanism
ABCEIILNOPRTU republication
ABCEIILNORSTY bacteriolysin
ABCEIILORSSTY bacteriolysis
ABCEIILPRSTTU subtriplicate
ABCEIILPSSTUY subspeciality
ABCEIIMNNOORT recombination
ABCEIIMOORRST isobarometric
ABCEIIMOSSTTY biosystematic
ABCEILLORSTTY obstetrically
ABCEILNNORSTU inconstruable
ABCEILNNOSTTY incontestably
ABCEILNORTTUU tuberculation
ABCEILOORSSTU strobilaceous
ABCEILORRRTUU arboriculture
ABCEILRRRTTUU tritubercular
ABCEIOOORRRTV corroborative
ABCEIOPRSSSUY presbyacousis
ABCELMMNORSUY commensurably
ABCELNNOQRUUY unconquerably
ABCFILMMORRUU umbraculiform
ABCFLMNNOORUY unconformably

ABCFLMNOORTUY	uncomfortably
ABCGGHINORRTU	turbocharging
ABCGHHNOOPRRY	bronchography
ABCGHIKLNSSUW	swashbuckling
ABCGIILLNNOOO	non-biological
ABCGILLMNOORU	macroglobulin
ABCHHINOOPRST	opisthobranch
ABCHIILLRSTUY	hubristically
ABCHIILOOOPRU	ailourophobic
ABCHILOOPRSTT	trophoblastic
ABCIIIILNOSTY	insociability
ABCIIIILNRTTU	tribuniticial
ABCIIIINNRTTU	tribunitician
ABCIIILLNOTUY	inoculability
ABCIIILMOPTTY	compatibility
ABCIIILNOSTUY	unsociability
ABCIILLMOSSTY	symbolistical
ABCIILLMOSTYY	symbiotically
ABCIILLMRSTUU	biculturalism
ABCIILMMOTTUY	commutability
ABCILLOPRSTUY	subtropically
ABCILNOORSTTU	obstructional
ABCINOOOORRRT	corroboration
ABCLRRSSTTUUU	substructural
ABCOOOORRRRTY	corroboratory
ABDDDEEILMNRU	muddle-brained
ABDDDEILMNORY	broadmindedly
ABDDEEEHLORTU	double-hearted
ABDDEEEIKLMRR	middlebreaker
ABDDEEEILMNOT	diamond-beetle
ABDDEEGILLNOU	double-dealing
ABDDEELNORTUU	double-natured
ABDDEGIINPRRY	bidding-prayer
ABDDEHIILMNRS	Hildebrandism
ABDDEHLNOORRS	no-holds-barred
ABDDEHMNOORUW	homeward-bound
ABDDEINORRRUY	boundary-rider
ABDDGILMNOORU	moulding-board
ABDEEEEILMRRS	irredeemables
ABDEEEFGINRST	breast-feeding
ABDEEEGILNOST	désobligeante
ABDEEEGKLLNOW	knowledgeable
ABDEEEHIRSTTW	white-breasted
ABDEEEHKNORRT	broken-hearted
ABDEEEHNRRRTU	thunder-bearer
ABDEEEIILMRTY	redeemability
ABDEEEIINNORT	Tenebrionidae
ABDEEEILLNRUV	undeliverable
ABDEEEILLNSSY	yieldableness
ABDEEEILNRSSS	desirableness
ABDEEELNNRSSU	endurableness
ABDEEELOSTTTT	estate-bottled
ABDEEFFILLNRS	snaffle-bridle
ABDEEFGHINRRT	finger-breadth
ABDEEFIIILRSV	diversifiable
ABDEEFIIILSTY	defeasibility
ABDEEGGNRSTTU	butter-and-eggs
ABDEEGIILNRST	disintegrable
ABDEEGILMNNOU	double-meaning
ABDEEGILNRSST	dressing-table
ABDEEGINNORSW	Swedenborgian
ABDEEGKLLNOWY	knowledgeably
ABDEEHILNSSTU	unestablished
ABDEEIILNNPSS	indispensable
ABDEEIILNNSSU	inaudibleness
ABDEEIILNOPRT	perditionable
ABDEEIILNPTXY	expendability
ABDEEIILNTTXY	extendability
ABDEEIILSTTTY	detestability
ABDEEIIMRTTXY	ambidexterity
ABDEEIKLNNRSS	drinkableness
ABDEEIKMMNRST	disembarkment
ABDEEILLNORRS	banderilleros
ABDEEILLOORTV	blood-relative
ABDEEILMNOPRS	imponderables
ABDEEILMRRSTU	master-builder
ABDEEIMORSTUX	ambidexterous
ABDEEINNSSSSU	unbiassedness
ABDEFIIINNORT	defibrination
ABDEFIILLORRT	defibrillator
ABDEFIILMORTY	deformability
ABDEFIILNNTUU	infundibulate
ABDEGGHNORSUY	horse-and-buggy
ABDEGGILLNOUZ	double-glazing
ABDEGHINOORSU	boarding-house
ABDEGIILNSSUU	undisguisable
ABDEGIILOOSTT	diabetologist
ABDEGILLLNORR	rollerblading
ABDEGILMOOSVY	viol-de-gamboys
ABDEGINNOORUV	overabounding
ABDEHILMNNSST	blandishments
ABDEHILNOORSU	dishonourable
ABDEIIIILQRSU	disequilibria
ABDEIILLNOSSV	indissolvable
ABDEIILLOPRTY	deplorability
ABDEIILNNPSSY	indispensably
ABDEIILNOPRTY	ponderability
ABDEIILPRRTUY	perdurability
ABDEIINNORSTU	insubordinate
ABDEIINNORTTW	rainbow-tinted
ABDEIINORSTUV	subordinative
ABDEILLNOOORT	blood-relation
ABDEILNORSTUY	subordinately
ABDELNNOPTUUW	unputdownable
ABDFGINNORSSU	brassfounding
ABDFIIILMORTY	formidability
ABDGIIILNOOST	disobligation
ABDGIIKNORRST	skirting-board
ABDGIILOORSTY	disobligatory
ABDGIINNORSTU	subordinating
ABDGILMNNORSU	Bildungsroman
ABDHIIINORSTY	hybridisation
ABDHIIINORTYZ	hybridization
ABDHILNOORSUY	dishonourably
ABDIIIILMSSTY	admissibility
ABDIIILNOSSUV	subdivisional
ABDIIILOPSSTY	disposability
ABDIIILPSTTUY	disputability
ABDIINNOORSTU	subordination
ABDILLMNNOPTU	platinum-blond
ABDLLMMNOOOSS	almond-blossom
ABEEEEFLNORSU	unforeseeable
ABEEEEGLMNRTU	beleaguerment
ABEEEEILMMPRS	semi-permeable

ABEEEEIRRRTVV	reverberative
ABEEEELNNRSSV	venerableness
ABEEEELNPRRST	representable
ABEEEEMNPSTTT	tempest-beaten
ABEEEFFILNNSS	ineffableness
ABEEEFHNNORTT	feather-bonnet
ABEEEFIILLMPX	exemplifiable
ABEEEGHHIMNTV	might-have-been
ABEEEGHIMORRV	megaherbivore
ABEEEGLMMNNRT	embranglement
ABEEEHILNPPRS	apprehensible
ABEEEHINRTTTW	weather-bitten
ABEEEIIKLMNRS	Berkeleianism
ABEEEIILLPRRV	irrepleviable
ABEEEIILRRRTV	irretrievable
ABEEEIKKRRRST	strikebreaker
ABEEEILMNRSSS	miserableness
ABEEEILNNRRSS	inerrableness
ABEEEILNPRRTT	interpretable
ABEEEILNPRRUV	unreprievable
ABEEEILNQSSTU	equitableness
ABEEEILNRSSTV	veritableness
ABEEEINORRRTV	reverberation
ABEEEJLNNOSSY	enjoyableness
ABEEELMMNORSS	memorableness
ABEEELMNPSSTT	temptableness
ABEEELNNNSSTU	untenableness
ABEEELNNPRSTU	unpresentable
ABEEELNNPRTUV	unpreventable
ABEEELNRSSTTU	utterableness
ABEEENOSSSTUU	beauteousness
ABEEEORRRRTVY	reverberatory
ABEEFGIILNRRR	irrefrangible
ABEEFGLNORTTU	unforgettable
ABEEFIILPRRTY	preferability
ABEEFILNRRRST	transferrible
ABEEGGHIOOPRR	biogeographer
ABEEGHHILNORT	breathing-hole
ABEEGHIIMNRTT	breathing-time
ABEEGHIKNORSU	house-breaking
ABEEGHINORRTV	over-breathing
ABEEGHLORSTTT	ghetto-blaster
ABEEGHMNORRRT	brother-german
ABEEGIINORRTV	verbigeration
ABEEGILLNORRR	roller-bearing
ABEEGILMOORST	metagrobolise
ABEEGILMOORTZ	metagrobolize
ABEEGILNNNOOT	non-negotiable
ABEEGILNORRVY	overbearingly
ABEEGILNOSSST	blastogenesis
ABEEHHMORRTTU	mouthbreather
ABEEHIILNSTUX	inexhaustible
ABEEHILLNSTUW	unwhistleable
ABEEHILMNSSTT	△establishment
ABEEHIMOPRSTT	Hemerobaptist
ABEEHLMNORSTU	unsmotherable
ABEEIILMPRTTY	temperability
ABEEIILNPRTTY	penetrability
ABEEIILNRRSST	irritableness
ABEEIILOPRRSV	proverbialise
ABEEIILOPRRVZ	proverbialize
ABEEIILQSTUYZ	squeezability
ABEEIILRRRTVY	irretrievably
ABEEIKLLSSTTT	table-skittles
ABEEIKNOPRRRS	prison-breaker
ABEEILLNPSSSU	plausibleness
ABEEILMMNOSSV	immovableness
ABEEILMMNSSTU	immutableness
ABEEILMNNNOTU	unmentionable
ABEEILMNPSSTU	imputableness
ABEEILNNRSSSS	brainlessness
ABEEILNNSTTUU	sublieutenant
ABEEILNPRSSSU	suprasensible
ABEEILNQSSTUU	subsequential
ABEEINNOSSSTT	obstinateness
ABEEKMNNORTUY	mountebankery
ABEELMOOORRST	morale-booster
ABEELMPPRRRUY	paper-mulberry
ABEELNNNORRTU	non-returnable
ABEELNNNSSTUU	untunableness
ABEENORRSSTUU	subterraneous
ABEFGIILNRRRY	irrefrangibly
ABEFGLNORTTUY	unforgettably
ABEFIIIILNSTY	infeasibility
ABEFIIIILRTVY	verifiability
ABEFIIILLRTTY	filterability
ABEFIIILNRTUV	unvitrifiable
ABEFIIJLNSTUU	unjustifiable
ABEFIILMORRTY	reformability
ABEFIMNOORRSU	neurofibromas
ABEFLLNOOPSTU	tablespoonful
ABEGGHILMNOSU	gambling-house
ABEGHIIIMMNRS	Birminghamise
ABEGHIIIMMNRZ	Birminghamize
ABEGHIILLNRTW	whirling-table
ABEGHILNORTTW	throwing-table
ABEGHILNOSTTW	washing-bottle
ABEGHINOOOPRT	gerontophobia
ABEGIIILNOTTY	negotiability
ABEGIIKNNOPRT	breaking-point
ABEGIILLOOPST	palebiologist
ABEGIILOOORST	aerobiologist
ABEGIKMNNNOTU	mountebanking
ABEGILMNNORTU	Grumbletonian
ABEGILNOPPRTT	blotting-paper
ABEGIMNOSSSUU	ambiguousness
ABEGLMNOOORSS	orange-blossom
ABEHHINNOORST	Heath-Robinson
ABEHHIOOPRRTY	erythrophobia
ABEHIIILPRSTY	perishability
ABEHIIINNORST	hibernisation
ABEHIIINNORTZ	hibernization
ABEHIILNSTUXY	inexhaustibly
ABEHIINOORRST	herborisation
ABEHIINOORRTZ	herborization
ABEHIIPRRRSST	barristership
ABEHIKMNOORST	thrombokinase
ABEHILNORRSTW	brothers-in-law
ABEHINNOOSTTT	ethnobotanist
ABEHINORSSSTT	basset-hornist
ABEHLLMOPSSUY	blasphemously
ABEIIIILMNNSZ	Leibnizianism
ABEIIIILNTTVY	inevitability
ABEIIIILLNRTUY	unreliability

ABEIIILMNORST	liberationism
ABEIIILMNRTTY	terminability
ABEIIILNOPRTY	inoperability
ABEIIILNOQRTU	equilibration
ABEIIILNORSTT	liberationist
ABEIIILNORTXY	inexorability
ABEIIILNPSTXY	expansibility
ABEIIIMMNNRSU	mini-submarine
ABEIILLNNRSST	brilliantness
ABEIILLNRTUVY	vulnerability
ABEIILLORSTVY	resolvability
ABEIILMNRSSST	transmissible
ABEIILMNRSTTT	transmittible
ABEIILMNRSTUY	mensurability
ABEIILMOPRRSV	proverbialism
ABEIILMPRTTUY	permutability
ABEIILNORSSTV	vibrationless
ABEIILNSSSTTU	subsistential
ABEIILOPRRSTV	proverbialist
ABEIILOPRTTXY	exportability
ABEIILRTTTUVY	attributively
ABEIIMNNOSSTT	abstentionism
ABEIIMNOSSSTU	ambitiousness
ABEIINNOORSTV	inobservation
ABEIINNORSSTT	baton-sinister
ABEIINNOSSTTT	abstentionist
ABEIINORRTTTU	reattribution
ABEIINRRSSTTU	tributariness
ABEIINSSSTTUV	substantivise
ABEIINSSTTUVZ	substantivize
ABEIKMMNNOSTU	mountebankism
ABEILLLMOTTUU	multilobulate
ABEILLNOOSSSY	obsessionally
ABEILNOORSSSU	laboriousness
ABEILNOPPRSTU	insupportable
ABEILNSSTTUVY	substantively
ABEIMNNOSSSUW	businesswoman
ABEINNORSTUVY	subventionary
ABEINOOPRRTTU	protuberation
ABEINORRSSUVY	subversionary
ABEKNOQRSTTUU	Quaker-buttons
ABELNOPPRSTUU	unsupportable
ABELNOPRRTTUY	protuberantly
ABEMOPRSSSTTU	sub-postmaster
ABFIIIILLLMNS	infallibilism
ABFIIIILLLNST	infallibilist
ABFIIIILLLNTY	infallibility
ABFIIILOPRTTY	profitability
ABFIIJLNSTUUY	unjustifiably
ABGGGIILLNORT	ballot-rigging
ABGGHIILNNRTW	night-warbling
ABGGIILOOORST	agrobiologist
ABGHIIMMNSSTW	swimming-baths
ABGHLMOOPRSYY	symbolography
ABGIIIILNNTTY	intangibility
ABGIIINORRSTU	subirrigation
ABGIIMNNORRST	brainstorming
ABGILLORRSUUY	burglariously
ABGILMNOSUUUY	unambiguously
ABHHIILMOOPRT	thrombophilia
ABHHIILOOPPSY	syphilophobia
ABHHIINOOOPRT	ornithophobia
ABHIIILNPSTUY	punishability
ABHIIILNRSTTY	labyrinthitis
ABHIIKMNNPRSS	brinksmanship
ABHIIMNOORRST	Romano-British
ABIIIIILMNTTY	inimitability
ABIIIILLNOTVY	inviolability
ABIIIILMPRTTY	impartibility
ABIIIILMPSSTY	impassibility
ABIIIILNOSTVY	insolvability
ABIIILMOPRTVY	improvability
ABIIILNOSSTTU	subtilisation
ABIIILNOSTTUZ	subtilization
ABIIILNSTTUUY	unsuitability
ABIIILRSTUVVY	survivability
ABIIINOORSSTT	sorbitisation
ABIIINOORSTTZ	sorbitization
ABIILMNNNTTUU	tintinnabulum
ABIILMNOOSSTY	symbolisation
ABIILMNOOSTYZ	symbolization
ABIILMNOSTUUY	unambitiously
ABIILMOOPRTTY	promotability
ABIILMORRTTUV	multivibrator
ABIINSSTTTUVY	substantivity
ABILLLMOPSSYY	polysyllabism
ABILLMMNOOSSY	monosyllabism
ABILNOOPPSTUU	subpopulation
ABILNOPPRSTUY	insupportably
ACCCCEIJMNRUY	circumjacency
ACCCCEIKKLLTY	clickety-clack
ACCCCILLLNOYY	concyclically
ACCCDEEEINNNS	incandescence
ACCCDEEILNOPY	encyclopaedic
ACCCDEHILNOSY	synecdochical
ACCCDGIILLOOO	codicological
ACCCEEELNNOSV	convalescence
ACCCEEILLNRTY	eccentrically
ACCCEEILMOSTU	cosmeceutical
ACCCEEKOOPPPR	peacock-copper
ACCCEELNNOSVY	convalescency
ACCCEGILMNNOO	meningococcal
ACCCEHIILMOPR	microcephalic
ACCCEHIINORTT	architectonic
ACCCEHILMMOOS	cosmochemical
ACCCEHINNOOSU	cinchonaceous
ACCCEIINOPSUU	pucciniaceous
ACCCEILNOOPRS	necroscopical
ACCCEIMMNOOOR	macroeconomic
ACCCEIMNRSSTU	circumstances
ACCCELOOOPRST	Protococcales
ACCCELOOPRSTT	streptococcal
ACCCENNOOOVVX	concavo-convex
ACCCGHIKLNOTW	clock-watching
ACCCGHILLNOOO	conchological
ACCCGIIKMNORR	microcracking
ACCCHILOOPSTY	staphylococci
ACCCIILMMOORS	microcosmical
ACCCIILMOOPRS	microscopical
ACCCILLOOOPPS	colposcopical
ACCDDEEEHHKLU	chuckle-headed
ACCDDEEHRRSTU	starch-reduced
ACCDDEHKOOOSW	woodcock's-head
ACCDEEEGHNORT	hedge-accentor

ACCDEEENNNRST	transcendence
ACCDEEENORRRT	catercornered
ACCDEEGGHIKNN	chicken-and-egg
ACCDEEGHLOPRU	charge-coupled
ACCDEEHHIKLPT	thick-pleached
ACCDEEHHORRST	scorched-earth
ACCDEEHIKNRRU	hurricane-deck
ACCDEEHLOOPRU	peach-coloured
ACCDEEIILNOST	occidentalise
ACCDEEIILNOTZ	occidentalize
ACCDEEILNNOPY	encyclopedian
ACCDEEINNOPRT	accident-prone
ACCDEEINORTUU	outrecuidance
ACCDEELMOORRU	cream-coloured
ACCDEEMNOPSST	compactedness
ACCDEENNNRSTY	transcendency
ACCDEENNORSTU	unconsecrated
ACCDEHHILLOOP	dolichocephal
ACCDEHHILOPRY	hydrocephalic
ACCDEHLNNORRY	corn-chandlery
ACCDEIIKLOOPS	kaleidoscopic
ACCDEIILMNOST	Occidentalism
ACCDEIILNNOOT	codeclination
ACCDEIILNORUU	Curculionidae
ACCDEIILNOSTT	Occidentalist
ACCDEIINOORTT	decortication
ACCDEIINORTTV	contradictive
ACCDEILMNOPTU	uncomplicated
ACCDEILNORSUY	cylindraceous
ACCDFIIILNOTU	dulcification
ACCDGHIKNORRY	hydrocracking
ACCDHHINOOPRY	hypochondriac
ACCDHIIINORST	diachronistic
ACCDHILLOOPYY	hypocycloidal
ACCDHIMNOPSYY	psychodynamic
ACCDIIILNNOOP	clinopinacoid
ACCDIIILNSSTY	syndicalistic
ACCDIIINORSTY	idiosyncratic
ACCDIILLLMOSU	molluscicidal
ACCDIILLLNRYY	cylindrically
ACCDIILLOSSYY	cyclodialysis
ACCDIIMMNNOOU	incommunicado
ACCDIINNOORTT	contradiction
ACCDINOORRTTY	contradictory
ACCDMNOORRTTU	tram-conductor
ACCEEEEHLLNOP	encephalocele
ACCEEEELMORRT	accelerometer
ACCEEEGILMNOU	leucaemogenic
ACCEEEHILLNPT	telencephalic
ACCEEEHILMNPS	mesencephalic
ACCEEEILLORST	ecclesiolater
ACCEEEILMMORS	commercialese
ACCEEEILNRSTX	excrescential
ACCEEFFIILRSS	self-sacrifice
ACCEEFKLOOPRW	peacock-flower
ACCEEGHIKLRRT	trickle-charge
ACCEEGHILLMOY	geochemically
ACCEEGHMNORTV	Congreve-match
ACCEEGHNNORTU	counterchange
ACCEEGHNORRTU	countercharge
ACCEEGILLOOOP	paleoecologic
ACCEEHHIOPSYZ	Schizophyceae

ACCEEHHLOOPRY	Chlorophyceae
ACCEEHHLOORST	schoolteacher
ACCEEHIILMMOS	semiochemical
ACCEEHIINNORT	coinheritance
ACCEEHILLNOTY	acetylcholine
ACCEEHILLOPPT	leptocephalic
ACCEEHILMOPRT	petrochemical
ACCEEHILNNSST	technicalness
ACCEEHIMMNSTU	catechumenism
ACCEEHIMNRRST	screech-martin
ACCEEHKNOOPRT	peacock-throne
ACCEEHLLNNOPS	splanchnocele
ACCEEHORRSTTY	oyster-catcher
ACCEEIILMMNSU	ecumenicalism
ACCEEIILMMORS	commercialise
ACCEEIILMMORZ	commercialize
ACCEEIIOPRRTV	reciprocative
ACCEEILLORSTY	ecclesiolatry
ACCEEILLORTTV	volta-electric
ACCEEILMNOORT	econometrical
ACCEEILNNRSST	centricalness
ACCEEILNOPSTU	conceptualise
ACCEEILNOPTUZ	conceptualize
ACCEEILNOSTUV	vice-consulate
ACCEEILNQSTUY	acquiescently
ACCEEILORSTTT	electrostatic
ACCEEIMMNOTUX	excommunicate
ACCEEIMORSSTT	microcassette
ACCEEINNORTTV	concentrative
ACCEEINOPRTTV	contraceptive
ACCEEINORTTUV	counteractive
ACCEEJKORRSST	jack-crosstree
ACCEELLMMOORU	macromolecule
ACCEELOOPRTUV	octave-coupler
ACCEEMNORRSTT	concertmaster
ACCEEMNORSTTU	accoustrement
	accouterments
	accoutrements
ACCEENNOORTTY	octocentenary
ACCEENORRSTTU	counter-caster
ACCEEOORRSSTU	stercoraceous
ACCEFFIIINOSU	inefficacious
ACCEFFIIINPRS	infraspecific
ACCEFFIILOSUY	efficaciously
ACCEFHILMOORR	cochleariform
ACCEFIIINOPST	specification
ACCEFIIINORTT	certification
	rectification
ACCEFIILMOORS	Scoleciformia
ACCEFIIORRTTY	certificatory
ACCEFINNOORTY	confectionary
ACCEGHHIOOPRR	choreographic
ACCEGHIILOPRX	lexicographic
ACCEGHILLNOOT	technological
ACCEGHILMOPYY	hypoglycaemic
ACCEGHILNNORY	encroachingly
ACCEGHILNOPTT	plectognathic
ACCEGHIOPRRVY	cervicography
ACCEGIILNQSUY	acquiescingly
ACCEGIINNNORT	concertinaing
ACCEGIINOPRRT	reciprocating
ACCEGILLNOOSY	synecological

ACCEGILMNOORT	conglomeratic
ACCEGIMNORSST	cross-magnetic
ACCEGINOORRTT	gerontocratic
ACCEHHIIOPSTT	Theopaschitic
ACCEHHILMOOPT	photochemical
ACCEHHILMOPTY	phytochemical
ACCEHHILOSSTZ	eschscholtzia
ACCEHHIMORSTT	chrestomathic
ACCEHHIMRRSSW	schwärmerisch
ACCEHIILLNSST	callisthenics
ACCEHIILPRRTY	hypercritical
ACCEHIIMRSSTT	chrematistics
ACCEHILLNOPRT	phallocentric
ACCEHILLNOPTY	polytechnical
ACCEHILMNOTYZ	zymotechnical
ACCEHILMOOSTT	cosmothetical
ACCEHILNOPRTY	pyrotechnical
ACCEHILOOPPRS	chorepiscopal
ACCEHIOOPSSTT	tachistoscope
ACCEHLLNOOPRR	pro-chancellor
ACCEIIIILNPPRV	vice-principal
ACCEIIIMNNORS	Ciceronianism
ACCEIIKLNOSTW	anticlockwise
ACCEIIKNNPRST	panic-stricken
ACCEIILMMMORS	commercialism
ACCEIILMMORRT	micrometrical
ACCEIILMMORST	commercialist
ACCEIILMMORTY	commerciality
ACCEIILMNOSSS	neoclassicism
ACCEIILMORSTV	viscometrical
ACCEIILNOSSST	neoclassicist
ACCEIILNRRSTT	transit-circle
ACCEIILOPRRTY	reciprocality
ACCEIILPRRSTU	supercritical
ACCEIIMMNOTUV	communicative
ACCEIINNNRSST	scintiscanner
ACCEIINOOPRRT	reciprocation
ACCEIINOORTTX	excortication
ACCEIIOPPRSSU	perspicacious
ACCEIKKKKNNRY	knick-knackery
ACCEILMMNNOOR	non-commercial
ACCEILMNNNOOP	non-compliance
ACCEILMNOPPSS	pencil-compass
ACCEILMNOPSTU	conceptualism
ACCEILNOPSTTU	conceptualist
ACCEILOOPRSTT	proteoclastic
ACCEINNNOORTT	concentration
ACCEINNOOPRTT	contraception
ACCEINNOORRTY	concretionary
ACCEINNOORSSY	concessionary
ACCEINNOORTTU	counteraction
ACCEINOOPPRTU	preoccupation
ACCEINOPPRSSU	percussion-cap
ACCEJLLNORTUY	conjecturally
ACCELLOORSSUU	sclerocaulous
ACCFGHHIKNRTU	chuck-farthing
ACCFHIIILNOTY	chylification
ACCFHIIIMNOTY	chymification
ACCFIIIINNOTZ	zincification
ACCFIIINNOORT	cornification
ACCFIIINOORST	scorification
ACCFIIINOOSTT	Scotification
ACCFIILLLNOOT	floccillation
ACCGHHHHIMNRU	High-Churchman
ACCGHHIKKMMUU	high-muck-a-muck
ACCGHHINORSST	cross-hatching
ACCGHHIOPPRSY	psychographic
ACCGHIILLOORT	trichological
ACCGHILLNOOOR	chronological
ACCGHILLOOPSY	psychological
ACCGHILOOPRSY	hygroscopical
ACCGHIMNNOORU	mourning-coach
ACCGHIMNORSST	cross-matching
ACCGHIOPPRRTY	cryptographic
ACCGIIIMNORRT	microgranitic
ACCGIILLMOOSU	musicological
ACCGIILLOOOTX	toxicological
ACCGIILMORRSU	microsurgical
ACCGIILNOORST	carcinologist
ACCGILLOOPRTY	cryptological
ACCGILNOOPRSY	laryngoscopic
ACCHHHIMNPRSU	churchmanship
ACCHHILOORSTY	charity-school
ACCHHIMMOOORT	homochromatic
ACCHHINOPRSTY	chrysophantic
ACCHIILMOSSST	scholasticism
ACCHIIMNOOPRT	actinomorphic
ACCHIINOPSTTY	antipsychotic
ACCHIINPPSSTY	panpsychistic
ACCHILMOOPRTY	polychromatic
ACCHIMMNOOORT	monochromatic
ACCHIMNOOPPST	phonocamptics
ACCHIMOOPSSTY	psychosomatic
ACCHIOOPRSSUZ	schizocarpous
ACCIIIILLNNSST	scintilliscan
ACCIIILNOORRT	onirocritical
ACCIIIMMNOOST	iconomaticism
ACCIILLNNQUUY	quincuncially
ACCIILLNRRTUU	criniculturaI
ACCIILLPRSTUU	piscicultural
ACCIILMNOOPRV	comprovincial
ACCIILMNOOPST	complications
ACCIILNORTTTY	contractility
ACCIIMMNNOOTU	communication
ACCIIMNOOSSTY	actinomycosis
ACCIINOOPRSST	cranioscopist
ACCIJLNNNOOTU	conjunctional
ACCILMNNOOTTY	concomitantly
ACCIMMNOORTUY	communicatory
ACCIMNOOPRSTU	pococurantism
ACCINNOOPRSTU	conspurcation
ACCINOOPRSTTU	pococurantist
ACCINPRSTTUUU	acupuncturist
ACCLLORRSSTUU	cross-cultural
ACDDEEEFHNRSU	schadenfreude
ACDDEEEHKKLNU	knuckle-headed
ACDDEEEINPRTU	undepreciated
ACDDEEFFILSTY	disaffectedly
ACDDEEGIKNNOR	dead-reckoning
ACDDEEHLLORTY	cold-heartedly
ACDDEEIIKLMNN	nickel-and-dime
ACDDEEIMNOOTY	adenoidectomy
ACDDEEIMOPRTU	computer-aided
ACDDEGIILNNPP	candle-dipping

ACDDEGILLNOOR dendrological
ACDDEGILNOORU dead-colouring
ACDDEGINORSUU undiscouraged
ACDDEHILMOSUY dichlamydeous
ACDDEHIMNOOPS dodecaphonism
ACDDEHINOOPST dodecaphonist
ACDDEHINOORSU deoch-an-doruis
ACDDEIIMNOORS androdioecism
ACDDEIINOSSTU undissociated
ACDDEINNOORTU uncoordinated
unco-ordinated
ACDDEJLOORSUU Judas-coloured
ACDDHIMNORSYY hydrodynamics
ACDEEEEILNRRV redeliverance
ACDEEEFHIKRST sick-feathered
ACDEEEFHILRSV cheval-de-frise
ACDEEEFINORTV confederative
ACDEEEGIKLNNP packing-needle
ACDEEEGKNPRSS deck-passenger
ACDEEEGNNRSUV unscavengered
ACDEEEHINRRUV underachiever
ACDEEEIIRSTTV carte-de-visite
ACDEEEIMNRSTV misadvertence
ACDEEEIOSSTTV videocassette
ACDEEEIPQRRSU square-pierced
ACDEEEKQRRRTU quarterdecker
ACDEEELMOPPRR emerald-copper
ACDEEELNOPRST preadolescent
ACDEEELNPRRSU supercalender
ACDEEENNOPPRR preponderance
ACDEEENNRSSTU uncreatedness
ACDEEFFLNNRSU candle-snuffer
ACDEEFGHILRSS self-discharge
ACDEEFHHIKNRS handkerchiefs
ACDEEFHNORRTW thenceforward
ACDEEFIIILNRT delirifacient
ACDEEFIIINORT re-edification
ACDEEFILNNOST self-contained
ACDEEFINNOORT confederation
ACDEEFLLMOORU flame-coloured
ACDEEFNORRRTW centre-forward
ACDEEGHIKNNRT kitchen-garden
ACDEEGHILLNRT candle-lighter
ACDEEGHNRRSTU draught-screen
ACDEEGIIILRRTT lattice-girder
ACDEEGILLLNPW dwelling-place
ACDEEGILMNRSU muscle-reading
ACDEEGILNPRTY deprecatingly
ACDEEGINOPRRT tape-recording
ACDEEGORRRSST cross-gartered
ACDEEHIILLNTX hexactinellid
ACDEEHIILLOTT △diotheletical
ACDEEHILLOTTY △dyotheletical
ACDEEHILORRTT tetrachloride
ACDEEHLNNOORR hole-and-corner
ACDEEHLNNOORS scalenohedron
ACDEEHMOPSSUY Scyphomedusae
ACDEEIIILMNRS decriminalise
ACDEEIIILMNRZ decriminalize
ACDEEIIJPRTUV prejudicative
ACDEEIILLRTTV verticillated
ACDEEIILNNSST identicalness
ACDEEIILNPSSU unspecialised
ACDEEIILNPSUZ unspecialized
ACDEEIILPRTUV reduplicative
ACDEEIILPRTVY predicatively
ACDEEIILRTTUV diverticulate
ACDEEIIMNNRTY indeterminacy
ACDEEIIMNOPRT premedication
ACDEEIINNORST inconsiderate
ACDEEIINNORTV revendication
ACDEEIINNOSST Ascensiontide
ACDEEIINOPRTT decrepitation
ACDEEIINORSTV considerative
ACDEEIINRSSTT Testicardines
ACDEEIKNQRSUW quick-answered
ACDEEILLNNSTY clandestinely
ACDEEILNOORST reconsolidate
ACDEEILNORSTY considerately
ACDEEILNPPRRU △perpendicular
ACDEEILOPRRTY deprecatorily
ACDEEIMNORSTU documentarise
ACDEEIMNORTUZ documentarize
ACDEEIMNOSTTU undomesticate
ACDEEINNORSSS secondariness
ACDEEINPRSUVY dispurveyance
ACDEEIOPPRSTU propaedeutics
ACDEELLOORSTU slate-coloured
ACDEEMNNOPSTU uncompensated
ACDEENNOPPRRY preponderancy
ACDEENORRSTTU unstercorated
ACDEFGILLRSUY disgracefully
ACDEFIIILNOST fictionalised
ACDEFIIILNOTZ fictionalized
ACDEFIIIMNTUV mundificative
ACDEFIILNNOSS non-classified
ACDEGHHHIMOST high-stomached
ACDEGHHOOPRTU thorough-paced
ACDEGHIIMNNRS merchandising
ACDEGHIIMNNRZ merchandizing
ACDEGHIMNORTY hydromagnetic
ACDEGIILLMRUY demiurgically
ACDEGIILNNPRW drawing-pencil
ACDEGILLMNOOO demonological
ACDEGILLNOOOT deontological
ACDEHHLOPRSUY hydrocephalus
ACDEHIILLOTTY △dyothelitical
ACDEHIILMOSTT Methodistical
ACDEHIILNOPRR perichondrial
ACDEHIIMRSSTT Christmas-tide
ACDEHIIOPSSTT sophisticated
ACDEHIKMOOOSU cook-housemaid
ACDEHILMORRTY hydrometrical
ACDEHILNOORST school-trained
ACDEHIMMNOPRS commandership
ACDEHIMMNORTY thermodynamic
ACDEHLLMNOOST old-clothesman
ACDEHLMOOPRSY chlamydospore
ACDEHOOOPRRTT protochordate
ACDEIIILOPRST periodicalist
ACDEIIINNORTV revindication
ACDEIIJLLPRUY prejudicially
ACDEIIJNOPRTU prejudication
ACDEIIKMNPRTY prick-me-dainty

ACDEIILNNOTTU	denticulation
ACDEIILNNSTTY	clandestinity
ACDEIILNOOSTV	consolidative
ACDEIILNOPRTU	reduplication
ACDEIILRSTTVY	distractively
ACDEIIMNNOORT	enantiodromic
ACDEIIMNOOSTT	domestication
ACDEIINNOORST	consideration
ACDEIINOQRSTU	quadrisection
ACDEIINORRSTY	discretionary
ACDEIINRSTTUV	adventuristic
ACDEIIOPSSTTU	disceptatious
ACDEILLPPSTYY	dyspeptically
ACDEILMNORTUY	documentarily
ACDEILMNOSTTU	documentalist
ACDEILNNORSTY	constrainedly
ACDEILNORSTTU	destructional
ACDEILOOPRRTU	parti-coloured
ACDEILOPRSSTY	perissodactyl
ACDEIMNNNOOPU	uncompanioned
ACDEIMNNOOTTU	documentation
ACDEIMNORSTTU	documentarist
ACDEINNNORSTU	unconstrained
ACDEIOOPRRRTT	tricorporated
ACDEIOPPRRSTU	Dipterocarpus
ACDELNOOOSTUY	acotyledonous
ACDELOOPRRTUY	party-coloured
ACDELOORRSTUW	straw-coloured
ACDEMMNNOSTUU	unconsummated
ACDFGIIIINNOT	dignification
ACDFIIIMNNOTU	mundification
ACDFILNNOSTUY	dysfunctional
ACDGHIIKLNRUY	hydraulicking
ACDGHINOOOPRT	gonadotrophic
ACDGIILNRSTTY	distractingly
ACDGIINNRSTTU	undistracting
ACDGIINOOSSTY	cytodiagnosis
ACDGILLNOOOOT	odontological
ACDGILLOORTTY	troglodytical
ACDGILMOSTYYZ	zygodactylism
ACDGINNNNOOPR	pro-and-conning
ACDGLOOSTUYYZ	zygodactylous
ACDHIILMNOORT	mitochondrial
ACDHIINOPSSTU	custodianship
ACDHIJOOPRSTU	coadjutorship
ACDHILOORSSUU	Dolichosaurus
ACDHIMNNOOOOP	companionhood
ACDHINOOPQRSU	quadrophonics
ACDIIIILMNOOT	domiciliation
ACDIIIKLNNOOP	clinopinakoid
ACDIIILLORSTY	dioristically
ACDIIIILNNOPTU	induplication
ACDIIILNORTVY	vindicatorily
ACDIIIMNORRST	discriminator
	doctrinairism
ACDIILLMOOSTY	sodomitically
ACDIILLNNOOTY	conditionally
ACDIILNNNOOTU	unconditional
ACDIILNNOOOST	consolidation
ACDIILNOOORST	discoloration
ACDIILNRSTTUY	translucidity
ACDIILPQRTUUY	quadruplicity
ACDIINNOORRTT	indoctrinator
ACDIINOORRRRT	corridor-train
ACDILLMOPSTYY	polydactylism
ACDINOOQRSSTU	conquistadors
ACDLLOOPSTUYY	polydactylous
ACDLMNOOOSTUY	condylomatous
	monodactylous
ACEEEEFKMNRRR	reference-mark
ACEEEEHLPRSST	steeplechaser
ACEEEELNPSSSS	peacelessness
ACEEEEPPRRSTW	carpet-sweeper
ACEEEFFGINOPR	peace-offering
ACEEEFFLNSSTU	effectualness
ACEEEFGIJKNRT	reefing-jacket
ACEEEFIKLOTTV	ticket-of-leave
ACEEEFILNORRT	coreferential
ACEEEFINOPRTT	perfectionate
ACEEEFLOPRRTT	polecat-ferret
ACEEEFLRSSSUV	surface-vessel
ACEEEFMORRRTT	refractometer
ACEEEGILLNRTY	energetically
ACEEEGLMNORTT	electromagnet
ACEEEGLMNORTY	laryngectomee
ACEEEGLNRSSSS	gracelessness
ACEEEGMNNORTU	encouragement
ACEEEHHOORTTT	toothache-tree
ACEEEHIKLLMNO	chameleon-like
ACEEEHILMNRTU	hermeneutical
ACEEEHINOSSST	coenaesthesis
ACEEEHLLNNOPT	telencephalon
ACEEEHLMNNOPS	mesencephalon
ACEEEHRRSSTTU	treasure-chest
ACEEEILLMPRST	capellmeister
ACEEEILMNNRTT	interlacement
ACEEEILNNNRTT	tercentennial
ACEEEILRRRRTT	letter-carrier
ACEEEINNRSSSS	necessariness
ACEEEINOSSTVV	evocativeness
ACEEEIOPRTTVX	expectorative
ACEEEIOQSSTUU	equisetaceous
ACEEELLNORTTV	electrovalent
ACEEELLOPRRTT	electroplater
ACEEELNSSSSSU	causelessness
ACEEENNORRRTT	contraterrene
ACEEFFHINNPRS	affenpinscher
ACEEFFILLNTUY	ineffectually
ACEEFGHLNNSSU	changefulness
ACEEFGHLOPRRT	reflectograph
ACEEFGIIMNRRT	ferrimagnetic
ACEEFGIINNOPR	pigeon-fancier
ACEEFGIMNNRST	fencing-master
ACEEFGIMNORRT	ferromagnetic
ACEEFGINNORRY	ferricyanogen
ACEEFGJLNOSTU	self-conjugate
ACEEFGNNOORRY	ferrocyanogen
ACEEFHHIRSTTT	feather-stitch
ACEEFHIIKMMRS	mischief-maker
ACEEFHIINNNTT	tenant-in-chief
ACEEFHIMNNRST	franchisement
ACEEFHLNSSSTU	scathefulness
ACEEFHMNOSTUV	vouchsafement
ACEEFILLNOPRW	pelican-flower

ACEEFILNNRSSU	self-insurance
ACEEFINORRSTU	nectariferous
ACEEFINOSSSTU	facetiousness
ACEEFMNORSTUU	frumentaceous
ACEEGGILNOTTT	telecottaging
ACEEGHHIOPRRR	cheirographer
ACEEGHHIRTTWW	weight-watcher
ACEEGHHMNRRRU	hunger-marcher
ACEEGHHOOPRRR	choreographer
ACEEGHIILLNOS	collieshangie
ACEEGHIIMNNSW	sewing-machine
ACEEGHILLOPSU	colleagueship
ACEEGHILMNOOT	homogenetical
ACEEGHILMPRYY	hyperglycemia
ACEEGHILNOPRS	selenographic
ACEEGHILOPRRX	lexicographer
ACEEGHILOPSTU	Galeopithecus
ACEEGHIMNNNRU	machine-gunner
ACEEGHINNPRTT	tent-preaching
ACEEGHINNRSSS	searchingness
ACEEGHIOPRRST	stereographic
ACEEGHLOPRRTY	electrography
ACEEGHMNRRSTU	surchargement
ACEEGIIKNOPSV	speaking-voice
ACEEGIILSTTUV	gesticulative
ACEEGIIMNNOST	miscegenation
ACEEGIIMNOPTZ	piezomagnetic
ACEEGIINNNRST	intransigence
ACEEGIINOPRRR	carrier-pigeon
ACEEGIKNNRRVW	nerve-wracking
ACEEGILLLNOOS	selenological
ACEEGILLLOOPS	speleological
ACEEGILLMORTY	geometrically
ACEEGILLNNOOT	non-collegiate
ACEEGILMMNORR	miracle-monger
ACEEGILMNNOQU	magniloquence
ACEEGILNNPRRS	spring-cleaner
ACEEGIMNOPRST	spermatogenic
ACEEGINOPPPRS	popping-crease
ACEEGINORRSTT	gastroenteric
ACEEGMRRSTTUU	megastructure
ACEEHHIILLPRS	helispherical
ACEEHHIILMPRS	hemispherical
ACEEHHILLORTT	heterothallic
ACEEHHILNPSSS	seneschalship
ACEEHHNRSTTTU	earth-chestnut
ACEEHIILLLNST	Hellenistical
ACEEHIILLMORT	heliometrical
ACEEHIILNOPRT	epitrachelion
ACEEHIIMOOPTT	hematopoietic
ACEEHIINNRSTV	even-Christian
ACEEHIKLMOTUY	leukocythemia
ACEEHIKNPSTUY	Kenyapithecus
ACEEHIKNRRSTT	heart-stricken
ACEEHIKNRSSST	heart-sickness
ACEEHILLNPRTY	phrenetically
ACEEHILLORTTY	theoretically
ACEEHILMMOPSS	mesocephalism
ACEEHILMPRRTY	hypermetrical
ACEEHILNPRSSS	sphericalness
ACEEHILOPRRST	terpsichoreal
ACEEHILOPRSTT	heteroplastic
ACEEHINOPRRST	terpsichorean
ACEEHINORSSTT	thoracentesis
ACEEHIPRRSSTY	secretaryship
ACEEHIPRSSTTY	cryptesthesia
ACEEHLLMOOORT	alcoholometer
ACEEHLLOPPSTU	leptocephalus
ACEEHLMNOOPTY	encephalotomy
ACEEHLMNORRTU	thermonuclear
ACEEHLMNSSSST	matchlessness
ACEEHLMOOPSSU	mesocephalous
ACEEHLORRSTUY	treacherously
ACEEHMNOPPRRT	rapprochement
ACEEHNPRRSSTU	purse-snatcher
ACEEHOOPRRSTU	heterocarpous
ACEEIIILLNNPS	penicillinase
ACEEIIIMNRRTV	recriminative
ACEEIIINPSSTT	antisepticise
ACEEIIINPSTTZ	antisepticize
ACEEIIIPPRTTV	precipitative
ACEEIIKLRSSTT	Rickettsiales
ACEEIILLMNRTT	intermetallic
ACEEIILLNRRTY	rectilinearly
ACEEIILMMNORS	ceremonialism
ACEEIILMNOPRS	semiporcelain
ACEEIILNORSTT	electrisation
ACEEIILNORTTZ	electrization
ACEEIILNPRTUV	plantie-cruive
ACEEIILPPRTTY	precipitately
ACEEIILPQSSTU	sesquiplicate
ACEEIILPRTTTY	rectipetality
ACEEIIMMORSTV	commiserative
ACEEIIMNNOSST	amniocentesis
ACEEIIMNNPRSS	Spencerianism
ACEEIIMNORRST	mercerisation
ACEEIIMNORRTZ	mercerization
ACEEIINNOPTTX	inexpectation
ACEEIINNOSSTT	necessitation
ACEEIINNRSSTT	intricateness
ACEEIIRSSTTUV	resuscitative
ACEEIJLNRRTTU	interjectural
ACEEILLLNOTUV	involucellate
ACEEILLLNPSTY	splenetically
ACEEILLLNRRTU	intercellular
ACEEILLLNSTTU	intellectuals
ACEEILLMNOSSU	miscellaneous
ACEEILLMNTTUU	multinucleate
ACEEILLNNNSSU	uncleanliness
ACEEILLNOPTXY	exceptionally
ACEEILLORRTVY	correlatively
ACEEILLPSTUVY	speculatively
ACEEILLRRSSTY	recrystallise
ACEEILLRRSTYZ	recrystallize
ACEEILMNNSSSU	masculineness
ACEEILMNOPTTV	contemplative
ACEEILNNOPRTV	convertiplane
ACEEILNNOPTUX	unexceptional
ACEEILNNOQSTU	consequential
ACEEILNNRSSUY	unnecessarily
ACEEILNOOPRSU	porcelaineous
ACEEILNOQSSUV	equivocalness
ACEEILNORSTTU	interosculate
ACEEILNOSTTUX	contextualise

ACEEILNOTTUXZ	contextualize
ACEEILNPSTUUV	unspeculative
ACEEILOPRSTTY	stereotypical
ACEEILORRTTVY	retroactively
ACEEILPPPRRST	carpet-slipper
ACEEIMMMOORTV	commemorative
ACEEINNNORSST	non-resistance
ACEEINNNOSTTY	consentaneity
ACEEINNNQRTUY	quincentenary
ACEEINNNRSSTU	uncertainness
ACEEINNNSSSST	incessantness
ACEEINNOORSVZ	conversazione
ACEEINNORRSUV	overinsurance
ACEEINNOSSSTU	tenaciousness
ACEEINOOPRSTU	proteinaceous
ACEEINOOPRTTX	expectoration
ACEEINOOPRTUV	uncooperative
	unco-operative
ACEEINOORRSTV	conservatoire
ACEEKLNRSSSST	tracklessness
ACEELLMOPRSUU	supramolecule
ACEELLNOOPRSU	porcellaneous
ACEELLOORRRST	rollercoaster
ACEELLOPRSSTU	supercollate
ACEELMMNOPRTY	complementary
ACEELNNRRRSTU	scarlet-runner
ACEELNOOPRRTU	counter-parole
ACEEMMNNOPSST	encompassment
ACEENNNOORTVY	novocentenary
ACEENNNOOSSTU	consentaneous
ACEENOOPRRSST	corporateness
ACEFFGIILNNNS	self-financing
ACEFFHLSSTTUZ	schutzstaffel
ACEFGGIINRSTU	figure-casting
ACEFGHIIKLNST	fishing-tackle
ACEFGIIIINSTV	significative
ACEFGIIKLNNPS	scalping-knife
ACEFGIILLNTTT	cattle-lifting
ACEFGIILMNNTY	magnificently
ACEFGILLNRTUY	centrifugally
ACEFGINOSSSUU	fugaciousness
ACEFHHIIINPST	chieftainship
ACEFHLLOPRRUY	reproachfully
ACEFHLNOPRRUU	unreproachful
ACEFIIIJSTTUV	justificative
ACEFIIILLMNOT	mellification
ACEFIIILNOSTT	felicitations
ACEFIIIMMNNTU	immunifacient
ACEFIIIMNORTT	metrification
ACEFIIINNORTU	reunification
ACEFIIINOPRTT	petrification
ACEFIIINORSTV	versification
ACEFIIINOSTTT	testification
ACEFIILLNOORT	refocillation
ACEFIILLPRSUY	superficially
ACEFIILNORSTY	forensicality
ACEFIINNNOORT	fonctionnaire
ACEFIIORSTTTY	testificatory
ACEFILLLMOPRS	scalpelliform
ACEFILLLOOORR	Corolliflorae
ACEFILLOORRSU	coralliferous
ACEFILNOORRRW	carrion-flower
ACEFINNOORSSY	confessionary
ACEFINNORRTTY	confraternity
ACEFINORSSSTU	fractiousness
ACEFINORSSSUU	furaciousness
ACEGGGHIINNNR	change-ringing
ACEGGHIINSTTW	casting-weight
ACEGGHILLLNNY	challengingly
ACEGGHIOOOPRZ	zoogeographic
ACEGGILLOOPTY	Egyptological
ACEGGILNNORUY	encouragingly
ACEGGILNOOSTY	gynaecologist
ACEGHHIMOPRRT	thermographic
ACEGHHNOOPRRR	chronographer
ACEGHHOOPRRSY	orchesography
ACEGHIILMOOTY	oligocythemia
ACEGHIILNNSTU	launching-site
ACEGHIILOPSTT	phlogisticate
ACEGHIIMMNNOW	mowing-machine
ACEGHIIMNPPRW	whipping-cream
ACEGHIIMOPRSS	seismographic
ACEGHIINOPTTY	pathogenicity
ACEGHILLLOOTY	ethologically
	theologically
ACEGHILLNOOPR	nephrological
	phrenological
ACEGHILLNOOSV	school-leaving
ACEGHILLNOOTU	untheological
ACEGHILLOOORT	heortological
ACEGHILLOOPPS	psephological
ACEGHILMORRTY	hygrometrical
ACEGHILNORSSU	soul-searching
ACEGHILOOSSTT	eschatologist
ACEGHILORRRTY	chlorargyrite
ACEGHILORRSTT	cloister-garth
ACEGHIMOOPRRT	ergatomorphic
ACEGHINNNOOPT	non-pathogenic
ACEGHINNOOPRT	anthropogenic
ACEGHINNOPRRU	unreproaching
ACEGHNOOPPRSY	pharyngoscope
ACEGHOPPRRRTY	cryptographer
ACEGHOPPRRSTY	spectrography
ACEGIIILNOOPT	geopolitician
ACEGIIINORTTY	iatrogenicity
ACEGIIKKLNTTW	walking-ticket
ACEGIIKKNPRTT	parking-ticket
ACEGIIKLLNNPT	nickel-plating
ACEGIILLLNOSS	illogicalness
ACEGIILLMOOSS	seismological
ACEGIILLNOOST	neologistical
ACEGIILLNRTUV	revictualling
ACEGIILLOSTTY	egotistically
ACEGIILMNOORT	goniometrical
ACEGIILNOSTTU	gesticulation
ACEGIINNNRSTY	intransigency
ACEGIKKLLNPSU	skulking-place
ACEGILLLOORSY	serologically
ACEGILLMNOOOT	entomological
ACEGILLMNOORU	numerological
ACEGILLMNOORY	ergonomically
ACEGILLNNOOTY	ontogenically
ACEGILLNOORSU	coralligenous
ACEGILLNOPTYY	genotypically

ACEGILLOOPRTY	geotropically
ACEGILMNOPSTY	salpingectomy
ACEGILMOOSSTU	cleistogamous
ACEGILNNOORSS	congressional
ACEGILNNORSTU	counter-signal
ACEGILNOPPPST	stopping-place
ACEGILNORRSUU	neurosurgical
ACEGILNPRSTTY	trysting-place
ACEGILORSTTUY	gesticulatory
ACEGIMNOOPSTT	magneto-optics
ACEGIMNOPRSTU	pneumogastric
ACEGIMNORSSTU	gastrocnemius
ACEGINOOPRSTT	prognosticate
ACEGLNOOOPSUY	polygonaceous
ACEGLOPPRSSST	prospect-glass
ACEGMNNOORSSW	Congresswoman
ACEHHIILMNNTT	anthelminthic
ACEHHIINOPRSZ	schizophrenia
ACEHHILPPRSYY	hyperphysical
ACEHHINOOPTTY	hypothecation
ACEHHIOPPRTTY	phreatophytic
ACEHHMMNRSTUY	chrysanthemum
ACEHHMOOOPRRT	chromatophore
ACEHHOPPRSTYY	psychotherapy
ACEHIIIKLNRST	Christianlike
ACEHIIILRSTTT	tritheistical
ACEHIIINNORST	corinthianise
ACEHIIINNORTZ	corinthianize
ACEHIIINNPRTT	antinephritic
ACEHIIINRRSST	christianiser
ACEHIIINRRSTZ	christianizer
ACEHIILLLMOTY	homiletically
ACEHIILLOOPRT	heliotropical
ACEHIILLRSTUY	heuristically
ACEHIILMNOPST	machine-pistol
ACEHIILMNSSSW	whimsicalness
ACEHIILOOPPRT	apheliotropic
ACEHIILOORSTT	orthosilicate
ACEHIILOPRRST	prehistorical
ACEHIIMMRSSTT	Christmas-time
ACEHIINNRSSST	Christianness
ACEHIINOOPRSY	Syrophoenicia
ACEHIIPRTTVYY	hyperactivity
ACEHIKLLNORSU	unscholarlike
ACEHILLLMOOPR	allelomorphic
ACEHILLLOPPST	phelloplastic
ACEHILLLOPRTY	plethorically
ACEHILLMNOOSU	melancholious
ACEHILLNORSSS	scholarliness
ACEHILLNSTTYY	synthetically
ACEHILLOPPRTY	prophetically
ACEHILMNOORRS	rhinoscleroma
ACEHILMOPRSTT	thermoplastic
ACEHILNNOOPTT	technopolitan
ACEHILNOOPPRS	cephalosporin
ACEHILNOPPRTU	unprophetical
ACEHILOPPRSTY	petrophysical
ACEHILORRSSTT	orchestralist
ACEHILPPRSSUY	superphysical
ACEHIMNPSTTUY	unsympathetic
ACEHIMOPRSTUY	musicotherapy
ACEHINOORRSTT	orchestration
ACEHINOPPRRST	copartnership
ACEHINOPSSTTU	pentastichous
ACEHIOPPRSSTT	spectatorship
ACEHIOPRRSSSY	hypersarcosis
ACEHIOPRRSSTT	stratospheric
ACEHIORSSTTTU	tetrastichous
ACEHLLMOOORTY	alcoholometry
ACEHLMNOOORSU	melanochroous
ACEHLOOOPRRSU	rhopalocerous
ACEHMMOPSTTYY	sympathectomy
ACEIIIILMPRST	imperialistic
ACEIIILLMPTVY	implicatively
ACEIIILMPSSST	pessimistical
ACEIIILNOPRSV	provincialise
ACEIIILNOPRVZ	provincialize
ACEIIILNOSTVV	vivisectional
ACEIIILQSTUVY	acquisitively
ACEIIIMNNORRT	recrimination
ACEIIIMNPSSTT	antisepticism
ACEIIINOPPRTT	precipitation
ACEIIINORSTTT	recitationist
ACEIILLMORSTY	isometrically
ACEIILLNNOORT	intercolonial
ACEIILLNOQTUY	equinoctially
ACEIILLNORRTY	acrylonitrile
ACEIILLNRSTXY	extrinsically
ACEIILMNOPSST	neoplasticism
	Neo-Plasticism
ACEIILMNORTUV	vermiculation
ACEIILMNOSSSU	maliciousness
ACEIILMNPRRSU	supercriminal
ACEIILNNOORTT	interlocation
ACEIILNNOPSST	non-specialist
ACEIILNNPPRSS	principalness
ACEIILNOPRRTT	intertropical
ACEIILNOPRSST	personalistic
ACEIILNPPRTTY	precipitantly
ACEIILNPQTTUU	quintuplicate
ACEIILORRTTVY	correlativity
ACEIIMMNOORST	commiseration
ACEIIMNNOOOST	economisation
ACEIIMNNOOOTZ	economization
ACEIIMNORRRTY	recriminatory
ACEIIMOORSTTU	autoeroticism
ACEIINNOOPRST	preconisation
ACEIINNOOPRTT	enantiotropic
ACEIINNOOPRTZ	preconization
ACEIINNOORSVZ	conversazioni
ACEIINOOPRRTV	incorporative
ACEIINOORRSTV	anticorrosive
ACEIINOORSSTT	sectorisation
ACEIINOORSTTV	vectorisation
ACEIINOORSTTZ	sectorization
ACEIINOORTTVZ	vectorization
ACEIINORSSSUV	vicariousness
ACEIINORSSTTU	resuscitation
ACEIINOSSSUVV	vivaciousness
ACEIINPRRSTTV	transcriptive
ACEIIORRTTTVY	retroactivity
ACEILLLLMRTUU	multicellular
ACEILLLPSTYY	sylleptically
ACEILLLMOTTUU	multiloculate

ACEILLLOPPRTY prolepticallyACEILLLOPPRTY prolepticallyACEILLLOPPRTY proleptically
ACEILLMMNOTYY metonymically
ACEILLMMRSTYY symmetrically
ACEILLMNOPRSU ceruloplasmin
ACEILLNNNOSSY nonsensically
ACEILLNNOOSTT constellation
ACEILLNOOPRRY incorporeally
ACEILLNOQUUVY unequivocally
ACEILMMNNORTU intercommunal
ACEILMMNOPRTY complimentary
ACEILMMNRSTUY unsymmetrical
ACEILMMOTTUVY commutatively
ACEILMNNOOPSS companionless
ACEILMNNOOPTT contemplation
ACEILMNNORRTU intercolumnar
ACEILMNOOPRSS compressional
ACEILMNOPSTTT contemplatist
ACEILMNOPTTUY pneumatolytic
ACEILNNOORSTY clay-ironstone
ACEILNNORSTTU interosculant
ACEILNOORRSTV controversial
ACEILOOPRRSTU prosecutorial
ACEILOOPRTVVY provocatively
ACEILOORRSTTW watercolorist
ACEIMMMNOOORT commemoration
ACEIMNNNOORTU connumeration
ACEIMNOOOOPTT onomatopoetic
ACEIMNORSSSTU customariness
ACEIMOOPRRRSS air-compressor
ACEINNNOORSTT consternation
ACEINNNOORTTV contravention
ACEINNNOORTVY conventionary
ACEINNOOORTTT contortionate
ACEINNOOPRSTT cornet-à-piston
ACEINOOPRRSSY processionary
ACEINOOPRTUVV unprovocative
ACEINOORSSSTU atrociousness
ACEINOORSSSUV voraciousness
ACEINOPRRSTTU perscrutation
ACEIOORRRSSTU stercorarious
ACEIOPRSSTUUU supercautious
ACELLMMNOOORU monomolecular
ACELLNNRSTTUY translucently
ACELLNOORSTTY constellatory
ACELMNOORSSSU clamorousness
ACELMNOPRRSUU supercolumnar
ACELMNORRSUUU neuromuscular
ACELMNSSTTUUU sustentaculum
ACELNOORSSSUU oraculousness
ACELOOPPRRTUY precopulatory
ACEMMMOOORRTY commemoratory
ACEMOOPRSTTTY prostatectomy
ACEOPPRRSSTTU streptocarpus
ACEOQRRRSSSTU cross-quarters
ACFFGHIILRSTT traffic-lights
ACFFGILNOSTUY suffocatingly
ACFFIIIILNOPST spifflication
ACFFIIINOORTT fortification
ACFGHHIINPRTT pitch-farthing
ACFGIIIILNNOT lignification
ACFGIIIINNNST insignificant
ACFGIIIINNOST signification
ACFGIIIILNNSTY significantly
ACFGIIIILNOORT glorification
ACFGIIIINORSTY significatory
ACFGIIILNNSTYY sanctifyingly
ACFGIINNOORTU configuration
ACFGILLOOOSTT olfactologist
ACFGILLOORTUU futurological
ACFHIIINORTTU thurification
ACFHIILLNOORY honorifically
ACFIIIIKNNOTZ zinkification
ACFIIIINNORTT nitrification
ACFIIIINORTTV vitrification
ACFIIIJLLNOOT jollification
ACFIIIJNOSTTU justification
ACFIIIILLMNOOT mollification
ACFIIIILLNNOTU nullification
ACFIIIILMOPRST simplificator
ACFIIIILNOOPRT prolification
ACFIIIILNOPTTY pontificality
ACFIIIMMMNOTU mummification
ACFIIIMNOORTT mortification
ACFIIIMNOSTTY mystification
ACFIIINOPPTUY yuppification
ACFIIINORSSTU Russification
ACFIIJORSTTUY justificatory
ACFIILLLORSTY floristically
ACFIILMNNOSTU functionalism
ACFIILMORRSTU formularistic
ACFIILNNOSTTU functionalist
ACFILLLLOOORR corollifloral
ACFILLLORRTUU floricultural
ACFILNNNNOOTU non-functional
ACFINNNOOORTT confrontation
ACGGHHILOPPRY glyphographic
ACGGHIKLNOSTU laughing-stock
ACGGHILOPPRTY glyptographic
ACGGILLLOOOSS glossological
ACGHHIIOPPRSY physiographic
ACGHHIIOPRRST chirographist
ACGHHIMNOOSTT shooting-match
ACGHHINOOPSTY onychophagist
ACGHIIILLOOPSY physiological
ACGHIIMOOPRST mastigophoric
ACGHILLLMOOOY homologically
ACGHILLMOOOPR morphological
ACGHILNOOPSSU sphagnicolous
ACGHIMNNOOOPT pathognomonic
ACGHIOOOPSTUX toxicophagous
ACGHLLNNOOPSY splanchnology
ACGHLOOOPTTYY cytopathology
ACGHMNOOPSSTU Compsognathus
ACGHNOOPPRSYY pharyngoscopy
ACGIIIILNNSTU linguistician
ACGIIILLLOSSTY syllogistical
ACGIIILLMMNOOU immunological
ACGIIILLMNNOPY complainingly
ACGIIILLMOOSTT climatologist
ACGIIILMNNNOPU uncomplaining
ACGIIILRRSTTUU agriculturist
ACGIIMMNOORRS micro-organism
ACGIIMNNNOOOT cognomination
ACGIINNNOSTUY consanguinity

ACGIINNOOPRRT	incorporating
ACGIKLMNNOORU	mourning-cloak
ACGILLLNOOOTY	ontologically
ACGILLLOOOPTY	topologically
ACGILLNOOOSTV	volcanologist
ACGILLNOOSTUV	vulcanologist
ACGILLNOOSTYY	glycosylation
ACGILNNOORTTU	conglutinator
ACGILNORSSTUV	cross-vaulting
ACGINNNOOOSTU	non-contagious
ACHHIIINNORST	ornithischian
ACHHIIINPPSSY	physicianship
ACHHIILLOOPPS	philosophical
ACHHIILNOPPRT	philanthropic
ACHHIINNNOSTU	Hutchinsonian
ACHHILMMOORSS	school-marmish
ACHHIMNOORSTX	xanthochroism
ACHHIMNOOSTTU	autochthonism
ACHHIOPPSSTTY	psychopathist
ACHHLLNOOOSTU	allochthonous
ACHHNOOORSTUX	xanthochroous
ACHHNOOOSTTUU	autochthonous
ACHIIILLOOPRU	ailourophilic
ACHIIILNPPPRS	principalship
ACHIIIMNNORTY	inharmonicity
ACHIILLOPSSTY	sophistically
ACHIILNNRSTUY	unchristianly
ACHIILNOPPRST	psilanthropic
ACHIIMMORRSTT	trichromatism
ACHIIMNNOOPPS	companionship
ACHIIMNNOORTT	ornithomantic
ACHIIOOPRSSTT	sophisticator
ACHILLORRTTUU	horticultural
ACHILMOPSTTYY	sympatholytic
ACHILNOPRSTTY	lycanthropist
ACHILOOOPSTTV	photovoltaics
ACHIMNOORSTTU	tautochronism
ACHIMOOOPRSTT	somatotrophic
ACHINNOOPRSSY	narcohypnosis
ACHMMNOOOORRT	monochromator
ACHNOOORSTTUU	tautochronous
ACIIIIMNOSTTV	victimisation
ACIIIIMNOTTVZ	victimization
ACIIILLLMOPTY	impolitically
ACIIILLNNOSTT	scintillation
ACIIILLNNRSTY	intrinsically
ACIIILLNOOPTT	pollicitation
ACIIILMNNORTU	anticlinorium
ACIIILMNOPRSV	provincialism
ACIIILMNORSTY	consimilarity
ACIIILNNOPRST	inscriptional
ACIIILNOPRSTV	provincialist
ACIIILNOPRTVY	provinciality
ACIIIMNNORRTY	incriminatory
ACIILLLMOOQSU	colloquialism
ACIILLLOOQSTU	colloquialist
ACIILLLSSTTYY	stylistically
ACIILLMOPRTTU	multiplicator
ACIILLNNSTTUY	instinctually
ACIILLNOORTUY	illocutionary
ACIILLNRSTTYY	crystallinity
ACIILMNOOOPST	compositional
ACIILMNOORSUY	acrimoniously
ACIILMNOORTTY	microtonality
ACIILMPRRSSTU	scripturalism
ACIILNNORSTTU	instructional
ACIILNOOORSTU	colourisation
ACIILNOOORTUZ	colourization
ACIILNORSTTUV	voluntaristic
ACIILPRRSSTTU	scripturalist
ACIIMMOOPRSTT	compatriotism
ACIIMNNOOSSTU	sanctimonious
ACIIMNOOPRTTU	protoactinium
ACIIMNOOSSTTU	customisation
ACIIMNOOSTTUZ	customization
ACIINNNOOPRTU	pronunciation
ACIINNOOOPRRT	incorporation
ACIINNOORSTTT	contristation
ACIINNOPRRSTT	transcription
ACILLLMRTTUUU	multicultural
ACILLLRSTUUVY	sylvicultural
ACILMNOSSSTTU	sansculottism
ACILMRRSSTTUU	structuralism
ACILNNNNOOSTY	inconsonantly
ACILNNOORSUVY	convulsionary
ACILNNPTTUUUY	unpunctuality
ACILNOORRSTUY	contrariously
ACILNOORRSUVY	carnivorously
ACILNOSSSTTTU	sansculottist
ACILRRSSTTTUU	structuralist
ACIMNOOORRTTT	motor-traction
ACINNOOPRSTTU	constupration
ACINNOPRSTTTU	contrapuntist
ACINORRSTTTUU	structuration
ACLMOOOOPPSTY	omoplatoscopy
ACLMORSSTTUUU	cumulostratus
	strato-cumulus
ACNNNOOOPSSTT	stop-consonant
ACNOOOPPRSSTT	contrappostos
ADDDDEEFFILLR	fiddle-faddler
ADDDDEEGHINPU	pudding-headed
ADDDEEEEHLLSW	swelled-headed
ADDDEEEFLRSSS	self-addressed
ADDDEEHIMNRSU	dunderheadism
ADDDEEHLNNRUY	underhandedly
ADDDEEIIMNOWW	maiden-widowed
ADDDEGGLLNOSY	daddy-long-legs
ADDDEIMNOOPRW	diamond-powder
ADDEEEEHNRRTT	tender-hearted
ADDEEEGHIKNOS	hide-and-go-seek
ADDEEEGHINPSS	pigheadedness
ADDEEEGHIRTTW	trade-weighted
ADDEEEGILNNNR	darning-needle
ADDEEEHLLNOSW	swollen-headed
ADDEEEHNNPPRU	unapprehended
ADDEEEILMNRST	Middle-Eastern
ADDEEELNRSSSS	dreadlessness
ADDEEENPPRRRU	underprepared
ADDEEFFHNNOSS	offhandedness
ADDEEFILNPRTT	fiddle-pattern
ADDEEGHLNORWY	wrong-headedly
ADDEEGIMNNOTU	maiden-tongued
ADDEEGNNRSSUU	unguardedness
ADDEEHIKLNRTY	kind-heartedly

ADDEEHIKNORSW	whiskerandoed
ADDEEHILMNRTY	earthly-minded
ADDEEHILNPPSS	spindle-shaped
ADDEEHNRRRTTU	thunder-darter
ADDEEILMOPPRR	pompier-ladder
ADDEEIMNNPRRU	unreprimanded
ADDEEIMNNSSSY	many-sidedness
ADDEEIMNRSTUV	misadventured
ADDEEINNSSSUV	unadvisedness
ADDEEMNOOPSSU	pseudomonades
ADDEENNNSSTUU	undauntedness
ADDEGIIKNRRST	redding-straik
ADDEGIIMMNNOT	Maginot-minded
ADDEGIIMNNNPX	mind-expanding
ADDEGINNNRSTU	understanding
ADDEGIOOPRRTW	partridge-wood
ADDEGLNOORTUY	good-naturedly
ADDEIIIILNSUV	individualise
ADDEIIIILNUVZ	individualize
ADDEIIINOOSTX	deoxidisation
ADDEIIINOOTXZ	deoxidization
ADDEIILNORSTY	disordinately
ADDEIINOOORST	deodorisation
ADDEIINOOORTZ	deodorization
ADDEIINOPRSTU	superaddition
ADDEIKLNNRTUY	kindly-natured
ADDEIMNNRSSTU	misunderstand
ADDGGILNNNORU	landing-ground
ADDHNNOOPSTUU	thousand-pound
ADDIIIILMNSUV	individualism
ADDIIIILNSTUV	individualist
ADDIIIILNTUVY	individuality
ADDIIIINNOTUV	individuation
ADDIINOOOPRTT	Diprotodontia
ADEEEEEHLLRRW	wheeler-dealer
ADEEEEGHLNRTT	gentle-hearted
ADEEEEGNNRRTU	unregenerated
ADEEEENPRSSST	desperateness
ADEEEFFGILNST	self-defeating
ADEEEFFIINRTT	differentiate
ADEEEFGGHILLT	eagle-flighted
ADEEEFHRRSTTU	feather-duster
ADEEEFILLNRTY	deferentially
ADEEEGGIMNNST	disengagement
ADEEEGGINORST	desegregation
ADEEEGHILNRST	single-hearted
ADEEEGHILNRTT	letter-heading
ADEEEGHILNRTW	leather-winged
ADEEEGHINOPRT	pigeon-hearted
ADEEEGHLLNRTU	leather-lunged
ADEEEGHLNOPSZ	lozenge-shaped
ADEEEGIINNORU	audio-engineer
ADEEEGINNNRSS	endearingness
ADEEEGIOPPRRS	pease-porridge
ADEEEGIORSSSU	grouse-disease
ADEEEGJMNSTTU	judgement-seat
ADEEEGLLLRTUW	well-regulated
ADEEEGMNRRRRY	gerrymanderer
ADEEEGNNRSSST	estrangedness
ADEEEGOPRRTUY	daguerreotype
ADEEEHHLORSUV	heave-shoulder
ADEEEHILMPRST	simple-hearted
ADEEEHINRRTVW	weather-driven
ADEEEHLNSSSST	deathlessness
ADEEEIILNRRST	intersidereal
ADEEEIIMMNSST	immediateness
ADEEEIIMNNRTT	indeterminate
ADEEEIIMNRTTV	determinative
ADEEEIIMPRTTV	premeditative
ADEEEIINPRSST	pedestrianise
ADEEEIINPRSTZ	pedestrianize
ADEEEIIORRTTV	deteriorative
ADEEEILMNRTTY	determinately
ADEEEILNOPRSS	depersonalise
ADEEEILNOPRSZ	depersonalize
ADEEEILOPRTTY	radioteletype
ADEEEIMNNRTTU	undeterminate
ADEEEIMNPRTTV	tamper-evident
ADEEEIMNRSTTU	underestimate
ADEEEIMNRSTTV	advertisement
ADEEEIMNRTTVZ	advertizement
ADEEEINNNRTTU	unentertained
ADEEEINNRSSST	sedentariness
ADEEEINOPQRTU	equiponderate
ADEEEJMNOSTWW	Jamestown-weed
ADEEELLMNOPTV	developmental
ADEEELMNRSSSS	dreamlessness
ADEEELNNNRSSU	unlearnedness
ADEEEMNNORTUV	endeavourment
ADEEEMNORSTUV	adventuresome
ADEEENPPRRTTU	unperpetrated
ADEEEORSSTUVW	sweet-savoured
ADEEFFIILSSST	self-satisfied
ADEEFGGILNRRS	self-regarding
ADEEFGINRRRTY	tarry-fingered
ADEEFGLNRRSSU	regardfulness
ADEEFHILNNSST	left-handiness
ADEEFHIORTUVW	white-favoured
ADEEFIILOQRUV	overqualified
ADEEFIILPRSSS	self-dispraise
ADEEFILMOSTTV	self-motivated
ADEEFILNOPPST	self-appointed
ADEEFILNSSSTU	self-sustained
ADEEFINOORSTT	deforestation
ADEEFIOPSSTTY	safety-deposit
ADEEGGHINNRTU	draught-engine
ADEEGHHORRTTU	thought-reader
ADEEGHIINNRST	disheartening
ADEEGHILMNOPT	dephlegmation
ADEEGHILNRSTY	near-sightedly
ADEEGHINNRRTW	night-wanderer
ADEEGHJLLMNTU	judgement-hall
ADEEGHLMNNOOT	gentlemanhood
ADEEGIIINRTTT	interdigitate
ADEEGIKNNRRRT	kindergärtner
ADEEGILLNRRST	drill-sergeant
ADEEGIMNNOSSY	dynamogenesis
ADEEGIMNNPRTU	unimpregnated
ADEEGIMORSTTU	deuterogamist
ADEEGINOPPRSV	eavesdropping
ADEEGINORSTTU	deuteragonist
ADEEGLLOOOPPY	paleopedology
ADEEGMMOPPRRR	preprogrammed
ADEEGNNORSSSU	dangerousness

ADEEGOPRRTUYY	daguerreotypy
ADEEHHILNNRST	Netherlandish
ADEEHHILNOOTT	toad-in-the-hole
ADEEHHIMOPRRT	hermaphrodite
ADEEHHLLOORTW	hollow-hearted
ADEEHIILMMNTY	dimethylamine
ADEEHIIRSSSTT	radiesthesist
ADEEHLMNORRSY	dysmenorrheal
ADEEHLNOPPSTU	pentadelphous
ADEEHMNOORRSY	dysmenorrhoea
ADEEHMNRRSTTU	thunder-master
ADEEHMPPRSTTU	trumpet-shaped
ADEEHNOOPRRTZ	trapezohedron
ADEEIIILNOSST	dieselisation
ADEEIIILNOSTZ	dieselization
ADEEIIIMNSSTV	disseminative
ADEEIILMNNOTY	demyelination
ADEEIILMNPSST	dissepimental
ADEEIILMNSTTT	dilettanteism
ADEEIIMNNORTT	determination
ADEEIIMNNOSTT	sedimentation
ADEEIIMNOPRTT	premeditation
ADEEIIMNORRTT	intermediator
ADEEIIMNPRSST	pedestrianism
ADEEIINOORRTT	deterioration
ADEEIINOPRTXY	expeditionary
ADEEIINORSSTT	desertisation
ADEEIINORSSTV	disseveration
ADEEIINORSTTZ	desertization
ADEEILLMNRTTY	detrimentally
ADEEILLNNRTTY	interdentally
ADEEILLNOPPTW	well-appointed
ADEEILMMNNSTT	dismantlement
ADEEILNNRTTVY	inadvertently
ADEEILNPRRSTZ	serpent-lizard
ADEEIMNNOPRRT	preordainment
ADEEIMNORSTTV	demonstrative
ADEEIMNRRSTUV	misadventurer
ADEEINNNSSTTU	untaintedness
ADEEINNOPQRTU	equiponderant
ADEEINOPRRSST	predatoriness
ADEEINOPRRSTT	predestinator
ADEEINOPRRSTU	superordinate
ADEEINPRSSTUU	unpasteurised
ADEEINPRSTUUZ	unpasteurized
ADEEIOPRSSSTW	power-assisted
ADEELLNOOPRRW	woollen-draper
ADEELNNSSSSTU	dauntlessness
ADEEMMOOSTUXY	myxoedematous
ADEEMOORRSTUX	xerodermatous
ADEENPPRRRSTU	understrapper
ADEFFHILLNOSU	full-fashioned
ADEFGHHILNOST	sleight-of-hand
ADEFGHINOORSW	foreshadowing
ADEFGIJLNSSTU	self-adjusting
ADEFGILNOORTW	waterflooding
ADEFHHINRTTUY	unthriftyhead
ADEFHILNOORSS	foolhardiness
ADEFIIILMMRTU	multiramified
ADEFIILLNQUUY	unqualifiedly
ADEFILLLORUVY	ill-favouredly
ADEFILLSSTTUY	distastefully
ADEFINNNOOTTU	foundation-net
ADEFMNNORRSTU	untransformed
ADEGGIILNNRSS	niggardliness
ADEGGINNOORVW	wood-engraving
ADEGHIILLLNRT	drilling-lathe
ADEGHIKNNORRW	work-hardening
ADEGHINNOORTY	hydrogenation
ADEGHINNOPPRS	pendragonship
ADEGHINOPRSWW	washing-powder
ADEGHLMNORRTY	grandmotherly
ADEGIIILMTTTU	multidigitate
ADEGIIINORSTV	disinvigorate
ADEGIILLNPSSY	displeasingly
ADEGIILMNTTUY	unmitigatedly
ADEGIILNNOTTU	deglutination
ADEGIILNNTUVY	undeviatingly
ADEGIIMNSSTTU	unstigmatised
ADEGIIMNSTTUZ	unstigmatized
ADEGIIMOOPRST	diageotropism
ADEGIINNNPRTU	underpainting
ADEGIINOOSTTU	auto-digestion
ADEGIINORRSTT	disintegrator
ADEGIKLNORRSW	walking-orders
ADEGILLMNOUZZ	muzzle-loading
ADEGILLNOSTUU	solidungulate
ADEGILMOORSTT	dermatologist
ADEGILNNOQRTU	grandiloquent
ADEGILNNQRSUY	squanderingly
ADEGILNNRSUVY	land-surveying
ADEGJLMNNNOTU	non-judgmental
ADEGLLMNORUWZ	mangold-wurzel
ADEGNOOOPSSTU	steganopodous
ADEGOOOPRSSTU	gasteropodous
ADEHHILOOORTU	Holothuroidea
ADEHIKLNNPSSS	spindle-shanks
ADEHILMNORXYY	hydroxylamine
ADEHILMORTTUU	multi-authored
ADEHILNNOPRSW	land-ownership
ADEHILOOPRSTT	strophiolated
ADEHIMMOOPPRS	paedomorphism
ADEHIMOOPRRST	moderatorship
ADEHLLOOPPSUY	polyadelphous
ADEHNORRSTTWW	north-westward
ADEHORSSTTUWW	south-westward
ADEIIILLMNSTU	disilluminate
ADEIIILMNORTY	meridionality
ADEIIILMSSTUV	dissimulative
ADEIIILNPSTTU	platitudinise
ADEIIILNPTTUZ	platitudinize
ADEIIILNRSSTU	industrialise
ADEIIILNRSTUZ	industrialize
ADEIIIMNNOSST	dissemination
ADEIIIMNOSSTT	disestimation
ADEIIINOOPRST	periodisation
ADEIIINOOPRTZ	periodization
ADEIIINOOPSTT	epidotisation
ADEIIINOOPTTZ	epidotization
ADEIIINORSTTV	derivationist
ADEIIINRSTTTU	attitudiniser
ADEIIINRTTTUZ	attitudinizer
ADEIILLMNNTUU	unilluminated
ADEIILMNPRSTU	prudentialism

ADEIILMNRRTUY	rudimentarily
ADEIILNOOSTTV	devotionalist
ADEIILNOOTTVY	devotionality
ADEIILNPRSTTU	prudentialist
ADEIILNPRTTUY	prudentiality
ADEIILNQSTTUY	equidistantly
ADEIILPSTTUVY	disputatively
ADEIIMNNOOPRT	preadmonition
	predomination
ADEIIMNNOORST	modernisation
ADEIIMNNOORTZ	modernization
ADEIIMNNOPSSU	unimpassioned
ADEIIMNNORSTT	anti-modernist
ADEIINNOOPRRT	preordination
ADEIINOPRSTTU	disreputation
ADEIIPPRRSTTY	party-spirited
ADEILLNRSTTUU	unillustrated
ADEILMMNOOPSY	polydaemonism
ADEILMNNOPRTY	predominantly
ADEILNOORTUVY	devolutionary
ADEIMNNOORSTT	demonstration
ADEIMNNOPRSTU	superdominant
ADEIMNNRSTTTU	untransmitted
ADEINOPRRRSUY	superordinary
ADEINOSSSSSUU	assiduousness
ADELNOPRRSTTY	transportedly
ADELNORSTUUVY	adventurously
ADEMNOORRSTTY	demonstratory
ADENNORSTUUUV	unadventurous
ADENOOPRRRSTU	proterandrous
ADFGIIILNQSUY	disqualifying
ADFGIIINORSTU	disfiguration
ADFIIIILMNOSS	solifidianism
ADGGGIILNNRSS	glass-grinding
ADGGGILNNNORU	ground-angling
ADGHHILLNOPTY	diphthongally
ADGHIIILNQSUW	washing-liquid
ADGHIILNNOPPS	island-hopping
ADGHIILNNORTU	hound-trailing
ADGHIINNNNOTU	Huntingdonian
ADGHIINNRTUWW	unwithdrawing
ADGHINNOOOPRT	gonadotrophin
ADGHMNNOOPRRY	gynandromorph
ADGIIIINNOPST	pidginisation
ADGIIIINNOPTZ	pidginization
ADGIIILNPRSSY	dispraisingly
ADGIIINNOPPST	disappointing
ADGIJLNOPPRWY	jawdroppingly
ADGILLMOOOPTY	diplomatology
ADGILNNOSTTUY	outstandingly
ADGILNOOOOSTT	odonatologist
ADGILNOOQRSUU	grandiloquous
ADHHIORRRSSTY	hydrarthrosis
ADHHLMOOPPSTU	podophthalmus
ADHIIKNOOOPRT	orthopinakoid
ADHIILLNOQRTU	quadrillionth
ADHIILMNOPRSU	dolphinariums
ADHIIMNOORSSU	disharmonious
ADHIMNOPRSSSW	swordsmanship
ADHINOOOPRSTT	prosthodontia
ADHINOORRSTWW	Wordsworthian
ADHIOOOPPRTTY	diaphototropy

ADHMOOORSSTUY	hydrosomatous
ADIIIILMNOSST	dissimilation
ADIIIILMRSSTY	dissimilarity
ADIIILMMOPRRS	primordialism
ADIIILMNOSSTU	dissimulation
ADIIILMNRSSTU	industrialism
ADIIILMOPRRTY	primordiality
ADIIILNOOPSST	dispositional
ADIIILNRSSTTU	industrialist
ADIILLMMOORST	stillroom-maid
ADIILMNRTTUUY	multitudinary
ADIILNNOSTTUU	undulationist
ADIILNOPSTTUU	platitudinous
AEEEEEFKMRRRT	free-marketeer
AEEEEEINPRRRS	arrière-pensée
AEEEEEMNPPTTZ	appeteezement
AEEEEFGHLNRRV	half-evergreen
AEEEEGGMNNPRT	pre-engagement
AEEEEHMOPPRRT	Ephemeroptera
AEEEEHMORRTTW	weatherometer
AEEEEILNRRSST	rensselaerite
AEEEEIMNPRSST	passementerie
AEEEEMMNRRSTU	remeasurement
AEEEEMNNPRRST	representamen
AEEEEMNPRSSTT	temperateness
AEEEFFGHINORV	heave-offering
AEEEFFLMMNRRW	Flammenwerfer
AEEEFGHHIRTTW	featherweight
AEEEFGHLNRTTU	feature-length
AEEEFGIIRRRTV	refrigerative
AEEEFGILLNRSV	self-revealing
AEEEFGILNPRST	self-repeating
AEEEFGLNNNSSW	newfangleness
AEEEFHHORRSST	horsefeathers
AEEEFILLNRRTY	referentially
AEEEFILLQRTUU	quatrefeuille
AEEEFILRSSSTV	self-assertive
AEEEFINQRTTUV	frequentative
AEEEFKMNNNRTT	frank-tenement
AEEEFLMNRSTTT	self-treatment
AEEEFNORRSTTW	water-softener
AEEEGGIMNOSST	gametogenesis
AEEEGHHINPRSS	sheepshearing
AEEEGHHIRRTTT	tithe-gatherer
AEEEGHILNPSST	sheep-stealing
AEEEGHIMNNRST	garnisheement
AEEEGHIMNOSST	hematogenesis
AEEEGHLNOPRRS	selenographer
AEEEGHMNOPRST	magnetosphere
AEEEGIKLLMNNT	gentlemanlike
AEEEGIKLMNRTT	telemarketing
AEEEGILLMNSTV	televangelism
AEEEGILLNSTTV	televangelist
AEEEGILMNNORT	noli-me-tangere
AEEEGILMNPRSS	passenger-mile
AEEEGILPRRSTT	register-plate
AEEEGINORRRTT	reinterrogate
AEEEGINORSSTT	teratogenesis
AEEEHHHLRRSTW	thresher-whale
AEEEHHIPRSSTY	hyperesthesia
AEEEHHLMORRTT	heterothermal
AEEEHHNOPRSST	asthenosphere

AEEEHIKNRSTVY	sneak-thievery
AEEEHILMMNPRT	penthemimeral
AEEEHILMNNOPS	phenomenalise
AEEEHILMNNOPZ	phenomenalize
AEEEHLMNSSSSS	shamelessness
AEEEHLNPSSSSS	shapelessness
AEEEHLNRSSSST	heartlessness
AEEEHMMNORTTV	earth-movement
AEEEHORRSSTUU	treasure-house
AEEEIILNRRRTV	irreverential
AEEEIIMNRTTVX	exterminative
AEEEIKLLMPRST	kapellmeister
AEEEILLNRRTVY	reverentially
AEEEILMNPRSSX	exemplariness
AEEEILMNPRTTY	intemperately
AEEEILNNSSSST	essentialness
AEEEILNPRTTVY	penetratively
AEEEILNRSSSTV	versatileness
AEEEIMMPRSTUY	empyreumatise
AEEEIMMPRTUYZ	empyreumatize
AEEEIMNNNRTTT	entertainment
AEEEIMNNRSTTT	reinstatement
AEEEIMNORSSSW	wearisomeness
AEEEIMNPRRSTV	imperseverant
AEEEINNNSSSST	insensateness
AEEEINNPSSSVX	expansiveness
AEEEINNSSSSTV	assentiveness
AEEEINNSSTTTV	attentiveness
	tentativeness
AEEEINOPRRSTV	perseveration
AEEEINOPRSSTV	operativeness
AEEEINPRSSSVV	pervasiveness
AEEEINRSSSSTV	assertiveness
AEEELNPRSTTTT	letters-patent
AEEELNSSSSSTT	statelessness
	tastelessness
AEEEMMNOPRTTU	pneumatometer
AEEEMNORSTTTV	overstatement
AEEEMNPRRSSTU	prematureness
AEEENNOPRSTTU	Enteropneusta
AEEEORRRSTTUV	treasure-trove
AEEFFGHHILRTT	flight-feather
AEEFFGHIMNRTT	affreightment
AEEFFLLLNNORW	flannel-flower
AEEFGGIINRUVW	figure-weaving
AEEFGHHINRRTT	three-farthing
AEEFGHILNORSV	half-sovereign
AEEFGHLLRSSTU	self-slaughter
AEEFGIINORRRT	refrigeration
AEEFGIIPRRTUV	prefigurative
AEEFGILNOPRST	self-operating
AEEFGILNRSSST	self-asserting
AEEFGIMNORRRT	interferogram
AEEFGINORRSTU	argentiferous
	garnetiferous
AEEFGINRRRSUY	sugar-refinery
AEEFGIORRRRTY	refrigeratory
AEEFGLNNPRSTU	self-repugnant
AEEFGNOOPRSST	foot-passenger
AEEFHHLLNSSTU	healthfulness
AEEFHIILMNNRS	line-fisherman
AEEFHILNSSSST	faithlessness
AEEFHIMNNORST	refashionment
AEEFHLMOOPRRT	mother-of-pearl
AEEFHLNOOPSTT	elephant's-foot
AEEFIILLNNRTY	inferentially
AEEFIILOPRRTV	proliferative
AEEFIINRRSSTT	fire-resistant
AEEFILLMORSTU	metalliferous
AEEFILNORSSST	self-assertion
AEEFILNRRSSTT	self-restraint
AEEFIMOPRRSSS	Passeriformes
AEEFINNNORSTU	antenniferous
AEEFINNOQRTTU	frequentation
AEEFINNORSSSU	nefariousness
AEEFINOORRSTT	reforestation
AEEFINOPRSTTU	superfetation
AEEFIOOPRRSST	professoriate
AEEFLLNORSTVW	fellow-servant
AEEFLLNSSSSTU	faultlessness
AEEFLMNRSSSTU	masterfulness
AEEFLNPRRSSUY	prayerfulness
AEEFLNRSSSTUW	wasterfulness
AEEFNNORSSTTU	fortunateness
AEEGGHILLNOTY	genethlialogy
AEEGGHOOOPRRZ	zoogeographer
AEEGGIILNNNRV	line-engraving
AEEGGINNOORSS	organogenesis
AEEGHHIOPRRSY	heresiography
AEEGHHMOPRRRT	thermographer
AEEGHIIKNNSSV	heaven-kissing
AEEGHILLLNPRS	pearl-shelling
AEEGHILMNNPST	gentlemanship
AEEGHILMOORST	isogeothermal
AEEGHILNNRTTY	threateningly
AEEGHIMOPRRSS	seismographer
AEEGHINOPRSST	taphrogenesis
AEEGHINORSTUW	watering-house
AEEGHLMNOOOTU	theologoumena
AEEGHLNORRRSW	horse-wrangler
AEEGIIINSTTVV	investigative
AEEGIILLLSTVY	legislatively
AEEGIILMNORSS	generalissimo
AEEGIILNNPSST	palingenesist
AEEGIIMNNORST	generationism
AEEGIIMNNORTT	regimentation
AEEGIIMNNRSTT	mainstreeting
AEEGIINNOORTT	renegotiation
AEEGIINNOPRRT	peregrination
AEEGIINNORRTT	reintegration
AEEGIINORRTTV	interrogative
AEEGIKLNRSTTW	streetwalking
AEEGILLLNPRST	selling-plater
AEEGILLNRSTVY	everlastingly
AEEGILLOOPSST	spelaeologist
AEEGILNNPRTTY	penetratingly
AEEGILNNTTUXY	extenuatingly
AEEGILNOOPRST	antigropeloes
AEEGILOPRRTVY	prerogatively
AEEGIMMNOOTTV	magnetomotive
AEEGIMNNNNSSU	unmeaningness
AEEGIMNNRTTUY	integumentary
AEEGINNNQRTUY	quingentenary
AEEGINNOSSUUX	exsanguineous

AEEGINNPPRRSV	preserving-pan
AEEGINNPPRSTT	step-parenting
AEEGINOPRRRTY	peregrinatory
AEEGINRRSSSTV	transgressive
AEEGIORRRSTTV	tergiversator
AEEGLLMNNNTUY	ungentlemanly
AEEGLLMNNOTWY	gentlewomanly
AEEGLMNNPSSTU	puss-gentleman
AEEGLMNOOPRRY	prolegomenary
AEEGNNQRRRTUU	quarter-gunner
AEEHHHKRRRSST	thresher-shark
AEEHHIINNOPTZ	phenothiazine
AEEHHILLLNOTW	hole-in-the-wall
AEEHHILMMNNTT	nemathelminth
AEEHHILNNSSTU	unhealthiness
AEEHHLMMOOORT	homoeothermal
AEEHHLMORRTTY	earth-motherly
AEEHHMNOOPRRY	hypomenorrhea
AEEHHMOPRRTTY	thermotherapy
AEEHIIIPPRSTT	perihepatitis
AEEHIIKNPRSTY	kinesitherapy
AEEHIILMNOSSS	leishmanioses
AEEHIILMNRTTY	triethylamine
AEEHIILPPRRTY	peripherality
AEEHIIMMNPRTY	pyrimethamine
AEEHIIMOOPSST	hematopoiesis
AEEHILMMNNOPS	phenomenalism
AEEHILMNNOPST	phenomenalist
AEEHILMNNOPTY	phenomenality
AEEHILNNRSSTU	unearthliness
AEEHIMNNPSSSS	misshapenness
AEEHIMNPRSSUU	superhumanise
AEEHIMNPRSUUZ	superhumanize
AEEHIMNQSSSSU	squeamishness
AEEHIMOPPRRTY	hypermetropia
AEEHINNOPRTTX	xanthopterine
AEEHINOPSSTTY	enhypostatise
AEEHINOPSTTYZ	enhypostatize
AEEHINORSSSTV	overhastiness
AEEHINORSSSTW	seaworthiness
AEEHIPRRRSSTU	treasurership
AEEHKLNNSSSST	thanklessness
AEEHLLORTTTVV	throttle-valve
AEEHLMNOOSSST	loathsomeness
AEEHLMORRSTWY	whoremasterly
AEEHLNORRSTTY	north-easterly
AEEHLORSSTTUY	south-easterly
AEEHMMOOPRSST	metamorphoses
AEEHMMOPSSTUY	emphysematous
AEEHMNOOPPRTU	pneumatophore
AEEHMOOPPRRST	spermatophore
AEEHMOPPRSTTY	spermatophyte
AEEHMORSSTTUY	erythematosus
AEEHOPPRRTTYY	pyretotherapy
AEEIIILMNPRRS	preliminaries
AEEIIIMNSSTTV	imitativeness
AEEIIKLLOPRRT	realpolitiker
AEEIILLLMNNPR	premillennial
AEEIILLNNPTTY	penitentially
AEEIILLNOPSTT	pelletisation
AEEIILLNOPTTZ	pelletization
AEEIILLNSTTXY	existentially
AEEIILMNOPRSS	impersonalise
AEEIILMNOPRSZ	impersonalize
AEEIILMNRTTVY	terminatively
AEEIILMOPRSTT	temporalities
AEEIILNNORRTT	interrelation
AEEIILNNOSSTV	inviolateness
AEEIILNNPSSTV	plaintiveness
AEEIILNNTTTVY	inattentively
AEEIILNOPQTTU	equipotential
AEEIILNOPRRTT	interpetiolar
AEEIILNOPRTTV	interpolative
AEEIILNORSTTV	revelationist
AEEIILNORSTVY	televisionary
AEEIILNPRRSTT	interpilaster
AEEIILNPRSTTY	presentiality
AEEIILNQSTTUY	sequentiality
AEEIILORRRTTX	exterritorial
AEEIIMMNORSST	mesmerisation
AEEIIMMNORSTZ	mesmerization
AEEIIMNNOPRTT	impenetration
AEEIIMNNORTTX	extermination
AEEIIMNPSSSSV	impassiveness
AEEIIMNQRSSTU	equestrianism
AEEIINNOORRTT	reorientation
AEEIINNOQRSTU	questionnaire
AEEIINOPRRTTY	repetitionary
AEEIIOPRRRSTY	prairie-oyster
AEEIKLNPRRSTW	water-sprinkle
AEEIKNOPRSSTT	streptokinase
AEEILLMNNSTTY	sentimentally
AEEILLMNPRSTY	sempiternally
AEEILLNNOPTXY	exponentially
AEEILLNNOSTXY	extensionally
AEEILLNORRSVY	reversionally
AEEILLNRRSTTY	interstellary
AEEILLPRSTUVY	superlatively
AEEILLQRTTTUY	letter-quality
AEEILLRRRSTTY	terrestrially
AEEILLRTTTTTT	tittle-tattler
AEEILMMNNPRTY	impermanently
AEEILMMNRSSTU	semimenstrual
AEEILMNNNORTV	environmental
AEEILMNNNSTTU	unsentimental
AEEILMOPRRTXY	extemporarily
AEEILMORRSTUY	temerariously
AEEILNNNOOPPS	Peloponnesian
AEEILNNNOPRST	anti-personnel
AEEILNNOPRRST	interpersonal
AEEILNNOPRSTT	septentrional
AEEILNNQQTUUV	quinquevalent
AEEILNNRSSSUV	universalness
AEEILNNSSSSST	stainlessness
AEEILNOOPRTTT	teleportation
AEEILNRRRSTTU	unterrestrial
AEEILNRRSTVVY	livery-servant
AEEILOPRSSTUY	erysipelatous
AEEILOPSTTUVX	expostulative
AEEILORRSTTVY	restoratively
AEEIMMNNORSST	momentariness
AEEIMNNOPPRTT	reappointment
AEEIMNNORSSTV	normativeness
AEEIMNOPRRSST	temporariness

AEEIMNORRSTTV	remonstrative
AEEIMNORRTTXY	exterminatory
AEEINNNRSSSTT	transientness
AEEINOOPRRTTX	re-exportation
AEEINOOPSSSST	possessionate
AEEINOPRRSSTY	arsenopyrites
AEEINOPRSSTTT	Protestantise
AEEINOPRSTTTZ	Protestantize
AEEINOQRSSTTU	sequestration
AEEINOSSSTUVX	vexatiousness
AEEIOOPPRSTTV	post-operative
AEEIPPRRSSSTT	asset-stripper
AEELLMOQRRSUY	quarrelsomely
AEELMNPPRSTUY	supplementary
AEELNOPRSTTTT	talent-spotter
AEEMNPRRRSUUY	supernumerary
AEEMOPRRSSTTU	posture-master
AEFFGHIKNNORT	thank-offering
AEFFGIMRSSTTU	suffragettism
AEFGGIINNRRSU	sugar-refining
AEFGHINNNPRTY	penny-farthing
AEFGHINNRRSTU	nursing-father
AEFGIIILNTTTT	tattie-lifting
AEFGIILMNQRTU	quilting-frame
AEFGIILNNSTVV	snifting-valve
AEFGIINOPRRTU	prefiguration
AEFGILLNNRTUY	unfalteringly
AEFGILNOPPRSV	self-approving
AEFGILNORRSUU	granuliferous
AEFGINOOPRRTW	waterproofing
AEFHHLLLNTUUY	unhealthfully
AEFHNOOSSSSTT	soothfastness
AEFIIIILMNNST	infinitesimal
AEFIIILNORSTT	fertilisation
AEFIIILNORTTZ	fertilization
AEFIILLLNNTUY	influentially
AEFIILLMMNTTU	multifilament
AEFIILLNNNTUU	uninfluential
AEFIILLOPPRSU	papilliferous
AEFIILMNORSUU	aluminiferous
AEFIILNOOPRRT	proliferation
AEFIILNOPRSTU	platiniferous
AEFIIMNNORTUV	uninformative
AEFIIMNOOPRRT	imperforation
AEFIIMNORSSTU	staminiferous
AEFIINRRSTTTY	interstratify
AEFILMNOPRSTT	self-important
AEFILNOOPRSSW	passion-flower
AEFILNRSSTUVY	transfusively
AEFIMNORRSTUU	frumentarious
AEFIOQRRSTUUZ	quartziferous
AEFLNNORTTUUY	unfortunately
AEGGHHLOPPRRY	glyphographer
AEGGHILNNOSTU	tongue-lashing
AEGGHILNOORTW	wool-gathering
AEGGHLOOPRRSS	glossographer
AEGGIINORRTTU	regurgitation
AEGGIMMNORSTY	gyromagnetism
AEGGIMNOOOSTU	geitonogamous
AEGGINNNOORSS	non-aggression
AEGHHILMNOSTU	lighthouseman
AEGHHINPPRRYY	hyperphrygian
AEGHHIOPPRRSY	physiographer
AEGHHMOOPPRRR	morphographer
AEGHIIKNNPRSS	pinking-shears
AEGHIIKNOTTTW	tattie-howking
AEGHIILNOOPRT	gerontophilia
AEGHIINNSTTUX	extinguishant
AEGHIINRRRSTT	heart-stirring
AEGHIIPRRRSST	registrarship
AEGHIKLNORSST	stalking-horse
AEGHIKNNRRSTT	knights-errant
AEGHILLOOORTY	aerolithology
AEGHILNOOPSTT	pantheologist
AEGHILNORSTUV	vaulting-horse
AEGHILNOSTUUV	vaulting-house
AEGHILOOPRSST	phraseologist
AEGHIMNORTTUW	mouthwatering
AEGHINNPRRSSU	pruning-shears
AEGHINOPRSSTT	stenographist
AEGHIOPRRSSTU	surrogateship
AEGHLMMNOOOOU	homologoumena
AEGHLMMOORTTY	thremmatology
AEGHLOPPRRTYY	pterylography
AEGHMNOOOPSTU	entomophagous
AEGHOOOPRSSTU	ostreophagous
AEGIIIILLMNRTT	time-trialling
AEGIIIMNORSTT	emigrationist
AEGIIINNOSTTV	investigation
	tenovaginitis
AEGIIIPRRSSTT	perigastritis
AEGIILLOPRSSS	aspergillosis
AEGIILMNORSYY	syringomyelia
AEGIILMOOSSST	semasiologist
AEGIILNNOOSST	signal-to-noise
AEGIILNNPPRRU	purple-in-grain
AEGIILNNPPRTT	plate-printing
AEGIILNOOPRRT	progenitorial
AEGIILNOSSTUU	ustilagineous
AEGIIMNOPRRTY	primogenitary
AEGIIMNRRSTTW	writing-master
AEGIINNOORRTT	interrogation
AEGIINNORRTUY	genito-urinary
AEGIINORSTTVY	investigatory
AEGIKLLNORRST	roller-skating
AEGILLLMNSSST	smelling-salts
AEGILLNOOPSTT	planetologist
AEGILNNNORSUY	unreasoningly
AEGILNOOPRRSS	progressional
AEGILNOPPPRTT	plotting-paper
AEGILNORRTTTW	otter-trawling
AEGIMMNORRSUW	measuring-worm
AEGIMNNOPRRRY	morning-prayer
AEGIMNOOPRSSU	angiospermous
AEGIMNOPRRSSU	superorganism
AEGIMOOOPPRST	apogeotropism
AEGINNNPRSSSU	unsparingness
AEGINNORRSSST	transgression
AEGINNPRSSSTU	untrespassing
AEGINOORRRTTY	interrogatory
AEGLMOOSSTTYY	systematology
AEGLNORRSSSUU	garrulousness
AEHHHINOPRRRY	herniorrhaphy
AEHHIIILMNSST	helminthiasis

AEHHIINNOPSTY	hyphenisation	AEIILLNQRRSTU	tranquilliser
AEHHIINNOPTYZ	hyphenization	AEIILLNQRRTUZ	tranquillizer
AEHHILLNOPTTY	anthophyllite	AEIILLORRRTTY	territorially
AEHHILMMOOORT	homoiothermal	AEIILMNNOOSST	solemnisation
AEHHIMNOPRSTT	theanthropism	AEIILMNNOOSTZ	solemnization
AEHHIMOOOPSTT	homoeopathist	AEIILMNOORSTT	tolerationism
AEHHINOPRSTTT	theanthropist	AEIILMNOPRRTX	interproximal
AEHHIOPPRSTYY	physiotherapy	AEIILMNOPRSTY	impersonality
AEHHLOOPPRSSY	phosphorylase	AEIILMNPRTTYY	amitryptyline
AEHHLOOPPRSTY	phosphorylate	AEIILNNNNOPRT	lantern-pinion
AEHHMNOOOPPST	monophosphate	AEIILNNNNOTTU	unintentional
AEHHNOOPPRTTY	anthropophyte	AEIILNNNORTTU	interlunation
AEHHNORSSTTUY	hysteranthous	AEIILNNNSSSTU	unsaintliness
AEHHOOPPPRSTY	pyrophosphate	AEIILNNOOPRTT	interpolation
AEHIIIKNPSSTT	kinesipathist	AEIILNNPRSTUY	peninsularity
AEHIIILMNOSSS	leishmaniosis	AEIILNNQQTUUV	quinquivalent
AEHIIKLNNPRST	skirl-in-the-pan	AEIILNOOPPRST	prepositional
AEHIIMNORTTTU	Titanotherium	AEIILNOOPSTTX	sexploitation
AEHIINNOOPSTT	phonetisation	AEIILNOORSTTT	tolerationist
AEHIINNOOPTTZ	phonetization	AEIILNOPRSTUV	pulverisation
AEHIINORRSSTW	airworthiness	AEIILNOPRTUVZ	pulverization
AEHILLOPPSSTY	Psilophytales	AEIILNORRTTTY	torrentiality
AEHILMMOOSSUX	homosexualism	AEIILNPRSSSTU	spiritualness
AEHILMOOSSTUX	homosexualist	AEIILOOPPRRRT	proprietorial
AEHILMOOSTUXY	homosexuality	AEIIMNNOOPRST	impersonation
AEHIMMNOPRTUY	immunotherapy	AEIIMNNOPRTTT	partitionment
AEHIMMOOPRSST	metamorphosis	AEIIMNOOPRSTT	temporisation
AEHIMNNOOPRTY	enantiomorphy	AEIIMNOOPRTTZ	temporization
AEHIMNNPRSSTT	transshipment	AEIIMNOPRSSSU	mispersuasion
AEHIMNPRSTUUY	superhumanity	AEIIMNOSSSTTY	systemisation
AEHINOPRRSTUW	nature-worship	AEIIMNOSSTTYZ	systemization
AEHINOPRSSSUV	vapourishness	AEIIMOOPRSSUV	semioviparous
AEHLLNOPRSUUY	sulphonylurea	AEIINNOOPPSTT	peptonisation
AEHLOQRRRTUUY	quarter-hourly	AEIINNOOPPTTZ	peptonization
AEHMNNOOORTTT	tooth-ornament	AEIINNOOSTTTU	Teutonisation
AEHMNOOPRRTTY	anthropometry	AEIINNOOTTTUZ	Teutonization
AEHMNOOPRSSSU	amorphousness	AEIINNOQRSTTU	quaternionist
AEIIILLLMNNST	millennialist	AEIINOOPPRRTX	expropriation
AEIIILLMMNNNS	millennianism	AEIINOOPRSTTX	extraposition
AEIIILLMMNNRS	millenniarism	AEIINOOPRSTTZ	posterization
AEIIILLMNORSS	millionairess	AEIINOORRRSTT	terrorisation
AEIIILLMNPRRY	preliminarily	AEIINOORRRTTZ	terrorization
AEIIILLMNRSTY	ministerially	AEIINOPRSSTTV	transpositive
AEIIILLMRRSTT	triliteralism	AEIINORRRSTTT	antiterrorist
AEIIILLMRRSVY	verisimilarly	AEIINORRSSSTT	transistorise
AEIIILMNNRSTU	unministerial	AEIINORRSSTTZ	transistorize
AEIIILNNOSTTU	luteinisation	AEIKKLMNNORUW	unworkmanlike
AEIIILNNOTTUZ	luteinization	AEIKLLNNPRRSW	lawn-sprinkler
AEIIILNORSSTT	sterilisation	AEIKLMNOPRSST	sportsmanlike
AEIIILNORSTTZ	sterilization	AEILLLMNOOSSS	salmonellosis
AEIIILPRRSSTU	spiritualiser	AEILLMMMNOOST	monometallism
AEIIILPRRSTUZ	spiritualizer	AEILLMMNOOSTT	monometallist
AEIIIMNOORSST	isomerisation	AEILLMNNOOTUY	unemotionally
AEIIIMNOORSTZ	isomerization	AEILMNNNOSSUW	unwomanliness
AEIIINNORSSSV	visionariness	AEILMNOPRTTUY	importunately
AEIIINNORSTTW	winterisation	AEILMNOPSSTUY	pneumatolysis
AEIIINNORTTWZ	winterization	AEILNNORSSTUV	voluntariness
AEIIINNOSSSTT	sensitisation	AEILNOOPRSTTT	tortoise-plant
AEIIINNOSSTTZ	sensitization	AEILNOOPSTTUX	expostulation
AEIILLNNNOTTY	intentionally	AEILNOORRTUVY	revolutionary
AEIILLNNORTVY	inventorially	AEILNOORSUVXY	over-anxiously
AEIILLNOQRTUV	ventriloquial	AEILNOPRRSTTU	perlustration

AEILOOOOPPPRS	prosopopoeial
AEILOOQRSTUUZ	Louis-Quatorze
AEIMNNOOPPRTT	apportionment
AEIMNNOORRSTT	remonstration
AEIMNOOOOPSST	onomatopoesis
AEIMNOPRSSTTT	Protestantism
AEIMORSSSSTTT	toastmistress
AEINNORSSSUUV	unsavouriness
AEINOOOPPRRTT	proportionate
AEINOOPRSSSSY	possessionary
AEINRRSSSTTTU	rust-resistant
AELLMNOPRRSUY	supernormally
AELMNNORRSTTY	remonstrantly
AELMNOPRSSTTU	postmenstrual
AELNNOOPSSTUY	spontaneously
AELOOPRSTTUXY	expostulatory
AEMMNNORSTUUV	verumontanums
AEMMNOOORSTTU	monotrematous
AEMNOOOPRSSZZ	mezzo-sopranos
AEMNOORRRSTTY	remonstratory
AENOOOPPRRTXY	proparoxytone
AFFGIIMNOSTUU	suffumigation
AFGHHIORRSTTT	straightforth
AFGHIILMNNOSS	salmon-fishing
AFGHIINOPRRST	profit-sharing
AFGIIILNNRTUY	infuriatingly
AFGIIKLNNNPPT	flint-knapping
AFGIILNNOOPTT	floating-point
AFGILNRRSTTUY	frustratingly
AFIIILNOOSSST	fossilisation
AFIIILNOOSSTZ	fossilization
AFIIINNOOPRST	infraposition
AFIILLORSTTUY	flirtatiously
AFIILOPRSSSUY	fissiparously
AGGHHIIPRSTTT	straight-pight
AGGHHMOPPRSYY	sphygmography
AGGHIILLNNSUY	languishingly
AGGHIKLNOOPPR	grappling-hook
AGGHILNOOPSST	sphagnologist
AGGIIILNNOSTU	isoagglutinin
AGGIIILNNSTTY	instigatingly
AGGIIINNORTTU	ingurgitation
AGGIILNNOPPRR	grappling-iron
AGGIILNQSSUZZ	quizzing-glass
AGGILLNOORSTY	laryngologist
AGGILOOORSSTT	agrostologist
AGHHIILLMNRST	thrashing-mill
AGHHIILMNRSTY	nightmarishly
AGHHIIMNNOSTU	mountains-high
AGHHIMNOORSTT	orthognathism
AGHHINOOPPRST	phonographist
AGHHINOOPRSST	sharpshooting
AGHHIOOPPRSTT	photographist
AGHHIOOPPRSTY	opisthography
AGHHIOOPRRSTT	orthographist
AGHHLLMOOOPTY	ophthalmology
AGHHLLOOPPSUY	phyllophagous
AGHHLMNNOOOPT	monophthongal
AGHHNOOORSTTU	orthognathous
AGHIIILNPRSTT	hair-splitting
AGHIILNNOSSTY	astonishingly
AGHIINNPPRSST	transshipping
AGHIMSSSTTUUU	tsutsugamushi
AGHINOOPSTTTT	Photostatting
AGHOOOPPPRRSY	prosopography
AGIIILLLNTTTY	titillatingly
AGIIILLMNRSTU	trilingualism
AGIIILNNNSTUY	insinuatingly
AGIIILNNORTUY	unoriginality
AGIIIMNNOOPRT	impignoration
AGIIINPPPRRST	spirit-rapping
AGIIILLNNOPRTY	rallying-point
AGIIILLNOOSSTY	syllogisation
AGIIILLNOOSTYZ	syllogization
AGIIILMOOPPRST	plagiotropism
AGIIILMOOPRSTT	primatologist
AGIIILNNOPRSTY	patronisingly
AGIIILNNOPRTYZ	patronizingly
AGIIILNPQRTTUY	quilting-party
AGIIILOORSSSTY	Assyriologist
AGIIMNOORRSUV	graminivorous
AGIINNOOOPPRT	oppignoration
AGIINNOPRSTTT	train-spotting
AGIINNOPRSTTY	star-ypointing
AGIINNOPRTTTY	potty-training
AGILMMNOOSTUY	numismatology
AGILMOOOPSSTU	plagiostomous
AGILMOORRSTTY	martyrologist
AGILNNOPPRUVY	unapprovingly
AGILOOOPPRSTU	plagiotropous
AGIMNOOOPRSUZ	zoosporangium
AGLLOOOSTTUUY	tautologously
AHHIKLNORTTWY	thankworthily
AHHILLMPPSTUY	spathiphyllum
AHHLLOPPRSYYY	hypsophyllary
AHHMNOOOPPRRT	anthropomorph
AHHMNOOOPPRTY	Pythonomorpha
AHHNOOOPPRSTY	anthroposophy
AHIIILNOOPRRT	horripilation
AHIIILNOPSSTY	syphilisation
AHIIILNOPSTTY	inhospitality
AHIIILNOPSTYZ	syphilization
AHIIJMNNNOOSS	Johnsonianism
AHIILNOOPRSTY	polyhistorian
AHIILNOORTTYZ	horizontality
AHIILNOPPRSTX	xiphiplastron
AHIIMNOPRSSTT	misanthropist
AHIINNOOPSTTY	hypnotisation
AHIINNOOPTTYZ	hypnotization
AHILLNOOPSSUY	anisophyllous
AHILMMOOPPSSU	psammophilous
AHIMNOOOPRSTT	somatotrophin
AHIMNOPPRSSST	sportsmanship
AHINOPPRRSSTT	transport-ship
AHKLNNOOPPTTY	phytoplankton
AHMOOOPRRSTUU	tauromorphous
AIIIILNNOQSTU	inquisitional
AIIIILNOQRSTU	inquisitorial
AIIILLMNNOSTU	illuminations
AIIILLMNPSTUY	pusillanimity
AIIILMNOPRSTY	postliminiary
AIIILNNOSTTTU	institutional
AIIIMMNNOORSS	Morisonianism
AIIIMMNNOSSST	Saint-Simonism

AIIIMNNOSSSTT Saint-Simonist
AIIIMNOOPPRRT impropriation
AIIIMNOOPRSTV improvisation
AIIIMOPRRSTVX improvisatrix
AIIINNNOOSTTV innovationist
AIIJNOOPSTTUX juxtaposition
AIILLMMNOOPSY polynomialism
AIILLMNOPSSUU pusillanimous
AIILLNNORTUVY involuntarily
AIILLNOOPRSVY provisionally
AIILLNPRSTUUY unspiritually
AIILMMPRSTTUY multipartyism
AIILNOOOPPRST propositional
AIILNOOPPSSTU suppositional
AIIMMNOOPSTTU impostumation
AIIMNOPSSSTTU Assumptionist
AIIMOOPRRSTVY improvisatory
AIINNOOPRSSTT transposition
AIINOPPPQRTUY appropinquity
AIIOOOPRSUVVV ovoviviparous
AILMOOOPSSSTX toxoplasmosis
AILORRSTTUUUV ultra-virtuous

B

BBCCEEJJOSTTU subject-object
BBCDGIIKLLNOU building-block
BBCEEHLORRRSY sherry-cobbler
BBCEEIORRSSUV oversubscribe
BBCEHMOORRSTU butcher's-broom
BBCEIILMNOSTU incombustible
BBCEIIRSTTTUU butter-biscuit
BBCGGHIILNNTU nightclubbing
BBCIILMNOSTUY incombustibly
BBDDEEGIILRRU bridge-builder
BBDDEELLOOORT blood-boltered
BBDEGIILNNOPU Bible-pounding
BBDIIILNOOSVY division-lobby
BBEEEEEEHIIJS heebie-jeebies
BBEEEEILLRSTT blister-beetle
BBEEEGILNRTUY burying-beetle
BBEGGIMNNORUY money-grubbing
BBEGHIILMNPTU Bible-thumping
BBEILMOORSTUY Bloomsburyite
BBHIIIILLMOPS bibliophilism
BBHIIIILLOPST bibliophilist
BCCCEIILNOPSU concupiscible
BCCCEIIMRRRSU circumscriber
BCCCHINOOOPRS bronchoscopic
BCCDELNOOOTUU double-coconut
BCCEEIILORRTT triboelectric
BCCEEIINRSTTY cyberneticist
BCCEEIKKKNORR △knickerbocker
BCCEEILORRTTU turbo-electric
BCCEFIIIINOST bioscientific
BCCEGILLNOOTX collecting-box
BCCEHIILLNRTU clincher-built
BCCEIIIJOSTTV objectivistic
BCCEIIILMMNOS incommiscible
BCCEIIILNNNOV inconvincible
BCCEIILLOOPSU ebullioscopic
BCCEILNORSTTU constructible
BCCENOORTTTUU coconut-butter
BCCGHIKLNOOPP chopping-block
BCDDDELLLOOOY cold-bloodedly
BCDDEEEILNNSU undescendible
BCDDEEEILNSSU deducibleness
BCDDEEHILNNOU double-chinned
BCDDEEINORRTU counterbidder
BCDDEIIILTTUY deductibility
BCDDGILLNOORU bloodcurdling
BCDEEEILNRSSU reducibleness
BCDEEFIIILTTY defectibility
BCDEEGIKNORST stockbreeding
BCDEEGINORRSS crossbreeding
BCDEEHNORRSTT stretcher-bond
BCDEEIIILNNRS indiscernible
BCDEEIIILPTTY deceptibility
BCDEEIILNNRSU undiscernible
BCDEEIKLNRSTY tickly-benders
BCDEELOORRSSU double-crosser
BCDEHILMOOORR chlorobromide
BCDEIIIILNRTY incredibility
BCDEIIILNNRSY indiscernibly
BCDEIILNNRSUY undiscernibly
BCDEIILNORTUY indolebutyric
BCDEIILNSSSUU undiscussible
BCDEIIMNOOSTY endosymbiotic
BCDIIILOPRTUY producibility
BCEEEEFFILRSV effervescible
BCEEEEHLRRSTU beetle-crusher
BCEEEFGIINNRR birefringence
BCEEEFIILMPRT imperfectible
BCEEEFPRRSTUU subprefecture
BCEEEGIINORST bioenergetics
BCEEEGILLNORT cobelligerent
BCEEEGILNOORS bernicle-goose
BCEEEHKNRRSTU trunk-breeches
BCEEEIILMPPRT imperceptible
BCEEEIJNOSSTV objectiveness
BCEEEINNNRRSU incense-burner
BCEEGIKLNRSUW swinge-buckler
BCEEIIIILPRTTY receptibility
BCEEIILMPPRTY imperceptibly
BCEEIILNNORTV inconvertible
BCEEIILNPSSTU insusceptible
BCEEIILPPRRST prescriptible
BCEEILMNOPSTT Contemptibles
BCEEILNNORTUV unconvertible
BCEEILNPSSTUU unsusceptible
BCEFFGIIKNOOO booking-office
BCEFFIOOPSSTU sub-post-office
BCEFIILLPSSTU self-publicist
BCEFIILLPSTUY self-publicity
BCEGHILNOOOTY biotechnology
BCEHHMMNOOOTY honeycomb-moth
BCEHILMRSTTUW tumbler-switch
BCEIILMNOOPSS incompossible
BCEIILNNORTVY inconvertibly
BCEIILNOPRRTU incorruptible
BCEIILNPSSTUY insusceptibly
BCEIINNOOORSV bioconversion
BCEIJLNSTUUVY subjunctively
BCEILMNOOPRYY polyembryonic
BCEILORSTTUVY obstructively

BCEINORSTTUUV unobstructive
BCGGIIKLNNOSW swinging-block
BCGHHILNOTTUU boulting-hutch
BCGHILNOOOORY chronobiology
BCGHILOOOPSYY biopsychology
psychobiology
BCGIIIILORRTY corrigibility
BCGIILOOORSTY cryobiologist
BCGIKLMNNOOTU mounting-block
BCGINOOSSTUUU subcontiguous
BCHIILLOOPPSY polyphloisbic
BCIIIIILMMSTY immiscibility
BCIIIIILNNTVY invincibility
BCIIILOORRSTY corrosibility
BCIILNOPRRTUY incorruptibly
BCIIMMNOOSSSU subcommission
BCILLNOOORTUU court-bouillon
BCINNOOSSTUUU subcontinuous
BDDEEEGGINNNR gender-bending
BDDEEEGJMNTTU judgement-debt
BDDEEFLNOORTU double-fronted
BDDEEFLNOOTUU double-founted
BDDEEGLNOOTUU double-tongued
BDDEEHLMOOTUU double-mouthed
BDDEEHLOOSTTU double-shotted
BDDEEIILNOSTY disobediently
BDDEEIIMMNOST disembodiment
BDDEEIJLNOOTU double-jointed
BDDEEILNNRSSU unbridledness
BDDEEILNOSTUY double-density
BDDEENNNOSSUU unboundedness
BDDEIINRSTTUU undistributed
BDDEILNNORSSW word-blindness
BDDEILNRSTUUY undisturbedly
BDEEEFGILNOTT feeding-bottle
BDEEEFLRTTUWY butterfly-weed
BDEEEFMMNORRU founder-member
BDEEEGIINNRRT interbreeding
BDEEEGILRRSTT trestle-bridge
BDEEEGIMOORSU embourgeoised
BDEEEHILLMNSU unembellished
BDEEEIILLNNSS indelibleness
BDEEEIILMPRRU empire-builder
BDEEEILLLLOWY yellow-bellied
BDEEEIMMMNRST dismemberment
BDEEELLMORSST bestsellerdom
BDEEELNNSSSSU unblessedness
BDEEELNPRSSTU suspender-belt
BDEEENOPSSSTT bespottedness
BDEEFFHLLOSUU double-shuffle
BDEEFIIILNSTY defensibility
BDEEGGHIILMRT thimblerigged
BDEEGHINNORUU unneighboured
BDEEGIILLNRWY bewilderingly
BDEEGIILMNOST disobligement
BDEEGINNNNSSU unbendingness
BDEEGINOOTTUU tongue-doubtie
BDEEHHLMMOTUU humble-mouthed
BDEEHLMMPRTUU rumbledethump
BDEEIIILNSSSV divisibleness
BDEEIIILNTTXY extendibility
BDEEIKLNRSTTY kittly-benders
BDEELLNOOSSSS bloodlessness
BDEELNNOSSSSU boundlessness
BDEFFIINOSTUU diffusion-tube
BDEFGGIIILNRT lifting-bridge
BDEGGINNOORVY governing-body
BDEGHHINOOORU neighbourhood
BDEGIIIILSTTY digestibility
BDEGIIJLNRRUY jerry-building
BDEGIILLMNSSY dissemblingly
BDEGIIMNNORRU mourning-bride
BDEHHMNOOORRS rhombohedrons
BDEHIIOPRSSTU subeditorship
BDEHJNOORRUUU bonheur-du-jour
BDEHNOOOPRSTU boustrophedon
BDEIIIIILNNTVY invendibility
BDEIIIILRTTVY divertibility
BDEILOOPRSSTU Lepidostrobus
BDEILOOQRSTUU double-or-quits
BDFFIIIILSTUY diffusibility
BDGGIIILLNOSY disobligingly
BDGGINNORRUUY burying-ground
BDHIIIIINNOST disinhibition
BDHIIIINORSTY disinhibitory
BDIIILLOSSTUY dissolubility
BEEEEFHINORRT thereinbefore
BEEEEGILLMNSW well-beseeming
BEEEEGIMNNSSS beseemingness
BEEEEHILNPRRS reprehensible
BEEEEHILNSTWW betweenwhiles
BEEEELLLRSSTT belles-lettres
BEEEGGGILNRTT begging-letter
BEEEGIILLLNSS illegibleness
BEEEGIIMNRTTT time-bettering
BEEEGILLLNRTY belligerently
BEEEGILMNNSUY unbeseemingly
BEEEGIMMNNRRU unremembering
BEEEGIMNORSSY embryogenesis
BEEEHILLMMNST embellishment
BEEEHILNPRRSY reprehensibly
BEEEIILNPRSSX inexpressible
BEEEIILPRRRSS irrepressible
BEEEILMMNRTTT embrittlement
BEEEILNPRSSSU supersensible
BEEEILNPRSSUX unexpressible
BEEEIMMNRRSTU reimbursement
BEEFGINORSTTT first-begotten
BEEFGINRRSTTU butter-fingers
BEEFHIMNRRSTU refurbishment
BEEFHOORRRSTT foster-brother
BEEFIIILLRTXY reflexibility
BEEFILLMORSUU umbelliferous
BEEGGHIILMRRT thimblerigger
BEEGGIIILMNTU time-beguiling
BEEGGIILNNNSS beginningless
BEEGHILNORSSU neighbourless
BEEGIIIILLRTY re-eligibility
BEEGIILLNNUVY unbelievingly
BEEHIKLNORRTU unbrotherlike
BEEHILLORSTWW whistle-blower
BEEHILNORRSST brotherliness
BEEHIPPRRSSTY presbytership
BEEIIIIILNSSST sensibilities

BEEIIILMMPRSS	impermissible
BEEIIILNNSSSV	invisibleness
BEEIIILNSTTXY	extensibility
BEEIIILRRSTVY	reversibility
BEEIILMNPRSSU	unimpressible
BEEIILNOPRRSS	irresponsible
BEEIILNORRSTV	introversible
BEEIILNPRSSXY	inexpressibly
BEEIILPRRRSSY	irrepressibly
BEEIILRRTTUVY	retributively
BEEILLNNOSSSU	insolubleness
BEEILNPRSSSUY	supersensibly
BEEILNRSSTUVY	subserviently
BEEILOQRSTUUU	turquoise-blue
BEEINOOQRSTUU	bone-turquoise
BEEINORSSSTUV	obtrusiveness
BEELLMOORSTUY	troublesomely
BEELPRSSTTUUY	supersubtlety
BEENNOOSSSTUU	bounteousness
BEFFGINNORRTU	burnt-offering
BEFFHILRSTTUY	butterfly-fish
BEFGIIILNRSTU	filibustering
BEFGILLOORSUU	globuliferous
BEFIIIILLNTXY	inflexibility
BEFIIILMRSSTU	filibusterism
BEFIILORSSTUU	filibusterous
BEFILNNOSSTUU	bountifulness
BEGGHIILNNTTU	lightning-tube
BEGGHMNOOORRU	borough-monger
BEGGIIIILLNTY	negligibility
BEGGILNOORTTT	globetrotting
BEGGINNNOORUU	bourguignonne
BEGHILNNORUUY	unneighbourly
BEGHIMNOPRSTW	bowstring-hemp
BEGIIIIILLNTY	ineligibility
BEGIILLMOPRTT	pilgrim-bottle
BEGILLMNNRTUY	untremblingly
BEHIIIIMNOSTX	exhibitionism
BEHIIIINOSTTX	exhibitionist
BEHIIILOPRTVY	prohibitively
BEHIMNOOSSSTY	tomboyishness
BEIIIILMRSSTY	remissibility
BEIIIILNNSSTY	insensibility
BEIIIILOPSSST	possibilities
BEIIIILRSSTTY	resistibility
BEIIILMMPRSSY	impermissibly
BEIIILNOSSTTY	ostensibility
BEIILNOOSSSUV	obliviousness
BEIILNOPRRSSY	irresponsibly
BEIILNORSTUVY	inobtrusively
BEIIOPRSSTTUU	subreptitious
BEILLMNOPSTUV	plumbisolvent
BEILNORSTUUVY	unobtrusively
BEIMNOPSSSTUU	bumptiousness
BEINNOOOSSSUX	obnoxiousness
BELLMNOOPSTUV	plumbosolvent
BELNOORSSSTUU	troublousness
BENOORRSTTTUU	trouser-button
BFILLOORSTUUU	tubuliflorous
BFILMMOORRSTU	strombuliform
BGHHNOORTTTUU	button-through
BGIIMNNORRRRU	burning-mirror
BHHMOOPPRRRYY	rhombporphyry
BHIIILMOPRSTT	timbrophilist
BHLMOOPRSTTUU	sulphur-bottom
BIIIILMMOPSSS	impossibilism
BIIIILMOPSSST	impossibilist
BIIIILMOPSSTY	impossibility
BIIILLMORRSUV	morbillivirus
BIILNNOOSTUUV	subinvolution
BILOOOPPRRSUY	opprobriously

C

CCCCEEINNOPSU	concupiscence
CCCCEGIIMNNOO	meningococcic
CCCCEIIKKLLTY	clickety-click
CCCCEIOOPRSTT	streptococcic
CCCDEEEENRRSU	recrudescence
CCCDEEENRRSUY	recrudescency
CCCDEEHIIOPRT	cercopithecid
CCCDEIIMNRSUU	uncircumcised
CCCDHIIOOOPRS	dichrooscopic
CCCDIIMNORTUU	circumduction
CCCDIMORRTUUY	circumductory
CCCEEEENNNOSS	consenescence
CCCEEEFIMNRRU	circumference
CCCEEEHILMORT	electrochemic
CCCEEENNNOSSY	consenescency
CCCEEFILMNRUU	circumfluence
CCCEEHHIRRSUV	church-service
CCCEEHIOPRSTU	Cercopithecus
CCCEEILOOPRST	electroscopic
CCCEFFHHIORRU	church-officer
CCCEFHKKOOORT	cock-of-the-rock
CCCEGIMNNOOSU	meningococcus
CCCEHIIMOSTYZ	schizomycetic
CCCEIIMMNOOOR	microeconomic
CCCEIINNORTTY	concentricity
CCCEIIORSSSTY	cysticercosis
CCCEILMPRSTUY	circumspectly
CCCEIOOPPRSST	spectroscopic
CCCEOOPRSSTTU	△streptococcus
CCCIIMNORSTUU	succinctorium
CCDDEEGINNNOS	condescending
CCDDEELLNOTUW	well-conducted
CCDEEEEEFNRSV	defervescence
CCDEEEEFNRSVY	defervescency
CCDEEEEILNQSU	deliquescence
CCDEEEFILNOST	self-conceited
CCDEEEFLLLOST	self-collected
CCDEEEILNNRTT	client-centred
CCDEEEINNOSST	conceitedness
CCDEEELLLORTY	recollectedly
CCDEEELLNNOTW	well-connected
CCDEEELLNORTU	unrecollected
CCDEEELLNOSST	collectedness
CCDEEENNNORSS	concernedness
CCDEEFILNOSTV	self-convicted
CCDEEHIILNNPY	phencyclidine
CCDEEHILORRTY	hydroelectric
CCDEEILMNOPSY	encyclopedism
CCDEEILNOPSTY	encyclopedist
CCDEEIMOORRTT	microdetector
CCDEEINNNOOSS	condescension

CCDEEINOOPRUW	owner-occupied
CCDEEINOORSST	cordocentesis
CCDEEINOPPRUU	unpreoccupied
CCDEEIOOPRSTU	deuteroscopic
CCDEEJNNORTUU	unconjectured
CCDEELNNNORUY	unconcernedly
CCDEELNOOPPRW	copple-crowned
CCDEGINNNOORT	connecting-rod
CCDEHKLNOORTU	round-the-clock
CCDEIINNNOOST	disconnection
CCDEIINNOORST	disconcertion
CCDEIMNOORSTU	semiconductor
CCDEIMOOSSTUY	discomycetous
CCDELMNOOOPUU	leuco-compound
CCDGINNNNOOTU	non-conducting
CCDHINOOPRSTU	conductorship
CCDIIMNNOOPUY	pycnoconidium
CCEEEEEFFNRSV	effervescence
CCEEEEFFLNORS	efflorescence
CCEEEEFFNRSVY	effervescency
CCEEEELMNORTT	electrocement
CCEEEFFIOSTTV	cost-effective
CCEEEFGINNRTU	centrifugence
CCEEEFILNNORS	inflorescence
CCEEEFILORRRT	ferroelectric
CCEEEFNOORRRT	ferroconcrete
CCEEEHHIIKNNR	chinkerinchee
CCEEEHIPRTTUY	hypereutectic
CCEEEHMOOPRRT	chemoreceptor
CCEEEIILOPRTZ	piezoelectric
CCEEEIINNNNOV	inconvenience
CCEEEILMNNORT	reconcilement
CCEEEILMORRTT	electrometric
CCEEEINNNOQSU	inconsequence
CCEEEINNRRRTU	intercurrence
CCEEFFIIINNSU	insufficience
CCEEFFIINOSTT	cost-efficient
CCEEFGIIINOST	geoscientific
CCEEFIIINPRST	interspecific
	prescientific
CCEEFINNOORTY	confectionery
CCEEGGILNNOOU	gluconeogenic
CCEEGHIINOSTZ	schizogenetic
CCEEGHINOPSTY	psychogenetic
CCEEGIIMNORST	geocentricism
CCEEGIINORTTY	egocentricity
CCEEHHHRRSSTU	screech-thrush
CCEEHHINOORRT	heterochronic
CCEEHIILLOPRT	electrophilic
CCEEHILOOPRTT	photoelectric
CCEEHIMMNNOST	mnemotechnics
CCEEHIMNNORRY	chimney-corner
CCEEHIMOSSTYZ	Schizomycetes
CCEEIILNOORST	isoelectronic
CCEEIILRRSTUU	sericiculture
CCEEIIMNRTUVV	circumventive
CCEEIINNNOSST	inconsistence
CCEEIINNOSTUV	inconsecutive
CCEEIJMNORSTU	misconjecture
CCEEILNOORTTU	electrocution
CCEEILNOSTUVY	consecutively
CCEEILOOPRSTT	electro-optics
CCEEIMOPRRSTT	spectrometric
CCEEINNOOPPRT	preconception
CCEEINNORRSST	incorrectness
CCEEINOOPRRTU	Europocentric
CCEEINOOPRRUW	owner-occupier
CCEEINORSTTTU	section-cutter
CCEEIOPRRSSTU	prosecutrices
CCEELLNOORRTT	rent-collector
CCEELLSSSSSUY	successlessly
CCEEMNNNNORTU	unconcernment
CCEENNOOOVVXX	convexo-convex
CCEENOPRRRTUY	petrocurrency
CCEFFIIINNSUY	insufficiency
CCEFIIILMORST	microfelsitic
CCEFIIILMRSST	self-criticism
CCEFIIINNNOST	non-scientific
CCEFIILMNORUX	circumflexion
CCEFILNOOSSSU	self-conscious
CCEGHINNORSSS	scorchingness
CCEGIIKKNOPPT	pocket-picking
CCEGIIKNNQSTU	quick-scenting
CCEGILOOOOTXY	ecotoxicology
CCEGINNNORSTY	constringency
CCEHHIINOPRSZ	schizophrenic
CCEHIIKNOPSTY	psychokinetic
CCEHIILOSSTTY	cholecystitis
CCEHILLOOPRST	collectorship
CCEHILMNOORTY	Chloromycetin
CCEHIMOPRRSTY	psychrometric
CCEHIMOPRSSTY	psychometrics
CCEHIMORSTTYY	cytochemistry
CCEHIOOPRRSTU	urethroscopic
CCEHIOPRSSSSU	successorship
CCEIIIMORSSTV	viscosimetric
CCEIIIOPRRRTY	irreciprocity
CCEIILNNNOSTY	inconsciently
CCEIIMNNNOOST	connectionism
CCEIIMNNOOPST	misconception
CCEIIMNNORTUV	circumvention
CCEIIMNOORRST	miscorrection
CCEIIMNOOSSSU	semiconscious
CCEIINNNOSSTY	inconsistency
CCEIINNOOPSTT	Conceptionist
CCEIINNOOSSST	concessionist
CCEIINNOOSSTU	conscientious
CCEIINOSSSSTU	successionist
CCEIJLNNOTUVY	conjunctively
CCEIJNNNOTUUV	unconjunctive
CCEIKLOOPSTTU	cuckoo-spittle
CCEILNNNOOSUV	non-conclusive
CCEIMMOOPRRTU	microcomputer
CCEINNOOSSSSU	consciousness
CCELMOOPRSSUY	cyclospermous
CCELOORRSSSST	cross-crosslet
CCENNNNOORRTU	non-concurrent
CCENOORRRSTTU	reconstructor
CCFKKKKNNOOOR	knock-for-knock
CCGHHHHIIMRSU	High-Churchism
CCGIIILOOOSST	sociologistic
CCGIIKNNOOPTT	cotton-picking
CCHHIILOPPRSY	psychrophilic
CCHHIMOOOPRST	photochromics

CCHHIOPPSSSYY	psychophysics
CCHIINNORSSTY	synchronistic
CCHIINNORSTYY	synchronicity
CCHILNOOORRRU	chlorocruorin
CCIILMOOOPSST	cosmopolitics
CCIIMOOOSSTXY	mycotoxicosis
CCIINNOOPSSUU	inconspicuous
CCILNNOOSSUUY	unconsciously
CCILNOOPSSUUY	conspicuously
CCIOORRRSSSSW	criss-cross-row
CDDDEEEGLNNOS	long-descended
CDDEEEENNPRTU	unprecedented
CDDEEEFFINNRU	undifferenced
CDDEEEFLMNNOS	self-condemned
CDDEEEGLNORST	golden-crested
CDDEEEHIORRTT	other-directed
CDDEEEHIRSTTW	wide-stretched
CDDEEEIINNRRT	inner-directed
CDDEEEMMNNORU	unrecommended
CDDEEFHIOOPRT	pitched-roofed
CDDEEHIIKMNNT	kitchen-midden
CDDEEIILLNORS	ill-considered
CDDEEIILOOPPS	dipleidoscope
CDDEEILNNRSUY	undiscernedly
CDDEEILNOOSTY	Dicotyledones
CDDEEINOSSSUU	deciduousness
CDDEELNNOSSUU	uncloudedness
CDDEFIIMNOSTU	undiscomfited
CDDEHHILOORRY	hydrochloride
CDDEHMOOORSST	odd-come-shorts
CDDEIIILNNPSU	undisciplined
CDDEIINNNOOTU	unconditioned
CDDIIMMOOOSSU	discommodious
CDEEEEELMORRT	decelerometer
CDEEEEFINSSTV	defectiveness
CDEEEEFLLNSSY	defencelessly
CDEEEEFLLORUW	flower-de-leuce
CDEEEEGLNNSST	neglectedness
CDEEEEHNORRRT	three-cornered
CDEEEEIINNPRX	inexperienced
CDEEEEINNPRUX	unexperienced
CDEEEEINPSSTV	deceptiveness
CDEEEELLPRSTW	well-respected
CDEEEFFILLSTU	self-deceitful
CDEEEFFLNOSSS	self-confessed
CDEEEFHKLNRSW	Schwenkfelder
CDEEEFIILNRTU	unelectrified
CDEEEFIINNSST	deficientness
CDEEEFILNOPST	self-deception
CDEEEFILNSSTU	deceitfulness
CDEEEGHIILNSW	weeding-chisel
CDEEEGHINOPST	pigeon-chested
CDEEEGILNORRT	telerecording
CDEEEIIMNNOTT	mine-detection
CDEEEIINPRSTV	vice-president
CDEEEIKMPQRTU	quick-tempered
CDEEEILMORRST	sclerodermite
CDEEEILNPRUVY	unperceivedly
CDEEEIMOPRSSV	decompressive
CDEEEINNNRSSU	underniceness
CDEEEINRSSTUV	reductiveness
CDEEEINSSSTUV	seductiveness
CDEEELMNOPSSX	complexedness
CDEEEMNNOPRSU	unrecompensed
CDEEENNNOSSTT	contentedness
CDEEENOORRSTV	seroconverted
CDEEENPSSSSTU	suspectedness
CDEEFFIILLNST	self-inflicted
CDEEFFILNNOST	self-confident
CDEEFGILNORRS	self-recording
CDEEFIILNORST	self-direction
CDEEFIILNSTUV	self-inductive
CDEEFILPRSSTU	disrespectful
CDEEFINNOORTV	over-confident
CDEEGIINNOORT	derecognition
CDEEHILMNNORW	women-children
CDEEHILNOORTU	leucitohedron
CDEEHIMMNOPRS	miscomprehend
CDEEHIMNORRSY	dysmenorrheic
CDEEHLLOOORUW	whole-coloured
CDEEHNNOOOPPS	phonendoscope
CDEEIIIMNRSTT	deterministic
CDEEIIKLQRSUV	quicksilvered
CDEEIILNORSST	directionless
CDEEIILNOSSSU	deliciousness
CDEEIILPRSTVY	descriptively
CDEEIIMNORSTT	densitometric
CDEEIINORRSTT	derestriction
CDEEIJNPRRSUU	jurisprudence
CDEEIKNORRTTY	kitty-cornered
CDEEILLOORRUV	liver-coloured
CDEEILLOPRRSU	supercollider
CDEEILNNOOPRS	scolopendrine
CDEEILNOPRRTW	triple-crowned
CDEEILOORRSUV	versicoloured
CDEEILORRTUVY	overcredulity
CDEEILRSTTUVY	destructively
CDEEIMMNOORST	endosmometric
CDEEIMNOOPRSS	decompression
CDEEINNNOSSTU	continuedness
CDEEINOPQSTTU	cinque-spotted
CDEEKKLNRSTUU	knuckleduster
CDEELLMNOOORU	lemon-coloured
CDEELMOOORSUU	mouse-coloured
CDEELMOORRSSU	sclerodermous
CDEELNOOORSTU	stone-coloured
CDEELNORSSSUU	credulousness
CDEELNPSSTUUY	unsuspectedly
CDEELOORRSUUV	overcredulous
CDEENNOOPRRST	correspondent
CDEFFGIILNNOS	self-confiding
CDEFFGINOORRU	ground-officer
CDEFFLNOORSUU	snuff-coloured
CDEFGIINNNOSS	confidingness
CDEFIILNNOSTU	self-induction
CDEFILNNOSTTU	discontentful
CDEGHHIKOSTTU	sick-thoughted
CDEGHIILNORST	riding-clothes
CDEGHILNNORTU	underclothing
CDEGIIKOPRRST	porridge-stick
CDEGIILNNORSY	consideringly
CDEGIIMMOOSTY	sigmoidectomy
CDEGIIMOOOPSS	sigmoidoscope
CDEGIINNNORSU	unconsidering

CDEGIINNNOSTT	discontenting
CDEGIINOOOSUY	gynodioecious
CDEGILNNOOORY	endocrinology
CDEGINNOOPRRS	corresponding
CDEGINORRSSSS	cross-dressing
CDEHHIMNNOOST	smooth-chinned
CDEHHIOOORRST	rhodochrosite
CDEHIIIOPRSTY	spheroidicity
CDEHIIKLTTTWY	thick-wittedly
CDEHIIKMNSTTU	stick-in-the-mud
CDEHIIKNORSTY	hydrokinetics
CDEHIIMNOPRRU	perichondrium
CDEHIIOOOPPRT	photoperiodic
CDEHIMOOPPRSU	pseudomorphic
CDEHIMOORTTYY	thyroidectomy
CDEHINNORSTUU	urchin-snouted
CDEHKNRRSTTUU	thunderstruck
CDEHNNOORSSSY	synchondroses
CDEIIIINNSTTV	indistinctive
CDEIIILMNOSTU	consimilitude
CDEIIILNOPSTY	epicondylitis
CDEIIILNSTTVY	distinctively
CDEIIIMPRSSTV	descriptivism
CDEIIINNSTTUV	undistinctive
CDEIIJLNSTUVY	disjunctively
CDEIIJNOSSSUU	judiciousness
CDEIIMNOOOPST	decomposition
CDEIINNRSSTUU	unscrutinised
CDEIINNRSTUUZ	unscrutinized
CDEIINOOPPRSY	pycnidiospore
CDEIINOPRTUWW	picture-window
CDEIINORSTTUU	rectitudinous
CDEIIRSSTTTUV	destructivist
CDEIIRSTTTUVY	destructivity
CDEILLMOORTUU	multicoloured
CDEILLNORSUUY	incredulously
CDEILMNOOPRSU	scolopendrium
CDEILMNOOPSUY	compendiously
CDEILNNOPRSTY	nondescriptly
CDEILNORSSSUU	ludicrousness
CDEINNOOPRTUV	non-productive
CDEINOOOPPRUW	porcupine-wood
CDEKLMNOOOPUU	leuko-compound
CDELMNNOOOOTY	monocotyledon
CDELOOORRTTUU	trout-coloured
CDELOOPRTTUUY	putty-coloured
CDELOORRSTUUY	rusty-coloured
CDEMNNNOOOPRU	non-compounder
CDEOOOPRRRSSW	word-processor
CDFGILNNNOOUY	confoundingly
CDFIIMNOORSTY	disconformity
CDGHIILOOORST	orchidologist
CDGIIILOOSSTU	suicidologist
CDGIIINOSTTUY	discontiguity
CDGIIMOOOPSSY	sigmoidoscopy
CDGIINOOSSTUU	discontiguous
CDHHIIIMORRTY	idiorrhythmic
CDHHIMNOOPRUY	hypochondrium
CDHIIMNNOOORT	mitochondrion
CDHILMOOOSTUY	dichotomously
CDHINNOORSSSY	synchondrosis
CDHMNOOOOPRTU	ortho-compound
CDIIIINNNOSTT	indistinction
CDIIIJLNOSUUY	injudiciously
CDIIIMMNOOSSS	discommission
CDIIINNOSTTUY	discontinuity
CDIIINOORSSSV	cross-division
CDIINNOOSSTUU	discontinuous
CDIMNNOOOPRTU	nitro-compound
CDINNNOOOPRTU	non-production
CEEEEEFLNRRSV	self-reverence
CEEEEEGHINNPT	eighteen-pence
CEEEEEILNORRT	electioneerer
CEEEEFFINSSTV	effectiveness
CEEEEFILNORST	free-selection
CEEEEFILNSSTX	self-existence
CEEEEFLPRRTTT	letter-perfect
CEEEEFMNNORRT	re-enforcement
CEEEEFPPRRRTT	preterperfect
CEEEEGHINORTT	heterogenetic
CEEEEGIINOPRT	epeirogenetic
CEEEEHLNRSSSS	cheerlessness
CEEEEHNPRRSTT	three-per-cents
CEEEEIMNNPRSU	supereminence
CEEEEINNNPPTY	tenpenny-piece
CEEEEINNPRSUV	supervenience
CEEEEINPRSSTV	receptiveness
CEEEEINRSSSSV	recessiveness
CEEEEINRSSSTV	secretiveness
CEEEEINSSSSVX	excessiveness
CEEEEIOPRTTVX	exteroceptive
CEEEEJNNRSTUV	rejuvenescent
CEEEELNORRTTV	teleconverter
CEEEFFIILNTVY	ineffectively
CEEEFGILNSTUX	self-executing
CEEEFHLNPSSSU	speechfulness
CEEEFIINNSSTV	infectiveness
CEEEFILORRSVW	flower-service
CEEEFIMNNORRT	reinforcement
CEEEFIMNPRSST	imperfectness
CEEEFINORRTTU	counterfeiter
CEEEFNNPRSSTU	unperfectness
CEEEGHIKNNOTU	tongue-in-cheek
CEEEGHILLNOPT	phellogenetic
CEEEGHIMNORTT	thermogenetic
CEEEGIIILNNRV	receiving-line
CEEEGIIINPSTT	epigeneticist
CEEEGIILLNNRT	intelligencer
CEEEHHIPRSTTY	hyperesthetic
CEEEHHKLRSTTU	Kletterschuhe
CEEEHILLLMOSU	hemicellulose
CEEEHILMNOPRT	nephelometric
CEEEHIMNOPRSV	comprehensive
CEEEHLMORRTTY	electrothermy
CEEEHLNORSSSU	lecherousness
CEEEHMMNOSTYY	Hymenomycetes
CEEEIILORSTTV	toilet-service
CEEEIIMNNRTTT	intermittence
CEEEIINOPRTTV	interoceptive
CEEEILMMORRST	electromerism
CEEEILMNPRSTU	multipresence
CEEEILMNRSSSS	mercilessness
CEEEILMOORTTV	electromotive
CEEEILNOSSSSV	voicelessness

CEEEILNPPRRSU	pluripresence
CEEEILNPRSSSS	pricelessness
CEEEILNSSSUVX	exclusiveness
CEEEILPPRSTVY	perspectively
CEEEINNNOORTV	conventioneer
CEEEINNOORRRT	reconnoiterer
CEEEINNOPPTWY	twopenny-piece
CEEEINOPSSTTX	post-existence
CEEEINRSSSUVX	excursiveness
CEEEIOPRRSTTV	retrospective
CEEELMNNOSSUW	unwelcomeness
CEEEMNOPRSTYY	Pyrenomycetes
CEEEOPRRRSSSV	process-server
CEEFFGHINOOSU	coffee-housing
CEEFFIIILNNTY	inefficiently
CEEFFIILNNOST	self-infection
CEEFFIOORRRRS	ferrosoferric
CEEFGIIKNRRST	grief-stricken
CEEFGIINNNOTU	eigenfunction
CEEFIIJLNNOST	self-injection
CEEFIIJLNNOTU	fuel-injection
CEEFIIKLNORSU	nickeliferous
CEEFIILLNOTWZ	fellow-citizen
CEEFIILNOSUVY	veneficiously
CEEFIIMNOPRST	perfectionism
CEEFIINOPRSTT	△perfectionist
CEEFILLLORSUU	celluliferous
CEEFILMOOPRST	telescopiform
CEEFILNOORRTT	retroflection
CEEFILNORTTUY	counterfeitly
CEEFINOORSSSU	ferociousness
CEEFLMOORRSST	recomfortless
CEEFLNORRTUUY	counter-fleury
CEEGGHLNOOOTY	geotechnology
CEEGHHIINPPRW	whipping-cheer
CEEGHHILNOPTT	Phlegethontic
CEEGHIIINPRSV	receiving-ship
CEEGHIIKLMTTU	Gemütlichkeit
CEEGHIIKLNPRR	pickle-herring
CEEGHIIKNRSTV	knight-service
CEEGHIIMOORST	isogeothermic
CEEGHIINOSSSZ	schizogenesis
CEEGHIIRRSTUW	cruiserweight
CEEGHIMNOOPRT	morphogenetic
CEEGHINOOPRTT	genetotrophic
CEEGHINOPSSSY	psychogenesis
CEEGHINORTTUW	counter-weight
CEEGIIMNNOPRU	mourning-piece
CEEGIIMNOORRV	receiving-room
CEEGILLNORSSV	level-crossing
CEEGILMMNOTTU	telecommuting
CEEGIMNNORRTY	retromingency
CEEHHIIMORRTU	Cheirotherium
CEEHHIMMOOORT	homoeothermic
CEEHHIMMORSTT	thermochemist
CEEHHIMOOPRRT	heteromorphic
CEEHHIOOPRRTT	heterotrophic
CEEHIIKLNRSSS	lickerishness
CEEHIIMMOPSTT	committeeship
CEEHIIMORTTXY	exothermicity
CEEHIINPRRSSV	scrivenership
CEEHIKLOPRSTU	prick-the-louse
CEEHIKNORSSSS	horse-sickness
CEEHILLNNOPSU	Punchinelloes
CEEHILOORSTTU	heteroclitous
CEEHILOPRTVYY	hypervelocity
CEEHIMMNNOSTT	mnemotechnist
CEEHIMMRSSSTT	Messerschmitt
CEEHIMNNOOPRS	comprehension
CEEHIMNNORSTT	ethnocentrism
CEEHIMNOPSSTU	Semnopithecus
CEEHIMOORSTTY	stoechiometry
CEEHIMOPPRRTY	hypermetropic
CEEHINNOPSSSY	synecphonesis
CEEHINNORRSSY	resynchronise
CEEHINNORRSYZ	resynchronize
CEEHINOPPRRST	precentorship
CEEHIOOPRRSTU	cheiropterous
CEEHLNOOOPRTT	photoelectron
CEEHLOOPRRSTU	electrophorus
CEEHNOOPRTTWW	twopenceworth
CEEHOOOPPRRTT	photoreceptor
CEEIIIMMMPRST	metempiricism
CEEIIIMMPRSTT	metempiricist
CEEIIIMORSTTT	meteoriticist
CEEIIKKLNPRSW	winkle-pickers
CEEIILMNNRSTY	reminiscently
CEEIILMNRSTTU	lectisternium
CEEIILRRSTTVY	restrictively
CEEIIMNNRTTTY	intermittency
CEEIIMNOPPRST	misperception
CEEIIMNOPTTUV	uncompetitive
CEEIIMPPRSSTV	perspectivism
CEEIINOPRSTTV	introspective
CEEIIPPRSSTTV	perspectivist
CEEILLMNOQTUU	multiloquence
CEEILLNSUUVXY	unexclusively
CEEILMNNOOQSU	somniloquence
CEEILMNNOPTTY	incompetently
CEEILMNOORSUY	ceremoniously
CEEILNNOOPRTU	nucleoprotein
CEEILNOOPRRST	scleroprotein
CEEILNOSSSTUY	necessitously
CEEILOPPRSTVY	prospectively
CEEILOPRSTTTY	electrotypist
CEEILORRSTTUU	ostreiculture
CEEILPQRSTUUY	picturesquely
CEEIMMNNOOPTT	omnicompetent
CEEIMNNOORSUU	unceremonious
CEEIMNOOPRRSS	recompression
CEEIMNOOPSSST	compositeness
CEEINNORSTTTU	reconstituent
CEEINOOPRRSSV	corresponsive
CEEINOOPRRSTT	retrospection
CEEINOORRSSSV	corrosiveness
CEEIOOPRSSSTT	stereoscopist
CEEIOPPPRRSTY	copper-pyrites
CEEIOPRRSSTUX	prosecutrixes
CEEJMNOPRRTUU	counter-jumper
CEEKMMNOORSSU	smoke-consumer
CEEKNOORRSTTU	counterstroke
CEEKOOPRRSTTU	trouser-pocket
CEELOOPPRSTTU	plectopterous
CEELOOPRRSSTT	protectorless

CEELPQRSSTUUU	sculpturesque
CEELRRSSSTTUU	structureless
CEEMMNNOOPTUY	pneumonectomy
CEEMNNNOOPRTU	pronouncement
CEEMNOOPRRTUU	neurocomputer
CEEMOPPRRSTUU	supercomputer
CEENOORSSSTUU	courteousness
CEEOOOOPPPRRS	pooper-scooper
CEFFFGIILNSSU	self-sufficing
CEFFGIKNNOORS	off-reckonings
CEFFIINOOSSSU	officiousness
CEFGHIIKNNOPP	chopping-knife
CEFGILMNNOSSU	self-consuming
CEFGINOORSSTT	soft-sectoring
CEFHIMMOORRRU	ferro-chromium
CEFHINOOPRSSS	confessorship
CEFIIILLMNOPR	penicilliform
CEFIINNNOOPRT	non-proficient
CEFIIOOPRSTTU	profectitious
CEFILMMNNOOSU	self-communion
CEFILNOPRRTUY	perfunctorily
CEGGHLNOOOORY	geochronology
CEGGIINNNORRT	groin-centring
CEGGIINNNORSU	unrecognising
CEGGIINNNORUZ	unrecognizing
CEGHHIILOPRSY	hieroglyphics
CEGHIIILLNNPS	spine-chilling
CEGHIILLNOOST	lichenologist
CEGHIILOOOSTY	stoicheiology
CEGHIINNNNPPY	penny-pinching
CEGHINNOOSTUU	counting-house
CEGHOPRRSSUYY	psychosurgery
CEGIIIKNRTTTW	ticket-writing
CEGIIILNOORST	coreligionist
CEGIIINNOORRT	irrecognition
CEGIILNOOSSTT	insectologist
	Scientologist
CEGIIMMNNOSTU	time-consuming
CEGIIMMNNOTTU	cummingtonite
CEGIIMNOORRTT	trigonometric
CEGIIMNORTTUY	tumorgenicity
CEGIINNOOPRSS	processioning
CEGIINNOPPRRT	intercropping
CEGIKLNOOSSST	stocking-soles
CEGILMMOORSTY	myrmecologist
CEGILMOOOSSTT	cosmetologist
CEGILOORSSTTU	Etruscologist
CEGIMMNNOOOSY	gynomonoecism
CEGINNOPRSTUY	counterspying
CEGINOPRRRSSS	cross-springer
CEGNNOOOPRSTY	röntgenoscopy
CEGNNOORSSSUU	congruousness
CEHHIIINNORTT	ornithichnite
CEHHIIIPSSTTY	physitheistic
CEHHIILOPRSTY	chrysophilite
CEHHIIMMOOORT	homoiothermic
CEHHIIMOOPRRT	theriomorphic
CEHHIMMOOOOPR	homoeomorphic
CEHHINOPRRTYY	phycoerythrin
CEHIIKNOPSSSY	psychokinesis
CEHIILMOSSUVY	mischievously
CEHIILNNOOSTT	coin-in-the-slot
CEHIIMMOOORST	homoeroticism
CEHIIMOORSTTY	stoichiometry
CEHIINOOOPRTT	iontophoretic
CEHIINOPPRSST	inspectorship
CEHIIOPRRSTTT	trichopterist
CEHILNOOPRSSU	counselorship
CEHILNOPSTTYY	polysynthetic
CEHIMOPRSSTTY	psychometrist
CEHIOOPPRRSST	prosectorship
CEHIOOPPRRSTT	protectorship
CEHIOOPRRSTTU	trichopterous
CEHIOOPRSSSTY	spherocytosis
CEHIOOPSSSTTT	stethoscopist
CEIIILMNOPSST	impoliticness
CEIIILNNSTTVY	instinctively
CEIIILNPRSTVY	inscriptively
CEIIIMNOPSTUY	impecuniosity
CEIIIMORSTUVV	vivisectorium
CEIIJNOOPRSTT	projectionist
CEIILLLNOOSTV	violoncellist
CEIILMNOPSUUY	impecuniously
CEIILNNNNOTTY	incontinently
CEIILNNOORTTU	interlocution
CEIILNOPSSSSU	suspicionless
CEIILNORRTTUX	interlocutrix
CEIILNRSTTUVY	instructively
CEIILOPPRSTUY	precipitously
CEIILPRRSTTUU	stirpiculture
CEIILRRSSTTUU	sericulturist
CEIIMNNORRTTU	micronutrient
CEIIMNNORSSSU	criminousness
CEIIMNOOOPRST	recomposition
CEIIMNOOPRSTT	protectionism
CEIINNNOOSTTV	conventionist
CEIINNNOPRTTU	interpunction
CEIINNOOPRSTT	introspection
CEIINNORSSSUU	incuriousness
CEIINNRSTTUUV	uninstructive
CEIINOOOPRSST	oneiroscopist
CEIINOOPRSSTT	retinoscopist
CEIINOOPRSTTT	protectionist
CEIINOORSSTUV	insectivorous
CEIINOORTTUXY	neurotoxicity
CEIINOPRSSSTU	percussionist
CEIIOOPRSSSTV	visceroptosis
CEILLMNOOSTTY	tonsillectomy
CEILMNNOOOSSU	mononucleosis
CEILMNOPSTUVY	consumptively
CEILNNOOSTTUY	contentiously
CEILNNORSSTUU	uncourtliness
CEILNOORRTTUY	interlocutory
CEILOPPRSSUUY	perspicuously
CEIMMMNOORSTY	monosymmetric
CEIMMMNOORSUU	Eurocommunism
CEIMMNOORSTUU	Eurocommunist
CEIMNNOOORTTU	countermotion
CEIMNORRSSSTU	Russocentrism
CEIMOOOPPSSTT	metoposcopist
CEINNNOOSSSUU	innocuousness
CEINNNOOSTTUU	uncontentious
CEINNOOOPRSTU	counter-poison
CEINNOPRRSSTU	incorruptness

CEINOOQRSSSTU	cross-question
CEINOORRSTTTV	controvertist
CEINORRSSSTTU	Russocentrist
CEIOOOPPPRRRT	proprioceptor
CEOOPPRRSSSSU	cross-purposes
CFFIIILNOOSUY	inofficiously
CFGHIILLNNNUY	unflinchingly
CFGHIMNNOORTU	unforthcoming
CFGIIIKMNOSST	kissing-comfit
CFGIKLNOOSTTU	floutingstock
CFGIMNNNNOOOR	nonconforming
CFHILMOOORRST	chloroformist
CFHNNOOORRSTW	crown-of-thorns
CFILNORSTUUUY	infructuously
CFIMNNNOOORST	△nonconformist
CFIMNNNOOORTY	nonconformity
CGGHIIILMNORT	microlighting
CGHHIILLOORSS	schoolgirlish
CGHHIILOOSTTY	ichthyologist
CGHHIKMNORSTU	mocking-thrush
CGHIIKNORSTTW	throwing-stick
CGHIILNOORSTW	writing-school
CGHIILOORSSTT	Christologist
CGHLNNOOORSYY	synchronology
CGHLOOOOPSYYZ	zoopsychology
CGIIIKNNOPSTT	sticking-point
CGIIILLOOOPST	oligopolistic
CGIIILMNOORST	criminologist
CGIIILMOOSTTV	victimologist
CGIIILNOOSSTU	sociolinguist
CGIIIMNNOPRRT	microprinting
CGIIJNNOORSTU	coursing-joint
CGIIKNNOOPSTT	pointing-stock
CGIJNNNOORTUW	grown-junction
CGILNNOORSUUY	incongruously
CHHIILNOOPPSU	unphilosophic
CHHIILOPRSTUU	thiosulphuric
CHHILMOOPPRTY	lymphotrophic
CHHILOPPRSUUY	hyposulphuric
CHHIMMOOOPRST	photochromism
CHHIOOORSSTTU	orthostichous
CHHIOOPRSSTYY	psychohistory
CHIIIIMNORSST	histrionicism
CHIIILNOPRTTT	lithontriptic
CHIIILOOPRSST	solicitorship
CHIIILOPPRSST	scripophilist
CHIILOORSSSTU	lissotrichous
CHIIOOOPRRSTT	proto-historic
CHIIOOPTTTXYY	phytotoxicity
CHILLMOOPRSUY	microphyllous
CHILNOOORSSUY	isochronously
CHILNOOPPRSSU	proconsulship
CHILOPPRRSUUY	pyrosulphuric
CHIMNOOOPRSST	monostrophics
CHLNNOORSSUYY	synchronously
CIIIINNSTTTVY	instinctivity
CIIILNRSTTUUV	viniculturist
CIIILRSTTTUUV	viticulturist
CIILLNOPSTUUY	punctiliously
CIILMMOOOPSST	cosmopolitism
CIILMNOOPSSTU	compulsionist
CIILNNOOSSTUV	convulsionist
CIIMNNOOOPSST	monopsonistic
CIIMNNOOORSTT	contortionism
CIIMNOPSTTUVY	consumptivity
CIIMOOOPRRSTY	microporosity
CIINNOOORSTTT	contortionist
CIINOOPPRSTTU	opportunistic
CIINOOPRRSTTU	corruptionist
CILMOOPRSSUUY	promiscuously
CILMOPRSSTUUY	scrumptiously
CIMMNNOOOPSTU	post-communion

D

DDDEEIINNSSUV	undividedness
DDDEEILNNOOPR	Lepidodendron
DDDEENNOORUWW	wonder-wounded
DDDEHIMOORSUY	hydromedusoid
DDDEIIKLNSTWY	tiddledywinks
DDDEILLMNORWY	worldly-minded
DDDIINOOOPRTT	diprotodontid
DDEEEEFLNNPST	self-dependent
DDEEEEILNNOPT	needle-pointed
DDEEEELLLOPVW	well-developed
DDEEEFILLRTVV	velvet-fiddler
DDEEEGGILLNPS	spindle-legged
DDEEEGHILNSST	delightedness
DDEEEGIILNNPP	dipping-needle
DDEEEGILNPSUV	pudding-sleeve
DDEEEHHNPRRSU	under-shepherd
DDEEEIINRSSTT	disinterested
DDEEEILNNNPTY	independently
DDEEEIMNPRSTU	undistempered
DDEEEINPRSSSS	dispersedness
DDEEFHIINNRSU	underfinished
DDEEFIIINRSUV	undiversified
DDEEGGINNRRRU	gerund-grinder
DDEEGHHINRTUW	hundredweight
DDEEGIINSSSSU	disguisedness
DDEEGINSSSSTU	disgustedness
DDEEHILNOOTWY	dyed-in-the-wool
DDEEIIKMNRRST	Kidderminster
DDEEIILNRSTUU	underutilised
DDEEIILNRTUUZ	underutilized
DDEFINOOPRRUV	unprovided-for
DDEGHIIINSSTU	distinguished
DDEGIIIILLNNTW	twiddling-line
DDEGIILNSSUUY	undisguisedly
DDEHHILOPRSUY	hydrosulphide
DDEHIIMOOSTTT	smooth-dittied
DDEHIKLNRSTUW	whistled-drunk
DDEHINNOORSUU	undishonoured
DDEIIIILMSSTU	dissimilitude
DDEIIILLNOSSU	disillusioned
DDEIIINOOPSST	dispositioned
DDEIMNOORSSTU	misunderstood
DDHIILMORRSTW	Third-Worldism
DEEEEEMPRSTTW	sweet-tempered
DEEEEFFGIRRRZ	fridge-freezer
DEEEEGILNNNTT	netting-needle
DEEEELLPRRSVW	well-preserved
DEEEELMNOPRTV	redevelopment
DEEEELNPPRSSX	perplexedness
DEEEEMNNORRST	re-endorsement

DEEEENNPRRSTU	unrepresented
DEEEFFIINQRTU	equidifferent
DEEEFFLOPRSSS	self-professed
DEEEFGHILPSST	selfe-despight
DEEEFGIILNNRR	life-rendering
DEEEFGILLNRRW	fringe-dweller
DEEEFGINNNSSU	unfeignedness
DEEEFGJLMNSTU	self-judgement
DEEEFGJMNORTU	forejudgement
DEEEFGKLLNOSW	self-knowledge
DEEEFGKLNOORW	foreknowledge
DEEEFHLNORSST	threefoldness
DEEEFIILMNPUX	unexemplified
DEEEFIINRSTTX	fixed-interest
DEEEFIMNNOORT	forementioned
DEEEFINPRRSSV	perfervidness
DEEEFLLLOPPRS	self-propelled
DEEEFLNORRTTU	letter-founder
DEEEFLNRRRSSU	self-surrender
DEEEFLOPSSSSS	self-possessed
DEEEGHILNNNTU	unenlightened
DEEEGIIILNORS	dereligionise
DEEEGIIILNORZ	dereligionize
DEEEGIILNOPRV	pigeon-livered
DEEEHILNNPRSU	unreplenished
DEEEHINPPRRST	pretendership
DEEEHMOPRRSTT	short-tempered
DEEEIILNNPTXY	inexpediently
DEEEIIMNRSTTV	divertisement
DEEEILLORSTUY	deleteriously
DEEEKLMMRRTTU	kettledrummer
DEEELLNNPRSTY	resplendently
DEEELNNSSSTTU	unsettledness
DEEEMOPSSSTTT	tempest-tossed
DEEENOPRRSUUX	underexposure
DEEENORSSSTUX	dexterousness
DEEFFIILNNRTY	indifferently
DEEFFIINSSSUV	diffusiveness
DEEFGGHIILNRT	light-fingered
DEEFGHIILLNSS	self-shielding
DEEFGHILNOORS	shingle-roofed
DEEFGIIMNRSTU	disfigurement
DEEFGILLNNSTU	self-indulgent
DEEFGILLNNSYY	self-denyingly
DEEFGILMNRRSU	self-murdering
DEEFGILMOPSTU	gumple-foisted
DEEFIIILMNOSS	field-emission
DEEFIIINNOPRT	predefinition
DEEFIILNNOOPS	self-opinioned
DEEFIKNNNORSU	unforeskinned
DEEFILNNOORYZ	ozone-friendly
DEEFILNOPRSSU	splendiferous
DEEFLNNORSSUW	wonderfulness
DEEFLOPPRSSTU	self-supported
DEEGGIIINNNNW	winding-engine
DEEGHILLNOSUW	dwelling-house
DEEGHILMOOSTY	demythologise
DEEGHILMOOTYZ	demythologize
DEEGIIKLNOPRW	dog-periwinkle
DEEGILMNOOSTY	sedimentology
DEEGILNNORTUV	overindulgent
DEEGILNNRSUVY	undeservingly
DEEGILNORSTUV	silver-tongued
DEEHHIOPPRRTY	hypertrophied
DEEHHNORRSTUW	thunder-shower
DEEHHOOPPRSTT	phosphoretted
DEEHHOPPRSTTU	phosphuretted
DEEHIINPPRSST	presidentship
DEEHIKNRRSTTU	thunderstrike
DEEHILMMNOSST	demolishments
DEEHILPRRSSUU	desulphuriser
DEEHILPRRSUUZ	desulphurizer
DEEHKNORRSTTU	thunder-stroke
DEEIIIMMNNRST	indeterminism
DEEIIIMNNRSTT	indeterminist
DEEIIINOQRSTU	derequisition
DEEIIINPRSSTT	serendipitist
DEEIIKLLNORSU	unsoldierlike
DEEIILLNORSSS	soldierliness
DEEIILMNNOSSS	dimensionless
DEEIILMNNSSTU	unlimitedness
DEEIILMOPRSSY	epidermolysis
DEEIILNORSSSU	deliriousness
DEEIILOPPRSTT	lepidopterist
DEEIILOPSTUXY	expeditiously
DEEIIMNNRTTTU	unintermitted
DEEIIMNNSSTTV	disinvestment
DEEIIMNOORSST	endometriosis
DEEIIMNOPRSTT	Redemptionist
DEEIINNSSTTTW	nitwittedness
DEEIINOOPRRSU	urediniospore
DEEIINOPRSSTU	serendipitous
DEEIINOSSSSTU	seditiousness
DEEILMMNOPSTY	disemployment
DEEILMNOOSSSU	melodiousness
DEEILMNORSTUV	silver-mounted
DEEILMORTTUUV	overmultitude
DEEILNNOSTTUY	tendentiously
DEEILNORSSSTU	desultoriness
DEEILNOSSSSTU	dissoluteness
DEEILNPRRTTUY	interruptedly
DEEILOOPPRSTU	lepidopterous
DEEIMMNRSSTUY	unsymmetrised
DEEIMMNRSTUYZ	unsymmetrized
DEEIMNOORSTTU	Deuteronomist
DEEIMOPRRRSSV	dress-improver
DEEINNOOPSSTT	post-tensioned
DEEINNPRRTTUU	uninterrupted
DEEIOPRSTTUVY	topside-turvey
DEEKLLOORTUWW	well-worked-out
DEELNNOPSSSUU	pendulousness
DEENNOOPRSSSU	ponderousness
DEENNOPSSSTTU	unspottedness
DEFFGIIKNNORR	drink-offering
DEFHIILLOPSSW	disfellowship
DEFHIMORRRTUU	rutherfordium
DEFIILLNOPSUU	filipendulous
DEFIILPRSTUUY	superfluidity
DEFILLRSSSTUY	distressfully
DEFILMNNNSSUU	unmindfulness
DEFILNNSSTUUU	undutifulness
DEFILOOORRSUY	odoriferously
DEGGHIKNNOORY	good-King-Henry
DEGGIILLNOPSS	disgospelling

DEGGINNOOPRWW powdering-gown
DEGHHILOPRTTT troth-plighted
DEGHIIILPRSTT light-spirited
DEGHIIINRSSTU distinguisher
DEGHIINNPRSTU hunting-spider
DEGHILLNORSTU shrill-tongued
DEGHILMOOOSTT methodologist
DEGHINNNOOSST do-nothingness
DEGHINNORSSTW downrightness
DEGHMNOOOSTTU smooth-tongued
DEGIIILNPSSTT side-splitting
DEGIIILNQSTUY disquietingly
DEGIIJMNPPRSU jumping-spider
DEGIILNRSSSTY distressingly
DEGIILOOPRSTT pteridologist
DEGIIMNOPPRRW priming-powder
DEGIINOPRSSTU true-disposing
DEGIKLNORSTTU skittle-ground
DEGIKNNOORRWW wonder-working
DEGIMNOOOPRRW powdering-room
DEHHIIOPRRSSY hyperhidrosis
DEHHILOORRSTW otherworldish
DEHHILOPRSTUY hydrosulphite
DEHIINOOPPSST deipnosophist
DEHINNOOORSTT odontornithes
DEIIIKLMNNOTT milk-dentition
DEIIILMNOOSTT demolitionist
DEIIILOPSSTVY dispositively
DEIIINNNNSTTU Nintendinitus
DEIIINNOSSSSU insidiousness
DEIIINNOSSSUV invidiousness
DEIIINOOPRSTT periodontitis
DEIILLNORSTWW trellis-window
DEIILMNOPRTVY improvidently
DEIILNNOPSTUU plenitudinous
DEIILNOORSSTU redissolution
DEIILNOOSTTUV devolutionist
DEIINNOOPRSUV unprovisioned
DEIINOOPSSSSS dispossession
DEILLNNORSSUW unworldliness
DEIMMMNOSTTUU mutton-dummies
DEIMMNOOPRSST post-modernism
DEIMNOOPRSSTT post-modernist
DEINNOOORSSSU inodorousness
DELNOPPRSTUUY unsupportedly
DFGGHIILLNOOT floodlighting
DFGGHIINNORSU fishing-ground
DFGINNOOOPRSU soundproofing
DFIINOORSTTUU fortitudinous
DFILLRSSTTUUY distrustfully
DGGHINNNORTUU hunting-ground
DGHHIILNNOTUW unwithholding
DGHIIIILMNNSY diminishingly
DGIIIILNPRSTY dispiritingly
DGIIIKNNNPPSY skinny-dipping
DGIIIMNORRRRV driving-mirror
DGIIINNPRSSTW winding-strips
DGIILNNOOOSST sindonologist
DGIILNOPRSTTW word-splitting
DGIINNOPPRRTU round-tripping
DGILLNOOSSUUU solidungulous
DGLMNOOOOSSTU odontoglossum
DHHIIIOOOPRST histiophoroid
DHIIIMMOOPRSS isodimorphism
DHIIMOOOPRSSU isodimorphous
DHNOOOOOPRSTU odontophorous
DIIIINNOOPSST indisposition
DIILMNOSTTUUU multitudinous
DIILNORSSTUUY industriously
DIINOOOPPRRST disproportion
DILLNOOPSSSYY spondylolysis
DLNOOOOPPRTTY polyprotodont
DMOOPRSTTUVYY topsy-turvydom

E

EEEEEGIMNRRSV semi-evergreen
EEEEENNPRRSTU entrepreneuse
EEEEFILNRSSVX reflexiveness
EEEEFILPRRRSV life-preserver
EEEEGHINNNPTY eighteen-penny
EEEEGHINORSST heterogenesis
EEEEGHINORTTY heterogeneity
EEEEGHNOORSTU heterogeneous
EEEEGIINOPRSS epeirogenesis
EEEEGIMNRRSSW messenger-wire
EEEEGINNRSTVY yesterevening
EEEEHINORRSVW whereinsoever
EEEEHKLLRRSTT helter-skelter
EEEEHLNNSTTVY seventeenthly
EEEEIIMMPRRST semiperimeter
EEEEINNPSSSVX expensiveness
EEEEINNRSSTTV retentiveness
EEEEINNSSSTVX extensiveness
EEEEINPQRSSTU sesquiterpene
EEEEINPRRSSTT preteriteness
EEEELLNPSSSSS sleeplessness
EEEELNNRSSSSV nervelessness
EEEELNNSSSSSS senselessness
EEEEMNNPRRSTT representment
re-presentment
EEEFFGILLLNOW fellow-feeling
EEEFFGILLNORY forefeelingly
EEEFFGILNRRRS self-referring
EEEFFINNOSSSV offensiveness
EEEFGILLLLNSV self-levelling
EEEFGILNNNSSU unfeelingness
EEEFGIMNPRRTU prefigurement
EEEFHIKOPSSUW housewifeskep
EEEFHKNORRSTU seek-no-further
EEEFIILLLLMSU millefeuilles
EEEFINNPRSSSU superfineness
EEEFJLMNNOSTY self-enjoyment
EEEFLLNORRTTU fortune-teller
EEEGGINORSSSU egregiousness
EEEGHILMNNNTT △enlightenment
EEEGHIMNORSST thermogenesis
EEEGIILMMNPSS seeming-simple
EEEGIIMNRRSST Meistersinger
EEEGILLNSSSSU guilelessness
EEEGILNOORSTV venereologist
EEEGILNPRRSVY perseveringly
EEEGIMMMNRSSU summer-seeming
EEEGINNNNSSUU ungenuineness
EEEGIORRRSSTV retrogressive

EEEGKLNOOSSTU	skeletogenous
EEEGNOQRSSSTU	grotesqueness
EEEHHINPRSTTY	hypersthenite
EEEHHIORRSTVW	whithersoever
EEEHHNNOPRRTT	threepenn'orth
EEEHILMNNPRST	replenishment
EEEHILMNOSSST	lithesomeness
EEEHILMOPRRTY	pyrheliometer
EEEHIMNNNOOPP	epiphenomenon
EEEHLLORRTTTV	throttle-lever
EEEHLMNNOOOPT	monotelephone
EEEHLMNOOOTTU	homeoteleuton
EEEHLMNOOSSSW	wholesomeness
EEEHOOPRRSTTU	heteropterous
EEEIIILLNPRTV	perivitelline
EEEIILNNPSVXY	inexpensively
EEEIIMNPRSTTX	experimentist
EEEIINNNSSSTV	intensiveness
EEEIINNNSSTVV	inventiveness
EEEIINNSSSSTV	sensitiveness
EEEIINQRSSSTU	requisiteness
EEEIINQSSSTUX	exquisiteness
EEEIIOQRSTUVX	over-exquisite
EEEILNNNPSSSS	pennilessness
EEEILNNOSSSSS	noiselessness
EEEILNNPSSSSS	spinelessness
EEEILNNPSUVXY	unexpensively
EEEILNOPSSSVX	explosiveness
EEEILNPRSSSUV	repulsiveness
EEEIMMOPRSSTY	sympiesometer
EEEIMNOOPRTTT	potentiometer
EEEINNOPRSSTT	septentriones
EEEINPRRRSSTT	interpretress
EEEKLMNOSSSSS	smokelessness
EEELLMORRSSSY	remorselessly
EEELLNPSSSSSU	pulselessness
EEELMMNOORTUV	volumenometer
EEELMNORRSSSU	unremorseless
EEELMNORSTUVY	venturesomely
EEELMNOSTTTTU	outsettlement
EEELNNOPSSSTU	plenteousness
EEELNOPRSSSSW	powerlessness
EEENNOORRSSSU	erroneousness
EEFFFGLLORSTU	self-forgetful
EEFFGLNORSSTU	forgetfulness
EEFFIILLRSTTY	self-fertility
EEFFIILNNOSVY	inoffensively
EEFGGILNNORSV	self-governing
EEFGHILNPRSSS	flesh-pressing
EEFGHILORSSST	foresightless
EEFGHILORSSTU	self-righteous
EEFGIIINRRSST	fire-resisting
EEFGIILLOOTTW	gillie-wetfoot
EEFGIILNNRRTY	interferingly
EEFGIINNOPRRT	finger-pointer
EEFGIINNOPRTZ	freezing-point
EEFGILLOORSTX	reflexologist
EEFGILNOPRRSV	self-reproving
EEFGINNOORSST	frontogenesis
EEFGINNORSSUV	unforgiveness
EEFGNNOORSSTT	forgottenness
EEFHHIILNOPST	ship-of-the-line
EEFHHIIOPSSUW	housewifeship
EEFHILNNSSSSU	unselfishness
EEFHILNSSSSST	shiftlessness
EEFHIORRSSTYY	oyster-fishery
EEFHNNORRTTUU	fortune-hunter
EEFIILLMNOSTU	feuilletonism
EEFIILLNNOSSX	inflexionless
EEFIILLNOSTTU	feuilletonist
EEFIILLRSSTTY	self-sterility
EEFIILOPRRSTU	reptiliferous
EEFIIMNORSTTU	fermentitious
EEFILLLLMNTUY	mellifluently
EEFILLNNPSSTU	plentifulness
EEFILNNOOSSSU	feloniousness
EEFILNRSSSSTU	fruitlessness
EEFILOOPRRSTU	petroliferous
EEFILOPRSSTUY	pestiferously
EEFLMNOORRSTT	self-tormentor
EEFLMOPRRTTUW	trumpet-flower
EEFLNNNSSTUUU	untunefulness
EEFLNNRSSSTUU	unrestfulness
EEFMNOORRSSTT	stern-foremost
EEGGHINNNRSTT	strengthening
EEGGHMNOOOPRY	geomorphogeny
EEGGIINNNNRTU	engine-turning
EEGGIJKOPRRYY	jiggery-pokery
EEGGJLLNNNOSY	Jenny-long-legs
EEGHHIILOPSVX	high-explosive
EEGHIILNNNPSW	spinning-wheel
EEGHIILOORSST	heresiologist
EEGHIIMNNOOTY	inhomogeneity
EEGHIINNOOSST	seine-shooting
EEGHIJNORTUWY	journey-weight
EEGHIKNRRRSTU	hunger-striker
EEGHILMNOSSST	lightsomeness
EEGHILMNOSSTU	smelting-house
EEGHILNSSSSST	sightlessness
EEGHILOOPRSTT	herpetologist
EEGHIMNNOOOSU	inhomogeneous
EEGHIMNOOPRSS	morphogenesis
EEGHIMNORSTTT	thermosetting
EEGHINORSSSTU	righteousness
EEGHLMNNOOOPY	phenomenology
EEGHLNOOORTUY	neuroethology
EEGIIIMNOPRTV	primogenitive
EEGIILLLNNTTY	intelligently
EEGIILLNNNTTU	unintelligent
EEGIILLNOSTUV	vitelligenous
EEGIILNNRSTTY	interestingly
EEGIILNORSSSU	religiousness
EEGIIMNOPRRTU	primogeniture
EEGIIMNORSSTU	tumorigenesis
EEGIIMNPRRTTT	pretermitting
EEGIINNNOSSSU	ingeniousness
EEGIINNNRSTTU	uninteresting
EEGILLNNNRTUY	unrelentingly
EEGILLNSSSSTU	guiltlessness
EEGILMOOORSTT	meteorologist
EEGILNNNPRTUY	unrepentingly
EEGILOPRRSSVY	progressively
EEGIMMNNORSTV	misgovernment
EEGIMNNORRSTY	yestermorning

EEGIMNPRSSSST	sempstressing
EEGINNNOSSSUU	ingenuousness
EEGINNNRSSSTT	stringentness
EEGINNNRSSSTU	unrestingness
EEGINNOPPSSTT	stepping-stone
EEGINOORRRSST	retrogression
EEGINOPPRSSSS	prepossessing
EEGINOPRRSSUV	unprogressive
EEGINORSTTTUW	tongue-twister
EEGLMNOOOPRSU	prolegomenous
EEGMMNORRSTYY	mystery-monger
EEHHIILLLMNPS	philhellenism
EEHHIILLLNPST	philhellenist
EEHHMMNOOOPPR	morphophoneme
EEHHMMOOORSTU	homeothermous
EEHHOOPRRSTTY	heterostrophy
EEHIIINPPRRST	perinephritis
EEHIIKNNSSSTT	kittenishness
EEHIILLMNORRS	horse-milliner
EEHIINOOPRRRT	heir-portioner
EEHIINOPRRSST	spheristerion
EEHILLNOSSSWY	yellowishness
EEHILLOORSSTT	tortoiseshell
EEHILMMNOOSTT	△monotheletism
EEHILMNRSSSST	mirthlessness
EEHILMORSSTTY	heterostylism
EEHILNNORRSST	northerliness
EEHILNORSSSTU	southerliness
EEHIMMNNOPRST	premonishment
EEHIMNOPTTTUU	up-to-the-minute
EEHIMORRSSSTW	whoremistress
EEHIMORSSSSTU	housemistress
EEHLLMNOOSUWY	unwholesomely
EEHLNORRSTTWY	north-westerly
EEHLNORSSSSTW	worthlessness
EEHLNRSSSSTTU	truthlessness
EEHLOORSSTTUY	heterostylous
EEHLORSSTTUWY	south-westerly
EEHMMNOOPTTTU	up-to-the-moment
EEHMNOOOSSSTT	toothsomeness
EEHMNOOPRSTUY	hymenopterous
EEHOOOPRRSSTU	heterosporous
EEIIILNNSSTVY	insensitively
EEIIIMNPRSSTV	primitiveness
EEIILLMNSSSST	limitlessness
EEIILMNNPRTTY	impertinently
EEIILMNPSSSUV	impulsiveness
EEIILMOOSSTTY	osteomyelitis
EEIILNOORSTUV	revolutionise
EEIILNOORTUVZ	revolutionize
EEIILNOQRSTUV	ventriloquise
EEIILNOQRTUVZ	ventriloquize
EEIILOPPRSTVY	prepositively
EEIILOPRSTTUY	repetitiously
EEIILPRSTUUVV	vivisepulture
EEIIMNOPRRSST	pretermission
EEIIMNOPRSSSU	imperiousness
EEIIMNOPRSSSX	△expressionism
EEIINNOPRRSST	interspersion
EEIINNRSSSTUV	intrusiveness
EEIINOPRSSSTX	expressionist
EEILLNOOSSWYY	linsey-woolsey
EEILMMMNOPSTY	misemployment
EEILMNNRTTTUY	unremittently
EEILMPPRSTUVY	presumptively
EEILNNOPSSSST	pointlessness
EEILNNOSSTTUY	sententiously
EEILNOPRSTTUY	pretentiously
EEILNPRRSTUUV	supervirulent
EEIMNOPSSSTUU	impetuousness
EEIMOOPRRSSTT	stereotropism
EEINNNOPRSSTT	non-persistent
EEINNOPRSSSUU	penuriousness
EEINNOPRSTTUU	unpretentious
EEINOOPPRSSSS	prepossession
EEINOPPRSSSUV	purposiveness
EEIOOOPRSSSTT	osteopetrosis
EEKNNOOPSSSTU	outspokenness
EEKNOOPPRSSSS	spokespersons
EELLNOOPPPRYY	polypropylene
EELLOPPRSSSUY	purposelessly
EELMNORSSSTUU	tremulousness
EELMOPSSTTUUY	tempestuously
EELNOQRSSSUUU	querulousness
EELNRSSSSSTTU	trustlessness
EEMMNNOOSSSTU	momentousness
EEMMPRRSSTUYY	supersymmetry
EENNOOPPRSSTU	opportuneness
EENNORSSSSTUU	strenuousness
EENNORSSSTUUV	venturousness
EFFGGILNNORSU	longsuffering
EFFGHILNRSSTU	frightfulness
EFFGIINNNOORT	non-forfeiting
EFFIILOORSSSU	fossiliferous
EFFILLMNNNOTU	non-fulfilment
EFGGHIIILNTTW	weight-lifting
EFGGHIIINPRTZ	prizefighting
EFGGHIILNNRTY	frighteningly
EFGHHLLOOTTUW	well-thought-of
EFGHIIILMNTWY	mini-flyweight
EFGHIIILNNSTT	thing-in-itself
EFGHILLNORSTU	flugelhornist
	flügelhornist
EFGIILNRSSUVV	self-surviving
EFGIKLNNOORWY	foreknowingly
EFGILLNOORVWY	overflowingly
EFGKLLMOOOTYY	folk-etymology
EFHIINNRSSTTU	unthriftiness
EFHILMNOPSSTY	self-hypnotism
EFHIOOPPRRSSS	professorship
EFHLNNRSSTUUU	unhurtfulness
EFIILLNOOPRSU	polliniferous
EFIILNNPSSTUU	unpitifulness
EFIILNOPRSSUU	spinuliferous
EFIKLLNNSSSUU	unskilfulness
EFILLLLMOSUUY	mellifluously
EFILLLNOOPSTU	self-pollution
EFILLOOPRRSUY	proliferously
EFILNOOORSSTU	stoloniferous
EFILNOOPPRRST	splinter-proof
EFILNOORSSSUV	frivolousness
EFLLOPRSSUUUY	superfluously
EFLNOORRSSSUW	sorrowfulness
EFLNOPRSSUUUU	unsuperfluous

Words marked △ may be spelled also with a capital letter

EGGHIIILMNTTT	light-emitting
EGGHINNOOPSSU	sponging-house
EGGHINNOPSSUU	spunging-house
EGGHLMOOOOPRY	geomorphology
EGGIIILNNNPST	spine-tingling
EGGIIMNOSSSTU	suggestionism
EGGIINOSSSTTU	suggestionist
EGGILNOOORSTT	gerontologist
EGHHIILLMNRST	threshing-mill
EGHHIILOPRSTY	hieroglyphist
EGHHILLMNOOTY	helminthology
EGHHLLOSSTTUY	thoughtlessly
EGHIIIKNNRSST	kiss-in-the-ring
EGHIILLNNRSST	thrillingness
EGHIILMNNOPSY	sphingomyelin
EGHIILNNOSTTU	ethnolinguist
EGHIILNNSSSTU	unsightliness
EGHIILNOPPSTU	tippling-house
EGHIILNPRSSST	sprightliness
EGHIINNNOPSSU	spinning-house
EGHIINNOPRSTU	printing-house
EGHILNORSTUUY	unrighteously
EGHILNPRSTTUU	sulphuretting
EGHILOPRSTUUY	uprighteously
EGIIIILNORRST	irreligionist
EGIIIKLNOOSST	kinesiologist
EGIIILLORRSUY	irreligiously
EGIIILNOSSSTU	litigiousness
EGIIIMNOPRRTX	primogenitrix
EGIIJNNNNNPSY	spinning-jenny
EGIILLLOOSTVX	vexillologist
EGIILLMNORSTT	△millstone-grit
EGIILLNNNSSUW	unwillingness
EGIILMNNRTTUY	unremittingly
EGIILMNOPRSTY	temporisingly
EGIILMNOPRTYZ	temporizingly
EGIILNNOPSSTT	listening-post
EGIILNNOQSTUY	questioningly
EGIILNNORSTUU	neurolinguist
EGIILNNRSSTUY	unresistingly
EGIILNOPSTTTV	vote-splitting
EGIILNORSTUVY	vertiginously
EGIILNRSSTTTY	trysting-stile
EGIILOOOSSTTV	△sovietologist
EGIIMNOORRSST	risorgimentos
EGIIMOPRRSSSV	progressivism
EGIINNNOQSTUU	unquestioning
EGIINNNSSTTUW	unwittingness
EGIINNOORRSST	introgression
EGIINNPPRRSST	printing-press
EGIIOPRRSSSTV	progressivist
EGIKLMNORSSTW	smelting-works
EGIKNNNNOSSUW	unknowingness
EGILLNPRSTTUY	splutteringly
EGILMMNOPRTUU	rumelgumption
	rumlegumption
EGILNNNRRTUUY	unreturningly
EGMMNOOPRSSUY	gymnospermous
EGNOOOPRRSTUY	proterogynous
EHHHIOOPPPSTY	hypophosphite
EHHIILOOPPRSS	philosophiser
EHHIILOOPPRSZ	philosophizer

EHHILMOOPRSTU	thermophilous
EHHIMMMOOOPRS	homeomorphism
EHHIOOOPPRSST	photophoresis
EHHMMOOOOPRSU	homeomorphous
EHHOOPPRRSTUY	hypertrophous
EHIIILPPRSTTY	perityphlitis
EHIIKLMOOPRTY	poikilothermy
EHIILLOPSSTWW	will-o'-the-wisps
	wills-o'-the-wisp
EHIILMMNOOSTT	△monothelitism
EHIILNOOOPSSU	eosinophilous
EHIIMNOOOPSST	photo-emission
EHIINOOOPRSST	iontophoresis
EHIKLORRSSTTW	silk-throwster
EHIKMMOOPRSSU	skeuomorphism
EHILLNNOOPQUY	phylloquinone
EHILMNOOOPSTU	entomophilous
EHILNOPSSSTYY	polysynthesis
EHIMMOOPRRSTT	thermotropism
EHINOPPRRSSUW	sunworshipper
EHIOOPPRSSSSS	possessorship
EHLLLOOPPSTUY	leptophyllous
EHLLNOOPSSTUY	stenophyllous
EHLLOPRSSUUUY	sulphureously
EHMMNOPRTTTUU	mutton-thumper
EHMMOOPSSTYYY	symphyseotomy
EHNNOOPRTTWWY	two-pennyworth
EIIIILNQSTUVY	inquisitively
EIIIINNQSTUUV	uninquisitive
EIIIINNSSTTVY	insensitivity
EIIILLMOOPSTY	poliomyelitis
EIIILNSTTTUVY	institutively
EIIIMMNOPRSSS	△impressionism
EIIIMNOPRSSST	△impressionist
EIIINNOOPRSTT	interposition
EIIJNNORSSSUU	injuriousness
EIILMNOOPRRTY	premonitorily
EIILMNOORSTUV	revolutionism
EIILMNOQRSTUV	ventriloquism
EIILMOORRSTUY	meritoriously
EIILNOORSTTUV	revolutionist
EIILNOQRSTTUV	ventriloquist
EIILNORRSSSTY	sinistrorsely
EIILOOPPRSSST	leptospirosis
EIINNNOOSSSUX	innoxiousness
EIINNOOSSTTVY	tenosynovitis
EIINOOPPRSSTU	superposition
EIINOOPPRSTTU	opportunities
EIINOPRSSSSTU	spiritousness
EIIOPRRSSTTUU	surreptitious
EIIOPRSSSTTUU	superstitious
EIJLNOOPPRSTU	jet-propulsion
EILNNOOPPRTUY	inopportunely
EILNOOQRSTUUV	ventriloquous
EILNORSSSUUUX	luxuriousness
EILOQRRSTTUUY	triquetrously
EINNOOOPSSSSU	poisonousness
EINNOOORSSSTU	notoriousness
EMNNOORSSSSTU	monstrousness
EMNOPSSSSTUUU	sumptuousness

Words marked △ may be spelled also with a capital letter

F

FFGIIILLMNORR fringilliform
FFGIMNNORSTUU mourning-stuff
FFLLLLNOOOORR roll-on-roll-off
FGHHLLOOORTUW follow-through
FGHIILLNORSUY flourishingly
FIIIMOORSSSST fortississimo
FILLMRSSTTUUY mistrustfully
FILMNRSSTTUUU unmistrustful

G

GGGHHINOOORTU thoroughgoing
GGHHIIIKNNRTT right-thinking
GGHIIINNPPRTT night-tripping
GGIILLNNPRSTU string-pulling
GHHIILNOPSSTW whistling-shop
GHIIKLNNNRSUY unshrinkingly
GHIILLOOPSSTY syphilologist
GHIILNOOORSTT ornithologist
GHIIMMOOPRSTT thigmotropism
GHIIMNOOPSSTY physiognomist
GHILOOOOPSYYZ zoophysiology
GIIIILNNPRSTY inspiritingly
GIIIKLLLMNSTU multiskilling
GIIILLMNSTTUU multilinguist
GIIILMNNOOSUY ignominiously
GIIIMNORRRRTW mirror-writing
GIILMNNOPRSUY unpromisingly
GIILMNRSSTTUY mistrustingly
GIINNOOOPPRRT proportioning
GIINOPRRSSTTW sportswriting
GILLLMOOPSSYY polysyllogism
GILLNNOOOPRST trolling-spoon
GILMMNNRRUUUY unmurmuringly

H

HHILLOOPPSUXY xiphophyllous
HHIMMOOOOPRSS homomorphosis
HHIMOOOOPPRSU ophiomorphous
HHIMOOOPRRSUZ rhizomorphous
HIIILLNNOQTTU quintillionth
HIIILOPRSTTTT lithotriptist
HIILNOOPRRTTT lithontriptor
HIIMMNOOPSSTY △monophysitism
HILORRSTTTUWY trustworthily
HIMMOOPSSTYYY symphysiotomy
HIMOOOPPRRSTT trophotropism
HNORRSTTTUUWY untrustworthy

I

IIILLMORSSSTU illustrissimo
IIILMNOOPSSTU postliminious
IIINOOOPPSSTT oppositionist
IILLLORSSTUUY illustriously
IIMNOOOPPRRST misproportion
IINNOOPPRTTUY inopportunity

14AAA

A

AAAAACGILMMNRT anagrammatical
AAAAAGGINNRRTT rangatiratanga
AAAABBIIMNRSST Sabbatarianism
AAAACCDEEEILPS Asclepiadaceae
AAAACCDEINORSU anacardiaceous
AAAACCEEEINRRS Sarraceniaceae
AAAACCEEGIMRRV Marcgraviaceae
AAAACCEEHIMNRT Marchantiaceae
AAAACCEHHLNOPT Acanthocephala
AAAACCILLPRTTY paratactically
AAAACCINNRSSTU transcaucasian
AAAACDEEEHILMM Hamamelidaceae
AAAACDEEGHILOR Haloragidaceae
AAAACDEEILLMRY Amaryllidaceae
AAAACDGIILMPRT paradigmatical
AAAACDIIMMNOST macadamisation
AAAACDIIMMNOTZ macadamization
AAAACEEGILNNPT Plantaginaceae
AAAACEGILLMMNO megalomaniacal
AAAACEHMNORSTU amaranthaceous
AAAACEIMNNRRST sacramentarian
AAAACHILPPRRST paraphrastical
AAAADEGINNQRRU quadragenarian
AAAAEEHIKNPRSS Shakespeariana
AAAAELLLOOPRTV palato-alveolar
AAAAFIILNNPRRS Infralapsarian
AAAAGHIMNOPRST phantasmagoria
AAAAGIMMPRRSTT paragrammatist
AAAAIILLNOPSTT palatalisation
AAAAIILLNOPTTZ palatalization
AAAAILNPPRRSSU Supralapsarian
AAAANNOPRRSSVW savanna-sparrow
AAABBBEEHKRRST Sabbath-breaker
AAABBCHHIOOPRT batrachophobia
AAABBCIIILLMNO bibliomaniacal
AAABBEEFKLRSTT breakfast-table
AAABBEGLLNOORR barrage-balloon
AAABCCEIILLMST acclimatisable
AAABCCEIILLMTZ acclimatizable
AAABCCILMNNOOY cyanocobalamin
AAABCDGHILNORY brachydiagonal
AAABCDHIINNRTU Nudibranchiata
AAABCEEGILMNPU Plumbaginaceae
AAABCEEILLMNRU bear-animalcule
AAABCEHILLLPTY alphabetically
AAABCEHILNOPPR inapproachable
AAABCEHLNOPPRU unapproachable
AAABCEILLNOOPT paleobotanical
AAABCEILMNRRTU interambulacra
AAABCELMMNNOUW ambulancewoman

AAABCGHHILPRTY	bathygraphical
AAABCGHINORTYZ	Zygobranchiata
AAABCHILNOPPRY	inapproachably
AAABCHLNOPPRUY	unapproachably
AAABDDEENRRRST	standard-bearer
AAABDEEFGINNNR	banana-fingered
AAABDHIMOPRSSS	ambassadorship
AAABDIILMNNORT	intra-abdominal
AAABDIINORSSTT	bastardisation
AAABDIINORSTTZ	bastardization
AAABEEEGLMNNSS	manageableness
AAABEEGILMNRRU	unmarriageable
AAABEEILNNSSTT	attainableness
AAABEGGIILNNPR	plea-bargaining
AAABEGIILLNOUV	bougainvillaea
AAABEIIILMNRSS	Rabelaisianism
AAABEIILMNNNTU	unmaintainable
AAABEILNOOPSTT	palaeobotanist
AAABEILRRRSTTW	barrister-at-law
AAABELLNNPRSTT	transplantable
AAABELLNNRSTTU	untranslatable
AAABIIILLNTUVY	unavailability
AAABIILNORSTTU	tabularisation
AAABIILNORTTUZ	tabularization
AAABLLNNRSTTUY	untranslatably
AAACCCEEHLOPTY	Phytolaccaceae
AAACCCEHILRSTT	catachrestical
AAACCCGHHILOPR	chacographical
AAACCDDEILNNOR	cardinal-deacon
AAACCDEFHINNNR	French-Canadian
AAACCDEIMNNOOR	adenocarcinoma
AAACCDEIOPPRSU	capparidaceous
AAACCDIILOPRTT	catadioptrical
AAACCDILORRSUV	cardiovascular
AAACCEEFIILOPR	Caprifoliaceae
AAACCEEHILMPRY	hypercalcaemia
AAACCEEINNQRTU	reacquaintance
AAACCEGHILLOOR	archaeological
AAACCEHILMPRTU	pharmaceutical
AAACCEHLLMRSSV	clash-ma-clavers
AAACCEIILLMOPT	palaeoclimatic
AAACCEILNNORTX	extracanonical
AAACCEINNNQTUU	unacquaintance
AAACCELMNOPSUU	campanulaceous
AAACCGHHILPRTY	tachygraphical
AAACCGHIILLLPR	calligraphical
AAACCGHILLNOOR	arachnological
AAACCGHILOPRRT	cartographical
AAACCGILLMNOOP	campanological
AAACCHIINORSST	saccharisation
AAACCHIINORSTZ	saccharization
AAACCHILLMORTY	achromatically
AAACCHILLNNORY	anachronically
AAACCHINORRSST	narcocatharsis
AAACCIIINNOPTT	incapacitation
AAACCIILORRSTT	aristocratical
AAACCILLORTTUY	autocratically
AAACCINNORSSTU	Transcaucasion
AAACCLMOORSSTU	malacostracous
AAACDDEGGKLNOR	cloak-and-dagger
AAACDEFGNORRUV	Grace-and-Favour
	grace-and-favour
AAACDEIILNPPRU	Appendicularia
AAACDEILLMOPRS	Camelopardalis
AAACDFHIMNNRST	handicraftsman
AAACDGMNORSSTU	coastguardsman
AAACDHIINOPRST	antaphrodisiac
AAACDHILNOOPRS	achondroplasia
AAACDIIILNORST	radicalisation
AAACDIIILNORTZ	radicalization
AAACDIILNNOSST	scandalisation
AAACDIILNNOSTZ	scandalization
AAACEEELNOPPRS	aerospace-plane
AAACEEFILOPRSS	Passifloraceae
AAACEEGIILNSTT	telangiectasia
AAACEEGIILNSTU	Ustilaginaceae
AAACEEGILNNPRT	captain-general
AAACEEIILNORST	aeroelastician
AAACEEIKLMNPRT	parliament-cake
AAACEEILNORSUV	valerianaceous
AAACEEIMMNNNNT	maintenance-man
AAACEFFGIMNRRT	traffic-manager
AAACEFGILLLMNO	flagellomaniac
AAACEFGIORSSUX	saxifragaceous
AAACEGHILLOPPR	paleographical
AAACEGHILMOPTT	apothegmatical
AAACEGIILMMPRT	epigrammatical
AAACEGIMMRRSTT	grammaticaster
AAACEHHINNNTTX	canthaxanthine
AAACEHIILMRRSV	air-vice-marshal
AAACEHIILNPTTT	antipathetical
AAACEHILLLMPRY	alphamerically
AAACEHILLMMTTY	mathematically
AAACEHILLMNPRU	alphanumerical
AAACEHILMMNTTU	unmathematical
AAACEHILMOOPPR	pharmacopoeial
AAACEHILNOPPRT	palaeanthropic
AAACEHILOPRRTX	extra-parochial
AAACEHIMNOOPPR	pharmacopoeian
AAACEHOOPRRTTT	Prototracheata
AAACEIIILLMNNRS	miscellanarian
AAACEIILMNORST	caramelisation
AAACEIILMNORTZ	caramelization
AAACEIIMMNNPRS	Pan-Americanism
AAACEILLMNNSTY	anamnestically
AAACEILLNORTUY	aeronautically
AAACEILMMNRSST	sacramentalism
AAACEILMNRSSTT	sacramentalist
AAACEIMNORSTTT	castrametation
AAACFIIINNORST	Africanisation
AAACFIIINNORTZ	Africanization
AAACFIILNSTTTY	fantasticality
AAACFIINNOSTTT	fantastication
AAACFIMNORRSTW	aircraftswoman
AAACGGHHIILOPR	hagiographical
AAACGHIILPRSTT	stratigaphical
AAACGHILMRTTUU	thaumaturgical
AAACGHILNOPPRT	pantographical
AAACGHILNOPRRU	uranographical
AAACGHIMNOPRST	phantasmagoric
AAACGIILLMSTTY	astigmatically
AAACGIILMPRTTY	pragmaticality
AAACGILLMNORTY	morganatically
AAACGILLNOPSTV	galvanoplastic

AAACGIMNOOPRRS macrosporangia
AAACGIMNOPPRTT pantopragmatic
AAACHIILMMRRST matriarchalism
AAACHIILMPRRST patriarchalism
AAACHIILNOPSTT chaptalisation
AAACHIILNOPTTZ chaptalization
AAACHIILNPRSTT antiphrastical
AAACHILLLLOPTY allopathically
AAACHILMMNNOPY nymphomaniacal
AAACIIILNOPSTT capitalisation
AAACIIILNOPTTZ capitalization
AAACIILNRRRTTU intra-articular
AAACILMNOOPRST paronomastical
AAADDDGNNORRST dragon-standard
AAADEEIKLLMNRS salamander-like
AAADEGHIMOPRRT dermatographia
AAADEGLNOSTUVY advantageously
AAADEHIMNORSTU adiathermanous
AAADEIILNNRTUV valetudinarian
AAADGHIOOPRRTU autoradiograph
radioautograph
AAADGLLNQRRUUY quadrangularly
AAADIIILNNRTTU altitudinarian
latitudinarian
AAADIIINNRTTTU attitudinarian
AAADIILNOOSTTV vasodilatation
AAADILOORSTTVY vasodilatatory
AAAEEEHILPPRRT Praeraphaelite
AAAEEGILNPPRRW wearing-apparel
AAAEEGINNPRSTU septuagenarian
AAAEEGMNRRSSTT sergeant-at-arms
AAAEEHHIINRRTV heavier-than-air
AAAEEHIMNPRRTY hypernatraemia
AAAEEJMNRRSSTT serjeant-at-arms
AAAEFGIMORRRUV marriage-favour
AAAEFIILMMRSST matresfamilias
AAAEFIILMPRSST patresfamilias
AAAEGHILOPPRST palaeographist
AAAEGIIILMNRST egalitarianism
AAAEGIMNNORSTT station-manager
AAAEGINOPRRSTT tetrasporangia
AAAEGMMNORRTTT △tetragrammaton
AAAEGNOPRSSSTU asparagus-stone
AAAEHIKLMNOPRX alexipharmakon
AAAEHIMOPRRSTT aromatherapist
AAAEHLNOPPRSTU Palaeanthropus
AAAEIILLNORSTT lateralisation
AAAEIILLNORTTZ lateralization
AAAEIILMPPRTTT palmatipartite
AAAEIILNNOPRRS pararosaniline
AAAEILMOPPPRRT malappropriate
AAAEIMMMNRRSTU armamentariums
AAAELLQQRSUUVY quaquaversally
AAAFGILNORSTTY stagflationary
AAAFIILLMNRRXY inframaxillary
AAAFIILLNNOPRT intrafallopian
AAAGHHLOPRSSTY thalassography
AAAGHHMOPRTTUY thaumatography
AAAGIILNNOORST organisational
AAAGIILNNOORTZ organizational
AAAGIIMNOPRSTT pragmatisation
AAAGIIMNOPRTTZ pragmatization
AAAGIINNNOOSTT antagonisation
AAAGIINNNOOTTZ antagonization
AAAIIIILNNOSTT Italianisation
AAAIIIILNNOTTZ Italianization
AAAIIIILNOPRSTT patrialisation
AAAIIIILNOPRTTZ patrialization
AAAIIIMNNQRSTU antiquarianism
AAAIILNNORSTTU naturalisation
AAAIILNNORTTUZ naturalization
AAAIIMNORSTTTU traumatisation
AAAIIMNORTTTUZ traumatization
AAAILNNORSTTUV transvaluation
AABBCCEEEGLTTU cabbage-lettuce
AABBCCHHIOOPRT batrachophobic
AABBCEEFINORST absorbefacient
AABBDDEENRRTTU bread-and-butter
AABBDEEELMRRST marble-breasted
AABBDGGIINNNOR △brobdingnagian
AABBEEELNNRSSU unbearableness
AABBEEGILNNPRT rabbeting-plane
AABBEEILMNNOSS abominableness
AABBEHIKORSUYZ Bashi-Bazoukery
AABBEIMMNNPSSY namby-pambiness
AABCCCDHILRTYY brachydactylic
AABCCCEHHILPRY brachycephalic
AABCCCGHIKNRST backscratching
AABCCDDEILLOSY dodecasyllabic
AABCCDEILNORTT contradictable
AABCCEEELNPSST acceptableness
AABCCEELNNORTU counterbalance
AABCCEHIIORRTT trichobacteria
AABCCEHILLMOPS accomplishable
AABCCEHNOOORSU orobanchaceous
AABCCEIIORSTTT bacteriostatic
AABCCEILMMRTUU circumambulate
AABCCEIMNORTUY cyanobacterium
AABCCIIILPRTTY practicability
AABCCIILLNOSTU actinobacillus
AABCCIILNOTTUY accountability
AABCDDEELLLOSY dodecasyllable
AABCDDEILMNOPR bladder-campion
AABCDEEHNNRUZZ △nebuchadnezzar
AABCDEEINRRSTT scatterbrained
AABCDEENNPRSUU superabundance
AABCDEENRSSSTT abstractedness
AABCDEGIKLNRRT blank-cartridge
AABCDEHIINNRTU nudibranchiate
AABCDEHOORRSST across-the-board
AABCDHIIKNOPRY brachypinakoid
AABCDHIILNOPRS cardinal-bishop
AABCDIILLQRSUY quadrisyllabic
AABCEEEGHLNNSS changeableness
AABCEEEGHLNRSS chargeableness
AABCEEEKKLMRRT black-marketeer
AABCEEGHINPRST breathing-space
AABCEEHILNRSST charitableness
AABCEEHILOPRRR irreproachable
AABCEEHLMNNRTU unmerchantable
AABCEEHLNPRSUU unpurchaseable
AABCEEHLORSSTT across-the-table
AABCEEILLLMMTY emblematically
AABCEEILLMNPSS implacableness

AABCEEIMNORSSZ semicarbazones
AABCEEKLNORRTW tabernacle-work
AABCEELLNNNORT cannonball-tree
AABCEELMNOPRSS comparableness
AABCEELNPRRTUU unrecapturable
AABCEFGIILORRT fibrocartilage
AABCEFIIINOTTU beautification
AABCEFIILLNSSU unclassifiable
AABCEFIINOPRRT prefabrication
AABCEGHHIIMNNT bathing-machine
AABCEGHINORTYZ zygobranchiate
AABCEGIILLOOOP palaeobiologic
AABCEGIILLOOOR aerobiological
AABCEGINNORRTU bargain-counter
AABCEHIILLRSTY Hebraistically
AABCEHIILMNORS Elasmobranchii
AABCEHIIMMOSTT biomathematics
AABCEHILLPRTYY hyperbatically
AABCEHILNNOOTT ethnobotanical
AABCEHILOPRRRY irreproachably
AABCEIILLOORTY aerobiotically
AABCEIILRTTTXY extractability
AABCEIIORSSSTT bacteriostasis
AABCEILLLRSSTY crystallisable
AABCEILLLRSTYZ crystallizable
AABCEILLMORRTY barometrically
AABCEILLNTTUUV uncultivatable
AABCEILMNOOPSS compassionable
AABCEILNNOORST torsion-balance
AABCEIMOORSSUU simaroubaceous
AABCELMNNORSTT marble-constant
AABCGGIILLOOOR agrobiological
AABCGHIILLMOOP amphibological
AABCGHIILLOPRY biographically
AABCGHIIOOPRTU autobiographic
AABCGHIMOOPRRR microbarograph
AABCHILOOPRSTU claustrophobia
AABCIIIJMNNOST anti-Jacobinism
AABCIIILLMPRSY imparisyllabic
AABCIIILNRTTTY intractability
AABCIILLLOPSTY collapsability
AABCIIMNORSSTT abstractionism
AABCIINOOSSSTU subassociation
AABCIINORSSTTT abstractionist
AABCILLLLOPSYY polysyllabical
AABCILLORRRTUU arboricultural
AABCILMNNOOTTU noctambulation
AABCILNNOSSTTU consubstantial
AABDDEELNNRSTU understandable
AABDDEFIIOPRRS bird-of-paradise
AABDDEGHILLNOT Gnathobdellida
AABDDEGIINOORT biodegradation
AABDDEIILRSSTY addressability
AABDEEEHNRRSST threadbareness
AABDEEELNNRSSU unreadableness
AABDEEELNRRSSW rewardableness
AABDEEHINRRSTT shatter-brained
AABDEELNNOPRSS pardonableness
AABDEFGIILLRTY deflagrability
AABDEFIIILLQSU disqualifiable
AABDEIIILMNOPR imponderabilia
AABDEIIKLLMRRR billiard-marker
AABDEIIKMNORST disembarkation
AABDEIILNOQRTU quodlibetarian
AABDEIIOPPRSTV disapprobative
AABDEILLLQRSUY quadrisyllable
AABDELOOPRRRRU parlour-boarder
AABDFFFFOOORWY off-off-Broadway
AABDGIIILNOSTY diagnosability
AABDGIIIMNOSTU disambiguation
AABDIIIILNSTVY inadvisability
AABDIIILNOTUVY unavoidability
AABDIINOOPPRST disapprobation
AABDIOOPPRRSTY disapprobatory
AABEEEEGMRRTTV megavertebrate
AABEEEEHHLRRTT heather-bleater
AABEEEHKLNRSTT bletheranskate
AABEEEKLMNRRSS remarkableness
AABEEEKLMNRSST marketableness
AABEEELMNNSSTU untameableness
AABEEELMNRSSSU measurableness
AABEEELNNORSSS reasonableness
AABEEELNNOSSSS seasonableness
AABEEFGHILNPRT finger-alphabet
AABEEFGILNNOST self-abnegation
AABEEFGILNSSTU fatiguableness
AABEEFLMNORTTY flamboyant-tree
AABEEFLNNRRSTU untransferable
AABEEFLNORSSUV favourableness
AABEEGHINRRTTW water-breathing
AABEEGIILMNNSS imaginableness
AABEEGIKMORRRR marriage-broker
AABEEGLMMOPRRR reprogrammable
AABEEHIIILRTTV rehabilitative
AABEEHIILMNSTZ Elizabethanism
AABEEIILNNRSSV invariableness
AABEEIILNNSSST insatiableness
AABEEIILNRRRST irrestrainable
AABEEILMNPSSSS impassableness
AABEEILNNRRSTU unrestrainable
AABEELNNPSSSSU unpassableness
AABEFIMNOORRTU neurofibromata
AABEGGGINORSTU subaggregation
AABEGHILLNNQTU banqueting-hall
AABEGHIOOPRRTU autobiographer
AABEGIIILMNNSS Albigensianism
AABEGIILLOOPST palaebiologist
AABEHIIILNORTT rehabilitation
AABEHILNNQSUUV unvanquishable
AABEHLLOPPRSTY blepharoplasty
AABEIIIILLNNTY inalienability
AABEIIILLNORST liberalisation
AABEIIILLNORTZ liberalization
AABEIIILLNRTTY inalterability
AABEIIILMNRRST libertarianism
AABEIIILNPRSTY inseparability
AABEIIILPRRRTY irreparability
AABEIILLLMNTUY unmalleability
AABEIILLNRTTUY unalterability
AABEIILMPTTTTY attemptability
AABEIILNNNTTTU tintinnabulate
AABEIILNSSSTTU substantialise
AABEIILNSSTTUZ substantialize
AABEILMNNRSTTU intransmutable

AABEILMNOORSTT	retinoblastoma	AACCEEILORSTTT	stereotactical
AABEILNNORSTTU	subalternation	AACCEEINNNORSS	reconnaissance
AABEILNOPRRTTU	perturbational	AACCEEINNRSSTU	inaccurateness
AABELMNNRSTTUU	untransmutable	AACCEELLNOOUVV	Convolvulaceae
AABELMNOORSSTU	neuroblastomas	AACCEEMNNNOOPR	non-compearance
AABFFIIIILLSTY	falsifiability	AACCEEMNOPRTTY	pancreatectomy
AABFIIILLMMNTY	inflammability	AACCEFHIORRSSU	sacchariferous
AABFIILLNPPTUY	unflappability	AACCEFILNOSSTU	self-accusation
AABGIIILNORSTY	organisability	AACCEFIMNNORRU	circumforanean
AABGIIILNORTYZ	organizability	AACCEFLORSSTUY	self-accusatory
AABHHINOOOPPRT	anthropophobia	AACCEGGILLNOOY	gynaecological
AABIIILNSSTTUY	sustainability	AACCEGHILLNOPY	coelanaglyphic
AABIILMNSSSTTU	substantialism	AACCEGHILLOOST	eschatological
AABIILNNNNTTTU	tintinnabulant	AACCEGHILNOPRS	scenographical
AABIILNNNRTTUY	tintinnabulary	AACCEGHILNRRST	clear-starching
AABIILNSSSTTTU	substantialist	AACCEGHLOORRTY	characterology
AABIILNSSTTTUY	substantiality	AACCEGIIILOOPTT	galactopoietic
AABIINNOSSTTTU	substantiation	AACCEGIIMNRTUV	circumnavigate
AABILLNSSTTUVY	substantivally	AACCEGINNOSTUY	nyctaginaceous
AABILMMNNOOSTU	somnambulation	AACCEHHIILLRRY	hierarchically
AACCCCEGLOORSY	sacrococcygeal	AACCEHHLOPPSSU	scaphocephalus
AACCCCENNOOOVV	concavo-concave	AACCEHIILMNORT	cheiromantical
AACCCILLNORTY	contracyclical	AACCEHIILOPPRS	archiepiscopal
AACCCDHIIOORRT	cardiothoracic	AACCEHIILQRRSU	squirearchical
AACCCEEHILLTTY	catechetically	AACCEHILLORTTY	theocratically
AACCCEEHILMNTU	catechumenical	AACCEHINOPPRRT	parthenocarpic
AACCCEEIILLSST	ecclesiastical	AACCEHLMOOPRSU	macrocephalous
AACCCEHHILOPPS	scaphocephalic	AACCEIILMNOOSS	semi-occasional
AACCCEHIIRRSTT	characteristic	AACCEIILNORRTT	recalcitration
AACCCEHLNOSTUY	cyclanthaceous	AACCEIIMNOPSTT	misacceptation
AACCCGIILLNOOR	carcinological	AACCEILLLOPPTY	apoplectically
AACCCHLLOOPSTY	staphylococcal	AACCEILLMTUUVY	accumulatively
AACCCNNOOSTTTU	cost-accountant	AACCEILPRSTTUY	spectacularity
AACCDDEEHKNNSS	cack-handedness	AACCELLMMOORRU	macromolecular
AACCDDEIMMOOST	disaccommodate	AACCELNNORSUUU	ranunculaceous
AACCDDEMMNOOTU	unaccommodated	AACCENNORSSSST	sacrosanctness
AACCDEEEHINOOP	Chenopodiaceae	AACCFFGIILMNRT	traffic-calming
AACCDEEHLNRRST	cradle-snatcher	AACCFIIILNOORT	calorification
AACCDEEIINRRST	disincarcerate	AACCFIIILNOSST	classification
AACCDEEILNNOPY	encyclopaedian	AACCFIIINNOSTT	sanctification
AACCDEGHIMOORR	echocardiogram	AACCFIILORSSTY	classificatory
AACCDEHILOPRSY	polysaccharide	AACCGHHIIILNOPR	ichnographical
AACCDEHIMNOORS	monosaccharide	AACCGHHILOOPRR	chorographical
AACCDEIILLOPTY	apodeictically	AACCGHHILOPRST	chalcographist
AACCDEIINNORTT	contraindicate	AACCGHIILNOPRZ	zincographical
AACCDEILLMORTY	democratically	AACCGHILMOOPRS	cosmographical
AACCDHIILLNORY	diachronically	AACCGIIILLLMOOT	climatological
AACCDHIMOPRSTY	psychodramatic	AACCGIILLMORTY	tragicomically
AACCDHLOPSTUYY	pachydactylous	AACCGILLLNOOOV	volcanological
AACCDIIINRSTTU	Traducianistic	AACCGILLLNOOUV	vulcanological
AACCDIINNNORTT	contraindicant	AACCHIILLMSSTY	schismatically
AACCDIINNOOOPR	piano-accordion	AACCHILLLOPTTY	phyllotactical
AACCDLMOORSTUY	macrodactylous	AACCHILLLOSSTY	scholastically
AACCEEEIIKRSTT	Rickettsiaceae	AACCHILNOPSTYY	psychoanalytic
AACCEEELNNOTYY	cyanoacetylene	AACCHILOOPTTTY	photocatalytic
AACCEEGHHILNRT	archgenethliac	AACCHINNOPSTTU	accountantship
AACCEEGIILNTTT	telangiectatic	AACCIIILMPRTTY	impracticality
AACCEEGILLOOOP	palaeoecologic	AACCIILLMNOSTU	miscalculation
AACCEEGILMNNRS	cleansing-cream	AACCIILMNRSTTU	circumstantial
AACCEEHIILMPST	mesaticephalic	AACCIILNNOOOST	consociational
AACCEEHILMORTT	tacheometrical	AACCIILNPRTTUY	unpracticality
AACCEEHILMOTUY	leucocythaemia	AACCIILOOPRSTV	vicar-apostolic

AACCIIMNOORSST	carcinomatosis
AACCILNOPRRSUU	corpuscularian
AACCINNOORRTTY	contractionary
AACCLLMNORSTYY	crystallomancy
AACDDEEEOPTTUV	advocate-depute
AACDDEEHINOOTT	Chaetodontidae
AACDDEEHIPRSTT	death-practised
AACDDEEIILMMNR	Middle-American
AACDDHILMNORYY	hydrodynamical
AACDEEEEINOPRT	Pontederiaceae
AACDEEEFHMNSSS	shamefacedness
AACDEEEGLMNNTT	gentleman-cadet
AACDEEGHIIMNNR	reading-machine
AACDEEGIPPRRRT	cartridge-paper
AACDEEHIILLNTX	Hexactinellida
AACDEEHIIMMSTT	mathematicised
AACDEEHIIMMTTZ	mathematicized
AACDEEHILMPSTU	sulphacetamide
AACDEEHIPRRTTY	Trachypteridae
AACDEEHLMMNOOY	Monochlamydeae
AACDEEILLMMNTY	medicamentally
AACDEEILLNQTUW	well-acquainted
AACDEEILOPPRTU	propaedeutical
AACDEEILPRRTTU	ultracrepidate
AACDEELNNNRSTT	transcendental
AACDEENORSSSUV	cadaverousness
AACDEFIIINNOTZ	denazification
AACDEFMNNRTUUU	unmanufactured
AACDEGHHOOPRRT	cathodographer
AACDEGHIMOPRRT	dermatographic
AACDEGILLMOORT	dermatological
AACDEGINOPRSST	data-processing
AACDEHIMOPRSSU	pseudo-archaism
AACDEHLLLNORTW	tallow-chandler
AACDEHLLMOTUWY	what-d'you-call-'em
AACDEHLNOOPRSU	androcephalous
AACDEHMOPRSTUY	pachydermatous
AACDEIIILLLSTY	idealistically
AACDEIIILMNOST	decimalisation
	medicalisation
AACDEIIILMNOTZ	decimalization
	medicalization
AACDEIIILMORST	isodiametrical
AACDEIIIMNORTU	audiometrician
AACDEIILNOSTTU	educationalist
AACDEIILNPRRST	cardinal-priest
AACDEIILOPRSTT	disceptatorial
AACDEIIMNORSTY	aerodynamicist
AACDEILLMOPRYY	polyacrylamide
AACDEILLNNRSTU	slantendicular
AACDEILMMNORTY	dynamometrical
AACDEILMNPSTTY	pentadactylism
AACDEILMNRTTUU	unmatriculated
AACDEILMOPRSTT	dermatoplastic
AACDEILOPRSSTY	Perissodactyla
AACDEIMNNNOTTU	uncontaminated
AACDEIMNNOORTT	decontaminator
AACDELNNOSSSSU	scandalousness
AACDELNOPSTTUY	pentadactylous
AACDELORSTTTUY	tetradactylous
AACDFIIIILNOPT	lapidification
AACDGHHILOPRRY	hydrographical
AACDGHILOPRTYY	dactyliography
AACDGIIILNNOOTT	antiodontalgic
AACDGIINOPPRST	propagandistic
AACDHIIILLOPTY	idiopathically
AACDHILLOTTUWY	what-d'you-call-it
AACDHIMMNNOPST	commandantship
AACDHIMOOPRTYY	cardiomyopathy
	myocardiopathy
AACDIIIILNNPRS	disciplinarian
AACDIIILNOPPST	disapplication
AACDIIINOOSSST	disassociation
AACDIILLLMOPTY	diplomatically
AACDIILLNNRSTU	slantindicular
AACDILNOOSSTUY	anisodactylous
AACEEEEIMMNPRS	Menispermaceae
AACEEEGILLLNTV	televangelical
AACEEEGKLRSTWY	greywacke-slate
AACEEEHLMOSTUY	thymelaeaceous
AACEEFFILNOTTY	affectionately
AACEEFGHLLOSTU	shelf-catalogue
AACEEGGGILRRRU	luggage-carrier
AACEEGGILLLNOY	genealogically
AACEEGGILORSTT	geostrategical
AACEEGHHINRRST	heart-searching
AACEEGHHLNOPPR	encephalograph
AACEEGHIIMNNPR	reaping-machine
AACEEGHILLLNTY	genethliacally
AACEEGHILMPRYY	hyperglycaemia
AACEEGHILNOPST	stegocephalian
AACEEGHLLOPYYZ	Zygophyllaceae
AACEEGIILLMNSV	evangelicalism
AACEEGIILLNNPT	palingenetical
AACEEGIILNSSTT	telangiectasis
AACEEGIINNNRST	intransigeance
AACEEGILLLOOPS	spelaeological
AACEEGILMNOSTT	magneto-elastic
AACEEGJLMNORRY	major-generalcy
AACEEHHINORRST	Archaeornithes
AACEEHHIOOPRRZ	Rhizophoraceae
AACEEHHLNOPPTY	encephalopathy
AACEEHIIMOOPTT	haematopoietic
AACEEHILLLPTTY	telepathically
AACEEHILMMNTTY	enthymematical
AACEEHILMNPSST	emphaticalness
AACEEHILNRSSTT	theatricalness
AACEEHILPRSTXY	hypercatalexis
AACEEHILRRTUVX	extravehicular
AACEEHIMORRSTT	archaeometrist
AACEEHIPRSSTTY	cryptaesthesia
AACEEHMNORSTUY	aerenchymatous
AACEEIIINPPRTV	inappreciative
AACEEIILOPRSTV	overcapitalise
AACEEIILOPRTVZ	overcapitalize
AACEEIILPPRTVY	appreciatively
AACEEIILPRTTUV	recapitulative
AACEEIIMNNNRST	centenarianism
AACEEIIMNNRSSS	necessarianism
AACEEIINPPRTUV	unappreciative
AACEEIJLMNSSST	majesticalness
AACEEILLLMSTTY	telesmatically
AACEEILMMNSSTU	immaculateness
AACEEILMMPRTUY	empyreumatical

AACEEILNRSSTTU	articulateness
AACEEINRSSTTTV	attractiveness
AACEELMMOOSSTU	melastomaceous
AACEELNNOPSTUU	pennatulaceous
AACEELOOPRRRTX	extracorporeal
AACEEMNNNOOPRT	contemporanean
AACEFIIILNRSST	artificialness
AACEFIILOOQSUU	aquifoliaceous
AACEFILLNOSSSU	fallaciousness
AACEGGHILLOPRY	geographically
AACEGGHINOPRST	steganographic
AACEGGIINPRRRS	spring-carriage
AACEGGILNNOORT	△congregational
AACEGHHIILLOPR	heliographical
AACEGHHIILOPRR	hierographical
AACEGHHIIMNNSW	washing-machine
AACEGHHILNOPRT	ethnographical
AACEGHHILOPRTY	hyetographical
AACEGHHIMOPPTT	apophthegmatic
AACEGHIIKLMNNT	talking-machine
AACEGHIILMNNNP	planing-machine
AACEGHIILMOOTY	oligocythaemia
AACEGHIIMMORRT	hierogrammatic
AACEGHILLLMPTY	phlegmatically
AACEGHILLMOPRT	metallographic
AACEGHILLOOPRS	phraseological
AACEGHILOPPRRT	petrographical
AACEGHILOPRTTU	telautographic
AACEGHIMNOPRTY	cinematography
AACEGHINNOPSWW	weaponschawing
AACEGHINNPPSWW	wappenschawing
AACEGHLNNSTUUW	Weltanschauung
AACEGHLOOOORYZ	archaeozoology
AACEGIILLLLSTY	legalistically
AACEGIILLMOOSS	semasiological
AACEGIILMOPRTY	Malacopterygii
AACEGIINOORSTT	categorisation
AACEGIINOORTTZ	categorization
AACEGIKMMNORRT	macro-marketing
AACEGILLLOOPTY	apologetically
AACEGILLMNOORT	organometallic
AACEGILMNOOPTT	magneto-optical
AACEGILNORTTUV	congratulative
AACEGILNRRTTUY	rectangularity
AACEHHILNNOPTY	phthalocyanine
AACEHIILLMRTTY	arithmetically
AACEHIILLNTTTY	antithetically
AACEHIILNSSTTU	enthusiastical
AACEHIILPPRRST	periphrastical
AACEHIIMNOSSTT	schematisation
AACEHIIMNOSTTZ	schematization
AACEHIIMNPRRST	Petrarchianism
AACEHIINNOTTTU	authentication
AACEHIINPRRSTT	Petrarchianist
AACEHILLMNNORY	enharmonically
AACEHILLMNOPTY	phonematically
AACEHILLMOPRSY	semaphorically
AACEHILLMOPRTY	metaphorically
AACEHILLMPSTYY	metaphysically
AACEHILMNOPRTU	unmetaphorical
AACEHILMNPSTUY	unmetaphysical
AACEHILNOOPPRT	paleoanthropic
AACEHKOOPPRRST	approach-stroke
AACEHLLOPPSTUY	platycephalous
AACEHLOPRRSSTY	sphaerocrystal
AACEHMNOPRSTUY	parenchymatous
AACEIIILNOPSST	specialisation
AACEIIILNOPSTZ	specialization
AACEIIILNPTTVY	anticipatively
AACEIIINNOPPRT	inappreciation
AACEIILLLMRTTY	altimetrically
AACEIILLNPSTTY	antiseptically
AACEIILLNRTTUY	inarticulately
AACEIILMNRRRTU	intramercurial
AACEIILNNORSTT	centralisation
AACEIILNNORSTU	nuclearisation
AACEIILNNORTTZ	centralization
AACEIILNNORTUZ	nuclearization
AACEIILNOOPPSU	papilionaceous
AACEIILNOPRTTU	recapitulation
AACEIILNORRTVY	early-Victorian
AACEIILNORSSTU	secularisation
AACEIILNORSTUZ	secularization
AACEIILOPSTTTT	petticoat-tails
AACEIIMNNRSSTU	unsectarianism
AACEIINORSSSUV	avariciousness
AACEILLLNOPSTY	pleonastically
AACEILLMMRSTYY	asymmetrically
AACEILLMNNOORT	nomenclatorial
AACEILLMNORRTU	intramolecular
AACEILLMRTTTUU	multarticulate
AACEILLMSSTTYY	systematically
AACEILMMNOORTT	commentatorial
AACEILMNNOOPST	compensational
AACEILMNOSSSTU	calamitousness
AACEILMNSSTTUY	unsystematical
AACEILNNNRSSTY	tyrannicalness
AACEILNNOORSTV	conservational
	conversational
AACEILNORSTTUX	exclaustration
AACEILNPRRSSTU	particularness
AACEILNRTTTUVY	unattractively
AACEILOPRRTTUY	recapitulatory
AACEINOORRRSTT	rostrocarinate
AACEKLNNORSTUY	cantankerously
AACELLMNOOPRRY	monocarpellary
AACELNNNOOPRST	preconsonantal
AACEMMNOPRSSTU	Castanospermum
AACENNOPRSSTTU	counter-passant
AACENNORSSTTUU	transcutaneous
AACFFGIILNRSST	traffic-signals
AACFGIIINNOSTU	sanguification
AACFGNOOORSTTT	contrafagottos
AACFIIIILLNRTY	inartificially
AACFIIIKNORSTT	karstification
AACFIIILLNRTUY	unartificially
AACFIIINNOOPST	saponification
AACFIIINNOQTTU	quantification
AACFIIINORSTTT	stratification
AACFIILLMORTTU	multifactorial
AACFIILMORSTTT	stalactitiform
AACFIILORSSTTY	satisfactorily
AACFIINNOSSTTU	unsatisfaction
AACFILMNNOOORT	conformational

Words marked △ may be spelled also with a capital letter

AACFINORSSTTUY	unsatisfactory
AACGGHHILOPRRY	hygrographical
AACGGILLLNOORY	laryngological
AACGGILLOOORST	agrostological
AACGHHIILLOPRT	lithographical
AACGHHILOOPPRT	photographical
AACGHHILOOPRRT	orthographical
AACGHHIOPPRRRY	rhyparographic
AACGHHMOOPRRTY	chromatography
AACGHILLLOOPTY	pathologically
AACGHILMOOPRST	pharmacologist
AACGHLOOOPRSTU	galactophorous
AACGHLOOPPRSYY	parapsychology
AACGHOOOPPRTUY	autocoprophagy
AACGIIILNPRSTU	paralinguistic
AACGIILNOOSTTV	Vaticanologist
AACGIIMNOOPRRS	microsporangia
AACGILLLOORSTY	astrologically
AACGILLLOOTTUY	tautologically
AACGILLLRRTUUY	agriculturally
AACGILLMOORRTY	martyrological
AACGILMOOPRRTU	compurgatorial
AACGILNNOORTTU	congratulation
AACGIMOORSSTTT	stomatogastric
AACGINNOORRTTT	contrarotating
AACGLNOORRTTUY	congratulatory
AACHHIIMNRRTTY	antiarrhythmic
AACHHIINORSTUY	ichthyosaurian
AACHHINOOPPRTT	anthropopathic
AACHIILLNNOPTY	antiphonically
AACHIILLNOOOST	alcoholisation
AACHIILLNOOOTZ	alcoholization
AACHIILLOPRSTY	aphoristically
AACHIILMNOPRST	misanthropical
AACHIIMMNNOOPR	morphinomaniac
AACHIIMNNORSTT	antimonarchist
AACHILLOPSTTYY	hypostatically
AACHILMOOPPRST	pharmacopolist
AACHILNOPSSSYY	psychoanalysis
AACHILOOPSSTTY	photocatalysis
AACHLLOOOPPPRY	Polyplacophora
AACHLMNOOOOPPR	Monoplacophora
AACIIILLLSTTVY	vitalistically
AACIIILLMMRSTU	multiracialism
AACIIILLNRSTTY	inartistically
AACIIILMNOPPST	misapplication
AACIIILNNORTTU	inarticulation
AACIIILNOPRTTY	anticipatorily
AACIIIMNOOSSST	associationism
AACIILLLRSTTUY	altruistically
AACIILLMMNOPTY	pantomimically
AACIILLMMNSTUY	numismatically
AACIILNOOPRRST	conspiratorial
AACIILNPRRSTTU	antiscriptural
AACIINNOOTTTUX	auto-intoxicant
AACILLLNORSTUY	ultrasonically
AACILLMNNORTUY	unromantically
AACILLMNOORSTY	astronomically
AACILLMOPSTTYY	asymptotically
AACILMOOPPRSTT	protoplasmatic
AACILNNNOORSTT	triconsonantal
AACILNNNOSTTUV	anticonvulsant
AACINOOPRRRSTT	procrastinator
AADDDFFILLNOWY	daffadowndilly
AADDEEHILNNORT	△neanderthaloid
AADDEELNOQRRSU	squadron-leader
AADDEINORSTTUW	outward-sainted
AADEEEGILMPRSS	spread-eagleism
AADEEEGKMNRRRT	market-gardener
AADEEEHIIMNRRT	maidenhair-tree
AADEEEHIMMNPTX	dexamphetamine
AADEEEHIPSSSTU	pseudaesthesia
AADEEEHLRRRSSS	dress-rehearsal
AADEEEILLLNPRV	parallel-veined
AADEEEILLLPPPR	parallelepiped
AADEEEINNQSSTU	inadequateness
AADEEFGHLPRSTU	flaughter-spade
AADEEFGILLLNOT	dinoflagellate
AADEEFHILNRTTY	faint-heartedly
AADEEFIILMNRST	anti-federalism
AADEEFIILNORST	federalisation
AADEEFIILNORTZ	federalization
AADEEFIILNRSTT	anti-federalist
AADEEGGIMNNRST	aggrandisement
AADEEGGIMNNRTZ	aggrandizement
AADEEGHILOPRRT	radiotelegraph
AADEEGHIPPPRSU	pseudepigrapha
AADEEGIIMNQRTU	quadrigeminate
AADEEGIMNNRRST	disarrangement
AADEEGLLOOOPPY	palaeopedology
AADEEHHIMPRSST	headmastership
AADEEHIIMNRTTY	diathermaneity
AADEEHLNOOPRRY	aerohydroplane
	hydro-aeroplane
AADEEIILMNRSTU	unmaterialised
AADEEIILMNRTUZ	unmaterialized
AADEEIILNPQSSU	sesquipedalian
AADEEIINNPRRST	predestinarian
AADEEILLLOPPPR	parallelopiped
AADEEILLNOPPRS	plane-polarised
AADEEILLNOPPRZ	plane-polarized
AADEEILMNORTTT	tatterdemalion
AADEEINNPRSSTT	antidepressant
AADEELLMNPRTTY	departmentally
AADEEPRRSSTTUU	supersaturated
AADEFIILMNORST	self-admiration
AADEFIIMNORSTU	diamantiferous
AADEFILMMNNSTU	fundamentalism
AADEFILMNNSTTU	fundamentalist
AADEFILMNNTTUY	fundamentality
AADEGGGIINORST	disaggregation
AADEGHILNRSTUW	daughters-in-law
AADEGIIIIMPRTT	imparidigitate
AADEGIILNNPTZZ	dazzle-painting
AADEGIINNORRTT	intergradation
AADEGINOORRRTT	retrogradation
AADEHIILLMNPSU	sulphanilamide
AADEHINNOPSSSU	diaphanousness
AADEHNORRSSTTW	north-eastwards
AADEHORSSSTTUW	south-eastwards
AADEIIIILNNOSST	desalinisation
AADEIIILNNOSTZ	desalinization
AADEIIILNOSTTV	devitalisation
AADEIIILNOTTVZ	devitalization

Words marked △ may be spelled also with a capital letter

AADEIIIMNORSST	nematodiriasis
AADEIIIMNRSTTV	administrative
AADEIILLLNTUVY	antediluvially
AADEIILMNNNOOT	denominational
AADEIILMNOORST	demoralisation
AADEIILMNOORTZ	demoralization
AADEIILNNOPSST	dispensational
AADEIILNOOPRST	depolarisation
AADEIILNOOPRTZ	depolarization
AADEIILNOORSTV	devalorisation
AADEIILNOORTVZ	devalorization
AADEIILNORSSTT	dissertational
AADEIINORRSSTT	radioresistant
AADEIIOPPPRRST	disappropriate
AADEILLMNRRTUY	intramedullary
AADEILNNORTUUV	undervaluation
AADEINOPPPRRTU	unappropriated
AADFFIIIILNOST	disaffiliation
AADFFIIIMNORST	disaffirmation
AADFIIILNNNOST	Finlandisation
AADFIIILNNNOTZ	Finlandization
AADGGHIILNSTVY	daylight-saving
AADGIIIILNOSTT	digitalisation
AADGIIIILNOTTZ	digitalization
AADGIIILNORRSTU	agroindustrial
AADIIILMNORSTT	traditionalism
AADIIILNNORSTU	solitudinarian
AADIIILNORRTTY	traditionarily
AADIIILNORSTTT	traditionalist
AADIIILNORTTTY	traditionality
AADIIIMNNORSTT	administration
AADIIIMNRRSTTX	administratrix
AADIMNOOORRSTY	radio-astronomy
AAEEEFGLMMNNST	self-management
AAEEEFGMNNORRS	ferro-manganese
AAEEEGHIMNOSST	haematogenesis
AAEEEGMNNPRRRT	prearrangement
AAEEEHHINRSSTV	heart-heaviness
AAEEEHHIPRSSTY	hyperaesthesia
AAEEEHILLMNPRT	parliament-heel
AAEEEHILMNORTU	eleutheromania
AAEEEIMNPPRRST	reappraisement
AAEEELPPPRRSTT	saltpetre-paper
AAEEENNPRRRSTU	superterranean
AAEEFGHILLNRRT	larger-than-life
AAEEFGILLNNTTU	flag-lieutenant
AAEEFGIMNNORRS	ferromagnesian
AAEEFHHORRSTTT	star-of-the-earth
AAEEFHNOPSSTTT	seat-of-the-pants
AAEEFILNNRRSTT	transferential
AAEEFNOORRSTUX	extraforaneous
AAEEGGHLOOPPRY	paleogeography
AAEEGGHNOPRRST	steganographer
AAEEGHIMMNOPSY	hypomagnesemia
AAEEGHLLMOPRRT	metallographer
AAEEGHNNOOPRTY	Neopythagorean
AAEEGIILLNORST	Anglo-Israelite
AAEEGIILNNORST	generalisation
AAEEGIILNNORTZ	generalization
AAEEGIILNNOSTV	evangelisation
AAEEGIILNNOTVZ	evangelization
AAEEGILLNRTVVW	travelling-wave
AAEEGILMMNOPST	paleomagnetism
AAEEGILMNQRTUV	gram-equivalent
AAEEGILNRSSTVY	asseveratingly
AAEEGIMMNNRRST	misarrangement
AAEEGLLQRRRTUY	quarter-gallery
AAEEGLMNPRSSTU	suprasegmental
AAEEGMNOPRSSSU	rampageousness
AAEEHIIMNSSTTT	antimetathesis
AAEEHIIMOOPSST	haematopoiesis
AAEEHILMPPRSSS	plasmapheresis
AAEEHIMNRSSSTU	amateurishness
AAEEHMOOPRRRST	spermatorrhoea
AAEEIILLMNNPRR	premillenarian
AAEEIILNNNORTT	Internationale
AAEEIILNNORSTT	eternalisation
AAEEIILNNORTTZ	eternalization
AAEEIILNOPRRST	proletarianise
AAEEIILNOPRRTZ	proletarianize
AAEEIINNPRRSTT	painter-stainer
AAEEILMNNOOPPR	paraleipomenon
AAEEILMNOPRRTU	Euro-Parliament
AAEEILMNRSTTTY	testamentarily
AAEEILNNOPRSTT	presentational
AAEEILNNPRRTTY	interplanetary
AAEEILNOOPPRRT	preoperational
AAEEINNOPSSSST	passionateness
AAEEINRRSSTTTW	water-resistant
AAEELNNNPSSSTU	unpleasantness
AAEEMNNOPPRSWW	newspaper-woman
AAEFFGILNOPTTU	palagonite-tuff
AAEFFIIILMORST	forisfamiliate
AAEFGIILNOSTTU	angustifoliate
AAEFIINNORRSTT	fraternisation
AAEFIINNORRTTZ	fraternization
AAEFIMNORRSTTV	transformative
AAEFLMNOOOPTTW	footplatewoman
AAEGGHIMNOPRTY	enigmatography
AAEGGIINNORRST	grangerisation
AAEGGIINNORRTZ	grangerization
AAEGGIMMNOPRSU	megasporangium
AAEGHHIILNRRTT	lighter-than-air
AAEGHHOPPRRRRY	rhyparographer
AAEGHIILLNRTXY	exhilaratingly
AAEGHIKMMNNPPR	knapping-hammer
AAEGHIMNOPRSTY	Pythagoreanism
AAEGHIMOOPPRRY	paroemiography
AAEGHLLOOOPPTY	paleopathology
AAEGHLNOOPPRTY	paleontography
AAEGIIILNNOSTT	gelatinisation
AAEGIIILNNOTTZ	gelatinization
AAEGIILLNOORST	allegorisation
AAEGIILLNOORTZ	allegorization
AAEGIILMNQQSUU	quinquagesimal
AAEGIILNORRSTU	regularisation
AAEGIILNORRTUZ	regularization
AAEGIILNQRTUUY	equiangularity
AAEGIIMNRRSTTV	transmigrative
AAEGIINNNOSTUX	exsanguination
AAEGIINNNRSSSU	sanguinariness
AAEGIINNOORRST	reorganisation
AAEGIINNOORRTZ	reorganization
AAEGINOPRRSTUY	sauropterygian

AAEHHILLOPSTUZ	sulphathiazole
AAEHIILMNORSTT	thermalisation
AAEHIILMNORTTZ	thermalization
AAEHILNOPPSSSY	psephoanalysis
AAEHIOOPPRRSTT	protospathaire
AAEHIPPQRRSTUZ	sapphire-quartz
AAEHLMNNOOSTUX	xanthomelanous
AAEHLNOOPPRSTU	Paleoanthropus
AAEHNNORRSSSTU	anarthrousness
AAEIIIILNRSTTU	utilitarianise
AAEIIIILNRTTUZ	utilitarianize
AAEIIIKNNORSTT	keratinisation
AAEIIIKNNORTTZ	keratinization
AAEIIILLMMNNRS	millenarianism
AAEIIILMNNORST	mineralisation
AAEIIILMNNORTZ	mineralization
AAEIIILNORSTTT	retaliationist
AAEIIILNORSTTV	revitalisation
AAEIIILNORTTVZ	revitalization
AAEIIINNNRSSST	insanitariness
AAEIIINNPPRTTT	pinnatipartite
AAEIIINNRRSTUV	universitarian
AAEIIINPRSSSTT	antiperistasis
AAEIILLMNRRTXY	intermaxillary
AAEIILLNPRSTTY	interspatially
AAEIILMNNOPRTT	reimplantation
AAEIILMNNOSSST	sensationalism
AAEIILMNOORRST	remoralisation
AAEIILMNOORRTZ	remoralization
AAEIILMNOPRRST	proletarianism
AAEIILNNORSTTU	neutralisation
AAEIILNNORTTUZ	neutralization
AAEIILNNOSSSTT	sensationalist
AAEIILNNOSSSTU	sensualisation
AAEIILNNOSSTUZ	sensualization
AAEIILNOORRSTV	revalorisation
AAEIILNOORRTVZ	revalorization
AAEIILNQTTTUVY	quantitatively
AAEIIMOPPPRRST	misappropriate
AAEIINNORSSSTT	stationariness
AAEIINNPPRRSTT	antiperspirant
AAEIINOPRSSTTU	pasteurisation
AAEIINOPRSTTUZ	pasteurization
AAEILLLLMORRST	lamellirostral
AAEILLLNPRRTTY	artillery-plant
AAEILMNRSSSTUX	transsexualism
AAEILMOOPPRSTT	spatiotemporal
AAEILNNNOOOPRT	non-operational
AAEILNNNPRTTUU	ultra-Neptunian
AAEILNORRRSTTT	transliterator
AAEILNORTTTTTY	yttro-tantalite
AAEILNRRSSTTVY	transversality
AAEILORRRRSSTT	serratirostral
AAEIMMNOPSSSTY	synaposematism
AAEIMNNOORSTTU	neuroanatomist
AAEINNNOPRSTUU	superannuation
AAELLNPRRSTUUY	supernaturally
AAELMNOOPPSSTU	postmenopausal
AAFIIIMNNORRTU	uniformitarian
AAFILMNNOOPRTT	plant-formation
AAFIMNNOORRSTT	transformation
AAGGHILMMNOPRY	lymphangiogram
AAGGIIILNNRTTY	ingratiatingly
AAGHHNOOPPRRTY	anthropography
AAGHIIILMOPSTT	stigmatophilia
AAGHIIINOPRSTT	graphitisation
AAGHIIINOPRTTZ	graphitization
AAGHIIPRRSSTTT	stratigraphist
AAGHIMMNNOORRU	organ-harmonium
AAGHOOPPRTTUYY	autotypography
AAGIIIMNNSSTUU	Augustinianism
AAGIIIMNOSSTTT	stigmatisation
AAGIIIMNOSTTTZ	stigmatization
AAGIIINNNOORST	inorganisation
AAGIIINNNOORTZ	inorganization
AAGIILMMMOPRST	lipogrammatism
AAGIILMMOPRSTT	lipogrammatist
AAGIILOOPRSSTT	parasitologist
AAGIIMNNORRSTT	transmigration
AAGIMNOOOSSTTU	angiostomatous
AAGIMNOOPRSSTU	potassium-argon
AAGIMNORRRSTTY	transmigratory
AAHILNOOOPRRTT	prothonotarial
AAHINOOOPRRTTT	prothonotariat
AAHLMOOPRRSSTV	provost-marshal
AAIIIIILNNOSTT	initialisation
AAIIIIILNNOTTZ	initialization
AAIIIILMNORSTT	militarisation
AAIIIILMNORTTZ	militarization
AAIIIILMNRSTTU	utilitarianism
AAIIIILNORSTTV	trivialisation
AAIIIILNORTTVZ	trivialization
AAIIIIMNNRRSTT	Trinitarianism
AAIIIILLNOOSTTV	volatilisation
AAIIIILLNOOTTVZ	volatilization
AAIIILMNNNOOST	nominalisation
AAIIILMNNNOOTZ	nominalization
AAIIILMNOOPSTT	optimalisation
AAIIILMNOOPTTZ	optimalization
AAIIINNORSSSTU	Russianisation
AAIIINNORSSTUZ	Russianization
AAIILLLNORSTTU	illustrational
AAIILLMNOOTTVY	motivationally
AAIILLNNORSTTY	transitionally
AAIILMNNORSSST	transmissional
AAIILMNNORSSTT	mistranslation
AAIILNOOPPRSTU	popularisation
AAIILNOOPPRTUZ	popularization
AAIIMNOORRSSTZ	Zoroastrianism
AAILMMNNORSTTU	ultramontanism
AAILMNNORSTTTU	ultramontanist
AAINNOOPRRSTTT	transportation
ABBBBEEILLPPRR	pribble-prabble
ABBBCDGINORRSU	scrubbing-board
ABBCCEILNOORTY	cyclobarbitone
ABBCDEEEHMORRS	robes-de-chambre
ABBCDEEEIORRSU	berberidaceous
ABBCDEEIILNRSS	indescribables
ABBCDEEIMOORST	discomboberate
ABBCDEILMOOSTU	discombobulate
ABBCDIKKKLNRSU	skunk-blackbird
ABBCEENORRSSTU	subarborescent
ABBCHIIIORRTTU	thiobarbituric
ABBDDEEELLORRU	double-barreled

ABBDDEEELORSTU	double-breasted
ABBDIIIILNTTUY	indubitability
ABBEEELNORSSSV	observableness
ABBEEHINNOOPRT	phenobarbitone
ABBEEIKKLLMMSS	skimble-skamble
ABBEEINNOOPRTT	pentobarbitone
ABBEENOPRRSSTU	superabsorbent
ABBEGILLMNRRTU	tumbling-barrel
ABBEIILQRRRSTU	rabbit-squirrel
ABBIIILMOOPRRS	probabiliorism
ABBIIILOOPRRST	probabiliorist
ABCCCEEEEENRSX	exacerbescence
ABCCCEEIIMMNRU	circumambience
ABCCCEIIMMNRUY	circumambiency
ABCCCEIORSTUUU	cucurbitaceous
ABCCCIILMOOTXY	coxcombicality
ABCCDEEIMNNRSU	disencumbrance
ABCCDEEIMOORSS	Scombresocidae
ABCCDEFIILOORS	blood-sacrifice
ABCCDEHILRRSTU	scratchbuilder
ABCCEEGHIILMOO	biogeochemical
ABCCEEIILLNORR	irreconcilable
ABCCEEILLNNORU	unreconcilable
ABCCEEILMMNOUX	excommunicable
ABCCEEILNNOORT	concelebration
ABCCEFHHNRSSTU	Burschenschaft
ABCCEHIINORSST	bronchiectasis
ABCCEIIILNOTVY	conceivability
ABCCEIILLNORRY	irreconcilably
ABCCEIILMMNNOU	incommunicable
ABCCEIILMRRSUV	cruciverbalism
ABCCEIILNNNOOS	inconscionable
ABCCEIILRRSTUV	cruciverbalist
ABCCEIJKNOOPRT	back-projection
ABCCEILLNNORUY	unreconcilably
ABCCEILMMNNOUU	uncommunicable
ABCCEILNNNOOSU	unconscionable
ABCCEOOOPPRSTT	tobacco-stopper
ABCCGIILLOOORY	cryobiological
ABCCGINNORSTTU	subcontracting
ABCCHILOOPRSTU	claustrophobic
ABCCIILMMNNOUY	incommunicably
ABCCILNNNOOSUY	unconscionably
ABCDDEEILMMNOS	discommendable
ABCDDEELMNOOPU	decompoundable
ABCDDEGIINNPTU	cabinet-pudding
ABCDEEEEILNSSV	deceivableness
ABCDEEEEKNRSTW	neck-sweetbread
ABCDEEEELLNSST	delectableness
ABCDEEEGHHJKTY	△jack-by-the-hedge
ABCDEEEHIILNPR	indecipherable
ABCDEEEHILNPRU	undecipherable
ABCDEEEIILRSSV	disserviceable
ABCDEEEILNPSSS	despicableness
ABCDEEEILNRSST	creditableness
ABCDEEEILPRSST	disrespectable
ABCDEEIIINNOTT	cabinet-edition
ABCDEEIILNNORS	inconsiderable
ABCDEEIILNORSV	indiscoverable
ABCDEEIIMOSSTY	Basidiomycetes
ABCDEEILMNOOPS	indecomposable
ABCDEEILNORSUV	undiscoverable
ABCDEEKLNNORRU	blockade-runner
ABCDEELMNOOPSU	undecomposable
ABCDEELNNORSTU	under-constable
ABCDEFILMNOORS	disconformable
ABCDEFILMOORST	discomfortable
ABCDEGHHOORRTU	thoroughbraced
ABCDEGIILLNSTU	castle-building
ABCDEHKLNORRTU	alder-buckthorn
ABCDEIIILPRTTY	predictability
ABCDEIIILNNORSY	inconsiderably
ABCDEIIILNNOSTY	condensability
ABCDEILNORSUVY	undiscoverably
ABCDENOOORRRTU	uncorroborated
ABCDGHILNOOORS	boarding-school
ABCDHILNOOORRT	broncho-dilator
ABCDIIIILOSSTY	dissociability
ABCEEEEILNRSSV	receivableness
ABCEEEFIILNNSS	beneficialness
ABCEEEIILPRSST	respectabilise
ABCEEEIILPRSTZ	respectabilize
ABCEEELNNRSSSU	censurableness
ABCEEFIIILNPRT	perfectibilian
ABCEEFILLMOPST	self-compatible
ABCEEGIILNORRS	irrecognisable
ABCEEGIILNORRZ	irrecognizable
ABCEEGIINORSUZ	zingiberaceous
ABCEEGILLNRSUY	subgenerically
ABCEEGILNNORSU	unrecognisable
ABCEEGILNNORUZ	unrecognizable
ABCEEHIOOPRSUU	euphorbiaceous
ABCEEHKLNNOSTU	luncheon-basket
ABCEEIIIILRSTVY	serviceability
ABCEEIIILLLRSTT	belletristical
ABCEEIIILLNNNSS	inclinableness
ABCEEIILORRTVY	recoverability
ABCEEIILPRSTTY	respectability
ABCEEIILRRSSTU	irresuscitable
ABCEEIINORSUZZ	zinziberaceous
ABCEEILMNOPSST	compatibleness
ABCEEILNNOSSSU	unsociableness
ABCEEILRRTTTUU	trituberculate
ABCEENORRTTTUY	counter-battery
ABCEFIIINNORTU	eburnification
ABCEGHHIKLNORT	knight-bachelor
ABCEGHIILMNNRU	burling-machine
ABCEGHIMNOSTTU	bathing-costume
ABCEGIILOORSTT	bacteriologist
ABCEGILNNORSUY	unrecognisably
ABCEGILNNORUYZ	unrecognizably
ABCEHHIILMRTUU	Baluchitherium
ABCEHILLLOPRYY	hyperbolically
ABCEHIMOPRSSTU	subatmospheric
ABCEIIIILNSTUXY	inexcusability
ABCEIIIILORRTVY	irrevocability
ABCEIILRRSSTUY	irresuscitably
ABCEIIMOSSSTTY	biosystematics
ABCEILLLNNOORT	incontrollable
ABCEILLMNOSSSY	symbolicalness
ABCEILMMNNOOTU	communion-table
ABCEILNNNOSTTU	subcontinental
ABCEINORRSTTUY	subcontrariety
ABCELLLNNOORTU	uncontrollable

Words marked △ may be spelled also with a capital letter

ABCELNOSSTUUUY	subcutaneously
ABCFIILMNOORTY	conformability
ABCGIIIILNOTTY	incogitability
ABCGIILLMOOOTY	bioclimatology
ABCGILLNNOOOTU	conglobulation
ABCHHINOOOPPRT	anthropophobic
ABCIIIILLLOPSTY	collapsibility
ABCIIILNRSTTUY	inscrutability
ABCIILMMNOSSTU	somnambulistic
ABCIILNORSTTUY	construability
ABCILLLNNOORTY	incontrollably
ABCILMNORSTUUY	rambunctiously
ABCLLLNNOORTUY	uncontrollably
ABDDDEEEHLORTU	double-threaded
ABDDEEEFGHINRT	featherbedding
ABDDEEEGKLNOSW	knowledge-based
ABDDEEEHLLNSSU	bull-headedness
ABDDEEHILLOSST	old-established
ABDDEEILMNNSTY	absent-mindedly
ABDDELNOORTUUY	roundaboutedly
ABDDHILLNRRSUY	drill-husbandry
ABDDIILMNOORST	Bristol-diamond
ABDEEEEELMNRSS	redeemableness
ABDEEEEFILNSSS	defeasibleness
ABDEEEEILNRSST	deliberateness
ABDEEEELNSSSTT	detestableness
ABDEEEGILNRSST	single-breasted
ABDEEEGINOPRST	pigeon-breasted
ABDEEEHILPRSST	pre-established
ABDEEEIILLRTVY	deliberatively
ABDEEEIILMNNRT	indeterminable
ABDEEEIINNOPZZ	benzodiazepine
ABDEEEILMNNRTU	undeterminable
ABDEEEILMNPRTU	unpremeditable
ABDEEEILNNNSSU	undeniableness
ABDEEEIMNNOOTV	above-mentioned
ABDEEELLLOPPRR	propeller-blade
ABDEEELLNOPRSS	deplorableness
ABDEEEMMNOPRSU	pseudomembrane
ABDEEEMNQRRSTU	Rembrandtesque
ABDEEFGHINRRST	fingers-breadth
ABDEEFIIILNNTU	unidentifiable
ABDEEFILMNORSS	formidableness
ABDEEGIPRRRRTY	partridge-berry
ABDEEHIIILRTTY	hereditability
ABDEEHRRSSTTTU	buttress-thread
ABDEEIIILLRTVY	deliverability
ABDEEIIILQRSTU	disequilibrate
ABDEEIILMNNRTY	indeterminably
ABDEEIILMNSSSS	admissibleness
ABDEEILMNNORST	indemonstrable
ABDEEILNOPSSSS	disposableness
ABDEEILNPSSSTU	disputableness
ABDEELMNNORSTU	undemonstrable
ABDEFIIILLNORT	defibrillation
ABDEFIINNOSTUU	subinfeudation
ABDEFINORSTUUY	subinfeudatory
ABDEGGIKNNORRU	groundbreaking
ABDEGHILNRRSTT	birth-strangled
ABDEGHLMNORTUU	rough-and-tumble
ABDEHIIILMNNSU	undiminishable
ABDEIIILMNOOST	demobilisation
ABDEIIILMNOOTZ	demobilization
ABDEIIILNPSSTY	dispensability
ABDEIIILNRSTUY	undesirability
ABDEIILNOORSTW	bowdlerisation
ABDEIILNOORTWZ	bowdlerization
ABDEILMNNORSTY	indemonstrably
ABDEILMORSTUXY	ambidextrously
ABDEKMMMNOOORU	memorandum-book
ABDENNOORSSTUU	roundaboutness
ABDFGHIINORSST	shifting-boards
ABDHILNNOORTTY	labyrinthodont
ABDIIIILMNOTTY	indomitability
ABDIIILLOSSTVY	dissolvability
ABDIIILNORSTTU	distributional
ABDIIINORSTTTU	disattribution
ABEEEELNNPRSST	penetrableness
ABEEEFFLNRSSSU	sufferableness
ABEEEFIILNNSSS	infeasibleness
ABEEEFIILORSTY	foreseeability
ABEEEHHILRRTTU	heather-bluiter
ABEEEHHLRRTTTU	heather-blutter
ABEEEHILNPRSSS	perishableness
ABEEEHLNRSSSST	breathlessness
ABEEEIILLPRRSV	irreplevisable
ABEEEIILNNPSSX	inexpiableness
ABEEEIILNNSSTV	inevitableness
ABEEEIKMOPRRRS	promise-breaker
ABEEEILLNNRSSU	unreliableness
ABEEEILMNNRSST	terminableness
ABEEEILNNOPRSS	inoperableness
ABEEEILNNORSSX	inexorableness
ABEEEIMNRRSTTU	turbine-steamer
ABEEELLNNRSSUV	vulnerableness
ABEEELNNOPRSSS	personableness
ABEEELNORRSSST	restorableness
ABEEFIILMNRTTY	fermentability
ABEEFILNOPRSST	profitableness
ABEEFKLNNOORUW	unforeknowable
ABEEGHHIILNRTW	breathing-while
ABEEGHIILNSTUX	extinguishable
ABEEGHIJNNORRS	Johannisberger
ABEEGHIKNNNRTT	knight-banneret
ABEEGIIKKNRRST	strikebreaking
ABEEGIILNNNSST	intangibleness
ABEEGMNORSSSUU	umbrageousness
ABEEGNOORRRTTU	turbo-generator
ABEEHIIINNSSTV	inhabitiveness
ABEEHILNOPSSST	hospitableness
ABEEHLNNOORSSU	honourableness
ABEEHLNNOPTUYZ	phenylbutazone
ABEEIIIILMMPRTY	impermeability
ABEEIIILMNNSST	inimitableness
ABEEIILLNNOSSV	inviolableness
ABEEIILMNOPRSS	impressionable
ABEEIILMNPSSSS	impassibleness
ABEEIILNPRSTTY	presentability
ABEEIILNPRTTVY	preventability
ABEEIILPRRSTVY	preservability
ABEEILLMRSSSTT	ballet-mistress
ABEEILLNNPRSTU	unsplinterable
ABEEILLPRRSSTT	blister-plaster
ABEEILLPRRSTYY	presbyterially

ABEEILMNNNOSTU unmentionables
ABEEILMNOPRSSV improvableness
ABEEILNNOQSTUU unquestionable
ABEEILNNSSSTUU unsuitableness
ABEEILRRRSSTTU subterrestrial
ABEEIMMORRSSTT strabismometer
ABEEIMNOSSSSTU abstemiousness
ABEEIMOOPRRSTT absorptiometer
ABEEINOPRSSSTV absorptiveness
ABEEKLNNNOSSUW unknowableness
ABEELMNOOPRTYY polyembryonate
ABEFGIIILNRRTY refrangibility
ABEFIIILRRTTUY irrefutability
ABEFIILLNORRRU neurofibrillar
ABEFILNOOPRSST self-absorption
ABEFLLNOOPSSTU tablespoonfuls
ABEGHILMNOOOXY oxyhaemoglobin
ABEGHLMNRRSSTU bremsstrahlung
ABEGIIILMNPRTY impregnability
ABEGIIKNNOPRRS prison-breaking
ABEGIILLOOOPST paleobiologist
ABEGIILNOORSST obligatoriness
ABEGIILORRSSTY gyrostabiliser
ABEGIILORRSTYZ gyrostabilizer
ABEGILMNRSTTUU Sturmabteilung
ABEHIIILSTTUXY exhaustibility
ABEHILLMMOOOST holometabolism
ABEHIMMOOPRSTY symmetrophobia
ABEHLLMOOOOSTU holometabolous
ABEIIIILLNRRTY inerrabilility
ABEIIIILMNNSTZ Leibnitzianism
ABEIIIILMNSTTY inestimability
ABEIIIILMPRTVY imperviability
ABEIIIILLNORTTY intolerability
ABEIIILMNNRTUY innumerability
ABEIIILMORRTVY irremovability
ABEIIILNPRSTUY insuperability
ABEIIILPRSSTUY persuasibility
ABEIIIMNRSSTUU subminiaturise
ABEIIIMNRSTUUZ subminiaturize
ABEIIMNOPRRTTU imperturbation
ABEIIMOPRSSTUU superambitious
ABEILMNNORSTUU insurmountable
ABEILNNOQSTUUY unquestionably
ABEILNOOOPPRRT proportionable
ABEILNORSSSSUU salubriousness
ABEINNORSSTUYZ Russo-Byzantine
ABELMNNORSTUUU unsurmountable
ABFGIIIILNNRTY infrangibility
ABFIIIIJLSTTUY justifiability
ABFIILNOOORTTV vibroflotation
ABGIIIIILMMTTY immitigability
ABHIIIKLNNTTUY unthinkability
ABHIIINOOPRRTY prohibitionary
ABHILMNOOPRSTT thromboplastin
ABIIIIIILLLMTTY illimitability
ABIIIILLMPSTUY implausibility
ABIIIILMMNOOST immobilisation
ABIIIILMMNOOTZ immobilization
ABIIIIMNNOSTTU bituminisation
ABIIIIMNNOTTUZ bituminization
ABIIIILLNOOSSTU solubilisation
ABIIIILLNOOSTUZ solubilization
ABIIIILNOORSSTT strobilisation
ABIIIILNOORSTTZ strobilization
ABIIIINNNOSSTUU subinsinuation
ABIIILLNORSSUUY insalubriously
ABIIILNNNOSTTUU tintinnabulous
ABIIILNOSSTTTUU substitutional
ABIJOQSSTTUUUU jusqu'auboutist
ABILMNNORSTUUY insurmountably
ABILNOOOPPRRTY proportionably
ACCCDEEILLNOPY encyclopedical
ACCCEEHILLNORV vice-chancellor
ACCCEEIILSSSTU Ecclesiasticus
ACCCEEILMOSSTU cosmeceuticals
ACCCEENNOOOVVX convexo-concave
ACCCEHHILMOPSY psychochemical
ACCCEHIINOORSS onchocerciasis
ACCCEHIINORSTT architectonics
ACCCEILLNNORTY concentrically
ACCCEIMMNOOORS macroeconomics
ACCCGINNOOSTTU cost-accounting
ACCCHLOOPSSTUY staphylococcus
ACCCILNOOSSSSU class-conscious
ACCDDDEKLOOOOO cock-a-doodle-doo
ACCDDEINNORTTU uncontradicted
ACCDEEEELNOPRS preadolescence
ACCDEEEHHIKNRT chicken-hearted
ACCDEEFIINRTTU uncertificated
ACCDEEFILNNSTU self-inductance
ACCDEEGHNNORTU counterchanged
ACCDEEHHIKNNNS hen-and-chickens
ACCDEEHILOSTUY lecythidaceous
ACCDEEILMNORTY dynamo-electric
ACCDEEILNOPSTY encyclopaedist
ACCDEEIMNOPPTY appendicectomy
ACCDEEINNNOSTU discountenance
ACCDEEINNOORST deconsecration
ACCDEEINOPRRTU unreciprocated
ACCDEEIOOORSSU dioscoreaceous
ACCDEEMNOSSSTU accustomedness
ACCDEENNORSSTT contractedness
ACCDEFHIORRRSU Crouched-friars
ACCDEFHIRRRSTU Crutched-friars
ACCDEFNNOORTUU unaccounted-for
ACCDEHHILLOOPY dolichocephaly
ACCDEHHIMNORSY hydromechanics
ACCDEHILMNOPSU unaccomplished
ACCDEIIILLNNOTY coincidentally
ACCDEIINNNOSTU discontinuance
ACCDEIMMNNOTUU uncommunicated
ACCDELMOOPRTUY pluto-democracy
ACCDGINNNORTUY country-dancing
ACCDHIMMNOORSY chromodynamics
ACCDHIMNNOORRU chondrocranium
ACCDHIMNOPSSYY psychodynamics
ACCDIINOORSTTU contradictious
ACCEEEFILNPTXY life-expectancy
ACCEEELLNORTVY electrovalency
ACCEEELMNOORTT electromotance
ACCEEFLLMNOPST self-complacent
ACCEEGHIKLRRRT trickle-charger
ACCEEGIINNORSS carcinogenesis

ACCEEGILLNORTY	geocentrically
ACCEEHHIILNNPR	rhinencephalic
ACCEEHHILMMORT	thermochemical
ACCEEHHILPRRTY	Charley-pitcher
ACCEEHHIMNPSTU	catechumenship
ACCEEHILNOPPRS	prosencephalic
ACCEEHIPRSTTTY	cryptaesthetic
ACCEEHKLNORRTU	rocket-launcher
ACCEEIIIKKNNNV	nievie-nick-nack
ACCEEIILMMNOSU	oecumenicalism
ACCEEIIMNNOORT	econometrician
ACCEEIINNOORSS	concessionaire
ACCEEIKKLLNNRR	crinkle-crankle
ACCEEILLLNORTY	electronically
ACCEEILLLOPSTY	telescopically
ACCEEILLOOPRTT	electro-optical
ACCEEILLRRTTTT	clitter-clatter
ACCEEILMOPRSTU	proceleusmatic
ACCEEILNOOPTUY	leucocytopenia
ACCEEILORSSTTT	electrostatics
ACCEEINNOORRST	reconsecration
ACCEELLNOOPTTY	cyclopentolate
ACCEFGIIIINNNS	insignificance
ACCEFIIILLNSTY	scientifically
ACCEFILMNOORSW	moccasin-flower
ACCEFMNNNNOOOR	non-conformance
ACCEGHHILNOOST	schoolteaching
ACCEGHIILLNNOU	hallucinogenic
ACCEGHINOPRRSS	preaching-cross
ACCEGHIOPPRRST	spectrographic
ACCEGIILNRTUXY	excruciatingly
ACCEGILLMMOORY	myrmecological
ACCEGILLOOPRST	spectrological
ACCEHHILLNOPRS	chancellorship
ACCEHIILMMMNOU	immunochemical
ACCEHIILMORSTT	stichometrical
ACCEHIILMRTUVY	clavicytherium
ACCEHIINNOPRTY	pyrotechnician
ACCEHIKLLMOORY	mock-heroically
ACCEHILMMNOPST	accomplishment
ACCEHILMNOORRT	chronometrical
ACCEHILMOOPRSU	microcephalous
ACCEHILMOPRSTY	psychometrical
ACCEHILMOPSUUY	sceuophylacium
ACCEIIILMMORSS	microseismical
ACCEIIILNNOORT	reconciliation
ACCEIIILNOORRT	oneirocritical
ACCEIILLLOSSTY	solecistically
ACCEIILLMRRSUY	semicircularly
ACCEIILLMRSSTY	semicrystallic
ACCEIILLNOPSST	scintillascope
ACCEIILNNOPTTU	centuplication
ACCEIILNOORRTY	reconciliatory
ACCEIINNOORSTT	concretisation
ACCEIINNOORTTZ	concretization
ACCEIINOPRSSSU	capriciousness
ACCEILLNOSSSUY	successionally
ACCEILMMNNOOSS	commonsensical
ACCEILMOOOPPST	metoposcopical
ACCEILNOORSSST	cross-sectional
ACCEIMMNOORTUX	excommunicator
ACCEIMNOOPRSTU	pococuranteism
ACCFFIIINORTTU	fructification
ACCFGIIIINNNSY	insignificancy
ACCFIIIIILNOST	silicification
ACCFIIIIKNNOTZ	zinckification
ACCFIIINOOSTTT	Scottification
ACCGHHIILLOOTY	ichthyological
ACCGHHIOPPRSSY	psychographics
ACCGHIILLOORST	Christological
ACCGIIILNNOPRT	calico-printing
ACCGIILLLMOORY	micrologically
ACCGIIMNORRTUY	circumgyration
ACCGIMNNOOTTTU	coconut-matting
ACCGIMORRRTUYY	circumgyratory
ACCHHIILMOORTT	lithochromatic
ACCHHILOPPSSYY	psychophysical
ACCHHIMOOORRTT	orthochromatic
ACCHIIIMNOOORV	Mohorovicician
ACCHIIINNNOOST	cinchonisation
ACCHIIINNNOOTZ	cinchonization
ACCHIILLOPRTYY	hypocritically
ACCHIILOOPRSTY	hypocoristical
ACCHILLNNORSYY	synchronically
ACCHIMOOPSSSTY	psychosomatics
ACCIIIMNORRSSU	Rosicrucianism
ACCIILLMOOOPST	cosmopolitical
ACCIILLMORRTTU	circumlittoral
ACCIILNNOOPRST	conscriptional
ACCIILNNOORTUY	unconciliatory
ACCIIMMNNOOSTU	communications
ACCIIMNNORTTUU	circumnutation
ACCIINNNOORSTT	triconsonantic
ACCIINNOOOSTTV	convocationist
ACCIKKMMNNRRUU	crinkum-crankum
ACCILLOPPRRTYY	procryptically
ACCILMNOOSTUUY	contumaciously
ACCILNNOORSTTU	constructional
ACCILOPRRSTUUY	corpuscularity
ACCIMMNNNNOOTU	non-communicant
ACCIMNORRTTUUY	circumnutatory
ACDDDEEIILMNST	middle-distance
ACDDEEEEHINRTV	heaven-directed
ACDDEEEFNNORTU	unconfederated
ACDDEEENNORSTX	extra-condensed
ACDDEEGIKLNOSW	disacknowledge
ACDDEEGKLNNOUW	unacknowledged
ACDDEEHMMOORRS	chordamesoderm
ACDDEEIILRTTUV	diverticulated
ACDDEEIMNOSTTU	undomesticated
ACDDEEINRSSSTT	distractedness
ACDDEHMOOPRSTU	proud-stomached
ACDDEIIINNOORT	air-conditioned
ACDDEIINOOORSU	androdioecious
ACDDEILNNOOSTU	unconsolidated
ACDDEILNRSTTUY	undistractedly
ACDEEEFFNNSSTU	unaffectedness
ACDEEEFHIRSUVX	chevaux-de-frise
ACDEEEHHIKNRSV	handkerchieves
ACDEEEILNOPRTU	Pleuronectidae
ACDEEEINNOPQRU	equiponderance
ACDEEEINORSSTV	decorativeness
ACDEEELNOPRRUW	nuclear-powered
ACDEEENRRRSTUY	under-secretary

ACDEEFFIMORRTT	diffractometer
ACDEEFHIINNRSS	disenfranchise
ACDEEFHIKLNNSW	Schwenkfeldian
ACDEEFILLMOPRS	self-proclaimed
ACDEEFINOQRRUY	radio-frequency
ACDEEFINOQRUUY	audio-frequency
ACDEEGHIILOOPT	galeopithecoid
ACDEEGHNNOORUY	ocean-greyhound
ACDEEGIILNPRTY	depreciatingly
ACDEEGIJKNRSST	dressing-jacket
ACDEEGIMNORSTU	discouragement
ACDEEGKLMNNOTW	acknowledgment
ACDEEGLNOOORRU	orange-coloured
ACDEEHIIINNRST	disinheritance
ACDEEHIIINRSST	dechristianise
ACDEEHIIINRSTZ	dechristianize
ACDEEHIINOORRT	Rhinocerotidae
ACDEEHILMNOSST	methodicalness
ACDEEHIMNNNSTT	disenchantment
ACDEEHINNRSSST	disenchantress
ACDEEHINOOPPRT	apprenticehood
ACDEEHINOPPRTY	cyproheptadine
ACDEEIILNNNSST	incidentalness
ACDEEILLMNTTUU	multinucleated
ACDEEILNOPSSST	despoticalness
ACDEEIMMMOPRRS	promise-crammed
ACDEEIMMNNOORT	recommendation
ACDEEINNNOORST	recondensation
ACDEEINNOORSST	co-ordinateness
ACDEEINOPRSSSU	predaciousness
ACDEELLMNNOTTY	malcontentedly
ACDEELMNNOPTTU	uncontemplated
ACDEELNNNRSTTY	transcendently
ACDEELNNOORTTV	lavender-cotton
ACDEEMMNOORRTY	recommendatory
ACDEFGHIILMNNO	folding-machine
ACDEFIIIINNOTT	identification
ACDEFIIINNOSTY	Disneyfication
ACDEFIIINOOTTX	detoxification
ACDEFIIINORRTT	denitrificator
ACDEFIILLNNOTY	confidentially
ACDEGHILLMOOOT	methodological
ACDEGHIMNORSTY	hydromagnetics
ACDEGHINNORSTU	countershading
ACDEGIILLOOSTT	dialectologist
ACDEGINNORRSSW	crossing-warden
ACDEGINNORRTTU	counter-trading
ACDEGMMNNOOORR	common-or-garden
ACDEHHIILMOPRT	edriophthalmic
ACDEHHIIMOPRRT	hermaphroditic
ACDEHHLOOPRSUY	hydrocephalous
ACDEHIIILOOPRT	diaheliotropic
ACDEHIILLMMOTY	immethodically
ACDEHIILNRSSTT	child-resistant
ACDEHIIMORRSTY	radiochemistry
ACDEHILLMOPRYY	hypodermically
ACDEHILLNOORRY	hydrocoralline
ACDEHIMMNORSTY	thermodynamics
ACDEHIMNOPRTUY	hydropneumatic
ACDEHINOORRSTT	trisoctahedron
ACDEHOORRRTTXY	hydroextractor
ACDEIIIIMNNRST	indiscriminate
ACDEIIIIMNRSTV	discriminative
ACDEIIILMNRSTY	discriminately
ACDEIIILNNORTU	unidirectional
ACDEIIILNORSTY	discretionally
ACDEIIILMMRSSTY	dissymmetrical
ACDEIIILMPSTTUU	multicuspidate
ACDEIIILNNOOST	decolonisation
ACDEIIILNNOOTZ	decolonization
ACDEIIILNOOORST	decolorisation
ACDEIIILNOOORTZ	decolorization
ACDEIIINOOPRRST	disincorporate
ACDEIKNOPRRTTV	davenport-trick
ACDEILLMNOOSTY	endosmotically
ACDEILLNOOSSTY	disconsolately
ACDEILLNRSSTUY	uncrystallised
ACDEILLNRSTUYZ	uncrystallized
ACDEILNOSSSTTU	sansculottides
ACDEIMMNNOOORS	andromonoecism
ACDEIMMNNOPSUY	pneumodynamics
ACDEINNOOPRRTU	unincorporated
ACDEINNORSTUUY	consuetudinary
ACDEINOOQRSSTU	conquistadores
ACDEIOOPPRRSTU	dipterocarpous
ACDELLMNOOORSU	salmon-coloured
ACDELLOOPSTTUY	leptodactylous
ACDFHIIIIMNOTU	humidification
ACDFIIIILNOOST	solidification
ACDGGIILNORSUY	discouragingly
ACDGHILLLOORYY	hydrologically
ACDGIIIIMNNRST	discriminating
ACDHHIMNOOPRSY	hypochondriasm
ACDHHINOOPRSTY	hypochondriast
ACDHIIOOOPPRTT	diaphototropic
ACDHILLNOOPRYY	hydroponically
ACDHIMNOOORSST	chondromatosis
ACDIIIILMNPRSU	disciplinarium
ACDIIIILNNNOST	disinclination
ACDIIIIMNNORST	discrimination
ACDIIIJLNORSTU	jurisdictional
ACDIIILNNOOTTY	conditionality
ACDIIILOSSTTUY	adscititiously
ACDIIIMNORRSTY	discriminatory
ACDIIINNNOOORT	inco-ordination
ACDIIINNNOORTT	indoctrination
ACDIILNNOOOSST	disconsolation
ACDIILNOOORSTU	discolouration
ACDIIOOPPRRSTY	cryptosporidia
ACDIMNOOPRSSTU	massproduction
ACEEEEFFFLMNST	self-effacement
ACEEEEFHHLNPRT	three-halfpence
ACEEEEGILLPTXY	epexegetically
ACEEEEHHILNRTW	Catherine-wheel
ACEEEFFLNSSSST	affectlessness
ACEEEFGLNNPRSU	self-repugnance
ACEEEFHIIIMNNX	examine-in-chief
ACEEEFLLORRTUW	fellow-creature
ACEEEFLNNSSSTU	self-sustenance
ACEEEGHIILNOPT	galeopithecine
ACEEEGHIINOSST	aesthesiogenic
ACEEEGHIJKNNRT	Jack-in-the-green
ACEEEGHILNPSST	steeplechasing
ACEEEGILLMNOTT	metallogenetic

ACEEEGILLNOORV	venereological
ACEEEGMORSSTTY	Gasteromycetes
ACEEEHHIPRSSTY	hyperaesthesic
ACEEEHHIPRSTTY	hyperaesthetic
ACEEEHILNORSST	cholinesterase
ACEEEHLLMORRTT	electrothermal
ACEEEHLOPRRTTY	electrotherapy
ACEEEHNPRSSTUY	hyperacuteness
ACEEEIILMNNNST	semi-centennial
ACEEEIILMNRRTT	recrementitial
ACEEEIILMNRTTX	excrementitial
ACEEEIILOPRSSV	overspecialise
ACEEEIILOPRSVZ	overspecialize
ACEEEILLPRSSTU	supercelestial
ACEEEILMORRSTT	stereometrical
ACEEEILNNQQUUV	quinquevalence
ACEEEIMNNPPRTT	apprenticement
ACEEEIMNORSVWX	ex-servicewoman
ACEEEMNOOPRSTV	overcompensate
ACEEEMNOPRRTTU	contemperature
ACEEEMNORRSTUU	countermeasure
ACEEENNORSSSTU	nectareousness
ACEEFFIILNTTUY	ineffectuality
ACEEFGHLOPRRTY	reflectography
ACEEFGIILNRSTU	centrifugalise
ACEEFGIILNRTUZ	centrifugalize
ACEEFGILLLOORX	reflexological
ACEEFGLNNRSSUU	ungracefulness
ACEEFHHIORRSTT	ostrich-feather
ACEEFHIIINORTT	etherification
ACEEFIIILPRSSU	superficialise
ACEEFIIILPRSUZ	superficialize
ACEEFIIINORSTT	esterification
ACEEFIKNRRSTTT	transfer-ticket
ACEEFILMNOPRST	self-importance
ACEEFINORRRSST	refractoriness
ACEEFMNNNOOPRR	non-performance
ACEEGGHIILLNOT	genethlialogic
ACEEGGHLMNOOTY	megatechnology
ACEEGGIMNNORRS	scaremongering
ACEEGHHINOPRSU	preaching-house
ACEEGHIINNPRST	speech-training
ACEEGHIKPRRRTT	prick-the-garter
ACEEGHILLNOPRY	hypoallergenic
ACEEGHILLOOPRT	herpetological
ACEEGHILNOPTTY	phytogenetical
ACEEGHLOOPSSTU	stegocephalous
ACEEGHMNRRTTTU	gutter-merchant
ACEEGIIMMOPRTT	micropegmatite
ACEEGIKLNPRSTU	plague-stricken
ACEEGILLLLOOTY	teleologically
ACEEGILLMOOORT	meteorological
ACEEGILLNOPRTT	electroplating
ACEEGILLOOOPST	paleoecologist
ACEEGILLPRRTUY	picture-gallery
ACEEGIMNNORSUV	misgovernaunce
ACEEGINNNORTTY	octingentenary
ACEEGLNOORRSTU	colour-sergeant
ACEEGNOORSSSUU	courageousness
ACEEHHILNNNOPR	rhinencephalon
ACEEHHMOOPRRST	chromatosphere
ACEEHIILLNNPST	Panhellenistic
ACEEHIIMNNSSTZ	Nietzscheanism
ACEEHIINPPPRST	apprenticeship
ACEEHILLLNOPTY	telephonically
ACEEHILLMNOOTT	△monotheletical
ACEEHILLMORTXY	exothermically
ACEEHILMMORRTT	thermometrical
ACEEHIMMNORSSV	servomechanism
ACEEHLNNOOPPRS	prosencephalon
ACEEIIILLLMPST	semi-elliptical
ACEEIIILMNNRST	reminiscential
ACEEIIILMNPPRR	prince-imperial
ACEEIIILNRRTTY	rectilinearity
ACEEIIIMPPRSTT	peripateticism
ACEEIIJLNNORTT	interjectional
ACEEIILLRRSTTV	verticillaster
ACEEIILMMORSST	seismometrical
ACEEIILMNOPSTX	exceptionalism
ACEEIILMNPRSTT	centripetalism
ACEEIILNNNNQTU	quincentennial
ACEEIILNNORSST	intercessional
ACEEIILNNORSTT	intersectional
ACEEIILNORRSST	intercessorial
ACEEIILNOSSTTY	coessentiality
ACEEIKLNNPRSTT	planet-stricken
ACEEIKLNOOPTUY	leukocytopenia
ACEEILLLLNTTUY	intellectually
ACEEILLLNNTTUU	unintellectual
ACEEILLMNORRTU	intermolecular
ACEEILMNOOOPSU	polemoniaceous
ACEEILNNOPSSTU	unpoeticalness
ACEEILNNORSTTU	counter-salient
ACEEILNOPSSTTT	Pentecostalist
ACEEILNORRRSTU	resurrectional
ACEEILNORSSTTU	sansculotterie
ACEEILNORSTVVY	conservatively
ACEEIMMNNORSTU	incommensurate
ACEEIMNNOOPRTT	contemperation
ACEEINNOORSSTT	contesseration
ACEEINNOORSSVZ	conversaziones
ACEEINNPRTTTUU	interpunctuate
ACEEINOPRRSSSU	precariousness
ACEEINOQQSTTUU	quinquecostate
ACEEINOQSSSSUU	sequaciousness
ACEELMMNORSTUY	commensurately
ACEELNOPRSTUUY	percutaneously
ACEEMNOOOPRSTU	cotemporaneous
ACEENNNOPSSTTY	pennystone-cast
ACEFFIIILLMOSY	semi-officially
ACEFFINRRRSTTU	traffic-returns
ACEFGGIINNNOPY	pigeon-fancying
ACEFGHIIIKMMNS	mischief-making
ACEFGIIINNORTT	gentrification
ACEFGIILLNORSU	fringillaceous
ACEFGIINNORTTU	centrifugation
ACEFHLMNOSSSTU	stomachfulness
ACEFHLNNSSTUUW	unwatchfulness
ACEFIIIILMPSTV	simplificative
ACEFIIIINNORST	resinification
ACEFIIIINORTVV	revivification
ACEFIIILMNOSTU	emulsification
ACEFIIILPRSTUY	superficiality
ACEFIIINOPRTTT	prettification

ACEFIINOSSSTTU	factitiousness
ACEFILMNOOPRSS	self-comparison
ACEFINNOORSSSU	facinorousness
ACEFINRRRSTTUU	infrastructure
ACEGGHHIINTTWW	weight-watching
ACEGGIILNNNPRS	spring-cleaning
ACEGGILLNOOORT	gerontological
ACEGGILLNOOSTY	geognostically
ACEGHHIILLOPRY	hieroglyphical
ACEGHHIIOPRRST	cheirographist
ACEGHIILLNOSTY	histogenically
ACEGHIILOOPSTT	hepaticologist
ACEGHIILOPRSTX	lexicographist
ACEGHILLLNOOTY	ethnologically
ACEGHILOPPRRTY	pterylographic
ACEGHINNPRSSTU	purse-snatching
ACEGHIOPPRRSSU	supercargoship
ACEGHLMOOPSTYY	metapsychology
ACEGHLNOOPSTTU	plectognathous
ACEGHMMOOPRSUY	myrmecophagous
ACEGIIILMNSTTU	metalinguistic
ACEGIIKMMNORRT	micro-marketing
ACEGIILLLOOPTY	geopolitically
ACEGIILLLOSTUY	eulogistically
ACEGIILLMNOORT	terminological
ACEGIILLOOORST	soteriological
ACEGIILLOOOSTV	△sovietological
ACEGIILLORSSUY	sacrilegiously
ACEGIILNNNOTUY	uncongeniality
ACEGIILNNOTTUV	conglutinative
ACEGIKMNORRSST	cross-marketing
ACEGILLLMOOTYY	etymologically
ACEGILLLNOORUY	neurologically
ACEGILLLOOPRTY	petrologically
ACEGILMNNOOORT	conglomeration
ACEGIMNNOORRST	cairngorm-stone
ACEGINNNOOSSUU	consanguineous
ACEGINNOOSSSTU	contagiousness
ACEGINNOPSSSUU	pugnaciousness
ACEGINNORSSSUU	ungraciousness
ACEGINOPPRRSSU	porcupine-grass
ACEHHIIILLOSST	cholelithiasis
ACEHHIIMOPSSTT	Theopaschitism
ACEHHIINOPRRTT	therianthropic
ACEHHILLOOPSTY	theosophically
ACEHHILLOPTTYY	hypothetically
ACEHHILOPPRRTY	hypertrophical
ACEHHIMOOPPRST	metaphosphoric
ACEHHLMOOOPPST	ophthalmoscope
ACEHHMOOOPRTTU	chemoautotroph
ACEHIIINNRSSTU	unchristianise
ACEHIIINNRSTUZ	unchristianize
ACEHIILLOPSTTY	polytheistical
ACEHIILLPSTUUY	euphuistically
ACEHIILMNOOSTT	monotheistical
ACEHIILNOOOPST	opisthocoelian
ACEHIILOOPRSTT	photorealistic
ACEHIIMNNOOPRT	enantiomorphic
ACEHIIMORRSTTY	iatrochemistry
ACEHIINNOOPRSY	Syrophoenician
ACEHIINNSSTTUU	unenthusiastic
ACEHIINNTTTUUY	unauthenticity
ACEHIINOOPRTTU	eutrophication
ACEHIINOPPRSST	spinthariscope
ACEHIINOPSSTTU	unsophisticate
ACEHIIOOPRSSST	spirochaetosis
ACEHILLLOPPSST	phelloplastics
ACEHILMNOOPRRZ	chlorpromazine
ACEHILMNOPTTYY	antilymphocyte
ACEHILNORSSSUV	chivalrousness
ACEHIMNOOPRRTT	anthropometric
ACEHIMOPPRSTTY	spermatophytic
ACEHINNORSSSTY	narcosynthesis
ACEHLLMOORSSTY	schoolmasterly
ACEHMOOORSTTTU	tetrachotomous
ACEIIIILNPPRST	principalities
ACEIIIINORSSTT	sericitisation
ACEIIIINORSTTZ	sericitization
ACEIIILLMPTTUV	multiplicative
ACEIIILNRRTUVY	curvilinearity
ACEIIILNRSSTUV	universalistic
ACEIIILNRSTTXY	extrinsicality
ACEIIIMMNOORSS	commissionaire
ACEIIIMMNORRTU	microminiature
ACEIIIMNNORSTT	interactionism
ACEIIINNOOSSTT	sectionisation
ACEIIINNOOSTTZ	sectionization
ACEIIINNOPSSTX	expansionistic
ACEIIINNORSTTT	interactionist
ACEIIINORSSTTU	securitisation
ACEIIINORSTTUZ	securitization
ACEIIJNOOPRSTT	projectisation
ACEIIJNOOPRTTZ	projectization
ACEIILLMNNOOOS	neocolonialism
ACEIILLMOOPRTT	metropolitical
ACEIILLMOPRTUV	pluviometrical
ACEIILLNNOOOST	neocolonialist
ACEIILMNNNOSTT	continentalism
ACEIILNNNOSSTY	nonsensicality
ACEIILNNNOSTTT	continentalist
ACEIILNNOOORST	recolonisation
ACEIILNNOOORTZ	recolonization
ACEIILNNORRSTU	insurrectional
ACEIILNNOSTUVV	anticonvulsive
ACEIILNOOPRRTY	incorporeality
ACEIILNOOPRRVY	ivory-porcelain
ACEIILNOPRSTUY	pertinaciously
ACEIILNOSSSSUV	lasciviousness
ACEIIMNOOORRTT	recitation-room
ACEIIMOOQRSTUV	vicesimo-quarto
ACEIINNOSSSTUU	incautiousness
ACEIINOOPRSTTV	contrapositive
ACEIINOPSSSSUU	auspiciousness
ACEILLLMORTUVY	volumetrically
ACEILLNNNOOTVY	conventionally
ACEILLNOPRSSUY	supersonically
ACEILMMOORRTTU	ultramicrotome
ACEILMNOOORTUV	macroevolution
ACEILMNORSSSUU	miraculousness
ACEILNNNNOOTUV	unconventional
ACEILNNOOOPRST	spironolactone
ACEILNOOPRRTUY	perlocutionary
ACEILNOOQSSSUU	loquaciousness
ACEILOORRSTTUW	watercolourist

ACEILORRRRSTUV	recurvirostral
ACEIMMNNOORSTU	commensuration
ACEIMNNNOOPRTU	pronunciamento
ACEIMNOORRSTUV	conservatorium
ACEIMNOQRSTTTU	quattrocentism
ACEINNNOOOOPRT	non-co-operation
ACEINNOOPRSSTT	cornet-à-pistons
ACEINOQRSTTTTU	quattrocentist
ACELRRRSTTTUUU	ultrastructure
ACEMNOOORSSTTU	entomostracous
ACFFIIINOORSTT	fortifications
ACFGIILMNNNOTU	malfunctioning
ACFIIIILMNOPST	simplification
ACFIIIINOQTUZZ	quizzification
ACFIIILNOSTTTU	stultification
ACFIIINOPRSSTU	Prussification
ACFIIMNORRSSTT	transformistic
ACGGHHIMOPPRSY	sphygmographic
ACGHHHIOOPSTUY	ichthyophagous
ACGHHIIOOPPRST	opisthographic
ACGHHINOOSSTUZ	schizognathous
ACGHIIILNOPSTT	antiphlogistic
ACGHIILLLLOOPY	philologically
ACGHIILLLOOSTY	histologically
ACGHIILLNOOORT	ornithological
ACGHIILMNOOPSY	physiognomical
ACGHILLLMOOTYY	mythologically
ACGIIIJLLNOSTY	jingoistically
ACGIIILLLNSTUY	linguistically
ACGIIILLLPSTUY	pugilistically
ACGIIILMNOSSTY	misogynistical
ACGIIINNNOTTUX	unintoxicating
ACGIILLNPPSTUY	supplicatingly
ACGIILNNNOOTTU	conglutination
ACGILLLOOOPRTY	tropologically
ACGILNOOPRSSTY	laryngoscopist
ACGINOOOPRRSTT	prognosticator
ACHHILLMNRTUYY	unrhythmically
ACHHILNOPSSTYY	sycophantishly
ACHHILOORSTTUY	ichthyolatrous
ACHHLMOOOPPSTY	ophthalmoscopy
ACHHMMNOOORRSU	mushroom-anchor
ACHIIIINNORSTT	trichinisation
ACHIIIINNORTTZ	trichinization
ACHIIILLNORSTY	histrionically
ACHIIILNOORSTT	chloritisation
ACHIIILNOORTTZ	chloritization
ACHIIILOSSSTTY	cystolithiasis
ACHIIIMNOORSST	trichomoniasis
ACHIIINOOPSSTT	sophistication
ACHIILLLOSTTYY	histolytically
ACHIIMMOPRSSSY	commissaryship
ACHIIOPRSSSTTY	astrophysicist
ACHIKNPSSSTTUU	Aussichtspunkt
ACHIMMMNOOORST	monochromatism
ACHIOOPPRRRSTU	procuratorship
ACHLMMNNOOOORS	non-chromosomal
ACHLNNOORSSUYY	asynchronously
ACIIIIILNNRSTTY	intrinsicality
ACIIIIILNOOPSTT	politicisation
ACIIIIILNOOPTTZ	politicization
ACIIIIILPRSSTTU	spiritualistic
ACIIILLLMPSSTY	simplistically
ACIIILLMNOPTTU	multiplication
ACIIILLMOPSTTY	optimistically
ACIIILNOPSSUUY	inauspiciously
ACIILNNOOSTTTU	constitutional
ACIIMMNOOPSTTU	miscomputation
ACIIMNNOPSTTUU	mispunctuation
ACIINNOOOPRSTT	contraposition
ACIINNOPSTTTUU	punctuationist
ACILLMMNNOOTTY	non-committally
ACILLNPRRSTUUY	unscripturally
ACILMMOORRTTUY	ultramicrotomy
ACILNOPRSSTUUY	transpicuously
ACLMOOOPPRSTUY	campylotropous
ADDDDEEEHLLMUY	muddleheadedly
ADDDDEFFGIILLN	fiddle-faddling
ADDDEEEGGLLRST	straddle-legged
ADDDEEINNOOORS	endoradiosonde
ADDEEEEFHNNRSS	free-handedness
ADDEEEEHNNNSSV	even-handedness
ADDEEEFHLNNSST	left-handedness
ADDEEEFILLPSSS	self-displeased
ADDEEEGGINNSSS	disengagedness
ADDEEEGHLNNOSS	long-headedness
ADDEEEGNRRTTUU	undergraduette
ADDEEEHILMNNVY	heavenly-minded
ADDEEEHIOPRRTY	Hydropterideae
ADDEEEHNNNOPSS	open-handedness
ADDEEEIKMNNSSW	weak-mindedness
ADDEEEILMPRTTY	premeditatedly
ADDEEEILNPSSSS	displeasedness
ADDEEEIMNPRTTU	unpremeditated
ADDEEFFHLRRUUY	furfuraldehyde
ADDEEGHHHINNSS	high-handedness
ADDEEHIKLNNPSS	spindle-shanked
ADDEEIIMNSSSSV	misadvisedness
ADDEELNOPPRTUU	underpopulated
ADDEFGILLRRSUY	disregardfully
ADDEFIILNNSSSU	disdainfulness
ADDEFIIMNOORSU	diamondiferous
ADDEGINNNRSSTU	understandings
ADDEHIIIMNOTYZ	azidothymidine
ADDEIIIMNOPSSS	disimpassioned
ADDEILMNNORRWY	narrow-mindedly
ADDEIMNNOOORTX	andromedotoxin
ADDEINORSSTUUV	disadventurous
ADEEEEEGNNRSST	degenerateness
ADEEEEGHILLNRW	wheeler-dealing
ADEEEEILMORRTT	radiotelemeter
ADEEEEIMNPRRTT	predeterminate
ADEEEFGLNNNSSW	newfangledness
ADEEEFHINRSSTV	fives-and-threes
ADEEEFILNRRSST	self-restrained
ADEEEFILRRSSTV	self-advertiser
ADEEEFIMNNOORT	aforementioned
ADEEEFIMNNORTT	after-mentioned
ADEEEFINNORSTT	defenestration
ADEEEGIKNNRRRT	kindergartener
ADEEEGILNNPPST	leaden-stepping
ADEEEGLNRRSSSS	regardlessness
ADEEEGOPRRRTUY	daguerreotyper
ADEEEHHLLORTWY	whole-heartedly

ADEEEHHLMORTTU	leather-mouthed
ADEEEHIINRRSST	hereditariness
ADEEEHILNOOPRT	radiotelephone
ADEEEIILLNPTXY	expedientially
ADEEEIILMNRTTY	intermediately
ADEEEIIMMQRSUV	demi-semiquaver
ADEEEIIMNSSTTV	meditativeness
ADEEEIINPRSTTV	predestinative
ADEEEIMMNORSST	immoderateness
ADEEEIMPRRSTTU	distemperature
ADEEEINNRRSSST	restrainedness
ADEEEINOOPRRTU	Neuropteroidea
ADEEEMNNRSTTTU	understatement
ADEEENNPPRRSSU	unpreparedness
ADEEENNSTTTWWY	sweet-and-twenty
ADEEFFFGHILRST	self-affrighted
ADEEFFIILLNRTY	differentially
ADEEFFIINORRTT	differentiator
ADEEFFLNOOSSTT	flat-footedness
ADEEFGHINRSSST	far-sightedness
ADEEFGHORRSTTU	foster-daughter
ADEEFGLLOOPRSU	gold-of-pleasure
ADEEFLLLMOORWY	follow-my-leader
ADEEGGHLNOOSTT	snaggletoothed
ADEEGHHILLRTTY	light-heartedly
ADEEGHHILNOSSY	highly-seasoned
ADEEGHIILLNRTW	willing-hearted
ADEEGHILNRSSTU	daughterliness
ADEEGHIPPPRSUY	pseudepigraphy
ADEEGIIINRSTTV	disintegrative
ADEEGIINNOPRST	predesignation
ADEEGIINNORRTT	redintegration
ADEEGIINORRSTT	deregistration
ADEEGILOOOSSST	Osteoglossidae
ADEEGINOORRSST	derogatoriness
ADEEGINOPRRSTY	predesignatory
ADEEGJLMNNNOTU	non-judgemental
ADEEGLLLMNNOTY	old-gentlemanly
ADEEHHIILMOPRS	hemispheroidal
ADEEHIIIPRSTTW	tide-waitership
ADEEHILMNNRSTT	disenthralment
ADEEHILNOOPRTY	radiotelephony
ADEEHLMNOORRSY	dysmenorrhoeal
ADEEHLORSTTTUY	stout-heartedly
ADEEHMNNNOSSSU	unhandsomeness
ADEEHNOOPRRSTZ	trapezohedrons
ADEEIIIMNNORTT	intermediation
ADEEIIINORSSST	radiosensitise
ADEEIIINORSSTV	radiosensitive
ADEEIIINORSSTZ	radiosensitize
ADEEIILMNNOTVY	denominatively
ADEEIILNPSSTVY	dispensatively
ADEEIILPQSSTUY	sesquipedality
ADEEIIMNNNRSTT	disentrainment
ADEEIIMNNOOSTT	demonetisation
ADEEIIMNNOOTTZ	demonetization
ADEEIIMNORRTTY	intermediatory
ADEEIINNNORSST	inordinateness
ADEEIINNOPRSTT	predestination
ADEEILLNNRSSTU	ill-naturedness
ADEEILNNOOSSTV	devotionalness
ADEEILNNRRSTUY	unrestrainedly
ADEEIMNNORRSST	arrondissement
ADEEIMNSSSTTUY	unsystematised
ADEEIMNSSTTUYZ	unsystematized
ADEELLNOOPRRWY	woollen-drapery
ADEELNNOPPRRTY	preponderantly
ADEELNNORSSSSU	slanderousness
ADEEMOOORSSTTU	osteodermatous
ADEFFHILLNOSUY	fully-fashioned
ADEFGHIMOORRTY	fairy-godmother
ADEFGIIMNORRST	transmogrified
ADEFGILLNORSUU	glanduliferous
ADEFIIINNOSSTT	disinfestation
ADEFIILMNORRTW	manifold-writer
ADEFIINNOOORRT	foreordination
ADEFIINOSSSSTU	fastidiousness
ADEGGHHINORTTU	thought-reading
ADEGGHIINNNRTW	night-wandering
ADEGGHIKNNORTU	kneading-trough
ADEGGIILNNRSST	leading-strings
ADEGHILNNOPRTU	hunting-leopard
ADEGHIMMOPRRRT	third-programme
ADEGIIIINNNOST	indigenisation
ADEGIIIINNNOTZ	indigenization
ADEGIIINNORSTT	disintegration
ADEGIIINNOSTTV	tendovaginitis
ADEGIILNNPRSUY	undespairingly
ADEGIIMNOQRSUU	quadrigeminous
ADEGILNOOORRUY	neuroradiology
ADEGINNPPRRSTU	understrapping
ADEHHIILNOOPRT	Ornithodelphia
ADEHILNNOSSSTU	outlandishness
ADEHILNOPRSTUU	desulphuration
ADEHIMOOOPPRSS	paedomorphosis
ADEHINOORRSSTW	roadworthiness
ADEHNORRSSTTWW	north-westwards
ADEHORSSSTTUWW	south-westwards
ADEIIILLNORSTT	redistillation
ADEIIILMNNORST	tridimensional
ADEIIINNOORSTT	disorientation
ADEIIINOPRSTTU	repudiationist
ADEIILLNOPRTVY	providentially
ADEIILMNNOOSTW	two-dimensional
ADEIILNOPRSSTY	dispensatorily
ADEIILNOSTTUVY	adventitiously
ADEIIMNNOPPSTT	disappointment
ADEILNNORSSTUW	untowardliness
ADEIMNORSSTUUV	misadventurous
ADEINOOORRTTTX	dextrorotation
ADEINOPRRRRSTT	transport-rider
ADELLOORRSSWWW	sword-swallower
ADELMNOOORSSSU	malodorousness
ADEOOORRRTTTXY	dextrorotatory
ADFGIKLNOOORRW	forward-looking
ADFIIIMNNOORST	disinformation
ADFINNOOOPSTTU	foundation-stop
ADGGHOOORSSSTT	dog's-tooth-grass
ADGGIMNNOPRSTU	stamping-ground
ADGGINNNOPRSUW	spawning-ground
ADGHLNNOORSSST	longs-and-shorts
ADGHMNNOOPRRYY	gynandromorphy
ADGIIIINNSTTTU	attitudinising
ADGIIIINNTTTUZ	attitudinizing

ADGIILLLNNOTUY	longitudinally
ADGIILMOOPRSTY	pyramidologist
ADGIILNOPPRSVY	disapprovingly
ADHIILMNOOPXYY	hypomixolydian
ADIIIILNOQSSTU	disquisitional
ADIIILLNORSSUY	disillusionary
ADIIILMNOOOSTT	dolomitisation
ADIIILMNOOOTTZ	dolomitization
ADIIIMNNNOOOPR	monoprionidian
ADIILNOPRSSTTU	postindustrial
ADIILOPSSTTUUY	disputatiously
ADIIMNOORRSTTU	radio-strontium
AEEEEEKLPRRSSU	pleasure-seeker
AEEEEFFIMNNSST	effeminateness
AEEEEGILNRRTVY	regeneratively
AEEEEGINSSTTVV	vegetativeness
AEEEEGNOQRRSUZ	orange-squeezer
AEEEEINNPRRTTT	interpenetrate
AEEEEINNRSSTTV	inveterateness
AEEEEINPRRSTTV	representative
AEEEELLNPRRTTW	water-repellent
AEEEFGGILNNRST	self-generating
AEEEFHHLNNPRTY	three-halfpenny
AEEEFHLNRSSSST	fatherlessness
AEEEFIILNNRRTT	interferential
AEEEFILLNORSTV	self-revelation
AEEEFILLNPRRTY	preferentially
AEEEFLMMNPRTTU	temperamentful
AEEEFLMOQRRTTU	letter-of-marque
AEEEGGILNNRSTV	steel-engraving
AEEEGGINRSSSSV	aggressiveness
AEEEGHHIOPRRRS	heresiographer
AEEEGHHNRRRTTU	hunter-gatherer
AEEEGHILMNPPRT	pamphleteering
AEEEGHILMNRSUW	measuring-wheel
AEEEGIILLRRSTY	siege-artillery
AEEEGIILMNSSTT	legitimateness
AEEEGIOPRRSTUV	supererogative
AEEEGLNOPPRRSU	general-purpose
AEEEHHHILMMPRT	hephthemimeral
AEEEHHHINNSSST	heathenishness
AEEEHHIMRRTTUX	heather-mixture
AEEEHHLLNSSSST	healthlessness
AEEEHIINNPPRSV	inapprehensive
AEEEHILNPPRSVY	apprehensively
AEEEHILNPRTTVY	hyperventilate
AEEEHINNPPRSUV	unapprehensive
AEEEHINSSSTUVX	exhaustiveness
AEEEIILLNPRTXY	experientially
AEEEIILLNRSSTT	illiterateness
AEEEIILMNNSSTT	sentimentalise
AEEEIILMNNSSTV	alimentiveness
AEEEIILMNNSTTZ	sentimentalize
AEEEIILNRRSSTV	irrelativeness
AEEEIINPRRTTTV	interpretative
AEEEILLMNPRTXY	experimentally
AEEEILLORSTTTT	ottrelite-slate
AEEEILMNNPRSTT	presentimental
AEEEILMNOPRTTU	Mitteleuropean
	Mittel-European
AEEEILNOPRSTUV	superelevation
AEEEILNPRSSSTU	superessential
AEEEIMMMNRSSTU	mismeasurement
AEEEIMNNRRTUUV	unremunerative
AEEEIMNOPRTTXY	extemporaneity
AEEEINNNPRRTTT	interpenetrant
AEEEINNOPRRSTT	representation
	re-presentation
AEEEINPRSSSSUV	persuasiveness
AEEEIOOPRRRTTV	retro-operative
AEEELLOPRSSSTU	Pasteurelloses
AEEELMOPRRTTUW	low-temperature
AEEELNNOPRSTTU	enteropneustal
AEEELNPRRSSSSY	prayerlessness
AEEEMNOOPRSTUX	extemporaneous
AEEENNORSSSTUX	extraneousness
AEEENQSSSSTTUU	statuesqueness
AEEFFFIMORRRRT	tariff-reformer
AEEFFGILLLNSTV	levelling-staff
AEEFFGILLLORSU	flagelliferous
AEEFFGILLNRSTT	self-flattering
AEEFGGILLNRSTU	self-regulating
AEEFGHHINRRSTT	three-farthings
AEEFGIILLNNPSX	self-explaining
AEEFGIIMMNRRST	ferrimagnetism
AEEFGIINRSSTUV	figurativeness
AEEFGILLNORSTU	self-regulation
AEEFGIMMNORRST	ferromagnetism
AEEFGLLORRSTUY	self-regulatory
AEEFGLNNRSSTUU	ungratefulness
AEEFHHLNNOPSVY	shove-halfpenny
AEEFIILMOPPRRW	power-amplifier
AEEFIILNNOPRRU	infopreneurial
AEEFIILNOQQTUU	quinquefoliate
AEEFIMNOOPRRRT	pre-Reformation
AEEFINOOPRSTTU	superfoetation
AEEFIOPRRRSSTU	ferroprussiate
AEEFLMNOOOPTTW	footplatewomen
AEEGGIILNPRSUV	pleasure-giving
AEEGGIINORSSTT	segregationist
AEEGGINORRSSSU	gregariousness
AEEGHHLOOPPRTT	phototelegraph
	telephotograph
AEEGHHLORSSTUU	slaughterhouse
AEEGHILNOOSSTY	anesthesiology
AEEGHINRSSTTTW	watertightness
AEEGHLLNOOOPTY	paleoethnology
AEEGIIILLLMTTY	illegitimately
AEEGIIILLLNNTT	intelligential
AEEGIIILLNNSTT	intelligentsia
AEEGIIILLNNTTZ	intelligentzia
AEEGIIINNORSST	greisenisation
AEEGIIINNORSTZ	greisenization
AEEGIILMNORSSS	generalissimos
AEEGIILNNNRTTY	entertainingly
AEEGIIMMNOPSTZ	piezomagnetism
AEEGIIMNNNORTU	mountaineering
AEEGIIMNOORSTT	geometrisation
AEEGIIMNOORTTZ	geometrization
AEEGIINNNNRTTU	unentertaining
AEEGIINNOOPRTT	prenegotiation
AEEGIINORRSTTV	tergiversation
AEEGILMNOPRTUV	Protevangelium
AEEGILNNOOSSSU	oleaginousness

AEEGIMNRRRTUWZ	Gewürztraminer
AEEGINOOPRRSTU	supererogation
AEEGINOORSTTTU	uterogestation
AEEGINOPRRRSSU	organiser-purse
AEEGINOPRRRSUZ	organizer-purse
AEEGIORRRSTTVY	tergiversatory
AEEGMNOOPRSSTU	spermatogenous
AEEGNOORSSSTUU	outrageousness
AEEGOOPRRRSTUY	supererogatory
AEEHHIIITTTTWW	whittie-whattie
AEEHHILLMORSTT	heterothallism
AEEHHLMMOOPRTT	ophthalmometer
AEEHHMNOOOPRRY	hypomenorrhoea
AEEHHOPPPRSSTU	superphosphate
AEEHIILMMNRTTY	trimethylamine
AEEHIILMNNPRTY	triphenylamine
AEEHIILNNPSTTU	lieutenantship
AEEHIINNNOPPRS	inapprehension
AEEHILLMRSSSTW	Wilhelmstrasse
AEEHILLNORSSSV	all-overishness
AEEHINPPPPRRSW	whippersnapper
AEEHLMNOORRTTT	thermotolerant
AEEHLOPPPRSSUY	pleurapophyses
AEEHMOOORSSTTU	heterosomatous
AEEIIILMNOSSTT	testimonialise
AEEIIILMNOSTTZ	testimonialize
AEEIIILMNSSTTX	existentialism
AEEIIILNNNORTT	interlineation
AEEIIILNSSTTTX	existentialist
AEEIIILORRRSTT	territorialise
AEEIIILORRRTTZ	territorialize
AEEIILLLNPSTTY	pestilentially
AEEIILLNNOPPTT	plenipotential
AEEIILLNNOPRTT	interpellation
AEEIILMMNNOPTT	implementation
AEEIILMMNNSSTT	sentimentalism
AEEIILMNNNPRSY	penny-a-linerism
AEEIILMNNOSSTX	extensionalism
AEEIILMNNSSTTT	sentimentalist
AEEIILMNNSTTTY	sentimentality
AEEIILNNOSTTXY	extensionality
AEEIILNNQSSTTU	quintessential
AEEIILNRSTTUXY	intersexuality
AEEIILPRTTUVVY	vituperatively
AEEIIMNNOORSTT	remonetisation
AEEIIMNNOORTTZ	remonetization
AEEIIMNOORSTTV	overestimation
AEEIINNOPPSSST	inappositeness
AEEIINNOPRRTTT	interpretation
AEEIINNORSSTTW	westernisation
AEEIINNORSTTWZ	westernization
AEEIINNRSSSTTV	transitiveness
AEEIJLLMNORSTU	telejournalism
AEEIJLLNORSTTU	telejournalist
AEEIKKLOOPSSTW	swoopstake-like
AEEILLNNRSSSTT	slatternliness
AEEILLOPRSSSTU	Pasteurellosis
AEEILLPPRRTTTT	prittle-prattle
AEEILMNNNNRSSU	unmannerliness
AEEILNOORTTTXY	extortionately
AEEIMNOQRSSTTU	question-master
AEEINNPPPPRRSS	snipper-snapper
AEEJKKOPRRUWYY	joukery-pawkery
AEELLLMNPPSTUY	supplementally
AEELLMNORSSSUV	marvellousness
AEFFGIILNSSSTY	self-satisfying
AEFFHILNNSSTUU	unfaithfulness
AEFFIIMNOORRSU	foraminiferous
AEFGGIIINNNPRT	finger-painting
AEFGHHINORSTTT	star-of-the-night
AEFGHILLLNNOTW	half-wellington
AEFGIILMNOSTTV	self-motivating
AEFGIILNNSSSTU	self-sustaining
AEFGIILNOSSSTU	flagitiousness
AEFGIIMORSSTTU	stigmatiferous
AEFGILLNNRTTUY	unflatteringly
AEFHHLNNOPRTWY	halfpennyworth
AEFHIILNNOPRTY	hyperinflation
AEFHIIMNOORSTT	hesitation-form
AEFHKLNNNSSTUU	unthankfulness
AEFIILLLMOOTTU	multifoliolate
AEFIILLMMNOOST	self-immolation
AEFIIMNOORRSTT	reformationist
AEFIINOQQRSUUU	quinquefarious
AEFILLNOOPRSSY	professionally
AEFILLOOPRRSSY	professorially
AEFILMNOPSSSTU	self-assumption
AEFILNNOOPRSSU	unprofessional
AEFIMNNOORRSTW	frontierswoman
AEFLLMNNOOSTWW	fellow-townsman
AEGGGIILLNNRSY	singing-gallery
AEGGHHOOPPRTYY	phytogeography
AEGGHIIINNRTTW	weight-training
AEGGHINNOOPRTV	photo-engraving
AEGGHINORRTTUW	watering-trough
AEGGHNNOOPRRTY	röntgenography
AEGGIILLNNNRWY	winning-gallery
AEGGILOOORSSTT	astrogeologist
AEGGINOOSSTTUU	auto-suggestion
AEGHHLMOPPRSTY	plethysmograph
AEGHIILLNOPSST	polishing-slate
AEGHIILLOPRSST	legislatorship
AEGHIILNNSTTUY	unhesitatingly
AEGHIILNOPPSST	polishing-paste
AEGHIIMNNOOOST	homogenisation
AEGHIIMNNOOOTZ	homogenization
AEGHIKNNRRRTTY	knight-errantry
AEGHILMOORSTTU	rheumatologist
AEGHILOOPPRSTY	epistolography
AEGHIMMMNORTUU	omnium-gatherum
AEGHINOOOPPRRS	sporangiophore
AEGHLLMOOPPRSY	megasporophyll
AEGHLLOOOPPTYY	paleophytology
AEGHLLORSSTUUY	slaughterously
AEGHLNOOOPRTUY	neuropathology
AEGHMMOOPRRTTY	photogrammetry
AEGIIIILLMNOTT	illegitimation
AEGIIIILMNOSTT	legitimisation
AEGIIIILMNOTTZ	legitimization
AEGIIIMNNORRTT	intermigration
AEGIIINNOORRTV	reinvigoration
AEGIIINNORSTTT	integrationist
AEGIILLLNNRTUY	interlingually
AEGIILLNTTTTTT	tittle-tattling

AEGIILNNNRSTTY	intransigently
AEGIIMOOQRSTUV	vigesimo-quarto
AEGIINNNPRRTTU	nature-printing
AEGIINNNPRSSSU	unaspiringness
AEGIINPPRSSSTT	asset-stripping
AEGILLLMNOOOPY	paleolimnology
AEGILLMNNOQTUY	magniloquently
AEGILLNOOOPSTT	paleontologist
AEGILLOOOOPSTZ	paleozoologist
AEGILMNOOORSTU	osmoregulation
AEGILMNOOPSTTU	pneumatologist
AEGILNNNOOPSTU	louping-on-stane
AEGILNNPPRSTTU	snapping-turtle
AEGIMMNOOPRSTU	spermatogonium
AEGIMNNNSSSSUU	unassumingness
AEGINNPRSSSSSU	surpassingness
AEGINOOOPPRRSS	sporangiospore
AEGINOOPRRRSSY	progressionary
AEGLNNOORSSSUU	languorousness
AEHHHILNOORTTU	holier-than-thou
AEHHHOOOPPRSTT	orthophosphate
AEHHIIILMPRSUX	xiphihumeralis
AEHHIILLLLRSSY	shilly-shallier
AEHHILMOPPRSTU	Periophthalmus
AEHHILOOPPRSST	philosophaster
AEHHLMMOOPRTTY	ophthalmometry
AEHHNNOORRSTTT	north-north-east
AEHHOOSSSTTTUU	south-south-east
AEHIIKLLMOOPRT	poikilothermal
AEHIILMNOORSTY	Hierosolymitan
AEHIILMOOPPRST	apheliotropism
AEHIILOPRRSTWY	praiseworthily
AEHIINNNOORSTT	enthronisation
AEHIINNNOORTTZ	enthronization
AEHIIOORRSSTTT	osteoarthritis
AEHILLLMMOOPRS	allelomorphism
AEHILOPPPRSSUY	pleurapophysis
AEHIMNNOORSSSU	harmoniousness
AEHIMOOPPPSSTU	hippopotamuses
AEHIMOPPRSSSTT	postmastership
AEHINOPRRSTUWY	unpraiseworthy
AEHIOOORRSSSTT	osteoarthrosis
AEHLMNOOOPSSTU	haplostemonous
AEHNOOPRSSTTUY	thysanopterous
AEIIIILMNRSSTT	ministerialist
AEIIIIMMNORSST	immiserisation
AEIIIIMMNORSTZ	immiserization
AEIIILMORRRSTT	territorialism
AEIIILNNNOTTTY	intentionality
AEIIILNNOOPTVY	opinionatively
AEIIILNNRSTTVY	intransitively
AEIIILNPRSSTUU	unspiritualise
AEIIILNPRSTUUZ	unspiritualize
AEIIILORRRSTTT	territorialist
AEIIILORRRTTTY	territoriality
AEIIINOQRRSTUY	requisitionary
AEIILLLMNNOPST	post-millennial
AEIILLLRSTTUVY	illustratively
AEIILLNNNQQUUY	quinquennially
AEIILMNOOPRSTY	polymerisation
AEIILMNOOPRTYZ	polymerization
AEIILMNOPRRSST	tripersonalism
AEIILMNRSSSTVY	transmissively
AEIILNOOPRSTTX	explorationist
AEIILNOPRRSSTT	tripersonalist
AEIILNOPRRSTTY	tripersonality
AEIIMMNORSSTTY	symmetrisation
AEIIMMNORSTTYZ	symmetrization
AEIIMNNORRSSST	retransmission
AEIIMNOOOOPSST	onomatopoiesis
AEIIMNOORRSSTT	restorationism
AEIIMNRSSSTTTV	transvestitism
AEIIMOOPRRSTVV	improvvisatore
AEIINNORRSSSTT	transitoriness
AEIINOORRSSTTT	restorationist
AEIINOPRRSSSTU	pressurisation
AEIINOPRRSSTUZ	pressurization
AEIINOPRSSSUVV	viviparousness
AEILLMNNRSTTUY	instrumentally
AEILLMNOSSTUUY	simultaneously
AEILMNOPRRSTUY	supernormality
AEILNNOOSSTTUY	enantiostylous
AEILNOOOPPRTUV	overpopulation
AEILNOOPRSTUUV	superovulation
AEILNOOSSTTTUY	ostentatiously
AEIMNOPPRRSTTU	superimportant
AEINNOOSSTTTUU	unostentatious
AEINOOPRRSSSUU	uproariousness
AEINOORRSSSTTU	traitorousness
AFFIILNNOOOPRT	inflation-proof
AFGGHIIMNNNOOS	fashionmonging
AFGHHILNOORRST	thrashing-floor
AFGHHINORRSTTW	farthingsworth
AFIIIMMNNOORST	misinformation
AFIILLMORSTUUY	multifariously
AFIINNORSSSTTU	transfusionist
AGGGGHHINNORTU	through-ganging
AGGLLNOOOORTYY	otolaryngology
AGHHIIOOPRRSTY	historiography
AGHHILOOOPSTTY	histopathology
AGHHLOOOPPTTYY	phytopathology
AGHHOOOPPPRRTY	pyrophotograph
AGHIIMNNPSSTUY	unsympathising
AGHIIMNNPSTUYZ	unsympathizing
AGHILLOOOPSSST	opisthoglossal
AGHILNOOOPRSTT	anthropologist
AGHIMOOOPRSSTU	mastigophorous
AGHLOOPPRRXYYY	xylopyrography
AGHLOOPPRTXYYY	xylotypography
AGIIIIILNOTTTV	vitilitigation
AGIIILLMNNNTUU	unilluminating
AGIIKLLMNOPRRU	milking-parlour
AGIILLMMNNOOSU	monolingualism
AGIILLNOORSUVY	vaingloriously
AGIINNOORSSUUV	sanguinivorous
AGILNNOPRRSTTY	transportingly
AGLMMOOOPSTTYY	symptomatology
AHHIILNOPPRSTT	philanthropist
AHHIMNOOPPRSTU	anthropophuism
AHIIIILLNOOPSTY	lyophilisation
AHIIILLNOOPTYZ	lyophilization
AHIILMNNOORSUY	inharmoniously
AHIILMNOPPRSST	psilanthropism
AHIILMOOPSSSST	histoplasmosis

AHIILNOPPRSSTT	psilanthropist
AHIILNOPRSSTUU	sulphurisation
AHIILNOPRSTUUZ	sulphurization
AHIIMMNOOPSTTU	imposthumation
AHILLOOOOPRSST	alloiostrophos
AHOPPQRRRTUYYZ	quartz-porphyry
AIIIILMNNOSTTU	intuitionalism
AIIIILNNOSTTTU	intuitionalist
AIIIILNOORSTTV	vitriolisation
AIIIILNOORTTVZ	vitriolization
AIIIIMNNOPRSST	inspirationism
AIIIINNOPRSSTT	inspirationist
AIIIINOOPRRSTT	prioritisation
AIIIINOOPRRTTZ	prioritization
AIIILMNNOOSTTY	mylonitisation
AIIILMNNOOTTYZ	mylonitization
AIIILOOPPRRTTY	propitiatorily
AIIIMNRSSSTTVY	transmissivity
AIIINNORSTTTUY	institutionary
AIILLNORRSSSTY	sinistrorsally
AIILMNOOPRSSUY	parsimoniously
AIILNOOOPPSSTT	postpositional
AIINOOPPRSSTUY	suppositionary
AIKKMMNNRRTTUU	trinkum-trankum
AILLNOOOPPRRTY	proportionally
AIMNNNOPPRSSSU	snip-snap-snorum

B

BBBCGHINRRSSUU	scrubbing-brush
BBBCGIIKLNOORS	scribbling-book
BBCCDEIIMNRSUU	circumbendibus
BBCGIKLLMNOSTU	stumbling-block
BBDDEEHHLMOOOY	hobbledehoydom
BBDDEELOOOPSTT	blood-bespotted
BBDDEGGIIILNRU	bridge-building
BBDEEHHHILOOSY	hobbledehoyish
BBDEEHHILMOOSY	hobbledehoyism
BBEEGHOORRSSUY	gooseberry-bush
BBEGIIILMRSTUY	submergibility
BBEIIILMRSSTUY	submersibility
BCCCIIMOOPRSSU	submicroscopic
BCCDDEEHLLOTUU	double-declutch
BCCDIIILNOTTUY	conductibility
BCCEEHMNNRRRUU	number-cruncher
BCCEEIIILORTTY	bioelectricity
BCCEEIKKKNORRS	knickerbockers
BCCEEJNORSTTUU	countersubject
BCCEIIIJSSTTUV	subjectivistic
BCCILNOOSSSUUY	subconsciously
BCDEEEEILRRSTT	street-credible
BCDEEEGHIINRRS	riding-breeches
BCDEEEIILNNRSS	incredibleness
BCDEEGIKLNRSUW	swindge-buckler
BCDEEIIILNPRST	indiscerptible
BCDEEIILNOORTU	ribonucleotide
BCDEEIILNRSTTU	indestructible
BCDEEIILOPRRRU	irreproducible
BCDEEILNOPRRUU	unreproducible
BCDEEMOOOPPRTT	copper-bottomed
BCDEGHINNORSTT	stretching-bond
BCDEHIINOORRRS	rhinoceros-bird
BCDEIIIILPRSTY	discerpibility
BCDEIIIILRRTUY	irreducibility
BCDEIIILPPRSTU	public-spirited
BCDEIILLNORSTU	bill-discounter
BCDEIILNRSTTUY	indestructibly
BCDEIKNOORRSTU	discount-broker
BCDGILMNNOOOSU	blood-consuming
BCDHHIIOOPRTYY	hydrophobicity
BCDIIILOPRTTUY	productibility
BCEEEEFILMNRST	fermentescible
BCEEEEGHINNSSS	beseechingness
BCEEEHILMNOPRS	comprehensible
BCEEEIJNSSSTUV	subjectiveness
BCEEEORRRRSTWY	worcesterberry
BCEEFIIILMPRST	perfectibilism
BCEEFIIILPRSTT	perfectibilist
BCEEFIIILPRTTY	perfectibility
BCEEFLRRSTTUWY	butterfly-screw
BCEEGHIKLNRRUY	huckleberrying
BCEEGILLOOORTY	electrobiology
BCEEGIMNNNOSSU	unbecomingness
BCEEHILMNOPRSY	comprehensibly
BCEEIIILNNNSSV	invincibleness
BCEEIIILPPRTTY	perceptibility
BCEEIILMNNOSTU	bioluminescent
BCEEIILMNOPRSS	incompressible
BCEEILNOORRTTV	controvertible
BCEEIMNNPRSTUU	superincumbent
BCEIIIILRSTTVY	vitrescibility
BCEIIILNORTTVY	convertibility
BCEIIILPSSTTUY	susceptibility
BCEIILMRRSTTUU	trituberculism
BCEILLMNOPSUVY	plumbisolvency
BCEILMOORTTTUY	yttro-columbite
BCEILNOORRTTVY	controvertibly
BCELLMNOOPSUVY	plumbosolvency
BCGIIILMOOORST	microbiologist
BCGIIILOOOOSST	sociobiologist
BCIIILMOOPSSTY	compossibility
BCIIILOPRRTTUY	corruptibility
BCIIMNOORSSTTU	obstructionism
BCIINOORSSTTTU	obstructionist
BDDEEEEFILLMNY	feeble-mindedly
BDDEEEFLLOORUW	double-flowered
BDDEEGGINNORRU	breeding-ground
BDDEEIKMNNOOSS	book-mindedness
BDDEFGIINNORSS	forbiddingness
BDEEEEILLRSSTT	blistered-steel
BDEEEFGIILMNNR	nimble-fingered
BDEEEFGINRRTTU	butter-fingered
BDEEEGIMMNOSTU	disemboguement
BDEEEIINNNORTZ	dinitrobenzene
BDEEEILMMNOSTW	disembowelment
BDEEGIIILMNPRU	empire-building
BDEEHIINOSTTUY	hebetudinosity
BDEEHLMMPRSTUU	rumbledethumps
BDEEIIIRRSTTUV	redistributive
BDEEILLNOSSSSU	dissolubleness
BDEGGILNNOOTUU	double-tonguing
BDEGHIILNNNSST	night-blindness
BDEGIIMNOORSTT	bed-sitting-room
BDEGILNOOPPSTU	double-stopping
BDEGIMNNOORRRU	mourning-border

BDEIIIILMQRSUU	disequilibrium
BDEIIIILNSSTTY	distensibility
BDEIIIILNNOSSSU	libidinousness
BDEIIILRSTTUVY	distributively
BDEIIINORRSTTU	redistribution
BDGHIILOOORSTY	hydrobiologist
BDGIILNNOOOOPS	blood-poisoning
BDHIILLOORSTTY	bloodthirstily
BDIIIIIILNSTVY	indivisibility
BEEEELMNORSTUV	bouleversement
BEEEFIILLNNSSX	inflexibleness
BEEEGGIIINNNOR	bioengineering
BEEEGILLNNNORT	non-belligerent
BEEEGINOORRSWY	gooseberry-wine
BEEEHILMNOSSST	blithesomeness
BEEEIILNNNSSSS	insensibleness
BEEEIILNPRSSSX	inexpressibles
BEEEILLNORSSSU	rebelliousness
BEEEILMNNNOOTV	omnibenevolent
BEEELMMNORSSSU	lumbersomeness
BEEELMNNRSSSSU	numberlessness
BEEFGLOOOORRSY	gooseberry-fool
BEEGGHIILNNTTT	belt-tightening
BEEGGHIILNOTTW	weighing-bottle
BEEGGIIMNOORSU	embourgeoising
BEEGHIILLLMNSY	embellishingly
BEEGHIILNNORSS	neighborliness
BEEGHMOOORRSTY	gooseberry-moth
BEEGIIILLLNNTU	unintelligible
BEEGILMOOOORTY	biometeorology
BEEHLOOORRSTTU	troubleshooter
BEEIIKLNNSSSUU	unbusinesslike
BEEIILNPPRSSSU	insuppressible
BEEIIMNSSSSSUV	submissiveness
BEEINOOQSSSSUU	obsequiousness
BEEINOORSSSSTU	boisterousness
BEELOOPRRSSTUY	obstreperously
BEGGGHIIILMNRT	thimblerigging
BEGGHHILNOORSU	borough-English
BEGGIIILSSTTUY	suggestibility
BEGHIILLNOSTWW	whistle-blowing
BEGIIILLLNNTUY	unintelligibly
BEGIILNOOORSTU	neurobiologist
BEGILMMNOPRTUU	rumblegumption
BEGILNORSSSUUU	lugubriousness
BEHHMNOOPPRRRY	rhombenporphyr
BEHHNOOOPPRRSZ	phosphor-bronze
BEIIIILMPRSSTY	impressibility
	permissibility
BEIIILLORRSTUY	irresolubility
BEIIILNOPRSSTY	responsibility
BEIIILNPSSSTUY	suspensibility
BEIILNPPRSSSUY	insuppressibly
BEIILSSTTTUUVY	substitutively
BEINOORSSSSTUU	robustiousness
BGHIILOOOOPSTT	photobiologist
BGIILLMMNNOOUU	immunoglobulin
BHIIIIMNOOPRST	prohibitionism
BHIIIINOOPRSTT	prohibitionist
BIIISSTTTTUUVY	substitutivity

C

CCCCIOOOPRSSTY	cryptococcosis
CCCDDEEEENNNOS	condescendence
CCCDEEHIIOOPRT	cercopithecoid
CCCDEFINNOOSST	soft-conscienc'd
CCCDGIILOOORTU	glucocorticoid
CCCEEEHHHIINNR	chincherinchee
CCCEEEILLNOQSU	colliquescence
CCCEEEILNNOSSS	conscienceless
CCCEEIIMPRSTUV	circumspective
CCCEENNNNOORRU	non-concurrence
CCCEHHINOPSSTY	psychotechnics
CCCEHIINORRSTT	Christocentric
CCCEIIILMRSSSU	circumscissile
CCCEIIMMNOOORS	microeconomics
CCCEIIMNOPRSTU	circumspection
CCCIIIMNNORSUU	uncircumcision
CCCIILMNOORTUU	circumlocution
CCCILMOORRTUUY	circumlocutory
CCDDEEILNNOSTY	disconnectedly
CCDEEEEIILLRST	diesel-electric
CCDEEEFFILNNOS	self-confidence
CCDEEEFGIINPRS	gender-specific
CCDEEEFINNOORV	over-confidence
CCDEEEHIIKLNRV	chicken-livered
CCDEEEIINPRSVY	vice-presidency
CCDEEELNOPRRTY	preconcertedly
CCDEEENNOOPRRS	correspondence
CCDEEGIMNNNOOO	non-comedogenic
CCDEEHILNOORTU	technicoloured
CCDEEIIMNOORTT	microdetection
CCDEEIMNNORSTT	disconcertment
CCDEENNOOPRRSY	correspondency
CCDEGIIMNNOSTU	semiconducting
CCDEIILMOORTTY	clitoridectomy
CCDEIIOOORRSTT	corticosteroid
CCDEINNOORSTTU	deconstruction
CCDENOOPRRSTUU	superconductor
CCDHIIMOPRRSTY	cryptorchidism
CCDIIIMOOSSSUV	mucoviscidosis
CCEEEEEFLNNORT	teleconference
CCEEEEEJNNRSUV	rejuvenescence
CCEEEEFNORRRSS	cross-reference
CCEEEEHIMOPRTV	chemoreceptive
CCEEEEMMMNNORT	recommencement
CCEEEFHIIOPRST	heterospecific
CCEEEFIIOPRSST	stereospecific
CCEEEHILMORRTT	electrothermic
	thermoelectric
CCEEEHILMORSTT	electrochemist
CCEEEILLLORTVY	recollectively
CCEEEIMMNNOOPT	omnicompetence
CCEEEINSSSSSUV	successiveness
CCEEELLORRTTUU	electroculture
CCEEFFNRSSTTUU	suffructescent
CCEEFGILNORRST	self-correcting
CCEEFHIILLNNOO	colonel-in-chief
CCEEFIMNORRRTU	circumferentor
CCEEFLNSSSSSUU	successfulness
CCEEGHINOPSSTY	psychogenetics

CCEEGIILLOOSST	ecclesiologist
CCEEGIINNOOSTT	oncogeneticist
CCEEGIINOSTTTY	cytogeneticist
CCEEHIIIPRRSTY	hypercriticise
CCEEHIIIPRRTYZ	hypercriticize
CCEEHIIKKPRRYY	hickery-pickery
CCEEHIILLMOPTU	multiple-choice
CCEEHIIMOORSTT	stoechiometric
CCEEIILNORRTTU	interlocutrice
CCEEIINORRTTUY	Eurocentricity
CCEEILNNOSSSUV	conclusiveness
CCEEILNOOOPRTT	optoelectronic
CCEEILNOSSSSSU	successionless
CCEEINNNOORRTT	interconnector
CCEEINOOORRRTV	overcorrection
CCEEINOOPRSSSU	precociousness
CCEEINORRSTTUV	reconstructive
CCEELNORRTTUUU	counter-culture
CCEENNORRRTTUU	counter-current
CCEFIILNNOOSTV	self-conviction
CCEFIINNOORSST	cross-infection
CCEFLLNSSSUUUY	unsuccessfully
CCEHHIILORSSTT	chlorite-schist
CCEHHIOOPSSUYZ	schizophyceous
CCEHIIIMOORSTT	stoichiometric
CCEHIIIMPRRSTY	hypercriticism
CCEHIILNOPSSUV	vice-consulship
CCEHIIMMORRSTY	microchemistry
CCEHIMMOORSSTY	cosmochemistry
CCEHIMOOSSTUYZ	schizomycetous
CCEHINOOPRSSUY	hyperconscious
CCEHINOOPRSTUY	psychoneurotic
CCEHLMOOOSTTYY	cholecystotomy
CCEIIIJMNNOORT	microinjection
CCEIILLNNOSUVY	inconclusively
CCEIILLNOOPSST	scintilloscope
CCEIIMNNOOOPTU	pneumoconiotic
CCEIINORSSSTUU	circuitousness
CCEIKLNOOPRSSU	percussion-lock
CCEILLOOSSTUYY	leucocytolysis
CCEILNORSTTUVY	constructively
CCEIMMNNOOOPRT	microcomponent
CCEIMOOOPRRRSS	microprocessor
CCEIMORRRSTTUU	microstructure
CCEINNOORRSTTU	△reconstruction
CCEIOOPPRSSSTT	spectroscopist
CCGHIIKNOSSTTT	stocking-stitch
CCGHIIOOPRSTYY	hygroscopicity
CCGIIKMNOOPSST	composing-stick
CCGIIMMNOOPRTU	microcomputing
CCHIINOOOPRRTT	corticotrophin
CCHILMMNNOOOTU	communion-cloth
CCHIOORRRSSSTW	Christ-cross-row
CCIIIIMNOORRST	onirocriticism
CCIIIJNNOSTTUV	conjunctivitis
CCIIILPRSSTTUU	pisciculturist
CCIIIMNOOPRSTU	circumposition
CCIILMNOORTUUV	circumvolution
CCIIMNORSSTTUV	constructivism
CCILMNOOPSTUUY	compunctiously
CDDEEEEEFLNNPS	self-dependence
CDDEEEHMNNOPRU	uncomprehended
CDDEEEHNNPRRTU	hundred-per-cent
CDDEEILNNOSTTY	discontentedly
CDDEHLMOOORSTY	odd-come-shortly
CDDEIIILLNNOOT	ill-conditioned
CDDEILNOOOSTUY	dicotyledonous
CDEEEEFMNNORRR	norm-referenced
CDEEEEIRRSSSTV	dessert-service
CDEEEELNOPRSTW	steeple-crowned
CDEEEENNPSSTUX	unexpectedness
CDEEEFGILLNNSU	self-indulgence
CDEEEFGINOPRSW	weeding-forceps
CDEEEFHINNRRRT	trencher-friend
CDEEEGIIMNPRRU	murdering-piece
CDEEEGIINORRRV	receiving-order
CDEEEGILNNORUV	overindulgence
CDEEEHIKLNNOTV	devil-on-the-neck
CDEEEHLLOOPRRW	Rochelle-powder
CDEEEHLOOOPRTT	photoelectrode
CDEEEIIINNSSSV	indecisiveness
CDEEEIINNRSSST	indiscreetness
	indiscreteness
CDEEEIIOPPRSTT	deposit-receipt
CDEEEINNNOORRU	neuroendocrine
CDEEFGHILORRRT	flight-recorder
CDEEFGIIKNRSTY	sticky-fingered
CDEEFGILMNNNOS	self-condemning
CDEEFIIILLNPSS	self-discipline
CDEEFINNOPRSTU	superconfident
CDEEGGHINOORRS	schooner-rigged
CDEEGGIILLNORT	electrogilding
CDEEGHINNOORSS	chondrogenesis
CDEEHIKLNPRRSU	under-clerkship
CDEEHIMNOORRSY	dysmenorrhoeic
CDEEHLLLOORSUY	hydrocellulose
CDEEIIINNNORRT	inner-direction
CDEEIIINNSSTVV	vindictiveness
CDEEIIMMNOORSS	decommissioner
CDEEIINRSSSSUV	discursiveness
CDEEIKNNORRSTW	wonder-stricken
CDEEILLNOOPTUY	polynucleotide
CDEEILNRRSTTUY	unrestrictedly
CDEEILOPRRTUVY	reproductively
CDEEIMNNNOSTTT	discontentment
CDEEINNOORSSSU	indecorousness
CDEEINNORSTTUV	non-destructive
CDEEINOPRSSTUV	productiveness
CDEEINPSSSTTUU	intussuscepted
CDEELLOOPPRRUU	purple-coloured
CDEENNOORRTTUV	uncontroverted
CDEFGLNOOOSSTU	slug-foot-second
CDEFLLNOOOORRT	food-controller
CDEGHHIIILNPPR	high-principled
CDEGHMNRRSTUUU	Durchmusterung
CDEGINOOPRRSSW	word-processing
CDEHHIILNOOPRT	ornithodelphic
CDEHHINNOOOPRR	chondrophorine
CDEHHINOOPRRTY	hydronephrotic
CDEHINOOORRSTY	hydrocortisone
CDEIIIILRSTTUV	diverticulitis
CDEIIILORSSTUV	diverticulosis
CDEIIIMNOPRSST	misdescription
CDEIIINNNSSSTT	indistinctness

CDEIILNORSSSUU	ridiculousness
CDEIINNOORRTTU	reintroduction
CDEIINNOPRSTUU	superinduction
CDEIINORSSTTTU	destructionist
CDEIIOPRRTTUVY	reproductivity
CDEILNOPRTUUVY	unproductively
CDEILOORSSTUUY	discourteously
CDEIMMNOOOSSSU	commodiousness
CDEINOOOPPRSSU	pseudoscorpion
CDEINOOOPRRTUV	overproduction
CDELLLNNOORTUY	uncontrolledly
CDFHKOORSSTTUU	futtock-shrouds
CDHHILOPRRSUUY	hydrosulphuric
CDHIIILNOOSTVY	school-divinity
CDHIKMNOOPRRTU	durchkomponirt
CDHINOOOPRSSTT	prosthodontics
CDIIJNNNNOOSTU	nondisjunction
CDIILMMNOOOSUY	incommodiously
CDIILNOORRTTUY	introductorily
CDIINOPRTTUUVY	unproductivity
CDINOOOPPRSTTU	post-production
CEEEEEILNPRSSX	experienceless
CEEEEFGINNQRUY	eigen-frequency
CEEEEFIINNPPVY	fivepenny-piece
CEEEEFILNRSSTV	reflectiveness
CEEEEGIILNNORT	electioneering
CEEEEGILNORSST	electrogenesis
CEEEEHIMNPRSWY	chimney-sweeper
CEEEEHLNPSSSSS	speechlessness
CEEEEINNORSSTT	enterocentesis
CEEEEINPPRSSTV	perceptiveness
CEEEELLNPRSTUX	superexcellent
CEEEFFGILNRSVY	effervescingly
CEEEFFHIKPRRSU	Kupferschiefer
CEEEFFLLPRSSTU	self-respectful
CEEEFGILNPRSST	self-respecting
CEEEFGLLNNSSTU	neglectfulness
CEEEFHIKNNORST	knotenschiefer
CEEEFHILMNNRST	self-enrichment
CEEEFHLNNRSSUU	uncheerfulness
CEEEFIILMPRTVY	imperfectively
CEEEFILLNORSST	reflectionless
CEEEFILOPRSTTV	self-protective
CEEEFIMNNORRST	reinforcements
CEEEFLNNOQSSTU	self-consequent
CEEEFLNPRSSSTU	respectfulness
CEEEFLOORRRRTT	retroreflector
CEEEGHIINORSUV	receiving-house
CEEEGHLORRSTTV	glove-stretcher
CEEEGILNOPRSST	teleprocessing
CEEEHIMORSSTTY	hysterectomise
CEEEHIMORSTTYZ	hysterectomize
CEEEHMMOPSSSTY	metempsychoses
CEEEHNOORRTTUV	over-the-counter
CEEEIIKNNPRSST	pernicketiness
CEEEIILPRRSTVY	irrespectively
CEEEIIMMOORRTT	micro-meteorite
CEEEIIMOORRSST	stereoisomeric
CEEEIKLNPSSSSY	sleepy-sickness
CEEEILMNNOPSST	incompleteness
CEEEIMMNNOPRTV	pincer-movement
CEEEIMNNORRSVY	money-scrivener
CEEEINOPRSSTTV	protectiveness
CEEEINPSSSSTUV	susceptiveness
CEEEIOOPRRTTVV	overprotective
CEEELLNNOORTTY	non-electrolyte
CEEFFFIILNSSTU	self-sufficient
CEEFFGIILNRSTY	self-rectifying
CEEFGILLNNRTUY	unreflectingly
CEEFGILMNOORRT	electroforming
CEEFGILNOPRSTT	self-protecting
CEEFHHILNOPRRS	French-polisher
CEEFIILLNNOSST	inflectionless
CEEFIINNOPRSTU	superinfection
CEEFIINNOSSSTU	infectiousness
CEEFILMMMNOSTT	self-commitment
CEEFILMNNRSSUU	unmercifulness
CEEFILMNOORSSS	frolicsomeness
CEEFILNNOSSSTT	self-consistent
CEEFILNOOPRSTT	self-protection
CEEFINOORSSSUV	vociferousness
CEEFINOPRSSSUU	percussion-fuse
CEEFLLMMNOOORW	fellow-commoner
CEEGGHIMNOOOPR	geomorphogenic
CEEGHHIKNNRRTT	trencher-knight
CEEGHLNOOORTTY	terotechnology
CEEGIIINNOPPRT	precipitinogen
CEEGIILNNNORTW	electrowinning
CEEGIILNNORRTY	nitroglycerine
CEEGIIMMNNOSTU	immunogenetics
CEEGILLLLNOOSU	lignocellulose
CEEGINNNOOPRTU	counter-opening
CEEGINOPRSSTTX	text-processing
CEEGNNOOPRRSSS	Congressperson
CEEHHIILMOPPST	Mephistophelic
CEEHHIILOOPSTY	heliosciophyte
CEEHHILMNORSTT	Trochelminthes
CEEHHIMNOORRST	heterochronism
CEEHHIMNOSSSTY	chemosynthesis
CEEHHIOOPRRSTT	heterostrophic
CEEHHMOOORRSTU	heterochromous
CEEHHNOOORRSTU	heterochronous
CEEHHNOOPPRSST	phosphorescent
CEEHIILMOPRRTY	pyrheliometric
CEEHIILNOPPRTY	pyelonephritic
CEEHIIMOORSTTY	stoicheiometry
CEEHIIMOPRSTYZ	piezochemistry
CEEHILMNOOPSTU	photoluminesce
CEEHIMMOPSSSTY	metempsychosis
CEEHIMOOOOPRST	oophorectomise
CEEHIMOOOOPRTZ	oophorectomize
CEEHIMOPRRSTTY	petrochemistry
CEEHINOQSSSTTU	coquettishness
CEEHNOOPRSSSUY	psychoneuroses
CEEIILLMNORSTT	scintillometer
CEEIILMORRSTUY	meretriciously
CEEIILNNNNOTVY	inconveniently
CEEIILNNOSSSTU	licentiousness
CEEIILNPSSTUVY	insusceptively
CEEIILPPRRSTVY	prescriptively
CEEIIMNOOPRTTT	potentiometric
CEEIINNNNOORTX	interconnexion
CEEIINNOPRSSSU	perniciousness
CEEIINNORRSTTV	non-restrictive

CEEIINNORSSTTU	neuroscientist
CEEIIOOPPPRRTV	proprioceptive
CEEIKNOPPRRSTU	counterskipper
CEEIKNORRRRSTT	terror-stricken
CEEILLLNOORSTU	nitrocellulose
CEEILLMNOOPSSX	complexionless
CEEILLMOTUVYZZ	muzzle-velocity
CEEILMNOSSSTUU	meticulousness
CEEILMOOORSSST	electro-osmosis
CEEILNNNOQSTUY	inconsequently
CEEILNNOSSSUVV	convulsiveness
CEEILNORRSSTTU	interlocutress
CEEIMMNNNOSTTT	miscontentment
CEEIMNOOQRRSUU	croque-monsieur
CEEINNNOPRSTTU	supercontinent
CEEINNOOORRSSV	seroconversion
CEEINNOORSSSSU	censoriousness
CEEINNOSSSSTUU	incestuousness
CEEINOOOPPRSTY	peritoneoscopy
CEEIPRRSSTTUUV	superstructive
CEEMNOOPRSTUYY	pyrenomycetous
CEEPRRRSSTTUUU	superstructure
CEFFGIIINNOPRT	printing-office
CEFFIIILNNSTUY	insufficiently
CEFGHIIKNORSST	night-fossicker
CEFIIIIILOPSTT	filiopietistic
CEGGHILMOOOOPR	geomorphologic
CEGGIIILNOSSTU	geolinguistics
CEGHHIILLMNOOT	helminthologic
CEGHIIILNOPRSS	rice-polishings
CEGHLNNNOOOOTY	nonotechnology
CEGHNNOOORSSUY	geosynchronous
CEGIIIKLNQRSUV	quicksilvering
CEGIIILNOORRST	correligionist
CEGIIIMMNNOTUY	immunogenicity
CEGIIIMNORTTUY	tumorigenicity
CEGIIINPRRTTUW	picture-writing
CEGIILMNNNORTU	microtunneling
CEGIINNOOORRTT	retrocognition
CEGIIOOPRRSSTY	Crossopterygii
CEGILNNPSSTUUY	unsuspectingly
CEGIMNNOOOOSUY	gynomonoecious
CEGIMNNOOPRTUU	neurocomputing
CEGINNOOSSSTUU	contiguousness
CEHHIIMORSSTTY	histochemistry
CEHHIMMNOOOPPR	morphophonemic
CEHHIMOOPRSTTY	photochemistry
CEHHINOOPSTTTY	photosynthetic
CEHHMOOPPSTYYY	hypophysectomy
CEHIIIKLMOOPRT	poikilothermic
CEHIIIKLQRSSUV	quicksilverish
CEHIIOPPRSSTTY	petrophysicist
CEHIKNOORRRRST	horror-stricken
CEHILLNOOPRRST	controllership
CEHILLNOOPRSSU	counsellorship
CEHILMMOOPRSUY	myrmecophilous
CEHILMOORSSSST	schoolmistress
CEHILOOOOPSSTU	opisthocoelous
CEHINOOPRSSSUY	psychoneurosis
CEHLLLOOPRSSUY	sclerophyllous
CEIIIINOSSTTVV	vivisectionist
CEIIIILNOOSTTUV	evolutionistic
CEIIIMPPRRSSTV	prescriptivism
CEIIINORRSSTTT	restrictionist
CEIIIPPRRSSTTV	prescriptivist
CEIILLOPRSSUUY	superciliously
CEIILMNOOORTUV	microevolution
CEIILNNNOSSTTY	inconsistently
CEIILNOOSSSSTU	solicitousness
CEIILOPPRRSTVY	proscriptively
CEIIMMNNNOORTU	intercommunion
CEIIMMNNORTTUY	intercommunity
CEIIMNNOOOPSSU	pneumoconiosis
CEIINNOORSTTTU	reconstitution
CEIINOORSSSTUV	victoriousness
CEIINOPPRRSSTU	superscription
CEIINOPSSSSSUU	suspiciousness
CEIKLLOOSSTUYY	leukocytolysis
CEILLMNOOSTUUY	contumeliously
CEILNOPRRSTUUV	proventriculus
CEILNORRSSSSUU	scurrilousness
CEINNNNOOOSTTU	non-contentious
CEINNNOOSSSTUU	continuousness
CEINOPRRSSTTUU	superstruction
CELMNOOPSTTUUY	contemptuously
CELNOPRSSSSUUU	scrupulousness
CELOOPRRSSUUUV	overscrupulous
CFGIILMNNOORSU	soul-confirming
CFIILLORRSTTUU	floriculturist
CFILLLOOOORRSU	corolliflorous
CGGIIKLNNOSSTW	swingling-stock
CGHIILNOPSSTUY	psycholinguist
CGIIILNNRSSTUY	scrutinisingly
CGIIILNNRSTUYZ	scrutinizingly
CGIIILNOOOPSST	oligopsonistic
CGIILNNOOQTTTU	quilting-cotton
CGIILNNOOSTUUY	incontiguously
CGIIMMNNOOPRSU	uncompromising
CHHHNOOOPRRSUY	rhynchophorous
CHHIIIILOOPPSST	philosophistic
CHHIILNOPRTTTY	lithonthryptic
CHHIIMNOOOPRRT	ornithomorphic
CHHIIOOPRSSTTY	trichophytosis
CHHIOOOPPPRRSY	pyrophosphoric
CHIILORRSTTTUU	horticulturist
CHIIOOOPRRSSST	sporotrichosis
CHIIOOORSSTTXY	thyrotoxicosis
CHILMOOORSTTUY	trichotomously
CHILOOOPPRRSTU	prolocutorship
CIIIMNNORSSTTU	misinstruction
CIILNOPSSSUUUY	unsuspiciously
CLLNOPRSSUUUUY	unscrupulously

D

DDDDEEIILNOOPR	lepidodendroid
DDDEEEELNOPRUV	underdeveloped
DDEEEEEGNRRSWY	dyer's-greenweed
DDEEEEFILMNRST	self-determined
DDEEEEIMNORRTV	over-determined
DDEEEEINNNPRTT	interdependent
DDEEEELMMNOSSS	meddlesomeness
DDEEEENNRSSSUV	undeservedness
DDEEEFINNNRSSU	unfriendedness
DDEEEGINNNSSSU	undesignedness

DDEEEIILMNNSSV	evil-mindedness
DDEEEIMNNNOPSS	open-mindedness
DDEEEIMNNNORTU	undermentioned
DDEEFGHINNORTU	night-foundered
DDEEGGIIIINNNV	dividing-engine
DDEEGHHIIMNNSS	high-mindedness
DDEEGHIIILMNPT	pig-in-the-middle
DDEEGILNNNOSSW	long-windedness
DDEEGNNNORSSUU	ungroundedness
DDEEHINNORRSUU	undernourished
DDEEIIINPRSSST	dispiritedness
DDEEIIJNNOSSST	disjointedness
DDEEIILNORRSSS	disorderliness
DDEEIINNOPSSSS	indisposedness
DDEGHLMOOORUUY	good-humouredly
DDEGIINNORSSWW	window-dressing
DEEEEFHLNORSTY	self-heterodyne
DEEEEFILNRSSTT	self-interested
DEEEEHILLOSTTT	stiletto-heeled
DEEEEHILNOOPTV	videotelephone
DEEEEILLMMOSSS	Mesdemoiselles
DEEEEILMNRSSSS	remedilessness
DEEEEINNRSSSTT	interestedness
DEEEELMNOPPRTV	predevelopment
DEEEENNRRSSSUV	unreservedness
DEEEFGILLNOPSV	self-developing
DEEEFIIINNNSST	indefiniteness
DEEEFIIINNSSTV	definitiveness
DEEEFILNNRSSSS	friendlessness
DEEEFILNPSSSTU	despitefulness
DEEEFNOORSSSTU	surefootedness
DEEEGHNNNRSTTU	unstrengthened
DEEEGIIKLNNNTT	knitting-needle
DEEEHHPPRRSSSU	shepherd's-purse
DEEEHIIKLNOOTT	kinetheodolite
DEEEIILLNNOSSV	love-in-idleness
DEEEIIMMNPRRST	predeterminism
DEEEIIMNRSSTTV	divertissement
DEEEIMMNORRSTY	memory-resident
DEEEINNNPRSTTU	superintendent
DEEELNNORSSSUV	unresolvedness
DEEEMNNORSSSTU	tremendousness
DEEENOPPRSSSSU	unprepossessed
DEEFFIIIMNNRST	indifferentism
DEEFFIIINNRSTT	indifferentist
DEEFGHILLNSSTU	delightfulness
DEEFGILNORSSTY	self-destroying
DEEFIILNNNRSSU	unfriendliness
DEEFIINOPRSSSU	perfidiousness
DEEFIKLLORRTWY	flowery-kirtled
DEEFILOORRSTUY	do-it-yourselfer
DEEGHHHILORSTU	shoulder-height
DEEGHHMOOORRST	horse-godmother
DEEGHIINNSTUUX	unextinguished
DEEGIIILMOOPST	epidemiologist
DEEGIIINNRRSTT	riding-interest
DEEGIIINNRSSTT	disinteresting
DEEGIILNNNSSUY	unyieldingness
DEEGIINNNPRSTU	superintending
DEEGILLOOSSTTY	dysteleologist
DEEGILMNNRSTTU	disgruntlement
DEEGILNNNPRTUY	unpretendingly
DEEGLNNORSSSSU	groundlessness
DEEGMNOPRTTTUU	trumpet-tongued
DEEHIILMNNPSST	displenishment
DEEHIILPQSSSUU	sesquisulphide
DEEHIMNOOPPRTY	Epidermophyton
DEEHNNOORRSSSU	horrendousness
DEEHNNORSSSTUU	thunderousness
DEEIIIILMRSTUV	verisimilitude
DEEIIILLNNNOTT	ill-intentioned
DEEIIILNOPRSTV	vespertilionid
DEEIIIMNNSSTUV	diminutiveness
DEEIIINRSSTTUV	disinvestiture
DEEIILLNPPRSST	tinsel-slipper'd
DEEIINOPSSSSTU	dispiteousness
DEEIMNOPPPPRRT	peppermint-drop
DEEMMOPRSSTUYY	pseudosymmetry
DEENNOPSSSSTUU	stupendousness
DEFGHILLOOOPSW	goodfellowship
DEFGILNSSSSTUU	disgustfulness
DEFHIIMNNRSSTU	disfurnishment
DEGGHILOOORSTY	hydrogeologist
DEGGIINNSSSSTU	disgustingness
DEGHHHIIOOPRST	high-priesthood
DEGHHILORSSTTY	short-sightedly
DEGHILOOOOTTTV	dogtooth-violet
DEGIIKLNNNOSSV	loving-kindness
DEGIILNNOSSUUY	disingenuously
DEGIINOOPRSSSU	prodigiousness
DEGILNOOOOPRTY	periodontology
DEGILNOORSSTUY	soul-destroying
DEHHINOOPRRSSY	hydronephrosis
DEHIIILOPPRSTT	pteridophilist
DEHIIMOOOPPRST	photoperiodism
DEHIMMOOPPRSSU	pseudomorphism
DEHMOOOPPRSSUU	pseudomorphous
DEIIIILLNOSSSU	disillusionise
DEIIIILLNOSSUZ	disillusionize
DEIIINOOPPRSST	predisposition
DEILMNOOOPSSTU	diplostemonous
DEILNOOOPSSTUU	pseudosolution
DEINNOOOPPRRTU	unproportioned
DELMNOOPSSUUYY	pseudonymously
DFGGHINNOOOORT	good-for-nothing
DGGHIIIINNSSTU	distinguishing
DGGHINNNORSTUU	hunting-grounds
DGHIINNOOPPSWW	window-shopping
DHHIIMOOPRSTYY	hypothyroidism
DHINOOOPRSSTTT	prosthodontist
DIIILMNOOSSSTU	dissolutionism
DIIILNOOSSSTTU	dissolutionist

E

EEEEELPRSTTTTY	Teletypesetter®
EEEEFGLNNRSSUV	revengefulness
EEEEFIMNNORRTV	over-refinement
EEEEFIMNORRRTT	interferometer
EEEEFKNNOPRSSS	free-spokenness
EEEEGHMMOORRTT	geothermometer
EEEEGINRRSSSSV	regressiveness
EEEEHILNPRRSVY	reprehensively
EEEEIINPRSSTTV	repetitiveness
EEEEILPRRTTTWY	teletypewriter

EEEEINNPRSSSTV	presentiveness
EEEEINNPRSSTVV	preventiveness
EEEEINPRSSSSVX	expressiveness
EEEELLNNRSSSST	relentlessness
EEEELMMNOSSSTT	mettlesomeness
EEEFGILNPRRSSV	self-preserving
EEEFGLMNNORSTV	self-government
EEEFILNOPRRSSS	self-repression
EEEFILNOPRSSSX	self-expression
EEEFIMNORRRTTY	interferometry
EEEFLLMMNOPSTY	self-employment
EEEFLMNORRSSSU	remorsefulness
EEEGGIMNNORRSV	verse-mongering
EEEGGINSSSSTUV	suggestiveness
EEEGHILNSSSSTW	weightlessness
EEEGIIKMNOPPRS	promise-keeping
EEEGIIMNOPRSSS	spermiogenesis
EEEGIIMNRRSSST	Meistersingers
EEEGINOQRRSTUU	turquoise-green
EEEHHILMOPPSST	Mephistopheles
EEEHIINNNOPPRR	norepinephrine
EEEHIINPRSSSTY	hypersensitise
EEEHIINPRSSTVY	hypersensitive
EEEHIINPRSSTYZ	hypersensitize
EEEHILLLMNOSST	shell-limestone
EEEHINNOORRSTT	norethisterone
EEEHIOPPRRRSTW	tree-worshipper
EEEHLMNOOOOTTU	homoeoteleuton
EEEIILMNPSTTVY	intempestively
EEEIILNPRRTTVY	interpretively
EEEIIMNNNRTTTW	intertwinement
EEEIIMNPRRRSTT	misinterpreter
EEEIIMNPRSSSSV	impressiveness
	permissiveness
EEEIINPRSSSTUV	supersensitive
EEEILMNNPRSTUY	supereminently
EEEILMNOSSSSTV	motivelessness
EEEILNOPRSSSSX	expressionless
EEEILNORRSSSTU	irresoluteness
EEEILNRSSSSSST	resistlessness
EEEIMNOPPRRSST	peremptoriness
EEEINNOPRSSSSV	responsiveness
EEEINOPPRSSSSV	oppressiveness
EEEINOPSSSSSSV	possessiveness
EEEIPPRRSTTTTY	pretty-pretties
EEELLNRSSSSSTU	resultlessness
EEFFFILLLMNSTU	self-fulfilment
EEFGGILNOSSSTU	self-suggestion
EEFGHHIINRRRSY	herring-fishery
EEFGHILPRSTUWY	super-flyweight
EEFGHINNOORRST	foreshortening
EEFGILLLNOPPRS	self-propelling
EEFGILLNNORTTU	fortune-telling
EEFGILMNNORSTT	self-tormenting
EEFHHILOORSSTW	two-for-his-heels
EEFHIIOPPRRRSW	fire-worshipper
EEFHILMNNPSSTU	self-punishment
EEFHILNRSSSSTT	thriftlessness
EEFILNOOPSSSSS	self-possession
EEFLLMNORRSUUY	unremorsefully
EEFLNOPPRSSSUU	purposefulness
EEGHHIILNPSSTW	sheep-whistling
EEGHIIMNNSTTUX	extinguishment
EEGHILLMNORVWY	overwhelmingly
EEGHINOOPPRRTY	porphyrogenite
EEGHIOORSTTYYZ	heterozygosity
EEGHLMNNOOOOTU	theologoumenon
EEGIILMNORTTUU	ultimogeniture
EEGIILMOOPSSTT	epistemologist
EEGIILNNNPRSTY	serpentiningly
EEGIILNNPRRSTY	enterprisingly
EEGIINNNPRRSTU	unenterprising
EEGILNOOPRRVWY	overpoweringly
EEHHILNPPRSTTU	hunt-the-slipper
EEHHILOOPPRSSS	philosopheress
EEHHIMMOOPRRST	heteromorphism
EEHHIOPPPPTTYY	hippety-hoppety
EEHHLLOOPRSTUY	heterophyllous
EEHHMMOOOORSTU	homoeothermous
EEHHMOOOPRRSTU	heteromorphous
EEHIILMNNQRSTU	relinquishment
EEHIILNOPPRSTY	pyelonephritis
EEHIIMMNOPRSTV	impoverishment
EEHIINOOPRRTTY	erythropoietin
EEHIINOOPSSSTT	photosensitise
EEHIINOOPSSTTV	photosensitive
EEHIINOOPSSTTZ	photosensitize
EEHIIOOPRRSSTY	erythropoiesis
EEHILNNNOPSTTY	penny-in-the-slot
EEHIMPPRSSSSST	sempstress-ship
EEHINNOORSSTTW	noteworthiness
EEHINNORSSSTWW	newsworthiness
EEHINOPPRRSSTW	serpent-worship
EEHMMNOORSSSUU	humoursomeness
EEIIIMNPSTTTVY	intempestivity
EEIILMNNRTTTTY	intermittently
EEIILNNRSSSSTU	unsisterliness
EEIILNOPRRSSVY	irresponsively
EEIILNPRRTTUVY	interruptively
EEIILNPRSSSSST	spiritlessness
EEIIMMMNOPRSTV	misimprovement
EEIIMNOPRSSSUV	imperviousness
EEILMNNNNOOTVV	non-involvement
EEILNNOPRSSUVY	unresponsively
EEIMNORSSSSTUY	mysteriousness
EEINOPRRSSSTUV	protrusiveness
EEIOPPRRSSSTTU	strepsipterous
EELNNOORSSSTUU	ultroneousness
EELOOPPRRSSTUY	preposterously
EENNOOOPPRRSST	person-to-person
EENNOOPRSSSTTU	portentousness
EENOOPPRRSSSSU	prosperousness
EENOORRSSSSTTU	stertorousness
EFFFGIILLLLNSU	self-fulfilling
EFFGHHLOORTTUU	forethoughtful
EFFGIIJLNSSTUY	self-justifying
EFFILNNRSSTUUU	unfruitfulness
EFGGHHIILLTTWY	light-flyweight
EFGGHIILNNORTW	night-flowering
EFGGIIINNNOPRT	finger-pointing
EFGGIIINNNPRRT	fingerprinting
EFGHHILNOORRST	threshing-floor
EFGHHINORRSSTT	forthrightness
EFGHHLNOSSTTUU	thoughtfulness

EFGHIILNOORRTW	withering-floor
EFGHILNNRSSTUU	unrightfulness
EFGHILNPRSSSTU	sprightfulness
EFGILNOPPRSSTU	self-supporting
EFHILMNOOOSSST	tomfoolishness
EFHILNOPRSSSUW	worshipfulness
EFHLNNRSSTTUUU	untruthfulness
EFILLNOOPPRSSU	self-propulsion
EFILOOOPRRSSUY	soporiferously
EFINOORSSSTTUU	fortuitousness
EGGIILNNOPRTTU	triple-tonguing
EGHHIMNNOOOPST	monophthongise
EGHHIMNNOOOPTZ	monophthongize
EGHHLLOOTTTUUW	well-thought-out
EGHIIILMNRSSTV	silversmithing
EGHIIKLNNNSSTU	unknightliness
EGHIIKNNNNSSTU	unthinkingness
EGHIIMOOQSTTUW	mosquito-weight
EGHIINOOPPRRST	progenitorship
EGHLNNOOOPRUYY	neurohypnology
EGHLOOOOPRRTTY	orthopterology
EGIIILNNNRTTWY	intertwiningly
EGIIIMNNNRTTTU	unintermitting
EGIIKLLMNOORST	Kremlinologist
EGIILNNOORSSSU	ingloriousness
EGIIMNOOPRRSSS	progressionism
EGIINNOPRRRSTU	interior-sprung
EGIINNPRRSSSSU	surprisingness
EGIINOOPRRSSST	progressionist
EGILMMMNOPRTUU	rummelgumption
	rummlegumption
EHHIIILMOPPSST	Mephistophilis
EHHIIMMOOPRRST	theriomorphism
EHHILMOOPPSSTU	Mephostophilus
EHHIMMMOOOOPRS	homoeomorphism
EHHIMMOOOORSTU	homoiothermous
EHHIMOOOPRRSTU	theriomorphous
EHHINOOOPPPRST	phosphoprotein
EHHINOOPSSSTTY	photosynthesis
EHHLLMOOPRSTUY	thermophyllous
EHHMMOOOOOPRSU	homoeomorphous
EHHNNOORRSTTTW	north-north-west
EHHOOSSSTTTUUW	south-south-west
EHIILMNOPRSTUW	multi-ownership
EHIILNNOOPRRTT	trinitrophenol
EHIIMMNOOPRSSU	immunophoresis
EHIIOOPPPRRRST	proprietorship
EHIIOPPRRSSSUV	supervisorship
EHILMNOPSSTTYY	polysynthetism
EHINOOOPRRSSTU	trophoneurosis
EIIIINNQRSTTUU	inquisiturient
EIIIINOQRSSTTU	requisitionist
EIIIMNORSSTTTU	restitutionism
EIIINNOQSSSTUU	iniquitousness
EIIINORSSTTTTU	restitutionist
EIIKMNNOOOPSSU	pneumokoniosis
EIIKMNNOORRTUW	munition-worker
EIILMNOOQRSUUY	querimoniously
EIILOOPPSSTTVY	postpositively
EIINNOOOPPRTTT	point-to-pointer
EIINNORSSSTTUU	nutritiousness
EIINOOPPPRSSTU	presupposition
EIINOOPPRSSSTU	propitiousness
EIINOPRSSSSTUU	spirituousness
EILMNNOOSSSUUV	voluminousness
EILNOOOPPRRSST	proportionless
EIMMNOPPRSSSUU	immunosuppress
EIMNNOOOPPRRTT	proportionment
EINOPRSSSTTUVY	topsy-turviness
ELMNOSSSTTUUUU	tumultuousness
ELMOPPRSSTUUUY	presumptuously
ELNOOPPRRSSUUY	unprosperously
ELNOOPSSSTUUUV	voluptuousness
EMNNNOOOOSSSTU	monotonousness
EMNNNOOSSSSUYY	synonymousness
EMNOPPRSSTUUUU	unpresumptuous

F

FGGHIIIILLNOPTW	pillow-fighting
FGHHLLNOTTUUUY	unthoughtfully

G

GGIIIKNNRSSSST	kissing-strings
GGIIIILLOORSTTU	liturgiologist
GHHIIIKLLNRRSS	shrill-shriking
GHHIILLNORSSTW	shillingsworth
GHIIKMNNNOOSTW	know-nothingism
GHILOOOOPSTTYZ	zoophytologist
GIIIINPRRRSSTT	spirit-stirring
GIILOOOPRSSTTT	protistologist
GILOOOOOPRSTTZ	protozoologist

H

HHIILNOOOPRSTU	ornithophilous
HHLOOPPRSSUUUY	hyposulphurous
HIIILNOPRSTTTT	lithontriptist

I

IIIOOPPSSSTTUU	supposititious
IILLNOOORRTTTU	trinitrotoluol
IILNOOPPRSTUUY	unpropitiously

A

AAAABCCHIILMNNS	bacchanalianism
AAAABCEHINRRTTT	Tetrabranchiata
AAAABCEILLNOOPT	palaeobotanical
AAAABEEHILMSSTT	beta-thalassemia
AAAACCCCCHHNSTT	catch-as-catch-can
AAAACCCILLLLTTY	catallactically
AAAACCDIIKLLLSY	lackadaisically
AAAACCEEEIILNPS	Caesalpiniaceae
AAAACCEFIIMNNRR	African-American
AAAACCEHHLNNOPT	acanthocephalan
AAAACEGHILLOPPR	palaeographical
AAAACEGIILRRRWY	railway-carriage
AAAACGHILLPPRRY	paragraphically
AAAAEIILMNNPRRT	parliamentarian
AAAAELMORRSSTTT	tarsometatarsal
AAAAGHILMNOPRST	phantasmagorial
AAABBBEGHIKNRST	Sabbath-breaking
AAABBDDEEFKNRST	bed-and-breakfast
AAABBEEGIMNNRST	bargain-basement
AAABBIIIILLOTVY	bioavailability
AAABCCCIKLLNOTU	back-calculation
AAABCCEEHLMNRSU	ambulance-chaser
AAABCCEHIINRTTT	Tectibranchiata
AAABCDEEEHILMNR	machine-readable
AAABCDEELLMNPRS	landscape-marble
AAABCEEHHILMNSW	machine-washable
AAABCEEHINRRTTT	tetrabranchiate
AAABCEEILNNRSTU	unascertainable
AAABCEFLMNNRSTU	blast-furnaceman
AAABCEILLLRSTTY	tetrasyllabical
AAABCEILLMNRRTU	interambulacral
AAABCHIILOPPRTY	approachability
AAABCIIILNNNOST	cannibalisation
AAABCIIILNNNOTZ	cannibalization
AAABEEILLNNSSUV	unavailableness
AAABEELNNRRSSTW	warrantableness
AAABEHIILNOPSTT	alphabetisation
AAABEHIILNOPTTZ	alphabetization
AAABELMNOORSTTU	neuroblastomata
AAABIIIILMNNTTY	maintainability
AAABIILMNPRSSSU	△sublapsarianism
AAABILNNRSSTTTU	transubstantial
AAACCCEEFILNPST	self-capacitance
AAACCCEEHIILLRT	Callitrichaceae
AAACCCEHHKMNNOY	hackney-coachman
AAACCCILLLMSTYY	cataclysmically
AAACCDEEHHILMRY	Archichlamydeae
AAACCDEEILOPSSU	asclepiadaceous
AAACCDEIMNNOORS	adenocarcinomas
AAACCEEEILNOORU	Eriocaulonaceae
AAACCEEHKNOPPST	peacock-pheasant
AAACCEEHLLOPRYY	Caryophyllaceae
AAACCEEINNPQRTU	preacquaintance
AAACCEEINORRSSU	sarraceniaceous
AAACCEFIIRRRRRT	aircraft-carrier
AAACCEGHILNOOPR	oceanographical
AAACCEHMNORTTTT	chemoattractant
AAACCEIIILLNPRTY	Capernaitically
AAACCEILLNNORTY	anacreontically
AAACCEMOPPRRSTU	carpometacarpus
AAACCHIILMNNORT	antimonarchical
AAACCIIILMNOSTT	acclimatisation
AAACCIIILMNOTTZ	acclimatization
AAACCIILLLSTTTY	stalactitically
AAACCIILLMNORTY	microanalytical
AAACCILLLOPPTYY	apocalyptically
AAACDEEEHHILLPP	Philadelphaceae
AAACDEEFFGHIRRS	chargé-d'affaires
AAACDEFGIORRRRW	carriage-forward
AAACDEFJKLLORST	Jack-of-all-trades
AAACDEGGIILNNRR	landing-carriage
AAACDEGIILLMNTY	diamagnetically
AAACDEHIILMMSSY	Michaelmas-daisy
AAACDEIILNNORST	calendarisation
AAACDEIILNNORTZ	calendarization
AAACDEIILNNPPRU	appendicularian
AAACDEIILNORSST	desacralisation
AAACDEIILNORSTZ	desacralization
AAACDEILLMNORYY	aerodynamically
AAACDEILLMORSUY	amaryllidaceous
AAACDEILNOPRSSX	paradoxicalness
AAACDIINNNNOTUY	Annunciation-day
AAACEEEEGILLLNS	Selaginellaceae
AAACEEGILNORTTV	lactovegetarian
AAACEEHIIMOPRST	spirochaetaemia
AAACEEHILLNSTTY	anaesthetically
AAACEEHIMMMSTTT	metamathematics
AAACEFHHIILMRRS	air-chief-marshal
AAACEFILNNSSSTT	fantasticalness
AAACEGILMNOPRTY	malacopterygian
AAACEGILMNPRSST	pragmaticalness
AAACEGILNNOPSTU	plantaginaceous
AAACEHHIILMPRTT	amphitheatrical
AAACEHHLLLOOPRS	alpha-chloralose
AAACEHIILNPRSSS	pharisaicalness
AAACEHILNOOPPRT	palaeoanthropic
AAACEHIMPPRSTTY	parasympathetic
AAACEIIILLMRSTT	materialistical
AAACEIIIMNNORST	Americanisation
AAACEIIIMNNORTZ	Americanization
AAACEIILNPRSSST	parasiticalness
AAACEILMNNOORTU	neuroanatomical
AAACGHHILOPRSST	thalassographic
AAACGHIILPRRSTT	stratigraphical
AAACGHILLOPRTUY	autographically
AAACGIIILLMNNST	anti-Gallicanism
AAACGIILLLMSTTY	stalagmitically
AAACGILLMMNRTUY	ungrammatically
AAACGILLMOORTTU	traumatological
AAACGIMNOPPRSTT	pantopragmatics
AAACHIIMNOORSTT	achromatisation
AAACHIIMNOORTTZ	achromatization
AAACIILLLMNOSTY	anomalistically
AAACIILNORSSTUV	vascularisation
AAACIILNORSTUVZ	vascularization
AAACILLNNOORTTV	contravallation
AAACILLNNORSTTY	transactionally
AAADDEFHNNRSSST	hard-and-fastness
AAADDEGINOSSTUV	disadvantageous
AAADDIINNORSSTT	standardisation
AAADDIINNORSTTZ	standardization
AAADEEEILLLPPPR	parallelepipeda

AAADEEFGIMORSWX	meadow-saxifrage
AAADEEGJLNNRTTU	adjutant-general
AAADGHIIIMPRSTT	diaphragmatitis
AAADGHIOOPRRTUY	autoradiography
AAADIIILNNPRTTU	platitudinarian
AAAEEFIILMMRSST	materfamiliases
AAAEEFIILMPRSST	paterfamiliases
AAAEEGGHLOOPPRY	palaeogeography
AAAEEGHIMMNOPSY	hypomagnesaemia
AAAEEGILMMNOPST	palaeomagnetism
AAAEEGLMMNNRSTT	Gentleman-at-arms
AAAEGHHLOPRRSST	thalassographer
AAAEGHLLOOOPPTY	palaeopathology
AAAEGHLNOOPPRTY	palaeontography
AAAEGIINNNQQRUU	quinquagenarian
AAAEHHLOPRSSTTY	thalassotherapy
AAAEHIIMMNOSTTT	mathematisation
AAAEHIIMMNOTTTZ	mathematization
AAAEHLNOOPPRSTU	Palaeoanthropus
AAAEIIILMNORSTT	materialisation
AAAEIIILMNORTTZ	materialization
AAAEIIILMNQRSTU	equalitarianism
AAAEIIILNORRSTT	arterialisation
AAAEIIILNORRTTZ	arterialization
AAAEIILLMNPRRTY	parliamentarily
AAAEIILMMNPRRST	parliamentarism
AAAEILMNNPRRTUY	unparliamentary
AAAEMORRSSSTTTU	tarsometatarsus
AAAGIILLNORTTVY	gravitationally
AAAGIINNOORSTTV	astronavigation
AAAHIIIMMNNRSTU	humanitarianism
AAAIIIINNNRRTTT	antitrinitarian
AAAIIILLMMNOSST	malassimilation
AAAIIILLMNNOPRS	Apollinarianism
AAAIIILMNORSTTT	totalitarianism
AAAIIILNNNOOSTT	nationalisation
AAAIIILNNNOOTTZ	nationalization
AAAIIILNNOORSTT	rationalisation
AAAIIILNNOORTTZ	rationalization
AAAIIIMNPPRSSST	Patripassianism
AAAILLLNNORSTTY	translationally
AAAILMNNORSTTTU	transmutational
AAAILNNNOPRSTTT	transplantation
AABBCGHIIILLOPR	bibliographical
AABBEHIIORRTTTU	thiobarbiturate
AABBEILNNORTTTU	non-attributable
AABBIINNORSSTUU	suburbanisation
AABBIINNORSTUUZ	suburbanization
AABBILNNORTTTUY	non-attributably
AABCCDEEHILLNSY	hendecasyllabic
AABCCDHLORSTUYY	brachydactylous
AABCCEEHIILMNRV	vice-chamberlain
AABCCEEHIINRTTT	tectibranchiate
AABCCEEILNPRSST	practicableness
AABCCEELNNOSSTU	accountableness
AABCCEELORRRSUV	cerebrovascular
AABCCEGIILLOORT	bacteriological
AABCCEGIILMNRUV	circumnavigable
AABCCEHHLOPRSUY	brachycephalous
AABCCGIIMMORSUU	circumambagious
AABCCIIIILLLNTUY	incalculability
AABCCIILNORTTTY	contractability
AABCDEEEGKLLNOW	acknowledgeable
AABCDEEEHLLLNSY	hendecasyllable
AABCDEEFIILMORT	democratifiable
AABCDEEGKLLNOWY	acknowledgeably
AABCDEELMNNORTU	countermandable
AABCDEHIINORRST	dorsibranchiate
AABCDEIINNOORST	decarbonisation
AABCDEIINNOORTZ	decarbonization
AABCDEIINORRSTU	decarburisation
AABCDEIINORRTUZ	decarburization
AABCDHIILLMRTYY	dithyrambically
AABCEEEELNNPSSU	unpeaceableness
AABCEEEGHILNNRT	interchangeable
AABCEEEGHLLLNNU	unchallengeable
AABCEEEGLLNNOSS	congealableness
AABCEEEHLNNSSTU	unteachableness
AABCEEFFIIILNTY	ineffaceability
AABCEEGHIILNTXY	exchangeability
AABCEEGHILNNRTY	interchangeably
AABCEEGHLLLNNUY	unchallengeably
AABCEEGIILLNOTY	abiogenetically
AABCEEILLNORTUV	countervailable
AABCEEILNNRSSTT	intractableness
AABCEEINOQRSSTU	sesquicarbonate
AABCEELNNRSSTTU	untractableness
AABCEGGHIILOOPR	biogeographical
AABCEGHIILNNTUY	unchangeability
AABCEGIIILLLOOOP	paleobiological
AABCEGILMNOPSUU	plumbaginaceous
AABCEHHIILMNPRS	chamberlainship
AABCEHHILNOOPRT	lophobranchiate
AABCEHILMNOPRTU	pulmobranchiate
AABCEILLLMOPRTY	problematically
AABCEILLLMORSTY	meroblastically
AABCEILMMNRRTUU	interambulacrum
AABCEILMNNNOOPU	uncompanionable
AABCEILMOPRSSTT	spermatoblastic
AABCEILNNNORSTU	unconstrainable
AABCEINNOSSTTTU	consubstantiate
AABCFIIILLNOSTY	syllabification
AABCHHIINOOPRST	Opisthobranchia
AABCHIIIMNOPRRS	Marsipobranchii
AABCIIIILLNPPTY	inapplicability
AABCIIILMNOPRTY	incomparability
AABCIILLLLRSTYY	trisyllabically
AABCIINOORSSTTU	bio-astronautics
AABDDEEGHLOOPRT	photodegradable
AABDEEFGHINORRT	feather-boarding
AABDEEFLMNNNOST	self-abandonment
AABDEEGHINORRTW	weatherboarding
AABDEEGIIILRSTY	disagreeability
AABDEEGIMMRRSST	gris-amber-steam'd
AABDEEIILNNSSSV	inadvisableness
AABDEEILNNOSSUV	unavoidableness
AABDEEILNNSSSUV	unadvisableness
AABDEIIILNORSTT	detribalisation
AABDEIIILNORTTZ	detribalization
AABDEINNSSTTTUU	unsubstantiated
AABDELNNPRSTUUY	superabundantly
AABDHIIIILNOSTT	dishabilitation
AABDINNOOORTTUU	roundaboutation
AABEEEFLMNORTTY	flamboyante-tree

AABEEEHILLNNPST	nepheline-basalt
AABEEEILLNNRSST	inalterableness
AABEEEILNNPRSSS	inseparableness
AABEEEILNPRRRSS	irreparableness
AABEEEKLNNPSSSU	unspeakableness
AABEEELLNNRSSTU	unalterableness
AABEEELLNPRSSSU	pleasurableness
AABEEELNNORSSST	treasonableness
AABEEFHILNNOSSS	fashionableness
AABEEFILLMMNNSS	inflammableness
AABEEFLNNRRRSTU	untransferrable
AABEEIIILLPRRTY	irrepealability
AABEEIILMNRTUVY	maneuverability
AABEEINNPPRRSTY	Pan-Presbyterian
AABEFGIIILRRRTY	irrefragability
AABEFIILNRRSTTY	transferability
AABEFILLNSSSTTU	self-substantial
AABEFILNOOPPRST	self-approbation
AABEGIILLOOOPST	palaeobiologist
AABEIILMNORTUVY	manoeuvrability
AABEILLNOORSTVY	observationally
AABEILNNSSSSTTU	substantialness
AABGHIIOPRRSTTY	biostratigraphy
AABGIILMMOPRRTY	programmability
AABHHHILMOOOPPT	ophthalmophobia
AABIILLNNSSTTUY	insubstantially
AABIILMNRSTTTUY	transmutability
AABIILNOPRSSTTY	transposability
AACCCDEEILLNOPY	encyclopaedical
AACCCDEFIIILNOT	decalcification
AACCCEEHILPRTTY	hypercatalectic
AACCCEHIIOPPRSY	archiepiscopacy
AACCCEIILLLSTYY	acetyl-salicylic
AACCCHIIMNOOORR	choriocarcinoma
AACCCHILLLOORTY	ochlocratically
AACCCILLMMOORSY	macrocosmically
AACCCILLMOOPRSY	macroscopically
AACCDDIIIMOSTTU	autodidacticism
AACCDEEEHILTTUV	vehicle-actuated
AACCDEEHHLOOPRT	cephalochordate
AACCDEEIOPRSSSU	peasecod-cuirass
AACCDEGHILNNRST	cradle-snatching
AACCDEHIIOSSTTU	autoschediastic
AACCDFIIMMOORRR	micromicrofarad
AACCDGILMMNOOTY	accommodatingly
AACCDGIMMNNOOTU	unaccommodating
AACCDHHILNOOPRY	hypochondriacal
AACCDHIIMOOSSST	sadomasochistic
AACCDHILNOOPRST	achondroplastic
AACCEEEGIILMNRR	marriage-licence
AACCEEGILLLOOOP	paleoecological
AACCEEGILNORSST	categoricalness
AACCEEHIIOPPRST	archiepiscopate
AACCEEHILMNORSV	servomechanical
AACCEEHNRRSSTTV	canvas-stretcher
AACCEFIILNRRSTU	interfascicular
AACCEFIILOOPRSU	caprifoliaceous
AACCEGHIILLOOPT	hepaticological
AACCEGHIILLOPRX	lexicographical
AACCEGHIIMNOPRT	cinematographic
AACCEHHHILNOPRY	Rhynchocephalia
AACCEHHILMNOOPT	photo-mechanical
AACCEHHILMORSTT	chrestomathical
AACCEHHLOOPPSSU	scaphocephalous
AACCEHIIKMNOPRT	pharmacokinetic
AACCEHIILLMNSTY	mechanistically
AACCEHIKLNOOSVZ	Czechoslovakian
AACCEHILLRRTTUY	architecturally
AACCEHINNNNOPTV	pantechnicon-van
AACCEHMNORSSTUY	sarcenchymatous
AACCEIIIILLMNRST	anticlericalism
AACCEIILLMNOSTY	encomiastically
AACCEIILMNPRSST	impracticalness
AACCEIIMNRSTTTU	circumstantiate
AACCEIINNOPSSSU	incapaciousness
AACCEILLMNNORTY	necromantically
AACCEILNNNNOSSU	uncanonicalness
AACCEILNNOOORST	consolation-race
AACCEILRRRRTUUX	extra-curricular
AACCGHHILOPPRSY	psychographical
AACCGHHIMOOPRRT	chromatographic
AACCGHIMNOOPRST	pharmacognostic
AACCGIIMNORRTUV	circumnavigator
AACCHIIILNOOSTT	△catholicisation
AACCHIIILNOOTTZ	△catholicization
AACCHIIIMNNORST	Monarchianistic
AACCHILLNOPSTYY	sycophantically
AACCIIILLLOSSTY	socialistically
AACCIIILPRRSTTU	particularistic
AACCIILLMNORTUV	circumvallation
AACCIILMNRSSTTU	circumstantials
AACCIKKKKNNORTY	knick-knackatory
AACDDEGGHILNRRT	great-grandchild
AACDDELLOOPRRRS	saddler-corporal
AACDEEEFLMNNSTV	self-advancement
AACDEEFFIINOSTT	disaffectionate
AACDEEHIIORRSTT	icositetrahedra
AACDEEHINNTTTUU	unauthenticated
AACDEEIILLNRTTT	Tetractinellida
AACDEEIIMNNOTTV	decontaminative
AACDEGHIILLOPRY	ideographically
AACDEHHIILNPRST	Christadelphian
AACDEHILLNOORRY	Hydrocorallinae
AACDEHILMMNORTY	thermodynamical
AACDEIIJLLRTUXY	extrajudicially
AACDEIIMNNNOOTT	decontamination
AACDEIIMNOORSTT	democratisation
AACDEIIMNOORTTZ	democratization
AACDEILLMORRTTU	courtmartialled
AACDFIIINOSSSTT	dissatisfaction
AACDFIIORSSSTTY	dissatisfactory
AACDGGHILLNNORW	all-changing-word
AACDGIIILLNRTUVY	victualling-yard
AACDHHILLOPRTYY	hydropathically
AACDHILLORSTTYY	hydrostatically
AACDIIIILLMNOTUY	unidiomatically
AACDIIIILNORSTTU	disarticulation
AACDIIIMNNORRST	doctrinarianism
AACDIIILNOPQRTUU	quadruplication
AACDIIMNORSSTTY	astrodynamicist
AACDIINNNOOTTUY	continuation-day
AACDIINOOORSSTW	word-association
AACDILMNOOPRRUY	cardiopulmonary
AACEEEGHIMOPRRT	Megacheiroptera

Words marked △ may be spelled also with a capital letter

AACEEEGILLNNSSV	evangelicalness
AACEEEGMNOPRSTU	pergamentaceous
AACEEEINRRSSSTT	crease-resistant
AACEEENNQRRTTUY	quatercentenary
AACEEFFHIMNNRST	affranchisement
AACEEFFIKLRRSTV	slave-trafficker
AACEEFIMMNRSTUU	semimanufacture
AACEEGGHILOOPPR	paleogeographic
AACEEGHHLNOPPRY	encephalography
AACEEGHILLLPRTY	telegraphically
AACEEGHILLNOPRS	selenographical
AACEEGHILOOOPSS	Ophioglossaceae
AACEEGHIMNOPRRT	cinematographer
AACEEGILLOOOPST	palaeoecologist
AACEEHHHLNOOPRX	hexachlorophane
AACEEHIILPPRRST	Pre-Raphaelistic
AACEEHIINORSTTT	catheterisation
AACEEHIINORTTTZ	catheterization
AACEEHILLMORTTY	theorematically
AACEEHILLNPRTTY	parenthetically
AACEEHILLPRTTUY	therapeutically
AACEEHILMOPSSTU	mesaticephalous
AACEEIIIMPPRSTV	misappreciative
AACEEILLNORSSTY	electroanalysis
AACEEILNNRRTTTU	intertentacular
AACEEIMNNOPRSST	castanospermine
AACEGGHIINNOPRY	cineangiography
AACEGGHILOOOPRZ	zoogeographical
AACEGHIILMOPRSS	seismographical
AACEGHILLMOORTU	rheumatological
AACEGHILLOOOPPT	paleopathologic
AACEGIIKLLMOORR	kilogram-calorie
AACEGIILLLMNORY	mineralogically
AACEGILLLNOOOPT	paleontological
AACEGILLLOOOOPZ	paleozoological
AACEGILLMNOOPTU	pneumatological
AACEHHILLMOOPTY	homeopathically
AACEHIILOOPPRRT	paraheliotropic
AACEHILLMOPRSTY	atmospherically
AACEHILLMPSTTYY	sympathetically
AACEIIILMNOPPSS	episcopalianism
AACEIIILNPRSTTT	antiperistaltic
AACEIIIMNNOPSTT	emancipationist
AACEIIIMNOPPRST	misappreciation
AACEIIINNORSSTT	canisterisation
AACEIIINNORSTTZ	canisterization
AACEIILLLPRSTTY	peristaltically
AACEIILLMNNRSTY	manneristically
AACEIILLMRTTTUU	multiarticulate
AACEIILMNOPRRTT	malpractitioner
AACEIILNOPRRTVX	extra-provincial
AACEIINNNOSTTTY	co-instantaneity
AACEIINOPRRSTTV	procrastinative
AACEIJLNORRTTUY	interjaculatory
AACEILLORRSSTTY	cross-laterality
AACEILMNOOPSSTY	compassionately
AACEIMNNOOPSSTU	uncompassionate
AACEINNNOOSSTTU	coinstantaneous
AACELLMMNOPRTTY	compartmentally
AACFGIIIINNORTT	granitification
AACFGIILNNOORTU	configurational
AACFIIINNOORSTT	fractionisation

AACFIIINNOORTTZ	fractionization
AACFILMMNNOOORT	malconformation
AACFILNNNOOORTT	confrontational
AACFILNRRRSTTUU	infrastructural
AACGGHHILNOOPRY	cholangiography
AACGGHILLLOOPRY	logographically
AACGGHILLOOPRSS	glossographical
AACGHHIILOPPRSY	physiographical
AACGHHINOOPPRTU	phonautographic
AACGHHMOOOPPRRT	photomacrograph
AACGHIILLLMORTY	logarithmically
AACGHILLMNOOPRY	gramophonically
	nomographically
AACGHILLNOOOPRT	anthropological
AACGHILLOOPPRTY	topographically
AACGHILLOPPRTYY	typographically
AACGHIMNNNOOOTT	thanatognomonic
AACGHIMNOOPRSST	pharmacognosist
AACGHLLOPRRSTYY	crystallography
AACGIIILNPRSSTU	paralinguistics
AACGIILLRRSTTUU	agriculturalist
AACGIILNORRSSWY	railway-crossing
AACGIINNOPRRSTT	procrastinating
AACGILNNOORSTTU	congratulations
AACGILNOORSSTUY	agranulocytosis
AACGIMMNOOPRRSU	macrosporangium
AACHHIILLNOPPRT	philanthropical
AACHIIILNNRSTTY	antichristianly
AACHIIILOQRSSTU	quasi-historical
AACHILLMOOPRTUY	automorphically
AACHILLOPPRSTYY	saprophytically
AACIIIILMNNORST	criminalisation
AACIIIILMNNORTZ	criminalization
AACIIIILNORRSTT	irrationalistic
AACIIILLLRSTTUY	ritualistically
AACIIIMNNOORSTT	romanticisation
AACIIIMNNOORTTZ	romanticization
AACIILLNOPRTTUY	unpatriotically
AACIILLNORSSTTY	crystallisation
AACIILLNORSTTYZ	crystallization
AACIILMMNNOOSTU	communalisation
AACIILMMNNOOTUZ	communalization
AACIILNNOPRRSTT	transcriptional
AACIINNOOPRRSTT	procrastination
AACILLLNOOPSTUY	unapostolically
AACILLMMOPSTTYY	symptomatically
AACILLMNNOPSTUY	uncomplaisantly
AACILLMNRRSTUUY	intramuscularly
AACINOOPRRRSTTY	procrastinatory
AACLNNNOOOPSSTT	postconsonantal
AADDDEIINNRRTVW	dividend-warrant
AADDEEEGLNRRSST	saddler-sergeant
AADDEEEHHNRRSST	hard-heartedness
AADDEEFGILNORST	self-degradation
AADDEIILNOPRSTU	superadditional
AADEEEEGILPRSSW	spread-eaglewise
AADEEEFHHLNRSST	half-heartedness
AADEEEHMNRRSSTW	warm-heartedness
AADEEEILMNPRSTT	departmentalise
AADEEEILMNPRTTZ	departmentalize
AADEEEIMNSTTTTV	testament-dative
AADEEFNNSSSSTTU	unsteadfastness

AADEEGGIKMNNRRT	market-gardening
AADEEGHIIIMNPRR	hearing-impaired
AADEEGHILOPRRTY	radio-telegraphy
AADEEGHLNOOPSUX	pseudohexagonal
AADEEGIIMNNOSTT	demagnetisation
AADEEGIIMNNOTTZ	demagnetization
AADEEHIIIMNRRST	hereditarianism
AADEEHIIINRRSTT	hereditarianist
AADEEHILMNPRRSY	hyperadrenalism
AADEEIILNOSSTUX	desexualisation
AADEEIILNOSTUXZ	desexualization
AADEEIINORRRSTX	extraordinaries
AADEEILLMNORTTT	tatterdemallion
AADEEILMMNPRSTT	departmentalism
AADEGHIMNOOOPRR	radio-gramophone
AADEGHIOOPRRRXY	xeroradiography
AADEGHMNOOPRRRT	ergatandromorph
AADEGIMNNRRSTTU	untransmigrated
AADEHHIIJNNNORY	Johnny-head-in-air
AADEHHIILMNOPRT	edriophthalmian
AADEHHLMNOPPTYY	lymphadenopathy
AADEHLNORRSTTWY	north-eastwardly
AADEHLORSSTTUWY	south-eastwardly
AADEIIIILMSSSTV	disassimilative
AADEIIILNNOSSTT	de-Stalinisation
AADEIIILNNOSTTZ	de-Stalinization
AADEIILNOPSSSTY	dispassionately
AADEIILNORRRTXY	extraordinarily
AADELNOPRSTTUUY	polyunsaturated
AADFGHIORRRSTTW	straightforward
AADFIIILNNORSTY	disinflationary
AADGHHIMNPRSSTU	draughtsmanship
AADGIIINNOORSST	disorganisation
AADGIIINNOORSTZ	disorganization
AADHILLNORRSTYY	synarthrodially
AADIIIILMNOSSST	disassimilation
AADIIINOPQRRTTU	quadripartition
AAEEEGGHLOOPPRR	paleogeographer
AAEEEGLNNORRTTY	Attorney-General
	attorney-general
AAEEEGMMNRRSSST	messenger-at-arms
AAEEEHHIMMMNPTT	methamphetamine
AAEEEHIILNORSTT	etherealisation
AAEEEHIILNORTTZ	etherealization
AAEEEHKMMORRTTT	katathermometer
AAEEEILMNNPTTTU	antepenultimate
AAEEELLMMNPRTTY	temperamentally
AAEEFFINOORRSTT	reafforestation
AAEEFGIMNNRRSST	fragmentariness
AAEEFHILRSSTTVV	harvest-festival
AAEEFIILLNORSST	self-realisation
AAEEFIILLNORSTZ	self-realization
AAEEFIILMNNOSTX	self-examination
AAEEFILNOPPRRST	self-preparation
AAEEFLLNOPRSTXY	self-explanatory
AAEEGHHIMOPPSTT	apophthegmatise
AAEEGHHIMOPPTTZ	apophthegmatize
AAEEGHHINRRSTTT	earthshattering
AAEEGHIILMNNPRT	parliament-hinge
AAEEGHILNOOSSTY	anaesthesiology
AAEEGHIMOOPPRRR	paroemiographer
AAEEGHLLNOOOPTY	palaeoethnology
AAEEGIIILMMNPSS	Semi-Pelagianism
AAEEGIIIMNNSSTV	imaginativeness
AAEEGIIILMNRSSST	magisterialness
AAEEGIILNNORSTV	evangelistarion
AAEEGIJLMNNNRSU	Jungermanniales
AAEEGILMNRTTUVY	argumentatively
AAEEHHIILPPRRST	Pre-Raphaelitish
AAEEHHINNOPSSTY	hypno-anesthesia
AAEEHIILMPPRRST	Pre-Raphaelitism
AAEEHILMNOPRSTU	parliament-house
AAEEIILNNORSTTX	externalisation
AAEEIILNNORTTXZ	externalization
AAEEIILNNPRRRTU	intrapreneurial
AAEEIINNOOPRSTU	Europeanisation
AAEEIINNOOPRTUZ	Europeanization
AAEEIKLMNNSSTTU	unstatesmanlike
AAEEILLLMORRSTT	lamellirostrate
AAEEILLRRSTTTUX	extra-illustrate
AAEEILMNNOPRSTT	malpresentation
AAEEILMNOOPRTTT	metropolitanate
AAEEILNOPRSTTUX	superexaltation
AAEEILNPRRSSTUU	supernaturalise
AAEEILNPRRSTUUZ	supernaturalize
AAEEIMNNPRRSSTT	semitransparent
AAEEIMNPRRSSTTT	tamper-resistant
AAEEINOOPPRRRTV	overpreparation
AAEEINOPPPRRSST	appropriateness
AAEELLNPRRRTTUY	preternaturally
AAEENNNPRRSSSTT	transparentness
AAEFFFIILMNORST	self-affirmation
AAEFGGILNOPPRST	self-propagating
AAEFGIIMORRRSTU	margaritiferous
AAEGGHINOPRSSTT	steganographist
AAEGHHILLMOOPPT	ophthalmoplegia
AAEGHHIMOPPSTTT	apophthegmatist
AAEGHHINOOPPRTT	anthropophagite
AAEGHHNOOOPPRST	organophosphate
AAEGHIIMMORRSTT	hierogrammatist
AAEGHLLOOOPPTYY	palaeophytology
AAEGIIILMNNTUVY	unimaginatively
AAEGIIILNNOORST	regionalisation
AAEGIIILNNOORTZ	regionalization
AAEGIIMNOOPRRRT	marriage-portion
AAEGILLLMNOOOPY	palaeolimnology
AAEGILLNOOOPSTT	palaeontologist
AAEGILLOOOOPSTZ	palaeozoologist
AAEGILLOPRRRTTY	portrait-gallery
AAEGILNNORRSSST	transgressional
AAEGIMNOPRRSTTU	tetrasporangium
AAEGINORRSSTTTU	angustirostrate
AAEHIILORTTTUVY	authoritatively
AAEHIINORTTTUUV	unauthoritative
AAEIIILMNNNORTT	interlamination
AAEIIILMNORSSTT	Aristotelianism
AAEIIILNNNORSTT	internalisation
AAEIIILNNNORTTZ	internalization
AAEIIILNPRSSSTT	antiperistalsis
AAEIIINOPRRSTTV	reprivatisation
AAEIIINOPRRTTVZ	reprivatization
AAEIIILLLMMRSTTU	multilateralism
AAEIIILLLMRSTTTU	multilateralist
AAEIIILLMNNOPRST	post-millenarian

AAEIILLMNNRSTTU	transilluminate
AAEIILLNNNORTTY	internationally
AAEIILMNNOORRST	renormalisation
AAEIILMNNOORRTZ	renormalization
AAEIILNNOOPRSST	personalisation
AAEIILNNOOPRSTZ	personalization
AAEIILNNORRSTTT	transliteration
AAEIILNOPPPRRTY	inappropriately
AAEIIMNOSSSTTTY	systematisation
AAEIIMNOSSTTTYZ	systematization
AAEIINOPPRRRTTT	portrait-painter
AAEILMNPRRSSTUU	supernaturalism
AAEILNNNOSSTTUY	instantaneously
AAEILNPRRSSTTUU	supernaturalist
AAEINOPRRSSTTUU	supersaturation
AAELNOPRRSTTTTU	ultra-Protestant
AAFGIINNORRSTTU	△transfiguration
AAFIILLNORRTTTU	ultrafiltration
AAFIILMNOORRSTU	formularisation
AAFIILMNOORRTUZ	formularization
AAFIIOOPRRSSTTW	two-pair-of-stairs
AAFILLMNOPRSTUY	slumpflationary
AAGHHNOOOPPRSTU	anthropophagous
AAGHIIIMNNNORST	nothingarianism
AAGHLNOOPRRSTUY	ultrasonography
AAGIIILNNORSSTU	singularisation
AAGIIILNNORSTTU	granulitisation
AAGIIILNNORSTUZ	singularization
AAGIIILNNORTTUZ	granulitization
AAGILMOOOPSSTTU	plagiostomatous
AAHHHLOPPRRSTYY	staphylorrhaphy
AAHHIILMNOPPSTT	panophthalmitis
AAHHIMNOOPPRSTT	anthropopathism
AAHIIIILMNNNOST	annihilationism
AAHIIILNOOPSSTT	hospitalisation
AAHIIILNOOPSTTZ	hospitalization
AAHIOOPPRRSSTTU	protospatharius
AAIIIILMNOSSSTT	assimilationist
AAIIIIMNNORSTTU	miniaturisation
AAIIIIMNNORTTUZ	miniaturization
AAIIILLNNOPRSTY	inspirationally
AAIIILMMNOORSTT	immortalisation
AAIIILMMNOORTTZ	immortalization
AAIIILMOOPRRSTV	improvisatorial
AAIIILNNOQRTTUZ	tranquilization
AAIIJLNOOPSTTUX	juxtapositional
AAIIKLMNOOSSSTY	ankylostomiasis
AAIILNNOOPRSSTT	transpositional
AAIIMNOOPRSSSTY	trypanosomiasis
AAIINNOOPPPQRTU	appropinquation
AAILLLNOOPSTTUY	postulationally
ABBCCCEIILMRRSU	circumscribable
ABBCEEIJLNNOOTU	unobjectionable
ABBCEEILMMOORRT	bomb-calorimeter
ABBCEGIILNPPRRS	scribbling-paper
ABBCEIJLNNOOTUY	unobjectionably
ABBDDEEELLLORRU	double-barrelled
ABBDEEIILNNSSTU	indubitableness
ABBDEIIILNRSTTU	indistributable
ABBEGHIILNSTTYY	shabby-gentility
ABBEIIILOPQRTUY	equiprobability
ABCCCHILNOOOPRS	bronchoscopical
ABCCDGHIILNRSTU	scratchbuilding
ABCCEEEILNNOSSV	conceivableness
ABCCEEIILLNNORU	unreconciliable
ABCCEEILLNOOPST	police-constable
ABCCEEIMNORRTUY	Corynebacterium
ABCCEFIIIJNOOTT	objectification
ABCCEFIILLPSSUY	subspecifically
ABCCEHHINOORRST	brachistochrone
ABCCEIIIILNSSTY	inaccessibility
ABCCEIIILLNORTY	reconcilability
ABCCEIILLLOOPSU	ebullioscopical
ABCCEIINORSSSSU	scribaciousness
ABCCGIIILLMOOOR	microbiological
ABCCGIIILLOOOOS	sociobiological
ABCCIIILMMNOTUY	communicability
ABCCIIILNORTTTY	contractibility
ABCDDEEEEILLOPS	peasecod-bellied
ABCDDEEEFLNOSSU	double-facedness
ABCDDEHHILLNORY	Rhynchobdellida
ABCDDEKLNORRSUW	sword-and-buckler
ABCDEEEILNPRSST	predictableness
ABCDEEELMMNNORU	unrecommendable
ABCDEEELMMNNOSS	commendableness
ABCDEEHIIILPRTY	decipherability
ABCDEEIIILNOSSSS	dissociableness
ABCDEIIIILLNNPS	indisciplinable
ABCDEIIIILLNNPSU	undisciplinable
ABCDEIIILMOOPSTY	decomposability
ABCDEIIMOOSSTUY	basidiomycetous
ABCDEILNOOORRUW	rainbow-coloured
ABCDGHIIILLOOORY	hydrobiological
ABCDIIIILRSTTTY	distractibility
ABCEEEEFLLMNRSS	self-resemblance
ABCEEEEHRRRRSTT	stretcher-bearer
ABCEEEEILNRSSSV	serviceableness
ABCEEEELNORRSSV	recoverableness
ABCEEEELNPRSSST	respectableness
ABCEEEILNNOPTUX	unexceptionable
ABCEEEILNNSSSUX	inexcusableness
ABCEEEILNORRSSV	irrevocableness
ABCEEELNNOQRSSU	conquerableness
ABCEEHHLMNNOOPR	rhombencephalon
ABCEEILMMNNORSU	incommensurable
ABCEEILNNOPTUXY	unexceptionably
ABCEEILNNRSSSTU	inscrutableness
ABCEEILNORSTTTU	reconstitutable
ABCEELNNNOOPRUU	unpronounceable
ABCEFLNOOOPRRRU	perfluorocarbon
ABCEGIILLNOOORU	neurobiological
ABCEIIIILLNPTXY	inexplicability
ABCEIILLNOPRSTU	public-relations
ABCEIILLOPRSSSY	perissosyllabic
ABCEIILNORSTTUU	tuberculisation
ABCEIILNORTTUUZ	tuberculization
ABCEILMMNNORSUY	incommensurably
ABCGGIIILLNOOOOT	gnotobiological
ABCGHHIOOPPRSYY	psychobiography
ABCGIIILLLLNTUV	victualling-bill
ABCGIILLNOOOTTY	gnotobiotically
ABCIIIILMNOPTTY	incompatibility
ABCIIIILNOSSTUV	subcivilisation
ABCIIIILNOSTUVZ	subcivilization

ABCIIILLNNOOSTY	inconsolability
ABCIIILMMNOTTUY	incommutability
ABCIILLLMOPSSYY	polysyllabicism
ABCIILLLNOORTTY	controllability
ABCIILORRRSTTUU	arboriculturist
ABCILLNOORSTTUY	obstructionally
ABDDDEEIMNNORSS	broadmindedness
ABDDDEHLNNOORTU	blood-and-thunder
ABDEEEEILMNPRRT	predeterminable
ABDEEEFIILNNNSS	indefinableness
ABDEEEHKLNORRTY	broken-heartedly
ABDEEEIIILMRRTY	irredeemability
ABDEEEILNNPSSSS	dispensableness
ABDEEEILNNRSSSU	undesirableness
ABDEEFIIIILNSTY	indefeasibility
ABDEEHILMOORTTW	Bartholomew-tide
ABDEEIIILMNRTTY	determinability
ABDEEIILMNNOSST	indomitableness
ABDEEILLNOSSSSV	dissolvableness
ABDEEINNORSSSTU	subordinateness
ABDEGGHHIILLNRV	high-gravel-blind
ABDEGHIIILNSSTU	distinguishable
ABDEGIIKLLNOTWY	knowledgability
ABDEIIILMNOPRTY	imponderability
ABDEIIILPRSTTUY	disreputability
ABDEIILMNORSTTY	demonstrability
ABDEIILNNORSTUY	insubordinately
ABDFFGIIIIILNRTY	diffrangibility
ABDGHIIILNSSTUY	distinguishably
ABDHHIMOOOPPRSY	dysmorphophobia
ABDIIIIILMNSSTY	inadmissibility
ABDIIIILNPSTTUY	indisputability
ABDIIILMNORSTTU	maldistribution
ABDIIINNNOORSTU	insubordination
ABDIILNOORTTUUY	roundaboutility
ABEEEEILMMNPRSS	impermeableness
ABEEEEILNNPRRTT	interpenetrable
ABEEEEILNRRSSTV	retrievableness
ABEEEELNNPRSSST	presentableness
ABEEEFGILNNRRSS	refrangibleness
ABEEEFILNRRSSTU	irrefutableness
ABEEEGINNORRSSV	overbearingness
ABEEEHHILOOPRTU	eleutherophobia
ABEEEHIILNNPPRS	inapprehensible
ABEEEHILMNRSSTT	re-establishment
ABEEEHILNNPPRSU	unapprehensible
ABEEEIILMNNSSST	inestimableness
ABEEEIILMNPRSSV	imperviableness
ABEEEIILNNQSSTU	inequitableness
ABEEEIINPRRSSTY	△presbyterianise
ABEEEIINPRRSTYZ	△presbyterianize
ABEEEILLNNORSST	intolerableness
ABEEEILMNNNRSSU	innumerableness
ABEEEILMNORRSSV	irremovableness
ABEEEILNNPRRTTU	uninterpretable
ABEEEILNNPRSSSU	insuperableness
ABEEFGIILNNNRSS	infrangibleness
ABEEFIIJLNSSSTU	justifiableness
ABEEFILNOORSSTV	self-observation
ABEEGHINNOQSTUU	banqueting-house
ABEEHILMNORSSTW	blameworthiness
ABEEHLLNOOOPPSY	polyphloesboean
ABEEHOPRRSSSTTU	substratosphere
ABEEIIILLLMNSST	illimitableness
ABEEIIILMNPRTTY	impenetrability
ABEEIIILLMNPSSSU	implausibleness
ABEEIILNNORSTUV	labour-intensive
ABEEIIMNPRRSSTY	△presbyterianism
ABEEINNSSSSTTUV	substantiveness
ABEELNOPPRSSSTU	supportableness
ABEELNORRSSTUUY	subterraneously
ABEFIIIIILNRTUVY	unverifiability
ABEFIILLNORRRUY	neurofibrillary
ABEGIIILNNPTUXY	inexpugnability
ABEHIIIILMPRSTY	imperishability
ABEHIINOOPPRRST	probationership
ABEHILMOOPRSSTY	strephosymbolia
ABEIIILLNNRTUVY	invulnerability
ABEIIILLORRSTVY	irresolvability
ABEIIILMMNRSTUY	immensurability
ABEIIILMNNRSSST	intransmissible
ABEIIILNOQSTTUY	questionability
ABEIILMNNRSSSTU	untransmissible
ABEIJMOQSSTUUUU	jusqu'auboutisme
ABEIJOQSSTTUUUU	jusqu'auboutiste
ABFIIILNOPRTTUY	unprofitability
ABGHILNOOOOPRTY	anthropobiology
ABHIIILNOPSTTYY	hypnotisability
ABHIIILNOPTTYYZ	hypnotizability
ABIINORSSTTTUUY	substitutionary
ACCCDDKLLNOOOUU	cloud-cuckoo-land
ACCCDEHHIILLOOP	dolichocephalic
ACCCDEHILLNOSYY	synecdochically
ACCCEEEELNNORSV	reconvalescence
ACCCEEEFLLMNOPS	self-complacence
ACCCEEEHILLMORT	electrochemical
ACCCEEFHILLLOOR	cholecalciferol
ACCCEEGIILLLOOS	ecclesiological
ACCCEEIIILMSSST	ecclesiasticism
ACCCEEILOORSTTU	acousto-electric
	electroacoustic
ACCCEFIIKNNOOTY	cockneyfication
ACCCEGIIINNORTY	carcinogenicity
ACCCEHHIILMOPSY	physicochemical
ACCCEIILNOPSTTU	conceptualistic
ACCCEILOOPPRSST	spectroscopical
ACCCIILLMOOPRSY	microscopically
ACCCILLLOOOPPSY	colposcopically
ACCDDEIMMNNNOOS	second-in-command
ACCDEEHINOOOPSU	chenopodiaceous
ACCDEEILMNORSTY	electrodynamics
ACCDEIIILNORTTVY	contradictively
ACCDEIILOPRSSTY	perissodactylic
ACCDEIOPPRRSTTU	picture-postcard
ACCDFHIIINNOORT	chondrification
ACCDIIILNOORRTTY	contradictorily
ACCEEEFINNORSTU	counterfeisance
ACCEEEFNNORSTUU	counterfesaunce
ACCEEEGILMNORTT	electromagnetic
	magneto-electric
ACCEEEHILORRTTY	heterocercality
ACCEEEHMNOOPRRT	mechanoreceptor
ACCEEEIILMNRSST	éclaircissement
ACCEEEILLMORRTT	electrometrical

ACCEEFFHIIOSTVZ	schizo-affective	ACCINOOORRSSTTV	vasoconstrictor
ACCEEFFIINOSSSU	efficaciousness	ACDDEEEELNPRRSU	supercalendered
ACCEEFHIIINOPST	speechification	ACDDEEEFFINSSST	disaffectedness
ACCEEFIIILNORTT	electrification	ACDDEEEHHIKNSST	thick-headedness
ACCEEFIILMNRRTU	circumferential	ACDDEEEHLNORSST	cold-heartedness
ACCEEGHILNOPSTY	psychogenetical	ACDDEEHIILLRSUY	diesel-hydraulic
ACCEEGILLNOTTYY	cytogenetically	ACDDEEINNOSSTTV	second-adventist
ACCEEHHIMOORRTT	heterochromatic	ACDDEIIMMNNOOST	discommendation
ACCEEHILOORRSTT	atherosclerotic	ACDDHIIMNORSTYY	hydrodynamicist
ACCEEHINOORSSTT	thoracocentesis	ACDDIIIIILNSTUV	individualistic
ACCEEIIMMNOTUVX	excommunicative	ACDEEEEFFHINPRS	phase-difference
ACCEEIINNNOORSS	concessionnaire	ACDEEEFGILNPRST	self-deprecating
ACCEEIIOPPRRTTY	cryoprecipitate	ACDEEEGHIKNNRRT	kitchen-gardener
ACCEFFGIIILNRSS	self-sacrificing	ACDEEEGILNORRRT	director-general
ACCEFFHIIINNORT	Frenchification	ACDEEEGKLMNNOTW	acknowledgement
ACCEFFIIILNOSUY	inefficaciously	ACDEEEHLLORTTUY	eleutherodactyl
ACCEFGIIIINOSTV	cosignificative	ACDEEEIIMNPRSSV	manic-depressive
ACCEFIMNOORRSUU	circumforaneous	ACDEEEILNNNSSST	clandestineness
ACCEGGHHILLNSTU	Gleichschaltung	ACDEEEIMNNNRSTT	disentrancement
ACCEGHIIILNNORT	anticholinergic	ACDEEEINNORSSST	considerateness
ACCEGHIIIMMNNPR	crimping-machine	ACDEEEIPRRRRSTU	scripture-reader
ACCEGHIIKNPSTTW	packet-switching	ACDEEFGILNRSSSU	disgracefulness
ACCEGHIILLOOOST	stoechiological	ACDEEFIIINORSTT	desertification
ACCEGHIIMNOPRRY	cinemicrography	ACDEEGHIILOPSTT	dephlogisticate
ACCEGHIIOPRRSTY	psychogeriatric	ACDEEGHIIPPPRSU	pseudepigraphic
ACCEGHILLLNOOTY	technologically	ACDEEGIIILLMOOP	epidemiological
ACCEGIIIMMOPRTT	micropegmatitic	ACDEEGILLLOOSTY	dysteleological
ACCEGILLLNOOSYY	synecologically	ACDEEHIMNOORSTU	echinodermatous
ACCEHHILLMNOOPR	chloramphenicol	ACDEEHLLOPPRRSU	shoulder-clapper
ACCEHHILNOOSSTU	health-conscious	ACDEEHLOORSTTUY	heterodactylous
ACCEHHIMOPRSTYY	chemopsychiatry	ACDEEIIINNSSTVV	vindicativeness
ACCEHIILLPRRTYY	hypercritically	ACDEEIILNNORSTY	inconsiderately
ACCEHIILNORSSTT	interscholastic	ACDEEIILNORSTVY	consideratively
ACCEHIIMNOPRSTY	psychometrician	ACDEEIINNOORRST	reconsideration
ACCEHIIMOOPRRRT	Microchiroptera	ACDEEILLNPPRRUY	perpendicularly
ACCEHILLNOPRTYY	pyrotechnically	ACDEEIMMNORSTUY	semidocumentary
ACCEHILMOPRRSTY	psychrometrical	ACDEEIMORRRRSUU	armoured-cruiser
ACCEHINNOOPRRTT	anthropocentric	ACDEEINNPRSSSTU	unpractisedness
ACCEHLLMNOOSTUY	collenchymatous	ACDEELMOORRSSTU	sclerodermatous
ACCEIIILMORSSTV	viscosimetrical	ACDEFIIIIMNNNOT	indemnification
ACCEIIILOSSTTVY	viscoelasticity	ACDEFIIIINNORTT	denitrification
ACCEIIIMMNNOTUV	incommunicative	ACDEFIIIINORSTV	diversification
ACCEIILMMNOTUVY	communicatively	ACDEFIIIINORTTV	devitrification
ACCEIILOPPRSSUY	perspicaciously	ACDEFIIILMNOSTU	demulsification
ACCEIIMMNNOOTUX	excommunication	ACDEFIIILNNOSTV	self-vindication
ACCEIIMMNNOTUUV	uncommunicative	ACDEFIIILNNOTTY	confidentiality
ACCEILMOOPRRSTU	ultramicroscope	ACDEFIIIMNOSTTY	demystification
ACCEIMMNOORTUXY	excommunicatory	ACDEGHIIILLMNNR	drilling-machine
ACCEINNOOOPRTUW	owner-occupation	ACDEGHILMOPRSTY	dermatoglyphics
ACCELLNOOOSUUVV	convolvulaceous	ACDEHHLMMOOOSUY	homochlamydeous
ACCFIIINOOOPRRT	corporification	ACDEHIILLMOSTTY	Methodistically
ACCGHIIILLOOOST	stoichiological	ACDEHIINOPSSTTU	unsophisticated
ACCGHILLLNOOORY	chronologically	ACDEHILLNOOPRTY	polychlorinated
ACCGHILLLOOPSYY	psychologically	ACDEHINOORRSSTT	trisoctahedrons
ACCGIILLLOOOTXY	toxicologically	ACDEHLMMNOOOSUY	monochlamydeous
ACCHHIILMOORSTT	lithochromatics	ACDEIIIILMNNOORT	omnidirectional
ACCHHILMOOOPPST	ophthalmoscopic	ACDEIIIILNORRSTY	discretionarily
ACCHHINOOPPRSTY	anthropopsychic	ACDEIIINNNOORST	inconsideration
ACCHIILNNORSSTY	synchronistical	ACDEIILNNOOORST	reconsolidation
ACCHIINOPRRSTTY	crypto-Christian	ACDEIILNOOORSTU	decolourisation
ACCIJLLNNNOOTUY	conjunctionally	ACDEIILNOOORTUZ	decolourization
ACCILMOOPRRSTUY	ultramicroscopy	ACDEILNNNORSTUY	unconstrainedly

ACDEIMNNOOOORSU	andromonoecious
ACDGHIMNNOOPRRY	gynandromorphic
ACDGIIIINNNOORT	air-conditioning
ACDGIILLLOSSTYY	dyslogistically
ACDHHIINOOPRSSY	hypochondriasis
ACDIIINNNOOSTTU	discontinuation
ACDIILLNNNOOTUY	unconditionally
ACEEEEGILNORTTV	electronegative
ACEEEFFILNNSSTU	ineffectualness
ACEEEFHIMNNNRST	enfranchisement
ACEEEFIIILMPTVX	exemplificative
ACEEEGHIMNNNRTT	interchangement
ACEEEGHINNOPRTT	parthenogenetic
ACEEEGHNOORRRTV	teacher-governor
ACEEEGIILLNORTT	intercollegiate
ACEEEGIINRRSSST	crease-resisting
ACEEEGIMNOPRSTT	spermatogenetic
ACEEEHHHLNOOPRX	hexachlorophene
ACEEEHILLMNRTUY	hermeneutically
ACEEEHILLMOORST	cholesterolemia
ACEEEHILNNPPRRS	pencil-sharpener
ACEEEHNORRSSSTU	treacherousness
ACEEEIILLLNSTTU	intellectualise
ACEEEIILLLNTTUZ	intellectualize
ACEEEILNORRSSTV	correlativeness
ACEEEILNPSSSTUV	speculativeness
ACEEEIMMNOPRSSU	menispermaceous
ACEEEINNNRSSSSU	unnecessariness
ACEEEINNQRSSTUY	sesquicentenary
ACEEEINOPRRSSTV	procreativeness
ACEEFGILMNNRSTU	smelting-furnace
ACEEFGILNRRTTUU	ultracentrifuge
ACEEFHIOOPRRTTV	photorefractive
ACEEFHLNOPRRSSU	reproachfulness
ACEEFIIILMNOPTX	exemplification
ACEEFIIINNOSTTX	extensification
ACEEFIILLNOPSTX	self-explication
ACEEFIILNPRSSSU	superficialness
ACEEFILNORSTTUU	tentaculiferous
ACEEGGHHIIIMNNW	weighing-machine
ACEEGGIILLNNORT	training-college
ACEEGHILLNOOOPT	paleoethnologic
ACEEGHLMOOPRRTY	electromyograph
ACEEGIILLMOOPST	epistemological
ACEEGILLNNOOTTY	ontogenetically
ACEEHHIILMMNNTT	nemathelminthic
ACEEHIILLLLNSTY	Hellenistically
ACEEHIILLMNRSTY	hemicrystalline
ACEEHIILLMPSTUY	euphemistically
ACEEHIILMNNOPST	phenomenalistic
ACEEHIKNOOPPSST	phenakistoscope
ACEEHILLNOPSSSU	lissencephalous
ACEEHILOORRSSST	atherosclerosis
ACEEHLMMNNOOTWW	new-Commonwealth
ACEEIIIILMOPRRST	isoperimetrical
ACEEIIINQSSSTUV	acquisitiveness
ACEEIIJNNORRTTY	interjectionary
ACEEIILLLMNSTTU	intellectualism
ACEEIILLLNSTTTU	intellectualist
ACEEIILLLNTTTUY	intellectuality
ACEEIILLMNRSSTY	semicrystalline
ACEEIILNNNOOSTV	conventionalise
ACEEIILNNNOOTVZ	conventionalize
ACEEIILNNNOQSTU	inconsequential
ACEEILLLMNOSSUY	miscellaneously
ACEEILLLMNOTTUU	multinucleolate
ACEEILLMMNOPRTY	complementarily
ACEEILLMNOPTTVY	contemplatively
ACEEILLNNOPTUXY	unexceptionally
ACEEILLNNOQSTUY	consequentially
ACEEILMMNNOOPTT	complementation
ACEEILMMNOPRTTY	complementarity
ACEEILMMNRSSSTY	symmetricalness
ACEEILNNNNOSSSS	nonsensicalness
ACEEILNOOPRTUVY	uncooperatively
	unco-operatively
ACEEIMNNOOPRTTY	contemporaneity
ACEEIMNNORRRSTU	resurrection-man
ACEEINOOPRSSTVV	provocativeness
ACEEINORRRRSTUY	resurrectionary
ACEEKLLLMOSSTUU	musculo-skeletal
ACEELLNOOPPRRRT	contrapropeller
ACEELNNNOOSSTUY	consentaneously
ACEEMNNOOOPRSTU	contemporaneous
ACEENNNNOOSSTUU	unconsentaneous
ACEFFIIINOORRTT	refortification
ACEFGIIIIINNSTV	insignificative
ACEFGIIIILNSTVY	significatively
ACEFHIILMNOQRSU	marsh-cinquefoil
ACEFIIIINNNOSTT	intensification
ACEFIIINNOOPRST	personification
ACEFIILMNNOOSSS	confessionalism
ACEFIILNNOOSSST	confessionalist
ACEGGHHIOOPPRTY	phytogeographic
ACEGGHIIIMNNNRW	wringing-machine
ACEGHHIIILMNNRW	whirling-machine
ACEGHHILLOOPTYY	paleichthyology
ACEGHHILNOSSTTW	swathing-clothes
ACEGHIIIKMNNNTT	knitting-machine
ACEGHIIILMMORST	semi-logarithmic
ACEGHIIIMNNNPRT	printing-machine
ACEGHIILMNNOSTT	slotting-machine
ACEGHILLLNOOPRY	phrenologically
ACEGHILMNOORSST	schoolmastering
ACEGHIMMOOPRRTT	photogrammetric
ACEGHLLOOPSUYYZ	zygophyllaceous
ACEGIIILMNSSTTU	metalinguistics
ACEGIIKLNPRSSTT	sticking-plaster
ACEGIILLMNOORTY	goniometrically
ACEGIILLNRSSTYY	synergistically
ACEGIILMNOORRTT	trigonometrical
ACEGIINOOPRSTTV	prognosticative
ACEGILLLMNOOOTY	entomologically
ACEGILMOORSTUVY	cytomegalovirus
ACEGIMNNOOSSUUU	mucosanguineous
ACEGINOOPRRSSTY	crossopterygian
ACEHHIILOOPSSTT	theosophistical
ACEHHILMOORSSST	schoolmasterish
ACEHHIMMMNOOPRS	mechanomorphism
ACEHHIMMOOORSST	hemochromatosis
ACEHHINOPPRSTTU	Pithecanthropus
ACEHHIOPPRSSTTY	psychotherapist
ACEHIIIKLNNRSTU	unchristianlike
ACEHIIILLNORSST	schillerisation

ACEHIIILLNORSTZ	schillerization
ACEHIIIMNNOOPST	phonemicisation
ACEHIIIMNNOOPTZ	phonemicization
ACEHIIINNOOPSTT	phoneticisation
ACEHIIINNOOPTTZ	phoneticization
ACEHIIINNORSTTY	Neo-Christianity
ACEHIIJKLNPPTTU	Jack-in-the-pulpit
ACEHIILLLOOPRTY	heliotropically
ACEHIILLOPRRSTY	prehistorically
ACEHIILOOPSTTTY	photoelasticity
ACEHIIMMMOPSTTY	sympathomimetic
ACEHIKNPSSSTTUU	Aussichtspunkte
ACEHILLLNOORSTY	holocrystalline
ACEHILLNOPSTTYY	polysynthetical
ACEHINOOPRRSSTV	conservatorship
ACEHINOOPRRSSTW	ancestor-worship
ACEHINOPRRSTUYY	neuropsychiatry
ACEHMNOOPRSSTUY	prosenchymatous
ACEIIIINNNOSTTV	incentivisation
ACEIIIINNNOTTVZ	incentivization
ACEIIIINNOSTTVV	antivivisection
ACEIIILLMPSSSTY	pessimistically
ACEIIILNNNRSSST	intrinsicalness
ACEIIILNNOPRRTV	interprovincial
ACEIIIMOPRRSTVV	improvvisatrice
ACEIILLLNNOORTY	intercolonially
ACEIILMNNNOOSTV	conventionalism
ACEIILNNNOOSTTV	conventionalist
ACEIILNNNOOTTVY	conventionality
ACEIILNNOORSTTU	interosculation
ACEIILNOOPRSSST	processionalist
ACEIILNPRRSTTVY	transcriptively
ACEIILPPRSSTTUY	superplasticity
ACEIIMNNOORSSSU	acrimoniousness
ACEIIMNNOORSSTV	conversationism
ACEIIMNOOPRSTTU	computerisation
ACEIIMNOOPRTTUZ	computerization
ACEIINNOORSSTTV	conservationist
	conversationist
ACEIINNORRRSTUY	insurrectionary
ACEIINNORRRTTTU	counterirritant
ACEILLLNOPRSTYY	polycrystalline
ACEILLMMNRSTUYY	unsymmetrically
ACEILLMNNOORSTY	monocrystalline
ACEILLNOORRSTVY	controversially
ACEILMMMNOORSTY	monosymmetrical
ACEILMMNNOPRTUY	uncomplimentary
ACEILNNOORRSTUV	uncontroversial
ACEIMNNNOOPRSTU	pronunciamentos
ACEINNOORRSSSUV	carnivorousness
ACELNOOOPPRRSTU	counter-proposal
ACELPRRRSSTTUUU	superstructural
ACFFHHIIMMNORST	Fifth-monarchism
ACFFHHIIMNORSTT	Fifth-monarchist
ACFGIIIILNNNSTY	insignificantly
ACGHHIIIOOPRRST	historiographic
ACGHHIMOOOPPRRT	microphotograph
	photomicrograph
ACGHHINOOOPPRTZ	photozincograph
ACGHHLMOOOPRRXY	chromoxylograph
ACGHHLOOOPPSTYY	psychopathology
ACGHIIILLNPSTUV	victualling-ship
ACGHIILLLOOPSYY	physiologically
ACGHILLNOSSTTUW	swathling-clouts
ACGHILLOOOOPTYZ	zoophytological
ACGHILOOPPRTXYY	xylotypographic
ACGIILLLLOSSTYY	syllogistically
ACGIILLLMMNOOUY	immunologically
ACGIILLMNNNOPUY	uncomplainingly
ACGIIMMNOOPRRSU	microsporangium
ACGIINNOOOPRSTT	prognostication
ACGILLMMOOOPSTY	symptomological
ACGILLOOOOOPRTZ	protozoological
ACHHHHMNOPRRSUY	Rhamphorhynchus
ACHHIILLLOOPPSY	philosophically
ACHHIILLNOOPPSU	unphilosophical
ACHHIINOOPRSSTY	psychohistorian
ACHHIMNOOOPPRRT	anthropomorphic
ACHHIOOPRRSTTYY	orthopsychiatry
ACHIIIMOOSSSSST	schistosomiasis
ACHIILLMOOOPRRT	allotriomorphic
ACHIIMNOOOPPSTT	compotationship
ACHIINNNOORSSTY	synchronisation
ACHIINNNOORSTYZ	synchronization
ACHMNNNOORRTTUY	north-countryman
ACIIIILLLNOSTVY	violinistically
ACIIILLLOPSSSTY	solipsistically
ACIIILNNOPQTTUU	quintuplication
ACIILMMNOOOPSST	cosmopolitanism
ACIILMNNOOSSTUY	sanctimoniously
ADDDEEEHNNNRSSU	underhandedness
ADDDEEFHILMOORT	middle-of-the-road
ADDDEIINOOOPRTT	Diprotodontidae
ADDEEEEHLNRRTTY	tender-heartedly
ADDEEEEILMNRRST	Middle-Easterner
ADDEEEGHHILNSST	light-headedness
ADDEEEGHNNORSSW	wrong-headedness
ADDEEEHIKNNRSST	kind-heartedness
ADDEEGHHINNRSST	right-handedness
ADDEEGNNOORSSTU	good-naturedness
ADDEEIIILNRSSTU	deindustrialise
ADDEEIIILNRSTUZ	deindustrialize
ADDEGILNNNRSTUY	understandingly
ADEEEEEFHNRRSST	free-heartedness
ADEEEEHNNOPRSST	open-heartedness
ADEEEEHNRRSSTTU	true-heartedness
ADEEEEIMNRRSTTV	readvertisement
ADEEEFGHLLRSSTU	self-slaughtered
ADEEEFIILLNQSTU	field-sequential
ADEEEGHILLNRSTY	single-heartedly
ADEEEGHINNRSSST	near-sightedness
ADEEEGIIMNNRRTT	rate-determining
ADEEEGIINNORSTT	degenerationist
ADEEEGILMNNNSTT	disentanglement
ADEEEGKLNNORTUW	natureknowledge
ADEEEGMMNRRRSTU	sergeant-drummer
ADEEEHIIOPRRSST	sphaerosiderite
ADEEEIILMNNRTTY	indeterminately
ADEEEIIMNNORRTT	redetermination
ADEEEIIMOORRSST	diastereoisomer
ADEEELLLMNOPTVY	developmentally
ADEEFFIIINNORTT	differentiation
ADEEFFIMNORSSTT	disafforestment
ADEEFIIINRRSTTT	interstratified

ADEEFIILNNOOPST	self-opinionated
ADEEFIILNNQSSUU	unqualifiedness
ADEEFIINNSSSSTU	unsatisfiedness
ADEEFILLNORSSUV	ill-favouredness
ADEEFILNSSSSTTU	distastefulness
ADEEFNOORRRSSVW	overforwardness
ADEEGGHINOPSSSU	pedagoguishness
ADEEGGMMNORRTTU	Götterdämmerung
ADEEGGNNOOORTUV	tongue-and-groove
ADEEGHIILNNRSTY	dishearteningly
ADEEGIILNNPSSSS	displeasingness
ADEEGIIMNOOORRT	radiogoniometer
ADEEGILLOOOPPST	paleopedologist
ADEEGIOPRRSTTUY	daguerreotypist
ADEEGKLNNORRUVW	Völkerwanderung
ADEEHHNOOPPSSYY	adenohypophyses
ADEEHHOOPPRSTTX	dextrophosphate
ADEEHIIILLMNNTY	dimethylaniline
ADEEHILLMNNRSTT	disenthrallment
ADEEIIILNORSSTV	desilverisation
ADEEIIILNORSTVZ	desilverization
ADEEIIILNRRSSTU	reindustrialise
ADEEIIILNRRSTUZ	reindustrialize
ADEEIIIMNNNORTT	indetermination
ADEEIIINNOSSSTT	desensitisation
ADEEIIINNOSSTTZ	desensitization
ADEEIIINORRTTVV	nitro-derivative
ADEEIIMNNNORTTU	undetermination
ADEEIIMNNOPRTTU	unpremeditation
ADEEIIMNNORSTTU	underestimation
ADEEIIMNNRRSSTU	rudimentariness
ADEEIINPSSSTTUV	disputativeness
ADEEILMNORSTTVY	demonstratively
ADEEIMNNORSTTUV	undemonstrative
ADEENNOPRRSSSTT	transportedness
ADEENNORSSSTUUV	adventurousness
ADEFFHINNOSSSST	standoffishness
ADEFGIIILLNQSTU	self-liquidating
ADEFIILMNNOORSU	four-dimensional
ADEFINNNOOOSTTU	foundation-stone
ADEGGGHINNORRTU	gathering-ground
ADEGHILNORRSTTW	world-shattering
ADEGHLLMORRTUYY	hydrometallurgy
ADEGIIIINNORTTT	interdigitation
ADEGIIIOPRRSTTT	prestidigitator
ADEGIINNORSSSTT	dressing-station
ADEGILLNNOQRTUY	grandiloquently
ADEGJLLMNNNOTUY	non-judgmentally
ADEHHIILNNOOPRT	ornithodelphian
ADEHHIIMMOPRRST	hermaphroditism
ADEHHILMOOPRSTU	edriophthalmous
ADEHHINOOPPSSYY	adenohypophysis
ADEHIIILMOOPRST	diaheliotropism
ADEHIIINOOPRSST	spheroidisation
ADEHIIINOOPRSTZ	spheroidization
ADEHIINNOOPSTTY	dehypnotisation
ADEHIINNOOPTTYZ	dehypnotization
ADEHLNORRSTTWWY	north-westwardly
ADEHLORSSTTUWWY	south-westwardly
ADEIIJLNPRRSTUU	jurisprudential
ADEIILMNNOORTTU	intermodulation
ADEIILNORRSSTTX	sinistrodextral
ADEIILNORRSTTVY	dorsiventrality
ADEIIMMOORSSTTY	dermatomyositis
ADEIINNOOPRRSTU	superordination
ADFGGHINOOPRRTU	draught-proofing
ADGHIIMNOORRTWW	withdrawing-room
ADGHIINNNOSTTTW	notwithstanding
ADGIIINNNOPPSTU	undisappointing
ADHIILMNOORSSUY	disharmoniously
ADHIIMOOOPPRSTT	diaphototropism
ADIIIINOQRSSTUY	disquisitionary
ADIILNOOOPPRRST	disproportional
ADILNOOOOPPRTTY	Polyprotodontia
ADMNOOOOOSSTTTU	odontostomatous
AEEEEGIKLNPRSSU	pleasure-seeking
AEEEEGLLNRRRYYY	greenery-yallery
AEEEEIILMNPRSTX	experimentalise
AEEEEIILMNPRTXZ	experimentalize
AEEEEIIMNPRTTVX	experimentative
AEEEEILNNPRRRTU	entrepreneurial
AEEEEIMNNPRSSTT	intemperateness
AEEEEINNPRSSTTV	penetrativeness
AEEEFIILMNPRRST	preferentialism
AEEEFIILNPRRSTT	preferentialist
AEEEFLLLLORRTVW	fellow-traveller
AEEEFLMOQRRSTTU	letters-of-marque
AEEEGGINNOPPRSS	passenger-pigeon
AEEEGGLNNOORRRV	governor-general
AEEEGHINNOPRSST	parthenogenesis
AEEEGIKLLMNNNTU	ungentlemanlike
AEEEGILLMNNNSST	gentlemanliness
AEEEGILMNNNRTTT	intertanglement
AEEEGILNNRSSSTV	everlastingness
AEEEGIMNOPRSSST	spermatogenesis
AEEEHHILMMNNSTT	Nemathelminthes
AEEEHHILMNOPPST	Mephistophelean
AEEEHIIMNPPRSSV	misapprehensive
AEEEHIKLMORRTUY	erythroleukemia
AEEEHILORSTTUXY	heterosexuality
AEEEIIILMNPRSTX	experientialism
AEEEIIILNPRSTTX	experientialist
AEEEIILMMNPRSTX	experimentalism
AEEEIILMNPRSTTX	experimentalist
AEEEIIMNNOPRTTX	experimentation
AEEEIINNNSSTTTV	inattentiveness
AEEEIINNOPRSSTV	inoperativeness
AEEEILNPRSSSTUV	superlativeness
AEEEIMNOPRRSSTX	extemporariness
AEEELMNOQRRSSSU	quarrelsomeness
AEEFFGHIINNORTT	fifth-generation
AEEFGIINNORRSTT	first-generation
AEEFGIMNNRRSTTU	transfigurement
AEEFHHLLNNSSTUU	unhealthfulness
AEEFIILNOOPRSSS	professionalise
AEEFIILNOOPRSSZ	professionalize
AEEFILMNNSSSTTU	self-sustainment
AEEFILOPRRRSTTU	self-portraiture
AEEFNNNORSSTTUU	unfortunateness
AEEGGHHOOPPRRTY	phytogeographer
AEEGGHLNNNOSTTU	tungsten-halogen
AEEGHHLOOPPRTTY	phototelegraphy
	telephotography
AEEGHHMOOPRRTTY	hyetometrograph

AEEGHIMNNORRSUZ	Erziehungsroman
AEEGHINNOOPRSST	anthropogenesis
AEEGHNNOOPRRTTY	röntgenotherapy
AEEGIILNORRTTVY	interrogatively
AEEGIINNOORRRTT	reinterrogation
AEEGIINORRSSTTT	gastroenteritis
AEEGILNOORRRSST	retrogressional
AEEGILNRRSSSTVY	transgressively
AEEGIMNNNOORSST	sensation-monger
AEEGMNNOPRRTTVY	party-government
AEEGNOOPRRSSTTV	provost-sergeant
AEEHHHILLNNOPPT	phenolphthalein
AEEHHIILMNOPPST	Mephistophelian
AEEHHILLMNPSTTY	Platyhelminthes
AEEHIILMOOPSTTU	epitheliomatous
AEEHIIMNNOPPRSS	misapprehension
AEEHIKLNNOPRTUY	phenylketonuria
AEEHINNORSSSTUW	unseaworthiness
AEEIIINNOSTTVXZ	extensivization
AEEIIINOORRSTTX	exteriorisation
AEEIIINOORRTTXZ	exteriorization
AEEIILMNOOPRSTT	metropolitanise
AEEIILMNOOPRTTZ	metropolitanize
AEEIILNNOPPRTTY	plenipotentiary
AEEIILNNOPRSSTT	septentrionalis
AEEIIMNNOPRSSTT	presentationism
AEEIIMNOOPRSTTX	extemporisation
AEEIIMNOOPRTTXZ	extemporization
AEEIINNOPRSSTTT	presentationist
AEEIINOPRRSSTTV	preservationist
AEEILLMNPPRSTUY	supplementarily
AEEILLNNOPRRSTY	interpersonally
AEEILLNNOPRSTTY	septentrionally
AEEILMNNOOPPRUU	pleuropneumonia
AEEILMNNOPPSTTU	supplementation
AEEIMNNOOPPRRTT	reapportionment
AEEIMNNOPRSSTTU	importunateness
AEEIMQRRRSSSTTU	quartermistress
AEEINNOPRSSTTTU	unprotestantise
AEEINNOPRSTTTUZ	unprotestantize
AEEINOQRRSSSSTU	quarter-sessions
AEENNNOOPSSSSTU	spontaneousness
AEFGHILLLNNOSTW	half-wellingtons
AEFHHIINORSSTTW	faithworthiness
AEFHIIILLMNOSTU	self-humiliation
AEFIIIILLMNNSTY	infinitesimally
AEFIILLLNNOOPST	self-pollination
AEFIILMNOOPRSSS	professionalism
AEFIIMMNOOPRRST	preformationism
AEFIIMNOOPRRSTT	preformationist
AEFIINOPRSSSSSU	fissiparousness
AEFILLMNOPRSTTY	self-importantly
AEFILNNNOOOPRSS	non-professional
AEFIMNOOOPRRSTT	post-Reformation
AEFLOOPPRSTTUUU	paulo-post-future
AEGHHIIMNNRSSST	nightmarishness
AEGHHIIOOPRRRST	historiographer
AEGIIIMNNNRSSTT	intransigentism
AEGIIINNNOORSTT	nitrogenisation
AEGIIINNNOORTTZ	nitrogenization
AEGIIINNNRSSTTT	intransigentist
AEGILMNNORRSTTY	remonstratingly
AEHHIIMNOPRRSTT	therianthropism
AEHHIIOPPRSSTTY	physiotherapist
AEHHIKNNORSSTTW	thankworthiness
AEHIIKNNRRSSSTT	shrink-resistant
AEHIILNNOOPTTVY	hypoventilation
AEHIIMMNNOOPRST	enantiomorphism
AEHILNNOPPRSUYZ	sulphinpyrazone
AEHIMNNOOOPRSTU	enantiomorphous
AEIILLLNOQRTUVY	ventriloquially
AEIIILLNNNNOTTUY	unintentionally
AEIIILLNOOPPRSTY	prepositionally
AEIIILLOOPPRRRTY	proprietorially
AEIILMMNNRSSTTU	instrumentalism
AEIIILMNNRSSTTTU	instrumentalist
AEIIILMNNRSTTTUY	instrumentality
AEIIILNNNORSSTUV	involuntariness
AEIIMNNNORSTTTU	instrumentation
AEIIMOPPRRSSTTU	superpatriotism
AEIKLMNNOPRSSTU	unsportsmanlike
AEILNOOOPPRRTTY	proportionately
AEINNOOOPPRRTTU	unproportionate
AFGGIIMNNORRSTY	transmogrifying
AFGIIKMNNNOOPRT	non-profit-making
AGHHHILOOOPPRTT	photolithograph
AGHHIILLLLNSSYY	shilly-shallying
AGHHILLMOOOPSTT	ophthalmologist
AGHHINOOOPSSTTU	opisthognathous
AGHHLOOOPPRTXYY	photoxylography
AGHHOOOPPPRRTYY	pyrophotography
AGHIIILMOPSSTTT	stigmatophilist
AGHIILMNOOOSTTY	mythologisation
AGHIILMNOOOTTYZ	mythologization
AGHILMMNOOOPTUY	immunopathology
AGIIIILLLMMNSTUU	multilingualism
AGIIILLNNQRTUYZ	tranquilizingly
AGIILMMNOOSSTTU	numismatologist
AHHILNOOOPPRSTY	phosphorylation
AHHINOOOPPRSSTT	anthroposophist
AHIIIMOPPRSTTUY	hypopituitarism
AHIJLMNOOOPRSTU	photojournalism
AHIJLNOOOPRSTTU	photojournalist
AIIIIILLNOQRSTUY	inquisitorially
AIIIIMMNNOOSTUZ	isoimmunization
AIIILLNNOSTTTUY	institutionally
AIIILNOOPPRSTTY	propylitisation
AIIILNOOPPRTTYZ	propylitization
AIILLLMNOPSSUUY	pusillanimously
AIILLNOOPPSSTUY	suppositionally
AIILNOOOPPRRTTY	proportionality

B

BBBBEEFGIIILRTT	flibbertigibbet
BBCDEEIILORSTTU	biodestructible
BBCEEILMNOSSSTU	combustibleness
BBDDEEHHHLOOOOY	hobbledehoyhood
BBEEEFHIILLORTY	Lob-lie-by-the-fire
BBEEEIILMMRSSSU	semisubmersible
BBEEEKKNOORRRST	kerbstone-broker
BBEHILMMMOOORST	thromboembolism
BCCCDEIIMNRRSUU	uncircumscribed
BCCEEEIILMNNOSU	bioluminescence
BCCEEEIMNNPRSUU	superincumbence

BCCEEIMNNPRSUUY	superincumbency
BCCEGHIMNNNRRUU	number-crunching
BCDDDEELLNOOOSS	cold-bloodedness
BCDDGILLLNOORUY	bloodcurdlingly
BCDEEEIILNRRSSU	irreducibleness
BCDEFHILORRTTUY	butterfly-orchid
BCDEIIIILRRTTUY	irreductibility
BCDEIIILRSTTTUY	destructibility
BCEEEEILMNNNOOV	omnibenevolence
BCEEEGIILLNNSTU	subintelligence
BCEEEGILLNNNORY	non-belligerency
BCEEEGILNNOOPST	boning-telescope
BCEEEHHILOOPRTU	eleutherophobic
BCEEEIIJNRSTTUV	intersubjective
BCEEEILMNORRTTV	convertible-term
BCEEEILNPSSSSTU	susceptibleness
BCEEEJLMMORRTUY	jerry-come-tumble
BCEEGHIIMOORSTY	biogeochemistry
BCEEGIIMMNNOSSS	misbecomingness
BCEEHHHIOPRRRST	herb-Christopher
BCEEIIILMPPRRST	imprescriptible
BCEEIILLNNOSTTU	subintellection
BCEEIJOPRRSSTUU	subject-superior
BCEEILNOPRRSSTU	corruptibleness
BCEFHILORRSTTUY	butterfly-orchis
BCEGHIILNOOOSTT	biotechnologist
BCEHIIIIINOSTTX	exhibitionistic
BCEIIILMNOPTTTY	contemptibility
BCEIIILMOPRSSTY	compressibility
BCEIIMMNOORSSSU	subcommissioner
BCGHIILOOOPSSTY	psychobiologist
BCGIIIIILNORRTY	incorrigibility
BCILLNOOORSSTUU	courts-bouillons
BCINNNOOORRTTUY	non-contributory
BDDEEEILMNNNOSS	noble-mindedness
BDDEEEIMNNORSSS	sober-mindedness
BDEEEEFIMNNOORT	before-mentioned
BDEEFIIIIILNNSTY	indefensibility
BDEEFLMMNOORRUY	ferro-molybdenum
BDEEIIIILNNSSSV	indivisibleness
BDEGGIIILNNOSSS	disobligingness
BDEGIIIIILNSTTY	indigestibility
BDEGIILLNOOSSTU	blood-guiltiness
BDFFIIILMNNORUU	infundibuliform
BDIIIILLNOSSTUY	indissolubility
BEEEEHIILNPRRRS	irreprehensible
BEEEGNOOORRSSTY	gooseberry-stone
BEEEHIILNPRRRSY	irreprehensibly
BEEEIINNNORRTTZ	trinitrobenzene
BEEELMNOORSSSTU	troublesomeness
BEEFFLLORRTTUWY	butterfly-flower
BEEGGGIINNOQSTU	question-begging
BEEGHIILNNORSSU	neighbourliness
BEEHIIINOPRSSTV	prohibitiveness
BEEIIIIILNNSTTXY	inextensibility
BEEIIIILRRRSTVY	irreversibility
BEEIINNORSSSTUV	inobtrusiveness
BEEINNORSSSTUUV	unobtrusiveness
BEFILMOORRSSTUU	strombuliferous
BEGHILNOOORSTTU	troubleshooting
BEGIIIIILLLNTTY	intelligibility
BEGIIILLNRSTTUU	subintelligitur
BEHHMNOOPPRRRYY	rhombenporphyry
BEIIIIILMRRSSTY	irremissibility
BEIIIIILRRSSTTY	irresistibility
BEIMOPRSSSSSTTU	sub-postmistress
BEINOOOPPRRSSSU	opprobriousness

C

CCCEEEHILNORSTT	electrotechnics
CCCEEEHLOORSTUU	eleutherococcus
CCCEEHHIIKKLRST	Schrecklichkeit
CCCEEHLMOOSTTYY	cholecystectomy
CCCEEIILMNOORRT	microelectronic
CCCEEIKLLOORTTT	ticket-collector
CCCEEIMNPRSSSTU	circumspectness
CCCEGIIIKNNOQUV	quick-conceiving
CCCEIIIMMOORRRU	micromicrocurie
CCCEIIIMNNORSSU	circumincession
CCCEIIIMPRRSTUV	circumscriptive
CCCEINNOOOSSSSU	coconsciousness
CCCIIIMNOPRRSTU	circumscription
CCDDEEGILNNNOSY	condescendingly
CCDEEEEFINNOORV	videoconference
CCDEEEEINNORTUV	counter-evidence
CCDEEEELLNORSST	recollectedness
CCDEEEFINNOPRSU	superconfidence
CCDEEENNNNORSSU	unconcernedness
CCDEEINOPRSTUUV	superconductive
CCDEENNORRSTTUU	unreconstructed
CCDEGINNOPRSTUU	superconducting
CCDEHINOOOPTTUV	photoconductive
CCDEIIIMNOORSST	microdissection
CCDGHINNOOOPTTU	photoconducting
CCEEEEELLNPRSUX	superexcellence
CCEEEEFLNNOQSSU	self-consequence
CCEEEFFGIIINORV	receiving-office
CCEEEHHNOOPPRSS	phosphorescence
CCEEEHILMORRSTT	electrothermics
CCEEEHILOOPRRTT	electrophoretic
CCEEEIIKLNORSTT	electrokinetics
CCEEEIILMNNORRT	irreconcilement
CCEEEILLMNOORST	mole-electronics
CCEEEINNOSSSTUV	consecutiveness
CCEEELNSSSSSSSU	successlessness
CCEEFFFIILNSSUY	self-sufficiency
CCEEFIIINOPRSTT	perfectionistic
CCEEFILNNOSSSTY	self-consistency
CCEEHHIINOPRSTZ	schizophrenetic
CCEEHIIIMOORSTT	stoicheiometric
CCEEHINOOPRRRTY	hypercorrection
CCEEHNORRSTTTUU	technostructure
CCEEIILOPRRTTYY	pyro-electricity
CCEEIINNNNOORTT	interconnection
CCEEIJNNNOSSTUV	conjunctiveness
CCEEILNOOOPRSTT	optoelectronics
CCEEINORRSTTUUY	counter-security
CCEFGINOOOPRRRT	proof-correcting
CCEFILNNOOSSSUU	unselfconscious
CCEGHILMNOOORTY	microtechnology
CCEGIILOOOOSTTX	ecotoxicologist
CCEGIIMNOOPRRSS	microprocessing
CCEHHIMOPRSSTYY	psychochemistry
CCEHIIMMOOPSSTY	psychosomimetic

CCEHIIMMOOPSTTY	psychotomimetic
CCEHILNOOOPRSST	school-inspector
CCEHLMOOOSSTTYY	cholecystostomy
CCEIIIIMNOORRST	oneirocriticism
CCEIIILRRSSTTUU	sericiculturist
CCEIIIMNNORSSSU	circuminsession
CCEIILNNOOSSTUY	conscientiously
CCEIINNNOOSSTUU	unconscientious
CCEINNNOOSSSSUU	unconsciousness
CCEINNOOPRRSTTU	preconstruction
CCEINNOOPSSSSUU	conspicuousness
CCGIIIILNOOSSTU	sociolinguistic
CCHHIIOPPSSSTYY	psychophysicist
CCHINOOOPRSSTYY	onychocryptosis
CCIIINNOOPRSSTT	conscriptionist
CCIILNNOOPSSUUY	inconspicuously
CCIIMNNOORSSTTU	constructionism
	misconstruction
CCIINNOORSSTTTU	constructionist
CCIMMNOOPRSTTUY	crypto-communist
CDDDEGIINNOOOOT	good-conditioned
CDDEEEEEINNNPRT	interdependence
CDDEEEELNNPRTUY	unprecedentedly
CDDEEEIIMNOPPRR	medicine-dropper
CDDEEFIIINNORRT	direction-finder
CDDEEIILLNNOOTW	well-conditioned
CDDEGHIIILMNSTT	middle-stitching
CDDEINNOOPRRTUU	under-production
CDDIILMMOOOSSUY	discommodiously
CDEEEEEFLNNSSSS	defencelessness
CDEEEEINNNPRSTU	superintendence
CDEEEFFIKNNSSST	stiff-neckedness
CDEEEFILRSSTTUV	self-destructive
CDEEEFLNOORRTUW	counter-flowered
CDEEEGINNORSTUU	secundogeniture
CDEEEHNNORRTTUU	under-the-counter
CDEEEIINNPRRSWW	windscreen-wiper
CDEEEIINPRSSSTV	descriptiveness
CDEEEIMNNPRSTUU	superinducement
CDEEEINNNPRSTUY	superintendency
CDEEEINRSSSTTUV	destructiveness
CDEEENNOPRSSTTU	unprotectedness
CDEEENNPSSSSTUU	unsuspectedness
CDEEFFILLNNOSTY	self-confidently
CDEEFGIILNNORSS	self-considering
CDEEFGILMNNOSTU	self-documenting
CDEEFILLPRSSTUY	disrespectfully
CDEEFILNORSSTTU	self-destruction
CDEEFILNOSSTTTU	self-constituted
CDEEGHIMNNNOPRU	uncomprehending
CDEEGIIIMMNORTT	riding-committee
CDEEGIILLNOOOTU	oligonucleotide
CDEEGILNOOPRSTW	powdering-closet
CDEEHIIKNSSTTTW	thick-wittedness
CDEEHIKNNRRSTTU	thunder-stricken
CDEEIIIINNSSSTTV	distinctiveness
CDEEIIKNQSSTTUW	quick-wittedness
CDEEILNNORSSSUU	incredulousness
CDEEIMNNOOPSSSU	compendiousness
CDEEINNNOPRSSST	nondescriptness
CDEELMNNOOOOSTY	Monocotyledones
CDEELNNOOPRRSTY	correspondently
CDEFILMNOOOPRRS	scolopendriform
CDEGHHMOOOPRSTU	through-composed
CDEGIIIMMNNNOOSS	decommissioning
CDEGIILMNOPRTUU	picture-moulding
CDEGILNNOOPRRSY	correspondingly
CDEHHIILOORTTUY	ichthyodorulite
CDEHHIILOORTTYY	ichthyodorylite
CDEHIKMNOOPRRTU	durchkomponiert
CDEIIIILNNSTTVY	indistinctively
CDEIIIJNNOSSSUU	injudiciousness
CDEIIMMNNNOOOSS	non-commissioned
CDHIILNOPRSTUUU	pulchritudinous
CDIIIINOSSSTUUV	vicissitudinous
CDIILNNOOSSTUUY	discontinuously
CDIIMOOPPRRSTUY	cryptosporidium
CDINOOOPSSSSTYY	pycnodysostosis
CEEEEELOOPRSSTT	telestereoscope
CEEEEFFGIINNRTY	energy-efficient
CEEEEFFIINNSSTV	ineffectiveness
CEEEEFILORRRTTV	retroreflective
CEEEEHHNOPRRTTW	threepenceworth
CEEEFGIMNNNORRR	norm-referencing
CEEEFIIMNORRRTT	interferometric
CEEEFLNORRSSSUU	resourcefulness
CEEEGGILNNOOSSU	gluconeogenesis
CEEEGHIQRRRSUUU	churrigueresque
CEEEGIIILLMNNST	misintelligence
CEEEGINOPRRSSSW	crossing-sweeper
CEEEHIIMNNOPRSV	incomprehensive
CEEEHIIMNOPRSSV	comprehensivise
CEEEHIIMNOPRSVZ	comprehensivize
CEEEHILMNOPRSVY	comprehensively
CEEEHILOOPRRSST	electrophoresis
CEEEHIMNNOPRSUV	uncomprehensive
CEEEHIMORRSSTTY	stereochemistry
CEEEIILOOPRSTTV	electropositive
CEEEIIMNOPSSTTV	competitiveness
CEEEIIMNORRSTTU	recrementitious
CEEEIIMNORSTTUX	excrementitious
CEEEIINOPRRRSTU	resurrection-pie
CEEEIINORRRSSTU	resurrectionise
CEEEIINORRRSTUZ	resurrectionize
CEEEILOPRRSTTVY	retrospectively
CEEEIMNNOORSSSU	ceremoniousness
CEEEINNOSSSSSTU	necessitousness
CEEEINOPPRSSSTV	prospectiveness
CEEEINPQRSSSTUU	picturesqueness
CEEEIOPRRRRSTTU	picture-restorer
CEEEMMNNOORTTUV	countermovement
CEEENOPRRRSSTUU	counter-pressure
CEEFHIIMNOPRSSS	Sphenisciformes
CEEFINNOPRRSSTU	perfunctoriness
CEEFLMNOORSSSST	comfortlessness
CEEHHIMMORRSTTY	thermochemistry
CEEHIIMNNNOOPRS	incomprehension
CEEHIIMNOSSSSUV	mischievousness
CEEHIKLNNOPRTUY	phenylketonuric
CEEHILNNOSSSTUY	nucleosynthesis
CEEHLLNOOOPPRRY	polychloroprene
CEEIIILLMMMORRT	micromillimetre
CEEIIINOPRSSSTX	expressionistic
CEEIIMNNOPSSSUU	impecuniousness

CEEIIMNORRRSSTU	resurrectionism
CEEIINNNOORRSTV	interconversion
CEEIINNRSSSTTUV	instructiveness
CEEIINOPPRSSSTU	precipitousness
CEEIINORRRSSTTU	resurrectionist
CEEIINPSSSTTUUV	intussusceptive
CEEIKNOPRRSTTVY	poverty-stricken
CEEILMNNOORSUUY	unceremoniously
CEEIMNNOPSSSTUV	consumptiveness
CEEINNNOOSSSTTU	contentiousness
CEEINOPPRSSSSUU	perspicuousness
CEFFIIINNOOSSSU	inofficiousness
CEFGHHIILNNOPRS	French-polishing
CEGGHILNOOOORST	geochronologist
CEGHIIILNNOSTTU	ethnolinguistic
CEGHILMNOOOSTUY	ethnomusicology
CEGHLNOOOPRSUYY	neuropsychology
CEGIIILNNORSTUU	neurolinguistic
CEGINNNOORSSSUU	incongruousness
CEHHIMMNOOOPPRS	morphophonemics
CEHHINOPSSSSTYY	psychosynthesis
CEHIILMNRRSSTTY	Christy-minstrel
CEHIIMMMNORSTUY	immunochemistry
CEHIINNOOPRSSSU	connoisseurship
CEHINNOOPRSSSTY	post-synchronise
CEHINNOOPRSSTYZ	post-synchronize
CEHNNNOORSSSSUY	synchronousness
CEIIIIMNOPRSSST	impressionistic
CEIIILNOQRSTTUV	ventriloquistic
CEIIIMNNORRSSTU	insurrectionism
CEIIINNORRSSTTU	insurrectionist
CEIILNNOPSSSTUU	punctiliousness
CEIILORRSSTTTUU	ostreiculturist
CEIINNOOPRSSTTU	introsusception
CEIINNOPSSSTTUU	intussusception
CEILLOPRRSTTUUW	pillow-structure
CGHILLNOOSSTTUW	swothling-clouts
CHHHINNOORRSTUY	ornithorhynchus
CHHHIOOOOPPRRST	orthophosphoric
CHILLMOOOPPRRSY	microsporophyll
CIIIMOORRSSTUVY	myristicivorous
CIIINNOOSSTTTTU	constitutionist

D

DDDEEHLNOORRSUU	round-shouldered
DDEEEEHINOPPRSU	pseudoephedrine
DDEEEEIIMNNNPST	semi-independent
DDEEEELLORSWWYY	dyer's-yellowweed
DDEEEGIILNPRRUV	under-privileged
DDEEEIILNRSSTTY	disinterestedly
DDEEGHIILMNNSST	light-mindedness
DDEEGHIIMNNRSST	right-mindedness
DDEEHILLOPPRSSU	shoulder-slipped
DDEGHIIINNSSTUU	undistinguished
DDEHILNOORTTUWW	world-without-end
DEEEEEHNNNRSTUV	seventeen-hunder
DEEEEFLLMNOPSTV	self-development
DEEEEHNOPRRSTUY	superheterodyne
DEEEEILNORSSSTU	deleteriousness
DEEEELMNOOPRTVV	overdevelopment
DEEEFGIILMNNRST	self-determining
DEEEHLLLOPRSTUW	well-upholstered
DEEEIILLNNNOTTW	well-intentioned
DEEEIINOPSSSTUX	expeditiousness
DEEEINNNOSSSTTU	tendentiousness
DEEELMMNNOPRTUY	underemployment
DEEFHLMNOOSSTUU	foul-mouthedness
DEEFILNRSSSSSTU	distressfulness
DEEFINOOORRSSSU	odoriferousness
DEEFLNOOPRSSSTU	dessertspoonful
DEEGGHILNNOSSST	long-sightedness
DEEGGIMNNNOORRW	wondermongering
DEEGIILMNOOSSTT	sedimentologist
DEEGILLOOOPPRTY	lepidopterology
DEEHHLNOORSSTTU	shoulder-shotten
DEEHIIKNNNNSSST	thin-skinnedness
DEEHIILOPPRRSVW	devil-worshipper
DEEIIIILNOPRSSTT	stilpnosiderite
DEEIILMNNRTTTUY	unintermittedly
DEEIILNOPRSSSTW	low-spiritedness
DEEIILNOPRSSTUY	serendipitously
DEEILNNPRRTTUUY	uninterruptedly
DEFGHILOPRSSTTY	softly-sprighted
DEFILNRSSSSTTUU	distrustfulness
DEGHIIIMNNSSTTU	distinguishment
DEGHIILNOOPPRSW	polishing-powder
DEHHIIMOPRRSTYY	hyperthyroidism
DEHHILNOOOPRSTU	ornithodelphous
DEIIILLMNNOSSTU	disillusionment
DEIIIMMNNOPRSST	disimprisonment
DEIIMNOOOPPRRST	misproportioned
DIILLMNOSTTUUUY	multitudinously
DIKNOOOPSSSSTYY	pyknodysostosis

E

EEEEGHLNOORSTUY	heterogeneously
EEEEIINNNPSSSVX	inexpensiveness
EEEEIINNRRSSTTV	irretentiveness
EEEELMNORRSSSSS	remorselessness
EEEEMNNORSSSTUV	venturesomeness
EEEFFIINNNOSSSV	inoffensiveness
EEEFGGIILNRRSST	self-registering
EEEFGIIMNRRTUXZ	freezing-mixture
EEEFGILNORSSTVY	self-sovereignty
EEEFHMMNOORRRST	refreshment-room
EEEFILMMNOPRSTV	self-improvement
EEEGHMNNOOOSSSU	homogeneousness
EEEGIINNNRSSSTT	interestingness
EEEGILNNNNRSSTU	unrelentingness
EEEGILORRRSSTVY	retrogressively
EEEGINOPRRSSSSV	progressiveness
EEEHHNNOPRRTTWY	threepennyworth
EEEHIIMPPRRSTUV	heir-presumptive
EEEHIINPPRRRSTT	interpretership
EEEHLMNNOOSSSUW	unwholesomeness
EEEIIINNNSSSSTV	insensitiveness
EEEIIMMOORRSSST	stereoisomerism
EEEIINOPRSSSTTU	repetitiousness
EEEINNNOSSSSTTU	sententiousness
EEEINNOPRSSSTTU	pretentiousness
EEELNOPPRSSSSSU	purposelessness
EEEMNOPSSSSTTUU	tempestuousness
EEFFFGLLLORSTUY	self-forgetfully
EEFFGIIILLNRSST	self-fertilising

EEFFGIIILLNRSTZ	self-fertilizing
EEFGHIIILLOOTTW	gillie-white-foot
EEFGIILNNOQSSTU	self-questioning
EEFIMNOORRSSSTU	mortiferousness
EEFLNOPRSSSSUUU	superfluousness
EEGGHIMNOOOPRST	geomorphogenist
EEGHHLNOSSSSTTU	thoughtlessness
EEGHILMNNOOOPST	phenomenologist
EEGHINNORSSSTUU	unrighteousness
EEGIIILNORRSSSU	irreligiousness
EEGIILNNNRSTTUY	uninterestingly
EEGIIMNNNRSSTTU	unremittingness
EEGIIMNORSSTUUV	seeming-virtuous
EEGIINNORSSSTUV	vertiginousness
EEGILNOPPRSSSSY	prepossessingly
EEGILNOPRRSSUVY	unprogressively
EEGINNOPPRSSSSU	unprepossessing
EEHHNOOPPRSSUYY	neurohypophyses
EEHIINOOPRSSSTT	photosensitiser
EEHIINOOPRSSTTZ	photosensitizer
EEHIINORRRSSTVW	riverworthiness
EEHLNOPRSSSSUUU	sulphureousness
EEIIIINNQSSSTUV	inquisitiveness
EEIIIMNNNORSTTV	interventionism
EEIIINNNORSTTTV	interventionist
EEIILNNOORRTTTU	trinitrotoluene
EEIIMNOORRSSSTU	meritoriousness
EEIINNNNNOORTTV	non-intervention
EEIMNNOOOPPPRRS	properispomenon
EEINNNOOPPRSSTU	inopportuneness
EFFIILNOORSSSUU	unfossiliferous
EFGGIINNNORSSUV	unforgivingness
EFGGILNNORTTTUU	flutter-tonguing
EFGHIIJLNORTUWY	junior-flyweight
EFHHHIMOOOPRSTT	shoot-from-the-hip
EFILMNRSSSSTTUU	mistrustfulness
EGGHILMOOOOPRST	geomorphologist
EGHHIILLMNOOSTT	helminthologist
EGHHIIMNORSTTTY	thirtysomething
EGHILNOOOPRSUYY	neurophysiology
EGIIILNNRSTTTWY	intertwistingly
EHHIIMOOOPRRSST	theriomorphosis
EHHINOOPPRSSUYY	neurohypophysis
EHIILLMOOPPRTTU	photomultiplier
EHINORRSSSTTTUW	trustworthiness
EIIIMNOOPPRSSTU	superimposition
EIILLMMNNOOORTT	montmorillonite
EIILLNORSSSSTUU	illustriousness
EIILOPRRSSTTUUY	surreptitiously
EIILOPRSSSTTUUY	superstitiously

G

GGGHHILNOOORTUY	thoroughgoingly
GHIILOOOOPSSTYZ	zoophysiologist

H

HHHOOOOPPPRSSUY	hypophosphorous
HILNORRSTTTUUWY	untrustworthily

I

IIINNNNOORSSTTU	non-intrusionist